A MODERN CHINESE-ENGLISH DICTIONARY

外研社·现代汉英词典

新版

本社辞书部 编

外语教学与研究出版社
FOREIGN LANGUAGE TEACHING AND RESEARCH PRESS

(京)新登字 155 号

图书在版编目(CIP)数据

外研社·现代汉英词典(新版)/本社辞书部编. －北京:外语教学与研究出版社,2001
ISBN 7－5600－2188－3

Ⅰ. 外… Ⅱ. 本… Ⅲ. ①英语－词典 ②词典－汉、英 Ⅳ. H316

中国版本图书馆 CIP 数据核字(2001)第 14042 号

外研社·现代汉英词典(新版)
本社辞书部 编
* * *
项目负责人: 刘相东 陈 忠
责任编辑: 陈 忠
助理编辑: 付分钗 骆 飞 赵海麟 陈海燕
出版发行: 外语教学与研究出版社
社 址: 北京市西三环北路 19 号 (100089)
网 址: http: //www. fltrp. com. cn
印 刷: 北京外国语大学印刷厂
开 本: 850×1168 1/32
印 张: 41.25
字 数: 2704 千字
版 次: 2001 年 7 月第 1 版 2002 年 4 月第 6 次印刷
书 号: ISBN 7－5600－2188－3/H·1168
定 价: 49.90 元
* * *

序

词典有小型的，中型的，大型的。小型的词典好比人的两条腿，很方便，哪里都可以去，可往往不够用；大型的词典好比汽车，能装许多东西，派大用场，但很占地方，再说又较贵；中型的词典则像自行车，用起来很方便，可以满足日常的需要，花费也不多。外研社的《朗文当代英语辞典》(英语版)和这部《现代汉英词典》，都是 32 开本的中型词典，最适合一般人放在手边，以备随时取用。

本词典是一部汉英语文工具书，主要收录常用的语文词条，同时酌收社会科学和自然科学各领域的基本词条，包括常见的最新科技词汇。另一方面，本词典所收虽以现代日常语词为主，但也兼收文言和书面语汇，因为它们是富含生命力的汉语数千年来的积淀。在实际语言运用中，语文和百科、口语和书面语往往没有明确的界限，这一语用事实反映到词典中，争取两相兼顾便是很自然的考虑。

汉英词典主要是给中国人学英语用的，特别是为中译英服务。但外国人也可以用它来学汉语。过去有的外国人说汉语没有语法，中国人自己也觉得“词无定类”，弄得汉语的字典词典大都不标注词性。现在不同了，人们都认识到汉语有语法，词也可以划类，只是兼类现象较多。本词典试给汉语的单音节词标注了词性，这样，读者在面对英汉两种语言的词类差异时，便能既知其然，又能说出个所以然。当然，词性问题相当复杂，如何处理双音节词和多音节词，还有待探索。

汉英词典的目标之一是跟进汉语词汇的发展，一方面删汰旧词、修订释义，另一方面尽可能多地收录新词新义。这个目标本来就不可能完全达到，在语言随社会变化、知识膨胀而迅速更新的当今更难以企及。鲜活的语言总是走在前头，把一切词典抛在后面，在这部词典问世的时候，编辑者也不得不承认已经落后于语言，需要着手下一步的修订工作了。

姚小平
北京外国语大学教授
博士生导师

前　言

本词典依据的蓝本为荣获国家辞书一等奖、第十届中国图书奖、全国优秀畅销书奖等国家级大奖的《汉英词典》(修订版)(外研社 1997 年版),在此基础上删去汉字国标码表中没有的字头,以及生僻、罕用的词条,并增补了一万余条新词(包括日常用语、成语、俗语、谚语、常用科技术语等)。增添的条目主要是常见于大众报刊、既流行又较稳定的词语,如商战、申办、套餐、体饰、乌龙球、语音信箱、远程教育等。近几年网络的飞速发展促成了许多与网络有关的词语,如网站、网页、网吧、网恋、网迷、网友等,在本词典中都已收录。

本词典的服务对象为国内的英语学习者,注意突出以下特点:

一、内容新。全书共收条目五万三千条,其中新增条目在一万以上,主要是改革开放以来出现的新词新语;不但有近年来出现在报刊、影视和网络等媒体中的新的词汇,也有寻常百姓所喜闻乐见的俗语、谚语。编者以自心度用者心,时时将读者的需求放在心中,常常为添加一个新词,甚至一个义项而查阅大量资料,以求准确无误。

二、范围广。现代汉英词典内容丰富,覆盖了政治、经济、文化、科技等许多方面。随着学科术语的不断普及,编者在新增的词汇中主要包括了读者日常阅读翻译会遇到的经贸、电子、社科类常见术语。相信一般使用者工作、学习中需要查找的条目、词组,多能在本词典里查到满意的解答。

三、体例醒目。为方便读者查阅,编者给词目添加了大量标注,详细标出学科、文体和修辞用法。与原本体例最大的不同在于,本词典给所有单字条目标明了词性,为此编者查阅了许多汉语资料并请教了多位专家,目的只有一个:为英语学习者提供更多的帮助。此外,本书参见详明,可使读者举一反三、触类旁通。

四、附录翔实丰富、实用性强。为满足不同读者的不同需要,本词典对原有附录进行了认真修订,除保留一些常见附录外,还增加了英文字母开头的词语,以及亲属关系等富有创新的内容。另外,本词典补充了有关形状、颜色和动植物名称的分类词汇。至于是否得当,有待于读者在实际使用中体会。

总之，本词典力求做到收词多、内容新、释义准、例句丰富、编排合理、实用性强、开本适中、字体醒目。但以上目标是否已经达到，还要由读者来检验。敬希读者不吝赐教，以便本书再版时更上一层楼。

外语教学与研究出版社

辞书部

目　录

用 法 说 明

Guide to the Use of the Dictionary

一 条目安排

Arrangement of Entries

1. 本词典所收条目分单字条目和多字条目;有些多字条目后有合成词。
2. 单字条目按汉语拼音字母顺序排列。同音异调的汉字按汉字声调顺序排列。同音同调的汉字按笔划多少排列。
3. 多字条目按第一个字分列于单字条目之下。同一个单字条目下的多字条目不止一条时,按第二个字的汉语拼音字母顺序和笔划多少排列。第二个字相同时,按第三个字排列,依此类推。儿化词注音中的 **r** 不计入顺序字母。如:托儿(tuōr)排在托(tuō)之后,托庇(tuōbì)之前;人缘儿(rényuánr)排在人员(rényuán)之后,人猿(rényuán)之前。
4. 单字或多字条目字形相同而音或调不同者,分立条目。如:答(dā)和答(dá);播种(bōzhǒng)和播种(bōzhòng)。分立的单字条目一般加注"另见"。如答(dá)后加注"另见 dā";反之亦然。
5. 轻声单字条目一般紧接在同形的非轻声单字条目之后;带轻声字的多字条目紧接在同形的无轻声字的多字条目之后。如:大方(dàfang)排在大方(dàfāng)之后;地道(dìdao)排在地道(dìdào)之后,地道战(dìdàozhàn)之前。
6. 在同一单字条目下,多字条目意义相同、用字略有差异者,一般只收录其中较常见者,并在条目后加"又作"。如:"百折不挠"(又作'百折不回')。
7. 多字条目能和其他条目组成习语者,最后加"另见",表示参看该习语条目。

二 注音

Pronunciation

本词典读者对象为国内英语学习者,为节省篇幅,多字条目后没有标注拼音。但有些多字词条有不同的读音,则标注拼音,以示区别。

三 释义

Definitions

1. 专业条目一般用中文注明所属专业或学科名称,详细的学科术语可参见"学科术语略语表”。

2. 单字条目标注词性。如果该字有多个词性,则用罗马数字 **I**、**II**、**III** 等表明,详细词性分类可参见“词类略语表”。多字条目不标词性。
3. 释义一般用对应的英语词语,无对应的词语时用英语解释。同一义项下有两个或两个以上解释时,用分号“;”隔开;一个条目有两个或两个以上义项时用❶❷❸等数码标出顺序。
4. 释义中的可替换词语放在圆括号“()”内,前面加“**or**”。如:群起而攻之:**all rise (or turn) against sb.**
5. 由于条目和英语对应词二者的词义范围不同,有的释义用英语加注补充性或限制性说明,放在圆括号内。如:

   嫁:**(of a woman) marry**

   马克:**mark (German monetary unit)**
6. 有关用法、语法特征等都用英语说明,放在圆括号内。
7. 某些条目先用英语作字面翻译,然后释义,二者之间加破折号“—”。如:

   舍车保帅:**give up a chariot to save the marshal (in Chinese chess) —make minor sacrifices to safeguard major interests**
8. 有的单字条目本身无意义,只是构词成分,释义用“(构词成分)见下”来表示。
9. 不在同一单字条目下的同义多字条目,一般只对较常见者释义,另一处用“同”表示。如:虎踞龙盘:同〖龙盘虎踞〗。
10. 释义时常用的英语词语有 **general name**(统称)、**common name**(通称)、**popular name**(俗称)、**old name**(旧称)、**another name**(别称)等。
11. 为避免重复,条目释义后的有些例词省略英文翻译,读者可参见其首字在正文中的相应条目。

四 例证

Examples

1. 例证前加冒号“:”。例证中的本条目用代词号“～”表示。例证的英语译文不止一个时,如果是词或词组,用分号隔开;如果是句子,用 **or** 隔开。例证与例证之间用斜线号“/”隔开。
2. 例证中可替换部分及其英译放在圆括号内。
3. 例证英译中替换词语放在圆括号内,前面加 **or**。

略 语 表

学科术语略语表

本词典学科标记	中文学科术语	术语英文对应词
[测]	测绘	surveying and drawing
[地理]	地理学	geography
[地质]	地质学	geology
[电]	电学;电工	electricity
[电影]	电影	film
[电子]	电子学	electronics
[动]	动物学	zoology
[法]	法律	legal
[纺]	纺织;纺织工程	textile
[工美]	工艺美术	arts & crafts
[航海]	航海	navigation
[航空]	航空	aviation
[航天]	航天	space
[化]	化学	chemistry
[化纤]	化学纤维	chemical fibre
[环保]	环境保护	environmental protection
[机]	机械	mechanics
[几何]	几何学	geometry
[计]	计算机	computer
[建]	建筑	architecture
[交通]	交通	transportation
[经]	经济;经济学	economics
[军]	军事	military

本词典学科标记	中文学科术语	术语英文对应词
[考古]	考古	archaeology
[矿]	矿物学;矿业	mining
[林]	林业	forestry
[逻]	逻辑学	logic
[美]	美术	arts
[牧]	畜牧业(学)	animal husbandry
[农]	农业;农学	agriculture
[气]	气象学	meteorology
[商]	商业	commerce
[摄]	摄影	photography
[生]	生物学	biology
[生化]	生物化学	biochemistry
[生理]	生理学	physiology
[史]	历史	history
[数]	数学	mathematics
[刷]	印刷	printing
[水]	水利	water
[体]	体育	sports
[天]	天文学	astronomy
[铁路]	铁路	railway
[统计]	统计	statistics
[外交]	外交	diplomacy
[微]	微生物学	bacteriology
[无]	无线电	radio
[物]	物理学	physics
[戏]	戏剧	theatre
[心理]	心理学	psychology
[药]	药物;药学	pharmacy
[冶]	冶金学	metallurgy

本词典学科标记	中文学科术语	术语英文对应词
[医]	医学	medicine
[音]	音乐	music
[油]	石油	petroleum
[渔]	渔业	fishery
[语]	语言学;语言	linguistics
[语音]	语音学	phonetics
[杂]	杂技	acrobatics
[哲]	哲学	philosophy
[植]	植物学	botany
[中]	中医、中药	Chinese medicine
[宗]	宗教	religion

修辞用语略语表

本词典略语标记	中文修辞术语	术语英文对应词
〈贬〉	贬抑	derogatory
〈粗〉	粗野话	vulgar
〈反〉	反义词	(as) opposed (to)
〈方〉	方言	dialect
〈古〉	古词、古义	archaic
〈诙〉	诙谐语	humorous
〈讳〉	讳言(骂人话)	offensive
〈旧〉	旧词	old
〈口〉	口语	informal
〈略〉	略语	abreviation
〈谦〉	谦辞	humble
〈书〉	书面语	formal
〈套〉	客套语	polite

本词典略语标记	中文修辞术语	术语英文对应词
〈婉〉	婉辞	euphemistic
〈文〉	文学语言	literary
〈语〉	语法	grammar
〈喻〉	比喻	figurative
〈字〉	字面意义	literal(ly)
〈尊〉	尊称	honorific

词类略语表

本词典词性标记	词性	英文对应词
代	代词	pronoun
动	动词	verb
副	副词	adverb
介	介词	preposition
连	连词	conjunction
量	量词	measure word
名	名词	noun
数	数词	numeral
叹	叹词	interjection
象	象声词	onomatopoeia
形	形容词	adjective
助	助词	particle

A

ā

阿 助〈方〉❶(a prefix used before pet names, monosyllabic surnames, or numbers denoting order of seniority in a family, to form terms of endearment):～宝 *A Bao* / ～唐 *A Tang; Tang* / ～大 *A Da; the eldest* ❷(a prefix used before kinship terms):～爸 *dad; pop; pa* / ～妹 *younger sister; sister* ——另见 ē

【阿的平】[药] atabrine

【阿斗】❶ the infant name of Liu Shan(刘禅,207-271), last emperor of Shu Han (蜀汉,221-263), known for his lack of ability and weakness of character ❷ a weak-minded and ne'er-do-well person; a failure (or fool):扶不起的～ *a disappointing person; a hopeless case*

【阿尔巴尼亚】Albania ◇～人 Albanian;～语 Albanian (language)

【阿尔卑斯山脉】the Alps

【阿尔法粒子】[物] alpha particle

【阿尔法射线】[物] alpha ray

【阿尔及利亚】Algeria ◇～人 Algerian

【阿飞】a young street rowdy; a (teenager) hoodlum (or hooligan)

【阿富汗】Afghanistan ◇～人 Afghan

【阿根廷】Argentina ◇～人 Argentine

【阿訇】[宗](伊斯兰教) ahung; imam (the officiating priest of a mosque)

【阿拉伯半岛】the Arabian Peninsula; Arabia

【阿拉伯国家】Arab countries (or states)

【阿拉伯国家联盟】the League of Arab States; the Arab League

【阿拉伯胶】gum arabic; gum acacia

【阿拉伯联合酋长国】the United Arab Emirates

【阿拉伯人】Arab

【阿拉伯数码】(又作'阿拉伯数字') Arabic numerals

【阿拉伯语】Arabic (language)

【阿曼】Oman ◇～人 Omani

【阿芒拿】[化] ammonal

【阿门】(used at the end of a Christian's prayer) amen

【阿米巴】amoeba ◇～痢疾 amoebic dysentery

【阿米妥】[药] amytal

【阿片】[药] Opium ◇～制剂 [药] Opiate

【阿奇】[电子] Archie

【阿司匹林】[药] aspirin

【阿托品】[药] atropine

【阿姨】❶〈方〉mother's sister; aunt ❷ a form of address for a woman of one's parents generation; auntie ❸ a nursemaid in a family or a childcare worker in a nursery school or kindergarten

【阿扎尼亚】Azania ◇～人 Azanian

啊 叹 (expressing surprise or admiration):～,出虹了! *Oh, there's a rainbow!* / ～,这菊花真美! *Ah, these chrysanthemums are simply gorgeous!*

锕 名 [化] actinium (Ac)

【锕系元素】[化] actinides

āi

哀 Ⅰ 形 grieved; sorrowful: 悲哀 Ⅱ 名 ❶ mourning: 志哀 ❷ pity: 哀怜

【哀兵必胜】An army burning with indignation is bound to win.

【哀愁】be distressed: 无限～ *be extremely distressed*

【哀辞】a formal expression of sorrow or mourning, esp. in verse; elegy

【哀悼】mourn for the deceased; grieve over sb.'s death; lament sb.'s death: 向死者家属表示深切的～ *express one's heartfelt condolences to the family of the deceased*

【哀而不伤】sorrow without self-injury

【哀告】beg piteously; supplicate

【哀歌】❶ dirge; elegy ❷ croon plaintively

【哀号】cry piteously; wail

【哀鸿遍野】famished refugees swarming over the land; disaster victims moaning everywhere

【哀怜】feel compassion for; pity

【哀鸣】whine plaintively: 那是天鹅临死前的～。*It's the plaintive call of the dying swan.* / 没落阶级的～ *lamentations of the declining classes*

【哀求】entreat; implore

【哀伤】be grieved and heartbroken

【哀思】sad memories (of the deceased); grief: 寄托～ *give expression to one's grief over sb.'s death*

【哀叹】sigh sorrowfully for; lament; bewail; bemoan: 他～自己命运不济。*He bemoaned his fate.* / 她的死讯引起一片～。*The news of her death caused widespread lamentation.*

【哀痛】mourn sorrowfully; grieve deeply for; lament: 我们～失去了一位亲密的战友。*We la-*

ment the death of a very close friend of ours.
【哀怨】aggrieved; resentful
【哀乐】funeral music; dirge

埃 名 ❶ 见〖尘埃〗❷［物］angstrom (Å)
【埃及】Egypt ◇～人 Egyptian
【埃塞俄比亚】Ethiopia ◇～人 Ethiopian

哎 叹 hey; ah
【哎哟】Oh, dear!; Ouch!; Ow!

挨 Ⅰ 动 be or get close to; be next to: ～着窗口坐 *sit by the window* / 那两家铺子紧～着。*The two shops are next to each other.* / 别挤了! 一个～一个进去。*Don't push. Go in one by one.* Ⅱ 介 follow a regular order or sequence; do sth. in sequence or by turns: ～家送牛奶 *go from house to house delivering milk* / 他就住在这一带,你～着门找找。*He lives somewhere around here. Try to find him by going from door to door.* ——另见 ái
【挨次】take turns (doing sth.); do sth. one after another or in turn: ～上车 *get on the bus one after another* / ～入场 *file in*
【挨个儿】〈口〉do sth. by turns or one by one: ～检查身体 *have medical check-ups in turn* / 把他们～找来问问。*Bring them here one at a time for questioning.*
【挨近】get close to; be near to: 别～我! 离我远点儿! *Don't come near me! Keep your distance!* / 我近视,要挨得很近才看得清。*I'm near-sighted and have to get very close in order to see things clearly.*
【挨门挨户】(又作'挨家挨户') go from house to house (or from door to door): ～搜查 *make a house-to-house search*

唉 叹 expressing sadness, weariness, regret or disappointment ——另见 ài
【唉声叹气】heave deep sighs (of grief, worry or anguish); moan and groan: 不要受了一点挫折就～。*Don't moan and groan because of a little setback.* / 她怎么整天～,愁眉苦脸的? *Why is she looking so depressed and sighing all the time?*

ái

挨 动 ❶ suffer; endure: ～饿 *suffer from hunger; go hungry* / ～骂 *get a scolding; get a dressing-down* / ～批评 *be criticized* / ～了一记耳光 *got a box on the ear* ❷ struggle to pull through (hard times); drag out: ～日子 *suffer day after day; drag out a miserable existence* / 咱们总算～过来了。*We've pulled through at long last.* ❸ delay; stall; put off: 快走吧,别～时间了。*Get going and stop dawdling.* or *Quit stalling.* / 为什么非要～到下个月不可? *Why must we put it off till next month?* ——另见 āi
【挨打】❶ take a beating; get a thrashing: 他挨了骂不算,还挨了一顿打。*On top of a tongue-lashing, he got a beating as well.* ❷ come under attack: 处于被动～的地位 *be passive and vulnerable to attack*
【挨批】be criticized; be denounced
【挨整】be in for criticism and denunciation

皑 形〈文〉pure white; snow white
【皑皑】(of snow, frost, etc.) pure white: 白雪～ *an expanse of white snow* / ～的雪山 *a snow-capped mountain*

癌 名 cancer; carcinoma: 肝癌
【癌变】canceration
【癌扩散】metastasis (or proliferation) of cancer
【癌切除术】carcinectomy; carcinomectomy
【癌细胞】cancer cell
【癌症】cancer

ǎi

矮 形 ❶ short (of stature): 我个子～。*I'm short.* / 他比他哥哥～一头。*He's a head shorter than his brother.* ❷ low: ～墙 *a low wall* ❸ low in rank or grade: 她在中学里比我～一级。*She was a grade lower than me in middle school.*
【矮凳】a low stool
【矮墩墩】pudgy; dumpy; stumpy
【矮杆品种】［农］short-stalked variety; short-straw variety
【矮个儿】(又作'矮个子') a low-built person; a short person
【矮林】coppice; brushwood
【矮胖】short and stout; squat; dumpy; roly-poly
【矮人】❶ a short person; dwarf ❷ Pigmy (or Pygmy)
【矮小】short and small; low and small; undersized: 身材～ *short and slight in figure* / ～的房屋 *a small, low house*
【矮星】［天］dwarf star; dwarf
【矮壮素】［农］cycocel
【矮子】a short person; dwarf
【矮子里拔将军】choose a general from among the dwarfs—pick the best out of a mediocre bunch

嗳 叹 (expressing disagreement or negation): ～,没有这回事。你别信他。*No, it isn't true. Don't believe what he says.* / ～,你搞混啦。*No, no, you're all mixed up.* ——另见 ài
【嗳气】belch; eructation

蔼 形 friendly; amiable: 和蔼
【蔼然可亲】kindly; amiable; affable

霭 名〈书〉mist; haze: 暮霭

ài

艾 Ⅰ 名［植］Chinese mugwort (Artemisia argyi) Ⅱ 动〈书〉end; stop

【艾灸】[中] moxibustion

【艾米奖】Emmy

【艾绒】moxa

【艾炷】moxa cone

【艾滋病】AIDS (acquired immune deficiency syndrome) ◇～携带者 AIDS carriers

砹 名 [化] astatine (At)

唉 叹 ❶(a sigh of sadness or regret): ～,要是老张在这儿该多好啊! *Oh, if only Lao Zhang were here.* / ～,谁能想到啊! *Well, who'd have thought of that?* / ～,真可惜! *What a pity!* ❷(a response to a call, order, etc.): 快开门去。—～。*Open the door, quick! —Right.* / 小王! —～,来啦。*Xiao Wang! —Yes. Coming.* ——另见 āi

爱 动 ❶ love: 他们俩相～已经多年。*They have been in love for a number of years.* / 他～上她了。*He has fallen in love with her.* ❷ like; be fond of; be keen on: ～游泳 *be fond of swimming* / ～干净 *like cleanliness* / 只～听恭维话,不～听批评话 *be fond of flattery but deaf to criticism* ❸ cherish; treasure; hold dear; take good care of: ～公物 *take good care of public property* ❹ be apt to; be in the habit of: 他～头疼。*He gets headaches easily.* / 我～晕车。*I'm apt to get carsick.* / 她老～发脾气。*She's always losing her temper.* / 铁～生锈。*Iron rusts easily.*

【爱不释手】be so fond of sth. that one will not let it out of one's hand: 她拿着那副耳环～。*The moment she got hold of those earrings, she took a fancy to them and wouldn't let go of them.*

【爱财如命】love money as one loves one's life; love money as much as life itself; be greedy for money; be a money-grubber

【爱称】term of endearment; pet name

【爱戴】love and esteem: 老师博得了同学们的～。*The teacher has won the love and esteem of his (or her) students.*

【爱尔兰】Ireland ◇～人 the Irish; Irishman; ～语 Irish (language); ～共和军 Irish Republican Army

【爱抚】show tender care for: 她用～的眼光看着那个婴儿。*She looked at the baby tenderly.*

【爱国】love one's country; be patriotic: 他很～。*He is very patriotic.* / ～同胞们! *Patriotic fellow-countrymen!* / ～华侨 *patriotic overseas Chinese* ◇～人士 patriotic personage; ～统一战线 the patriotic united front; ～卫生运动 the patriotic health campaign; ～心 patriotic feeling; patriotism; ～者 patriot; ～主义 patriotism

【爱好】❶ take great pleasure in; have sth. as a hobby; be keen on: ～音乐 *like music* / ～京剧 *be keen on Beijing opera* / ～体育 *go in for sports* ❷ interest; hobby: 她的～是多方面的。*She has a wide range of interests.* / 你在文娱方面有什么～? *What kind of recreation do you go in for?*

【爱好者】lover (of art, sports, etc.); enthusiast; fan: 音乐～ *music-lover* / 体育～ *sports enthusiast; sports fan*

【爱护】cherish; treasure; take good care of: ～公物 *take good care of public property* / ～儿童 *take good care of children; bring up children with loving care*

【爱克斯光】X ray; Roentgen ray: 照～ *take an X-ray; have an X-ray taken* ◇～机 X-ray apparatus; ～透视 fluoroscopy; X-ray examination; ～照片 roentgenogram; X-ray; radiograph; ～诊断 X-ray diagnosis; roentgen diagnosis

【爱理不理】(又作'爱答不理') look cold and indifferent; be standoffish: 我去向他请教,他～的,不太愿意帮助我。*I went to consult him, but he was cold and indifferent and not very willing to help me out.*

【爱怜】show tender affection for: 她用～的目光看着那些孤儿。*She looked at the orphans with love and sympathy.*

【爱恋】be in love with; feel deeply attached to: 他深深地～着那位姑娘。*He is head over heels in love with the girl.* / 对乡土的～ *attachment to one's native soil*

【爱美】set great store by one's appearance; love to make up and wear beautiful clothes

【爱面子】be concerned about face-saving; be sensitive about one's reputation

【爱莫能助】be willing to help but unable to do so: 对不起,实在～! *I'm sorry. I'd love to help you but my hands are tied.*

【爱慕】adore; admire: 相互～ *adore each other* / ～虚荣 *be vain; be given to vanity*

【爱鸟周】Bird Protection Week

【爱琴海】Aegean Sea

【爱情】love (between man and woman): 他们之间已经有了很深的～。*They have a deep love for each other already.* / ～专一 *be constant in love*

【爱人】❶ husband or wife: 您～好吗? *How is your husband (or wife)?* / 你不知道他们是～关系吗? *Don't you know they are husband and wife?* ❷sweetheart; lover

【爱沙尼亚】Estonia ◇～人 Estonian; ～语 Estonian (language)

【爱神】god of love; Cupid

【爱斯基摩人】Eskimo

【爱屋及乌】love for a person extends even to the crows on his roof; love me, love my dog

【爱惜】value highly and use prudently; treasure: ～人才 *treasure men of talent* / ～时间 *make the best use of one's time; use time efficiently*

【爱心】love; sympathy; compassion: 让世界充满～。*Fill the world with love.* / 人人献出一片～。*Everybody offered his or her loving care.*

【爱憎分明】understand what to love and what to hate; know whom to love and whom to hate

隘 Ⅰ 形 narrow: ～巷 *a narrow lane; alley* Ⅱ 名

a narrow pass：要隘

【隘口】mountain pass

【隘路】defile；narrow passage

碍 动 hinder；obstruct；be in the way of：在这儿呆着吧，你～不着我。*Stay where you are. You're not in my way.* / 有～团结 *be harmful (or detrimental) to unity*

【碍口】be too embarrassing to mention：这事有点～，不好说。*It's rather embarrassing；I don't know how to bring it up.*

【碍面子】spare sb.'s feelings：碍着他爸爸的面子，我不好说什么。*I didn't say anything for fear of hurting his father's feelings.*

【碍事】〈口〉❶ be in the way；be a hindrance：这桌子放在门口太～了。*This table is too close to the door, it gets in the way.* ❷ (usu. used in the negative) be of consequence；matter：这不～。*It doesn't matter.* or *It's of no consequence.* / 她来不了不～。*It doesn't matter if she can't come.*

【碍手碍脚】be in the way；be a hindrance：你走开，别在这儿～的！*Get out of the way!* / 过道里放满了自行车，～的。*The corridor is crowded with bikes which get in everybody's way.*

【碍眼】be unpleasant to look at；offend the eye；be an eyesore：那些广告牌真～。*Those billboards are a real eyesore.*

【碍于情面】for fear of hurting sb.'s feelings；out of consideration for sb.'s feelings

嗳 叹 (expressing regret or annoyance)：～，早知道就好了。*Oh! If only I'd known sooner.* ——另见 ǎi

暧 形〈书〉(of daylight) dim

【暧昧】❶ ambiguous；equivocal：态度～ *assume an ambiguous attitude* ❷ shady；dubious：关系～ *dubious relationship*

ān

安 Ⅰ 形 ❶ peaceful；at ease；undisturbed；tranquil；calm：～睡 *sleep peacefully* ❷ safe；secure；in good health：～抵拉萨 *arrive in Lhasa safely (or safe and sound)* Ⅱ 动 ❶ set (sb.'s mind) at ease；calm：安神 ❷ rest content；be satisfied：安于现状 ❸ place in a suitable position；find a place for：把我～在哪儿都行。*I'll be happy with any job I'm assigned to.* or *I'll fit in contentedly anywhere.* ❹ install；fix；fit：～电灯 *install electric lights* / 窗玻璃～上了。*The windowpanes have been put in.* ❺ set up：咱们这儿～上电视转播站了。*A TV relay station has been set up here.* ❻ bring (a charge against sb.)；give (sb. a nickname)：～罪名 *bring charges against；put the blame on* / 我连去都没去，这个罪名可～不到我的头上。*I wasn't even there. There's no way to put the blame on me.*

【安邦定国】(of a ruler) bring peace and stability to the country

【安不忘危】mindful of possible danger in times of peace

【安步当车】stroll over instead of riding in a carriage；walk rather than ride

【安插】❶ place (sb.) in a certain position；assign to a job：这么多人叫我往哪儿～？*Where can I find positions for so many people?* / ～亲信 *put one's trusted followers in key positions* ❷ insert (an episode, etc.) into a story, play, article, etc.：作者在这里～了一段倒叙。*At this point the writer puts in a flashback.*

【安常处顺】stick to the status quo；go along with things as they are

【安道尔】Andorra ◇～人 Andorran

【安定】❶ stable；quiet；settled：～的生活 *a stable (or settled) life* / ～的社会环境 *a stable social environment* ❷ stabilize；maintain：～社会秩序 *maintain social order* / ～人心 *reassure the public；set people's minds at rest* ❸［药］diazepam

【安定团结】stability and unity：～的政治局面 *political stability and unity*

【安顿】❶ help settle down (or in)；get sth. or everything arranged；find a place for：家里都～好了吗？*Have you got everything settled at home?* / 妈妈把女儿～在托儿所里。*The woman found a place for her daughter in a nursery.* ❷ undisturbed；peaceful：病人吃了药，睡觉～多了。*The patient slept much better after taking the medicine.*

【安放】put in a proper place；lay：把仪器～好。*Put the instruments in their proper places.* / 这张两用沙发没有合适的地方～。*There's nowhere to put the sofa bed.*

【安分】not go beyond one's bounds；be law-abiding；know one's place：这孩子在课堂上一点也不～，老要搞小动作。*The boy doesn't behave himself in class；he's always playing some prank or other.*

【安分守己】abide by the law and behave oneself；be content with one's lot and act one's part；know one's place：我知道你是个老实人，你是～的。*I know you are an honest man, content with your lot and not causing any trouble.*

【安抚】aid and comfort (or console)；reassure and pacify；appease：～伤员 *aid and comfort the wounded* / ～人心 *reassure and pacify the public* / ～政策 *a policy aimed at appeasing the people*

【安哥拉】Angola ◇～人 Angolan

【安好】safe and sound；well：全家～，请勿挂念。*You will be pleased to know that everyone in the family is well.*

【安家】❶ settle down：他们在新疆安了家。*They settled in Xinjiang.* ❷ set up a home；get married：他收入不高，还没有条件～。*He isn't earning enough to get married and start a family.*

【安家费】allowance for setting up a home in a new

place；settling-in allowance；family allowance

【安家落户】make one's home (or take up residence) in a new place；settle：他们已经在海南岛～。*They have settled in Hainan*.

【安静】❶ quiet；peaceful：病人需要～。*The patient needs peace and quiet*. / 保持～！*Keep quiet*！❷ calm；undisturbed：周围安安静静的，没有任何异常情况。*Everything around was still and quiet. Nothing unusual happened*. ❸ quiet down：大幕一拉开，观众顿时～下来。*As soon as the curtain rose, the audience quieted down*.

【安居】settle down (in a place) ◇～房 low-cost apartments provided by the government；～工程 housing project for low-income urban residents；low-cost housing project；affordable housing project

【安居乐业】live and work in peace and contentment

【安康】in good health：祝您～！*Wishing you the best of health*！

【安乐】peaceful and happy；free from worry

【安乐死】mercy killing；euthanasia

【安乐窝】cosy nest：夫妇俩一直梦想着为自己建立一个～。*The couple always dreamed of building a cosy nest for themselves*.

【安乐椅】easy chair

【安理会】(〈略〉全称为'联合国安全理事会') the (U.N.) Security Council

【安眠】sleep peacefully ◇～酮［药］methaqualone；hyminal；～药 sleeping pill (or tablet)；soporific

【安民】pacify the people；reassure the public：～政策 *policies to reassure the public* ◇～告示 a notice to reassure the public；advance notice (of an agenda, etc.)

【安乃近】［药］analgin

【安宁】❶ peaceful；tranquil：两口子成天吵架，闹得左邻右舍不得～。*The couple are always bickering. They give their neighbours no peace*. ❷ calm；composed；free from worry：心里很不～ *feel rather worried*

【安宁片】［药］meprobamate

【安排】arrange (matters)；plan in detail；dispose (manpower)：为外宾～参观游览 *arrange visits and sightseeing trips for foreign guests* / 妥善～时间 *budget one's time well* / 合理～人力 *dispose available manpower rationally*

【安培】［电］Ampere ◇～计 ammeter；amperemeter；～小时 ampere-hour

【安全】safe；secure：～操作 *safe operation* / ～停车距离 *safe stopping distance* / ～高度 *safe altitude* / ～措施 *safety measures* / ～设施 *safety devices* / ～规程 *safety regulations* / 交通～ *traffic safety* / ～第一！*Safety first*！/～测验 *safety test* ◇～避孕法 rhythm method；～玻璃 safety glass；～带 safety belt；seat belt；～岛 safety island；pedestrian island；～感 sense of security；～简便 safe and handy；safe and simple；～帽 safety helmet；～门 exit；～期 safe period；～锁 safety lock；～套 condom；～梯 emergency staircase；fire escape；～剃刀 同〖保险刀〗；～通行证 safe-conduct；～网 safety netting；～系数 safety coefficient (or factor)；～月 the Safety Month

【安全灯】❶［矿］safety lamp ❷［摄］safelight

【安全理事会】the (U.N.) Security Council

【安然】❶ safe：～脱险 *be out of danger* ❷ be free from worry；feel at ease：～入睡 *go to sleep peacefully* / 只有把这件事告诉他，他心里才会～。*He will never feel at ease unless we tell him about this*.

【安然无恙】safe and sound；(escape) unscathed

【安如磐石】as firm (or solid) as a rock

【安如泰山】as solid as Mount Tai；as firm (or solid) as a rock

【安设】install；set up：在山顶上～一个气象观测站 *set up a weather station on the mountaintop*

【安身】have a roof over one's head；take shelter：无处～ *have no roof over one's head；have nowhere to live；be homeless and shelterless*

【安身立命】*settle down and get on with one's work*

【安神】❶ calm (or soothe) the nerves ❷［中］relieve uneasiness of body and mind ◇～药［中］sedative；tranquillizer

【安生】❶ peaceful；restful：过～日子 *live a peaceful and restful life* / 那帮小青年吵得邻居们不得～。*Those youngsters raised such a ruckus. They gave their neighbours no peace*. ❷ (usu. of children) quiet；still；untroublesome：这孩子即便睡觉也不～。*The kid won't keep still, not even in sleep*.

【安适】quiet and comfortable：～的环境 *a quiet and comfortable environment*

【安替比林】［药］antipyrine

【安土重迁】love one's homeland and not wish to leave it；hate to leave one's native land

【安危】safety and danger；safety：不顾个人～ *be heedless of one's personal safety*

【安慰】❶ be comforted；feel encouraged：我听了这些话心里很～。*I felt much comforted at hearing these words*. ❷ comfort；console：我～了他几句。*I said a few words to comfort him (or gave him a few words of comfort)*. / 自我～ *console oneself* ❸ consolation；comfort：孩子成了她惟一的～。*The child became her only consolation*. ◇～剂［医］placebo；～奖 consolation prize；～赛［体］consolation event (or match)

【安稳】❶ smooth and steady：船走得很～ *The boat sailed smoothly*. / 睡得很～ *sleep peacefully* ❷〈方〉calm and poised

【安息】❶ rest；go to sleep ❷ rest in peace：烈士们，～吧！*May the revolutionary martyrs rest in peace*！❸ Parthia (an ancient country) ◇～日 Sabbath (day)；～香 benzoin (the plant, the resin, or the perfume)

【安闲】peaceful and carefree；relaxed；leisurely：～自在 *leisurely and carefree* / ～的心情 *a relaxed mood*

【安详】serene; composed; unruffled: 举止～ *behave with composure* / 在那危急的时刻，他还保持着～的神态。*At the critical juncture, he still kept his composure.*

【安歇】go to bed; retire for the night

【安心】❶ feel at ease; be relieved; set one's mind at rest: 他怎么也安不下心来做事。*He simply can't set his mind to work.* ❷ keep one's mind on sth.: ～工作 *keep one's mind on one's work; work contentedly*

【安逸】easy and comfortable; easy: ～的生活 *an easy life*

【安营】pitch a camp; camp: 大军在那片树林里～造饭。*The army camped in the forest and started to prepare food.* ◇ ～扎寨 pitch a camp; camp

【安于】be content or satisfied with a state of affairs: ～落后，不求上进 *be quite satisfied with one's backward state (or be satisfied with oneself) and not wish to do any better* ◇ ～现状 be content with things as they are; be satisfied with the existing state of affairs

【安葬】bury (the dead): 把他的遗骸送回去～ *escort his remains back to his home town for burial* / 举行了隆重的～仪式。*A solemn burial service was held.*

【安枕】arrange the pillow—go to bed: 祸根不除，大家不得～。*We can't rest in peace if this evil is not eradicated.*

【安之若素】❶ bear (hardship, etc.) with equanimity ❷ regard (wrongdoing, etc.) with indifference

【安置】find a suitable place, position, job, etc. for; arrange for the placement of: 把行李～好 *put the luggage in the right place* / 我们把家～好了再说。*We'll see about it after we have set up our home.* ◇ ～费 placement or settlement allowance

【安装】install; fix; set up: ～电话 *install a telephone* / ～机器 *install machinery* / ～扩音器 *set up a megaphone*

桉 名 [植] eucalyptus

【桉树】eucalyptus

【桉油】volatile oil extracted from eucalyptus' leaves or twigs

氨 名 [化] ammonia: 合成～ *synthetic ammonia*

【氨苯磺胺】[药] sulfanilamide

【氨茶碱】[药] aminophylline

【氨化】ammoniation

【氨基】amino; amino-group

【氨基比林】[药] aminopyrine

【氨基酸】amino acid

【氨碱法】[化] ammonia soda process

【氨硫脲】[药] thiacetazone

【氨溶液】ammonia solution

【氨水】ammonia solution; ammonia (water); aqua ammoniae

谙 动〈书〉know well: 不～水性 *not know how to swim* / 素～针灸之术 *be highly skilled in administering acupuncture and moxibustion*

【谙练】〈书〉conversant; skilled; proficient

【谙熟】be proficient in; be conservant with: ～汉语 *be well versed in the Chinese language*

庵 名 ❶〈书〉hut: 草～ *a thatched hut* ❷ nunnery; Buddhist convent

【庵堂】〈方〉nunnery; Buddhist convent

鹌 (构词成分)见下

【鹌鹑】quail (a bird)

鞍 名 saddle

【鞍部】a ridge connecting two higher elevations; saddle (of a hill or mountain)

【鞍点】saddle point ◇ ～定理 saddle point theorem

【鞍环】handle; pommed

【鞍马】❶ [体] pommelled horse; side horse ❷〈书〉saddle and horse—horseback riding: ～生活 *life on horseback—soldiering*

【鞍子】saddle

ǎn

铵 名 [化] ammonium

揞 动 apply medicinal powder to (a wound): 你手上的伤口比较深，最好～上一点儿消炎粉。*The cut in your hand is rather deep. You'd better apply some powder to it.*

àn

岸 Ⅰ 名 bank; shore; coast: 江～ *the bank of a river; river bank* / 上～ *go ashore* / 小河两～柳树成行。*On either bank of the stream stand rows of willow trees.* Ⅱ 形〈书〉❶ lofty; tall and big: 伟岸 ❷ proud: 傲岸

【岸标】shore beacon

【岸然】〈书〉in a solemn manner

【岸上交货价格】landed terms

【岸线】water front

按 Ⅰ 动 ❶ press; push down: ～电钮 *press (or push) a button* / ～门铃 *ring a doorbell* / ～手印 *put one's fingerprint on (a document, etc.)* / 把他～倒在地 *push him down on the ground* ❷ leave aside; shelve: ～下此事不提 *leave this aside for the moment* ❸ restrain; control: ～不住心头怒火 *be unable to restrain (or control) one's anger* ❹ keep one's hand on; keep a tight grip on: ～住操纵杆 *keep a tight grip on the control lever* ❺〈书〉check; refer to: 有原文可～。*There's the original to refer to.* Ⅱ 介 according to; in accordance with; in the light of; on the basis of：～比例发展 *develop in proportion*；*proportional development* / ～年代顺序排列 *arrange in chronological order* Ⅲ 名 (of an editor or author) make a comment：编者～ *editor's note*

【按比例】pro rata；in proportion

【按兵不动】❶ hold one's troops where they are；not throw one's troops into battle ❷ take no action；bide one's time：大家都干起来了，你怎么还～呢？*Everybody else has started work. Why do you sit there doing nothing?*

【按部就班】follow the prescribed order；keep to conventional ways of doing things：学习应该～，循序渐进。*In studying it is imperative to follow the proper order and advance step by step.*

【按成】according to percentage；proportionately：～计算 *reckon in terms of percentages* / ～分配红利 *distribute the bonuses proportionately*

【按方配药】have a prescription filled at the pharmacy；make up a prescription

【按股分红】share profits according to contribution；sharing profits according to contributions

【按键】button：波段选择～ *push-button for selecting wavebands* /重放～ *playback button* /倒带～ *re-wind button* /录音～ *record button* /抹音～ *erase cut-out button* /暂停～ *pause button*

【按件计工】reckon by the piece：实行～ *adopt the piecework system*

【按揭】(usu. used in real estate) mortgage：～购房 *take out a mortgage to buy a house*；*buy a house on time* / ～贷款 *mortgage loan* / ～利率 *mortgage (interest) rate* / 首期～ *down-payment* / 从事～业务 *be in the house-mortgaging business*

【按劳分配】distribution according to work ——另见〖各尽所能，按劳分配〗

【按理】(又作'按理说') according to principle or reason；in the ordinary course of events；normally：这种病～不该有并发症。*Normally there are no complications with this illness.* / ～不应当这么办。*Logically, it shouldn't be done this way.*

【按脉】feel (or take) the pulse

【按摩】massage ◇ ～疗法 massotherapy；～器 massager；～师 massager；massagist

【按捺】(又作'按纳') restrain；control

【按捺不住】cannot control (or contain) oneself：～激动的心情 *be unable to suppress one's excitement* / ～心中的仇恨 *be unable to suppress any longer the bitterness in one's heart*

【按年摊付】yearly installments

【按钮】push button ◇～控制 push button control；dash control；～战争 press-button warfare

【按期】on schedule；on time：这项工作我们必须～完成。*We must complete this job on schedule.* / ～交货 *deliver goods on schedule*

【按时】on time；on schedule：～到达 *arrive on time* / 我们一定～开会，不要迟到。*We will begin the meeting at the appointed hour. Don't be late.*

【按说】in the ordinary course of events；ordinarily；normally：～这时候该下雪了。*Ordinarily it should be snowing at this time of the year.*

【按图索骥】look for a steed with the aid of its picture—❶ try to find sth. by following up a clue ❷ deal with (or handle) a matter in a mechanical way

【按蚊】anopheles；malarial mosquito

【按下葫芦浮起瓢】hardly has one gourd been pushed under water when another bobs up - solve one problem only to find another cropping up

【按需分配】distribution according to need ——另见〖各尽所能，按需分配〗

【按压】❶ press down with one's hand：他作了个往下～的手势。*He made a gesture with his hand pressing downward.* ❷ suppress；restrain：～不住心头怒火 *can't suppress one's anger*

【按语】a note or comment (by an author or editor on a piece of writing or certain parts of it)

【按照】according to；in accordance with；in the light of；on the basis of：～宪法规定的基本原则 *according to the fundamental principles laid down in the constitution* / ～等价交换的原则 *in accordance with the principle of exchange of equal values*

【按质分等】grade according to the quality

案 名 ❶ an old-fashioned long, narrow table or desk：条案 ❷ a long board propped up to serve as a table or counter：～上摆着各色日用小百货。*A variety of small articles of daily use are displayed on the propped-up counter.* ❸ law case；case：破案 ❹ record；file：在案 ❺ a plan submitted for consideration；proposal：提案

【案板】kneading (or chopping) board (usu. rectangular)

【案秤】counter scale

【案牍】〈书〉official documents or correspondence

【案犯】[法] case criminal：～全部抓获。*The criminals in the case have all been captured.*

【案件】law case；case：刑事～ *a criminal case*

【案卷】records；files；archives

【案例】[法] case：～分析 *case analysis*

【案情】details of a case；case：了解～ *investigate the details of a case* / ～相当复杂。*The case is quite complicated.*

【案头】on the table or desk：这项计划还剩下一些～工作要做。*There is still some desk work to be done before we can finish the project.* ◇～日历 desk calendar

【案验】〈书〉investigate the evidence of a case

【案由】the main points (or a brief summary) of a case；brief

【案语】同〖按语〗

【案子】❶ a long, narrow table or a long board propped up to serve as a table or counter：乒乓球～ *ping-pong table* / 肉～ *meat counter* ❷

〈口〉law case；case

胺 名［化］amine

【胺化】amination

【胺盐】amine salt

暗 Ⅰ形 ❶ dark；dim；dull：天色渐渐～下来了。*It's getting dark.* / 灯光很～。*The light is rather dim.* / 这间屋子光线太～。*This room is too dark.* / ～紫色 *dull purple* / ～绿 *dark green* ❷ unclear；hazy：若明若暗 Ⅱ副 hidden；secret：～下决心 *make up one's mind secretly*

【暗暗】secretly；inwardly；to oneself：～跟踪 *secretly follow sb.* / 我～吃了一惊。*I was startled but didn't show it.*

【暗堡】［军］bunker

【暗病】同〖暗疾〗

【暗藏】hide；conceal：～枪枝 *conceal firearms；illegally possess firearms*

【暗娼】a disguised prostitute；unlicensed (or unregistered) prostitute

【暗潮】〈喻〉undercurrent

【暗处】❶ a dark place：猫头鹰白天躲在～。*Owls stay in dark places in the daytime.* ❷ a secret place；a covert place；cover

【暗袋】［摄］camera bag (for changing film)

【暗淡】dim；faint；dismal；gloomy：～的颜色 *a dull colour* / ～的景象 *a dismal picture* / 屋里灯光～。*The room is dimly lit.*

【暗地里】(又作'暗地') secretly；inwardly；on the sly：～做了些不可告人的事 *do something secretly which cannot be told to anybody* / ～捣鬼 *secretly make trouble* / 我们～替他高兴。*We inwardly rejoiced for him.*

【暗渡陈仓】(of a man and a woman) enter into a secret liaison ——另见〖明修栈道，暗渡陈仓〗

【暗访民情】make secret inquires into the condition of the people

【暗沟】underground drainage ditch；underground drain

【暗害】❶ kill secretly ❷ stab in the back

【暗含】imply：他的回答～着对我们工作的批评。*His reply implied a criticism of our work.*

【暗号】a secret signal (or sign)；countersign；watchword

【暗合】be in complete agreement without prior consultation；(happen to) coincide

【暗河】underground river

【暗盒】［摄］magazine；cassette

【暗疾】a disease one is ashamed of；unmentionable disease

【暗记儿】secret mark

【暗间儿】inner room (usu. used as a bedroom or storeroom)

【暗箭】an arrow shot from hiding—an attack by a hidden enemy；a stab in the back

【暗箭伤人】stab sb. in the back；injure sb. by underhand means

【暗箭难防】hidden arrows are difficult to guard

【暗礁】❶ submerged reef (or rock) ❷ latent obstacle

【暗流】undercurrent

【暗码锁】combination lock

【暗盘】〈旧〉secretly negotiated price

【暗器】hidden weapon (as darts hidden inside sleeves)

【暗杀】assassinate

【暗伤】❶ internal (or invisible) injury ❷ indiscernible damage

【暗射】insinuate

【暗射地图】a map with locations marked but not labelled (a teaching aid to train learners in identifying places on a map)

【暗示】❶ drop a hint；hint；suggest：他～我快走开。*He hinted that he wanted me to leave at once.* / 她没有懂我的～。*She didn't take my hint.* ❷［心理］suggestion

【暗事】clandestine or illicit action：明人不做暗事

【暗室】［摄］darkroom

【暗适应】［心理］dark adaptation

【暗送秋波】make eyes at sb.；give sb. the glad eye；ogle；make secret overtures to sb.

【暗算】plot against：遭人～ *fall a prey to a plot* / ～别人 *plot against sb.*

【暗锁】built-in lock

【暗滩】hidden shoal

【暗探】secret agent；spy

【暗无天日】complete darkness—total absence of justice

【暗喜】feel pleased but not show it：不由得心中～ *cannot help feeling secretly pleased*

【暗线光谱】［物］dark-line spectrum

【暗箱】［摄］camera bellows；camera obscura

【暗想】muse；ponder；turn over in one's mind

【暗笑】laugh in one's sleeve；snigger；snicker

【暗影】❶ shadow ❷［天］umbra

【暗语】code word

【暗喻】metaphor

【暗中】❶ in the dark：我在～什么也看不见。*I couldn't see anything in the dark.* ❷ in secret；on the sly；surreptitiously：～操纵 *pull strings from behind the scenes* / ～策划 *plot in the dark* /～支持 *give secret support to* / ～串通 *collude with；conspire* /～行贿 *cross sb's hand with silver* /～摸索 *grope in the dark*

【暗转】［戏］blackout in the middle of a scene or act (to indicate either a change in time, or, with a quick change of setting, a change in place)

【暗自】inwardly；to oneself；secretly：～落泪 *cry to oneself；shed a tear in secret*

【暗自庆幸】congratulate oneself；consider oneself lucky

黯 形 dim；gloomy

【黯然】〈书〉❶ dark and dim-looking：工地上千万盏电灯光芒四射，连天上的星月也～无光。*The worksite was ablaze with thousands of lights so that even the moon and the stars appeared lustre-*

less in comparison. ❷ dejected; low-spirited; downcast: 神色～ *appear dejected* / 听到那消息，她不禁～泪下。*The news dampened her spirits and set tears rolling down her cheeks*.

【黯然神伤】feel dejected (or depressed)

【黯然失色】be cast into the shade; be overshadowed; be eclipsed; pale into insignificance

āng

肮 (构词成分)见下

【肮脏】❶ dirty; filthy: ～的衣服 *dirty clothes* / ～的阴沟 *a filthy sewer* / 这孩子浑身上下肮里肮脏的。*The boy was covered all over with dirt*. ❷ vile; mean; foul; dirty: ～的勾当 *dirty work*; *a foul deed* / ～的政治交易 *a dirty political deal*

áng

昂 Ⅰ 动 hold (one's head) high: ～起头，挺起胸 *hold up one's head and throw out one's chest*; *chin up and chest out* Ⅱ 形 high; soaring: 战天斗地志气～ *battle against nature with high resolve*

【昂昂】high-spirited; brave-looking

【昂贵】expensive; costly: 价格～ *be high-priced* / ～的首饰 *costly jewels*

【昂然】chin up and chest out; upright and unafraid: 他～直入。*He strode in, chin up and chest out*.

【昂首】hold one's head high

【昂首阔步】stride along with one's chin up; stride proudly ahead

【昂扬】high-spirited: ～的歌声 *spirited singing*

àng

盎 Ⅰ 名 an ancient vessel with a big belly and a small mouth Ⅱ 形〈书〉brimming; abundant

【盎然】abundant; full; exuberant: 趣味～ *be full of interest*

【盎司】(又作'盎斯') ounce

āo

凹 形 concave; sunken; dented: ～鼻梁儿 *a flat nose*

【凹岸】concave bank

【凹版】[刷] intaglio; gravure: 照相～ *photogravure* ◇ ～印刷 intaglio (or gravure) printing; ～印刷机 intaglio (or gravure) press; ～制版 gravure plate-making

【凹槽】beard; fillister

【凹地】concave ground; depression

【凹度】concavity

【凹面镜】concave mirror

【凹透镜】concave lens

【凹凸不平】full of bumps and holes; uneven

【凹凸轧花】[纺] embossing

【凹凸印刷】embossing; die stamping

【凹凸印刷机】embossing (or die stamping) press

【凹陷】cave in; sink: 地面～。*The ground caved in*. / 双颊～ *have sunken (or hollow) cheeks*

【凹纹印刷】spanishing

【凹字】characters cut in bas-relief

熬 动 stew (vegetables, etc.) in water: ～白菜 *stewed cabbage* / 豆腐～好了没有? *Has the bean curd been stewed long enough*? ——另见 áo

áo

遨 动 stroll; saunter

【遨游】go on a pleasure tour; travel: ～海上 *go on a cruise* / ～太空 *travel through space*

嗷 (构词成分)见下

【嗷嗷】the sound of crying (of certain birds or animals, or of human beings in pain or suffering): 疼得～叫 *howl with pain* / 雁群～地飞过。*Flocks of honking geese flew past*.

【嗷嗷待哺】(of starving people or young animals) cry piteously for food

熬 动 ❶ cook (cereals, etc.) into porridge or thick soup: ～粥 *make gruel* / ～一锅汤 *prepare a pot of soup* / 汤快～干了。*The soup is overstewed*; *it's nearly dried up*. / 用微火～ *simmer* ❷ extract sth.'s essence by long boiling: ～药 *decoct Chinese medicine by boiling and simmering medicinal herbs, etc. in water* ❸ endure (distress, hard times, etc.); hold out: 他眼睛都～红了。*His eyes are bloodshot through staying up late all night*. / 他的病怕～不过冬天了。*I doubt if he will live through the winter*. ——另见 āo

【熬煎】suffering; torment; torture: 受尽～ *be subjected to all kinds of sufferings (or afflictions)* / 她经不住这样的～，过早地离开了人世。*Unable to endure such torments, she came to an untimely end*.

【熬夜】stay up late (or all night): 天天～，谁受得了? *Who can keep on staying up late night after night*?

螯 名 chela; pincers (of crustaceans, etc.)

翱 动〈书〉take wing

【翱翔】hover; soar: 海鸥在惊涛骇浪上～。*Seagulls hover over the surging waves*. / ～长空的女飞行员 *women pilots soaring in the skies* ◇ ～机 sailplane

鏖 动〈书〉engage in fierce battle

【鏖战】〈书〉fight hard; engage in fierce battle: 两军～三日。*The two armies were fiercely engaged for three days*. / 两队～九十分钟，不分胜负。*Af-*

ter a fierce 90-minute contest, the score was even.

ǎo

袄 名 a lined Chinese-style coat or jacket：小～ *a short close-fitting jacket*

ào

坳 名 low-lying land between or amidst higher points in a mountain range；col：珠峰北～ *the North Col of Mount Qomolangma (Mount Everest)*

拗 动 defy；disobey：违拗 ——另见 niù

【拗口】be hard to pronounce (esp. rapidly)；be awkward reading：这两句念起来～。*These two lines do not read smoothly.* ◇～令 tongue twister

傲 Ⅰ形 proud；haughty：这个人～得很，可不好接近了。*That fellow is extremely haughty and standoffish.* Ⅱ动 refuse to yield to；brave；defy：红梅～雪凌霜开。*Braving snow and frost, the plum trees blossomed defiantly.*

【傲岸】〈书〉proud；haughty：～的青松 *a proud and towering pine tree* ◇～不群 haughty and standoffish；proud and aloof

【傲骨】unbending backbone—lofty and unyielding character：他生就一身～，宁折不弯。*A man of unyielding character, he would rather break than bend.*

【傲慢】arrogant；haughty；overbearing：态度～ *be arrogant；put on airs；give oneself airs；hold one's nose in the air* / 他的～无礼激起了大家的愤怒。*His overbearing insolence angered everyone.*

【傲气】❶ air of arrogance；haughtiness：～十足 *full of arrogance；extremely haughty* ❷ arrogant；haughty：她可～了。*She's very haughty.*

【傲然】lofty and proud-looking；unyielding：～挺立的山峰 *a mountain peak towering proudly into the skies*

【傲视】regard with disdain；turn up one's nose at；show disdain for

奥 Ⅰ形 profound and difficult to understand；abstruse：深奥 Ⅱ名〈书〉the southwestern corner or the innermost part of a house

【奥比奖】Obie

【奥地利】Austria ◇～奥地利人 Austrian

【奥林匹克运动会】Olympic Games

【奥纶】［纺］orlon

【奥秘】profound mystery：探索宇宙的～ *probe the mysteries of the universe*

【奥妙】profound and subtle：神奇～ *mysterious and profound* / ～无穷 *extremely subtle* / 不难看出其中的～。*It's not difficult to see what's behind it.*

【奥氏体】［冶］austenite：～钢 *austenitic steel*

【奥斯特】［物］oersted (Oe)

【奥斯卡金像奖】Oscar (award for film)

【奥陶纪】［地质］the Ordovician Period

【奥委会】Olympic Committee

【奥运会】〈略〉见〖奥林匹克运动会〗

【奥运实况转播】a telecast live on TV for the Olympic Games

澳 名 ❶ (usu. used as part of a place name) an inlet of the sea；bay：三都～ *Sandu Bay* ❷〈略〉见〖澳门〗：港～同胞 *compatriots in Hong Kong and Macao* ❸〈略〉见〖澳大利亚〗

【澳大利亚】Australia ◇～人 Australian

【澳抗】Australia antigen；hepatitis-associated antigen (HAA)

【澳门】Aomen (Macao) ◇～特别行政区 the Macao Special Administrative Region；～特别行政区基本法 the Basic Law of Macao Special Administrative Region

懊 形 ❶ regretful；remorseful：懊悔 ❷ annoyed；vexed：懊恼

【懊悔】feel remorse；repent；regret：我～不该错怪了她。*I regretted having blamed her unjustly.* / 现在你不好好学习，将来你自会～的。*If you don't study hard now, you will regret it in the future.*

【懊恼】be annoyed, vexed or upset；fret：他工作没做好，心里很～。*He was quite upset at not having done his work well.* / 她正为自己丢失了钱包而～呢。*She's fretting over the loss of her purse.*

【懊丧】feel dejected (or depressed)

B

bā

八 数 eight：～公斤 *eight kilos* / ～个班 *eight classes* / ～班 *the eighth class*；*class 8*
【八宝】eight treasures (choice ingredients of certain special dishes)
【八宝菜】eight-treasure pickles；assorted soy-sauce pickles
【八宝饭】eight-treasure rice pudding (steamed glutinous rice with bean paste，lotus seeds，preserved fruits，etc.)
【八宝山】Eight-Treasure Mountain (or Babaoshan— a place in western Beijing，known for its cemetery)：上～ *go to Babaoshan* (*Cemetery*)—*die*
【八辈子】〈口〉of long standing；of the worst kind：我倒了～霉了。*I couldn't have worse luck*. or *I'm up to my neck in trouble*.
【八倍体】octoploid
【八成】❶ eighty per cent：～新 *eighty per cent new*；*practically new* / 事情有了～啦。*It's almost as good as settled*. or *There's a fair chance of success*. ❷ most probably；most likely：～儿他不来了。*Most probably he isn't coming*.
【八度】octave
【八方】the eight points of the compass；all directions：一方有难，～支援。*When trouble occurs at one spot*，*help comes from all quarters*. ——另见〖四面八方〗
【八方呼应】responses from every direction；cooperation from all
【八分音符】quaver；eighth note
【八分之一决赛】eighth-finals
【八哥儿】myna
【八股】❶ eight-part essay ❷ stereotyped writing
【八卦】the Eight Trigrams
【八级风】［气］force 8 wind；fresh gale
【八级工】eight-grade worker (highest on the eight-grade wage scale)；top-grade worker
【八角】❶ anise；star anise ❷ aniseed
【八角枫】alangium
【八角帽】octagonal cap
【八角形】octagon
【八进位制】octal (number) system
【八九不离十】about right；pretty close；very near：猜个～ *make a very close guess* / 这些估计虽然不是绝对保险，但也～。*These calculations*，*though not always one hundred percent accurate*，*were never far out*.
【八开】［刷］octavo；8vo ◇ ～本 octavo
【八路军】the Eighth Route Army
【八面玲珑】be smooth and slick (in establishing social relations)
【八面威风】an aura of awesome might；a commanding presence
【八旗】the "Eight Banners"
【八色联合印花机】8-color combined printing machine
【八仙过海，各显神通】like the Eight Immortals crossing the sea，each one showing his or her special prowess：没有统一计划，你们就～吧。*There's no unified plan*，*so you'll all be on your own resources and prove your worth*.
【八仙桌】Eight Immortals table—an old-fashioned square table for eight people
【八小时工作制】eight-hour day
【八音盒】(又作'八音匣子') music box；musical box
【八月】❶ August ❷ the eighth month of the lunar year；the eighth moon ◇ ～节 the Mid-Autumn Festival (the 15th day of the 8th lunar month)
【八折】20 per cent discount：打～ *give* 20 *per cent discount*；*charge* 80 *per cent of the original price* / 这是～买的。*This was bought at* 20 *per cent discount*.
【八珍】eight delicacies：～蛇羹 *snake potage with eight delicacies*
【八字】Eight Characters ◇ ～步 a measured gait with the toes pointing outwards；～胡 mustache shaped like character；～脚 splayfoot；～眉 slanted eyebrows
【八字还没一撇儿】there's not even the first stroke of the character 八—things aren't even starting to take shape yet；there's not the slightest sign of success yet：你的喜事准备得怎么样了？——～呢。*How are the wedding preparations going*？—*Oh*，*we haven't even got off the ground yet*.
【八字帖儿】a card with the horoscope of a boy or girl sent as a proposal for betrothal

巴 Ⅰ 动 ❶ hope earnestly；wait anxiously：巴望 ❷ cling to；stick to：爬山虎～在墙上。*The ivy clings to the wall*. / 粥～了锅了。*The porridge has stuck to the pot*. ❸〈方〉be close to；be next to：前不巴村，后不巴店 Ⅱ 名 ❶ crust：锅巴 ❷［物］bar：微～ *microbar*

【巴巴多斯】Barbados ◇～人 Barbadian
【巴比伦】Babylon
【巴比特合金】babbitt (metal)
【巴比妥】[药] barbitone; barbital
【巴布亚新几内亚】Papua New Guinea ◇～人 Papua New Guinean
【巴不得】〈口〉be only too anxious (to do sth.); eagerly look forward to; earnestly wish: 我～天快晴。*I wish it would clear up soon.* / 这是～的好事。*This is the best thing we can wish for.*
【巴斗】同〖笆斗〗
【巴豆】[植] (purging) croton
【巴豆霜】[中] defatted croton seed powder
【巴儿狗】pekingese; sycophant; toady
【巴尔干半岛】the Balkan Peninsula
【巴尔干国家】Balkan states; the Balkans
【巴哈马】the Bahamas ◇～人 Bahamian
【巴基斯坦】Pakistan ◇～人 Pakistani
【巴结】fawn on; curry favour with; make up to: ～阔人 *fawn on rich people*
【巴拉圭】Paraguay ◇～人 Paraguayan
【巴勒斯坦】Palestine ◇～人 Palestinian
【巴勒斯坦解放组织】the Palestine Liberation Organization (PLO)
【巴黎公社】the Paris Commune
【巴黎绿】[化] Paris green
【巴林】Bahrain ◇～人 Bahraini
【巴龙霉素】[药] paromomycin
【巴拿马】Panama ◇～人 Panamanian; ～运河 the Panama Canal
【巴士】bus (a transliteration)
【巴士底狱】the Bastille
【巴望】〈方〉❶ look forward to; hope: 我真～我们再也不分开了。*I hope we'll never separate again.* ❷ good prospects: 这事总算有了～了。*Things are looking up now.*
【巴西】Brazil ◇～人 Brazilian
【巴掌】palm; hand: 拍～ *clap one's hands* / 打他一～ *give him a slap* / 现在连～大的地方都利用上了。*Now, every square inch of land is utilized.*

扒 动 ❶ hold on to; cling to: 孩子们～着窗台看游行队伍。*Holding on to the windowsill, the children watched the parade.* ❷ dig up; rake; pull down: ～土 *rake earth* / ～了旧房盖新房 *pull down the old house to build a new one in its place* / 城墙～了个豁口。*A breach was made in the city wall.* ❸ push aside: ～开芦苇 *push aside the reeds* ❹ strip off; take off: ～兔皮 *skin a rabbit* ——另见 pá
【扒车】climb onto a slow-going train, etc.
【扒钉】cramp
【扒拉】push lightly: 把压在苗上的土～开 *flick the earth off the seedlings* / ～算盘子儿 *move the beads of an abacus up and down; click away at an abacus*

芭 名 a fragrant plant (mentioned in ancient texts)
【芭蕉】plantain; Chinese banana
【芭蕾舞】ballet: 跳～ *dance ballet* ◇～剧 ballet; ～迷 balletomane; ～设计 choreography; ～演员 ballet dancer

吧 Ⅰ 象 ～的一声,弦断了。*The string broke with a snap.* / ～～两声枪响。*Crack! Crack! Two shots rang out.* Ⅱ 名 bar
【吧嗒】(bādā) patter; splatter: ～一声,门关上了。*The door clicked shut.*
【吧嗒】(bāda) ❶ smack one's lips (in surprise, alarm, etc.): 他～了一下嘴。一声也不言语。*He smacked his lips but did not utter a word.* ❷ 〈方〉pull at (a pipe, etc): 他～着叶子烟打主意。*He puffed at his pipe as he wondered what to do.*
【吧女】barmaid; bar girl

疤 名 scar: 刀伤在他的膝盖上留下了一个～。*The cut left a scar on his knee.* / 香烟在桌面上烧了一个～。*The burning cigarette left a mark on the top of the table.*
【疤瘌】(又作'疤拉') scar: ～脸 *scarred face*
【疤痕】scar

笆 名 basketry: 竹篾～ *bamboo basketry*
【笆斗】round-bottomed basket

bá

拔 动 ❶ pull out; pull up: ～草 *pull up weeds; weed* / ～麦子 *harvest wheat (by pulling it up)* / ～牙 *pull out (or extract) a tooth* / ～剑 *draw one's sword* ❷ suck out; draw: 把火～一～。*Put a chimney on the stove to make the fire draw.* ❸ choose; select; pick: 选拔 ❹ lift; raise: ～起嗓子直嚷 *shout at the top of one's voice* ❺ stand out among; surpass: 海拔 ❻ capture; seize
【拔除】pull out; remove
【拔萃】〈书〉stand out from one's fellows; be out of the common run: ～出群 *stand head and shoulders above others; be outstanding*
【拔刀相助】unsheathe one's sword and go to the rescue of another (for the sake of justice); take up the cudgels against an injustice: 路见不平,～。*When a man sees somebody being wantonly attacked on the road, he will immediately go to his rescue.*
【拔钉锤】claw hammer
【拔毒】[中] draw out pus by applying a plaster to the affected part
【拔高】❶ raise: 他～嗓子喊叫。*He shouted at the top of his voice.* ❷ deliberately boost (sb. or sth.); play up: ～人物 *make a character (in a novel, etc.) larger than life; make a person better than he or she actually is* / 对这部电视系列片的评价,显然有故意～的倾向。*There is apparently a tendency to overrate this TV series.*
【拔罐子】[中] cupping

【拔河】tug-of-war
【拔火罐儿】(又作'拔火筒') detachable stove chimney
【拔尖儿】〈口〉❶ tiptop; top-notch: 他的学习成绩是～的。*He is a top-notch student*. ❷ push oneself forward; be pushy
【拔节】[农] jointing: ～期 *jointing* (*or elongation*) *stage*
【拔锚】weigh anchor
【拔苗助长】try to help the shoots grow by pulling them upward—spoil things by excessive enthusiasm
【拔染】[纺] discharge: ～剂 *discharging agent*; *discharge*
【拔丝】❶ [机] wire drawing: ～机 *wire drawing bench* (*or machine*) ❷ candied floss: ～山药 *hot candied yam*
【拔腿】❶ lift the foot (and begin to run, chase, etc.): ～就跑 *start running away at once*; *immediately take to one's heels* / ～就追 *give instant chase* ❷ leave (one's work); get away; free oneself: 他事情太多,拔不开腿。*He is too busy with his work to get away*.
【拔牙】extract teeth: 我拔去两颗牙。*I had two teeth pulled out*.
【拔秧】[农] pull up seedlings (for transplanting)
【拔营】[军] strike camp

跋 Ⅰ 动 cross mountains Ⅱ 名 postscript (to a book)
【跋扈】domineering; bossy
【跋山涉水】scale mountains and ford streams—travel afar under difficult conditions
【跋涉】trudge; trek
【跋文】postscript (to a book)

bǎ

把 Ⅰ 动 ❶ hold; grasp: ～住栏杆 *hold on to a railing* / ～着手教 *take sb. by the hand and teach him how to do sth*. / ～犁 *handle a plough* ❷ hold (a baby while it relieves itself): 给孩子～尿 *hold a baby out to let it urinate* ❸ guard; watch Ⅱ 名 ❶ handle (of a pushcart, etc.): 自行车～ *the handlebars of a bicycle* ❷ bundle; bunch: 草～ *a bundle of straw* Ⅲ 量 ❶ (for sth. with a handle): 一～刀 *a knife* / 一～茶壶 *a teapot* / 一～扇子 *a fan* ❷ handful of: 一～米 *a handful of rice* / 一～花 ❸ a bunch of flowers (for certain abstract ideas): 有一～年纪 *be getting on in years* / 有～力气 *be quite strong* / 加～劲 *make an extra effort*; *put on a spurt* / 一～好手 ❹ an efficient or skillful worker (for sth. done with the hand): 拉他一～ *give him a tug*; *give* (*or lend*) *him a hand* Ⅳ 介 (used to shift the object to before the verb, which must be reduplicated or accompanied by some other word or expression): ～衣服洗洗 *have the clothes washed* / ～头一扭 *toss one's head* / ～衣服撕了个口子 *tear a hole in one's jacket* Ⅴ 助 (used after 百,千,万,里,丈,顷,斤,个,etc., the combination admitting of no numeral) about; or so: 个～月 *about a month*; *a month or so* / 百～人 *some hundred people* ——另见 bà
【把柄】handle: 给人抓住～ *give sb. a handle* (*against oneself*) / 他抓住了你什么～? *What hold does he have on you*? / 不要给别人留下～。*Don't do anything that others can hold against you*.
【把持】❶ 〈贬〉 dominate; monopolize: ～一切 *monopolize everything* / ～一部分权力 *seize a certain amount of power* ❷ control (one's feelings, etc.)
【把舵】hold the rudder; hold (or take, be at) the helm; steer
【把关】❶ guard a pass ❷ check on: 层层～ *make checks at all levels* / 把好质量关 *guarantee the quality* (*of products*)
【把酒】❶ raise one's wine cup ❷ fill a wine cup for sb.
【把脉】〈方〉feel the pulse
【把企业搞活】enliven enterprises
【把企业推向市场】encourage the enterprises to compete in the market; push enterprises to (the) market
【把势】(又作'把式') ❶ 〈口〉 wushu(武术); martial arts: 练～ *practise wushu* ❷ 〈口〉 a person skilled in wushu; a person skilled in a trade: 论庄稼活,他可真是个好～。*He's a highly skilled farmer*. ❸〈方〉 skill: 学会木工的全套～ *learn all the skills of carpentry*
【把守】guard: ～城门 *guard a city gate* / 分兵～ *divide up one's forces for defence*
【把手】〈方〉 ❶ shake hands ❷ handle; grip; knob
【把水搅浑】muddy the water —create confusion
【把头】labour contractor; gangmaster
【把稳】〈方〉 trustworthy; dependable: 他办事很～。*He is dependable in what he does*.
【把握】❶ hold; grasp: 司机～着方向盘。*The driver was holding the steering wheel*. / 透过现象,～本质 *see through the phenomena to grasp the essence* / ～时机 *seize the opportunity*; *seize the right time* ❷ assurance; certainty: 他很有～地回答了所有的问题。*He answered all the questions with assurance*. / 做这项工作,他很有～。*He's quite sure he can do this job*.
【把戏】❶ acrobatics; jugglery: 耍～ *play tricks*; *juggle* ❷ cheap trick; game: 不知道他玩的是什么～。*I wonder what trick he is up to*. / 他玩的～我都看穿了。*I saw through his game*.
【把兄弟】sworn brothers

钯 名 [化] palladium (Pd)

靶 名 target: 打中了～ *hit the target*
【靶场】shooting range; range
【靶船】target ship

【靶壕】marking pit; pit
【靶机】target drone
【靶心】centre of a target; bull's-eye
【靶纸】target sheet
【靶子】target

bà

把 名 ❶ grip; handle: 茶壶～儿 *the handle of a teapot* / 枪～儿 *rifle butt* ❷ stem (of a leaf, flower or fruit): 花～儿 *a flower stem* ——另见 bǎ
【把子】handle

坝 名 ❶ dam ❷ dyke; embankment ❸〈方〉sandbar ❹ (usu. used as part of a place name) flatland; plain

爸 名〈口〉pa; dad; father
【爸爸】papa; dad; father

耙 Ⅰ 名 harrow Ⅱ 动 draw a harrow over (a field); harrow: 那块地已经～过两遍了。*That piece of land has already been harrowed twice.* ——另见 pá

罢 动 ❶ stop; cease: 欲罢不能 ❷ dismiss: 罢官 ❸〈方〉finish: 说～,他就走了。*With these words he left.*
【罢黜】〈书〉❶ dismiss from office ❷ ban; reject
【罢工】strike; go on strike: 号召～ *call for a strike* / 工人已经罢了三天工了。*The workers have been on strike for three days now.*
【罢官】dismiss from office
【罢教】teachers' strike
【罢课】students' strike
【罢了】(bàle) (used at the end of a declarative sentence) that's all; nothing else: 这没有什么,我不过做了我应该做的事～。*It's nothing. I've only done what I ought to do.*
【罢了】(bàliǎo) let it pass; be done with it: 他不愿意来也就～。*Let him stay away if he wishes.* / 他不肯也～,连个回信也不给。*I wouldn't have minded his refusing, but he didn't even answer my letter.*
【罢论】abandoned idea: 此事已作～。*The idea has already been dropped.*
【罢免】recall: 常委由代表大会选举或者～。*Members of the standing committee are elected and subject to recall by the congress.* ◇ ～权 right of recall; recall
【罢市】shopkeepers' strike
【罢手】give up: 不试验成功,我们决不～。*We will never stop until the experiment succeeds.*
【罢休】(usu. used in the negative) give up; let the matter drop: 不达目的,决不～。*We'll not stop until we reach our goal.*
【罢职】dismiss from office; remove form a position

霸 Ⅰ 名 ❶ leader of feudal lords: 春秋五～ *the Five Overlords of the Spring and Autumn Period* (770-476 *B. C.*) ❷ tyrant; despot; bully: 他是地方一～。*He is a local despot.* ❸ hegemonist power; hegemonism; hegemony: 争霸 Ⅱ 动 dominate; lord it over; tyrannize over: 军阀割据,各～一方。*The country was torn by warlordism, with each warlord dominating a region.*
【霸道】(bàdào) ❶ (in ancient political thought) rule by force ❷ overbearing; high-handed; unreasonable: 他这个人很～,你没法儿跟他说。*That guy is very unreasonable; there's no use arguing with him.*
【霸道】(bàdao) (of liquor, medicine, etc.) strong, potent: 这酒真～,少喝点吧。*This liquor is pretty strong; you'd better go easy.*
【霸权】hegemony; supremacy
【霸权主义】hegemonism
【霸王】❶ Hegemon King (a title assumed by Xiang Yu 项羽, 232-202 B. C.) ❷ overlord; despot
【霸王鞭】❶ a rattle stick used in folk dancing ❷ rattle stick dance
【霸业】achievements of a leader of feudal lords
【霸占】forcibly occupy; seize: ～别国领土 *forcibly occupy the territory of another country*
【霸主】❶ a powerful leader of feudal lords (of the Spring and Autumn Period, 770-476 B. C.) ❷ overlord; hegemon: 海上～ *maritime overlord*

bāi

掰 动 break off with the fingers and thumb: 把饼～成两半 *break the cake in two* / ～玉米 *break off corncobs* / 一分钱～成两半花 *watch every penny* / ～着手指算 *count on one's fingers*
【掰腕子】hand wrestling

bái

白 Ⅰ 形 ❶ white: 几根～发 *a few white (or grey) hairs* / 皮肤～ *have a fair complexion* ❷ clear: 真相大白 ❸ pure; plain; blank: ～纸 *a blank sheet of paper* ❹ (of a Chinese character) wrongly written or mispronounced: 我把这字念～了。*I've mispronounced the character.* Ⅱ 副 ❶ in vain; to no purpose; for nothing: ～忙了半天 *go to a lot of trouble for nothing* / ～跑一趟 *make a fruitless trip* ❷ free of charge; gratis: ～看戏 *go to a theatre free of charge* / ～送 *give away free (of charge)* / ～给我也不要。*I wouldn't take it even as a gift.* Ⅲ 动 ❶ look at sb. with the white of the eye—give sb. a supercilious look; throw a cold glance at sb.: 我～了他一眼。*I gave him a supercilious look.* ❷ state; explain: 表白

【白矮星】[天] white dwarf
【白白】in vain; to no purpose; for nothing: 我～浪费了精力。*I made my effort in vain.* / 不要～放过大好时机。*Don't let a golden opportunity slip through your fingers.* / 他～忙了一阵子。*He busied himself for quite some time for nothing.*
【白班】〈口〉day shift: 上～ *be on day shift*
【白报纸】newsprint
【白璧微瑕】a slight flaw in white jade—a minor blemish in a thing of beauty; a slight defect in a person of integrity
【白璧无瑕】flawless white jade—impeccable moral integrity
【白醭】mould (on the surface of vinegar, soy sauce, etc.)
【白布】plain white cloth; calico
【白菜】Chinese cabbage
【白痴】❶ idiocy ❷ idiot
【白炽】同〖白热〗◇～电灯 incandescent lamp
【白醋】light-coloured vinegar
【白搭】〈口〉no use; no good: 和他辩也是～。*It's no use arguing with him.*
【白大褂】white gown (worn by medical personnel): 穿～的 *doctor or nurse*
【白带】[医] leucorrhoea; whites
【白蛋白】[生化] albumin
【白道】[天] moon's path
【白癜风】[医] vitiligo
【白度】[物] degree of whiteness
【白俄罗斯】Belarus
【白垩】chalk (a type of limestone)
【白垩纪】[地质] the Cretaceous Period
【白矾】alum
【白匪】White bandits
【白费】waste: ～力气 *waste one's energy* / ～心思 *bother one's head for nothing* / 再等下去是～时间。*It's waste of time to wait any longer.*
【白费唇舌】同〖徒费唇舌〗
【白粉病】[农] powdery mildew
【白宫】the White House
【白姑鱼】white Chinese croaker
【白骨精】❶ White Bone Demon (in the novel Pilgrimage to the West《西游记》) ❷ sinister and ruthless woman
【白果】[植] ginkgo; gingko
【白鹤】[动] white crane
【白喉】[医] diphtheria
【白狐】arctic fox
【白化病】albinism: ～人 *albino*
【白话】vernacular ◇～诗 free verse written in the vernacular; ～文 writings in the vernacular; ～文运动 the Vernacular Movement (1917-1919)
【白桦】[植] white birch
【白芨】[中] the tuber of hyacinth bletilla (Bletilla striata)
【白僵蚕】[中] the larva of a silkworm with batrytis
【白金】platinum: ～手表 *platinum watch*
【白净】(of skin) fair and clear: 这孩子长得白白净净的。*The child has a fair complexion.*
【白酒】spirit (usu. distilled from sorghum or maize); white spirit
【白驹过隙】a glimpse of a white colt flashing past a chink in a wall (said of the fleeting of time)
【白卷】a blank examination paper; an examination paper unanswered ——另见〖交白卷〗
【白开水】plain boiled water
【白口铁】white iron
【白蜡】white wax; insect wax ◇～虫 wax insect
【白兰地】brandy (a transliteration)
【白痢】❶ [中] dysentery characterized by white mucous stool ❷ [牧] husbandry white diarrhoea
【白鲢】silver carp
【白脸】white face, face painting in Beijing opera, etc., traditionally for the villain ——另见〖唱白脸〗
【白磷】[化] white phosphorus
【白蛉】(又作'白蛉子') sand fly ◇～热 [医] sandfly fever
【白领】white-collar: ～工人 *white collar worker* / ～阶级 *white collar workers*
【白榴石】leucite (a mineral)
【白鹭】egret
【白马王子】prince riding a white horse-Prince Charming
【白茫茫】(of mist, snow, oodwater, etc.) a vast expanse of whiteness: 下了一场大雪,田野上～一片。*After the heavy snow, the fields were a vast expanse of whiteness.*
【白猫黑猫论】theory (first put forward by Deng Xiaoping) that it doesn't matter if a cat is black or white as long as it catches mice
【白茅】[植] cogongrass (Imperata cylindrica) ◇～根 [中] cogongrass rhizome
【白煤】❶〈方〉anthracite; hard coal ❷ white coal; waterpower
【白米】(polished) rice: ～饭 (*cooked*) *rice*
【白棉纸】stencil tissue paper
【白面】wheat flour; flour
【白面书生】pale-faced scholar; pasty-faced bookworm
【白描】❶ line drawing in traditional ink and brush style ❷ simple, straightforward style of writing
【白名单】white list
【白木耳】tremella
【白内障】[医] cataract: ～摘除术 *cataract extraction*
【白砒】[化] white arsenic; arsenic trioxide
【白皮书】white paper; white book
【白皮松】(又作'白果松') lacebark pine
【白屈菜】[植] greater celandine
【白热】white heat; incandescence
【白热化】turn white-hot: 争论达到了～的程度。*The debate became white-hot.*
【白人】white man or woman
【白刃】naked sword ◇～战 bayonet charge; hand-to-hand combat
【白日做梦】spin daydreams; indulge in wishful

thinking; build castles in the air
【白肉】plain boiled pork
【白色】❶ white (colour) ❷ White (as a symbol of reaction):～据点 *White stronghold*; *stronghold of reaction* / ～政权 *White regime*
【白色恐怖】White terror
【白色人种】the white race
【白色体】[植] leucoplast
【白色污染】white pollution
【白砂糖】refined white (granulated) sugar
【白芍】[中] (peeled) root of herbaceous peony (Paeonia lactiflora)
【白食】free food; free meal:我不喜欢那些吃～的人。*I don't like those who are prone to live off other people*.
【白手起家】(又作'白手成家') build up from nothing; start from scratch:他～开了这家饭馆。*He started his restaurant from scratch*.
【白首】〈书〉hoary head; old age
【白薯】sweet potato
【白苏】[植] common perilla (Perilla frutescens)
【白糖】(refined) white sugar
【白陶】[考古] white pottery (of the Shang Dynasty, c. 16th-11th century B.C.)
【白体】[刷] lean type
【白天】daytime; day:～我睡不着。*I cannot sleep in the daytime*. / 冬季～时间短。*The day is shorter in winter*.
【白条】❶ unofficial receipt (in financial transactions); IOU:打～ *give an IOU* (*instead of paying cash*) ❷ slaughtered poultry or animal, stripped of hairs or feathers, or with head, feet and entrails removed:～猪 *pig carcass*
【白铁】common name for 镀锌铁 ◇～皮 tinplate; galvanized iron sheet
【白铜】copper-nickel alloy; paktong
【白头】❶ hoary head; old age ❷ unsigned; anonymous
【白头翁】❶ [动] Chinese bulbul ❷ [中] the root of Chinese pulsatilla
【白头偕老】live in conjugal bliss to a ripe old age; remain a devoted couple to the end of their lives; remain happily married to a ripe old age
【白钨矿】scheelite
【白皙】〈书〉(of skin) fair and clear:皮肤～ *have a fair complexion*; *be fair-complexioned*
【白细胞】[生理] white blood cell; leucocyte
【白鲜】[植] shaggy-fruited dittany (Dictamnus dasycarpus) ◇～皮 [中] the root bark of shaggy-fruited dittany
【白鹇】[动] silver pheasant
【白熊】polar bear; white bear
【白絮】❶ white cotton (fibre) ❷ 〈文〉 cotton fluff—snowflake
【白血病】leukaemia
【白血球】[生理] white blood cell; leucocyte
【白鲟】Chinese paddlefish
【白眼】supercilious look:～看人 *treat people superciliously*; *look upon people with disdain* / 遭人～ *be treated with disdain*
【白眼珠】〈口〉the white of the eye
【白杨】[植] white poplar
【白药】[中] baiyao, a white medicinal powder for treating haemorrhage, wounds, bruises, etc.
【白夜】[天] white night
【白衣天使】〈喻〉nurse
【白衣战士】warrior in white; medical worker
【白蚁】termite; white ant
【白银】silver
【白鱼】whitefish
【白云母】muscovite; white mica (a mineral)
【白云石】dolomite (a mineral)
【白噪声】white noise
【白纸黑字】(written) in black and white:这些条件～,一清二楚,想抵赖是抵赖不掉的。*These terms are clearly written in black and white. You can never deny them*.
【白种】the white race
【白昼】daytime; day
【白字】a character misused or mispronounced through confusion with one that sounds or looks like it:写(读)～ *write a wrong character* (*pronounce a character wrongly*) *in mistake for one that resembles it*
【白字连篇】reams of wrong characters; (of speech or writing) full of mispronounced or wrong words:这篇文章～。*There're so many wrong characters in this piece*.

bǎi

百 Ⅰ [数] hundred Ⅱ [形] numerous; all kinds of:～花盛开 *a hundred flowers in bloom* / ～忙之中 *in the midst of pressing affairs*; *despite many claims on one's time*
【百儿八十】〈口〉about a hundred; a hundred or so
【百般】in a hundred and one ways; in every possible way; by every means:～咒骂 *abuse in every possible way*; *heap abuse on* / ～抵赖 *try by every means to deny* / ～奉承 *flatter sedulously*
【百般刁难】create obstructions of every description; put up innumerable obstacles; raise all manner of difficulties
【百倍】a hundredfold; a hundred times:展望未来,信心～ *look to the future with full confidence*
【百病】all kinds of diseases and ailments:～不生 *be immune from disease* / 包治～ (*of a quack*) *cure all*; *guarantee to put right all troubles*
【百步穿杨】shoot an arrow through a willow leaf at a hundred paces; split a willow wand at a hundred paces; shoot with great precision
【百尺竿头,更进一步】make still further progress; further improve one's work
【百出】〈贬〉full of; innumerable:错误～ *full of errors* / 漏洞～ *plenty of loopholes* / 洋相～ *make a terrible spectacle* (*or fool*) *of oneself*
【百川归海】all rivers flow to the sea —all things

tend in one direction; everyone turns to sb. for guidance

【百读不厌】be worth reading a hundred times; can be read a hundred times with delight: 这本书～。*You never get tired of reading this book.*

【百端待举】A hundred things remain to be done; Numerous tasks have yet to be undertaken.

【百发百中】A hundred shots, a hundred bull's-eyes; Every shot hits the target; shoot with unfailing accuracy; be a crack shot: 他是我们班里的神枪手,打靶时总是～。*He's the crack shot of our squad and never misses the bull's-eye in target practice.*

【百废俱兴】(又作'百废具兴') All neglected tasks are being undertaken; All that was left undone is now being undertaken.

【百分比】percentage: 失业～ *unemployment percentage* / 按～计算 *in terms of percentage* / 癌症病人的～在不断上升。*The percentage of cancer patients keeps rising.*

【百分点】one percentage point: 增加一个～ *an increase of one percentage point*

【百分率】percentage; per cent

【百分之百】hundred-percent; out and out; absolutely: 有～的把握 *be a hundred per cent sure; be absolutely certain* / 这是～的谎话! *That's an out-and-out lie!*

【百分制】hundred-mark system

【百感交集】all sorts of feelings well up in one's heart

【百合】[植] lily ◇ ～病 lily disease

【百花奖】the Hundred Flowers Award

【百花齐放】let a hundred flowers bloom —free development of different forms and styles in the arts

【百花齐放,百家争鸣】let a hundred flowers blossom and a hundred schools of thought contend

【百花齐放,推陈出新】let a hundred flowers blossom, weed through the old to bring forth the new

【百花争艳】(又作'百花争妍') a hundred flowers contend in beauty; the flowers are a riot of colour

【百货】general merchandise: 日用～ *articles of daily use* ◇ ～公司 department store; ～商店 general store; department store

【百家姓】the Book of Family Names

【百科全书】encyclopaedia

【百孔千疮】riddled with gaping wounds; afflicted with all ills

【百口难辩】difficult to get at the truth

【百老汇】Broadway: ～大街 *Broadway Street (running northwest and southeast through New York City)* / ～剧院 *Broadway Theater (in New York City)*

【百里挑一】one in a hundred; cream of the crop: ～的美人 *an exceptional beauty*

【百炼成钢】be tempered into steel

【百灵】lark

【百米赛跑】100-metre dash

【百慕大】Bermuda ◇ ～人 Bermudan; ～三角 Bermuda Triangle; Devil's Triangle

【百年】❶ a hundred years; a century: ～大业 *a cause of vital and lasting importance* ❷ lifetime: 祝你们～好合。*Wishing you life-long happiness and perfect harmony.* ◇～不遇 not seen once in a hundred years; ～纪念 centenary; centennial

【百年大计】a matter of fundamental importance for generations to come; a project of vital and lasting importance; a major project: 基本建设是～,要求质量第一。*Capital construction projects, which are to last for generations, call above all for good quality.*

【百年树人】it takes a hundred years to make education bear fruit: 十年树木,～。*It takes ten years to grow trees but a hundred years to rear people.*

【百日咳】whooping cough; pertussis: ～疫苗 *pertussis vaccine*

【百十】a hundred or so: ～户人家 *about a hundred households*

【百事可乐】Pepsi (Pepsi-cola)

【百事通】❶ knowledgeable person ❷ know-all

【百思不解】still puzzled after pondering a hundred times; remain perplexed despite much thought

【百听不厌】worth hearing a hundred times: 这个故事～。*You never get tired of hearing this story.*

【百万】million ◇～吨级 megaton; ～富翁 millionaire; ～雄师 a million bold warriors; a mighty army

【百闻不如一见】It is better to see once than to hear a hundred times; Seeing for oneself is better than hearing from others.

【百无禁忌】all taboos in abeyance (a magic formula credited with the power of neutralizing offences against taboos)

【百无聊赖】bored to death; bored stiff; overcome with boredom: ～时我就随手抓过一本书来,强迫自己看下去。*In times of sheer boredom I would pick up a book and force myself to read.*

【百无一失】no danger of anything going wrong; no risk at all; perfectly safe; surefire

【百姓】common people

【百业凋敝】all business declining

【百叶】louver

【百叶窗】shutter; blind; jalousie

【百叶箱】[气] thermometer screen

【百依百顺】docile and obedient; all obedience: 这位当妈妈的宠爱儿子,对他可真是～。*The mother doted on her son so much that she complied with all his whims.*

【百用不厌】never get tired of using; worth using a hundred times

【百战百胜】fight a hundred battles, win a hundred victories—emerge victorious in every battle; be ever-victorious

【百折不挠】(又作'百折不回') keep on fighting in

spite of all setbacks; be undaunted by repeated setbacks; be dauntless; be indomitable; be unrelenting: ～的努力 *unrelenting effort* / 用～的毅力去克服所有的困难 *overcome all difficulties with an indomitable will*
【百周年纪念】centenary; centennial; centenary celebration; one hundredth anniversary
【百子莲】African agapanthus
【百足之虫,死而不僵】A centipede does not topple over even when dead; A centipede dies but never falls down; Old institutions die hard.

柏 名 cypress
【柏树】cypress
【柏油】common name for 沥青
【柏子仁】[中] the seed of Oriental arborvitae

摆 Ⅰ 动 ❶ put; place; arrange: 把药瓶～在架子上 *put the medicine bottles on the shelf* / 把碗筷～好 *set* (*or lay*) *the table* ❷ lay bare; state clearly: ～矛盾 *lay bare the contradictions* / 把有利和不利的条件～一～ *set forth the advantages and disadvantages* ❸ put on; assume: ～威风 *give oneself airs; put on airs* / ～出一副吓人的架势 *assume an intimidating posture* ❹ sway; wave: 钟摆～来～去。*The pendulum swung backwards and forwards*. Ⅱ 名 [物] pendulum: 单摆
【摆布】❶decorate; arrange: 这间屋子～得十分雅致。*The room is tastefully furnished*. ❷ order about; manipulate: 任人～ *allow oneself to be ordered about; be at the mercy of others*
【摆荡吊环】[体] swinging rings
【摆地摊】set up a temporary stall or simply lay out various items on a newspaper, cloth, etc. to sell on the street
【摆动】swing; sway: 柳条迎风～。*The willows swayed in the breeze*. / 指示针来回～。*The pointer flickered* ◇～额 swing limit; ～信贷 swing credit; ～账户 swing account
【摆渡】❶ cross a river by boat; ferry ❷ ferryboat; ferry
【摆放】lay; place; put in a certain place: 屋里～着新家具。*The room is furnished with new furniture*.
【摆好】enumerate sb.'s merits; commend; praise: 评功～ *enumerate sb.'s merits; speak of sb. in glowing terms*
【摆架子】put on airs; give oneself airs: 摆出一副大官的架子 *affect the pose of a high official*
【摆阔】parade one's wealth; be ostentatious and extravagant
【摆擂台】❶make open challenges to fights ❷make challenges to a contest
【摆龙门阵】〈方〉chat; gossip; spin a yarn
【摆轮】(又作'摆盘') balance (of a watch or clock); balance wheel
【摆门面】put up a front; maintain an outward show; keep up appearances
【摆弄】❶ move back and forth; fiddle with: 你别来回～那几盆花了。*Don't move those flower pots back and forth*. ❷ order about; manipulate
【摆平】be fair to; be impartial to: ～关系 *be impartial in dealings with people* / 两边要～ *must be fair to both parties*
【摆谱儿】〈方〉❶ keep up appearances; show off: 爱～的人 *showy person* / 她经济本来不宽裕,可是硬要～。*Though she is not well-off, she tries to keep up appearances*. ❷ put on airs; throw one's weight about: 提升以后,他就跟原来的同事们～了。*After his promotion, he began to throw his weight about* (*or put on airs*) *before his former colleagues*.
【摆设】furnish and decorate (a room): 屋子里～得很整齐。*The room is decorated neatly*.
【摆设儿】❶ ornaments; decorations: 客厅里的～朴素大方。*The decorations in the drawing-room are simple but in good taste*. ❷ objects or articles merely for show
【摆事实,讲道理】present the facts and reason things out
【摆手】❶ shake one's hand in admonition or disapproval ❷ beckon; wave: 她向我摆了摆手,要我跟着她。*She beckoned me to follow her*. / 他～叫我走开。*He waved me away*.
【摆摊子】(又作'摆摊儿') ❶ set up a stall ❷ maintain a large staff or organization
【摆脱】shake off; cast off; break away from; free (or extricate) oneself from: ～贫穷落后的状态 *be lifted out of poverty and backwardness* / ～困境 *extricate oneself from a predicament*
【摆尾】wag the tail
【摆样子】do sth. for show: 他的自我批评是认真的,不是～的。*His self-criticism was serious and not made for show*.
【摆针】pointer (on a meter, scales, etc.)
【摆钟】pendulum clock
【摆轴】balance staff (of a balance wheel)
【摆子】〈方〉malaria

bài

败 Ⅰ 动 ❶ be defeated; lose: 这次比赛他～了。*He was beaten in the contest*. / 主队以二比三～于客队。*The home team lost to the visitors 2 to 3*. ❷ defeat; beat: 击败 ❸ fail: 成败 ❹ spoil: 事情可能就～在他手里。*He may spoil the whole show*. ❺ counteract Ⅱ 形 decayed; withered: 枯枝～叶 *dead twigs and withered leaves* / 开不～的花朵 *a flower that will not fade*
【败北】〈书〉suffer defeat; lose a battle
【败笔】❶ a faulty stroke in calligraphy or painting ❷ a faulty expression or flaw in writing: 电影里这段三角恋爱故事是个～。*The love triangle in this film is a flaw in an otherwise very good plot*.
【败兵】a defeated army; an army in flight; defeated troops

【败坏】ruin; corrupt; undermine: ～名誉 *discredit; defame* / 道德～ *morally degenerate* / ～风俗 *corrupt morals; exert a bad moral influence* / ～社会风气 *corrupt social values*
【败火】[中] relieve inflammation or internal heat
【败绩】〈书〉be utterly defeated; be routed: 屡遭～ *be badly defeated again and again; have sustained severe defeats time and again*
【败家】dissipate a family fortune
【败家子】spendthrift; wastrel; prodigal
【败局】lost game; losing battle: ～已定。*The game is as good as lost.*
【败类】scum of a community; degenerate: 民族～ *scum of a nation*
【败露】(of a plot, etc.) fall through and stand exposed: 阴谋终于～。*In the end the conspiracy was brought to light.*
【败落】decline (in wealth and position): 这部小说反映了一个封建家庭的～。*This novel reflects the decline of a feudal family.*
【败诉】lose a lawsuit
【败退】retreat in defeat
【败胃】spoil one's appetite (by eating certain food or taking certain medicines)
【败兴】have one's spirits dampened; feel disappointed ◇ ～而归 come back disappointed —— 另见〖乘兴而来〗
【败血症】[医] septicaemia
【败叶】fallen leaf; withered leaf: 枯枝～ *dead twigs and withered leaves*
【败仗】lost battle; defeat: 打～ *be defeated in battle; suffer a defeat* / 吃了个大～ *have suffered a crushing defeat*
【败阵】be defeated on the battlefield or be beaten in a contest: ～而逃 *lose the field and take to flight* / 败下阵来 *lose a battle or be beaten in a contest*

拜 动 ❶ do obeisance: 拜佛 ❷ pay a courtesy call: 回拜 ❸ congratulate (on a certain occasion): 拜年 ❹ visit; pay a visit: 新搬来的张同志刚才～街坊来了。*The new neighbour, Comrade Zhang, came to visit us.* ❺ confer a title on sb.; appoint: ～相 *confer the title of Prime Minister on sb.; appoint sb. as Prime Minister* ❻ acknowledge sb. as one's master, godfather, etc.: 我～他为师学钢琴。*I became a piano student of his.* ❼〈套〉(used before a verb): ～谢 *express one's thanks*
【拜把子】become sworn brothers
【拜别】(又作'拜辞')〈套〉take leave of
【拜倒】prostrate oneself; fall on one's knees; grovel: ～在某人脚下 *grovel (or lie prostrate) at the feet of sb.*
【拜读】〈套〉read with respect; have the pleasure of reading an essay, etc.: ～大作 *have the pleasure of perusing your work*
【拜访】pay a visit; call on: 正式～ *formal visit* / 专程～ *make a special trip to call on sb.* / ～亲友 *pay a visit to one's relatives and friends*
【拜佛】prostrate oneself before the image of Buddha; worship Buddha
【拜会】(usu. used on diplomatic occasions) pay an official call; call on: 告别～ *farewell call* / 礼节性～ *courtesy call* / 私人～ *personal visit (or call)*
【拜火教】Zoroastrianism; Mazdaism
【拜见】❶ pay a formal visit; call to pay respects ❷ meet one's senior or superior
【拜金主义】money worship
【拜客】pay visits; make calls
【拜年】pay a New Year call; wish sb. a Happy New Year: 给您拜个早(晚)年。*Let me wish you an early (a belated, late) Happy New Year.*
【拜师】formally become a pupil to a master
【拜寿】congratulate an elderly person on his birthday; offer birthday felicitations
【拜堂】〈旧〉(of bride and groom) make ceremonial obeisances—perform the marriage ceremony
【拜托】〈套〉request sb. to do sth.: ～您捎个信给他。*Would you be kind enough to take a message to him?*
【拜物教】fetishism: 商品～ *commodity fetishism*
【拜谒】〈书〉❶ pay a formal visit; call to pay respects ❷ pay homage (at a monument, mausoleum, etc.)
【拜祖先】ancestor worship

稗 Ⅰ 名 barnyard grass Ⅱ 形〈书〉insignificant; unofficial: 稗史
【稗官野史】books of anecdotes
【稗子】[植] barnyard grass; barnyard millet

bān

扳 动 pull; turn: ～倒 *pull down* / ～枪栓 *pull back the bolt of a rifle* / ～道岔 *pull railway switches* / ～着指头算 *count on one's fingers* / ～成平局 *equalize the score*
【扳不倒儿】〈口〉tumbler; roly-poly
【扳道员】pointsman; switchman
【扳机】trigger
【扳手】❶ spanner; wrench ❷ lever (on a machine)
【扳子】spanner; wrench

班 Ⅰ 名 ❶ class; team: 甲～ *class A* / 作业～ *work team* / ～上有十五个学生。*There're fifteen students in the class.* ❷ shift; duty: 三～倒 *work in three shifts* / 今天晚上是我的～儿。*I'll be on duty tonight.* ❸ [军] squad Ⅱ 量 ❶ a group of people: 这～年轻人真了不起。*They're a fine bunch of young people.* ❷ a trip by bus, boat, etc.: 搭下一～火车 *take the next train* / 一路公共汽车每隔三分钟就有一～。*There's a Number One bus every three minutes.* Ⅲ 形 regularly-run; regular; scheduled: 班机
【班禅喇嘛】the Panchen Lama

【班车】regular bus (service)

【班次】❶ order of classes or grades at school：在学校时，她～比我高。*At school she was in a higher class than me*. ❷ number of runs or flights：增加货车～ *increase the number of runs of freight trains*

【班底】❶ ordinary members of a theatrical troupe ❷ core members of an organization

【班房】〈口〉jail：坐～ *be (put) in jail*

【班费】activities fee (for school classes, usually paid by the students)

【班会】class meeting (in schools)

【班机】airliner；regular air service：京沪～ *scheduled flights between Beijing and Shanghai* / 两国首都之间有～来往。*There's a regular air service between the two capitals*.

【班级】classes and grades in school：我们在中学是同一个～。*We used to be in the same class when at high school*. /～教育 *class teaching*

【班轮】regular passenger or cargo ship；regular steamship service

【班门弄斧】show off one's skill with the axe before Lu Ban (鲁班), the master carpenter—display one's slight skill before an expert：在你面前～，太不好意思了。*I'm making a fool of myself trying to show off before an expert like you*.

【班期】schedule (for flights, voyages, etc.)：～表 *a table of scheduled flights, voyages, etc.*；*timetable*

【班师】〈书〉withdraw troops from the front；return after victory

【班图人】Bantu

【班图语】Bantu (language)

【班长】❶ class monitor ❷［军］squad leader ❸ (work) team leader

【班主任】a teacher in charge of a class (in a primary or middle school)；form master

【班子】❶〈旧〉theatrical troupe ❷ organized group：生产～ *a team in charge of production* / 专业～ *a special, full-time group*

【班组】teams and groups (in factories, etc.)：～竞赛 *emulation between teams or groups*；*emulation at the team or group level*

般 助 same as；just like：闪电～地 *like lightning* / 暴风雨～的掌声 *stormy (or thunderous) applause* / 兄弟～的情谊 *fraternal feelings*

【般配】be well matched (as in marriage)；match each other：他俩是挺～的一对儿。*The two of them can make a very good couple*.

颁 动 promulgate；issue

【颁布】promulgate；issue；publish：～法令 *promulgate (or issue) a decree*

【颁发】❶ issue；promulgate：～嘉奖令 *issue an order of commendation* ❷award：～奖章 *award a medal*

【颁奖】give out an award：向劳模～ *give out awards to model workers*

【颁行】issue for enforcement

斑 Ⅰ 名 spot；speck；speckle；stripe：油～ *oil stains*；*grease spots* Ⅱ 形 spotted；striped：斑马

【斑白】grey；grizzled：头发～ *with grizzled hair*；*grey-haired*

【斑斑】full of stains or spots：血迹～ *bloodstained*

【斑鬓】greying hair on the temples

【斑驳陆离】of many colours；many-hued

【斑翅山鹑】partridge

【斑点】spot；stain；speckle

【斑鸠】turtledove

【斑斓】〈书〉gorgeous；bright-coloured；multicoloured：五彩～ *a riot of colour* / ～的玛瑙 *gorgeous agates*

【斑羚】goral

【斑马】zebra

【斑马线】zebra crossing

【斑蝥】［动］Chinese blister beetle；cantharides

【斑铜矿】bornite

【斑纹】stripe；streak：斑马有黑白相间的～。*A zebra has black and white stripes*.

【斑岩】［地质］porphyry

【斑疹】［医］macula ◇ ～伤寒 typhus

【斑竹】mottled bamboo

搬 动 ❶ take away；move；remove：把桌子～走 *take the table away* / 把小说里的故事～到舞台上 *adapt a story for performance on the stage*；*dramatize a novel* ❷ move (house)：他早就～走了。*He moved out long ago*. ❸ apply indiscriminately；copy mechanically：生搬硬套

【搬兵】call in reinforcements；ask for help：眼见施工任务完不成，他赶紧去～。*Realizing that the construction project might not be completed as scheduled, he lost no time in trying to get outside help*.

【搬家】❶ move (house)：我们下星期～。*We're moving next week*. ❷ remove；move：把这个箱子搬搬家，别挡路。*Please move the box out of the way*. / ～公司 *removing company*

【搬弄】❶ move sth. about；fiddle with：别～枪栓。*Don't fiddle with the rifle bolt*. ❷ show off；display：～学问 *parade one's erudition* / 他总好～自己的那点儿知识。*He is apt to show off what he knows*. ❸ instigate；sow discord

【搬弄是非】sow discord；tell tales；make mischief：～的人 *a talebearer*

【搬迁】move；transfer；remove：我们的办事处从西区～到东区了。*Our office has moved from the west to the east district*. /～减价 *removal sale*

【搬迁户】a relocated unit (or household)

【搬运】carry；transport：～货物 *transport goods* / ～工人 *porter (at a railway station)*；*docker (at a seaport)* /～费 *transportation charges*

瘢 名 scar

【瘢痕】scar

bǎn

板 Ⅰ名 ❶ board; plank; plate: 切菜～ *chopping block* / 混凝土～ *concrete slab* ❷ shutter: 铺子都上了～儿了。*The shops have all put up the shutters.* ❸ table tennis bat ❹［音］clappers ❺ an accented beat in traditional Chinese music; time; measure: 板眼 Ⅱ形 ❶hard: 地～了,锄不动。*The ground is too hard to hoe.* ❷ stiff; unnatural: 我这张照片照得太～了。*I look too stiff in this picture.* Ⅲ动 stop smiling; look serious: ～起面孔 *put on a stern expression* / ～着脸 *keep a straight face*

【板壁】wooden partition

【板擦儿】blackboard eraser

【板车】a flatbed cart

【板锉】flat file

【板凳】wooden bench or stool

【板斧】broad axe

【板鼓】a small drum for marking time

【板规】［机］plate gauge

【板胡】a bowed stringed instrument with a thin wooden soundboard

【板结】harden: ～的土壤 *hardened and impervious soil*

【板块】［地质］plate ◇～构造学［地质］platetectonics

【板蓝根】［中］Radix Isatidis, Chinese herbal medicine for treating colds

【板栗】Chinese chestnut

【板梁桥】plate girder bridge

【板皮】［林］slab

【板球】❶ cricket ❷ cricket ball

【板书】❶ write on the blackboard ❷ words written on the blackboard; blackboard writing: 这位老师的～漂亮。*The teacher writes a beautiful hand on the blackboard.*

【板刷】scrubbing brush

【板条】［建］lath

【板条箱】crate

【板鸭】pressed (or dried) salted duck

【板牙】❶〈方〉front tooth; incisor ❷〈方〉molar ❸［机］screw die; threading die

【板牙扳手】stock and die

【板烟】plug (of tobacco)

【板岩】［地质］slate

【板眼】❶［音］accented and unaccented beats in traditional Chinese music; measure; time: 一板三眼 *one accented beat and three unaccented beats in a bar, similar to 4/4 time* ❷ orderliness; system; method: 她做事很有～。*There is method in what she does.* or *She is very methodical in her work.* ——另见〖有板有眼〗

【板油】leaf fat; leaf lard

【板羽球】❶ battledore and shuttlecock ❷ shuttlecock

【板纸】paperboard; board: 草～ *straw board* / 牛皮～ *kraft board*

【板桩】［建］sheet pile

【板子】❶ board; plank ❷ bamboo or birch for corporal punishment

版 名 ❶ printing plate (or block): 铜版 ❷ edition: 新～ *new edition* /《现代汉英词典》(新～) *Modern Chinese-English Dictionary (New Edition)* / 香港～ *Hong Kong edition* ❸ page (of a newspaper): 第四～ *Page 4* / 国内新闻～ *home news section*

【版本】edition (as in different forms, bindings, etc. or by different publishers): 这本书有三个～。*This book has three editions.*

【版次】the order in which editions are printed

【版画】a picture printed from an engraved or etched plate; print

【版刻】carving; engraving

【版权】copyright: 此书～归出版社所有。*The publisher has the copyright of the book.* / ～所有,不准翻印。*All rights reserved.* /～保护 *copyright protection* /～法 *copyright law* /～转让 *assignment of copyright* ◇ ～页 copyright page; colophon

【版式】format

【版税】royalty (on books)

【版图】domain; territory: ～辽阔 *vast in territory*

bàn

办 动 ❶ do; handle; manage; tackle; attend to: 我该怎么～? *What shall I do?* / 你看着～吧。*Do whatever you think is best.* / 缺少经费,这事没法～。*It is impossible to do the job without the necessary funds.* ❷ set up; run: ～工厂 *run a factory* / ～教育 *carry out education* ❸ buy a fair amount of; get sth. ready: ～年货 *do New Year shopping; do shopping for the Spring Festival* / ～酒席 *prepare a feast* / 他们刚～完喜事。*They've recently got married.* ❹ punish (by law); bring to justice: ～了几个为首的 *have punished the ringleaders*

【办案】❶ handle a legal case ❷ apprehend (a criminal)

【办报】run a newspaper

【办法】way; means; measure: 找出克服困难的～ *find a way to overcome a difficulty* / 他这个人～多。*He is resourceful.* / 借钱不是个～。*Borrowing money is no way out.*

【办公】handle official business; work (usu. in an office): ～时间 *office hours* / 你在什么地方～? *Where do you work?* or *Where is your office?* ◇ ～费 administrative expenses; ～室 office; ～厅 general office; ～桌 desk; bureau

【办公室自动化】office automation(OA)

【办理】handle; conduct; transact: ～进出口业务 *handle imports and exports* / ～手续 *go through the formalities (or procedure)*

【办事】handle affairs；work：～公正 *be fair and just in handling affairs* / ～认真 *be conscientious in one's work* / 按原则～ *act according to principles* ◇ ～处 office；agency；～机构 administrative body；working body；～员 office worker；～组 administrative group

【办喜事】manage a wedding；prepare for a happy occasion

【办学】run a school：～方针 *guiding principle for running a school*

【办罪】punish sb.（for a crime）

半 Ⅰ[数] half；semi-：～小时 *half an hour* / 一个～月 *a month and a half*；*one and a half months* / ～年 *six months*；*half a year* / ～机械化 *semi-mechanized* / 增加一倍～ *increase by* 150% Ⅱ[形] ❶ in the middle；halfway：～山腰 *halfway up a hill* ❷ very little；the least bit：他连～句话都不说。*He wouldn't breathe a word*. Ⅲ[副] partly；about half：～开玩笑地说 *say sth. half jokingly* / 房门～开着。*The door was left half open*.

【半百】fifty（years of age）：年近～ *getting on for fifty*；*approaching fifty*

【半…半…】（used before two antonyms indicating the simultaneous existence of two states）：半文半白 *half literary*，*half vernacular* / 半饥半饱 *underfed* / 半心半意 *half-hearted*

【半半拉拉】〈口〉incomplete；unfinished：这点活儿干完算了，别剩下～的。*Let's finish the job off*. *Don't leave a lot of loose ends hanging over*.

【半包装】semi-packed

【半辈子】half a lifetime：我活了～了，还不知道这个吗？*How can a person of my age be ignorant of such a thing*？

【半壁江山】（又作'半壁河山'）half of the country（usu. referring to the unoccupied part of an invaded country）

【半边】half of sth.；one side of sth.：～身子 *left or right side of the body* / 这个苹果～儿红，～儿绿。*One half of the apple is red*，*the other half is green*.

【半边莲】［中］Chinese lobelia（Lobelia chinensis）

【半边天】❶ half of the sky：夕阳映红了～。*The setting sun tinted half of the sky with a reddish hue*. or *Half the sky shone red in the glow of the sunset*. ❷ women of the new society；womenfolk（from Mao Zedong's saying 妇女能顶～。Women can hold up half of the sky.）

【半…不…】（used in the same way as 半…半…）：半明不暗 *not very bright*；*dimly lit*

【半场】［体］❶ half of a game or contest：上～ *the first half*（*of a game*）❷ half-court：（*in basketball*）～紧逼 *half-court press*/～线 *half count line*

【半成品】semi-manufactured goods；semi-finished articles；semi-finished products

【半导体】semiconductor：～存储器 *semiconductor store*（*or memory*）/ ～集成电路 *semiconductor integrated circuit* ◇ ～收音机 transistor radio（or receiver）

【半岛】peninsula

【半地下室】semi-basement

【半点】the least bit：没有～慌张 *not the least bit flurried* / 这是一个科学问题，来不得～虚伪。*This is a matter of science*，*which permits no dishonesty*.

【半吊子】❶ dabbler；smatterer ❷ tactless and impulsive person

【半蹲】parallel squat；half kneebend

【半封建】semi-feudal

【半工半读】part work，part study；work-study programme

【半公开】semi-overt；more or less open

【半官方】semi-official：据～人士称 *according to semi-official sources* /～机构 *semi-official institution*

【半价】half price：～出售 *sell at half price*

【半截】half（a section）：～香肠 *half of a sausage* / 话只说了～儿 *finish only half of what one has to say* / 把这两～儿粘上 *stick the two halves together*

【半截入土】with one foot in the grave

【半斤八两】six of one and half a dozen of the other；not much to choose between the two；two of a kind：他们俩的技术～，差不多。*So far as their skills are concerned*，*it's six of one and half a dozen of the other*.

【半径】radius：爆炸声在～十公里范围内都能听到。*The explosion could be heard within a radius of ten kilometres*.

【半决赛】［体］semi-finals

【半空中】〈口〉in midair；in the air：悬在～ *hang in midair*

【半劳动力】（又作'半劳力'）one able to do light manual labour only；semi-ablebodied or part-time（farm）worker

【半老徐娘】（又作'徐娘半老'）woman of fading charms：徐娘半老，风韵犹存。*Though a middle-aged woman*，*she was not without*（*her*）*charms*.

【半连续信道】semi-continuous channel

【半流体】semifluid

【半路】halfway；midway；on the way：走到～，天就黑了。*We had got only halfway when it began to get dark*. / ～上遇到熟人 *run into a friend on the way*

【半路出家】become a monk or nun late in life—switch to a job one was not trained for

【半路夫妻】couple married halfway through life（usu. after a previous marriage）

【半卖半送】sell goods at rock-bottom prices

【半耐用品】semi-durable goods

【半票】half-price ticket；half fare

【半瓶醋】〈口〉half a bottle of vinegar—dabbler；smatterer：他的法文是半瓶子醋。*He has a smattering of French*.

【半破产状态】semi-bankrupty

【半旗】half-mast

【半球】hemisphere：东～ *the Eastern Hemisphere* /

北～ *the Northern Hemisphere*

【半人半鬼】half man, half ghost —an inhuman person or one living in conditions that are inhuman

【半人马座】[天] Centaurus

【半日制学校】half-day (or double-shift) school

【半身不遂】[医] hemiplegia

【半身像】❶ half-length photo or portrait ❷ bust

【半生】half a lifetime：～戎马 *led a soldier's life for many years*

【半失业】semi-employed; partly employed; underemployed

【半熟练】semi-skilled

【半数】half the number; half：～以上 *more than half; majority*

【半衰期】[物] half-life

【半死】half-dead：被打个～ *be beaten within an inch of one's life* / 气得～ *be half-dead from anger; nearly faint with rage* / 庄稼旱得～。*The drought nearly ruined the crops.*

【半死不活】half-dead; more dead than alive

【半天】❶ half of the day：前～ *morning* / 后～ *afternoon* ❷ a long time; quite a while：他～说不出话来。*He remained tongue-tied for a long time.*

【半透明】translucent; semitransparent ◇ ～体 [物] translucent body; ～纸 onionskin

【半途】〈书〉halfway; midway：～折伙 *part company halfway*

【半途而废】give up halfway; leave sth. unfinished：改革必须坚持到底,不能～。*Reforms must be carried through to the end and not abandoned halfway.*

【半推半就】yield with a show of reluctance; give way after making a show of declining：说了几句客气话,他也就～地把礼物收下了。*He accepted the gift after making a polite show of declining.*

【半脱产】partly released from productive labour; partly released from one's regular work

【半文盲】semiliterate

【半夏】[中] the tuber of pinellia (Pinellia ternata)

【半信半疑】half-believing, half-doubting; not quite convinced：他抱着～的态度去试一试。*Not quite convinced, he went to try it himself.* / 她～地摇摇头。*Still a little sceptical, she shook her head.*

【半夜】midnight; in the middle of the night：会议一直开到～。*The meeting went on far into the night.*

【半夜三更】in the depth of night; late at night：～的,你起来干什么? *Why are you getting up at this time of night?*

【半音】[音] semitone ◇ ～音阶 [音] chromatic scale

【半影】[物] penumbra：～锥 *penumbra cone*

【半元音】[语音] semivowel

【半圆】semicircle

【半月瓣】[生理] semilunar valve

【半月刊】semimonthly (a periodical); fortnightly

【半载】[交通] half load

【半真半假】❶ half-genuine, half-sham; partly true, partly false ❷ half in jest, half in earnest

【半支莲】[植] sun plant

【半殖民地】semi-colony：～半封建社会 *semi-colonial, semi-feudal society*

【半制浆】paper making half stuff; semi-pulp

【半制品】同〖半成品〗

【半中间】middle; halfway：他一气儿游到河的～。*He swam halfway across the river at a stretch.* / 这事～出了岔儿。*Something went wrong when the work was in progress.*

【半中腰】〈口〉middle; halfway：山的～有一座亭子。*A pavilion is halfway up the hill.* / 他的话说到～就停住了。*He broke off in the middle of a sentence.*

【半主权国】half-sovereign state

【半自动】semi-automatic ◇ ～步枪 semi-automatic rifle; ～化 semi-automatization; ～信息转接站 semi-automatic message switching centre

【半自耕农】semi-tenant peasant; semi-owner peasant

【半字节】(四位元)nibble(or nybble)

扮 动 ❶ be dressed up as; play the part of; disguise oneself as：他在戏里～一位老贫农。*In the opera he plays the part of an old poor peasant.* ❷ put on (an expression)：～鬼脸 *make grimaces; make faces*

【扮相】the appearance of an actor or actress in costume and makeup：～好 *cut a good figure when in costume and makeup*

【扮演】play the part of; act

【扮装】(of an actor, etc.) put on makeup; make up

伴 Ⅰ 名 companion; partner：我得找个～儿一块儿去。*I have to find someone to go with me.* / 跟我一起旅游的都是挺不错的～儿。*My fellow tourists were all good companions.* Ⅱ 动 accompany：行政命令必须～之以说服教育。*Administrative regulations must be accompanied by persuasion and education.*

【伴唱】❶ vocal accompaniment ❷ accompany (a singer)

【伴读】accompany one's spouse who is studying abroad

【伴侣】companion; mate; partner

【伴娘】bridesmaid

【伴生气】[油] associated gas

【伴随】accompany; follow：肖邦的夜曲～我度过了这个晚上。*Chopin's nocturnes accompanied me throughout the night.*

【伴舞】❶ accompanying dancer ❷ (hired) dancing girl; escort

【伴星】[天] companion (star)

【伴音信号】sound signal

【伴奏】accompany (with musical instruments)：钢琴～ *piano accompaniment* / 手风琴～：张小芳

Accompanied on the accordion by Zhang Xiaofang / ～者 *accompanist*

拌 动 mix：～匀 *mix thoroughly* / ～饲料 *mix fodder* / ～鸡丝 *shredded chicken salad* / ～黄瓜 *cucumber salad* / 香椿～豆腐 *bean curd and toon buds salad* / ～海蜇皮 *jellyfish salad*

【拌和】mix and stir；blend

【拌面】noodles served with soy sauce，sesame butter，etc.

【拌种】[农] seed dressing ◇ ～机 seed dresser

【拌嘴】bicker；squabble；quarrel：我一时忍不住，和她拌了几句嘴。*I couldn't control myself and exchanged a few hot words with her.*

绊 动 (cause to) stumble；trip：他被树根～了一下。*He stumbled over the root of a tree.* / 差点儿～了我一跤。*I tripped and almost fell.* / 别让日常事务把你～住了。*Don't get yourself bogged down in routine work.* / ～手～脚 *be in the way*

【绊脚石】stumbling block；obstacle：害怕批评是进步的～。*Your fear of criticism is an obstacle to your ideological progress.*

【绊腿】trip；tie up person's movements

瓣 Ⅰ 名 ❶ petal：这朵花儿掉了一个～儿。*This flower has lost one petal.* ❷ segment or section (of a tangerine，etc.)；clove (of garlic) ❸ valve；lamella：三尖瓣 / 鳃瓣 ❹ fragment；piece：摔成几～ *be broken into several pieces* Ⅱ 量 一～儿蒜 *a clove of garlic*

【瓣膜】[生理] valve

bāng

邦 名 nation；state；country：邻邦

【邦交】relations between two countries；diplomatic relations：建立（断绝，恢复）～ *establish (sever，resume) diplomatic relations*

【邦联】confederation

帮 Ⅰ 动 ❶ help；assist；aid：你～我翻译一下这首诗好吗？*Will you please help me to translate this poem?* / 我～他搬了行李。*I helped him with his luggage.* ❷ be hired：～短工 *serve as a seasonal labourer* Ⅱ 名 ❶ side (of a boat，truck，etc.) or upper (of a shoe)：鞋帮 ❷ outer leaf (of cabbage，etc.) ❸ gang；band；clique：匪帮 ❹ secret society；underworld gang Ⅲ 量 group：来了一～孩子。*Here comes a group of children.*

【帮办】❶ 〈旧〉assist in managing：～军务 *assist in handling military affairs* ❷ deputy：副国务卿～ *Deputy Under Secretary (of the U. S. Department of State)* / 助理国务卿～ *Deputy Assistant Secretary (of the U. S. Department of State)*

【帮厨】help in the mess kitchen

【帮倒忙】be more of a hindrance than a help；do sb. a disservice：她替儿子做作业，反而帮了倒忙。*She did her son a disservice by doing his homework for him.*

【帮工】❶ help with farm work ❷ casual labourer (in pre-liberation countryside)；seasonal labourer；helper

【帮会】secret society；underworld gang

【帮教】help and educate：对失足青少年进行～工作 *help and educate young people who have gone astray*；*help and educate delinquent youth*

【帮忙】help；give (or lend) a hand；do a favour；do a good turn：～把这封信寄一下好吗？*Will you do me a favour and mail this letter?* / 我能帮什么忙吗？*Can I be of any assistance?*

【帮派】faction：～体系 *factionalist setup*

【帮腔】❶ [音] vocal accompaniment in some traditional Chinese operas ❷ speak in support of sb.；echo sb.；chime in with sb.：他看见没有人～，也就不再坚持了。*When he saw nobody supporting him，he no longer insisted.*

【帮手】helper；assistant

【帮闲】❶ hang on to and serve the rich and powerful by literary hack work，etc. ❷ literary hack ◇ ～文人 literary hack

【帮凶】accomplice；accessary

【帮助】help；assist；aid：～消化 *aid digestion* / 他～我学外文。*He helped me learn a foreign language.* / 希望你从思想上多给我～。*I hope you will give me as much help as you can to improve myself.*

【帮子】❶ outer leaf (of cabbage，etc.) ❷ upper (of a shoe)

梆 Ⅰ 名 watchman's clapper Ⅱ 象 rat-tat；rat-a-tat：～～～的敲门声 *a rat-a-tat at the door*

【梆子】❶ watchman's clapper ❷ [音] wooden clappers with bars of unequal length

bǎng

绑 动 ❶ bind；tie：～个三脚架 *tie three sticks together to make a tripod* ❷ bind sb.'s hands behind him；truss up

【绑匪】kidnapper

【绑架】❶ kidnap ❷ [农] stake：下午咱们给黄瓜～。*We're going to stake the cucumbers this afternoon.*

【绑票】kidnap (for ransom)

【绑腿】leg wrappings；puttee

榜 名 a list of names posted up：发榜

【榜样】example；model：～的力量是无穷的。*A fine example has boundless power.*

膀 名 ❶ upper arm；arm ❷ shoulder：肩膀 ❸ wing (of a bird)：翅膀 ——另见 páng

【膀臂】❶ 〈方〉upper arm；arm ❷ capable assistant；reliable helper；right-hand man

【膀子】❶ upper arm；arm：光着～ *be stripped to the waist* ❷ wing (of a bird)：鸭～ *duck wings*

bàng

蚌 名 freshwater mussel; clam

谤 动〈书〉slander; defame; vilify: 诽谤

傍 动 ❶ be close to (in distance); draw near: 船～了岸。*The boat drew alongside the bank.* ❷ close to (in time): 傍晚

【傍大款】(of girls) attach to money bags; to accompany a rich man; to rely on someone with a lot of money

【傍晚】toward evening; at nightfall; at dusk

【傍系】coset: a subset of a mathematical group

棒 Ⅰ 名 stick; club; cudgel: 木～ *wooden stick* / 垒球～ *softball bat* Ⅱ 形〈口〉good; fine; excellent; strong: 字写得～ *write a good hand* / 庄稼长得真～。*The crops are excellent.* / ～小伙子 *a strong young fellow* / 你干得～极了。*You've done a first-rate job.*

【棒槌】❶ wooden club (used to beat clothes in washing) ❷〈方〉clumsy, awkward

【棒磨机】[矿] rod mill

【棒球】baseball: ～场 *baseball field*

【棒杀】"kill with the club"—cause sb. to fail by open attack: 对于年轻有为的作家,既不要"～",也不要"捧杀"。*It is essential to prevent the suppression of promising young writers by harsh criticism, as well as their corruption by flattery.*

【棒糖】lollipop; sucker

【棒针】thick knitting needle

【棒子】❶ stick; club; cudgel ❷〈方〉maize; corn ❸〈方〉ear of maize (or corn); corncob ◇ ～面 cornmeal; corn flour

磅 Ⅰ 量 ❶ pound (a measure of weight) ❷ [刷] point (type): 六～字太小了。*6-point type is too small.* Ⅱ 名 scales: 把行李搁在～上看有多重。*Put the luggage on the scales and see how much it weighs.* Ⅲ 动 weigh: ～体重 *weigh oneself or sb. on the scales* ——另见 páng

【磅秤】platform scale; platform balance

镑 量 pound (a currency): 英镑

bāo

包 Ⅰ 动 ❶ wrap: 把东西～起来 *wrap things up* / ～书 *wrap up a book in a piece of paper; put a jacket (or cover) on a book* / ～饺子 *make jiaozi (dumplings)* ❷ surround; encircle; envelop: 浓雾～住了群山。*The hills were enveloped in dense fog.* ❸ include; contain: 包含 ❹ undertake the whole thing: 这事～在我身上。*Just leave it all to me.* ❺ assure; guarantee: ～你满意。*You'll like it, I assure you.* or *Satisfaction guaranteed.* ❻ hire; charter: ～一只船 *hire (or charter) a boat* / ～三桌酒席 *reserve three banquet tables* Ⅱ 名 ❶ bundle; package; pack; packet; parcel: 邮包 ❷ bag; sack: 书包 ❸ protuberance; swelling; lump: 脑门上碰了个～ *have (or get) a bump on one's forehead* / 腿上起了个～ *have a swelling in the leg* ❹ yurt Ⅲ 量 package; bundle: 一大～衣服 *a big bundle of clothes* / 一～香烟 *a packet (or pack) of cigarettes*

【包办】❶ take care of everything concerning a job: 这件事你一个人～了吧。*You'd better do the whole job yourself.* ❷ run the whole show; monopolize everything ◇ ～代替 take away sb. else's work; run things all by oneself without consulting others; ～婚姻 an arranged marriage

【包庇】shield; harbour; cover up: 互相～ *shield each other* / ～坏人坏事 *harbour evildoers and cover up their evil deeds*

【包藏】contain; harbour; conceal: 大海～着许多秘密。*The sea contains many mysteries.* ◇ ～祸心 harbour evil intentions

【包产】make a production contract; take full responsibility for output quotas: ～合同 *contract for fixed output* / ～指标 *targets stated in a contract for fixed output*

【包产到户】fixing of farm output quotas for each household

【包场】book a whole theatre or cinema; make a block booking

【包车】❶ vehicle hired by an individual or institution for a certain period of time; chartered car or bus: 拉～ *pull a rickshaw exclusively for sb.* / ～夫 *rickshaw coolie in sb.'s employ* / 门前挤满了各公司的～。*Lines of cars or buses chartered by companies are parked in front of the door.* ❷ be responsible for the use and maintenance of a locomotive, bus or trolley: ～组 *team responsible for such a vehicle; responsible crew* ❸ hire a car for a period of time; charter: 包一辆车 *charter a car*

【包抄】out flank; envelop: 从两翼～逃敌 *out flank the fleeing enemy on both wings* / 骑兵分三路～过去。*The cavalry closed in on the enemy in a three-pronged attack.*

【包乘】charter (a plane, ship, etc.) ◇～制[交通] responsible crew system; ～组 [交通] (responsible) crew

【包虫病】echinococcosis; hydatid disease

【包饭】❶ get or supply meals at a fixed rate; board: 在附近的饭馆里～ *board at a nearby restaurant* ❷ meals thus arranged

【包房】❶ rent a hotel room for a period of time ❷ hotel room thus rented

【包袱】❶ cloth-wrapper ❷ a bundle wrapped in cloth ❸ millstone round one's neck; load; weight; burden: 思想～ *a load (or weight) on one's mind* / 不要把成绩当～ *not allow one's merits to become a hindrance to one's progress*

【包干】be responsible for a task until it is completed：分片～ *divide up the work and assign a part to each individual or group*
【包干制】a system of payment partly in kind and partly in cash
【包工】❶（又作'包活'）undertake to perform work within a time limit and according to specifications；contract for a job ❷ contractor ◇～包料 contract for labor and materials of work contracted；fixing the amount of materials in accordance with the amount；～头 labour contractor
【包购包销】exclusive right to purchase and sell
【包管】assure；guarantee：～退换。*Merchandise will be exchanged if found unsatisfactory.* / 吃这个方子，～你三天痊愈。*If you take this prescription, you are sure to fully recover within three days.*
【包裹】❶ wrap up；bind up：用布把伤口～起来。*Bandage up the wound.* ❷ bundle；package；parcel：今天上午我收到一个邮寄来的～。*I got a parcel in the post this morning.* ◇～单 parcel form
【包含】contain；embody；include：他的建议～不少合理的因素。*His proposal contains much that is reasonable.* / 这句话～好几层意思。*This statement has quite a few implications.*
【包涵】〈套〉excuse；forgive；bear with：我唱得不好，请多多～。*Excuse (me for) my poor singing.*
【包换】guarantee to accept the return or exchange (of products that do not meet standards)：商品不合格～。*Exchange or return is guaranteed if the commodity does not meet the standards.*
【包机】❶ charter a plane ❷ a chartered plane
【包金】cover with gold leaf；gild
【包茎】phimosis
【包括】include；consist of；comprise；incorporate：他的报告～三个方面。*His report contained three aspects.*
【包揽】undertake the whole thing；take on everything：这样多的事，一个人～不了。*No one person can take on so much work.*
【包揽词讼】engage in pettifoggery
【包罗】include；cover；embrace：民间艺术～甚广。*Folk art covers a wide range.*
【包罗万象】all-embracing；all-inclusive
【包络】envelope ◇～检波 envelope detection
【包赔】guarantee to pay compensations
【包皮】❶ wrapping；wrapper ❷［生理］prepuce；foreskin ◇～环切术［医］circumcision
【包票】old name for 保单 ——另见〖打包票〗
【包容】❶ pardon；forgive ❷ contain；hold
【包身工】indentured labourer
【包退】money back guarantee ◇～包换 guarantee change of article or refund if unsatisfactory；refund or change for a better one；guarantee exchange if returned as unsuitable
【包围】surround；encircle：亭子被茂密的松林～着。*The pavilion is surrounded by a thick pine forest.* ◇～圈 ring of encirclement
【包线制】［交通］responsibility system by line
【包厢】box (in a theatre or concert hall)
【包销】❶ have exclusive selling rights ❷ be the sole agent for a production unit or a firm
【包圆儿】〈口〉❶ buy the whole lot：你少算一点的话，这些我～了。*If you give me a reduction, I'll buy the whole lot.* ❷ finish up (or off)：剩下的活儿我一个人～了。*I'll finish off what's left of the work.*
【包扎】wrap up；bind up；pack：～伤口 *bind up (or dress) a wound* / 待运的自行车已经～好了。*The bicycles to be transported are packed.*
【包扎艺术品】empaquetage
【包治百病】guarantee a cure for all ills；be guaranteed to cure all ills：～的药方 *a remedy for all ills；panacea；cure-all*
【包装】pack (commodities)；package ◇～标志 packing mark；～标准 standardization of packing；～车间 packing department；～多样 diversified packing；～设计 packing design；～箱 packing box (or case)；～纸 wrapping (or packing) paper
【包子】steamed stuffed bun
【包租】❶〈旧〉rent land or a house for subletting ❷〈旧〉fixed rent for farmland (to be paid no matter how bad the harvest might be) ❸ hire (a car, boat, etc.) for a period of time；charter

苞 Ⅰ 名 bud：花苞 Ⅱ 形〈书〉luxuriant；profuse；thick：竹～松茂 *bamboos and pines growing in profusion*

孢（构词成分）见下
【孢子】［植］spore：～体 *sporophyte* ◇～生殖［植］sporogony；～植物 cryptogam

炮 动 ❶ quick-fry；sauté：～羊肉 *quick-fried mutton* ❷ dry by heat：湿衣服搁在热炕上，一会儿就～干了。*Put the damp clothes on a hot kang and they'll soon dry.* ——另见 páo；pào

胞 Ⅰ 名（human）afterbirth Ⅱ 形 born of the same parents：～兄弟 *full (or blood) brothers*
【胞衣】［中］(human) afterbirth

剥 动 shell；peel；skin：～花生 *shell peanuts* / ～香蕉 *peel a banana* / ～兔皮 *skin a rabbit* ——另见 bō

龅（构词成分）见下
【龅牙】bucktooth

褒 Ⅰ 动 praise；honour；commend：褒扬 Ⅱ 形〈书〉(of clothes) loose；large：～衣博带 *a loose gown with wide girdle*
【褒贬】❶ pass judgment on；appraise：～人物 *pass judgment on people* / 不加～ *make no comment, complimentary or otherwise；neither praise nor censure* ❷speak ill of；cry down：别在背地里～人。*Don't speak ill of anybody behind*

his back.
【褒奖】praise and honour; commend and award
【褒扬】praise; commend
【褒义】commendatory (or complimentary) sense: "崇高"总带有～。*The word 崇高 is always commendatory*. ◇～词 commendatory term

báo

雹 名 hail
【雹暴】hailstorm
【雹灾】disaster caused by hail
【雹子】hail; hailstone
薄 形 ❶ thin; flimsy: ～纸 *thin paper* / ～布 *flimsy cloth* ❷ weak; light: 酒味很～。*This is a light wine*. ❸ lacking in warmth; cold: 待他不～ *treat him quite well* ❹ infertile; poor: ～地 *poor land* ——另见 bó; bò
【薄板】[冶] sheet metal; sheet: 不锈钢～ *stainless sheet steel* / ～轧机 *sheet rolling mill*
【薄饼】thin pancake
【薄钢板】sheet steel
【薄壳结构】[建] shell structure
【薄呢】woollenette
【薄纱】chiffon
【薄页纸】❶ tissue paper ❷ flimsy

bǎo

宝 Ⅰ 名 treasure: 粮食是～中之～。*Grain is the treasure of treasures*. Ⅱ 形 ❶ precious; treasured ❷〈尊〉your: ～眷 *your wife and children*; *your family* / ～号 *your firm*; *your shop*
【宝宝】(a pet name for a child) darling; baby ◇～装 infant clothes
【宝贝】❶ treasured object; treasure ❷ darling; baby ❸ (used ironically) good-for-nothing or queer character: 这人真是个～! *What a fellow!* ◇～疙瘩〈方〉darling child
【宝刹】❶ pagoda in a temple ❷〈尊〉your temple (or monastery)
【宝刀不老】the man is old, but not his sword—he is still at the height of his powers
【宝典】a treasured book; a revered book
【宝贵】❶ valuable; precious: ～意见 *valuable suggestion* / ～经验 *valuable experience* / ～文物 *precious cultural relics* ❷ value; treasure; set store by: 你不希罕, 他可是～得很。*You don't care for it, but he treasures it dearly*.
【宝剑】a double-edged sword
【宝库】treasure-house: 中国医药学是一个伟大的～。*Chinese medicine and pharmacology are a great treasure-house*.
【宝蓝】sapphire blue
【宝石】precious stone; gem ◇～学 gemology
【宝塔】pagoda ◇～菜 [植] Chinese artichoke; ～筒子 [纺] cone
【宝物】treasure
【宝藏】precious (mineral) deposits: 发掘地下～ *unearth buried treasure*; *tap mineral resources* / 民间艺术的～真是无穷无尽。*Folk art is a truly inexhaustible treasure trove*.
【宝座】throne
饱 Ⅰ 形 ❶ have eaten one's fill; be full: 吃～喝足 *eat and drink one's fill* / 我～了。一点也吃不下了。*I've had enough. I can't eat any more*. ❷ full; plump: 谷粒很～。*The grains are quite plump*. Ⅱ 副 fully; to the full: ～览海岛的美丽风光 *drink in the beauty of the island scenery* / 她的眼眶里～含着幸福的热泪。*Her eyes filled with tears of joy*. Ⅲ 动 satisfy: 饱眼福
【饱餐】eat one's full; feast one's eyes on: ～了一顿狍子肉 *eat roe deer meat to one's heart's content* / ～秀色 *feast one's eyes on beautiful scenery (or the beauty of a girl)*; *enjoy the beautiful scenery very much*.
【饱尝】❶ enjoy to the full: ～美味 *have one's fill of delicate dishes* ❷ experience (or suffer): ～艰辛 *endure all hardships* / ～人世的痛苦 *experience all the agonies of life* / ～铁窗风味 *have a full taste of life behind bars*
【饱汉不知饿汉饥】The well-fed don't know how the starving suffer.
【饱和】saturation: ～点 *saturation point* / 相对湿度为百分之百时空气即呈～。*When the relative humidity reaches 100 per cent the air is saturated*. ◇～差 [气] saturation deficit (or deficiency); ～轰炸 saturation bombing; ～剂 [化] saturant; ～器 saturator; ～溶液 [化] saturated solution; ～压力 saturation pressure; ～值 saturation value
【饱经沧桑】have experienced many vicissitudes of life: 她一生～。*She has experienced the vicissitudes of life*.
【饱经风霜】weather-beaten; having had one's fill of hardships: ～的面容 *a weather-worn face* / 一位～的老渔民 *an old fisherman who has survived the hardships of life*
【饱满】full; plump: 颗粒～的小麦 *plump-eared wheat* / 精神～ *full of vigour (or vitality)*; *energetic* ◇～度 [农] *plumpness (of seeds)*
【饱食终日, 无所用心】*eat all day without exerting one's mind*; *eat three square meals a day and do no work*; *be sated with food and lead an idle life*
【饱私囊】*line one's pocket*; *swell personal fortunes*; *commit embezzlement*; *line one's pockets*; *feather one's nest*
【饱学】*learned*; *erudite*; *scholarly* ◇～之士 *an erudite person*; *a learned scholar*; *a man of learning*
【饱眼福】*feast one's eyes on sth.*; *enjoy to the full (watching a show, scene, etc.)*
保 Ⅰ 动 ❶ protect; defend: ～家卫国 *protect our homes and defend our country* ❷ keep;

maintain; preserve: 这种热水瓶能～暖二十四小时。*This kind of thermos flask keeps water hot for 24 hours.* ❸ guarantee; ensure: 旱涝～收 *ensure stable yields despite drought or waterlogging* / 西瓜～甜。*Watermelon sweetness guaranteed.* ❹ stand guarantor (or surety) for sb.; bail: 他把儿子从派出所～了出来。*He bailed his son out from the police substation.* Ⅱ 名 guarantor: 作保

【保安】❶ ensure public security ❷ ensure safety (for workers engaged in production): ～措施 *security measures* / ～规程 *safety regulations* / ～装置 *protective device* ◇～人员 security personnel

【保本】protect any investment or deposit against possible loss; keep the capital intact: ～保值 *protect (bank deposits, etc.) from declining in value (as a result of inflation)* / 这笔生意仅仅～而已。*I only broke even on the deal.*

【保镖】bodyguard

【保不住】most likely; more likely than not; may well: 这个天儿很难说, ～会下雨。*The weather is rather uncertain; most likely it's going to rain.*

【保藏】keep in store; preserve: 食品～ *food preservation* / 把这幅画好好～起来。*Preserve the painting carefully.*

【保持】keep; maintain; preserve: ～安静 *keep quiet* / ～冷静的头脑 *keep a cool head; keep cool* / ～中立 *remain neutral; maintain neutrality* / ～警惕 *maintain vigilance; be on the alert* / ～跳高记录 *retain the high jump record*

【保存】preserve; conserve; keep: ～实力 *preserve one's strength; conserve one's forces* / 这批文物～得很完好。*These cultural relics are well preserved.* ◇～期 retention period

【保单】guarantee slip; warranty

【保底】❶ protect an investment or deposit against currency depreciation ❷ guarantee a minimum sum; ensure a basic figure: 上不封顶, 下不～ *set no maximum or minimum; impose no ceiling or floor figure*

【保兑文句】confirming clause

【保兑信用证】confirming credit

【保兑银行】confirming bank

【保费】insurance fee

【保付支票】certified check

【保管】❶ take care of: 图书～工作 *the care of library books* / 这个仓库的粮食～得很好。*The grains in this barn are well preserved.* ❷ warehouseman; storeman; storekeeper ❸ certainly; surely: 他～不知道。*He certainly doesn't know.* / 你只要努力, ～能学好汉语。*I assure you that you can learn Chinese if you make the effort.* ◇～费 storage charges; storage fee; ～室 storeroom; ～员 warehouseman; storeman; storekeeper

【保函】[经]letter of guarantee (L/G)

【保护】protect; safeguard: ～眼睛 *protect one's eyes* / ～环境, 防止污染 *protect the environment against pollution* / ～现场 *keep intact the scene of a crime or accident* ◇～地 protectorate; dependent territory; ～关税 protective tariff; ～关税政策 policy of protective tariffs; ～国 protectorate; ～剂 protectant; preservative; ～价 protective pricing; price set to protect the manufacturers or producers; ～贸易政策 policy of protection; ～鸟 protected birds; ～人 guardian; ～伞 protective umbrella (a protecting power); ～色 protective coloration; ～涂剂 protective coating; ～知识产权 protect intellectual property rights; ～主义 protectionism

【保护性关税】protective duty

【保护性拘留】protective custody; protective detention

【保护性贸易】protective trade

【保皇党】royalists

【保加利亚】Bulgaria ◇ ～人 Bulgarian; ～语 Bulgarian (language)

【保驾】〈诙〉escort the Emperor: 放心吧, 我给你～。*Don't worry. I'll escort you.*

【保健】health protection; health care: 妇幼～ *maternal and child hygiene; mother and child care* ◇～按摩 keep-fit massage; ～操 setting-up exercises; ～产品 health products; ～费 health subsidies; ～食品 health food; ～网 health care network; ～箱 medical kit; ～员 health worker; ～站 health station (or centre); ～珍品 health treasure; ～组织 health organizations

【保洁】keep the environment clean; do sanitation work: 加强公园的～工作 *step up the sanitation work in parks*

【保洁箱】litter-bin

【保龄球】❶ tenpin bowling; tenpins; bowling ❷ bowling ball

【保留】❶ continue to have; retain: 这个地方还～着原来的面貌。*The place still looks the same as before.* ❷ hold (or keep) back; reserve: 持～意见 *have reservations* / 有意见都谈出来, 不要～。*Don't hold back anything you want to say.* ◇～剧目 repertory; repertoire; ～条款 reservation clause

【保留地】reservation (as Indian reservations in the U.S.)

【保媒】〈旧〉be a matchmaker (or go-between); arrange a match

【保密】maintain secrecy; keep sth. secret: 这事绝对～。*This must be kept absolutely secret.* or *This is strictly confidential.* / 我说的事儿你可要～。*Keep mum about what I said.* ◇～级别 security classification; ～码 secret code; ～条例 security regulations; ～文件 classified document

【保苗】[农] keep a full stand of seedlings

【保姆】❶ housemaid; housekeeper ❷ (children's) nurse

【保暖防风】warm and windproof

【保全】❶ save from damage; preserve: ～名誉 *preserve one's reputation* / ～面子 *save face* ❷ maintain; keep in good repair: ～工 *maintenance worker*

【保释】release on bail; bail: 准予(不准)～ *accept* (*refuse*) *bail* ◇～保证书 bail bonds

【保守】❶ guard; keep: ～国家机密 *guard state secrets* ❷ conservative: ～观点 *conservative point of view* / ～思想 *conservative ideas* (*or thinking*) / ～的估计 *a conservative estimate* / ～派 *conservatives* / 这计划定得有些～。*This is rather a conservative plan*. ◇～党 Conservative Party (as in Britain); ～疗法[医] conservative treatment; ～主义 conservatism

【保税】bonded: ～仓库 *bonded warehouse* / ～货物 *bonded goods* / ～区 *bonded area* / ～运输 *bonded transportation*

【保送】recommend sb. for admission to school (without taking the entrance examination), etc.: ～留学生 *a student recommended to study abroad*

【保胎】prevent miscarriages

【保泰松】[药] phenylbutazone

【保外就医】[法] be released on bail for medical treatment; remain out of custody and obtain medical treatment

【保卫】defend; safeguard: ～祖国 *defend one's country* / ～国家主权和领土完整 *safeguard state sovereignty and territorial integrity* ◇～部门 public security bodies; ～工作 security work; ～科 security section (of an organization)

【保温】heat preservation: 积雪可以～保墒。*A layer of snow can preserve soil moisture and prevent it from freezing*. / 这个暖瓶不～。*This thermos flask doesn't keep the heat well*. ◇～杯 thermos mug; ～材料 thermal insulation material; ～层[建] (thermal) insulating layer; ～车[铁路] refrigerator wagon (or car); ～瓶 vacuum flask (or bottle); thermos

【保息股票】guaranteed stock

【保鲜】keep vegetables, fruit, etc. fresh; preserve freshness: ～包装 *fresh-keeping packaging*; *keep fresh package* ◇～剂 antistaling agent; ～膜 clingfilm; plastic wrap; ～期 length for preservation

【保险】❶ insurance: 人寿(海损)～ *life* (*maritime*) *insurance* / 你的汽车保了险没有? *Is your car insured*? / 保了火险 *have insured against fire* ❷ safe: 骑车太快可不～。*It's not safe to cycle too fast*. / 你还是带上雨衣吧,～点儿。*You'd better take your raincoat just to be on the safe side*. ❸ be sure; be bound to: 他明天～会来。*He is sure to come tomorrow*. / ～能行! *It's bound to work*. / 你依我的话,～不会出错。*If you follow my advice, then I can assure you that nothing will go wrong*. ◇～代理人 insurance agent; ～带 safety belt; ～刀 safety razor; ～范围 insurance coverage; ～费 insurance premium; ～粉 sodium hydrosulphite; ～杆 bumper bar; ～杠 bumper (on a car); ～公司 insurance company; ～柜 strongbox; safe; ～国有化 nationalization of insurance; ～盒 fuse box; ～回扣 insurance rebate; ～机 safety (of a firearm); ～金 insurance amount; insurance money; ～金额 insurance amount; ～经纪人 insurance broker; ～客户 policy holder; ～赔偿金 insurance indemnity; ～凭证 C/T(certification of insurance); ～期 insurance period; ～契约 contract of insurance; ～人 the insurer; assurer; ～丝 fuse; fuse-wire; ～索赔 insurance claim; ～弹簧 relief spring; ～箱 strongbox; safe; ～证明书 insurance certificate; ～装置 safety device

【保修】guarantee to keep sth. in good repair: 这只表～一年。*There is a year's guarantee with this watch*. or *This watch is guaranteed for a year*. ◇～期 guarantee period

【保养】❶ take good care of (or conserve) one's health: 他很会～,六十岁了,还显得很年轻。*He certainly knows how to take care of himself, looking so young at the age of* 60. ❷ maintain; keep in good repair: 机器～ *maintenance* (*or upkeep*) *of machinery* / 这条路～得很好。*This road is in good repair*. ◇～费 maintenance cost; upkeep; ～工 maintenance worker

【保佑】bless and protect: 我们相信人定胜天,不靠老天～。*We believe in man's conquest of nature and don't rely on blessings from heaven*.

【保幼人员】daycare workers

【保育】child care; child welfare ◇～员 child-care worker; nurse; ～院 nursery school

【保障】ensure; guarantee; safeguard: ～人民言论自由 *guarantee freedom of speech for the people* / 在这里职业有～。*Jobs are secure here*.

【保真度】fidelity: 高～ *high fidelity*

【保证】pledge; guarantee; assure; ensure: 我～说到做到。*I assure you I'll do what I say*. / ～供应。*There's a guaranteed supply*. ◇～单位 guarantor unit

【保证金】❶ earnest money; cash deposit ❷ [法] bail

【保证人】[法] ❶ guarantor ❷ bail

【保证书】written pledge; guarantee; guaranty; letter of guarantee

【保值】be inflation-proof in value ◇～储蓄 inflation-proof savings deposit; value-ensured savings deposit

【保职停薪】(又作'留职停薪'或'停薪留职') to retain the job but suspend the salary

【保质保量】guarantee both quality and quantity

【保质期】quality guarantee period

【保重】(used in expressing one's concern about sb.'s health) take care of oneself: 多多～。*Take good care of yourself*. or *Look after yourself*.

鸨 名 ❶ [动] bustard ❷ procuress: 老鸨

【鸨母】(又作'鸨儿') a woman running a brothel; procuress; madam

葆 动 〈书〉preserve; nurture: 永～青春 *keep alive the fervour of youth*

堡 名 fort; fortress: 地堡
【堡礁】barrier reef
【堡垒】fort; fortress; stronghold; blockhouse: ～是最容易从内部攻破的。*The easiest way to capture a fortress is from within.* ◇～战 blockhouse warfare

bào

报 Ⅰ 动 ❶ report; announce; declare: ～公安局 *report to the public security bureau* / ～上级批准 *report* (*or submit*) *sth. to the higher authorities for approval* ❷ reply; respond; reciprocate: ～友人书 *a* (*letter in*) *reply to a friend* / ～以热烈的掌声 *respond with warm applause* ❸ recompense; requite: 无以为～ *be unable to repay a kindness* ❹ revenge: 报仇 Ⅱ 名 ❶ retribution; judgment ❷ newspaper: 日报 ❸ periodical; journal: 画报 ❹ bulletin; report: 战报 ❺ telegram; cable: 发报
【报案】report a case to the security authorities
【报表】forms for reporting statistics, etc.; report forms ◇～生成 reports generation
【报偿】repay; recompense
【报仇】revenge; avenge: 为父～ *avenge one's father* / 报私仇 *settle personal scores*
【报仇雪恨】avenge oneself; take revenge
【报酬】reward; remuneration; pay: 不计～ *not concerned about pay; irrespective of remuneration* / 工作很累，～不多 *get very little in reward for one's hard work*
【报答】repay; requite: 我怎么也～不了您的恩情。*How can I ever repay you for your kindness?*
【报单】taxation form; declaration form
【报到】report for duty; check in; register: 向大会秘书处～ *check in at the secretariat of the congress* / 新生已开始～。*The new students have started registering.*
【报道】(又作'报导') ❶ report (news); cover: 据～ *it is reported that* / 各报都在第一版～了这个消息。*This was front-paged in all the papers.* ❷ news report; story: 一篇关于奥运会的～ *a news report about the Olympic Games*
【报恩】pay a debt of gratitude
【报废】❶ report sth. as worthless ❷ discard as useless; reject; scrap: 使～矿井复生 *reopen an abandoned mine* / 这架机器太旧，快～了。*This machine is so old it will soon have to be scrapped.*
【报分】[体] call the score
【报复】make reprisals; retaliate: 图谋～ *nurse thoughts of revenge* / ～性打击 *vindictive blow; retaliatory strike* / 杀害人质作为～ *retaliate by killing hostages* ◇～关税 retaliatory duties
【报告】❶ report; make known: ～大家一个好消息。*Here's a piece of good news for us all.* / 现在～新闻。*Here is the news.* ❷ report; speech; talk; lecture: 作～ *give a talk or lecture* / 总结～ *summing-up report* / 动员～ *mobilization speech* / ～会 *public lecture* / ～人 *speaker; lecturer* ◇～文学 reportage
【报关】declare sth. at customs; apply to customs: 你有什么东西要～吗? *Have you got anything to declare?* / 进出口货物～ *customs declaration for imports and exports* ◇～表 declaration form; customs declaration; ～代理行 customs house broker; ～代理人 customs agent; ～费 customs clearing fee; ～行 customs agency; ～人 declarant; ～手续 customs formalities; ～单 quotation list
【报馆】popular name for 报社
【报国】dedicate oneself to the service of one's country: 以身～ *lay down one's life for one's country*
【报户口】apply for a residence permit: 报临时户口 *apply for a temporary residence permit* / 给新生婴儿～ *register the birth of a child*
【报话机】handie-talkie
【报价】[经] quoted price ◇～单 quotation of prices
【报捷】report a success; announce a victory
【报界】the press; journalistic circles; the journalists: 向～发表谈话 *make a statement to the press*
【报警】❶ report (an incident) to the police: 报火警 *report a fire* ❷ give an alarm: 鸣钟～ *sound the alarm bell* / ～系统 *warning system* / ～显示 *alarm display* ◇～器 alarm; warner; warning device; ～信号 alerting signal
【报刊】newspapers and periodicals; the press
【报考】enter oneself for an examination: ～清华大学 *register for the entrance examinations to Qinghua University; apply for entrance to Qinghua University*
【报名】enter one's name; sign up: ～参加百米赛跑 *enter one's name for the 100-metre dash* / 他已在夜大学～了。*He has signed up for the evening university.*
【报幕】announce the items on a (theatrical) programme: ～员 *announcer*
【报批】submit to a higher authority for approval: 履行～手续 *go through the formalities to secure approval* / 层层～ *report to the higher authorities at different levels for examination and approval*
【报社】general office of a newspaper; newspaper office: 他在一家～工作。*He works for a newspaper.*
【报失】report the loss of sth. to the authorities concerned: 已向保卫部门～。*The loss has been reported to the security department.*
【报时】give the correct time ◇～器 chronopher; ～台 (telephone) time inquiry service
【报数】number off: ～! (*word of command*) *Count off!*
【报税】declare dutiable goods; make a statement of dutiable goods ◇～单 taxation form

【报摊】news-stand; news stall
【报头】masthead (of a newspaper, etc.); nameplate
【报务员】telegraph operator; radio operator
【报喜】announce good news; report success：我给大家～来了。*I've come with good news for all of you.*
【报喜不报忧】report the good news but not the bad; hold back unpleasant information
【报销】❶ submit an expense account; apply for reimbursement：向财务科～ *submit an expense account to the treasurer's office* / 旅费凭票～。*Travelling expenses can be reimbursed on handing in the tickets.* ❷ hand in a list of expended articles ❸〈口〉write off; wipe out
【报晓】(of a cock, bell, etc.) herald the break of day; be a harbinger of dawn：晨鸡～。*The crowing of roosters at dawn heralded the break of day.* / 远处传来～的钟声。*From afar came the chimes of a bell announcing the break of day.*
【报效】render service to repay sb's kindness：我参军是为了～祖国。*I enlisted in order to serve my country.*
【报谢】express appreciation (for sb.'s kindness or hospitality); acknowledge
【报信】notify; inform：赶快给他报个信儿。*Let him know as soon as possible.*
【报修】report to the relevant office and request the repair of something
【报业巨子】press baron
【报应】❶［宗］(佛教) retribution; judgment ❷ due punishment：这是他应得的～。*He's getting what he deserves.* / 他净干坏事，现在可遭～了。*He's getting paid back for all the bad things he's done.*
【报章】newspapers：～杂志 *newspapers and magazines*
【报账】render an account; submit an expense account; apply for reimbursement：修理费用可以～。*Costs of repairs may be reimbursed.*
【报支】file a request for reimbursement of expenses
【报纸】❶ newspaper：～夹 *newspaper holder* ❷ newsprint

刨 Ⅰ 动 plane sth. down; plane：～木板 *plane a board* Ⅱ 名 plane; planer; planing machine ——另见 páo

【刨冰】water ice (powdered or in shavings)
【刨程】［机］planing length
【刨齿】［机］gear-shaping：～机 *gear shaper*
【刨床】planer; planing machine
【刨刀】［机］❶ planer tool ❷ plane iron
【刨工】❶ planing ❷ planing machine operator; planer
【刨花】wood shavings ◇～板［建］shaving board
【刨刃儿】(又作'刨铁') plane iron
【刨式磨床】planer-type grinder
【刨式铣床】planer-type miller
【刨子】plane (a carpenter's tool)

抱 Ⅰ 动 ❶ hold or carry in the arms; embrace; hug：把小孩子～起来 *take a child in one's arms* / 不要～住错误观点不放。*Don't stick to your wrong views.* ❷ have one's first child or grandchild：她快～孙子了。*She'll soon be a grandmother.* ❸ adopt (a child)：他的女儿是～的。*His daughter is adopted.* ❹〈方〉hang together：～成一团 *gang up; hang together* ❺ cherish; harbour：～很大希望 *entertain high hopes* / ～正确的态度 *adopt (or take) a correct attitude* / 不～幻想 *cherish no illusions* Ⅱ 量 armful of：一～草 *an armful of hay* / 这棵树有一～粗。*You can just get your arms around this tree trunk.*

【抱病】be ill; be in bad health：～工作 *go on working in spite of ill health*
【抱不平】be outraged by an injustice (done to sb. else)：有人替他～。*Some felt indignant on his behalf.* ——另见〖打抱不平〗
【抱残守缺】cherish the outmoded and preserve the outworn—be conservative; be an anachronism
【抱粗腿】(又作'抱大腿') latch on to the rich and powerful; throw oneself under the protection of someone of influence or power
【抱佛脚】clasp Buddha's feet—profess devotion only when in trouble; make a hasty last-minute effort ——另见〖急来抱佛脚〗
【抱负】aspiration; ambition：很有～ *have high aspirations; cherish high ambitions*
【抱恨】have a gnawing regret
【抱恨终天】feel bitter regret to the end of one's days; have an aching void in one's heart
【抱愧】feel ashamed
【抱歉】be sorry; feel apologetic; regret：叫你久等了，很～。*Very sorry to have kept you waiting.* / 这书晚还了两天，很～。*I apologize for keeping the book two days overdue.*
【抱屈】feel wronged
【抱头鼠窜】cover the head and sneak away like a rat; scurry (or scamper) off like a frightened rat
【抱头痛哭】weep in each other's arms; cry on each other's shoulders
【抱窝】sit (on eggs); brood; hatch：母鸡～了。*The hen is sitting.*
【抱薪救火】carry faggots to put out a fire —adopt a wrong method to save a situation and end up by making it worse; do something counterproductive
【抱养】adopt (a child)
【抱怨】complain; grumble：不要总是～别人对你帮助不够。*Don't always complain that you haven't been given enough help.* / 他～自己的工资低。*He grumbled about his low pay.*

豹 名 leopard; panther

【豹猫】leopard cat

鲍 名 见〖鲍鱼〗

【鲍鱼】❶〈书〉salted fish ❷ abalone
【鲍鱼之肆】a shop which sells salted fish ——另见〖如入鲍鱼之肆〗

暴 Ⅰ形 ❶ sudden and violent ❷ cruel；savage；fierce：残暴 ❸ short-tempered；hot-tempered：脾气～ *have a hot temper* Ⅱ动 ❶ stick out；stand out；bulge：急得头上的青筋都～出来了 *be so agitated that the veins on one's forehead stand out* ❷〈书〉waste；ruin；spoil：自暴自弃
【暴病】sudden attack of a serious illness：得～ *be suddenly seized with a severe illness* / ～而死 *die of a sudden illness*
【暴跌】steep fall (in price)；slump：股票价格～。*There was a slump in share prices.*
【暴动】insurrection；rebellion；riot：举行～ *raise an insurrection；stage a riot*
【暴发】❶ break out：山洪～。*Torrents of water rushed down the mountain.* ❷〈贬〉suddenly become rich or important；get rich quick：～户 *upstart*
【暴风】❶ storm wind ❷ storm (force 11 wind)
【暴风雪】snowstorm；blizzard
【暴风雨】rainstorm；storm；tempest：遇上～ *be caught in a storm* / ～般的掌声 *thunderous applause*
【暴风骤雨】violent storm；hurricane；tempest：其势如～ *with the force of a hurricane*
【暴富】suddenly become rich；get rich quick
【暴光】同〖曝光〗
【暴洪】a sudden，violent flood；flash flood
【暴君】tyrant；despot
【暴力】violence；force：～行为 *an act of violence* / 电影里的～镜头 *violence (or violent scenes) shown in films* / ～革命 *violent revolution* ◇ ～工具 means of violence
【暴利】sudden huge profits
【暴戾】〈书〉ruthless and tyrannical；cruel and fierce
【暴戾恣睢】cruel and despotic；tyrannical
【暴烈】violent；fierce：性情～ *have a fiery temper*
【暴露】expose；reveal；lay bare：～思想 *lay bare one's thoughts* / ～目标 *give away one's position* / ～在光天化日之下 *be exposed to the light of day* ◇ ～文学 literature of exposure (exposing the dark side of a society)；～无遗 be thoroughly exposed
【暴乱】riot；rebellion；revolt
【暴怒】violent rage；fury
【暴虐】brutal；tyrannical
【暴殄天物】a reckless waste of the products of nature
【暴跳如雷】stamp with fury；fly into a rage：气得～ *stamp frantically in anger* / 他～地发了一顿脾气。*He stormed and raged in a fit of temper.*
【暴徒】ruffian；thug
【暴行】savage act；outrage；atrocity
【暴雨】torrential rain；rainstorm：下了一阵～。*There was a heavy downpour.*
【暴躁】irascible；irritable：脾气～ *be irritable by nature；be hot-tempered*
【暴涨】(of floods，prices，etc.) rise suddenly and sharply：河水～。*The river suddenly rose.* / 物价～。*Prices soared (or skyrocketed).*
【暴政】tyranny；despotic rule
【暴卒】die of a sudden illness；die suddenly

爆 动 ❶ explode；burst：车胎～了。*The tyre's burst.* / 子弹打在石头上，～起许多火星。*The bullet hit the rock and sent sparks flying from it.* ❷ quick-fry；quick-boil：葱～牛肉 *quick-fried beef with scallions*
【爆发】erupt；burst out；break out：火山～ *volcanic eruption* / 战争～。*War broke out.* / 人群中～出一片欢呼声。*The crowd burst into cheers.* ◇ ～力［体］explosive force
【爆管】cartridge igniter；squib
【爆花】❶ snuff (of a wick) ❷ 同〖爆米花儿〗
【爆冷门】(of a contest，etc.) produce an unexpected winner；a dark horse bobbing up
【爆裂】burst；crack：豌豆过熟就会～。*Pea pods burst open when overripe.*
【爆满】❶ (of a theatre，cinema，etc.) have a full house；house full ❷ (of a stadium，etc.) be filled to capacity
【爆米花儿】❶ puffed rice ❷ popcorn
【爆破】blow up；demolish；dynamite；blast：连续～ *successive demolitions* / ～敌人的碉堡 *blow up an enemy's pillbox* ◇ ～弹 blasting cartridge；～手 dynamiter；～筒 bangalore (torpedo)；～英雄 demolition hero；ace dynamiter；～炸弹 demolition bomb；～组 demolition team
【爆音】［航空］sonic boom；shock-wave noise
【爆炸】explode；blow up；detonate：～力 *explosive force* / 炸弹～了。*A bomb exploded.* / ～性新闻 *shocking news* ◇ ～极限 explosive limit；～物 explosive
【爆竹】(又作'爆仗') firecracker：放～ *let off firecrackers* / ～没响。*The firecracker didn't go off.*

曝 (构词成分)见下
【曝光】❶［摄］exposure：多次～ *multiple exposure* / ～表 *exposure meter* / ～宽容度 *exposure latitude* ❷ make (sth. bad) public；expose

bēi

杯 Ⅰ名 cup：玻璃～ *glass* / 高脚～ *goblet* ❷ (alcoholic) drink：咱们喝一～。*Let's have a drink.* / 多喝了几～ *have a drop (or glass) too much* ❸ (prize) cup；trophy：世界～ *World Cup* Ⅱ量 cup：一～茶 *a cup of tea*
【杯弓蛇影】mistake the reflection of a bow in the cup for a snake—beset with imaginary fears；extremely suspicious
【杯盘狼藉】wine cups and dishes strewn in disorder (after a feast)

【杯水车薪】try to put out a blazing cartload of faggots with a cup of water—an utterly inadequate measure

【杯子】cup；glass

卑 形 ❶ low：地势～湿 *low-lying and damp* ❷ inferior：自卑 ❸〈书〉modest；humble

【卑鄙】base；mean；contemptible；despicable：～行为 *a base (or mean) action；sordid conduct；abject behaviour* / ～手段 *contemptible means；dirty tricks* / ～勾当 *a dirty deal*

【卑鄙无耻】base and shameless

【卑躬屈节】(又作'卑躬屈膝') bow and scrape；cringe；act servilely (or obsequiously)

【卑贱】❶ lowly；humble ❷ mean and low

【卑劣】base；mean；despicable：～手法 *a mean (or despicable) trick* ◇～行径 base conduct；dishonourable behaviour

【卑怯】mean and cowardly；abject：～行为 *abject behaviour*

【卑下】base；low

背 动 ❶ carry on the back：～着孩子 *carry a baby on one's back* ❷ bear；shoulder：我怕～不起这样的责任。*I'm afraid I can't shoulder such a responsibility.* ——另见 bèi

【背包】❶knapsack；rucksack；infantry (or field) pack；backpack ❷［军］blanket roll

【背包袱】carry baggage—have a weight (or load) on one's mind：你不要因此～。*Don't let it weigh on your mind.*

【背带】❶ braces；suspenders ❷ sling (for a rifle)；straps (for a knapsack)

【背负】bear；carry on the back；have on one's shoulder：～着衣包 *carry a bundle of clothes on one's back* / ～着人民的希望 *with people's expectations always on one's mind*

【背黑锅】〈口〉be made a scapegoat；be unjustly blamed：他倒称心如意了，却叫我一人～。*He got what he wanted and left me in the lurch as a scapegoat.*

【背篓】a basket carried on the back

【背头】swept-back hair

【背债】be in debt；be saddled with debts：背了一屁股债 *be heavily in debt；be up to one's eyes in debt*

悲 形 ❶ sad；sorrowful；melancholy：～不自胜 *be overcome with grief* ❷ compassionate：慈悲

【悲哀】grieved；sorrowful

【悲惨】miserable；tragic：～的遭遇 *a tragic experience* / ～的过去 *the bitter past*

【悲从中来】feel sadness welling up

【悲悼】mourn；grieve over sb.'s death

【悲愤】grief and indignation ◇～填膺 be filled with grief and indignation

【悲歌】❶ sad melody；stirring strains ❷［音］elegy；dirge；threnody ❸ sing with solemn fervour

【悲哽】choke with grief：说到这里，她满眼泪花，声音～，不能说下去了。*At this point her eyes filled with tears, and her voice choked with sobs, she was unable to go on.*

【悲观】pessimistic：～情绪 *pessimism* / ～厌世 *be pessimistic and world-weary* / 持～看法 *take a pessimistic (or gloomy) view* / ～失望 *pessimistic and despondent；disheartened* / ～主义 *pessimism* / ～主义者 *gloomster*

【悲欢离合】joys and sorrows, partings and reunions—vicissitudes of life

【悲剧】tragedy

【悲鸣】utter sad calls；lament

【悲泣】weep with grief

【悲伤】sad；grieved；sorrowful：人生的欢乐和～ *the joys and sorrows of life*

【悲叹】sigh mournfully；lament

【悲天悯人】bemoan the state of the universe and pity the fate of mankind：装出一副～的样子 *pretend to bewail the times and pity the people；be sanctimonious；assume a compassionate tone*

【悲痛】grieved；sorrowful：感到深切的～ *be deeply grieved；be filled with deep sorrow* / 化～为力量 *turn grief into strength*

【悲喜交集】mixed feelings of grief and joy；grief and joy intermingled；joy tempered with sorrow：两人久别重逢，～。*The reunion after a long separation brought mixed feelings of joy and sorrow to both of them.*

【悲喜剧】tragicomedy

【悲壮】solemn and stirring；moving and tragic：～的歌曲 *a solemn and stirring song*

碑 名 an upright stone tablet；stele：立一块～纪念死者 *put up a tablet (or erect a monument) in memory of the dead*

【碑额】the top part of a tablet

【碑记】a record of events inscribed on a tablet

【碑帖】a rubbing from a stone inscription (usu. as a model for calligraphy)

【碑文】an inscription on a tablet

běi

北 Ⅰ 名 north：城～ *north of the city* / ～屋 *a room with a southern exposure* / 往～走 *go north* Ⅱ 动〈书〉be defeated：连战皆～ *be defeated in one battle after another；suffer repeated defeats*

【北半球】the Northern Hemisphere

【北冰洋】the Arctic (Ocean)

【北大荒】the Great Northern Wilderness (in northeast China)

【北斗星】the Big Dipper；the Plough

【北伐军】the Northern Expeditionary Army

【北伐战争】the Northern Expedition (1926-1927)

【北方】❶ north：～刮来的风沙 *sand blown from the north* ❷ the northern part of the country, esp. the area north of the Huanghe River；the North：～话 *northern dialect* / ～人 *Northerner*

【北国】〈文〉the northern part of the country；the North：好一派～风光！*What magnificent northern scenery*！
【北海】the North Sea
【北寒带】the north frigid zone
【北回归线】the Tropic of Cancer
【北货】delicacies from north China（such as dried persimmons，etc.）
【北极】❶ the North Pole；the Arctic Pole ❷ the north magnetic pole ◇～光［天］northern lights；aurora borealis；～狐 another name for 白狐；～圈 the Arctic Circle；～星 Polaris；the North Star；the polestar；～熊 polar bear
【北京猿人】（又作'北京人'）［考古］Peking Man（Sinanthropus pekinensis）
【北美洲】North America
【北美自由贸易区】the North American Free Trade Zone
【北温带】the north temperate zone
【北洋军阀】the Northern Warlords（1912-1927）
【北约】the North Atlantic Treaty Organization ◇～主义 Natoism

bèi

贝 名 ❶ shellfish ❷ cowrie：虎斑～ *tiger cowrie*
【贝雕】［工美］shell carving：～画 *shell picture*；*shell mosaic*
【贝壳】shell（of shellfish）◇～学 conchology
【贝雷帽】beret
【贝类】shellfish；molluscs
【贝母】［中］the bulb of fritillary（Fritillaria thunbergii）
【贝宁】Benin ◇～人 Beninian
【贝丘】［考古］shell mound

备 Ⅰ 动 ❶ be equipped with；have：各种农业机械无一不～ *be equipped with all sorts of farm machinery* / ～有样品。*Samples are available*. ❷ prepare；get ready：把料～齐 *get all the materials ready* ❸ provide（or prepare）against；take precautions against：以～万一 *prepare against all eventualities* Ⅱ 名 equipment：设备 Ⅲ 副 fully；in every possible way：～受虐待 *be subjected to every kind of maltreatment* / 艰苦～尝 *suffer untold hardships* / ～受欢迎 *enjoy great popularity*；*be very popular*
【备案】put on record（or on file）；enter（a case）in the records
【备查】for future reference：所有重要文件都要存档～。*All important documents should be kept on file for reference*.
【备而不用】have sth. ready just in case；keep sth. for possible future use
【备份】［计］backup
【备耕】make preparations for ploughing and sowing
【备荒】prepare against natural disasters
【备件】spare parts
【备考】（an appendix，note，etc.）for reference
【备课】（of a teacher）prepare lessons
【备料】❶ get the materials ready ❷ prepare feed（for livestock）
【备取】be on the waiting list（for admission to a school）
【备忘录】［外交］❶ memorandum；aide-mémoire ❷ memorandum book
【备选】be an alternative；be on the short list（for further screening）：～案文 *alternative text* / ～方案 *alternative proposal*（*or scheme*）
【备用】reserve；spare；alternate：～物资 *reserve goods and materials* / ～轮胎 *spare tyre* / ～款项 *reserve funds* / ～航空站 alternate airport / ～机器 *standby machine*
【备有现货】in stock
【备战】❶ prepare for war：扩军～ *arms expansion and war preparations* ❷ be prepared against war
【备至】to the utmost；in every possible way：颂扬～ *praise profusely*
【备注】remarks ◇～栏 remarks column

背 Ⅰ 名 ❶ the back of the body：～痛 *backache* ❷ the back of an object：椅～ *the back of a chair* / 墨透纸～。*The ink blotted on the paper*. Ⅱ 动 ❶ with the back towards：～着太阳坐 *sit with one's back to the sun* / ～着手 *with one's hands clasped behind one's back* / ～山面海 *with hills behind and the sea in front* ❷ turn away：把脸～过去 *turn one's face away* ❸ leave；go away：背井离乡 ❹ hide sth. from；do sth. behind sb.'s back：～着人说话 *talk behind sb.'s back* / 没有什么～人的事 *have nothing to hide from anyone* ❺ recite from memory；learn by heart（or by rote）：～台词 *speak one's lines* / 书～熟了。*I've learnt the lesson by heart*. or *I have the lesson off pat*. ❻ act contrary to；violate；break：～着良心说话 *talk against good conscience* Ⅲ 形 ❶ out-of-the-way：～街 *back street*；*side street* / 那地方很～。*It is an out-of-the-way place*. or *That place is off the beaten track*. ❷〈口〉unlucky：手气～ *have bad luck*（*at mahjong playing*，*etc*.）❸ hard of hearing：耳朵有点～ *be a bit hard of hearing* ——另见 bēi
【背城借一】make a last-ditch stand before the city wall；fight to the last ditch；put up a desperate struggle
【背道而驰】run in the opposite direction；run counter to：同改革的要求～ *contradict the whole purpose of reforms* / 和他们的愿望～ *run counter to their intentions*
【背地里】behind sb.'s back；privately；on the sly：他当着面恭维你，～净使坏。*He flatters you to your face while playing dirty tricks behind your back*.
【背风】out of the wind；on the lee side；leeward：～处 *lee side*；*sheltered side*

【背光】be in a poor light; do sth. with one's back to the light; stand in one's own light
【背后】❶ behind; at the back; in the rear: 门～ *behind the door* / 房子～ *at the back of the house* ❷ behind sb.'s back: 当面不说,～乱说 *say nothing to people to their faces but gossip about them behind their backs* / ～捣鬼 *plot (or scheme) behind the scenes; play underhand tricks* / ～下毒手 *stab in the back*
【背井离乡】leave one's native place (esp. against one's will); be away from home
【背景】background; backdrop: 这幅画的～是一片森林。*The painting shows the woods in the background.* / 历史～ *historical background (or setting)* / ～光 *background light* / ～音乐 *background music*
【背静】quiet and secluded
【背靠背】❶ back to back: ～坐着 *sit back to back* ❷ criticize or expose sb. without his knowledge
【背离】deviate from; depart from: ～奥林匹克精神 *deviate from the Olympic spirit* / ～社会主义的言论 *views departing from socialism*
【背面】the back; the reverse side; the wrong side: 信封的～ *the back of an envelope* / 请阅～ *please turn over (P.T.O.); see overleaf*
【背叛】betray; forsake: 忘记过去就意味着～。*Forgetting the past means betrayal.*
【背鳍】[动] dorsal fin
【背弃】abandon; desert; renounce: ～原来的立场 *abandon one's original stand* / ～自己的诺言 *go back on one's word*
【背山面海】with hills behind and sea in front
【背时】〈方〉❶ behind the times ❷ unlucky
【背书】❶ recite a lesson from memory; repeat a lesson ❷ [经] endorsement (on a cheque): ～责任 *liability for endorsement* /～支票 *endorse a check*
【背水一战】fight with one's back to the river—fight to win or die
【背诵】recite; repeat from memory
【背斜】[地质] anticline: ～层 *anticlinal strata*
【背心】a sleeveless garment: 西服～ *waistcoat* / 毛～ *sleeveless woollen sweater* / 棉～ *cotton-padded waistcoat*
【背信弃义】break faith with sb.; be perfidious: ～的行为 *a breach of faith; perfidy* / ～地撕毁协定和合同 *perfidiously tear up agreements and contracts*
【背阴】in the shade; shady: ～处 *shady spot*
【背影】a view of sb.'s back; a figure viewed from behind: 凝望着他逐渐消失的～ *gaze at his receding figure*
【背约】break an agreement; go back on one's word; fail to keep one's promise
【背运】❶ bad luck; ill luck: 走～ *go through an unlucky period* ❷ have bad luck; be out of luck

悖

Ⅰ **动** 〈书〉be contrary to; go against: 悖理 Ⅱ **形** perverse; erroneous: 悖谬

【悖理】〈书〉contrary to reason
【悖谬】〈书〉absurd; preposterous
【悖逆】〈书〉disloyal; treasonable; rebellious
【悖入悖出】ill-gotten, ill-spent

被

Ⅰ **名** quilt: 做一床～ *make a new quilt* Ⅱ **动** 〈书〉❶ cover (with) ❷ suffer: ～灾 *suffer from a disaster* Ⅲ **介** (used in a passive sentence to introduce either the doer of the action or the action if the doer is not mentioned): 他～对手击倒。*He was knocked down by his opponent.* / 那棵树～大风刮倒了。*The tree was uprooted by the gale.* / 她～选为主席。*She was elected chairwoman.* Ⅳ **助** (used to form a set phrase with a passive meaning): ～捕 *be arrested; be under arrest*

【被保护国】protectorate
【被保护人】insurant; the insured; insured person
【被保险人】❶ the insured; ❷ policy holder
【被剥削阶级】exploited class
【被乘数】[数] multiplicand
【被除数】[数] dividend
【被传出庭】be summoned to appear in count; be subpoenaed
【被袋】bedding bag
【被单】(又作'被单子') (bed) sheet ◇～布 sheeting
【被担保人】guaranteed person
【被动】passive: 陷于～地位 *land oneself in a passive position; be thrown into passivity* / 变～为主动 *regain the initiative* ◇～式 [语] passive form; ～吸烟 passive smoking; secondhand smoking; ～语态 [语] passive voice
【被服】bedding and clothing (esp. for army use): ～厂 *clothing factory*
【被俘】be captured; be taken prisoner
【被告】[法] (又作'被告人') defendant; the accused ◇～席 defendant's seat; dock
【被管制人】[法] person under public surveillance
【被害人】[法] the injured party; the victim
【被加数】[数] summand
【被减数】[数] Minuend
【被里】the underneath side of a quilt
【被面】the facing of a quilt: 绣花～ *an embroidered quilt cover*
【被难】be killed in a disaster, political incident, etc.
【被迫】be compelled; be forced; be constrained: ～承认错误 *be forced to admit one's mistakes*
【被侵略者】victim of aggression
【被褥】bedding; bedclothes
【被上诉人】[法] appellee
【被套】❶ bedding bag ❷ (bag-shaped) quilt cover; slipcover for a quilt ❸ cotton wadding for a quilt
【被统治者】the ruled
【被窝儿】a quilt folded to form a sleeping bag
【被卧】quilt
【被选举权】the right to be elected

【被压迫民族】oppressed nation
【被罩】(bag-shaped) quilt cover; slipcover for a quilt
【被子】quilt
【被子植物】angiosperm

倍 Ⅰ名 times; -fold: 四～ *four times; fourfold* / 二的五～是十。*Five times two is ten.* / 十是五的两～。*Ten is twice as much as five.* / 大一～ *twice as big; twice the size* Ⅱ形 double; twice as much: 勇气～增 *with redoubled courage*
【倍频器】[电子] frequency multiplier
【倍数】[数] multiple
【倍塔】beta ◇ ～粒子 [物] beta particle; ～射线 [物] beta ray
【倍增器】[电子] multiplier: 光电～ *photoelectric multiplier*

焙 动 bake over a slow fire: ～干 *dry over a fire* / ～制 *cure sth. by drying it over a fire*
【焙烧】roast; bake: ～炉 *roaster*

辈 名 ❶ people of a certain kind; the like: 无能之～ *people without ability* ❷ generation: 他比我长(小)一～。*He's one generation my senior (junior).* / 他俩同～。*They belong to the same generation.* ❸ lifetime: 后半～儿 *the latter part of one's life*
【辈出】come forth in large numbers: 英雄～的时代 *an age of heroes*
【辈分】(又作'辈行') order of seniority in the family or clan; position in the family hierarchy: 她的～比我小。*She ranks as my junior in the clan.*
【辈子】all one's life; lifetime: 她家三～都当工人。*Hers has been a working-class family for three generations.*

惫 形 exhausted; fatigued: 疲惫

蓓 (构词成分)见下
【蓓蕾】bud

bēn

奔 动 ❶run quickly: ～马 *a galloping horse* ❷ hurry; hasten; rush ❸ flee: 东奔西跑 ——另见 bèn
【奔波】rush about; be busy running about: 为了生计,他不得不经常在外～。*In order to make a living, he had to go from place to place hunting for jobs.*
【奔驰】run quickly; speed: 骏马在草原上～。*Sturdy steeds gallop on the grasslands.* / 火车向前～。*The train sped on.*
【奔窜】run helter-skelter
【奔放】bold and unrestrained; untrammelled: 豪爽～的性格 *a forthright and uninhibited nature* / ～不羁的风格 *a bold and flowing style* / 李白的诗潇洒～。*Li Bai's poems are known for their freedom and naturalness of expression.*
【奔赴】hurry to (a place); rush to: ～前线 *hurry to the front*
【奔流】❶ flow at great speed; pour: ～入海 *flow into the sea* / 铁水～ *molten iron pouring out in a stream* ❷ racing current
【奔忙】be busy rushing about; bustle about: 他似乎一天到晚～不休。*He seems to be on the move all day long.*
【奔命】rush about on errands; be kept on the run ——另见 bènmìng
【奔跑】run: 一路～去请医生 *run all the way to fetch a doctor* / 母亲一喊,孩子们都～过来。*The children came running when their mother called them.*
【奔丧】hasten home for the funeral of a parent or grandparent
【奔逃】flee; run away: 四散～ *flee in all directions; flee helter-skelter; stampede*
【奔腾】❶ gallop: 那马～疾驰而去。*The horse galloped off at full speed.* ❷ surge forward; roll on in waves: 浩浩长江,～不息。*The mighty waters of the Changjiang roll on incessantly.*
【奔腾芯片】[计] Pentium chip
【奔袭】[军] long-range raid
【奔泻】(of torrents) rush down; pour down: 怒涛滚滚,～千里。*An angry torrent rolls thunderously on for a thousand li.*
【奔走】❶ run ❷ go around (in order to accomplish certain goals); rush about; be busy running about: 我父亲一生辛苦,～于外。*My father had a hard life going from place to place all the year round.*
【奔走呼号】go around crying for help or campaigning for a cause: ～,为灾民募款 *go around trying to raise a relief fund for the victims of the disaster*
【奔走相告】run around spreading the news; lose no time in telling each other the news: 喜讯传来,人们～。*On hearing the good news, they lost no time telling everybody.*

贲 (构词成分)见下
【贲门】[生理] cardia

běn

本 Ⅰ名 ❶ the root or stem of a plant: 水有源,木有～。*A stream has its source; a tree has its roots.* ❷ foundation; basis; origin: 兵民是胜利之～。*The army and the people are the foundation of victory.* ❸ capital; principal: 还本 ❹ book: 笔记本 ❺ manuscript; copy: 抄本 ❻ script: 剧本 ❼ edition; version: 普及本 Ⅱ形 ❶ principal; major; central: 本部 ❷ one's own; native: ～厂 *this factory* ❸current; this; present: ～周 *this week; the current week* / ～决议 *this resolution* Ⅲ副 originally; at first: 我～想

不去。*Originally I didn't want to go*. Ⅳ量（for books, parts of a serial, etc.）：两～书 *two books* / 这部电影有十二～。*This is a twelve-reel film*.

【本本主义】book worship；bookishness

【本币】〈略〉见〖本位货币〗

【本部】headquarter：校～ *main campus*

【本草】a class of traditional Chinese medical literature consisting of herbals which focus ondescriptions of individual drugs ◇ ～纲目 Compendium of Materia Medica（by Li Shizhen 李时珍 1518-1593）

【本初子午线】the first meridian；the prime meridian

【本底】[物] background：放射性～ *radioactive background* ◇ ～噪声 background noise

【本地】this locality：～风光 *local colour* / ～口音 *local accent* / ～货 *local（or native）goods* / 我是～人。*I'm a native of this place*. or *I was born here*.

【本分】❶ one's duty：尽～ *do one's duty（or bit）* ❷ honest；decent：～人 *an honest person* / 他这个人很～。*He never goes beyond what is proper*. or *He's a decent person*.

【本固枝荣】when the root is firm, the branches flourish

【本国】one's own country：～资源 *national resources* /～语 *native language；mother tongue*

【本行】one's line；one's own profession：搞建筑是他的～。*Architecture is his line*.

【本家】a member of the same clan；a distant relative with the same family name

【本届】current；this year's：～联合国大会 *the current session of the U. N. General Assembly* / ～毕业生 *this year's graduates*

【本金】capital；principal

【本科】（as distinguished from a preparatory course, a correspondence course, etc.）regular college course；undergraduate course ◇ ～学生 undergraduate

【本来】❶ original：～的意思 *original meaning（or intention）* / 事物～的辩证法 *the dialectics inherent in things* ❷ originally；at first：大会～定星期五举行。*The meeting was originally fixed for Friday*. / 他～身体很瘦弱。*He used to be thin and weak*. ❸ it goes without saying；of course：～就该这样办。*Of course it should be handled that way*. / 你～用不着着急。*You needn't have worried about it*.

【本来面目】true colours；true features：认清他们的～ *see them in their true colours* / 还其～ *reveal sth. in its true colours*

【本垒】[体] home base；home plate；home；the plate

【本利】principal and interest

【本领】skill；ability；capability：他的～很大。*He's very capable*. / 凡是他要的东西他都有～弄到手。*He is resourceful enough to get whatever he is after*.

【本命年】every 12th year after the year of one's birth ——另见〖生肖〗

【本末】❶ the whole course of an event from beginning to end；ins and outs：详述～ *tell the whole story from beginning to end* ❷ the fundamental and the incidental

【本末倒置】take the branch for the root；put the incidental before the fundamental：强调方法而忽视内容是～。*To put emphasis on method at the expense of content is to put the cart before the horse*.

【本能】instinct：出于～ *by instinct* / 大多数动物都有保护幼仔的～。*Most animals have an instinct to protect their young*.

【本能行为】instinctive behaviour：～障碍 *instinctive behaviour disturbance*

【本年度】this year；the current year：～计划 *this year's plan* / ～国家预算 *the national budget for this fiscal year*

【本票】cashier's cheque

【本钱】❶ capital：没～做生意 *have no capital to start a business* ❷ what is capitalized on；sth. used to one's own advantage

【本轻利重】the capital is small, but the profit remarkable；low cost great profit；the cost being low but the profit being great

【本人】❶ I（me, myself）：～认为 *in my opinion* ❷ oneself；in person：必须你～来。*You must come in person*.

【本色】（běnsè）true（or inherent）qualities；distinctive character：劳动人民的～ *the true qualities of the labouring people*

【本色】（běnshǎi）natural colour ◇ ～布 unbleached and undyed cloth；grey cloth

【本身】itself；in itself：院子里杂草丛生，但房子～完好无损。*The yard is full of weeds, but the house itself is in good condition*. / 条约～ *the treaty per se*

【本生灯】Bunsen burner

【本事】（běnshì）source material；original story：这些诗词的～，年久失考。*The original story these poems were based on has long been lost*. / 电影～ *synopsis of a film*

【本事】（běnshi）同〖本领〗

【本题】the subject under discussion；the point at issue：请不要离开～。*Please keep（or stick）to the point*. / 这跟～无关。*This has nothing to do with the point at issue*. or *This is quite irrelevant*.

【本体】❶ [哲] noumenon；thing-in-itself ❷ main part of a machine or a project ◇～论 [哲] ontology

【本土】❶ one's native country（or land）❷ metropolitan territory

【本位】❶ [经] standard：金本位 ❷ one's own department or unit：～工作 *the work of one's own department；one's own job（or work）* ◇ ～号 [音] natural（♮）；～货币 the basic monetary unit of a country's currency (e. g. yuan of China, dollar of the U. S.)

【本位主义】selfish departmentalism; departmental selfishness

【本文】❶ this text, article, etc.: ～谈的是我国经济方面的一些问题。*This article deals with certain problems in our national economy.* ❷ the original text; the original

【本息】principal (or capital) and interest

【本乡本土】native soil; native land; home village: 大家都是～的，有话好说嘛。*As we're all natives of this village, no problems are too difficult to settle among us.*

【本小利微】small capital and little gain—a small business: 我们～，实在周转不过来。*Ours is a very small business, and we just don't have enough cash to carry on.*

【本性】natural instincts (or character, disposition); nature; inherent quality: ～好战 *be belligerent by nature*

【本性难移】it is hard to change one's nature; the leopard can't change his spots ——另见〖江山易改,本性难移〗

【本义】original meaning; literal sense: "兵"字的～是武器。*The original meaning of "兵" is weapon.* / 这个词不能按～去理解。*This word should not be taken in its literal sense.*

【本意】original idea; real intention: 我看这不是她的～。*I don't think that is her real intention.* / 他～是好的，只是说话方式不好。*He meant well, though he said it in an inappropriate way.*

【本影】[物] umbra

【本源】origin; source

【本着】in line with; in conformity with; in the light of: ～我们一贯的立场 *in line with our consistent stand* / ～增进两国之间友好关系的愿望 *actuated by a desire to promote friendly relations between our two countries*

【本职】one's job (or duty): 做好～工作 *do one's own job well*

【本质】essence; nature; innate character; intrinsic quality: ～方面 *an essential aspect* / 非～方面 *a nonessential aspect* / ～差别 *an essential distinction* / 透过现象看～ *see through the appearance to the essence*

【本子】❶ book; notebook: 改～ *go over students' written exercises; correct papers* ❷ edition: 这两个～都是宋本。*Both of these are Song Dynasty block-printed editions.*

【本族语】native language; mother tongue

苯 名 [化] benzene; benzol: ～中毒 *benzene poisoning; benzolism*

【苯胺】[化] aniline ◇～革 aniline leather; ～染料 aniline dyes; ～印刷 aniline printing; flexography; ～紫 mauve

【苯巴比妥】[药] phenobarbital; phenobarbitone; luminal

【苯酚】[化] phenol

【苯海拉明】[药] diphenhydramine; benadryl

【苯甲酸】[化] benzoic acid

【苯妥英纳】[药] phenytoin sodium; dilantin

【苯乙烯】[化] styrene

畚 Ⅰ 名 a bamboo or wicker scoop Ⅱ 动〈方〉 scoop up with a dustpan

【畚箕】〈方〉❶ a bamboo or wicker scoop ❷ dustpan

bèn

奔 Ⅰ 动 ❶ go straight towards; head for: 直～实验室 *head straight for the laboratory* / 这条路～天津。*This road goes (or leads) to Tianjin.* ❷ approach; be getting on for: 他是～六十的人了。*He's getting on for sixty.* Ⅱ 介 towards: 汽车～广场驶去。*The car sped by towards the square.* ——另见 bēn

【奔命】〈口〉 be in a desperate hurry ——另见 bēnmìng

【奔头儿】sth. to strive for; prospect: 大有～ *have a bright prospect*

笨 形 ❶ stupid; dull; foolish: ～人 *a stupid person; fool* / 脑子～ *stupid; slow-witted* ❷ clumsy; awkward: 我的手太～，干不了这活。*I'm all thumbs and no good for this.* ❸ cumbersome; awkward; unwieldy: 这把锄头太～。*This is an awkward hoe.* / 这大柜子太～了。*This cabinet is too large and clumsy.*

【笨蛋】〈讳〉 fool; idiot: 真是个大～! *What a fool!*

【笨口拙舌】awkward in speech; slow of speech; inarticulate

【笨鸟先飞】clumsy birds have to start flying early—the slow need to start early (usu. said self-depreciatingly)

【笨手笨脚】clumsy; awkward: 他这人～。*He is clumsy.* or *His fingers are all thumbs.*

【笨重】heavy; cumbersome; unwieldy: ～的家具 *heavy (or cumbersome) furniture*

【笨拙】clumsy; awkward; stupid: 动作～ *clumsy (or awkward) in movement* / ～的伎俩 *stupid tricks*

bēng

崩 动 ❶ collapse: 山崩 ❷ burst: 把气球吹～了 *burst a balloon* / 他们谈～了。*Their negotiations broke down.* ❸ (of sth. bursting) hit sb. or sth.: 爆竹～了他的手。*The firecracker went off in his hand.* ❹〈口〉 execute by shooting; shoot ❺ (of an emperor) die: 驾崩

【崩溃】❶ collapse; crumble; fall apart: 殖民主义的～ *the collapse of colonialism* ❷ crash

【崩裂】burst (or break) apart; crack: 炸药轰隆一声，山石～。*Boom! The dynamite sent the rocks*

flying.
【崩漏】[中] uterine bleeding
【崩塌】collapse; crumble
【崩陷】fall in; cave in

绷 动 ❶ stretch (or draw) tight: 在绷子上～块绸子 *stretch a piece of silk on an embroidery frame* / 弓弦一定要～紧。*The bowstring must be drawn tight*. ❷ spring; bounce: 盒子一打开,弹簧就～出来了。*When the box was opened, the spring jumped out*. ❸ baste; tack; pin: ～着金字的横幅红布 *a red cloth streamer with golden papercut characters pinned on it* ——另见 běng; bèng
【绷带】bandage
【绷簧】〈方〉spring
【绷子】embroidery frame; hoop; tambour

嘣 象 the sound of palpitations or explosions: 我心里～～直跳。*My heart is thumping*. / 爆竹～地一响。*The firecracker went bang*.

béng

甭 副〈方〉don't; needn't: ～再说了。*Don't say any more*. / 有这样好的徒工,老师傅～提有多高兴了。*Needless to say, the old master worker was happy to have such good apprentices*. / 你～管! *None of your business*! / 您～管了。*Don't bother. Leave it to me*.

běng

绷 动〈口〉❶ look serious: ～着脸 *look displeased; pull a long face* ❷ strain oneself: 咬住牙～住劲 *clench one's teeth and strain one's muscles* ——另见 bēng; bèng

bèng

迸 动 spout; spurt; burst forth: 火星乱～ *sparks flying in all directions* / 他怎么突然～出这句话来? *What made him blurt out such a remark*?
【迸发】burst forth; burst out: 锤子打在岩石上,～了好些火星儿。*Sparks flew out as the sledge hammer hit the rock*. / 大厅里～出一阵笑声。*There was an outburst of laughter in the hall*.
【迸裂】split; burst (open): 脑浆～ *have one's brains dashed out*

泵 Ⅰ 名 pump: 高扬程～ *high lift pump* Ⅱ 动 pump (in or out)
【泵房】pump house
【泵排量】pumpage; pump delivery

绷 Ⅰ 动 split open; crack: 玻璃～了一条缝儿。*The glass has a crack in it*. Ⅱ 副〈口〉(used before certain adjectives) very: ～脆 *very crisp* / ～硬 *hard as a rock; stiff as a board* / ～直 *exceptionally straight* / ～亮 *shining bright* ——另见 bēng; běng

蹦 动 leap; jump; spring: 他使劲一～就过了沟。*With one powerful leap he crossed the ditch*. / 这件事还没处理完,那件事又～出来了。*One problem had scarcely been solved when another cropped up*.
【蹦蹦车】〈口〉small motorized three-wheel transport vehicles
【蹦蹦跳跳】bouncing and vivacious: 孩子们～地进了教室。*The children bounced into the classroom*.
【蹦迪】disco dancing
【蹦豆儿】〈方〉❶ roasted broad beans ❷ little child: 这是大的,家里还有个小～。*This is the older one; there's a little one at home*.
【蹦极】bungee jumping

bī

逼 动 ❶ force; compel; press: ～对方取守势 *force one's opponent onto the defensive* / ～某人招供 *try to force sb. to talk* /他拿枪～着她交出钱来。*He forced her at gun point to give him her money*. ❷ press for; extort: 逼债 ❸ press on towards; press up to; close in on: 直～城下 *press up to the city wall*
【逼宫】(of ministers, etc.) force the king or emperor to abdicate
【逼供】extort a confession: 严刑～ *extort a confession by cruel torture*
【逼近】press on towards; close in on; approach; draw near: 天色已经～黄昏。*Dusk is closing in*.
【逼良为娼】force a girl of good family or woman of virtue to engage in prostitution; force an honest person to do sth. dishonest
【逼迫】force; compel; coerce: 他们～他辞职。*They forced him to resign*.
【逼人】pressing; threatening: 形势～。*The situation spurs us on*. / 寒气～。*There is a cold nip in the air*. ◇ ～太甚 press (or push) people too hard
【逼上梁山】be driven to revolt
【逼视】look at from close-up; watch intently: 光采夺目,不可～。*At close range the glare dazzles one's eyes*.
【逼死】hound sb. to death
【逼问】❶ force sb. to answer ❷ question closely
【逼肖】〈书〉bear a close resemblance to; be the very image of
【逼债】press for payment of debts; dun
【逼真】❶ lifelike; true to life: 这幅湘竹画得十分～。*This painting of mottled bamboos is really true to life*. ❷ distinctly; clearly: 听得～ *hear*

distinctly / 看得～ *have a clear view of sth*. ◇～度［电子］fidelity

【逼租】press for payment of (land) rent

bí

荸（构词成分）见下

【荸荠】water chestnut (Eleocharis tuberosa), the plant or its tuber

鼻 名 ❶ nose ❷〈书〉start; initiation: 鼻祖

【鼻成形术】rhinoplasty

【鼻儿】❶ a hole in an implement, utensil, etc., for sth. to be inserted into; eye: 门鼻儿 ❷〈方〉whistle: 火车拉～了。*The engine is whistling*.

【鼻翅儿】common name for 鼻翼

【鼻窦】paranasal sinus ◇～炎 nasosinusitis

【鼻化元音】［语音］nasalized vowel

【鼻尖】(又作'鼻子尖儿') tip of the nose

【鼻镜】［医］rhinoscope: 电光～ *nasoscope*

【鼻孔】nostril

【鼻梁】bridge of the nose

【鼻腔】［生理］nasal cavity

【鼻青脸肿】a bloody nose and a swollen face; badly battered: 被打得～ *have one's face bashed in; be beaten black and blue*

【鼻塞】have a stuffy nose

【鼻饲】［医］nasal feeding

【鼻涕】nasal mucus; snivel: 流～ *have a running nose*

【鼻烟】snuff ◇～盒 snuffbox; ～壶 snuff bottle

【鼻炎】［医］rhinitis

【鼻眼净】［药］naphazoline

【鼻翼】the alae of the nose

【鼻音】［语音］nasal sound: 说话带～ *speak with a twang* / ～化 *nasalize*

【鼻渊】［中］nasosinusitis

【鼻韵母】［语音］(in Chinese pronunciation) a vowel followed by a nasal consonant (e.g. an, ian, en, in, un, ang, ing, ong, etc.)

【鼻针疗法】［中］nose-acupuncture therapy

【鼻中隔】［生理］nasal septum

【鼻子】nose: 高～ *high-bridged nose; high nose* / 塌～ *snub nose; pug nose* / 不要只顾～底下的小事。*Don't get bogged down in trivial matters*. ——另见〖哭鼻子〗;〖牵鼻子〗;〖有鼻子有眼儿〗

【鼻祖】the earliest ancestor; originator (of a tradition, school of thought, etc.)

bǐ

匕 名 an ancient type of spoon

【匕首】dagger

比 Ⅰ 动 ❶ compare; contrast: ～得上 *can compare with; compare favourably with* / 想想过去, ～～现在 *recall the past and contrast it with the present* ❷ emulate; compete; match: 这家旅馆的服务质量谁也～不上。*This hotel can't be matched for its good service*. / 咱俩～一～, 看谁高。*Let's stand back to back and see who is taller*. ❸ gesture; gesticulate: 连说带～ *gesticulate as one talks* ❹〈方〉aim at; direct towards: 警察用枪～着罪犯。*The policeman pointed his gun at the criminal*. ❺ copy; model after: ～着旧衣裁新衣 *pattern a new garment on an old one* / 用尺～着画。*Use a ruler when drawing this*. ❻ draw an analogy; liken to; compare to: 我们这小小的公司可以～作一个大家庭。*Our little company can be likened to a big family*. Ⅱ 名 ratio; proportion: 这里小麦同水稻的年产量约为一与三之～。*Here the annual yield of wheat and rice is in a ratio of about one to three*. Ⅲ 介 ❶ to (in a score): 甲队以二～一胜乙队。*Team A beat team B (by a score of) two to one*. / 现在几～几? *What's the score?* ❷ than: 我～你早来一个钟头。*I came an hour earlier than you did*. Ⅳ 形〈书〉close together; next to

【比比皆是】can be found everywhere; such is the case everywhere: 好人好事, ～。*Good people and good deeds can be found everywhere*.

【比方】❶ analogy; instance: 打～ *draw an analogy* / 拿盖房子作～ *take for instance the building of a house* / 这不过是个～。*This is only by way of analogy*. ❷ suppose: 听说他待人热情, ～我求他帮个忙。他不会拒绝吧? *I hear he's very warm-hearted, so I don't suppose he would refuse me help if I ask him*. ❸ 同〖比如〗

【比分】［体］score: 双方～十分接近。*It's a close game*. / ～领先 *(to) outscore; score in one's favour* / ～落后 *score against one*

【比画】(又作'比划') gesture; gesticulate: 他～着讲。*He made himself understood with the help of gestures*.

【比基尼】bikini

【比价】❶ price relations; parity; rate of exchange: 英镑和美元的～ *the rate of exchange between the pound sterling and the U.S. dollar* / 粮棉～ *the price ratios between grain and cotton* ❷ compare bids or prices

【比较】❶ compare; contrast: 有～才能鉴别。*Only by comparing can one distinguish the difference*. / 把译文和原文～一下 *check the translation against the original* ❷ (used to compare a difference in degree): ～去年有显著的增长 *show a marked increase over last year* ❸ fairly; comparatively; relatively; quite; rather: ～快 *relatively fast* / 两个都可以, 不过这个～好一点儿。*Either will do, but this one is a bit better*. ◇～法 comparative method; comparative approach; ～级［语］comparative degree; ～文学 comparative literature

【比利时】Belgium ◇～人 Belgian

【比例】❶ proportion: 不合～ *out of proportion* / 按～发展 *develop in proportion; proportionate development* ❷ scale: 按～绘制 *be drawn to scale* / 这个模型是按准确的～做的。*This model is made exactly to scale.*

【比例尺】❶ scale：这张地图的～是四十万分之一。*The scale of the map is* 1∶400,000. ❷ architect's scale; engineer's scale

【比例失调】be out of proportion

【比例税】proportional tax ◇ ～率 flat rate

【比量】❶ take rough measurements (with the hand, a stick, string, etc.) ❷ make gestures

【比邻】❶ neighbour; next-door neighbour ❷ near; next to：跟车站～的那个工厂 *the factory next to the railway station*

【比邻星】[天] the self-luminous star nearest to the sun

【比率】ratio; rate

【比美】compare favourably with; rival

【比目鱼】flatfish; flounder

【比拟】❶ compare; draw a parallel; match：难以～ *beyond compare* ❷ analogy; metaphor

【比丘】[宗](佛教) monk

【比丘尼】[宗](佛教) nun

【比热】[物] specific heat

【比容】[物] specific volume

【比如】for example; for instance; such as

【比赛】match; competition：足球～ *football match* / 自行车～ *bicycle race* / 射击～ *shooting contest* / 象棋～ *chess tournament* / ～规则 *rules of a game; rules of a contest* ◇ ～项目 event

【比色分析】[化] colorimetric analysis

【比色计】[化] colorimeter

【比上不足,比下有余】not up to those above, but above those below—middling; passable; tolerable

【比湿】[气] specific humidity

【比试】❶ have a competition：不信咱俩～～。*If you don't believe me, let's have a competition and see.* ❷ make gestures：两个小演员拿长枪一～,就开始对打起来。*With a flourish of their spears, the two little performers started sparring with each other.*

【比武】take part in a wushu contest

【比学赶帮超】emulate, learn from, catch up with, help and in turn surpass each other

【比翼】fly wing to wing：～齐飞 *pair off wing to wing; fly side by side* ◇～鸟 fabulous birds that had only one wing each and thus had to fly in pairs (used in poetry as an epithet for a loving couple)

【比喻】metaphor; analogy; figure of speech：这只是一个～的说法。*This is just a figure of speech.*

【比照】❶ according to; in the light of：我们可以～其它厂的做法拟定计划。*We can draw up our plan in the light of the experience of other factories.* / ～着实物绘图 *draw with an object as a model* ❷ contrast：两相～ *contrasting the two*

【比值】ratio; rate

【比重】❶ [物] specific gravity ❷ proportion：工业在整个国民经济中的～ *the proportion of industry in the national economy as a whole* ◇ ～计 hydrometer; ～选种[农] specific gravity selection (of seeds)

妣 名〈书〉one's deceased mother

彼 代 ❶ that; those; the other; another：～时 *at that time* ❷ the other party：要知己知～。*You must know both your opponent and yourself.*

【彼岸】❶ [宗](佛教) Faramita ❷ the other side or bank of a river; the opposite shore：太平洋的～ *the opposite shore of the Pacific*

【彼此】❶ each other; one another：～呼应 *support each other; act in coordination with each other* / ～之间无话不谈 *be so intimate as to keep no secrets from each other* ❷〈套〉(used in reduplication as a reply) me too or you too：您辛苦啦！—～～！*You must have taken a lot of trouble.—So must you!*

【彼一时,此一时】that was one situation, and this is another; times have changed：～,不要拿老眼光看新事物。*Times have changed, you know, so don't judge new things by old standards.*

秕 形 (of grain) not plump; blighted：～粒 *blighted seeds*

【秕糠】❶ chaff ❷ worthless stuff

【秕子】blighted grain

笔 Ⅰ 名 ❶ pen, pencil or writing brush：一枝～ *a pen or pencil* / 一管～ *a writing or painting brush* ❷ technique of writing, calligraphy or drawing：文笔 ❸ stroke; touch：这里再添几～,情节就更生动了。*Add a few touches here and the episode will be more lively.* / 你给他写信时,替我带一～。*Please remember me to him when you write.* Ⅱ 动 write：～之于书 *put down in black and white* Ⅲ 量 ❶ (for sums of money, financial accounts, debts, etc.)：一～钱 *a sum of money; a fund* / 我们有三～账要算。*We have three scores to settle.* ❷ (for skill in callighraphy or painting)：写得一～好字 *write a good hand* / 能画几～山水画 *be a landscape painter of sorts*

【笔答】give a written answer; answer in writing：最后一道题必须～。*The final question should be answered in writing.*

【笔底下】ability to write：～不错 *write well* / ～来得快 *write with ease (or facility)*

【笔调】(of writing) tone; style：讽刺的～ *a satirical tone* / 他用通俗的～写了许多科学读物。*He wrote many books on science in a popular style.*

【笔法】technique of writing, calligraphy or drawing

【笔锋】❶ the tip of a writing brush ❷ vigour of style in writing; stroke; touch：～犀利 *write in an incisive style; wield a pointed pen*

【笔杆子】(又作'笔杆儿') ❶ the shaft of a pen or writing brush; penholder ❷ pen：耍～ *wield the pen* ❸ a facile writer; a literary spokesman：他

是编辑部的～。*He is the most effective writer of the editorial department*.

【笔画】strokes of a Chinese character

【笔会】❶ forum in writing：文艺评论～ *written forum on literary criticism* ❷ association (or club) of writers：国际～ *PEN* (*International Association of Poets, Editors, Essayists, and Novelists*)

【笔迹】a person's handwriting; hand：对～ *identify sb's handwriting* ◇～鉴定 handwriting verification

【笔记】❶ take down (in writing) ❷ notes：记～ *take notes* ❸ pen jottings (a type of literature consisting mainly of short sketches)：《阅微草堂～》*Jottings from the Thatched Abode of Close Observations* ◇～本 notebook；～本电脑 notebook computer；～小说 literary sketches; sketchbook

【笔架】pen rack; penholder

【笔尖】❶ nib; pen point ❷ the tip of a writing brush or pencil

【笔力】vigour of strokes in calligraphy or drawing; vigour of style in literary composition：～雄健 *powerful strokes* / 这篇文章没有表现出作者平素的～。*This essay lacks the vigour and vitality which characterize the author's usual style*.

【笔录】❶ put down (in writing); take down ❷ notes; record

【笔帽】the cap of a pen, pencil or writing brush

【笔名】pen name; pseudonym

【笔墨】pen and ink; words; writing：我们激动的心情难以用～来形容。*Words can hardly describe how excited we were*. / 把无关紧要的话删去，不要浪费～。*To save space, leave out superfluous words and sentences*. ◇～官司 written polemics (or controversy); a battle of words

【笔石】graptolite

【笔试】written examination

【笔顺】order of strokes observed in calligraphy

【笔算】❶ do a sum in writing ❷ written calculation

【笔谈】❶ conversation by writing ❷ comment in writing; give a written statement ❸ pen conversations (often used in book titles)：《梦溪～》*Dream Pool Essays*

【笔体】writing style; calligraphy; handwriting; hand：我认得出他的～。*I can identify his handwriting*.

【笔挺】❶ (standing) very straight; straight as a ramrod; bolt upright：战士们～地站着，听候发令。*The soldiers stood at attention, waiting for orders*. ❷ well-ironed; trim：穿着一身～的制服 *be dressed in a trim uniform*

【笔筒】pen container; brush pot

【笔头儿】❶ 同〖笔尖〗❷ ability to write; writing skill：你～快，你写吧。*You're good at writing. You do it*. ❸ written; in written form：～练习 *written exercises*

【笔误】❶ make a slip in writing ❷ a slip of the pen

【笔下】❶ 同〖笔底下〗❷ the wording and purport of what one writes

【笔下超生】(of a judge) spare a life by a stroke of the brush; refrain from passing a death sentence

【笔下留情】be charitable in writing critical comments

【笔心】(又作'笔芯') ❶ pencil lead ❷ refill (for a ball-point pen)

【笔译】written translation

【笔友】pen-friend; pen pal

【笔战】written polemics

【笔者】the present writer; the author

【笔直】perfectly straight; straight as a ramrod; bolt upright：～的马路 *straight avenues* / ～走 *go straight on* (*or ahead*) / 身子挺得～ *stand straight as a ramrod; draw oneself up to one's full height*

鄙 形 ❶ low; mean; vulgar：粗鄙 ❷〈谦〉my：～意 *my humble opinion; my idea* ❸〈书〉despise; disdain; scorn：可～ *despicable*

【鄙薄】〈书〉despise; scorn：不应～技术工作。*One should not despise technical work*.

【鄙陋】superficial; shallow：～无知 *shallow and ignorant*

【鄙弃】disdain; loathe：～这种庸俗作风 *disdain such vulgar practices*

【鄙人】〈谦〉your humble servant; I

【鄙视】despise; disdain; look down upon：有些人～体力劳动者。*Some people look down on manual workers*.

【鄙俗】vulgar; philistine

bì

币 名 money; currency：外币

【币值】currency value：～稳定 *a stable currency*

【币制】currency (or monetary) system ◇～改革 currency (or monetary) reform

必 副 ❶ certainly; surely; necessarily：我明天下午三点～到。*I'll definitely be there at 3 p.m. tomorrow*. / 你们这次访问～将增强两国人民之间的友谊。*Your visit will certainly strengthen the friendship between our two peoples*. ❷ must; have to：～读书目 *a list of required reading* / 事物的发展～有一定的条件。*Things can only develop under certain conditions*.

【必不可少】absolutely necessary; indispensable; essential

【必得】must; have to：你～去一趟。*You simply must go*.

【必定】❶ must; have to：他～知道。*He must have known it*. ❷ be bound to; be sure to：明天我们～把图纸送到。*We'll be sure to send you the blueprints tomorrow*.

【必恭必敬】reverent and respectful; extremely

deferential：～听着 *listening with the utmost deference*

【必然】❶ inevitable；certain：～结果 *an inevitable outcome* / ～趋势 *an inexorable trend* / ～的结论 *a logical conclusion* ❷ be bound to；be sure to：他～失败。*He's bound to fail*. ❸［哲］necessity ◇ ～规律 inexorable law；～王国［哲］realm of necessity；～性 necessity；inevitability；certainty

【必修课】a required (or obligatory) course

【必须】must；have to：～指出 *it must be pointed out that* / ～厉行节约。*It is imperative to practise economy*.

【必需】essential；indispensable：发展工业所～的原料 *raw materials essential for industrial development*

【必需品】necessities；necessaries

【必要】necessary；essential；indispensable：～条件 *essential condition*；*prerequisite* / 没有～再讨论了。*There's no need to discuss it any more*. ◇ ～产品［经］necessary product；～劳动 necessary labour；～前提 prerequisite；precondition；～性 necessity

【必由之路】the road one must follow or take；the only way

闭 动 ❶ shut；close：～门 *shut the door* / ～上眼 *close one's eyes* / ～嘴！*Hold your tongue*！or *Shut up*！/ 他笑得～不上嘴。*He just couldn't stop laughing*. ❷ stop up；obstruct：闭气

【闭关锁国】cut off one's country from the outside world

【闭关政策】closed-door policy

【闭关自守】close the country to international intercourse；follow a policy of national isolation；adopt a closed-door policy：独立自主并不意味着～。*Independence does not mean isolation from other countries*.

【闭合】close ◇ ～电路 closed circuit；～度［地质］Closure；～生态［航天］closed ecology

【闭会】lose (or end, adjourn) a meeting：委员会～期间 *when the committee is not in session*

【闭经】［医］amenorrhoea

【闭卷】closed-book：～考试 *closed-book examination* (*during which examinees are not allowed to use any reference*)

【闭口不谈】refuse to say anything about；avoid mentioning

【闭口无言】remain silent；be tongue-tied；be left speechless

【闭路电视】closed-circuit television；closed circuit

【闭路系统】closed-circuit system

【闭门羹】deny or be denied entrance：飨以～ *shut the door in sb.'s face—refuse to receive sb.* / 吃～ *find the door closed on one—be denied a reception*

【闭门思过】shut oneself up and ponder over one's mistakes；ponder over one's mistakes in seclusion

【闭门谢客】close the door to visitors；stop receiving visitors

【闭门造车】make a cart behind closed doors—work behind closed doors；divorce oneself from the masses and from reality；act blindly

【闭目塞听】shut one's eyes and stop one's ears—cut oneself off from reality

【闭幕】❶ the curtain falls；lower the curtain：在观众热烈掌声中～。*The curtain fell to the loud applause of the audience*. ❷ close；conclude：会议已胜利～。*The conference has come to a successful close*. ◇ ～词 closing address (or speech)；～式 closing ceremony

【闭气】❶ stop breathing：他跌了一跤，闭住气了。*He fell over and almost stopped breathing*. ❷ hold one's breath：护士放轻脚步闭住气走近病人床前。*The nurse held her breath and walked quietly towards the patient's bed*.

【闭塞】❶ stop up；close up：鼻孔～ *with one's nose stuffed up* ❷ hard to get to；out-of-the-way；inaccessible：以前这一带交通～。*In the past this district was very hard to get to*. ❸ unenlightened：消息～ *ill-informed* ❹［电］blocking ◇～信号［铁路］block signal

【闭塞眼睛捉麻雀】try to catch sparrows with one's eyes blindfolded —act blindly

【闭音节】［语音］closed syllable

【闭元音】［语音］closed vowel

【闭月羞花】(of feminine beauty) outshine the moon and put the flowers to shame ——另见〖沉鱼落雁〗

毕 Ⅰ 动 finish；accomplish；conclude：阅～请放回原处。*Please replace after reading*. Ⅱ 副〈书〉fully；altogether；completely

【毕恭毕敬】同〖必恭必敬〗

【毕竟】after all；all in all；when all is said and done；in the final analysis：这部书虽然有缺页，但～是珍本。*This book is a rare edition, though there are several pages missing*.

【毕其功于一役】accomplish the whole task at one stroke

【毕生】all one's life；lifetime：～事业 *lifework*；*work of a lifetime*

【毕肖】〈书〉resemble closely；be the very image of：画得神情～ *paint a lifelike portrait of sb*.

【毕业】graduate；finish school：还有一年，他就大学～了。*He'll graduate from college next year*. ◇ ～班 graduating class；～典礼 graduation (ceremony)；commencement；～分配 job assignment on graduation；～论文 graduation thesis (or dissertation)；～设计 graduation project；～实习 graduation field work；～证书 diploma；graduation certificate

【毕业生】graduate

庇 动 shelter；protect；shield：包庇

【庇护】shelter；shield；put under one's protection；take under one's wing ◇ ～权 right of asylum；

～所 sanctuary; asylum
【庇荫】❶ (of a tree, etc.) give shade ❷ shield
陛 名〈书〉a flight of steps leading to a palace hall
【陛下】❶ Your Majesty ❷ His or Her Majesty
毙 动 ❶ die; get killed: 倒毙 ❷〈口〉kill or execute by shooting; shoot: 愤怒的群众要求～了这个杀人犯。*The angry masses demanded that the murderer be shot.* ❸〈书〉fall down
【毙命】〈贬〉meet a violent death; get killed: 两名匪徒当场～。*Two of the bandits were killed on the spot.*
铋 名 [化] bismuth (Bi)
秘 (构词成分) ——另见 mì
【秘鲁】Peru ◇～人 Peruvian
敝 形 ❶〈书〉shabby; worn-out; ragged: ～衣 *ragged clothing; shabby (or worn-out) clothes* ❷〈谦〉my; our; this: ～处 *my place* / ～校 *my school* / ～姓陈。*My name is Chen.*
【敝帚自珍】value one's own old broom —cherish sth. of little value simply because it is one's own (usu. used as a self-depreciatory expression)
婢 名 slave girl; servant-girl: 奴婢
【婢女】slave girl; servant-girl
筚 名 a bamboo or wicker fence: 蓬门筚户
【筚路蓝缕】drive a cart in ragged clothes to break fresh ground—endure hardships in pioneer work
裨 名〈书〉benefit; advantage: 无～于事。*It won't help matters.* or *It won't do any good.*
【裨益】〈书〉benefit; advantage; profit: 大有～ *be of great benefit*
蓖 (构词成分)见下
【蓖麻】[植] castor-oil plant ◇～蚕 castor silkworm; ～油 castor oil; ～子 castor bean
辟 Ⅰ 名〈书〉monarch; sovereign: 复辟 Ⅱ 动〈书〉ward off; keep away ——另见 pì
【辟邪】exorcise evil spirits
碧 Ⅰ 名〈书〉green jade Ⅱ 形 bluish green; blue: ～海 *the blue sea* / ～空 *a clear blue sky; an azure sky*
【碧蓝】dark blue: ～的海洋 *the blue sea*
【碧绿】dark green: ～的田野 *green fields*
【碧瓦】green, glazed tile
【碧血】blood shed in a just cause ◇～丹心 loyalty unto death
【碧玉】jasper
蔽 动 cover; shelter; hide: ～风雨 *shelter from the wind and rain* / 浮云～日。*The clouds shut out the sun.*
弊 名 ❶ fraud; abuse; malpractice: 舞弊 ❷ disadvantage; harm: ～多利少。*The disadvantages outweigh the advantages.*
【弊病】❶ malady; evil; malpractice: 资本主义所固有的社会～ *social evils inherent in capitalism* ❷ drawback; disadvantage: 这种做法～不少。*This method has quite a few drawbacks (or disadvantages).*
【弊端】malpractice; abuse; corrupt practice
避 动 ❶ avoid; evade; shun: ～而不谈 *evade the question; avoid the subject; keep silent about the matter* / ～而不答 *avoid making a reply* / ～雨 *seek shelter from the rain* ❷ prevent; keep away; repel: 避孕
【避弹坑】foxhole
【避弹衣】flak jacket
【避风】❶ take shelter from the wind ❷ (又作'避风头') lie low; stay away from trouble: 避一避风头 *lie low until it blows over* ◇～港 haven; harbour
【避讳】(bìhuì) avoid a taboo (on the personal names of emperors, one's elders, etc.)
【避讳】(bìhui) (又作'避忌') ❶ a word or phrase to be avoided as taboo; taboo ❷ evade; dodge: ～这个问题 *evade the issue*
【避坑落井】dodge a pit only to fall into a well; out of the frying pan into the fire
【避雷器】lightning arrester
【避雷针】lightning rod
【避免】avoid; refrain from; avert: ～错误 *avoid mistakes* / ～轻率行动 *refrain from any rash action* / 设法～了一场事故 *succeed in averting an accident*
【避难】take refuge; seek asylum ◇～港 port of refuge; ～所 refuge; sanctuary; haven
【避人耳目】avoid being noticed; elude observation
【避其锐，击其惰归】avoid the enemy when he is fresh, strike him when he is tired and withdraws
【避实就虚】stay clear of the enemy's main force and strike at his weak points
【避世】retire from the world; withdraw from society
【避暑】❶ be away for the summer holidays; spend a holiday at a summer resort: 暑假我们将去海边～。*We're going to spend our summer holidays at a seaside resort.* ❷ prevent sunstroke ◇～胜地 summer resort; ～药 medicine for preventing sunstroke; preventive against sunstroke
【避税】tax avoidance
【避蚊胺】Metadelphene
【避蚊剂】mosquito repellent
【避嫌】avoid doing anything that may arouse suspicion; avoid arousing suspicion
【避孕】contraception ◇～栓 contraceptive suppository; ～套 condom; ～丸药 the pill; ～药膏 contraceptive jelly; ～用品 contraceptives
【避重就轻】evade major responsibility and take minor; avoid the important and dwell on the trivial

璧 名 ❶ wall ❷ sth. resembling a wall：细胞壁 ❸ cliff：峭壁 ❹ rampart；breastwork

【壁报】wall newspaper：办～ *put up a regular wall newspaper*

【壁橱】a built-in wardrobe or cupboard；closet

【壁灯】wall lamp；bracket light

【壁挂】(wall) hanging

【壁虎】［动］gecko；house lizard

【壁画】mural (painting)；fresco：敦煌～ *the Dunhuang murals*

【壁垒】rampart；barrier：贸易～ *trade barrier* / ～分明 *be diametrically opposed；be sharply divided*

【壁垒森严】❶ closely guarded；strongly fortified ❷ sharply divided；rival camps confronting each other

【壁立】(of cliffs, etc.) stand like a wall；rise steeply：～千尺 *a sheer rise of a thousand feet* / ～的山峰 *a sheer cliff*

【壁炉】fireplace ◇ ～台 mantelpiece

【壁球】squash rackets；squash

【壁虱】❶ tick ❷〈方〉bedbug

【壁毯】tapestry (used as a wall hanging)

【壁纸】wallpaper

臂 名 ❶ arm：左～ *the left arm* ❷ upper arm

【臂膀】arm

【臂纱】(black) armband：戴～ *wear a black armband*

【臂章】❶ armband；armlet ❷［军］shoulder emblem (or patch)

璧 名 a round flat piece of jade with a hole in its centre (used for ceremonial purposes in ancient China)

【璧还】〈套〉❶ return (a borrowed object) with thanks ❷ decline (a gift) with thanks

【璧谢】〈套〉decline (a gift) with thanks

biān

边 名 ❶ side (of a geometrical figure)：三角形的一～ *one side of a triangle* ❷ side；margin；edge；brim；rim：街道两～ *both sides of the street* / 宽～草帽 *broad-brimmed hat* / 衬衣的～ *the hem of a shirt* ❸ border；frontier；boundary ❹ limit；bound：外层空间没个～儿。*Outer space is boundless.* / 这话可太没～儿了。*That's just absurd.* ❺ the place next to a person or thing：身边 ❻(suffix of nouns of locality) side：东～ *east side*

【边隘】frontier pass

【边鄙】〈书〉frontier region；remote district

【边…边…】(used with two verbs to indicate the simultaneous progression or development of two actions)：他边唱歌边工作。*He sang as he worked.* / 边干边学 *learn while working；learn on the job*

【边陲】〈书〉border area；frontier

【边带】sideband

【边地】border district；borderland

【边防】frontier (or border) defence ◇ ～部队 frontier guards；～检查 frontier inspection；～军 frontier force；～哨 border sentry；～战士 frontier guard

【边关】frontier pass：镇守～ *guard a frontier pass；hold a frontier command*

【边际】limit；bound；boundary：绿色的田野，望不到～。*Before me is a boundless stretch of green fields.* ◇～效用论［经］the theory of marginal utility

【边际效益】marginal benefit

【边疆】border area；borderland；frontier；frontier region：支援～建设 *support the construction of the border areas* / 保卫～ *guard the frontier*

【边角料】leftover bits and pieces (of industrial material)

【边界】boundary；border：越过～ *cross a boundary；cross the border* ◇～层 boundary layer；～实际控制线 line of actual control on the border；～事件 border incident；～谈判 border talks；～线 boundary line；～现状 status quo on the border；status quo of the boundary；～协定 boundary agreement；～争端 boundary dispute；～走向 alignment of the boundary line

【边境】border；frontier ◇ ～冲突 border clash (or conflict)；～交货 delivered at frontier (D. A. F.)；～经济合作区 border economic cooperative zone；～贸易 frontier trade；～贸易额 border trade volume；～贸易市场 border trade market；～贸易中心 border trade centre；～事件 border incident；～市镇 border town；～易货贸易 border barter trade

【边框】frame；rim：镜子的～ *the rim of a mirror*

【边门】side door；wicket door (or gate)：请走～。*Side door, please.*

【边民】people living on the frontiers；inhabitants of a border area

【边卡】border checkpoint

【边区】border area (or region)

【边塞】frontier fortress

【边线】❶［体］sideline ❷［体］(垒球) foul line ◇ ～裁判员 linesman

【边沿】edge；fringe：森林～ *the edge (or fringe) of a forest* / 市镇～地带 *the periphery of a town*

【边音】［语音］lateral (sound)

【边缘】❶edge；fringe；verge；brink；periphery：在特区的～ *on the border of the special administrative zone* / 悬崖的～ *the edge of a precipice* / 临近经济破产的～ *on the verge of economic bankruptcy* ❷ marginal；borderline ◇ ～地区 border district；borders；～海 marginal sea；～科学 frontier science

【边远】far from the centre；remote；outlying：～省份 *remote border provinces* / ～地区 *an outlying district*

【边寨】borderland village

砭 Ⅰ名 a stone acupuncture needle (used in ancient times) Ⅱ动 ❶perform acupunctures with stone needles (as in ancient times) ❷〈喻〉pierce：冷风～骨。*The cold wind cuts one to the marrow.* / 痛～时弊 *castigate the abuses of the time*

编 Ⅰ动 ❶ weave；plait：～柳条筐 *weave wicker baskets* / ～辫子 *plait one's hair* ❷ organize；group；arrange：～班 *group into classes* / 把他～在我们组吧。*Put him in our group.* ❸ edit；compile：～教材 *compile teaching material* / ～杂志 *edit a magazine；work in the editorial department of a magazine* ❹ write；compose：～剧本 *write a play* / ～儿童歌曲 *compose songs for children* ❺ fabricate；invent；make up；cook up：这事儿是他～出来的。*He made the whole thing up.* Ⅱ名 (often used in book titles) book；copy：人手一～。*Everyone has a copy.* /《故事新～》*A New Book of Stories*

【编程】[计]program ◇ ～员 programmer

【编次】order of arrangement

【编导】❶ write and direct (a play, film, etc.)：这个话剧是由两位青年作家～的。*The play was written and directed by two young writers.* ❷ playwright-director (of a play)；choreographer-director (of a ballet)；scenarist-director (of a film)

【编订】(又作'编定') compile and edit：鲁迅～了《唐宋传奇集》. *Lu Xun compiled and edited the Literary Tales of the Tang-Song Period.*

【编队】❶ form into columns；organize into teams ❷ formation (of ships or aircraft) ◇～飞行 formation flight (or flying)；～轰炸 formation bombing

【编发】edit and release (manuscript, news, etc.)：新华社～了大会消息。*The Xinhua News Agency released dispatches about the conference.*

【编号】❶ number：给树苗～ *number the saplings* ❷ serial number

【编辑】❶ edit；compile：～图书索引 *compile an index (of books)* ❷ editor；compiler：总～ *editor-in-chief；chief editor* ◇～部 editorial department；～人员 editorial staff；～委员会 editorial board

【编剧】❶ write a play, scenario, etc. ❷ playwright ❸ screenwriter；scenarist

【编码】coding ◇ ～程序 builder；～机 code machine；～器 coder；～员 coder；～指令 coded order

【编目】❶ make a catalogue；catalogue：新到的图书正在～。*The new books are being catalogued.* ❷ catalogue；list ◇ ～部 cataloguing department；～员 cataloguer

【编年史】annalistic history；annals；chronicle

【编年体】annalistic style (in historiography)

【编排】arrange；lay out：文字和图片的～ *the layout of pictures and articles* / 课文要按难易程度～。*The texts should be graded in order of difficulty.*

【编审】❶ read and edit ❷ senior editor

【编外】(of personnel) not on the permanent staff；not on the regular payroll：～人员 *personnel not on the permanent staff；personnel not on the regular payroll*

【编委】editorial member

【编写】❶ compile：～教科书 *compile a textbook* ❷ write；compose：～歌剧 *compose an opera* / ～剧本 *write a play*

【编选】select and edit；compile

【编演】write and produce (a play, etc.)

【编译】❶ translate and edit ❷ translator-editor ◇ ～程序 compiling routine；compiler program；compiler；～自动化 compiling automation

【编印】compile and print；publish

【编造】❶ compile；draw up；work out：～预算 *draw up a budget* / ～表册 *compile statistical tables* ❷ fabricate；invent；concoct；make up；cook up：～谎言 *fabricate lies* / ～情节 *falsify the details of an event；invent (or make up) a story* ❸ create out of the imagination：古代人民～的神话 *myths invented by the ancients*

【编者】editor；compiler

【编者按】(又作'编者案') editor's note；editorial note

【编织】weave；knit；plait；braid：～地毯 *weave a rug* / ～草席 *weave a straw mat* / ～毛衣 *knit a sweater*

【编制】❶ weave；plait；braid：～竹器 *weave bamboo articles* ❷ work out；draw up：～生产计划 *work out a production plan* / ～教学大纲 *draw up a teaching programme*/～程序 *program composition* ❸ authorized strength；establishment：部队～ *establishment (for army units)*/ 控制人员～ *control the manning quotas；limit the size of the personnel force*

【编钟】a set of bells；chimes

【编著】compile；write

【编撰】compile；write

【编组】❶ organize into groups ❷[铁路] marshalling：～场 *marshalling (or classification) yard*

【编纂】compile：～词典 *compile a dictionary*

蝙 (构词成分)见下

【蝙蝠】bat (an animal)

【蝙蝠衫】an upper outer garment with batwing sleeves

鳊 名 bream

【鳊鱼】bream

鞭 Ⅰ名 ❶ whip；lash ❷ an iron staff used as a weapon in ancient China ❸ sth. resembling a whip：教鞭 ❹ a string of small firecrackers：放～ *let off firecrackers* / 一挂～ *a string of firecrackers* Ⅱ动〈书〉flog；whip；lash：～马 *whip a horse*

【鞭策】spur on; urge on
【鞭长莫及】beyond the reach of one's power (or authority); too far away to be helped
【鞭笞】〈书〉flog; lash
【鞭虫】whipworm
【鞭打】whip; lash; flog; thrash
【鞭痕】welt; whip scar; lash mark
【鞭毛】[动] flagellum ◇ ～虫 flagellate
【鞭炮】❶ firecrackers ❷ a string of small firecrackers
【鞭辟入里】(又作'鞭辟近里') penetrating; trenchant; incisive
【鞭挞】〈书〉lash; castigate
【鞭子】whip

biǎn

贬 动 ❶ (in imperial times) demote; relegate: ～为庶民 *be degraded to commoner status* ❷ reduce; devalue: ～价出售 *sell at a reduced price* ❸ censure; depreciate: ～得一钱不值 *condemn as worthless*
【贬斥】❶〈书〉demote ❷ denounce
【贬词】同〖贬义词〗
【贬低】belittle; depreciate; play down: ～其重要性 *belittle the importance of sth.* / 她想～他在这件事里起的作用,夸大自己的作用。*She tried to play down his part in the affair and play up her own.*
【贬价】reduce the price; mark down: ～出售 *sell at a reduced price*
【贬义】derogatory sense: 这个词常用于～。*This word is often used in a derogatory sense.* ◇～词 derogatory term; expression of censure
【贬抑】belittle; depreciate
【贬值】[经] ❶ devalue; devaluate: 中国政府承诺人民币不～。*The Chinese government promised not to devalue Renminbi.* ❷ depreciate: 由于恶性通货膨胀,该国货币大大～了。*Owing to runaway inflation, that country's currency has greatly depreciated.*
【贬职】demote

扁 形 flat: 一只～盒子 *a flat case; a shallow box* / 纸箱子压～了。*The cardboard box was crushed.* ——另见 piān
【扁虫】flatworm
【扁蝽】flat bug
【扁担】carrying pole; shoulder pole
【扁豆】hyacinth bean: 小～ *lentil*
【扁钢条】flat steel bar
【扁骨】[生理] flat bone
【扁坯】[冶] slab
【扁平足】同〖平足〗
【扁桃】❶ almond tree ❷ almond ❸〈方〉flat peach
【扁桃体】(又作'扁桃腺') [生理] tonsil ◇ ～肥大 hypertrophy of tonsils; ～切除术 tonsillectomy
【扁形动物】flatworm; platyhelminth
【扁圆】oblate

匾 名 ❶ a horizontal inscribed board ❷ a silk banner embroidered with words of praise: 绣金～ *embroidering a silk banner with words of gold* ❸ a big round shallow basket
【匾额】a horizontal inscribed board

褊 形〈书〉narrow; cramped
【褊急】〈书〉narrow-minded and short-tempered
【褊狭】〈书〉narrow; cramped: 居处～ *live in cramped quarters* / 气量～ *small-minded*

biàn

弁 名 ❶ a man's cap used in ancient times ❷〈旧〉a low-ranking military officer
【弁言】〈书〉foreword; preface

苄 名 [化] benzyl

变 Ⅰ 动 ❶ become different; change: 情况～了。*The situation has changed.* / 这地方～了样了。*The place looks quite different now.* ❷ change into; become: 天气～暖和了。*The weather became warmer.* / 旱地～水田。*Dry land has been turned into paddy fields.* / 牛奶～酸了。*The milk has gone sour.* ❸ transform; change; alter: ～废为宝 *change waste material into things of value; recycle waste material* / ～害为利 *turn bane into boon* ❹ sell off (one's property): 变产 Ⅱ 形 changeable; changed: 变态 Ⅲ 名 an unexpected turn of events: 事变
【变把戏】perform conjuring tricks; conjure; juggle: ～的 *conjurer; magician*
【变本加厉】become aggravated; be further intensified
【变产】sell off one's property
【变成】change into; turn into; become; transform into: 在一定的条件下,坏事能够～好事。*Under given conditions, bad things can be turned into good things.*
【变电站】(transformer) substation
【变调】❶ [语音] tone sandhi ❷ 同〖转调〗
【变动】❶ alteration; change: 文字上作一些～ *make some changes (or alterations) in the wording* / 人事没有什么～。*There is not much change of personnel.* ❷ change: 你安排得不错,不用～了。*Your arrangement is not bad. There is no need to change it.*
【变法】[史] introduce institutional reforms: 王安石～,推行新政。*Wang Anshi introduced reforms and initiated new policies.*
【变分法】[数] calculus of variations
【变分方程】variation equation
【变分原理】variation principle
【变革】transform; change: ～自然 *transform nature* / 社会～ *social change*

【变更】change; alter; modify: ～作息时间 *alter the daily timetable* / 我们的计划稍有～。*We have modified our plan.* ◇ ～记录 change record

【变工】exchange work (or labour) ◇ ～队 work-exchange team (an agricultural producers' mutual-aid organization)

【变故】an unforeseen event; accident; misfortune: 发生了～。*Something quite unforeseen has happened.*

【变卦】go back on one's word; break an agreement: 昨天说得好好的,怎么～了? *Yesterday you agreed. What made you change your mind?*

【变化】change; vary: 气温的～ *variations (or fluctuations) of temperature* / ～无常 *constantly changing; changeable; capricious*: 高山天气～。*In high mountains the weather is changeable.*

【变幻】change irregularly; fluctuate ◇ ～莫测 changeable; unpredictable

【变换】vary; alternate: ～手法 *vary one's tactics* / ～位置 *shift one's position* ◇ ～电子 conversion electron; ～器 convertor

【变价】appraise at the current rate: ～出售 *sell at the current price*

【变焦距镜头】[摄] zoom lens

【变节】make a political recantation; turn one's coat ◇ ～分子 recanter; turncoat

【变脸】suddenly turn hostile: 他跟我～了。我哪儿得罪他了? *He turned on me. What did I do to offend him?*

【变量】[数] variable

【变流器】[电] converter

【变卖】sell off (one's property): ～产业 *sell off one's estate*

【变频】[电子] frequency conversion: ◇ ～管 converter tube; ～器 converter; ～增益 conversion gain

【变迁】changes; vicissitudes: 人事～ *the vicissitudes of life* / 时代～ *the changes of the times*

【变色】❶ change colour; discolour: 这种墨水不会～。*This ink will not change colour.* / 脸不～心不跳 *one's face does not change colour, nor does one's heart beat faster—without a trace of fear* ❷ change countenance; become angry ◇ ～镜 light-sensitive glasses; ～滤光器 variable-color filter; metachromatic filter

【变色龙】❶ chameleon ❷ a changeable or fickle person (esp. in politics)

【变数】[数] variable

【变速】[机] speed change; gearshift ◇ ～比 gear ratio; ～车道 speed change lane; ～传动装置 speed transforming transmission; variable-speed drive device; ～器 gearbox; transmission; ～运动 [物] variable motion

【变态】❶ [生] metamorphosis ❷ abnormal; anomalous ◇ ～反应 [医] allergy; ～心理 abnormal psychology; ～心理学 abnormal psychology (a science)

【变天】❶ change of weather: 太闷热了,看来要～。*The weather is bound to change soon, it's so close.* ❷ change of heavens—restoration of reactionary rule

【变通】be flexible; accommodate (or adapt) sth. to circumstances: ～办法 *accommodation; adaptation* / 根据不同情况作适当的～ *make appropriate adaptations in the light of specific conditions*

【变为】change into; turn into: 把荒漠～绿色的原野 *turn the wilderness into green fields*

【变温层】another name for 对流层

【变温动物】poikilothermal (or coldblooded) animal

【变戏法】perform conjuring tricks; conjure; juggle

【变相】in disguised form; covert: ～体罚 *corporal punishment in disguised form* / ～的剥削行为 *a covert act of exploitation* / ～涨价 *disguised price increases*

【变心】cease to be faithful; change loyalties; break faith

【变星】[天] variable (star)

【变形】be out of shape; become deformed: 这箱子压得～了。*The box has been crushed out of shape.* / 病人的脊椎骨已经～。*The patient has a deformed spine.* ◇ ～镜头 anamorphic lense; ～体 plasmodium

【变形虫】amoeba ◇ ～痢疾 amoebic dysentery

【变形金刚】transformer (called in the U.S.)

【变性】[化] ❶ denaturation ❷ change sex ◇ ～蛋白质 denatured protein; ～酒精 denatured alcohol; ～人 transsexual; ～手术 transsexual operation

【变压器】[电] transformer

【变样】change in shape or appearance: 几年没见,你还没～。*You haven't changed any since I saw you last.* / 这个地方已经大～了。*This place has changed a lot.*

【变异】[生] variation: ～性 *variability*

【变质】❶ go bad; deteriorate: 这肉～了。*The meat has gone bad.* ❷ [地质] metamorphism ◇ ～岩 [地质] metamorphic rock

【变种】❶ [生] mutation; variety ❷ variety; variant: 机会主义的～ *a variety of opportunism*

【变奏】[音] variation: ～曲 *variations (on a theme)*

【变阻器】[电] rheostat

便 Ⅰ **形** ❶ convenient; handy: 近便 ❷ informal; plain; ordinary: 便饭 Ⅱ **名** ❶ a convenient situation or time: 得便 ❷ piss or shit; urine or excrement: 粪便 Ⅲ **动** relieve oneself: 大便 / 小便 Ⅳ **副** ❶ soon afterwards: 车开不久,天～亮了。*It was light soon after the train had started.* ❷ in that case; then: 这几天不是刮风,～是下雨。*During the last few days, if it was not blowing, then it was raining.* Ⅴ **连** even if: ～是累了,我也要来。*I'll come even if I'm tired.* ——另见 pián

【便步走】[军] march at ease; route step: ～! (*word of command*) *At ease, march!* or *Route step, march!*

【便车】sb.'s car in which one may have a ride: 我要找个～带我进城。*I'm looking for a ride to town.* or *I'm looking for someone who can give me a lift to town.*

【便池】urinal

【便当】❶ convenient; handy; easy: 房子里家具不多,收拾起来很～。*There isn't too much furniture in the room. We can easily tidy it up.* ❷ fast food in box

【便道】❶ shortcut: 抄～走 *take a shortcut* ❷ pavement; sidewalk: 行人走～。*Pedestrians walk on the pavement.* ❸ makeshift road

【便饭】an ordinary meal; a simple meal; potluck: 跟我们一块儿吃顿～吧。*Come along and take potluck with us.*

【便服】❶ everyday clothes; informal dress ❷ civilian clothes

【便函】an informal letter sent by an organization

【便壶】(bed) urinal; chamber pot

【便笺】❶ (informal) note ❷ notepaper; memo; memo pad

【便捷】❶ convenient ❷ quick; nimble

【便览】brief guide: 交通～ *roadbook* / 旅游～ *guidebook*

【便利】❶ convenient; easy: 交通～ *have convenient communications; have good transport facilities; be conveniently located* ❷ facilitate: 为～居民,新盖了一个副食商场。*A new food market has been built for the convenience of the residents.*

【便路】shortcut: 走～ *take a shortcut*

【便帽】cap

【便门】side door; wicket door

【便秘】comstipation

【便民】for the convenience of the people: ～措施 *facilities for the convenience of the people* / ～商店 *convenience shop*

【便溺】urinate or defecate; relieve oneself

【便盆】bed pan

【便桥】temporary (or makeshift) bridge

【便人】somebody who happens to be on hand for an errand: 如有～,请把那本书捎来。*Please send the book by anyone who happens to come this way.*

【便士】penny ◇ ～股票 penny stock

【便条】(又作'便签') (informal) note

【便桶】chamber pot

【便鞋】cloth shoes; slippers

【便携式】portable ◇ ～电视接收机 portable television receiver; ～录像机 portable videotape recorder; ～摄像机 portable video camera; ～终端装置 portable terminal

【便血】[医] have (or pass) blood in one's stool

【便宴】informal dinner: 设～招待 *give a dinner for sb.*

【便衣】❶ civilian clothes; plain clothes: ～警察 *plainclothes policeman* / ～公安人员 *plainclothes public security personnel; public security personnel in plain clothes* ❷ plainclothesman

【便宜行事】(authorized to) act at one's discretion; act as one sees fit

【便于】easy to; convenient for: ～携带 *easy to carry*

【便中】at one's convenience; when it's convenient: 我替你捎来一双鞋,望～来取。*I've brought you a pair of shoes. Please come for them whenever it's convenient.*

遍 Ⅰ 副 all over; everywhere: 我找～了也没找着。*I have looked everywhere, but I can't find it.* / 走～全省 *travel all over the province* / 我们的朋友～天下。*We have friends all over the world.* Ⅱ 量 (for actions) once through; a time: 这本书我从头到尾看过两～。*I've read the book twice from cover to cover.* / 请再说一～。*Please say it again.*

【遍布】be found everywhere; spread all over: 乡镇企业～全国。*Enterprises run by townships and villages can be found all over the country.*

【遍地】all over the place; everywhere ◇ ～开花 blossom everywhere; spring up all over the place

【遍及】extend (or spread) all over

【遍体鳞伤】be covered all over with cuts and bruises; be beaten black and blue; be a mass of bruises

辨 动 differentiate; distinguish; discriminate: 不～真伪 *fail to distinguish between truth and falsehood; be unable to tell the true from the false*

【辨别】differentiate; distinguish; discriminate: ～真假 *distinguish the true from the false* / ～方向 *take one's bearings* ◇ ～力 ability to see things in their true light; discerning power

【辨认】identify; recognize: 他的笔迹容易～。*His handwriting is easy to identify.* / 相片已经模糊,不能～。*The photo has faded beyond recognition.*

【辨析】differentiate and analyse; discriminate: 同义词～ *synonym discrimination*

【辨正】determine and rectify

【辨证论治】(又作'辨证施治') [中] diagnosis and treatment based on an overall analysis of the illness and the patient's condition

辩 动 argue; dispute; debate: 真理愈～愈明。*The more truth is debated, the clearer it becomes.*

【辩白】offer an explanation; plead innocence; try to defend oneself

【辩驳】dispute; refute: 无可～ *beyond all dispute; indisputable; irrefutable*

【辩才】〈书〉eloquence: 颇有～ *be quite eloquent; have a silver tongue*

【辩辞】(又作'辩词') explanation; argument

【辩护】❶ speak in defence of; argue in favour of; defend: 不要替他～了。*Don't try to defend him.* ❷ [法] plead; defend: 为被告人～ *plead for the accused* / 出庭～（*of a lawyer*）*defend a case in court* / 被告人有权获得～。*The accused has the right to defence*. ◇ ～权 right to defence；～人 defender；counsel；～士 apologist

【辩解】provide an explanation；try to defend oneself：错了就错了，不要～。*A mistake is a mistake. Don't try to explain it away.*

【辩论】argue；debate：～个水落石出 *argue the matter out* ◇～会 a debate

【辩证】❶ investigate；authenticate ❷ dialectical：～的统一 *dialectical unity* / ～地看问题 *look at things dialectically* ◇ ～法 dialectics；～逻辑 dialectical logic

【辩证唯物主义】dialectical materialism

辫 名 plait；braid；pigtail：蒜～ *a braid of garlic*

【辫子】❶ plait；braid；pigtail：梳～ *braid one's hair* / 留～ *wear one's hair in braids* ❷ a mistake or shortcoming that may be exploited by an opponent；handle ——另见〖梳辫子〗；〖抓辫子〗

biāo

标 Ⅰ 名 ❶ mark；sign：路标 ❷ prize；award：夺标 ❸ outward sign；symptom：治标 ❹ tender；bid：招标 Ⅱ 动 put a mark，tag or label on；label：～上号码 *put a number on* / ～界 *demarcate a boundary* / 商品都～了价格。*Every article has a price tag on it.*

【标榜】❶ flaunt；advertise；parade：～自由平等 *flaunt the banner of liberty and equality* ❷ boost；excessively praise：互相～ *boost each other；exchange excessive praise*

【标本】❶ specimen；sample：昆虫～ *insect specimen* ❷［中］the root cause and symptoms of a disease：～同治 *treat a disease by looking into both its root cause and symptoms*

【标本虫】［动］spider beetle

【标兵】❶ parade guards（usu. spaced out along parade routes）❷ example；model；pacesetter：树立～ *set sb. up as a pacemaker*

【标尺】❶ surveyor's rod；staff ❷〈水〉staff gauge ❸ common name for 表尺

【标灯】❶ beacon light；beacon ❷ sign lamp（as outside a post office，chemist，etc. at night）

【标底】base number of a tender

【标的】❶ target ❷ aim；purpose ❸ common objectives of both parties to a commercial contract with regard to their rights and duties in the execution of the project

【标点】❶ punctuation ❷ punctuate ◇ ～符号 punctuation mark

【标定】❶ demarcate：～边界线 *demarcate a boundary by setting up boundary markers*（*done jointly by the two parties concerned*）❷ standardize ❸ check according to set standards ❹ standard；standardized

【标杆】❶ surveyor's pole ❷ model；example

【标高】elevation；level

【标号】grade：水泥～ *grade of cement* / 高～水泥 *high-grade cement*

【标记】sign；mark；symbol：探清地雷，作出～ *locate the landmines and mark their location*

【标价】❶ mark a price ❷ marked price

【标量】［物］scalar quantity

【标明】mark；indicate：货箱上～"小心轻放"。*The crate is marked "Handle with care".*

【标签】label；tag：贴上～ *stick on a label* / 价目～ *price tag*

【标枪】javelin

【标书】❶（papers for）invitation to bidding ❷ bidding papers

【标题】title；heading；headline；caption ◇ ～新闻 the headlines；～音乐 programme music

【标新立异】start sth. new just in order to be different；do sth. unconventional or unorthodox；create sth. new and original

【标音】transcription：宽式～ *broad transcription* / 严式～ *narrow transcription*

【标语】slogan；poster：张贴～ *put up slogans*（*or posters*）◇ ～牌 placard

【标志】（又作'标识'）❶ sign；mark；symbol：兴旺发达的～ *a sign of vigour and prosperity* ❷ indicate；mark；symbolize：中华人民共和国的成立，～着我国新的历史阶段的开始。*The founding of the People's Republic of China marked the beginning of a new historical period in our country.* ◇ ～层［地质］marker bed

【标致】（usu. of women）beautiful；handsome

【标注】mark

【标桩】（marking）stake

【标准】❶ standard；criterion：合乎～ *up to standard* / 按我们的～来看 *by our standards* ❷ serving as or conforming to a standard ◇～测试 standard testing；～层［地质］key bed；～差 standard deviation；～大气压［物］standard atmosphere；～化 standardize；～化试题 standardization test(paper)；～集装箱 standard container；～局 bureau of standards；～时 standard time；～像 official portrait；～音 standard pronunciation；～语 standard speech（or language）

彪 名〈书〉a young tiger

【彪炳】〈书〉shining；splendid

【彪炳千古】shine through the ages：其功业将～。*The glory of his achievements will shine through the ages.*

【彪悍】intrepid；doughty；valiant

【彪形大汉】burly chap；husky fellow；hefty fellow

膘 名 fat（of a domestic animal）：牲口～肥体壮。*The animals are plump and sturdy.* / 这块肉～厚。*This piece of meat has got a lot of fat on it.*

镖 名 a dartlike weapon（used in former times）

【镖局】（in former times）a professional establish-

ment which provided armed escorts
【镖客】(又作'镖师')(in former times) armed escort (of travellers or merchants' caravans)

飙 名〈书〉violent wind; whirlwind: 狂飙
【飙升】rocket; rise quickly: 资产价格大幅~。*The price of assets is rocketing*.

biǎo

表 Ⅰ 名 ❶ surface; outside; external: 表面 ❷ the relationship between the children or grandchildren of a brother and a sister or of sisters: 表哥 ❸ model; example: 表率 ❹ table; form; list: 价目~ *price list* / 登记~ *registration form* ❺meter; gauge: 水表 ❻ watch (a timepiece) Ⅱ 动 ❶ show; express: 深~同情 *show deep sympathy* / ~决心 *express* (*or declare*) *one's determination* ❷ [中] administer medicine to bring out the cold
【表白】express or state clearly; explain; clarify; explain oneself: ~诚意 *assert one's sincerity* / 我们看一个人,不是根据他的~,而是根据他的行动。*We judge a person not by what he says but by what he does*.
【表报】statistical tables and reports
【表册】statistical forms; book of tables or forms: 公文报告~ *documents, written reports and statistical forms*
【表层】surface layer
【表尺】[军] rear sight ◇ ~座 rear sight base
【表达】express; convey; voice: 我激动的心情难以用语言来~。*Words can hardly express my excitement*.
【表带】watchband; watch strap
【表弟】younger male cousin; cousin
【表哥】older male cousin; cousin
【表格】form; table: 填写~ *fill in a form*
【表功】❶ brag about one's deeds ❷〈书〉praise; commend
【表观】[物] apparent ◇ ~运动 apparent motion; ~质量 apparent mass
【表姐】older female cousin; cousin
【表决】decide by vote; vote: 投票~ *decide* (*or vote*) *by ballot* / 举手~ *vote by a show of hands* / 唱名~ *vote by roll call; roll-call vote* / 口头~ *voice vote; vote by "yes" and "no"* / 起立~ *vote by sitting and standing* / ~通过 *be voted through* ◇~程序 voting procedure; ~机器 voting machine; ~指示牌 vote indicator
【表决权】the right to vote; the vote: 行使~ *exercise the right to vote* / 有(无)~ *have the right* (*no right*) *to vote*
【表里】❶ outside and inside; one's outward show and inner thoughts: ~为奸 *collusion between those within and those without* ❷ [中] exterior and interior ◇~不一 think one way and act another; ~如一 think and act in one and the same way
【表链】watch chain
【表露】show; reveal: 他很着急,但并没有~出来。*He was very worried, but didn't show it*.
【表妹】younger female cousin; cousin
【表蒙子】watch glass; crystal
【表面】❶ surface; face; outside; appearance: 地球的~ *the surface of the earth* / 你不能只看事情的~。*You must not look only at the surface of things*. / 他~上好像很和气。*He seems very friendly on the surface*. ❷〈方〉dial plate; dial ◇ ~处理 surface treatment; ~价值 face value; ~现象 superficial phenomenon; ~硬化 [冶] case-hardening; ~张力 [物] surface tension
【表面光】attractive on the surface; cheaply showy: 这产品~,质量却很差。*This product looks nice, but proves to be poor in quality*.
【表面化】come to the surface; become apparent: 矛盾~了。*The contradiction has become apparent*.
【表面文章】show; ostentation: 他那番话不过是~。*He was merely paying lip service*.
【表明】make known; make clear; state clearly; indicate: ~立场 *make known one's position; declare one's stand* / 有迹象~会谈即将恢复。*There are indications that the talks will be resumed soon*.
【表盘】dial plate; dial
【表皮】[生] epidermis; cuticle
【表亲】❶ cousin ❷ cousinship
【表情】❶ express one's feelings: 她演戏善于~。*Her acting is very expressive*. ❷ expression: 她唱歌很有~。*She sings with great expression*. / 面部~ *facial expression* / ~不自然 *look awkward; wear an unnatural expression*
【表示】❶ show; express; indicate: ~关切 *show concern* / ~愤慨 *voice* (*or express*) *one's indignation* / ~热烈欢迎 *extend a warm welcome* ❷ expression; indication: 友好的~ *an expression of friendship; a friendly gesture*
【表述】explain; state: ~己见 *state* (*or air*) *one's views*
【表率】example; model: 老师要做学生的~。*A teacher must set an example* (*or a good example*) *to his students*.
【表态】make known one's position; declare where one stands; commit oneself: 明确~ *take a clearcut stand*
【表土】surface soil; topsoil
【表现】❶ show; display; manifest: 他心里很不高兴,可是没有~出来。*He was unhappy, but he didn't show it*. ❷ expression; manifestation; display: 这是他无知的又一种~。*This is yet another manifestation of his ignorance*. ❸ behaviour; performance: 他在工作中的~很好。*He is doing very well in his work*. ❹ show off: 好~ *like to show off* ◇~手法 technique of expression; ~形式 form of expression; manifestation; ~型 [生] phenotype; ~主义 expressionism

【表象】～型［生］phenotype；［心理］［哲］presentation

【表兄】同〖表哥〗

【表演】❶ perform；act；play：～节目 *give a performance*；*put on a show* / 她～得很好。*She performed very well*. ❷ performance；exhibition：杂技～ *acrobatic performance* / 体育～ *sports exhibition* / 航空模型～ *model planes exhibition* ❸ demonstrate：～新操作方法 *demonstrate new techniques of operation* ◇～唱 singing with actions；～赛 exhibition match

【表扬】praise；commend：～好人好事 *praise good people and good deeds* / 大会～了十个先进集体。*The conference commended ten advanced units*. ◇～信 commendatory letter

【表意文字】ideograph；ideogram；ideography

【表音文字】phonography

【表语】［语］predicative

【表彰】cite (in dispatches)；commend：为了～他生前的事迹 *in recognition of his deeds in his lifetime*

婊

（构词成分）见下

【婊子】prostitute；whore

裱

动 ❶ mount (a picture, etc.)：把画拿去～一下。*Go and have the painting mounted*. ❷ paper (a wall, ceiling, etc.)

【裱褙】（又作'裱贴'）mount (a picture, etc.)

【裱糊】paper (a wall, ceiling, etc.)

biē

憋

动 ❶ suppress；hold back：～不住 *be unable to hold oneself back*；*can't contain oneself* / ～住气 *hold one's breath* / ～了一肚子火 *be filled with pent-up anger* ❷ suffocate；feel oppressed：心里～得慌 *feel very much oppressed* / 屋里太闷，～得人透不过气来。*The room was so stuffy, one could hardly breathe*.

【憋闷】feel oppressed；be depressed；be dejected

【憋气】❶ feel suffocated (or oppressed) ❷ choke with resentment；feel injured and resentful：憋着一肚子气 *have pent-up grievances*

瘪

（构词成分）见下 ——另见 biě

【瘪三】〈方〉a wretched-looking tramp who lives by begging or stealing

鳖

名 soft-shelled turtle

【鳖甲】［中］turtle shell

【鳖裙】（又作'鳖边'）calipash

bié

别

Ⅰ 动 ❶ leave；part：～故乡 *leave one's native place* ❷ differentiate；distinguish：～其真伪 *determine whether it's true or false* ❸ fasten with a pin or clip：把表格～在一起 *pin* (*or clip*) *the forms together* ❹ stick in：腰里～着旱烟袋 *with a pipe stuck in one's belt* / 把门～上。*Bolt the door*. Ⅱ 代 other；another：～处 *another place*；*elsewhere* Ⅲ 名 ❶ difference；distinction：男女有～ *make a distinction between the sexes* ❷ classification；category：性别 Ⅳ 副 ❶ (used in giving commands or advice) don't；had better not：～忘了。*Don't forget*. / ～忙。*No hurry*. or *Take your time*. ❷ (used in expressing anxiety that sth. bad may happen)：明天可～下雨。*I hope it won't rain tomorrow*. / 他～睡过头了，误了火车。*Maybe he's overslept and missed the train*. ——另见 biè

【别称】another name；alternative name：湘是湖南的～。*Xiang is another name for Hunan*.

【别出心裁】adopt an original approach；try to be different

【别处】other places；elsewhere：咱们到～看看。*Let's take a look at other places*. or *Let's take a look around elsewhere*.

【别动队】❶ special detachment；commando ❷ an armed secret agent squad

【别管】no matter (who, what, etc.)：～是谁，一律按原则办事。*No matter who it is, we'll act according to principle*.

【别号】〈旧〉another name；alias：李白，字太白，～青莲居士。*Li Bai, whose courtesy name was Taibai, was also known as the Hermit of Green Lotus*.

【别家】other stores, shops, factories, etc.：你要的型号已售完，请到～去看看吧。*The goods of your specifications are all sold out. Please try* (*your luck in*) *some other stores*.

【别具匠心】show ingenuity；have originality：园中布置～。*The layout of the garden shows the designer's ingenuity*.

【别具一格】have a style of one's own；have a unique (or distinctive) style：这个舞蹈刚健清新，～。*There is something unique about the liveliness and vigour of the dance*.

【别开生面】start sth. new (or original)；break a new path；break fresh ground：这首诗可谓命意新奇，～。*This poem can be considered fresh and original, quite a new approach to the subject*.

【别来无恙】I trust all has been well with you since we last saw each other

【别离】take leave of；leave：～家乡，踏上征途 *leave home and start on a long journey*

【别论】another or a different matter：又当～ *should be regarded as a different matter*

【别名】another name；alternative name：铁牛是拖拉机的～。*Iron-ox is another name for tractor*.

【别人】other people；others；people：认真考虑～的意见 *consider other people's suggestions seriously* / ～恐怕不这样看。*People won't view it this way, I'm afraid*.

【别树一帜】set up a new banner；found a new

school of thought; have a style of one's own
【别墅】villa
【别说】to say nothing of; not to mention; let alone: 这种动物我连听也没听说过,～见过了。*I haven't even heard of such an animal, let alone seen it.*
【别提】〈口〉no need to mention; you can well imagine: 他那个高兴劲儿啊,就～了。*You can well imagine how happy he was.*
【别体】a varied form of a Chinese character
【别无长物】have nothing other than: 他是一介寒士,除书以外,～。*A poor scholar, he possessed nothing but his books.*
【别无他图】have no other intentions: 他说他除了要把事做得更好外～。*He said he had no other aim than to do a better job of it.*
【别绪】sorrow of separation
【别有风味】have a distinctive flavour
【别有天地】a place of unique beauty; scenery of exceptional charm; an altogether different world
【别有用心】have ulterior motives; have an axe to grind
【别针】❶ safety pin; pin ❷ brooch
【别致】unique; unconventional: 天坛的建筑结构非常～。*The architecture of the Temple of Heaven is unique.*
【别字】❶ 同〖白字〗❷ 同〖别号〗

蹩 动 〈方〉sprain (one's ankle or wrist)
【蹩脚】〈方〉inferior; shoddy: ～的宣传家 *an incompetent propagandist* / 他的英语很～。*His English is very poor.* ◇ ～货 inferior goods; poor stuff; shoddy work

biě

瘪 Ⅰ 形 shrivelled; shrunken: ～花生 *blighted peanuts* / 没牙～嘴儿 *have a toothless, sunken mouth* Ⅱ 动 become hollow, sink down: 车胎～了。*The tyre is flat.* ——另见 biē

biè

别 动 〈方〉persuade sb. to change his opinion or give up his idea (usu. used in 别不过): 我想不依他,可是又～不过他。*I'd hate to let him have his own way, but I can't talk him round.* ——另见 bié
【别扭】❶ awkward; difficult; uncomfortable: 这个人真～。*That chap is really difficult to deal with (or is really contrary).* ❷ not see eye to eye; disagree: 两个人素来有些别别扭扭的。*The two of them often have difficulty with each other.* ❸ (of speech or writing) unnatural; awkward: 这句话听起来有点～。*This sentence sounds a bit awkward.* ——另见〖闹别扭〗

bīn

宾 名 guest: 贵宾
【宾词】[逻] predicate
【宾格】[语] the objective case
【宾馆】guesthouse
【宾客】guests; visitors ◇ ～盈门 a house always full of visitors
【宾朋】friends and guests; guests: ～满座。*There was a houseful of guests.* or *Visitors filled all the seats.*
【宾语】[语] object
【宾至如归】where guests feel at home (said of a hotel, etc.); a home from home: 在这家饭店住宿的旅客都有～的感觉。*All travellers find this hotel a home from home.*
【宾主】host and guest: ～频频举杯。*Host and guests proposed repeated toasts.*

彬 (构词成分) 见下
【彬彬】〈书〉refined
【彬彬有礼】refined and courteous; urbane: 他扣上上衣的扣子,～地走上一步。*He buttoned up his jacket and moved forward with ceremonious deference.*

傧 (构词成分) 见下
【傧相】attendant of the bride or bridegroom at a wedding

滨 Ⅰ 名 bank; brink; shore: 湘江之～ *on the banks of the Xiangjiang River* Ⅱ 动 be close to (the sea, a river, etc.); border on: ～海城市 *a city bordering on the sea* / ～海地区 *a coastal region* / ～江公园 *a riverside park*

缤 (构词成分) 见下
【缤纷】〈书〉in riotous profusion: 五彩缤纷

槟 (构词成分) 见下 ——另见 bīng
【槟子】a species of apple which is slightly sour and astringent

镔 (构词成分) 见下
【镔铁】wrought iron

濒 动 ❶ be close to (the sea, a river, etc.); border on: ～湖 *border on the shores of a lake* / 东～大海 *face the sea on the east* ❷ be on the brink of; be on the point of
【濒临】be close to; border on; be on the verge of: 河北省～渤海。*Hebei Province is on the Bohai.* / 春秋末期奴隶社会～瓦解。*By the end of the Spring and Autumn Period slave society was on the verge of disintegration.*
【濒危】〈书〉❶ be in imminent danger: 我国有354种珍稀植物～。*In our country 354 species of rare plants are on the brink of extinction (or are dying out).* ❷ be critically ill

【濒于】be on the brink of：～破产 *be on the brink of bankruptcy* / ～崩溃 *verge on collapse* / ～灭亡 *near extinction* / ～绝境 *face an impasse*

bìn

摈 动〈书〉discard；get rid of：～而不用 *reject* / ～诸门外 *shut (or lock) sb. out*

【摈斥】〈书〉reject；dismiss：～异己 *dismiss those who hold different opinions*

【摈除】discard；get rid of；dispense with：～繁文缛节 *dispense with all unnecessary formalities*

【摈弃】abandon；discard；cast away：～陈旧的道德观念 *cast away antiquated moral values*

殡 动 ❶ lay a coffin in a memorial hall ❷ carry a coffin to the burial place：出殡

【殡车】hearse

【殡殓】a corpse and carry it to the grave

【殡仪馆】the undertaker's；funeral parlour (or home)

【殡葬】funeral and interment

髌 名 kneecap；patella

【髌骨】kneecap；patella

鬓 名 temples；hair on the temples：双～斑白 *greying at the temples*

【鬓发】hair on the temples：～苍白 *greying at the temples*

【鬓角】(又作'鬓脚') temples；hair on the temples

bīng

冰 Ⅰ 名 ice Ⅱ 动 ❶put on the ice；ice：把那瓶啤酒～上。*Ice the bottle of beer*. ❷ feel cold：这水～手。*This water is freezing cold*.

【冰棒】〈方〉同〖冰棍儿〗

【冰雹】hail；hailstone：下～了。*It's hailing*.

【冰场】skating (or ice) rink；ice stadium；ice arena

【冰川】glacier ◇～湖 glacial lake；～期 glacial epoch；ice age；～舌 glacier tongue；～学 glaciology；～作用 glaciation

【冰醋酸】[化] glacial acetic acid

【冰镩】ice chisel

【冰袋】[医] ice bag

【冰蛋】frozen eggs

【冰刀】[体] (ice) skates

【冰岛】Iceland ◇～人 Icelander；～语 Icelandic (language)

【冰灯】ice lantern

【冰点】[物] freezing point ◇～测定器 cryoscope

【冰雕】❶ ice carving ❷ carved ice；ice sculpture

【冰冻】❶ freeze ❷〈方〉ice ◇～季节 freezing season；～疗法 ice therapy；～区 frost zone；～食物 frozen foods

【冰冻三尺，非一日之寒】it takes more than one cold day for the river to freeze three chi deep—the trouble has been brewing for quite some time

【冰斗】cirque

【冰毒】ice—a deadly stimulant drug

【冰帆】❶ iceboat ❷ [体] iceboating

【冰封】❶ (of a river, lake, etc.) freeze over；be blocked up with ice：这湖～了，可以在上面走。*The lake has frozen over；you can walk on it*. ❷ icebound：～的港口 *an icebound harbour*

【冰盖】[地质] ice sheet

【冰糕】〈方〉❶ 同〖冰激凌〗❷ 同〖冰棍儿〗

【冰镐】ice axe

【冰柜】freezer；refrigerator

【冰棍儿】ice-lolly；popsicle；ice-sucker；frozen sucker

【冰河】同〖冰川〗◇～时代 同〖冰川期〗

【冰花】❶ frost (on windows)；frostwork ❷ (soft) rime

【冰激凌】ice cream

【冰肌玉骨】flesh of ice and bones of jade—❶ a beautiful woman ❷ noble and unsullied

【冰窖】icehouse

【冰晶】[气] ice crystal

【冰晶石】cryolite

【冰景】icescape

【冰冷】ice-cold

【冰凉】ice-cold：～的酸梅汤 *ice-cold sweet-sour plum juice* / 他两手冻得～。*His hands were freezing*.

【冰凝器】[物] cryophorus

【冰排】ice raft；ice floe

【冰片】[中] borneol

【冰期】同〖冰川期〗

【冰淇淋】同〖冰激凌〗

【冰碛】[地质] moraine：～物 *till* / ～岩 *tillite*

【冰橇】led；sledge；sleigh

【冰清玉洁】同〖玉洁冰清〗

【冰球】[体] ❶ ice hockey ❷ puck

【冰染染料】azoic dyes

【冰人】〈书〉matchmaker；go-between

【冰山】❶ an icy mountain ❷ iceberg ❸ an individual or a group not to be relied upon for long

【冰上表演】ice show

【冰上溜石】curling

【冰上赛车】icekhana

【冰上运动】ice-sports：～会 *ice-sports meet*

【冰释】〈书〉(of misgivings, misunderstandings, etc.) disappear；vanish；be dispelled：涣然冰释

【冰霜】〈书〉ice and frost—❶ moral integrity ❷ austerity

【冰塔】[地质] serac

【冰炭不相容】as incompatible (or irreconcilable) as ice and hot coals

【冰糖】crystal sugar；rock candy ◇～葫芦 candied haws on a stick

【冰天雪地】a world of ice and snow

【冰隙】[地质] crevasse

【冰箱】icebox；refrigerator；freezer

【冰消瓦解】melt like ice and break like tiles—dis-

integrate；dissolve；be dispelled：通过谈心，他们两人之间的误会已经～。*The misunderstandings between the two of them were cleared up*（*or removed*）*after a heart-to-heart talk*.
【冰鞋】skating boots；skates
【冰心】moral purity
【冰雪聪明】extremely intelligent；remarkably bright；brilliant
【冰镇】iced：～西瓜 *iced watermelon* / ～汽水 *iced soda water*
【冰洲石】Iceland spar
【冰柱】icicle
【冰砖】ice-cream brick
【冰锥】（又作'冰锥子'）同〖冰柱〗

兵 名 ❶ weapons；arms ❷ soldier：当兵 ❸ rank-and-file soldier；private：官兵 ❹ army；troops：骑兵 ❺ military：纸上谈兵 ❻ pawn，one of the pieces in Chinese chess
【兵败如山倒】an army in flight is like a landslide
【兵变】mutiny
【兵不血刃】with blades innocent of blood—win victory without shedding a drop of blood or firing a shot
【兵不厌诈】there can never be too much deception in war；all's fair in war
【兵车】❶〈旧〉(war) chariot ❷ military vehicle
【兵船】man-of-war；naval vessel；warship
【兵多将广】a very large army with many able generals—very powerful military forces
【兵法】art of war；military strategy and tactics
【兵符】❶（in former times）military tally（used as evidence of authority）❷ 同〖兵书〗
【兵戈】〈书〉❶ weapons；arms：不动～ *without resorting to force* ❷ fighting；war：～扰攘 *war-torn*
【兵工厂】munitions（or ordnance）factory；arsenal
【兵贵神速】speed is what counts in war；in war it's speed that counts
【兵荒马乱】the turmoil and chaos of war
【兵家】❶ military strategist in ancient China ❷ military commander；soldier：～必争之地 *a place contested by all strategists*；*strategic point*
【兵舰】warship
【兵精粮足】have well-trained troops and abundant supplies
【兵来将挡，水来土掩】confront soldiers with generals and stem water with earth—take such measures as the situation calls for
【兵力】ilitary strength；armed forces；troops：～对比 *relative military strength* / 分散～ *disperse one's troops*；*spread one's forces too thin* / ～不足 *be short of men*（*or armed forces*）
【兵连祸结】ravaged by successive wars；war-torn；war-ridden
【兵临城下】The enemy host has reached the city gates；The city is under siege.
【兵乱】turmoil caused by war
【兵马】troops and horses；military forces
【兵马未动，粮草先行】food and fodder should go ahead of troops and horses —proper preparations should be made ahead of time
【兵马俑】terra cotta soldiers and horses；wood or clay figures of warriors and horses buried with the dead
【兵痞】army riffraff；army ruffian；soldier of fortune
【兵器】weaponry；weapons；arms
【兵强马壮】strong soldiers and sturdy horses—a well-trained and powerful army
【兵权】military leadership；military power：掌握～ *hold military power*
【兵戎】arms；weapons ◇ ～相见 resort（or appeal）to arms；open hostilities；cross swords with；meet on the battleground
【兵士】rank-and-file soldiers；privates
【兵书】a book on the art of war
【兵团】large（military）unit；formation；corps
【兵械】ordnance；armament
【兵役】military service：服～ *serve in the army*；*perform military service* ◇ ～法 military service law；～制 system of military service
【兵营】military camp；barracks
【兵员】soldiers；troops：五十万～500，000 *troops*；*an army* 500，000 *strong*
【兵源】manpower resources（for military service）；sources of troops
【兵站】army service station；military depot
【兵种】a combat branch of one of the armed forces；arm：步兵是陆军～之一。*The infantry is one of the arms of the army*.
【兵卒】〈旧〉soldiers

槟（构词成分）见下 ——另见 bīn
【槟榔】areca；betel palm

bǐng

丙 Ⅰ 名 the third of the ten Heavenly Stems（天干）（另见〖干支〗）Ⅱ 数 third：～等 *the third grade*；*grade C* / ～种维生素 *vitamin C*
【丙纶】［纺］polypropylene fibre
【丙酮】［化］acetone ◇～树脂 acetone resin
【丙烯酸】［化］acrylic acid
【丙种射线】［物］gamma ray

秉 动 ❶〈文〉grasp；hold：～笔 *hold a pen* / ～烛 *hold a candle* ❷〈书〉control；preside over：～政 *hold political power*；*be in power*
【秉承】〈书〉take（orders）；receive（commands）
【秉赋】❶ possess；be endowed with ❷ natural endowment；gift
【秉公】justly；impartially ◇ ～办理 handle a matter impartially；act with justice
【秉性】同〖禀性〗
【秉政】〈书〉be at the helm of the state；be in power；be in office
【秉直】〈书〉honest；upright

【秉烛夜游】wander about at night carrying a lamp—make merry while one may

炳 形〈书〉bright；splendid；remarkable：彪炳

柄 名 ❶ handle：刀～ *the handle of a knife* / 斧～ *the shaft of an axe*；*helve* ❷ stem (of a flower, leaf or fruit)：花～ *the stem of a flower* ❸ anything affording an advantage or pretext to an opponent：话柄

【柄臣】〈书〉a powerful minister (of a monarchy)

【柄权】〈书〉be in power；exercise control

饼 名 ❶ a round flat cake：月饼 ❷ sth. shaped like a cake：柿饼

【饼铛】baking pan

【饼肥】cake (fertilizer)

【饼干】biscuit；cracker

【饼子】(maize or millet) pancake

屏 动 ❶ hold (one's breath)：～着呼吸 *hold one's breath* ❷reject；get rid of；abandon：屏除——另见 píng

【屏除】get rid of；dismiss；brush aside：～杂念 *dismiss distracting thoughts*

【屏绝】dismiss；brush aside；abandon

【屏气】hold one's breath：他放轻脚步屏住气向病房走去。*Holding his breath, he stepped lightly towards the ward.*

【屏气凝神】hold one's breath in concentration：～地听讲 *listen with rapt attention*

【屏弃】discard；reject；throw away；abandon

【屏息】hold one's breath：～静听 *listen with bated breath*

禀 动〈书〉report (to one's superior or senior)；petition

【禀报】〈书〉report (to one's superior or senior)

【禀承】同〖秉承〗

【禀复】〈书〉report back (to one's superior or senior)

【禀赋】natural endowment；gift：～聪明 *be gifted with keen intelligence*

【禀告】〈书〉report (to one's superior or senior)

【禀明】explain (to one's superior or senior)

【禀性】natural disposition：～纯厚 *be simple and honest by nature*

bìng

并 Ⅰ 动 ❶combine；merge；incorporate：几个小厂～成一个大厂。*Several small factories merged into a big one.* ❷ stand or place side by side：并肩 Ⅱ 副 ❶side by side；equally；simultaneously：并存 ❷(used to reinforce a negative) actually；definitely：你以为他糊涂，他～不糊涂。*You thought he was foolish, but actually he isn't.* Ⅲ 连 and；besides：我完全同意～拥护这个报告。*I fully agree with and endorse this report.*

【并存】exist side by side：多种经济成份～。*Multiple sectors of the economy exist side by side.* / 两说～。*The two statements are compatible.*

【并蒂莲】twin lotus flowers on one stalk—a devoted married couple

【并发】be complicated by；erupt simultaneously

【并发症】［医］complication

【并股】［经］reverse stock split

【并轨】combination of two (methods, systems, etc.)

【并激】［电］shunt excitation ◇ ～电动机 shunt motor；～绕组 shunt winding

【并驾齐驱】run neck and neck；keep abreast of sb.；keep pace with sb.；be on a par with sb.

【并肩】shoulder to shoulder；side by side；abreast：四人～而行。*The four of them walked abreast.* ◇ ～作战 fight side by side；fight shoulder to shoulder

【并进】advance side by side：齐头并进

【并举】carry on (two things) at the same time；develop concurrently

【并卷机】［纺］ribbon lap machine

【并立】exist side by side；exist simultaneously

【并联】［电］parallel connection：～电路 *parallel circuit* ◇～谐振 parallel resonance

【并列】stand side by side；be juxtaposed：～第二名 *be both runners-up*；*tie for second place* ◇ ～分句［语］coordinate clause；～句［语］compound sentence

【并拢】close up；join together

【并排】side by side；abreast：不要～骑车。*Don't all cycle abreast.*

【并且】and；besides；moreover；furthermore：这本书内容好，～写得很生动。*This book is sound in content and lively in style.*

【并入】merge into；incorporate into

【并纱】［纺］doubling：～机 *doubling winder*

【并条】［纺］drawing：～机 *drawing frame*

【并吞】swallow up；annex；absorb：大垄断资本集团～中小企业。*Big monopoly capitalist groups swallow up medium and small enterprises.*

【并网】merge and synchronize two or more power grids

【并行】❶ walk abreast；run side by side ❷ carry on (two things) at the same time ◇～操作 concurrent operation；～处理 parallel processing；～外部操作 concurrent peripheral operations

【并行不悖】both can be accomplished without coming into conflict；not be mutually exclusive

【并用】use two things simultaneously：手脚～ *use both hands and feet*

【并重】lay equal stress on；pay equal attention to：预防和治疗～ *lay equal stress on prevention and cure*

病 Ⅰ 名 ❶ disease；illness；sickness：他有～。*He is ill.* / 他的～已经好了。*He is well again.* ❷ malady；evil：弊病 ❸ fault；defect：不足为～ *can't count as a fault* Ⅱ 动 ill；sick：他～了。

He is ill. / 他～得很厉害。*He is seriously ill*.

【病案】同〖病历〗

【病包儿】〈口〉a person who is always falling ill; chronic invalid

【病变】pathological changes

【病病歪歪】weak or unsteady from illness; in bad shape

【病程】course of disease

【病虫害】plant diseases and insect pests

【病床】❶ hospital bed: 这所医院有三百张～。*The hospital has three hundred beds*. ❷ sickbed: 我在他～旁边守了好几夜。*I watched beside his sickbed for several nights*.

【病从口入,祸从口出】Disease goes in by the mouth and trouble comes out of the mouth; Illness comes from food and trouble from speech.

【病倒】be down with an illness; be laid up

【病毒】［医］virus ◇～病 virosis; ～性肝炎 viral hepatitis; ～学 virology

【病笃】〈书〉be critically ill; be terminally ill

【病房】ward (of a hospital); sickroom: 隔离～ *isolation ward* / 内科～ *medical ward*

【病夫】sick man

【病根】❶ an incompletely cured illness; an old complaint ❷ the root cause of trouble: 他犯错误的～在于私心太重。*His error stems from selfishness*.

【病故】die of illness

【病害】(plant) disease

【病号】sick personnel; person on the sick list; patient: 老～ *one who is always ill*; *chronic invalid* ◇～饭 patient's diet; special food for patients

【病患】disease; illness; sickness

【病急乱投医】men at death's door will turn in desperation to any doctor—men in a desperate plight will try anything

【病家】❶ a patient and his family ❷ patient

【病假】sick leave: 请～ *ask for sick leave* / 休～ *be on sick leave* / 给三天～ *grant three days' sick leave* ◇ ～条 certificate for sick leave

【病句】a faulty sentence (grammatically or logically)

【病菌】pathogenic bacteria; germs

【病况】state of an illness; patient's condition

【病来如山倒,病去如抽丝】sickness comes like an avalanche but goes like reeling silk; illness strikes like a landslide, recovery is as slow as reeling silk; agues come on horseback, but go away on foot

【病理】pathology ◇～学 pathology

【病历】medical record; case history: ～室 *records room*

【病例】case (of illness): 流感～ *a case of influenza*

【病魔】the demon of disease—serious illness: ～缠身 *be possessed by the demon of disease—be afflicted with a lingering disease*

【病情】*state of an illness*; *patient's condition*: 孩子的～有好转。*The child's condition took a favourable turn*. or *The child's condition was improving*. ◇ ～公报 medical bulletin

【病人】❶ a sick person; invalid: 他是～。*He's a sick man*. / 我家有～。*Someone in my family is ill*. / 重～ *a serious case* ❷ patient: 这家医院医生不够,～太多。*This hospital has not enough doctors and too many patients*.

【病容】sickly look: 面带～ *look ill*; *look unwell*

【病入膏肓】the disease has attacked the vitals—beyond cure

【病史】medical history; case history

【病势】degree of seriousness of an illness; patient's condition: 针灸以后,～略为减轻。*The patient became a bit better after the acupuncture treatment*.

【病逝】〈书〉die of illness

【病死】die of illness

【病榻】〈书〉sickbed

【病态】morbid (or abnormal) state ◇～心理 morbid psychology (or mentality)

【病痛】slight illness; indisposition; ailment

【病危】be critically ill; be terminally ill

【病象】symptom (of a disease)

【病休】be on sick leave

【病因】cause of disease; pathogeny

【病友】a friend made in hospital or people who become friends in hospital; wardmate

【病愈】recover (from an illness)

【病员】sick personnel; person on the sick list; patient

【病原】cause of disease; pathogeny ◇ ～体 pathogen; ～学 aetiology

【病院】a specialized hospital

【病征】symptom (of a disease)

【病症】disease; illness

【病重】be seriously ill

【病株】diseased or infected plant

【病状】symptom (of a disease)

摒 动 get rid of; brush aside; dismiss ——另见〖屏〗bǐng

【摒绝】get rid of; dismiss; brush aside: ～杂念 *dismiss distracting thoughts*

【摒弃】discard; reject; throw away; abandon

bō

波 名 ❶ wave: 水波 ❷ ［物］wave: 声波 ❸ an unexpected turn of events: 风波

【波长】wavelength ◇～常数 wave-length constant; ～计 wavemeter; cymometer

【波茨坦公告】Potsdam Proclamation (1945)

【波荡】heave; surge: 海水～。*The sea surges*.

【波导】［物］wave guide ◇ ～管 wave guide; ～通信 wave guide communication

【波动】❶ undulate; fluctuate: 物价～ *price fluctuation* / 情绪～ *in an anxious state of mind* ❷ ［物］wave motion ◇ ～汇率 fluctuating rate; ～

说［物］wave theory
【波段】［无］wave band：～开关 *band switch*；*waver* ◇ ～覆盖 band coverage；～划分 band division；～选择 band select
【波多黎各】Puerto Rico ◇～人 Puerto Rican
【波尔多液】［农］Bordeaux mixture
【波尔卡】polka（a dance）
【波峰】［物］wave crest
【波幅】［物］amplitude：～失真 *amplitude distortion*
【波谷】［物］trough
【波黑共和国】Republic of Bosnia-Herzegovena
【波及】spread to；involve；affect：经济危机～整个资本主义世界。*The economic crisis affected the entire capitalist world*.
【波兰】Poland ◇ ～人 Pole；～语 Polish（language）
【波澜】great waves；billows
【波澜起伏】（of a piece of writing）with one climax following another
【波澜壮阔】surging forward with great momentum；unfolding on a magnificent scale：一首～、气势磅礴的史诗 *a mighty and magnificent epic*；*an epic of magnificent sweep*
【波浪】wave：～起伏 *waves rising and falling* / ～式前进 *advance wave upon wave*
【波利尼西亚】Polynesi ◇～人 Polynesian；～语 Polynesian（language）
【波罗的海】the Baltic（Sea）
【波美比重计】（又作'波美表'）Baumé hydrometer
【波美度】［化］Baumé degrees
【波谱】［物］spectrum
【波束】［物］beam ◇ ～展宽 beam-broadening；～制导计算机 beam-controlling computer；～转换 beam switching
【波斯】Persia ◇ ～猫 Persian cat；Persian；～湾 Persian Gulf；～语 Persian（language）
【波速】［物］wave velocity
【波涛】great waves；billows：～滚滚 *waves rolling* /～汹涌 *waves surging turbulently*；*waves running high*
【波特】［通信］baud ◇～码 baudot code
【波纹】❶ ripple ❷ corrugation ◇～管［机］bellows；corrugated pipe；～铁 corrugated iron；～纸板 corrugated cardboard
【波音】❶［音］mordent：逆～ *inverted mordent* ❷ Boeing：～747 *Boeing 747*
【波折】twists and turns：事情发生了～。*Events took an unexpected turn*.
【波状热】［医］undulant fever；brucellosis
【波状云】［气］undulatus

拨 Ⅰ 动 ❶ move or adjust with the hand，the foot，a stick，etc.：～算盘 *move the beads on an abacus* / ～火 *poke a fire* / ～钟 *set a clock* / ～电话号码 *dial a telephone number* / ～到北京电台 *tune in to Radio Beijing* ❷ set aside；assign；allocate：～两间房子给词典组 *set aside two rooms for the dictionary group* ❸ turn round：～转马头 *turn the horse round* Ⅱ 量（for people）group；batch：民工分成两～儿挖渠道。*The labourers divided themselves into two groups for digging the channel*.
【拨发】transfer；deliver；set aside；appropriate：～救济粮 *set aside relief grains for delivery*
【拨付】appropriate（a sum of money）：～经费 *appropriate funds*
【拨号】［通信］dial a number；dial：～系统 *dial system*
【拨号盘】（telephone）dial
【拨火棍】poker
【拨开】push aside
【拨款】❶ appropriate money：市政府～筹建一所新中学。*The municipal government appropriated money for a new middle school*. ❷ money appropriated：军事～ *military appropriations* / 财政～ *financial allocations*
【拨浪鼓】a drum-shaped rattle（used by pedlars or as a toy）；rattle-drum
【拨乱反正】bring order out of chaos；set to rights what has been thrown into disorder；restore things to order
【拨弄】❶ move to and fro with the hand，the foot，a stick，etc.；fiddle with：～火盆里的木炭 *poke the charcoal in the brazier* / ～琴弦 *pluck the strings of a fiddle* ❷ stir up：～是非 *stir things up*
【拨冗】〈套〉find time in the midst of pressing affairs：务希～出席。*Your presence is cordially requested*.
【拨弦乐器】plucked string（or stringed）instrument；plucked instrument
【拨云见日】（又作'拨云见天'）〈喻〉dispel the clouds and see the sun：得蒙先生指教，如～，感激不尽。*You have dispelled the clouds to let me see the sun，sir. I can't say how grateful I am for your advice*.
【拨正】set right；correct：～航向 *correct the course*
【拨子】❶［音］plectrum；pick ❷（for people）group；batch：刚才有一～队伍从这里过去了。*A group of soldiers passed by just now*.
【拨奏】［音］pizzicato

玻（构词成分）见下
【玻利维亚】Bolivia ◇ ～人 Bolivian
【玻璃】❶ glass ❷〈口〉nylon；plastic ◇ ～板 glass plate；plate glass；glass top（of a desk）；～版［刷］collotype；～杯 glass；tumbler；～布 glass cloth；～厂 glassworks；～刀 glass cutter；glazier's diamond；～粉 glass dust；～钢 glass fibre reinforced plastic；～棉（又作'玻璃绒'）glass wool；～片 sheet glass；～纱 organdy；～丝 glass silk；～体［生理］vitreous body；～纤维 glass fibre；～纸 cellophane；glassine；～砖 glass block
【玻意耳定律】［物］Boyle's law

剥 动（同〖剥〗bāo，limited to use in compound

words and idiomatic phrases) ——另见 bāo
【剥采比】[矿] stripping-to-ore ratio; stripping ratio
【剥夺】deprive; expropriate; strip: ～公民权 *deprival of civil right; disfranchisement* / ～权益 *outlawry* / ～自由 *deprivation of freedom* / ～人身自由 *deprivation of personal liberty* / ～所有权 *expropriate*
【剥茧抽丝】reel silk from a cocoon—seek out a clue from a confused or chaotic situation
【剥离】(of tissue, skin, covering, etc.) come off; peel off; be stripped: 表土～ *topsoil stripping*
【剥落】come off; peel off: 门上的漆已～了。*The paint on the door has peeled off.*
【剥皮】skin; peel off the skin
【剥蚀】❶(侵蚀)denude; corrode; erode; wear away: 由于风雨～,碑文已无法辨认。*Owing to the ravages of wind and rain, the inscription on the stone tablet is already undecipherable.* ❷ erode: 冰川～ *glacial erosion* ◇～作用[地质] denudation
【剥削】exploit ◇～收入 income from exploitation; ～阶级 exploiting class
【剥削者】exploiter: ～与被剥削者 *exploiter and exploited*

钵
名 ❶earthen bowl ❷ alms bowl (of a Buddhist monk)
【钵盂】alms bowl (of a Buddhist monk)

饽
(构词成分)见下
【饽饽】〈方〉❶ pastry ❷ (steamed) bun; cake: 玉米～ *maize cake*

菠
(构词成分)见下
【菠菜】spinach
【菠萝】pineapple

播
动 ❶ sow; seed: 夏～ *summer sowing* ❷ broadcast: ～出音乐 *broadcast music*
【播发】broadcast: ～新闻 *broadcast news*
【播放】❶ broadcast ❷ broadcast a TV programme
【播讲】talk over the radio: ～故事 *tell a story over the radio* / ～卫生常识 *give a radio talk on health and hygiene*
【播弄】❶ order sb. about ❷ stir up ◇～是非 stir things up; stir up trouble; sow dissension; tell tales
【播送】broadcast; transmit; beam: ～新闻 *broadcast news* / ～电视节目 *broadcast a TV programme* / 向东南亚～的节目 *programme beamed to Southeast Asia*
【播音】transmit; broadcast: 这次～到此结束。*That concludes our programme for this transmission.* ◇～室 broadcasting studio; ～员 announcer
【播种】(bōzhǒng) sow seeds; sow; seed ◇～机 seeder; planter; grain drill
【播种】(bōzhòng) sowing; seeding ◇～面积 sown area; seeded area; ～期 sowing (or seeding) time

bó

伯
名 ❶father's elder brother; uncle ❷ the eldest among brothers: ～兄 *the eldest brother* ❸ earl; count: 伯爵
【伯伯】〈口〉❶ father's elder brother; uncle: 二～ *second uncle* ❷ a term of address for a man of one's father's generation who is older than one's father; uncle: 张～ *Uncle Zhang*
【伯父】❶ father's elder brother; uncle ❷ a term of address for a man of one's father's generation who is older than one's father; uncle
【伯爵】earl; count ◇～夫人 countess
【伯乐】❶ a legendary connoisseur of horses ❷ a good judge of talent
【伯母】wife of father's elder brother; aunt
【伯仲】〈书〉the first and the second brother—not much difference: 相～ *about the same*
【伯仲叔季】eldest, second, third and youngest of brothers; order of seniority among brothers
【伯仲之间】almost on a par; about the same; equally matched

驳
Ⅰ 动 ❶refute; contradict; gainsay: 他老～我。*He's always contradicting me.* / 他的建议被～回来了。*His proposal was rejected.* / 真理不怕人～。*Truth fears no refutation.* ❷ transport by lighter: 起驳 Ⅱ 形 parti-coloured; variegated: 斑驳 Ⅲ 名 barge; lighter: 油驳
【驳岸】a low stone wall built along the water's edge to protect an embankment; revetment
【驳斥】refute; rebut; contradict: ～谬论 *refute a fallacy*
【驳船】barge; lighter
【驳倒】demolish sb.'s argument; refute; argue sb. down; outargue: 我一句话把他～了。*I refuted him in one sentence.*
【驳回】reject (an appeal, request, proposal, etc.); turn down; overrule: ～上诉 *reject an appeal* / 法院～了他的无理要求。*The court overruled his unreasonable claim.*
【驳壳枪】Mauser pistol
【驳面子】not spare sb.'s sensibilities; not show due respect for sb.'s feelings
【驳运】transport by lighter; lighter ◇～费 lighterage
【驳杂】multifarious; heterogeneous: 这本书三分历史,七分科学,内容非常～。*This book is a heterogeneous mass of information, being three parts history and seven parts science.*

泊
动 ❶ be at anchor; moor; berth: ～岸 *anchor alongside the shore* / 船～港外。*The ship was lying at anchor outside the harbour.* ❷ stay for a time; stop ——另见 pō
【泊位】berth (for a ship): 深水～ *deepwater berth* ◇～费 berthage

帛 名〈书〉silks
【帛画】painting on silk
【帛书】a book copied on silk
勃 形〈书〉vigorous；thriving：蓬勃
【勃勃】thriving；vigorous；exuberant：生气勃勃
【勃发】〈书〉❶ thrive；prosper：生机～ *full of life* / 英姿～ *dashing and spirited* / 游兴～ *be seized with a desire to travel* ❷ break out：战争～。*War broke out.*
【勃郎宁】Browning (a type of automatic pistol)
【勃起】have an erection；erect；erection
【勃然】❶ agitatedly；excitedly：～变色 *agitatedly change colour；be visibly stung* ❷ vigorously：第三世界～兴起。*The Third World is rising as a vigorous new force.* ◇～大怒 fly into a rage；flare up
【勃兴】〈书〉rise suddenly；grow vigorously：一个工业城市的～ *the vigorous growth of an industrial town*
钹 名［音］cymbals
铂 名［化］platinum (Pt)
舶 名 oceangoing ship：巨～ *a huge ship*
【舶来品】imports
脖 名 ❶ neck ❷ sth. shaped like a neck：这个瓶子～儿长。*The bottle has a long neck.*
【脖颈儿】(又作'脖梗儿') back of the neck；nape
博 Ⅰ 形 ❶ rich；abundant；plentiful：渊博 ❷〈书〉loose；big：宽衣～带 *in loose garments* Ⅱ 动 ❶erudite；well-informed：博古通今 ❷ win；gain：聊～一笑 *just for your entertainment*
【博爱】universal fraternity (or brotherhood)；universal love：自由、平等、～ *liberty, equality, and fraternity*
【博采众议】adopt good advice from all quarters
【博茨瓦纳】Botswana ◇～人 (sing.) Motswana；(pl.) Batswana
【博大精深】have extensive knowledge and profound scholarship
【博导】(〈略〉全称为'博士生导师') tutor of a Ph. D. student
【博得】win；gain：～同情 *win sympathy* / ～全场喝采 *draw loud applause from the audience；bring the house down* / ～好评 *have a favourable reception*
【博而不精】have wide but not expert knowledge；know something about everything
【博古】❶ conversant with things of the past ❷ paintings of ancient objects
【博古通今】possess a wide knowledge of things ancient and modern—erudite and informed
【博览】read extensively (or widely)：～群书 *be well-read*
【博览会】(international) fair
【博取】try to gain；court：～同情 *seek (or enlist) sb.'s sympathy* / ～欢心 *curry favour* / ～信任 *try to win sb.'s confidence*
【博识】learned；erudite：多闻～ *well-informed and learned*
【博识洽闻】experienced and knowledgeable；erudite
【博士】❶ doctor：哲学～ *Doctor of Philosophy (Ph. D.)* / 张～ *Doctor Zhang* / 念～ *study (or read) for a doctorate* ❷ court academician
【博士后】❶ postdoctoral student or researcher ❷ postdoctoral study or research ❸ postdoctoral；postdoctorate：～科研 *postdoctoral research* / ～科研人员 *postdoctoral researchers*
【博士学位】doctor's degree；doctorate：念～ *study (or read) for a doctorate*
【博闻强记】(又作'博闻强识'，'博闻强志') possessed of wide learning and a powerful memory；have encyclopaedic knowledge
【博物】old general name for zoology, botany, mineralogy, physiology, etc.
【博物馆】museum：中国革命～ *the Museum of the Chinese Revolution* ◇～学 museology
【博物院】museum
【博学】learned；erudite：～之士 *learned scholar；erudite person* ◇～多才 learned and versatile
【博雅】learned：～之士 *a scholar of profound knowledge*
【博奕】〈书〉play chess；have a game of chess
【博引】quote extensively：旁征～ *well-provided with a wide range of authoritative quotations；well-documented*
鹁 (构词成分) 见下
【鹁鸽】pigeon
【鹁鸪】wood-pigeon
搏 Ⅰ 动 ❶ wrestle；fight；combat；struggle：肉搏 ❷ pounce on：恶狼～羊。*The wolf pounced on the sheep.* Ⅱ 名 beat；throb：脉搏
【搏动】(of the heart, the blood, or the pulse) beat rhythmically；throb；pulsate
【搏斗】wrestle；fight；struggle：他同歹徒进行了～。*He struggled with the ruffian.* / 与风浪～ *battle with the winds and waves* / 生死～ *a life-and-death struggle*
【搏击】struggle with；fight with：～风浪 *battle with the winds and waves*
【搏杀】❶ fight with a weapon ❷ (in chess games) be locked in a fierce contest
箔 名 ❶ screen (of reeds, sorghum stalks, etc.)：苇箔 ❷ a bamboo tray for rearing silkworms：蚕箔 ❸foil；tinsel：金箔 ❹ paper tinsel burnt as offerings to the dead：锡箔
膊 名 arm：赤膊
薄 Ⅰ 形 ❶ slight；meagre；small：～酬 *small reward；meagre remuneration* ❷ ungenerous；unkind；mean：薄待 ❸ frivolous：轻薄 Ⅱ 动 ❶

despise; belittle: 鄙薄❷〈书〉approach; near: 日薄西山 ——另见 báo; bò

【薄产】a small property

【薄脆】crisp fritter

【薄脆饼】wafer; waffle; snap

【薄待】treat sb. ungenerously

【薄厚】(又作'厚薄')(treat) casually or with kindness: 亲戚有远近,相待难免有～。*There are close and distant relatives, and it's natural some are treated with more cordiality than others.*

【薄酒】light wine (said by a host of his own wine)

【薄礼】〈谦〉my small (or unworthy) gift

【薄利】small profits: ～多销 *small profits but quick turnover*

【薄命】(usu. of women) born under an unlucky star; born unlucky

【薄膜】❶ membrane ❷ film: 塑料～ *plastic film* ◇～电阻 film resistor

【薄暮】〈文〉dusk; twilight

【薄片】thin slice; thin section ◇～分析［地质］thin section analysis

【薄情】inconstant in love; fickle: ～郎 *a heartless (man) lover*

【薄弱】weak; frail: 意志～ *weak-willed* / 能力～ *lacking in ability* / 技术力量～ *lack qualified technical personnel* / ～环节 *weak link; vulnerable spot*

【薄胎瓷器】eggshell china

【薄雾】mist; haze

【薄幸】〈书〉inconstant in love; fickle; heartless: ～贼! *You heartless brute!*

【薄油层】［油］oil sheet

【薄葬】simple burial: 提倡厚养～ *advocate good care of one's parents (while they are alive) and simple burials for them (when they are dead)*

bǒ

跛 形 lame: ～了一只脚 *lame in one leg* / 一颠一～ *walk with a limp; limp along*

【跛鳖千里】a lame tortoise can walk a thousand li—success can be gained by steady continuous effort

【跛脚】lame

【跛子】a lame person; cripple

簸 动 winnow with a fan; fan: ～谷 *winnow away the chaff; fan the chaff* ——另见 bò

【簸荡】roll; rock: 船～得很厉害。*The ship was rolling heavily.*

【簸动】❶ jolt; bump; toss ❷〈旧〉strike (a gong)

【簸箩】shallow basket

【簸扬】winnow

bò

薄 (构词成分)见下 ——另见 báo; bó

【薄荷】field mint; peppermint ◇～醇(又作'薄荷脑')［化］menthol; peppermint camphor; ～糖 peppermint drops; ～酮 menthone; ～油 peppermint oil

簸 (构词成分)见下 ——另见 bǒ

【簸箕】❶ dustpan ❷ winnowing fan ❸ loop (of a fingerprint)

bǔ

卜 动 ❶ divine; tell fortunes: ～卦 *divine by the Eight Trigrams* ❷〈书〉foretell; predict: 生死未～。*It is hard to tell whether the person is alive or not.* / 行期未～。*The date of departure remains undecided.*

【卜辞】oracle inscriptions of the Shang Dynasty (16th-11th century B.C.) on tortoiseshells or animal bones

【卜卦】a system of divination

【卜筮】divination; fortune-telling

补 Ⅰ 动 ❶ mend; patch; repair: ～衣服 *mend (or patch) clothes* / ～鞋 *repair (or mend) shoes* / ～袜子 *darn socks* / ～车胎 *mend a puncture* / 修桥～路 *build bridges and repair roads* ❷ fill; supply; make up for: 把漏了的字～上 *supply the missing words* / 我们还得～两个人。*We have two vacancies to be filled.* or *We need two more people.* ❸ nourish: ～身体 *build up one's health (with nourishing food or tonics)* Ⅱ 名〈书〉benefit; use; help

【补白】filler (in a newspaper or magazine)

【补报】❶ make a report after the event; make a supplementary report: 调查结果以后～。*Findings will be reported later.* ❷ repay a kindness

【补编】supplement:《现代汉语词典～》*Supplement to A Dictionary of the Modern Chinese Language*

【补仓】variation call; margin call; cover

【补差】make up a deficiency; pay for those who continue working after retirement; make up pay for difference between former pay and retirement

【补偿】compensate; make up: ～所受的损失 *compensate sb. for a loss* / ～差额 *make up a deficiency* ◇～电容器 compensation condenser; ～费 compensatory payment; compensation; ～关税 compensation tariff; ～贸易 compensation trade

【补充】❶ replenish; supplement; complement; add: ～人力 *replenish manpower* / ～兵员 *fill up (an army unit) to full strength; replace losses* / ～库存 *replenish the stock* ❷ additional; complementary; supplementary: ～规定 *additional regulations* / ～说明 *additional remarks* / ～读物 *supplementary reading material* / ～决议 *supplementary resolution* / ～条款 *subsidiary; supplementary terms* / ～投资 *additional investment*

【补丁】(又作'补钉') patch: 打～ *put (or sew) a*

patch on; *patch up*
【补发】supply again (sth. lost, etc.); reissue; pay retroactively: 材料丢失,不予~。*The material will not be reissued if lost*. / ~增加的工资 *pay increased wages retroactively*
【补过】make amends for one's faults ——另见〖将功补过〗
【补花】[工美] appliqué
【补给】[军] supply ◇~点 supply point; ~品 supplies; ~线 supply line; ~站 depot
【补假】days off for having worked overtime
【补角】[数] supplementary angle
【补救】remedy: ~办法 *remedial measure*; *remedy* / 无可~ *be past* (*or beyond*) *remedy*; *irremediable*; *irreparable*
【补考】make-up examination
【补课】❶ make up a missed lesson: 教师给学生~。*The teacher helped his pupils make up the lesson they had missed*. ❷ do over again sth. not well done
【补亏】the state subsidizing deficit enterprises: 凡属经营性亏损的,国家不再~。*All losses arising from management will no longer be subsidized by the state*.
【补炉】[冶] fettling
【补苗】[农] fill the gaps with seedlings
【补偏救弊】remedy defects and rectify errors; rectify a deviation and correct an error
【补票】buy one's ticket after the normal time
【补品】tonic
【补缺】fill a vacancy; supply a deficiency ◇ ~选举 by-election
【补色】complementary colour
【补税】❶ pay a tax one has evaded ❷ pay an overdue tax
【补台】help sb. strengthen his position; boost sb.: 同事之间,要相互~,不要拆台。*Colleagues should support*, *not sabotage*, *each other*.
【补体】[医] complement (in blood serum): ~结合试验 *complement fixation test*
【补贴】❶ subsidize: 由国家给予~ *be subsidized by the state* ❷ subsidy; allowance: 粮食~ *grain subsidy* / 价格~ *price subsidy* / 出口~ *export subsidy* / 生活~ *living allowances*; *subsistence allowances*
【补习】take lessons after school or work; take a make-up course ◇~学校 continuation school
【补休】take a deferred leave or holiday
【补选】by-election: ~人民代表 *hold a by-election for a people's deputy*
【补血】build (or enrich) the blood: 猪肝据说能~。*Pork liver is said to be a blood-builder*. ◇ ~剂 blood (or haematic) tonic
【补牙】fill a tooth; have a tooth stopped
【补养】take a tonic or nourishing food to build up one's health
【补药】tonic
【补液】❶ [医] fluid infusion ❷ (liquid) tonic: 营养~ *nutritious drink*; *tonic*
【补遗】addendum; supplement: 《文选》~ *Supplement to the Wenxuan* (*a book title*)
【补益】〈书〉❶ benefit; help: 有所~ *be of some help* (*or benefit*) ❷ be of help (or benefit)
【补语】[语] complement
【补种】reseed; resow; replant
【补助】❶ help financially; subsidize ❷ subsidy; allowance: 实物~ *subsidy in kind* / 煤火~ *heating allowance* ◇~金 grant-in-aid; subsidy
【补缀】mend (clothes); patch: 缝连~ *mend and darn* / ~成文 *put together some sort of an article*; *produce a patchwork of an article*
【补足】bring up to full strength; make up a deficiency; fill (a vacancy, gap, etc.): ~缺额 *fill all the vacancies*

捕 动 catch; seize; arrest: ~鸟 *catch birds* / 被~ *be arrested*; *be under arrest*
【捕虫叶】[植] insect-catching leaf
【捕风捉影】chase the wind and clutch at shadows—speak or act on hearsay evidence
【捕俘】[军] capture enemy personnel (for intelligence purposes)
【捕获】catch; capture; seize: 当场~ *catch sb. redhanded* ◇ ~法 [法] law of prize; ~量 catch (of fish, etc.)
【捕鲸船】whaler; whale catcher
【捕快】(in former times) a yamen officer charged with hunting down criminals; constable; sheriff
【捕捞】fish for (aquatic animals and plants); catch: ~对虾 *catch prawns* ◇ ~控制 fishing control; ~能力 fishing capacity
【捕猎】catch (wild animals); hunt
【捕拿】arrest; apprehend; capture; catch
【捕杀】catch and kill
【捕食】❶ (of an animal) hunt for food; prey: 猫头鹰在夜间~。*Owls prey at night*. ❷ (of an animal) hunt and eat (another animal); prey on: 猫头鹰~鼠、麻雀等小动物。*Owls prey* (*or feed*) *on mice*, *sparrows*, *and other small animals*.
【捕鼠器】mousetrap
【捕蝇器】flytrap
【捕头】police officer (in former foreign concessions)
【捕鱼】catch fish; fish: 出海~ *go fishing on the sea*
【捕捉】hunt; chase; catch; seize: ~战机 *seize the opportunity for battle*; *seize the right moment to strike* / ~镜头 *catch a good shot*; *take a candid shot* / ~信息 *hunt for information*

哺 Ⅰ 动 formalfeed (a baby); nurse Ⅱ 名 the food in one's mouth
【哺乳】breast-feed; suckle; nurse ◇~室 nursing room
【哺乳动物】mammal: ~学 *mammalogy*
【哺养】〈书〉feed; rear
【哺育】❶〈书〉feed: ~雏鸟 (*of mother birds*) *feed little birds* ❷ nurture; foster

bù

不 副 ❶ (used before verbs, adjectives, and other adverbs; never before 有) not; won't; not want to: 他的病～(很)严重。*His illness is not (very) serious.* / 他～是学生。*He isn't a student.* / 我～会。*I don't know how.* ❷ (used before certain nouns to form an adjective) un-; in-: 不法/ 不轨 ❸ (used by itself or with a particle in responses) not so; no: 他知道吗? —～, 他不知道。*Does he know? —No, he doesn't.* / 他不知道吧? —～, 他知道。*He doesn't know, does he? — Yes, he does.* ❹ 〈方〉 (used at the end of a sntence to indicate that it is a question): 他现在身体好～? *Is he in good health now?* ❺ (used between a verb and its complement) cannot: 进～去 *cannot go in* / 拿～动 *find sth. too heavy to carry* ❻ (inserted within a reduplication, usu. preceded by 什么) no matter (how, where, etc.): 什么学历～学历,要有真才实学才行。*It doesn't matter how much formal schooling you've had; what matters is whether you have real ability and learning.* ❼ (used correlatively with 就) if not... (then...): 他这会儿～是在教室,就是在图书馆。*He's now either in the classroom or in the library.* ❽ (used in polite formulas only) don't; needn't: 不谢

【不安】❶ intranquil; unpeaceful; unstable: 动荡不安 ❷ uneasy; disturbed; restless: 听了这消息我心里很～。*I was rather disturbed by the news.* ❸ 〈套〉 sorry: 老来麻烦您,真是～。*I'm sorry to trouble you so often.*

【不安定因素】factors leading to social instability

【不白之冤】unrighted wrong; unredressed injustice: 蒙受～ *be grievously wronged*

【不败之地】invincible position

【不卑不亢】同〖不亢不卑〗

【不备】❶ unprepared; off guard: 乘其～ *catch sb. off guard* / 伺其～ *watch for a chance to take sb. by surprise* ❷ 〈书〉 (used at the end of a letter) there is more than I can tell you in this letter

【不比】unlike: 北方～南方,春天老刮风。*The north of China, unlike the south, is windy in spring.*

【不比不知道,一比吓一跳】If you don't compare, you're in the dark; The moment you do, you get a shock.

【不必】need not; not have to: ～担心(惊慌)。*There is no need to worry (panic).* / 你～去了。*You don't have to go now.*

【不避艰险】shrink (or flinch) from no difficulty or danger; make light of difficulties and dangers

【不变成本】constant cost

【不变价格】fixed price; constant price: 国民收入按～计算增加了 1.31 倍。*National income increased by 131% at constant prices.*

【不变美元价值】constant-dollar values

【不变资本】[经] constant capital

【不便】❶ inconvenient; inappropriate; unsuitable: 交通～ *have poor transport facilities; not be conveniently located* / 给治疗带来～ *hamper medical treatment* ❷ 〈口〉 short of cash: 手头～ *be short of cash; be hard up*

【不辨菽麦】be unable to tell beans from wheat—have no knowledge of practical matters

【不…不…】❶ (used with two words or expressions which are similar in meaning; an emphatic negative form): 不理不睬 *take no notice of; ignore* ❷ (used with two words or expressions which are opposite in meaning) neither... nor...: 不大不小 *neither too big nor too small; just right* / 不多不少 *neither too much nor too little; just right* ❸ if not... then not...: 他不吃饭不喝酒。*He won't drink unless he's eating.* or *He only drinks at meals.*

【不才】〈书〉〈谦〉I (〈字〉"without ability")

【不测】accident; mishap; contingency: 以防～ *be prepared for any contingency* / 如有～ *if anything untoward should happen* / 险遭～ *have a narrow escape*

【不曾】never (have done sth.): 我～到过那里。*I have never been there.*

【不成】❶ won't do: 只说不做,那是～的。*Mere talk and no action won't do.* ❷ (used at the end of a rhetorical question beginning with 难道 or 莫非): 难道就这样算了～? *How can we let it go at that?*

【不成材】(又作'不成器') good-for-nothing; worthless; ne'er-do-well

【不成体统】most improper; downright outrageous

【不成文法】[法] unwritten law

【不承认主义】policy of nonrecognition

【不逞之徒】desperado; the unruly

【不齿】〈书〉 despise; hold in contempt: 为世人所～ *held in contempt by the people*

【不耻下问】not feel ashamed to ask one's subordinates or people below

【不啻】〈书〉 ❶ not less than: 工程所需,～万金。*The project requires a tremendous amount of money.* ❷ as; like; as good as: ～沧海一粟 *like a drop in the ocean* / ～是当头一棒 *like a blow on the head*

【不出所料】as expected: ～,她轻而易举地通过了考试。*As expected, she passed the exam easily.*

【不揣冒昧】I venture to; may I take the liberty of

【不辞而别】go away without taking leave; leave without saying goodbye

【不辞辛苦】spare no effort; take pains; take the trouble to; go to the trouble of doing sth.: 感谢同志们～来支援我们。*Thank you comrades for all the trouble you have taken to help us.*

【不错】❶ correct; right: 这个答案一点儿～。*This answer is perfectly correct.* ❷ (used by itself to express agreement) yes: ～,他是这么说的。*Yes, that's what he said.* ❸〈口〉 not bad; pretty good：这个主意～。*This idea is not bad*. / 这个录音～。*The recording is pretty good*.

【不打不成器】spare the rod and spoil the child

【不打不相识】out of blows friendship grows；no discord，no concord

【不打自招】confess without being pressed；make a confession without duress；give oneself away

【不大】❶ not very；not too：～好 *not very good* / ～清楚 *not too clear* ❷ not often：他最近～来。*He hasn't been coming around much recently*. / 我～吃鱼。*I don't eat fish often*. or *I'm not too keen on fish*.

【不大离儿】〈口〉❶ pretty close；just about right：你这个子打篮球还～。*You're about the right height for a basketball player*. ❷ not bad：这块地的麦子长得～。*The wheat on this field is not bad*.

【不待说】needless to say；it goes without saying

【不丹】Bhutan ◇～人 Bhutanese；～语 Bhutanese (language)

【不单】❶ not the only：获奖的～是这几部影片。*These are not the only films that have won the prizes*. ❷ not merely；not simply

【不但】(used correlatively with 而且，并且，也 or 还) not only：我们的产品～要求数量多，而且要求质量好。*In production，we demand not only quantity but also quality*.

【不当】unsuitable；improper；inappropriate：处理～ *not be handled properly* / 措辞～ *inappropriate wording*

【不倒翁】self-righting doll；tumbler；roly-poly

【不到长城非好汉】If you fail to reach the Great Wall，you are not a man.

【不到黄河心不死】not stop until one reaches the Huanghe River—not stop until one reaches one's goal；refuse to give up until all hope is gone

【不道德】immoral；unethical：拆阅别人信件是～的。*Opening other people's letters and reading them is unethical*.

【不得】(bùdé) must not；may not；not be allowed：～将参考书携出阅览室。*Reference books may not be taken out of the reading room*. / ～有误。*Let there be no mistake*.

【不得】(bude) (used after a verb) must not：去～ *must not go* / 马虎～ *mustn't* (*or can't afford to*) *be careless* / 这件事你做～。*You must never do this*.

【不得不】have no choice (or option) but to；cannot but；have to：我～去。*There's nothing I can do but go*. / 铁证如山，那个坏家伙～低头认罪。*Confronted with ironclad evidence the scoundrel had to plead guilty*.

【不得而知】unknown；unable to find out：作者是谁，～。*The name of the author is unknown*. / 情况如何，～。*We are unable to find out how things stand*.

【不得劲】❶〈口〉awkward；unhandy：这把铁锹使起来～。*This is an awkward spade*. ❷〈口〉be indisposed；not feel well：我今天有点～儿。*I'm not feeling too well today*. ❸〈方〉feel embarrassed：大家都看着他，弄得他怪～儿的。*He was embarrassed by so many people staring at him*.

【不得了】❶ no way out；no end of trouble：让人口这样增长下去，那可～。*If population is allowed to grow like this，disaster will overtake us*. ❷ (used after 得 as a complement) extremely；exceedingly：高兴得～ *be extremely happy*；*be wild with joy* / 坏得～ *be very bad*；*couldn't be worse* / 后悔得～ *regret it very much*；*be overcome with remorse*

【不得其门而入】can't find the door and get in；can't find one's way in；can't gain admission

【不得人心】not enjoy popular support；be unpopular：这个政策很～。*This policy is very unpopular*.

【不得要领】fail to grasp the main point；not see what sb. is driving at：他讲了半天，我还是～。*He talked at great length，but I just couldn't see what he was driving at*.

【不得已】act against one's will；have no alternative but to；have to：实在～，她只好请几天假。*She had no alternative but to ask for a few days' leave*. / 他们这样做是出于～。*They did it that way because they had no choice*.

【不得已而求其次】have to be content with the second best

【不得已而为之】do sth. against one's will；have no alternative but to do sth.

【不登大雅之堂】too low to enter polite company；not appeal to refined taste；be unrefined；be unpresentable

【不等】vary；differ：数量～ *vary in amount* / 大小～ *differ* (*or vary*) *in size*

【不等边三角形】[数] scalene triangle

【不等号】[数] sign of inequality

【不等价交换】[经] exchange of unequal values

【不等式】[数] inequality

【不抵抗主义】policy of nonresistance

【不迭】(used after a verb) ❶ cannot cope；find it too much：忙～ *hasten* (*to do sth*.) / 后悔～ *too late for regrets* ❷ incessantly：称赞～ *praise profusely*

【不丁点儿】very few or very small

【不定】❶ hard to say；hard to predict：事情还～怎么样呢。*It's hard to predict how things will turn out*. ❷ indefinite；indeterminate ◇～变异[生] indeterminate variation；～方程[数] indeterminate equation；～根[植] adventitious root；～冠词[语] indefinite article；～式[语] infinitive

【不定度】uncertainty

【不定额抵押】open-end mortgage

【不定积分】[数] indefinite integral

【不定期航班】nonregular service

【不定芽】[植] adventitious bud

【不动产】real estate；immovable property；immovables ◇～保险 immovables insurance；～税 real estate tax；～所有权 title to real estate；～投

资信托 real estate investment trusts

【不动声色】(又作'不露声色') maintain one's composure; stay calm and collected; not turn a hair; not bat an eyelid:他～,镇静如常。*He remained unperturbed and was as calm as usual.*

【不冻港】ice-free port; open port

【不独】not only:养猪～可以改善人民生活,还能多积肥料。*Pig-breeding not only improves the people's diet, it makes more manure available.*

【不端】improper; dishonourable:品行～ *having bad conduct; ill-behaved*

【不断】unceasing; uninterrupted; continuous; constant:人类社会总是～进步的。*Human society makes unceasing progress.* / 使针刺麻醉～完善 *bring about steady improvement in acupuncture anaesthesia*

【不对】❶ incorrect; wrong:这样做～。*It's wrong to act like that.* / 他没有什么～的地方。*He's not in the wrong.* ❷ (used by itself to express disagreement) no:～,我没有那么说。*No, I didn't say that.* ❸ amiss; abnormal; queer:这机器声音～。*The machine makes a queer noise.* / 她今天神色有点儿～。*She doesn't quite look her usual self today.* ❹ be in disagreement; be at odds:他们俩素来～。*The two of them have always been in disagreement.*

【不对头】同〖不对〗❶❸❹

【不…而…】do... without doing...:不战而胜 *win without fighting a battle; win hands down*

【不二法门】the one and only way; the only proper course to take

【不二价】fixed prices; uniform prices

【不发达国家】an underdeveloped country

【不乏】〈书〉there is no lack of ◇～其人 such people are not rare; there is no lack of such people; ～先例 there is no lack of precedents

【不法】lawless; illegal; unlawful:～行为 *unlawful practice; an illegal act* / ～商人 *lawbreaking merchants* ◇～收益 illegal interest; ～之徒 a lawless person

【不凡】out of the ordinary; out of the common run:自命不凡

【不妨】there is no harm in; might as well:你～现在就告诉他。*You might as well tell him right now.* / ～一试。*There is no harm in trying.*

【不费吹灰之力】as easy as blowing off dust; as easy as falling off a log

【不分彼此】make no distinction between one's own and sb. else's; share everything; be on very intimate terms:如果你要用钱,我可以给你,我们姐妹俩还分什么彼此。*If you need money, I'll give you some. You and I are sisters—what's the difference between yours and mine?*

【不分敌我】not distinguish between the enemy and ourselves

【不分高低】be equally matched

【不分亲疏】irrespective the degree of intimacy

【不分青红皂白】(又作'不分皂白') make no distinction between right and wrong; indiscriminately:如果～,一概拒绝向外国学习,就只能使中国永远处于落后地位。*If we indiscriminately refused to learn anything from foreign countries, China would remain backward forever.*

【不分胜负】tie; draw; come out even:一场～的比赛 *a drawn game* / 两队～。*The two teams tied.* or *The two teams came out even.*

【不孚众望】not inspire popular confidence

【不服】refuse to obey (or comply); refuse to accept as final; remain unconvinced by; not give in to:～指导 *refuse to obey instructions* / ～裁判 *refuse to accept the referee's ruling*

【不服水土】(of a stranger) not accustomed to the climate of a new place; not acclimatized

【不符】not agree (or tally, square) with; not conform to; be inconsistent with:言行～ *deeds not matching words* / 名实～ *have an undeserved reputation*

【不复】no longer:～存在 *no longer exist*

【不干不净】unclean; filthy:嘴里～ *be foul-mouthed*

【不干涉】noninterference; nonintervention ◇～政策 policy of noninterference (or nonintervention)

【不甘】unreconciled to; not resigned to; unwilling ◇～寂寞 hate to be neglected or overlooked; ～落后 not content to lag behind; ～示弱 unwilling to be outshone; not to be outdone

【不甘心】not reconciled to; not resigned to:～于自己的失败 *will not take one's defeat lying down* / 我们输给那么个队,我真～。*We lost to such a team—I simply can't take it.*

【不敢】❶ not dare to do sth. ❷ 同〖不敢当〗

【不敢当】〈套〉(used in reply to a compliment or a complimentary gesture) I really don't deserve this; it's too much of an honour; I'm overwhelmed; I'm much obliged; you flatter me:您中国话说得真好。—～。*You speak Chinese very well. — I'm flattered.* / 请上坐。—～。*Please take the seat of honour. — I really don't deserve it.*

【不敢问津】not dare to inquire (as about the price of expensive goods)

【不敢越雷池一步】not dare to go one step beyond the limit

【不更事】have not seen the world; have not experienced life; be inexperienced ——另见〖少不更事〗

【不公】unjust; unfair:办事～ *be unfair in handling matters*

【不攻自破】collapse of itself:这种谣言在事实面前将～。*These rumours will declare their own bankruptcy when confronted with the facts.* or *Facts will eventually scotch these rumours.*

【不恭】disrespectful:言词～ *use disrespectful language*

【不共戴天】will not live under the same sky (with one's enemy)—absolutely irreconcilable:～的敌人 *a sworn enemy; a mortal foe* / ～之仇 *invet-*

erate hatred

【不苟】not lax; not casual; careful; conscientious ◇～言笑 reserved; reticent; taciturn; sober; sedate

【不够】not enough; insufficient; inadequate: 分析～深入。*The analysis lacks depth.* / 准备～ *be inadequately prepared*

【不顾】in spite of; regardless of: ～后果 *regardless of the consequences* / ～事实 *fly in the face of the facts; have no regard for the truth* / ～大局 *show no consideration for the general interest; ignore the larger issues* / ～信义 *be guilty of bad faith*

【不关】have nothing to do with

【不关痛痒】of no consequence; immaterial

【不管】regardless of; no matter (what, who, etc.): ～他来不来，我们得走了。*No matter whether he comes or not, we've got to leave.*

【不管部部长】minister without portfolio

【不管三七二十一】casting all caution to the winds; regardless of the consequences; recklessly: ～，我要照计划行事。*I'll carry out the plan, regardless of the consequences.*

【不光】〈口〉❶ not the only one: 报名参加的～是他一个人。*He was not the only one to sign up.* ❷ not only: 我们县～出煤，而且出铁。*Our county produces not only coal, but iron.*

【不光彩】disgraceful; dishonoeable; ignominious

【不规则】irregular: 这种结晶体呈～菱形。*This kind of crystal takes the shape of an irregular rhombus.* ◇～动词［语］irregular verb

【不轨】against the law or discipline

【不过】❶ (used as an intensifier after an adjective): 那就再好～了！*It couldn't be better!* or *That would be superb!* ❷ only; merely; no more than ❸ but; however; only: 病人精神还不错，～胃口不大好。*The patient feels pretty well, but he hasn't much of an appetite.*

【不过尔尔】not better than that—only just so-so; merely mediocre; just middling

【不过如此】only just so-so

【不过意】be sorry; feel apologetic: 叫您受累了，真～。*I'm terribly sorry to have given you such a lot of trouble.*

【不含糊】〈口〉❶ unambiguous; unequivocal; explicit: 以毫～的语言作出回答 *answer in clear and unequivocal terms; answer in explicit language* ❷ not ordinary; really good: 他那手乒乓球可～。*He is a very good table-tennis player.* / 他这活儿做得真～。*He's really made a good job of it.* ❸ not be afraid of: ～你们。*I am not afraid of you.*

【不含咖啡因的】noncaddein; containing no caffein

【不含油腻】greaseless; without grease

【不含脂肪】fat free; no fat

【不寒而栗】shiver all over though not cold —tremble with fear; shudder

【不好惹】not to be trifled with; not to be pushed around; stand no nonsense: 他这个人可是～的。*He's not a man to be trifled with.*

【不好意思】❶ feel embarrassed; be ill at ease: 她被夸得～了。*She felt embarrassed by so much praise.* / 让你久等了，真～。*I'm sorry to have kept you waiting.* ❷ find it embarrassing (to do sth.): ～推辞 *find it difficult to refuse* / ～再问 *hesitate to ask again*

【不合】❶ not conform to; be unsuited to; be out of keeping with: 脾气～ *be temperamentally incompatible* / ～她的口味 *not be to her taste; not appeal to her* / ～当地习俗 *not conform to the customs of the locality* ❷〈书〉should not; ought not: 早知如此，当初～叫他去。*Had we foreseen that, we would not have let him go.* ❸ not get along well; be on bad terms

【不合格】unqualified; substandard

【不合理】unreasonable; irrational: ～的规章制度 *irrational rules and regulations* /～的推论 *illogical deduction*

【不合时宜】be out of keeping with the times; be incompatible with present needs; be inopportune or inappropriate

【不合作】uncooperative; noncooperative

【不和】❶ not get along well; be on bad terms; be at odds: 兄弟～ *brothers on bad terms with each other* ❷ discord: 制造～ *sow discord*

【不怀好意】harbour evil designs; not with the best of intentions

【不欢而散】part on bad terms: 会议～。*The conference broke up in discord.*

【不慌不忙】unhurried; calm; leisurely: 他慢慢地，～地从椅子上站起来，然后开始讲话。*Slowly and deliberately he rose from his chair and began to speak.*

【不讳】〈书〉❶ without concealing anything: 直言不讳 ❷〈婉〉die

【不会】❶ be unlikely; will not (act, happen, etc.): 她～不知道。*It's not likely that she doesn't know.* / 人～多的。*There won't be too many people.* ❷ have not learned to; be unable to: 我～游泳。*I don't know how to swim.* / 谢谢你，我～抽烟。*No, thanks. I don't smoke.* ❸ (used to express reproach for the non-performance of an action): 你就～打个电话问一问？*Couldn't you have phoned up and asked?*

【不惑】〈书〉be free from doubts (used esp. in): ～之年 *the age of forty (from Confucius' saying* 四十而不惑 *"At forty I came to be free from doubts")* / 年逾～ *be over forty*

【不及】❶ not as good as; inferior to: 这台录音机～那台好。*This recorder is not as good as that one.* ❷ find it too late: 躲避～ *too late to dodge* / 后悔～ *too late for regrets*

【不及格】fail; flunk

【不及物动词】〈语〉intransitive verb

【不即不离】be neither familiar nor distant; keep sb. at arm's length

【不急之务】a matter of no great urgency; business requiring no immediate attention

【不计其数】countless; innumerable: 每日过往客人～。*There are countless travellers coming and going every day.*

【不记名投票】secret ballot

【不济】not good; of no use: 我眼力～了。*My eyesight is failing.*

【不济事】no good; of no use; not of any help: 这是项突击任务,人少了～。*This is a shock task. It'll be no good to be short of hands.*

【不假辞色】look at sb. with a solemn mien and speak harshly; be severe in speech and countenance

【不假思索】(又作'不加思索')(act, respond, etc.) without thinking; without hesitation; readily; offhand: 这些句子是摇笔即来,～的。*Such phrases flow unsought at the flourish of a pen.*

【不检】be indiscreet (in one's speech and conduct); be careless (about one's words and acts): 行为～ *depart from correct conduct*

【不减当年】just like one's old self (in appearance, bearing, etc.): 他的精力～。*He is as energetic as ever.*

【不简单】❶ not simple; rather complicated: 这事～,需要进一步调查。*The matter is not so simple; it requires further investigation.* ❷ remarkable; marvellous: 他有这么大的进步真～。*It's remarkable he's made such good progress.*

【不见】not see; not meet: 好久～。*Haven't seen you for a long time.* / 这孩子一年～,长这么高了。*It's only a year since I last saw the child and he's grown so tall.*

【不见不散】(let's) not leave without seeing each other (said when making an appointment): 咱们两点钟左右在大门口碰头,～。*Let's meet at the gate around two o'clock and not leave without seeing each other.*

【不见得】not necessarily; not likely: ～对 *not necessarily correct* / 他今晚～会来。*He's not likely to come tonight.*

【不见棺材不落泪】not shed a tear until one sees the coffin—refuse to be convinced until faced with grim reality

【不见经传】not found in the classics—not authoritative; unknown: 此人名～。*He is not a well-known figure.* or *He is a nobody.*

【不骄不躁】not conceited or rash; free from arrogance and rashness

【不结盟】nonalignment ◇～国家 nonaligned countries; ～国家首脑会议 the Summit Meeting of Non-aligned Countries; ～运动 non-aligned movement; ～政策 nonalignment policy

【不解】❶ not understand: ～其意 *not understand what he means* ❷ indissoluble

【不解之谜】an unsolved riddle (or puzzle); enigma; mystery

【不解之缘】an indissoluble bond; an irrevocable commitment: 他早年就和文学结下了～。*Early in his life he was irrevocably committed to literature.*

【不禁】can't help (doing sth.); can't refrain from: 看他那滑稽的样子,我～笑了起来。*He looked so funny that I couldn't help laughing.*

【不仅】❶ not the only one: 这～是我一个人的看法。*I'm not the only one who holds this view.* ❷ 同〖不但〗

【不进则退】move forward, or you'll fall behind ——另见〖逆水行舟〗

【不近人情】not amenable to reason; unreasonable

【不经一事,不长一智】You can't gain knowledge without practice; Wisdom comes from experience.

【不经意】carelessly; by accident: 他～把茶杯碰倒了。*He accidentally knocked over a cup.*

【不经之谈】absurd statement; cock-and-bull story

【不景气】❶ [经] depression; recession; slump ❷ in a depressed state: 最近生意～。*Business is bad these days.*

【不胫而走】get round fast; spread like wildfire: 此书一经问世,～。*As soon as it was published, the book had a big circulation.*

【不久】❶ soon; before long: 水库～就能完工。*The reservoir will soon be completed.* ❷ not long after; soon after: 插完秧～就下了一场雨。*It rained soon after we had transplanted the rice seedlings.*

【不咎既往】(又作'不究既往') forgive sb.'s past misdeeds; not censure sb. for his past misdeeds

【不拘】❶ not stick to; not confine oneself to: 字数～。*No limit is set on the length (for an article).* ❷ no matter (what, who, etc.); whatever: ～什么任务,只要对人民有益的,我都愿意接受。*I'm ready to accept any job whatever, so long as it is in the interest of the people.*

【不拘小节】not bother about trifles; not niggling

【不拘形迹】without formality; not standing on ceremony

【不拘形式】not particular about form; informal: 请你给墙报写些东西。～,文章、诗,都可以。*Please write something for the wall newspaper. Any form will do—poetry or prose.*

【不拘一格】not stick to one pattern; not limited to one type (or style): ～选拔人才 *recruit all kinds of talented people (or talent of all sorts)*

【不倦】tireless; untiring; indefatigable: 诲人不倦

【不绝如缕】❶ hanging by a thread; very precarious; almost extinct ❷ (of sound) linger on faintly

【不堪】❶ cannot bear; cannot stand: ～其苦 *cannot bear the hardships* ❷ (used after words of bad meaning) utterly; extremely: 疲惫～ *be in a state of utter exhaustion; be dog-tired* / 穿得破烂～ *be dressed in rags (or tatters)* ❸ extremely undesirable: 他这个人太～了。*He is impossible.*

【不堪回首】cannot bear to look back on; find it unbearable to recall

【不堪入耳】intolerable to the ear; revolting; disgusting

【不堪入目】most unsightly; not fit to be seen; revolting; disgusting

【不堪设想】too ghastly (or dreadful) to contemplate: 后果将～。*The consequences would be too ghastly to contemplate.* or *The consequences would be disastrous.*

【不堪一击】cannot withstand a single blow; collapse at the first blow

【不看僧面看佛面】not for the monk's sake, but for the Buddha's—(do sth. for a person) out of deference to sb. else

【不亢不卑】neither haughty nor humble; neither supercilious nor obsequious; neither overbearing nor servile

【不可】❶ cannot; should not; must not: 你～随便说话。*You cannot say whatever you wish.* / ～一概而论 *must not make sweeping generalizations* ❷ (used in 非…～): 非你去～。*It won't do unless you go (with stress on "you").*

【不可比因素】incomparable factor; factor not subject to comparison

【不可多得】hard to come by; rare: ～的佳作 *a rare specimen of good writing* / ～的人才 *a man of rare ability*

【不可分割】inseparable: 社会主义民主和社会主义法制～。*Socialist democracy is inseparable from a socialist legal system.* / ～的一部分 *an integral part*

【不可告人】not to be divulged; hidden: ～的动机 *motives that cannot bear the light of day; ulterior motives* / ～的勾当 *a sinister trick*

【不可估量】inestimable; incalculable; immeasurable; beyond measure: ～的损失 *an immeasurable loss*

【不可或缺】indispensable

【不可救药】incurable; incorrigible; hopeless: 人总是要犯错误的,但～的却很少。*Everyone makes mistakes, but few are incorrigible.*

【不可开交】(used as a complement after 得 to indicate a hopeless state of affairs): 忙得～ *be up to one's eyes in work; be awfully (or terribly) busy*

【不可抗力】[法] force majeure

【不可理喻】be impervious to reason; won't listen to reason

【不可名状】(又作'不可言状') beggar description; be indescribable; be beyond description

【不可磨灭】indelible: ～的印象 *an indelible impression* / ～的贡献 *an everlasting contribution* / ～的功绩 *ineffaceable merit; unforgettable meritorious deeds*

【不可逆转】irreversible: ～的历史潮流 *an irreversible trend of history*

【不可偏废】cannot do one thing and neglect the other

【不可企及】matchless; inimitable

【不可侵犯权】[外交] inviolability

【不可胜数】countless; innumerable: 缴获的武器装备～。*The military equipment captured was beyond counting.*

【不可收拾】irremediable; unmanageable; out of hand; hopeless: 事情到了～的地步。*The situation got out of hand.*

【不可思议】inconceivable; unimaginable; unthinkable: 不久以前,登月旅行还是～的事情。*Travel to the moon was inconceivable until recently.*

【不可同日而语】cannot be mentioned in the same breath; there's no comparison between them

【不可望其项背】can't (or not be fit to) hold a candle to sb.

【不可一世】consider oneself unexcelled in the world; be overweeningly (or insufferably) arrogant: 声势汹汹,～ *bluster and swagger like a conquering hero* / 他晋级以后,盛气凌人,～。*As soon as he was promoted, he began to act high-and-mighty.*

【不可逾越】impassable; insurmountable; insuperable: ～的鸿沟 *an impassable chasm; an unbridgeable gulf* / ～的障碍 *an insurmountable (or insuperable) barrier*

【不可知论】[哲] agnosticism: ～者 *agnostic*

【不可终日】be unable to carry on even for a single day; be in a desperate situation ——另见〖惶惶不可终日〗

【不可转让】non-assignable; non-transferable; unalienable: ～的义务 *non-assignable duty* / ～的债券 *non-transferable bond*

【不可转移性】untransferability: 恶债的特点在于它的～。*The characteristic of odious debts lies in their untransferability.*

【不可捉摸】difficult to ascertain; unpredictable; elusive: ～的概念 *an elusive concept* / ～的哲理文章 *intangible philosophical essays* / 情况～。*The situation is hard to size up.*

【不克】be unable to; cannot: ～胜任 *be unequal to the job*

【不客气】❶ impolite; rude; blunt: 说句～的话 *to put it bluntly* / 你再这样,我可就要～了。*If you go on like this, I won't be so easy on you.* ❷ 〈套〉 you're welcome; don't mention it; not at all ❸ 〈套〉 please don't bother; I'll help myself

【不快】❶ be unhappy; be displeased; be in low spirits: 心中～ *feel unhappy* / 精神～ *feel depressed* ❷ be indisposed; feel under the weather; be out of sorts

【不愧】be worthy of; deserve to be called; prove oneself to be: 她～是律师的女儿。*She was not the daughter of an attorney for nothing.*

【不扩散核武器条约】the Treaty on the Non-proliferation of Nuclear Weapons

【不赖】〈方〉 not bad; good; fine: 今年的庄稼可真～。*This year's crops are really fine.*

【不稂不莠】(又作'不郎不秀') useless; worthless; good-for-nothing

【不劳而获】reap without sowing; profit by or reap the fruits of other people's toil

【不理】refuse to acknowledge; pay no attention to; take no notice of; ignore: 见了人～ *cut sb. dead* / 别～他,要帮助他。*Don't ignore him;*

help him. / 我才～那些闲话呢。*I don't pay attention to such gossip*.

【不力】not do one's best; not exert oneself: 办事～ *not do one's best in one's work*; *be slack in one's work* / 领导～ *not exercise effective leadership*

【不利】❶ unfavourable; disadvantageous; harmful; detrimental: 化～因素为有利因素 *turn unfavourable factors into favourable ones* ❷ unsuccessful: 首战～ *lose the first battle*

【不良】bad; harmful; unhealthy: ～倾向 *harmful trends* / ～现象 *unhealthy tendencies* / ～影响 *harmful* (*or adverse*) *effects* / 存心～ *harbour evil intentions*; *have ulterior motives*

【不了】(used after a verb plus 个) without end: 一天到晚忙个～ *busy from morning till night* / 大雨下个～。*The rain kept pouring down*.

【不了了之】settle a matter by leaving it unsettled; end up with nothing definite: 这件案子因证据不足,也就～了。*Prosecution of the case fizzled out for lack of conclusive evidence*.

【不料】unexpectedly; to one's surprise: 早上天气还好好的,～下午竟下起雹子来了。*It was so fine this morning. Who would have thought it would hail in the afternoon*!

【不吝】〈套〉(used in asking advice) not stint; not grudge; be generous with

【不吝指教】not be stinting with comments or criticism: 尚希～。*We hope that you will not spare your comments*. or *We hope that you will not be stinting with your criticism*.

【不灵】not work; be ineffective: 这机器～了。*The machine doesn't work*. / 老太太手脚有点～了。*The old lady has trouble moving about*.

【不留情面】not spare sb.'s sensibilities; be not afraid to hurt sb.'s feelings: 他这个人办事铁面无私,从来～。*Impartial and upright*, *he has never stretched a point to spare people's sensibilities*.

【不留意】careless: 路那么滑,稍～就会跌倒。*The road is so slippery that if you are off guard the least bit*, *you'll slip and fall*.

【不留余地】leave no room; make no allowance: 说话～往往会陷入被动。*You'll land yourself in a difficult position if you make no allowances in your statement*.

【不露声色】not show (or betray) one's feelings, intentions, etc.: 他～地说… *He said without any change of expression* (*or without betraying what was going through his mind*)...

【不伦不类】neither fish nor fowl; nondescript: ～的比喻 *an inappropriate metaphor*; *a far-fetched analogy*

【不论】(often used correlatively with 都 or 总) no matter (what, who, how, etc.); whether... or...; regardless of: ～性别年龄 *regardless* (*or irrespective*) *of sex and age*

【不落窠臼】not follow the beaten track; have an original style; show originality; be unconventional: 不落前人窠臼 *depart from the beaten track of one's predecessors*

【不落俗套】conform to no conventional pattern; depart from convention

【不买账】not buy it, not go for it

【不满】resentful; discontented; dissatisfied: 心怀～ *nurse a grievance* / 他对这件事,非常～。*He is very unhappy about this matter*.

【不忙】there's no hurry; take one's time: 这件事你先去调查一下,～表态。*Don't be in a hurry to say what you think about this. First find out the facts*.

【不毛之地】barren land; desert

【不免】cannot avoid; cannot help but: 谁碰到这种事也～要发牢骚。*Anyone in such a situation cannot help but complain*.

【不妙】(of a turn of events) not too encouraging; far from good; anything but reassuring: 情况～。*Things are none too encouraging*.

【不名一文】(又作'不名一钱') without a penny to one's name; penniless

【不名誉】disreputable; disgraceful

【不明】❶ not clear; unknown: 失踪的渔船至今下落～。*The whereabouts of the missing fishing boat is still unknown*. ❷ fail to understand: ～事理 *lack common sense* / ～是非 *confuse right and wrong* / ～真相 *be unaware of the truth*; *be ignorant of the facts*

【不明不白】obscure; doubtful; dubious: 死得～ *meet a mysterious death*

【不明飞行物】unidentified flying object (UFO); the flying saucer

【不谋而合】agree without prior (or previous) consultation; happen to hold the same view: 我们的意见～。*Our views happened to coincide*.

【不能】cannot; must not; should not: 我～收这份儿礼。*I cannot accept this gift*. / 我们决～一见成绩就自满起来。*We must not become complacent the moment we have some success*.

【不能不】have to; cannot but: ～表示惋惜 *cannot but express regret* / ～指出 *it must be pointed out that*

【不能自拔】unable to extricate oneself (from one's plight): 他染上了吸毒的恶习,～。*He cannot extricate himself from the drug habit*.

【不能自已】cannot control oneself; lose self-control; can't help; be beside oneself: 度假日即将到来,她兴奋得～。*She was beside herself with excitement as the day of her holiday approached*.

【不念旧恶】not bear a grudge; forgive and forget

【不佞】〈书〉〈谦〉I

【不怕不识货,就怕货比货】don't worry about not knowing much about the goods; just compare them and you will see which is better

【不怕官,只怕管】It is not the official, but the clerk, that is to be feared; It is the person in direct control, however low his position, that has to be reckoned with; fear no oficials, except those who officiate over you

【不配】❶ be unworthy of; not deserve; be unqualified for: 她～当翻译。*She is not a qualified interpreter.* / 他～得金牌。*He didn't deserve the gold medal he got.* ❷ not match: 这一对儿真有点～。*They are not a well-matched pair.* / 领带颜色与上装～。*The colour of the tie doesn't match that of the jacket.*

【不偏不倚】even-handed; impartial; unbiased

【不平】❶ injustice; unfairness; wrong; grievance ❷ indignant; resentful: 消除心中的～ *allay one's resentment*

【不平等条约】unequal treaty

【不平衡】disequilibrium: 工农业发展～ *the disequilibrium between the development of industry and agriculture*

【不平则鸣】injustice provokes outcry; where there is injustice, there will be protest

【不破不立】there is no construction without destruction; there's no making without breaking; to make you must break

【不期而遇】meet unexpectedly (or by chance); have a chance encounter

【不起眼】〈方〉not attract attention; not be noticeable; not be attractive: 别看这人～儿，人家可是一肚子学问。*He is not taken much notice of, but he is a very learned man.*

【不巧】unfortunately; as luck would have it: 我到那儿，～他刚走。*As luck would have it, he had just left when I arrived.*

【不切实际】unrealistic; unpractical; impracticable: ～的计划 *an impracticable plan* / ～的幻想 *unrealistic notions; fanciful ideas*

【不求甚解】not seek deep understanding; be content with a superficial understanding; not seek to understand things thoroughly

【不屈】unyielding; unbending: 坚强～ *iron-willed and unyielding*

【不屈不挠】unyielding; indomitable; dauntless: ～，前仆后继 *dauntlessly step into the breach as others fall*

【不然】❶ not so: 其实～。*Actually this is not so.* ❷ (used at the beginning of a sentence to express disagreement) no: ～，事情没有那样简单。*No, it's not as simple as that.* ❸ or else; otherwise; if not: 我得早点去，～就赶不上火车了。*I've got to leave a bit early, otherwise I'll miss the train.*

【不人道】inhuman: 那些战俘受到了～的待遇，世界舆论为之震惊。*Inhuman treatment of the prisoners of war shocked world opinion.*

【不仁】❶ not benevolent; heartless ❷ numb: 麻木不仁

【不忍】cannot bear to: 我～看到老年人生活穷困，无人照料。*I cannot bear to see old people living in poverty and neglect.* ◇～坐视 cannot bear to stand idly by

【不日】〈书〉within the next few days; in a few days' time: 我～到京，请准备住处。*I'll be in Beijing in a few days. Please find me accommodation.*

【不容】not tolerate; not allow; not brook: ～外国干涉 *tolerate no foreign interference* / ～耽搁 *allow of no delay* / ～歪曲 *brook no distortion* / ～怀疑 *admit of no doubt* ◇～置辩 indisputable; incontestable; ～置疑 allow (or admit) of no doubt; not be open to doubt; be beyond doubt

【不如】❶ not equal to; not as good as; inferior to: 论手巧，一般人都～她。*Few can equal (or compare with) her in manual dexterity.* ❷ it would be better to: 要是这样我还～呆在家里。*In that case I might as well stay at home.*

【不入虎穴，焉得虎子】how can you catch tiger cubs without entering the tiger's lair; nothing venture, nothing gain (or have)

【不三不四】❶ dubious; shady: ～的人 *a person of dubious (or shady) character* / 交些个～的朋友 *make friends with a lot of dubious characters* ❷ neither one thing nor the other; neither fish nor fowl; nondescript: 自己生造的～的词句 *nondescript expressions of one's own coinage* / 说些～的话 *make frivolous remarks; talk twaddle*

【不善】❶ bad; ill: 来意～ *come with ill intent* / 处理～ *not handle properly; mishandle* ❷ (又作'不善于') not good at: ～管理 *not good at managing things*

【不上不下】be suspended in mid air; be in a fix

【不上市股票】unlisted stock

【不上市的证券】unlisted securities

【不设防城市】open city

【不甚了了】not know much (about sth.); not be too clear (about sth.)

【不声不响】quiet; silent: 这小伙子平时～，只是埋头工作。*The young man was usually very quiet and devoted to his work.* / 他～地走进屋来。*He slipped into the room without a word.*

【不胜】❶ cannot bear (or stand); be unequal to: 体力～ *be physically unequal to (a task); be physically incapable of coping with (a job)* ❷ (used between two identical verbs to indicate difficulty or impossibility of fulfilment): 看～看 *find it difficult to read so many books, etc.* ❸ (used in expressing feelings) very; extremely: ～遗憾 *be very sorry; much to one's regret* / ～感激 *be very much obliged; be deeply grateful*

【不胜枚举】too numerous to mention individually (or one by one): 诸如此类的事情，～。*Things like these defy enumeration.*

【不胜其烦】be pestered beyond endurance

【不失时机】not let the opportunity slip; seize the opportune moment; lose no time: 用兵贵在～。*The great thing in war is to seize your opportunities before they're gone.*

【不失为】can yet be regarded as; may after all be accepted as: 这～一个办法。*This, after all, is one way of doing it.*

【不识大体】fail to see the larger issues; ignore the general interest

【不识时务】❶ show no understanding of the times

❷ lack judgment

【不识抬举】fail to appreciate sb.'s kindness; not know how to appreciate favours

【不时】❶ frequently; often: 他～来看我。*He comes to see me from time to time.* ❷ at any time: 不时之需

【不时之需】a possible period of want or need: 以备～ *for emergency needs; provide against a rainy day*

【不食人间烟火】not interested in, or out of touch with, mundane affairs; above the material attractions of the world

【不是玩儿的】〈口〉it's no joke: 你正在养伤,受了寒可～! *It's no joke catching a chill when you are recovering from an injury.*

【不是味儿】(又作'不是滋味儿')〈口〉❶ not the right flavour; not quite right; a bit off: 这个菜炒得～。*This dish doesn't taste quite right.* / 他的京剧唱得～。*The way he sings Beijing opera is a bit off.* ❷ fishy; queer; amiss: 他的作风,我越看越～。*I feel more and more that there's something wrong with his way of doing things.* ❸ feel bad; be upset: 听了他的话,我心里感到～。*I was upset by what he said.*

【不是冤家不聚头】only the ones with mutual bonds will be thrown together; enemies and lovers are destined to meet

【不是】(bùshi) fault; blame: 落个～ *get blamed in the end* / 这就是你的～了。*It's your fault.* or *You're to blame.*

【不适】unwell; indisposed; out of sorts: 胃部～ *have a stomach upset* / 略感～ *feel a bit unwell*

【不受欢迎的人】[外交] persona non grata

【不受理】❶ [法] reject a complaint ❷ [外交] refuse to entertain (a proposal)

【不爽】❶not well; out of sorts; in a bad mood ❷ without discrepancy; accurate: 丝毫～ *not deviate a hair's breadth; be perfectly accurate; be right in every detail*

【不死不活】neither dead nor alive; half dead; lifeless; lethargic

【不死心】unwilling to give up; unresigned: 失败了还～ *not be reconciled to one's failure*

【不送】〈套〉don't bother to see me out

【不送气】[语音] unaspirated: ～音 *unaspirated sound (e.g. Chinese b, d, g, z, zh, j)*

【不速之客】uninvited (or unexpected) guest; gatecrasher

【不随意肌】[生理] involuntary muscle

【不碎玻璃】shatterproof (or safety) glass

【不通】❶ be obstructed; be blocked up; be impassable: 管子～。*The pipe is blocked.* / 电话～。*The line's dead.* ❷ not make sense; be illogical; be ungrammatical: 文章写得～。*The article is badly written.*

【不同】not alike; different; distinct: 在～的程度上 *to varying degrees*

【不同凡响】(usu. of literary and artistic works) outstanding; out of the ordinary; out of the common run

【不痛不痒】scratching the surface; superficial; perfunctory: ～的批评 *superficial criticism* / 讲些～的话 *make some perfunctory remarks*

【不透明】opaque ◇～色 body colour; ～体 opaque body; ～性 opacity

【不透气】airtight: 尼龙布～。*Nylon cloth is airtight.* / 屋里～。*The room is stuffy.*

【不透水】waterproof; watertight; impermeable ◇～层 [地质] impermeable stratum; impervious bed

【不图】❶ not seek; not strive for: ～名利 *not seek fame or gain* ❷ 〈书〉unexpectedly; contrary to expectation

【不吐气】同〖不送气〗

【不妥】not proper; inappropriate: 这样处理,恐怕～。*I'm afraid this isn't the proper way to handle the case.* / 觉得有些～ *feel that something is amiss*

【不外】(又作'不外乎') not beyond the scope of; nothing more than: ～两种可能。*There are only two possibilities.*

【不完全的信托】imperfect market

【不完全统计】incomplete statistics: 据～ *according to incomplete statistics*

【不完全叶】[植] incomplete leaf

【不完全中立】[法] imperfect neutrality

【不为已甚】not go too far; refrain from going to extremes; never go beyond reasonable limits

【不闻不问】not bother to ask or to listen; show no interest in sth.; be indifferent to sth.: 采取～的态度 *adopt a "none of my business" attitude*

【不稳平衡】[物] unstable equilibrium

【不问】❶ pay no attention to; disregard; ignore: ～年龄大小 *irrespective of age* / ～事实真相 *ignore the facts* / ～是非曲直 *make no distinction between right and wrong; not look into the rights and wrongs of the case* ❷ let go unpunished; let off: 胁从～。*Those who acted under duress shall go unpunished.*

【不无小补】not be without some advantage; be of some help

【不务正业】❶ not do honest work; not live by honest labour ❷ ignore one's proper occupation; not attend to one's duties

【不惜】❶ not stint; not spare: ～一切代价 *at all costs; at any cost* ❷ not hesitate (to do sth.); not scruple (to do sth.)

【不惜工本】spare no expense

【不暇】have no time (for sth.); be too busy (to do sth.): ～顾及 *be too busy to attend to sth.*

【不下于】❶ (又作'不下') as many as; no less than: 展出的新产品～二百种。*There are as many as 200 new products on show.* ❷ not inferior to; as good as; on a par with: 这个街道小厂的产品,质量～一些国营大厂。*The products of this small neighbourhood factory are as good as those turned out by some large state-run plants.*

【不相干】be irrelevant; have nothing to do with:

～的话 *irrelevant remarks* / 那件事跟你～。*That has nothing to do with you.*

【不相容】incompatible

【不相上下】equally matched; about the same; almost on a par: 能力～ *of about equal ability; equally able*

【不详】〈书〉❶ not well known; not quite clear: 吴承恩生卒年月～。*Wu Cheng'en's dates are unknown.* / 言之～ *be stated too briefly; not be given in detail* ❷ (used in letters) no need to go into details; let me spare you the details

【不祥】ominous; inauspicious ◇～之兆 an ill (or evil) omen

【不像话】❶ unreasonable: 要你们自己掏钱就～了。*It would be unreasonable for you to pay out of your own pockets.* ❷ shocking; outrageous: 这种行为真～。*Such behaviour is really shocking.*

【不像样】❶ in no shape to be seen; unpresentable: 这活儿～,拿不出手。*This is a shoddy piece of work, it's hardly presentable.* ❷ (used as a complement after 得) beyond recognition: 瘦得～ *extremely thin; worn to a mere shadow* / 破得～ *worn to shreds*

【不肖】〈书〉(of children) unworthy: ～子 *an unworthy son* ◇～子孙 unworthy descendants

【不孝】be an unfilial son or daughter; act contrary to filial piety

【不屑】(又作'不屑于') disdain to do sth.; think sth. not worth doing; feel it beneath one's dignity to do sth.: ～答复 *disdain to reply* ◇ ～一顾 will not spare a glance for; regard as beneath one's notice

【不谢】〈套〉don't mention it; not at all

【不懈】untiring; unremitting; indefatigable: 作～的努力 *make unremitting efforts; make a sustained effort*

【不信任案】no-confidence motion

【不信任投票】vote of no-confidence

【不信邪】not believe in heresy; refuse to be taken in by fallacies; not be scared by evil forces

【不兴】❶ out of fashion; outmoded: 现在～中山装了。*The Chinese tunic suit is out of fashion now.* ❷ impermissible; not allowed: ～这样做。*That's not allowed.* ❸ (only used in a rhetorical question) can't: 你干吗嚷嚷,就～小点儿声吗? *Why shout? Can't you lower your voice a little?*

【不行】❶ not be allowed; won't do; be impossible: 开玩笑可以,欺负人可～。*To have a joke is all right, but to bully people just won't do.* ❷ be no good; won't work: 这个方法～。*This method just won't work.* / 我的脑子～,还不大懂。*My mind is no good; I still don't quite understand.* ❸ not be good; be poor: 料子不错,手工～。*The material is fine, but the workmanship is poor.* ❹ (used as a complement after 得) awfully; extremely: 大街上热闹得～。*The streets are awfully busy.* / 我可困得～了。*I'm terribly sleepy.*

【不行了】on the point of death; dying: 病人快要～。*The patient is failing fast.*

【不省人事】lose consciousness; be unconscious; be in a coma

【不幸】❶ misfortune; adversity: 遭～ *meet with a misfortune* ❷ unfortunate; sad: ～的消息 *sad news* ❸ unfortunately: 他～以身殉职。*To our great sorrow, he died at his post.*

【不幸言中】the prophecy unfortunately comes true: 现在怎么样? ～了吧。*Now, you see what has happened. Unfortunately my prediction has come true.*

【不休】(used as a complement) endlessly; ceaselessly: 争论～ *argue endlessly; keep on arguing*

【不修边幅】not care about one's appearance; be slovenly

【不朽】immortal: ～的著作 *an immortal masterpiece* / ～的功勋 *immortal deeds*

【不锈钢】stainless steel

【不虚此行】the journey has not been made in vain; the journey has been well worthwhile; it's been a worthwhile journey

【不许】❶ not allow; must not: ～说谎。*You mustn't tell lies.* / 熄灯后～说话。*No talking after lights out.* ❷〈口〉(used in a rhetorical question) can't: 何必非等我,你就～自己去吗? *Why wait for me? Can't you go yourself?*

【不宣而战】open hostilities without declaring war; start an undeclared war

【不学无术】have neither learning nor skill; be ignorant and incompetent

【不逊】〈书〉rude; impertinent

【不雅观】offensive to the eye; unbecoming: 随地吐痰既～也不卫生。*Spitting in public places is not only unbecoming but also unsanitary.*

【不言不语】not say a word; keep silent

【不言而喻】it goes without saying; it is self-evident

【不厌】not mind doing sth.; not tire of; not object to

【不厌其烦】not mind taking the trouble; take great pains; be very patient

【不厌其详】go into details; dwell at length upon: 她～地向她朋友诉说她的遭遇。*She told her friend in detail all the things she'd gone through.*

【不扬】not good-looking: 其貌不扬

【不要】don't: ～麻痹大意。*Don't slacken your vigilance.* / ～总是以为自己对。*Don't think you are always right.*

【不要紧】❶ it's not serious; it doesn't matter; never mind: 有点伤风,～。*Just a slight cold, nothing serious.* ❷ it looks all right, but: 你这一嚷～,把大家都吵醒了。*You may think it's all right for you to shout, but you've woken everybody up.*

【不要脸】〈讳〉have no sense of shame; shameless: 只有～的人才能做出这样～的事。*Only those who have no sense of shame can do such shameful things.* / 真～! *What a nerve!*

【不一】vary; differ: 质量～ *vary in quality* / 长短～ *differ in length*

【不一而足】no isolated case; numerous: 凡此种种, ～。*There are countless similar cases.* or *Such instances are legion.*

【不依】❶ not comply; not go along with: 我们劝他休息, 他怎么也～。*We advised him to have a rest, but he simply wouldn't hear of it.* ❷ not let off easily; not let sb. get away with it: 你要是再这样, 我可～你。*If you do this again, I won't let you off so easily.*

【不宜】not suitable; inadvisable: 这一点～过分强调。*It's inadvisable to overemphasize this point.* / 这种土壤～种花生。*This kind of soil is not suitable for growing peanuts.*

【不遗余力】spare no pains (or effort); do one's utmost

【不已】endlessly; incessantly: 赞叹～ *praise again and again*

【不以为意】pay no attention to; take no notice of; not mind

【不义之财】ill-gotten wealth (or gains)

【不亦乐乎】(used as a complement after 得) extremely; awfully: 忙得～ *be awfully (or terribly) busy*

【不易之论】perfectly sound proposition; undeniable truth; irrefutable argument

【不意】〈书〉❶ unexpectedly: ～大雨如注, 无法启程。*Unexpectedly it poured with rain and it was impossible to start off.* ❷ unawareness; unpreparedness: 利用敌人的错觉和～来争取自己的主动 *exploit the enemy's misconceptions and unpreparedness to gain the initiative*

【不翼而飞】❶ (of an object) disappear without trace; vanish into thin air: 他一掏口袋, 皮夹子已～。*He reached into his pocket for the wallet only to find it was missing.* ❷ spread fast as if on wings; spread like wildfire: 这消息传得这样快, 简直是～。*The news has spread fast, as if on wings.*

【不阴不阳】neither yin nor yang — assume an ambiguous (or equivocal) attitude

【不用】need not: ～着急。*You needn't worry.* or *There is no need to worry.* / ～说 *it goes without saying; needless to say*

【不由得】can't help; cannot but: 他说得这么透彻, ～你不信服。*He spoke so cogently that you couldn't help being convinced.*

【不由分说】(又作'不容分说') allowing no explanation; without so much as a "by your leave"; without listening to sb.'s protests: 他们把他抓住, ～, 痛打一顿。*They seized him, and without waiting for an explanation gave him a severe beating.*

【不由自主】can't help; involuntarily: ～地流下了眼泪 *cannot help shedding tears; be unable to hold back one's tears; shed tears in spite of oneself*

【不予】not grant: ～批准 *not grant approval* / ～考虑 *refuse to take into consideration; will not consider*

【不育性】(又作'不孕性')[农] sterility

【不育症】[医] sterility; barrenness

【不远千里】make light of travelling a thousand li; make light of travelling from afar; go to the trouble of travelling a long distance

【不约而同】do or think the same without prior consultation; happen to coincide: 她一讲完, 大家～都鼓起掌来。*Spontaneous applause broke out as soon as she finished speaking.*

【不悦】displeased; annoyed

【不在】not be in; be out: 你找老王吗? 他～。*Are you looking for Lao Wang? He's out.*

【不在乎】见〖在乎〗❶

【不在话下】be nothing difficult; be a cinch: 她摩托车都会骑, 自行车更～了。*She can ride a motorcycle, to say nothing of a bicycle.*

【不在了】〈婉〉be dead: 他爷爷早就～。*His grandfather has been dead a long time.*

【不在其位, 不谋其政】He who holds no rank in a state does not discuss its policies.

【不在意】❶ pay no attention to; take no notice of; not mind: 别人背后议论, 他毫～。*He doesn't care at all what people say behind his back.* ❷ negligent; careless: 人家托你的事, 你别～。*When people ask you to do something, you should take it seriously.*

【不赞一词】not say a word; keep silent; make no comment: 我对这个问题不清楚, 只能～。*I'm not clear about this matter, so I had better keep quiet.*

【不择手段】by fair means or foul; by hook or (by) crook; unscrupulously: 他为了达到个人目的可以～。*He'd stop at nothing (or stoop to anything) to get what he wants.*

【不怎么】not very; not particularly: 这块地～大。*This plot isn't very big.* / 我～想去。*I'm not particularly keen on going.* / 他～爱说话。*He doesn't talk much.*

【不怎么样】not up to much; very indifferent: 这幅画画得～。*This isn't much of a painting.* / 他的英语怎么样? —～。*Is his English any good? — It doesn't amount to much.*

【不战不和】no war, no peace: ～的局面 *a stalemate of "no war, no peace"*

【不折不扣】❶ hundred-percent; to the letter ❷ out-and-out: ～的伪君子 *an out-and-out hypocrite* / ～的老实人 *an honest man through and through*

【不争气】be disappointing; fail to live up to expectations: 他这个人真～。*This chap has let us down.* / 我这腿～, 最后一圈跑不动了。*My legs failed me and I wasn't able to run the last lap.*

【不正当的手段】dishonest methods

【不正当的职业】illegitimate occupation

【不正当竞争】illicit competition

【不正当收入】illegitimate income

【不正之风】unhealthy tendency; malpractice: 纠正行业～ *correct malpractices in all trades and* professions

【不知不觉】unconsciously; unwittingly: ～已过了三个月。*Before we knew it three months had passed.*

【不知分寸】lack tact; have no sense of propriety: 说话～ *talk tactlessly*

【不知好歹】(又作'不识好歹') can't tell good from bad; not know what's good for one

【不知进退】have no sense of propriety; not know where to stop

【不知死活】act recklessly; do sth. regardless of danger

【不知所措】be at a loss; be at one's wits' end: 茫然～ *be at a complete loss what to do*

【不知所云】❶ scarcely know what one has said ❷ not understand what sb. is driving at: 他说了半天,听的人还是～。*He talked on and on, but the audience couldn't make out what he was driving at.*

【不知天高地厚】not know the height of the heavens or the depth of the earth—have an exaggerated opinion of one's abilities; not understand things

【不值】not worth: 我看～那么多。*I don't think it's worth that much.* / 跑这一趟～。*The trip is not worthwhile.* ◇ ～一驳 not worth refuting; ～一提 not worth mentioning; ～一文 utterly worthless

【不止】❶ incessant; without end: 愚公毫不动摇,每天挖山～。*Unshaken in his conviction, the Foolish Old Man kept on digging at the mountain every day.* / 大笑～ *roar with laughter* ❷ more than; not limited to: ～一次 *more than once; not just once* / 他恐怕～六十岁了。*He is probably over sixty.*

【不只】not only; not merely: 河水～可供灌溉,且可用来发电。*River waters can be used not only for irrigation but also for the generation of electricity.*

【不至于】cannot go so far; be unlikely: 他～连这一点道理也不明白。*He must have more sense than that.*

【不治之症】incurable disease

【不致】not in such a way as to; not likely to: 事先做好准备,就～临时手忙脚乱了。*If you arrange everything in advance, you won't be in a rush at the last moment.*

【不置可否】decline to comment; not express an opinion; be noncommittal; hedge: 你是负责人,你怎么能对这个问题～? *You are in charge of the job. How could you evade the issue?*

【不中用】unfit for anything; no good; useless: 这铁锹～,我去换一把吧。*This spade is no good. I'll go and get another one.* / 老了,～啦。*I'm getting old and useless.*

【不周】not attentive and satisfactory; thoughtless; inconsiderate: 计划～ *not well planned; not planned carefully enough* / 招待～ *not be attentive enough to guests*

【不周延】[逻] undistributed

【不准】not allow; forbid; prohibit: 此处～吸烟。*Smoking is not allowed here.* or *No Smoking!* / ～停车。*No parking!* / ～入内。*No admittance.*

【不着边际】not to the point; wide of the mark; neither here nor there; irrelevant: ～的长篇大论 *a long rambling talk* / 他越讲越～。*The more he talked, the further he strayed from the point.*

【不着痕迹】leave no trace

【不着陆飞行】nonstop flight

【不自量】not take a proper measure of oneself; overrate one's own abilities

【不自量力】not have a proper measure of oneself; overrate one's own abilities; overreach oneself

【不自由,毋宁死】Give me liberty, or give me death.

【不足】❶ not enough; insufficient; inadequate: 资源～ *inadequate resources* / 给养～ *be short of supplies* / 人手～ *be shorthanded; be understaffed* ❷ not worth ❸ cannot; should not: 非团结～图存。*We cannot survive unless we unite.*

【不足道】not worth mentioning; inconsiderable; of no consequence: 我这方面的这点知识是～的。*What little I know on the subject is not worth mentioning.*

【不足挂齿】not worth mentioning; nothing to speak of

【不足轻重】worthless; negligible

【不足为凭】cannot be taken as evidence; afford little or no evidence

【不足为奇】not at all surprising; nothing to be surprised at

【不足为训】not fit to serve as a model; not to be taken as an example; not an example to be followed; not to be taken as authoritative: 书本上讲的也有～的。*What is stated in books is not always true.*

【不足为外人道】This is not to be mentioned to outsiders; This is strictly between ourselves.

【不足与谋】not worth consulting with: 此人胆小怕事,～。*He is so overcautious and timid that we had better not consult with him.*

【不做声】keep silent; not say a word

布

Ⅰ 名 ❶ cotton cloth; cloth: 把车用块干净的～擦一擦。*Wipe the car with a clean cloth.* ❷ an ancient coin Ⅱ 动 ❶ declare; announce; publish; proclaim ❷ spread; disseminate ❸ dispose; ❹ arrange; deploy: ～好阵势 *deploy the troops in battle formation*

【布帛】cloth and silk; cotton and silk textiles

【布帛菽粟】cloth, silk, beans and grain—food and clothing; daily necessities

【布达拉宫】the Potala (the former palace of the Dalai Lamas, in Lhasa, Xizang)

【布道】preach the Gospel; evangelize

【布店】cloth store; draper's; piece-goods store

【布丁】pudding

【布尔乔亚】bourgeoisie (a transliteration)

【布尔什维克】Bolshevik ◇～主义 Bolshevism
【布防】place troops on garrison duty；organize a defence
【布告】notice；bulletin；proclamation：张贴～ *paste up a notice* ◇～栏 notice board；bulletin board
【布谷鸟】cuckoo
【布基纳法索】Burkina Faso
【布景】❶ composition (of a painting) ❷［戏］setting：～设计师 *set designer*
【布局】❶ overall arrangement；layout；distribution：新市区的～ *the layout of a new urban district* / 合理调整城乡经济～ *make rational adjustments in the distribution of urban and rural economies* ❷ composition (of a picture，piece of writing，etc.) ❸ position (of pieces on a chessboard)
【布控】have (sb.) under surveillance：对作案对象进行了严密～ *have the suspects under strict surveillance*
【布莱尔盲字】Braille
【布朗运动】［物］Brownian movement
【布雷】lay mines；mine：在港口～ *mine a harbour* ◇～舰艇 minelayers；～区 minefield
【布隆迪】Burundi ◇ ～人 Burundian
【布鲁氏菌】brucella ◇～病 brucellosis；undulant fever
【布面】cloth cover (of a book) ◇～精装本 clothbound de luxe edition
【布匹】cloth；piece goods ◇～染色 piece dyeing
【布设】lay；make arrangement：～ 地雷 *lay (sour) mines* / ～圈套 *set (or lay) a trap*
【布施】〈书〉alms giving；charitable
【布头】❶leftover of a bolt of cloth ❷ odd bits of cloth
【布网船】［军］netlayer
【布纹纸】wove paper
【布线】［电］wiring ◇ ～图 wiring diagram
【布鞋】cloth shoes
【布衣】❶ cotton clothes ❷〈古〉commoner
【布衣蔬食】coarse clothes and simple fare—a thrifty and simple life
【布展】to set up an exhibition ～水平 caliber of the exhibition /书展的布展方式很有特色。*The set-up of the book exhibition is very distinctive.*
【布置】❶ fix up；arrange；decorate：～会场 *fix up a place for a meeting* / ～展品 *arrange exhibits* ❷ assign；make arrangements for；give instructions about：～工作 *assign work*；*give instructions about an assignment*

步

Ⅰ 名 ❶ step；pace：只有几～路了。*It's only a few steps away.* / 大～前进 *advance with big strides* / 走一～棋 *make a move (in chess，etc.)* ❷ stage；step：下一～怎么办？*What's the next step (or move)?* / 这只好一～一～地去做。*This will have to be done step by step.* ❸ condition；situation；state：事情怎么发展到这一～？*How did things get into such a state?* Ⅱ 动 walk；go on foot：～入会场 *walk into the assembly hall*
【步兵】❶ infantry；foot ❷ infantryman；foot soldier
【步步】step by step；at every step：～进逼 *press forward steadily*
【步步为营】advance gradually and dig in at every step；consolidate at every step；act cautiously
【步测】measure by paces；pace out
【步调】pace；step：统一～ *concert action* ◇～一致 march in step；keep in step；act in unison
【步伐】step；pace：加快～ *quicken one's steps (or pace)* / ～整齐 *(march) in step* / 跟上时代的～ *keep pace with the times*
【步法】footwork (in dancing，sports，etc.)
【步话机】walkie-talkie
【步犁】walking plough
【步履】〈书〉walk
【步履蹒跚】walk haltingly；hobble along
【步履维艰】have difficulty walking；walk with difficulty
【步枪】rifle
【步人后尘】follow in sb.'s footsteps
【步哨】sentry；sentinel
【步行】go on foot；walk◇～街 vehicle free promenade (or street)
【步行虫】ground beetle
【步韵】use the rhyme sequence of a poem (when replying to it)
【步骤】step；move；measure：采取适当的～ *take proper steps* / 这是增产的一个具体～。*This is a practical move to increase production.*
【步子】step；pace：～轻快 *walk with springy steps* / 队伍的～走得很整齐。*The soldiers marched in step.*

怖

动 fear；be afraid of：恐怖

钚

名［化］plutonium (Pu)

部

Ⅰ 名 ❶ part；section：分为三～ *divide into three parts (or sections)* / 南～ *the southern part* ❷unit；ministry；department；board：解放军某～ *a certain PLA unit* ❸ headquarters ❹ troops；forces Ⅱ 动〈书〉control；command Ⅲ 量 ❶(for books and films)：两～字典 *two dictionaries* / 一～电影 *a film* ❷〈方〉(for machines and vehicles)：一～机器 *a machine* / 两～汽车 *two cars*
【部队】❶ army；armed forces ❷ troops；force；unit：通讯兵～ *signal troops* / 这是一支野战～。*This is a field army unit.* ◇～代号 code designation (of a military unit)
【部分】part；section；share：我们看问题，不但要看到～，而且要看到全体。*In approaching a problem we should see the whole as well as the parts.* ◇～赔付 partial settlement
【部件】parts；components；assembly ◇～分解图 exploded view
【部将】〈旧〉officers under one's control
【部类】category；division

【部落】tribe ◇～社会 tribal society

【部门】department；branch：政府各～ *various government departments* / 工业和农业是国民经济的两个重要～。*Industry and agriculture are the two important sectors of the national economy.*

【部首】radicals by which characters are arranged in traditional Chinese dictionaries

【部属】❶ 同〖部下〗❷ affiliated to a ministry：～机构 *organizations affiliated to the ministry*

【部署】dispose；deploy：～兵力 *dispose* (*or deploy*) *troops for battle* / 改革的～和实施 *the planning and implementation of the reform*

【部委】ministries and commissions：国务院各～ *ministries and commissions under the State Council*

【部位】(usu. used of parts of the human body) position；place：发音时舌的～ *the position of the tongue in pronunciation*；*tongue position* / 受伤～ *the location of an injury*

【部下】❶ troops under one's command ❷ subordinate

【部优】ministry-recognized quality product

【部优产品】ministry prize product

【部长】minister；head of a department (under the Party Central Committee)：外贸部～ *Minister of Foreign Trade* / 省委宣传部～ *Director of the Propaganda Department of a provincial Party committee* ◇～会议 Council of Ministers；～级会议 conference at ministerial level；～助理 assistant minister

埠

名 ❶ wharf；pier ❷ port

【埠头】〈方〉wharf；pier

簿

名 notebook；book：账簿

【簿册】books for taking notes or keeping accounts

【簿籍】account books，registers，records，etc.

【簿记】bookkeeping：复(单)式～ *double-entry* (*single-entry*) *bookkeeping*

【簿子】notebook；book

C

cā

擦 动 ❶ rub：～根火柴点烟 *strike a match and light a cigarette* / 他～伤了膝盖。*He skinned his knee.* / 没关系，就～破了一点皮。*Nothing serious; just a scratch.* ❷ wipe：～桌子（地板，玻璃，自行车）*wipe a table (mop the floor, clean a pane of glass, clean a bike)* / 你～～汗吧，这儿有毛巾。*Wipe the sweat away, here's a towel.* / 他的皮鞋～得很亮。*His shoes are well shined.* ❸ apply or spread sth. on：～药水或药膏 *apply medicinal lotion or ointment (to an affected spot)* / ～粉 *powder one's face* / 我的皮鞋该～点儿油了。*My shoes need a shine.* ❹ touch lightly or come close to in passing; shave; brush：他～着我的肩膀走过去了。*He brushed past me.* / 飞机～着山顶飞过。*The plane swept the hilltops.* ❺ scrape into shreds：把萝卜～成丝儿。*Shred the turnips.*

【擦棒球】foul tip (in baseball, soft ball, etc.)

【擦边球】[体]（乒乓球）edge ball; touch ball

【擦亮】scour：把铜像～ *shine the bronze statue*

【擦亮眼睛】remove the scales from one's eyes; sharpen one's vigilance：我们要～识破他们的阴谋。*We should sharpen our vigilance and guard against their schemes.*

【擦伤】abrasion; gall; scotch; scratch

【擦屁股】clear up the mess left by sb. else

【擦拭】wipe clean; cleanse：～枪支 *clean firearms*

【擦网球】net ball (in table tennis, volleyball, etc.)

【擦洗】clean (with water or alcohol)：这个手表该～了。*This watch needs cleaning.*

【擦音】[语音] fricative

【擦澡】rub oneself down with a wet towel

cāi

猜 动 ❶ guess; conjecture; speculate：你～谁来了？*Guess who's here.* / 他准～不着。*He's sure to guess wrong.* / 这个谜语真难～。*This riddle is really difficult to solve.* ❷ suspect：我～他和这件事有点牵连。*I suspect that he is somewhat involved in the affair.*

【猜不透】unable to guess; unable to make out

【猜测】guess; conjecture; surmise：那都是～。*That's pure conjecture.* / 妄加～ *make wild guesses*

【猜度】*surmise; conjecture*：他心里在～，这位老人家是谁？*He was wondering who that old man could be.*

【猜忌】be suspicious and jealous：自己没有私心，就不会～别人。*If you didn't have selfish motives, you wouldn't be suspicious and jealous of others.*

【猜奖】guessing game with prizes for winners

【猜谜儿】❶ guess a riddle ❷ guess：快说吧，别让我们～了。*Now out with it. Don't keep us guessing.*

【猜拳】同〖划拳〗

【猜透】guess right：他的意图我早就～了。*I guessed his intentions long ago.* / 我猜不透她的心事。*I can't figure out what's on her mind.*

【猜想】suppose; guess; suspect：我～他病了。*I suspect he is ill.* / 你这种～不一定正确。*This supposition of yours might be wrong.*

【猜疑】harbour suspicions; be suspicious; have misgivings：不要随便～。*Don't let your suspicions get out of hand.*

【猜中】guess right：谁～这个谜语可得奖。*Whoever guesses the riddle will get a prize.*

cái

才 Ⅰ 名 ❶ ability; talent：才能 ❷ a capable person：人才 ❸ people of a certain type：奴才 Ⅱ 副 ❶ a moment ago; just：你怎么～来就要走？*You've only just come. Why do you want to leave so soon?* ❷ (preceded by an expression of time) not until：他九点钟～来，太晚了。*He didn't come until 9 o'clock. That was too late.* / 大风到晚上～住了。*The gale didn't stop until evening.* ❸ (preceded by an expression of reason or condition) not unless; not until; then and only then; for no other reason：经他解释之后，我～明白是怎么回事。*I didn't understand what was going on until he explained it to me.* / 他说行～行。*It's OK only if he says so.* ❹ (followed by a numerical expression) only：这孩子～五岁，已经认得不少字了。*The child is only five, and he already knows quite a few characters.* ❺ (used in an assertion or contradiction, emphasizing what comes before 才, usu. with 呢 at the end of the sentence) actually; really：这～好呢！*Now this is really good!* / 你以为他傻吗？他～不傻

呢！*You think he's stupid? Not him!*

【才干】ability；competence：长～ *enhance one's abilities* / 他很有～。*He is very capable.* / 这件事充分显示了他的～。*This fully shows his ability.*

【才高八斗】be endowed with unusual literary talents

【才华】literary or artistic talent：她是一位很有～的青年作家。*She is a gifted young writer.* ◇～横溢 brim with talent；have superb talent

【才略】ability and sagacity (in political and military affairs)：雄才大略

【才貌】talent and appearance ◇～出众 of exceptional talent and distinguished appearance；～双全 be endowed with both beauty and talent

【才能】ability；capability；talent：有～ *have ability；be capable* / 在工厂的经营管理方面，她显示出非凡的～。*She shows rare capability in factory management.*

【才女】a gifted female scholar

【才气】同〖才华〗◇～横溢 同〖才华横溢〗

【才识】ability and insight：～过人 *be gifted with talent and insight far beyond the average person*

【才疏学浅】〈套〉have little talent and less learning

【才思】imaginative power and creativeness (in writing)：～敏捷 *have a facile imagination*

【才学】talent and learning；scholarship：他读书万卷，～出众。*He's read volumes and is an outstanding scholar.*

【才智】ability and wisdom：充分发挥人民群众的聪明～ *give full play to the wisdom and creativity of the people* / ～过人 *far surpass others in ability and wisdom*

【才子】a talented scholar ◇～佳人 genius and beauty

材 名 ❶ timber：木材 ❷ coffin：寿材 ❸ material：教材 ❹ ability；talent；aptitude：因材施教 ❺ a capable person：成材

【材积】[林] volume of timber

【材料】❶ material：做个书架需要些什么～？*What materials do you need to make a bookcase?* ❷ data；material：学习～ *material for study* / 档案～ *archival material* / 调查～ *data；findings* / 搜集～ *gather material；collect data* ❸ makings；stuff：她不是演戏的～。*She hasn't the makings of an actress.* ◇～科学 material science；～力学 mechanics of materials

财 名 wealth；money：财政

【财宝】money and valuables

【财帛】wealth；money

【财产】property：公共～ *public property* / 国家～ *state property* / 私人～ *private property* / ～保险 *property insurance* ◇～抵押权 encumbrance；～估价 assessment；～管理 administration of assets；～继承 inheritance of property；～留置权 possessory lien；encumbrance；～权 property right；～使用权 right to the use of property；～税 property tax；～转让 transfer of property；～转让书 assurance

【财大气粗】he who has wealth speaks louder than others

【财东】〈旧〉❶ shopowner；store owner ❷ moneybags

【财阀】financial magnate；plutocrat；tycoon

【财富】wealth；riches：自然～ *natural wealth* / 精神～ *spiritual wealth* / 物质～ *material wealth*

【财经】finance and economics：～工作 *work in the field of finance and economics* / ～学校 *schools of finance and economics* / ～纪律 *financial discipline*

【财力】financial resources (or capacity)：～雄厚 *have abundant financial resources* / ～不足 *have insufficient financial resources* / ～有限 *have limited financial resources*

【财路】means to acquire wealth：广开～ *open (or exploit) all possible avenues for wealth*

【财贸】finance and trade (or commerce)

【财迷】moneygrubber；miser：他是个老～。*He's an old miser.*

【财迷心窍】be mad about money；be money-grubbing

【财权】❶ ownership of property；property right ❷ financial power；control over money matters：她在单位里是掌～的。*She has control over financial matters in her unit (or organization).*

【财神】(又作'财神爷') the God of Wealth：请～ *invoke the God of Wealth*

【财势】wealth and influence：依仗～ *count on one's or sb. else's wealth and influence*

【财税】finance and taxation：～秩序混乱 *chaos in finance and taxation* / ～制度 *financial and taxation system (or regime)*

【财团】financial group：国际～ *consortium*

【财务】financial affairs：～报告 *financial statement (or report)* / ～行政 *financial administration* ◇～补偿 financial indemnity；～监督 financial supervision；～会计 financial accounting；～科 finance section

【财物】money and goods；property (estate not included)：个人～ *personal property；personal effects* / 公共～ *public property*

【财源】financial resources；source of revenue：～茂盛 *rich in financial resources* / 广开～ *explore all possible ways of bringing in money or revenue*

【财运】luck in making money：他～不错，一下子赚了十几万。*He's very lucky, and has made over a hundred thousand yuan in one deal.*

【财政】(public) finance：～危机 *financial crisis* / ～收入 *revenue* / ～支出 *expenditure* / ～收支平衡 *balance of revenue and expenditure* / ～政策 *financial (or fiscal) policy* / ～机关 *financial organ or administration；fiscal organ or administration* ◇～包干 fiscal responsibility system；～补贴 financial subsidies；financial subsidy；～部 the Ministry of Finance；～赤字 financial deficits；～关税 financial duty；～基金 financial funds；～监督 financial supervision；～困难 in financial difficulties；～年度 financial (or fiscal) year；～预算 financial budget；～资本 financial capital

【财主】rich man；moneybags：他是本地有名的～。*He's one of the well-known rich men in these parts.*

裁 Ⅰ 动 ❶ cut (paper, cloth, etc.) into parts：把一张纸～成条儿 *cut a sheet of paper into strips* / ～件新衣服 *cut out a new garment* / 这块料子可以～两套衣服。*Two suits can be cut out of this piece of material.* ❷ reduce；cut down；dismiss：这家公司去年～了十个人。*This company dismissed ten people last year.* ❸ judge；decide：裁决 Ⅱ 名 ❶ check；sanction：制裁 ❷ mental planning：别出心裁

【裁并】cut down and merge (organizations)：这个科已～到总务处。*This section has been merged into the general affairs department.*

【裁撤】dissolve (an organization)：这个机构应该～。*This organization should be dissolved.* / 我们已经～了两个科室。*We have dissolved two offices already.*

【裁处】consider and solve；decide and take action：这件事由你～。*This matter will be left in your hands.* / 这事太复杂，一时很难～。*This is too complicated a matter to be settled right away.*

【裁定】[法] decide or declare judicially；rule：法官～他的证词有效。*The judge ruled that his testimony was valid.*

【裁断】consider and decide：此事如何处理，请您～。*Please consider the problem and decide how to handle it.*

【裁夺】同〖裁断〗

【裁缝】tailor；dressmaker

【裁剪】cut out (a garment)：我这件大衣请你照这个式样～。*Please cut out my overcoat according to (or after) this pattern.*

【裁减】reduce；cut down：～机关工作人员 *reduce (or cut down) the staff of an organization* / ～军备 *reduce armaments*

【裁决】adjudicate；rule：依法～ *adjudicate according to law* / 会议主席作出了～。*A ruling was given by the chairman.*

【裁军】reduce armaments：～谈判 *disarmament talks*

【裁判】❶ [法] judge ❷ [体] act as referee ❸ [体] referee；judge；umpire：他应邀为这场排球赛担任～。*He is asked to referee this volleyball match.*

【裁判权】jurisdiction：有～ *have jurisdiction* / 取消～ *deprive sb. of his jurisdiction*

【裁判员】同〖裁判〗❸

【裁判长】[体] head referee；head judge

【裁员】cut down the number of persons employed；reduce the staff：这家饭店已～二十人。*The hotel has dismissed twenty people from its staff.*

【裁纸刀】paper cutter；paper knife

【裁纸机】paper cutter；(paper) trimmer

cǎi

采 Ⅰ 动 ❶ pick, pluck or gather：～茶 *pick tea* / ～药 *gather medicinal herbs* / 潜水～珠 *dive for pearls* ❷ mine；extract：采煤 / 采油 ❸ choose；select：采取 / 采用 Ⅱ 名 manner, air or spirit (of a person)：神采 ——另见 cài

【采办】select and purchase on a considerable scale (esp. for a special occasion)：～年货 *make special purchases for the Spring Festival*

【采编】gather and edit (news material)：新闻～ *news coverage and editing* / ～人员 *reporters and editors；staff writers*

【采场】[矿] stope

【采伐】cut timber；lumber：～原始森林 *open up a primeval forest for logging* / 他从事～多年。*He has been engaged in the lumbering business for years.* ◇～迹地 cutover；～量 (timber) cut

【采访】❶ hunt for and collect：图书～工作 *the work of finding and collecting books for libraries* ❷ gather news；cover：～新闻 *cover a news item* / ～一位名演员 *interview a famous actor*

【采风】collect folk songs and tales

【采购】make purchases for an organization or enterprise；purchase：～建筑材料 *purchase building materials* ◇～价 procurement price；～员 purchasing agent；～站 purchasing station

【采光】[建] (natural) lighting；daylighting

【采集】gather；collect：～标本 *collect specimens* / 原始部落靠渔猎～为生。*Primitive tribes lived by fishing, hunting and gathering.*

【采掘】[矿] excavate：～设备 *equipment for excavation*

【采矿】mining：露天～ *opencut (or opencast) mining* / ～工程 *mining engineering* / ～工业 *mining (industry)*

【采录】collect and record：～民歌 *collect and record folk songs*

【采买】❶ select and purchase ❷ purchasing agent：我可以当～。*I can handle the purchasing job.* or *I can do all the purchasing for the occasion.*

【采煤】coal mining；coal extraction；coal cutting：～工作面 *coal face* / ～回收率 *coal recovery*

【采棉机】cotton picker (farming machine)

【采纳】accept (opinions, suggestions, requests, etc.)：～群众建议 *accept suggestions made by the masses*

【采暖】heating：蒸气～ *steam heating* / ～设备 *heating equipment (or facilities)*

【采取】adopt；assume or take：～紧急措施 *take emergency measures* / ～主动 *take the initiative* / ～攻势 *take the offensive*

【采石场】stone pit；quarry

【采撷】〈书〉❶ pick；pluck ❷ gather

【采样】[矿] sampling

【采用】select and use；adopt：～新技术 *adopt new techniques* / ～有效的工作方法 *use effective work methods*

【采油】［油］oil extraction；oil recovery：二次～ *secondary recovery* ◇～队 oil production crew

【采摘】pick (fruit, flowers, leaves, etc.)；pluck：～苹果(棉花) *pick apples (cotton)*

【采制】gather and process：～中草药 *gather medicinal herbs and prepare them for use*

【采种】［农］seed collecting

彩 名 ❶ colour：彩色 ❷ applause；cheer ❸ variety；brilliance；splendour：丰富多彩 ❹ prize：中彩 ❺ blood from a wound：挂彩 ❻ coloured silk；variegated silk：张灯结彩

【彩蚌】［工美］painted clam shell (a clam shell with a colour painting done on its inside)

【彩笔】colour pencil；crayon

【彩车】❶ float (in a parade) ❷ bridal car

【彩绸】coloured silk

【彩带】coloured ribbon (or streamer)

【彩蛋】❶［工美］painted eggshell (an emptied eggshell with a colour painting done on its outside, with or without decorative silk tassels) ❷〈方〉preserved egg

【彩弹游戏】paintball

【彩灯】coloured lights

【彩电】colour television set；colour TV：一台 20 英寸～ *a 20″ colour TV*

【彩号】a soldier wounded in action

【彩虹】rainbow

【彩绘】coloured drawing or pattern：～磁器 *porcelain decorated with coloured drawings* / ～陶俑 *painted pottery figurine*

【彩卷】［摄］colour film

【彩扩】(〈略〉见〖彩色扩印〗)［摄］make enlargements of 135 colour films

【彩礼】betrothal gifts (from the bridegroom to the bride's family)；bride-price：要(收，送)～ *ask for (accept, present) betrothal gifts*

【彩练】coloured ribbon

【彩排】dress rehearsal：明天晚上进行～。*We are having a dress rehearsal tomorrow evening.*

【彩票】lottery ticket

【彩旗】coloured banner；bunting

【彩球】coloured silk ball (for decorative purposes)

【彩券】lottery ticket

【彩色】multicolour；colour：～铅笔 *colour pencil；crayon* ◇～编码器 colour coder；～玻璃 stained glass；～电视机 colour television set；colour TV；～胶卷 colour film；～解码器 colour decoder；～平衡 colour balance；～摄像机 colour video camera；～失真 colour distortion；～显示屏幕 colour display screen；～显像管 colour display tube；～印刷 colour printing

【彩陶】painted pottery (of a Neolithic culture)

【彩头】good luck in business, contests or lotteries

【彩霞】rosy (or pink) clouds

【彩印】〈略〉见〖彩色印刷〗

【彩釉陶】glazed coloured pottery

【彩照】［摄］colour picture；colour photo

【彩纸】❶ coloured paper ❷［摄］colour photographic paper

睬 动 pay attention to；take notice of：别～他。*Take no notice of him.* or *Ignore him.* / 嘿，人家对你说话呢，你怎么能～也不～？*Hey, he's talking to you. How can you pay no attention to what he says?*

踩 动 step on；trample：对不起，～了您的脚。*Sorry for stepping on your toe!* / 他～在凳子上挂窗帘。*He stepped onto the stool to put up the curtains.* / 不小心一脚～到烂泥里了。*I stepped into the mud before I knew it.*

【踩水】［体］tread water

【踩线】［体］❶ foot fault ❷ commit a foot fault；footfault

cài

采 (构词成分)见下 ——另见 cǎi

【采地】(又作'采邑')fief；vassalage

菜 名 ❶ vegetable；greens：种～ *grow vegetables* ❷ (non-staple) food：上街买～ *go to the market to buy food* ❸ dish；course：一道～ *a course* / 川～ *Sichuan dishes；Sichuan cuisine* / 做～ *prepare the dishes；do the cooking* / 做四道～ *prepare a four-course meal* ❹ (edible) wild herbs：吃糠咽～ *barely keep alive on chaff and wild herbs*

【菜板】chopping board

【菜帮】outer leaves (of a cabbage, etc.)

【菜场】food market

【菜畜】livestock (raised for meat)

【菜单】menu；bill of fare

【菜刀】kitchen knife

【菜地】vegetable plot

【菜豆】kidney bean

【菜粉蝶】cabbage butterfly

【菜瓜】snake melon

【菜馆】〈方〉restaurant

【菜花】❶ cauliflower ❷ rape flower

【菜窖】vegetable cellar

【菜篮子】❶ shopping basket (for food)；food basket ❷ food supply：关心人民群众的～ *see that the people have plenty to eat*

【菜篮子工程】shopping basket programme—a programme for increasing food production

【菜牛】beef cattle

【菜农】vegetable grower

【菜谱】❶ menu；bill of fare ❷ cookery book

【菜畦】small sections of a vegetable plot；vegetable bed

【菜青】dark greyish green

【菜青虫】cabbage caterpillar

【菜色】a sickly pallor of one living on wild herbs；

a famished (or emaciated) look：面有～ *look famished*

【菜市】food market

【菜蔬】❶ vegetables or greens ❷ (vegetable and meat) dishes prepared for a meal or a feast

【菜薹】tender flower stalk (of garlic, rape, mustard, etc.)

【菜摊】vegetable stall

【菜心】heart (of a cabbage, etc.)

【菜肴】cooked dishes

【菜油】rapeseed oil; rape oil

【菜园】vegetable garden; vegetable farm

【菜子】(又作'菜籽') ❶ vegetable seeds ❷ rapeseed ◇ ～饼 rapeseed cake (usu. used as a fertilizer)；～油 同〖菜油〗

cān

参 动 ❶ join; enter; take part in：参战 ❷ refer; consult ❸call to pay one's respects to：参谒 / 参拜 ——另见 cēn；shēn

【参拜】❶ pay one's respects to (a superior)；present oneself to：大礼～ *present oneself to sb. ceremoniously* ❷ pay homage to sb. (before his tomb or image)

【参半】half; half-and-half：疑信～ *half believing, half doubting*

【参禅】(of Buddhists) sit in deep meditation

【参股】purchase of shares in enterprises

【参观】visit; have a look around：～工厂 *visit a factory* / ～名胜古迹 *go on sightseeing trips to scenic spots and historical monuments* / ～游览 *visit places of interest; go sightseeing* / 欢迎～。*Visitors are welcome*. ◇～团 visiting group

【参加】❶ join (a group, organization, etc.)；take part in (an activity)：～晚会 *go to an evening party* /～管理国家大事 *participate in the management of state affairs* ❷ give (advice, suggestion, etc.)：这件事你也来～点儿意见吧? *Come and give us your view on the matter, won't you?*

【参见】❶see (used in references)：～第九章。*See Chapter 9*. ❷pay one's respects to (a superior, etc.)

【参军】join the army; join up; enlist：这个青年要报名～。*That boy wants to enlist*.

【参看】❶ see (used in references)：～下面注释。*See the note below*. / ～第二十二页。*See page 22*. ❷ read sth. for reference; consult：他～了不少有关书刊。*He consulted a number of relevant books and periodicals*.

【参考】❶ consult; refer to：～历史文献 *consult historical documents* ❷reference：仅供～。*For reference only*. ◇～书 reference book；～书目 a list of reference books; bibliography；～资料 reference material

【参谋】❶［军］staff officer ❷ give advice：请你给我们～～看怎么办才好。*Please give us some advice as to what is the best way to do it*. ◇ ～长［军］chief of staff

【参评】be sent in for public appraisal or competitive selection：这次图书奖评比，他有两本著作～。*He has two of his works nominated for appraisal and selection for the Book Awards*.

【参赛】participate in a match or contest：～选手 *contestant*

【参事】counsellor; adviser

【参试】❶ take part in an experiment：～的科研人员 *scientific research personnel who take part in the experiment* ❷ take or sit for an exam：报员～ *sign up for the exam* / ～者达万人。*Around 10,000 people took the exam*.

【参数】［数］parameter

【参天】(of trees, etc.) reach to the sky; tower：～古树 *towering old trees*

【参谒】〈书〉❶ pay one's respects to (a superior) ❷ pay homage to sb. (before his tomb or image)

【参选】❶ enter into an election contest; run in an election：～的政界头面人物 *prominent political figures running in the election* ❷ enter a contest for public appraisal：～作品 *works entered for appraisal and selection (in a contest)*

【参议】〈书〉counsel; advise ◇～员 senator；～院 senate

【参与】(又作'参预') participate in; have a hand in; involve oneself in：～其事 *have a hand in the matter* / ～制订计划 *participate in the drawing up of a plan*. ◇ ～放款 participation loan；～意识 sense of participation

【参杂】mix; mingle

【参赞】❶ counsellor; councilor：商务～ *commercial counsellor* / 文化～ *cultural attaché* ❷〈书〉participate in planning; serve as an adviser：～军务 *participate in military planning*

【参展】supply exhibits for an exhibition; participate in an exhibition：～作品 *works on display (at an exhibition)* / ～厂家 *factories and enterprises participating in the exhibition*

【参战】enter a war; take part in a battle ◇ ～国 belligerent state

【参照】consult and follow：～原文作必要的修改 *consult the original and make some necessary changes* / 翻译这个句子非～上下文不可。*We can't translate this sentence without reference to the context*. ◇ ～物 object of reference

【参政】participate in government and political affairs ◇ ～议政 participate in the deliberation and administration of state affairs

【参酌】consider (a matter) in the light of actual conditions; deliberate：以上意见仅供～，切勿机械执行。*The afore-mentioned suggestions are for your consideration only. They are not to be followed blindly*.

餐 Ⅰ 动 eat：聚餐 Ⅱ 名 food; meal：西餐 / 中餐 Ⅲ 量 (for meals)：一日三～ *three meals a day*

【餐车】restaurant car; dining car; diner：列车上有

一节～。*There is a dining car on the train.*
【餐风宿露】同〖风餐露宿〗
【餐馆】restaurant
【餐盒】dining box; dinner pail
【餐巾】table napkin ◇～纸 napkin paper; paper napkin; serviette
【餐具】tableware; dinner service; dinner set
【餐厅】❶ dining room; dining hall ❷ restaurant
【餐位】seating in a restaurant or dining hall
【餐饮】food and drink: 提供～ *provide food and drinks* ◇～业 catering (trade)
【餐桌】dining table ◇ ～转盘 Lazy Susan

cán

残 Ⅰ 形 ❶ incomplete; deficient: ～稿 *an incomplete manuscript* / 这部书很好,可惜～了。*It is a very good book, but unfortunately it's incomplete.* ❷ remnant; remaining: ～敌 *remnants of the enemy forces* / ～冬 *the last days of winter* ❸ cruel; savage; barbarous; ferocious: 残暴 Ⅱ 动 injure; damage: 身～志不～ *broken in health but not in spirit*
【残暴】cruel and ferocious; brutal; savage
【残杯冷炙】the crumbs which fall from one's master's table; leftovers from a rich man's table
【残兵败将】remnants of a routed army: 收拾～,企图东山再起 *muster the remnants of the army, intending to stage a comeback*
【残部】remnants of sb.'s defeated troops
【残次】defective or substandard: ～品 *defective product* / 用～零件拼装的计算机 *computer assembled with substandard parts*
【残存】be left alive; survive: 大熊猫是一种～的古动物。*The giant panda is one of the surviving ancient animal species.*
【残废】❶ become disabled; be crippled: 他的双腿去年就～了。*He lost the use of both legs last year.* ❷ a disabled person; cripple ◇～军人 disabled armyman; ～证 certificate of disability
【残羹剩饭】(又作'残茶剩饭') remains of a meal; leftovers; crumbs from the table: 她把～倒进垃圾桶里。*She dumped the leftovers into the rubbish bin.*
【残骸】remains (of a person or animal); wreckage (of a building, machine, vehicle, etc.): 敌机～ *the wreckage of an enemy plane*
【残害】cruelly injure or kill: ～肢体 *cause bodily injury* / 侵略者到处～无辜老百姓。*Wherever they went the invaders slaughtered innocent civilians.*
【残花败柳】faded flowers and withered willows—fallen women
【残货】damaged or substandard goods; shopworn goods
【残疾】deformity: 他的腿有～,行动不便。*He's got a deformed leg, so he has difficulty getting about.* ◇～人 a disabled (or handicapped) person; ～人奥运会 Paralympics
【残迹】a remaining trace, sign, etc.; vestiges
【残局】❶ the final phase of a game of chess ❷ the situation after the failure of an undertaking or after social unrest: 收拾～ *clear up the mess; pick up the pieces*
【残酷】cruel; brutal; ruthless: ～的剥削 *ruthless exploitation* / ～的殖民统治 *brutal colonial rule* / ～的现实 *the harsh reality* / ～地杀害 *kill sb. in cold blood*
【残联】association of physically challenged persons
【残留】remain; be left over: 这里还～着战争的痕迹。*Traces of war still remain here.*
【残年】❶ the evening of life; declining years ❷ the last days of the year
【残篇断简】同〖断编残简〗
【残品】damaged article; defective goods
【残破】broken; dilapidated: 有些器皿在出土时已经～。*Some utensils were already broken when they were unearthed.*
【残缺】incomplete; with parts missing: 迄今仍未发现竹简的～部分。*The missing parts of the inscribed bamboo slips have not yet been discovered.*
【残缺不全】incomplete; fragmentary: 一套～的茶具 *an incomplete tea set* / 那套书已～。*That set of books is no longer complete.*
【残忍】cruel; ruthless: 他这样对待老年人,太～了。*It's really cruel of him to treat old people like that.*
【残杀】murder in cold blood; slaughter: ～无辜 *kill the innocent*
【残生】❶ one's remaining years ❷ one's wretched life
【残阳】the setting sun
【残余】remnants; remains; survivals; vestiges: 封建～ *remnants of feudalism; feudal remnants* / ～势力 *remaining (or surviving) forces*
【残垣断壁】broken walls
【残月】❶ the waning moon ❷ the setting moon: 晓风～ *breezes at dawn and the fading moon*
【残渣余孽】dregs of the old society
【残照】sunset glow; evening glow: 天边只留下一抹～。*There was only a trace of sunset glow left on the horizon.*

蚕 名 silkworm: 养～ *raise silkworms*
【蚕箔】a bamboo tray for breeding silkworms
【蚕蔟】a small bundle of straw, etc., for silkworms to spin cocoons on
【蚕豆】broad bean (the plant, the pod or the seed)
【蚕蛾】silk moth
【蚕茧】silkworm cocoon
【蚕眠】the inactive state of the silkworm before it sheds its skin
【蚕农】silkworm breeder; sericulturist
【蚕桑】silkworm breeding and mulberry growing (as an industry)
【蚕沙】silkworm excrement

【蚕山】〈方〉a cone-shaped bundle of straw, etc., for silkworms to spin cocoons on

【蚕食】nibble：～别国领土 *nibble at another country's territory* ◇ ～政策 the policy of nibbling at another country's territory

【蚕食鲸吞】nibble away like a silkworm or swallow like a whale—seize another country's territory by piecemeal encroachment or wholesale annexation

【蚕丝】natural silk; silk

【蚕蚁】newly-hatched silkworm

【蚕蛹】silkworm chrysalis

【蚕纸】silkworm egg sheet (a sheet of paper on which silk moths have laid eggs)

【蚕子】silkworm egg

惭 形 feel ashamed：惭愧

【惭愧】be ashamed：我没有完成任务，感到很～。*I feel quite ashamed that I have not fulfilled the task.*

cǎn

惨 形 ❶ miserable; tragic：他死得很～。*He died a tragic death.* ❷ cruel; brutal; merciless：～遭杀害 *be murdered in cold blood; be brutally killed* ❸ to a serious degree; disastrously：他们愈是捣乱，就失败得愈～。*The more trouble they make, the worse will be their downfall.*

【惨案】massacre：五卅～ *the May 30th Massacre (1925, in Shanghai)*

【惨白】deathly pale：脸色～ *look deathly pale*

【惨败】be crushingly (or disastrously) defeate

【惨不忍睹】too horrible (or tragic) to look at

【惨淡】❶ gloomy; dismal; dim：在～的星光下 *in the dim starlight* / 天色～。*It was gloomy weather.* / 市面～。*Business was dull.* ❷ take great pains：惨淡经营

【惨淡经营】keep (an enterprise, etc.) going by painstaking effort; take great pains to carry on one's work under difficult circumstances

【惨祸】a horrible disaster; a frightful calamity：球迷们疯狂地争斗起来，看台倒坍，酿成～。*When the football fans got into a frenzied fight, the spectators' stand collapsed and a horrible disaster occurred.*

【惨叫】give a horrible shriek; give a blood-curdling scream

【惨境】an extremely miserable condition; dire straits

【惨剧】a dreadful, fatal event; a tragic event; calamity; disaster：渡船翻了，一场～发生了。*The ferry capsized and a disaster occurred.*

【惨绝人寰】tragic beyond compare in this human world; extremely tragic：～的暴行 *an atrocity of unparalleled savagery* / 一场～的浩劫 *a holocaust tragic beyond compare*

【惨然】saddened; grieved：他听到这个不幸的消息，不禁～。*He couldn't but feel deeply grieved at this sad news.*

【惨杀】massacre; murder

【惨死】die a tragic death：他～于车祸。*He died a tragic death in a traffic accident.*

【惨痛】distressingly grievous; excruciatingly painful; bitter; agonizing：～的教训 *a bitter lesson* / 一起～的事件 *a most distressing incident*

【惨无人道】inhuman; brutal：遭受～的迫害 *be subjected to inhuman persecution*

【惨笑】a sad smile

【惨遭不幸】die a tragic death; meet a sad end

【惨重】heavy; grievous; disastrous：损失～ *suffer heavy (or grievous) losses* / ～失败 *a disastrous defeat* / 伤亡～ *suffer heavy casualties*

【惨状】a miserable condition; a pitiful or horrible sight：一声爆炸，霎时间血肉横飞，其～不忍卒睹。*A loud explosion sent flesh and blood flying in every direction—a sight too horrible to look at.*

càn

灿 (构词成分)见下

【灿烂】magnificent; brilliant; resplendent; splendid：～的阳光 *the bright sun; brilliant sunshine* / ～的民族文化 *splendid national culture* / 我们的前途光辉～。*Our prospects are bright.*

【灿然】bright; brilliant; resplendent

cāng

仓 名 storehouse; warehouse：粮食满～。*The granary is bursting with grain.*

【仓储】keep grain, goods, etc. in a storehouse：尽量避免商品在～过程中的损耗。*Avoid as much as possible the spoilage of goods during storage.*

【仓储式超市】warehouse-type supermarket

【仓储销售】cash and carry：～商店 *cash-and-carry store*

【仓促】(又作'仓猝','仓卒') hurried; hasty：我走得太～。*I left in too great a hurry.* / ～应战 *accept battle in haste* / 不要～下结论。*Don't jump to conclusions.* / 时间～，咱们还是马上出发边走边谈的好。*Time is pressing. We'd better leave right now and talk it over on our way.*

【仓房】warehouse; storehouse

【仓皇】(又作'仓黄') in a flurry; in panic：～逃窜 *flee in confusion; flee in panic; flee helter-skelter* / ～退却 *retreat in haste* ◇ ～失措 be scared out of one's wits; be panic-stricken

【仓库】warehouse; storehouse; depository：清理～ *take stock; check warehouse stocks* ◇ ～保管员 warehouseman

【仓鼠】hamster

【仓租】warehouse storage charges

伧 形 rude; rough

【伧俗】vulgar

沧 形 (of the sea) deep blue

【沧海】the deep blue sea; the sea

【沧海横流】the seas in turbulence—the country or the world in chaos

【沧海桑田】from seas into mulberry fields and from mulberry fields into seas—time brings great changes to the world

【沧海一粟】a drop in the ocean

【沧桑】〈略〉见〖沧海桑田〗

苍 形 ❶ dark green or blue: ～松 *green pines* ❷ grey; ashen: ～髯 *a grey beard*

【苍白】❶ pale; pallid; wan: 她脸色～。*She looks pale*. ❷ lifeless; flat: 这篇文章～无力。*This article is flat writing*.

【苍苍】〈文〉❶ grey: 他年近七十,两鬓～。*He is nearly seventy and greying at the temples*. ❷ dark blue: 天～,野茫茫。*The sky is blue, blue; and the steppe wide, wide*. ❸ luxuriant

【苍翠】(of trees, grass, etc.) green; verdant: 山峦～。*The hills are verdant*.

【苍耳】Siberian cocklebur (Xanthium sibiricum)

【苍黄】❶ greenish yellow: 病人面色～。*The patient has a sallow complexion*. ❷〈书〉black or yellow —changeable

【苍劲】❶ (of trees) old and hardy: 古松～挺拔。*The sturdy old pines stand tall and straight*. ❷ (of calligraphy or painting) vigorous; bold: 笔力～ *write or paint in bold, vigorous strokes* / 他的书法～有力。*His calligraphy is bold and vigorous*.

【苍老】❶ old (in appearance); hoary; (of an old man's voice) hoarse: 他显得～多了。*He looks much older than before*. / "谁呀?"一个～的声音从室内传出来。"*Who is it?" An old man's voice was heard from the room*. ❷ (of calligraphy or painting) vigorous; forceful: 这幅画笔势～遒劲,显出画家功力深厚。*This painting exhibits a force and vigour characteristic of a master's hand*.

【苍凉】desolate; bleak: 过去满目～的乡村,现在已经完全变了样。*The once desolate countryside has changed entirely*.

【苍鹭】heron

【苍茫】❶ vast; boundless: ～大地 *boundless land* / ～的大海 *vast seas* / 一片～的海天景色 *a vast expanse of sea and sky* ❷ indistinct: 夜色～。*The shades of dusk are deepening*.

【苍穹】〈文〉the vault of heaven; the firmament

【苍生】〈书〉the common people

【苍术】❶ [植] Chinese atractylodes (Atractylodes chinensis) ❷ [中] the rhizome of Chinese atractylodes

【苍天】Heaven

【苍鹰】goshawk

【苍蝇】fly; housefly ◇～拍(又作'苍蝇拍子') flyswatter

舱 名 ❶ cabin (of an airplane or ship): 客舱 ❷ module (of a spacecraft): 指挥舱

【舱口】hatchway; hatch ◇～盖 hatch door; hatch cover

【舱门】hatch door; cabin door

【舱面】deck ◇～货 deck cargo

【舱内货】underdeck cargo

【舱位】❶ cabin seat or berth ❷ shipping space

cáng

藏 动 ❶ hide; conceal: 钱～在箱子里。*The money was hidden in a trunk*. / 这人肚子里～不住话。*This chap can't keep anything to himself*. ❷ store; lay by: 阁楼上可以～好多东西。*We can store a lot of things in the attic*. ——另见 zàng

【藏垢纳污】(又作'藏污纳垢') shelter evil people and countenance evil practices: ～之所 *a sink of iniquity*

【藏奸】❶ harbour evil intentions: 笑里～ *hide one's evil intentions behind one's smiles* ❷〈方〉be unwilling to help others

【藏龙卧虎】(used esp. in) ～之地 *a place where dragons and tigers are hiding—a place where people of unusual ability are to be found*

【藏匿】conceal; hide; go into hiding: 那个罪犯在一个远房亲戚家里～了三个星期。*The criminal remained in hiding at a distant relative's place for three weeks*.

【藏身】hide oneself; go into hiding: 无处～ *have no place to hide* / ～之处 *hiding-place; hideout*

【藏书】❶ collect books: 他有～的爱好。*His hobby is book-collecting*. ❷ a collection of books; library: 他有很多珍贵的～。*He has a large collection of valuable books*.

【藏头露尾】hide the head but show the tail—hide one part of sth. only to reveal another

【藏掖】❶ try to cover up: 他做错了事,从不～躲闪。*He never tries to cover up or explain away his mistakes*. ❷ cover-up: 我全说了,没有一点儿～。*I've told you everything, I haven't held anything back*.

【藏拙】hide one's inadequacy by keeping quiet

【藏踪】conceal one's tracks

cāo

糙 形 rough; coarse: ～纸不好写字。*Rough paper is no good for writing*. / 这活儿做得太～。*This is very slipshod work*.

【糙粮】〈方〉coarse food grain

【糙米】brown rice; unpolished rice

【糙皮病】pellagra

操 I 动 ❶ grasp; hold: 他～刀就砍了过去。*He grabbed a knife and struck with it*. ❷ do; operate：操劳 / 操作 ❸ speak (a language or dialect)：～本地口音 *speak with a local accent* / 他～一口流利的英语。*He speaks fluent English*. Ⅱ 名 ❶ conduct；behaviour：操行 ❷ drill；exercise：体操

【操办】manage affairs；make preparations or arrangements for：～婚事 *make preparations for a wedding*

【操场】playground；sports ground；drill ground

【操持】manage；handle：～家务 *manage household affairs* / 这件事由你～。*I'll leave the matter in your hands*.

【操典】[军] drill regulations；drill manual；drill book

【操舵室】wheelhouse；pilothouse；steering room

【操劳】❶ work hard：她～过度，病倒了。*She overworked herself and fell ill*. ❷ take care；look after：这事请您多～。*Would you mind looking after this?*

【操练】drill；train

【操切】rash；hasty：不要～从事。*Don't act with undue haste*.

【操心】worry；take trouble；take pains：这件事你不必～了。*You needn't worry about it*. / 多少父母为子女操碎了心。*Many parents go to a lot of trouble for their children*.

【操行】behaviour or conduct (usu. of a student at school)

【操演】drill：学生在为运动会开幕式加紧～。*The students are drilling hard for the opening ceremony of the coming sports meet*.

【操之过急】act with undue haste：这事不可～。*This shouldn't be done in haste*. / 不宜～。*It's no good being overhasty (or overzealous)*.

【操纵】❶ operate；control：培养～新机器的工人 *train workers to operate the new machines* / 无线电～ *radio control* ❷ manipulate；rig：～市场 *rig the market* / ～表决机器 *tamper with the voting machine；manipulate the voting* / 幕后～ *manipulate from behind the scenes；pull strings* ◇～杆 operating lever；control rod；control stick；～价格 administered price；～室 control room；～台 control panel

【操作】operate；manipulate：避免～上的疏忽。*Avoid carelessness in manipulation*. / 他能独立～了。*He can operate the machines by himself*. ◇～程序 operation sequence；～程序图 flow diagram；flow chart；～代码 operation code；～规程 operating rules and regulations；～顺序 operations sequence；～系统 operating system；～性能 [机] serviceability

cáo

嘈

形 noisy

【嘈杂】noisy：人声～ *a hubbub of voices* / 机器声～刺耳。*The machine makes a deafening noise*.

槽

名 ❶ trough：水～ *water trough* ❷ groove；notch：开个～ *cut a notch* / 这个～挖得太深了。*The groove is made too deep*.

【槽床】troughstand

【槽坊】〈旧〉brewery；distillery

【槽钢】(又作'槽铁')[冶] channel iron

【槽谷】[地质] trough valley

【槽距】[机] slot pitch

【槽口】[机] notch

【槽探】[矿] trenching

【槽头】trough (in a livestock shed)：～兴旺 *a manger full of sturdy livestock*

【槽牙】molar

cǎo

草

Ⅰ 名 ❶ grass：羊在山上吃～。*The sheep are grazing on the hillside*. ❷ straw：～可以做饲料，也可以造纸。*Straw can be used both for fodder and for papermaking*. ❸ draft：草拟 Ⅱ 形 ❶ careless；rough：这几个字写得太～。*These characters are written in a sloppy hand*. ❷〈口〉female livestock or poultry：草鸡 / 草驴

【草案】draft (of a plan, law, etc.)：拟订一个计划～ *make out a draft plan*

【草包】❶ straw bag；straw sack ❷ a bungling oaf

【草本】herbaceous ◇～植物 herbs

【草草】carelessly；hastily：今天的报纸我只～地看过一遍。*I've only skimmed through today's newspapers*. ◇～了事 get a job done any old way；～收场 hastily wind up a matter

【草测】make a preliminary survey

【草叉】pitch-fork

【草场】meadow；pasture；grassland

【草创】start (an enterprise, etc.)：～时期 *initial (or pioneering) stage*

【草丛】a thick growth of grass

【草地】❶ grassland；meadow；pasture ❷ lawn ◇～网球 lawn tennis；

【草甸子】〈方〉grassy marshland

【草垫子】straw mattress；pallet

【草垛】haystack；hayrick

【草房】thatched cottage

【草稿】rough draft；preliminary draft：打个～ *make a rough draft*

【草根阶层】people at the grass roots；people of lower classes

【草菇】straw mushroom

【草荒】neglected farmland with more weeds than crops

【草灰】❶ plant ash ❷ ash grey

【草菅人命】treat human life as if it were not worth a straw；act with utter disregard for human life

【草浆】straw pulp (for making paper)

【草芥】trifle；mere nothing；trash：视如～ *regard as worthless；treat like dirt*

【草寇】〈旧〉robbers in the greenwood；brigands

【草兰】cymbidium；orchid
【草料】forage；fodder：我去给马喂点～。*I'll go and feed the horse.*
【草履虫】paramecium
【草绿】grass green
【草莽】❶ a rank growth of grass ❷ uncultivated land；wilderness ◇ ～英雄 a hero of the greenwood
【草帽】straw hat
【草帽缏】（又作'草帽辫'）plaited straw（for making hats，baskets，etc.）
【草莓】strawberry（the plant or the fruit）
【草棉】the cotton plant
【草木】grass and trees；plants and trees
【草木灰】plant ash
【草木皆兵】every bush and tree looking like an enemy soldier—a state of extreme suspicion and fear：你们不要神经过敏，弄得～了。*Don't be oversensitive and suspect everybody.* ——另见〖风声鹤唳，草木皆兵〗
【草木犀】［植］sweet clover
【草拟】draw up；draft：请你～一个开会通知。*Please draft a notice for the meeting.*
【草棚】a thatched shack；a thatched shed
【草皮】sod；turf（used for making lawns or protecting dams，banks，etc.，or as fertilizer）
【草坪】lawn
【草签】initial：～协定 *initial an agreement* / 协议书已由双方代表～。*Representatives from both sides have initialled the agreement.* ◇ ～合同 sign a referendum contract；～文本 initialed text
【草裙舞】hula；hula-hula
【草石蚕】［植］❶ Chinese artichoke（Stachys sieboldii）❷ the plant's pagoda-shaped stem tuber（popularly known as 宝塔菜）
【草食】herbivorous：～动物 *herbivorous animal；herbivore*
【草书】（in Chinese calligraphy）cursive script
【草率】sloppy；careless；slapdash；perfunctory：这件事你做得太～了。*You did a sloppy job.* ◇ ～从事 act rashly；take hasty action
【草酸】［化］oxalic acid
【草头王】king of the bushes—a bandit chief
【草图】sketch
【草屋】thatched hut
【草席】straw mat
【草鞋】straw sandals：打一双～ *weave a pair of straw sandals*
【草药】herbal medicine
【草鱼】grass carp
【草原】grasslands；prairie
【草约】draft treaty；draft agreement；protocol
【草纸】❶ rough straw paper ❷ toilet paper
【草子】grass seed

cè

册 Ⅰ 名 volume；book：装订成～ *be bound into book form* Ⅱ 量 copy；volume：这本书已销售十万～。*100,000 copies of the book have been sold.* / 这部书一共六～。*This book is in six volumes.*
【册封】（of a king，emperor，etc.）confer a title upon sb.：皇帝～她为贵妃。*The emperor bestowed on her the title of imperial concubine of the highest rank.*
【册页】an album of paintings or calligraphy
【册子】book；volume

厕 名 lavatory；toilet；washroom；W.C.：男～ *men's（room or toilet）* / 女～ *women's（room or toilet）*
【厕所】lavatory；toilet；W.C.

侧 Ⅰ 名 side：左（右）～ *the left（right）side* / 公路两～种着杨树。*Poplars are planted on both sides of the highway.* Ⅱ 动 incline to one side：～着身子睡 *sleep on one's side*
【侧柏】［植］oriental arborvitae
【侧吹转炉】［冶］side-blown converter
【侧耳】incline the ear；strain one's ears：～而听 *listen attentively；be all ears*
【侧根】［植］lateral root
【侧航】crabbing
【侧击】make a flank attack
【侧记】（usu. used in news report headings）sidelights：《出口商品展览会～》*Sidelights on the Export Commodities Exhibition*
【侧力】side force；lateral force
【侧门】side door；side entrance：入场请走正门，退场请走～。*Please enter through the main entrance and exit through the side doors.*
【侧面】side；flank；aspect：我们要从～了解一下情况。*We should find out about the situation from indirect sources.* / 这篇短篇小说反映了当前农村改革的一个～。*This short story presents one aspect of the present agricultural reform.* ◇ ～像 profile
【侧目】cast sidelong glances（with fear or indignation）：权尊势重，朝野～。*Exalted and powerful，he was feared by officials and common citizens alike.* ◇～而视 look askance at sb.（with fear or indignation）
【测评】to observe and evaluate
【侧身】turn or move sideways：你侧着身就能挤过去。*You can squeeze through sideways.* / 战士们～匍匐前进。*The soldiers advanced crawling on their sides.*
【侧石】kerbstone；kerb
【侧视】look sideways ◇ ～图 side view；profile
【侧室】side room—a concubine
【侧手翻】［体］cartwheel；turn a cartwheel
【侧卫】［军］flank guard
【侧卧】lie on one's side
【侧线】lateral line（of fishes，amphibians，round worms，etc.）
【侧旋】［体］sidespin；cut a sidespin
【侧压力】［物］lateral pressure

【侧芽】［植］axillary bud
【侧翼】［军］flank
【侧影】profile；silhouette
【侧泳】［体］sidestroke；do the sidestroke
【侧重】lay special emphasis on：这篇文章～讨论交通运输问题。*In this article, special emphasis is laid on problems of communications and transportation.*

测

动 ❶ survey；fathom；measure：～雨量 *gauge rainfall* / ～温度 *gauge temperature* / ～风向 *determine the wind direction* / ～深浅 *measure the depth of*；*fathom* ❷ infer；conjecture：变幻莫测
【测程仪】mileage meter；(navigation) log
【测电笔】test pencil (for detecting and measuring electricity)
【测定】ascertain by measuring or surveying；determine：～船只方位 *take a ship's bearings* / 航线已经～。*The route (of a ship or plane) has been surveyed and determined.* ◇～结果 result of determination
【测度】estimate；infer：根据风向～，今天不会下雨。*Judging by the direction of the wind, it won't rain today.*
【测风经纬仪】pilot balloon theodolite
【测风气球】pilot balloon
【测杆】surveying rod；measuring staff
【测候】［气］astronomical and meteorological observation
【测候网】［气］reseau
【测谎器】polygraph；lie detector
【测绘】survey and drawing；mapping；cartography：地形～ *topographical survey* ◇～飞机 air-mapping plane；～卫星 cartographic satellite；～员 surveyor-draftsman；surveyor-cartographer
【测井】［油］well logging
【测距仪】range finder
【测力计】［物］dynamometer
【测量】survey；measure；gauge：～地形 *survey the topography* / ～河道 *survey the river course* / 大地～ *geodetic survey* / 航空～ *air survey* / ～仪器 *surveying instrument* ◇～学 surveying；～员 surveyor
【测漏】track down a leak
【测评】observe and evaluate
【测深仪】fathometer；depth-sounder
【测试】❶ test (a machine, meter or apparatus)：产品须经～方能出厂。*All products must be tested before leaving the factory.* ❷ test (a student's proficiency)：～英语水平 *give (students) an English proficiency test* ◇～报告 test report；～程序 test program；～技术 testing technique
【测算】measure and calculate
【测向仪】goniometer
【测斜仪】inclinometer
【测验】❶ put to the test；test：～机器的性能 *test the performance of a machine* / 老师～学生的拼写。*The teacher tested the students in spelling.* ❷ test；quiz：算术～ *an arithmetic test (or quiz)*
【测云气球】［气］ceiling balloon
【测云器】［气］nephoscope
【测震学】seismometry
【测字】fortune-telling by analysing the component parts of a Chinese character；glyphomancy ◇～先生 glyphomancer
【测醉器】drunkometer

恻

形 sorrowful；sad
【恻隐】〈书〉feel compassion for sb.
【恻隐之心】compassion：～，人皆有之。*Compassion is common to all men.* / 他对那个孤儿起了～。*His heart went out to the orphan.*

策

Ⅰ 名 ❶ bamboo or wooden slips used for writing on in ancient China ❷ questions on current affairs set for the imperial examinations ❸ plan；scheme：献计献～ *suggest ways and means* Ⅱ 动 whip (a horse) with a riding crop：～马前进 *whip a horse on*
【策动】instigate；engineer；stir up：～政变 *plot to stage a coup d'état* / ～农民造反 *engineer a peasant rebellion*
【策反】instigate rebellion within the enemy camp；incite defection
【策划】plan；plot；scheme：～作战方案 *make a battle plan* / ～阴谋 *hatch a plot* / 幕后～ *plot behind the scenes*
【策励】encourage；spur on：时刻～自己 *constantly spur oneself ahead*
【策略】❶ tactics：制订对敌斗争的～ *work out the tactics of our struggle against the enemy* ❷ tactful：这样做很不～。*That's not a very tactful way to do it.*
【策论】an essay on current affairs presented to the emperor as advice on government policy
【策士】counsellor
【策应】［军］support by coordinated action
【策源地】place of origin；source (of a war or a social movement)：战争～ *a source of war*；*a hotbed of war*

cēn

参

(构词成分)见下 ——另见 cān；shēn
【参差】uneven；not uniform
【参差不齐】uneven；not uniform：同学们的汉语水平～。*The students have different levels of proficiency in Chinese.*

céng

层

Ⅰ 量 ❶ storey；floor：十五～大楼 *a fifteen-storey building* / 我住一～。*I live on the ground floor.* / 她住二～。*She lives on the first floor.* ❷ a component part in a sequence：这段文章有两

～意思。*This article has two levels of discourse.* / 他这话还有一～意思。*What he said has further implications.* ❸ layer; stratum: 桌上积了厚厚的一～灰尘。*The desk is covered with a thick layer of dust.* / 湖上结了一～薄冰。*A thin layer of ice formed on the lake.* Ⅱ 名 level: 层次 Ⅲ 形 one on top of another; overlapping: 层峦叠嶂

【层报】report a matter to the higher authorities level by level: 此事已经～备案。*The matter has been reported to our superiors at each level for the record.*

【层层】layer upon layer; ring upon ring: ～包围 *surround ring upon ring* / ～设防 *set up successive lines of defence; erect defensive works in depth* / ～把关 *check at each level*

【层出不穷】*emerge in an endless stream*: 新生事物～。*New things are emerging one after another.*

【层次】❶ arrangement of ideas (in writing or speech): 这篇文章～不清。*This article lacks unity and coherence.* ❷ administrative levels: 为了提高工作效率，必须减少办事机构的～，精简人员。*To raise efficiency, we should simplify the administrative structure and reduce the staff.* ❸ [摄] gradation

【层叠】one on top of another: 层层叠叠的雪峰 *range upon range of snow-capped mountains*

【层高】the number of stories and the height of a building

【层见叠出】occur frequently; appear repeatedly

【层理】[地质] bedding; stratification

【层流】[物] laminar flow

【层峦】range upon range of hills: ～叠翠 *range upon range of green hills* / ～起伏 *range upon range of undulating hills*

【层峦叠嶂】peaks rising one upon another; range upon range of hills

【层压】[化] lamination

【层云】[气] stratus

【层子】[物] straton ◇ ～模型 [物] straton model

曾 副 (indicating that an action once happened or a state once existed): 几年前我～见过她一面。*I met her once several years ago.* / 我未～听说过这样的事。*I've never heard of such a thing.* ——另见 zēng

【曾经】(indicating that an action once happened or a state once existed): 她～参加过校队。*She once played for the school team.* / 我～在美国住过两年。*I lived in the United States for two years.*

【曾经沧海】have sailed the seven seas—have much experience of life; have seen much of the world

【曾经沧海难为水】one who has seen the ocean thinks nothing of mere rivers—to a sophisticated person there is nothing new under the sun

cèng

蹭 动 ❶ rub; scrape; scratch: 小猫在桌子腿上～痒痒。*The kitten is scratching its back against the table leg.* / 我的手～破了皮。*I grazed my hand.* ❷ rub against sth. and get stained: 油漆没干，留神别～了。*The paint is not dry. Be careful that you don't stain your clothes.* / 你上哪儿去了？～了一身泥。*Where have you been? Your clothes are all muddy.* ❸ move slowly: 他的腿疼得厉害，只能一步一步地往前～。*His legs hurt terribly. He could only drag himself along inch by inch.* / 快干吧！别～时间了。*Get on with your work. Don't dawdle.* ❹〈方〉cadge; scrounge: 他常～吃～喝。*He's always cadging meals and drinks.* / 坐～车 *go on a bus or train without buying a ticket*

chā

叉 Ⅰ 名 ❶ fork: 钢～ *steel fork* / 干草～ *hayfork; pitchfork* / 餐～ (*table*) *fork* ❷ X-sign; cross: 在每个错别字上打个～ *put a cross above each wrongly written word* Ⅱ 动 work with a fork; fork: ～草上垛 *pitch hay onto a stack* / ～鱼 *spear fish* ——另见 chǎ

【叉车】forklift

【叉烧】grill (marinated pork): ～肉 *grilled pork* / ～包 *steamed buns stuffed with diced grilled pork*

【叉手】raise one's folded hands to one's chin to salute sb.

【叉腰】akimbo: 她双手～站着。*She stood with arms akimbo.*

【叉子】fork

杈 名 wooden fork; hayfork; pitchfork ——另见 chà

差 Ⅰ 名 ❶ difference; dissimilarity: 差别 ❷ [数] difference Ⅱ 副〈书〉only just; barely: ～可 *barely passable* ——另见 chà; chāi; cī

【差别】difference; disparity: 年龄～ *disparity in age* / 数量与质量上的～ *quantitative and qualitative differences* ◇ ～关税 differential rates of duty; differential duties; ～汇率 differential tax rates; ～阈限 difference limen (or threshold)

【差错】❶ mistake; error; slip: 她抄的这个文件没有一点儿～。*There is not a single mistake in the paper she copied.* ❷ mishap; accident: 万一这孩子出了～怎么办？*What if anything should happen to the child?*

【差动】[机] differential: ～齿轮 *differential gear* / ～滑轮 *differential pulley*

【差额】difference; differential; balance; margin: 补足～ *make up the balance* (*or difference*) ◇ ～税 variable levies; ～选举 multi-candidate election

【差价】price difference: 地区～ *regional price differences* / 季节～ *seasonal price differences; seasonal variations in price* ◇ ～关税 variable import levy

【差距】❶ gap; disparity: 在成绩面前找~。*Try to find out where you fall short when you have achieved success.* ❷［机］difference: 检测工件与设计标准之间的~ *see if there's any difference between the part and the set standard*
【差强人意】just passable
【差误】mistake; error; slip
【差异】difference; divergence; discrepancy; diversity: 这两个地区气候~很大。*These two regions differ greatly in climate.*
【差之毫厘，谬以千里】(又作'差之毫厘，失之千里') An error the breadth of a single hair can lead you a thousand li astray.

插 动 ❶ stick in; insert: 把插头~上 *insert the plug in a socket; plug in* / 把双手~在口袋里 *put one's hands in one's pockets* / 把门~上 *bolt the door* / 山峰高~入云。*The peaks penetrate into the clouds.* ❷ interpose; insert: 他说个没完，别人半句话也~不进。*He talked on and on and nobody else could get a word in.*
【插班】(of a new or transferred student) join a class in the middle of the course; be placed in an appropriate class
【插翅难飞】(又作'插翅难逃') unable to escape even if given wings: 密密层层的天罗地网，我看他~。*He's closely hemmed in on all sides. I don't think he could possibly get away even if he grew wings.*
【插杠子】poke one's nose into sb.'s business; meddle; butt in: 别到处~! *Don't poke your nose in everybody's business.* / 我没想到他会在我们中间~。*Little did I imagine that he would try to drive a wedge between us.*
【插管】［医］intubate ◇ ~法［医］intubation
【插花】❶ arrange flowers in a vase, basket, etc. ❷ insert sth. amidst things of another kind; mix; mingle
【插话】❶ interpose a remark, etc.; chip in: 这时老张插了话，补充了一些新例子。*At this point Lao Zhang chipped in with some fresh examples.* ❷ a remark interposed ❸ digression; episode: 这一段~使她的报告生动多了。*This digression added to the liveliness of her talk.*
【插科打诨】(of actors) make impromptu comic gestures and remarks; make gags
【插口】［电］socket; jack
【插屏】［工美］table plaque
【插曲】❶［音］interlude ❷ a song in a film or play ❸ episode; interlude: 双方谈判中的一个~ *an episode in the negotiations between the two parties*
【插入】❶ insert: 这本书再版时~了新的一章。*A new chapter is included in the second edition.* ❷［电］plug in: ~部件 *plug-in unit* ◇ ~程序 plugged program; ~镜头 cut-in; interscene
【插入式耳机】insert earphone
【插入语】［语］parenthesis
【插身】❶ squeeze in; edge in: 很难~ *difficult to squeeze in* ❷ take part in; get involved in: 他不想~在这场纠纷中间。*He doesn't want to get involved in this dispute.*
【插手】❶ take part; lend a hand: 人够多了，您就不用~了。*You don't have to join in, there are more than enough people on the job already.* ❷ have a hand in; poke one's nose into; meddle in: 想不到她会插上一手。*We never thought she would poke her nose into this.*
【插条】❶ transplant a cutting ❷ cutting
【插头】［电］plug: 三脚~ *a three-pin plug*
【插图】illustration (artistic or scientific in nature); plate: 书中有几幅彩色~。*The book has several colour plates.* ◇ ~本 illustrated edition
【插销】❶ bolt (for a door, window, etc.) ❷［电］plug
【插叙】narration interspersed with flashbacks
【插秧】transplant rice seedlings (or rice shoots) ◇ ~机 rice transplanter
【插页】insert; inset
【插足】put one's foot in
【插嘴】interrupt; chip in: 别人说话，你别~。*You shouldn't interrupt when others are talking.* / 她真爱~。*She always loves to chip in her own two cents' worth.*
【插座】［电］socket; outlet: 弹簧~ *cushion socket*

喳 (构词成分)见下 ——另见 zhā
【喳喳】whisper: 她在她妈妈耳边~了两句。*She whispered a few words in her mother's ear.*

chá

茬 名 ❶ stubble: 麦~ *wheat stubble* ❷ crop: 这块菜地一年种几~? *How many crops can this vegetable plot produce a year?* / 二~韭菜 *the second crop of Chinese chives*
【茬口】❶ crops for rotation: 选好~，实行合理轮作 *select the right crops and rotate them rationally* ❷ soil on which a crop has been planted and harvested: 西红柿~壮，种白菜挺合适。*A crop of tomatoes enriches the soil and makes it suitable for growing cabbage.*

茶 名 ❶ tea (the plant or its leaves): 种~ *grow tea* / 采~ *pick tea (leaves)* / 这儿产~。*Tea is produced here.* ❷ tea (the drink): 沏~ *make tea* / 浓(淡)~ *strong (weak) tea* / 咱们喝点儿~吧。*Let's have some tea.* / 请你给我倒杯~。*Please give me a cup of tea.* ❸ certain kinds of drink or liquid food: 杏仁~ *almond paste*
【茶杯】teacup
【茶场】tea plantation
【茶匙】teaspoon
【茶点】tea and pastries; refreshments
【茶碟儿】saucer (for holding a teacup)
【茶饭】tea and rice—food and drink; food: 不思~ *have no appetite*

【茶房】〈旧〉waiter (who serves tea and does odd jobs in a hotel, teahouse, or theatre, or on a ship or train)
【茶缸子】mug
【茶倌】〈旧〉teahouse waiter
【茶馆】teahouse：开～ *run a teahouse*
【茶褐色】dark brown
【茶壶】teapot
【茶花】camellia
【茶话会】a tea party at which the participants chat or give talks
【茶会】tea party
【茶几】tea table; teapoy; side table
【茶晶】citrine; yellow quartz
【茶具】tea set; tea-things; tea service
【茶客】❶ customer of a teahouse ❷〈旧〉tea dealer; tea merchant
【茶楼】a teahouse with two or more storeys
【茶末】tea dust
【茶农】tea grower
【茶盘】(又作'茶盘子') tea tray; teaboard
【茶钱】❶ payment for tea (in a teahouse) ❷〈旧〉tip
【茶色】dark brown：～玻璃 *brown-coloured glass*
【茶食】cakes and sweetmeats
【茶树】tea shrub; tea tree
【茶水】tea or plain boiled water (supplied to walkers, trippers, etc.) ◇～站 tea-stall set up for an occasion
【茶摊】roadside tea-stall：那姑娘摆过～，卖过大碗茶。*That girl once set up a roadside stall and sold big bowls of tea to passersby.*
【茶亭】tea-booth; tea-kiosk
【茶托】saucer (for holding a teacup)
【茶碗】(handleless) teacup; tea-bowl
【茶锈】tea stain
【茶叶】tea leaves; tea：买一百克～ *buy 100 grams of tea* ◇～蛋 tea eggs；～罐 tea caddy; tea canister
【茶役】同〖茶房〗
【茶油】tea-seed oil; tea oil
【茶余饭后】(又作'茶余酒后') over a cup of tea or after a meal：这些轶事可作～的谈助。*These anecdotes are good topics for after-dinner conversation.*
【茶园】❶ tea plantation ❷ a place where tea and soft drinks are served; tea garden
【茶盅】handleless teacup
【茶砖】tea brick
【茶座】❶ tea-stall with seats：树阴下面有～儿。*There's a tea-stall with seats under the shady trees.* ❷ seats in a teahouse or tea garden：这家茶馆有五十多个～儿。*There are over fifty seats in this teahouse.*

查 动 ❶ check; examine：～卫生 *make a public health and sanitation check (or inspection)* / ～血 *have a blood test* ❷ look into; investigate：～一～事故的原因 *find out the cause of an accident* / ～过他的履历吗？*Have you looked into his antecedents?* or *Have you checked his curriculum vitae?* ❸ look up; consult：～字典 *look up a word in the dictionary; consult a dictionary* / ～资料 *consult reference materials (on a subject)*
【查办】investigate and deal with accordingly：撤职～ *dismiss (or discharge) sb. from his post and prosecute him*
【查抄】make an inventory of a criminal's possessions and confiscate them
【查处】investigate and prosecute
【查档】consult the files
【查点】check the number or amount of; make an inventory of：～出席人数 *check the number of people present; check the attendance* / ～存货 *make an inventory of the goods in stock; take stock*
【查对】check and verify：～材料 *check the data* / ～原文 *check against the original (text, manuscript, etc.)* / ～数字 *verify the figures* / ～无误 *examined and found correct; verified*
【查房】(of doctors, nurses, etc.) make (or go) the rounds of the wards：值班护士每夜查两次房。*Nurses on duty make two rounds of the wards during the night.*
【查访】go around and make inquiries; investigate：～案情 *investigate the details of a crime*
【查封】seal up; close down：～伪政府大楼 *seal up the office building of the puppet government* / ～敌产 *seal up and confiscate enemy property*
【查号台】(at a telephone exchange) directory inquiries; information
【查户口】check residence cards; check on household occupants
【查获】hunt down and seize; ferret out; track down：～逃犯 *track down a fugitive criminal* / ～大批走私毒品 *track down and seize a large shipment of smuggled drugs*
【查禁】ban; prohibit; suppress：依法～淫秽书刊 *have pornographic literature banned according to law* / 严格～走私活动 *rigorously suppress smuggling*
【查究】investigate; try to ascertain (cause, responsibility, etc.); look into and find out：～责任 *find out who should be held responsible*
【查勘】survey; prospect：～地形 *survey the terrain* / ～地界 *survey the boundaries of a piece of land* / ～矿产资源 *prospect for mineral deposits*
【查看】look over; examine：～证件 *check the certificates* / ～账目 *examine the accounts* / ～水情 *look into the water or flood situation*
【查考】investigate; try to ascertain; do research on：～中国古时有关地震的全部文献 *study all available literature about earthquakes in ancient China*
【查明】prove through investigation; find out; ascertain：～事实真相 *find out the truth; ascertain the facts* / ～起因 *find out the cause* / 现已

～ *it has been established that; investigation reveals that*

【查票】examine (or check) tickets

【查铺】[军] go the rounds of the beds (in barracks) at night; bed check: 干部坚持～制度。*The officers make it a regular practice to go the rounds of the men's beds at night.*

【查讫】checked

【查清】make a thorough investigation of; check up on: ～某人的来历 *find out sb.'s background; check up on sb.* / ～一件事情的来龙去脉 *find out how sth. started and developed*

【查哨】[军] go the rounds of guard posts; inspect the sentries

【查收】(usu. used in a letter, note, etc.) check and accept (what is sent herewith): 寄上样品十种,请～。*Please find ten samples enclosed herewith.*

【查税】make a tax inspection

【查问】❶ inquire about ❷ question; interrogate: ～证人 *interrogate a witness* / ～口令 *challenge for a password*

【查无实据】investigation reveals no evidence (against the suspect): 事出有因,～。*An investigation was called for, but no evidence was found.*

【查询】inquire about: ～地址 *inquire about sb.'s address* / ～行李下落 *inquire about the whereabouts of the luggage*

【查验】check; examine: ～护照 *examine a passport* / 海关凭原入境申报单～放行。*Customs clearance shall be based on inspection of the original declaration made at the time of entry.*

【查夜】❶ go the rounds at night ❷ night patrol

【查阅】consult (books, magazines, papers, etc.); look up: ～技术资料 *consult technical data; look up technical literature*

【查账】check (or audit) accounts: 下星期要查你们单位的账。*We'll start to audit your accounts next week.*

【查找】look for: ～失主 *try to find the owner of the lost property* / ～资料 *gather data*

【查照】〈书〉please note (and act accordingly): 希～办理。*Please note and take appropriate action.*

【查证】investigate and verify; check: 证据必须～核实。*Evidence must be examined and verified.* / ～属实 *be checked and found to be true; be verified*

搽 动 put (powder, ointment, etc.) on the skin; apply: ～雪花膏 *put on vanishing cream* / ～药 *apply ointment, lotion, etc.* / ～粉 *powder one's face, etc.*

楂 名 ❶ short, bristly hair or beard; stubble: 胡子～ *a stubbly beard* ❷ 同〖茬〗——另见 zhā

察 动 examine; look into; scrutinize: 观察

【察访】make firsthand observations and inquiries; make an investigation trip: 暗中～ *make a secret investigation trip*

【察觉】be conscious of; become aware of; perceive: ～到一个盗窃国家机密的阴谋 *discover a plot to steal government secrets* / 开始我没有～到他有病。*At first I wasn't aware that he was ill.*

【察看】watch; look carefully at; observe; inspect: ～风向 *watch which way the wind is blowing* / ～现场 *inspect the scene*

【察探】investigate; detect; scout: ～敌情 *scout an area to obtain information about the enemy; gather intelligence about the enemy*

【察言观色】carefully weigh up a person's words and closely watch his expression; watch a person's every mood: 她善于～,理会经理的心思。*She is good at watching the manager's every mood and guessing his thoughts.*

碴 动〈方〉be cut (by broken glass, china, etc.): 小心别让碎玻璃～了手! *Mind you don't cut yourself on the broken glass!*

【碴儿】❶ broken pieces; fragments: 冰～ *small pieces of ice* / 玻璃～ *fragments of glass* ❷ sharp edge of broken glass, china, etc.: 碰到碗～上,手指头拉了个口子。*I happened to touch the sharp edge of the broken bowl and cut my finger.*

檫 名 sassafras (a tree)

chǎ

叉 动 part so as to form a fork; fork: ～着腿站着 *stand with one's legs apart* ——另见 chā

镲 名 small cymbals

chà

汊 名 a branch of a river

杈 名 (tree) branch: 树杈 ——另见 chā

【杈子】(tree) branch

岔 Ⅰ 名 ❶ branching off; forked: 岔路 ❷ 同〖岔子〗 Ⅱ 动 turn off the main road: 自行车下了公路～上了小道。*The cyclist turned off the highway onto a side road.*

【岔开】❶ branch off; diverge: 线路在这儿～了。*The line branches here.* ❷ diverge to (another topic); change the subject (of conversation): 两个人正要争吵,我给～了。*A quarrel was starting between the two of them, but I headed it off.* ❸ stagger: 把休假日～ *stagger the days off*

【岔口】fork (in a road): 他们一直把他送到～。*They saw him straight to the fork in the road.*

【岔路】(又作'岔道儿') branch road; byroad; side road

【岔气】feel a pain in the chest when breathing

【岔子】❶ 同〖岔路〗❷ accident; trouble: 他开了好几年卡车,从没有出过~。*He has been a truck driver for years and never had an accident.* / 你放心吧,出不了~。*Don't worry, nothing will go wrong.*

诧 动 be surprised: 诧异

【诧异】be surprised; be astonished: ~的神色 *a surprised look* / 听到这个突如其来的消息,我们都十分~。*We were all astonished at the unexpected news.*

衩 名 vent or slit in the sides of a garment

刹 名 Buddhist temple or monastery: 古~ *an ancient Buddhist temple* ——另见 shā

【刹那】(又作'刹时') instant; a split second: 一~ *in an instant; in a flash; in the twinkling of an eye* / ~间,他倒在地上,不省人事。*Suddenly he collapsed and lost consciousness.*

姹 形 〈文〉beautiful

【姹紫嫣红】deep purples and bright reds —beautiful flowers: 公园里百花盛开,~,十分绚丽。*With lovely flowers everywhere, the park is a blaze of colour.*

差 Ⅰ 动 ❶ differ from; fall short of: 我们离父母的要求还~得远。*We still fall far short of what our parents expect of us.* ❷be less than; be short of: 一个月~两天 *two days less than a month* / ~七天不到一年 *seven days short of a year* / ~十分四点 *ten (minutes) to four* / ~两个人 *two people short* Ⅱ 形 ❶wrong: 这你可说~了。*You're wrong there.* ❷ not up to standard; poor: 成绩不算太~。*The results are by no means poor.* / 这个街道工厂设备~,可是产品并不~。*The neighbourhood factory's equipment is not up to much, but its products are not at all bad.* ——另见 chā; chāi; cī

【差不多】❶ about the same; similar: 姐妹俩长相~。*The two sisters look very much alike.* / 他们俩高矮~。*The two of them are about the same height.* ❷ just about right; just about enough; not far off; not bad: 麦子熟得~了,该割了。*The wheat is just about ripe enough to be cut.* ❸ almost; nearly: 我~等了两个小时。*I waited for nearly two hours.* / 你比我~高一头。*You're almost a head taller than me.* / ~一半同学都学过英语。*Nearly half the students have learned some English before.*

【差不多的】the average person: ~都知道这件事了,你还不知道? *Practically everyone knows all about it, and you don't?*

【差点儿】❶ not quite up to the mark; not good enough: 她的技术还~。*Her technique is not quite up to the mark.* / 这支笔比那支笔~。*This pen is not as good as that one.* ❷ almost; nearly; on the verge of: 我~没赶上车。*I almost missed the bus.* / 那个问题可难了,我~没答上来。*The question was so difficult I almost failed to answer it.*

【差劲】(of quality, ability, etc.) no good; disappointing: 这条路坑坑洼洼的,太~了。*The road is no good, it's rough and full of holes.* / 你这人真~,说话不算数。*You didn't keep your word; you disappointed me.*

【差生】slow student; poor student: 帮助~补习功课 *help a slow student with his lessons*

chāi

拆 动 ❶ tear open; take apart: ~信 *open a letter* / ~机器 *disassemble a machine; take a machine apart; strip a machine* / 把这个组~了。*Break up the group.* ❷ pull down; dismantle: ~房子 *pull down a house* / ~桥 *dismantle a bridge* / ~帐篷 *strike a tent* / 把旧毛衣~了重新织一下 *unravel an old sweater and reknit it*

【拆白党】〈方〉a gang of swindlers

【拆除】dismantle; tear down; demolish: ~城墙 *tear down (or demolish) a city wall* / ~破房子 *pull down a dilapidated old house*

【拆穿】expose; unmask: ~骗局 *expose a fraud* ◇ ~西洋镜 strip off the camouflage; expose sb.'s tricks

【拆东墙,补西墙】tear down the east wall to repair the west wall—reinforce one place at the expense of another; rob Peter to pay Paul

【拆封】open up a seal (of a door, a letter, etc.)

【拆股】dissolve a partnership

【拆毁】demolish; pull down; tear down: 侵略军强行~民房。*The invading troops tore down the people's houses.*

【拆伙】dissolve a partnership; part company

【拆借】〈方〉a short-term loan made at a daily interest

【拆开】take apart; open; separate: 把机器~ *disassemble a machine* / 他能摸着黑儿把机枪~再装上。*He can strip and reassemble a machine gun in the dark.*

【拆迁】have an old building pulled down and its occupants move elsewhere ◇ ~户 households or units relocated due to building demolition

【拆墙脚】undermine; pull away a prop: 投机倒把是拆社会主义的墙脚。*Speculation undermines socialism.*

【拆散】(chāisǎn) break (a set): 这是整套的,别~了。*These pieces belong together, don't break the set.*

【拆散】(chāisàn) break up (a marriage, family, group, etc.)

【拆台】cut the ground from under sb.'s feet; pull away a prop: 工作要互相支持,不要互相~。*We should help and not hinder each other in our work.* / 你一定来,可别拆我的台。*Be sure to come, don't let me down.*

【拆洗】wash after removing the padding or lining;

take apart and clean：～棉被 *wash a quilt after removing the padding* / ～打字机 *take apart and clean a typewriter*
【拆线】take out stitches (in surgery) ◇ ～刀 seam ripper
【拆卸】dismantle；disassemble；dismount
钗 名 hairpin (formerly worn by women for adornment)：金～ *a gold hairpin*
差 Ⅰ 动 send on an errand；dispatch：～人去送封信 *send a letter by messenger* / ～他去办件事 *send (or dispatch) him on an errand* Ⅱ 名 errand；job ——另见 chā；chà；cī
【差旅费】allowances for a business trip
【差遣】send sb. on an errand or mission；dispatch；assign：听候～ *await assignment* / 我听候您的～。*I'm at your disposal.*
【差使】(chāishǐ) send；dispatch；assign
【差使】(chāishi) official post；billet；commission；job：我一点也不喜欢我这新～。*I don't like this new job of mine at all.*
【差事】❶ errand；assignment：给你们一件～。*Here's a job for you.* ❷ 同〖差使〗
【差役】❶ corvée ❷ runner or bailiff in a yamen

chái

柴 名 firewood
【柴草】faggot；firewood
【柴扉】〈书〉wicker gate
【柴胡】❶ [植] Chinese thorowax (Bupleurum chinense) ❷ [中] the root of Chinese thorowax
【柴火】faggot；firewood
【柴鸡】small-bodied chicken (usu. raised by househdds)
【柴米油盐】fuel，rice，oil and salt—chief daily necessities
【柴油】diesel oil
【柴油机】diesel engine：船用～ *marine diesel engine* / 陆用～ *stationary diesel engine*
豺 名 jackal
【豺狼】jackals and wolves—cruel and evil people
【豺狼当道】jackals and wolves hold sway—the cruel and the wicked are in power：～，安问狐狸。*When the wolf is rampant，why pick on the fox.*

chān

掺 同〖搀〗❷
搀 动 ❶support sb. by the arm；support sb. with one's hand：把盲人～过马路 *help a blind person across the street* / 这位老先生太胖，我一个人～不起他来。*The old gentleman was too heavy，I wasn't able to help him up alone.* ❷mix：往沙子里～石灰 *mix lime into sand* / 油和水～不到一块儿。*Oil and water do not mix.*
【搀兑】mix different substances (esp. liquids)：把酒精跟水～起来。*Mix the alcohol with water.*
【搀扶】support sb. by the arm
【搀和】❶ mix：粗粮细粮～着吃 *have a mixed diet of fine and coarse grain* ❷ meddle；disturb；cause trouble：别人正忙着呢，你别在这儿瞎～。*We are busy. Don't hang around interfering.*
【搀假】adulterate：这批中草药～了。*This batch of herbal medicine has been adulterated.*
【搀水股】[经] water stock
【搀杂】mix up；jumble up：别把这两种菜籽～在一起。*Don't mix up these two kinds of vegetable seeds.*

chán

婵 (构词成分)见下
【婵娟】〈文〉❶ (of a woman) lovely；beautiful；❷ the moon
谗 动 slander；backbite
【谗害】calumniate or slander sb. in order to have him persecuted；frame sb. up
【谗言】slanderous talk；calumny
馋 形 greedy；gluttonous：别这么～，留点儿给大家吃吧。*Don't be so greedy—leave some of the food for the rest of us.* / 看见下棋他就～得慌。*His fingers itch at the sight of a game of chess.*
【馋涎欲滴】mouth drooling with greed：使他～ *make his mouth water* / 他那贪婪的眼光露出～的神情。*There was a look of unrestrained greed in his covetous eyes.*
【馋嘴】❶ gluttonous ❷ glutton；a greedy eater：你这～，把个苹果派全吃了！*You've eaten the whole apple pie，you glutton!*
孱 形 frail；weak
【孱弱】〈书〉❶ frail (of physique)；delicate in health：体质～ *have a frail constitution* ❷ weak and incompetent ❸ insubstantial；thin
禅 名 [宗](佛教) ❶ prolonged and intense contemplation；deep meditation；dhyana：坐禅 ❷ relating to Buddhism；Buddhist：禅堂 / 禅杖 ——另见 shàn
【禅房】❶ Buddhist monks' living quarters ❷ Buddhist temple
【禅机】Buddhist allegorical word or gesture
【禅林】Buddhist temple
【禅师】honorific title for a Buddhist monk
【禅堂】a room or hall in a Buddhist monastery set apart for meditation；meditation room or hall
【禅心】meditative mind
【禅杖】a Buddhist monk's staff
【禅宗】the Chan sect；Dhyana；Zen
缠 动 ❶ twine；wind：把线～在线轴上。*Wind*

the thread onto the reel. / 把毛线～成球。*Wind the knitting wool into balls.* / 他手上～着绷带。*His hand was bandaged.* ❷ tangle; tie up; pester: 这两股线～在一起了。*The two threads got tangled up.* / 这孩子真～人。*That kid is a real pesterer* (*or pest, nuisance*). ❸〈方〉deal with: 这人真难～。*This fellow is really hard to deal with.*

【缠绵】❶ (of an illness or emotion) be lingering: ～病榻 *be bedridden with a lingering disease* / 乡思～ *be tormented by homesickness* ❷ melodious and moving: 歌声是那样柔和～。*The singing was so soft and sweet.*

【缠绵悱恻】(of a story, poem, etc.) exceedingly sentimental; full of pathos

【缠磨】〈口〉pester; bother: 这孩子老～人。*The child is really a pest.* / 许多事情～着他,搞得他老是晕头转向的。*He's got so much on his plate he's always in a muddle.*

【缠绕】❶ twine; bind; wind: 大树上～着藤萝。*There is a wisteria twining round the big tree.* ❷ pester; bother; harass: 孩子们～着我不让我走。*The children kept pestering me and would not let me go.*

【缠绕植物】twining plant; twiner

【缠手】(of a matter) be troublesome; be hard to deal with; (of an illness) be hard to cure: 这件事有些～。*That's a rather troublesome matter.* / 这病真～。*This is a very difficult case.*

【缠足】同〖裹脚〗

蝉 名 cicada

【蝉联】continue to hold (a post or title): 多次～全国冠军 *win the national championship several times running*

【蝉蜕】❶ cicada slough (used as a Chinese medicine) ❷〈书〉free (or extricate) oneself

【蝉翼】cicada's wings: 薄如～的轻纱 *gauze as thin as a cicada's wings*

【蝉翼纱】[纺] organdie

潺 (构词成分)见下

【潺潺】murmur; babble; purl: ～流水 *a murmuring stream*

蟾 名〈略〉见〖蟾蜍〗

【蟾蜍】❶ toad ❷ the fabled three-legged toad in the moon ❸〈文〉the moon

【蟾宫】〈文〉Toad Palace—the moon

【蟾宫折桂】pluck the laurel branch from Toad Palace—obtain a jinshi (进士) degree

【蟾酥】the dried venom of toads; toad-cake (used as a Chinese medicine)

巉 形〈书〉dangerously steep; precipitous

【巉峻】〈书〉steep and precipitous: ～的悬崖 *a sheer overhanging cliff*

【巉岩】〈书〉an overhanging rock: ～林立 *a forest of precipitous rocks*

chǎn

产 Ⅰ 动 ❶ give birth to; be delivered of: 蚕蛾～卵了。*The silk moths are laying eggs.* ❷ produce; yield: ～油 *produce oil* / ～煤 *produce coal* / 水稻主要～在南方。*Rice is grown chiefly in the south.* Ⅱ 名 ❶ product; produce: 土产 / 特产 ❷ property; estate: 房地产

【产床】obstetric table

【产蛋鸡】laying hen; layer

【产地】place of production (or origin); producing area: 甘蔗～ *a sugarcane growing area* / 原料～ *sources of raw materials* ◇ ～证明书 certificate of origin

【产犊】[牧] calving

【产儿】❶ newborn baby ❷ result; product: 这种新工具正是技术革新运动的～。*This new kind of implement is a product of the technical innovation drive.*

【产房】delivery room

【产妇】a lying-in woman; a woman in childbirth; puerpera

【产羔】[牧] lambing; kidding

【产后】postnatal; postpartum: ～护理 *postnatal care; puerperal care* ◇ ～出血 postpartum haemorrhage

【产假】maternity leave

【产驹】[牧] foaling

【产科】❶ obstetrical department; maternity department ❷ obstetrics ◇ ～病房 obstetrical ward; maternity ward

【产量】output; yield: 今年煤的～ *this year's output of coal* / 杂交水稻的亩～超过普通水稻的百分之十五至二十。*The per mu yield of hybrid rice exceeds that of ordinary rice by 15 to 20 percent.*

【产卵】(of birds) lay eggs; (of fishes, frogs, etc.) spawn; (of insects) oviposit

【产品】product; produce: ～质量 *the quality of products* ◇ ～包装 the packaging of product; ～保证书 product warranty; ～定型 type approval; ～返销 product buy-back; ～积压 stockpiling; ～检验 product inspection; ～结构 product structure; ～设计 product design; ～责任 product responsibility; ～质量认证 product quality authentication; ～专利 product patent

【产婆】〈旧〉midwife

【产前】antenatal; prenatal; antepartum ◇ ～检查 antenatal (or prenatal) examination

【产前、产中和产后】service before, during and after the production process

【产钳】obstetric forceps

【产权】(〈略〉全称为'财产权') property right: ～要求 *property claim* ◇ ～拍卖 equity auctioning; ～转让 transfer of property right.

【产褥期】[医] puerperium

【产褥热】puerperal fever; childbed fever

【产生】(used with immaterial things) give rise to;

bring about; evolve; emerge; come into being: ～好的结果 *produce good results* / ～很大的影响 *exert a great influence* / 最近我对围棋～了很大的兴趣。*I've become very interested in go recently.*

【产物】outcome; result; product

【产销】production and marketing: ～平衡 *coordination of production and marketing* / ～两旺。*Both production and marketing are thriving.* ◇～见面 link production with sale; ～结合 coordination between production and marketing

【产需】production and demand: ～平衡 *production-demand balance*

【产业】❶ estate; property: 他们祖上传下来的～早就变卖掉了。*They sold their ancestral estate long ago.* ❷ industry: 第三产业 *tertiary industry* ◇～革命 *the Industrial Revolution*; ～工人 *industrial worker*; ～后备军 *industrial reserve army; reserve army of labour*; ～结构 *industrial structure; structure of production*; ～结构升级 *upgrading of an industrial structure*; ～结构重组 *reorganization of an industrial organization*; ～界 industrial circles; ～军 the army (or body) of industrial workers; ～税［经］industrial tax; ～循环 business cycle; ～资本 industrial capital

【产值】value of output; output value

【产仔】(of a mammal) give birth to its young: 熊猫每胎～一到二只。*A female panda bears only one or two young per litter.* / 大白猪～了。*The big white sow is farrowing.*

谄 动 fawn on; curry favour with; toady to

【谄媚】fawn on; toady to; curry favour with

【谄上欺下】be servile to one's superiors and tyrannical to one's subordinates; fawn on those above and bully those below

【谄笑】give an ingratiating smile; smile obsequiously

铲 Ⅰ 名 shovel; spade: 锅铲 Ⅱ 动 work with a shovel or spade: ～煤 *shovel coal* / 把地～平 *scrape the ground even; level the ground with a spade*

【铲车】forklift truck

【铲除】root out; uproot; eradicate: ～杂草 *root out weeds; weed* / ～封建旧习俗 *eradicate old feudal customs*

【铲土机】spading machine; earth-scraper

【铲运机】carry-scraper; scraper

【铲子】shovel; spade

阐 动 explain

【阐发】elucidate: 这篇文章～了在我国发展商品经济的意义。*This article elucidates the significance of developing a commodity economy in our country.*

【阐明】expound; clarify: ～社会发展规律 *expound the laws of social development* / ～观点 *clarify one's views*

【阐释】explain; expound; interpret: 她对各项规定作了明确的～。*She gave a clear explanation of each of the rules and regulations.*

【阐述】expound; elaborate; set forth: 进行系统的～ *make a systematic exposition* / 各方～了自己对这一问题的立场。*Each side set forth its position on this question.*

【阐扬】expound and propagate: ～教义 *expound and propagate religious doctrines*

chàn

忏 动 repent

【忏悔】❶ repent; be penitent ❷ confess (one's sins) to God or to a priest

颤 动 quiver; tremble: 她的手～得厉害。*Her hands shook violently.* / 我两腿直～。*My legs kept shaking.*

【颤动】vibrate; quiver: 声带～ *vibration of the vocal chords* / 树叶在微风中～。*The leaves quivered in the breeze.*

【颤抖】shake; tremble; quiver; shiver: 冻得全身～ *shiver all over with cold* / 吓得两腿～ *shake in one's shoes*

【颤巍巍】(usu. of aged people) tottering; faltering: 老太太～地走出屋来。*The old lady came tottering out of her room.*

【颤音】❶［语音］trill ❷［音］trill; shake

【颤悠】shake; quiver; flicker: ～的灯光 *a flickering light* / 这块桥板直～。*This board on the bridge is shaky.*

chāng

伥 名 the ghost of one devoured by a tiger, who helps the tiger to devour others: 为虎作伥

【伥鬼】同〖伥〗

昌 形 prosperous; flourishing

【昌明】(of government, culture, etc.) flourishing; thriving; well-developed; advanced: 科学～。*Science is flourishing.*

【昌盛】prosperous: 建设一个繁荣～的社会主义国家 *build a prosperous socialist country*

猖 形〈书〉ferocious

【猖獗】rampant; raging; running wild: ～多年的天花，终于灭迹了。*Smallpox, rampant for ages, has at last been eliminated.*

【猖獗一时】be rampant for a while; run wild for a time

【猖狂】savage; furious: ～的挑衅 *reckless provocation* / ～的攻击 *a furious attack*

娼 名 prostitute

【娼妇】〈讳〉bitch; whore

【娼妓】prostitute; streetwalker

鲳 名 silvery pomfret; butterfish

【鲳鱼】silvery pomfret; butterfish

cháng

长 Ⅰ形 (of space or time) long: 这条河很～。*This is a long river.* / 夏季昼～夜短。*In summer the days are long and the nights short.* / ～～的柳条垂到湖面。*The long willow twigs hang low, brushing against the surface of the lake.* Ⅱ名 ❶ length: 南京长江大桥全～六千七百七十二米。*The overall length of the Changjiang River Bridge at Nanjing is 6,772 metres.* ❷ strong point; forte: 取人之～,补己之短 *overcome one's shortcomings by learning from others' strong points* Ⅲ动 be good at; be proficient in: 她～于刺绣。*She is good at embroidery.* or *Embroidery is her forte.* ——另见 zhǎng

【长臂猿】[动] gibbon

【长波】long wave ◇ ～通讯 long-wave communication

【长城】❶ the Great Wall ❷ impregnable bulwark

【长抽短吊】(in table tennis, badminton, etc.) combine long drives with drop shots

【长处】good qualities; strong points: 他有许多～。*He has many good qualities.* / 国无大小,都各有～和短处。*Every nation, big or small, has its strong and weak points.*

【长传】(in ball games) throw a long pass

【长蝽】chinch bug (an insect): 高粱～ *sorghum chinch bug*

【长此以往】(又作'长此下去') if things go on like this; if things continue this way: 这些青少年不好好念书,却成天玩牌,～,怎么得了? *These teenagers don't work hard at their studies; instead, they play cards all the time. If they go on like this, what will become of them?*

【长存】live forever

【长凳】backless bench

【长笛】flute

【长度】length: 两者～相同。*The two are of equal length.* / 这条跑道的～是多少? *What is the length of the track?*

【长短】❶ length: 这两条扁担～差不多。*The two carrying poles are about the same length.* / 这件上衣～正合适。*This coat is just the right length.* ❷ accident; mishap: 万一这孩子的母亲有个～,怎么办? *What if anything should happen to the child's mother?* ❸ right and wrong; strong and weak points: 背地里议论别人～是不应该的。*It is not right to gossip about a person behind his back.*

【长吨】long ton

【长方体】rectangular parallelepiped; cuboid

【长方形】rectangle: ～的脸 *a long, squarish face*

【长庚】[天] ancient Chinese name for Venus

【长工】farm labourer hired by the year; longterm hired hand

【长骨】[生理] long bone

【长鼓】a long drum, narrowing towards the middle, used by the Korean and Yao ethnic group

【长号】[音] trombone

【长河】long river—endless flow: 历史的～ *the long process (or span) of history*

【长话短说】to make a long story short

【长假】long leave of absence; resignation: 请～ *ask for a long leave of absence; hand in one's resignation*

【长江】the Changjiang (Yangtze) River: ～后浪推前浪,一代更比一代强。*As in the Yangtze River the waves behind drive on those before, so each new generation excels the last one.* ◇ ～三峡工程 the Three Gorges Projects

【长颈鹿】giraffe

【长久】for a long time; permanently: 他打算在这儿～住下去。*He's thinking of living here permanently.* / 这种发夹外形美观,但用不～。*These hairpins look nice but won't last.*

【长久之计】a long-term plan; a permanent solution: 不是～ *not a permanent solution; just a makeshift arrangement*

【长距离】long distance: ～赛跑 *a long-distance race*

【长空】the vast sky: 万里～ *the vast expanse of the sky*

【长裤】trousers; slacks; pants

【长廊】❶ a covered corridor or walk; gallery ❷ the Long Corridor (of the Summer Palace in Beijing)

【长龙】long queue: 买火车票的人排成～。*People stood in a long queue to buy train tickets.*

【长矛】long spear; lance

【长眠】〈婉〉 have an eternal sleep; be dead: ～地下 *be dead and buried*

【长年】all the year round: 筑路工人～奋战在风雪高原。*The road builders brave the wind and snow on the plateaus all the year round.*

【长年累月】year in year out; over the years: 他～在大西北从事野外工作。*Year in year out he has been doing fieldwork in the Northwest.*

【长袍儿】long gown (worn by men)

【长跑】long-distance running; long-distance race: 他每天～。*He goes long-distance running every day.* / 这次运动会,我参加了五千米～。*I ran the 5,000-metre race at the sports meet.*

【长篇大论】a lengthy speech or article: 注意简明扼要,不要～。*Be sure to make it clear and concise and avoid long-windedness.*

【长篇小说】novel

【长期】over a long period of time; long-term; long-lasting: ～规划 *a long-term plan* / ～天气预报 *a long-range weather forecast* / ～存在的问题 *a long-standing problem* ◇ ～保险 long-term insurance; ～亏损 run at a loss for years; ～利率 long term interest rate; ～市场前景 long-term market outlook; ～债券 long-term bond

【长期共存，互相监督】long-term coexistence and mutual supervision
【长枪】❶ spear ❷ long-barrelled gun；rifle
【长驱】(of an army) make a long drive；push deep：～千里 *make a long drive of* 1,000 *li*
【长驱直入】drive straight in：我军～，所向披靡。*Our army drove straight in, carrying everything before it.*
【长衫】unlined long gown (worn by men)
【长舌】long tongue—a gossipy person；gossip-monger：～妇 *a gossipy woman*
【长蛇阵】single-line battle array：排成一字～ *deploy the troops in a long line；string out in a long line*
【长蛇座】[天] Hydra
【长生不老】live forever and never grow old：～药 *elixir of life*
【长石】feldspar (a mineral)
【长逝】pass away；be gone forever
【长寿】a long life；longevity：祝您健康～。*I wish you good health and a long life.*
【长丝】[纺] filament
【长叹】deep sigh：～一声 *heave a deep sigh*
【长条校样】[刷] galley proof
【长统皮靴】high boots
【长统袜】stockings
【长途】❶ a long distance：经过～飞行 *after a long-distance flight* ❷〈略〉见〖长途电话〗◇～跋涉 make a long, arduous journey；trudge a long distance；trek a long way；～奔袭[军] make a long-distance raid；～电话 long-distance telephone call；～电话局 long-distance telephone exchange；～电信局 long-distance telecommunications bureau；～汽车 long-distance bus；coach；～运输 long-distance transport
【长物】❶ surplus ❷ a presentable thing：身无长物
【长线】(of products) be in oversupply：～产品 oversupplied products
【长项】sth. one is good at；one's strong point
【长效】enduring effect：～磺胺 *sulphamethoxypyridazine (SMP)*
【长吁短叹】utter sighs and groans；moan and groan：他在床上翻来覆去，不时地～。*He tossed about in bed, moaning and groaning from time to time.*
【长须鲸】finback (a whale)
【长夜】〈文〉❶ eternal night ❷ all night：作～饮 *carouse all night long*
【长于】be good at；be adept in：她～绘画。*She is good at painting.* / 他～舞蹈。*He is adept in dancing.*
【长元音】[语音] long vowel
【长圆】oval；egg-shaped
【长远】long-term；long-range：～的利益 *long-term interests* / ～规划 *a long-term (or long-range) plan* / ～目标 *long-range objectives*
【长斋】a Buddhist's permanent abstention from meat, fish, etc.
【长征】❶ expedition；long march ❷ the Long March
【长治久安】a long period of peace and order；lasting political stability
【长住】live in a place for long；settle
【长足】〈书〉leaps and bounds：有了～的进展 *have made considerable progress* / ～进步 *make great strides；make rapid progress*

场 Ⅰ名 ❶ a level open space (often used as a threshing ground, etc.)：麦子已经上～。*The wheat has been taken to the threshing ground.* ❷〈方〉country fair；market：赶场 Ⅱ量 spell；period：那是一～硬仗。*That was a hard battle.* / 昨夜下了一～大雪(雨)。*There was a heavy fall of snow (rain) last night.* / 她害了一～大病。*She was seriously ill.* ——另见 chǎng
【场院】threshing ground

肠 名 intestines：大～ *large intestine* / 小～ *small intestine*
【肠穿孔】intestinal perforation；enterobrosis
【肠断】〈文〉heartbroken
【肠肥脑满】同〖脑满肠肥〗
【肠梗阻】intestinal obstruction
【肠激酶】[生化] enterokinase
【肠结核】tuberculosis of the intestines
【肠扭转】volvulus
【肠儿】sausage
【肠套叠】intussusception
【肠胃】intestines and stomach；stomach；belly：～不好 *suffer from stomach trouble*
【肠胃炎】enterogastritis
【肠炎】enteritis
【肠衣】casing for sausages
【肠子】intestines

尝 Ⅰ动 taste；try the flavour of：～～味道。*Try it and see if it tastes all right.* / ～到甜头 *become aware of the benefits of；come to know the good of* Ⅱ副 ever；once：何尝
【尝鼎一脔】try one morsel and you'll know the whole potful—get to know the whole from sampling a part
【尝试】attempt；try：为了增产，他们曾～过各种方法。*They have tried various ways to increase production.* / 最后一次～成功了。*The last try was a success.*
【尝受】have a personal experience of (hardship, misery, etc.)；taste (the bitterness of life, etc.)
【尝味】try the flavour；taste；savour：这是一道名菜，你一定要～一下。*Do have a taste of this well-known dish.*
【尝鲜】have a taste of a delicacy；have a taste of what is just in season
【尝新】have a taste of what is just in season

常 Ⅰ形 ❶ ordinary；common；normal：人情之～ *natural and normal* ❷ constant；invariable：冬夏～青 *remain green throughout the year；evergreen* Ⅱ副 frequently；often；usually：～来～

往 *exchange frequent visits; pay frequent calls* / 她～去听音乐会。*She goes to concerts quite often.* / 我们～见面。*We see quite a lot of each other.*
【常备不懈】always be on the alert; be ever prepared (against war)
【常备军】standing army
【常常】frequently; often; many a time; more often than not: 她～工作到深夜。*She often works far into the night.* / 他俩～通信,交换学术上的看法。*The two of them frequently write to each other, exchanging views on academic questions.*
【常春藤】［植］Chinese ivy
【常规】❶ convention; common practice; routine: 按照～办事 *follow the old routine* / 打破～ *break with convention* ❷［医］routine: 血～ *routine blood test* / 尿～ *routine urine test* ◇ ～裁军 conventional disarmament; ～疗法［医］routine treatment; ～能源 conventional source of energy; ～武器 conventional weapons; ～战争 conventional war
【常轨】normal practice (or course): 这类事情,可以遵循～解决。*We can follow the usual procedures when dealing with this sort of thing.*
【常衡】(又作'常衡制')avoirdupois (weight)
【常会】regular meeting; regular session: 委员会每半年举行一次～。*The committee holds regular meetings once every six months.*
【常见】be common: 这儿的春天,风沙是～的。*Duststorms are common here in spring.* / ～病 *common disease; common ailment*
【常客】a frequent guest or customer; frequenter (of a theatre, restaurant, ballroom, etc.)
【常理】general rule; what is normal: 按～ *normally*
【常例】common practice
【常量】［物］constant
【常绿植物】evergreen plants; evergreens
【常年】❶ throughout the year; year in year out: ～坚持体育锻炼 *persist in physical training all the year round* ❷ an average year: 这儿小麦～亩产三百公斤。*In this area the per mu yield of wheat for an average year is* 300 *kilograms.*
【常青】evergreen: 四季～ *have green leaves throughout the year* / 冷杉和松树是～树。*Firs and pines are evergreens.*
【常情】reason; sense: 按照～,他会提出这个问题同你讨论的。*It stands to reason that he will take up the matter with you.* / 既然这事合乎～,我不反对。*Since this is a sensible thing to do, I have no objections.*
【常人】ordinary person; the man in the street
【常任】permanent; standing: 安理会～理事国 *permanent member of the Security Council* / ～代表 *permanent representative* ◇ ～理事 permanent council member
【常山】❶［植］antipyretic dichroa (Dichroa febrifuga) ❷［中］the root or leaves of antipyretic dichroa
【常设】(of an organization) standing; permanent: ～机构 *standing body; permanent organization* / ～秘书处 *permanent secretariat* / ～委员会 *permanent committee*
【常胜将军】an ever-victorious general
【常识】❶ general knowledge; elementary knowledge: 卫生～ *elementary knowledge of hygiene and sanitation* / 科学～ *general knowledge of science* / ～课 *general knowledge course* ❷ common sense: 天冷了要穿得暖一点儿,这是～。*It's common sense to dress more warmly when it gets cold.*
【常数】［数］constant
【常态】normal behaviour or conditions; normality; normalcy: 恢复～ *return to normal (or normalcy)* ◇ ～分布 normal distribution; ～曲线 normal curve
【常委】〈略〉见〚常务委员〛
【常温】❶ normal atmospheric temperature (between 15° and 25℃) ❷［动］homoiothermy ◇ ～动物 homoiothermal animal; homoiotherm
【常务】day-to-day business; routine: 主持～ *in charge of day-to-day business* ◇ ～理事 managing director; ～委员 member of the standing committee; ～委员会 standing committee
【常言】saying: ～道 *as the saying goes* / ～说得好 *as the saying aptly puts it; it is well said that...*
【常用】in common use: ～药材 *medicinal herbs most in use* ◇～词语 everyday expressions
【常住】❶ permanently reside at a place: 有～户口 *be a permanent resident* ❷［宗］(佛教) changeless; permanent
【常驻】resident; permanent: ～联合国代表团 *a permanent mission to the United Nations* ◇ ～大使 resident ambassador; ～代表 permanent representative; ～记者 resident correspondent

偿 动 ❶ repay; compensate for: ～债 *pay (or discharge) a debt* ❷ meet; fulfil: 得～夙愿 *have fulfilled one's long-cherished wish*
【偿付】pay back; pay: 延期～ *delay the payment of a debt*
【偿还】repay; pay back: ～债务 *pay a debt* / 如数～ *pay back the exact amount*
【偿命】pay with one's life (for a murder); a life for a life
【偿清】pay back in full; clear (a debt): ～债务 *clear one's debts*
【偿债基金】［经］sinking fund

倘 (构词成分)见下
【倘佯】〈书〉wander about unhurriedly; roam leisurely

嫦 (构词成分)见下
【嫦娥】the Lady in the Moon

chǎng

厂 名 ❶ factory; mill; plant; works: 鞋～ *shoe*

factory / 面粉～ *flour mill* / 机床～ *machine tool plant* / 钢铁～ *iron and steel works* / 制糖～ *sugar refinery* / 造船～ *shipyard* / ～办食堂 *factory-run canteen* ❷ yard; depot: 煤～ *coal yard*

【厂房】❶ factory building ❷ factory workshop

【厂风】overall management and working style of a factory

【厂家】factory; mill: 有些～濒临破产。*Some of the factories are verging on bankruptcy.*

【厂矿】factories and mines ◇～企业 factories, mines and other enterprises; industrial enterprises

【厂牌政策】brand policy

【厂商】❶ factory owner: 承包～ *contractor* ❷ factories and stores

【厂校挂钩】establish a hookup between a school and a factory

【厂休】a factory's day of rest (usu. on a weekday): 今天我们～。*Today is our factory's day of rest.*

【厂长】factory director ◇～负责制 the responsibility system of factory directors

【厂址】the site (or location) of a factory: 选择～ *choose a site for building a factory*

【厂主】factory owner; millowner

场 Ⅰ 名 ❶ a large place used for a particular purpose: 操场 ❷ stage: 开场 ❸ [戏] scene: 第二幕第三～ *Act II, Scene iii* ❹ [物] field: 电场 / 磁场 Ⅱ 量 (for recreational or sports activities): 一～电影 *a film show* / 一～球赛 *a match; a ball game* / 加演一～ *give an extra performance or show* / 第二～两点开始。*The second show starts at two.* ——另见 cháng

【场磁铁】[电] field magnet

【场次】the number of showings of a film, play, etc.

【场地】space; place; site: 体育比赛～ *sports arena; sports ground; court* / 施工～ *construction site* ◇～使用权 right to the use of site

【场合】occasion; situation: 外交～ *a diplomatic occasion* / 这种～你不能穿得太随便。*You should be properly dressed for such an occasion.*

【场记】❶ log (for film shooting, theatrical performance, etc.) ❷ log keeper

【场界灯】boundary lights (in an airfield)

【场景】❶ [戏][电影] scene: 富有特色的～ *scene with special features of its own; scene with a distinctive flavour* ❷ sight; scene; picture: 热火朝天的劳动～ *picture of overflowing labour enthusiasm* / 依依惜别的～ *sentimental parting scene*

【场面】❶ scene (in drama, fiction, etc.); spectacle: 电影里的动人～ *a moving scene in a film* / 作者很善于描写大的～。*The author is adept in depicting grand scenes.* ❷ occasion; scene: 盛大的～ *a grand occasion* / 热烈友好的～ *a scene of warm friendship* ❸ appearance; front; facade: 撑场面场内交易 *floor trading* ◇～话 polite platitude for the occasion; civil banalities; unctuous words; ～人 man about town; very sociable person; person of prestige; celebrity; ～上 on social occasions; in social life

【场内交易】transaction on exchange

【场内经纪人】floor broker; board broker

【场所】place; arena: 公共～ *a public place* / 娱乐～ *place of recreation* / 这里通常是举行纪念活动的～。*This is the usual place for commemorative activities.*

【场外交易】ex-pit; kerb transaction ◇～市场 over the counter market; ～证券 off-board securities

【场外下注】off-track betting

【场子】a place where people gather for various purposes (e.g. theatre, hall, sports ground, etc.): 这个～够大，可是音响效果不好，不适合用来开音乐会。*The place is big enough, but the acoustics are not good enough for a concert.*

敞 Ⅰ 形 (of a house, courtyard, etc.) spacious; roomy: 这屋子太～。*This room is too big.* Ⅱ 动 open; be uncovered: ～着门 *leave the door open; with the door open*

【敞车】❶ open wagon; open freight car ❷ a railway flatcar

【敞怀】have one's shirt unbuttoned; bare one's chest

【敞开】open wide: 把门～ *open the door wide* / 大门～着。*The gate was left wide open.* / ～思想 *say what's in (or on) one's mind; get things off one's chest*

【敞亮】❶ light and spacious: 这间屋子很～。*This room is light and spacious.* ❷ (of one's thinking) clear

【敞篷车】open car

【敞胸露怀】bare one's chest

氅 〈旧〉名 cloak: 大氅

chàng

怅 形 disappointed; sorry: 惆怅

【怅然】disappointed; upset: ～而返 *come away disappointed*

【怅惘】distracted; listless: 轮船在远处消失了，而她仍然～地站在江边。*Even after the steamship had sailed out of sight, she still stood in a daze on the pier.*

畅 形 ❶ smooth; unimpeded: 流畅 ❷ free; uninhibited

【畅达】fluent; smooth: 译文～。*The translation reads smoothly.* / 交通～ *have a good transport and communications network*

【畅快】free from inhibitions and happy; carefree: 心情～ *have ease of mind; be carefree and happy* / 大家都玩得非常～。*We all had a wonderful time.*

【畅所欲言】pour out all that one wishes to say; speak without any inhibitions; speak one's mind freely; speak out freely

【畅谈】talk freely and to one's heart's content: ～国内外大好形势 *speak glowingly of the excellent situation at home and abroad*

【畅通】unimpeded; unblocked: 前面道路～无阻。*The road ahead is clear of obstructions.* or *Open road ahead.* / 这里过去很偏僻,现在铁路公路都～了。*This formerly inaccessible place can now be easily reached by road and rail.*

【畅销】sell well; have a ready market; be in great demand: 中国丝绸～国外。*Chinese silk fabrics sell well on foreign markets.* / 秋天是毛织品～的季节。*Autumn is a lively season for the wool market.* ◇ ～书 best seller

【畅行无阻】pass unimpeded; proceed without hindrance

【畅叙】chat cheerfully (usu. about old times): ～友情 *relive an old friendship*

【畅游】❶ have a good swim: ～长江 *have a good swim in the Changjiang River* ❷ enjoy a sightseeing tour: ～名胜古迹 *enjoy a trip to places of historic interest*

倡 动 initiate; advocate: 倡议

【倡导】initiate; propose: ～和平共处五项原则 *initiate the Five Principles of Peaceful Coexistence*

【倡始】initiate; start; found ◇ ～人 initiator; founder

【倡言】〈书〉propose; initiate

【倡议】propose; initiate: ～召开国际会议 *propose the calling of an international conference* / 他的～得到了大家一致的赞同。*His proposal met with unanimous approval.* ◇ ～权 diplomacy initiative; ～书 written proposal; proposal; ～者 initiator

唱 Ⅰ 动 ❶ sing: ～国歌 *sing the national anthem* / ～女高音 *sing the soprano* ❷ call; cry: 鸡～三遍。*The cock has crowed for the third time.* Ⅱ 名 a song or a singing part of a Chinese opera

【唱白脸】wear the white mask of the villain — play the villain; pretend to be harsh and severe (often used in contrast to 唱红脸)

【唱本】the libretto or script of a ballad-singer

【唱词】libretto; words of a ballad

【唱独角戏】(又作'唱独脚戏') put on a one-man show; go it alone

【唱段】aria: 京剧～ *an aria from a Beijing opera*

【唱对台戏】put on a rival show; enter into rivalry with sb.

【唱反调】sing a different tune; speak (or act) contrary to

【唱高调】mouth high-sounding words; say fine-sounding things; affect a high moral tone: 少～,你要是能干,就来试试。*None of your high-sounding words. If you can do it, come and have a try.*

【唱歌】sing (a song): 她很会～。*She is a good singer.*

【唱工】(又作'唱功')[戏] art of singing; singing

【唱和】❶ one singing a song and the others joining in the chorus: 此唱彼和。*When one starts singing, another joins in.* ❷ an exchange of poems

【唱红脸】wear the red mask of the hero — play the hero; pretend to be generous and kind (often used in contrast to 唱白脸): 一个～,一个唱白脸。*One coaxes, the other coerces.*

【唱机】phonograph; record player; gramophone

【唱空城计】perform The Stratagem of the Empty City—present a bold front to conceal a weak defence; have an absentee staff

【唱名】❶ read out a list of names ❷ [音] sol-fa syllables (*do*, *re*, *mi*, *fa*, *sol*, *la* and *ti*) ◇ ～表决 vote by roll call; roll-call vote

【唱名法】[音] sol-fa; solmization: 固定～ *fixed-do system* / 首调～ *movable-do system*

【唱片】phonograph (or gramophone) record; disc: 放～ *play a phonograph record* / 灌～ *cut a disc*

【唱票】call out the names of those voted for while counting ballot-slips ◇ ～人 teller

【唱腔】vocal music in a Chinese opera

【唱诗班】choir

【唱双簧】❶ give a two-man comic show (with one speaking or singing while hiding behind the other who gesticulates) ❷ collaborate with each other

【唱头】pickup (of a phonograph)

【唱戏】〈口〉sing and act in a traditional opera: 她从小就跟她爸爸学～。*She began to learn opera singing and acting from her father when she was a mere child.*

【唱针】gramophone needle; stylus

【唱主角】play the leading role: 这个课题组由你来～。*You'll play the leading role in this research team.*

【唱做念打】singing, gesticulating, elocution and acrobatics—elements of the art of acting in traditional opera

chāo

抄 动 ❶ copy; transcribe: ～书 *copy from a book* / 请把稿件～一下。*Please make a fair copy of the manuscript.* / 照～原文 *make a verbatim transcription of the original* ❷ plagiarize; lift: ～别人的文章 *plagiarize (from) somebody else's writing* / 逐字逐句地～人家的作业 *copy another student's written work word by word* ❸ search and confiscate; make a raid upon: ～土匪的老窝 *destroy the bandits' den* ❹ take a shortcut: ～到他们前面 *outstrip them by taking a shortcut* ❺ fold (one's arms): ～着手站在一边 *stand by with folded arms* ❻ grab; take up: ～起一把铁

锹就干 *take up a spade and plunge into the job* / 谁把我的字典～走了? *Who's gone off with my dictionary?*

【抄本】hand-copied book; transcript:《红楼梦》～ *a handwritten copy of A Dream of Red Mansions*

【抄道】❶ take a shortcut ❷〈口〉shortcut: 走～去要近两公里路。*If you take the shortcut, it will be two kilometres closer.*

【抄后路】outflank and attack (the enemy) in the rear; turn the enemy's rear

【抄获】search out; ferret out

【抄家】search sb.'s house and confiscate his property

【抄件】duplicate; copy: 现将报告的～转发给你们。*A copy of the report is forwarded herewith.*

【抄录】make a handwritten copy of; copy: 这段引文是从报上～来的。*This quotation is copied (or taken) from a newspaper article.*

【抄身】search a person; frisk

【抄送】make a copy for; send a duplicate to

【抄网】dip net

【抄袭】❶ plagiarize; lift: ～行为 *(an act of) plagiarism* ❷ borrow indiscriminately from other people's experience ❸ launch a surprise attack on the enemy by making a detour

【抄写】copy (by hand); transcribe ◇ ～员 copyist

吵 (构词成分)见下 ——另见 chǎo

【吵吵】〈方〉make a row; kick up a racket: 一个一个说; 别～。*Speak one at a time; don't make such a row.*

钞 名 bank note; paper money: 现～ *cash*

【钞票】bank note; paper money; bill: 一张五元的～ *a five-yuan bill*

绰 动 grab; take up: ～起一根棍子 *grab a stick* / ～起活儿就干 *plunge right into the job* ——另见 chuò

焯 动 dip vegetables in boiling water for a few seconds; scald: 先把菠菜～一下。*First, scald the spinach.*

超 Ⅰ 动 ❶ exceed; surpass; overtake: 赶先进, ～先进 *catch up with and surpass the advanced* / 亩产～千斤 *produce over 1,000 jin per mu; exceed 1,000 jin in per mu yield* ❷ transcend; go beyond: ～现实 *transcend realism* Ⅱ 形 ultra; super; extra: 超高温

【超薄】ultra-thin: ～磁带 *ultra-thin magnetic tape* / ～镜片 *ultra-thin glasses* / ～切片 *ultra-thin section* / ～式手表 *ultra-thin watch*

【超编】overstaff: ～人员 *excess personnel*

【超标】surpass the set standard; exceed a quota: 因～占用住房而受到批评 *be criticized for moving into an apartment in excess of the set standard of floor space due to one*

【超产】overfulfil a production target (or quota): ～百分之二十 *exceed the production quota by 20%*

【超常】*be above average; be above the common run*: 智力～ *be a person of extraordinary intelligence* ◇ ～儿童 a suppernormal child

【超车】overtake (a car, a person in a car, etc.): 别～,对面来车了! *Don't try to overtake— there's a car coming the other way.* / 不准～! *No overtaking!* or *No passing!*

【超尘拔俗】avoid earthly concerns and hold oneself aloof from the vulgar

【超出】overstep; go beyond; exceed: ～范围 *go beyond the scope (or bounds)* / ～定额 *exceed the quota* / ～预料 *exceed one's expectations*

【超导】[物] superconduction ◇ ～材料 superconductor; ～存储器 superconductivity memory; ～电性 superconductivity; ～技术 superconducting technology; ～体 superconductor

【超等】of superior grade; extra fine: ～质量 *extra good quality; superfine*

【超低空飞行】minimum altitude flying; hedgehopping

【超低温】ultralow temperature

【超度】redeem lost souls by making offerings and saying prayers

【超短波】ultrashort wave

【超短裙】miniskirt

【超额】above quota: ～完成生产指标 *overfulfil the production quota; surpass the production target* ◇ ～保险 excess insurance; ～利润 superprofit; ～剩余价值 excess surplus value

【超凡】❶ transcend the worldly ❷ out of the ordinary; extraordinary; uncommon

【超负荷】excess load; overload ◇ ～运转 overloading operation

【超高频】ultrahigh frequency (UHF): ～变压器 *ultrahigh-frequency transforme*

【超高速巨型计算计】giant ultra-high-speed computer

【超高温】superhigh temperature

【超高压】❶ [物] superhigh pressure ❷ [电] extrahigh voltage (or tension): ～线路带电作业 *working on live extrahigh tension power lines*

【超购加价】additional prices for above quota purchase

【超过】outstrip; surpass; exceed: ～规定的速度 *exceed the speed limit* / ～限度 *go beyond the limit* / ～历史最高水平 *top all previous records* / ～世界先进水平 *surpass advanced world levels*

【超级】super: ～间谍 *superspy* ◇ ～磁泡 superbubble; ～大国 superpower; ～大学 megaversity; ～公路 superhighway; ～计算机 super computer; ～市场 supermarket; ～油轮 supertanker

【超计划生育】have more children than what the plan allows

【超假】overstay one's leave

【超经济剥削】extraeconomic exploitation

【超巨星】[天] supergiant star

【超绝】unique; superb; extraordinary: 技艺～ *exhibit superb skill*

【超空间】hyperspace
【超龄】overage：因为她已～，那家公司没有要她。*The company wouldn't have her because she was overage.*
【超媒体】hypermedia
【超期服役】[军] extended active duty；extended service in the army
【超前】❶ ahead of times；aiming at the future ❷ surpassing past generations ❸ [电] lead ◇～消费 excessive consumption
【超群】head and shoulders above all others；pre-eminent：武艺～ *be extremely skilful in martial arts*
【超然】aloof；detached：他对那件事持～的态度。*He took a detached attitude to the matter.* ◇～科学 pataphysics
【超然物外】hold oneself aloof from the world；be above worldly considerations；stay away from the scene of contention
【超人】❶ be out of the common run：～的记忆力 *exceptionally good memory* ❷ superman (as defined by Nietzsche)
【超生】❶ [宗](佛教) be reincarnated ❷ spare sb.'s life；be merciful ❸ unplanned birth
【超声波】ultrasonic (wave)；supersonic (wave)：～探伤仪 *ultrasonic flaw detector* ◇～疗法 ultrasonic therapy
【超声物理学】ultrasonic physics
【超声学】ultrasonics
【超市】〈略〉见〖超级市场〗
【超速】❶ exceed the speed limit ❷ hypervelocity ◇～粒子 [物] hypervelocity particle
【超脱】❶ unconventional；original：他的字，信笔写来，十分～。*His effortless calligraphy has an unconventional grace of its own.* ❷ be detached；stand (or hold, keep) aloof：～现实是不可能的。*It's impossible to detach oneself from reality.*
【超外差】[电子]superheterodyne；superhet ◇～式收音机 superheterodyne (radio set)
【超微粒胶片】superfine grain film
【超文本传输协议】hypertext transfer protocol (http)
【超现实主义】surrealism
【超线】superstring
【超小型计算计】microminicomputer
【超小型管】[电子] subminiature tube
【超新星】[天] supernova
【超星团】supercluster
【超逸】unconventionally graceful；free and natural
【超音速】supersonic speed ◇～喷气机 superjet；～战斗机 supersonic fighter-plane；supersonic fighter
【超铀元素】transuranic (or transuranium) element
【超越】surmount；overstep；transcend；surpass：～障碍 *surmount an obstacle* / ～职权范围 *go beyond one's terms of reference；overstep one's authority* ◇～射击 [军] overhead fire
【超载】[交通] overload：～能力 *overload capacity*
【超支】overspend：从不～ *never live beyond one's income*
【超重】❶ overload ❷ overweight：～信件 *overweight letter* / ～行李 *excess luggage*
【超重量级】[体] super-heavy weight ◇～拳击 super heavy weight boxing；～柔道 super weight judo
【超轴】[铁路] over haulage：～牵引 *trains hauling above-normal tonnage*
【超子】[物] hyperon
【超自然】supernatural

cháo

巢 名 nest (of birds, ants, etc.)：小鸟回～了。*The bird has returned to the nest.*
【巢菜】common vetch
【巢蛾】ermine moth
【巢居】dwell in trees
【巢鼠】harvest mouse
【巢穴】lair；den；nest；hideout：匪徒的～ *a bandits' lair*

朝 Ⅰ 名 ❶ royal court；government ❷ dynasty：唐～ *the Tang Dynasty* ❸ (a sovereign's) reign：康熙～ *the reign of Emperor Kangxi* ❹ an assembly held by a sovereign；court：早～ *a morning court held by a sovereign* Ⅱ 动 make a pilgrimage to：朝圣 Ⅲ 介 facing；towards：～南走 *go southward* / 他背～我站着。*He stood there with his back towards me.* / 这门是～里开还是～外开？*Does the door open inwards or outwards?* ——另见 zhāo
【朝拜】❶ make obeisances to (a sovereign) ❷ pay religious homage to；worship：这座寺庙常有善男信女来～。*Devotees often come to this temple to worship.*
【朝代】dynasty
【朝服】court dress
【朝贡】(of envoys from a vassal state or a foreign country) present tribute to an emperor
【朝见】have an audience with a sovereign：进宫～皇上 *be presented at court*
【朝觐】❶〈书〉have an audience with a sovereign ❷ go on a pilgrimage to a shrine or a sacred place
【朝山】(of Buddhists) make a pilgrimage to a temple on a famous mountain
【朝圣】(of religious people) make a pilgrimage to a sacred place
【朝廷】❶ royal or imperial court ❷ royal or imperial government
【朝鲜】Korea ◇～人 Korean；～语 Korean (language)
【朝鲜族】❶ the Korean ethnic group, or the Koreans, distributed over Jilin, Heilongjiang and Liaoning Provinces ❷ the Koreans (of Korea)
【朝向】turn towards；face：向日葵总是～太阳。*Sun flowers always turn towards the sun.*

【朝阳】(cháoyáng) have a sunny, usu. southern, exposure: 这间屋～。*The room has a southern exposure*. ——另见 zhāoyáng

【朝野】❶ the court and the commonalty ❷ the government and the public

【朝政】(in imperial times) court administration; affairs of state

潮 Ⅰ 名 ❶ tide: 早～ *morning tide* / 花如海,歌如～。*A sea of flowers; a tidal wave of songs*. ❷ social upsurge; current; tide: 思潮 Ⅱ 形 damp; moist: 火柴～了。*The matches have got damp*. / 这屋子太～。*The room is too damp*.

【潮呼呼】damp; dank; clammy: 下了七八天雨,屋子里什么都是～的。*After a week's rain, everything in the house became damp and clammy*.

【潮解】[化] deliquescence

【潮流】❶ tide; tidal current ❷ trend: 历史～ *historical trend* / 顺应世界之～ *adapt oneself to (or go along with) world trends*

【潮气】moisture in the air; humidity: 仓库里～太大,粮食就容易发霉。*The grain is liable to mildew when the humidity in the barn is too high*.

【潮热】[中] hectic fever

【潮湿】moist; damp: 这间屋子太～,不适宜住人。*This room is too damp to live in*.

【潮水】tidewater; tide: ～上涨了。*The tide is coming in*. / 欢乐的人群～般地涌向天安门广场。*Crowds of joyous people streamed into Tian'anmen Square from all directions*.

【潮位】the level of the tidal current at its flow or ebb; tidemark

【潮汐】morning and evening tides ◇ ～表 tide table; ～测站 tide station; ～电站 tidal power stations; ～能 tidal energy

【潮涌】roll like the tide: 心事如～ *one's mind seething with all kinds of thoughts*

嘲 动 ridicule; deride: 嘲弄

【嘲讽】sneer at; taunt: 她带着～的神情斜了他一眼。*She gave him a sideway glance with a sneering look on her face*.

【嘲弄】mock; poke fun at: ～历史的人必将被历史所～。*Those who mock history will be mocked by history*.

【嘲笑】ridicule; deride; jeer at; laugh at: 反正我觉得该做的就做,不怕别人～。*I will do what I think I should do and fear no ridicule*.

chǎo

吵 动 ❶ make a noise: 别～! *Don't make so much noise!* / 瞧,孩子被你们～醒了。*Look! You've woken the child*. / 别～他。*Don't disturb him*. ❷ quarrel; wrangle; squabble: 不要为一点小事就～起来。*Don't squabble over trifles*. / 我不跟他～。*I will not quarrel with him*. / ～翻了天 *kick up a terrific row* ——另见 chāo

【吵架】quarrel; have a row; wrangle: 我跟他～了。*I had a quarrel with him*.

【吵闹】❶ wrangle; kick up a row: 他们俩各不相让,～不休。*As neither of them was willing to give ground, they quarrelled on and on*. ❷ harass; disturb: 这孩子～得我整整一上午不得安宁。*The child has been harassing me all morning*. ❸ din; hubbub: 院子里一片～声。*A hubbub was heard in the courtyard*.

【吵嚷】make a racket; shout in confusion; clamour

【吵嘴】quarrel; bicker: 她从来不跟别人～。*She has never quarrelled with anybody*.

炒 动 ❶ stir-fry; sauté: ～肉丝 *stir-fried shredded pork* / ～黄瓜 *sautéed cucumber* / ～鸡蛋 *scrambled eggs* ❷ roast while stirring: 糖～栗子 *chestnuts roasted (in sand) with brown sugar* / ～花生 *roasted peanuts* ❸ 〈口〉 speculate (on the stock exchange, etc.): ～股票(汇) *speculate in shares (foreign exchange)* ❹ profiteer through buying and selling commodities in rapid succession ❺ mount aggressive publicity, thereby raise the popularity of someone (e. g. a performer): 新闻媒介爆～歌星。*The news media is awash with publicity for a certain singer*.

【炒菜】❶ make dishes: 我～,你做饭。*I'll make the dishes while you cook the rice*. ❷ a stir-fried dish: 我要了两个～一个汤。*I ordered two dishes and soup*.

【炒股】profiteer with stocks

【炒汇】buying and selling foreign currency

【炒货】roasted seeds and nuts

【炒冷饭】stir-fry leftover rice—say or do the same old thing; dish up the same old stuff; rehash

【炒买炒卖】stir-fry in buying and selling

【炒米】❶ parched rice ❷ millet stir-fried in butter (staple food of the Mongolians)

【炒米花】puffed rice

【炒面】❶ fried noodles with shredded meat and vegetables; chow mein ❷ parched flour

【炒勺】round-bottomed frying pan; wok

【炒鱿鱼】〈口〉 give sb. the sack; sack; fire: 被～ *get the sack*

【炒作】profiteering activities

chào

耖 名 ❶a harrow-like implement for pulverizing soil ❷ level land with such an implement

chē

车 Ⅰ 名 ❶ vehicle: ～已经开了。*The car (bus, etc.) has already left*. / 骑～ *ride a bike* ❷ a wheeled instrument: 水车 ❸ machine: 这台～停了。*This machine has stopped*. Ⅱ 动 ❶ lathe; turn: ～机器零件 *lathe a machine part* / ～光

smooth sth. on a lathe ❷ lift water by waterwheel：把河里的水～到稻田里。*Lift some water from the river into the paddy fields.* ——另见 jū

【车把】handlebars（of a bicycle，motor cycle，etc.）；shaft（of a wheelbarrow，handcart，etc.）

【车把式】（又作'车把势'）cart-driver；carter

【车床】lathe：多刀～ *multicut lathe*

【车次】❶ train number ❷ coach number（indicating order of departure）

【车刀】lathe tool；turning tool：木工～ *wood turning tool*

【车到山前必有路】the cart will find its way round the hill when it gets there—things will eventually sort themselves out

【车道】（traffic）lane；roadway

【车灯】general name for lights on a vehicle（e.g. headlights，bicycle lamp，etc.）

【车队】motorcade

【车匪路霸】train and highway bandits and robbers

【车费】（passenger's）fare：到动物园～多少？*What's the fare to the Zoo?*

【车夫】〈旧〉carter；driver；rickshaw puller；chauffeur

【车工】❶ lathe work ❷ turner；lathe operator：～车间 *turning shop*

【车钩】［铁路］coupling

【车轱辘】〈口〉wheel（of a vehicle）

【车号】license number（of a vehicle）

【车祸】traffic accident；road accident：昨天出了两起～，死伤四人。*There were two traffic accidents yesterday，with four casualties.*

【车技】［杂］trick-cycling

【车架】frame（of a car，bicycle，etc.）

【车间】workshop；shop ◇ ～主任 workshop director

【车库】garage

【车辆】vehicles：来往～ *traffic* / 铁路机车及～ *rolling stock* ◇ ～周转率［铁路］average turnround rate of rolling stock

【车流】❶ traffic：～不息 *an incessant stream of vehicles—heavy traffic* ❷ the rate of traffic flow

【车轮】wheel（of a vehicle）

【车轮战】the tactic of several persons taking turns in fighting one opponent to tire him out

【车马费】travel allowance

【车牌】license plate

【车篷】awning for a vehicle

【车皮】railway wagon or carriage；flatcar or freight car：两～货物 *two freight cars of goods*

【车票】train or bus ticket；ticket

【车身】the body of a vehicle

【车水马龙】an incessant stream of horses and carriages—heavy traffic：那天真是～，游览的人络绎不绝。*The tourist traffic was very busy that day. There was an endless stream of visitors.* / 门前～。*The courtyard was thronged with visitors.*

【车速】speed of a motor vehicle：～太快！*The car is going too fast!* / 现在～为每小时五十公里。*The car is travelling at 50 km per hour.*

【车胎】tyre

【车头】❶ the front of a vehicle ❷ engine（of a train）；locomotive

【车帷】curtain in a carriage

【车位】parking place：这个停车场有五十个～。*The parking lot has fifty parking places.*

【车厢】railway carriage；railroad car

【车削】［机］turning

【车辕】shaft（of a cart，etc.）

【车载斗量】enough to fill carts and be measured by the bushel—common and numerous：在我们那里像我这样的人～，不可胜数。*Where I come from，people like me come by the bushel.*

【车闸】brake（of a car，bicycle，etc.）：我的～不灵，要修理一下。*My brakes don't work very well and need to be fixed.*

【车站】station；depot；stop

【车照】driving license

【车辙】rut

【车轴】axletree；axle

【车子】❶ a small vehicle（such as a car，pushcart，etc.）❷〈方〉bicycle

chě

扯 动 ❶ pull：～着他的袖子 *pull him by the sleeve* / ～住绳子不放 *hold onto the rope* / ～着嗓子喊 *shout at the top of one's voice* ❷ tear：把信～得粉碎 *tear the letter to pieces* / ～下假面具 *tear off the mask* ❸〈口〉buy（cloth，thread，etc.）：～三尺布 *buy three chi of cloth* ❹ chat；gossip：别～远了。*Don't wander from the subject.* or *Stick to the point.*

【扯淡】〈方〉talk nonsense：别瞎～！*Don't talk nonsense!*

【扯后腿】hold sb. back（from action）；be a drag on sb.；be a hindrance to sb.：他要去参军，你不要扯他的后腿。*He wants to enlist. Don't try to hold him back.*

【扯谎】tell a lie or fib；lie：我对他扯了个谎，他真信了。*I told him a fib，and he swallowed it whole.*

【扯家常】talk about everyday matters；engage in small talk；chitchat

【扯皮】dispute over trifles；argue back and forth；bicker：政府机构互相～ *government organizations pass the buck to each other*

chè

彻 形 thorough；penetrating：彻骨

【彻底】thorough；thoroughgoing：屋子打扫得很～。*The room has been given a thorough cleaning.* / ～失败 *end in utter failure* / ～性 *(degree of) thoroughness*

【彻骨】penetrate to the bone：寒风～。*The bitter wind chills one to the bone.*

【彻头彻尾】out and out; through and through; downright: ～的坏蛋 *an out-and-out villian* / ～的骗局 *a downright (or sheer) fraud*; *deception from beginning to end* / ～的谎言 *an absolute lie*

【彻夜】all night; all through the night; from dusk to dawn: ～不眠 *lie awake all night* / 工地上灯火～通明。*The lights were ablaze at the worksite all through the night.*

坼 动 〈书〉split open; crack: 天旱地～。*The ground cracked after a long drought.*

【坼裂】〈书〉split open; crack

掣 动 ❶ pull; tug: 掣肘 ❷ draw: 他赶紧～回手去。*He quickly drew back his hand.* ❸ flash past: 电～雷鸣。*Lightning flashed and thunder rolled.*

【掣肘】hold sb. back by the elbow—impede sb. from doing sth.: 这件事办得很顺利,没有人～。*As there was no one making things difficult for us, we settled the matter smoothly.*

澈 形 (of water) clear; limpid: 清澈

撤 动 ❶ remove; take away: 把障碍物～了 *remove the obstacle* / 把盘子、碗～了 *clear away the dishes* ❷ dismiss: 他的职务给～了。*He was dismissed from his post.* ❸ withdraw; evacuate: 向后～ *withdraw*; *retreat* / 把伤员～走 *evacuate the wounded*

【撤兵】withdraw troops

【撤除】remove; dismantle: ～军事设施 *dismantle military installations* / 外国空军基地应立即～。*Foreign air bases should be removed immediately.*

【撤防】withdraw a garrison; withdraw from a defended position

【撤换】dismiss and replace; recall; replace

【撤回】❶ recall; withdraw: ～军队 *recall troops* / ～步哨 *withdraw the guard* ❷ revoke; retract; withdraw: ～起诉 *withdraw charges*; *revoke a court action* / ～提案 *withdraw a proposal*

【撤军】withdraw troops

【撤离】withdraw from; leave; evacuate: ～阵地 *abandon a position* / ～现场 *quit the scene* / ～一座城市 *evacuate a city*

【撤诉】(of the plaintiff) withdraw an accusation; drop a lawsuit

【撤退】withdraw; pull out: 向安全地区～ *withdraw to a safe place* / ～方向 *the line of withdrawal* / 安全～ *make good one's retreat*

【撤席】clear the table (after a feast): ～以后,端上水果。*Fruits were served after the table was cleared.*

【撤消】(又作'撤销') cancel; rescind; revoke: ～职务 *dismiss sb. from his post* / ～一项决议 *annul a decision* / ～处分 *rescind (or annul) a penalty*

【撤职】dismiss (or discharge) sb. from his post; remove sb. from office: ～查办 *discharge sb. from his post and prosecute him*

【撤走】withdraw; leave: ～军用物资 *withdraw and transfer military supplies* / ～使馆人员家属 *withdraw the families of the embassy staff*

chēn

抻 动 〈口〉pull out; draw out; stretch: 把你的衣服～一～。*Stretch and smooth out your clothes.*

【抻面】❶ hand-pulled noodles ❷ make noodles by drawing out the dough by hand: 他～抻得好极了。*He's really good at making hand-pulled noodles.*

嗔 动 〈书〉❶ be angry; be displeased: 生～ *get angry* ❷ be annoyed (with sb.)

【嗔怪】blame; rebuke

【嗔怒】get angry

【嗔色】an angry or sullen look: 微露～ *look somewhat displeased* / 她面带～。*She looks sullen.* or *She's wearing a sullen expression.*

chén

尘 名 ❶dust; dirt: 灰尘 ❷this world: 红尘

【尘埃】dust ◇ ～传染[医] dust infection

【尘暴】dust storm

【尘肺】[医] pneumoconiosis

【尘封】be covered with dust; be dust-laden

【尘垢】dust and dirt; dirt

【尘世】this world; this mortal life

【尘俗】❶ this world; this mortal life ❷ mundane affairs

【尘土】dust: 卡车开过,～飞扬。*The truck stirred up a cloud of dust as it drove by.* / 满身～ *be covered all over with dust*

【尘烟】(又作'尘雾') ❶ a cloud of dust: ～滚滚 *clouds of dust churning* ❷ smoke and dust: ～弥漫 *be heavy with smoke and dust*

【尘缘】the bonds of this world; carnal thoughts: ～未断 *have not broken free the bonds of this world*

臣 名 ❶ an official under a feudal ruler; subject; minister: 君～ *the monarch and his subjects* ❷ your servant (a form of self-address used by a subject when speaking to a ruler)

【臣服】〈书〉❶ submit oneself to the rule of; acknowledge allegiance to ❷ serve a ruler as his subject

【臣民】subjects of a feudal ruler

【臣子】an official in feudal times

沉 Ⅰ 动 ❶ sink: 船～了。*The boat sank.* / ～底儿 *sink to the bottom* / 月落星～。*The moon is down and the stars have set.* ❷ 〈喻〉keep down; lower; sink: ～下脸来 *pull a long face*; *put on a serious expression* / 我的心直往下～。*My heart*

sank. ❸ feel heavy：我觉得头有点～。*My head feels a bit heavy.* / 胳膊～ *have a stiff arm* / 两条腿～得迈不动步。*My legs were heavy and I could hardly move a step.* Ⅱ 形 ❶ deep；profound：睡得很～ *be in a deep sleep；be fast asleep；sleep like a log；sleep soundly* ❷ heavy：这只箱子很～。*This trunk is very heavy.*

【沉沉】❶ heavy：穗子～地垂下来。*The ears hang heavy on the stalks.* ❷ deep：～入睡 *sink into a deep sleep* / 暮霭～。*Dusk is falling.*

【沉甸甸】heavy：～的谷穗 *heavy ears of millet* / 任务还没有完成，我心里老是～的。*The thought of the unfinished task weighed heavily on my mind.*

【沉淀】form a sediment；precipitate：墨水～了。*There is some sediment in the ink.* / 水太浑啦，～一下再用。*The water is muddy，let it settle for a while.* ◇ ～池 precipitating tank；～剂 precipitating agent；～物 sediment；precipitate

【沉浮】❶ sink and rise；bob on water ❷ ups and downs of fortune；vicissitudes：宦海～ *vicissitudes of an official career*

【沉积】❶ deposit：泥沙～河底。*The silt is deposited in the riverbed.* ❷［地质］(又作'沉积作用') sedimentation：～旋回 *cycle of sedimentation* ◇ ～物 deposit；sediment；～岩 sedimentary rock

【沉寂】❶ quiet；still：～的深夜 *in the still of (the) night* / 入夜后，四野一片～。*Night fell，and it was all quiet in the open country.* ❷ no news：消息～。*There has been no news whatsoever.*

【沉降】subside ◇ ～缝 settlement joint

【沉浸】be immersed in；be steeped in；be permeated with：～在幸福的回忆中 *be immersed in happy memories*

【沉井】［建］open caisson

【沉静】❶ quiet；calm：夜深了，村子里～下来。*It was late at night，and all was quiet in the village.* ❷ calm；serene；placid：～的神色 *a serene look* / 这姑娘性格～。*She is a placid girl.*

【沉沦】sink into vice，degradation，depravity，etc.

【沉闷】❶ (of weather，atmosphere，etc.) dreary；gloomy；oppressive；depressing：那里的气氛太～了，令人无法忍受。*The atmosphere there is unbearably oppressive.* ❷ depressed；in low spirits：心情～ *feel depressed* ❸ not outgoing；withdrawn：他这个人很～。*He's rather withdrawn.*

【沉迷】be confused；be bewildered

【沉湎】〈书〉indulge in；wallow in；be given to：～于酒 *be given to heavy drinking*

【沉没】sink；founder：军舰被鱼雷击中，立即～。*The warship was torpedoed and sank at once.* / 渔船于暴风雨中～。*The fishing boat foundered in a hurricane.*

【沉默】❶ reticent；taciturn；uncommunicative：从此，他变得更～了。*He has become even more reticent since then.* ❷ silent：保持～ *remain silent* / 他～了一会儿又继续说下去。*After a moment's silence he went on.* ◇ ～寡言 reticent；taciturn；uncommunicative

【沉溺】wallow or indulge in (vices，etc.)：～于声色 *wallow in sensual pleasures*

【沉砂池】［环保］grit chamber

【沉睡】be sunk in sleep；be fast asleep；be sound asleep

【沉思】ponder；meditate；be lost in thought：他为这个问题～了好久。*He pondered over this problem for a long time.* / 陷入～之中 *be lost in thought；be deep in meditation*

【沉痛】❶ with a deep feeling of grief or remorse；heavy at heart：怀着～的心情 *be deeply grieved* ❷ deeply felt；bitter：应该接受这个～的教训。*It is necessary to learn a lesson from this bitter experience.*

【沉稳】❶ steady；staid；sedate：这个人很～，处理问题细密周到。*A sober and steady type，he is meticulous and thoughtful in handling matters.* ❷ untroubled；sound：睡得很～ *sleep soundly (or peacefully)*

【沉陷】❶ sink；cave in：地震后路基～了。*The earthquake made the roadbed cave in.* ❷ settlement：不均匀～ *unequal settlement*

【沉香】［植］agalloch eaglewood (Aquilaria agallocha；Aquilaria sinensis)

【沉箱】［建］caisson

【沉毅】steady and strong：这位将军～果断。*The general was steady and resolute.*

【沉吟】mutter to oneself，unable to make up one's mind：他～了一会儿才去打电话。*He hesitated for a while before he made the phone call.*

【沉吟不决】hesitate；be irresolute；be undecided

【沉鱼落雁】(of feminine beauty) make fish sink and birds alight

【沉郁】depressed；gloomy

【沉冤】gross injustice；unrighted wrong：他的十年～终于得到昭雪。*After being a victim of gross injustice for ten long years，he was finally rehabilitated.*

【沉冤莫白】grievous wrongs that can never be redressed

【沉渣】❶ sediment；dregs ❷ dregs of society

【沉重】❶ heavy：～的脚步 *heavy steps* / ～的打击 *a heavy blow* / 心情～ *with a heavy heart* ❷ serious；critical：病情～ *critically ill*

【沉住气】keep calm；keep cool；be steady：不要一听到不同意见就沉不住气。*Don't get excited the moment you hear a differing opinion.*

【沉着】cool-headed；composed；steady；calm：勇敢～ *brave and steady* / ～应战 *meet the attack calmly*

【沉子】sinker

【沉醉】〈喻〉get drunk；become intoxicated：～在节日的欢乐里 *be intoxicated with the spirit of the festival*

忱 名〈书〉sincere feeling；true sentiment：热忱

辰 名 ❶ celestial bodies：星辰 ❷ any of the traditional twelve two-hour periods of the day：时辰 ❸ time；day；occasion：寿辰

【辰砂】cinnabar；vermillion

【辰时】the period of the day from 7 a.m. to 9 a.m.

陈 Ⅰ 动 ❶ lay out；put on display：陈列 ❷ state；explain：此事当另函详～。*The matter will be explained in detail in a separate letter.* Ⅱ 形 old；stale：～米 *old rice*

【陈兵】mass (or deploy) troops：～边境 *mass troops along the border* / ～百万 *deploy a million troops*

【陈陈相因】follow a set routine；stay in the same old groove

【陈词滥调】hackneyed and stereotyped expressions；clichés

【陈醋】mature vinegar

【陈废率】rate of obsolescence

【陈腐】old and decayed；stale；outworn：～的词句 *stale phrases* / 重男轻女的～观念 *the outworn concept of regarding men as superior to women*

【陈规】outmoded conventions：打破～ *break with outmoded conventions* ◇ ～陋习 outmoded regulations and irrational practices；bad customs and habits

【陈货】old stock；shopworn goods

【陈迹】a thing of the past

【陈酒】old wine；mellow wine

【陈旧】outmoded；obsolete；old-fashioned；out-of-date：～的观点 *an outmoded notion* / ～的设备 *outdated equipment* / ～的词语 *obsolete words and expressions*

【陈列】display；set out；exhibit：玻璃柜里～着各种矿物标本。*Ore specimens are on display in showcases.* ◇ ～馆 exhibition hall；～柜 showcase；～品 exhibits；articles on display；～室 exhibition room；showroom

【陈年】of long standing；preserved for a long time：～老酒 *old vintage wine* / ～老账 *an old (or longstanding) debt*

【陈皮】[中] dried tangerine or orange peel

【陈设】❶ display；set out：屋子里～着几件工艺品。*There is some artware set out in the room.* ❷ furnishings：房间里的～朴素大方。*The room was furnished simply and in good taste.*

【陈述】state：～自己的意见 *state one's views* ◇ ～句 [语] declarative sentence

【陈说】state；explain：～利害 *explain the advantages and disadvantages (of a situation, course of action, etc.)*

【陈诉】state；recount：～委屈 *state one's grievances*

晨 名 morning：清晨

【晨操】morning exercises

【晨光】the light of the early morning sun；dawn ◇ ～熹微 the first faint rays of dawn

【晨练】morning exercise；morning practice

【晨夕】morning and evening：～相处 *be together from morning till evening；be very close*

【晨曦】the first rays of the morning sun

【晨星】❶ stars at dawn ❷ [天] morning star

chèn

衬 Ⅰ 动 ❶ line；place sth. underneath：～着驼绒的大衣 *a fleece-lined overcoat* / ～上一层纸 *put a piece of paper underneath* / 里面～一件背心 *wear a vest underneath* ❷ provide a background for；set off；serve as a foil to：白雪～着红梅，景色十分美丽。*The red plum blossoms set off by the white snow were a beautiful sight.* Ⅱ 名 lining；liner：领～ *collar lining* / 袖～ *cuff lining* / 钢～ *steel liner* / ～管 *liner tube*

【衬布】lining cloth

【衬裤】underpants；pants

【衬里】lining

【衬裙】underskirt；slip；petticoat

【衬衫】❶ shirt ❷ blouse

【衬托】set off；serve as a foil to：红花要有绿叶～。*Red flowers must have green leaves as a foil.*

【衬衣】❶ underclothes；undergarments ❷ shirt

【衬纸】slip sheet；interleaving paper

【衬字】word inserted in a line of verse for balance or euphony

称 动 fit；match；suit：对称 ——另见 chēng

【称身】(of a garment) fit：这件外套你穿了挺～的。*This coat fits you perfectly.*

【称体裁衣】同〖量体裁衣〗

【称心】find sth. satisfactory；be gratified：这孩子一不～就发脾气。*The child will kick up a row if he doesn't get his own way.* / 这老人晚年过得很～。*The man spent his old age in contentment.*

【称心如意】after one's own heart；very gratifying and satisfactory：～的工作 *a most satisfying job* / 天底下的事未必都那么～。*In this world, things don't always turn out the way you want.*

【称愿】be gratified (esp. at the misfortune of a rival)

【称职】prove oneself competent at one's job；fill a post with credit；be well qualified for a post：他在公司里担任过好几种职务，都很～。*He has held several different posts in the firm and proved himself competent at all of them.*

趁 Ⅰ 动 take advantage of (time, opportunity, etc.)；avail oneself of：我想～这个机会讲几句话。*I'd like to take this opportunity to say a few words.* Ⅱ 介 while：这面～热吃吧。*Eat the noodles while they are hot.* / ～风起帆 *set sail when the wind is fair*

【趁便】when it is convenient；at one's convenience：你回去的时候，～给我带个口信。*W'* you go back, would you take a message for me?

【趁火打劫】loot a burning house —take advantage of sb.'s misfortune to do him harm; fish in troubled waters

【趁机】take advantage of the occasion; seize the chance: ～捣乱 *seize the opportunity to make trouble*

【趁空】use one's spare time; avail oneself of leisure time: 我～去看了看老王。*I went to see Lao Wang when I happened to have a few minutes to spare.*

【趁钱】〈方〉have lots of money; be rich: 他的老板很～。*His boss is rolling in money.*

【趁热打铁】strike while the iron is hot

【趁势】take advantage of a favorable situation: 他越过对方后卫,～把球踢入球门。*He dribbled past the full back and scored a goal.*

【趁早】as early as possible; before it is too late; at the first opportunity: 咱们～动身,争取十点以前赶到。*Let's start off early and try to get there by ten.* / 你脸色不好,～去看看吧。*You don't look well. You'd better go and see a doctor right away.*

chēng

称 Ⅰ动 ❶ call: 我们都～他老李。*We all call him Lao Li.* ❷ say; state: 据外交部发言人～ *according to the Foreign Ministry spokesman* ❸〈书〉commend; praise: 称许 ❹ weigh: 用秤～一～。*Weigh it in the balance.* / 给我～一公斤苹果。*I'd like one kilo of apples, please.* Ⅱ名 name: 俗～ *popular name* / 青藏高原素有世界屋脊之～。*The Qinghai-Xizang Plateau has long been known as the roof of the world.* ——另见 chèn

【称霸】seek hegemony; dominate: ～世界 *dominate the world*

【称便】find sth. a great convenience: 商店日夜服务,群众无不～。*Shops that stay open twenty-four hours a day are a great convenience to the public.*

【称病】claim to be ill; offer illness as an excuse; plead illness: ～辞职 *resign on grounds of ill health*

【称臣】declare oneself a vassal or subject; acknowledge one's allegiance to a ruler

【称道】speak approvingly of; praise; acclaim: 值得～ *be praiseworthy* / 无足～ *not worth mentioning; of no consequence*

【称得起】deserve to be called; be worthy of the name of: 他～一位伟大的改革家。*He deserves to be called a great reformer.*

【称帝】proclaim oneself emperor

【称孤道寡】style oneself king— act like an absolute monarch

【称号】title; name; designation: 她获得了先进工作者的～。*She has won the title of advanced worker.*

【称呼】❶ call; address: 我该怎么～她? *What should I call her? or How should I address her?* ❷ a form of address

【称快】express one's gratification; express joy and jubilation

【称量】weigh ◇ ～体重[体] weigh in

【称奇】speak admiringly of; regard as amazing: 啧啧～ *praise sb. profusely (for his superb ability, skill or performance)*

【称颂】praise; extol; eulogize: 人人～他的崇高品德。*Everyone extols his noble qualities.*

【称王】proclaim oneself king

【称王称霸】act like an overlord; lord it over; domineer

【称为】call or be called; be known as: 食盐在化学上～氯化钠。*Sodium chloride is the chemical term for table salt.*

【称谓】appellation; title

【称羡】express one's admiration or envy: ～不已 *express profuse admiration*

【称谢】express one's thanks; thank: ～不止 *thank sb. again and again*

【称兄道弟】call each other brothers; be on intimate terms

【称雄】hold sway over a region; rule the roost: 割据～ *break away from central authority and exercise local power; set up separationist rule*

【称许】praise; commendation: 他的工作博得普遍的～。*His work received high praise from everyone.*

【称誉】sing the praises of; praise; acclaim

【称赞】praise; acclaim; commend: 我们都～她办事公道。*We all praise her for her impartiality.*

蛏 名 razor clam

【蛏干】dried razor clam

【蛏子】razor clam

撑 Ⅰ动 ❶ prop up; support: 两手～着下巴 *rest one's chin in both hands* ❷ push or move with a pole; pole: ～船 *pole a boat; punt* ❸ maintain; keep up: 他～不住,笑了。*He could not help laughing.* ❹ open; unfurl: ～伞 *open an umbrella* / 把麻袋～开 *hold open the sack* ❺ fill to the point of bursting: 我已经有点～,不能再吃了。*I'm rather full and can't eat any more.* / 别装得太多,把口袋～破了。*Don't stuff the sack too full, or it'll burst.* Ⅱ名 [机] brace; stay: 角～ *corner brace*

【撑臂】[机] brace

【撑场面】(又作'撑门面')keep up appearances: 他们为了～,借了很多钱大摆喜筵。*In order to keep up appearances, they borrowed a lot of money to give a big wedding party.*

【撑持】prop up; shore up; sustain: ～局面 *shore up a shaky situation*

【撑杆】vaulting pole ◇ ～跳高 pole vault; pole jump

【撑条】[机] stay：斜～ *diagonal stay* / 横～ *cross stay*

【撑腰】support；back up；bolster up：有他给你～，你还怕什么？*He's backing you up，so what's there to fear？* ◇ ～打气 bolster and pep up

瞠 动〈书〉stare

【瞠乎其后】stare helplessly at the vanishing back of the runner ahead—despair of catching up

【瞠目】stare（in alarm，embarrassment，confusion，etc.）：～不知所答 *stare blankly，at a loss for a suitable reply* / ～相视 *stare fixedly in each other's face*

【瞠目结舌】stare tongue-tied；stare dumbfounded

chéng

丞 名 an assistant to an official（in ancient China）：县～ *county magistrate's assistant*

【丞相】prime minister（in ancient China）；chief minister

成 Ⅰ 动 ❶ accomplish；succeed：事～之后 *after this is achieved* / 他～不了大事。*He can't accomplish anything significant.* ❷ become；turn into：两个人～了好朋友。*The two of them became good friends.* / 雪化～水了。*The snow melted into water.* / 绿树～荫。*The trees give welcome shade.* ❸〈口〉all right；O.K.：～！就这么办吧。*O.K. Go ahead.* / 你不去可不～。*No，you must go.* / 什么时候都～。*Any time will do.* Ⅱ 名 achievement；result：坐享其成 Ⅲ 形 ❶ fully developed or fully grown：成人 / 成虫 ❷ established；ready-made：成规/ 成药 ❸ in considerable numbers or amounts：～排的新房 *row upon row of new houses* / 产量～倍增长。*Output has doubled and redoubled.* ❹ capable；able：说起口译，他可真～！*When it comes to oral interpretation，he really knows his job.* Ⅳ 量 one tenth：增产两～ *a 20% increase in output；output increased by 20 per cent*

【成败】success or failure：～在此一举。*Success or failure hinges on this one action.*

【成本】cost：生产～ *production cost* / 固定～ *fixed cost* / 可变～ *variable cost* / 直接(间接)～ *direct（indirect）cost* ◇ ～法 law of cost；～分配 cost distribution；～核算 cost accounting；～加运费价格 cost and freight（C.& F.）；～价格 cost price；～会计 cost accounting；～膨胀 cost inflation；～效率 cost performance；～账 cost accounts；～指数 cost index number

【成材】❶ grow into useful timber：这棵树已经～了。*This tree has grown to full size.* ❷ become a useful person：不让孩子经风雨见世面，怎么能～呢？*How can a child grow up to be useful if he is not allowed to face the world and brave the storm？*

【成材林】standing timber；mature timber

【成虫】[动] adult insect；imago

【成簇处理】[计] in-line processing

【成堆】form a pile；be in heaps：菜市场门外摆着～的蔬菜。*Vegetables are piled（or heaped）up outside the food market.* / 我们不要等问题成了堆才去解决。*We shouldn't wait until problems pile up before we try to solve them.*

【成方】[中] set prescription

【成分】(又作‘成份’) ❶ composition；component part；ingredient：化学～ *chemical composition* / 肥料的～ *the composition of a fertilizer* ❷ one's class status；one's profession or economic status：定～ *determine sb.'s class status*

【成风】become a common practice；become the order of the day：国内旅游～。*Tourism has become very popular in this country.*

【成个儿】❶ grow to a good size：苹果已经～了。*The apples have grown to a good size.* ❷ be well formed；be in the proper form：他的字写得不～。*His handwriting lacks form.*

【成功】succeed；be a success：大会开得很～。*The congress was a great success.* / 试验～了吗？*Did the experiment come off all right？*

【成规】established practice；set rules；groove；rut

【成果】achievement；fruit；gain；positive result：科研～ *achievements in scientific research* / 劳动～ *the fruits of labour* / 改革的～ *successes scored in reform*

【成婚】get married

【成活】survive：新栽的树苗都已～。*The new seedlings have all survived.* ◇ ～率 survival rate

【成绩】result（of work or study）；achievement；success：取得很大～ *achieve great successes* / 在比赛中取得良好的～ *get good results in a tournament* / 学习～不太好 *not do very well in one's studies* ◇ ～报告 score reporting；～评定 achievement evaluation

【成绩单】school report；report card；transcript

【成家】(of a man) get married：他还没有～。*He's not married yet.* ◇ ～立业 marry and embark on a career

【成见】preconceived idea；prejudice：有～ *be prejudiced* / ～很深 *be deeply prejudiced* / 消除～ *dispel prejudices*

【成交】strike a bargain；conclude a transaction；clinch a deal ◇ ～额 volume of business

【成角透视】angular perspective

【成就】❶ achievement；success；attainment；accomplishment：他是个很有～的科学家。*He is an accomplished scientist.* / 没什么～ *haven't achieved anything* / 剧本的艺术～ *artistic merits of a play* ❷ achieve；accomplish

【成矿作用】mineralization

【成立】❶ found；establish；set up：～一所学校 *set up（or establish）a school* / 举行～大会 *hold an inaugural meeting* ❷ be tenable；hold water：这个论点不能～。*That argument is untenable（or does not hold water）.*

【成例】precedent；existing model：这件事没有～

可援。*There is no precedent for this.* / 有～可循。*There is a precedent to follow.* / 援引～ *cite a precedent*

【成殓】〈书〉be encoffined

【成龙配套】fill in the gaps to complete a chain (of equipment, construction projects, etc.); link up the parts to form a whole: 使排灌设备～ *complete a drainage and irrigation network*

【成眠】〈书〉fall asleep; go to sleep: 夜不～ *lie awake all night*

【成名】become famous; make a name for oneself: 他早就成了名。*He made a name for himself long ago.*

【成名成家】establish one's reputation as an authority in one's field

【成命】an order already issued: 收回成命

【成年】❶ grow up; come of age: ～人 *grown-ups; adults* / ～树 *full-grown trees* / 尚未～ *be under age; have not grown up yet* ❷〈口〉all year: ～在外 *be away from home all year* ◇ ～累月 year in year out; for years on end

【成批】group by group; in batches: ～的新钢材 *batches of new-type steel products* / ～生产 *serial production; mass production* ◇ ～处理 batch processing

【成品】end product; finished product

【成气候】(usu. used in the negative) make good: 成不了什么气候 *will not get anywhere*

【成器】grow up to be a useful person: 他那儿子将来成不了器。*His boy will never come to anything.*

【成千上万】(又作'成千成万','成千累万') thousands and tens of thousands; thousands upon thousands: ～的人 *tens of thousands of people*

【成亲】get married: 他们是去年成的亲。*They got married last year.*

【成全】help sb. achieve his aim

【成群】in groups; in great numbers: ～的牛羊 *herds (or droves) of cattle and sheep* / ～的狼(猎狗) *packs of wolves (hounds)* ◇ ～结队 in crowds

【成人】❶ be grown up; become full-grown: 长大～ *be grown to manhood* ❷ adult; grown-up ◇ ～电影 adult film; ～高等教育 adult higher education; ～高考 entrance examination to institute of higher education for adults; ～高校 institution of higher education for adults; ～教育 adult education

【成人之美】help sb. to fulfil his wish; aid sb. in doing a good deed: 君子～。*A gentleman is always ready to help others attain their aims.*

【成仁】〈书〉die for a righteous cause: 不成功,便～。*Fulfil your mission or, failing that, lay down your life.*

【成色】❶ the percentage of gold or silver in a coin, etc.; the relative purity of gold or silver: 这条金项链～好。*This is a fine gold necklace.* ❷ quality: 看～定价钱 *fix the prices according to the quality*

【成事】❶ accomplish sth.; succeed: 你这样做成不了事,只会误事。*If you go at it this way you'll never succeed. Instead you'll make a mess of things.* ❷〈书〉a thing that is past or finished ◇ ～不足,败事有余 unable to accomplish anything but liable to spoil everything; never able to achieve, always able to ruin; never make, but always mar

【成书】❶ be published in book form ❷ a book already in circulation

【成熟】ripe; mature: 桃子快～了。*The peaches will soon be ripe.* / 她到十六岁发育～。*She had reached maturity by the time she was sixteen.* ◇ ～林 mature forest; ～期 mature period; maturity

【成双】form a pair

【成说】an accepted theory or formulation: 进行科学研究,不能囿于～,要敢于创新。*In scientific research, one should break new paths and not be fettered by accepted theories.*

【成诵】〈书〉be able to recite; be able to repeat from memory: 熟读～ *read again and again until one knows by heart; learn by rote*

【成俗】become social custom

【成算】a preconceived idea or plan: 我是走一步看一步,心里没什么～。*I am just groping along without any preconceived plans.*

【成套】form a complete set: ～家具 *complete sets of furniture* / ～设备 *complete sets of equipment; complete plants and equipment*

【成天】〈口〉all day long; all the time: ～忙忙碌碌 *be kept busy all day long* / ～不在家 *be out all the time*

【成为】become; turn into: ～工程师 *become an engineer* / 把我国建设～社会主义的现代化强国 *build China into a powerful modern socialist country*

【成文】❶ existing writings: 抄袭～ *copy exist-ing writings; follow a set pattern* ❷ writtn: 规则已经归纳～。*The rules are all put together in written form.* ◇ ～法 written laws; statute law; statutory law

【成问题】be a problem; be open to question (or doubt, objection): 雨再不停,明天的比赛就要～了。*If the rain doesn't stop, I doubt if we can have the game tomorrow.*

【成仙】become an immortal

【成象】[物] formation of image; imagery

【成效】effect; result: ～显著 *produce a marked effect; achieve remarkable success* / ～甚少 *achieve little* / 初见～ *win initial success*

【成心】intentionally; on purpose; with deliberate intent: 别生气,他不是～的。*Don't be angry. He didn't mean it.* / 他～让我难堪。*He purposely embarrassed me.*

【成形】❶ take shape: 我们的计划开始～了。*Our plan is beginning to take shape.* ❷ shaping; forming: 爆炸～ *explosive forming* / 冷滚～ *cold roll forming*

【成型】(of workpieces or products) be in finished form

【成性】by nature; become sb.'s second nature: 好斗～ *be belligerent by nature* / 这家伙盗窃～。*Stealing has become that rascal's second nature.*

【成药】pharmacist-prepared medicine; patent medicine

【成衣】❶〈旧〉tailoring ❷ ready-made clothes; ready-to-wear ◇ ～铺〈旧〉tailor's shop; tailor's; dress-maker's

【成议】an agreement already reached: 此事已有～。*An agreement has already been reached on this issue.*

【成因】cause of formation; contributing factor: 海洋的～ *the origin of seas and oceans*

【成鱼】adult fish

【成语】set phrase (usu. composed of four characters); idiom

【成员】member (of a group or family): 正式～ *a full member* / 家庭主要～ *the chief members of a family* / 全社会～ *every member of society* ◇ ～国 member state

【成约】a signed treaty or agreement; an existing agreement

【成灾】cause disaster; result in disaster: 暴雨～。*The heavy rainstorm caused a disastrous flood.*

【成则为王,败则为寇】(又作'成者为王,败者为寇') The winner is the king, the loser a bandit; Losers are always in the wrong; nothing succeeds like success.

【成长】grow up; grow to maturity: 果树正茁壮～。*The fruit trees are growing well.* / 关心年轻一代的健康～ *take an active interest in the healthy growth of the younger generation*

【成竹在胸】同〖胸有成竹〗

呈 Ⅰ **动** ❶ assume (form, colour, etc.): 叶～椭圆形。*The leaf is oval in shape.* ❷ submit or present (a report, etc.) to a superior Ⅱ **名** petition; memorial

【呈报】submit a report; report a matter (to a superior): ～上级机关备案 *report the matter to a higher level for the record*

【呈递】present; submit: ～国书 *present credentials (or letters of credence)*

【呈览】submit sth. to a higher authority for perusal

【呈请】apply (to the higher authorities for consideration or approval): ～上级审批 *apply to the higher level for approval*

【呈文】a document submitted to a superior; memorial; petition

【呈现】present (a certain appearance); appear; emerge

【呈献】respectfully present: ～花圈 *lay a wreath with due formality*

诚 Ⅰ **形** sincere; honest: 诚心 Ⅱ **副**〈书〉really; actually; indeed: ～非易事。*It is by no means easy.* / ～有此事。*There actually was such a thing.*

【诚笃】〈书〉sincere and earnest: 他为人～,可以信赖。*He's sincere and earnest, and so can be trusted.*

【诚服】submit oneself willingly (to sb.): 心悦诚服

【诚惶诚恐】with reverence and awe; in fear and trepidation

【诚恳】sincere: 态度～ *be sincere in what one does and says* / ～地接受别人的意见 *listen to other people's criticisms with an open mind*

【诚朴】honest; sincere and simple: 一个～的青年 *an honest youth* / ～的工作作风 *a simple and honest work style*

【诚然】❶ truly; really: 她喜爱她的小狗,那小狗也～可爱。*She loves her puppy, and the puppy is really lovable.* ❷ (used correlatively with 但是) no doubt; to be sure; it is true: 旱情～是严重的,但是它吓不倒我们。*True, the drought is serious, but it can't scare us.*

【诚实】honest: ～可靠 *honest and dependable* / ～劳动 *honest work*

【诚心】❶ sincere desire; sincerity; whole-heartedness: 一片～ *in all sincerity* ❷ sincere and earnest; devout: 她长年吃斋念佛,可～了。*Over the years she's been abstaining from meat and praying to Buddha. She's such a devout Buddhist.*

【诚心诚意】earnestly and sincerely: 我们要～地积极帮助少数民族发展经济建设和文化建设。*We must sincerely and actively help the minority nationalities to develop their economy and culture.*

【诚意】good faith; sincerity: 表明～ *show one's good faith* / 缺乏～ *lack sincerity* / 谁也不怀疑你的～。*No one doubts your sincerity.*

【诚挚】sincere; cordial: ～友好的气氛 *a sincere and friendly atmosphere* / 致以～的谢意 *extend one's heartfelt thanks to sb.*

承 **动** ❶ bear; hold; carry: 那座木桥～得住这样重的卡车吗? *Can that wooden bridge carry such heavy trucks?* ❷ undertake; contract (to do a job): ～印名片 *undertake the printing of visiting cards* ❸〈书〉be indebted (to sb. for a kindness); be granted a favour: ～您过奖。*You flatter me.* ❹ continue; carry on: 继承

【承办】undertake: ～土木工程 *undertake civil engineering projects* / 这件事由他一手～。*He has taken the whole task upon himself.* ◇ ～者 contractor

【承包】contract: ～桥梁工程 *contract to build a bridge* / ～一万吨水泥的供应 *contract for the supply of ten thousand tons of cement* ◇ ～合同 contract; ～经营责任制 managerial responsibility system of contractor; ～商 contractor; ～责任制 responsibility system of operation on contracting basis; ～制 contract system; contracting out system

【承保】undertake to provide insurance; accept insurance：这家公司为工矿企业～火险。*The company undertakes to provide fire insurance for factories, mines and other enterprises.* ◇ ～单［经］open cover；～范围 insurance coverage；～人 insurer

【承保通知书】cover note

【承担】bear；undertake；assume：～一切费用 *bear all the costs* / ～义务 *undertake the obligation* ◇ ～法律责任 bear legal liability；～风险 acceptance of risk；bear the risks；～责任 shoulder (or bear) the responsibility

【承当】❶ bear；take on：一切责任由我～。*I'll bear all the responsibility.* ❷〈方〉agree (to do sth.)；promise

【承兑】honour；accept：～支票 *honour a cheque* / ～汇票 *accept a bill* ◇ ～交单 documentary against acceptance；～票据 acceptance bill；～人 acceptor

【承继】❶ be adopted as heir to one's uncle ❷ adopt one's brother's son (as one's heir)

【承建】(of a project) contract to construct：宾馆由建筑公司～。*A construction company has contracted to build the guesthouse*

【承接】❶ hold out a vessel to have a liquid poured into it ❷ continue；carry on：～上文 *continued from the preceding paragraph* ❸ undertake the task of；contract to accept：～来料加工 *accept customers' materials for processing；undertake the processing of supplied materials*

【承揽】contract to do a whole job；undertake an entire project：～物资运输业务 *undertake the transportation of materials* ◇ ～合同 contract of work；contractor's agreement

【承蒙】〈套〉be accorded (a kindness)；be granted (a favour)：～照顾，十分感谢。*I am very grateful to you for the kind treatment you accorded me.*

【承诺】promise to undertake；undertake to do sth.：我无法作出肯定的～。*I can't make a definite promise.*

【承情】〈套〉be much obliged；owe a debt of gratitude

【承认】❶ admit；acknowledge；recognize：～错误 *admit one's mistake；acknowledge one's fault* / 大家都～这个规划还很不完善。*Everybody agreed that the plan was far from perfect.* ❷ give diplomatic recognition；recognize：～中华人民共和国政府为中国的惟一合法政府 *recognize the Government of the People's Republic of China as the sole legal government of China*

【承上启下】(又作'承上起下') form a connecting link between what comes before and what goes after (as in a piece of writing, etc.)

【承受】❶ bear；support；endure：这桥～得住很大的重量。*The bridge can bear a tremendous weight.* / ～住种种考验 *be able to stand every kind of trial* ❷ inherit (a legacy, etc.)

【承袭】❶ adopt；follow (a tradition, etc.)：～旧制 *follow the old system* ❷ inherit (a peerage, etc.)

【承先启后】(又作'承前启后') inherit the past and usher in the future；serve as a link between past and future

【承销】act as sales agent ◇ ～人 sales agent；salesman

【承运】❶〈书〉(of a ruler) be ordained by Heaven ❷undertake the transportation of (goods) ◇ ～人 carrier

【承载】bear the weight of：～能力 *bearing (or carrying) capacity；load-bearing capacity*

【承重】load-bearing；bearing ◇ ～墙［建］bearing (or load-bearing) wall

【承转】assume the responsibility of forwarding (a document) to the level above or below

城

城 名 ❶ city wall；wall：～外 *outside the city wall；outside the city* ❷ city：外～ *outer city* / 内～ *inner city* / 东～ *the eastern part of the city* ❸ town

【城邦】city-state

【城堡】castle

【城池】〈书〉city wall and moat；city

【城防】city defence：～巩固。*The city is closely guarded.* / ～部队 *city garrison* / ～工事 *defence works of a city*

【城府】〈书〉a mind hard to fathom；subtle thinking：～很深 *shrewd and deep；subtle*

【城根】sections of a city close to the city wall

【城关】the area just outside a city gate

【城隍】town god (in Taoist legend) ◇ ～庙 town god's temple

【城际】inter-city ◇ ～快车 inter-city express (buses, trains, etc.)

【城郊】outskirts of a town

【城里】inside the city；in town：～人 *city dwellers；townspeople* / ～很热闹。*The city is bustling with activity.*

【城楼】a tower over a city gate；gate tower：在天安门～上 *on the rostrum of Tian An Men*

【城门】city gate

【城门失火，殃及池鱼】When the city gate catches fire, the fish in the moat come to grief—innocent people suffering from what happens to others

【城墙】city wall

【城区】the city proper：～和郊区 *the city proper and the suburbs*

【城市】town (or city)：～规划 *city planning* / ～环境 *urban environment* / ～居民 *city dwellers；urban population* ◇ ～发展 urban development；～高速铁路 rapid transit；～公共设施规划 urban public facilities planning；～建设 urban construction；city building；～旧区改造 makeover for an old downtown area；～垃圾 municipal refuse；～贫民 urban poor；city poor；～社会学 urban sociology；～污染 municipal pollution；～学 urbanology；～学专家 urbanologist；～与区域计划学 ekistics；～综合开发 urban comprehensive development; city building

【城乡结合】integration of town and country

【城乡贸易】urban and rural trade

【城头】❶ the top of a city wall: ～飘扬着红旗。*Red flags are flying on top of the city wall.* ❷ gate tower

【城下之盟】a treaty concluded with the enemy who have reached the city wall; terms accepted under duress; a treaty signed under coercion

【城乡】town and country; urban and rural areas; the city and the countryside: ～居民 *urban and rural residents* / ～差别 *the difference between town and country*

【城运会】(〈略〉全称为'城市运动会') city sports meet

【城镇】cities and towns ◇～污水 town sewage

乘 动 ❶ ride: ～公共汽车 *ride in a bus; go by bus* / ～出租汽车到火车站去 *take a taxi to the railway station* / ～火车(飞机、轮船)旅行 *travel by train (plane, boat)* / 他们～车前往宾馆。*They drove to the guesthouse.* ❷ take advantage of; avail oneself of: ～夜出击 *attack under cover of night* / ～敌不备 *take the enemy unawares* ❸[数] multiply: 五～三等于十五。*Five times three is fifteen.* or 5 *multiplied by* 3 *is* 15.

【乘便】when it is convenient; at one's convenience: 请你～把那本书带给我。*Please bring me the book whenever it's convenient.*

【乘法】[数] multiplication ◇～表 multiplication table

【乘方】❶ involution ❷ power: *n* 的五次～ *the fifth power of n; n (raised) to the power of 5;* n^5

【乘风破浪】ride the wind and cleave the waves; brave the wind and the waves

【乘机】seize the opportunity: ～反攻 *seize the opportunity to counterattack*

【乘积】[数] product

【乘警】train police

【乘客】passenger

【乘凉】enjoy the cool; relax in a cool place

【乘龙快婿】an excellent or ideal son-in-law (usu. of high social or official position)

【乘幂】[数] power

【乘人之危】take advantage of sb.'s precarious position

【乘胜】exploit (or follow up) a victory: ～追击 *follow up a victory with hot pursuit* / ～前进 *advance on the crest of a victory; push on in the flush of victory*

【乘数】[数] multiplier

【乘务员】attendant on a train

【乘隙】take advantage of a loophole; turn sb.'s mistake to one's own account: ～突围 *an opportunity to break through the encirclement (or siege)* / 乘敌之隙 *exploit the enemy's blunder*

【乘兴】while one is in high spirits: ～作了一首诗 *improvise a poem while in a joyful mood*

【乘兴而来】arrive in high spirits; set out cheerfully / ～,兴尽而返 *arrive in high spirits and depart well content* / ～,败兴而归 *set out cheerfully and come back disappointed*

【乘虚】take advantage of a weak point (or an opening) in an opponent's defence; act when sb. is off guard

【乘虚而入】(又作'乘隙而入') break through at a weak point; act when one's opponent is off guard; exploit one's opponent's weakness: 我军～,势如破竹。*Our troops took advantage of the enemy's weakened position and cut in like a knife slicing down a length of bamboo.*

盛 动 ❶ fill; ladle: ～饭 *fill a bowl with rice* / 把菜～出来 *ladle food from the pot; dish out food* / ～汤 *ladle out soup* / 缸里～满了酒。*The crock is filled with wine.* ❷ hold; contain: 这间屋子太小,～不了这么多东西。*The room is too small to hold all these things.* / 这个礼堂能～一千人。*This hall is big enough for a thousand people.* ——另见 shèng

程 名 ❶ rule; regulation: 章程 ❷ order; procedure: 议程 ❸ journey; stage of a journey: 送他一～ *accompany him part of the way* / 送了一～又一～ *accompany (a guest, traveller, etc.) league after league before parting* ❹ distance: 行程

【程度】❶ level; degree: 文化～ *level of education; degree of literacy* ❷ extent; degree: 在很大(一定)～上 *to a great (certain) extent* / 在不同～上 *in varying degrees*

【程控】〈略〉见〖程序控制〗

【程控电话】program-controlled telephone ◇～网络 programme-controlled phone network

【程控网】program-controlled network

【程式】form; pattern; formula: 公文～ *forms and formulas of official documents* / ～动作 *stylized movements (as in Beijing opera)* ◇～化 stylize

【程序】❶ order; procedure; course; sequence: 工作～ *working procedure* / 法律～ *legal procedure* / ～事项 *procedural matters* ❷ automation program: 编～ *write programs for computers; program* ◇～存储器 program memory; ～法 procedural law; ～分析员 analyst-programer; ～计算器 program counter; ～教学 programmed instruction or learning; ～控制 programmed control; ～库 program library; ～流程图 program flow chart; ～设计 automation programming; ～设计语言 programming language; program language; ～设计员(又作'程序员') programmer; ～装入 program loading

【程仪】〈书〉a gift of money for a friend going on a journey

惩 动 punish; penalize: 惩罚

【惩办】punish: 依法～ *punish according to law* / 严加～ *punish severely* / ～和宽大相结合 *com-*

bine punishment with leniency

【惩处】penalize; punish: 依法～ *punish in accordance with the law*

【惩恶劝善】punish evil-doers and encourage people to do good

【惩罚】punish; penalize: 受到一次严厉的～ *pay a severe penalty*

【惩戒】punish sb. to teach him a lesson; discipline sb. as a warning; take disciplinary action against: 吊销执照,以示～ *revoke sb.'s licence as a punishment*

【惩前毖后】learn from past errors to avoid future mistakes: ～,治病救人 *learn from past mistakes to avoid future ones, and cure the sickness to save the patient*

【惩一儆百】(又作'惩一警百') punish one to warn a hundred; make an example of sb.: 重办这个为首的,～。*Severely punish the ringleader as a warning to the rest.*

【惩治】punish; mete out punishment to ◇ ～腐败 fight against corruption; ～贪污条例 Regulation for Suppression of Corruption

澄 Ⅰ 形 (of water, air, etc.) clear; transparent; limpid Ⅱ 动 clear up; clarify ——另见 dèng

【澄碧】lear blue: 湖水～。*The lake water is a clear blue.*

【澄清】❶ clear; transparent: 湖水碧绿～。*The water of the lake is green and clear.* ❷ clear up; clarify: ～误会 *clear up a misunderstanding* / ～事实 *clarify some facts* / 要求～ *demand clarification* ——另见 dèngqīng

橙 名 ❶ orange (the tree and the fruit): 甜～ *sweet orange* ❷ orange colour

【橙黄】orange colour

【橙子】orange (the fruit)

chěng

逞 动 ❶ show off; aunt: ～英雄 *pose as a hero* / ～威风 *show off one's strength or power; swagger about* ❷ carry out (an evil design); succeed (in a scheme): 得逞 ❸ indulge; give free rein to

【逞能】show off one's skill or ability; parade one's ability: 他的缺点是好～。*The trouble with him is that he likes to show off.*

【逞强】aunt one's superiority: ～好胜 *parade one's superiority and strive to outshine others*

【逞凶】act violently; act with murderous intent

骋 动 〈书〉❶ gallop: 驰骋 ❷ give free rein to

【骋目】〈书〉look as far as the eye can see; look into the distance: ～远眺 *scan distant horizons*

chèng

秤 名 balance; steelyard: 拿～称称 *weigh it in a balance (or on the scales)* / 一杆～ *a steelyard*

【秤锤】the sliding weight of a steelyard

【秤杆】the arm (or beam) of a steelyard

【秤钩】steelyard hook

【秤盘】❶ the pan or dish of a steelyard ❷ either of the pans or dishes of a balance; scale

【秤砣】〈口〉the sliding weight of a steelyard

【秤星】gradations marked on the beam of a steelyard

chī

吃 动 ❶ eat; take: ～苹果 *eat an apple* / ～药 *take medicine* / ～糖 *have some sweets* / ～得很饱 *have eaten one's fill* ❷ have one's meals; eat somewhere: ～食堂 *have one's meals in the mess* ❸ live on (or off): ～利钱 *live on interest* / ～劳保 *live on labour insurance* ❹ annihilate; wipe out: ～掉敌军一个师 *annihilate an enemy division* / ～一个子儿 *take a piece (in chess)* ❺ exhaust; be a strain on: 吃力 ❻ absorb; soak up: 这种纸不～墨水。*This kind of paper does not absorb ink.* / 茄子很～油。*Eggplant calls for a lot of oil in cooking.* ❼ suffer; bear; incur: 腿上～了一枪 *get wounded by a shot in the leg* / 连～败仗 *suffer one defeat after another* / 我可不～这一套。*I won't take all this lying down.*

【吃白食】eat food that isn't earned; not earn an honest living; live off others: 他不务正业,惯～。*He does not do any honest work and lives off others.*

【吃饱了撑的】restless from overeating (said of sb. doing sth. silly or senseless)

【吃不饱】❶ not have enough to eat ❷ (of factories, etc.) cannot operate at full capacity; operate under capacity: 由于原料缺乏,我们厂长期处于～状态。*Owing to a constant shortage of raw materials, our factory has not been running at full capacity.*

【吃不开】be unpopular; won't work: 这种工作作风到哪儿都～。*Such a work style isn't popular anywhere.*

【吃不来】not be fond of certain food: 芥末我～。*I'm not especially fond of mustard.* / 很多南方人～生蒜。*Many southerners do not eat raw garlic.*

【吃不了】cannot finish (all the food): 这么一大碗面条我实在～。*I really can't finish such a bowlful of noodles.*

【吃不了兜着走】get more than one bargained for; land oneself in serious trouble: 这件事你如果说出去,我叫你～。*If you let this leak out, I'll make you sorry for it!*

【吃不上】❶ be unable to get something to eat: ～一顿饱饭 *be unable to get a square meal* ❷ miss a meal: 快走吧,再晚就什么也～了。*Hurry up, or we'll be too late to get anything to eat.*

【吃不下】not feel like eating; be unable to eat any more: 他不太舒服,～饭。*He's not very well and doesn't feel like eating.* / 谢谢,我实在～了。*Thanks, but I really can't eat any more.* or *Thanks, I've really had enough.*

【吃不消】be unable to stand (exertion, fatigue, etc.): 走这么多的路恐怕你～。*It may be too much for you to walk such a long way.* / 这文章写得又长又难懂,真让看的人～。*No reader can put up with such a long-winded article.*

【吃不住】be unable to bear or support: 机器太沉,这个架子～。*The stand is not strong enough for this heavy machine.*

【吃穿】food and clothing: ～不愁 *not have to worry about food and clothing* / 她很讲究～。*She's fastidious about her food and clothing.*

【吃醋】be jealous (usu. of a rival in love): 他不过请你女朋友跳了两次舞,你干吗～啊! *He's only had a couple of dances with your girlfriend. Why should you eye him with such jealousy?*

【吃大锅饭】❶ eat in the cafeteria the same as everyone else; mess together ❷ eat from the same big pot—get the same reward or pay as everyone else regardless of one's performance in work

【吃大户】mass seizure and eating of food in the homes of landlords during famines (as in pre-liberation China)

【吃刀】[机] (of the cutting tool on a lathe, etc.) penetrate a certain depth into a workpiece

【吃得苦中苦,方为人上人】Only by standing the hardest of hardships can you hope to rise in society.

【吃得开】be popular; be much sought after: 只要技术好,到哪儿都～。*A person who has expertise is welcome anywhere.*

【吃得来】be able to eat; not mind eating: 辣椒我～,但不特别喜欢。*I can eat red pepper, though I'm not overfond of it.*

【吃得上】❶ be able to get sth. to eat; can afford to eat: 鱼塘和鸡场多了,大家都～鲜鱼、鲜蛋了。*There are plenty of fish ponds and chicken farms, supplying everybody with fresh fish and eggs.* ❷ be in time for a meal; be able to get a meal: 十二点半以前赶回去还～饭。*If we get back before twelve thirty, we won't be too late for lunch.*

【吃得下】be able to eat: 还有一点,你～吗? *There's still a bit left. Can you eat some more?* / 她已经好多了,饭也～了。*She's much better; she's got an appetite now.*

【吃得消】be able to stand (exertion, fatigue, etc.): 再干一个夜班,我也完全～。*I can easily stand working another night shift.* or *I'm certainly good for another night shift.*

【吃得住】able to bear or support: 再重的卡车,这座桥也～。*This bridge can bear the weight of the heaviest lorry.*

【吃豆腐】〈方〉❶ flirt with a woman: 你别想吃她豆腐! *Don't try to flirt with her.* ❷ crack a joke ❸ visit the bereaved to offer one's condolences

【吃耳光】〈方〉get a slap in the face

【吃饭】❶ eat; have a meal: 吃了饭再走吧! *Don't go. Stay for dinner.* / 吃过饭了吗? (〈字〉"*Have you eaten?*") *Hello!* ❷ keep alive; make a living: 靠打猎～ *make a living by hunting*

【吃官司】〈口〉get into trouble with the law; serve a jail term

【吃馆子】〈口〉eat in a restaurant; dine out: 他要请我们～。*He's going to invite us out to dinner.* / 我难得～。*I seldom dine out.*

【吃喝风】the practice of dining and wining on public funds

【吃喝嫖赌】go dining, wining, whoring and gambling—lead a dissipated life

【吃喝玩乐】eat, drink and be merry—idle away one's time in pleasure-seeking

【吃黑枣儿】〈口〉eat a black date—get shot

【吃后悔药】feel remorse; regret: 你要先考虑好再去,免得～。*Think it over before you go so that you won't regret it later.*

【吃花酒】go to a dinner party with singsong girls in attendance

【吃回扣】get commission

【吃荤】eat meat: 胃口不好,不想～ *have no appetite for meat*

【吃紧】be critical; be hard pressed: 形势～。*The situation was critical.* / 前后方都～ *be hard pressed both at the front and in the rear*

【吃惊】be startled; be shocked; be amazed; be taken aback: 大吃一惊 *be flabbergasted* / 他那坚强的毅力使人～。*His will power is amazing.*

【吃苦】bear hardships: 怕～,就干不成大事。*Those who fear hardships will not accomplish anything great.* / ～耐劳 *bear hardships and stand hard work; work hard and endure hardships*

【吃苦在前,享乐在后】be the first to bear hardships and the last to enjoy comforts

【吃亏】❶ suffer losses; come to grief; get the worst of it: 机械地搬用外国的东西是要吃大亏的。*Mechanical copying of things foreign would be disastrous.* ❷ be at a disadvantage; be in an unfavourable situation: 他跑得不快,踢足球～。*He can't run fast and that puts him at a disadvantage as a footballer.*

【吃劳保】live on labour security funds

【吃老本】live off one's past gains; rest on one's laurels

【吃里爬外】live off one person while secretly helping another

【吃力】❶ entail strenuous effort; be a strain: 他身体好,干这点儿活不算～。*He's strong; this bit of work won't be too much for him.* ❷〈方〉tired; fatigued: 我跑了一天路,感到很～。*After a long day's journey, I felt exhausted.* ◇ ～不讨好 同〖费力不讨好〗

【吃奶】suck the breast: ～的孩子 *a sucking child; suckling* / 使尽～的力气 *strain every muscle*

【吃偏饭】(又作'吃偏食') eat better-than-average meals in the mess; enjoy special privilege: 这孩子是个长跑的好苗子,教练何不给他吃点偏饭? *The child has great potential for long-distance running. Why doesn't the coach give him some special training?*

【吃请】accept an invitation to dinner (extended as a bribe)

【吃软不吃硬】be open to persuasion, but not to coercion

【吃食】(of animals or birds) feed：小鸡正在～。*The chickens were feeding.*

【吃水】❶〈方〉drinking water：过去这里～很困难。*It used to be difficult to get drinking water here.* ❷ absorb water：这块地不～。*This plot of land absorbs little water.* / 这种大米～。*You need a lot of water in cooking this kind of rice.* ❸［航海］have a draught (or draft) of：这船～三米。*The ship has a draught of 3 metres.* / 满载～ *load draught* / 空载～ *light draught* ◇ ～线［航海］waterline

【吃素】abstain from eating meat；be a vegetarian

【吃透】understand thoroughly；have a thorough grasp of sth.：吃得透 *be able to understand correctly (or thoroughly)* / 吃不透 *fail to understand correctly；cannot quite see；be not sure*

【吃闲饭】lead an idle life；be a loafer or sponger

【吃现成饭】(又作'吃现成') eat what is already prepared—enjoy the fruits of others' work

【吃香】〈口〉be very popular；be much sought after；be well-liked：这种花布在群众中很～。*This kind of cotton print is very popular.*

【吃小灶】eat at a small mess where better food is served—enjoy some privelege：给困难学生～ *give problem students special tutorials*

【吃一堑,长一智】A fall into the pit, a gain in your wit.

【吃硬不吃软】be open to coercion, but not to persuasion

【吃斋】practise abstinence from meat (as a religious exercise)；be a vegetarian for religious reasons

【吃重】❶ arduous；strenuous：这个任务很～。*This is a hard job.* or *The task is arduous.* ❷ carrying (or loading) capacity：这辆卡车～多少？*What's the carrying capacity of this truck?*

笞 动〈书〉beat with a stick, cane, etc.：鞭笞

【笞刑】flogging as a punishment

痴 形 ❶ silly；idiotic ❷ crazy about sb. or sth. ❸〈方〉insane；mad

【痴呆】❶ dull-witted；stupid ❷［医］dementia

【痴楞】dumbstruck；in a daze；in a trance：她～地望着她妈,半晌说不出话来。*She stared blankly at her mother, speechless.*

【痴迷】infatuated；obsessed；crazy

【痴情】❶ unreasoning passion；infatuation ❷ be infatuated

【痴人说梦】idiotic nonsense；lunatic ravings

【痴想】wishful thinking；illusion

【痴心】infatuation：一片～ *sheer infatuation* / ～女子负心汉 *an innocent girl infatuated with a heartless man (the common theme of many old love stories)*

【痴心妄想】wishful thinking；fond dream

嗤 动〈书〉sneer

【嗤笑】laugh at；sneer at：为人～ *be sneered at*

【嗤之以鼻】give a snort of contempt；turn up one's nose at；despise

chí

池 名 ❶ pool；pond：养鱼～ *fishpond* ❷ an enclosed space with raised sides：花池子 ❸ stalls (in a theatre)；orchestra ❹〈书〉moat：城池

【池塘】pond；pool

【池盐】lake salt

【池鱼之殃】a disaster for the fish in the moat—trouble not of one's own making ——另见〖城门失火,殃及池鱼〗

【池沼】a large pond

【池子】〈口〉❶ pond ❷ common bathing pool (in a bathhouse) ❸ dance floor (in a ballroom) ❹ stalls (in a theatre)；orchestra

【池座】stalls (in a theatre)；orchestra

弛 动〈书〉relax；slacken：松弛

【弛缓】relax；calm down：他听了这一番话,紧张的心情渐渐～下来。*On hearing this he calmed down.* / 局势渐趋～。*Things are easing up.*

【弛张热】［医］remittent fever

驰 动 ❶ (of vehicles, horses, etc.) speed；gallop：飞驰 ❷ spread：驰名 ❸〈书〉(of thoughts) turn eagerly towards：心驰神往

【驰骋】gallop：～在辽阔的原野上 *gallop across the vast plain* / ～文坛 *play an outstanding role in the literary world；bestride the literary stage*

【驰名】be known far and wide；be famous；be renowned：世界～的万里长城 *the world-famous Great Wall* / ～中外 *be renowned at home and abroad* ◇ ～商标 famous trademark；well-known trademark

【驰驱】❶ gallop ❷ do one's utmost in sb.'s service

【驰援】rush to the rescue

迟 形 ❶ slow；tardy：～于作复,歉甚。*I'm sorry I have not been able to reply sooner.* ❷ late：对不起,来～了。*I'm sorry I'm late.*

【迟迟】slow；tardy：～不表态 *not state one's position even after stalling for a long time* / 他为什么～不来？*Why is he taking so long to come?*

【迟到】be (or come, arrive) late：～五分钟 *be five minutes late* / 上班从不～ *never be late for work*

【迟钝】slow (in thought or action)；obtuse：反应～ *be slow in reacting；react slowly*

【迟缓】slow；tardy；sluggish：进展～ *make slow progress* / 行动～ *act slowly* / 这件事要赶快办,不能～。*This must be done at once. There must* be no delay.

【迟脉】［中］retarded pulse (less than 60 beats per minute)

【迟误】delay; procrastinate: 不得～ *admit of no delay*

【迟延】delay; retard: 毫不～地执行命令 *carry out orders without delay*

【迟疑】hesitate: 毫不～地接受了任务 *accept an assignment without hesitation*

【迟疑不决】hesitate to make a decision; be irresolute; be undecided: 你要是再～，就失去机会了。*If you remain undecided, you'll let the chance slip.*

【迟早】sooner or later: 他～会来的。*He will come sooner or later.*

【迟滞】❶ slow-moving; sluggish: 河道淤塞，水流～。*The river is silted up and the water flows sluggishly.* ❷［军］delaying (action)

持 动 ❶ hold; grasp: ～枪 *hold a gun* / ～相反意见 *hold a contrary opinion* / ～保留态度 *have reservations* ❷ support; maintain: 支持 ❸ manage; run: 主持 ❹ oppose: 相持

【持币抢购】rushing to buy with cash in hand

【持不同政见者】dissident

【持股公司】holding company

【持家】run one's home; keep house: ～有方 *be good at running one's home*

【持久】lasting; enduring; protracted: 作～打算 *plan on a long-term basis* / ～和平 *lasting peace* / 他们之间的感情是不会～的。*Their love won't last.* ◇ ～力 staying power; stamina; endurance; ～战 protracted war; protracted warfare

【持论】present an argument; put a case; express a view: ～公平 *state a case fairly* / ～有据 *put forward a well-grounded argument*

【持票人】bearer (of a cheque, etc.)

【持平】unbiased; fair ◇ ～之论 a fair argument; an unbiased view

【持球】［体］holding

【持续】continue; sustain: 使国民经济～稳定增长 *bring about a sustained, stable growth in the national economy*

【持有】hold: ～护照 *hold a passport* / ～不同意见 *hold differing views*

【持之以恒】persevere: 刻苦学习，～ *study assiduously and perseveringly*

【持之有故】have grounds for one's views

【持重】prudent; cautious; discreet

匙 名 spoon: 汤匙

【匙子】spoon

踟 (构词成分) 见下

【踟蹰】(又作'踟躇') hesitate; waver ◇ ～不前 hesitate to move forward

chǐ

尺 Ⅰ 量 ❶ chi, a traditional unit of length ❷ 〈略〉见〖市尺〗 Ⅱ 名 ❶ rule; ruler: 尺子 ❷ an instrument in the shape of a ruler: 计算尺

【尺寸】❶ measurement; dimensions; size: 衣服的～ *measurements of a garment* / 量～ *take sb.'s measurements* ❷〈口〉proper limits for speech or action; sense of propriety: 他办事很有～。*He knows what to do and what not to do.*

【尺动脉】［生理］ulnar artery

【尺牍】❶ a model of epistolary art ❷ correspondence (of an eminent writer)

【尺度】yardstick; measure; scale: 检验真理的～ *yardstick of truth*

【尺短寸长】〈略〉见〖尺有所短，寸有所长〗

【尺幅千里】a thousand-mile view on a one-foot scroll—rich content within a small compass

【尺骨】［生理］ulna

【尺蠖】［动］looper; inchworm; measuringworm; geometer: 桑～ *mulberry looper* ◇ ～蛾［动］geometrid moth

【尺码】size; measures: 你穿多大～的鞋？*What size shoes do you wear?*

【尺有所短，寸有所长】sometimes a foot may prove short while an inch may prove long—everyone has his strong and weak points

【尺子】rule; ruler

齿 Ⅰ 名 ❶ tooth ❷ a tooth-like part of anything ❸〈书〉age: 稚～ *very young* / ～德俱尊 *advanced in age and moral integrity* Ⅱ 动〈书〉mention: 不足～数 *not worth mentioning*

【齿冷】〈书〉laugh sb. to scorn

【齿轮】gear wheel; gear: 正～ *spur gear* / 斜～ *helical gear* / 伞～ *bevel gear* / ～传动 *gear drive* / ～间隙 *gear clearance* / ～箱 *gear box* / ～组 *gear cluster*

【齿条】［机］rack

【齿音】［语音］dental sound

【齿龈】［生理］gums

侈 形〈书〉❶ wasteful; extravagant: 奢侈 ❷ exaggerate: 侈谈

【侈谈】talk glibly about; prate about; prattle about: ～永久和平 *prate about eternal peace*

耻 名 shame; disgrace; humiliation: 引以为～ *regard as a disgrace*

【耻骨】［生理］pubic bones; pubis

【耻辱】shame; disgrace; humiliation

【耻笑】hold sb. to ridicule; sneer at; mock

褫 动〈书〉strip; deprive: ～职 *deprive sb. of his post; remove sb. from office*

【褫夺】strip; deprive: ～公权 *deprive sb. of civil rights*

chì

叱 动〈书〉loudly rebuke; shout at

【叱呵】(又作'叱喝') shout at; bawl at

【叱骂】scold roundly；curse；abuse

【叱责】scold；upbraid；rebuke

【叱咤】〈书〉shout or bawl angrily

【叱咤风云】commanding the wind and the clouds；shaking heaven and earth；all-powerful：～的英雄气概 *earthshaking heroism*

斥 动 ❶ upbraid；scold；denounce；reprimand：痛斥 ❷ repel；exclude；oust：同电相～。*Two like electric charges repel each other.* ❸〈书〉open up；expand：～地 *expand territory*

【斥革】〈书〉dismiss from office

【斥力】［物］repulsion

【斥骂】reproach；upbraid；scold

【斥退】❶〈旧〉dismiss sb. from his post ❷〈旧〉expel from a school ❸ shout at sb. to go away

【斥责】reprimand；rebuke；denounce：厉声～ *severely reprimand*；*excoriate*

【斥逐】expel；oust；drive away

【斥资】〈书〉furnish funds for；fund：～创办医院 *furnish funds for setting up hospitals*

赤 形 ❶ red：～色 *red colour* ❷〈旧〉revolutionary；Communist ❸ loyal；sincere；single-hearted：赤心 ❹ bare：赤膊／赤脚

【赤背】barebacked

【赤膊】barebacked：打～ *be stripped to the waist*

【赤膊上阵】go into battle stripped to the waist—throw away all disguise；come out into the open

【赤诚】absolutely sincere：～待人 *treat people with absolute sincerity*

【赤胆忠心】utter devotion；whole-hearted dedication；ardent loyalty：～为人民 *serve the people with utter devotion*

【赤道】❶ the equator ❷［天］the celestial equator ◇～几内亚 Equatorial Guinea；～几内亚人 Equatorial Guinean；～面 the equatorial plane；～无风带 the equatorial calm belt；～仪 equatorial telescope

【赤地千里】a thousand li of barren land—a scene of utter desolation（after a drought or an insect plague）：那年，华北平原大旱，～。*That year the North China Plain was visited by a great drought that seared vast expanses of farmland.*

【赤豆】〈方〉red bean

【赤褐色】russet

【赤红】crimson

【赤脚】barefooted；barefoot：赤着脚在稻田里干活 *work barefooted in the paddy fields* ／打～ *go barefoot* ◇～医生 barefoot doctor

【赤金】pure gold；solid gold

【赤痢】［中］dysentery characterized by blood in the stool

【赤磷】red phosphorus

【赤露】bare：～着胸口 *with bared chest*

【赤裸】❶ bare：～着上身 *barebacked*；*stripped to the waist* ／全身～ *stark naked* ❷ undisguised

【赤裸裸】❶ without a stitch of clothing；stark naked ❷ undisguised；naked；out-and-out：～的勾结 *undisguised collusion* ／～的强盗行径 *plain robbery*

【赤霉素】［生化］gibberellin

【赤贫】in abject poverty；utterly destitute

【赤芍】［中］the（unpeeled）root of herbaceous peony（Paeonia lactiflora）

【赤身】naked

【赤身露体】stark naked；not wearing a stitch

【赤手空拳】bare-handed；unarmed：巡捕用警棍对付～的示威学生。*The police in the foreign concessions used truncheons against the unarmed demonstrating students.*

【赤松】Japanese red pine（Pinus densiflora）

【赤陶】terra-cotta

【赤条条】have not a stitch on；be stark naked

【赤铁矿】red iron ore；hematite

【赤铜矿】red copper ore；cuprite

【赤心】sincere heart；genuine sincerity；whole-hearted devotion：～相待 *treat sb. with all sincerity*

【赤血盐】［化］potassium ferricyanide；red prussiate of potash

【赤眼蜂】trichogramma

【赤子】❶ a newborn baby ❷〈书〉the people：海外～ *overseas compatriots* ◇～之心 the heart of a newborn babe—utter innocence

【赤字】deficit：～开支 *deficit spending* ／财政（贸易）～ *financial*（*trade*）*deficit* ／弥补～ *make up*（*or meet*）*a deficit*

【赤足】barefooted；barefoot

饬 〈书〉Ⅰ 动 put in order；readjust：整饬 Ⅱ 形 orderly；well-behaved Ⅲ 名（usu. used in official documents）order：严～ *issue strict orders*

【饬令】（usu. used in official documents）order

炽 形 flaming；ablaze

【炽烈】burning fiercely；flaming；blazing：炉火～。*The stove is burning fiercely.* ／～的气氛 *a fervent atmosphere*

【炽热】❶ red-hot；blazing：～的钢水 *red-hot molten steel* ／～的阳光 *a blazing sun* ❷ passionate：～的情感 *passionate feelings*

【炽盛】flaming；ablaze；flourishing：火势～。*The fire is blazing.*

翅 名 ❶ wing ❷ shark's fin

【翅膀】wing

【翅果】［植］samara

【翅脉】vein（of the wings of an insect）

敕 名 imperial order；edict

【敕封】appoint sb. to a post or confer a title on sb. by imperial order

【敕令】（又作'敕命'）imperial order；edict

chōng

冲 Ⅰ 名 ❶ thoroughfare；important place：要冲

❷〈方〉a stretch of flatland in a hilly area ❸［天］opposition Ⅱ 动 ❶ charge；rush；dash：他～进着火的房子，救出了两个小孩。*He dashed into the burning house and rescued two children*. ❷ clash；collide：冲突 ❸ pour boiling water on：～茶 *make tea* ❹ rinse；flush：把盘子～一～。*rinse the plates* / 便后～水。*Flush the toilet after use*. ❺［摄］develop：～胶卷 *develop a roll of film* ——另见 chòng

【冲程】［机］stroke：四～发动机 *four-stroke engine*

【冲冲】in a state of excitement：怒气～ *in a great rage*

【冲出亚洲，走向世界】Break Asian records and set sights on world level in sports.

【冲刺】［体］spurt；sprint：向终点线～ *make a spurt* (*or dash*) *towards the tape* / 最后～ *a final sprint*；*a sprint at the finish* / ～速度 *dash speed*

【冲淡】❶ dilute：把溶液～ *dilute the solution* ❷ water down；weaken；play down：～戏剧效果 *weaken the dramatic effect* / 不要因次要问题而～了中心任务。*Don't stress minor issues at the expense of the central task*.

【冲动】❶ impulse：出于一时～ *act on impulse* ❷ get excited；be impetuous：他很容易～。*He easily gets excited*.

【冲断层】［地质］thrust fault

【冲犯】offend；affront：他控制不住自己，说了几句话，～了他叔父。*He forgot himself and said something that offended his uncle*.

【冲锋】charge；assault：打退敌人的～ *beat back the enemy assault* / 在改革中，他们～在前。*They are in the vanguard of the movement for reform*. ◇ ～号 a bugle call to charge；～枪 submachine gun；tommy gun

【冲锋陷阵】charge and shatter enemy positions；charge the enemy lines；charge forward：冒着枪林弹雨～ *charge under a hail of bullets*；*charge under heavy fire*

【冲服】take (medicine) after mixing it with water, wine, etc.

【冲昏头脑】turn sb.'s head：胜利～ *be dizzy with success*；*be carried away by success*

【冲击】❶ lash；pound：海浪～着礁石，飞起像珠子般的水花。*The waves lashed at the rocks, sending up pearly spray*. ❷ charge；assault：向世界纪录展开猛烈～ *make vigorous attempts to break the world records* ◇ ～波 shock wave；blast wave；

【冲积】［地质］alluviation ◇ ～层［地质］alluvium；～平原 alluvial plain；～扇［地质］alluvial fan；～土 alluvial soil

【冲剂】medicine to be taken after being mixed with boiling water, wine, etc.

【冲决】burst；smash：～堤防 *burst the dykes* / ～束缚他们的罗网 *smash the trammels that bind them*

【冲口而出】say sth. unthinkingly；blurt out

【冲垮】burst；shatter：洪水～了堤坝。*The flood waters burst the dykes*. / ～敌军防线 *shatter the enemy lines*

【冲浪】❶［体］surfing；surfboarding：～板 *surfboard* ❷［计］surf (the web)；surfing

【冲力】impulsive force；momentum

【冲凉】〈方〉have a shower

【冲量】［物］impulse

【冲破】break through；breach：～重重障碍 *break through one barrier after another*；*surmount all obstacles* / ～传统观念的束缚 *smash the bonds of tradition*

【冲散】break up；scatter；disperse：～人群 *disperse a crowd* / 游行队伍让马队给～了。*The demonstrators were scattered by the mounted police*.

【冲杀】charge；rush ahead：在枪林弹雨中～ *charge head-on against a hail of bullets*

【冲沙闸】scouring sluice

【冲晒】［摄］develop and print

【冲刷】❶ wash and brush；wash down：把汽车～得干干净净 *give the car a thorough wash-down* ❷ erode；wash away：岩石上有被洪水～过的痕迹。*The rocks carry marks left by a flood*.

【冲塌】(of floodwater, etc.) cause to collapse；burst：～堤坝 *burst dykes and dams* / ～房屋 *dash against the houses and wash them away*

【冲天】towering；soaring：～干劲 *boundless enthusiasm* / 怒气～ *be in a towering rage*

【冲突】conflict；clash：武装～ *an armed conflict* / 边境～ *a border clash* / 利害～ *conflict of interests* / 避免～ *avoid clashes* / 这两个会的时间～了。*The two meetings clash*.

【冲洗】❶ rinse；wash：用消毒药水～伤口 *wash a wound with a disinfectant* ❷［摄］develop：～照片 *develop prints*

【冲要】(of a place) strategically important

【冲澡】〈口〉take a shower：我冲个澡再走。*I'll take a shower before I leave*.

【冲账】［经］❶ strike a balance ❷ reverse an entry

【冲撞】❶ collide；bump；ram：渔船遭到敌舰的～。*The fishing boat was rammed by an enemy warship*. ❷ give offence；offend：我没想到这句话竟～了他。*I didn't expect him to take offence at that remark*.

充

Ⅰ 形 sufficient；full：充分 Ⅱ 动 ❶ fill；stuff：充电 / 充塞 ❷ serve as；act as：～向导 *serve as a guide* ❸ pretend to be；pose as；pass sth. off as：～内行 *pretend to be an expert* / ～好汉 *pose as a hero*

【充斥】〈贬〉flood；congest；be full of：市场上～着外国商品。*The markets were flooded with foreign goods*.

【充当】serve as；act as；play the part of：～翻译 *act as interpreter* / ～辩护士 *play the part of an apologist*

【充电】charge (a battery)：～器 *charger*

【充耳不闻】stuff one's ears and refuse to listen；

turn a deaf ear to：对于别人的批评，他们是～的。*They turned a deaf ear to other people's criticisms.*

【充分】❶ full；ample；abundant：～协商 *full consultation* / ～证据 *ample evidence* / 我们有～理由相信这消息是可靠的。*We have every reason to believe that the news is true.* ❷ to the full；as fully as possible：～利用 *fully utilize*；*make full use of*

【充公】confiscate：他受贿的财物全部充了公。*The bribes and gifts that he took were all confiscated.*

【充饥】challay (or appease) one's hunger：靠野菜～ *allay one's hunger with wild herbs*

【充军】be transported to a distant place for penal servitude；banish

【充满】❶ fill：欢呼声～了会场。*Loud cheers filled the assembly hall.* ❷ be filled with；be full of；brim with；be permeated (or imbued) with：屋子里～着阳光。*The room is full of sunshine.* / 大厅里～了孩子们的欢笑声。*The hall resounded with the laughter of children.*

【充沛】plentiful；abundant；copious：雨水～ *abundant rainfall*

【充其量】(又作'充其极') at most；at best：这点给养～只够维持三天。*The provisions can last three days at most.*

【充气电池】aeration (oxygen) cell

【充任】fill the post of；hold the position of：聘请老工程师～顾问 *ask senior engineers to be our advisers* / 他～经理很合适。*He's well suited for the position of manager.*

【充塞】fill (up)；cram：我心里～着喜悦的情绪。*My heart is filled with joy.*

【充实】❶ substantial；rich：内容～ *substantial in content* ❷ substantiate；enrich；replenish：～论据 *substantiate one's argument* / ～库存 *replenish the stocks*

【充数】make up the number；serve as a stopgap：参加你们队，我只能充个数。*I'll only be an also-ran in your team.*

【充血】[医] hyperaemia；congestion

【充溢】be full to the brim；be exuberant；be overflowing：孩子们的脸上～着幸福的笑容。*The children's faces beamed with happy smiles.*

【充裕】abundant；ample；plentiful：时间～ *have ample (or plenty of) time* / 经济～ *well-off*

【充足】adequate；sufficient；abundant；ample：经费～ *have sufficient (or ample) funds* / 阳光～ *full of sunshine*；*sunny*

忡 (构词成分)见下

【忡忡】laden with anxiety；careworn

舂 动 pound (in a mortar)；pestle：～米 *husk rice with mortar and pestle* / ～药 *pound medicinal substances into powder*

憧 (构词成分)见下

【憧憧】flickering；moving to and fro：树影～ *flickering shadows of trees* / 人影～ *shadows of people moving about*

【憧憬】yearn for；long for；look forward to：～着更为美好的未来 *yearning for a better and brighter future* / 青年的～ *yearnings of young people*

chóng

虫 名 insect or worm

【虫草】〈略〉见〖冬虫夏草〗

【虫害】insect pest

【虫胶】shellac ◇ ～清漆 shellac (varnish)

【虫媒花】[植] entomophilous flower

【虫蚀】worm-eaten；moth-eaten

【虫牙】popular name for 龋齿

【虫瘿】gall (on plants)

【虫灾】a plague of insects

【虫子】insect or worm

重 Ⅰ 动 repeat；duplicate：这两个例子～了。*These two examples duplicate each other.* / 书买～了。*Two copies of the same book have been bought by mistake.* Ⅱ 副 again；once more：～启战端 *renew hostilities* / 把生词～抄一遍。*Copy the new words over again.* Ⅲ 量 layer：越过万～山 *climb over countless mountains* / 突破一～又一～的障碍 *break through barrier after barrier* ——另见 zhòng

【重版】❶ (of books, periodicals, etc.) be republished ❷ republication

【重播】❶ rebroadcast a programme (from the same station) ❷ resow (the same field)

【重操旧业】resume one's old profession；take up one's old trade again

【重唱】an ensemble of two or more singers, each singing one part：四～ (*vocal*) *quartet*

【重重】layer upon layer；ring upon ring：陷入～包围之中 *be encircled ring upon ring* / 克服～困难 *overcome one difficulty after another*；*surmount numerous difficulties*

【重蹈覆辙】follow the track of the overturned cart—follow the same old road to ruin

【重叠】one on top of another；overlapping：山峦～ *range upon range of mountains* / 精简～的行政机构 *streamline (or simplify) overlapping administrative organizations*

【重发球】[体] let service；let

【重返】return：～前线 *go back to the front* / ～家园 *return to one's homeland* ◇ ～大气层 reentry (of a spaceship, rocket, etc.)

【重犯】repeat (an error or offence)：吸取教训，避免～错误 *draw a lesson from past errors so as to prevent their recurrence*

【重逢】meet again；have a reunion：旧友～ *reunion of old friends*

【重复】repeat；duplicate：避免不必要的～ *avoid unnecessary repetition* / 他一再～他的观点。*He reiterated his views over and over again.* ◇～建设

duplicated proeict；～利用 recycle
【重估】re-evaluate；re-estimate；re-calculate
【重合】［数］coincide
【重婚】［法］（commit）bigamy
【重见天日】once more see the light of day—be delivered from oppression or persecution
【重建】rebuild；reconstruct；reestablish；rehabilitate：战后的～工作 *postwar reconstruction* / ～家园 *rehabilitate one's homeland*；*rebuild one's home village or town*.
【重起炉】begin all over again；make a fresh start
【重申】reaffirm；reiterate；restate：～前令 *reaffirm an existing decree* / ～我国政府的一贯立场 *reiterate the consistent stand of our government*
【重审】［法］retrial
【重施故技】play the same old trick；repeat a stock trick
【重孙】〈口〉son's grandson；great-grandson
【重孙女】son's granddaughter；great-granddaughter
【重弹老调】同〖老调重弹〗
【重提】bring up again：旧事～ *bring up an old case*；*recall past events*
【重围】tight encirclement：杀出～ *break through a tight encirclement*
【重温】review：～第二次世界大战的历史 *review the history of World War II*
【重温旧梦】revive an old dream；relive an old experience
【重现】reappear：当年的战斗场面又～在他眼前。*The battle scenes of those years reappeared in his mind's eye*.
【重新】again；anew；afresh：～考虑 *reconsider* / ～部署 *rearrange*；*redeploy* / ～发起进攻 *launch a fresh offensive* /～做人 *start one's life afresh*；*turn over a new leaf*◇～启动键［计］reset button(or key)；～组合 recombination；
【重修旧好】renew cordial relations；become reconciled；bury the hatchet
【重檐】［建］double-eaved roof
【重演】❶ put on an old play，et. ❷ recur；reenact；repeat：历史的错误不许～。*Past mistakes should not be repeated*.
【重洋】the seas and oceans
【重译】retranslate
【重印】reprint ◇ ～本 reprint
【重振军威】restore the prestige of an army；make an army's might felt once again
【重整旗鼓】rally one's forces（after a defeat）
【重奏】［音］an ensemble of two or more instrumentalists，each playing one part：四～（*instrumental*）*quartet*

崇 Ⅰ 形 high；lofty；sublime：崇山峻岭 Ⅱ 动 esteem；worship：尊崇
【崇拜】worship；adore：她很～她父亲。*She worships her father*. / ～偶像 *worship of idols*；*idolatry*
【崇奉】believe in（a religion）；worship
【崇高】lofty；sublime；high：～的理想 *a lofty ideal* / ～的威望 *high prestige* / 顺致最～的敬意。*I avail myself of this opportunity to renew to you the assurances of my highest consideration*.
【崇敬】esteem；respect；revere：我很～这位老教授。*I have great respect for the old professor*. / 怀着十分～的心情 *cherish a feeling of great reverence for*
【崇山峻岭】lofty ridges and towering mountains
【崇尚】uphold；advocate：～勤俭 *advocate industry and thrift*
【崇洋媚外】worship foreign things and toady to foreign powers

chǒng

宠 动 dote on；bestow favour on：他太～小女儿了。*He dotes on his youngest daughter too much*. / 别把孩子～坏了。*Don't spoil the child*.
【宠爱】make a pet of sb.；dote on：奶奶特别～小孙儿。*Grandma dotes on her little grandson*.
【宠儿】pet；favourite；darling：命运的～ *the darling of fortune* / 时代的～ *the idol of the day*
【宠辱不惊】remain indifferent whether favoured or humiliated
【宠物】pet（e.g. a cat or a dog）◇ ～店 pet shop
【宠信】be specially fond of and trust unduly（a subordinate）

chòng

冲 Ⅰ 形〈口〉❶ with vim and vigour；with plenty of dash；vigorously：这小伙子干活儿真～。*This young fellow does his work with vim and vigour*. / 水流得很～。*The water flows with great force*. / 他说话很～。*He speaks bluntly*. ❷（of smell）strong；pungent：这药味很～。*This medicine has a strong smell*. Ⅱ 介〈口〉❶ facing；towards：窗户～南开。*The window faces south*. / 这话是～他说的。*That remark was aimed at him*. ❷ on the strength of；on the basis of；because：～他们这股子干劲儿，没有克服不了的困难。*With such drive，there's no difficulty that they can't overcome*. Ⅲ 动［机］punching：冲压 ——另见 chōng
【冲床】［机］punch（press）；punching machine
【冲劲儿】❶ vim and vigour；dash ❷ strength（of liquor）；kick：这二锅头～大。*This erguotou has a lot of kick in it*.
【冲孔】［机］❶ punching ❷ punched hole
【冲模】［机］die ◇ ～插床［机］die slotting machine
【冲头】［机］drift；punch pin
【冲压】［机］stamping；punching ◇ ～机 another name for 冲床
【冲子】punching pin（a tool）

chōu

抽 动 ❶ take out (from in between): 从文件夹里～出一份申请书 *take an application out of the file* ❷take (a part from a whole): 把他～出来管仓库 *release him from his job and put him in charge of the warehouse* / 开会前请～时间把文件看一下。*Try and find time to read the document before the meeting.* ❸ (of certain plants) put forth: ～枝 *branch out*; *sprout* / 小树～出了嫩芽。*The saplings are budding.* ❹ obtain by drawing, etc.: ～血 *draw blood (for a test or transfusion)* ❺ shrink: 这种布一洗就～。*This cloth shrinks in the wash.* ❻ lash; whip; thrash: ～陀螺 *whip a top* / ～牲口 *lash a draught animal* ❼ [体] drive

【抽测】spot check: 在两个小时的～中,有十个超速驾驶的司机被罚款。*Ten drivers were fined who exceeded the speed limit during a two-hour spot check.*

【抽查】carry out selective examinations; make spot checks; spot-check

【抽搐】❶ twitch ❷ [医] tic

【抽打】lash; whip; thrash: 农奴主用皮鞭～农奴。*The serf owner lashed the serf with a whip.*

【抽搭】〈口〉sob: 抽抽搭搭地哭了起来 *break into sobs*

【抽调】transfer (personnel or material): ～部分兵力向北增援 *move part of the troops to the north as reinforcements*

【抽动】twitch; have a spasm; jerk spasmodically

【抽肥补瘦】take from the fat to pad the lean; take from those with much and give to those with little

【抽风】❶ [医] convulsions ❷〈口〉go crazy; lose one's senses: 别～了! *Don't be crazy!*

【抽检】spot check: ～合格 *pass a spot check* / 在同类产品～中,被评为优等品 *be evaluated as of excellent quality during a spot check of similar products*

【抽奖】draw lots (to give out prizes); draw a winning number (for lottery, sweeptake, etc.): ～活动 *activity with prizes to be given out by drawing lots* /～仪式 *ceremony for drawing lots to choose winners*/ 抽了一个头奖 *have won first prize (in the sweep-take)*

【抽筋】❶pull out a tendon ❷〈口〉cramp: 腿～ *have a cramp in the leg*

【抽空】manage to find time: 他工作很忙,可是还～学习英语。*Despite the pressure of work, he manages to find time to study English.* / 抽不出空来 *be unable to find time*

【抽气机】air exhauster; air extractor; air pump

【抽泣】sob: 低声～ *weep in choking sobs*

【抽签】draw (or cast) lots

【抽球】[体] drive

【抽取】draw; collect: ～版税 *receive a royalty* / ～百分之三佣金 *charge a commission of 3%*

【抽纱】[工美] drawnwork

【抽身】leave one's work; extricate oneself; get away: 及早～ *hasten to extricate oneself from a difficult situation*

【抽水】draw (or pump) water: 从河里～ *pump water from a river* ◇ ～机 water pump; ～马桶 flush toilet; water closet; ～站 pumping station

【抽税】levy a tax

【抽丝】reel off raw silk from cocoons

【抽穗】(of cereal plants) put forth ears; ear: 小麦正在～。*The wheat is in the ear.* ◇ ～期 earing stage (or period); heading stage (or period)

【抽缩】shrink; contract

【抽薹】(of garlic, chives, rape, etc.) bolt: 油菜～了。*The rape is bolting.*

【抽提】[化] extraction: ～蒸馏 *extractive distillation*

【抽屉】drawer

【抽头】❶ take a percentage (or cut) of the winnings in gambling ❷ [电] tap: ～电路 *tap circuit*

【抽闲】manage to find time: 我们～去十三陵玩玩。*Let's find time for a trip to the Ming Tombs.*

【抽象】❶ abstract: ～的概念 *an abstract concept* / 科学的～ *scientific abstraction* / 不要这样～地谈问题。*Don't speak in such abstract terms.* ❷ form a general idea from particular instances: 从客观事物中～出正确的结论 *draw a correct conclusion from objective facts* ◇ ～表现派 action painting; ～劳动 abstract labour; ～名词 abstract noun; ～派 abstractionist school; ～数 abstract number; ～思维 abstraction; ～艺术 abstract art

【抽薪止沸】take out the fuel to stop the pot boiling—take drastic measures to stop sth.

【抽绣】[工美] punchwork

【抽芽】put forth buds; bud; sprout: 柳树开始～了。*The willow trees have begun to bud.*

【抽烟】smoke (a cigarette or a pipe): 你～吗? *Do you smoke?* / 请～。*Have a smoke.* / 抽一袋烟 *smoke a pipe*

【抽验】sample testing; spot check: ～时,发现该产品绝缘性能差。*During a sample testing, it was found that the product had poor insulation.*

【抽样】ampling (in statistics and research) ◇ ～调查[统计] sample survey; sampling; ～分布 [统计] sampling distribution; ～分析 sampling analysis; ～误差 [统计] sampling error

【抽噎】sob: 一个小姑娘坐在角落里～着。*A little girl sat sobbing in the corner.*

【抽印】offprint: ～学报的头一篇文章 *offprint the first article of the journal* / ～三百份 *offprint 300 copies (of an article, etc.)*; *make 300 offprints* ◇ ～本 offprint

【抽油泵】oil-well pump

【抽油烟机】range hood

chóu

仇 名 ❶ enemy; foe: 仇敌 ❷ hatred; enmity;

有～ *have a score to settle* / 这～一定要报。*This wrong must be avenged.*
【仇敌】foe; enemy
【仇恨】❶ hatred; enmity; hostility: 满腔～ *seething with hatred* ❷ feel great enmity towards; hate
【仇家】personal enemy
【仇人】personal enemy ◇ ～相见,分外眼红 when enemies come face to face, their eyes blaze with hate
【仇杀】kill in revenge
【仇视】regard as an enemy; look upon with hatred; be hostile to
【仇隙】〈书〉bitter quarrel; feud

惆 形 sad; disappinted
【惆怅】sad; disconsolate; melancholy: 他这一走,她似乎有些～。*She seems rather melancholy now that he has gone away.*

绸 名 silk fabric; silk: 那连衣裙是～的。*The dress is made of silk.*
【绸缎】silks and satins
【绸缪】〈书〉❶ be sentimentally attached: 情意～ *be head over heels in love* ❷ 见〖未雨绸缪〗
【绸子】silk fabric

畴 名〈书〉❶ farmland: 平～千里 *a vast expanse of cultivated land* ❷ kind; division: 范畴
【畴辈】〈书〉people of the same generation

愁 动 worry; be anxious: 不～吃,不～穿 *not have to worry about food and clothing* / 你别～,病人很快会好的。*Don't worry. The patient will soon recover.* / 这件事可把我～死了。*This is really worrying me to death.*
【愁肠百结】with anxiety gnawing at one's heart; weighed down with anxiety
【愁苦】anxiety; distress
【愁眉】knitted brows; worried look
【愁眉不展】with a worried frown; with knitted brows: 她成天～,唉声叹气的。*She looked terribly distressed and was sighing all the time.*
【愁眉苦脸】wear a worried look; pull a long face: 我看你这两天～的,有什么心事吧? *I've noticed these last few days that you've been looking rather unhappy. There must be something worrying you.*
【愁眉锁眼】with knitted brows and lowered eyes; wearing a deep frown on one's face: 大家以为有了出路,～的姿态为之一扫。*There is a general feeling that a way out of the impasse has been found, and people no longer knit their brows in despair.*
【愁闷】feel gloomy; be in low spirits; be depressed: 他工作不顺利,心里十分～。*He was very cast down by setbacks in his work.*
【愁容】worried look; anxious expression: ～满面 *look extremely worried* / 面带～ *look rather worried*
【愁绪】〈书〉gloomy mood: 小女儿的欢笑使他～全消。*His little daughter's bright smiles dispelled all his gloom.*

稠 形 ❶ thick: 粥很～。*The porridge is very thick.* ❷ dense: 地窄人～ *small in area but densely populated*
【稠密】dense: 人口～ *densely populated; populous* / 交通网～ *a dense communications network*
【稠人广众】a large crowd; a big gathering: 在～面前说话,她还是第一回呢。*It was the first time she had ever spoken before such a big audience.*

酬 Ⅰ 动 ❶〈书〉propose a toast; toast ❷ friendly exchange: 应酬 ❸ fulfil; realize: 壮志未酬 Ⅱ 名 reward; payment
【酬报】requite; reward; repay; recompense
【酬宾】bargain sales ◇ ～展销 show for sale with gifts to customers
【酬答】❶ thank sb. with a gift ❷ respond with a poem or speech
【酬金】monetary reward; remuneration: 优厚的～ *a generous remuneration*
【酬劳】❶ repay; reward; recompense: 他们辛苦了一天,得好好～他们一下。*We should reward them generously for a hard day's work.* ❷ repayment; reward; recompense: 我自愿帮忙,不要任何～。*I volunteered to help and expected no reward.*
【酬谢】thank sb. with a gift: 他帮了我们大忙,我不知道该怎么～他才好。*He has given us a lot of help. I don't know what to give him to express my thankfulness.*
【酬应】同〖应酬〗❶

筹 Ⅰ 名 chip; counter: 竹筹 Ⅱ 动 prepare; plan: ～款 *raise money (or funds)*
【筹办】make preparations; make arrangements: ～国家行政学院 *make preparations to found a state administrative college* / 这次越野赛跑由我们厂负责～。*Our factory is to make arrangements for the cross-country race.*
【筹备】prepare; arrange: ～工作 *preparatory work; preparations* / ～会议 *preparatory (or preliminary) meeting* / ～委员会 *preparatory committee*
【筹措】raise (money): ～旅费 *raise money for travelling expenses*
【筹划】plan and prepare: 这里正在～建设一座水力发电站。*Plans are being drawn up to build a hydroelectric station here.*
【筹集】accumulate; raise (money): ～基金 *raise funds*
【筹建】prepare to construct or establish sth.: ～研究所 *make preparations for the setting up of a research institute*
【筹款】raise funds; raise money
【筹码】chip; counter: 麻将～ *mahjong counters* / 政治交易的～ *bargaining counters in political*

deals

【筹募】collect (funds)：～福利基金 *collect welfare funds*

【筹商】(又作'筹议') discuss；consult：～对策 *discuss what countermeasures to take*

【筹委会】(〈略〉全称为'筹备委员会') preparatory committee

【筹资】fund raising

踌 (构词成分)见下

【踌躇】hesitate；shilly-shally ◇ ～不决 hesitating；irresolute；～不前 hesitate to move forward；hesitate to make a move

【踌躇满志】enormously proud of one's success；smug；complacent

chǒu

丑 形 ❶ ugly；unsightly；hideous：长得不～ *not bad-looking* ❷ disgraceful；shameful；scandalous：这种事太～了，不要说出去。*This is really disgraceful. Don't breathe a word of it to anyone.*

【丑八怪】〈口〉a very ugly person

【丑表功】brag shamelessly about one's deeds；claim undeserved credit：他做了一点儿事，就到处～。*He always swaggers around boasting about any little thing he has done.*

【丑恶】ugly；repulsive；hideous：～表演 *a disgusting performance* / 露出～的嘴脸 *show one's ugly face；reveal one's hideous features* ◇ ～灵魂 an ugly soul；～面目 ugly features

【丑化】smear；uglify；defame；vilify

【丑话】❶ vulgar language；abusive words ❷ blunt words：我把～说在前头，事情办糟了你可得负责。*I must tell you bluntly that should anything go wrong you will be held responsible.*

【丑剧】farce

【丑角】❶comic role ❷ (in real life) clown；comedian；buffoon

【丑陋】ugly

【丑事】a disgraceful affair；scandal

【丑态】ugly (or ludicrous) performance；buffoonery：～百出 *act like a buffoon；cut a contemptible figure* / ～毕露 *be utterly shameless；be extremely nauseating*

【丑闻】scandal：水门事件是1972年发生在美国的一件政治～。*The Watergate affair was a U.S. political scandal that broke in 1972.*

【丑媳妇总得见公婆】an ugly daughter-in-law will have to face her parents-in-law sooner or later—whatever its faults or shortcomings, one's work must be shown to others

【丑星】clown；buffoon

瞅 动〈方〉look at：让我～～。*Let me have a look.* / 她～了我一眼。*She took a look (or glance) at me.*

【瞅见】〈方〉see：你～他没有？*Did you see him?* / 啥也瞅不见 *can't see anything*

chòu

臭 Ⅰ 形 smelly；foul；stinking：～味儿 *stink；offensive odour；foul smell* / ～鸡蛋 *a rotten egg* / ～不可闻 *give off an unbearable stink* Ⅱ 动 discredit：他的名声早就～了。*He has long been discredited.* Ⅲ 副 severely：被～骂了一顿 *get a tongue-lashing；get a dressing down* / 挨了一顿～打 *get a good beating* ——另见 xiù

【臭虫】bedbug

【臭椿】[植] tree of heaven (Ailanthus altissima)

【臭豆腐】strong-smelling preserved bean curd

【臭烘烘】stinking；foul-smelling；smelly

【臭美】〈口〉show off shamelessly；be disgustingly smug：你看她打扮得花里胡哨的，真～！*Look how gaudily she is dressed；what a shameless display!* / 你摇头晃脑的，～什么劲儿？*What makes you so smug, swaggering like that?*

【臭名昭著】of ill repute；notorious

【臭气】bad (or offensive) smell；stink：～熏天 *stink to high heaven*

【臭味相投】be birds of a feather；be two of a kind

【臭氧】[化] ozone ◇ ～层 ozonosphere；ozone layer

【臭鼬】[动] skunk

chū

出 Ⅰ 动 ❶ go or come out：～城 *go out of town* / ～站 *come out of the station* ❷ exceed；go beyond：～月 *after this month；next month* / 不～三年 *within three years* / 球～了边线。*The ball went beyond the sideline.* ❸ issue；put out：～证明 *issue a certificate* / ～杂志 *publish a magazine* / ～主意 *offer advice；supply ideas；make suggestions* / ～布告 *post an announcement；put up a notice* ❹ produce；turn out：多～煤，～好煤。*Produce more coal, and good coal, too.* / 要多～人才。*We must turn out a greater number of qualified personnel.* ❺ arise；happen：这事～在三十年前。*It happened thirty years ago.* / ～问题 *go wrong；go amiss* / 防止～事故 *prevent accidents* ❻ put forth；vent：树上～了不少花蕾。*The tree has put forth many buds.* / ～疹子 *have measles* ❼ rise well (with cooking)；grow in volume：出数儿 ❽ pay out；expend：量入为出 Ⅱ 量 (for operas or plays)：一～戏 *an opera；a play*

【出版】come off the press；publish；put out (or come out)：这本书什么时候～？*When will the book be published?* / ～自由 *freedom of the press* ◇ ～社 publishing house；～物 publication

【出榜】❶ publish a list of successful candidates or examinees：考试后三日～。*The list of successful examinees will be published three days after the* exams. ❷〈旧〉put up a notice：～安民 *put up a notice to reassure the public*

【出奔】leave one's home or country under compulsion; run away; flee

【出殡】carry a coffin to the cemetery; hold a funeral procession

【出兵】dispatch (or send) troops

【出操】go out for drill or a workout：每周出两次操 *have two workouts every week*

【出差】go or be away on official business; go or be on a business trip：去上海～ *go on a business trip to Shanghai* / 出了几天差 *have been away a few days on business* / ～费 *allowances for a business trip*

【出产】❶ yield or manufacture; produce：江西景德镇～精美的瓷器。*Jindezhen in Jiangxi Province produces fine porcelain.* ❷ product; produce

【出厂】(of products) be dispatched from the factory：～价格 *producer price*；*ex-factory price* / ～日期 *date of production (or manufacture)* / ～检验 *delivery inspection*

【出场】❶ come on the stage; appear on the scene：她一～，台下就响起了热烈的掌声，*There was enthusiastic applause as soon as she came on the stage.* ❷ enter the arena：～的运动员名单 *list of players for the match* / 他～准赢。*If he enters the contest, he's sure to win.*

【出超】favourable balance of trade; export surplus

【出车】❶ dispatch a vehicle：公共汽车早五点～。*Bus service starts at 5 a.m.* ❷ be out driving a vehicle：老王～去了。*Lao Wang is out with the car.*

【出丑】make a fool of sb. or oneself：上次我已经出过一回丑，今天我可不唱了。*I sang and made a fool of myself last time. I'm not going to sing again today.*

【出处】source (of a quotation or allusion)：注明～ *indicate the source*；*give references* / 查明引文～ *find out the source of a quotation* / 你知道这个典故的～吗？*Do you know the original source of this allusion?*

【出错】make a mistake：他管账很少～。*He seldom makes a mistake in the accounts.* / 用典～ *make mistakes in using allusions*

【出单公司】issuing company

【出道】(formerly of an apprentice) start working as a journeyman after serving one's apprenticeship; make one's début in society; embark on one's career; become known：～前她也拍过电视剧。*She played some parts in TV plays before she became known (as a film star, etc.).*

【出点子】offer advice; make suggestions：怎么办？大家来出出点子。*What's to be done? Let's put our heads together.* / 有人在背后出坏点子。*Someone is directing the show from behind the scenes.*

【出动】❶ set out; start off：小分队提前～了。*The detachment set off ahead of schedule.* / 待命～ *await orders to set out (or go into action)* ❷ send out; dispatch：～军舰 *dispatch warships* / ～飞机二十架次 *fly 20 sorties* / ～医护人员 *send out medical personnel*

【出尔反尔】go back on one's word; contradict oneself：你怎么说话不算数，～？*Why do you go back on your word? Doesn't what you promised still count?*

【出发】❶ set out; start off：部队于拂晓前～。*The troops set out before dawn.* / 医疗队今天就要～了。*The medical team is leaving tonight.* ❷ take... as a starting point in consideration; proceed from：从国家利益～ *proceed from the considerations of national interests* / 从长远的观点～ *from a long-term point of view*

【出发点】❶ the starting point of a journey ❷ starting point (in a discussion, argument, etc.); point of departure：研究问题的～ *the starting point for a study of the problem*

【出发港】port of departure

【出发信号】starting signal

【出访】go abroad on an official visit：～西欧四国 *go on an official visit to four Western European countries*

【出风头】(又作'出锋头') seek (or be in) the limelight：喜欢～ *like to be in the limelight*；*seek the limelight*；*enjoy being the centre of attention* / 出够了风头 *have been in the limelight enough*

【出伏】the fu days end; the hottest days of the year are over：今天～。*The fu days end today.* / 出了伏，天气就明显地凉快起来。*The weather gets noticeably cooler when the fu days are over.* ——另见〖三伏〗

【出钢】tap molten steel; produce steel：这座平炉年底可以～。*This open-hearth furnace will be ready to produce steel by the end of the year.*

【出港】clear a port; leave port ◇ ～呈报表 bill of clearance; ～证 clearance papers; clearance

【出阁】〈书〉(of a girl) get married; marry

【出格】❶ be out of the ordinary; be outstanding ❷ overstep the bounds; exceed what is proper：他这样做太～了。*What he's doing is most improper.* / 你这话有点～了。*That's going a bit too far.*

【出工】show up for work; go to work：准时～ *show up on time for work*

【出恭】go to the lavatory (for a bowel movement)

【出乖露丑】make an exhibition of oneself

【出轨】❶ go off the rails; be derailed ❷ overstep the bounds; exceed what is proper：～行为 *improper behaviour*

【出国】go abroad：～旅行 *go travelling abroad* / ～留学 *go abroad to study* / 他出过两次国。*He has been abroad twice.* ◇ ～热 craze of going abroad

【出海】go to sea; put out to sea：～捕鱼 *go fishing on the sea* / 货轮已经～。*The freighter has put out to sea.*

【出汗】perspire; sweat：我热得直～。*I'm so hot*

that I'm dripping with sweat. / 出一身汗 *break into a sweat; sweat all over*

【出航】(of a ship or plane) set out on a voyage or flight: 飞机～侦察。*The plane set out on a reconnaissance flight*. / 班轮按时～。*The liner set sail on schedule*.

【出乎意料】exceeding one's expectations; contrary to one's expectations; unexpectedly: 这件事出乎我的意料。*This is something quite contrary to my expectations*. / ～之外,却在情理之中 *unexpected but not surprising*

【出活】yield results in work; get a lot done: 这样干～快。*We'll get quicker results if we do it this way*. / 我们下午虽然只干了两个钟头,可是很～。*We worked only two hours in the afternoon, but we accomplished a lot*.

【出击】❶ launch an attack; hit out; make a sally: 四面～ *hit out in all directions* ❷ fight against (evil, crime, etc.)

【出家】renounce the family (to become a monk or nun)

【出价】offer a price; bid: 你出个价吧! *Would you name a price for it?* / 你～多少? *How much would you pay for it?*

【出嫁】(of a woman) get married; marry

【出界】[体] out-of-bounds; outside; out

【出借】lend (things other than money)

【出境】❶ leave the country: 限期～ *leave the country within the specified time* / 办理～手续 *go through exit formalities* / ～登记 *departure registration* / ～签证 *exit visa* / ～许可证 *exit permit* ❷ leave a certain region

【出局】out (in baseball, soft ball, etc.)

【出口】❶ speak; utter: 这话我很难～。*I'd be too embarrassed to bring that up*. ❷ (of a ship) leave port: 证件不齐,这条船不能～。*Since the necessary papers are not in order, the ship cannot yet leave port*. ❸ export: ～大米 *export rice* / ～信贷担保 *export credit guarantee* / ～产业和产品 *export-oriented industries and products* ❹ exit: 地铁～ *subway exit* / 剧场的～ *theatre exit* ◇～包装 export packing; ～报单 entry outward; ～补贴 export subsidy; ～创汇 earn foreign exchange through export; ～刺激 export incentives; ～代理 export agent; ～单据 export documents; ～额 value of export; ～发票 export invoice; ～管制 export control; ～货 exported goods; exports; outbound freight; exportation; ～货物 export commodities; ～加工区 export processing zones; ～价格 export price; ～检验 export inspection; ～检疫 export quarantine; ～净值 net export value; ～量 export volume; ～贸易 export trade; ～商 exporter; ～商品 export commodities; ～收入 export earnings; ～税 export duties; ～特许证 special permission export; ～推销 export drive; ～信贷 export credit; ～许可证 export permit; export license; ～证书 export certification; ～转内销 export goods for sale

【出口成章】words flow from the mouth as from the pen of a master; talk in literature

【出口伤人】say things that will hurt others' feelings; speak bitingly

【出来】❶ come out: 太阳～了。*The sun has come out*. / 你～,我跟你说句话。*Come out, will you? I have something to tell you*. ❷ emerge; arise; appear: 要是～新问题怎么办? *What should we do if a new problem crops up?*

【出类拔萃】stand out from one's fellows; be out of the common run; be pre-eminent: ～的人物 *an outstanding figure*

【出力】put forth one's strength; exert oneself: 每人多出把力,任务就可以提前完成。*If everyone puts in a bit more effort, the job will be finished ahead of time*.

【出列】[军] leave one's place in the ranks: ～! (*word of command*) *Fall out!*

【出猎】go on a hunting trip

【出笼】❶ come out of the steamer: 刚～的包子 *hot stuffed buns just out of the steamer* ❷〈贬〉come forth; appear: 那本坏书是什么时候～的? *When did that filthy book come out?*

【出娄子】〈方〉get into trouble; go wrong: 你这样下去非～不可。*You are bound to get (or run) into trouble if you go on like this*.

【出炉】〈字〉to come out of the stove—〈喻〉to make something known to the public: 投资保护法细则将在年底之前～。*The detailed rules and regulations of the Investment Protection Law will be promulgated before the end of the year*.

【出路】❶ a way out; outlet: 他们在森林里迷失了方向,找不到～。*They lost their bearings in the forest and couldn't find their way out*. / 给以生活～ *provide sb. with the opportunity to earn a living* ❷ an outlet for goods: 给滞销商品找个～ *find an outlet for unsalable goods*

【出乱子】go wrong; get into trouble: 你放心,出不了什么乱子。*Don't worry. There won't be any trouble*.

【出落】(of a young person, esp. a young girl) grow (prettier, etc.): 三年不见,这姑娘～得更漂亮了。*The girl has grown prettier than ever since I last saw her three years ago*.

【出马】go into action; take the field: 亲自～ *take up the matter oneself; attend to the matter personally; take personal charge of the matter*

【出卖】❶ offer for sale; sell ❷ sell out; betray: ～原则 *barter away principles* / ～民族利益 *betray the interests of the nation*

【出毛病】be or go out of order; malfunction: 机器～了。*The machine is out of order*. or *There's some trouble with the machine*. / 汽车～了。*Something has gone wrong with the car*.

【出门】❶ go out: 他刚～,一会儿就回来。*He's just gone out, he'll be back soon*. ❷ leave home; go on a journey: ～在外,要多加小心。*Look after yourself when you're away from home*. / 我年纪

大了,不能出远门了。*I'm too old to go on long trips any more*. ❸〈方〉(of a woman) get married; marry

【出面】appear personally; act in one's own capacity or on behalf of sb.: ～调停 *act as a mediator* / 我愿出力,不愿～。*I'm willing to help out but not to act on anyone's behalf*.

【出苗】(of seedlings) emerge; come out; sprout ◇ ～率［农］the rate of emergence

【出名】❶ be famous; be well known: 四川菜在国内外都很～。*Sichuan cuisine is famous both at home and abroad*. ❷ lend one's name (to an occasion or enterprise); use the name of: 今天由学生会～,召开迎新晚会。*This evening the Students' Union will give a party to welcome the new students*.

【出没】appear and disappear; haunt: 大熊猫～于川西山区。*The mountainous areas of western Sichuan are the haunt of the giant panda*. /～无常 *appear and disappear unexpectedly; come and go unpredictably*

【出谋划策】give counsel; mastermind: 躲在背后～ *mastermind a scheme from behind the scenes*

【出纳】❶ receipt and payment of money or bills ❷ cashier; teller ❸ lending and receiving books ◇ ～员 cashier; teller

【出纳台】❶ cashier's (or teller's) desk ❷ circulation desk (in a library);

【出票日】date of draft

【出品】❶ make; produce; manufacture: 光明化工厂～ *manufactured (or made) by Guangming Chemical Plant* ❷ product: 这是本厂的新～。*This is a new product of our factory*.

【出其不意】take sb. by surprise; catch sb. unawares

【出奇】unusual; extraordinary: 今年夏天热得～。*It's unusually hot this summer*. / 那天清晨,大海～地宁静。*The sea was extraordinarily calm that morning*.

【出奇制胜】defeat one's opponent by a surprise move: 我们不是冒险,是～! *We wouldn't be running any risk; we'd be winning by means of a surprise attack!*

【出气】give vent to one's anger; vent one's spleen: 是她得罪了你,可别在我身上～。*She's the one who offended you. Don't take it out on me*. ◇ ～口 gas outlet; air vent; ～筒〈方〉〈喻〉punching bag

【出勤】❶ turn out for work: 她已经三天没～了。*She's been absent from work for three days*. / 全体～ *full attendance* ❷ be or go out on business ◇ ～率 attendance rate; attendance

【出去】go out; get out: ～走走 *go out for a walk (or stroll)* / 他刚～。*He's just gone out*. / 门口太拥挤,一时出不去。*The exit is too crowded for us to get out yet*.

【出缺】(of a high post) fall vacant

【出让】sell (one's own things): 自行车减价～ *sell one's bicycle at a reduced price*

【出人头地】rise head and shoulders above others; stand out among one's fellows

【出人意料】(又作'出人意表') exceeding all expectations; beyond all expectations: 疗效之佳～。*The curative effect exceeded all expectations*.

【出任】〈书〉take up the post of: ～县长 *take up the post of county magistrate* / 你们准备推荐谁～此职? *Who are you going to recommend for the post?*

【出入】❶ come in and go out: 机房不能随便～。*You can't come in and go out of the motor room as you please*. / ～大门请下车! *Cyclists please dismount at the gate*. ❷ discrepancy; divergence: 他说的和你说的有～。*There's some discrepancy between your account and his*. ◇ ～手续 entry and exit procedures; ～证 pass (identifying a staff member, etc.)

【出赛】［体］take part in a sports competition

【出色】outstanding; remarkable; splendid: 干得很～ *do a remarkable job; acquit oneself splendidly* / 他们～地完成了任务。*They accomplished their task with flying colours*.

【出山】❶ leave a hilly region ❷〈喻〉enter politics as a government official; take up a post or task

【出身】❶ be descended from; come of (or from): ～书香门第 *come from a family of scholars* ❷ family background; (class) origin: 咱俩都是穷苦～。*We are both from poor families*. ❸ one's previous experience or occupation: 那位将军是铁匠～。*The general began life as a blacksmith*.

【出神】be spellbound; be in a trance; be lost in thought: 青年钢琴家的演奏使她听得出了神。*She was held spellbound by the performance of the young pianist*. / 他坐在那里～。*He sat there, lost in thought*.

【出神入化】reach the acme of perfection; be superb: 他的表演艺术～。*His performance was superb*.

【出生】be born: 我是 1930 年～的。*I was born in 1930*. / 他～在美国。*He was born in the United States*. / ～登记 *registration of birth* / ～日期 *date of birth* ◇ ～地 birthplace; ～率 birthrate; ～证 birth certificate

【出生入死】go through fire and water; brave untold dangers; at the risk of life and limb: 革命战争中～的战士 *a fighter who risked death in the revolutionary wars*

【出师】❶ complete one's apprenticeship ❷〈书〉dispatch troops to fight; send an army to battle: ～不利 *lost the first battle or game; meet with initial setbacks*

【出使】serve as an envoy abroad; be sent on a diplomatic mission: ～西班牙 *be sent as an envoy to Spain; be accredited to Spain*

【出示】❶ show; produce: 请～车票。*Please show your ticket*. / ～证件 *produce one's papers* ❷〈书〉put up a notice: ～安民 *put up a notice to reassure the public*

【出世】❶ come into the world; be born; come into being: 他～才三天，他妈妈就去世了。*His mother died three days after he was born.* ❷ renounce the world; keep aloof from worldly affairs ❸ rise high above the world

【出事】meet with a mishap; have an accident: 飞机～了。*The plane crashed.* / 出了什么事? *What's wrong?* or *What's happening?* / ～地点 *the site of an accident*

【出手】❶ get (hoarded goods, etc.) off one's hands; dispose of; sell: 货物已经～了。*The goods have been disposed of.* ❷ give out: 他相当大方，一～就给了一百块。*He was quite generous and gave* 100 *yuan offhand.* ❸ skill displayed in making opening moves (in wushu, chess, etc.)

【出手不凡】make skilful (or masterly) opening moves (in wushu, chess, etc.)

【出售】offer for sale; sell

【出数儿】〈口〉(of rice) rise well with cooking: 这种米做饭很～。*This kind of rice rises well when it's cooked.*

【出水芙蓉】同〖芙蓉出水〗

【出台】❶ appear on the stage ❷ make a public appearance

【出逃】flee: ～国外 *flee the country*

【出题】❶ set a question; set a test paper ❷ set a topic

【出挑】❶ 见〖出落〗❷ develop (in skill, etc.): 不满一年，他就～成一个好司机。*In less than a year he developed into a good driver.*

【出铁】tap molten iron; tap a blast furnace: 新炉～了。*They have started tapping the new blast furnace.* / 出一炉铁 *tap a heat of molten iron* ◇ ～口 [冶] taphole; iron notch

【出庭】appear in court: ～作证 *appear in court as a witness*

【出头】❶ hold up one's head; free oneself (from misery, persecution, etc.): 穷苦人有了～的日子。*Poor people can now hold up their heads.* ❷ appear in public; come forward: 他要肯～，咱们这件事准能成功。*If he's willing to come forward on our behalf, we're sure to succeed.* ❸ (used after a round number) a little over; odd: 他三十～了。*He's a little over thirty.* / 三百～ *three hundred odd*

【出头露面】appear in public; be in the limelight: ～的人物 *a public figure* / 喜欢～ *be fond of being in the limelight; enjoy being the centre of attention*

【出头鸟】〈字〉the head of a bird first appeared; 〈喻〉someone who stands out from the crowd or who leads a flock

【出土】❶ be unearthed; be excavated: ～文物 *unearthed artifacts; archaeological finds* ❷ come up out of the ground: 小苗刚～。*The sprouts have just come up.*

【出脱】❶ manage to sell; dispose of: 那批货一时～不了。*We can't sell off those goods just now.* ❷ 同〖出落〗❸ acquit; absolve: 你的罪名无法～。*You can never clear yourself of that charge.*

【出亡】〈书〉flee from one's home or country; go into exile

【出污泥而不染】emerge unstained from the filth

【出息】❶ prospects; a bright future: 有～ *have prospects of success in life; show promise* / 这人真没～。*This chap is a good-for-nothing.* ❷〈方〉make good progress: 这孩子比去年～多了。*The boy is doing much better than he did last year.*

【出席】be present (at a meeting, social gathering, etc.); attend: ～会议 *attend a meeting* / ～宴会 *be present at a banquet* / ～人数 *number of persons present; attendance*

【出险】❶ be or get out of danger: 救人～ *rescue sb. from danger* ❷ (of dykes, dams, etc.) be in danger; be threatened: 河堤～，全村的人都赶去抢修。*When the dyke was in danger, the whole village rushed out to repair it.*

【出现】appear; arise; emerge: 天上～一片乌云。*Black clouds appeared in the sky.* / 她的～使人感到意外。*Her appearance was quite unexpected.* / ～了新情况。*A new situation arose.*

【出项】item of expenditure; expenses; outlay

【出血】❶ lose blood; bleed: 她出了大量的血。*She's lost a lot of blood.* ❷ [医] haemorrhage; bleeding: 大(内、胃)～ *massive (internal, gastric) haemorrhage*

【出巡】go on an inspection tour

【出芽】put forth buds; bud; sprout

【出言不逊】make impertinent remarks; speak insolently

【出演】❶ 同〖演出〗❷ play the part of; act

【出洋】〈旧〉go abroad: ～留学 *go abroad to study*

【出洋相】make an exhibition of oneself; make a spectacle of oneself

【出以公心】keep the public interest in mind; act without selfish considerations

【出迎】go or come out to meet

【出油井】[油] producing well

【出游】go on a sightseeing tour

【出于】start from; proceed from; stem from: ～自愿 *on a voluntary basis; of one's own accord* / ～无奈 *as it cannot be helped; there being no alternative*

【出狱】be released from prison

【出院】(of an inpatient) leave hospital: 病愈～ *be discharged from hospital after recovery* / ～证明 *hospital discharge certificate*

【出渣口】[冶] slag notch; cinder notch

【出账】❶ enter an item of expenditure in the accounts ❷〈方〉items of expenditure

【出诊】(of a doctor) visit a patient at home; pay a home visit; make a house call

【出征】go on an expedition; go out to battle: ～的战士 *soldiers sent on an expedition*

【出众】be out of the ordinary; be outstanding: 人才～ *a person of exceptional ability* / 成绩～ *get outstanding results in study (or work)*

【出资】provide funds or capital: 此项工程由市政

府～兴建。*The municipal government is going to provide funds for this construction project.*
【出走】leave one's home or country under compulsion; run away; flee：仓卒～ *leave in a hurry*
【出租】hire out; rent; let：游船按小时～。*Rowboats for hire by the hour.* / 房屋～。*Houses to let.* / 这家公司～汽车、大轿车。*This company has cars and buses for hire.* /～柜台 *rent out counters*

初 Ⅰ **名** the beginning of; the early part of：八月～ *early in August*; *in early August* / 本世纪～ *the beginning of this century* Ⅱ **形** ❶ first (in order)：～雪 *first snow* / ～战 *first battle* / ～一(五、十) *the first (fifth, tenth) day of the lunar month* ❷ elementary; rudimentary：初级 / 初等 ❸ original：和好如～ *become good friends again*; *become reconciled* Ⅲ **副** for the first time; just beginning：感冒～起 *with the first symptoms of a cold* / ～具规模 *be just beginning to take shape*
【初版】❶ first edition ❷ be first published：这部词典于1978年～。*This dictionary was first published in* 1978.
【初步】initial; preliminary; tentative：～方案 *a tentative programme* / ～设想 *a tentative idea* / ～估计 *preliminary estimates*
【初产妇】primipara
【初潮】first menses
【初出茅庐】just come out of one's thatched cottage—at the beginning of one's career; young and inexperienced：～的电视节目主持人 *a fledgling TV host*
【初创】newly established：～阶段 *initial stage*
【初春】early spring; first spring month (i. e. the first month of the lunar year)
【初次】the first time：～见面 *see sb. for the first time* / ～登台 *appear for the first time on the stage*; *make one's début*
【初等】elementary; primary：～数学 *elementary mathematics* ◇～教育 elementary education
【初冬】early winter; first winter month (i. e. the tenth month of the lunar year)
【初犯】❶ first offender ❷ first offence
【初伏】❶ the first fu—the first of the three ten-day periods of the hot season ❷ the first day of the first fu (falling in mid-July) ——另见〖三伏〗
【初稿】first draft; draft
【初会】first encounter; first meeting
【初婚】❶ first marriage ❷ newly married
【初级】elementary; primary：～产品 *primary products* / ～读本 *primer* ◇～线圈 primary coil;～小学 lower primary school;～中学 junior middle school
【初级阶段】primary stage：社会主义～ *the primary stage of socialism*
【初加工】preliminary working
【初见成效】achieve an initial success
【初交】new acquaintance：我和他是～，对他还不太了解。*We've just got acquainted, so I don't know much about him.*
【初具规模】begin to take shape
【初亏】[天] first contact (the beginning of an eclipse) ——另见〖食相〗
【初恋】❶ first love：一个人的～是最难以忘怀的。*One can never forget one's first love.* ❷ the first stage of falling in love：他们老两口儿还像～那会儿那样亲昵。*The old couple still dote on each other just as when they first fell in love.*
【初露锋芒】display one's talent for the first time
【初露头角】begin to show ability or talent：～的新作家 *budding writers*
【初年】the first years of a historical period：民国～ *in the first years of the Republic*
【初评】preliminary appraisal; first round of evaluation：进行～ *make preliminary appraisal*
【初期】initial stage; early days：战争～ *in the early days of the war* / 解放～ *during the initial post-liberation period*; *just (or right) after liberation*
【初秋】early autumn; first autumn month (i. e. the seventh month of the lunar year)
【初赛】preliminary contest; preliminary
【初审】[法] trial of first instance; first trial：～案件 *case of first instance* / ～法庭 *court of first instance*
【初生之犊不怕虎】newborn calves are not afraid of tigers—young people are fearless
【初始】initial; first; primary
【初试】❶ first try ❷ preliminary examination
【初速度】[物] initial velocity
【初夏】early summer; first summer month (i.e. the fourth month of the lunar year)
【初选】primary election
【初学】begin to learn; be a beginner：我是～，还不会拉曲子。*I'm just a beginner; I can't play a tune yet.*
【初叶】early years (of a century)：二十世纪～ *early in the twentieth century*
【初夜】❶ early evening ❷ wedding night ◇～权 right of first night
【初诊】one's first visit to a doctor or hospital
【初值】[数] initial value
【初中】〈略〉见〖初级中学〗
【初衷】one's original intention：虽经挫折，不改～ *will not change one's original intention despite the setbacks one has suffered*

chú

刍 Ⅰ **名**〈书〉hay; fodder：反刍 Ⅱ **动** cut grass
【刍秣】〈书〉fodder; forage
【刍议】〈书〉(my) modest proposal; (my) tentative suggestion：考试制度改革～ *a modest proposal (or tentative suggestions) for the reform of the examination system*

除 Ⅰ **动** ❶ get rid of; eliminate; remove：除草

/ 铲除 ❷［数］divide：八～以四得二。*8 divided by 4 is 2*. / 二～六得三。*2 goes into 6 three times*. / 十能被五～尽。*10 divides by 5*. or *5 goes into 10*. Ⅱ 介 ❶except：～此而外 *with the exception of this*；*excepting this* ❷ besides：～水稻外，我们还种棉花和小麦。*Besides rice, we grow cotton and wheat*.

【除暴安良】get rid of bullies and bring peace to good people

【除草】remove weeds；weed ◇ ～机 weeder；～剂 weed killer；herbicide

【除尘器】dust remover：真空～ *vacuum cleaner*

【除虫菊】Dalmatian chrysanthemum

【除恶务尽】one must be thorough in exterminating an evil

【除法】［数］division

【除非】❶（used correlatively with 才）only if；only when：～他做不了，他才会找我帮忙。*Only when he can't do it does he ask me for help*. ❷（usu. used correlatively with 否则，不然，or 要不然）(not)... unless：～你跟我去，否则我不去。*I won't go unless you go with me*. ❸（preceded by a clause with 要）must needs；necessarily：要想取得第一手资料，～你亲自去作调查。*If you want firsthand information, you'll have to find out for yourself*.

【除根】dig up the roots；cure once and for all；root out：斩草必须～。*When you're weeding, you must dig up the roots*. / 这病很难～。*It's difficult to find a permanent cure for this disease*.

【除号】division sign（÷）

【除旧布新】get rid of the old to make way for the new；do away with the old and set up the new

【除旧更新】replace the old with the new

【除了】❶ except：～这位老猎人，那条山路谁也不熟悉。*Nobody knows the mountain path well except the old hunter*. ❷（used correlatively with 还，也，etc.）besides；in addition to：懂日语的，～我还有两个人。*There are two others besides me who know some Japanese*. ❸（used correlatively with 就是）if not...（then...）；either ...（or...）：刚生下来的孩子，～吃就是睡。*If a newborn baby isn't eating, then it's sleeping*. / 这几天～刮风，就是下雨。*Recently we've been having either windy or rainy days*.

【除名】remove sb.'s name from the rolls；strike sb.'s name off the rolls；expunge sb.'s name from a list

【除数】［数］divisor

【除霜】defrost：自动～ *auto-defrosting* / 手动～ *manual defrosting* / 快速～ *fast defrosting* ◇ ～器 defroster

【除四害】eliminate the four pests（usu. referring to rats，bedbugs，flies and mosquitoes）

【除外】except；not counting；not including：展览会每天开放，星期一～。*The exhibition is open every day except Monday*. / 一共五件行李，药箱～。*There are five pieces of luggage, not counting the medical kit*.

【除夕】New Year's Eve

【除莠剂】herbicide

厨 名 kitchen：下～ *go to the kitchen（to do cooking）*

【厨房】kitchen：～用具 *kitchen（or cooking）utensils*

【厨师】cook；chef

【厨艺】culinary art

锄 Ⅰ 名 hoe Ⅱ 动 ❶do hoeing：～草 *hoe up weeds*；*weed with a hoe* ❷ uproot；eliminate；wipe out：锄奸

【锄地】hoe the fields；do hoeing：锄玉米地 *hoe the cornfields*

【锄奸】eliminate traitors；ferret out spies：～工作 *elimination of traitors*；*anti-espionage work*

【锄强扶弱】suppress the strong and aid the weak

【锄头】❶ pickaxe（used in southern China）❷〈方〉hoe

雏 形 young（bird）：～燕 *young swallow*

【雏儿】〈口〉❶ a young bird；nestling：燕～ *young swallow* / 鸭～ *duckling* ❷ a young，inexperienced person；fledgling

【雏鸟】nestling；fledgling

【雏形】❶ a rudimentary，undeveloped form of an organism；an embryonic form：蛹显示出成虫的触角、腿、翅膀的～。*The undeveloped forms of the adult insect's antennae, legs and wings are embodied in the pupa*. ❷ miniature

橱 名 cabinet；closet；wardrobe：～顶上放着两只皮箱。*There are two suitcases on the top of the wardrobe*. / 玻璃～里放着许多小摆设。*A lot of bric-a-brac is displayed in the glass-fronted cabinet*.

【橱窗】❶ show（or display）window；showcase；shopwindow ❷ glass-fronted billboard

【橱柜】❶ cupboard ❷ a cupboard that also serves as a table；sideboard

chǔ

处 动 ❶〈书〉dwell：穴居野处 ❷ get along（with sb.）：容易相～ *easy to get along with* / 他们俩～得很好。*They get along quite well*. / 这个人不好～。*This fellow is hard to get along with*. ❸ be situated in；be in a certain condition：我们正～在一个伟大的历史时代。*We are living in a great historic era*. ❹ manage；handle；deal with：处事 ❺ punish；sentence：～以两年徒刑 *sentence sb. to two years' imprisonment* ——另见 chù

【处罚】punish；penalize

【处方】❶ write out a prescription；prescribe ❷ prescription；recipe ◇ ～药 prescription drug；prescription medicine

【处分】❶ take disciplinary action against；punish：

免予～ *exempt sb. from punishment* / 党内～ *disciplinary action within the Party* / 行政～ *administrative disciplinary measure* ❷〈书〉handle; manage; deal with

【处境】unfavourable situation; plight: ～困难 *be in a sorry plight*; *be in a predicament*; *be in a difficult situation* / ～危险 *be in a dangerous (or precarious) situation*; *be in peril*

【处决】❶ put to death; execute: 依法～ *put to death in accordance with the law* / 被秘密～ *be executed in secret* ❷ manage and make decisions: 大会休会期间，一切事项由常委会～。*When the Congress is not in session, all affairs are handled by the standing committee.*

【处理】❶ handle; deal with; dispose of: ～国家大事 *conduct state affairs* / ～日常事务 *handle day-to-day work*; *deal with routine matters* ❷ treat (a workpiece or product) by a special process: 用硫酸～ *treat with sulphuric acid* ❸ sell at reduced prices: ～积压商品 *sell old stock at reduced prices* / ～价格 *reduced price*; *bargain price* ◇ ～程序 processing design

【处理机】processor: 数据～ *data processor* / 文字～ *word processor* / 中央～ *central processor*

【处理品】goods (usu. shopworn or substandard) sold at reduced prices

【处女】virgin; maiden ◇ ～地 virgin land (or soil); ～航 maiden voyage or flight; ～膜［生理］hymen; ～作 maiden work; first effort

【处身】place oneself; settle: ～在异常艰险的环境中 *place oneself amid great hardships and dangers* / ～涉世 *the way one conducts oneself in society*

【处士】recluse

【处世】conduct oneself in society: ～哲学 *philosophy of life*

【处事】handle affairs; deal with matters: 他～严肃，态度却十分和蔼。*He handles affairs in a businesslike yet friendly way.*

【处暑】❶ the End of Heat—the 14th of the 24 solar terms ❷ the day marking the beginning of the 14th solar term (Aug. 22, 23, or 24, when summer is really over) ——另见〖节气〗

【处死】put to death; execute

【处心积虑】〈贬〉deliberately plan (to achieve evil ends); incessantly scheme: ～地破坏革命队伍的团结 *be bent on undermining the unity of the revolutionary ranks*

【处刑】［法］condemn; sentence

【处于】be (in a certain condition): ～有利的地位 *find oneself in an advantageous position* / ～平等地位 *be on an equal footing* / ～优势 *have the advantage* / ～昏迷状态 *be in a coma*

【处之泰然】take things calmly; remain unruffled

【处治】punish

【处置】❶ handle; deal with; manage; dispose of: 妥善地～各种复杂情况 *handle complex situations aptly* / ～失当 *mismanage*; *mishandle* ❷ punish

【处子】〈书〉virgin

杵 Ⅰ 名 ❶ pestle: ～臼 *mortar and pestle* ❷ a wooden club used to beat clothes in washing Ⅱ 动 poke: 用手指头～他一下 *give him a poke* / 把纸～个窟窿 *poke a hole in the paper*

础 名 plinth: ～石 *the stone base of a column*; *plinth*

储 动 store up: ～粮备荒 *store up grain against natural disasters* / 冬～白菜 *cabbages stored for the winter*

【储备】❶ store for future use; lay in; lay up: ～过冬饲料 *lay up fodder for the winter* / ～粮食 *store up grain*; *build up supplies of grain* ❷ reserve: 黄金～ *gold reserve* / 外汇～ *foreign exchange reserve* ◇ ～寸头 reserve position; ～基金 reserve fund; ～粮 grain reserves; ～银行 savings bank

【储藏】❶ save and preserve; store; keep: 鲜果～ *preservation (or storage) of fresh fruit* ❷ deposit: 我国有丰富的石油～。*Our country abounds in oil deposits.* ◇ ～量 reserves; ～室 storeroom

【储存】lay in; lay up; store; stockpile; deposit: 把钱～在银行里 *deposit the money in a bank*

【储放】store; leave in sb.'s care: 把行李～在寄存处 *check one's luggage at the checkroom*

【储户】depositor

【储积】❶ store up; save: ～余粮，以备急需 *store up surplus grain for use in time of need* ❷ stock; savings

【储集】store up; save ◇ ～层［油］reservoir bed

【储君】crown prince

【储量】［矿］reserves: 远景～ *prospective reserves* / 探明～ *proved reserves* / 可采～ *recoverable (or workable) reserves* / ～等级 *ore reserve classification*

【储气】gas storage ◇ ～构造 gas-bearing structure

【储气罐】gas tank

【储蓄】save; deposit: 提倡～ *encourage saving* / 城乡～迅速增加。*Savings deposits in both urban and rural areas have shown a rapid increase.* ◇ ～存款 savings deposit; ～代办所 savings agency; ～额 total savings deposits; ～所 savings bank

【储油】［油］oil storage ◇ ～构造［油］oil-bearing structure

【储油罐】［油］oil storage tank; oil tank

【储运】store up and transport: ～网 *storage and transport network* / ～站 *storage and transport depot*

楚 Ⅰ 形 clear; neat: 清楚 Ⅱ 名 ❶〈书〉pang; suffering: 苦楚 ❷ one of the Warring States into which China was divided during the Eastern Zhou period (770-256 B.C.), occupying what is now Hubei and northern Hunan ❸ a name for what is now Hubei and Hunan (esp. the former)

【楚材晋用】the talents of Chu used by Jin—the intellectual resources of one country used by another

【楚楚】❶ tidy; neat; spotlessly clean ❷ delicate; dainty

【楚楚可怜】(of a young woman) delicate and charming

chù

处 Ⅰ名 ❶ place: 别～ *another place; elsewhere* / 停车～ *parking place; car park* ❷ point; part: 有相同之～ *bear a resemblance; have something in common* ❸department; office: 总务～ *general affairs department* Ⅱ量 (for places or for occurrences or activities in different places): 几～人家 *several homesteads* / 发现两～印刷错误 *find two misprints*——另见 chǔ

【处处】everywhere; in all respects: ～严格要求自己 *set strict demands on oneself in all respects* / ～关心同学 *show the students every consideration*

【处所】place; location

【处长】the head of a department or office; section chief

绌 形〈书〉inadequate; insufficient: 相形见绌

畜 名 domestic animal; livestock: 牲畜——另见 xù

【畜肥】animal manure

【畜类】domestic animals

【畜力】animal power: ～车 *animal-drawn cart* / ～农具 *animal-drawn farm implements*

【畜生】❶ domestic animals ❷〈诋〉beast; dirty swine

【畜疫】epidemic disease of domestic animals

触 动 ❶ touch; contact: ～到痛处 *touch a sore spot; touch sb. to the quick* ❷ strike; hit: ～雷 *strike (or touch off) a mine* ❸ move sb.; stir up sb.'s feelings: ～起前情 *awaken one's old love*

【触电】get an electric shock: 小心～! *Danger! Electricity!* or *Danger! Live wire!*

【触动】❶ touch sth., moving it slightly: 他在暗中摸索着,忽然～了什么东西。*Groping in the dark, he suddenly touched something.* ❷ move sb.; stir up sb.'s feelings: 有所～ *be somewhat moved* / 这句话～了他的心事。*That remark reminded him of something he'd had on his mind for a long time.*

【触发】detonate by contact; touch off; spark; trigger: ～热核聚变 *trigger thermonuclear fusion* / ～乡思 *touch off a train of home thoughts; provoke nostalgic longing* ◇ ～地雷 contact mine; ～电路 trigger circuit; ～器 trigger

【触犯】offend; violate; go against: ～法律 *violate (or break) the law* / ～人民利益 *encroach on the interests of the people* / 我什么地方～了你? *What have I done to offend you?*

【触击】❶ strike: 钢镚儿～的声音 *the sound of coins striking against each other; the jingling of coins* ❷[体] bunt

【触及】touch: ～人们的灵魂 *touch people to their very souls* / ～事物的本质 *get to the essence of a matter*

【触礁】run (up) on rocks; strike a reef (or rock)

【触角】[动] antenna; feeler

【触景生情】the sight strikes a chord in one's heart: 他～,想起家乡,不觉泪下。*He was moved by the occasion to thoughts of home, and despite himself he began to weep.*

【触觉】[生理] tactile (or tactual) sensation; sense of touch ◇ ～器官 tactile organ

【触类旁通】grasp a typical example and you will grasp the whole category; comprehend by analogy

【触媒】[化] catalyst; catalytic agent

【触摸】touch; feel: 请勿～展品。*Please don't touch the exhibits.*

【触目】❶ meet the eye ❷ eye-catching; striking; conspicuous: ～的广告 *eye-catching posters* / ～皆是 *can be seen everywhere; be everywhere in evidence*

【触目惊心】startling; shocking

【触怒】make angry; infuriate; enrage

【触杀剂】contact insecticide

【触手】[动] tentacle

【触痛】❶ touch a tender (or sore) spot; touch sb. to the quick ❷[医] tenderness

【触网】[体] touch net

【触须】[动] cirrus: 鱼类～ *barbel* / 无脊椎动物～ *palp*

【触诊】[医] palpation

黜 动〈书〉remove sb. from office; dismiss

【黜免】〈书〉dismiss (a government official)

矗 动〈书〉stand tall and upright

【矗立】stand tall and upright; tower over sth.: 人民英雄纪念碑～在天安门广场上。*The Monument to the People's Heroes towers aloft in Tian'anmen Square.*

chuāi

揣 动 hide or carry in one's clothes: ～在怀里 *hide in the bosom; tuck into the bosom* / 这封信一直～在我口袋里。*The letter has been in my pocket all this time.* ——另见 chuǎi

【揣手儿】tuck each hand in the opposite sleeve

搋 动 ❶ rub; knead: ～面 *knead dough* / 这衣服没洗干净,再～两下。*These clothes haven't been washed clean, Let me give them another rub or two.* ❷ clear a drain with a suction pump

chuǎi

揣 动〈书〉estimate; surmise; conjecture: 揣测

——另见 chuāi

【揣测】guess; conjecture: 据我～,他已经离开太原了。*My guess is that he's already left Taiyuan.*

【揣度】〈书〉estimate; appraise; conjecture: ～敌情 *make an appraisal of the enemy's situation*

【揣摩】try to fathom; try to figure out: 我始终～不透他的用意。*I simply couldn't figure out his intention.*

【揣想】guess; think: 她心里～着接下去会发生什么情况。*She was trying to figure out what would happen next.*

chuài

踹 动 ❶ kick: 一脚把门～开 *kick the door open* ❷ tread; stamp: 一脚～在水坑里 *step in a puddle*

chuān

川 名 ❶ river: 高山大～ *high mountains and big rivers* ❷ plain: 米粮川

【川贝】[中] tendril-leaved fritillary bulb of Sichuan origin

【川流不息】flowing past in an endless stream; never-ending: 顾客～。*Customers came in an endless stream.* or *Customers kept pouring in.*

【川芎】[中] the rhizome of chuanxiong (Ligusticum wallichii)

【川资】travelling expenses

氚 名 [化] tritium (T or H^3)

【氚核】[物] triton

穿 动 ❶ pierce through; penetrate: ～个窟窿 *pierce (or bore) a hole* / 鞋底磨～了。*The sole of the shoe was worn through.* ❷ pass through; cross: 飞机～云下降。*The plane descended through the clouds.* ❸ wear; put on; be dressed in: ～灰大衣的那个女的 *the woman in a grey overcoat* / 衣服～旧了。*The clothes show signs of wear.* / 这种鞋小点不要紧,～～就大了。*It doesn't matter if the shoes feel a bit tight. They'll stretch with wearing.* ❹ string together: 用珠子～成一串项链 *string the beads into a necklace*

【穿插】❶ alternate; do in turn: 施肥和除草～进行 *do manuring and weeding in turn* ❷ weave in; insert: 他在报告中～了一些生动的例子。*His talk was spiced with vivid examples.* ❸ subplot; interlude; episode ❹ [军] thrust deep into the enemy forces: 打～ *fight a deep-thrust battle* / ～分割敌人 *penetrate and cut up the enemy forces* ◇ ～营 [军] deep-thrust battalion

【穿刺】[医] puncture: 肝(腰椎)～ *liver (lumbar) puncture*

【穿戴】apparel; dress: ～整齐 *be neatly dressed and adorned* / 不讲究～ *not be particular about one's dress*

【穿过】go across or through; cross; penetrate: ～马路 *cross a street* / 从人群中～去 *thread one's way through the crowd* / 子弹～头盔射入他的头部。*The bullet penetrated his helmet and hit his head.*

【穿甲弹】armour-piercing projectile; armour-piercing shell or bullet; armour piercer

【穿卡机】punched-card machine

【穿孔】❶ bore (or punch) a hole; perforate: ～卡片 *punched card* / ～纸带 *punched tape* ❷ [医] perforation: 胃(阑尾)～ *gastric (appendicular) perforation*

【穿孔机】punch; perforator

【穿筘机】[纺] reeding machine

【穿山甲】❶ [动] pangolin ❷ [中] pangolin scales

【穿梭】shuttle back and forth: ～轰炸 *shuttle bombing* / ～外交 *shuttle diplomacy*

【穿堂风】draught

【穿堂门】passageway; alley gate

【穿透】pierce through; run through: 钉子～了木板。*The nail ran through the board.*

【穿小鞋】(usu. used in) 给某人～ *give sb. tight shoes to wear—make things hard for sb. by abusing one's power; make it hot for sb.*

【穿孝】be in mourning; wear mourning: 为母亲～ *wear mourning for one's mother*

【穿心莲】[中] creat

【穿新鞋,走老路】tread the same old path in new shoes—do sth. old in a new form; old wine in a new bottle: 这家工厂的改革有～之嫌。*The reform of this factory looks like going through the motions.*

【穿一条裤子】share the same pair of trousers—band together; collude; gang up

【穿衣镜】full-length mirror

【穿越】pass through; cut across: 铁路～原始森林。*The railway cuts through a primeval forest.* / ～国境 *cross the border*

【穿凿】give a farfetched (or strained) interpretation; read too much into sth. ◇ ～附会 give strained interpretations and draw farfetched analogies

【穿针】thread a needle

【穿针引线】act as a go-between

【穿着】dress; apparel: ～朴素整洁 *be plainly but neatly dressed*

chuán

传 动 ❶ pass; pass on: 此件请按名单顺序向下～。*Please pass on this document in the order of the name list.* ❷ hand down: 这种药方没能～下来。*That herbal prescription has been lost to posterity.* ❸ pass on (knowledge, skill, etc.); impart; teach: 老师傅把他的技术全～给徒弟了。*The old master passed all his skills on to his apprentices.* ❹ spread: 消息很快～开了。*The news spread quickly.* or *The news soon got around.* /

这个秘密是他～出去的。*He's the one who let out the secret*. ❺ transmit; conduct: ～热 *transmit heat* / 铜～电。*Copper conducts electricity*. ❻ convey; express: 传神/ 传情 ❼ summon: ～证人 *summon a witness* ❽ infect; be contagious: 小心别让你孩子～上流感。*Mind that your children don't catch the flu*. ——另见 zhuàn

【传帮带】(of experienced people) pass on experience, help and guide new hands (in their work)

【传播】❶ disseminate; propagate; spread: ～花粉 *carry pollen (from flower to flower)*; *pollinate* / ～知识(消息) *spread knowledge (news)* / 制止疾病的～ *check the spread of the disease* ❷ [物] propagation: 直线～ *rectilinear propagation* / 散射～ *scatter propagation* ◇ ～媒介 mass media; the media

【传布】disseminate; propagate; spread: ～基督教 *spread Christianity*

【传抄】make private copies of (a manuscript, document, etc. which is being circulated)

【传出神经】[生理] efferent nerve

【传达】❶ pass on (information, etc.); transmit; relay; communicate: ～命令 *transmit an order* / 听～报告 *hear a relayed report* ❷ reception and registration of callers at a public establishment ❸ janitor ◇ ～室 reception office; janitor's room

【传代】pass on from generation to generation

【传单】leaflet; handbill

【传导】❶[物] conduct (heat, electricity, etc.): 金属都有～作用。*All metals are conductive*. / 热的～ *the conduction of heat* ❷ [生理] transmit: 神经纤维把外界的刺激～给大脑。*Nerve fibres transmit external stimuli to the brain*.

【传道】❶ deliver a sermon; preach ❷ propagate Confucianist doctrines

【传递】transmit; deliver; transfer: ～信件 *deliver mail* / ～信息 *transmit messages*

【传动】[机] transmission; drive: 变速～ *change drive* / 齿轮～ *gear drive (or transmission)* ◇ ～比 drive ratio; ratio of transmission; transmission ratio; ～齿轮 transmission (or drive) gear; ～带 transmission belt; ～箱 transmission case; ～轴 transmission shaft; ～装置 gearing

【传粉】[植] pollination: ～媒介 *pollination medium*

【传感器】[电] sensor; transducer: 激光～ *laser sensor*

【传呼】(of a trunk-line operator or public telephone custodian) pass on a telephone message or call sb. to answer the phone ◇ ～电话 neighbourhood telephone service; ～服务 paging service; ～机 beeper

【传话】pass on a message

【传唤】[法] summon to court; subpoena

【传家宝】❶ family heirloom: 这块玉佩是咱们家的～。*This jade pendant is our family heirloom*. ❷ a cherished tradition or heritage: 艰苦朴素的作风是中国人民的～。*Hard work and plain living is a cherished heritage of the Chinese people*.

【传教】do missionary work ◇ ～士 missionary

【传令】transmit (or dispatch) orders: ～嘉奖 *cite sb. in a dispatch*

【传媒】❶ 〈略〉见〖传播媒介〗 ❷ media; vehicle

【传票】❶ [法] (court) summons; subpoena: 发出～ *issue a summons* ❷ accounting voucher

【传奇】❶ tales of the marvellous (short stories of the Tang-Song period, written in the literary style ❷ a form of drama of the Ming-Qing period, immensely long with an average of forty or more scenes ❸ legend; romance: ～式的人物 *a legendary figure*

【传情】express amorous feelings: 借诗～ *convey one's feelings through a poem*

【传球】pass the ball to a teammate

【传染】infect; be contagious: 接触～ *contagion* / 空气～ *infection through air* / 水～ *waterborne infection* / 这病不～。*This disease is not contagious (or infectious)*. / 感冒很容易～。*Colds are highly infectious*. ◇ ～病 infectious (or contagious) disease; ～病院 hospital for infectious diseases; isolation hospital; ～性 infectiousness; contagion

【传入神经】[生理] afferent nerve

【传神】vivid; lifelike: 他的画很能～。*His paintings are lifelike*. / ～之笔 *a vivid touch (in writing or painting)*

【传声器】microphone

【传声清晰度】[无] articulation

【传声筒】❶ megaphone; loud hailer ❷ one who parrots another; sb.'s mouthpiece

【传世】be handed down from ancient times: ～珍宝 *a treasure handed down from ancient times* / 他有两部作品～。*Two of his works have been handed down to posterity*.

【传授】pass on (knowledge, skill, etc.); impart; teach: ～知识 *impart knowledge to*; *teach* / 向年轻人～技术 *teach young people skills*; *give technical instruction to young people*

【传输】[电] transmission: ～损耗 *transmission loss* ◇ ～线[电] transmission line; transmission control

【传说】❶ pass from mouth to mouth; it is said; they say: 村里～他叔要从国外回来了。*The villagers are all saying that his uncle is soon coming home from abroad*. ❷ legend; tradition: 鲁班的～ *the legend of Lu Ban* / 民间～ *folklore*; *popular legend*

【传诵】be widely read; be on everybody's lips: 为世人所～ *be read with admiration by people all over the world* / ～一时 *be on everybody's lips at the time*

【传送】convey; deliver: ～信息 *convey information* / 村里的邮件都由他～。*He's the postal delivery man in his village*. ◇ ～带 [机] conveyer belt

【传颂】be told from mouth to mouth with approbation; be on everybody's lips

【传统】tradition：发扬优良～ *carry on a fine tradition* / ～友谊 *traditional (ties of) friendship* / ～观念 *traditional ideas* / ～剧目 *traditional theatrical pieces* ◇ ～产业 traditional industries；～教育 traditional education；～商品 traditional commodities

【传闻】❶ it is said；they say ❷ hearsay；rumour；talk：这只是～，我不相信。*That's only hearsay. I don't believe it.* / ～失实。*The rumour was unfounded.*

【传销】multi-layer transit sale or a method of direct marketing

【传讯】［法］summon for interrogation or trial；subpoena；cite：～有关人员 *summon the persons concerned for interrogation*

【传言】❶ hearsay；rumour：不可轻信～！*Give no credence to rumours!* / ～非虚。*It's not just hearsay.* ❷ pass on a message：我不愿给人家～送语，你自己找他说去。*I don't like to act as a messenger. Go and speak to him yourself.*

【传扬】spread (from mouth to mouth)：～四方 *spread far and wide* / 这件事不要～出去。*Don't let a word of this get around.*

【传译】translate one language into another：同声～ *simultaneous interpretation*

【传阅】pass round (or circulate) for perusal：这篇稿子请大家～。*Please pass the draft round.*

【传真】❶ portraiture ❷ facsimile；fax：无线电～ *radio facsimile*；*radiophotography* ◇ ～电报 phototelegraph；～机 facsimile equipment；fax；～记录法 facsimile recording；～信号 facsimile signal；～照片 wirephoto；radiophoto

【传旨】deliver an imperial order：～嘉奖 *deliver an imperial commendation*

【传宗接代】produce a male heir to continue the family line

船 名 boat；ship：上～ *board a ship*；*go on board*；*embark* / 乘～去大连 *go to Dalian by boat*；*embark (on a ship) for Dalian*

【船板】deck of a small wooden boat

【船帮】❶ the side of a boat；shipboard ❷ merchant fleet

【船舶】shipping；boats and ships ◇ ～登记证书 ship's certificate of registry；～证书 ship's papers

【船边交货】free alongside ship (F.A.S.)

【船边提货】alongside delivery；shipside delivery

【船埠】wharf；quay

【船舱】❶ ship's hold ❷ cabin

【船次】❶ number indicating a ship's order of departure ❷ number of voyages taken by a ship

【船到桥头自然直】you will cross the bridge when you get to it.

【船队】fleet；flotilla

【船方】［经］the ship：～不负担装货费用 *free in (F.I.)* / ～不负担卸货费用 *free out (F.O.)* / ～不负担装、卸、理仓费用 *free in and out and stowed (F.I.O.S.)*

【船夫】〈旧〉boatman ◇ ～曲 boatmen's song

【船工】❶ boatman；junkman ❷ boatwright

【船级】ship's classification (or class) ◇ ～社 (ships') classification society；～证书 ship's classification certificate

【船籍】the nationality of a ship

【船籍港】port of registry；home port

【船家】〈旧〉one who owns a boat and makes a living as a boatman；boatman

【船检】inspect ships

【船脚】❶ boatman；junkman ❷shipping freight

【船壳】hull

【船老大】〈方〉❶ the chief crewman of a wooden boat ❷ boatman

【船篷】❶ the mat or wooden roofing of a boat ❷ sail

【船票】steamer ticket：预订去青岛的～ *book one's passage to Qingdao*

【船期】sailing date ◇ ～表 sailing schedule

【船桥】(ship's) bridge

【船蛆】shipworm

【船艄】stern

【船上交货】ex ship；free on board ◇ ～价 free on board (F.O.B.)

【船身】hull (of a ship)：～倾斜。*The boat is tilted to one side.*

【船首】stem；bow；prow ◇ ～楼 forecastle

【船台】(building) berth；shipway；slipway；slip：干式～ *dry shipway*

【船台周期】berth period

【船体】the body of a ship；hull

【船尾】stern ◇ ～部 quarter；～楼 poop

【船位】❶ accommodation on a ship：订～ *book one's passage (on a ship)* ❷ ship's position：测定～ *fix a ship's position (at sea)*；*position finding* / ～推算法 *dead reckoning*

【船坞】dock；shipyard：浮～ *floating dock* / 干～ *dry (or graving) dock* ◇ ～费 dockage

【船舷】side (of a ship or boat)

【船小好调头】〈口〉it is easier for a small boat to turn round—it is easier for a small enterprise to change its line of products or a small company to change its business orientation

【船用油】bunker oil

【船员】(ship's) crew

【船闸】(ship) lock

【船长】captain；skipper

【船只】shipping；vessels：往来～ *shipping traffic* / 载货～ *carrying vessels* / ～失事 *shipwreck*

【船主】❶ the captain of a vessel；skipper ❷ the owner of a boat or ship

椽 名 rafter

【椽子】rafter

chuǎn

喘 Ⅰ 动 breathe heavily；gasp for breath；pant

Ⅱ 名［医］asthma

【喘气】❶ breathe (deeply)；pant；gasp：喘不过气来 *gasp for breath*；*be out of breath* / 大口大口地～ *puff and blow* ❷ take a breather：喘口气儿再干。*Let's take a breather before we go on*.

【喘息】❶ pant；gasp for breath ❷ breather；breathing spell；respite：～未定 *before catching one's breath*；*before one has a chance to catch one's breath*

【喘吁吁】puff and blow

chuàn

串 Ⅰ 动 ❶ string together：把鱼～起来 *string the fish together* ❷ conspire；gang up：串通 ❸ get things mixed up：电话～线 *get the (telephone) lines crossed* / (收音机)～台 *get two or more (radio) stations at once* / 字印得太小，很容易看～行。*The print is too small, you can easily miss (or skip) a line*. ❹ go from place to place；run about；rove：到处乱～ *run about aimlessly* / ～亲戚 *go visiting one's relatives* ❺ play a part (in a play)；act：客串 Ⅱ 量 (for a string of things) string；bunch；cluster：一～珠子 *a string of beads* / 一～钥匙 *a bunch of keys* / 一～葡萄 *a cluster of grapes*

【串并联】［电］series-parallel connection

【串处理语言】［电］string processing language

【串供】act in collusion to make each other's confessions tally

【串行】(chuànháng) (in reading or typing) skip a line；confuse two lines：字印得太小，很容易看～。*The print is so small that you can easily miss (or skip) a line*. ——另见 chuànxíng

【串讲】❶ explain a text sentence by sentence ❷ give a summing-up of a text after going over it paragraph by paragraph

【串联】❶ establish ties；contact ❷［电］series connection：～电池组 *series battery* / ～电阻 *series resistance*

【串亲戚】go visiting one's relatives：春节期间人们相互～。*Relatives pay calls on each other (or exchange visits) during the Spring Festival*.

【串通】gang up；collaborate；collude

【串通一气】gang up；collaborate；work hand in glove；collude：两人～，互相包庇。*Acting in collaboration, the two of them shielded each other*. / 你们～来算计我！*You're all in league against me*！

【串味儿】absorb the smell of sth.；become tainted inflavour：茶叶与化妆品放在一起就会～。*Tea stored close to cosmetics will become tainted in flavour*.

【串行】(chuànxíng)［计］series：～计算机 *series machine* / ～成批处理系统 *serial batch system* / ～处理系统 *serial processing*——另见 chuànháng

【串演】play (or act) the role of

【串珠】a string of beads

chuāng

创 Ⅰ 名 wound：创伤 Ⅱ 动 deal sb. a fatal or decisive：重创 ——另见 chuàng

【创痕】scar

【创口】wound；cut：～很大 *a gaping wound*

【创伤】wound；trauma：精神上的～ *a mental scar*；*a traumatic experience* / 医治战争的～ *heal the wounds of war*

疮 名 ❶ sore；skin ulcer：我手上长的～挺疼的。*The sore on my hand hurts*. ❷ wound：刀～ *a sword wound*

【疮疤】scar：脸上的～ *a scar on the face*

【疮痂】［医］scab

【疮口】the open part of a sore

【疮痍】〈书〉wounds；traumata—devastation caused by a war or a natural calamity：～满目 everywhere a scene of devastation meets the eye

窗 名 window：开～ *open the window* / 看～外 *look out of the window*

【窗玻璃】windowpane

【窗洞】an opening in a wall (to let in light and air)

【窗格子】window lattice

【窗户】window；casement

【窗花】paper-cut for window decoration

【窗口】window：坐在～ *sit at (or by) the window* / 在对外开放中发挥～作用 *serve as a window open to the outside world*

【窗口行业】service trades (e. g. commerce, catering, public transport, etc.)

【窗框】window frame

【窗帘】window curtain

【窗明几净】with bright windows and clean tables；bright and clean

【窗纱】gauze for screening windows；window screening

【窗扇】casement

【窗台】windowsill

【窗沿】windowsill

【窗子】window

chuáng

床 Ⅰ 名 ❶ bed：小孩～ *child's cot*；*baby's crib* / 躺在～上 *lie in bed* / 卧病在～ *take to one's bed*；*be laid up* ❷ sth. shaped like a bed：河床 Ⅱ 量 (for bedding)：一～被子 *one quilt* / 两～毯子 *two blankets* / 三～铺盖 *three sets of bedding*

【床单】sheet

【床垫】mattress

【床架】bedstead

【床铺】bed

【床身】［机］lathe bed

【床头】the head of a bed；bedside ◇ ～灯 bedside

lamp；～柜 bedside cupboard；～箱［机］headstock

【床位】berth；bunk；bed

【床沿】the edge of a bed

【床罩】bedspread；counterpane

【床笫】〈书〉bed mat—the bed as a place of conjugal intimacies ◇ ～之言 private talk between husband and wife；pillow talk

幢 名 a pennant or streamer used in ancient China——另见 zhuàng

【幢幢】(of shadows) flickering；dancing：人影～ *shadows of people moving about* / 树影～ *the dancing shadows of the trees*

chuǎng

闯 动 ❶ rush；dash；charge：～进来 *rush in*；*break in*；*force one's way in* ❷ temper oneself (by battling through difficulties and dangers)；venture out into the world：他是自己～出来的。*He has hewed out his path on his own.* / 我们必须～出一条新路子。*We must break a new path.*

【闯荡】make a living away from home

【闯红灯】❶ go against a red light；jump a red light ❷ violate law and descipline；break down a barrier or limit

【闯祸】get into trouble；bring disaster：你～了。*Look what you've done!* / 你开车要小心，千万别～。*Drive carefully and be sure not to have an accident.*

【闯江湖】(又作'闯荡江湖') make a living wandering from place to place (as a fortune-teller, acrobat, quack doctor, etc.)

【闯将】a daring general；pathbreaker：他是技术革新的～。*He's a pathbreaker in technical innovation.*

【闯劲】the spirit of a pathbreaker；pioneering spirit：搞改革就要有一股不怕困难的～。*To go in for reforms, one must have the fearless spirit of a pathbreaker.*

【闯练】leave home to temper oneself；be tempered in the world：让青年人到社会上去～～。*Let young people temper themselves in society.*

【闯南走北】同〖走南闯北〗

chuàng

创 动 start (doing sth.)；achieve (sth. for the first time)；creat (sth. new)：～记录 *set a record*；*chalk up a record* / 该厂钢产量～历史最高水平。*The plant's steel output was an all-time high.* ——另见 chuāng

【创办】establish；set up：～利润 *promoter's profit* / ～人股份 *founder's shares*；*promoter's stocks*

【创汇】earn foreign exchange：出口～能力 *capacity to earn foreign exchange through export* ◇ ～产品 foreign exchange-earning export products

【创见】original idea：有～的思想家 *an original thinker*

【创建】found；establish：～一个政党 *found a (political) party* / 这所学校是1978年冬～的。*This school was set up in the winter of 1978.*

【创举】pioneering work (or undertaking)：伟大的～ *a great beginning*

【创刊】start publication：～号 *first issue (or number)*

【创立】found；originate：～新学派 *found a new academic school*

【创利】make or earn a profit

【创设】❶ found；create；set up：～一个新的研究所 *set up a new research institute* ❷ create (conditions, etc.)：为我们的学习～有利的条件 *create favourable conditions for our studies*

【创始】originate；initiate；found：处在～阶段 *be in the initial stage* / 中国是联合国的～会员国之一。*China is a founding member of the United Nations.* ◇ ～人 founder；originator；initiator

【创收】create income

【创新】bring forth new ideas；blaze new trails：在艺术上不断～ *constantly bring forth new ideas in the arts* / 勇于实践，大胆～。*Be bold in putting things into practice and blazing new trails.* ◇ ～精神 enterprising spirit；

【创业】start an undertaking；do pioneering work

【创意】original idea

【创优】create excellence

【创造】create；produce；bring about：～有利条件 *create favourable conditions* / ～优异成绩 *produce excellent results* / ～新记录 *set (or create) a new record* / ～奇迹 *create miracles*；*work wonders*；*achieve prodigious feats* ◇ ～力 creative power (or ability)；～性 creativeness；creativity

【创作】❶ create；produce；write：～技巧 *artistic technique*；*craftsmanship* / ～经验 *creative experience* / ～思想 *ideas guiding artistic or literary creation* ❷ creative work；creation：文艺～ *literary and artistic creation* / 划时代的～ *epoch-making creative work*

chuī

吹 动 ❶ blow；puff：～火 *blow a fire* / 把灯～灭 *blow out the lamp* / ～一口气 *give a puff* / 门～开了。*The door blew open.* / 什么风把你给～来了？*What brings you here?* ❷ play (wind instruments)：～笛子 *play the flute* / ～起床号 *sound the reveille* ❸〈口〉boast；brag：先别～，做出具体成绩来再说，*Don't brag about what you're going to do. Get something done.* / ～得天花乱坠 *boast in the most fantastic terms* ❹〈口〉break off；break up；fall through：他们俩～了。*That couple have broken up.*

【吹吹打打】beating drums and blowing trumpets；piping and drumming

【吹吹拍拍】boasting and toadying：这个人～，到处钻营。*That man is given to boasting and flattering, trying to secure personal gain wherever he goes.*

【吹打乐】［音］an ensemble of Chinese wind and percussion instruments

【吹风】❶ be in a draught；catch a chill：你病还没有好，不要～。*Don't get in a draught, you aren't well yet.* ❷ dry（hair，etc.）with a blower；blow-dry ❸ blow-dryer；blower（for drying hair）❹〈口〉let sb. in on sth. in advance：下次会要讨论什么，你给我们吹吹风吧。*Will you give us some idea of what will be taken up at the next meeting?* ◇ ～会 briefing

【吹风机】❶ blower（for drying hair）；blow-dryer ❷ air-blower；blower

【吹拂】❶（of a breeze）sway；stir：晨风～着垂柳。*The morning breeze is swaying the weeping willows.* ❷〈书〉praise and recommend sb.

【吹鼓手】❶ music makers at old-time weddings or funerals ❷〈贬〉eulogist

【吹管】［机］blowpipe：氢氧～ *oxyhydrogen blowpipe* / 氧乙炔～ *oxyacetylene blowpipe*

【吹胡子瞪眼】froth at the mouth and glare with rage；foam with anger

【吹灰之力】the effort needed to blow away a speck of dust；just a small effort ——另见〖不费吹灰之力〗

【吹拉弹唱】blow，bow，pluck，and sing —be very musical：～他样样都会。*He plays every instrument of the band and sings as well.*

【吹冷风】blow a cold wind over；throw cold water on；make discouraging remarks

【吹炼】［冶］blowing

【吹毛求疵】find fault；pick holes；nitpick：总的说来，这是一本好书，若对不足之处过多指摘，未免～。*On the whole it's a good book; and it would be nitpicking to dwell on those small defects.*

【吹牛】boast；brag；talk big：他就爱～。*He's a boastful person.*

【吹牛拍马】boast and flatter

【吹捧】flatter；laud to the skies；lavish praise on：互相～ *flatter each other*

【吹嘘】lavish praise on oneself or others；boast

【吹奏】play（wind instruments）◇ ～乐 band music；wind music

炊 动 cook a meal：无米之炊

【炊饼】〈旧〉steamed cake

【炊具】cooking utensils

【炊事】cooking；kitchen work：～用具 *kitchen (or cooking) utensils* ◇ ～班 cookhouse（or mess，kitchen）squad；～员 a cook or the kitchen staff

【炊烟】smoke from kitchen chimneys

【炊帚】a brush for cleaning pots and pans；pot-scouring brush

chuí

垂 Ⅰ 动 ❶ hang down；droop；let fall：～泪 *shed tears; weep* ❷〈书〉bequeath to posterity；hand down：功～竹帛 *be recorded in history in letters of gold* / ～法后世 *set an example for posterity* ❸〈书〉〈套〉（of one's elders or superiors）condescend：～问 *condescend to inquire* / ～念 *show kind concern for（me）* Ⅱ 副〈书〉nearing；approaching：～亡 *be dying out*

【垂钓】fish with a hook and line；go angling

【垂帘听政】（of an empress regent）sit behind a screen to receive ministerial reports；hold court from behind a screen（an empress regent was supposed to be concealed from the sight of ministers at audience）

【垂柳】weeping willow

【垂落】hang down；drop down；fall：她两行眼泪簌簌地～下来。*Tears streamed down her cheeks.* / 夜幕～。*Night has fallen.*

【垂暮】〈书〉dusk；towards sunset；just before sundown：～之年 *in old age*

【垂盆草】［植］stringy stonecrop（Sedum sarmentosum）

【垂青】〈书〉show appreciation for sb.；look upon sb. with favour

【垂手】with one's hands at one's side：～侍立 *stand respectfully in attendance*

【垂手可得】extremely easy to obtain

【垂死】moribund；dying：～的命运 *approaching doom*

【垂死挣扎】be in one's death throes；put up a last-ditch（or deathbed）struggle

【垂体】［生理］hypophysis；pituitary body（or gland）◇ ～后叶素［药］pituitrin

【垂头】hang（or bow）one's head：～叹息 *hang one's head and sigh*

【垂头丧气】be crestfallen；be dejected

【垂危】❶ be critically ill；be at one's last gasp ❷（of a nation）be in great peril

【垂涎】drool；slaver；covet ◇ ～三尺 spittle three feet long —drool with envy；～欲滴 同〖馋涎欲滴〗

【垂直】perpendicular；vertical：～平面 *vertical plane* / ～发射 *vertical firing（or launching）* / ～俯冲 *steep dive; nose dive* / ～降落 *vertical landing* / ～起飞 *vertical takeoff*

陲 名〈书〉frontiers；borders：边陲

捶 动 beat（with a stick or fist）；thump；pound：～背 *pound sb.'s back（as in massage）* / ～鼓 *beat a drum* / ～门 *bang on the door*

【捶打】beat；pound；thump：～衣服 *beat clothes（when washing them）* / 用榔头～铁板 *hammer away at the iron plate* / ～凸纹 *hammer repousse*

【捶胸顿足】beat one's breast and stamp one's feet

(in sorrow, etc.)

槌 名 mallet; beetle: 棒槌

锤 Ⅰ名 ❶ hammer: 铁～ *iron hammer* / 手～ *hand hammer* ❷ mace ❸weight: 调节～ *governor weight* / 平衡～ *balance weight* Ⅱ动 hammer into shape: ～金箔 *hammer gold into foil*

【锤骨】[生理] malleus; hammer

【锤光】[机] planish

【锤炼】❶ hammer into shape ❷ temper oneself; steel oneself ❸ (of an artist, writer, etc.) try to perfect one's skill or technique by strenuous effort; hammer out; polish: ～钢琴演奏技巧 *work hard to perfect one's piano technique* / ～词句 *polish a piece of writing*

【锤子】hammer

chūn

春 名 ❶ spring: 温暖如～ *as warm as spring* ❷ love; lust: 春心 ❸ life; vitality: 枯木逢春

【春播】spring sowing: ～作物 *spring-sown crops*

【春分】❶ the Spring Equinox—the 4th of the 24 solar terms ❷ the day marking the beginning of the 4th solar term (March 20 or 21)

【春风】❶ spring breeze ❷ a kindly and pleasant countenance

【春风得意】be flushed with success

【春风化雨】life-giving spring breeze and rain—salutary influence of education

【春风满面】beaming with satisfaction; radiant with happiness

【春耕】spring ploughing: ～大忙季节 *busy spring ploughing season*

【春宫】❶ living quarters of the crown prince ❷ pornographic pictures

【春灌】[农] spring irrigation

【春光】sights and sounds of spring; spring scenery

【春光明媚】a sunlit and enchanting scene of spring

【春寒料峭】there is a chill in the air in early spring

【春华秋实】spring flowers and fall fruit —literary talent and moral integrity

【春化】[农] vernalization

【春季】spring; springtime

【春假】spring holidays

【春节】the Spring Festival

【春卷】spring roll (a thin sheet of dough, rolled, stuffed and fried)

【春困】feeling of lethargy that comes over many people in spring; drowsiness on spring dars

【春雷】spring thunder

【春雷霉素】[药] kasugarnycin

【春联】Spring Festival couplets (pasted on gateposts or door panels conveying one's best wishes for the year); New Year couplets

【春令】❶ spring ❷ spring weather: 冬行～ *a springlike winter; a very mild winter*

【春梦】spring dream—transient joy

【春暖花开】spring has come and the flowers are in bloom

【春情】stirrings of love

【春秋】❶ spring and autumn; year: ～多佳日。*There are many fine days in spring and autumn.* / 几度～ *several years* ❷ age: ～已高 *be advanced in years* ❸ annals; chronicle: 《海岛～》 *The Chronicle of an Island (a short story)* ◇ ～衫 jackt suitable for spring or autumn

【春色】❶ spring's colours; spring scenery: 水乡～ *spring in a waterside village* / ～恼人。*Spring's hues are teasing.* ❷ joyful look; wine-flushed face

【春色满园】spring's colours fill the garden

【春笋】bamboo shoots in spring

【春天】spring; springtime

【春宵】spring night: ～苦短。*A spring night is rather too short.*

【春小麦】spring wheat

【春心】thoughts of love; stirrings of love; budding love: 动了～ *feel the first stirrings of love*

【春汛】❶ spring flood ❷[渔] spring (fishing) season

【春药】aphrodisiac

【春意】❶ spring in the air; the beginning (or awakening) of spring: 树梢发青,现出了几分～。*The tops of the trees are turning green; spring is in the air.* ❷ thoughts of love: ～盎然 *spring is in the air* / ～阑珊 *spring is on the wane*

【春游】spring outing

【春雨贵如油】rain in spring is as precious as oil

【春运高峰期】the spring peak transport period

【春种】spring sowing: ～秋收 *spring sowing and autumn harvest*

【春装】spring clothing; spring costume

椿 名 [植] ❶ Chinese toon ❷ tree of heaven

【椿象】stinkbug; shieldbug

chún

纯 Ⅰ 形 ❶ pure; unmixed: ～毛 *pure wool* / ～金 *pure (or solid) gold* / ～白 *pure white* / ～黑 *all black* ❷ skilful; practised; well versed: 功夫不～ *not skilful enough* Ⅱ 副 purely; sheerly; wholly: 这件事的发生～属偶然。*It all happened by sheer chance.*

【纯粹】❶ pure; unadulterated: 陶器是用比较～的黏土制成的。*Pottery is made from unadulterated clay.* / 一个～的人 *a pure person* ❷ purely; sheerly; wholly: 我帮助她～是为了友谊。*I helped her purely out of friendship.* / 那～是浪费时间。*It was a sheer waste of time.*

【纯度】degree of purity

【纯化】purification

【纯碱】[化] soda ash; sodium carbonate

【纯洁】❶ pure; clean and honest: 心地～ *be pure of heart* ❷ purify: ～组织 *purify an organiza-*

tion

【纯净】pure; clean: ～的水是透明的。*Pure water is transparent.*

【纯利】(又作'纯利润') net profit

【纯朴】honest; simple; unsophisticated: ～敦厚 *simple and honest* / ～爽朗 *honest and frank* / 文风～ *simplicity of style*

【纯收入】net income

【纯熟】skilful; practised; well versed: 技术～ *highly skilled*

【纯损】net loss

【纯文学】pure literature; belles-lettres

【纯一】single; simple: 目标～ *singleness of purpose*

【纯音】[物] pure (or simple) tone

【纯真】pure; sincere: ～无邪 *pure and innocent*

【纯正】pure; unadulterated: 动机～ *have pure motives* / 他说的是～的普通话。*He speaks pure putonghua.*

【纯种】thoroughbred; purebred: ～马 *thoroughbred horse* / ～牛 *purebred cattle; pedigree cattle*

唇 名 lip: 上～ *upper lip* / 下～ *lower lip*

【唇齿音】[语音] labiodental (sound)

【唇膏】lipstick

【唇裂】harelip; cleft lip

【唇枪舌剑】cross verbal swords; engage in a battle of words

【唇舌】words; argument

【唇亡齿寒】If the lips are gone, the teeth will be cold; If one (of two interdependent things) falls, the other is in danger; share a common lot

【唇音】[语音] labial (sound)

莼 (构词成分)见下

【莼菜】[植] water shield

淳 形〈书〉pure; honest

【淳厚】pure and honest; simple and kind

【淳朴】honest; simple; unsophisticated: ～的庄稼人 *an honest peasant; unsophisticated countryfolk*

鹑 名 quail

醇 Ⅰ 名 ❶〈书〉mellow wine; good wine ❷ [化] alcohol Ⅱ 形〈书〉pure; unmixed

【醇和】(of quality, taste, etc.) mellow; pure

【醇厚】❶ mellow; rich: 酒味～。*The wine is (or tastes) mellow.* ❷ 同〖淳厚〗

【醇化】❶ refine; purify; perfect ❷ [化] acoholization ◇ ～物 alcoholate

【醇解】[化] alcoholysis

【醇酸】[化] alcohol (or alcoholic) acid ◇ ～树脂 alkyd resin

chǔn

蠢 Ⅰ 动〈书〉wriggle Ⅱ 形 stupid; foolish; dull; clumsy

【蠢笨】clumsy; awkward; stupid

【蠢材】〈诽〉idiot; fool

【蠢蠢欲动】ready to start wriggling—ready to make trouble

【蠢动】❶ wriggle ❷ create disturbances; carry on disruptive activities

【蠢货】〈诽〉blockhead; dunce; idiot

【蠢驴】〈诽〉idiot; donkey; ass

【蠢人】fool; blockhead

【蠢事】a stupid thing: 我再也不干那种～了。*I will never do such a stupid thing again.*

【蠢头蠢脑】stupid-looking

【蠢猪】〈诽〉idiot; stupid swine; ass

chuō

戳 动 ❶ jab; poke; stab: 小心! 你的竹竿儿别～了他的眼睛。*Be careful! Don't jab his eye out with your bamboo pole.* / 在纸上～了一个洞 *poke a hole in the paper* / 一～就破 *break at the slightest touch* ❷〈方〉sprain; blunt: 打排球～了手 *sprain one's wrist while playing volleyball* / 钢笔尖儿～了。*The nib is blunted.*

【戳穿】❶ puncture: 笔尖把纸～了。*The sharp nib scratched through the paper.* ❷ lay bare; expose; explode: ～谣言和诡辩 *lay bare sb.'s lies and sophistry*

【戳记】stamp; seal

【戳子】(又作'戳儿')〈口〉stamp; seal: 在文件上盖个～ *put a seal (or stamp) on a document* / 橡皮～ *rubber stamp*

chuò

啜 动〈书〉❶ sip; suck: ～茗 *sip tea* ❷ sob

【啜泣】sob

绰 形〈书〉ample; spacious ——另见 chāo

【绰绰有余】(又作'绰有余裕') more than sufficient; enough and to spare

【绰号】nickname: 他的～叫小老虎。*He has got the nickname of "Young Tiger".* or *He is nicknamed "Young Tiger".*

【绰约】〈书〉(*of a girl*) *graceful* ◇ ～多姿 (of a girl) graceful

辍 动〈书〉stop; cease: ～工 *stop work* / 时作时～ *on and off; by fits and starts*

【辍笔】stop in the middle of writing or painting

【辍学】discontinue one's studies; drop out of school

cī

刺 象 sound of tearing, friction, bursting etc.: ～的一声, 他滑了一个跟头。*Swish! He slipped*

and fell. / 花炮点着后，～～地直冒火星。*The firecracker spattered sparks the moment it was lit*. ——另见 cì

【刺啦】the sound of ripping, tearing, or scratching：～一声，她划着了火柴。*Scratch! She struck a match*.

【刺溜】the sound of slipping, sliding, etc.：～一下滑倒了 *slip and fall* / 子弹～～地从他耳边擦过去。*The bullets whistled past his ears*.

疵 名 flaw; defect; blemish：小～ *a trifling defect* / 无～ *flawless; impeccable*

【疵点】flaw; fault; defect

差 （构词成分）见〖参差〗(cēncī) ——另见 chā; chà; chāi

cí

词 名 ❶ word; term：这个～略带贬义。*This word is slightly derogative*. / 调子我记得，可是～儿我忘了。*I remember the tune all right, but I've forgotten the words*. ❷ speech; statement：开幕词 ❸ ci, poetry written to certain tunes with strict tonal patterns and rhyme schemes, in fixed numbers of lines and words, originating in the Tang Dynasty (618-907) and fully developed in the Song Dynasty (960-1279)

【词不达意】(又作'辞不达意') The words fail to convey the idea.

【词典】dictionary ◇ ～学 lexicography

【词法】[语] morphology

【词干】[语] stem

【词根】[语] root

【词汇】vocabulary; words and phrases：常用～ *common words* ◇ ～表 word list; vocabulary; glossary; ～学 lexicology

【词句】words and phrases; expressions：空洞的～ *empty phrases*

【词类】[语] parts of speech

【词库】lexicon; word bank

【词素】[语] morpheme

【词头】[语] prefix

【词尾】[语] ❶ suffix ❷ inflectional ending

【词形】[语] morphology：～变化 *morphological changes; inflections*

【词性】[语] syntactical functions and morphological features that help to determine a part of speech

【词序】[语] word order

【词义】[语] the meaning (or sense) of a word

【词语】words and expressions; terms

【词源】[语] the origin of a word; etymology

【词藻】同〖辞藻〗

【词缀】[语] affix

【词组】[语] word group; phrase

祠 名 ancestral hall (or temple); memorial temple：宗祠

【祠堂】ancestral hall (or temple); memorial temple

茨 名〈书〉❶ thatch (a roof) ❷ [植] puncture vine

瓷 名 porcelain; china：～碗 *china bowl* / 细～ *fine china*

【瓷雕】porcelain carving

【瓷漆】enamel paint; enamel

【瓷器】porcelain; chinaware

【瓷实】〈方〉solid; firm; substantial：他身体很～。*He is solidly built*.

【瓷土】porcelain clay; china clay

【瓷砖】ceramic tile; glazed tile

辞 Ⅰ 名 ❶ diction; phraseology：修辞 ❷ a type of classical Chinese literature：《楚～》*The Songs of Chu* ❸ a form of classical poetry：《木兰～》*The Ballad of Mulan* Ⅱ 动 ❶ take leave：告辞 ❷ decline; resign：他～了科长的职务。*He resigned his post of section chief*. / 固～ *firmly decline* ❸ dismiss; discharge：老板把他给～了。*His boss dismissed him*. ❹ shirk：不辞辛苦

【辞别】bid farewell (to); say goodbye (to); take one's leave (of)：～父母 *say goodbye to one's parents*

【辞呈】(written) resignation：提出～ *submit (or hand in) one's resignation*

【辞典】dictionary

【辞工】❶ dismiss (a labourer or employee); discharge：老板辞了他的工。*The boss dismissed him*. ❷ quit one's job; resign：他～不干了。*He's quit his job*.

【辞令】language appropriate to the occasion：外交～ *diplomatic language* / 善于～ *be gifted with a silver tongue*

【辞让】politely decline：他～了一番，才在前排就座。*After first politely declining, he eventually took a seat in the front row*.

【辞世】depart this life; pass away

【辞书】dictionary; lexicographical work (e. g. wordbook, etc.)

【辞岁】bid farewell to the outgoing year; see the old year out; celebrate the lunar New Year's Eve

【辞退】dismiss; discharge

【辞谢】politely decline; decline with thanks

【辞行】say goodbye (to one's relatives, friends, etc.) before setting out on a journey

【辞藻】flowery language; rhetoric; ornate diction：堆砌～ *string together ornate phrases*

【辞章】❶ poetry and prose; prose and verse ❷ art of writing; rhetoric

【辞职】resign; hand in one's resignation

慈 Ⅰ 形 kind; loving：心～ *tenderhearted; kindhearted* Ⅱ 名〈书〉mother

【慈爱】love (of an older person for a younger one); affection; kindness

【慈悲】mercy; benevolence; pity：发～ *have pity*;

be merciful
【慈姑】[植] arrowhead (the plant or its edible corm)
【慈和】kindly and amiable
【慈眉善目】a benign countenance
【慈母】loving mother; mother
【慈善】charitable; benevolent; philanthropic: ～机关 *charitable institution* (*or organization*) / ～事业 *charities*; *good works*; *philanthropy* ◇ ～家 philanthropist
【慈祥】kindly: ～的面容 *a kindly face*

磁 名 ❶ [物] magnetism: 磁场 ❷ 同〖瓷〗
【磁暴】[物] magnetic storm: ～记录器 *magnetic storm monitor*
【磁北】the magnetic north
【磁场】[物] magnetic field ◇ ～强度 [物] magnetic field intensity
【磁带】(magnetic) tape ◇ ～存储器 (magnetic) tape storage; tape-memory; ～录音机 tape recorder; ～文件 magnetic tape file
【磁道】track
【磁感应】[物] magnetic induction
【磁钢】magnet steel
【磁化】[物] magnetization ◇ ～杯 magnetic cup (cup made of magnetic material, said to be good for health); ～率 [物] magnetic susceptibility; ～器 magnetizer
【磁极】[物] magnetic pole ◇ ～强度 magnetic pole strength
【磁卡】magnetic card ◇ ～电话 card phone; ～锁 magnetic card lock
【磁力】[物] magnetic force: ～测定 *magnetometry* / ～勘探 *magnetic prospecting* / ～选矿 *magnetic dressing* ◇ ～探矿仪 magnetic detector (for ore deposits); ～探伤器 magnetic flaw detector; magnetic fault finder; ～线 [物] magnetic line of force; ～仪 magnetometer
【磁疗】magnet therapy
【磁盘】[计] magnetic disk ◇ ～操作系统 disk operating system (DOS); ～存储器 computer magnetic disk memory; ～驱动器 disk drive; ～文件 disk file
【磁偏角】[物] magnetic declination
【磁石】❶ magnetite ❷ [电] magnet ◇ ～发电机 magneto; ～检波器 magneto detector
【磁体】[物] magnetic body; magnet
【磁铁】[物] magnet: 马蹄形～ *horseshoe magnet* / 永久～ *permanent magnet* ◇ ～矿 magnetite
【磁通量】[物] magnetic flux
【磁头】magnetic head (of a recorder)
【磁心】[计] (magnetic) core ◇ ～存储器 [计] core memory
【磁性】[物] magnetism; magnetic ◇ ～水雷 magnetic mine; ～炸弹 magnetic bomb
【磁悬浮列车】magnetic suspension train
【磁选】[矿] magnetic separation: 湿法～ *wet magnetic separation* / ～厂 *magnetic ore dressing plant*
【磁针】magnetic needle
【磁子】[物] magneton

雌 形 female
【雌花】[植] female (or pistillate) flower
【雌黄】❶ orpiment ❷ 见〖信口雌黄〗
【雌蕊】[植] pistil
【雌性】female
【雌雄】❶ male and female ❷ victory and defeat ◇ ～同体 [动] hermaphroditism; monoecism; ～同株 [植] monoecism; ～异体 [动] gonochorism; dioecism; ～异株 [植] dioecism

糍 (构词成分) 见下
【糍粑】cooked glutinous rice pounded into paste; glutinous rice cake

cǐ

此 代 ❶ this: ～处 *this place*; *here* / ～等 *this kind*; *such as these* / 由～往南 *go south from here* ❷ here and now: 从此
【此岸】[宗] (佛教) this shore; temporality
【此地】this place; here: ～人 *local people*
【此地无银三百两】no 300 taels of silver buried here (the sign put up by the man in the folk tale over the place where he had hidden some money)—a clumsy denial resulting in self-exposure
【此后】after this; hereafter; henceforth
【此呼彼应】as one calls out, another responds; echo and reecho: 口号声～。*Shouts of slogans resounded back and forth.*
【此间】around here; here: ～已有传闻。*It has been so rumoured here.*
【此刻】this moment; now; at present
【此路不通】dead end; blind alley: ～! (*street sign*) *Not a Through Road.*
【此起彼伏】as one falls, another rises; rise one after another: ～的农民起义 *repeated peasant uprisings* / 欢呼声～。*Loud cheers rang out continuously.*
【此时】this moment; right now: ～此刻 *at this very moment* / ～此地 *here and now*
【此外】besides; in addition; moreover: 他一生就写过这两部书，～没有别的著作了。*Besides these two books, he didn't produce any other work during his lifetime.*
【此一时，彼一时】同〖彼一时，此一时〗

cì

次 Ⅰ 名 order; position in a series; place in a sequence: 车次 Ⅱ 形 ❶ second; next: ～子 *second son* / ～年 *the next year* ❷ second-rate; inferior: ～棉 *poor quality cotton* / 这本书真～。*This book is really no good.* / 我的字写得可～了。*My handwriting is terrible.* ❸ [化] hypo-: ～氯酸 *hypochlorous acid* Ⅲ 量 occurrence;

time：三～ *three times* / 首～ *first time*；*first* / 进行几～会谈 *hold several talks*
【次大陆】subcontinent
【次等】second-class；second-rate；inferior
【次第】❶ order；sequence ❷ one after another：～入座 *take seats one after another*
【次货】inferior goods；substandard goods
【次级线圈】［电］secondary coil
【次品】substandard products；defective goods
【次轻量级】weight lifting featherweight
【次生】［地质］secondary：～矿床 *secondary deposit* / ～矿物 *secondary mineral*
【次声】（又作'次声波'）［物］infrasonic sound；infrasonic wave
【次数】number of times；frequency：～不多 *not very often* / 练习的～越多，熟练的程度越高。*The more you practise，the more skilful you'll become.*
【次序】order；sequence：按～入场 *enter in proper order* / 文件的～不对。*The papers are not in the right order.*
【次要】less important；secondary；subordinate；minor：～问题 *secondary questions* / ～矛盾 *secondary contradiction*
【次音速】subsonic
【次之】take second place：该省矿藏，以锡最多，铜～。*Among the mineral deposits of the province，tin occupies first place*；*copper comes second.*
【次中音号】［音］tenor horn
【次重量级】weight lifting middle heavyweight
【次最轻量级】weight lifting flyweight

伺

（构词成分）见下 ——另见 sì
【伺候】wait upon；serve：难～ *hard to please*；*fastidious*

刺

Ⅰ 名 thorn；splinter：手上扎了个～ *get a thorn*（*or splinter*）*in one's hand* / 他说话总带～儿。*There's always a sting in his words.* Ⅱ 动 ❶ stab；prick：～伤 *stab and wound* ❷ assassinate：被～ *be assassinated* ❸ irritate；stimulate：～鼻 *irritate the nose*；*assail one's nostrils* ❹ pry；spy：刺探 ❺ criticize：讽刺 ——另见 cī
【刺柏】Chinese juniper；Taiwan juniper
【刺刺不休】talk incessantly；chatter on and on
【刺刀】bayonet：上～！（*order of command*）*Fix bayonets*！/ 下～！（*order of command*）*Unfix bayonets*！/ 拼～ *bayonet-fighting*
【刺耳】grating on the ear；jarring；ear-piercing；harsh：这声音太～。*The sound is too piercing.* / ～的话 *harsh words*；*sarcastic remarks*
【刺骨】piercing to the bones；piercing；biting：寒风～。*The cold wind chills one to the bone.*
【刺槐】locust（tree）
【刺激】❶ stimulation；stimulus；incentive：强～ *a strong stimulus* / 竞争给产业以有力的～。*Competition is a strong incentive to industry.* ❷ stimulate；urge on；encourage：咖啡能～神经。*Coffee can stimulate one's nerves.* ❸ provoke；irritate；upset：别～他。*Don't provoke him.* / 这一不幸的消息给了她很大的～。*She was badly upset by the sad news.* ◇ ～反应 stimulus-response；～物 stimulus；stimulant；～性毒剂 irritant agent
【刺客】assassin
【刺杀】❶ assassinate ❷［军］bayonet charge：练～ *practise bayonet fighting*
【刺探】make roundabout or secret inquiries；pry；spy：～军情 *spy out military secrets*；*gather military intelligence*
【刺网】［渔］gill net：三层～ *trammel net*
【刺猬】hedgehog
【刺绣】❶ embroider ❷ embroidery ◇ ～品 embroidery
【刺眼】dazzling；offending to the eye：亮得～ *dazzlingly bright* / 打扮得～ *be loudly dressed*
【刺字】❶ tattoo ❷（in former times）brand a criminal by tattooing

赐

动 ❶ bestow；confer：～恩 *bestow favours* / ～爵 *confer a title of nobility* / ～福 *bless* ❷〈套〉favour；grant：请即～复。*Please favour me with an early reply.* / 盼～示。*I await your instructions.*
【赐福】blessing
【赐教】〈套〉condescend to teach；grant instruction：不吝～ *please favour*（*or enlighten*）*me with your instructions*；*be so kind as to give me a reply*
【赐予】grant；bestow

cōng

匆

副 hastily；hurriedly
【匆匆】hurriedly：～吃了一顿饭 *take a hurried meal*；*hurry through a meal* /来去～ *come and go in a hurry*
【匆促】hastily；in a hurry：～起程 *set out hastily* / 时间～ *be pressed for time*
【匆忙】hastily；in a hurry：～作出决定 *make a hasty decision* / 临行～，未能向你告别。*I left in such a hurry that I didn't have time to say goodbye to you.*

枞

名［植］fir

葱

Ⅰ 名 onion；scallion Ⅱ 形 green：葱绿
【葱白】very light blue
【葱白儿】scallion stalk
【葱翠】fresh green；luxuriantly green：～的竹林 *a green bamboo grove*
【葱花】chopped green onion ◇ ～饼 green onion pancake
【葱茏】verdant；luxuriantly green：草木～ *luxuriant vegetation*
【葱绿】pale yellowish green；light green；verdant：～的田野 *verdant fields* / 麦苗一片～。*The wheat shoots are a lush green.*
【葱头】onion

【葱郁】verdant；luxuriantly green：～的松树林 *a verdant pine wood*

聪 Ⅰ名〈书〉faculty of hearing：左耳失～ *become deaf in the left ear* Ⅱ形 acute hearing：耳聪目明

【聪慧】bright；intelligent

【聪明】intelligent；bright；clever：～能干 *bright and capable* / 这孩子很～。*This child is very clever*. ◇ ～才智 intelligence and wisdom

【聪明反被聪明误】clever people may be victims of their own cleverness；cleverness may overreach itself

【聪明一世，糊涂一时】clever all one's life but stupid this once；smart as a rule，but this time a fool

【聪颖】〈书〉intelligent；bright；clever：～过人 *far surpass others in intelligence*；*be exceptionally bright*

cóng

从 Ⅰ动 ❶ follow；comply with；obey：～俗 *follow the general custom*；*conform to custom* ❷ join；be engaged in：从军 ❸ in a certain manner；according to a certain principle：～宽处理 *handle leniently*；*treat with leniency* / ～轻发落 *deal with an offender leniently* Ⅱ名 follower；attendant：随从 Ⅲ形 ❶ secondary；accessary：从犯 ❷ relationship between cousins，etc. of the same paternal grandfather or great-grandfather：～兄弟 *cousins on the paternal side*；*cousins* Ⅳ介 ❶ from（a time，a place，or a point of view）：～上海到北京 *from Shanghai to Beijing* / ～现在起 *from now on* / ～全局出发 *proceed from the situation as a whole* / ～根本上说 *essentially*；*in essence* ❷ via，through，or past（a place）：～门缝里往外看 *peep outside through a crevice in the door* / ～学校门前经过 *pass the school gate* Ⅴ副（followed by a negative）ever：～没听说过。*Never heard of it*. / 她在成绩面前～不骄傲。*Her head was never turned by success*.

【从长计议】give the matter further thought and discussion；take one's time in reaching a decision

【从此】from this time on；from now on；from then on；henceforth；thereupon

【从…到…】from... to...：从上到下 *from top to bottom*；*from the higher levels to the grass roots* / 从无到有 *grow out of nothing* / 从早到晚 *from dawn to dusk*；*from morning till night* / 从古到今 *from ancient times to the present*；*from time immemorial*

【从动】[机] driven：～齿轮 *driven gear* / ～构件 *driven member*

【从而】thus；thereby

【从犯】accessary criminal；accessary

【从价税】[经] ad valorem duties

【从简】conform to the principle of simplicity：一切～ *dispense with all unnecessary formalities*

【从教】be engaged in the teaching profession；be a teacher：给～三十年的教工颁奖。*Awards are conferred on those who have been engaged in educational work for thirty years*.

【从井救人】jump into a well to save sb. who's fallen in—(originally) try to do a good deed in the wrong way；try to save sb.'s life at the risk of one's own

【从句】〈语〉subordinate clause

【从军】join the army；enlist

【从来】from the past till the present；always；at all times；all along：我～没有见过他。*I've never seen him before*.

【从良】(of a prostitute) get married and start a new life

【从量税】[经] specific duties

【从略】be omitted：此处引文～。*The quotation is omitted here*.

【从命】do sb.'s bidding；comply with sb.'s wish；obey an order：欣然～ *gladly comply with sb.'s wish*

【从前】before；formerly；in the past：咱们村跟～大不一样了。*Our village is very different from what it was before*.

【从权】as a matter of expediency：～处理 *do what is expedient*

【从群众中来，到群众中去】come from the masses，go among the masses

【从戎】〈书〉join the army；enlist

【从容】❶ calm；unhurried；leisurely：举止～ *deport oneself in a calm，unhurried manner* ❷ plentiful：时间很～。*There's still plenty of time*. / 手头～ *be quite well off at the moment*

【从容不迫】calm and unhurried：他～，面带笑容。*He was calm and unhurried and wore a smiling face*.

【从善如流】follow what is right as a stream follows its course；readily accept good advice

【从事】❶ go in for；be engaged in：～科学研究工作 *be engaged in scientific research* / ～文学创作 *take up writing as a profession*；*be engaged in literary work* / ～技术革新 *work on technical innovations* ❷ deal with：慎重～ *act cautiously*；*steer a cautious course* / 军法～ *deal with according to military law*；*court-martial*

【从属】subordinate：～地位 *subordinate status* / ～关系 *relationship of subordination* ◇ ～信用证 subsidiary credit

【从速】as soon as possible；without delay：～处理 *deal with the matter as soon as possible*；*settle the matter quickly* / 存书无多，欲购～。*Only a few copies left. Buy now，while they last*.

【从天而降】descend from heaven：灾祸～。*A disaster descended from heaven (i.e. befell sb. unexpectedly)*.

【从头】❶ from the beginning：～做起 *start from the very beginning* ❷ anew；once again：～再来 *start afresh*；*start all over again*

【从小】from childhood; as a child
【从刑】[法] accessary punishment
【从业】obtain employment: ～机会 *job openings*
【从业人员】the employed
【从业员】employees in commerce and in the service trades
【从一而终】be faithful to one's husband to the end
【从中】out of; from among; therefrom: ～渔利 *profit from; cash in on* / ～作梗 *hinder sb. from carrying out a plan; place obstacles in the way; put a spoke in sb.'s wheel*
【从众】follow the populace; follow public opinion: ～行事 *act in conformity with the majority (or most of the people)*

丛 Ⅰ 动 crowd together: 丛生 Ⅱ 名 ❶ clump; thicket; grove: 草丛 ❷ crowd; collection: 人～ *a crowd of people* / 论～ *a collection of essays; collected essays*
【丛集】❶ crowd together; pile up: 百感～ *all sorts of feelings welling up* / 债务～ *debts piling up* ❷ collected writings
【丛刊】(often used in series titles) a series of books; collection: 《四部～》*Collected Writings of the Four Basic Branches of Literature*
【丛林】jungle; forest: ～战 *jungle warfare* ◇ ～热 [医] jungle fever
【丛生】❶ (of plants) grow thickly: 荆棘～ *be overgrown with brambles* ❷ (of diseases, evils, etc.) break out: 百病～ *all kinds of diseases and ailments breaking out*
【丛书】a series of books; collection: 《青年自学～》*Young People's Self-Study Series*
【丛杂】motley

淙 (构词成分)见下
【淙淙】gurgling: 流水～ *a gurgling stream*

còu

凑 动 ❶ gather together; pool; collect: ～足人数 *gather together enough people; get a quorum* / ～情况 *pool information* ❷ happen by chance; take advantage of: 正～上是个星期天。*It happened to be a Sunday.* / ～空儿 *try to find time (to do sth.)* ❸ move close to; press near: ～近点儿。*Move closer, please.*
【凑份子】club together (to present a gift to sb.)
【凑合】❶ gather together; collect; assemble: 昨天下班后大伙儿～在一起练歌。*Yesterday we gathered after work to practise singing.* ❷ improvise: 请大家会前作好发言准备,不要临时～。*Please prepare before coming to the meeting. Don't speak offhand.* ❸ make do: 他没有学过会计,但还能～着记记账。*He isn't a trained accountant, but he manages to keep simple accounts.* ❹ passable; not too bad: 这本小说怎么样? —— 还～。*What do you think of this novel? —Not too bad.*
【凑集】gather together: ～图书建立街道儿童阅览室 *pool books to form a neighbourhood children's reading room*
【凑钱】pool money
【凑巧】luckily; fortunately; as luck would have it: 搬家的那一天,～赶上下雨。*As luck would have it, it rained the day we moved.* / 真不～! 他出去了。*What bad luck! He's not at home.*
【凑趣儿】❶ join in (a game, etc.) just to please others: 他也说了几句玩笑话,凑了个趣儿。*He also cracked a few jokes to make everybody happy.* ❷ make a joke about; poke fun at: 别拿我～。*Don't poke fun at me.*
【凑热闹】❶ join in the fun ❷ add trouble to: 我们够忙的了,别再来～了。*We're busy enough as it is, don't give us more trouble.*
【凑手】at hand; within easy reach: 一时不～,我拿不出那么多钱来。*It happens I haven't got so much money on me at the moment.*
【凑数】make up the number or amount; serve as a stopgap

cū

粗 Ⅰ 形 ❶ wide (in diameter); thick: 一条～绳 *a thick rope* / 这棵树很～。*This tree has a thick trunk.* ❷ coarse; crude; rough: ～沙 *coarse sand; grit* / ～盐 *crude salt* / 这个活儿太～了。*This is too slovenly a piece of work.* ❸ gruff; husky: ～嗓子 *a husky voice* / ～声大气 *a deep, gruff voice* ❹ careless; negligent: 粗心 ❺ rude; unrefined; vulgar: 说话很～ *speak rudely; use coarse language* Ⅱ 副 roughly; slightly: ～知一二 *have a rough idea; know a little*
【粗暴】rude; rough; crude; brutal: ～的态度 *a rude attitude* / ～的行为 *crude behaviour* / ～地违反国际惯例 *gross violation of international practice*
【粗笨】clumsy; unwieldy: 动作～ *clumsy* / ～的家具 *unwieldy furniture*
【粗鄙】vulgar; coarse: 言语～ *vulgar in speech*
【粗布】❶ coarse cloth ❷ homespun cloth
【粗糙】❶ coarse; rough: 皮肤～ *rough skin* ❷ crude: 手工～ *crudely made; of poor workmanship*
【粗茶淡饭】plain tea and simple food; homely fare
【粗大】❶ thick; bulky: ～的手 *big strong hands* ❷ loud: ～的嗓门 *a loud voice* / ～的鼾声 *thunderous snoring*
【粗放】❶ free and easy: ～的笔触 *a free and easy style of writing or painting* ❷ careless; slipshod ❸ [农]extensive: ～耕作 *extensive cultivation* / ～经营 *extensive farming*
【粗犷】❶ rough; rude; boorish ❷ straightforward and uninhibited; bold and unconstrained; rugged
【粗豪】❶ forthright; straightforward: ～坦率 *forthright and candid* ❷ raucous; gruff; strident
【粗花呢】[纺] tweed

【粗话】vulgar language
【粗活】heavy manual labour; unskilled work
【粗加工】[机] rough machining; roughing ◇ ～制成品 roughly processed products
【粗具规模】be roughly in order; be roughly in shape
【粗粮】coarse food grain (e. g. maize, sorghum, millet, etc. as distinct from wheat flour and rice)
【粗劣】of poor quality; cheap; shoddy: ～的赝品 *a cheap imitation*
【粗陋】coarse and crude: 这所房子盖得很～。*This is a crudely built house.*
【粗鲁】(又作'粗卤') rough; rude; boorish: 态度～ be *rude*
【粗略】rough; sketchy: ～估计 *a rough estimate* / ～一看 *on cursory examination*
【粗麻布】burlap; gunny; sacking
【粗毛羊】coarse-wooled sheep
【粗眉大眼】bushy eyebrows and big eyes; heavy features
【粗浅】superficial; shallow; simple: ～的体会 *a superficial understanding* / ～的道理 *a simple truth*
【粗人】❶ a rough fellow; a rash person ❷ an unrefined person; boor: 我是个～,说话直来直去,你可别见怪。*I'm a bit of a boor, so I hope you won't mind if I speak bluntly.*
【粗纱】[纺] roving
【粗纱机】[纺] fly frame
【粗梳毛纺】[纺] woollen spinning
【粗梳棉纱】[纺] carded yarn
【粗疏】careless; inattentive
【粗率】rough and careless; ill-considered: ～的决定 *an ill-considered decision*
【粗饲料】coarse fodder; roughage
【粗俗】vulgar; coarse: 说话～ *use coarse or vulgar language*
【粗算】rough estimate or calculation
【粗纹唱片】coarse groove record
【粗通】have a rough idea; know a little: ～文墨 *be just able to read and write*
【粗细】❶ (degree of) thickness: 碗口～的钢管 *steel tubes as big as the mouth of a bowl* / 这样～的沙子最合适。*Sand this fine will be just right.* ❷ crudeness or fineness; degree of finish; quality of work: 庄稼长得好坏,也要看活儿的～。*Whether the crops grow well or not depends also on how the work is done.*
【粗线条】❶ thick lines; rough outline: ～的描写 *a rough sketch* ❷ rough-and-ready; slapdash: 我不喜欢他那～的工作方法。*I don't like his slapdash way of doing things.*
【粗心】careless; thoughtless
【粗心大意】negligent; careless; inadvertent
【粗野】rough; boorish; uncouth: 举止～ *behave boorishly* / 比赛中动作～ *play rough*
【粗轧】[冶] roughing (down) ◇ ～机 roughing mill
【粗支纱】[纺] coarse yarn
【粗枝大叶】crude and careless; sloppy; slapdash: ～的工作作风 *a crude and careless style of work*
【粗制滥造】manufacture in a rough and slipshod way
【粗制品】semifinished product
【粗中有细】there is finesse in sb.'s roughness; usually careless, but sometimes sharp; crude in most matters, but subtle in some
【粗重】❶ (of voice, etc.) loud and jarring: ～的嗓音 *a gruff voice* / ～的喘息声 *loud breathing* ❷ big and heavy; bulky: ～的钢管 *big and heavy steel tubes* ❸ thick and heavy: 眉毛浓黑～ *bushy black eyebrows* ❹ strenuous; heavy: ～的活计 *heavy work; heavy manual labour*
【粗壮】❶ sturdy; thickset; brawny: ～的小伙子 *a sturdy lad* / ～的胳臂 *brawny arms* ❷ thick and strong: ～的树干 *a thick tree trunk* ❸ deep and resonant: 声音～ *have a deep, resonant voice*

cù

促 Ⅰ 形 (of time) short; hurried; urgent: 气～ *breathe quickly; be short of breath; pant* Ⅱ 动 ❶ urge; promote: ～其实现 *help to bring it about* ❷〈书〉close to; near: 促膝(谈心)
【促成】help to bring about; facilitate: ～那对情人的婚事 *help to bring about a happy union of the lovers* / 这桩生意希望您大力～。*We hope you'll do your best to see that this deal comes off.*
【促进】promote; advance; accelerate: ～两国关系的正常化 *promote the normalization of relations between the two countries* /～相互理解 *further mutual understanding*
【促销】promote the sale (of goods); sales promotion
【促使】impel; urge; spur: 对外开放～许多人学习外语。*The policy of opening the country to the outside world spurs many people on to study foreign languages.*
【促膝谈心】sit side by side and talk intimately; have a heart-to-heart talk

猝 形〈书〉sudden; abrupt; unexpected: ～不及防 *be taken by surprise*
【猝倒病】[农] damping off: 松苗～ *damping off of pine see dlings*
【猝然】suddenly; abruptly; unexpectedly: ～决定 *make a sudden decision*
【猝死】[医] sudden death

酢 名 同〖醋〗
【酢浆草】[植] creeping oxalis (Oxalis corniculata)

醋 名 ❶ vinegar ❷ jealousy (as in a love affair)
【醋罐子】(又作'醋坛子') a jealous person
【醋海生波】waves in a sea of jealousy—storms

raised by a jealous woman
【醋精】vinegar concentrate
【醋栗】gooseberry (the plant or its fruit)
【醋酸】[化] acetic acid ◇ ～酐 acetic oxide; ～盐 acetate
【醋酯纤维】acetate fibre

簇 Ⅰ名〈书〉form a cluster; pile up: 花团锦簇 Ⅱ量 cluster; bunch: 一～鲜花 *a bunch of flowers* / 一～～灿烂的礼花 *clusters of brilliant fireworks*
【簇居】live in a community
【簇射】[物] shower: 宇宙线～ *cosmic-ray shower* / 高能～ *energetic shower*
【簇生】(of plants, flowers, etc.) grow in clusters
【簇新】brand new
【簇拥】cluster round: 前后～着一大群人 *escorted by big crowds in front and behind*

蹙 Ⅰ形〈书〉pressed; cramped: 穷～ *in dire straits* Ⅱ动 knit (one's brows): ～额 *knit one's brows; frown*

蹴 动〈书〉❶ kick ❷ tread: 一蹴而就

cuān

汆 动 quick-boil: ～丸子 *quick-boiled meat balls with soup*
【汆子】a small, cylindrical metal pot which can be thrust into a fire to boil water quickly

镩 动 cut or break (ice) with an ice pick
【镩子】ice pick

蹿 动 ❶ leap up: 他往上一～,把球接住。*He leapt up and caught the ball.* / 猫～到树上去了。*The cat leapt up into the tree.* ❷〈方〉spray; spurt: 我鼻子～血了。*Blood spurted from my nose.*
【蹿房越脊】(of swordsmen, robbers, etc. in old Chinese novels) leap from roof to roof

cuán

攒 动 collect together; assemble: 自己～一辆自行车 *assemble a bicycle oneself* ——另见 zǎn
【攒动】(used esp. in) 人头～ *a mass of bobbing heads*
【攒聚】(又作'攒集') gather closely together
【攒三聚五】(of people) gather in knots; gather in threes and fours

cuàn

窜 动 ❶ flee; scurry: 鼠窜 ❷〈书〉exile; expel ❸ change (the wording in a text, manuscript, etc.); alter
【窜犯】raid; make an inroad into: ～边境的匪徒已全部就歼。*All the bandits that invaded the border area have been wiped out.*
【窜改】alter; tamper with; falsify: ～原文 *alter the original text* / ～记录 *tamper with the minutes* / ～账目 *falsify accounts; manipulate accounts*
【窜扰】harass: ～活动 *harassment*
【窜逃】flee in disorder; scurry off

篡 动 usurp; seize: ～权 *usurp power*
【篡夺】usurp; seize: ～政权 *usurp state power*
【篡改】distort; misrepresent; tamper with; falsify: ～历史 *distort history* / 事实不容～,谎言必须戳穿。*Facts cannot be altered; lies must be exposed.*
【篡国】usurp state power
【篡位】usurp the throne

cuī

催 动 ❶ urge; hurry; press: ～办 *press sb. to do sth.* / 扬鞭～马 *urge one's horse on with a whip; whip one's horse on* / 去～他一下。*Go and hurry him up.* ❷ hasten; expedite; speed up: 春风～绿。*The spring wind speeds the greening of the plants.*
【催逼】press (for payment of debt, etc.)
【催产】expedite child delivery; hasten parturition; induce labour (by artificial means) ◇ ～药 [药] oxytocic
【催促】urge; hasten; press: 我们～她尽快来成都。*We urged her to come to Chengdu as soon as possible.*
【催肥】[牧] fatten
【催化】[化] catalysis: ～促进剂 *catalytic promoter* / ～反应 *catalytic reaction* / ～裂化 *catalytic cracking* ◇ ～剂 catalyst; catalytic agent
【催款单】[经] prompt; prompt-note
【催泪弹】tear bomb; tear-gas grenade
【催眠】lull (to sleep); hypnotize; mesmerize ◇ ～曲 lullaby; cradlesong; ～术 hypnotism; mesmerism
【催奶】stimulate the secretion of milk; promote lactation ◇ ～剂 galactagogue
【催青】[农] hasten the hatching of silkworms (by adjusting temperature and humidity)
【催生】❶ (of an expectant mother's family) send gifts over to convey best wishes ❷ 同〖催产〗
【催熟】[农] accelerate the ripening (of fruit)
【催吐剂】[药] emetic
【催醒剂】[药] analeptic: 中药～ *herbal analeptic*
【催租】press a tenant to pay rent; press for payment of rent

摧 动 break; destroy: 坚不可摧
【摧残】wreck; destroy; devastate: 他的身体受到严重的～。*His health was ruined.* / ～民主 *trample on democracy*

【摧毁】destroy; smash; wreck
【摧枯拉朽】(as easy as) crushing dry weeds and smashing rotten wood
【摧眉折腰】bowing and scraping
【摧折】〈书〉❶ break; snap ❷ setback

cuǐ

璀 (构词成分)见下
【璀璨】〈书〉bright; resplendent: ～夺目 *dazzling*

cuì

脆 形 ❶ fragile; brittle: 这纸太～。*This kind of paper is too fragile.* / ～金属 *brittle metal* ❷ crisp: 这种梨又甜又～。*These pears are sweet and crisp.* ❸ (of voice) clear; crisp: 听她的嗓音多～! *What a crisp voice she has!*
【脆骨】gristle (as food)
【脆弱】fragile; frail; weak: 感情～ *be easily upset*
【脆性】[冶] brittleness
淬 动 temper (a metal workpiece) by dipping in water, oil, etc.; quench
【淬火】quench: ～硬化 *quench hardening* ◇ ～剂 hardening agent; quenching liquid
【淬砺】〈书〉temper oneself through severe trials
萃 Ⅰ 动〈书〉come together; assemble: 荟萃 Ⅱ 名 a gathering of people or a collection of things: 出类拔萃
【萃萃蝇】tsetse fly
【萃集】gather; assemble: 港口船舶～ *ships gathering in harbour*
【萃聚】gather; assemble: 群英～ *heroes of our time getting together*
【萃取】[化] extraction
啐 动 spit; expectorate: ～他一口 *spit at him* / ～一口唾沫 *throw out some spittle*
瘁 形〈书〉overworked; tired: 心力交瘁/ 鞠躬尽瘁
粹 Ⅰ 形 pure: ～白 *pure white* / ～而不杂 *pure and unadulterated* Ⅱ 名 essence; the best: 精粹
【粹美】〈书〉perfect; flawless: 品学～ *a man of flawless character and eminent scholarship*
翠 Ⅰ 形 emerald green; green: ～竹 *green bamboos* Ⅱ 名 ❶ kingfisher ❷ jadeite: 珠翠
【翠菊】[植] China aster (Callistephus chinensis)
【翠蓝】bright blue; azure: ～的天空 *the azure sky*
【翠绿】emerald green; jade green
【翠鸟】kingfisher

cūn

村 Ⅰ 名 village; hamlet: 渔～ *a fishing village* / 一个小～儿 *a hamlet* Ⅱ 形 rustic; boorish: 村野
【村办企业】village industry
【村夫】villager; countryman
【村姑】village girl; country wench
【村口】entrance to a village
【村落】village; hamlet
【村民】villager; village people
【村舍】cottage
【村野】❶ villages; countryside ❷ rustic; countrified
【村寨】stockaded village; village: ～相望 *neighbouring villages within sight of each other*
【村长】village head
【村镇】villages and small townships
【村庄】village; hamlet
【村子】village; hamlet
皴 动 (of skin) be chapped from the cold: 孩子的手～了。*The child's hands were chapped from the cold.*
【皴裂】(of skin) be chapped from the cold: 手足～。*Both one's hands and feet were chapped from the cold.*

cún

存 动 ❶ exist; live; survive: 父母俱～。*Both parents are still living.* ❷ store; keep: ～粮 *store up grain* / 新水库～了大量的水。*A large quantity of water is stored in the new reservoir.* / 天气热,西红柿～不住。*Tomatoes won't keep in hot weather.* ❸ accumulate; collect: 一下雨,洼地里就～了好些水。*Whenever it rains, a lot of water accumulates in the low-lying land.* ❹ deposit: 把钱～在银行里 *deposit money in a bank* ❺ leave with; check: 行李先～在这里,回头再来取。*Let's check our luggage here and come back for it later.* / ～自行车 *leave one's bicycle in a bicycle park* ❻ reserve; retain: 他有什么说什么,肚子里～不住话。*He always says what he thinks; he can't hold anything back.* ❼ remain on balance; be in stock: 收支相抵,净～两千元。*The accounts show a surplus of 2,000 yuan.* ❽ cherish; harbour: ～着很大的希望 *cherish high hopes* / 不～幻想 *harbour no illusions*
【存案】register with the proper authorities
【存查】file for reference
【存车处】parking lot (for bicycles); bicycle park (or shed)
【存储】[电子] memory; storage: ～二极管 *storage diode* / ～容量 *memory capacity* / ～元件 *memory element* / ～器 *memory (of a computer)* ◇

～按钮 store key；～程序 stored (or saved) program

【存单】deposit receipt：定期～ *time certificate (bearing specific maturity date)*

【存档】keep in the archives；place on file；file

【存底儿】keep the original draft；keep a file copy

【存而不论】leave the question open

【存放】❶ leave with；leave in sb.'s care：我把箱子～在朋友那里了。*I've left my suitcase with a friend of mine*. ❷ deposit (money)：把节余的钱～在银行里。*Put your savings in the bank*.

【存根】counterfoil；stub：支票～ *cheque stub*

【存户】depositor

【存货】❶ stock up ❷ goods in stock；existing stock

【存取方式】access mode

【存取控制】access control

【存取周期】access cycle

【存款】❶ deposit money (in a bank) ❷ deposit；bank savings：个人～ *personal savings account* ◇ ～不足 insufficient funds；～单 certificate of deposit

【存栏】[牧] livestock on hand：牲畜～总头数比去年增加了一倍。*The total livestock number is twice as large as it was last year*.

【存身】take shelter；make one's home：无处～ *find no shelter*；*have no place to call one's home*

【存食】suffer from indigestion

【存亡】live or die；survive or perish：抗日战争是一场关系民族～的战争。*The War of Resistance Against Japan was a life-and-death struggle for the Chinese nation*.

【存项】credit balance；balance

【存心】❶ cherish certain intentions：～不良 *cherish evil designs (or intentions)* / 他说这番话，不知存着什么心。*It's hard to say what his intentions were in saying that*. ❷ intentionally；deliberately；on purpose：我不是～这么做的。*I didn't do it on purpose*.

【存疑】leave a question open；leave a matter for future consideration：这件事情暂时～吧。*Let's put this matter aside for the time being*.

【存在】exist；be：那个问题已经不～了。*That problem no longer exists*. / 矛盾～于一切事物发展的过程中。*Contradiction is present in the process of development of all things*.

【存折】deposit book；bankbook

【存执】counterfoil；stub

cǔn

忖 动 turn over in one's mind；ponder；speculate

【忖度】speculate；conjecture；surmise

【忖量】❶ think over；turn over in one's mind：她～了半天，还拿不定主意。*She turned the matter over in her mind for a long while but still could not come to a decision*. ❷ conjecture；guess：我一边走，一边～着他说的那番话的意思。*As I walked along I kept wondering what he really meant*.

cùn

寸 Ⅰ 量 ❶ a traditional unit of length ❷〈略〉见〖市寸〗 Ⅱ 形 very little；very short；small

【寸步】a tiny step；a single step

【寸步不离】follow sb. closely；keep close to sb.；be always at sb.'s elbow

【寸步不让】refuse to yield an inch；not budge an inch

【寸步难行】be unable to move even a single step—be unable to do anything：市场困难，头寸短少，真是～。*Markets were difficult, ready cash was in short supply—in fact it was impossible to do anything*.

【寸草不留】leave not even a blade of grass；be devastated

【寸金难买寸光阴】Money can't buy Time；Time is more precious than gold.

【寸进】a little progress；a small advance：略有～ *have made just a little progress* / ～尺退 *advance by inches, retreat by feet*；*more regressing than progressing*

【寸土必争】fight for (or contest) every inch of land

【寸心】❶ feelings：聊表～ *as a small token of my feelings*；*just to show my appreciation* ❷ heart；mind：～不忘 *bear it in mind*

cuō

搓 动 ❶ rub with the hands：～手取暖 *rub one's hands together to warm them* / ～麻绳 *make cord by twisting hemp fibres between the palms* / 这件上衣太脏了，洗时要多～～。*This jacket is very dirty*；*give it a good scrubbing*. ❷ [体] (in tennis, table tennis, cricket, etc.) chop：一板一板地把球～过去 *return every shot with a chop*

【搓板】washboard

【搓球】[体] chopping

【搓揉】rub；knead；twist：她把那封信～成一团，扔进了字纸篓。*She crumpled the letter into a ball and threw it into the wastepaper basket*.

【搓手顿脚】wring one's hands and stamp one's feet—get anxious and impatient

【搓澡】give or get a rubdown with a damp towel

磋 动 consult

【磋商】consult；exchange views：与各有关部门进行～ *hold consultations with all departments concerned*

撮 Ⅰ 动 ❶〈书〉gather；bring together ❷ scoop up (with a dustpan or shovel)：～起一簸箕土

scoop up a dustpan of dirt ❸〈方〉pick up or hold (dust, powder, etc.) between the thumb and the first finger：～一点儿盐 *take a pinch of salt* ❹ extract；summarize：撮要 Ⅱ 量 ❶〈方〉pinch：一～盐 *a pinch of salt* / 一～儿米 *a small pinch of rice* ❷ handful (of bad people)：一小～法西斯匪徒 *a handful of fascist gangsters* ——另见 zuǒ

【撮合】make a match；act as go-between

【撮弄】❶ make fun of；play a trick on；tease ❷ abet；instigate；incite

【撮要】❶ make an abstract；outline essential points：把工作情况～上报 *submit an outline report on one's work* ❷ abstract；synopsis；extracts：论文～ *an abstract of a thesis*

蹉（构词成分）见下

【蹉跌】〈书〉trip and fall—make a slip

【蹉跎】waste time：一再～ *let one opportunity after another slip away*

【蹉跎岁月】let time slip by accomplishing nothing；idle away one's time

cuó

痤（构词成分）见下

【痤疮】acne (a skin disease)

cuò

挫 动 ❶ defeat；frustrate：受挫 ❷ subdue；lower：～敌人的锐气，长自己的威风 *deflate the enemy's arrogance and boost one's own morale* / ～其锋芒 *blunt the edge of sb.'s advance*

【挫败】frustrate；foil；defeat：遭到严重的～ *suffer a serious defeat* / ～扩张主义者的阴谋 *foil the schemes of the expansionists*

【挫伤】❶［医］contusion；bruise ❷ dampen；blunt；discourage：不要～群众的积极性。*Don't dampen the enthusiasm of the masses.*

【挫折】setback；reverse：屡遭～ *suffer repeated setbacks (or reverses)*

厝 动〈书〉❶ lay；place ❷ place a coffin in a temporary shelter pending burial

【厝火积薪】a fire beneath a pile of faggots—a hidden danger

措 动 ❶ arrange；manage；handle：惊慌失措 ❷ make plans：筹措

【措辞】wording；diction：～不当 *inappropriate wording* / ～严厉 *couched in harsh terms* / ～强硬 *strongly worded*

【措施】measure；step：采取重大～ *adopt an important measure*

【措手不及】be caught unprepared；be caught unawares：打他个～ *make a surprise attack on them*

【措置】handle；manage；arrange ◇ ～得当 handle properly

锉 Ⅰ 名 file：方～ *square file* / 圆～ *round file* / 木～ (*wood*) *rasp* Ⅱ 动 make smooth with a file；file：～光 *file sth. smooth*

【锉刀】file

【锉屑】filing

错 Ⅰ 形 ❶ interlocked and jagged；intricate；complex：交错 / 错落 ❷ wrong；mistaken；erroneous：你弄～了。*You've got it wrong.* / 拿～东西 *take sth. by mistake* / 从头～到底 *completely wrong* ❸ (used in the negative) bad；poor：今年的收成～不了。*This year's harvest is sure to be good.* Ⅱ 动 ❶ grind；rub：～牙 *grind one's teeth (in one's sleep)* ❷ make way；move out of the way：劳驾往那边～一～。*Would you mind making room for me?* ❸ alternate；stagger：这两个会不能同时开，得～一下。*We can't hold the two meetings at the same time. We must stagger them.* ❹ be out of alignment：这行没排齐，中间～进去了一点儿。*This line is not straight. It's a little crooked in the middle.* Ⅲ 名 fault；demerit：这是他的～，不怨你。*You are not to blame. It's his fault.*

【错爱】〈套〉undeserved kindness or favour

【错案】［法］misjudged case

【错别字】wrongly written or mispronounced characters

【错车】one vehicle gives another the right of way：地方太小，错不开车。*The space is too narrow for vehicles to make way for each other.*

【错处】fault；demerit

【错怪】blame sb. wrongly

【错过】❶ miss；let slip：～机会 *miss an opportunity* / ～这趟汽车，今天就走不成了。*If we miss this bus, we won't be able to go today.* ❷ 同〖过错〗

【错角】［数］alternate angle

【错金】inlay with gold：～器皿 *gold-inlaid ware；metal-inlaid ware*

【错觉】illusion；misconception；wrong impression：这样会给人造成～。*This will give people a false impression.*

【错开】stagger：把日子～ *stagger the days off* / 三场球赛应～进行。*We should stagger the three ball games.*

【错乱】in disorder；in confusion；deranged：颠倒～ *topsy-turvy*

【错落】in disorderly profusion：～不齐 *disorderly and uneven* / ～有致 *in picturesque disorder*

【错位】［医］dislocation：肘关节～ *dislocation of the elbow*

【错误】❶ wrong；mistaken；erroneous：～思想 *wrong thinking；a mistaken idea* / ～的结论 *wrong conclusion* / ～路线 *an erroneous line* ❷ mistake；error；blunder：犯～ *make a mistake；commit an error* / ～百出 *riddled with errors；*

full of mistakes◇ ～分析 error analysis；～校正 error correction (EC)；～校正码 error correcting code

【错字】❶ wrongly written character ❷ misprint

【错综】crisscross；intricate

【错综复杂】intricate；complex：这部小说的情节～，引人入胜。*The plot of the novel is intricate and fascinating.*

D

dā

耷 名〈书〉big ear

【耷拉】droop; hang down: ～着脑袋 *hang one's head* / 他眼皮～下来,一会儿就睡着了。*His eyelids drooped and he was soon asleep.*

搭 动 ❶ put up; build: ～一个临时舞台 *put up a makeshift stage* / ～窝 *build a nest* / ～帐篷 *pitch a tent* ❷ hang over; put over: 把洗好的衣服～在绳上 *hang the washing on a line* / 他肩膀上～着一块毛巾。*He had a towel over his shoulder.* ❸ come into contact; join: 那两根电线～上了。*The two wires are touching.* / ～上关系 *strike up a relationship with; establish contact with* ❹ throw in more (people, money, etc.); add: 你忙不过来,给你～个人吧。*You're terribly busy. We'll send someone to help you.* / 为了救他,我差点儿把命都～进去了。*In trying to save him I nearly lost my own life, too.* ❺ lift sth. together: 帮我把这包大米～上卡车。*Help me lift the bag of rice onto the truck.* / 咱们俩把这筐土～走。*Let's carry this basket of earth away.* ❻ take (a ship, plane, etc.); travel (or go) by: ～轮船去上海 *go to Shanghai by boat* / ～飞机 *go by plane* / ～长途汽车 *travel by coach* / ～他们的车走 *get a lift in their car*

【搭班子】set up a (work) team or group: 把领导班子搭起来 *form a leading group; get a leading group set up*

【搭伴】join sb. on a trip; travel together: 他也到新疆去,你们搭个伴儿吧。*He's going to Xinjiang too, so you may as well travel together.*

【搭乘】travel by (plane, car, ship, etc.)

【搭档】❶ cooperate; work together: 咱俩～吧。*Let us two team up.* ❷ partner: 老～ *old partner; old workmate*

【搭话】❶ make conversation; get a word in: 十几个年轻人围着他,抢着跟他～。*About a dozen boys and girls crowded round him, all trying to enter into a conversation with him.* ❷ send word

【搭伙】❶ join as partner: 他们明天去参观故宫,我也想～去。*They're going to visit the Palace Museum tomorrow and I'd like to join them.* ❷ eat regularly in (a mess, etc.): 我们都在厂里食堂～。*We all eat in the factory cafeteria.*

【搭架子】❶ build a framework; get (an undertaking, etc.) roughly into shape: 先搭好架子,再充实内容。*First make an outline, then fill in the content.* ❷〈方〉put on airs; assume great airs

【搭肩】❶ help to shoulder sth. heavy ❷ stand on another's shoulders

【搭救】rescue; go to the rescue of: ～落水儿童 *rescue a drowning child*

【搭客】❶ passenger ❷〈方〉take on passengers

【搭拉】同〖耷拉〗

【搭理】同〖答理〗

【搭卖法】tie-in sale

【搭配】❶ arrange in pairs or groups: 她和小王～参加混合双打。*She paired up with Xiao Wang in the mixed doubles.* ❷［语］collocation: 这两个词～不当。*These two words don't collocate.* / ～简单 *a simple matching*

【搭腔】❶ answer; respond: 我问了两遍,没人～。*I repeated my question, but nobody answered.* ❷ talk to each other: 以前他俩合不来,彼此不～。*In the past the two of them did not get on at all well; they weren't even on speaking terms.*

【搭桥】build bridge; act as a go-between

【搭桥牵线】(又作'牵线搭桥') act as a go-between; bring (people, etc.) into contact

【搭讪】(又作'搭湗') strike up a conversation with sb.; say sth. to smooth over an embarrassing situation: 他很尴尬,～着走开了。*Feeling embarrassed, he muttered a few words and walked off.* / 他总是一边卖东西一边和顾客～。*While doing business, he would strike up a conversation with his customers.*

【搭售】pair unsalable goods up with goods that sell well, making the purchase of the former compulsory for anyone who wants to buy the latter

答 (构词成分)见下 ——另见 dá

【答理】(usu. used in the negative) acknowledge (sb.'s greeting, etc.); respond; answer: 我跟他打招呼,他没～我。*I greeted him but he didn't respond.* / 不爱～人 *be standoffish* / 他生气地坐在那里,谁也不～。*She sat there sulking and wouldn't speak to anyone.*

【答谢词】speech of thanks; thank-you speech

【答应】❶ answer; reply; respond: 敲了半天门没人～。*I knocked again and again but there was no answer.* / 我在楼下喊你半天,你怎么不～? *I kept calling to you from downstairs* —how come you didn't answer? ❷ agree; promise; comply with: 我们请他来参加座谈会,他已经～了。*We asked him to attend our discussion, and he agreed to come.* / 他～八点半到。*He promised to be here at* 8:30.

褡 (构词成分)见下

【褡包】(又作'褡膊'、'褡布') a long, broad girdle

【褡裢】❶ a long, rectangular bag sewn up at both ends with an opening in the middle (usu. worn round the waist or across the shoulder) ❷ a jacket, made of several layers of cloth, worn by wrestlers

dá

打 量 dozen: 一～铅笔 *a dozen pencils* / 论～出售 *sell by the dozen* ——另见 dǎ

达 Ⅰ 动 ❶ extend: 四通八达 ❷ reach; attain; amount to: 我们不～目的决不罢休。*We will never cease our efforts until we achieve our aim.* / 听众鼓掌～两分钟之久。*The audience applauded for two whole minutes.* ❸ understand thoroughly: 通达 ❹ express; communicate: 传达 Ⅱ 形 eminent; distinguished: 达官贵人

【达标】reach a set standard

【达成】reach (agreement): 双方就会议议程～协议。*The two parties reached agreement on the agenda of the meeting.* / ～交易 *strike a bargain* / ～谅解 *come to anunderstanding*

【达旦】until dawn: 通宵达旦

【达到】achieve; attain; reach: ～目的 *achieve (or attain) the goal* / ～高潮 *reach a high tide; come to a climax* / ～世界先进水平 *come up to advanced world standards* / 你要求太高,我恐怕达不到。*Your expectations are too high. I'm afraid I can't live up to them.* / 货物运输量将～四千万吨。*The volume of freight handled will amount to* 40 *million tons.*

【达尔文主义】Darwinism

【达观】take things philosophically

【达官贵人】high officials and noble lords; VIPs: 周旋于～之间 *move in high society*

【达赖喇嘛】the Dalai Lama

【达姆弹】[军] dumdum (bullet)

【达人】〈书〉❶ an intelligent, well-informed person ❷ a person who takes everything philosophically

【达意】express (or convey) one's ideas: 抒情～ *express one's thoughts and feelings*

【达因】[物] dyne

沓 量 pile (of paper, etc.); pad: 一～报纸 *a pile of newspapers* / 一～信纸 *a pad of letter paper* / 一～钞票 *a wad of bank notes* ——另见 tà

【沓子】pile (of paper, etc.); pad: 一大～十元钞票 *a thick wad of* 10-yuan notes

答 动 ❶ answer; reply; respond: 一问一～ *one asking and the other answering* / 这个问题他～不上来。*He couldn't answer the question.* ❷ return (a visit, etc.); reciprocate: ～礼 *return a salute* ——另见 dā

【答案】answer; solution; key: 找不到问题的～ *find no solution to the problem* / 练习的～ *key to an exercise*

【答拜】pay a return visit (or call)

【答辩】reply (to a charge, query or an argument): 保留公开～的权利 *reserve the right of public reply* / 进行论文～ *defend one's thesis*

【答词】thank-you speech; answering speech; reply

【答对】(usu. used in the negative) answer sb.'s question; reply: 被问得没法～ *be baffled by the question*

【答非所问】give an irrelevant answer

【答复】answer; reply: ～他的询问 *reply to his inquiry*

【答话】(usu. used in the negative) answer; reply: 人家问你,你怎么不～? *I've asked you a question, Why don't you answer?*

【答卷】❶ answer the questions or solve the problems in a test paper ❷ an answered test paper: 标准～ *standard answers to a test paper*

【答数】answer (to an arithmetic problem)

【答题卡】response card

【答问】❶ answer a question ❷ a question-and-answer form of writing

【答谢】express appreciation (for sb.'s kindness or hospitality); acknowledge: 我们简直不知道怎样～你们的热情招待。*We simply don't know how to repay your kind hospitality.* ◇ ～宴会 return banquet

【答疑】(of a teacher, speaker, etc.) answer questions: 留下半小时～ *set aside half an hour for questions and answers (or for answering questions)*

鞑 (构词成分)见下

【鞑靼】Tartar

dǎ

打 Ⅰ 动 ❶ strike; hit; knock: ～门 *knock at the door* / ～稻子 *thresh rice* / 钟～了十下。*The clock struck ten.* ❷ break; smash: 我～了一个碗。*I broke a bowl.* / 窗玻璃～破了。*The windowpane is broken.* ❸ beat; fight; attack: 不许～他! *You mustn't beat him!* / 两个人～了起来。*The two men came to blows.* ❹ deal with sb. or sth.: 打交道 / 打官司 ❺ construct; build: ～坝 *construct a dam* / ～田埂 *build low ridges between paddy fields* ❻ make (articles of daily use or food): ～一把刀 *forge a knife* / ～家具 *make furniture* / ～烧饼 *make sesame seed cakes* ❼ mix; stir; beat: ～鸡蛋 *beat eggs* / ～糨子 *mix paste* ❽ tie up; pack: ～行李 *pack one's luggage; pack up* / ～成一捆 *tie (things) up in a bundle* / ～裹脚 *wind a puttee* ❾ knit; weave:

～草鞋 *weave straw sandals* / ～毛衣 *knit a sweater* ⑩ draw; paint; make a mark on: ～方格儿 *draw squares* / ～手印 *put one's fingerprint on a document* / ～一个问号 *put a question mark; put a query* ⑪ spray; spread: ～农药 *spray insecticide* / 在地板上～蜡 *wax the floor* ⑫ open; dig: ～井 *dig (or sink) a well* / ～炮眼 *drill a blasting hole* ⑬ hold up; hoist; raise: ～灯笼 *carry a lantern* / ～伞 *hold up an umbrella* / ～起精神来 *raise one's spirits; cheer up* ⑭ send; dispatch; project: ～电报 *send a telegram* / ～电话 *make a phone call* / ～信号 *give a signal; signal* / ～炮 *fire a cannon* / ～手电 *flash a torch* ⑮ issue or receive (a certificate, etc.): ～介绍信 *write a letter of introduction (for sb.); get a letter of introduction (from one's organization)* ⑯ remove; get rid of: ～蛔虫 *take medicine to get rid of roundworms; take worm medicine* ⑰ ladle; draw: ～粥 *ladle gruel* / ～一盆水 *fetch a basin of water* / 从井里～水 *draw water from a well* ⑱ buy: ～酱油 *buy soy sauce (in a small quantity with one's own container)* / ～票 *buy a (train, bus, etc.)* ticket ⑲ catch; hunt: ～鱼 *catch fish* / ～鸟 *shoot birds* / ～野鸭 *go duck-hunting* ⑳ gather in; collect; reap: ～柴 *gather firewood* / ～了八百斤麦子 *get in 800 jin of wheat* ㉑ estimate; calculate; reckon: 成本～二百块钱 *estimate (or reckon) the cost at 200 yuan* / 损耗已经～进去了。*Allowances have been made for damages.* ㉒ work out: ～草稿 *work out a draft* ㉓ do; engage in: ～短工 *work as a day or seasonal labourer; be a temporary worker* / ～夜班 *go on night shift* ㉔ play: ～篮球 *play basketball* / ～扑克 *play cards* / ～秋千 *have a swing* ㉕ go through (some physical action): ～手势 *make a gesture; gesticulate* / ～喷嚏 *sneeze* / ～个跟斗 *turn (or do) a somersault* ㉖ adopt; use: ～个比方 *draw an analogy* ㉗ (used to give a clue to the answer when setting a riddle): 画时圆,写时方;寒时短,热时长。—— ～一字。(谜底:日) *When drawn it is round, but when written it is square; in cold weather it is short, and in hot weather long. — A character. (Answer: the character* 日 *"sun, day")* Ⅱ 介 from; since: ～那以后 *since then* / 你～哪儿来? *Where have you come from?* / 他～门缝里往外看。*He looked out through the crack in the door.* / 他～心眼里感到高兴。*It warmed the cockles of his heart.* ——另见 dá

【打靶】target (or shooting) practice ◇ ～场 target range

【打白条】write IOUs (instead of paying cash): 收购粮食不准～。*It is prohibited to write IOUs instead of paying the farmers when purchasing their grain.*

【打摆子】〈方〉suffer from malaria

【打败】❶ defeat; beat; worst ❷ suffer a defeat; be defeated

【打扮】❶ dress up; make up; deck out: 孩子们～得像春天的花朵一样。*The gaily-dressed children looked like spring flowers.* ❷ way or style of dressing: 学生～ *be dressed like a student*

【打包】❶ bale; pack: ～费 *packing charges* ❷ unpack ◇ ～机 baling press

【打包票】(又作'打保票') vouch for; guarantee: 这件事你可不能给人～。*This is not a matter in which you can vouch for other people.* / 他最适合做这件事,我敢～。*He's the right man for this job, I can give you my word.*

【打苞】(of wheat, sorghum, etc.) form ears; ear up

【打抱不平】take up the cudgels for the injured party; defend sb. against an injustice; be the champion of the oppressed: 他是个爱～的人。*He was always ready to defend the weak and helpless.*

【打边鼓】(又作'敲边鼓') say sth. from the sidelines: 这件事由你去跟领导说,我～。*You take this matter up with the leadership and I'll put in a word or two for you from the sidelines.*

【打草惊蛇】beat the grass and startle the snake—act rashly and alert the enemy

【打杈】prune: 给棉花～ *prune cotton plants* / 打旁杈 *prune the side branches*

【打岔】interrupt; cut in: 他们在谈正经事儿,别～。*Don't interrupt them; they're talking business.* / 我说话的时候你别～。*Don't butt in while I'm talking.*

【打场】thresh grain (on the threshing ground)

【打成一片】become one with; identify oneself with; merge with: 和群众～ *be (or become) one with the masses*

【打冲锋】❶ charge (in a battle) ❷ be in the vanguard

【打虫药】parasiticide

【打虫子】get rid of intestinal parasites or worms by taking medicine

【打出水平,打出风格】be at one's best in skill and style of play

【打打闹闹】have boisterous fun; horseplay

【打蛋器】egg-whisk; whisk

【打倒】overthrow: ～帝国主义! *Down with imperialism!*

【打得火热】be very thick with each other; be as thick as thieves: 两人正在谈情说爱,～。*The two of them were billing and cooing together; they were obviously very engrossed.*

【打的】〈口〉go by taxi; take a taxi

【打底】❶ eat sth. before having a drink ❷ feel secure: 心里不～ *feel insecure* ❸ 同〖打底子〗❹ [纺] bottoming ◇ ～机 padding machine

【打底子】❶ sketch a plan, picture, etc.: 这篇文章我先打个底子,再请你修改。*I'll make a draft of the essay and then ask you to revise it.* ❷ lay a foundation: 学英语应该在小学就打好底子。*Learners of English should be given a good grounding in primary school.*

【打地铺】sleep on the floor; have a shakedown on

the floor or on the ground：我可以打个地铺。*I can have a shakedown on the floor*.

【打点】❶ get (luggage, etc.) ready：～行李，准备出发。*Pack the luggage and make ready to depart*. ❷ bribe officials

【打点滴】(in nursing) put on a drip：手术后他一直在～。*He has been on a drip since the surgery (or operation)*.

【打掉】destroy；knock out；wipe out：把敌人的探照灯～ *knock out the enemy's searchlight* / ～敌人一个师 *wipe out an enemy division*

【打动】move；touch：这番话～了他的心。*He was moved (or touched) by these words*.

【打赌】bet；wager：我敢～他明天准来。*I bet he'll come tomorrow*.

【打断】❶ break：他的腿给弹片～了。*A shrapnel broke his leg*. ❷ interrupt；cut short：～思路 *interrupt sb.'s train of thought* / 别～他，让他说完。*Don't cut him short；let him finish*. / 他的讲话不时被热烈的掌声～。*His speech was punctuated with warm applause*.

【打盹儿】doze off；take (or have) a nap：午饭后他总要打个盹儿。*He always takes (or has) a nap after lunch*.

【打耳光】box sb.'s ears；slap sb. in the face

【打发】❶ send；dispatch：赶快～人去请大夫。*Send for a doctor at once*. ❷ dismiss；send away：他把孩子们～走了，坐下来工作。*He sent the children away and sat down to work*. ❸ while away (one's time)

【打翻】overturn；strike down：一个大浪把小船～了。*A huge wave overturned the boat*. / 把人～在地 *strike sb. down*

【打榧子】〈方〉snap the fingers

【打分】give a mark；mark students' papers, etc.

【打稿】(又作'打稿子') work out a draft

【打嗝儿】〈口〉❶ hiccup ❷ belch；burp

【打更】sound the night watches

【打埂】［农］ridging

【打工】hire out for work；do manual work (for sb. temporarily)；work part-time：给老板～ *work for a boss*/～糊口 *make a living by manual labour*/他在国外靠～上学。*While abroad, he had to work part-time to support himself at college*. ◇ ～妹 employed female worker (usu. referring to a rural girl working in a city)；～仔 employed labourer (usu. referring to a rural young man working in a city)

【打躬作揖】bow and raise one's clasped hands in salute；fold the hands and make deep bows；bow and scrape

【打谷场】threshing ground (or floor)

【打鼓】❶ beat a drum ❷ feel uncertain (or nervous)：心里直～ *feel extremely diffident*

【打官腔】speak in a bureaucratic tone；talk like a bureaucrat；stall with official jargon

【打官司】❶ go to court (or law)；engage in a lawsuit ❷〈口〉squabble：打不完的官司 *endless squabbles*

【打光棍】remain a bachelor：你快结婚吧，哪能打一辈子光棍。*You'd better get married soon. How could you be a bachelor all your life?* / 他决心打一辈子光棍。*He's a confirmed bachelor*.

【打滚】roll about：小毛驴在地上～。*The little donkey rolled on the ground*. / 疼得直～ *writhe with pain*

【打棍子】beat with a big stick—criticize unsparingly or unfoundedly

【打哈哈】make fun；crack a joke：别拿我～。*Don't make fun of me*. / 这是正经事，可别～。*This is a serious matter；let's not joke about it*.

【打哈欠】(又作'打呵欠') yawn

【打鼾】snore

【打夯】ramming；tamping ◇ ～机 ramming machine；rammer；tamper

【打滑】❶ skid around：我们的车陷在泥坑里，车轮直～。*Our car got stuck in the mud and the wheels just skidded around*. ❷ slip (on slippery ground)

【打火】strike sparks from a flint；strike a light

【打火机】lighter

【打诨】(as of a clown in a traditional opera) make a joke

【打击】hit；strike；attack：～投机倒把活动 *crack down on speculation and profiteering* / ～报复 *make vindictive attacks on sb.；retaliate* / ～经济犯罪 *crackdown on serious criminal activities in the economic field*

【打击乐器】percussion instrument

【打家劫舍】loot；plunder

【打假】mount an attack on producers of counterfeit products

【打架】come to blows；fight；scuffle

【打尖】❶ stop for refreshment when travelling；have a snack (at a rest stop) ❷［农］topping；pinching

【打江山】fight to win state power

【打浆】paper making beating：～机 *beating engine；beater*

【打交道】come into (or make) contact with；have dealings with：两个厂经常～。*The two factories maintain frequent contacts*. / 我没跟他打过交道。*I've never had any dealings with him*.

【打搅】disturb；trouble：人家正在工作，别去～他了。*He's working. Don't disturb him*. / 对不起，～您了！*Sorry to have bothered you*. / ～您一下。*May I trouble you a minute?*

【打劫】rob；plunder；loot ——另见〖趁火打劫〗

【打结】tie a knot：打个结 *tie a knot* / 眉头～ *knit one's brows* / 舌头～ *be tongue-tied* ◇ ～器［化］fibre knotter

【打卡】punch card：～机 *punch-card machine；punched-card machine*/这种～上夜班的生活他习惯了。*He got used to working on night shift and punching in regularly*.

【打开】❶ open；unfold：把门～ *open the door* / ～盖子 *take off the lid* / ～包袱 *untie a bundle* /

～缺口 *make a breach* / ～眼界 *widen one's horizon* / ～局面 *open up a new prospect*; *make a breakthrough* ❷ turn on; switch on: ～收音机（电灯）*turn on the radio* (*light*)

【打开天窗说亮话】frankly speaking; let's not mince matters; let's be frank and put our cards on the table

【打瞌睡】doze off; nod

【打孔机】card punch

【打垮】defeat completely; rout: 把敌军的精锐部队～ *put the enemy's crack troops to rout*

【打捞】❶ get out of the water; salvage: ～沉船 *salvage a sunken ship* / ～尸体 *retrieve a corpse from the water* ❷［油］fishing: ～工具 *fishing tool* ◇～公司 salvage company; wrecking company

【打雷】thunder: 远处在～。*It's thundering in the distance.*

【打擂】join in an open competition or contest

【打冷枪】❶ shoot from a hiding-place; snipe ❷ attack in a sly way

【打量】❶ measure with the eye; look sb. up and down; size up: 门卫上下～着那个陌生人。*The sentry looked the stranger up and down.* ❷ think; suppose; reckon: 你～她这点事都干不了? *Do you think she can't do a little job like that?*

【打猎】go hunting

【打卤面】noodles served with thick gravy as sauce

【打乱】throw into confusion; upset: ～计划 *disrupt a plan*; *upset a scheme* / 他的突然到来把一切都给～了。*His unexpected arrival threw everything into confusion.*

【打落水狗】beat a drowning dog —completely crush a defeated enemy

【打马虎眼】〈方〉pretend to be ignorant of sth. (in order to gloss it over); act dumb

【打埋伏】❶ lie in ambush; set an ambush; ambush ❷ hold sth. back for one's own use; keep sth. in reserve

【打闷棍】❶ (of a robber) give sb. a staggering blow with a cudgel ❷〈喻〉give sb. a stunning blow

【打磨】polish; burnish; shine

【打牌】❶ play cards or mahjong: 打了通宵的牌 *play mahjong* (*or cards*) *all night long* ❷ (in international or domestic politics) exploit for one's own end: 打"民意"牌 *exploit "public opinion" for one's own end*; *play the "public opinion" card* / 中国不打别国牌，也不允许别人打中国牌。*China does not play any other country as a card and will not allow other people to play the China card.*

【打破】break; smash: ～僵局 *break a deadlock*; *find a way out of a stalemate* / ～记录 *break a record* / ～界线 *break down barriers* / ～平衡 *upset a balance* / ～条件分割 *dismantle the barriers between regions* / ～铁饭碗 *break the iron rice bowl*

【打破砂锅问到底】insist ongetting to the bottom of the matter: 小明老爱问为什么，老爱～。*Xiaoming always asks why and he'll never be satisfied until he knows everything.*

【打气】❶ inflate; pump up: 给车胎～ *inflate* (*or pump up*) *a tyre* ❷ bolster up (or boost) the morale; encourage; cheer up: 给他打打气 *try to encourage him* ◇ ～筒 inflater; tyre pump

【打钎】drill a blasting hole in rock with a hammer and a drill rod

【打前失】(of horses or mules) stumble

【打前站】act as an advance party; set out in advance to make arrangements

【打情骂俏】fool around and banter in flirtation

【打秋风】try to sponge on people

【打趣】banter; tease; make fun of

【打圈子】circle: 飞机在机场上空～。*The plane circled over the airfield.* / 不要在枝节问题上～。*Don't get bogged down in minor issues.*

【打拳】shadowbox

【打群架】engage in a gang fight

【打入冷宫】banish (a queen or concubine) to the cold palace—consign to limbo; put on the back shelf

【打入十八层地狱】banish to the lowest depths of hell—condemn to eternal damnation

【打散】reak up; scatter: 把原来的组～重编 *break up the existing groups to form new ones*

【打扫】sweep; clean: ～房间 *clean a room* / ～垃圾 *sweep away rubbish* / ～战场 *clean up the battlefield* / 把院子～干净 *sweep the courtyard clean*

【打闪】(of lightning) flash: 打了两个闪。*Lightning flashed twice.*

【打食】❶ (of birds and beasts) seek food ❷ use medicine to aid digestion or ease constipation

【打手】hired roughneck (or thug); hatchet man: 充当反动派的～ *serve as a hatchet man for the reactionaries*

【打水漂儿】play ducks and drakes;〈喻〉squander: 一群小孩在江边～。*A group of children were playing ducks and drakes by the river.* / 不要拿着钱来～。*Don't play loose with your money.*

【打算】plan; intend: 他～当教师。*He intends to become a teacher.* / 作最坏的～ *be prepared for the worst* / 各有各的～。*Each has a plan of his own.* or *Each has his own calculations.*

【打算盘】❶ calculate on an abacus ❷ calculate; scheme: 打小算盘 *be calculating*; *be petty and scheming* / 打错算盘 *miscalculate*

【打碎】break into pieces; smash; destroy: 玻璃杯～了。*The glass is smashed to pieces.*

【打胎】have an (induced) abortion

【打天下】❶ (of rebels) seize state power ❷ win success in a big enterprise

【打铁】forge iron; work as a blacksmith: ～先得本身硬 *if you want to work with iron, you must be tough yourself—one must be ideologically sound and professionally competent to do arduous work*

【打听】ask about; inquire about: 跟您～一件事。*I'd like to ask you about something.* / ～战友的消息 *inquire about one's comrades-in-arms*

【打通】get through; open up: 电话打不通 *be unable to get through (on the telephone)* / 两家的院墙～了。*An opening has been made in the wall between the two courtyards.*

【打头】take the lead: 老师傅～,青年人跟着上。*The old worker took the lead and the youngsters followed suit.*

【打头炮】fire the first shot; be the first to speak or act

【打头阵】fight in the van; spearhead the attack; take the lead

【打退】beat back (or off); repulse: ～敌人的进攻 *repulse an enemy attack*

【打退堂鼓】retreat; withdraw: 不能遇到点困难就～呀。*You can't give up the moment you run up against difficulty.* / 你既然答应了,就别～。*You've given your word; don't try to back out.*

【打围】encircle and hunt down (animals)

【打先锋】fight in the van; be a pioneer

【打响】❶ start shooting; begin to exchange fire: 武昌起义～了推翻封建朝廷的第一枪。*The Wuchang Uprising fired the first shot against the feudal imperial regime.* ❷ win initial success: 这一炮～了,下一步就好办了。*Success at this stage will make the next step easier.*

【打消】give up (an idea, etc.); dispel (a doubt, etc.): 她～了春节回家的念头。*She gave up the idea of going home for the Spring Festival.* / ～顾虑 *dispel misgivings*

【打小报告】be an informer

【打雪仗】have a snowball fight; throw snowballs

【打眼】❶ punch (or bore) a hole; drill ❷〈方〉catch the eye; attract attention

【打掩护】provide cover for: 为主力部队～ *provide cover for the main force*

【打样】❶ draw a design ❷［刷］make a proof ◇ ～机［刷］proof press

【打烊】〈方〉(of shops) put up the shutters; close for the night

【打印】❶ put a seal on; stamp ❷ cut a stencil and mimeograph; mimeograph ❸print out◇ ～格式 print format; ～件 mimeographed copy

【打印机】printer ◇ ～接口 printer port; ～驱动器程式 printer driver; ～终端 typewriter terminal

【打油诗】doggerel; ragged verse

【打游击】❶ fight as a guerrilla: 上山～ *join the guerrillas in the mountains; wage guerrilla warfare in the mountains* ❷〈诙〉operate like a guerrilla—work, eat, sleep, etc. at no fixed place

【打预防针】have a preventive injection—take precautions against sth.; caution against: 我说的这些话,就算是给你～吧。*Let these words of mine serve as a warning to you.*

【打圆场】mediate a dispute; smooth things over

【打援】attack (or ambush) enemy reinforcements: 围点～ *besiege an enemy stronghold in order to strike at the reinforcements*

【打杂儿】do odds and ends: 我不会做菜,只能在厨房打打杂儿。*I can't cook, so I can only do odds and ends in the kitchen.*

【打砸抢】beating, smashing and looting: 严禁～。*Acts of smashing and grabbing are strictly forbidden.* ◇ ～者 smash-and-grabber

【打颤】(又作'打战') shiver; tremble; shudder: 浑身～ *shiver all over* / 冷得我直～。*I was so cold that I kept shivering.*

【打仗】fight; go to war; make war

【打招呼】❶ greet sb.; say hello: 他俩见面不～,仿佛谁也不认得谁。*The two of them never greet each other and behave as if they were strangers.* ❷ notify; let sb. know: 你什么时候去开封,给我打个招呼。*When you go to Kaifeng, please let me know.* ❸ warn; remind: 事先已跟他们打过招呼了。*I've already warned them.*

【打折扣】❶ sell at a discount; give a discount ❷ fall short of a requirement or promise: 说到做到,不～ *carry out one's pledge to the letter*

【打针】give or have an injection

【打制】make (by hammering, chipping, etc.): ～镰刀 *make sickles*

【打制石器】［考古］chipped stone implement

【打肿脸充胖子】slap one's face until it's swollen in an effort to look imposing—puff oneself up to one's own cost

【打中】hit the mark (or target); hit: ～一艘敌舰 *hit an enemy vessel* / ～要害 *hit on the vital spot; hit where it really hurts*

【打主意】❶ think of a plan; evolve an idea: 打定主意 *make up one's mind* / 打错主意 *miscalculate; make a wrong decision* ❷ try to obtain; seek: 他们正在打你的主意,要你帮忙呢。*They are thinking of asking you to help.*

【打住】come to a halt; (in speech or writing) stop: 他说到这儿突然～了。*He suddenly stopped when he came to that point.*

【打转】spin; rotate; revolve: 卡车轮子在烂泥里直～。*The truck's wheels kept spinning in the mud.*

【打桩】pile driving; piling ◇ ～机 pile driver

【打字】typewrite; type ◇ ～带 typewriter ribbon; ～稿 typescript; ～机 typewriter; ～员 typist; ～纸 typing-paper

【打嘴巴】slap sb.'s face: 我打了他一嘴巴。*I gave him a slap on the cheek.* / 打自己的嘴巴 *slap one's own face—be self-contradictory*

【打坐】(of a Buddhist or Taoist monk) sit in meditation

dà

大 Ⅰ 形 ❶ big; large; great: ～城市 *big city* / ～眼睛 *big eyes* / ～救星 *great liberator* / 这张照片不够～。*The picture isn't large enough.* ❷ heavy (rain, etc.); strong (wind, etc.): 雪下得很~。*The snow is falling heavily.* / 风太~,你没法放风筝。*The wind is too strong to fly your kite.* / 外面风~。*It's blowing hard.* / 团结起来力量~。*Unity is strength.* ❸ loud: 声音太~ *too loud* / 收音机开~点。*Turn the radio up a bit louder.* ❹ general; main; major: ~马路 *main street* / ~问题 *major issue; big problem* / ~手术 *major operation* / ~反攻 *general counteroffensive* ❺ size: 那间屋子有这间两个~。*That roomis twice the size of this one.* / 你穿多~的鞋? *What size shoes do you wear?* ❻ age: 你的孩子多~了? *How old is your child?* / 他~我两岁。*He's two years my senior.* ❼ eldest: ~哥 *eldest brother* / ~房 *senior branch of a family* ❽〈尊〉your: ~札 *your letter* / ~作 *your writing* ❾ (used before a time word, etc. to show emphasis): ~清早 *early in the morning* Ⅱ 副 ❶ greatly; fully: ~长中国人民的志气 *greatly heighten the morale of the Chinese people* / ~笑 *laugh heartily* / 天已~亮。*It's already broad daylight.* ❷ in a big way; on a big (or large) scale; with all-out efforts; vigorously: ~删~改 *do a thorough job in revising* / ~搞农田水利 *go all out with irrigation and water conservancy* Ⅲ 名〈方〉❶ father ❷ father's brother; uncle ——另见 dài

【大案要案】major cases

【大白】❶〈方〉whiting: ~浆 *whitewash* ❷ come out; become known: 真相已~于天下。*The truth has become known to all.*

【大白菜】Chinese cabbage

【大白话】colloquial speech

【大白天】broad daylight; daytime

【大白天说梦话】daydream talk; sheer nonsense

【大败】❶ defeat utterly; put to rout: ~敌军 *inflict a crushing defeat on the enemy* ❷ suffer a crushing defeat

【大班】❶〈方〉big boss (a term for the manager of a foreign firm in old China); compradore; taipan ❷ the top class in a kindergarten

【大板车】large flatbed tricycle

【大办】go in for sth. in a big way (or on a big scale)

【大半】❶ more than half; the greater part; most; more often than not: ~天 *the greater part of a day; most of the day* ❷ most probably; most likely: 他~不来了。*Most probably he isn't coming.* / 这火车~要晚点了。*The train will most likely be late.*

【大包干】all-round contract system

【大爆炸宇宙论】Big Bang Theory

【大本营】❶ supreme headquarters ❷ base camp: 登山队~ *the base camp of a mountaineering expedition*

【大便】❶ defecate; have a bowel movement; shit: ~不通 (*suffer from*) *constipation* / 通~ *ease constipation* ❷ stool; human excrement; shit; faeces: 去化验~ *have one's stool examined*

【大兵】common soldier

【大兵团】large troop formation: ~作战 *large formation warfare; grand (or major) tactics*

【大饼】a kind of large flatbread

【大伯】❶ father's elder brother; uncle ❷ uncle (a polite form of address for an elderly man)

【大不了】❶ at the worst; if the worst comes to the worst: ~我们走着回去。*If the worst comes to the worst, we'll walk back.* ❷ (usu. used in the negative) alarming; serious: 划破点皮,没有什么~的。*It's nothing serious; just a scratch.*

【大步流星】with vigorous strides: 他在这条小路上~地走着。*He strode along the path.*

【大部】the greater part: 歼敌~ *annihilate the greater part of the enemy*

【大部头】voluminous work: ~的小说 *novel in several volumes; long novel*

【大材小用】large material put to small use—one's talent wasted on a petty job; not do justice to sb.'s talents

【大菜】❶ the last course of a feast (usu. a whole chicken or duck, or a leg of pork) ❷〈旧〉Western-style food

【大操大办】make large-scale arrangements (for a marriage or funeral)

【大肠】[生理] large intestine ◇ ~杆菌 colon bacillus

【大氅】overcoat; cloak; cape

【大潮】spring tide

【大车】❶ cart ❷ a respectful term for an engine driver or the chief engineer of a ship

【大车店】an inn for carters

【大臣】minister (of a monarchy)

【大乘】Great Vehicle (a school of Buddhism); Mahayana

【大吃大喝】(又作'大吃八喝') eat and drink to one's heart's content; eat and drink extravagantly: 反对~,注意节约。*Oppose extravagant eating and drinking and pay attention to thrift and economy.*

【大吃一惊】be greatly surprised; be quite taken aback

【大虫】〈方〉tiger

【大酬宾】give a large discount

【大出血】❶ [医] massive hemorrhage ❷〈喻〉bargain sale; big spending: ~价 *bargain price* / 这回我就~,为乡亲们修条路。*I'll dig deep into my pocket to pay for the construction of a road for the village.*

【大处落墨】(又作'大处着墨') concentrate on the key points

【大处着眼,小处着手】keep the general goal in sight while taking hold of the daily tasks

【大吹大擂】make a great fanfare; make a big noise; beat the drum

【大锤】sledgehammer

【大醇小疵】sound on the whole though defective in details

【大词】[逻] major term
【大慈大悲】infinitely compassionate and merciful
【大葱】green Chinese onion
【大错特错】completely mistaken; absolutely wrong
【大打出手】come to blows; get into a fight
【大大】greatly; enormously: 生产效率～提高。*Productivity has risen greatly.*
【大…大…】(used before nouns, verbs, or adjectives to show a high degree): 大鱼大肉 *plenty of meat and fish; rich food* / 大红大绿 *loud colours* / 大吵大闹 *kick up a row; make a scene*
【大大咧咧】〈方〉careless; casual: 别看他～的,什么事他都很在心。*He seems unconcerned, but nothing escapes his attention.*
【大袋鼠】kangaroo
【大胆】bold; daring; audacious: ～的革新 *a bold innovation* / ～! *How dare you!*
【大刀】broadsword
【大刀阔斧】bold and resolute; drastic: ～地进行改革 *carry out drastic reforms*
【大道理】major principle; general principle; great truth: 这些～人人都懂,真正做到可不容易啊! *These general principles are widely known, but it isn't easy to live up to them.*
【大灯】headlight (of a car)
【大敌】formidable enemy; archenemy / ～当前 *a formidable enemy stands before one; be faced with a formidable foe*
【大抵】generally speaking; in the main; on the whole: ～相同 *basically the same; more or less alike*
【大地】earth; mother earth: 阳光普照～。*The sun illuminates every corner of the land.* / ～回春。*Spring returns to the earth.* or *Spring is here again.* / 走遍祖国～ *travel all over the land* ◇～测量学 geodesy; ～构造学 geotectology; tectonics; ～水准面 geoid
【大典】❶ grand ceremony: 开国～ *founding ceremony (of a state)* ❷ a body of classical writings; canon:《永乐～》*Yongle Canon*
【大调】[音] major: C～奏鸣曲 *sonata in C major*
【大订单】maxi-order
【大动干戈】go to war; get into a fight
【大动肝火】fly into a rage; be furious; be very angry
【大动脉】❶[生理]main artery; aorta ❷ main line of communication; main communications artery: 南北交通的～ *the main artery of communications between north and south*
【大豆】soybean; soya bean
【大毒枭】drug baron
【大度】〈书〉magnanimous: ～包容 *regard with kindly tolerance; be magnanimous and tolerant; be magnanimous*
【大端】〈书〉main aspects (or features); salient points: 仅举其～ *merely point out the main features*
【大队】❶ a military unit corresponding to the battalion or regiment; group ❷ production brigade (of a rural people's commune); brigade ❸ a large body of: ～人马 *a large contingent of troops; a large body of marchers, paraders, etc.*
【大多】for the most part; mostly: 树上的苹果～已经成熟。*Most of the apples on the tree have ripened.* / 现代音乐～难以欣赏。*Most modern music is difficult to appreciate.*
【大多数】great majority; vast majority; the bulk: 为中国和世界的～人谋利益 *work for the interests of the vast majority of the people of China and of the whole world*
【大而无当】large but impractical; unwieldy: ～的计划 *a grandiose but impractical plan*
【大发雷霆】be furious; fly into a rage; bawl at sb. angrily: 他～,跳起脚来骂我。*He flew into a rage and jumped up and shouted at me.*
【大法】fundamental laws and principles (of a state); constitution
【大凡】generally; in most cases: ～坚持锻炼的,身体抵抗力都比较强。*Generally those who exercise regularly have high resistance to disease.*
【大方】❶〈书〉expert; scholar: 贻笑大方 ❷ generous; liberal ❸ natural and poised; easy; unaffected: 举止～ *have an easy manner; have poise; carry oneself with ease and confidence* ❹ in good taste; tasteful: 这种料子的颜色和花样很～。*The pattern and colour of this fabric are in good taste.*
【大方向】general orientation
【大放厥词】talk a lot of nonsense; spout a stream of empty rhetoric
【大粪】human excrement; night soil
【大风】❶ [气] fresh gale ❷ gale; strong wind: 外面刮着～。*There's a gale blowing.* or *It's blowing hard.*
【大风大浪】wind and waves; great storms: 人类社会是从～中发展起来的。*It is amid great storms that human society progresses.*
【大风子】[植] chaulmoogra (Hydnocarpus anthelmintica): ～油 *chaulmoogra oil*
【大夫】a senior official in feudal China ——另见 dàifu
【大幅度】by a wide margin; by a big margin; substantially: ～持续增产 *large continuous increase of crops* / ～提高 *be increased by a big margin* / ～增长 *increase by a wide margin; rise by a big margin*
【大副】first (or chief) mate; mate; chief officer
【大腹贾】potbellied merchant; rich merchant
【大腹便便】potbellied; big-bellied
【大概】❶ general idea; broad outline: 我只知道个～。*I have only a general idea.* / 我～跟他说了说。*I told him briefly.* ❷ general; rough; approximate: 作一个～的分析 *make a general analysis* / ～的数字 *an approximate figure* / ～的估计 *a rough estimate* ❸ probably; most likely; presumably: 会议～要延期。*The meeting will probably be postponed.* / 你～知道他吧。*Pre-*

sumably you know him.

【大干】work energetically; go all out; make an all-out effort ◇ ～快上 get going and go all out

【大纲】outline: 世界史～ *an outline history of the world* /《土地法～》*Outline Land Law*

【大哥】❶ eldest brother ❷ elder brother (a polite form of address for a man about one's own age)

【大哥大】❶ popular name for 移动电话 ❷〈口〉man with power; boss

【大革命】❶ great revolution: 法国～ *the French Revolution* ❷ the Great Revolution in China (1924-1927)

【大公】grand duke ◇ ～国 grand duchy

【大公无私】❶ selfless; unselfish ❷ perfectly impartial

【大功】great merit; extraordinary service: 立了～ *have performed exceptionally meritorious services*

【大功告成】be brought to successful completion; be accomplished; be crowned with success

【大功率】[电] high-power: ～可控硅 *high-power silicon controlled rectifier*

【大姑子】〈口〉husband's elder sister; sister-in-law

【大骨节病】Kaschin-Beck disease

【大鼓】❶[音] bass drum ❷ dagu, versified story sung to the accompaniment of a small drum and other instruments

【大褂】unlined long gown

【大观】grand sight; magnificent spectacle: 蔚为大观

【大规模】large-scale; extensive; massive; mass: ～生产 *large-scale production* / ～兴修水利 *launch a large-scale (or extensive) water conservancy project* / ～进攻 *launch a massive attack* ◇ ～集成 large scale integration; ～集成电路[电子] large-scale integrated circuit; LSI circuit; ～开发 large-scale development

【大锅饭】food prepared in a large canteen cauldron; mess ——另见〖吃大锅饭〗

【大国沙文主义】(又作'大国主义') great-nation chauvinism

【大国外交】great-power politics

【大国一致原则】principle of unanimity of the Five Powers (i.e. the five permanent members of the Security Council of the United Nations)

【大过】serious offence: 记～一次 *record a serious mistake*

【大海捞针】fish for a needle in the ocean; look for a needle in a haystack

【大寒】Greater Cold—the last of the 24 solar terms

【大喊大叫】❶ shout at the top of one's voice ❷ conduct vigorous propaganda

【大汉族主义】Han chauvinism

【大旱望云霓】long for a rain cloud during a drought—look forward to relief from distress

【大好】very good; excellent: 形势～。*The situation is very good*. / ～时机 *opportune moment*; *golden opportunity*; *finest hour* ◇ ～河山 beautiful rivers and mountains (of a country); one's beloved country

【大号】❶ large size: ～的鞋 *large-size shoes* ❷ [音] tuba; bass horn ❸〈尊〉your (given) name

【大和民族】Japanese nation; Yamato

【大合唱】antata; chorus:《黄河～》*The Yellow River Cantata*

【大亨】〈旧〉big shot; bigwig; magnate

【大轰大嗡】make a terrific din; raise a hue and cry

【大红】bright red; scarlet

【大后方】❶ rear area ❷ the area under KMT rule during the War of Resistance Against Japan

【大后年】three years from now

【大户】❶ rich and influential family ❷ large family ❸ (formerly) big clans such as wealthy, landlord families ❹ (now) households or units with large-scale enterprises; large-scale purchasers ◇ 盈利～ profit-making large-scale enterprise; 用水～ big water consumer

【大花脸】❶[戏] character with painted facial make-up in traditional Chinese opera, specializing in singing ❷ dirty funny face; besmirched face

【大话】big (or tall) talk; boast; bragging: 说～ *talk big*; *brag*

【大黄蜂】hornet

【大黄鱼】large yellow croaker

【大茴香】[植] anise; star anise

【大会】❶ plenary session; general membership meeting: 党支部～ *a general membership meeting of a Party branch* ❷ mass meeting; mass rally: 庆祝～ *a celebration meeting*

【大伙儿】(又作'大家伙儿')〈口〉we all; you all; everybody

【大祸临头】disaster is imminent; disaster is hanging over one

【大惑不解】be extremely puzzled; be unable to make head or tail of sth.

【大集体】big collective

【大吉大利】good luck and great prosperity (an expression of good wishes)

【大计】a major programme of lasting importance; a matter of fundamental importance: 共商～ *discuss matters of vital importance*

【大蓟】[植] setose thistle (Cephalanoplos setosum)

【大家】❶ a great master; authority: 书法～ *a great master of calligraphy*; *a noted calligrapher* ❷ all; everybody: 你给～弹肖邦的曲子。*Please play Chopin for us*. / 明天咱们～开个会谈谈。*We'll have a meeting to discuss it tomorrow*.

【大家闺秀】a girl from a good family; a well-bred girl; lady

【大家庭】big family; community: 李家是个～,有三代人。*The Lis are a big family with three generations*.

【大驾】〈尊〉you: 恭候～ *wait respectfully for your gracious presence*/有劳～ *have to rely on your efforts*; *have to ask you to take the trouble*

【大减价】sale; sale price; big bargain price; inflation busters

【大奖】grand prize；top prize；big award or prize：以～招揽顾客 *attract customers with big prizes* / 这项发明获得～。*The invention was awarded the grand prize*. ◇ ～赛 prize-giving competition

【大将】❶ senior general ❷ high-ranking officer

【大教堂】cathedral

【大街】main street；street：逛～ *go window-shopping*；*stroll around the streets*

【大街小巷】streets and lanes：～彩旗飘扬。*The streets and lanes are decked with bunting*.

【大节】political integrity

【大捷】great victory

【大姐】❶ eldest sister ❷ elder sister（a polite form of address for a woman about one's own age）

【大姐大】〈口〉woman with power；boss

【大解】go to the lavatory（to defecate）；have a bowel movement

【大襟】the front of a Chinese garment which buttons on the right

【大惊失色】turn pale with fright

【大惊小怪】be surprised or alarmed at sth. quite normal；make a fuss about nothing：有什么值得～的？*What's there to be surprised at*？/ 是什么要紧的事，这么～！*Why get so excited over a little thing like this*？

【大净】[宗]（伊斯兰教）Ghusl

【大静脉】[生理] vena cava

【大舅子】〈口〉wife's elder brother；brother-in-law

【大局】overall（or general，whole）situation：事关～。*It's an issue that concerns the overall situation*. / ～已定。*The outcome is a foregone conclusion*.

【大举】carry out（a military operation）on a large scale：～进攻 *mount a large-scale offensive*；*attack in force*

【大军】❶main forces；army：我们是先头部队，～随后就到。*We are the advance detachment*. *The main forces will be here soon*. ❷ large contingent：筑路～ *a large contingent of road builders* / 百万～ *an army a million strong*

【大卡】[物] kilocalorie；large（or great）calorie

【大楷】❶ regular script in big characters，as used in Chinese calligraphy exercises ❷ block letters；blockwriting

【大考】end-of-term examination；final exam

【大课】a lecture given to a large number of students；enlarged class

【大跨径桥】long-span bridge

【大快人心】（usu. of the punishment of an evil-doer）affording general satisfaction；most gratifying to the people；to the immense satisfaction of the people

【大块头】〈方〉a fat person；a person of big build；fatty

【大款】〈口〉tycoon；moneybags

【大括弧】brace

【大牢】〈口〉prison；jail

【大老粗】uncouth fellow；uneducated person；rough and ready fellow

【大礼拜】〈口〉two-day weekend（in contrast with one day off）

【大礼堂】big assembly hall；auditorium

【大理石】marble

【大力】energetic；vigorous：～发展教育事业 *devote major efforts to developing education* ◇ ～扣杀 hammer

【大力士】a man of unusual strength，esp. a weight-lifter

【大丽花】dahlia

【大殓】encoffining ceremony

【大梁】ridgepole；ridgepiece

【大龄青年】unmarried men or women of the age group between 28 and 35

【大量】❶ a large number；a great quantity：为国家积累～资金 *accumulate large funds for the state* / 收集～科学资料 *collect a vast amount of scientific data* / ～财富 *enormous wealth*；*large fortune* / ～事实 *a host of facts* / ～库存 *huge stocks* ❷ generous；magnanimous

【大料】〈方〉aniseed

【大溜】main current；main trend；greater number（of persons）；majority（of the people）：随～ *follow the crowd*；*conform to the majority*；*follow the trend*

【大楼】multi-storied building：居民～ *apartment house*；*block of flats*

【大陆】continent；mainland：中国～ *the mainland of China* ◇ ～架 continental shelf；～隆 [地质] continental rise；～漂移 continental drift；～坡 continental slope；～桥 continental bridge；～性气候 continental climate

【大路】main road；highway

【大路货】popular goods of dependable quality

【大略】❶ general idea；broad outline：我只知道个～。*I have only a general idea*. / 时间不多了，你～说说吧。*There isn't much time left*. *Could you speak just briefly*？❷ bold vision

【大妈】❶ father's elder brother's wife；aunt ❷ aunt（an affectionate or respectful form of address for an elderly woman）

【大麻】❶ hemp ❷ marijuana ◇ ～文化 pot culture

【大麻哈鱼】（又作'大马哈鱼'）chum salmon；dog salmon

【大麦】barley

【大满贯】Grand Slam

【大忙】very busy：～季节 *rush*（*or busy*）*season* ◇ ～人 busy bee

【大猫熊】giant panda

【大帽子】a big hat—an exaggerated epithet used to categorize a person；unwarranted charge；political label：别拿～压人。*Don't you try to intimidate people by pinning political labels on them*.

【大门】entrance（or front）door；gate

【大米】（husked）rice

【大面儿】〈方〉general appearance；surface：～上

还过得去。*It's basically all right*.

【大民族主义】big-nationality chauvinism

【大名】❶ one's formal personal name ❷〈尊〉your (given) name

【大名鼎鼎】famous; celebrated; well-known: 他已经是～的人物了。*He has become a celebrity*.

【大螟】pink rice borer (Sesamia inferens)

【大谬不然】entirely wrong; grossly mistaken

【大模大样】in an ostentatious manner; with a swagger: 我看见他穿着一身新衣服～地在街上走。*I saw him swaggering along the street in his new suit*.

【大拇指】〈口〉thumb: 竖起～叫好 *hold up one's thumb in approval*

【大拿】〈口〉❶ person with power; boss: 我们这里厂长说了算,他是～。*The director has the final say here. He is the boss*. ❷ expert; authority: 在力学方面,他是我们这里的～。*In mechanics, he is the expert (or an authority)*.

【大男子主义】male chauvinism

【大难】catastrophe; disaster

【大难不死,必有后福】After surviving a great disaster, one is bound to have good fortune in later years.

【大难临头】with great disaster hanging over one; be faced with imminent disaster

【大脑】[生理] Cerebrum ◇ ～半球 cerebral hemisphere; ～脚 cerebral peduncle; ～皮层 cerebral cortex

【大鲵】[动] giant salamander

【大逆不道】treason and heresy; worst offence; greatest outrage

【大年】❶ good year; bumper year; (for fruit trees) on-year ❷ a lunar year in which the last month has 30 days ❸ the Spring Festival

【大年初一】〈口〉first day of the lunar year; lunar New Year's Day

【大年夜】〈方〉lunar New Year's Eve

【大娘】〈口〉❶ wife of father's elder brother; aunt ❷ aunt (a respectful form of address used for an elderly woman)

【大排档】side walk snack eatery

【大炮】❶ artillery; big gun; cannon ❷〈口〉one who speaks boastfully or forcefully; one who noisily overstates things

【大陪审团】grand jury

【大篷车】❶ (covered) wagon ❷ covered truck or lorry (for carrying goods); caravan: 组织～送货下乡 *send goods into the country in caravans*

【大批】❶ large quantities (or numbers, amounts) of: ～轻工业品运往农村。*Large quantities of light industrial products are transported to the countryside*. ❷ mass

【大披肩】(in ancient Greece or Rome) pallium

【大屏幕投影电视机】large-screen television projector

【大谱表】[音] great stave

【大起大落】great fluctuations

【大气】❶ [气] atmosphere; air ❷ heavy breathing: 跑得直喘～ *breathe heavily from running* / 吓得连～也不敢出 *catch (or hold) one's breath in fear* ◇ ～层 atmospheric layer; atmosphere; ～电 atmospheric electricity; ～干扰 atmospheric interference; ～环流 atmospheric circulation; general circulation of atmosphere; ～科学 atmospheric sciences; ～磅礴 of great momentum; powerful; grand and magnificent; ～污染 air (or atmospheric) pollution; ～压 atmospheric pressure; atmosphere; ～折射 atmospheric (or astronomical) refraction

【大气候】general tendency; general political climate

【大器晚成】great vessels take years to produce—great minds mature slowly

【大千世界】the boundless universe

【大前年】three years ago

【大前提】[逻] major premise

【大前天】(又作'大前儿') three days ago

【大庆】❶ grand celebration of an important event; great occasion: 十年～ *the festive occasion of the 10th anniversary* ❷ the birthday of an old person who commands respect: 七十～ *the seventieth birthday*

【大秋】❶ harvest season in autumn ❷ crops harvested in autumn; autumn harvest ◇ ～作物 crops sown in spring and reaped in autumn; autumn-harvested crops

【大曲】❶ yeast for making hard liquor ❷ a hard liquor made with such yeast

【大趋势】general trend of events

【大权】power over major issues; authority: ～在握 *hold power in one's hands*

【大权独揽】centralize power in one person's hands; have sole power; arrogate all authority to oneself

【大权旁落】lose one's power to others (usu. one's subordinates)

【大犬座】[天] Canis Major

【大人】❶〈旧〉〈尊〉(used in a letter to address one's parents or people of an older generation): 父亲～ *Dear Father* ❷ adult; grown-up ❸〈旧〉Your Excellency or His Excellency

【大人物】important person; great personage; big shot; VIP

【大撒把】totally laissez-faire

【大扫除】general cleaning; thorough cleanup: 节日～ *thorough cleanup before a holiday*

【大嫂】❶ eldest brother's wife; sister-in-law ❷ elder sister (a polite form of address for a woman about one's own age)

【大杀风景】(又作'大煞风景') utterly spoil the fun

【大厦】❶ large building ❷ mansions (used in names of large buildings): 上海～ *Shanghai Mansions*

【大厦将倾】a great mansion on the point of collapse—the situation is hopeless

【大少爷】❶ eldest son (of a rich family) ❷ a spoilt son of a rich family; spendthrift: ～作风

behaviour typical of the spoilt son of a rich family; *extravagant ways*

【大舌头】〈口〉a thick-tongued person; one who lisps; lisper

【大赦】amnesty; general pardon

【大婶儿】aunt (an affectionate or respectful form of address for a woman about one's mother's age)

【大声疾呼】raise a cry of warning; loudly appeal to the public

【大牲口】(又作'大牲畜') draught animal

【大失所望】greatly disappointed; to one's great disappointment

【大师】❶ great master; master: 国画～ *a great master of traditional Chinese painting* ❷ Great Master (a courtesy title used to address a Buddhist monk)

【大师傅】cook; chef

【大使】ambassador: 特命全权～ *ambassador extraordinary and plenipotentiary* ◇ ～馆 embassy; ～级会谈 talks at ambassadorial level; ambassadorial talks; ～衔 ambassadorial rank

【大事】❶ great (or major) event; important matter; major issue: 头等～ *a matter of prime (or paramount) importance* / 关心国家～ *concern oneself with affairs of state* / 当前国际政治中的一件～ *a major event in current international politics* ❷ overall (or general) situation: ～不好。*A disaster is imminent.* ❸ in a big way: ～渲染 *enormously exaggerate*; *play up* ◇ ～记 chronicle of events

【大事化小,小事化了】reduce major issues to minor ones and minor ones to nothing; turn big problems into small ones and small ones into no problems at all

【大势】general trend of events

【大势所趋】the trend of the times; the general trend: ～,人心所向 *the trend of the times and the desire of the people*; *the general trend and popular feeling*

【大势已去】the situation is hopeless; the game is as good as lost; it's all up with sb.

【大是大非】major matters of principle; cardinal questions of right and wrong: 分清～ *draw clear distinctions concerning cardinal issues of right and wrong*; *distinguish between right and wrong on cardinal issues*

【大手笔】❶ the work of a well-known writer ❷ a well-known writer

【大手大脚】wasteful; extravagant: 他是～过惯了的。*He has been used to extravagance.* / 现在人们好像都变得～了。*It seems people have become very free with their money these days.*

【大书特书】record in letters of gold; write volumes about

【大叔】❶ younger brother of one's father; uncle ❷ uncle (a polite form of address for a man about one's father's age)

【大暑】Greater Heat—the 12th of the 24 solar terms

【大树底下好乘凉】〈口〉A big tree affords good shade; An influential friend, relative or mentor provides protection and help.

【大水】flood; floodwater

【大肆】without restraint; wantonly: ～攻击 *wantonly vilify*; *launch an unbridled (or all-out) attack against*

【大苏打】[化] sodium thiosulfate; sodium hyposulfite; hypo

【大蒜】garlic: 一头～ *a head of garlic*

【大踏步】in big strides: ～前进 *stride along*

【大堂】lobby (of a hotel): ～经理 *manager on duty*

【大…特…】(with a word repeated for emphasis): 大改特改 *make drastic changes (in writing, etc.)*

【大特写】big close-up (BCU)

【大提琴】violoncello; cello

【大体】❶ cardinal principle; general interest: 识～,顾大局 *have the cardinal principles in mind and take the overall situation into account* ❷ roughly; more or less; on the whole; by and large; approximately: ～相同 *more or less alike*; *about the same* / 收支～平衡。*Income and expenditure roughly balance.*

【大田】land for growing field crops ◇ ～作物 field crop

【大厅】hall

【大庭广众】(before) a big crowd; (on) a public occasion: ～之中 *in public*; *before a large audience*

【大同】Great Harmony (an ideal or perfect society)

【大同小异】much the same but with minor differences; alike except for slight differences; very much the same

【大头】❶ head mask ❷ the bigger end; the main part: 抓～儿 *grasp the main part* ❸〈贬〉spendthrift; wastrel: 拿～ *sponge on a spendthrift*

【大头菜】[植] rutabaga

【大头针】pin

【大团圆】❶ happy reunion ❷ happy ending

【大腿】thigh

【大腕】〈口〉❶ star (usu. referring to actors, singers, etc.) ❷ past master; master-hand

【大腕儿】big finesse

【大尉】senior captain

【大无畏】dauntless; utterly fearless; indomitable: ～的英雄气概 *dauntless heroism*

【大西洋】the Atlantic (Ocean)

【大喜】〈口〉❶ great rejoicing: 在这～的日子里 *in these days of great rejoicing* / 您～啦! *Congratulations!* ❷ wedding: 哪天是你们～的日子? *When will your wedding take place?*

【大喜过望】be delighted that things are better than one expected

【大戏】❶ a full-scale traditional opera ❷〈方〉Beijing opera

【大虾】prawn

【大显身手】display one's skill to the full; give full play to one's abilities; distinguish oneself; give a good account of oneself: 你～的时机到啦! *Now's your chance to distinguish yourself*.

【大显神通】give full play to one's remarkable skill (or abilities); display one's prowess

【大相径庭】widely divergent; entirely different; poles apart

【大小】❶ big or small: ～水库十座 *ten reservoirs of varying sizes* / 国家不论～,应该一律平等。*All countries, big or small, should be equal*. ❷ size: 这双鞋我穿上～正合适。*These shoes are just my size*. ❸ degree of seniority: 说话没个～ *speak impolitely to elderly people* ❹ adults and children: 全家～五口。*There are five people in the family altogether*. / ～平安。*All's well in the family*.

【大校】senior colonel

【大协作】large-scale cooperation; a major pooling of efforts

【大写】❶ the capital form of a Chinese numeral: ～金额 *amount in words* ❷ capitalization: ～字母 *capital letter* ◇ ～锁定[计] caps lock

【大兴】go in for sth. in a big way: ～调查研究之风 *energetically encourage the practice of conducting investigations and studies*

【大兴土木】go in for large-scale construction; be busy putting up buildings

【大兴问罪之师】angrily point an accusing finger at; scathingly condemn

【大猩猩】gorilla

【大行星】[天] major planet

【大型】large-scale; large: ～企业 *large enterprise* / ～彩色记录片 *full-length colour documentary film* / ～运输机 *giant transport aircraft; air freighter* / ～轧钢厂 *heavy steel rolling plant* ◇ ～客机 air liner

【大熊猫】giant panda

【大熊座】[天] Ursa Major; the Great Bear

【大修】[机] overhaul; heavy repair

【大选】general election

【大学】university; college

【大学生】university (or college) student

【大雪】Greater Snow—the 21st of the 24 solar terms

【大循环】[生理] systemic circulation

【大牙】❶ molar ❷ front tooth ——另见〖笑掉大牙〗

【大雅】elegance; refinement; good taste——另见〖不登大雅之堂〗

【大烟】common name for 鸦片 ◇ ～鬼 opium addict

【大言不惭】brag unblushingly; talk big

【大盐】crude salt

【大雁】wild goose

【大洋】❶ ocean ❷ silver dollar

【大洋洲】Oceania; Oceanica

【大样】❶ [刷] full-page proof ❷ [建] detail drawing

【大摇大摆】strutting; swaggering: 显然小偷是从这里～出去的。*Obviously the thief had simply walked out this way as bold as brass*.

【大要】main points; gist: 文章的～ *the gist of an article*

【大爷】〈口〉❶ father's elder brother; uncle ❷ uncle (a respectful form of address for an elderly man)

【大业】great cause; great undertaking: 创～ *become pioneers in a great undertaking*

【大衣】overcoat; topcoat

【大姨】〈口〉mother's eldest sister; aunt

【大姨子】〈口〉wife's elder sister; sister-in-law

【大义】cardinal principles of righteousness; righteous cause: 深明～ *be deeply conscious of the righteousness of a cause*

【大义凛然】inspiring awe by upholding justice; with stern righteousness

【大义灭亲】place righteousness above loyalty to one's family; sacrifice ties of blood to righteousness

【大意】❶ general idea; main points; gist; tenor: 段落～ *the gist of a paragraph* / 把他讲话的～记下来就行了。*Just jot down the main ideas (or points) of what he says*. ❷ careless; negligent; inattentive: 千万不可粗心～ *must never on any account be negligent* / 他真～,竟把她的地址给丢了。*He was so careless that he lost her address*.

【大音阶】[音] major scale

【大印】great seal—the seal of power

【大油】〈口〉lard

【大有】❶ there is much: ～区别。*There is a great difference* / ～希望。*There is great promise for the future*. ❷〈书〉abundance: ～之年 *a year of abundance*

【大有可为】be well worth doing; have bright prospects: 淡水养鱼～。*There are bright prospects for freshwater fish farming*.

【大有人在】there are plenty of such people; such people are by no means rare

【大有文章】there's something behind all this; there's more to this than meets the eye

【大有作为】have full scope for one's talents; be able to develop one's ability to the full; have great possibilities: 青年人在这里是可以～的。*There are plenty of opportunities for young people here*.

【大雨】heavy rain: ～如注 *the rain is pouring down; it's raining cats and dogs; it's raining in torrents*

【大元帅】generalissimo

【大员】〈旧〉high-ranking official: 委派～ *appoint high-ranking officials*

【大院】courtyard; compound: 居民～ *residential compound*

【大约】❶ approximately; about: ～有十二个人。*There were around a dozen people*. / ～一小时的路程。*It's about an hour's journey*. ❷ probably:

他～是到车间去了。*He has probably gone to the workshop*.

【大月】greater month—a solar month of 31 days; a lunar month of 30 days

【大跃进】the Great Leap Forward (1958)

【大运河】the Grand Canal

【大杂烩】hodgepodge; hotchpotch

【大杂院儿】a compound occupied by many households

【大灶】ordinary mess

【大张旗鼓】on a grand scale; in a big way：～地宣传新时期的总任务 *give wide publicity to the general task in the new period*

【大丈夫】true man; real man; man

【大政方针】fundamental policy (of a state); major policy

【大指】thumb

【大志】high aim; lofty aim; exalted ambition; high aspirations：胸怀～ *cherish high ideals; have lofty aspirations*

【大治】great order：～之年 *a year of great order*

【大致】roughly; approximately; more or less：～相同 *roughly (or about) the same* / 这项工程～两年可以完工。*This project will take about two years to complete*.

【大智若愚】a man of great wisdom often seems slow-witted

【大中型】large-and-medium-sized：

【大众】the masses; the people; the public; the broad masses of the people：～歌曲 *popular songs* / ～文艺 *art and literature for the masses; popular literature* ◇～传播 mass communication; ～媒体 mass media; ～消费品 large-scale goods

【大众化】popularize：～的饭菜 *popular low-priced dishes* / 语言～ *use the language of the ordinary people*

【大众汽车公司】(Germany) Volkswagen Automobile Plant; Volkswagenwerk AG

【大洲】continent

【大主教】archbishop

【大专院校】universities and colleges; institutions of higher education

【大资产阶级】the big bourgeoisie

【大自然】nature：征服～ *conquer nature*

【大宗】❶ a large amount (or quantity)：～款项 *a large amount of money; large sums* ❷ staple：～产品 *staple product* / 本地出产以棉花为～。*Cotton is the staple crop here*.

【大作】❶〈尊〉your writing：拜读～ *have the pleasure of perusing your work* ❷ spring up; break out：霎时狂风～。*A violent wind suddenly sprang up*. / 枪声～。*Shots rang out*.

dāi

呆 Ⅰ 形 ❶ slow-witted; dull：这孩子大病之后变～了。*After recovering from a serious illness, the child became slow-witted*. / 这人怎么那么～！*What a silly man*！❷ blank; wooden：～～地望着 *stare at sth. blankly* / 吓～了 *be stupefied; be scared stiff; be dumbstruck* Ⅱ 动〈口〉stay：～在家里 *stay at home* / 我在那家饭店～了三个晚上。*I stayed three nights at that hotel*.

【呆板】stiff and awkward; rigid; not natural; inflexible：动作～ *stiff and awkward movements* / 表情～ *a stony expression* / 这个人真～。*This person is inflexible*.

【呆若木鸡】dumb as a wooden chicken; dumbstruck; transfixed (with fear or amazement)：他站在那里，吓得～。*He stood there transfixed with horror*.

【呆头呆脑】stupid-looking

【呆小症】[医] cretinism

【呆性物质】[化] inert material

【呆账】bad debt

【呆滞】❶ dull：两眼～无神 *with a dull look in one's eyes* / 她注视着远方，目光是～的。*She gazed into the distance with her eyes blank*. ❷ idle：避免资金～ *prevent capital from lying idle* ◇～贷款 dead loan; bad loan; ～库存 inert inventory; inactive stock; ～商品 unsalable commodity; drug on the market; ～市场 stagnant market; sluggish market

【呆子】idiot; simpleton; blockhead

dǎi

歹 形 bad; evil; vicious：为非作歹

【歹毒】〈方〉sinister and vicious

【歹人】〈方〉villain; gangster or robber

【歹徒】scoundrel; ruffian; evildoer

【歹心】(又作'歹意') malice; malicious intent：把别人的好心当作歹意 *take sb.'s goodwill for evil intent*

逮 动 capture; catch：猫～老鼠。*Cats catch mice*. ——另见 dài

dài

大 形 (义同"大"(dà)，用于"大夫、大黄、大王") ——另见 dà

【大夫】〈口〉doctor; physician ——另见 dàfū

【大黄】[植] Chinese rhubarb

【大王】great king (a term of address for a king or a bandit cheif, used in traditional operas and novels)

代 Ⅰ 动 ❶ take the place of; be in place of：请～我向他致意。*Please give him my regards*. ❷ acting：～部长 *acting minister* Ⅱ 名 ❶ historical period：汉～ *the Han Dynasty* ❷ [地质] era：古生代 ❸ generation：～～相传 *pass on (or hand down) from generation to generation* / 一～新人在成长。*A new generation is growing up*.

【代办】❶ do sth. for sb.; act on sb.'s behalf: 这件事请你～吧。*Could you do this for me?* or *Could you act on my behalf?* ❷［外交］chargé d'affaires: 临时～chargé d'affaires ad interim ◇～处［外交］Office of the Chargé d'Affaires

【代办进口】importing on customer's behalf

【代办律师】commission merchant

【代办所】agency: 储蓄～ *savings agency* / 邮政～ *postal agency*

【代笔】write (a letter, etc.) for sb.; be a ghost writer: 老太太求我～给她儿子写封信。*The old woman asked me to write a letter for her to her son.*

【代表】❶ deputy; delegate; representative: 全国人大～ *deputy to the National People's Congress* / 常驻～ *permanent representative* (*or delegate*) ❷ represent; stand for: 这三个人～三种不同性格。*These three persons represent three different types of character.* / ～时代精神 *embody the spirit of the era* ❸ on behalf of; in the name of: ～我国政府表示衷心的感谢 *express heartfelt thanks on behalf of our government* ◇～大会 congress; representative assembly (or conference); ～权 representation; ～人物 representative figure (or personage); typical representative; leading exponent; ～团 delegation; mission; deputation; ～性 representativeness; ～资格 qualifications of a representative; ～资格审查委员会 (delegates') credentials committee; ～作 representative work

【代步】〈书〉ride instead of walk

【代词】〈语〉pronoun

【代沟】generation gap

【代购】buy on sb.'s behalf; act as a purchasing agent: 本店为顾客办理～业务。*This store will act as a purchasing agent for customers.* ◇～代销点 purchasing and marketing agency

【代号】code name

【代价】price; cost: 不惜任何～ *prepared to pay any price; at any cost; at all costs* ◇～券 scrip

【代课】take over a class for an absent teacher

【代劳】do sth. for sb.; take trouble on sb.'s behalf: 这事请你老李～吧。*Will you do this for us, Lao Li?*

【代理】❶ act on behalf of sb. in a responsible position: 总经理病了，工作由他～。*He acted for the general manager who was ill.* / ～厂长 *acting manager of a factory* ❷ act as agent (or proxy, procurator) ◇～关系 agency relation; ～权 agency right; procuration; power of attorney; ～人 agent; deputy; proxy; procurator; attorney; ～人酬金 agent's remuneration; ～业 factorage; ～制 agent system

【代码】code ◇～检验 code file; ～图像 code image; ～文件 code file; ～系统 coding system

【代名词】❶ 同〖代词〗❷ synonym: 诸葛亮在民间传说中成了智慧的～。*Zhuge Liang is a synonym for wisdom in folklore.*

【代庖】〈书〉do what is sb. else's job; act in sb.'s place

【代培】train on contract

【代培生】student recruited or trained for an organization

【代乳粉】milk powder substitute

【代售】be commissioned to sell sth. (usu. as a sideline): 此处～邮票。*Stamps sold here.*

【代数】algebra ◇～方程 algebraic equation; ～式 algebraic expression

【代替】replace; substitute for; take the place of: 用国产品～进口货 *substitute homemade products for imported goods* / 有些外科手术可用针麻～药麻。*In some surgical operations, acupuncture anaesthesia may be used instead of medicinal anaesthetics.*

【代为】(used before verbs) on behalf of; for (sb.): ～说项 *put in a good word for sb.* / 请～致意。*Please give him my regards.*

【代销】sell goods (for the state) on a commission basis; be commissioned to sell sth. (usu. as a sideline); act as a commission agent: ～店 *shop commissioned to sell certain goods; commission agent*

【代谢】❶ supersession: 新旧事物的～ *the supersession of the old by the new* ❷［生］metabolize: 分解～ *catabolism* / 组成～ *anabolism* ◇～病 metabolic disease; ～期［生］metabolic stage; ～物［生］metabolite; ～作用［生］metabolism —— 另见〖新陈代谢〗

【代行】act on sb.'s behalf: ～职权 *function in an acting capacity*

【代序】an article used in lieu of a preface (or by way of introduction)

【代言人】spokesman; mouthpiece

【代议制】the representative system (of government): ～机构 *representative institution*

【代用】substitute: ～材料 *substitute* (*or ersatz*) *materials* ◇～品 substitute; ersatz

【代孕】surrogacy ◇～母亲 foster

【代职】hold a position in an acting capacity

【代字号】swung dash (～)

迨 〈书〉Ⅰ【动】wait till Ⅱ【介】before sth. happens: ～天之未阴雨 *before it rains*

玳 (构词成分)见下

【玳瑁】［动］hawksbill turtle

带 Ⅰ【名】❶ belt; girdle; ribbon; band; tape: 皮带 / 丝带 / 磁带 ❷ tyre: 自行车～ *bicycle tyre* ❸ zone; area; belt: 他在这一～打过游击。*He used to be a guerrilla fighter in these parts.* Ⅱ【动】❶ take; bring; carry: 我可以～多少行李? *How much luggage can I take?* / 别忘了～雨衣。*Don't forget to take your raincoat along.* ❷ do sth. incidentally: 上街时给～点茶叶来。*When you go out, get me some tea.* / 你出去请把门～上。*Please pull the door to when you go out.* ❸ bear; have: ～有时代的特点 *bear the imprint of the* *times* / 面～笑容 *wear a smile* / ～刺的灌木 *a thorny bush* / 一项～根本性的措施 *a measure of fundamental importance* ❹ having sth. attached; simultaneous: ～叶的橘子 *tangerines with their leaves on* / ～电脑的收录机 *a programmable cassette recorder* ❺ lead; head: ～队 *lead (or be the leader of) a group of people* / ～兵 *lead (or be in command of) troops* / ～研究生 *direct (or be a tutor of) postgraduates* ❻ look after; bring up; raise: ～孩子 *look after children* ❼ drive; spur on; bring along: 他这样一来～得大家都勤快了。*His example has spurred everybody on to work harder.*

【带病】in spite of illness: 他～坚持工作。*He went on working in spite of his illness.*

【带材】[冶] Strip

【带操】[体] gymnastics with ribbons

【带处理装置】tape processing unit

【带穿孔机】tape punch

【带电】electrified; live; charged: ～导线 *live wire* ◇ ～粒子 [物] charged particle; ～体 charged (or electrified) body; ～作业 live-wire work

【带动】drive; spur on; bring along: 抓好典型，～全局 *take firm hold of typical examples to promote the work as a whole* / 改革～了生产。*The reforms have given an impetus to production.*

【带钢】strip steel

【带劲】❶ energetic; forceful: 他干起活来可～了。*He works like a horse.* / 这篇文章写得真～。*This is a very forceful piece of writing.* ❷ interesting; exciting; wonderful: 这场比赛真～。*This is really a terrific match.* / 下棋不～，咱们游泳去吧。*Chess is no fun; let's go swimming.*

【带锯】[机] band saw

【带菌者】[医] carrier

【带累】implicate; involve; get sb. into trouble: 我病成这样，可不能再～你了。*I'm so ill. I shouldn't trouble you any more.*

【带领】lead; guide: 他～全家出海捕鱼。*He led the whole family out to sea to catch fish.* / 老师～同学们去参观中国历史博物馆。*The teacher took the pupils to the Museum of Chinese History.*

【带路】(又作'带道') show (or lead) the way; act as a guide: 老猎户给我们～。*The old hunter acted as our guide.*

【带路人】guide

【带式干燥器】belt drier ; band drier

【带式提升机】belt elevator; band elevator

【带速】tape speed

【带头】take the lead; be the first; take the initiative; set an example: ～发言 *be the first to speak; break the ice* / 带个好头 *set a good example* ◇ ～人 foregoer; person who plays a leading role or sets an example

【带头羊】bellwether

【带徒弟】train (or take on) an apprentice

【带孝】wear mourning for a parent, relative, etc.; be in mourning: 给母亲～ *wear mourning for one's mother* / 带了一个月的孝 *have been in mourning for one month*

【带信儿】take or bring a message: 请你带个信儿给我妈，说我今天要晚点儿回去。*Please tell my mother that I'll be home late tonight.*

【带音】[语音] voiced

【带鱼】hairtail

【带职】retain one's post during absence from duty: ～学习 *go on a study course without being formally relieved of one's post ; go on as training course as a mid-career student* / ～培训 *in-service training*

【带状疱疹】[医] herpes zoster; zoster

【带子】belt; girdle; ribbon; band; tape

殆 〈书〉 Ⅰ 名 dangerous; perilous: 危殆 Ⅱ 副 nearly; almost: 敌人伤亡～尽。*The enemy were practically wiped out.*

待 动 ❶ treat; deal with: ～人诚恳 *treat people sincerely; be sincere with people* / 他们～我如家人。*They treated me as one of the family.* ❷ entertain: ～客 *entertain a guest* ❸ wait for; await: ～机 *await an opportunity; bide one's time* / 尚～解决的问题 *a problem awaiting solution; an outstanding issue* ❹ need: 自不待言 ❺ going to; about to: 我正～出门，有人来了。*I was about to go out when someone came.*

【待到】by the time; when: ～来年冰雪消融时，我们再相会。*Let's meet again when the thaw comes in.*

【待岗】be on a waiting post; unemployed and waiting for a new post

【待价而沽】wait to sell at a good price; wait for the highest bid

【待考】need checking; remain to be verified: 此说是否正确～。*Whether or not this is true remains to be verified.*

【待命】(又作'待令') await orders: ～出发 *await orders to set off* / 原地～ *stay where one is, pending orders; stand by*

【待聘人员】the members waiting for engagement

【待人处世】the way one treats people and conducts oneself in society

【待人接物】the way one gets along with people

【待续】to be continued

【待业】job-waiting; unemployed: ～青年 *job-waiting youth* / ～人员 *job-waiting people; the unemployed* ◇ ～保险 unemployment insurance; insurance for awaiting occupation

【待遇】❶ treatment; reception: 冷淡的～ *cold reception; cold shoulder* / 受到良好～ *have received good treatment* / 政治～ *political treatment* ❷ remuneration; pay; wages; salary: 优厚～ *excellent pay and conditions* / 这家公司～很高。*This company pays very high salaries.*

【待字闺中】(of a girl) staying in the boudoir waiting to be betrothed—not yet betrothed

贷 Ⅰ 名 loan: 农贷 Ⅱ 动 ❶ borrow or lend: 银

行～给工厂大量款项。*The bank granted a large loan to the factory.* ❷ shift (responsibility); shirk: 责无旁贷 ❸ pardon; forgive: 严惩不贷

【贷方】bookkeeping credit side; credit

【贷款】❶ provide (or grant) a loan; extend credit to; make an advance to: 银行给他们贷了款。*The bank granted a loan to them.* / 向银行～ *ask for a bank loan* ❷ loan; credit: 无息～ *interestfree loans* / 未偿～ *outstanding loans* / ～对象 *prospective borrower* / ～计划 *borrowing plan* / ～利率 *interest rate on a loan* / ～期限 *terms of a loan* / ～条件 *conditions for a loan* / ～账户 *a loan account* ◇ ～规模 volume of credit; ～结构 loan mix; ～凭单 credit memo; ～人 accommodator; ～协议 loan agreement; ～业务 lending propramme; ～种类 types of loans

怠 形 idle; remiss; slack: 懈怠

【怠惰】idle; lazy; indolent

【怠工】slow down; go slow

【怠慢】❶ cold-shoulder; slight: 不要～了客人。*See that none of the guests are neglected.* ❷〈套〉(used by the host at the end of a reception, etc.): ～了! *I'm afraid I have been a poor host.*

袋 Ⅰ 名 bag; sack; pocket; pouch: 旅行袋 / 工具袋 / 口袋 Ⅱ 量 一～面粉 *a sack of flour* / 一～烟的功夫 *time needed to smoke a pipe*

【袋泡茶】teabag

【袋传送器】pocket conveyor

【袋兽】marsupial

【袋鼠】kangaroo

【袋装】in bags: ～奶粉 *milk powder in bags*; ～糖 bagged sugar

【袋子】sack; bag

逮 动 ❶〈书〉reach: 力有未～ *beyond one's reach (or power)* ❷ arrest ——另见 dǎi

【逮捕】arrest; take into custody: ～法办 *arrest and deal with according to law; bring to justice* / 你被～了。*You are under arrest.*

【逮捕证】arrest warrant

戴 动 ❶ put on; wear: ～上手套 *put on one's gloves* / ～眼镜 *wear glasses* ❷ respect; honour: 爱戴

【戴高帽子】❶ flatter; lay it on thick: 爱～ *be fond of flattery* / 他爱给有钱有势的人～。*He is always ready to flatter rich and influential people.* ❷ wear a tall paper hat (as a mark of shame); wear a dunce's cap

【戴绿帽】(又作'戴绿头巾') be a cuckold

【戴帽子】be branded as; be labelled

【戴胜】[动] hoopoe

【戴罪立功】atone for one's crimes by doing good deeds; redeem oneself by good service

黛 名 a black pigment used by women in ancient times to paint their eyebrows

【黛绿】〈书〉dark green

dān

丹 Ⅰ 形 red: ～枫 *a flaming maple* Ⅱ 名 [中] pellet or powder

【丹顶鹤】red-crested crane; red-crowned crane

【丹毒】[医] erysipelas

【丹方】同〖单方〗

【丹凤眼】slanting eyes: 一双～,两道柳叶眉 *with slanting eyes and arched brows*

【丹桂】[植] orange osmanthus

【丹麦】Denmark ◇ ～人 Dane; ～语 Danish (language)

【丹皮】[中] the root bark of the tree peony

【丹青】〈文〉red and green colours—painting: ～妙笔 *superb artistry (in painting); the superb touch of a great painter; the touch of a master*

【丹田】the pubic region: ～之气 *deep breath controlled by the diaphragm*

【丹心】a loyal heart; loyalty

单 Ⅰ 形 ❶ one; single: ～扇门 *a single-leaf door* ❷ odd: ～只袜子 *an odd sock* ❸ single; solitary ❹ simple: 简单 ❺ thin; weak: 单薄 ❻ unlined (clothing): 单衣 Ⅱ 副 only; alone: 我～看见小李。*I only saw Xiao Li.* / ～她一个人就拿了三块金牌。*She alone won 3 gold medals.* / 把这几件东西～放在一个地方。*Keep these things in a separate place.* Ⅲ 名 ❶ sheet: 床单 ❷ bill; list: 名单 / 菜单

【单摆】[物] simple pendulum

【单板】veneer

【单帮】a travelling trader working on his own: 跑～ *travel around trading on one's own*

【单倍体】[生] monoploid; haploid

【单本位制】[经] monometallic standard; monometallism

【单边】[经] unilateral: ～进(出)口 *unilateral import (export)* ◇ ～贸易 unilateral trade

【单薄】❶ (of clothing) thin: 穿得～ *be thinly clad* ❷ thin and weak; frail: 身体～ *have a poor physique* ❸ insubstantial; flimsy; thin: 论据～ *a feeble argument*

【单产】per unit area yield

【单车】〈方〉bicycle

【单程】one way: ～车票 *one-way (or single) ticket* ◇ ～清棉机 [纺] single process scutcher

【单纯】❶ simple; pure: 思想～ *pure in mind; unsophisticated* / 问题决不像我们当初想象的那么～。*The problem is by no means as simple as we first thought.* ❷ alone; purely; merely: 不～追求数量 *not concentrate on quantity alone* ◇ ～词 [语] single-morpheme word

【单词】❶ individual word; word ❷ 同〖单纯词〗

【单打】[体] singles: 男子(女子)～ *men's (women's) singles* / 少年男子(女子)～ *boys' (girls') singles* / 她只参加～。*She's only playing in the singles.*

【单打一】❶ concentrate on one thing only ❷ have a one-track mind

【单单】only；alone：别人都来了，～他没来。*He's the only one absent. Everybody else is here.* or *Everybody has come except him.*

【单刀】❶ short-hilted broadsword ❷ single-broadsword event

【单刀直入】come straight to the point；speak out without beating about the bush：我～地问他到底要干什么。*I asked him point-blank what he wanted to do.* / 他说话喜欢～，不绕弯子。*He likes to come straight to the point without beating about the bush.*

【单调】monotonous；dull；drab：声音～ *in a monotonous tone* / 色彩～ *dull colouring* / 昨天的节目比较～。*Yesterday's programme was rather dull.*

【单独】alone；by oneself；on one's own；single-handed；independent：采取～行动 *take independent action* / 她～住一间屋子。*She has a room to herself.* / 我要和他～谈一谈。*I want to have a talk with him alone.* ◇ ～包装 individually wrapped；～法人 corporation sole

【单发】［军］single shot：～射击 *single shot*

【单方】folk prescription；home remedy ◇ ～行为 unilateral transaction, unilateral juristic act

【单方面】one-sided；unilateral：～撕毁协定 *unilaterally tear up an agreement*

【单飞】［航空］solo flight

【单峰驼】one-humped camel；dromedary；Arabian camel

【单幅】［纺］single width

【单干】❶ work on one's own；go it alone；work by oneself；do sth. single-handed ❷ individual farming：～户 *a peasant family still farming on its own after agricultural cooperation*

【单杠】［体］❶ horizontal bar ❷ horizontal bar gymnastics

【单个儿】❶ individually；alone：最好集体去，不要～去。*We'd better go in a group, not individually.* ❷ an odd one：这副手套只剩下～了。*There's only an odd glove left.* / ～棋子不卖。*Chessmen aren't sold by the piece.*

【单轨】single track

【单号】odd numbers (of tickets, seats, etc.)

【单簧管】［音］clarinet

【单级火箭】single-stage rocket

【单季稻】single cropping of rice

【单价】❶［经］unit price ❷［化］［生］univalent

【单间儿】separate room (in a hotel, restaurant, etc.)

【单键】［化］single bond

【单脚跳】［体］hop

【单晶硅】［电子］monocrystalline silicon

【单晶体】［物］monocrystal

【单句】［语］simple sentence

【单据】documents attesting to the giving or receiving of money, goods, etc., such as receipts, bills, vouchers and invoices：货运～ *shipping documents*

【单卡】single cassette deck

【单孔目】［动］Monotremata：～动物 *monotreme*

【单口相声】one-man comic talk

【单跨】［建］single span

【单利】［经］simple interest

【单恋】unrequited love

【单轮射箭】［体］single round archery：女子三十米～ *women's 30-metre single round archery event*

【单宁酸】［化］tannic acid

【单片处理机】single-chip processor

【单片眼镜】monocle

【单枪匹马】（又作'单人独马'）single-handed；all by oneself；alone

【单亲】single parent ◇ ～家庭 one-parent family；～领养 solo adoption

【单人床】single bed

【单人房】single-bed room

【单人舞】solo dance：跳～ *dance a solo*

【单日】odd-numbered days (of the month)

【单弱】thin and weak；frail

【单色】monochromatic：～电视 *monochrome television* ◇ ～光［物］monochromatic light；～画 monochrome (painting)；～胶印机 single-colour offset press

【单身】❶ unmarried；single ❷ not be with one's family；live alone：～在外 *live alone away from home* ◇ ～贵族 single aristocrat；～汉 unmarried man；bachelor；bachelor quarters；～母亲 bachelor mother；～宿舍 quarters for unmarried men or women

【单生花】［植］solitary flower

【单式】bookkeeping single entry

【单数】❶ odd number ❷〈语〉singular number

【单丝】［纺］monofilament

【单丝不成线，孤树不成林】one strand of silk doesn't make a thread；one tree doesn't make a forest

【单瘫】［医］monoplegia

【单糖】［化］monose；monosaccharide

【单体】［化］monomer ◇ ～计算机 all-in-one computer

【单条】a vertically-hung scroll of painting or calligraphy (not in a set)；wall scroll

【单位】❶ unit (as a standard of measurement)：长度～ *a unit of length* / 货币～ *monetary unit* / ～面积产量 *yield per unit area* / 以秒为～计算时间 *measure time by the second* ❷ unit (as an organization, department, division, section, etc.)：行政～ *administrative unit* / 生产～ *production unit* / 基层～ *basic (or grass-roots) unit* ◇ ～价值 unit profit；～利润 unit profit；～圆［数］unit circle；～制 system of unit

【单细胞】unicellular ◇ ～动物 unicellular animal

【单弦儿】danxianr, story-telling to musical accompaniment

【单线】❶ single line ❷ one-way (contact)；single-line (link)：做地下工作时，他和我～联系。*When we were doing underground work, he was my on-*

ly contact. ❸［交通］single track ◇ ～铁路 single-track railway；single-track line
【单相思】unrequited love
【单向】one-way；unidirectional：～电路 *one-way circuit* / ～交通 *one-way traffic*
【单项】［体］individual event：～比赛 *individual competition*
【单相】single-phase；monophase：～电动机 *single-phase motor* / ～合金 *single-phase alloy*
【单斜】［地质］monocline：～层 *monoclinal stratum*
【单行本】❶ separate edition ❷ offprint
【单行法规】special (or separate) regulations
【单行条例】specific regulations
【单行线】one-way road
【单性花】［植］unisexual flower
【单性生殖】［生］parthenogenesis；parthenogenetic propagation (or reproduction)
【单眼】［动］simple eye
【单眼皮】single-edged eyelid
【单叶】［植］simple leaf
【单一】single；unitary：管理方式陈旧～。*The methods of management are outdated and simplistic*. ◇ ～标志商店 only shop；～汇率 unified foreign exchange rate；～货币 single currency；～经济 single-product economy；～市场 single market；～税 single tax ；～种植 monoculture；one-crop farming
【单衣】unlined garment
【单翼机】monoplane
【单音词】［语］monosyllabic word；monosyllable
【单元】unit：运算～ *arithmetic unit* / 三号楼丙～四号 *No. 4，Entrance C，Building 3* ◇ ～楼 apartment building；block of flats
【单渣操作】［冶］single-slag practice
【单子】❶ list；bill；form：开个～ *make out a list* / 填写～ *fill in a form* ❷ bed sheet：床～ *bed sheet*
【单子叶植物】monocotyledon
【单字】❶ individual character (of the Chinese language) ❷ separate word (of a foreign language)
【单座飞机】single-seater (aeroplane)

担 动 ❶ carry on a shoulder pole：～水 *carry water (with a shoulder pole and buckets)* ❷ take on；undertake：咱们把任务～起来。*Let's take on the job*. / 不怕～风险 *be ready to face any danger；not be afraid of running risks* ——另见 dàn
【担保】assure；guarantee；vouch for：这事交给她办，～错不了。*I assure you that she can be trusted to do the work well*. or *I'll vouch for her as the best person for the job*. / 出口信贷～ *export credit guarantees* ◇ ～承兑 acceptance on security；～金 bail；bond；～期 period of guarantee；～企业 guarantor enterprise；～人 guarantor；guarantee；～书 deed of security；～信贷 secured credit
【担不起】❶ be unable to shoulder (the responsibility)；be unequal to (a task)：我～如此重任。*I am unequal to such a responsible task*. ❷〈谦〉I really don't deserve this；you flatter me：对我这样夸奖，我可～。*I really don't deserve such praise*.
【担不是】take the blame：出了问题，由我一个人～。*If anything goes wrong，I'll take the blame*.
【担待】〈口〉❶ be magnanimous；be tolerant ❷ bear the responsibility：你放心吧，一切由我～。*Have no fear. I'll bear all the responsibility*.
【担当】take on；undertake；assume：～重任 *take on heavy responsibilities* / 无论什么工作，他都敢于～。*He's willing to take on any kind of job*.
【担负】bear；shoulder；take on；be charged with：～责任 *shoulder responsibility* / ～费用 *bear an expense* / ～领导工作 *hold a leading post*
【担搁】同〖耽搁〗
【担架】stretcher；litter：～队 *stretcher-team* / ～员 *stretcher-bearer*
【担惊受怕】feel alarmed；be in a state of anxiety
【担任】assume the office of；hold the post of：他～外交部长。*He assumed office as Foreign Minister*. / 她～什么职务？*What office does she hold?*
【担心】worry；feel anxious：我真～她的健康。*I do worry about her health*. / 快给老大娘写信，免得她～。*Write to the old lady at once so as to set her mind at rest*.
【担忧】worry；be anxious：不要为我的身体～。*Don't worry about my health*.

耽 动 ❶ delay：耽误 ❷〈书〉abandon oneself to；indulge in：～乐 *indulge in pleasure*
【耽搁】❶ stop over；stay：我去天津途中可能在济南～一下。*I may have a stopover at Jinan on my way to Tianjin*. / 我不打算在这里～多久。*I won't be here for long*. ❷ delay：毫不～ *without delay* / 不得～ *admit of no delay* / 一分钟也不能～。*Not a single minute is to be lost*.
【耽误】delay；hold up：～了整个工程 *hold up (or delay) the whole project* / ～功夫 *waste time* / 把～的时间夺回来 *make up for lost time*

殚 动〈书〉use up；exhaust：～心 *devote one's entire mind*
【殚精竭虑】(又作'殚思极虑') tax one's ingenuity；rack (or cudgel) one's brains

箪 名〈古〉a bamboo utensil for holding cooked rice
【箪食壶浆】(welcome an army with) food and drink

dǎn

胆 名 ❶ gallbladder ❷ courage；guts；bravery：壮胆 ❸ a bladder-like inner container：热水瓶～ *the glass liner of a vacuum flask*

【胆大】bold；audacious：～包天 *audacious in the extreme* / ～妄为 *bold and reckless*；*daredevil* / ～心细 *bold but cautious*
【胆矾】[化] chalcanthite；blue vitriol
【胆敢】dare；have the audacity to
【胆固醇】biochem cholesterol
【胆管】[生理] bile duct ◇ ～炎 cholangitis；～造影 cholangiography
【胆寒】be terrified；be struck with terror
【胆红素】[生化] bilirubin
【胆碱】[生化] choline
【胆量】courage；guts；pluck；spunk：很有～ *have plenty of guts* (*or spunk*)
【胆略】courage and resourcefulness：～过人 *have unusual courage and resourcefulness*
【胆囊】[生理] gallbladder ◇ ～炎 cholecystitis
【胆怯】timid；cowardly：他不喜欢自己的工作，可又～，不敢另找一个。*He does not like his job, but is too timid to try to find another.*
【胆石】[医] cholelith；gallstone ◇ ～病 cholelithiasis
【胆识】courage and insight
【胆酸】[生化] cholic acid
【胆小】timid；cowardly：这孩子～，怕黑。*The timid child was afraid of the dark.* ◇ ～鬼 coward
【胆小如鼠】as timid as a mouse；chicken-hearted：表面上气壮如牛，实际上～ *outwardly fierce as a bull, but inwardly timid as a mouse*
【胆战心惊】tremble with fear；be terrorstricken：使人～ *strike terror into sb.*；*be terrifying*
【胆汁】[生理] bile
【胆子】courage；guts；nerve：放开～ *pluck up courage*；*stop being afraid* / 好大的～！ *What a nerve!* / 你大着～去，不要怕。*Go right ahead and don't be afraid.*

掸 动 brush lightly；whisk：～掉身上的雪花 *brush* (*or whisk*) *the snow off one's coat* / ～～衣服 *brush the dust off one's clothes* / 墙壁和天花板都～得很干净。*The walls and the ceiling were all dusted clean.*
【掸子】duster (usu. made of chicken feathers or strips of cloth)：鸡毛～ *feather duster*

dàn

石 量 a unit of dry measure for grain (= 1 hectolitre) ——另见 shí

旦 名 ❶〈书〉dawn；daybreak：通宵达旦 ❷ day：元旦 ❸ female role ❹ [纺] denier
【旦夕】〈书〉this morning or evening—in a short while
【旦夕之间】between morning and evening —in a day's time；overnight

但 Ⅰ 连 but；yet；still；nevertheless：这孩子用功～不怎么聪明。*He's a hardworking but not very intelligent boy.* / 他早已年过六十，～毫不见老。*He's well over sixty, but he doesn't look at all old.* Ⅱ 副 only；merely：明哲保身，～求无过 *be worldly-wise and play safe and seek only to avoid blame*
【但凡】in every case；without exception；as long as：～过路的人，没有一个不停下来欣赏这儿的风景的。*Whoever passes here stops to admire the scenery.*
【但是】but；yet；still；nevertheless：一个宏大～不切实际的计划 *a grandiose but impracticable plan* / 他虽然很能干，～这个问题太难，他也不好解决。*He's an able man, but the problem is too hard for him.*
【但书】[法] proviso
【但愿】if only；I wish：～天气赶快放晴。*If only it would clear up soon!*

担 Ⅰ 量 ❶ a unit of weight (= 50 kilograms) ❷ shoulder-pole load：一～水 *two buckets of water* (*carried on a shoulder pole*) Ⅱ 名 a carrying (or shoulder) pole and the loads on it；load；burden：货郎担 ——另见 dān
【担担面】〈方〉street vendor's noodles (served with sauce only)
【担子】❶ a carrying (or shoulder) pole and the loads on it；load；burden ❷ task：我们不怕～重，一定要把事情办好。*We're not afraid of the heavy task and are determined to do a good job.*

诞 Ⅰ 名 ❶ birth：诞辰 ❷ birthday：华～ *your birthday* Ⅱ 形 absurd；fantastic：荒诞
【诞辰】〈书〉birthday
【诞生】be born；come into being；emerge：新中国的～ *the birth of New China* ◇ ～地 birthplace

淡 形 ❶ thin；light：～酒 *light wine* / 云～风轻。*The clouds are pale and a light breeze is blowing.* ❷ bland；tasteless；weak；without enough salt：～茶 *weak tea* / ～酒 *weak wine* / 这个汤太～。*There's not enough salt in this soup.* or *This soup is too bland for me.* ❸ (of colour) light；pale：～黄 *light yellow* / ～紫 *pale purple*；*lilac* ❹ indifferent；cool：淡然 ❺ slack；dull：淡季 ❻〈方〉meaningless；trivial：扯淡
【淡泊】〈书〉not seek fame and wealth：他一生～，生活简朴。*All through the years he led a simple life without worldly desires.*
【淡泊明志】show high ideals by simple living
【淡薄】❶ thin；light：朝雾渐渐地～了。*The morning mist gradually thinned.* ❷ tasteless；weak：酒味～。*The wine tastes weak.* ❸ become indifferent；flag：他对象棋的兴趣逐渐～了。*His interest in chess has begun to flag.* ❹ faint；dim；hazy：时间隔得太久，印象也就～了。*With the passage of time, these impressions became dim.*
【淡菜】同〖贻贝〗
【淡出】fade out
【淡淡】❶ thin；light；pale：～的浮云 *thin clouds*

floating in the sky / ～的香水味 *a faint smell of perfume* ❷ indifferent; cool: ～地答应了一声 *answer drily* ❸〈文〉(of ripples) undulating gently

【淡化】desalinate: 海水～ *desalination of sea water*

【淡积云】[气] cumulus humilis

【淡季】slack (or dull, off) season: 争取做到蔬菜～不淡,旺季不烂 *strive for an ample supply of vegetables in the off seasons and avoid waste in the peak periods*

【淡漠】❶ indifferent; apathetic; nonchalant ❷ faint; dim; hazy: 这件事在我脑子里已很～了。*The event has left only faint memories in my mind.*

【淡墨】light ink

【淡青】light greenish blue

【淡然】indifferent; cool: ～一笑 *smile drily* / ～地回答 *answer drily* (*or coolly*)

【淡然处之】treat with indifference; regard coolly

【淡入】fade in

【淡市】bear market

【淡水】fresh water: ～养鱼 *freshwater fish-farming* ◇ ～湖 freshwater lake; ～鱼 freshwater fish; ～资源 fresh-water clause

【淡忘】fade from one's memory: 这件事我早已～。*It has long since faded from my memory.*

【淡味烟】mild-strength tobacco

【淡雅】simple but elegant; quietly elegant; unadorned and in good taste: 衣着～ *be tastefully dressed in a simple style*; *be dressed with sober refinement*

【淡竹】[植] henon bamboo (phyllostachys nigra var. henonis)

【淡妆】be lightly made up

啖 动〈书〉❶ eat ❷ feed ❸ entice; lure

蛋 名 ❶ egg ❷ an egg-shaped thing: 泥～儿 *mud ball*

【蛋白】❶ egg white; albumen ❷ protein ◇ ～疗法 protein therapy

【蛋白石】opal

【蛋白质】protein: ～塑料 *protein plastics* ◇ ～工程 protein engineering

【蛋粉】powdered eggs; egg powder

【蛋糕】cake

【蛋羹】egg custard

【蛋黄】yolk

【蛋鸡】laying hen; layer

【蛋壳】eggshell

【蛋品】egg products

【蛋青】pale blue

【蛋清】〈口〉egg white

【蛋用鸡】layer (a hen)

【蛋子】an egg-shaped thing

弹 名 ❶ ball; pellet: 泥～儿 *mud ball* ❷ bullet; bomb: 燃烧弹 ——另见 tán

【弹道】trajectory: 内(外)～ *interior* (*exterior*) *ballistics* ◇ ～弧线 ballistic curve; ～火箭 ballistic rocket; ～式导弹 ballistic missile; ～学 ballistics

【弹弓】catapult; slingshot

【弹痕】bullet or shell hole; shot mark: ～累累 *be riddled with bullets*

【弹夹】(cartridge) clip; charger

【弹尽粮绝】run out of ammunition and provisions

【弹壳】shell case; cartridge case

【弹坑】(shell) crater

【弹幕】arrage

【弹盘】cartridge drum; magazine

【弹片】shell fragment (or splinter); shrapnel

【弹膛】chamber (of a gun)

【弹头】bullet; projectile nose; warhead

【弹丸】❶ pellet; shot; bullet ❷〈文〉(of a place) very small; tiny: ～小邑 *a very small town*

【弹丸之地】a tiny little place

【弹匣】[军] magazine

【弹药】ammunition ◇ ～库 ammunition depot (or storehouse); ～手 ammunition man (or bearer); ～所 ammunition supply (or refilling) point; ～箱 ammunition chest; cartridge box

【弹着】[军] impact: ～点 *point of impact*; *hitting point* / ～角 *angle of impact* / ～区 *impact* (*or objective*) *area*

【弹子】❶ a pellet shot from a slingshot ❷ marble: 打～ *play marbles* ❸〈方〉billiards: ～房 *billiard room*

氮 名 [化] nitrogen (N)

【氮肥】nitrogenous fertilizer

dāng

当 Ⅰ 动 ❶ be equal to: 门当户对 ❷ ought to; should; must: 能省的就省,～用的还是得用。*Save what you can, but use what you must.* ❸ work as; serve as; be: 选他～组长 *elect him group leader* / 我长大要～飞行员。*I want to be a pilot when I grow up.* ❹ bear; accept; deserve: 敢做敢～ *dare to act and to take the consequences* / 我可～不起这样的夸奖。*I just don't deserve such praise.* ❺ direct; manage; be in charge of: 当家 ❻ in sb.'s presence; to sb.'s face: ～着大家谈一谈。*Speak out in the presence of everyone.* Ⅱ 介 just at (a time or place) Ⅲ 象 the sound of a gong or a bell: ～～的钟声 *the tolling of a bell* ——另见 dàng

【当班】be on a shift: 他病了,我得替他去～。*He's ill, so I've got to work his shift.*

【当兵】be a soldier; serve in the army

【当场】on the spot; then and there: ～拒绝他们的要求 *turn down their request on the spot* / ～抓住 *catch red-handed* (*or in the act*)

【当场出彩】❶ make a spectacle of oneself ❷ give the show away on the spot

【当初】originally; at the outset; in the first place;

at that time：～打算在这儿盖一座大楼。*It was originally planned to put up a big building here.* / 早知今日，何必～？*If I had known it would come to this, I would have acted differently.*

【当代】the present age; the contemporary era：毛泽东是～最伟大的人物之一。*Mao Zedong was one of the greatest men of our time.* / ～著名作家 *a famous contemporary writer* ◇ ～文化 contemporary culture；～意识 modernism

【当道】❶ blocking the way：别在～站着。*Don't stand in the way.* ❷〈贬〉be in power; hold sway：坏人～，好人受害。*When evildoers are in power, good people suffer.*

【当地】at the place in question; in the locality; local：～土特产 *special local products* / ～人民 *local people; local inhabitants* / ～时间 *local time* ◇ ～法律豁免 exemption from local law；～公司 domestic corporation

【当断不断】fail to make a decision when one should; hesitate when decision is needed

【当归】［中］Chinese angelica

【当机立断】decide quickly; make a prompt decision：情况紧急，需要我们～！*In this crisis we've got to make a quick decision.*

【当即】at once; right away：～表示同意 *give one's consent right away*

【当家】manage (household) affairs：我妻子很会～。*My wife is a very good housekeeper.*

【当家作主】be master in one's own house; be the master of one's own affairs (or destiny)：人民～。*The people are the masters of their own country.*

【当街】❶ facing the street ❷〈方〉in the street

【当今】❶ now; at present; nowadays：～之世 *in the world of today; at the present time* ❷ old the emperor on the throne; the reigning emperor

【当局】the authorities：政府(学校)～ *the government (school) authorities*

【当局者迷，旁观者清】The spectators see the chess game better than the players; The onlooker sees most of the game.

【当空】high above in the sky：明月～。*A bright moon is shining in the sky.*

【当口儿】〈口〉this or that very moment：就在这～ *at the very moment; just at that time*

【当啷】clank; clang

【当量】［化］equivalent (weight)：电化～ *electrochemical equivalent* / 克～ *gram equivalent* / ～比例定律 *the law of equivalent proportions* / ～浓度 *equivalent concentration*

【当令】in season：现在是伏天，西瓜正～。*These are the dog days; watermelons are just in season.*

【当面】to sb.'s face; in sb.'s presence：～撒谎 *tell a barefaced lie* / ～弄清楚 *straighten things out face to face* / 信是我～交给主任的。*I handed the letter to the director personally.*

【当面锣对面鼓】direct confrontation and face-to-face argument

【当面说好话，背后下毒手】say nice things to sb.'s face, then stab him in the back

【当年】❶ in those years (or days)：～家里穷，无力抚养孩子。*In those years we were too poor to bring up our children properly.* ❷ the prime of life：他正在～。*He is in his prime.* ——另见 dàngnián

【当前】❶ before one; facing one：一事～，应该先想到国家的利益。*Whenever something crops up, one should first think of the interests of the state.* ❷ present; current：～的中心任务 *the central task at present* / ～世界的主要倾向 *the main trend in the world today* / ～利益 *immediate interests* / ～的国际形势 *the current (or present) international situation* ◇ ～用户 active user

【当权】be in power; hold power：～派 *person in power; people in authority*

【当然】❶ without doubt; certainly; of course; to be sure：这样做～最好。*Of course this is the best way to do it.* / 借你的笔用一下可以吗？—～可以。*May I borrow your pen? —Certainly! (or Sure!)* ❷ natural：～同盟军 *natural ally* / 你取得成功是～的。*It is quite natural that you should succeed.* ❸ ex officio：～成员 *an ex officio member (of a committee, etc.)* / ～继承人 *heir apparent*

【当仁不让】not decline to shoulder a responsibility; not leave to others what one ought to do oneself; not pass on to others what one is called upon to do：那件事你可～啊！*That's what you should do by rights.*

【当日交易人】day trade

【当时】then; at that time：～我并不知道。*I didn't know then.* ——另见 dàngshí

【当事】❶ be in charge; be in control：坏人～，好人倒霉。*When bad people are in control, good people suffer.* ❷ concerned; involved ❸ the authorities or the parties concerned

【当事国】the state directly involved; the country concerned

【当事人】❶［法］party (to a lawsuit); litigant ❷ person (or party) concerned; interested parties：经济合同～ *parties to an economic contract*

【当头】❶ right overhead; right on sb.'s head; head on：烈日～照。*The hot sun is shining right overhead.* / 给他～一瓢冷水 *pour cold water on him* ❷ facing (or confronting) one; imminent：那时候正是国难～，爱国青年都纷纷到抗敌前线去。*The country was in imminent danger, and large numbers of patriotic young people left for the front to fight the enemy.*

【当头棒喝】a blow and a shout—a sharp (or severe) warning

【当头炮】direct criticism

【当头一棒】(又作'当头棒') a head-on blow

【当务之急】the most pressing matter of the moment; a top priority task; urgent matter

【当下】instantly; immediately; at once：我一听这话，～就警惕起来了。*Hearing this, I was instantly on the alert.*

【当下手】work as sb.'s subordinate or assistant; serve under sb.：他这个人很自负，不愿给人家～。*As he is arrogant and opinionated, he does not want to take orders from anybody.*

【当先】in the van; in the front ranks; at the head：奋勇～ *fight bravely in the van*

【当心】take care; be careful; look out：～别把试管打碎了。*Take care not to break the test tube.* / ～路滑。*Watch your step. The road is slippery.*

【当选】be elected：他～为全国人大代表。*He was elected a deputy to the National People's Congress.*

【当一天和尚撞一天钟】同〖做一天和尚撞一天钟〗

【当政】be in power; be in office

【当之无愧】fully deserve (a title, an honour, etc.); be worthy of

【当中】❶ in the middle; in the centre：河～水流最急。*The current is swiftest in the middle of the river.* / 坐在主席台～ *be seated in the centre of the rostrum* ❷ among

【当众】in the presence of all; in public：～认错 *acknowledge one's mistakes in public*

【当众出丑】make an exhibition of oneself

裆 名 ❶ crotch (of trousers) ❷［生理］crotch

dǎng

挡 Ⅰ 动 ❶ keep off; ward off; block：～雨 *keep off the rain; shelter one from the rain* / ～风 *shelter sth. from (or keep out) the wind* ❷ block; get in the way of：～路 *be (or get) in the way* / ～光 *be (or get) in the light* Ⅱ 名 ❶ fender; blind：炉～儿 *(fire) fender; fire screen* / 窗～子 *window blind (or shade)* ❷ gear (of a car)：前进(倒)～ *forward (reverse) gear* / 高速(低速)～ *top (bottom) gear*

【挡车】be in charge of looms and check the quality and quantity of the products

【挡风玻璃】windshield; wind screen

【挡驾】〈婉〉turn away a visitor with some excuse; decline to receive a guest

【挡箭牌】❶ shield ❷ excuse; pretext

【挡泥板】mudguard (of a car); fender

【挡土墙】［建］retaining wall

党 名 ❶ political party; party ❷ the Party (the Communist Party of China)：～的生活 *Party life* ❸ clique; faction; gang：死党 ❹〈书〉be partial to; take sides with：党同伐异 ❺〈书〉kinsfolk; relatives：父党

【党八股】stereotyped Party writing; Party jargon

【党报】❶ party newspaper (or organ) ❷ the organ of the Chinese Communist Party; the Party organ

【党代表】Party representative (a political worker of the Chinese Communist Party in the Red Army before 1929)：～制 *the system of Party representatives*

【党费】party membership dues

【党风】a party's work style; party members' conduct

【党纲】party programme

【党棍】a dirty politician who uses his party membership as a means in promoting self-interest

【党籍】party membership：开除～ *expel from the party*

【党纪】party discipline ◇ ～国法 Party discipline and the law of the land

【党课】Party class; Party lecture：听(讲)～ *attend (give) a Party lecture*

【党魁】〈贬〉party chieftain (or chief, boss)

【党龄】party standing：多年～的老党员 *a Communist Party member of many years' standing*

【党内】within (or inside) the party; inner-party：～斗争 *inner-party struggle* / ～民主 *democracy within the Party; inner-Party democracy*

【党派】political parties and groups; party groupings：～关系 party affiliation

【党旗】party flag

【党人】❶ members of a political party ❷〈书〉partisans

【党同伐异】defend those who belong to one's own faction and attack those who don't; be narrowly partisan

【党徒】〈贬〉❶ member of a clique or a reactionary political party ❷ henchman

【党团】❶ political parties and other organizations ❷ the Chinese Communist Party and the Chinese Communist Youth League; the Party and the League：～员 *Party and League members* ❸ parliamentary group of a political party

【党外】outside the party：～人士 *non-Party personages*

【党委】Party committee：～制 *the Party committee system (a system for ensuring collective leadership in the Party)*

【党务】party work; party affairs

【党小组】Party group (a small group under a branch committee in the Party)

【党校】Party school

【党性】Party spirit; Party character：～不纯的表现 *a sign of impurity in Party spirit*

【党羽】〈贬〉members of a clique; adherents; henchmen

【党员】party member：～大会 *general membership meeting of a party organization; meeting of all party members*

【党章】party constitution

【党证】party card

【党政分开】separation of the functions of the Pary and the government (an important element of China's political reform)

【党支部】Party branch：～书记 *Party branch secretary*

【党中央】the Party Central Committee; the central leading body of the Party

【党总支】general Party branch
【党组】leading Party members' group (in a state organ, of ministerial level)

dàng

当 Ⅰ形 proper; right; appropriate: 以上意见～否,请批示。*We are awaiting your comment on the proposals set forth above.* Ⅱ动 ❶ match; equal to: 他一个人能～两个人用。*He can do the work of two persons put together.* ❷ treat as; regard as; take for: 不要把支流～主流。*Don't take minor aspects for major ones.* ❸ think: 我～你不知道。*I thought you didn't know.* ❹ pawn: ～衣服 *pawn one's clothes; put one's clothes in pawn* Ⅲ名 sth. pawned; pawn; pledge: 赎当 Ⅳ代 that very (day, etc.)——另见 dāng
【当成】regard as; treat as; take for
【当年】the same year; that very year ——另见 dāngnián
【当票】pawn ticket
【当铺】pawnshop: ～老板 *pawnbroker*
【当日】the same day; that very day: ～有效 *good for the date of issue only*
【当时】right away; at once; immediately: 他一接到电报,～就赶回去了。*He hurried back the moment he received the telegram.* / 她一听到这消息～就晕倒了。*She fainted on hearing the news.* ——另见 dāngshí
【当天】the same day; that very day: 你可以～来回。*You can go and come back on the same day.* / ～的事～做完。*Today's work must be done today.*
【当真】❶ take seriously: 我只是开个玩笑,何必～呢? *I was only joking. Why take it seriously?* ❷ (really) true: 这话～? *Is it really true?* ❸ really; sure enough: 他说要来,～来了。*He said he would come and, sure enough, he did.*
【当做】treat as; regard as; look upon as: 农奴主把农奴～会说话的牲口。*Serf owners regarded their serfs as animals that could talk.*

宕 动〈书〉delay: 延宕

荡 Ⅰ动 ❶ swing; sway; wave: ～秋千 *play on a swing* / ～桨 *pull on the oars* ❷ loaf about: 游荡 ❸ rinse ❹ clear away; sweep off: 扫荡 Ⅱ形 loose in morals: 淫荡 Ⅲ名 a shallow lake; marsh: 芦苇～ *a reed marsh*
【荡船】swingboat
【荡涤】cleanse; clean up; wash away
【荡妇】〈书〉❶ a loose woman ❷ prostitute
【荡平】wipe out; quell; stamp out
【荡气回肠】同〖回肠荡气〗
【荡然无存】all gone; nothing left: 大火之后,庙里过去那些雄伟建筑～。*After the fire, nothing remained of the once magnificent temple buildings.*
【荡漾】ripple; undulate: 湖水～。*There were ripples on the lake.* / 歌声～。*The song rose and fell like waves.* / 金黄的小麦在微风中～。*The golden wheat rippled in the breeze.*

档 名 ❶ shelves (for files); pigeonholes: 归档 ❷ files; archives: 查档 ❸ crosspiece (of a table, etc.) ❹ grade: 这一～的羊毛可低价出售。*This grade of wool can be sold at a lower price.*
【档案】files; archives; record; dossier: ～管理员 *archivist* ◇ ～馆 archives; ～柜 filing cabinet
【档次】grade: 拉开职工收入的～ *widen the difference between the income brackets of workers and staff members* / ～较高的消费品 *high-grade (or better quality) consumer goods*

dāo

刀 Ⅰ名 ❶ knife; sword ❷ [机] cutting tool; tool ❸ sth. shaped like a knife: 冰～ *ice skates* Ⅱ量 one hundred sheets (of paper)
【刀把子】(又作'刀把儿') ❶ the handle of a knife ❷ (sword) hilt ❸ military power; power ❹ 〈方〉sth. that may be used against one; a handle
【刀背】the back of a knife blade
【刀笔】writing of indictments, appeals, etc.; pettifoggery: ～吏 *petty official who draws up indictments, etc.; pettifogger*
【刀兵】❶ weapons; arms ❷ fighting; war: 动～ *resort to arms; resort to force*
【刀叉】knife and fork
【刀豆】sword bean (the plant or the pods it bears)
【刀锋】the point or edge of a knife
【刀斧手】〈旧〉executioner; headsman
【刀耕火种】slash-and-burn cultivation: 那个偏僻山区,过去是～。*In those remote mountains people used to farm by the slash-and-burn method.*
【刀光剑影】the glint and flash of daggers and swords
【刀痕】a mark or scar left by a knife-cut
【刀架】[机] tool carrier; tool carriage
【刀具】[机] cutting tool; tool
【刀口】❶ the edge of a knife ❷ where a thing can be put to best use; the crucial point; the right spot: 把劲儿使在～上 *bring efforts to bear on the right spot* / 钱要花在～上。*Use your money where it's needed most.* ❸ cut; incision
【刀片】❶ razor blade ❷ [机] (tool) bit; blade
【刀枪】sword and spear; weapons
【刀枪不入】(of a human body) arms-proof
【刀枪入库,马放南山】put the weapons back in the arsenal and graze the war horses on the hillside—relax vigilance against war
【刀鞘】sheath; scabbard
【刀刃】❶ the edge of a knife ❷ where a thing can be put to best use; the crucial point
【刀山火海】a mountain of swords and a sea of flames—most dangerous places; most severe tri-

als：刀山敢上，火海敢闯 *dare to climb a mountain of swords or plunge into a sea of flames*；*be ready to undergo the most severe trials*

【刀伤】a wound inflicted with a knife or sword; gash or stab

【刀子嘴，豆腐心】〈口〉(have) a sharp tongue but a soft heart

叨 (构词成分)见下 ——另见 tāo

【叨叨】talk on and on; chatter away：别一个人～了，听听大家的意见吧。*Don't say the same thing over and over again. Listen to what other people have to say.*

【叨唠】〈口〉talk on and on; chatter away：他～了半天，人都不爱听。*He chattered for a long time and bored everybody.*

氘 名［化］deuterium (H^2 or D)

【氘核】［化］deuteron

dǎo

导 动 ❶ lead; guide：～淮入海 *channel the Huaihe River into the sea* ❷ transmit; conduct：导电 ❸ instruct; teach; give guidance to：教导

【导播】compile and broadcast (a program on radio or TV) ◇ ～控制室 production control room

【导弹】guided missile：反辐射～ *anti-radiation missile* / 反坦克～ *anti-tank missile* / 空中截击～ *air intercept missile* ◇ ～发射场 missile (launching) site; launching site; ～发射井 launching silo; ～发射器 missile launcher; ～发射台 (missile) launching pad; ～核潜艇 nuclear submarine armed with guided missiles; ～基地 missile base; ～驱逐舰 guided missile destroyer; ～巡洋舰 guided missile cruiser

【导电】transmit electric current; conduct electricity：～性 *electric conductivity*

【导风板】［航空］baffle

【导购】provide guidance for purchase：～小姐 *sales girl*; *shopping guide*

【导管】❶［机］conduit; pipe; duct：冷却～ *cooling duct* / 金属～ *metal conduit* ❷［生］vessel; duct

【导轨】［机］slideway; guide：刀架～ *tool guide* ◇ ～磨床［机］slideway grinder

【导航】navigation：无线电（雷达、天文）～ *radio (radar, celestial) navigation* ◇ ～台 guidance station; nondirection radio beacon (NDB)

【导火索】［军］(blasting) fuse

【导火线】❶ (blasting) fuse ❷ a small incident that touches off a big one：战争的～ *an incident that touches off a war*

【导流】［水］diversion：～隧洞 *diversion tunnel*

【导轮】［机］guide pulley; pilot wheel

【导论】introduction (to a thesis, etc.); introductory remarks

【导尿】［医］catheterization

【导盘】［化纤］godet

【导热】［物］conduct heat ～系数 thermal conductivity

【导师】❶ tutor; teacher ❷ guide of a great cause; teacher

【导数】［数］derivative

【导体】［物］conductor

【导线】［电］lead; (conducting) wire：玻璃纤维～ *fibreglass wire* / ～管 *conduit*

【导向】❶ direct sth. towards：这次会谈～两国关系的正常化。*These talks were directed towards the normalization of the relations between the two countries.* ❷ direct the course of sth.; guide：舆论～ *the guidance of public opinion (as by news media)*

【导言】introduction (to a piece of writing); introductory remarks

【导演】❶ direct (a film, play, etc.) ❷ director ◇ ～控制台 production control desk; ～椅 director's chair

【导游】❶ conduct a sightseeing tour ❷ tourist guide ❸ guidebook：～图 *tourist map* ◇ ～证书 tourist guide certificate

【导源】❶ (of a river) have its source：黄河～于青海。*The Huanghe River rises in Qinghai Province.* ❷ originate; derive：认识～于实践。*Knowledge derives from practice.*

【导致】lead to; bring about; result in; cause：～第二次世界大战的一些事件 *the events that led up to World War II* / 理论上的错误必然～实践上的失败。*Errors in theory inevitably result in failures in practice.*

岛 名 island

【岛国】country consisting of one or more islands; island country

【岛屿】islands and islets; islands

倒 动 ❶ fall; topple：摔～ *fall over* / 风把树刮～了。*The gale uprooted the tree.* / 我～在床上就睡着了。*I threw myself down on the bed and fell asleep immediately.* ❷ collapse; fail：内阁～了。*The cabinet collapsed.* ❸ close down; go bankrupt; go out of business：这家公司～了。*The company went bankrupt.* ❹ (of voice) become hoarse：他的嗓子～了。*He has lost his voice.* ❺ change; exchange：～肩 *shift a burden from one shoulder to the other* / 请你们两位把座位～一下。*Will you two please swop (or change) seats?* ❻ move around：地方太小，～不开身。*There is no room to move around.* ——另见 dào

【倒把】engage in profiteering; speculate

【倒班】change shifts; work in shifts; work by turns：昼夜～ *work in shifts round the clock*

【倒闭】close down; go bankrupt; go into liquidation：企业～ *bankruptcy of an enterprise*

【倒毙】drop dead：～街头 *drop dead in the street*

【倒伏】(of crops) lodging：抗～力强的稻种 *a strain of rice with strong resistance to lodging*

【倒戈】change sides in a war; turn one's coat;

transfer one's allegiance

【倒换】❶ rotate; take turns: 几种作物～着种 *rotate several crops* / ～着看护伤员 *take turns looking after the wounded* ❷ rearrange (sequence, order, etc.); replace

【倒汇】deal illegally in foreign currency; resell the foreign exchange at a profit

【倒买倒卖】speculative buying and selling

【倒卖】resell at a profit; scalp: ～火车票 *scalp train tickets* ◇ ～票证 trade in coupons

【倒霉】(又作'倒楣') have bad luck; be out of luck; be down on one's luck: 真～,赶到车站车刚开走。*What lousy luck! When I reached the station, the train had just left.*

【倒嗓】(of a singer) lose one's voice

【倒手】(of merchandise, etc.) change hands: 这批货他一～就赚了一千元。*As soon as this batch of goods passed through his hands, he made a 1,000-yuan profit.*

【倒塌】(又作'倒坍') collapse; topple down

【倒台】fall from power; downfall

【倒腾】〈口〉❶ rummage; move; shift: 那小孩最喜欢的事是～他妈妈的手提包。*Nothing delighted the child more than to turn out his mother's handbag.* ❷ replace; exchange; rearrange: 人手少,事情多,～不开。*It is hard to cope, with so few hands and so much to do.* ❸ buy in and sell out; deal in; trade in: 他～旧家具。*He deals (or trades) in second-hand furniture.*

【倒头】touch the pillow; lie down: ～就睡 *tumble into bed*

【倒胃口】spoil one's appetite: 这东西吃多了容易～。*Too much of this food will spoil your appetite.* / 这样的电视剧真叫人～。*I've no stomach for such TV dramas.*

【倒休】(of workers and staff) exchange working days and holidays; stagger holidays

【倒爷】profiteer

【倒运】❶〈方〉have bad luck; be out of luck; be down on one's luck ❷ profiteer by buying cheap and selling dear

【倒账】a bad debt

捣 动 ❶ pound with a pestle, etc.; beat; smash: ～药 *pound medicine in a mortar* / ～米 *husk rice with a pestle and mortar* / ～衣 *beat clothes (in washing)* / 他用胳膊肘～了我一下。*He poked me with his elbow.* ❷ harass; disturb

【捣蛋】make (or cause) trouble: 这孩子老在班上～。*The boy is always making trouble in class.*

【捣动】❶ turn over ❷〈方〉stir up; incite

【捣固】make firm by ramming or tamping

【捣鼓】〈方〉move back and forth; fiddle with

【捣鬼】play tricks; do mischief: 你别跟我～,我要知道事情的真相。*Don't play tricks on me—I want to know the truth.* / 你在捣什么鬼? *What mischief are you up to?*

【捣毁】smash up; demolish; destroy: ～敌军据点 *destroy enemy strongpoints*

【捣乱】make (or cause) trouble; create a disturbance: 有人想在会上～。*Some people tried to make trouble at the meeting.* / 他专门～。*He's a real troublemaker.* / 叔叔忙着呢,你别～。*Uncle's busy. Don't disturb him.*

【捣碎】pound to pieces

祷 动 ❶ pray: 祈祷 ❷ (used in an old-style letter) ask earnestly; beg

【祷告】pray; say one's prayers

【祷文】prayer

蹈 动 ❶〈书〉tread; step: 赴汤蹈火 ❷ skip; trip: 舞蹈

【蹈常袭故】go on in the same old way; get into a rut; follow a set routine

【蹈袭】follow slavishly: ～前人 *slavishly follow one's predecessors*

dào

到 Ⅰ 动 ❶ arrive; reach: 火车～站了。*The train has arrived at the station.* / ～了多少人? *How many people were present?* / 时间～了。*Time's up.* / ～! *(answer to roll call) Here!* ❷ go to; leave for: ～兰州去 *go to Lanzhou* / ～群众中去 *go among the masses; go into the midst of the masses* ❸ (used as a verb complement to show the result of an action): 办得～ *can be done* / 说～做～ *be as good as one's word* Ⅱ 介 up until; up to: 从星期三～星期五 *from Wednesday to Friday* / ～目前为止 *up to the present; until now; so far* / 工作～深夜 *work late into the night* Ⅲ 形 thoughtful; considerate: 不～之处请原谅。*Please excuse me if I have been inconsiderate in any way.*

【到岸价格】[经] cost, insurance and freight (C. I. F.)

【到场】be present; show up; turn up: 市长～为展览会剪了彩。*The mayor was present and cut the ribbon for the exhibition.*

【到处】at all places; everywhere: 烟头不要～乱扔。*Don't drop cigarette ends about.* / ～碰壁 *run into snags everywhere*

【到达】arrive; get to; reach: 代表团于今晨～广州。*The delegation arrived in Guangzhou this morning.* / 按现在的速度,我们三点以前可以～。*We can get there before three o'clock at this speed.* ◇ ～港 port of arrival; ～站 destination

【到底】❶ to the end; to the finish: 打～ *fight to the finish* / 将革命进行～。*Carry the revolution through to the end.* ❷ at last; in the end; finally ❸ (used in a question for emphasis): 你～是什么意思? *What on earth do you mean?* / 你那样干～是为什么? *What in the world did you do that for?* ❹ after all; in the final analysis: 他～是新手,干活还不熟练。*After all, he's new to the work and isn't very skilful at it yet.*

【到顶】reach the summit (or peak, limit); cannot be improved

【到会】be present at a meeting; attend a meeting: ～人数很多。*There was a large attendance.*

【到货通知】arrival note

【到家】reach a very high level; be perfect; be excellent: 这活儿做得很～。*This is excellent workmanship.* / 他这笔字写得还不～。*His calligraphy is far from perfect.*

【到来】arrival; advent: 迎接技术革新高潮的～ *hail the arrival of a high tide of technical innovation*

【到期】become due; mature; expire: 这本书已经～了。*This book is due for return.* / 这张票据什么时候～? *When does this bill mature (or become due)?* / 签证下月～。*The visa expires next month.*

【到任】take office; arrive at one's post

【到手】in one's hands; in one's possession

【到头】to the end; at an end: 这条街走～就有一个邮局。*There's a post office at the end of the street.*

【到头来】in the end; finally: 不老实的人～总是要栽跟头的。*Dishonest people are bound to come a cropper in the end.*

【到位】attain a predetermined position; specifically fulfill a policy (or measure)

【到职】take office; arrive at one's post

倒 Ⅰ **动** ❶ upside down; inverted; inverse; reverse: 次序～了。*The order is reversed.* / 小孩把画挂～了。*The child hung the picture upside down.* ❷move backwards; turn upside down: 火车～回去了。*The train backed up.* ❸ pour; tip: ～一杯茶 *pour a cup of tea* / ～垃圾 *tip (or dump) rubbish* / 他把一肚子冤屈都～了出来。*He poured out all his grievances* Ⅱ **副** ❶ (indicating sth. unexpected): 你还有什么要说的,我～要听听。*I'd like to hear what else you've got to say.* ❷ (indicating contrast): 你说得～容易,做起来可不容易。*It's easy for you to say that, but it's not so easy to do it.* or *That's easier said than done.* ❸ (indicating concession): 我跟他认识～认识,就是不太熟。*Yes, I know him, but not very well.* / 那本书好～是好,可是太贵。*That book is good all right, but it's too expensive.* ❹ (used to press sb. for an answer): 你～去不去呀! *Do you want to go or don't you?* / 你～是说话呀! *Can't you say something?* ——另见 dǎo

【倒背如流】can recite sth. backwards — know sth. by heart

【倒背手】with one's hands behind one (when pacing to and fro or strolling)

【倒不如】it would be better to

【倒彩】booing; hooting; catcall: 喝～ *make catcalls; boo and hoot*

【倒插门】(of a man) marry into the wife's family: ～女婿 *a live-in son-in-law*

【倒车】back a car: 他倒着车开进车库。*He backed his car into the garage.*

【倒春寒】a cold wave coming after the onset of warm spring weather

【倒刺】hangnail; agnail

【倒打一耙】make unfounded counter-charges; put the blame on one's victim; recriminate: 他自己错了不承认,反而～。*So far from admitting his own mistake, he falsely accused his critic.*

【倒带】rewind(REW)

【倒挡】reverse gear

【倒放速度】reverse speed

【倒飞】[航空] inverted (or upside down) flight ◇ ～筋头 inverted loop

【倒钩】overhead hook

【倒挂金钟】[植] fuchsia

【倒灌】(of floodwaters, tidal currents, etc.) flow from a lower to a higher place; (of smoke) pour in down a chimney

【倒睫】[医] trichiasis

【倒经】[医] vicarious menstruation

【倒立】❶ stand upside down: 宝塔的影子～在水里。*The pagoda is reflected upside down in the water.* ❷ [体] handstand ◇ ～转体 handstand turn

【倒流】flow backwards: 河水不能～。*Rivers don't flow backwards.* / 防止商品运输上的～ *avoid transporting goods back to their place of origin*

【倒赔】lose money instead of making money

【倒片】film rewind: ～机 *rewinder*

【倒摄遗忘】[心理] retroactive (or retrograde) amnesia

【倒摄抑制】retroactive inhibition

【倒收付息】[经] negative interest

【倒数】(dàoshǔ) count from bottom to top or from rear to front; count backwards: ～第三行 *the third line from the bottom* / 我住在这条胡同里～第二家。*I live in the last house but one in this lane.*

【倒数计时】countdown

【倒数】(dàoshù) [数] reciprocal

【倒算】seize back confiscated property ——另见〖反攻倒算〗

【倒锁】lock sb. in: 她把小孩儿～在屋里,出门去买东西。*She locked her baby in the room and went shopping.*

【倒贴】❶ pay instead of getting paid ❷ (of a woman) pay for the upkeep of her paramour; keep a gigolo

【倒退】go backwards; fall back: 迎面一阵狂风把我刮得～了好几步。*A gust of strong wind pushed me a few steps backwards.* / ～三十年,我也是个壮小伙子。*Thirty years ago, I was a strapping young fellow too.* / 坚持进步,反对～ *persist in progress and oppose retrogression*

【倒相器】inverted amplifier unit; phase reverser

【倒像】[物] inverted image

【倒行逆施】❶ go against the trend of the times; try to put the clock back; push a reactionary policy ❷ perverse acts: 反动派的～从反面教育了人

民。*The perverse acts of the reactionaries taught the people by negative example.*

【倒许】but perhaps; or maybe: 她对学外语不感兴趣,让她学学绘画看,～合适。*She is not interested in foreign languages. Let her try painting; maybe she has an aptitude for that.*

【倒叙】flashback

【倒序词典】reversal dictionary

【倒悬】〈书〉hang by the feet—be in sore straits

【倒因为果】take cause for effect

【倒影】inverted image; inverted reflection in water

【倒栽葱】fall head over heels; fall headlong: 飞机引擎失灵,一个～掉到海里了。*The engine failed and the plane fell headlong into the sea.*

【倒置】place upside down; invert ◇ ～汽缸 inverted cylinder

【倒转】turn the other way round; reverse: ～来说,也是这样。*The same is true the other way round.*

【倒装词序】〈语〉inverted word order

悼 动 mourn; grieve: 哀悼

【悼词】memorial speech: 致～ *deliver a memorial speech*

【悼念】mourn; grieve over: 沉痛～ *mourn with deep grief*

盗 Ⅰ 动 steal; rob: 被～ *be stolen* Ⅱ 名 thief; robber: 强盗

【盗版】illegal copy; pirate copy; piracy: ～小说 *illegally copied novel; pirate copy of a novel* / ～影碟 *illegally copied video disc; pirated video disc* / ～现象 *phenomenon of illegal copying; illegal copying; (copy) piracy*

【盗伐】fell trees unlawfully: ～森林 *surreptitious felling of a forest; illegal lumbering*

【盗匪】bandits; robbers: 肃清～ *exterminate banditry*

【盗汗】[医] night sweat

【盗卖】steal and sell (public property)

【盗名欺世】同〖欺世盗名〗

【盗墓】rob a tomb (or grave): ～人 *grave robber*

【盗窃】steal: ～国家机密 *steal state secrets* ◇ ～犯 thief; ～罪 [法] larceny

【盗用】embezzle; usurp: ～公款 *embezzle public funds* / ～名义 *usurp a name*

【盗贼】robbers; bandits

道 Ⅰ 名 ❶ road; way; path: 这是往古北口去的～儿。*This road goes (or leads) to Gubeikou.* / 山间小～ *a mountain path* ❷ channel; course: 河道 ❸ way; method: 养生之道 ❹ doctrine; principle; the Tao; the Way: 孔孟之道 ❺ Taoism; Taoist: 道士 ❻ superstitious sect: 会道门 ❼ line: 画一条斜～儿 *draw a slanting line* Ⅱ 量 ❶ (for long and narrow objects): 一～河 *a river* / 万～金光 *myriads of golden rays* / 一～缝儿 *a crack* ❷ (for doors, walls, etc.): 两～门 *two successive doors* / 三～防线 *three lines of defence* ❸ (for orders, questions, etc.): 一～命令 *an order* / 出五～题 *set five questions (for an examination, etc.)* ❹ (for courses in a meal, stages in a procedure, etc.): 上四～菜 *serve four courses* / 省一～手续 *save one step in the process* / 上三～漆 *apply three coats of paint* Ⅲ 动 ❶ say; talk; speak: 能说会道 ❷ say (polite words): 道谢 ❸ say (the words quoted): 她笑～:"你说对了!" *She said with a smile, "You're right!"* ❹ think; suppose: 我～是老周呢,原来是你。*So it's you! I thought it was Lao Zhou.*

【道白】spoken parts in an opera

【道班】railway or highway maintenance squad

【道别】bid farewell; say goodbye

【道不拾遗】no one picks up what's left by the wayside—honesty prevails throughout society: ～,夜不闭户。*People do not take any articles left by the wayside and doors are not bolted at night.*

【道不同,不相为谋】there is no point in people taking counsel together who follow different ways

【道岔】railway switch; points

【道场】❶ Taoist or Buddhist rites (performed to save the souls of the dead) ❷ place where such rites are performed

【道床】railway roadbed: 整体～ *monolithic roadbed*

【道道儿】〈方〉way; method: 找到增产的新～ *find new ways of increasing production* / 说出个～来 *give a convincing explanation*

【道德】morals; morality; ethics: ～品质 *moral character* / ～教育 *education in ethics* / 体育～ *sportsmanship* / ～败坏 *morally degenerate* / 商业～ *business ethics* ◇ ～法庭 court of conscience

【道德经】the Classic of the Virtue of the Tao

【道钉】railway (dog) spike

【道高一尺,魔高一丈】as virtue rises one foot, vice rises ten; the more illumination, the more temptation

【道姑】Taoist nun

【道观】Taoist temple

【道号】Taoist name

【道贺】congratulate

【道家】Taoist school (a school of thought in the Spring and Autumn and Warring States Periods, 770-221 B.C.); Taoists

【道教】the Taoist religion; Taoism

【道具】stage property; prop

【道理】❶ principle; truth; hows and whys: 言语不多～深。*The words were few, but they contained profound truth.* / 我自有～。*I shall find a way.* ❷ reason; argument; sense: 你的话很有～。*What you said is quite reasonable (or right).* / 讲不出一点～ *unable to come up with any convincing argument; unable to justify oneself in any way*

【道林纸】glazed printing paper

【道路】road; way; path: ～泥泞。*The road is*

muddy. / 走前人没有走过的～ *break paths none have explored before* / 为两国首脑会谈铺平～ *pave the way for summit talks between the two countries*

【道貌岸然】pose as a person of high morals; be sanctimonious: 好一个～的伪君子! *What a sanctimonious hypocrite!*

【道袍】Taoist robe

【道破】point out frankly; lay bare; reveal: 一语道破

【道歉】apologize; make an apology: 你把她的生日给忘了,应该向她～。*You should apologize to her for forgetting her birthday.* / 我得向你～。*I owe you an apology.*

【道琼斯股票价格平均数】Dow Jones Stock average

【道琼斯商品行情指数】Dow Jones Commodity Index

【道琼斯指数】Dow Jones Index

【道士】Taoist priest

【道听途说】hearsay; rumour; gossip: 这是～,不足为信。*This is only hearsay, and is not to be taken seriously.*

【道谢】express one's thanks; thank

【道行】〈口〉the attainments of a Taoist priest

【道学】❶ 同〖理学〗 ❷ rigidly and stubbornly adhering to outworn rules and ideas; pedantic: ～先生 *a scholar rigidly adhering to principles, esp. Confucian principles; pedant*

【道义】morality and justice: ～上的支持 *moral support*

【道砟】railway ballast

稻

稻 名 rice; paddy

【稻白叶枯病】bacterial blight of rice

【稻苞虫】rice plant skipper

【稻草】rice straw ◇ ～人 scarecrow

【稻恶苗病】Bakanae disease of rice

【稻谷】paddy

【稻糠】rice chaff

【稻壳】rice husk (or hull)

【稻烂秧】seedling blight of rice

【稻螟虫】rice borer

【稻田】(rice) paddy; rice field; paddy field ◇ ～皮炎［医］paddy-field dermatitis

【稻瘟病】(又作'稻热病') rice blast

【稻纹枯病】sheath and culm blight of rice

【稻秧】rice seedlings; rice shoots

【稻子】〈口〉rice; paddy

dé

得 Ⅰ 动 ❶ get; obtain; gain: ～第一名 *get a first; win first place* / ～了一大笔钱 *have obtained a large sum of money* / 这次选举他只～了五票。*He only received (or got) 5 votes at the election.* ❷ (of a calculation) result in: 二三～六。*Twice three is six.* ❸ fit; proper: 得用 ❹ 〈书〉satisfied; complacent: 自得 ❺〈口〉be finished; be ready: 饭～了。*Dinner is ready.* Ⅱ 叹 〈口〉❶ (expressing approval or prohibition): ～,就这么办。*All right! Just go ahead.* / ～了,别再说了。*That's enough. Let it go at that.* ❷ (expressing helplessness or frustration): ～,又搞错了! *Look! I've got it wrong again!* ——另见 de; děi

【得便】when it's convenient: 这几样东西,请你～捎给他。*Please take these things to him whenever it's convenient.*

【得病】fall ill; contract a disease: 突然～ *be suddenly taken ill* / 得了重病 *be seriously ill* / 得了传染病 *contract a contagious disease*

【得不偿失】the loss outweighs the gain; the game is not worth the candle: 不打～的消耗战。*Avoid battles of attrition in which we lose more than we gain.*

【得逞】〈贬〉have one's way; prevail; succeed: 阴谋未能～。*The plot fell through.*

【得宠】〈贬〉find favour with sb.; be in sb.'s good graces

【得出】reach (a conclusion); obtain (a result)

【得寸进尺】reach for a yard after getting an inch; give him an inch and he'll take a yard (or a mile, an ell); be insatiable

【得当】apt; appropriate; proper; suitable: 安排～ *be properly arranged* / 措词～ *aptly worded; appropriate wording*

【得到】get; obtain; gain; receive: ～及时治疗 *get timely medical treatment*

【得道多助,失道寡助】A just cause enjoys abundant support while an unjust cause finds little; A a just cause gains great support, an unjust one gains little.

【得法】do sth. in the proper way; get the knack: 管理～ *be properly managed* / 讲授不甚～ *not teach in the right (or proper) way*

【得分】score: 客队的六号～最多。*Player No. 6 of the visiting team scored the most points.* / 连得四分 *win four points in a row*

【得过且过】get by however one can; muddle along; drift along: 敷衍了事,～ *work perfunctorily and muddle along* / 像他这样～,有什么出息? *What future will a man ever have if he keeps dragging along like this?*

【得计】succeed in one's scheme

【得奖】win (or be awarded) a prize: ～人 *prizewinner* / ～单位 *prizewinning unit*

【得劲】❶ feel well: 他这几天身体不大～。*He hasn't been feeling well for the last few days.* ❷ fit for use; handy: 这把锹我用起来很～。*This spade is just right for me.*

【得救】be saved (or rescued): 病人～了。*The patient was saved.*

【得空】have leisure; be free: 老想来看你,总不～。*I've been meaning to come and see you but haven't had the time.*

【得了】❶ (expressing a suggestion): 你走～,剩下

的事我干。*You just go, and I'll finish the rest.* ❷ that's enough; that's that: ～,我才不信呢! *That's enough! I don't believe a word of it.*

【得力】❶ benefit from; get help from: ～于平时勤学苦练 *profit from diligent study and practice* / 我得他的力很不小。*I benefited a lot from his help.* ❷ capable; competent: ～助手 *capable assistant; right-hand man* / ～干部 *competent cadre* / 办事～ *do things efficiently*

【得陇望蜀】covet Shu after getting Long—have insatiable desires

【得人心】have the support of the people; be popular: 他做那件事很～。*That was a very popular move on his part.*

【得胜】win a victory; triumph: ～归来 *return in triumph; return with flying colours*

【得失】❶ gain and loss; success and failure: ～相当 *gains and losses balance each other; break even* ❷ advantages and disadvantages; merits and demerits: 两种办法各有～。*Each of the two methods has its advantages and disadvantages.*

【得势】❶ be in power ❷ get the upper hand; be in the ascendant

【得手】go smoothly; come off; do fine; succeed

【得体】befitting one's position or suited to the occasion; appropriate: 讲话～ *speak in appropriate terms* / 她打扮得很～。*She was suitably dressed.*

【得天独厚】be richly endowed by nature; abound in gifts of nature; enjoy exceptional advantages: 长江三角洲是～的鱼米之乡。*The Changjiang Delta, richly endowed by nature, is a land of plenty.*

【得悉】hear of; learn about: ～病体康复,不胜欣慰。*I rejoice to hear of your recovery.*

【得闲】have leisure; be free: 病中～ *have a little leisure when convalescing*

【得心应手】❶ with facility; with high proficiency: 他画起马来真可谓～。*He is in his element when painting horses.* ❷ serviceable; handy: 这支笔写起来～。*This pen writes very well.*

【得宜】proper; appropriate; suitable: 措置～ *handle properly*

【得以】so that...can (or may)...: 为求本联合声明～有效执行 *with a view to the effective implementation of this joint declaration*

【得益】benefit; profit: 读者的意见使他～不少。*He benefits considerably from the readers' comments.*

【得意】proud of oneself; pleased with oneself; complacent: 对自己取得的成功感到～ *be proud of one's success*

【得意门生】a favourite pupil

【得意忘形】grow dizzy with success; have one's head turned by success: 工作有了成绩,可不能～。*We mustn't let our achievements turn our heads.* / ～地吹嘘 *boast elatedly*

【得意扬扬】(又作'得意洋洋') be immensely proud; look triumphant

【得鱼忘筌】forget the trap as soon as the fish is caught; forget the means by which the end is attained; forget the things or conditions which bring one success

【得志】achieve one's ambition; have a successful career: 少年～ *enjoy success when young*

【得罪】offend; displease: 不怕～人 *not be afraid of giving offence* / 我的话把他给～了。*My words offended him.*

德 名 ❶ virtue; morals; moral character: 品德 ❷ heart; mind: 同心同德 ❸ kindness; favour: 以怨报德

【德才兼备】have both ability and integrity

【德高望重】(of an old person) be of noble character and high prestige; enjoy high prestige and command universal respect

【德国】Germany ◇ ～人 German

【德行】❶ moral integrity; moral conduct ❷ 〈方〉 disgusting; shameful: 那个家伙真～。*That fellow is really disgusting.*

【德语】German (language)

【德育】moral education; education in ethics

【德政】benevolent rule

【德治】rule of virtue

【德智体全面发展】all round development of morality, intelligence and physique

de

地 助 (用在状语的后面): 实事求是～处理问题 *handle problems in a practical and realistic way* / 天渐渐～冷了。*The weather is getting cold.* ——另见 dì

的 助 (用在定语的后面) ❶ (used after an attribute): 铁～纪律 *iron discipline* / 已经站起来～中国人民 *the Chinese people who have stood up* / 我～母亲 *my mother* ❷ (used to form a noun phrase or nominal expression): 赶大车～ *a carter* / 我爱吃辣～。*I like hot (or peppery) food.* / 无缘无故～,你着什么急? *why do you get excited for no reason at all?* / 这里用不着你,你只管睡你～去。*We don't need you here. You just go to bed.* ❸ (used after a verb or between a verb and its object to stress an element of the sentence): 谁买～? *Who bought it?* / 你嗓子怎么哑了? 一唱～。*Why are you so hoarse? —From singing.* ❹ (used at the end of a declarative sentence for emphasis): 你们这两天真够辛苦～。*You've really been working hard the past few days.* ——另见 dí; dì

【的话】(used to express a condition): 如果你有事～,就不要来了。*Don't come if you're busy.* / 如果我是你～,我绝对不干。*If I were you, I definitely wouldn't do it.*

得 助 (用在动词或形容词)❶ (used after a verb

or an adjective to express possibility or capability)：吃～ *eatable* / 做不～ *must not be done* / 这双鞋穿～。*These shoes fit well.* / 这个人批评不～。*He's not a man to criticize.* ❷ (inserted between a verb and its complement to express possibility or capability)：我拿～动。*I can carry it.* / 那办～到。*That can be done.* / 他做～好做不好？*Can he do it well?* ❸ (used to link a verb or an adjective to a complement which describes the manner or degree)：写～非常好 *very well written* / 唱～不好 *not sing well* / 冷～打哆嗦 *shiver with cold* / 笑～肚子痛 *laugh till one's sides split* ——另见 dé；děi

děi

得 动〈口〉❶ need：这个工程～三个月才能完。*This project will take three months to complete.* ❷ must；have to：有错误就～批评。*Wherever mistakes occur, they must be criticized.* ❸ certainly will：要不快走，我们就～迟到了。*We'll be late if we don't hurry.* ——另见 dé；de

dēng

灯 名 ❶ lamp；lantern；light：突然所有的～都灭了。*Suddenly all the lights went out.* ❷ valve；tube：五～收音机 *a five-valve radio set* ❸ burner：酒精灯

【灯标】beacon light；beacon；light buoy

【灯彩】❶ coloured-lantern making ❷ coloured lanterns (formerly used on the stage)

【灯草】rush (used as lampwick)

【灯船】lightship；light vessel

【灯光】❶ the light of a lamp；lamplight：～很暗。*The light is rather dim.* ❷ (stage) lighting：～渐暗 *lights slowly dim；lights fade to dark* / 舞台～ *stage lights；lighting* ◇ ～球场 floodlit (or illuminated) court, field, etc.

【灯红酒绿】red lanterns and green wine—feasting and revelry

【灯花】snuff (of a candlewick)

【灯火】lights：～熄了。*The lights went out.* ◇ ～管制 blackout (enforced during wartime)；～辉煌 brilliantly illuminated；blaze with lights

【灯节】the Lantern Festival (the 15th of the first lunar month)

【灯具】lamps and lanterns

【灯笼】lantern：点～ *light a lantern* / 打～ *carry a lantern* / 挂～ *hang a lantern*

【灯笼裤】knee-length or ankle-length sports trousers；knickerbockers

【灯谜】riddles written on lanterns；lantern riddles：猜～ *guess a lantern riddle*

【灯泡】〈口〉(electric) bulb；light bulb：螺口(卡口)～ *screw- (bayonet-) socket bulb* / 乳白～ *opal bulb*

【灯丝】filament (in a light bulb or valve)

【灯塔】lighthouse；beacon

【灯台】lampstand

【灯头】❶ lamp holder；electric light socket：螺口～ *screw socket* / 开关～ *switch socket* ❷ a holder for the wick and chimney of a kerosene lamp

【灯心】lampwick；wick

【灯心草】[植] rush

【灯心绒】[纺] corduroy

【灯油】lamp-oil；kerosene；paraffin oil

【灯语】lamp signal

【灯座】lampstand

登 动 ❶ ascend；mount；scale (a height)：～上讲台 *mount the platform* / ～上峰顶 *reach the summit* ❷ publish；record；enter：～账 *enter an item in an account book* / ～广告 *advertise (in a newspaper)* ❸ be gathered and taken to the threshing ground：五谷丰登 ❹ press down with the foot；pedal；treadle：～三轮车 *pedal a pedicab* ❺ step on；tread：～在窗台儿上擦玻璃 *step onto the sill to clean the window* ❻〈方〉put on (shoes or trousers)：～上鞋 *put one's shoes on* / 脚～高跟鞋 *wearing high-heeled shoes*

【登岸】go ashore；land

【登报】publish in the newspaper：～声明 *make a statement in the newspaper*

【登场】❶ be gathered and taken to the threshing ground：小麦已经～。*The wheat has been carried to the threshing ground.* ❷ come on stage ◇ ～人物 characters in a play；dramatis personae

【登峰造极】reach the peak of perfection；have a very high level (of scholastic attainment or technical skill)；reach great heights：他的人物画在当时可谓～。*His painting of people attained a level never known before.*

【登高】❶ ascend a height：～远眺 *ascend a height to enjoy a distant view* ❷ climb hills or mountains on the Double Ninth Festival (重阳节)

【登革热】[医] dengue fever

【登广告】advertise

【登机牌】boarding card

【登机入口】boarding gate

【登基】ascend the throne；be enthroned

【登记】register；check in；enter one's name：结婚～ *marriage registration* / 向有关部门～ *register with the proper authorities* / 在旅馆～住宿 *check in at a hotel* ◇ ～簿 register；registry；～处 registration (or registry) office；～股东 stockholder of record

【登临】❶ climb a hill, a tall building, etc. which commands a broad view ❷ visit famous mountains, places of interest, etc.

【登录】[计] entry

【登陆】land；disembark：盟军在诺曼底海滩～。*The Allied troops landed on the beaches of Normandy.* / 台风将于明晨～。*The typhoon will land tomorrow morning.* ◇ ～部队 landing force；～场 beachhead；～车 lander；～地点 debarkation（or landing）point；～舰 landing ship；～母舰 landing-craft carrier；～艇 landing craft；～作战 landing operations

【登门】call at sb.'s house：～拜访 *pay sb. a visit*

【登山】mountain-climbing；mountaineering：～队 *mountaineering party*（*or expedition*）◇ ～鞋 climbing（or mountaineering）boot；～运动 mountaineering；～员 mountaineer

【登时】immediately；at once；then and there：说干就干，大家～动起手来了。*Once agreed, everyone set to work straight away.*

【登台】mount a platform；go up on the stage：想～表演一番 *strive to take the stage and perform*

【登堂入室】pass through the hall into the inner chamber—reach a higher level in one's studies；become more proficient in one's profession

【登月舱】lunar module

【登月飞船】lunar excursion vehicle

【登载】publish（in newspapers or magazines）；carry：各报在显著位置～了这条消息。*The newspapers gave prominent coverage to the news.*

噔 象 thump；thud：听见楼梯上～～～的脚步声 *hear heavy footsteps on the stairs*

蹬 动 press down with the foot；pedal；treadle ——另见 dèng

【蹬技】［杂］juggling with the feet

【蹬腿】❶ kick one's legs ❷〈口〉〈诙〉kick the bucket；turn up one's toes

děng

等 Ⅰ 量 ❶ class；grade；rank：分为三～ *classify into three grades* ❷ kind；sort：这～事 *this sort of thing* / 此～人 *this kind of person* Ⅱ 形 equal：相等 Ⅲ 动 wait；await：～车 *wait for a train, bus, etc.* / ～上级批准 *await approval by the higher authorities* / 请～一下。*Would you mind waiting a minute, please.* Ⅳ 介 when；till：～我做完再走。*Stay till I'm through.* Ⅴ 助 ❶〈书〉（used after a personal pronoun or a personal name to show plurality）：我～ *we* / 彼～ *they* / 该犯～ *the aforesaid criminals* ❷ and so on；and so forth；etc.：购置书籍、纸张、文具～ *buy books, stationery and so on* ❸（indicating the end of an enumeration）：长江、黄河、黑龙江、珠江～四大河流 *the four large rivers—the Changjiang, the Huanghe, the Heilongjiang and the Zhujiang*

【等边三角形】equilateral triangle

【等差】〈书〉place in a series；grade

【等次】place in a series；grade：产品按质量划分～。*The products are graded according to quality.*

【等待】wait；await：～时机 *await a favourable opportunity*；*wait for a chance*；*bide one's time* / 抓紧时间，不要～。*Don't waste time. Go ahead.* ◇ ～状态［计］wait state

【等到】by the time；when

【等额分期付款】equal amount instalment payment

【等额选举】single-candidate election

【等等】❶ and so on；and so on and so forth；etc.：标点符号有逗号，句号、冒号～。*Punctuation marks are commas, full stops, colons, etc.* ❷ wait a minute

【等而下之】from that grade down；lower down：好的尚且如此，～的就不必谈了。*Even those higher up are not worth much, to say nothing of those lower down.*

【等份】equal divisions；equal portions

【等风速线】［气］isotach

【等高线】［地质］contour（line）：～地图 *contour map*

【等号】［数］equal-sign；equality sign

【等候】wait；await；expect：～命令 *wait for instructions*；*await orders*

【等级】❶ grade；rank：棉花按～收购 *pay for cotton according to its grade* ❷ order and degree；social estate；social stratum：封建社会～森严。*Feudal society was rigidly stratified.* ◇ ～制度 hierarchy；social estate system

【等价】of equal value；equal in value：～交换 *exchange of equal values*；*exchange at equal value* / ～有偿的原则 *principle of making compensation for equal value* ◇ ～物［经］equivalent

【等距离】equidistance：*A* 和 *B* 同 *C* 是～。*Points A and B are equidistant from C.* ◇ ～外交 equidistant diplomacy

【等离子体】［物］plasma：～激光器 *plasma laser* / ～加速器 *plasmatron* ◇ ～物理学 plasma physics

【等量齐观】equate；put on a par：这两部小说差得太远了，怎么能～呢？*There is a world of difference between these two novels. How can you equate one with the other?*

【等日照线】［气］isohel

【等深线】［地理］isobath

【等式】［数］equality

【等同】equate；be equal：你不能把现象和本质～起来。*You must not equate the appearance with the essence.* ◇ ～语 equivalent word；equivalent

【等外】substandard：～品 *substandard product*

【等温线】［气］isotherm

【等闲】〈书〉❶ ordinary；unimportant ❷ aimlessly；thoughtlessly：大好时光，不可～度过。*Don't fritter away your precious time.*

【等闲视之】regard as unimportant；treat lightly（or casually）：这样的违法行为不可～。*Such an illegal act should not be treated lightly.*

【等效】［电］equivalent：～电抗 *equivalent reactance* / ～天线 *equivalent antenna*

【等压面】［气］isobaric surface；constant pressure surface

【等压线】［气］isobar；isobaric line

【等腰三角形】isosceles triangle

【等音】［音］enharmonic
【等于】❶ equal to；equivalent to：一公里～二华里。*One kilometre is equal to two li.* / 三加二～五。*Three plus two is five.* ❷ amount to；be tantamount to：这～拒绝执行命令。*This is tantamount to refusal to carry out orders.* / 抓而不紧，～不抓。*Not to grasp firmly is not to grasp at all.*
【等雨量线】［气］isohyet
【等震线】［地质］isoseismal line；isoseismal；isoseismic line
【等值线】［气］isopleth；isoline；isogram：～图 *isogram*

戥 动 weigh with a small steelyard
【戥子】a small steelyard for weighing precious metal，medicine，etc.

dèng

凳 名 stool or bench：方～ *square stool* / 长～ *bench*
【凳子】stool

澄 动（of a liquid）settle ——另见 chéng
【澄清】（of a liquid）settle；become clear：这水太浑，等～了再用。*This water is too muddy. Wait till it has settled before you use it.* ——另见 chéngqīng

瞪 动 open（one's eyes）wide；stare；glare：他注视着这个景象，眼睛都～圆了。*He gazed at the scene with round eyes.* / 她不高兴地～着他。*She glared at him with displeasure.*
【瞪眼】❶ open one's eyes wide；stare；glare：别瞪着眼叫那流氓溜了。*Don't let the hooligan get away from right under your nose.* ❷ glower and glare at sb.；get angry with sb.：我生气地瞪了他一眼。*I gave him an angry look.* ——另见〖干瞪眼〗

镫 名 stirrup
【镫骨】［生理］stapes；stirrup bone

磴 Ⅰ 名 stone steps Ⅱ 量（for steps or stairs）：这楼梯有三十来～。*This flight of stairs has about thirty steps.* ——另见 dēng

dī

低 Ⅰ 形 low：～水位 *low water level* / 情绪～ *be low-spirited* / 压～嗓门 *lower one's voice* / 我比他～一年级。*I am one grade below him.* Ⅱ 动 let droop；hang down：他把头～了下来。*He hung his head.*
【低标准】low level
【低产】low yield：～田 *low-yield（or low-yielding）land* / ～作物 *low-yielding crop* ◇ ～井［油］stripper well；stripped well
【低潮】low tide；low ebb：处于～ *be at a low tide*；*be at a low ebb* / ～线 *low water mark*
【低沉】❶ overcast；lowering：～的天空 *an overcast sky* ❷（of voice）low and deep ❸ low-spirited；downcast
【低成本】low cost ◇ ～高收益投资 low-cost high-return investment
【低垂】hang low：乌云～。*Black clouds hang low.*
【低档】❶ low gear ❷ low grade：～商品 *low-grade goods*；*cheap goods*
【低等动物】lower animal；invertebrate
【低地】lowland
【低调】❶ low-key ❷［摄］low tone ◇ ～演说 low-keyed address
【低度啤酒】non alcohol beer
【低飞】low-altitude flight
【低工资职工】low-paid workers
【低估】underestimate；underrate：这篇她翻译得不错，过去我们～了她的英语水平。*She translated this piece quite well，We had underestimated her English level.*
【低谷】all-time low
【低轨道卫星】lower-orbiting satellite
【低耗】low cost；low operation cost
【低合金钢】［冶］low-alloy steel
【低回】（又作'低徊'）〈书〉❶ pace up and down ❷ linger；be loath to part
【低级】❶ elementary；rudimentary；lower ❷ vulgar；low ◇ ～趣味 vulgar interests；bad taste
【低贱】low and degrading；humble
【低空】low altitude；low level ◇ ～导弹［军］low-level missile；low-altitude missile；～飞行 low-altitude（or low-level）flying；～轰炸 low-level bombing；～扫射 low-level strafing；ground strafing
【低栏】［体］low hurdles
【低廉】cheap；low：价格～。*Prices are low.*
【低劣】inferior；low-grade：质量～ *of inferior quality*
【低龄】young in age（compared to the norm），lower than normal age
【低龄化】become lower in age
【低落】low；downcast：情绪～ *be low-spirited*
【低眉顺眼】be submissive and servile
【低能】mental deficiency；feeble-mindedness ◇ ～儿 imbecile；retarded child
【低频】low frequency：～变压器 *low-frequency transformer* / ～放大器 *low-frequency amplifier* ◇ ～扬声器 woofer
【低聘】a person who had had a high professional position being hired for an inferior position
【低气压】［气］low pressure；depression
【低人一等】inferior to others：～的工作 *inferior jobs*
【低三下四】❶ lowly；humble；degrading：他们不是什么～的人家。*Theirs is a respectable family.* ❷ servile；obsequious；cringing：从来没有向人～ *have never gone crawling to anyone* / ～地求情 *go bowing and scraping to sb. for a favour*

【低烧】[医] low fever; slight fever
【低声】in a low voice; under one's breath; with bated breath
【低声波】[物] infrasonic wave
【低声下气】speak humbly and under one's breath; be meek and subservient; be obsequious: ～地乞求施舍 *humbly beg for alms*
【低首下心】bow and scrape; be obsequiously submissive
【低碳钢】[冶] low-carbon steel
【低头】❶lower (or bow, hang) one's head: ～默哀 *bow one's head in silent mourning* ❷ yield; submit: 决不向困难～ *never bow to difficulties* ◇ ～认罪 hang one's head and admit one's guilt; plead guilty
【低洼】low-lying: ～地 *low-lying land*
【低微】❶ (of a voice or sound) low: ～的呻吟 *low groans* ❷ lowly; humble: 出身～ *of humble origin*
【低温】❶low temperature ❷ [气] microtherm: ～气候 *microthermal climate* ❸ [医] hypothermia: ～麻醉 *hypothermic anaesthesia* ◇ ～恒温器 [物] cryostat; ～生物学 cryobiology; ～学 cryogenics
【低下】(of status or living standards) low; lowly: 经济地位～ *be of low economic status*
【低消耗】low consumption (of raw materials, fuel, etc.): 保持高产、优质、～ *maintain a record of high production, good quality and low consumption*
【低血糖】[医] hypoglycemia
【低血压】[医] hypotension
【低血脂】[医] hypolipemia
【低压】❶ [物] low pressure ❷ [电] low tension; low voltage: ～水银蒸气灯 *low-tension mercury-vapour lamp* ❸ [气] low pressure; depression: ～气流 *low-pressure air current* ❹ [医] minimum pressure ◇ ～槽 [气] trough
【低腰紧身裤】hip-huggers
【低音提琴】double bass; contrabass
【低音控制】bass control
【低云】[气] low clouds

堤 名 dyke; embankment
【堤岸】embankment
【堤坝】dykes and dams
【堤防】dyke; embankment: 加固～ *strengthen the dykes* / ～工程 *dyke building; embankment project*

提 动 (构词成分)见下 ——另见 tí
【提防】take precautions against; be on guard against; beware of: ～恐怖主义分子的破坏 *guard against sabotage by terrorists*
【提溜】〈方〉carry: 他手里～着一个小提包。*He was carrying a small bag.*

滴 Ⅰ 动 drip: 他脸上的汗水直往下～。*Sweat kept dripping from his face.* / 往轴承里～油 *put a few drops of lubricating oil in the bearings; oil the bearings* / ～眼药 *put drops in one's eyes* Ⅱ 量 drop: 一～水 *a drop of water*
【滴鼻剂】nose drops; collunarium
【滴虫】trichomonad ◇ ～病 trichomoniasis
【滴答】(又作'滴嗒') ❶ drip: 屋顶上的雪化了,～着水。*The snow on the roof melted and dripped down.* ❷ tick; ticktack; ticktock: 夜很静,只有钟摆～～地响。*The night was very quiet except for the ticktack of the clock.*
【滴滴涕】DDT (dichloro-diphenyl-trichloroethane)
【滴定】[化] titration: 比浊～ *heterometric titration* / 碘量～ *iodometry* / ～度 *titre* / ～管 *burette* / ～剂 *titrant*
【滴管】dropper
【滴灌】[农] drip irrigation; trickle irrigation
【滴漏】water clock; clepsydra; hourglass
【滴滤池】[环保] trickling filter
【滴色画】drip painting
【滴水不漏】❶ watertight ❷〈喻〉tightly packed or completely enclosed
【滴水成冰】(so cold that) the water freezes as it drips; freezing cold: ～的天气 *freezing weather*
【滴水穿石】同〖水滴石穿〗
【滴水石】dripstone
【滴水瓦】drip-tile (placed at either end of an eaves)
【滴眼剂】eye drops

嘀 (构词成分)见下 ——另见 dí
【嘀嗒】同〖滴答〗

镝 名 [化] dysprosium (Dy) ——另见 dí

dí

的 Ⅰ 形 true; really: 的确 Ⅱ 名〈口〉taxi ——另见 de; dì
【的确】indeed; really: 听到这消息我～很高兴。*I was indeed very glad to hear the news.* / 我～不知道。*I really don't know.*
【的哥】〈口〉taxi driver brother; male taxi driver
【的姐】〈口〉taxi driver sister; female taxi driver
【的士】taxi
【的士高酒吧】disco-pub
【的士高女郎】discogirl
【的士高乐队】discoset
【的确良】dacron; terylene
【的站】taxi station; taxi stop

迪 动〈书〉enlighten; guide: 启迪
【迪斯科】disco (a transliteration): ～舞厅 *discotheque*
【迪斯尼乐园】Disneyland
【迪斯尼式的】Disneyesque

敌 Ⅰ 名 enemy; foe Ⅱ 动 ❶oppose; fight; resist: 与人民为～的人绝不会有好下场。*Those who oppose the people will come to no good end.*

❷match；equal：军民团结如一人，试看天下谁能～？*If the army and the people are united as one，who in the world can match them?*

【敌百虫】［农］dipterex

【敌稗】［农］Stam F-34（dichloropropionanilide）

【敌敌畏】DDVP；dichlorvos

【敌对】hostile；antagonistic：～阶级 *antagonistic （or hostile） classes* / ～行为 *a hostile act* / ～行动 *hostilities* / ～分子 *a hostile element* / ～情绪 *hostility；enmity* / ～双方 *opposing sides；parties to hostilities*

【敌国】enemy state

【敌后】enemy's rear area：深入～ *penetrate into the enemy's rear area* / 建立～根据地 *establish base areas behind the enemy lines*

【敌军】enemy troops；the enemy；hostile forces

【敌忾】〈书〉hatred towards the enemy ——另见〖同仇敌忾〗

【敌情】the enemy's situation：侦察～ *make a reconnaissance of the enemy's situation*

【敌人】enemy；foe

【敌视】be hostile （or antagonistic） to；adopt a hostile attitude towards

【敌手】❶ match；opponent；adversary ❷ enemy hands：落入～ *fall into enemy hands*

【敌台】enemy broadcasting station

【敌探】enemy spy

【敌特】enemy spy；enemy agent

【敌伪】the enemy and the puppet regime（during the War of Resistance Against Japan）：～人员 *enemy and puppet personnel* / ～时期 *the period of Japanese occupation；during the Japanese occupation*

【敌我矛盾】contradictions between ourselves and the enemy

【敌意】hostility；enmity；animosity

涤 动〈书〉wash；cleanse：洗涤

【涤除】wash away；do away with；eliminate：～旧习 *do away with old customs*

【涤荡】wash away；clean up；cleanse

【涤纶】［纺］polyester fibre：～长丝 *polyester filament* / ～短纤维 *polyester staple fibre* / ～絮棉 *polyester cotton*

【涤瑕荡垢】（又作‘涤瑕荡秽’）remove the stains and cleanse the filth—eradicate bad habits and customs

笛 名 ❶ bamboo flute ❷ whistle：汽笛

【笛子】bamboo flute

嘀 （构词成分）见下 ——另见 dī

【嘀咕】❶ whisper；talk in whispers：两个女孩子嘀嘀咕咕地不知谈些什么。*The two girls were talking in whispers；I couldn't hear a word.* ❷ have misgivings about sth.；have sth. on one's mind：我心里直～这件事。*It's been on my mind all the while.*

嫡 Ⅰ 名 of or by the wife（as distinguished from a concubine under the feudal-patriarchal system）：～长子 *the wife's eldest son* Ⅱ 形 of lineal descent；closely related

【嫡传】be handed down in a direct line from the master

【嫡派】❶ 同〖嫡系〗❷ disciples taught by the master himself

【嫡亲】blood relations；close paternal relations：～弟兄 *blood brothers；whole brothers*

【嫡堂】relationship between cousins of the same paternal grandfather：～兄弟（*male*）*cousins of the same paternal grandfather*

【嫡系】❶ direct line of descent ❷ one's own clique：～部队 *troops under one's direct control；one's own （or personal） troops*

镝 名〈书〉arrowhead：鸣～ *whistling arrow* ——另见 dī

dǐ

诋 动〈书〉slander；defame

【诋毁】slander；vilify；calumniate；defame

邸 名 the residence of a high official：官邸

底 名 ❶ bottom；base：井～ *the bottom of a well* ❷ the heart of a matter；ins and outs：交底 ❸ rough draft ❹ a copy kept as a record：留个～儿 *keep a copy on file；duplicate and file （a letter，etc.）* ❺ end of a year or month：年底 ❻ ground；background；foundation：白～红花 *red flowers on a white background*

【底版】photographic plate；negative

【底本】❶ a copy for the record or for reproduction；master copy ❷ a text against which other texts are checked；original text

【底册】a bound copy of a document kept on file

【底层】❶ （British） ground floor；（American） first floor ❷ bottom；the lowest rung

【底肥】base fertilizer

【底稿】draft；manuscript

【底火】❶ the fire in a stove before fuel is added ❷［军］primer；ignition cartridge

【底价】base price

【底架】［机］chassis

【底孔】［水］bottom outlet

【底牌】cards in one's hand；hand：亮～ *show one's hand*

【底盘】chassis（of a car）

【底片】photographic plate；negative

【底栖生物】benthon

【底漆】priming paint；primer

【底气】lung power：～足 *have good lungs*

【底色】［纺］bottom

【底墒】［农］soil moisture（before sowing or planting）

【底视图】［机］bottom view

【底数】❶ the truth or root of a matter；how a

matter actually stands：心中有～ *know how the matter stands* ❷［数］base number
【底霜】cream base
【底图】［地理］base map
【底细】ins and outs；exact details：我们不了解这件事的～。*We don't know the ins and outs of the matter*.
【底下】❶ under；below；beneath：树～ *under the tree* / 手～工作多 *have one's hands full* / 笔～不错 *write well* ❷ next；later；afterwards：他们～说的话我就听不清了。*I didn't catch what they said next*. / ～再交换意见吧。*We can exchange views after the meeting*.
【底线】❶ 同〖端线〗❷ under thread ❸ a planted agent
【底子】❶ bottom；base：鞋～ *the sole of a shoe* ❷ foundation：～薄 *have a poor foundation to start with* / 他的英文～好。*He has a good grounding in English*. ❸ rough draft or sketch：画画儿要先打个～。*When drawing a picture, first make a rough sketch*. ❹ a copy kept as a record：发出的文件要留个～。*Keep a copy of each document sent out*. ❺ remnant：货～ *remnants of stock*
【底座】base；pedestal；foundation

抵 动 ❶ support；sustain；prop：用手～着下巴颏儿 *prop one's chin in one's hands* / 用东西把门～住，别让风刮开。*Prop something against the door so that it won't blow open*. ❷ resist；withstand：～住来自外面的压力 *withstand the pressure from outside* ❸ compensate for；make good：抵命 ❹ mortgage：用房屋做～ *mortgage a house* ❺ balance；set off：以定金～作价款 *balance the deposit against the price* ❻ be equal to：干活他一个能～我们两个。*He can do the work of two of us* ❼〈书〉reach；arrive at：日内～京 *will arrive in Beijing in a day or two*
【抵偿】compensate for；make good；give sth. by way of payment for：用货物～欠款 *give merchandise in payment for a debt* / ～损失 *compensate for (or make good) a loss*
【抵触】conflict；contradict：与法律相～ *contravene (or go against) the law* / ～情绪 *resentment；resistance*
【抵达】arrive；reach：总理及其一行于昨天～巴黎。*The Premier and his party arrived in Paris last night*.
【抵挡】keep out；ward off；check；withstand：～风寒 *keep out the wind and the cold* / ～洪水 *keep the flood in check* / ～突然袭击 *withstand a sudden attack*
【抵换】substitute for；take the place of
【抵近射击】［军］point-blank firing
【抵抗】resist；stand up to：奋起～ *rise in resistance* / 增强对疾病的～力 *build up one's resistance to disease*
【抵赖】deny；disavow：不容～ *brook no denial* / 事实是～不了的。*Denying the facts is futile*. or *Facts cannot be denied*.
【抵命】pay with one's life (for a murder, etc.)；a life for a life
【抵数】make up the number；serve as a stopgap
【抵消】offset；cancel out；counteract：～影响 *offset an influence* / ～药物的作用 *counteract the effect of a medicine* ◇ ～记人 cross entry；～权 right of set-off；～税 countervailing duty
【抵押】mortgage：以某物作～ *raise a mortgage on sth.*；leave sth. as a pledge ◇ ～承包 mortgage to contract；～法 law of mortgages；～放款 mortgage loan；secured loan；loan on security；～负债 mortgage debt；～合同 mortgage contract；～货款 mortgage financing；mortgage loan；～经纪人 mortgage middleman；～品 security；pledge；～权 mortgage holdings；～市场 mortgage market；～诉讼 mortgage action；～险 hypothecation insurance；～银行 mortgage bank；～债券 mortgage bond；～资产 mortgage assets
【抵御】resist；withstand：～侵略 *resist aggression* / ～自然灾害 *withstand natural calamities* / 建立防风林带～风沙的侵袭 *build a shelter belt against sandstorms*
【抵债】pay a debt in kind or by labour
【抵制】resist；boycott：～会议 *boycott a meeting*
【抵罪】be punished for a crime

砥 名〈书〉whetstone
【砥砺】❶ temper：～革命意志 *temper one's revolutionary will* ❷ encourage：互相～ *encourage each other*
【砥柱】mainstay：中流砥柱

骶（构词成分）见下
【骶骨】［生理］sacrum

dì

地 名 ❶ the earth：大地 ❷ land；soil：山地 ❸ fields：在～里干活儿 *work in the fields* / 麦～ *wheat field* ❹ ground；floor：水泥～ *cement floor* ❺ place；locality：每到一～ *wherever one goes* / ～处山区 *be located in a mountain area* ❻ position；situation：不败之地 ❼ background；ground：一块白～黑字的木牌 *a board with black characters on a white background* ❽ distance travelled (measured in li 里 or stops 站)：学校离村子有一里～。*The school is one li away from the village*. / 我家离工厂只有两站～。*My home is only a couple of bus stops from the factory*. ——另见 de
【地巴唑】［药］dibazol
【地板】❶ floor board ❷ floor：水泥～ *cement floor* ◇ ～革 plastic flooring；～蜡 floor wax
【地堡】［军］bunker；blockhouse；pillbox
【地表】the earth's surface ◇ ～水［地质］surface water
【地鳖虫】［中］ground beetle (Eupolyphage sinen-

sis)

【地步】❶ condition; plight: 你怎么闹到这样的～? *How did you get into such a mess?* / 事情到了不可收拾的～。*The situation got out of hand.* ❷ extent: 发展到公开对抗的～ *develop to the point of an open clash* / 兴奋到不能入睡的～ *be so excited that one can't get to sleep* ❸ room for action: 留～ *leave room for manoeuvre; have some leeway; give oneself elbowroom*

【地蚕】〈方〉❶ cutworm ❷ grub

【地槽】[地质] geosyncline ◇ ～学说 theory of geosyncline

【地层】[地质] stratum; layer: ～层序 *stratigraphic succession (or sequence)* / ～对比 *stratigraphic correlation* / ～图 *stratigraphic map* ◇ ～学 stratigraphy

【地产】landed estate; landed property; real estate ◇ ～公司 real estate agency; ～经纪人 real estate broker; ～市场 market of real estate; the real estate market; ～税 tax on urban land

【地秤】weighbridge

【地磁】[物] terrestrial magnetism; geomagnetism: ～场 *terrestrial magnetic field; geomagnetic field* ◇ ～暴 geomagnetic storm; ～极 geomagnetic pole; ～记录仪 magnetograph; ～仪 magnetometer; ～异常 magnetic anomaly

【地大物博】vast territory and abundant resources; a vast land with rich resources; a big country abounding in natural wealth: 中国～,人口众多。*China is a vast country with a large population and abundant resources.*

【地带】district; region; zone; belt: 沙漠(森林)～ *a desert (forest) region* / 危险～ *a danger zone*

【地道】(dìdào) tunnel

【地道战】tunnel warfare

【地道】(dìdao) ❶ from the place noted for the product; genuine: ～的吉林人参 *genuine Jilin ginseng* ❷ pure; typical: 她的上海话说得真～。*She speaks pure Shanghai dialect.* / 讲一口～的英语 *speak idiomatic English* ❸ well-done; thorough: 他干的活儿真～。*He does excellent work.*

【地地道道】out-and-out; outright; hundred-percent: ～的伪君子 *a thoroughgoing hypocrite*

【地点】place; site; locale: 开会～ *place for a meeting; venue* / 故事发生的～ *the locale (or scene) of a story* / 在这里建个百货商店,～倒适中。*This would be a suitable site for a new department store.*

【地电】terrestrial electricity

【地动】〈口〉earthquake; quake: ～山摇 *earthshaking* ◇ ～仪 seismograph

【地洞】a hole in the ground; burrow

【地段】a sector (or section) of a town, etc.; area: 这个～商店多。*There're quite a few shops in this area.*

【地对地导弹】ground-to-ground (guided) missile; surface-to-surface missile

【地对空导弹】ground-to-air (guided) missile; surface-to-air missile

【地盾】[地质] shield

【地方】(dìfāng) ❶ locality (as distinct from the central administration): 充分发挥中央和～两个积极性 *give full play to the initiative of both central and local authorities* ❷ local: ～政权机关 *local state organs* / ～武装 *local armed forces* / ～观念 *localistic way of thinking; localism* / ～军 *local forces; regional troops* ◇ ～病 endemic disease; ～工业 local industry; ～国有 state-owned but locally-administered; ～民族主义 local nationalism; local-nationality chauvinism; ～气候 microclimate; ～时间 local time; ～税 local taxes; ～戏 local opera; local drama; ～志 local chronicles; annals of local history; ～主义 regionalism; localism

【地方】(dìfang) ❶ place; space; room: 你是什么～人? *Where are you from?* / 这张桌子太占～。*That desk takes up too much space (or room).* ❷ part; respect: 你说的话有对的～,也有不对的～。*What you say is partly right and partly wrong.*

【地瓜】〈方〉❶ yam bean ❷ sweet potato

【地光】ashes of light preceding an earthquake

【地广人稀】a vast but thinly populated area; a vast territory with a sparse population: 那个边区～,只有五十万人口。*The border region has only* 500,000 *inhabitants, a small population for so large an area.*

【地滚球】❶ baseball ground ball; grounder ❷ 同〖保龄球〗

【地核】[地质] the earth's core

【地黄】[植] glutinous rehmannia (Rehmannia glutinosa)

【地基】❶ ground ❷ foundation

【地极】[地理] terrestrial pole

【地级市】prefecture-level city

【地价】land price ◇ ～测算 land price estimating

【地脚】lower margin (of a page)

【地脚螺栓】[机] foundation bolt

【地窖】cellar

【地界】the boundary of a piece of land

【地块】[地质] massif

【地蜡】earth wax; ozocerite: 纯～ *ceresin wax*

【地牢】dungeon

【地老虎】cutworm

【地雷】(land) mine: 埋～ *plant (or lay) mines* / 防坦克～ *antitank mine* ◇ ～场 minefield; ～战 (land) mine warfare

【地垒】[地质] horst

【地理】❶ geographical features of a place: 熟悉～民情 *be familiar with the place and its people* ❷ geography: 自然(经济)～ *physical (economic) geography* / ～发现 *geographical discovery* / ～分布 *geographical distribution* / ～环境 *geographical conditions* / ～特点 *geographical features* / ～位置 *geographical position* ◇ ～先生 geomancer; ～学 geography; ～坐标 geographical coordinates

【地力】soil fertility; ～保持 preservation of fertility

【地利】❶favourable geographical position；topographical advantages ❷land productivity

【地沥青】asphalt；bitumen

【地裂】the ground cleaves：山崩地裂

【地龙】［中］earthworm

【地龙墙】［建］sleeper wall

【地漏】［建］floor drain

【地幔】［地质］（the earth's）mantle

【地貌】the general configuration of the earth's surface；landforms ◇～图 geomorphologic map；～学 geomorphology；～学家 geomorphologist

【地面】❶ the earth's surface；ground：高出～两米 *two metres above ground level* ❷［建］ground；floor：水磨石～ *terrazzo floor* ❸〈口〉region；area；territory：这里已经进入山东～。*We're now in the Province of Shandong.* ◇ ～部队 ground forces；～沉降［地质］surface subsidence；～辐射［气］terrestrial surface radiation；～灌溉 surface irrigation；～通讯设备 ground communication equipment（GCE）；～卫星站（又作'地面站'）ground satellite station；～遥测装置 ground telemetering equipment；～砖［建］floor tile

【地名】place name：～辞典 *dictionary of place names*；*gazetteer* ◇ ～学 toponomy；toponymy

【地膜】〈口〉plastic sheets used for covering the ground in agriculture ◇ ～覆盖 covering with ground sheeting

【地盘】territory under one's control；domain：军阀互相争夺～。*The warlords competed for spheres of influence.*

【地皮】❶ land for building ❷ ground：雨停了，～还没有干。*The ground is still wet after the rain.*

【地痞】local ruffian；local riffraff

【地平经度】［天］azimuth

【地平经纬仪】［天］altazimuth

【地平纬度】［天］altitude

【地平线】horizon

【地平坐标】［天］horizontal coordinates

【地铺】shakedown：用稻草和毯子在地板上打个～ *make a shakedown of straw and blankets on the floor*

【地契】（又作'地券'）title deed for land

【地堑】［地质］graben

【地壳】［地质］the earth's crust ◇ ～均衡 isostasy；～运动 crustal movement

【地勤】［航空］ground service：～人员 *ground crew*；*ground personnel*

【地球】the earth；the globe ◇ ～保护日 Earth Day；～村 global village；～化学 geochemistry；～环境 global environment；～科学 geoscience；～日 Earth Day（April 22）；～探测火箭 geoprobe；～同步卫星 geostationary satellite；synchronous satellite；～卫星 earth satellite；～物理学 geophysics；～仪（terrestrial）globe；～资源卫星 earth resources satellite

【地区】❶ area；district；region：北京～ *the Beijing area* / 多山～ *a mountainous district* / 这个～最适宜种小麦。*This area is most suitable for growing wheat.* ❷ prefecture：河北省保定～ *the Baoding Prefecture of Hebei Province* ◇ ～差价 regional price differences；～冲突 regional conflict；～封锁 barriers between the regions；～合作 regional cooperation；～间经济协调 economic coordination among regions；～经济 regional economy

【地权】land ownership：平均～ *equalization of land ownership*

【地热】（又作'地下热'）［地质］the heat of the earth's interior；terrestrial heat ◇ ～电厂 geothermal power plant；～电力 geothermal power；～能源 geothermal energy resources；～学 geothermics；～资源 geothermal resources

【地声】earthquake sounds

【地史学】historical geology

【地势】physical features of a place；relief；terrain；topography：～险要。*The terrain is strategically situated and difficult of access.*

【地税】land tax

【地摊】roadside stall：摆～ *set up a stall on the street*

【地毯】carpet；rug

【地毯式轰炸】carpet bombing

【地铁】〈略〉见〖地下铁道〗

【地头】❶ edge of a field：在～休息一会儿 *rest for a moment at the edge of a field*（*while doing farm work*）❷〈方〉destination ❸〈方〉the place：你～熟悉，联系起来方便。*You know the place well, so you can easily make contacts there.*

【地头蛇】a snake in its old haunts—local villain（or bully）

【地图】map ◇ ～集 atlas；～投影 map projection；～学 cartography

【地外文明】extraterrestrial civilization

【地委】prefectural Party committee

【地位】❶ position；standing；place；status：政治～ *political position*（*or standing*）/ 国际～ *international standing* / 经济～ *economic status* / 社会～ *social position*（*or status*）❷ place（as occupied by a person or thing）

【地温】［气］ground（or earth）temperature ◇～表 ground（or earth）thermometer；～梯度 geothermal gradient

【地文学】physical geography；physiography

【地物】surface features（usu. man-made features of a region）

【地峡】isthmus：巴拿马～ *the Isthmus of Panama*

【地下】❶ underground；subterranean：～仓库 *underground storehouse* / ～宫殿 *underground palace* ❷ secret（activity）；underground：转入～ *go underground* / 被打入～ *be driven underground* / 搞～工作 *do underground work* / ～党 *underground Party*；*underground Party organization* ❸ on the ground：掉在～ *fall on the ground* / 从～捡起 *pick up from the ground* ◇ ～餐馆 caveteria；basement restaurant；～车间 subterranean garage；～发射井 underground launching silo；～工厂 underground factories；～构造 subsurface structure；～管道 underground piping；～河流 subterranean river (or stream)；～核试验 underground nuclear test；～交易 covert transaction；～茎［植］subterranean stem；～刊物 underground publications；illegal publications；～人行道 underground pedestrian walk ways；～渗流 underground percolation；～室 basement；～水 groundwater；～水位 groundwater level；water table；～铁道 underground (railway)；tube；subway；～停车场 subterranean parking

【地线】［电］ground (or earth) wire

【地心】the earth's core ◇～引力 terrestrial gravity；gravity

【地形】topography；terrain：～优越 *enjoy topographical advantages* / 中国～复杂。*China has a varied topography.* / ～测量 *topographic survey* / ～侦察 *terrain reconnaissance* ◇～图 topographic map；relief map；～学 topography；～雨［气］orographic rain；～云［气］orographic cloud

【地衣】［植］lichen

【地应力】［地质］crustal stress：～场 (*crustal*) *stress field*

【地狱】hell；inferno

【地域】region；district：～辽阔 *vast in territory* / ～观念 *regionalism*

【地缘政治学】geopolitics

【地震】earthquake；seism：这次～为里氏七点一级。*The shock was of 7.1 magnitude on the Richter scale.* / ～观测 *seismological observation* / ～活动 *seismic activity* / ～勘探 *seismic prospecting* ◇～波 seismic (or earthquake) wave；～带 seismic belt；～海啸 seismic sea wave；tsunami；～检波器 geophone；～烈度 earthquake intensity；～区 seismic area (or region)；～台站 seismograph (or seismic) station；～学 seismology；～仪 seismograph；～预报 earthquake prediction；earthquake forecasting；～震级 (earthquake) magnitude

【地址】address：回信～ *return address* ◇～变数 address modifier；～常数 address constant；～存储器 addressed memory；～计数器 address counter；～空间 address space

【地志学】topology

【地质】geology：～调查 *geological survey* ◇～构造 geological structure；～勘探 geological prospecting；～力学 geomechanics；～年代学 geochronology；～时代 geologic age (or period)；～图 geologic map；～学 geology

【地中海】the Mediterranean (Sea)

【地轴】the earth's axis

【地主】❶landlord ❷host：尽～之谊 *perform the duties of the host* ◇～阶级 the landlord class

【地租】land rent；ground rent；rent：～剥削 *exploitation through land rent*

弟

名 ❶younger brother ❷〈谦〉(used between male friends, usu. in old-style letters) I

【弟弟】younger brother；brother

【弟妇】younger brother's wife；sister-in-law

【弟妹】❶ younger brother and sister ❷〈口〉younger brother's wife；sister-in-law

【弟兄】brothers：亲～ *blood brothers*

【弟子】disciple；pupil；follower

的

名 target；bull's-eye：目的 ——另见 de；dí

帝

名 ❶ the Supreme Being；god：上帝 ❷ emperor：称帝 ❸〈略〉见〖帝国主义〗

【帝俄】tsarist Russia

【帝国】empire：英～ *the British Empire*

【帝国主义】imperialism：～分子 *imperialist element*；*imperialist* / ～者 *imperialist*

【帝王】emperor；monarch

【帝制】autocratic monarchy；monarchy

递

Ⅰ 动 hand over；pass；give：把报～给我。*Hand me the newspaper, please.* / 给他～个口信 *take a message to him* Ⅱ 副 successively；in the proper order

【递补】fill vacancies in the proper order

【递归程序】recursive program

【递加】progressively (or successively) increase；increase by degrees

【递减】decrease progressively (or successively)；decrease by degrees：产品的成本随着生产率提高而～。*Increase in productivity is accompanied by a progressive decrease in production costs.* ◇～累进税 degressive tax；regressive tax；degressive taxation

【递交】hand over；present；submit：～国书 (*of an ambassador*) *present one's credentials* / ～抗议书 *lodge a protest* / ～一份声明 *send in a statement* / ～入党申请书 *submit an application for Party membership*

【递解】escort (a criminal) from one place to another：～回籍 *send (a convict, etc.) to his native place under escort*

【递进】❶ go forward one by one ❷ increase progressively；increase by degrees

【递送】send；deliver：～情报 *send out (or pass on) information* / ～信件 *deliver letters*

【递推公式】［数］recurrence formula

【递延贷款】deferred credit

【递延股息】deferred dividends

【递眼色】tip sb. the wink；wink at sb.：他给我递了个眼色，要我保持沉默。*He winked at me to keep silent.*

【递增】increase progressively；increase by degrees：产量平均每年～百分之十五。*The output increased at an average rate of 15 per cent a year.* or *The output showed a yearly average increase of 15 per cent.* ◇～率 increasing rate

谛

Ⅰ 副〈书〉carefully；attentively：～听 *listen attentively* / ～视 *examine closely*；*scrutinize* Ⅱ 名 meaning；significance：真谛

第

Ⅰ 助 (used before numerals to form ordinal numbers)：《～五交响曲》*The Fifth Symphony*；

Symphony No.5 / 宪法～三条 *Article 3 of the Constitution* Ⅱ 名 ❶〈书〉grades into which successful candidates in the imperial examinations were placed：及第 ❷ the residence of a high official：府第

【第二产业】secondary industry

【第二次世界大战】the Second World War (1939-1945)；World War II

【第二次鸦片战争】the Second Opium War (1856-1860)

【第二课堂】the second classroom—referring to teaching activity outside the classroom

【第二审】［法］second instance：～法院 *court of second instance*

【第二世界】the second world

【第二信号系统】［生理］the second signal system

【第二性】［哲］secondary

【第二梯队】second echelon；the second echelon-referring to middle-aged leaders

【第二优先股】second-preferred

【第二宇宙速度】second cosmic velocity

【第二职业】a second occupation，the second job；second job；sparetime work

【第六感觉】the sixth sense

【第三产业】tertiary industry；the service sector

【第三纪】［地质］the Tertiary Period

【第三世界】the third world

【第三梯队】the third echelon-referring to young cadres who will be future leaders

【第三者】❶ third party (to a dispute)：这件事的是非曲折，可向～了解。*Ask a third party for the rights and wrongs of the case*. ❷ person having an affair with either the husband or the wife；third party：他的悲剧是由～的插足造成的。*His tragedy was caused by the involvement of a third party in his family life*.

【第四纪】［地质］the Quaternary Period

【第五纵队】fifth column

【第一】first；primary；foremost：～号种子选手 *No.1 seeded player* / 获得～名 *win first place；get a first；win a championship* / 他跑百米得了～。*He came in first in the 100-metre dash*.

【第一把手】first in command；number one man；a person holding primary responsibility

【第一产业】primary industry

【第一次世界大战】the First World War (1914-1918)；World War I

【第一夫人】the First Lady (wife of head of state)

【第一家庭】First Family (family of head of state)

【第一轮投票】first round of voting

【第一审】［法］first instance：～法院 *court of first instance*

【第一世界】the first world

【第一手】firsthand：～材料 *firsthand material*

【第一梯队】the first echelon-referring to veteran leaders

【第一线】forefront；front line；first line：生产～ *the forefront of production* / 教学～ *the first-line work of a school teaching* ◇ ～飞机 first-line aircraft

【第一信号系统】［生理］the first signal system

【第一性】［哲］primary：物质是～的，意识是第二性的。*Matter is primary and consciousness is secondary*.

【第一优先留置权】first and paramount lien

蒂 名 the base of a fruit：并蒂莲

缔 动 form (a friendship)；conclude (a treaty)

【缔交】❶ establish diplomatic relations ❷ form (or contract) a friendship

【缔结】conclude；establish：～条约 *conclude a treaty* / ～邦交 *establish diplomatic relations*

【缔盟】form an alliance

【缔约】conclude (or sign) a treaty：～双方 *both contracting parties* ◇ ～国 signatory (state) to a treaty；party to a treaty；(high) contracting party

【缔造】found；create：～者 *founder*

碲 名［化］tellurium (Te)

diān

掂 动 weigh in the hand：～～这有多重。*Weigh this in your hand*.

【掂斤播两】(又作'掂斤簸两') engage in petty calculations；be calculating in small matters

【掂量】〈方〉❶ weigh in the hand：你～一下有多重。*Try to feel its weight*. ❷ think over；weigh up：你～着办得了。*Just do as you think fit*.

【掂算】estimate；calculate；weigh

颠 Ⅰ 名 ❶crown (of the head) ❷ top；summit：山～ *mountain top* / 塔～ *the top of a pagoda* Ⅱ 动 ❶ jolt；bump：路不平，卡车～得厉害。*As the road was rough，the truck jolted badly*. ❷ fall；turn over；topple down：颠覆 ❸〈方〉run；go away：整天跑跑～～ *be on the go all day long* / 对不起，我得～儿了。*Sorry，I've got to be on my way*.

【颠簸】jolt；bump；toss：卡车在土路上～着前进。*The truck bumped along the dirt road*. / 风更大了，船身～起来。*As the wind grew stronger，the boat was tossed about by the waves*.

【颠倒】❶ put (or turn) upside down；transpose；reverse；invert：这一头朝上，别放～了。*This is the top；don't put it upside down*. / 把这两个字～过来句子就顺了。*Transpose these two words and the sentence will read right*. ❷ confused；disordered

【颠倒黑白】confound black and white；confuse right and wrong；stand facts on their heads

【颠倒是非】confound (or reverse) right and wrong；confuse truth and falsehood；turn things upside down

【颠覆】overturn；subvert：火车出轨～了。*The train derailed and overturned*. / ～活动 *subver-*

sive activities; *subversion*

【颠来倒去】over and over：就那么点事，他却～说个没完。*It was only a small matter but he kept harping on it*. / 如果一篇文章～总是那么几个词，人家就不愿看。*No one cares to read an article that merely rings the changes on a few terms*.

【颠连】〈书〉❶ hardship；trouble；difficulty ❷ peak upon peak

【颠沛流离】drift from place to place，homeless and miserable；wander about in a desperate plight；lead a vagabond life

【颠扑不破】be able to withstand heavy battering；irrefutable；indisputable：～的真理 *irrefutable truth*

【颠茄】［药］belladonna

【颠三倒四】incoherent；disorderly；confused

巅 名 mountain peak；summit：泰山之～ *the summit of Mount Tai*

【巅峰】summit；peak；pinnacle：我们的运动员正处于～状态。*Our athletes are in top form*.

癫 形 mentally deranged；insane：疯癫

【癫狂】❶ demented；mad；insane ❷ frivolous

【癫痫】［医］epilepsy

diǎn

典 Ⅰ 名 ❶ standard；law；canon：典范 ❷ standard work of scholarship：词典 ❸ allusion；literary quotation：用～ *use allusions* ❹ ceremony：盛典 Ⅱ 动 ❶〈书〉be in charge of：典狱 ❷ mortgage；pawn

【典当】mortgage；pawn ◇ ～商 pawn operator

【典范】model；example；paragon

【典故】allusion；literary quotation

【典籍】ancient codes and records；ancient books and records：先秦～ *pre-Qin books and records*

【典礼】ceremony；celebration

【典卖】mortgage

【典契】deed of mortgage

【典型】❶ typical case (or example)；model；type：抓～ *grasp typical cases* / 理论与实践相结合的～ *a model of the integration of theory and practice* ❷typical；representative：～人物 *a typical character* / ～事例 *a typical instance* (*or case*)

【典押】mortgage；pawn

【典雅】(of diction，etc.) refined；elegant

【典狱】prison warden

【典狱官】custodial officer

【典章】institutions；decrees and regulations

【典质】mortgage；pawn

【典制】laws and institutions

点 Ⅰ 名 ❶ drop (of liquid)：雨点 ❷ spot；dot；speck：墨～ *ink spots* ❸ dot stroke (in Chinese characters) ❹［数］point：两～成一直线。*A line is formed by connecting two points*. ❺ place；point：突破一～ *make a breakthrough at one point* ❻ aspect；feature：从这～上看 *viewed from this aspect* / 对这一～没人怀疑。*Nobody has any doubt about that*. ❼ appointed time ❽ refreshments：茶点 Ⅱ 量 ❶ decimal point；point：三～儿五 *three point five* (3.5) ❷ a little；a bit；some：给我～纸。*Give me some paper*，*will you*？/ 他今天好～了。*He's feeling a bit better today*. ❸ (for items)：我有几～不成熟的想法。*I have some tentative suggestions*. ❹ o'clock：上午九～钟 *nine o'clock in the morning* / 现在几～了？*What time is it now*？Ⅲ 动 ❶ put a dot：～三个点表示省略 *put three dots to show that something has been omitted* ❷ touch on very briely；skim：他用篙一～就把船撑开了。*He pushed the boat off with a shove of the pole*. / 她发言时～了这件事。*She touched on the matter in her speech*. ❸ drip：～眼药 *put drops in the eyes* ❹ sow in holes；dibble：～豆子 *dibble beans* ❺ check one by one：请你把钱～一～。*Please check and see if the money is right*. / ～货 *check over goods*；*take stock* ❻ select；choose：他～了牛排。*He ordered a steak*. ❼ hint；point out：一～他就明白了。*He quickly took the hint*. ❽ light；burn；kindle：～灯 *light a lamp* / 他是火爆性子，一～就着。*He's got a fiery temper and ares up at the slightest provocation*. ❾ embellish；decorate：装点

【点播】request a programme from a radio station：听众～的节目 *a programme by request*；(listeners') request / 听众～的爵士乐 *jazz for the asking*

【点拨】〈口〉give directions；show how (to do sth.)；coach

【点菜】choose dishes from a menu；order dishes (in a restaurant)

【点唱】(of an audience) request a number (a song，an aria from a traditional opera，etc.)

【点钞机】money-counting machine (for bills only)

【点穿】bring sth. out into the open；lay bare

【点滴】❶ a bit：这批资料是点点滴滴积累起来的～ *This fund of information has been accumulated bit by bit*. ❷［医］intravenous drip：打葡萄糖～ *have an intravenous glucose drip*

【点定】〈书〉make corrections in a piece of writing

【点对点传输】［计］point to point transmission

【点焊】spot (or point) welding

【点火】❶ light a fire ❷ ignition ❸ stir up trouble ◇ ～试验 firing run；～线圈 ignition coil

【点货】check over goods；tally the cargo

【点饥】have a snack to stave off hunger

【点击】click

【点将】❶ (in traditional operas) call the muster roll of officers and assign them tasks ❷ name a person for a particular job

【点交】hand over item by item

【点金成铁】touch gold and turn it into iron—miscorrect a piece of writing

【点睛】(〈略〉见『画龙点睛』，used in) ～之笔 *a finishing touch added to a painting*；*an apt word*

added to clinch the point
【点名】❶ call the roll：晚～ *evening roll call* / 老师点了名。*The teacher called the roll.* / 我到的时候刚要～。*I arrived just before roll call.* ❷ mention sb. by name：他～要你去。*He named you as the one he wanted.* / ～攻击 *attack sb. by name* / ～批判 *criticize sb. by name* ◇ ～册 roll book；roll
【点明】point out；put one's finger on：～问题所在 *put one's finger on the cause of the trouble*
【点破】bring sth. out into the open；lay bare；point out bluntly：我没有～他的真实意图。*I didn't point out what he was really after.*
【点燃】light；kindle；ignite：～火把 *light a torch* / ～革命之火 *kindle the ames of revolution*
【点染】❶ add details to a painting ❷ touch up (or polish) a piece of writing
【点射】[军] ❶ fixed fire ❷ firing in bursts
【点石成金】touch a stone and turn it into gold—turn a crude essay into a literary gem
【点收】check and accept：按清单～货物 *acknowledge receipt of goods after checking them against a list*
【点数】check the number (of pieces, etc.)；count：找你的钱别忘了点点数。*Don't forget to count your change.*
【点题】bring out the theme
【点头】nod one's head；nod：～同意 *nod assent* / ～打招呼 *nod to sb. (as a greeting)* / ～示意 *signal by nodding* / 他已经～了。*He's already given the go-ahead.* or *He's already OK'd it.*
【点头哈腰】〈口〉bow unctuously；bow and scrape
【点头之交】nodding (or bowing) acquaintance：我和他只是～。*I have only a nodding acquaintance with him.* or *He and I are only nodding acquaintances.*
【点心】light refreshments；pastry
【点穴】(in Chinese boxing) touch vital points on the adversary's body to cause internal injury
【点验】examine item by item
【点阵】[物] lattice ◇ ～打印机 dot-matrix printer
【点种】dibble in the seeds
【点缀】❶ embellish；ornament；adorn ❷ use sth. merely for show：贴几张标语～～ *put up some slogans for more atmosphere*
【点字】braille
【点子】❶ drop (of liquid)：雨～ *raindrops* ❷ spot；dot；speck：油～ *grease spot* ❸ beat (of percussion instruments)：鼓～ *drumbeat* ❹ key point：这话说到～上了。*This remark gets to the heart of the matter.* ❺ idea；pointer：他～多。*He's full of ideas.* ——另见〖出点子〗
【点子公司】ideas company

碘 名 [化] iodine (I)
【碘酊】[药] tincture of iodine
【碘仿】[化] iodoform
【碘化银】silver iodide
【碘酒】同〖碘酊〗

踮 动 stand on tiptoe：他得～着脚才够得着架子。*He had to stand on tiptoe to reach the shelf.* / 护士～着脚走到病人床边。*The nurse tiptoed to the bedside of the patient.*

diàn

电 Ⅰ 名 ❶ electricity ❷ telegram；cable Ⅱ 动 ❶ give or get an electric shock：电门有毛病，～了我一下。*There was something wrong with the switch and I got a shock.*
【电霸】electricity tyrants
【电棒】〈方〉(electric) torch；flashlight
【电报】telegram；cable：无线～ *radiotelegram* / 有线～ *wire telegram* / 打～ *send a telegram；cable* / 打～让他回来 *wire him to come back* ◇ ～等级 telegram message precedence；～挂号 cable address；telegraphic address；～机 telegraph；～局 telegraph office；～音响器 telegraph sounder
【电笔】popular name for〖测电笔〗
【电表】❶ any meter for measuring electricity, such as ammeter or voltmeter ❷ kilowatt-hour meter；watt-hour meter；electric meter
【电冰箱】(electric) refrigerator；fridge；freezer：单门～ *single-door refrigerator* / 双门～ *double-door refrigerator*
【电波】同〖电磁波〗
【电铲】power shovel
【电场】electric field：～强度 *electric field intensity*
【电唱机】electric gramophone (or phonograph)；record player
【电唱头】pickup (of a record player)
【电唱针】(gramophone) stylus；needle
【电车】❶ tram；tramcar；streetcar ❷ trolleybus；trolley
【电池】(electric) cell；battery：干～ *dry cell* / 太阳能～ *solar cell* / ～组 *battery* ◇ ～充电器 battery charger
【电传】telex ◇ ～打字电报机 teletypewriter；teleprinter
【电磁】electromagnetism ◇ ～波 electromagnetic wave；～感应 electromagnetic induction；～铁 electromagnet；～学 electromagnetics
【电大】college courses broadcast on television
【电导】conductance：～仪 *conductivity gauge*
【电灯】electric lamp；electric light：偏僻的山村现在有了～。*Electric light has now reached remote mountain villages.* ◇ ～泡 electric (light) bulb
【电动】motor-driven；power-driven；poweroperated；electric：～泵 *motor-driven pump；electric pump* / ～车 *electrically operated motor car* / ～发电机 *motor generator* / ～割草机 *power-operated mower* / ～葫芦 *electric hoist (or block)* / ～回转罗盘 *electric gyro-compass* / ～记分牌 *electric scoreboard* ◇ ～机 (electric) motor；～计分器 electric scoring apparatus；～力学 electrody-

namics；～势 electro-motive force (EMF)；～剃刀 electric shaver；～玩具 battery operated toy
【电度表】kilowatt-hour meter；watt-hour meter；electric meter
【电镀】electroplate：无氰～ *electroplating without using cyanide*
【电饭煲】〈方〉(electric) rice cooker
【电饭锅】(electric) rice cooker
【电风扇】同〖电扇〗
【电感】inductance：～电桥 *inductance bridge*
【电工】❶ electrical engineering：～技术 *electrotechnics* / ～器材 *electrical appliances* ❷ electrician ◇ ～学 electrical engineering；electrotechnics
【电功率】electric power：～计 *electrodynamometer*
【电灌站】electric pumping station (or house)
【电光】light produced by electricity；lightning ◇ ～工艺［纺］schreinering
【电棍】electric prod
【电焊】electric welding：～机 *electric welding machine*；*electric welder* ◇ ～工 electric welder；～条 welding electrode；welding rod
【电贺】telegraph one's congratulations to sb.；cable a message of congratulations
【电荷】electric charge；charge：正(负)～ *positive (negative) charge*
【电弧】electric arc：～割切机 *arc cutting machine* / ～炉 *arc furnace* ◇ ～焊接 (electric) arc welding
【电化当量】electrochemical equivalent
【电化教育】education with electrical audio-visual aids；audio-visual education programme
【电化学】electrochemistry
【电话】❶ telephone；phone：请别把～挂上。*Hold the line, please.* / 他把～挂了。*He's hung up.* ❷ phone call：打～ *make a phone call*；*phone sb.*；*call (or ring) sb. up*；*give sb. a ring* / 他正在打～。*He's on the phone.* / 有你的～。*There's a phone call for you.* or *You're wanted on the phone.* ◇ ～簿 telephone directory (or book)；～传真 telefacsimile；～分机 extention (telephone)；～号码 telephone number；～会议 telephone conference；teleconference；～机 telephone (set)；～间 telephone box (or booth, kiosk)；call box；～交换台 telephone exchange (or switchboard)；～局 telephone office (or exchange)；～卡 telephone card；～亭 telephone booth；telephone kiosk；call box；～用户 telephone subscriber；～增音机 telephone repeater
【电汇】telegraphic money order；remittance by telegram；telegraphic transfer：～汇价 *rate for telegraphic transfer*
【电火花】electric spark：～加工 *electric spark machining*
【电机】electrical machinery：～厂 *electrical machinery plant* / ～工程 *electrical engineering*
【电机车】electric locomotive
【电积】［冶］electrodeposition
【电吉他】［音］electric guitar
【电极】electrode：阳～ *anode*；*positive electrode* / 阴～ *cathode*；*negative electrode*
【电价键】［化］electrovalent bond
【电键】telegraph key；key；button
【电教】〈略〉见〖电化教育〗◇ ～馆 the hall for education with electrcal audio-visual aids (or A/V) centre
【电解】electrolysis ◇ ～质 electrolyte
【电介质】dielectric
【电锯】electric saw
【电抗】reactance：～器 *reactor*
【电缆】electric cable；cable
【电老虎】electricity tiger
【电烙铁】❶ electric iron ❷ electric soldering iron
【电离】ionization ◇ ～层［气］ionosphere
【电力】electric power；power：～工程 *electric power project* / ～工业 *power industry* / ～供应 *supply of electricity* / ～机械 *electrical power equipment* / ～系统 *power system* / ～消耗 *power consumption* ◇ ～捕鱼 electrofishing；～机车 electric locomotive；～网 power network；～线 power line；electric line of force
【电疗】［医］electrotherapy：短波～ *shortwave therapy* / 超短波～ *ultrashort-wave therapy*
【电料】electrical materials and appliances
【电铃】❶ electric bell ❷ doorbell
【电流】electric current：载波～ *carrier current* / 反向～ *reverse current* / ～强度 *current intensity* ◇ ～表 同〖安培计〗；～计 galvanometer
【电炉】❶ electric stove；hot plate ❷ electric furnace：～钢 *electric steel* / ～炼钢法 *electric furnace process*
【电路】(electric) circuit
【电路图】circuit diagram
【电码】(telegraphic) code：莫尔斯～ *Morse code* / ～本 *code book*
【电门】(electric) switch
【电木】［化］bakelite ◇ ～粉 phenolic moulding powder
【电纳】［物］susceptance
【电脑】'electronic brain'—computer ◇ ～病毒 computer virus；～犯罪 computer crime；～顾问 computer adviser；～红娘 computer dating；～记事簿 personal digital assistant；PDA；～恐惧症 cyberphobia；～盲 computer illiteracy；～迷 computerites；～文化 cyberculture；～验光 computer optometry；～游戏 computer game；～中心 electronic computer center
【电钮】push button；button：按～ *press (or push) a button*
【电瓶】common name for〖蓄电池〗◇ ～车 storage battery car；electromobile
【电气】electric：～机车 *electric locomotive* / ～设备 *electrical equipment*；～系统 electrical system
【电气化】electrify：全国铁路系统几乎全部～了。*The national railway system has nearly all been electrified.* / 农业～ *electrification of agriculture* / ～铁路 *electric railway*
【电气石】tourmaline

【电器】electrical equipment (or appliance): 家用～ *household (electrical) appliances* ◇ ～店 electric appliances shop

【电热】electric heat; electrothermal ◇ ～杯 electric heating jug; ～器 electric heater; ～丝 heating wire; ～毯 electric blanket; ～针灸 electrothermal acupuncture

【电容】electric capacity; capacitance: ～率 permittivity ◇ ～传声器 condenser microphone

【电容器】condenser; capacitor

【电熔炼】[冶] electric smelting

【电扇】electric fan

【电渗析】[化] electrodialysis

【电石】[化] calcium carbide

【电石气】同〖乙炔〗

【电视】television; TV: 看～ *watch television* / 彩色(黑白,立体)～ *colour (black-and-white, stereoscopic) television* ◇ ～车 TV jeep; television car; ～大学 TV university; ～电话 video telephone; video-phone; ～电影 tele cine; ～发射机 television transmitter; ～广播 television broadcasting; telecasting; videocast; ～广告 television advertising; ～机柜 television board; ～讲座 telecourse; ～接收机 television receiver; television set; ～剧 TV drama; TV play; ～雷达导航仪 teleran; ～连续剧 TV series; television serial; TV play series; ～录像 television recording; ～片 telefilm; ～频道 television channel; ～屏幕 television screen; ～摄影机 television camera; telecamera; ～实况转播 live television coverage; live telecast; ～塔 television tower; ～台 television station; ～套 TV set cover; ～网 television network; ～卫星中继 television relay by satellite; ～文化 TV culture; ～信号 television signal; ～转播 television relay; ～转播车 telecruiser; outside broadcast van ; ～转播卫星 television transmission satellite

【电视购物】teleshopping

【电枢】armature: ～绕组 *armature winding*

【电刷】[机] brush: ～触点 *brush contact*

【电台】❶ transmitter-receiver; transceiver ❷ broadcasting (or radio) station

【电烫】permanent hair styling (or waving); permanent wave; perm

【电梯】lift; elevator: ～司机 *lift operator*; *elevator runner*

【电筒】(electric) torch; flashlight

【电网】electrified wire netting; live wire entanglement

【电位】(electric) potential: ～差 *potential difference*

【电线】(electric) wire: ～杆子 *(wire) pole*; *telephone pole*

【电信】telecommunications: ～业务 *telecommunication service* ◇ ～局 telecommunication bureau

【电刑】❶ torture by electricity ❷ electrocution; the electric chair; the chair

【电学】electricity (as a science)

【电讯】❶ (telegraphic) dispatch: 世界各地发来的～ *dispatches from all parts of the world* ❷ telecommunications: ～设备 *telecommunication equipment*

【电压】voltage ◇ ～表(又作'电压计') voltmeter

【电眼】electric eye; magic eye

【电唁】send a telegram (or message) of condolence

【电冶金】electrometallurgy

【电椅】electric chair

【电影】film; movie; motion picture: 有声(无声)～ *sound (silent) film* / 彩色(黑白)～ *colour (black-and-white) film* / ～发行公司 *film distribution corporation* / ～译制厂 *film dubbing studio* / ～制片厂 *(film) studio* ◇ ～放映机 (film) projector; cineprojector; ～剪辑机 film editing machine; ～胶片 cinefilm; motion-picture film; ～节 film festival; ～界 film (or movie) circles; ～剧本 scenario; ～明星 film star; movie star; ～摄像机 cinecamera; film camera; ～摄影师 cinematographer; cameraman; ～说明书 film synopsis; ～演员 film actor (or actress); ～院 cinema; movie (house); ～招待会 film reception; ～周 film week; ～字幕 (film) caption

【电泳】[物] electrophoresis

【电玉粉】[化] urea-formaldehyde moulding powder

【电源】power supply; power source; mains: 接上～ *connect with the mains* ◇ ～变压器 power transformer; mains transformer; ～线 power cord

【电灶】electric cooking stove (or range)

【电渣炉】[冶] electroslag furnace

【电闸】main switch; master switch

【电针疗法】[中] acupuncture with electric stimulation; galvano-acupuncture

【电针麻醉】[中] galvano-acupuncture anaesthesia

【电钟】electric clock

【电铸版】[刷] electrotype

【电子】electron: 热～ *thermal electron* / 正～ *positron* / 负～ *negatron* / ～工业 *electronics industry* / ～器件 *electronic device* ◇ ～百科全书 electrnic encyclopedia; ～秤 electronic-weighing system; ～传递 electron transfer; ～词典 electronic dictionary; ～点火装置 electric ignition device; ～伏特 electron-volt; ～公告栏[计] bulletin board system (BBS); ～管 electron tube; valve; ～管收音机 valve radio set; ～光学 electron optics; ～回旋加速器 betatron; ～货币 electronic money; ～计时器 electronic timer; ～计算机 electronic computer; ～计算器 electronic calculator; ～警报系统 electronic alarm system; ～壳层 electron shell; ～刻版机 [刷] electronic engraving machine; ～排版 computer composition; ～枪 electron gun; ～琴 electronic organ; electronic keyboard; ～世界 electronic world; ～束 electron beam; ～图书 electronic books; ～图书馆 electronic library; ～玩具 electronic toys; ～望远镜 electron telescope; ～物理学 electron physics; ～显微镜 electron microscope; ～学 electronics；～游戏 video game；TV game；～信箱 electronic mail box；～音乐 electronic music ～银行 electronic banking；～邮件 email；～邮箱 email box；～游戏机 video game player；TV game player；～云 electron cloud；～战 electronic warfare；～照相术 electro photography

【电阻】［电］resistance：～率 *resistivity*；*specific resistance*

【电钻】electric drill

佃 动 rent land (from a landlord)

【佃户】tenant (farmer)

【佃农】tenant peasant；tenant farmer

【佃租】land rent

店 名 ❶ shop；store：服装～ *clothing store* / 文具～ *stationer's* ❷ inn：住～ *stop at an inn*

【店铺】shop；store

【店堂】the business quarter of a shop (or store)；commodity section

【店员】shop assistant；salesclerk；clerk；salesman (or saleswoman)

玷 Ⅰ 名 a flaw in a piece of jade Ⅱ 动 blemish；disgrace：玷污

【玷辱】bring disgrace on；be a disgrace to

【玷污】stain；sully；tarnish

垫 Ⅰ 动 ❶ put sth. under sth. else to raise it or make it level；fill up；pad：～路 *repair a road by filling the holes* / 桌子腿底下～点儿纸就平了。*Put a wad of paper under the leg of the table to make it level*. ❷ pay for sb. and expect to be repaid later：你先给我～上，以后再还你。*Would you mind paying for me? I'll pay you back later*. Ⅱ 名 pad；cushion；mat：椅～ *chair cushion*

【垫背】〈方〉act as a cushion—bear the blame for others；be made a scapegoat

【垫付】(又作'垫支') pay for sb. and expect to be repaid later

【垫肩】shoulder pad (or padding)

【垫脚石】stepping-stone

【垫圈】(diànjuàn) bed down the livestock；spread earth in a pigsty，cowshed，etc. ——另见 diànquān

【垫款】money advanced for sb. to be paid back later

【垫密片】［机］gasket：气缸～ *cylinder gasket*

【垫球】under pass；under toss

【垫片】［机］❶ spacer：绝缘～ *insulation spacer* ❷ shim：轴承～ *bearing shim*

【垫平】level up：把篮球场～ *level a basketball court*

【垫圈】(diànquān)［机］washer：毡～ *felt washer* / 锁紧～ *locking washer* / 开口～ *snap washer* ——另见 diànjuàn

【垫上运动】［体］mat tumbling；mat work

【垫子】mat；pad；cushion：蹭鞋～ *doormat* / 体操～ *gym mat* / 沙发～ *sofa cushion* / 弹簧～ *spring mattress* / 茶杯～ *teacup mat*；*coaster*

淀 Ⅰ 动 form sediment；settle；precipitate Ⅱ 名 (usu. used as part of a place name) shallow lake：白洋～ *Baiyangdian Lake* (*in Hebei Province*)

【淀粉】starch；amylum

【淀粉酶】［生化］amylase

【淀积作用】［地质］illuviation

惦 动 remember with concern；be concerned about；keep thinking about：我一直～着这件事。*I've been thinking about that all the time*.

【惦记】remember with concern；be concerned about；keep thinking about：她老～着给孩子打件毛衣。*She's always thinking of knitting a sweater for her child*.

【惦念】(又作'惦挂') keep thinking about；be anxious about；worry about：我一切都好，请您不要～。*Everything's fine with me. Don't worry*.

奠 动 ❶ establish；settle：奠都 ❷ make offerings to the spirits of the dead：祭奠

【奠定】establish；settle：～基础 *lay a foundation*

【奠都】establish (or found) a capital：太平天国～南京。*The Taiping Heavenly Kingdom made Nanjing its capital*.

【奠基】lay a foundation：～礼 *foundation stone laying ceremony* / ～人 *founder* / ～石 *foundation stone*；*cornerstone*

【奠仪】a gift of money made on the occasion of a funeral

殿 Ⅰ 名 hall；palace；temple：太和～ *the Hall of Supreme Harmony* (*in the former Imperial Palace*) Ⅱ 动 march at the rear：殿后 Ⅲ 形 at the rear：殿军

【殿后】bring up the rear

【殿军】❶ rearguard ❷ a person who comes last in a contest or last among the winners；the last of the successful candidates

【殿堂】palace or temple hall：音乐～ *palace of music*；艺术～ *palace of art*；知识～ *palace of knowledge*；文学～ *palace of literature*

【殿下】〈尊〉Your Highness；His (or Her) Highness

靛 名 ❶ indigo ❷ indigo-blue

【靛蓝】indigo：～色 *indigo-blue*

【靛青】❶ indigo-blue ❷〈方〉indigo

癜 名 purplish or white patches on the skin：紫癜

diāo

刁 形 tricky；artful；sly：放刁

【刁悍】cunning and fierce

【刁滑】cunning；crafty；artful

【刁民】〈旧〉unruly people

【刁难】create difficulties; make things difficult: 故意～ *deliberately make things difficult for others*

【刁钻】cunning; artful; wily: 发球～ *tricky service*

【刁钻古怪】sly and capricious: ～的人 *a strange crafty person* / ～的脾气 *a strange cranky temper*

叼 动 hold in the mouth: 嘴里～着烟卷 *with a cigarette dangling from one's lips* / 黄鼠狼～走一只小鸡。*A weasel ran off with a chick in its mouth.*

凋 动 wither: 苍松翠柏，常绿不～。*The pine and the cypress remain green all the year round.*

【凋敝】❶ (of life) hard; destitute ❷ (of business) depressed

【凋零】❶ (of flowers and plants) wither ❷ decline; be on the wane: 百业～。*All business languished.* ❸ die: 老辈～。*The older generation is dying off.*

【凋落】wither and fall

【凋谢】❶ wither and fall ❷ die of old age

貂 名 marten

【貂皮】fur or pelt of marten; marten

【貂裘】marten coat

【貂熊】同〖狼獾〗

碉 (构词成分)见下

【碉堡】pillbox; blockhouse

【碉楼】watchtower

雕 Ⅰ 动 carve; engrave: 这个像是用大理石～成的。*This statue is carved out of marble.* Ⅱ 名 [动] vulture

【雕虫小技】insignificant skill (esp. in writing); the trifling skill of a scribe; literary skill of no high order

【雕花】❶ carve patterns or designs on woodwork ❷ carving: ～家具 *carved furniture* ◇ ～玻璃 cut glass

【雕刻】carve; engrave: 玉石～ *jade carving* / ～刀 *carving tool; burin* / ～品 *carving* / ～工艺 *artistic carving*

【雕梁画栋】carved beams and painted rafters—a richly ornamented building

【雕漆】carved lacquerware

【雕塑】sculpture

【雕像】statue: 大理石～ *marble statue* / 半身～ *bust* / 小～ *statuette*

【雕琢】❶ cut and polish (jade, etc.); carve ❷ write in an ornate style

鲷 名 porgy

diào

吊 Ⅰ 动 ❶ hang; suspend: 门前～着两盏红灯。*There were two red lanterns hanging over the door.* ❷ lift up or let down with a rope, etc.: 把和好的水泥～上去。*Hoist up the mixed cement.* ❸ put in a fur lining: ～皮袄 *line a coat with fur* ❹ revoke; withdraw: 吊销 ❺ condole; mourn: 吊丧 Ⅱ 名 crane: 塔吊

【吊膀】(又作'吊膀子')〈方〉(of a man) try to get fresh with a woman; flirt

【吊钹】[音] suspension cymbal

【吊车】crane; hoist: ～梁 *crane beam*

【吊床】hammock

【吊打】hang up and beat sb.

【吊灯】pendent lamp

【吊斗】cableway bucket

【吊儿郎当】〈口〉careless and casual; slovenly: 他从来不干什么工作，整天～的。*He never does any work; he just fools around all day long.*

【吊杆】❶〈口〉well-sweep; sweep ❷ [机] boom; jib: 起重机～ *crane boom* / (船用)起重～ *derrick*

【吊杠】[体] trapeze

【吊钩】[机] (lift) hook; hanger

【吊古】visit a historical site and muse over the past

【吊环】[体] rings: 摆荡(静止)～ *swinging (still) rings*

【吊货盘】platform (or tray) sling

【吊货网】cargo net

【吊架】[机] hanger: 平衡～ *balance hanger*

【吊景】[戏] drop scene

【吊兰】Chlorophytum comosum

【吊雷】[军] hanging mine

【吊链】chain sling; sling chain

【吊楼】(又作'吊脚楼')〈方〉house projecting over the water

【吊铺】hanging bed; hammock

【吊桥】❶ suspension bridge ❷ drawbridge

【吊丧】visit the bereaved to offer one's condolences; pay a condolence call

【吊嗓子】train (or exercise) one's voice

【吊扇】ceiling fan

【吊死】hang by the neck; hang oneself

【吊索】sling: 钢丝～ *wire sling* / 绳～ *rope sling*

【吊桶】well-bucket; bucket

【吊袜带】garters; suspenders

【吊胃口】tantalize

【吊慰】(又作'吊问') offer condolences

【吊线】plumb-line

【吊销】revoke; withdraw: ～驾驶执照 *revoke a driving licence* / ～护照 *withdraw a passport* ◇ ～签证 cancel a visa already issued

【吊孝】〈口〉visit the bereaved to offer one's condolences; pay a condolence call

【吊唁】condole; offer one's condolences: ～函电 *messages of condolence*

【吊钟花】another name for〖倒挂金钟〗

【吊装】[建] hoisting

钓 动 ❶ fish with a hook and line; angle: 你今天～了几条? *How many fish did you catch today?* ❷ pursue (personal fame and gain): 沽名

钓誉
【钓饵】bait
【钓竿】fishing rod
【钓钩】fishhook
【钓具】fishing tackle
【钓丝】fishline；fishing-line
【钓鱼】go fishing；angle

调 Ⅰ 动 transfer；shift；move：～干部 *transfer cadres* / ～挡 *shift gears* / 她～到这个小组来了。*She has been transferred to this group*. Ⅱ 名 ❶ accent：这人说话带山东～儿。*This person speaks with a Shandong accent*. ❷［音］key：C～ *the key of C* ❸ air；tune；melody：～寄《沁园春》*to the tune of Qinyuanchun* ❹［语音］tone；tune：升调 / 降调 ——另见 tiáo
【调包】同〖掉包〗
【调兵遣将】❶ dispatch officers and men；move troops；deploy forces ❷ muster and organize manpower (according to needs)
【调拨】allocate and transfer (goods or funds)；allot：～款项购置图书 *allocate funds for books*
【调查】investigate；inquire into；look into；survey：作社会～ *make a social investigation* / ～原因 *investigate the cause* / 农村～ *rural survey* / ～报告 *findings report*
【调查问卷】questionnaire：发出～ *distribute questionnaires* / 回答～ *respond to a questionnaire* / 设计～ *formulate a questionnaire*
【调车场】［铁路］switchyard
【调档】transfer the files；examine sb's record
【调动】❶ transfer；shift：～工作 *transfer sb. to another post* ❷ move (troops)；manoeuvre；muster：部队～频繁。*There have been numerous troop movements*. ❸ bring into play；arouse；mobilize：～一切积极因素 *bring every positive factor into play*
【调度】❶ dispatch (trains, buses, etc.) ❷ dispatcher：他是电车公司的～。*He is a dispatcher at the trolleybus company*. ❸ manage；control：生产～ *production management* ◇ ～程序 dispatcher；scheduler；～室 dispatcher's office；control room；～员 dispatcher；controller
【调防】［军］relieve a garrison
【调号】❶［语音］tone mark ❷［音］key signature
【调虎离山】lure the tiger out of the mountains—lure the enemy away from his base
【调换】同〖掉换〗
【调换债券】refunding bonds
【调回】recall (troops, etc.)：把某人～北京 *recall sb. to Beijing* / ～驻外使节 *recall a diplomatic envoy (stationed overseas)*
【调集】assemble；muster：～兵力 *assemble forces* / ～二十个师 *concentrate twenty divisions*
【调离】be transferred from one place or job (to another)：他已～该厂。*He has been transferred from this factory (to another place)*.
【调令】transfer order：她的～已到。*The order for her transfer has arrived*.
【调门儿】〈口〉❶ pitch：请把～定低点儿。*Please pitch the tune in a lower key*. / 他说话～高。*He has a high-pitched voice*. ❷ point of view；argument
【调派】send；assign
【调配】allocate；deploy：～原材料 *allocation of raw materials* / 合理～劳动力 *rational deployment of manpower* ——另见 tiáopèi
【调遣】dispatch；assign：～军队 *dispatch troops* / 听从～ *(be ready to) accept an assignment*
【调任】be transferred to another post：他已～车间主任。*He has been transferred to be head of a workshop*.
【调式】［音］mode
【调用】transfer (under a unified plan)：～干部 *transfer cadres (to a specific job)* / ～物资 *allocate materials* ◇ ～程序 calling program；～序列 calling sequence
【调运】allocate and transport：～大批工业品到农村 *allocate and ship large quantities of industrial products to the rural areas*
【调值】［语音］tone pitch
【调职】be transferred to another post
【调子】❶ tune；melody：这个～倒挺熟的。*The tune is quite familiar*. / 两个人唱的是一个～。*Both men sang the same tune*. ❷ tone (of speech)；note：定～ *set the tone (or keynote)*

掉 动 ❶ fall；drop；shed；come off：～下几滴眼泪 *shed a few tears* ❷ fall behind：他脚上打了泡，～在后面了。*He got blisters on his feet, so he lagged behind*. ❸ lose；be missing：我把钥匙～了。*I've lost my key*. / 这本书～了两页。*Two pages are missing from the book*. ❹ reduce；drop：他得了一场大病，体重～了十多斤。*During his serious illness he lost over ten jin*. ❺ wag；swing：～尾巴 *wag the tail* / ～臂而去 *leave in a flurry* ❻ turn：把车头～过来 *turn the car round* ❼ change；exchange：～座位 *change (or exchange) seats*；*swop places with sb*. ❽ (used after certain verbs to indicate removal)：洗～ *wash out* / 扔～ *throw away* / 擦～ *wipe off* / 改～坏习气 *correct bad habits*
【掉包】stealthily substitute one thing for another
【掉队】drop out (or off)；fall behind：在三天的急行军中，没有一个～的。*No one dropped out in the three days' forced march*.
【掉换】exchange；change；swop：咱们俩的上班时间～一下好吗？*Would you mind swopping shifts with me?* / ～工作 *be assigned a new job*；*be transferred to another post*
【掉魂】be frightened out of one's wits
【掉价】fall (or drop) in price；go down in price：西红柿～了。*The price of tomatoes has come down*.
【掉色】lose colour；fade：这种料子不～。*This material won't fade*. or *This material is colourfast*.
【掉书袋】a walking satchel—a person who lards his speech with quotations and allusions

【掉头】turn round; turn about: 这地方太窄，汽车不好～。*The place is too narrow for the truck to turn around.*

【掉以轻心】lower one's guard; relax one's vigilance; treat sth. lightly: 大敌当前，我们决不可～。*Faced with a formidable enemy, we must not lower our guard.*

【掉转】turn round; make a U-turn: ～身子 *turn round* / ～枪口 *turn one's gun (against one's superiors or old associates)*

diē

爹 名〈口〉father; dad; daddy; pa: ～娘 *father and mother; mum and dad; ma and pa; parents*

跌 动 ❶ fall; tumble: 他～伤了。*He fell down and injured himself.* / ～进泥坑 *fall into a quagmire* ❷ drop; fall: 跌价

【跌打损伤】injuries from falls, fractures, contusions and strains

【跌宕】(又作'跌荡')〈文〉❶ free and easy; bold and unconstrained ❷ flowing rhythm

【跌倒】fall; tumble: 他滑了一下，～在地。*He slipped and fell over.* / 在哪儿～就从哪儿爬起来。*Pick yourself up from where you fell—correct your mistake where you made it.*

【跌跌撞撞】dodder along; stagger along: 他～地出了门。*He staggered out of the house.*

【跌幅】size of decrease

【跌价】fall (or drop) in price; go down in price: 收音机～了。*The prices of radio sets have gone down.*

【跌交】❶ trip (or stumble) and fall; fall: 跌了一交 *have a fall* ❷ make a mistake; meet with a setback

【跌落】fall; drop

【跌停板】limit down

dié

迭 Ⅰ 动 alternate; change: 更迭 Ⅱ 副 ❶ repeatedly; again and again: ～挫强敌 *inflict repeated reverses on a formidable enemy* / 近二十年来，地下文物～有发现。*Over the last 20 years, archaeological finds have been made one after another.* ❷ in time for: 不迭

【迭代操作】iterative operation

【迭次】repeatedly; again and again: ～磋商 *repeatedly consult each other*

【迭起】occur repeatedly; happen frequently: 入冬以来，车祸～。*Since winter began, there have been frequent traffic accidents.*

谍 名 ❶ espionage: 谍报 ❷ intelligence agent; spy: 间谍

【谍报】information obtained through espionage; intelligence report; intelligence: ～员 *intelligence agent; spy*

喋 (构词成分)见下

【喋喋不休】chatter away; rattle on; talk endlessly

【喋血】〈文〉bloodshed; bloodbath

牒 名 an official document or note; certificate: 通牒

叠 动 ❶ pile up; repeat: 重叠 ❷ fold: 把信～好 *fold the letter* / ～被子 *fold up a quilt; make the bed (after getting up)*

【叠床架屋】pile one bed upon another or build one house on top of another—needless duplication: 这样～，文章就太啰嗦了。*So much needless repetition makes the article long-winded.*

【叠句】reiterative sentence

【叠罗汉】[体] pyramid

【叠韵】[语] rhyming compound (a compound consisting of two syllables that rhyme with one another; e.g. 徘徊，宛转)

【叠字】[语] reduplicated word; reduplication (e.g. 皎皎，年年，妹妹，坛坛罐罐)

碟 名 small plate; small dish: 一～炒黄豆 *a dish of fried soya beans*

【碟子】small dish; small plate

蝶 名 butterfly: 蝴蝶

【蝶骨】[生理] sphenoid bone

【蝶形花】papilionaceous flower

【蝶泳】butterfly stroke

dīng

丁 Ⅰ 名 ❶ man ❷ members of a family; population: 添丁 ❸ a person engaged in a certain occupation: 园丁 ❹ small cubes of meat or vegetable; cubes: 黄瓜～儿 *diced cucumber* ❺ the fourth of the ten Heavenly stems (天干) Ⅱ 数 fourth: ～等 *the fourth grade; grade D* / ～种维生素 *vitamin D*

【丁当】ding-dong; jingle; clatter: 碟子碗碰得丁丁当当的。*The dishes and bowls slid together with a clatter.* / 铃儿～响。*The bell jingled.* / 穷得～响 *be penniless; be broke*

【丁点儿】〈方〉a tiny bit: 这套茶具连一～毛病都没有。*There isn't the slightest flaw in this tea set.* / 这～事不必放在心上。*Don't bother about such trifles.*

【丁东】(又作'丁冬') tinkle

【丁克族】DINKS (a short term for 'dual income, no kids')

【丁零】tinkle; jingle: ～～的自行车铃声 *the jingling of bicycle bells*

【丁零当郎】cling-clang

【丁是丁，卯是卯】(又作'钉是钉，铆是铆') keep ding (a Heavenly Stem) distinct from mao (an

Earthly Branch)—be meticulous; be precise; be unaccommodating: 他办起事来~，从不含糊。*He is very exacting in his work*.

【丁烷】[化] butane: ~气 *butagas*

【丁烯】[化] butene

【丁香】[植] ❶ lilac ❷ clove: ~油 *clove oil*

【丁字】T-shaped ◇ ~尺 T-square; ~钢(又作'丁字铁') T-steel; ~街 T-shaped road junction; ~形 T-shaped

叮 动 ❶ sting; bite: 腿上叫蚊子~了一下 *get a mosquito bite on the leg* ❷ say or ask again to make sure: 我~了他一句，他才说了真话。*I asked him again, and at last he came out with the truth*.

【叮嘱】urge again and again; warn; exhort: 父亲再三~我们要谦虚谨慎。*Father urged us again and again to be modest and prudent*.

玎 (构词成分)见下

【玎玲】clink; jingle; tinkle

疔 名 malignant boil (or furuncle)

【疔疽】miliary vesicle under the nose or on either side of the mandible

盯 动 fix one's eyes on; gaze at; stare at: 他两眼~着雷达荧光屏。*His eyes were fixed on the radar screen*. / ~住这个坏蛋。*Keep a close watch on the scoundrel*.

【盯梢】同〖钉梢〗

钉 Ⅰ 名 nail; tack: 螺丝钉 Ⅱ 动 ❶ follow closely; tail: 紧紧~住敌长机 *keep on the tail of the enemy's lead plane* ❷ urge; press: 你要~着他吃药，别让他忘了。*You must remind him to take his medicine, in case he forgets*. ——另见 dìng

【钉齿耙】spike-tooth harrow

【钉锤】nail hammer; claw hammer

【钉螺】[动] oncomelania (a kind of freshwater snail, which is the intermediate host of the blood fluke); snail

【钉帽】the head of a nail

【钉耙】(iron-toothed) rake

【钉人】[体] watch (or mark) an opponent in a game: ~防守 *man-for-man* (*or man-to-man*) *defence*

【钉梢】shadow sb.; tail sb.: 他觉得有人钉他的梢。*He felt he was being shadowed*.

【钉鞋】spiked shoes; spikes

【钉子】❶ nail ❷ saboteur: 安插~ *plant a saboteur* ◇ ~户 tartar ——另见〖碰钉子〗

【钉子精神】spirit of the nail—make the best use of one's time and work persistently to achieve one's purpose

耵 (构词成分)见下

【耵聍】earwax; cerumen

酊 名 tincture: 碘酊 ——另见 dǐng

【酊剂】[药] tincture

dǐng

顶 Ⅰ 名 ❶ the crown of the head: 秃顶 ❷ top: 此山之~有一古庙。*There is an old temple at the top of the mountain*. Ⅱ 动 ❶carry on the head: 头上~着一罐水 *carry a pitcher of water on one's head* ❷gore; butt: 这牛爱~人。*This bull gores people*. ❸go against: ~风雪，战严寒 *face blizzards and brave severe cold* ❹push from below or behind; push up; prop up: 嫩芽把土~起来了。*The sprouts have pushed up the earth*. / 用千斤顶把汽车~起来 *jack up a car* ❺ retort; turn down: 我~了他几句。*I said a few words to him in retort*. / 把抗议~回去 *reject a protest* ❻ cope with; stand up to: 负担虽重，他们两个也~下来了。*The load was heavy, but the two of them coped with it all right*. ❼take the place of; substitute; replace: ~别人的名字 *assume sb. else's name* / 不能拿次货~好货卖。*You shouldn't pass inferior goods off as high-quality goods and sell them*. ❽ equal; be equivalent to Ⅲ 量 (for things which have a top): 一~帽子 *a cap; a hat* / 一~帐子 *a mosquito net* Ⅳ 副 very; most; extremely: ~有用 *very useful* / ~小的那个孩子 *the youngest* (*or smallest*) *child* / 我~喜欢贝多芬的音乐。*I'm very fond of Beethoven's music*.

【顶班】❶ work on regular shifts; work full time ❷ work as a substitute for sb. absent

【顶板】[矿] roof: 直接~ *immediate* (*or nether*) *roof* / ~下沉 *roof-to-floor convergence; roof convergence*

【顶部掘进法】top cut method

【顶吹】[冶] top-blown: ~转炉 *top-blown converter*

【顶灯】dome light (of a car)

【顶点】❶ apex; zenith; acme; pinnacle ❷ [数] vertex; apex

【顶端】❶ top; peak; apex ❷ end: 我们走到大桥的~。*We walked to the end of the bridge*.

【顶多】at (the) most; at best: 屋里~不过十个人。*There were at most ten people in the room*.

【顶风】❶ against the wind: ~骑车 *cycle against the wind* / 开~船 *sail against the wind* ❷ head wind

【顶峰】peak; summit; pinnacle

【顶骨】[生理] parietal bone

【顶呱呱】(又作'顶刮刮') tip-top; first-rate; excellent

【顶好】❶ very good ❷ had better; it would be best: 我们~现在就动身回去。*We'd better be starting back now*.

【顶尖】topmost; top level: ~科学家 *top level scientist* / ~人物 *topmost figure*

【顶交】[农] topcross

【顶角】[数] vertex angle

【顶礼】prostrate oneself before sb. and press one's

head against his feet (a Buddhist salute of the highest respect)

【顶礼膜拜】〈贬〉prostrate oneself in worship; make a fetish of; pay homage to

【顶门儿】the front top of the head

【顶命】a life for a life; pay with one's life (for a first-degree murder)

【顶牛儿】lock horns like bulls; clash; be at loggerheads: 他们两人一谈就～。*The two of them began to wrangle the moment they got talking.*

【顶盘】highest quotation

【顶棚】ceiling

【顶球】[体] head (a ball)

【顶少】at (the) least: 这～得五块钱。*It costs at least 5 yuan.*

【顶事】be useful; serve the purpose: 这孩子可～啦! *The boy is a great help!*

【顶替】❶ take sb.'s place; replace: 他走了谁来～他? *Who's going to take his place after he leaves?* ❷ get a job at one's parent's place of work when the parent retires or dies

【顶天立地】of gigantic stature; of indomitable spirit; dauntless: 做一个～的英雄汉 *be a dauntless hero*

【顶头】❶ coming directly towards one: ～风 *head wind* ❷ top; end: 这条胡同的～有个公用电话。*There is a public telephone (booth) at the end of this lane.*

【顶头上司】〈口〉one's immediate (or direct) superior

【顶芽】[植] terminal bud

【顶用】be of use (or help); serve the purpose: 等她毕了业就～了。*She'll be a help when she finishes school.* / 我去也不～。*I can't be of any help even if I go.*

【顶针】thimble

【顶住】withstand; stand up to; hold out against: ～压力 *withstand pressure* / ～逆流 *stand up against an adverse current* / ～风浪 *weather a storm*

【顶撞】contradict (one's elder or superior): ～父母 *contradict one's parents*

【顶嘴】〈口〉reply defiantly (usu. to one's elder or superior); answer back; talk back: 你不该跟你奶奶～。*You shouldn't talk back to your grandmother.*

酊 见〖酩酊大醉〗——另见 dīng

鼎 Ⅰ 名 ❶ an ancient cooking vessel with two loop handles and three or four legs: 三足～ *tripod* / 四足～ *quadripod* ❷〈方〉pot Ⅱ 形〈书〉enter upon a period of: 鼎盛

【鼎鼎大名】同〖大名鼎鼎〗

【鼎沸】〈书〉like a seething cauldron; noisy and confused: 人声鼎沸

【鼎革】〈书〉change of dynasty or regime; dynastic change

【鼎力】〈套〉your kind effort: 多蒙～协助,无任感谢。*We are extremely grateful to you for the trouble you have taken on our behalf.*

【鼎立】(of three antagonists confronting one another) stand like the three legs of a tripod; tripartite confrontation; tripartite balance of forces

【鼎盛】in a period of great prosperity; at the height of power and splendour: ～时期 *a period of full bloom; prime; heyday*

【鼎新】〈书〉make innovations: 革故鼎新

【鼎足】the three legs of a tripod—three rival powers: 势成～ *a situation of tripartite confrontation*

【鼎足之势】tripartite balance of forces; triangular balance of power: 赤壁之战决定了魏、蜀、吴三国～。*The battle of the Red Cliffs determined the triangular balance of power of the three kingdoms, Wei, Shu, and Wu.*

dìng

订 动 ❶ conclude; draw up; agree on: ～条约 *conclude a treaty* / ～合同 *enter into (or make) a contract* / ～计划 *draw up (or work out) a plan* / ～日期 *fix (or agree on) a date* / ～生产指标 *set a production target* ❷ subscribe to (a newspaper, etc.); book (seats, tickets, etc.); order (merchandise, etc.): ～《中国日报》*subscribe to China Daily* / ～房间 *make room (or hotel) reservations* / ～座 *make reservations for seats (in a restaurant, theatre, etc.)* ❸ make corrections; revise: 修订 ❹ staple together: 他把两封信～在一起。*He stapled the two letters together.*

【订单】order for goods; order form

【订费】subscription (rate)

【订购】order (goods); place an order for sth.: ～一套家具 *order a set of furniture* / 欢迎～。*Customers are welcome to place orders.*

【订户】❶ subscriber (to a newspaper or periodical) ❷ a person or household with a standing order for milk, etc.

【订婚】be engaged (to be married); be betrothed

【订货】order goods; place an order for goods: ～确认书 *confirmation of order* ◇ ～代理人 indent agent; ～单 order list; ～付款 cash with order (CWO); ～合同 goods-ordering contract; order contract; ～会 meeting for the placement of orders; order-placing meeting; ～量 quantity (or size) of order

【订交】pledge friendship; establish friendly relations with each other

【订金】an initial payment; earnest

【订立】conclude (a treaty, agreement, etc.); make (a contract, etc.): ～收购合同 *conclude a purchasing contract*

【订书机】❶ stapler; stapling-machine ❷ bookbinding machine

【订约】conclude a contract or treaty

【订阅】subscribe to (a newspaper, periodical, etc.)

【订正】make corrections; emend: ～了第一版中的错误。*Corrections have been made to the first edition*.

钉 动 ❶ nail: ～马掌 *nail on horseshoes* / ～钉子 *drive in a nail* / 把窗子～死 *nail up a window* ❷ sew on: ～扣子 *sew a button on* ——另见 dīng

定 Ⅰ 形 ❶ calm; stable: 天下大～。*General stability has been achieved in the country*. ❷ fixed; settled; established: 定见 Ⅱ 动 ❶ decide; fix; set: 开会时间～在明天上午。*The meeting is fixed for tomorrow morning*. / 代表团～于今日离京。*The delegation is due to leave Beijing today*. / ～方针 *decide on a policy* / ～计划 *make a plan* ❷ subscribe to (a newspaper, etc.); book (seats, tickets, etc.); order (merchandise, etc.) Ⅲ 副〈书〉surely; certainly; definitely: ～可取胜 *be sure to win*

【定案】❶ decide on (or pass) a verdict; reach a conclusion on a case ❷ verdict; final decision

【定比定律】[化] the law of definite (or constant) proportions

【定单】order for goods; order form

【定点厂】designated factory; factory designated by the state to make a particular product

【定点企业】a specialized enterprise

【定点运算】fixed-point arithmetic

【定调子】set the tone (or keynote)

【定都】choose a site for the capital; establish a capital: ～北京 *make Beijing the capital*; *decide on Beijing as the capital*

【定夺】make a final decision; decide: 讨论后再行～。*We won't make any decision until after the discussion*.

【定额】quota; norm: 生产～ *production quota* ◇ ～分配制 the quota system; ～管理 quota managemant

【定岗】set work requiremants for a position

【定高气球】constant-level balloon

【定稿】❶ finalize a manuscript, text, etc. ❷ final version or text

【定格镜头】freeze shot

【定购】❶ order (goods); place an order for sth. ❷ a system of fixed quotas for purchasing ◇ ～定销 fixed quotas for purchasing and marketing; ～粮 quota grain to be sold by peasants to the state at fixed price

【定冠词】[语] definite article

【定规】❶ established rule or practice; set pattern: 并无～。*There's no hard and fast rule*. ❷〈方〉be bent on; be determined

【定婚】be engaged (to be married); be betrothed

【定货】同〖订货〗

【定级】decide grade and level

【定计】devise a stratagem; work out a scheme

【定价】❶ fix a price: 你给这批货定个价吧。*Could you set a price for this batch of goods, please?* ❷ fixed price: 这种衬衫每件～十元。*The marked price of these shirts is* 10 *yuan each*. ❸ list price

【定见】definite opinion; set view: 这事儿请你们讨论,我没有～。*Please discuss the matter among yourselves. I have no definite opinion about it*.

【定界】determination of boundaries

【定金】deposit (put down on sth. for future purchase)

【定睛】fix one's eyes upon: ～细看 *look fixedly and scrutinize*

【定居】settle down: 回乡～ *return to settle in one's native place* / 我决定在北京～。*I've decided to settle down in Beijing*. ◇ ～点 settlement (of herdsmen, fishermen, etc.)

【定局】❶ foregone conclusion; inevitable outcome: 今年丰收已成～。*It's a foregone conclusion that we'll have a bumper harvest this year*. ❷ settle finally: 事情还没有～,明天可以再议。*The matter isn't settled yet. We can take it up again tomorrow*.

【定理】theorem: 基本～ *fundamental theorem*

【定例】usual practice; set pattern; routine: 每星期六我们学校总要放场电影,这已成～了。*It's a usual practice in our school to have a film shown every Saturday*.

【定量】❶ fixed quantity; ration: ～供应 *rationing* ❷ determine the amounts of the components of a substance ◇ ～分析 [化] quantitative analysis

【定量供应商品】goods on ration

【定律】(scientific) law: 万有引力～ *the law of universal gravitation*

【定论】final conclusion: 这个问题尚无～。*No final conclusion has yet been reached on this matter*. or *This is still an open question*.

【定苗】[农] final singling (of seedlings)

【定名】name; denominate

【定期】❶ fix (or set) a date ❷ regular; at regular intervals; periodical: ～体格检查 *regular physical checkups* / ～轮换 *rotate at regular intervals* / ～汇报工作 *regularly report back on one's work* / ～刊物 *periodical publication*; *periodical* / 不～刊物 *nonperiodic publication* ◇ ～班车 routine car; ～保险 term insurance; ～存款 fixed deposit; time deposit; ～贷款 term loan; time loan; time money; ～抵押 term mortgage; ～货款 time mortgage loan; ～汇票 date draft; time draft; time bill; ～信用证 time letter of credit; ～债券 fixed-maturity bonds; term bond; ～租船 time charter

【定钱】deposit; earnest (money): ～已付。*Earnest money is paid*. / 租房子要先付～。*One has to pay a deposit when renting a house*.

【定亲】engagement (usu. arranged by parents); betrothal: 她已跟李家的儿子定了亲。*She is betrothed to a son of the Li family*.

【定情】pledge love
【定然】certainly; definitely: 这件事他～不会同意。*He definitely won't agree to it.*
【定神】❶ collect oneself; compose oneself; pull oneself together: 一开头她吓坏了,后来才定下神来。*At first she was terrified, then she pulled herself together.* ❷ concentrate one's attention: 听见有人叫我,～一看,原来是小李。*I heard someone calling me and, looking hard, saw that it was Xiao Li.*
【定时开关】time switch
【定时器】timer
【定时炸弹】time bomb
【定位】❶ fixed position; location; orientation ❷ orientate; position ◇ ～器[矿] positioner
【定息】fixed interest
【定弦】❶ tune a stringed instrument ❷〈方〉make up one's mind
【定向】directional ◇ ～爆破 directional blasting; ～地雷 oriented mine; ～培育[农] directive breeding; ～天线 directional antenna; ～仪[气] direction finder
【定心】❶[机] centering: ～装置 *centering device* ❷ feel relieved; feel at ease: 那笔钱找到了,这一下她可～了。*Now that the money was found, she could feel relieved.* ◇ ～丸 sth. capable of setting sb.'s mind at ease
【定形】❶[化] fibre setting: 热～ *heat setting* ❷ knitting boarding: ～机 *boarding machine*
【定型】finalize the design; fall into a pattern
【定向分配】fixed direction allocation
【定向培养】train professional personnel for a certain area or work unit
【定向销售】fixed direction marketing
【定向招生】directioned recruitment of students; enroll students who are pre-assigned specific posts or areas
【定性】❶ determine the nature (of an offence or a case) ❷ determine the chemical composition of a substance ◇ ～分析[化] qualitative analysis
【定义】definition: 下～ *give a definition; define*
【定音鼓】[音] kettledrums; timpani
【定影】[摄] fixing; fixation: ～罐 *fixing tank* / ～剂 *fixer* / ～液 *fixing bath*
【定语】[语] attribute: ～从句 *attributive clause*
【定员】fixed number of staff members or passengers: 这节车厢～一百二十人。*This carriage has a seating capacity of 120 people.*
【定则】[物] rule: 左手(右手)～ *left-hand (right-hand) rule*
【定植】[植] field planting (or setting)
【定址】addressing ◇ ～方式 addressing mode
【定制】❶ have sth. made to order; have sth. custom-made: ～家具 *have furniture made to order* / 欢迎选购和～。*Orders for ready-made or custom-made articles are welcome.* ❷ an established rule or practice
【定子】[电] stator: ～绕组 *stator winding*
【定罪】declare sb. guilty; convict sb. (of a crime)
【定做】have sth. made to order (or measure): ～的衣服 *tailor-made clothes; clothes made to measure* / 这双鞋是～的。*This pair of shoes was made to order.*

锭 Ⅰ 名 ❶ ingot-shaped tablet (of medicine, metal, Chinese ink, etc.) ❷[纺] spindle Ⅱ 量 (for ingot-shaped objects): 一～墨 *an ink stick*
【锭剂】[药] lozenge; pastille; troche
【锭模】[冶] ingot mould
【锭子】[纺] spindle

diū

丢 动 ❶ lose; mislay: 这套书～了一本。*There's a book missing from the set.* / 我把钳子～哪儿了? *Where have I left my pliers?* ❷ throw; cast; toss: 把菜帮子～给小兔吃 *throw the outer leaves to the rabbit* / 不要随地～果皮。*Please don't litter.* ❸ put (or lay) aside: ～在脑后 *let sth. pass out of one's mind; clean forget; completely ignore* / 我的法语～了好几年了,都忘得差不多了。*I haven't used my French for years and have forgotten almost all of it.*
【丢丑】lose face; be disgraced: 简直是～! *It's really a disgrace!*
【丢掉】❶ lose: 我～了一支笔。*I've lost my pen.* ❷ throw away; cast away; discard: ～幻想 *cast away illusions* / ～错误观点 *discard mistaken views* / ～官气 *shed one's bureaucratic airs*
【丢饭碗】lose one's job
【丢盔卸甲】(又作'丢盔弃甲') throw away one's helmet and coat of mail; throw away everything in headlong flight
【丢脸】lose face; be disgraced: 这不是～的事。*There's nothing to be ashamed of.*
【丢面子】lose face: 有了错误要作自我批评,不要怕～。*Criticize yourself when you've made a mistake. Don't be afraid of losing face.*
【丢弃】abandon; discard; give up
【丢人】lose face; be disgraced: 真～! *What a disgrace!*
【丢人现眼】make a fool of oneself; make a spectacle of oneself
【丢三落四】forget this and that; be always forgetting things: 他老是这么～的。你看,又把房门钥匙锁在屋子里了。*He's so scatterbrained. Look, he's locked his key inside his room again.*
【丢失】lose
【丢手】wash one's hands of; give up: 他～不管了。*He washed his hands of the matter.*
【丢眼色】wink at sb.; tip sb. the wink: 他朝我丢了个眼色,转身走了。*He winked at me, turned, and left.*
【丢卒保车】give up a pawn to save a chariot—sacrifice minor things to save major ones

铥 名[化] thulium (Tm)

dōng

东 名 ❶ east：城～ *east of the city* / ～城 *the eastern part of the city* / ～郊 *eastern suburbs* ❷ master；owner：房东 ❸ host：今天是我的～。*I'll be the host today*. or *It's my treat today*.

【东半球】the Eastern Hemisphere

【东北】❶ northeast ❷ northeast China；the Northeast

【东奔西跑】run around here and there；bustle about；rush about (or around)：为找职业而～ *be driven from pillar to post seeking employment*

【东窗事发】the plot has come to light；the secret is out

【东倒西歪】leaning；unsteady；tottering：三间～的屋子 *three tumbledown rooms* / 这个醉鬼～地在马路上走。*The drunk man staggered along the road*.

【东道】(又作'东道主') one who treats sb. to a meal；host：做～*play the host*；*stand treat* ◇ ～国 host country

【东方】❶ the east：～欲晓。*Dawn is breaking*. ❷ the East；the Orient ◇ ～航空公司 China Eastern Airlines；(US) Eastern Air Lines Inc.；～明珠 oriental pearl

【东风】❶ east wind；spring wind ❷ driving force of revolution ◇ ～带［气］easterlies

【东风吹马耳】like the east wind blowing at the ear of a horse—go in one ear and out the other

【东郭先生】Master Dongguo (the soft-hearted scholar who narrowly escaped being eaten by a wolf which he had helped to hide from a hunter)—a naive person who gets into trouble through being soft-hearted to evil people

【东海】the Donghai Sea；the East China Sea

【东家】a form of address formerly used by an employee to his employer or a tenant-peasant to his landlord；master；boss

【东经】［地理］east longitude：北京位于～116度，北纬40度。*Beijing is located at 40°N and 116°E*.

【东拉西扯】drag in irrelevant matters；talk at random；ramble：他做起报告来，～不着边际。*When he lectures he often strays from the subject*.

【东鳞西爪】odds and ends；bits and pieces；fragments：～地收集材料 *glean scraps of information*

【东盟】〈略〉见〖东南亚国家联盟〗

【东南】❶ southeast ❷ southeast China；the Southeast

【东南亚】Southeast Asia

【东南亚国家联盟】the Association of Southeast Asian Nations (ASEAN)

【东欧】Eastern Europe

【东跑西颠】rush here and hurry there；rush about

【东拼西凑】scrape together；knock together：他～地借到了一笔钱。*He scraped together a sum of money by borrowing left and right*. / 那篇文章是～来的。*That article is just scissors-and-paste work*.

【东山再起】stage a comeback；resume one's former position

【东施效颦】Dongshi，an ugly woman，knitting her brows in imitation of the famous beauty (西施)，only to make herself uglier—crude imitation with ludicrous effect

【东西】❶ east and west ❷ from east to west：这地方～三里，南北五里。*This district is three li across from east to west and five li from north to south*. ❸ thing：他收拾好～就走了。*He packed his things and left*. / 一成不变的～是没有的。*Nothing is immutable*. ❹ (referring to a person or animal) thing；creature：这小～真可爱。*What a sweet little thing*! / 真不是～！ *What a despicable creature*!

【东…西…】here ... there：东一个，西一个 (*of things*) *be scattered here and there* / 东一句，西一句 *talk incoherently*

【东西对话】East-West dialogue

【东亚】East Asia

【东张西望】gaze (or peer) around；glance this way and that；look in every direction：她在车站外～了一会，看不见有接她的人。*She stood outside the station，looking round in all directions，but apparently no one had come to meet her*.

【东正教】the Orthodox Eastern Church

冬 Ⅰ 名 winter：～寒 *winter cold* Ⅱ 象 the sound of beating a drum，knocking at a door，etc.；rub-a-dub；rat-tat；rat-a-tat

【冬菜】preserved，dried cabbage or mustard greens

【冬虫夏草】［中］Chinese caterpillar fungus (Cordyceps sinensis)

【冬储】store away in winter

【冬耕】winter ploughing

【冬菇】dried mushrooms (picked in winter)

【冬瓜】wax gourd；white gourd

【冬灌】［农］winter irrigation

【冬烘】shallow but pedantic

【冬候鸟】winter bird

【冬季】winter ◇ ～施工 winter construction；～体育运动 winter sports

【冬季作物】winter crops

【冬眠】［生］winter sleep；hibernation

【冬青】［植］Chinese ilex

【冬笋】winter bamboo shoots

【冬天】winter

【冬汛】［渔］winter fishing season

【冬衣】winter clothes

【冬泳】winter outdoor swimming

【冬至】the Winter Solstice—the 22nd of the 24 solar terms

【冬装】winter dress (or clothes)

氡 名［化］radon (Rn)

dǒng

董 Ⅰ **动**〈书〉direct；superintend；supervise：～其成 *supervise the project until its completion* Ⅱ **名** director；trustee

【董事】director；trustee

【董事会】board of directors (in an enterprise)；board of trustees (in an educational institution)

【董事长】chairman (or president) of the board of directors

懂 **动** understand；know：～英语 *know English* / ～礼貌 *have good manners* / 不要不～装～。*Don't pretend to know (or understand) when you don't.* / 他的话我听～了。*I understand what he said.*

【懂得】understand；know；grasp：这一事件使我们更清楚地～了问题的复杂性。*This incident brought home to us the complex nature of the problem.* / 用群众所熟悉和～的词句 *use words which are familiar and intelligible to the masses*

【懂行】〈方〉know the business；know the ropes

【懂事】sensible；intelligent：～的孩子 *a sensible child* / 你怎么这样不～？*How can you be so thoughtless?*

dòng

动 **动** ❶ move；stir：他扭了腰，～不了。*He's strained his back and can't move.* / 微风吹～树叶。*A breeze stirred the leaves.* ❷ act；get moving：经过动员，群众普遍地～起来了。*After the mobilization meetings, the masses all got moving.* ❸ change；alter：这句话只要～一两个字就顺了。*Just change one or two words and the sentence will read smoothly.* ❹ use：～脑筋 *use one's head* ❺ touch (one's heart)；arouse：～了公愤 *have aroused public indignation* / ～感情 *be carried away by emotion；get worked up* / 不为甜言蜜语所～ *not be swayed by fine words* ❻〈方〉(usu. used in the negative) eat or drink：不～荤腥 *never touch meat or fish；be a vegetarian*

【动笔】take up the pen；start writing：他最近很少～。*He hasn't done much writing recently.* / 想清楚了再～。*Think it all out before you start writing.*

【动宾词组】[语] verb-object word group

【动不动】easily；frequently；at every turn：～就感冒 *catch cold easily* / ～就发脾气 *be apt to lose one's temper；often get into a temper* / 他～就训人。*He is always lecturing people.*

【动产】movable property；movables；personal property ◇ ～抵押 chattel mortgage

【动产和不动产】movable and immovable property

【动词】[语] verb：～不定式 *infinitive*

【动荡】turbulence；upheaval；unrest：～的局势 *a turbulent situation*

【动荡不安】turbulent；in turmoil：世界局势～。*The world situation is characterized by turbulence and intranquility.*

【动电学】electrokinetics

【动肝火】get angry；flare up

【动工】❶ begin construction；start building：新的电视塔～了。*Construction of the new television tower has started.* ❷ construct：这里正在～，车辆不能通过。*Construction site ahead. No thoroughfare.*

【动画片】animated cartoon (or drawing)；cartoon

【动火】〈口〉get angry；flare up

【动机】motive；intention：出于自私的～ *be actuated by selfish motives* / ～不纯 *have impure motives* / 他的～是好的。*His intentions are good.* or *He means well.*

【动静】❶ the sound of sth. astir：屋子里静悄悄的，一点～也没有。*It was quiet in the room, nothing was stirring.* ❷ movement；activity：发现可疑～ *spot something suspicious*

【动力】❶ motive power；power ❷ motive (or driving) force；impetus：社会发展的～ *the motive force of the development of society* / 改革是推进一切工作的～。*Reform motivates us in all our work.* ◇ ～反应堆 power reactor；power pile；～机械 motive power machine；～学 dynamics；kinetics

【动量】[物] momentum：广义～ *generalized momentum* / ～矩 *moment of momentum* ◇ ～守恒定律 [物] the law of conservation of momentum

【动令】[军] command of execution

【动乱】turmoil；disturbance；upheaval；turbulence：～时期 *a time of turmoil；a time of storm and stress* / 社会～ *social upheaval* / ～年代 *years of upheaval*

【动脉】[生理] artery：～脉搏 *arterial pulse* ◇ ～弓 arch of aorta；～血压 arterial pressure；～脉炎 arteritis；～硬化 arteriosclerosis；～粥样硬化 atherosclerosis

【动名词】[语] gerund

【动能】[物] kinetic energy

【动怒】lose one's temper；flare up

【动气】〈口〉take offence；get angry

【动情】❶ get worked up；become excited ❷ become enamoured；have one's (sexual) passions aroused

【动人】moving；touching：～的情景 *a moving scene* / ～的事迹 *stirring deeds* / ～的故事 *a touching story*

【动人心弦】tug at one's heartstrings；be deeply moving

【动身】go (or set out) on a journey；leave (for a distant place)：行李都打好了，我们明天早上就～。*We've already packed and will leave tomorrow morning.*

【动手】❶ start work；get to work：早点儿～，早点儿完成。*The sooner we start, the sooner we fin-*

ish. ❷ touch; handle: 爱护展品,请勿～。*Please don't touch the exhibits*. ❸ raise a hand to strike; hit out: 谁先动的手? *Who struck the first blow?* ◇ ～动脚 get fresh with sb.

【动手术】❶ perform an operation; operate on sb. ❷ have an operation; be operated on

【动态】❶ trends; developments: 科技新～ *recent developments in science and technology* ❷ dynamic state: ～电阻 *dynamic resistance* ◇ ～范围 dynamic range; ～分析 dynamic analysis; ～经济学 dynamic economics; ～平衡[物] dynamic equilibrium; ～数据互换 dynamic data exchange(DDE); ～特性[电] dynamic characteristic; ～再定位 dynamic reloction

【动弹】move; stir: 机器不～了。*The machine has stopped*. ◇ ～不得 cannot move

【动听】interesting or pleasant to listen to: 他能把极平常的事儿说得很～。*He can make ordinary things sound interesting*. / 她唱得很～。*She sings beautifully*.

【动土】break ground; start building

【动窝】〈方〉start moving; make a move: 不管你说什么,他就是不～。*No matter what you say, he just won't stir*.

【动武】use force; start a fight; come to blows

【动物】animal: ～界 *the animal kingdom* ◇ ～蛋白因子 animal protein factor; ～胶[化] animal size (or glue); ～区系 fauna; ～权益维护者 animal rightist; ～生态学 animal ecology; ～学 zoology; ～油 animal oil; ～园 zoo; zoological garden; ～志 fauna

【动向】trend; tendency: 新～ *new trends*

【动心】one's mind is perturbed; one's desire, enthusiasm or interest is aroused

【动刑】subject sb. to torture; torture

【动眼神经】oculomotor nerve

【动摇】shake; vacillate; waver: 环境再艰苦也～不了他们征服自然的决心。*No difficulties can shake their resolve to conquer nature*.

【动议】motion: 紧急～ *an urgent motion* / 提出一项～ *put forward a motion*

【动用】put to use; employ; draw on: ～大量人力 *employ a tremendous amount of manpower* / ～库存 *draw on stock*

【动员】mobilize; arouse: 整个医院都～起来,抢救伤员。*The whole hospital was galvanized into action to save the wounded*. ◇ ～报告 mobilization speech; ～大会 mobilization meeting; ～令 mobilization order

【动植物检疫】quarantine of animals and plants

【动辄】〈书〉easily; frequently; at every turn: ～发怒 *fly into a rage on the slightest provocation*

【动辄得咎】be constantly taken to task; be blamed for whatever one does

【动作】❶ movement; motion; action: ～敏捷(缓慢) *quick (slow) in one's movements* / 优美的舞蹈～ *graceful dance movements* ❷ act; start moving: 且看他下一步如何～。*Let's see how he acts next*.

冻 Ⅰ 动 ❶ freeze: 水管里的水～了。*The water in the pipes froze*. ❷ feel very cold; freeze; be frostbitten: 多穿些,别～着了。*Put on more clothes so you don't catch cold*. / 她手都～了。*Her hands were frostbitten*. / 真～得够戗! *Brr, I'm freezing!* Ⅱ 名 jelly: 肉冻

【冻冰】freeze: 河上～了。*The river is frozen*.

【冻疮】chilblain: 生～ *have chilblains*

【冻豆腐】frozen bean curd

【冻害】[农] freeze injury

【冻僵】frozen stiff; numb with cold

【冻结】❶ freeze; congeal ❷ (of wages, prices, etc.) freeze: 工资～ *wage freeze* / ～的资产 *frozen assets*; ◇ ～账目 frozen account; ～资金 frozen fund; blocked fund

【冻凝】congeal: ～点 *congealing point*

【冻伤】frostbite

【冻死】freeze to death; freeze and perish; die of frost: 昨天来寒流时,～了两只小羊。*When the cold snap set in yesterday, two lambs froze to death*.

【冻土】frozen earth (or ground, soil) ◇ ～学 cryopedology

【冻雨】[气] sleet

【冻原】another name for 〖苔原〗

洞 Ⅰ 名 hole; cavity: 城门～儿 *archway of a city gate* / 衬衣破了一个～ *have a hole in one's shirt* Ⅱ 副 〈书〉penetratingly; thoroughly: 洞晓

【洞察】see clearly; have an insight into: ～力 *insight; discernment; acumen* / ～是非 *see clearly the rights and wrongs of the case* / ～一切 *have a keen insight into matters*

【洞彻】understand thoroughly; see clearly: ～事理 *be sensible and perfectly aware*

【洞穿】❶ pierce: 一颗子弹～他的右肺。*A bullet pierced his right lung*. ❷ have an insight into; understand fully

【洞达】understand thoroughly: ～事理 *be sensible*

【洞房】bridal (or nuptial) chamber

【洞房花烛】wedding festivities; wedding

【洞若观火】see sth. as clearly as a blazing fire

【洞天】cave heaven—fairyland; a heavenly abode: 别有～ *a place of unique, enchanting beauty*

【洞悉】know clearly; understand thoroughly

【洞箫】a vertical bamboo flute

【洞晓】have a clear knowledge of: ～其中利弊 *have a clear understanding of the advantages and disadvantages*

【洞穴】cave; cavern ◇ ～墓 catacomb

【洞烛】see through; discern clearly: ～其阴谋 *see through his scheme*

【洞烛其奸】see through sb.'s tricks

恫 动 〈书〉fear

【恫吓】threaten; intimidate

栋 Ⅰ 名 〈书〉ridgepole Ⅱ 量 (for buildings): 一～楼房 *a building*

【栋梁】ridgepole and beam—pillar of the state ◇ ～之材 one with the makings of a statesman

dōu

都 副 ❶ all：大家～到了吗？*Is everybody here?* / 我父母～不在了。*My parents are both dead.* / 什么～行。*Anything will do.* ❷ (used with 是 to show the cause)：～是你老磨蹭，害得我们迟到了。*It was all because of your dawdling that we were late.* / ～是你，把他灌成这样。*It's all your fault; you made him drunk.* ❸ even：今天天气真怪，中午比早晨～冷。*Strange weather we're having today, It's even colder at noon than it was early in the morning.* / 连他～不知道。*Even he doesn't know it.* ❹ already：他～八十岁了，身子骨还那么硬朗。*He's already eighty but still going strong.* ——另见 dū

兜 Ⅰ 名 pocket; bag：他站着，两手插在～里。*He stood with his hands in his pockets.* / 钥匙在我上衣～里。*The key is in my coat pocket.* Ⅱ 动 ❶ wrap up in a piece of cloth, etc.：用毛巾～着几个鸡蛋 *carry a few eggs wrapped up in a towel* ❷ move round：我们乘车在城里～了一圈。*We went for a drive around in town.* ❸ canvass; solicit：～了一号买卖 *have convassed a business order* ❹ take upon oneself; take responsibility for sth.：没关系，出了问题我～着。*Don't worry. If anything goes wrong, I'll take responsibility for it.*

【兜捕】surround and seize; round up：～一伙走私犯 *close in on the gang of smugglers*

【兜抄】close in from the rear and both flanks; round up

【兜底】〈口〉reveal all the details (of a person's disreputable background, etc.); disclose the whole inside story：千万别兜他的底儿！*Don't you bring up anything about his past!*

【兜击】furning attack

【兜风】❶ catch the wind：帆破了～兜不住风。*The sails are torn; they won't catch the wind.* ❷ 〈方〉go for a drive, ride or sail; go for a spin：在河边骑车兜兜风，很有意思。*It's fun to take a spin on your bicycle along the riverbank.*

【兜揽】❶ canvass; solicit：～生意 *solicit custom; drum up trade* ❷ take upon oneself (sb. else's work, etc.)：这是你～来的事，我不管。*You've taken this on yourself. I'm not going to get involved in it.*

【兜圈子】❶ go around in circles; circle：飞机在森林上空～。*The aeroplane circled over the forest.* ❷ beat about the bush

【兜售】peddle; hawk：～劣货 *hawk low-quality goods* / ～军火 *peddle munitions*

【兜子】pocket; bag

dǒu

斗 Ⅰ 量 a unit of dry measure for grain (= 1 decalitre) Ⅱ 名 ❶ a dou measure ❷ an object shaped like a cup or dipper：漏斗 ❸ (〈略〉见〖北斗星〗) the Big Dipper; the Dipper——另见 dòu

【斗车】trolley (in a mine or at a construction site); tram

【斗胆】〈谦〉make bold; venture：我～说一句，这件事您做错了。*May I make bold to suggest that you were wrong to do so.*

【斗拱】(in monumental buildings) sets of brackets on top of the columns supporting the beams within and roof eaves without (each set consisting of tiers of outstretching arms called gong, cushioned with trapezoidal blocks called dou)

【斗箕】(又作'斗记') fingerprint

【斗笠】bamboo hat

【斗篷】❶ cape; cloak ❷ [方] bamboo hat

【斗渠】[水] lateral canal

【斗式提升机】[机] bucket elevator

【斗烟丝】pipe tobacco

抖 动 ❶ tremble; shiver; quiver：浑身直～ *tremble all over* ❷ shake; jerk：把衣服上的雪～掉 *shake the snow off one's clothes* / ～一～缰绳 *give the reins a jerk* ❸ rouse; stir up：～起精神 *pluck up one's spirits* ❹ (used sarcastically) get on in the world

【抖动】shake; tremble; vibrate

【抖搂】〈方〉❶ shake off; shake out of sth.：把包里的东西～出来 *shake a bag to empty it* ❷ expose; bring to light：把她干的那些坏事给大伙～～。*Let everyone know all the wicked things she has done.*

【抖擞】enliven; rouse：精神抖擞 ◇ ～精神 brace up; pull oneself together

【抖威风】throw one's weight about

陡 Ⅰ 形 steep; precipitous：山～路险。*The hill is steep, and the climb is dangerous.* Ⅱ 副 suddenly; unexpectedly; abruptly：天气～变。*The weather changed suddenly.* / 狂风～起。*A sudden gale struck.*

【陡槽】[水] chute

【陡度】[物] gradient：压力～ *pressure gradient*

【陡峻】high and precipitous

【陡立】rise steeply

【陡坡】steep slope

【陡峭】recipitous：～的山崖 *a sheer precipice*

【陡然】suddenly; unexpectedly; abruptly：～下降 *fall suddenly*

dòu

斗 动 ❶ fight; tussle：拳～ *fist fight; fisticuffs* ❷ struggle against; denounce ❸ contest with;

contend with：很少人～得过他。*Few people can get the better of him*. / 狐狸再狡猾也～不过好猎手。*The craftiest fox can't escape the skilled hunter*. ❹ make animals fight (as a game)：～蛐蛐 *hold a cricketfight* ❺ fit together：～榫 *fit the tenon into the mortise；dovetail* / 大家～一～情况。*Let's pool our information and size up the situation*. ——另见 dǒu

【斗法】❶ exercise magic powers against each other ❷ use stratagems

【斗牛】bullfight ◇ ～士 bullfighter；matador

【斗殴】fight；scuffle

【斗气】quarrel or contend with sb. on account of a personal grudge

【斗心眼儿】fight a battle of wits

【斗争】❶ struggle；fight；combat：新与旧的～ *conflict between the new and the old* ❷ accuse and denounce at a meeting ❸ strive for；fight for：为完成五年计划而～ *strive for the fulfilment of the five-year plan* ◇ ～性 fighting spirit；militancy

【斗志】will to fight；fighting will：～昂扬 *have high morale；be full of fight；be militant*

【斗智】fight a battle of wits

【斗嘴】❶ quarrel；bicker；squabble ❷ banter

豆 名 pod-bearing plant or its seeds：扁豆

【豆瓣酱】thick broad-bean sauce

【豆包】steamed bun stuffed with sweetened bean paste

【豆饼】[农] soya-bean cake；bean cake

【豆豉】fermented soya beans，salted or otherwise

【豆腐】bean curd ◇ ～房 bean-curd plant；～干 dried bean curd；～脑儿 jellied bean curd；～皮 skin of soya-bean milk；～乳 fermented bean curd

【豆腐渣工程】construction project with building materials like bean dregs；project built with skimped materials

【豆荚】pod

【豆浆】soya-bean milk

【豆角儿】〈口〉fresh kidney beans

【豆秸】beanstalk (left after threshing)

【豆科】[植] the pulse family；bean (or pea) family ◇ ～植物 legume；leguminous plant

【豆蔻】[植] round cardamom (Amomum cardamomum)

【豆蔻年华】(of a girl) in one's early teens

【豆绿】(又作'豆青') pea green

【豆面】bean flour

【豆娘】[动] damselfly

【豆萁】〈方〉beanstalk

【豆蓉】fine bean mash，used as stuffing in cakes

【豆沙】sweetened bean paste

【豆象】[动] bean weevil

【豆芽儿】bean sprouts

【豆雁】[动] bean goose

【豆油】soya-bean oil

【豆渣】residue from beans after making soyabean milk；bean dregs

【豆汁】❶ a fermented drink made from ground beans ❷〈方〉soya-bean milk

【豆制品】bean products

【豆子】❶ pod-bearing plant or its seeds ❷ bean-shaped thing

逗 Ⅰ 动 ❶ tease；play with：～孩子玩 *play with a child* / 别～了。*You're kidding*! ❷ provoke (laughter，etc.)；amuse：这小女孩～人喜欢。*She's a lovable little girl*. ❸ stay；stop：逗留 Ⅱ 形〈方〉funny：这话真～！*What a funny remark*!

【逗哏】[戏] provoke laughter with funny remarks (esp. in a comic dialogue)

【逗号】comma (，)

【逗留】(又作'逗遛') stay；stop：他们中途在西安～了几天。*They stopped over in Xi'an for several days*. / 禁止～！*No loitering*!

【逗弄】tease；kid；make fun of：他～你呢。*He's kidding you*.

【逗趣儿】〈方〉set people laughing (by funny remarks，etc.)；amuse：他真会～！*He's really very amusing*!

【逗笑儿】〈方〉amusing

【逗引】tease：～孩子玩儿 *amuse oneself by teasing with the kids* / 这孩子被～哭了。*The child has been teased to tears*.

痘 名 ❶ smallpox ❷ smallpox pustule ❸ (bovine) vaccine：种痘

【痘苗】(bovine) vaccine

窦 名 ❶ hole ❷ [生理] sinus：鼻窦

dū

都 名 ❶ capital (of a country)：建都 ❷ big city；metropolis：鞍山是我国的钢～。*Anshan is our country's steel metropolis*. ——另见 dōu

【都城】capital (of a country)

【都督】❶ commander-in-chief in ancient China ❷ provincial military governor in the early Republican period who was also in charge of civil administration

【都会】a big city；metropolis

【都市】a big city；metropolis ◇ ～化 urbanization；～化地区 urbanized areas

嘟 Ⅰ 象 toot；honk：汽车喇叭～～响。*The car tooted*. Ⅱ 动〈方〉pout：生气地～起了嘴 *pout sulkily*

【嘟噜】〈口〉❶ bunch；cluster：一～葡萄 *a bunch of grapes* / 一～钥匙 *a bunch of keys* ❷ hang down in a bunch ❸ trill；打～儿 *pronounce with a trill；trill*

【嘟囔】(又作'嘟哝') mutter to oneself；mumble：他嘴里嘟嘟囔囔的，也不知道在说什么。*He was mumbling to himself and was barely intelligible*.

督 动 superintend and direct：～战 *supervise (military) operations*

【督察】superintend；supervise

【督促】supervise and urge：已经布置了的工作，应当认真～检查。*We must supervise and speed up fulfilment of assigned tasks.*

【督导】supervise and direct：～人员 *supervisory personnel* / ～培训班 *course for training supervisors*

【督军】provincial military governor in the early Republican period

【督励】urge and encourage

【督学】〈旧〉educational inspector

dú

毒 Ⅰ 名 ❶ poison；toxin：服毒 ❷ narcotics；(narcotic) drugs：吸毒 Ⅱ 形 ❶ poisonous；noxious；poisoned：～蜘蛛 *poisonous spider* / 有～气体 *noxious gas* / ～箭 *a poisoned arrow* ❷ malicious；cruel；fierce：他的心肠真～！*How cruel he is!* / 那时太阳正～，晒得他汗珠直往下滚。*The sun was at its fiercest and beads of sweat kept rolling down his face.* / ～打 *beat up* Ⅲ 动 ❶ kill with poison；poison：～老鼠 *poison rats* ❷ poison (sb.'s mind)：毒害

【毒扁豆】[植] calabar bean ◇ ～碱 [药] physostigmine；eserine

【毒草】❶ poisonous weeds ❷ harmful speech, writing, etc.

【毒蛾】tussock moth

【毒饵】poison bait

【毒谷】poison grains (planted with seeds to kill harmful insects)

【毒害】❶ murder by poisoning；poison ❷ poison (sb.'s mind)

【毒化】poison；spoil：～会谈的气氛 *poison the atmosphere of the talks* / ～社会风气 *debase social morality*

【毒计】venomous scheme；deadly trap

【毒剂】toxic；toxicant

【毒辣】sinister；diabolic：阴险～ *sinister and ruthless* / 手段～ *vicious means*

【毒瘤】malignant tumour；cancer

【毒品】narcotics；(narcotic) drugs

【毒气】poisonous (or poison) gas ◇ ～弹 gas shell；gas bomb；～室 gas chamber

【毒区】contaminated area (in chemical warfare)；gassed area

【毒杀】kill with poison；poison

【毒杀芬】[农] toxaphene；octachlorocamphene

【毒蛇】poisonous (or venomous) snake；viper

【毒手】violent treachery；murderous scheme —— 另见〖下毒手〗

【毒死】kill with poison；poison：这药～了三个人。*Three people were poisoned by this chemical.*

【毒素】❶ [生] toxin ❷ poison：清除封建～ *eliminate feudal poison*

【毒瓦斯】poisonous (or poison) gas

【毒物】poisonous substance；poison

【毒腺】[动] poison gland

【毒枭】big drug trafficker

【毒刑】cruel corporal punishment；horrible torture

【毒性】toxicity；poisonousness

【毒蕈】poisonous fungus；toadstool

【毒牙】poison (or venom) fang

【毒药】poison；toxicant

【毒液】venom

【毒瘾】drug addiction

【毒汁】venom

独 Ⅰ 形 only；single：～子 *only son* Ⅱ 副 ❶ solely；only：大家都到了，～有他还没来。*He's the only one who isn't here yet.* ❷ alone；by oneself；in solitude：～居 *live a solitary existence* / ～坐 *sit alone* Ⅲ 名 old people without offspring；the childless：鳏寡孤独

【独霸】dominate exclusively；monopolize ◇ ～一方 lord it over a district；be a local despot

【独白】soliloquy；monologue

【独步】be unrivalled：～文坛 *be the unrivalled literary colossus of the age*

【独裁】dictatorship；autocratic rule：～者 *autocrat；dictator* / ～政治 *autocracy*

【独唱】(vocal) solo ◇ ～会 recital (of a vocalist)

【独出心裁】show originality；be original

【独创】original creation：～精神 *creative spirit* / ～性 *originality* / ～一格 *create a style all one's own；have a unique (or distinctive) style*

【独此一家】the only authentic one (brand, store etc)

【独词句】[语] one-member sentence

【独当一面】take charge of a department or locality；assume responsibility for a certain sector：他成长很快，已经可以～了。*He's matured quickly, He can now take charge of the whole locality.*

【独到】original：～的见解 *original view* ◇ ～之处 distinctive qualities；specific characteristics

【独断】arbitrary；dictatorial

【独断独行】(又作'独断专行') make arbitrary decisions and take peremptory action；act arbitrarily

【独家】sole；the only one；exclusive：～经销 *sole agent* ◇ ～出口 the sole export；～代理 sole agency；～代理人 sole agent；～经销 exclusive sell；～经营 engage in a line of business without competion；～新闻 Journalism exclusive；～主顾 monospony

【独角戏】(又作'独脚戏') monodrama；one-man show

【独具匠心】show ingenuity；have originality

【独具只眼】be able to see what others cannot；have exceptional insight

【独来独往】coming and going all alone— unsociable；aloof：她老是～的。*She kept pretty much to herself.*

【独揽】arrogate；monopolize：～大权 *arrogate all powers to oneself*

【独力】by one's own efforts；on one's own：～经营 *manage affairs on one's own*

【独立】❶ stand alone：～山巅的苍松 *a pine tree standing alone on a mountain peak* ❷ independence：宣布～ *proclaim independence* ❸ independent；on one's own：～营（团、师）*independent battalion*（*regiment*，*division*）/ ～分析问题和解决问题的能力 *ability to analyse and solve problems on one's own* ◇ ～成分［语］independent element；～法人 independent legal person；～国 independent state；～核算 keep separate accounts；practise independent accounting；～核算单位 independent accounting unit；～核算自负盈亏 independent accounting and assume sole responsibility for its profits losses；～经营承包商 independent contractor；～王国〈喻〉independent kingdom；～自主的和平外交政策 independent foreign policy of peace

【独立性】independent character；independence：闹～ *assert one's "independence"—refuse to obey the leadership*

【独立自主】maintain independence and keep the initiative；act independently and with the initiative in one's own hands

【独联体】the Commonwealth of Independent States

【独轮车】wheelbarrow

【独门独院】a single house which has its own entrance and courtyard

【独苗】（又作'独苗苗'）only son and heir

【独木不成林】one tree doesn't make a forest—one person alone can't accomplish much

【独木难支】one log can't prop up a tottering building—one person alone can't save the situation

【独木桥】❶ single-plank（or single-log）bridge ❷ difficult path

【独木舟】dugout canoe

【独幕剧】one-act play

【独辟蹊径】open a new road for oneself；develop a new style or a method of one's own

【独善其身】maintain one's own integrity

【独身】❶ separated from one's family：～在外 *be away from home and family* ❷ unmarried；single：她现在还是～。*She's still single*. ◇ ～主义 celibacy

【独生女】only daughter

【独生子】only son

【独生子女】only child ◇ ～费 the only-child allowance

【独树一帜】fly one's own colours —develop a school of one's own

【独特】unique；distinctive：～的风格 *a unique style*

【独吞】take exclusive possession of sth.

【独舞】solo dance

【独行其是】do what one thinks is right regardless of others' opinions

【独眼龙】〈贬〉a person blind in one eye；one-eyed person

【独一无二】unique；unparalleled；unmatched

【独占】have sth. all to oneself；monopolize

【独占鳌头】come out first；head the list of successful candidates；be the champion

【独占资本】［经］monopoly capital

【独资】exclusive investment ◇ ～经营 single proprietorship；sole proprietorship；～企业 exclusive investment in enterprises；enterprises solely owned by sb.

【独自】alone；by oneself：他～一人走向公园。*He walked on alone towards the park*.

【独奏】（instrumental）solo：钢琴～ *piano solo* ◇ ～会 recital（of an instrumentalist）

读 动 ❶ read；read aloud：这部小说值得一～。*This novel is worth reading*. / ～报 *read the newspaper aloud* / 老师～一句，同学们跟着～一句。*The students read after the teacher sentence by sentence*. ❷ attend school：～完大学 *finish college* ——另见 dòu

【读本】reader；textbook：汉语～ *a Chinese reader*

【读出装置】reading machine；readout unit

【读卡机】card reader

【读书】❶ read；study：～是学习，使用也是学习，而且是更重要的学习。*Reading is learning，but applying is also learning and the more important kind of learning at that*. / 她～很用功。*She studies hard*. ❷ attend school ◇ ～班 study class

【读书笔记】reading notes

【读数】reading：温度计～ *thermometer reading* / 标度～ *scale reading*

【读图】interpret blueprints；interpret drawings

【读物】reading matter（or material）：儿童～ *children's books* / 通俗～ *popular literature*

【读写磁头】read write head

【读写存储器】read write memory

【读音】pronunciation：他把这个字的～忘了。*He forgot the pronunciation of this word*.

【读者】reader（of a book，newspaper，etc.）◇ ～来信 readers' letters；letters to the editor；～文摘 Reader's Digest（a popular American magazine）

渎 动〈书〉show disrespect or contempt：亵渎

犊 名 calf：初生之犊不畏虎

牍 名 ❶ wooden tablets or slips for writing（in ancient times）❷ documents；archives；correspondence：文牍

黩 动〈书〉❶ blacken；defile ❷ act wantonly

【黩武】〈书〉militaristic；warlike；bellicose：穷兵黩武 ◇ ～主义 militarism

dǔ

肚 名 tripe：拌～丝儿 *slices of pork tripe and*

cucumber in soy sauce ——另见 dù
【肚子】(dǔzi) tripe ——另见 dùzi

笃 形 ❶ sincere; earnest: 感情弥～ *have an ever deeper affection for each other*; *be more passionately attached to each other* ❷ (of an illness) serious; critical: 病笃
【笃厚】sincere and magnanimous
【笃实】❶ honest and sincere ❷ solid; sound: 学问～ *sound scholarship*
【笃信】sincerely believe in; be a devout believer in
【笃学】diligent in study; devoted to study; studious

堵 Ⅰ动 ❶ stop up; block up: 把老鼠洞～死 *stop up mouseholes* / 我鼻子～了。*My nose is all blocked up*. / 别～着门! *Don't stand in the doorway*! ❷ stifled; suffocated; oppressed: 胸口～得慌 *feel suffocated*; *feel a tightness in the chest* / 心里～得难受 *have a load on one's mind* Ⅱ名〈书〉wall: 观者如～。*There was a crowd of spectators*. Ⅲ量 (used of walls): 一～墙 *a wall*
【堵击】intercept and attack: ～逃敌 *intercept the fleeing enemy*
【堵截】intercept: ～不明国籍的飞机 *intercept an unidentified airplane*
【堵塞】stop up; block up: 交通～ *traffic jam* / ～漏洞 *stop up a loophole*; *plug a hole*
【堵嘴】gag sb.; silence sb.: 你别想堵住我的嘴。*You can't stop me from speaking out*.

赌 动 ❶ gamble: ～了个通宵 *gamble all night* ❷ bet: 打赌
【赌本】❶ money to gamble with ❷ resources for risky ventures
【赌博】gambling
【赌场】gambling house
【赌风】the common and unhealthy practice of gambling
【赌棍】hardened (or professional) gambler
【赌局】gambling party; gambling joint
【赌具】gambling paraphernalia; gambling device
【赌窟】gambling-den
【赌气】feel wronged and act rashly: 他觉得受了委屈,一～就走了。*Feeling he had been wronged, he went off in a fit of pique*.
【赌钱】gamble
【赌徒】gambler
【赌债】a gambling debt
【赌咒】take an oath; swear
【赌注】stake

睹 动 see: 目睹
【睹物思人】seeing the thing one thinks of the person—the thing reminds one of its owner

dù

杜 Ⅰ名 birch-leaf pear Ⅱ动 shut out; stop; prevent: 以～流弊 *so as to put an end to abuses*
【杜蘅】(又作'杜衡')[植] wild ginger
【杜渐防微】同〖防微杜渐〗
【杜鹃】❶ [动] cuckoo ❷ [植] azalea
【杜绝】stop; put an end to: ～弊端 *stop all corrupt practices* / ～浪费 *put an end to waste*
【杜康】❶ legendary figure who first distilled liquor ❷〈喻〉wine (or liquor): 何以解忧? 惟有～。*There is nothing but wine to assuage my sorrow*.
【杜梨】birch-leaf pear
【杜灭芬】[药] domiphen
【杜松子酒】gin
【杜宇】[动] cuckoo
【杜仲】[中] the bark of eucommia (Eucommia ulmoides) ◇ ～胶 gutta-percha
【杜撰】fabricate; make up: 他讲的是真有其事,不是～的。*The story he told is true, not made up*.

肚 名 belly; abdomen; stomach ——另见 dǔ
【肚带】bellyband; girth
【肚皮】〈方〉belly
【肚脐】(又作'肚脐眼儿') navel; belly button
【肚子】(dùzi) ❶ belly; abdomen: ～疼 *have a stomachache*; *suffer from abdominal pain* / 笑得～疼 *laugh till one's sides split* / 一～气 *absolutely exasperated*; *full of pent-up anger* ❷ a belly-shaped thing: 腿肚子 ——另见 dǔzi

妒 动 be jealous (or envious) of; envy: 同行相～ *professional jealousy*
【妒忌】be jealous (or envious) of; envy
【妒贤嫉能】be jealous of the worthy and the able
【妒意】feeling of jealousy; jealousy: 满脸～ *very image (or picture) of jealousy*

度 Ⅰ名 ❶ linear measure: 度量衡 ❷ degree of intensity: 硬度/ 湿度 ❸ limit; extent; degree: 将玻璃管加热,以能弯曲为～。*Heat the glass tube to the point that it can bend*. ❹ tolerance; magnanimity: 度量 ❺ consideration: 置之度外 Ⅱ量 ❶ a unit of measurement for angles, temperature, etc.; degree: 直角为九十～。*A right angle is an angle of 90 degrees*. / 北纬三十八～ *latitude 38° N*. ❷ [电] kilowatt-hour (kwh) ❸ occasion; time: 一年一～ *once a year* Ⅲ动 spend; pass: 在农村～过童年 *spend one's childhood in the countryside* ——另见 duó
【度荒】tide over a lean year
【度假】spend one's holidays (or vacation); go vacationing ◇ ～村 vacational village; holiday village
【度量】tolerance; magnanimity: ～大 *broadminded*; *magnanimous* / ～小 *narrow-minded*
【度量衡】length, capacity and weight; weights and measures ◇ ～学 metrology
【度日】subsist (in hardship); eke out an existence: 过去他靠什么～的? *What did he do for a living in the old days*?
【度日如年】one day seems like a year; the days

drag on like years

【度数】number of degrees；reading：那个表上的～是多少？*What does that meter read?*

渡 Ⅰ 动 ❶ cross (a river, the sea, etc.)：～河 *cross a river* / 飞～太平洋 *fly (across) the Pacific* ❷ tide over；pull through：～过难关 *tide over a difficulty；pull through* ❸ ferry (people, goods, etc.) across Ⅱ 名 (usu. used as part of a place name) ferry crossing：深～(*in Anhui Province*)

【渡槽】aqueduct

【渡场】［军］crossing site

【渡船】ferryboat；ferry

【渡河点】point of crossing

【渡口】ferry crossing

【渡轮】ferry steamer；ferryboat

【渡鸦】［动］raven

镀 动 plating：～镍 *nickel-plating* / ～铝钢 *aluminium-plated steel*

【镀金】❶ gold-plating；gilding ❷ get gilded (formerly said of students who went abroad to study in order to enhance their social status)

【镀锡】tin-plating；tinning ◇ ～铁 tinplate

【镀锌】zinc-plating；galvanizing ◇ ～铁 galvanized iron

【镀银】silver-plating；silvering

蠹 Ⅰ 名 a kind of insect that eats into books, clothing, etc.；moth：书～ *bookworm* Ⅱ 动 moth-eaten；worm-eaten：流水不腐，户枢不蠹

【蠹虫】❶ a kind of insect that eats into books, clothing, etc.；moth ❷ a harmful person；vermin

【蠹鱼】silverfish；fish moth

duān

端 Ⅰ 名 ❶ end；extremity：两～ *both ends* / 岛的南～ *the southern tip (or end) of the island* ❷ beginning：开端 ❸ point；item：举其一～ *for instance；just to mention one example* ❹ reason；cause：无端 Ⅱ 形 upright；proper：～坐 *sit up straight* Ⅲ 动 hold sth. level with both hands；carry：～盘子 *carry a tray* / ～饭上菜 *serve a meal* / ～进两杯茶来 *bring in two cups of tea*

【端点用户】an end user

【端丽】comely；graceful：姿容～ *have comely features* / 字体～ *write a graceful hand*

【端量】look sb. up and down

【端倪】❶ clue；inkling：略有～ *have an inkling of the matter* ❷ predict：千变万化，不可～。*Things are constantly changing and unpredictable.*

【端午节】the Dragon Boat Festival (the 5th day of the 5th lunar month)

【端线】［体］end line

【端详】❶ details：细说～ *give a full and detailed account；give full particulars* ❷ dignified and serene：举止～ *behave with serene dignity* ❸ look sb. up and down：我～了半天，才认出来她是小张。*I looked her over for a long time before I recognized her as Xiao Zhang.*

【端绪】inkling；clue：我们谈了半天，仍然毫无～。*We talked the matter over for quite some time but didn't get anywhere.*

【端正】❶ upright；regular：五官～ *have regular features* / 把画像端端正正地挂起来 *hang the portrait straight* ❷ proper；correct：品行～ *having good conduct；well-behaved* ❸ rectify；correct：～社会风气 *improve general social conduct* / ～思想 *correct one's thinking；straighten out one's ideas* / ～学习态度 *take a correct attitude towards study*

【端庄】dignified；sedate

duǎn

短 Ⅰ 形 short；brief：她头发剪得～～的。*She had her hair cut short.* / 这条路最～。*This is the shortest way.* / 冬季日～夜长。*In winter the days are short and the nights long.* Ⅱ 动 lack；owe：一个月～两天 *two days short of a month；a month less two days* / 别人都来了，就～他一个。*All the others are here；he's the only one missing.* / ～你三块钱。*I owe you three yuan.* Ⅲ 名 weak point；fault：揭短

【短兵相接】fight at close quarters；engage in hand-to-hand fighting (or close combat)

【短波】shortwave

【短不了】❶ cannot do without：人～水。*Man cannot do without water.* ❷ cannot avoid；have to：以后～还要请你帮忙。*Most likely I'll have to ask you for help again.*

【短程】short distance；short range ◇ ～小客机 air-taxi

【短处】shortcoming；failing；fault；weakness

【短传】［体］short pass

【短促】of very short duration；very brief：呼吸～ *be short of breath；gasp；pant* / 舒伯特～的一生里，六百多首歌曲从他的笔端流泻出来。*During Schubert's brief life, more than 600 songs poured from his pen.*

【短大衣】short overcoat；car coat

【短笛】［音］piccolo

【短吨】short ton

【短工】casual labourer；seasonal labourer

【短骨】［生理］short bone

【短号】［音］cornet

【短见】❶ shortsighted view ❷ suicide：自寻～ *attempt suicide；commit suicide*

【短斤缺两】同〖缺斤短两〗

【短距离】short distance ◇ ～赛跑 short-distance run；dash；sprint

【短裤】shorts

【短路】［电］short circuit
【短命】die young；be short-lived
【短跑】short-distance run；dash；sprint：～运动员 *dash man*；*sprinter*
【短篇小说】short story
【短片】short film；short
【短平快】short，adaptable and fast
【短评】short commentary；brief comment
【短期】short-term：在～内 *in a short time*；*in a brief space of time* / ～贷款 *short-term loan* / ～轮训 *short-term training in rotation* / ～周转资金 *short-term revolving fund* ◇ ～保险 short-term insurance；～公债 short-term public loan；～国库券 short-term treasury bond；～汇率 short quotation；short exchange；～趋势 short swings；～投资 short-term investment；liquid investment；～行为 short-term behavior；short-term action；～预测 short-term forecasting
【短浅】narrow and shallow：见识～ *lacking knowledge and experience*；*shallow*
【短欠】❶ owe；be in arrears ❷ be short of
【短枪】short arm；handgun
【短缺】shortage：～产品 *products in short supply* / 资金～ *short of funds*
【短少】deficient；short；missing：～一页。*There is one page missing*.
【短时记忆】［心理］short-term memory
【短视】❶ nearsightedness；myopia ❷ lack foresight；be shortsighted
【短寿】be short-lived；die young
【短统靴】ankle boots
【短途】short distance：～运输 *short-distance transport*；*short haul*
【短袜】socks
【短尾猴】stump-tailed macaque（or monkey）
【短纤维】❶ short-staple：～棉花 *short-staple cotton* ❷［纺］staple（fibre）：～切断器 *staple cutter*
【短线产品】goods in short supply；goods in great demand；undersupplied product
【短小】short and small；short；small：身材～ *of small stature* / ～的序幕 *a brief prologue*
【短小精悍】❶ not of imposing stature but strong and capable ❷（of a piece of writing）short and pithy；terse and forceful
【短效】short-term effects：～口服避孕药 *contraceptive pills with a short-term effect*
【短卸】short-landed
【短讯】news in brief；brief dispatch
【短训】short-term training training；short training
【短语】［语］phrase
【短元音】［语音］short vowel
【短暂】of short duration；transient；brief：她的一生是～而光荣的一生。*Her life was short but glorious*.
【短装】be dressed in a Chinese-style jacket and trousers

duàn

段 Ⅰ 量 section；segment；part：一～铁路 *a section of railway* / 一～衣料 *a length of dress material* / 这～历史 *this phase of history* / 一～时间 *a period of time* / 边界东～ *the eastern sector of the boundary* Ⅱ 名 paragraph；passage：另起一～ *start a new paragraph* / 这是钢琴五重奏《鳟鱼》里我最喜欢的一～。*That is my favourite passage from the piano quintet，the Trout*.
【段表】segment table
【段落】❶ paragraph：这篇文章～清楚。*This article is well paragraphed*. ❷ phase；stage：第一期工程已经告一～。*The first phase of the project has been completed*.

断 Ⅰ 动 ❶ break；snap：喀嚓一声，～成两截 *break in two with a snap* / 他给小提琴调弦的时候，E 弦～了。*When he was tuning his violin，the E string snapped*. ❷ break off；cut off；stop：～水 *cut off the water supply* ❸ give up；abstain from：～烟 *give up*（*or quit*）*smoking* ❹judge；decide：诊断 Ⅱ 副〈书〉（usu. used in the negative）absolutely；decidedly：～不可信 *absolutely incredible* / ～无此理 *absolutely untenable*（*or unreasonable*）；*the height of absurdity*
【断案】❶ settle a lawsuit ❷［逻］conclusion（of a syllogism）
【断壁】❶ dilapidated walls：残垣断壁 ❷ cliff；precipice；steep
【断编残简】（又作'断简残编'）stray fragments of text
【断层】［地质］fault：倾向（走向）～ *dip*（*strike*）*fault* / ～带 *fault zone* / ～面 *fault plane* / ～作用 *faulting* ◇ ～地震［地质］fault earthquake；～湖［地质］fault lake；～山［地质］fault mountain
【断肠】heartbroken
【断炊】run out of rice and fuel；can't keep the pot boiling；go hungry
【断代】division of history into periods：文学史的～研究 *the study of the history of literature by period* ◇ ～史 dynastic history
【断档】be out of stock；be sold out
【断点】breakpoint；breaking point
【断定】conclude；form a judgment；decide；determine：我们有理由可以～，会议推迟了。*We may reasonably conclude that the meeting has been postponed*.
【断断】（usu. used in the negative）absolutely：～使不得。*That will never do*. or *That simply won't do*.
【断断续续】off and on；intermittently：～读过四年书 *had four years of schooling off and on* / ～地说 *speak haltingly*
【断顿】can't afford the next meal；go hungry

【断根】❶ be completely cured; effect a permanent cure ❷ have no heir; have no progeny
【断后】❶〈旧〉bring up the rear; cover a retreat ❷ have no progeny
【断乎】(usu. used in the negative) absolutely: ～不可 *absolutely impermissible*
【断交】❶ break off a friendship ❷ sever (or break off) diplomatic relations
【断句】❶ make pauses in reading unpunctuated ancient writings ❷ punctuate
【断绝】break off; cut off; sever: ～外交关系 *sever (or break off) diplomatic relations* / ～交通 *stop traffic*
【断粮】run out of grain (or food)
【断流器】[电] cutout: 安全～ *safety cutout*
【断路】❶ [电] open circuit; broken circuit: ～器 *circuit breaker* ❷ waylay; hold up: 一伙武装匪徒～拦劫旅客的钱财。*A band of armed bandits held up the passengers and took all their money.*
【断面】surveying & drawing section: ～图 *sectional drawing; section*
【断奶】(又作'断乳') wean: 给孩子～ *wean a child* / 宝宝已经断了奶,改吃固体食物了。*The baby has been weaned on to solid foods.*
【断片】part; passage; extract; fragment
【断然】❶ resolute; drastic: 采取～措施 *take drastic measures* ❷ absolutely; flatly; categorically: ～不能接受 *absolutely inacceptable* / ～拒绝 *flatly refuse* / ～否认 *categorically deny*
【断送】forfeit (one's life, future, etc.); ruin: 这件丑闻～了他的前程。*The scandal ruined his career.*
【断头】[纺] ❶ broken end ❷ end breaking: ～率 *end breaking rate*
【断头台】guillotine
【断弦】snap the lute string—lose one's wife
【断线】❶ a string being broken: 啊唷,风筝～啦! *Oh, the (kite's) string is broken!* ❷ disconnect; sever; break off: 有的学科后继乏人,面临～的危险。*Certain disciplines lack successors and face the danger of being discontinued.*
【断线风筝】a kite with a broken string—gone beyond recall
【断言】say (or state) with certainty; assert categorically; affirm
【断语】conclusion; judgment: 遽下～ *jump to conclusions*
【断章取义】quote out of context; garble a statement, etc.
【断肢再植】[医] replantation of a severed limb
【断子绝孙】〈讳〉may you die sonless (or without sons); may you be the last of your line

缎 名 satin: 绸缎
【缎纹】satin weave
【缎子】satin

煅 动 ❶ forge: ～铁 *forge iron* ❷ calcine
【煅烧】calcine

椴 名 [植] (Chinese) linden

锻 动 forge
【锻锤】forging hammer
【锻工】❶ forging: ～车间 *forging shop; forge* ❷ forger; blacksmith ◇ ～钳 band jaw tongs
【锻件】forging
【锻接】forge welding
【锻炼】❶ take exercise; have physical training: 每天～半小时 *take half an hour's exercise every day* / 在大江大海中游泳,既可以～身体,又可以～意志。*Swimming in big rivers and seas helps to build up both physical strength and willpower.* ❷ temper; steel; toughen: 劳动～ *temper oneself through manual labour*
【锻炉】forge
【锻铁】❶ wrought iron ❷ forge iron
【锻压机】forging press ◇ ～械 metal forming machine
【锻造】forging; smithing: 压力～ *press forging*

duī

堆 Ⅰ 动 pile up; heap up; stack: 把麦秸～在场上 *stack the wheat-stalks on the threshing ground* / 桌上～满了书。*The desk was piled with books.* Ⅱ 名 heap; pile; stack: 柴火～ *a pile (or stack) of firewood* / 土～ *mound* / 草～ *haystack* Ⅲ 量 heap; pile; crowd: 一～垃圾 *a garbage (or rubbish) heap* / 一～人 *a crowd of people*
【堆存】store up
【堆垛机】(hay) stacker
【堆放】pile up; stack: 库房里～着许多农具。*A lot of farm tools are piled in the storehouse.*
【堆肥】[农] compost
【堆积】❶ pile up; heap up: 工地上建筑材料～如山。*Building materials are piled up mountain-high on the construction site.* ❷ [地质] accumulation
【堆垒数论】[数] additive theory of numbers
【堆漆】embossed lacquer
【堆砌】❶ pile up (hewn rocks, etc. to build sth.) ❷ load one's writing with fancy phrases: ～辞藻 *string together ornate phrases*
【堆石坝】[水] rock-fill dam
【堆笑】put on a smile; wear a grin from ear to ear: 满脸～ *be all smiles; one's face is wreathed in smiles*
【堆栈】storehouse; warehouse

duì

队 Ⅰ 名 ❶ a row of people; line: 排成两～ *fall into two lines* ❷ team; group: 篮球～ *basketball team* ❸ (〈略〉全称为'少年先锋队') Young Pioneers Ⅱ 量: 一～战士 *a file of soldiers*
【队部】the office or headquarters of a team, etc.:

勘探队～ *the prospecting team headquarters*

【队列】formation：～教练（*military*）*drill*；*formation drill*

【队旗】［体］team pennant：互赠～ *exchange team pennants*

【队伍】❶ troops：～就要出发了。*The troops are about to set out*. ❷ ranks；contingent：游行～ *contingents of marchers*；*procession*；*parade*

【队形】formation：成战斗～ *in battle formation* / 以密集（散开）～前进 *advance in close*（*open*）*order*

【队友】fellow player；fellow member of a group or team

【队员】team member

【队长】❶［体］captain：排球队～ *the captain of a volleyball team* ❷ team leader：生产队～ *production team leader*

对

Ⅰ 动 ❶ answer；reply：无言以～ *have nothing to say in reply* ❷ treat；cope with；counter：刀～刀，枪～枪 *sword against sword and spear against spear* ❸ be trained on；be directed at：枪口～着敌人 *train the gun on the enemy* / 她的话不是～着你的。*What she said was not directed at you*. ❹ bring（two things）into contact；fit one into the other：～暗号 *exchange code words* / 这个榫头～不上。*This tenon won't fit*. ❺ suit；agree；get along：～心眼儿 *suit one down to the ground* / ～胃口 *suit one's taste* ❻ compare；check；identify：～笔迹 *identify the handwriting* / ～号码 *check numbers* ❼ set；adjust：～表 *set one's watch*；*synchronize watches* / ～好望远镜的距离 *adjust the focus of a telescope* ❽ mix；add：茶太浓了，给我～点儿水。*Add some water to the tea*, *it's too strong for me*. Ⅱ 副 ❶ mutual；face to face：～骂 *call each other names* / ～坐 *sit facing each other* / ～饮（*two people*）*have a drink together* ❷ divide into halves：～股劈 *go halves*；*split fifty-fifty* Ⅲ 形 ❶ opposite；opposing：～岸 *the opposite bank*；*the other side of the river* ❷ right；correct：猜～了 *guess right* / 这事你做得～。*You did the right thing*. / 你说得很～。*What you say is quite true*. Ⅳ 名 antithetical couplet；couplet：喜～ *wedding couplet* Ⅴ 量 pair；couple：一～花瓶 *a pair of vases* / 一～夫妇 *a married couple* Ⅵ 介 with regard to；concerning；to：～敌狠，～己和 *ruthless to the enemy*，*kind to one's comrades* / ～这个问题的不同意见 *different views on this question*

【对氨水杨酸钠】［药］sodium para-aminosalicylate（PASNa）

【对案】diplomacy counterproposal

【对白】dialogue

【对半】❶ half-and-half；fifty-fifty：～儿分 *divide half-and-half*；*go halves* ❷ double：～儿利 *a double profit*

【对比】❶ contrast；balance：今昔～ *contrast the present with the past* / 构成鲜明的～ *form a sharp contrast* ❷ ratio：双方人数～是一对四。*The ratio between the two sides*（*or parties*）*is one to four*. ◇ ～度 contrast ratio；contrast；～剂［医］contrast medium

【对不起】（又作‘对不住’）❶〈套〉I'm sorry；sorry；excuse me；pardon me；I beg your pardon：～，给你添麻烦了。*Sorry to have given you so much trouble*. ❷ let sb. down；be unworthy of；do a disservice to；be unfair to：球队输了球，大伙儿觉得～教练。*The team lost and felt they had let the coach down*.

【对策】the way to deal with a situation；countermeasure；countermove

【对策论】［数］game theory

【对唱】musical dialogue in antiphonal style；antiphonal singing

【对称】symmetry

【对答】answer；reply：～不上来 *can't answer the question*

【对答如流】answer fluently；answer questions without hesitation

【对待】treat；approach；handle：正确地～群众 *adopt a correct attitude towards the masses*

【对得起】（又作‘对得住’）not let sb. down；treat sb. fairly；be worthy of：你要我做的事情我都做了，我总算～你了。*I've done everything you asked me to do*. *I didn't let you down in the least*.

【对等】reciprocity；equity：在～的基础上 *on the basis of reciprocity*；*on a reciprocal basis* ◇ ～货样 counter sample；～贸易 counter-trade

【对调】exchange；swop：～工作 *exchange jobs* / ～座位 *exchange*（*or swop*）*seats*

【对顶角】［数］vertical angles

【对方】the other（or opposite）side；the other party：～付费电话 *collect call*

【对付】❶ deal with；cope with；counter；tackle：那人好～。*That man is easy to deal with*. ❷ make do：这把锹你先～着用吧。*Try to make do with this spade for now*.

【对歌】singing in antiphonal style

【对光】［摄］set（or focus）a camera：自动～ *automatic focusing* / 对好光再拍照。*Focus the camera before you take the picture*.

【对过】opposite；across the way：他就住在～。*He lives just across the way*. / 我家～就是邮局。*The post office is just opposite my house*.

【对号】❶ check the number：～入座 *take one's seat according to the number on the ticket*；*sit in the right seat* ❷ fit；tally：这张图纸有几个数据对不上号。*There are a few figures on this blueprint that don't tally*. / 他说的和做的不～。*His deeds don't match his words*. ❸ check mark（√）；tick

【对话】dialogue：两国政府已开始～。*The two governments have opened a dialogue*. / 南北～ *North-South dialogue* ◇ ～框［计］dialog box

【对换】change or exchange

【对讲电话】intercommunicating telephone set

【对讲机】walkie-ralkie；intercom
【对角线】［数］diagonal (line)
【对接】［航天］dock
【对接焊】［机］butt welding
【对襟】a kind of Chinese-style jacket with buttons down the front
【对劲儿】❶ be to one's liking；suit one：这把锄我使着很～。*This hoe suits me very well*. ❷ normal；right：这件事我越想越觉得不～。*The more I think of it, the more I'm convinced there's something fishy about it*. ❸ get along (well)：他们俩一向很～。*The two of them have always got along very well*.
【对进突击】［军］two-pronged assault from opposite directions
【对局】play a game of chess, etc.：我跟他对了一局，输了。*I played a game of chess with him and lost*.
【对开】❶ (of trains, buses or ships) run from opposite directions ❷ divide into two halves；go fifty-fifty ❸［刷］folio；◇ ～信用证 reciprocal credit；counter credit
【对抗】❶ antagonism；confrontation：阶级～ *class antagonism* / 两国之间的～ *confrontation between two states* ❷ resist；oppose ◇ ～刺 opposition thrust；time thrust；～赛［体］dual meet
【对抗性】antagonism ◇ ～矛盾 antagonistic contradiction
【对空射击】antiaircraft firing
【对口】❶ (of two performers) speak (or sing) alternately ❷ be geared to the needs of the job；fit in with one's vocational training (or speciality)：～训练 *training geared to the needs of the job* /专业～ *a job suited to one's special training* ❸ counterpart ◇ ～唱 musical dialogue in antiphonal style；antiphonal singing；～疮［中］a boil on the nape；～词 rhymed dialogue；～会谈 talks between representatives of similar organizations of two countries；counterpart conversations；～赛 emulation between counterpart organizations；～相声 cross talk；comic dialogue；～型 lip-sync
【对垒】stand facing each other, ready for battle；be pitted against each other：两军～ *two armies pitted against each other*
【对立】oppose；set sth. against；be antagonistic to：消灭城乡～ *abolish the antithesis between town and country* / ～情绪 *antagonism*
【对立面】［哲］opposite；antithesis：矛盾着的～ *the opposites in a contradiction* / 为自己树立～ *create one's own antithesis*
【对立统一】［哲］unity of opposites：～规律是宇宙的根本规律。*The law of the unity of opposites is the fundamental law of the universe*.
【对联】antithetical couplet (written on scrolls, etc.)
【对流】［物］convection ◇ ～层［气］troposphere；～雨［气］convective rain
【对路】❶ satisfy the need：这种货到农村正～。*These goods are the very thing the countryside needs*. ❷ be to one's liking；suit one：一句话不～，两个人就要拌嘴。*One word out of turn, the two of them would quarrel*.
【对门】❶ (of two houses) face each other ❷ the building or room opposite：照相馆～是家餐厅。*Opposite the photo studio is a restaurant*.
【对面】❶ opposite：他家就在我家～。*His house is opposite mine*. ❷ right in front：～来了一位解放军。*A PLA man came towards us*. ❸ face to face：这事儿得他们本人～儿谈。*They should talk about this face to face*. / 他俩～坐着。*The two of them sat facing each other*.
【对内】internal；domestic；at home：～政策 *domestic (or internal) policy* / ～搞活经济 *enliven the domestic economy*
【对牛弹琴】play the lute to a cow—address the wrong audience；talk over sb.'s head
【对偶】❶ antithesis ❷［数］dual：～运算 *dual operations*
【对偶原理】［数］principle of duality
【对瓶】a twin vase
【对日照】［天］counterglow
【对生】［植］opposite：～叶 *opposite leaf*
【对事不对人】concern oneself with facts and not with individuals (when trying to settle a question)
【对手】❶ opponent；adversary ❷ match；equal：他不是你的～。*He's no match for you*.
【对数】［数］logarithm：～函数 *logarithmic function* ◇ ～表 logarithmic table
【对台戏】rival show：演～ *put on a rival show* ——另见〖唱对台戏〗
【对头】❶ correct；on the right track：方法～，效率就高。*When the method is correct, efficiency is high*. or *Good methods make for high efficiency*. ❷ (usu. used in the negative) normal；right：你的脸色不～。*You're not looking well*. ❸ (usu. used in the negative) get on well；hit it off：过去他俩不大～，现在却合得来了。*The two didn't get along in the past but now they hit it off well*. ❹enemy：死～ *sworn enemy* ❺ opponent；adversary
【对外】external；foreign：～工作 *external work；work in the field of external relations* / ～关系 *external (or foreign) relations* / ～援助 *aid to foreign countries* /～政策 *external (or foreign) policy* ◇ ～贸易仲裁委员会 (China) Foreign Trade Arbitration Commission (FTAC)；～投资 investment abroad
【对外开放】(the policy of) opening to the outside world；the open policy：～，对内搞活经济 *open to the outside and invigorate the economic domestically*
【对外贸易】foreign trade：～逆差 *foreign trade deficit；unfavourable balance of trade* / ～顺差 *foreign trade surplus；favourable balance of trade* ◇ ～额 value of foreign trade；～资金融通 foreign trade financing

【对位】［音］counterpoint
【对味儿】❶ to one's taste；tasty ❷（usu. used in the negative）seem all right：他的发言不大～。*What he said didn't sound quite right.*
【对物权】right rem
【对虾】prawn
【对象】❶ target；object：革命～ *targets of the revolution* / 研究～ *an object of study* ❷ boy（or girl）friend：找～ *look for a partner in marriage* ——另见〖搞对象〗
【对消】offset；cancel each other out
【对眼】cross-eye
【对应】corresponding；homologous：～物 *homologue* ◇ ～原理［物］correspondence principle
【对照】contrast；compare：～原文修改译文 *check the translation against the original and make corrections* / 英汉～读本 *an English-Chinese bilingual textbook*
【对折】50% discount
【对着干】❶ adopt a confrontational approach；set oneself against ❷ compete with sb. in work
【对证】verify；check：～事实 *verify the facts*
【对症下药】suit the medicine to the illness；suit the remedy to the case；prescribe the right remedy for an illness
【对质】confrontation（in court）：让被告与原告～ *confront the accused with his accuser*
【对峙】stand facing each other；confront each other：两山～。*The two mountains stand facing each other.* / 武装～ *military confrontation*
【对撞机】collider
【对准】❶ aim at：把枪口～敌人 *aim a gun at the enemy* ❷［机］alignment：轴～ *shaft alignment*
【对子】❶ a pair of antithetical phrases，etc.：对～ *supply the antithesis to a given phrase，etc.* ❷ 同〖对联〗

兑 动 ❶ exchange；convert：用纸币～黄金 *convert notes into gold* ❷ add（water，etc.）：这酒是～了水的。*The wine has been watered.*
【兑付】cash（a cheque，etc.）：～人民币 *cash（a cheque，etc.）in Renminbi*
【兑换】exchange；convert：把外币～成人民币 *exchange foreign money for Renminbi* ◇ ～率 rate of exchange（between two currencies）；～券 bank draft；money order
【兑现】❶ cash（a cheque，etc.）❷ honour（a commitment，etc.）；fulfil；make good：说话不～ *not live up to one's promise；fail to make good one's promise* ◇ ～支票 cash check

dūn

吨 量 ton（t.）
【吨公里】ton kilometre
【吨海里】ton sea（or nautical）mile
【吨时】ton hour
【吨位】tonnage

敦 形 honest；sincere：敦请
【敦促】urge；press：～他早日启程 *urge him to start on his journey early*
【敦厚】honest and sincere：质朴～ simple and honest；unsophisticated
【敦煌石窟】the Dunhuang Caves
【敦煌学】study of the Dunhuang Caves
【敦睦】〈书〉promote friendly relations：～邦交 *promote friendly diplomatic relations between two countries*
【敦请】cordially invite；earnestly request
【敦实】stocky：他长得很～。*He's stockily built.* / 这个坛子真～。*This jar is rather squat.*

墩 Ⅰ 名 ❶ mound：土～ *mound* ❷ a block of stone or wood：树墩/ 桥墩 Ⅱ 量 cluster：栽稻秧三万～ *transplant* 30，000 *clusters of rice seedlings*
【墩布】mop；swab
【墩子】a block of wood or stone：菜～ *chopping block*

蹲 动 ❶ squat on the heels：两人～下就聊起来了。*Squatting down，the two of them started to have a chat.* ❷ stay：他在实验室里一～就是好几个小时。*He would stay for hours at a stretch in the laboratory.*
【蹲班房】〈口〉be put in jail；be imprisoned
【蹲膘】（of cattle，etc.）fatten in the shed
【蹲点】（of cadres）stay at a selected grass-roots unit to help improve its work and gain firsthand experience for guiding overall work
【蹲苗】restrain the growth of seedlings（for root development）

dǔn

盹 名 short light sleep；doze：打盹儿

趸 Ⅰ 名 wholesale：趸批 Ⅱ 动 buy wholesale：～货 *buy goods wholesale*
【趸船】landing stage；pontoon
【趸批】wholesale：～买进（卖出）*buy（sell）wholesale*

dùn

囤 名 a grain bin ——另见 tún

炖 动 ❶ stew：～一只鸡 *stew a chicken* ❷ warm sth. by putting the container in hot water：～酒 *warm（up）wine*

砘 动 ram the loose soil with a stone-roller after sowing

盾 名 shield
【盾牌】❶ shield ❷ pretext；excuse

钝 形 ❶ blunt；dull：刀～了。*The knife is blunt.* ❷ stupid；dull-witted：迟钝

【钝化】［化］passivation；inactivation：～剂 *passivator*

【钝角】［数］obtuse angle：～三角形 *obtuse triangle*

【钝性物质】［化］inactive substance

顿 Ⅰ动 ❶ pause：他～了一下，又接着往下说。*After a short pause，he went on.* ❷ (in Chinese calligraphy) pause in writing in order to reinforce the beginning or ending of a stroke ❸ arrange；settle：安顿 ❹ touch the ground (with one's head) ❺ stamp (one's foot) Ⅱ副 suddenly；immediately；at once：～悟 *suddenly realize the truth，etc.*；attain enlightenment Ⅲ量 (used to indicate frequency)：一天三～饭 *three meals a day* / 说了他一～ *give him a dressing down* Ⅳ形 fatigued；tired：劳顿

【顿挫】pause and transition in rhythm or melody

【顿号】a slight-pause mark used to set off items in a series (、)

【顿河】the Don

【顿开茅塞】suddenly see the light；be suddenly enlightened：闻兄大教，～。*Your excellent advice has opened my eyes.*

【顿时】suddenly；immediately；at once：喜讯传来，人们～欢呼起来。*People broke into cheers as soon as they heard the good news.*

【顿悟学习】insight learning

【顿足捶胸】同〖捶胸顿足〗

【顿钻钻井】churn drilling；percussion drilling；cable tool drilling

遁 动 escape；flee；fly：远～ *flee to a far-away place*

【遁词】subterfuge；quibble

【遁入空门】become a monk or nun

duō

多 Ⅰ形 ❶ many；much；more：很～人 *many people* / 要办的事情很～。*There are many things to attend to.* / 时间紧迫，我不能～考虑。*Time is running out，I can't give it much thought.* / 请～～帮助。*Please give me all the help you can.* ❷ excessive：～疑 *oversensitive；oversuspicious；given to suspicion* Ⅱ动 ❶ have (a specified amount) more or too much：这个句子～了一个字。*There is one word too many in this sentence.* / 班上～了三个新同学。*There are three more new students in the class.* ❷ have sth. in abundance：南方～水，利于灌溉。*Irrigation is easy in the South because of the abundance of water.* /这里春天～风，夏天～雨。*Here we have a lot of wind in spring and a lot of rain in summer.* /夏天～痢疾。*There is a high incidence of dysentery in summer.* Ⅲ助 over a specified amount；and more：三个～月 *more than three months；three months and more* / 六十～岁 *over sixty years old* / 十斤～ *ten jin and more* Ⅳ副 ❶ (used in questions) to what extent：他～大年纪了？*How old is he?* / 天安门有～高？*How high is Tian'anmen?* / ～厚的木板才能做桌面呢？*How thick must a piece of wood be if it is to be made into a table top?* ❷ (used in exclamations) to what an extent：这天儿～闷哪！*How sultry it is!* / 看她～漂亮！*Look how pretty she is!* ❸ to an unspecified extent：有～大劲儿使～大劲儿。*Put out all the strength you have.*

【多半】❶ the greater part；most；more often than not：星期天他～上这儿来。*He comes over on Sunday more often than not.* ❷ most probably；very likely：他这会儿还不来，～不来了。*Since he hasn't come yet，he probably isn't coming.*

【多倍体】［生理］polyploid：～植物 *polyploid plant*

【多臂机】［纺］dobby

【多边】multilateral：～会谈 *multilateral talks* / ～贸易 *multilateral trade* / ～条约 *multilateral treaty* ◇ ～关税谈判 multilateral tariff negotiations；～合作 multi-lateral cooperation；～贸易协定 multilateral trade agreement；～条约 multilateral treaty

【多边外交】multilateral diplomacy

【多边形】［数］polygon

【多变】changeable；changeful；varied：～的战术 *varied tactics* /山区气候～，小心感冒。*The weather in the mountains is very changeable. Be careful not to catch cold.*

【多才多艺】versatile；gifted in many ways：一位～的表演艺术家 *a versatile performer*

【多层次推销】multilevel marketing

【多产】❶ prolific：～作家 *a prolific writer* ❷［医］multiparity：～妇 *a multiparous woman*

【多吃多占】eat or take more than one is entitled to；grab more than one's share

【多此一举】make an unnecessary move：何必～？*Why take the trouble to do that?*

【多次】many times；time and again；repeatedly；on many occasions：她曾～访问中国。*She's visited China many times.*

【多重处理】multiprocessing

【多愁善感】sentimental and susceptible

【多弹头】multiple warhead：～导弹 *multiple warhead missile* / ～分导重返大气层运载工具 *multiple independently targeted reentry vehicle (MIRV)*

【多党制】multiparty system；multi-party system

【多刀切削】［机］multiple cut；multicut

【多道程序】multiprogramming

【多动症】hyperactivity

【多多益善】the more the better

【多发病】frequently-occurring disease

【多方】in many ways；in every way：～设法 *try all possible means；make every effort* / ～协助 *render all manner of help*

【多方面】many-sided；in many ways

【多哥】Togo ◇ ～人 Togolese

【多功能】multi-functional; multi-(or all-) purpose: ～收录机 *multi-functional tape recorder* / ～、现代化的经济中心 *a modern, multi-functional economic centre* / ～厅 *multi-purpose hall* ◇ ～显示器 multi-function display

【多寡】number; amount: ～不等 *vary in amount (or number)*

【多管】[军] multibarrel: ～高射机关炮 *pompom* / ～火箭炮 *multibarrel (rocket) launcher* / ～炮 *multibarreled gun*

【多国公司】multinational corporation

【多铧犁】multishare (or multifurrow) plough

【多会儿】〈口〉❶ when: 你是～来的? *When did you come?* ❷ ever; at any time: 我～有空～去。*I'll go there when I'm free.*

【多级火箭】multistage rocket

【多级管理】multiple management

【多极】[电] multipolar: ～发电机 *multipolar generator* ◇ ～化 multipolarization

【多晶硅】[电子] polycrystalline silicon

【多晶体】[物] polycrystal

【多孔】porous ◇ ～动物 porifera; ～砖 porous brick; perforated brick

【多口相声】cross talk (or comic dialogue) performed by more than two persons

【多跨】[建] multispan: ～结构 *multispan structure* / ～桥 *multiple span bridge*

【多快好省】more, faster, better, cheaper—achieve greater, faster, better and more economical results

【多亏】thanks to; luckily: ～你的帮助 *thanks to your help* / ～你给我们带路。*We were lucky to have you as our guide.*

【多劳多得,少劳少得】more pay for more work and less pay for less work

【多路转换器】multiplexer

【多买多送】buy more and get more free

【多媒体】multimedia ◇ ～电脑 multi-media computer; ～教学法 multimedia approach; ～信息中心 multimedia information centers

【多么】❶ (used in exclamations) to what an extent: ～新鲜的水果啊! *How fresh the fruit is!* or *What fresh fruit!* / 这是～高尚的精神! *What a noble spirit this is!* ❷ to an unspecified extent: 不管天～冷,他都坚持户外锻炼。*However cold it was, he never stopped taking outdoor exercise.*

【多米尼加】Dominica ◇ ～共和国 the Dominican Republic; ～人 Dominican

【多米诺骨牌】dominoes

【多米诺骨牌理论】the domino theory

【多米诺效应】domino effect

【多面手】a many-sided person; a versatile person; an all-rounder

【多面体】[数] polyhedron

【多民族国家】a multi-nationality country

【多谋善断】resourceful and decisive; sagacious and resolute

【多幕剧】a play of many acts; a full-length drama

【多难兴邦】Much distress regenerates a nation; Deep distress resurrects a nation.

【多瑙河】the Danube

【多年生】[植] perennial: ～植物 *perennial plant*

【多尿症】polyuria

【多配偶】polygamy

【多普勒效应】[物] Doppler effect

【多情】full of tenderness or affection (for a person of the opposite sex): 他对她很是～。*He feels great affection for her.*

【多刃刀具】[机] multiple-cutting-edge tool; multipoint tool

【多如牛毛】as many as the hairs on an ox; countless; innumerable

【多色】polychrome: ～染料 *polygenetic dyes* / ～印刷 *polychrome printing*

【多少】❶ number; amount: ～不等 *vary in amount (or number)* ❷ somewhat; more or less; to some extent: ～有点失望 *feel somewhat disappointed* / 他讲的～有点道理。*There's something in what he says.* ❸ how many; how much: 这一班有～学生? *How many pupils are there in this class?* / 这药我每次吃～? *How much of the medicine do I take each time?* ❹ (expressing an unspecified amount or number): 我跟你说过不知～次了。*I've told you I don't know how many times.* / 我知道～说～。*I'll tell all I know.*

【多神教】polytheism

【多声道盒式录音机】multi-channel cassette recorder

【多时】a long time: 等候～ *have waited a long time*

【多事】❶ meddlesome: 怪我～。*I shouldn't have poked my nose into this.* or *I shouldn't have interfered.* ❷ eventful

【多事之秋】an eventful period or year; troubled times

【多数】majority; most: 绝对～ *an overwhelming majority* / 微弱的～ *a small majority* / 必要的～ *the requisite majority* / 简单～ *a simple majority* / 相对～ *a relative majority* / 特定～ *a qualified majority* ◇ ～表决 decision by majority; ～党 the majority party; the majority; ～党领袖 the majority leader; ～票 majority vote

【多速】multi-speed

【多肽】[生化] polypeptide: ～酶 *polypeptidase*

【多糖】[化] polysaccharide; polysaccharose: ～酶 *polysaccharase; polyase*

【多头】❶ (on the stock exchange) bull; long ❷ many chiefs or bosses: 领导～ *with too many bosses* ◇ ～市场 long market; bull market; ～政治 polyarchy

【多退少补】(in subscribing to sth. or doing business) refund for any overpayment or demand a supplemental payment for any difference in price

【多细胞生物】multicellular organism

【多相】[化] heterogeneous: ～催化 *heterogeneous*

catalysis / ～聚合 *heterogeneous polymerization*
【多项变压器】polyphase transformer
【多项式】［数］multinomial；polynomial
【多项选择题】multiple-choice question
【多谢】〈套〉many thanks；thanks a lot
【多心】oversensitive；paranoid：你别～，我只是就一般而论。*Don't get me wrong；I'm speaking in general.* / 他听了这话～了。*He became paranoid when he heard this.*
【多芯电缆】multicore cable
【多学科的】multidisciplinary
【多样】diversified：形式～ *diversified in form*
【多样化】diversify；make varied：使农作物～ *diversify the crops* / ～的艺术风格 *a variety of artistic styles*
【多一事不如少一事】the less trouble the better；avoid trouble whenever possible
【多义词】［语］polysemant
【多余】unnecessary；surplus；superfluous；uncalled-for：删掉～的词语 *cut out superfluous words and phrases* / 把～的农产品卖给国家 *sell surplus farm products to the state*
【多元论】［哲］pluralism：～历史观 *the pluralistic concept of history*
【多元模式】plural patterns
【多元酸】［化］polybasic acid
【多元文化的】multicultural
【多源的】multi-source
【多云】［气］cloudy
【多中心主义】polycentrism
【多种多样】varied；manifold：满足人民群众～的需要 *meet the manifold needs of the people* / 音乐创作的形式是～的。*The forms of musical composition are many and varied.*
【多种经济】diversified economy
【多种经营】diversified economy；diversification：～方式 *various methods of business operation*
【多足动物】myriopod
【多嘴】speak out of turn；shoot off one's mouth：～多舌 *gossipy and meddlesome；long-tongued* / 要不是他～，事情也不至于搞僵。*If he hadn't shot his mouth off，things wouldn't have been so awkward.*

咄 叹 tut-tut
【咄咄逼人】overbearing；aggressive：他说话时的神气～。*He spoke with an overbearing air.*
【咄咄怪事】monstrous absurdity：岂非～？*Isn't it absurd?* or *Isn't it a strange business?*

哆 (构词成分)见下
【哆嗦】tremble；shiver：气得直～ *tremble with rage* /冷得打～ *shiver with cold*

掇 动 pick up：拾掇
【掇弄】〈方〉❶ fix up：经他一～机器就好了。*The machine worked again after he fixed it up.* ❷ stir up (trouble，etc.)；incite

duó

夺 动 ❶ take by force；seize；wrest：从暴徒手上～下刀子 *wrest a knife from a hooligan* / 从甲队手里～走冠军 *take the championship from team A* ❷ force one's way：～门而出 *force open the door and rush out；force one's way out* / 眼泪～眶而出。*Tears started from one's eyes.* ❸ contend for；compete for；strive for：～得冠军 *carry off the first prize* ❹ deprive：剥夺
【夺标】❶ win the championship：～呼声很高 *be a likely champion* ❷ have one's tender accepted
【夺佃】eviction of peasants from land leased to them by landlords or rich peasants
【夺冠】(又作'夺魁') carry off the first prize；win first place；win the championship
【夺回】recapture；retake；seize back：～阵地 *recapture a position* / ～一局 *win a game (after losing one or more)；pull up by a game* / ～发球权 *win back service* / ～失去的时间 *make up for lost time*
【夺目】dazzle the eyes：光彩夺目
【夺取】❶ capture；seize；wrest：～主动权 *seize the initiative* / 武装～政权 *seize state power by armed force* ❷ strive for
【夺权】seize power；take over power

度 动〈书〉surmise；estimate：揣度 ——另见 dù
【度德量力】estimate one's own moral and material strength；make an appraisal of one's own position

踱 动 pace；stroll：～来～去 *pace to and fro；pace up and down* / ～方步 *walk with measured tread*

duǒ

朵 量 一～花 a flower / 一～云 *a cloud*
【朵儿】flower

垛 名 ❶ buttress ❷ battlements ——另见 duò
【垛口】(又作'垛堞') crenel
【垛子】❶ buttress ❷ battlements：城垛子

躲 动 ❶ hide (oneself)：～进深山老林 *hide in a mountain forest* / 我去～在门背后。*I'll hide behind the door.* / 你快～起来！*Quick，hide yourself!* ❷ avoid；dodge：你怎么老～着他？*Why do you keep avoiding him?*
【躲避】❶ hide (oneself)：这几天他好像有意～我。*He seems to have been hiding from me these days.* / 你还是～起来为好。*You had better hide.* ❷ avoid；elude；dodge：～困难 *avoid difficulties*
【躲藏】❶ hide (or conceal) oneself；go into hiding：他～在哪儿？*Where is he hiding?* / 他被迫～起来。*He was forced to go into hiding.* / 被赶

得没处～ *be so hounded that one can find no place to hide* ❷ avoid；dodge：暴风雨快要来了，鸟儿都～起来。*As the storm approached, the birds were seeking shelter.*

【躲躲闪闪】be evasive；hedge；equivocate

【躲懒】shy away from work；shirk

【躲闪】dodge；evade：小王～不及，和我撞了个满怀。*It was too late for Xiao Wang to dodge and I bumped into him.*

【躲债】avoid a creditor

duò

驮 （构词成分）见下 ——另见 tuó

【驮子】❶ a load carried by a pack-animal；pack ❷ used of caravan goods：三～货 *three packs of goods*

剁 动 chop；cut：把柳条～成三段 *chop a willow branch into three pieces* / ～肉馅 *chop up* (*or mince*) *meat*

垛 Ⅰ 动 pile up neatly；stack：把木头～起来 *pile up the logs* Ⅱ 名 pile；stack：柴火～ *a pile of faggots* / 麦～ *a stack of wheat* ——另见 duǒ

舵 名 rudder；helm：方向舵

【舵工】（又作‘舵公’）steersman；helmsman

【舵轮】（又作‘舵盘’）steering wheel

【舵手】steersman；helmsman

堕 动 fall；sink：～地 *fall on the ground*

【堕落】degenerate；sink low：走上～、犯罪的道路 *embark on the road of degeneration and crime* / 政治上～ *be politically degenerate* / ～成罪犯 *degenerate into a common criminal*

【堕入】sink (or lapse) into；land oneself in：～陷阱 *fall into a trap*

【堕胎】❶ induced abortion ❷ have an (induced) abortion ◇ ～药 aborticide；pellentia

惰 形 lazy；indolent：懒惰

【惰性】inertia ◇ ～气体[化] inert gas；～元素[化] inert element

跺 动 stamp (one's foot)：气得直～脚 *stamp one's foot with fury*

E

ē

阿 动 play up to; pander to: 法不～贵。*The law cannot fawn on the noble*. ——另见 ā

【阿胶】[中] E-gelatin (a traditional Chinese tonic for nourishing the blood, named after its place of origin, Dong E County of Shandong Province)

【阿弥陀佛】❶ [宗](佛教) Amitābha Buddha (who presides over the Western Paradise and whose name is used as an incantation repeated by the faithful) ❷ (used as an exclamation) may Buddha preserve us; Buddha be praised

【阿魏】[中] asafoetida (a gum resin obtained from the roots of the plant Ferula asafoetida)

【阿谀奉承】flatter; toady to

婀 (构词成分)见下

【婀娜】(of a woman's carriage) lithe and graceful; supple and graceful: 体态～ *have a supple, graceful carriage*

é

讹 Ⅰ 形 erroneous; mistaken: ～字 *wrong words (in a text)* Ⅱ 动 extort under false pretences; blackmail: 这不是～人吗? *Isn't this blackmail!*

【讹传】false (or unfounded) rumour

【讹误】error (in a text)

【讹诈】extort under false pretences; blackmail: ～钱财 *extort money under false pretences*

俄 Ⅰ 副 very soon; presently; suddenly: 俄顷 Ⅱ 名 ❶〈略〉见〖俄罗斯帝国〗❷〈略〉见〖俄罗斯联邦〗

【俄罗斯帝国】the Russian Empire (1721-1917)

【俄罗斯联邦】the Russian Federation

【俄罗斯人】Russian

【俄罗斯族】❶ the Russian nationality (or the Russians) ❷ the Russians (of Russia)

【俄顷】〈书〉in a moment; presently

【俄语】Russian (language)

娥 名 a pretty young woman: 宫娥

【娥眉】〈文〉❶ the beautiful eyebrows of a woman ❷ a beautiful woman ——另见〖蛾眉〗

鹅 名 goose

【鹅黄】light yellow

【鹅颈管】[机] gooseneck

【鹅口疮】thrush

【鹅卵石】cobblestone; cobble

【鹅毛】❶ goose feather ❷ sth. as light as a goose feather: 下了一场～大雪。*Snow fell in big feathery flakes*.

【鹅绒】goose down

【鹅行鸭步】waddle along like a duck (or a goose)

【鹅掌楸】Chinese tulip tree

锇 名 [化] osmium (Os)

蛾 名 moth

【蛾眉】〈文〉❶ moth eyebrows—the fine and delicate eyebrows of a woman (suggesting the dainty sweep of a moth's antennae) ❷ a beautiful woman

【蛾子】moth

额 名 ❶ forehead ❷ a horizontal tablet; a horizontal inscribed board ❸ a specified number or amount: 贸易～ *volume of trade*

【额定功率】rated power

【额定马力】rated horsepower

【额定输出】nominal output

【额度】specified number or amount; guota

【额骨】[生理] frontal bone

【额角】frontal eminence

【额手称庆】raise one's hand to one's forehead in joy—be overjoyed

【额数】a specified number, figure or amount

【额头】forehead

【额外】extra; additional; added: ～开支 *extra expenses* / ～收入 *additional income* / ～负担 *added burden*

ě

恶 (构词成分)见下 ——另见 è; wù

【恶心】❶ feel like vomiting; feel nauseated; feel sick: 我一坐海船就感到～。*I always feel sick (or nauseated) at sea*. ❷ be nauseating; disgust: 看了这事真～。*It was a disgusting sight to see*. ❸〈方〉rotten; lousy: 他的棋下得可～。*He is a lousy chess-player*.

è

厄 Ⅰ名 ❶〈书〉a strategic point：险～ *a strategic pass* ❷ adversity；disaster；hardship：遭～ *meet with disaster* Ⅱ动 be in distress；be stranded：渔船～于风暴。*The fishing boat was caught in a storm.*

【厄尔尼诺现象】［气］El Niño phenomenon

【厄瓜多尔】Ecuador ◇ ～人 Ecuadorian

【厄境】a difficult situation；adversity：处于～ *be in a difficult situation* / 在～中保持乐观 *remain cheerful in adversity*

【厄运】adversity；misfortune

扼 动〈书〉❶ clutch；grip：～住他的咽喉 *clutch at his throat* ❷ guard；control：扼制

【扼流圈】［电］choke

【扼杀】strangle；smother；throttle：～在摇篮里 *strangle in the cradle* / ～在萌芽状态中 *nip in the bud* / ～新生事物 *stifle new things*

【扼守】hold (a strategic point)；guard：战士们～住山口，打退了敌人的进犯。*The soldiers held the mountain pass and beat back the intruders.*

【扼死】strangle；throttle

【扼要】to the point：简明～ *brief and to the point* / 请～说明。*Please explain the main points briefly.*

【扼制】control；restrain；check；bring under control ◇ ～经济过热 curb an overheated economy

呃 象 hiccups

【呃逆】hiccups

苊 名［化］acenaphthene

轭 名 yoke

垩 Ⅰ名 chalk (a soft, white, powdery limestone) Ⅱ动 whiten with chalk

恶 形 ❶ evil；vice；wickedness：罪大恶极 ❷ fierce；ferocious：一场～战 *a fierce battle* / ～骂 *vicious abuse* / ～狗 *a ferocious (or vicious) dog；cur* ❸ bad；evil；wicked：～行 *evil (or wicked) conduct* / ～势力 *evil forces* ——另见 ě；wù

【恶霸】local tyrant (or despot) ◇ ～地主 despotic landlord

【恶报】retribution for evildoing；judgment

【恶病质】cachexia (general ill health with emaciation, due to a serious chronic disease like cancer)

【恶臭】a foul smell；stench：伤口溃烂，散发出一股～。*The wound is festering and stinking.*

【恶毒】vicious；malicious；venomous：～的诬蔑 *venomous slander* / ～攻击 *viciously attack* / ～的语言 *vile language* / 用心极其～ *entertain most evil designs*

【恶感】ill feeling；malice：我对他并无～。*I bear him no malice.*

【恶贯满盈】be guilty of countless crimes and deserve to come to judgment；be steeped in evil and deserve damnation

【恶鬼】❶ evil spirit ❷〈讳〉devil

【恶棍】ruffian；scoundrel；bully

【恶果】evil consequence；disastrous effect：不注意环境保护造成的～ *the evil consequences of the neglect of environmental protection*

【恶狠狠】fierce；ferocious：她～地瞪了他一眼。*She gave him a ferocious stare.*

【恶化】worsen；deteriorate；take a turn for the worse：他的病情～了。*His condition has worsened.* / 局势愈来愈～。*The situation is getting worse and worse.*

【恶疾】a foul (or nasty) disease

【恶劣】odious；abominable；disgusting：～作风 *abominable behaviour* / ～行径 *disgusting conduct* / 手段～ *mean (or dirty) tricks* / ～环境 *adverse circumstances* / 品质～ *unprincipled；base*

【恶露】［医］lochia

【恶眉恶眼】a very fierce expression

【恶梦】nightmare

【恶名】a bad name；a bad reputation；infamy

【恶魔】demon；devil；evil spirit

【恶气】❶ a bad odor；a foul smell ❷ insult；outrage ❸ grievance；resentment：出口～ *vent one's grievance* ❹ anger；fury：恶声恶气

【恶人】an evil person；a vile creature；villain ◇ ～先告状 the villain sues his victim before he himself is prosecuted；the guilty party files the suit

【恶少】a young ruffian：洋场～ *a young rake in a gay cosmopolitan city (as in preliberation Shanghai)*

【恶声恶气】angry voices and hard words

【恶事传千里】bad news spreads far and wide

【恶习】a bad (or pernicious) habit：染上～ *contract a bad habit；fall into evil ways* / ～不改 *persist in one's evil ways*

【恶性】malignant；pernicious；vicious：～事故 *a fatal accident* / ～通货膨胀 *galloping (or runaway) inflation* ◇ ～贫血 pernicious anaemia；～循环 vicious circle；～肿瘤 malignant tumour

【恶言】rude language；abusive language：～相向 *exchange hot words* / 口出～ *use abusive language；wag one's vicious tongue*

【恶意】evil (or ill) intentions；ill will；malice：～攻击 *malicious attacks* / 她对你并无～。*She bore you no malice (or ill will).*

【恶语中伤】viciously slander；calumniate

【恶运】bad luck：我交了～。*Luck is against me.*

【恶兆】ill (or bad) omen

【恶浊】foul；filthy：空气～ *foul air* / ～的社会环境 *a very bad social environment*

【恶作剧】a practical joke；a mischievous prank；mischief：这孩子十分淘气，喜欢～。*The child is* very naughty and likes to play practical jokes. / 别～了！No more of your practical jokes!

饿 Ⅰ 形 hungry：挨～ go hungry / 孩子～了。The child is hungry. / 可把我～坏了。I feel famished. or I'm starving. Ⅱ 动 cause to starve; starve：别～着小猪。Don't starve the piglets. / 好好～他一顿就好了。He'll feel better if you let him miss a meal.

【饿饭】〈方〉go hungry; go without food

【饿虎扑食】like a hungry tiger pouncing on its prey：守门员来了个～，把球扑住了。The goalkeeper pounced like a tiger and caught the ball.

【饿殍】〈书〉bodies of the starved ◇ ～遍野 the fields strewn with the bodies of the starved

愕 形 stunned; astounded

【愕然】stunned; astounded：～四顾 look around in astonishment / 消息传来，大家为之～。Everyone was stunned by the news.

萼 名 [植] calyx

【萼片】[植] sepal

遏 动 check; hold back：怒不可遏

【遏抑】suppress; restrain：不可～的怒火 uncontrollable fury

【遏止】check; hold back：一股无法～的激情 an uncheckable wave of emotion / 不可～的改革洪流 the irresistible tide of reform

【遏制】keep within limits; contain：～不住的笑声 uncontrollable laughter / ～愤怒的情绪 check one's anger / 不可～的欲望 an irrepressible desire ◇ ～政策 policy of containment

腭 名 [生理] palate：硬腭 / 软腭

【腭裂】cleft palate

鹗 名 osprey; fish hawk; sea eagle

颚 名 ❶ mandibles (of arthropods) ❷ 同〖腭〗

噩 形 shocking; upsetting

【噩耗】sad news of the death of a beloved person：～传来，犹如晴天霹雳。The grievous news came like a bolt from the blue.

【噩梦】a frightening (or horrible) dream; nightmare：这一切犹如一场～。The whole thing was a nightmare.

鳄 名 crocodile; alligator

【鳄鱼】crocodile; alligator ◇ ～眼泪 crocodile tears

ēn

恩 名 kindness; favour; grace：施～ bestow favours

【恩爱】(of a married couple) be deeply in love with each other：～夫妻 an affectionate couple / 小两口儿十分～。The young couple love each other tenderly.

【恩赐】❶ bestow (favours, charity, etc.) ❷ favour; charity：大自然的～ the bounty of Nature

【恩德】benevolence; favour; kindness; grace

【恩典】❶ favour; grace：这是皇上的～。This is an imperial favour. ❷ bestow (favours)：求老爷～～！I beg your excellency's grace.

【恩惠】a favour bestowed or received; bounty

【恩将仇报】requite kindness with enmity; return hate for love; bite the hand that feeds one

【恩情】loving-kindness：我一辈子也忘不了义母对我的～。I shall never forget my foster mother's loving-kindness to me as long as I live.

【恩人】benefactor

【恩深义重】a great debt of gratitude

【恩同再造】a favour tantamount to giving sb. a new lease of life

【恩威并用】make a combined use of favour and disfavour (as in controlling one's subordinates); use both the mailed fist and the velvet glove

【恩怨】❶ feeling of gratitude or resentment：～分明 know clearly to whom to show gratitude and against whom to feel resentment ❷ resentment; grievance; old scores：不计较个人～ not allow oneself to be swayed by personal feelings

【恩重如山】Sb.'s great kindness is as weighty as a mountain.

蒽 名 [化] anthracene

【蒽酸】anthroic acid

èn

摁 动 press (with the hand or finger)：～电钮 press (or push) a button / ～住不放 press sth. down and hold it there / ～电铃 ring an electric bell

【摁钉儿】〈口〉drawing pin; thumbtack

【摁扣儿】〈口〉snap fastener

ér

儿 Ⅰ 名 ❶ child：婴儿 ❷ youngster; youth (esp. a young man)：健儿 / 男儿 ❸ son：他有一～一女。He has a son and a daughter. Ⅱ 形 male：儿马 Ⅲ (后缀，注音作 r)

【儿茶】❶ [植] Acacia catechu ❷ [中] catechu

【儿歌】children's song; nursery rhymes

【儿皇帝】puppet emperor

【儿科】(department of) paediatrics ◇ ～医生 paediatrician

【儿女】❶ sons and daughters; children：～都已长大成人。The children have all grown up. ❷ young man and woman (in love)

【儿女情长】love between man and woman is long：英雄气短，～。Brief is the spirit of a hero, but love between man and woman is long (said of a *man who turns from duty for the sake of love*).

【儿孙】children and grandchildren; descendants; posterity: ～满堂 *with generations of offspring filling the house* (*formerly regarded as a sign of prosperity*)

【儿童】children ◇ ～节 (International) Children's Day (June 1); ～剧 children's drama; ～团 the Children's Corps; ～文学 children's (or juvenile) literature; ～心理学 child psychology; ～学步车 go-car; walker; babywalker; ～医院 children's hospital; ～娱乐中心 Children's Amusement Centre

【儿媳妇儿】daughter-in-law

【儿戏】trifling matter: 这样重要的工作可不能当～。*You shouldn't regard such important work as a trifling matter.* / 视同～ *regard as a mere trifle*

【儿子】son

而 连 ❶ and; as well as: 伟大～艰巨的任务 *a great and arduous task* / 这篇文章长～空。*This article is long-winded and lacks substance.* ❷ and yet; but; while on the other hand: 有其名～无其实 *in name but not in reality* / 你喜爱体育运动,～我呢,情愿看书。*You like sports, while I'd rather read.* ❸ so that; in order to: 不要因失败～灰心,也不要因成功～骄傲。*Don't be discouraged by failure or get dizzy with success.* ❹ (used with 由,从,自, etc.) to: 由南～北 *from south to north* / 自远～近 *approach from a distance* / 由童年～少年,～壮年 *from childhood to teenage, then to middle age* ❺ (connecting an adverbial element to a verb): 匆匆～去 *leave in haste* / 顺流～下 *go down the stream* / 盘旋～上 *spiral up*

【而后】after that; then: 先小组酝酿～由大会讨论。*First exchange ideas in small groups and then hold a general discussion.*

【而今】now; at the present time

【而立】〈书〉(used esp. in): ～之年 *the age of thirty* (*from Confucius' saying* 三十而立 "*At thirty I took my stand*") / 年近～ *be nearly thirty*

【而且】❶ and also: 这屋子很宽敞,～光线充足。*The room is spacious and bright.* ❷ but also

【而已】that is all; nothing more: 我不过是个学生～。*I'm just a student, that's all.* / 如此～,岂有他哉! *That's all there is to it!*

鸸 (构词成分)见下

【鸸鹋】[动] emu

ěr

尔 代〈书〉❶ thou; you: 非～之过。*It's not your fault.* or *You are not to blame.* ❷ like that; so: 果～ *if so* ❸ that: ～日 *that day* / ～时 *at that time*

【尔代节】another name for 开斋节

【尔格】[物] erg

【尔后】〈书〉thereafter; subsequently; hence-forth: ～的战斗 *the subsequent battles*

【尔虞我诈】(又作'尔诈我虞') each trying to cheat the other: 各派勾心斗角,～。*All the factions intrigued against each other, resorting to deception and fraud.*

耳 Ⅰ 名 ❶ ear: 内耳 / 外耳 ❷ any ear-like thing: 鼎～ *the ears of a tripod* ❸ on both sides; flanking; side Ⅱ 助〈书〉only; just: 距此不过五里～。*It is only five li from here.* / 想当然～。*It is mere conjecture.*

【耳背】be hard of hearing: 老太太有点儿～,你说话大声点儿。*The old lady is a bit hard of hearing. Louder, please.*

【耳鼻喉科】❶ E. N. T. (ear-nose-throat) department; otolaryngological department ❷ otolaryngology ◇ ～医生 E. N. T. specialist; otolaryngologist

【耳边风】a puff of wind passing the ear—unheeded advice: 当作～ *let sth. go in one ear and out the other; turn a deaf ear to sth.*

【耳鬓厮磨】ear to ear and temple to temple—(of a boy and a girl) have close childhood friendship

【耳沉】(又作'耳朵沉')〈方〉be hard of hearing

【耳垂】[生理] earlobe

【耳聪目明】have good ears and eyes — have a clear understanding (of the situation)

【耳朵】ear: ～尖 *have sharp ears* / 穿～ *have one's earlobes pierced* (*for wearing earrings*) ◇ ～软 credulous; easily influenced; susceptible to flattery

【耳福】the good fortune of hearing sth. rare or beautiful: 大饱～ *enjoy to the full listening to music, singing, etc.*

【耳根清净】peace of heart or mind attained by staying away from, or shutting one's ears to, worldly discord

【耳垢】earwax

【耳鼓】同〖鼓膜〗

【耳光】(又作'耳光子') a slap in the face; a box on the ear: 打～ *slap sb.'s face; box sb.'s ears* / 我了他一个～。*I gave him a box on the ear.* / 事实给了他们一记响亮的～。*The facts have given them a slap in the face.*

【耳环】earrings

【耳机】earphone; earpiece: 戴上～ *put on the earphones*

【耳镜】[医] otoscope

【耳聋】be deaf

【耳轮】[生理] helix

【耳鸣】have a ringing sensation in the ears; tinnitus: 我～。*My ears are ringing.*

【耳膜】tympanic membrane; eardrum

【耳目】❶ what one sees and hears; knowledge; information: ～不广 *not well-informed* ❷ one who spies for sb. else: 他～众多。你说话要小

心。*His men are everywhere. Be careful what you say.*

【耳目闭塞】ill-informed; uninformed; ignorant

【耳目所及】from what one sees and hears; from what one knows: 就～,只觉得这几年的变化可真不小。*From what I hear and see, things have changed a lot in these last few years.*

【耳目一新】find everything fresh and new: 他们一到那里就感到～。*They found themselves in an entirely new world the moment they arrived.*

【耳屏】[生理] tragus

【耳濡目染】be imperceptibly influenced by what one sees and hears

【耳软心活】credulous and pliable

【耳塞】earplug

【耳生】unfamiliar to the ear; strange-sounding: 外面说话的声音听着～。*The voice outside sounds unfamiliar to me.*

【耳屎】〈口〉earwax: 挖～ *pick one's ears*

【耳熟】familiar to the ear: 这个名字好～,好像在广播里听到过。*The name sounds so familiar, I seem to have heard it mentioned over the radio.*

【耳熟能详】What's frequently heard can be repeated in detail.

【耳提面命】pour earnest advice into sb.'s ears; give earnest exhortations

【耳听为虚,眼见为实】What you hear may be false, what you see is true.

【耳挖子】earpick

【耳闻】hear of (or about): 这事略有～,详细情况不很清楚。*I've heard a little about it, but I don't know the details.*

【耳闻不如目见】Seeing for oneself is better than hearing from others.

【耳闻目睹】(又作'耳闻目击') what one sees and hears: 其间～的事,算起来也很不少。*During that time I witnessed or heard about a lot of things.*

【耳蜗】[生理] cochlea; acoustic labyrinth

【耳咽管】[生理] Eustachian tube; auditory tube

【耳语】whisper in sb.'s ear; whisper: 大夫看了看我的伤口,跟护士～了几句便出去了。*After examining my wound, the doctor whispered something in the nurse's ear and left.*

【耳针疗法】[中] auriculotherapy; ear-acupuncture therapy

【耳坠子】(又作'耳坠儿')〈口〉eardrops

迩 形〈书〉near; close: 遐迩闻名

饵 Ⅰ 名 ❶ cakes; pastry: 果～ *candies and cakes; confectionery* ❷ (fish) bait Ⅱ 动〈书〉entice: ～以重利 *use great wealth as a bait; entice sb. with prospects of great wealth*

【饵敌】set a trap for the enemy

【饵子】(fish) bait

铒 名 [化] erbium (Er)

èr

二 Ⅰ 数 two: ～公斤 *two kilograms* / ～～得四。*Twice two is four.* / 第～遍 *the second time* / ～路公共汽车 *No. 2 bus* / ～哥 *one's second elder brother* / ～层楼 *(British) first floor; (American) second floor* Ⅱ 形 different: 二心

【二八】sixteen: 年方～ *be only sixteen years of age*

【二把刀】〈方〉❶ have a smattering of a subject ❷ smatterer

【二把手】the second toppest leader of a unit

【二百二】(又作'二百二十') common name for 汞溴红

【二百五】❶〈口〉a stupid person: 他是个～。*He's a rather stupid person.* or *He's not all there.* ❷〈方〉dabbler; smatterer

【二倍体】[生] diploid

【二部制】two-shift system (in schools); two part-time shifts: ～学校 *a school with two part-time shifts; two-shift school*

【二重唱】[音] (vocal) duet

【二重性】dual character (or nature); duality

【二重奏】[音] (instrumental) duet

【二传】second pass; toss

【二传手】setter (in volleyball)

【二次方程】[数] quadratic equation

【二次曲面】[数] quadratic surface

【二次分频电路】divide-by-two circuit

【二次能源】secondary energy source (such as electricity, steam, etc.)

【二次曲线】[数] conic section

【二次调制】secondary modulation

【二道贩子】a person who resells at inflated prices

【二等】second-class; second-rate ◇ ～兵 private; ～残废军人 disabled soldier, second class; ～舱 second-class cabin; ～功 Merit Citation Class II; ～公民 sub-citizen; ～奖 second prize; ～秘书 diplomacy Second Secretary; ～品 second-class (or inferior) goods; seconds

【二叠纪】[地质] the Permian Period

【二分点】[天] the equinoxes

【二分音符】[音] minim; half note

【二副】second mate; second officer

【二锅头】a strong, colourless liquor distilled from sorghum (so called because it is distilled twice)

【二胡】erhu, a two-stringed bowed instrument with a lower register than jinghu (京胡)

【二化螟】striped rice borer (Chilo suppressalis)

【二话】(often used in the negative) demur; objection: ～不说 *without demur* / 需要他干什么,他就干什么,从来没有～。*Whatever he is required to do, he does it readily.*

【二黄】(又作'二簧') [戏] erhuang, one of the two chief types of music in traditional Chinese operas

【二级反馈系统】second order feed-back system

【二级风】[气] force 2 wind; light breeze

【二极管】[电子] diode ◇ ～检波器 diode detector

【二级子程序】second-order subroutine
【二尖瓣】［生理］mitral valve ◇ ～狭窄 mitral stenosis
【二阶环路】second-order loop
【二进宫】❶〈婉〉detained (or sentenced) for a second time; in and out of prison twice ❷〈诙〉do sth. for a second time：他这次～，又来学英文了。This is his second stint at the college to learn English.
【二进码】binary code
【二进制】binary system
【二进制标度】binary scale
【二进制数】binary number
【二进制数字】binary digit
【二郎腿】〈方〉a sitting posture with the legs crossed and one foot poised in the air：跷起～ *sit cross-legged, poising one foot in the air*
【二愣子】a rash fellow
【二流子】loafer; idler; bum
【二硫化物】［化］bisulphide
【二面角】［数］dihedral angle
【二名法】［生］binomial nomenclature
【二年生】［植］biennial ◇ ～植物 biennial plant
【二全音符】［音］breve
【二十四节气】the twenty-four solar terms
【二十四史】❶ the Twenty-Four Histories (dynastic histories from remote antiquity till the Ming Dynasty) ❷ a long intricate story：一部～，不知从何说起。*It's such a long and complicated story, I hardly know where to start.*
【二手】❶ assistant：让我给你当～怎么样？*Will you take me as your assistant?* ❷ secondhand：～资料 *secondhand materials* / ～货 *secondhand goods*
【二四滴】［农］2,4-D; 2,4-dichlorophenoxyacetic acid
【二踢脚】〈口〉double-kick (popular name for 双响)
【二五眼】〈方〉❶ of inferior ability or quality ❷ an incompetent person
【二项式】［数］binomial
【二象性】［物］dual property; duality：物质的～ *the dualistic nature of matter* / 波粒～ *wave-particle duality*
【二心】❶ disloyalty ❷ halfheartedness
【二氧化物】［化］dioxide (e.g. 二氧化碳 carbon dioxide; 二氧化硅 silicon dioxide; silica)
【二一添作五】go halves; go fifty-fifty
【二元】❶［数］duality ❷［化］binary
【二元论】［哲］dualism
【二月】❶ February ❷ the second month of the lunar year; the second moon
【二者必居其一】either one or the other：或者把老虎打死，或者被老虎吃掉，～。*Either kill the tiger or be killed by him—one way or the other.*
【二至点】［天］the solstices

贰 Ⅰ 数 two (used for the numeral 二 on cheques, banknotes, etc. to avoid mistakes or alterations) Ⅱ 形 disloyal：贰臣
【贰臣】an official who retains his position after capitulating to the new dynasty; turncoat official
【贰心】同〖二心〗

F

fā

发 Ⅰ 动 ❶ send out; issue; emit; give forth; shoot: ～电报 *send a telegram* / ～传单 *distribute leaflets* / ～命令 *issue an order* / ～信号 *give a signal* ❷ utter; express: ～一通议论 *speak at length* ❸ come or bring into existence: 发电 / 发芽 ❹ become; come to be: 脸色～白 *become pale; lose colour* / 树叶～黄了。*The leaves are turning yellow.* / 肉～臭了。*The meat smells a bit off.* or *The meat smells bad.* ❺ (of foodstuffs) rise or expand when leavened or soaked: 面～起来了。*The dough has risen.* / ～海参 *puff up dried sea cucumbers* (*by soaking them in water*) ❻ develop; expand: 发育 ❼ open up; expose: 发掘 ❽ feel; have a feeling: 嘴里～苦 *have a bitter taste in the mouth* / ～麻 *tingle* / ～痒 *itch* ❾ start; set out: 车船齐～。*All the boats and carts set out at the same time.* Ⅱ 量 (for bullets and shells): 一～炮弹 *one shell* / 两百～子弹 *two hundred rounds of ammunition; two hundred cartridges* ——另见 fà

【发案】(of a case) occur; take place: ～率 *incidence* (*of criminal cases*) / ～时间 *time of the occurrence of a case*

【发榜】publish a list of successful candidates (or applicants): 高考过后,同学们都焦急地等待着～。*After the college entrance examinations, the students were all waiting anxiously for the results to be published.*

【发报】transmit messages by radio, telegraphy, etc. ◇ ～机 [无] transmitter

【发标】issue of bidding documents

【发表】publish; issue: ～声明 *issue* (*or make*) *a statement* / ～文章 *publish an article* / ～意见 *express an opinion; state one's views*

【发病】(of a disease) come on: 他是昨天半夜发的病,现在还在抢救。*He came down with the illness about midnight and is still under emergency treatment.* ◇ ～率 incidence of a disease

【发布】issue; release: ～命令 *issue orders* / ～新闻 *release news*

【发财】get rich; make a fortune; make a pile: 他做股票生意发了大财。*He made a fortune buying and selling stocks.*

【发潮】become damp: 衣服有点儿～。*The clothes feel a bit damp.*

【发车场】[铁路] departure track; departure yard

【发愁】worry; be anxious: 不要为这事～。*Don't worry about it.* / 你发什么愁啊? *What are you so anxious about?*

【发出】issue; send out; give out: ～警报 *sound the alarm* / ～警告 *send out a warning* / ～阵阵清香 *send forth wafts of delicate fragrance* / ～指示 *issue a directive*

【发达】❶ developed; flourishing: 肌肉～ *have well-developed muscles* / 交通～ *have a well-developed transportation system* / 工商业很～。*Industry and commerce are flourishing.* ❷ promote; develop: ～贸易 *develop* (*or promote*) *trade* ◇ ～国家 developed country

【发呆】stare blankly; be in a daze; be in a trance: 他话也不说,坐在那里～。*He said nothing but sat there staring blankly.* or *He said nothing but sat there as if in a trance.*

【发电】generate electricity (or electric power)

【发电厂】power plant; power station: 水力(火力)～ *hydraulic* (*thermal*) *power plant* / 地热～ *geothermal power plant* / 原子能～ *atomic power plant* / ～容量 *station capacity*

【发电机】generator; dynamo: 双水内冷汽轮～ *turbogenerator with inner water-cooled stator and rotor* / 永磁～ *magneto generator* / ～容量 *generator capacity* / ～组 *generating set*

【发电站】power station

【发动】❶ start; launch: ～机器 *start a machine; set a machine going* / ～战争 *launch* (*or unleash*) *a war* ❷ call into action; mobilize; arouse: ～群众 *arouse the masses to action; mobilize the masses*

【发动机】engine; motor

【发抖】shiver; shake; tremble: 冷得～ *shiver* (*or shake*) *with cold* / 吓得～ *tremble with fear; shake in one's shoes* / 气得～ *tremble with anger*

【发端】make a start

【发反手上旋球】backhand backspin service

【发放】provide; grant; extend: ～贷款 *grant a loan*

【发奋】❶ work energetically ❷ 同〖发愤〗

【发愤】make a firm resolution; make a determined effort: ～工作 *put all one's energies into one's work* ◇ ～图强 work with a will to make the country strong

【发疯】go mad; go crazy; become insane; be out of one's mind

【发福】〈套〉(usu. said to older people) grow

stout；put on weight：您～了。*You have put on weight*.

【发糕】steamed sponge cake

【发稿】❶ distribute news dispatches ❷ send manuscripts to the press

【发给】issue；distribute；grant：～护照 *issue a pass-port*

【发光】❶ give off light；shine；be luminous：～发热 *emit light and heat* / 群星闪闪～。*The stars twinkled*. ❷［物］luminescence：场致～ *electroluminescence* / ～度 *luminosity* ◇ ～漆 luminous paint；～体 luminous body；luminary；luminophor

【发汗】induce perspiration (as by drugs)；diaphoresis ◇ ～药 sudorific；diaphoretic

【发号施令】issue orders；order people about：你有什么资格向别人～？*What right have you to order people about?*

【发狠】❶ make a determined effort：他们一～，三天的任务一天就完成了。*With a determined effort, they finished the three-day task in a single day*. ❷ be angry

【发花】(of the eyes) grow dim；see things in a blur

【发还】return sth. (usu. to one's subordinate)；give (or send) back：把作业～给学生 *return the homework to the pupils*

【发慌】feel nervous；get flustered；get flurried：她虽是第一次当众讲话，却一点都不～。*She didn't feel a bit nervous though it was the first time she'd spoken in public*.

【发挥】❶ bring into play；give play to；give free rein to：～想像力 *give free rein to one's imagination* / 我们没有充分～他的才干。*We're not doing justice to his talents*. ❷ develop (an idea, a theme, etc.)；elaborate：这一论点有待进一步～。*This point needs further elaboration*. ◇ ～潜力 bring potential into play

【发昏】❶ feel giddy (or dizzy)：我的头有点儿～。*I feel a bit giddy*. ❷ lose one's head；become confused：你～啦！*Are you out of your mind?*

【发火】❶ catch fire；ignite ❷ detonate；go off：他打了一枪，没有～。*He pulled the trigger but the gun didn't go off*. ❸ get angry；flare up；lose one's temper：你别～，咱们慢慢儿谈。*Don't get excited. Let's talk it over calmly*. ◇ ～点［物］ignition point

【发货】send out goods；deliver goods ◇ ～单 dispatch list；～人 consignor；shipper

【发急】become impatient or excited：等得～ *wait impatiently* / 他一输棋，就会～。*Every time he lost a game of chess, he got excited*.

【发迹】(of a poor man) gain fame and fortune；rise to power and position

【发家】build up a family fortune ◇ ～致富 build up a family fortune

【发奖】award prizes：～仪式 *prize-giving ceremony*

【发酵】ferment ◇ ～饲料 fermented feed

【发酒疯】get drunk and behave sillily；have a drunken fit

【发觉】find；detect；discover；realize：错误一经～，就应改正。*Mistakes should be corrected as soon as they are detected*.

【发掘】excavate；unearth；explore：～古墓 *excavate an ancient tomb* / ～文物 *unearth cultural relics* / ～人才 *seek gifted (or talented) people*

【发刊词】foreword (or introduction) to a periodical

【发狂】go mad；go crazy

【发困】〈口〉feel sleepy (or drowsy)

【发懒】feel lazy (or sluggish)

【发冷】feel cold (or chilly)：我有点～，没准儿发烧了。*I feel chilly, maybe I am running a fever*.

【发楞】〈口〉stare blankly；be in a daze；be in a trance

【发亮】shine：把机器擦得～ *polish the machine till it shines* / 东方～了。*The gleam of dawn shimmered in the east*.

【发令】❶ issue an order；give orders ❷ give a password ◇ ～枪［体］starting gun (or pistol)；～员 starter

【发落】deal with (an offender)：从轻～ *deal with sb. leniently*

【发霉】go mouldy；become mildewed

【发面】❶ leaven dough ❷ leavened dough：～饼 *leavened pancake*

【发明】❶ invent：印刷术是中国首先～的。*Printing was first invented by the Chinese*. ❷ invention：最新～ *the latest invention* ❸〈书〉expound：本书对《老子》的哲理颇多～。*This book does much to expound the philosophy of the Lao Zi*.

【发明权】patent rights of an inventor

【发难】❶ rise in revolt；launch an attack ❷ 同〖问难〗

【发怒】get angry；flare up；lose one's temper

【发排】send a manuscript to the compositor

【发盘】offer ◇ ～附样品 offer sample

【发胖】put on (or gain) weight；get fat：我近来好像～了。*I seem to have put on some weight lately*.

【发配】〈旧〉be transported to a distant place for penal servitude

【发脾气】lose one's temper；get angry：有理慢慢儿说，何必～。*Speak calmly if you think you're in the right；there's no need to get angry*. / 他从来没发过脾气。*He has never lost his temper*.

【发票】(又作'发货票') invoice：开～ *make an invoice*

【发起】❶ initiate；sponsor：这次会议是由十四个国家～的。*The meeting was sponsored by 14 countries*. / 这个歌咏队是我们～成立的。*This singing group was formed on our initiative*. ❷ start；launch：～反攻 *launch a counterattack* ◇ ～国 sponsor nation；～人 initiator；sponsor

【发情】［动］❶ oestrus：同步～ *synchronization of oestrus* ❷ be in heat ◇ ～期 heat period；oestrus；～周期 oestrous cycle

【发球】serve a ball：该谁～？*Whose service is it?* /

～得分 *ace* / ～不过网 *serve a ball into the net* / 他～发得好。*He has a very good serve.* / 他发了一个怪球。*He made a tricky serve.* ◇ ～擦网 service touching the net；～次序 service order；～犯规 fault；～区 service area；～权 right to serve；～失误 missed service

【发热】❶ have (or run) a fever；have (or run) a temperature：我好像有点儿～。*I feel as if I'm running a fever.* ❷ give out heat；generate heat：恒星本身发光～。*A fixed star can emit light and heat by itself.* ❸ be hotheaded；be impetuous：别头脑～！*Don't be so impetuous!* ◇ ～量［化］calorific capacity

【发人深省】(又作'发人深醒'；'发人深思') set people thinking；call for deep thought；provide food for thought

【发散】❶ (of rays, etc.) diverge ❷［中］disperse the internal heat with sudorifics：吃点药～一下 *take a sudorific to sweat out a cold* ◇ ～思维 divergent thinking

【发丧】❶ announce a death；send out an obituary ❷ arrange a funeral

【发上手旋球】overhand float serve

【发烧】have (or run) a fever；have (or run) a temperature ◇ ～友 fan；audiophile

【发射】❶ launch；project；discharge；shoot；fire：～导弹 *launch a guided missile* / ～人造卫星 *launch a man-made satellite* / ～炮弹 *fire shells* ❷［物］transmit；emit ◇ ～场 launching site；～光谱 emission spectrum；～架 launcher；～井 launching silo；～时限 launch window；～台 launching stand；launching (or firing) pad

【发神经】go mad；go crazy；be out of one's mind

【发生】happen；occur；take place：～了意外。*Something unexpected happened.* / 那里～了强烈地震。*A violent earthquake occurred there.*

【发生器】［化］generator：氨～ *ammonia generator*

【发声】sound production

【发誓】vow；pledge；swear：他们～要为死难烈士报仇。*They vowed to avenge the martyrs.*

【发售】sell；put on sale：这些杂志在全国各地书店均有～。*These magazines are sold at bookstores throughout the country.* / 新的纪念邮票将于下星期～。*The new commemorative stamps will be put on sale next week.*

【发水】flood：过去一下暴雨，这条河就发大水。*This river used to get flooded whenever there was a rainstorm.*

【发送】❶ transmit by radio：～密码电报 *transmit a coded message* ❷ dispatch (letters, etc.)

【发酸】❶ turn sour；taste sour：牛奶～了。*The milk has turned sour.* ❷ feel a tingle in one's eyes or nose (when about to break down and weep)：她觉得两眼～，泪水止不住流了下来。*She felt a tingle in her eyes and could hardly keep from shedding tears.* ❸ ache slightly：腰有点～ *have a slight backache*

【发条】［机］spiral power spring；clockwork spring

【发文】outgoing message；dispatch：～簿 *register of outgoing documents (or letters, etc.)*

【发问】ask (or pose, raise) a question

【发现】❶ discover；find：一四九二年哥仑布～美洲。*Columbus discovered America in 1492.* ❷ discovery；find：物理学方面一个划时代的～ *an epoch-making discovery in physics* / 考古方面的重大～ *important archaeological finds* ❸ find；realize；perceive；notice：我们～他有神经病。*We found him to be a mental case.* / 我～他好像有什么心事。*I noticed that he seemed to have something on his mind.*

【发祥地】place of origin；birthplace：黄河流域是我国古代文化的～。*The Yellow River Basin was the birthplace of China's ancient culture.*

【发笑】burst into laughter；laugh：令人～ *make one laugh；provoke laughter；be ridiculous*

【发泄】give vent to；let off：～不满情绪 *express one's discontent；air one's grievances* / 有气就～出来比闷在心里要好得多。*It's much healthier to give vent to your anger than to try to control it.*

【发信】post a letter：我接连发了两封信，催他快来。*I sent off two letters in succession, urging him to come at once.* / ～人 *addresser*

【发行】issue；publish；distribute；put on sale：～货币(债券，股票) *issue currency (bonds, stocks)* / ～书刊 *publish books and magazines* / ～影片 *release a film* / ～者 *publisher* ◇ ～公债 issue of government bonds；～银行 bank of issue

【发虚】❶ feel apprehensive；feel diffident ❷ feel feeble and weak

【发芽】germinate；sprout：种子还没有～。*The seeds haven't sprouted yet.* / ～率 *germination percentage* / ～试验 *germination test*

【发言】speak；make a statement or speech；take the floor：他在会上～了吗？*Did he speak at the meeting?* / ～稿 *the text of a statement (or speech)*

【发言权】right to speak：我们对这事当然有～。*Of course we have a say in this matter.* / 他们对这个问题最有～。*They are best qualified to speak on this question.* / 没有调查就没有～。*No investigation, no right to speak.*

【发言人】spokesman；spokeswoman：政府～ *government spokesman (or spokeswoman)*

【发炎】［医］inflammation：伤口～了。*The wound has become inflamed.*

【发扬】❶ develop；carry on (or forward)：～民主作风 *develop a democratic style of work* / ～正气，打击歪风。*Encourage healthy trends and combat unhealthy ones.* ❷ make the most of；make full use of：～火力，消灭敌人 *make full use of firepower to destroy the enemy*

【发扬光大】carry forward；develop；enhance

【发疟子】have an attack of malaria；suffer from malarial fever

【发音】pronounce；enunciate：这个字怎么～？*How do you pronounce this word?* / 她～清晰。*She enunciates her words clearly.* / 他～不清楚。

His articulation is poor. ◇ ～部位 points of articulation；～困难［医］dysphonia；～器官 vocal organs；speech organs

【发育】grow；develop：～健全 *physically well developed* / 婴儿～情况良好。*The baby is coming along well*. ◇ ～不全［医］hypoplasia；～异常［医］dysplasia

【发源】rise；originate：一切真知都是从直接经验～的。*All genuine knowledge originates in direct experience*. ◇ ～地 place of origin；source；birthplace

【发晕】feel dizzy (or giddy)

【发展】❶ develop；expand；grow：用～的眼光看人 *look at a person with an eye on the course of his development* / ～经济，保障供给。*Develop the economy and ensure supplies*. / ～多种经营 *develop diversified* ❷ recruit；admit：～新党员 *recruit new party members* ◇ ～经济学 development economics；～外向型经济 develop an export-oriented economy

【发展中国家】developing country

【发胀】❶ swell：肚子～ *feel bloated* / 头脑～ *have a swelled head* ❷ feel distended (under acupuncture treatment)

【发作】❶ break out；show effect：昨天她的心脏病又～了。*She had another heart attack yesterday*. / 酒性开始～。*The liquor began to show its effect*. ❷ have a fit of anger；flare up：他有些生气，但当着大家的面又不好～。*He was angry, but with everybody present, he could not very well show it*. / 歇斯底里大～ *have a bad fit of hysterics*

fá

乏 Ⅰ 动 lack：不乏其人 Ⅱ 形 tired；weary：走～了 *be tired from a long walk*

【乏味】dull；insipid；drab；tasteless：语言～ *dull (or drab) language* / 这项工作枯燥～。*This is dull and tedious work*.

伐 动 ❶ fell；cut down：～了几棵树 *cut down a few trees* ❷ send an expedition against；strike；attack：讨伐

【伐木】lumbering；felling；cutting：～工人 *lumberman* ◇ ～业 lumbering

【伐区】［林］cutting area；felling area

罚 动 punish；penalize：挨～ *be punished* / ～他唱个歌。*Let him sing a song as a forfeit*.

【罚不当罪】the punishment exceeds the crime；be punished too severely

【罚出场】［体］be ordered off the field for foul play；foul out

【罚界外球】throw-in

【罚金】fine；forfeit：处以～ *impose a fine on sb.*；*fine sb*.

【罚酒】be made to drink as a forfeit：我打赌输了，被罚了两大杯酒。*I lost the bet and had to drink two glassfuls of wine as a forfeit*.

【罚款】❶ impose a fine or forfeit：违反交通规则要～。*Fines are imposed for breaches of traffic rules*. ❷ fine；forfeit；penalty

【罚球】(in basketball) foul shot；free throw；(in football) penalty kick ◇ ～点 penalty spot；～区 penalty area；～线 penalty line

阀 名 ❶ a powerful person or family：财阀 ❷［机］valve：安全阀

【阀门】［机］valve

筏 名 raft：橡皮～ *rubber raft* / 竹～ *bamboo raft*

【筏道】log chute；logway

【筏子】raft

fǎ

法 Ⅰ 名 ❶ law：守法 ❷ method；way；mode：教～ *teaching method* / 表达～ *mode of expression* ❸ standard；model：法书 ❹［宗］(佛教) the Law；dharma ❺ magic arts：作法 Ⅱ 动 follow；model after：效法

【法案】proposed law；bill

【法办】deal with according to law；punish by law；bring to justice：将贪污分子逮捕～ *have the grafters arrested and brought to justice*

【法宝】❶［宗］(佛教) the Sutras ❷ a magic weapon or formula

【法场】〈旧〉execution ground：押赴～ *be taken under escort to the execution ground* / 劫～ *raid an execution ground to rescue the condemned*

【法典】code；statute book

【法定】legal；statutory：按照～手续办理 *do sth. according to legal procedure* ◇ ～贬值 official devaluation；～代理人 legal representative；～股本 authorized stock；～汇兑平价 official par of exchange；～汇率 official rate (of exchange)；pegged rate of exchange；pegged exchange parity；～货币 legal tender；～假期 official holiday；～年龄 lawful (or legal) age；～期限［法］Prescription；～人数 quorum；～税率 national tariff；statutory tariff；～最低资本额 minimal capital required by law

【法官】judge；justice

【法规】laws and regulations；statutes：经济～ *economic statutes*

【法国】France ◇ ～大革命 the French Revolution (1789-1799)；～人 the French；Frenchman

【法国梧桐】plane tree

【法纪】law and discipline：目无～ *act in utter disregard of law and discipline*；*flout law and discipline* / 遵守～ *observe law and discipline*

【法警】bailiff

【法拉】［物］farad

【法拉第定律】［物］Faraday's law

【法兰】［机］flange

【法兰盘】flange plate
【法兰绒】flannel
【法兰西银行】La Banque de France
【法郎】franc
【法老】Pharaoh (the title of the ruler of ancient Egypt)
【法理】legal principle；theory of law ◇ ～学 jurisprudence
【法力】❶ power of the Buddhist doctrine；dharma power ❷ magic power：使～ *exercise one's magic power*
【法令】laws and decrees；decree：政府～ *government decree*
【法律】law；statute：～保护 *legal protection* / ～地位 *legal status* / ～根据 *legal basis* / ～规定 *legal provisions* / ～手续 *legal procedure* / ～制裁 *legal sanction* / ～面前人人平等。*All are equal before the law*. ◇ ～承认 de jure recognition；～顾问 legal adviser；～实体 judicial entity；～行为 legal activities
【法螺】❶［动］triton (shell) ❷ conch：自吹～ *blow one's own trumpet*
【法盲】a person ignorant of the law；one who lacks legal knowledge
【法门】❶［宗］(佛教) gateway to the Law：～寺 *the Temple of the Law Gate* ❷ way；method
【法名】religious name (the name one adopts on becoming a Buddhist monk or nun)
【法器】musical instruments used in a Buddhist or Taoist mass
【法人】［法］person；artificial person；corporation ◇ ～身份 status of a legal person；～团体 body corporate
【法师】Master of the Law (a title of respect for a Buddhist or Taoist priest)
【法书】❶ model calligraphy ❷〈套〉your calligraphy
【法术】magic arts
【法庭】court；tribunal ◇ ～保释 court bond insurance
【法统】legally constituted authority
【法网】the net of justice；the arm of the law：逃不出人民的～ *be unable to escape the net of justice spread by the people*
【法西斯】fascist：～化 *fascistization*
【法西斯主义】fascism
【法学】the science of law；law ◇ ～家 jurist
【法眼】同〖慧眼〗
【法衣】garments worn by a Buddhist or Taoist priest at a religious ceremony
【法医】legal medical expert
【法医学】medical jurisprudence；forensic medicine
【法语】French (language)
【法院】court of justice；law court；court
【法则】❶ rule；law：自然～ *law of nature* ❷〈书〉laws and regulations ❸〈书〉model
【法治】rule by law ◇ ～国家 a country under the rule of law
【法制】legal system；legal institutions；legality：～教育 *education in legality* ◇ ～观念 awareness of the legal system；～建设 the building of the legal system
【法子】way；method：我们得想个～解决这个问题。*We'll have to think of a way to solve the problem*. or *We must find a way out*.

砝 (构词成分)见下
【砝码】weight (used on a balance)

fà

发 名 hair：白～ *white hair* ——另见 fā
【发辫】plait；braid；pigtail
【发髻】hair worn in a bun or coil
【发夹】hairpin；bobby pin
【发胶】hair spray
【发蜡】pomade
【发廊】hairdresser's；beauty parlor (for women)；barber's or barbershop (for men)
【发卡】hairpin
【发乳】hair cream；pomade
【发刷】hairbrush
【发网】hairnet
【发屋】同〖发廊〗
【发型】hairstyle；hairdo；coiffure：～美观大方 *a tasteful hairstyle* / 流行～ *a stylish coiffure* ◇ ～师 hairtician
【发癣】ringworm of the scalp；tinea capitis
【发油】hair oil
【发指】one's hair bristling up with anger

珐 (构词成分)见下
【珐琅】enamel
【珐琅质】enamel (of the teeth)

fān

帆 名 sail：把～扯起来。*Raise the sails*.
【帆板】windsurfer；sailboard
【帆板运动】windsurfing；sailboarding
【帆布】canvas：～包 *canvas bag*；*kit bag* / ～床 *cot*；*campbed* / ～篷 *canvas roof*；*awning* / ～鞋 *plimsolls*；*sneakers*
【帆船】sailing boat or ship；sailboat；junk ◇ ～运动 sailboating；sailing

番 Ⅰ 名 ❶ aborigines ❷ foreign；barbarian ❸ (used in names for certain plants originally introduced from abroad)：番茄 / 番薯 Ⅱ 量 ❶ (for actions，deeds，etc.)：下过一～功夫 *have put in a lot of time and effort* / 费了一～口舌才使他回心转意。*It took a lot of talking to bring him round*. / 她上上下下打量了我一～。*She looked me up and down*. ❷ (used with the numeral 一 only) kind：洞里别有一～天地。*The cave is an altogether different world*. ❸ (used after the verb 翻) times；-fold：翻番

【番号】the designation of a military unit
【番木瓜】papaya (the tree or its fruit)
【番茄】tomato：～酱 *tomato ketchup* (*or catsup*)；*tomato sauce* / ～汁 *tomato juice*
【番薯】〈方〉sweet potato

幡 名 a long narrow flag；streamer
【幡儿】funeral streamer

藩 名 ❶ hedge；fence：藩篱 ❷〈书〉screen；barrier：屏藩
【藩篱】hedge；fence；barrier
【藩属】vassal state

翻 动 ❶ turn upside down or inside out；turn over：～谷子 *turn over the grain* (*to dry*) / 船～了。*The ship capsized*. / 车～了。*The cart overturned*. / 我把茶杯碰～了。*I knocked the teacup over*. ❷ look through；search：～参考书 *look through reference works* / 抽屉我都～遍了，还是找不到。*I rummaged all the drawers, but still couldn't find it*. ❸ reverse：翻案 ❹ cross；get over：～过山头 *cross a mountaintop* / ～墙 *climb over a wall* ❺ multiply；double：翻番 ❻ translate：把英文～成中文 *translate the English into Chinese* / ～电报 *decode a telegram* ❼〈口〉fall out；break up：他们闹～了。*They fell out*. / 谁把他惹～了？*Who made him so angry*?
【翻案】reverse a verdict
【翻白眼】show the whites of one's eyes (as from emotion or illness)：她以为我们在议论她，直朝我们～。*She kept glaring at us, thinking that we had been talking about her*.
【翻版】reprint；reproduction；refurbished version
【翻场】turn over the grain on the threshing ground
【翻车】❶ (of a car) overturn：在公路拐弯处发生了一起～事故。*A car turned over at the road bend*. ❷ run into difficulties ◇ ～机［矿］tipper；dumper；tipple
【翻地】turn up the soil；plough up the fields
【翻斗】tipping bucket；skip bucket ◇ ～车 skip car；tipcart；～卡车 tipping lorry；tip lorry；tip truck
【翻番】increase by a specified number of times
【翻覆】❶ turn over；turn upside down：车辆～。*Cars turned over*. / 天地～ *heaven and earth turning upside down—cataclysmic changes* ❷ toss and turn：～不能眠 *toss and turn in bed, being unable to sleep*
【翻改】remake (old clothes)
【翻盖】rebuild or renovate (a house)
【翻杠子】［体］do gymnastics on a horizontal bar (or on parallel bars)
【翻跟头】turn a somersault；loop the loop：飞机连翻了三个跟头。*The plane looped the loop three times*.
【翻供】withdraw a confession；retract one's testimony
【翻滚】❶ seethe；churn：白浪～。*The waves rolled and foamed*. ❷ roll about；toss about：痛得不住地～ *writhe in pain*
【翻悔】back out (of a commitment, promise, etc.)：一经答应，就别～。*Once you've given your word, don't try to back out*.
【翻江倒海】holding back rivers and overturning seas—overwhelming；tremendous；earth-shaking：以～之势 *with the momentum of an avalanche*
【翻浆】(of road surfaces) burst and become muddy when a thaw sets in
【翻来覆去】❶ toss and turn；toss from side to side：他在床上～睡不着。*He tossed and turned in bed, unable to sleep*. ❷ again and again；repeatedly：这种话，她～不知说过多少遍了。*This is what she has been saying over and over again—I don't know how many times*.
【翻老账】(又作'翻旧账') rake up old scores (or grievances)
【翻脸】fall out；suddenly turn hostile：他俩从来没有翻过脸。*The two of them have never quarrelled*. / ～不认人 turn against a friend
【翻脸无情】turn against a friend and show him no mercy；be treacherous and ruthless
【翻两番】quadruple
【翻领】turndown collar
【翻录】pirate recordings
【翻然】(change) quickly and completely
【翻然悔悟】wake up to one's error；make an effort to atone for one's misdeeds
【翻砂】［机］❶ founding ❷ moulding；casting ◇ ～车间 foundry shop；～工 foundry worker；caster
【翻山越岭】cross over mountain after mountain；tramp over hill and dale
【翻身】❶ turn (the body) over：他翻了个身又睡着了。*He turned over in bed and fell asleep again*. / 一～从床上爬起来 *roll off the bed* ❷ free oneself；stand up：～农奴 *emancipated serfs* / ～做主人 *stand up and be master of one's fate*
【翻腾】❶［体］tuck dive：向内(前)～两周半 *backward* (*forward*) *tuck dive with two-and-a-half somersaults* ❷ seethe；rise；churn：波浪～ *seething* (*or turbulent*) *waves* / 许多问题在他脑子里～着。*His mind was seething with problems*. ❸ turn sth. over and over：几个箱子都～遍了也没有找到。*I rummaged through all the boxes but still could not find it*. / 过去的事，别再去～了。*Don't rake up the past*.
【翻天覆地】earth-shaking；world-shaking：～的变化 *an earth-shaking change*
【翻胃】同〖反胃〗
【翻箱倒柜】(又作'翻箱倒箧') rummage through chests and cupboards；ransack boxes and chests
【翻新】renovate；recondition；make over：旧大衣可以～。*Old overcoats can be reconditioned*. / ～车胎 *retread a tyre* ——另见〖花样翻新〗
【翻修】rebuild or renovate：～房屋 *have the house rebuilt or renovated* / ～地板 *relay a wooden*

floor / ～马路 *repair the roads*

【翻译】❶ translate; interpret: 这部书早就～成中文了。*This book was translated into Chinese a long time ago.* / ～电码 *decode; decipher* ❷ translator; interpreter: 担任～ *act as interpreter* ◇～本 translation; ～片 dubbed film; ～器 interpreter

【翻印】reprint; reproduce

【翻阅】leaf through; thumb through; look over; glance over: ～报章杂志 *look over newspapers and magazines* / ～目录 *glance through a catalogue*

【翻云覆雨】produce clouds with one turn of the hand and rain with another—be given to playing tricks; keep shifting one's ground

fán

凡 Ⅰ形 commonplace; ordinary: 非凡 Ⅱ名 this mortal world; the earth: 下凡 Ⅲ副〈书〉❶ all; every; any: ～属我国文化遗产中有用的东西,都应当继承。*All of our cultural heritage which is useful should be inherited.* ❷ altogether; in all: 全书～二十卷。*The set consists of 20 volumes altogether.*

【凡尘】this world; this mortal life

【凡夫俗子】ordinary people; the common herd

【凡例】notes on the use of a book etc.; guide to the use of a book, etc.

【凡人】❶〈书〉ordinary person ❷ mortal

【凡士林】vaseline; petrolatum

【凡事】everything: ～应该用脑筋好好想一想。*We should always use our brains and think everything over carefully.*

【凡是】every; any; all: ～正义的事业都是不可战胜的。*A just cause is invincible.* / ～认识他的人,没有不称赞他的。*All who know him speak highly of him.*

【凡庸】(usu. of humans) commonplace; ordinary: ～之辈 *the common herd*

矾 名[化] vitriol

【矾土】alumina (a mineral): ～水泥 *alumina cement*

钒 名[化] vanadium (V): ～钢 *vanadium steel*

烦 Ⅰ形 ❶ be vexed; be irritated; be annoyed: 孩子老哭,真～人! *How annoying it is to have a kid crying all the time!* / 你～什么? *What are you getting so annoyed about?* ❷ be tired of: 这话我都听～了。*I'm fed up with this kind of talk.* ❸ superfluous and confusing: 要言不烦 Ⅱ动〈套〉trouble (sb. to do sth.); bother: ～交某人 *please forward this to so-and-so* / ～您给她捎个信儿。*May I trouble you to pass on a message to her?*

【烦劳】❶ trouble (sb. to do sth.): ～您带几本书给他。*Would you mind taking a few books to him?* ❷ depressed; feeling low

【烦闷】be unhappy; be depressed; be moody: 雨下个不停,真叫人～。*When will the rain ever stop? How depressing!* / 你干吗这样～? *Why are you so unhappy?*

【烦恼】vexed; worried: 何必为这些小事～? *Why should you fret over such trifles?*

【烦扰】❶ bother; disturb ❷ feel disturbed

【烦冗】❶ (of one's affairs) diverse and complicated ❷ (of speech or writing) lengthy and tedious; prolix

【烦神】spend time and energy; take great trouble: 这些事就不用您～了。*You needn't trouble yourself about these things.*

【烦琐】loaded down with trivial details: ～的手续 *overelaborate procedure; tedious formalities* / ～的考证 *pedantic textual criticism; overelaborate research* / 这篇文章写得太～。*This article is too long and wordy.*

【烦琐哲学】❶ scholasticism ❷〈口〉over-elaboration; hairsplitting

【烦嚣】〈书〉noisy and annoying: 住在乡间,城里～的声音一点也听不到了。*As I live out of the city, I'm not harrassed by the racket of urban life.*

【烦心】annoying; vexatious; troublesome: 她从不把～的事对人讲。*She never confides her troubles to anybody.*

【烦躁】fidgety; agitated: 某些动物～不安可能是地震临震前的预兆。*Agitated activity by certain animals may be a sign of an impending earthquake.*

蕃 Ⅰ形 (of trees, grass, etc.) luxuriant; thriving: ～茂 *luxuriant; lush* Ⅱ动 multiply; proliferate

樊 名〈书〉fence

【樊篱】❶ fence ❷ barriers; restriction: 冲破～ *break down barriers; cast off trammels*

【樊笼】〈喻〉bird cage

繁 Ⅰ形 in great numbers; numerous; manifold: ～星满天 *a starry sky* Ⅱ动 propagate; multiply: 农场自～自养的牲畜 *livestock bred and reared by the farm itself*

【繁多】various: 花色～ *a great variety*

【繁分数】[数] complex fraction

【繁复】heavy and complicated: 有了计算机,～的计算工作在几秒钟之内就可以完成。*A computer does complicated calculations in a few seconds.*

【繁华】flourishing; bustling; busy: 城里最～的地区 *the busiest section of town; the downtown district*

【繁忙】busy: ～的收获季节 *the busy harvest season* / 工作～ *be very busy with one's work; be busily engaged*

【繁茂】lush; luxuriant: 草木～ *a lush growth of trees and grass* / 枝叶～ *with luxuriant foliage*

【繁密】dense: 林木～ *densely wooded* / ～的鞭炮

声 *the sound of firecrackers going off uninterruptedly*

【繁难】hard to tackle; troublesome: 校对是一件～的工作。*Proofreading is a troublesome task.*

【繁荣】❶ flourishing; prosperous; booming: ～的文化事业 *flourishing cultural undertakings* / ～富强 *rich, strong and prosperous* / 经济～。*The economy is booming.* / 市场～。*The market is brisk.* ❷ make sth. prosper: ～经济 *bring about a prosperous economy; promote economic prosperity* / ～文学创作 *promote literary creation* ◇ ～兴旺 brisk and flourish; flourishing; prosperous; rich and vigorous; thriving

【繁荣昌盛】thriving and prosperous: 祝贵国～,人民幸福。*We wish your country prosperity and her people happiness.*

【繁盛】thriving; flourishing; prosperous: 这个城市越来越～了。*The city is becoming more and more prosperous.*

【繁体字】the original complex form of a simplified Chinese character

【繁文缛节】unnecessary and overelaborate formalities; red tape

【繁细】overloaded with details; excessively detailed

【繁衍】〈书〉multiply; increase gradually in number (or quantity)

【繁育】breed: ～优良品种 *breed good strains*

【繁杂】many and diverse; miscellaneous: ～的日常事务 *daily chores of all sorts*

【繁殖】breed; reproduce; propagate: 自我～ *self-reproduction; autosynthesis* / ～牲畜 *breed livestock* / 靠种子～的植物 *plants which propagate themselves by seeds* ◇ ～力 reproductive capacity; fecundity; fertility; ～率 rate of reproduction; breeding rate

【繁重】heavy; strenuous; onerous: ～的劳动 *strenuous labour* / 任务～。*The tasks are arduous.*

fǎn

反 Ⅰ 副 ❶ in an opposite direction; reverse; inside out: 你的袜子穿～了。*You have put your socks on inside out.* / ～绑着手 *with one's hands tied behind one's back* / 这件上衣正～两面都可以穿。*This coat is reversible, you can wear it inside out.* ❷ on the contrary; instead: 他不但不支持我,～把我批评了一顿。*Instead of supporting me, he criticized me.* / 这样做不但于事无补,～会把事情弄糟。*This won't do any good; on the contrary, it will make things even worse.* Ⅱ 动 ❶ turn over; reverse: 反败为胜 ❷ return; counter: 反击/ 反问 ❸ revolt; rebel; turn against: ～朝廷 *rebel against the imperial government* ❹ oppose; combat: ～贪污 *combat corruption* / ～侵略 *oppose aggression*

【反霸】❶ struggle against local despots (in land reform) ❷ oppose hegemonism

【反败为胜】turn defeat into victory; turn the tide

【反比】inverse relation; inverse proportion: 与…成～ *be inversely proportional to...; be in inverse proportion to...*

【反比例】[数] inverse ratio; inverse proportion: 分数值与分母值成～。*The value of a fraction is inversely proportional to that of the denominator.*

【反病毒软件】[计] anti-virus (software)

【反驳】refute; rebut: 作出强有力的～ *refute (or rebut) with convincing arguments* / ～对方的指责 *refute the other party's accusations*

【反差】[摄] contrast

【反常】unusual; abnormal; strange: 最近天气有点儿～。*The weather is a bit unusual these days.* / 他昨天的表现有点儿～。*His behaviour yesterday was a bit strange.*

【反潮流】go against the tide; swim against the stream: ～而动 *act against the prevailing mood (or current)*

【反衬】set off by contrast; serve as a foil to

【反冲】recoil; kick ◇ ～核 [物] recoil nucleus; ～力 [物] recoil

【反刍】ruminate; chew the cud

【反刍动物】ruminant

【反唇相讥】answer back sarcastically

【反导弹导弹】antimissile missile

【反倒】〈口〉on the contrary; instead

【反帝】oppose imperialism; be anti-imperialist: ～斗争 *anti-imperialist struggle*

【反动】❶ reactionary: ～势力 *reactionary forces* ❷ reaction: 他弃家出走,是对旧社会婚姻压迫的～。*He finally left home in an effort to counter the tyranny of arranged marriage in the old society.* ◇ ～分子 reactionary element; reactionary; ～派 reactionaries

【反对】oppose; be against; fight; combat: ～种族歧视 *oppose racial discrimination* / ～官僚主义 *combat bureaucracy* / ～贪污浪费 *fight against corruption and waste* / 有～意见吗? *Any objections?* ◇ ～党 opposition party; the Opposition; ～派 opposition faction; ～票 dissenting vote; negative vote

【反而】on the contrary; instead: 风不但没停,～更大了。*Instead of going down, the wind blew even harder.*

【反封建】anti-feudal; against feudalism

【反腐败斗争】the fight against corruption

【反复】❶ repeatedly; again and again: ～解释 *explain over and over again* / ～思考 *think a lot about sth; turn sth. over in one's mind again and again* ❷ back out; chop and change: 说一是一,说二是二,决不～。*I mean what I say and I'll never go back on my word.* / 他的态度反反复复,叫人难以捉摸。*He's always chopping and changing, and you just can't tell where he stands.* ❸ reversal; relapse: 思想上有～ *have ideological relapses*

【反复无常】behave capriciously; blow hot and cold; chop and change: 这个人～,很不可靠。*This fellow is always chopping and changing; he's very unreliable.*

【反感】be disgusted with; be averse to; dislike; take unkindly to: 我对他的话很～。*I'm disgusted with what he said.* / 对这种人极其～ *have a strong aversion to such people; feel a repugnance to such people*

【反戈一击】turn one's weapon around and strike—turn against one's own side

【反革命】❶ counterrevolutionary: ～罪行 *a counterrevolutionary crime* ❷ a counterrevolutionary: 镇压～ *suppress counterrevolutionaries*

【反攻】launch a counteroffensive; counterattack: 敌人已无力～。*The enemy hasn't the strength to counterattack.* / 发动猛烈的～ *launch a fierce counterattack (on sb.)*

【反攻倒算】(of members of an overthrown reactionary class) counterattack to settle old scores; launch a vindictive counterattack; retaliate

【反躬自问】examine oneself; examine one's conscience

【反顾】〈书〉look back; turn back: 义无反顾

【反光】❶ reflect light: 白墙～,屋里显得很敞亮。*With the white walls reflecting the light, the room looks bright and spacious.* ❷ reflection of light: 湖面上的～把我的眼睛都照花了。*The reflections of sunlight in the lake dazzled my eyes.* ◇ ～灯 reflector lamp; ～镜 reflector; ～照明 reflect lighting

【反函数】[数] inverse function

【反核子】antinucleon

【反话】an ironic remark; irony

【反悔】go back on one's word (or promise): 一言为定,决不～。*I give you my word and I'll never go back on it.*

【反汇编程序】disassembler

【反击】strike back; beat back; counterattack: 自卫～ *counterattack in self-defence* / 对挑衅给予有力的～ *answer provocation with a vigorous counterblow*

【反剪】❶ have one's hands tied behind one's back ❷ hold one's hands behind one's back

【反间】sow distrust or dissension among one's enemies; set one's enemies at odds (by spreading rumours, etc.)

【反间计】a stratagem of sowing distrust or discord among one's enemies: 不要中了敌人的～。*Don't fall into the enemy's plot of sowing discord among us.*

【反诘】ask in retort; counter with a question

【反抗】revolt; resist: ～侵略 *resist aggression* / ～精神 *spirit of revolt; rebellious spirit* / 哪里有压迫,哪里就有～。*Where there is oppression, there is resistance.*

【反客为主】turn from guest into host—gain the initiative

【反科学】antiscience

【反空降】[军] anti-airborne defence

【反恐怖主义】counterterrorism

【反馈】❶ [电子] feedback: 正(负)～ *positive (negative) feedback* ❷ feedback (a response): 公司欢迎消费者对他们产品的～。*The company welcomes feedback from consumers who use their products.* ◇ ～控制系统 feedback control systems; ～信息 feedback informaton; ～抑制 [生理] feedback inhibition

【反粒子】[物] antiparticle

【反例证】counter-example

【反面】❶ reverse side; wrong side; back: 唱片的～ *the reverse side of a disc* / 料子的～ *the wrong side of the cloth* ❷ the reverse side of a state of affairs, a problem, etc. ❸ opposite; negative side: 走向～ *change (or turn) into one's opposite* / ～的教训 *a lesson learnt from negative (or bitter) experience; wisdom won from hard knocks* ◇ ～教材 negative example which may serve as a lesson; bad experience which teaches us what not to do; ～教员 teacher by negative example; ～人物 villain; negative character; negative role

【反目】(usu. of husband and wife) fall out; have a falling-out

【反派】villain (in drama, etc.); negative character: 演～人物 *act the part of the villain; play a negative role*

【反叛】revolt; rebel: ～朝廷 *rebel against the imperial government*

【反批评】counter-criticism

【反聘】rehire after retirement

【反扑】pounce on sb. again after being beaten off; launch a counteroffensive to retrieve lost ground

【反其道而行之】act in a diametrically opposite way; do exactly the opposite

【反气旋】[气] anticyclone

【反潜】defend (maritime space) against enemy submarines ◇ ～导弹 antisubmarine missiles; ～机 antisubmarine plane; ～舰艇 antisubmarine vessels

【反倾销】anti-dumpling

【反射】❶ reflect (light, heat, sound, etc.): 镜子能～光线。*Mirrors reflect light.* ❷ [生理] reflex ◇ ～比 [物] reflectance; ～测云器 reflecting nephoscope; ～弧 [生理] reflex arc; ～计 reflectometer; ～镜 reflector; ～炉 reverberatory furnace; ～望远镜 reflecting telescope

【反身代词】[语] reflexive pronoun

【反手】backhand: ～抽球 *backhand drive* / ～接住飞盘 *catch the Frisbee backhand (or backhanded)*

【反水】〈方〉turn one's coat; defect

【反思】self-examination; infrospection

【反诉】[法] countercharge; counterclaim

【反贪】combat graft

【反坦克炮】antitank gun

【反特】prevent or thwart enemy espionage; engage in counterespionage: ～影片 *spy film;*

counterespionage film
【反题】[哲] antithesis
【反铁电现象】antiferroelectricity
【反围盘】[机] reverse repeater (used in steel rolling)
【反胃】have a gastric disorder; feel nauseated; feel queasy
【反问】❶ ask a question in reply ❷ [语] rhetorical question
【反响】repercussion; echo; reverberation: 在世界上引起广泛的～ *evoke worldwide repercussions* / 在很多人心中引起～ *find an echo in the hearts of many people*
【反向】opposite direction; reverse ◇ ～铲 backhoe; ～电流 reverse current; ～技术转让 reverse transfer of technology; ～卫星 retrograde satellite
【反斜面】[军] reverse slope; rear slope
【反信风】[气] antitrades
【反省】engage in introspection, self-examination or soul-searching: 停职～ *be temporarily relieved of one's post for self-examination*
【反宣传】❶ counterpropaganda ❷ slander campaign
【反咬一口】trump up a countercharge against one's accuser; make a false countercharge
【反义词】[语] antonym
【反应】❶ response; repercussion; reaction: ～不一。*Reactions vary.* / 作出～ *make a response* / ～冷淡。*The response was far from warm.* ❷ react; respond: 他对你的建议～怎么样? *How did he react to your suggestion?* / 对老师的提问,他～很快。*He responds very quickly to the teacher's questions.* ❸ [生理][医] reaction: 过敏～ *allergic reaction* / 阳性(阴性)～ *positive (negative) reaction* / 病人打针(化验)以后的～ *a patient's reaction to an injection (a medical test)* ❹ [化][物] reaction: 链式反应 ◇ ～本领 [物] reaction capacity; ～塔 reaction tower; ～物 [化] reactant
【反应堆】[物] reactor: 高温～ *high-temperature reactor* / 浓缩铀～ *enriched uranium reactor* / 增殖～ *breeder reactor* / 石墨减速～ *graphite-moderated reactor* / 热中子～ *thermal reactor* / 轻水慢化～ *light-water-moderated reactor*
【反映】❶ reflect; mirror: 这张报纸～知识分子的看法和意见。*The newspaper reflects the intellectuals' views and opinions.* / 这部小说真实地～了拓荒者的生活。*This novel gives a faithful representation of (or is a mirror of) the life of the pioneers.* ❷ report; make known: 向上级～ *report to the higher level* / 把群众的呼声及时地～上去 *transmit the voices of the people to the leading bodies without delay*
【反映论】[哲] theory of reflection
【反语】irony
【反正】❶ come over from the enemy's side ❷ (often used correlatively with 不管,无论, etc.) in any case; at any rate; anyway: 不管怎么样, ～工作不能停。*Come what may, the work must go on.* / 无论你怎么说, ～我不答应。*No matter what you say, I won't agree.* ❸ since; as: ～得去一个人,就让我去吧! *Since someone has to go anyway, let me go.*
【反证】disproof; counterevidence ◇ ～法 reduction to absurdity; reductio ad absurdum
【反之】〈书〉 whereas; on the other hand; conversely
【反殖】anti-colonialist
【反质子】[物] antiproton
【反中子】[物] antineutron
【反主流文化】counterculture
【反转】reverse
【反转片】reversal film
【反坐】[法] sentence the accuser to the punishment facing the person he falsely accused
【反作用】counteraction; reaction: 你要起好作用,不要起～。*You should set a good example, not a bad one.* ◇ ～力 [物] reacting force

返 动 return; come or go back: ～沪 *return to Shanghai*
【返潮】get damp: 雨季里东西容易～。*Things get damp easily in the rainy season.*
【返防】[军] return to stations
【返工】do poorly done work over again: 这项工作必须～。*This job will have to be done over again.* / 当初要是听了我的意见,今天哪至于～呢! *If you had listened to me, you wouldn't have to do it all over again.*
【返航】(of ships, planes, etc.) return to base (or port): 在～途中 *on the homebound voyage (or flight)* / 这支舰队在完成任务后,已安然～。*After completing its voyage, the fleet safely returned to base.*
【返回】return; come or go back: ～原地 *return to the starting point* / ～港口 *put back to port* / 使人造地球卫星～地面 *recover a man-made earth satellite* / ～工作岗位 *return to one's post* ◇ ～卫星 recoverable satellite; return satellite; ～指令 link order
【返老还童】recover one's youthful vigour; feel rejuvenated
【返璞归真】one's original simplicity; return to one's original nature
【返青】[农] (of winter crops or transplanted seedlings) turn green
【返销】(of state-purchased grain) be sold back to a grain-producing area (in cases of natural disaster, etc.): 吃～粮 *eat "resold grain"*
【返校】(of students) return to school: ～日 *a day set for schoolchildren to return to school during the vacation to have homework checked*
【返祖现象】(又作'返祖遗传') [生] atavism; reversion

fàn

犯 I 动 ❶ violate; offend (against the law,

etc.)：～纪律 *violate discipline* / ～校规 *offend (or break) a school rule* ❷ attack; invade; work against ❸ have a recurrence of (an old illness); revert to (a bad habit)：他的气喘病又～了。*He's got another attack of asthma.* / ～脾气 *get angry; fly into a temper; be in a bad temper* ❹ commit (a mistake, crime, etc.)：～错误 *make a mistake* / ～官僚主义 *commit the error of bureaucracy* Ⅱ 名 criminal：战犯

【犯案】(of a criminal) be found out and brought to justice

【犯病】have an attack of one's old illness：她妈又～了。*Her mother is ill again.* / 这孩子三天两头～。*This child gets ill too often.* / 别理他，他又～了。*Leave him alone! He's in one of his moods again.*

【犯愁】worry; be anxious：你犯什么愁？*What are you worrying about?*

【犯法】violate (or break) the law：～行为 *an offence against the law* / 重婚是～的。*Bigamy is against the law.*

【犯规】❶ break the rules ❷［体］foul：侵人～ *personal foul* / 三号队员已经犯了四次规。*Player No. 3 has already fouled four times in the game.*

【犯忌】violate a taboo：几年前～的话题，我们现在可以谈论了。*Now we can discuss topics that would have been taboo a few years ago.*

【犯禁】violate a ban (or prohibition)

【犯人】prisoner; convict

【犯上】go against the king or emperor (in former times); defy one's elders, superiors, etc.

【犯上作乱】defy one's superiors and start a rebellion; rebel：你一放松，他们就～无所不为了。*Once the lid is loose, there'll be a deluge of rebellion and they'll take the law into their own hands.*

【犯嫌疑】arouse suspicion; come under suspicion

【犯疑】(又作'犯疑心') become suspicious

【犯罪】commit a crime (or an offence)：～分子 *offender; criminal* / ～团伙 *a criminal gang* / ～行为 *a criminal offence* / 浪费这么好的粮食简直是～。*It's a crime to waste such good food.* ◇ ～侦查学 criminalistics

泛 Ⅰ 动 ❶〈书〉float：～舟西湖 *go boating on the West Lake* ❷ drift out; spread out：从厨房里～出阵阵香味。*Delicious aromas wafted out of the kitchen.* / 她的脸色黑里～红。*She has a tanned and glowing face.* / 脸上～出红晕 *with one's cheeks suffused with blushes* ❸ flood; inundate：黄泛区 Ⅱ 形 extensive; general; nonspecific：泛读

【泛称】general term

【泛读】extensive reading

【泛泛而谈】speak in general terms; talk in generalities

【泛泛之交】casual acquaintance

【泛非主义】Pan-Africanism ◇ ～者 Pan-Africanist

【泛光灯】floodlight

【泛函分析】［数］functional analysis

【泛滥】be in flood; overflow; inundate：河水～。*The river was flooding.* or *The river overflowed its banks.* / 不能让错误思想自由～。*Under no circumstances should erroneous ideas be allowed to spread unchecked.*

【泛滥成灾】flood; run rampant; run wild：江水决堤，～。*The river overflowed its banks and caused serious flooding.* / 表格之多，闹得～。*There is such a flood of statistical forms that they become a scourge.*

【泛美主义】Pan-Americanism

【泛神论】［哲］pantheism

【泛音】［音］overtone; harmonic ◇ ～列［音］harmonic series

【泛指】make a general reference; be used in a general sense：他的发言是～一般情况，不是针对某一个人的。*His statement refers to people in general, not to anyone in particular.*

饭 名 ❶ cooked rice or other cereals：小米～ *(cooked) millet* ❷ meal：～前洗手。*Wash your hands before meals.*

【饭菜】❶ meal; repast：～可口，服务周到 *tasty food and good service* ❷ dishes to go with rice, steamed buns, etc.

【饭店】❶ hotel：北京～ *Beijing Hotel* ❷〈方〉restaurant

【饭馆】(small) restaurant; eating house：下～ *eat (or dine) in a restaurant*

【饭锅】❶ pot for cooking rice; rice cooker ❷ means of living; livelihood：砸～ *lose one's livelihood; lose one's job*

【饭盒】lunch-box; mess tin; dinner pail

【饭局】dinner party; feast

【饭来张口，衣来伸手】have only to open one's mouth to be fed and hold out one's arms to be dressed—lead an easy life, with everything provided; be waited on hand and foot

【饭量】appetite：～很大 *have an enormous appetite; be a big eater* / 她的～比你小多了。*She eats much less than you do.*

【饭票】meal ticket; mess card

【饭铺】(small) restaurant; eating house

【饭食】food provided by a canteen, restaurant, boarding house, etc. (esp. with regard to its quality); fare：那儿的～挺不错。*You get pretty good food there.*

【饭厅】dining hall; dining room; mess hall：这个～可容三百人就餐。*The dining hall can seat 300 people.*

【饭桶】❶ rice bucket ❷ a big eater; a piggish eater ❸ fathead; good-for-nothing

【饭碗】❶ rice bowl ❷〈口〉job; means of livelihood：丢～ *lose one's job* / 找～ *hunt for a job* / 你要加倍小心，这事弄不好会把你的～砸了。*Be extra cautious. It may cost you your job if anything goes wrong.*

【饭庄】(又作'饭庄子')(big) restaurant
【饭桌】dining table

范 名 ❶〈书〉mould; matrix; pattern ❷ model; example: 典范 ❸ limits: 就范 ❹〈书〉restriction: 防范
【范本】a model for calligraphy or painting: 习字～ *a model for calligraphy*
【范畴】❶ category: 这些概念属于美学的～。*These concepts belong in the field of aesthetics.* ❷ type; scope
【范例】example; model: 这是厉行节约的一个出色～。*This is an outstanding example of strict economy.*
【范式】canonical form; normal form
【范围】limits; scope; range: 在法律许可～内 *within the limits permitted by law* / 国家管辖～ *the limits of national jurisdiction* / 势力～ *sphere of influence* / 我们谈话的～很广。*Our talk covered a wide range of subjects.*
【范文】model essay; anthology piece

贩 Ⅰ 动 (of traders) buy to resell: ～牲口 *buy and sell draught animals* Ⅱ 名 trader; monger; pedlar (or peddler): 小贩
【贩毒】traffic in narcotics
【贩卖】traffic; peddle; sell: ～腐朽思想 *peddle decadent ideas* / ～军火 *traffic in arms* / ～皮货 *be in the fur trade* ◇ ～人口 traffic in human beings; human traffic
【贩私】traffic in smuggled goods
【贩运】transport goods for sale; traffic: 在广州和东北之间搞长途～ *transport goods for sale between Guangzhou and the Northeast*
【贩子】trader; monger: 马～ *horse trader* / 鱼～ *fishmonger*

梵 名 ❶ of ancient India: 梵文 ❷ Buddhist: ～刹 *Buddhist temple*
【梵蒂冈】the Vatican
【梵文】Sanskrit
【梵语】Sanskrit

fāng

方 Ⅰ 名 ❶ square: 这块板子是～的。*This is a square board.* ❷ [数] involution; power: 二的四次～是十六。*The fourth power of 2 is 16.* / 三的三次～是二十七。*The third power (or cube) of 3 is 27.* ❸ direction: 东方 ❹ side; party: 我～ *our side* ❺ place; region; locality: 远方 ❻ method; way: 有方 ❼ prescription: 这～儿专治腰痛。*This prescription is especially good for backaches.* Ⅱ 量 ❶ (for square things): 三～图章 *three seals* / 一～手帕 *a handkerchief* ❷ short for square metre or cubic metre: 一～木材 *a cubic metre of lumber* / 铺地板十五～ *lay 15 square metres of floorboards* Ⅲ 形 upright; honest: 方正 Ⅳ 副〈书〉❶ just when; at the time when: 方今 ❷ only; just: 年～二十 *be just twenty years old*
【方案】scheme; plan; programme: 提出初步～ *put forward a preliminary plan*
【方便】❶ convenient: 这儿交通～。*Transportation is convenient here.* / 什么时候～,什么时候来。*Drop in whenever it's convenient.* / 这件事让我去办很～。*It's quite convenient for me to do that.* ❷ make things convenient for sb.: ～群众 *make things convenient for the people* ❸〈婉〉have money to spare or lend: 手头不～ *have little money to spare* ❹〈婉〉〈口〉go to the lavatory: 你要不要～一下? *Do you want to use the lavatory (or wash your hands)?* ◇ ～米 instant rice; ～面 instant noodles; ～食品 convenience food
【方便之门】convenience: 大开～ *do everything to suit sb.'s convenience*
【方步】measured steps: 迈～ *walk with measured steps*
【方才】❶ just now: ～的情形,你都知道了。*You know what has just happened.* ❷ (only) just; not until: 等到天黑,他～回来。*He didn't come back until after dark.*
【方程】[数] equation: 三次～ *cubic equation* / 高次～ *equation of higher degree* / 线性～ *linear equation*
【方程式】❶ 同〖方程〗❷ (chemical) equation ◇ ～赛车 formula
【方寸】❶ square cun (=1/9 *square decimetre*) ❷〈字〉heart
【方法】method; way; means: 学习～ *study method* / 看问题的～ *the way one approaches a problem (or looks at things)* / 用各种～ *in all sorts of ways; by every means* / 用某种～ *by some means or other; one way or another* ◇ ～工程 methods engineering
【方法论】[哲] methodology
【方钢】[冶] square steel
【方格】a pattern of squares; check: ～桌布 *a checked (or check) tablecloth* / ～纹 *trellis design* / ～纸 *squared paper; graph paper*
【方根】[数] root
【方剂】[中] prescription; recipe
【方济各会】the Franciscan Order
【方尖碑】obelisk
【方解石】calcite (a mineral)
【方块字】square-shaped characters—Chinese characters
【方框】square frame
【方括号】square brackets ([ ])
【方略】general plan: 建国～ *a general plan for national reconstruction*
【方面】respect; aspect; side; field: 在这～ *in this respect* / 在工业、商业、财政～ *in the fields of industry, commerce and finance* / 站在我们这～ *stand on our side; take our side* / 考虑各～的意见 *consider opinions from different quarters*

【方铅矿】galena
【方士】❶ necromancer ❷ alchemist
【方式】way; fashion; pattern: 生活～ *way (or mode) of life; life-style* / 斗争～ *form of struggle*
【方糖】sugar cube; lump sugar
【方位】❶ points of the compass: 东、南、西、北为基本～。*East, west, north and south are the cardinal points of the compass.* ❷ direction and position; bearings: 确定～ *find one's bearings* ◇ ～词 [语] noun of locality; localizer; ～角 [天] azimuth; ～罗盘 surveying azimuth compass; ～天文学 positional astronomy; ～物 [军] topographic marker; landmarker
【方向】direction; orientation: 他朝学校的～走了。*He went in the direction of the school.* / 她深信已在生活中找到了新的～。*She is confident that she has found a new orientation in life.* ◇ ～舵 rudder (of an airplane); ～盘 steering wheel; ～整流器 direction rectifier
【方兴未艾】be fast unfolding; be in the ascendant: 这场运动～。*The movement is now in the ascendant.*
【方形】square-shaped; square
【方言】dialect ◇ ～学 dialectology
【方圆】❶ neighbourhood; vicinity: ～左近的人,他都认识。*He knows everyone in the neighbourhood.* ❷ circumference: 那个湖～八百公里。*The lake has a circumference of 800 kilometres.*
【方丈】❶ Buddhist abbot ❷ abbot's room
【方针】policy; guiding principle: 基本～ *fundamental policy (or principle)* / ～政策 *general and specific policies*
【方正】❶ upright and foursquare: 字要写得～。*In writing, make the characters square and upright.* ❷ straightforward; upright; righteous: 他为人～。*He is an upright man.*
【方志】local records
【方子】❶ prescription: 开～ *write out a prescription* ❷ directions for mixing chemicals; formula
【方钻杆】[油] kelly (bar)

坊 名 ❶ lane (usu. as part of a street or lane name): 白纸～ *White Paper Lane (a street in Beijing)* ❷ 见〖牌坊〗——另见 fáng
【坊本】〈旧〉block-printed edition prepared by a bookshop
【坊间】in the streets (esp. with reference to the bookshops): 此书～少见。*This book is rarely seen in the bookshops.*

芳 形 ❶ sweet-smelling; fragrant: ～草 *fragrant grass* ❷ good (name or reputation); virtuous: 流芳百世
【芳菲】〈书〉❶ the fragrance of flowers and plants ❷ flowers and plants
【芳龄】〈旧〉the age of a young woman
【芳名】〈旧〉❶ the name of a young woman ❷ a good reputation
【芳烃】[化] aromatic hydrocarbon
【芳香】(esp. of flowers or plants) fragrant ◇ ～剂 an aromatic drug; aromatic
【芳心】the heart of a young woman
【芳族】[化] aromatics: ～化合物 *aromatic compound*; *aromatic* / ～酸 *aromatic acid*

钫 名 [化] francium (Fr)

fáng

防 Ⅰ 动 ❶ guard against; provide against: ～病 *prevent disease* / ～霜冻 *protect plants against severe frosts* ❷ defend: 国防/ 防御 Ⅱ 名 dyke; embankment: 堤防
【防暴】riot protection ◇ ～队 riot protection team; ～警察 riot police; riot squad; ～车 anti-riot vehicle
【防弹车】bubble car
【防弹汽车】bulletproof car
【防备】guard against; take precautions against: 他们事先没有一点～。*They didn't take any precautions whatever.* or *They threw precautions to the winds.*
【防波堤】breakwater; mole
【防不胜防】hard to guard against; cannot reckon with all eventualities: 他的球路多变,打得对手～。*His opponent couldn't stand up to his varied and fast-changing tactics.*
【防潮】❶ dampproof; moistureproof: ～纸 *moistureproof paper; tarred paper* / ～砖 *moisture-proof brick* ❷ give protection against the tide: ～堰堤 *tidal barrage* ◇ ～层 [建] dampproof course; damp course; ～火药 moistureproof powder; nonhygroscopic powder
【防尘】dustproof ◇ ～圈 [机] dust ring; ～罩 dust cover
【防磁】[物] protect against magnetization; be antimagnetic: ～表 *antimagnetic watch*
【防弹】bulletproof; shellproof: ～背心 *bulletproof vest* / ～玻璃 *bulletproof glass*
【防盗】guard against theft; take precautions against burglars
【防地】[军] defence sector; station (of a unit)
【防冻】prevent frostbite: ～药品 *frostbite preventive* ◇ ～剂 antifreezing agent; freeze proof agent; ～液 antifreeze solution
【防毒】protect (men or animals) against poisonous substances; protect against poison gas: ～器材 *gas protection equipment* / ～衣 *protective clothing* ◇ ～面具 gas mask
【防范】be on guard; keep a lookout: 严加～ *take strict precautions*
【防风】protect against the wind; provide shelter from the wind ◇ ～林 windbreak forest
【防辐射】protect against radiation
【防腐】❶ antiseptic: ～纱布 *antiseptic gauze* ❷ antirot: ～材料 *antirot material* ◇ ～剂 antisep-

tic; preservative

【防寒服】cold-resistant clothing

【防旱】take precautions against drought

【防洪】prevent or control flood: ～措施 *flood control measures* / ～工程 *flood control works*

【防护】protect; shelter: 人体～ *physical protection* / ～涂层 *protective coating*

【防护堤】(protection) embankment

【防护林】shelter-forest: ～带 *shelterbelt*

【防滑链】tyre chain; skid chain

【防化学兵】(又作'防化兵') antichemical warfare corps

【防患未然】(又作'防患于未然') take preventive measures; provide against possible trouble

【防火】❶ prevent fires ❷ fireproof: ～油漆 fire-retardant paint ◇ ～隔离线[林] fire lane; ～墙 fire wall

【防空】air defence: ～导弹 *air defence missile*; *interceptor missile* / ～演习 *air defence exercise*; *air-raid drill* ◇ ～部队 air defence forces; ～洞 air-raid shelter; ～壕 air-raid dugout; ～警报 air-raid warning; air-raid siren

【防涝】prevent waterlogging

【防凌】reduce the menace of ice run

【防窃听电话】scrambler phone

【防区】defence; area; garrison area

【防染剂】[纺] resist

【防沙林】sand-break forests

【防身】defend oneself against violence: ～武器 *weapons for self-defence*

【防守】defend; guard: ～阵地 *defend one's position (in battle)*

【防暑】prevent heatstroke (or sunstroke): ～措施 *measures taken to prevent heatstroke* / ～药 *heatstroke preventive*

【防水】waterproof: ～表 *waterproof watch* / ～布 *waterproof cloth* / ～水泥 *waterproof cement* ◇ ～层[建] waterproof layer

【防缩】[纺] shrinkproof: ～整理 *shrinkproof finish*; *shrinkage control finish*

【防坦克】antitank defence: ～地雷 *antitank mine* / ～壕 *tank (or antitank) ditch* / ～炮 *antitank gun* / ～阵地 *antitank position*

【防特】guard against enemy agents

【防微杜渐】nip in the bud; check at the outset

【防卫】defend: ～作战能力 *defence capability*

【防污染】anti-pollution

【防务】matters pertaining to defence; defence

【防线】line of defence: 突破敌人～ *break through the enemy's line of defence*

【防锈】rust-resist; rustproof: 不要让自行车在雨里淋,注意～。*Don't leave the bike in the rain and let it rust.* / ～漆 *antirust paint* / ～脂 *antirust grease* ◇ ～剂 rust inhibitor; antirust agent

【防汛】flood prevention or control: 组成一支～大军 *organize an army of flood-fighters* / ～指挥部 *flood-control headquarters*

【防疫】epidemic prevention ◇ ～站 epidemic prevention station; ～针 (prophylactic) inoculation

【防雨布】waterproof cloth; tarpaulin

【防御】defend; guard: 积极(消极)～ *active (passive) defence* / 纵深～ *defence in depth* / 加强～力量 *strengthen defence capabilities* / 由～转入进攻 *go over from the defensive to the offensive* ◇ ～部队 defending force (or troops, unit); ～部署 defensive disposition; ～措施 defensive measure; ～工事 defences; fortifications; defence works; ～区 defensive area; ～武器 weapons of defence; ～战 defensive warfare; ～阵地 defensive position; defended post; ～正面 frontage in defence; front of defence

【防灾】take precautions against natural calamities

【防震】❶ shockproof: ～表 *shockproof watch* ❷ take precautions against earthquakes: ～措施 *precautions against earthquakes* ◇ ～棚 temporary shelter for earthquake

【防止】prevent; guard against; forestall; avoid: ～交通事故 *try to forestall traffic accidents* / ～经济过热。*Prevent the economy from becoming over heated.* ◇ ～核扩散 nonproliferation of nuclear weapons

【防治】provide prevention and cure; administer prophylaxis and treatment: ～血吸虫病 *the prevention and cure of schistosomiasis* / ～病虫害 *the prevention and control of plant diseases and elimination of pests*

【防皱】crease-proof; crease-resist

坊

名 handicraftsmen's workplace; workshop; mill: 油坊 —— 另见 fāng

妨

动 ❶ hinder; hamper; impede; obstruct: 妨碍 ❷ (used in the negative or interrogative) harm: 不妨

【妨碍】hinder; hamper; impede; obstruct: ～团结 *hinder unity* / ～交通 *block traffic* / ～生产的发展 *hamper the growth of production* / 这不～我们按期动工。*This won't stop us from starting the project on schedule.* ◇ ～公务 interference with public function; ～婚姻家庭罪 crimes of interference with the family

【妨害】impair; jeopardize; be harmful to: 吃得不好会～健康。*A poor diet is harmful to one's health.*

房

名 ❶ house: 一所砖～ *a brick house* ❷ room; bedroom: 三间～ *three rooms* / 两～一厅 *two bedrooms and a living room* ❸ a house-like structure: 莲～ *lotus pod*

【房舱】passenger's cabin in a ship

【房产】house property

【房地产】real estate: ～经纪人 *estate agent*; *house agent*; *realtor* ◇ ～公司 real estate agency; ～交易 real estate transaction; ～交易中心 real estate exchange centre; ～经营 real estate business; ～经营管理 real estate operation and management; ～开发 real estate development; ～市场 real estate market; ～税 housing and land

tax；real estate tax
【房顶】roof
【房东】the owner and lessor of a house or room；landlord or landlady
【房改】housing reform；reform of the housing problem ◇ ～方案 housing reform program；～房 housing reform houses
【房管】real estate management
【房管所】urban real estate management organs
【房荒】housing shortage
【房基】foundations (of a building)
【房间】room：一套～ *a suite*；*an apartment*；*a flat*
【房客】tenant (of a room or house)；lodger
【房契】title deed (for a house)
【房事】〈婉〉sexual intercourse (usu. between a married couple)
【房市】housing market
【房贴】rental allowance
【房屋】house (or building)；housing
【房檐】eaves
【房主】house-owner
【房子】❶ house；building ❷ room，apartment，etc.：我弄到了一套两室一厅的～。*I've got a flat with two bedrooms and a living room.*
【房租】rent (for a house，flat，etc.)；rental

fǎng

访 动 ❶ visit；call on：～友 *call on a friend* ❷ seek by inquiry or search；try to get：采访 / 访求
【访查】go about making inquiries；investigate
【访求】search for：～民间丹方 *search for folk remedies*
【访谈】interview and discuss ◇ 焦点～ an interview discussion；～录 record of an interview discussion
【访问】visit；call on；interview：～亲友 *call on friends and relatives* / 正式(非正式)～ *an official (unofficial) visit* / 国事～ *a state visit* / 进行一次亲善～ *pay a goodwill visit* ◇ ～学者 visiting scholar

仿 Ⅰ 动 ❶ imitate；copy：仿造 ❷ resemble；be like：相仿 Ⅱ 名 characters written after a calligraphy model：写一张～ *write a page of characters after a calligraphy model*
【仿单】instructions for use (of a commodity，esp. a medicine)
【仿佛】❶ seemingly；as if：这事她～已经知道了。*She seems to know about it already.* / 他的身体，看外表～很好，其实有高血压病。*He appears to be healthy，but has high blood pressure.* ❷ be more or less the same；be alike：这两个人的年纪相～。*These two persons are about the same age.* / 他的模样还和十年前相～。*He looks about the same as he did ten years ago.*
【仿古】modelled after an antique；in the style of the ancients：～青铜器 *an imitation of an ancient bronze*
【仿生机器人】bio-robot
【仿生计算机】bionic computer
【仿生学】bionics
【仿效】imitate；follow the example of：他～那位名歌唱家的唱法，已经达到无懈可击的地步。*His imitation of that famous singer is perfect.*
【仿形】[机] profile modelling：～车床 *copying lathe*；*repetition lathe* / ～机械 *profiling mechanism*
【仿造】copy；be modelled on
【仿照】imitate；follow：这个办法很好，各地可以～办理。*This is a good method. It might well be adopted by other localities.*
【仿真】simulation；emulation；phantom
【仿制】copy；imitate；be modelled on ◇ ～品 an imitation；replica；copy

纺 Ⅰ 动 spin：把棉花～成纱 *spin cotton into yarn* Ⅱ 名 a thin silk cloth
【纺车】spinning wheel
【纺绸】a soft plain-weave silk fabric
【纺锤】spindle
【纺纱】spinning：～工人 *spinner* / ～机 *spinning machine*
【纺丝】[化] fibre spinning：～泵 *spinning pump* / ～罐 *spinning box* / ～机 *spinning machine* / ～浴 *spinning bath*
【纺织】spinning and weaving：～厂 *textile mill* / ～工人 *textile worker* / ～工业 *textile industry*
【纺织娘】[动] katydid；long-horned grasshopper
【纺织品】textile；fabric

舫 名 boat：画舫

fàng

放 动 ❶ let go；set free；release：～他走 *let him go* / 抓住绳子不～ *won't let go of the rope* / 把俘虏～了 *release the captives* / 把游泳池里的水～掉 *let the water out of the swimming pool* ❷ give way to；let oneself go：放胆 ❸ put out to feed：～牛 *put cattle out to pasture*；*graze cattle* / ～鸭子 *put ducks out to feed in a pond，stream，etc.* ❹ let off；give off or out：～枪 *fire a gun* / ～箭 *shoot an arrow* / ～爆竹 *set off firecrackers* / ～风筝 *fly a kite* ❺ show (a film，etc.)；play (a record，etc.)：～录音 *play back a recording* / ～录像 *play a video tape* / ～幻灯片 *show some lantern slides* / ～点儿音乐听听 *play some music records or tapes* / ～电视 *switch on the TV* ❻ light；kindle：放火 ❼ lend (money) at interest；loan：他的钱全～出去了，一时收不回来。*All his money has been loaned out. He can't get it back for the moment.* ❽ make larger or longer；let out；let down：～几张相片 *have a few photos enlarged* / 把这条裙子～长一点儿。

Let out the hem on this skirt a little. / 裤腰要～一厘米。*Please let these trousers out* 1 cm. *at the waist*. ❾ moderate (one's action, attitude or behaviour): ～老实点儿! *You behave yourself*! / ～明白些。*Be sensible*. / 请你脚步～轻些! *Tread softly, please*. ❿ (of flowers) blossom; open: 百花齐放 / 心花怒放 ⓫ put; place; lay: 把书～在桌上。*Put the book on the desk*. / 你来～碗筷。*Will you set the table for dinner*? ⓬ 〈口〉 cause sth. or sb. to fall to the ground: 上山～树 *go to the mountains to fell trees* / 他三下两下就把那个坏蛋～倒了。*With just a few blows, he knocked the hooligan down to the ground*. ⓭ lay aside; store away (for future use); keep long: 这事不急,～一～再说。*It's not an urgent matter. Let's lay it aside for the moment*. / 鲜牛奶不能～得太久。*Fresh milk won't keep long*.

【放长线,钓大鱼】throw a long line to catch a big fish—adopt a long-term plan to secure sth. big

【放大】enlarge; magnify; amplify: 把照片～ *make enlargements of a photograph*; *have a photo enlarged* ◇ ～尺 pantograph; ～机 [摄] enlarger; ～镜 magnifying glass; magnifier; ～率 magnifying power; ～器 [电子] amplifier; ～照片 enlarged photograph; enlargement; blowup; ～纸 [摄] enlarging paper; bromide paper

【放胆】act boldly and with confidence: 你尽管～去干! *Don't hesitate to forge ahead*!

【放诞】wild in speech and behaviour

【放荡】❶ dissolute; dissipated: 她决不是一个～的女人。*She's definitely not a woman of easy virtue*. ❷ unconventional

【放荡不羁】unconventional and unrestrained

【放电】[物] (electric) discharge: 火花～ *spark discharge* / 尖端～ *point discharge* / 闪电是自然界的～现象。*Lightning is a natural discharge of electricity*.

【放刁】make difficulties for sb.; act in a rascally manner

【放毒】❶ put poison in food, water, etc.; poison ❷ make vicious remarks; spread poisonous ideas

【放风】❶ let in fresh air ❷ let prisoners out for exercise (or relieve themselves) ❸ leak certain information; spread news or rumours

【放高利贷】lend money at an excessively high rate of interest; practise usury

【放工】get out of work; knock off: 我们是下午六点钟放的工。*We got out of work at six o'clock in the afternoon*. / 大多数工厂五点～。*Most factories knock off work at five*.

【放过】let sb. off; let sth. slip by: 我们决不冤枉一个好人,也决不～一个坏人。*We will never wrong a single good person nor let off a single bad one*. / 这是个好机会,不要～。*Don't let this good opportunity slip by*.

【放虎归山】同〖纵虎归山〗

【放火】❶ set fire to; set on fire; commit arson: 游击队～烧了敌人的仓库。*The guerrillas burned down the enemy's depot*. ❷ create disturbances ◇ ～犯 arsonist

【放假】have a holiday or vacation; have a day off: 你们什么时候放暑假? *When is your summer vacation*?

【放开】have a free hand in doing sth.: 让外贸企业～经营 *give foreign trade enterprises full authority over management* ◇ ～价格 relax price control

【放空炮】talk big; spout hot air; indulge in idle boasting: 不要～,拿出行动来。*Now, none of your empty talk. Let's see how you act*.

【放空气】drop a hint; spread word; create an impression: 放出紧张空气 *try to create the impression that the situation is tense*

【放宽】relax restrictions; relax: ～尺度 *relax the requirements* / ～期限 *extend a time limit* / ～条件 *soften the terms* ◇ ～限制 relaxation of restrictions; ～政策 introduce more flexible policies

【放款】make loans; loan: 短(中,长)期～ *short-term (medium-term, long-term) loan*

【放浪】〈书〉 ❶ unrestrained ❷ dissolute

【放浪形骸】refuse to be bound by convention; be defiant of convention

【放疗】〈略〉见〖放射疗法〗

【放牧】put out to pasture; graze; herd: ～牛羊 *herd (or graze) sheep and cattle* ◇ ～期 grazing season

【放排】❶ set a raft going (downstream): ～喽! *Here goes the raft*! ❷ rafting (a way of transporting logs)

【放盘】〈旧〉 (of a shop) sell at reduced prices or buy in at raised prices

【放炮】❶ fire a gun: 放三炮 *fire three gunshots* ❷ set off firecrackers ❸ blast: ～,危险! *Danger*! *Blasting in progress*! ❹ (of a tyre, etc.) blow out: 车胎～了! *The tyre's had a blowout*. ❺ shoot off one's mouth: 不了解情况不要乱～! *Don't shoot off your mouth if you don't know the facts*.

【放屁】❶ break wind; fart ❷ 〈讳〉 talk nonsense: ～! *Shit*! or *What crap*!

【放弃】abandon; give up; renounce: ～原来计划 *abandon the original plan* / ～表决权 *abstain from voting* / ～原则 *forsake one's principles*

【放情】to one's heart's content; as much as one likes

【放晴】clear up (after rain): 天一～咱们就开镰收麦子。*We'll begin harvesting the wheat as soon as it clears up*.

【放权】delegate power to the lower levels; forsake one's power; transfer power to a lower level

【放热】[化] exothermic ◇ ～反应 [化] exothermic reaction

【放任】❶ not interfere; let alone ❷ noninterference; laissez-faire: 采取～态度 *take a laissez-faire attitude*

【放任自流】let things drift (or slide)

【放散】(of smoke, scent, etc.) diffuse; disperse; dissipate

【放哨】be on sentry or on patrol：站岗～ *stand sentry*；*stand sentinel*；*go on sentry duty* / 巡逻～ *go on patrol*；*patrol*

【放射】radiate：初升的太阳～出万道金光。*The rising sun radiated myriads of golden rays*. ◇～病 radiation sickness；～疗法 radiotherapy；～线 radioactive rays；～现象［物］radioactivity

【放射性】［物］radioactivity；activity ◇～衰变 radioactive decay；～碳素断代法［考古］radiocarbon dating；～同位素 radio isotope；～微尘 radioactive dust；fallout；～污染 radioactive pollution；～物质 radioactive materials；～元素 radioactive element；radioelement；～沾染 radioactive contamination；～战剂 radioactive agent

【放生】free captive animals；(of Buddhists) buy captive fish or birds and set them free

【放手】❶ let go；let go one's hold：他一～，笔记本就掉了。*He let go his hold and the notebook dropped to the ground*. / 你抓紧，我要～了。*Hold tight*. *I'm going to let go*. ❷ have a free hand；go all out：让他们～工作 *give them a free hand in their work* ❸ release one's control；hand over to sb. else：我要他交给小张去办，可他就是不～。*I told him to let Xiao Zhang take over the job*, *but he refused to hand it over*.

【放水】❶ turn on the water：给浴缸里放上水。*Turn on the water in the bathtub*. ❷ draw off some water (from a reservoir, etc.)

【放肆】unbridled；wanton：～的行为 *unbridled behaviour* / ～诬蔑 *wantonly vilify* / 极为～ *throw all restraint to the winds* / 胆敢如此～！*How dare you take such liberties*!

【放松】relax；slacken；loosen：～鞋带 *loosen up the shoelaces* / ～肌肉 *relax one's muscles* / ～警惕 *relax one's vigilance*

【放送】broadcast；send out (over a loudspeaker, etc.)：～大会实况录音 *broadcast the live recording of the conference*

【放下】lay down；put down：～手头的工作 *put aside the work on hand* / ～包袱 *cast off mental burdens*；*get rid of the baggage*；*lay down one's burden*

【放下屠刀，立地成佛】drop one's cleaver and become a Buddha—achieve salvation as soon as one gives up evil

【放线菌】［微］actinomyces

【放心】❶ set one's mind at rest；be at ease；rest assured；feel relieved：你～，一切都会安排好的。*You can rest assured that everything will be all right*. ❷ have confidence in sb.；trust sb.：我对他不大～。*I don't quite trust him*. / 你怎么老不～别人？*Why do you have no confidence in others*?

【放行】let sb. or sth. pass：申请～ *request clearance* / 免税～ *tax-free clearance*

【放学】❶ classes are over；school lets out：他们学校下午五点～。*Their school lets out* (*or closes*) *at five p.m.*. / 孩子们都～回家了。*The children have all left school and gone home for the day*. ❷ have a holiday or vacation

【放血】phlebotomy；bloodletting：大夫给他放了血，他感觉好多了。*He felt much better after the doctor did a phlebotomy on him*.

【放眼】take a broad view；scan widely：他～远望，只见万里长江，奔腾东去。*He looked ahead and saw the mighty Changjiang rolling and surging towards the east*.

【放眼世界】have the whole world in view；open one's eyes to the whole world：胸怀祖国，～ *have the whole country in mind and the whole world in view*

【放羊】❶ graze sheep；pasture sheep；look after sheep：～娃 *shepherd boy* ❷〈贬〉be reinless；throw (the) reins off；drift along

【放养】put (fish, insects, etc.) in a suitable place to breed：水库里～了许多种鱼。*Various kinds of fish are being bred in the reservoir*.

【放鹰】❶ go hawking；hunt with falcons ❷〈喻〉lose everything；lose completely：他的钱全都放了鹰了。*He lost all his money*. or *He went clean broke*.

【放映】show (a film)；project：剧院有时也用来～电影。*Occasionally theatres are used for film shows*. ◇～队 film projection team；～机 (film) projector；～室 projection room；～员 projectionist

【放债】(又作'放账') lend money at interest

【放之四海而皆准】universally applicable；valid everywhere：～的普遍真理 *universally applicable truth*

【放置】lay up；lay aside：～不用 *lay up* (*machinery*, *equipment*, *etc.*)；*lie idle*

【放逐】send into exile；exile；banish

【放纵】❶ let sb. have his own way；indulge：你太～孩子了。*You are too indulgent with your child*. ❷ self-indulgent；undisciplined

fēi

飞 Ⅰ 动 ❶ (of birds or insects) fly；flit：小鸟～了。*The bird flew away*. / 老鹰～得高。*Eagles fly high*. / 蜜蜂在花丛中～来～去。*Bees are flitting from flower to flower*. ❷ (of an aircraft or its occupants) fly：我明天～广州。*I'm flying to Guangzhou tomorrow*. / 那架飞机从北京直～广州。*That plane flies nonstop from Beijing to Guangzhou*. ❸ hover or flutter in the air：～鸢 *a hovering kite* / ～絮 *willow catkins fluttering in the air* / ～雪花了。*It's snowing*. ❹〈口〉disappear through volatilization：樟脑丸放久了会～净的。*Camphor balls will disappear as time goes on*. Ⅱ 副 (move) swiftly Ⅲ 形 unexpected；accidental；unfounded；groundless：～祸 *unexpected disaster*

【飞镖】❶ a dartlike weapon ❷ darts (a game)

【飞车走壁】acrobatics stunt cycling, driving or

motorcycling on the inner surface of a cylindrical wall
【飞驰】(of trains, cars, horses, etc.) speed along：火车～而过。*A train sped by*.
【飞虫】winged insect
【飞船】❶ airship；dirigible ❷ spaceship；spacecraft
【飞弹】❶ missile ❷ stray bullet
【飞地】❶ land of one province or county enclosed by that of another ❷ enclave；exclave
【飞碟】❶［体］skeet shooting；skeet；trapshooting ❷ flying saucer；UFO ◇ ～学 ufology
【飞短流长】spread embroidered stories and malicious gossip
【飞蛾投火】(又作'飞蛾扑火') a moth darting into a flame—bring destruction upon oneself；seek one's own doom
【飞鸽牌】❶ Flying Pigeon (a bicycle brand) ❷〈喻〉〈口〉person ready to shift from one job to another
【飞花】❶ showing cotton wad (of worn-out or torn cotton-padded clothes, shoes, etc.) ❷［纺］flyings；fly
【飞黄腾达】make rapid advances in one's career；have a meteoric rise
【飞蝗】migratory locusts
【飞机】aircraft；aeroplane；plane：我坐～去上海。*I'll go to Shanghai by plane*. ◇ ～场 airfield；airport；aerodrome；～乘客保险 aircraft passanger insurance；～库 hangar；～上交货物 free on plane；free on aircraft；～修理 aircraft repair；～制造业 aircraft industry；aviation industry
【飞溅】splash：浪花～到甲板上。*The waves splashed on the deck*. / 钢花～ *sparks flying off molten steel*
【飞快】❶ very fast；at lightning speed：以～的速度前进 *forge ahead at full speed* / 他～地向出事地点奔去。*He tore along to the site of the accident*. ❷ extremely sharp；razorsharp：把镰刀磨得～。*Sharpen the sickles till they are like razors*.
【飞轮】❶［机］flywheel ❷ free wheel (of a bicycle)
【飞毛腿】❶ fleet-footed；swift of foot ❷ a fleet-footed runner ◇ ～导弹 Scud Missile
【飞沫传染】［医］infection through breathing in flying particles of the saliva or phlegm of a sick person
【飞盘】Frisbee disk；frisbee：孩子们玩～，大人聊天。*Kids flip frisbees while their elders chat*.
【飞泉】cliffside spring
【飞人】❶ trapeze：空中～ *flying trapeze* ❷ fastest runner；best sprinter；best athlete：亚洲女～ *best woman sprinter in Asia*
【飞散】❶ (of smoke, mist, etc.) disperse；dissipate ❷ (of birds) fly away in different directions；scatter；disperse：麻雀听到枪声而～。*The sparrows scattered at the sound of the gun*.
【飞沙走石】sand flying about and stones hurtling through the air (as in a windstorm)
【飞鼠】flying squirrel
【飞速】at full speed：列车在～前进。*The train is running at express speed*.
【飞腾】fly swiftly upward；soar：烟雾～。*A smoke-laden fog rose quickly and soon filled the air*.
【飞天】［工美］flying Apsaras (as in the frescoes of the Dunhuang Caves)
【飞艇】airship；dirigible
【飞腿】fly kick
【飞吻】blow a kiss
【飞舞】dance in the air；flutter：雪花～。*Snowflakes are dancing in the air*. / 蝴蝶在花丛中～。*Butterflies fluttered about among the flowers*.
【飞翔】circle in the air；hover：展翅～ *spread wings and fly* / 雄鹰在山谷中～着。*An eagle was hovering over the valley*.
【飞行】(of an aircraft, missile, etc. or of a pilot) fly；make a flight：～速度 *flying speed* / ～表演 *demonstration (or exhibition) flight* ◇ ～半径 flying radius；～服 flying suit；～管制 air traffic control；～记录簿 flight log；～帽 aviator's helmet；～器 aircraft；～人员 aircrew；aircrewman；～员 pilot；aviator；flyer
【飞檐】［建］upturned eaves
【飞檐走壁】(of swordsmen, etc. in old Chinese novels) leap onto roofs and vault over walls
【飞眼】make eyes；ogle：她直向他～。*She kept making eyes at him*.
【飞扬】fly upward；rise：尘土～ *clouds of dust flying up* / 到处～着欢乐的歌声。*Songs of joy were floating in the air*.
【飞扬跋扈】arrogant and domineering
【飞鱼】flying fish ◇ ～导弹 Exocet
【飞跃】❶ leap：我国的石油工业正～地发展。*China's oil industry is developing by leaps and bounds*. ❷［哲］leap：认识过程的一次～ *a leap in the process of cognition*
【飞灾】unexpected disaster
【飞贼】❶ a burglar who makes his way into a house over walls and roofs ❷ an intruding enemy airman；air marauder (or pirate)
【飞涨】(of prices, water level, etc.) soar；shoot up；skyrocket：物价～。*Prices were skyrocketing*.
【飞针走线】ply one's needle nimbly；do skilful needlework：她那～的手艺，见到的人无不惊叹。*The skill with which she plied her needle astounded all who saw her*.

妃 名 ❶ imperial concubine ❷ the wife of a prince
【妃红】light pink
【妃色】light pink
【妃子】imperial concubine

非 Ⅰ 名 ❶ wrong；wrongdoing：是非 ❷〈略〉见〖非洲〗Ⅱ 动 ❶ not conform to；run counter to：

非法 ❷ censure; blame: 无可厚非 ❸〈书〉be not: 当时的情景～言语所能形容。*The occasion defies description*. / 这件事～你我所能解决。*This cannot be decided by either you or me*. Ⅲ 助 (前缀)(表示否定或不属于某种范围) non-: ～党员 *non-Party member* / ～无产阶级思想 *non-proletarian ideology* (*or ideas*) Ⅳ 副〈口〉have got to; simply must: 不行,我今天～去! *No, I simply must go there today*. / 他不来就算了,为什么～叫他来? *If he doesn't want to come, that's fine. Why should we insist on him coming?* / 干这种活儿～要有耐心才成。*You've got to have patience in doing this kind of work*.

【非保兑信用证】unconfirmed letter of credit

【非比寻常】unusual; out of the ordinary

【非病原菌】nonpathogenic bacteria

【非常】❶ extraordinary; unusual; special: ～会议 *extraordinary session* / ～支出 *a special expenditure* / ～措施 *emergency measures* ❷ very; extremely; highly: ～必要 *highly necessary* / ～重要 *extremely important* / ～精彩 *simply marvellous*

【非常任】nonpermanent: ～代表 *nonpermanent representative* / 安理会～理事国 *nonpermanent member of the UN Security Council*

【非常时期】time of emergency

【非此即彼】either this or that; one or the other

【非但】not only: 他～自己干得好,还肯帮助别人。*He not only does his own work well, but is also ready to help others*.

【非得】(followed by 不 or 才) have got to; must: 做校对工作～仔细才行。*You've got to be very careful when you do proofreading*. / 这病～马上开刀不可。*This disease calls for an immediate operation*.

【非独】〈书〉not merely: ～无益,而且有害 *not merely useless, but harmful*

【非对抗性】nonantagonistic: ～矛盾 *nonantagonistic contradiction*

【非法】illegal; unlawful; illicit: ～活动 *unlawful* (*or illegal*) *activities* / ～收入 *illicit income* / ～入境 *illegal entry* (*into a country*) / 被宣布为～ *be outlawed; be declared illegal; be illegalized* ◇ ～倒卖 profiteering; illegal buying and selling; ～交易 illegal deal; ～经商 unlawful trade; ～刊物 illegal publication; ～同居 illicit cohabitation

【非凡】outstanding; extraordinary; uncommon: ～的成就 *outstanding achievements; extraordinary successes*

【非分】overstepping one's bounds; assuming; presumptuous: ～的要求 *presumptuous demands*

【非分之想】inordinate ambitions

【非公莫入】no admittance except on business

【非挂牌股票】unlisted stock

【非挂牌证券】unlisted securities; over-the-counter

【非官方】unofficial: ～消息 *news from unofficial sources* / ～机构 *unofficial or nongovernmental institution*

【非会员银行】nonmember bank

【非婚生子女】children born out of wedlock; illegitimate children

【非婚性行为】extra-marital sexual activity

【非交战国】nonbelligerent

【非借入储备】non-borrowed reserves

【非金属】nonmetal: ～材料 *nonmetallic materials* / ～元素 *nonmetallic elements*

【非晶质】[化] noncrystalline; amorphous

【非军事化】demilitarize: ～计划 *demilitarization programme*

【非军事区】demilitarized zone

【非军事人员】civilian personnel

【非驴非马】neither ass nor horse—neither fish, flesh, nor fowl

【非卖品】(articles) not for sale

【非贸易外汇收入】foreign exchange earned from sources other than trade

【非难】(usu. used in the negative) blame; censure; reproach: 他的品德是无可～的。*His character is irreproachable*.

【非亲非故】neither relative nor friend; neither kith nor kin: 我跟他～,跟你也无冤无仇,我不偏向哪个,只说几句良心话。*He's not my relative, and you are not my enemy. I don't favour either one of you. I only want to say a few honest words*.

【非人】❶〈书〉not the right person: 所用～ *choose the wrong person for a job* ❷ inhuman: ～待遇 *inhuman treatment*

【非生产部门】nonproductive departments

【非生产劳动】nonproductive labour

【非生产性】unproductive; nonproductive: ～开支 *nonproductive* (*or unproductive*) *expenditure*

【非条件反射】[生理] unconditioned reflex

【非同小可】no small (or trivial) matter: 这件事～,我们一定要抗议! *This is no trivial matter; we must raise our voices against it*.

【非线性分析】nonlinear analysis

【非刑】brutal torture (not permitted by the law) ◇ ～拷打 put sb. to the torture

【非议】(usu. used in the negative) reproach; censure

【非银行背书】non-bank endorsement

【非约束性条款】permissive provision

【非战斗人员】[军] noncombatant

【非正规军】irregular troops; irregulars

【非正式】unofficial; informal: ～译文 *unofficial translation* / ～访问 *unofficial* (*or informal*) *visit* / ～会议 *informal meeting*

【非正统】unorthodox

【非正义战争】an unjust war

【非职务发明】non-service invention

【非洲】Africa

【非洲统一组织】the Organization of African Unity (OAU)

【非主要矛盾】nonprincipal contradiction

菲 Ⅰ 形 (of flowers and grass) luxuriant and rich with fragrance: 芳菲 Ⅱ 名 [化] phenanthrene ——另见 fěi

【菲菲】〈文〉❶ luxuriant and beautiful ❷ richly fragrant

【菲律宾】the Philippines ◇ ～人 Filipino

绯 形 red

【绯红】bright red; crimson; scarlet: ～的晚霞 *rosy evening clouds* / 脸羞得～ *blush with shame*

扉 名〈书〉door leaf: 柴～ *faggot door*

【扉页】[刷] title page

蜚 〈书〉同〖飞〗——另见 fěi

【蜚短流长】同〖飞短流长〗

【蜚声】〈书〉make a name; become famous: ～文坛 *be famous in literary circles* / 我国的工艺美术品～海外。*China's arts and crafts enjoy a high reputation abroad.*

霏 形〈字〉❶ (of rain or snow) fall thick and fast: 雨(yù)雪其～。*It's snowing thick and fast.* ❷ thin, floating clouds; mist: 夕～ *evening mist*

【霏霏】〈字〉(of rain, snow, mist, cloud, etc.) thick and fast; heavy: 淫雨～。*It has been raining heavily for days.* / 云～。*Clouds are gathering thick and fast.*

鲱 名 Pacific herring

féi

肥 Ⅰ 形 ❶ fat: ～猪 *a big porker* / 这肉太～了。*The meat is too fat.* ❷ fertile; rich: 这里的地～极了。*The soil here is extremely fertile.* ❸ loose-fitting; loose; large: 这条裤子太～了。*These trousers are too baggy.* Ⅱ 动 ❶ fertilize: 肥田粉 ❷ become rich by illegal means or income Ⅲ 名 fertilizer; manure: 上点儿～ *spread some manure on the soil* / 这些花缺～。*The flowers are in need of fertilizer.*

【肥大】❶ loose; large: ～的衣服 *a loose garment* ❷ fat; plump; corpulent: ～的鲤鱼 *a fat carp* / 果实～ *lush and plump fruit* ❸ [医] hypertrophy: 心脏(扁桃体)～ *hypertrophy of the heart (tonsils)*

【肥分】[农] (the percentage of) nutriment in a fertilizer

【肥厚】❶ plump; fleshy: 果肉～。*The pulp is full and fleshy.* / 嘴唇～ *have thick lips* ❷ thick and fertile: 土层～ *thick and fertile topsoil*

【肥力】[农] fertility (of soil)

【肥料】fertilizer; manure: 有机～ *organic fertilizer* / 细菌～ *bacterial fertilizer*

【肥美】❶ fertile; rich: ～的土地 *rich soil; fertile land* ❷ luxuriant; plump; fleshy; fat: 水草～牛羊壮 *rich pastures and thriving herds* / ～的北京鸭 *plump, tender-fleshed Beijing ducks*

【肥胖】fat; corpulent ◇ ～病 obesity

【肥缺】a lucrative post

【肥实】❶ fat; stout: 这匹马很～。*This is a stout horse.* ❷ rich in fat: 这块肉很～。*The meat is fatty.*

【肥水不流外人田】〈方〉No rich water should be let out of one's own fields. *or* One should always keep all benefits for one's own people.

【肥硕】❶ (of fruit) big and fleshy ❷ (of limbs and body) large and firm-fleshed

【肥田】❶ fertile land: 五亩～ *five mu of fertile land* ❷ fertilize (or enrich) the soil: 草木灰可以用来～。*Plant ash can be used to fertilize the soil.* ◇ ～粉〈口〉ammonium sulphate

【肥沃】fertile; rich: 这里土地～。*The land here is rich and fertile.*

【肥效】[农] fertilizer efficiency (or effect)

【肥育】[牧] fatten ◇ ～期 [牧] stage of fattening

【肥源】[农] source of manure

【肥皂】soap: ～泡 *soap bubble* ◇ ～粉 soap powder; ～剧 soap opera; ～片 soap flakes; ～水 soapsuds

【肥壮】stout and strong: 牛羊～ *thriving herds of sheep and cattle*

腓 名 calf (of the leg)

fěi

诽 动 slander

【诽谤】slander; calumniate; libel: 我要以～罪控告你。*I'll sue you for libel.* ◇ ～罪 crime of defamation

匪 Ⅰ 名 bandit; brigand; robber: 土匪 Ⅱ 副〈书〉not: 获益～浅 *reap no little benefit*

【匪帮】bandit gang; a felonious political gang: 法西斯～ *the Fascist gangsters*

【匪巢】bandits' lair

【匪患】the evil of banditry; banditry

【匪军】bandit troops

【匪窟】bandits' lair

【匪首】bandit chieftain (or chief)

【匪徒】gangster; bandit

【匪夷所思】〈书〉(of ideas) unimaginably queer; fantastic

悱 形〈书〉be at a loss for words

【悱恻】〈书〉laden with sorrow; sad at heart

菲 Ⅰ 名〈古〉radish or its like Ⅱ 形〈谦〉poor; humble; unworthy: ～材 *my humble talent* ——另见 fēi

【菲薄】❶ humble; poor: ～的礼物 *a small gift* ❷ belittle; despise

【菲仪】(又作'菲敬')〈谦〉my small (or unworthy) gift

斐 形〈书〉(of literary talent) striking; brilliant

【斐济】Fiji ◇ ～人 Fijian; ～语 Fijian (language)

【斐然】〈书〉striking; brilliant; splendid: 文采～ *with striking* (*or brilliant*) *literary talent* / 成绩～ (*achieve*) *splendid results*

【斐然成章】show striking literary merit

蜚 名〈古〉an insect ——另见 fēi

【蜚蠊】another name for 蟑螂

翡 名〈古〉a kind of bird with red feathers

【翡翠】❶ halcyon (a bird) ❷ jadeite (a mineral)

榧 名 Chinese torreya (tree)

【榧子】[植] ❶ Chinese torreya (tree) ❷ Chinese torreya nut

fèi

吠 动 (of a dog) bark; yap; yelp: 狂～ *bark furiously*

【吠影吠声】(又作'吠形吠声') when one dog barks at a shadow all the others join in—blindly follow others

沸 动 boil: ～油 *boiling oil* / ～水 *boiling water*

【沸点】boiling point

【沸沸扬扬】bubbling and gurgling; in a hubbub: 大家～地嚷起来。*A general hubbub arose.* / 消息～地传开了。*The news spread like wildfire.*

【沸泉】[地质] near-boiling spring (a spring with waters hotter than 80℃)

【沸石】another name for 泡沸石

【沸腾】❶ [物] boiling; ebullition ❷ seethe with excitement; boil over: 大会主席宣布选举结果后,全场顿时～起来。*When the chairman announced the election results, the whole assembly clapped and cheered.*

废 Ⅰ 动 give up; abandon; abolish; abrogate: 不以人～言 *not reject an opinion because of the speaker* / 把条约～了 *abrogate* (*or nullify*) *the treaty* Ⅱ 形 ❶ waste; useless; disused: ～热 *waste heat* / ～棉 *cotton waste* / ～井 *a disused well* / ～矿 *an abandoned mine* ❷ disabled; maimed: ～疾 *disability*

【废弛】(of a law, custom, discipline, etc.) cease to be binding; become lax

【废除】abolish; abrogate; annul; repeal: ～一切不平等条约 *abrogate all unequal treaties* / ～烦琐的礼节 *do away with tedious formalities* / ～领导干部终身制 *abolish the system of life-long tenure in leading*

【废黜】dethrone; depose: ～王位 *dethrone* / ～国王 *dethrone the king* / 太子被～了。*The crown prince was deposed* (*by the emperor*).

【废话】superfluous words; nonsense; rubbish: 我说的也可能是～,不过还是请你再考虑考虑。*What I said may seem superfluous, but I do hope you'll give it a little more thought.*

【废话连篇】pages of nonsense; reams of rubbish: 这篇文章简直是～。*This article is just so much nonsense.*

【废料】waste material; waste; scrap: ～堆 *scrap heap; waste heap* ◇ ～处理 waste treatment; ～艺术 junk art

【废票】❶ invalidated ticket ❷ invalidated ballot

【废品】❶ waste product; reject: ～率 *reject rate* ❷ scrap; waste: 你可以把这东西当～卖。*You could sell it for scrap.* ◇ ～雕塑家 junk sculpture; ～回收 waste recovery; salvage of waste material; ～收购站 salvage station

【废气】waste gas or steam ◇ ～净化设备 gas-cleaning facilities

【废弃】discard; abandon; cast aside: ～陈规旧习 *discard outdated regulations and customs* / ～多年的旧机器零件 *old machine parts discarded for years*

【废寝忘食】forget to eat and sleep: ～地工作 *forget to eat and sleep while working*

【废人】❶ disabled person ❷ good-for-nothing

【废水】waste water; liquid waste: ～渗透 *waste water infiltration* ◇ ～处理场 waste water processing station; ～处理池 purification tank for liquid waste

【废丝】[纺] waste silk

【废铁】scrap iron

【废物】(fèi wù) waste material; trash: ～利用 *make use of waste material; convert waste into useful material* ◇ ～袋 litter bag; ～回收 waste recovery

【废物】(fèi wu)〈讳〉good-for-nothing: 他什么事也不会干,简直是个～! *He's really a good-for-nothing!*

【废渣】waste residue

【废止】nullify; annul; abolish (a law, decree, regulation, etc.): 科举制是在1905年～的。*The imperialist examinations system was abolished in* 1905. / 这个法令早就～了。*This decree has long been annulled.*

【废纸】waste paper: 不要乱扔～。*Don't litter the place with waste paper.* / 他们的那个条约不过是一张～而已。*That treaty of theirs is a mere scrap of paper.*

【废置】put aside as useless: 这样珍贵的资料竟被～在一边,真是太可惜了。*It's a great pity such precious documents should be cast aside as useless.*

狒 名 baboon

【狒狒】baboon (a mammal)

肺 名 lung

【肺癌】carcinoma of the lungs; lung cancer

【肺病】〈口〉pulmonary tuberculosis (TB)

【肺腑】the bottom of one's heart: 出自～ *straight from the heart; from the depths of one's heart*

【肺腑之言】words from the bottom of one's heart

【肺活量】vital capacity
【肺结核】pulmonary tuberculosis (TB)
【肺静脉】[生理] pulmonary vein
【肺痨】〈口〉consumption; tuberculosis
【肺脓肿】pulmonary abscess
【肺泡】[生理] pulmonary alveolus
【肺气肿】pulmonary emphysema
【肺切除术】pneumonectomy
【肺吸虫】(又作'肺蛭') lung fluke
【肺循环】[生理] pulmonary circulation
【肺炎】pneumonia
【肺叶】[生理] a lobe of the lung
【肺脏】lungs

费 Ⅰ 名 fee; dues; expenses; charge: 生活～ *living expenses* / 订报～ *subscription for a newspaper* / 医药～ *medical expenses* Ⅱ 动 ❶ cost; spend; expend: 买这部电影机～了我们不少钱。*This projector cost us a lot of money.* / 买东西～时间。*Shopping takes time.* ❷ consume too much; expend sth. too quickly; be wasteful: 这部汽车～油。*This car consumes too much gasoline.* / 这孩子穿鞋太～。*This child wears out his shoes much too quickly.*

【费工】take a lot of work; require much labour: 这种活儿～。*This is a difficult job.* / 做这样的衣裳不太～。*This kind of dress isn't too hard to make.*

【费工夫】(又作'费功夫') take time and energy; be time-consuming; be exacting; be demanding: 他费了好多工夫才把电视机修好。*It took him a lot of time to get the TV set repaired.*

【费话】take a lot of talking or explaining: 一说她就明白,用不着人～。*Just mention it and she'll catch on. It won't take much talking.*

【费解】hard to understand; obscure; unintelligible: 这段文章实在～。*This passage is really hard to understand.*

【费尽心机】rack one's brains (in scheming); tax one's ingenuity

【费劲】〈口〉need or exert great effort; be strenuous: 安装这台机器真～。*It really took a lot of effort to install this machine.* / 他看英文参考书一点不～。*He can read reference books in English without difficulty.*

【费力】need (or exert) great effort; be strenuous: 我们费了大力才把这件事办好。*It took us a lot of effort to get this done.*

【费力不讨好】❶ work hard but get little result; do a hard but thankless job ❷ arduous but fruitless: ～的差使 *a tough but thankless job*; *an exacting but unrewarding task*

【费钱】cost a lot; be costly: 做广告挺～。*Advertising costs a good deal of money.*

【费神】❶ need (or exert) great mental effort: 孩子进了幼儿园以后,你就不用那么操心～了。*It will be a load off your mind when your child enters kindergarten.* ❷〈套〉(used in making a request or giving thanks) may I trouble you (to do sth.); would you mind (doing sth.): 我这篇稿子您～给看看好吗? *Would you mind going over this article for me?* / 让您～了,多谢,多谢! *Thanks a lot for the trouble you've taken to help us!*

【费时】take time; be time-consuming: 手工操作既～又费力。*It takes both time and effort to do it by hand.*

【费事】give or take a lot of trouble: 别给我们烧水了,太～了。—一点儿也不～。*Don't bother to boil any water for us. —Oh, it's no trouble at all.*

【费心】❶ give a lot of care; take a lot of trouble: 她为这些孩子可费了不少心。*She devoted a lot of care to these children.* ❷〈套〉(used in making a request or giving thanks) may I trouble you (to do sth.); would you mind (doing sth.): 您见到他时,～把这封信交给他。*Will you be so kind as to give him this letter when you see him?*

【费用】cost; expenses: 生产～ *production cost* / 这笔～由我们负担。*We'll bear the expenses.*

痱 名 prickly heat

【痱子】[医] prickly heat ◇ ～粉 prickly-heat powder

镄 名 [化] fermium (Fm)

fēn

分 Ⅰ 动 ❶ divide; separate; part: 一年～四季。*The year is divided into four seasons.* / 一条河把那个县城～成两部分。*A river divides the county town into two parts.* / ～阶段实行 *carry out stage by stage* ❷ distribute; assign; allot: 音乐会的票都已经～完了。*The tickets for the concert have all been distributed.* / 把这个任务～给我们吧。*Assign (or Give) this task to us, please.* ❸ distinguish; differentiate: 是非不～ *make no distinction between right and wrong* Ⅱ 名 ❶ branch (of an organization): 新华社上海～社 *the Shanghai Branch of the Xinhua News Agency* ❷ fraction: 分母 Ⅲ 量 ❶ (used in spoken forms of fractions and percentages): 三～之一 *one-third* / 十～之七 *seven-tenths* / 百～之四 *four per cent* ❷ one tenth (of certain units of the metric system): 分克 / 分米 / 分升 ❸ fen, equal to one hundredth of a yuan 元: 六元三角五～ 6.35 *yuan* ❹ minute, equal to one sixtieth of an hour ❺ minute, equal to one sixtieth of a degree of angle or arc: 成36度30～角 *form an angle of 36 degrees 30 minutes* (36°30′) / 东经129度15～ *129 degrees 15 minutes* (129°15′) east longitude ❻ point; mark: 60～为及格。*Sixty is the passing mark.* ❼ (for nonphysical things) one-tenth: 七～成绩,三～错误 *70 per cent achievements, 30 per cent mistakes*——另见 fèn

【分包商】sub-contractor

【分保】reinsurance ◇ ～接受人 reinsurer
【分贝】[物] decibel (db) ◇ ～计 decibelmeter; level-measuring set
【分崩离析】disintegrate; fall to pieces; come apart
【分辨】❶ distinguish; differentiate; tell: ～真假 *distinguish truth from falsehood* / 很难～谁是谁非。*It's hard to tell who is right and who is wrong*. ❷ [物] resolution: ～率 *resolving power* ❸ defend oneself (against a charge); offer an explanation: 不容～ *allowing no explanation to be offered*
【分别】❶ part; leave each other: 我们～快两年了。*It's almost two years since we parted*. / 他们～不久又见面了。*They met again after a short separation*. ❷ distinguish; differentiate: ～善恶 *distinguish good from evil* ❸ difference: 两者之间没有任何～。*There is no difference between the two*. ❹ in different ways; differently: 对他们两人应该～对待。*You should treat the two of them differently*. ❺ separately; individually; respectively: 你还是～跟他们谈谈的好。*You'd better have a talk with each of them separately*.
【分兵】divide forces: ～把守 *divide the forces for defence* / ～两路前进。*The troops separated and advanced by two different routes*.
【分布】be distributed (over an area); be dispersed; be scattered: 彝族主要～在云南、四川、贵州三省。*The Yis are distributed mainly over Yunnan, Sichuan and Guizhou Provinces*.
【分册】a separately published part of a book; fascicle: 第二～ *Book Two*
【分层开采法】bench method; slicing
【分杈】[农] ❶ branching ❷ branch
【分成】divide into tenths; share: 四六～ *divide into two shares of four and six tenths (with one party getting 40% and the other 60%)*
【分词】[语] participle: 现在(过去)～ *present (past) participle* / ～短语 *participial phrase*
【分寸】proper limits for speech or action; sense of propriety; sense of proportion: 他说话很有～。*He knows what to say and what not to say*. / 她说话做事都没有～。*She has no sense of propriety in what she does or says*. / 批评要注意掌握～。*Don't go too far in criticism*.
【分担】share responsibility for: ～费用 *shoulder part of the expenses; share the expenses*
【分道】[体] lane: 第一～ *the first lane*
【分道扬镳】go different ways; part company
【分等】grade; classify: 产品按质～ *grade products according to quality* / 商品～论价 *grade commodities and fix prices accordingly; fix prices according to the different grades of commodities*
【分店】branch (of a shop) ◇ ～经理 branch manager
【分队】a troop unit corresponding to the platoon or squad; element
【分而治之】divide and rule
【分发】❶ distribute; hand out; issue (to individuals): 把课本～给同学们 *hand out textbooks to the students* / 给优胜者～奖品 *distribute prizes to the winners* / ～证件 *issue certificates individually* ❷ assign to a post; appoint to a job
【分肥】share out ill-gotten gains; divide booty
【分赴】leave for different destinations: ～不同的工作岗位 *go to take up different posts*
【分割】cut apart; break up; carve up: 民主和集中这两方面,任何时候都不能～开。*Democracy and centralism can at no time be separated*.
【分隔】separate; divide: 把一间房～成两小间 *partition a room into two small ones*
【分工】division of labour: ～负责 *division of labour with individual responsibility* / 咱们怎么～? *How shall we divide up the work?* / 社会～ *social division of labour*
【分工合作】share out the work and help one another
【分公司】branch office (or company)
【分管】be assigned personal responsibility for; be put in charge of
【分光吃光】total distribution and total consumption
【分光计】[物] spectrometer
【分光镜】[物] spectroscope
【分行】branch (of a bank, business firm, etc.): 国内～ *home (or domestic) branch* / 国外～ *overseas branch*
【分毫】fraction; iota: 不差～ *without the slightest error; just right*
【分号】❶ semicolon (;) ❷ branch (of a shop, firm, etc.): 本店只此一家,别无～。*Our shop is the only one bearing the name; there are no branches*.
【分红】draw (or receive) dividends; share profits: 股份～ *dividends on shares; dividends to the shareholders*
【分洪】flood diversion: ～工程 *flood-diversion project* ◇ ～区 flood-diversion area; ～闸 flood-diversion sluice
【分户账】ledger
【分化】❶ become divided; break up: 随着私有制的产生,人类便～为阶级。*With the emergence of private ownership, humanity was divided into classes*. ❷ split up: 把一部分人从敌人营垒中间～出来 *split off a number of people from the enemy camp* ❸ [生] (of cells or tissues) differentiate
【分化瓦解】disintegrate; divide and demoralize
【分会】branch (of a society, committee, association, etc.); chapter
【分机】(telephone) extension
【分级】grade; classify: 这几筐苹果还没～。*These baskets of apples have not been graded yet*. ◇ ～管理 manage by different levels; ～核算 business accounting at different levels
【分级机】[农] grader; sorter: 水果～ *fruit grader* / 马铃薯～ *potato sorter*
【分家】❶ divide up family property and live

apart; break up the family and live apart ❷ separate; break up: 咱俩分工不～。*Let's divide the work but still work together.*

【分解】❶［物］［数］resolve: 力的～ *the resolution of forces* / ～成因式 *resolve into factors* ❷［化］decompose; resolve: 水可以～为氢和氧。*Water can be decomposed (or resolved) into hydrogen and oxygen.* ❸ explain (used in traditional novels) ◇ ～代谢［生］catabolism; ～反应［化］decomposition reaction; ～剂 disintegrant; ～热［化］decomposition heat

【分界】❶ have as the boundary; be demarcated by: 这两个县以运河～。*The two counties have the canal as their common boundary.* ❷ dividing line; line of demarcation: 这两块地之间有一排大树作为～。*There is a row of trees on the line of demarcation between the two pieces of land.*

【分界线】line of demarcation; boundary: 军事～ *a military demarcation line*

【分进合击】［军］concerted attack by converging columns

【分镜头】story board ◇ ～剧本 continuity; shooting script

【分居】❶ (of family members) live apart: 她的兄弟都成了家，～各地。*All her brothers are married and live in different parts of the country.* ❷ (of husband and wife) live separately; separate: 他们夫妻结婚十年就～了。*They separated after ten years of marriage.*

【分句】［语］clause

【分开】❶ come apart; separate; part: 弟兄俩～已经三年了。*It is three years since the two brothers parted.* / 他们结婚才一年就～了。*They separated after only one year's marriage.* ❷ cause to separate; sort: 把好的和坏的～ *sort out the good ones from the bad*

【分类】classify: 把这些资料加以～ *classify the data* / 按题材～ *classify according to subjects* ◇ ～财务报表 classified financial statement; ～程序 sorter; ～法 classification; ～广告 classified advertisement; classified advertising; ～机 sequencer; sorter; ～数字 breakdown figures; ～索引 classified index; ～学 taxology; taxonomy; systematics; ～账 ledger

【分离】❶ (of things) separate; sever: 医院决定对这对连体婴儿作～手术。*The hospital decided to perform a separation operation on the Siamese twins.* ❷ (of people) leave; part; separate: ～多年的好友又重逢了，他们非常高兴。*The friends were glad to meet after so long a separation.* ◇ ～器［化］separator

【分理处】a small local branch (of a bank)

【分力】［物］component (of force)

【分列式】［军］march-past

【分裂】❶［生］［物］fission: 核～ *nuclear fission* / 细胞～ *cell division* ❷ split; divide; break up: ～革命队伍 *split the revolutionary ranks* / 这些人是从保守党～出来加入民主党的。*These people broke away from the Conservative Party to join the Democratic Party*

【分裂主义】splittism: ～分子 *splittist*

【分流】❶ distributary; split-flow: ～河道 *distributary channel* ❷ split-flow of human resources: 我国青少年从中学阶段开始～，初中毕业生一部分升入高中，一部分进入职业学校。*The split-flow of the youth in our country starts in secondary school years. Of the junior secondary school leavers, some go to senior secondary schools, some to vocational schools.* ❸ (of communications and transport) split-flow; diversion: 铁路客运～业务 *railway passenger split-flow operation* / 开辟客运～线路 *open up a passenger diversion line* ❹ (in economic restructuring) repositioning of redundant personnel

【分馏】［化］fractional distillation; fractionation ◇ ～塔 fractionating tower; fractional column

【分路】❶ go along separate routes or from several directions: ～前进 *advance along separate routes* / ～出击 *attack from several directions* ❷［电］shunt: ～电流 *branch current* / ～电阻 *shunt resistance*

【分袂】〈书〉leave each other; part company; part

【分门别类】put into different categories; classify

【分米】decimetre (dm.)

【分泌】［生］secrete: ～胃液 *secrete gastric juice* ◇ ～物 secretion

【分娩】childbirth; parturition

【分秒】every minute and second; instant: 时间不饶人，～赛黄金。*Time waits for no man; every minute is as precious as gold.*

【分秒必争】seize every minute and second; every second counts; not a second is to be lost

【分明】❶ be clear; be distinct; be unmistakable: 这件事情是非～，无可争辩。*The rights and wrongs of the case are perfectly clear and admit of no dispute.* ❷ clearly; evidently; obviously: ～是你不对。*Obviously you are in the wrong.*

【分母】［数］denominator

【分蘖】［农］tiller: 有效～ *effective tillering* / 麦子正在～。*The wheat is tillering.* ◇ ～节 tillering node; ～期 tillering stage

【分派】assign (to different persons or groups); apportion

【分配】❶ distribute; allot: ～土地 *distribute land* / ～住房 *allot dwelling houses* ❷ assign; dispose: 合理～劳力 *rational disposition of manpower* ❸［经］distribution: ～制度 *distribution system* ◇ ～结构 distribution structures; ～律［数］distributive law; ～渠道 distribution channel

【分批】in batches; group by group; in turn: ～轮流参加训练班 *go to a training course in turn*

【分屏】［计］split screen

【分片包干】divide up the work and assign a part to each

【分期】by stages: ～实行 *implement by stages* / ～分批 *by stages and in groups; group after group at different times* ◇ ～交货 delivery by instalments

【分期付款】payment by instalments; hire purchase; instalment plan

【分歧】difference; divergence: 意见～ *divergence of views*; *differences of opinion* / 原则～ *a difference in principle* / 制造～ *sow discord*; *create dissension* / 消除～ *iron out differences*

【分清】distinguish; draw a clear distinction between; draw a clear line of demarcation between: ～是非 *distinguish right from wrong* / 分不清真假 *cannot distinguish between genuine and sham*

【分权】a division of power or authority

【分群】(of bees) hive off

【分散】❶ scattered; dispersed; diverted; decentralized: ～的落后的个体经济 *a scattered and backward individual economy* / 注意力～ *with one's attention diverted* (*or distracted*) *to something else* ❷ disperse; distribute: ～传单 *disperse handbills* ◇ ～剂[化] dispersing agent; ～染料 disperse dyes; ～数据处理 decentralize data processing; ～学习 dipersed learning; ～主义 decentralism

【分色机】[刷] colour scanner

【分身】(usu. used in the negative) spare time from one's main work to attend to sth. else: 他实在太忙,无法～。*He is really too busy to attend to anything else*.

【分神】〈套〉give some attention to: 请～照顾一下这孩子。*Would you mind keeping an eye on the child?*

【分时】time-sharing ◇ ～电脑系统 time-sharing computer system

【分手】part company; say good-bye: 我们是在车站～的。*We said good-bye to each other at the station*. / 他们因意见分歧而～了。*They parted company due to a difference of opinion*.

【分数】❶ [数] fraction ❷ mark; grade ◇ ～线 minimum passing score

【分水岭】❶ [地质] watershed; divide ❷ line of demarcation; dividing line

【分水闸门】[水] bifurcation gate

【分税制】a system of tax distribution: 实行中央和地方～ *institute a system of tax distribution between the central and local authorities*

【分说】〈书〉defend oneself (against a charge); explain matters

【分送】send; distribute

【分摊】apportion; share: ～费用 *share the expenses* ◇ ～成本 apportioned cost

【分庭抗礼】stand up to sb. as an equal; act independently and defiantly

【分头】❶ separately; severally: 这事咱们～去做吧。*Let's go about the work separately*. ❷ parted hair: 他理了个小～。*He has a new hair parting*.

【分文】a single cent (or penny): 身无～ *have not a penny to one's name*

【分文不取】not take (or charge) a cent; free of charge

【分析】analyse: ～句子成分 *parse a sentence* / 培养～问题和解决问题的能力 *cultivate the ability to analyse and solve problems* ◇ ～方法 analytical method; ～化学 analytical chemistry; ～试剂 analytical reagent; ～天平[化] analytical balance; ～研究 analytical investigation; ～语[语] analytical language

【分线规】dividers

【分享】share (joy, rights, etc.); partake of: ～胜利的喜悦 *share the joys of victory*

【分相】[电] split phase ◇ ～器 phase splitter

【分销店】retail shop

【分晓】❶ (usu. used after 见) outcome; solution: 此事明天就见～。*We'll know the outcome of the whole affair tomorrow*. ❷ sth. seen or understood clearly: 问个～ *inquire about and get to the bottom of a matter*

【分校】a branch school

【分心】❶ divert (or distract) one's attention: 她工作起来,什么事也不能使她～。*Nothing can divert her attention once she starts working*. ❷〈套〉may I trouble you (to do sth.); would you mind (doing sth): 这件事您多～吧。*Would you be kind enough to take care of the matter?*

【分压器】[电] voltage divider

【分野】dividing line

【分忧】share sb.'s cares and burdens; help sb. to get over a difficulty: 孩子懂事了,学会为妈妈～了。*The boy has really grown up and is beginning to share his mother's worries*.

【分赃】divide the spoils; share the booty (or loot): 他们由于～不均而争吵。*They quarrelled over the spoils*.

【分针】minute hand (of a clock or watch)

【分支】subdivision; branch: 银行的～机构 *branches of a bank* ◇ 程序 branched program

【分子】❶ [数] numerator (in a fraction) ❷ [化] molecule ◇ ～病 molecular disease; ～仿生学 molecular bionics; ～结构 molecular structure; ～量 molecular weight; ～溶液[化] molecular solution; ～筛 molecular sieve; ～生物学 molecular biology; ～式 molecular formula; ～遗传学 molecular genetics ——另见 fènzǐ

【分组】divide into groups: ～讨论 *discuss in groups*; *group discussion*

芬

名 sweet smell; fragrance

【芬达汽水】Fanta

【芬芳】❶ sweet-smelling; fragrant: ～的花朵 *sweet-smelling flowers* ❷ sweet smell; fragrance: 空气里弥漫着玫瑰的～。*The sweet smell of roses fills the air*.

【芬兰】Finland ◇ ～人 Finn; Finlander; ～语 Finnish (language)

吩

(构词成分)见下

【吩咐】〈口〉❶ tell; instruct: 父亲～孩子好生照看小马驹。*The father told his son to take good care of the foal*. / 我们该做什么,请您～。*Please tell us what we should do*. ❷ instructions：听候～ *await instructions* / 您有什么～？*Have you any instructions to give?*

纷 形 ❶ confused；tangled；disorderly：纷扰 ❷ many and various；profuse；numerous：纷飞

【纷繁】numerous and complicated：头绪～ *have too many things to take care of*；*have too many irons in the fire*；*be highly complicated*

【纷纷】❶ numerous and confused：落叶～。*Leaves fell in profusion*. / 敌军～逃窜。*The enemy troops fled pell-mell*. ❷ one after another；in succession：世界各地～来电祝贺。*Congratulatory telegrams poured in from all parts of the world*.

【纷乱】numerous and disorderly；helter-skelter；chaotic：～的脚步声 *hurried footsteps* / ～的局面 *a state of chaos*

【纷扰】confusion；turmoil：内心的～使他无法入睡。*His mind was in such a turmoil that he couldn't get to sleep*.

【纷纭】diverse and confused：头绪～ *have too many things to attend to*

【纷争】dispute；wrangle：～不已 *endless dispute*

【纷至沓来】come in a continuous stream；come thick and fast；keep pouring in

氛 名 atmosphere：气氛

【氛围】atmosphere：人们在欢乐的～中迎来了新的一年。*People saw in the New Year in a happy and gay atmosphere*.

酚 名［化］phenol

【酚醛】［化］phenolic aldehyde ◇ ～树脂 phenolic resin；～塑料 phenolic plastics；phenolics；phenoplast

【酚酞】［化］phenolphthalein ◇ ～试纸 phenolphthalein test paper

fén

坟 名 grave；tomb

【坟地】（又作'坟场'）graveyard；cemetery

【坟墓】grave；tomb

【坟头】grave mound

【坟茔】❶ grave；tomb ❷ graveyard；cemetery

焚 动 burn：～香 *burn incense*

【焚风】［气］foehn

【焚化】incinerate；cremate ◇ ～炉 incinerator；cremator

【焚毁】destroy by fire；burn down

【焚烧】burn；set on fire：起义农民～了地主庄园。*The peasant rebels burned down the manor houses*.

【焚尸扬灰】burning the corpse and scattering the ashes（considered a most merciless treatment of the dead in feudal times）

【焚书坑儒】burning books and burying Confucian scholars alive（by Qin Shi Huang 秦始皇，the First Emperor of Qin）

fěn

粉 Ⅰ 名 ❶ powder：磨成～ *grind into powder or flour* ❷ cosmetics in powder form：脸上擦～ *put on face powder*；*powder one's nose* ❸ noodles or vermicelli made from bean or sweet potato starch：菠菜炒～ *bean noodles stir-fried with spinach* Ⅱ 动 ❶〈方〉become powder ❷〈方〉whitewash：墙刚～过。*The wall has just been whitewashed*. Ⅲ 形 ❶ white：～底布鞋 *cloth shoes with white soles* ❷ pink：～色 *pink colour* / 系上～绸带 *tie with a pink ribbon*

【粉笔】chalk：两支～ *two chalks* ◇ ～画 chalk drawing；crayon

【粉彩】arts and crafts mixed glaze

【粉刺】common name for 痤疮

【粉底霜】foundation cream

【粉蝶】［动］white（butterfly）：菜～ *cabbage butterfly*

【粉红】pink；rosy：一张～的圆脸 *a round face with rosy cheeks* / 一条～色的裙子 *a pink skirt*

【粉剂】❶［医］powder ❷［农］dust

【粉领族】pink-collar（tribe）

【粉瘤】sebaceous cyst

【粉末】powder

【粉墨登场】make oneself up and go on stage—embark upon a political venture

【粉皮】sheet jelly made from bean or sweet potato starch

【粉扑】powder puff

【粉墙】plaster wall

【粉身碎骨】have one's body smashed to pieces and one's bones ground to powder；die the most cruel death

【粉饰】gloss over；whitewash ◇ ～太平 present a false picture of peace and prosperity

【粉刷】❶ whitewash：～一新 *take on a new look after whitewashing* ❷〈方〉plaster

【粉丝】vermicelli made from bean starch，etc.

【粉碎】❶ broken to（or into）pieces：茶杯摔得～。*The cup was smashed to pieces*. ❷ smash；shatter；crush：～经济封锁 *smash an economic blockade*

【粉碎机】pulverizer；grinder；kibbler：饲料～ *fodder grinder* / 球磨～ *ball mill pulverizer*

【粉碎性骨折】comminuted fracture

【粉头】〈旧〉prostitute

【粉线】tailor's chalk line

【粉装玉琢】silvery white（said of a snow scene）：大雪整整下了一夜，晨起一看窗外变成了一个～的世界。*It snowed all night, and looking out of the window in the morning, I found a world of silvery white*.

fèn

分 Ⅰ 名 ❶ component：盐～ *salt content* ❷ what is within one's rights or duty：过分 Ⅱ 动〈书〉think；expect：自～不能肩此重任 *be aware of one's inability to shoulder such a heavy responsibility* ——另见 fēn

【分量】weight：给足～ *give full measure* / ～给得不足 *give short measure* / 称称～ *weigh it* / 这个铺盖卷没多少～，我拿得动。*This bedding roll isn't heavy at all, I can manage it.*

【分内】one's job or duty：这是我～的工作。*This is my share of the work.*

【分外】❶ particularly；especially：～高兴 *particularly happy* / ～香 *especially fragrant* ❷ not one's job or duty：不要把帮助别人看作～的工作。*Don't think that helping others is not one's job.* or *Never say "Helping others is not my job".*

【分子】member；element ——另见 fēnzǐ

份 Ⅰ 名 ❶ share；part；portion：把钱平分成三～。*Divide the money into three equal shares.* / 这一～是你的。*This share is yours.* ❷ (combined with 年，月，省 or 县 to form units for differentiation)：月份 / 省份 Ⅱ 量 part；portion：送一～礼去 *send a gift* / 为祖国出一～力量 *do one's bit for one's country*

【份额】share；portion

【份儿饭】table d'hote；set meal

【份子】❶ one's share of expenses for a joint undertaking, as in buying a gift for a mutual friend ❷ a gift of money

奋 动 ❶ exert oneself；act vigorously：振奋 ❷ raise；lift：～臂高呼 *raise one's arm and call out aloud* / ～笔疾书 *wield one's brush furiously*

【奋不顾身】dash ahead regardless of one's safety

【奋斗】struggle；fight；strive：～到底 *struggle to the end* / ～目标 *the objective of a struggle*

【奋发】rouse oneself；exert oneself：一个～有为的青年 *a promising enterprising youth*

【奋发图强】go all out to make the country strong；work hard for the prosperity of the country

【奋力】do all one can；spare no effort：骑兵战士冲入敌群，～砍杀。*The cavalrymen charged into the enemy ranks, slashing furiously.* / ～实现生产指标 *do all one can to fulfil the production quota*

【奋勉】make a determined effort

【奋乃静】［药］perphenazine

【奋起】❶ brace up；exert oneself；rise with force and spirit：～抗敌 *rise against the enemy* / ～自卫 *rise in self-defence* ❷ raise or lift sth. with all one's strength：～直追 *do all one can to catch up*

【奋勇】summon up all one's courage and energy：～前进 *advance bravely*；*forge ahead courageously*

【奋战】fight bravely；work strenuously：～到底 *fight to the bitter end* / ～七天 *fight for seven days on end*；*work without a letup for seven days*

粪 Ⅰ 名 excrement；faeces；dung；droppings Ⅱ 动〈书〉apply manure：～田 *manure the fields*

【粪便】excrement and urine；night soil：～检查 *stool examination*

【粪车】dung-cart；night-soil cart

【粪池】manure pit

【粪堆】dunghill；manure pile (or heap)

【粪肥】muck；manure；dung

【粪坑】manure pit

【粪筐】manure basket

【粪桶】night-soil bucket；manure bucket

【粪土】dung and dirt；muck

愤 名 indignation；anger；resentment：气愤

【愤愤不平】be indignant；feel aggrieved；be resentful：人们为他受到的不公正待遇～。*People are indignant at the unfair treatment he received.* / 他还是有些～的情绪。*He was still smouldering with indignation.*

【愤恨】indignantly resent；detest

【愤慨】〈书〉(righteous) indignation：表示～ *express one's indignation* / 这起儿子虐待老人的事件，引起了群众的极大～。*The maltreatment of the old man by his son aroused great public indignation.*

【愤懑】〈书〉depressed and discontented；resentful

【愤怒】indignation；anger；wrath

【愤世嫉俗】detest the world and its ways；be cynical

fēng

丰 形 ❶ abundant；plentiful：丰收 ❷ great：丰功伟绩 ❸ fine-looking；handsome

【丰碑】❶ monument：❷ monumental work：这部著作不愧为中国新文化运动的～。*This book is a monumental work worthy of China's new cultural movement.*

【丰产】high yield；bumper crop：～田 *a highyield plot* / ～经验 *experience in getting bumper crops*

【丰登】bumper harvest

【丰富】❶ rich；abundant；plentiful：资源～ *rich in natural resources* / 积累～的资料 *accumulate a wealth of data* ❷ enrich：～自己的生活经验 *enrich one's experience of life* / 向各方面学习，～自己的知识 *learn from every possible source to widen one's knowledge*

【丰富多彩】rich and varied；rich and colourful：～的节日活动 *varied and colourful festival activities*

【丰功伟绩】great achievements；signal contributions

【丰厚】❶ thick：绒毛～ *rich and thick fur* ❷ rich and generous：～的礼品 *generous gifts*

【丰满】❶ plentiful：粮仓～。*The granaries are full*. ❷ full and round；well-developed；full-grown：～的脸盘 *a chubby (or plump) face* / 体态～ *have a well filled-out figure* / 她比去年生病的时候～多了。*She's rounded out quite a bit since she fell ill last year*.

【丰茂】luxuriant；lush

【丰美】lush：水草～ *lush pasture*

【丰年】a bumper harvest year；a good year

【丰饶】rich and fertile：～的草原 *fertile grassland*

【丰润】plump and smooth-skinned：肤色～ *have smooth and velvety skin*

【丰盛】rich；sumptuous：～的酒席 *a sumptuous feast*

【丰收】bumper harvest：连年～ *bumper harvests for years running* / ～在望。*A good harvest is in sight*.

【丰硕】plentiful and substantial；rich：取得～的成果 *reap rich fruits；score great successes*

【丰衣足食】have ample food and clothing；be well-fed and well-clothed：过着～的生活 *live a life of plenty*

【丰盈】❶ full and round；well-developed：体态～ *have a full figure* ❷ plentiful：衣食～ *have plenty to eat and wear*

【丰裕】well provided for；in plenty：生活～ *live in plenty；be comfortably off*

【丰足】abundant；plentiful：衣食～ *have plenty of food and clothing*

风 Ⅰ 名 ❶ wind：一阵～ *a gust of wind* / 起～了。*The wind is rising*. / ～停了。*The wind has stopped*. ❷ practice；custom；tendency：此～不可长。*This tendency is not to be encouraged*. ❸ scene；view：风光 ❹ style；attitude：文风 ❺ news；information：他刚听见一点～儿就来打听。*He came to ask the moment he got wind of it*. Ⅱ 动 air-dry；winnow：晒干～净 *sun-dried and well winnowed* / ～鸡 *air-dried chicken* / ～肉 *air-dried meat* Ⅲ 形 rumoured；unfounded：风闻

【风暴】❶ windstorm；storm：海上～ *a storm at sea* ❷ a violent commotion；storm；tempest：革命～ *the storm of revolution*

【风泵】❶ air pump ❷ air compressor

【风痹】［中］wandering arthritis

【风标】weathercock；weather vane

【风波】〈字〉wind and waves；〈喻〉disturbance；storm：～迭起。*Disturbances arose repeatedly*. / 平地起～ *a storm out of nowhere*

【风采】❶〈书〉elegant demeanour；graceful bearing：～动人 *have a strikingly elegant and graceful bearing* ❷〈书〉literary grace

【风餐露宿】eat in the wind and sleep in the dew—endure the hardships of an arduous journey

【风潮】agitation；unrest：闹～ *agitate (for a strike, etc.)*

【风车】❶ windmill ❷ winnower；winnow ❸ pinwheel (a child's toy)

【风尘】❶ wind and dust—travel fatigue：满面～ *travel-stained* ❷ hardships or uncertainties in an unstable society，esp. in the officials' circle ❸ the life of a prostitute：沦落～ *be driven to prostitution*

【风尘仆仆】have endured the hardships of a long journey；be travel-stained；be travel-worn and weary

【风驰电掣】swift as the wind and quick as lightning：列车～般闪过。*The train flashed past*.

【风传】(of news or rumours) get about (or round)；be rumoured (or said)；they say：～内阁即将改组。*The rumour is getting about that there's going to be a reshuffle of the cabinet*.

【风吹草动】the rustle of leaves in the wind—a sign of disturbance or trouble：不要一有～就惊慌失措。*Don't fly into a panic at the mere rustle of leaves in the wind*.

【风吹浪打】be beaten by wind and waves；be battered by a storm：～不动摇 *never waver in the storm and stress of struggle*

【风吹雨打】be buffeted by wind and rain；be exposed to the weather：经不起～ *cannot withstand natural calamities*

【风挡】automobile windscreen；windshield

【风笛】bagpipes；pipes

【风动工具】pneumatic tools

【风洞】［航空］wind-tunnel

【风斗】wind scoop

【风度】demeanour；bearing：有～ *have poise* / ～大方 *have an easy manner* / 他的举止动作完全是军人～。*He carries himself every inch like a soldier*.

【风度翩翩】(of a young man) have an elegant and smart carriage

【风发】❶ swift as the wind ❷ energetic

【风帆】❶ sail：扬起～ *unfurl the sails* ❷ sailing boat or ship

【风范】〈书〉❶ demeanour；bearing；poise ❷ style；manner；air

【风干】air-dry：木材经过～可以防止腐烂。*Air-drying can prevent wood rotting away*. / ～栗子 *air-dried chestnuts* / ～腊肉 *air-dried bacon*

【风镐】pneumatic pick；air pick

【风格】style；manner；mode：～高 *behave in a generous manner* / 作者的～是喜爱作细腻的描述。*The author's style is characterized by a fondness for detailed descriptions*.

【风骨】❶ strength of character ❷ vigour of style (in writing，painting or of calligraphy)

【风光】❶ scenery；scene；view；sight：北国～ *typical northern scenery* / 青山绿水好～ *a splendid view of green mountains and blue waters* ❷〈方〉grand；impressive；in style ◇ ～片 scenic film

【风害】damage caused by a windstorm

【风寒】chill；cold：只是受了点儿～。*It's nothing but a chill*. / 经常洗冷水澡可以抵御～。*Taking cold baths regularly can heighten one's resistance to colds.*

【风和日丽】(又作'风和日暖') a bright sun and a gentle breeze; warm and sunny weather: 又是～、万木争荣的时节了。*It was a time of sunshine and gentle breezes, of trees and shrubs bursting into glorious blossom.*

【风花雪月】wind, flowers, snow and the moon—referring originally to certain types of literary works and later to effete and sentimental writings in general

【风华】〈书〉elegance and intellectual brilliance

【风华正茂】at life's full flowering; in one's prime

【风化】❶ morals and manners; decency: 有伤～ *an offence against decency* ❷［地质］weathering ❸［化］efflorescence

【风级】［气］wind scale: ～表 *wind scale; Beaufort scale*

【风纪】conduct and discipline; discipline

【风井】［矿］ventilating shaft; air shaft

【风景】scenery; landscape: 欣赏～ *admire the scenery* / 桂林以～优美著称。*Guilin is famous for its scenic beauty.* ◇ ～画 landscape painting; ～林 scenic forest; ～区 scenic spot; ～线 scenic view; attractive scenery or phenomenon

【风镜】goggles

【风卷残云】a strong wind scattering the last clouds—make a clean sweep of sth.

【风口】❶ a place where there is a draught: 别站在～上,小心着凉。*Don't stand in the draught. You may catch cold.* ❷［地质］wind gap ❸［冶］(blast) tuyere: 渣～ *slag tuyere*

【风口浪尖】where the wind and the waves are highest—where the struggle is fiercest

【风浪】❶ stormy waves; storm: ～大,船颠簸得很利害。*There was a heavy sea and the ship tossed terribly.* ❷ a stormy experience: 久经～ *have weathered many a storm*

【风雷】wind and thunder; tempest: 革命的～ *the storm of revolution* ◇ ～激荡 a storm raging in all its fury

【风力】❶ wind-force: 测试～大小 *gauge the wind's intensity* ❷ wind power: 以～为动力 *wind-powered; wind-driven* ◇ ～发电机 wind-driven generator; windmill generator; ～发电站 wind power station; ～输送机 pneumatic conveyor; ～提水机 wind-driven water pump; wind pump

【风凉】cool: 大家坐在～的地方休息。*All of us were sitting in a cool place for a rest.*

【风凉话】irresponsible and sarcastic remarks: 说～ *make sarcastic comments*

【风铃】wind-bells (hung on the eaves of pagodas or temple buildings)

【风流】❶ refined and tasteful ❷ unrestrained in spirit and behaviour ❸ romantic; amorous; licentious: ～年少 *a romantic young man* / ～才子 *a gallant young scholar* / ～寡妇 *a merry widow* / ～韵事 *romantic deeds; amorous encounters*

【风流云散】dispersed by the wind and scattered like the clouds—(usu. of old companions) separated and scattered

【风马牛不相及】have nothing to do with each other; be totally unrelated: 这和我们的谈话内容,有点～啊! *I don't see it has anything to do with what we're talking about.*

【风帽】❶ a cowl-like hat worn in winter ❷ hood

【风貌】❶ style and features: 民间艺术的～ *the style and features of folk art* ❷ view; scene: 农村新～ *the new look of the countryside* ❸ elegant appearance and bearing

【风媒传粉】wind pollination

【风媒花】［植］anemophilous flower

【风门】❶［矿］air door; ventilation door ❷ storm door (put up in winter in northern China)

【风靡】be fashionable: 今夏超短裙又～京沪了。*Miniskirts have become fashionable again in Beijing and Shanghai this summer.*

【风靡一时】become fashionable for a while; be all the rage at the time

【风磨】windmill (for grinding grain)

【风能】wind energy source

【风派】(又作'风派人物') timeserver; trimmer

【风平浪静】the wind has dropped and the waves have subsided; calm and tranquil: ～的海面 *an unruffled sea* / 他的生活总是～的。*His life had been uneventful.*

【风起云涌】winds rising and clouds scudding; rolling on with full force; surging forward

【风气】general mood; atmosphere; common (or established) practice: 促进整个社会～的改变 *help to change the general mood of society*

【风琴】organ: 弹～ *play the organ*

【风情】❶ information about wind direction, wind-force, etc. ❷〈书〉bearing; demeanour ❸〈书〉feelings ❹ amorous feelings; flirtatious expressions: 卖弄～ *play the coquette; coquet; flirt* ❺ local conditions and customs

【风趣】humour; wit: 他是一个很有～的人。*He is a man of charm and wit.* / 她说话很有～。*She is a witty talker.*

【风圈】solar or lunar halo

【风骚】❶〈书〉literary excellence ❷ coquettish; flirtatious: 卖弄～ *play the coquette; coquet; flirt*

【风色】❶ how the wind blows: ～突然变了,由南往北刮。*The wind suddenly veered round to the north.* ❷ how things stand: ～不对。*Things are going against one.* ——另见〖看风色〗

【风沙】sand blown by the wind: 这里春天～很大。*It's very windy and dusty here in spring.*

【风扇】electric fan; fan: 散热～ *radiator fan* / 通风～ *draught fan*

【风尚】prevailing custom (or practice, habit): 勤俭节约的新～ *a new habit of diligence and frugality* / 时代～ *the vogue of the day*

【风声】❶ the sough of the wind: ～萧萧。*The wind is soughing.* ❷ rumour: 听到～ *get wind of sth*. / ～很紧。*The situation is getting tense*.

【风声鹤唳,草木皆兵】scared by the moan of the wind and the cry of the cranes, and seeing the enemy in every bush and tree (said of the extreme nervousness of a fleeing army)

【风湿】[医] rheumatism

【风湿性关节炎】rheumarthritis

【风蚀】[地质] wind erosion; deflation

【风霜】wind and frost—hardships of a journey or of one's life

【风水】the location of a house or tomb, supposed to have an influence on the fortune of a family; geomantic omen: 这栋房子～好。*The site of this house is of high geomantic quality*. or *This house is favourably sited in terms of geomantic quality*. ◇ ～先生 geomancer

【风俗】custom: ～习惯 *customs and habits* ◇ ～画 genre painting; genre

【风速】wind speed; wind velocity ◇ ～表 anemometer; ～计 anemograph; registering anemometer; ～器 wind gauge

【风瘫】common name for 瘫痪

【风调雨顺】good weather for the crops; favourable weather: ～,五谷丰登。*Good weather brings good harvests*. / ～,国泰民安。*The elements were propitious, the country prospered and the people were at peace*.

【风头】❶ the way the wind blows: 船老大仔细观察～和水势。*The boatman kept a sharp eye on the wind and water*. ❷ the trend of events (as affecting a person): 避避～ *lie low until sth. blows over* / 看～办事 *act according to circumstances* ❸ (usu. 〈贬〉) the publicity one receives: ～十足 *be very much in the limelight*

【风土】natural conditions and social customs of a place ◇ ～人情 local conditions and customs

【风土驯化】[农] acclimatization

【风味】special flavour; local colour (or flavour): 家乡～ *the pleasing taste of the cooking of one's native place; local flavour* / 这首诗有民歌～。*This poem has a distinctive balladic air*. ◇ ～菜 typical local dishes; local delicacies

【风味小吃】local delicacies: 中国每个地区都有自己的～。*Each region of China boasts its local delicacies*.

【风闻】learn through hearsay; get wind of

【风险】risk; hazard: 冒～ *take risks* / 要改革就不怕担～。*A true reformist fears no dangers*. / ～补偿 *income to compensate for risk-taking* ◇ ～报酬 risk premium; ～补贴 danger money; ～分担 allocation of risks; ～合同 risk contract; ～基金 risk fund; ～企业 venture business; ～投资 risk investment; venture capital; venture investment; ～意识 sense of risk

【风箱】bellows

【风向】wind direction ◇ ～标 wind vane; ～袋 wind sleeve; wind sock; wind cone; ～计 registering weather vane; ～图 wind rose; ～仪 anemoscope

【风信子】[植] hyacinth

【风行】be in fashion (or vogue); be popular: ～全国 *be popular all over the country*

【风行一时】be popular for a while; be all the rage for a time

【风选】[农] selection by winnowing (or wind)

【风选机】winnowing machine; winnower

【风压】[气] wind pressure

【风雅】❶ literary pursuits ❷ elegant; refined: 举止～ *have refined manners*

【风言风语】groundless talk; slanderous gossip

【风衣】windcheater; windbreaker; wind-jacket

【风油精】essential balm

【风雨】wind and rain; the elements; trials and hardships: 迎着～去战斗 *go into battle braving wind and rain*

【风雨交加】It's raining and blowing hard; It's wet and windy.

【风雨飘摇】swaying in the midst of a raging storm; precarious; tottering: ～的年代 *precarious times; troubled times*

【风雨如晦】wind and rain sweeping across a gloomy sky—a grim situation

【风雨同舟】in the same storm-tossed boat—stand together through thick and thin

【风雨无阻】stopped by neither wind nor rain—regardless of the weather; rain or shine: 我们郊游的日期已定,～。*We've fixed the date for the outing and we'll go regardless of wind or rain*.

【风雨衣】a rainproof windcheater; mackintosh

【风云】wind and cloud—a stormy or unstable situation

【风云变幻】constant change of events; a changeable situation: ～的时代 *an age of rapid change* / 国际政治～。*World politics are constantly changing*.

【风云人物】man of the hour

【风云突变】a sudden change in the situation

【风韵】(usu. a woman's) graceful bearing; charm

【风灾】disaster caused by a windstorm: 遭受～ *be hit by a windstorm*

【风闸】[机] pneumatic brake

【风障】[农] windbreak

【风疹】[医] nettle rash; urticaria

【风筝】kite: 放～ *fly a kite*

【风烛残年】old and ailing like a candle guttering in the wind

【风姿】graceful bearing; charm: ～秀逸 *have elegant bearing*

【风钻】pneumatic drill

枫 ❶ 名 同〖枫树〗❷ maple

【枫树】(又作'枫香树') Chinese sweet gum (Liquidambar formosana)

【枫叶】leaves of Chinese sweet gum, maple, etc. which turn red in autumn

疯 Ⅰ 形 mad; insane; crazy: 他～了。*He's gone mad*. Ⅱ 副 (of a plant, grain crop, etc.) spin-

dly and not likely to bear much fruit or seed：这些棉花长～了。*These cotton-plants are growing too tall and spindly* (*or are overgrowing*).
【疯疯癫癫】mentally deranged；acting like a lunatic；flighty
【疯狗】mad dog；rabid dog
【疯狂】❶ insane ❷ frenzied；unbridled：～咒骂 *frenzied vilification* / ～反扑 *a desperate counterattack* / ～掠夺 *unbridled plunder* / ～叫嚣 *frenzied clamouring*
【疯牛病】mad cow disease
【疯人院】madhouse；lunatic asylum
【疯瘫】同〖风瘫〗
【疯长】［农］overgrowing；spindling：防止～ *prevent spindling*
【疯子】lunatic；madman

封 Ⅰ动 ❶ confer (a title，territory，etc.) upon：～王 *be made a prince* / 分～诸侯 *grant titles and territories to the nobles* ❷ seal：把信～上 *seal a letter* / 大雪纷飞，江河冰～。*It is snowing hard，and rivers and streams have frozen over.* ❸bank (a fire)：炉子～了吗？*Have you banked up the fire?* Ⅱ名 wrapper；envelope：赏～ *an envelope with money reward sealed in*；*an enveloped money reward* Ⅲ量 (for sth. enveloped)：一～信 *a letter*
【封闭】❶ seal：用蜡～瓶口 *seal a bottle with wax* ❷ seal off；close：～机场 *close an airport* / ～的社会 *a closed society* ◇ ～层［油］confining bed；～港 closed port；～疗法 block therapy；～式公司 closed corporation
【封存】seal up for safekeeping
【封袋机】bag seating machine；bagger
【封底】［刷］back cover
【封地】fief；feud；manor
【封顶】❶ (of a plant) cease growing any taller ❷ impose a ceiling (on prices，wages，bonuses，etc.)：奖金不～。*There is no ceiling on bonuses.*
【封冻】(of a river，the ground，etc.) freeze ◇ ～期 a period of freezing weather；freeze
【封二】［刷］inside front cover (also called 封里)
【封港】close a port or harbour
【封官许愿】〈贬〉offer official posts and make lavish promises；promise high posts and other favours
【封罐机】tin seamer；can seamer
【封火】bank a fire
【封建】❶ the system of enfeoffment ❷ feudalism ❸ feudal；feudalistic：头脑～ *feudal-minded*
【封建割据】feudal separationist rule
【封建社会】feudal society
【封建主】feudal lord
【封建主义】feudalism
【封镜】finish making a film：这部影片已经～。*They have finished making the film.*
【封口】❶ seal：这封信还没～。*The letter hasn't been sealed yet.* ❷ heal：腿上的伤已经～了。*The leg wound has healed.* ❸ say sth. definitive so as to prevent further discussion
【封蜡】sealing wax
【封里】［刷］❶ inside front cover ❷ inside back cover
【封面】［刷］❶ the title page of a thread-bound book ❷ the front and back cover of a book ❸ front cover
【封泥】❶ sealing clay ❷［冶］lute
【封皮】〈方〉❶ paper wrapping ❷ envelope
【封妻荫子】(of the emperor) confer titles of honour on the wife of a deserving official and hereditary ranks on his descendants
【封三】［刷］inside back cover (also called 封里)
【封杀】strangle；smother：这股歪风一冒头即遭～。*That unhealthy trend was nipped in the bud.*
【封山】seal (or close) a mountain pass：大雪～。*Heavy snow has sealed the mountain passes.* ◇ ～育林 close hillsides (to livestock grazing and fuel gathering) to facilitate afforestation
【封四】［刷］back cover (also called 封底)
【封锁】block or seal off (through military or other compulsory means)；blockade：～港口 *blockade a port* / ～边境 *close the border* / ～消息 *block the passage of information* / 经济～ *economic blockade* ◇ ～线 blockade line；blockade
【封套】big envelope (for holding documents，books，etc.)
【封条】a strip of paper used for sealing (doors，drawers，etc.)；paper strip seal
【封网】［体］(网) block：她那一下～可精彩了！*She made a brilliant block.*
【封一】［刷］front cover (also called 封面)
【封印】seal (on mail)
【封嘴】❶ speak with a tone of finality ❷ seal sb.'s lips

峰 Ⅰ名 ❶ peak；summit；crest：孤～ *a solitary peak* / 浪～ *the crest of a wave* ❷ hump：驼峰 Ⅱ量 (only for camels)：四～骆驼 *four camels*
【峰巅】mountain peak；summit
【峰回路转】amidst surrounding elevations and winding roads
【峰会】summit (meeting)：五国～昨已开幕。*The summit meeting of the five countries began yesterday*
【峰峦】ridges and peaks
【峰态】［数］kurtosis
【峰值】［电］peak value；crest value

烽 名 beacon
【烽火】❶ beacon-fire (used to give border alarm in ancient times)；beacon ❷ flames of war
【烽火连天】flames of battle raging everywhere
【烽火台】beacon tower
【烽烟】beacon-fire；beacon

锋 名 ❶ a sharp point or cutting edge (of a knife，sword，etc.)：刀锋 ❷ vanguard：先锋 ❸

[气] front

【锋钢】high-speed steel; rapid steel

【锋利】❶ sharp; keen: ～的钢刀 *a sharp knife* ❷ incisive; sharp; poignant: ～泼辣的笔调 *a sharp and pungent style*

【锋芒】(又作'锋铓') ❶ cutting edge; spearhead: 斗争的～ *the spearhead of struggle* ❷ talent displayed; abilities: 不露～ *refrain from showing one's ability; be able but modest*

【锋芒毕露】make a display of one's abilities

【锋面】[气] frontal surface ◇ ～低压 [气] frontal low

蜂

Ⅰ 名 ❶ bee; honeybee ❷ wasp Ⅱ 副 in swarms

【蜂巢】honeycomb

【蜂刺】the sting of a bee (or wasp)

【蜂毒】bee venom

【蜂房】any of the six-sided wax cells in a honeycomb

【蜂糕】steamed sponge cake (made of wheat or rice flour)

【蜂蜡】beeswax

【蜂蜜】honey

【蜂鸣器】buzzer

【蜂鸟】hummingbird

【蜂群】(bee) colony

【蜂乳】royal jelly

【蜂王】❶ queen bee ❷ queen wasp

【蜂王精】royal jelly

【蜂窝】❶ common name for 蜂巢 ❷ a honeycomb-like thing; honeycomb ◇ ～炉 honeycomb briquet stove; ～煤 honeycomb briquet (or briquette); ～织炎 [医] cellulitis; phlegmon; phlegmona; ～组织 [生理] cellular tissue; areolar tissue

【蜂箱】beehive; hive

【蜂拥】swarm; flock: 车门一开,乘客～而上。*As soon as the door opened, passengers swarmed onto the bus.*

【蜂拥而来】come swarming; swarm forward: 四面八方的人向广场～。*People came swarming into the square from all directions.*

féng

逢

动 meet; come upon: ～人便问 *ask whoever happens to come one's way* / ～双(单)日开放 *open on even (odd) days of the month*

【逢场作戏】join in the fun on occasion: 咱们搞这行的只不过是"～"嘛。*We of this trade know too well that we are only playing a game.*

【逢集】market day: 我们进村的那天正好～。*The day we arrived at the village happened to be market day.*

【逢年过节】on New Year's Day or other festivals: ～我总回家。*On New Year's Day and other festivals, I always go back home.*

【逢山开路,遇水搭桥】cut paths through mountains and build bridges across rivers

【逢凶化吉】ill luck turns into good: 因为他在外边的朋友多,遇啥事都能～。*He has many connections, and he can always find some way of tiding over a crisis.*

【逢迎】make up to; fawn on; curry favour with: 百般～上司 *curry favour with one's superior sedulously*

缝

动 stitch; sew: ～被子 *stitch a quilt cover on* / ～扣子 *sew a button on* / 刀口刚～好。*The incision has just been stitched up.* ——另见 fèng

【缝补】sew; mend (by sewing): ～衣服 *mend clothes*

【缝合】[医] suture; sew up: ～伤口 *sew up (or suture) a wound* ◇ ～线 another name for 缝线

【缝纫】sewing; tailoring: ～车间 *tailoring shop* ◇ ～机 sewing machine

【缝线】[医] suture: 吸收性～ *absorbable suture* / 羊肠～ *catgut suture*

fěng

讽

动 ❶ satirize; mock: 嘲讽 ❷ 〈书〉 chant; intone: 讽诵

【讽刺】❶ satirize: 这是一部～封建文人的作品。*This is a satire on feudal scholars.* ❷ ridicule; taunt; mock: 别～他了。*Don't ridicule him.* / 我受不了这种～。*I can't stand such taunts (or sarcasm).* ◇ ～画 caricature; ～诗 satirical poem; ～文学 satire; ～小品 satirical essay

【讽诵】〈书〉 read with intonation and expression

【讽喻】parable; allegory ◇ ～诗 allegorical poem

唪

动 chant in a loud voice

【唪经】(of Buddhists or Taoists) recite (or chant) the scriptures in a loud voice

fèng

凤

名 phoenix: 凤凰

【凤凰】phoenix (凤 being the male and 凰 being the female) ◇ ～木 royal poinciana (Delonix regia); flamboyant (tree); ～座 [天] Phoenix

【凤凰竹】hedge bamboo (Bambusa multiplex)

【凤梨】pineapple (the plant and its fruit)

【凤毛麟角】(precious and rare as) phoenix feathers and unicorn horns; rarity of rarities

【凤尾鱼】common name for 鲚

【凤尾竹】fernleaf hedge bamboo (Bambusa multiplex var. nana)

【凤仙花】garden balsam; balsam

奉

动 ❶ give or present with respect: 双手～上 *present respectfully with both hands* / ～上新书一册。*I am forwarding you a new book.* ❷ receive (orders, etc.): ～上级指示,暂停开放。

Temporarily closed on orders from above. ❸ esteem; revere: ～为典范 *look upon as a model* ❹ believe in: 素～佛教 *have always believed in Buddhism* ❺ wait on; attend to: 侍奉

【奉承】flatter; fawn on; toady to: 许多人～他就因为他有钱。*Many people fawn on him only because of his wealth.* ◇ ～话 flattery

【奉告】〈套〉let sb. know; inform: 详情容后～。*I'll give you the details later.*

【奉公守法】be law-abiding

【奉还】〈套〉return sth. with thanks

【奉命】(又作'奉令') receive orders; act under orders: ～出发 *receive orders to set off* / ～于危难之间 *be entrusted with a mission at a critical and difficult moment*

【奉命唯谨】obey orders scrupulously

【奉陪】〈套〉keep sb. company: 恕不～。*Sorry I won't be able to keep you company.*

【奉陪到底】have the honour of keeping sb. company until the end: 今天晚上来和我们玩桥牌,好吗? —好极啦,我一定～。*Will you come and join us at a bridge party this evening? — Yes, I'll be glad to, and I'll stay at the party until the very end.*

【奉劝】〈套〉may I offer a piece of advice: ～你少喝点儿酒。*I'd like to advise you not to drink too much.*

【奉若神明】worship sb. or sth.; make a fetish of sth.

【奉送】〈套〉offer as a gift; give away free

【奉为楷模】hold up as a model

【奉献】offer as a tribute; present with all respect ◇ ～精神 spirit of utter devotion

【奉行】pursue (a policy, etc.): ～不结盟政策 *pursue a policy of nonalignment*

【奉行故事】follow established practice

【奉养】support and wait upon (one's parents, etc.)

【奉旨】by order of the emperor; by imperial decree

俸 名 pay; salary: 薪俸

【俸禄】〈旧〉an official's salary; government salary

缝 名 ❶ seam: 缭～儿 *sew a seam* ❷ crack; crevice; fissure: 院墙上裂了一道～儿。*There is a crack in the courtyard wall.* ——另见 féng

【缝隙】chink; crack; crevice

fó

佛 名 ❶ Buddha ❷ Buddhism: 信～ *believe in Buddhism* ❸ an image of Buddha; Buddha: 一尊铜～ *a bronze statue of Buddha* / 大殿上塑着三尊～。*There are three Buddhas in the main hall of the temple.*

【佛得角】Cape Verde ◇ ～人 Cape Verdean

【佛法】❶ Buddha dharma; Buddhist doctrine: 传布～ *spread Buddhism* ❷ power of Buddha

【佛法僧】Buddha-dharma-sangha ——另见〖三宝〗

【佛教】Buddhism ◇ ～徒 Buddhist

【佛经】Buddhist Scripture; Buddhist sutra; Buddhist sacred literature

【佛龛】a niche for a statue of Buddha

【佛口蛇心】a Buddha's mouth but a viper's heart—honeyed words but evil intent

【佛门】Buddhism: ～弟子 *followers of Buddhism; Buddhists* / 皈依～ *be converted to Buddhism*

【佛事】Buddhist ceremony (or service)

【佛手】[植](又作'佛手柑') Buddha's hand; fingered citron

【佛堂】family hall for worshipping Buddha

【佛头着粪】smear Buddha's head with dung—desecrate

【佛陀】Buddha—a title for Sakyamuni or a person who has attained enlightenment

【佛像】an image of Buddha; Buddha

【佛学】Buddhist philosophy

【佛牙】sacred tooth relic of Buddha

【佛争一柱香,人争一口气】As Buddha needs incense, so man needs self-respect.

【佛珠】beads; rosary

【佛祖】Buddhist patriarch

fǒu

否 Ⅰ 动 ❶ negate; deny: 否认 ❷〈口〉turn down: 我的建议被他～了。*He turned down my offer.* Ⅱ 副 ❶〈书〉nay; no: 这是妥当的办法吗? ～! *Is that the right way to do it? No!* / 你这样说合适吗? ～! *Is it right for you to say so? No!* ❷〈书〉(used at the end of a sentence to indicate that the sentence is a question): 知其事～? *Do you know anything about it?* ❸ (used with 是,能,可,etc.) whether or not: 明日能～出发须视天气而定。*Whether or not we can start off tomorrow will depend on the weather.* ——另见 pǐ

【否定】❶ negate; deny: 你不能～他的话是合乎事实的。*You cannot deny the truth of his statement.* ❷ negative: ～的答复 *a negative answer; an answer in the negative* ❸ [哲] negation: ～之～ *the negation of negation*

【否决】vote down; veto; overrule: ～提案 *veto a proposal* / 提议被大会～了。*The motion was voted down at the assembly.* or *The assembly rejected the motion.* ◇ ～权 veto power; veto

【否认】deny; repudiate: 他～做过任何违法的事。*He denied doing anything illegal.*

【否则】otherwise; if not; or else: 快点走,～要迟到了。*Hurry up, or we'll be late.*

fū

夫 名 ❶ husband: 夫妻 ❷ man: 匹夫 ❸ a manual worker: 渔夫 ❹ (in former times) a conscripted labourer：拉夫

【夫唱妇随】the husband sings and the wife follows—domestic harmony；conjugal felicity

【夫妇】husband and wife：新婚～ *a newly married couple*；*newlyweds*

【夫妻】husband (or man) and wife

【夫妻店】a small shop run by husband and wife

【夫权】authority of the husband

【夫人】❶ a lady of high rank；the wife of a feudal lord；the wife of a high official ❷ the wife of a diplomat：各国使节和～ *foreign diplomatic envoys and their wives* ❸ Mrs.；Madame (Mme)；Lady：张～ *Madame Zhang* / 第一～ *First Lady* ❹〈套〉wife：您的～好吗？*How is your wife?*

【夫子】❶〈旧〉(a respectful term of address for a scholar or a teacher) master：孔～ *Master Kong*；*Confucius* ❷〈旧〉my husband ❸ pedant：～气 *pedantry*

【夫子自道】what the Master says is a description of himself (said of a person criticizing others when he himself is open to the same charge)

呋 (构词成分)见下

【呋喃】[化] furan

【呋喃妥英】[药] nitrofurantoin

【呋喃西林】[药] nitrofurazone；furacin

肤 名 skin：皮肤

【肤泛】superficial；shallow：～之论 *shallow views*

【肤觉】[生理] dermal sensation

【肤皮潦草】cursory；casual；perfunctory

【肤浅】superficial；shallow：我对这个问题的认识很～。*I have only a superficial understanding of the problem.*

【肤色】colour of skin：不同国度、不同～的运动员欢聚一堂。*Players from different lands and of different colours were gathered happily in the same hall.* / 不论种族、信仰或～ *without regard to race, creed, or colour*

麸 名 (wheat) bran

【麸皮】(wheat) bran ◇ ～面包 whole wheat bread；brown bread

【麸子】(wheat) bran

跗 名 instep (i.e. the arching area of the middle of the human foot)

【跗骨】[生理] tarsus；tarsal bones

【跗面】instep (i.e. the upper surface of the arching area of the human foot)

孵 动 hatch；brood；incubate：～小鸡 *hatch chicks* / ～出来了十只小鸭子。*Ten ducklings have hatched.*

【孵化】hatch；incubate：这台孵卵器一次能～的蛋要比一百只母鸡还多。*This incubator can hatch more eggs at a time than a hundred hens.* ◇ ～场 hatchery (for poultry, etc.)；～池 hatchery (for fish, etc.)

【孵卵】brood；hatch；incubate：～鸡 *brooding hen* ◇ ～期 incubation period；～器 incubator

敷 动 ❶ apply (powder, ointment, etc.)：～粉 *apply powder* / 在创口上～药膏 *dress the wound with ointment* ❷ spread；lay out：敷设 ❸ be sufficient for：入不敷出

【敷料】[医] dressing

【敷设】❶ lay (pipes, etc.)：～管道 *lay pipelines* / ～铁轨 *lay a railway track* / ～电缆 *lay electricity cables* ❷ lay (mines)：～水雷 *lay mines in water*

【敷衍】❶ act in a perfunctory manner；go through the motions；do just enough to satisfy sb.：他做事老是采取～的态度，很不认真。*He's in the habit of working perfunctorily and half-heartedly.* ❷ barely get by；just manage：这几个钱只够我～几天的。*This money is barely enough for me to get by (or manage) a few days.*

【敷衍了事】muddle through one's work：她办事认真，从不～。*She is very conscientious and never skimps her work.*

【敷衍塞责】perform one's duty in a perfunctory manner

弗 副〈书〉not：自愧～如 *feel ashamed of one's inferiority*

fú

伏 Ⅰ 动 ❶lean over；bend over：～几而卧 *fall asleep against a table* ❷ lie prostrate：～地不动 *lie still on the ground, face downwards* ❸ subside；go down：起伏 ❹ hide：昼～夜出 *hide by day and come out at night* ❺ yield；admit (defeat, guilt, etc.)：伏输❻ subdue；vanquish：降龙伏虎 Ⅱ 名 ❶the hottest days of the year：初伏 ❷〈略〉见〖伏特〗

【伏安】[电] volt-ampere

【伏案】bend (or lean) over a table：～读书(作画) *bend over one's desk reading (painting)* / ～入睡 *fall asleep against a table*

【伏笔】a hint foreshadowing later developments in a story, essay, etc.；foreshadowing：这件事为以后故事情节的发展埋下了～。*This episode carries a foreshadowing of what is to follow later on in the story.*

【伏兵】troops in ambush；ambush

【伏尔加河】the Volga

【伏法】be executed；be put to death

【伏击】ambush：遭到～ *fall into (or get caught in) an ambush* / 进行～ *attack from (an) ambush* / ～敌人 *ambush the enemy*

【伏击圈】ambush ring

【伏流】[地质] subterranean drainage；underground stream

【伏侍】同〖服侍〗

【伏输】同〖服输〗

【伏暑】the torrid weather of the year's hottest

days

【伏特】[电] volt

【伏特计】voltmeter

【伏特加】vodka

【伏天】the fu days—the hottest days of the year ——另见〖三伏〗

【伏帖】❶ at ease; content; comfortable: 心里很～ *feel perfectly content* ❷ fit perfectly: 这身衣服穿着很～。*This suit fits perfectly*.

【伏卧】lie prostrate; take a prone position; lie on one's stomach

【伏羲】a legendary ruler of great antiquity, the first of the Three August Ones (三皇), credited with the invention of hunting and fishing and the domestication of animals

【伏汛】summer flood (or freshet)

【伏诛】〈书〉be executed

【伏罪】同〖服罪〗

凫 ❶ wild duck ❷ swim: ～水 *swim*

【凫翁】[动] water cock

扶 动 ❶ support with the hand; place a hand on sb. or sth. for support: ～着栏杆上楼 *walk upstairs with one's hand on the banisters* / 你～着点梯子,我上去。*Hold the ladder while I climb up*. ❷ help sb. up; straighten sth. up: ～苗 *straighten up the seedlings* / 护士～起伤员,给他换药。*The nurse propped up the wounded soldier and changed the dressing on his wound*. ❸ help; assist; support: 扶持

【扶病】(do sth.) in spite of illness: ～出席会议 *go to a meeting in spite of one's illness*

【扶持】❶ support sb. with one's hand; help sb. to stand or walk: 伤员们互相～着练习走路。*Leaning on each other for support, the wounded men practised walking*. ❷ help sustain; give aid to; support: 荷花虽好,也要绿叶～。*For all its beauty the lotus needs its green leaves to set it off*.

【扶老携幼】holding the old by the arm and the young by the hand; bringing along the old and the young

【扶贫】aid-the-poor programme (a government programme for providing assistance for poor areas of the country)

【扶弱抑强】同〖抑强扶弱〗

【扶手】❶ handrail; rail; banisters ❷ armrest ◇～椅 armchair

【扶疏】〈书〉luxuriant and well-spaced: 枝叶～。*The branches and leaves are luxuriant but well-spaced*.

【扶梯】❶ staircase ❷〈方〉ladder

【扶危济困】help those in distress and aid those in peril

【扶养】❶ provide for; support and assist: 夫妻间有互相～的义务。*Husband and wife have the duty to support and assist each other*. ❷ 同〖抚养〗◇～费 payment for support and assistance (for one's former spouse); alimony

【扶摇直上】soar on the wings of a cyclone; rise steeply; skyrocket

【扶植】foster; prop up: ～新生力量 *foster new rising forces* / ～傀儡政权 *prop up a puppet regime*

【扶助】help; assist; support: ～老弱 *help the old and the weak*

芙 (构词成分)见下

【芙蓉】[植] ❶ cottonrose hibiscus ❷ another name for 荷花

【芙蓉出水】a lotus flower just appearing above the water (said of a beautiful poem or painting or of a beautiful woman)

孚 动 inspire confidence in sb.: 深～众望 *enjoy great popularity; enjoy high prestige*

拂 动 ❶ stroke: 春风～面 *a spring breeze stroking the face* ❷ whisk; flick: ～去桌上的尘土 *whisk the dust off the desk* ❸ go against (sb.'s wishes)

【拂尘】horsetail whisk

【拂动】brush against; stroke; caress: 和风～着姑娘的披肩秀发。*A gentle breeze brushed against (or caressed) the girl's beautiful long hair*.

【拂拭】whisk or wipe off

【拂晓】daybreak; dawn: ～出发 *set off at dawn* / ～前发起总攻 *start the general offensive before dawn*

【拂袖而去】leave with a flick of one's sleeve —go off in a huff

服 Ⅰ 名 ❶ clothes; dress: 工作服 ❷ mourning apparel: 有～在身 *be wearing mourning clothes; be in mourning* Ⅱ 动 ❶ wear or put on (clothes): 服丧 ❷ take (medicine): 日～三次,每次两片。*To be taken three times a day, two (tablets) each time*. ❸ serve: ～兵役 *serve in the army; perform military service* ❹ be convinced; obey: 你说得有道理,我～了。*What you've said is reasonable. I'm convinced*. ❺ be accustomed to: 不服水土——另见 fù

【服从】obey; submit (oneself) to; be subordinated to: ～命令 *obey orders* / 少数～多数。*The minority should submit to the majority*.

【服毒】take poison: ～自杀 *commit suicide by taking poison*

【服法】❶ submit to the law: 认罪～ *admit one's guilt and submit oneself to the law* ❷ directions about how to take a medicine

【服气】be convinced: 他批评得对,你别不～。*His criticism is justified. You shouldn't take it amiss*.

【服丧】be in mourning (for the death of a kinsman, etc.)

【服饰】dress and personal adornment; dress

【服侍】(又作'服事') wait upon; attend: ～父母 *attend one's parents* / 他生病的时候,同志们轮流来～他。*His comrades took turns looking after him when he was ill*.

【服输】admit (or acknowledge) defeat

【服帖】❶ docile; obedient; submissive: 他对老板很～。*He is obedient to his boss*. ❷ appropriate; fitting; well arranged: 把事情都弄得服服帖帖的 *arrange everything smoothly*

【服务】give service to; be in the service of; serve: 为人民～。*Serve the people*. / ～周到 *provide good service* / 提高～质量 *improve one's service* ◇ ～程序 service routine; ～费 service fee; ～上门 door-to-door service; ～台 service desk (or counter); information and reception desk; ～态度 attitude in attending to or waiting on guests, customers, etc.; ～行业 service trades; ～性租赁 service leases; ～一条龙 a series of service; ～员 attendant; ～站 service centre

【服刑】serve a sentence: ～期满 *complete a term of imprisonment* / 他已～三年。*He has served three years in prison*.

【服药】take medicine

【服役】❶ be on active service; enlist in the army: 他在海军～。*He's serving in the Navy*. / ～期间 *during one's term of military service; during the period of enlistment* / ～期满 *complete one's term of service* ❷ (in former times) do corvée labour

【服用】❶〈书〉clothing and articles for daily use: ～甚俭 *be frugal in one's habits* ❷ take (medicine)

【服装】dress; clothing; costume: ～整齐 *be neatly dressed* / 民族～ *national or ethnic costume* / 她负责保管这出戏的～。*She's the wardrobe mistress of this play*. ◇ ～表演 fashion show; ～店 clothes shop; clothing store; ～工业 the clothing industry; ～设计 dress designing

【服罪】plead guilty; admit one's guilt: 不～ *plead not guilty*

茯

(构词成分)见下

【茯苓】fuling (Poria coccus, an edible fungus, often used as a herbal medicine)

氟

名 [化] fluorine (F)

【氟化氢】[化] hydrogen fluoride

【氟化物】[化] fluoride

【氟利昂】[化] freon

【氟石】fluorite; fluorspar (a mineral)

俘

Ⅰ 动 capture; take prisoner: 被～ *be taken prisoner* Ⅱ 名 prisoner of war; captive: 遣～ *repatriate prisoners of war*

【俘获】❶ capture; seize: 我军～甚众。*Our army captured a lot of enemy soldiers and weapons*. ❷ [物] capture: 中子～ *neutron capture* / 裂变～ *fission capture*

【俘虏】❶ capture; take prisoner: 那一仗他们～敌军一千二百名。*They captured twelve hundred enemy soldiers in that battle*. ❷ captive; captured personnel; prisoner of war (P.O.W.): 执行宽待～的政策 *carry out the policy of lenient treatment of prisoners of war*

浮

Ⅰ 动 ❶ float: 木头能～在水面上。*Wood floats on water*. / 潜水员～上来了。*The diver has emerged*. / 她脸上～起了笑容。*A faint smile played on her face*. ❷〈方〉swim: 他一口气～到了对岸。*He swam across at one go*. Ⅱ 形 ❶ on the surface; superficial: 浮土 ❷ movable ❸ temporary; provisional: ～支 *expenditure not in the regular account* ❹ shallow and frivolous; superficial: 他这个人太～,办事不踏实。*He is too frivolous to do solid work*. ❺ hollow; inflated: 浮夸 ❻ excessive; surplus: ～额 *surplus number*

【浮报】give inflated figures in a report

【浮标】buoy

【浮冰】floating ice; (ice) floe

【浮尘】floating dust; surface dust

【浮尘子】[动] leafhopper

【浮沉】now sink, now emerge; drift along: 宦海～ *the ups and downs in officialdom; the vicissitudes of an official career*

【浮船坞】floating dock; floating dry dock

【浮荡】float in the air: 歌声在空中～。*The air resounded with singing*.

【浮雕】relief (sculpture): ～群像 *a relief sculpture of a group of people*

【浮吊】[机] floating crane

【浮动】❶ float; drift: 树叶在水面上～。*Leaves were floating on the water*. ❷ be unsteady; fluctuate: 物价飞涨,人心～。*With the soaring of prices, there was a growing feeling of insecurity*. ❸ [经] float: 货币共同～ *a joint currency oat* ◇ ～工资 floating wages; ～汇率 floating exchange rate; ～价格 floating prices; ～利率 floating interest rate; ～轴 [机] floating axle

【浮法玻璃】float glass

【浮泛】❶〈书〉float about: 轻舟～ *a light boat gliding past* ❷ reveal; display: 她的脸上～着愉快的神情。*Her face beamed with joy*. ❸ superficial; too abstract: 他的发言内容～。*His speech was superficial and full of generalities*.

【浮光掠影】skimming over the surface; hasty and casual; cursory

【浮华】showy; ostentatious; flashy: 文辞～ *florid language; an ornate style* / ～的生活 *a showy and luxurious life style*

【浮记】keep a tally of a transaction before entering it in the regular accounts; keep a temporary account

【浮夸】boastful; exaggerating: ～作风 *proneness to boasting and exaggeration*

【浮雷】[军] floating mine

【浮力】[物] buoyancy

【浮码头】floating pier

【浮面】surface: 把～的一层泥铲掉 *scrape the mud off the surface* / 汤一开锅就把～的油撇掉。*Skim the grease from the soup when it starts to boil*.

【浮名】an empty name：～身后有谁知？*After death who remembers an empty name?*
【浮皮儿】❶ outer skin ❷ surface
【浮皮蹭痒】scratching the surface；superficial
【浮萍】[植] duckweed
【浮浅】superficial；shallow：一种～的看法 *a superficial view*
【浮桥】pontoon bridge；floating bridge
【浮生若梦】this fleeting life of ours is like an empty dream
【浮石】pumice (stone)
【浮筒】float；pontoon；buoy
【浮屠】[宗](佛教)(又作'浮图') ❶ 同〚佛陀〛❷ a title applied by Buddhists to a monk ❸ Buddhist pagoda or stupa：救人一命胜造七级～。*There is greater merit in saving one life than in building a seven-tier pagoda.*
【浮土】dust collected on furniture, clothing, etc.；surface dust
【浮文】verbiage；padding
【浮现】appear before one's eyes：往事～在我眼前。*Scenes of the past rose before my eyes.* or *The past came back to my mind.*
【浮想】❶ thoughts flashing across one's mind ❷ recollections
【浮想联翩】thoughts thronging one's mind：～，夜不能寐。*Thoughts thronged my mind and I could not sleep.*
【浮选】[矿] flotation ◇ ～剂 flotation agent
【浮游】❶ swim；float ❷〈书〉go on a pleasure trip
【浮游生物】plankton
【浮游资金】floating fund
【浮云】floating clouds
【浮躁】impetuous；impulsive
【浮渣】[冶] dross
【浮肿】dropsy；edema
【浮子】❶ float (in fishing) ❷ carburettor float (in automobile)

符 Ⅰ 名 ❶ a tally issued by a ruler to generals, envoys, etc., as credentials in ancient China：兵符 ❷ symbol：音符 ❸ magic figures drawn by Taoist priests to invoke or expel spirits and bring good or ill fortune：画了一张～ *draw a magic figure* Ⅱ 动 tally with；accord with：与事实不～ *not tally with the facts*
【符号】❶ symbol；mark：注音～ *phonetic symbol* / 标点～ *punctuation mark* / 代数～ *algebraic symbol* ❷ insignia ◇ ～地址 symbolic address；～学 semiology
【符合】❶ accord with；tally with；conform to；be in keeping with：～要求 *accord with the demands* / ～实际情况 *tally with the actual situation；conform to reality* ❷ [物] coincidence ◇ ～摆 [物] coincidence pendulum
【符咒】Taoist magic figures or incantations

幅 Ⅰ 名 ❶ width of cloth：宽～白布 *extra wide white cloth* ❷ size：大～照片 *a large-sized photo* Ⅱ 量 (for cloth, picture, etc.)：一～画 *a picture；a painting* / 一～布 *a breadth of cloth*
【幅度】range；scope；extent：病人血压变化的～不大。*The patient's blood pressure fluctuates within a narrow range.*
【幅面】width of cloth
【幅员】the area of a country's territory；the size of a country：～广大 *vast in territory*
【幅员辽阔】have a vast territory：～的国家 *a country with a vast territory*

福 Ⅰ 名 good fortune；blessing；happiness：～寿双全 *enjoy both happiness and longevity* Ⅱ 动 (of a woman in former times) make a curtsy：～了一～ *make a curtsy*
【福尔马林】[化] formalin
【福分】〈口〉good luck；good fortune；a happy lot：我们可没有你这样的～。*We don't have such good luck as you do.*
【福利】material benefits；well-being；welfare：为人民谋～ *work for the well-being of the people* ◇ ～费 welfare funds；～国家 welfare state；～基金 welfare fund；～设施 welfare facilities；～事业 welfare project (or services)
【福气】good luck；good fortune；a happy lot：这位老太太有～，儿女都很孝顺。*The old lady is fortunate in having such dutiful children.*
【福如东海】happiness as boundless as the eastern seas (a stock term of congratulations)：爷爷！祝您老人家～，寿比南山！*I wish you long life and happiness, Grandpa!*
【福无双至，祸不单行】Blessings never come in pairs；misfortunes never come singly.
【福相】a face showing good fortune
【福星】lucky star；mascot：～高照。*The lucky star is in the ascendant.*
【福音】❶ [宗](基督教) Gospel：～书 *the Gospels (in the Bible)* ❷ glad tidings
【福至心灵】When good fortune comes, the mind works well.

辐 名 spoke (of a wheel)
【辐散】[气] divergence：～场 *divergence field*
【辐射】❶ radiate (from a central point)：八条大道从广场呈～形伸展出去。*Eight roads radiate from the square.* ❷ [物] radiation：热～ *thermal radiation* / 电磁～ *electromagnetic radiation* / 受激～ *stimulated radiation* / 自发～ *spontaneous radiation* ◇ ～带 [气] radiation zone；～电阻 radiation resistance；～计 radiometer；～剂量 radiation dosage；～能 radiant energy；～频率 radiation frequency；～强度 radiation intensity；～容限 radiotolerance；～体 radiant body；～学 radiology；～育种 [农] radioactive breeding；～源 radiant
【辐条】〈口〉spoke (of a wheel)
【辐照】[物] irradiation ◇ ～度 [物] irradiance

蜉 (构词成分)见下

【蜉蝣】［动］mayfly

蝠 名［动］bat：蝙蝠

fǔ

抚 动 ❶ comfort；console：安抚 ❷ nurture；foster：抚养 ❸ stroke：～琴 *play the zither* ❹ 同〖拊〗

【抚爱】caress；fondle

【抚躬自问】同〖反躬自问〗

【抚今追昔】recall the past and compare it with the present；reflect on the past in the light of the present

【抚摩】stroke：他轻轻地～着我的头发。*He was gently stroking my hair.*

【抚弄】stroke；fondle：她双手不停地～着她的辫子。*She kept on stroking her braids.*

【抚慰】comfort；console；soothe：～灾区人民 *console the people in afflicted areas*

【抚恤】comfort and compensate a bereaved family

【抚恤金】pension for the disabled or for the family of the deceased

【抚养】foster；raise；rear；bring up：父母对子女有～教育的义务。*Parents have the duty to rear and educate their children.* / 她一人把那三个孤儿～成人。*She brought up the three orphans all by herself.*

【抚养费】payment for the upbringing of one's children (as after divorce)

【抚育】foster；nurture；tend：～烈士子女 *bring up the children of revolutionary martyrs* / 森林～ *the tending of woods*

【抚掌】clap one's hands

府 名 ❶ seat of government；government office：政府 ❷〈旧〉government repository：府库 ❸ official residence；mansion：总统府 ❹〈尊〉your home：贵～ *your home*

【府绸】poplin：山东～ *Shandong pongee*；*shantung pongee*

【府第】(又作'府邸') mansion (of nobles，high officials，big landlords，etc.)；mansion house

【府库】government repository (in former times)

【府上】〈尊〉❶ your home；your family：改日再来～拜访。*I'll pay a visit to your home some other day.* / ～都好吗？*How is everybody in your family?* ❷ your native place：您～哪里？*Where are you from?*

斧 名 axe；hatchet

【斧头】axe；hatchet

【斧正】(又作'斧政')〈套〉(please) make corrections

【斧子】axe；hatchet

拊 动〈书〉clap：～手 *clap hands*

【拊掌】〈书〉clap hands：～大笑 *clap hands and laugh heartily*

釜 名 a kind of cauldron used in ancient China

【釜底抽薪】take away the firewood from under the cauldron—take drastic measures to deal with an emergency

【釜底游鱼】a fish swimming in the bottom of a cauldron—a person whose fate is sealed

俯 Ⅰ 动 bow (one's head)：俯视 Ⅱ 副〈套〉〈旧〉(used in official documents or letters) condescend to：～允 *condescend to give permission* / ～察 *deign to examine*

【俯冲】［航空］dive：～轰炸 *dive-bomb* ◇ ～飞行 diving flight；～角 dive angle

【俯伏】lie prostrate；lie prone

【俯角】angle of depression

【俯就】❶〈套〉condescend to accept (a job) ❷ adapt oneself to；make the best of；make do with

【俯瞰】look down at；overlook：从飞机上～海面 *look down at the sea from a plane*

【俯瞰摄影】［摄］crane shot；boom shot

【俯拍】take a crane (or boom) shot

【俯身】bend over；bend down：她～亲亲睡在摇篮里的孩子。*She bent down to kiss the baby in the crib.*

【俯拾即是】be found everywhere；be extremely common：这类事例～。*Such instances are extremely common.*

【俯视】look down at；overlook：站在山上～蜿蜒的公路 *stand on the top of the hill looking down at the winding highway below* ◇ ～图 vertical view

【俯首】bow one's head (in submission)：～就范 *meekly submit*；*surrender without a struggle*

【俯首甘为孺子牛】head bowed，like a willing ox I serve the children ——另见〖横眉冷对千夫指，俯首甘为孺子牛〗

【俯首帖耳】be docile and obedient；be all obedience；be servile：我知道这是他拉拢我，好让我～地为他效劳。*I knew he was trying to wheedle me into being at his beck and call.*

【俯卧】lie prostrate；lie face down (on the ground)

【俯卧撑】［体］push-up

【俯仰】〈书〉a bending or lifting of the head—a simple move or action：随人～ *be at sb.'s beck and call* ◇ ～角［航空］angle of pitch；～运动［机］pitching movement

【俯仰由人】be at others' beck and call

【俯仰之间】in the twinkling of an eye；in an instant；in a flash

脯 名 ❶ dried meat：鹿～ *dried venison* ❷ sun-dried candied fruit；preserved fruit：桃脯——另见 pú

辅 动 assist；complement；supplement：自力更生为主，争取外援为～ *rely mainly on one's own efforts while making external assistance subsidiary*

【辅币】fractional currency (or money)：硬～ *sub-*

sidiary coin; minor coin

【辅车相依】as dependent on each other as the jowls and the jawbone; as close as the jowls and the jaws

【辅导】give guidance in study or training; coach: 个别～ *individual coaching (or tutorial)* / ～报告 *guidance lecture (supplementary lecture on background, study method, etc.)* / ～材料 *guidance material* ◇ ～班 tutorial class

【辅导员】(political and ideological) assistant; instructor: 政治～ *political assistant* / 理论～ *instructor in political theory*

【辅课】subsidiary course

【辅音】[语音] consonant

【辅助】❶ assist: 多加～ *assist (sb.) as much as possible* ❷ supplementary; auxiliary; subsidiary: ～劳动 *auxiliary labour (or jobs)* / ～仪器 *supplementary instruments* ◇ ～存储器 auxiliary memory; ～机构 auxiliary body; ～舰船 auxiliary vessels; ～人员 auxiliary staff members; ～设备 auxiliary equipment; ～授粉 [农] supplementary pollination

【辅佐】(又作'辅翼')〈书〉assist a ruler in governing a country

腐 Ⅰ 形 rotten; putrid; stale; corroded: ～肉 *rotten meat* Ⅱ 名 tofu; beancurd

【腐败】❶ rotten; putrid; decayed: ～的食物 *putrid food* / 油漆涂在木材上,可以防止～。*Paint is put on wood as a protection against rotting.* ❷ corrupt; rotten: ～无能 *corrupt and incompetent* / 消除～现象 *put an end to corrupt dealings* / 政治～ *political corruption*

【腐臭】emitting a smell of decay; decaying and stinking; smelly

【腐化】❶ degenerate; become corrupt, dissolute or depraved: 生活～ *lead a dissolute (or dissipated) life* ❷ rot; decay; decompose ◇ ～堕落 degenerate and decadent; leading a dissolute (or dissipated) life; ～分子 degenerate; a depraved person

【腐烂】❶ decompose; become putrid (or rotten): 一大批水果～了。*A large supply of fruit rotted.* / ～的树叶是好肥料。*Decomposed leaves make good fertilizer.* ❷ corrupt; rotten

【腐泥煤】sapropelic coal

【腐乳】fermented tofu (or beancurd)

【腐生】[生] living on nonliving organic matter; saprophytic: ～细菌 *saprophytic bacteria* / ～植物 *saprophyte*

【腐蚀】❶ [化] corrode; etch ❷ corrupt; corrode: ～性 *corrosiveness* ◇ ～版 [刷] etched plate; ～机 [刷] etching machine; ～剂 [化] corrosive; corrodent

【腐朽】❶ rotten; decayed: 这些木材已经～了。*The timber has rotted.* ❷ decadent; degenerate: ～庸俗的作风 *decadent and philistine ways*

【腐殖煤】humic coal

【腐殖酸】[农] humic acid: ～类肥料 *humic acid fertilizers*

【腐殖土】[农] humus soil

【腐殖质】humus

【腐竹】dried rolls of bean milk cream

fù

父 名 ❶ father: ～与子 *father and son* ❷ male relative of a senior generation: 祖父

【父辈】people of father's generation

【父本】[植] male parent: ～植株 *paternal plant*

【父党】father's kinsfolk

【父老】elders (of a country or district): ～兄弟 *elders and brethren*

【父母】father and mother; parents

【父母之命,媒妁之言】the command of parents and the good offices of a go-between—(in former times) the proper way of contracting a marriage

【父亲】father

【父权制】patriarchy

【父系】❶ paternal: ～亲属 *paternal relatives* ❷ patrilineal: ～家族制度 *patrilineal family system* / ～氏族公社 *patrilineal clan commune*

【父兄】❶ father and elder brothers ❷ head of a family

【父执】〈书〉father's friends

【父子】father and son: 他们家～四人都是教师。*The father and his three sons are all schoolteachers.*

讣 名 ❶ announce sb.'s death ❷ obituary

【讣告】❶ announce sb.'s death ❷ obituary

【讣闻】(又作'讣文') obituary

付 动 ❶ hand (or turn) over to; commit to: ～表决 *put to the vote; take a vote on* / ～诸实施 *put into effect* ❷ pay: ～房租 *pay rent (for a house, flat or room)* / ～税 *pay taxes* / 票钱已经～了。*I've paid for the tickets.*

【付出】pay; expend: ～现款 *pay in cash* / ～代价 pay a price

【付定金】pay earnest money

【付方】[经] credit side; credit

【付刊】send to the press; put into print

【付款】pay a sum of money: 货到～ *cash on delivery (C.O.D.)* / 凭单～ *cash against documents* / ～办法 *methods of payment* ◇ ～保证银行 certifying bank; ～方式 type of payment; ～凭单 warrant; paying certificate; ～凭证 payment voucher; ～人 payer; drawee; ～条件 terms of payment; ～通知 advice of payment; payment order; ～银行 paying bank

【付排】[刷] send to the compositor

【付讫】(of a bill) paid

【付清】pay in full; pay off; clear (a bill): 一次～ *pay off in one lump sum*

【付托】put sth. in sb.'s charge; entrust: ～重任 charge sb. with a heavy responsibility / 他把家

产～给他的好友照管。*He entrusted his best friend with the care of his property.*

【付息】pay interest

【付现】pay in cash

【付印】❶ send to the press ❷ turn over to the printing shop (after proofreading)

【付邮】send by post; take to the post; post; mail: 贺年片本周内必须全部～。*All the New Year cards must be posted off this week.*

【付账】pay a bill: 我付过账了。*I've already paid the bill.*

【付之一炬】commit to the flames

【付之一笑】dismiss with a laugh

【付诸东流】(又作'付之东流','付之流水') thrown into the eastward flowing stream—all one's efforts wasted; irrevocably lost

负 Ⅰ 动 ❶〈书〉carry on the back or shoulder: ～薪 *carry firewood on one's back* ❷ shoulder; bear: 身～重任 *shoulder an important task* / ～责任 *assume the responsibility* ❸ have at one's back; rely on: ～险固守 *put up a stubborn defence by relying on one's strategic position* ❹ suffer: 负伤 ❺ enjoy: 久～盛名 *have long enjoyed a good reputation* ❻ owe: 负债 ❼ fail in one's duty, obligation, etc.; betray: 负约 ❽ lose (a battle, game, etc.); be defeated: 一比二～于对方 *lose the match* 1:2 / 该队以两胜一～的成绩取得小组第二名。*The team finished second in its group with two wins and one loss.* Ⅱ 形 ❶［数］less than zero; minus; negative: ～乘～得正。*A negative number multiplied by another negative number makes the product positive.* / ～一点五 *minus one point five* (−1.5) ❷［电］negative: 负极

【负担】❶ bear (a burden); shoulder: 旅费由东道国～。*All the travelling expenses will be borne by the host country.* ❷ burden; load; encumbrance: 财政～ *financial burden* / 家庭～ *family burden (esp. financial)* / 工作～ *workload* / 思想～ *a load on one's mind; mental burden* / 减轻学生～ *lighten the students' load* / 解除精神～ *free one's mind of encumbrances*

【负电荷】negative (electric) charge

【负电极】negative electrode; cathode

【负电子】electron; negatron

【负电阻】negative resistance

【负反馈】negative feedback

【负号】［数］negative sign

【负荷】❶〈书〉carry on one's back and shoulder; bear; shoulder: ～重任 *shoulder important responsibilities* ❷ load (that a person or machine is expected to perform); work load: 满～ *full-load* / 超～ *overload*

【负极】［电］negative pole

【负加速度】［物］negative acceleration

【负荆请罪】proffer a birch and ask for a flogging—offer a humble apology

【负疚】〈书〉feel apologetic; have a guilty conscience

【负离子】［物］anion

【负面效应】negative effects

【负片】［摄］negative

【负气】do sth. in a fit of pique: ～而去 *leave in a fit of pique*

【负伤】be wounded; be injured: 负重伤 *be badly wounded* / 光荣～ *be wounded in action*

【负数】［数］negative number

【负像】［物］negative image

【负心】ungrateful (esp. in love); untrue; heartless

【负隅顽抗】(of an enemy or a robber) fight stubbornly with one's back to the wall; put up a desperate struggle

【负约】❶ break a promise; go back on one's word ❷ fail to keep an appointment

【负载】［电］［机］load: 高峰～ *peak load* / 工作～ *operating load* / ～调整 *load regulation*

【负责】❶ be responsible for; be in charge of: 由此产生的一切后果由你方～。*Your side will be held responsible for all the consequences arising therefrom.* ❷ conscientious: 她对工作很～。*She is very conscientious in her work.* ◇ ～人 person in charge; leading cadre

【负债】❶ be in debt; incur debts: 她～从来不还。*She never repays her debts.* / 他负了上千元的债。*His debts amount to nearly a thousand yuan.* ❷ liabilities: 资产与～ *assets and liabilities* ◇ ～累累 be heavily in debt; be up to one's ears in debt; ～证明书 certificate of indebtedness

【负重】❶ carry a heavy load on one's back ❷ shoulder a heavy task ◇ ～训练 weight training

【负重致远】bear a heavy burden and go a long way—shoulder heavy responsibilities

【负资产】negative asset

【负罪】〈书〉bear the blame

妇 名 ❶ woman: 妇孺 ❷ married woman: 少妇 ❸ wife: 夫妇

【妇产科】(department of) gynaecology and obstetrics

【妇产医院】a hospital for gynaecology and obstetrics

【妇代会】(〈略〉全称为'妇女代表大会') conference of women representatives; women's conference

【妇道人家】〈贬〉women; womenfolk

【妇科】(department of) gynaecology ◇ ～医生 gynaecologist

【妇联】〈略〉见『妇女联合会』

【妇女】woman: ～队长 *woman leader (in charge of women's affairs in a production team)* ◇ ～病 gynaecological (or women's) disease; ～联合会 the Women's Federation

【妇人】married woman

【妇孺】〈书〉women and children: ～皆知 *known even to women and children*

【妇婴】women and infants; mothers and babies: ～卫生 *maternity and infant hygiene*

【妇幼】women and children: ～保健站 *health cen-*

tre for women and children; maternity and child-care centre / ～卫生 *maternity and child hygiene*

附 动 ❶ add; attach; enclose: ～上一笔 *add a word or two (in a letter, etc.)* / ～表三张 *with three lists or charts attached* / ～寄照片四张,希查收。*Please find enclosed four snapshots.* ❷ get close to; be near: ～在耳边低声说话 *whisper in sb.'s ear* ❸ depend on; rely on; comply with: 附议

【附笔】additional remarks (in a letter, document, etc.): 内人～问好。*I'd like to add that my wife asked to be remembered to you.*

【附带】❶ in passing: ～说一下 *mention in passing; by the way; incidentally* ❷ attach: 我们提供的援助不～任何条件。*The aid we provide has no strings attached.* ❸ subsidiary; supplementary: 从事～劳动 *do supplementary labour*

【附点】[音] dot: ～音符 *dotted note*

【附耳】move close to sb.'s ear: ～低语 *whisper in sb.'s ear* / 他们俩～谈了几句。*They whispered a few words to each other.*

【附睾】[生理] epididymis ◇ ～炎 [医] epididymitis

【附和】echo; chime in with: ～别人的意见 *echo other people's views*

【附会】draw wrong conclusions by false analogy; strain one's interpretation

【附加】❶ add; attach: 文件后面～两项说明。*The document has two explanatory notes attached to it.* ❷ additional; attached; appended ◇ ～费 extra charge; surcharge; ～工资 supplemental wage; extra wage; ～税 surtax; additional tax; supertax; ～条款 additional article; memorandum clause; ～文件 diplomacy appended document; ～议定书 diplomacy additional protocol

【附件】❶ appendix; annex: 作为调查报告的～ *as an appendix to the investigation report* ❷ enclosure ❸ [机] accessories; attachment: 车床～ *lathe accessories* / 铲工～ *backing-off attachment*

【附近】❶ nearby; neighbouring: ～地区 *nearby regions* / ～的城市 *neighbouring (or adjacent) towns* ❷ in the vicinity of; close to: 住在工厂～ *live close to the factory* / ～有没有邮局? *Is there a post office near here?* / 就在～,几分钟就可走到。*It's only a few minutes' walk from here.*

【附录】appendix (to a book): 词典的十二个～ *the twelve appendices to the dictionary*

【附上】be enclosed herewith: 随信～商品目录一份。*A catalogue of commodities is enclosed herewith.* / ～样稿一份,请查收。*Enclosed please find a set of sample sheets.*

【附设】have as an attached institution: 这个学院～一所中学。*There is a middle school attached to the institute.*

【附生植物】[植] epiphyte; air plant

【附属】subsidiary; auxiliary; attached; affiliated: 医学院～医院 *a hospital attached to a medical college* / ～机构 *subsidiary body* ◇ ～公司 subcompany; ～国 dependency; ～品 accessory; appendage; ～小学 attached primary school; ～中学 attached middle school

【附图】attached map or drawing; figure: 见～一。*See Figure 1.*

【附息贷款】lend money on interest

【附言】postscript (P. S.)

【附议】second a motion; support a proposal: 我～! *I second the motion!*

【附庸】❶ dependency; vassal ❷ appendage: 语言文字学在清代还只是经学的～。*During the Qing Dynasty, philology was a mere handmaid of classical studies.*

【附庸风雅】(of landlords, merchants, etc.) mingle with men of letters and pose as a lover of culture

【附则】supplementary articles (appended to a treaty, decree, etc.)

【附中】(〈略〉全称为'附属中学') attached (or affiliated) secondary school: 北师大二～ *No. 2 Secondary School attached to the Beijing Normal University*

【附注】notes appended to a book, etc.; annotations

【附赘悬疣】swelling tumours and protruding wens—superfluities

【附着】adhere to; stick to: 地衣～在岩石、树干上。*Lichens adhere to rocks and tree trunks.* / 这种病菌～在病人使用过的东西上。*This germ is found on the things used by the patients.* ◇ ～力 [物] adhesive force; adhesion

【附子】[中] monkshood

服 量 (for Chinese medicine) dose: 一～中药 *a dose of Chinese medicine* ——另见 fú

驸 名 a horse hitched up by the side of the shaft-horse (to assist the pulling of a vehicle)

【驸马】husband of an emperor's daughter or sister; emperor's son-in-law or brother-in-law

赴 动 go to; attend: 离京～美 *leave Beijing for U.S.A.*

【赴会】attend a meeting; keep an appointment (to meet sb.)

【赴难】go to the aid of one's country; go to help save the country from danger

【赴任】go to one's post; be on the way to one's post

【赴汤蹈火】go through fire and water; defy all difficulties and dangers

【赴宴】go to a feast; attend a banquet

【赴约】keep an appointment

复 Ⅰ 形 ❶ duplicate: 复写 ❷ compound; complex: ～光谱 *complex spectrum* Ⅱ 动 ❶ turn round; turn over: 反复无常 ❷ reply; answer: 请即电～。*Cable reply immediately.* ❸ recover; resume: 复职 ❹ revenge: 报复 Ⅲ 副 again: 复查

/ 复活

【复背斜】[地质] anticlinorium

【复本】duplicate

【复本位制】[经] bimetallism

【复辟】restore a dethroned monarch (or the old order): 1814 年波旁王朝在法国～。*The Bourbons were restored to power in France in* 1814. / ～活动 *restorationist activities (or manoeuvres)*

【复波】[物] complex wave

【复查】check; reexamine: 一个月后到医院～。*Come back to the hospital for a check in a month's time.*

【复仇】revenge; avenge: ～心理 *vindictiveness; a desire for revenge* / 他发誓要～。*He vowed to avenge himself.* ◇ ～主义 revanchism

【复穿孔】pang-punch

【复电】❶ send a telegram in reply: 我已给家里复了电。*I've already telegraphed my family in reply.* ❷ a telegram in reply: ～已发。*A telegram has been sent in reply to the one received.*

【复调音乐】[音] polyphony

【复读】(students destined to graduate from elementary or secondary schools) repeat the last year of schooling due to the next level

【复读生】student retaking classes after failing a college entrance examination

【复发】have a relapse; recur: 旧病～ *have an attack of an old illness; have a relapse* / 他的关节炎～了。*He's suffering from arthritis again.*

【复方】❶ [中] a prescription composed of two or more recipes of herbal medicines ❷ [医] medicine made of two or more ingredients; compound: ～阿斯匹林 *aspirin compound (APC)* / ～甘草合剂 *brown mixture*

【复分解反应】[化] double decomposition reaction

【复根】[化] compound radical

【复工】return to work (after a strike or layoff)

【复古】restore ancient ways; return to the ancients ◇ ～主义 the doctrine of "back to the ancients"

【复关】re-enter GATT

【复合】compound; complex; composite ◇ ～磁头 combined record; ～词 [语] compound word; compound; ～电路 compound circuit; ～肥料 compound fertilizer; ～句 [语] compound or complex sentence; ～量词 [语] compound classifier; ～元音 [语音] diphthong (as ei, uo) or triphthong (as uai, iao)

【复核】❶ check: 把数字～一下 *check the figures* ❷ [法] (of the Supreme People's Court) review a case in which a death sentence has been passed by a lower court

【复婚】(of a divorced couple) remarry each other

【复活】❶ come back to life; revive: 防止法西斯主义～ *guard against the revival of fascism* ❷ [宗] (基督教) Resurrection

【复活节】[宗] (基督教) Easter

【复激】[电] compound excitation: ～发电机 *compound generator*

【复交】❶ resume (once broken) relations ❷ diplomacy reestablish (or resume) diplomatic relations

【复进口】re-import

【复旧】restore (or revive) old ways; return to the past

【复句】[语] a sentence of two or more clauses

【复卷机】papermaking rewinding machine; rewinder

【复刊】(of magazines or newspapers) resume publication

【复课】resume classes: 实习完毕, 明日～。*The field work is completed, and classes will begin again tomorrow.*

【复利】[经] compound interest

【复明】recover lost eyesight

【复命】report back after carrying out an order

【复赛】[体] intermediary heat; semi-finals

【复审】❶ reexamine ❷ [法] review a case

【复生】come back to life

【复式】[经] double entry: ～税则 *double tariff*

【复式车床】[机] double lathe

【复式住宅】a type of residential housing that maximizes usage space by increasing the number of two-storey buildings

【复试】reexamination; final examination

【复述】❶ repeat: ～命令 *repeat an order* ❷ retell (in language learning): 把故事～一遍 *retell a story*

【复数】❶ [语] plural (number) ❷ [数] complex number

【复丝】[化] fibre multifilament

【复苏】❶ come back to life or consciousness; resuscitate ❷ recovery; resurgence: 经济～ *economic resurgence*

【复位】❶ [医] reduce ❷ be restored to the throne ◇ ～术 [医] reduction

【复习】review; revise: ～功课 *review (or revise) lessons* ◇ ～提纲 outline for review

【复线】[交通] multiple track ◇ ～铁路 double-tracking railways

【复向斜】[地质] synclinorium

【复写】make carbon copies; duplicate ◇ ～纸 carbon paper

【复信】❶ write a letter in reply; reply: 我给他复了三封信, 他说都没收到。*He says he has received none of the three letters I wrote back to him.* ❷ a letter in reply

【复兴】revive; rejuvenate: 民族～ *national rejuvenation* / ～国家 *rejuvenate one's country*

【复姓】compound surname; two-character surname: 司马在汉族姓氏里是～。司马 (Sīmǎ) *is a compound surname among Chinese surnames.*

【复学】go back to school (after prolonged absence for health reasons, etc.); resume one's interrupted studies

【复盐】[化] double salt

【复眼】[动] compound eye (of insects)

【复业】❶ take up one's old trade again ❷ reopen or restart business

【复叶】[植] compound leaf
【复议】reconsider (a decision)
【复音】[物] complex tone
【复音词】disyllabic (or polysyllabic) word
【复印】xerox; duplicate: ～文件 *xerox (or duplicate) documents* ◇ ～机 xerox (machine); duplicator; ～纸 duplicating paper
【复员】❶ return to peacetime conditions ❷ (of servicemen) be demobilized: 小王是1982年从部队～的。*Xiao Wang was demobilized from the army in* 1982. ◇ ～费 demobilization pay; ～军人 a demobilized serviceman; an ex-serviceman; ～令 demobilization order
【复原】❶ (又作'复元') recover from an illness; be restored to health: 他身体已经～了。*He's already recovered*. ❷ be restored; be rehabilitated: 这座在战争中惨遭破坏的城市已经～。*The city, which was destroyed in the war, has been restored*.
【复圆】[天] fourth contact of a total eclipse; last contact of a partial eclipse; end of an eclipse
【复杂】complicated; complex: 情况～。*The situation is complicated*. / 故事情节～。*The story is very complicated*. / ～的心情 *mixed feelings*
【复照】[外交] a note in reply
【复诊】further consultation (with a doctor); subsequent visit
【复职】resume one's post; be reinstated
【复制】duplicate; reproduce; make a copy of: ～模型 *reconstructed model* ◇ ～片 duplicated film; copy of a film; ～品 replica; reproduction
【复种】[农] multiple cropping ◇ ～面积 multiple cropping area; ～指数 multiple crop index

副 Ⅰ **形** ❶ deputy; assistant; vice-: ～主席 *vice-chairman* / ～总理 *vice-premier* / ～部长 *vice-minister* / ～主任 *deputy director* / ～经理 *deputy manager* / ～主编 *associate editor in chief* / ～司令员 *assistant commanding officer (or commandant)* / (飞机)～驾驶员 *copilot* ❷ auxiliary; subsidiary; secondary: ～泵 *auxiliary pump* Ⅱ **名** assistant post; a person who takes an assistant post: 大副 Ⅲ **动** correspond to; fit: 名不副实 Ⅳ **量** ❶ for a set of sth.: 一～手套 *a pair of gloves* ❷ for facial expression: 一～笑脸 *a smiling face* / 装出一～庄严的面孔 *put on solemn looks; assume a solemn face*
【副本】duplicate; transcript; copy
【副标题】subheading; subtitle
【副产品】(又作'副产物') by-product
【副赤道带】[气] subequatorial belt
【副词】❶ [语] adverbial word, any of a class of words that are used mainly to modify a verb or an adjective ❷ [语] adverb
【副歌】[音] refrain
【副官】adjutant; aide-de-camp
【副虹】[气] secondary bow
【副交感神经】[生理] parasympathetic nerve
【副教授】associate professor
【副井】[矿] auxiliary shaft
【副刊】supplement: 文学～ *literary supplement*
【副品】substandard goods
【副热带】another name for 亚热带
【副伤寒】[医] paratyphoid (fever)
【副神经】[生理] accessory nerve
【副食】non-staple food ◇ ～品 non-staple food (or foodstuffs)
【副食商店】grocer's; grocery
【副手】assistant
【副署】countersign
【副研】(〈略〉全称为'副研究员') associate professor
【副业】sideline; side occupation: ～生产 *sideline (or supplementary, subsidiary) production* / 家庭～ *household sideline production*
【副翼】[航空] aileron
【副油箱】[航空] ❶ auxiliary tank ❷ drop tank
【副职】the position of a deputy to the chief of an office, department, etc.
【副轴】[机] countershaft; layshaft
【副作用】❶ side effect; by-effect: 麻醉药物的～ *side effects from the use of anaesthetics* / 这种新药已经发现有～。*The new drug was found to have harmful side effects*. ❷ [机] secondary action

富 Ⅰ **形** ❶ rich; wealthy; abundant: 他不是很～的。*He is not very rich*. / ～日子当穷日子过。*Be thrifty even in days of abundance*. ❷ be rich in: ～于养分 *be rich in nutrition* / ～于自我批评精神 *be imbued with the spirit of self-criticism* / ～于创造性 *be highly creative* Ⅱ **名** resource; property: 财富
【富贵】riches and honour; wealth and rank: ～人家 *a rich and powerful family*
【富贵病】a rich man's disease (i.e. one which calls for a long period of rest and an expensive diet)
【富国】❶ rich nation ❷ make a nation rich and powerful ◇ ～强兵 enrich the nation and strengthen the military; make one's country rich and build up its military might; ～利民 enrich the nation and bring benefits to the people
【富豪】rich and powerful people
【富矿】[矿] rich ore; high-grade ore ◇ ～体 ore shoot
【富丽堂皇】beautiful and imposing; in majestic splendour; sumptuous: ～的建筑 *magnificent buildings*
【富民】make the people rich and prosperous
【富民政策】policy of enriching people; policy to enrich people
【富农】rich peasant
【富强】(of a country) prosperous and strong: 使祖国更加繁荣～ *make our country more prosperous and powerful*
【富饶】richly endowed; fertile; abundant: 美丽～的国家 *a beautiful and richly endowed country* / ～的土地 *fertile land*

【富士山】Fujiyama
【富庶】rich and populous
【富翁】man of wealth; moneybags
【富有】❶ rich; wealthy: 他家非常～。*His family is very rich.* ❷ be rich in; be full of: ～经验 *be rich in experience; be very experienced*
【富裕】prosperous; well-to-do; well-off: 日子过得挺～ *lead a well-to-do life*
【富余】have more than needed; have enough and to spare: 我们还～两张票。*We have two tickets to spare.* / 你有～的钱吗? *Have you any money to spare?* / 粮食有～。*There is a surplus of grain.*
【富源】natural resources
【富足】plentiful; abundant; rich

赋 Ⅰ 动 ❶〈书〉bestow; grant ❷ compose (verses): ～诗 *compose verses* / ～诗一首 *compose a poem* Ⅱ 名 ❶〈旧〉land tax ❷ an intricate literary form combining elements of poetry and prose
【赋格曲】[音] fugue
【赋税】taxes ◇ ～减免 tax remission
【赋闲】be out of office; be out of employment
【赋形剂】[药] excipient
【赋性】inborn nature: ～刚强 *be strong by nature; be of an unyielding nature*
【赋役】taxes and corvée
【赋有】be endowed with (qualities or characteristics): 劳动人民～忠厚质朴的性格。*Working people are endowed with an honest, kindly nature.*
【赋予】entrust (an important task) to sb.

傅 Ⅰ 名 teacher; instructor: 师傅 Ⅱ 动 ❶〈古〉lay on; apply: ～彩 *lay on colours* / ～粉 *put powder on; powder (the face, etc.)* ❷ teach; instruct
【傅科摆】Foucault pendulum

腹 名 ❶ belly (of the body); abdomen; stomach ❷ belly (of a bottle, etc.): 一个～大颈细的瓶子 *a narrow-necked, big-bellied bottle*
【腹背受敌】be attacked front and rear
【腹地】hinterland
【腹诽】(又作'腹非')〈书〉unspoken criticism
【腹稿】a draft worked out in one's mind: 打～ *work out a draft in one's mind*
【腹股沟】[生理] groin
【腹膜】[生理] peritoneum ◇ ～炎 [医] peritonitis
【腹鳍】[动] ventral fin
【腹腔】[生理] abdominal cavity ◇ ～镜 [医] peritoneoscope
【腹水】[医] ascites: 抽～ *tap the abdomen*
【腹痛】abdominal pain
【腹泻】diarrhoea
【腹胀】abdominal distension
【腹足】[动] abdominal leg; proleg
【腹足类】[动] gastropod

缚 动 tie up; bind fast: 手脚都被～住 *have one's hands and feet tied up*

鲋 名 crucian carp ——另见〖涸辙之鲋〗

蝮 (构词成分)见下
【蝮蛇】Pallas pit viper

覆 动 ❶〈书〉cover: 种子播下后～土大约要十厘米厚。*The sown seeds shall be covered with about 10cm of soil.* ❷〈书〉overturn; upset: ～舟 *capsized boat*
【覆巢无完卵】when the nest is overturned no egg stays unbroken—when disaster befalls a family, etc., no member can escape unscathed
【覆盖】❶ cover: 积雪～着地面。*The ground is covered with snow.* ❷ plant cover; vegetation: ～率 *rate of coverage* ❸ [计] overwrite ◇ ～层 [地质] overburden
【覆灭】destruction; complete collapse
【覆没】❶〈书〉(of a ship) capsize and sink ❷ (of an army) be overwhelmed; be annihilated
【覆盆之冤】a wrong that can never be righted; irremediable wrong
【覆盆子】[中] Korean raspberry
【覆水难收】spilt water can't be gathered up—what is done can't be undone
【覆亡】fall (of an empire, nation, etc.)
【覆辙】the track of an overturned cart

馥 名〈书〉fragrance
【馥郁】〈书〉strongly fragrant; sweet-scented; sweet-smelling: ～的花香 *the sweet scent of flowers*

G

gā

夹 （构词成分）见下 ——另见 jiā；jiá

【夹肢窝】armpit

旮 （构词成分）见下

【旮旯儿】〈方〉❶ nook；corner：墙～ *a corner formed by two walls*；*corner* ❷ out-of-the-way place：山～ *a mountain recess*

伽 （构词成分）见下 ——另见 jiā；qié

【伽马射线】［物］gamma ray

咖 （构词成分）见下 ——另见 kā

【咖喱】curry：～牛肉 *beef curry* / ～粉 *curry powder*

嘎 象 a loud，high-pitched sound：汽车～的一声刹住了。*The car screeched to a halt*.

【嘎巴】❶ a cracking or snapping sound：手杖～一声断成两截了。*Crack! The stick broke in two*. ❷〈方〉form into a crust；crust：瞧，浆糊都～在你袖子上了。*Look，the paste has crusted on your sleeve*. ❸ crust：粥～儿 *porridge crust*

【嘎嘎】the quacking sound made by a duck；quack

【嘎吱】(usu. reduplicated) the creaking sound of objects that are under great stress：行李压得扁担～～直响。*The shoulder pole creaked under the weight of the luggage*.

gá

钆 名［化］gadolinium (Gd)

gāi

该 Ⅰ 动 ❶ ought to be；should be：按岁数排，～老潘排第一。*By seniority，first place goes to Lao Pan*. ❷ be sb.'s turn，duty，or lot：这回～我了吧？*It's my turn now，isn't it*？/ 下一个～谁发言？*Who's the next speaker*？❸ (used alone) deserve the punishment；serve sb. right：～！谁叫他不守纪律。*It serves him right；he shouldn't have broken the rules*. ❹ must；should；ought to：我～走了。*I must be off now*. / 我不～来。*I shouldn't have come*. ❺ (no negative form；not to be used alone in answering a question) will probably；can be reasonably or naturally expected to：他是昨天动的身，今天～到了。*He started out yesterday，so he ought to get here today*. ❻ owe (money or debt)：这钱是～你的。*I owe you this money*. Ⅱ 副 (used in exclamatory sentences)：等这些树木都长大成林，风景～(有)多美！*When these trees grow into a forest，how beautiful the scenery will be*！Ⅲ 代〈书〉this；that；the said；the above-mentioned：～厂 *this (or the said) factory* / ～校 *that (or the above-mentioned) school* / ～项工作 *the job (or work) in question*

【该当】❶ deserve：～何罪？*What punishment do you think you deserve*？❷ should：集体的事，我们～尽力。*It's for the collective and we should do our best*.

【该死】〈口〉(used to show one's abomination or anger)：～的天气！*What wretched weather*！/ ～！我又忘了带钥匙了。*Oh，no！I've forgotten my key again*.

【该账】be in debt：他在银行还该一笔账呢。*He still owes the bank a sum*. / ～该多了，就不好还了。*If you run up your bills，you'll have difficulty paying them*.

赅 Ⅰ 形〈书〉complete；full：言简意赅 Ⅱ 动 include in；embrace

gǎi

改 动 ❶ change；transform：几年没来，这儿完全～样了。*I've been away for only a few years，but the place has completely changed*. / ～洼地为稻田 *transform lowlands into paddy fields* ❷ alter；revise：他写完这篇文章以后，又～了～。*After he finished writing the essay he made a few more changes in it*. ❸ correct；rectify；put right：～作业 *correct students' homework or papers* / 有错误一定要～。*Any mistakes you've made must be corrected*. ❹ (followed by a verb) switch over to (doing sth. else)：～用良种 *begin to use improved varieties* / 他现在～踢左后卫。*He's playing left-back now*.

【改版】［刷］correcting

【改编】❶ adapt；rearrange；revise：这支歌已～成小提琴曲。*The music of the song has been rearranged (or adapted) for the violin*. / 根据这本小

说～的剧本 *a stage version of the novel* ❷ reorganize; redesignate: 把七个师～为六个师 *reorganize seven divisions into six*

【改变】change; alter; transform: ～主意 *change one's mind* / 人们的精神面貌～了。*People's spiritual complexion has changed.*

【改朝换代】change of dynasty or regime; dynastic changes

【改道】❶ change one's route: 他们决定～先去延安。*They decided to change their route and go to Yan'an first.* ❷ (of a river) change its course: 历史上,黄河曾多次～。*The Huanghe River has changed its course many times over the centuries.*

【改掉】give up; drop: 睡懒觉的坏习惯我已经～了。*I've given up the bad habit of getting up late.*

【改订】reformulate; rewrite: ～规章制度 *draw up new rules and regulations*

【改动】change; alter; modify: 这篇文章我只～了一些词句。*I just polished a few sentences in this essay.*

【改恶从善】abandon evil and do good; turn over a new leaf; mend one's ways

【改革】reform: ～经济管理体制 *reform the economic management system* / 工具～ *improvement of tools* ◇ ～进程 the course of reform; ～开放 reform and open; ～学制 reform educational (school) system

【改观】change the appearance (or face) of: 第二次世界大战后,世界的面貌大大～了。*The face of the world has changed greatly since the Second World War.*

【改过】mend one's ways; correct one's mistakes: 勇于～ *have the courage to correct one's mistakes*

【改过自新】correct one's errors and make a fresh start; mend one's ways; turn over a new leaf

【改行】change one's profession (or occupation, trade): 他原先在学校教书,后来～当记者。*He started off as a schoolteacher, but later left the professions and became a journalist.*

【改换】change over to; change: ～名称 *rename* / 这句话不好懂,最好～一个说法。*This sentence is difficult to understand. You'd better try to put it another way.*

【改悔】repent: 毫无～之意 *show not the least sign of repentance; be absolutely unrepentant*

【改嫁】(of a woman) remarry: 丈夫死了以后,她～了。*She got remarried after her husband's death.*

【改建】reconstruct; rebuild: 把仓库～为厂房 *remodel a storehouse for use as a workshop* ◇ ～扩建工程 projects for renovation and expansion

【改进】improve; make better: ～工作作风 *improve one's work style* / 服务态度有很大的～。*The service has improved a lot.*

【改口】withdraw or modify one's previous remark; correct oneself: 他发现自己说错了,连忙～。*He corrected himself as soon as he realized he'd made a mistake.* / 他原来是那么说的,现在～了。*That's what he said at first, but he's changed it now.*

【改良】❶ improve; ameliorate: ～土壤 *improve (or ameliorate) the soil* / ～家畜品种 *improve the breed of domestic animals* ❷ reform

【改良主义】reformism

【改判】[法] change the original sentence; commute; amend a judgment: 由死刑～无期徒刑 *commute the death sentence to life imprisonment*

【改期】change the date (usu. to a later date); postpone: 会议～举行。*The meeting has been put off.* / 由于下大雨,足球赛不得不～。*The soccer match had to be postponed because of heavy rain.*

【改任】change to another post: 他从上月起～车间主任。*He has been at his new post as workshop superintendent since last month.*

【改日】同〖改天〗

【改善】improve; ameliorate: 两国关系有所～。*The relations between the two countries have shown some improvement.* ◇ ～经营管理 improve management and administration

【改天换地】transform heaven and earth; change the world: 以～的气概 *in a spirit of changing heaven and earth*

【改头换面】change the appearance but not the essence; dish up the same old stuff in a new form: 他把别人著作中的话～算作自己的意见。*He took pieces of another author's works, changed them around a little, and then tried to pass them off as his own ideas.*

【改弦更张】adopt new ways; make a fresh start

【改弦易辙】change one's course; strike out on a new path

【改邪归正】give up vice and return to virtue; turn over a new leaf

【改写】rewrite; adapt: 经过～,文章生动多了。*Rewriting has livened up the article.* / 这篇课文是根据《中国文学》上的一个故事～的。*This text is adapted from a story in Chinese Literature.*

【改选】reelect: 班委会每年～一次。*A new class committee is elected every year.*

【改元】change the designation of an imperial reign; change the title of a reign

【改造】transform; reform; remould; remake: ～自然 *remake nature* / 把罪犯～成新人 *reform a criminal, making a new man out of him*

【改正】correct; amend; put right: ～错误 *correct one's mistakes* ◇ ～液 correction fluid

【改装】❶ change one's costume or dress ❷ repackage; repack ❸ reequip; refit: ～一辆卡车 *refit a truck*

【改锥】screwdriver

【改组】reorganize; reshuffle: ～管理机构 *reorganize the management* / ～内阁 *reshuffle the cabinet* / ～现有企业 revamping existing enterprises

gài

丐 Ⅰ 动 〈书〉beg Ⅱ 名 beggar

芥（构词成分）见下 ——另见 jiè

【芥菜】［植］leaf mustard ——另见 jiècài

【芥蓝】［植］cabbage mustard

钙［化］calcium（Ca）

【钙化】［医］calcify

【钙镁磷肥】calcium magnesium phosphate

盖 Ⅰ名 ❶ lid；cover：茶壶～ *teapot lid* / 轴承～ *bearing cap*（*or cover*）❷ shell（of a tortoise，crab，etc.）❸ canopy：华盖 Ⅱ动 ❶put a cover on；cover：盖儿～得不紧。*The lid isn't on tight*. / 用塑料薄膜～住秧苗 *cover the seedlings with plastic sheeting* / 箱子没～严。*The lid of the box hasn't been put on right*. or *The box isn't closed properly*. ❷ affix（a seal）：盖戳 ❸ surpass；top：大桥通车了，欢庆的锣鼓声～过了江上的浪涛声。*When the bridge was opened to traffic，the joyful sounds of gongs and drums drowned the roar of the river*. ❹build：～新房 *build new houses* / 这栋楼～得真漂亮。*This building is really nice-looking*. Ⅲ副〈书〉approximately；about；around：与会者～一千人。*About a thousand people attended the meeting*.

【盖菜】leaf mustard（a vegetable）

【盖戳】〈口〉affix one's seal；put a stamp on

【盖棺论定】final judgment can be passed on a person only when the lid is on his coffin；no final verdict can be pronounced on a man until after his death

【盖帽儿】❶block a shot（in basketball）❷〈口〉great；bad；totally awesome；fantastic；marvellous

【盖然性】［逻］probability

【盖世】〈书〉unparalleled；matchless；peerless：～无双 *unparalleled anywhere on earth*；*matchless throughout the world*；*peerless*；*unrivalled*

【盖世太保】Gestapo

【盖世英雄】a peerless（or matchless）hero

【盖章】affix one's seal；seal；stamp：由本人签字～ *to be signed and sealed by the recipient or applicant* / 这份合同他已盖过章了。*He has affixed his seal to the contract*.

【盖盅儿】（又作'盖杯'）teacup with a lid

【盖子】❶ lid；cover；cap；top：水壶～ *the lid of a kettle* / 瓶～ *bottle top* ❷ shell（of a tortoise，etc.）——另见〖捂盖子〗

概 Ⅰ名 ❶ general idea；broad outline：梗概❷ the manner of carrying oneself；deportment：气概 Ⅱ副 ❶generally；approximately：～而论之 *generally speaking* ❷ without exception；categorically：～不追究 *no action will be taken*（*against sb. for his past offences*）/ 货物售出，～不退换。*Goods sold are not returnable*.

【概况】general situation；survey：我把这里的～介绍一下。*I'll give a brief account of how things are in this place*. /《非洲～》*A Survey of Africa*

【概括】❶ summarize；generalize；epitomize：这部小说的优点～起来有以下几方面。*The good points of the novel may be summarized as follows*. / ～起来说 *to sum up* / 高度的艺术～ *a highly artistic condensation* ❷ brief and to the point：～地说 *to put it briefly* / 请把你的看法～地讲一讲。*Please give your views in broad outline*.

【概括性】generality：最后这段话～很强。*The last paragraph is a succinct summary*.

【概率】［数］probability ◇ ～论 probability；～预算 probabilistic budget

【概略】outline；summary：这只是故事的～。*This is only an outline of the story*.

【概论】（usu. used in book titles）outline；introduction：《地质学～》*An Introduction to Geology*

【概貌】general picture：反映人民生活的～ *give a general picture of the life of the people*

【概莫能外】admit of no exception whatsoever：古今中外，～。*There is no exception to this in modern times or ancient，in China or abroad*.

【概念】concept；conception；notion；idea：基本～ *fundamental concept*；*basic concept* / 玩弄～游戏 *juggle with concepts* / 我对汉语语法只有一点模糊的～。*I have only a hazy idea about Chinese grammar*. ◇ ～艺术 conceptual art

【概念化】deal in generalities；write or speak in abstract terms：公式化、～的作品 *literary works which tend to formularize and generalize*

【概述】give a brief account of（an event，etc.）

【概数】approximate number；round number

【概算】［经］budgetary estimate

【概要】（usu. used in book titles）essentials；outline：《汉语语法～》*Essentials of Chinese Grammar* /《汉语方言～》*Outline of Chinese Dialects*

gān

干 Ⅰ动 ❶〈书〉offend：干犯 ❷ have to do with；be concerned with；be implicated in：与你何～? *What has this to do with you*? / 这事与我无～。*It has nothing to do with me*. or *It's none of my business*. Ⅱ形 ❶ dry：这天气洗衣服～得慢。*The washing dries slowly in this weather*. / 池塘快～了。*The pond is drying up*. / 口～ *feel thirsty* / 油漆未～。*Wet paint*. ❷ empty；hollow；dry：钱都花～了。*All the money has been spent*. / ～号 *cry aloud but shed no tears*；*affected wailing* ❸ taken into nominal kinship：干亲 Ⅲ名 dried food：萝卜～儿 *dried radish* / 牛肉～儿 *dried beef*；*jerked beef* Ⅳ副 in vain；to no purpose；for nothing：他们上午不来，咱们别～等了。*They're not coming this morning*. *Let's not waste time waiting for them*. ——另见 gàn

【干巴巴】dull and dry；insipid；dryasdust；dull as ditchwater：～的土地 *parched land* / 文章写得～的。*The article is dull*. / 这个人～的，毫无意思。*The man is so insipid—not the slightest bit interesting*.

【干板】[摄] dry plate
【干杯】drink a toast：为我们的合作成功干一杯！*Let's drink a toast to the success of our cooperative effort!*
【干贝】dried scallop (adductor)
【干瘪】❶ dry：墙上挂着的丝瓜都已经给风吹～了。*The towel gourds hanging on the wall have been dried out by the wind.* ❷ shrivelled；wizened：～老太婆 *a wizened old woman* ❸ (of writing) dull；drab；dryasdust
【干冰】[化] dry ice
【干菜】dried vegetable
【干草】hay：～垛 *haystack*
【干柴烈火】dry wood near a fierce fire—❶ a man and a woman burning with passion ❷ an explosive situation
【干醋】jealousy about something that is none of one's business；vicarious jealousy：吃～ *experience uncalled-for (or vicarious) jealousy*
【干脆】❶ clear-cut；straightforward：他回答得很～。*His answer was simple and straightforward.* or *He gave a clear-cut reply.* ❷ simply；just；altogether：你～说"行"还是"不行"。*Just say yes or no.* / 她～不承认有这回事。*She simply denied that such a thing had ever happened.*
【干打雷,不下雨】all thunder but no rain—much noise but no action
【干瞪眼】〈口〉stand by anxiously, unable to help；look on in despair：他气得说不出话来，只会～。*He was speechless with anger, and could only stand by helplessly.*
【干电池】dry cell：～组 *dry battery*
【干爹】(nominally) adoptive father；godfather
【干儿子】(nominally) adopted son
【干犯】〈书〉offend；encroach upon：～法纪 *break the law and violate discipline*
【干饭】cooked rice
【干纺】dry spinning：～纱 *dry-spun yarn*
【干戈】weapons of war—war：动～ *take up arms；go to war*
【干果】❶ dry fruit (e. g. nuts) ❷ dried fruit
【干旱】(of weather or soil) arid；dry
【干涸】dry up；run dry：河道～。*The river dried up.*
【干货】dried food and nuts (as merchandise)
【干季】dry season
【干结】dry and hard：大便～ *constipated*
【干净】❶ clean；neat and tidy：把院子扫～ *sweep the yard clean* / 他穿得干干净净的。*His clothes are neat and tidy.* ❷ complete；total：忘得干干净净 *have completely forgotten；clean forgot*
【干净利落】neat and tidy；neat；efficient：他办事～。*He's very efficient.* / 这一仗打得～。*The battle was neatly won.*
【干咳】have a dry cough
【干枯】dried-up；withered；shrivelled；wizened：～的树木 *withered trees* / ～的皮肤 *wizened skin* / 小河～了。*The stream has dried up.*
【干酪】cheese
【干酪素】同〖酪素〗
【干冷】dry and cold (weather)
【干粮】solid food (prepared for a journey)；field rations；rations for a journey：明天郊游，请自带～。*Bring your own food on tomorrow's outing.* / ～袋 *haversack；ration bag*
【干裂】crack because of dryness；be dry and cracked：嘴唇～ *parched lips*
【干馏】[化] dry distillation
【干妈】(nominally) adoptive mother；godmother
【干女儿】(nominally) adopted daughter
【干呕】[医] retch
【干亲】nominal kinship：认～ *enter into an adoptive relationship*
【干扰】❶ disturb；interfere；obstruct：把收音机开小点儿，别～人家。*Turn down the radio, or you'll disturb people.* ❷ [无] interference；jam：～台 *jamming station*
【干鞣法】leather dry tannage
【干涉】❶ interfere；intervene；meddle：外来～ *external interference* / 武装～ *armed intervention* / 互不～内政 *noninterference in each other's internal affairs* ❷ relation：二者了无～。*There is no relation whatsoever between the two.* ❸ [物] interference：相长(相消)～ *constructive (destructive) interference*
【干涉仪】interferometer
【干湿表】[气] psychrometer
【干瘦】skinny and wizened；bony
【干洗】dry-clean
【干系】responsibility；implication：逃脱不了～ *cannot shirk the responsibility* / 他同这桩案子有～。*He is implicated in the case.*
【干鲜果品】composite term for dried and fresh fruit
【干笑】laugh hollowly；force a smile
【干薪】salary drawn for a sinecure：领～ *hold a sinecure*
【干选】[矿] dry separation
【干预】(又作'干与') intervene；interpose；meddle：这是你们内部的事情，我们不便～。*This is your internal affair；it is not for us to interfere.*
【干燥】❶ dry；arid：气候～ *arid climate* / 大便～ *constipated；costive* ❷ dull；uninteresting：～无味 *dryasdust；dull* ◇ ～剂 drier；drying agent；desiccating agent；～器 [化] desiccator
【干着急】be anxious but unable to do anything：他什么事也不会干，只会～！*He could do nothing but worry.* / 这件事她～没办法。*She had to stand by helplessly and couldn't do anything about it.*
【干支】the Heavenly Stems (天干) and Earthly Branches (地支) (two sets of signs, with one being taken from each set to form 60 pairs, designating years, formerly also months and days)

甘 Ⅰ 形 sweet；pleasant：～泉 *sweet spring water* Ⅱ 副 willingly；of one's own accord：～当群众的小学生 *be a willing pupil of the masses*

【甘拜下风】candidly acknowledge one's inferiority (in knowledge, ability, etc.); bow to sb.'s superiority
【甘草】[中] licorice root
【甘汞】[化] calomel; mercurous chloride: ～电池 *calomel cell*
【甘结】(in former times) a written pledge given to the government authorities
【甘居中游】be resigned to mediocrity; be content to stay mediocre
【甘苦】❶ sweetness and bitterness; joys and sorrows; weal and woe: 同～ *share the joys and sorrows* ❷ hardships and difficulties experienced in work: 没有搞过这种工作,就不知道其中的～。*You don't know how difficult the job is, unless you have done it yourself.*
【甘蓝】[植] wild cabbage
【甘霖】a good rain after a long drought; timely rainfall
【甘露】❶ sweet dew ❷ [药] manna
【甘美】sweet and refreshing: 泉水～。*The spring water is sweet and refreshing.*
【甘薯】sweet potato ◇ ～黑斑病 sweet potato black rot; ～软腐病 sweet potato soft rot
【甘甜】sweet: ～可口 *sweet and delicious*
【甘心】❶ do sth. willingly; be ready and willing ❷ be reconciled to; resign oneself to; be content with: 敌人对于他们的失败是不会～的。*The enemy will not resign themselves to defeat.*
【甘心情愿】willingly and gladly
【甘休】be willing to give up: 不试验成功,决不～。*We won't give up until the experiment succeeds.*
【甘油】[化] glycerine
【甘油炸药】dynamite
【甘于】be willing to; be ready to; be happy to: ～牺牲个人利益 *be ready to sacrifice one's personal interests*
【甘愿】do sth. willingly; be ready and willing: 谁也没有强迫他,是他～这么做的。*Nobody forced him to do it; he did it of his own free will.*
【甘蔗】sugarcane: ～渣 *bagasse* / ～渣浆厂 *bagasse-pulp mill* ◇ ～板[建] cane fibre board
【甘之如饴】enjoy sth. bitter as if it were malt sugar—gladly endure hardship

杆 名 pole; staff: 旗杆——另见 gǎn
【杆子】pole: 电线～ *wire pole; telephone pole*

肝 名 liver
【肝癌】cancer of the liver
【肝肠寸断】be heartbroken; be deeply grieved
【肝胆】❶ open-heartedness; sincerity ❷ heroic spirit; courage
【肝胆过人】far surpass others in daring
【肝胆相照】(of friends) treat each other with all sincerity; be devoted to each other heart and soul
【肝功能】liver function: ～试验 *liver function test* / ～正常。*The liver is functioning normally.*
【肝火】irascibility: ～旺 *hot-tempered; irascible*
【肝脑涂地】spill one's liver and brains on the ground—lay down one's life (in fighting for one's sovereign)
【肝气】❶ [中] diseases with such symptoms as costal pain, vomiting, diarrhoea, etc. ❷ irritability
【肝素】[药] heparin
【肝泰乐】[药] glucurolactone; glucurone
【肝吸虫】liver fluke
【肝炎】hepatitis
【肝硬变】(又作'肝硬化') cirrhosis (of the liver)
【肝脏】liver
【肝蛭】another name for 肝吸虫
【肝肿大】hepatomegaly

泔 名 swill; slops; hogwash
【泔水】swill; slops; hogwash

矸 (构词成分)见下
【矸石】waste (rock)
【矸子】common name for 矸石

坩 (构词成分)见下
【坩埚】[化] crucible: 石墨～ *graphite (or carbon) crucible*
【坩埚炉】[冶] crucible furnace

柑 名 mandarin orange
【柑橘】❶ oranges and tangerines ❷ citrus ◇ ～酱 marmalade
【柑子】mandarin orange

竿 名 pole; rod: 钓～ *fishing rod*
【竿子】bamboo pole

尴 (构词成分)见下
【尴尬】❶ (of the situation one is in) awkward; hard to deal with: 处境～ *in an awkward position; in a dilemma* / 他觉得去也不好,不去也不好,实在～。*He felt it would be bad to go and bad not to go. He was in a real quandary.* ❷ 〈方〉 embarrassed: 样子十分～ *look very much embarrassed*

gǎn

杆 Ⅰ 名 the shaft or arm of sth.: 钢笔～儿 *penholder* / 枪～ *the barrel of a rifle* Ⅱ 量 (for a long and thin cylindrical object): 一～秤 *a steelyard* / 一～枪 *a rifle* / 一～红旗 *a red flag* ——另见 gān
【杆秤】steelyard
【杆菌】bacillus: ～载体 *bacillus carrier*

秆 名 stalk: 高粱～ *sorghum stalk* / 麻～ *hemp stalk*

赶 Ⅰ 动 ❶ catch up with; overtake: ～先进 *catch up with the advanced* / 落在后面的人～上

来了。*Those who lagged behind have caught up.* ❷ try to catch; make a dash for; rush for: ～头班车 *catch the first bus* / 火车七点三十分开,我们～得及吗? *The train leaves at 7:30. Can we make it?* ❸ hurry (or rush) through: ～任务 *rush through one's job* ❹ drive: ～大车 *drive a cart* / 把羊～到山上去放。*Herd the sheep up the hill to graze.* ❺ drive away; expel: ～苍蝇 *whisk the flies off*; *brush away a fly* ❻ happen to; find oneself in (a situation); avail oneself of (an opportunity): ～上一场雨 *run into a rain* Ⅱ **介** till: 咱俩的婚事～年下再办吧。*Let's put off our wedding till the Spring Festival.* / ～晌午我就走。*I'll be leaving at noon.* / 这事～以后再谈吧。*Let's discuss the matter later.*

【赶不及】there's not enough time (to do sth.); it's too late (to do sth.): 火车七点开,动身晚了就～了。*The train leaves at seven, and we won't catch it if we start off too late.*

【赶不上】❶ be unable to catch up with: 他已经走远了,～了。*He's pretty far away by now and we won't be able to catch up with him.* ❷ there's not enough time (to do sth.); it's too late (to do sth.): 离开车只有十分钟,恐怕～了。*The train is going to leave in ten minutes. I'm afraid we'll be too late.*

【赶场】❶〈方〉go to the village fair or market ❷ (of a performer) hurry from one performance to a second one in another place

【赶超】catch up with and surpass: ～世界先进水平 *catch up with and surpass the advanced world level*

【赶得及】there is still time; be able to do sth. in time; be able to make it: 马上就动身还～。*There's still time if we start at once.*

【赶得上】❶ be able to catch up: 你先走吧,我～你的。*You go first. I'll be able to catch up with you.* ❷ there is still time; be able to do sth. in time; be able to make it: 他们还没有走,你现在去还～和他们告别。*They haven't left yet. If you go there right away, you'll be just in time to say good-bye to them.*

【赶集】go to market; go to a fair

【赶紧】hastily; without losing time: ～刹车 *quickly put on the brakes* / ～解释 *hasten to explain*

【赶尽杀绝】kill all; wipe out the whole lot; spare none; be ruthless

【赶考】take the imperial examinations: 进京～ *go to the capital to sit for the imperial examinations*

【赶快】at once; quickly: ～跟我走。*Come along with me at once.* / ～把这块地收完。*Let's finish harvesting this plot quickly.* / ～! *Be quick!* or *Hurry up!*

【赶浪头】follow the trend

【赶路】hurry on with one's journey: 快休息吧,明天一早还要～呢。*Let's go to bed right away. We must push on with our journey early tomorrow morning.* / 赶了一天路,累了吧? *Aren't you tired after such a hard day's journey?*

【赶忙】hurriedly; hastily: 他从自行车上摔下来,我～过去把他扶了起来。*He fell off his bicycle and I hurried over to help him up.* / 他～道歉。*He hastened to apologize.*

【赶前不赶后】it's better to hurry at the beginning than to rush at the last moment

【赶巧】happen to; it so happened that: 上午我去找他,～他不在家。*I went to see him this morning, but he happened to be away.*

【赶上】❶ overtake; catch up with; keep pace with: ～先进单位 *catch up with the advanced units* / ～时代的发展 *keep abreast of the times* ❷ run into (a situation); be in time for: 我到北京那天正～过国庆。*It happened to be National Day when I arrived in Beijing.*

【赶时髦】follow the fashion; try to be in style

【赶鸭子上架】drive a duck onto a perch—try to make sb. do sth. entirely beyond him: 我不会唱,你偏叫我唱,这不是～吗? *I can't sing. But if you insist on my singing, it'll be like driving a duck onto a perch.*

敢 Ⅰ **形** bold; courageous; daring: 勇敢 Ⅱ **动** ❶ be brave enough; dare: ～想、～说、～干 *dare to think, dare to speak and dare to act* / 过去连想都不～想的事,现在变成了现实。*What one couldn't even imagine in the past has now become reality.* ❷ have the confidence to; be certain; be sure: 我～说他一定乐于接受这个任务。*I'm confident he will be willing to undertake the task.* / 我不～说他究竟哪一天来。*I'm not sure just what day he will come.* ❸〈书〉〈套〉make bold; venture: ～问 *I venture to ask*; *may I ask*

【敢怒而不敢言】be forced to keep one's resentment to oneself; choke with silent fury

【敢死队】dare-to-die corps; suicide squad

【敢于】dare to; be bold in; have the courage to: ～斗争,～胜利 *dare to struggle and dare to win*

【敢作敢当】have the courage to take the blame for what one does

【敢作敢为】bold and decisive in action

感 Ⅰ **动** ❶ feel; sense: 身体略～不适 *not feel very well*; *be under the weather*; *be out of sorts* ❷ move; touch; affect: 深有所～ *be deeply moved*; *be greatly touched* ❸ be grateful; be obliged: 请早日寄下为～。*I should be grateful if you would send it to me at an early date.* ❹［中］be affected: 外感 ❺［摄］sensitize: 感光 Ⅱ **名** sense; feeling: 民族自豪～ *a sense of national pride* / 读后～ *reaction to (or impressions of) a book or an article* / 给人以一种新鲜～ *engender a feeling of freshness*

【感触】thoughts and feelings; feeling: 深有～地说 *say with deep feeling* / 故乡的巨大变化引起了我很多～。*Great changes in my home village give me much food for thought.*

【感到】feel; sense: ～疲倦 *feel tired* / ～幸福 *feel*

happy / 这件事结局没想到是这样，我真～遗憾。*I never thought it would turn out this way. I do regret it.* / 我胸部～疼痛。*I have a pain in my chest.* / 他～自己错了。*He sensed that he himself was wrong.*

【感动】move; touch: ～得流下眼泪 *be moved to tears* / 深为他的精神所～。*be deeply touched by his spirit* / 他的话深深地～了在座的人。*What he said deeply moved everyone present.*

【感恩】feel grateful; be thankful: ～不尽 *be extremely grateful*

【感恩戴德】be deeply grateful; be overwhelmed with gratitude

【感恩节】Thanksgiving Day

【感恩图报】be grateful to sb. and seek ways to return his kindness

【感奋】be moved and inspired; be fired with enthusiasm

【感官】〈略〉见〖感觉器官〗

【感光】［摄］sensitize: ～度 (*light*) *sensitivity* / ～计 *sensitometer* / ～纸 *sensitive paper* ◇ ～测定 sensitometry

【感荷】be thankful for; feel gratitude for

【感化】help (a misguided or erring person) to change by persuasion, setting an example, etc.

【感怀】❶ recall with emotion: ～往事 *recall past events with deep feeling* ❷ reflections; thoughts; recollections: 新春～ *thoughts on the Spring Festival*

【感激】feel grateful; be thankful; feel indebted: 不胜～ *be deeply grateful*; *feel very much indebted* / 很～你给我的帮助。*I'm very grateful for your help.*

【感激涕零】shed grateful tears; be moved to tears of gratitude

【感觉】❶ sense perception; sensation; feeling: 这只是我个人的～。*That's only my personal feeling.* / 他给人以亲切的～。*He gives you the impression that he's a very kind man.* ❷ feel; perceive; become aware of: 一场秋雨过后就～有点冷了。*I felt a little bit cold after the autumn rain.* ◇ ～论［哲］sensualism; ～器官 sense (or sensory) organ; ～神经 sensory nerve; ～艺术品 feelie; ～阈限［心理］sense limen; sense threshold

【感慨】sigh with emotion: 提起过去那段经历，他无限～。*When he spoke of those hard times, he sighed a great sorrow.* ◇ ～万端 all sorts of feelings well up in one's mind; ～系之 sigh with deep feeling

【感抗】inductive reactance

【感冒】❶common cold: 患～ *catch cold*; *have a cold* ❷ be interested in; enthusiastic about: 郭嫂对女儿每几个月就换男朋友带回家来的做法不～。*Aunt Guo was not happy about her daughter's practice of bringing a new boyfriend home every few months.*

【感念】remember with gratitude; recall with deep emotion: ～不忘 *always recall sb. with deep emotion*

【感情】❶ emotion; feeling; sentiment: 动～ *be carried away by one's emotions*; *get worked up* / 伤～ *hurt sb.'s feelings* ❷ affection; attachment; love: 这些年来，她对他产生了～。*She formed an attachment for him over the years.* / 他对母亲的～很深。*He has a deep love for his mother.* ◇ ～投资 invest in human relations; ～线 heart line

【感情用事】be swayed by one's emotions; act impetuously

【感染】❶ infect: 细菌～ *bacterial infection* / 手术后～ *postoperative infection* / 身体不好，容易～流行性感冒。*If one is feeling physically low, it's easy to catch the flu.* ❷ influence; infect; affect: 她的乐观态度～了周围的人。*Her optimism was infectious.* / 诗人的激情～了每一个读者。*The poet's passion affected all his readers.* ◇ ～区 infected area

【感染力】power to move the feelings; appeal: 艺术～ *artistic appeal*

【感人】touching; moving: ～的故事 *a moving story* / 他的先进事迹十分～。*His meritorious deeds are very moving.*

【感人肺腑】touch one to the depths of one's soul; move one deeply

【感伤】sad; sorrowful; sentimental

【感生电流】同〖感应电流〗

【感受】❶ be affected by: ～风寒 *be affected by the cold*; *catch cold* ❷ experience; feel ◇ ～器［生理］receptor

【感叹】sigh with feeling ◇ ～词 interjection; exclamation; ～号 exclamation mark; exclamation point (!); ～句 exclamatory sentence

【感同身受】〈套〉I shall appreciate it as a personal favour (often said when making a request on behalf of a friend)

【感悟】come to realize

【感想】impressions; reflections; thoughts: 请你谈谈看了这部影片后的～。*Please tell us your impressions of the film.* or *Tell us what you think of the film.*

【感谢】thank; be grateful: 表示衷心的～ *express heartfelt thanks* / 非常～你的帮助。*Thank you very much for your help.* ◇ ～信 letter of thanks

【感性】(sense) perception: 认识的～阶段 *the perceptual stage of cognition* ◇ ～认识［哲］perceptual knowledge; ～运动［生］nastic movement; ～知觉［心理］sense impressions

【感应】❶ response; reaction; interaction: 凡是动物都有对外界的刺激发生比较灵敏的～的特性。*Reaction to strong stimuli from the outside world is a characteristic of all animals.* ❷［生］irritability ❸［电］induction: 电磁～ *electromagnetic induction* / 静电～ *electrostatic induction* / ～干扰 *inductive interference* / ～式话筒 *inductor microphone* ◇ ～场 induction field; ～电动机 induction motor; ～电流 induced current; ～电压调节器 induction-voltage regulator; ～率 inductivity；～圈 induction coil；inductor

【感召】move and inspire；impel

【感知】mental perception through sensory organs

橄（构词成分）见下

【橄榄】［植］❶ Chinese olive（Canarium album）；the fruit of the canary tree ❷ olive ◇ ～绿 olive green；～石 olivine（a mineral）；～岩［地质］Peridotite；～油 olive oil；～枝 olive branch—a symbol of peace

【橄榄球】［体］rugby；American football

擀 动 roll（dough，etc.）：～饺子皮 *roll out dumpling wrappers* / ～面条 *make noodles*

【擀面杖】rolling pin

gàn

干 Ⅰ 名 ❶ trunk；main part：骨干 ❷〈略〉见〖干部〗Ⅱ 动 ❶ do；work：咱们～吧！*Let's get cracking*! or *Let's get started*! / 叫我～什么都行。*I'll do whatever job I'm given*. ❷ work as；go in for：他～过队长。*He used to be a team leader*. Ⅲ 形 capable；able：～员 *a capable official* ——另见 gān

【干部】cadre：各级领导～ *leading cadres at all levels* / ～政策 *policy towards cadres*；*cadre policy* ◇ ～学校 a school for cadres；cadre school

【干才】❶ ability；capability：这个人还有点～。*The man is quite capable*. ❷ a capable（or able）person：他是个～。*He's a capable person*.

【干掉】〈口〉kill；get rid of；put sb. out of the way：先～敌人的哨兵。*Get rid of the enemy sentry first*.

【干活】work；work on a job：～去吧。*Let's get to work*. / 他们都在～呢。*They are all at work*. or *They are all on the job*. / 今儿你干什么活啊？*What's your job for today*?

【干家】capable person

【干架】❶ quarrel ❷ come to blows

【干将】capable person；go-getter

【干劲】drive；vigour；enthusiasm：鼓～ *rouse one's enthusiasm* / ～十足 *be full of vigour*（*or drive*）

【干警】police officers；cadres and police

【干练】capable and experienced：他的确是一个精明～的人才。*He's a really bright and capable man*.

【干流】trunk stream；mainstream

【干吗】〈口〉❶ why on earth；whatever for：～这么大规矩？*Why all this formality*? ❷ what to do：今儿下午～？*What are we going to do this afternoon*? / 你想～？*What are you up to*?

【干渠】trunk canal；main canal

【干事】a secretary（or clerical worker）in charge of sth.：文娱～ *person in charge of recreational activities*

【干线】main line；trunk line；artery：公路～ *arterial or main highway* / 交通～ *main lines of communication*（*or transportation*）

【干休所】sanatorium for retired cadres

绀 名 dark purple；dark red

【绀青】dark purple；prune purple

gāng

冈 名 ridge（of a hill）：景阳～ *the Jingyang Ridge*

【冈比亚】the Gambia ◇ ～人 Gambian

扛 动 ❶ lift with both hands ❷〈方〉（of two or more people）carry together ——另见 káng

刚 Ⅰ 形 firm；strong；indomitable：他的性情太～。*He has a very strong character*. / 她的舞蹈柔中有～。*There is strength as well as grace in her dancing*. Ⅱ 副 ❶ just；exactly：这双鞋大小～合适。*This pair of shoes is just the right size*. or *This pair of shoes fits perfectly*. ❷ barely；only；just：我参加八路军时，～跟枪一般高。*When I joined the Eighth Route Army*，*I was barely the height of a rifle*. ❸ only a short while ago；just：她～走。*She just left*. / 她～来过。*She was here just now*.

【刚愎自用】self-willed；headstrong；opinionated

【刚才】a moment ago；just now：别把～跟你说的事忘了。*Don't forget what I told you just now*. / 他～还说要去呢。*He was saying only a moment ago that he wanted to go*.

【刚刚】❶ just；only；exactly：上次讨论会到现在～一个月。*It's only a month since the last discussion*. / 那时候天～亮。*It was just beginning to get light*. ❷ a moment ago；just now：报纸～到。*The newspaper came just now*. / 他～走，你快去追吧！*He left just a minute ago*. *Run and try to catch him*.

【刚果】the Congo ◇ ～河 the Congo（River）；～红 Congo red；～人 Congolese；～语 Congolese（language）

【刚好】❶ just；exactly：我们～赶上末班车。*We just managed to catch the last bus*. / 这件上衣你穿着不大不小，～。*This jacket fits you beautifully*. ❷ by chance；by coincidence：～校长在这儿，你就跟他谈谈吧。*The Chancellor happens to be here*. *You'd better talk it over with him*.

【刚架】［建］rigid frame：～结构 *rigid-framed structure*

【刚健】vigorous；energetic；robust：～的舞姿 *vigorous movements of a dancer*

【刚劲】bold；vigorous；sturdy：笔力～ *write in a bold hand* / ～的松枝 *sturdy boughs of a pine*

【刚…就】as soon as；no sooner than；immediately：刚过立春，天气就异乎寻常地热。*It got unusually hot just after the Beginning of Spring*.

【刚烈】fiery and forthright；upright and unyielding

【刚强】firm; staunch; unyielding: 性格～ *be of firm character*
【刚柔相济】couple hardness with softness (in dealing with people); temper toughness with gentleness
【刚体】[物] rigid body
【刚性】[物] rigidity: ～结构 *rigid structure*
【刚毅】resolute and steadfast: 在斗争中表现得非常～和机智 *display both fortitude and resourcefulness in the struggle*
【刚玉】corundum (a mineral)
【刚正】upright; honourable; principled
【刚正不阿】upright and above flattery
【刚直】upright and outspoken

纲 名 ❶ the headrope of a fishing net ❷ key link; guiding principle: 纲举目张 ❸ outline; programme: 总纲 ❹ [生] class: 哺乳动物～ *the class of mammals* / 亚～ *subclass*
【纲纪】〈书〉law and order; discipline
【纲举目张】once the headrope of a fishing net is pulled up, all its meshes open—once the key link is grasped, everything falls into place
【纲领】programme; guiding principle: ～性文件 *programmatic document*
【纲目】(usu. used in book titles) detailed outline (of a subject); outline; compendium: 《本草～》 *Compendium of Materia Medica*
【纲要】❶ outline; sketch: 他把意见写成～，准备在会上发言。*He made an outline of his views and got ready to present them at the meeting.* ❷ (usu. used in book titles) essentials; compendium: 《英语语法～》 *Essentials of English Grammar*

肛 名 anus: 脱肛
【肛裂】[医] anal fissure
【肛瘘】[医] anal fistula
【肛门】anus

缸 名 ❶ vat; jar; crock: 水～ *water vat* / 一～咸菜 *a jar of salted vegetables* / 金鱼～ *goldfish bowl* / 一口大～ *a big vat* ❷ a compound of sand, clay, etc. for making earthenware: 缸盆 ❸ a jar-shaped vessel: 汽缸
【缸管】earthen pipe
【缸盆】glazed earthen basin
【缸瓦】a compound of sand, clay, etc. for making earthenware
【缸砖】clinker (tile); quarry tile
【缸子】mug; bowl: 茶～ *(tea) mug* / 糖～ *sugar bowl*

钢 名 steel: ～是用铁炼成的。*Steel is made from iron.* ——另见 gàng
【钢板】❶ steel plate; plate: 锅炉～ *boiler plate* / 造船～ *ship plate* ❷ spring (of a motorcar, etc.) ❸ stencil steel board
【钢笔】pen; fountain pen ◇ ～画 pen-and-ink drawing; ～水〈口〉ink
【钢材】steel products; steels; rolled steel
【钢尺】steel rule
【钢锭】steel ingot
【钢骨水泥】reinforced concrete
【钢管】steel tube (or pipe): 无缝～ *seamless steel tube* / 焊接～ *welded steel pipe*
【钢轨】rails (for trains, etc.); tracks ◇ ～探伤仪 rail flaw detector
【钢号】[冶] steel grade
【钢花】spray (or sparks) of molten steel
【钢化玻璃】toughened glass
【钢结构】[建] steel structure
【钢筋】reinforcing bar
【钢筋混凝土】reinforced concrete
【钢精】(又作'钢种') aluminium (as used for utensils): ～锅 *aluminium pan*
【钢锯】hacksaw: ～架 *hacksaw frame* / ～条 *hacksaw blade*
【钢盔】(steel) helmet
【钢坯】[冶] billet: 大～ *bloom*
【钢片琴】[音] celesta
【钢钎】drill rod; drill steel
【钢琴】piano: 大～ *grand piano* / 竖式～ *upright piano* / ～家 *pianist*
【钢水】[冶] molten steel: ～包 *steel ladle*
【钢丝】(steel) wire: ～垫子 *spring mattress* ◇ ～床 spring bed; ～锯 fret saw; scroll saw; ～录音机 wire recorder; ～钳 combination pliers; cutting pliers; ～绳 steel cable; wire rope
【钢铁】❶ iron and steel; steel: ～厂 *steelworks* / ～工业 *iron and steel industry* / ～公司 *iron and steel company* / ～联合企业 *integrated iron and steel works; iron and steel complex* ❷ strong; firm; staunch: ～意志 *iron will* / ～运输线 *an unbreakable transportation line*
【钢印】❶ steel seal; embossing seal ❷ embossed stamp
【钢珠】steel ball (in a ball bearing); ball bearing; ball

罡 (构词成分)见下
【罡风】❶ Taoism winds in the empyrean ❷ strong winds

gǎng

岗 名 ❶ hillock; mound: ～峦起伏 *undulating hills* ❷ ridge; welt; wale: 他眉毛脱了，只剩下两道肉～儿。*Only the two superciliary ridges are left there since his eyebrow hair fell out.* ❸ sentry; post: 布～ *post sentries*
【岗警】policeman on point duty
【岗楼】watchtower
【岗哨】❶ lookout post ❷ sentry; sentinel: 设置～ *post sentries*
【岗亭】sentry box; police box
【岗位】post; station: 坚守～ *stand fast at one's post; stick to one's guns* / 走上新的～ *take up a*

new post; *take on a new job* ◇ ～津贴 job subsidies; subsidies appropriate to particular jobs; ～培训 on-the job training; pre-job training; ～责任 post responsibility

【岗位责任制】system of personal responsibility (for each section of a production line, etc.)

【岗子】❶ hillock; mound: 土～ *earth hillock* ❷ ridge; wale; welt: 他胸口上肿起一道～。*There's a welt on his chest*.

港 名 ❶ port; harbour: 天然～ *natural harbour* / 停靠～ *port of call* ❷〈略〉见〖香港〗

【港澳同胞】compatriots from (in) Hong kong and Macao

【港币】Hong Kong dollar

【港汊】branching stream

【港督】governor of Hong Kong

【港府】Hong Kong government

【港客】visitors and guests from Hong Kong region

【港口】port; harbour: 沿海～ *coastal port* / ～规章 *harbour regulations* / ～吞吐量 *traffic* (*of a port*) / ～税 *port dues* ◇ ～建设 port construction

【港人】Hong Kong residents

【港商】Hong Kong businessman

【港式】Hong Kong style

【港台】Hong Kong and Taiwan

【港湾】harbour

【港务费】harbour dues

【港务监督】harbour superintendency administration

【港务局】port office

【港至港提单】port to port bill of landing

gàng

杠 Ⅰ 名 ❶ a thick stick ❷ [体] bar: 单杠/ 双杠 ❸ rod-like spare parts used for machine tools: 丝杠 ❹ stout poles used to carry a coffin Ⅱ 动 cross out; delete: 她把草稿中不必要的词句都～掉了。*She crossed out all the superfluous words and phrases in the draft*.

【杠棒】a stout carrying pole

【杠杆】lever: ～臂 *lever arm* / ～原理 *lever principle* / ～率 *leverage* / 经济～ *economic levers*

【杠铃】[体] barbell: ～片 *disc* (*of a barbell*)

【杠子】❶ a thick stick; a stout carrying pole ❷ thick line (drawn beside or under words in reading, correcting papers, etc.)

钢 动 ❶ sharpen; whet; strop: ～菜刀 *sharpen a kitchen knife* / ～镰刀 *whet a sickle* / ～剃刀 *strop a razor* ❷ reinforce the edge (of a knife, etc.) by adding steel and retempering: 这口铡刀该～了。*The fodder chopper needs to be reinforced*. ——另见 gāng

【钢刀布】(razor) strop

gāo

高 形 ❶ tall; high: 这里地势很～。*The terrain here is very high*. / 她比小红～一头。*She is a head taller than Xiao Hong*. ❷ of a high level or degree; above the average: ～速度 *high speed* / ～年级 *higher* (*or senior*) *grades* / ～质量 *high* (*or good*) *quality* / 体温～ *have a fever* ❸ loud: 嗓门～ *have a loud voice* / ～喊 *shout loudly*; *raise a cry* ❹ high-priced; dear; expensive: 要价太～ *ask too high a price* ❺〈尊〉your: 高见

【高矮】height: 这两棵树～差不多。*The two trees are about the same height*.

【高昂】❶ hold high (one's head, etc.): 骑兵队伍～着头通过了广场。*The mounted troops passed the square with their heads held high*. ❷ high; elated; exalted: 情绪～ *be in high spirits* ❸ dear; expensive; exorbitant

【高傲】❶ supercilious; arrogant; haughty ❷ proud; self-respecting; high-minded

【高保真】high fidelity; hi-fi ◇ ～度接收机 high fidelity receiver

【高标号】high grade: ～水泥 *high-grade cement*

【高不成,低不就】❶ be unfit for a higher post but unwilling to take a lower one ❷ be unable to achieve one's heart's desire but unwilling to accept less

【高不可攀】too high to reach; unattainable

【高才生】(又作'高材生') a brilliant (or outstanding) student

【高层云】[气] altostratus

【高产】high yield; high production: ～品种 *high-yield variety* / ～田 *high-yield field* / ～作物 *high-yield crop*; *highly productive crop*

【高唱】❶ sing loudly; sing with spirit: ～战歌 *sing battle songs* ❷ talk glibly about; call out loudly for

【高超】superb; excellent: 技艺～ *superb skill* / 见解～ *excellent ideas*

【高超音速】[物] hypersonic speed: ～火箭 *hypersonic rocket*

【高潮】❶ high tide; high water: ～线 *high-water mark* (*or line*) ❷ upsurge; high tide ❸ (of fiction, drama and films) climax: 全剧的～ *the climax of the play*

【高大】❶ tall and big; tall: 身材～ *be of tall and sturdy stature* / ～的建筑物 *tall buildings* / ～明亮的车间 *a big, bright, high-ceilinged workshop* ❷ lofty: 革命英雄的～形象 *the lofty image of a revolutionary hero*

【高蛋白】high protein

【高档】high (or top) grade; superior quality: ～服装 *superior quality clothing* ◇ ～耐用消费品 durable high-priced consumer; ～商品 expensive commodities, high-grade products

【高等】higher: ～哺乳动物 *higher mammal* ◇ ～教育 higher education; ～数学 higher mathematics；～学校 institutions of higher learning；colleges and universities

【高低】❶ height：山崖的～ *the height of a cliff* / 声调的～ *the pitch of a voice* ❷ relative superiority or inferiority：争个～ *vie with each other to see who is better* / 难分～ *hard to tell which is better* ❸ sense of propriety；discretion：不知～ *not know what's proper*；*have no sense of propriety*

【高低杠】［体］uneven（parallel）bars

【高低角】［军］angle of site

【高地】❶ highland；upland；elevation：～田 *an upland field* ❷［军］height：拿下 332～ *capture Height* 332

【高调】❶ lofty tone；high-sounding words ❷［摄］high tone ——另见〖唱高调〗

【高度】❶ altitude；height：飞行～ *flying altitude* / 山的～ *the height of a mountain* ❷ a high degree：～赞扬 *pay high tribute to*；*speak highly of* ◇ ～表（又作'高度计'）altimeter；～差 altitude difference；～通货膨胀 hyperinflation

【高额利润】huge profit

【高尔夫球】❶ golf：～场 *golf course*；*golf links* ❷ golf ball

【高尔基体】［生］golgiosome

【高分低能】high scores and low ability

【高分子】［化］high polymer；macromolecule：～化学（*high*）*polymer chemistry* ◇ ～化合物 macromolecular compound；high-molecular compound；～聚合物 high polymer

【高风亮节】noble character and sterling integrity

【高峰】peak；summit；height：珠穆朗玛峰是世界第一～。*Mount Qomolangma*（*Everest*）*is the world's highest peak*. / 攀登科学的～ *scale the heights of science* / 人口出生～期 *a baby boom* ◇ ～会议 summit meeting

【高峰时间】peak-hour；rush hour

【高干】high-ranking official；senior cadres：～病房 *wards*（*in hospital*）*for high-ranking officials*（*or cadres*）/ ～子弟 *children of senior cadres*

【高高在上】set oneself high above the masses；be far removed from the masses and reality

【高歌猛进】stride forward singing songs of triumph；advance triumphantly

【高个儿】（又作'高个子'）a tall person

【高跟鞋】high-heeled shoes

【高工】senior engineer

【高官厚禄】high position and handsome salary；high position with high pay

【高贵】❶ morally elevated；magnanimous；noble：～品质 *noble quality* ❷ highly privileged；elitist

【高积云】［气］altocumulus

【高级】❶ senior；high-ranking；high-level；high：～将领 *high-ranking general officers* / ～官员 *high-ranking official* ❷ high-grade；high-quality；advanced：～染料 *high-grade dyestuff* / ～墨水 *high-quality ink* / ～读本 *advanced reader* / 这个旅馆真～！*This hotel is really first-class*. ◇ ～干部 senior cadre；～会晤 summit talk；～经理 senior manager；～跑车 Gran turismo；～人民法院 higher people's court；～神经活动［生理］higher nervous activity；～特技飞行 advanced aerobatics；～小学 higher primary school；～斜纹呢 himalaya；～研究员 senior research fellow；～语言 high-level language；～知识分子 higher intellectual；～职称 title of a senior post；～中学 senior middle school

【高技术】high-technology；high-tech

【高技术产品】high-tech products

【高技术产业】high-tech industry

【高技术领域】fields of high technology

【高加索山脉】the Caucasus Mountains

【高价】high price：～收买 *buy over at a high price* / ～货物 *expensive goods* ◇ ～出售 sell something at a high price；sell sth. at a high price；～收购 offer high price for（something）

【高架桥】viaduct

【高架铁道】overhead railway；elevated railway

【高见】〈尊〉your brilliant idea；your opinion：有何～？*What do you think about it*？

【高洁】noble and unsullied

【高精尖】high-grade，precision and advanced（industrial products）

【高就】〈套〉move up to a higher position（usu. in another place）：哎哟！怎么你要～了！*Oh！So you're moving up*！/ 另有～ *have landed a better job*

【高举】hold high；hold aloft：他～着奖杯向观众致意。*He held the cup high for all the audience to see*.

【高聚物】［化］high polymer

【高踞】stand above；set oneself above；lord it over

【高峻】high and steep

【高亢】❶ loud and sonorous；resounding：～的歌声 *sonorous singing* ❷（of terrain）high ❸〈书〉supercilious；arrogant；haughty

【高考】（〈略〉全称为'高等学校招生考试'）college entrance examination

【高科技】high technology；high-level science and technology ◇ ～产品 high-tech products；～开发试验区 high-tech industrial development and experimental zone；～企业 high-tech enterprises

【高空】high altitude；upper air：～飞行 *high-altitude flight* / ～核试验 *high-altitude nuclear test* / ～适应 *high-altitude adaptation* ◇ ～病 altitude sickness；～气象学 aerology；～作业 work high above the ground

【高栏】［体］high hurdles

【高丽参】Korean ginseng

【高利贷】usury；usurious loan：放～ *practise usury* / ～者 *usurer*；*loan shark* / ～资本 *usurer's capital*

【高粱】kaoliang；Chinese sorghum ◇ ～酒 spirit distilled from sorghum；～米 husked kaoliang

【高粱饴】sweets（or candy）made of sorghum syrup；sorghum candy

【高龄】〈套〉advanced age（usu. over 60）；venerable age：八十～ *the venerable age of* 80

【高岭石】kaolinite
【高岭土】kaolin
【高楼大厦】high buildings and large mansions
【高炉】［冶］blast furnace：～利用系数 *capacity factor of a blast furnace* / ～煤气 *blast furnace gas* / ～寿命 *life of a blast furnace*
【高氯酸】［化］perchloric acid
【高论】〈套〉enlightening remarks；brilliant views
【高帽子】❶ tall paper hat（worn as a sign of humiliation）；dunce's cap ❷ flattery ——另见〖戴高帽子〗
【高锰酸钾】［化］potassium permanganate
【高妙】ingenious；masterly：手艺～ *masterly craftsmanship* / 笔法～ *masterly writing skills*
【高明】❶ brilliant；wise：群众比我们～。*The masses are wiser than we are*. / 他这一手一点也不～。*This move of his is not at all clever*. / 见解～ *brilliant ideas* ❷ a wise person：另请高明
【高难】（of technology）high caliber and high degree of difficulty ◇ ～动作 difficult movements that require superior skills；～技巧 a superior and difficult technique
【高能】high energy：～粒子 *high-energy particle*；*energetic particle* ◇ ～燃料 high-energy fuel；～物理学 high-energy physics
【高攀】make friends or claim ties of kinship with someone of a higher social position：不敢～。*I dare not be so presumptuous as to make friends with someone so high up*.
【高抛式发球】high toss service
【高朋满座】a great gathering of distinguished guests
【高频】［无］high frequency：甚～ *very high frequency*（VHF）/ 超～ *ultrahigh frequency*（UHF）/ ～扬声器 *tweeter* ◇ ～电波 high-frequency electric wave；～放大器 high-frequency potency amplifier；radio-frequency amplifier
【高品位】high-grade
【高聘】be appointed to a high position
【高气压】high atmospheric（or barometric）pressure：～区 *high-pressure area*；*region of high barometric pressure*
【高强】excelling in：武艺～ *excel in martial arts*
【高强度】high strength：～钢 *high-strength steel*；*high-tensile steel*
【高跷】stilts：踩～ *walk on stilts*
【高清晰度电视】high definition television（HDTV）
【高清晰度兼容数码】high definition compatible digital
【高球】［体］high ball；lob：放～ *send a ball in a lob*；*lob*
【高热】同〖高烧〗
【高人】❶ a man of noble character；a man of great sanctity ❷ a man of superior attainments；past master；master-hand
【高人一等】a cut above other people：他老以为自己～。*He always thinks he's a cut above others*. / 他看问题确是～。*He stood head and shoulders above others in the way he looked at problems*.
【高僧】eminent monk
【高山病】mountain sickness
【高山反应】altitude reaction
【高山滑雪】alpine skiing
【高山流水】high mountains and flowing waters— ❶ sublime music ❷ understanding friends（a reference to an anecdote of the two great friends 伯牙 and 钟子期）
【高山植物】alpine plant
【高尚】❶ noble；lofty：～的人 *a noble-minded person* / ～的理想 *lofty ideals* ❷ meaningful；not in poor taste：～的娱乐 *tasteful entertainment*
【高烧】high fever：发～ *have*（*or run*）*a high fever*
【高射机关枪】antiaircraft machine gun
【高射炮】antiaircraft gun（or artillery）
【高深】advanced；profound；recondite：～的学问 *great learning*（*or scholarship*）
【高深莫测】同〖莫测高深〗
【高升】be promoted
【高视阔步】carry oneself proudly；strut；swagger；prance
【高手】past master；master-hand；ace：象棋～ *master*（*Chinese*）*chess player* / 他在外科手术上是有名的～。*He's a well-known master-hand in surgery*.
【高寿】❶ longevity；long life ❷〈套〉your venerable age：老大爷，您今年～？*May I ask how old you are*，*Grandpa*？
【高耸】（stand）tall and erect；towering：～入云 *reach to the sky*；*tower into the clouds* / ～的纪念碑 *a towering monument*
【高速】high speed：～前进 *advance at high speed* / ～发展 *develop by leaps and bounds*；*develop at top speed* / ～转弯很危险。*It's dangerous to turn a corner at high speed*. ◇ ～存储器 high-speed memory；～打印机 high-speed printer；～挡 top gear；high gear；～电影摄影机 high-speed motion picture camera；～钢 high-speed steel；rapid steel；～缓冲存储器 cache；cache memory；～公路 expressway；freeway；～摄影 high-speed photography
【高抬贵手】be magnanimous；be generous；not be too hard on sb.
【高谈阔论】indulge in loud and empty talk；talk volubly or bombastically
【高碳钢】［冶］high-carbon steel
【高汤】❶ soup-stock ❷ thin soup
【高堂】❶ big hall；main hall ❷〈书〉one's parents
【高危】high and dangerous
【高纬度】high latitudes
【高温】high temperature：～计 *pyrometer* / ～气候 *megathermal climate* ◇ ～切削［机］high-temperature machining；～作业 high-temperature operation
【高屋建瓴】pour water off a steep roof—sweep down irresistibly from a commanding height；operate from a strategically advantageous posi-

tion

【高下】relative superiority or inferiority：两个人的技术不分～。*The two of them are equally matched in their skills.*

【高消费】high level of consumption

【高效节能】energy-efficient

【高校】(〈略〉全称为'高等学校') institutions of higher education；universities and colleges

【高新技术】advanced high technology；hi-tech

【高薪】high salary；high pay

【高兴】❶ glad；happy；cheerful：看到孩子们有进步，心里很～。*He was very pleased to see that the kids had made progress.* ❷ be willing to；be happy to：他就是～看电影，看戏不感兴趣。*He's fond of seeing films, and not at all interested in watching plays.* / 你不～去就甭去了。*You needn't go if you don't feel like it.*

【高血压】[医] hypertension；high blood pressure

【高压】❶ [物] [气] high pressure ❷ [电] high tension；high voltage：～电力网 *high-tension network* ❸ [医] maximum pressure ❹ high-handed (persecution)：反动政权的～政策 *the high-handed policy of a reactionary regime* ◇ ～泵 [机] high-pressure pump；～电缆 high-tension cable；～锅 pressure cooker；～脊 [气] ridge of high pressure；pressure ridge；～灭菌器 autoclave；～水龙 water cannon；～线 high-tension line (or wire)

【高雅】refined；elegant

【高研】(〈略〉全称为'高级研究员') high-level researcher

【高眼鲽】[动] plaice

【高音喇叭】tweeter

【高原】plateau；highland；tableland：青藏～ *the Qinghai-Xizang Plateau*

【高瞻远瞩】stand high and see far；take a broad and long view；show great foresight

【高涨】rise；upsurge；run high：群众热情～。*The enthusiasm of the masses ran high.* / 物价～。*Prices were skyrocketing.*

【高招】(又作'高着儿') 〈口〉 clever move；brilliant idea：我看他也没有什么～。*I don't think he can come up with any clever move.* / 你有什么～，快说说。*What have you got up your sleeve? Out with it!*

【高枕无忧】shake up the pillow and have a good sleep；sit back and relax

【高知】(〈略〉全称为'高级知识分子') high-level intellectual

【高指标】high targets in production

【高姿态】lofty stance；magnanimous attitude

【高足】〈尊〉 your brilliant disciple；your pupil

【高祖】(paternal) great-great-grandfather

【高祖母】(paternal) great-great-grandmother

羔 名 lamb；kid；fawn：羊羔

【羔皮】lambskin；kidskin；kid

【羔羊】lamb—an innocent and helpless person or a scapegoat

【羔子】lamb；kid；fawn：小猪～ *piglet*

膏 名 ❶ fat；grease；oil：春雨如～。*Rain in spring is as precious as oil.* ❷ paste；cream；ointment：雪花膏——另见 gào

【膏剂】[药] medicinal extract；electuary

【膏粱】〈字〉 fat meat and fine grain；rich food：居处于～锦绣之中 *living in the lap of luxury* ◇ ～子弟 good-for-nothing sons of the idle rich

【膏药】[中] medicated plaster；plaster：贴～ *apply a plaster to*

【膏腴】〈书〉 fertile：～之地 *fertile land*

睾 (构词成分)见下

【睾丸】testis；testicle ◇ ～炎 orchitis

糕 名 cake；pudding

【糕点】cake；pastry

【糕干】sweetened rice flour (sometimes fed to infants as a substitute for powdered milk)

篙 名 punt-pole

gǎo

搞 动 ❶ do；carry on；be engaged in：～调查研究 *do some investigation and study*；*do surveys* / ～改革 *carry on reforms* ❷ make；produce；work out：～个计划 *draw up a plan* / 我们～一点核武器完全是为了自卫。*It is purely for self-defence that we have produced some nuclear weapons.* ❸ set up；start；organize：这家工厂是由一个个体户～起来的。*This factory was started by a self-employed worker.* ❹ get；get hold of；secure：你去给我们～点吃的来。*Go and get us something to eat.* / ～钱 *raise money*；*make money* ❺ (followed by a complement)：把事情～糟了 *have made a mess of things* / 把某人～臭 *make sb.'s name stink*；*discredit sb.*

【搞对象】go steady

【搞鬼】play tricks；be up to some mischief：提防有人暗中～。*Beware of foul play!* / 你究竟在搞什么鬼？这么神秘。*What on earth are you up to? You're being so mysterious.*

【搞好】make a good job of；do well：～团结 *strengthen unity* / ～军民关系 *build good relations between the army and the people*

【搞活】vitalize；enliven：～国营大中型企业 *invigorate large and medium-sized state-owned enterprises* / ～经济 *enliven the economy* / ～流通 *stimulate commodity circulation* / ～企业 *invigorate the enterprises* / ～市场 *enliven the market*

【搞特殊化】*use ones position to pursue personal perquisites and privileges*

缟 名 a thin white silk used in ancient China

【缟素】white mourning apparel

槁 形 withered：枯槁

【槁木】a withered tree

【槁木死灰】dead trees and cold ashes—complete apathy

稿 名 ❶〈书〉stalk of grain; straw ❷ draft; sketch: 先打个～儿再画 *make a sketch before painting* ❸ a rough draft (of a document); draft: 拟～ *make a draft*

【稿本】manuscript (of a book, etc.)

【稿费】payment for an article or book published; contribution fee; author's remuneration: 这家出版社的～标准较高。*This publisher offers a better rate of remuneration.*

【稿件】manuscript; contribution

【稿约】notice to contributors (to a magazine, etc.)

【稿纸】standardized writing paper with squares or lines

【稿子】❶ draft; sketch: 起个～ *make a draft* ❷ manuscript; contribution: 给黑板报写～ *write sth. for the blackboard newspaper* / 这篇～是谁写的? *Who wrote this article?* ❸ idea; plan: 我心里还没个准～。*I haven't got any definite plan yet.*

镐 名 pick; pickaxe

【镐头】pick; pickaxe

gào

告 动 ❶ tell; inform; notify: 何时启程,盼～。*Please inform me of your date of departure.* ❷ go to law against sb.; sue; take sb. to court: 到法院去～他。*Go to court and sue him.* ❸ ask for; request; solicit: 告假 ❹ declare; announce: 不～而别 *go away without taking leave; leave without saying good-bye* ❺ reach (a particular state): ～一段落 *come to the end of a stage; be brought to a temporary close*

【告白】a public notice or announcement

【告别】❶ leave; part from: 我们～了这个地方,继续向前进。*We left the place and went on with our journey.* ❷ bid farewell to; say good-bye to: 挥手～ *wave farewell* / 我向你～来了。*I've come to say good-bye to you.* / 向遗体～ *pay one's last respects to the deceased* ◇ ～词 farewell speech; valediction; ～宴会 farewell banquet; ～仪式 farewell ceremony

【告病】ask for sick leave: 他～未出席会议。*He was not present at the meeting on account of illness.*

【告成】(of a major task or project) be completed or accomplished: 这部巨著历时十年方始～。*This magnum opus took ten years to complete.*

【告吹】〈口〉fizzle out; fail: 由于资金不足,计划～。*The plan fizzled out due to lack of funds.*

【告辞】take leave (of one's host): 我怕耽误他的时间,谈了一会儿就～了。*I took leave after a brief talk so as not to take up too much of his time.*

【告贷】ask for a loan: 四处～ *borrow money from everyone* / 奔走～ *run around trying to raise money* / ～无门 *be unable to get a loan from any source*

【告发】report (an offender); inform against; lodge an accusation against: 向政府～了他的卖国罪行 *report his treasonous act to the government* / 他逃税漏税的事早就被人～了。*He has already been reported concerning his tax-evasion.*

【告急】❶ be in a state of emergency: 洪水猛涨,大坝～。*The dam was in danger because of the rising flood.* ❷ report an emergency; ask for emergency help: 前线频频～。*The front-line units repeatedly signalled for help.*

【告假】ask for leave: 告三天假 *ask for a three-day leave*

【告捷】❶ win victory (in war or games): 首战～ *win in the very first battle or game* ❷ report a victory

【告诫】warn; admonish; exhort: 他再三～自己,不要轻举妄动。*Again and again, he cautioned himself against rashness.*

【告警】report an emergency; give (or sound) an alarm

【告老】retire on account of age

【告老还乡】〈旧〉(of a government official) retire and return to one's native place

【告密】inform against sb.: 他做地下工作时,曾因叛徒～而被捕。*When he was doing underground work he was arrested because a renegade informed against him.* / ～者 *informer*

【告罄】run out; be exhausted: 弹药～。*Ammunition has run out.* / 库存～ *be out of stock*

【告饶】beg for mercy; ask pardon: 求情～ *plead for mercy*

【告示】❶ notify; announce: 我们按照海报上～的钟点,准时进入会场。*We went to the meeting hall at the time as announced in the poster.* ❷ official notice; bulletin; placard ❸〈旧〉slogan; poster

【告诉】tell; let know: ～他们别等了。*Tell them not to wait.* / 有什么消息,～我一声。*Let me know if there's any news.* / 我～你,下回可不许这样。*Let me tell you, don't do it again.*

【告退】ask for leave to withdraw from a meeting, etc.: 兄弟在此不便久留,就此～。*I should not stay here too long. I wish you good day.* / 随着仪式结束,客人全部～。*As the ceremony came to a close, all the guests departed.*

【告御状】accuse sb. before the emperor; complain or report to the higher authorities (over one's immediate bosses, etc.)

【告枕头状】complain (about sb. or sth.) to one's spouse when in bed; pillow-talk; give a curtain lecture

【告知】inform; notify: 他问起许多老同学的近况,我一一～。*He inquired about many of our old* classmates, and I told him about each of them. / 我将这事～了有关人员。*I informed those concerned of this matter*.

【告终】come to an end; end up: 以失败～ *end in failure* / 以损人开始,以害己～ *start with the aim of harming others and end up by harming oneself*

【告状】❶ go to law against sb.; bring a lawsuit against sb. ❷ lodge a complaint against sb. with his superior: 他在老师面前告了我一状。*He lodged a complaint against me with the teacher*.

诰 名 ❶〈古〉(of superiors) admonish; enjoin ❷〈古〉a written admonition ❸ imperial mandate: 诰封

【诰封】the conferment of honorary titles by imperial mandate

【诰命】❶ imperial mandate ❷〈旧〉a titled lady

锆 名 [化] zirconium (Zr)

【锆鞣】zirconium tanning: ～革 *zirconium tanned leather*

【锆石】zircon (a mineral)

膏 动 ❶ lubricate: ～车 *lubricate the axle of a cart* / 在轴上～点儿油 *put some lubricant on the axle* ❷ dip a writing brush in ink and smooth it on an inkstone before writing: ～笔 *smooth a (ink-dipped) writing brush on the edge of an inkstone* ——另见 gāo

gē

戈 名 dagger-axe (an ancient weapon)

【戈壁】❶ [地质] gobi ❷ the Gobi Desert

圪 (构词成分)见下

【圪哒】(又作'圪塔') ❶ 同〖疙瘩〗❷ mound; knoll

疙 (构词成分)见下

【疙瘩】❶ a swelling on the skin; pimple; lump ❷ lump; knot: 线结成了～。*The thread has got tangled (or got into a knot)*. ❸ a knot in one's heart; hang-up: 解开心上的～ *get rid of one's hang-up*

【疙疙瘩瘩】(又作'疙里疙瘩')〈口〉rough; knotty; bumpy: 路上净是石头子儿,～的,差点绊倒。*The road was full of gravel and very bumpy. I almost stumbled*. / 这事情～的,很不好办。*It was a tricky problem to deal with*.

咯 (构词成分)见下 ——另见 kǎ

【咯噔】click: ～～的皮靴声 the click of boots (on a floor)

【咯咯】❶ the sound made by a hen; cluck; chuckle; cackle: 母鸡下完蛋后,～地叫个不停。*The hen started clucking after she laid an egg*. ❷ the sound of laughing; chuckle; titter: 她～地笑个不停,眼泪都笑出来了。*She chuckled herself to tears*.

【咯吱】creak; groan: 扁担压得～～地直响。*The carrying pole creaked under the load*.

哥 名 ❶ (elder) brother: 大～ *the eldest of one's brothers* ❷ a friendly term of address for male older acquaintances: 李二～ *Brother Li'er*

【哥德巴赫猜想】[数] Goldbach's conjecture

【哥哥】(elder) brother

【哥伦比亚】Colombia ◇ ～人 Colombian

【哥儿们】〈口〉❶ brothers ❷ buddies; pals: 穷～ *we, the poor* / ～义气 *brotherhood loyalty; gang spirit*

【哥斯达黎加】Costa Rica ◇ ～人 Costa Rican

【哥特式】[建] Gothic: ～教堂 *Gothic cathedral (or church)*

【哥特体】[刷] gothic (type)

胳 (构词成分)见下

【胳臂】arm

【胳膊】arm ◇ ～腕子 wrist; ～肘儿 elbow

【胳膊扭不过大腿】the arm is no match for the thigh—the weaker can't contend with the stronger

【胳膊肘儿往外拐】one's elbow turns to the wrong side; side with outsiders instead of one's own people

鸽 名 pigeon; dove: 家鸽

【鸽哨】a whistle tied to a pigeon

【鸽子】pigeon; dove: ～笼 *dovecote; pigeon house; loft*

割 动 cut: ～麦子 *cut (or reap) wheat* / ～草 *cut grass; mow* / ～破手指 *cut one's finger*

【割爱】give up what one treasures; part with some cherished possession: 这盘磁带请你～让给我吧。*Would you be willing to part with this cassette and give it to me please?*

【割草机】mower

【割除】cut off; remove; excise: ～肿瘤 *remove a tumour*

【割断】sever; cut off: ～电话线 *cut telephone wires* / 我们不能～历史看问题。*We mustn't consider a question apart from its historical context*.

【割胶】tap rubber

【割炬】[机] cutting torch

【割据】set up a separatist regime by force of arms: 封建～ *feudal separatist rule* / 军阀～ *separatist warlord regimes* / 诸侯～称雄的封建国家 *a feudal state torn apart by rival principalities*

【割捆机】[农] self-binder; binder

【割礼】[宗] circumcision

【割裂】cut apart; separate; isolate: 这两点是互相联系的,不能～。*The two points are related and cannot be taken separately*.

【割让】cede: ～领土 *cession of territory*

【割晒机】[农] swather; windrower

【割舍】give up; part with: 难以～ *find it hard to part with*

【割线】［数］secant

搁 动 ❶ put：把箱子～在行李架上。*Put the suitcase on the luggage-rack*. / 你把东西～下。*Put down your things*. ❷ put aside；leave over；shelve：这件事得～一～再办。*We'll have to put the matter aside for the time being*. ——另见 gé

【搁笔】lay down the pen or brush；stop writing or painting

【搁浅】❶ run aground；be stranded：船～了。*The ship got stranded (or ran aground)*. ❷ reach a deadlock：谈判～了。*The negotiations have come to a deadlock*.

【搁置】shelve；lay aside；pigeonhole：～一项动议 *shelve a motion* / 他要出国留学，婚事只好～不提。*Since he was going abroad to study, he had to shelve his marriage plans*.

歌 Ⅰ 名 song：唱支～儿 *sing a song* Ⅱ 动 sing

【歌本】songbook

【歌唱】❶ sing：尽情～ *sing to one's heart's content* / ～家 *singer*；*vocalist* ❷ praise (through songs, poems, etc.)：～祖国的繁荣昌盛 *sing (in praise) of the prosperity of our country*

【歌词】words of a song

【歌功颂德】eulogize sb.'s virtues and achievements；sing the praises of sb.

【歌喉】(singer's) voice；singing voice：～婉转 *have a sweet (or beautiful) voice*

【歌后】most accomplished female singer；singing queen

【歌剧】opera：小～ *operetta* / ～剧本 *libretto* / ～团 *opera troupe (or company)* / ～院 *opera house*

【歌诀】formulas or directions put into rhyme

【歌迷】song fan or devotee

【歌片儿】song sheet

【歌谱】music score of a song；music of a song

【歌曲】song

【歌声】sound of singing；singing：～四起。*Sounds of singing were heard from all around*.

【歌手】singer；vocalist

【歌颂】sing the praises of；extol；eulogize

【歌坛】the circle of singers：～新秀 *a new singing star*

【歌舞】song and dance ◇ ～伎 kabuki (a popular Japanese dramatic form)；～剧 song and dance drama；～片 musical；～团 song and dance ensemble (or troupe)

【歌舞升平】sing and dance to extol the good times—put on a show of peace and prosperity

【歌星】a singing star

【歌谣】ballad；folk song；nursery rhyme：民间～ *folk songs*；*popular ballads*

【歌咏】singing：～比赛 *singing contest* / ～队 *singing group*；*chorus*

gé

革 Ⅰ 名 leather；hide：皮革 Ⅱ 动 ❶ change；transform：变革 ❷ remove sb. from office；expel：革职

【革除】❶ abolish；get rid of；eliminate：～陈规陋习 *abolish outmoded regulations and eliminate irrational practices* ❷ expel；dismiss；remove sb. from office

【革故鼎新】discard the old and introduce the new

【革履】leather shoes

【革命】❶ cause great social change；rise in revolt；take part in revolution：～到底 *carry the revolution through to the end*；*remain a revolutionary to the end of one's life* ❷ revolution：技术～ *technological revolution* / ～理论 *revolutionary theory* ◇ ～化 revolutionize；do things in a revolutionary way；～回忆录 reminiscences of earlier revolutionary times；～家 revolutionary；revolutionist；～浪漫主义 revolutionary romanticism；～人道主义 revolutionary humanitarianism；～现实主义 revolutionary realism；～性 revolutionary character (or quality, spirit)；～英雄主义 revolutionary heroism

【革新】innovate；improve：技术～ *technological innovation* / 传统的手工艺技术不断～。*Traditional handicraft techniques are being steadily improved*.

【革职】remove sb. from office；dismiss sb. from his post；cashier：他因贻误军机被朝廷～查办。*The imperial court removed him from office and prosecuted him for delaying the fulfilment of a military plan*.

阁 名 ❶ pavilion (usu. two-storeyed) ❷ cabinet (of a government)：组阁 ❸〈旧〉boudoir：出阁 ❹〈书〉shelf：束之高阁

【阁楼】attic；loft；garret

【阁下】〈尊〉Your Excellency or His or Her Excellency：大使～ *Your Excellency Mr. Ambassador* or *His Excellency the Ambassador*

【阁员】member of a cabinet

格 Ⅰ 名 ❶ squares formed by crossed lines；check：把字写在～儿里。*Write the characters in the squares*. / 在纸上打～儿 *square off the paper* ❷ division (horizontal or otherwise)：横～纸 *ruled paper* / 四～儿的书架 *a bookcase with four shelves* / 每服一小～。*Dose one measure each time*. ❸ standard；pattern；style：合格 ❹〈语〉case：主～ *the nominative case* / 宾～ *the objective case* Ⅱ 动〈书〉impede；obstruct；bar：～于成例 *be hindered by conventions*

【格调】❶ (literary or artistic) style：～豪放 *a vigorous and flowing style* / 这首诗～很老成。*This poem is written in a grand style*. ❷〈书〉one's style of work as well as one's moral quality：他这个人～不高。*He's rather vulgar*.

【格斗】grapple；wrestle；fistfight：徒手～ *fight with bare fists*

【格格不入】incompatible with；out of tune with；out of one's element；like a square peg in a round hole：他的计划和我的意图是～的。*His plan is incompatible with my intentions.*

【格局】pattern；setup；structure：外交～ *the pattern of a country's foreign affairs*

【格莱梅奖】Grammy；Grammys or Grammies

【格林纳达】Grenada ◇ ～人 Grenadian

【格林威治时间】Greenwich mean time（GMT）

【格陵兰】Greenland

【格鲁吉亚】Georgia

【格律】rules and forms of classical poetic composition（with respect to tonal pattern，rhyme scheme，etc.）

【格杀勿论】（又作‘格杀不论’）kill on the spot with the authority of the law

【格式】form；pattern：公文～ *the form（or standardized style）of an official document*

【格外】❶ especially；particularly；all the more：雪地上骑车要～小心。*You've got to be especially careful when you cycle on snow.* ❷ additionally：卡车装不下，～找了一辆大车。*As the truck couldn't hold all the goods，an additional cart was ordered.*

【格物致知】to investigate things is to attain knowledge

【格言】maxim；motto；aphorism

【格子】squares formed by crossed lines；check；chequer：用尺打～ *square（the page）off with a ruler* ◇ ～布 checked fabric；check；～窗 lattice window；～花呢 tartan

葛 名 ❶［植］kudzu vine ❷ poplin ——另见 gě

【葛布】ko-hemp cloth

【葛根】［中］the root of kudzu vine

蛤 名 clam ——另见 há

【蛤蜊】clam

搁 动 bear；stand；endure：～不住压 *cannot stand crushing* ——另见 gē

隔 动 ❶separate；cut off；partition：把一间屋～成两间 *partition a room into two* ❷ be apart from；be at a distance from：相～千里 *be a thousand li away from each other* / 每棵树苗要～开五米。*The saplings should be five metres apart.* /你～两天再来吧。*Come back in two days' time.*

【隔岸观火】watch a fire from the other side of the river—look on at sb.'s trouble with indifference

【隔壁】next door：～邻居 *next-door neighbour* / 住在～ *live next door* / ～第二间 *next door but one*

【隔断】❶ cut off；separate；obstruct：洪水把村子同县城的交通～了。*The flood cut the village off from the county town.* ❷［建］partition（wall，board，etc.）

【隔行如隔山】different trades are separated as by mountains（i.e. the outsider knows no more of the secrets of the craft than he knows of another country）

【隔阂】❶ estrangement；misunderstanding：制造～ *foment feelings of estrangement* ❷ barrier：语言的～ *language barrier*

【隔绝】cut off；separate；obstruct：和外界～ *be cut off from the outside world* / 他走了以后就与我们音信～了。*He has never been heard of since he left us.* or *There's been no news of him since he left.*

【隔离】keep apart；isolate；segregate：种族～ *racial segregation；apartheid* / 病人已经～了一周。*The patient has been in isolation for a week.* ◇ ～病房 isolation ward；～带 dividing strip，specifically the lines separating fast and slow lanes on a road；～审查（during political movements）isolate and interrogate；～栅 isolated gate

【隔膜】❶ lack of mutual understanding：他们之间有些～。*They are somewhat estranged from each other.* ❷ be unfamiliar with：我对那里的情况很～。*I know very little about the situation there.*

【隔片】［机］spacer

【隔墙】［建］partition（wall）

【隔墙有耳】walls have ears；beware of eavesdroppers

【隔热】［建］insulate against heat

【隔扇】partition board

【隔声】［建］insulate against sound：～板 *sound insulating board* / ～材料 *sound insulator*

【隔靴搔痒】scratch an itch from outside one's boot—fail to get to the root of the matter；fail to strike home；take totally ineffective measures

【隔夜】of the previous night：把～的菜热一热 *warm up last night's leftovers* / ～的茶最好别喝。*You'd better not drink last night's tea.*

【隔音】give sound insulation ◇ ～符号 syllable-dividing mark（'）；～室 soundproof room

嗝 名 ❶ hiccup ❷ belch；burp

膈 名 diaphragm

【膈膜】diaphragm

镉 名［化］cadmium（Cd）

gě

舸 名〈字〉barge

葛（构词成分）见下 ——另见 gé

【葛仙米】［植］nostoc

gè

个 Ⅰ 名 size，height：个儿/个头儿 Ⅱ 量 ❶（before nouns without special measure words of their own）：三～苹果 *three apples* / 一～故事 *a story* / 两～星期 *two weeks；a fortnight* / 一～心眼儿 *be of one mind* / 第五～年头 *the fifth year* ❷（used to replace certain measure words）：

一～(or 所)学校 *a school* / 一～(or 家)工厂 *a factory* / 两～(or 只)耳朵 *two ears* ❸(before an approximate number): 他每星期来～一、两趟。*He comes here once or twice every week.* ❹(between a verb and its object): 洗～澡 *have a bath* / 睡～好觉 *have a good sleep* Ⅲ 助 ❶(between a verb and its complement): 砸～稀巴烂 *smash sth. to smithereens* / 忙～不停 *be as busy as a bee* ❷(used as a suffix after 些): 那些～花儿 *all those flowers* / 这些～书哪能看完? *How can I finish reading so many books?* Ⅳ 形 individual: 个别 / 个人

【个案】(individual or special) case: ～研究 *case study*

【个把】one or two; a couple of: 多～人也住得下。*There is enough room to put up one or two more people.* / 再过～月,我就要回国了。*In a couple of months, I'll be going back to my country.*

【个别】❶ individual; specific: ～辅导 *individual coaching* / ～照顾 *special consideration for individual cases* ❷ very few; one or two: 只有～人请假。*Only one or two people asked for leave.* / 这是极其～的事例。*Such instances are very rare.* / 这是～情况。*These are isolated cases.* ◇ ～差异[心理] individual differences; ～教学法 individualized introduction; ～许可证 individual licence

【个儿】size, height: ～高 *tall*

【个个】*each and every one; all*: 这些战士～都是好样的。*Each and every one of these soldiers has proved his mettle.*

【个股】individual share

【个人】❶ individual (person): ～利益 *personal interests* / 用他～的名义 *in his own name* ❷ I: ～认为 *in my opinion* / 我～并不反对你这样干。*Personally I see no objection to your doing so.* ◇ ～崇拜 deify and worship an individual (national leader, etc.); individual superstition; ～存款 individual deposits; ～电脑 personal computer; PC; ～冠军 individual championship; ～技术 personal skill; ～迷信 cult of the individual; personality cult; ～所得税 personal income tax; ～投资 individual investment; ～项目[体] individual events; ～信用 personal credit; ～野心 personal ambition; ～英雄主义 individualistic heroism; ～主义 individualism

【个体】individual: ～农业经营 *individual farming* ◇ ～户 privately owned small enterprise; self-employed labourer (or worker); ～经济 individual economy; ～经营 individually-owned business; ～劳动者 a person who works on his own; self-employed labourer (or worker); ～劳动协会 self-employed laborer's association; ～企业 private enterprise; private firm; individual enterprise; ～商贩 individual traders and peddlers; businessman; ～商业 trade run by individuals; ～生产者 individual producer; ～所有制 individual (or private) ownership

【个头儿】〈方〉size, height

【个性】individual character; individuality; personality: 共性和～ *the general and specific character of sth.* / 这孩子～很强。*The boy has a strong character.* ◇ ～转变期 identity crisis

【个中】〈书〉therein: ～奥妙 *the inside story; the secret of it* ◇ ～人 a person in the know

【个子】height; stature; build: 高～ *a tall person* / 小～ *a small fellow; a short person*

各 Ⅰ 代 each; every; various; different: ～人有～人的优点。*Each has his merits.* / ～式糕点 *various kinds of cakes and pastries* Ⅱ 副 variously; respectively: 这三人～按其能力分配了工作。*The three men were given work according to their respective abilities.* / 两侧～有一门。*There's a door on either side.*

【各半】half and half; fifty-fifty: 成败的可能性～。*The chances of success are fifty-fifty.*

【各奔前程】each pursues his own course; each goes his own way

【各别】❶ distinct; different: ～对待 *treat differently; treat each on its (his, etc.) own merits* ❷〈方〉out of the ordinary; peculiar: 这只闹钟式样很～。*This alarm clock is quite unusual-looking.* ❸ odd; eccentric; funny: 这人的脾气真～。*He's a really eccentric character.*

【各不相让】neither is willing to give ground; each is trying to outdo the other

【各持己见】(又作'各执己见') each sticks to his own view.

【各打五十大板】punish the wronged and the wrong-doer alike; punish the guilty and the innocent alike; blame both sides without discrimination

【各得其所】each is in his proper place; each is properly provided for; each has a role to play

【各个】❶ each; every; various: ～厂矿 *each factory and mine* / ～方面 *all the various aspects* / 社会上的～阶级 *the various classes in society* ❷ one by one: ～解决 *resolve problems one at a time*

【各行各业】all trades and professions; all walks of life

【各级】all or different levels: ～领导机关 *leading organizations at all levels* / ～人民代表大会 *the people's congresses at different levels* ◇ ～政府 government at all levels

【各界】all walks of life; all circles: ～人士 *personages of various circles*

【各尽所能】each doing his best; from each according to his ability

【各尽所能,按劳分配】from each according to his ability, to each according to his work—the socialist principle of distribution

【各尽所能,按需分配】from each according to his ability, to each according to his needs—the communist principle of distribution

【各就位】[体](word of command) on your marks

【各取所需】each takes what he needs

【各人自扫门前雪】each one sweeps the snow from his own doorstep—each one minds his own business：～，莫管他家瓦上霜。*Each one sweeps the snow from his own doorstep and heeds not the frost on his neighbour's roof.*

【各色】of all kinds；of every description；assorted：商店里～货物，一应俱全。*The shop is well stocked with goods of all kinds.*

【各抒己见】each airs his own views

【各司其职】each does his or her duty；each performs his or her own functions

【各位】❶ everybody（a term of address）：～请注意！*Attention please，everybody.* ❷ every：～代表 *fellow delegates*

【各向同性】［物］isotropy

【各向异性】［物］anisotropy

【各行其是】each does what he thinks is right；each goes his own way

【各有千秋】each has something to recommend him；each has his strong points

【各有所长】each has his own strong points

【各有所好】each has his likes and dislikes；each follows his own bent

【各执一词】each sticks to his own version or argument

【各自】each；respective：散会的时候已经很晚了，大家就～回家了。*When the meeting ended，it was already very late，so everyone just went home.*

【各自为政】each does things in his own way

铬 名［化］chromium（Cr）

【铬钢】［冶］chromium steel；chrome steel

【铬镍钢】chrome-nickel steel

【铬鞣】chrome tanning：～革 *chrome leather*

【铬铁】ferrochrome ◇ ～矿 chromite

硌 动〈口〉（of sth. hard or bulging）press or rub against：褥子没有铺平，躺在上面～得难受。*That rumpled mattress was terribly uncomfortable.* / 鞋里有砂子，～脚。*There's some grit in the shoe，and it hurts my foot.*

gěi

给 Ⅰ 动 ❶give；grant：我哥～了我一块表。*My brother gave me a watch.* / 公司～他一个月的假。*The company granted him a month's leave.* / 杭州～我的印象很好。*Hangzhou left a very good impression on me.* ❷ let；allow；make：～我看看。*Let me have a look.* / 开完运动会，～我累得够呛。*After the sports meet，I was tired out.* Ⅱ 介 ❶ for the benefit of；for the sake of；for：她～旅客送水倒茶。*She brought drinking water and tea for the passengers.* / 我～你当翻译。*I'll act as interpreter for you.* ❷（used to introduce the recipient of an action）for，to：他～我道歉了。*He's apologized to me.* / 小朋友～老师行了礼。*The children saluted their teacher.* Ⅲ 助 ❶〈口〉（used before a verb for emphasis）：质量不合格～换。*Substandard products will be exchanged.* / 把纸收起来，别叫风～刮散了。*Put away all the paper. Don't let it get blown about.* / 我差点儿把这事～忘了。*I almost forgot that.* ❷（used after a verb indicating the handing over of sth.）：信已经交～他了。*I've handed the letter to him.* ——另见 jǐ

【给出路】give sb. a way out

【给脸】do sb. a favour；save sb.'s face：董事长来打了个照面儿，也算是～了。*As a favour，the president put in a brief appearance.*

【给脸不要脸】be fool enough to reject a face-saving offer

【给小鞋穿】give sb. tight shoes to wear—make things difficult for sb. by abusing one's power；make sb. feel the pinch：你敢提意见，老板就给你小鞋儿穿。*If you dare to make a complaint the boss will give you a hard time.*

【给颜色看】make it hot for sb.：你如果不安分，他就要给你颜色看。*If you go on making trouble，he'll show（or tell）you a thing or two.*

【给以】（usu. with abstract nouns as direct object）give；grant：～充分的重视 *pay ample attention to* / ～适当照顾 *show due consideration for*

gēn

根 Ⅰ 名 ❶ root（of a plant）：树～ *roots of a tree* ❷ descendants；offspring：单～独苗 *the sole male descendant（or heir）* ❸［数］solution of an algebraic equation ❹［化］radical：酸～ *acid radical* ❺ root；foot；base：舌～ *the root of the tongue* / 城墙～ *the foot（or base）of a city wall* ❻ cause；origin；source；root：我们是老街坊，彼此都知～知底的。*We are old neighbours，so we know each other's background very well.* Ⅱ 副 thoroughly；completely：根除 Ⅲ 量（for long，thin objects）：一～火柴 *a match* / 一～小绳子 *a piece of string*

【根本】❶ foundation；base：千头万绪抓～。*Faced with a great variety of problems，one must concentrate on what is of basic importance.* ❷ basic；fundamental；essential；cardinal：～原因 *basic reason；root cause* / ～原则 *cardinal principle* / 一件带～性的大事 *a major measure of fundamental importance* ❸（usu. used in the negative）at all；simply：我～就不赞成你的主张。*I don't agree with you at all.* ❹ radically；thoroughly：问题已经得到～解决。*The problem has been settled once and for all.*

【根本法】fundamental law（i.e. a constitution）：宪法是国家的～。*The Constitution is the fundamental law of the state.*

【根本性逆差】fundamental deficit

【根除】thoroughly do away with；eradicate；root out；eliminate：～一切形式的殖民主义 *eradicate all forms of colonialism* / ～水患 *eliminate the scourge of floods*

【根底】❶ foundation：～浅 *have a shaky foundation* / 他的英文～很好。*He has a solid foundation in English*. ❷ cause；root：追问～ *inquire into the cause of the matter* / 你了解这个人的～吗？*Do you know that fellow's background*？

【根雕】tree-root carving (a handicraft)

【根腐病】[农] root rot

【根冠】[植] root cap

【根号】[数] radical sign

【根基】❶ foundation；basis：打好～ *lay a solid foundation* / ～牢固 *a firm foundation* / ～动摇 *be shaken to the very foundations* ❷ property accumulated over a long time；resources：公司刚成立，～还很差。*The company has just been established and is still on unsound footing*.

【根茎】(又作'根状茎') [植] rhizome

【根究】make a thorough investigation of；get to the bottom of；probe into：～缘由 *probe into the cause*

【根据】❶ on the basis of；according to；in the light of；in line with：～天气预报，明天要下雨。*According to the weather forecast, it's going to rain tomorrow*. ❷ basis；grounds；foundation：说话要有～。*One should avoid making assertions without good grounds*. / 毫无～ *utterly groundless* / ～情节轻重。*According to the seriousness of the case*

【根据地】base area；base

【根绝】stamp out；eradicate；exterminate：～血吸虫病 *stamp out snail fever* / ～事故 *eliminate accidents*

【根瘤】[植] root nodule ◇ ～菌 nodule bacteria

【根毛】[植] root hair

【根苗】❶ root and shoot ❷ source；root ❸〈旧〉(usu. male) offspring

【根深蒂固】(又作'根深柢固') deep-rooted；ingrained；inveterate：～的偏见 *deep-rooted (or inveterate) prejudice*

【根深叶茂】have deep roots and luxuriant leaves—be well eatablished and vigorously developing

【根式】[数] radical (expression)

【根外追肥】[农] foliage dressing；foliage spray

【根由】cause；origin：追问～ *make detailed inquiries about the cause of sth*.

【根源】❶ source；origin；root：实践是一切科学知识的～。*Practical experience is the source of all scientific knowledge*. ❷ originate；stem from：经济危机～于资本主义制度。*Economic crisis originates in the capitalist system*.

【根植】take root

【根治】effect a radical cure；cure once and for all；bring under permanent control：～支气管炎 *effect a radical cure of bronchitis*

【根治手术】[医] radical operation

【根轴系】[植] root system

【根子】〈口〉❶ root (of a plant) ❷ cause；origin；source；root

跟 Ⅰ 名 heel：脚跟 Ⅱ 动 follow：～我来。*Come along with me*. or *Follow me*. / 紧～形势 *keep abreast of the current situation* Ⅲ 介 ❶ (used to indicate accompaniment, relationship, involvement, etc.) with：～父母住一块儿 *live with one's parents* ❷ (used to introduce the recipient of an action)：我有几句话～你讲。*There's something I want to talk to you about*. ❸ (used to show comparison)：今天的活儿～往常一样。*Our job today is the same as before*. / ～去年相比，产量增加了百分之十。*Output has increased by 10% over last year*. Ⅳ 连 and：他～我都是四川人。*He and I are both from Sichuan*.

【跟班】❶ join a regular shift or class：～劳动 (*of a leading comrade*) *go to work in a workshop for a specified period of time* / ～听课 *audit a class* ❷ (又作'跟班儿的') 〈旧〉 footman

【跟单承兑】documentary acceptance

【跟单汇兑】documentary remittance

【跟单信用证】documentary credit

【跟脚】〈方〉❶ (of shoes) fit well ❷ close upon sb.'s heels：你刚走，他～儿就来找你。*He came to see you just after you left*. ❸ wait upon one's master when going out：～的 *footman* ❹ (of children) not be willing to leave one's parents

【跟屁虫】〈方〉〈贬〉 persistent follower；shadow；pest

【跟前】the area in front of sb. or sth.：他把我叫到～又讲了几句。*He told me to come closer and said a few more words*. / 桌子～靠着一支猎枪。*A shotgun leans against the table*.

【跟上】keep pace with；catch up with；keep abreast of：快～！*Hurry and catch up*！/ 跟不上形势的需要 *fall short of the demands of the times* / 跟不上形势的发展 *cannot keep up with the changing situation*

【跟随】❶ follow：这条狗紧紧～在主人身后。*The dog followed closely behind his master*. ❷ retinue：他每次出门，后面总有一大批～。*Whenever he goes out, he always has a whole entourage following him*.

【跟头】❶ tumble；fall：摔～ *have a fall* ❷ somersault：翻个～ *turn a somersault*

【跟头虫】wiggler；wriggler

【跟踪】follow the tracks of：雪地～ *follow sb.'s tracks in the snow* / ～追击 *go in hot pursuit of* / ～敌舰 *shadow the enemy warships* ◇ ～程序 tracing routine；～搜索 [电子] tack-while-scan

gén

哏 形 〈方〉❶ amusing；comical；funny：这段相声真～。*This comic dialogue is really funny*. / 这孩子笑的样子真有点儿～。*The way the child laughs is quite funny*. ❷ clownish speech or behaviour；clowning；antics：他说话带～。*There's humour in his words*.

gěn

艮 形〈方〉blunt；straightforward；forthright：这人真～！*That fellow is really blunt*. / 他说的话太～。*He put it too sharply*.

gèn

亘 动 extend；stretch：绵亘

【亘古未有】no such thing from days of old—unheard-of；unprecedented

gēng

更 Ⅰ 动 ❶ change；replace：变更 ❷〈书〉experience：少不更事 Ⅱ 名 one of the five two-hour periods into which the night was formerly divided；watch：打更 ——另见 gèng

【更迭】alternate；change：内阁～ *a change of cabinet*

【更动】change；alter：人事～ *personnel changes* / 图案已有所～。*The design has been altered*.

【更番】by turns；alternately：～出差 *go on business trips by turns*

【更夫】〈旧〉night watchman

【更改】change；alter：不可～的决定 *an unalterable decision* / 由于天气恶劣，飞机不得不～航线。*Owing to bad weather the plane had to change its course*.

【更换】change；replace：～位置 *change places* / ～衣裳 *change one's clothes* / 农展馆的展品常有～。*The exhibits in the agricultural exhibition centre keep changing*.

【更年期】climacteric or menopause；change of life

【更仆难数】too many to count；innumerable；countless

【更深人静】deep is the night and all is quiet：在～的时候 *at dead of night*；*in the quiet of the night*

【更生】❶ regenerate；revive：自力更生 ❷ renew：可～和不可～的海洋资源 *renewable and nonrenewable marine resources*

【更生霉素】［药］actinomycin D

【更替】replace：生产方式的～ *the replacement of one mode of production by another*

【更新】❶ replace：设备～ *renewal of equipment* / 渔船在不断～。*Old fishing vessels are continually being replaced by new ones*. ❷ (of forest, plants, etc.) renew；rejuvenate：他们采用科学方法～草场。*They have adopted scientific methods to rejuvenate the pastures*.

【更新伐】［林］regeneration felling (or cutting)

【更新改造项目】projects of equipment renewal and technological transformation

【更新观念】change one's concepts；renew ideas

【更新换代】replace the old with the new

【更新投资】replacement investment

【更新造林】reforestation

【更衣】change one's clothes ◇ ～室 changing room；locker room

【更正】make corrections (of errors in published statements or articles)：文章有了错误，应当在报纸上～。*If there is a mistake in any of the articles*, *the newspaper should correct it*.

庚 名 ❶ the seventh of the ten Heavenly Stems (天干) ❷ age：年庚——另见〖干支〗

耕 动 plough；till：春耕

【耕畜】farm animal

【耕地】❶ plough；till：耕了两亩地 *plough two mu of land* ❷ cultivated land：～面积 *area under cultivation*；*cultivated area*

【耕具】tillage implements

【耕牛】farm cattle

【耕耘】plough and weed；cultivate：一分～，一分收获。*The more ploughing and weeding*, *the better the crop*. —*No gains without pains*.

【耕者有其田】land to the tiller

【耕种】till；cultivate

【耕作】tillage；cultivation；farming ◇ ～方法 methods of cultivation；farming methods；～机械 tillage machinery；～技术 farming technique；～园田化 garden-style cultivation of farmland；gardenization；～制度 cropping system

羹 名 a thick soup：鸡蛋～ *egg custard* (*usu. salty*)

【羹匙】soup spoon；tablespoon

gěng

埂 名 ❶ a low bank of earth between fields：田埂 ❷ a long, narrow mound：山～ *a hill mound* ❸ an earth dyke (or embankment)

耿 形 ❶〈文〉bright ❷ honest and just；upright

【耿耿】❶〈文〉bright：～星河 *the bright Milky Way* ❷ devoted；dedicated：忠心～为革命 *be dedicated heart and soul to the revolution* ❸ having sth. on one's mind；worried：～不寐 *lose sleep over sth*.

【耿耿于怀】brood on (an injury, one's neglected duty, etc.)；take sth. to heart

【耿直】honest and frank；upright：秉性～ *be upright by nature* / 他是个～人，一向知无不言，言无不尽。*He is honest and frank*, *and always says everything he knows without reserve*.

哽 动 choke (with emotion)；feel a lump in one's throat：他心里一酸，喉咙～得说不出话来。*He felt a pang of sadness*, *and got so choked up he couldn't speak*.

【哽咽】choke with sobs：她怎么也忍不住，～了一声泪水便夺眶而出。*Unable to control herself any longer, she began to sob and her tears fell in torrents.* /她用～了的嗓音苦苦哀求。*She implored piteously, in a voice choked with sobs.*

梗 Ⅰ名 ❶ stalk; stem: 荷～ *lotus stem* / 菠菜～儿 *spinach stalk* ❷ a slender piece of wood or metal: 火柴～ *matchstick* Ⅱ动 ❶straighten: ～着脖子 *straightening up one's neck* ❷ obstruct; block: 梗塞

【梗概】broad outline; main idea; gist: 故事的～ *the gist of a story; synopsis*

【梗塞】❶ block; obstruct; clog: 交通～ *traffic jam* ❷［医］infarction

【梗死】［医］infarction: 心肌～ *myocardial infarction*

【梗阻】❶ block; obstruct; hamper: 山川～ *be separated by mountains and rivers; be far away from each other* / 横加～ *unreasonably obstruct or raise obstacles* ❷［医］obstruction: 肠～ *intestinal obstruction*

鲠 名 ❶ fishbone ❷ (of a fishbone) get stuck in one's throat: 如～在喉 *like having a fishbone caught in one's throat (said of a person who has a criticism that he must express)*

gèng

更 副 ❶ more; still more; even more: 他没有放慢速度,反而把车开得～快了。*He didn't slow down. On the contrary, he drove faster.* / 刮了一夜北风,天～冷了。*The weather has got even colder since the north wind blew all night.* ❷〈书〉further; furthermore; what is more: ～进一步地阐明观点 *go still one step further to explain one's position* / ～有甚者 *what is more* ——另见 gēng

【更加】(又作'更其') more; still more; even more: 问题～复杂了。*The problem became even more complicated.* / 天色渐亮,星星～稀少。*The stars faded as day dawned.*

gōng

工 Ⅰ名 ❶ worker; workman; the working class: 女工 ❷ work; labour: 上～ *go to work* / 既省料又省～ *save both material and labour* ❸ (construction) project: 动工 ❹ industry: ～交战线 *the industry and communications front; industry and communications* ❺ man-day: 这项工程需要五千个～。*This project will take 5,000 man-days to complete.* ❻ skill; craftsmanship: 唱工 Ⅱ动 be versed in; be good at: ～诗善画 *be well versed in painting and poetry* Ⅲ形 exquisite; fine: 工巧

【工本】cost (of production)

【工笔】traditional Chinese realistic painting characterized by fine brushwork and close attention to detail

【工兵】engineer (in an army): 坑道～ *sapper* / 轻～ *pioneer*

【工部】the Board of Works

【工厂】factory; mill; plant; works: 铁～ *iron works* / ～区 *factory district* ◇ ～自动化 factory automation

【工场】workshop

【工潮】workers' demonstration or protest movement; strike movement: 闹～ *go on strike*

【工尺】a traditional Chinese musical scale

【工尺谱】［音］a traditional Chinese muscial notation

【工程】❶ engineering: 土木(机械,电机,采矿)～ *civil (mechanical, electrical, mining) engineering* ❷ project: 水利～ *water conservancy project* / ～浩大 *a gigantic project; a tremendous amount of work* ◇ ～兵 engineer (in an army); ～车 machineshop car; ～贷款 financing of projects; ～地质学 engineering geology; ～队 construction brigade; ～技术人员 engineers and technicians; ～经济学 value engineering; engineering economics; ～师 engineer; ～塑料 engineering plastics; ～验收［建］acceptance of work; ～语言学 engineering linguistics; ～造价 cost of construction

【工党】the Labour Party

【工地】building site; construction site: ～上一片繁忙景象。*The construction site was a scene of bustling activity.*

【工读学校】reform school; approved school

【工段】❶ a section of a construction project ❷ workshop section ◇ ～长 section chief

【工蜂】worker (bee)

【工夫】❶ time: 他三天～就学会了滑冰。*It took him only three days to learn to skate.* / 她去了没多大～就回来了。*She didn't take long to get there and come back.* ❷〈方〉at that time: 我当闺女那～,连大门都不敢出。*When I was a girl, I didn't even dare to go outdoors.* ❸ workmanship; skill; art: 练～ *(of actors, athletes, etc.) practise* / 这位杂技演员可真有～! *The acrobat's skill is really superb!* ❹ effort; work: 花了好大～ *put in a lot of work*

【工行】(〈略〉全称为'工商银行') the Industrial and Commercial Bank

【工会】trade union; labour union

【工间操】work-break exercises

【工件】workpiece; work: ～夹具 *workpiece holder; (work) fixture*

【工匠】*craftsman; artisan*

【工交】(〈略〉全称为'工业和交通运输业') industry and communications: ～战线职工 *staff and workers of industrial and communication sectors*

【工具】tool; instrument; implement; means: 木工～ *carpenter's tools* / 生产～ *implements of production* / 运输～ *means of transport* / 爱护～ *take good care of the tools.* ◇ ～车床 toolmaker lathe; ～袋 kit bag; workbag; ～房 toolhouse;

tool storeroom；～钢 tool steel；～书 reference book；～箱 toolbox；tool kit；workbox

【工科】engineering course：～大学 *college of engineering*

【工力】❶ skill；craftsmanship：～深厚 *remarkable craftsmanship* / 颇见～ *show the hand of a master* ❷ manpower（needed for a project）

【工联主义】（又作'工会主义'）（trade）unionism

【工料】labour and materials（for a building project）

【工龄】length of service；standing；seniority：一个有三十年～的老工人 *an old worker of thirty years' standing*

【工贸】industry and trade

【工农】workers and peasants

【工农差别】the difference between industry and agriculture

【工农联盟】alliance of workers and peasants；worker-peasant alliance

【工农业总产值】gross output value of industry and agriculture

【工棚】❶ builders' temporary shed ❷ work shed

【工期】time limit for a project：提高效率，缩短～。*Increase efficiency and shorten the time limit for the project.*

【工钱】❶ money paid for odd jobs；charge for a service：做这套衣服要多少～？*How much should I pay for having the suit made?* ❷〈口〉wages；pay

【工巧】exquisite；fine

【工区】work area（a grass-roots unit of an industrial enterprise）

【工人】worker；workman：产业～ *industrial worker* ◇ ～贵族 labour aristocracy；aristocrats of labour；～阶级 the working class；～纠察队 workers' pickets；～运动 labour（or workers'）movement

【工伤】injury suffered on the job；industrial injury：～事故 *industrial accident*

【工商界】industrial and commercial circles；business circles

【工商联】〈略〉见〖工商业联合会〗

【工商税】industry and commercial income tax

【工商银行】the Industrial and Commercial Bank

【工商业】industry and commerce：私营～ *privately owned industrial and commercial enterprises* / ～者 *industrialists and businessmen*（*or merchants*）

【工商业联合会】association of industry and commerce

【工时】man-hour

【工事】fortifications；defence works：修筑～ *build fortifications*（*or defence works*）

【工头】foreman；overseer

【工团主义】syndicalism

【工效】work efficiency：提高～ *raise*（*or improve*）*work efficiency*

【工薪阶层】salaried workers；wage-earners

【工薪族】wage-earners

【工休日】day off；holiday

【工序】working procedure；process

【工业】industry ◇ ～病 professional diseases of industrial workers；～布局 distribution of industry；～产权 industrial property right；～废水 industrial wastewater；～粉尘 industrial dust；～革命 the Industrial Revolution；～国 industrialized（or industrial）country；～化 industrialize；～基地 industrial base；～酒精 industrial alcohol；～品 industrial products；manufactured goods；～企业 industrial enterprise；～气压 technic atmosphere；～体系 industrial system；～总产值 gross value of industrial output

【工艺】technology；craft：手工艺 ◇ ～流程 technological process；～美术 industrial art；arts and crafts；～品 handicraft article；handiwork；handicraft；～设计 technological design；～水平 technological level；～要求 technological requirements

【工友】a manual worker such as janitor，cleaner，etc. in a school or government office

【工于心计】adept at scheming；very calculating

【工欲善其事，必先利其器】a workman must first sharpen his tools if he is to do his work well

【工贼】scab；blackleg

【工长】section chief（in a workshop，or on a building site）；foreman

【工整】careful and neat：字迹～ *neatly lettered* / 他把自己的名字工工整整地写在书的衬页上。*He carefully wrote his name on the flyleaf.*

【工致】exquisite；delicate：那幅花鸟画画得很～。*The flower-and-bird painting was executed with great delicacy.*

【工种】type of work in production

【工转干】change of one's status from worker to cadre

【工装裤】overalls

【工资】wages；pay ◇ ～表 payroll；pay sheet；～袋 pay packet；～改革 reform of the wage system；～级别 wage scale；～率 wage rate；～制 wage system

【工字钢】I-steel

【工字形】I-shaped

【工作】❶ work；operate：努力～ *work hard* / 机器正在～。*The machine is in operation.* ❷ work；job：分配～ *assign jobs*（*or work*）/ 做研究～ *do research work* / 懂外语的人比较容易找到～。*People who know a foreign language can find jobs more easily.* / 他是做消防～的。*He works in the fire brigade.* ◇ ～本 working copy；～表 worksheet；～餐 working dinner；～场所程序图 workplace chart；～单位 an organization in which one works；place of work；～队 work team；working force；～服 work clothes；boiler suit；～会议 working conference；～量 amount of work；work load；～母机 machine tool；～人员 working personnel；staff member；functionary；～日 workday；working day；～台［机］working table；bench；～样片 film rushes；～证

employee's card; I. D. Card; ～周期［机］action cycle

【工作面】❶［矿］face: 采煤～ *coal face* / 回采～ *stope* / ～运输机 *face conveyor* ❷［机］working surface

【工作语言】working language

【工作者】worker: 教育～ *educational worker* / 文艺～ *literary and art workers; writers and artists* / 美术～ *art worker; artist* / 音乐～ *musician* / 新闻～ *journalist*

弓 Ⅰ名 ❶ bow: 用～和箭射鹿 *shoot a deer with a bow and arrow* ❷ anything bow-shaped: 弹棉花用的绷～儿 *bow used to tease cotton* ❸ wooden land-measuring dividers Ⅱ动 bend; arch; bow: ～着背 *arch one's back; bend low* / ～着腿坐着 *sitting with arched legs*

【弓箭】bow and arrow ◇ ～步 forward lunge (in wushu 武术 or gymnastics)

【弓弦】bowstring ◇ ～乐器 bowed stringed (or string) instrument; bowed instrument

【弓形】❶［数］segment of a circle ❷ bowshaped; arched; curved

【弓腰】bend over; bend down

【弓子】❶ bow (of a stringed instrument) ❷ anything bow-shaped

公 Ⅰ形 ❶ public; state-owned; collective: ～私要分清 *make a clear distinction between public and private interests* ❷ common; general: ～分母 *common denominator* ❸ of the world; international; universal: 公海 ❹ equitable; impartial; fair; just: 公买公卖 ❺ male (animal): ～象 *male (or bull) elephant* / 这只小鸡是～的。*It's a cockerel.* / 你的狗是～的还是母的? *Is your dog a he or a she?* / ～狼 *he-wolf* Ⅱ名 ❶ public affairs; official business: 因～外出 *be away on official business* ❷ duke: 公爵 ❸ (a respectful term of address for an elderly man): 张～ *the revered Mr. Zhang* ❹ husband's father; father-in-law Ⅲ动 make public: 公之于世

【公安】public security: ～人员 *public security officer (or man)* / ～部队 *public security troops* / ～机关 *public security organs* ◇ ～部 the Ministry of Public Security; ～干警 public security police; ～局 public security bureau

【公案】〈旧〉❶ court table (used by a judge) ❷ a complicated legal case ❸ a much discussed issue; a sensational affair

【公办】government administered; state-run: ～企业 *government run enterprise* / ～学校 *state school*

【公报】communiqué; bulletin: 新闻～ *press communiqué* / 政府～ *(government) bulletin*

【公报私仇】avenge personal wrongs in the name of public interests; abuse public power to retaliate against a personal enemy

【公倍数】［数］common multiple: 最小～ *least (or lowest) common multiple*

【公布】promulgate; announce; publish; make public: ～法令 *promulgate a decree* / ～罪状 *announce sb.'s crimes* / ～名单 *publish a name list* / ～账目 *publish the accounts*

【公厕】(〈略〉全称为'公共厕所') public toilets

【公差】(gōngchā) ❶［数］common difference ❷［机］tolerance: 制造(安装)～ *manufacturing (location) tolerance*

【公差】(gōngchāi) ❶ public errand; official business; noncombatant duty: 出～ *go on a public errand; go on official business; perform noncombatant duty* ❷ a person on a public errand (or noncombatant duty)

【公产】public property

【公车】❶ public (as opposed to private) vehicles; ❷ (in Taiwan) buses

【公称】［机］nominal: ～尺寸 *nominal dimension*

【公尺】metre (m.)

【公出】be away on official business

【公畜】male animal (kept for breeding); stud

【公担】quintal (q.)

【公道】(gōngdào) justice: 主持～ *uphold justice*

【公道】(gōngdao) fair; just; reasonable; impartial: 说句～话 *to be fair; in fairness to sb.* / 价钱～。*The price is reasonable.* / 办事～ *be even-handed; be impartial*

【公德】public morality (concerned with a regulated behaviour pattern in a community); social ethics ◇ ～心 public spirit

【公敌】public enemy: 人民～ *an enemy of the people; a public enemy*

【公牍】〈书〉official document

【公断】❶ arbitrate: 听候众人～ *await the verdict of the public* ❷ consider and decide impartially ◇ ～人 umpire; arbitrator

【公吨】metric ton (MT)

【公而忘私】so devoted to public service as to forget private interests; selfless

【公法】［法］public law

【公方】state ownership (in a joint state-private enterprise): ～代表 *representatives of state ownership (in a joint state-private enterprise)*

【公费】(at) public (or state) expense: ～留学 *study abroad on state scholarship* ◇ ～旅游 travel at public expense; ～医疗 free medical service (or care); public health services

【公分】❶ centimetre (cm.) ❷ gram (g.)

【公愤】public indignation; popular anger: 激起～ *arouse public indignation*

【公干】official business: 有何～? *What important business brings you here?*

【公告】announcement; proclamation

【公共】public; common; communal: ～财产 *public property* / ～场所 *public places* / ～建筑 *public buildings* / ～食堂 *canteen; mess; cafeteria* ◇ ～厕所 public conveniences; public latrine; ～积累 common accumulation; accumulation fund; ～汽车 bus; ～卫生 public health (or hygiene); ～责任保险 public liability insurance ; ～秩序

public order

【公共关系】public relations ◇ ～学 the study of public relations

【公共课】common required course

【公公】❶ husband's father; father-in-law ❷〈方〉(paternal) grandfather ❸〈方〉(maternal) grandfather ❹ (a respectful term of address for an elderly man) grandpa; grandad: 刘～ *Grandpa Liu* ❺〈旧〉a form of address for a court eunuch

【公股】government share (in a joint state-private enterprise)

【公关】〈略〉见〖公共关系〗◇ ～部 public relations department; ～部主任 public relations manager; ～小姐 PR ladies; public relations girl

【公馆】〈旧〉residence (of a rich or important person); mansion

【公国】duchy; dukedom

【公海】high seas

【公害】social effects of pollution; environmental pollution

【公函】official letter

【公鸡】cock; rooster

【公积金】accumulation fund (of a socialist economic collective)

【公祭】public memorial ceremony

【公家】〈口〉the state; the public; the organization: ～的财产就是人民的财产。*Public property is the people's property*.

【公检法】public security organs, procuratorial organs and people's courts

【公教人员】〈旧〉government employees and teachers

【公斤】kilogram (kg.); kilo

【公爵】duke ◇ ～夫人 duchess

【公开】❶ open; overt; public: ～论战 *open polemics* / ～审判 *public* (*or open*) *trial* / ～的秘密 *an open secret* ❷ make public; make known to the public: 把事情～出去 *make the matter known to the public* ◇ ～报价 public offer; ～拍卖 public auction; sell by public auction; ～赛 open tournament; ～投标 open bidding; public bidding; ～招标 competitive bidding; competitive tender; ～招聘 publicly engage

【公开化】come out into the open; be brought into the open

【公开信】open letter

【公筷】serving chopsticks; chopsticks for serving food

【公款】public money (or fund)

【公里】kilometre (km.)

【公理】❶ generally acknowledged truth; self-evident truth ❷［数］axiom

【公历】the Gregorian calendar

【公立】established and maintained by the government; public

【公粮】agricultural tax paid in grain; grain delivered to the state; public grain: 交～ *deliver tax grain to the state*

【公量】［纺］conditioned weight

【公路】highway; road: ～交通 *highway communication* / ～运输 *highway* (*or road*) *transportation* ◇ ～桥 highway bridge; ～容量 highway capacity

【公论】public opinion; verdict of the masses

【公买公卖】be fair in buying and selling; buy and sell at reasonable prices

【公民】citizen: 中华人民共和国～ *a citizen of the People's Republic of China* ◇ ～权 civil rights; citizen's rights; ～投票 referendum; plebiscite; ～义务 civil duty; civil obligation

【公亩】are (a.)

【公墓】cemetery

【公牛】bull

【公派】be sent (abroad to study, to work, etc.) by the state

【公平】fair; just; impartial; equitable: ～合理 *fair and reasonable* / 买卖～ *be fair in buying and selling; buy and sell at reasonable prices* / ～交易 *fair deal* ◇ ～称 fair scales—scales provided by markets for consumers to verify accuracy of purchase weight; ～竞争 fair play; fair competition; ～原则 equitable principles

【公婆】husband's father and mother; parents-in-law

【公仆】public servant: 人民的～ *a servant of the people*

【公切线】［数］common tangent

【公勤人员】service personnel in an office; office attendants

【公顷】hectare (ha.)

【公然】〈贬〉openly; undisguisedly; brazenly: ～背叛 *openly betray* / ～撕毁协议 *brazenly tear up an agreement*

【公认】generally acknowledge (or recognize); (universally) accept; establish: ～的国际关系原则 *generally recognized principles governing international relations*

【公设】［数］postulate

【公社】❶ primitive commune ❷ commune: 巴黎～ *the Paris Commune* ❸ people's commune

【公审】［法］public (or open) trial

【公升】litre

【公使】envoy; minister: ～衔参赞 *counsellor with the rank of minister; minister-counsellor* ◇ ～馆 legation

【公式】formula ◇ ～翻译 formula translator

【公式化】❶ formulism (in art and literature) ❷ formulistic; stereotyped

【公事】public affairs; official business (or duties): 还是～要紧。*Public affairs should come first*. / 我还有很多～要办。*I still have a lot of official duties to attend to*. ◇ ～包 briefcase; portfolio; ～房 office (room or building)

【公事公办】do official business according to official principles; not let private affairs interfere with public duty; business is business

【公署】government office

【公说公有理,婆说婆有理】each says he/she is right; both parties claim to be in the right

【公司】company; corporation: 钢铁～ *iron and steel company* / 进出口～ *import and export corporation* ◇ ～模型 company models

【公私】public and private: ～兼顾 *give concurrent consideration to public and private interests* / ～两利 *benefit both public and individual interests* / ～分明 *make (or draw) a clear distinction between public and private interests*

【公私合营】joint state-private ownership (the principal form of state capitalism adopted during the socialist transformation of capitalist enterprises in China)

【公诉】[法] public prosecution: 对罪犯提起～ *institute legal proceedings against an offender* ◇ ～人 public prosecutor; the prosecution

【公堂】❶〈旧〉law court; tribunal ❷ ancestral hall (or temple); memorial temple

【公推】recommend by general acclaim

【公文】official document: ～程式 *forms and formulas of official documents* ◇ ～袋 document envelope; ～纸 paper for copying official documents

【公务】public affairs; official business: 办理～ *handle official business* / 执行国家～ *perform official duties* ◇ ～车 service car; ～护照 service passport; ～人员 government functionary; ～员 government office worker; civil servant

【公物】public property

【公休】general holiday; official holiday

【公演】perform in public; give a performance: 青年剧院下月～曹禺名剧《日出》。*The Youth Theatre is presenting Cao Yu's famous play Sunrise next month.*

【公羊】ram

【公议】have a public or mass discussion: 自报～ *self-assessment and public discussion* / 交由群众～ *pass on to the masses for discussion*

【公益】public good; public welfare: 热心～ *be public-spirited* ◇ ～广告 public-interest ads; ～金 public welfare fund (of a socialist economic collective); ～劳动 volunteer labor; ～事业 cause of public good

【公意】public will; will of the public

【公因子】[数] common factor: 最大～ *greatest common factor (or divisor)*

【公营】publicly-owned; publicly-operated; public: ～经济 *the public sector of the economy; public economy* / ～企业 *public enterprise*

【公用】for public use; public; communal: ～电话 *public telephone* / 这个操场是两校～的。*This sports ground is shared by the two schools.* ◇ ～语言 common language; ～事业 public utilities

【公有】publicly-owned; public: ～财产 *public property* ◇ ～化 transfer to public ownership; socialize; ～制 public ownership (of means of production)

【公寓】❶ block of flats; apartment house ❷〈旧〉lodging house

【公元】the Christian era: ～一二〇〇年 *A.D. 1200* / ～前二二一年 *221 B.C.*

【公园】park

【公约】❶ convention; pact: 日内瓦～ *Geneva Convention* ❷ joint pledge: 爱国卫生～ *patriotic public health pledge* / 服务～ *service pledge (given by workers in the service trades)*

【公约数】[数] common divisor: 最大～ *greatest common divisor*

【公允】just and sound; fair and equitable; even-handed: 持论～ *be just and fair in argument*

【公债】(government) bonds: 经济建设～ *economic construction bonds* ◇ ～发行 public subscription; ～券 government securities debentures; government bond

【公章】official seal: 盖～ *affix an official seal*

【公正】just; fair; impartial; fair-minded: ～的舆论 *fair-minded public opinion* / 有个裁判不～。*One of the judges was partial.* / 历史将对这些人作出最～的判决。*History will pass the fairest judgment on such people.*

【公证】notarization ◇ ～处 notary office; ～人 notary public; notary

【公证手续】notarial acts

【公证委托书】letter of commitment

【公之于世】(又作'公之于众') make known to the world; reveal to the public

【公职】public office; public employment: 担任～ *hold public office* / 开除～ *discharge sb. from public employment; take sb.'s name off the books* ◇ ～人员 civil servant

【公制】the metric system: ～尺寸 *metric size* ◇ ～螺纹 [机] metric thread

【公众】the public: ～领袖 *leader of the public* / 制造谎言欺骗～ *fabricate lies to deceive the public* / ～妨害 *public mischief*

【公诸同好】share enjoyment with those having similar tastes

【公猪】boar

【公主】princess

【公转】[天] revolution

【公子】son of a feudal prince or high official

【公子哥儿】a pampered son of a wealthy or influential family

功 名 ❶ meritorious service (or deed); merit; achievement: 他的～大于过。*His achievements outweighed his errors.* ❷ result; effect; success: 教育之～ *the fruits of education* ❸ skill: 基本功 ❹ [物] work: 机械～ *mechanical work*

【功败垂成】fail on the verge of success; suffer defeat when victory is within reach

【功臣】a person who has rendered outstanding service: 治淮～ *meritorious workers in harnessing the Huaihe River* / 开国～ *founders of a state* / 不要以～自居。*Don't give yourself the airs of a hero.*

【功成不居】claim no credit for one's service

【功成名遂】(又作'功成名立') be successful and famous
【功成身退】retire after winning merit
【功成业就】(of a person's career) be crowned with success
【功到自然成】constant effort yields sure success
【功德】❶ merits and virtues：歌颂人民英雄的～ *extol the merits and virtues of the people's heroes* ❷ ［宗］(佛教) charitable and pious deeds; benefaction; beneficence; works
【功德无量】boundless beneficence; great service：谁要是能够找到治疗癌症的方法，那真是～。*Whoever finds a cure for cancer will render a great service to mankind.*
【功底】grounding in basic skills：～扎实 *have a good grounding* (*or be well grounded*) *in basic skills*
【功夫片】martial arts movie
【功过】merits and demerits; contributions and blunders
【功过是非】merits and demerits, right and wrong
【功绩】merits and achievements; contribution
【功课】❶ schoolwork; homework：做～ *do homework* ❷ a school subject：他在学校里门门～都很好。*He does well in every subject at school.*
【功亏一篑】fail to build a mound for want of one final basket of earth—fall short of success for lack of a final effort
【功劳】contribution; meritorious service; credit：她的～可不小啊！*She has certainly made no small contribution!* or *She has rendered great service.*
【功劳簿】record of merits：不要躺在自己的～上。*Don't rest on your laurels.*
【功利】utility; material gain ◇ ～主义 utilitarianism：～者 *utilitarian*
【功率】［物］power：～计 *dynamometer*
【功名】scholarly honour or official rank (in feudal times)：上京赶考，求取～ *go to the capital to take the imperial examination in the hopes of winning an official rank*
【功名利禄】position and wealth
【功能】function：～锻炼 *functional training* / ～性障碍 *functional disorder* / 这种机器具有多种～。*This gadget can perform many different functions.* / 肝～正常。*The liver is functioning normally.* ◇ ～法 functional approach; ～各异 different in function; ～键 function key; ～失调 functional disturbance
【功效】efficacy; effect：此药～非常显著。*This medicine is most efficacious.*
【功勋】exploit; meritorious service：～卓著 *notable exploits*
【功业】exploits; achievements
【功用】function; use

攻 动 ❶ attack; take the offensive：～城 *attack a city* / ～入敌阵 *storm into the enemy position* / 进攻受阻，～不进去。*The attack hit a snag and made no headway.* / 全～型选手 *an all-out attack player* ❷ accuse; charge：群起而攻之 ❸ study; specialize in：专攻
【攻城略地】attack cities and seize territories
【攻打】attack; assault：～一座城市 *attack a city*
【攻读】❶ assiduously study; diligently study：刻苦～ *study assiduously* ❷ specialize in：～法律 *study law* / ～博士学位 *study for a doctorate*
【攻关】❶ storm a strategic pass ❷ tackle key problems：攻下这一关，其他问题就好办了。*Once this difficulty is overcome, other problems will be easy to solve.*
【攻击】❶ attack; assault; launch an offensive：发起总～ *launch a general offensive* ❷ accuse; charge; vilify：恶毒～ *viciously attack* / 无端的～ *groundless charges* / 人身～ *personal attack*
【攻击机】another name for 强击机
【攻击型选手】aggressive player(s)
【攻击性言论】attack line
【攻坚】storm fortifications; assault fortified positions：～部队 *assault troops* ◇ ～战 storming of heavily fortified positions
【攻克】capture; take：～敌军据点 *capture an enemy stronghold* / ～技术难关 *surmount* (*or overcome*) *a technical difficulty*; *solve a difficult technical problem*
【攻破】make a breakthrough; breach：～敌军防线 *break through* (*or penetrate*) *the enemy defence lines* / 这个堡垒是攻不破的。*This is an impregnable fortress.*
【攻其不备】strike where or when the enemy is unprepared; take sb. by surprise; catch sb. unawares
【攻其一点，不及其余】pounce on one point and ignore all others—attack sb. for a single fault without considering his other aspects
【攻取】storm and capture; attack and seize：～据点 *capture a stronghold*
【攻势】offensive：采取～ *take the offensive* / 政治～ *political offensive* / 客队～凌厉。*The visiting team maintained a powerful offensive.*
【攻守同盟】an offensive and defensive alliance—an agreement between partners in crime not to give each other away; a pact to shield each other
【攻丝】［机］tapping：～机 *tapping machine*
【攻无不克】all-conquering; ever-victorious：战无不胜，～ *take every objective one attacks and win every battle one fights*
【攻陷】capture; storm
【攻心】❶ attack the mind; make a psychological attack：政策～ *try to win over or obtain a confession from a person by explaining the Party's policy* ❷ ［中］be in a coma or remain in a stupor (because of sorrow or hatred), or be in danger of dying (from severe burns or gangrene)
【攻心为上】psychological offensive is the best of tactics：用兵之道，～，攻城为下。*In war, to attack the mind is first, to attack a city second.*
【攻占】attack and occupy; storm and capture

供 动 ❶ supply; feed: ～不上 *run out*; *be in short supply* / ～不起 *unable to meet the demand*; *unable to afford the cost* ❷ provide sb. with sth. (for the use or convenience of): 仅～参考 *for your reference only* / 这个饭厅可～五百人同时用饭。*This dining hall can accommodate five hundred people at a time*. ——另见 gòng

【供不应求】supply falls short of demand; demand exceeds supply

【供电】supply electricity; supply power: ～调度员 *load dispatcher* / ～干线 *supply main* ◇ ～局 power supply bureau; ～系统 同〖电力网〗

【供过于求】supply exceeds demand

【供给】supply; provide; furnish: 原料由国家～。*Raw materials are provided by the state*. ◇ ～制 the supply system—a system of payment in kind

【供暖】heating: 热水～ *hot water heating* / 蒸汽～ *steam heating* / 这幢楼正在安装～设备。*A heating system is being installed in this building*. ◇ ～系统 heating system

【供气】[机] air feed

【供求】supply and demand: ～关系 *the relation between supply and demand* / 调剂市场物资,使商品～平衡 *redistribute goods and materials in the market in order to strike a balance between supply and demand*

【供销】supply and marketing ◇ ～合作社 (又作'供销社') supply and marketing cooperative

【供养】provide for (one's parents or elders); support: ～老人 *support the elders* (*esp*. *one's aged parents or grandparents*)

【供应】supply: 大量～ *supply in large quantity* / 计划～ *planned supply* / 市场～ *supply of commodities*; *market supplies* ◇ ～点 supply centre; ～线 supply line

肱 名 〈书〉the upper arm; arm: 曲～而枕 *sleep with one's head resting on one's bent arm*

【肱骨】[生理] humerus

宫 名 ❶ imperial palace ❷ a house in which supernatural beings live; heavenly palace: 天宫 ❸ temple (used in a name): 雍和～ *the Lama Temple of Peace and Harmony* (*in Beijing*) ❹ a place for cultural activities and recreation: 工人文化～ *the Workers' Cultural Palace* ❺ [生理] womb; uterus

【宫灯】palace lantern

【宫殿】palace: ～式建筑 *palatial architecture*

【宫调】[音] modes of ancient Chinese music

【宫内节育器】intrauterine device (IUD)

【宫女】a maid in an imperial palace; maid of honour

【宫阙】imperial palace

【宫廷】❶ palace ❷ royal or imperial court; court ◇ ～秘方 imperial secret recipe, palace recipe; ～政变 palace coup

【宫外孕】[医] ectopic pregnancy; extrauterine pregnancy

【宫闱】〈书〉palace chambers: ～秘事 *palace secrets*

【宫刑】castration (a punishment in ancient China)

恭 形 respectful; reverent: ～而有礼 *be polite and respectful* / 执礼甚～ *treat sb*. *with great respect*

【恭贺】〈套〉congratulate: ～新禧 *Happy New Year*

【恭候】〈套〉await respectfully: ～光临。*We request the pleasure of your company*.

【恭谨】respectful and cautious

【恭敬】respectful: 学生们恭恭敬敬地向老师行了个礼。*The students bowed respectfully to their teacher*.

【恭敬不如从命】〈套〉it is better to accept deferentially than to decline courteously (on accepting gifts, etc. from one's elders)

【恭请】〈套〉invite respectfully: ～光临。*We request the honour of your presence*.

【恭顺】respectful and submissive

【恭桶】closestool; nightstool; commode

【恭维】(又作'恭惟') flatter; compliment: ～话 *flattery*; *compliments* / 我～了他几句。*I said a few words complimenting him*. / 他那几句英语,我实在不敢～。*I can't compliment him on his English*.

【恭喜】〈套〉congratulate: ～! ～! ～你们试验成功! *Congratulations*! *Congratulations*! *I congratulate you on the success of your experiment*. / ～发财! *Congratulations and may you be prosperous*! or *Wishing you happiness and prosperity*! (a Spring Festival greeting)

躬 Ⅰ 形 〈书〉personally: ～行实践 *practise what one preaches* Ⅱ 动 bend forward; bow: ～身 *bend at the waist*

【躬逢其盛】be present in person on the grand occasion

【躬亲】attend to personally: 事必躬亲

觥 名 an ancient bronze wine vessel in the shape of a composite animal

【觥筹交错】wine cups and mora chips lying about in disorder—a hilarious party

gǒng

巩 动 consolidate: 巩固

【巩固】❶ consolidate; strengthen; solidify: ～阵地 *consolidate a position* / ～政权 *consolidate political power* ❷ consolidated; strong; solid; stable: ～的国防 *strong national defence* / 两国人民的友谊是～的。*The people of the two nations have strong ties of friendship*.

【巩膜】[生理] sclera

【巩膜炎】scleritis

汞 名 [化] mercury; hydrargyrum (Hg)

【汞弧灯】mercury-arc lamp
【汞化】［化］mercurate；mercurize：～物 *mercuride*
【汞溴红】［药］mercurochrome

拱 Ⅰ动 ❶ cup one hand in the other before the chest (in salutation)：拱手 ❷ surround：四山环～的大湖 *a large lake surrounded by mountains* ❸ hump up；arch：猫～了～腰。*The cat arched its back.* ❹ push with the shoulders or head：用肩膀把门～开 *push the door open with one's shoulder* ❺ sprout up through the earth：苗儿～出土了。*The sprouts are coming out of the earth.* Ⅱ名［建］arch：～道 *archway* / ～式涵洞 *arch culvert*
【拱坝】［水］arch dam
【拱抱】surround：群峰～的山坞 *a cove surrounded by cliffs*
【拱点】［天］apsis；apse
【拱顶】［建］vault
【拱门】［建］arched door
【拱桥】［建］arch bridge：双曲～ *double-curvature arch bridge*
【拱手】make an obeisance by cupping one hand in the other before the chest：两人～作别，互道珍重。*The two men bid farewell to each other with a cupped-hand salute, each asking the other to take good care of himself.*
【拱手让人】surrender sth. submissively；hand sth. over on a silver platter
【拱卫】surround and protect
【拱形建筑】arch；arched construction
【拱券】［建］arch

珙 名〈书〉a kind of jade
【珙桐】［植］dove tree

gòng

共 Ⅰ形 common；general：共性 Ⅱ动 share：～命运 *share a common fate；throw in one's lot with sb.* Ⅲ副 ❶ together；in company：～进午餐 *have lunch together* ❷ altogether；in all；all told：这个集子～收小说十二篇。*There are altogether twelve short stories in this collection.* / 我们小组～有十人。*There are ten of us in the group.*
【共产党】the Communist Party：～人 *Communist* / ～员 *member of the Communist Party；Communist；Party member*
【共产国际】the Communist International (1919-1943)；Comintern
【共产主义】communism：～道德 *communist morality* / ～风格 *communist style (or spirit)* / ～觉悟 *communist consciousness* / ～人生观 *communist outlook on life* / ～者 *communist*
【共产主义青年团】the Communist Youth League
【共处】coexist：每一个矛盾的两个方面～于一个统一体中。*The two aspects of every contradiction coexist in a single entity.*
【共存】coexist
【共电制】common-battery system：～电话机 *common-battery telephone* / ～电话局 *common-battery telephone exchange*
【共度】spend (an occasion) together：～佳节 *celebrate a festival together*
【共轭】［数］［物］conjugate ◇ ～点［数］conjugate point；～角［数］conjugate angles；～象［物］conjugate image
【共发射极】［电子］common emitter
【共犯】［法］accomplice
【共管】〈略〉见〖国际共管〗
【共和】republicanism；republic
【共和党】the Republican Party (in U. S.)
【共和国】republic
【共基极】［电子］common base
【共计】amount to；add up to；total：两项开支～三十元。*These two items of expenditure come to thirty yuan.* / 参观展览会的～二十万人。*Altogether 200,000 people visited the exhibition.*
【共价】［化］*covalence*：～键 *covalent bond*
【共聚】［化］copolymerization：～物 *copolymer*
【共聚一堂】gather in the same hall；gather together：各族人民的代表～，商讨国家大事。*Representatives of different nationalities gather in the same hall to discuss affairs of state.*
【共勉】encourage each other：愿～之。*Let us encourage each other in our endeavours.* / 毕业时同学们互相题词～。*At graduation the students presented each other with valedictory inscriptions.*
【共鸣】❶［物］resonance：～器 *resonator* ❷ sympathetic response：引起～ *arouse sympathy；strike a sympathetic chord*
【共栖】［生］commensalism
【共青团员】member of the Communist Youth League；League member
【共生】❶［地质］intergrowth；paragenesis ❷［生］symbiosis：～细菌 *symbiotic bacteria* ◇ ～次序［地质］paragenesis；～矿 mineral intergrowth
【共识】common understanding
【共事】work together (at the same organization)；be fellow workers：～多年 *have been colleagues for many years*
【共通】applicable to both or all：这两者之间有～的道理。*The same argument applies to both cases.*
【共同】❶ shared；common：～语言 *common language* / ～敌人 *common enemy* / ～关心的问题 *matters of common concern；issues of common interest* / 有～之处 *have something in common* ❷ together；jointly：～战斗 *fight side by side* / ～努力 *make joint efforts* / ～对敌 *join forces to oppose the enemy* / ～行动 *act in concert* ◇ ～保险 co-insurance；～承兑人 co-acceptor；～点 common ground；～对外关税 common external tariff (CET)；～过失 joint negligence；～配额

common quotas；～市场 the Common Market

【共同体】community：欧洲经济～ *the European Economic Community (EEC)* / 加勒比～ *the Caribbean Community (CARICOM)*

【共析】［冶］eutectoid：～钢 *eutectoid steel*

【共享】enjoy together；share：～胜利的喜悦 *share the joys of victory* ◇～软件 shareware

【共性】general character；generality

【共用天线】common antenna

【共振】［物］resonance：～器 *resonator* / ～腔 *resonant cavity* / ～示波器 *resonoscope*

【共轴】coaxial

贡 动 tribute：进贡

【贡品】articles of tribute；tribute

【贡税】tribute and taxes

【贡献】❶ contribute；dedicate；devote：他把自己的全部藏书都～给了图书馆。*He contributed all his collections of books to the library.* ❷ contribution；dedication；devotion：中国应当对人类有更大的～。*China ought to make a greater contribution to humanity.*

供 Ⅰ 动 ❶ present (offerings)：遗像前～着鲜花。*Fresh flowers were laid out before the portrait of the deceased.* ❷ confess；own up：据该犯～称 *as was confessed by the culprit* / 他～出了主犯的名字。*He gave the name of the chief culprit.* Ⅱ 名 ❶ offerings：上供 ❷ confession；deposition：问了半天也问不出～来。*No confession was forthcoming during the lengthy interrogation.* ——另见 gōng

【供词】a statement made under examination；confession

【供奉】❶ enshrine and worship；consecrate ❷ actors who gave command performances (in the Qing Dynasty)

【供具】sacrificial vessel

【供品】offerings

【供认】confess

【供认不讳】candidly confess；confess everything

【供职】hold office

【供状】written confession；deposition

【供桌】altar table

gōu

勾 Ⅰ 动 ❶ cancel；cross out；strike out；tick off：把他的名字～掉 *cross out his name；strike his name off the register* / ～了这笔账 *cancel the debt* / 把重要的项目～出来 *tick off the important items* ❷ delineate；draw：～出一个轮廓 *draw an outline* ❸ fill up the joints of brickwork with mortar or cement；point：～墙缝 *point a brick wall* ❹ thicken：～芡 *thicken soup* ❺ induce；evoke；call to mind：这件事～起了我对童年的回忆。*This evoked memories of my childhood.* ❻ collude with；gang up with：他们这帮人怎么～上的？*How did these people come to form a gang?* Ⅱ 名 old name for the shorter leg of a right triangle ——另见 gòu

【勾搭】❶ gang up with：这四个坏家伙～上了。*The four scoundrels ganged up.* / 那家伙跟投机倒把分子勾勾搭搭。*That fellow works hand in glove with speculators.* ❷ carry on (or have a carry-on) with sb.：她丈夫和隔壁那个女人勾勾搭搭的。*Her husband is carrying on with the woman next door.*

【勾动】stir up (sb.'s feeling)；move；arouse；cause：～食欲 *arouse (or whet) one's appetite* / ～思乡之情 *make sb. homesick*

【勾股定理】［数］the Pythagorean theorem (or proposition)

【勾画】draw the outline of；delineate；sketch：寥寥数笔，就把这高利贷者贪婪的嘴脸～出来了。*A few words successfully bring out the greediness of the usurer.*

【勾魂】captivate sb.'s soul—enchant；bewitch

【勾魂摄魄】(of a woman) have the power to bewitch men；cast a spell (on)；lay an enchantment (on)

【勾结】collude with；collaborate with；gang up with：与敌人相～ *collude with the enemy*

【勾勒】❶ draw the outline of；sketch the contours of：他只用简单的几笔就～出了马的轮廓。*He sketched the outline of a horse with just a few rapid strokes.* ❷ give a brief account of；outline

【勾通】collude with；work hand in glove with

【勾引】tempt；entice；seduce：～少女 *seduce young girls*

沟 名 ❶ ditch；channel；trench：排水～ *drainage ditch；drain* / 交通～ *communication trench* ❷ groove；rut；furrow：开～播种 *make furrows for sowing seeds* / 拖拉机在泥路上轧出两道～。*The tractor made ruts in the dirt road.* ❸ gully；ravine：七～八梁 *seven gullies and eight ridges；full of gullies and ridges* / 乱石～ *boulder-strewn gully*

【沟灌】［农］furrow irrigation

【沟壑】gully；ravine：～纵横 *a crisscross network of gullies*

【沟渠】irrigation canals and ditches：田野上～纵横。*The fields are crisscrossed by irrigation canals and ditches.*

【沟通】link up：～南方各省的新铁路 *the new railways that link up the southern provinces* / ～两大洋的运河 *an interoceanic canal* / ～思想 *promote mutual understanding*

【沟沿儿】banks of a ditch or canal

佝 (构词成分)见下

【佝偻病】rickets

钩 Ⅰ 名 ❶ hook：钓鱼～ *fishhook* / 挂衣～ *clothes-hook* ❷ hook stroke (in Chinese characters) ❸ check mark；tick Ⅱ 动 ❶ secure with a hook；hook：杂技演员用脚～住绳圈儿。*The acrobat hooked his foot into the loop*. ❷ crochet：～花边 *crochet lace* ❸ sew with large stitches：～贴边 *sew on an edging*

【钩虫】hookworm ◇ ～病 hookworm disease；ancylostomiasis

【钩端螺旋体病】leptospirosis

【钩吻】［植］elegant jessamine

【钩心斗角】intrigue against each other；jockey for position

【钩针】crochet hook

【钩子】❶ hook：有挂衣服的～吗？*Is there a hook to hang my coat on?* ❷ a hook-like thing：蝎子的～有毒。*The sting of a scorpion is poisonous*.

篝 名〈书〉cage

【篝火】bonfire；campfire：举行～晚会 *give a campfire party* / 宿营地上燃起熊熊的～。*A bright bonfire was built at camp*.

gǒu

苟 Ⅰ 形 careless；negligent；indifferent（to right or wrong）：不苟 Ⅱ 连〈书〉if：～能坚持，必将胜利。*If you can persist, you are sure to win*. or *Given persistence, victory is certain*.

【苟安】seek a moment's peace however one can；be content with temporary ease and comfort

【苟合】illicit sexual relations

【苟活】drag out an ignoble existence；live on in degradation

【苟且】❶ drift along；be resigned to circumstances ❷ perfunctory；careless：～了事 *dispose of sth. perfunctorily* / 他做翻译，一字一句都不敢～。*In doing translation work, he chose every word with great care*. ❸ illicit（sexual relations）；improper

【苟且偷安】seek a moment's peace however one can；be content with temporary ease and comfort

【苟且偷生】drag out an ignoble existence

【苟全】aimlessly preserve（one's own life）

【苟全性命】barely manage to survive：～于乱世 *barely secure personal safety in a troubled age*

【苟同】〈书〉（usu. used in the negative）agree without giving serious thought；readily subscribe to（sb.'s view）：不敢～ *beg to differ；cannot agree*

【苟延残喘】be on one's last legs；linger on in a steadily worsening condition

狗 Ⅰ 名 dog Ⅱ 形〈诋〉damned；cursed：～东西 *that son of a bitch*

【狗宝】［中］the stone of a dog's gallbladder，kidney or bladder

【狗吃屎】〈诙〉fall flat on the face；fall down heavily：跌了个～ *stumble and fall flat on one's face*

【狗胆包天】monstrously audacious

【狗苟蝇营】同〖蝇营狗苟〗

【狗獾】badger

【狗急跳墙】a cornered beast will do something desperate

【狗脊蕨】［植］chain fern

【狗拿耗子，多管闲事】a dog trying to catch mice—poke one's nose into other people's business

【狗皮膏药】［中］❶ dogskin plaster（a plaster for rheumatism，strains，contusions，etc.，formerly spread on dogskin，but now usu. on cloth）❷ quack medicine ——另见〖卖狗皮膏药〗

【狗屁】〈诋〉horseshit；rubbish；nonsense

【狗屁不通】unreadable rubbish；mere trash：这篇文章写得～。*This article is mere trash*.

【狗食袋】doggy bag

【狗屎】dog's droppings — worthless stuff：～不如 *utterly worthless*

【狗头军师】❶ a person who offers bad advice；inept adviser ❷ villainous adviser

【狗腿子】〈口〉hired thug；lackey；henchman

【狗尾草】［植］green bristlegrass

【狗尾续貂】a dog's tail joined to sable—（of a literary work）a wretched sequel to a fine work

【狗窝】kennel；doghouse：房间里乱得像～。*The room is such a mess that it resembles a doghouse*.

【狗血喷头】（usu. used in 骂得～）let loose a stream of abuse against sb.；pour out a flood of invective against sb.

【狗熊】❶ black bear ❷ coward

【狗眼看人低】be a bloody snob

【狗咬狗】dog-eat-dog：傀儡集团内部～的斗争 *a dog-eat-dog struggle within a puppet clique*

【狗咬吕洞宾】snarl and snap at Lü Dongbin（one of the eight immortals in Chinese mythology）—wrong a kind-hearted person

【狗蝇】dog louse fly

【狗鱼】pike（a fish）

【狗崽子】〈诋〉son of a bitch

【狗仔队】paparazo(sing.)；paparazzi(pl.)

【狗蚤】dog flea

【狗仗人势】like a dog threatening people on the strength of its master's power—be a bully with the backing of a powerful person

【狗彘不如】worse than a cur or a swine

【狗嘴里吐不出象牙】no ivory issues from the mouth of a dog；a filthy mouth can't utter decent language；what can you expect from a dog but a bark

枸（构词成分）见下 ——另见 jǔ

【枸骨】［植］Chinese holly

【枸杞子】［中］the fruit of Chinese wolfberry（Lycium chinense）

gòu

勾（构词成分）见下 ——另见 gōu

【勾当】〈贬〉business；deal：罪恶～ *criminal activities* / 肮脏～ *a dirty deal*

构 Ⅰ 动 ❶ construct; form; compose: ～词 *form a word* ❷ fabricate; make up: 虚构 Ⅱ 名 literary composition: 佳～ *a good piece of writing*

【构成】constitute; form; compose; make up: ～威胁 *constitute (or pose) a threat* / 西沙群岛是由珊瑚礁～的。*The Xisha Archipelago is formed of coral reefs.* / ～部分 *component part*

【构词法】[语] word-building; word-formation

【构答反映】constructed response

【构件】❶ [建] (structural) member; component ❷ [机] component (part)

【构思】(of a writer or artist) work out the plot of a story or the composition of a painting: 他正在～一部小说。*He is working out the plot of a novel.*

【构图】composition (of a picture)

【构想】idea; conception; concept: 我有个经济体制改革的～。*I have an idea for restructuring the economy.*

【构造】❶ structure; construction: 人体～ *the structure of the human body* / 句子的～ *the structure of a sentence* / 这种机器～简单,使用方便。*This machine is simple in construction and easy to handle.* ❷ [地质] tectonic; structural: ～体系 *structural system* / ～序次 *structural generation* ◇ ～地震 tectonic earthquake; ～地质学 structural geology; ～运动 [地质] tectonic movement

【构筑】construct (military works); build: ～工事 *construct field works (or fortifications)*; build defences; dig in ◇ ～物 [建] structures

购 动 purchase; buy: 此书～于北京新华书店。*The book was bought in the Beijing Xinhua Bookstore.*

【购股单】stock purchase warrent

【购货单】order form; order

【购货合同】purchase contract

【购货券】a purchase coupon

【购买】purchase; buy: 实验室计划～大量设备。*The laboratory plans to buy a lot of equipment.* ◇ ～动机 buying motive

【购买力】purchasing power ◇ ～平价 purchasing power parity

【购买税】purchase tax

【购物手推车】push cart

【购物天堂】a shopping kingdom

【购物指南】shopping guide

【购物中心】shopping centre

【购销】purchase and sale; buying and selling: ～两旺 *brisk buying and selling*

【购置】purchase (durables): ～农具 *purchase farm implements* / 学校～了大量的实验设备。*Our school bought a large amount of lab equipment.*

诟 Ⅰ 名 〈书〉 shame; humiliation: ～感之情 *sentiments of shame and thankfulness* Ⅱ 动 revile; talk abusively: 诟病

【诟病】〈书〉 denounce; castigate: 为世～ *become an object of public denunciation*

【诟骂】〈书〉 revile; abuse; vilify: 当众～ *vilify sb. in public*

垢 名 ❶ 〈书〉 dirty; filthy: 蓬头垢面 ❷ dirt; filth: 油～ *grease stain* ❸ 〈书〉 disgrace; humiliation: 含垢忍辱

够 Ⅰ 形 enough; sufficient; adequate: 你钱～不～? *Do you have enough money?* / 我吃～了。*I've had enough.* / 这里只举一个例子就～了。*Here a single example will suffice.* Ⅱ 副 enough (to reach a certain extent); sufficiently: ～好了。*It's good enough.* / 今儿～冷的。*It's quite cold today.* / 今天你们可～辛苦了。*You've really done a hard day's work.* Ⅲ 动 ❶ reach (sth. by stretching): 你～得着那些桑葚儿吗? *Can you reach those mulberries?* / 我～不着书架的最上一层。*I can't reach the top shelf of the bookcase.* ❷ reach (a standard or level): ～标准 *be up to standard* / ～资格 *be qualified*

【够本】❶ make enough money to cover the cost; break even ❷ the gains balancing the losses

【够格】be qualified; be up to standard: 当代表,他满～。*He's well qualified to be a representative.*

【够劲儿】〈口〉 ❶ (of an onerous task, etc.) almost too much to cope with: 他一个人担任那么多工作,真～。*He really has a tough job having to attend to so many things.* ❷ strong (in taste, strength, etc.): 这辣椒真～。*This pepper is really hot.* / 这茅台酒真～。*This maotai is certainly powerful stuff.*

【够朋友】〈口〉 deserve to be called a true friend; be a friend indeed

【够戗】(又作'够呛')〈方〉 unbearable; terrible: 疼得～ *unbearably painful* / 她的脚冻得～。*Her feet were terribly frostbitten.* / 他的伤势怎么样? —～! *How's his wound? —Pretty bad!* / 这家伙真～! *He's simply impossible.*

【够瞧的】really awful; too much: 天热得真～。*The weather is terribly hot.* or *The weather is really scorching.*

【够受的】quite an ordeal; hard to bear: 累得～ *be dog-tired* / 他这一跤摔得真～。*He had a really bad fall.*

【够数】sufficient in quantity; enough: 你领的镰刀不～。*You didn't get enough sickles to go round.*

【够味儿】〈口〉 just the right flavour; just the thing; quite satisfactory: 最后这两句你唱得真～! *The way you sang the last two lines was just superb!*

【够意思】❶ really something; terrific: 这场球赛可真～。*That was a really terrific game.* ❷ generous; really kind: 不～ *unfriendly; ungrateful*

媾 动 〈书〉 ❶ wed: 婚～ *marriage* ❷ reach an

agreement：媾和 ❸ coition：交媾

【媾和】make peace：单独～ *make peace without consulting one's allies*；*make a separate peace*

gū

估 动 estimate；appraise：你～一～这堆西红柿有几斤。*Can you tell how many jin of tomatoes there are in this heap?*

【估产】❶ estimate the yield：这块地～八百斤。*The estimated yield of this plot of land is 800 jin*. ❷ appraise the assets；assess

【估计】estimate；appraise；reckon：清醒地～当前的形势 *make a clearheaded appraisal of the present situation* / ～错误 *miscalculate* / 过高～ *overestimate* / 过低～ *underestimate*

【估计残值】estimated scrap value

【估价】❶ appraise；evaluate：这件家具请你估一估价。*Evaluate this piece of furniture, please*. ❷［经］appraised price ◇ ～惯例 valuation convention

【估量】appraise；estimate；assess；reckon：～双方力量的对比 *assess the balance of strength between the two sides* / 你～他挣多少？*How much do you reckon he earns?*

【估摸】〈口〉reckon；guess：我～着她月底就能回来。*I reckon she'll be back by the end of this month*.

【估税】tax assessment ◇ ～人 assessor

【估算】estimate；appraise；reckon：～产量 *estimate the yield* / ～到几种可能性 *reckon with several possibilities*

沽 动〈书〉❶ buy：～酒 *buy wine* ❷ sell：待价而沽

【沽名钓誉】fish for fame and compliments

咕 象 the clucking of a hen；the cooing of a pigeon：鸽子一边儿吃，一边儿～～地叫。*The pigeon was eating and cooing at the same time*.

【咕咚】the sound of a heavy thing falling down；thud；splash；plump：大石头～一声掉到水里去了。*The rock fell into the water with a splash*. / 他～一声倒在地上了。*He fell to the ground with a thud*.

【咕嘟】❶ bubble；gurgle：泉水～～地往外冒。*The spring kept bubbling up*. / 他端起一碗水，～～地喝了下去。*He took up a bowl of water and gulped it down*. ❷ boil for a long time：白菜早就～烂了。*The cabbage is overcooked*. ❸〈方〉purse (one's lips)：不高兴地～着嘴 *purse one's lips in displeasure*

【咕唧】(又作'咕叽') ❶ a squelching sound：水牛拉着犁，在稻田里～～地走着。*The water buffalo squelched up and down the paddy fields, pulling the plough*. ❷ (又作'咕叽') whisper；murmur：他俩～了半天。*They whispered to each other for a long time*.

【咕隆】rumble；rattle；roll：远处雷声～～地响。*Thunder rumbled in the distance*. / 行李车在月台上～～地跑着。*The luggage trolley rattled along the platform*.

【咕噜】rumble；roll：他的肚子～～直响。*His stomach kept rumbling*. / 粗大的圆木～～地从山坡上滚下来。*Large logs came rolling down the slope*.

【咕哝】murmur；mutter；grumble：他在～些什么？*What is he muttering about?*

呱（构词成分）见下 ——另见 guā

【呱呱】〈书〉the cry of a baby：～而泣 *mewl* ——另见 guāguā

【呱呱坠地】(of a baby) come into the world with a cry；raise the first cry of life；be born

孤 形 ❶ (of a child) fatherless or orphaned：孤儿 ❷ solitary；isolated；alone：～雁 *a solitary wild goose*

【孤傲】proud and aloof：去掉～习气 *rid oneself of aloofness and arrogance*

【孤本】the only copy extant；the only existing copy

【孤残】the orphaned and disabled：～儿童 *orphaned and disabled children*

【孤单】❶ alone；lonely：孤孤单单一个人 *all alone*；*all by oneself*；*a lone soul* / 感到～ *feel lonely* ❷ weak：力量～ *weak and helpless*

【孤胆】fighting single-handed：～英雄 *a lone fighter*

【孤岛】an isolated island

【孤独】lonely；solitary：过着～的生活 *live in solitude* / 同学们都回家去了，剩下自己一个人不免感到～、烦闷。*The other students have all gone home, leaving me here all alone, and I can't help feeling lonely and depressed*.

【孤独症】autism

【孤儿】❶ a fatherless child ❷ orphan ◇ ～寡妇 (又作'孤儿寡母') a widow and her child；～院 orphanage

【孤芳自赏】a solitary flower in love with its own fragrance；a lone soul admiring his own purity；indulge in self-admiration

【孤寡】❶ 同〖孤儿寡妇〗❷ lonely；solitary：家里只剩下她一个～老婆儿。*The old woman is the only one left in the family*.

【孤寂】lonely

【孤家寡人】a person who is utterly isolated

【孤军】an isolated force ◇ ～深入 an isolated force penetrating deep into enemy territory；～作战 fight in isolation；fight a lone battle

【孤苦伶仃】orphaned and helpless；alone and uncared for；friendless and wretched

【孤老院】old folks' home；home for the aged

【孤立】❶ isolated：处境～ *find oneself in an isolated position* / ～无援 *isolated and cut off from help* / 任何事物都不是～地存在着的。*Nothing exists in isolation*. ❷ isolate：～敌人 *isolate the enemy*

【孤零零】solitary；lone；all alone
【孤陋寡闻】ignorant and ill-informed
【孤僻】unsociable and eccentric：性情～ *of an uncommunicative and eccentric disposition*
【孤身】alone：～前往 *go there alone* / 他哥哥去世后，家里只剩下他～一人了。*After the death of his brother，he was the only one left in the family.*
【孤行己见】follow one's bigoted course
【孤掌难鸣】it's impossible to clap with one hand—it's hard to succeed without support
【孤注一掷】stake all on a single throw；risk everything on a single venture；put all one's eggs in one basket

姑

Ⅰ**名** ❶ father's sister；aunt ❷ husband's sister；sister-in-law ❸〈古〉husband's mother；mother-in-law ❹ nun：尼姑 Ⅱ**副**〈书〉tentatively；for the moment：～置勿论 *leave sth. aside for the moment*
【姑表】the relationship between the children of a brother and a sister；cousinship：～兄弟 *male cousins（the father of one and the mother of the other being brother and sister）*
【姑夫】（又作'姑父'）the husband of one's father's sister；uncle
【姑姑】〈口〉father's sister；aunt
【姑老爷】a form of address for a man used by members of his wife's family
【姑妈】〈口〉father's (married) sister；aunt
【姑母】father's (married) sister；aunt
【姑奶奶】〈口〉❶ married daughter ❷ the sister of one's paternal grandfather；grandaunt ❸ your grandaunt (used by a woman in mentioning herself when quarrelling)
【姑娘】❶ girl ❷〈口〉daughter
【姑且】tentatively；for the moment：你～试一试。*Have a try，anyhow.* or *Suppose you give it a try.* / 我这里有支钢笔，你～用着。*I have a pen here. You can use it for the moment.*
【姑嫂】a woman and her brother's wife；sisters-in-law
【姑妄听之】see no harm in hearing what sb. has to say
【姑妄言之】tell sb. sth. for what it's worth
【姑息】appease；indulge；tolerate：不应该～他的错误。*We shouldn't be indulgent towards his mistakes.*
【姑息疗法】［医］palliative treatment
【姑息养奸】to tolerate evil is to abet it
【姑嫜】〈书〉a woman's parents-in-law
【姑丈】the husband of one's father's sister；uncle

轱

（构词成分）见下
【轱辘】（又作'轱轳'）❶〈口〉wheel ❷ roll：把桶推一下就～过来了。*Give the barrel a push and it'll roll over here.* ◇ ～鞋 roller skates

骨

（构词成分）见下 ——另见 gǔ
【骨朵儿】〈口〉flower bud
【骨碌】roll：皮球在地上～。*The ball is rolling on the ground.* / 他一～从床上爬起来。*He rolled out of bed.*

菇

名 mushroom：香菇

辜

名 guilt；crime：无辜
【辜负】let down；fail to live up to；be unworthy of；disappoint

箍

Ⅰ**动** bind round；hoop：用铁丝把桶～上 *bind a bucket with wire* / 他头上～着条毛巾。*He had a towel wound round his head.* Ⅱ**名** hoop；band：铁～ *iron hoop*
【箍桶匠】cooper；hooper

gǔ

古

形 ancient；age-old；palaeo-：～时候 *in ancient times；in olden days* / ～画 *ancient paintings* / ～瓷 *old china* / 这座庙～得很。*This temple is very old.*
【古奥】(usu. of writing) archaic and abstruse
【古巴】Cuba ◇ ～人 Cuban
【古板】old-fashioned and inflexible
【古刹】an ancient temple
【古代】❶ the period in Chinese history from remote antiquity down until the mid-19th century ❷ the age of slave society；ancient times；antiquity：～文化 *ancient civilization* / ～史 *ancient history*
【古道热肠】warm-hearted and compassionate
【古典】❶ classical allusion ❷ classical：～作品 *classic* ◇ ～文学 classical literature；～音乐 classical music；～主义 classicism
【古董】❶ antique；curio：～鉴赏家 *connoisseur of curios* ❷ old fogey
【古动物学】palaeozoology
【古都】ancient capital
【古尔邦节】［宗］（伊斯兰教）Corban
【古风】❶ ancient customs；antiquities ❷ 同〖古体诗〗
【古怪】eccentric；odd；strange：～脾气 *eccentric character* / 样子～ *odd-looking*
【古汉语】archaic Chinese
【古话】old saying：～说，有志者事竟成。*As the old saying goes，where there's a will there's a way.*
【古籍】ancient books
【古迹】historic site；place of historic interest
【古今中外】ancient and modern，Chinese and foreign；at all times and in all lands
【古旧】antiquated；archaic：～词语 *archaic words and expressions；archaisms*
【古柯】［植］Coca ◇ ～碱 another name for 可卡因
【古兰经】［宗］（伊斯兰教）the Koran
【古老】ancient；age-old：～的传说 *legend* / ～的文明 *an old civilization* / ～的风俗 *ancient (or old) customs* / ～的中国变年轻了。*Old China has been rejuvenated.*

【古朴】(of art, architecture, etc.) simple and unsophisticated; of primitive simplicity
【古人】the ancients; our forefathers
【古人类学】palaeoanthropology: ～家 *palaeoanthropologist*
【古色古香】(又作'古香古色') antique; quaint: 这个鼎土花斑驳，～。*This tripod has a beautiful patina and an air of great antiquity.*
【古生代】[地质] the Palaeozoic Era
【古生界】[地质] Palaeozoic Erathem
【古生物学】palaeontology
【古诗】ancient poetry
【古书】ancient books
【古塔胶】[化] gutta-percha
【古体诗】a form of pre-Tang poetry, usu. having five or seven characters to each line, without strict tonal patterns or rhyme schemes
【古铜色】bronze-coloured; bronze
【古玩】antique; curio: ～店 *antique shop*
【古往今来】throughout the ages; from time immemorial
【古为今用】make the past serve the present: ～，洋为中用。*Make the past serve the present and foreign things serve China.*
【古文】❶ prose written in the classical literary style; ancient Chinese prose ❷ Chinese script before the Qin Dynasty (221-206 B.C.)
【古文字】ancient writing ◇ ～学 palaeography
【古物】ancient objects; antiquities: ～陈列馆 *museum of antiquities*
【古稀】seventy years of age: 年近～ *getting on for seventy*
【古雅】(of material things, literary works, etc.) of classic beauty and in elegant taste; of classic elegance
【古植物学】palaeobotany
【古装】ancient costume ◇ ～戏 costume play

汩 象〈书〉(of running water) gurgle
【汩汩】gurgle: 渠水～地流入稻田。*Gurgling water flowed from the irrigation ditch into the paddy fields.*

谷 名 ❶ valley; gorge: 深～ *a deep valley; gorge* ❷ cereal; grain ❸ millet ❹〈方〉unhusked rice
【谷氨酸】[药] glutamic acid
【谷仓】granary; barn
【谷草】❶ millet straw ❷〈方〉rice straw
【谷底】bottom of a valley: 这次衰退已经到过～。*The present recession has touched bottom.*
【谷蛾】grain moth
【谷坊】[水] check dam
【谷贱伤农】low prices for grain hurt the peasants; cheap grain harms the peasants
【谷壳】husk (of rice)
【谷物】cereal; grain ◇ ～干燥机 grain dryer; ～交易所 corn exchange
【谷雨】Grain Rain—the 6th of the 24 solar terms
【谷子】❶ millet ❷〈方〉unhusked rice ◇ ～白发病[农] downy mildew of millet

股 Ⅰ 名 ❶ thigh ❷ section (of an office, enterprise, etc.): 人事～ *personnel section* ❸ strand; ply: 三～的绳子 *a three-strand rope* / 双～的毛线 *two-ply wool* / 把线捻成～儿。*Twist the threads into yarn.* ❹ share in a company or one of several equal parts of property: 分～ *divide into equal parts* / 每～五百元。*Five hundred yuan for each share.* Ⅱ 量 ❶ for a long, narrow thing: 一～线 *a skein of thread* / 一～泉水 *a stream of spring water* / 上山有两～道。*There are two roads (or paths) going up the hill.* ❷ for strength, smell, etc.: 一～香味 *a whiff of fragrance* / 一～热气 *a stream (or puff) of hot air* / 一～劲 *a burst of energy* ❸〈贬〉for a group of people: 两～土匪 *two gangs of bandits* / 一～敌军 *a horde of enemy soldiers; an enemy detachment*
【股本】capital stock ◇ ～折价 stock discount; discount on capital stock
【股东】shareholder; stockholder ◇ ～大会 stockholders' meeting; ～分户账 stock ledger; ～权益 stockholder's equity; ～优先认购权 privileged allocation of insurance to stockholders
【股份】(又作'股分') share; stock ◇ ～保险 joint stock insurance; ～不定投资公司 open-end investment company; ～合作制 stock cooperative system; ～红利 dividend on shares; stock dividend; stock bonus; ～制 shareholding system
【股份公司】joint-stock company; stock company
【股份有限公司】limited-liability company; limited company (Ltd.)
【股份资本】share capital
【股肱】〈书〉right-hand man
【股骨】[生理] thighbone; femur
【股金】money paid for shares (in a partnership or cooperative)
【股民】person who buys and sells stocks
【股票】share certificate; share; stock ◇ ～持有人 shareholder; ～抵押借款 stock collateral loans; ～发行 bond issue; stock issue; issuance; ～分割 stock split; ～行市 current prices of stocks; quotations on the stock exchange; ～过户 stock transfer; ～价格限制 stock price restraint; ～价格指数 stock price index; ～交易 buying and selling of stocks; ～交易所 stock exchange; ～经纪人 stockbroker; stockjobber; ～票面价值 face value of share; ～平均价格 stock price averages; ～升水 premium on capital stock; ～市场 stock market; ～投资信托 stock investment trust; ～指数 stock index
【股票行情】stock quotation ◇ ～看跌 beating tendency; ～看涨 bullish tendency
【股权】stock ownership; stockholder's right
【股市】(〈略〉全称为'股票市场') stock market: 香港～ *Hong Kong Stock Market* / ～暴跌。*The stock market fell abruptly.* / ～崩溃。*The stock*

market crashed.

【股息】dividend ◇ ～限度 dividend limitation

【股线】［纺］plied yarn

【股长】section chief

【股指】stock market index：～快速下探。*The stock market index is falling rapidly*.

【股子】❶ share in a company ❷（for strength, smell, etc.）：这小伙子有一～使不完的劲。*The youngster just doesn't know what it is to be tired*.

牯

名 bull

【牯牛】bull

骨

名 ❶ bone ❷ skeleton；framework：伞～ *umbrella frame*；*the ribs of an umbrella* ❸ character；spirit：媚骨——另见 gū

【骨刺】［医］spur

【骨粉】（又作'骨肥'）bone meal；bone dust

【骨干】❶［生理］diaphysis ❷ backbone；mainstay：起～作用 *be a mainstay* / 科技队伍的～力量 *the backbone of the scientific and technological contingents* ◇ ～分子 core member；key member

【骨干企业】key enterprises

【骨骼】［生理］skeleton ◇ ～肌 skeletal muscle

【骨鲠在喉】（like）having a fishbone caught in one's throat：如～，不吐不快 *feel as if one has a fishbone in one's throat and be unable to rest until one has spat it out*；*have a criticism that one must express*

【骨骺】［生理］epiphysis

【骨化】［生理］ossify

【骨灰】❶ bone ash ❷ ashes of the dead ◇ ～盒 cinerary casket

【骨架】skeleton；framework：房屋的～ *the framework of a house* / 小说的～已经有了。*The framework of the novel has been worked out*.

【骨胶】［化］bone glue

【骨节】［生理］joint

【骨结核】bone tuberculosis；TB bone

【骨科】（department of）orthopaedics ◇ ～医生 orthopaedist

【骨刻】bone sculpture（or carving）

【骨痨】［中］tuberculosis of bones and joints

【骨料】［建］aggregate：轻～ *light aggregate*

【骨瘤】［医］osteoma

【骨膜】［生理］periosteum ◇ ～炎 periostitis

【骨牌】dominoes

【骨盆】［生理］pelvis

【骨气】strength of character；moral integrity；backbone：有～的人 *a man of integrity* / 我们中国人是有～的。*We Chinese have backbone*.

【骨器】bone object；bone implement

【骨肉】flesh and blood；kindred：亲生～ *one's own flesh and blood* / ～情谊 *kindred feelings*；*feelings of kinship* ◇ ～团聚 a family reunion；～相连 as closely linked as flesh and blood；～兄弟 blood brothers；one's own brothers；～之亲 blood relations

【骨软化】［医］osteomalacia

【骨瘦如柴】lean as a rake；worn to a shadow；a mere skeleton；a bag of bones：他渐渐饮食不进，～。*Gradually he lost his appetite and wasted away till he was nothing but skin and bones*.

【骨髓】［生理］marrow ◇ ～炎 osteomyelitis

【骨炭】bone black；animal charcoal

【骨头】❶ bone ❷ moral character：他～很硬。*He is a person of great moral integrity*. ❸〈方〉sharpness；bitterness：他话里有～。*His words had a bite to them*.

【骨头架子】〈口〉❶ skeleton：瘦得只剩个～ *be reduced to a skeleton*；*be all skin and bones* ❷ a very thin person

【骨学】osteology

【骨折】［医］fracture：粉碎性～ *comminuted fracture* / 开放性～ *open*（*or compound*）*fracture* / 他摔了一交，右臂～了。*He fell and fractured his right arm*.

【骨质疏松】［医］osteoporosis

【骨质增生】［医］osteoproliferation

【骨子】frame；ribs：伞～ *umbrella frame*；*the ribs of an umbrella*

【骨子里】〈贬〉in the bones—beneath the surface；in one's innermost nature；in substance：他表面上和和气气，～却阴险狠毒。*He had a frank friendly look, but at heart he was crafty and ruthless*.

贾

〈书〉Ⅰ 名 merchant Ⅱ 动 ❶ engage in trade ❷ buy ❸ sell；afford：余勇可贾

钴

名［化］cobalt（Co）

蛊

名 a legendary venomous insect

【蛊惑】poison and bewitch

【蛊惑人心】confuse and poison people's minds；resort to demagogy：～的口号 *demagogic slogans*

鼓

Ⅰ 名 ❶ drum：打～ *beat a drum* / ～声 *drumbeats* ❷ a thing like a drum：耳鼓 Ⅱ 动 ❶ beat；strike；sound：～琴 *play the zither* ❷ blow with bellows, etc.：～风 *work a bellows* ❸ rouse；agitate；pluck up：～起勇气 *pluck up*（*or muster*）*one's courage* ❹ bulge；swell：钱包很～。*The purse is bulging*. / 把口袋塞得～～的 *fill one's pockets till they bulge* / ～着嘴 *pout*

【鼓板】［音］clappers

【鼓吹】❶ advocate：～革命 *advocate revolution* ❷〈贬〉preach；advertise；play up

【鼓槌】drumstick

【鼓捣】〈方〉❶ tinker with；fiddle with：他最爱～收音机。*He likes to tinker with radios*. ❷ egg on；incite：在背后～ *egg on from behind the scenes* / ～别人去干坏事 *incite people to do evil*

【鼓点子】❶ drumbeats ❷ clapper beats which set the tempo and lead the orchestra in traditional Chinese operas

【鼓动】❶ agitate；arouse：做宣传～工作 *conduct propaganda and agitation* / ～群众 *arouse the* masses ❷ instigate; incite: 这些坏事是谁～你干的? *Who put you up to all these dirty tricks?*

【鼓风】[冶] (air) blast: 富氧～ *oxygen-enriched (air) blast* ◇ ～机 air-blower; blower; ～炉 blast furnace

【鼓鼓囊囊】bulging: 背包里装满了工具,～的。*The backpack is bulging with tools.*

【鼓劲】rouse one's enthusiasm

【鼓励】encourage; urge: 老师～大家学习英语。*Our teacher encouraged us to learn English.*

【鼓楼】drum-tower

【鼓膜】[生理] tympanic membrane; eardrum ◇ ～穿孔[医] perforation of the tympanic membrane

【鼓弄】〈口〉fiddle with; play with

【鼓室】[生理] tympanum

【鼓手】drummer

【鼓舞】inspire; encourage; hearten: ～士气 *boost the morale of the soldiers* / 形势令人～。*The present state of affairs is quite heartening.*

【鼓舞人心】inspiring; heartening: ～的消息 *most heartening news*

【鼓乐】strains of music accompanied by drumbeats: ～齐鸣,万众欢腾。*The cheers of the jubilant crowds mingled with crescendos of music.*

【鼓噪】make an uproar; raise a hubbub; clamour: ～一时 *make a great to-do about sth. for a time*

【鼓掌】clap one's hands; applaud: 热烈～ *warmly applaud* / ～通过 *approve by acclamation*

【鼓足干劲】go all out

毂 名 hub

臌 (构词成分)见下

【臌胀】[中] distension of abdomen caused by accumulation of gas or fluid due to dysfunction of liver and spleen; tympanites

gù

固 Ⅰ 形 solid; firm: 基础已～。*The foundation is solid.* Ⅱ 动 solidify; consolidate; strengthen: ～堤 *strengthen the dyke* Ⅲ 副 ❶ firmly; resolutely: ～辞 *resolutely refuse; firmly decline* / ～请 *insistently request* ❷ originally; in the first place; as a matter of course: ～当如此。*It is just as it should be.* Ⅳ 连 (used in the same way as 固然): 乘车～可,乘船亦无不可。*Admittedly we can make the journey by train, but there is no harm in our travelling by boat.*

【固步自封】同〖故步自封〗

【固氮菌】[微] nitrogen-fixing bacteria; azotobacter

【固氮作用】[农] nitrogen fixation; azofication

【固定】❶ fixed; regular: ～职业 *permanent occupation* / ～价格 *fixed price* / 电台的～节目 *a regular (or scheduled) radio programme* / 不要用～眼光看问题。*Don't take a static view of things.* ❷ fix; regularize: 把灯座～在车床上 *fix the lampstand on the lathe* / 把业务学习时间～下来 *set a regular time for vocational study* ◇ ～负债 fixed liability; ～工资制 fixed-wage system; ～汇率 fixed (exchange) rate; ～机库 permanent hangar; ～基金 fixed fund; ～价格 fixed price; ～平价 fixed parity; ～式平炉 stationary open-hearth furnace; ～投入 fixed input; ～资本 fixed capital

【固定资产】fixed assets ◇ ～投资 fixed investments

【固化】[化] solidify: ～酒精 *solidified alcohol*

【固件】computer firmware

【固井】[油] well cementation

【固然】(admitting a point that goes or does not go against the main argument of the sentence) though of course; admittedly; no doubt; it is true: 这样办～稳当些,可就是要慢一些。*No doubt it would be safer to do it that way, but it would be slower.*

【固若金汤】strongly fortified; impregnable

【固沙林】sand-fixation forest; dune-fixing forest

【固守】❶ defend tenaciously; be firmly entrenched in: ～阵地 *tenaciously defend one's position* ❷ stick to: ～老一套的办法 *stick to the old ways*

【固态】[物] solid state ◇ ～物理学 solid-state physics

【固体】solid body; solid ◇ ～废物 solid waste; ～酱油 solidified soy sauce

【固体燃料】solid fuel ◇ ～发动机 solid propellant engine; solid engine

【固体水库】solid reservoir

【固有】intrinsic; inherent; innate: ～的属性 *intrinsic attributes* / 人的正确思想不是自己头脑里～的。*Correct ideas are not innate in the mind.*

【固执】❶ obstinate; stubborn: 她很～,不会改变主意的。*She's very obstinate and won't change her mind.* ❷ persist in; cling to

【固执己见】stubbornly persist in one's opinions: ～,拒不接受别人的经验 *adhere stubbornly to one's own opinions and reject other people's experience*

故 Ⅰ 名 ❶ incident; happening: 事故 ❷ reason; cause: 该生不知何～缺席。*The reason for the student's absence remains unknown.* ❸ friend; acquaintance Ⅱ 副 on purpose; intentionally: ～作镇静 *pretend to be calm* / ～作惊讶 *put on a show of surprise; feign surprise* Ⅲ 连 hence; therefore; so; for this reason: 无私～能无畏。*Fearlessness stems from selflessness.* Ⅳ 形 former; old: 黄河～道 *the old course of the Yellow River* Ⅴ 动 (of people) die; dead: 他父母早～。*His parents died when he was very young.* or *He was left an orphan when very young.*

【故步自封】stand still and refuse to make progress; be complacent and conservative

【故地】an old haunt: ～重游 *revisit an old haunt*

【故都】onetime capital
【故而】and so; therefore; hence
【故宫】the Imperial Palace (in Beijing) ◇ ～博物院 the Palace Museum (in Beijing)
【故国】〈字〉native land; native soil; native place
【故伎】(又作'故技') stock trick; old tactics
【故伎重演】be up to one's old tricks; play the same old trick
【故旧】old friends and acquaintances
【故居】former residence (or home): 鲁迅～ *the former residence of Lu Xun*
【故里】native place; hometown: 荣归～ *return home with honours*
【故弄玄虚】purposely make a mystery of simple things; be deliberately mystifying
【故去】(of one's elders) die; pass away: 他父亲早就～了。*His father passed away a long time ago.*
【故人】an old friend
【故杀】[法] premeditated (or wilful) murder
【故事】❶ story; tale: 讲～ *tell a story* / 红军长征的～ *stories about the Long March of the Red Army* / ～员 *storyteller* ❷ plot: 这部小说～性很强。*The novel has an interesting plot.* ◇ ～会 a gathering at which stories are told; story-telling session; ～片 feature film
【故态复萌】slip back into one's old ways
【故土】native land; native place; birthplace; hometown: 怀念～ *long for home*
【故乡】old home; native place; birthplace: 北京已经成了我的第二～。*Beijing has become a second home to me.*
【故意】intentionally; wilfully; deliberately; on purpose: 他～让我生气。*He made me angry on purpose.* / 他是～侮辱人。*His insults were deliberate.* / 对不起,我不是～的。*I'm sorry, I didn't do it on purpose.* or *I'm sorry, I didn't mean it.* / ～刁难 *place obstacles in sb.'s way* ◇ ～犯规 intentional foul
【故障】hitch; breakdown; stoppage; trouble: 排除～ *fix a breakdown; clear a stoppage* / 发动机出了～。*The engine has broken down.* or *The engine is out of order.* / 出了什么～? *What's gone wrong?* ◇ ～自动分析 automatic malfunction analysis
【故纸堆】〈贬〉a heap of musty old books or papers: 他埋头于～中,不问世事。*He buried himself in his musty old books and took no notice of the outside world.*
【故作高深】pretend to be learned and profound
【故作姿态】strike a pose; put on airs

顾 I 动 ❶ turn round and look at; look at ❷ attend to; take into consideration: 你别只～自己。*Don't just think of yourself.* / 这么多事你一个人～得过来吗? *You've got so many things to attend to. Can you manage all by yourself?* ❸ visit; call on: 三顾茅庐 II 名 customer: 主顾
【顾此失彼】cannot attend to one thing without neglecting the other; have too many things to take care of at the same time
【顾大局,识大体】bear the overall situation in mind and put the general interest above all else
【顾及】take into account; attend to; give consideration to: 无暇～ *have no time to attend to the matter* / 事前应该～事后的效果。*Before taking an action, one should consider what effect it may have.*
【顾忌】scruple; misgiving: 毫无～ *without scruple; have no scruples* / 不能不有所～ *have to think twice (before doing sth.); be unable to overcome certain misgivings*
【顾家】look after one's family: 他工作太忙,很少～。*He's so busy at work that he hardly looks after his family.*
【顾客】customer; shopper; client: ～至上。*Customers First.* ◇ ～心理学 consumer psychology
【顾虑】misgiving; apprehension; worry: 打消～ *dispel one's misgivings (or worries)* / 你不必有任何～。*You needn't have any misgivings whatsoever.* / 他毫无～地谈出了自己的想法。*He spoke his mind without the slightest hesitancy.*
【顾虑重重】have no end of worries; be full of misgivings
【顾面子】❶ save face; keep up appearances ❷ spare sb.'s feelings: 为了顾她的面子,我没有说她这事做得有多糟。*I tried to spare her feelings by not telling her what a poor job she had done.*
【顾名思义】seeing the name of a thing one thinks of its function; just as its name implies; as the term suggests: 心理学,～,是研究人们心理的科学。*Psychology is by definition the scientific study of the mind.*
【顾盼】〈书〉look around: 左右～ *glance right and left*
【顾盼自雄】look about complacently
【顾前不顾后】drive ahead without considering the consequences; act rashly
【顾全】show consideration for and take care to preserve ◇ ～大局 take the interests of the whole into account; consider the situation as a whole
【顾问】adviser; consultant: 法律～ *legal adviser* ◇ ～公司 consulting firm; ～委员会 consultative (or advisory) committee
【顾惜】value; care for: ～自己的身体 *look after one's health*
【顾影自怜】❶ look at one's reflection and admire oneself ❷ look at one's shadow and lament one's lot
【顾主】customer; client; patron

梏 名〈书〉wooden handcuffs: 桎梏

雇 动 hire; employ: 我们大家～了一只船。*We hired a boat between us.* / 我想～个保姆。*I want to hire a maid.* / 他家里～了好些用人。*Many servants were employed in his house.*
【雇工】❶ hire labour; hire hands ❷ hired labou-

rer (or hand, worker) ❸ 同〖雇农〗

【雇农】farmhand; farm labourer

【雇佣】employ; hire ◇ ～合同 employment contract

【雇佣兵役制】mercenary system

【雇佣观点】hired-hand mentality—the attitude of one who won't do more than he is paid for: 抱有～的人，决不可能干好工作。*Those with a hired-hand mentality will never do a good job.*

【雇佣军】mercenary army (or troops); mercenaries

【雇佣劳动者】wage labourer

【雇佣奴隶】wage slave

【雇员】employee

【雇主】employer

痼 形 chronic; inveterate: 痼疾

【痼疾】chronic (or obstinate) illness: 医学的发达，使很多所谓～都能治好。*Advances in medical science have made it possible to cure many so-called chronic diseases.*

【痼癖】addiction

【痼习】inveterate (or confirmed) habit: ～难改。*Confirmed habits are difficult to break.*

锢 动 ❶ plug with molten metal; run metal into cracks ❷〈书〉hold in custody; imprison

【锢囚】［气］occlusion: ～气旋 *occluded cyclone*

guā

瓜 名 melon, gourd, etc.

【瓜分】cut up a melon—carve up; dismember; partition; divide up: 几个战胜国无情地～了这个战败国，各自攫取了同样大小的一片土地。*The victors mercilessly carved up the defeated country, each taking an equal share.*

【瓜葛】connection; implication; association: 他跟投机倒把分子有～。*He's got mixed up with speculators.*

【瓜葛亲】distant relatives

【瓜皮帽】a kind of skullcap resembling the rind of half a watermelon; skullcap

【瓜熟蒂落】when a melon is ripe it falls off its stem—things are easily settled once conditions are ripe

【瓜田李下】in a melon patch or under a plum tree—in suspicious circumstances or surroundings

【瓜子】melon seeds: 嗑～儿 *crack melon seeds*

【瓜子脸】an oval face

呱（构词成分）见下 ——另见 gū

【呱嗒】（又作'呱哒'）❶ clip-clop; clack: 她在人行道上走着，脚底下～～地响。*Her heels clacked as she walked on the pavement.* ❷(used in): ～着脸 *pull a long face*

【呱呱】*the quacking of a duck; the croaking of a frog; the cawing of a crow*: 鸭子～地叫。*A duck quacks.* ——另见 gūgū

【呱呱叫】〈口〉tiptop; top-notch

【呱唧】the sound of hands being clapped

刮 动 ❶ scrape; shave: 把墙上的漆～下去 *scrape the paint off the wall* / ～锅子 *scrape a pot clean* / ～鱼鳞 *scale a fish* / ～胡子 *shave the beard* / 就～破一点皮。*It's only a scratch.* ❷ smear with (paste, etc.): ～糨子 *stiffen (cloth) by spreading paste over it* ❸ plunder; fleece; extort: 他当知县时～了不少的钱。*While holding office as county magistrate, he made a lot of money by extortion.* ❹(of the wind) blow: ～大风了。*It's blowing hard.* or *There's a gale blowing.* / 土～得满天飞。*Dust was blown into the air.*

【刮刀】scraping cutter; scraper: 三角～ *triangular scraper*

【刮地皮】scrape off the earth—(of reactionary rulers) extort money from the people

【刮宫】［医］dilatation and curettage (D. and C.)

【刮垢磨光】scrape and polish—❶ take pains to teach and train a person or to improve oneself ❷ be meticulous and painstaking

【刮脸】shave (the face): 我天天早上～。*I shave every morning.* ◇ ～刀 razor; ～皮〈方〉rub the forefinger against one's own cheek (to indicate scorn for sb.); point the finger of scorn at sb.

【刮目相看】（又作'刮目相待'）look at sb. with new eyes; treat sb. with increased respect

【刮痧】［中］a popular treatment for sunstroke by scraping the patient's neck, chest or back

【刮削】scrape: ～器 *scraper*

guǎ

剐 动 ❶ cut to pieces (a form of capital punishment in ancient times); dismember: 千刀万剐 ❷ cut; slit: 手上～了个口子 *cut one's hand*

寡 形 ❶ few; scant: 以寡敌众 ❷ bland; tasteless: 清汤寡水 ❸ widowed: 鳏～ *widowers and widows*

【寡不敌众】be hopelessly outnumbered; fight against hopeless odds

【寡妇】widow

【寡廉鲜耻】lost to shame; shameless

【寡人】I, your unworthy king (corresponding to the English "royal we")

【寡头】oligarch: 金融～ *financial oligarch; financial magnate* / ～垄断 *oligopoly* ◇ ～政治 oligarchy

【寡言】taciturn: 沉默寡言

guà

卦 名 divinatory symbols: 占卦

挂 Ⅰ 动 ❶ hang; put up: 把地图～在墙上。*Put*

(*or Hang*) *the map up on the wall*. / 天上~着一轮明月。*A bright moon hung in the sky*. / 把这件事先~一~再说。*Let's leave the matter aside for the moment*. ❷ hang up; ring off: 我还没有来得及问他名字,他就把电话~了。*He hung up* (*or rang off*) *before I could ask his name*. / 你先别~,等我查一下。*Hold the line while I find out*. ❸〈方〉call (or phone, ring) up; put sb. through to: 我呆会儿再给他~电话。*I'll ring him up again*. ❹ hitch; get caught: 把拖车~上。*Hitch up the trailer*. / 她的衣服给钉子~住了。*Her dress got caught on a nail*. ❺〈方〉be concerned about: 时刻把群众的利益~在心上 *always have the welfare of the masses at heart* ❻〈方〉be covered with; be coated with: 他脸上~了一层尘土。*His face was covered with dust*. / 瓦盆里面~一层釉子。*The earthen pot is glazed inside*. ❼ register (at a hospital, etc.): 我要~外科。*I want to register for surgery*. or *Surgery, please*. Ⅱ 量 a set or string (of things): 一~大车 *a horse and cart* / 十多~鞭炮 *a dozen strings of firecrackers* / 一~珠子 *a string of pearls*

【挂表】〈方〉pocket watch

【挂不住】〈方〉lose control of one's feelings (in embarrassment)

【挂彩】❶ decorate with coloured silk festoons; decorate for festive occasions ❷ be wounded in action: 他在战争中挂了两回彩。*He was wounded twice in the war*.

【挂车】trailer

【挂齿】mention: 何足挂齿

【挂挡】put into gear: 挂高速挡 *change to* (*or put into*) *high gear* / 挂头挡 *engage the first gear*

【挂钩】❶［交通］couple (two railway coaches); articulate ❷ link up with; establish contact with; get in touch with: 产销直接~,减少中间环节。*With direct contact between producing and marketing departments, the number of intermediate steps are reduced*.

【挂冠】〈旧〉resign from office

【挂号】❶ register (at a hospital, etc.): 请排队~。*Please queue* (*or line*) *up to register*. / 你挂的是几号? *What's your registration number*? ❷ send by registered mail: 你这封信要不要~? *Do you want to have this letter registered*? ◇ ~处 registration office; ~费 registration fee; ~信 registered letter (or mail)

【挂花】be wounded in action: 他腿上挂过两次花。*He was twice wounded in the leg*.

【挂记】worry about; be anxious about; keep thinking about

【挂靠】become attached to another unit

【挂历】monthly calender hung up on the wall; wall calender

【挂零】odd: 这个人看样子顶多不过四十~。*This man is about forty odd at most*. / 到会人数五百~。*Five hundred odd were present at the meeting*.

【挂虑】be anxious about; worry about: 孩子由她姥姥照看,用不着~。*The child is being looked after by his grandmother, so there's no need to worry*.

【挂面】fine dried noodles; vermicelli

【挂名】titular; nominal; only in name: 我只是~委员,没有什么事儿干。*I'm only a titular committee member, having little or nothing to do*. ◇ ~股东 nominal partner; ostensible partner

【挂念】worry about sb. who is absent; miss: ~亲人 *miss one's folks at home* / 我身体很好,请勿~。*I'm in good health. Please don't worry*.

【挂拍】end a career as player of one of the racket games (i.e. table tennis, badminton, etc.); end of a racket game competition: 全国少年乒乓球赛~。*The National Youth Table Tennis Championship came to an end*.

【挂牌】hang out one's shingle; put up one's brass plate: 他行医多年,在天津和北京都挂过牌。*He practised medicine for many years and opened clinics of his own in both Tianjin and Beijing*. ◇ ~股票 listed stock; ~上市公司 listed company; quoted company; ~证券 quoted securities

【挂屏】a set of hanging scrolls of painting or calligraphy

【挂失】report the loss of (identity papers, cheques, etc.): 他存折丢了,赶紧去银行~。*He lost his bankbook, and hurried to the bank to report it*.

【挂帅】be in command; assume (or take) command; assume leadership: 所长亲自~进行这项工作。*The director himself took charge of the project*.

【挂锁】padlock

【挂毯】tapestry

【挂图】❶ wall map ❷ hanging chart

【挂线疗法】［中］ligating method for treating anal fistula

【挂心】be on one's mind

【挂靴】(又作'挂鞋')(of a footballer) retire

【挂羊头,卖狗肉】hang up a sheep's head and sell dogmeat—try to palm off sth. inferior to what it purports to be

【挂一漏万】for one thing cited, ten thousand may have been left out—the list is far from complete

【挂衣钩】clothes-hook

【挂账】buy or sell on credit suspend repayment: ~停息 *suspend repayment of bank loans and interest*

【挂职】suspend duties; retain one's position while working temporarily elsewhere: 她参加了学校组织的暑期~实习。*She took part in the summer internship program organized by the school but retained her current job*.

【挂钟】wall clock

【挂轴】hanging scroll (of Chinese painting or calligraphy)

褂 名 a Chinese-style unlined garment; gown:

短～儿 *short gown*

【褂子】a Chinese-style unlined upper garment; short gown

guāi

乖 形 ❶ (of a child) well-behaved; good: 真是个～孩子。*There's a dear*. ❷ clever; shrewd; alert: 学～了 *become a little wiser* ❸ perverse; contrary to reason: 有～常理 *run counter to reason*

【乖乖】❶ well-behaved; obedient: 孩子们都～儿地坐着听老师讲故事。*The children all sat quietly listening to the teacher telling stories*. ❷ (to a child) little dear; darling ❸ good gracious

【乖觉】alert; quick: 松鼠～得很,听到一点儿响声就溜跑了。*The squirrel is very alert, and will run away as soon as it hears the slightest sound*.

【乖戾】perverse; unreasonable; disagreeable

【乖谬】absurd; abnormal

【乖僻】eccentric; odd

【乖巧】❶ clever; ingenious ❷ cute; lovely

【乖张】eccentric and unreasonable; perverse; recalcitrant

掴 动 slap; smack: ～耳光 *box sb.'s ears; slap sb. on the face*

guǎi

拐 Ⅰ 动 ❶ turn: ～过墙角 *turn the corner of a house* / ～进一条胡同 *turn into an alley* / 往左～ *turn to the left* / 前面走不通了,咱们～回去吧。*We can't get through here, let's turn back*. ❷ limp: 他一～一～地走。*He limped along*. or *He walked with a limp*. ❸ swindle; make off with: ～款潜逃 *abscond with funds* ❹ abduct; kidnap Ⅱ 名 ❶〈方〉corner; turning: 墙～ *a corner formed by two walls* ❷ crutch: 走路架着双～ *walk on crutches*

【拐脖儿】elbow (of a stove pipe)

【拐带】kidnap (women or children); abduct

【拐棍】walking stick: 拄着～ *leaning on a stick*

【拐角】corner; turning: 胡同～有个邮筒。*There is a postbox at the street corner*.

【拐卖】kidnap and sell; engage in slavery: ～妇女儿童 *abduct and sell women and children*

【拐骗】abduct; swindle: ～钱财 *swindle money (out of sb.)*

【拐弯】❶ turn a corner; make a turn: ～要慢行。*Slow down when turning a corner*. / 往前走向左一～就到了。*Go straight ahead, turn left and you'll be there*. ❷ change one's opinion to another point of view; pursue a new course: 他思想一时还拐不过弯来。*He hasn't straightened out his thoughts yet*. ❸ corner; turning

【拐弯抹角】talk in a roundabout way; beat about the bush: 说话不要～。*Get to the point. Don't beat about the bush*. / 他～地提到这件事。*He referred to it obliquely*.

【拐杖】walking stick

【拐子】❶〈口〉cripple ❷ I-shaped spool or reel ❸ crutch ❹ abductor; swindler

guài

怪 Ⅰ 形 strange; odd; queer; bewildering: ～现象 *something quite unusual* / 你说～不～? *Isn't this strange?* / 他这个人真～! *He's rather odd*. Ⅱ 动 ❶ find sth. strange; wonder at: 那有什么可～的? *Is that anything to be surprised at?* ❷ blame: 不能～他们。*They're not to blame*. or *It's not their fault*. / ～我没讲清楚。*I'm to blame for not having made it clearer*. Ⅲ 副〈口〉quite; rather: ～不好意思的 *feel rather embarrassed* / 箱子～沉的。*The suitcase is rather heavy*. Ⅳ 名 monster; demon; evil being: 鬼怪

【怪不得】❶ no wonder; so that's why; that explains why: ～多一张票,她把自己的让出来了。*So that's why (or No wonder) there's an extra ticket. She has given hers up*. ❷ not to blame: 他来晚了,～他,因为开会时间通知错了。*He's not to blame for arriving late. He was told the wrong time for the meeting*.

【怪诞】weird; strange: ～的传说 *a strange legend* ◇～不经 weird and uncanny; fantastic

【怪话】cynical remark; grumble; complaint: 说～ *make cynical remarks*

【怪里怪气】eccentric; peculiar; queer: ～的人 *an eccentric fellow* / 她的声音～的。*Her voice sounds queer*.

【怪模怪样】queer-looking; grotesque: 这条小狗长得～的。*The little dog is queer-looking*. / 你穿着这衣服显得～的。*You look grotesque in those clothes*.

【怪僻】eccentric: 性情～ *eccentric*

【怪圈】strange phenomenon which is hard to explain ; vicious circle

【怪声怪气】(speak in) a strange voice or an affected manner

【怪事】strange thing: 我的表刚才还在桌上的呢,怎么转眼就不见了,真是～! *Strange! My watch was on the desk a minute ago, and now it has disappeared*.

【怪胎】monster; teratism

【怪物】❶ monster; monstrosity; freak ❷ an eccentric person; a queer bird; oddball

【怪异】❶ monstrous; strange; unusual: 听到一些～的声音我吃了一惊。*Queer noises startled me*. ❷ strange phenomenon; portent; prodigy

【怪罪】blame sb.

guān

关 Ⅰ 动 ❶ shut; close: 把门～上。*Shut the*

door. / 这扇窗户～不上。*This window won't shut.* ❷ turn off: ～收音机 *turn (or switch) off the radio* / ～电灯 *turn off the light* ❸ shut in; lock up: 别把孩子们整天～在屋里。*Don't keep the children inside all day.* ❹ (of a business) close down: 镇上～了好几家店铺。*Quite a few shops in the town closed down.* Ⅱ 名 ❶ mountain pass; a guarded passage: 玉门～ *the Yumen Pass* ❷ customs house: 海关 ❸ barrier; a critical juncture: 大考是一～。*The final exam is a barrier to be passed.* / 只要突破这一～,就好办了。*Once we have got over this difficulty, it will be plain sailing.*

【关爱】concern and care; love and care: 老师们的深切～,使她很受感动。*The love and care shown by the teachers moved her greatly.*

【关隘】〈书〉(mountain) pass

【关闭】❶ close; shut: 门窗都紧紧～着。*The doors and windows were all tightly closed.* ❷ (of a shop or factory) close down; shut down: 那家工厂无人订货,被迫～。*The factory had to close down through lack of orders.*

【关岛】Guam

【关东】east of the Pass (i. e. 山海关 "Pass Between Mountain and Sea")—the Northeast; Northeast China ◇ ～糖 a kind of malt candy (originating in the Northeast)

【关防】❶ security measures: ～严密 *tight security measures* ❷〈旧〉government or army seal (usu. rectangular in shape)

【关怀】show loving care for; show solicitude for: 在老师的～下,这次考试我取得了良好的成绩。*Thanks to my teacher's concern I got good results in the exam.*

【关怀备至】show the utmost solicitude

【关键】❶ door bolt; door bar ❷ key; hinge; crux: 问题的～ *the key to the question; the crux (or heart) of the matter* / ～时刻 *a critical (or crucial) moment* / ～的一年 *a year of crucial importance*

【关节】❶［生理］joint: 指～ *finger joints* ❷ a key (or crucial) link; a key (or crucial) point: 应该注意那些涉及全局的重要～。*Attention should be centred on the links that have a bearing on the situation as a whole.* ◇ ～炎 arthritis

【关口】❶ strategic pass ❷ juncture

【关联】be related; be connected: 国民经济各部门是互相～互相依存的。*The various branches of the national economy are interrelated and interdependent.* / 数学和天文学是互相～的科学。*Mathematics and astronomy are cognate sciences.*

【关贸总协定】General Agreement on Tariffs and Trade (GATT) ◇ ～缔约国 a contracting party to GATT

【关门】❶ (of a shop, etc.) close: 展览馆下午六点半～。*The exhibition centre closes at 6:30 p.m.* ❷〈口〉(of a business) close down: 公司因为管理不善,最后只好～。*The company had no choice but to close down in the end due to mismanagement.* ❸ refuse discussion or consideration; slam the door on sth.: 对方在谈判中还没有～。*The other side hasn't yet slammed the door on further negotiations.* / 采取～态度 *adopt a closed-door attitude* ❹ be behind closed doors: 我们不能～办报。*We must not run a newspaper behind closed doors.*

【关门打狗】bolt the door and beat the dog—block the enemy's retreat and then destroy him

【关门大吉】〈诙〉(of a factory, business, etc.) close down for good

【关内】inside the Pass—the area to the west of Shanhaiguan (山海关) or to the east of Jiayuguan (嘉峪关)

【关卡】an outpost of a tax office; checkpoint

【关切】❶ considerate; thoughtful: 他待人非常和蔼、～。*He's very kind and thoughtful.* ❷ be deeply concerned; show one's concern over: 感谢同志们对我的～。*I'm grateful to you comrades for your deep concern.*

【关税】customs duty; customs; tariff: 这种东西～很重。*The duty on this sort of goods is awfully high.* ◇ ～壁垒 tariff barrier; ～法 tariff act; ～负担 incidence of duty; ～豁免 exemption from customs duties; ～减让 concession of tariff; ～配额 customs quota; tariff quota; ～升级 tariff escalation; ～税则 customs tariff; tariff schedule; ～同盟 customs (or tariff) union; ～优惠 tariff preference; ～政策 tariff policy; customs policy; ～制度 tariff system; ～自主 tariff autonomy

【关停并转】closure, suspension of production, merger and conversion (spec. Unprofitable enterprises or heavily polluting ones)

【关头】juncture; key moment: 在革命的重要～ *at important junctures of the revolution* / 生死存亡的紧要～ *a critical moment of life-and-death importance*

【关外】outside the Pass (another name for 关东)

【关系】❶ connections; relations; relationship: 夫妻～ *relations between husband and wife* / 家庭～ *family connections* / 社会～ *social connections* ❷ relevance; bearing; influence; significance: 这件事跟我没有～。*This matter has nothing to do with me.* / 你回答的话跟他所问的我看不出有什么～。*I don't see any connection between your answer and his question.* ❸ (usu. used with 由于 or 因为 to indicate cause or reason): 由于时间～,就谈到这里吧。*Since time is limited, I'll have to stop here.* ❹ credentials showing membership in or connection with an organization: 党员调动工作时要转党的～。*When a Party member is transferred to another place of work, his Party credentials are sent there.* ❺ concern; affect; have a bearing on; have to do with: 农业～国计民生极大。*Agriculture is of vital importance to the nation's economy and the people's livelihood.*

【关系户】parties of connection; connections

【关系网】relative network；a well-connected network

【关系学】〈诙〉the art of cultivating good personal relations

【关心】be concerned about；show solicitude for；care for；be interested in：我很～你。*I'm very concerned about you.* / 我们要～国家大事。*We should concern ourselves with affairs of state.*

【关押】lock up；put under detention；put in prison：～犯人 *put a criminal in prison*

【关于】about；on；with regard to；concerning：这是一个～龙的故事。*This is a story about dragons.* / 他读了几本～政治经济学的书。*He read a few books on political economy.* / ～这件事我没有意见。*I have no suggestions concerning this.*

【关张】〈方〉(of a shop) close down；go out of business

【关照】❶ (often used in asking or thanking sb. for help) look after；take care of；keep an eye on：我走后，这里的工作就靠你多～了。*When I'm gone, you'll have to look after the work here.* ❷ notify by word of mouth；tell：你走的时候请～一声。*Please let me know when you're ready to go.* / 医生再三～不许你再抽烟。*The doctor ordered you again and again to stop smoking.*

【关注】follow with interest；pay close attention to；show solicitude for：我们对那个地区的局势十分～。*We're paying a good deal of attention to what's going on in that area.*

观

Ⅰ 动 look at；watch；observe：登泰山～日出 *ascend Taishan Mountain to see the sunrise* Ⅱ 名 ❶ sight；view：奇观 ❷ outlook；view；concept：世界观 ——另见 guàn

【观测】❶ observe and survey：～气象 *make weather observations* / 气球～ *balloon observation* ❷ observe；watch：～敌情 *watch enemy movements* ◇ ～站 observation station

【观察】observe；watch；survey：～地形 *survey the terrain* / ～动静 *watch what is going on* / 这个病人需要住院～。*This patient should be hospitalized for observation.* ◇ ～机 observation aircraft；～家 observer (a pseudonym used by a political commentator)；～所［军］observation post；～员［外交］observer (who has the right to make a speech, but not to vote)

【观潮派】a person who takes a wait-and-see attitude；onlooker；bystander

【观点】point of view；viewpoint；standpoint：阶级～ *class viewpoint* / 马克思列宁主义的～ *Marxist-Leninist standpoint* / 阐明～ *explain one's position*

【观风】be on the lookout；serve as a lookout

【观感】impressions；observations：对新中国的～ *impressions of New China* / 我就自己～所及，写了一篇通讯。*I wrote a news report based on my own observations.*

【观光】go sightseeing；visit；tour：～市容 *tour the city* / 南京长江大桥建成后有不少外宾前来～。*Many foreign visitors have come to see the Nanjing Changjiang Bridge since its construction.* / ～者 *sightseer* ◇ ～团 sightseeing party；tour group

【观看】watch；view：～排球比赛 *watch a volleyball match* / ～话剧《茶馆》(舞剧《天鹅湖》) *see the play Teahouse (the ballet Swan Lake)*

【观礼】attend a celebration or ceremony：国庆～代表 *a representative attending National Day celebrations* ◇ ～台 reviewing stand；visitors' stand

【观摩】inspect and learn from each other's work；view and emulate：～演出 *give a performance before fellow artists for the purpose of discussion and emulation* / ～教学 *learn how to teach by observing other teachers' classes and emulating their teaching methods*

【观念】sense；idea；concept：组织～ *sense of organization* / 私有～ *private ownership mentality* / 破除旧的传统～ *break away from outdated traditional modes of thought* ◇ ～形态 同〖意识形态〗

【观赏】view and admire；enjoy the sight of：我们～了几位名演员的表演。*We watched with enjoyment the performances of several famous actors.* ◇ ～艺术 the visual arts；～鱼 fishes for display (e.g. goldfish)；～植物 ornamental (or decorative) plant

【观通站】［军］observation and communication post (of the naval service)

【观望】❶ wait and see；look on (from the sidelines)：采取～态度 *take a wait-and-see attitude* ❷ look around：四下～ *look around*

【观象台】observatory

【观音】(又作'观世音')［宗］(佛教) Guanyin；the Goddess of Mercy；(Sanskrit) Avalokitesvara (〈字〉"looking on or hearing the voices of the suffering")

【观音竹】fernleaf hedge bamboo (Bambusa multiplex var. nana)

【观瞻】the appearance of a place and the impressions it leaves；sight；view

【观战】❶ watch a battle；watch other people fight ❷ watch a match or contest

【观众】spectator；viewer；audience

【观众席】auditorium (of a theatre)；grandstand (of a stadium)

官

Ⅰ 名 ❶ government official；officer；officeholder：大～ *a high official* / 他做过什么～？*What official positions has he held?* ❷ organ (a part of the body)：感官 Ⅱ 形 governmental；official：官办

【官办】run by the government；operated by official bodies：～企业 *state enterprise*

【官报私仇】同〖公报私仇〗

【官本位】official rank or status taken as the only criterion for judging one's social worth；official rank standard ◇ ～意识 rank consciousness；～

制 system of ranking of officials
【官逼民反】oppressive government drives the people to rebellion
【官兵】❶ officers and men：～一致 *unity between officers and men* ❷〈旧〉government troops
【官场】〈贬〉officialdom；official circles
【官倒】official-speculator
【官邸】official residence；official mansion：首相～ *prime minister's residence*
【官方】of the government；official：～人士 *government officials* / ～消息 *news from government sources；official sources* / 以～身分 *in an official capacity* / ～宣传 *official propaganda；government publicity* ◇ ～统计 official statistics；～外汇市场 official exchange market；～外汇资产 official foreign assets；～文件 official documents；patent；～注册 official register
【官府】〈旧〉❶ local authorities ❷ feudal official
【官复原职】restore an official to his original post；be reinstated
【官官相护】officials protect each other；bureaucrats shield one another
【官宦】〈旧〉government official
【官价】official price (or rate)
【官架子】the airs of an official；bureaucratic airs：摆～ *put on bureaucratic airs*
【官阶】an official's rank
【官吏】〈旧〉government officials
【官僚】bureaucrat：封建～ *feudal bureaucrat* / 清除～习气 *get rid of bureaucratic practices* / 这人真～！ *What a bureaucrat that fellow is!* ◇ ～机构 bureaucratic apparatus；～主义 bureaucracy；bureaucratism；～资本 capital owned by the bureaucrat-capitalist class；bureaucratic capital；～资产阶级 the bureaucrat-capitalist class
【官了】settle according to policy and law
【官迷】a person who hankers after public office；office seeker
【官能】(organic) function；sense：视、听、嗅、味、触这五种～ *the five senses of sight, hearing, smell, taste and touch* ◇ ～团［化］functional group；～症 functional disease
【官气】bureaucratic airs；bureaucratism：～十足 *full of bureaucratic airs*
【官腔】bureaucratic tone；official jargon ——另见〖打官腔〗
【官商】❶ government commerce；state-operated commerce ❷ government merchant；a bureaucratic operator of a commercial enterprise：～作风 *the style of government merchants；a bureaucratic way of handling commerce*
【官司】〈口〉lawsuit
【官衔】official title
【官样文章】officialese；bureaucratic red tape；mere formalities
【官瘾】〈贬〉love for public office；anxiety to be an official
【官员】official：外交～ *diplomatic official*
【官运】official career；fortunes of officialdom
【官运亨通】have a successful official career
【官职】government post；official position

冠 名 ❶ hat：衣冠 ❷ corona；crown：树冠 ❸ crest；comb：鸡冠 ——另见 guàn
【冠盖如云】(又作'冠盖云集') a large gathering of high officials
【冠盖相望】constant exchange of high officials' visits between two nations
【冠冕】❶ royal crown；official hat ❷ stately；ceremonious
【冠冕堂皇】highfalutin；high-sounding：～的理由 *high-sounding excuses* / 他说得～，干的却是种种见不得人的事。*He talks in a dignified, high-sounding way, but engages in all sorts of underhand activities.*
【冠心病】coronary heart disease
【冠周炎】pericoronitis
【冠状动脉】coronary artery ◇ ～硬化 coronary arteriosclerosis
【冠子】crest；comb：鸡～ *cockscomb*

倌 名 ❶ a keeper of domestic animals；herdsman：马～儿 *groom* ❷〈旧〉a hired hand in certain trades：堂倌

棺 名 coffin：棺材
【棺材】coffin
【棺床】［考古］coffin platform
【棺椁】［考古］inner and outer coffins
【棺架】bier
【棺木】coffin

鳏 形 wifeless；widowered：～居 *live as a widower*
【鳏夫】〈书〉an old wifeless man；bachelor or widower
【鳏寡孤独】widowers, widows, orphans and the childless—those who have no kith and kin and cannot support themselves

guǎn

馆 名 ❶ accommodation for guests：旅馆 ❷ embassy；legation or consulate：使馆 ❸ (of service trades) shop：茶馆 ❹ a place for cultural activities：博物馆
【馆子】restaurant；eating house：下～ *eat at a restaurant*

管 Ⅰ 名 ❶ tube；pipe：钢管 ❷ wind instrument：单簧管 ❸［电子］valve；tube：电子管 Ⅱ 量 (for long, thin cylinder-shaped things)：一～毛笔 *a writing brush* / 一～牙膏 *a tube of toothpaste* Ⅲ 动 ❶ manage；run；control；take care of；be in charge of：～家务 *manage a household；run a house* / ～孩子 *take care of children* ❷ have jurisdiction over；administer：这个市～着十个县。*This city has jurisdiction o-*

ver ten counties. ❸ discipline (children or students): 孩子要~,但更要引导。*Children need discipline, but they need guidance even more.* ❹ be concerned about; care about; bother about; intervene: 他只~自己,不~别人。*He's only concerned about himself, not about others.* ❺ provide; guarantee: ~吃~住 *provide meals and accommodation* Ⅳ 介 〈口〉(used in the pattern 管…叫"call sb. sth., address sb., as sth.") Ⅴ 连 〈方〉no matter (who, what, how, etc.): ~你怎么说,我也要再试一下。*No matter what you say, I'll try again.* / ~它下不下雨,我们都得马上出发。*We've got to be off immediately, whether it rains or not.*

【管保】guarantee; assure: 我~你吃了这药就好。*I guarantee that if you take this medicine, you'll soon get well.* / 他~不知道。*I'm sure he doesn't know.*

【管不了】(又作'管不住') be unable to control or manage: 这孩子非常淘气,连他父亲都~他。*The child is very naughty and even his father cannot manage him.*

【管不着】have no right to interfere; (it's) none of your concern (or business): 这是我们家里事,你~! *This is something within the family, and you have no right to interfere.*

【管道】pipeline; piping; conduit; tubing: 煤气~ *gas piping* / ~安装 *piping erection*

【管得宽】make everything one's own business: 我去哪儿你都要问,你也管得太宽了。*Whenever I go out, you always ask where I'm going. You bother about too many things.*

【管风琴】[音] pipe organ; organ

【管家】❶ manage a household; run a house ❷ 〈旧〉steward; butler ❸ manager (of a work unit); housekeeper

【管见】〈谦〉my humble opinion; my limited understanding: 容陈~。*Let me state my humble opinion.*

【管教】discipline (children or students); correct: 他母亲经常~他。*His mother corrects him from time to time.* / 她从不~孩子,现在管不住了。*She never disciplines her children and they are uncontrollable.*

【管教所】reformatory

【管界】(又作'管片') ❶ area or land under control; sphere of jurisdiction; jurisdiction zone: 事件发生在这个派出所的~内。*It took place in an area under the jurisdiction of this police station.* ❷ border of a jurisdiction zone

【管井】[水] tube well

【管窥】look at sth. through a bamboo tube —have a restricted view: ~所及 *in my humble opinion*

【管窥蠡测】look at the sky through a bamboo tube and measure the sea with a calabash—be restricted in vision and shallow in understanding

【管理】❶ manage; run; administer; govern; take care of: ~财务 *be in charge of financial affairs* / ~图书 *take care of the library books* / ~群众生活 *look after the everyday life of the masses* / 工商~ *industrial and commercial management* / 城市~ *city government* / 加强企业~ *strengthen the management (or administration) of enterprises* / 因为~不善,销路日减。*Sales have been falling off due to mismanagement.* ❷ control (people or animals): ~罪犯 *keep criminals under control* / ~牲口 *tend and control draught animals* ◇ ~程序 supervisory routine; ~处 administrative (or management) office; ~当局 routine management process; ~方法 office procedure; ~费 management expenses; costs of administration; ~阶层 management echelon; ~科学 management science; ~模式 management model; management pattern; ~系统 management system; ~委员会 management committee; board of management; ~员 a person managing some aspect of daily work within an organization; ~职能 management function

【管路】[机] pipeline: ~铺设 *pipe laying* / ~输送能力 *carrying capacity of a pipeline; delivery capacity*

【管事】❶ run affairs; be in charge: 这里谁~? *Who's in charge here?* ❷ 〈口〉of use; effective: 这药很~儿。*This medicine helps a lot (or is very effective).* / 找他不~。*It's no use asking him.* / 他说的话不~。*What he says doesn't count for much.* ❸ 〈旧〉manager; steward

【管束】restrain; check; control: 严加~ *keep sb. under strict control*

【管辖】have jurisdiction over; exercise control over; administer: 在~范围之内 *come within the jurisdiction of* / 这个市由中央直接~。*This municipality is directly under the Central Government.* ◇ ~权 jurisdiction

【管闲事】be meddlesome; be a busybody: 他爱~。*He's a real busybody.* / 这是他们内部问题,你别~。*This is their own problem, keep your nose out of it.*

【管弦乐】orchestral music ◇ ~队 orchestra

【管押】take sb. into custody; keep in custody; detain

【管用】同〖管事〗

【管乐队】wind band; band

【管乐器】wind instrument

【管制】❶ control: ~物价 *control prices* / ~灯火 *enforce a blackout* / 军事~ *military control* / 外汇~ *foreign exchange control* ❷ put (a criminal, etc.) under surveillance: 交群众~ *put sb. under public surveillance* / ~劳动 *labour under surveillance* ◇ ~股 controlled stock

【管中窥豹,可见一斑】look at one spot on a leopard and you can visualize the whole animal; conjure up the whole thing through seeing a part of it

【管状花】[植] tubular flower

【管子】tube; pipe: 自来水~ *tap water pipe*

【管子工】plumber; pipe fitter

guàn

观 名 Taoist temple：白云～（*White Cloud*）*Temple*（*in Beijing*）——另见 guān

贯 Ⅰ动 ❶ pass through；pierce：纵贯 ❷ be linked together；follow in a continuous line：贯珠 Ⅱ量〈旧〉（a string of 1,000 cash）

【贯彻】carry out；carry through；go through with；put into effect；implement：～党的路线 *implement the Party line* / ～十三大精神 *act in the spirit of the thirteenth Party Congress* / ～群众路线 *follow the mass line*

【贯穿】❶ run through；penetrate：这条公路～十几个县。*This highway runs through a dozen counties*. ❷ permeate：友爱的精神～在我们的班里。*Our class is permeated with the spirit of camaraderie*. ◇ ～辐射 penetrating radiation

【贯串】spread through；run through；permeate：事物发展的每一过程都～着矛盾。*Each phase of the development of any phenomenon is permeated with contradictions*.

【贯通】❶ have a thorough knowledge of；be well versed in：～中西医学 *have a thorough knowledge of both Western and traditional Chinese medicine* ❷ link up；thread together：大运河～五大河流。*The Grand Canal links up five big rivers*. / 这条铁路已全线～。*The whole railway line has been linked up*.

【贯众】［中］the rhizome of cyrtomium（Cyrtomium fortunei）

【贯珠】〈书〉a string of pearls：声如～。*The notes rang out like a string of pearls*.

【贯注】❶ concentrate on；be absorbed in：把精力～在工作上 *concentrate one's energy on one's work* ❷ be connected in meaning or feeling：这两句是一气～下来的。*These two sentences are closely connected*. or *These two sentences hang together*.

冠 Ⅰ动 ❶〈书〉put on a hat ❷ precede；crown with：英语的名词可以～以一个叫做"冠词"的单音节词。*In English a noun may be preceded by a monosyllable called 'article'*. Ⅱ名 first place；the best：这里的棉花产量为全国之～。*This area ranks first in the whole country for cotton output*. ——另见 guān

【冠词】〈语〉article

【冠军】champion ◇ ～赛 another name for 锦标赛

惯 名 ❶ be used to；be in the habit of：这里空气比较稀薄，～了就好了。*The air is rather thin here, but you'll get used to it in time*. ❷ indulge；spoil：他爷爷奶奶～着他，他要什么就给什么。*His grandparents indulge him by giving him anything he asks for*. / 别把孩子～坏了。*Don't spoil the child*.

【惯犯】habitual offender；hardened criminal；recidivist；repeater

【惯匪】hardened bandit；professional brigand

【惯技】〈贬〉customary tactic；old trick

【惯例】convention；usual practice：按照国际～ *according to international practice* / 打破～ *do away with convention*；*break with usual practice* / 因循～ *follow convention or usual practice* ◇ ～集团 managerial body

【惯量】［物］inertia

【惯偷】hardened thief

【惯性】［物］inertia：～矩 *moment of inertia* ◇ ～定律 the law of inertia；～飞行导弹 coasting missile；coaster；～领航 inertial navigation

【惯用】〈贬〉❶ habitually practise；consistently use：～两面派的手法 *consistently use double-faced tactics* ❷ habitual；customary：～伎俩 *customary tactics*；*old tricks* / ～手法 *habitual practice*

掼 动〈方〉❶ throw；toss；cast：～手榴弹 *throw a hand grenade* / ～稻 *thresh rice* ❷ fall；throw down：他～了一个跟头。*He had a fall*. / 他把对手～倒在地。*He flung his opponent down on the ground*.

【掼纱帽】〈方〉throw away one's official's hat in a huff；resign in resentment；quit office

盥 动〈书〉wash（the hands or face）

【盥漱】wash one's face and rinse one's mouth

【盥洗】wash one's hands and face：～用具 *toilet articles* ◇ ～室 washroom；～台 washstand

灌 动 ❶ irrigate：～田 *irrigate the fields* ❷ pour；fill：把剩下的牛奶～到那个瓶里。*Pour the rest of the milk into that bottle*. / ～药 *pour medicine down the throat* ❸ record（sound，music，etc. on a tape or disc）：～唱片 *make a gramophone record*；*cut a disc*

【灌肠】❶［医］give an enema（or clyster）❷ sausage

【灌溉】irrigate：～农田 *irrigate the fields* / 提水～ *irrigation by pumping* ◇ ～面积 area under irrigation；irrigated area；～渠 irrigation canal；～网 irrigation network；～系统 irrigation system

【灌浆】❶［建］grout ❷［农］（of grain）be in the milk ❸［医］form a vesicle（during smallpox or after vaccination）

【灌录】make a recording

【灌迷魂汤】try to ensnare sb. with honeyed words

【灌米汤】lay it on thick；butter sb. up

【灌木】bush；shrub：～丛 *shrubbery*

【灌区】irrigated district

【灌输】❶ divert running water for use elsewhere ❷ instil into；inculcate；imbue with：向农民～科学知识 *imbue the peasants with scientific knowledge* / 给学生～爱国思想 *instil patriotism into the students*

【灌音】have one's voice recorded

【灌制】tape-record；record：～唱片 *cut a disc* / 把

课文～在磁带上 *record the texts on tape*
【灌注】pour into：把铁水～到砂型里 *pour molten iron into a sand mould*

鹳 名 stork

罐 名 ❶ jar; pot; tin：一～苹果酱 *a jar of apple jam* / 茶叶～ *tea caddy* / 水～ *water pitcher* ❷［矿］coal tub
【罐车】tank car; tank truck; tanker
【罐笼】［矿］cage
【罐头】❶〈方〉pot; jar; pitcher; jug ❷ tinned (or canned) food：吃～ *eat tinned (or canned) food* / ～牛肉 *tinned (or canned) beef* ◇ ～食品 tinned (or canned) food (or goods)
【罐装】canning
【罐子】pot; jar; pitcher; jug：这个～是空的。*The caddy is empty.* / 两～水 *two jugs of water*

guāng

光 Ⅰ 名 ❶ light：太阳～ *the light of the sun; sunlight* / 就着蜡烛～看书 *read by the light of a candle* / ～很暗。*The light is dim.* ❷ scenery：风光 ❸ honour; glory：儿子没出息，父母脸上也无～。*A worthless son is a disgrace to his parents.* ❹ brightness; lustre：两眼无～ *dull-eyed* Ⅱ 动 ❶〈书〉glorify; bring honour to ❷ bare; be naked：别～着脚走。*Don't walk around barefoot.* / ～着膀子 *be stripped to the waist* Ⅲ 形 ❶ bare; naked：～脚 barefoote ❷ smooth; glossy; polished：这个桌子面儿很～。*The surface of this table is smooth.* ❸ all gone; used up; nothing left：他的钱都～了。*All his money is gone.* / 墨水用～了。*The ink's used up.* / 把敌人消灭～ *wipe out the enemy* Ⅳ 副 only; alone：她～笑不说话。*She just smiled and said nothing.* / ～你一个人没法儿抬这架钢琴。*You can't lift the piano alone.*
【光斑】［天］facula
【光板儿】❶ worn-out fur ❷ (in former times) a copper coin without a distinctive stamp
【光泵】optical pump
【光笔】light pen
【光标】cursor
【光波】light wave
【光彩】❶ lustre; splendour; radiance：～绚丽的贝雕吸引了许多观众。*The brilliant lustre of the shell carving attracted many visitors.* ❷ honourable; honoured; glorious：扮演一个极不～的角色 *play a most inglorious part*
【光大】〈书〉❶ glorify; carry forward; develop：发扬光大 ❷ wide; extensive
【光导纤维】another name for 光学纤维
【光点】［计］light spot
【光电】［物］photoelectricity：～发射 *photoelectric emission; photoemission* ◇ ～导体 photoconductor; ～管 photocell; phototube; ～效应 photoelectric efficiency; ～子［物］photoelectron
【光度】［物］luminosity ◇ ～计 photometer
【光辐射】ray radiation：～伤害 *ray radiation injury*
【光复】recover (lost territory); restore (old glory, etc.)
【光杆儿】❶ a bare trunk or stalk：～牡丹 *peony on a bare stalk* ❷ a man who has lost his family ❸ a person without a following
【光杆司令】a general without an army; a leader without a following
【光顾】〈套〉(used by a shop owner or a shop assistant) patronize：如蒙～，无任欢迎。*Your patronage is cordially invited.*
【光怪陆离】grotesque in shape and gaudy in colour; bizarre and motley：～的广告 *grotesque and gaudy advertisements*
【光棍】❶ ruffian; hoodlum ❷〈方〉a clever (or wise) person：～不吃眼前亏。*A wise man doesn't fight agaist impossible odds.*
【光合作用】［植］photosynthesis
【光华】brilliance; splendour：日月～ *the brilliance of the sun and the moon*
【光滑】smooth; glossy; sleek：这个桌子面儿很～。*The surface of this table is very smooth.* / 她的皮肤～细腻。*Her skin is smooth and delicate.* / 她在地板上打蜡，让它～美观。*She waxed the floor to give it a nice gloss.*
【光化】［化］❶ actinic：～射线 *actinic ray* ❷ photochemical ◇ ～作用 photochemical action
【光环】❶ a ring of light (round a planet)：土星周围沿赤道面有三个～。*Saturn is encircled by a system of three rings lying in the plane of its equator.* ❷ halo (round the head of a holy person)
【光辉】❶ radiance; brilliance; glory：太阳的～ *the brilliance of the sun* ❷ brilliant; magnificent; glorious：～形象 *a glorious image* / ～典范 *a glorious model* / ～榜样 *a shining example* / ～的一生 *a glorious life*
【光辉灿烂】glorious and magnificent; brilliant and dazzling
【光洁】bright and clean：在灯光照耀下，平滑的大理石显得格外～。*In the lamp light the smooth marble looks especially bright and clean.* ◇ ～度［机］smooth finish
【光介子】［物］photomeson
【光景】❶ scene：看到这排窑洞，当年延安的～又重现在眼前。*The sight of the caves brought back scenes of our life at Yan'an.* ❷ situation; circumstances; conditions：他的～挺不错。*He's quite comfortably off.* ❸ (used after time and numerical expressions) about; around：离这儿有十里～。*It's about 10 li away from here.*
【光刻】［物］photoetching
【光缆】optical cable
【光亮】bright; luminous; shiny：～的窗子 *bright windows* / 这套家具油漆得挺～。*This set of furniture has a very shiny coat of paint.*
【光疗】［医］phototherapy

【光临】〈套〉(of a guest or visitor) honour sb. with one's presence：欢迎你们～指导。*We welcome you and would appreciate your advice.* / 敬请～。*Your presence is cordially requested.*

【光溜溜】❶ smooth；slippery：～的大理石地面 *a smooth marble floor* / 她走在～的冰上有点害怕。*She was a bit nervous walking on the slippery ice.* / 她把头梳得～的。*She combed her hair smooth.* ❷ bare；naked：孩子们脱得～的在河里游泳。*The children stripped off their clothes and swam naked in the river.*

【光芒】rays of light；brilliant rays；radiance：旭日东升，～四射。*The morning sun rises in the east, shedding its rays in all directions.*

【光芒万丈】shining with boundless radiance；gloriously radiant；resplendent

【光敏】［物］photosensitive ◇ ～电阻 photoresistance；～二极管 photodiode

【光明】❶ light：黑暗中的一线～ *a streak of light in the darkness* ❷ bright；promising：世界的前途是～的。*The future of the world is bright.* / 社会主义的～大道 *the bright road of socialism* ❸ openhearted；guileless：心地～ *upright and pure in mind*

【光明磊落】open and aboveboard

【光明正大】just and honourable；open and aboveboard：这件事我认为～，可以跟任何人谈。*This business is quite open and aboveboard so far as I'm concerned. I don't care who knows.*

【光年】［天］light-year

【光盘】opticasl disk；compact disc (CD) ◇ ～驱动器 CD-ROM driver；disc drive

【光票】clean bill；clean draft ◇ ～托收 collection on clean bill

【光谱】［物］spectrum：明(暗)线～ *bright-line (dark-line) spectrum* / 太阳～ *solar spectrum* ◇ ～比较仪 spectrocomparator；～分析 spectrum (or spectral) analysis；～学 spectroscopy

【光气】［化］phosgene

【光球】［天］photosphere

【光圈】(又作'光孔'，'光阑')［摄］diaphragm；aperture；stop：你用多大～？*What aperture are you using?* / 比 f / 3.5 大一档的～是 f / 2。*The next stop smaller than f / 3.5 is f / 2.*

【光荣】❶ honourable；honoured；glorious：～传统 *a glorious tradition* / ～的行为 *a glorious deed* / 他有这么好的儿子，觉得很～。*He feels very proud having such a wonderful son.* ❷ honour；glory；credit：～归于祖国。*The honour (or credit) goes to the country.* / 我们国家的～ *the glory of our country* ◇ ～榜 honour roll；a roster of honour；～花 rosette；～院 institutes for the glorious；mursing homes；～之家 an honourable family

【光荣院】institutes for the glorious；nursing homes

【光润】(of skin) smooth

【光扫描】photoscanning；optical scanning

【光栅】［物］grating

【光渗】［物］irradiation

【光束】［物］light beam：参考～ *reference beam*

【光速】［物］velocity of light

【光天化日】broad daylight；the light of day：一起抢劫案竟在～之下发生在一条热闹大街上。*A holdup took place in broad daylight in a crowded street.* / 我要把他们的伪善面貌暴露在～之下。*I'll expose their hypocrisy to the light of the day.*

【光通量】［物］luminous flux

【光头】❶ bare one's head：他不习惯戴帽子，一年四季总光着头。*He is not used to wearing a hat and goes bareheaded all year round.* ❷ shaven head：剃个～ *have one's head shaved*

【光秃秃】bare；bald：～的山坡 *bare hillsides* / ～的树枝 *naked branches*

【光纤】〈略〉见〖光学纤维〗◇ ～通讯 fibre communication optical

【光线】light；ray：这间屋子～不够。*There's not enough light in this room.* / 别在～不好的地方看书。*Don't read in poor light.*

【光行差】［天］aberration

【光学】optics：几何～ *geometrical optics* / 非线性～ *nonlinear optics* / ～影象 *optical image* ◇ ～玻璃 optical glass；～录音 optical recording；～容限［物］optical tolerance；～纤维 light guide；optical fibre；～仪器 optical instrument

【光焰】radiance；flare

【光耀】❶ brilliant light；brilliance：～夺目 *dazzling* ❷ honour；glory；credit ❸ glorify；carry forward；develop：～祖国 *bring honour to one's country*

【光阴】time available；time：～很宝贵。*Time is precious.* / ～荏苒，不觉又过了两年。*Little by little time slipped away, and two more years passed by unnoticed.*

【光阴似箭】time flies like an arrow；how time flies：～，不觉残年将尽。*Time went by like an arrow, and before I knew it the year was drawing to a close.*

【光源】［物］light source；illuminant

【光泽】lustre；gloss；sheen：这些珍珠的～都很好。*These pearls have a fine lustre.* / 经过半年疗养，他脸上有了～。*After a six months' recuperation, his cheeks were glowing with health.*

【光照】［植］illumination：～阶段 *photostage*

【光制】［机］finishing：最后～ *final finishing* / ～品 *finished product*

【光质子】［物］photoproton

【光子】(又作'光量子')［物］photon：～火箭 *photon rocket*

【光宗耀祖】bring honour to one's ancestors

咣 象 bang：～的一声，关上了大门。*The door closed with a bang.*

桄 (构词成分)见下

【桄榔】［植］gomuti palm

guǎng

广 Ⅰ 形 ❶ wide；broad；vast；extensive：知识

面～ *have a wide range of knowledge* / 他见识很～。*He's a man of wide experience*. / 她兴趣相当～。*Her interests are fairly broad*. / 交游甚～ *have a large circle of friends* ❷ numerous: 大庭广众 Ⅱ 动 expand; spread: 以～流传 *so that it may spread far and wide*

【广板】[音] largo

【广播】❶ broadcast: 那个电台每天～二十四小时。*That radio station broadcasts* (*or is on the air*) 24 hours a day. / 开始(停止)～ *go on* (*off*) *the air* ❷ [无] broadcast: 我每天晚上听新闻～。*I listen to the news broadcast every evening*. / 实况～ *live broadcast*; *live transmissions over the radio or television* / 听北京台～ *tune in to Radio Beijing* ◇ ～电视大学 radio and television university; college on the air; ～电台 broadcasting (or radio) station; ～电影电视部 the Ministry of Radio Film and TV; ～稿 broadcast script; ～讲话 broadcast speech; radio talk; ～教学 distance teaching; ～节目 broadcast (or radio) programme; ～剧 radio play; ～喇叭 loudspeaker; ～时间 air time; ～室 broadcast; ～体操 setting-up (or callisthenic) exercises to radio music; ～网 rediffusion (or broadcasting) network; ～卫星 broadcasting satellite; ～员 (radio) announcer; broadcaster; ～站 broadcasting station (of a factory, school, etc.); rediffusion station;

【广播找人】page: 现在～，詹姆斯·史密斯先生，请到服务台去。*Attention please, paging Mr. James Smith, would you please go to the reception desk*.

【广博】(of a person's knowledge) extensive; broad; wide: 知识～ *have extensive knowledge*; *be erudite*

【广场】public square; square: 天安门～ *Tian'anmen Square*

【广大】❶ (of an area or space) vast; wide; extensive: 幅员～ *vast in territory* / ～地区 *vast areas*; *extensive regions* / ～农村 *the vast countryside*; *extensive rural areas* ❷ large-scale; widespread: 掀起～的增产节约运动 *set off a large-scale emulation drive to increase production and practise economy* ❸ (of people) numerous: ～官兵 *the broad ranks of officers and men* / ～读者 *the reading public*

【广度】scope; range: 这篇文章讲国民经济，具有一定的～和深度。*This article is a fairly comprehensive and in-depth study of the national economy*.

【广而告之】give extensive publicity; spread far and wide: 电视台新节目:"～"。*A new TV series "Spread Far and Wide" is now showing*.

【广而言之】speaking generally; in a general sense

【广泛】broad; extensive; wide-ranging; widespread: ～的兴趣 *wide interests* / ～而深入的影响 *a widespread and profound influence* / ～的统一战线 *a broad united front*

【广柑】a kind of orange (produced in Guangdong, Sichuan and Taiwan Provinces)

【广告】advertisement: 登～ *put an advertisement in a newspaper, magazine, etc*. / 做～ *advertise* / 贴～ *post a bill* ◇ ～策划 advertisement scheme; ～代理人 advertising agent; ～费 advertising expenses; advertising fee; ～歌曲 commercial song; ～公司 advertising firm; ～价格 advertising rates; ～片 advertising film; ～画 poster; ～栏 advertisement column (in a newspaper, etc.); ～牌 billboard; ～色 poster colour; ～文化 advertisement culture; ～预算 advertising budget

【广寒宫】the Moon Palace (the mythical palace in the moon)

【广交会】the Guangzhou Export Commodities Fair

【广角镜头】wide-angle lens

【广开才路】open all avenues for people of talent

【广开言路】provide wide opportunities for airing views; encourage the free airing of views

【广阔】vast; wide; broad: ～的前景 *broad prospects* / 交游～ *have a wide circle of acquaintances*; *have a large circle of friends* / 中国国土～，资源丰富。*China is a vast country abundant in natural resources*.

【广漠】vast and bare: 在～的沙滩上 *on the bare expanse of the beach*

【广木香】[中] costusroot (Saussurea lappa)

【广延】[物] extension: ～量 *extensive quantity*

【广义】❶ broad sense: ～地说 *in a broad sense*; *broadly speaking* / "古典音乐"这个名称有～和狭义之分。*The term "classical music" can be used in a broad and a narrow sense*. ❷ [物] generalized: ～空间 *generalized space* / ～坐标 *generalized coordinates*

【广域信息服务系统】Wide Area Information Server (WAIS)

【广种薄收】extensive cultivation

犷 形〈书〉rustic; uncouth; boorish: 粗犷

【犷悍】tough and intrepid

guàng

逛 动 stroll; ramble; roam: ～公园 *go for a walk in the park* / ～大街 *stroll around the streets*; *go window-shopping* / 咱们今天下午到城里～去，看商店有什么东西卖。*Let's just roam around the town this afternoon, looking in the shop windows*.

【逛荡】〈贬〉loiter; loaf about

【逛窑子】〈旧〉〈方〉visit a brothel

guī

归 Ⅰ 动 ❶ go back to; return: 归期 ❷ give back to; return sth. to: 物归原主 ❸ converge; come together: 把性质相同的问题～为一类 *group together problems of a similar nature* ❹ turn over to; put in sb.'s charge: 颗粒～仓 *every grain to the granary* / 消防工作～我们管。*We are in charge of fire fighting.* ❺ (used between two identical verbs) regardless of; despite: 玩笑～玩笑，事情可得认真去办。*It's all right to crack jokes but you must do your job seriously.* Ⅱ 名［数］division on the abacus with a one-digit divisor

【归案】bring to justice: 缉拿～ *arrest and bring to justice*

【归并】❶ incorporate into; merge into: 这个厂后来～到另一个工厂里去了。*This factory was later incorporated into another one.* / 把两组～成一组 *merge the two groups into one* ❷ lump together; add up: 这三笔账～起来是四百五十元。*The three accounts add up to 450 yuan.*

【归程】*return journey*

【归档】*place on file; file away*: 把文件～ *place a document on file; file a document* / 那封信你～了吗? *Did you file that letter?*

【归队】❶ rejoin one's unit: 他的伤已经好了，可以～了。*Now that his wound has healed, he can go back to his unit.* ❷ return to the profession one was trained for: 前几年改行做其他工作的教师，现在逐渐～了。*Those teachers who went in for other jobs during the past few years are now gradually returning to their teaching posts.*

【归附】submit to the authority of another: ～国法 *obey the law of the state*

【归根结底】(又作'归根结柢') in the final analysis; fundamentally

【归功】give the credit to; attribute the success to: 教练把球队的胜利～于平时的训练。*The coach attributed the team's victory to training and practice.*

【归国】return to one's country: ～观光 *return to one's homeland on a sightseeing tour* ◇ ～华侨 returned overseas Chinese

【归航】［航空］homing: ～飞行 *homing flight* / ～台 *homer*

【归还】return; revert: 向图书馆借书要按时～。*Books borrowed from the library should be returned on time.*

【归结】❶ come to a conclusion; sum up; put in a nutshell: 原因很多，～起来不外三个方面。*There is a variety of reasons, which can be summed up in three points.* ❷ end (of a story, etc.): 剧本是以主人公之死作为～的。*The play ends with the hero's death.*

【归咎】impute to; attribute a fault to; put the blame on: 不要把你的错误都～于客观原因。*Don't attribute all your mistakes to objective causes.*

【归类】sort out; classify: 请你把这些文件整理～，分别存档。*Please sort out, classify and file these documents.*

【归拢】put together: 你把工具～一下。*Please put the tools together.*

【归谬法】reduction to absurdity; reductio ad absurdum: 他用～驳斥了这个观点。*He refuted the view by reducing it to absurdity.*

【归纳】induce; conclude; sum up: 请你把这篇文章的大意～一下。*Will you please sum up the main ideas of this article?* ◇ ～法 the inductive method; induction

【归期】date of return

【归侨】〈略〉见〖归国华侨〗

【归入】classify; include: 这些问题可～一类。*These questions may be included in the same category.*

【归属】belong to; come under the jurisdiction of: 无所～ *belong nowhere* / 该岛的～早已确定无疑。*The ownership of the island has long been established beyond dispute.*

【归顺】come over and pledge allegiance

【归宿】a home to return to; a permanent home; a final settling place

【归天】〈婉〉pass away; die

【归途】homeward journey; one's way home

【归降】surrender

【归心似箭】with one's heart set on speeding home; impatient to get back; anxious to return

【归于】❶ belong to; be attributed to: 光荣～伟大的祖国。*Glory to the great motherland.* ❷ result in; end in: 经过长时间的辩论，大家的意见～一致。*The long debate finally ended in agreement.* or *Agreement was reached after a long debate.*

【归置】〈口〉put in order; tidy up: 把东西～～，马上就要动身了。*Put everything in order. We'll be starting out soon.*

圭 名 an elongated pointed tablet of jade held in the hands by ancient rulers on ceremonial occasions

【圭表】an ancient Chinese sundial consisting of an elongated dial (gui) and one or two gnomons (biao), used for measuring the length of the year and of the 24 solar terms

【圭臬】〈书〉criterion; standard

【圭亚那】Guyana ◇ ～人 Guyanese

龟 名 tortoise; turtle: 乌龟 —— 另见 jūn

【龟板】［中］tortoise plastron

【龟背】［中］curvature of the spinal column

【龟甲】tortoise-shell

【龟缩】huddle up like a turtle drawing in its head and legs; withdraw into passive defence; hole up: 敌人～在几个孤立的据点里。*The enemy was holed up in a few isolated strongholds.*

【龟头】［生理］glans penis

规 Ⅰ 名 ❶ compasses; dividers: 圆规 ❷ regulation; rule: 校规 ❸［机］gauge: 线规 Ⅱ 动 ❶ admonish; advise: 规劝 ❷ plan; map out: 规划

【规避】evade; dodge; avoid: ～问题的实质 *evade the substance of the issue*

【规程】rules; regulations: 操作～ *rules of opera-*

tion

【规定】❶ stipulate；provide；prescribe：学校～不许抽烟。*The school made a regulation forbidding smoking*. ❷ rule；regulation；stipulation：关于出国留学问题，最近有了某些新～。*Certain new regulations concerning study abroad have been laid down recently*. ◇ ～动作［体］compulsory exercise；～数额［经］quota

【规范】standard；norm：合乎～ *conform to the standard* / 这个词的用法不～。*This is not the normal way of using the word*. ◇ ～化 standardize

【规费收入】income from the payment of stipulated fees

【规格】specifications；standards；norms：统一的～ *unified standards* / 不合～ *not be up to standard；fall short of specifications*；～化 standardize

【规划】❶ programme；plan：城市～ *city planning* / 长远～ *a long-term programme；long-term planning* ❷ make a programme；draw up a plan：兴修水利，应当全面～。*An overall plan should be made for the construction of water conservancy projects*. ◇ ～目标 object of planning

【规矩准绳】compasses，set square，spirit level and plumb line—standards；norms；criteria

【规矩】❶ rules of a community or organization；established practice；custom：损坏东西要赔，是我们解放军的老～。*To pay compensation for damage done is an old rule in our PLA*. ❷ customary rules of good behaviour；social etiquette；manners：守～ *abide by the rules；behave oneself* / 这个孩子没～。*This child has no manners*. ❸ proper in behaviour；well-behaved；well-disciplined：你（放）～点儿。*Behave properly*. / 他这个老头儿不～。*He's an old man of loose morals*. / 规规矩矩 *well-behaved；law-abiding*

【规律】law；regular pattern：客观～ *objective law* / 历史发展的～ *law of the development of history* / 自然界的～ *the laws of nature* / 生活有～ *live a regular life* ◇ ～性 regularity；law

【规模】❶ scale；scope；extent；dimensions：那个公司的～很大。*The scope of that company is very extensive*. / 这个工程～宏大。*The project is of a grand scale*. ❷ large-scale：～经济 *large-scale production*

【规劝】admonish；advise：好意～ *give well-meaning advice*

【规行矩步】❶ behave correctly and cautiously ❷ stick to established practice；follow the beaten track

【规约】stipulations of an agreement

【规则】❶ rule；regulation：交通～ *traffic regulations* / 篮球比赛～ *basketball competition rules* ❷ regular：这条河流的水道原来很不～。*The course of this river used to be quite irregular*.

【规章】rules；regulations：～制度 *rules and regulations*

皈
（构词成分）见下

【皈依】❶ the ceremony of proclaiming sb. a Buddhist ❷ be converted to Buddhism or some other religion：他晚年退隐山林，～佛教。*In his later years he retired from public life，went into the mountains and was converted to Buddhism*.

闺
名 ❶〈古〉a small door ❷ lady's chamber；boudoir：深闺

【闺房】〈旧〉lady's chamber；boudoir

【闺女】❶ girl；maiden ❷〈口〉daughter

硅
名［化］silicon（Si）

【硅肺】［医］silicosis

【硅钢】［冶］silicon steel

【硅华】［地质］siliceous sinter；silica sinter

【硅胶】［化］silica gel

【硅可控整流器】［电子］silicon-controlled rectifier；thyristor

【硅铝带】［地质］sial

【硅镁带】［地质］sima

【硅锰钢】silico-manganese steel

【硅石】silica

【硅酸】［化］silicic acid ◇ ～钠［化］sodium silicate

【硅酸盐】［化］silicate：～砖 *silicate brick*

【硅铁】ferrosilicon

【硅藻】［植］diatom ◇ ～土 diatomaceous earth；diatomite

【硅砖】silica brick

瑰
形〈书〉rare；marvellous

【瑰宝】rarity；treasure；gem：敦煌壁画是我国古代艺术中的～。*The Dunhuang frescoes are gems of ancient Chinese art*.

【瑰丽】surpassingly beautiful；magnificent：南京长江大桥的夜景雄伟～。*The view of the Nanjing Changjiang bridge at night is magnificent*.

【瑰玮】（又作'瑰伟'）〈书〉❶（of one's character）remarkable ❷（of language or style）ornate

鲑
名 salmon

guǐ

轨
名 ❶ rail；track：铁轨 ❷ course；path：正轨

【轨道】❶ track：地铁～ *underground railway track* ❷ orbit；trajectory：人造卫星已进入～。*The man-made satellite is now in orbit*. ❸ the proper way of doing things；a proper course：工作已走上～。*The work has got onto the right track*. ◇ ～变换［航天］orbital transfer；～衡［铁路］track scale；～火箭 orbital rocket；～交角［航天］orbit inclination；～空间站［航天］orbital space station；～平面［航天］orbit plane；～运动［天］orbital motion

【轨范】standard；criterion

【轨迹】❶［数］locus ❷［天］orbit ◇ ～球［计］

trackball

【轨距】［铁路］gauge：标准～ *standard gauge*

【轨枕】［铁路］sleeper；tie：纵向～ *longitudinal sleeper* / ～板 *concrete slab sleeper*

诡 形 ❶ deceitful；tricky；cunning：诡诈 ❷〈书〉weird；eerie：诡异

【诡辩】❶ quibble；indulge in sophistry ❷ sophistry；sophism；quibbling：～改变不了事实。*Sophistry won't alter facts.* ◇ ～术 sophistry

【诡称】falsely allege；pretend

【诡计】a crafty plot；a cunning scheme；trick；ruse

【诡计多端】have a whole bag of tricks；be very crafty

【诡谲】〈书〉❶ strange and changeful ❷ weird；eccentric；odd：言语～ *speak cryptically* ❸ crafty；cunning；treacherous

【诡雷】［军］booby mine；booby trap

【诡秘】furtive；surreptitious；secretive：行踪～ *surreptitious in one's movements*

【诡异】（又作'诡奇'）strange；abnormal

【诡诈】crafty；cunning；treacherous

癸 名 the last of the ten Heavenly Stems（天干）

鬼 Ⅰ 名 ❶ ghost；spirit；apparition：不信～，不信神 *believe in neither ghosts nor gods* ❷〈讳〉：懒～ *lazy bones* / 讨厌～ *a bore* ❸ sinister plot；dirty trick：有鬼 Ⅱ 形 ❶ stealthy；surreptitious：鬼鬼祟祟 ❷ terrible；damnable：～天气 *terrible weather* / ～地方 *a damnable place* ❸〈口〉clever；smart；quick：这家伙真～。*He's an artful devil.*

【鬼把戏】sinister plot；dirty (or underhand) trick：耍～ *play dirty tricks*

【鬼点子】〈方〉wicked idea；devilish trick：出～ *give devilish advice*；*make a wicked suggestion* / 他～多。*He's full of wicked ideas.* or *He's always got some trick or other up his sleeve.*

【鬼斧神工】uncanny workmanship；superlative craftsmanship

【鬼怪】ghosts and monsters；monsters of all kinds；forces of evil：妖魔鬼怪

【鬼鬼祟祟】sneaking；furtive；stealthy：这家伙～的，想干什么？*What's that fellow up to，sneaking around like that?* / 两个人～的，不知说什么。*Goodness knows what they're being so secretive about.*

【鬼话】false words；lies：说～ *tell lies* ◇ ～连篇 a pack of lies；lies from start to finish

【鬼魂】ghost；spirit；apparition

【鬼混】lead an aimless or irregular existence；fool around：和不三不四的人～ *hang around with shady characters*

【鬼火】popular name for 磷火

【鬼哭狼嚎】wail like ghosts and howl like wolves；let loose wild shrieks and howls

【鬼脸】❶ funny face；wry face；grimace：做～ *make a wry face*；*make faces*；*make grimaces* ❷ a mask used as a toy

【鬼魅】〈书〉ghosts and goblins；forces of evil

【鬼门关】the gate of hell—a danger spot；a trying moment：穷人进了收租院，就象进了～。*For the poor peasants，to enter that rent-collection courtyard was like entering the gate of hell.*

【鬼迷心窍】be possessed；be obsessed

【鬼使神差】doings of ghosts and gods —unexpected happenings；a curious coincidence

【鬼胎】sinister design；ulterior motive；dark scheme

【鬼头鬼脑】thievish；stealthy；furtive：有两个人～地从山洞里钻了出来。*Two suspicious-looking people sneaked out of the cave.* / ～的！走开！*Get out of here! Peeping and prying like that!*

【鬼蜮】evil spirit；demon；treacherous person

【鬼蜮伎俩】a devilish stratagem；evil tactics；dirty underhanded tricks

【鬼针草】［植］beggar-ticks (Bidens bipinnata)

【鬼主意】evil plan；wicked idea：打～ *form an evil plan*

【鬼子】devil (a term of abuse for foreign invaders)

晷 名 ❶〈书〉a shadow cast by the sun —time：余晷 ❷ sundial

guì

刽 动〈古〉cut off；chop off

【刽子手】❶ executioner；headsman ❷ slaughterer；butcher

柜 名 ❶ cupboard；cabinet：碗柜 ❷ cashier's office in a shop；shop cashier：现款都交了～了。*The cash has all been handed in to the cashier.*

【柜房】cashier's office in a shop；shop cashier

【柜台】counter；bar ——另见〖站柜台〗

【柜员】counter clerk ◇ ～机 automated teller machine (ATM)

【柜子】cupboard；cabinet

贵 形 ❶ expensive；costly；dear：这本书不～。*This book is not expensive.* / 丝绸比棉布～。*Silk is more expensive than cotton.* / 我买～了。*I paid too much for it.* ❷ highly valued；valuable：兵～精，不～多。*Troops are valued for their quality，not their number.* ❸ of high rank；noble：～妇人 *a noble lady* ❹〈尊〉your：～国 *your country* / 您～姓？*May I ask your name?* or *What's your name，please?*

【贵宾】honoured guest；distinguished guest ◇ ～席 seats for distinguished guests；distinguished visitors' gallery；～休息室 reserved lounge (for honoured guests)

【贵妃】highest-ranking imperial concubine：杨～ *Lady Yang*

【贵干】〈套〉honourable business；noble errand：有何～？*What honourable business (or noble er-*

rand) *brings you here*?

【贵金属】noble (or precious) metal

【贵客】honoured guest

【贵人】❶ a high official ❷ a high-ranking imperial concubine

【贵人多忘事】a man of your eminence has a short memory (said with good-natured sarcasm); important people have short memories: 你是"～",哪里还能记得我呀? *The higher the rank, the worse the memory. How could you remember me*?

【贵重】valuable; precious: ～物品 *valuables* / ～药品 *costly* (*or expensive*) *medicines* / 他送了一份儿～的礼物。*He gave a valuable present*.

【贵族】noble; aristocrat: 封建～ *feudal nobles* / 精神～ *intellectual aristocrats* / ～老爷式的态度 *an aristocratic attitude*

桂 名 ❶ cassia ❷ laurel; bay tree ❸ sweet-scented osmanthus

【桂冠】laurel (as an emblem of victory or distinction): 该队以七战七胜的成绩摘取了本届篮球大赛的～。*With seven wins and no losses, the team won the championship of the basketball tournament*.

【桂花】[植] sweet-scented osmanthus ◇ ～酒 wine fermented with osmanthus flowers

【桂皮】❶ cassia-bark tree; Chinese cinnamon tree ❷ cassia; cassia bark; Chinese cinnamon

【桂圆】longan: ～肉 *dried longan pulp*

【桂枝】[中] cassia twig

桧 名 [植] Chinese juniper

跪 动 kneel: ～下 *kneel down*; *go* (*or get*) *down on one's knees* / ～着祈祷 *be kneeling in prayer* / 他的腿都～麻了。*His legs were numb from kneeling*. / ～一条腿 *go down on one knee*

【跪拜】worship on bended knees; kowtow: 行～礼 *perform the kowtow*; *perform the prostration ceremony*

【跪倒】throw oneself on one's knees; prostrate oneself; grovel: ～在敌人脚下的可耻叛徒 *a shameless renegade who prostrated himself before the enemy* / 双膝～在地 *get down on one's knees*

【跪射】[军] kneeling fire

【跪姿】kneeling position: ～射击 *shoot from a kneeling position*

鳜 名 mandarin fish

gǔn

衮 名 ceremonial dress for royalty

【衮衮】〈古〉❶ continual ❷ numerous

【衮衮诸公】❶ high-ranking officials; government dignitaries ❷〈诙〉Your Excellencies

绲 Ⅰ 名 ❶ ribbon; band; tape ❷ string; cord Ⅱ 动 bind; trim: 袖口上～一条边儿 *bind the cuffs* / 用红绦子在领口上～一道边儿 *bind the collar with a red silk ribbon* / 裙子～上花边 *trim the skirt with lace*

【绲边】(又作'绲条') an embroidered border

辊 名 [机] roller

【辊筒印花】[纺] roller printing

滚 动 ❶ roll; trundle: 一个球在地上～。*A ball is rolling on the ground*. / 一块石头从山坡上～下来。*A stone came rolling down the slope*. ❷ get away; beat it: ～出去! *Get out of here*! / 你给我～! *Get lost*! ❸ boil: 水～了。*The water is boiling*.

【滚槽机】[机] channelling machine

【滚齿机】[机] gear-hobbing machine; hobbing machine

【滚存资金】deferred assets

【滚蛋】〈讳〉beat it; scram: 滚你的蛋吧! *Get lost*!

【滚刀】[机] hobbing cutter; hob

【滚刀肉】(又作'滚刀筋')〈方〉unreasonable troublemaker; annoying person; nuisance

【滚动】roll; trundle ◇ ～摩擦 [物] rolling friction; ～轴承 [机] rolling bearing

【滚翻】[体] roll: 侧～ *sideward roll*

【滚瓜烂熟】(recite, etc.) fluently; (know sth.) by heart: 背得～ *memorize sth. thoroughly*; *have* (*or know*) *sth. off pat*

【滚滚】roll; billow; surge: ～的浓烟 *billowing smoke* / 历史车轮～向前。*The wheel of history rolls on*.

【滚开】〈讳〉beat it; scram: ～,要不我揍你! *Beat it, or I'll hit you*! / 这儿没你的事儿,～! *You're not wanted here, so scram*!

【滚雷】[军] rolling mine

【滚轮】[体] gyro wheel; hoop

【滚热】piping hot; burning hot; boiling hot: 刚出锅的～的汤 *boiling hot soup just from the pot* / 他脑袋～,一定在发高烧。*His forehead feels scalding hot; he must be running a very high fever*.

【滚水坝】[水] overflow dam

【滚烫】boiling hot; burning hot

【滚筒】cylinder; roll ◇～印刷机 cylinder press

【滚雪球】(of a business, project, etc.) get bigger and bigger as it proceeds; snowball: 放高利贷是～,连本带利,越滚越多。*When practising usury, the capital and interest can have a snowball effect*. / 他的买卖近来像～似的,越做越大。*His business has snowballed recently*.

【滚圆】round as a ball: 腰身～的母牛 *a round-bellied cow* / 她的两只眼睛睁得～的。*She opened her eyes wide and round*.

【滚轧】[机] rolling: ～机 *rolling mill*

【滚针轴承】needle bearing

【滚珠】[机] ball

【滚珠轴承】ball bearing

【滚柱轴承】roller bearing

【滚装码头】ro-ro dock；roll-on-roll-off dock
【滚子链】roller chain
磙 Ⅰ 名 roller：石～ *stone roller* Ⅱ 动 level (ground, etc.) with a roller：～地 *roll the ground*
【磙子】❶ stone roller ❷ roller

gùn

棍 名 ❶ rod；stick：木～ *a wooden stick* / 小～儿 *a small stick* ❷ scoundrel；rascal：恶棍
【棍棒】❶ club；cudgel；bludgeon ❷ a stick or staff used in gymnastics
【棍子】rod；stick ——另见〖打棍子〗

guō

郭 名 the outer wall of a city：东～ *the east wall of a city*
聒 形 noisy：聒耳
【聒耳】grate on one's ears：蝉声～。*The shrilling of the cicadas grated on my ears.*
【聒噪】〈方〉noisy；clamorous
锅 名 ❶ pot，pan，boiler，cauldron，etc.：两口大～ *two cauldrons* / 炒菜～ *wok* ❷ bowl (of a pipe，etc.)：烟锅
【锅巴】crust of cooked rice；rice crust
【锅铲】slice (a kitchen utensil)
【锅盖】the lid of a cooking pot
【锅炉】boiler：火管～ *fire tube boiler* / 水管～ *water tube boiler* / ～给水 *boiler feedwater* ◇ ～防垢剂 boiler compound；～房 boiler room
【锅台】the top of a kitchen range：围着～转 *be tied to the kitchen sink* / 我不想当家庭妇女，一辈子围着～转。*I don't want to be a housewife slaving away at a hot stove all my life.*
【锅贴儿】lightly fried dumpling
【锅驼机】portable steam engine；locomobile
【锅烟子】soot on the bottom of a pan
【锅子】❶ bowl (of a pipe，etc.) ❷ chafing dish
蝈 (构词成分)见下
【蝈蝈儿】katydid；long-horned grasshopper

guó

国 Ⅰ 名 country；nation；state：大～ *a big country* / 强～ *a powerful nation* / 诸侯～ *feudal states* / 此河流经数～。*That river flows through several countries.* Ⅱ 形 ❶ of the state；national：国花 ❷ of our country；Chinese：国画
【国奥队】(〈略〉全称为'国家奥林匹克队') the National Olympics Team
【国宝】national treasure：熊猫号称是中国的～。*The Giant Panda is known as the national treasure of China.*
【国宾】state guest ◇ ～馆 state guesthouse
【国策】the basic policy of a state；national policy
【国产】made in our country；made in China：～远洋货轮 *Chinese-built oceangoing freighter* / ～影片 *a homemade film*
【国耻】national humiliation：洗雪～ *wipe out a national humiliation*
【国粹】the quintessence of Chinese culture
【国道】national road；national highway
【国都】national capital；capital：北京是中华人民共和国的～。*Beijing is the capital of the People's Republic of China.*
【国度】country；state；nation
【国法】the law of the land；national law；law：～难容 *punishable by law*
【国防】national defence：巩固～ *strengthen the national defence* / 建设强大的～ *build up a strong national defence* / ～力量 *defence capability* ◇ ～部 the Ministry of National Defence；～军 national defence troops (or forces)；～科工委 the Commission of Science Technology and Industry for National Defence；～前哨 national defence outpost；～委员会 the National Defence Council；～线 national defence line；～支出 expenditure on national defence；defence spending
【国父】father of a republic (formerly an epithet for 孙中山 Dr. Sun Yat-sen)
【国歌】national anthem：中国～叫《义勇军进行曲》。*The Chinese national anthem is called March of the Volunteers.*
【国格】national prestige：不做有损～的事 *do nothing that would undermine national prestige*
【国号】the title of a reigning dynasty (e. g. 元 Yuan，明 Ming，清 Qing，etc.)
【国花】national flower (as an emblem)
【国画】traditional Chinese painting：～家 *a painter in the traditional Chinese style*
【国徽】national emblem
【国会】parliament；(in the U. S.) Congress；(in Japan) the Diet
【国货】China-made goods；Chinese goods
【国籍】nationality；citizenship：你是哪国～？*What's your nationality?* / 他是中国～。*He has Chinese nationality (or is of Chinese nationality).*
【国计民生】the national economy and the people's livelihood：轻工业和农业关系～极大。*Light industry and agriculture are of vital importance to the nation's economy and the people's livelihood.*
【国际】international：～地位 *international status (or standing)* / ～合作 *international cooperation* / ～问题 *international problem*；*foreign relations issue* / ～形势 *the international (or world) situation* / ～影响 *international repercussions*；*impact abroad* / 带有～性 *have an international character* ◇ ～标准规格 international standards；～标准书号 international standard book number (ISBN)；～博览会 international fair；～裁判

international referee；～驰名 world-famous；～储备货币 international reserve currency；～单位制 international system of units；～电信联盟 International Telecommunication Union（ITU）；～儿童节 International Children's Day (June 1)；～法院 the International Court of Justice；the World Court；～分工 international division of labour；～妇女节 International Women's Day（March 8）；～歌 The Internationale；～公法（public）international law；the law of nations；～公约 international convention；～公制 the metric system；～共产主义运动 the international communist movement；～共管 condominium；～关系 international relations；～惯例 international practice；～航道 international waterway（or sea-lane）；～和平年 Interational Year of Peace；～化 internationalize；～环境日 World Environment Day；～机场 international airport；～机构 international machinery；～技术转让 international transfer of technology；～结算 international clearing；～经济合作 international economic co-operation；～经济秩序 international economic order；～劳动节 International Labour Day；May Day（May 1）；～联盟 the League of Nations（1920-1946）；～列车 international train；～垄断同盟 international monopoly combines ；～垄断组织 international monopoly；～贸易 international trade（or commerce）；world trade；～贸易政策 international trade policy；～贸易中心 international trade centre；～日期变更线 international date line；～扫盲年 International Literacy Year；～商业机器(万国商业机器) International Business Machine Corporation(IBM)；～社会 international community；～市场 international market；～市场价格 world (international)market price；～事务 international (or world) affairs；～水道 international waterway；international watercourse；～水域 international waters；～私法 private international law；～铁路联运 international railway through transport；～通用商标 international brand；～象棋 chess；～刑警组织 interpol；～音标 the International Phonetic Symbols (or Alphabet)；～友人 foreign friends；～舆论 world（public）opinion；～原子能组织 International Atomic Energy Agency；～争端 international dispute；～制裁 international sanctions；～主义 internationalism；～住房年 International Year of Shelter for the Homeless；～纵队 the International Brigade（in the Spanish civil war of 1936-1939）

【国际奥林匹克委员会】the International Olympic Committee（IOC）

【国际货币】convertible foreign exchange；international currency ◇ ～基金组织 International Monetary fund（IMF）

【国际收支】balance of（international）payments：～不平衡 *disequilibrium of balance of payments* / ～逆差 *international payments deficit*；*unfavourable balance of payments* / ～顺差 *international payments surplus*；*favourable balance of payments* / ～危机 *international payments crisis*

【国家】country；nation；state：在我国，母亲和儿童受～的保护。*In our country, mothers and children are protected by the state.* / ～至上。*The state above all.* or *The state is supreme.* ◇ ～裁判 state (or national) referee；～储备金 state reserve funds；～大事 national (or state) affairs；～典礼 state functions；～队 national team；～法 constitutional law；the law of the state；～副主席（Chinese）vice-president；～工作人员 personnel of organs of state；state personnel；～机关 state organs；government offices；～机器 state apparatus（or machinery）；～技术监督局 the State Bureau of Technical Supervision；～决算 final accounts of state revenue and expenditure；final state accounts；～领导人 state leaders；～垄断资本主义 state monopoly capitalism；～权力 state power；～所有制 state ownership；～统计局 the state Statistic Bureau；～外汇储备 state foreign exchange reserves；～学说 theory of the state；～一级企业 state first-level enterprises；～银行 state bank；～预算 state budget；～元首 head of state；～政权 state power；～职能 functions and powers of the state；～重点工程 the country's key projects；～主席（Chinese）president；～资本主义 state capitalism；～自然保护区 state nature reserves；

【国家兴亡，匹夫有责】every man has a share of responsibility for the fate of his country

【国交】diplomatic relations

【国脚】〈口〉player of the national football team；footballer of the national team

【国教】state religion

【国界】national boundaries

【国境】national territory：偷越～ *cross the border illegally* ◇ ～线 the boundary (line) of a country

【国库】national (or state) treasury；exchequer：充实～ *augment the national treasury* / ～空虚。*The national treasury is depleted.*

【国库券】State treasury bond；treasury bill

【国力】national power（or strength，might）：～雄厚 *have solid national strength*

【国立】state-maintained；state-run：～大学 *national university*

【国门】〈书〉the gateway of a country ：御敌于～之外 *turn the enemy back at the border* / 这是我第一次跨出～，踏上异国土地。*This is the first time I have left my country and set foot on foreign soil.*

【国民】a member of a nation；national；the people of a nation ◇ ～生产总值 gross national product（GNP）；～收入 national income

【国民经济】national economy：～有计划按比例的发展 *planned and proportionate development of the national economy*

【国民党】the Kuomintang（KMT）

【国难】national crisis（esp. as brought on by foreign aggression）：～当头。*A national crisis is imminent.* / 共赴～ *unite to meet the national*

crisis
【国内】internal; domestic; home: ～市场 *domestic (or home) market* / ～贸易 *domestic trade* / ～新闻 *home news* / ～革命战争 *revolutionary civil war* / ～形势 *the domestic situation; internal conditions* / ～外形势 *the situation at home and abroad* ◇ ～生产总值 gross domestic product (GDP); ～消费水平 domestic consumption level
【国破家亡】country conquered and family ruined
【国旗】national flag
【国企】state enterprise: ～税负十分沉重。*The tax burden of state enterprises is extremely heavy.*
【国情】the condition (or state) of a country; national conditions ◇ ～咨文 (in the U.S.) State of the Union Message
【国庆】(又作'国庆节') National Day (in China observed on October 1)
【国人】〈书〉compatriots; fellow countrymen; countrymen: ～皆曰可杀。*The whole country says that the man deserves death.*
【国色天香】ethereal colour and celestial fragrance (said of the peony or a beautiful woman)
【国事】national (or state) affairs ◇ ～访问 state visit
【国手】national champion (in chess, etc.); grand master
【国书】letter of credence; credentials: 这位新任驻华大使向中华人民共和国政府主席递交～。*The new ambassador to China presented his credentials to the President of the People's Republic of China.*
【国术】traditional Chinese martial arts
【国税】national tax ◇ ～局 National Tax Bureau
【国泰民安】the country is prosperous and the people live in peace: 风调雨顺，～。*The elements were propitious, the country prospered and the people were at peace.*
【国体】❶ state system ❷ national prestige: 有辱～ *bring disgrace to national prestige*
【国土】territory; land: 神圣～ *our sacred land* / 捍卫每一寸～ *defend every inch of our territory*
【国外】external; overseas; abroad: ～事务 *external affairs* / ～来信 *letter from abroad* / ～市场 *overseas (or foreign) market* / ～投资 *investment in foreign countries*
【国王】king
【国威】international prestige of a state; national power and influence: 大振～ *greatly enhance (or boost) a country's national power and influence (or international prestige)*
【国务】state affairs ◇ ～会议 state conference; ～卿 (in the U.S.) Secretary of State; ～委员 a member of the State Council; State Councillor; ～院 the State Council
【国玺】❶ imperial seal ❷ national seal
【国宴】state banquet
【国营】state-operated; state-run: ～工商业 *state-operated industry and commerce* / ～牌价 *state-set prices* ◇ ～经济 state sector of the economy; state-owned economy; ～农场 state farm
【国营企业】state enterprise
【国优】(of a product) national best
【国有】belonging to the nation (or the state); state-owned: 土地～ *nationalization of land* / 将私营企业收归～ *bring private enterprises under state control* ◇ ～大中型企业 state-run large and medium-sized enterprises; ～化 convert to national ownership; nationalize
【国运】the fortunes or destiny of a nation: ～昌盛 *a nation growing in prosperity*
【国葬】state funeral: 举行～ *hold a state funeral for sb.*
【国债】national debt
【国子监】the Imperial College (the highest educational administration in feudal China)
【国嘴】a top-ranking broadcaster in the country

guǒ

果 Ⅰ 名 ❶ fruit: 水果 ❷ result; consequence: 结果 Ⅱ 形 resolute; determined: 果敢 Ⅲ 副 really; as expected; sure enough: ～不出所料 *just as one expected* Ⅳ 连 if indeed; if really: ～能如此 *if things can really turn out that way; if that is so*
【果不其然】just as expected; sure enough: 他经常酒后开车，早晚得出事。～！*He often drove when drunk, sooner or later I knew something would happen. Wasn't I right?*
【果茶】❶ fruit drinks ❷ hawthorn juice
【果冻】jelly
【果断】resolute; decisive; determined: 办事～ *handle affairs in a decisive manner* / ～地作出决定 *resolutely make a decision* / 采取～措施 *take decisive measures*
【果脯】preserved fruit; candied fruit
【果腹】〈书〉fill the stomach; satisfy one's hunger: 食不～ *not have enough food in one's belly; be starving*
【果敢】courageous and resolute; resolute and daring: 采取～的行动 *take resolute action* / 她～地跳入水中，救起溺水的孩子。*Without hesitation, she leapt into the water and saved the drowning child.*
【果酱】jam (as made of preserves)
【果料儿】raisins, kernels, melon seeds, etc. used in making cakes, buns, etc.: ～面包 *raisin bread*
【果木】fruit tree ◇ ～园 orchard
【果农】fruit grower
【果盘】fruit bowl; fruit tray
【果皮】the skin of fruit; peel; rind ◇ ～箱 litterbin
【果品】fruit: 干鲜～ *fresh and dried fruit*
【果然】❶ really; as expected; sure enough: ～你说对了。*As expected, what you said proved to be correct.* / ～名不虚传。*A really well-deserved*

reputation. ❷ if indeed; if really: 事情～是那样,那就好办了。*If that's really the way things are, there should be no difficulty.*

【果仁儿】❶ kernel ❷ shelled peanut; peanut kernel

【果肉】the flesh of fruit; pulp

【果实】❶ fruit: ～累累 *fruit growing in close clusters; fruit hanging heavy on the trees* ❷ gains; fruits: 劳动～ *fruits of labour* / 胜利～ *fruits of victory* / 保卫革命～ *guard the gains of the revolution*

【果树】fruit tree: ～栽培 *fruit growing; pomiculture*

【果糖】[化] fructose; levulose

【果园】orchard

【果真】❶ really; as expected; sure enough: 说来,他～来了。*He came just as expected.* / 这一回男排～夺到了冠军。*The men's volleyball team did win the title this time.* ❷ if indeed; if really: ～如此,我就放心了。*If this is really true, it'll take a load off my mind.*

【果珍】a kind of powdered fruit drink

【果汁】fruit juice

【果枝】❶ fruit-bearing shoot; fruit branch ❷ boll-bearing branch (of the cotton plant)

【果子】fruit ◇ ～酒 fruit wine

【果子狸】another name for 花面狸

【果子露】fruit syrup

裹 动 bind; wrap: 把伤口～好 *bind up (or bandage) the wound* / 头上～着毛巾 *have one's head wrapped in a towel; wear a towel turban* / 我～了一条毯子。*I wrapped a blanket around myself.*

【裹脚】(又作'裹脚布') bandages used in binding women's feet in feudal China

【裹腿】puttee; leggings

【裹胁】force to take part (in bad things); coerce: 把敌军中被～的人争取过来 *win over those who joined the enemy army under duress*

【裹足不前】hesitate to move forward

guò

过 Ⅰ 动 ❶ cross; pass: 长征途中,红军爬雪山,～草地。*On the Long March, the Red Army climbed snow-topped mountains and plodded through grasslands.* ❷ spend (time); pass (time): 假期～得怎样? *How did you spend your holiday?* / 日子越来越好～了。*Life is getting better and better.* ❸ go beyond (a certain point of time): ～了好几个月我才收到他的信。*Several months passed before I heard from him.* ❹ undergo a process; go through; go over: ～了筛子又～箩 *sifted again and again; carefully screened* / 咱们把这篇稿子再～一遍。*Let's go over the draft once again.* ❺ exceed; go beyond: 亩产～千斤。*The yield is over 1,000 jin per mu.* / 树长得～了房。*The tree has grown taller than the house.* ❻ (used after a verb plus 得 or 不 to indicate winning or deserving): 要说跑,咱们谁也比不～他。*None of us can run as fast as he can.* / 这样的大学生,我们信得～。*We have faith in college students of this sort.* Ⅱ 副 too; unduly; excessively: 雨水～多 *excessive rainfall; too much rain* / ～早 *too early; premature* / ～长 *too long; unduly long* Ⅲ 名 fault; mistake: 苟有～,人必知之。*Whenever I make a mistake, other people are sure to notice it.* Ⅳ 助 ❶ (used after a verb to indicate the completion of an action): 我吃～午饭就去。*I'll go right after lunch.* / 桃花都已经开～了。*The peach blossoms are over.* ❷ (used after a verb or an adjective to indicate a past action or state): 你去～韶山吗? *Have you ever been to Shaoshan?* / 我以前没看～这个戏。*I've never seen this opera before.*

【过半】more than half: 敌兵伤亡～。*Over half the enemy soldiers were wounded or killed.*

【过磅】weigh (on the scales): 你的行李在机场得～。*You must have your luggage weighed at the airport.*

【过饱和】[化] supersaturation; oversaturation: ～溶液 *supersaturated solution*

【过不去】❶ cannot get through; be unable to get by: 前面正在修路,～。*As the road ahead is under repair, you can't get through.* ❷ be hard on; make it difficult for; embarrass: 人家批评你,并不是跟你～。*People didn't mean to be hard on you when they criticized you.* ❸ feel sorry: 费了你这么多时间,我心里真～。*I'm sorry for having taken up so much of your time.*

【过场】❶ [戏] interlude ❷ [戏] cross the stage ❸ 见〖走过场〗

【过程】course; process: 在讨论～中 *in the course of the discussion* / 缩短制作～ *shorten the process of manufacture*

【过秤】weigh (on the steelyard): 他们把摘下的水果过了过秤。*They weighed the fruit they had picked.*

【过从】〈书〉have friendly intercourse; associate: ～甚密 *be in close association with sb.*

【过错】fault; mistake: 这不是你一个人的～,我也有责任。*It's not all your fault. I'm also responsible.*

【过道】passageway; corridor

【过得去】❶ be able to pass; can get through: 这条胡同儿很宽,汽车～。*The lane is wide enough for a car to get through.* ❷ passable; tolerable; so-so; not too bad: 我身体还～。*My health is not too bad.* ❸ (used in a rhetorical question) feel at ease: 叫你一趟一趟地跑,我怎么～呢? *I'm terribly sorry to have kept you on the go like this.*

【过电影】〈喻〉go over past scenes in one's mind; recall; recollect; bring to mind: 早上发生的事情在他脑海里一幕一幕～。*He went over in his mind what happened this morning.*

【过冬】pass the winter; winter: 把羊群赶到山坳里去～ *herd the sheep into the valley for the winter* / 这种鸟在哪儿～? *Where do these birds winter?*

【过度】❶ excessive; undue; over-: 饮酒～对身体有害。*Excessive drinking is harmful to the health.* / ～兴奋 *be overexcited* / ～疲劳 *be overtired* ❷ transition; interim: ～措施 *interim measure* / 从社会主义～到共产主义 *transition from socialism to communism* ◇ ～飞行 transition flight; ～过程 transient process; ～内阁 caretaker cabinet or government; ～时期 transition period

【过分】excessive; undue; over-: ～的要求 *excessive demands* / ～强调 *put undue stress on; overemphasize* / 做得太～ *go too far; overdo sth.*

【过关】❶ pass a barrier; go through an ordeal ❷ pass a test; reach a standard: 过技术关 *be technically up to standard; be technically proficient* / 这项新产品的质量已经～。*The quality of this new product is up to standard.*

【过河拆桥】pull down the bridge after crossing the river—drop one's benefactor once his help is not needed; kick down the ladder

【过后】afterwards; later: 他起初同意,～又翻悔了。*At first he agreed, but later he backed out.* / 我先去通知了他,～才来通知你的。*I first went to tell him, and then came to tell you.*

【过户】[法] transfer ownership; change the name of the owner in a register: 车辆转让必须到市公安局办理～手续。*If you want to transfer ownership of a vehicle, you must go to the municipal public security bureau to do the required paper work.*

【过话】〈方〉❶ exchange words; talk with one another: 我跟他不在一个单位,所以很少～。*We don't work in the same outfit, so we haven't talked much.* ❷ send word; pass on a message: 请你替我过个话,就说我明天不去找他了。*Would you mind giving him a message? Just say I won't call on him tomorrow.*

【过火】go too far; go to extremes; overdo: ～的行动 *excesses* / 这话说得太～了。*It's going too far to say that.*

【过激】too drastic; extremist: ～的言论 *extremist opinions*

【过继】❶ adopt a young relative ❷ have one's child adopted by a relative

【过家家】〈方〉play house (a children's game)

【过奖】〈套〉overpraise; give undeserved compliment: 您的英语说得真好。——您～了。*You speak very good English. —Thank you. You flatter me.*

【过街老鼠】a rat crossing the street—a person or thing that provokes a hue and cry ——另见〖老鼠过街,人人喊打〗

【过街天桥】overhead pedestrian crossing; overpass

【过节】(guòjié) celebrate a festival: ～后咱们就开始做新的工作。*After the Festival, we'll start doing new work.*

【过节儿】(guòjiér) grudge; hard feelings; ill will: 听说他们之间有点～。*I hear there is a feeling of animosity between them.*

【过境】pass through the territory of a country; be in transit ◇ ～货物 transit cargo; ～旅游 cross-border tourism; ～贸易 transit trade; ～签证 transit visa; ～权 right of passage; ～手续 transit formalities; ～税 transit duty

【过客】passing traveller; transient guest: 匆匆来去的～ *travellers coming and going hurriedly*

【过来】❶ come over; come up: 快～! *Come over here, quick!* / 有个人～向我打听去火车站的路。*A man came up and asked me the way to the railway station.* ❷ (used after a verb plus 得 or 不 to indicate the sufficiency or insufficiency of time, capability or quantity): 你一个人忙得～吗? *Can you manage by yourself?* ❸ (used after a verb to indicate motion towards the speaker): 一队士兵正朝我们走～。*A contingent of soldiers was marching towards us.* ❹ (used after a verb to indicate turning around towards the speaker): 他转过脸来,我才认出是位老同学。*He turned around, and then I recognized him as a former classmate of mine.* ❺ (used after a verb to indicate a return to the normal state): 醒～ *wake up; sober up; come to*

【过来人】a person who has had some experience: 作为～,我可以讲讲我的体会。*As one who has had experience in this respect, let me tell you how I feel about it.*

【过冷】[物] super-cooling

【过梁】lintel

【过量】excessive; over-: 饮食～ *excessive eating and drinking* / 这种药千万不能服～。*Whatever happens, never take an overdose of this medicine.*

【过磷酸钙】calcium superphosphate

【过路】pass by on one's way: 我是个～的人,对这儿的情况完全不了解。*I'm only a passerby and know nothing at all about this place.*

【过路财神】a temporary God of Wealth—a person temporarily handling large sums of money

【过虑】be overanxious; worry overmuch; worry unnecessarily: 问题会得到解决的,你不必～。*The problem will be solved. You needn't be overanxious.* / 孩子不会出什么事的,你也太～了。*No harm will come to the child. You worry too much.*

【过滤】filter; filtrate ◇ ～器 filter; ～嘴 filter tip (of a cigarette)

【过门】(of a woman) go over to a man's house — get married

【过门儿】[音] ❶ opening bars ❷ short interlude between verses

【过敏】[医] allergy: 皮肤～ *skin allergy* / 他对鸡蛋(青霉素)～。*He is allergic to eggs (penicillin).* ◇ ～性反应 [医] allergic reaction

【过目】look over (papers, lists, etc.) so as to

check or approve：名单已经排好，请您～。*Here's the list for you to go over.* / 账算好了，你要过过目吗？*The accounts have been worked out. Do you want to have a look?*

【过目不忘】learn sth. by heart after reading it once; have a photographic (or very retentive) memory

【过目成诵】be able to recite sth. after reading it once; have a photographic (or very retentive) memory

【过年】celebrate the New Year or the Spring Festival; spend the New Year or the Spring Festival：他今年回家～。*He'll be home for the New Year holiday.* / 快～了。*It'll soon be New Year.*

【过期】exceed the time limit; be overdue：你借的书已经～。*The book you borrowed is overdue.* / ～作废 *become invalid after the specified date* ◇ ～胶卷 expired film; ～提单 stale bill of lading; ～杂志 back number of a magazine

【过谦】too modest：这件事你办最合适，不必～了。*You are the best person for the job. Don't be so modest.*

【过去】❶ (in or of) the past; formerly; previously：～我没见过他。*I have never seen him before.* / 这个地方～流行的一些疾病已经基本消除。*Diseases formerly prevalent here have been mostly eradicated.* ❷ go over; pass by：你在这里等着，我～看看。*You wait here, I'll go over and see.* / 一辆公共汽车刚～。*A bus has just passed by.* ❸ (used after a verb to indicate motion away from the speaker)：把车开～。*Drive the car over (there).* / 一只燕子飞～了。*A swallow flew past.* ❹ (used after a verb to indicate turning away from the speaker)：先别把这一页翻～。*Don't turn over the page yet.* ❺ (used after a verb to indicate a departure from the normal state)：病人晕～了。*The patient has fainted.*

【过热】overheated：经济～ *overheated economic growth*

【过人】surpass; excel：精力～ *surpass many others in energy* / 勇气～ *excel in courage* / ～的记忆力 *a remarkable memory* / ～之处 *the things one excels in; one's forte*

【过日子】live; get along：勤俭～ *live industriously and frugally* / 挺会～ *can manage to get along quite well*

【过筛】sift out

【过甚】exaggerate; overstate ◇ ～其词 give an exaggerated account; overstate the case

【过剩】excess; surplus：生产～ *overproduction* / 资本～ *surplus of capital* / 商品～ *a glut of goods*

【过失】❶ fault; slip; error：那算不上什么错误，只是一种～罢了。*That wasn't really a mistake; it was only a slip.* ❷ [法] Negligence ◇ ～犯罪 [法] offence through negligence; unpremeditated crime; ～杀人 [法] manslaughter

【过时】out-of-date; outmoded; obsolete; antiquated; out of fashion：～的设备 *outmoded (or obsolete) equipment* / 这种观点早就～了。*That kind of viewpoint has long been considered antiquated.*

【过时不候】no waiting after the set time：校车六点开车，～。*The school bus leaves at six sharp and won't wait.*

【过世】die; pass away

【过手】take in and give out (money, etc.); receive and distribute; handle：银钱～，当面点清。*Count the money on the spot.* / 他～信件千千万，但没有错过一件。*He handled thousands and thousands of letters without making a single mistake.*

【过数】take a count; count：这是付给你的三万元，请你过过数。*This is your 30,000 yuan. Please count it.*

【过堂风】wind coming through a passageway; draught

【过头】go beyond the limit; overdo：菜煮～了。*The food is overcooked.* / 批评他是可以的，不过你说得～了。*It was all right to criticize him, but you overdid it.* / 聪明～ *be too clever by half*

【过屠门而大嚼】start munching when passing the butcher's—feed on illusions

【过往】❶ come and go：～的行人 *pedestrian traffic* / ～的车辆 *vehicular traffic* ❷ have friendly intercourse with; associate with：他们俩是老同学，～很密。*The two of them have been friends since school days and see much of each other.*

【过问】concern oneself with; take an interest in; bother about：亲自～ *take up a matter personally; take a personal interest in a matter* / 无人～ *not be attended to by anybody; be nobody's business* / 这事你不必～了。*You needn't bother about this.*

【过细】meticulous; care too much：～地做工作 *work with meticulous care*

【过眼云烟】as transient as a fleeting cloud

【过夜】❶ pass the night; put up for the night; stay overnight：附近的旅馆都客满，只好到朋友家～。*All the hotels in the area are full. We'll have to go spend the night in a friend's home.* ❷ of the previous night

【过意不去】feel apologetic; feel sorry：这事给你添了不少麻烦，真～。*I'm very sorry to have put you to so much trouble.*

【过瘾】satisfy a craving; enjoy oneself to the full; do sth. to one's heart's content：今天我一口气游了两千米，真～。*Today I really swam to my heart's content. I did 2,000 metres at a stretch.* / 这段唱腔听起来很～。*This aria is a joy to hear.*

【过硬】have a perfect mastery of sth.; be really up to the mark; be able to pass the stiffest test：～的操作技术 *a perfect mastery of operational technique* / 苦练～的本领 *train hard to perfect one's skill*

【过犹不及】going too far is as bad as not going far

enough

【过于】too; unduly; excessively: ～劳累 *overtired* / 你不必～为我们担心。*You needn't worry too much about us*.

【过载】❶ transship ❷ overload

【过账】transfer items (as from a daybook to a ledger); post

【过重】(of luggage, letters, etc.) overweight: 这个包裹～一公斤。*This parcel is overweight by one kilo*. / ～加费 *overweight charge*

H

hā

哈 Ⅰ 动 breathe out (with the mouth open)：眼镜上～点儿气再擦。*Breathe on your glasses before wiping them.* Ⅱ 象 (usu. reduplicated) the sound of laughing：～～大笑 *laugh heartily; roar with laughter* Ⅲ 叹 (usu. reduplicated, expressing self-pride or satisfaction)：～～,我猜着了。*Aha, I've got (or guessed) it.* / ～～,小鬼,这下子可跑不了啦。*Aha, you can't get away from me this time, you little devil.* ——另见 hǎ; hà

【哈哈镜】distorting mirror

【哈吉】[宗](伊斯兰教) haji (a title of honour for a Moslem who has made a pilgrimage to Mecca)

【哈喇子】〈方〉dribble; drivel; drool：流～ *slobber* / 宝宝流～,围嘴儿都湿了。*The baby has slobbered its bib.*

【哈雷彗星】Halley's Comet; the Halley Comet

【哈里发】[宗](伊斯兰教) caliph

【哈密瓜】Hami melon (a variety of muskmelon)

【哈乃斐派】[宗](伊斯兰教) the Hanafite school

【哈欠】yawn：他太困了,～连天的。*He kept yawning for he was too sleepy.*

【哈萨克斯坦】Kazakhstan

【哈萨克族】the Kazak (Kazakh) ethnic group, or the Kazaks (Kazakhs), distributed over the Xinjiang Uygur Autonomous Region and the Gansu and Qinghai Provinces

【哈腰】〈口〉❶ bend one's back; stoop：我一～把钢笔掉在地上了。*As I bent over, my fountain pen fell to the ground.* ❷ bow slightly：点头哈腰

铪 名 [化] hafnium (Hf)

há

蛤 (构词成分)见下 ——另见 gé

【蛤蟆】❶ frog ❷ toad

hǎ

哈 动 〈方〉scold：我～了他一顿。*I gave him a good scolding (or lecturing).* ——另见 hā; hà

【哈巴狗】❶ Pekinese (a breed of dog) ❷ toady; sycophant

【哈达】a piece of silk (usu. white in colour) used as a greeting gift among the Zang and Monggol nationalities：献～ *present a hada*

hà

哈 (构词成分)见下 ——另见 hā; hǎ

【哈什蚂】Chinese forest frog (Rana temporaria chensinensis) ◇ ～油 [中] the dried oviduct fat of the forest frog

hāi

咳 叹 (expressing sadness, regret or surprise)：～,我怎么这么糊涂! *Dammit! How stupid I was!* / ～,真有这种怪事儿! *What! That's really strange!* ——另见 ké

【咳声叹气】heave deep sighs; sigh in despair; moan and groan

嗨 (构词成分)见下

【嗨哟】heave ho; yo-heave-ho; yo-ho

hái

还 副 ❶ still; yet：夜深了,他～在学习。*It was late at night and he was still studying.* / ～有一些具体问题要解决。*Some specific problems have yet to be solved.* ❷ even more; still more：今年的收成比去年～要好。*This year's harvest is even better than last year's.* ❸ also; too; as well; in addition：这本书我～想看一遍。*I want to read the book once more.* ❹ passably; fairly：屋子不大,收拾得倒～干净。*The room is small, but it's kept quite tidy.* / 这张画儿画得～可以。*The painting wasn't done too badly.* or *This painting's not too bad.* ❺ even：你跑那么快～赶不上他,何况我呢? *If a good runner like you can't catch up with him, how can I?* ❻ (used for emphasis)：这～了得! *This is the limit!* or *This is simply atrocious!* ❼ (expressing realization or discovery)：他～真有办法。*You've got to admit he's resourceful.* or *He really is resourceful.* / 下这么大的雨,没想到你～真准时到了。*I didn't expect you'd arrive on time as it's raining so hard.* ——另见 huán

【还好】❶ not bad; passable：你今天感觉怎样? —

～。*How are you feeling today? —Not so bad.* / 你最近很忙吧? —～。*Are you very busy these days? —So so.* ❷ fortunately: ～,这场大水没有把堤坝冲坏。*Fortunately, the flood did not break the dyke.* / ～,电话总算打通了。*I was fortunate enough to get through finally.*

【还是】❶ still; yet: 废物～可以利用。*Waste materials can still be made use of.* / 这次～他做我们的向导。*He is still our guide for this trip.* ❷ (expressing a preference for an alternative): 天冷了,你～多穿点儿吧。*It's getting cold, you'd better put on more clothes.* ❸ (expressing realization or discovery): 这个人～真了不起。*This chap is really great.* / ～利害的人有办法。*It's the pushing type that gets on.* ❹ or: 你去,～他去? *Are you going or is he?* / 先去上海～先去西安没有最后定。*We haven't decided yet whether we go to Shanghai or Xi'an first.* ❺ no matter what, how etc.; whether... or...; regardless of: 无论唱歌～跳舞,她都行。*Singing or dancing, she is good at them all.*

孩 名 child: 小孩儿

【孩儿参】[中] caryophyllaceous ginseng (Pseudostellaria heterophylla)

【孩提】〈书〉early childhood; infancy: 我在故乡度过了～时代。*I spent my childhood in my hometown.*

【孩子】❶ child: 男～ *boy* / 女～ *girl* ❷ son or daughter; children: 她有两个～。*She has two children.*

【孩子话】silly childish talk: 别说～了! *Don't say such silly childish things!*

【孩子气】childish: 你已经16啦,别这么～! *You shouldn't be so childish, you're sixteen now!* / 他一脸的～。*He still looks so childish.*

骸 名 ❶ bones of the body; skeleton: 四肢百～ *all the limbs and bones* ❷ body: 形骸

【骸骨】bones of the dead

hǎi

海 Ⅰ名 ❶ sea or lake: 大～ *the sea* / 洱～ *Erhai Lake (in Yunnan Province)* ❷ a great number of people or things coming together: 林海 Ⅱ副〈方〉randomly or aimlessly: ～骂 *shout at no one in particular* / ～找 *look high and low (for sth.)* / 他有钱就～吃～喝。*Whenever he has some money, he squanders it on food and drink.* Ⅲ形 extra large; of great capacity

【海岸】seacoast; coast; seashore

【海岸炮】coast gun: ～兵 *coast (or seacoast) artillery* / ～台 *coast battery*

【海岸线】coastline ◇ ～效应 coast-line effect

【海拔】height above sea level; elevation: ～四千米 4,000 *metres above sea level; at an elevation of* 4,000 *metres*

【海百合】[动] *sea lily; crinoid*

【海报】playbill: 贴～ *put up a playbill* / 电影～ *a film bill*

【海豹】seal

【海滨】seashore; seaside: ～疗养院 *a seaside sanatorium* / ～风景游览区 *a seashore scenic and tourist area*

【海波】common name for 大苏打

【海菜】edible seaweed

【海产】marine products

【海昌蓝】[纺] hydron blue

【海潮】(sea) tide

【海程】distance travelled by sea; voyage

【海船】seagoing vessel

【海带】kelp

【海胆】sea urchin

【海岛】island (in the sea)

【海盗】pirate; sea rover: ～行为 *piracy* / 这一海域经常有～出没。*That sea is infested with pirates.* ◇ ～船 pirate (ship); sea rover

【海堤】sea wall

【海底】the bottom of the sea; seabed; sea floor ◇ ～采矿 undersea mining; offshore mining; ～电报 submarine telegraph; cablegram; ～电缆 submarine cable; ～勘察 submarine exploration; ～矿 submarine mine; ～山 seamount; ～水雷 ground mine (or torpedo); ～峡谷 submarine canyon; ～油田 offshore oilfield; ～资源 seabed resources; submarine resources

【海底捞月】try to fish out the moon from the bottom of the sea—strive for the impossible or illusory: ～一场空 *as futile as fishing for the moon in the sea*

【海底捞针】fish for a needle in the ocean; look for a needle in a haystack: 要在茫茫人海中找到他,就像～一样难。*Trying to find him in such a huge crowd of people is as difficult as looking for a needle in a haystack.*

【海地】Haiti ◇ ～人 Haitian

【海防】coast defence: ～前哨 *outpost of coastal defence* / ～前线 *coastal front* ◇ ～部队 coastal defence force; ～艇 coastal defence boat

【海风】sea breeze; sea wind

【海港】seaport; harbour: ～设备 *harbour installations*

【海沟】(oceanic) trench

【海狗】fur seal; ursine seal

【海关】customhouse; customs ◇ ～仓库 customs warehouses; ～担保 customs guarantee; ～登记 customs entry; ～发票 customs invoice; ～官员 customs house officer; ～缉私官员 customs preventive officer; ～检疫 customs quarantine control; ～申报单 customs declaration; ～手续 customs formalities; ～税则 customs tariff; ～通行证 customs pass; ～统计 customs statistics; ～总署 customs head office; ～组织 customs organization

【海关检查】customs inspection (or examination): 通过～ *go through customs* / ～站 *customs inspection post*

【海龟】green turtle (Chelonia mydas)
【海涵】〈套〉be magnanimous enough to forgive or tolerate (sb.'s errors or shortcomings)：招待不周，还望～。*Please forgive us if we have not looked after you well*. or *Please forgive us for our poor hospitality*.
【海魂衫】sailor's striped shirt
【海货】marine products
【海鲫】Japanese seaperch
【海疆】coastal areas and territorial seas
【海角】cape; promontory
【海角天涯】同〖天涯海角〗
【海禁】ban on maritime trade or intercourse with foreign countries (as during the Ming and Qing dynasties)
【海景】seascape
【海鸠】guillemot
【海军】navy ◇ ～航空兵 naval air force; ～基地 naval base; ～陆战队 marine corps; marines; ～呢 navy cloth; ～武官［外交］naval attaché; ～学校 naval academy
【海口】❶ seaport ❷ (usu. used in) 夸～ boast about what one can do; talk big
【海枯石烂】(even if) the seas run dry and the rocks crumble：～心不变。*The seas may run dry and the rocks may crumble, but our hearts will always remain loyal*.
【海葵】［动］sea anemone
【海阔天空】as boundless as the sea and the sky; unrestrained and far-ranging：～地聊个没完 *have a rambling chat about everything under the sun* / ～地谈一通，不解决任何实际问题 *indulge in far-ranging rambling discourse without solving any practical problems*
【海蓝】sea green; sea blue
【海蓝宝石】aquamarine
【海狸】old name for 河狸
【海狸鼠】coypu; nutria
【海里】nautical mile; sea mile
【海量】❶〈套〉magnanimity：对不住的地方，望您～包涵。*I hope you will be magnanimous enough to excuse any incorrect behaviour on my part*. ❷ great capacity for liquor：您是～，再来一杯。*Have another one. You can hold your liquor*.
【海流】ocean current
【海龙】❶〈口〉sea otter ❷ pipefish
【海路】sea route; sea-lane; seaway：走～ *travel by sea*
【海轮】seagoing (or oceangoing) vessel
【海螺】conch
【海洛因】heroin
【海马】sea horse
【海鳗】conger pike
【海米】dried shrimps
【海绵】❶ sponge ❷ foam rubber or plastic; sponge ◇ ～垫 foam rubber cushion
【海绵球拍】foam-rubber (or sponge) table-tennis bat：正(反)贴～ *outward* (*inward*) *pimpled rubber bat spongy soil*
【海绵铁】sponge iron
【海面】sea surface
【海难】perils of the sea ◇ ～救助 *salvage at sea*
【海内】within the four seas; throughout the country：他的书画～知名。*He's known throughout the country for his calligraphy and painting*.
【海内存知己，天涯若比邻】if in this world an understanding friend survives, then the ends of the earth seem like next door; a bosom friend afar brings a distant land near
【海鲇】sea catfish
【海牛】manatee; sea cow
【海鸥】sea gull
【海盘车】［动］starfish
【海泡石】sepiolite; sea-foam (a mineral)
【海平面】sea level
【海区】［军］sea area
【海群生】［药］hetrazan
【海鳃】［动］sea pen; sea feather
【海商法】maritime law
【海上】at sea; on the sea：～风暴 *a storm at sea* / ～作业 *operation on the sea* / ～空间 *air space above the sea* / ～霸权 *maritime* (*or naval*) *hegemony* ◇ ～保险 marine (or maritime) insurance; ～补给 sealift; seaborne supply; ～封锁 naval blockade; ～交通 maritime traffic; ～贸易 marine trade; ～油田 offshore oil field; ～遇险信号 signal of distress; GMDSS; ～运输 marine transportation
【海蛇】sea snake
【海参】sea cucumber; sea slug; trepang
【海狮】sea lion
【海事】maritime affairs ◇ ～法庭 admiralty court; maritime court; ～仲裁 maritime arbitration
【海誓山盟】(make) a solemn pledge of love
【海市蜃楼】❶ mirage ❷ illusion
【海水】seawater; brine; the sea ◇ ～淡化 desalination sea water; ～工业 marine industry; ～浴 seawater bath; sea bathing
【海水不可斗量】the sea cannot be measured with a bushel—great minds cannot be fathomed
【海损】［经］average：共同(单独)～ *general* (*particular*) *average* / ～理算 *average adjustment*
【海獭】sea otter
【海滩】seabeach; beach：孩子们喜欢在～上玩耍。*Children love playing on the beach*.
【海棠】Chinese flowering crabapple
【海塘】seawall
【海桐花】tobira
【海退】［地质］regression
【海豚】dolphin ◇ ～泳［体］dolphin butterfly; dolphin fishtail; dolphin
【海外】overseas; abroad：扬名～ *known the world over* / 中国丝绸畅销～。*Chinese silk is sold all over the world*. / 他在～住了几十年。*He lived abroad for scores of years*. / ～华侨 *overseas Chinese; Chinese nationals residing abroad* / ～侨胞 *countrymen residing abroad* ◇ ～版 overseas

edition；～关系 relatives abroad；～奇谈 a strange story from over the seas；a traveller's tale；a tall story；～市场 overseas market
【海湾】bay；gulf ◇ ～国家 Gulf States
【海王星】Neptune
【海味】choice seafood
【海峡】strait；channel：台湾～ *the Taiwan Straits* / 英吉利～ *the English Channel*
【海峡群岛】the Channel Islands
【海鲜】seafood
【海相】［地质］marine (or sea) facies ◇ ～沉积［地质］marine deposit
【海象】walrus；morse
【海啸】tsunami；seismic sea wave
【海蟹】sea crab
【海星】starfish：*sea star*
【海熊】fur seal；ursine seal
【海寻】nautical fathom
【海牙】The Hague ◇ ～仲裁公约 Hague Arbitration Convention
【海盐】sea salt
【海蜒】dried anchovy
【海燕】(storm) petrel
【海洋】seas and oceans；ocean ◇ ～动物 marine animal；～法 law of the sea；～工程 oceanics industries；～公约 maritime convention；～环境 marine environment；～气象船 ocean weather ship；～气象学 marine meteorology；～权 marine rights；～生物 marine organisms；～特别保护区 special marine protection area；special marine reserve；～性冰川 marine glacier；～性气候 maritime (or marine) climate；～学 oceanography；oceanology；～渔业 sea fishery；～资源 marine resources；～自然资源保护区 marine nature conservation area；marine nature reserve
【海洋石油】offshore oil：～采油平台 *offshore oil extraction platform* / ～勘探 *offshore oil exploration* / ～资源 *offshore petroleum resources* / ～钻井船 *offshore oil drilling rig* / ～钻井平台 *offshore oil drilling platform*
【海域】sea area；maritime space：南海～ *Nanhai Sea waters*
【海员】seaman；sailor；mariner：～俱乐部 *seamen's club* / ～用语 *nautical expression*
【海运】sea transportation；ocean shipping ◇ ～保险商 underwriter；underwriting agent；～承运人 ocean carrier；～代理商 ocean shopping agents；～合同 contract of ocean carriage；～货物保险单 cargo policy；～业 sea-carrying trade；shipping industry
【海葬】sea-burial
【海枣】［植］date palm；date
【海藻】marine alga；seaweed
【海战】sea warfare；naval battle
【海蜇】jellyfish
【海震】［地质］seaquake
【海蜘蛛】sea spider

胲 名 ［化］hydroxylamine

hài

亥 名 the last of the twelve Earthly Branches (地支)
【亥时】the period of the day from 9 p.m. to 11 p.m.

骇 动 be astonished；be shocked：惊骇
【骇怪】be shocked；be astonished
【骇惧】be frightened；be terrified
【骇然】gasping with astonishment；struck dumb with amazement
【骇人听闻】shocking；appalling：～的暴行 *horrifying atrocities* / ～的纵火事件 *a shocking case of arson*
【骇异】be shocked；be astonished

害 Ⅰ 名 evil；harm；calamity：～多利少 *more disadvantages than advantages*；*more harm than good* Ⅱ 形 harmful；destructive；injurious：害鸟 Ⅲ 动 ❶ do harm to；impair；cause trouble to：你把地址搞错了，～得我白跑一趟。*You gave me the wrong address and made me go all that way for nothing.* ❷ kill；murder：谋财害命 ❸ contract (an illness)；suffer from：害病 ❹ feel (ashamed, afraid, etc.)：害羞
【害病】fall ill：害了一场大病 *have been seriously ill*
【害虫】injurious (or destructive) insect；pest
【害处】harm：吸烟过多对身体有～。*Excessive smoking is harmful to one's health.*
【害鸟】harmful (or destructive) bird
【害怕】be afraid；be scared：没有什么可～的。*There's nothing to be afraid of.* / ～得要命 *be scared to death*；*be mortally afraid*
【害群之马】an evil member of the herd；one who brings disgrace on his group；a black sheep
【害人不浅】no small harm is done；do people great harm
【害人虫】an evil creature；pest；vermin
【害人之心不可有，防人之心不可无】one should never intend to harm others；nor should one forget to guard against others' evil intentions.
【害臊】〈口〉feel ashamed；be bashful；be shy：替他～ *be ashamed of him* / 真不～。*You've got some nerve!*
【害羞】be bashful；be shy：她是第一次当众讲话，有些～。*This was the first time she had spoken before many people, so she was a bit shy.*
【害眼】have eye trouble

氦 名 ［化］helium (He)

hān

顸 形 〈方〉thick：这线太～了，有细的吗？*This thread is too thick. Have you got anything finer?*

/他的胳膊真～。*He has thick and muscular arms.*

蚶 名［动］blood clam

【蚶子】［动］blood clam

酣 形（drink, etc.）to one's heart's content：～歌 *sing to one's heart's content*

【酣畅】❶ merry and lively (with drinking) ❷ sound (sleep) ❸ with ease and verve; fully：笔墨～ *write with ease and verve*

【酣畅淋漓】heartily; to one's heart's content：这首诗～地抒发了作者的革命豪情。*This poem fully expresses the author's revolutionary fervour.*

【酣梦】a sweet dream

【酣睡】sleep soundly; be fast asleep：闹钟的响声将我从～中惊醒。*The alarm clock roused me from my deep sleep.*

【酣饮】drink to the full; carouse

【酣战】hard-fought battle：两军～ *two armies locked in fierce battle*

【酣醉】be dead drunk

憨 形 ❶ foolish; silly ❷ straightforward; naive; ingenuous：憨直

【憨厚】straightforward and good-natured; simple and honest

【憨态可掬】charmingly naive

【憨笑】smile fatuously; simper

【憨直】honest and straightforward：为人～ *be honest and straightforward towards others*

鼾 名 snore：打鼾

【鼾声】sound of snoring：从屋里传来连续不断的～。*The continuous sound of snoring was heard from the room.*

【鼾声如雷】snore thunderously

【鼾睡】sound, snoring sleep

hán

含 动 ❶ keep in the mouth：嘴里～着止咳糖 *with a cough drop in one's mouth* / 此丸宜～服。*This pill is to be sucked, not swallowed.* ❷ contain：～多种矿物 *contain several kinds of minerals* / ～泪 *with tears in one's eyes* / ～硫污水 *sulphur bearing waste water* / 这种梨～的水分很多。*These pears are very juicy.* / ～沙量 *silt content* ❸ nurse; cherish; harbour：含恨

【含苞】〈书〉in bud

【含苞待放】a bud just ready to burst

【含垢忍辱】endure contempt and insults; bear shame and humiliation

【含恨】nurse a grievance or hatred

【含糊】（又作'含胡'）❶ ambiguous; vague：他的话很～，我不明白是什么意思。*He was rather vague. I don't know what he really meant.* ❷ careless; perfunctory：这事一点儿也不能～。*We'll have to handle the matter with meticulous care.* ❸ 见〖不含糊〗

【含糊其词】talk ambiguously; equivocate：～的答复 *an equivocally worded reply*

【含混】indistinct; ambiguous：言词～，令人费解 *speak so ambiguously as to be barely intelligible* / 发音～不清 *unclear articulation*

【含金量】❶ gold content：矿石的～ *gold content of ore* ❷ real worth or value：同是奖牌，足球冠军比有些球的～可大多了。*As first prize, the championship for soccer is worth much more than those for some other ball games.*

【含量】content：牛奶的乳糖～ *the lactose content of the milk*

【含硫量】sulphur content

【含怒】be in anger

【含情脉脉】(soft eyes) exuding tenderness and love

【含沙射影】innuendo; insinuations：采用～的卑劣手法 *resort to insinuation* / ～，恶语中伤 *vilify sb. by insinuation*

【含漱剂】［药］gargle

【含水】containing water or moisture ◇ ～层［地质］water-bearing stratum; aquifer; ～率 moisture content

【含笑】have a smile on one's face：～点头 *nod with a smile*

【含辛茹苦】endure suffering; bear hardships

【含羞】with a shy look; bashfully

【含羞草】［植］sensitive plant

【含蓄】❶ contain; embody ❷ implicit; veiled：～的批评 *implicit criticism* / 这首诗简短而～。*The poem is brief and pregnant with meaning.* ❸ reserved：他是个很～的人。*He is a very reserved person.*

【含血喷人】make slanderous accusations; make vicious attacks

【含饴弄孙】play with grandchildren with candy in mouth—enjoy happy old age

【含义】meaning; implication：这个词用在不同场合有不同的～。*The meaning of this word varies with different contexts.* / 这句话～深刻。*This remark has profound implications.*

【含英咀华】relish the joys of literature

【含油层】［油］oil-bearing formation (or stratum)

【含冤】suffer a wrong：～死去 *die uncleared of a false charge*

【含怨】bear a grudge; nurse a grievance

函 名 ❶〈书〉case; envelope：镜～ *a case for a mirror* / 这部《全唐诗》分成十二～。*This set of Complete Tang Poems is in twelve cases.* ❷ letter：来函

【函大】〈略〉见〖函授大学〗

【函电】letters and cables

【函购】purchase by mail; mail order：～部 *mail-order department*

【函件】letters; correspondence

【函授】teach by correspondence; give a correspondence course：～部 *correspondence department*

(*of a school*)
【函授大学】correspondence university
【函授教学】correspondence instruction
【函授学校】correspondence school
【函数】[数] function
【函索】request by letter：～即寄 *be sent on application*；*be available on request*

涵 Ⅰ 动 contain：海涵 Ⅱ 名 culvert：桥涵
【涵洞】culvert
【涵养】❶ ability to control oneself；self-restraint：他从不发火，很有～。*He has self-control and never loses his temper*. ❷ conserve：用造林来～水源 *conserve water through afforestation*

焓 名 [物] enthalpy；total heat

寒 形 ❶ cold：～夜 *a cold night* / 受了一点～ *catch a slight cold* ❷ tremble (with fear)：胆寒 ❸ poor；needy：贫寒 ❹〈谦〉my：寒舍
【寒痹】[中] arthritis (aggravated by cold)
【寒潮】[气] cold wave
【寒碜】(又作'寒伧')〈口〉❶ ugly；unsightly：长得不～ *not bad-looking* / 穿得～死了 *be distastefully dressed* ❷ shabby；disgraceful：你说出这样的话来也不嫌～！*Aren't you ashamed of yourself for saying such a thing*? ❸ ridicule；make fun of：叫人～了一顿 *be ridiculed by sb*.
【寒窗】a cold window—the difficulties of a poor student
【寒带】frigid zone
【寒冬腊月】severe winter；dead of winter
【寒风】cold wind：～凛冽 *a piercing wind* / ～刺骨。*The cold wind chilled one to the bone*.
【寒假】winter vacation
【寒噤】shiver (with cold or fear)：他打了个～。*A shiver ran over his body*. or *A chill shot through him*.
【寒来暑往】as summer goes and winter comes—as time passes；with the passage of time
【寒冷】cold；frigid：气候～。*The climate is cold*.
【寒流】[气] cold current
【寒毛】fine hair on the human body：吓得我～直竖。*My hair stood on end with fright*.
【寒门】〈书〉❶ a poor and humble family ❷〈谦〉my family
【寒气】cold air；cold draught；cold：～逼人。*There is a nip in the air*.
【寒热】[中] chills and fever：～往来 *alternating spells of fever and chill* / 发～ *have* (*or run*) *a fever*；*have* (*or run*) *a temperature*
【寒舍】〈谦〉my humble home (or abode)
【寒士】〈书〉a poor scholar
【寒暑】❶ cold and heat ❷ winter and summer—a year：经历了几十个～ *after scores of years*
【寒暑表】thermometer
【寒酸】(usu. of a poor scholar) shabby and miserable：一副～相 *look shabby and miserable*
【寒腿】〈口〉rheumatism in the legs
【寒武纪】[地质] the Cambrian Period
【寒心】❶ be bitterly disappointed：令人～ *bitterly disappointing* ❷ be afraid；fear
【寒暄】exchange of conventional greetings；exchange of amenities (or compliments)：他们～了几句就转入正题。*After exchanging a few words of greetings they got down to business*.
【寒鸦】jackdaw
【寒衣】winter clothing
【寒意】a nip (or chill) in the air：初春季节仍有～。*It's spring but there's still a chill in the air*.
【寒战】(又作'寒颤') shiver (with cold or fear)：迎面吹来一阵冷风，她禁不住打了个～。*She couldn't help shivering in the face of a gust of cold wind*.
【寒症】[中] symptoms caused by cold factors (e.g. chill, slow pulse, etc.)

hǎn

罕 副 rarely；seldom：希罕
【罕百理派】[宗](伊斯兰教) the Hanbalite school
【罕觏】〈书〉rarely seen
【罕见】seldom seen；rare：一场～的洪水 *an exceptionally serious flood*
【罕事】a rare event
【罕物】a rare thing：拜送～ *present sb. with a rare and valuable thing*
【罕有】very rare

喊 动 ❶ shout；cry out；yell：～口号 *shout slogans* / 把嗓子～哑了 *shout oneself hoarse* / "站住！"他大～一声。"*Halt*！" *he cried*. / ～救命 *cry* "*Help*！ *Help*！" ❷ call (a person)：你走以前～他一声。*Give him a shout before you go*.
【喊话】❶ propaganda directed to the enemy at the front line：对敌人～ *shout propaganda at enemy troops across the lines* ❷ communicate by tele-equipment：向团部～ *establish radio contact with the regimental headquarters*
【喊叫】shout；cry out：他疼得大声～。*He screamed with pain*.
【喊冤叫屈】cry out about one's grievances；complain loudly about an alleged injustice

hàn

汉 名 ❶ the Han Dynasty (206 B.C. – A.D. 220) ❷ the Han nationality：汉人 ❸ Chinese (language)：～英词典 *a Chinese-English dictionary* ❹ man：老汉
【汉白玉】white marble
【汉堡包】hamburger
【汉化】[计] Chinese localisation
【汉奸】traitor (to China)：～卖国贼 *traitor and collaborator*
【汉人】❶ the Hans；the Han people ❷ people of

the Han Dynasty

【汉显】(〈略〉全称为'汉字显示')［通信］showing Chinese characters on the screen (of a pager): ～呼机 *pager which shows Chinese characters on it*

【汉学】❶ the Han school of classical philology ❷ Sinology: ～家 *Sinologist*

【汉语】Chinese (language) ◇ ～拼音方案 the Scheme for the Chinese Phonetic Alphabet; ～拼音字母 the Chinese phonetic alphabet; ～水平考试 HSK—test of Chinese language ability (for foreigners)

【汉子】❶ man; fellow ❷〈方〉husband

【汉字】Chinese character: ～改革 *reform of Chinese characters* / ～简化方案 *the Scheme for Simplifying Chinese Characters* / ～注音 *phonetic annotation of Chinese characters* ◇ ～编码 encoding of Chinese characters; ～操作系统 Chinese characters disk operating system (CCDOS)

【汉族】the Han ethnic group, China's main nationality, or the Hans, distributed all over the country

汗 名 sweat; perspiration: ～如雨下 *dripping with perspiration*

【汗斑】❶ sweat stain ❷ 同〖花斑癣〗

【汗背心】sleeveless undershirt; vest; singlet

【汗碱】sweat stain

【汗脚】feet that sweat easily; sweaty feet

【汗孔】［生理］pore

【汗淋淋】dripping with perspiration; soaked with sweat

【汗流浃背】sweat streaming down and drenching one's back; soaked with sweat: 他大惊失色，～。*He turned pale with fright and sweat broke out all over his body.*

【汗马功劳】❶ distinctions won in battle; war exploits: 立下了～ *win glory in battle; perform deeds of valour in battle* ❷ one's contributions in work; render great services: 她为女排夺得冠军立下了～。*She distinguished herself in winning the championship for the woman's volleyball team.*

【汗毛】fine hair on the human body

【汗牛充栋】enough books to make the pack-ox sweat or to fill a house to the rafters—an immense collection of books

【汗青】❶ sweating green bamboo strips—completion of a literary undertaking (reference to the ancient practice of drying green bamboo strips on the fire before writing on them) ❷ historical records; chronicles; annals

【汗衫】❶ undershirt; T-shirt ❷〈方〉shirt

【汗水】sweat (esp. in large amounts): ～湿透了他的衣衫。*His shirt was soaked through with sweat.*

【汗腺】sweat gland

【汗颜】〈书〉blush with shame; feel deeply ashamed

【汗珠子】beads of sweat

【汗渍】❶ sweat stain ❷ be soaked with sweat

旱 Ⅰ 名 ❶ dry spell; drought: 抗～ *combat drought.* ❷ dryland: 旱稻 ❸ on land: 旱路 Ⅱ 形 dry; arid: 旱季

【旱冰】［体］roller-skating ◇ ～场 roller rink; ～鞋 roller skates

【旱船】land boat, a model boat used as a stage prop in some folk dances

【旱稻】upland rice; dry rice

【旱地】nonirrigated farmland; dry land: ～耕作 *dry farming*

【旱季】dry season

【旱金莲】(又作'旱莲花')［植］nasturtium

【旱井】❶ water-retention well ❷ dry well (used to store vegetables in winter)

【旱涝保收】ensure stable yields despite drought or excessive rain; make gains no matter what happens; ensure a safe income

【旱柳】dryland willow (salix matsudana)

【旱路】overland route: 走～ *travel by land*

【旱年】year of drought

【旱桥】viaduct; overpass; flyover

【旱情】damage to crops by drought; ravages of a drought: ～严重 *be afflicted with a severe drought* / ～缓和了。*The drought has become less serious.*

【旱伞】〈方〉parasol

【旱生动物】xerophilous animal

【旱生植物】xerophyte

【旱獭】marmot

【旱田】dry farmland; dry land

【旱象】signs of drought: 普降喜雨，～解除。*A welcome rain fell, ending all signs of drought.*

【旱鸭子】❶ ducks raised on dry land as opposed to ducks raised by rivers and ponds ❷ non-swimmer

【旱烟】tobacco (smoked in a long-stemmed Chinese pipe): ～袋 *long-stemmed Chinese pipe*

【旱灾】drought

悍 形 ❶ brave; bold: 一员～将 *a brave warrior* ❷ fierce; ferocious: 凶悍

【悍妇】a shrewish woman; shrew

【悍然】outrageously; brazenly; flagrantly: ～入侵 *outrageously invade* / ～撕毁协议 *flagrantly scrap an agreement*

捍 动 defend; guard: 捍卫

【捍卫】defend; guard; protect: ～祖国 *defend one's motherland* / ～国家主权 *uphold state sovereignty* / ～民族经济权益 *protect national economic rights and interests*

焊 动 weld; solder: 把断了的车轴～起来 *weld the pieces of the broken axle*

【焊缝】welding seam; weld line

【焊工】❶ welding; soldering ❷ welder; solderer

【焊接】weld; solder: 电弧～ *(electric) arc welding* / ～钢管 *welded steel pipe*

【焊料】solder
【焊枪】welding torch; (welding) blowpipe
【焊条】welding rod
【焊锡】soldering tin; tin solder
【焊液】welding fluid; soldering fluid
【焊油】soldering paste

颔〈书〉Ⅰ名 chin Ⅱ动 nod
【颔首】〈书〉nod: ～微笑 *nod smilingly* / ～致意 *nod in greeting*

憾 名 regret: 死而无～ *die without regret*
【憾事】a matter for regret: 行前未及告别,至今引为～。*I didn't find time to say good-bye to you before I left. I regret it to this day.*

撼 动 shake: 震撼
【撼动】shake; vibrate
【撼天动地】shake heaven and earth

翰 名〈书〉❶ writing brush ❷ writing
【翰林】member of the Imperial Academy ◇ ～院 the Imperial Academy (in feudal China)
【翰墨】〈书〉brush and ink—writing, painting, or calligraphy

瀚 形〈书〉vast: 浩瀚
【瀚海】〈书〉big desert

hāng

夯 Ⅰ名 rammer; tamper Ⅱ动 ❶ ram; tamp; pound: 把土～实 *ram the earth* ❷〈方〉strike heavily
【夯歌】rammers' work chant
【夯具】rammer; tamper
【夯土机】rammer; tamper

háng

行 Ⅰ名 line; row: 第三～ *the third line* / 排成两～ *fall into two lines* / 杨柳成～ *lined with rows of willows* ❷ seniority among brothers and sisters: 你～几? —我～三。*Where do you come among your brothers and sisters? —I'm the third.* ❸ trade; profession; line of business: 他干哪～? *What's his line?* / 干一～爱一～ *love whatever job one takes up* ❹ business firm: 银行 Ⅱ量 (used to refer to anything that forms a line): 一～树 *a row of trees* / 四～诗句 *four lines of verse* ——另见 xíng
【行当】❶〈口〉trade; profession; line of business: 干我们这个～,吃不得苦可不行。*People of our profession must endure a lot of hardships.* ❷ type of role (in traditional Chinese operas)
【行贩】pedlar
【行规】〈旧〉guild regulations
【行行出状元】every profession produces its own leading authority
【行话】professional jargon; cant
【行会】〈旧〉guild: ～制度 *the guild system*
【行家】❶ expert; connoisseur: 老～ *an old hand* ❷〈方〉(used in the affirmative) be expert at sth.: 你对吃挺～嘛。*You are quite a connoisseur of food!*
【行间】❶〈书〉in the ranks ❷ between lines: 字里行间 ❸ between rows: 栽种向日葵的～距离要宽。*Leave a wide space between the rows when planting sunflowers.*
【行距】[农] row spacing
【行列】ranks: 排成整齐的～ *be drawn up in orderly ranks* / 参加革命～ *join the ranks of the revolution*
【行列式】[数] determinant
【行频】TV line frequency
【行情】quotations (on the market); prices: ～见涨。*A rising market is expected.* ◇ ～表 quotations list
【行市】quotations (on the market); prices: 一天一个～。*The prices change from day to day.* ◇ ～标准 basis of quotation; ～记录 quotation record; ～坚稳 firm in the undertone; ～上涨 higher in quotation
【行同步脉冲】horizontal synchronization pulse
【行伍】〈旧〉the ranks: ～出身 *rise from the ranks* / 投身～ *join the army*
【行业】trade; profession; industry ◇ ～语 professional jargon; cant
【行长】president (of a bank)

吭 名 throat: 引吭高歌 ——另见 kēng

杭 名 Hangzhou (capital of Zhejiang Province)
【杭纺】a silk fabric produced in Hangzhou
【杭育】heave ho; yo-heave-ho; yo-ho: 拉纤的船夫在河岸上一步步挣扎着前进,一面有节奏地齐声哼着"～! ～!" *As they inched forward, step by step, on the banks of the river, the boat-pullers kept up a constant rhythmical "Heave ho! Heave ho!"*

绗 动 sew with long stitches: ～被子 *sew on the quilt cover with long stitches*

航 Ⅰ名 boat; ship Ⅱ形 navigate (by water or air): 民航
【航班】scheduled flight; flight number
【航标】navigation mark
【航测】〈略〉见〖航空测量〗
【航程】voyage; passage; range: ～记录器 *odograph*
【航船】boat that plies regularly between inland towns
【航次】❶ the sequence of voyages or flights; voyage or flight number ❷ the number of voyages or flights made
【航道】channel; lane; course: 主～ *the main channel* ◇ ～疏浚 water way dredging
【航海】navigation: ～仪器 *nautical instrument* /

～用语 *nautical term* ◇ ～法规 navigation law；～罗盘 mariner's compass；～日志 logbook；log；～天文历 nautical almanac；～天文学 nautical astronomy

【航迹】［航空］flight path；track

【航空】aviation：～发动机 *aero-engine*；*aircraft engine* / ～工程 *aeronautical engineering* / ～货运 *airfreight* / ～机械员 *aircraft mechanic* / ～联运 *through air transport* / ～汽油 *aviation gasoline* / ～器材 *air material* / ～燃料 *aviation* (*or aircraft*) *fuel* / ～通信 *air communications* / ～运输 *air transportation* ◇ ～版 airmail edition；～保险 aviation insurance；～标塔 airway beacon；～病 airsickness；～测量 aerial survey；～磁测 aeromagnetic survey；～地图 aeronautical chart；aerial map；～电子学 avionics；～法 air law；～港 air harbour；～公司 airline company；airways；～力学 aeromechanics；～模型 model airplane；～母舰 aircraft carrier；～气象台 air weather station；aeronautical meteorological station；～气象学 aeronautical meteorology；～器 air vehicle；aircraft；～日志 aircraft logbook；～人身意外保险 aviation personal accident insurance；～探矿 mineral exploration aviation；aerial prospecting；～体育运动 air sports；flying sports；～天文历 air almanac；～协定 air transport agreement；～信 airmail letter；air letter；airmail；～学 aeronautics；aviation；～学校 aviation (or flying) school；～学院 aeronautical engineering institute

【航空兵】❶ air arm ❷ airman：～部队 *air unit*

【航空照相】aerial photography：～机 *aerocamera*；*aerial camera*

【航模】❶〈略〉见〖航空模型〗❷ model of a ship

【航区】navigation area

【航速】speed of a ship or plane

【航天】spaceflight：～技术 *space technology* / ～通信 *space communication* (*SPACECOM*) ◇ ～舱 space capsule；～飞机 space shuttle；～器 spacecraft；space vehicle；～站 spaceport

【航图】chart

【航务】navigational matters

【航线】air or shipping line；route；course：内河～ *inland navigation line*

【航向】course (of a ship or plane)：改变～ *change course*；*tack* / 右～ *starboard tack* / 左～ *port tack* / 误差～ *course error* / ～指示器 *direction* (*or heading*) *indicator*

【航行】❶ navigate by water；sail：内河～ *inland navigation* ❷ navigate by air；fly：空中～ *aerial navigation* ◇ ～半径 navigation radius；～灯 navigation light；～权 right of navigation

【航运】shipping ◇ ～保险 shipping insurance；～公司 shipping company

hàng

沆 名〈书〉a vast expanse of water

【沆瀣】〈书〉evening mist

【沆瀣一气】❶ be congenial to each other ❷ act in collusion with；wallow in the mire with

巷 名 tunnel ——另见 xiàng

【巷道】［矿］tunnel：～掘进机 *tunnelling machine*

hāo

蒿 名 wormwood artemisia

【蒿目】gaze into the distance

【蒿目时艰】watch the country's ills with deep concern

【蒿子】wormwood；artemisia

【蒿子杆儿】crown daisy chrysanthemum (as a vegetable)

薅 动 ❶ pull up (weeds, etc.) ❷〈方〉pull；tug；drag

【薅草】weeding

háo

号 动 ❶ howl；yell：怒号 ❷ wail：哀号 ——另见 hào

【号叫】howl；yell：他疼得～起来。*He yelled* (*or cried out*) *with pain*. / 救火车～着开来了。*The fire engine came with its siren screaming*.

【号哭】wail：一个妇女在一座墓前～。*A woman was weeping and wailing at a grave*.

【号啕】cry loudly；wail：～大哭 *cry loudly*；*weep and wail*

蚝 名 oyster

【蚝油】oyster sauce

毫 Ⅰ 名 ❶ fine long hair：羊毫 ❷ writing brush：挥毫 ❸ one of the two or three loops on a steelyard for hanging from the user's hand：头(二)～ *first* (*second*) *loop* Ⅱ 副 (used in the negative) in the least；at all：～不足怪 *not at all surprising* / ～不动摇 *not waver in the least*；*be unswerving* / ～无道理 *utterly unjustifiable*；*for no reason whatsoever* / ～无顾虑 *free from all inhibitions* Ⅲ 量 milli-：毫米

【毫安】［电］milliampere：～表 *milliammeter*

【毫巴】［气］millibar

【毫不利己，专门利人】utter devotion to others without any thought of self

【毫法】［电］millifarad

【毫发】〈书〉(usu. used in the negative) a hair；the least bit；the slightest：～不差 *not deviate a hair's breadth*；*be perfectly accurate*

【毫发不爽】not deviating a hair's breadth；without the slightest error

【毫伏】［电］millivolt：～计 *millivoltmeter*

【毫克】milligram (mg.)

【毫厘】the least bit；an iota：～不差 *without the*

slightest error; just right

【毫毛】soft hair on the body: 那些诬蔑无损于我们一根～。*Those slanders can't harm a single hair of our head.* / 谁敢动他一根～? *Who would dare touch a hair of his?*

【毫米】millimetre (mm.): ～波 *millimetre wave*

【毫秒】millisecond

【毫升】millilitre (ml.)

【毫微程序】nanoprogram

【毫微法】[电] millimicrofarad

【毫微米】millimicron (mμ)

【毫微秒】nanosecond; millimicrosecond

【毫无二致】without the slightest difference; just the same; identical: 在这一点上,他们～。*On this point they are entirely at one.*

嗥 动 (of a jackal or wolf) howl

貉 (构词成分)见下 ——另见 hé

【貉绒】racoon dog fur

【貉子】racoon dog

豪 Ⅰ 名 a person of extraordinary powers or endowments: 文豪 Ⅱ 形 ❶bold and unconstrained; forthright; unrestrained: 豪迈 ❷ despotic; bullying: 土豪

【豪放】bold and unconstrained: 性情～ *a bold and uninhibited character*

【豪放不羁】bold and uninhibited

【豪富】❶ powerful and wealthy ❷ the rich and powerful

【豪横】despotic; bullying

【豪华】luxurious; sumptuous; splendid: ～的生活 *a life of luxury; luxurious living* / ～的住宅 *a magnificent house* / ～的陈设 *sumptuous furnishings* / ～的饭店 *a luxury hotel* / ～型汽车 *a de luxe model of a car* / ～版 *deluxe edition*

【豪杰】person of exceptional ability; hero

【豪举】❶ a bold move ❷ a munificent act

【豪迈】bold and generous; heroic: ～的誓言 *a bold pledge* / ～的气概 *heroic spirit* / ～地说 *say with pride* / 以～的步伐跨入新的一年 *stride into the new year with pride and confidence*

【豪门】rich and powerful family; wealthy and influential clan: ～大族 *powerful families and great clans* / ～子弟 *sons of the rich*

【豪气】heroism; heroic spirit

【豪强】❶ despotic; tyrannical ❷ despot; bully

【豪情】lofty sentiments ◇ ～满怀 full of pride and enthusiasm; full of spirit; ～壮志 lofty sentiments and high aspirations

【豪商】a wealthy and powerful merchant

【豪绅】despotic gentry

【豪爽】bold and uninhibited

【豪侠】❶ gallant ❷ a gallant man

【豪兴】exuberant spirits; exhilaration; keen interest: 虽到老年,他仍吟诗作画,～不减。*As an old man, he continued to compose verses and paint pictures, his exuberant spirits undiminished.*

【豪言壮语】brave words; proud words

【豪饮】rink with abandon; drink heavily

【豪雨】torrential rain

【豪语】brave words; bold promise

【豪猪】porcupine

【豪壮】grand and heroic: ～的事业 *a grand and heroic cause* / ～的声音 *a firm, strong voice*

壕 名 ❶ moat ❷ trench: 防空壕

【壕沟】❶ [军] trench ❷ ditch

【壕堑】同〖堑壕〗

嚎 动 ❶ howl: 一声长～ *give a long howl* ❷ wail

【嚎啕】(又作'嚎咷')同〖号啕〗

hǎo

好 Ⅰ 形 ❶ good; fine; nice: ～人 *a nice person* / 天气真～。*The weather's really nice.* ❷ friendly; kind: ～朋友 *a good (or great) friend* / 他们对我真～。*They are really kind to me.* ❸ be in good health; get well: 我的病～了。*I'm well (or all right) now.* / 你～哇! *How are you?* ❹ be ready; done: 饭～了。*The food (or rice) is ready.* ❺ used after verbs to indicate finishing or finishing satisfactorily: 这件事他做不～。*He can't do that job well.* Ⅱ 副 ❶ (used before verbs) be good to; be easy to: 这个问题～回答。*This question is easy to answer.* / 这本书可不～买。*This book is not easily available.* / 暖瓶放在这儿～拿。*It's handy to have the thermos here.* ❷ the better to; in order to; so that: 今儿早点睡,明儿～早起赶火车。*Let's turn in early, so as to get up early tomorrow to catch the train.* / 把她的地址告诉我,我～找她。*Tell me her address so that I can go and see her.* ❸(used before adjectives with exclamatory force) very; quite; so: 今天～冷。*Today is quite cold.* / 你～大胆子。*You are so daring.* / ～大的工程! *What a huge project!* ❹(used before adjectives in the same way as 多) to what extent; how: 火车站离这儿～远? *How far is the railway station from here?* ❺(used before indefinite numbers) quite a few: ～几个 *quite a few* / ～几天 *quite a few days* / ～半天 *quite a while* Ⅲ 叹 (used at the beginning of a sentence or clause, to express agreement, disapproval, surprise, etc.): ～,就这么办。*O.K., it's settled.* ——另见 hào

【好办】easy to handle: 这事不～。*This is no easy matter.* or *This is rather a headache.* / 这件事～。*That can be easily arranged.*

【好比】can be compared to; may be likened to; be just like

【好不】(used with exclamatory force) very; quite; so: 人来人往,～热闹! *What a busy place, with so many people coming and going.* / 他们见了面,～欢喜。*How happy they were to see each other.*

【好不容易】(又作'好容易') not at all easy; very difficult:你～来一次,多待一会儿再走。*It's not at all easy for you to come. Stay a little longer before you go.*

【好处】❶ good; benefit; advantage:你每天做点户外运动,会有～。*Some outdoor exercises every day will do you good.* ❷ gain; profit:他从这里捞不到任何～。*He can gain nothing from this.*

【好处费】pickings

【好歹】❶ good and bad; what's good and what's bad ❷ mishap; disaster:万一她有个～,这可怎么办? *What if something should happen to her?* ❸ in any case; at any rate; anyhow:～试试看。*Let's try, anyhow.* ❹ no matter in what way; anyhow:别再做什么了,～吃点儿就得了。*Don't cook us anything more. We'll have whatever there is.*

【好端端】in perfectly good condition; when everything is all right:～的,怎么生起气来了? *Why are you angry when everything is perfectly all right?*

【好多】❶ a good many; a good deal; a lot of:还有～问题没解决。*There are still lots of problems to be solved.* ❷〈方〉how many; how much:今天到会的人有～? *How many came to the meeting today?*

【好感】good opinion; favourable impression:对他有～ *be well disposed towards him; have a good opinion of him* / 给人～ *make a good impression on people*

【好钢用在刀刃】use the best steel to make the knife's edge — use material where it is needed most; use the best material at the key point

【好汉】brave man; true man; hero

【好汉不吃眼前亏】a wise man will not fight when the odds are obviously against him; a wise man doesn't fight against impossible odds:别惹他们。这一帮人不好惹,～。*Don't get on the wrong side of them. People like that can be nasty if you annoy them. Only a fool goes looking for trouble.*

【好汉不提当年勇】a hero is silent about his past glories

【好汉做事好汉当】a true man has the courage to accept the consequences of his own actions:～,我死就死,决不连累旁人。*Come what may, I'll brace myself and face the music. I'd rather die than implicate others!*

【好好先生】one who tries not to offend anybody; Mr. Agreeable; Mr. Goody-goody

【好话】❶ a good word; word of praise:给他说句～ *put in a good word for him* / 不要听了一些～就沾沾自喜。*Don't become complacent when you hear a few words of praise.* ❷ fine words

【好话说尽,坏事做绝】say every fine word and do every foul deed

【好家伙】good god; good lord; good heavens:～,他们一天足足走了一百里! *Good lord, they walked a hundred li in a day!*

【好借好还】make it a point to return or repay what one has borrowed:～,再借不难。*It's easy to get a loan again if one returns (or repays) what one has borrowed in time.* or *Return (or repay) what you borrow in time and you'll be welcome the next time.*

【好景不长】good times don't last long

【好久】❶ a long time:～以前 *a long time ago; long ago* / ～没见。*I haven't seen you for a long time.* ❷〈方〉how long:你学英语学了～了? *How long have you been learning English?*

【好看】❶ good-looking; nice:这花布做裙子一定很～。*This piece of cotton print would surely make a very beautiful skirt.* / 你戴那顶帽子很～。*That hat looks nice on you.* ❷ interesting:这本小说很～。*This novel is very interesting.* ❸ honoured; proud:儿子立了功,我这做娘的脸上也～。*My son has won distinction; as his mother, I share the honour.* ❹ in an embarrassing situation; on the spot:等着吧,有他的～。*You can be sure he'll soon find himself on the spot.* / 让我上台表演,这不是要我的～吗? *Me, on the stage? Do you want me to make a fool of myself?*

【好莱坞】Hollywood(centre of US movie industry located close to Los Angeles):～明星 *Hollywood star*

【好了疮疤忘了疼】forget the pain once the wound is healed—forget the bitter past when released from one's suffering

【好男不跟女斗】a gentleman doesn't fight women

【好评】favourable comment; high opinion:对他颇有～ *have a rather high opinion of him* / 博得读者～ *be well received by the readers*

【好球】well played; good shot; bravo

【好人】❶ a good (or fine) person:他是个～。*He's a good man.* ❷ a healthy person:他身体不好,别把他当～使。*He's in poor health; don't work him as you would a healthy person.* ❸ a soft person who tries to get along with everyone (often at the expense of principle):她只想做个～,连说句话也怕得罪人。*She's out to please everyone, and she takes care that whatever she says offends no one.*

【好人好事】good people and good deeds; fine people and fine deeds

【好日子】❶ auspicious day:他们拣个～开张。*They chose an auspicious day to start the business.* ❷ wedding day:今天是他们的～。*Today is their wedding day.* ❸ good days; happy life:过～ *live a happy life; live well; live in happiness*

【好善乐施】(又作'乐施好善') enjoy helping those in need; be generous in one's charity; be philanthropic:老先生～而闻名遐尔。*The old gentleman was renowned far and wide for his philanthropic generosity.*

【好生】❶ quite; exceedingly:～奇怪! *What an exceedingly strange thing!* / 这个人～面熟。*That person looks quite familiar.* ❷〈方〉carefully; properly:～想一想。*Think it over carefully.* /

～拿着。*Mind how you carry it.*

【好声好气】〈口〉in a kindly manner; gently: 他说话从来不～,总是板着脸训人。*He never has a kind word for anyone, and is always pulling a long face and lecturing others.*

【好使】be convenient to use; work well: 这把剪刀不～。*This pair of scissors doesn't work well.*

【好事】(hǎoshì) ❶ good deed; good turn: 为群众做～ *do people good turns* ❷ an act of charity; good works ❸〈书〉happy event; joyous occasion ——另见 hàoshì

【好事不出门,恶事传千里】good news never goes beyond the gate, while bad news spreads far and wide

【好事多磨】❶ the road to happiness is strewn with setbacks ❷ the course of true love never did run smooth

【好手】good hand; past master: 做针线活儿,她可是把～。*She is adept at needlework.*

【好受】feel better; feel more comfortable: 我吃了药以后～多了。*I felt much better after taking the medicine.* / 白天太热,夜里还～点。*It's terribly hot during the day but a bit better at night.*

【好说】❶〈套〉(used in answer to praises or thanks): ～,～!您太夸奖了。*It's very good of you to say so, but I don't deserve such praise.* or *You flatter me. I wish I could deserve such compliments.* ❷ no problem: 关于费用问题,～。*The expenses are no problem.*

【好说歹说】try every possible way to persuade sb.: 我～,他总算答应了。*He agreed, but only after I had pleaded with him in every way I could.*

【好说话儿】good-natured; open to persuasion: 王大爷～,求求他准行。*Uncle Wang is very obliging. He's sure to help if you ask him.*

【好死不如赖活】even a good death is not like a wretched existence

【好似】seem; be like: 大坝～铜墙铁壁,顶住了洪水的冲击。*Like an iron bastion, the dam withstood the rushing floodwaters.*

【好天儿】fine day; lovely weather: 这些衣服～要拿出去晒晒。*These clothes should be put out to air on a sunny day.*

【好听】pleasant to hear: ～的话 *fine words* / 这支歌很～。*This is a very pleasant song.* / 他说的比唱的还～。*His glib talk sounds as sweet as a song.*

【好玩儿】amusing; interesting: 颐和园～极了。*The Summer Palace is a most delightful place.* / 这小娃娃挺～。*The baby is very cute.* / 这可不是～的!*This is no joking matter.*

【好闻】smell good; smell sweet: 茉莉花挺～。*Jasmine flowers smell sweet.*

【好戏】❶ good play ❷ great fun (used sarcastically): 这回可有～看了!*We're going to see some fun!* / ～还在后头呢!*The worst is yet to come!*

【好像】seem; be like: ～要下雪。*It looks like snow.* / ～谁也没听见铃响。*No one seems to have heard the bell.* / 他们～是多年的老朋友了。*They seem to have been close friends for many years.*

【好笑】laughable; funny; ridiculous: 有什么～的?*What's so funny?* / 又好气又～ *be annoying and amusing at the same time*

【好些个】(又作'好些') quite a lot; a good deal of: 他有～朋友。*He has quite a lot of friends.*

【好心】good intention: 一片～ *with the best of intentions* / ～没好报 *get no thanks for one's good intentions*

【好心当作驴肝肺】take an honest man's heart for a donkey's liver and lungs—take sb.'s goodwill for ill intent

【好样儿的】〈口〉(of a man or woman) fine example; great fellow: 是～,就站出来说吧!*If you are man enough, come out with what you have to say!*

【好一个】(又作'好个') what a (used in praise or in condemnation): ～幽雅去处!*What a quiet, elegant spot!* / ～投手,一人得了40分!*What a shooter! He scored 40 points all by himself.*

【好意】good intention; kindness: ～相劝 *give well-intentioned advice* / 谢谢您的～。*Thank you for your kindness.*

【好意思】how can one have the face (or nerve) to do sth.: 人家请我喝酒,我～不喝吗?*When he offered me a drink, how could I have the face to refuse it?*

【好在】fortunately; luckily: ～他伤势不重。*Luckily he was not very seriously wounded.* / 我可以再去一趟,～路不远。*Luckily it's not very far. I can easily go there again.*

【好转】take a turn for the better; take a favourable turn; improve: 形势～。*The situation took a favourable turn.* / 病情～。*The patient is on the mend.*

【好自为之】look out for yourself: 有这样的机会不容易,希望你～。*An opportunity like this is not easy to come by, so I hope you'll make best use of it.*

【好走】〈方〉goodbye

hào

号 Ⅰ **名** ❶ name: 绰号 ❷ assumed name; alternative name; literary name; sobriquet: 苏轼字子瞻,～东坡。*Su Shi, styled Zizhan, was also known by his literary name Dongpo ("Eastern Slope").* ❸ business house: 银号 ❹ mark; sign; signal: 暗号 ❺ number: 五～楼 *Building No. 5* ❻ size: 大(中,小)～ *large (medium, small) size* / 这鞋小了两～。*These shoes are two sizes too small.* ❼ date: 今天几～?—13～。*What date is it today?—The 13th.* ❽ personnel: 病号 ❾ order: 发号施令 ❿ any brass-wind instrument: 小号 Ⅱ **量** (for workmen): 今天有一百多～人出工。*Over a hundred people went to work* today. Ⅲ 动 examine (the pulse): 号脉——另见 háo

【号称】❶ be known as: 四川～天府之国。*Sichuan is known as a land of plenty.* ❷ claim to be: ～五十万大军 *an army claiming to be half a million strong*

【号角】❶ bugle; horn ❷ bugle call: 吹响战斗的～ *sound a bugle call for battle*

【号令】verbal command; order

【号码】number: 电话～ *telephone number* ◇ ～机 numbering machine

【号脉】[中] feel the pulse

【号手】bugler; trumpeter

【号外】extra (of a newspaper)

【号型】size (of shoes, clothes, etc.)

【号衣】〈旧〉livery or army uniform

【号召】call; appeal: ～人们参军 *call on the people to enlist* ◇ ～书 appeal

【号子】a work song sung to synchronize movements, with one person leading

好 动 ❶ like; love; be fond of: ～说话 *like to talk* / ～表现 *like to show off* / ～跳舞 *love dancing* / ～喝酒 *be fond of drinking* / ～管闲事 *meddlesome; officious* ❷ be liable to: ～晕船 *be liable to seasickness; be a bad sailor* / ～伤风 *be subject to colds; catch cold easily* ——另见 hǎo

【好吃懒做】be fond of eating and averse to work; be gluttonous and lazy

【好大喜功】crave for greatness and success; have a fondness for the grandiose

【好高务远】(又作'好高骛远') reach for what is beyond one's grasp; aim too high

【好客】be hospitable; keep open house: 他这个人热情～。*He is a good-natured and hospitable man.*

【好奇】be curious; be full of curiosity: 孩子们都很～。*Children are very curious.* ◇ ～心 curiosity

【好强】eager to do well in everything

【好色】love woman's beauty; be fond of women ◇ ～之徒 lecher; libertine

【好胜】love to outshine others; seek to do others down

【好事】(hàoshì) meddlesome; officious ◇ ～之徒 busybody ——另见 hǎoshì

【好为人师】like to lecture people; be given to laying down the law

【好恶】likes and dislikes; taste: 人各有～。*Everyone has his likes and dislikes.* / 翻译时不应根据自己的～改变原文意思。*In doing translation, one should not alter the meaning of the original to suit one's own taste.*

【好学】be fond of learning; be eager to learn: 聪明～ *be intelligent and fond of learning*

【好逸恶劳】love ease and hate work

【好战】bellicose; warlike: ～分子 *bellicose (or warlike) elements*

【好整以暇】remain calm and composed while handling pressing affairs

耗 Ⅰ 动 ❶ consume; cost: 这汽车～油。*This car uses a lot of petrol.* / ～了不少粮食 *have consumed much grain* / 锅里的水快～干了。*The pot is boiling dry.* ❷ waste time; dawdle: 别～着了,快走吧。*Stop dawdling and get going.* Ⅱ 名 bad news: 噩耗

【耗电】consume electricity ◇ ～量 power consumption

【耗费】consume; expend: ～时间、金钱 *expend time and money*

【耗减优惠】depletion allowance

【耗竭】exhaust; use up: 人力～ *be drained of manpower*

【耗尽】exhaust; use up: ～心血 *exhaust all one's energies* / ～体力 *use up all one's strength*

【耗能量】quantity of energy consumption

【耗散】[物] dissipation: 功率～ *power dissipation*

【耗损】consume; waste; lose: 减少水果在运输中的～ *reduce the wastage of fruit in transit*

【耗油量】oil consumption

【耗资】cost (a large sum of money): ～百万 *cost a million yuan*

【耗子】〈方〉mouse; rat ◇ ～药 ratsbane

浩 形 ❶ great; vast; grand: 浩繁 ❷ many; much: 浩博

【浩博】extensive; wide-embracing

【浩荡】vast and mighty: ～的长江 *the mighty Changjiang River* / 东风～。*The east wind blows with mighty power.*

【浩繁】vast and numerous: ～的开支 *heavy expenditure*

【浩瀚】〈书〉vast: ～的沙漠 *a vast expanse of desert* / 典籍～ *a vast accumulation of ancient literature* / ～的大海 *a boundless sea*

【浩浩荡荡】vast and mighty: ～的革命大军 *an enormous and powerful revolutionary army; mighty revolutionary contingents*

【浩劫】great calamity; catastrophe: 空前～ *an unheard-of calamity*

【浩淼】(of water) extending into the distance; vast

【浩气】noble spirit: ～长存 *a noble spirit that will never perish*

【浩然之气】noble spirit; moral force

【浩如烟海】vast as the open sea—a tremendous amount (of literature, data, etc.)

【浩叹】❶ heave a deep sigh; sigh deeply ❷ be greatly touched

皓 形 ❶ white: 皓齿 ❷ bright; luminous: 皓月当空

【皓齿】white teeth ——另见〖明眸皓齿〗

【皓矾】[化] zinc sulphate

【皓首】〈书〉hoary head: ～穷经 *continue to study even in old age*

【皓月当空】a bright moon hung in the sky

hē

诃 动 scold

【诃子】[植] myrobalan (Terminalia chebula)

呵 动 ❶breathe out (with the mouth open): ～一口气 *give a puff* / 他一边写,一边～手。*As he wrote, he kept breathing on his hands to warm them*. ❷ scold: 呵责

【呵斥】(又作'呵叱') berate; excoriate

【呵呵】the sound of laughing: ～大笑 *laugh loudly; roar with laughter*

【呵护】〈书〉bless

【呵欠】yawn

【呵责】berate; excoriate

喝 动 ❶ drink: ～茶 *drink tea* / ～汤 *drink soup* ❷ drink alcoholic liquor: 爱～两盅 *be fond of drinking* / ～醉了 *be drunk*——另见 hè

【喝墨水】drink ink—go to school: 他没喝过几年墨水。*He's had only a few years of school*.

【喝水不忘掘井人】when you drink the water, think of those who dug the well

【喝西北风】drink the northwest wind—live on air; have nothing to eat

嗬 叹 ah; oh: ～,这小伙子真棒! *Oh, what a fine young chap*! / ～,真了不得了! *Oh, how terrible*! / ～,怎么这么贵! *Wow, how expensive*!

hé

禾 名 standing grain (esp. rice)

【禾本科】[植] the grass family

【禾草类】[植] grass

【禾场】〈方〉threshing floor

【禾苗】seedlings of cereal crops

合 Ⅰ 动 ❶ close; shut: 把书～上 *close the book* / 笑得～不上嘴 *grin from ear to ear* ❷ join; combine: 合办 ❸ suit; agree: ～胃口 *suit one's taste; be to one's taste* / 正～我意。*It suits me fine*. ❹ be equal to; add up to: 一公顷～15 市亩。*A hectare is equal to 15 mu*. / 这件上衣连工带料～多少钱? *How much will this coat cost, including material and tailoring*? ❺〈书〉be proper: 理～声明。*I deem it appropriate to make a statement*. Ⅱ 形 whole: ～村 *the whole village* Ⅲ 名 [气] conjunction

【合办】operate or run jointly: ～企业 *a joint enterprise; a joint venture*

【合瓣】[植] sympetalous; gamopetalous: ～花 *sympetalous flower* / ～花类 *metachlamydeae; sympetalae*

【合璧】(of two different things) combine harmoniously; match well: 中西～ *a good combination of Chinese and Western elements*

【合编】❶ compile in collaboration with: 这本书是他们两位～的。*They are the two joint compilers of this book*. ❷ merge and reorganize (army units, etc.): 两支军队～后,兵力达万人。*A merging of the two army units brought the strength up to 10,000 men*.

【合并】❶ merge; amalgamate: 五个组～为两个组了。*The five groups have merged into two*. ❷ (of an illness) be complicated by another illness ◇ ～程序 merging program; ～分类 merge sort

【合不来】not get along well; be incompatible

【合唱】chorus: 混声～ *mixed chorus* ◇ ～曲 (music for) chorus; ～团 chorus (a group of singers)

【合成】❶ compose; compound: 由两部分～ *be composed of two parts* / 力的～ *composition of forces* ❷ [化] synthetize; synthesize ◇ ～氨 [化] synthetic ammonia; ～词 [语] compound word; ～革 synthetic leather; ～结晶牛胰岛素 synthetic crystalline bovine insulin; ～酶 [生化] synzyme; ～器[计] synthesizer; ～树脂 synthetic resin; ～洗涤剂 synthetic detergent; ～纤维 synthetic fibre; ～橡胶 synthetic rubber

【合得来】get along well; be compatible

【合订本】one-volume edition; bound volume

【合二而一】[哲] two combine into one

【合法】legal; lawful; legitimate; rightful: 惟一～政府 *the sole legal government* / ～地位 *legal status* / ～斗争 *legal struggle* / ～继承人 *rightful heir* / ～权利 *legitimate right; lawful right* / ～权益 *legitimate rights and interests* / ～收入 *lawfully earned income* / ～途径 *legal means* ◇ ～经营 lawful operation; ～化 legalize; legitimize

【合格】qualified; up to standard: ～的司机 *a qualified driver* / 产品～。*The product is up to standard*. / 我们保证质量～。*We can vouch for the quality*. ◇ ～技术人员 qualitified technicians; ～证 certificate of inspection; certificate of quality

【合股】❶ pool capital; form a partnership ❷ [纺] plying: ～线 *ply (or plied) yarn* ◇ ～企业 joint stock enterprises

【合乎】conform with (or to); correspond to; accord with; tally with: ～人民的利益 *conform with the interests of the people* / ～实际 *conform to the actual situation* / ～历史发展的规律 *be in conformity with the law of historical development*

【合欢】❶ conjoined happiness—sexual pairing ❷ [植] silk tree

【合伙】form a partnership: ～经营 *run a business in partnership* / 两人～买下了这家公司。*The two of them formed a partnership and bought the company*.

【合击】make a joint attack on: 分进～ *concerted attack by converging columns*

【合计】(héjì) amount to; add up to; total: 这两项开支～一千元。*The cost of the two items amounts to 1,000 yuan*. / 把这一栏的数字～一

下。*Add up the figures in this column*.

【合计】(héji)〈方〉❶ héji think over; figure out: 他心里老～这件事。*He kept thinking it over*. ❸ consult: 大家～～该怎么办。*Let's put our heads together and see what's to be done*.

【合剂】[药] mixture

【合家】the whole family: ～团圆 *a reunion of the whole family*

【合金】alloy: 二元(三元)～ *binary* (*ternary*) *alloy* ◇ ～钢 alloy steel; ～元素 alloying element

【合刊】combined issue (of a periodical)

【合口】❶(of a wound) heal up ❷(of a dish) be to one's taste: 你做的菜很～。*The dishes you make are very much to my taste*.

【合理】rational; reasonable; equitable: 收费～ *reasonable charges* / 时间安排～ *a well worked out timetable* / ～分工 *rational division of labour* / ～利用资源 *put resources to rational use; make rational use of resources*

【合理化】rationalize: ～建议 *rationalization proposal*

【合力】❶ join forces; pool efforts: ～修建水库 *pool efforts to build a reservoir* ❷ [物] resultant of forces

【合流】❶ flowing together; confluence: 永定河和大清河在天津附近～。*The Yongding and Daqing rivers meet near Tianjin*. ❷ collaborate; work hand in glove with sb.

【合龙】❶ closure (of a dam, dyke, etc.) ❷ join the two sections of a bridge, etc.

【合霉素】[药] syntomycin

【合谋】❶ conspire; plot together; connive ❷ [法] conspiracy

【合拍】in time; in step; in harmony: 与时代潮流～ *in step with the trend of the times*

【合情合理】fair and reasonable; fair and sensible: 这个建议～。*The proposal is fair and reasonable*.

【合群】❶ get on well with others; be sociable ❷ be gregarious

【合身】fit: 这件上衣很～。*This jacket fits well*.

【合十】put the palms together before one (a Buddhist greeting)

【合时】fashionable; in vogue: 穿戴～ *dress fashionably*

【合适】(又作'合式') suitable; appropriate; becoming; right: 这双鞋我穿着正～。*These shoes fit me beautifully*. / 星期五对我最～。*Friday suits me best*.

【合算】❶ paying; worthwhile ❷ reckon up

【合题】[哲] synthesis

【合同】contract: 订立～ *conclude* (*or make*) *a contract* / 撕毁～ *tear up a contract* / ～期限 *contract period* ◇ ～法 contract law; ～工 contract worker; ～婚姻 contract marriage; ～纠纷 contract dispute; ～满期 termination of the contract; ～医院 assigned hospital; ～制 contract system; ～仲裁机构 contract arbitration committee

【合围】surround

【合演】appear in the same play, dance, etc.; co-star

【合叶】(又作'合页') hinge

【合宜】suitable; appropriate; becoming; right: 他担任这个工作倒很～。*He's just the right man for the job*.

【合议庭】[法] collegiate bench (of judges, or of a judge and people's assessors); collegial panel: 由审判员一人,人民陪审员二人组成的～ *a collegial panel composed of one judge and two people's assessors*

【合议制】[法] collegiate system (a judicial system according to which justice is administered by a collegiate bench of judges, or by a judge and people's assessors)

【合意】suit; be to one's liking (or taste): 这个合你的意吗? *Does this suit you*? / 你说的正合我意。*You took the very words out of my mouth*.

【合营】jointly owned; jointly operated: ～期满 *termination of agreement of a joint venture* / 公私～企业 *enterprises under joint public and private ownership*

【合影】❶ take a group photo (or picture): ～留念 *have a group photo taken to mark the occasion* ❷ group photo (or picture)

【合用】❶ share: 两家～一个厨房。*Two families share a kitchen*. ❷ of use: 绳子太短,不～。*The rope is too short to be of any use*.

【合约】contract

【合葬】(of husband and wife) be buried in the same grave

【合账】〈口〉make up accounts; figure out accounts

【合辙】❶ in rhyme ❷ in agreement: 两人一说就～。*The moment they started talking they found themselves in complete agreement*.

【合资】pool capital; enter into partnership

【合资经营】jointly owned; jointly operated: 中外～企业 *a Chinese-foreign joint venture* / ～各方 *parties to a venture*

【合奏】instrumental ensemble

【合作】cooperate; collaborate; work together: 互相～ *cooperate with each other* / 这幅画是他们～的。*This painting is their joint work*. / 南南～ *South-South cooperation*

【合作化】(a movement to) organize cooperatives

【合作经营】jointly operated; cooperative management; cooperative business operation

【合作社】cooperative; co-op

【合作项目】cooperative projects; cooperative project

【合作医疗】cooperative medical service

【合作银行】cooperative bank

何 代〈书〉what; which; how; why: ～人 *who* / ～时 *what time; when* / ～处 *what place; where* / ～往 *whither* / 从～而来? *Where from*? / ～济于事? *Of what avail is it*? / 有～不可? *Why not*?

【何必】there is no need; why: ～去那么早。*There*

is no need to go so early. / 开个玩笑嘛，～当真呢？*I was only joking. Why take it so seriously*?

【何不】why not：～早说？*Why didn't you say so earlier*?

【何尝】(used in rhetorical questions) ever so：我～不想去，只是没工夫罢了。*Not that I don't want to go; I just haven't got the time*.

【何等】❶ what kind：你知道他是～人物？*Do you know what kind of person he is*? ❷ (used in exclamations) what; how：这是～高超的技术！*What consummate skill*!

【何妨】why not; might as well：～一试？*Why not have a try*? or *You might as well have a try*. / 人少不热闹，～多请些人？*The more the merrier—why not invite some more people*?

【何故】*why*：不知～。*I don't know why*.

【何苦】why bother; is it worth the trouble：你～在这些小事上伤脑筋？*Why bother your head about such trifles*?

【何况】❶ much less; let alone：这根木头连小伙子都抬不动，～老人呢？*The log is too heavy even for a young fellow to lift, let alone an old man*. ❷ moreover; besides; in addition：我不喜欢那所房子，～价钱也太高。*I don't like the house, and moreover, the price is too high*.

【何乐而不为】why not do it; one would be only too glad to do it

【何其】(used in exclamations to express disapproval) what; how：～愚蠢！*What a fool*! / ～荒唐！*How absurd*!

【何去何从】what course to follow：～，速作抉择。*What course to follow—that is a question you must quickly decide for yourselves*.

【何如】〈书〉❶ how about：请君一试，～？*How about you having a try*? ❷ wouldn't it be better：与其强攻，～智取。*It would be better to use strategy than to attack by force*.

【何首乌】［中］the tuber of multiflower knotweed (Polygonum multiflorum)

【何谓】〈书〉what is meant by; what is the meaning of：～灵感？*What is meant by inspiration*? / 此～也？*What does it mean*? or *What do you mean*?

【何许】〈书〉what kind of; what：～人 *what sort of person*

【何以】〈书〉how; why：～自解？*How are you to explain yourself*? / ～见得？*What makes you think so*?

【何在】〈书〉where：困难～？*Wherein lies the difficulty*? / 原因～？*What is the reason for it*?

【何止】far more than：例子～这些。*There are far more instances than we have just enumerated*.

【何足挂齿】〈套〉not worth mentioning; don't mention it：区区小事，～。*Such a trifle is not worth mentioning*.

河 名 ❶ river ❷ the Milky Way system ❸ the Huanghe River; the Yellow River

【河岸】river bank

【河川】rivers and creeks

【河床】(又作'河槽'；'河身') riverbed

【河道】river course

【河堤】river embankment

【河东狮吼】the roar of the lioness from the east side of the River (said of sb.'s dominating wife in a temper)

【河防】flood-prevention work done on rivers, esp. the Huanghe River

【河港】river port

【河沟】brook; stream

【河谷】river valley

【河口】river mouth; stream outlet：～湾 *estuary*

【河狸】beaver

【河流】rivers ◇ ～沉积 fluvial (or fluviatile) deposit；～污染 stream pollution；～袭夺［地质］river capture; river piracy

【河马】hippopotamus; hippo; river horse

【河鳗】river eel

【河泥】river silt; river mud

【河清海晏】the Yellow River is clear and the sea is calm—the world is at peace

【河曲】bend (of a river); meander

【河渠】rivers and canals; waterways：～纵横 *be crisscrossed by rivers and canals*

【河山】rivers and mountains; land; territory

【河滩地】flood land

【河套】❶ the bend of a river ❷ the Great Bend of the Huanghe River

【河豚】globefish; balloonfish; puffer

【河外星云】(又作'河外星系')［气］extragalactic nebula

【河网】a network of waterways：～化 *build a network of waterways*

【河蟹】river crab

【河源】river head (or source)

【河运】river transport

和 Ⅰ 形 ❶ gentle; mild; kind：温和 ❷ harmonious; on good terms：～为贵。*Harmony is what matters*. Ⅱ 名 ❶ peace：讲和 ❷［数］sum：两数之～ *the sum of the two numbers* / ～国际惯例接轨。*conform to international practice* Ⅲ 动［体］draw; tie：那盘棋～了。*That game of chess ended in a draw*. Ⅳ 介 ❶ together with：和衣 ❷ (indicating relationship, comparison, etc.)：～这件事没有关系 *have nothing to do with the matter; bear no relation to it* / 他～我一样高。*He's the same height as I*. Ⅴ 连 and：工人～农民 *workers and peasants* / 你～我 *you and I* ——另见 hè; huó; huò

【和蔼】kindly; affable; amiable：态度～ *amiable* ◇ ～可亲 affable; amiable; genial

【和畅】(of a wind) gentle and pleasant：惠风～ *a gentle and pleasant breeze*

【和风】❶ soft (or gentle) breeze：～拂面 *a gentle breeze caressing one's face* / ～丽日 *a gentle breeze and a bright sun; fine weather* ❷［气］moderate breeze

【和风细雨】like a gentle breeze and light rain—in a gentle and mild way
【和服】kimono
【和光同尘】soften one's glare and move along old ruts—swim with the tide
【和好】become reconciled：他们吵过架，现在～了。*They had a quarrel but have made it up now.* / ～如初 *be on good terms again；restore good relations*
【和缓】❶ gentle；mild：水流～ *gentle flow of a stream* / 态度～ *adopt a mild attitude* ❷ ease up；relax：～一下气氛 *relieve the tension a little*
【和会】peace conference
【和奸】commit adultery
【和解】become reconciled：两国开始对话，表示愿意～。*The two countries started to hold dialogues and showed a willingness to conciliate.* / 采取～的态度 *adopt a conciliatory attitude*
【和局】drawn game；draw；tie：三盘棋却有两盘是～。*Two of the three chess games ended in draws.*
【和美】harmonious and happy：～的家庭 *happy family* / 和和美美过日子 *live happily together；live in happy harmony*
【和睦】harmony；concord；amity：～相处 *live in harmony* / 民族～ *national concord* / 家庭～ *family harmony；domestic peace* / 友好～关系 *friendly and harmonious relations*
【和暖】pleasantly warm；genial：天气～ *warm，genial weather* / ～的阳光 *genial sunshine*
【和盘托出】reveal everything；hold nothing back：把自己的想法～ *reveal everything on one's mind*
【和平】❶ peace：～倡议 *peace proposals* / ～环境 *peaceful environment* / ～利用原子能 *peaceful utilization of atomic energy；use of atomic energy for peaceful purposes* / ～解决边界争端 *peaceful settlement of a boundary dispute* ❷ mild：药性～。*The medicine is mild.* ◇ ～队 Peace Corps；～鸽 dove of peace；～攻势 peace offensive；～共处 peaceful coexistence；～过渡 peaceful transition；～竞赛 peaceful competition；～谈判 peace negotiations；peace talks；～演变 peaceful evolution (from socialism back to capitalism)；～中立政策 policy of peace and neutrality
【和平共处五项原则】the Five Principles of Peaceful Coexistence (mutual respect for territorial integrity and sovereignty，mutual non-aggression，non-interference in each other's internal affairs，equality and mutual benefit，and peaceful coexistence)
【和平主义】pacifism：～者 *pacifist*
【和棋】a draw in chess or other board games
【和气】❶ gentle；friendly；polite；amiable：对人～ *be friendly to people* / 他们彼此很～。*They are very friendly with each other.* / 说话～ *speak politely (or gently)；be soft-spoken* / 和和气气 *polite and amiable* ❷ harmony；friendship：咱们别为那件小事儿伤了～。*Don't let that unpleasantness end our friendship.*
【和气生财】amiability begets riches (a motto for businessmen)：买卖买卖，～。*Do business with a smile，and you'll make a pile.*
【和亲】(of some feudal dynasties) attempt to cement relations with rulers of minority nationalities in the border areas by marrying daughters of the Han imperial family to them
【和善】kind and gentle；genial
【和尚】Buddhist monk
【和尚头】〈口〉shaven head：剃个～ *have one's head shaved*
【和声】[音] harmony
【和事老】peacemaker (esp. one who is more concerned with stopping the bickering than settling the issue)
【和数】[数] sum
【和谈】〈略〉见〖和平谈判〗
【和弦】[音] chord
【和谐】harmonious：音调～ *in perfect harmony；melodious；tuneful* / 颜色搭配得很～。*The colours match quite well.* / ～的气氛 *a harmonious atmosphere*
【和煦】pleasantly warm；genial：～的阳光 *genial sunshine* / 春风～。*The spring breeze is warm and gentle.*
【和颜悦色】have a kind face；have a genial expression
【和衣】(sleep) with one's clothes on：～而卧 *sleep with one's clothes on*
【和约】peace treaty
【和衷共济】work together with one accord (in time of difficulty)

劾 动 expose sb.'s misdeeds or crimes：弹劾

阂 动 cut off from；not in communication with：隔阂

荷 名 lotus ——另见 hè
【荷包】❶ small bag (for carrying money and odds and ends)；pouch ❷ pocket (in a garment)
【荷包蛋】poached or fried eggs
【荷尔蒙】hormone (old name for 激素)
【荷花】lotus
【荷兰】the Netherlands (Holland) ◇ ～人 the Dutch；Dutchman；～语 Dutch (language)
【荷叶】lotus leaf

核 Ⅰ 名 ❶ pit；stone：桃～ *peach-pit；peach-stone* / 无～蜜桔 *pipless tangerine* / 无～葡萄干 *seedless raisins* ❷ nucleus：细胞核 ❸ atomic nucleus Ⅱ 动 examine；check：核准 ——另见 hú
【核安全】nuclear security；nuclear safety：～标准 *nuclear safety standard* / ～保障 *nuclear safeguard*
【核保护伞】nuclear umbrella
【核爆幸存者】hibakusha
【核爆炸】nuclear explosion
【核备战】preparation for nuclear war
【核裁军】nuclear disarmament

【核查】examine and verify；check
【核尘】nuclear dust
【核磁共振】nuclear magnetic resonance
【核打击力量】nuclear strike capability (or force)
【核大国】nuclear power
【核蛋白】［生化］nucleoprotein
【核弹头】nuclear warhead
【核导弹】nuclear missile
【核电站】nuclear power plant
【核定】check and ratify；appraise and decide ◇ ～承兑汇票 approved acceptance；～概算 (to) approve estimates；～股本 authorized stock
【核冬天】nuclear winter
【核动力】nuclear power
【核对】check：～数字 *check figures* / ～账单 *check a bill* / ～事实 *check the facts*
【核讹诈】nuclear blackmail
【核发】approve and issue：～驾驶执照 *approve and issue a driving license*
【核反应】nuclear reaction ◇ ～堆 nuclear reactor
【核废料】nuclear waste
【核辐射】nuclear radiation
【核苷】［生化］nucleoside：～酸 *nucleotide*
【核果】［植］drupe
【核黄素】riboflavin；lactoflavin
【核火箭】nuclear rocket
【核计】assess；calculate：～成本 *assess the cost*
【核价】verify prices：这个食品公司春节期间出售的货品将按有关规定～，以防乱涨价。*To prevent random price hikes, the prices of goods sold by this company during the Spring Festival will be verified in accordance with the regulations.*
【核聚变】nuclear fusion
【核扩散】nuclear proliferation
【核理论】nuclear theory
【核裂变】nuclear fission
【核垄断】nuclear monopoly
【核能】(又作'核子能') nuclear energy
【核潜艇】nuclear-powered submarine
【核燃料】nuclear fuel
【核仁】❶［生］nucleolus ❷ kernel (of a fruit-stone)
【核实】verify；check：～的产量 *verified output* / 请把这些数字～一下。*Please check these figures.*
【核事故】nuclear accident
【核试验】nuclear test：大气层(高空，地下)～ *atmospheric (high-altitude, underground) nuclear test*
【核衰变】nuclear disintegration
【核素】❶［化］nuclein ❷［物］nuclide
【核酸】［生化］nucleic acid：～酶 *nuclease* / ～内切酶 *endonuclease*
【核算】❶ examine and calculate；assess：～生产成本 *work out the costs of production* ❷ business accounting
【核算单位】accounting unit：基本～ *basic accounting unit* / 独立～ *independent accounting unit*
【核糖】［生化］ribose
【核糖核酸】［生化］ribonucleic acid；RNA：脱氧～ *deoxyribonucleic acid；DNA* / 信息～ *messenger ribonucleic acid；m-RNA*
【核桃】walnut ◇ ～仁 walnut meat
【核威慑力量】nuclear deterrent (power)
【核威胁】nuclear threat
【核微粒沾染】contamination from nuclear fallout
【核武库】nuclear arsenal
【核武器】nuclear weapon：～储备 *stockpiling of nuclear weapons；nuclear weapons stockpile*
【核销】cancel after verification
【核心】nucleus；core；kernel：领导～ *the core of leadership* / ～力量 *force at the core* / ～人物 *key person；key figure* / 起～作用 *play a key role* / 抓住问题的～ *get to the heart of the matter* / 辩证法的～ *the kernel of dialectics* ◇ ～家庭 nuclear family；～课程 core curriculum；～内阁 inner cabinet；～小组 core group
【核优势】nuclear superiority
【核战争】nuclear war (or warfare)
【核装置】nuclear device
【核准】examine and approve；check and approve：经主管部门～后，发给营业执照。*Business licences shall be issued after examination and approval by the department concerned.*
【核资】verify capital or asset：清产～ *check-up of assets*
【核子】［物］nucleon ◇ ～学 nucleonics

涸 动〈书〉dry up：干涸
【涸竭】dried up；exhausted
【涸泽而渔】同〖竭泽而渔〗
【涸辙之鲋】a fish stranded in a dry rut—in a desperate situation

盒 名 box；case：一～火柴 *a box of matches*
【盒饭】box lunch
【盒式磁带】cassette tape ◇ ～录音机 cassette tape recorder；～录像机 video cassette recorder
【盒子】box；case；casket

颌 名 jaw：上(下)～ *the upper (lower) jaw*

阖 Ⅰ 形〈书〉entire；whole：～城 *the whole town* Ⅱ 动 shut；close：～户 *close the door*
【阖府】(又作'阖第')〈尊〉your whole family：敬请～光临。*The presence of your whole family is cordially requested.*
【阖家】the whole family
【阖眼】close one's eyes

貉 名 racoon dog ——另见 háo

hè

吓 Ⅰ 动 threaten；intimidate Ⅱ 叹 (showing disapproval)：～，怎么能干这种事呢？*Tut-tut, how could you do that?* ——另见 xià

和 动 ❶ join in the singing：一唱百和 ❷ compose a poem in reply：奉～一首 *write a poem in*

reply (*to one sent by a friend*, *etc*., *using the same rhyme sequence*) ——另见 hé; huó; huò

贺 动 congratulate: 道贺

【贺匾】congratulatory plaque

【贺词】speech (or message) of congratulation; congratulations; greetings: 致～ *give a speech of congratulation*

【贺电】message of congratulation; congratulatory telegram: 发～ *send a congratulatory telegram*

【贺卡】greeting card

【贺礼】congratulatory gift

【贺年】extend New Year greetings or pay a New Year call

【贺年片】New Year card

【贺岁片】New Year greeting film

【贺喜】congratulate sb. on a happy occasion (e.g. a wedding, the birth of a child, etc.); offer congratulations

【贺信】(又作'贺函') congratulatory letter; letter of congratulation

荷 Ⅰ 动〈书〉carry on one's shoulder or back: ～锄 *carry a hoe on one's shoulder* Ⅱ 名 burden; responsibility: 重荷 ——另见 hé

【荷负】〈书〉bear; shoulder

【荷枪实弹】(of soldiers or policemen) carry loaded rifles—ready for an emergency

【荷载】load

【荷重】the weight a building can bear; load

喝 动 shout loudly: 大～一声 *give a loud shout* ——另见 hē

【喝彩】acclaim; cheer; shout "bravo!": 齐声～ *cheer in chorus*; *cheer with one accord* / 博得全场～ *bring the house down*

【喝倒彩】make catcalls; hoot; boo: 观众～, 这位喜剧演员下了场。*The comedian left the stage because of the catcalls of the audience*.

【喝令】shout an order (or command)

【喝问】shout a question to

褐 Ⅰ 名〈书〉coarse cloth or clothing Ⅱ 形 brown

【褐斑病】[植] brown spot

【褐煤】(又作'褐炭') brown coal; lignite

【褐色土】drab soil

【褐铁矿】brown iron ore; limonite

【褐藻】brown alga

赫 Ⅰ 形 conspicuous; grand: 显赫 Ⅱ 名 (〈略〉见〖赫兹〗)

【赫赫】illustrious; very impressive: ～战功 *illustrious military exploits*; *brilliant military success*

【赫赫有名】distinguished; illustrious: ～的人物 *an illustrious personage*

【赫然】❶ impressively; awesomely: 一只猛虎～出现在山坡上。*To his consternation*, *a fierce tiger suddenly appeared on the mountain slope*. ❷ terribly (angry): ～震怒 *get into a terrible temper*; *fly into a violent rage*

【赫兹】[电] hertz

鹤 名 crane

【鹤发童颜】white hair and ruddy complexion—healthy in old age; hale and hearty

【鹤立鸡群】like a crane standing among chickens—stand head and shoulders above others

【鹤嘴镐】pick; pickaxe; mattock

壑 名 gully; big pool: 千山万～ *innumerable mountains and valleys*

hēi

黑 形 ❶ black: ～发 *black hair* ❷ dark: ～屋子 *a dark room* / 天～了。*It's dark*. ❸ secret; shady: ～交易 *shady deal* ❹ wicked; sinister: 黑心 ❺ reactionary Ⅱ 动 ❶ blackmail: ～了他一把。*He was blackmailed*. ❷ hack: 网站被～ *The website was hacked*.

【黑暗】dark: 山洞里一片～。*It's all darkness in the cave*. / ～统治 *dark rule*; *reactionary rule* / ～面 *a dark aspect*; *the seamy side* / ～势力 *forces of darkness*; *reactionary forces*

【黑白】❶ black and white: ～花儿 *a black-and-white pattern* ❷ right and wrong ◇ ～电视 black-and-white television; ～片 black-and-white film

【黑白分明】with black and white sharply contrasted; in sharp contrast: 两种态度, ～。*The two attitudes stand in sharp contrast*.

【黑斑病】[植] black spot

【黑板】blackboard ◇ ～报 blackboard newspaper; blackboard bulletin

【黑板擦】(blackboard) eraser

【黑帮】reactionary gang; sinister gang; cabal

【黑不溜秋】〈方〉swarthy: 他长得～的。*He is dark and swarthy*. / 这件上衣～的, 一点也不好看。*This jacket is too dark and doesn't look nice at all*.

【黑潮】[地理] black stream; Kuroshio; Japan Current (or Stream)

【黑船】ships used for smuggling and other illegal acts: 这条运"人蛇"的～在纽约港被扣住。*The ship carrying illegal immigrants was detained at New York harbor*.

【黑道】❶ dark road: 拿着电筒, 省得走～。*Take a torch*, *or you'll be groping your way in the dark*. ❷ dark deeds (as of robbers)

【黑灯瞎火】〈口〉dark; unlighted: ～的, 小心别走错路了。*It's dark outside*. *Mind you don't get lost*.

【黑点】stain; blemish; smirch

【黑店】〈旧〉an inn run by brigands

【黑貂】sable: ～皮 *sable fur*

【黑鲷】black porgy

【黑洞】[天] black hole; collapsar

【黑豆】black soya bean

【黑非洲】Black Africa
【黑粉病】同〖黑穗病〗
【黑粪】［医］melaena
【黑钙土】同〖黑土〗❶
【黑咕隆咚】〈口〉very dark；pitch-dark：天还～的，他就起来了。*He got up when it was still pitch-dark*.
【黑光】black light
【黑海】the Black Sea
【黑糊糊】（又作'黑忽忽'；'黑乎乎'）❶ black；blackened：满手油泥，～的 *hands dirty with grease* / 墙熏得～的。*The wall was blackened by smoke*. ❷ rather dark；dusky：屋子里～的。*It's rather dark in the room*. ❸ indistinctly observable in the distance：远处是一片～的树林。*A dark mass of trees loomed in the distance*.
【黑胡椒】black pepper (Piper nigrum)
【黑户】❶ unregistered household；unregistered resident ❷ a shop without a license；an illegal shop
【黑话】❶ (bandits') argot；(thieves') cant ❷ double-talk；malicious words
【黑鲩】another name for 青鱼
【黑会】a clandestine meeting
【黑货】smuggled goods；contraband
【黑胶布】［电］black tape；friction tape
【黑客】hacker (person who tampers with other people's computers through the Internet)：电脑～ *computer hacker* / 该国的军事情报网络曾被～渗透。*The military information networks of the country were penetrated (or breached, or broken into) by hackers*.
【黑牢】dark prison cell
【黑里康大号】［音］helicon
【黑里俏】a dark beauty
【黑瘤】［医］melanoma
【黑马】dark horse—little-known person who unexpectedly becomes successful or prominent：这次竞选中，除了目前领先的候选人以外，还可能出现一两名～。*Apart from the front-runners, there may yet appear one or two dark horses in the election campaign*.
【黑麦】rye
【黑面包】black bread；brown bread；rye bread
【黑名单】blacklist：上了～ *be blacklisted*
【黑木耳】edible black fungus
【黑幕】inside story of a plot, shady deal, etc.：揭穿～ *expose a sinister project；tell the inside story of a plot, etc*.
【黑啤酒】dark beer；black beer；stout
【黑钱】ill-gotten money
【黑枪】❶ illegally possessed firearms ❷ a shot fired from a hiding-place：打～ *fire shots from a hiding-place；snipe*
【黑热病】kala-azar
【黑人】Black people；Black：美国～ *Afro-American；Black American*
【黑色】black (colour) ◇ ～火药 black powder；～金属 ferrous metal；～人种 the black race；～素［生化］Melanin
【黑色星期一】Black Monday(1987年10月19日星期一，这天纽约金融市场出现世界性的股票暴跌。)
【黑色幽默】black humour
【黑纱】black armband
【黑社会】the underworld
【黑市】black market ◇ ～汇兑 black market exchange；～价 black rate；～交易 off-the-books deal；～投机买卖 black market；speculative trading；～票 scalping ticket
【黑手】a vicious person manipulating sb. or sth. from behind the scenes；evil backstage manipulator
【黑手党】Mafia
【黑死病】the plague
【黑穗病】［农］smut
【黑索金】hexogen；cyclonite；RDX
【黑桃】spade (in cards)
【黑陶】black pottery (of a late Neolithic culture) ◇ ～文化 the black pottery culture (another name for 龙山文化)
【黑体】❶［物］blackbody ❷［刷］boldface：～字 *boldface type*
【黑天】night；nightfall：我等她等到～，也没见她来。*I waited until after dark, but she didn't show up*.
【黑土】❶ chernozem；black earth ❷ opium
【黑钨矿】wolframite
【黑匣子】black box
【黑箱】black box ◇ ～理论 black box theory
【黑心】black heart；evil mind
【黑信】〈口〉poison-pen letter
【黑猩猩】chimpanzee
【黑熊】black bear
【黑压压】（又作'黑鸦鸦'）a dense or dark mass of：广场上～地挤满了人。*The square was thronged with a dense crowd*. / 远处～的一片，看不清是些什么东西。*One couldn't make out what the dark mass was from a distance*.
【黑眼镜】sunglasses
【黑眼珠】iris
【黑曜岩】obsidian
【黑夜】night：他们昨天～到了上海。*They arrived in Shanghai last night*. / ～笼罩着大地。*Night enshrouded the earth*.
【黑影儿】a dark shadow；shadow：他一回头，只见有个～一晃而过。*He turned round and saw a shadow flit by*.
【黑油油】jet-black；shiny black：～的头发 *shiny black hair*
【黑黝黝】❶ 同〖黑油油〗❷ dim；dark：四周～的。*It's dark all around*.
【黑鱼】snakeheaded fish；snakehead
【黑云】black clouds；dark clouds
【黑云母】black mica；biotite
【黑枣】dateplum persimmon (Diospyros lotus)
【黑芝麻】Semen sesame nigrum
【黑子】❶〈书〉black mole (on the skin) ❷［天］sunspot

【黑字】surplus：日本将向发展中国家提供几百亿美元的贷款，以便将～还流到"南方"。*Japan is to provide the developing nations with billions of dollars in loans, so that its trade surpluses will flow back to the South.*

嘿 叹 hey；why：～，我说的你听见没有？*Hey! Did you hear what I said?* / ～！快走吧！*Hey, hurry up!* / ～，咱们生产的机器可真不错呀！*Hey, the machine we made is really not bad.* / ～，下雪了！*Why, it's snowing!* / ～，真没想到！*Well, what do you know?*

hén

痕 名 mark；trace：刀痕

【痕迹】mark；trace；vestige：轮子的～ *wheel tracks* / 旧社会的～ *vestiges of the old sociey* / 罪犯没有留下任何作案的～。*The criminal didn't leave behind any trace of his crime.*

【痕量】（又作'痕迹量'）［化］trace：～元素 *trace elements* / ～杂质 *trace impurity*

hěn

很 副 very；very much；quite：我家离学校～近。*I live quite near the school.* / 这故事发生在～久～久以前。*The story took place a long long time ago.* / 这几天热得～。*It's been very hot these last few days.*

狠 Ⅰ 形 ❶ ruthless；relentless：比豺狼还～ *more savage than a wolf* ❷ firm；resolute；severe：我把他～～打了一顿。*I gave him a good beating.* / ～批了他一顿。*He was severely criticized.* / ～～打击歪风邪气 *take vigorous measures to counter evil trends* Ⅱ 动 harden (the heart)；suppress (one's feelings)：狠心

【狠毒】vicious；venomous：用心～ *with vicious intent*

【狠命】〈方〉go all out

【狠心】❶ harden one's heart；make a painful decision：我一～，打了他一顿。*I hardened my heart and gave him a beating.* / 我狠不下心去。*I can't make such a painful decision.* ❷ cruel；heartless；callous：你真～。*You are being rather callous.*

hèn

恨 动 ❶ hate：她～你就因为你说了那句话。*She hates you for saying that.* ❷ regret：遗恨

【恨不得】（又作'恨不能'）one wishes one could；one would if one could；be dying to：我～立刻就去。*I wish I could go immediately.* / 我～立刻就认识他。*I'm dying to meet him.*

【恨铁不成钢】wish that iron could turn straight into steel—be anxious for sb. to improve

【恨之入骨】hate sb. to the marrow of one's bones；bear a bitter hatred for sb.；bitterly hate

hēng

亨 形 go smoothly：亨通

【亨利】［电］henry：微～ *microhenry*

【亨通】go smoothly；be prosperous：万事～。*Everything is going smoothly.*

哼 动 ❶ groan；snort：痛得直～～ *groan with pain* / 轻蔑地～了一声 *give a snort of contempt* ❷ hum；croon：他一边走，一边～着曲子。*He was humming a tune as he walked along.* / ～着歌儿哄孩子睡觉 *croon the baby to sleep* ——另见 hng

【哼哧】puff hard：他跑得～～地直喘。*He was puffing and blowing from running.*

【哼哈二将】a pair of fierce men serving one master or acting in collusion with each other

【哼唧】mutter；hum

【哼儿哈儿】hem and haw：他总是～的，就是不说句痛快话。*He hemmed and hawed but wouldn't say anything definite.*

【哼唷】heave ho；yo-heave-ho；yo-ho

héng

恒 Ⅰ 形 ❶ permanent；lasting：永恒 ❷ usual；common；constant：恒言 Ⅱ 名 perseverance：有恒

【恒齿】（又作'恒牙'）permanent tooth

【恒等】［数］identically equal；identical：～式 *identical equation；identity*

【恒定】constant

【恒河沙数】as numerous as the sands of the Ganges；innumerable；countless

【恒久】permanent；lasting；enduring

【恒量】［物］constant

【恒流调节器】［电］constant current regulator

【恒生】Hang Sang：～银行 *Hang Sang Bank* / ～指数 *Hang Sang Index*

【恒温】constant temperature：～器 *thermostat* ◇ ～动物 homoiothermal (or warm-blooded) animal；～箱［医］incubator；thermostated container

【恒心】perseverance；constancy of purpose：你要是没有～可学不好。*Unless you persevere with a subject you can't hope to master it.*

【恒星】(fixed) star ◇ ～年［天］sidereal year；～日［天］sidereal day；～时［天］sidereal time；～天文学［天］stellar astronomy；～物理学［天］stellar physics；～系［天］stellar system；galaxy；～月［天］sidereal month；～云［天］star cloud

【恒压器】barostat

【恒言】common saying

【恒阻网络】constant resistance network

珩 名 the top gem of a girdle-pendant (as worn by aristocrats and high officials in ancient China)

桁 名［建］purlin

【桁架】［建］truss：～桥 *truss bridge*

【桁条】［建］purlin

横 Ⅰ形 ❶ horizontal; transverse：～线 *a horizontal line* ❷ from east to west or from west to east：横贯 ❸ crosswise; sideways：中文也能～着写。*Chinese can also be written across the page.* / 一棵倒了的树～在马路上。*A fallen tree lay across the road.* ❹ at a right angle to：横剖面 Ⅱ动 place sth. crosswise or horizontally：把扁担～过来。*Put the carrying pole in a horizontal position.* / 把这个桌子～过来。*Turn this table and place it crosswise.* / ～刀跃马 *gallop ahead with sword drawn* Ⅲ副 unrestrained; turbulent：蔓草～生 *overgrown with creepers* / 老泪～流 *tears flowing from aged eyes* Ⅳ名 horizontal stroke (in a Chinese character) ——另见 hèng

【横波】［物］transverse wave

【横冲直撞】push one's way by shoving or bumping; jostle and elbow one's way; dash around madly; barge about; charge about

【横穿】cross：～马路 *cross a street*

【横档】crosspiece (of a table, etc.)

【横倒竖歪】in disorder; higgledy-piggledy

【横笛】bamboo flute

【横渡】cross a river, etc.：～太平洋的飞行 *a trans-Pacific flight*

【横断面】同〖横剖面〗

【横队】rank; row：排成三列～ *line up three deep*

【横幅】❶ horizontal scroll of painting or calligraphy ❷ banner; streamer：欢迎群众举着～标语。*The welcoming crowd carried banners with slogans on them.*

【横杆】cross bar; beam

【横杠】wippletree; wiffletree

【横格纸】lined paper

【横膈膜】［生理］diaphragm

【横亘】lie across; span：一座雄伟的大桥～在江上。*A magnificent bridge spans the river.*

【横贯】pass through from east to west or from west to east; traverse：黄河～本省。*The Yellow River flows through this province from west to east.* / 这条铁路～五省。*The railway traverses five provinces.*

【横巷】［矿］crosscut

【横祸】unexpected calamity; sudden misfortune

【横加】do sth. to sb. unreasonably, forcibly, wilfully, etc.：～指责 *make unwarranted charges* / ～干涉 *flagrantly interfere* / ～阻挠 *wilfully obstruct*

【横结肠】［生理］transverse colon

【横跨】stretch over or across：一道彩虹～天际。*A rainbow arched across the sky.* / ～长江的大桥 *a gigantic bridge spanning the Changjiang River*

【横梁】❶［建］crossbeam ❷ cross member (of a car)

【横眉】frown in anger; scowl

【横眉冷对千夫指，俯首甘为孺子牛】fierce-browed, I coolly defy a thousand pointing fingers; head bowed, like a willing ox I serve the children

【横眉怒目】with frowning brows and angry eyes; darting fierce looks of hate

【横眉竖眼】glare in anger

【横拍握法】tennis grip; handshake grip

【横批】a horizontal scroll bearing an inscription (usu. hung over a door and flanked by two vertical scrolls forming a couplet)

【横披】a horizontal wall inscription; a horizontal hanging scroll

【横剖面】cross (or transverse) section

【横七竖八】in disorder; at sixes and sevens; higgledy-piggledy：满院子～的绳子上，晒着各家的破衣破被。*Lines are strung across here and there on which the families have hung out their old and tattered clothes and bedding to dry.* / 屋子里～地堆放着许多杂物。*The room was cluttered with all sorts of things.*

【横切】crosscut

【横肉】fierce-looking：一脸～ *look ugly and ferocious*

【横扫】❶ sweep across; sweep away; make a clean sweep of：～一切 *sweep everything away; be overwhelming* ❷ glance quickly from side to side：他向大家～了一眼，才开口讲话。*He threw a glance across the room before he started to speak.*

【横生】❶ grow wild：蔓草～ *be overgrown with weeds* ❷ be overflowing with; be full of ❸ happen unexpectedly：～是非 *a dispute unexpectedly broke out*

【横生枝节】raise unexpected difficulties; deliberately complicate an issue

【横竖】〈口〉in any case; anyway：～我要去的，不用给他打电话了。*No need to ring him up. I'll be going there anyway.*

【横挑鼻子竖挑眼】〈口〉find fault in a petty manner; pick holes in sth.; nitpick

【横尾翼】［航空］tail plane; horizontal stabilizer

【横纹肌】striated muscle

【横向】horizontal; crosswise：发展沿海开放城市同内地的～经济联合 *expand the horizontal economic collaboration (or ties) of the open coastal cities with the interior areas* ◇ ～联合 horizontal linkage

【横心】steel one's heart; become desperate：横下一条心 *resolve to do sth. in desperation*

【横行】run wild; run amuck; be on a rampage：盗匪～。*Banditry was rife.*

【横行霸道】ride roughshod over; trample on; tyrannize; domineer：～，为所欲为 *act like an overlord and do whatever one wishes*

【横行无忌】run wild; run amuck

【横行一时】run wild for a time

【横移】sidesway

【横溢】❶(of a river) overflow; be in flood: 江河～ *turbulent waters overflowing their banks* ❷(of talent, enthusiasm, etc.) brimming; overflowing; abundant: 才气～ *brimming with talent* / 热情～ *overflowing with enthusiasm*

【横征暴敛】extort excessive (or heavy) taxes and levies; levy exorbitant taxes: 利用独裁权力～ *use one's dictatorial powers to extort taxes and levies*

【横轴】[机] cross axle (or shaft)

【横坐标】[数] abscissa

衡

Ⅰ 名 ❶ the graduated arm of a steelyard ❷ weighing apparatus Ⅱ 动 weigh; measure; judge: 衡量

【衡量】weigh; measure; judge: 用政治标准来～ *measure sth. or judge sb. by political criteria* / 请你～一下这件事该怎么办。*Will you please consider what to do about it?* / ～得失 *weigh up the gains and losses*

【衡器】weighing apparatus

【衡情度理】considering the circumstances and judging by common sense; all things considered

hèng

横

形 ❶ harsh and unreasonable; perverse: ～话 *harsh, unreasonable words* ❷ unexpected: ——另见 héng

【横暴】perverse and violent

【横财】ill-gotten wealth (or gains): 发～ *get rich by foul means*

【横死】die a violent death; meet with a sudden death

【横议】〈书〉comment without reserve; make unbridled criticism

hng

哼

叹 (expressing disapproval or suspicion) humph: ～，谁信你的！*Humph! Who believes what you say?* ——另见 hēng

hōng

轰

Ⅰ 象 bang; boom: ～的一声，敌人的碉堡给炸飞了。*The enemy pillbox was blown up with a bang.* / ～！～！～！一连串爆破声震撼山谷。*Boom! Boom! Boom! A series of explosions shook the valley.* Ⅱ 动 ❶ rumble; bombard; explode: 雷～电闪。*Thunder rumbled and lightning flashed.* / 万炮齐～ *ten thousand cannons booming* ❷ shoo away; drive off: ～麻雀 *shoo away the sparrows* / ～下台 *hoot sb. off the platform; oust sb. from office (or power)* / 把他～出去。*Throw him out.*

【轰动】cause a sensation; make a stir: ～全国 *cause a sensation throughout the country* / 全场～ *make a stir in the audience (or in the hall)* ◇ ～效应 sensational effect

【轰动一时】create a furore; make a great stir; cause a great sensation: ～的谋杀案 *a sensational murder case* / 这部电影曾～。*The film was a great hit.*

【轰赶】shoo away; drive off: ～鸡 *shoo the chickens away* / ～苍蝇 *whisk the flies off*

【轰轰烈烈】on a grand and spectacular scale; vigorous; dynamic: ～的群众运动 *vigorous mass movements*

【轰击】❶ shell; bombard: ～敌人阵地 *shell enemy positions* ❷ [物] bombard: 中子～ *neutron bombardment*

【轰隆】rumble; roll: 雷声～～地响。*Thunder rumbled.* / ～的机器声 *the hum of machines*

【轰鸣】thunder; roar: 马达～。*Motors roared.* / 雷声～。*There was a peal of thunder.*

【轰撵】force out, expel: 买卖房屋的任何一方不得～住户搬家。*Both parties to a housing-contract are forbidden to evict the current occupant of the house.*

【轰然】with a loud crash (or bang)

【轰响】roar; rumble: 大炮～。*The cannons roared.* / 货车～着开过去了。*The lorry roared past.*

【轰炸】attack with bombs; bomb: ～陆地目标 *bomb targets on the ground* / 昨天有五架敌机前来～。*Five enemy planes came to bomb us yesterday.* ◇ ～机 bomber; ～瞄准具 bombsight; ～误差 bombing error

哄

Ⅰ 象 roars of laughter Ⅱ 动 hubbub ——另见 hǒng; hòng

【哄传】(of rumours) circulate widely: 这个消息很快就～开了。*It was not long before the news was widely circulated.*

【哄抢】(of a crowd of people) make a mad rush for; make a scramble for (public property, goods, etc.)

【哄然】boisterous; uproarious: ～大笑 *burst into uproarious laughter* / 舆论～。*There was a public outcry.*

【哄抬】drive up (prices)

【哄堂大笑】the whole room rocking with laughter: 引起听众～ *make the audience roar with laughter* / 众人听了，～起来。*The whole party exploded in fits of mirth.*

烘

动 ❶ dry or warm by the fire: ～手 *warm one's hands at the fire* / 把湿衣服～一～ *dry wet clothes by the fire* / ～面包 *bake bread* ❷ set off: 烘托

【烘焙】cure (tea or tobacco leaves)

【烘干】❶ dry over heat: 把湿衣服～ *dry wet clothes over the fire* ❷ [化] stoving

【烘缸】dryer

【烘烘】the sound of a roaring fire
【烘烤】toast；bake：～面包 *bake bread* / 大家围着火堆，～着冻得发僵的手。*Everybody sat round the fire, warming their frozen hands.*
【烘漆】baking finish；stoving finish
【烘丝机】cut-tobacco drier
【烘托】❶（in Chinese painting）add shading around an object to make it stand out ❷ set off by contrast；throw into sharp relief：～出音乐的主题 *set off the leitmotiv by contrast*
【烘箱】oven
【烘相器】［摄］print drier
【烘云托月】paint clouds to set off the moon；provide a foil for a character or incident in a literary work：收到了～的艺术效果 *achieve the artistic effect of prominence through contrast*

hóng

弘 Ⅰ 形 great；grand；magnificent Ⅱ 动 enlarge；expand
【弘扬】carry forward；develop；enhance：～五四精神 *carry forward the spirit of the May 4th Movement*

红 Ⅰ 形 ❶ red：～墙绿瓦 *a red ochre wall with green tiles* / 他的眼睛都熬～了。*His eyes become bloodshot from lack of sleep.* / 脸上～一阵白一阵 *flush and turn pale by turns* ❷ revolutionary；red：～五月 *the red month of May* ❸ successful：他是个很～的歌星。*He's a very popular singer.* Ⅱ 名 ❶ red cloth，bunting，etc. used on festive occasions：披红 ❷ bonus；dividend：分红
【红白喜事】weddings and funerals：什么～，讨媳妇，死了人，大办酒席，实在可以不必。*When people wear red or white, that is, at weddings or funerals, the practice of giving lavish feasts can well be dispensed with.*
【红斑】［医］erythema ◇ ～狼疮 lupus erythematosus
【红榜】honour roll（or board）
【红包】a red paper envelope containing money as a gift，tip，or bonus
【红宝石】ruby
【红菜头】beetroot
【红茶】black tea
【红场】Red Square（in Moscow）
【红潮】❶ blush；flush：人家一夸，她脸上就泛起～。*She blushes when praised.* ❷［生］red tide；red water
【红尘】the world of mortals；human society
【红丹】［化］red lead；minium ◇ ～漆 red lead paint
【红得发紫】（of a person）extremely popular：三十年代他～，战后就默默无闻了。*He reached the height of his popularity in the thirties, and was all but forgotten after the war.*
【红灯区】red-light district
【红电气石】［矿］rubellite
【红豆】❶ ormasia ❷ love pea
【红粉】rouge and powder-women
【红汞】［药］mercurochrome
【红骨顶】［动］moorhen
【红光满面】one's face glowing with health；in the pink
【红果】〈方〉the fruit of large Chinese hawthorn；haw
【红海】the Red Sea
【红鹤】ibis
【红狐】red fox
【红花】［中］safflower
【红货】〈旧〉pearls and jewels；jewelry
【红火】〈方〉flourishing；prosperous：石榴花越开越～。*The pomegranate flowers were more and more flourishing.* / 他们的日子越过越～。*Their days are becoming better and better.* / 晚会开得很～。*The evening party was a great success.*
【红极一时】be well-known for a time；enjoy popularity for a time
【红脚鹬】redshank
【红军】❶ the Chinese Workers' and Peasants' Red Army（1928—1937）；the Red Army ❷ Red Army man ❸ Soviet Union army before 1946
【红利】bonus；extra dividend ◇ ～分配 profit sharing；～股 bonus dividend；bonus stock
【红脸】❶ blush：这小孩跟生人说话爱～。*This child often blushes when speaking to strangers.* ❷ flush with anger；get angry：他俩从来没有红过脸。*There has never been a cross word between the two of them.* ❸ red face，face painting in Beijing opera，etc.，traditionally for the heroic or the honest ——另见〖唱红脸〗
【红磷】red phosphorus
【红铃虫】pink bollworm
【红领巾】❶ red scarf（worn by Young Pioneers）❷ Young Pioneer
【红领章】red collar tab（as formerly on PLA uniforms）
【红绿灯】traffic light；traffic signal
【红麻】［植］bluish dogbane（Apocynum venetum）
【红媒】matchmaker；go-between
【红霉】erythromycin
【红焖】stew in soy sauce：～鸡 *stewed chicken*
【红米】red rice
【红模子】a sheet of paper with red characters printed on it，to be traced over with a brush by children learning calligraphy
【红木】padauk；mahogany：～家具 *mahogany furniture*
【红男绿女】young men and women in love：公园里一对对～，牵手偕行。*Gaily dressed young couples walked hand in hand in the park.*
【红娘】go between；matchmaker
【红娘鱼】sea robin；red gurnard
【红牌】［体］red card
【红喷喷】reddish；with a red tint：～的苹果 *red apples* / 姑娘脸颊～的，挂着微笑。*The girl had*

rosy cheeks, brightened by a smile.

【红皮书】red paper; red book

【红扑扑】flushed: 喝了几杯酒,脸上~的。*After a few drinks his face flushed.*

【红旗】red flag or banner (often as a symbol of the proletarian revolution or of an advanced unit): 在~下长大 *be brought up under the red flag; grow up in socialist society* ◇ ~单位 red-banner unit; advanced unit; ~手 red-banner pacesetter; advanced worker

【红壤】(又作'红土') red soil (or earth)

【红人】a favourite with sb. in power; fair-haired boy: 部长的~ *a favourite with the Minister*

【红润】ruddy; rosy: 脸色~ *ruddy complexion; rosy cheeks*

【红三叶】red clover

【红色】❶ red ❷ revolutionary; red: ~政权 *red political power*

【红色警戒】red alert

【红杉】Chinese larch

【红烧】braise in soy sauce: ~肉 *pork braised in brown sauce; red-cooked pork*

【红十字会】the Red Cross

【红树】mangrove

【红松】Korean pine

【红糖】brown sugar

【红桃】heart (in cards)

【红陶】red pottery; terra-cotta

【红藤】Sargent gloryvine (Sargentodoxa cuneata)

【红彤彤】(又作'红通通') bright red; glowing: ~的火苗 *glowing red flames* / 他脸儿晒得~的。*His face is aglow from exposure to the sun.*

【红外线】(又作'红外光','热线') infrared; infrared ray ◇ ~辐射 infrared radiation; ~扫描装置 infrared scanner; ~探测器 infrared detector; 遥感技术 infrared remote sensing technique; ~照相 infrared photography

【红外照相】infrared photography

【红头文件】official documents with the name of the issuing department printed in red: 老罗觉得他什么都不信,只认~。*Old Luo said he only believes in official documents.*

【红细胞】red blood cell; erythrocyte: ~计数 *red cell count*

【红小豆】red bean

【红心】a red heart—a heart loyal to the cause of proletarian revolution: 一颗~为人民 *with a red heart always loyal to the people*

【红星】red star (a symbol of the proletarian revolution): ~帽徽 *red star cap insignia (of PLA soldiers)*

【红学】studies of the Hongloumeng (《红楼梦》, A Dream of Red Mansions); Hongloumeng scholarship; Red-ology: ~家 *Hongloumeng scholar*

【红血球】red blood cell; erythrocyte

【红颜】〈文〉a pretty face—a beautiful woman

【红颜薄命】beautiful women suffer unhappy fates

【红眼】❶ become infuriated; see red: 别再跟他闹了,再闹,他可要~了。*Don't tease him any more or he'll see red in a minute.* ❷〈方〉be envious; be jealous of: 一见别人收入比他多,他就~。*He is always jealous of people who earn more than he does.*

【红眼病】❶ popular name for 结膜炎 ❷ envy; jealousy

【红艳艳】brilliant red: ~的杜鹃花 *bright red azaleas*

【红药水】mercurochrome

【红叶】red autumnal leaves (of the maple, etc.)

【红衣主教】[宗](基督教) cardinal

【红缨枪】red-tasselled spear

【红鱼】(red) snapper

【红运】good luck: 走~ *have a spate of good luck*

【红晕】blush; flush: 脸上泛出~ *one's face blushing scarlet*

【红枣】red date

【红藻】red alga

【红蜘蛛】〈方〉red spider (mite); spider mite

【红肿】red and swollen

【红柱石】[地质] andalusite

【红装】(又作'红妆')〈文〉❶ gay feminine attire ❷ young woman

【红装素裹】clad in white, adorned in red (said of a sunlit snow scene)

宏

形 great; grand; magnificent

【宏程序】macroprogram

【宏大】grand; great: 规模~ *on a grand scale* / ~的计划 *a great plan* / ~的志愿 *great aspirations*

【宏代码】macro-code

【宏观】❶ [物] macroscopic ❷ macro: ~经济效益 *macroeconomic results* / 越是搞活经济,越要重视~调节。*The more the economy is enlivened, the more attention we should pay to macroeconomic regulation.* / 把~管理和微观搞活结合起来。*Combine macro-control and micro-flexibility.* ◇ ~结构 macrostructure; ~经济管理 macro-economic management; macro-economic control; ~经济调控 macro-economic regulation and control; ~经济调整 macro-economic regulation; macro-economic adjustment; ~经济效益 macro-economic results; ~经济学 macroeconomics; ~世界 macrocosm; ~决策 macro-level policy making

【宏论】informed opinion; intelligent view

【宏图】great plan; grand prospect: 发展国民经济的~ *great plans for developing the national economy*

【宏伟】magnificent; grand: ~的人民大会堂 *the magnificent Great Hall of the People* / ~的前景 *grand prospects* / 一项~壮丽的事业 *a magnificent undertaking*

【宏愿】great aspirations; noble ambition: 改造自然的~ *the great aspirations to reshape nature* / 中国女排实现了三连冠的~。*The Chinese women's volleyball team realized their great ambition of winning the world championship three times in succession.*

【宏旨】main theme; leading idea of an article
【宏指令】macro instruction

泓 Ⅰ 形〈书〉(of water) deep Ⅱ 量 (used of clear water): 一～清泉 *a clear spring* / 一～秋水 *an expanse of limpid water in autumn*

洪 Ⅰ 形 ❶ big; vast: 洪亮 Ⅱ 名 flood: 防洪
【洪大】loud: ～的回声 *resounding echoes*
【洪都拉斯】Honduras ◇ ～人 Honduran
【洪泛区】floodplain; flooded area
【洪峰】flood peak
【洪福齐天】limitless blessing
【洪荒】chaotic state-primeval times: ～时代 *primeval ages; remote antiquity*
【洪亮】loud and clear; sonorous: 嗓音～ *a sonorous voice*
【洪量】❶ magnanimity; generosity ❷ great capacity for liquor
【洪流】mighty torrent; powerful current: 木筏顺着～远下。*The mighty torrent carried the raft far downstream.* / 时代的～ *the powerful current of the times*
【洪炉】great furnace: 在革命的～里锻炼成长 *be tempered in the mighty furnace of revolution*
【洪脉】[中] pulse beating like waves; full pulse
【洪水】flood; floodwater: ～位 *flood level*
【洪水猛兽】fierce floods and savage beasts-great scourges
【洪讯】flood information; flood message
【洪灾】a big flood; inundation
【洪钟】〈书〉large bell: 声如～ *have a stentorian (or sonorous) voice*

虹 名 rainbow
【虹彩】old name for 虹膜
【虹膜】[生理] Iris ◇ ～炎 fliritis
【虹吸管】siphon
【虹吸现象】siphonage
【虹雉】monal

鸿 Ⅰ 名 ❶swan goose ❷〈书〉letter Ⅱ 形 great; grand
【鸿沟】wide gap; chasm; gulf
【鸿鹄】❶ swan ❷ a person of noble aspirations; a person with lofty ideals
【鸿鹄之志】lofty ambition; high aspirations
【鸿毛】〈文〉goose feather-something very light or insignificant
【鸿门宴】Hongmen feast—a meeting contrived as a trap
【鸿篇巨制】a monumental work
【鸿雁】swan goose
【鸿运】good luck

hǒng

哄 动 ❶ fool; humbug: 你这是～我。我不信。*You're kidding me; I don't believe it.* ❷ keep (esp. a child) in good humour; coax: ～孩子 *keep a child in good humour* ——另见 hōng; hòng
【哄逗】keep (esp. a child) in good humour; coax: 她很会～孩子。*She knows how to handle children.* or *She has a way with children.*
【哄骗】cheat; humbug; hoodwink: 他编了一套假话来～人。*He made up a string of lies to hoodwink people.*
【哄劝】coax: ～孩子吃药 *coax a child to take medicine*

hòng

哄 名 uproar; horseplay: 起哄 ——另见 hōng; hǒng
【哄场】make catcalls; hoot; boo——另见 hóng

hóu

侯 名 ❶ marquis: 侯爵 ❷ a nobleman or a high official: 侯门似海
【侯爵】marquis ◇ ～夫人 marquise
【侯门似海】the gate of a noble house is like the sea—impassable to the common man

喉 名 larynx; throat
【喉擦音】[语音] guttural fricative
【喉急】〈方〉feel anxious; feel worried
【猴儿精】〈方〉❶ astute; shrewd; smart: 这小子～的。*That fellow is awfully shrewd.* ❷ clever and mischievous person; mischief-maker: 这孩子是个～。*The boy is a mischief-maker.*
【喉结】[生理] Adam's apple
【喉镜】[医] laryngoscope: ～检查 *laryngoscopy*
【喉咙】throat: ～痛 *have a sore throat* / 他～叫哑了。*He shouted himself hoarse.* / 我渴得～里冒烟。*My throat feels parched.*
【喉塞音】[语音] glottal stop
【喉痧】[中] scarlet fever
【喉舌】mouthpiece: 人民的～ *the mouthpiece of the people*
【喉头】larynx; throat
【喉炎】laryngitis

猴 Ⅰ 名 monkey Ⅱ 形〈方〉naughty (boy)
【猴面包树】[植] monkey-bread tree; baobab
【猴皮筋儿】(又作'猴儿筋')〈口〉rubber band
【猴年马月】impossible date; day that will never come: 那要等到～! *I'm afraid we'll be waiting for all eternity!*
【猴拳】[体] monkey boxing (in wushu): 打～ *play monkey boxing*
【猴头】[植] hedgehog hydnum (Hydnum erinaceus)
【猴戏】a show by a performing monkey; monkey show: 耍～ *give a monkey show*
【猴子】monkey

瘊 (构词成分)见下

【瘊子】common name for 疣

hǒu

吼 动 roar; howl: 狮～ *the roar of a lion* / 汽笛长～了一声。*The siren sounded loud and long.* / 远方传来大炮的～声。*Guns rumbled in the distance.* / 示威群众愤怒的～声 *the angry shouts of the demonstrators*

【吼叫】roar; howl; shout: 伤员痛楚地～。*The wounded soldier shouted in pain.* / 狂风～着穿过树林。*The wind howled through the trees.*

hòu

后 名 ❶ behind; back; rear: 村前村～ *in front of and behind the village* / 屋～ *behind (or at the back of) a house* ❷ after; afterwards; later: 课～ *after class* ❸ last: ～五名 *the last five (persons)* ❹ offspring: 无后 ❺ empress; queen

【后半生】(又作'后半辈子') the latter half of one's life

【后半天】afternoon

【后半叶】latter half of a century: 十九世纪～ *the latter half of 19th century*

【后半夜】the second half of the night; the small hours

【后备】reserve: 留有～ *keep sth. in reserve* / ～力量 *reserve forces* / ～基金 *reserve fund* ◇ ～部队[军] reserve units; ～干部 reserve cadre; cadres in support; ～军 reserve force

【后背】❶ back (of the body): 他～上长了个疮。*He has a boil on his back.* ❷ 〈方〉 at the back; in the rear: 从～袭击敌人 *attack the enemy from the rear*

【后辈】❶ younger generation; juniors ❷ posterity

【后步】room for manoeuvre: 留～ *leave sufficient room for manoeuvre*

【后场】backcourt

【后尘】〈书〉 dust kicked up by sb. walking in front

【后处理】❶ [化] aftertreatment ❷ [纺] finishing

【后代】❶ later periods (in history); later ages ❷ later generations; descendants; posterity: 为～着想 *for the sake of future generations; in the interest of future generations* ❸ [生] progeny

【后灯】taillight (of a car); tail lamp

【后爹】〈口〉 stepfather

【后盾】backing; backup force: 坚强的～ *powerful backing*

【后发制人】gain mastery by striking only after the enemy or adversary has struck: 有的时候,我们可以～。*Sometimes we may subdue the enemy by striking after he has struck the first blow.*

【后方】❶ rear: ～工作 *rear-area work; work in the rear* / ～勤务 *rear service; logistics (service)* / ～医院 *base (or rear) hospital* ❷ behind

【后福】❶ future blessings ❷ blessings in one's old age

【后跟】heel (of a shoe or sock)

【后宫】❶ imperial harem; palace of imperial concubines ❷ imperial concubines

【后工业化】postindustrialism

【后顾】❶ turn back (to take care of sth.): 无暇～ *have no time to look after things one has left behind* ❷ look back (on the past): ～与前瞻 *look back to the past and ahead into the future*

【后顾之忧】fear of disturbance in the rear; trouble back at home: 孩子有人照管,父母上班没有～。*With the baby well cared for, the parents will be free of worries at work.*

【后滚翻】[体] backward roll

【后果】consequence; aftermath: 承担～ *accept the consequences* / ～不堪设想。*The consequences would be too ghastly to contemplate.* or *The consequences would be disastrous.*

【后花园】back garden

【后话】part of a story to be recounted later; part of a story that is to come: 这是～,暂且不提。*That's what happened later, so no more of it now.*

【后患】future trouble: 根除～ *dig up the root of (or remove the cause of) future trouble*

【后患无穷】no end of trouble for the future

【后悔】regret; repent: ～不已 *be overcome with regret* / 我很～当初没有听他的话。*I regret that I didn't heed his advice.*

【后悔莫及】too late to repent: 你会感到～。*You will find it too late for regrets.*

【后会有期】we'll meet again some day: ～,请多保重。*We shall meet again. Till then take good care of yourself.*

【后记】postscript (added to a finished book, etc.)

【后继】succeed; carry on

【后继无人】leave no successor (to carry on a tradition, transmit an art or craft, etc.)

【后继有人】there is no lack of successors; there's another generation to carry on

【后脚】❶ the rear foot (in walking): 前脚一滑,～也站不稳。*As the front foot slipped, the rear foot became unsteady.* ❷ (used after 前脚) close behind: 我前脚到车站,他～就赶到了。*Immediately after I got to the station, he arrived.*

【后襟】the back of a Chinese robe or jacket

【后进】❶ lagging behind; less advanced; backward: 见～就帮 *ready to help those who lag behind* / ～赶先进 *the less advanced striving to catch up with the more advanced* ❷ juniors

【后劲】❶ delayed effect; aftereffect: 这酒～大。*This wine has a strong delayed effect.* ❷ reserve strength; stamina: 他干活有～。*He has staying power when he's doing a job.* / 长跑运动员～得足。*Long-distance runners require plenty of stamina.*

【后景】background (of a picture)

【后空翻】[体] backward somersault
【后来】afterwards; later: ～怎么样? *What happened afterwards?* / ～的情况好多了。*Things got much better later on.*
【后来居上】the latecomers surpass the old-timers
【后来人】successors: 革命自有～。*There is no lack of successors to carry on the revolutionary cause.*
【后浪推前浪】the waves behind drive on those before: 长江～,一代更比一代强。*As in the Changjiang River the waves behind drive on those before, so each new generation excels the last one.*
【后路】❶ communication lines to the rear; route of retreat: 抄～ *attack from the rear* / 切断敌人～ *cut off the enemy's route of retreat* ❷ room for manoeuvre; a way of escape
【后掠角】[航空] sweep angle; sweepback
【后掠翼】[航空] swept-back wing
【后轮】rear wheel
【后妈】〈口〉stepmother
【后门】❶ back door (or gate): 大院的～ *the back gate of a compound* ❷ backdoor (or backstairs) influence
【后面】❶ at the back; in the rear; behind: ～还有座位。*There are vacant seats at the back.* ❷ later: 这个问题我～还要讲。*I'll come back to this question later.*
【后母】stepmother
【后脑】hindbrain; rhombencephalon ◇ ～勺子(又作'后脑勺儿')〈方〉the back of the head
【后年】the year after next
【后娘】〈口〉stepmother
【后怕】fear after the event: 事过之后,我倒真有些～。*After it was all over, I became really scared.*
【后排】back row: ～座位 *back row seats*
【后期】later stage; later period: 解放战争～ *the later stage of the War of Liberation* / 十九世纪四十年代～ *the late 1840s*
【后起】(of people of talent) of new arrivals; of the younger generation: ～的乒坛好手 *the younger generation of crack table-tennis players* / ～的青年作家 *budding young writers*
【后起之秀】an up-and-coming youngster; a promising young person
【后桥】rear (or back) axle (of a car): ～壳 *rear axle housing*
【后勤】rear service; logistics: ～部 *rear-service department; logistics department (or command)* / ～部队 *rear-service units; rear services* / ～机关 *rear-service establishments* / ～基地 *logistics base; rear supply base* / ～人员 *rear-service personnel* / ～支援 *logistic support*
【后人】❶ later generations ❷ posterity; descendants
【后任】successor (to a post)
【后三角队形】[军] V formation
【后身】❶ the back of a person: 我只看见个～,认不清是谁。*I couldn't make out who he was as I only saw his back.* ❷ the back of a garment: 这件衬衫的～太长了。*The back of the shirt is too long.*
【后生】〈方〉❶ young man; lad ❷ having a youthful appearance: 他长得～,看不出是四十岁的人。*He's forty but looks much younger.*
【后生可畏】a youth is to be regarded with respect
【后世】❶ later ages: 《诗经》对～的文学有很大的影响。*The Book of Songs had great influence on the literature of later ages.* ❷ later generations: ～子孙 *descendants; posterity*
【后事】❶ (usu. used in traditional novels) what happened afterwards: 欲知～如何,且听下回分解。*If you want to know what happened afterwards, read the next chapter.* ❷ funeral affairs
【后视镜】rearview (or rear-vision) mirror (as inside a car)
【后视图】[机] back view; rearview
【后手】❶〈旧〉successor ❷ defensive position (in chess): 这一着儿一走错,你就变成～了。*By this false move you've forced yourself into the defensive.* ❸ room for manoeuvre; a way of escape
【后手翻】back handspring
【后送】[军] evacuation
【后台】❶ backstage ❷ backstage supporter; behind the scenes backer: ～很硬 *have very strong backing* ◇ ～程序 background program; ～老板 backstage boss; backstage supporter; behind-the-scenes backer
【后天】❶ (又作'后日') day after tomorrow ❷ postnatal; acquired: 知识是～获得的,不是先天就有的。*Knowledge is acquired, not innate.*
【后天免疫缺损综合症】acquired immunodeficiency syndrome; acquired immune deficiency syndrome (Aids)
【后头】❶ at the back; in the rear; behind ❷ later; future: 吃苦还在～呢。*The worst is yet to come.*
【后腿】hind legs
【后退】draw back; fall back; retreat: 主动～,以便歼灭更多敌人 *retreat on one's own initiative in order to wipe out more enemy troops* / 遇到困难决不～ *never shrink from difficulties*
【后卫】❶ [军] rear guard: ～战斗 *rear-guard action* ❷ [体](足球) full back; defender ❸ [体](篮球) guard
【后现代主义】post-modernism
【后项】[数] consequent
【后续】❶ follow-up: ～部队 *follow-up units* / ～会议 *follow-up meeting* ❷〈方〉remarry after the death of one's wife
【后悬】rear overhang (of a car)
【后腰】〈口〉the small of the back
【后遗症】❶ sequelae: 脑震荡～ *sequelae of cerebral concussion* ❷ aftereffect; aftermath
【后裔】descendant (of a dead person); offspring
【后影】the shape of a person or thing as seen from the back: 看～像是小李。*From the back view I thought he must be Xiao Li.*
【后援】reinforcements; backup force; backing

【后院】backyard
【后者】the latter
【后肢】hind legs (of an animal)
【后轴】rear axle
【后缀】suffix
【后坐力】recoil
【后座议员】backbencher

厚 Ⅰ 形 ❶ thick：～木板 *a thick plank* / ～棉衣 *a heavy padded coat* / 一尺～的雪 *snow one chi deep* ❷ deep；profound：交情很～ *profound friendship* ❸ kind；magnanimous：忠厚 ❹ large；generous：厚利 ❺ rich or strong in flavour：酒味很～。*The wine tastes strong.* Ⅱ 动 favour；stress：厚此薄彼
【厚爱】〈套〉your kind thought；your kindness：承蒙～，赠我画册，十分感谢。*Thank you for your kindness in giving me this lovely collection of paintings.*
【厚薄】thickness：～合适。*It's just the right thickness.*
【厚薄规】[机] feeler (gauge)
【厚此薄彼】favour one and be prejudiced against the other；favour one and discriminate against the other
【厚道】honest and kind
【厚度】thickness
【厚墩墩】very thick：～的棉大衣 *a heavy padded overcoat*
【厚古薄今】stress the past，not the present
【厚积薄发】be versed in a subject；be well-grounded；be well-prepared：只有对西方哲学做到～，才能写出这样的好论文。*Only when well grounded in Western philosophy can one write such an excellent thesis.*
【厚今薄古】stress the present，not the past
【厚礼】generous gifts
【厚利】large profits
【厚脸皮】(又作'厚脸') thick-skinned；brazen；cheeky：厚着脸皮说 *have the nerve to say*
【厚禄】handsome salary；high government pay
【厚漆】paste paint
【厚实】❶〈口〉thick：这布挺～。*This cloth is very thick.* / ～的被褥 *thick，heavy quilts and mattresses* ❷〈方〉abundant；rich：储备～ *abundant reserves* / 家底～ *a family with substantial resources*
【厚望】great expectations：不负～ *live up to sb.'s expectations；not let sb. down* / 寄予～ *place high hopes on*
【厚颜无耻】impudent；brazen；shameless
【厚意】kind thought；kindness：多谢你的～。*Thank you for your kindness.*
【厚葬】❶ bury with full honours ❷ a lavish funeral
【厚重】❶ thick and heavy ❷ rich and generous：～的礼物 *generous gifts* ❸〈书〉kind and dignified

候 Ⅰ 动 ❶ wait；await：请稍～一会儿。*Please wait a moment.* / ～领 *to be kept until claimed* ❷ inquire after：问候 Ⅱ 名 ❶ time；season：时候 ❷ condition；state
【候补】be a candidate (for a vacancy)；be an alternate：中共中央政治局～委员 *an alternate member of the Political Bureau of the Central Committee of the CPC*
【候车】wait for a train，bus，etc. ◇ ～室 waiting room (in a railway or bus station)
【候机室】airport lounge or waiting room
【候教】〈套〉await your instructions：本星期日下午在舍下～。*I'll be expecting you at my place this coming Sunday afternoon.*
【候鸟】migratory bird；migrant
【候审】[法] await trial
【候选人】candidate：提出～ *nominate candidates* / ～名单 *list of candidates* / ～资格 *qualifications for standing for election*
【候诊】wait to see the doctor ◇ ～室 waiting room (in a hospital)

hū

乎 Ⅰ 助 (expressing doubt)〈书〉：成败之机，其在斯～？*Does not success or failure hinge on this?* Ⅱ (verb suffix)：超～寻常 *be out of the ordinary* Ⅲ (suffix of an adjective or adverb)：巍巍～ *towering；lofty* / 确～重要 *very important indeed*

呼 Ⅰ 动 ❶ breathe out；exhale：～出二氧化碳 *exhale carbon dioxide* ❷ shout；cry out：～口号 *shout slogans* ❸ call：直～其名 *address sb. disrespectfully (by name)* ❹ beep；page：有人在～我。*Somebody is paging me.* / ～一下王大夫！*Call Dr. Wang on his beeper!* Ⅱ 象 the sound of wind etc.：北风～～地吹。*A north wind is whistling.*
【呼哧】(又作'呼蚩') the sound of panting：～～直喘 *puff and blow*
【呼叱】(又作'呼斥') berate；excoriate；shout at (sb.)
【呼风唤雨】summon wind and rain-exercise magic powers；stir up trouble：～，驾雾腾云 *command the wind and rain，ride on the mists and clouds*
【呼喊】call out；shout：大声～ *shout at the top of one's voice*
【呼号】❶ wail；cry out in distress ❷ call sign；call letters ❸ catchword (of an organization)
【呼唤】call；shout to：我们在门外～了半天，他才开门。*We called at the door for a long time before he opened it.* / 祖国在～我们！*Our country is calling us.*
【呼机】〈口〉(又作'传呼机') beeper；pager
【呼叫】❶ call out；shout ❷ telecommunications call：～灯 *calling lamp* / ～信号 *calling signal*
【呼救】call for help；send out SOS signals
【呼拉圈】hula hoop

【呼噜】〈口〉snore：打～ *snore*

【呼朋引类】gang up：～，聚众闹事 *gang up to make trouble*

【呼请】call for (a doctor)：现在急诊科有了呼救权，可直接点名～有关专家。*The emergency ward can now call directly for the competent specialist.*

【呼扇】〈口〉❶ shake：过木桥时，木板直～。*The planks shook as I crossed the wooden bridge.* ❷ fan：他摘下草帽不停地～。*He took off his straw hat and fanned himself with it.*

【呼哨】whistle：打～ *give a whistle*

【呼声】cry；voice：群众的～ *the voice of the masses* / 世界舆论的强大～ *the powerful voice of world opinion* / 在几个候选人中，他的～最高。*He is the most likely of all the candidates.*

【呼天抢地】lament to heaven and knock one's head on earth-utter cries of anguish

【呼吸】breathe；respire：～新鲜空气 *have a breath of fresh air* / ～急促 *be short of breath* / ～困难 *breathe with difficulty*；*lose one's breath* / 停止～ *stop breathing*；*die* ◇ ～道 respiratory tract；～率 respiratory rate；～器 respirator；～器官 respiratory apparatus；～系统 respiratory system；～相通 share the same sentiments and fate；be bound together by common interests

【呼啸】whistle；scream；whizz：子弹～而过。*A bullet whizzed past.* / 寒风～。*A cold wind is whistling.*

【呼幺喝六】❶ shout for numbers in throwing dice-noisy shouting in gambling ❷〈方〉shouting right and left-arrogant

【呼应】echo；work in concert with：互相～ *echo each other*

【呼吁】appeal；call on：～团结 *appeal for unity* ◇ ～书 letter of appeal；appeal

【呼之即来，挥之即去】have sb. at one's beck and call

【呼之欲出】(of lifelike figures in pictures or vivid characters in novels) ready to come out at one's cal—be vividly portrayed

忽 Ⅰ 动 neglect；overlook；ignore：忽视 Ⅱ 副 suddenly；all of a sudden：～见前面一个人影。*All of a sudden, I saw a figure in front of me.*

【忽而】now..., now...：～哭，～笑 *cry and laugh by turns* / ～主张这个，～主张那个 *advocate one thing today and another tomorrow*

【忽略】neglect；overlook；lose sight of：我们～了一个重要的细节。*We overlooked an important detail.*

【忽然】suddenly；all of a sudden：他正要出去，～下起大雨来了。*It suddenly started pouring just as he was going out.*

【忽闪】(of the eyes, etc.) sparkle；flash：小姑娘～着大眼睛看着妈妈。*The little girl stared at her mother, her big eyes flashing.*

【忽视】ignore；overlook；neglect：不可～的力量 *a force not to be ignored*；*a force to be reckoned with* / 不应～困难。*We should not overlook the difficulties.* / 不要强调一面而～另一面。*Don't stress one aspect to the neglect of another.*

【忽悠】〈方〉flicker：渔船上的灯火～～的。*Lights flickered on the fishing boats.* / 大旗叫风吹得直～。*The flag fluttered in the wind.*

【忽左忽右】suddenly left, suddenly right—now one extreme, now the other

烀 动 stew in shallow water

糊 动 plaster：用灰把墙缝～上 *plaster up cracks in the wall* / ～一层泥 *spread a layer of mud* ——另见 hú；hù

hú

囫 (构词成分)见下

【囫囵】whole：～吞下 *swallow sth. whole*

【囫囵吞枣】swallow a date whole-lap up information without digesting it；read without understanding：读这份材料要细嚼慢咽，不能～。*You must read the texts carefully, and not gloss over them without properly digesting them.*

狐 名 fox

【狐步】foxtrot (a ballroom dance)

【狐臭】(又作'狐臊') body odour；bromhidrosis

【狐假虎威】the fox borrows the tiger's fierceness (by walking in the latter's company)—bully people by flaunting one's powerful connections

【狐狸】fox ◇ ～精 fox spirit—a seductive woman

【狐狸尾巴】fox's tail—something that gives away a person's real character or evil intentions；cloven hoof：～总是要露出来的。*A fox cannot hide its tail.* or *The devil can't hide his cloven hoof.* / 抓住阴谋家的～ *seize hold of the evidence which gives the conspirator away*

【狐媚】bewitch by cajolery；entice by flattery

【狐裘】fox-fur robe

【狐群狗党】(又作'狐朋狗党') a pack of rogues；a gang of scoundrels

【狐疑】doubt；suspicion：满腹～ *be full of misgivings*；*be very suspicious*

弧 名 ❶［数］arc ❷〈古〉bow

【弧度】［数］radian

【弧光】arc light；arc：～灯 *arc lamp*；*arc light*

【弧菌】vibrio

【弧圈球】［体］(乒乓球) loop drive

【弧线】pitch arc

【弧形】arc；curve：～闸门 *radial gate*

胡 Ⅰ 名 ❶ non-Han ethnic groups living in the north and west in ancient times ❷ introduced from the northern and western ethnic groups or from abroad：胡萝卜 ❸ moustache, beard or whiskers：胡须 Ⅱ 副 recklessly；wantonly；outrageously：～编 *cook up*；*concoct* Ⅲ 副〈书〉why：～不归？*Why not return?*

【胡扯】talk nonsense；chatter idly：～！*Nonsense*！or *That's a lie*！/ 别～了，快干活吧。*Stop chattering and get on with your work*. / 这纯粹是～。*This is sheer nonsense*.

【胡吃海塞】recklessly stuff oneself with food

【胡吹】boast outrageously；talk big

【胡蝶】同〖蝴蝶〗

【胡匪】〈方〉bandit

【胡蜂】wasp；hornet

【胡搞】❶ mess things up；meddle with sth. ❷ carry on an affair with sb.；be promiscuous

【胡话】ravings；wild talk：烧得直说～ *be delirious from fever*

【胡椒】pepper

【胡椒鲷】［动］grunt（Plectorhynchus cinctus）

【胡搅】❶ pester sb.；be mischievous ❷ argue tediously and vexatiously；wrangle

【胡搅蛮缠】argue tediously and vexatiously；plague sb. with unreasonable demands

【胡来】❶ mess things up；fool with sth.：你要是不会修就别～。*If you don't know how to repair it*，*don't fool with it*（*or mess it up*）. ❷ run wild；act irresponsibly or recklessly：他溜冰溜到了冰层很薄的地方，真是～。*It was reckless of him to skate out onto the thin ice*.

【胡乱】carelessly；casually；at random：～吃了点饭 *eat a hasty meal*；*grab a quick bite* / ～写了几行 *scribble a few lines* / ～猜测 *make wild guesses*

【胡萝卜】carrot ◇ ～素［生化］carotene

【胡闹】run wild；be mischievous；make trouble：他喝酒喝多了就～。*When he drinks too much he makes trouble*. / 我们在谈正经事。你别～。*We're discussing something serious*. *Don't talk nonsense*.

【胡琴】a general term for certain two-stringed bowed instruments，such as erhu（二胡），（京胡），etc.

【胡说】❶ talk nonsense；drivel：你再～，我从此不理你。*If you utter any more nonsense*，*I'm not going to pay any attention to you*. ❷ nonsense

【胡说八道】talk nonsense；sheer nonsense；rubbish：你要是～我就不听。*If you're going to talk nonsense*，*I won't listen*. / 这部电视剧是～。*This TV drama is nonsense*.

【胡思乱想】go off into flights of fancy；give way to foolish fancies；let one's imagination run away with one：无根据地～ *disregard reality and indulge in flights of fancy*

【胡同】lane；alley

【胡颓子】［植］thorny elaeagnus（Elaeagnus pungens）

【胡须】beard，moustache or whiskers

【胡言乱语】talk nonsense；rave

【胡杨】［植］diversiform-leaved poplar（Popular diversifolia）

【胡枝子】［植］shrub lespedeza（Lespedeza bicolor）

【胡诌】fabricate wild tales；cook up：～了一大堆理由 *cook up a lot of excuses*

【胡子】❶ beard，moustache or whiskers ❷ 同〖胡匪〗

【胡子工程】project or engineering work that proceeds very slowly or is delayed：这个道路"～"终于今年开工。*This long-delayed road project will finally begin this year*.

【胡子拉碴】a stubbly beard；a bristly unshaven chin

【胡作非为】act wildly in defiance of the law or public opinion；commit all kinds of outrages；run amuck

壶 名 ❶ kettle；pot：～里是开水 *There's boiled water in the pot*. ❷ bottle；flask：行军壶

核（构词成分）见下 ——另见 hé

【核儿】〈口〉❶ stone；pit；core：杏～ *apricot stone* / 梨～ *pear core* ❷ sth. resembling a fruit stone：煤～ *partly-burnt coals or briquets*；*cinders*

斛 名 a dry measure used in former times，originally equal to 10 dou（斗），later 5 dou

湖 名 lake

【湖笔】writing brush produced in Huzhou（湖州），Zhejiang Province

【湖滨】lakeside

【湖光山色】a beautiful scenery of lakes and mountains

【湖泊】lakes

【湖色】light green

【湖田】land reclaimed from a lake；shoaly land

【湖心亭】a pavilion in the middle of a lake；midlake pavilion

【湖泽】lakes and marshes

【湖沼学】limnology

葫（构词成分）见下

【葫芦】bottle gourd；calabash：拿～装酒 *have a gourd filled with wine* / 他的～里到底卖的是什么药？*What has he got up his sleeve*？

猢（构词成分）见下

【猢狲】macaque；monkey

鹄 名 swan

【鹄候】〈书〉await respectfully；expect：～回音。*I am awaiting your reply*.

【鹄立】〈书〉stand erect

【鹄望】〈书〉eagerly look forward to

煳 动（of food）burnt：饭～了。*The rice is burnt*.

【煳锅】burnt in a pot：肉都～了。*The meat is burnt*.

糊 动 stick with paste；paste：～窗户 *paste a sheet of paper over a lattice window or seal with paper the cracks around a window*——另见 hū，

hù
【糊精】[化] dextrin; artificial gum
【糊里糊涂】muddle-headed; mixed up: 他觉得自己有点～。*He felt rather confused.* / 我～地跑到这儿。*Somehow I stumbled here in a daze.*
【糊涂】❶ muddled; confused; bewildered: ～观念 *a muddled idea* / 他越想越～。*The more he thought the more confused he became.* / 我真～，把信忘在家里了。*How careless of me to have left the letter at home.* ❷〈方〉blurred; indistinct ——另见〖装糊涂〗
【糊涂】muddled; confused; bewildered: ～观念 *a muddled idea* / 他越想越～。*The more he thought the more confused he became.* ◇ ～虫 blunderer; bungler
【糊涂账】chaotic accounts; a mess

槲 名 [植] Mongolian oak (Quercus dentata)
【槲寄生】[植] mistletoe (Viscum coloratum)
【槲栎】[植] oriental white oak (Quercus aliena)

蝴 (构词成分)见下
【蝴蝶】butterfly
【蝴蝶花】fringed iris
【蝴蝶结】bowknot; bow
【蝴蝶衫】butterfly-sleeved
【蝴蝶效应】butterfly effect

hǔ

虎 Ⅰ 名 tiger: 幼～ *a tiger cub* Ⅱ 形 brave; vigorous: 虎将 Ⅲ 动〈方〉look ferocious: 他突然～起脸对我吼起来。*He suddenly turned ferocious and shouted at me.*
【虎背熊腰】have a back like a tiger's and a waist like a bear's-tough and stocky
【虎骨酒】tiger-bone liquor
【虎虎有生气】be full of vim and vigour
【虎将】a brave general
【虎劲】dauntless drive; dash: 有一股子～ *be full of drive and daring; have plenty of dash*
【虎口】❶ tiger's mouth-jaws of death: 把同志救出～ *save one's comrade from the jaws of death* ❷ part of the hand between the thumb and the index finger
【虎口拔牙】pull a tooth from the tiger's mouth—dare the greatest danger
【虎口余生】be saved from the tiger's mouth—have a narrow escape from death; be snatched from the jaws of death
【虎狼】tiger and wolf-cruel and ruthless: ～之性 *voracious and wolfish nature* / ～之国 *a nation of savages*
【虎里虎气】(usu. of a young man) strong and vigorous; strapping
【虎钳】vice: 台～ *bench vice* / 万能～ *universal vice* / ～口 *vice jaw*
【虎鲨】bullhead shark
【虎视眈眈】glare like a tiger eyeing its prey; eye covetously or menacingly
【虎头虎脑】(usu. of a boy) looking strong and good natured: 你儿子长得～，非常可爱。*Your son's a lovely boy, so strong and good natured.*
【虎头蛇尾】a tiger's head and a snake's tail—a fine start and a poor finish; in like a lion, out like a lamb
【虎威】(of a military officer) valiant and awe-inspiring
【虎穴】tiger's den—a danger spot: ～追踪 *track the tiger to its lair*
【虎牙】〈口〉protruding canine teeth

浒 名 waterside:《水～传》(*name of a novel*) *Water Margin; Outlaws of the Marsh*

唬 动〈口〉bluff: 你别～人。*Quit bluffing.* / 她没被～住。*She wasn't intimidated.*

琥 (构词成分)见下
【琥珀】amber: ～油 *amber oil*

hù

户 名 ❶ door: 足不出～ *never step out of doors; confine oneself within doors* ❷ household; family: 全村共三十～。*There are thirty households in the village.* / 无房～ *residents who do not have their own living quarters* ❸ family status: 门当户对 ❹ (bank) account: 开户
【户籍】❶ census register; household register ❷ registered permanent residence ◇ ～警 policeman in charge of household registration
【户均】per household; per family: ～收入 *per household income; average family income*
【户口】❶ number of households and total population ❷ registered permanent residence: 他在北京没～。*He's an unregistered resident in Beijing.* ◇ ～簿(又作'户口本') (permanent) residence booklet ◇ ～清册 census record
【户枢不蠹】a doorhinge never becomes wormeaten—constant activity staves off decay ——另见〖流水不腐，户枢不蠹〗
【户头】(bank) account: 开～ *open an account*
【户外】outdoor: ～运动 *outdoor games; outdoor sports*
【户限为穿】a threshold worn low by visitors—an endless flow of visitors
【户主】head of a household

互 副 mutually; each other: ～不干涉内政 *non-interference in each other's internal affairs* / ～为条件 *mutually conditional; interdependent* / ～通情报 *exchange information; keep each other informed* / ～派常驻使节 *exchange resident envoys; mutually accredit resident envoys*
【互补】mutually complementary: ～性 *complementarity* / 我们两国的经济是～的。*Our two countries are mutually complementary in econo-*

my.

【互不侵犯条约】nonaggression treaty (or pact)

【互导】[电] mutual conductance; transconductance

【互动】mutual; reciprocal: ～关系 *reciprocal effect*

【互访】exchange visits: 两国体育代表团的～ *exchange of sports delegations between two countries*

【互感应】(又作'互感')[电] mutual inductance

【互换】exchange: ～批准书 *exchange instruments of ratification* / ～记者 *exchange correspondents*

【互惠】mutually beneficial; reciprocal: 在～的基础上 *on a mutually beneficial basis* / 贸易～ *reciprocity in trade* ◇ ～待遇 reciprocal treatment; ～关税 mutually preferential tariff; ～条约 reciprocal treaty

【互见】❶ cross-reference ❷ (of two contrasting things) exist side by side

【互利】mutually beneficial; of mutual benefit ◇ ～互惠 mutual benefit and reciprocity; offer mutual benefit and achieve common progress

【互联网】[计](又作'英特网')Internet

【互让】yield to each other; give in to each other

【互生】[植] alternate: ～叶 *alternate leaf*

【互调干扰】intermodulation interference

【互通有无】each supplies what the other needs; supply (or meet) each other's needs: ～, 调剂余缺 *each making up the other's deficiency from his own surplus*

【互为因果】interact as both cause and effect

【互相】mutually; each other: ～依存 *depend on each other for existence; be interdependent* / ～排斥 *be mutually exclusive* / ～配合 *work in coordination* / ～利用 *each using the other for his own ends* / ～掣肘 *hold each other back* / ～勾结 *work in collusion*

【互相扯皮】buck-passing; will not serve as a precedent; engage in endless haggling and shifts of responsibility

【互助】help each other: ～合作 *mutual aid and cooperation*

【互助会】credit union (financial aid society organized by workers or staff members on a voluntary basis)

【互助组】❶ mutual aid group: 学习～ *mutual help study group* ❷ mutual aid team (an elementary form of organization in China's agricultural cooperation): 临时～ *temporary mutual aid team* / 常年～ *all-the-year-roud mutual aid team*

护

动 ❶ protect; guard; shield: ～厂 *guard a factory* / 在敌机扫射时,她用自己的身子～住伤员。*She shielded the wounded soldier from the strafing of the enemy plane with her own body.* ❷ be partial to; shield from censure: 别～着自己的孩子。*Don't be partial to your own child.*

【护岸】bank revetment ◇ ～林 protective belt (of trees) along an embankment

【护庇】shield; put under one's protection; take under one's wing

【护城河】city moat

【护持】shield and sustain

【护短】shield a shortcoming (or fault): 做母亲的对孩子～没什么好处。*It does no good to a child to have his faults shielded by his mother.*

【护耳】earflaps; earmuffs

【护发素】hair conditioner

【护封】book jacket; jacket

【护肤霜】face cream

【护航】escort; convoy: 由五艘军舰～ *be convoyed by five warships; have an escort of five warships* / ～部队 *escort force* / ～飞机 *escort aircraft* / ～舰 *convoy ship; escort vessel*

【护肩】〈方〉shoulder pad (or padding)

【护颈】camail

【护壳】[机] protective case (or shell)

【护理】nurse; tend and protect: ～伤病员 *nurse the sick and the wounded* / 精心～小麦越冬 *take good care of the wheat through the winter* ◇ ～人员 nursing staff

【护林】protect a forest

【护路】❶ patrol and guard a road or railway ❷ road maintenance ◇ ～林 protective belt (of trees) along a road

【护面】[体] mask

【护目镜】goggles

【护青】〈方〉keep watch over the ripening crops

【护秋】keep watch over the autumn harvest

【护身符】❶ amulet; protective talisman ❷ (又作'护符') a person or thing that protects one from punishment or censure; shield

【护士】(hospital) nurse ◇ ～学校 nurses' school; ～长 head nurse

【护手盘】[体] hand guard

【护送】escort; convoy: ～伤员去后方医院 *escort wounded men to a rear hospital* / ～救灾物资 *convoy vehicles bringing relief to a disaster-stricken area*

【护腿】[体] shinguard

【护腕】wristlet; bracer

【护卫】❶ protect; guard: 他在保卫人员的～下离开了机场。*He left the airport under the protection of the security guards.* ❷ bodyguard ◇ ～舰 escort vessel; corvette; ～艇 another name for 炮艇

【护膝】[体] kneepad; kneecap

【护胸】[体] chest protector

【护袖】〈方〉oversleeve

【护养】❶ cultivate; nurse; rear: ～秧苗 *cultivate seedlings; nurse young plants* / ～仔猪 *rear (or look after) piglets* ❷ maintain: ～公路 *maintain a highway*

【护照】passport: 外交～ *diplomatic passport* / 公务～ *service passport*

【护肘】elbow guard

怙

动〈书〉rely on

【怙恶不悛】be steeped in evil and refuse to repent;

remain impenitent：～，继续做坏事 *remain impenitent and keep up one's evildoing* / ～的罪犯 *an incorrigible criminal*

戽 Ⅰ 名 bailing bucket Ⅱ 动 bail：～水灌田 *bail water to irrigate fields*

【戽斗】bailing bucket

笏 名 a tablet held before the breast by officials when received in audience by the emperor

扈 名〈书〉retinue

【扈从】〈书〉retinue；retainer

糊 名 paste：辣椒～ *chilli paste* / 玉米～ *(cornmeal) mush* ——另见 hū；hú

【糊弄】〈方〉❶ fool；deceive；palm sth. off on：你别～我。*Don't try to fool me.* ❷ go through the motions；be slipshod in work：这可是细活，不能瞎～。*This is a delicate job. It mustn't be done carelessly.*

huā

花 Ⅰ 名 ❶ flower；blossom；bloom：一朵～ *a flower* ❷ anything resembling a flower：雪花 ❸ fireworks：放～ *let off fireworks* ❹ pattern；design：白底红～ *red flowers on a white background* ❺ cream；essence：文艺之～ *the cream of literature and art* ❻ used metaphorically for courtesans or prostitutes：寻花问柳 Ⅱ 形 ❶ multicoloured；coloured；variegated：～衣服 *bright-coloured clothes* / ～蝴蝶 *variegated butterfly* / 小～狗 *spotted puppy* / 布染～了。*The cloth is dyed unevenly.* ❷ flower-decorated；coloured：花篮 ❸ blurred；dim：看书看得眼睛都～了 *read until the print looks blurred* ❹ fancy；florid；flowery；showy：你的字太～了。*Your handwriting is too fancy.* Ⅲ 动 spend；expend：～不少钱 *spend a lot of money* / 很～时间 *take a lot of time；be time-consuming*

【花白】(of hair or beard) grey；grizzled：头发～ *with grey (or grizzled) hair；grey-haired*

【花斑】piebald：～马 *a piebald horse*

【花斑癣】［医］tinea versicolour

【花瓣】petal

【花苞】(flower) bud

【花被】［植］perianth；floral envelope

【花边】❶ decorative border：瓶口上有一道～。*There is a floral border round the mouth of the vase.* ❷ lace：～装饰 *lace trimmings* / 在衣服上镶一条～ *trim a dress with lace* ❸［刷］fancy borders in printing

【花边新闻】titbits (of news)；interesting sidelights

【花布】cotton print；print

【花菜】〈方〉cauliflower

【花草】❶ flowers and plants ❷〈方〉Chinese milk vetch

【花插】any container for cut flowers

【花插】crisscross

【花茶】scented tea：茉莉～ *jasmine tea*

【花厂】〈旧〉flower shop；florist's

【花车】festooned vehicle

【花池子】flower bed

【花虫】〈方〉pink bollworm

【花丛】flowering shrubs；flowers in clusters

【花大姐】［动］potato ladybird

【花旦】female role in traditional opera

【花道】ikebana

【花灯】festive lantern (as displayed on the Lantern Festival) ◇ ～戏 local opera popular in Yunnan and Sichuan Provinces

【花缎】figured satin；brocade

【花朵】flower：盛开的～ *flowers in full bloom* / 儿童是祖国的～。*Children are the flowers of our country.*

【花萼】calyx

【花房】greenhouse

【花肥】fertilizers for potted flowers

【花费】❶ spend；expend；cost：～金钱 *spend money (on a project, etc.)* / ～时间 *spend time；take time* / ～心血 *take pains* ❷ money spent；expenditure；expenses：这笔～我担负不了。*I can't afford the expense.*

【花粉】［植］pollen：～管 *pollen tube*

【花粉食品】pollen food

【花岗岩】(又作'花岗石') ❶ granite ❷ incorrigibly obstinate：～脑袋 *a granite-like skull；ossified thinking* ◇ ～化［地质］granitize

【花格窗】lattice window

【花梗】pedicel

【花工】worker employed in a plant nursery；flower grower

【花骨朵】common name for 花蕾

【花鼓】flower-drum，a folk dance popular in the Changjiang valley ◇ ～戏 flower-drum opera，popular in Hunan，Hubei and Anhui

【花冠】❶ corolla：合瓣～ *gamopetalous corolla* / 离瓣～ *choripetalous corolla* ❷ an ornamental crown worn by a bride on her wedding day in former times

【花好月圆】(usu. used as a congratulatory message for sb.'s marriage) blooming flowers and full moon-perfect conjugal bliss

【花红】❶［植］Chinese pear-leaved crabapple ❷ gift for a wedding，etc. ❸ bonus

【花红柳绿】red flowers and green willows—a beautiful spring scene

【花候】［植］flowering season

【花花肠子】〈方〉❶ cunning；trickery；deceit：一肚子～ *be full of cunning* ❷ a cunning person

【花花公子】playboy；dandy；coxcomb；fop

【花花绿绿】brightly coloured；colourful：穿得～的 *be colourfully dressed* / ～的招贴画 *poster in colour*

【花花世界】the dazzling human world with its myriad temptations；this mortal world：大都市这～使他感到眼花缭乱。*He was dazzled by the gaiety and splendour of the metropolis.*

【花环】garland; floral hoop

【花卉】❶ flowers and plants ❷ painting of flowers and plants in traditional Chinese style: ～画 *flower-and-plant painting*

【花会】flower fair

【花鸡】bramble finch; brambling

【花甲】a cycle of sixty years: ～之年 *sixty (years of age)* / 年逾～ *over sixty years old*

【花架子】showy postures of martial arts—a thing that is showy but of no practical use: 要练好基本功,别尽学～。*You should spend time on basic training, not on those flourishes.*

【花剑】[体] foil: ～运动员 *foil fencer; foilsman*

【花键】[机] spline: ～轴 *spline shaft* / ～座 *splined hub*

【花匠】gardener

【花椒】Chinese prickly ash

【花轿】bridal sedan chair

【花秸】chopped straw

【花街柳巷】streets of ill repute; red-light district

【花镜】presbyopic glasses

【花酒】a dinner party with singsong girls in attendance

【花卷】fancy-shaped (or plaited, twisted) steamed roll; steamed twisted roll

【花篮】❶ a basket of flowers ❷ gaily decorated basket

【花蕾】(flower) bud

【花里胡哨】❶ gaudy; garish; showy: 穿得～的 *be gaudily dressed* ❷ without solid worth: 他吹得～的,不能信。*Don't believe his florid words.*

【花鲢】variegated carp

【花脸】[戏] male character in Chinese opera with a painted face

【花柳病】venereal disease (V. D.)

【花露】(medicinal) liquid distilled from honeysuckle flowers or lotus leaves

【花露水】toilet water

【花蜜】[植] nectar

【花面狸】masked civet; gem-faced civet

【花苗】flower seedling

【花名册】register (of names); membership roster; muster roll

【花呢】fancy suiting

【花鸟】painting of flowers and birds in traditional Chinese style: ～画 *flower-and-bird painting*

【花农】flower grower

【花盘】❶ [植] flower disc ❷ [机] disc chuck; faceplate

【花炮】fireworks and firecrackers: 放～ *let off fireworks*

【花盆】flowerpot

【花瓶】❶ flower vase; vase ❷ a woman who only knows how to make herself up and can do no useful work

【花圃】flower nursery

【花期】florescence

【花旗】〈旧〉 star-spangled banner—the United States ◇ ～银行 the First National City Bank of New York

【花前月下】amidst flowers and in the moonlight—an ideal setting for amorous dalliance

【花枪】❶ a short spear used in ancient times ❷ trickery: 耍～ *play tricks*

【花腔】❶ florid ornamentation in Chinese opera singing; coloratura ❷ guileful talk: 耍～ *speak guilefully* ◇ ～女高音 coloratura soprano; coloratura

【花墙】lattice wall

【花青】[化] cyanine: ～染料 *cyanine dyes* ◇ ～素 [化] anthocyanidin

【花圈】(floral) wreath

【花拳绣腿】showy but not practical martial arts; any showy but not practical skill

【花容月貌】flower-like features and moonlike face—a great beauty

【花蕊】stamen or pistil

【花色】❶ design and colour: 这布的～很好看。*This cloth is beautiful in both design and colour.* ❷ (of merchandise) variety of designs, sizes, colours, etc.: 新的～ *latest designs* / ～繁多 *a great variety*

【花色品种】variety of colours and designs: 增加～ *increase the variety of colours and designs*

【花纱布】a collective name for cotton, cotton yarn and cloth

【花哨】❶ garish; gaudy: 她打扮得太～。*She was gaudily dressed.* ❷ full of flourishes; flowery: 他鼓点子敲得又响亮又～。*He beat the drum loudly and with a lot of flourishes.*

【花生】peanut; groundnut ◇ ～饼 [农] peanut cake; ～豆儿〈方〉shelled peanut; peanut kernel; ～黑斑病 cercospora black spot of peanut; ～酱 peanut butter; ～米(又作'花生仁') shelled peanut; peanut kernel; ～糖 peanut brittle; ～油 peanut oil

【花市】flower market

【花饰】ornamental design

【花式跳水】fancy diving

【花式游泳】fancy synchronized swimming

【花鼠】Siberian chipmunk; chipmunk

【花束】a bunch of flowers; bouquet

【花丝】❶ [植] filament ❷ [工美] filigree

【花坛】(raised) flower bed; flower terrace

【花天酒地】indulge in dissipation; lead a life of debauchery

【花厅】reception room or parlour (usu. in a garden or side courtyard)

【花筒】tube-shaped fireworks

【花团锦簇】bouquets of flowers and piles of silks—rich multi-coloured decorations: 打扮得～ *be splendidly dressed*

【花托】[植] receptacle

【花纹】decorative pattern; figure: 各种～的地毯 *carpets of different patterns* / 这些瓷盘的～很别致。*These porcelain plates have rather original designs on them.* / ～玻璃 *figured glass*

【花线】❶ coloured thread ❷［电］flexible cord; flex

【花消】（又作'花销'）〈口〉cost; expense: 他抽烟喝酒的～大。*He spends a lot on smoking and drinking.*

【花序】［植］inflorescence

【花絮】titbits (of news); interesting sidelights: 运动会～ *sidelights on the sports meet*

【花芽】(flower) bud

【花言巧语】sweet words; fine words; flattery; blandishments: 他们的一切～都是骗人的。*All their fine words are nothing but humbug.*

【花眼】❶ presbyopia ❷ be dazzled: 挑来挑去挑～了 *be dazzled by so many varieties to choose from*

【花样】❶ decorative pattern; variety: ～繁多 *a great variety* ❷ trick: 玩～ *play tricks* / 他又在闹什么新～。*I wonder what he's up to now.* ◇～滑冰 figure skating; ～滑水 figure water skiing; acrobatic water skiing; ～游泳 water ballet; synchronized swimming

【花样翻新】❶ innovations in pattern or design ❷ old things in a new guise

【花药】［植］anther

【花椰菜】cauliflower

【花叶病】［农］mosaic (disease): 甜菜～ *beet mosaic*

【花园】（又作'花园子'）flower garden; garden ◇～城市 garden city

【花账】padded accounts or bills: 开～ *make out a padded account; pad accounts*

【花招】（又作'花着'）❶ showy movement in wushu (武术); flourish ❷ trick; game ——另见〖耍花招〗

【花枝招展】(of women) be gorgeously dressed: 打扮得～的 *freshly made up and as pretty as a flower*

【花轴】（又作'花茎'）［植］floral axis

【花烛】candles with dragon and phoenix patterns used in the bridal chamber on the wedding night: ～之夜 *the wedding night*

【花柱】［植］style

【花砖】ornamental slab for paving the floor

【花子】beggar

哗 象 the sound of water flowing, raining etc.: 铁门～的一声拉上了。*The iron gate was pulled to with a clang.* / 溪水～～地流。*The stream went gurgling on.* ——另见 huá

【哗啦】（又作'哗啦啦'）: 风吹得树叶～～地响。*The leaves rustled in the wind.* / 墙～一声倒了。*The wall fell with a crash.* / 雨～～地下个不停。*The rain kept pouring down.*

huá

划 动 ❶ paddle; row: ～船 *paddle (or row) a boat* ❷ be to one's profit; pay: 划得来 ❸ scratch; cut the surface of: ～玻璃 *cut a piece of glass* / ～火柴 *strike a match* / 她手～破了。*Her hands were scratched.* / 几道闪电～破长空。*Flashes of lightning streaked across the sky.* ——另见 huà

【划不来】（又作'划不着'）be not worth it; do not pay: 这么好的地，种饲料～。*It doesn't pay to grow feed crops on such good soil.*

【划船运动】boating

【划得来】（又作'划得着'）be worth it; pay: 还是买质量好的东西～。*It always pays to buy good quality products (or goods).*

【划拳】play the finger-guessing game

【划水】strike water with one's arms in swimming

【划算】❶ calculate; weigh: 下星期要花多少钱我得～一下。*I must calculate how much money I'll spend next week.* ❷ be to one's profit; pay: ～不～，不能只从本单位的利益考虑。*One mustn't consider whether or not it pays simply from the standpoint of one's own unit.*

【划艇】canoe: ～运动 *canoeing*

【划子】small rowboat

华 Ⅰ 形 ❶ magnificent; splendid: 华丽 ❷ prosperous; flourishing: 繁华 ❸ flashy; extravagant: 浮华 ❹ grizzled; grey: 华发 Ⅱ 名 ❶ best part; cream: 精华 ❷ China: 华北 ❸ Chinese (language): ～俄词典 *a Chinese-Russian dictionary*

【华北】North China, area including Hebei, Shanxi and the municipalities of Beijing and Tianjin: ～平原 *North China Plain*

【华表】ornamental columns erected in front of palaces, tombs, etc.

【华达呢】gabardine

【华灯】colourfully decorated lantern; light: ～初上 *when the evening lights are lit*

【华而不实】flashy and without substance; superficially clever

【华尔街】Wall Street: ～财阀 *Wall Street magnates*

【华尔兹】waltz

【华发】〈书〉grey hair: 满头～的老人 *grey-haired old man (or woman)* / 早生～ *have grey hair at an early age (or prematurely)*

【华盖】❶ canopy (as over an imperial carriage) ❷ ancient name for a certain star considered unlucky

【华贵】❶ luxurious; sumptuous; costly: ～的地毯 *luxurious carpet* ❷ wealthy: ～之家 *a wealthy family*

【华里】li, a unit of distance (=1/2 kilometre)

【华丽】magnificent; resplendent; gorgeous: ～的宫殿 *a magnificent palace* / 服饰～ *gorgeously dressed and richly ornamented* / ～的词藻 *flowery language*

【华美】magnificent; resplendent; gorgeous

【华侨】overseas Chinese

【华人】Chinese: 美籍～ *an American Chinese*

【华沙条约】the Warsaw Treaty (1955): ～组织

the Warsaw Treaty Organization
【华氏温度计】the Fahrenheit thermometer
【华夏】archaic name for 中国
【华夏系构造】[地质] Cathaysian (structural) system
【华裔】foreign citizen of Chinese origin：～美国人 *an American of Chinese descent*
【华语】Chinese (language)

哗 形 noisy；clamourous：喧哗 ——另见 huā
【哗变】mutiny
【哗然】in an uproar；in commotion：举座～。*The audience burst into an uproar.* / 舆论～。*There was a public outcry.*
【哗笑】uproarious laughter
【哗众取宠】try to please the public with claptrap：无实事求是之意，有～之心 *have no intention of seeking truth from facts, but only a desire to curry favour by claptrap*

铧 名 ploughshare：双～犁 *double-shared plough；double-furrow plough*

滑 Ⅰ形 ❶ slippery；smooth：又圆又～的小石子 *smooth, round pebbles* / 路～。*The road is slippery.* ❷ cunning；crafty；slippery：又奸又～ *mean and crafty* Ⅱ动 slip；slide：～倒 *slip and fall* / 在错误的道路上越～越远 *slide further and further down the wrong road*
【滑板】❶[机] slide ❷[体](乒乓球) feint play ❸ skateboard
【滑冰】ice-skating；skating ◇ ～场 skating rink
【滑车神经】[生理] trochlear nerve
【滑道】chute；slide
【滑动】[物] slide ◇ ～摩擦[物] sliding friction；～轴承[机] sliding bearing
【滑竿】a kind of litter
【滑旱冰】roller-skate
【滑稽】❶ funny；amusing；comical：这个丑角的表演非常～。*The clown gave a very funny performance.* / 他样子很～。*He is funny-looking.* ❷ comic talk ◇ ～戏 farce
【滑精】[中] involuntary emission；spermatorrhoea
【滑溜】(huáliū) sauté with starchy sauce：～里脊 *sauté fillet with thick gravy*
【滑溜】(huáliu)〈口〉slick；smooth；slippery：这块绸子摸着挺～。*This piece of silk feels very smooth.*
【滑轮】(又作'滑车') pulley；block ◇ ～组 assembly pulley
【滑脉】[中] smooth pulse
【滑面】[机] sliding surface；slide face
【滑腻】(of the skin) satiny；velvety；creamy
【滑坡】❶ landslide；landslip ❷ be on the slippery slope；decline；come down；drop：财政收入连续两年～。*State revenue declined for two years in succession.*
【滑润】smooth；well-lubricated
【滑石】talcum；talc ◇ ～粉 talcum powder
【滑水】[体] water skiing ◇ ～板 aquaplane；hydro-ski
【滑膛枪】smoothbore (gun)；musket
【滑梯】(children's) slide
【滑天下之大稽】be the biggest joke in the world；be the laughingstock of the world；be the object of universal ridicule
【滑头】❶ slippery fellow；sly customer ❷ slippery；shifty；slick：～滑脑 *crafty；artful；slick*
【滑翔】glide ◇ ～机 glider；sailplane
【滑行】slide；coast：冰上～ *slide on the ice* / ～下坡 *coast down a slope* / 飞机在跑道上～。*The plane taxied along the runway.*
【滑雪】[体] skiing：～板 *skis* / ～鞋 *ski boots* / ～杖 *ski pole；ski stick* / ～衫 *ski suit；down garment*
【滑移】slide；slip：山～约 5 万立方米。*There was landslide of over 50,000 cubic meters of earth.*
【滑音】❶[语音] glide ❷[音] portamento
【滑脂枪】[机] grease gun

猾 形 cunning；crafty；sly：～吏 *a cunning and unscrupulous official*

huà

化 Ⅰ动 ❶ change；turn；transform：～害为利 *turn harm into good；turn a disadvantage into an advantage* / ～公为私 *appropriate public property* ❷ convert；influence：感化 ❸ melt；dissolve：雪～了。*The snow has melted.* / 他把药片用水～开。*He dissolved the pills in water.* ❹ digest ❺ burn up：焚化 ❻[宗] die：坐化 ❼ (of Buddhist monks or Taoist priests) beg alms：化斋 Ⅱ名〈略〉见〖化学〗 Ⅲ(动词后缀)-ize；-ify：绿化
【化悲痛为力量】turn grief into strength (usu. used in a memorial speech)
【化除】eliminate；dispel；remove：～成见 *dispel prejudices*
【化冻】thaw；melt：冰冻的食品必须化了冻才能煮。*Frozen food must be thawed before cooking.* / 湖上的冰已经～了。*The ice on the lake has melted.*
【化肥】〈略〉见〖化学肥料〗
【化粪池】septic tank
【化腐朽为神奇】turn the foul and rotten into the rare and ethereal—❶ turn bad into good ❷ change waste material into things of value
【化干戈为玉帛】turn hostility into friendship；bury the hatchet
【化工】〈略〉见〖化学工业〗 ◇ ～厂 chemical plant；～仪表 chemical instruments；～原料 industrial chemicals
【化公为私】turn public property into private property；line one's pocket with public funds；embezzle public property
【化合】[化] chemical combination：～反应 *combination reaction* ◇ ～价[化] valence；～物 chem-

ical compound

【化解】ease off; reconcile; resolve: ～矛盾 *ease contradictions*

【化境】sublimity; perfection: 这幅山水画已臻～。*This landscape painting is a consummate work of art.*

【化疗】〈略〉见〖化学疗法〗

【化名】❶ use an assumed name ❷ assumed name; alias

【化脓】fester; suppurate: 伤口～了。*The wound is festering.*

【化身】incarnation; embodiment: 智慧和勇敢的～ *the embodiment of wisdom and courage* / 魔鬼的～ *the devil incarnate* / 这部小说的主人公正是作者自己的～。*The hero of this novel is a portrait of the author himself.*

【化石】fossil: 整理～ *dress fossils* / 标准～ *index fossil* / 指相～ *facies fossil* / 微体～ *microfossil* / ～作用 *fossilization*

【化痰】reduce phlegm: ～止咳 *reduce phlegm and relieve coughing*

【化铁炉】[冶] cupola furnace

【化为乌有】melt into thin air; vanish; come to naught

【化纤】〈略〉见〖化学纤维〗

【化险为夷】turn danger into safety; head off a disaster

【化学】❶ chemistry: 应用～ *applied chemistry* / 理论～ *theoretical chemistry* ❷〈口〉celluloid: 这把梳子是～的。*This comb is made from celluloid.* ◇ ～变化 chemical change; ～成分 chemical composition; ～处理 chemical treatment; ～弹头 chemical warhead; ～当量 chemical equivalent; ～反应 chemical reaction; ～方程式 chemical equation; ～肥料 chemical fertilizer; ～符号 chemical symbol; ～工业 chemical industry; ～疗法 chemotherapy; ～试剂 chemical reagent; ～武器 chemical weapons; ～纤维 chemical fibre; ～性质 chemical property; ～元素 chemical element; ～炸药 chemical explosive; ～战争 chemical warfare; ～作用 chemical action

【化验】chemical examination; laboratory test: ～单 *laboratory test report* / ～室 *laboratory* / ～员 *laboratory technician (or assistant)* ◇ ～样品 assay sample

【化油器】[机] carburettor

【化缘】(of Buddhist monks or Taoist priests) beg alms

【化雨春风】同〖春风化雨〗

【化斋】(of Buddhist monks or Taoist priests) beg a vegetarian meal

【化整为零】break up the whole into parts

【化妆】❶ (of actors) make up ❷ put on makeup; make up: 年轻妇女多喜欢～。*Most young ladies like to use makeup.* ◇ ～品 cosmetics; ～室 dressing room; ～水 beauty water; ～用品小镜匣 cosmetic case

【化装】❶ (of actors) make up ❷ disguise oneself: ～侦察 *go reconnoitring in disguise* / 他～成商人,混过了封锁线。*He disguised himself as a merchant and managed to pass through the blockade line.* ◇ ～师 makeup man; ～室 dressing room; ～舞会 fancy dress ball; masked ball; masquerade

划 动 ❶ delimit; differentiate: ～界 *delimit a boundary* / ～成分 *determine class status* / ～为右派 *be branded as a Rightist* ❷ transfer; assign: ～款 *transfer money* / 他把试验田～给这个小组负责。*He assigned the experimental plot to that group.* ❸ plan: 筹划 ——另见 huá;

【划拨】❶ transfer: 这笔款子由银行～。*The money will be transferred through the bank.* ❷ assign; allocate: 把节余的钢材～给农具厂。*Allocate the spare steel to the Farm Tools Factory.*

【划等号】equate one thing with another: 弃权票不能和反对票～。*An abstention is not equivalent to a negative vote.*

【划定】delimit; designate: ～捕鱼区 *delimit fishing areas* / ～边界 *delimit a boundary line* / 在～的区域内游泳 *swim in the designated areas*

【划分】❶ divide: ～行政区域 *divide a country into administrative areas* ❷ differentiate

【划归】put under (sb.'s administration, etc.); incorporate into: 这个企业已～地方管理。*The enterprise has been put under local administration.*

【划价】have a prescription priced (in a hospital dispensary)

【划框框】set limits; place restrictions

【划清】draw a clear line of demarcation; make a clear distinction: ～是非 *make a clear distinction between right and wrong*

【划时代】epoch-making: 具有～的意义 *have epoch-making significance* / ～的宣言 *a declaration that is a landmark in history; an epoch-making declaration*

【划线】delineate (esp. into political camps during the Cultural Revolution): 提升应看人的才能,而不能以新老来～。*Promotion should be based on merit, not seniority.*

【划一】❶ standardized; uniform: ～的模式 *a uniform model* ❷ standardize: ～这本词典的体例 *standardize the layout of the dictionary*

【划一不二】fixed; unalterable; rigid: 价钱～ *fixed price (not subject to bargaining)* / 写文章没有～的公式。*There's no hard and fast rule for writing.*

话 Ⅰ 名 word; talk: 说几句～ *say a few words* / ～不能这么说! *I wouldn't say that.* Ⅱ 动 talk about; speak about: 话别

【话把儿】〈方〉subject for ridicule; handle: 抓别人的～做文章 *seize sb.'s mistake to make an issue of it*

【话本】printed versions of the prompt-books used by popular storytellers in Song and Yuan times

【话别】say a few parting words; say good-bye: 他们在车站～。*They said their good-byes at the sta-*

tion.

【话柄】subject for ridicule; handle: 留下了～ *leave behind a subject for ridicule*

【话不投机半句多】if there's no common ground, a single word is a waste of breath

【话茬儿】(又作'话碴儿')〈方〉❶ thread of discourse: 接上～ *take up the thread of a conversation* ❷ tone of one's speech: 听他的～,这件事不好办。*From what he says, that can't be easily done.* ❸ a cause for dispute; quarrel: 他正找不到～呢,别惹他。*He's trying to pick a quarrel, so it's better to leave him alone.*

【话锋】thread of discourse; topic of conversation: 把～一转 *switch the conversation to some other subject*

【话家常】chitchat; exchange small talk

【话旧】talk over old times; reminisce

【话剧】modern drama; stage play ◇ ～团 modern drama troupe; theatrical company

【话里有话】the words mean more than they say; there's more to it than meets the ear

【话梅】preserved plum

【话题】subject of a talk; topic of conversation: 他见有人进来,马上转了～。*He changed the subject as soon as he saw someone coming in.*

【话亭】telephone booth; telephone kiosk; telephone box; call box

【话筒】❶ microphone ❷ telephone transmitter ❸ megaphone

【话头】thread of discourse: 打断～ *interrupt sb.; cut sb. short* / 拾起～ *take up the thread of a conversation* / 他知道越解释越糟,马上拨转～谈别的了。*Knowing that any explanation would only make matters worse, he hastened to change the subject.*

【话务员】(telephone) operator

【话匣子】〈方〉❶ gramophone ❷ radio receiving set ❸ chatterbox: 这人是个～。*That fellow is a chatterbox.* / 他打开～就没个完。*Once he opens his mouth, he never stops.*

【话音】❶ one's voice in speech: ～儿未落 *when one has hardly finished speaking* ❷〈口〉tone; implication: 听他的～儿,准是另有打算。*His tone suggests that he has something else in mind.*

【话语】what one says; words: 他～不多,可句句中听。*His words are few, but everything he says makes good sense.*

【话中有刺】(there are) hidden barbs in one's words; have a sting in the tail; sarcastic remark: 他听出她～,不觉脸带愠色。*He could not help looking annoyed when he detected there was a catch in her remarks.*

画 Ⅰ 动 ❶ draw; paint: ～一个圈 *draw (or describe) a circle* / ～一张草图 *make a sketch* ❷ draw; mark; sign: ～线 *draw a line* Ⅱ 名 ❶ drawing; painting; picture: 一张～ *a picture* ❷ stroke (of a Chinese character): "人"字有两～。*The character 人 is made up of two strokes.* Ⅲ 形 decorated with paintings or pictures: 画屏

【画板】drawing board

【画报】illustrated magazine or newspaper; pictorial

【画笔】painting brush; brush

【画饼充饥】draw cakes to allay hunger —feed on illusions

【画布】canvas (for painting)

【画册】an album of paintings; picture album

【画地为牢】draw a circle on the ground to serve as a prison—restrict sb.'s activities to a designated area or sphere

【画法】technique of painting or drawing: ～新颖 *a novel technique in painting or drawing*

【画舫】gaily-painted pleasure-boat

【画风】style of painting: 南方～ *style of painting typical of South China*

【画幅】❶ picture; painting: 美丽的田野是天然的～。*The beautiful open country is a painting done by nature.* ❷ size of a picture: ～虽然不大,所表现的天地却十分广阔。*The picture is small but it shows broad vistas.*

【画稿】rough sketch (for a painting)

【画工】artisan-painter

【画虎类狗】(又作'画虎不成反类犬') try to draw a tiger and end up with the likeness of a dog—attempt sth. over-ambitious and end in failure

【画家】painter; artist

【画夹】painting folder

【画架】easel

【画匠】❶ artisan-painter ❷ inferior painter

【画境】picturesque scene: 如入～ *feel as though one were in a landscape painting*

【画具】painter's paraphernalia

【画卷】❶ picture scroll ❷ magnificent scenery or stirring battle scene

【画绢】silk for drawing on; drawing silk

【画刊】❶ pictorial section of a newspaper ❷ pictorial

【画框】frame (for a picture)

【画廊】❶ painted corridor ❷ (picture) gallery

【画龙点睛】bring a picture of a dragon to life by putting in the pupils of its eyes—add the touch that brings a work of art to life; add the finishing touch; add an apt word to clinch the point

【画龙画虎难画骨】in drawing a tiger or dragon, it is easy to show its skin or scales, but not its bones: ～,知人知面不知心。*As you can draw a tiger's skin but not its bones, so you can know a man's face but not his heart.*

【画眉】❶[动] a kind of thrush ❷ blacken eyebrows; draw eyebrows

【画面】❶ general appearance of a picture; tableau ❷ film frame

【画皮】disguise or mask of an evildoer: 剥～ *rip off sb.'s mask*

【画片】a miniature reproduction of a painting

【画屏】painted screen

【画谱】a book on the art of drawing or painting

【画圈儿】〈口〉draw a circle round one's name on a document submitted for approval to show that one has read it
【画蛇添足】draw a snake and add feet to it—ruin the effect by adding sth. superfluous
【画师】❶ painter; artist ❷ artisan-painter
【画十字】❶ mark a cross (on a document in place of a signature by sb. who cannot write) ❷ cross oneself
【画室】studio
【画坛】art circle
【画帖】a book of model paintings or drawings
【画图】❶ draw designs, maps, etc. ❷〈喻〉picture: 这些诗篇构成了一幅农村生活多彩的～。*These poems give a colourful picture of country life.*
【画外音】film offscreen voice
【画像】❶ draw a portrait; portray: 给孩子画个像 *draw a portrait of the child* / 让人～ *sit for one's portrait* ❷ portrait; portrayal: 巨幅～ *a huge portrait*
【画像石】stone relief (on ancient Chinese tombs, shrines, etc.)
【画押】make one's cross (or mark); sign
【画页】page with illustrations (in a book or magazine); plate
【画展】art exhibition; exhibition of paintings
【画轴】painted scroll; scroll painting: 山水～ *a scroll of landscape painting*

桦 名 [植] birch

huái

怀 Ⅰ 名 ❶ bosom: 小孩儿在妈妈的～里睡着了。*The baby fell asleep in its mother's arms.* ❷ mind: 襟怀 Ⅱ 动 ❶ keep in mind; cherish: ～着真诚的愿望 *cherish sincere hopes* / ～着深厚的感情 *with deep feelings* / 少～大志 *harbour lofty ambition when still young* ❷ think of; yearn for: ～友 *think of a friend* / ～乡 *yearn for one's native place; be homesick* ❸ conceive (a child): ～了孩子 *become pregnant; be with child*
【怀抱】❶ hold or carry in the arms: ～着婴儿 *carry a baby in one's arms* ❷ bosom: 她把孩子搂在～里。*She held the child to her bosom.* / 回到祖国的～ *return to the embrace of one's homeland* ❸ cherish: ～远大的理想 *cherish lofty ideals*
【怀表】pocket watch
【怀才不露】refrain from showing one's abilities; sheathe or hide one's talents; be modest about one's learning
【怀才不遇】have unrecognized talents
【怀春】〈书〉harbour the amorous thoughts of spring—(of a young girl) have thoughts of love
【怀古】recall antiquity; meditate on the past (often used in titles of poems which are reflections on historical events)
【怀鬼胎】have evil intentions; harbour sinister designs
【怀恨】nurse hatred; harbour resentment: ～在心 *nurse a hatred*
【怀旧】remember past times or old acquaintances (usu. with kindly thoughts) ◇ ～情结 retrocomplex; ～热 retro boom; ～文化 retroculture
【怀恋】think fondly of (past times, old friends, etc.); look back nostalgically: 他深深地～童年的生活。*He felt a great nostalgia for his childhood.*
【怀炉】handwarmer (small aluminum box burning a special kind of coal for warming the hands or stomach)
【怀念】cherish the memory of; think of: ～革命先烈 *cherish the memory of revolutionary martyrs* / ～远方的友人 *think of an absent friend who is far away* / ～故乡 *yearn for one's hometown*
【怀柔】(of feudal rulers) make a show of conciliation in order to bring other nationalities or states under control: ～政策 *policy of control through conciliation; policy of mollification*
【怀胎】be (or become) pregnant
【怀疑】doubt; suspect: 引起～ *raise doubts; arouse suspicion* / 消除～ *dispel doubts; clear up suspicion* / 受到～ *come under suspicion* / ～他的动机 *suspect his motives* / 持～态度 *take a sceptical attitude* ◇ ～论 [哲] scepticism
【怀孕】(又作'怀妊') be pregnant: ～五个月了 *be five months pregnant; be five months gone* / ～期 *period of pregnancy; gestation period*

槐 名 Chinese scholartree
【槐角】[中] the pod of Chinese scholartree

踝 名 ankle
【踝骨】anklebone

huài

坏 Ⅰ 形 ❶ bad; harmful: ～习惯 *bad habit* / ～透了 *downright bad; rotten to the core* / ～天气 *foul weather* / ～书 *a harmful book* ❷ (used after certain verbs or adjectives) extremely: 吓～了 *be badly scared* / 气～了 *be beside oneself with rage* / 乐～了 *be wild with joy* / 累～了 *be dead tired; be dog-tired* Ⅱ 动 become or make bad; ruin; spoil: 鱼～了。*The fish has gone bad.* / 身体～ *be in poor health* / 他胃口～了。*He has lost his appetite.* Ⅲ 名 evil idea; dirty trick: 使坏
【坏处】harm; disadvantage: 一点～也没有。*There's no harm in it at all.* or *There's nothing bad about it.* / 从～着想,往好处努力。*Prepare for the worst; strive for the best.*
【坏蛋】〈口〉bad egg; scoundrel; bastard
【坏东西】bastard; scoundrel; rogue

【坏分子】[法] bad element; evildoer

【坏话】❶ malicious remarks; vicious talk: 讲别人～ *speak ill of others* ❷ unpleasant words: 好话～都要让人讲完。*One should let others finish what they have to say whether it sounds pleasant or unpleasant.*

【坏疽】[医] gangrene

【坏人】bad person; evildoer; scoundrel

【坏事】❶ bad thing; evil deed: 向坏人～作斗争 *struggle against evildoers and evil deeds* ❷ ruin sth.; make things worse: 急躁只能～。*Impetuosity will only make things worse.* / ～了! *Something terrible has happened.* / 他太粗心了! 结果坏了事。*He was so careless that he made a hash of it.*

【坏水】〈口〉evil trick; deceit; craft and guile: 使～ *play evil tricks; use deceit* / 蔫儿不唧地冒～ *be full of tricks though quiet* / 别信她! 这个女人可是一肚子～! *Don't trust her. She's full of craft and guile.*

【坏死】[医] necrosis: 局部～ *local necrosis* / 牙～ *dental necrosis*

【坏心眼儿】〈口〉evil intention; ill will: 他没有～，完全是为了你好。*He meant no harm, what he did was for your benefit.*

【坏血病】scurvy

【坏账】a bad debt

huān

欢 形 ❶ joyous; merry; jubilant: 联欢 ❷〈方〉vigorously; with great drive; in full swing: 这些小青年干得可～呢! *How vigorously these lads work!*

【欢蹦乱跳】healthy-looking and vivacious: 幼儿园里的孩子个个都是～的。*The children in the kindergarten were healthy and lively.*

【欢畅】thoroughly delighted; elated

【欢唱】sing merrily

【欢度】spend (an occasion) joyfully: ～佳节 *celebrate a festival with jubilation*

【欢呼】hail; cheer; acclaim: 人们在街道两旁列队,向归来的英雄们～。*The people lined the streets to hail the returning heroes.* / ～胜利 *hail the victory* ◇ ～雀跃 shout and jump for joy; be elated

【欢聚】happy get-together; happy reunion: 春节到了,全家老小～在一起。*The whole family got together happily for the Spring Festival.*

【欢聚一堂】happily gather under the same roof: 不同国度、不同肤色的运动员～。*Athletes from different lands and of different colours were gathered happily together.*

【欢快】cheerful and light-hearted; lively: ～的心情 *in a cheerful mood* / ～的曲调 *a lively melody* / 随着音乐～地起舞 *dance cheerfully to the music*

【欢乐】happy; joyous; gay: ～的人群 *happy crowds* / ～的景象 *a scene of great joy* / 给节日增添了～气氛 *add to the gaiety of the festival*

【欢洽】friendly; congenial: 两人谈得十分～。*The two of them talked very congenially.*

【欢庆】celebrate joyously: ～五一 *celebrate May Day*

【欢声雷动】cheers resound like peals of thunder: 全场～。*The audience broke into deafening cheers.*

【欢声笑语】happy laughters and cheerful voices

【欢送】see off; send off: 热烈～毕业生到祖国需要的地方去 *give a warm send-off to graduates going to where the country needs them* / ～会 *farewell meeting; send-off meeting* / ～仪式 *seeing-off ceremony*

【欢腾】great rejoicing; jubilation: 喜讯传来,举国～。*There was nationwide rejoicing at the good news.* / 广场上一片～。*The square was astir with jubilant crowds.*

【欢天喜地】with boundless joy; wild with joy; overjoyed: ～地迎接国庆 *greet National Day with boundless joy*

【欢喜】❶ joyful; happy; delighted: 满心～ *be filled with joy* / 欢欢喜喜过春节 *spend a joyful Spring Festival* ❷ like; be fond of; delight in: 她～拉手风琴。*She likes to play the accordion.* ◇ ～冤家 quarrelsome and loving couple; quarrelsome lovers

【欢笑】laugh heartily

【欢心】favour; liking; love: 想博取～ *try to win sb.'s favour*

【欢欣鼓舞】be filled with exultation; be elated: 捷报传来,全国人民无不～。*The good tidings filled the whole nation with joy.* or *The good tidings elated the whole nation.* / ～地跨入了新的一年 *stride into the new year in high spirits*

【欢宴】entertain sb. to dinner on some happy occasion

【欢迎】❶ welcome; greet: ～大家批评 *Criticisms are welcome.* / 我们受到了非常热烈的～。*We received a very warm welcome.* /～惠顾。*Your patronage is welcome.* ❷ be well received: 这部电影深受群众～。*The film has been well received by the people.*

【欢愉】happy; joyous; joyful: 人们都沉浸在节日的～之中。*Everybody was in a happy festive mood.*

獾 名 [动] badger

【獾油】badger fat (for treating burns)

huán

还 动 ❶ go (or come) back: 还乡 ❷ give back; return; repay: 这几本是到期要～的书。*These books are due for return.* / 下个月～你钱。*I'll pay you back next month.* ❸ give or do sth. in return: 还价 ——另见 hái

【还本】repayment of principal (or capital)：～付息 *repay capital with interest*
【还耕】restore abandoned land to cultivation；reclaim：有一千多亩废弃地已～。*More than 1 000 mu of abandoned land has been reclaimed.*
【还魂】revive after death；return from the grave
【还击】❶ fight back；return fire；counterattack：进行自卫～ *fight in self-defence* / ～敌人 *hit back at the enemy* ❷ fencing riposte
【还价】counter-offer；counter-bid
【还口】answer back；retort：骂不～ *not retort when sworn at*
【还款信用状】[经] reimbursement letter of credit
【还礼】❶ return a salute ❷ send a present in return；present a gift in return
【还清】pay off：～债务 *pay off one's debts*
【还情】repay a favour
【还手】strike (or hit) back
【还俗】(of Buddhist monks and nuns or Taoist priests) resume secular life
【还席】give a return banquet or dinner：礼尚往来嘛，对他的盛情，我们自当～。*Courtesy demands reciprocity, so we shall certainly invite him to dinner in return for his hospitality.*
【还乡】return to one's native place
【还原】❶ return to the original condition or shape；restore ❷ [化] reduction：～剂 *reducing agent*；*reductant* / ～酶 *reductase*
【还愿】❶ redeem a vow to a god ❷ fulfil one's promise：说话要算数，不能光许愿不～。*You should do what you say；you can't go on making promises and not keeping them.*
【还债】pay one's debt；repay a debt
【还账】pay one's debt；settle accounts
【还嘴】〈口〉answer (or talk) back；retort：不许和奶奶～，这不礼貌。*Don't answer back to your grandmother；it's not polite.*

环 Ⅰ 名 ❶ ring；hoop：在窗帘上缝几个～儿。*Sew a few rings on the curtain.* ❷ link：一～套一～ *all linked with one another*；*wheels within wheels* / 最薄弱的一～ *the weakest link* ❸ [体] ring：命中九～ *hit the nine-point ring* / 在射箭中取得 342～的成绩 *score 342 points in archery* Ⅱ 动 surround；encircle；hem in
【环靶】[体] round target
【环保】〈略〉见〖环境保护〗
【环抱】surround；encircle；hem in：群山～的村庄 *a village nestling among the hills*
【环比指数】[经] chain index
【环城】around the city：～赛跑 *round-the-city race* / ～公路 *ring road*；*belt highway*；*beltway*
【环带】[动] clitellum
【环岛】[交通] rotary island；roundabout
【环顾】〈书〉look about (or round)：～四周 *look all round* / ～国际局势 *take stock of the world situation*
【环海】be surrounded by sea
【环化】[化] cyclization：～橡胶 *cyclized rubber*；*cyclorubber* / ～橡胶树脂 *cyclized rubber resin*
【环礁】[地质] atoll
【环节】❶ link；sector：减少～，提高效率 *reduce the number of intermediate links and raise efficiency* / 不少～上存在着问题。*Problems exist in many sectors.* / 主要～ *a key link* / 生产～ *links in the production chain* ❷ [动] segment ◇ ～动物 annelid
【环颈雉】[动] ring-necked pheasant
【环境】environment；surroundings；circumstances：如～许可 *if circumstances permit* / 创造适宜的经济和社会～ *create a favourable economic and social environment* / 改善投资～ *improve the investment environment* ◇ ～监测系统 environmental monitoring system；～净化 depollution of environment；～科学 environmental science；～空气质量 ambient air quality；～生态学 environmental ecology；～试验 environmental test；～退化 environmental degradation；～卫生 environmental sanitation；general sanitation；～污染 pollution of the environment；environmental pollution
【环境保护】environmental protection ◇ ～法 law of environmental protection
【环流】[气] circulation
【环路】roundabout；traffic circle；ring highway；circular road：北京的三～ *the Third Ring Road of Beijing*
【环幕电影】panorama film；circular movie
【环球】❶ round the world：～旅行 *travel round the world*；*a round-the-world tour* ❷ the earth；the whole world ◇ ～定位系统 global positioning system (GPS)；～飞行 circumaviation
【环绕】surround；encircle；revolve around：大院的四周，绿树～。*The compound is surrounded by trees.* / 月亮～着地球转动。*The moon revolves around the earth.* / ～着中心任务 *centre around the main task* ◇ ～速度 [天] circular (or orbital) velocity；first cosmic velocity ——另见〖宇宙速度〗
【环山】❶ around a mountain：～公路 *a road circumscribing (or going around) a mountain* ❷ be surrounded by mountains：这村子四面～。*The village is surrounded (or hemmed in) by mountains.* or *There are mountains all round the village.*
【环蛇】krait
【环食】[天] annular eclipse (of the sun)
【环视】look around：我～车站四周，那位朋友毫无踪影。*I looked around the station but couldn't see my friend anywhere.*
【环太平洋】circum-Pacific：～地区 *circum-Pacific region*；*Pacific Basin* / ～地震带 *circum-Pacific seismic belt* / ～构造带 *circum-Pacific tectonic belt*
【环烃】[化] cyclic hydrocarbon
【环烷】[化] cycloalkanes；cycloparaffin；naphthene
【环卫】(〈略〉全称为'环境卫生') environmental

sanitation：～部门 *public sanitation department* / ～工人 *sanitation worker*

【环线】circular road；circular track；belt；loop line：地铁～ *subway circular line*

【环行】going in a ring：～一周 *make a circuit* / ～公共汽车 *bus with a circular route*/～公路 *ring road*；*belt highway*；*beltway* / ～铁路 *circuit railway*；*belt line* ◇ ～天线 loop antenna

【环形】annular；ringlike ◇ ～山［天］ring structure；lunar crater；～铁路 circular railway

【环氧树脂】［化］epoxy resin

【环游】tour around（a place）：～世界 *take a round-the-world tour*

【环宇】（又作'寰宇'）entire world：轰动～ *raise a worldwide sensation*

【环状】cyclic；annular；ring-like；loop-like

【环子】ring；link

寰 名 extensive region：人寰

【寰球】the earth；the whole world

【寰宇】〈书〉the earth；the whole world

huǎn

缓 Ⅰ形 ❶ slow；unhurried：～流 *flow slowly* ❷ not tense；relaxed Ⅱ动 ❶ delay；postpone；put off：～办 *postpone doing sth*. / 这事～几天再说。*Let's put it off for a couple of days*. ❷ not tense；relaxed recuperate；revive；come to：过了好一阵他才～过来。*It was a long time before he came to*. / ～过劲儿来 *feel refreshed after a breathing spell*

【缓兵之计】measures to stave off an attack；a stratagem to gain a respite：这不过是～而已。*These are nothing but stalling tactics*.

【缓不济急】slow action cannot save a critical situation

【缓步】walk unhurriedly

【缓冲】❶ buffer；cushion：弹性～ *elastic buffer* / 起～的作用 *produce a cushioning effect*；*absorb the shock* / ～的余地 *leeway*；*room for manoeuvre* ❷［化］buffer：～剂 *buffer* ◇ ～存储器 buffer storage；～地带 buffer zone；～放大器 buffer amplifier；～国 buffer state；～器［机］buffer；bumper；～区 buffer area；buffer zone；～文化 buffer culture

【缓和】❶ relax；ease up；mitigate；alleviate：风势渐趋～。*The wind is subsiding*. / ～矛盾 *mitigate（or alleviate）a contradiction* ❷ détente：两国关系出现了一定程度的～。*Some relaxation of tensions has been brought about between the two countries*. ◇ ～剂［物］moderator

【缓急】❶ pressing or otherwise；of greater or lesser urgency ❷ emergency ◇ ～相助 help each other in time of need

【缓减】abate；relieve；ease；subside：～紧张局势 *relieve a tense situation*

【缓建】postpone construction

【缓解】relieve；alleviate；ease：～疼痛 *relieve（or ease）the pain* / ～住房（供应）紧张情况 *alleviate（or ease）the housing（food）shortage*

【缓慢】slow：动作～ *slow in action*；*slowmoving* / 进展～ *make slow progress*

【缓聘】defer employment：目前财政有困难，只好对新职工～。*Present financial difficulties will defer employment of new staff*.

【缓坡】gentle slope

【缓期】postpone a deadline；suspend：～付款 *delay（or defer）payment* / 判处死刑，～二年执行 *condemned to death with the sentence suspended for two years*；*sentenced to death with a two-year reprieve*

【缓气】get a breathing space；have a respite；take a breather：他实在太忙了，连缓口气的工夫都没有。*He was so busy that he didn't even have a chance to take a breather*. / 我跑不动了，让我缓缓气。*I'm shagged out! Let me get my breath back*.

【缓行】❶ move，drive or walk slowly：拄杖～ *walk slowly with a stick（or cane）* / 弯道～。*（road sign）Zigzag ahead，drive slowly*. ❷ put off；postpone：计划～。*The programme has been postponed*.

【缓刑】［法］temporary suspension of the execution of a sentence；reprieve；probation：～二年 *two years' probation*

【缓役】［军］deferment（of service）

【缓征】postpone the imposition of a tax or levy

【缓滞】moderate；abate：工程完成后，可大大～上游洪峰，减弱下游压力。*Once the project is completed，flood peaks can be controlled on the upper reaches，thus relieving pressure on the lower reaches of the river*.

huàn

幻 形 ❶ unreal；imaginary；illusory：虚幻 ❷ magical；changeable：变幻

【幻灯】❶ slide show：放～ *show slides* / 看～ *watch a slide show* ❷ slide projector ◇ ～机 slide projector；epidiascope；～片（lantern）slide

【幻化】magically change：雪后的山谷～成一个奇特的琉璃世界。*The snow changed the valley into a strange glazed world*.

【幻景】illusion；mirage

【幻境】dreamland；fairyland

【幻觉】hallucination；illusion ◇ ～重现（hallucination）flashback

【幻梦】illusion；dream

【幻灭】vanish into thin air：他的希望～了。*His hopes were dashed*.

【幻视】［医］photism

【幻术】magic；conjuring

【幻听】［医］phonism

【幻想】❶ imagine；dream：自古以来，人们就～能在天空飞行。*People have dreamed of flying ever since ancient times*. ❷ illusion; fancy; fantasy: 抱有～ *cherish illusions* / 丢掉～ *cast away illusions* / 沉湎于～ *indulge in fantasy*; *be lost in reverie* / 生活在～的世界里 *live in a world of fantasy*

【幻想曲】[音] fantasia:《韩德尔主题～》*Fantasia on a Theme of Handel*

【幻象】mirage; phantom; phantasm

【幻影】unreal image

宦 名 ❶ official: 宦海 ❷ be an official; fill an office: 仕宦 ❸ eunuch

【宦官】eunuch

【宦海】officialdom; official circles: ～沉浮 *the ups and downs in officialdom*; *the vicissitudes of an official career*

【宦途】〈书〉official career

浣 Ⅰ 动 wash: ～衣 *wash clothes* Ⅱ 名〈旧〉any of the three ten-day divisions of a month: 上～ *the first ten days of a month*

【浣熊】racoon

涣 动 melt; vanish

【涣然】(of misgivings, doubts, etc.) melt away; disappear; vanish

【涣然冰释】melt away; disappear; vanish: 他的疑虑～。*All his misgivings vanished*.

【涣散】lax; slack: 纪律～ *be lax in discipline* / ～斗志 *sap sb.'s morale* (*or fighting will*)

换 动 ❶ exchange; barter; trade: 以兽皮～工业品 *exchange* (*or barter*) *furs for industrial products* / 用鲜血～来的教训 *a lesson paid for in blood* ❷ change: ～衣服 *change one's clothes* / 他～工作了吗? *Has he changed his job*? / ～乘火车 *change to a train* / 出去走一下,～～脑筋。*Let's go for a walk and give our minds a rest*. ❸ exchange; convert: 把美元～成人民币 *convert* (*or change*) *U. S. dollars into Renminbi*

【换班】❶ change shifts: 日班和夜班的工人正在～。*Daytime and nighttime workers are changing shifts now*. ❷ relieve a person on duty ❸ [军] changing of the guard

【换边】[体] change sides

【换步】[军] change step

【换茬】[农] change of crops

【换车】change trains or buses: 从学校回家一路上要换四趟车。*I have to change buses four times going home from school*.

【换代】replace; regenerate: 产品更新～ *replace the older generations of products by new ones*

【换挡】[机] shift gears

【换道】change of lanes (tracks)

【换发球】[体] change of service

【换防】[军] relieve a garrison

【换房】exchange houses: ～站 *housing exchange office*

【换俘协定】agreement for exchange of prisoners; cartel

【换岗】relieve a sentry (or guard)

【换工】exchange labour

【换汇】earn foreign exchange, exchange for foreign currencies: 出口～ *earn foreign exchange through exports*

【换货】exchange goods; barter: ～和付款协定 *goods exchange and payments agreement* / ～协定 *barter agreement*

【换机放映】film changeover

【换季】change garments according to the season; wear different clothes for a new season

【换肩】shift the carrying pole onto the other shoulder

【换届】replace (a leading group whose term has expired): ～选举 *end-of-term* (*regular*) *election*; *elect successors*

【换句话说】in other words

【换脑筋】❶ remould one's ideology ❷ change habitual ways of thinking; change one's mindset: 时代变了。该～! *Times have changed*, *we need new ways of thinking*!

【换能器】[物] transducer

【换气】take a breath (in swimming) ◇ ～扇 ventilation fan

【换钱】❶ change money (or bills) ❷ sell: 废铁也可以～。*Scrap iron can be sold for money*.

【换亲】(of two families) take each other's daughters as daughters-in-law

【换取】exchange (or barter) sth. for; get in return: 用工业品～农产品 *exchange* (*or barter*) *industrial products for farm produce* / ～外汇 *gain foreign exchange* / 以较小的代价～更大的收益 *get greater gains at smaller cost*

【换人】[体] substitution (of players) ◇ ～暂停 time-out for substitution

【换算】conversion: ～表 *conversion table*

【换汤不换药】the same medicine with a different name—the same old stuff with a different label; a change in form but not in content (or essence)

【换文】exchange of notes (or letters): 建立外交关系的～ *an exchange of notes on the establishment of diplomatic relations*

【换洗】change clothes (for washing): 带一套～的衣服。*Take along a change of clothes*.

【换型】change the model (of a product); remodel; replace the old model by a new one

【换血】〈字〉change blood;〈喻〉reshuffle (usu. sports team): ～后的新成员 *new blood*; *young member*

【换休】change the day off: 那个工厂实行～制。*That factory is implementing the system of changing the day off*.

【换牙】(of a child) grow permanent teeth

【换样】vary: 顿顿吃面条,就不能换个样儿? *Can't we vary our diet a bit instead of having noodles all the time*?

【换药】change bandage; use fresh dressing for a wound

【换羽】moult

【换约】exchange of notes (or letters)
【换装站】[铁路] transshipment station

唤 动 call out：呼唤
【唤起】❶ arouse：～民众 *arouse the masses of the people* ❷ call；recall：有必要～人们注意这个事实。*It is necessary to call attention to this fact.* / ～对往事的回忆 *evoke past memories*
【唤醒】wake up；awaken：他睡得正香，我不愿～他。*I didn't want to wake him from his sound sleep.* / ～人民 *arouse the people*

焕 形 shining；glowing
【焕发】shine；glow；irradiate：～精神，努力工作 *call forth all one's vigour and work with redoubled efforts*
【焕然一新】take on an entirely new look (or aspect)；look brand-new：这个老港经过改造和建设，面貌～。*After renovation and reconstruction the old port has changed beyond recognition.*

患 Ⅰ 名 ❶trouble；peril；disaster：水患 ❷ anxiety；worry Ⅱ 动 contract；suffer from：～肝炎 *contract (or have) hepatitis*
【患病】suffer from an illness；fall ill；be ill
【患处】affected part (of a patient's body)
【患得患失】worry about personal gains and losses；be swayed by considerations of loss and gain
【患难】trials and tribulations；adversity；trouble：可与共～，不可与共安乐 *can share distress with others，but not happiness*
【患难夫妻】husband and wife who have gone through difficult times together
【患难与共】go through thick and thin together；share weal and woe
【患难之交】friends in adversity；tested friends
【患者】sufferer；patient：结核病～ *a person suffering from tuberculosis；a TB patient*

豢 (构词成分)见下
【豢养】feed；groom；keep

huāng

荒 Ⅰ 形 ❶ waste：地～了。*The land lies waste.* ❷ desolate；barren：荒村 ❸ famine；crop failure：荒年 ❹ unreasonable：荒谬 Ⅱ 名 wasteland；uncultivated land：垦荒 Ⅲ 动 neglect；be out of practice：别把功课～了。*Don't neglect your lessons.* / 好久不下棋，～了。*It's a long time since I played chess. I'm out of practice.* / 他的英语～掉了。*His English is rusty.*
【荒草】weeds
【荒村】a deserted village
【荒诞】fantastic；absurd；incredible：～的想法 *a fantastic idea* / ～的情节 *an incredible plot*
【荒诞不经】preposterous；fantastic；absurd：《聊斋志异》所记鬼怪故事诚属～，然而却能引人入胜，多年来为无数读者所喜爱。*Though admittedly wild and fanciful，the ghost stories of the Liao Zhai Zhi Yi have a beauty that has captivated countless readers over the years.*
【荒诞无稽】fantastic；absurd；incredible：～之谈 *a tall story；a preposterous statement*
【荒岛】a desert (or uninhabited) island
【荒地】wasteland；uncultivated (or undeveloped) land
【荒废】❶ leave uncultivated；lie waste：我们村里没有一亩地是～的。*Not a single mu of land in our village lies waste.* ❷ fall into disuse (or disrepair)：这所别墅～已久。*This villa has long fallen into disuse.* ❸ waste (time)：她一边说话一边干活，不肯～半点功夫。*She worked while she chatted，not wasting a single moment.* ❹ neglect；be out of practice：～学业 *neglect one's studies*
【荒瘠】wild and barren；desolate and infertile
【荒郊】desolate place outside a town；wilderness
【荒凉】bleak and desolate；wild：一片～ *a scene of desolation* / 过去这里是～的穷山沟。*This used to be a bleak and barren gully.* / ～的景色 *wild scenery*
【荒乱】in great disorder；in turmoil
【荒谬】absurd；preposterous：～的说法 *an absurd formulation*
【荒谬绝伦】utterly absurd；absolutely preposterous：这种评论～。*This comment is absolutely preposterous.*
【荒漠】❶ desolate and boundless：～的草原 *desolate and boundless grasslands* ❷ bleak and boundless desert；wilderness
【荒年】famine (or lean) year
【荒僻】desolate and out-of-the-way：～的山区 *a desolate mountain area*
【荒歉】crop failure；famine
【荒山】a barren hill
【荒时暴月】a time of dearth；a lean year；hard times：～，他们就向亲友乞哀告怜。*In hard times，they piteously beg help from relatives and friends.*
【荒疏】out of practice；rusty：好多年不拉提琴了，现在都已～了。*I'm out of practice since I haven't played the violin for many years.* / 因为长期居住国外，我的汉语有点～了。*My Chinese is a little rusty after a long residence abroad.*
【荒唐】❶ absurd；fantastic；preposterous：～可笑 *ridiculous；absurd* / ～透顶 *absolutely ridiculous；preposterous* ❷ dissipated；loose；intemperate
【荒无人烟】desolate and uninhabited：～的地带 *a region with no sign of human habitation*
【荒芜】lie waste；go out of cultivation：由于连年战乱，百姓流离，田园～。*Owing to long years of war，people left their homes and the land was allowed to lie waste.*
【荒野】wilderness；the wilds
【荒淫】dissolute；licentious；debauched
【荒淫无耻】shamelessly dissipated：过着～的生活

lead a life of shameless dissipation

【荒原】wasteland；wilderness

【荒置】leave unused；desert；abandon：有些设备一次未用就被～在露天里。*Some equipment was dumped in the open and never used.*

慌 形 ❶ flurried；flustered；confused：沉住气，别～！*Keep calm！Don't panic！*／～了手脚 *be alarmed and confused；be flustered*／～作一团 *be thrown into utter confusion* ❷（huang）〈口〉(used after 得 as a complement) awfully；unbearably：心里闷得～ *be bored beyond endurance*／累得～ *be tired out；be dog-tired；be played out*

【慌不择路】flee along any path one stumbles upon；seize on any solution when hard pressed：～，饥不择食。*You'll take any road when you're panicky and any food when you're hungry.*

【慌里慌张】（又作'慌慌张张'）in a hurried and confused manner；all in a fluster；in a flurry：这个小伙子总是～的，老叫人不放心。*The young man is always in a fluster and doesn't seem to be very dependable.*

【慌乱】flurried；alarmed and bewildered：作好充分准备，免得临时～ *make ample preparations so as not to be in a rush at the last moment*

【慌忙】in a great rush；in a flurry；hurriedly：～赶到现场 *rush to the spot*／～起身迎客 *hurriedly rise to greet one's guest*

【慌神儿】be scared out of one's wits；panic：进考场不能～。*Be sure to remain coolheaded in the examination room*

【慌手慌脚】in a rush；in a flurry

【慌张】flurried；flustered；confused：神色～ *look flurried (or flustered)*／为什么这样慌慌张张的？*Why are you so flustered?*

huáng

皇 Ⅰ 形〈书〉grand；magnificent：堂皇 Ⅱ 名 emperor；sovereign：女皇

【皇朝】feudal dynasty

【皇储】crown prince；designated heir to the throne

【皇带鱼】oarfish

【皇帝】emperor

【皇宫】(imperial) palace

【皇冠】imperial crown

【皇后】empress

【皇家】imperial family (or house)：～卫队 *imperial guards*

【皇历】〈口〉almanac

【皇陵】imperial mausoleum

【皇亲国戚】relatives of the emperor

【皇权】imperial power (or authority)

【皇上】❶ the emperor；the throne；the reigning sovereign ❷ Your Majesty or His Majesty

【皇室】imperial family (or house)

【皇太后】empress dowager

【皇太子】crown prince

【皇天】Heaven (personified)；High Heaven

【皇天不负苦心人】Providence doesn't let down a man who does his best

【皇族】people of imperial lineage；imperial kinsmen

黄 Ⅰ 形 yellow；sallow：～沙 *yellow sands*／脸色发～ *a sallow face* Ⅱ 名（〈略〉见〖黄河〗）the Yellow River：治～ *harness the Yellow River* Ⅲ 动〈口〉fizzle out；fail；come to nothing；fall through：那笔买卖～了。*The deal is off.*

【黄斑】❶［生］yellow spot；macula lutea retinae ❷ yellow stain；fox mark：旧报纸上满是～。*The old newspaper was full of fox marks.*

【黄包车】〈方〉rickshaw

【黄檗】（又作'黄柏'）［中］the bark of a cork tree (Phellodendron)

【黄灿灿】bright yellow；golden：～的稻子 *golden rice*

【黄刺玫】yellow rose (Rosa xanthina)

【黄疸】［医］jaundice：肝原性～ *hepatogenous jaundice*／阻塞性～ *obstructive jaundice*／～指数 *icterus index*

【黄道】［天］ecliptic：～光 *zodiacal light*／～星座 *zodiacal constellation*／～座标 *ecliptic coordinates* ◇ ～带 zodiac；～十二宫 the 12 signs of the zodiac；zodiacal signs

【黄道吉日】（又作'黄道日'）a propitious (or auspicious) date；a lucky day：挑个～娶亲 *choose an auspicious day for wedding*

【黄澄澄】glistening yellow；golden：～的麦穗儿 *golden ears of wheat*

【黄帝】Huangdi or Yellow Emperor—legendary ruler and ancestor of the Chinese nation

【黄鲷】yellow porgy

【黄豆】soya bean；soybean

【黄泛区】areas formerly flooded by the Huanghe River；the Yellow River Inundated Area

【黄蜂】wasp

【黄姑鱼】spotted maigre

【黄瓜】cucumber

【黄海】the Huanghai Sea；the Yellow Sea

【黄河】the Huanghe River；the Yellow River

【黄褐色】yellowish-brown；tawny

【黄花】❶ chrysanthemum ❷ day lily ❸〈口〉virgin

【黄花菜】day lily

【黄花女儿】virgin；maiden

【黄花鱼】yellow croaker

【黄昏】dusk ◇ ～恋 love of the elderly

【黄酱】salted and fermented soya paste

【黄金】gold：～储备 *gold reserve (or stock)* ～价格 price of gold；gold rate／～市场 *gold market*／～总库 *gold pool* ◇ ～地带 golden area

【黄金分割】［数］golden section

【黄金海岸】Gold Coast

【黄金时代】golden age：唐朝是诗的～。*The Tang Dynasty is the golden age of Chinese poetry.*

【黄金时间】prime time；peak viewing time：～的广告费是很贵的。*Prime-time advertising rates are very high*.

【黄金水道】gold water route—referring to much-used water route

【黄金外汇储备】gold and foreign exchange reserves

【黄荆】［植］five-leaved chaste tree（Vitex negundo）

【黄精】［中］sealwort（Polygonatum sibiricum）

【黄酒】yellow rice or millet wine；Shaoxing（绍兴）wine

【黄鹂】oriole：黑枕～ *black-naped oriole*

【黄历】同〖皇历〗

【黄连】［中］the rhizome of Chinese goldthread（Coptis chinensis）

【黄连木】［植］Chinese pistache

【黄粱美梦】Golden Millet Dream（from the story of a poor scholar who dreamt he had become an official but awoke to find the pot of millet still cooking on the fire）—pipe dream

【黄磷】［化］yellow phosphorus

【黄栌】smoke tree（Cotinus coggygria）

【黄麻】［植］（roundpod）jute：～袋 *gunnysack*；*gunny-bag*；*gunny* / ～袋布 *gunny*（*cloth*）

【黄毛丫头】a chit of a girl；a silly little girl

【黄梅季】（又作'黄梅天'）the rainy season，usu. in April and May，in the middle and lower reaches of the Changjiang River

【黄梅戏】a form of regional drama popular in central Anhui Province

【黄梅雨】intermittent drizzles in the rainy season in the middle and lower reaches of the Changjiang River

【黄米】glutinous millet

【黄鸟】common name for 金丝雀

【黄牛】❶ ox；cattle ❷〈方〉scalper of tickets，etc.

【黄牌】［体］yellow card ◇ ～警告 a yellow card warning

【黄袍加身】be draped with the imperial yellow robe by one's supporters—be acclaimed emperor；seize political power after a coup

【黄芪】［中］the root of membranous milk vetch（Astragalus membranaceus）

【黄芩】［中］the root of large-flowered skullcap（Scutellaria baicalensis）

【黄泉】the Yellow Springs—the world of the dead；the underworld；the nether world：命赴～ *go to the Yellow Springs—die*

【黄雀】siskin

【黄壤】yellow earth；yellow soil

【黄热病】yellow fever

【黄色】❶ yellow ❷ decadent；obscene；pornographic：～电影 *pornographic movie*；*sex film* / ～书刊 *pornographic books and periodicals* / ～小说 *pornographic novel* / ～新闻 *yellow journalism* / ～音乐 *decadent music*

【黄色工会】yellow union；scab union

【黄色人种】the yellow race

【黄色炸药】❶ trinitrotoluene（TNT）❷ common name for 苦味酸

【黄鳝】ricefield eel；finless eel

【黄熟】［农］yellow maturity

【黄鼠】ground squirrel；suslik

【黄鼠狼】another name for 黄鼬

【黄鼠狼给鸡拜年，没安好心】the weasel goes to pay his respects to the hen—not with the best of intentions

【黄水疮】common name for 脓疱病

【黄体】［生理］corpus luteum ◇ ～酮［药］progesterone

【黄铁矿】pyrite

【黄铜】brass：～管 *brass pipe*（*or tube*）◇ ～矿 chalcopyrite

【黄土】［地理］loess ◇ ～高原 loess plateau

【黄萎病】［农］verticillium wilt：棉～ *verticillium wilt of cotton*

【黄癣】［医］favus

【黄羊】Mongolian gazelle

【黄杨】［植］Chinese littleleaf box

【黄莺】同〖黄鹂〗

【黄油】❶［化］grease：～枪 *grease gun* ❷ butter

【黄鼬】yellow weasel

【黄鱼】yellow croaker

【黄玉】topaz（a mineral）

【黄种】the yellow race

隍 名 dry moat outside a city wall

惶 形 fearful；afraid；anxious：惊惶

【惶惶】in a state of anxiety；on tenterhooks；alarmed

【惶惶不可终日】be in a constant state of anxiety；be on tenterhooks

【惶惑】perplexed and alarmed；apprehensive：～不安 *perplexed and uneasy*

【惶遽】〈书〉frightened；scared：神色～ *look scared*

【惶恐】terrified：～万状 *be seized with fear*；*be frightened out of one's senses*

【惶恐不安】in a state of alarm（or trepidation）

煌 形 bright；brilliant：辉煌

【煌斑岩】［地质］lamprophyre

蝗 名 locust

【蝗虫】locust

【蝗蝻】the nymph of a locust

【蝗灾】plague of locusts

篁 名〈书〉❶ bamboo grove ❷ bamboo：修～ *tall bamboos*

磺 名 sulphur：硫磺

【磺胺】［药］sulphanilamide（SN）

【磺化】sulphonate：～剂 *sulphonating agent*

【磺酸盐】［化］sulphonate

【磺酰胺】［化］sulphonic acid amide

簧 名 ❶［音］reed ❷ spring：闹钟的～断了。*The main spring of the alarm clock is broken.*

【簧风琴】reed organ；harmonium

【簧片】［音］reed

【簧乐器】reed instrument

huǎng

恍 副 ❶ all of a sudden；suddenly ❷（used together with 如，若，etc.）seem；as if：～如梦境 *as if in a dream*

【恍惚】（又作'恍忽'）❶ in a trance；absentminded：精神～ *be in a trance* ❷ dimly；faintly；seemingly：我～听见他进屋去了。*I was faintly aware that he entered the room.*

【恍然大悟】suddenly see the light；suddenly realize what has happened：经他一指点，我才～，原来是我错了。*When he dropped the hint，it suddenly dawned on me that I was wrong.*

【恍如隔世】there seems to be an interval of a whole generation (said on finding things greatly changed)

晃 动 ❶ dazzle：明晃晃 ❷ flash past：窗外有个人影儿一～就不见了。*A figure flashed past the window.* ——另见 huàng

【晃眼】❶ dazzle：亮得～ *be dazzlingly bright* ❷ twinkling：一～十年过去了。*Ten years have passed in a twinkling.*

谎 名 lie；falsehood：撒谎

【谎报】lie about sth.；give false information；start a canard：～年龄 *lie about one's age* ◇ ～军情 make a false report about the (military) situation

【谎称】falsely claim to be；pretend to be：他～自己是记者，混了进来。*He pretended to be a reporter and managed to get in.*

【谎话】lie；falsehood：说～ *tell a lie*；*lie* / ～连篇 *a pack of lies*

【谎骗】deceive；cheat；dupe

【谎言】lie；falsehood：墨写的～掩盖不了血写的事实。*Lies written in ink cannot cover up facts recorded in blood.*

幌 名〈书〉heavy curtain

【幌子】❶ shop sign；signboard ❷ pretence；cover；front：打着"援助"的～ *under the pretence of aid*；*in the guise of aid* / 骗人的～ *a facade*；*a front*

huàng

晃 动 shake；sway：他～～手说："不去了"。*With a sweep of his hand he said，"I won't go."* / 他一朗读就爱～脑袋。*He has a habit of swaying his head when he reads aloud.* ——另见 huǎng

【晃荡】rock；shake；sway：小船在江面上～。*The small boat is rocking on the river.* / 桶里水很满，一～就出来了。*The bucket was so full that it overflowed at the slightest motion.* / 风吹得马灯不停地～。*The barn lantern kept swaying in the wind.*

【晃动】rock；sway：别～这船。*Don't rock the boat.* / 车轮有点～。*The wheels wobble a bit.*

【晃梯】［杂］balancing on an upright ladder

【晃悠】shake from side to side；wobble；stagger：树枝在风中来回～。*The branches of the trees are swaying in the wind.* / 他晃晃悠悠地往前走。*He was staggering along.*

huī

灰 Ⅰ 名 ❶ ash：烧成～ *be burnt to ashes* ❷ dust：积了厚厚的一层～ *accumulate a thick layer of dust* / 看你弄了一脸的～。*Look at your face! It's all covered with dust.* ❸ lime；(lime) mortar：～墙 *plastered wall* / 和～ *mix mortar* Ⅱ 形 ❶grey：～马 *a grey horse* ❷disheartened；discouraged：心灰意懒

【灰暗】murky grey；gloomy：～的天空 *a gloomy (or murky grey) sky* / 他脸色～，象有什么大病。*His face is grey and he looks very ill.*

【灰白】greyish white；ashen；pale：～的鬓发 *greying temples* / 脸色～ *look pale*

【灰不喇唧】（又作'灰不溜丢'）〈方〉dull grey：这条裤子怎么变得这么～的了。*How did this pair of trousers get so faded?*

【灰尘】dust；dirt：大风过后，桌上落了一层～。*After the wind，there was a layer of dust on the desk.* / 掸掉桌上的～ *dust the table*

【灰沉沉】gloomy；leaden：天空～的 *a gloomy sky*；*a leaden sky*

【灰飞烟灭】become ashes and smoke；vanish like so much smoke

【灰分】［矿］ash content

【灰姑娘】Cinderella

【灰鹤】grey crane

【灰黄霉素】［药］griseofulvin

【灰浆】［建］mortar

【灰烬】ashes：化为～ *be reduced to ashes*

【灰口铁】（又作'灰铁'）grey (pig) iron

【灰领工人】gray-collar

【灰溜溜】❶ dull grey ❷ gloomy；dejected；crestfallen：他看起来有点～的样子。*He looked a little crestfallen (or depressed).* / 老李，别那么～的。*Cheer up，Lao Li.*

【灰蒙蒙】dusky；overcast：～的夜色 *a dusky night scene* / 天色～的。*The sky was overcast.*

【灰锰氧】common name for 高锰酸钾

【灰泥】［建］plaster

【灰雀】bullfinch

【灰壤】［农］podzol

【灰色】❶ grey；ashy：一件～上衣 *a grey jacket* ❷

pessimistic; gloomy: ～人生观 *a pessimistic (or grey) outlook on life* / ～的作品 *a literary work pessimistic in tone* ❸ obscure; ambiguous ◇ ～市场 [经] grey market (unofficial market in shares before regular distribution); ～系统理论 grey systems theory

【灰沙】dust and sand

【灰沙燕】sand martin

【灰鼠】squirrel

【灰心】lose heart; be discouraged: 这个队一场都没赢,队长都感到～了。*The team had won no games and the captain lost heart.* / 成功不骄傲,失败不～。*When you succeed don't get conceited; when you fail don't be dejected.*

【灰心丧气】be disheartened; get discouraged; lose heart: 他一遇上困难就～。*He's easily disheartened by difficulties.*

【灰指甲】common name for 甲癣

【灰质】[生理] grey matter

诙 动 〈书〉 ❶ banter; crack jokes ❷ ridicule; laugh at

【诙谐】humorous; jocular: 谈吐～ *be witty in conversation*

【诙谐曲】[音] humoresque

恢 形 extensive; vast: 恢恢

【恢复】❶ resume; renew: ～邦交 *resume diplomatic relations* / ～正常 *return to normal* / ～行使主权 *resume the exercise of sovereignty (over a place)* ❷ recover; regain: 他的身体～了没有? *Is he fully recovered?* / ～镇静 *regain one's composure* / ～知觉 *recover consciousness; come to* ❸ restore; reinstate; rehabilitate: ～民族权利 *restoration of national rights* / ～名誉 *rehabilitation (of a person's reputation)* / ～失地 *restore lost land; recover lost territory*

【恢复期】[医] convalescence

【恢弘】(又作'恢宏')〈书〉 ❶ broad; extensive; magnanimous: 气度～ *broad-minded; magnanimous* ❷ develop; carry on (or forward)

【恢恢】〈书〉 extensive; vast

挥 动 ❶ wave; wield: 他把手一～,上马驰骋而去。*With a wave of his hand, he mounted the horse and galloped away.* / ～刀 *wield a sword* / ～笔 *wield the brush; put pen to paper* ❷ wipe off: 挥泪 ❸ command (an army): 指挥 ❹ scatter; disperse: 发挥

【挥动】brandish; wave: ～大棒 *brandish a big stick* / ～旗子 *wave a flag* / ～拳头 *shake one's fist*

【挥发】volatilize: 瓶盖没拧紧,里面的酒精都～光了。*Because the top is loose, the alcohol inside has volatilized.* / ～性 *volatility* ◇ ～油 volatile oil

【挥戈】brandish one's weapons: ～东进 *march eastward*

【挥汗如雨】dripping with sweat

【挥毫】〈书〉 wield one's writing brush; write or draw a picture (with a brush)

【挥霍】spend freely; squander: ～公款。*Squander public funds.* / ～浪费 *spend extravagantly; wantonly squander* / ～无度 *spend without restraint*

【挥金如土】throw money about like dirt; spend money like water

【挥泪】wipe away tears; wipe one's eyes: ～而别 *take a tearful leave*

【挥手】wave one's hand; wave: ～致意 *wave greetings to; wave to sb. in acknowledgment* / ～告别 *wave farewell; wave good-bye to sb.*

【挥舞】wave; wield; brandish: ～花束表示欢迎 *wave bouquets in welcome* / ～指挥棒 *brandish the baton—order sb. about*

辉 名 ❶ brightness; splendour: 光辉 ❷ shine: 与日月同～ *shine for ever like the sun and the moon*

【辉长岩】[地质] gabbro

【辉光】[电] glow: ～灯 *glow lamp* / ～放电 *glow discharge* / ～放电管 *glow discharge tube*

【辉煌】brilliant; splendid; glorious: ～的战果 *a brilliant military victory* / ～的文化 *splendid civilization* / ～的一生 *a glorious life*

【辉绿岩】[地质] diabase

【辉钼矿】molybdenite

【辉砷钴矿】cobaltite

【辉石】[地质] pyroxene; augite

【辉锑矿】stibnite

【辉铜矿】chalcocite

【辉银矿】argentite

【辉映】shine; reflect

麾 〈书〉Ⅰ 名 standard of a commander (used in ancient times) Ⅱ 动 command: ～军前进 *command an army to march forward*

【麾下】〈书〉 ❶ under sb.'s command ❷ (a respectful title) general; commander

徽 Ⅰ 名 emblem; badge; insignia: 国徽 Ⅱ 形 fine; glorious: 徽号

【徽标】emblem; badge; insignia

【徽号】title of honour; good name

【徽记】mark; sign; logo; insignia: 这架飞机不带任何～。*The plane has (or carries) no insignia on it.*

【徽章】badge; insignia

huí

回 Ⅰ 动 ❶ circle; wind: 巡回 ❷ return; go back: ～家 *go back home* / ～到原地 *return to where one came from* / ～到生产第一线 *go back to one's post on the production front* ❸ turn round: ～过身来 *turn round* ❹ answer; reply: 回信 ❺ report back (to one's superior): 回禀 ❻ decline (an invitation, etc.); refuse; cancel;

dismiss Ⅱ量 ❶chapter：这部小说共112～。*This novel has 112 chapters.* ❷time；occasion：来过一～ *have been here once* / 有一～我在路上碰到他。*Once, I ran into him in the street.* / 完全是两～事 *two entirely different matters*

【回拜】pay a return visit

【回报】❶ report back on what has been done ❷ repay；requite；reciprocate：～他的盛情 *repay him for his hospitality (or kindness)* ❸ retaliate；get one's own back

【回避】❶ evade；dodge；avoid (meeting sb.)：～要害问题 *evade (or sidestep) the crucial question* / ～困难 *dodge difficulties* / 他～我的问题，不作答复。*He avoided answering my questions.* ❷［法］withdraw：如果审判员是案件的当事人，应当自行～。*If the judge is a party to the case, he should withdraw of his own accord.* ◇ ～制度［法］system of withdrawal

【回禀】report back (to one's superior)

【回波】［电子］echo：～脉冲 *echo pulse*

【回驳】refute：当面～ *refute sb. immediately to his face*

【回采】［矿］stoping；extraction：～工作面 *stope* / ～率 *percentage of recovery；recovery* / ～损失 *mining loss*

【回差现象】backlash phenomena

【回肠】❶［生理］ileum ❷〈书〉worried；agitated；anxious

【回肠荡气】(of music, poems, etc.) soul-stirring；thrilling；inspiring

【回肠九转】with anxiety gnawing at one's heart；weighed down with grief

【回潮】❶ (of dried things) get damp again ❷ resurgence；reversion：思想～ *an ideological relapse (or retrogression)* / 农村迷信活动有所～。*There is a revival of superstitious practices in the countryside.*

【回潮率】［纺］(moisture) regain

【回车键】［计］return key；enter key

【回程】❶ return trip ❷［机］return (or back) stroke

【回春】❶ return of spring ❷ bring back to life：～灵药 *a miraculous cure；a wonderful remedy*

【回答】answer；reply；response：请～我的问题。*Answer my question, please.* / 从理论上～了这个问题 *furnish a theoretical answer to this question*

【回荡】resound；reverberate：欢呼声在山谷间～。*Shouts of joy reverberated in the valleys.* / 她美妙的歌声依然～在我的耳际。*Her beautiful songs still ring in my ears.*

【回电】❶wire back：请即～。*Wire reply immediately.* ❷ a telegram in reply

【回跌】(of prices) go down after a rise

【回动】［机］reverse：～机构 *reversing mechanism* / ～弹簧 *return spring*

【回访】pay a return visit

【回风道】［矿］air return way

【回复】❶ reply (to a letter) ❷ return to normal state

【回顾】look back；review：～长征 *look back on the Long March* / 1991年的～ *1991 in retrospect*

【回顾展】retrospective exhibition：中国电影～ *a retrospective exhibition of Chinese films*

【回光返照】❶ the last radiance of the setting sun ❷ momentary recovery of consciousness just before death；a sudden spurt of activity prior to collapse

【回归】❶［统计］regression ❷return：～故里 *return to one's homeland* ❸draw back；fall back；retreat ◇ ～分析 regression analysis；～年［天］tropical year；solar year；～热［医］relapsing fever；～线［地理］tropic

【回锅】❶ heat up (a cooked dish) ❷ cook again ◇ ～肉 twice-cooked pork (often with chilli seasoning)

【回国】return to one's country or native land：～留学生 *student who has returned from abroad；returned student*

【回航】return to base or port

【回合】round；bout：他在第二个～中被击倒。*He was knocked out in the second round.* / 第一个～的胜利 *a first-round victory*

【回话】reply；answer：请你给他带个～。*Please take a message to him by way of reply.* / 后天给你～。*I'll give you an answer the day after tomorrow.*

【回火】［机］tempering：～脆性 *temper brittleness*

【回击】fight back；return fire；counterattack：给以有力的～ *strike a powerful counterblow；hit back hard*

【回见】〈口〉see you later (or again)；cheerio

【回降价格】roll back price

【回交】［生］backcross

【回教】［宗］(伊斯兰教) Island

【回敬】❶ return a compliment；do or give sth. in return：～一杯 *drink a toast in return* ❷ give sb. tit for tat：他先动手，我～了他一拳。*He hit me first, and I hit him back.*

【回绝】decline；refuse：一口～ *flatly refuse* / 她婉言～了他的邀请。*She declined his invitation politely.*

【回空】(of vehicles and ships) make the return trip empty (without passengers or cargo)

【回扣】sales commission

【回来】❶return；come back；be back：他马上就～。*He'll be back in a minute.* ❷ (used after a verb) back (here)：跑～ *run back* / 把借出去的书要～。*Recall the books on loan.* / 可把你盼～了。*Thank heavens, you're finally back.*

【回廊】winding corridor

【回老家】❶ revisit one's native town：他刚回了一趟老家。*He returned to his hometown recently* ❷ (usu. jocular or mocking) die；be no more：再不老实就送你～。*I'll send you to the next world, if you don't behave yourself.*

【回礼】❶ return a salute ❷ send a present in return；present a gift in return：他送了礼给我，我

得回他一份礼。*He sent me a gift; I should give him something in return.*

【回笼】❶ steam again：把凉馒头回回笼。*Heat up the cold steamed buns.* ❷ withdrawal (of currency) from circulation

【回笼觉】fall asleep again after waking up in the morning

【回炉】❶ melt down：废铁～ *melt down scrap iron; use scrap iron for smelting* ❷ bake (cakes, etc.) again

【回路】［电］return circuit；return；loop：～增益 *loop gain*

【回落】(of water levels, prices, etc.) fall after a rise

【回马枪】back thrust：杀他个～ *give sb. a back thrust; swing round and catch sb. off guard*

【回民】Hui people；Hui：～餐馆 *Moslem restaurant* / 他是～。*He is a Hui.*

【回眸】〈文〉(of a woman) glance back

【回娘家】❶ (of a married woman) return to her mother's house；❷〈喻〉go back to one's old job

【回暖】get warm again after a cold spell

【回聘】engage again (retired people, usu. by their former work units)：许多老技术员被～。*Many retired technicians have been rehired.*

【回迁】(of those who have been removed to make way for a project, or evacuated during an emergency) move back；return：心楼盖好后,居民又～了。*The inhabitants moved back when the new building was completed.*

【回青】〈方〉(of winter crops or transplanted seedlings) turn green

【回请】return hospitality；give a return banquet

【回去】❶ return；go back；be back：他明天回杭州去。*He will return to Hangzhou tomorrow.* / 他离开家乡十年,从未～过。*He has never been back to his birthplace since he left it ten years ago.* ❷ (used after a verb) back (there)：请把这封信给他退～。*Please return the letter to him.* / 昨天我是走～的。*I went back on foot yesterday.*

【回扫】［电子］flyback ◇ ～率 retrace ratio；～期 flyback time；retrace time

【回升】rise again (after a fall)；pick up：气温～。*The temperature has gone up again.* / 指数～。*The index is picking up.* / 价格又～了。*Prices rose again.*

【回生】❶ bring back to life ❷ forget through lack of practice；get rusty：几年不用,我的法语又～了。*I haven't used my French for years and it's getting rusty.*

【回声】echo：孩子们在山洞里高声喊叫,想听听～。*The children shouted loudly in the cave so that they could hear the echoes of their voices.*

【回收】retrieve；recover；reclaim：～贵重金属 *retrieve rare metals* / 发射和～卫星 *launch and retrieve satellites* / 余热～ *recovery of waste heat* ◇ ～率 rate of recovery (or reclamation)；～塔［化］recovery tower；～站 (waste materials) collection depot；～装置 retrieving device

【回手】❶ turn round and stretch out one's hand：他走出了屋子,～把门带上。*He went out of the room and closed the door behind him.* ❷ hit back；return a blow

【回首】❶ turn one's head；turn round ❷〈书〉look back；recollect：～往事 *recall the past*

【回溯】recall；look back upon：～革命战争的岁月 *look back upon the years of revolutionary war*

【回顺】roll back and rationalize：原料价格～后,有关问题可获缓解。*When prices of raw materials are rolled back and rationalized, some related problems will be alleviated.*

【回天乏术】unable to save the situation

【回天之力】power capable of saving a desperate situation；tremendous power

【回填】［建］backfill：～土 *backfill*

【回条】a short note acknowledging receipt of sth.；receipt

【回帖】〈旧〉a money order receipt to be signed and returned to the sender

【回头】❶ turn one's head；turn round：他～往后看。*He turned his head and looked back.* ❷ repent：及早～ *repent before it is too late* ❸〈口〉later：～再谈。*We'll talk it over later.*

【回头见】〈口〉see you later (or again)；cheerio

【回头路】the road back to one's former position；the road of retrogression：走～ *take the road back; backtrack*

【回头客】〈口〉frequent customer：他是饭店的～。*He is a frequent customer at this restaurant.*

【回头是岸】turn the head and the shore is at hand—repent and be saved：劝说他良心发现,～ *try to persuade him to recover his conscience and turn from his evil ways* ——另见〖苦海无边,回头是岸〗

【回味】❶ aftertaste ❷ call sth. to mind and ponder over it：～他说的话 *ponder over what he has said*

【回乡】return to one's home village：～探亲 *go home to visit one's family and relatives* / ～知识青年 (*before* 1978) *a school graduate who returns to work in his or her home village*

【回响】reverberate；echo；resound：雷声在山谷里激起了～。*Thunder reverberated in the valley.* / 他的亲切教导仍在我的耳边～。*His earnest instructions still ring in my ears.*

【回想】think back；recollect；recall：这首歌使我～起在中国的留学生活。*The song brought back to my mind the days when I was studying in China.* / 他确切的话我已～不起来了。*I can no longer recall his exact words.*

【回心转意】change one's mind；come around；have a change of heart：我晓得,这不过是你的气话,你会～的。*I know you're talking in anger and you'll come round.*

【回信】❶ write in reply；write back：我回了他一封信。*I wrote him a reply.* / 望早日～。*I'm looking forward to hearing from you soon.* ❷ a letter in reply ❸ a verbal message in reply；reply：

事情办妥了,我给你个～儿。*I'll let you know when I'm through with it.*

【回旋】❶ circle round:飞机在上空～。*The aeroplane is circling overhead.* ❷ (room for) manoeuvre ◇ ～加速器 [物] cyclotron;～曲 [音] rondo

【回旋余地】room for freedom of action; room for manoeuvre; leeway; latitude:留点儿～,别把话说死了。*Don't make it so definite — allow a little latitude.*

【回忆】call (or bring) to mind; recollect; recall:他的脸我还认得,可是他的名字我却～不起来了。*I remember his face, but I can't call his name to mind.* / 战争年代的～ *reminiscences of the war years* / 童年的～ *recollections of childhood; childhood memories* ◇ ～对比 recall the past and contrast it with the present;～录 reminiscences; memoirs; recollections

【回音】❶ echo ❷ reply:立候～ *hoping for an immediate reply* / 我去过三封信,但一直没有～。*I've written him three letters but haven't heard anything from him yet.* ❸ [音] turn:逆～ *inverted turn*

【回音壁】the Echo Wall (in the Temple of Heaven in Beijing)

【回应】answer; respond:我在窗外喊他,他没～。*I called to him at the window but he didn't answer.*

【回赠】send a present in return; present a gift in return

【回涨】(of water levels, prices, etc.) rise again after a fall:物价～。*Prices are rising again.*

【回执】a short note acknowledging receipt of sth.; receipt

【回注】[油] recycle

【回柱】[矿] prop drawing:～机 *prop drawer; post puller*

【回转】turn round:～马头 *turn the horse round* ◇ ～半径 [航海] radius of gyration;～工作台 [机] rotary table;～炉 [冶] rotary furnace;～式钻床 rotary drill;～体 [数] solid of revolution;～仪 [天] gyroscope; gyro

【回族】Hui ethnic group inhabiting the Ningxia Hui Autonomous Region mainly, but also distributed over other parts of China.

【回嘴】answer (or talk) back; retort

茴

(构词成分)见下

【茴香】[植] ❶ fennel:～油 *fennel oil* ❷〈方〉aniseed:～豆 *beans flavoured with aniseed*

蛔

(构词成分)见下

【蛔虫】roundworm; ascarid:～病 *roundworm disease; ascariasis*

huǐ

悔

动 regret; repent:～之晚矣 *too late to repent* / ～不该听信了他的话。*I shouldn't have believed him.*

【悔不当初】regret having done sth.:早知今日,～。*If I'd known then what was going to happen, I wouldn't have done as I did.*

【悔改】repent and mend one's ways:毫无～之意 *have no intention of mending one's ways; show no sign of repentance* / 表示愿意～ *show willingness to mend one's way*

【悔过】repent one's error; be repentant:有～表示 *show signs of repentance* / 诚恳～ *sincerely repent one's error; show sincere repentance* / ～书 *a written statement of repentance*

【悔过自新】repent and turn over a new leaf; repent and make a fresh start:停止作恶,～ *stop doing evil, repent and start anew*

【悔恨】regret deeply; be bitterly remorseful:～终身 *eternal regret*

【悔婚】break a pledge of marriage; break off an engagement

【悔棋】retract a false move in a chess game

【悔悟】realize one's error and show repentance

【悔之无及】too late to repent; too late for regrets:再要推延,就会～了。*With further delay it will be too late to repent.*

【悔罪】show repentance; show penitence:确有～表现 *show real repentance*

毁

动 ❶ destroy; ruin; damage:森林为大火所～。*The forest was destroyed by fire.* / 这场雹子把庄稼～了。*The hailstorm ruined the crops.* / 她的一生给～了。*She was ruined for life.* ❷ burn up:烧毁 ❸ defame; slander:毁谤

【毁谤】slander; malign; calumniate:这纯系～。*This is slander, pure and simple.*

【毁害】destroy; damage

【毁坏】destroy; damage:旋风～了好几十户人家。*The cyclone destroyed dozens of houses.* / 洪水～了铁路。*The flood damaged the railway.* / ～名誉 *ruin sb.'s reputation*

【毁家纾难】*give the family fortune to the state in a time of crisis*

【毁灭】destroy; exterminate:旧唐山在1976年的一场地震中～。*The old city of Tangshan was destroyed in an earthquake in 1976.* / 给侵略者以～性打击 *deal the aggressors a crushing (or devastating) blow*

【毁弃】scrap; annul:敌军逃跑时沿途～了许多武器。*The fleeing enemy abandoned and destroyed many weapons along the road.*

【毁容】disfigure one's face

【毁伤】injure; hurt; damage

【毁损】damage; impair:很多古代建筑遭到～。*Many ancient buildings have been damaged.*

【毁于一旦】be destroyed in one day; be destroyed in a moment:十年心血～! *The fruits of ten years' labours destroyed in one day!*

【毁誉】praise or blame; praise or condemnation:不计～ *be indifferent to people's praise or blame* / ～不一。*Evaluations differ widely.*

【毁誉参半】be as much censured as praised; get both praise and blame; find a mixed reception

【毁约】❶ break one's promise ❷ scrap a contract or treaty

huì

汇 Ⅰ 动 ❶converge: ～成巨流 *converge into a mighty torrent* ❷ gather together: ～印成书 *have (articles on a given subject) collected and published in book form* ❸remit: 给家里～点钱 *remit money to one's family; send some money home* Ⅱ 名 things collected; assemblage; collection: 词汇

【汇报】report; give an account of: ～调查结果 *report the findings of an investigation* / ～会 *a report-back meeting* ◇ ～演出 report-back performance

【汇编】compilation; collection; corpus: 资料～工作 *compilation of reference material* / 文件～ *a collection of documents* / 语言学研究资料～ *a corpus of philological data* ◇ ～程序 assembler program; assembler; assembly routine; ～语言[计] assembler language; ～指令 assembler instruction

【汇单】money order; remittance slip

【汇兑】remittance: 国内～ *domestic remittance* / ～网 *remittance network* ◇ ～银行 exchange bank

【汇费】(又作'汇水') remittance fee

【汇合】converge; join: 这两条河在什么地方～? *Where do the two rivers join?* / ～成一支巨大的力量 *unite to form a gigantic force*

【汇集】❶ collect; compile: ～材料 *collect all relevant data* / ～经济信息 *collect economic information* ❷ come together; converge; assemble: 游行队伍从四面八方～到天安门广场上。*The paraders converged on Tian'anmen Square from all directions.*

【汇寄】remit: 通过邮局～款项 *remit (or send) money by post* / 你需要钱我～给你。*If you need money I'll send it.*

【汇价】exchange rate; conversion rate

【汇款】❶ remit money; make a remittance: 他到银行～去了。*He went to the bank to remit some money.* / ～单 *money order* / ～人 *remitter* ❷ remittance: 收到一笔～ *receive a remittance* / 邮政～ *postal remittance*

【汇流】converge; flow together ◇ ～点[地质] confluence; ～条[电] busbar

【汇拢】❶ come together; gather; assemble ❷ collect; compile

【汇率】(又作'汇价') exchange rate: 固定～ *fixed (exchange) rate* / 浮动～ *floating (exchange) rate* / 中心～ *central rate*

【汇票】draft; bill of exchange; money order: 银行～ *bank draft* / 邮政～ *postal money order*

【汇算】settle accounts; wind up an account ◇ ～清缴 make the final settlement

【汇总】gather; collect; pool: 把材料～上报 *collect data for the higher level; present an itemized report to the higher level*

卉 名 (various kinds of) grass: 奇花异卉

会 Ⅰ 动 ❶ get together; assemble: 聚会 ❷ meet; see: 昨天我没有～着他。*I didn't see him yesterday.* ❸understand; grasp: 误会 ❹know: 我～英语,不～日语。*I know English but don't know Japanese.* / 他还～两出京戏。*He's able to sing a few airs of Beijing Opera.* ❺ can; be able to: ～滑冰 *can skate* / 这孩子刚～走路,还不大～说话。*The baby has just learnt to walk but has't learnt to speak yet.* ❻ be good at; be skilful in: ～修各种钟表 *be skilled in repairing all kinds of clocks and watches* / 很～这一套 *be a past master of this sort of game* ❼ be likely to; be sure to: 他～在家吗? *Is he likely to be at home?* / 他～来的。*He's sure to come.* / 没想到～这么顺利。*I didn't expect things would go off so smoothly.* ❽ pay (or foot) a bill: 饭钱我～过了。*I've paid for the meal.* Ⅱ 名 ❶ meeting; gathering; party; get-together; conference: 晚上有个全组～。*There's going to be a meeting of the whole group tonight.* ❷association; society; union: 帮会 ❸a temple fair: 庙会 ❹chief city; capital: 都会 ❺〈口〉a moment: 一会儿 ——另见 kuài

【会标】emblem of a sports meet, etc.

【会餐】dine together; have a dinner party

【会场】meeting-place; conference (or assembly) hall

【会道门】superstitious sects and secret societies: 反动～ *reactionary secret societies*

【会费】membership dues

【会风】style of meeting: ～不正 *unhealthy style of meeting*

【会馆】〈旧〉guild hall; provincial or county guild

【会海】〈贬〉sea of meetings—numerous meetings: 文山～ *piles of official papers and endless meetings*

【会合】join; meet; converge; assemble: 两军～后继续前进。*The two armies joined forces and marched on.*

【会合点】[军] meeting point; rallying point; rendezvous

【会话】conversation (as in a language course)

【会徽】emblem of a sports meet, etc.

【会籍】membership (of an association)

【会见】meet with (esp. a foreign visitor)

【会聚】assemble; flock together: 游园群众～于各个公园,欢庆五一节。*Holidaymakers flocked to the parks to celebrate May Day.*

【会聚透镜】[物] convergent lens

【会刊】❶ proceedings of a conference, etc. ❷ the journal of an association, society, etc.

【会考】general examination (an examination for

the graduating students of all schools in a locality)

【会客】receive a visitor (or guest): ～时间 *the time for receiving visitors; visiting hours* / 现在开会，不～。*No visitors. Meeting in progress.* ◇ ～室 reception room

【会面】meet: 我约定了星期天和他～。*I have an appointment to meet him on Sunday.* / 我和他才会过一次面。*I met him only once.*

【会期】❶ the time fixed for a conference; the date (or time) of a meeting ❷ the duration of a meeting: ～定为三天。*The meeting is scheduled to last three days.*

【会齐】get together; assemble: 明晨七时在门口～。*We'll assemble at the gate at 7 o'clock tomorrow morning.*

【会旗】the banner of a meeting

【会签】(of two or more than two units) jointly sign an official document

【会商】hold a conference or consultation: ～解决办法 *consult to find a solution*

【会审】❶ joint hearing (or trial) ❷ make a joint checkup: ～施工图纸 *have a joint checkup on the blueprints for a project*

【会师】join forces; effect a junction

【会所】the office of an association

【会谈】talks: 双边～ *bilateral talks* / ～纪要 *minutes of talks; notes on talks; summary of a conversation*

【会堂】assembly hall; hall: 人民大会堂

【会同】(handle an affair) jointly with other organizations concerned: 这件事由计委～经委审批。*This matter is subject to joint examination and approval by the Planning Commission and the Economic Commission.*

【会务】day-to-day work of a conference; routine affairs of a conference: ～费 *registration fee for a conference* / 主持～ *be in charge of the conference's day-to-day work*

【会晤】meet: 两国外长定期～。*The foreign ministers of the two countries meet regularly.*

【会心】understanding; knowing: ～的微笑 *an understanding smile* / 露出～的表情 *with a knowing look*

【会演】joint performance (by a number of theatrical troupes, etc.): 文艺～ *theatrical festival*

【会厌】[生理] epiglottis

【会议】❶ meeting; conference: 正式～ *official meeting* / 全体～ *plenary session* / ～地点 *meeting-place; venue* / ～日程表 *the daily agenda of a conference* / ～室 *meeting (or conference) room; council chamber* / ～厅 *conference (or assembly) hall* ❷ council; congress

【会意】同〖会心〗

【会阴】[生理] perineum

【会员】member: 工会～ *a member of the trade union* / 正式～ *full (or full-fledged) member* / ～人数 *membership* ◇ ～国 member state (or nation); ～证 membership card; ～资格 the status of a member; membership

【会战】❶ [军] meet for a decisive battle ❷ launch a mass campaign; join in a battle

【会章】❶ the constitution (or statutes) of an association, society, etc. ❷ the emblem of an association, society, etc.

【会长】the president of an association or society

【会账】pay (or foot) a bill

【会诊】[医] consultation of doctors; (group) consultation: 中西医～ *hold group consultations of doctors practising Chinese and Western medicine* / 几位大夫对这个病人进行了～。*Several doctors consulted about the case.*

【会址】❶ the site of an association or society ❷ the site of a conference or meeting

讳 Ⅰ 动 avoid as taboo: 直言不讳 Ⅱ 名 ❶ forbidden word; taboo: 犯了他的～了。*Something was said that happened to be taboo with him.* ❷ the name, regarded as taboo, of a deceased emperor or head of a family

【讳疾忌医】hide one's sickness for fear of treatment—conceal one's fault for fear of criticism

【讳莫如深】closely guard a secret; not breathe a word to a soul; not utter a single word about sth.

【讳言】dare not or would not speak up: 毫不～ *make no attempt to conceal the truth; confess freely*

诲 动 teach; instruct: 教诲

【诲人不倦】be tireless in teaching; teach with tireless zeal: ～的教师 *an indefatigable teacher* / 学而不厌，～。*have never grown tired of learning nor wearied of teaching others what one has learnt*

【诲淫诲盗】propagate sex and violence; stir up the base passions

荟 形〈书〉luxuriant growth (of plants)

【荟萃】(of distinguished people or exquisite objects) gather together; assemble: ～一堂 *gather together in one hall*

【荟集】gather; assemble; collect

绘 动 paint; draw: 描绘

【绘画】drawing; painting

【绘声绘色】(又作'绘声绘影'；'绘影绘声') vivid; lively: ～的描述 *a vivid description (or portrayal)*

【绘图】同〖制图〗◇ ～板 drawing board

【绘制】draw (a design, etc.): ～图表 *draw up a table*

烩 动 ❶ braise: ～虾仁 *braised shrimp meat* ❷ cook (rice or shredded pancakes) with meat, vegetables and water

贿 名 ❶〈书〉wealth ❷ bribe: 受贿 / 行贿

【贿赂】❶ bribe ❷ bribery

【贿买】buy over; suborn

【贿选】practise bribery at an election; get elected by bribery

彗 名〈书〉broom

【彗尾】the tail of a comet

【彗星】comet

晦 Ⅰ名 ❶ the last day of a lunar month ❷night Ⅱ形 dark; obscure; gloomy

【晦暗】dark and gloomy

【晦明】〈书〉night and day; gloomy and bright

【晦气】unlucky: 碰到这种事真是～! *What rotten luck to have this happen to me!*

【晦涩】(of literary writing, music, etc.) hard to understand; obscure: 文辞～ *obscure language (in poetry, drama, etc.)*

秽 名 ❶ dirty: 污秽 ❷ ugly; abominable: 秽行

【秽气】stink; bad (or offensive) smell: ～冲天 *stink to high heaven*

【秽土】rubbish; refuse; dirt

【秽闻】〈书〉ill repute (referring to sexual behaviour); reputation for immorality

【秽亵】〈书〉❶ filthy; foul ❷ obscene; salacious; bawdy

【秽行】〈书〉debauched behaviour; immoral conduct

【秽语】obscene words; lewd speech

惠 Ⅰ名 favour; kindness; benefit: 受惠 Ⅱ形〈套〉kind; gracious

【惠存】〈套〉please keep (this photograph, book, etc. as a souvenir); to so-and-so

【惠而不费】beneficial and not costly

【惠风】gentle breeze; soft breeze

【惠顾】〈套〉your patronage: 欢迎～。(*used by shopkeepers*) *Your patronage is solicited.*

【惠临】〈套〉your gracious presence: 敬请～。*Your presence is requested.*

喙 名〈书〉❶ beak or snout: 长～ *a long beak* ❷ mouth

慧 形 intelligent; bright: 智慧

【慧根】[宗](佛教) talent to thoroughly comprehend Buddhist teachings; innate intelligence

【慧黠】〈书〉clever and artful; shrewd

【慧心】wisdom

【慧眼】❶ [宗](佛教) a mind which perceives both past and future ❷ mental discernment (or perception); insight; acumen: 独具～ *have exceptional insight*

【慧中秀外】(又作'秀外慧中') intelligent within and beautiful without; both intelligent and beautiful

蕙 名[植] orchid

【蕙兰】a species of orchid

【蕙心】〈书〉pure heart of a woman

hūn

昏 Ⅰ名 dusk: 晨～ *at dawn and dusk* Ⅱ形 ❶ dark; dim: 天昏地暗 ❷confused; muddled: 昏头昏脑 Ⅲ动 lose consciousness; faint: ～倒 *fall into a swoon; go off into a faint; fall unconscious*

【昏暗】dim; dusky: ～的灯光 *a dim light* / 太阳下山了,屋里渐渐～起来。*The sun was setting, and the room was getting darker and darker.*

【昏沉】❶ murky: 暮色～ *murky twilight* ❷ dazed; befuddled: 我昨晚没睡好,头脑昏昏沉沉的。*I feel in a daze because I didn't sleep well last night.*

【昏黑】dusky; dark

【昏花】dim-sighted

【昏黄】pale yellow; faint; dim: 月色～ *faint moonlight* / ～的灯光 *a dim light*

【昏昏欲睡】drowsy; sleepy: 这出戏太沉闷,观众都～。*This dull play is sending the audience to sleep.*

【昏厥】faint; swoon: ～过去 *fall into a coma; faint away*

【昏君】a fatuous and self-indulgent ruler

【昏聩】(又作'昏愦') decrepit and muddleheaded: ～无能 *muddleheaded and incompetent*

【昏乱】❶ dazed and confused; befuddled ❷〈书〉benighted and disorderly

【昏迷】stupor; coma: 处于～状态 *be in a state of unconsciousness; be in a coma* / 她～过去了。*She went into a coma.* / ～不醒 *remain unconscious*

【昏睡】lethargic sleep; lethargy

【昏死】faint; fall into a coma

【昏天黑地】❶ heaven and earth in darkness: 到了晚上,～的,就更不好走了。*Night fell and, as darkness closed in, the going became even harder.* ❷ be in a state of delirium; lose consciousness: 当时我流血过多,觉得～的。*I blacked out through loss of blood.* ❸ dissipated: 过着荒淫无耻、～的生活 *lead an immoral life, given to dissipation and sensuality* ❹ dark rule and social disorder: 当时军阀混战,盗贼横行,真是～。*Ridden with warlordism and banditry, the country was then in a dark, troubled period of its history.*

【昏头昏脑】(又作'昏头胀脑') dizzy; muddle-headed; absent-minded

【昏头转向】同〖晕头转向〗

【昏星】evening star

【昏眩】dizzy; giddy: 一阵～ *a spell of giddiness*

【昏庸】fatuous; muddleheaded; stupid: 老朽～ *senile and fatuous*

荤 名 ❶ meat or fish: 三～一素 *three meat dishes and one vegetable dish* / 她不吃～。*She doesn't eat meat.* or *She's a vegetarian.* ❷

strong-smelling vegetables forbidden to Buddhist vegetarians, such as onions, leeks, garlic, etc.
【荤菜】meat dish
【荤腥】meat or fish
【荤油】lard

婚 Ⅰ 动 wed; marry: 未婚 Ⅱ 名 marriage; wedding: 婚姻
【婚变】divorce; extramarital affair (that disrupts a marriage): 不久有了～,两人分手了。*Their marriage broke up not long after. They each went their own way.*
【婚假】marriage leave
【婚嫁】marriage
【婚检】physical check-up before marriage
【婚礼】wedding ceremony; wedding: 星期天举行～。*The wedding will take place on Sunday.*
【婚恋】fall in love and get married: 这些民族有着不同的～风情。*These ethnic groups all have their own customs of courtship and marriage.*
【婚龄】(legally) marriageable age: 法定～ *legally marriageable age*
【婚内强奸】rape inside marriage
【婚配】married: 子女两人,均未～。*Both son and daughter are unmarried.*
【婚期】wedding day
【婚娶】(of a man) get married; take a wife
【婚生子女】[法] children born in wedlock; legitimate children
【婚事】marriage; wedding: 操办～ *prepare a wedding*
【婚书】〈旧〉marriage certificate
【婚外恋】an extramarital affair
【婚姻】marriage; matrimony: ～自由 *freedom of marriage* / ～纠纷 *matrimonial dispute*
【婚姻法】marriage law
【婚姻介绍所】matrimonial agency
【婚姻状况】marital status
【婚育期】marriageable and child-bearing age: 进入～ *reach the marriageable and child-bearing age.*
【婚约】marriage contract; engagement: 解除～ *break off one's engagement*

hún

浑 形 ❶ muddy; turbid: 水～得很。*The water is very muddy.* ❷ foolish; stupid ❸ simple and natural; unsophisticated: 浑朴 ❹ whole; all over: 浑身
【浑蛋】〈讳〉blackguard; wretch; scoundrel; bastard; skunk
【浑厚】❶ simple and honest ❷ (of writing, painting, etc.) simple and vigorous: 笔力～ *(of handwriting) bold and vigorous strokes* / 他的声音～洪亮。*He has a deep and rich voice.*
【浑话】impudent remark
【浑浑噩噩】muddle-headed and ignorant
【浑金璞玉】同〖璞玉浑金〗
【浑朴】simple and honest: 性格～ *simple and honest in nature; of simple and honest character* / 画风～ *paint in a plain and simple style* / ～的语言 *plain and simple language*
【浑球儿】(又作'混球儿')〈方〉rascal; wretch; skunk; son of a bitch
【浑然一体】one integrated mass; a unified entity; an integral whole
【浑身】from head to foot; all over: 吓得～发抖 *tremble all over with fear* / ～疼痛 *aching all over* / ～是劲 *brimming with energy; bursting with energy*
【浑身是胆】be every inch a hero; be the embodiment of valour
【浑水摸鱼】fish in troubled waters: 挑拨离间,制造混乱,以便～ *sow discord and create confusion so as to fish in troubled waters*
【浑天仪】[天] ❶ armillary sphere ❷ celestial globe
【浑象】[天] celestial globe
【浑仪】[天] armillary sphere
【浑圆】perfectly round: ～的珍珠 *a perfectly round pearl* / ～的月亮 *full moon*
【浑浊】muddy; turbid: ～的水 *turbid water* / ～的空气 *foul (or stale) air*

馄 (构词成分)见下
【馄饨】won ton; dumpling soup

魂 名 ❶ soul: 灵魂 ❷ mood; spirit: 神魂 ❸ the lofty spirit of a nation: 民族～ *national spirit*
【魂不附体】feel as if one's soul had left one's body: 吓得～ *be scared out of one's wits*
【魂不守舍】be scared out of one's wits; have lost one's mind
【魂飞魄散】be scared out of one's wits; be half dead with fright
【魂灵】〈口〉soul
【魂牵梦萦】miss very much; pine for: 这便是他日夜思念,～的恋人。*She is the woman he has been yearning for by day and dreaming about at night.*
【魂魄】soul

hùn

诨 名 joke; jest
【诨名】(又作'诨号') nickname

混 Ⅰ 动 ❶ mix; confuse: ～在一起 *mix things up* / 这是两码事,不要搞～了。*They're two entirely different matters; don't mix them up.* ❷ pass for; pass off as: 混充 ❸ muddle along; drift along: 连口饭都～不上 *can hardly make a living* / 我是～一天算一天。*I just manage to get by from day to day.* ❹ get along with sb.: 同他们～得很熟 *be quite familiar with them* Ⅱ 副 thoughtlessly; recklessly; irresponsibly: ～出主意 *put forward irresponsible suggestions*

【混充】pass oneself off as; palm sth. off as
【混沌】❶ Chaos (the primeval state of the universe according to folklore): ～初开 *when earth was first separated from heaven* ❷ ignorant; simple-minded; muddle-headed
【混饭吃】engage in a job for the sake of making a living (without having any real interest in it): 这种工作还有什么意思呢? 我只是在那儿混碗饭吃。*What interest could there possibly be in such a job? I'm just working there for the sake of making a living.*
【混纺】[纺] blending: ～织物 *blend fabric* / ～毛线 *blended wool*
【混合】mix; blend; mingle: 客货～列车 *mixed train* ◇ ～编队 [军] composite formation; ～器 [化] mixer; ～色 secondary colour; ～授粉 [农] mixed pollination; ～双打 [体] mixed doubles; ～物 mixture; ～岩 [地质] migmatite
【混混儿】〈方〉rascal; scoundrel
【混交林】mixed forest
【混进】(又作'混入') infiltrate; sneak into; worm one's way into: 他随着人流～会场。*He mixed with the crowd and gate-crashed the meeting.*
【混乱】confusion; chaos: 思想～ *ideological confusion* / 交通～ *chaotic traffic conditions* / 语言造成的～严重影响人们的生活。*The confusions created by language deeply affect men's lives.* / 管理～ *bad management*
【混凝剂】[化] coagulant
【混凝土】concrete: ～搅拌机 *concrete mixer* / ～结构 *concrete structure* / ～振捣器 (*concrete*) *vibrator*
【混频管】[电子] mixer tube
【混频器】mixer
【混日子】drift along aimlessly
【混世魔王】world-wrecking demon king —an evil man who disturbs the peace of the world; human fiend; devil incarnate
【混双】[体] (〈略〉全称为'混合双打') mixed doubles
【混同】confuse; mix up: 不要把诗和词～起来。*Don't confuse poetry of regular metre with poetry with irregular metre.*
【混为一谈】lump (or jumble) together; confuse sth. with sth. else: 把正义战争与非正义战争～ *lump together just wars and unjust wars*
【混响】[物] reverberation ◇ ～室 reverberation chamber
【混淆】obscure; blur; confuse; mix up: ～敌友 *confuse friend with foe* / ～两类不同性质的矛盾 *mix up the two different types of contradictions*
【混淆黑白】mix up black and white; confound right and wrong: 颠倒是非～ *confound right and wrong and turn things upside down*
【混淆是非】confuse right and wrong
【混淆视听】mislead the public; confuse public opinion
【混血儿】a person of mixed blood; half-breed
【混一】amalgamation
【混杂】mix; mingle: 不要把不同的种子～在一起。*Don't mix up different kinds of seeds.*
【混战】tangled warfare: 军阀～ *tangled warfare among warlords; tangled fighting between warlords* / 球门前一场～,球被捅进了球门。*In a scramble in front of the goal, the ball was kicked in.*
【混帐】〈讳〉scoundrel; bastard; son of a bitch ◇ ～话 impudent remark
【混浊】muddy; turbid: ～的水 *turbid water* / ～的空气 *foul* (*or stale*) *air* / 两眼～ *bleary-eyed* / 小便～ *cloudy urine*

huō

劐 动〈口〉❶ slit or cut with a knife: 把鱼肚子～开 *slit open the fish* ❷ hoe

豁 动 ❶ slit; break; crack: 墙上～了一个口子。*There is a breach in the wall.* ❷ give up; sacrifice: ～出三天时间,也要把它做好。*Even if it takes us three whole days, we must get the job done.* ——另见 huò
【豁出去】go ahead regardless; be ready to risk everything: 我们～了,决心跟他们干到底。*We are resolved to fight it out with them at all costs.*
【豁口】opening; break; breach: 城墙～ *an opening in the city wall*
【豁嘴】❶〈口〉harelip ❷ a harelipped person

huó

和 动 mix (powder) with water, etc.: ～点儿灰泥把洞堵上。*Prepare some plaster to fill the hole.* ——另见 hé, hè, huò
【和面】knead dough ◇ ～机 flour-mixing machine

活 Ⅰ 动 ❶ live: 她～到 80 岁。*She lived to be eighty.* / 鱼在水里才能～。*Fish can only live in water.* ❷ save (the life of a person): ～人无算 (*of a good doctor, etc.*) *save countless lives* Ⅱ 形 ❶ alive; living: 在他～着的时候 *during his lifetime* / ～老虎 *a live tiger* ❷ vivid; lively: 把这个角色演～了 *give a vivid portrayal of the character* / 把经济搞～ *reinvigorate the economy* / 脑子很～ *have a quick mind* / 把会开得～点 *make the meeting more lively* ❸ movable; moving: 活结 Ⅲ 副 exactly; simply: 活像 Ⅳ 名 ❶ work: 我的～儿干完了。*I have finished the work.* ❷ product: 这批～儿做得好。*This batch of products is well made.*
【活靶】[军] manoeuvring target
【活靶子】a live target
【活版】(又作'活字版') [刷] typography; letterpress
【活版印刷】typographic printing; typography; letterpress printing: ～机 *letterpress* (*printing*) *machine*

【活瓣】［生理］valve

【活宝】a bit of a clown；a funny fellow

【活报剧】living newspaper；skit；street performance

【活蹦乱跳】skip and jump about；gambol；frolic：孩子们在雪地里～。*The children were frolicking happily in the snow.*

【活标本】living specimen

【活茬】〈口〉farm work

【活到老，学到老】one is never too old to learn；keep on learning as long as you live

【活地图】walking map：老人是～，对这一带地形熟极了。*The old man is such a competent guide, familiar with every nook and cranny of this area.*

【活地狱】hell on earth

【活动】❶ move about；exercise：站起来～。*stand up and move about* / ～一下筋骨 *limber up the joints*；*limber oneself up* ❷ shaky；unsteady：这把椅子直～。*The chair is rick-ety.* / 这颗牙～了。*This tooth's loose.* ❸ movable；mobile；flexible：口气有点～ *sound less adamant*；*begin to relent a little* ❹ activity；manoeuvre：政治～ *political activities* / ～余地 *room for manoeuvre* ❺ use personal influence or irregular means：替他～ *put in a word for him*；*use one's influence on his behalf* ❻［心理］behaviour ◇ ～坝［水］movable dam；～扳手［机］adjustable spanner (or wrench)；～房屋 movable house；～家 activist；public figure；～桥 movable bridge；～资本 liquid capital

【活度】［化］activity：～系数 *activity coefficient*

【活泛】〈口〉flexible：办事别那么死板，心眼放～点。*Don't be so rigid. Be more flexible.*

【活佛】❶ Living Buddha ❷ (in Lamaism) a Buddha incarnate

【活该】〈口〉it serves sb. right：～，谁叫你不听我的话。*It serves you right. You should have listened to me.* / 罚了他五块钱，～。*They fined him five yuan. It serves him right.* / 这家伙落得如此下场，～。*The fellow got what he deserved.*

【活工资】unfixed wage；conditional wage

【活广告】stand messenger

【活荷载】［交通］［建］live load

【活化】［化］activation：～剂 *activator* / ～吸附 *activation adorption*

【活化石】living fossil

【活话】indefinite, vague, or open-ended remark；non-committal words：他临走前留下一句～，说可能还会回来。*He left, right before departure, a vague message, saying that he might come back later.*

【活活】while still alive：～烧死 *be burnt alive* / ～打死 *be beaten to death* / ～气死 *die from anger*

【活火山】active volcano

【活计】❶ handicraft work；manual labour：针线～ *needlework* / 把～统一安排一下。*Make an overall arrangement of the work.* ❷ handiwork；work：她拿着～给大家看。*She showed her work to everybody.*

【活见鬼】sheer nonsense；utterly impossible；simply absurd

【活教材】persons or things that can serve to educate people

【活结】a knot that can be undone by a pull；slipknot

【活口】❶ a survivor of a murder attempt ❷ a prisoner who can furnish information ❸ keep body and soul together；eke out an existence ❹ flexible tone；flexible words

【活扣】〈口〉a knot that can be undone by a pull；slipknot

【活力】vigour；vitality；energy：他是个小伙子，充满～。*He is a young lad with plenty of vigour.*

【活灵活现】（又作'活龙活现'）vivid；lifelike：说得～ *give a vivid description*；*make it come to life*

【活路】❶ means of subsistence；way out：旧社会哪有咱穷人的～。*What way out was there for us poor folk in the old society?* ❷ workable method

【活络】〈方〉❶ loose：牙齿有点～。*The tooth has become a bit loose.* ❷ noncommittal；indefinite：他说得很～。*He was rather noncommittal.*

【活埋】bury alive

【活门】［机］valve

【活命】❶ earn a bare living；scrape along；eke out an existence：过去他靠卖艺～。*In the old days he scraped along as a street entertainer.* ❷〈书〉save sb.'s life：～之恩 *indebtedness to sb. for saving one's life* ❸ life

【活泼】❶ lively；vivacious；vivid：天真～的孩子 *lively children* / 文字～ *written in a lively style* ❷［化］reactive

【活菩萨】living Bodhisattva—an epithet for a person who is full of compassion for the needy and the suffering

【活期】current：～储蓄 *current deposit*；*demand deposit* / ～存款账户 *current account*

【活气】lively atmosphere：大地充满了一片春耕的～。*The land is alive with spring sowing activities.*

【活钱儿】〈口〉❶ ready money；cash ❷ extra income

【活塞】［机］piston：～杆 *piston rod* / ～圈 *piston ring*

【活神仙】living immortal—an epithet for a man noted for his longevity or supposed to have clairvoyance

【活生生】❶ real；living：～的例子 *a living example* / 这篇小说里的人物都是～的，有血有肉的。*The characters in the novel are all vividly portrayed.* ❷ while still alive：万恶的封建礼教把这个年轻的妇女～地折磨死了。*The barbarous feudal ethical code literally snuffed out her young life.*

【活受罪】〈口〉suffer a living hell；have a hell of a life：听那又臭又长的报告，简直是～。*It was a real torture to listen to that long-winded dull speech.*

【活水】owing water；running water
【活死人】〈方〉〈讳〉a living corpse—a slow-witted，clumsy person
【活体解剖】vivisection
【活现】appear vividly；come alive
【活像】look exactly like；be the spit and image of；be an exact replica of：这孩子长得～他父亲。*The child is the very spit（or image）of his father.*
【活性】［化］active；activated ◇ ～酵母 activated dry yeast；～染料 reactive dyes；～炭［化］active（or activated）carbon
【活学活用】live learning，live usage
【活血】［中］invigorate the circulation of blood
【活阎王】devil incarnate；tyrannical ruler
【活样板】live model
【活页】loose-leaf：～笔记本 *loose-leaf notebook* / ～夹 *loose-leaf binder*；*spring binder* / ～文选 *loose-leaf selections* / ～纸 *paper for a loose-leaf notebook* ◇ ～乐谱 sheet assets
【活用】apply flexibly；apply with imagination and ingenuity
【活跃】❶ brisk；active；dynamic：市场～。*Business is brisk.* / 听到这消息，大家顿时～起来。*Everybody got excited at the news.* ❷ enliven；animate；invigorate：～文娱生活 *liven up cultural and recreational activities* / ～会场气氛 *enliven the atmosphere of the meeting*
【活捉】capture alive
【活字】［刷］type；letter：～盘 *type case*；*letter board*
【活字典】a walking dictionary
【活罪】（endure）hardships，tortures，etc.，while alive；bitter sufferings：死罪可免，～难逃 *exemptible from the death penalty but hardly from punishment*

huǒ

火 Ⅰ 名 ❶ fire：这屋里有～。*There's a fire in the room.* ❷ firearms；ammunition：军火 ❸［中］internal heat—one of the six causes of disease：败火 ❹ anger；temper：心头～起 *flare up in anger* / 你怎么这么大的～儿？*Why are you in such a temper?* Ⅱ 动 lose one's temper，get angry：他～儿了。*He flared up.* Ⅲ 形 ❶ fiery；flaming：火红 ❷ urgent；pressing：火速
【火把】torch
【火棒】lighted torch（used in acrobatics）
【火暴】（又作'火爆'）〈方〉❶ fiery；irritable：～性子 *a hot temper* ❷ vigorous；exuberant；lively：牡丹开得真～。*The peonies are in full bloom.* / 这出戏的场面很～。*The play is full of action and excitement.*
【火并】open fight between factions：军阀内部的～ *an open factional fight within the warlords*
【火柴】match：划根～ *strike a match* / ～盒 *matchbox*
【火场】the scene of a fire
【火车】train：乘～ *go by train* / ～票 *railway ticket* / ～时刻表 *railway timetable*；*train schedule* / ～司机 *engine driver*；（*locomotive*）*engineer* / ～站 *railway station* ◇ ～交货价 free on rail；～轮渡 train ferry；～座 booth（in a restaurant）
【火车头】（railway）engine；locomotive
【火成岩】［地质］igneous rock
【火法冶金】［冶］pyrometallurgy
【火攻】fire attack（using fire as a weapon against enemy personnel and installations）
【火罐儿】［中］upping jar（or glass）
【火光】flame；blaze：～冲天。*The flames lit up the sky.*
【火锅】chafing dish
【火海】a sea of flames：阵地上成了一片～。*The battlefield became a sea of flames.*
【火红】red as fire；fiery；flaming：～的太阳 *a flaming sun* / 医生摸了摸病人～发烫的脸颊。*The doctor felt the patient's fiery cheek.*
【火候】❶ duration and degree of heating，cooking，smelting，etc.：炒菜掌握～很重要。*Heat control is very important in stir-frying.* ❷ level of attainment：他的书法到～了。*He has matured as a calligrapher.*
【火狐】red fox
【火花】spark：～四溅 *sparks flying off in all directions* / 生命的～ *the sparks of life—exuberant vitalit* ◇ ～塞［机］sparking plug；spark plug；ignition plug
【火化】cremate
【火鸡】turkey
【火急】urgent；pressing：十万火急
【火碱】caustic soda
【火箭】rocket：发射～ *fire*（*or launch*）*a rocket* / ～部队 *rocket troops* / ～发射场 *rocket launching site* / ～发射台 *rocket launching pad*；*rocket mount* / ～技术 *rocketry* / 水下～ *submarine rocket* ◇ ～弹 rocket projectile；rocket shell；～炮 rocket gun；～喷焰 exhaust；～筒 rocket launcher（or projector）；bazooka
【火警】fire alarm
【火炬】torch：～赛跑 *torch race* / ～游行 *torchlight parade*
【火炬计划】Torch Programme，a plan to develop new and high technology
【火炕】heated *kang*；heated brick bed
【火坑】fiery pit；pit of hell；abyss of suffering：跳出～ *escape from the living hell*
【火辣辣】burning：～的太阳 *a scorching sun* / 疼得～的 *a searing pain* / 脸上觉得～的 *feel one's cheeks burning*（*as with shame*）/ 心里～的 *burning with anxiety*
【火力】［军］firepower；fire：～掩护 *fire cover* / ～侦察 *reconnaissance by firing*（*to observe enemy reactions*）/ ～支援 *support fire*；*fire support*
【火力发电】thermal power generation：～厂 *thermal power plant*
【火烈鸟】flamingo

【火流星】[天] bolide; fireball
【火龙】❶ fiery dragon—a procession of lanterns or torches ❷〈方〉an air channel from a brick kitchen stove to a chimney; flue
【火炉】(又作'火炉子') (heating) stove
【火冒三丈】fly into a rage; flare up
【火棉】guncotton; pyroxylin
【火苗】(又作'火苗子') a tongue of flame; flame: ~蹿上来了。*The flames leapt up.*
【火捻】❶ kindling ❷ fuse
【火炮】cannon; gun
【火盆】fire pan; brazier
【火拼】同〖火并〗
【火漆】sealing wax
【火气】❶ [中] internal heat (as a cause of disease) ❷ anger; temper: ~很大 *have a bad temper* / 压不住心头的~ *can hardly contain one's anger; cannot hold back one's rage*
【火器】[军] firearm
【火枪】firelock
【火墙】a wall with flues for space heating
【火情】the condition of a fire
【火热】❶ burning hot; fervent; fiery: ~的太阳 *a burning sun* / ~的心 *a fervent heart* / ~的斗争 *fiery struggles* ❷ intimate: 打得火热
【火绒】tinder
【火伞高张】a fully spread umbrella of fire—scorching sunlight in summer
【火山】volcano: ~喷发 *volcanic eruption* / ~灰 *volcanic ash* / ~口 *crater* / ~砾 *lapillus* / ~作用 *volcanism* ◇ ~岛 volcanic island; ~地震 volcanic earthquake; ~学 volcanology
【火伤】burn (caused by fire)
【火上加油】(又作'火上浇油') pour oil on the flames; add fuel to the flames: 她听了这些话,像是~。*These words only added fuel to the flames of her anger.*
【火烧】baked wheaten cake
【火烧火燎】❶ feeling terribly hot: 他身上每处伤口都疼得~。*His every wound began to burn like fire.* ❷ restless with anxiety: 孩子有病,妈妈急得~的。*The mother was filled with anxiety about her child's illness.*
【火烧眉毛】the fire is singeing the eyebrows—a desperate situation: ~的事儿 *a matter of the utmost urgency*
【火烧油层】[油] combustion (of oil) in situ
【火烧云】red clouds (at sunset or sunrise)
【火舌】tongues of fire: 房子起了火,~正在吞没屋顶。*The flames were licking the roof of the burning building.*
【火绳】a rope of plaited plants burnt as a mosquito repellent
【火石】flint
【火势】the intensity of a fire: ~很猛。*The fire burned fiercely.*
【火速】at top speed; posthaste: ~增援 *rush up reinforcements* / 任务十分紧急,必须~完成。*It's an urgent task and must be completed at once.* / 警察~赶到现场。*The police rushed to the scene.*
【火炭】burning charcoal or faggot
【火头】❶ flame: 油灯的~儿太小。*The flame of the lamp is too low.* ❷ duration and degree of heating, cooking, smelting, etc.: ~儿不到,饼就烙不好。*You can't bake a cake properly if the fire is not right.* ❸ anger: 你先把~压一压,别着急。*Don't fly off the handle. Calm down.*
【火头军】〈诙〉army cook
【火腿】ham
【火网】[军] network of fire; fire net
【火险】fire insurance
【火线】❶ battle (or firing, front) line: ~入党 *join the Party at the battlefront* / 轻伤不下~ *refuse to leave the front because of minor wounds* / ~抢救 *frontline first aid* ❷ [电] live wire
【火硝】common name for 硝酸钾
【火星】❶Mars ❷ spark: 铁锤打在石头上,迸出不少~。*Sparks flew up when the hammer struck the rock.* / 他气得两眼直冒~。*His eyes flashed with anger.* ◇ ~卫星 Martian satellite
【火眼】[医] pinkeye
【火眼金睛】fiery eyes and diamond pupils—discerning eyes: ~识真假。*Fiery eyes and diamond pupils are able to discern truth and falsehood.*
【火焰】flame ◇ ~光谱 flame spectrum; ~喷射器 flamethrower
【火药】gunpowder; powder: ~库 *powder magazine* / ~桶 *powder keg*
【火药味】〈喻〉the smell of gunpowder: 他的发言~很浓。*He made a very aggressive speech.* / 这是一篇充满~的声明。*This statement has a strong smell of gunpowder.*
【火印】a mark burned on bamboo or wooden articles; brand
【火油】〈方〉kerosene
【火源】burning things which may cause a fire disaster
【火灾】fire (as a disaster); conflagration
【火葬】cremation ◇ ~场 crematorium; crematory
【火中取栗】pull sb.'s chestnuts out of the fire; be a cat's-paw
【火种】❶ kindling material; kindling; tinder ❷ live cinders kept for starting a new fire: 革命的~ *sparks of revolution; seeds of revolution*
【火烛】things that may cause a fire: 小心~。*Be careful about fires!*
【火主】the owner of the house where a fire started; the person responsible for the starting of a fire
【火砖】refractory brick; firebrick

伙 Ⅰ 名 ❶ mess; board; meals: 入伙 ❷ partner; mate: 同伙 ❸ partnership; company: 合伙 Ⅱ 量 group; crowd; band: 三个一群,五个一~ *in small groups; in knots; in twos and threes* / 一~强盗 *a band of robbers* Ⅲ 动 combine; join: ~买 *club together to buy sth.* / ~着用 *share in the use of sth.*

【伙伴】partner；companion：我小时候的～ *a childhood pal of mine* / 贸易～ *trade partner*
【伙犯】accomplice
【伙房】kitchen (in a school, factory, etc.)
【伙夫】〈旧〉mess cook
【伙计】❶ partner ❷〈口〉fellow；mate：他是我的老～。*He's an old pal of mine*. / ～，上哪儿去？*Where are you going, mate?* ❸〈旧〉salesman；salesclerk；shop assistant；farm labourer
【伙食】mess；food；meals：～补助 *food allowance* / ～费 *money spent on meals*；*board expenses* / ～节余 *mess savings* ◇ ～科 catering office
【伙同】in league with；in collusion with

钬 名［化］holmium (Ho)

huò

或 Ⅰ 副 perhaps；maybe；probably：代表团明晨～可到达。*The delegation may arrive tomorrow morning*. Ⅱ 连 ❶or；either... or...：这块地可以种高粱～玉米。*We can grow sorghum or maize on this plot*. ❷no matter what, how, etc.：无论唱～跳，她都行。*She is good at both singing and dancing*.
【或…或…】or；either... or...：或去或留 *go or stay* / 或胜或负 *either win or lose* / 或迟或早 *sooner or later*
【或然】probable
【或许】perhaps；maybe：他～没有赶上火车。*Perhaps he has missed the train*. / 她～能来。*She might be able to come*.
【或则】or；either... or...：～你来，～我去，请你决定。*Either you come or I go, you just say the word*.
【或者】❶ perhaps；maybe：快点走，～还赶得上他。*Hurry up, we may catch up with him yet*. ❷ or；either... or...：请你把这本书交给小王～小李。*Please give this book to either Xiao Wang or Xiao Li*. ❸ no matter what, how, etc.：不论大事～小事，大家都愿意找他商量。*Everybody likes to consult with him about their problems no matter what kind of problem it is*.

和 Ⅰ 动 mix；blend：豆沙里～点儿糖 *mix a little sugar into the bean paste* / 油和水～不到一块儿。*Oil and water do not mix*. Ⅱ 量 a washing (of clothes)；a decocting (of medicinal herbs)：衣裳已经洗了三～。*The clothes have been rinsed three times*. / 二～药 *second decoction* (*of medicinal herbs*)——另见 hé；hè；huó
【和弄】〈方〉❶ stir；agitate；mix ❷ instigate；incite；sow discord
【和稀泥】try to mediate differences at the sacrifice of principle；try to smooth things over

货 Ⅰ 名 ❶ money：通货 ❷ goods；commodity：中国～ *Chinese goods* ❸〈讳〉(used in offensive terms)：蠢货 Ⅱ 动〈书〉sell：～卖 *sell commodities*
【货比三家】shop around to get a good buy
【货币】money；currency：储备～ *reserve currency* / 周转～ *vehicle currency* / 自由兑换～ *convertible currency* ◇ ～贬值 (currency) devaluation；(currency) depreciation；～存量 money stock；～单位 monetary unit；～地租 money rent；～工资 money wages；～回笼 withdrawal of currency from circulation；～交换 exchange through money；～流量分析 money flow analysis；～流通量 currency (or money) in circulation；money supply；～平价 currency parity；par value of currency；～升值 (currency) revaluation；(currency) appreciation；～危机 monetary crisis；～信用 confidence in the currency；～战 monetary war；～政策 monetary policy；～主义 monetarism；～资本 money-capital
【货舱】(cargo) hold；cargo bay (of a plane)
【货场】goods (or freight) yard
【货车】❶ goods train；freight train ❷ goods van (or wagon)；freight car (or wagon) ❸ lorry；truck
【货船】freighter；cargo ship；cargo vessel：定期～ *cargo liner*
【货单】manifest；waybill；shipping list
【货到付款】cash on delivery (COD)
【货柜】❶ counter；bar ❷ another name for 集装箱
【货好客自来】good wine needs no bush；good foods need no advertisement；quality goods sell themselves
【货机】cargo aircraft (or plane)；air freighter
【货价】commodity price；price of goods
【货架子】goods shelves：～上摆满各种商品。*The shelves are stocked full*.
【货款】money for buying or selling goods；payment for goods
【货郎】itinerant pedlar；street vendor ◇ ～担 street vendor's load (carried on a shoulder pole)
【货轮】freighter；cargo ship；cargo vessel
【货品】kinds or types of goods
【货色】❶ goods：～齐全。*Goods of every description are available*. / 上等～ *first-class goods*；*quality goods* ❷〈贬〉stuff；trash；rubbish：那本杂志登的尽是这种～。*That magazine is nothing but a load of such trash*. / 那是小报上的～。*That's just tabloid rubbish*.
【货摊】stall；stand
【货物】goods；commodity；merchandise ◇ ～税 commodity tax
【货箱】packing box
【货样】sample goods；sample
【货源】source of goods；supply of goods：～充足 *an ample supply of goods* / 开辟～ *find* (*or open up*) *new sources of goods*
【货运】freight transport：～业务 *cargo service* ◇ ～单 waybill；～费 shipping cost；freight (charges)；～量 volume of goods transported；volume of rail freight；volume of road haulage；～列车

goods train; freight train; ～周转量 rotation volume of goods (or freight) transport

【货栈】warehouse

【货真价实】❶ genuine goods at a fair price ❷ through and through; out-and-out; dyed-in-the-wool: ～的骗子 *an out-and-out swindler* / ～的伪君子 *a dyed-in-the-wool hypocrite*

【货主】owner of cargo

获 动 ❶ capture; catch: 捕获 ❷ obtain; win; reap: ～一等奖 *win the first prize* ❸ reap; harvest; gather in: 收获

【获得】gain; obtain; acquire; win; achieve: ～第一名 *win first place; get a first; win a championship* / ～好评 *win acclaim; earn favourable comment*

【获得性】[生] acquired character ◇ ～免疫 [医] acquired immunity

【获奖】win a prize; be awarded a prize: ～作品 *an award-winning work* / 这部影片获奥斯卡奖。*The film won an Oscar.*

【获救】be rescued

【获利】make a profit; reap profits

【获取】procure; obtain; gain; reap: ～暴利 *reap staggering (or colossal) profits*

【获胜】win victory; be victorious; triumph: 甲队以五比二～。*Team A won the match five to two.* ◇ ～率 average of wins

【获释】be released (from prison)

【获悉】(又作'获知')〈书〉learn (of an event)

【获选】be elected; win an election

【获准】secure approval; get permission: 开业申请业已～。*Our application for opening the business has been approved (or granted).*

祸 Ⅰ 名 misfortune; disaster; calamity: 惹祸 Ⅱ 动 bring disaster upon; ruin: 祸国殃民

【祸不单行】misfortunes never come singly; it never rains but it pours

【祸从口出】trouble comes out of the mouth (i.e. from a loose tongue)

【祸从天降】a disaster descends from heaven (i.e. befalls sb. unexpectedly)

【祸端】〈书〉the source of the disaster; the cause of ruin

【祸根】the root of the trouble; the cause of ruin; bane: 埋下～ *lay up trouble for the future*

【祸国殃民】bring calamity to the country and the people: 一小撮～的民族败类 *dregs of the nation who wreck the country and ruin the people*

【祸害】❶ disaster; curse; scourge: 黄河在历史上经常引起～。*Throughout the ages the Yellow River was a scourge of the nation.* ❷ damage; destroy: 防止野猪～庄稼。*Don't let the boars damage the crops.*

【祸患】disaster; calamity

【祸起萧墙】trouble arises behind the walls of the home—trouble arises within the family; there is internal strife afoot

【祸事】disaster; calamity; mishap

【祸首】chief culprit (or offender)

【祸水】a person (esp. a woman) who is the source of trouble

【祸胎】the root of the trouble; the cause of the disaster

【祸兮福所倚,福兮祸所伏】good fortune lieth within bad, bad fortune lurketh within good

【祸心】evil intent

惑 动 ❶ be puzzled; be bewildered: 智者不～。*The wise are free from perplexities.* ❷ delude; mislead: 造谣惑众

【惑乱】delude and confuse: ～人心 *confuse and poison people's minds* / ～军心 *undermine the morale of an army*

霍 副 suddenly; quickly

【霍地】suddenly: ～立起身来 *suddenly stand up; spring to one's feet*

【霍霍】❶ the sound of sharpening knives etc.: ～的磨刀声 *the scrape, scrape of a sword being sharpened* ❷ flash: 电光～。*The lightning flashed.*

【霍乱】❶ cholera ❷ [中] acute gastroenteritis

【霍然】suddenly; quickly: 手电筒～一亮。*Suddenly somebody flashed an electric torch.*

豁 Ⅰ 形 clear; open; open-minded; generous Ⅱ 动 exempt; remit: 豁免 ——另见 huō

【豁达】sanguine; optimistic

【豁达大度】open-minded and magnanimous

【豁亮】❶ roomy and bright: 这屋子又干净,又～。*The room is clean, bright and spacious.* ❷ sonorous; resonant: 嗓音～ *have a sonorous voice*

【豁免】exempt (from taxes or from customs inspection, etc.); remit: ～捐税 *exempt sb. from taxes; remit taxes*

【豁然贯通】suddenly see the whole thing in a clear light

【豁然开朗】❶ 见〖开朗〗❷ suddenly see the light; be suddenly enlightened

藿 名〈书〉leaves of pulse plants

【藿香】[中] wrinkled giant hyssop (Agastache rugosa)

J

jī

几 Ⅰ名 a small table：茶几 Ⅱ副〈书〉nearly；almost；practically：到会者～三千人。*Nearly* 3,000 *people came to the meeting*. ——另见 jǐ

【几乎】almost；nearly；practically：他～一夜没睡。*He lay awake almost the whole night*. / 我在物理学方面的知识，～等于零。*My knowledge of physics is practically nil*. / 你比我～高了一头。*You're nearly a head taller than I*.

【几近】be close to；be on the verge of：这种动物已～灭绝。*This species of animal is on the verge of extinction*.

【几率】同〖概率〗

【几维鸟】kiwi

讥 动 ridicule；mock；satirize：反唇相讥

【讥讽】ridicule；satirize：这是～，不是善意的批评。*This is sarcasm*，*not constructive criticism*.

【讥笑】ridicule；jeer；sneer at；deride：他毫不理睬某些人的～，继续进行试验。*Completely ignoring some people's sneers*，*he went on with his experiments*. / 他们～她穿得破旧。*They sneered at her old*，*worn-out clothes*.

击 动 ❶ beat；hit；strike：～鼓 *beat a drum* ❷ attack；assault：袭击 ❸ come in contact with；bump into：撞击

【击败】defeat；beat；vanquish：他以三比一～了对手。*He beat his opponent* 3 *to* 1.

【击毙】shoot dead：四名匪徒被当场～。*Four bandits were shot dead on the spot*.

【击沉】bombard and sink；send (a ship) to the bottom：～敌舰三艘 *sink three enemy warships*

【击穿】[电] puncture；breakdown

【击发】❶ pull the trigger (of a gun) ❷ [军] percussion：～装置 *percussion lock* (*or mechanism*)

【击毁】smash；wreck；shatter；destroy：～坦克二十四辆 *destroy* 24 *tanks*

【击剑】[体] fencing ◇ ～场 fencing strip；fencing terrian；～服 fencing clothes；～馆 fencing gall；～裤 fencing breeches；～上衣 fencing jacket；～手套 fencing glove；～运动员 fencer

【击落】shoot down；bring down；down：～敌机七架 *bring down seven enemy planes*

【击破】break up；destroy；rout：各个击破

【击球】batting (in baseball or softball)：～员 *batter*；*batsman*

【击伤】wound (a person)；damage (a plane，tank，etc.)

【击退】beat back；repel；repulse：～敌军几次进攻 *repulse several enemy assaults*

【击弦乐器】hammered string instrument

【击乐器】percussion instrument

【击掌】clap one's hands：～为号 *signal by clapping hands*

【击中】hit the target：他一枪～了目标。*He hit the target with one shot*. / ～无效部位。*Foul touch*.

【击中要害】hit the nail on the head；hit sb.'s vital point；hit home：你批评得对，击中了我的要害。*You're right in your criticism*. *You've pinpointed my main weakness*.

叽 象 the sound of a bird chirping：小鸟～～叫。*Little birds were chirping*.

【叽咕】talk in a low voice；whisper；mutter：他们俩叽叽咕咕地说些什么？*What are those two whispering to each other about*?

【叽叽喳喳】同〖唧唧喳喳〗

【叽里咕噜】the sound of sb. talking indistinctly or of sth. rolling around：他们～地说了半天。*They gabbled away for a long time*. / 石块～滚下山去。*Rocks went tumbling down the hill*.

【叽哩呱啦】the sound of loud talk or chatter：他～地说个没完。*He talked loudly and endlessly*.

饥 Ⅰ形 hungry；starved；famished Ⅱ名 famine；crop failure：大～之年 *a year of great famine*

【饥不择食】a hungry person is not picky and choosy：～，寒不择衣。*When one's hungry one eats what there is*；*when one's cold one wears what one has*.

【饥肠】〈文〉empty stomach

【饥肠辘辘】one's stomach rumbling with hunger

【饥饿】hungry；starved：挣扎在～线上 *struggling along on the verge of starvation*

【饥寒交迫】suffer from hunger and cold；live in hunger and cold；be poverty-stricken：陷入～的困难境地 *suffer the terrible hardship of hunger and cold*

【饥荒】❶ famine；crop failure：一九三四年中国发生过一次大～。*In* 1934，*there was a severe famine in China*. ❷〈口〉be hard up；be short of money：解放前我家月月闹～。*Before liberation my family ran short of cash month after month.* ❸〈方〉debt

【饥渴】hunger and thirst：～难耐 *unbearable hunger and thirst*

【饥民】famine victim；famine refugee

芨 (构词成分)见下

【芨芨草】splendid achnatherum（Achnatherum splendens）

机 Ⅰ 名 ❶ machine；engine：打字机 ❷ aircraft；aeroplane；plane：客机 ❸ crucial point：转机 ❹ chance；occasion；opportunity：时机 ❺ organic：有机 Ⅱ 形 flexible；quick-witted：机智

【机变】❶ flexible ❷ sly

【机播】machine sowing of crops

【机不可失，时不再来】don't let slip an opportunity as it may never come again；opportunity knocks but once

【机舱】❶ engine room（of a ship）❷ passenger compartment（of an aircraft）；cabin

【机插】machine transplanting of rice；mechanical rice transplanter

【机场】airport；airfield；aerodrome：～标志 *aerodrome markings* / ～待战 *ground alert* / ～灯标 *airport beacon*

【机车】locomotive；engine ◇ ～车辆厂 rolling stock plant；～组 locomotive crew

【机船】motor vessel

【机床】machine tool：木工～ *woodworking machine tool* / 数字程序控制～ *numerical controlled machine tool*

【机电】mechanical and electrical：～设备 *mechanical and electrical equipment*

【机动】❶ power-driven；motorized：～车 *motor-driven*（*or motor*）*vehicle* / ～炮 *mobile artillery* / ～自行车 *moped*；*autocycle* ❷ flexible；expedient；mobile：你可以根据情况～灵活地处置。*You can deal with it flexibly as you see fit.* ❸ in reserve；for emergency use：拨出五十元作为～开支 *allot* 50 *yuan for extras* / 不要把日程排得满满的，要留些～时间。*Don't arrange such a tight schedule. Leave some time to spare.* ◇ ～力量 reserve force；～粮 grain reserve for emergency use

【机动财力】financial resources for unforeseen expenditures；contingency reserve（or fund）

【机动性】mobility；manoeuvrability；flexibility：这条规定并不那么死板，有一定的～。*These rules aren't totally rigid. They are flexible within certain limits.*

【机断】act on one's own judgment in an emergency：～行事 *act promptly at one's own discretion*

【机帆船】motor sailboat；motorized junk

【机房】❶ generator or motor room ❷ engine room（of a ship）

【机耕】tractor-ploughing：～面积 *area ploughed by tractors* ◇ ～船 boat tractor；wet-field tractor

【机工】mechanic；machinist

【机构】❶［机］mechanism：传动～ *transmission mechanism* / 分离～ *disengaging mechanism* ❷ organization；setup：政府～ *government organization* / 国家～ *state institution* / 外交代表～ *diplomatic mission* / 领事～ *consular mission* / 商务～ *commercial organization* ❸ the internal structure of an organization：调整～ *adjust the organizational structure* / ～重叠 *organizational overlapping* / ～臃肿 *an overstaffed organization* ◇ ～改革 organizational reform；reform of organization

【机关】❶［机］mechanism；gear：起动～ *starting gear* ❷ machine-operated：～布景 *machine-operated stage scenery* ❸ office；organ；body：领导～ *leading bodies* / 党政～ *Party and government organizations* / 文化教育～ *cultural and educational institutions* ❹ stratagem；scheme；intrigue：识破～ *see through a trick* ◇ ～报 the official newspaper of a political party，a government，etc.；organ；～干部 government functionary；office worker；～刊物 the official publication of a party，government，etc.；～炮 cannon；～枪 machine gun

【机会】chance；opportunity：错过（抓住）～ *miss*（*seize*）*a chance* / 千载一时的好～ *a golden opportunity*；*the chance of a lifetime*

【机会成本】opportunity cost ◇ ～价值 opportunity cost value

【机会均等】equal opportunities

【机会主义】opportunism：～路线 *opportunist line* / ～者 *opportunist*

【机件】［机］parts；works：钟表的～ *the works of a clock or watch*

【机井】motor-pumped well

【机警】alert；sharp-witted；vigilant：游击队～地监视敌人的动静。*The guerrillas kept a close watch on the movements of the enemy.*

【机具】machines and tools：农业～ *farm implements*

【机库】hangar

【机理】mechanism：腐蚀～ *corrosion mechanism* / 结晶～ *crystallization mechanism* / 分娩～ *mechanism of labour*

【机灵】（又作'机伶'）clever；smart；sharp；intelligent：这孩子怪～的。*This child's very smart.* / 她有一双～的大眼睛。*She has large，intelligent eyes.* ◇ ～鬼 a clever person

【机率】probability：统计～ *statistical probability* / 50% 的～ *fifty percent likelihood*

【机米】machine-processed rice

【机密】❶ secret；classified；confidential：这个计划很～，不得向任何人泄露。*The plan is top-secret and we can't allow it to be leaked to anyone.* / ～文件 *classified papers*；*confidential documents* ❷ sth. secret；secret：严守国家～ *strictly guard state secrets*

【机敏】alert and resourceful：她在紧急关头总是沉着～。*She is calm and resourceful in an emergen-*

cy.

【机能】［生理］function：心脏的～ *the function of the heart* / ～障碍 *a functional obstruction* / 他下肢瘫痪，两腿丧失～。*His lower body was paralyzed, so he lost the use of his legs.*

【机器】machine；machinery；apparatus：安装新～ *install new machinery* / ～造型 *machine moulding* / ～制造 *machine building* ◇ ～翻译 machine translation；～脚踏车〈方〉motocycle；～码 machine code；～人 robot；～油 lubricating oil；lubricant；～语言 machine language (ML)

【机枪】〈略〉见〖机关枪〗◇ ～手 machine gunner

【机巧】adroit；ingenious：她对记者的回答很～。*She gave the newsman an adroit reply.* / 他～地避开了记者提出的这个敏感问题。*He adroitly avoided the sensitive question which the reporter raised.*

【机群】a group of planes：大～ *air armada*；*air fleet*

【机上导弹】air-launched missile

【机身】fuselage

【机师】❶ engineer ❷〈方〉air pilot

【机头】nose (of an aircraft) ◇ ～炮 nose gun (of a fighter)

【机尾】tail (of an aircraft)

【机务人员】❶ maintenance personnel ❷ ground crew

【机械】❶ machinery；machine；mechanism：～故障 *mechanical failure* (*or breakdown*) ❷ mechanical；inflexible；rigid：别人的经验不能～地照搬。*Other people's experience should not be applied mechanically.* / 你这样来理解他的话就太～了。*You're taking his words too literally.* ◇ ～动力学 mechanical kinetics；～功 mechanical work；～工程学 mechanical engineering；～工业 machine building；～加工 machining；～论 同〖机械唯物主义〗；～能［物］mechanical energy；～师 machinist；～手［机］manipulator；～运动［物］mechanical movement；～制图 mechanical drawing

【机械化】mechanize：农业～ *mechanization of agriculture*；*mechanization of farm work* ◇ ～部队 mechanized force (or troops, unit)

【机械唯物主义】mechanical materialism

【机心】❶ diabolical scheme；cunning idea ❷ inner works (of a watch, etc.)

【机型】❶ type (of an aircraft) ❷ model (of a machine)

【机要】confidential：～部门 *departments in charge of confidential or important work* / ～工作 *confidential work* ◇ ～秘书 confidential secretary

【机宜】principles of action；guidelines

【机翼】wing (of an aircraft)

【机油】engine oil；machine oil

【机遇】favourable circumstances；opportunity：他的成功是靠他的努力和一定的～。*His success was brought about by hard work and a certain amount of good luck.*

【机缘】good luck；lucky chance：～凑巧 *as luck would have it*；*by a lucky coincidence*；*by chance* / 由于一个偶然的～，我和她相识了。*I met her because of a lucky coincidence.*

【机长】aircraft (or crew) commander

【机罩】bonnet (of an aircraft)

【机制】❶ machine-processed；machine-made：～糖 *machine-processed sugar* / ～纸 *machine-made paper* ❷ mechanism：激发～ *excitation mechanism* / 建立富有活力的管理体制和运行～ *establish dynamic management systems and operating mechanisms*

【机智】quick-witted；resourceful：～勇敢的侦察兵 *brave and resourceful scouts* / 领航员～地带领船只通过险滩。*The navigator skillfully guided the ship over the dangerous shoals.*

【机组】❶［机］unit；set：发电～ *generating unit* (*or set*) ❷ aircrew；flight crew

肌

名 muscle；flesh：随意肌

【肌肤】〈书〉(human) skin and muscle

【肌腱】tendon

【肌理】〈书〉skin texture：～细腻 *fine-textured skin*

【肌肉】muscle：举重运动员～发达。*Weight lifters are muscular.* ◇ ～肿瘤 muscle tumor；～注射 intramuscular injection

【肌体】human body；organism

【肌萎缩】muscular dystrophy；amyotrophy

鸡

名 chicken：公～ *cock*；*rooster* / 母～ *hen* / 雏～ *chick*；*chicken* / ～鸣而起 *rise at cockcrow*

【鸡巴】〈粗〉cock (penis)

【鸡蛋】(hen's) egg

【鸡蛋糕】(sponge) cake

【鸡蛋里挑骨头】look for a bone in an egg—look for a flaw where there's none to be found；find fault；nitpick

【鸡蛋碰石头】(like) an egg striking a rock—attack sb. far stronger than oneself；court destruction

【鸡飞蛋打】the hen has flown away and the eggs in the coop are broken—all is lost

【鸡冠】cockscomb

【鸡冠花】cockscomb (a flower)

【鸡冠石】realgar

【鸡霍乱】fowl cholera

【鸡奸】sodomy；buggery

【鸡肋】〈文〉chicken ribs—things of little value or interest：味同～ *taste like chicken ribs—be of little or no value*

【鸡零狗碎】in bits and pieces；fragmentary

【鸡毛】chicken feather

【鸡毛掸子】feather duster

【鸡毛蒜皮】chicken feathers and garlic skins —trifles；trivialities：你何苦为这点～的事跟他吵呢？*Why quarrel with him over such a trifle?*

【鸡鸣狗盗】(ability to) crow like a cock and snatch like a dog—get up to mean or petty tricks：～之徒 *mean people who resort to petty tricks*

【鸡鸣犬吠】the crowing of cocks and the barking of dogs—country sounds
【鸡内金】［中］the membrane of a chicken's gizzard
【鸡皮疙瘩】gooseflesh：冻得我直起～。*It was so cold that I was gooseflesh all over.* / 想起那可怕的情景，我浑身都起～。*The thought of that horrible scene made my flesh crawl.*
【鸡皮鹤发】wrinkled skin and white hair—advanced in age
【鸡犬不留】even fowls and dogs are not spared—ruthless mass slaughter
【鸡犬不宁】even fowls and dogs are not left in peace—general turmoil：闹得家里～ *stir the whole family into a tempest*
【鸡犬升天】见〖一人得道，鸡犬升天〗
【鸡肉】chicken (as food)
【鸡尾酒】cocktail ◇ ～会 cocktail party
【鸡瘟】chicken pest
【鸡窝】chicken coop；henhouse；roost
【鸡窝里飞出金凤凰】a golden phoenix flying out of a henhouse—a person of humble origin rising to prominence
【鸡血藤】reticulate millettia (Millettia reticulata)
【鸡心】❶ chicken's heart ❷ heart-shaped：～领 *V-neck* ❸ a heart-shaped pendant
【鸡胸】［医］pigeon breast；chicken breast
【鸡眼】［医］corn；clavus：～膏 *corn plaster*
【鸡杂】chicken giblets

奇 Ⅰ 形 odd (number) Ⅱ 名〈书〉a fractional amount (over that mentioned in a round number)；odd lots：五十有～ *fifty odd* ——另见 qí
【奇偶校验】parity check
【奇数】［数］odd number

唧 动 spurt；squirt：～了我一身水。*The water squirted all over me.*
【唧唧】the sound of insects chirping：蟋蟀在草丛里～地叫。*Crickets are chirping in the grass.*
【唧唧喳喳】the sound of birds chirping or people talking rapidly and indistinctly：这几个女孩儿碰到一起就～说个没完。*Whenever these girls get together, they chatter away nonstop.*
【唧哝】talk in a low voice；whisper：那孩子在妈妈耳边～了几句就跑出去了。*The boy whispered in his mother's ear and ran out of the room.*
【唧筒】pump

积 Ⅰ 动 amass；store up；accumulate：～粮 *store up grain* / ～几十年的经验 *accumulate experience over scores of years* / ～小胜为大胜 *Many small victories add up to a big one.* Ⅱ 形 long-standing；long-pending；age-old：积案 Ⅲ 名 ❶［中］indigestion (in infants and children)：这孩子有～了。*The child is suffering from indigestion.* ❷［数］product：求～ *find the product by multiplication*
【积案】a long-pending case(〈反〉'现案')
【积弊】age-old malpractice；long-standing abuse：这种迷信的风俗存在了很长的时间，～很深，改革起来比较复杂。*This form of superstition has existed for ages and is deeply rooted, so it's not so easy to bring about reform.*
【积不相能】have always been at variance；have never been on good terms；be always at loggerheads
【积储】store up；lay up；stockpile
【积存】store up；lay up；stockpile：～的物资 *goods in stock*
【积德】accumulate merit (by good works)
【积淀】accumulate and take form (usu. the gradual formation of ideology, culture, customs, etc.)：文化的～ *formation of culture*
【积非成是】同〖习非成是〗
【积肥】collect (farmyard) manure
【积分】❶［数］integral：定(不定)～ *definite (indefinite) integral* ❷ accumulated points：足球联赛中，两队～相同。*The league football matches.* ◇ ～方程 integral equation；～学 integral calculus；～仪［数］integrator
【积谷防饥】store up grain against famine
【积毁销骨】repeated calumny can bring about one's ruin
【积极】❶ positive：只有调动一切～因素，我们才能做好这项工作。*We can do the work well only by mobilizing all positive factors.* ❷ active；energetic；vigorous：他锻炼身体一向很～。*He has always been very keen on doing physical exercises.* / 采取～措施 *adopt vigorous measures*
【积极分子】activist；active element；enthusiast：体育运动的～ *sport enthusiast*
【积极性】zeal；initiative；enthusiasm：这样的天气去游泳，孩子们～并不高。*The children are not enthusiastic about swimming in such weather.*
【积久】accumulate in the course of time：～成习 *form a habit (or custom) through long-repeated practice*
【积聚】gather；accumulate；build up：他把零用钱～起来，想买件礼物。*He saved up his pocket money in order to buy a gift.* / 资本～ *concentration of capital*
【积劳成疾】fall ill from constant overwork
【积累】❶ accumulate：他在工作中～了丰富的经验。*He has accumulated a wealth of experience in his work.* / 渊博的知识是一点点～起来的。*Profound knowledge is accumulated little by little.* ❷［经］accumulation (for expanded reproduction)：逐年增加公共～和个人收入 *increase public accumulation and personal income year by year* / ～与消费 *accumulation and consumption* / ～率 *rate of accumulation*
【积木】building blocks；toy bricks
【积年累月】for years on end；year after year
【积欠】❶ have one's debts piling up：我要尽快还清～的各种债务。*I want to clear up all my outstanding debts as soon as possible.* ❷ outstanding debts；arrears：还清～ *clear up all outstanding*

debts

【积善】accumulation of good deeds; performance of one good deed after another

【积少成多】many a little makes a mickle

【积习】old habit; long-standing practice: ～难除。*It is difficult to get rid of deep-rooted habits.* or *Old habits die hard.*

【积蓄】❶ put aside; save; accumulate: ～力量 *accumulate strength* ❷ savings: 她从不乱花钱,月月有～。*She is never extravagant and saves some money every month.* / 他把～拿出来送给了这个老人。*He took out his savings and gave it to the old man.*

【积雪】accumulated snow: 路上～很深。*The roads are deep in snow.*

【积压】keep long in stock; overstock: 因为质量不好,所以产品～,卖不出去。*The goods have been piling up in stock and can't be sold because of poor quality.* ◇ ～滞销 overstocking and sluggish

【积雨云】[气] cumulonimbus

【积怨】accumulated rancour; piled-up grievances: 他一贯欺压邻里,～甚多。*He always rode roughshod over his neighbours and incurred widespread resentment.*

【积云】[气] cumulus

【积攒】save (or collect) bit by bit: ～邮票 *collect stamps* / 这家业是一点一滴地～起来的。*The family fortune has been accumulated bit by bit.* / 他省吃俭用,～学费。*He economized on food and clothing to save for his tuition.*

【积重难返】bad old practices die hard; ingrained habits are hard to change

【积铢累寸】save every tiny bit; accumulate bit by bit

屐 名 ❶ clogs: 木屐 ❷ shoes in general: 草～ *straw sandals*

姬 名 ❶ a complimentary term for women used in ancient China ❷ a name used in ancient China for a concubine: ～妾 *concubines* / 宠～ *a concubine in high favour* ❸〈古〉a professional female singer: 歌～ *singing girl*; *female entertainer* / 舞～ *a professional female dancer*

【姬蜂】*ichneumon wasp*

基 Ⅰ 名 ❶ base; foundation: 路基 ❷ [化] radical; base; group: 自由～ *free radical* / 石蜡～ *paraffin base* Ⅱ 形 basic; key; primary; cardinal: 基调

【基本】❶ foundation: 人民是国家的～。*The people are the foundation of a nation.* ❷ basic; fundamental; elementary: 他们之间存在着～分歧。*Fundamental differences exist between them.* / ～原则 *basic principles* / ～观点 *basic concept* / ～知识 *elementary (or rudimentary) knowledge* ❸ main; essential: 这个车间一个技术人员也没有,不具备生产的～条件。*There's not one trained technician in the whole workshop, so it doesn't have the basic conditions necessary for production.* ❹ basically; in the main; on the whole; by and large: 那项工程已～完工。*The project has been basically completed.* / 这部电影～上是好的。*This film is good on the whole.* / 情况～属实。*It has been found to be basically true.* ◇ ～词汇 basic vocabulary; basic word-stock; ～法 basic law; ～费 minimum fare; ～工资 basic wage (or salary); ～规则 ground rule; primitive rule; ～国策 basic policy of the country; ～粒子 [物] elementary particle; ～路线 basic line; ～矛盾 fundamental contradiction

【基本功】basic training; basic skill; essential technique: 练好～ *have a thorough training in basic skills*; *master the basic skills* / 他的语言～很扎实。*He has a solid mastery of basic language skills.*

【基本建设】capital construction: ～的规模要和国力相适应。*The scale of capital construction must be suited to the overall capabilities of the nation.*

【基层】basic level; primary level; grass-roots unit: ～单位 *basic unit*; *grass-roots unit*; *unit at the grass-roots level* / ～干部 *cadre at the basic (or grass-roots) level* / ～选举 *elections at the basic level* ◇ ～党组织 grassroots party cells

【基础】❶ foundation; base; basis: 工人们正在为新校舍打～。*The workmen are laying the foundations of the new school.* / 物质～ *material base* / 理论～ *theoretical basis* ❷〈略〉见『经济基础』◇ ～代谢 [生] basal metabolism; ～工业 basic industry; ～教育 elementary education; ～科学 basic science; ～课 basic courses (of a college curriculum); ～理论 basic theory; ～设施 infrastructure; ～知识 rudimentary (or elementary) knowledge

【基带】base band

【基地】❶ base: 商品粮～ *marketable grain base* / 原料～ *source of raw materials* ❷ centre: 建立科研～ *set up scientific research centres*

【基点】❶ basic point; starting point: 分析问题是解决问题的～。*The analysis of a problem is the starting point for its solution.* ❷ [测] base point (BP)

【基调】❶ [音] fundamental key; main key ❷ keynote: 他讲话的～是团结。*The keynote of his speech was unity.* ❸ [摄] key tone

【基督】Christ

【基督教】the Christian religion; Christianity

【基督教青年会】the Young Men's Christian Association (Y M C A)

【基督徒】Christian

【基肥】base manure; base fertilizer

【基干】backbone; hard core: ～民兵 *primary militia*; *core members of the militia*

【基极】[电子] base

【基价】base price

【基建】〈略〉见『基本建设』

【基金】fund: 积累(消费)～ *accumulation (con-*

sumption) fund / 福利～ *welfare fund* / 教育～ *education fund* / 救济～ *fund for relief* / 专用～ *fund for special use*

【基金会】foundation：残疾人福利～ *welfare foundation for the disabled*

【基里巴斯】Kiribati

【基期】[统计] base period

【基色】primary colours

【基石】foundation stone；cornerstone：剩余价值学说是马克思经济理论的～。*The doctrine of surplus value is the cornerstone of Marx's economic theory.*

【基数】❶ [数] cardinal number ❷ statistics base：以一九六五年的产量为～ *taking the output of 1965 as the base*

【基线】[测] datum line

【基业】property，inheritance，family estate，etc.，considered as a foundation on which to build

【基因】[生] gene：等位～ *allele* / 显性～ *dominant gene* / 隐性～ *recessive gene* / ～突变 *gene mutation* / ～型 *genotype* ◇～工程（又作'遗传工程'）genetic engineering；～库 gene bank；gene pool；～学说 gene theory；～移殖 gene transplantation；implantation of genes；～增殖 gene amplification；～治疗 gene therapy；～转换 gene transfer；～组合 gene combination；～作用 action of a gene；genefic effect

【基音】[音] fundamental tone

【基于】because of；in view of：～目前这种情况，我们不得不修改原来的计划。*In view of the present situation, we'll have to revise our original plan.*

【基准】❶ [测] datum：～点（面，线）*datum point (plane, line)* ❷ standard；criterion ◇～兵 [军] guide；base marker；～测试（计）benchmark test；～汇率 benchmark exchange rate

犄（构词成分）见下

【犄角】❶〈口〉horn：牛～ *ox horn* / 鹿～ *antler* ❷〈口〉corner：桌子～ *the corner of a table* / 屋子～里有一个衣架。*A clothes tree stands in a corner of the room.*

缉 动 seize；arrest：通缉 ——另见 qī

【缉捕】seize；arrest：公安人员在～逃犯。*The police are pursuing the escaped prisoner.*

【缉查】search；ransack：挨户～ *make a house-to-house search*

【缉毒】drug control：～队 *narcotics squad* / ～警察 *narcotics agent*；*narcocop*

【缉拿】seize；arrest；apprehend：～凶手 *apprehend the murderer* / 已将叛乱分子一一～归案。*All the rebels have been brought to justice.*

【缉私】seize smugglers or smuggled goods；suppress smuggling ◇～船 anti-smuggling patrol boat；coast guard vessel；～人员 anti-contraband personnel

跻 动〈书〉ascend；mount：使中国科学～于世界先进科学之列 *enable China's science to rank among the world's most advanced*

【跻身】ascend；mount：中国队又夺得四枚金牌，～世界四强。*The Chinese team captured another four gold medals which put them in the ranks of the top four.*

畸 形 ❶ lopsided；unbalanced ❷ irregular；abnormal：畸形

【畸变】[无] distortion

【畸轻畸重】attach too much weight to this and too little to that；lopsided；now too much，now too little

【畸形】❶ [医] deformity；malformation：先天～ *congenital malformation* / 肢体发育～ *have deformed limbs* / ～儿 *a congenitally deformed baby* ❷ lopsided；unbalanced；abnormal：这种经济～发展的现象被纠正了。*The occurrence of that type of lopsided economic development has been checked.*

【畸形发展】deformed development

箕 名 ❶ dustpan：簸箕 ❷ winnowing basket；winnowing fan ❸ loop (of a fingerprint)

稽 动 ❶ check；examine；investigate：有案可稽 ❷ recriminate；argue；dispute ❸〈书〉delay；procrastinate

【稽查】❶ check (to prevent smuggling，tax evasion，etc.) ❷ an official engaged in such work；customs officer

【稽核】check；examine：～账目 *audit accounts*

【稽考】〈书〉ascertain；verify：这个名称起于何时，已经无从～了。*The date of origin of this name is unascertainable.*

【稽留】〈书〉delay；detain：他因事在沪～，不能如期归来。*He will not be able to return from Shanghai on schedule because he was detained on business.*

【稽留热】[医] continued fever

齑〈书〉Ⅰ 形 fine；powdery：齑粉 Ⅱ 名 finely chopped ginger，garlic，etc.

【齑粉】〈书〉fine powder；broken bits：碾成～ *be ground to dust*

激 Ⅰ 动 ❶ swash；surge；dash：海水冲击礁石，～起高高的浪花。*Swashing against the rocks, the breakers sent up a fountain of spray.* ❷ arouse；stimulate；excite：～起公愤 *arouse public indignation* / ～起强烈的反抗 *evoke strong opposition* / ～起了一场风波 *cause a commotion* ❸ fall ill from getting wet：他叫雨～着了。*He caught a chill from getting wet in the rain.* Ⅱ 形 sharp；fierce；violent：激战

【激昂】excited and indignant；roused：群情～。*Public feeling was aroused (or ran high).* / 会场上响起～嘹亮的歌声。*The meeting hall resounded with impassioned, lusty singing.*

【激变】change violently：政局发生～，他在这里呆不下去了。*The political situation changed drasti-*

cally, and he couldn't stay here any longer.

【激波】[物] shock wave

【激荡】agitate; surge; rage: 海水～。*The sea surged.* / 他的呼唤在山谷里～。*His shout echoed across the mountain valley.* / 知道这消息以后,她心潮～。*When she heard the news, her heart leapt.*

【激动】excite; stir; agitate: 受到这样的屈辱,他情绪～,气得发抖。*Being slandered that way made his blood boil, and he shook with anger.*

【激发】❶ arouse; stimulate; set off: 这出戏～了观众的爱国心。*This play aroused the audience's patriotism.* ❷ [物] excite: 热～ *thermal excitation* / ～机制 *excitation mechanism* / ～能级 *excitation level* / ～态 *excited state* ◇ ～电流 excitation current; ～电压 excitation voltage

【激奋】rouse sb. to action: 好消息传来,人心～。*When we heard the good news, everyone felt encouraged.*

【激愤】wrathful; indignant: 心情～ *be filled with indignation*

【激光】laser: ～波束制导武器 *laser beam riding weapon* / ～唱机 *compact disc player* / ～唱片 *compact disc (CD)* / ～测距仪 *laser range finder* / ～测云仪 *laser ceilometer* ◇ ～打印机(雷射印表机) laser printer; ～扫描 laser scanning

【激化】sharpen; intensify; become acute: 两国之间的矛盾进一步～。*The contradictions between the two countries are intensifying.*

【激活】[物] activation: ～剂 *activator* / ～媒质 *active medium* / ～能 *activation energy*

【激将法】prodding (or goading) sb. into action (as by ridicule, sarcasm, etc.): 他故意说我球打得很差,想用～使我同意和他比赛。*He tried to goad me into playing a match with him by taunting me and saying that I was a terrible player.*

【激进】radical: 他主张马上来个彻底改变,我觉得这意见太～了。*He advocates making immediate drastic changes, but I think this idea is too radical.* ◇ ～派 radicals

【激励】❶ encourage; impel; urge: 为国争光的志愿～运动员刻苦训练。*The desire to win glory for their country impels the athletes to train diligently.* ❷ [电子] drive; excitation: ～器 *driver; exciter*

【激烈】intense; sharp; fierce; acute: ～的争论 *heated argument* / 一场～的比赛 *a closely fought game; a gruelling match* / 争吵得很～ *quarrel bitterly*

【激流】torrent; rapids; turbulent current: 这里到处是～险滩,行船要加倍留意。*There are rapids and dangerous shoals throughout the area, so boats must be navigated with the utmost care.*

【激怒】enrage; infuriate; exasperate: 种族主义者的暴行～了人民。*The atrocities committed by the racists enraged the people.* / ～之下,他一甩门走了。*Infuriated, he slammed the door and left.* / 他一顶嘴更把父亲～了。*His back talk further infuriated his father.*

【激起】arouse; evoke; cause; stir up: ～众怒 *arouse popular indignation; stir up public wrath*

【激切】〈书〉(of language) impassioned; vehement: 言辞～ *impassioned language*

【激情】intense emotion; fervour; passion; enthusiasm: 他们的演出充满了爱国～。*Their performance was permeated with patriotic fervour.* / 他满怀～,歌唱着自己美丽的家乡。*He passionately sang a song of his beloved hometown.*

【激素】hormone

【激扬】❶ drain away the mud and bring in fresh water; drive out evil and usher in good ❷ excited and high-spirited; vehement: ～的歌声 *spirited singing* ❸ encourage; urge: ～士气 *boost the morale*

【激越】intense; vehement; loud and strong: 草原上扬起清亮～的歌声。*Songs were heard ringing loud and clear over the grasslands.*

【激增】increase sharply; soar; shoot up: 经济危机加剧,失业人数～。*With the deepening of the economic crisis, unemployment shot up.*

【激战】fierce fighting

【激浊扬清】drain away the mud and bring in fresh water—drive out evil and usher in good; eliminate vice and exalt virtue

【激子】[物] exciton

羁 Ⅰ **名** 〈书〉 bridle; headstall: 无～之马 *a horse without a bridle—running wild* Ⅱ **动** ❶ control; restrain: 放荡不羁 ❷ stay; delay; detain: 事务～身 *be detained by one's duties*

【羁绊】〈书〉trammels; fetters; yoke: 她为家务所～,未能前往。*She was tied up with housework and couldn't go.*

【羁留】❶ stay (in a strange place); stop over: 在穗～三日 *stop over in Guangzhou for three days* ❷ keep in custody; detain

【羁旅】〈书〉stay long in a strange place; live in a strange land

【羁押】〈书〉detain; take into custody

jí

及 Ⅰ **动** ❶ reach; come up to: 目力所～ *as far as the eye can reach* / 水深～腰。*The water came up to one's waist (or was waist-deep).* ❷ be in time for: 及时 Ⅱ **连** and; as well as: 图书、仪器～其他 *books, instruments and other things* / 句子的主要成分～其语法功能 *major sentence elements and their grammatical functions*

【及第】pass an imperial examination

【及格】pass a test, examination, etc.; pass: 他的历史课考试～了。*He passed the history test.* / 中国学校一般采用百分制,六十分为～。*Most schools in China use the hundred percentage point system, with 60 percent as the passing grade.* ◇ ～赛 qualification contest

【及时】❶ timely; in time; seasonable: 要～下种。*Sowing must be done at the right time.* / 这场雪很～。*This snow has come at the right time.* ❷ promptly; without delay: ～纠正错误 *correct a mistake promptly* / ～汇报 *report without delay*

【及时行乐】enjoy life while ye may

【及时雨】timely rain—help rendered in the nick of time; timely help

【及物动词】〈语〉transitive verb

【及早】at an early date; as soon as possible; before it is too late: 有病要～治。*When you are ill, see the doctor as soon as possible.* / 一有消息,请～通知我。*As soon as you get any news, please let me know.*

汲 动 draw (water): 从井里～水 *draw water from a well*

【汲取】draw; derive: 植物通过根部～养分。*Plants assimilate nutriment through their roots.* / 我们可以～其他地方的经验。*We can draw on the experience of other regions.*

吉 形 lucky; auspicious; propitious: 万事大吉

【吉卜赛人】Gypsy

【吉布提】Djibouti ◇ ～人 Djiboutian

【吉尔吉斯斯坦】Kirghizstan

【吉光片羽】fragment of a highly treasured relic

【吉利】lucky; auspicious; propitious: 门上贴个"喜"字,取个～。*Put the character* 喜 *on the door for good luck.*

【吉尼斯世界纪录】Guiness World Records

【吉普车】jeep

【吉庆】an auspicious occasion; a happy occasion

【吉庆有余】auspicious happiness in overmeasure (or in superabundance)

【吉人天相】Heaven stands by the good man

【吉日】auspicious day; lucky day

【吉他】guitar

【吉祥】lucky; auspicious; propitious: 过年了,按老风俗,见面都要说一些～话。*It's the lunar New Year. According to the old custom, when you meet someone, you should say a few auspicious words.*

【吉祥物】mascot

【吉星高照】be blessed by a lucky star

【吉凶】good or ill luck

【吉凶未卜】one's fate is in the balance; fate unknown: 他们在海上遇上了大风暴,至今尚无消息,～。*They've met with a storm at sea, and we haven't had any news of them yet. Their fate is still unknown.*

【吉言】auspicious remarks; blessing: 借你的～,这件事我干了! *With your blessing I shall go ahead with it.*

【吉兆】good omen; propitious sign: 今年一月份买卖就不错,这是个～。*This year began auspiciously with good trade figures for January.* / 妈妈听见喜鹊在房上叫,觉得是个～。*Mother heard a magpie call from the roof and took it for a good omen.*

岌 形〈书〉(of a mountain) lofty; towering

【岌岌可危】in imminent danger

级 Ⅰ 名 ❶ level; rank; grade: 各～党组织 *party organizations at all levels* / 大使～会谈 *talks at ambassadorial level* / 甲～产品 *grade A products; first-class products* / 三～工 *grade-3 worker* / 一～战备 *No. 1 alert* / 七～地震 *an earthquake of magnitude 7* (on the Richter scale) / 七～风 *force 7 wind (on the Beaufort scale)* ❷ any of the yearly divisions of a school course; grade; class; form: 同～不同班 *be in different classes of the same grade* ❸ step: 石～ *stone steps* / 拾～而登 *follow the steps up* ❹ [语] degree: 比较～ *the comparative degree* / 最高～ *the superlative degree* Ⅱ 量 (for steps, etc.): 十几～台阶 *a flight of a dozen steps*

【级别】rank; level; grade; scale: 外交～ *diplomatic rank* / 工资～ *wage scale; grade on the wage scale* / 她的～比我高。*She is above me in rank.* / 她是什么～的干部? *What rank of cadre is she?*

【级差地租】differential (land) rent

【级间分离】[航天] stage separation

【级数】[数] progression; series

极 Ⅰ 名 ❶ the utmost point; extremity: 愚蠢之～ *be the height of folly* / ～而言之 *talk in extreme terms* ❷ pole: 极地 Ⅱ 副 extremely; to the greatest extent; exceedingly: ～好(快、慢) *extremely good (fast, slow)* / ～重要 *of the utmost importance* / ～少数 *a tiny minority; only a few; a handful*

【极板】[电] plate

【极大】[数] maximum: ～值 *maximum (value)*

【极地】polar region: ～航行 *arctic navigation; polar air navigation*

【极点】the limit; the extreme; the utmost: 感动到了～ *be extremely moved* / 蛮横无理到了～ *reach the height of truculence*

【极度】❶ extremely; exceedingly; to the utmost: 他～兴奋,一夜没睡着。*He was so elated that he couldn't sleep all night.* / ～疲劳 *be extremely tired; be overcome with fatigue* ❷ the limit; the extreme; the utmost

【极端】❶ extreme: 对他的能力应该有个正确的估价,不要从一个～走到另一个～。*You should make a correct evaluation of his ability. Don't go from one extreme to the other.* ❷ extremely; exceedingly: ～困难 *exceedingly difficult* / ～贫困 *in dire poverty* / ～腐败 *rotten to the core* / ～个人主义者 *out-and-out egoist* / ～民主化 *ultra-democracy*

【极光】[天] aurora; polar lights—另见〖北极光〗;〖南极光〗

【极化】[物] polarization: ～张量 *polarization tensor*

【极乐鸟】bird of paradise
【极乐世界】[宗](佛教) the Land of Ultimate Bliss
【极力】do one's utmost; spare no effort: 我们将~避免发生事故。*We'll do our utmost to avoid accidents.* / ~劝阻 *try very hard to dissuade sb. from doing sth.* / ~吹捧 *laud sb. to the skies*
【极量】[医] maximum dose
【极目】look as far as the eye can see: ~远眺 *gaze far into the distance (from a high place, as a mountaintop)*
【极品】〈书〉highest grade; best quality: ~绿茶 *best quality green tea* / 关东人参号称~。*The ginseng of northeast China is known to be the best.*
【极谱】[物] polarogram: ~分析 *polarographic analysis* / ~仪 *polarograph*
【极其】most; extremely; exceedingly: 他对这个问题的看法~荒唐。*His views on this subject are absolutely ridiculous.* / 吸烟对身体~有害。*Smoking is extremely harmful to your health.* / 他的评论~深刻。*His comments were most penetrating.*
【极圈】polar circle ——另见〖北极圈〗;〖南极圈〗
【极权主义】totalitarianism
【极盛】the highest (point of development): 在古埃及文明的~时期 *at the height of ancient Egyptian civilization* / 在他精力~的时期 *in the prime of his life*
【极限】❶ the limit; the maximum: 这辆卡车的载重量已达到了~。*This truck has already reached the limit of its load capacity.* / ~负载 [电] *limit load* / ~压力 [物] *limiting pressure* ❷ [数] limit ◇ ~概率 limiting probabilities
【极刑】capital punishment; the death penalty: 处以~ *sentence sb. to death*
【极夜】polar night
【极右】ultra-Right: ~势力 *ultra-Right forces*
【极值】[数] extreme value
【极昼】polar day
【极"左"】ultra-"Left": 以~的面貌出现 *put on an extremely "Left" front* / ~分子 *ultra-"Leftist"* / ~思潮 *ultra-"Left" trend of thought*
【极坐标】polar coordinate: ~曲线 *polar curve* / ~图 *polar diagram* / ~导航系统 [航海] *polar-coordinate navigation system*

即 Ⅰ 动 ❶ approach; reach; be near: 可望而不可即 ❷ assume; undertake: 即位 ❸ be; mean; namely: 春节~农历新年。*The Spring Festival is the lunar New Year.* / 非此~彼。*It must be either this or that.* Ⅱ 形 ❶ at present; in the immediate future: 在即 ❷ prompted by the occasion: 即兴 Ⅲ 副 promptly; at once: 闻过~改 *correct one's mistake as soon as it is pointed out* / 招之~来 *be on call at any hour* Ⅳ 连 even; even if: ~遇困难,亦应按期完成任务。*We should fulfill the mission even if we run up against difficulties.*
【即便】even; even if; even though: ~你有理,也不应该发火啊! *You shouldn't have lost your temper even if you were in the right.*
【即将】be about to; be on the point of; soon: 比赛~开始。*The match is about to begin.* / 水电站~竣工。*The hydroelectric station is nearing completion.*
【即景】〈文〉(of a literary or artistic work) be inspired by what one sees: 西湖~ *glimpses of the West Lake*
【即景生情】the scene touches a chord in one's heart: 他~,赋诗一首。*The scene moved him to compose a poem.*
【即景诗】extempore verse
【即刻】at once; immediately; instantly: 警察~出发,火速赶到出事现场。*The police left immediately, and rushed to the scene of the accident.*
【即令】even; even if; even though
【即期】[经] immediate; spot: ~付现 *immediate (or prompt) cash payment* / ~外汇 *spot exchange* / ~汇价 *spot rate* ◇ ~承兑 immediate acceptance; ~存款 deposit at call; demand deposit; ~信用证 sight letter of credit; ~债务 debt at call
【即日】〈书〉❶ this or that very day: 本条例自~起施行。*The regulations come into force (or go into effect) as of today.* ❷ within the next few days: 本片~放映。*The film will be shown within the next few days.*
【即时】immediately; forthwith ◇ ~重播 instant replay
【即食麦片】granola
【即使】even; even if; even though: ~下雨我也去。*I'll go anyway even if it rains.* / ~条件再好,也还要靠自己努力。*No matter how favourable the conditions are, we'll still rely on our own efforts.*
【即位】〈书〉ascend the throne: 清德宗 1875 年~,定年号为光绪。*The Emperor Dezong of the Qing Dynasty ascended the throne in 1875, and chose the reign title of Guangxu.*
【即席】〈书〉❶ impromptu; extemporaneous: ~赋诗一首 *compose a poem impromptu; improvise a poem* / ~讲话 *speak impromptu; make an impromptu (or extemporaneous) speech* ❷ take one's seat (at a dinner table, etc.)
【即兴】impromptu; extemporaneous: ~之作 *an improvisation* ◇ ~买主 impulse buyer; ~曲 [音] impromptu; ~诗 extempore verse
【即以其人之道,还治其人之身】deal with a man as he deals with you; pay a person back in his own coin

亟 副〈书〉urgently; anxiously; earnestly: ~盼 *earnestly hope* / ~欲 *desire most ardently; want very much* / ~待解决的重大问题 *important problems demanding prompt solution* / ~须纠正 *must be speedily put right*

急 Ⅰ 形 ❶ impatient; anxious: ~着要出发 *be*

impatient to set out ❷ irritated; annoyed; nettled: 你老唠叨他，会把他弄～的。*If you keep nagging him, you'll make him very annoyed.* / 我没想到他真～了。*I didn't expect him to get angry.* ❸ fast; rapid; violent: 水流很～。*The current is swift.* or *It's a strong current.* / 雨下得正～。*It's raining hard.* / ～转弯 *make a sharp turn* ❹ urgent; pressing: 事情很～，必须立即处理。*The matter is pressing (or urgent) and must be dealt with at once.* / 他走得很～。*He left in a hurry.* Ⅱ 动 ❶ worry: 你怎么来得这么晚，真把人～死啦！*Why are you so late? We were worried to death about you.* ❷ be eager to help: ～人之难 *be eager to help those in need* / ～病人之所急 *be eager to meet the needs of the patients; put oneself in a patient's position* Ⅲ 名 urgency; emergency: 应急

【急板】[音] presto

【急病】acute disease

【急不可待】too impatient to wait; extremely anxious: 他一拿到信，在路上就～地拆开看了。*As soon as he was handed the letter, he anxiously ripped it open and read it right on the street.*

【急促】❶ hurried; rapid: ～的脚步声 *hurried footsteps* / ～的枪声 *rapid gunfire* / 呼吸～ *be short of breath* / 脉搏～ *have a short, quick pulse* ❷ (of time) short; pressing: 时间很～，不要再犹豫了。*Time is running short. Stop hesitating (or dithering).*

【急电】urgent telegram; urgent cable

【急风暴雨】violent storm; hurricane; tempest: 这场农民运动如～，势不可挡。*This peasant movement carried all before it like a hurricane.*

【急腹症】[医] acute abdominal disease; acute abdomen

【急公好义】zealous for the common weal; public-spirited: 这位老人历来～，为全村老百姓办了不少好事。*This old man has always been public-spirited, and has done a lot of good things for the community.*

【急功近利】eager for instant success and quick profits: 制定政策不能～，要有长远的观点。*In formulating policies, we must not be seeking short-term successes and quick profits. We should take a long-range view of things.*

【急件】an urgent document or dispatch

【急惊风】[中] acute infantile convulsions

【急救】first aid; emergency treatment: 有十几个人食物中毒，立刻送医院～。*Ten or so victims of food poisoning were sent to the hospital for emergency treatment.* ◇ ～包 first-aid dressing; ～车 breakdown van; emergency ambulance; ～人员 first-aid personnel; ～药品 first-aid medicine; ～药箱 first-aid kit; ～站 first-aid station; ～中心 first-aid centre

【急就章】hurriedly-written essay; hasty work; improvisation

【急剧】rapid; sharp; sudden: ～的变化 *rapid change* / ～转折 *abrupt turn* / 物价～上升。*There was a steep rise in prices.* / 气温～下降。*There was a sudden drop in the temperature.*

【急遽】rapid; sharp; sudden: ～的敲门声把她吓了一跳。*A sudden sharp knock on the door startled her.*

【急来抱佛脚】clasp Buddha's feet when in trouble—seek help at the last moment; make a frantic last-minute effort

【急流】❶ torrent; rapid stream; rapids: ～滚滚 *a torrent surging ahead* / 闯过～险滩 *sweep over rapids and shoals* ❷ [气] jet stream; jet flow

【急流勇进】forge ahead against a swift current; press on in the teeth of difficulties

【急流勇退】resolutely retire at the height of one's official career

【急忙】in a hurry; in haste; hurriedly; hastily: 你干吗这样急急忙忙的？*Why are you in such a hurry?* / 他起晚了，没吃早饭就～向学校跑去。*He got up late and hurriedly ran off to school without eating any breakfast.*

【急迫】urgent; pressing; imperative: 这是当前最～的任务。*This is the most pressing task at present.* / 事情很～，得赶快处理。*The matter is urgent and something's got to be done about it at once.*

【急起直追】rouse oneself to catch up; do one's utmost to overtake: 我们要～，迎头赶上。*We must do our utmost to catch up with the foremost.*

【急切】❶ eager; impatient: 她用～的目光注视着我，希望得到我的同意。*She looked at me intently; hoping that I would give her my consent.* / 我们～地盼望他早日归来。*We are eagerly awaiting his early return.* ❷ in a hurry; in haste: ～间找不着适当的人 *cannot find the right person on such short notice*

【急如星火】extremely pressing; most urgent; posthaste: 灾区需用医药，～。*Medical aid must be sent to the stricken area posthaste.*

【急刹车】❶ slam the brakes on ❷ bring to a halt: 工程进行得很顺利，突然上面下达命令，来了个～。*The project was going ahead smoothly when suddenly orders came from above to bring the whole thing to a halt.*

【急速】very fast; rapid: 汽车～地向前行驶。*The car was running at high speed.* / 他的病情～恶化。*His condition rapidly worsened.* / 情况～变化。*The situation changed quickly.*

【急湍】〈书〉swift (or rushing) current; gurgling rapids: 清流～ *clear streams and gurgling rapids*

【急弯】sharp turn: 拐了个～ *made a sharp turn* / 前有～，行车小心。*Sharp turn ahead. Drive carefully.*

【急务】urgent task: 因有～在身，不敢在此逗留。*I have an urgent task to attend to, so I can't make a stop-over here.*

【急先锋】❶ daring vanguard ❷ most aggressive, adventurous henchman

【急行军】rapid march; forced march: 部队～，一

夜走了一百里。*The detachment made a rapid march of 100 li in one night.*

【急性】acute：～阑尾炎 *acute appendicitis* / ～传染病 *acute infectious disease*

【急性病】❶［医］acute disease ❷ impetuosity：要周密计划后再开始做，不要犯～。*You must plan carefully before you begin. Don't make the mistake of being too impetuous.*

【急性子】❶ of impatient disposition；impetuous ❷ an impetuous person：他是个～，不把这件事干完是不肯歇的。*He's an impatient man. He won't rest until after he's finished the job.*

【急需】❶ be badly in need of：～帮助 *be in need of immediate help* / 提供～的资金 *provide much-needed funds* ❷ urgent need：以应～ *meet a crying need*

【急眼】〈方〉be taken aback；feel anxious：进屋一看，孩子不见了，她～了。*When she came into the room and saw that her child was nowhere to be seen, she became very anxious.*

【急用】urgent need：节约储蓄，以备～ *practise economy and save money against a rainy day* / 请把材料赶紧送来，有～。*Please send us the material at once; it's urgently needed.*

【急于】eager；anxious；impatient：～完成任务 *eager to fulfil a task* / ～表态 *impatient to state one's position* / 没准备好，就不要～开会。*Don't call the meeting till we're ready.*

【急于求成】overanxious for quick results；impatient for success：为什么有些作品不成熟呢？因为～。*Some works are immature owing to undue haste.*

【急躁】❶ irritable；irascible：他性情～。*He has an irascible temperament.* / 一听说事情还没办，他就～起来。*As soon as he heard that the matter hadn't been taken care of yet, he got very irritable.* ❷ impetuous；rash；impatient：防止～情绪 *guard against impetuosity* / 产生～情绪 *give way to impatience* / ～冒进 *advance impetuously*

【急诊】emergency call；emergency treatment：这病不能耽误，上医院看～吧。*This kind of illness allows no delay. Go right to hospital for emergency treatment.* ◇ ～病人 emergency case；～室 emergency room

【急症】sudden attack (of illness)；acute disease；emergency case

【急智】nimbleness of mind in dealing with emergencies；quick-wittedness

【急中生智】hit upon a plan in desperation；show resourcefulness in an emergency；suddenly hit on a way out of a predicament

【急转直下】(of the march of events, etc.) take a sudden turn and then develop rapidly

疾

Ⅰ**名** ❶ disease；sickness；illness：痼疾 ❷ suffering；pain；difficulty：疾苦 Ⅱ**动** hate；abhor：疾恶如仇 Ⅲ**形** ❶ fast；quick：～走 *walk quickly；march swiftly* ❷ vigorous；strong：疾风

【疾病】disease；illness：防治～ *prevention and treatment of disease* ◇ ～保险 sickness insurance

【疾恶如仇】hate evil like an enemy：他的绝对公正和～赢得了群众的信任和拥护。*His absolute fairness and abhorrence of evil won him the confidence and support of the masses.*

【疾风】❶ strong wind；gale ❷［气］moderate gale

【疾风扫落叶】like a strong wind sweeping away dead leaves—carrying everything before one

【疾风知劲草，烈火见真金】sturdy grass withstands high winds；true gold stands the test of fire—strength of character is tested in a crisis

【疾苦】sufferings；hardships：关心人民的～ *be concerned about the weal and woe of the people*

【疾驰】(of vehicles) speed along：～而去 *speed past*

【疾首蹙额】with aching head and knitted brows—frowning in disgust；with abhorrence

【疾言厉色】harsh words and stern looks：他对人很和蔼，从不～。*He is always affable and never brusque with people.*

棘

名 ❶ sour jujube ❷ thorn bushes；brambles ❸［动］spine；spina

【棘皮动物】echinoderm

【棘手】thorny；troublesome；knotty：～的问题 *a knotty problem* / 这件事情很～。*This is a sticky business.*

【棘爪】［机］pawl；detent：止回～ *check pawl*

集

Ⅰ**动** gather；collect：聚集 / ～各家之长 *incorporate the strong points of different schools* Ⅱ**名** ❶ country fair；market：这个镇每三天一个～，今天逢～。*An outdoor market is held every three days in this town, and today happens to be a market day.* ❷ collection；anthology：画～ *an album of paintings* ❸ volume；part：这些文章分三～出版。*These articles will be published in three volumes.* / 这部影片分上、下两～。*This film is in two parts.*

【集材】［林］logging；skidding；yarding

【集尘器】［机］dust arrester；dust collector；duster

【集成】❶ (usu. Used in book titles) collection ❷［电子］integration：计算机～制造 *CIM (computer integrated manufacturing)*

【集成电路】［电子］integrated circuit：～晶体管 *integrated circuit transistor*

【集大成】gather together all that is good；synthesize；be the culmination of；be a comprehensive expression of

【集电极】［电子］collecting electrode；collector

【集股】collect capital；form a stock company

【集管】［机］header

【集合】gather；assemble；muster；call together：～！(*word of command*) *Fall in!* / 紧急～ *emergency muster* / ～地点 *assembly place；rendezvous* / 命令全排战士～。*Order the whole platoon to fall in.* ◇ ～号 bugle call for fall-in；assembly；～论［数］set theory；～名词〈语〉collective noun；～体［矿］aggregate

【集会】assembly; rally; gathering; meeting: ～结社自由 *freedom of assembly and association* / 举行群众～ *hold a mass rally*

【集结】(esp. of troops) mass; concentrate; build up: ～军队 *mass troops*; *concentrate forces* / ～力量 *build up strength* / ～待命 *assemble and await orders* ◇ ～地域[军] assembly area

【集锦】(usu. used in book titles) a collection of choice specimens: 儿童画～ *outstanding examples of children's drawings*

【集句】a poem made up of lines from various poets

【集聚】gather; collect; assemble: ～资金 *accumulate funds*

【集刊】collected papers (of an academic institution)

【集流环】[电] slip ring

【集贸市场】fair trade market—a town or country market at which various products are sold and bought

【集纳】gather; assemble: 文章～了他一生的经历。*The article described all his life experiences.*

【集权】centralization of state power: 中央～的封建帝国 *a centralized feudal empire*

【集日】market day: 镇上每逢～,四乡农民都带着土特产前来赶集。*Whenever market day comes round, the farmers of the surrounding countryside all come to town, bringing their special produce for the market.*

【集散地】collecting and distributing centre; distributing centre: 该市位居南北交通枢纽,为各种重要物资的～。*This city, situated at the transportation hub between north and south, is a distribution centre for all kinds of important goods and materials.*

【集市】country fair; market ◇ ～贸易 country fair trade; open market

【集束】❶ tied in a bundle: ～炸弹 *cluster bomb* / ～式弹头 *cluster warhead* ❷ compile; compilation; collection: 科技新闻～ *collection of scientific news*

【集思广益】draw on collective wisdom and absorb all useful ideas; pool the wisdom of the masses

【集体】collective: ～的智慧 *collective wisdom* / ～创作 *collective effort in literary or artistic creation* / ～观念 *collective spirit* ◇ ～婚礼 mass wedding; ～经济 collective economy; ～领导 collective leadership; ～农庄 collective farm; ～企业 collectively—owned enterprise; ～生产劳动 collective productive labour; ～宿舍 dormitory; ～所有制 collective ownership; ～舞 group dancing; ～主义 collectivism; ～主义教育 education to foster a community spirit

【集体户】❶ collective ownership of an enterprise ❷ living place of a group of educated youth settled in the countryside (during the Cultural Revolution)

【集体化】collectivize: 农业～ *the collectivization of agriculture* / 走～的道路 *follow (or take) the road of collectivization*

【集团】group; clique; circle; bloc: 七十七国～ *the Group of 77* / 统治～ *the ruling clique*; *the ruling circle* / 军事～ *a military bloc* / 货币～ *monetary bloc* / 小～ *a small clique* ◇ ～军 group army; army

【集团购买力】the purchasing power of institutions; institutional purchases: 压缩～ *cut down the purchasing power of institutions*

【集团消费】institutional spending: 政府已采取一些措施防止～增长过快。*The government has taken measures to avoid excessive rapid increase in institutional spending.*

【集训】assemble for training: 干部轮流～。*Cadres take turns to receive training at a given place.*

【集训队】[体] team of athletes in training

【集腋成裘】the finest fragments of fox fur, sewn together, will make a robe—many a little makes a mickle

【集邮】stamp collecting; philately ◇ ～爱好者 stamp-collector; philatelist; ～簿 stamp-album

【集约】[农] intensive: ～经营 *intensive farming* ◇ ～投资 intensive investment

【集约化】intensify: 渔业生产开始转向～。*Fish farming is beginning to be intensified.*

【集约型增长】intensive mode of economic development

【集运】transport sth. containerized

【集镇】town; market town

【集中】concentrate; centralize; focus; amass; put together: ～精力 *concentrate one's energy* / ～火力 *concentrate fire (on a target)* / ～目标 *concentrate on the same target* / ～管理 *centralized management* / ～指挥 *centralized direction (or command)* / 思想不～ *be absent-minded* ◇ ～供热 central heating; ～轰炸 mass bombing; ～营 concentration camp

【集注】❶ focus: 代表们的眼光都～在大会主席台上。*All eyes at the conference were focused on the rostrum.* ❷ (usu. used in book titles) collected commentaries; variorum: 朱熹《四书章句～》*Zhu Xi's Collected Commentaries on the "Four Books"* ◇ ～本 variorum edition

【集装箱】container: ～船 *container ship* / ～化 *containerize* / ～码头 *container terminal* / ～运输 *containerized traffic*

【集资】raise funds; collect money; pool resources: 这座大桥由当地农民～兴建,没花国家一分钱。*This bridge was built with funds pooled by the local farmers. Not a cent of state money was spent.*

【集子】collection; collected works; anthology: 这个～里收有二十篇小说。*This anthology consists of 20 novels.*

辑 Ⅰ 动 collect; compile; edit: 编辑 Ⅱ 名 part; volume; division: 新闻简报第一～ *Newsreel No.1* / 这部丛书分三～,每～五本。*This set of books are in three parts, and each part is in five volumes.*

【辑集】collect and edit; compile

【辑录】compile：这个集子～了这位已故作家的所有来往信件。*All the letters of the late writer are compiled in this collection.*
【辑要】summary；abstract

蒺 (构词成分)见下
【蒺藜】［植］puncture vine

嫉 动 ❶ be jealous；be envious ❷ hate
【嫉妒】同〖忌妒〗
【嫉恨】envy and hate；hate out of jealousy
【嫉贤妒能】be envious of people of worth and ability

瘠 形〈书〉❶ lean；thin and weak ❷ barren；poor；lean：～土 *poor soil；lean soil；barren land*
【瘠田】infertile land

籍 名 ❶ book；record：古籍 ❷ registry；roll：户籍 ❸ native place；home town；birthplace：祖籍 ❹ membership：国籍
【籍贯】the place of one's birth or origin；native place

jǐ

几 代 ❶ how many：～点了？*What's the time?* or *What time is it?* / 你～号？*What's your number?* / 四乘六等于～？*What's four times six?* ❷ a few；several；some：说～句话 *say a few words* / 他过不了～天就会回来的。*He'll be back in a couple of days.* / ～十 *tens；dozens；scores* ——另见 jī
【几次三番】time and again；repeatedly：～地前来寻衅 *come repeatedly to pick a quarrel*
【几分】a bit；somewhat；rather：有～醉意 *a bit merry；a bit tipsy* / 让他～ *humour him a little*
【几何】❶〈书〉how much；how many：不知尚有～ *be uncertain how much is left or how many are left* ❷ geometry ◇ ～级数 geometric progression；geometric series；～失真 geometric distortion；～图形 geometric figure；～学［数］geometry
【几经】several times；time and again：这堵墙已～倒塌，～修补。*The wall has collapsed and been rebuilt several times.* / 这件事～周折才办成。*The matter was settled after a lot of bother.*
【几内亚】Guinea ◇ ～人 Guinean
【几内亚比绍】Guinea-Bissau
【几时】❶ what time；when：你们～走？*What time are you leaving?* / 不知～咱们才能再见面！*Who knows when we'll meet again?* ❷ any time；when：你～有空～来。*Come when you are free.* / 你们～见到他代我问好。*Please remember me to him when you meet him.*

己 代 oneself；one's own；personal：舍～为公 *make personal sacrifices for the public good*
【己不正，难正人】one who lacks moral integrity cannot expect to correct others' misdeeds；a person lacking moral integrity is in no position to help others correct their behavior；"Physician, heal thyself!"
【己方】one's own side
【己任】〈书〉one's duty：这批青年将建设边疆引为～。*These young people regard the construction of the borderland as their duty.*
【己所不欲，勿施于人】do not impose on others what you yourself do not desire；do not unto others as you would not have them do unto you

虮 (构词成分)见下
【虮子】the egg of a louse；nit

济 (构词成分)见下 ——另见 jì
【济济】(of people) many；numerous：人才济济
【济济一堂】gather together under the same roof：代表们～，进行了热烈的讨论。*The representatives gathered together and had a lively discussion.*

挤 动 ❶ squeeze；press：把水～掉 *squeeze the water out* / ～时间 *try and find time to do sth.；find time* ❷ jostle；push against：～进去 *force (or elbow, shoulder, push) one's way in；squeeze in* / ～上前去 *push to the front* / 别～。*Don't push.* / 人们互相～来～去。*People jostled each other.* ❸ crowd；pack；cram：～做一团 *pressed close together；packed like sardines* / 小屋～不下那么多人。*It's impossible to pack so many people into the small room.*
【挤兑】a run on a bank
【挤眉弄眼】make eyes；wink
【挤奶】milk (a cow, etc.) ◇ ～机 milking machine；milker
【挤压】［冶］extruding：～机 *extrusion press；extruder*
【挤牙膏】squeeze toothpaste out of a tube—be forced to tell the truth bit by bit：审问这个惯犯就跟～一样。*To interrogate this hardened criminal, you have to squeeze every word out of him.*
【挤眼】wink：他意味深长地向她挤挤眼。*He winked meaningfully to her.*
【挤占】occupy：～私房 *seize private housing* / ～绿化田地 *encroach upon a green belt*

给 Ⅰ 动 supply；provide：自给自足 Ⅱ 形 ample；well provided for：家给人足 ——另见 gěi
【给水】❶［建］watersupply：～工程 *watersupply engineering* ❷［机］feed water：锅炉～ *boiler feed water* / ～器 *water feeder*
【给养】provisions；victuals：～充足 *be abundantly provisioned* / ～不足 *be short of provisions* / 补充～ *replenish the provisions*
【给予】〈书〉give；render：～支持 *give support to* / ～协助 *render assistance to* / ～正式承认 *give official recognition to*

脊 名 ❶ spine；backbone ❷ ridge：山脊

【脊背】back (of a human being or any other vertebrate)

【脊梁】〈方〉back (of the human body)：光着～ *bare-backed*

【脊梁骨】backbone；spine：戳～ *criticize sb. behind him；backbite*

【脊鳍】[动] dorsal fin

【脊神经】spinal nerve

【脊髓】spinal cord ◇ ～灰质炎 poliomyelitis；polio；～炎 myelitis

【脊索】[动] notochord ◇ ～动物 chordate (animal)

【脊柱】spinal column；vertebral column；backbone；spine

【脊椎】vertebra ◇ ～动物 vertebrate；～骨 vertebra；spine

麂 名 muntjac

【麂皮】chamois (leather)；chammy

【麂子】〈口〉muntjac

jì

计 Ⅰ 动 ❶ count；compute；calculate；number：外币贷款按外币～收利息。*Interest on a foreign currency loan shall be computed and charged in foreign currency.* ❷ (usu. used in the negative) haggle over：工作不～时间 *be ready to work longer hours than required；not mind working extra hours* / 不～报酬 *not be concerned about pay* ❸ (only used in the pattern "为……计") for the purpose of；in order to：为长远～ *from a long-term point of view* Ⅱ 名 ❶ idea；ruse；stratagem；plan：退敌之～ *a stratagem to repulse the enemy* / 作归～ *plan to go home* / 他们一～不成，又生一～。*Their first ruse having failed, they tried another.* ❷ meter；gauge：体温计

【计策】stratagem；plan：定下了诱敌深入的～ *make a plan to lure the enemy in*

【计程表】taximeter；meter

【计程仪】[航海] log

【计酬】work out or calculate payment：按件～ *pay by the piece* / 按钟点～ *pay by the hour*

【计出万全】make a perfectly safe plan

【计划】❶ plan；project；programme：切实可行的～ *a feasible (or workable) plan* / 宏伟的～ *a magnificent project* / ～外的商品 *goods produced over and above the plan* / ～外项目 *projects outside the plan* ❷ map out；plan：～好了再动手干。*Map it out before you start.* / 我们～下周出发。*We plan to leave next week.* ◇ ～调拨 planned allocation；～供应 planned supply；～经济 planned economy；～评审技术 program evaluation and review technique；～生产 planned production；～外生育 unplanned birth

【计划生育】family planning；birth control ◇ ～宣传月 the Family Planning Month

【计划外】in excess of planned quotas；outside the plan：～价格 *prices for products in excess of planned quotas* / ～生产资料 *capital goods not covered by the plan*

【计价】valuate：固定资产的～，应当以原价为准。*The valuation of fixed assets shall be based on the original cost.* / ～过低 *undervaluation* / ～过高 *overvaluation*

【计件】reckon by the piece ◇ ～工资 piece rate wage；～工作 piecework

【计较】❶ haggle over；fuss about：～小事 *be too particular about trifles* / 他不～个人得失。*He gives no thought to personal gains or losses.* ❷ argue；dispute：我不同你～，等你气平了再说。*I won't argue with you now. Let's talk it over when you've calmed down.* ❸ think over；plan：先安排一周的活儿，以后再作～。*We'll arrange a week's work first and think about the rest afterwards.*

【计量】measure；calculate；estimate：这项发明影响之大不可～。*The influence of the invention is inestimable.* ◇ ～学 metrology

【计谋】scheme；stratagem

【计日程功】estimate exactly how many days are needed to complete a project；have the completion of a project in sight

【计生委】(〈略〉全称为'计划生育委员会') family planning commission

【计时】reckon by time ◇ ～工资 payment by the hour；time wage；～工作 timework；～器 hourmeter；hour counter

【计数】count

【计数器】counter：盖革～ *Geiger counter* / 闪烁～ *scintillation counter*

【计算】❶ count；compute；calculate：～出席人数 *count the number of people present* / ～产值 *calculate the output value* / 以人民币为～单位 *be computed in terms of Renminbi* ❷ consideration；planning：做事不能没个～。*We shouldn't do anything without a plan.* ❸ scheme；plot

【计算尺】slide rule

【计算机】computer；calculating machine：机械～ *mechanical computer* / 电子～ *electronic computer* / 模拟～ *analogue computer* / 微型～ *microcomputer* / 超高速巨型～ *giant ultra-high-speed computer* ◇ ～病毒 computer virus；～程序 computer program；～程序设计 computer programming；～存储器 computer memory；computer storage；～代码 computer code；～动画 computer-animation；～断层扫描 computed tomography (popularly called CT 扫描)；～辅助设计 computer-aided design (CAD)；～辅助语言教学 computer-assisted language learning (CALL)；～辅助制造 computer-aided manufacturing (CAM)；～监控系统 computer supervisory control system；～教育 education for computer；～科学 computer science；～控制 computer control；～模拟 computer simulation；～排字 computer typesetting；～配置 computer configuration；～情报检索 information retrieval by computer；～软件 computer software；～网络 computer network；～网络设备 computer network facilities；～文化 computer culture；～效益 computer utility；～应用 computer application；computer utility；～硬件 computer hardware；～语言 computer language；～指令 computer instruction；～专家 computernik

【计算器】electronic calculator

【计算语言学】computational linguistics

【计算中心】computing center

【计议】deliberate；talk over；consult：二人～已定。*The two of them settled on a scheme.*

记 Ⅰ**动** ❶ remember；bear in mind；commit to memory：～错了 *remember wrongly* / ～不清 *cannot recall exactly；remember only vaguely* / 牢牢地～在心上 *keep firmly in mind* ❷ write (or jot，take) down；record：～在笔记本上 *write it down in a notebook* / 把结果～下来 *record the results* / ～下电话号码 *jot down the telephone number* Ⅱ**名** ❶notes；record：大事记 ❷ mark；sign：暗～儿 *secret mark* ❸birthmark：他左腿有块～。*There is a birthmark on his left leg.* Ⅲ**量**〈方〉(used to count actions) slap：一～耳光 *a slap in the face*

【记仇】bear grudges；harbour bitter resentment：他可不～。*He's not the sort of person to bear a grudge.* / 她心胸狭隘，好～。*She is narrow-minded and tends to bear grudges.*

【记大过】record a serious offence

【记得】remember：～他的模样儿 *remember what he looked like* / 我完全记不得了。*I simply don't remember it.* / 我不～他有多大年纪了。*I don't remember how old he is.*

【记分】❶ keep the score；record the points (in a game) ❷ register a student's marks ❸ record workpoints ◇ ～牌 scoreboard；～员 scorekeeper；scorer；marker

【记功】cite sb. for meritorious service；record a merit：记一等功 *award sb. a Citation for Merit, First Class*

【记挂】〈方〉be concerned about；keep thinking about；miss：她一心～着生病的孩子，一下班就往家跑。*She was worried about her sick child, so she hurried home immediately after work.*

【记过】record a demerit：违反校规者将给予～处分。*Whoever violates the school regulations will be given a demerit.*

【记号】mark；sign：做个～ *make a sign；mark out* / 联络～ *mark for contact* / 我们按他在树干上做的～往前走。*We followed the marks he had made on the tree trunks.*

【记恨】bear grudges：她年轻不懂事，您别～她。*She is young and ignorant, so you shouldn't bear her any grudge.*

【记录】❶ take notes；keep the minutes；record：把发言的主要内容～下来 *note down the main points of the speeches* / ～在案 *place on record；as a matter of record* ❷ minutes；notes；record：会议～ *the minutes of a meeting* / 会谈～ *a transcript of talks* / 正式～ *official records* / 逐字～ *verbatim record* / 摘要～ *summary record* ❸ notetaker：这次讨论请你做～好吗？*Would you take the minutes of the discussion?* ❹ record：创～ *set a record；chalk up a record* / 世界～ *world record* ◇ ～本 minute book；～片 documentary film；documentary；～员 notetaker；stenographer；reporter

【记名】put down one's name (on a cheque，etc. to indicate responsibility or claim)；sign ◇ ～债券 registered bond；～证券 inscribed security；～支票 order cheque

【记谱法】［音］musical notation

【记取】remember；bear in mind：～这个血的教训 *bear firmly in mind this lesson learned at the cost of blood* / ～正反两方面的经验 *draw on experience both positive and negative*

【记时仪】［天］chronograph

【记事】❶ keep a record of events；make a memorandum：刻木结绳～ *keep records by notching wood or tying knots* ❷ account；record of events；chronicles

【记事儿】(of a child) begin to remember things：那时我只有五岁，才～。*I was then only five years old and had just begun to remember things.*

【记述】record and narrate：该书前言～了作者生平。*The preface of the book includes an account of the author's life.* / 这次庆祝活动没有什么可以～的。*The celebration has nothing worth recording.*

【记诵】commit to memory and be able to recite；learn by heart

【记性】memory：～好 *have a good memory* / ～坏 *have a poor (or short) memory*

【记叙】narrate：这篇文章～了他的先进事迹。*The article tells about his exemplary deeds.* ◇ ～文 narrative writing

【记忆】❶ remember；recall：就我～所及 *so far as I can remember* ❷ memory：你们的深情厚谊将永远留在我们的～中。*Your warm friendship will always remain in our memory.*

【记忆力】the faculty of memory；memory：～衰退 *one's memory is failing* / ～强(弱) *have a good (poor) memory*

【记忆犹新】remain fresh in one's memory

【记载】❶ put down in writing；record：详细地～事情经过 *record the incident in detail* / 有文字～的历史 *recorded history* ❷ record；account：地方志中有关于这次旱灾的～。*There is an account of this drought in the local chronicles.*

【记账】❶ keep accounts ❷ charge to an account：请把这笔开支记在我账上。*Please charge the expenses to my account.* ◇ ～交易 transaction for account

【记者】reporter；correspondent；newsman；journalist：新华社～ *Xinhua correspondent；reporter of the Xinhua News Agency* / 本报～ *staff reporter*; *staff correspondent* ◇ ～席 press gallery; ～协会 journalists' association; ～招待会 press conference; ～证 press card

【记住】remember; learn by heart; bear in mind: 把这首诗～ *learn the poem by heart* / 你记得住这些数字吗? *Can you carry all these figures in your head?*

纪 Ⅰ 名 ❶ discipline: 军纪 ❷ age; epoch: 中世～ *the Middle Ages* ❸ [地理] period: 震旦～ *the Sinian Period* Ⅱ 动 put down in writing; record

【纪检】inspect discipline

【纪录】同〖记录〗

【纪录片】同〖记录片〗

【纪律】discipline: 遵守～ *keep discipline*; *observe discipline* / ～严明 *highly disciplined* / 给予～处分 *take disciplinary measures against sb.* ◇ ～检查委员会 commission for inspecting discipline

【纪年】❶ a way of numbering the years: 阴历用干支～。*In the lunar calendar, the years are designated by the Heavenly Stems and Earthly Branches.* ❷ chronological record of events; annals

【纪念】❶ commemorate; mark: 人们集会～这位伟大的音乐家。*People held a meeting to commemorate the great musician.* / ～活动 *commemorative activities* ❷ souvenir; keepsake; memento: 留个～ *keep sth. as a souvenir* / 给你这张照片作个～。*Have this picture for a souvenir.* ❸ commemoration day; anniversary: 十周年～ *the tenth anniversary* ◇ ～币 commemorative coin; ～册 autograph book; autograph album; ～封 (stamp collecting) commemorate envelope; ～日 commemoration day; ～塔 memorial tower; monument; ～堂 memorial hall; commemoration hall; ～邮票 commemorative stamp; ～章 souvenir badge

【纪念碑】monument; memorial: 人民英雄～ *the Monument to the People's Heroes* / 建立革命烈士～ *erect a memorial to the revolutionary martyrs*

【纪念馆】memorial hall; museum in memory of sb.: 鲁迅～ *the Lu Xun Museum*

【纪念品】souvenir; keepsake; memento ◇ ～商店 souvenir shop

【纪实】record of actual events; on-the-spot report: 会议～ *an on-the-spot report of the meeting* ◇ ～文学 documentary literature

【纪委】〈略〉见〖纪律检查委员会〗

【纪行】(usu. used in book titles) travel notes: 《陕北～》*Notes On a Trip to Northern Shaanxi*

【纪要】summary of minutes; summary: 会谈～ *summary of conversations* (*or talks*) / 座谈会～ *summary of a forum or panel discussion*

【纪元】❶ the beginning of an era (e. g. an emperor's reign) ❷ epoch; era: 开辟了世界历史的新～ *usher in a new era in world history*

【纪传体】history presented in a series of biographies

伎 名 ❶ skill; ability; trick: 故伎重演 ❷ a professional female dancer or singer in ancient China

【伎俩】trick; intrigue; manoeuvre: "分而治之"是帝国主义者惯用的～。"*Divide and rule*" *has long been a favourite trick of the imperialists.* / 玩弄卑劣的～ *play a nasty trick*

技 名 skill; ability; trick: 一技之长

【技法】skill and technique (in painting, sculpture, etc.)

【技改】technical upgrading; technological change: ～项目 *technological transformation project*

【技工】❶ 〈略〉见〖技术工人〗 ❷ mechanic; technician ◇ ～学校 technical school

【技能】technical ability; mastery of a skill or technique: 生产～ *skill in production*

【技巧】skill; technique; craftsmanship: 写作～ *writing technique* / 艺术～ *artistry* / 精湛的玉雕～ *superb skill in jade carving*

【技巧运动】acrobatic gymnastics

【技穷】exhaust one's whole bag of tricks; come to the end of one's rope

【技师】technician

【技术】technology; skill; technique: 科学～ *science and technology* / 提高～水平 *increase technical competence* / ～要求很高 *demand high-level technology* / 重大～改革 *key technological transformations* / ～密集 *skill-intensive*; *technology-intensive* ◇ ～兵种 technical arms (or troops); ～服务 technical service; ～改造 technical transformation; technological transformation; ～革命 technological revolution; ～革新 technological innovation; technical innovation; ～工人 skilled worker; ～管理 technical management; ～规范 technical specification; technological specification; ～合同法 technological contract law; ～化社会 technopolis; ～鉴定 technical appraisement; ～诀窍协议 technical know-how agreement; ～开发 technological development; ～力量 technical force; technical personnel; ～密集型产业 technology-intensive industry; ～名词 technical term; ～评估 technological assessment; ～人员 technical personnel (or staff); ～市场 technology exchange market; ～手册 technical manual; technological manual; ～推广站 technical advice station; ～学校 technical school; ～研究所 technological research institute; ～员 technician; ～知识 technological know-how; technical knowledge; ～职称 titles for technical personnel; ～转让 technology transfer; ～装备 technical equipment; ～资料 technical data; technological data; ～咨询 technical advice

【技术科学】同〖应用科学〗

【技术性】technical; of a technical nature: ～问题 *technical matters* / 这工作～很强。*This job is highly technical.* ◇ ～贸易壁垒 technical barriers trade

【技术指导】❶ technological (or technical) guidance ❷ technical adviser

【技痒】itch to exercise one's skill：他看到孩子们打乒乓，不觉～。*Seeing the children playing ping-pong, he itched to have a go.*

【技艺】skill; artistry：～精湛 *highly skilled; masterly*

系 动 tie; fasten; do up; button up：～鞋带 *tie shoe laces* / 把衣服扣子～上 *button up a jacket* / 把晾衣绳～在树上 *fasten a clothesline between two trees* / 少先队员都～着红领巾。*The Young Pioneers all wear red scarves.* / 她～上围裙下厨房了。*She put on her apron and went to the kitchen.* ——另见 xì

【系泊】moor (a boat) ◇ ～浮筒 mooring buoy

【系船索】mooring rope; mooring line

【系留】moor (a balloon or airship) ◇ ～塔 mooring mast; mooring tower

忌 动 ❶ be jealous of; envy：～才 *be jealous of other people's talent; resent people more able than oneself* ❷ fear; dread; scruple：横行无忌 ❸ avoid; shun; abstain from：孕妇～服 *not to be taken by pregnant women* / ～生冷 *avoid cold and uncooked food* ❹ quit; give up：～酒 *give up alcohol; abstain from wine* / ～烟 *quit smoking*

【忌辰】the anniversary of the death of a parent, ancestor, or anyone else held in esteem

【忌惮】dread; fear; scruple：她破口大骂，毫无～。*She shouted abuse without any restraint.* ——另见〖肆无忌惮〗

【忌妒】be jealous (or envious) of; envy：她～她姐姐，因为她姐姐比她漂亮得多。*She is jealous of her sister because her sister is much prettier than herself.*

【忌讳】❶ taboo：犯～ *violate (or break) a taboo; offend a person's sensitivity; touch a person's sore spot* ❷ avoid as taboo：老张～人家叫他的外号。*Lao Zhang resents being called by his nickname.* ❸ avoid as harmful; abstain from：得了痢疾～吃生冷油腻。*People suffering from dysentery must avoid raw, cold or greasy food.*

【忌刻】(又作'忌克') jealous and mean; jealous and malicious

【忌口】avoid certain food (as when one is ill); be on a diet：我现在～，不能吃辣的。*I'm on a diet now and can't eat anything hot.*

【忌日】同〖忌辰〗

【忌食】❶ avoid certain food for health reasons or because of medical treatment：～生冷 *avoid cold and uncooked food* ❷ avoid certain food out of religious beliefs：印度教徒～牛肉。*Hindus avoid beef.*

际 名 ❶ border; boundary; edge：水～ *the edge of a body of water; waterside* ❷ between; among; inter-：春夏之～ *between spring and summer* / 校～比赛 *interschool matches; intercollegiate games* ❸ inside：脑～ *in one's head (or mind)* ❹ occasion; time：在代表大会召开之～ *on the occasion of the convening of the congress* / 临别之～ *at the time of parting* ❺ on the occasion of：～此盛会 *on the occasion of this grand gathering* ❻ one's lot; circumstances：遭际

【际遇】〈书〉favourable turns in life; spells of good or bad fortune：他～好，很快就提升了。*Fortune smiled on him and he was soon promoted.*

妓 名 prostitute

【妓女】prostitute

【妓院】brothel

季 Ⅰ 名 ❶ season：四季 ❷ the last month of a season ❸ the fourth or youngest among brothers：～弟 *the fourth or youngest brother* Ⅱ 量 the yield of a product in one season; crop：由种一～改为种两～ *reap two crops a year instead of one*

【季度】quarter (of a year)：～报告 *a quarterly report* / 我这份报纸是按～订的。*I subscribed to the newspaper by the quarter.*

【季风】(又作'季候风')〔气〕monsoon ◇ ～气候 monsoon climate; ～雨 monsoon rain

【季节】season：农忙～ *a busy farming season* / 收获～ *harvest season; harvest time* / 旅游～ *tourist season* ◇ ～差价 seasonal variations in price; ～失业 seasonal unemployment; ～工 seasonal worker; ～回游 seasonal migration (of fish, etc.)

【季节性】seasonal：～工作 *seasonal work; seasonal jobs*

【季军】third place (in sports contest, etc.)：她在 3,000 米跑中夺得～。*She came third in the 3,000-meter race.*

【季刊】quarterly publication; quarterly

剂 Ⅰ 名 a pharmaceutical or other chemical preparation：麻醉剂 Ⅱ 量 (for herbal medicine)：一～中药 *a dose of Chinese herbal medicine*

【剂量】〔医〕dosage; dose

【剂型】〔医〕the form of a drug (e.g. liquid, powder, pill, etc.)

济 动 ❶ cross a river：同舟共济 ❷ aid; relieve; help：缓不济急 ❸ be of help; benefit：无济于事 ——另见 jǐ

【济贫】aid the poor; relieve the poor

【济事】(usu. used in the negative) be of help (or use)：空谈不～。*Empty talk doesn't help matters.* ——另见〖不济事〗

荠 (构词成分)见下

【荠菜】shepherd's purse

迹 名 ❶ mark; trace：足迹 ❷ remains; ruins; vestige：遗迹 ❸ an outward sign; indication：～近剽窃 *an act verging on plagiarism*

【迹象】sign; indication：这是一种不寻常的～。

This is an unusual sign. / 有～表明两国将改善关系。*There are indications that the two countries are going to improve their relations.*

既 Ⅰ 副 already：濈洗～毕 *having performed one's ablutions* / ～得权利 *vested right* Ⅱ 连 ❶ since；as；now that：他～如此坚决，我也不便多说。*Since he is so determined, I consider it wise not to say any more.* ❷（used correlatively with 且，又，也，etc.）both...and；as well as：这间屋子～宽敞，又亮堂。*The room is both light and spacious.* / ～不实用，又不美观 *neither useful nor attractive*

【既成事实】accomplished fact；fait accompli：造成～ *present a fait accompli*；*make sth. an accomplished fact* / 承认～ *accept a fait accompli*

【既得利益】vested interest ◇ ～集团 vested interests

【既定】set；fixed；established：～目标 *set objective*；*fixed goal* / 就按～方案办吧，不要再改了。*Let's do it according to the existing plan. Don't make any further changes.*

【既来之，则安之】since you are here，you may as well stay and make the best of it

【既然】since；as；now that：～如此 *since it is so*；*such being the case*；*under these circumstances* / 你～表示了决心，就应该见之于行动。*Now that you have expressed your determination, you should act.*

【既是】since；as；now that：～天气不好，那就不去了吧。*Since the weather is bad, let's call off the trip.*

【既遂】［法］accomplished offence

【既往不咎】forgive sb.'s past misdeeds；not censure sb. for his past misdeeds：过去的事情～，以后你可得注意。*We'll overlook what you've done in the past but you'd better watch out in the future.*

觊 动〈书〉covet

【觊觎】〈书〉covet；cast greedy eyes on：～别国领土 *covet another country's territory*

继 Ⅰ 动 continue；succeed；follow：～踵 *follow close on sb.'s heels* / ～成昆铁路之后，我国西南又一条铁路建成通车了。*Following the Chengdu-Kunming Railway another new railway in Southwest China was completed and opened to traffic.* Ⅱ 副 then；afterwards：初感头晕，～又呕吐 *feel dizzy and then begin to vomit*

【继承】❶ inherit：夫妻有相互～遗产的权利。*Husband and wife have the right to inherit each other's property.* ❷ carry on：～优良传统 *carry forward the good traditions* ◇ ～法 law of succession；succession act；inheritance law

【继承权】right of succession；right of inheritance：非婚生子女享有与婚生子女同等的～。*Children born out of wedlock enjoy the same right of inheritance as children born in lawful wedlock.* / 剥夺～ *disinherit sb.*

【继承人】heir；successor；inheritor：直系～ *lineal successor* / 王位～ *successor to the throne* / 法定～ *heir at law*；*legal heir* / 那老人收养了这孩子并确定他为～。*The old man adopted the boy and made him his heir.*

【继承税】inheritance tax

【继电器】［电］relay

【继而】then；afterwards

【继父】stepfather

【继进】go on；continue the process

【继母】stepmother

【继女】stepdaughter

【继任】succeed sb. in a post：～首相 *succeed sb. as prime minister*

【继嗣】〈书〉❶ adopt a son ❷ heir

【继往开来】carry forward the cause and forge ahead into the future

【继位】succeed to the throne：乔治六世死后，伊丽莎白二世～。*When George VI died, Elizabeth II succeeded to the throne.*

【继续】❶ continue；go on：～工作 *continue working* / ～有效 *remain valid*；*remain in force* / ～执政 *continue in office*；*remain in power* / 会议～到深夜。*The meeting went on till late at night.* ❷ continuation：中国革命是伟大的十月革命的～。*The Chinese revolution is a continuation of the great October Revolution.*

【继子】stepson

寄 Ⅰ 动 ❶ send；post；mail：～信 *post a letter*；*mail a letter* / ～包裹 *send a parcel by post* / ～钱 *remit money* ❷ entrust；deposit；place：～希望于人民 *place hopes on the people* / 别～希望于他的帮助。*Don't count on him to help you.* ❸ depend on；attach oneself to：寄居 Ⅱ 形 adopted

【寄存】deposit；leave with；check：把大衣～在衣帽间 *check one's overcoat at the cloakroom*

【寄存器】computer register：变址～ *index register* / 进位～ *carry storage register*

【寄放】leave with；leave in the care of：把箱子～在朋友家里 *leave a suitcase with a friend* / 他把书～在哥哥家了。*He left his books in his brother's keeping.*

【寄费】postage

【寄件人】sender

【寄居】live away from home：从小～在舅父家里 *live from childhood with one's uncle*

【寄居蟹】hermit crab

【寄卖】（又作'寄售'）consign for sale on commission；put up for sale in a secondhand shop：把自行车放在委托商店里～ *put a bicycle on sale in a secondhand shop* ◇ ～品 consignment merchandise；～商店 commission shop；secondhand shop

【寄人篱下】live under another's roof；depend on sb. for a living：他想尽快找个工作，摆脱～的生活。*He was most anxious to find a job so as not to have to depend on others.*

【寄生】❶［生］parasitism ❷ parasitic：过着～生

活 *lead a parasitic life* ◇ ～虫 parasite；～虫病 parasitic disease；parasitosis；～虫学 parasitology；～动物 parasitic animal；～植物 parasitic plant

【寄售】consignment sales ◇ ～合同 agreement on consignment；consignment contract；～商店 consignment store

【寄宿】❶ lodge：～在朋友家里 *lodge (or put up) at a friend's house* ❷ (of students) board ◇ ～生 resident student；boarder；～学校 boarding school；residential college

【寄托】❶ entrust to the care of sb.；leave with sb.：把孩子～在邻居家里 *entrust one's child to the care of a neighbour* ❷ place (hope, etc.) on；find sustenance in：精神有所～ *have spiritual sustenance* / 他把希望全～在儿子身上。*He places all his hopes on his son.*

【寄销】commission sale；sell on commission

【寄信人】sender

【寄养】entrust one's child to the care of sb.；ask sb. to bring up one's child：把孩子～在亲戚家里 *leave a child in the care of a relative*

【寄予】❶ place (hope, etc.) on：党对青年一代～很大的希望。*The Party places great hopes on the youth.* ❷ show；give；express：～深切的同情 *show heartfelt sympathy to*

【寄语】〈书〉send word：～亲人报喜讯。*Send our dear ones the happy news.*

【寄主】［生］host (of a parasite)

寂 Ⅰ 形 quiet；still；silent：～无一人 *quiet and deserted* Ⅱ 副 lonely；lonesome；solitary

【寂静】quiet；still；silent：在～的深夜里 *in the still of the night* / ～的山村，顿时沸腾起来。*The quiet mountain village suddenly became astir.*

【寂寞】❶ lonely；lonesome：我在这里又交了新朋友，一点也不～。*I don't feel lonely as I've made new friends here.* ❷ quiet；still；silent：～的原野 *a quiet open country*

悸 动〈书〉(of the heart) throb with terror；palpitate：惊悸

【悸动】palpitate from nervousness

绩 名 ❶ twist hempen thread ❷ achievement；accomplishment；merit：战绩

【绩优股】(又作'蓝筹股')blue chip stocks

祭 动 ❶ hold a memorial ceremony for ❷ offer a sacrifice to：～天 *offer a sacrifice to Heaven；worship Heaven* ❸ wield：～起法宝 *wield a magic wand*

【祭奠】hold a memorial ceremony for

【祭礼】❶ sacrificial rites ❷ memorial ceremony ❸ sacrificial offerings

【祭品】sacrificial offerings；oblation

【祭器】sacrificial utensil

【祭祀】offer sacrifices to gods or ancestors

【祭坛】(又作'祭台')sacrificial altar

【祭文】funeral oration；elegiac address

蓟 名［植］setose thistle

霁 动 ❶ cease raining or snowing；clear up after rain or snow：雪～。*It's stopped snowing and is clearing up.* ❷ calm down after being angry：～颜 *calm down after a fit of anger；appear mollified*

稷 名 ❶ millet ❷ the god of grains worshipped by ancient emperors

鲫 名 crucian carp

【鲫鱼】crucian carp

髻 名 hair worn in a bun or coil

冀 动〈书〉hope；long for；look forward to：～其成功 *look forward to the success of sb. or sth.*

【冀望】〈书〉hope for；long for

jiā

加 动 ❶ add；plus：二～三等于五。*Two plus three makes five.* or *Two and three is five.* ❷ increase；augment：～工资 *increase (or raise) sb.'s wages* / ～件衣服再出去。*Put on more clothes before you go out.* / ～大油门 *open the throttle；step on the gas* ❸ put in；add；append：汤里～点盐 *put some salt in the soup* / 往威士忌里～水 *add water to whisky* / ～注解 *append notes to* ❹ (used in the same way as 加以 usu. after a monosyllabic adverb)：大～赞扬 *praise highly；lavish praise on* / 不～考虑 *not consider at all* / 严～处分 *punish severely*

【加班】work overtime；work an extra shift：今天晚上我们得加个班，不能去看电影。*We've got to work overtime tonight, so we can't go to the movies.* ◇ ～费 overtime pay；～加点 work extra shifts or extra hours；put in extra hours

【加倍】double；redouble：今天路滑，开车要～小心。*The roads are slippery today, so you'll have to be doubly careful driving the car.*

【加餐】snack：小学生课间有～。*School boys and girls have snacks between classes.*

【加车】(put on) extra buses or trains

【加成】［化］addition：～化合物 *additive compound；addition compound*

【加法】［数］addition ◇ ～器 adder

【加封】grant additional titles and territories (to the nobles)

【加工】❶ process：食品～ *food processing* / ～中草药 *process medicinal herbs* / ～厂 *processing factory* / 粗～制成品 *extensively processed products* / 精～制成品 *intensively processed products* ❷［机］machining；working：冷～ *cold working* / 机～ *machining* ❸ improve；polish (writings)；put final touches to：这篇文章需要～。*This article needs polishing.* ◇ ～出口 export processing；～订货 place orders with enterprises for processing materials or supplying manufactured goods；～ 贸易 processing trade

【加固】reinforce；consolidate：～堤坝 *reinforce dykes and dams* / ～工事 *improve defence works*

【加官晋爵】be promoted to a higher office and rank

【加害】injure；do harm to：～于人 *do harm to sb.*；*do sb. an injury*

【加号】plus sign（+）

【加黑】(粗体字)［计］boldface

【加急电】urgent telegram；urgent cable

【加价】price markup

【加紧】step up；speed up；intensify：～生产 *step up production* / ～准备 *speed up preparation* / 登山队～训练。*The mountaineering party intensified its training.*

【加劲】put more energy into；make a greater effort：加把劲儿！*Put your back into it*！or *Put on a spurt*！

【加剧】aggravate；intensify；exacerbate：～紧张局势 *aggravate tension* / 矛盾正在～。*The contradictions are sharpening.* / 病势～。*The patient's condition has taken a turn for the worse.*

【加快】quicken；speed up；accelerate；pick up speed：～步子 *quicken one's steps* / ～改革 *expedite reform*

【加宽】broaden；widen：～路面 *widen the road* / 适当～某些专业培养内容 *appropriately broaden the training in some specialities*

【加勒比共同体】the Caribbean Community（CARICOM）

【加勒比海】the Caribbean Sea

【加力】［航空］thrust augmentation；afterburning：～俯冲 *afterburning dive*

【加料】❶ feed in raw material：自动～ *automatic feeding* ❷ reinforced：～药酒 *reinforced tonic wine*

【加仑】gallon

【加码】❶〈旧〉raise the price of commodities；overcharge ❷ raise the stakes in gambling ❸ raise the quota：层层～ *raise the quota at each level*

【加盟】become a member of an alliance or union

【加密】❶［计］encrypt；encryption：～技术 *encryption technique* / ～文本 *encrypted text* ❷ set up a secret number（code）

【加冕】coronation ◇ ～日 Coronation Day

【加拿大】Canada ◇ ～人 Canadian

【加纳】Ghana ◇ ～人 Ghanaian

【加捻】［纺］twisting

【加农炮】cannon；gun

【加蓬】Gabon ◇ ～人 Gabonese

【加气】［建］air entrainment：～混凝土 *aero-crete* / ～水泥 *air entraining cement*

【加强】❶ strengthen；enhance；augment；reinforce：～行业管理。*Strengthen the trade management.* / ～宏观经济调控。*Strengthen macroeconomic control.* / ～精神文明建设。*Work for material improvement.* ❷ reinforced：～排（连、营）*reinforced platoon*（*company*，*battalion*）

【加氢】［化］hydrogenization；hydrogenation：～精制 *hydrofining* / ～裂化 *hydrocracking*

【加热】heating：～炉 *heating furnace* / ～器 *heating apparatus*；*heater*

【加入】❶ add；mix；put in ❷ join；accede to：～共产党 *join the Communist Party* / ～条约 *accede to a treaty* ◇ ～国 acceding（or adhering）state；～书 instrument of accession

【加塞儿】〈口〉push into a queue out of turn；jump a queue

【加上】❶ add；give：～种种罪名 *level all sorts of charges against sb.* / 给自己～新的头衔 *confer a new title on oneself* ❷ moreover；in addition：办个企业本来就不容易，～这些没完没了的烦琐手续，工作就更加困难了。*It isn't easy to start a business in the first place*，*but with all this endless red tape*，*it is all the more difficult.*

【加深】deepen：～河道 *deepen the channel of a river* / ～理解 *get a deeper understanding*

【加湿器】humidifier

【加时赛】［体］overtime

【加试】add（more items）to an examination：今年高考要～体育。*Physical education has been added to this year's college entrance examination.*

【加数】［数］addend

【加速】quicken；speed up；accelerate；expedite：～资本周转 *accelerate capital turnover*/ 队伍～前进。*The contingent quickened its advance.* ◇ ～器［物］accelerator

【加速度】［物］acceleration：重力～ *acceleration of gravity*

【加温】〈字〉heat up；raise the temperature；〈喻〉stimulate（of economy，project）

【加线】［音］ledger line；leger line

【加薪】increase the salary；raise the pay

【加压】pressurization；compression；pressure：～淬火 *pressure quenching* / ～气焊 *pressure-gas welding* / ～铸焊 *pressure thermite welding* / ～密封 *pressure seal* / ～蒸煮器 *pressure-cooker* / ～蒸馏器 *pressure-still* / ～氧化 *pressure oxidation*

【加压舱】compressing chamber

【加以】❶（used before a disyllabic verb to indicate that the action is directed towards sth. or sb. mentioned earlier in the sentence）：不合理的规定必须～改革。*The irrational rules must be changed.* ❷ in addition；moreover：这种鞋结实耐穿，～价格便宜，很受群众欢迎。*These shoes are very popular. They're sturdy and*，*what's more*，*they're cheap.*

【加意】with special care；with close attention：对这些犯人，你们必须～提防。*You must keep a close watch on the prisoners.* / ～保护 *protect with special care*

【加油】❶ oil；lubricate：这台机器该～了。*This*

machine needs oiling. ❷ refuel：飞机要在上海降落～。*The plane will land in Shanghai for refuelling.* / 空中～ *in-flight* (*or air*) *refuelling* ❸ make an extra effort：～干 *work with added vigour* / ～！～！*Come on! Come on!* / 观众为运动员～。*The spectators cheered the players on.* ◇～车 refuelling truck; refueller; ～飞机 tanker aircraft; ～站 filling (or petrol, gas) station

【加重】❶ make or become heavier; increase the weight of：～任务 *add to one's tasks* / ～思想负担 *add to one's worries* / ～语气 *say sth. with emphasis* ❷ make or become more serious; aggravate：～危机 *aggravate the crisis* / 病情～。*The patient's condition worsened.*

夹 Ⅰ 动 ❶ press from both sides; place in between：把相片～在书里 *put the photos in between the leaves of a book* / 鞋子～脚。*The shoe pinches.* ❷ mix; mingle; intersperse：～在人群里 *mingle with the crowd* / 狂风～着暴雨 *a violent wind accompanied by a torrential rain* ❸ carry sth. under one's arm：～着皮包 *carry a briefcase under one's arm* Ⅱ 名 clip, clamp, folder, etc.：纸～ *paper clip* / 发～ *hairpin* / 文件～ *folder* ——另见 gā; jiá

【夹板】❶ boards for pressing sth. or holding things together ❷ [医] splint：上～ *put* (*a limb, etc.*) *in splints* / 石膏～ *plaster splints*

【夹鼻眼镜】pince-nez

【夹层】double layer：～墙 *a double-layered wall*

【夹带】❶ carry secretly; smuggle：邮寄包裹不能～信件。*Don't put letters into a parcel.* ❷ notes smuggled into an examination hall

【夹道】❶ a narrow lane; passageway ❷ line both sides of the street：～欢迎贵宾 *line the street to welcome a distinguished guest*

【夹缝】a narrow space between two adjacent things; crack; crevice

【夹攻】attack from both sides; converging attack; pincer attack：受到两面～ *be under a pincer attack; be caught in a two-way squeeze* / 前后～ *attack from the front and the rear simultaneously* / 内外～ *attack from both within and without*

【夹击】converging attack; pincer attack

【夹剪】tweezers; tongs

【夹具】[机] clamping apparatus; fixture; jig

【夹克】(又作'茄克''甲克') jacket：皮～ *leather jacket*

【夹七夹八】incoherent; confused; cluttered (with irrelevant remarks)：他～地说了许多话，我也没听懂是什么意思。*He rambled on at great length but I couldn't make head or tail of what he said.*

【夹生】(of food) half-cooked; (of a job) not well done; (of facts or knowledge) not quite assimilated

【夹生饭】❶ half-cooked rice ❷ a job not thoroughly done

【夹馅】stuffed (pastry, etc.)

【夹心】with filling：果酱～糖 *sweets with jam centre* ◇～饼干 sandwich biscuits

【夹叙夹议】narration interspersed with comments：他的游记写得～，谈了不少自己的看法。*His travel sketch was written as a narrative interspersed with comments. In it he gave voice to many of his personal views.*

【夹杂】be mixed up with; be mingled with：他说话～着南方口音。*He speaks with a slight southern accent.* / 文章里～着不少生造的词语。*The article is cluttered up with unclear coined expressions.*

【夹杂物】[冶] inclusion

【夹竹桃】(sweet-scented) oleander

【夹注】interlinear notes

【夹子】❶ clip; tongs：弹簧～ *spring clip* / 点心～ *cake tongs* / 衣服～ *clothes-peg; clothespin* ❷ folder; wallet：文件～ *folder; binder* / 皮～ *wallet; pocketbook*

佳 形 good; fine; beautiful：～景 *fine landscape; beautiful view* / 成绩甚～ *achieve very good results*

【佳宾】honored (transit) guest

【佳话】a deed praised far and wide; a story on everybody's lips; a much-told tale

【佳节】happy festival time; festival：中秋～ *the joyous Mid-Autumn Festival* / 欢度国庆～ *celebrate the joyous festival of National Day*

【佳境】〈书〉the most enjoyable or pleasant stage

【佳句】beautiful line (in a poem); well-turned phrase

【佳丽】〈书〉❶ (of looks, scenery, etc.) beautiful ❷ a beautiful woman

【佳偶】〈书〉a happily married couple

【佳品】excellent product; famous produce：枸杞是滋补～。*Chinese wolfberry is an excellent tonic.*

【佳期】wedding (or nuptial) day

【佳人】〈书〉a beautiful woman; beauty

【佳肴】delicacies：美味～ *delicious food*

【佳音】〈书〉welcome news; good tidings; favourable reply：静候～。*I am awaiting the news of your success.*

【佳作】a fine piece of writing; an excellent work

茄 (构词成分)见下 ——另见 qié

【茄克】jacket

枷 名 cangue

【枷锁】yoke; chains; shackles; fetters：精神～ *spiritual shackles* / 摆脱殖民主义的～ *shake off the yoke of colonialism*

家 Ⅰ 名 ❶ family; household：他全～都是工人。*They're all workers in his family.* / 张～和王～ *the Zhangs and the Wangs* ❷ home：回～ *go home* / 不在～ *not be in; be out* / 上我～去吧。*Come to my place.* ❸ a person or family engaged in a certain trade：船家 ❹ a specialist in a certain field：科学家 ❺ a school of thought; school Ⅱ 代 〈谦〉my (used in speaking of relatives older than oneself)：家父 Ⅲ **形** domestic; tame：家兔 Ⅳ **量** (for families or business establishments)：两～人家 *two families* / 三～商店 *three shops* / 一～电影院 *a cinema*

【家蚕】silkworm

【家产】(又作'家财') family property

【家常】the daily life of a family; domestic trivia ◇ ～菜 home cooking; ～话 small talk; chitchat

【家常便饭】❶ homely food; simple meal：在这儿吃午饭吧，～。*How about staying for lunch? Just potluck.* ❷ common occurrence; routine; all in the day's work：搬家对勘探队员来说，简直是～。*To the members of a prospecting team, moving from place to place is all in the day's work.*

【家丑】family scandal; the skeleton in the cupboard (or closet)

【家丑不可外扬】the disgrace of a family should never be spread without; do not give publicity to family scandals; don't wash your dirty linen in public

【家畜】domestic animal; livestock ◇ ～繁育 animal breeding

【家传】handed down from the older generations of the family：他们全家都爱好音乐，～的。*All of them are music lovers—it runs in the family.* ◇ ～秘方 a secret recipe handed down in the family

【家当】〈口〉family belongings; property：我们这个润滑油厂创办的时候，全部～就是三口大锅。*When we first set up this lubricant factory, all we had was three cauldrons.*

【家道】family financial situation：～小康 *be comfortably off* / ～中落。*The family fortunes declined.* or *The family fortunes were at a low ebb.*

【家底】family property accumulated over a long time; resources：～薄 *without substantial resources; not financially solid* / 把咱们的～清理清理。*Let's take stock of what we've got.*

【家电】〈略〉见〖家用电器〗

【家法】❶ theory and methods of academic studies handed down from a master to his disciples ❷ domestic discipline exercised by the head of a clan or household ❸ rod or stick for punishing children or servants in a traditional household

【家访】a visit to the parents of schoolchildren or young workers：她工作认真，下课后又去～了。*She was very conscientious. After school, she went to visit her students' parents.*

【家风】family custom and style; family tradition

【家父】〈谦〉my father

【家鸽】pigeon

【家规】domestic discipline and family rules

【家和万事兴】if the family lives in harmony, all affairs will prosper; harmony in the family leads to prosperity in all undertakings

【家伙】〈口〉❶ tool; utensil; weapon：不要打架，更不能动～。*You shouldn't fight, still less use weapons.* / 这把～挺好使。*This is a very handy tool.* ❷ fellow; guy：小～ *little chap; kid* / 那个～是谁？*Who's that fellow?* / 你这～真会开玩笑。*What a joker you are!*

【家给人足】each family is provided for and every person is well-fed and well-clothed; all live in plenty

【家计】〈书〉family livelihood

【家家户户】each and every family; every household：～有电脑。*Every household has a computer.* / 村里～都装上了电话。*Telephones have been installed in every house of the village.*

【家家有本难念的经】every family has some sort of trouble; every family has its own hard nut to crack

【家教】❶ family education; upbringing：没有～ *not properly brought up; ill-bred* / ～严 *be strict with one's children* ❷ private tutor (for a school child, etc.); private tutoring：请～ *engage a private tutor*

【家境】family financial situation; family circumstances：～贫寒 *with one's family in straitened circumstances* / ～好 *come from a well-to-do family*

【家居】residence; the term also refers to family life

【家具】furniture：几件～ *several pieces of furniture* / 一套～ *a set of furniture*

【家眷】❶ wife and children; one's family ❷ wife

【家里】in the family; at home：～来了客人。*There is a guest in my home*

【家门】❶ house gate; home：好多天没出～ *have not stepped out of the house for days; have been staying indoors for days* ❷〈书〉family：有辱～ *bring disgrace to the family* ❸〈方〉member of the same clan：他是我的～堂兄弟。*He is my cousin and we are of the same clan.* ❹ family background：自报～ *give one's family background; tell about one's family*

【家培】cultivate：～蘑菇 *cultivated mushroom*

【家贫如洗】utterly destitute; penniless

【家破人亡】(又作'家败人亡') with one's family broken up, some gone away, some dead

【家谱】family tree; genealogical tree; genealogy

【家禽】domestic fowl; poultry

【家人】❶ family member ❷ servant

【家史】family history

【家事】family matters; domestic affairs

【家室】❶ wife：他已有～。*He is married.* ❷ family

【家什】〈口〉utensils, furniture, etc.：厨房里的～擦得很干净。*The kitchen furnishings have all been wiped clean.*

【家书】❶ a letter home ❷ a letter from home

【家书抵万金】a letter from home is worth ten thousand pieces of gold

【家属】family members; (family) dependents：死者及其～ *the deceased and his bereaved family* ◇ ～工厂 factory run by family members of workers, cadres, armymen, etc.

【家私】〈口〉family property

【家庭】family; household: 他有一个美满幸福的～。*He has a happy family.* / 现在差不多每个～都有电冰箱了。*Now almost every household owns a fridge.* ◇ ～背景 family background; ～病床 hospital bed at home; ～财产保险 household property insurance; ～成员 family member; ～出身 class status of one's family; family origin; ～服务 domestic help; servant; maid; ～妇女 housewife; ～副业 household sideline production; ～顾问 home consultant; ～观念 attachment to one's family; ～教师 private teacher; tutor; ～教育 family education; home education; ～纠纷 family quarrel; domestic discord; ～联产承包责任制 household contract responsibility system with remuneration linked to output; ～生活 home life; family life; ～舞会 home party; ～影院 home theater; ～作业 homework
【家徒四壁】have nothing but the bare walls in one's house—be utterly destitute
【家兔】rabbit
【家务】household duties: ～劳动 *housework*; *household chores* / ～总也做不完。*Household chores never get completely finished.* or *There is no end to household chores.*
【家乡】hometown; native place ◇ ～话 native dialect
【家小】〈口〉❶ wife and children ❷ wife
【家信】❶ a letter home ❷ a letter from home
【家宴】❶ family reunion feast ❷ family feast
【家燕】house swallow
【家业】family property; property: 不要以为我们厂～大,浪费一点不算啥。*Don't think, just because our factory is big and well-off, that we can waste things.*
【家蝇】housefly
【家用】family expenses; housekeeping money: 贴补～ *help out with the family expenses* ◇ ～电器 electrical home appliances; electrical household appliances
【家喻户晓】known to every household; widely known; known to all: 做到～,人人明白 *make known to every household and individual*
【家园】home; homeland: 重建～ *rebuild one's homeland*; *rebuild one's village or town* / 重返～ *return to one's homeland*
【家贼】a thief within a house
【家贼难防】a thief within a house is hard to guard against
【家长】❶ the head of a family; patriarch ❷ the parent or guardian of a child: 学校里明天开～会。*There will be a parents' meeting in our school tomorrow.*
【家长式】patriarchal: ～统治 *paternalism*; *arbitrary rule as by a patriarch* / 封建、～的领导 *leadership characterized by feudal, patriarchal practices*
【家长制】patriarchal system
【家长作风】a high-handed way of dealing with people; patriarchal behaviour
【家珍】family heirloom: 如数～ *as if enumerating one's family treasures—have an intimate knowledge of the subject*
【家政】❶ household management ❷ home economics ◇ ～学 home economics
【家装】home decoration: ～公司 *home decoration company*
【家族】clan; family

痂 名 scab; crust: 结痂

袈 (构词成分)见下
【袈裟】kasaya (a patchwork outer vestment worn by a Buddhist monk)

嘉 Ⅰ 形 good; fine: 嘉宾 Ⅱ 动 praise; commend: 精神可～ *a praiseworthy spirit*
【嘉宾】honoured guest; welcome guest
【嘉奖】commend; cite: 这个士兵因为作战英勇而受到～。*The soldier was cited for his bravery.* ◇ ～令 citation
【嘉勉】〈书〉praise and encourage
【嘉许】〈书〉praise; approve

镓 名 [化] gallium (Ga)

jiá

夹 形 double-layered; lined: ～袄 *lined jacket* ——另见 gā; jiā

荚 名 pod: 结～ *bear pods*; *pod*
【荚果】pod; legume

戛 动 〈书〉knock gently; tap
【戛然】〈文〉the loud cry of a bird: ～长鸣 *long and loud cries*
【戛然而止】(of a sound, etc.) cease abruptly; come to an abrupt end

颊 名 cheek: 两～红润 *with rosy cheeks* / 双～凹陷 *sunken (or hollow) cheeks*
【颊骨】cheekbone
【颊囊】[动] cheek pouch

jiǎ

甲 Ⅰ 数 first: ～级 *first rate*; *Class A* Ⅱ 名 ❶ (used for an unspecified person or thing): 某～与某乙 *Mr. A and Mr. B* / ～方和乙方 *the first party and the second party* / ～队和乙队 *team A and team B* ❷ shell; carapace: 龟甲 ❸ nail: 指甲 ❹ armour: 装甲车
【甲板】deck
【甲苯】[化] toluene; methylbenzene
【甲虫】beetle
【甲醇】[化] methyl alcohol; methanol; wood spirit; wood alcohol
【甲酚】[化] cresol

【甲肝】〈略〉见〖甲型肝炎〗
【甲睾酮】[药] methyltestosterone
【甲沟炎】[医] paronychia
【甲骨文】inscriptions on bones or tortoise shells of the Shang Dynasty (c. 16th-11th century B.C.)
【甲基】methyl ◇ ～纤维素 [药] methylcellulose
【甲级股】[经] Alpha Stock
【甲级战犯】top war criminal
【甲壳】crust ◇ ～动物 crustacean
【甲醛】[化]〈书〉dehyde ◇ ～水 [化] formalin
【甲酸】[化] formic acid; methanoic acid
【甲烷】[化] methane
【甲午战争】the Sino-Japaness War of 1894-1895 (launched by Japanese imperialism to annex Korea and invade China)
【甲型肝炎】hepatitis A
【甲癣】onychomycosis; ringworm of the nails
【甲氧胺】[药] methoxamine
【甲鱼】soft-shelled turtle
【甲状腺】[生理] thyroid gland ◇ ～功能亢进 hyperthyroidism; ～切开术 thyroidectomy; ～素 thyroxine; ～炎 [医] thyreoitis; thyroiditis; strumitis; ～肿 goitre
【甲子】a cycle of sixty years ——另见〖干支〗
【甲紫】gentian violet

岬 名 ❶ (usu. used as part of a place name) cape; promontory: 成山～ *Chengshanjia* (*in Shandong Province*) ❷ a narrow passage between mountains
【岬角】cape; promontory

胛 (构词成分)见下
【胛骨】[生理] shoulder blade

钾 名 [化] potassium (K)
【钾肥】potash fertilizer
【钾碱】potash
【钾盐】sylvite

假 Ⅰ 形 false; fake; sham; phoney; artificial: ～腿 *artificial leg* / ～民主 *bogus democracy*; *sham democracy* / ～和平 *phoney peace* Ⅱ 连 if; in case; suppose Ⅲ 动 borrow; avail oneself of: 久～不归 *keep putting off returning sth. one has borrowed*; *appropriate sth. borrowed for one's own use* ——另见 jià
【假案】[法] fabricated case; slanderous case
【假扮】disguise oneself as; dress up as
【假币】counterfeit money; fake money; forged money
【假钞】counterfeit money
【假充】pretend to be; pose as: ～内行 *pretend to be an expert*
【假传圣旨】deliver a false imperial edict—give a fake order
【假大空】(〈略〉全称为'弄虚作假，说大话而不办实事') lying, boasting and making empty promises
【假道】via; by way of: 代表团～欧洲去联合国。*The delegation went to the United Nations via Europe.*
【假定】❶ suppose; assume; grant; presume: ～有这么一回事 *suppose it really happened* / ～这是真的，也影响不了大局。*Even if this is the case, it will not affect the whole situation.* ❷ hypothesis
【假发】wig
【假分数】[数] improper fraction
【假根】[植] rhizoid
【假公济私】use public office for private gain; jobbery
【假果】[植] pseudocarp; spurious fruit
【假花】artificial flower
【假话】lie; falsehood: 说～ *tell lies*
【假货】fake products
【假借】make use of: ～外力 *make use of outside forces* / ～名义 *under the guise of*; *in the name of*; *under false pretences*
【假冒】pass oneself off as; palm off (a fake as genuine): 谨防～。*Beware of imitations.* ◇ ～产品 fake products; phony products; ～伪劣产品 fake quality commodity
【假寐】〈书〉catnap; doze
【假面具】mask; false front: 他戴了个～，我没认出他来。*He was wearing a mask and I didn't recognize him.* / 撕下伪君子的～ *unmask a hypocrite*
【假面舞会】masked ball; masquerade
【假名】❶ pseudonym ❷ kana (Japanese syllabic script)
【假漆】varnish
【假仁假义】pretended benevolence and righteousness; hypocrisy
【假如】if; supposing; in case: ～有这必要，就这么干吧。*Do so, if necessary.* / ～明天开会，准备工作来得及吗? *Supposing we hold the meeting tomorrow, will there be enough time to prepare?*
【假若】if; supposing; in case: ～我来不了，我会通知你的。*If I should be unable to come, I'll let you know.* / ～情况是这样，我就同意。*If that is the case, I'll agree.*
【假嗓子】falsetto
【假山】rockery
【假设】❶ suppose; assume; grant; presume ❷ hypothesis: 科学～ *a scientific hypothesis* ◇ ～成交 assumptive close (of a deal)
【假声】[音] falsetto
【假使】if; in case; in the event that: ～他不同意，那就作罢。*If he disagrees, let the matter drop.* / ～他到这儿来，通知我一下。*Let me know should he come here.*
【假释】[法] release on parole (or on probation) ◇ ～犯 [医] parolee
【假手】do sth. through sb. else; make a cat's-paw of sb.
【假手于人】(achieve one's end) through the instrumentality of sb. else
【假说】hypothesis
【假死】❶ [医] suspended animation ❷ play dead;

feign death; play possum

【假托】❶ on the pretext of: 他～有病没来开会。*He absented himself from the meeting on the pretext of illness*. ❷ under sb. else's name: 这篇文章不是他写的，是别人～他的名义发表的。*He didn't write the essay; somebody else did, and published it under his name*. ❸ by means of; through the medium of

【假想】❶ imagination; hypothesis; supposition ❷ imaginary; hypothetical; fictitious: 这个故事里的人物都是～的。*The characters in this story are all fictitious*. ◇ ～敌［军］imaginary enemy; hypothetical enemy

【假象】❶(又作'假相') false appearance: 制造～ *create a false impression; put up a false front* / 不要被～所迷惑。*Don't be misled by appearances*. ❷［地理］pseudomorph

【假小子】tomboy

【假惺惺】hypocritically; unctuously: ～地表示愿意支持 *hypocritically express willingness to support* / ～地宣称 *declare unctuously*

【假性近视】pseudomyopia

【假牙】dental prosthesis; false tooth; denture

【假眼】ocular prosthesis; artificial eye; glass eye

【假药】imitation medicine; fake medicine

【假意】❶ unction; insincerity; hypocrisy ❷ pretend; put on: ～奉承 *cheap flattery*

【假造】❶ forge; counterfeit: ～证件 *forge a certificate* / 这张钞票是～的。*This banknote is a forgery*. or *This is a forged banknote*. ❷ invent; fabricate: ～理由 *invent an excuse* / ～罪名 *cook up a false charge against; frame up*

【假正经】be hypocritical; pretend to be a saint

【假肢】artificial limb

【假支票】forged check; stumer

【假植】［农］heel in

【假装】pretend; feign; simulate; make believe: 他～生病。*He pretended illness*. / ～不知道 *feign ignorance*

jià

价 名 ❶ price: 买之前，你该问问～。*Before buying it you should ask the price*. ❷ value: 等价交换 ❸［化］valence: 氢是一～的元素。*Hydrogen is a one-valence element*.

【价拨】undersell; sell at a reduced price; discount: ～给每人一箱苹果 *sell everyone a carton of apples at a cheap rate*

【价差】price differential

【价格】price: 标明～ *mark (goods) with a price tag; have goods clearly priced* / ～管理 *price control* / ～政策 *price policy* ◇ ～标签 price tag; ～标准 price standards; ～波动 fluctuations in price; ～补贴 price subsidies (from the state); state subsidies to off-set price; ～差别 price discrimination; ～低廉 low in price; ～放开 lifting of control over prices; ～公道 at fair price; ～结构 price mechanism; ～扭曲 price distortion; ～体制 price system; ～调整 price readjustment; price regulation; ～协定(卡特尔) price cartel; ～战 price war; ～指数 price index

【价款】money paid for sth. purchased or received for sth. sold; cost

【价廉物美】(of a commodity) cheap but good; inexpensive but elegant

【价码】〈口〉listed price; marked price

【价目】marked price; price ◇ ～表 price list

【价钱】price: 讲～ *haggle over the price; bargain* / ～公道 *a fair (or decent, reasonable) price* / 西红柿什么～? *How much are the tomatoes?* / ～在涨。*The prices are rising*.

【价位】standard price; level of a price

【价值】❶［经］value ❷ worth; value: ～五百万元的设备 *five million yuan worth of equipment; equipment worth (or valued at) five million yuan* / 毫无～ *completely worthless* ◇ ～尺度 measure of value; ～工程 value engineering; ～规律［经］law of value; ～决定 determination of value; ～量［经］magnitude of value; ～形态［经］form of value

【价值观念】values: 社会～ *social values* / 他的～跟我不一样。*He has different values than I do*.

驾 Ⅰ 动 ❶ harness; draw (a cart, etc.): ～上牲口耕地 *harness cattle to plough the fields* ❷ drive (a vehicle); pilot (a plane); sail (a boat) Ⅱ 名 ❶〈尊〉you: 劳驾 ❷ the emperor: 驾崩

【驾崩】(of an emperor) pass away; die

【驾临】〈套〉your arrival; your esteemed presence: 恭候～。*Your presence is requested*.

【驾轻就熟】drive a light carriage on a familiar road—handle a job with ease because of previous experience; do a familiar job with ease

【驾驶】drive (a vehicle); pilot (a ship or plane): ～拖拉机 *drive a tractor* ◇ ～舱［航空］control cabin; cockpit; pilot's compartment; ～杆［航空］control stick (or column); joystick; ～盘 steering wheel; ～室 driver's cab; ～台 bridge (of a ship); ～员 driver (of a vehicle); pilot (of an airplane); ～执照 driving (or driver's) license

【驾校】driving school

【驾驭】(又作'驾御') ❶ drive (a cart, horse, etc.): 这匹马不好～。*This horse is hard to control*. ❷ control; master: ～自然 *tame nature* / 能够～复杂的局势 *be able to cope with complicated situations*

【驾照】(〈略〉全称为'驾驶执照') driving license

架 Ⅰ 名 ❶ frame; rack; shelf; stand: 房～ *the frame of a house* / 工具～ *tool rack* / 黄瓜～ *cucumber trellis* / 钢～桥 *steel-framed bridge* ❷ fight; quarrel: 打架 Ⅱ 动 ❶ put up; erect: 把梯子～在墙上。*Put up the ladder against the wall*. / ～起机枪 *mount a machine gun* ❷ fend off; ward off; withstand: 他一刀砍来，我拿枪～住。*I fended off his sword thrust with my spear*. ❸ support; prop; help: 他扭了脚脖子,我们只得把他~回去。*He sprained his ankle and had to be helped home*. ❹ kidnap; take sb. away forcibly: 强行~走 *carry sb. away by force; kidnap* Ⅲ量 (for machines, airplanes, and instruments which rest on a tripod or stand): 一~收音机 *a radio set* / 几百~飞机 *several hundred planes* / 一~照像机 *a camera* / 一~钢琴 *a piano*

【架不住】〈方〉❶ cannot sustain (the weight); cannot stand (the pressure); cannot stand up against: 他开始不想来,~我一说,也就来了。*At first he didn't feel like coming, but I persuaded him to*. ❷ be no match for; cannot compete with: 主队虽然技术不错,也~客队合作得好。*The home team displayed great skill but were no match for the visitors in teamwork*.

【架次】sortie: 出动四批飞机共六十~ *fly sixty sorties in four groups*

【架得住】〈方〉be able to bear or endure: 小学生怎么~这么多家庭作业? *How can the pupils cope with so much homework?*

【架空】❶ built on stilts: 这里的竹楼都是~的。*The bamboo huts here are all built on stilts*. ❷ impracticable; unpractical: 不采取相应的措施,计划就会~。*Unless we adopt the necessary measures the plan will come to nothing*. ❸ make sb. a mere figurehead ◇ ~管道 overhead pipe

【架设】erect (above ground or water level, as on stilts or posts): 这儿正在~一座天桥。*A platform bridge is being erected here*.

【架势】(又作'架式')〈方〉posture; stance; manner: 摆出一副海上霸主的~ *assume the posture of lord of the seas* / 看他们的~,是来找碴打架的。*They seem to have come only to pick a quarrel with us*.

【架子】❶ frame; stand; rack; shelf: 脸盆~ *washstand* ❷ framework; skeleton; outline: 写文章要先搭好~。*Make an outline before you start writing*. ❸ airs; haughty manner: 没有~ *be modest and unassuming; be easy of approach* / 放下~ *get down from one's high horse* ❹ posture; stance: 他拉开~,打起了太极拳。*He adopted a stance and began to do Taiji shadowboxing*. ——另见〖摆架子〗;〖拿架子〗

【架子工】scaffolder

假 名 ❶ holiday; vacation ❷ leave of absence; furlough: 病假 ——另见 jiǎ

【假期】vacation; holiday; period of leave

【假日】holiday; day off

【假条】❶ application for leave ❷ leave permit: 病~ *doctor's certificate (for sick leave)*

嫁 动 ❶ (of a woman) marry: 她~了个编辑。*She married an editor*. ❷ marry off a daughter: 她把女儿~给一名教师。*She married her daughter to a teacher*. ❸ shift; transfer: 转嫁

【嫁祸于人】shift the misfortune onto sb. else; put the blame on sb. else

【嫁鸡随鸡,嫁狗随狗】follow the man you marry, be he fowl or cur

【嫁接】[植] grafting

【嫁娶】marriage

【嫁人】〈口〉(of a woman) get married; marry

【嫁妆】dowry; trousseau

稼 Ⅰ动 sow (grain) Ⅱ名 cereals; crops: 庄稼

jiān

尖 Ⅰ名 ❶ point; tip; top: 钢笔~ *the point of a pen* / 铅笔~ *the tip of a pencil* / 指~ *fingertip* / 塔~ *the pinnacle of a pagoda* ❷ the best of its kind; the pick of the bunch; the cream of the crop: 全班学生中他是个~儿。*He is a top-notch student in the class*. Ⅱ形 ❶ pointed; tapering: ~下巴 *a pointed chin* / 把铅笔削~ *sharpen a pencil* ❷ shrill; piercing: ~声~气 *in a shrill voice* / ~叫 *scream* ❸ sharp; acute: 耳朵~ *have sharp ears; be sharp-eared* / 眼 ~ *have sharp eyes; be sharp-eyed* / 鼻子~ *have an acute (or sharp) sense of smell*

【尖兵】❶ [军] point ❷ trailblazer; pathbreaker; pioneer; vanguard: 他是开拓石油工业的~。*He was a pioneer in developing the oil industry*.

【尖刀】sharp knife; dagger

【尖顶】pinnacle

【尖端】❶ pointed end; acme; peak: 标枪的~ *the point of a javelin* ❷ most advanced; sophisticated: ~产品 *highly sophisticated products* ◇ ~技术 sophisticated technique; ~科学 most advanced branches of science; frontiers of science; ~武器 sophisticated weapons

【尖叫】shriek; scream; yell; whoop: 到处是~声,掌声和口哨声。*There were whooping, clapping and whistling everywhere*.

【尖刻】acrimonious; caustic; biting: 说话~ *speak with biting sarcasm*

【尖括号】angle brackets (〈 〉)

【尖利】❶ sharp; keen; cutting: ~的钢刀 *a sharp knife* / 眼光~ *sharp-eyed* ❷ shrill; piercing: ~的叫声 *a shrill cry*

【尖脐】❶ the narrow triangular abdomen of a male crab ❷ male crab

【尖锐】❶ sharp-pointed ❷ penetrating; incisive; sharp; keen: ~的对比 *a sharp contrast* / ~的批评 *incisive (or sharp) criticism* ❸ shrill; piercing: ~的哨声 *the shrill sound of a whistle* ❹ intense; acute; sharp: ~的思想斗争 *sharp mental conflicts* / ~对立 *be diametrically opposed to each other* ◇ ~化 sharpen; intensify; become more acute

【尖酸】acrid; acrimonious; tart

【尖酸刻薄】tart and mean; bitterly sarcastic: 这人说起话来老这么~。*He is given to making scathing remarks*.

【尖子】❶ the best of its kind; the pick of the

bunch；the cream of the crop：他是班上的～。*He's one of the top students in the class*. ❷ a sudden rise in pitch（in opera singing）◇ ～班 class of top students；class of talents

【尖嘴薄舌】have a caustic and flippant tongue

【尖嘴猴腮】have a mouth that sticks out and a chin like an ape's—have a wretched appearance

奸 Ⅰ形 ❶ wicked；evil；treacherous：奸计 ❷〈口〉self-seeking and wily：这个人才～哪，总想占便宜。*He's a self-seeker*；*he's always on the make*. Ⅱ名 ❶traitor：汉奸 ❷illicit sexual relations：通奸

【奸臣】treacherous court official

【奸党】clique or people disloyal to the country or monarch；cabal：～弄权，天下大乱。*As a wicked clique held power*，*the land was thrown into turmoil*.

【奸夫】adulterer

【奸妇】adultress

【奸猾】（又作'奸滑'）treacherous；crafty；deceitful

【奸计】an evil plot

【奸佞】〈书〉❶ crafty and fawning ❷ crafty sycophant

【奸情】adulterous affair

【奸人】evildoer；malefactor

【奸商】unscrupulous merchant；profiteer

【奸尸】necrophilia

【奸污】rape（or seduce）

【奸细】spy；enemy agent

【奸险】wicked and crafty；treacherous；malicious

【奸笑】sinister（or villainous）smile

【奸邪】〈书〉❶ crafty and evil；treacherous ❷ a crafty and evil person

【奸雄】a person who achieves high position by unscrupulous scheming；arch-careerist

【奸淫】❶ illicit sexual relations；adultery ❷ rape（or seduce）

【奸淫掳掠】rape and loot：～，无恶不作 *rape and pillage and commit all kinds of atrocities*

【奸贼】traitor；conspirator

【奸诈】fraudulent；crafty；treacherous

间 Ⅰ名 ❶ between；among：师生之～ *between teacher and pupil* / 同志之～ *among comrades* ❷ within a definite time or space：世间 ❸ room：衣帽间 Ⅱ量 ❶（for rooms）：一～卧室 *a bedroom* / 四～屋子 *four rooms* ❷（for room space）a section of a room or the lateral space between two pairs of pillars：三～门面 *a three-bay shop front* ——另见 jiàn

【间冰期】［地理］interglacial stage；interglacial

【间不容发】not a hair's breadth apart or away—extremely critical

【间架】❶ framework of a house ❷ form of a Chinese character ❸ structure of an essay

【间奏曲】［音］❶ entr'acte ❷ intermezzo

歼 动 annihilate；wipe out；destroy：～敌五千 *annihilate* 5,000 *enemy troops*

【歼击】attack and wipe out ◇ ～机 fighter plane；fighter；pursuit plane

【歼灭】annihilate；wipe out；destroy：～敌人有生力量 *wipe out the enemy's effective strength* / ～性的打击 *a crushing blow*；*a smashing blow* ◇ ～战 war（or battle）of annihilation

坚 Ⅰ形 hard；solid；firm；strong：～冰 *solid ice*；*hard ice* / 身残志～ *broken in body but firm in spirit* Ⅱ副 firmly；steadfastly；resolutely：～拒 *flatly refuse* / ～称 *state insistently*；*insist* Ⅲ名 a heavily fortified point；fortification；stronghold：攻坚

【坚壁清野】strengthen defence works，evacuate noncombatants，and hide provisions and livestock；strengthen the defences and clear the fields

【坚不可摧】indestructible；impregnable；indomitable：～的堡垒 *an indestructible bulwark*

【坚持】persist in；persevere in；uphold；insist on；stick to；adhere to：～原则 *adhere*（*or stick*）*to principle* / ～己见 *hold on to one's own views* / ～错误 *persist in one's errors*

【坚持不懈】unremitting；persistent：作～的努力 *make unremitting efforts*

【坚持不渝】persistent；persevering

【坚持改革开放】persevere in reform and opening polily

【坚持四项基本原则】adhere to the four cardinal principles

【坚定】❶ firm；staunch；steadfast：～的立场 *a firm stand* / ～的意志 *constancy of purpose* ❷ strengthen：～了攀登科学技术新高峰的决心 *strengthen one's resolve to scale new heights of science and technology*

【坚定不移】firm and unshakable；unswerving；unflinching：～的信念 *an impregnable belief*；*an unshakable faith*

【坚固】firm；solid；sturdy；strong：～耐用 *sturdy and durable* / ～的家具 *solid furniture*

【坚果】［植］nut

【坚决】firm；resolute；determined：～支持 *firmly support*；*stand firmly by* / ～反对 *resolutely oppose* / 态度～ *a determined attitude*；*a firm position*

【坚苦卓绝】showing the utmost fortitude：～的斗争 *an extremely hard and bitter struggle*；*a most arduous struggle* / ～的战斗 *a hard-fought battle*

【坚牢度】［纺］fastness：耐日光～ *fastness to sunlight*；*sunfastness* / 耐洗～ *washfastness*

【坚强】❶ strong；firm；staunch：～的意志 *strong will* / ～的领导 *firm leadership* / 一个性格～的人 *a person of strong character* ❷ strengthen

【坚忍】steadfast and persevering（in face of difficulties）

【坚韧】❶ tough and tensile ❷ firm and tenacious：运动员在比赛中表现出～的斗志。*The athletes displayed great tenacity throughout the contest*.

【坚韧不拔】firm and indomitable; persistent and dauntless: ～的革命精神 *indomitable revolutionary spirit* / ～的毅力 *an inflexible will*
【坚如磐石】solid as a rock; rock-firm
【坚实】❶ solid; substantial: 他做的家具相当～。*The furniture he made is quite sturdy.* / ～的基础 *a solid foundation* ❷ strong; robust: ～的年轻人 *a robust young man*
【坚守】stick to; hold fast to; stand fast: ～岗位 *stand fast at one's post* / ～阵地 *hold fast to one's position; hold one's ground*
【坚挺】[经] strong: 美元～。*The dollar was getting stronger.* / ～的市场价格 *a strong market* / 石油价格趋向～。*The oil price is tending upwards.*
【坚信】firmly believe: 他们～一定能获得胜利。*They are fully confident that they will win.*
【坚信不疑】firmly believe; have not the slightest doubt
【坚毅】firm and persistent; with unswerving determination; with inflexible will
【坚硬】hard; solid: ～的岩石 *solid rock*
【坚贞】faithful; constant
【坚贞不屈】remain faithful and unyielding

肩 Ⅰ 名 shoulder: ～并～ *shoulder to shoulder; side by side* / 耸耸～ *shrug one's shoulders* Ⅱ 动 take on; undertake; shoulder; bear: 身～重任 *shoulder heavy responsibilities*
【肩膀】shoulder
【肩负】take on; undertake; shoulder; bear: ～重荷 *bear a heavy burden; shoulder heavy loads*
【肩胛骨】[生理] scapula; shoulder blade
【肩摩毂击】shoulder to shoulder and hub to hub—crowded with people and vehicles
【肩头】❶〈书〉on the shoulders ❷〈方〉shoulders
【肩章】❶ shoulder loop; shoulder strap ❷ epaulet
【肩周炎】[医] periarthritis

艰 形 difficult; hard
【艰巨】arduous; formidable: ～的工作 *arduous work* / 这个工程非常～。*This is a formidable project.*
【艰苦】arduous; difficult; hard; tough: ～的生活 *hard life* / ～的工作 *a tough job*
【艰苦备尝】have experienced all hardships; have suffered untold hardships
【艰苦朴素】hard work and plain living: 平生～ *live simply and work hard all one's life*
【艰难】difficult; hard: 行动～ *walk with difficulty* / 生活～ *live in straitened circumstances* / ～的岁月 *difficult days; hard times; arduous years*
【艰难困苦】difficulties and hardships: 不论多么～,我们都要继续战斗下去。*No matter what the difficulties and hardships, we will fight on.*
【艰难曲折】difficulties and setbacks: 经过无数～ *experience countless difficulties and setbacks*
【艰难险阻】difficulties and obstacles: 路上遇着了说不尽的～。*We encountered untold difficulties and dangers on the way.*
【艰涩】involved and abstruse; intricate and obscure: 文词～ *involved and abstruse writing*
【艰深】difficult to understand; abstruse
【艰危】difficulties and dangers (confronting a nation)
【艰险】hardships and dangers: 不避～ *brave hardships and dangers*
【艰辛】hardships: 他们历尽～,方取得胜利。*They achieved success only after experiencing all kinds of hardships.*

兼 Ⅰ 形 double; twice Ⅱ 副 simultaneously; concurrently: 任总理～外交部长 *be Premier and concurrently Minister of Foreign Affairs* / ～管 *be concurrently in charge of; also look after* / 身～数职 *hold several posts simultaneously*
【兼备】have both... and... : 德才兼备
【兼并】annex (territory, property, etc.): 用武力～邻国领土 *annex the territories of a neighbouring country by force*
【兼程】travel at double speed: ～前进 *advance at the double* / 日夜～ *travel day and night*
【兼而有之】have both at the same time
【兼顾】give consideration to (or take account of) two or more things: 发展生产和改善人民生活二者必须～。*Consideration must be given to both the development of production and the improvement of the people's livelihood.*
【兼课】❶ do some teaching in addition to one's main occupation ❷ hold two or more teaching jobs concurrently
【兼任】❶ hold a concurrent post ❷ part-time
【兼容】compatible: ～制电视 *compatible television* ◇ ～信息系统 compatible information system; ～性 compatibility
【兼容并包】all-embracing; all-inclusive
【兼收并蓄】incorporate things of diverse nature; take in everything: 在继承古代文化上,我们决不能无批判地～。*In inheriting our old culture, we should never swallow anything and everything uncritically.*
【兼听则明,偏信则暗】listen to both sides and you will be enlightened; heed only one side and you will be benighted
【兼优】be good in more than one field: 品学～ (*of a student*) *of good character and scholarship*; (*of a person*) *of integrity and learning*
【兼职】❶ hold two or more posts concurrently: ～过多 *hold too many posts at the same time* ❷ concurrent post; part-time job: 辞去～ *resign one's concurrent job* ◇ ～教师 part-time teacher

监 Ⅰ 动 supervise; inspect; watch: 监督 Ⅱ 名 prison; jail: 收监 ——另见 jiàn
【监测】monitor: ～新药的副作用 *monitor the side effects of new drugs* / 加强环境～ *intensify monitoring of the environment*
【监测器】monitor: 污染～ *contamination monitor*
【监察】supervise; control: 加强对行政工作人员的

～ *strengthen supervision over administrative personnel* ◇ ～委员会 control commission; supervisory committee; ～员 supervisor; controller; ～制度 supervisory system

【监场】invigilate or monitor at an examination

【监督】❶ supervise; superintend; control: 加强质量～和财务～ *exercise effective supervision with regard to quality and finances* / 国际～ *international control; international supervision* ❷ supervisor ◇ ～程序 monitor program; ～电话 complaint hot-line; ～机关 supervisory institution; ～劳动 do penal labour under surveillance; ～权 authority to supervise; right of supervision; ～员 intendant; supervisor; monitor

【监犯】prisoner; convict

【监工】❶ supervise work; oversee ❷ overseer; supervisor

【监管】supervise; keep watch on: 海关对商品和货物出口执行～。*The customs office supervises the export of commodities and goods.* / ～人犯 *supervise and control offenders*

【监护】[法] guardianship

【监护人】[法] guardian: 责令他的～加以管教。*The guardian is to be ordered to subject him to discipline.*

【监禁】take into custody; imprison; put in jail (or prison)

【监考】❶ invigilate ❷ invigilator

【监控】monitor and control: 使用电子计算机对电网运行状况进行～。*Computers are employed to monitor and control the power grid.*

【监牢】〈口〉prison; jail

【监视】keep watch on; keep a lookout over: ～敌人的行动 *keep watch on the movements of the enemy* ◇ ～雷达 surveillance radar; ～器 monitor; ～哨 [军] lookout post; lookout; ～人 guard; sentinel

【监守】have custody of; guard; take care of

【监守自盗】steal what is entrusted to one's care; embezzle; defalcate

【监听】monitor ◇ ～器 monitor; ～无线电台 monitoring station

【监外执行】[法] execute (a sentence) outside prison

【监狱】prison; jail ◇ ～长 warden

【监制】supervise the manufacture of

笺 名 ❶ writing paper: 信笺 ❷ letter ❸〈书〉annotation; commentary

【笺注】〈书〉notes and commentary on ancient texts

菅 名 [植] villous themeda (Themeda gigantea var. villosa)

犍 名 bullock

【犍牛】bullock

缄 动 seal; close: 信封上写着"刘～"。*On the envelope is written: "from Liu".*

【缄口】〈书〉keep one's mouth shut; hold one's tongue; say nothing

【缄默】keep silent; be reticent

煎 I 动 ❶ fry in shallow oil without stirring: ～鸡蛋 *fried eggs* ❷ simmer in water; decoct: ～药 *decoct medicinal herbs* II 量 (for herb medicine) decoction: 头(二)～ *first (second) decoction* / 吃一～药就会好的。*One decoction will put you right.*

【煎熬】suffering; torture; torment: 由于长期生病,他受尽～。*He suffered severely from the lingering illness.*

【煎饼】thin pancake made of millet flour, etc.

鲣 名 oceanic bonito; skipjack (tuna)

jiǎn

拣 动 choose; select; pick out: 把最好的西红柿～出来 *pick out the best tomatoes* / ～要紧的说。*Say what you think is most urgent.*

【拣便宜】get a bargain; gain a small advantage

【拣选】select; choose

茧 名 cocoon: 这是蚕结的～。*It's a silkworm cocoon.*

【茧绸】pongee

【茧子】〈方〉silkworm cocoon

柬 名 card; note; letter: 请柬

【柬埔寨】Cambodia ◇ ～人 Cambodian

【柬帖】note; short letter

俭 形 thrifty; frugal: 省吃俭用

【俭朴】thrifty and simple; economical: 生活～ *lead a thrifty and simple life* / 衣着～ *dress simply* / 她是个～的主妇。*She is a thrifty housewife.*

【俭省】economical; thrifty: 过日子～ *live a frugal life; live economically* / 用钱～点。*Be sparing in your use of money.*

捡 动 pick up; collect; gather: ～麦穗 *pick up ears of wheat; glean a wheat field* / ～到一支钢笔 *find a fountain pen* / ～了一条命 *barely escape death*

【捡了芝麻,丢了西瓜】pick up the sesame seeds but overlook the watermelons—concentrate on minor matters to the neglect of major ones

【捡漏】repair the leaky part of a roof; plug a leak in the roof

【捡破烂儿】pick odds and ends from refuse heaps

【捡拾压捆机】[农] pick-up bale; pick-up press

检 动 ❶ check up; inspect; examine ❷ restrain oneself; be careful in one's conduct: 不检

【检波】[电子] detection: ～管 *detection tube* / ～器 *detector*

【检测】test; examine; check up: 利用电脑装置～

交通 *check traffic with computerized devices*

【检查】❶ check up; inspect; examine: ~工作 *check up on work* / ~质量 *check on the quality of sth*. ❷ self-criticism: 作~ *criticize oneself* / 写~ *write a self-criticism* ◇ ~哨 checkpost; ~团 inspection party; ~站 checkpoint; checkpost; inspection station

【检察】procuratorial work: 加强对经济犯罪行为的~工作 *strengthen the procuratorial work in dealing with economic crimes* ◇ ~官 public procurator (or prosecutor); ~机关 procuratorial organ; ~院 procuratorate; ~长 chief procurator; public procurator-general

【检尝】examine and taste: 对中秋月饼进行外观和内质的~。*Moon cakes are carefully examined for appearance and tasted for flavor*.

【检点】❶ examine; check: ~一下行李,看是不是都齐了。*Check the luggage and see if everything is there*. ❷ be cautious (about what one says or does): 他后悔自己说话不~。*He regrets his inappropriate remarks*. / 言行有失~ *be careless about one's words and acts; be indiscreet in one's speech and conduct*

【检定】examine and determine: 药品~ *test drugs*

【检获】search and seize; capture: 香港警方日前在一次行动中~了一批色情录影带。*The Hong Kong Police seized a number of pornographic video tapes in a recent sweep*.

【检举】report (an offence) to the authorities; inform against (an offender); accuse: ~特务 *inform against a secret agent* / ~失实 *accusation at variance with the facts* ◇ ~人 accuser; ~箱 a box for accusation letters; ~信 letter of accusation; written accusation

【检控】❶ investigate (criminal activities) ❷ inform against; accuse; charge: 有人~他挪用公款。*He was charged with embezzling public funds*.

【检漏】[电] leak hunting: ~器 *leak detector; leak localizer*

【检票】❶ examine tickets (or ballots) ❷ check in

【检视】check up; examine: 地勤人员正在~将要起飞的飞机。*Ground personnel are examining the plane that is going to take off*.

【检试】(of machines, facilities, installations, etc.) test; examine; inspect

【检索】refer to; look up: 资料按音序排列便于~。*For convenience of reference, the materials are arranged in pinyin order*. / 资料~系统 *data retrieval system*

【检讨】❶ self-criticism: 作~ *make a self-criticism* / ~自己的错误 *examine one's mistakes* / 书面~ *a written self-criticism* ❷ 〈书〉 examine; inspect

【检修】examine and repair; overhaul: ~汽车 *overhaul a car* / ~汽车引擎 *overhaul the engine of a car*

【检验】test; examine; inspect: 严格~产品质量 *strictly examine the quality of the products* / 商品~ *commodity inspection* ◇ ~费 survey fees; ~员 inspector; inspecting officer

【检疫】quarantine: 卫生~ *health quarantine* / 动植物~ *the quarantine of animals and plants* / ~对象 *objects subject to quarantine* / ~范围 *quarantine range* ◇ ~旗 quarantine flag; yellow flag; ~员 quarantine officer; ~站 quarantine station; ~证明书 quarantine certificate; vaccination certificate; yellow book

【检阅】review (troops, etc.); inspect: ~仪仗队 *review a guard of honour* / 对科研新成果的一次~ *a review of recent achievements in scientific research* ◇ ~台 reviewing stand

【检字表】word index (in a dictionary)

【检字法】the way in which Chinese characters are arranged and are to be located (as in a dictionary); indexing system for Chinese characters

剪 Ⅰ 名 scissors; shears; clippers Ⅱ 动 ❶ cut (with scissors); clip; trim: 别把头发~得太短了。*Don't cut the hair too short*. / 把图片从杂志上~下来 *cut the pictures out of the magazine* / ~指甲 *trim one's nails* / ~羊毛 *shear a sheep* ❷ wipe out; exterminate: 剪除

【剪报】newspaper cutting (or clipping)

【剪裁】❶ cut out (a garment); tailor: ~服装 *cut out dresses* ❷ cut out unwanted material (from a piece of writing); prune: 写文章要下一番~的工夫。*In writing an essay one must do a lot of pruning*.

【剪彩】cut the ribbon at an opening ceremony: 为展览会~ *cut the ribbon at the opening of an exhibition*

【剪草机】grass mower; grass-mowing machine; lawn mower

【剪除】wipe out; annihilate; exterminate

【剪床】[机] shearing machine

【剪刀】scissors; shears: 一把~ *a pair of scissors*

【剪刀差】scissors movement of prices; scissors differential (or difference); price scissors: 我们对于工农业产品的交换是缩小~,而不是扩大~。*In the exchange of industrial products for agricultural products, we try to narrow the price scissors, not widen them*.

【剪辑】❶ film montage; film editing ❷ editing and rearrangement: 话剧录音~ *highlights of a live recording of a play*

【剪接】film montage; film editing

【剪毛】[牧] shearing; clipping

【剪票】punch a ticket ◇ ~铗 conductor's punch

【剪切】[机] shearing: ~刀具 *shearing tool* / ~机 *shearer* / ~模 *shearing die* / ~作业线 *cutting line; shear line*

【剪秋萝】[植] senno campion (Lychnis senno)

【剪贴】❶ clip and paste (sth. out of a newspaper, etc.) in a scrapbook (or on cards) ❷ cutting out (as school-children's activity) ◇ ~簿 scrapbook

【剪影】❶ paper-cut silhouette ❷ outline; sketch

【剪应力】[机] shearing stress

【剪纸】paper-cut；scissor-cut
【剪子】scissors；shears；clippers

减 动 ❶ subtract：九～四得五。*Nine minus four is five*. or *Four from nine is five*. ❷ reduce；decrease；cut：工作热情有增无～ *work with ever increasing zeal*
【减半】reduce by half：儿童票价～ *half-price fare for children* / ～征收所得税 *be allowed a 50% reduction of income tax*
【减编】staff reduction
【减产】reduction of output；drop in production：～百分之十。*Output dropped by ten per cent*.
【减低】reduce；lower；bring down；cut：～速度 *lower (or slacken) speed；slow down* / 耗煤率～了百分之五。*Consumption of coal went down by 5%*.
【减法】subtraction
【减肥】reduce weight；slim：我不敢多吃，我想～。*I mustn't eat too much. I'm trying to slim*. / 医生要他～。*The doctor told him to reduce weight*. / ～体操 *slimming exercises* ◇ ～茶 weight-reducing tea；～中心 weight-control center
【减幅】range of decrease；decrease；amount of cut：燃料价格～在一成以上。*The price of fuel will be cut more than 10%*.
【减号】minus sign（－）
【减河】［水］distributary
【减缓】retard；slow down：～进程 *slow down the pace (or progress)*
【减价】reduce (or lower) the prices；mark down：～出售 *sell at a reduced prices* / ～一成 *be marked down by 10%*
【减亏】reduce a deficit；deficit reduction
【减免】❶ mitigate or annul (a punishment) ❷ reduce or remit (taxation, etc.)：成绩好的学生可以～学费。*Students with high marks can enjoy a partial or total tuition waiver*.
【减摩】［机］antifriction：～合金 *antifriction alloy (or metal)* / ～轴承 *antifriction bearing* / ～涂层 *triction coat*
【减轻】lighten；ease；alleviate；mitigate：～病人的痛苦 *alleviate (or ease) a patient's suffering* / ～处分 *mitigate a punishment*
【减弱】weaken；abate：体力大大～ *be much weakened physically* / 风势～了。*The wind has subsided*.
【减色】lose lustre；impair the excellence of；detract from the merit of：音响效果不好，使演出大为～。*Poor acoustics spoilt the performance*.
【减色法】subtractive process (in cinematography)
【减少】reduce；decrease；lessen；cut down：～非生产性开支 *reduce nonproductive expenditure* / 精简机构，～层次 *simplify the administrative structure and eliminate duplication*
【减声器】［机］muffler
【减数】［数］subtrahend
【减税】tax reduction ◇～让利 reduce taxes and allow enterprises to keep more profits
【减速】slow down；decelerate；retard ◇～度 deceleration；～副翼［航空］deceleron；～火箭 retro-rocket；～剂［物］moderator；～伞［航空］drag (or deceleration) parachute；～运动［物］retarded motion
【减缩】reduce；cut down；retrench：～开支 *reduce expenditure*
【剪贴】［计］cut and paste
【剪贴板】［计］clipboard
【减退】drop；go down：视力（记忆力）～。*One's eyesight (memory) is failing*. / 雨后炎热～了许多。*After the rain, the heat abated considerably*.
【减薪】reduce salary：裁员～ *cut down the number of employees and reduce the salary*
【减刑】［法］reduce a penalty；reduce a sentence；commute (or mitigate) a sentence
【减压】reduce pressure；decompress：～器 *pressure reducer；decompressor*
【减员】depletion of numbers (in the armed forces, etc.)：这个单位将补充自然～约百人。*About 100 persons will replace those who retire or cannot work for various reasons in this unit*.
【减灾】reduce natural disasters
【减震】shock absorption；damping：～器 *shock absorber；damper*

睑 名 eyelid
【睑腺炎】［医］sty

简 Ⅰ 形 simple；simplified；brief：从简 Ⅱ 名 ❶ bamboo slips (used for writing on in ancient times) ❷ letter：书简 Ⅲ 动〈书〉select；choose：简拔
【简拔】〈书〉select and promote
【简报】bulletin；brief report：会议～ *conference bulletin；brief reports on conference proceedings*
【简本】concise edition
【简编】(usu. used in book titles) short course；concise edition：《中国文学史～》*A Short History of Chinese Literature*
【简便】simple and convenient；handy：～的方法 *a simple and convenient method；a handy way* / 操作～ *easy to operate* / ～的手续 *simple procedures*
【简称】the abbreviated form of a name；abbreviation
【简单】❶ simple；uncomplicated：～明了 *simple and clear；concise and explicit* / 这机器构造～。*The machine is simple in structure*. ❷ oversimplified；casual：～粗暴 *do things in an oversimplified and crude way* / 不能用～的方法去解决这个问题。*This matter cannot be settled in a summary fashion*. ◇ ～多数 simple majority
【简单化】oversimplify：看问题～ *take a naive view；oversimplify a problem*
【简单再生产】［经］simple reproduction
【简短】brief：他的发言～有力。*His speech was brief and forceful*.
【简而言之】in brief；in short；to put it in a nut-

shell

【简化】simplify：～工序 *simplify working processes* / ～手续 *simplify the procedure*；*simplify the formalities*

【简化汉字】❶ simplify Chinese characters (i.e. reduce the number of strokes and eliminate complicated variants) ❷ simplified Chinese characters

【简洁】succinct；terse；pithy：～生动的语言 *terse and lively language* / 文笔～ *written in a pithy style*

【简捷】(又作'简截') simple and direct；forthright

【简介】brief introduction；synopsis；summarized account：剧情～ *the synopsis of a drama*

【简括】brief but comprehensive；compendious

【简历】biographical notes；curriculum vitae；résumé

【简练】terse；succinct；pithy：内容丰富，文字～ *rich in content and succinct in style*

【简陋】simple and crude：设备～ *simple and crude equipment* / ～的小木屋 *a crude log cabin*

【简略】simple (in content)；brief；sketchy：他提供的材料过于～。*The material he supplied is too sketchy.* / ～地拟出计划要点 *sketch out the main points of the plan*

【简慢】negligent (in attending to one's guest)

【简明】simple and clear；concise：《～汉英词典》*A Concise Chinese-English Dictionary*

【简明扼要】brief and to the point；concise：讲话、演说、写文章和写决议案，都应当～。*Talks, speeches, articles and resolutions should all be concise and to the point.*

【简明新闻】news in brief

【简朴】simple and unadorned；plain：生活～ *a simple and frugal life*；*plain living* / ～的语言 *plain language* / 衣著～ *be simply dressed*

【简谱】[音] numbered musical notation

【简体字】simplified Chinese character

【简图】sketch；diagram

【简谐运动】[物] simple harmonic motion

【简写】❶ write a Chinese character in simplified form ❷ simplify a book for beginners ◇ ～本 simplified edition

【简讯】news in brief

【简要】concise and to the point；brief：～的介绍 *a brief introduction*；*briefing* / ～记录 *a summary record*

【简仪】[天] abridged armilla

【简易】❶ simple and easy：～的办法 *a simple and easy method* ❷ simply constructed；simply equipped；unsophisticated ◇ ～病房 simply equipped ward；～读物 easy reader；～房 lightly constructed and simply equipped building；～公路 simply-built highway；～机场 airstrip；～楼 economy building

【简约】brief；concise；sketchy

【简章】general regulations

【简政放权】streamline administration and institute decentralization

【简直】simply；at all：这消息～好得叫人不敢相信。*The news is almost too good to be true.* / 我～不能相信自己的耳朵。*I could hardly believe my ears.*

【简装】simple packing

碱 名 ❶ alkali ❷ soda：洗涤～ *washing soda*

【碱处理】alkali treatment

【碱地】alkaline land

【碱化】alkalization；basification

【碱金属】alkali (or alkaline) metal

【碱式盐】[化] basic salt

【碱土金属】alkaline-earth metal

【碱性】basicity；alkalinity：～染料 *basic dyes* / ～土 *alkaline soil*

【碱性反应】alkaline reaction

jiàn

见 Ⅰ 动 ❶ see；catch sight of：从来没～过这种鸟。*I've never seen a bird like that before.* / 只～一个人影闪过墙角 *catch sight of sb. turning the corner* ❷ meet with；be exposed to：这种药怕～光。*This medicine is not to be exposed to daylight.* / 冰～热就化。*Ice melts with heat.* ❸ show evidence of；appear to be：并不～瘦 *not seem to be any thinner* / ～之于行动 *be translated into action* ❹ refer to；see；vide：～第三十六页 *see page 36* ❺ meet；call on；see：待会儿～。*See you later.* / 你～到他了没有？*Did you meet him?* / 我不想～他。*I don't wish to see him.* / 她今天下午要来～你。*She'll call on you this afternoon.* Ⅱ 名 view；opinion：依我之～ *in my opinion*；*to my mind* Ⅲ 助〈书〉(used before a verb to indicate the passive)：见笑 ——另见 xiàn

【见报】appear in the newspapers：有关这次会议的报道明日即可～。*Reports on this conference will appear in tomorrow's newspapers.*

【见不得】❶ not to be exposed to；unable to stand：～阳光 *not to be exposed to the sunlight* ❷ not fit to be seen or revealed：我没有做～人的事。*I've done nothing I am ashamed of.*

【见财起意】entertain evil thoughts at the sight of money

【见长】be good at；be expert in：她以写作～。*She is good at writing.* ——另见 jiànzhǎng

【见地】insight；judgment：很有～ *have keen insight*；*show sound judgment*

【见多识广】experienced and knowledgeable：他去过许多地方，～。*He is well-travelled, and is a man of wide experience.*

【见方】〈口〉square：这张桌子三尺～。*The table is 3 chi square.*

【见分晓】be clear；be sorted out；clear up (a matte or doubts)；find a solution：事情明日即～。*The outcome of the whole affair will be clear tomorrow.*

【见风是雨】take wind as the forerunner of rain—jump to hasty conclusions
【见风转舵】trim one's sails
【见缝插针】stick in a pin wherever there's room—make use of every bit of time or space
【见怪】mind; take offence: 菜做得不好,请不要~。*I hope you won't mind my poor cooking*. / 批评得不对,可别~。*Don't take offence if my criticism is incorrect*.
【见怪不怪,其怪自败】face the fearful with no fears, and its fearfulness disappears
【见鬼】❶ fantastic; preposterous; absurd: 手套怎么不见了? 真~! *That's funny! What have I done with my gloves?* ❷ go to hell: 让他的那套理论~去吧! *To hell with that theory of his!*
【见好】(of a patient's condition) get better; mend: 她的病~。*She's on the mend*.
【见机】as the opportunity arises; as befits the occasion; according to circumstances
【见机行事】act according to circumstances; do as one sees fit; use one's discretion
【见教】〈套〉favour me with your advice; instruct me: 有何~? *Is there something you want to see me about?*
【见解】view; opinion; understanding: 抱有不同~ *hold different views* / 一篇很有~的文章 *an article with original ideas* / 这只是我个人的~。*That's just my own opinion*.
【见景生情】have one's emotion aroused by the scene
【见老】be aged: 十年没见,你还那个样子,一点不~。*You haven't aged at all and still look the same as ten years ago when we last met*.
【见利忘义】forget what is right at the sight of profit
【见谅】〈套〉excuse me; forgive me: 务希~。*I sincerely hope you'll excuse me*.
【见猎心喜】thrill to see one's favourite sport and itch to have a go
【见马克思】〈婉〉(often used by Chinese revolutionary veterans) go to see Marx—breathe one's last; pass away: 他已去~了。*He has breathed his last*.
【见面】meet; see: 他俩经常~。*They see a lot of each other*. / 要使产销直接~ *establish direct links between the producer and the seller* ◇ ~礼 a present given to sb. on first meeting him
【见面熟】〈口〉hail-fellow-well-met
【见票即付】[经] payable at sight; payable to bearer
【见钱眼开】be wide-eyed at the sight of money—greedy
【见仁见智】different people, different views; opinions differ
【见上】see above; vide supra
【见上帝】〈婉〉go to see God—go the way of all flesh; die
【见世面】see the world; enrich one's experience: 这回到化工厂去参观,可见了世面了。*The trip to the chemical works was a real eye-opener*.
【见识】❶ widen one's knowledge; enrich one's experience: 到各处走走,~~也是好的。*It's not a bad idea to go around a bit and gain experience*. ❷ experience; knowledge; sensibleness: 长~ *widen one's knowledge; broaden one's horizons* / 他那样对待你是不对的,你别和他一般~。*He's behaved badly towards you, but a sensible person like you shouldn't want to take him up on it*.
【见树不见林】not see the wood for the trees
【见死不救】not try to save sb. who is in mortal danger; be impervious to other people's misfortunes or disasters
【见所未见】see what one has never seen before: 许多奇事,~,闻所未闻。*I saw and heard of many strange things of which I had hitherto been unaware*.
【见外】regard sb. as an outsider: 你我老朋友还那么客气干什么? 太~了。*Why all this formality between old friends like us? Anybody would think we were strangers!* / 到了我这儿可别~。*Just make yourself at home*.
【见危授命】be ready to die for one's country when it is in danger
【见微知著】from the first small beginnings one can see how things will develop; from one small clue one can see what is coming
【见闻】what one sees and hears; knowledge; information: 增长~ *add to one's knowledge* / ~广 *well-informed; knowledgeable*
【见物不见人】see things but not people; see only material factors, not human ones
【见习】learn on the job; be on probation ◇ ~技术员 technician on probation; ~领事 student consul; ~生 probationer; ~医生 intern
【见下】see below; vide infra
【见贤思齐】when you meet someone better than yourself, turn your thoughts to becoming his equal
【见效】become effective; produce the desired result: 这药吃下去就~。*This medicine produces an instant effect*. / 这些企业投资少,~快。*These enterprises call for small investments and yield quick returns*.
【见笑】❶ laugh at (me or us): 我刚开始学,您可别~。*Now don't laugh at me. I'm only a beginner*. ❷ incur ridicule (by one's poor performance): 写得不好,~,~。*Excuse my poor writing*.
【见血封喉】[植] upas
【见义勇为】see what is right and have the courage to do it; be ready to take up the cudgels for a just cause
【见异思迁】change one's mind the moment one sees something new; be inconstant
【见长】grow perceptibly: 下了一场雨,麦苗立刻~。*The wheat sprouts grew perceptibly after the rain*. / 这孩子不~。*The child doesn't seem to be growing*. ——另见 jiàncháng

【见证】witness; testimony: 警察找不到任何人作～。*The police could find no eyewitnesses.* / 历史是最好的～。*History is the most telling witness.*

【见证人】eyewitness; witness: 被告的～ *a witness for the defence*

件 Ⅰ量 ❶ (for matters in general): 一～事 *a matter; a thing* / 一～工作 *a piece of work; a job* ❷ (for clothing, furniture, luggage, etc.): 一～大衣 *an overcoat* / 一～家具 *a piece of furniture* / 三～行李 *three pieces of luggage* Ⅱ名 ❶ single item: 工件 / 零件 ❷ letter; correspondence; paper; document: 来件 / 密件

间 Ⅰ名 space in between; opening: 无间 Ⅱ动 ❶separate: 相间 ❷sow discord: 离间 ❸thin out (seedlings): 间苗 ——另见 jiān

【间谍】spy ◇ ～飞机 spy plane; ～网 espionage network; ～卫星 spy satellite

【间断】be disconnected; be interrupted: 他坚持锻炼,几年来从不～。*He has kept up physical training for several years without interruption.*

【间断性】[哲] discontinuity: 不～ *continuity*

【间隔】interval; intermission: 两次会议～才二十天。*There was an interval of only twenty days between the two conferences.*

【间隔号】separation dot, a punctuation mark separating the day from the month, as in 一二·九运动(the December 9th Movement), or separating the parts of a person's name, as in 诺尔曼·白求恩(Norman Bethune)

【间或】occasionally; now and then; sometimes; once in a while: 大家很安静地听着,～有人提一两个问题。*Everybody listened in silent attention, with occasional questions from the floor.*

【间接】indirect; secondhand: 这消息我是～听来的。*I heard the news indirectly.* ◇ ～宾语 [语] indirect object; ～地址 indirect address; ～肥料 indirect fertilizer; ～接触 [医] mediate contacts; ～经验 indirect experience; ～贸易 indirect trade; ～税 indirect tax; ～损害 indirect damage; ～推理 [逻] mediate inference; ～消费 indirect consumption; ～选举 indirect election; ～证据 circumstantial evidence

【间苗】thin out seedlings (or young shoots)

【间隙】❶ interval; gap; space: 利用工作～收集些资料 *find free time to gather material* ❷ [机] clearance: 齿轮～ *gear clearance*

【间歇】intermittence; intermission: ～性的精神病人 *a person whose mental illness is of an intermittent nature* ◇ ～喷泉 geyser; ～泉 intermittent spring; ～热 [医] intermittent fever

【间杂】be intermingled; be mixed

【间作】[农] intercropping: 实行玉米和大豆～ *intercrop maize and soya beans*

饯 动 ❶ give a farewell dinner: 饯行 ❷ preserve (fruits): 蜜饯

【饯别】give a farewell dinner: ～友人 *give a friend a farewell dinner*

【饯行】give a farewell dinner: 我们将设宴为他～。*We'll give a farewell dinner for him.*

建 动 ❶ build; construct; erect: ～电站 *build a power station* / ～桥工地 *the construction site of the bridge* ❷ establish; set up; found: ～社 *set up a people's commune (or a cooperative)* / ～新功 *make new contributions* ❸ propose; advocate: 建议

【建材】〈略〉见〖建筑材料〗

【建党】❶ found (or form) a political party ❷ build up the Party: ～路线 *line for Party building*

【建点】lay foundations; set up (an organization); do pioneering work: 刚～的机构 *recently established organization*

【建都】found a capital; make (a place) the capital: 唐代～长安。*The Tang Dynasty made Chang'an its capital.*

【建功】do a deed of merit; perform meritorious service: ～立业 *render meritorious service and make a distinguished career*

【建构】frame; construct (usu.〈喻〉): 在我们的社会中每个人都应重视自己心灵的～和陶冶。*Everyone in our society should cultivate their mind and spirit.*

【建国】❶ found (or establish) a state: 像这样的大会还是～以来第一次。*This congress is the first of its kind since the founding of our People's Republic.* ❷ build up a country: ～宏图 *a grand project for national reconstruction*

【建行】(〈略〉全称为'建设银行') the Construction Bank

【建交】establish diplomatic relations: ～联合公报 *a joint communiqué on the establishment of diplomatic relations*

【建军】❶ found an army ❷ build up the Army (i.e. the Chinese People's Liberation Army): ～路线 *line for army building* / ～原则 *principles of army building*

【建军节】Army Day (1 August)

【建兰】sword-leaved cymbidium (Cymbidium ensifolium)

【建立】build; establish; set up; found: ～友好关系 *build friendly relations* / ～外交关系 *establish diplomatic relations* / ～信心 *build up one's confidence* / ～功勋 *perform meritorious deeds*

【建设】build; construct: 把我国～成为社会主义的现代化强国 *build China into a powerful modern socialist country*

【建设性】constructive: ～的意见 *constructive suggestions* / 起～的作用 *play a constructive role* / 这次会谈富有～。*The talks were very constructive.*

【建设周期】construction cycle

【建树】〈书〉make a contribution; contribute: 人类认识史上的重大～ *major attainments in the his-*

tory of human knowledge / 他在任职期间毫无～。*He did nothing noteworthy during his tenure*.

【建议】❶ propose; suggest; recommend: 他们～休会。*They propose that the meeting be adjourned*. ❷ proposal; suggestion; recommendation: 提～ *offer suggestions*

【建造】build; construct; make: ～房屋 *build houses*

【建账】keep accounts

【建制】organizational system: 部队～ *the organizational system of the army* / ～部队 *organic unit*

【建筑】❶ build; construct; erect: ～铁路 *build a railway* / 你不能把自己的幸福～在别人的痛苦上。*You shouldn't build your happiness on the suffering of other people*. ❷ building; structure; edifice: 古老的～ *an ancient building* / 宏伟的～ *a magnificent structure* ❸ architecture: 他是学现代～的。*His speciality is modern architecture*. / ～设计 *architectural design* ◇ ～材料 building materials; ～工程学 architectural engineering; ～工地 building site; construction site; ～工人 building worker; builder; ～红线 property line; ～面积 built-up area; floorage ; ～群 architectural complex; ～设计 architectural design; ～师 architect; ～物 building; structure; ～学 architecture; ～业 building industry; ～造价 construction costs

剑 名 sword; sabre: ～柄 *the handle of a sword*; *hilt* / ～鞘 *scabbard*

【剑拔弩张】with swords drawn and bows bent; at daggers drawn

【剑客】chivalrous swordsman (in old novels)

【剑麻】sisal hemp

【剑眉】straight eyebrows slanting upwards and outwards; dashing eyebrows

【剑术】swordsmanship; fencing skill

【剑侠】chivalrous swordsman (in old novels)

荐 Ⅰ 动 recommend: 推荐 Ⅱ 名 〈书〉 ❶ grass; straw ❷ straw mat

【荐举】propose sb. for an office; recommend: 发现和～年轻的优秀管理人才 *discover and recommend excellent young managers*

【荐贤】recommend persons of virtue and ability

【荐引】〈书〉 recommend; introduce

贱 形 ❶ low-priced; inexpensive; cheap: ～卖 *sell cheap* ❷ lowly; humble: 贫贱 ❸ low-down; base; despicable: 她很～! *She's cheap*! ❹ 〈谦〉 my: 贱内

【贱骨头】〈讳〉 miserable (or contemptible) wretch

【贱货】❶ cheap goods ❷ 〈讳〉 miserable (or contemptible) wretch

【贱民】❶ people of the lowest social strata ❷ untouchables

【贱内】〈旧〉 my (humble) wife

【贱人】〈旧〉〈讳〉 slut

涧 名 ravine; gully

舰 名 warship; naval vessel; man-of-war

【舰队】fleet; naval force: 东海～ *the Dong Hai Sea Fleet*; *the East China Sea Fleet* / 联合～ *a combined fleet*

【舰对空导弹】ship-to-air missile

【舰首炮】bow chaser

【舰艇】naval ships and boats; naval vessels

【舰尾炮】stern chaser

【舰载】carrier-borne; carrier-based; ship-based: ～导弹 *ship-based missile* / ～飞机 *shipboard aircraft*; *deck-landing aircraft*

【舰长】captain (of a warship)

【舰只】warships; naval vessels: 海军～ *naval vessels*

监 名 an imperial office: 钦天～ *Board of Astronomy* ——另见 jiān

健 Ⅰ 形 healthy; strong Ⅱ 动 ❶ strengthen; toughen; invigorate: ～胃 *be good for the stomach*; *aid digestion* / ～脾 *invigorate the function of the spleen* ❷ be strong in; be good at: 健谈

【健步】walk with vigorous strides: ～登上主席台 *mount the rostrum in vigorous strides*

【健步如飞】walk as if on wings; walk fast and vigorously

【健儿】❶ valiant fighter ❷ good athlete: 乒坛～ *skilful ping-pong players*

【健将】master sportsman, top-notch player: 运动～ *master of sports*; *master sportsman* / 足球～ *top-notch footballer*

【健康】❶ health; physique: ～状况 *state of health*; *physical condition* / 人民的～水平有了很大提高。*The general level of the people's health has markedly improved*. ❷ healthy; sound: 运动正在～地发展。*The movement is developing healthily*. / 情况基本上是～的。*The situation is basically sound*. ◇ ～证明书 health certificate

【健美】❶ strong and handsome; vigorous and graceful: ～的体操表演 *a vigorous and graceful performance of callisthenics* ❷ body-building: 越来越多的人喜欢上了～运动。*More and more people go in for body-building*. ◇ ～比赛 body-building competition; ～操 aerobics dancing; ～体操 callisthenics; ～运动 bodybuilding

【健全】❶ sound; perfect: 身心～ *sound in mind and body* / 头脑～的人 *a person in his or her right mind* ❷ strengthen; amplify; perfect: ～合理的规章制度 *amplify necessary rules and regulations*

【健身】keeping fit; body-building ◇ ～操 circuit; body building exercise; 〈口〉 daily dozen; ～器[体] fitness (or body-building) equipment; ～运动 body-building

【健身房】gymnasium; gym

【健谈】be a good talker; be a brilliant conversationalist

【健体】be healthy and strong; strengthen the body
【健忘】forgetful; having a bad memory ◇ ～症 amnesia
【健旺】healthy and vigorous
【健在】〈书〉(of a person of advanced age) be still living and in good health: 她本人已年过七十,而她的父母还～。*She is over seventy and her parents are still alive.*
【健壮】healthy and strong; robust: ～的小伙子 *a robust young man* / 像马一样～ *as strong as a horse*

渐 副 gradually; by degrees: 天气～冷。*The weather is getting cold.*
【渐次】〈书〉gradually; one after another
【渐渐】gradually; by degrees; little by little: 天气～转暖。*The weather is getting warm.* / 路上的行人～少了。*The number of pedestrians gradually dwindled.* / 雨～小了。*The rain is beginning to let up.*
【渐进】advance gradually; progress step by step: 实现这目标是一个～过程。*The attainment of this goal is an evolutionary process.*
【渐入佳境】(of a situation) be improving; be getting better
【渐缩管】[机] reducing pipe
【渐显】[摄] fade in
【渐隐】[摄] fade out

溅 动 splash; spatter: ～一身泥 *be spattered with mud* / 钢花四～ *sparks of molten steel flying in all directions*
【溅落】(of a space vehicle, etc.) splash down ◇ ～点 splash point

践 动 ❶ trample; tread ❷ act on; carry out: 实践
【践踏】tread on; trample underfoot: 请勿～草地。*Keep off the grass.* / 肆意～别国主权 *wantonly trample on the sovereignty of other countries*
【践约】keep a promise; keep an appointment

腱 名 [生理] tendon
【腱鞘】[生理] tendon sheath ◇ ～炎 [医] tenosynovitis
【腱子】(beef or mutton) shank

毽 名 shuttlecock
【毽子】shuttlecock: 踢～*kick the shuttlecock (as a game)*

鉴 Ⅰ 名 ❶ mirror (made of bronze or brass in ancient times) ❷ warning; object lesson Ⅱ 动 ❶ reflect; mirror: 水清可～。*The water is so clear that you can see your reflection in it.* ❷ inspect; scrutinize; examine: 鉴定 ❸〈套〉(usu. used in the opening phrase in letters): 某先生台～。*Dear Mr. so-and-so: May I draw your attention to the following.*
【鉴别】distinguish; differentiate; discriminate: 他可以～这块宝石是不是真的。*He can judge whether the stone is genuine.* / 有比较才能～。*Only by comparing can one distinguish.* / ～文物 *make an appraisal of a cultural relic* ◇ ～器 [电] discriminator
【鉴定】❶ appraisal (of a person's strong and weak points): 毕业～ *graduation appraisal* ❷ appraise; identify; authenticate; determine: ～产品质量 *appraise the quality of a product* / ～文物年代 *determine the date of a cultural relic* ❸ [法] expert evaluation: ～人 *expert witness*
【鉴定书】[经] testimonial; written appraisal: 专家～ *expert's report*
【鉴戒】warning; object lesson: 我们应当把这次挫折引为～。*We should take warning from this setback.* ◇ ～会 appraising meeting
【鉴评】appraise, judge: 专家～ *expert appraisal*
【鉴认】authenticate; verify: ～名画的真假 *verify the authenticity of celebrated paintings*
【鉴赏】appreciate: ～能力 *ability to appreciate (painting, music, etc.); connoisseurship* / 对音乐颇有～力 *have a good ear for music* / 对文学有～力 *have a discriminating taste in literature*
【鉴于】in view of; seeing that: ～情况紧急,我们立即作出决定。*We made up our minds at once in view of the urgency of the case.*
【鉴证】appraise and verify: 作为合同～人的工商行政部门要认真负责进行监督。*The Administrative Department for Industry and Commerce which appraises and verifies contracts, should carefully supervise their execution.*

键 名 ❶ [机] key: 轴～ *shaft key* ❷ key (of a typewriter, piano, etc.) ❸ [化] bond
【键槽】[机] keyway; key slot; key seat
【键控穿孔】key-punch
【键盘】keyboard; fingerboard
【键盘乐器】keyboard instrument
【键入】(又作'输入','敲入') key in

僭 动〈书〉overstep one's authority
【僭越】〈书〉overstep one's authority

箭 名 arrow
【箭靶子】target for archery
【箭步】a sudden big stride forward: 他一个～蹿上前去。*He leapt up with a big stride.*
【箭杆】arrow shaft
【箭楼】an embrasured watchtower over a city gate
【箭筒】quiver (for arrows)
【箭头】❶ arrowhead ❷ arrow (as a sign)
【箭在弦上,不得不发】an arrow fitted to the bowstring cannot avoid being discharged—one cannot but go ahead; one has reached the point of no return
【箭猪】porcupine
【箭镞】metal arrowhead

jiāng

江 名 ❶ river ❷ the Changjiang River

【江岸】river bank
【江北】north of the River—a region including parts of Jiangsu and Anhui which are north of the Changjiang (Yangtze)
【江河日下】go from bad to worse; be on the decline
【江湖】❶ rivers and lakes—all corners of the country; the wide world: 流落～ *live a vagabond life* ❷ rivers and lakes—people wandering from place to place and living by their wits, e. g. fortune-tellers, quack doctors, itinerant entertainers, etc., considered as a social group
【江湖好汉】a good fellow of the rivers and lakes; a bravo of river and lake
【江湖骗子】swindler; charlatan
【江湖气】〈贬〉worldly-wise; slippery; sleek
【江湖医生】quack; mountebank
【江湖艺人】itinerant entertainer
【江郎才尽】a writer written out
【江轮】river steamer
【江米】polished glutinous rice ◇ ～酒 fermented glutinous rice
【江南】south of the River—a region in the lower Changjiang (Yangtze) valley, including southern Jiangsu and Anhui and northern Zhejiang (much celebrated in poetry for its beauties and joys)
【江山】❶ rivers and mountains; land; landscape: ～如画 *a picturesque landscape; beautiful scenery* ❷ country; state power: 保卫人民的～ *safeguard the people's state power*
【江山易改,本性难移】it's easy to change rivers and mountains but hard to change a person's nature
【江豚】(又作'江猪') black finless porpoise
【江洋大盗】a great robber
【江珧】[动] pen shell ◇ ～柱 the dried adductor of a pen shell

将 Ⅰ 动 ❶〈书〉support; take; bring: ～幼弟而归 *bring home one's little brother* / 相～而去 *go off supporting each other* ❷ Chinese chess check: ～! *Check!* / 他连～我三次。*He checked me three times in a row.* ❸ incite sb. to action; challenge; prod: 他已拿定主意不参加比赛了,你再～他也没用。*It's no use egging him on; he's made up his mind not to join in the tournament.* Ⅱ 介 ❶ with; by means of; by: ～开水沏茶 *make tea with boiling water* ❷ (used in the same way as 把Ⅳ): ～他请来 *invite him to come over* / ～革命进行到底。*Carry the revolution through to the end.* Ⅲ 副 ❶ be going to; be about to; will; shall: 我们～制定一个长远规划。*We are going to draw up a long-range plan.* / 天～黄昏。*It's almost dusk.* ❷ certainly; no doubt: 如不刻苦钻研,则～一事无成。*You will certainly achieve nothing unless you study assiduously.* Ⅳ 助〈方〉(used between a verb and its complement of direction): 唱～起来 *start to sing* / 传～出去 (*of news, etc.*) spread abroad / 赶～上去 *hurry to catch up* / 打～起来 *start to fight* ——另见 jiàng
【将错就错】leave a mistake uncorrected and make the best of it
【将功补过】make amends for one's faults by good deeds
【将功赎罪】atone for a crime by good deeds; expiate one's guilt by good deeds.
【将计就计】meet plot with plot; turn sb.'s trick against him; beat sb. at his own game
【将近】close to; nearly; almost: 这个国家有～四千年有记载的历史。*This country has nearly 4,000 years of recorded history.*
【将就】make do with; make the best of; put up with: 这件大衣稍微短一点,你～着穿吧。*This coat may be a bit too short for you, but perhaps you could make do with it.* / 哄着他点儿,～～他吧。*Humour him a little and bear with him.*
【将军】❶ general ❷ Chinese chess check: 他将了我两次军。*He checked me twice in a row.* ❸ put sb. on the spot; embarrass; challenge: 他们要我唱歌,这可将了我一军。*They embarrassed me by calling on me to sing.* ◇ ～肚 pot belly; big belly; beer belly
【将来】future: 在不远的～ *in the not too distant future; before long* / 在可以预见的～ *in the foreseeable future*
【将勤补拙】make up for lack of skill with or by industry
【将心比心】put oneself in sb.'s shoes; think of others; be empathic
【将心换心】to win other people's hearts by one's sincerity
【将信将疑】half believing, half doubting: 对他的话～ *take him half seriously and half sceptically; only half believe what he says*
【将养】rest; recuperate: 医生说你再～一个礼拜就可以好了。*The doctor says you ought to be well again after another week's rest.*
【将要】be going to; will; shall: 他～到西藏去工作。*He's going to work in Tibet.*
【将欲取之,必先与之】give in order to take

姜 名 ginger
【姜还是老的辣】old ginger is hotter than new—veterans are abler than recruits
【姜黄】[植] turmeric
【姜片虫】fasciolopsis: ～病 *fasciolopsiasis*
【姜汤】ginger tea

豇 (构词成分)见下
【豇豆】cowpea

浆 Ⅰ 名 thick liquid: 糖浆 Ⅱ 动 starch: ～衣服 *starch clothes*
【浆果】[植] berry
【浆纱】[纺] sizing
【浆洗】wash and starch
【浆纸机】papermaking coating machine

僵 Ⅰ形 ❶stiff; numb：他的脚冻～了。*His feet were numb with cold*. ❷ deadlocked：他把事情搞～了。*He's brought things to a deadlock*. Ⅱ动〈方〉stop smiling; look serious：他～着脸。*He kept a straight face*. or *He pulled a long face*.

【僵持】(of both parties) refuse to budge：双方～好久。*For quite some time, neither party was willing to budge from its original position*. / 谈判处于～状态。*The negotiations are now in a stalemate*.

【僵化】become rigid; ossify; stereotyped：思想～ *a rigid* (*or ossified*) *way of thinking*; *stereotyped thinking* / 冲破～的经济体制 *break down the rigid economic structures*

【僵局】deadlock; impasse; stalemate：打破～ *break a deadlock*

【僵尸】corpse：政治～ *a political mummy*

【僵死】dead; ossified

【僵硬】❶ stiff：觉得四肢～ *feel stiff in the limbs* ❷ rigid; inflexible：～的公式 *a rigid formula* / 工作方法太～ *work in a mechanical way* / 政策～ *an inflexible policy*

缰 名 reins; halter

【缰绳】reins; halter

疆 名 boundary; border

【疆场】battlefield

【疆界】boundary; border

【疆土】territory

【疆域】territory; domain

jiǎng

讲 动 ❶ speak; say; tell：～英语 *speak English* / ～故事 *tell stories* / ～几句话 *say a few words* ❷ explain; make clear; interpret：把道理～清楚 *state the reasons clearly* / 我来～～今天开会的目的。*Let me explain the purpose of today's meeting*. ❸ discuss; negotiate：～条件 *negotiate the terms*; *insist on the fulfilment of certain conditions* ❹ stress; pay attention to; be particular about：～卫生 *pay attention to hygiene* / ～质量 *stress quality* / ～排场 *go in for ostentation and extravagance*; *go in for showy display*; *be ostentatious* / 不～情面 *have no consideration for anyone's sensibilities* ❺ as far as sth. is concerned; when it comes to; as to; as regards：～能力，她不如你。*As to ability, she is not your match*.

【讲法】❶ the way of saying a thing; wording：这个意见你如果换一个～就不会惹他生气了。*If you had put your idea in a different way, he wouldn't have been offended*. ❷ statement; version; argument：按他的～办吧。*Do as he says*.

【讲稿】the draft or text of a speech; lecture notes

【讲和】make peace; settle a dispute; become reconciled：现在我们不能跟他们～。*We cannot make peace with them now*.

【讲话】❶ speak; talk; address：对着话筒～ *speak into a microphone* / 他在会上讲了话。*He spoke at the meeting*. or *He addressed the meeting*. ❷ speech; talk：鼓舞人心的～ *an inspiring speech* ❸ talks (used in titles of books that set out basic information)：《语法修辞～》*Talks on Grammar and Rhetoric*

【讲价】(又作'讲价钱') ❶ haggle over the price; bargain ❷ negotiate the terms; insist on the fulfilment of certain conditions

【讲解】explain：他指着示意图给来宾～远景规划。*Pointing at a sketch map, he explained the long-term plan to the visitors*. ◇ ～员 guide; announcer; narrator; commentator

【讲究】❶ be particular about; pay attention to; stress; strive for：她太～吃穿。*She is too fastidious about her food and clothing*. ❷ exquisite; tasteful：宾馆布置得很～。*The guesthouse is tastefully furnished*. ❸ careful study：翻译技巧大有～。*The art of translation calls for careful study*. or *Translation is quite an art*. / 其中大有～。*There's an art to it*.

【讲课】teach; lecture：他讲数学课。*He gives lessons in mathematics*. / ～时数 *teaching hours*

【讲理】❶ reason with sb.; argue：咱们跟他～去。*Let's go and argue it out with him*. ❷ listen (or be amenable) to reason; be reasonable; be sensible：这人没法跟他～。*He is utterly unreasonable*. or *He is impervious to reason*.

【讲明】explain; make clear; state explicitly：～立场 *explain* (*or state*) *one's stand*

【讲排场】put up a show; go in for ostentation and extravagance; be ostentatious; go in for pomp：结婚不要～。*One should not hanker after pomp and extravagance in a wedding*.

【讲评】comment on and appraise：～学生的作业 *comment on the students' work*

【讲情】intercede; plead for sb.：为他～ *plead for him* / 向他为我～ *intercede with him for me*

【讲求】be particular about; pay attention to; stress; strive for：～效率 *strive for efficiency* / ～实效 *lay stress on practical results*

【讲师】lecturer ◇ ～团 lecturers' group

【讲授】lecture; instruct; teach：他～哲学。*He teaches philosophy*. / ～提纲 *an outline for a lecture*; *teaching notes*

【讲述】tell about; give an account of; narrate; relate：故事～两姐妹在恋爱和婚姻中的遭遇。*The story tells about the fortunes of two sisters in love and marriage*.

【讲台】platform; dais; rostrum

【讲坛】❶ (speaker's) platform; rostrum ❷ forum (for public discussion)

【讲堂】lecture room; classroom

【讲题】topic of a lecture

【讲习】lecture and study ◇ ～班 study group; ～所 institute (for instruction or training)

【讲学】give lectures; discourse on an academic

subject：应邀来华～ *be invited to give lectures in China*

【讲演】❶give a speech or lecture ❷speech；lecture：他的～你听了没有？*Did you attend his lecture?*

【讲义】(mimeographed or printed) teaching materials

【讲义气】set store by personal loyalty or friendship：他太～，损害了原则。*He values personal loyalty at the expense of principles.*

【讲桌】lectern

【讲座】a course of lectures：英语广播～ *English lessons over the radio*；*English by radio*

奖 Ⅰ 动 encourage；praise；reward：有功者～。*Those who have gained merit will be rewarded.* / ～勤罚懒，～优罚劣 *reward the diligent and good and punish the lazy and bad* Ⅱ 名 award；prize；reward：得～ *win a prize* / 一等～ *first prize*

【奖杯】cup (as a prize)

【奖惩】rewards and punishments；rewards and penalties

【奖次】level of prize：照～分奖 *award different prizes*

【奖金】money award；bonus；premium ◇ ～分配制度 reward distribution system

【奖励】encourage and reward；award；reward：精神～ *moral encouragement* / 物质～ *material reward* / ～发明创造 *encourage innovations by giving awards* ◇ ～工资 incentive premium wages；～制度 system of reward

【奖牌】medal：～获得者 *medalist*

【奖品】prize；award；trophy

【奖旗】banner (as an award)

【奖勤罚懒】reward the diligent and punish the lazy

【奖券】lottery ticket

【奖赏】award；reward：他因学习成绩优秀而受到～。*He was awarded a prize for excellence in his studies.*

【奖售】encourage sales to the state

【奖台】temporary platform (or stage) on which prizes are awarded to the winners；presentation stage (or platform)

【奖学金】scholarship；exhibition

【奖掖】〈书〉reward and promote；encourage by promoting and rewarding

【奖优罚劣】reward the good and punish the bad

【奖章】medal；decoration

【奖状】certificate of merit

桨 名 oar

jiàng

匠 名 craftsman；artisan：铁匠

【匠气】unimaginative craftsmanship

【匠人】artisan；craftsman

【匠心】〈书〉ingenuity；craftsmanship

【匠心独运】consummate craftsmanship

降 动 ❶ fall；drop：温度～到摄氏零下十度。*The temperature dropped to minus ten degrees centigrade.* ❷ lower；reduce；cut down：把价钱～下来 *lower the price*——另见 xiáng

【降半旗】hoist a flag at half-mast：～致哀 *fly a flag at half-staff as a sign of mourning*

【降低】reduce；cut down；drop；lower：气温～了。*The temperature dropped.* / ～半个音。*make the note a semitone lower* / ～生产成本 *reduce production costs*；*lower production costs* / ～定额 *reduce the quota* (*or norm*) ◇ ～成色 debasement

【降调】[语音] falling tune；falling tone

【降幅】(of prices，profits，income，etc.) range of decrease：今年蔬菜价格～很大。*The prices of vegetables have fallen by a big margin this year.*

【降格】lower one's standard or status：两国关系～ *lower the level of diplomatic relations between two countries*

【降格以求】fall back on sth. inferior to what one hoped for；settle for a second best

【降号】[音] flat (b)

【降耗】reduce consumption；cut down on consumption：节能～ *conserve energy and reduce consumption*

【降级】❶ reduce to a lower rank；demote：这个军官因行为不端而被～。*The officer was demoted for misconduct.* ❷ send (a student) to a lower grade

【降价】reduce (or lower) the prices

【降临】〈书〉befall；arrive；come：灾难～了。*A disaster has befallen us.* / 夜色～。*Night fell.*

【降落】descend；land：大型飞机的起飞和～ *the take-off and landing of big aircraft* ◇ ～场 landing field；～伞 parachute

【降旗】lower a flag

【降生】〈书〉(of the founder of a religion，etc.) be born

【降水】[气] precipitation

【降水量】[气] precipitation：南方的年～比北方大。*The annual precipitation is greater in the south than in the north.*

【降温】❶ lower the temperature (as in a workshop) ❷ [气] drop in temperature

【降压】[电] step-down：～变电站 *step-down substation* / ～变压器 *step-down transformer*

【降压片】[药] hypertension pill

【降雨】a fall of rain；rainfall

【降雨量】rainfall：年～ *annual rainfall*

【降旨】issue an imperial edict

绛 形 deep red；crimson

【绛紫】dark reddish purple

将 Ⅰ 名 ❶ general：上将 ❷ commander in chief，the chief piece in Chinese chess Ⅱ 动〈书〉command；lead：～兵 *command troops* ——另见 jiāng

【将材】(又作'将才') a man with military talent; a man born to command troops
【将官】general
【将领】high-ranking military officer; general
【将令】order (issued by the commanding general): 传～ *issue the commanding general's order; pass on the commanding general's order*
【将门无犬子】a general's family will not produce a mongrel of a son
【将士】〈书〉officers and men
【将帅】high commanding officer: ～之才 (*man with*) *talent to be a good general; makings of a good commander*
【将相】〈旧〉generals and ministers of state
【将遇良材】meet one's equal; find one's own match; diamond cuts diamond: 棋逢对手,～。*As an ace chess player meets his peer, so a general finds his own match in military talent.*
【将在外,君命有所不受】a general in the field is not bound by orders from his sovereign

强 形 stubborn; unyielding ——另见 qiáng; qiǎng
【强嘴】reply defiantly; answer back; talk back

酱 名 ❶ a thick sauce made from soya beans, flour, etc. ❷ cooked or pickled in soy sauce ❸ sauce; paste; jam: 苹果～ *apple jam*
【酱菜】vegetables pickled in soy sauce; pickles
【酱豆腐】fermented bean curd
【酱缸】jar or vat for making or keeping soybean paste, pickled vegetables, etc.
【酱肉】pork cooked in soy sauce; braised pork seasoned with soy sauce
【酱色】dark reddish brown
【酱油】soy sauce; soy
【酱园】(又作'酱坊') a shop making and selling sauce, pickles, etc.; sauce and pickle shop
【酱紫】dark reddish purple

犟 形 obstinate; stubborn; self-willed: 这人真～。*He is a pigheaded* (*or bullheaded*) *person.* or *He is as stubborn as a mule.*
【犟劲】obstinacy; stubbornness

糨 形 thick: 粥熬得太～了。*The porridge is too thick.*
【糨糊】paste

jiāo

交 Ⅰ 动 ❶ hand over; give up; deliver: ～还 *give back; return* / ～会费 *pay membership dues* / 把任务～给我们实验室吧。*Assign the task to our laboratory.* ❷ (of places or periods of time) meet; join: 春夏之～ *when spring is changing into summer* ❸ reach (a certain hour or season): ～冬以后 when winter has set in / 明天就～夏至了。*Tomorrow will be the Summer Solstice.* / ～了好运气 *have good luck* ❹ cross; intersect: 这两条直线～于P点。The two lines intersect at P. ❺ associate with: ～朋友 *make friends* ❻ have sexual intercourse ❼ mate; breed: 杂交 Ⅱ 形 mutual; reciprocal; each other: 交换 Ⅲ 副 together; simultaneous: 饥寒交迫 Ⅳ 名 ❶ business transaction; deal; bargain: 成交 ❷ friend; acquaintance; friendship; relationship: 邦交 ❸ 同〖跤〗
【交白卷】❶ hand in a blank examination paper ❷ completely fail to accomplish a task: 咱们得把情况摸清楚,要不回去就得～。*We must find out exactly how things stand here, or we'll have nothing to report.*
【交班】hand over to the next shift
【交保】release on bail: ～释放 *release on bail*
【交杯酒】mutual toasting by bridegroom and bride by drinking from each other's cup at a wedding ceremony
【交兵】〈书〉(of two or more parties) be at war; wage war
【交叉】❶ intersect; cross; crisscross: 两条铁路在此～。*The two railways cross here.* ❷ overlapping: 两个提案中～的部分 *the overlapping parts of the two proposals* ❸ alternate; stagger: ～进行 *do alternately* ◇ ～报酬率 intersection rate of return; ～点 intersection; ～发价 cross offer; ～感染 cross infection; ～汇率 cross rate; ～火力［军］cross fire; ～科学 intersecting sciences
【交差】report to the leadership after accomplishing a task: 你不开收据,我们回去怎么～? *If you don't give us a receipt, how are we going to account for it?*
【交出】surrender; hand over: ～武器 *surrender one's weapons*
【交存】deposit; hand in for safekeeping: ～批准书 *deposit instruments of ratification*
【交错】❶ interlock; crisscross: 沟渠～。*Ditches and canals crisscross.* ❷［机］staggered: ～气缸 *stag-gered cylinder*
【交代】(又作'交待') ❶ hand over: ～工作 *hand over work to one's successor; brief one's successor on handing over work* ❷ explain; make clear; brief; tell: 作者对此未作进一步～。*The author makes no further reference to this.* ❸ account for; justify oneself: 这个问题你怎么～? *How are you going to account for this?* / ～不过去 *be unable to justify an action* ❹ confess: ～罪行 *confess a crime* / 彻底～ *make a clean breast of*
【交底】tell sb. what one's real intentions are; put all one's cards on the table
【交点】❶［数］point of intersection ❷［天］node: ～月 *nodical month*
【交锋】cross swords; engage in a battle or contest: 这两支足球队将在明天～。*The two football teams will face each other tomorrow.*
【交付】❶ pay: ～租金 *pay rent* ❷ hand over; de-

liver; consign: ～表决 *put to the vote* / 新建的楼房已经～使用。*The new building has been made available to the users.*

【交感神经】[生理] sympathetic nerve

【交割】complete a business transaction: 此项货款业已～。*The money for this consignment has already been paid.* ◇ ～延期费 backwardation

【交工】hand over a completed project

【交公】hand over to the collective or the state

【交媾】sexual intercourse; copulation

【交好】(of people or states) be on friendly terms

【交互】❶ each other; mutual: 学生～批改作业。*Students corrected each other's papers.* / ～校订译文 *check each other's translations* ❷ alternately; in turn: 两种策略～使用 *use the two tactics alternately* / 他两手～地抓住野藤爬上崖顶。*Holding on to the creepers, he climbed hand over hand to the top of the cliff.* ◇ ～处理 interactive processing; ～系统 interactive system; ～式 [计] interactive

【交还】give back; return: 他把书～给图书馆了。*He has returned the book to the library.*

【交换】exchange; swop: ～意见 *exchange views; compare notes* / ～场地[体] *change of courts, goals or ends* / ～文本 *exchange of texts (or copies)* ◇ ～齿轮 change gear; ～分保 exchange of reinsurance; ～价值 [经] exchange value; ～器 [电] converter

【交火】exchange shots; fight

【交货】delivery: 即期～ *prompt delivery* / 近期～ *near delivery* / 远期～ *forward delivery* / 分批～ *delivery by instalments; partial delivery* / 仓库～ *ex warehouse* / 船上～ *ex ship* / 铁路旁～ *ex rail* ◇ ～单 delivery order (D/O); ～港 port of delivery; ～期 date of delivery; ～前付款 cash before delivery; ～收据 delivery receipt

【交集】(of different feelings) be mixed; occur simultaneously ——另见〖百感交集〗;〖悲喜交集〗

【交际】social intercourse; communication: 语言是人们～的工具。*Language is the means by which people communicate with each other.* / 她～很广。*She has a large circle of acquaintances.* ◇ ～花 social butterfly; society woman; ～舞 (又作'交谊舞') ballroom dance; social dance

【交加】〈书〉(of two things) accompany each other; occur simultaneously: 雷电～ *lightning accompanied by peals of thunder; there was thunder and lightning* / 风雪～ *a raging snowstorm*

【交角】[数] angle of intersection

【交接】❶ join; connect: 夏秋～的季节 *when summer is changing into autumn* ❷ hand over and take over: ～班 *relief of a shift* / ～手续(仪式) *handing over procedure (ceremony)* ❸ associate with: 他所～的朋友 *the people he associates with; the friends he has made*

【交界】(of two or more places) have a common boundary: 三省～的地方 *a place where three provinces meet; the juncture of three provinces*

【交警】(〈略〉见〖交通警〗) traffic police; traffic policeman

【交卷】❶ hand in an examination paper ❷ fulfil one's task; carry out an assignment

【交口称誉】unanimously praise

【交流】exchange; interflow; interchange: ～经验 *exchange experience; draw on each other's experience* / 城乡物资～ *flow of goods and materials between city and country* / 国际文化～ *international cultural exchange* / 经济和技术～ *economic and technical interchange* ◇ ～电 alternating current (AC); ～发电机 alternating current generator; alternator; ～学者 visiting scholar under an exchange program

【交纳】pay (to the state or an organization); hand in: ～会费 *pay membership dues* / 照章～税款 *pay customs duty according to the regulation*

【交配】mating; copulation ◇ ～期 mating season

【交朋友】make friends: 与约翰～ *make friends with John* / 我们交了许多新朋友。*We have made a lot of new friends.*

【交浅言深】have a hearty talk with a casual acquaintance; give sincere advice to people one knows only slightly

【交情】friendship; friendly relations: 老～ *long-standing friendship* / 讲～ *do things for the sake of friendship* / 他们两人～不错。*The two of them are on very good terms.* ——另见〖套交情〗

【交融】blend; mingle ——另见〖水乳交融〗

【交涉】negotiate; make representations: 办～ *carry on negotiations with; take up a matter with* / 口头～ *verbal representations* / 经过～,问题解决了。*The problem was solved through negotiations.*

【交手】fight hand to hand; be engaged in a hand-to-hand fight; come to grips: 一言不合,两人交起手来。*The two came to grips after an exchange of hot words.* / 听说你棋下得不错,很想什么时候和你交交手。*I hear you are very good at chess. I'd like to play with you sometime.*

【交售】sell (to the state): 踊跃向国家～油菜籽 *enthusiastically sell rapeseed to the state*

【交税】pay tax: 他从不误～。*He is never late for paying tax.*

【交谈】talk with each other; converse; chat: 自由～ *a freewheeling conversation* / 他们就广泛的问题进行了友好的～。*They had a friendly conversation on a wide range of subjects.*

【交替】❶ supersede; replace: 新旧～。*The new replaces the old.* / 新旧体制的～ *in the transition from the old structure to the new* ❷ alternately; in turn: ～演奏两国乐曲 *play music of the two countries alternately*

【交通】❶ be connected; be linked: 阡陌～。*Linking paths lead everywhere.* ❷ traffic; communications: 公路～ *highway traffic* / 陆上～ *land traffic* / 市区～ *urban traffic* / ～便利 *have transport facilities* / 妨碍～ *interfere with the traffic* ❸ liaison; liaison man: ～员 *liaison man; underground messenger* ◇ ～安全 traffic safety; ～标线 traffic marking; ～标志 traffic sign; ～部 the Ministry of Communications; ～车 special bus (service); ～干线 main line of communication; main communications artery; ～高峰 traffic peak; rush hour; peak hour; ～工具 means of transportation; ～管理 traffic control; ～规则 traffic regulations; ～壕 [军] communication trench; ～警 traffic police; ～量 volume of traffic; ～流量 traffic flow; ～事故 traffic (or road) accident; ～网 network of communication lines; ～线 communication lines; communication routes; ～信号 traffic signal; ～要道 vital communication line; ～运输 communications and transportation; ～阻塞 traffic jam (or block)

【交头接耳】speak in each other's ears; whisper to each other

【交往】association; contact: 我和他～，得益不少。*I have gained a lot by associating with him.* / 两人～甚密。*The two of them often got together* / 他不大和人～。*He is unsociable.*

【交尾】mating; pairing; coupling

【交恶】fall foul of each other; become enemies: 自此两人～。*After that they grew to hate each other.*

【交相辉映】enhance each other's beauty: 湖光山色，～。*The lake and the hills enhance each other's beauty.*

【交响曲】[音] symphony

【交响诗】[音] symphonic poem; tone poem

【交响乐】[音] symphony; symphonic music ◇ ～队 symphony orchestra; philharmonic orchestra

【交心】lay one's heart bare; open one's heart to: 互相～ *have a heart-to-heart talk*

【交学费】❶〈字〉pay tuition fees ❷〈喻〉price paid for mistakes or losses: 难道我们～不够吗? 应该有些长进了! *Surely we've paid dearly for our mistakes and should have learnt something from them!*

【交验】hand over for examination (or checking): 必须向海关～许可证。*The licence must be produced for the customs office to examine.*

【交椅】❶ an ancient folding chair ❷ armchair: 坐第二把～ *occupy the second highest post; be second in command*

【交易】business; deal; trade; transaction: 现款～ *cash transaction* / 赊账～ *credit transaction* / 期货～ *dealing in futures* / ～额 *volume of trade* ◇ ～会 trade fair; commodities fair; ～量 volume of business, volume of trade; ～市场 the trading market; ～税 trade tax; transaction tax

【交易所】exchange ◇ ～经纪人费用 exchange brokerage; ～术语 stock exchange expression; stock exchange parlance

【交谊】〈书〉friendship; friendly relations

【交谊舞】"friendship dance"—social dance; ballroom dance

【交游】〈书〉make friends: ～甚广 *have a large circle of friends*

【交战】be at war; fight; wage war: ～状态 *state of war; belligerency* / ～行为 *belligerent act* / ～的一方 *a belligerent* / ～双方 *the two belligerent parties* ◇ ～国 belligerent countries (or states, nations)

【交账】❶ hand over the accounts ❷ account for: 把小孩冻坏了，我们怎么向他母亲～? *If the child catches a chill, what are we going to say to its mother?*

【交织】interweave; intertwine; mingle: 用羊毛和蚕丝～ *interweave wool with silk* / 惊异和喜悦的感情～在一起。*Joy mingled with surprise.*

郊 名 suburbs; outskirts: 京～ *the suburbs of Beijing* / 西～ *the western suburbs*

【郊区】suburban district; suburbs; outskirts

【郊外】the countryside around a city; outskirts

【郊县】suburbs and counties under the jurisdiction of a large city: 北京的～ *suburbs and counties of Beijing*

【郊游】outing; excursion

茭 名〈书〉hay

【茭白】(又作'茭瓜')[植] wild rice stem

浇 动 ❶ pour liquid on; sprinkle water on: 大雨～得他全身都湿透了。*He was drenched with rain.* ❷ irrigate; water: ～花 *water flowers* / ～地 *irrigate the fields* ❸ [刷] cast: ～铅字 *type casting; type founding*

【浇版】[刷] casting: ～机 *casting machine*

【浇灌】❶ water; irrigate ❷ pour: ～混凝土 *pour concrete*

【浇口】[冶] runner

【浇注】❶ pour (melted metal, cement mixed with water, etc.) into a mould ❷ devote (one's energies, etc.) to: 他把全部心血都～在事业上。*He put his heart and soul into advancing the cause.*

【浇铸】[冶] casting; pouring: ～机 *casting machine*

娇 Ⅰ 形 ❶ tender; lovely; charming: 嫩红～绿 *tender blossoms and delicate leaves* ❷ fragile; frail; delicate: 这孩子身体太～。*The child's health is fragile.* ❸ squeamish; finicky: 她才走几里地就叫苦，未免太～了。*She started grumbling after walking only a few li. She's really too soft.* Ⅱ 动 pamper; spoil: 别把你的小女儿～坏了! *Don't pamper your little daughter.*

【娇嗔】grumble in a flirtish manner

【娇滴滴】delicately pretty; affectedly sweet: ～的声音 *a sweet and charming voice*

【娇惯】pamper; coddle; spoil: ～孩子 *pamper a child*

【娇贵】❶ spoiled; coddled ❷ delicate and fragile: 仪表～，要小心轻放。*The apparatus is fragile and should be handled with care.*

【娇憨】lovely and innocent

【娇客】❶ son-in-law ❷ a pampered person
【娇媚】❶ coquettish; flirtatious ❷ sweet and charming: ～的牡丹，在百花丛中最鲜艳。*The sweet and charming peony is the most beautiful among the flowers.*
【娇嫩】❶ tender and lovely ❷ fragile; delicate: ～的幼苗 *delicate seedlings* / ～的身子 *delicate health*
【娇娘】beautiful young lady
【娇妻】a beloved wife; a pretty young wife
【娇气】❶ fragile; delicate: 你的身子也太～了，淋这么几滴雨就感冒。*You're really too delicate, catching cold from just a few drops of rain.* ❷ squeamish; finicky: 粗粮细粮一样吃，别那么～。*Coarse grain is just as good as fine. Don't be so finicky.* / 去掉～ *get rid of squeamishness*
【娇娆】enchantingly beautiful
【娇弱】tender and delicate; frail and delicate: ～的姑娘 *frail and delicate girl* / ～的声音 *tender and weak voice*
【娇生惯养】have been delicately brought up; be pampered and spoiled: 她自幼～，未受过一日委屈。*She's always lived in comfort, never had to put up with a single day's bad treatment.*
【娇态】sweet and charming manner: 故作～ *put on a sweet and charming air*
【娇小】petite; delicate: ～的女孩子 *a cute little girl*
【娇小玲珑】delicate and exquisite; petite and dainty: 这姑娘长得～。*She is a dainty little girl.*
【娇艳】delicate and charming; tender and beautiful: ～的桃花 *delicate and charming peach blossoms*
【娇纵】indulge (a child); pamper; spoil

骄 形 ❶ proud; arrogant; conceited: 骄傲 ❷ 〈文〉fierce; intense: 骄阳
【骄傲】❶ arrogant; conceited: 我们永远不能～，不能翘尾巴。*We should never become arrogant and cocky.* ❷ be proud; take pride in: 老科学家为青年同志的成就感到～。*The old scientist takes pride in the achievements of his young colleagues.* ❸ pride: 民族的～ *the pride of the nation*
【骄傲自大】self-important; conceited and arrogant
【骄傲自满】conceited and self-satisfied; arrogant and complacent
【骄兵必败】an army puffed up with pride is bound to lose
【骄横】arrogant and imperious; overbearing
【骄矜】〈书〉self-important; proud; haughty: 他为人谦逊，毫无～之态。*He is modest, and never puts on airs.*
【骄气】overbearing airs; arrogance
【骄奢淫逸】lordly, luxury-loving, loose-living and idle; wallowing in luxury and pleasure; extravagant and dissipated
【骄阳】〈文〉blazing sun: ～似火 *a scorching sun beating down*
【骄子】favourite son (usu.〈喻〉): 天之骄子
【骄纵】arrogant and wilful

姣 形 〈文〉handsome; beautiful-looking
【姣好】〈文〉beautiful and charming

胶 Ⅰ 名 ❶ glue; gum ❷ rubber Ⅱ 动 stick with glue; glue Ⅲ 形 gluey; sticky; gummy
【胶版】offset plate ◇ ～打样机 offset proof press; ～纸 offset paper
【胶版印刷】offset printing; offset lithography; offset: ～机 *offset press*; *offset (printing) machine*
【胶布】❶ rubberized fabric ❷〈口〉adhesive plaster ◇ ～带［电］rubberized tape; adhesive tape
【胶带】rubberized tape; adhesive tape
【胶合】glue together; veneer ◇ ～板 plywood; veneer board
【胶结】glued; cemented ◇ ～材料 cementing material; ～剂 cementing agent
【胶卷】roll film; film
【胶轮】rubber tyre: ～大车 *rubber-tyred cart*
【胶木】bakelite
【胶囊】capsule
【胶泥】❶ clay ❷［化］daub
【胶粘剂】adhesive
【胶凝作用】［化］gelation
【胶皮】❶ (vulcanized) rubber ❷〈方〉rickshaw
【胶片】film: 正色～ *orthochromatic film* / 缩微～ *microfiche* ◇ ～阅读器 film reader
【胶乳】［化］latex: 硫化～ *vulcanized latex*; *vultex*
【胶水】mucilage; glue
【胶体】［化］colloid ◇ ～化学 colloid chemistry
【胶鞋】rubber overshoes; galoshes; rubbers
【胶靴】high rubber overshoes; galoshes
【胶着】deadlocked; stalemated: ～状态 *deadlock*; *stalemate*; *impasse*

教 动 teach; instruct: 她～我们做实验。*She taught us how to conduct experiments.* ——另见 jiào
【教书】teach school; teach: 在小学～ *teach in a primary school*
【教书匠】〈贬〉pedagogue
【教书先生】school teacher
【教书育人】impart knowledge and educate people
【教学】teach

焦 Ⅰ 形 ❶ burnt; scorched; charred: 饼烤～了。*The pancake is burnt.* / 树被烧～了。*The trees are charred.* ❷ worried; anxious: 心焦 Ⅱ 名 coke: 炼焦
【焦脆】❶ (of food) turn crisp after being baked or fried: ～的麻花 *crisp fried dough twist* ❷ (of a voice, sound, etc.) clear; crisp: ～的枪声 *clear shots*
【焦比】［冶］coke ratio
【焦点】❶［物］focal point; focus: 主～ *prime (or principal) focus* / 虚～ *virtual focus* ❷ central

issue; point at issue: 这就是问题的～。*That is the heart of the matter.* / 争论的～ *the point at issue*

【焦耳】[物] joule

【焦黑】burned black

【焦化】[化] coking: 延迟～ *delayed coking*

【焦黄】sallow; brown: 脸色～ *a sallow face* / 把馒头烤得～ *toast a steamed bun brown*

【焦急】anxious; worried: 你不必为钱～。*You need not worry yourself about money.* / 大家都在～地等着他。*Everyone is waiting for him anxiously.*

【焦痂】[医] eschar

【焦距】[物] focal distance; focal length

【焦渴】terribly thirsty; parched

【焦枯】shrivelled; dried up; withered

【焦虑】feel anxious; have worries and misgivings: 我为她的健康感到～。*I am anxious about her health.*

【焦煤】coking coal

【焦炭】coke

【焦头烂额】in a sorry plight; in a terrible fix: 麻烦事一大堆,弄得他～。*He was in a sorry plight, weighed down by numerous troublesome problems.*

【焦土】scorched earth—ravages of war ◇ ～政策 scorched earth policy

【焦心】〈方〉feel terribly worried

【焦油】[化] tar

【焦躁】restless with anxiety; impatient: 克服～情绪 *curb one's impatience*

【焦灼】〈书〉deeply worried; very anxious

椒 名 any of several hot spice plants: 辣椒 / 胡椒

【椒盐】a condiment made of roast prickly ash and salt; spiced salt

蕉 名 any of several broadleaf plants: 香蕉

【蕉麻】abaca; Manila hemp

跤 名 fall: 摔了一～ have a fall

礁 名 reef

【礁石】reef; rock

jiáo

嚼 动 masticate; chew; munch: 吃东西好好～,容易消化。*If you chew your food properly it is easier to digest.* ——另见 jué

【嚼舌】(又作'嚼舌头';'嚼舌根') ❶ wag one's tongue; chatter; gossip: 别在背后～。*Don't gossip behind people's backs.* ❷ argue meaninglessly; squabble: 没功夫跟你～。*I've got no time to argue with you.*

【嚼烟】chewing tobacco

【嚼子】bit (of a bridle)

jiǎo

角 Ⅰ 名 ❶ horn: 牛～ *ox horn* ❷ bugle; horn: 号角 ❸ sth. in the shape of a horn: 菱角 ❹ cape; promontory; headland: 好望～ *the Cape of Good Hope* ❺ corner: 桌子～儿 *the corner of a table* / 信息～ *information corner* / 英语～ *English corner* ❻ [数] angle: 三十度的～ *an angle of 30 degrees* Ⅱ 量 a fractional unit of money in China (= 1 / 10 *of a yuan or* 10 *fen*)——另见 jué

【角尺】angle square

【角动量】[物] angular momentum

【角度】❶ [数] angle: 撑条和横梁之间～太大。*The brace is at too big an angle with the beam.* ❷ point of view; angle: 从各个～来研究问题 *examine the matter from various angles*

【角度计】goniometer; angle gauge

【角钢】angle iron

【角弓反张】[医] opisthotonos

【角规】angle gauge

【角砾岩】breccia

【角楼】a watchtower at a corner of a city wall; corner tower; turret

【角落】corner; nook: 在院子的一个～里 *in a corner of the courtyard* / 找遍每一个～ *search every nook and cranny; search high and low* / 躲在阴暗的～里搞阴谋诡计 *plot in a dark corner*

【角马】gnu

【角门】side gate

【角膜】[生理] cornea ◇ ～混浊 opacity of the cornea; ～炎 keratitis; ～移植术 corneal transplantation; keratoplasty

【角球】[体](足球) football corner (kick)

【角鲨】spiny dogfish

【角闪石】hornblende

【角速度】[物] angular velocity

【角铁】同〖角钢〗

【角质】[生] cutin: ～层 *cuticle (of plants)*

【角柱体】prism

【角锥体】pyramid

侥 (构词成分)见下

【侥幸】lucky; by luck; by a fluke: ～取胜 *gain victory by sheer good luck; win by a fluke* / ～心理 *the idea of leaving things to chance; trusting to luck*

佼 形 〈书〉handsome; beautiful

【佼佼】〈书〉above average; outstanding: ～者 *an outstanding figure; a giant among dwarfs*

狡 形 crafty; foxy; cunning

【狡辩】quibble; indulge in sophistry: 任何～都不能掩盖事实真相。*No amount of sophistry can cover up the truth.*

【狡猾】sly; crafty; cunning; tricky

【狡计】crafty trick; ruse

【狡赖】deny (by resorting to sophistry): 证据确凿,不容～。*It's no use denying it; the evidence is conclusive.*
【狡兔三窟】a wily hare has three burrows —a crafty person has more than one hideout
【狡黠】〈书〉sly; crafty; cunning
【狡诈】deceitful; crafty; cunning

绞 Ⅰ 动 ❶ twist; wring; entangle: 把几股铁丝～在一起 *twist several strands of wire together* / 把衣服～干 *wring out wet clothes* / 心如刀～ *feel as if a knife were being twisted in one's heart* ❷ wind: ～动辘轳 *wind a windlass* ❸ hang by the neck ❹ [机] bore with a reamer; ream: ～孔 *ream a hole* Ⅱ 量 skein; hank: 一～毛线 *a skein of woollen yarn*
【绞肠痧】[中] dry cholera
【绞车】winch; windlass
【绞刀】[机] reamer
【绞架】gallows
【绞尽脑汁】rack one's brains
【绞盘】capstan
【绞肉机】meat mincer; mincing machine
【绞杀】strangle
【绞纱】[纺] skein: ～染色 *skein dyeing*
【绞索】(the hangman's) noose
【绞痛】[医] angina: 肚子～ *abdominal angina; colic*
【绞刑】death by hanging: ～架 *gallows*

饺 名 dumpling: 水饺
【饺子】dumpling (with meat and vegetable stuffing): ～皮 *dumpling wrapper* / ～馅 *filling for dumplings; stuffing*

皎 形 clear and bright: ～月当空。*A bright moon hung in the sky.*
【皎皎】very clear and bright; glistening white
【皎洁】(of moonlight) bright and clear

铰 动〈口〉cut with scissors: ～一件男衬衣 *cut out a shirt* / ～成两半 *cut in two; cut into halves; cut in half*
【铰接】[机] join with a hinge; articulate: ～式大客车 *articulated bus*
【铰链】hinge: ～接合 *hinge joint*

脚 名 ❶ foot: 看他那两只～。*Look at his two feet.* ❷ base; foot: 墙脚
【脚背】instep
【脚本】script; scenario: 电影～ *film script*
【脚脖子】〈方〉ankle
【脚步】step; pace: 加快～ *quicken one's pace* / 放轻～ *walk softly* / ～声 *footfall; footsteps*
【脚灯】[戏] footlights
【脚蹬子】pedal; treadle
【脚底板】〈方〉sole (of the foot)
【脚垫】callus on the sole (of the foot)
【脚法】kicking skill
【脚夫】〈旧〉❶ porter ❷ one who hires out his donkey or horse to riders and leads or follows it on foot
【脚跟】(又作'脚根') heel
【脚光】footlight
【脚后跟】heel
【脚尖】the tip of a toe; tiptoe: 踮着～走 *walk on tiptoe*
【脚劲】〈方〉strength of one's legs
【脚力】strength of one's legs: 他一天能走一百里,～真好。*He's really got strong legs to be able to walk 100 li a day.*
【脚镣】fetters; shackles
【脚炉】foot warmer; foot stove
【脚轮】castor (on furniture, luggage, etc.)
【脚面】instep
【脚盆】a basin for washing feet
【脚蹼】flippers
【脚气】❶ [医] beriberi ❷〈口〉athlete's foot
【脚手架】scaffold; scaffolding
【脚踏板】treadle (of a sewing machine, etc.)
【脚踏车】〈方〉bicycle
【脚踏两只船】straddle two boats—have a foot in either camp; sit on the fence
【脚踏实地】have one's feet planted on solid ground—earnest and down-to-earth: 既要有远大的理想,又要～地干 *have both an ambitious goal and a down-to-earth style of work*
【脚踏脱粒机】pedal thresher
【脚踏游艇】pedal boat
【脚心】the underside of the arch (of the foot); arch
【脚癣】ringworm of the foot; tinea pedis; athlete's foot
【脚丫子】(又作'脚鸭子')〈方〉foot
【脚印】footprint; footmark; track: 侦察兵在雪地上发现了可疑的～。*The scouts discovered suspicious footprints in the snow.*
【脚掌】sole (of the foot)
【脚正不怕鞋歪】a straight foot is not afraid of a crooked shoe—an upright man fears no gossip
【脚指甲】toenail
【脚指头】〈口〉toe
【脚趾】toe
【脚注】footnote
【脚镯】ankle bangle

矫 Ⅰ 动 ❶ rectify; straighten out; correct: 矫正 ❷ pretend; feign; dissemble: ～命 *counterfeit an order; issue false orders* Ⅱ 形 strong; brave: ～若游龙 *as powerful as a flying dragon; as strong and brave as a lion*
【矫健】strong and vigorous: ～的步伐 *vigorous strides*
【矫捷】vigorous and nimble; brisk
【矫情】〈书〉be affectedly unconventional
【矫揉造作】affected; artificial: ～的姿态 *affected manners*
【矫饰】feign in order to conceal sth.; dissemble: 这篇文章语言质朴,毫无～。*This article is writ-*

ten in a simple style, free from any kind of affectation.

【矫枉过正】exceed the proper limits in righting a wrong; overcorrect

【矫形】[医] orthopaedics ◇ ～术 orthopaedics; ～外科 orthopaedic surgery; ～医生 orthopaedist

【矫正】correct; put right; rectify: ～发音 *correct sb.'s pronunciation mistakes* / ～偏差 *correct a deviation* / ～口吃 *correct a stammer* / ～视力 *correct defects of vision*

【矫直机】[冶] straightening machine; straightener

搅 动 ❶ stir; mix: 把粥～一～ *give the porridge a stir* ❷ disturb; annoy: 她在工作，别～她。*She's working. Don't disturb her.*

【搅拌】stir; agitate; mix: 把农药和种子～在一起 *mix insect powder with seed* ◇ ～机 mixer; ～器 stirrer; agitator

【搅棒】string rod

【搅动】mix; stir: 拿棍子～灰浆 *stir the plaster with a stick*

【搅浑】stir and make muddy; deliberately create confusion ——另见〖把水搅浑〗

【搅混】〈口〉mix; blend; mingle: 歌声和笑声～成一片。*Singing and laughing were mingled together.*

【搅和】〈口〉❶ mix; blend; mingle: 这是两码事，别～在一起。*They are two different matters. Don't mix them up.* ❷ mess up; spoil: 事情都让他～糟了。*He's messed everything up.* or *He's made a mess of everything.*

【搅局】upset the apple cart; make a mess of sth.: 这个人爱～，谁都不愿同他共事。*As he is a troublemaker, no one likes to work together with him.*

【搅乱】confuse; throw into disorder: 这消息～了她的心。*The news disturbed her very much.*

【搅扰】disturb; annoy; bother: 你姐姐在做功课，别去～。*Your sister is doing her homework. Don't disturb her.* / 对不起，～了。*Sorry to have bothered you.*

剿 动 send armed forces to suppress; put down

【剿除】exterminate; wipe out

【剿匪】suppress bandits

【剿灭】exterminate; wipe out: 土匪都～了。*The bandits were all wiped out.*

缴 动 ❶ pay; hand over; hand in: ～税 *pay taxes* ❷ capture: 他们～了三挺机枪。*They captured three machine guns.*

【缴获】capture; seize: ～很多战利品 *seize a lot of booty* / 一切～要归公。*Turn in everything captured.*

【缴枪】❶ (of enemy) hand over arms; surrender: ～不杀! *Lay down your arms and we'll spare your lives!* ❷ capture the enemy's guns: 缴了十支枪 *have captured ten rifles*

【缴销】*hand in for cancellation*: ～营业执照 *hand in the business licence for cancellation*

【缴械】❶ disarm: 他从后面悄悄爬过来，缴了那人的械。*He crept up from behind and managed to disarm the man.* ❷ surrender one's weapons; lay down one's arms: ～投降 *lay down one's arms and surrender*

jiào

叫 Ⅰ 动 ❶ cry; shout: 大～一声 *give a loud cry; shout; cry out loudly* / 汽笛在～。*The steam whistle is blowing.* ❷ call; greet: 外边有人～你。*Somebody outside is calling you.* / 你的电话～通了。*Your call has been put through.* / 这孩子腼腆，不爱～人。*The child is shy and doesn't like to greet people.* ❸ hire; order: ～个出租汽车 *hire (or call) a taxi* / ～二百斤煤 *order 200 jin of coal* ❹ name; call: 人们～他小张。*People call him Xiao Zhang.* / 他～什么名儿? *What's his name?* ❺ ask; order: ～他进来吗? *Shall I ask him (to come) in?* / 医生～她卧床休息。*The doctor ordered her to stay in bed.* ❻ permit; allow: 他哥哥不～他去。*His brother did not allow him to go.* Ⅱ 介 (used in a passive sentence to introduce the doer of the action): ～你猜着了。*You've guessed right.* / 你～雨淋湿了吗? *Did you get wet?*

【叫菜】choose dishes from a menu; order dishes (in a restaurant)

【叫喊】shout; yell; howl: 高声～ *shout at the top of one's voice* / 他把嗓子都～哑了。*He shouted himself hoarse.*

【叫好】applaud; shout "bravo!"; shout "well done!"

【叫号】❶ call a number: 看病的人都坐在门外等候护士～。*Registered patients are all waiting outside of the door for the nurse to call their numbers.* ❷〈方〉sing a work song to synchronize movements, with one person leading: 几个小伙子叫着号把大木头抬起来。*Several young fellows managed to lift the big woodblock by chanting a work song.* ❸〈方〉provoke by words; challenge: 他这样说简直是在～。*He is deliberately trying to kick up a row.*

【叫花子】(又作'叫化子')〈口〉beggar

【叫唤】❶ cry out; call out: 疼得直～ *cry out with pain* / 咬紧牙关，一声也不～ *clench one's teeth and not utter a sound* ❷ (of animals, birds, insects, etc.) cry; call: 小鸟儿在树上叽叽喳喳地～。*Birds are chirping in the tree.*

【叫价】bid

【叫绝】applaud as the very best (one has seen, etc.); shout "Bravo!": 拍案～ *applaud by thumping the table; thump the table and shout "Bravo!"*

【叫苦】complain of hardship or suffering; moan and groan: 暗暗～ *groan inwardly*

【叫苦不迭】complain incessantly; pour out endless

grievances

【叫苦连天】complain to high heaven; complain bitterly

【叫骂】shout curses: 他在一片～声中跑掉了。*He ran off amid shouts of cursing.*

【叫卖】cry one's wares; peddle; hawk: 沿街～ *hawk one's wares in the streets*

【叫门】call at the door to be let in

【叫牌】make a bid at bridge; bid: 你～了没有? *Have you bid yet?* / 该谁～? *Whose call is it?*

【叫屈】complain of being wronged; protest against an injustice

【叫嚷】shout; howl; clamour

【叫嚣】clamour; raise a hue and cry: 发出战争～ *clamour for war* / 大肆～ *raise a terrific hue and cry*; *raise a hullabaloo*

【叫醒】wake up; awaken

【叫阵】challenge an opponent to a fight when two armies meet

【叫座】draw a large audience; draw well; appeal to the audience; be a box-office success: 这出戏很～。*The play is a great box-office success.*

【叫做】(又作'叫作') be called; be known as: 这种机器～起重机。*This machine is called a crane.* / 你这～自作自受,没人可怜你。*This is what I call stewing in your own juice. Nobody feels sorry for you.*

觉 名 sleep: 一～醒来 *wake from one's sleep* ——另见 jué

校 动 check; proofread; collate: ～长条样 *read galley proofs* / 四～ *the fourth proof*; *proofread for the fourth time* ——另见 xiào

【校次】number of times a proof is read before publishing: 第三～ *The third proof*, *proofread for the third time*

【校订】check against the authoritative text

【校对】❶ proofread; proof ❷ proofreader ❸ check against a standard; calibrate: 一切计量器都必须～合格才可以出厂。*All measuring instruments must be calibrated before leaving the factory.* ◇ ～符号 proofreader's mark; ～机 collator

【校改】read and correct proofs

【校勘】collate ◇ ～学 textual criticism

【校样】proof sheet; proof: 已看完～ *have read the proofs* / 付印～ *final proof* / 长条～ *galley proof*

【校阅】read and revise

【校正】proofread and correct; rectify: ～错字 *correct misprints*

【校准】[机] calibration: 方位～ *bearing calibration* / ～器 *calibrator*

较 Ⅰ 动 ❶ compare; contrast: 相较 ❷〈书〉dispute: 锱铢必较 Ⅱ 介 (used to compare a difference in degree): 工作～前更为努力 *work even harder than before* Ⅲ 副 comparatively; relatively; fairly; quite; rather: ～好 *fairly good*; *quite good* / ～差 *relatively poor* / 有～大的进步 *have made considerable progress* Ⅳ 形〈书〉clear; obvious; marked: 二者～然不同。*There is a marked difference between the two.*

【较比】〈方〉comparatively; relatively; fairly; quite

【较劲】〈方〉match strength: 较一较劲儿 *have a trial of strength*

【较量】❶ measure one's strength with; have a contest; have a trial (or test) of strength: 经过反复的～ *after repeated trials of strength* ❷ haggle; argue; dispute

【较为】comparatively; relatively; fairly: 这本书～便宜。*This book is comparatively cheap.*

【较真】(又作'叫真')〈方〉serious; earnest: 老王干活可～儿啦,你可别马马虎虎的。*Lao Wang is very serious with work, so don't be lackadaisical.*

轿 名 sedan (chair): 花轿

【轿车】❶〈旧〉(horse-drawn) carriage ❷ bus or car: 大～ *bus*; *coach* / 小～ *car*; *limousine*; *sedan*

【轿夫】〈旧〉sedan-chair bearer

【轿子】sedan (chair) ——另见〖抬轿子〗

教 Ⅰ 动 ❶ teach; instruct: 受～于名师 *be taught by a great master* / ～子务农 *encourage one's children to go in for farming* Ⅱ 名 religion: 信～ *believe in a religion*; *be religious* ——另见 jiāo

【教案】teaching plan; lesson plan

【教本】textbook

【教鞭】(teacher's) pointer

【教材】teaching material

【教参】(〈略〉全称为'教学参考资料') reference material used in teaching: ～销售量最大。*The sales volume of reference material for teaching is the largest.*

【教程】❶ course of study ❷ (published) lectures: 《近代史～》*A Course in Modern History*

【教导】❶ instruct; teach; give guidance ❷ teaching; guidance: 师长的～记心间 *bear in mind the teacher's instructions* ◇ ～员 (battalion) political instructor

【教德】teaching ethics; ethics of the teaching profession

【教范】[军] manual: 兵器～ *a manual of arms*; *manual*

【教父】godfather

【教改】educational reform

【教工】teaching and administrative staff (of a school)

【教官】〈旧〉drillmaster; instructor

【教规】rules of a religion; canon

【教化】〈书〉enlighten by education

【教皇】pope; pontiff ◇ ～通谕 Papal Encyclical

【教会】(the Christian) church ◇ ～学校 missionary school

【教诲】〈书〉teaching; instruction: 谆谆～ *earnest*

teachings

【教籍】teaching post：他辞去了美术学院的～。*He resigned his teaching post at the Academy of Fine Arts.*

【教具】teaching aid

【教科书】textbook

【教练】❶ train；drill；coach：持枪～ *drill with weapons* / 徒手～ *drill without weapons* ❷ coach；instructor；trainer：足球～ *football coach* / ～兼队员 *playing coach* / 主～ *head coach* ◇ ～车 learner-driven vehicle；～船 training ship；～弹 practice projectile；dummy projectile；dummy；～机 trainer aircraft；trainer；～员 coach；instructor；trainer

【教龄】length of service as a teacher：有四十年～的教员 *a teacher of* 40 *years' standing*

【教母】godmother

【教派】religious sect；denomination

【教区】parish；diocese

【教师】teacher；schoolteacher ◇ ～节 Teacher's Day (Sept. 10，initiated in 1985)

【教士】priest；clergyman；Christian missionary

【教室】classroom；schoolroom

【教授】❶ professor ❷ instruct；teach：～历史 *teach history* ◇ ～法 teaching methods；pedagogics

【教唆】instigate；abet；put sb. up to sth.：谁～他们这样做的呢? *Who instigated them to do this?* / ～不满十八岁的人犯罪的，应当从重处罚。*One who instigates a person under the age of eighteen to commit a crime shall be given a heavier punishment.* ◇ ～犯 abettor；instigater；～罪 guilt of instigation to a crime

【教堂】church；cathedral

【教条】dogma；doctrine；creed；tenet

【教条主义】dogmatism；doctrinairism：～者 *dogmatist*；*doctrinaire*

【教廷】the Vatican；the Holy See ◇ ～大使 nuncio；～公使 internuncio

【教徒】believer (or follower) of a religion

【教委】commission of education

【教务】educational administration ◇ ～处 Dean's Office；～长 Dean of Studies

【教学】❶ teaching；education：～内容 *content of courses* ❷ teaching and studying ❸ teacher and student ◇ ～测试 instructional testing；～大纲 teaching programme；syllabus；～法 teaching methods；pedagogics；～方针 principles of teaching；～改革 transformation of education；reform in education；educational reform；～节目 teaching program；～设计 instructional design

【教学相长】teaching benefits teacher and student alike；teaching benefits teachers as well as students

【教训】❶ lesson；moral：血的～ *a lesson paid for with blood*；*lesson written in blood* / 吸取～ *draw a lesson (or moral) from sth.*；*take warning from sth.* ❷ chide；teach sb. a lesson；give sb. a talking-to；lecture sb. (for wrongdoing, etc.)：他～了儿子一顿。*He gave his son a lecture.*

【教研室】teaching and research section

【教研组】teaching and research group

【教养】❶ bring up；train；educate ❷ breeding；upbringing；education；culture：他是个很有～的人。*He is a man of fine breeding.* / 他家的孩子都很有～。*All his children are well brought up.*

【教养所】penitentiary where those who have committed misdemeanors that are not serious enough for a jail sentence are reeducated through labor ——另见〖劳动教养〗

【教养员】kindergarten teacher

【教义】religious doctrine；creed

【教益】〈书〉benefit gained from sb.'s wisdom；enlightenment

【教友会】the Society of Friends；the Quakers

【教育】❶ education：他受过大学～。*He has had a college education.* / 他没受过什么～。*He didn't receive much education.* ❷ teach；educate；inculcate：她～孩子懂礼貌。*She teaches her children to have good manners.* / 那本书起了巨大的～作用。*That book has played a great educative role.* ◇ ～程度 level of education；～电视 educational television；～方针 policy for education；educational policy；～革命 revolution in education；～家 educationist；educator；～界 educational circles；～投资 educational investment；～心理学 educational psychology；～学 pedagogy；pedagogics；education；～哲学 educational philosophy；～制度 system of education

【教员】teacher；instructor：汉语～ *a teacher of Chinese* ◇ ～休息室 staff room；common room

【教长】religion imam；dean：坎特伯雷～ *Dean of Canterbury*

【教长国】[宗](伊斯兰教) imamate

【教职员】teaching and administrative staff

【教主】the founder of a religion

窖 Ⅰ 名 cellar or pit for storing things：这个～是用来储存蔬菜的。*This cellar is used for storing vegetables.* Ⅱ 动 store sth. in a cellar or pit

【窖藏】store sth. in a cellar or pit

酵 名 ferment；leaven

【酵母】yeast ◇ ～菌 saccharomycete

【酵素】[化] ferment；enzyme

jiē

节 (构词成分)见下 ——另见 jié

【节骨眼】〈方〉critical juncture；vital link：就在这个～上，援军赶到了。*At this critical moment reinforcements rushed up.* / 你回来得正是～上! *You've come back in the nick of time!*

阶 名 ❶ steps；stairs：台阶 ❷ rank：官阶

【阶层】(social) stratum：社会～ *social stratum* / 特权～ *privileged stratum*

【阶地】[林] terrace

【阶段】❶ stage; phase: 过渡～ *transitional stage* / 战役的最后～ *the final phase of the campaign* ❷ [矿] level: ～高度 *level interval*

【阶级】❶〈书〉steps; stairs ❷ (social) class ◇ ～报复 class vengeance; ～本能 class instinct; ～本质 class nature; ～成分 class status; ～斗争 class struggle; ～队伍 class ranks; ～分化 class polarization; ～分析 class analysis; ～感情 class feeling; ～根源 class origin; ～观点 class viewpoint; ～教育 class education; ～觉悟 class consciousness; ～烙印 brand of a class; ～立场 class stand; ～路线 class line; ～矛盾 class contradictions; ～社会 class society; ～性 class character; class nature; ～异己分子 alien-class element; individual from an alien class; ～阵线 class alignment

【阶梯】a flight of stairs; ladder: 进身的～ *stepping stone* ◇ ～教室 lecture theatre

【阶下囚】prisoner; captive

疖 名 furuncle; boil

【疖子】furuncle; boil

皆 副〈书〉all; each and every: 人人～知。*It is known to all.* or *It is public knowledge.*

【皆大欢喜】everybody is happy; to the satisfaction of all

结 动 bear (fruit); form (seed): 这些花～子儿了。*These flowers have gone to seed.* ——另见 jié

【结巴】❶ stammer; stutter ❷ stammerer; stutterer

【结果】(jiēguǒ) bear fruit; fructify: 这棵树去年结了好多果儿。*This tree bore a lot of fruit last year.* ——另见 jiéguǒ

【结实】❶ solid; sturdy; durable: 一双～的鞋子 *a durable pair of shoes* / 这张桌子很～。*This is a very solid table.* / 拴～点儿。*Tie it fast.* ❷ strong; sturdy; tough: 个子不高但是长得很～ *short but sturdy*

接 动 ❶ come into contact with; come close to: 邻接 ❷ connect; join; put together; continue: ～电线 *connect wires* / ～关系 *establish contact (as in underground work)* ❸ catch; take hold of: ～球 *catch a ball* ❹ receive: ～到一封信 *receive a letter* / ～电话 *answer the phone* ❺ meet; welcome: 到车站～人 *go to the station to meet sb.* ❻ take over: ～工作 *take over a job*

【接班】take one's turn on duty; take over from; succeed; carry on: 谁接你的班? *Who comes on duty after you?* or *Who takes over from you?* ◇ ～人 successor

【接办】accept and handle: ～案件 *accept and hear legal cases* / 由青年人～的上海"大世界"游乐中心 *the Great World recreational center managed by young people*

【接产】❶ practise midwifery ❷ deliver animals of their young

【接触】❶ come into contact with; get in touch with: 她的手～了硫酸,烧伤了。*Her hand came into contact with sulphuric acid and was burned.* ❷ engage: 与敌人～ *engage the enemy* / 小规模～ *a minor (or small-scale) engagement* ❸ [电] contact: ～不良 *loose (or poor) contact* / ～故障 *contact fault* ◇ ～传染 [医] contagion; ～炉 [化] contact furnace; ～眼镜 contact lens

【接待】receive; admit: ～外宾 *receive foreign guests* / 这饭店可以～八百位客人。*This hotel can accommodate 800 guests.* ◇ ～单位 host organization; ～人员 reception personnel; ～室 reception room; ～站 reception centre

【接待日】reception day

【接地】❶ [电] ground connection; grounding; earthing: ～线 *ground wire*; *earth lead* ❷ [航空] touchdown; ground contact: ～迎角 *landing angle*

【接点】[电] contact

【接二连三】one after another; in quick succession: 捷报～地传来。*Reports of victory came in one after another.*

【接发球】[体] receive; return of service

【接防】relieve a garrison; relieve: ～部队 *relieving unit*

【接风】give a dinner of welcome (to a visitor from afar)

【接羔】[牧] deliver lambs: ～房 *lamb-delivery room* / ～季节 *lambing season*

【接骨】set a (broken) bone; set a fracture

【接管】take over control; take over: ～产业 *take over the estate* / 在他～之前,那个部门是一团糟。*The department was in utter chaos until he took charge.*

【接轨】be in line with; be in agreement with

【接合】[机] joint: 气密～ *airtight joint* / 水密～ *watertight joint* / 螺栓～ *bolted joint* / ～器 *adapter* ◇ ～点 [军] junction point

【接活】accept work; receive an order

【接火】〈口〉❶ start to exchange fire: 先头部队跟敌人～了。*The advanced detachment has started to exchange fire with the enemy.* ❷ [电] energize: 电灯安好了,可还没～呢。*The lights have been fixed, but not yet connected to the mains.*

【接获】receive: ～订单 *receive orders for ...* / ～举报 *receive reports (on offences)*

【接济】give material assistance to; give financial help to: 他在困难的日子里生活靠朋友～。*In his difficult days, he relied on friends for financial assistance.*

【接见】receive sb.; grant an interview to: ～外宾 *receive foreign guests* / ～记者 *give an interview to reporters*

【接近】be close to; near; approach: ～国际水平 *approach the international level* / 该项工程～完成。*The project is nearing completion.* / 比分很～。*It was a close game.*

【接客】❶ (of a hotel, etc.) receive lodgers or

guests ❷ (of a prostitute) receive or sleep with a patron

【接口】interface

【接力】work by relays ◇ ～棒 relay baton；～赛跑 relay race；relay

【接连】on end；in a row；in succession：～好几天 *for days on end* / ～三小时 *for three hours at a stretch* / ～提出许多问题 *raise one question after another*

【接龙】(in cards or dominoes) build up a sequence

【接木】［植］grafting

【接目镜】eyepiece；ocular

【接纳】admit (into an organization)：～新会员 *admit new members* / ～某国加入联合国 *admit a state to membership in the United Nations*

【接片】splicing (of pieces of film)：～机 *splicer*

【接气】coherent：这一段跟上一段不太～。*This paragraph doesn't quite hang together with the preceding one.*

【接洽】take up a matter with；arrange (business, etc.) with；consult with：请同有关部门～。*Please take up the matter with the department concerned.*

【接壤】〈书〉border on；be contiguous to；be bounded by：法国和瑞士～。*France borders on Switzerland.* / ～地区 *contiguous areas*

【接任】take over a job；replace；succeed：她将～校长。*She will replace the present chancellor.*

【接生】deliver a child；practise midwifery ◇ ～婆〈旧〉midwife；～员 midwife

【接收】❶ receive：～礼物 *receive gifts* ❷［无］receive：～无线电信号 *receive radio signals* / ～机 *receiver* / ～天线 *receiving antenna*；*receiving aerial* ❸ take over (property, etc.)；expropriate：我们把他们的房子～过来了。*We've taken over their house.* ❹ admit：～新会员 *recruit new members*

【接手】❶ take over (duties, etc.)：这项工作我刚～，还不熟悉。*I'm new to the job*；*in fact, I've just taken over.* ❷［体］catcher

【接受】accept：～邀请 *accept an invitation* / ～辞职 *accept a resignation* / ～任务 *accept an assignment* / ～意见 *take sb.'s advice* / ～群众的监督 *subject oneself to supervision by the masses* / ～贿赂 *accept (or take) bribes* / 附保留～ *acceptance under reserve* ◇ ～国 accepting state；receiving state；～书 instrument of acceptance；～条款 acceptance clause

【接送】pick up

【接穗】［植］scion

【接替】take over；replace：已经派人来～他的工作。*A new person has been appointed to take over his work.* / 他～他父亲任商行经理。*He succeeded his father as manager of the firm.*

【接听】answer the phone

【接通】put through：电话～了吗？*Have you got through?*

【接头】❶ connect；join；joint ❷［纺］piecing；tying-in ❸〈口〉contact；get in touch with；meet：我找谁～？*Who shall I get in touch with?* / ～地点 *contact point*；*rendezvous* ❹ have knowledge of；know about：这事我不～。*I know nothing about it.*

【接吻】kiss

【接物镜】objective lens；objective

【接线】［电］wiring：～图 *wiring diagram*；*connection diagram* / ～箱 *junction box* / ～柱 *terminal*；*binding post* ◇ ～生〈旧〉switch board operator

【接续】continue；follow：此段应～前页末行。*This paragraph should follow the last line of the previous page.*

【接应】❶ come to sb.'s aid；coordinate with；reinforce：一排冲上去了，二排随后～。*Platoon One charged and was soon followed by Platoon Two.* ❷ supply：水泥一时～不上。*Cement was in short supply at the time.*

【接站】meet somebody at the station：去北京前她给家里发了个电报叫他们来～。*Before leaving for Beijing, she telegraphed her family to meet her at the station.*

【接着】❶ catch：给你一个苹果，～！*Here's an apple for you. Catch!* ❷ follow；carry on：一个～一个 *one after another* / 我～刚才的讲下去。*I'll continue from where I left off a moment ago.* ❸ after that；and then：～我们又讨论了明年的计划。*Next (or Then, After that), we discussed plans for the following year.*

【接诊】(of a doctor) see and treat patients；be consulted by patients

【接枝】［植］grafting

【接踵】〈书〉following on sb.'s heels

【接踵而来】(又作'接踵而至') follow hard at heel：来访者～。*Visitors came one after another.* / 水旱灾害～。*Flood and drought came one after the other.*

【接种】have an inoculation；inoculate：～防霍乱疫苗 *inoculate sb. against cholera* / ～牛痘疫苗 *be vaccinated*

秸 名 stalks left after threshing；straw：麦秸

【秸秆】straw：～肥 *compost made of stalks*

揭 动 ❶ tear off；take off：把墙上那幅画～下来。*Take that picture off the wall.* ❷ uncover；lift (the lid, etc.) ❸ expose；show up；bring to light：～矛盾，找差距 *expose contradictions and find out where one is lagging behind* ❹〈书〉raise；hoist：～竿为旗 *raise a bamboo pole to serve as a standard of revolt*

【揭榜】❶ announce the results of an examination ❷ tear off (or take off) a notice inviting applications for jobs, etc., from a wall as a sign of accepting the invitation

【揭不开锅】have nothing in the pot；have nothing to eat；go hungry：他们昨晚上就～了。*They have run out of food since last night.*

【揭穿】expose；lay bare；show up：～谎言 *expose*

a lie / ～假面具 *tear the mask off sb.'s face*; *unmask sb.* / ～骗局 *show up the fraud* / ～阴谋 *lay bare an evil plot*.

【揭底】reveal the inside story：揭了他的老底 *exposed his old secret*; *dragged the skeleton out of his closet*

【揭短】rake up sb.'s faults, shortcomings or weaknesses

【揭发】expose; unmask; bring to light：根据已经～的材料 according to facts already revealed / 我们～自己工作中的错误。目的是为了改正。*We expose mistakes in our work in order to correct them.*

【揭盖子】take the lid off sth.; bring sth. into the open

【揭竿而起】raise the standard of revolt; start an uprising; rise in rebellion：公元前209年，陈胜、吴广～，领导了中国历史上第一次农民大起义。*In 209 B. C. Chen Sheng and Wu Guang raised the standard of revolt and led China's first great peasant uprising.*

【揭开】uncover; reveal; open：～宇宙的奥秘 *reveal the secrets of the universe* / ～两国关系史上的新篇章 *open a new chapter in the annals of relations between the two countries*

【揭老底】reveal the inside story; disclose sb.'s unsavoury past; dredge up embarrassing facts about sb.'s past：老板尽可能地避开他的前妻，生怕她～儿。*The boss goes out of his way to avoid his ex-wife for fear that she might disclose his unsavoury past.*

【揭露】expose; unmask; ferret out：～阴谋 *expose the plot* / ～其真面目 *expose sb.'s true colours*; *show sb. up for what he is*

【揭秘】break a secret; unveil a mystery：由于有人～，丑闻才暴露于光天化日之下。*The scandal did not see the light of day until somebody disclosed some secret dealings.*

【揭幕】unveil (a monument, etc.); inaugurate：市长为展览会～。*The mayor inaugurated the exhibition.* ◇ ～式 unveiling ceremony

【揭示】❶ announce; promulgate ❷ reveal; bring to light：小说作者深刻地～了人物的内心世界。*The novelist subtly delineates the inner world of his characters.*

【揭帖】〈旧〉notice, poster

【揭晓】announce; make known; publish：选举结果已经～。*The result of the election has been published.*

嗟 动〈书〉sigh; lament：悲～ *sigh in sorrow*

【嗟来之食】food handed out in contempt; handouts

街 名 ❶ street ❷〈方〉country fair; market：赶～ *go to a fair*; *go to market*

【街道】❶ street ❷ residential district; neighbourhood ◇ ～办事处 subdistrict office; ～服务站 street service stations; ～工厂 neighbourhood factory; ～居民委员会 neighbourhood committee; residents' committee; ～企业 street-enterprises

【街灯】street lamp：几个老头在～下下棋。*Several old men were playing chess under a street lamp.*

【街坊】〈口〉neighbour：我们是～。*We are neighbours.*

【街垒】street barricade

【街貌】appearance of streets

【街面儿上】〈口〉❶ (activities, etc.) in the street：镇子不大，～倒挺热闹。*Small as the town is, it has a busy street.* or *Though small, the town boasts a busy street.* ❷ neighbourhood：～都知道他会修收音机。*Everybody in the neighbourhood knows he can repair radios.*

【街市】downtown streets

【街谈巷议】street gossip; the talk of the town：我会到各方面的人，听到许多的～。*I met all sorts of people and picked up a good deal of gossip.*

【街头】street corner; street：流落～ *tramp the streets*; *be down and out in a city* / 涌上～ *pour into the streets* ◇ ～剧 street-corner skit; street performance; ～时装表演 street fashion show

【街头巷尾】streets and lanes：～，到处都是欢乐的人群。*There are happy crowds in all the streets and lanes.* / ～议论纷纷。*You hear the affair discussed on the street corners everywhere and by everybody.*

【街心公园】parks at the intersections

jié

孑 形〈书〉lonely; all alone：孑然

【孑然】solitary; lonely; alone：◇ ～一身 *all alone in the world*

节 Ⅰ 名 ❶ joint; node; knot：竹～ *bamboo joint* / ～材 *nodal wood* ❷ division; part：音节 ❸ festival; red-letter day; holiday：过节 ❹ item：细节 ❺ moral integrity; chastity：气节 ❻ [航海] knot：现在船的速度是十八～。*The ship is making 18 knots* Ⅱ 代 section; length：一～铁管 *a length of iron pipe* / 两～课 *two periods*; *two classes* / 八～车厢 *eight railway coaches* / 第一章第二～ *Chapter One, Section Two* Ⅲ 动 ❶ abridge：节译 ❷ economize; save：～电 *economize on electricity* / ～煤 *economize on coal*; *save coal.* ——另见 jiē

【节哀】〈书〉restrain one's grief (used in offering one's condolences)

【节本】abridged edition; abbreviated version

【节操】〈书〉high moral principle; moral integrity

【节点】[电] node; panel point

【节电】save electricity

【节徽】emblem or motif of a festival or special occasion

【节汇】(〈略〉全称为'节约外汇') save foreign exchange：由于更多地使用国产零部件，北京今年预计可～两亿美元。*It's estimated that 200 million US dollars of foreign exchange will be saved this year in Beijing due to the increasing use of home-made parts.*

【节假日】festivals and holidays

【节俭】thrifty；frugal：提倡～ *encourage frugality* / 她是个很～的主妇。*She is a very thrifty housewife.*

【节节】successively；steadily：～胜利 *win many victories in succession；go from victory to victory* / ～败退 *retreat in defeat again and again；keep on retreating* / 产量～上升。*Production rose steadily.*

【节理】［林］joint：倾向(走向)～ *dip (strike) joint*

【节令】climate and other natural phenomena of a season：七月是西瓜上市的～。*Watermelons are in season in July.* / 今年冬天～不正。*We are having unseasonable winter weather.*

【节流】❶ reduce expenditure：开源节流 ❷［机］throttle：全～ *full throttle*

【节录】extract；excerpt：我从收音机里听到过这本小说的～。*I have heard excerpts from the novel on the radio.*

【节律】the rhythm and pace of moving things

【节目】programme；item (on a programme)；number：晚会的～安排得不够紧凑。*The programme for the evening party was not well organized.* / 下一个～ *the next item (or number)* ◇ ～单 programme；playbill；～导演 program director (PD)；～主持人 host (of a radio or TV show)；compère；master of ceremonies

【节能】save energy ◇ ～灯 energy-saving stove

【节拍】［音］metre ◇ ～器［音］metronome

【节气】solar term or period

【节日】festival；red-letter day；holiday：庆祝～ *celebrate (or observe) a festival* / ～气氛 *festive air* / 致以～的祝贺 *extend holiday greetings* / 穿上～的盛装 *in one's holiday best；in gala dress*

【节省】economize；save；use sparingly；cut down on：～时间 *save time* / ～篇幅 *save space* / ～人力物力 *use manpower and material resources sparingly*

【节食】be moderate in eating and drinking；be (or go) on a diet：她要保持身材苗条就不得不～。*She has to diet to stay slim.* ◇ ～者 dieter

【节水】save water ◇ ～器 water-saving device

【节外生枝】❶ side issues (or new problems) crop up unexpectedly ❷ raise obstacles；deliberately complicate an issue：快要达成协议时，对方又～。*An agreement was about to be reached when the other side raised new issues (or caused complications).*

【节选】excerpts；extracts：一本书的～ *extracts (or excerpts) from a book*

【节衣缩食】economize on food and clothing；live frugally：他们～，但是仍然供不起儿子上学。*They scraped and saved, but still couldn't pay for their son's education.*

【节译】abridged translation

【节油器】fuel economizer

【节余】❶ save：就这一项，我们～了一万余元。*We saved over ten thousand yuan on this item alone.* ❷ surplus (as a result of economizing)

【节育】birth control ◇ ～环 intrauterine device (IUD)；the loop；～手术 birth control surgery

【节欲】restrain one's carnal desires；check one's selfish desire

【节约】practise thrift；economize；save：～原料 *economize on raw materials* / ～人力物力 *economize on manpower and material resources*

【节肢动物】arthropod

【节支】❶ cut down expenses；reduce expenses；retrench ❷［经］balance；money saved

【节制】❶ control；check；be moderate in：～饮食 *be moderate in eating and drinking；be (or go) on a diet* ❷ temperance；abstinence ◇ ～闸［水］check gate

【节资】economize the use of funds；use funds conservatively

【节奏】❶ rhythm：～明快 *lively rhythm* / 有～地鼓掌 *clap hands rhythmically* ❷ tempo：生活～ *the tempo of life*

劫 Ⅰ 动 ❶ rob；plunder；raid：打劫 ❷ coerce；compel：劫持 Ⅱ 名 calamity；disaster；misfortune：浩劫

【劫持】kidnap；hold under duress；hijack：～飞机(船舰、火车、汽车) *hijack an aeroplane (a ship, a train, a motor vehicle)* / ～者 *hijacker*

【劫道】waylay；hold up；mug：他被～了。*He was waylaid by bandits.* or *He was mugged.*

【劫夺】seize (a person or his property) by force

【劫匪】highwayman；robber：他是个作案多起的～。*He is a highwayman of many crimes.*

【劫富济贫】rob the rich to give to the poor

【劫后余生】be a survivor of a disaster

【劫机】hijack a plane ◇ ～犯 hijacker

【劫掠】plunder；loot

【劫难】disaster；calamity：屡遭～ *have experienced many disasters*

【劫数】inexorable doom；predestined fate

【劫营】raid the enemy camp

【劫狱】break into a jail and rescue a prisoner：他是聚众～的首要分子。*He is the ringleader in the prison raid.*

杰 Ⅰ 形 outstanding；prominent：杰作 Ⅱ 名 outstanding person；hero：豪杰

【杰出】outstanding；remarkable；prominent：～贡献 *a brilliant contribution* / ～的画家 *an outstanding painter*

【杰作】masterpiece

诘 动〈书〉closely question；interrogate：盘诘

【诘问】〈书〉closely question；interrogate；crossexamine

【诘责】〈书〉censure；rebuke；denounce

洁 形 clean：整洁
【洁白】spotlessly white；pure white：～的桌布 *a spotlessly white tablecloth* / ～的心灵 *a pure mind*
【洁肤霜】cleansing cream
【洁净】clean；spotless：他房间里的东西都收拾得很～。*He kept everything clean in his room*.
【洁具】sanitary ware
【洁癖】an unhealthy obsession with cleanliness；mysophobia
【洁身自好】❶ refuse to be contaminated by evil influence；preserve one's purity ❷ mind one's own business in order to keep out of trouble

拮（构词成分）见下
【拮据】in straitened circumstances；short of money；hard up

结 Ⅰ 动 ❶ tie；knit；knot；weave：～网 *weave a net* ❷ congeal；form；forge；cement：牛奶上面～了一层皮。*A skin has formed on the milk*. / ～下深厚的友谊 *forge a profound friendship* ❸ settle；conclude：这不～了吗？*That's that!* Ⅱ 名 ❶ knot：我解不开这个～。*I can't untie this knot*. ❷ written guarantee；affidavit ❸［电子］junction：*p-n*～ *p-n junction* / 生长～ *grown junction* ❹［生理］node：淋巴结 ——另见 jiē
【结案】wind up a case
【结疤】become scarred
【结拜】become sworn brothers or sisters
【结伴】go with：～而行 *go or travel in a group*
【结冰】freeze；ice up；ice over
【结彩】adorn (or decorate) with festoons：这店新开张，门口结了彩。*The shop is newly opened and the shop front is decorated with festoons*. ——另见〖张灯结彩〗
【结草衔环】pay a debt of gratitude
【结肠】［生理］colon ◇ ～炎 colitis
【结成】form：～同盟 *form an alliance*；*become allies* / ～一伙 *gang up*；*band together*
【结仇】start a feud；become enemies
【结存】❶ cash on hand；balance：现金～ *cash balance* / 银行存款～ *bank balance* / 财政年度年终～ *balance at the end of a fiscal year* ❷ goods on hand；inventory
【结党营私】form a clique to pursue selfish interests；band together for selfish purposes
【结缔组织】［生理］connective tissue
【结对子】become a partner of；partner somebody；associate with
【结发夫妻】husband and wife by the first marriage
【结构】❶ structure；composition；construction：经济～ *economic structure* / 所有制～ *the structure of ownership* / 产品～ *product mix* / 产业～ *the structure of production*；*industrial set-up* ❷［建］structure；construction：钢～ *steel structure* / 钢筋混凝土～ *reinforced concrete structure* / 铆合（焊接）～ *riveted* (*welded*) *construction* ❸［地理］texture：斑状～ *porphyritic texture* / 致密～ *compact texture* ◇ ～钢 structural steel；～工资制 structural wage system；～力学 structural mechanics；～流程图 structure flow chart；～式［化］structural formula；～调整 structural readjustment；～图 structural drawing；～心理学 structural psychology；～语言学 structural linguistics；～主义 structuralism；～主义学派 structuralists；～主义语法 structural grammar
【结关】customs clearance ◇ ～费 customs clearing charges；～证 clearance；clearance papers
【结果】(jiēguǒ) ❶ result；outcome：必然～ *inevitable result* / 会谈的～ *the outcome of the talks* / 这样瞎吵下去不会有什么～。*Squabbling like this won't get you anywhere*. ❷〈旧〉kill；finish off ——另见 jiēguǒ
【结合】❶ combine；unite；integrate；link：理论与实践相～ *combine theory with practice* / ～具体情况进行处理 *deal with sth. in the light of specific conditions* ❷ be united in wedlock
【结核】❶［医］tubercle ❷［医］tuberculosis：肺结核 ❸［矿］nodule：锰～ *manganese nodule* ◇ ～杆菌 tubercle bacillus；～菌素 tuberculin
【结核病】tuberculosis：～院 *tuberculosis hospital*；*tuberculosis sanatorium*
【结喉】［生理］Adam's apple
【结汇】settlement of exchange
【结婚】marry；get married；be married：她～了吗？*Is she married*？/ 她跟谁～了？*Who did she marry*？/ 她是什么时候结的婚？*When did she get married*？/ 她结过两次婚了。*She's been married twice*. ◇ ～登记 marriage registration；～证书 marriage certificate；marriage lines
【结集】❶ concentrate；mass：～兵力 *concentrate troops* ❷ collect articles，etc. into a volume：～付印 *compile a collection of writings and send it to the press*
【结痂】form a scab；crust
【结交】make friends with；associate with：他～的朋友大多是青年工人。*He associates mostly with young workers*.
【结节】［生］tubercle；node ◇ ～虫 nodular worm
【结晶】❶ crystallize ❷ crystal：盐～ *salt crystals* / ～岩石 *crystalline rock* / ～水 *water of crystallization*；*crystal water* ❸ crystallization：智慧的～ *a crystallization of wisdom* / 劳动的～ *the fruit of labour* ◇ ～化学 crystal chemistry；～学 crystallography
【结局】final result；outcome；ending：小说的～ *the ending of a novel*
【结块】agglomerate；curdle
【结论】❶［逻］conclusion (of a syllogism) ❷ conclusion；verdict：得出～ *draw* (*or come to*，*reach*) *a conclusion* / 不要忙于下～。*Don't jump to conclusions*.
【结盟】form an alliance；ally；align
【结膜】［生理］conjunctiva ◇ ～炎 conjunctivitis
【结欠】balance due
【结亲】❶〈口〉marry；get married ❷ (of two

families) become related by marriage
【结清】settle; square up: ～账目 *square accounts (with sb.)* / ～债务 *settle a debt by payment*
【结球甘蓝】cabbage
【结舌】unable to say anything because of terror or lack of argument; tongue-tied: 瞠目～ *stare tongue-tied; stare dumbfounded* / 张口～ *be agape and tongue-tied; be at a loss for words*
【结社】form an association ◇ ～自由 freedom of association
【结绳】tie knots: ～记事 *keep records by tying knots (in primitive times before the invention of writing)*
【结石】[医] stone; calculus: 排出～ *discharge of stones; pass stones*
【结识】get acquainted with sb.; get to know sb.: ～了很多新朋友 *have made a lot of new friends* / 有幸～了一位大人物 *have the honour of making the acquaintance of a VIP*
【结束】end; finish; conclude; wind up; close: ～讲话 *wind up a speech* / ～战争状态 *terminate the state of war* / 代表团～了对我国的访问。*The delegation has concluded its visit to China.*
【结束语】concluding remarks
【结算】settle accounts; close (or wind up) an account: 用人民币计价～ *use Renminbi for quoting prices and settling accounts* / 记账～ *settlement on account* ◇ ～价格 settlement price
【结为】enter into a specified relationship: ～夫妻 *become husband and wife*
【结尾】❶ ending; winding-up stage: ～工程 *the winding-up work of a project* / 文章的～很有力量。*The article has a forceful ending.* ❷ [音] coda
【结业】complete a course; wind up one's studies
【结余】cash surplus; surplus; balance
【结缘】form ties (of affection, friendship, etc.); become attached to: 他从小就和音乐结了缘。*He developed a liking for music even as a boy.*
【结怨】contract enmity; incur hatred
【结扎】[医] ligation; ligature: ～血管 *ligature (or tie up) blood vessels* / 输卵管～术 *ligation of oviduct* / 输精管～术 *vasoligation*
【结账】settle (or square) accounts; balance the books
【结转】carry-over; carry down

桔
(构词成分)见下 ——另见 jú
【桔梗】[中] the root of balloon flower (Platycodon grandiflorum)

桀
名 the name of the last ruler of the Xia Dynasty (c. 21st—c. 16th century B.C.), traditionally considered a tyrant
【桀骜不驯】stubborn and intractable; obstinate and unruly
【桀犬吠尧】the tyrant Jie's cur yapping at the sage-king Yao—the underling of an evil man will attack whoever he is told to attack

捷
Ⅰ 形 prompt; nimble; quick: 敏捷 Ⅱ 名 victory; triumph: 连战皆～ *win a series of victories*
【捷报】news of victory; report of a success ◇ ～频传 news of victory keeps pouring in
【捷径】shortcut: 走～ *take a shortcut*
【捷克】Czech ◇ ～人 Czech; ～语 Czech (language)
【捷足先登】the swift-footed arrive first; the early bird catches the worm

睫
名 eyelash; lash
【睫毛】eyelash; lash ◇ ～油 mascara

竭
动 exhaust; use up: 衰竭
【竭诚】wholeheartedly; with all one's heart: ～拥护 *give wholehearted support*
【竭尽】use up; exhaust: ～造谣诬蔑之能事 *stop at nothing in spreading lies and slanders*
【竭尽全力】spare no effort; do one's utmost; do all one can
【竭力】do one's utmost; use every ounce of one's energy; try by every possible means: ～支持 *give all-out support* / ～反对 *actively oppose* / ～鼓吹 *boost with all one's might; energetically advocate*
【竭泽而渔】drain the pond to get all the fish; kill the goose that lays the golden eggs

截
Ⅰ 动 ❶ cut; sever: ～成两段 *cut in two* ❷ stop; check; stem: 把惊马～住 *stop a bolting horse* / ～球 *intercept a pass* Ⅱ 量 section; chunk; length: 一～儿木头 *a log* Ⅲ 介 by (a specified time); up to: 截至
【截长补短】take from the long to add to the short; draw on the strength of each to offset the weakness of the other
【截断】❶ cut off; block: ～敌人的退路 *cut off the enemy's retreat* / ～河流 *dam a river* ❷ cut short; interrupt: 电话铃声～了他的话。*He was interrupted by the telephone.*
【截稿】stop accepting incoming articles or contributions: ～日期 *closing date; deadline for contributions*
【截获】intercept and capture: 游击队～了敌人一辆卡车。*The guerrillas intercepted and captured an enemy truck.*
【截击】intercept: ～敌增援部队 *intercept the enemy's reinforcements* ◇ ～导弹 interceptor (or interception) missile; ～机 interceptor
【截流】dam a river ◇ ～井 catch basin
【截留】intercept and hold on to; retain for one's own use; withhold: ～国家收入 *withhold state funds* / ～上交利润 *retain profits which ought to be turned over to the state*
【截煤机】[矿] coalcutter; cutter
【截面】section: 横～ *cross section* / 正～ *normal section*
【截取】cut off a section of sth.
【截然】sharply; completely: ～对立 *be diametri-*

cally opposed / 同他们以前的谈话～相反 *completely contradict their previous statement*

【截然不同】completely different; different as black and white; poles apart: 孩子的世界,与成人～。*The child's world is completely different from that of a fully grown man*.

【截瘫】[医] paraplegia

【截肢】[医] amputation

【截止】❶ end; close: 登记已经～了。*Registration has closed*. / 申请到本月二十日～。*The 20th of this month is the closing day for applications*. / ～日期 *closing date* ❷ [电] cut-off: ～电平 *cut-off level*

【截至】by (a specified time); up to: ～本月底 *by the end of this month* / ～目前为止 *up to now*

碣 名 stone tablet: 墓～ *tombstone*

羯 (构词成分)见下

【羯羊】wether

jiě

姐 名 ❶ elder sister; sister ❷ a general term for young women

【姐夫】elder sister's husband; brother-in-law

【姐姐】elder sister; sister

【姐妹】❶ sisters: 她没有～,只有一个哥哥。*She has a brother but no sisters*. ❷〈方〉brothers and sisters: 你们～几个? *How many brothers and sisters are there in your family*? ◇～城 sister cities; ～学校 sister schools; sister universities

解 Ⅰ 动 ❶ separate; divide: 溶解 ❷ untie; undo: ～缆 *untie the mooring rope* / ～鞋带 *undo shoelaces* ❸ allay; dispel; dismiss: ～油腻 *cut the grease of a rich meal (as with a cup of tea, etc.)* ❹ explain; interpret; solve: 此字作何～? *What does this word mean*? / 新～ *a new interpretation* ❺ understand; comprehend: 令人不～ *puzzling*; *incomprehensible* ❻ relieve oneself: 大解 Ⅱ 名 [数] solution: 求解 ——另见 jiè

【解表】[中] induce sweat; diaphoresis: ～药 *diaphoretic*

【解馋】satisfy a craving for good food

【解嘲】try to explain things away when ridiculed ——另见〖聊以解嘲〗;〖自我解嘲〗

【解除】remove; relieve; get rid of: ～职务 *remove sb. from his post*; *relieve sb. of his office* / ～合同 *rescind a contract*; *terminate a contract* / ～武装 *disarm* / ～禁令 *lift a ban* / ～婚约 *renounce an engagement*

【解除警报】❶ sound the all-clear ❷ all-clear

【解答】answer; explain: ～疑难问题 *answer difficult questions* / 习题的～ *key to an exercise*

【解冻】❶ thaw; unfreeze: ～季节 *thawing season* / 两国关系～ *a thawing of the relations between the two countries* ❷ unfreeze (funds, assets, etc.)

【解毒】❶ [医] detoxify; detoxicate ❷ [中] relieve internal heat (or fever:) ～药 *antidote*

【解饿】satisfy one's hunger

【解乏】❶ recover from fatigue: 他得好好睡一觉,才能～。*He needs a good long sleep to get over his fatigue*. / 烫烫脚～。*Bathe your feet in hot water and you won't feel so tired*. ❷ refreshing

【解法】[数] solution

【解放】❶ liberate; emancipate: 民族～运动 *the national liberation movement* / 妇女～ *the emancipation of women* ❷ Liberation (signifying the termination of Kuomintang rule in mainland China in 1949) ◇～区 liberated area; ～思想 emancipate the mind; free oneself from old ideas

【解放军】❶ liberation army ❷〈略〉见〖中国人民解放军〗❸ PLA man

【解放战争】❶ war of liberation ❷ China's War of Liberation (1945-1949)

【解疙瘩】solve a problem that is on sb.'s mind; get rid of a hang-up: 郭主任这回可没解开她心头上的疙瘩。*Director Guo failed to cut (or untangle) the knot in her mind this time*.

【解构】[哲] deconstructionism

【解雇】discharge; dismiss; fire ◇～费 severance pay; ～通知书 pink slip

【解恨】vent one's hatred; have one's hatred slaked: 这坏蛋打他一顿也不～。*Thrashing this scoundrel wouldn't be enough to slake our hatred for him*.

【解惑】〈书〉resolve (or remove, dispel) doubts

【解甲归田】take off one's armour and return to the land; be demobilized

【解禁】lift a ban

【解救】save; rescue; deliver: 通货膨胀政策～不了经济危机。*Inflationary policies are no remedy for an economic crisis*.

【解决】❶ solve; resolve; settle: ～争端 settle a dispute / ～困难 *overcome a difficulty*; *find a way out of a difficulty* / ～问题 *solve a problem*; *settle a question (or an issue)*; work out a solution ❷ dispose of; finish off: 这一仗把敌人完全～了。*In that battle we finished off all the enemy troops*.

【解开】untie; undo: ～头巾 *untie a kerchief* / ～上衣 *unbutton one's jacket* / ～这个谜 *find a clue to the mystery* / ～疑团 *clear up suspicions* / ～疙瘩 *get rid of a hang-up*

【解渴】quench one's thirst: 这西瓜真～。*This watermelon really quenches your thirst*.

【解扣】[电] trip: 自动～ *automatic trip*

【解扣儿】❶ unbutton; undo a button ❷〈喻〉sink a feud; get rid of a hang-up; remove ill will; overcome difficulties

【解困】overcome difficulties

【解困房】problem-solving houses

【解铃还是系铃人】(又作'解铃系铃') let him who tied the bell on the tiger take it off—whoever started the trouble should end it

【解码】decipher；decode
【解闷】divert oneself (from boredom)
【解密】［电子］deciphering
【解囊】〈书〉open one's purse (to help sb. with money) ——另见〖解囊相助〗；〖慷慨解囊〗
【解囊相助】help sb. generously with money
【解聘】dismiss an employee (usu. at the expiration of a contract)
【解剖】dissect：我们上生物课时～了一只青蛙。*We dissected a frog in biology class.* / 严于～自己 *be strict in dissecting oneself ideologically*；*be strict in appraising oneself* ◇ ～刀 scalpel；～学 anatomy
【解剖麻雀】dissect a sparrow—analyze a typical case
【解气】vent one's spleen；work off one's anger
【解热】allay a fever
【解散】❶ dismiss：队伍～后，战士们都在操场上休息。*After they were dismissed, the soldiers had a rest on the drill ground.* / ～！(*word of command*) *Dismiss*！❷ dissolve；disband：～组织 *disband an organization*
【解释】explain；expound；interpret：～一个新词 *explain a new word* / ～法律 *interpret laws* / 这些事实不能有别的～。*The facts admit of no other explanation.* ◇ ～权 right to interpret
【解释性】explanatory；interpretative：～规定 *interpretative provision* / ～声明 *interpretative declaration (or statement)*
【解手】relieve oneself；go to the toilet (or lavatory)
【解说】explain orally；comment：向观众～这种卡车的构造和性能 *explain to the visitors the structure and performance of this type of truck* ◇ ～词 (oral) commentary；(written) caption；～员 announcer；narrator；commentator
【解题】solve a (mathematical, etc.) problem
【解体】disintegrate：原始社会的～ *the disintegration of primitive society*
【解脱】❶ free (or extricate) oneself：从困境中～出来 *extricate oneself from a predicament* / 从世间烦恼中～出来 *free oneself from worldly worries* ❷ absolve；exonerate
【解围】❶ force an enemy to raise a siege；rescue sb. from a siege ❷ help sb. out of a predicament；save sb. from embarrassment：他们拿我开玩笑，你怎么不来给我～？*Why didn't you come to my rescue when they were making fun of me?*
【解析几何学】analytic geometry
【解严】declare martial law ended；lift a curfew
【解译】decipher；decode；figure out a message：～失事飞机的黑盒子 *decode the black box from a plane crash*
【解约】terminate an agreement；cancel (or rescind) a contract
【解职】dismiss from office；discharge；relieve sb. of his post

jiè

介 Ⅰ 动 ❶ be situated between；interpose：这座山～于两县之间。*The mountain lies between two counties.* ❷ take seriously；take to heart；mind：～意 *take offense*；*mind* Ⅱ 量〈书〉(now usu. used in) 一～书生 *a mere scholar* / 一～武夫 *a plain soldier*
【介词】［语］preposition
【介电常数】dielectric constant
【介壳】shell (of oysters, snails, etc.) ◇ ～虫 scale insect
【介入】intervene；interpose；get involved：不～无原则争论 *not get involved in unprincipled disputes* / ～两国之间的纷争 *be involved in the disputes and conflicts between two countries*
【介绍】❶ introduce；present：作自我～ *introduce oneself* / ～对象 *introduce sb. to a potential marriage partner*；*find sb. a boy or girl friend* ❷ recommend；suggest 我给你～一本书。*I'll recommend you a book.* ❸ let know；brief：～情况 *brief sb. on the situation*；*put sb. in the picture*；*fill sb. in* / ～经验 *pass on experience*
【介绍人】❶ one who introduces or recommends sb.；sponsor ❷ matchmaker
【介绍信】letter of introduction；reference
【介形虫】mussel-shrimp
【介意】(又作'介怀') (usu. used in the negative) take offence；mind：我是开玩笑，你可别～呀。*I was only joking. I hope you won't take offence.* / 即使有些批评过头了，他也不～。*He didn't mind even when some criticisms were excessive.*
【介质】［物］medium：工作～ *actuating medium*
【介子】［物］meson；mesotron

芥 名 mustard ——另见 gài
【芥菜】leaf mustard ◇ ～疙瘩 rutabaga——另见 gàicài
【芥蒂】〈书〉ill feeling；unpleasantness；grudge：心存～ *bear a grudge*
【芥末】mustard
【芥子】mustard seed
【芥子气】［化］mustard gas

戒 Ⅰ 动 ❶ guard against：～浮夸 *avoid boasting and exaggeration* ❷ exhort；admonish；warn：引以为戒 ❸ give up；drop；stop：～荤腥 *go on a vegetarian diet* Ⅱ 名 ❶ Buddhist monastic discipline：受戒 ❷ (finger) ring：钻～ *diamond ring*
【戒备】guard；take precautions；be on the alert：处于～状态 *be on the alert* ◇ ～森严 tight security is in force
【戒除】give up；drop；stop：～恶习 *give up a bad habit*
【戒毒】quit drug abuse
【戒毒中心】drug rehabilitation contre
【戒骄戒躁】guard against arrogance and rashness；

be on one's guard against conceit and impetuosity: ～,永远保持谦虚进取的精神 *guard against conceit and rashness, always remain modest and keep forging ahead*

【戒酒】give up drinking; swear off drinking

【戒律】religious discipline; commandment

【戒心】vigilance; wariness: 对某人怀有～ *be on one's guard against someone; keep a wary eye on someone*

【戒烟】give up smoking; swear off smoking: 抽一支烟吧? —谢谢,我～了。*Cigarette? —No thanks, I've sworn off smoking.* / ～糖(茶) *habit-breaking candy (tea) for smokers*

【戒严】enforce martial law; impose a curfew; cordon off an area: 宣布～ *proclaim martial law* / 警察在车站～,搜捕逃犯。*The police cordoned off the railway station to search for the escape prisoner.* ◇ ～令 proclamation of martial law

【戒指】(finger) ring: 戴～ *wear a ring* / 订婚～ *engagement ring* / 结婚～ *wedding ring* / 钻石～ *diamond ring*

届 Ⅰ 动 fall due Ⅱ 量 (for meetings, graduating classes, etc.): 第五～全国人民代表大会 *the Fifth National People's Congress*

【届满】at the expiration of one's term of office: 任期～。*The term of office has expired.*

【届期】when the day comes; on the appointed date

【届时】when the time comes; at the appointed time; on the occasion: 大桥下月竣工,～将举行通车典礼。*There will be an opening ceremony next month when the bridge is completed.*

疥 名 scabies

【疥虫】[医] sarcoptic mite

【疥疮】scabies

【疥螨】itch mite

【疥癣】mange: 羊～ *sheep scab*

诫 Ⅰ 动 warn; admonish: 告诫 Ⅱ 名 commandment: 十～ *the Ten Commandments*

界 名 ❶ boundary: 山西和陕西以黄河为～。*The boundary between Shanxi and Shaanxi is the Huanghe River.* ❷ scope; extent: 眼界 ❸ circles: 新闻界 ❹ primary division; kingdom: 动(植,矿)物～ *the animal (vegetable, mineral) kingdom* ❺ [地理] earthern: 古生界 ❻ [数] bound: 上(下)～ *upper (lower) bound*

【界碑】boundary tablet; boundary marker

【界标】boundary mark

【界尺】ungraduated ruler

【界段】area under a person's administration

【界定】specify the limits; delimit; define: 这个词的含义缺少精确的～。*There is no clear definition for the meaning of this word.*

【界河】boundary river

【界面】interface

【界内球】[体] in bounds; in

【界石】boundary stone (or tablet)

【界外球】[体] out-of-bounds; out

【界限】❶ demarcation line; dividing line; limits; bounds: 打破行业～,实行大协作 *break the bounds of different trades and go in for extensive coordination* ❷ limit; end

【界线】❶ boundary line ❷ 同〖界限〗❶

【界址】location of a dividing line (of land): 清查～ *find out where the dividing line lies*

【界桩】boundary marker

借 动 ❶ borrow: 跟人～钱 *borrow money from sb.* / 从图书馆～书 *borrow a book from the library* ❷ lend: 把自行车～给我骑一下好吗? *Could you lend me your bicycle?* ❸ make use of; take advantage of (an opportunity, etc.): 火～风势,越烧越旺。*Fanned by the wind, the fire burned more and more furiously.* ❹ use as a pretext: ～"援助"之名,行掠夺之实 *use "aid" as a pretext for plunder*

【借词】[语] loanword; loan

【借贷】❶ borrow or lend money ❷ debit and credit sides ◇ ～股票 lending stock; loan stocks; ～资本 loan capital

【借刀杀人】kill sb. by another's hand; make use of one person to get rid of another

【借调】temporarily transfer; loan: 他～到旅行社去工作了。*He's on loan to the Travel Service.*

【借东风】〈字〉taking advantage of the east wind; 〈喻〉with sb's help

【借读】study at a school on a temporary basis

【借端】use as a pretext: ～生事 *find an excuse to make trouble; avail oneself of a pretext to stir up trouble*

【借方】[经] debit side; debit

【借风使船】sail the boat with the help of the wind—achieve one's purpose through the agency of sb. else

【借古讽今】use the past to disparage the present

【借故】find an excuse: ～推托 *find an excuse to refuse* / 他～走了。*He found an excuse and left.*

【借光】〈套〉excuse me: ～,去百货大楼怎么走啊? *Excuse me, but can you direct me to the Department Store?*

【借花献佛】present Buddha with flowers given by another—make a gift of sth. given by another

【借火】ask for a light: 劳驾,借个火儿。*Excuse me. Would you mind giving me a light?*

【借鸡下蛋】borrow a hen to lay an egg—use external conditions to advance one's own project

【借鉴】(又作'借镜') use for reference; draw lessons from; draw on the experience of: 他们的做法有许多值得我们～的地方。*There's much in their method that we can make use of.* / ～外国的经验 *use the experience of other countries for reference*

【借酒浇愁】drown one's sorrows in liquor

【借据】receipt for a loan (IOU)

【借口】❶ use as an excuse (or pretext): 他～另有约会,提前走了。*He left early, on the pretext of having another appointment*. ❷ excuse; pretext: 找～ *find an excuse* (*or pretext*) / 制造～ *invent an excuse*; *cook up a pretext*

【借款】❶ borrow or lend money; ask for or offer a loan ❷ loan ◇ ～契约 loan agreement

【借尸还魂】(of a dead person's soul) find reincarnation in another's corpse—(of sth. evil) revive in a new guise

【借书处】loan desk (of a library)

【借书证】library card

【借水行舟】sail the boat with the help of the current—achieve one's purpose through the agency of sb. else

【借宿】stay overnight at sb. else's place; put up for the night: 勘探队员在牧民家里～了一夜。*Members of the prospecting team put up for one night in the homes of the herdsmen*.

【借题发挥】make use of the subject under discussion to put over one's own ideas; seize on an incident to exaggerate matters

【借条】receipt for a loan (IOU)

【借位】borrow ten (in subtraction)

【借问】〈套〉may I ask

【借以】so as to; for the purpose of; by way of: 试举数例，～说明问题的严重性。*Let me give a few examples to show how serious the problem is*.

【借用】❶ borrow; have the loan of: ～一下你的铅笔。*May I use your pencil?* ❷ use sth. for another purpose: ～一句古诗表达自己的心情 *quote a line from classical poetry to express one's feelings*

【借阅】borrow and read; lend: 她只管报纸～。*She is only responsible for lending newspapers*.

【借债】borrow money; raise (or contract) a loan: ～度日 *live by borrowing* ◇ ～抵押品 security for a loan

【借支】ask for an advance on one's pay

【借重】rely on for support; enlist sb.'s help: 以后要～您的地方还多着呢。*We'll need a lot more of your help in the future*.

【借住】stay at sb. else's place: 下周四我们能在你那里～一晚吗? *Can you put us up next Thursday night?*

【借助】have the aid of; draw support from: ～望远镜观察天体 *observe the celestial bodies with the aid of a telescope*

解 动 send under guard: 犯人已～到县里了。*The prisoner has been sent to the county seat under guard*. ——另见 jiě

【解送】send under guard

jīn

巾 名 a piece of cloth (as used for a towel, scarf, kerchief, etc.): 毛巾

【巾帼】❶ ancient woman's headdress ❷ woman ◇ ～英雄 a heroic woman; heroine

今 名 ❶ modern; present-day ❷ now; the present: 从～以后 *from now on*; *henceforth* / ～胜于昔。*The present is superior to the past*. ❸ of today; of this year: ～冬 *this* (*coming*) *winter*

【今非昔比】no comparison between past and present; the past cannot be compared with the present

【今后】from now on; in the days to come; henceforth; hereafter; in future: ～的十年内 *in the next decade*; *in the coming ten years* / ～的任务 *the tasks ahead*

【今年】this year

【今日】❶ this day; today ❷ present; now: ～中国 *China now*; *China today*

【今生】this life

【今世】❶ this life ❷ this age; the contemporary age

【今是昨非】today right, yesterday wrong (i.e. what I do today is right, what I did yesterday was wrong; said of repentance and reformation)

【今天】❶ this day; today: ～上午(下午) *this morning* (*afternoon*) / 一年前的～ *a year ago today* ❷ the present time or age; today: ～的青年有不同的道德观念。*Young people today* (*or of today*) *have different moral values*.

【今晚】this evening; tonight

【今昔】the present and the past; today and yesterday: 西安的～ *Xi'an past and present*; *Xi'an yesterday and today*

【今昔对比】contrast the past with the present

【今夜】this evening; tonight

【今译】modern translation; modern-language version: 古诗～ *ancient poems rendered into modern Chinese*

【今朝】❶〈方〉today ❷ the present; now

【今朝有酒今朝醉】drink today while drink you may

斤 量 a traditional unit of weight ——另见〖市斤〗

【斤斗】〈方〉❶ fall ❷ somersault

【斤斤】be particular (about small matters): ～于表面形式 *be particular about matters of form*

【斤斤计较】haggle over every ounce; be calculating: ～个人得失 *be preoccupied with one's personal gains and losses*

【斤两】weight: ～不足 *short weight*; *under-weight* / 他的话很有～。*What he said should not be taken lightly*. or *What he said carried a lot of weight*.

金 Ⅰ 名 ❶ metals: 五金 ❷ money: 现金 ❸ ancient metal percussion instruments: 鸣金收兵 ❹［化］gold (Au) Ⅱ 形 ❶ golden: 红底～字 *golden characters on a red background* ❷ highly respected; precious: 金口玉言

【金榜】a list of successful candidates in the imperial examinations: ～题名 *succeed in the imperial examinations*

【金杯】golden cup; gold cup
【金本位】[经] gold standard
【金笔】(quality) fountain pen
【金币】gold coin
【金碧辉煌】(of a building, etc.) looking splendid in green and gold; resplendent and magnificent
【金边证券】gilt-edged securities; gilts
【金箔】goldleaf; gold foil
【金不换】not to be exchanged even for gold; invaluable; priceless ——另见〖浪子回头〗
【金蝉脱壳】slip out of a predicament like a cicada sloughing its skin; escape by cunning manoeuvring
【金唱片】golden disc; gold record
【金城汤池】ramparts of metal and a moat of boiling water—an impregnable fortress
【金翅雀】greenfinch
【金疮】[中] metal-inflicted wound; incised wound
【金殿】imperial palace
【金额】〈书〉amount (or sum) of money
【金饭碗】〈字〉golden rice bowl; 〈喻〉secure and well-paid job: 时代变了,不能再靠~过日子。*Times have changed, one can no longer expect a secure and well-paid job forever.*
【金粉】❶ lead powder ❷ pollen ❸ gold bits
【金刚】Buddha's warrior attendant
【金刚努目】(又作'金刚怒目') glare like a temple door-god—be fierce of visage
【金刚砂】emery; corundum; carborundum: ~磨床 *emery grinder*
【金刚石】diamond
【金刚钻】diamond: ~钻头 *diamond bit*
【金戈铁马】golden spears and armoured horses—war or warriors
【金工】metalworking; metal processing: ~机械 *metalworking machinery*
【金箍棒】golden cudgel (weapon used by the Monkey King in the novel Pilgrimage to the West)
【金股】[经] golden share
【金光】golden light (or ray): 万道~ *myriad golden rays* / ~闪闪 *glittering; glistening*
【金光大道】golden road; bright broad highway
【金龟】tortoise
【金龟婿】rich son-in-law
【金龟子】scarab
【金合欢】sponge tree
【金衡】troy weight; troy
【金红】golden red
【金红石】rutile
【金花菜】(California) bur clover
【金黄】golden yellow; golden: 菜花一片~ *a vast stretch of golden rape flowers*
【金汇兑本位】[经] gold exchange standard
【金婚】golden wedding
【金鸡】golden pheasant
【金鸡独立】standing on one leg like a cock (a posture in Chinese boxing)
【金鸡奖】the Gold Rooster Award—the Chinese film award
【金鸡纳树】cinchona
【金鸡纳霜】quinine
【金奖】gold medal; highest award; first prize
【金交椅】〈贬〉extremely important post or position: 勾心斗角二十年,他才爬上了这把极有权势的~。*Only after twenty years' jockeying for power did he attain this position of great influence.*
【金橘】kumquat
【金卡】[经] gold card
【金科玉律】golden rule and precious precept: 奉为~ *accept as an infallible law*
【金口玉言】a golden mouth and pearly words—precious words; utterances that carry great weight
【金库】national (or state) treasury; exchequer
【金块】gold bullion
【金矿】goldmine: ~区 *goldfield*
【金兰之交】intimate friendship; sworn brotherhood
【金绿宝石】chrysoberyl
【金銮殿】the Hall of Golden Chimes (a popular name for the emperor's audience hall, e.g. the Hall of Great Harmony 太和殿 in the Imperial Palace)
【金霉素】aureomycin
【金牛座】[天] Taurus
【金瓯无缺】territorial integrity unimpaired
【金牌】gold medal
【金漆】gold lacquer: ~镶嵌制品 *inlaid gold lacquerware*
【金器】gold vessel
【金钱】money
【金钱豹】leopard
【金钱挂帅】money (money-making) in command
【金枪鱼】tuna
【金秋】autumn
【金曲】great hit
【金融】finance; banking: ~货币危机 *financial and monetary crises* / ~机构 *banking institution* / ~机关 *financial institution* ◇ ~财团 financial syndicate; ~改组 financial reorganization; ~寡头 financial oligarch (or magnate); ~汇率 financial rate; ~集团 financial clique; ~家 financier; ~界 financial circles; ~巨头 financial magnate; shark of high finance; financial tycoon; ~媒介 financial intermediation; ~市场 money (or financial) market; ~体制 banking system; ~危机 financial crisis; ~信息中心 financial information centre; ~业务 financial business; ~政策 financial policy; ~中心 financial (or banking) centre; ~资本 financial capital
【金三角】Golden Triangle, an area between Burma, Thailand and Laos, notorious for its drug production and trafficking
【金嗓子】beautiful voice; sweet, mellow voice: 她天生一副~,从小就喜欢唱歌。*Born with a sweet voice, she has liked singing from childhood.*
【金色】golden: ~的朝阳 *golden rays of the morning sun; golden dawn*

【金石】❶〈书〉metal and stone—a symbol of hardness and strength：精诚所至，金石为开 ❷ inscriptions on ancient bronzes and stone tablets ◇ ～学 the study of inscriptions on ancient bronzes and stone tablets；epigraphy

【金饰】gold ornament

【金属】metal ◇ ～工艺品 metal handicrafts；～加工 metal processing；metalworking；～结构 metal structure；～模 metal pattern；～疲劳 metal fatigue；～探伤 metal defect detection；crack detection；～陶瓷 cermet；～涂料 metallic paint；～性 metallicity

【金丝猴】golden monkey；snub-nosed monkey

【金丝雀】canary

【金丝镶嵌】gold filigree

【金丝燕】esculent swift

【金条】gold bar

【金童玉女】the Golden Boy and the Jade Maiden (attendants of the Taoist immortals)

【金文】inscriptions on ancient bronze objects

【金屋藏娇】live with one's young concubine in a plush house；keep a mistress in a love nest；take a concubine

【金无足赤】gold can't be hundred percent pure：～，人无完人。*Gold can't be pure and man can't be perfect.* or *There are spots even on the sun.*

【金线鱼】red coat；golden thread

【金相学】metallography

【金小蜂】tiny golden wasp；ptermalid

【金星】❶[天] Venus ❷ golden star (an object or figure) ❸ flashes of light that one seems to see (as from dizziness or a blow on the head)

【金钥匙】golden key—the best solution to a problem：自学是打开知识宝库的一把～。*Self-study is the golden key to the treasure-trove of knowledge.*

【金要足赤，人要完人】gold must be pure and man must be perfect—perfectionism

【金银财宝】gold，silver，treasures，and jewels — riches

【金银花】honeysuckle ◇ ～露 [中] distilled liquid of honeysuckle

【金樱子】[中] the fruit of Cherokee rose (Rosa laevigata)

【金鱼】goldfish

【金鱼缸】goldfish bowl；goldfish basin

【金玉】〈书〉gold and jade—valuable；precious

【金玉良言】golden sayings；invaluable advice

【金玉满堂】a hall filled with gold and jade—wealthy；learned

【金玉其外，败絮其中】rubbish coated in gold and jade；fair without，foul within

【金云母】phlogopite

【金盏花】pot marigold (Calendula officinalis)

【金针】❶ acupuncture needle ❷ dried day lily flower

【金针菜】day lily

【金针虫】wireworm

【金枝玉叶】golden branches and jade leaves —people of imperial lineage；royalty

【金字塔】pyramid ◇ ～式控制股权 pyramid golding；～式推销 pyramid selling

【金字招牌】a gold-lettered signboard —a vainglorious title

【金子】gold

津 名 ❶ saliva：生～止渴 *help produce saliva and slake thirst* ❷ sweat：遍体生～ *perspire all over* ❸ ferry crossing；ford：要津

【津巴布韦】Zimbabwe

【津津乐道】take delight in talking about；dwell upon with great relish

【津津有味】with relish；with gusto；with keen pleasure：吃得～ *eat with great relish* / 讲得～ *talk with gusto* / 这个故事他们听得～。*They listened to the story with great interest.*

【津贴】❶ financial aid；subsidy；allowance：出差～ *travel subsistence allowance* / 伙食～ *food allowance* / 生活～ *living allowance* / 岗位～ *subsidies appropriate to particular jobs* ❷ give financial aid；subsidize

【津要】〈书〉❶ key place ❷ key post

【津液】❶ [中] body fluid ❷ saliva

矜 Ⅰ 动 pity；sympathize with Ⅱ 形 ❶ self-important；conceited：骄矜 ❷ restrained；reserved：矜重

【矜持】restrained；reserved：举止～ *have a reserved manner*

【矜夸】conceited and boastful

【矜重】reserved and dignified

筋 名 ❶ muscle ❷〈口〉tendon；sinew ❸〈口〉veins that stand out under the skin：青筋 ❹ anything resembling a tendon (or vein)：叶～ *ribs of a leaf* / 芹菜太老，有很多～。*This celery is too old；it's very stringy.*

【筋道】〈方〉❶ (of food) tough and chewy：抻面吃到嘴里挺～。*Hand-pulled noodles are very chewy.* ❷ sturdy (old man)：这老头儿倒很～。*This old man is quite hale and hearty.*

【筋斗】〈方〉❶ somersault：翻～ *turn a somersault* ❷ fall；tumble (over)：摔了个～ *fall；have a fall；tumble over*

【筋骨】bones and muscles—physique：武术可以锻炼～。*Practising wushu strengthens the physique.*

【筋疲力尽】(又作'筋疲力竭') exhausted；played out；worn out；tired out；all in；dead-beat；dog-tired

【筋肉】muscles

禁 动 ❶ bear；stand；endure：这布～洗吗？*Will this cloth stand a lot of washing？* / 这鞋～穿。*These shoes are durable.* / 黑颜色～脏。*Black colour doesn't show dirt easily.* ❷ contain (or restrain) oneself：不禁

【禁不起】be unable to stand (tests，trials，etc.)：～严峻考验 *fail to stand rigorous tests*

【禁不住】❶ be unable to bear (or endure): 这种植物～冻。*This plant can't stand frost*. ❷ can't help (doing sth.); can't refrain from: ～笑了起来 *can't help laughing; burst out laughing*.

【禁得起】be able to stand (tests, trials, etc.): ～艰苦环境的考验 *be able to stand the test of hardships*

【禁得住】be able to bear (or endure): 这把椅子～我坐吗? *Will this chair hold me?* / 河上的冰已经～人走了。*The ice on the river is thick enough to walk on*.

【禁受】bear; stand; endure: 这些建筑～了时间的考验。*These buildings have stood the test of time*.

襟 名 ❶ front of a garment ❷ brothers-in-law whose wives are sisters: ～兄 *husband of one's wife's elder sister; brother-in-law*

【襟怀】〈书〉bosom; (breadth of) mind

【襟怀坦白】open-hearted and aboveboard; honest and straightforward

【襟翼】[航空] (wing) flap

jǐn

仅 副 only; merely; alone: ～次于 *second only to* / ～一人缺席。*Only one is absent*. / ～该市一地死于吸烟者已达数千人。*Smoking has caused thousands of deaths in this city alone*.

【仅供参考】just for reference; for reference only

【仅仅】only; merely; alone: 这～是开始。*This is only the beginning*. / 他解这道题～用了十分钟。*It took him only ten minutes to solve the problem*.

尽 Ⅰ 副 ❶ to the greatest extent: ～早 *as early as possible; at the earliest possible date* ❷ (used before a noun of locality) furthest; extreme: ～北边 *the northernmost end, etc*. / ～底下 *at the very bottom* / 他家住在村子～西头。*He lives at the western end of the village*. Ⅱ 介 be within the limits of: ～着三天把事情办好。*Get the job done in three days at the outside*. / ～着一百块钱花。*Don't spend more than* 100 *yuan*. Ⅲ 动 give priority to: ～着年纪大的坐。*Let the older people sit down first*. ——另见 jìn

【尽管】❶ feel free to; not hesitate to: 有什么问题～问。*If you have any questions, don't hesitate to ask them*. ❷ though; even though; in spite of; despite: 他～身体不好, 仍然坚持工作。*Though he's not in good health, he still keeps on working*. / 我喜欢这个工作, ～报酬很低。*I like the job, even though it's badly paid*.

【尽可能】as far as possible; to the best of one's ability: ～早点儿来 *come as early as possible* / 我～做好。*I'll do it to the best of my ability*.

【尽快】as quickly (or soon, early) as possible: 请～答复。*Please reply at your earliest convenience*.

【尽量】to the best of one's ability; as far as possible: ～采用先进技术 *make the widest possible use of advanced technology* ——另见 jìnliàng

【尽先】give first priority to: 我们都饿坏了, 得～解决吃饭问题。*We are starving—see to our meals first*.

【尽早】as soon as possible: 字典用毕, 请～送还。*Please return the dictionary as soon as you finish using it*. / 请～答复。*Please give us a reply at your earliest convenience*.

紧 Ⅰ 形 ❶ tight; taut; close: 把绳子拉～ *pull the rope taut* / 把螺丝拧～ *tighten the screw* / ～握手中枪 *hold the gun tight in one's hands* / 这双鞋太～。*These shoes are too tight*. or *These shoes pinch*. ❷ urgent; pressing; tense: 任务～。*The task is urgent*. / 风声～。*Things are tense*. / 雨下得正～。*It was raining hard*. ❸ strict; stringent: 管得～ *exercise strict control; be strict with* ❹ hard up; short of money: 手头～ *be short of money; be hard up* / 银根～。*Money is tight*. Ⅱ 动 tighten: ～一～背包带 *tighten the knapsack straps*

【紧巴巴】❶ tight: 我这条裤子穿着～的。*My trousers are too tight*. ❷ hard up; short of money: 日子过得～的 *be in financial straits* / 手头～的 *be short of money; be hard up*

【紧绷绷】❶ tightly drawn: 皮带系得～的 *with a belt fastened tight* ❷ (of one's facial expression) taut: 他脸～的, 像很生气的样子。*He had a taut expression on his face, apparently very angry*.

【紧逼】press hard; close in on: 步步～ *press on at every stage*

【紧凑】compact; terse; well-knit: 影片情节～。*The film has a well-knit plot*. / 活动安排得很～ *have a tight schedule*

【紧跟】follow closely; keep in step with: ～时代的步伐 *keep in step with the times* / ～形势 *keep abreast of the situation*

【紧箍咒】the Incantation of the Golden Hoop — inhibition

【紧急】urgent; pressing; critical: 发出～呼吁 *issue an urgent appeal* / 情况～。*The situation is critical*. / ～行动起来 *act promptly; take immediate action* / ～任务 *an urgent task* ◇ ～出口 emergency exit; ～措施 emergency measures; ～法令 emergency act; ～会议 emergency meeting; ～集合 emergency muster; ～降落 emergency landing; ～警报 emergency (air-raid) alarm; ～起飞 scramble; ～信号 emergency (or distress) signal; ～援助 (～救济) bailout; emergency aid; ～闸 emergency brake; ～状态 state of emergency

【紧紧】closely; firmly; tightly: ～相连 *closely linked* / ～盯着 *watch closely; stare fixedly; gaze steadfastly* / 他～抓住这个贼, 不让他跑掉。*He grasped the thief firmly to stop him running away*.

【紧邻】close neighbour; next-door neighbour
【紧锣密鼓】a wild beating of gongs and drums—an intense publicity campaign (usu. in preparation for some sinister undertaking)
【紧密】❶ close together; inseparable: ～团结 *be closely united* / ～合作 *close cooperation* / ～联系 *close contact* ❷ rapid and intense: 枪声～。*There was rapid, intense firing.*
【紧迫】pressing; urgent; imminent: 时间～ *be pressed for time* / 我有更～的事情要做。*I have more pressing things to attend to.* / 形势很～。*The situation is critical.* ◇ ～感 a feeling of urgency; a sense of urgency
【紧俏】(of consumer goods) in great demand but short supply ◇ ～商品 hard-to-get commodities; high demand merchandise
【紧缺】in short supply; badly needed: ～商品 *goods in short supply* / ～人才 *badly-needed professionals*
【紧日子】an austere life: 过～ *tighten one's belt; practice austerity*
【紧身短上衣】coatee
【紧身衣】tights
【紧缩】reduce; retrench; tighten: ～编制 *reduce staff* / ～开支 *cut down expenses; retrench; curtail outlay* / ～贷款 *decrease credit* / ～包围圈 *tighten the ring of encirclement*
【紧要】critical; crucial; vital: ～关头 *critical moment (or juncture); crucial moment* / 这一点十分～。*That's an extremely important point.* or *That's a vital point.*
【紧张】❶ nervous; keyed up: 神情～ *look nervous* / 慢慢讲,别～。*Speak slowly and don't be nervous.* ❷ tense; intense; strained: ～局势 *a tense situation* / ～气氛 *a tense atmosphere* ❸ in short supply; tight: 这几天鸡蛋供应有点～。*Eggs have been in rather short supply for the last few days.* or *There's been rather a shortage of eggs lately.* /目前这里住房相当～。*Accommodation here is pretty tight at present.*
【紧追】in hot pursuit: 小偷往街上跑,警察在后面～。*The thief ran down the street with a policeman in hot pursuit.*

堇 (构词成分)见下
【堇菜】[植] violet
【堇青石】cordierite
【堇色】violet (colour)

锦 Ⅰ名 brocade Ⅱ形 bright and beautiful: ～霞 *rosetinted clouds*
【锦标】prize; trophy; title
【锦标赛】championship contest; championships: 世界乒乓球～ *the World Table Tennis Championships*
【锦缎】brocade
【锦鸡】golden pheasant
【锦葵】[植] high mallow
【锦纶】polyamide fibre
【锦囊妙计】instructions for dealing with an emergency; wise counsel
【锦旗】silk banner (as an award or a gift)
【锦上添花】add flowers to the brocade—make what is good still better
【锦绣】as beautiful as brocade; beautiful; splendid
【锦绣河山】a land of splendours; a land of charm and beauty; a beautiful land
【锦绣前程】a glorious future
【锦衣玉食】live in luxury

谨 形 ❶ careful; cautious; circumspect: ～记在心 *bear in mind* / ～守规则 *strictly adhere to the rules* ❷ solemnly; sincerely: ～致谢意。*Please accept my sincere thanks.* / 我～代表全体职工,向你们表示热烈的欢迎。*On behalf of the staff and workers, I wish to extend to you our warmest welcome.*
【谨防】guard against; beware of: ～扒手。*Beware of pickpockets.* / ～假冒。*Beware of imitations.*
【谨上】(又作'谨启') (used after the signature in a formal letter) yours respectfully
【谨慎】prudent; careful; cautious; circumspect: 说话～ *be guarded in one's speech* / ～从事 *act with caution*
【谨小慎微】overcautious in small matters; overcautious
【谨严】careful and precise: 治学～ *careful and exact scholarship* / 文章结构～。*The article is compact and carefully constructed.*
【谨言慎行】speak and act cautiously; be discreet in word and deed
【谨赠】with the compliments of: 北京外国语大学～。*With the compliments of the Beijing Foreign Studies University.*

jìn

尽 Ⅰ动 ❶ exhausted; finished: 想～各种方法 *try all possible means* ❷ to the utmost; to the limit: 尽善尽美 ❸ use up; exhaust: 一饮而～ *empty a glass at one gulp; drain the cup with one gulp* ❹ try one's best; put to the best use: ～最大努力 *do one's best; exert one's utmost effort* Ⅱ形 all; exhaustive: 不可～信 *not to be believed word for word; to be taken with a grain of salt* / ～收眼底 *have a panoramic view* ——另见 jǐn
【尽处】terminal point; end: 山峡～,豁然开朗。*One suddenly sees broad light at the end of the mountain valley.*
【尽瘁】〈书〉do one's utmost; spare no effort; do all one can
【尽欢】enjoy oneself to the full: ～而散 (*of a party*) *break up after everyone has enjoyed himself to the full*
【尽力】do all one can; try one's best: 我们一定～支援。*We'll do our best to help.*
【尽力而为】do one's best; do everything in one's

power

【尽量】(drink or eat) to the full ——另见 jǐnliàng

【尽其所有】give everything one has; give one's all

【尽情】to one's heart's content; as much as one likes: ～欢呼 *cheer heartily* / ～歌唱 *sing to one's heart's content*

【尽然】(used in the negative) exactly like this: 你以为他说的都是真事,恐怕未必～吧! *You thought what he said was the truth, but that might not be the case.*

【尽人皆知】be known to all; be common knowledge

【尽人事】do what one can (to save a dying person, etc.); do all that is humanly possible (though with little hope of success)

【尽如人意】just as one wishes; entirely satisfactory: 哪能事事～? *How can you expect everything to turn out just as you wish?*

【尽善尽美】the acme of perfection; perfect

【尽是】full of; all; without exception: 这儿原来～石头。*This place used to be full of boulders.* / 这里展出的～新产品。*All the exhibits here are new products.*

【尽收眼底】have a panoramic view: 飞机在重庆上空徐徐降落,美丽的山城～。*The entire beautiful mountain city of Chongqing came into view as the plane slowly made its landing.*

【尽头】end: 路的～ *the end of the road* / 学问是没有～的。*There is no limit to knowledge.*

【尽心】with all one's heart: 医护人员为照看受伤的工人真是尽了心。*The doctors and nurses did their utmost to tend the injured workers.* / 这些年青人干活可～呢。*These young people are really conscientious in their work.*

【尽孝】be filial to one's parents; be a filial son (or daughter)

【尽心竭力】(do sth.) with all one's heart and all one's might

【尽兴】to one's heart's content; enjoy oneself to the full: ～而归 *return after thoroughly enjoying oneself*

【尽义务】❶ do one's duty; fulfil one's obligation: 尽公民的义务 *do one's duty as a citizen* ❷ work for no reward

【尽责】try one's best to fulfil one's responsibility; do one's duty

【尽职】fulfil one's duty: 他工作一向很～。*He has always been a conscientious worker.*

【尽忠】❶ be utterly loyal ❷ be faithful unto death

进 动 ❶ advance; move forward; move ahead: 向前～ *move forward* ❷ enter; come (or go into); get into: ～屋 *enter a house (or room)* / ～大学 *enter college* / 请～! *Come in!* ❸ receive; admit: 我们单位～了一个新打字员。*Our unit has taken on a new typist.* ❹ eat; drink; take: 进餐 ❺ submit; present: ～一言 *give a word of advice* ❻ (used after a verb) into; in: 走～车间 *walk into the workshop* / 把子弹压～弹匣 *press the cartridges into the magazine* / 住～新楼 *move into a new building* ❼ [体] score a goal: ～了! *It's in!* or *Goal!* / 这球没～。*He's missed it.*

【进逼】close in on; advance on; press on towards

【进兵】dispatch troops to attack (a place); (of troops) march on (a place)

【进补】take tonic; take extra nourishment: 冬令～ *take tonic in winter*

【进步】❶ advance; progress; improve: 两国关系向前进了一步。*The relationship between the two nations has moved a step formard.* / 你的发音很有～。*Your pronunciation has greatly improved.* ❷ (politically) progressive: 思想～ *have progressive ideas* / ～人士 *progressive personages* / ～势力 *progressive forces*

【进餐】〈书〉have a meal: 共进午餐 *have lunch together*

【进场】❶ march into the arena ❷ [航空] approach: ～失败 *missed approach*

【进城】go into town; go to town

【进程】course; process; progress: 历史～ *the course of history*

【进尺】[矿] footage: 掘进(凿岩,开拓)～ *drifting (drilling, tunnelling) footage*

【进出】❶ pass in and out: 这儿进进出出的人真多。*What a lot of people are coming in and out of here.* / 车辆由此～。*Vehicles this way!* ❷ (business) turnover: 这个商店每天有好几千元的～。*This store has a daily turnover of several thousand yuan.*

【进出口】❶ exits and entrances; exit ❷ imports and exports: ～公司 *import and export corporation* / ～商品 *import and export commodities* ◇ ～贸易 import and export trade; foreign trade; ～商品检验 import-export commodity inspection; ～许可证 import-export licence

【进刀】[机] feed: ～装置 *feed arrangement*; *feed gear*; *feeder*

【进度】❶ rate of progress (or advance): 加快～ *quicken the pace (or tempo)* ❷ planned speed; schedule: 我们已按照～完成了这道工序。*We have finished this part of the process according to plan.* ◇ ～表 progress chart

【进而】and then; after that: 我们工厂准备首先实现半自动化,～实现完全自动化。*Our factory plans first to achieve semiautomation and then proceed to complete automation.*

【进发】set out; start: 列车向北京～。*The train started for Beijing.*

【进犯】intrude into; invade

【进风井】[矿] downcast (shaft)

【进宫】❶ (in feudal times) enter imperial palace ❷〈诙〉be detained or imprisoned by police

【进攻】attack; assault; offensive: 做好～准备 *get ready to take the offensive* / 发起全面～ *launch an all-out offensive* ◇ ～性武器 offensive weapon

【进贡】❶ pay tribute (to a suzerain or emperor) ❷ grease (or oil) sb.'s palm

【进化】evolution：人是从类人猿～而来的。*Man evolved from the anthropoid ape.* ◇～论 the theory of evolution；evolutionism

【进货】stock (a shop) with goods；lay in a stock of merchandise；replenish one's stock：这家商店进了一批货。*The shop laid in a new stock of goods.*

【进见】call on (sb. holding high office)；have an audience with

【进京】go to the capital of the country：～开会 *go to the capital for a meeting*

【进军】march；advance：向西北～ *march into the Northwest* / 吹响～的号角 *sound the bugle to advance；sound the advance* / 号召向沙漠～ *a call to conquer the desert* ◇～号 bugle to advance

【进口】❶ entrance ❷ enter port ❸ import ◇～报单 import declaration；consumption entry；～报关 customs entry；～壁垒 import barrier；～补贴 import subsidy；～承诺 import commitment；～代办行 import commission；～代理商 import agent；～附加税 import surcharge；～港 port of entry；～管制 import control；～货 imported goods；imports；～检疫 import quarantine；～商 importer；～申报 declaration for import；～税 import duties；～替代 import substitution；～限额 import quota；～许可证 import license；～原料 imported materials

【进款】〈口〉income；receipts

【进来】❶ come (or get) in；enter：让他～。*Let him in.* / 进屋来吧，外面太冷了。*Do come in, it's cold outside.* ❷ (used after a verb) in (here)：她气喘吁吁地走～，浑身湿透了。*She came in panting and soaked to the skin.* / 从窗口飞～一只燕子。*A swallow flew in through the window.*

【进门】❶ go in；pass the gate：～之前要查看通行证。*Your pass will be checked at the gate.* ❷ learn the rudiments of sth.；cross the threshold：师傅领～，修行看各人。*The master initiates the apprentices, but their skill depends on their own efforts.* ❸ (of a woman) get married and move into the bridegroom's family：她是刚～的媳妇。*She has just married into the family.* or *She's the new bride.*

【进取】keep forging ahead；be eager to make progress；be enterprising：永远保持谦虚和～的精神 *always remain modest and keep forging ahead* ◇～心 enterprising spirit；initiative；gumption；push

【进去】❶ go in；get in；enter：你～看看，我在门口等着。*Go in and have a look, and I'll wait for you at the gate.* ❷ (used after a verb) in (there)：把桌子搬～ *move the table in* / 冲～ *rush in* / 从旁门走进几个人去了。*Some people went in through the side door.*

【进入】enter；get into：～阵地 *get into position* / ～决赛阶段 *enter the finals* / 运动已～高潮。*The movement has reached a high tide.* ◇～角色 get inside the character that one is playing；enter into the spirit of a character；live one's part；～系统 log in(on)

【进身之阶】stepping-stone (in one's official career)

【进食】take food；have one's meal

【进士】a successful candidate in the highest imperial examinations

【进水闸】intake work；intake

【进退】❶ advance and retreat：～自如 *free to advance or retreat (in a battle or game)；have room for manoeuvre* ❷ sense of propriety

【进退两难】find it difficult to advance or to retreat—be in a dilemma

【进退维谷】in a dilemma；between the devil and the deep blue sea

【进位】[数] carry (a number, as in adding)

【进献】offer or present (to one's superior)

【进香】(of Buddhists or Taoists) go on a pilgrimage to a temple；offer incense；worship：近几年，到杭州灵隐寺～的善男信女真不少。*These years, there has indeed been a large number of devout men and women going on pilgrimages to the Ling Yin Temple in Hangzhou.* ◇～客 Buddhist pilgrim

【进项】income；receipts

【进行】❶ be in progress；be underway；go on：工作～得怎么样？*How are you getting on with your work?* / 勘探工作已经在～。*Prospecting is already in progress.* / 手术～了六个小时。*The operation lasted six hours.* ❷ carry on；carry out；conduct：～实地调查 *make on-the-spot investigations* / ～科学实验 *engage in scientific experiment* ❸ be on the march；march；advance

【进行曲】[音] march

【进修】engage in advanced studies；take a refresher course：出国～ *go abroad for advanced studies* / 教师的业务～ *teachers' vocational studies* ◇～班 class for advanced studies；～生 graduate student

【进一步】go a step further；further：有了～的了解 *have a better understanding* / ～改善 *make further improvements* / ～开放 *open the door wider*

【进展】make progress；make headway：～神速 *advance at a miraculous pace* / 事情～如何？*How are things going?* / 谈判毫无～。*The talks have made no headway.*

【进占】march on and take (a place)

【进站】(of a train) get into (or draw into, pull into) a station：火车正在～，我们快点儿还来得及。*The train is just getting into (or drawing into, pulling into) the station. If we hurry we can catch it.*

【进账】income；receipts

【进驻】❶ enter and be stationed in；enter and garrison：部队已～该市。*Troops have been garrisoned in that city.* ❷ (of a working group) sent by a higher authority to investigate or resolve problems：省政府派小组～县政府调查贪污现象。*Provincial authorities sent a group to the county to investigate corruption.*

近 形 ❶ near; close: 歌声由远而～。*The singing came closer and closer*. / 离国庆节很～了。*National Day is drawing near*. or *It'll soon be National Day*. ❷ approaching; approximately; close to: 年～六十 *approaching sixty*; *getting on for sixty* / 观众～万人。*There were nearly* 10,000 *spectators*. ❸ intimate; closely related: 两家走得挺～。*The two families are on intimate terms*. ❹ easy to understand: 浅近

【近便】close and convenient: 咱们找个～的饭馆吃点吧。*Let's have a snack at the nearest restaurant*.

【近程】short range: ～雷达 *short-range radar*

【近处】vicinity; place nearby: ～没有客店。*There isn't any inn close by* (*or in the neighbourhood*).

【近代】modern times: ～史 *modern history*

【近道】shortcut

【近地点】[天] perigee

【近东】the Near East

【近海】coastal waters; inshore; offshore: 我国～有丰富的水产资源。*Our country has rich offshore aquatic resources*. / ～渔业 *inshore fishing* ◇ ～工程 offshore engineering

【近乎】❶ close to; little short of: ～荒谬的论点 *an argument little short of being ridiculous*; *an argument bordering on the absurd* / 他已～破产。*He is on the verge of bankruptcy*. ❷〈方〉intimate; friendly: 他们关系一直很～。*They have been intimate friends*. ——另见〖套近乎〗

【近郊】outskirts of a city; suburbs; environs

【近景】[摄] close shot

【近况】recent developments; how things stand: 中东～ *recent developments in the Middle East*

【近来】recently; of late; lately: ～她身体很不好。*Recently she has been rather unwell*.

【近邻】near neighbour: 他家和我家是～。*His family and mine are close neighbours*.

【近路】shortcut: 走～ *take a shortcut*

【近年】in recent years: ～获奖的影片不少。*Quite a few films have won prizes in recent years*.

【近旁】nearby; near: 屋子～ *near the house*

【近期】in the near future: ～内无大雨。*There won't be heavy rain in the coming few days*. / ～预报 *short-term forecast* / ～目标 *immediate objective*

【近亲】close relative; near relation ◇ ～繁殖 inbreeding; ～婚姻 consanguineous marriage

【近日】❶ recently; in the past few days: ～未曾见到他。*I haven't seen him recently*. ❷ within the next few days: 这项工程～即将完工。*The project will be completed within the next few days*.

【近日点】[天] perihelion

【近视】myopia; nearsightedness; shortsightedness: 她稍微有点～。*She is slightly myopic*. or *She is a bit nearsighted*. ◇ ～眼 myopia; nearsightedness; shortsightedness; ～眼镜 spectacles for nearsighted person

【近水楼台】waterside pavilion—a favourable position

【近水楼台先得月】a waterside pavilion gets the moonlight first—a person in a favourable position gains special advantages

【近似】approximate; similar: 这两幅画有些～。*These two paintings are somewhat similar*. ◇ ～读数 approximate reading; ～计算 approximate calculation; ～商 approximate quotient; ～值 approximate value

【近台防守】[体] close-table defence

【近台快攻】[体] close-table fast attack

【近义词】near synonym

【近因】immediate cause

【近于】bordering on; little short of: ～荒唐 *little short of preposterous*; *bordering on the absurd*

【近月点】[航天] perilune

【近在咫尺】close at hand; well within reach

【近战】fighting at close quarters; close combat

【近朱者赤,近墨者黑】he who stays near vermilion gets stained red, and he who stays near ink gets stained black—one takes on the colour of one's company

劲 名 ❶ strength; energy: 他～儿大。*He has great strength*. / 这酒～儿大。*This liquor is quite strong*. / 我烧是退了,可身上还是没～儿。*My temperature is down, but I'm still feeling weak*. ❷ vigour; spirit; drive; zeal: 他跟我别着～哪!能听我的吗? *How can you expect him to listen to me, when he's still in a huff with me?* ❸ air; manner; expression: 你这骄傲～儿得好好改改。*You've got to get rid of your arrogant ways*. / 瞧他那高兴～儿。*See how happy he looks*. ❹ interest; relish; gusto: 打扑克没～,咱们去游泳吧。*Playing cards is no fun; let's go swimming*. ——另见 jìng

【劲射】[体] (足球) a sudden shot at the goal: ～破门 *to make a sudden shot at the goal* / 起脚～入网 *to suddenly kick right into the net*

【劲头】〈口〉❶ strength; energy ❷ vigour; spirit; drive; zeal: 工作有～ *be full of drive in one's work* / 小伙子们～十足。*The young fellows are all enthusiasm*.

【劲舞】rap dancing

浸 动 soak; steep; immerse: 把衣服放在肥皂水里～一会儿再洗。*Soak the clothes in soapy water for a while before you wash them*. / 他的衣服让汗～湿了。*His clothes were soaked with sweat*.

【浸膏】[药] extract

【浸灌】❶ (as of floodwater) come in; spread out; flood: 海水～ *sea water spreading over* ❷ irrigate: 放水～秧田 *irrigate the rice seedling bed*

【浸剂】[药] infusion

【浸礼】[宗] (基督教) Christianity baptism; immersion

【浸礼会】the Baptist Church; the Baptists

【浸没】❶ submerge; flood; immerse: ～透镜 *im-*

mersion lens / ～折射计 *immersion refractometer* / ～式加热器 *immersion heater* / 整个村庄被洪水～。*The whole village was submerged in the flood*. ❷ be immersed in; be permeated with: 伟人逝世，人们～在悲痛之中。*People were immersed in grief at the passing away of the great man*.

【浸泡】soak; immerse: ～棉籽 *soak cottonseed*

【浸染】❶ be contaminated; be gradually influenced ❷ soak; infiltrate ❸ dip-dye

【浸软】macerate

【浸透】soak; saturate; steep; infuse: 汗水～了他的衣裳。*His clothes were soaked with sweat*. / 他伤口出的血～了绷带。*The blood from his wound has soaked right through the bandage*.

【浸种】[农] seed soaking (in water): 温汤～ *hot water treatment*

【浸渍】soak; ret; macerate: 亚麻～ *flax retting* / ～剂 *soaker* / ～液 *maceration extract*

烬 名 cinder: 灰烬

晋 动 ❶ enter; advance: 晋见 ❷ promote: 加官晋爵

【晋级】〈书〉rise in rank; be promoted

【晋见】call on (sb. holding high office); have an audience with

【晋升】〈书〉promote to a higher office

【晋谒】〈书〉call on (sb. holding high office); have an audience with

缙 名〈书〉red silk

【缙绅】(in former times) government official; government official in retirement

禁 Ⅰ 动 ❶ prohibit; forbid; ban: 严禁 ❷ imprison; detain: 监禁 Ⅱ 名 ❶ what is forbidden by law or custom; a taboo: 入国问禁 ❷ forbidden area ——另见 jīn

【禁闭】confinement (as a punishment): 关～ *be placed in confinement*

【禁地】forbidden area; restricted area; out-of-bounds area

【禁毒】ban drugs; drug control: ～法律 *laws banning drugs* / ～宣传 *publicity against drugs* / 政府～机构 *government drug enforcement agency*

【禁赌】ban gambling

【禁伐林】forest reserve where lumbering is prohibited

【禁方】[中] secret medicinal recipe

【禁飞区】no fly zone

【禁锢】❶ debar from holding office (in feudal times) ❷ keep in custody; imprison ❸ confine: 历代封建统治阶级都力图用礼教把妇女～起来。*All through the feudal ages the ruling class did their best to shackle women with Confucian ethics*.

【禁果】〈字〉forbidden fruit; 〈喻〉make love for the first time: 第三次约会，他们就吃～。*They made love for the first time on their third date*.

【禁忌】❶ taboo ❷ avoid; abstain from: ～辛辣油腻 *abstain from peppery or greasy food* ❸ [医] contraindication

【禁酒】prohibition on alcoholic drinks

【禁例】prohibitory regulations; prohibitions

【禁猎】prohibit hunting: ～期 *a period when hunting is prohibited* / ～区 *an area where hunting is prohibited*

【禁令】prohibition; ban

【禁区】❶ forbidden zone; restricted zone: 空中～ *restricted airspace* / 针灸～ *forbidden zone of acupuncture* / 那里是～，不准过去。*You can't go there. That place is out-of-bounds*. ❷ (wildlife or plant) preserve; reserve; natural park ❸ football penalty area ❹ basketball restricted area

【禁赛】banned from competition

【禁食】fast: 穆斯林在斋月的时候要～。*Muslims fast during the festival of Ramadan*. / 她在开刀前得～一天。*She had to fast for one day before her operation*.

【禁食疗法】fasting treatment; starvation cure

【禁书】banned book

【禁卫军】imperial guards

【禁线】restraining line

【禁烟】ban on opium-smoking and the opium trade ◇ ～区 no-smoking area

【禁渔】prohibit fishing: ～季 *closed fishing season* / ～区 *forbidden fishing zone*

【禁欲】be ascetic ◇ ～主义 asceticism

【禁运】embargo: 战时～品 *contraband of war* / 实行～ *lay (or put, place) an embargo on (sth.)* / 解除～ *lift (or remove) the embargo on (sth.)* / 属～之列 *under an embargo* ◇ ～品 contraband

【禁止】prohibit; ban; forbid: 医生～他抽烟。*The doctor forbids him to smoke*. / ～砍伐树木。*Felling trees is forbidden*. / ～入内。*No admittance*. / ～停车。*No parking*. / ～通行。*No thoroughfare*. or *Closed to traffic*. / ～倒垃圾。*No garbage here*. / ～招贴。*Post no bills*. / ～拍照。*Cameras are forbidden*.

【禁制品】articles the manufacture of which is prohibited except by special permit; banned products

【禁阻】prohibit; ban; forbid; prevent; stop

觐 动 ❶ present oneself before (a monarch) ❷ go on a pilgrimage

【觐见】present oneself before (a monarch); go to court; have an audience with

噤 动 ❶〈书〉keep silent ❷ shiver: 寒噤

【噤若寒蝉】as silent as a cicada in cold weather—keep quiet out of fear

jīng

泾 名 (or 泾河) a river rising in Ningxia and

flowing into central Shaanxi where it empties into the Weihe (渭河)

【泾渭不分】fail to distinguish between the good and the bad ——另见〖泾渭分明〗

【泾渭分明】as different as the waters of the Jinghe and the Weihe—entirely different

京 名 ❶ the capital of a country：进～ *go to the capital* ❷ short for Beijing

【京城】〈旧〉the capital of a country

【京都】〈旧〉the capital of a country

【京官】〈旧〉government officials in the capital of the country

【京胡】jinghu, a two-stringed bowed instrument with a high register; Beijing opera fiddle

【京剧】Beijing opera

【京腔】〈旧〉Beijing accent：撇～ *affect a Beijing accent*

【京味】of special Beijing flavour; with Beijing characteristics：～小吃 *snacks of Beijing flavour* / 这个戏的～儿很浓。*The play is rich in Beijing ambience (or flavour).*

【京戏】〈口〉Beijing opera

茎 Ⅰ 名 ❶ stem (of a plant); stalk ❷ a thing like a stem or stalk：刀～ *the handle of a knife* / 剑～ *the hilt of a sword* Ⅱ 量〈书〉(for long, narrow things)：数～小草 *a few small blades of grass* / 数～白发 *a few white hairs*

经 Ⅰ 名 ❶［纺］warp ❷［中］channels ❸ scripture; sutra; canon; classic：《孝～》*The Classic of Filial Piety* /《金刚～》*The Diamond Sutra* ❹ menses; menstruation ❺［地理］longitude：东经 / 西经 Ⅱ 动 ❶ manage; deal in; engage in：经商 ❷ pass through; undergo; experience：我这辈子可～了不少事。*I have seen quite a lot in my life.* ❸ stand; bear; endure：～得起时间的考验 *can stand the test of time* Ⅲ 形 constant; regular：经常 Ⅳ 介 as a result of; after; through：～检查，产品质量合格。*Examination confirmed that the quality of the products was up to specification.* ——另见 jìng

【经办】handle; deal with：这件事是他～的。*He managed that affair.*

【经闭】［中］amenorrhoea

【经编】［纺］warp knitting：～针织物 *warpknitted fabric*

【经常】❶ day-to-day; everyday; daily：～工作 *day-to-day work* / ～开支 *running expenses* ❷ frequently; constantly; regularly; often：这类问题是～发生的。*This kind of problem frequently crops up.* or *This sort of thing is a common occurrence.*

【经典】❶ classics ❷ scriptures：佛教～ *Buddhist scriptures* ❸ classical：马列主义～著作 *Marxist-Leninist classics; classical works of Marxism-Leninism* ◇ ～力学［物］classical mechanics；～作家 author of a classic; classic

【经度】longitude

【经费】funds; outlay：～不足 *be short of funds*

【经风雨，见世面】see the world and brave the storms：让孩子一个人出去闯一闯，经经风风雨雨，见见世面，这对他会有好处的。*Let the child leave home to venture out himself. It will do him good to see life and stand its tests.*

【经管】be in charge of：～财务 *be in charge of financial affairs*

【经过】❶ pass; go through; undergo：这汽车～动物园吗？*Does this bus pass the Zoo?* ❷ as a result of; after; through：～充分讨论，大家取得了一致意见。*After thorough discussion unanimity was achieved.* ❸ process; course：事件的全部～ *the whole course of the incident; the whole process from beginning to end* / 事情的～是这样的。*This is how it happened.*

【经互会】〈略〉见〖经济互助委员会〗

【经纪】❶ manage (a business) ❷ manager; broker

【经纪人】broker; middleman; agent：房地产～ *estate agent* / 外汇～ *foreign exchange broker* ◇ ～留置权 broker's lien

【经济】❶ economy：发展社会主义～ *develop the socialist economy* / 混合～ *mixed economy* / ～部门 *branches of the economy; economic departments* / ～地位 *economic status; economic position* ❷ of industrial (or economic) value; economic：经济植物 ❸ financial condition; income：～宽裕 *well-off; well-to-do* / ～拮据 *be hard up* ❹ economical; thrifty：～实惠 *economical and practical* / ～地使用 *use economically* / 不～ *costing too much; uneconomical* ◇ ～舱 economy class；～承包责任制 economic responsibility system with contracted jobs；～地理学 economic geography；～动物 economic animal；～发展战略 strategy for the development of economy; the economic development strategy；～法规 laws and regulations pertaining to the economy; economic statutes；～法庭 economic tribunal；～繁荣 economic prosperity；～犯罪 economic crimes；～封锁 economic blockade；～复苏 economic resurgence; economic recovery；～改革 economic reform；～杠杆 economic lever；～过热 economic over-heating; the overheated economy；～互助委员会 the Council of Mutual Economic Assistance (CMEA); Comecon (now dissolved)；～滑坡 economic decline；～基础 economic base; economic basis；～技术开发区 economic and technological development zone；～开放区 open economic region；～恐慌 economic crisis；～昆虫 economic insects；～立法 economic legislation；～联合体 economic association；～林 economic forest；～命脉 economic lifeline; economic arteries; key branches of the economy；～模式 economic mould；～圈 economic circle；～渗透 economic penetration; economic infiltration；～失调 economic ailment; dislocation of economy；～实力 economic strength；～适用房

economic houses；～特区 special economic zone；～腾飞 economic take-off；～萎缩 economic contraction；～萧条 economic depression (or slump)；～效益 economic performance；economic results；economic effectiveness；～援助 economic aid；～责任 financial responsibility；～增长点 growth engines；～账 financial considerations；～振兴 vigorous economic growth；～支柱 economic pillars；～植物 economic plants；～指数 economic index number；～制裁 economic sanctions；～制度 economic system；～主义 economism；～自由化 ligeralization of the economy；～总量 total supply and demand；～作物 industrial crop；cash crop

【经济成分】sector of the economy；economic sector：发展多种～ *develop diverse sectors of the economy*

【经济合同】economic contract：～仲裁委员会 *economic contract arbitration committee*

【经济核算】economic accounting；business accounting：～单位 *business accounting unit*

【经济环境】economic environment：治理～ *improve the economic environment*

【经济实体】economic entity：所有企业都应办成自主经营的～。*All enterprises should be turned into economic entities operating independently.*

【经济体制】economic structure：～改革 *reform of the economic structure；economic restructuring* / 集中统一的～ *a unified and centralized economic structure*

【经济危机】economic crisis：～周期 *economic crisis cycle*

【经济学】economics：～家 *economist*

【经济运行机制】economic mechanism；economic operation mechanism

【经济杂交】［牧］commercial crossbreeding

【经济秩序】economic order：整顿～ *rectify the economic order* / 新的国际～ *new international economic order*

【经久】❶ prolonged ❷ durable：～耐用 *durable；able to stand wear and tear*

【经久不息】prolonged：～的掌声 *prolonged applause*

【经理】❶ handle；manage ❷ manager；director ◇ ～身份 managership

【经历】❶ go through；undergo；experience：现代科学技术正在～着一场伟大的革命。*Modern science and technology are undergoing a great revolution.* ❷ experience：他这人～多，见识广。*He's a man of wide knowledge and experience.* / 个人～ *personal experiences* / 生活～ *life experience*

【经脉】［中］passages through which vital energy circulates，regulating bodily functions

【经贸】economy and trade：～政策 *policies for economic and trade activities*

【经密】［纺］warp density；ends per inch

【经年累月】for years and years；year in year out

【经期】(menstrual) period

【经纱】［纺］❶ warp ❷ end

【经商】engage in trade；be in business

【经手】handle；deal with：～公款 *handle public money* / 这件事是他～的。*He's the one who handled this matter.* / ～人 *person handling a transaction，particular job，etc.*

【经受】undergo；experience；withstand；stand；weather：～挫折 *go through setbacks* / 这些花～不住寒气。*These flowers cannot stand the cold.*

【经售】sell on commission；deal in；distribute；sell：这家农村商店～邮票。*The village shop sells postage stamps.* / ～处 *agency*

【经纬】❶ meridian and parallel (lines) ❷ main threads；orderliness；reason：～万端 *have too many things to attend to* / 他如今说话越发没了～。*He has become even more senseless in his speech now.* ❸〈书〉plan and administer：～天下 *attend to state affairs；order and regulate affairs of state*

【经纬度】［地理］latitude and longitude

【经纬仪】theodolite；transit：～测量 *transit survey*

【经文】scripts；passages from the Confucian classics or religious scriptures

【经线】❶［纺］warp ❷ meridian (line)

【经销】同〖经售〗◇ ～品牌 dealer brand；～商 distributor；～专业户 households specializing in marketing

【经心】careful；mindful；conscientious：～搜集各种资料 *take great care to collect all kinds of data* / 干什么工作都要～。*One should be conscientious in any kind of work.*

【经验】❶ experience：～丰富 *have rich experience；be very experienced* / ～不足 *lack experience；not be sufficiently experienced* / 直接(间接)～ *direct (indirect) experience* ❷ go through；experience：我从来没～过这样的艰难。*I have never experienced such hardships.*

【经验之谈】the wise remark of an experienced person；remark made by one who has had experience

【经验主义】empiricism：～者 *empiricist*

【经营】manage；operate；run；engage in：统一(分散)～ *unified (decentralized) management* / ～少量家庭副业 *engage in limited household sideline production* / 发展多种～ *promote a diversified economy* ◇ ～承包制 management contract system；～方向 management direction；～方针 managerial principles；～权 power of management；managerial authority；～思想 management philosophy；～性亏损 losses of a management nature；～责任制 responsibility system for operation；～资金 operation fund；floating capital；～作风 management style

【经由】via；by way of：～武汉去重庆 *be bound for Chongqing via Wuhan*

【经院哲学】scholasticism

【经轴】［纺］warp beam

【经传】❶ Confucian classics and commentaries on them；Confucian canon ❷ classical works；classics ——另见〖不见经传〗

荆 名 chaste tree; vitex

【荆棘】thistles and thorns; brambles; thorny undergrowth: ～丛生 *overgrown with brambles*

【荆棘载途】a path overgrown with brambles —a path beset with difficulties

【荆芥】[中] jingjie (Schizonepeta tenuifolia)

【荆条】twigs of the chaste tree (used for weaving baskets, etc.)

旌 名 an ancient type of banner hoisted on a featherdecked mast

【旌旗】banners and flags

惊 动 ❶ start; be frightened: 听到大坝出现险情,她心里一～。*She started at the news that the dyke was in danger*. / ～呆了 *be stupefied* ❷ surprise; shock; alarm: 惊动 ❸ shy; stampede: 马～了。*The horse shied*. / 大雷雨～了牛群。*The thunderstorm stampeded the cattle*.

【惊诧】surprised; amazed; astonished

【惊呆】stunned; stupefied: 看到孩子摔得鼻青脸肿,他～了。*He was stupefied at the sight of the badly bruised child*.

【惊动】alarm; alert; disturb: 枪声～了森林中的鸟兽。*The report of a gun startled the birds and animals in the forest*. / 别为这么点儿小事～他。*Don't trouble him about such a trifling matter*.

【惊愕】〈书〉stunned; stupefied

【惊风】[中] infantile convulsions: 急～ *acute infantile convulsions*

【惊弓之鸟】a bird that starts at the mere twang of a bow-string—a badly frightened person

【惊骇】〈书〉frightened; panic-stricken

【惊呼】cry out in alarm: 他～:"大事不好!" *He cried out in alarm*: "*Oh, calamity!*"

【惊慌】(又作'惊惶') alarmed; scared; panic-stricken: ～不安 *jittery*; *nervy* / ～的神色 *frightened looks* / 没有半点～ *not in the least scared*

【惊慌失措】frightened out of one's wits; seized with panic; panic-stricken

【惊魂未定】not yet recovered from a fright; still badly shaken

【惊悸】〈书〉palpitate with fear

【惊叫】cry in fear; scream

【惊厥】❶ faint from fear ❷ [医] convulsions

【惊恐】alarmed and panicky; terrified; panic-stricken; seized with terror: ～失色 *pale with fear*

【惊恐万状】in a great panic; convulsed with fear

【惊雷】frightening thunder; loud clap of thunder; thunderous warning or awakening: 一声震天动地的～ *sudden clap of a shattering thunder* / 于无声处听～。*You could hear thunderous warning in that dead silence*.

【惊奇】wonder; be surprised; be amazed: 孩子睁大眼睛,～地望着魔术师。*The child stared with wonder at the magician*.

【惊人】astonishing; amazing; alarming: ～的成就 *astonishing (or amazing) achievements* / ～的毅力 *amazing willpower* / 交通事故多得～。*There is a horrifying number of traffic accidents*.

【惊人之举】masterstroke; coup de maitre

【惊世骇俗】astound the world with an extraordinary idea, etc.: 你的高见,真可谓～。*Your idea was really amazing*.

【惊叹】wonder at; marvel at; exclaim (with admiration): 这些精美的牙雕,使大家～不已。*The exquisite ivory carvings won everybody's admiration*.

【惊叹号】exclamation mark (!)

【惊堂木】(又作'惊堂板') (in former times) a wooden block used by a magistrate to strike the table in calling for attention or order

【惊涛骇浪】(usu. 〈喻〉) terrifying waves; a stormy sea: 充满～的一生 *a life full of hazards*

【惊天动地】shaking heaven and earth; earthshake; world-shake: ～的伟业 *a magnificent and earth-shake feat*

【惊悉】be shocked to learn: ～某人不幸逝世 *be distressed to learn of the passing away of sb*.

【惊喜】pleasantly surprised: ～地叫了起来 *call out in happy astonishment*

【惊吓】frighten; scare: 这孩子受了～,睡得不安稳。*The child has had a shock and isn't sleeping well*.

【惊险】alarmingly dangerous; breathtaking; thrilling: ～动作 *astounding feat* / ～的表演 *breathtaking performance* / ～的场面 *thrilling scene*

【惊险片】thriller

【惊心动魄】soul-stirring; profoundly affecting: ～的革命运动 *stirring revolutionary movements*

【惊醒】(jīngxǐng) ❶ wake up with a start ❷ rouse suddenly from sleep; awaken: 一声巨响把他从睡梦中～。*He was awakened by a terrific bang*.

【惊醒】(jīngxing) sleep lightly; be a light sleeper: 他睡觉很～,有点响动都知道。*He's a very light sleeper; any little noise disturbs him*.

【惊讶】surprised; amazed; astonished; astounded: 他的无知令人～。*His ignorance is astonishing*.

【惊疑】surprised and bewildered

【惊异】surprised; amazed; astonished; astounded

菁 (构词成分)见下

【菁华】essence; cream; quintessence

晶 Ⅰ 形 brilliant; glittering: 晶莹 Ⅱ 名 ❶ quartz; (rock) crystal: 茶晶 ❷ any crystalline substance: 晶体

【晶格】[物] (crystal) lattice: 面心～ *face-centred lattice* / 体心～ *body-centred lattice*

【晶粒】[物] crystalline grain; grain

【晶石】spar

【晶体】crystal

【晶体管】transistor: 硅～ *silicon transistor* / 锗～ *germanium transistor* / ～收音机 *transistor ra-*

dio

【晶莹】sparkling and crystal-clear; glittering and translucent: 草上的露珠～发亮。*The grass glistened with dewdrops*. / 她有一颗～的心。*She has a pure crystal-like heart*.

【晶状体】[生理] crystalline lens

腈 名 [化] nitrile

【腈纶】acrylic fibres

粳 名 同〖粳稻〗

【粳稻】round-grained nonglutinous rice; japonica rice

【粳米】polished round-grained nonglutinous rice

睛 名 eyeball: 定睛

精 Ⅰ 形 ❶ refined; picked; choice: 精盐 ❷ perfect; excellent: 精良/ 精彩 ❸ meticulous; fine; precise: 那个裁缝的手工很～。*That tailor does skilful work*. / 这花瓶工艺很～。*This vase is a piece of exquisite workmanship*. ❹ smart; sharp; clever; shrewd: 这小鬼真～。*That's a really smart kid*. / 他做生意很～。*He is a shrewd businessman*. / 小算盘打得～ *be selfish and calculating* ❺skilled; conversant; proficient: ～于绘画 *skilled in painting* Ⅱ 名 ❶ essence; extract: 杏仁儿～ *almond extract* ❷ energy; spirit: 精疲力竭 ❸ sperm; semen; seed: 受精 ❹ goblin; spirit; demon: 狐狸精

【精兵】picked troops; crack troops

【精兵简政】better troops and simpler administration; better staff and simpler administration; streamlined administration

【精彩】brilliant; splendid; wonderful: ～的表演 *a brilliant performance* / 发言中最～的地方 *most interesting parts of a speech* / 这场球打得真～。*This is an exciting game*.

【精巢】[生理] spermary; testis; testicle

【精诚】〈书〉absolute sincerity; good faith: ～合作 *sincerely cooperate*

【精诚所至,金石为开】complete sincerity can affect even metal and stone

【精虫】[生理] spermatozoon

【精纯】consummate; superb: 技艺～ *consummate skill*

【精粹】succinct; pithy; terse

【精打细算】careful calculation and strict budgeting: 对人力物力的使用要～。*We must be meticulous in planning the use of men and material*.

【精当】precise and appropriate: 用词～ *precise and appropriate wording; masterly choice of words*

【精雕细刻】(又作'精雕细镂') work at sth. with the care and precision of a sculptor; work at sth. with great care

【精读】❶ read carefully and thoroughly ❷ intensive reading

【精度】(〈略〉见〖精密度〗) precision: 这台机床的～达到国家标准。*The precision of this lathe is up to state requirements*. / 高～ *high precision*

【精干】❶ (of a body of troops, etc.) small in number but highly trained; crack: 一支～的小分队 *a small detachment of picked troops* ❷ keen-witted and capable: 队长虽然年轻,但很～。*Young as he is, the team leader is very capable*.

【精耕细作】intensive and meticulous farming; intensive cultivation

【精光】❶ with nothing left: 票不到一个钟头就卖得～。*All the tickets sold out in an hour*. / 把衣服脱个～ *strip off one's clothes* ❷ bright and clean; shiny: 锅擦得～发亮。*The pot was polished to a high shine*.

【精悍】❶ capable and vigorous ❷ pithy and poignant

【精华】cream; essence; quintessence: 我国民族文化的～ *the cream of our national culture* / 去其糟粕,取其～ *discard the dross and select the essence*

【精加工】[机] finish machining; precision work

【精简】retrench; simplify; cut; reduce: ～节约 *simplify administration and practise economy* / ～开支 *cut expenses; retrench* / ～会议 *cut (the number of) meetings to a minimum* / ～编制 *reduce the staff* / ～机构 *simplify (or streamline) the administrative structure*

【精讲】present briefly and succinctly: 老师～文件内容。*The teacher gave a succinct talk on the document*.

【精矿】[矿] concentrate

【精力】energy; vigour; vim: 集中～解决主要矛盾 *concentrate one's effort on solving the main contradiction*

【精力充沛】full of vim and vigour; vigorous; energetic

【精练】concise; succinct; terse: 语言～ *succinct language*

【精炼】❶ [冶] refine; purify: 火法～ *fire refining* / 真空～ *vacuum refining* ❷ 同〖精练〗

【精良】excellent; superior; of the best quality: 制作～ *of excellent workmanship* / 装备～ *well-equipped*

【精料】refined fodder

【精灵】❶ spirit; demon ❷ 〈方〉(of a child) clever; smart; intelligent

【精馏】[化] rectification: ～酒精 *rectified alcohol* / ～塔 *rectifying (or fractionating) tower*

【精美】exquisite; elegant: ～的刺绣 *elegant embroidery* / 包装～ *beautifully packaged* / ～的食品 *delicacies*

【精米】polished rice

【精密】❶ precise; accurate: ～的观察 *accurate (or close) observation* ❷ precision: ～机床 *precision machine tool* / ～仪器 *precision instrument* / ～铸造 *precision casting*

【精密度】precision: 机床的～ *the precision of lathes*

【精明】astute; shrewd; sagacious: ～的政治家 *an*

astute statesman / ～的小伙子 *a bright young fellow* / 你骗不了他；他～着呢，不会上当。*You can't fool him; he's much too clever for that.*

【精明强干】intelligent and capable; able and efficient

【精囊】[生理] seminal vesicle

【精疲力竭】(又作'精疲力尽') exhausted; worn out; tired out; spent

【精辟】penetrating; incisive: 进行～的分析 *make a penetrating analysis* / ～的论述 *a brilliant exposition*

【精品】❶ fine works (of art): 艺术～ *art treasures* ❷ quality goods; articles of fine quality

【精巧】exquisite; ingenious: ～的牙雕 *exquisite ivory carving* / 构造～ *ingeniously constructed*

【精确】accurate; exact; precise: ～的统计 *accurate statistics* / 下一个～的定义 *give a precise definition* / 这个回答大致不差，但不～。*This answer is only approximate, not exact.*

【精气神儿】〈口〉vigour; energy; drive: 他睡了一会儿，～又来了。*He was refreshed and energetic after a short nap.*

【精肉】〈方〉lean meat

【精锐】crack; picked: ～部队 *crack troops; picked troops*

【精深】profound: ～的理论 *a comprehensive and profound theory*

【精神】❶ spirit; mind; consciousness: ～上的负担 *a load on one's mind* / ～支柱 *spiritual (or ideological) prop* / ～财富 *spiritual wealth* / ～空虚 *be spiritually barren* ❷ essence; gist; spirit: 译者没有体会原文的～。*The translator failed to capture the spirit of the original.* ❸ vigour; vitality; drive: ～饱满 *full of vigour (or vitality)*; energetic / 没有～ *listless; languid* / 振作～ *bestir oneself; summon up one's energy; get up steam* ❹ lively; spirited; vigorous; smart: 他穿上军装显得格外～。*The army uniform made him look especially impressive.* ◇ ～产品 intellectual products; ～错乱 mentally deranged; insane; ～抖擞 full of energy (or vitality); vigorous; ～分裂症 schizophrenia; ～公害 public spiritual poison; ～鼓励 moral encouragement; ～贵族 intellectual aristocrats; ～焕发 be in high spirits; one's spirits rise; ～枷锁 spiritual (or mental) shackles; ～疗法 psychotherapy; ～面貌 mental attitude; mental outlook; ～生活 cultural life; ～失常 have bats in the belfry; have lost one's marbles; have a screw loose; be deranged; ～食粮 nourishment for the mind; spiritual food; ～世界 inner world; mental world; ～衰弱 psychasthenia; ～鸦片 mental or spiritual opium (sth. that corrupts people's mind); ～状态 state of mind; mental outlook

【精神分析】psychoanalysis: ～学家 *psychoanalyst*

【精神文明】spiritual civilization: 促进社会主义物质文明和～的建设 *promote the construction of socialist material and spiritual civilization*

【精神污染】spiritual contamination; cultural contamination; ideological pollution

【精神支柱】moral pillars; spiritual (ideological)

【精瘦】skinny; skin and bones: 浑身～ *bag of bones* / 饿得～ *be bony from hunger* / ～的小猪 *skinny piglet* / ～的衣裳 *extremely slim dress*

【精梳】[纺] combing: ～机 *comber* / ～毛纺 *worsted spinning* / ～纱 *combed yarn*

【精饲料】concentrated feed; concentrate

【精髓】marrow; pith; quintessence: 马克思主义的～ *the quintessence of Marxism*

【精通】be proficient in; have a good command of; master: ～业务 *be proficient in professional work* / ～英语 *have a good command of English*

【精卫填海】the mythical bird jingwei trying to fill up the sea with pebbles—dogged determination to achieve one's purpose

【精细】meticulous; fine; careful: 考虑问题很～ *think matters over carefully; be circumspect* / 这件上衣做工～。*This jacket is well-tailored.* ◇ ～化工 fine chemicals

【精心】meticulously; painstakingly; elaborately: ～护理 *nurse with the best of care* / ～设计，～施工 *be meticulous in design and construction; painstakingly design and carefully construct*

【精选】❶ [矿] concentration ❷ carefully chosen; choice: 用～的原料制成 *made of choice material*

【精盐】refined salt; table salt

【精液】[生理] seminal fluid; semen

【精益求精】constantly improve sth.; keep improving: 对技术～ *be constantly improving (or perfecting) one's skill*

【精英】essence; cream; flower: 周代青铜器是我国古代艺术的～。*Zhou bronzes are the finest specimens of ancient Chinese art.* / 当代青年的～ *the flower of modern youth* / 象棋～ *chess master*

【精轧】[冶] finish rolling: ～机 *finishing mill; finisher*

【精湛】consummate; exquisite: ～的技巧 *consummate skill; superb technique* / 工艺～ *exquisite workmanship; perfect craftsmanship*

【精制】make with extra care; refine: ～品 *highly finished products; superfines*

【精致】fine; exquisite; delicate: ～的丝织品 *fine silks* / ～的烟盒 *an exquisite cigarette case*

【精装】(of books) clothbound; hardback; hardcover ◇ ～本 de luxe edition

【精壮】able-bodied; strong

【精子】[生理] sperm; spermatozoon ◇ ～库 sperm bank

兢 (构词成分)见下

【兢兢业业】cautious and conscientious: 多少年来，他工作一直～。*He'd been doing his job conscientiously for many years.*

鲸 名 whale: 雌～ *cow whale* / 雄～ *bull whale* / 幼～ *whale calf*

【鲸目动物】cetacean

【鲸吞】swallow like a whale; annex (territory)

——另见〖蚕食鲸吞〗
【鲸须】baleen; whalebone
【鲸油】whale oil; blubber: 割～ *flench*
【鲸鱼】whale
【鲸仔】whale calf

jǐng

井 Ⅰ 名 ❶ well: 一口～ *a well* / 打～ *sink a well; drill a well* ❷ sth. in the shape of a well: 油井 Ⅱ 形 neat; orderly: 井然
【井场】[油] well site
【井底】❶ the bottom of a well ❷ [矿] shaft bottom; pit bottom: ～车场 *shaft station* / ～矿仓 *shaft pocket*
【井底之蛙】a frog in a well—a person with a very limited outlook
【井灌】well irrigation
【井架】❶ [油] derrick: 轻便～ *portable derrick (or mast)* ❷ [矿] headframe; headgear; pit-headframe
【井井有条】in perfect order; shipshape; methodical: ～地工作 *work methodically* / 各种仪器、工具摆得～。*All the instruments and tools are kept in perfect order.*
【井口】❶ the mouth of a well ❷ [矿] pithead ❸ [油] wellhead: ～气 *wellhead gas; casinghead gas* / ～装置 *wellhead assembly*
【井喷】[油] blowout
【井然】〈书〉orderly; neat and tidy; shipshape; methodical: 秩序～ *in good order*
【井然有序】in good order; orderly; methodical
【井水不犯河水】well water does not intrude into river water—I'll mind my own business, you mind yours
【井台】a raised platform around a well
【井筒】[矿] pit shaft: ～隔间 *shaft compartment* / ～掘进 *shaft excavation*
【井下】in the pit; under the shaft: ～作业 *operation in the pit; underpit operation* / 他在～工作。*He works at (or down) the pit.*
【井斜】[油] well deflection; well deviation: 第一口井～是 1.7 度。*The first well had a deviation of 1.7 degrees from the vertical.*
【井盐】well salt

阱 名 trap; pitfall; pit: 陷阱

肼 名 [化] hydrazine

颈 名 neck
【颈动脉】carotid
【颈项】neck
【颈椎】cervical vertebra

景 Ⅰ 名 ❶ view; scenery; scene: 雪～ *a snow scene* / 西湖十～ *the ten sights of the West Lake* ❷ situation; condition: 背景 ❸ scenery (of a play or film): 换～ *change of scenery* Ⅱ 动 admire; revere; respect: 景慕
【景点】scenic spot
【景观】landscape: 自然～ *natural landscape* / 岩溶～ *karst landscape*
【景况】situation; circumstances: 她家的～越来越好了。*Things are getting easier and easier for her family.*
【景慕】〈书〉esteem; revere; admire
【景片】a piece of (stage) scenery; flat
【景气】prosperity; boom ——另见〖不景气〗
【景色】scenery; view; scene; landscape: 深秋～ *a late autumn scene* / 南方～ *southern landscape* / 海上看日出,～特别美丽。*At sea one can get a particularly beautiful view of the sunrise.*
【景深】[摄] depth of field
【景泰蓝】cloisonné enamel; cloisonné
【景天】[植] red-spotted stonecrop (Sedum erythrostictum)
【景物】scenery: 站在山上眺望山下的～ *stand on the top of the hill looking down at the scenery below*
【景象】scene; sight; picture: 一派丰收～ *one vast panorama of bumper crops*
【景仰】respect and admire; hold in deep respect: 怀着无限～的心情 *with boundless respect and admiration*
【景致】view; scenery; scene: 从塔顶可以看到全城的～。*The tower commands a view of the whole town.* / 一下雪,这里的～就更美了。*This place looks even more beautiful after a fall of snow.*

儆 动 warn; admonish: 惩一儆百
【儆戒】warn; admonish; exhort

警 Ⅰ 形 alert; vigilant: 警戒 Ⅱ 动 warn; alarm: 警告 Ⅲ 名 alarm: 火警
【警报】alarm; warning; alert: 拉～ *sound the alarm (or siren)* / 台风～ *a typhoon warning* / 战斗～ *combat alert* ◇ ～器 siren; alarm
【警备】guard; garrison: ～森严 *be heavily guarded* / ～区 *garrison command* / ～司令部 *garrison headquarters*
【警察】police; policeman: 女～ *policewoman* ◇ ～局 police headquarters; police station; ～巡逻车 radio car; radio patrol car; patrol car
【警车】police car; police van
【警笛】❶ police whistle ❷ siren
【警匪片】"cops and robbers" feature film
【警服】police uniform
【警告】❶ warn; caution; admonish: 我～你,你再这样就没你的好。*I'm warning you, if you do that again there'll be trouble.* ❷ warning (as a disciplinary measure): 给予～处分 *give sb. a disciplinary warning*
【警告信号】[交] warning signal
【警官】police officer
【警棍】policeman's baton; truncheon
【警花】police woman
【警徽】police emblem: 珍视～ *treasure the police*

emblem

【警戒】❶ warn; admonish ❷ be on the alert against; guard against; keep a close watch on: 采取～措施 *take precautionary measures* / 沿公路放出～ *post guards along the highway* / ～部队 *outpost troops; security force (or detachment)* ◇ ～色［动］warning (or aposematic) coloration; ～水位 warning water level; warning stage; ～线 cordon; security line; ～状态 state of alert

【警句】aphorism; epigram

【警觉】vigilance; alertness: 海防战士～地注视着出现在海面上的黑点。*The coastal guard kept a watchful eye on the black spot that had appeared out at sea.*

【警力】police strength: 联防巡逻队的建立,大大缓解了～不足的矛盾。*Setting up the joint patrol has greatly eased the strain on police strength.*

【警铃】alarm bell

【警民】the police and the people ◇ ～共建 police and civilians working together to build a society with a high cultural and ideological level

【警犬】police dog

【警示】lesson; warning: 该案件给我们的干部以有益的～。*The case is a lesson to our cadres.*

【警探】police detective

【警惕】be on guard against; watch out for; be vigilant: 丧失～ *drop one's guard; be off one's guard* / ～性 *vigilance*

【警亭】police box

【警卫】(security) guard: 执行～任务 *be on guard duty* / ～人员 *security personnel* / ～室 *guardroom* / ～团 *guards regiment* / ～员 *bodyguard*

【警务】police affairs; police service

【警衔】police rank (in the Chinese People's Military Police)

【警钟】alarm bell; tocsin ——另见〖敲警钟〗

jìng

劲 形 strong; powerful; sturdy: ～松 *sturdy pines* —— 另见 jìn

【劲敌】formidable adversary; strong opponent (or contender)

【劲风】a strong wind

【劲旅】〈书〉strong contingent; crack force: 这个厂的篮球队可算是全市的一支～。*This factory's basketball team is one of the strongest in the city.*

净 Ⅰ 形 ❶ clean: ～水 *clean water* / 擦～ *wipe sth. clean* / 这件褂子没洗～。*This jacket hasn't been properly washed.* ❷(used after a verb) finished; with nothing left: 钱都用～了。*The money is all used up.* / 把药喝～。*Drink your medicine up.* ❸ net: ～收入 *net income* / ～出口 *net export* / ～进口 *net import* Ⅱ 动 make clean: ～一～桌面儿。*Clean the top of the table.* Ⅲ 副 ❶ all; all the time: ～说不干 *all talk, no action* / 他～说瞎话。*He lies all the time.* / 别～打岔。*Don't keep interrupting.* ❷ only; merely; nothing but: ～吃肉不行。*It's not good to eat only meat.* / 他～说好听的。*He talks about nothing but pleasant things.*

【净菜】cleaned vegetables (readied for market)

【净产值】net output value

【净额】net amount

【净高】［建］clear height

【净荷载】net load

【净化】purify: ～空气 *purify the air* / ～废水 *purify liquid waste* / ～灵魂 *purify one's soul* / ～塔 *purifying column*

【净价】net price

【净街】close a street to traffic

【净面】wash one's face: 清水～ *wash one's face with water*

【净身】(of a man) be castrated

【净水厂】water treatment plant

【净桶】〈婉〉nightstool; closestool; commode

【净土】the Pure Land (a paradise into which anyone is reborn who calls on the name of the Buddha Amitabha with sincere devotion and in which one can attain final Enlightenment)

【净心】❶ free from care: 过几天～的日子 *free oneself from care for several days* ❷ have a peaceful and quiet mind; feel completely at ease: 难得有～。*It is difficult to have one's mind entirely at peace with itself.*

【净余】net balance; remainder; surplus: 除去开支,～二百元。*After deducting expenses, we have 200 yuan left.*

【净增】net increase; net growth: 人口～率 *net growth rate of population*

【净值】net worth; net value: 出口～ *net export value* / 进口～ *net import value*

【净重】net weight

【净赚】make a net profit of; clear: 他的买卖每月～一万元。*His business clears ten thousand yuan a month.*

径 Ⅰ 名 ❶ footpath; path; track: 山～ *a mountain path* ❷ way; means: 捷径 ❸(〈略〉见〖直径〗) diameter: 口径 / 半径 Ⅱ 副 straight; directly; straightaway: ～行办理 *deal with the matter straightaway* / ～回广州 *go straight back to Guangzhou*

【径迹】［物］track: 蜕变～ *decay track* / ～起点 *track origin*

【径流】runoff: 地表～ *surface runoff* / 地下～ *groundwater runoff*

【径情直遂】as smoothly as one would wish: 战胜困难的过程往往不是～的。*The process of overcoming a difficulty is usually not as direct and smooth as one would wish.* /

【径赛】［体］track: ～项目 *track events*

【径庭】〈书〉very unlike: 大相径庭

【径向】［物］radial: ～间隙 *radial clearance* / ～轴承 *radial bearing*

【径直】straight; directly; straightaway: 登山队员

～向主峰进发。*The mountaineers made straight for the summit.* / 飞机将～飞往昆明。*The plane will fly nonstop to Kunming.*

【径自】without leave; without consulting anyone: 会没开完,他～走了。*He left abruptly in the middle of the meeting.*

经 名 [纺] warping ——另见 jīng

胫 名 [生理] shin

【胫骨】shin bone; tibia

痉 (构词成分)见下

【痉病】[中] febrile disease with symptoms such as convulsions, opisthotonos, trismus, etc.

【痉挛】convulsion; spasm: 食管～ *spasm of the esophagus; esophagospasm*

竞 Ⅰ 动 compete; contend; vie Ⅱ 形 〈书〉 strong; forceful

【竞标】competitive bidding; competitive tender

【竞猜】compete to answer (in contest)

【竞渡】❶ boat race: 龙舟～ *dragon boat regatta* ❷ swimming race

【竞技】sports; athletics: ～场 *arena*

【竞技状态】form (of an athlete): ～好 *in good form; in top form* / ～不好 *not in good form; out of form; off one's game*

【竞价】bid (in auction)

【竞赛】contest; competition; emulation; race: 体育～ *athletic contest (or competition)* / 军备～ *arms (or armament) race*

【竞投】compete in bidding (for a contract, etc.)

【竞相】compete; vie: 两国正在～部署中程导弹。*The two powers are competing in the deployment of intermediate-range missiles.* / ～效尤 *vie with each other in following a bad example*

【竞选】enter into an election contest; campaign for (office); run for: ～总统 *run for the presidency* / ～活动 *electioneering* / ～演说 *election speech* / ～运动 *election campaign*

【竞争】compete: 市场～ *competition for markets* / 自由～ *free competition* / ～能力 *competitive power* / ～优势 *competitive edge* / 富有～力 *(of a price, product, etc.)* highly competitive ◇ ～机制 mechanism of competition; ～价格 competitive price

【竞争性】competitiveness: ～贬值 *competitive depreciation (or devaluation)*

【竞走】heel-and-toe walking race

竟 Ⅰ 动 finish; complete: 未～之业 *unaccomplished cause; unfinished task* Ⅱ 形 throughout; whole: ～夜 *the whole night; throughout the night* Ⅲ 副 ❶〈书〉in the end; eventually: 有志者事竟成 ❷unexpectedly; actually: 这么陡的峭壁,谁知他～爬上去了。*Who would have expected that he could climb up that steep cliff?* ❸ go so far as to; go to the length of; have the impudence (or effrontery) to

【竟敢】actually dare; have the audacity; have the impertinence: 你～跟我讲这种话! *How dare you say that to me!*

【竟然】❶ unexpectedly; to one's surprise; actually: 这样宏伟的建筑,～只用十个月的时间就完成了。*To think that such a magnificent building was completed in ten months!* ❷ go so far as to; go to the length of; have the impudence (or effrontery) to: ～不顾事实 *go so far as to disregard the facts*

【竟自】unexpectedly; to one's surprise; actually: 虽然没有人教他,他摸索了一段时间,～学会了。*Though nobody taught him, he learnt it all by himself through trial and error.*

敬 Ⅰ 名 respect: 致敬 Ⅱ 副 respectfully: 敬请 Ⅲ 动 offer politely: ～茶 *serve tea (to a guest)* / ～烟 *offer a cigarette (to a guest)* / ～你一杯! *To your health!*

【敬爱】respect and love: ～的领袖 *esteemed (or respected) and beloved leader; beloved leader*

【敬辞】term of respect; polite expression

【敬而远之】stay at a respectful distance from sb.

【敬奉】❶ piously worship ❷ offer respectfully; present politely

【敬告】〈套〉beg to inform: ～读者 *notice to readers*

【敬鬼神而远之】keep one's distance from the gods and spirits while showing them respect—stay at a respectful distance from sb.

【敬贺】〈套〉congratulate with respect; send respectful greetings to

【敬候】〈套〉await respectfully: ～佳音。*We are waiting to hear the good news.*

【敬酒】propose a toast; toast

【敬酒不吃吃罚酒】refuse a toast only to drink a forfeit—submit to sb.'s pressure after first turning down his request; be constrained to do what one at first refused to

【敬老爱幼】respect the aged and cherish the young

【敬老院】home of respect for the aged; old folks' home

【敬礼】❶ salute; give a salute ❷〈套〉(used at the end of a letter): 此致～ *salutations; with high respect; withbest wishes*

【敬慕】respect and admire

【敬佩】esteem; admire: 我对他的文才非常～。*I have the highest esteem for his literary ability.* / 大家以～的目光望着他。*Everybody looked at him admiringly.*

【敬请】〈套〉invite respectfully: ～光临。*Your presence is cordially requested.* / ～指教。*Kindly give me your advice.*

【敬上】(又作'敬启')(used after the signature in a letter to one's senior or superior) yours respectfully; yours sincerely

【敬挽】(used on funeral scrolls) with deep condolences from sb.

【敬畏】hold in awe and veneration; revere

【敬献】〈尊〉present politely; offer respectfully: ～鲜花 *present fresh flowers*

【敬仰】revere; venerate: 深受人民的爱戴和～ *command deep love and reverence among the people*

【敬业】dedicate oneself to one's studies: ～爱岗 *love and dedicate oneself to one's work*

【敬意】respect; tribute: 表示衷心的～ *extend one's heartfelt respects; pay sincere tribute* / 不成～ *just a small token of my regard (said when presenting a gift)*

【敬语】words spoken out of respect or courtesy; respectful remarks

【敬赠】(used when sending a gift) with compliments: 某某～ *with compliments from so-and-so* / 作者～ *with the author's compliments*

【敬重】deeply respect; revere; honour: 大家都十分～这位老红军战士。*We all have great respect for the veteran Red Army man.*

【敬祝】〈套〉(used at the end of a letter) I wish you: ～身体健康。*I wish you the best of health.*

靖 Ⅰ 形 quiet; peaceful; tranquil Ⅱ 动 〈书〉make tranquil; pacify: ～乱 *quell (or put down) a rebellion* / ～边 *pacify the border region*

【靖国神社】(Japan) Yasukuni Shrine (Japanese shrine for the war-dead built in Tokyo in 1869, including war criminals of WWII): ～法案 *Yasukuni Shrine Bill* / 参拜～ *pay homage to Yasukuni Jinja*

境 名 ❶ border; boundary: 在本省～内 *within the boundaries of this province* ❷ place; area; territory: 敌～ *enemy territory* ❸ condition; situation; circumstances: 困境

【境地】condition; circumstances: 处于狼狈的～ *be in a sorry plight; be in a predicament* / 陷入完全孤立的～ *land oneself in utter isolation*

【境界】❶ boundary ❷ extent reached; plane attained; state; realm: 理想～ *ideal state; ideal* / 他的诗有时达到了晚清诗人的～。*His poetry sometimes rises to the level of the late Qing poets.*

【境况】(financial) condition; circumstances: ～不佳 *in straitened circumstances* / ～不错 *be well-off; be comfortably off*

【境外企业】business (enterprises) outside national boundary

【境域】❶ condition; circumstances ❷ area; realm: 大同～ *the realm of Great Harmony*

【境遇】circumstances; one's lot: 极困难的～ *extremely adverse circumstances* / 悲惨的～ *a hard lot*

静 形 still; quiet; calm: ～～地躺着 *lie motionless* / 海浪～下来了。*The sea is now calm.* / 请～一～。*Please be quiet.*

【静电】static electricity: ～除尘器 *electrostatic precipitator* / ～纺纱 *electrostatic spinning* / ～感应 *electrostatic induction*

【静观】watch quietly: ～默察 *sit back and watch*

【静荷载】[建] dead load

【静候】quietly await: ～佳音 *quietly awaiting the good news*

【静力学】[物] statics: 气体～ *aerostatics*

【静脉】[生理] vein ◇ ～点滴 intravenous drip; ～曲张 varix; varicosity; ～炎 phlebitis; ～注射 intravenous injection

【静谧】〈书〉quiet; still; tranquil

【静默】❶ become silent: 会场上又是一阵～。*Another spell of silence fell upon the meeting room.* ❷ mourn in silence; observe silence: 为悼念革命先烈,全体起立,～致哀。*All rose in silent tribute to the memory of the revolutionary martyrs.*

【静穆】solemn and quiet

【静悄悄】very quiet: 屋子里～的。*It was very quiet in the room.*

【静态】[物] static state: ～电阻 *static resistance* / ～平衡 *static equilibrium* / ～特性 *static characteristic* ◇ ～经济学 static economic

【静听】listen attentively and quietly: 屏息～ *listen with bated breath*

【静物】still life: ～写生 *paint still life* ◇ ～画 still-life picture; still life

【静养】rest quietly to recuperate; convalesce: 希望你安心～。*I hope you'll set aside your worries and have a good rest.*

【静止】static; motionless; at a standstill: 相对～的状态 *a state of relative rest* / 生活永远不是～的。*Life is never at a standstill.* ◇ ～图像 still picture

【静坐】❶ sit quietly ❷ sit still as a form of therapy ❸ sit-down; sit-in: ～罢工 *sit-down (strike)* / ～示威 *sit-in (demonstration); sit-down (protest)*

镜 名 ❶ looking glass; mirror: 湖平如～。*The lake is as smooth as a mirror.* ❷ lens; glass: 放大镜

【镜花水月】flowers in a mirror or the moon in the water—an illusion

【镜框】❶ picture frame ❷ spectacles frame

【镜片】lens

【镜台】dressing table

【镜头】❶ camera lens: 远摄～ *telephoto lens* / 可变焦距～ *zoom lens* / 长焦距～ *telelens; long focus lens* ❷ shot; scene: 特写～ *close-up (shot)* / 伪装～ *process shot*

【镜匣】a wooden case with a looking glass and other toilet articles; dressing case

【镜像】[物] mirror image

【镜子】❶ mirror; looking glass ❷ 〈口〉glasses; spectacles

jiǒng

迥 副〈书〉widely different: 他病前病后～若两人。*He doesn't look like the same person after his*

illness.

【迥然】far apart；widely different

【迥然不同】utterly different；not in the least alike

【迥异】totally different：他们二人性情～。*They are diametrically opposed in temperament*.

炯 (构词成分)见下

【炯炯】〈书〉(of eyes) bright；shining：他的一双眼睛～发光。*He has a pair of bright piercing eyes*.

【炯炯有神】(of eyes) bright and piercing：他矮而且瘦，可是目光～。*He was short and thin, with, however, a pair of gleaming, penetrating eyes*.

窘 Ⅰ 形 ❶ in straitened circumstances；hard up：他一度生活很～。*He was rather hard up for a time*. ❷ awkward；embarrassed；ill at ease：他唱着唱着走了调，～得不敢往台下看。*He began to sing out of tune and he was too embarrassed to look at the audience*. Ⅱ 动 embarrass；disconcert：这个问题～得他无言可答。*The question embarrassed him so much that he was quite at a loss for an answer*.

【窘境】awkward situation；predicament；plight

【窘况】awkward situation；predicament；plight

【窘迫】❶ poverty-stricken；very poor：生活～ *live in poverty* ❷ hard pressed；embarrassed；in a predicament：处境～ *find oneself in a predicament*

【窘态】an embarrassed look：～百出 *be most embarrassed；to one's great embarrassment*

jiū

纠 动 ❶ entangle：纠缠 ❷ gather together：纠合 ❸ correct；rectify：有错必纠

【纠察】❶ maintain order at a public gathering ❷ picket：～队 *pickets* / ～线 *picket line*

【纠缠】❶ get entangled；be in a tangle：防止在枝节问题上～不休 *avoid endless quibbling over side issues* ❷ nag；worry；pester：他忙着呢，别～他了。*He's busy. Stop pestering him*.

【纠缠不清】too tangled up to unravel：问题～。*The problem has been made very complicated*.

【纠纷】dispute；issue：无原则～ *an unprincipled dispute* / 国与国之间的～ *disputes between countries* / 调解～ *mediate an issue* / 挑起～ *stir up trouble*

【纠葛】entanglement；dispute：他们之间发生了一点～。*There's a dispute between them*.

【纠合】〈贬〉gather together：～一伙流氓 *get together (or round up) a bunch of hoodlums* / ～党羽，图谋不轨 *gather together one's followers for criminal purposes*

【纠集】〈贬〉get together；muster：～一批打手 *gather together a bunch of thugs* / ～残部 *muster the remaining forces*

【纠结】intertwine；entangle

【纠偏】rectify a deviation；correct an error

【纠正】correct；put right；redress：～错误 *correct a mistake；redress an error* / ～姿势 *correct sb.'s posture* / ～不正之风 *check unhealthy tendencies*

究 Ⅰ 动 study carefully；go into；investigate：～其根源 *trace sth. to its source* Ⅱ 副〈书〉actually；really；after all：～应如何办理？*How should this really be dealt with?*

【究办】investigate and deal with：依法～ *investigate and deal with according to law*

【究竟】❶ outcome；what actually happened：大家都想知道个～。*Everybody wants to know what actually happened*. / 不管什么事，他总爱问个～。*He always likes to get to the heart of a matter, whatever it may be*. ❷ (used in questions to press for an exact answer) actually；exactly：明天的会～谁去参加？*Who is actually going to the meeting tomorrow?* / 你们～要什么？*What exactly do you want?* ❸ after all；anyway；finally：他～经验丰富，让他负责这项工作最合适。*After all, he is very experienced, so it is only suitable to put him in charge of the job*.

鸠 名 turtledove：绿～ *green pigeon*

【鸠形鹄面】gaunt and emaciated

赳 (构词成分)见下

【赳赳】valiant；gallant

【赳赳武夫】a stalwart, martial man

阄 名 lot：抓阄儿

揪 动 ❶ hold tight；seize：他～着绳子不撒手。*He held tightly to the rope and wouldn't let go*. / 他～着他的领子打他。*He seized him by the collar and hit him*. ❷ pull；tug；drag：～花 *pluck flowers* / 别那么使劲～绳子。*Don't pull so hard at the rope*.

【揪辫子】seize sb.'s queue—seize upon sb.'s mistakes or shortcomings；capitalize on sb.'s vulnerable point

【揪出】uncover；ferret out：～幕后操纵者 *uncover (or ferret out) the wirepuller*

【揪痧】[中] a popular treatment for sunstroke or other febrile diseases by repeatedly pinching the patient's neck, etc. to achieve congestion

【揪心】〈方〉❶ anxious；worried：小杨到现在还没有回来，真叫人～。*Xiao Yang's still not back. I'm really getting worried*. ❷ heartrending；agonizing；gnawing：伤口痛得～。*There was a gnawing pain from the wound*.

jiǔ

九 Ⅰ 数 nine：～车间 *No. 9 Workshop* / ～连 *the Ninth Company* Ⅱ 名 each of the nine nine-day periods beginning from the day after the Winter Solstice Ⅲ 形 many；numerous：三弯～转 *many twists and turns* / ～曲桥 *a zigzag bridge*

【九大行星】［天］nine principal planets (of the solar system：水星 Mercury，金星 Venus，地球 Earth，火星 Mars，木星 Jupiter，土星 Saturn，天王星 Uranus，海王星 Neptune，冥王星 Pluto)
【九段】ninth-dan (highest grade in go or weiqi)
【九级风】［气］force 9 wind；strong gale
【九节狸】zibet；large Indian civet
【九九表】multiplication table
【九九归一】when all is said and done；in the last analysis；after all：～，还是他的话对。*All things considered, what he says is right.*
【九牛二虎之力】the strength of nine bulls and two tigers—tremendous effort：费了～ *strain oneself to the limit；use every ounce of one's strength；make herculean efforts*
【九牛一毛】a single hair out of nine ox hides—a drop in the ocean
【九泉】〈文〉the Nine Springs—the nether world；grave：含笑于～ *rest happy in one's grave*
【九死一生】a narrow escape from death；survival after many hazards
【九天】〈文〉the highest heavens；heaven
【九霄云外】beyond the highest heavens—far，far away：把个人安危抛到～ *cast personal safety to the winds；disregard one's safety* / 他把那事丢到了～了。*He has forgotten completely about it.*
【九月】❶ September ❷ the ninth month of the lunar year；the ninth moon
【九州】❶ the nine divisions of China in remote antiquity ❷ a poetic name for China

久 副 ❶ for a long time；long：我们～不见面了。*We haven't seen each other for a long time.* / 很～以前 *long ago* ❷ of a specified duration：两个月之～ *for as long as two months* / 来了有多～？*How long have you been here?*
【久别重逢】meet again after a long separation；reunite after a long parting
【久病成医】prolonged illness makes a doctor of a patient
【久病床前无孝子】in cases of chronic sickness，there are no dutiful children at the bedside
【久等】wait for a long time：对不起，让你～了。*Sorry to have kept you waiting.*
【久而久之】in the course of time；with the lapse of time；as time passes：只要你注意搜集，～，资料就丰富了。*If you keep on collecting, in time you'll have a wealth of data.*
【久旱逢甘雨】have a welcome rain after a long drought—have a long-felt need satisfied
【久后】long afterwards；in the future
【久假不归】put off indefinitely returning sth. one has borrowed；appropriate sth. borrowed
【久经考验】long-tested；seasoned：他是一个～的战士。*He is a seasoned soldier.*
【久久】for a long，long time：他知道这消息后心里很难过，～不能平静。*He was deeply grieved to learn the news, and it was a long time before he calmed down.*
【久留】stay long：有要事在身，不敢～。*I can't stay long because I have some important business to attend to.*
【久违】〈套〉how long it is since we last met；I haven't seen you for ages
【久闻大名】I've long heard about your great name (used when meeting sb. for the first time) —— 另见〖如雷贯耳〗
【久仰】〈套〉I've heard about you for a long time (used when meeting sb. for the first time)；I've long been looking forward to meeting you；I'm very pleased to meet you
【久远】far back；ages ago；remote：年代～ *of the remote past；age-old；time-honoured*

灸 名［中］moxibustion

韭 名 fragrant-flowered garlic；(Chinese) chives：青～ *young chives；chive seedlings*
【韭菜】fragrant-flowered garlic；(Chinese) chives
【韭黄】hotbed chives

酒 名 alcoholic drink；wine；liquor；spirits
【酒吧间】bar；barroom
【酒保】〈旧〉bartender；barkeeper
【酒杯】wine cup or glass
【酒不醉人人自醉】liquor does not intoxicate，one intoxicates oneself
【酒菜】❶ food and drink ❷ food to go with wine or liquor
【酒厂】brewery；winery；distillery
【酒池肉林】lakes of wine and forests of meat—unbridled debauchery and licentiousness
【酒刺】acne
【酒店】❶ wineshop；public house ❷ hotel (used in names of hotels)
【酒饭】food and drink
【酒疯】the silly behaviour of a person when drunk；a drunken fit：发酒疯
【酒逢知己千杯少，话不投机半句多】for a congenial friend a thousand toasts are too few；in a disagreeable conversation one word more is too many
【酒馆】public house；pub
【酒鬼】❶〈诋〉drunkard；sot ❷ winebibber；toper
【酒酣耳热】warmed with wine；mellow with drink
【酒后】after drinking；under the influence of wine (or alcohol)：～失言 *make an indiscreet remark under the influence of alcohol*
【酒后开车】driving a car under the influence of alcohol；drunk driving
【酒后吐真言】wine in，truth out
【酒壶】wine pot；flagon
【酒花】［植］hops
【酒会】cocktail party
【酒家】❶〈旧〉wineshop；tavern ❷ restaurant (used in names of restaurants)：广东～ *Guangdong Restaurant*
【酒窖】wine cellar
【酒精】ethyl alcohol；alcohol ◇ ～比重计 spirit

gauge；～灯 spirit lamp；alcohol burner；～发酵 alcoholic fermentation；～含量 alcohol content；～酵母 distillery yeast；～炉 alcohol heater；～中毒 alcoholism

【酒具】drinking set

【酒力】❶ capacity for liquor：他不胜～，喝一点儿就醉。*He can't hold much liquor, and will get drunk after drinking a bit.* ❷ stimulating effect of wine；influence of alcohol：几杯酒下肚，不一会儿～发作，浑身焦热。*After drinking several cups of wine, he began to feel its effect and became uncomfortably hot all over.*

【酒量】capacity for liquor：他～很大。*He's a heavy drinker.* or *He can hold a lot of liquor.* / ～不济 *have little capacity for wine; not be a good drinker*

【酒令】drinkers' wager game

【酒楼】restaurant (used in names of restaurants)：广东～ *Guangdong Restaurant*

【酒囊饭袋】wine skin and rice bag—a good-for-nothing

【酒酿】(又作'酒娘') fermented glutinous rice

【酒钱】tips

【酒肉朋友】wine-and-meat friends；fair-weather friends

【酒色财气】wine，women，wealth，and temper—generally considered to be the four archevils of life

【酒色之徒】debauchee；libertine

【酒石酸】tartaric acid：～锑钾 *antimony potassium tartrate*

【酒窝】(又作'酒涡') dimple：她笑起来脸上有个～。*She has a dimple in her cheek when she smiles.*

【酒席】feast；banquet

【酒心巧克力】liqueur

【酒醒】awake from a drunken sleep (or a drunken stupor)

【酒兴】elation caused by intoxicants；rapture with wine：～正浓 *be buoyant with drunken elation*

【酒宴】feast；banquet

【酒药】yeast for brewing rice wine or fermenting glutinous rice

【酒意】a tipsy feeling：已有几分～ *be slightly tipsy; be mellow*

【酒糟】distillers' grains

【酒糟鼻】acne rosacea；brandy nose

【酒盅】(又作'酒钟') a small handleless wine cup

【酒足饭饱】have drunk and eaten to one's heart's content

【酒醉】be drunk：～失言 *make an indiscreet remark under the influence of alcohol*

jiù

旧 Ⅰ 形 ❶ past；bygone；old：～社会 *the old society* / ～时代 *former times* / ～思想 *old way of thinking; timeworn ideas* / ～的传统观念 *outdated conventional ideas* ❷ used；worn；old：～衣服 *used (or old) clothes* / 买～的 *buy sth. secondhand* / 你的鞋～了，买一双新的吧。*Your shoes are worn. Buy a new pair.* ❸ former；one-time：旧都 Ⅱ 名 old friendship；old friend：故旧

【旧案】❶ a court case of long standing：积年～都已经清理完毕。*Court cases of many years' standing have now been cleared.* ❷ old regulations；former practice

【旧病复发】❶ have a recurrence of an old illness；have an attack of a recurrent sickness；have a relapse ❷ relapse into one's old bad habits；slip back into one's bad old ways：他发过誓不再偷了，可不久又～，走上了犯罪道路。*He swore that he would never steal again, but soon relapsed into a life of crime.*

【旧部】former subordinate

【旧地】place where one went or stayed before；once familiar place；old haunt

【旧地重游】revisit a once familiar place

【旧调重弹】同〖老调重弹〗

【旧都】former capital

【旧恶】old grievance；old wrong

【旧房改造】old housing renovation

【旧观】former appearance；former state：北京许多古建筑已经修缮一新，恢复了～。*Many old buildings in Beijing have been renovated and restored to their former glory (or splendour).*

【旧恨新仇】new hatred piled on old

【旧货】secondhand goods；junk：我买的是～。*I bought it secondhand.* ◇ ～店 secondhand shop；junk shop；～市场 flea market

【旧交】old acquaintance；old friend

【旧金山】San Francisco

【旧居】former residence；old home

【旧历】the old Chinese calendar；the lunar calendar

【旧梦重温】同〖重温旧梦〗

【旧年】❶ the lunar New Year：很多中国人还是过～。*Many Chinese still celebrate the lunar New Year.* ❷ 〈方〉 last year

【旧瓶装新酒】new wine in old bottles—new content in old form

【旧情】old or former friendship；former affection

【旧日】former days；old days

【旧诗】old-style poetry；classical poetry ——另见〖古体诗〗

【旧石器时代】the Old Stone Age；the Paleolithic Period

【旧时】old times；old days

【旧式】old type；old style：～文人 *old-type scholars* / ～婚姻 *old-style marriage*

【旧事】an old matter or affair；a past event：～重提 *bring up a matter of the past*

【旧书】❶ secondhand book；used (or old) book ❷ ancient book；ancient text ◇ ～店 secondhand bookstore

【旧俗】old customs：破～，立新风 *do away with old customs and introduce new ones*

【旧习】old habit and custom：～难改。*It's difficult to change old habits and customs.*

【旧业】❶ old trade (or profession)：重操旧业 ❷ ancestral estate；family fortune：～荡然无存 *a goodly family fortune all dissipated*

【旧约】the Old Testament

【旧宅】old residence；old house

【旧账】old debt；old score；old feud：这些陈年～就不要算了。*we may just as well forget about those old scores.*

【旧址】site (of a former organization, building, etc.)：这是我们机关的～。*Here's where our organization used to be.*

【旧制】❶ old system；old practice：概依～ *act in strict accordance with old practices* ❷ China's old system of weights and measures：现在市尺和市斤已成～。Nowadays chi and jin belong to the old system of weights and measures.

臼

名 ❶ mortar：石～ *stone mortar* ❷ any mortar-shaped thing ❸ joint (of bones)：脱臼

【臼齿】molar

疚

形〈书〉remorse：内疚

咎

Ⅰ 名 fault；blame：归咎 Ⅱ 动 censure；punish；blame：既往不咎

【咎由自取】have only oneself to blame

柩

名 a coffin with a corpse in it：灵柩

【柩车】hearse

桕

名 Chinese tallow tree

救

动 ❶ rescue；save：他跳进急流，把孩子～了出来。*He jumped into the torrent and rescued the child from drowning.* / ～溺水儿童 *save a drowning child* ❷ save sb. from；relieve (distress, etc.)：救亡 / 救灾

【救兵】relief troops；reinforcements：搬～ *call in reinforcements*

【救复】repair (instrument, equipment)

【救国】save the nation：上中学时，他就参加了抗日～运动。*As a middle-school student he joined in the movement to resist Japanese aggression and save the country.*

【救护】relieve a sick or injured person；give first-aid；rescue：～伤员 *give first-aid to the wounded* / 奋勇～战友 *valiantly go to the rescue of one's comrade-in-arms* ◇ ～车 ambulance；～船 ambulance ship；～队 ambulance corps；～飞机 ambulance aircraft；～所 medical aid station (or point)；～站 first-aid station

【救荒】send relief to a famine area；help to tide over a crop failure：生产～ *tide over a crop failure by production*

【救活】bring sb. back to life；resuscitate：他们把一个几乎淹死了的人～了。*They resuscitated a man who had almost drowned.*

【救火】fight a fire；try to put out a fire：消防队员正在～。*The firemen are fighting the fire.* ◇ ～车 fire engine；～队 fire brigade；～队员 fireman；fire fighter

【救急】help sb. to cope with an emergency；help meet an urgent need：你们支援我们这些材料，可真～了。*You gave us this material just when we needed it most.*

【救济】extend relief to；relieve the distress of：～难民 *give relief to refugees* / ～灾区人民 *provide relief to the people in a disaster area* / 社会～事业 *social relief facilities*

【救驾】save the emperor from danger—save sb. from an awkward situation：多亏你救了我的驾！*Thanks a lot for rescuing me from embarrassment!*

【救苦救难】help the needy and relieve the distressed：～的观世音 *the benevolent Goddess of Mercy*

【救命】save sb.'s life：～！*Help!* ◇ ～稻草 a straw to clutch at；～恩人 saviour

【救难】help sb. out of distress

【救球】[体] follow the ball

【救人一命胜造七级浮屠】saving one life is better than building a seven-tiered pagoda

【救生】save life (esp. through the prevention of drowning)：～设备 *lifesaving appliance；life preserver* ◇ ～带 life belt；～圈 life buoy；～艇 lifeboat；～衣 life jacket；～员 lifeguard；lifesaver

【救世主】the Saviour；the Redeemer

【救死扶伤】heal the wounded and rescue the dying：～，实行革命的人道主义。*Heal the wounded, rescue the dying, practise revolutionary humanitarianism.*

【救亡】save the nation from extinction：～图存 *save the nation from doom and ensure its survival* ◇ ～运动 national salvation movement

【救险车】wrecking truck；wrecking car

【救星】liberator；emancipator；saviour

【救援】rescue；come to sb.'s help

【救灾】provide disaster relief；send relief to a disaster area；help the people tide over a natural disaster

【救治】bring a patient out of danger；treat and cure：大批医务人员奔赴灾区～伤病员。*Large numbers of medical workers hurried to the disaster area to give treatment to the sick and wounded.*

【救助】help sb. in danger or difficulty；succour ◇ ～条款 salvage clause

厩

名 stable；cattle-shed；pen

【厩肥】barnyard manure

就

Ⅰ 动 ❶ come near；move towards：我们～着路灯下棋。*We played chess by the light of a street lamp.* / 你～着桌子吃西瓜。*Eat your watermelon over the table.* ❷ undertake；engage in；enter upon：就业 / 就职 ❸ accomplish；make：这

个鼎是青铜铸～的。*This tripod is made of bronze*. ❹ take advantage of; accomodate oneself to: 我们～这个机会谈谈。*We'll take this opportunity to have a talk*. ❺ be eaten with; go with: 炒鸡蛋～饭 *have some scrambled eggs to go with the rice* / 他用花生～酒。*He has peanuts with his drinks*. Ⅱ **介** with regard to; concerning; on: ～我所知 *so far as I know* / 双方～共同关心的问题进行了会谈。*The two sides held talks on questions of common interest*. Ⅲ **副** ❶ at once; right away: 我～来。*I'll come right away*. / 我这～去。*I'll be going right away*. / 一会儿～得。*It'll be ready in a minute*. ❷ as early as; already: 今天我七点钟～来了。*I was here as early as 7 o'clock today*. / 我星期一～给你钱。*I'll pay you right on Monday*. ❸ as soon as; right after: 我一见他～生气。*As soon as I see him, I get angry*. / 说干～干 *act without delay* ❹ in that case; then: 要是你来,我～高兴了。*If you come, (then) I'll be very happy*. ❺ as much as; as many as: 光衬衫他～有二十件。*He has as many as 20 shirts*. ❻ only; merely; just: ～这一本了,看完请马上还。*This is the only copy left. Please return it as soon as you finish reading it*. ❼ just; simply: 我～不信我们妇女干不了这一行。*I just wouldn't believe that we women couldn't do this sort of work*. / 我不知道为什么,我～不喜欢他。*I don't know why, I just don't like him*. ❽ exactly; precisely: 你～是我要找的那个人。*You are precisely the person I'm looking for*. / 医务室～在这儿。*This is where the clinic is*. Ⅳ **连** even if: 你～不说,我也会知道的。*Even if you won't tell me, I'll know anyway*. / 你～生气也没用。*Even if you get angry, it won't help*.

【就伴】keep sb. company; accompany sb.: 你一个人在家多闷得慌,我来和你～吧。*Don't you feel bored staying at home all alone? Let me come and keep you company*.

【就便】at sb.'s convenience; while you're at it: ～也替我买一本。*While you're at it (or about it), buy me a copy too*.

【就餐】〈书〉have a meal; eat; dine: 客队在第一食堂～。*The visiting team are to dine in the No.1 dining-hall*.

【就此】at this point; here and now; thus: 讨论～结束。*The discussion was thus brought to a close*.

【就地】on the spot: ～解决问题 *settle the problem on the spot* / ～免职 *relieve sb. of his post then and there*

【就地取材】obtain materials from local sources; use local materials; draw on local resources

【就地视察】on-site-inspection

【就地正法】execute (a criminal) on the spot

【就读】〈书〉attend school: 他早年～于师范学校。*He attended a normal school in his early years*.

【就范】submit; give in: 迫使～ *compel sb. to submit* / 不肯～ *refuse to submit to control; refuse to give in*

【就近】(do or get sth.) nearby; in the neighbourhood; without having to go far: ～找个住处 *find accommodation in the neighbourhood*

【就寝】retire for the night; go to bed

【就让】〈口〉even if: ～他来,也晚了。*Even if he comes it will be too late*.

【就任】take up one's post; take office

【就势】making use of momentum: 对手扑过来,我～把他摔倒在地。*As my opponent threw himself at me, I made use of his momentum to fling him to the ground*.

【就事论事】consider sth. in isolation or out of context; deal with a matter on its merits: 我不清楚这件事的背景,只能～地谈谈。*I don't know the whole background, so I can only judge the case as it stands*.

【就是】❶ (used, usu. with 了, at the end of a sentence to give force to the statement): 他想要点儿钱～了。*He wants some money, that's all*. / 你说～了。*Just say it!* ❷ yes, that's right; exactly; precisely: 这是不是你说的那个? —～。*Is that what you were talking about? —Yes, that's it*. ❸ (used correlatively with 也) even if: 你～不愿意去,也得打个电话。*Even if you don't want to go, you still have to make a phone call*.

【就是说】that is to say; in other words; namely

【就手】while you're at it: 你～把这个也洗洗。*Please wash this too while you are washing the other things*. / ～把门关上。*Close the door behind you*.

【就算】〈口〉even if; granted that: ～你工作干得不错,也不应该骄傲吧。*Granted you have not done badly, still there is no reason to be conceited*.

【就位】take one's place

【就席】take one's seat (at a banquet, etc.); be seated at the table

【就绪】be in order; be ready: 一切都已～。*Everything is ready (or in order)*. / 准备工作已经大致～。*The preparations are more or less completed*.

【就要】be about to; be going to; be on the point of: 火车～开了。*The train is about to start*. or *The train is starting in a minute*.

【就业】obtain employment; take up an occupation; get a job: 充分～ *full employment* / ～不足 *underemployment* ◇ ～保险 employment security; ～技能培训 pre-job training; ～门路 job opportunities

【就医】seek medical advice; go to a doctor

【就义】be executed for championing a just cause; die a martyr

【就诊】see a doctor; seek medical advice

【就正】solicit comments (on one's writing): ～于读者 *request (or invite) the readers to offer their criticisms*

【就职】assume office: 宣誓～ *take the oath of office; be sworn in* ◇ ～典礼 inaugural ceremony; inauguration; ～演说 inaugural speech

【就座】(又作'就坐') take one's seat; be seated: 在主席台前列～的有… *seated in the front row on the rostrum were...* / 贵宾们依次～。*The honoured guests took their seats in due order.*

舅 名 ❶ mother's brother; uncle ❷ wife's brother; brother-in-law

【舅父】mother's brother; uncle

【舅舅】〈口〉mother's brother; uncle

【舅母】wife of mother's brother; aunt

【舅子】〈口〉wife's brother; brother-in-law

鹫 名 vulture

jū

车 名 chariot, one of the pieces in Chinese chess ——另见 chē

拘 Ⅰ 动 ❶ arrest; detain: 昨天晚上闹事的足球迷给～起来了。*The football fans who made trouble last night were detained.* ❷ restrain; restrict; constrain: 拘谨 Ⅱ 形 inflexible: 拘泥

【拘捕】arrest; take into custody

【拘谨】overcautious; reserved: 初次见面时,他有些～,不大爱说话。*At the first meeting he was rather reserved and withdrawn.*

【拘禁】take into custody; detain

【拘礼】be punctilious; stand on ceremony: 熟不～ *be too familiar with each other to stand on ceremony*

【拘留】detain; hold in custody; intern ◇ ～所 house of detention; lockup; ～证 detention warrant

【拘拿】arrest; take into custody

【拘泥】be a stickler for (form, etc.); rigidly adhere to (formalities, etc.): ～于形式 *rigidly adhere to form; be formalistic* / ～于细节 *be very punctilious* / ～成说 *rigidly adhere to accepted theories*

【拘票】arrest warrant; warrant

【拘守】❶ hold fast to; stick to: ～成规 *hold fast to convention* / ～绳墨 *stick to the rules* ❷〈书〉imprison

【拘束】❶ restrain; restrict: 不要～孩子们的正当活动。*Don't restrict the proper activities of children.* ❷ constrained; awkward; ill at ease: 在生人面前显得～ *look ill at ease in the presence of strangers* / 不要～。*Make yourself at home.*

【拘押】take into custody; detain

【拘役】[法] criminal detention: ～的期限为十五日以上,六个月以下。*The term of criminal detention is not less than fifteen days and not more than six months.*

狙 Ⅰ 名 a kind of monkey mentioned in ancient texts Ⅱ 动〈书〉watch for

【狙击】snipe ◇ ～手 sniper; ～战 sniping action

居 Ⅰ 动 ❶ reside; dwell; live: 侨居 ❷ be (in a certain position); occupy (a place): ～世界首位 *occupy first place in the world; rank first in the world* / 身～要职 *hold an important post* ❸ claim; assert: 自居 ❹ store up; lay by: 居奇 ❺ stay put; be at a standstill: 岁月不居 Ⅱ 名 residence; house: 故居

【居安思危】think of danger in times of safety; be vigilant in peace time

【居多】be in the majority: 我们球队里北方人～。*Most of the players in our team are northerners.*

【居高临下】occupy a commanding position (or height)

【居功】claim credit for oneself

【居功自傲】become arrogant because of one's achievements; claim credit and put on airs

【居家】live at home; run a household: ～过日子 *keep house (economically and efficiently)*

【居间】(mediate) between two parties: ～调停 *mediate between two parties; act as mediator* ◇ ～人 intermediary; mediator

【居留】reside: 在国外～ *reside abroad* / 长期～ *permanent residence* ◇ ～权 right of residence; ～证 residence permit

【居民】resident; inhabitant: 城镇～ *residents in cities and towns; urban residents* ◇ ～储蓄 household saving; ～点 residential area; ～身份证 resident's identification card; ～委员会 (or residents') committee

【居奇】hoard and speculate: 囤积居奇

【居然】❶ unexpectedly; actually; to one's surprise: 真没想到他～会做出这种事来。*Who would have thought he could do such a thing?* / 你怎么～相信这种谣言? *How could you believe such a rumour?* ❷ go so far as to: ～当面撒谎 *go so far as to tell a bare-faced lie*

【居室】room: 三～ *a three-room flat*

【居首】occupy first place; rank first

【居心】harbour (evil) intentions: 他们～何在? *What are they up to?*

【居心不良】harbour evil intentions

【居心叵测】with hidden intent; with ulterior motives

【居于】occupy (a certain position): ～领导地位的干部 *cadres in leading positions*

【居中】❶ (mediate) between two parties: ～斡旋 *mediate between disputants* ❷ be placed in the middle: 小标题一律～。*Subheads should be placed in the middle of the column.* or *Centre the subheads.*

【居住】live; reside; dwell: 他家一直～在乡下。*His family have always lived in the country.* / 苗族～地区 *a region inhabited by the Miao nationality* / ～条件 *housing conditions* ◇ ～面积 living space; floor space; ～期限 length of residence; ～小区 residential district; ～证 residence permit

驹 名 ❶ colt ❷ foal: 怀～ *be in (or with) foal* / 小驴～儿 *foal*

【驹子】foal

疽 名［中］subcutaneous ulcer; deep-rooted ulcer

掬 动 hold with both hands：以手～水 *scoop up some water with one's hands*

锔 动 mend (crockery) with cramps：～碗（缸）*mend a bowl (jar) with cramps* ——另见 jú

【锔子】a cramp used in mending crockery

鞠 动〈书〉rear; bring up

【鞠躬】bow：～致谢 *bow one's thanks* / 行个～礼 *salute by making a bow* / 深深地鞠一个躬 *make a deep bow; bow low*

【鞠躬尽瘁】bend oneself to a task and exert oneself to the utmost; spare no effort in the performance of one's duty

【鞠躬尽瘁，死而后已】bend one's back to the task until one's dying day; give one's all till one's heart stops beating

jú

局 名 ❶ chessboard：棋局 ❷ game; set; innings：第一～（*in table tennis, etc.*）the first game; the first set; (in shuttlecock, baseball and softball) the first innings ❸ situation; state of affairs：全局 ❹ gathering：赌局 ❺ ruse; trap：骗局 ❻ part; portion：局部 ❼ bureau; office：教育～ *bureau of education* / 邮政～ *post office* ❽ (used in shop names) shop：书局

【局部】part：～必须服从全局。*The part must be subordinated to the whole.* / ～地区 *some areas; parts of an area* / ～利益 *partial and local interests* ◇ ～麻醉 local anaesthesia；～认付 partial acceptance；～要价 partial bid；～战争 local war; partial war

【局促】❶ narrow; cramped：这地方～，走动不便。*This place is rather cramped; there's little room for free movement.* ❷〈方〉(of time) short：三天太～，恐怕办不成。*I'm afraid three days is not long enough for us to get it done.* ❸ feel (or show) constraint

【局促不安】ill at ease：他跟不认识的人在一起感到～。*He was ill at ease with people whom he didn't know.*

【局面】aspect; phase; situation：出现了崭新的～。*Things have taken on a new aspect.* / 打开～ *open up a new prospect; make a breakthrough*

【局内人】a person in the know; insider

【局势】situation：国际～ *the international situation* / 紧张～ *a tense situation; tension*

【局外人】a person not in the know; outsider：～不得而知 *unknown to an outsider*

【局限】limit; confine：颇有～ *be rather limited (in outlook, etc.); have many limitations* / 他的报告不～于教学法问题。*His talk wasn't confined to teaching methods.*

【局限性】limitations

【局域网】［计］local area network (LAN)

桔 名 a popular form for 橘 ——另见 jié

菊 名 chrysanthemum

【菊花】chrysanthemum

【菊科】［植］the composite family

【菊展】chrysanthemum show：每年秋季北京中山公园都举办～。*There is a chrysanthemum show every autumn in the Dr. Sun Yatsen Memorial Park of Beijing.*

焗 动〈方〉❶ steam food in a sealed container：全～鸡 *a whole steamed chicken* ❷ feel smothered; be stifling

【焗油】❶ treatment of the hair with a cream to make it soft and shiny ❷ hair treatment cream

锔 名［化］curium (Cm) ——另见 jū

橘 名 tangerine

【橘红】❶ tangerine (colour); reddish orange ❷［中］dried tangerine peel

【橘黄】orange (colour)

【橘汁】orange juice

【橘子】tangerine

jǔ

沮 动 ❶〈书〉stop; prevent：～其成行 *stop sb. from going* ❷ turn gloomy; turn glum：沮丧

【沮丧】❶ dejected; depressed; dispirited; disheartened：敌人士气～。*The enemy's morale is low.* ❷ depress; dispirit; dishearten：～敌人的精神 *demoralize the enemy*

咀 动 chew：含英咀华

【咀嚼】❶ masticate; chew ❷ mull over; ruminate; chew the cud：演员对每句台词都要反复吟咏、～，才能进入角色，*An actor must rehearse his lines again and again, chewing on them so to speak, before he can hope to get inside the character that he is playing.*

举 Ⅰ 动 ❶ lift; raise; hold up：他～起棍子，打了下来。*Raising his staff, he chopped down.* / ～枪瞄准 *level one's gun at the target* ❷ start：举义 ❸ elect; choose：我们～他当主席。*We elected him as chairman.* ❹ cite; enumerate：我可以～出好几件事来说明。*I can cite quite a few instances to illustrate.* / 你能～出什么理由来吗？*Can you give any reason for it?* Ⅱ 名 act; deed; move：国家安危，系于此～。*The entire safety of our country depends upon this one move.* Ⅲ 形〈书〉whole; entire：举座

【举哀】❶ wail in mourning ❷ go into mourning：宣布全国～三天 *declare three days national mourning*

【举案齐眉】holding the tray level with the brows—husband and wife treating each other with courtesy

【举办】conduct；hold；run：～训练班 *conduct a training course* / ～音乐会 *give a concert*

【举报】report (an offender)；inform against ◇ ～中心 centre to receive reports, denunciations of corruption

【举步】〈书〉take a step：～向前 *take a step forward* / ～维艰 *have difficulty in taking a step*

【举措】move；act

【举措失当】make an ill-advised move：敌军调动慌忙，～。*The enemy manoeuvred his troops in a disorderly way and made false moves.*

【举动】movement；move；act；activity：轻率的～ *a rash act* / 他年迈体衰，～越来越缓慢。*He's old and infirm, and his movements are getting slower and slower.* / 你有什么～要先告诉我一声。*Let me know before you make a move.*

【举度】manner：～潇洒 *debonair；carefree*

【举国】the whole nation：～欢腾。*The whole nation is jubilant.*

【举国上下】the whole nation from top to bottom；from the leaders of the nation to all the people：～团结一致。*There is solid unity throughout the nation.*

【举家】whole family：～老小 *all members of the family, old and young* / ～迁蜀。*The whole family moved to Sichuan.*

【举荐】recommend (a person)

【举例】give an example：举个例 *give an example* / ～说明 *illustrate with examples*

【举目】〈书〉raise the eyes；look：～四望 *look round* / ～远眺 *look into the distance*

【举目无亲】be away from all one's kin；be a stranger in a strange land；have no one to turn to (for help)

【举棋不定】hesitate about (or over) what move to make；be unable to make up one's mind；vacillate；shilly-shally：接受好还是不接受好，他～。*He vacillated between accepting and not accepting.*

【举世】throughout the world；universally：～皆知 *known to all* / ～公认 *universally acknowledged* ◇ ～闻名 of world renown；world-famous；～无双 unrivalled；matchless；～瞩目 attract worldwide attention；become the focus of world attention

【举手】raise (or put up) one's hand or hands：赞成的请～。*Those in favour please put up their hands.* / 举起手来！*Hands up!* / ～表决 *vote by a show of hands* ◇ ～礼 hand salute

【举手之劳】lift a finger：你不用谢我，这不过是～。*No need to thank me；it's nothing.*

【举行】hold (a meeting, ceremony, etc.)：～会谈 *hold talks* / ～宴会 *give (or host) a banquet* / ～罢工 *stage a strike* / 你们几时～婚礼？*When are you going to have your wedding?*

【举一反三】draw inferences about other cases from one instance

【举债】〈书〉borrow money；raise (or contract) a loan ◇ ～筹资 debt financing

【举止】bearing；manner；mien：～庄重 *deport oneself in a dignified manner；carry oneself with dignity* / ～大方 *have poise；have an easy manner；be gentle of mien*

【举重】weight lifting：～运动员 *weight lifter* ◇ ～台 platform

【举足轻重】hold the balance；prove decisive：一支～的力量 *a decisive force* / 处于～的地位 *occupy a pivotal position*

枸

(构词成分)见下 ——另见 gǒu

【枸橼】citron ◇ ～酸 citric acid；～酸钠 sodium citrate

矩

名 ❶ carpenter's square；square：矩尺 ❷ rules；regulations：循规蹈矩 ❸ [物] moment：力矩

【矩臂】[物] moment arm

【矩尺】carpenter's square

【矩形】rectangle

【矩阵】[数] matrix

龃

(构词成分)见下

【龃龉】〈书〉the upper and lower teeth not meeting properly—disagreement；discord：双方发生～。*The two parties quarrelled.*

jù

巨

形 huge；tremendous；gigantic：～幅标语 *a huge poster* / ～型运输机 *a giant transport plane* / 为数甚～ *a huge sum*

【巨变】a great change；a tremendous change：山村～ *tremendous changes in a mountain village*

【巨擘】❶ thumb ❷ authority in a certain field：医界～ *a leading medical authority*

【巨大】huge；tremendous；enormous；gigantic；immense：～的胜利 *a tremendous victory* / ～的力量 *tremendous force；immense strength* / ～的工程 *a giant project*

【巨额】a huge amount；a huge sum：积累了～财富 *have accumulated a huge amount of wealth* / ～投资 *huge investments* / ～利润 *enormous profits* / ～赤字 *huge financial deficits*

【巨富】❶ immense wealth ❷ a man of immense wealth；multimillionaire：美国石油～ *a U. S. oil tycoon*

【巨奸大猾】an arrant swindler

【巨匠】〈书〉great master；consummate craftsman；giant：文坛～ *a literary giant*

【巨款】a huge sum of money

【巨浪】billow；surge；mountainous waves

【巨流】〈喻〉a mighty current：汇成一股～ *converge into a mighty current*

【巨轮】〈喻〉❶ a large wheel：历史的～是拖不回来的。*The wheel of history cannot be turned* back. ❷ a large ship：远洋～ *a large oceangoing ship*

【巨人】giant；colossus ◇ ～症 gigantism

【巨商】big businessman；business tycoon：港澳～ *big businessmen from Hong Kong and Macao*

【巨头】magnate；tycoon：金融～ *financial magnate；shark of high finance；financial tycoon*

【巨无霸】the giant；the extra large

【巨细】big and small：事无～ *all matters，big and small* / ～毕究 *let nothing pass unnoticed*

【巨星】〔天〕giant star；giant

【巨型超市】hypermarket

【巨著】monumental work：历史～ *a magnum opus of historic significance*

【巨子】magnate；tycoon；giant：实业界～ *a business tycoon* / 文坛～ *a literary giant*

句 Ⅰ名 sentence：这～我不懂。*I don't understand this sentence.* / 我来说几～。*Let me say a few words.* Ⅱ量 sentence：一～话 *a sentence* / 两～诗 *two lines of verse* / 我一～话也没说。*I didn't say a word.* / 他说的一～实话也没有。*There's not a word of truth in what he says.*

【句读】the period and the comma；sentences and phrases

【句法】❶ sentence structure ❷〈语〉syntax

【句号】full stop；full point；period（。）(.)

【句型】sentence pattern

【句子】sentence ◇ ～成分 sentence element；member of a sentence

拒 动 ❶ resist；repel：～敌 *resist the enemy；keep the enemy at bay* ❷ refuse；reject：～不接受 *refuse to accept*

【拒捕】resist arrest

【拒发签证】refusal to issue a visa

【拒付】refuse payment；dishonour (a cheque)

【拒谏饰非】reject representations and gloss over errors；reject criticisms and whitewash one's mistakes

【拒绝】❶ refuse：～参加 *refuse to participate* / ～发表意见 *refuse to comment* ❷ reject；turn down；decline：～无理要求 *turn down (or reject) unreasonable demands* / ～别人的批评 *reject other people's criticism* ◇ ～承兑 non-acceptance

【拒聘】turn down an appointment；refuse an engagement

【拒人于千里之外】keep people at a distance of 1,000 li—be arrogant and unapproachable

【拒收】rejection

具 Ⅰ名 utensil；tool；implement：雨具 Ⅱ量〈书〉(for coffins，dead bodies，and certain instruments or machines)：一～尸体 *a corpse* / 座钟一～ *a desk clock* Ⅲ动 ❶possess；have：初～规模 *begin to take shape* ❷〈书〉provide；furnish：谨～薄礼 *allow me to present to you this trifling gift*

【具备】possess；have；be provided with：申请贷款者应～上述条件。*Those who ask for loans should satisfy the conditions listed above.*

【具名】put one's name to a document，etc.；affix one's signature

【具体】concrete；specific；particular：她谈得非常～。*She spoke in very concrete terms.* / ～日期未定。*No exact date has been set.* / 方案尚待～化。*Details of the plan have yet to be worked out.*

【具体而微】small but complete；miniature

【具体劳动】〔经〕concrete labour

【具文】mere formality；dead letter：一纸～ *a mere scrap of paper*

【具有】have (sth. immaterial)；possess：建设～中国特色的社会主义 *build a socialism with Chinese characteristics*

炬 名 ❶ torch：火炬 ❷ fire：付之一炬

俱 副〈书〉all；complete：罪证～在。*All the evidence of the crime is available.*

【俱乐部】club

【俱全】complete in all varieties：样样～。*Everything necessary is available.*

剧 Ⅰ名 theatrical work；drama；play；opera：这个～是谁主演的？*Who is the leading actor in the play?* Ⅱ形 acute；severe；intense：产量～增 *a sharp increase in output*

【剧本】❶ drama；play ❷ script；scenario；libretto：分镜头～ *shooting script* / ～创作 *play writing；script writing*

【剧变】a violent (or drastic) change

【剧场】theatre

【剧毒】hypertoxic

【剧减】dramatic reduction

【剧烈】violent；acute；severe；fierce：～运动 *strenuous exercise* / ～的对抗 *acute antagonism* / ～的社会变动 *radical social changes*

【剧目】a list of plays or operas

【剧评】a review of a play or opera；dramatic criticism

【剧情】the story (or plot) of a play or opera：～简介 *synopsis*

【剧痛】a severe pain

【剧团】theatrical company；opera troupe；troupe

【剧务】❶ stage management ❷ stage manager

【剧院】theatre

【剧增】increase drastically or sharply

【剧照】stage photo；still

【剧中人】characters in a play or opera；dramatis personae

【剧终】the end；curtain

【剧种】type (or genre) of drama

【剧组】cast，director and stage hands in a drama production

【剧作】drama；play ◇ ～家 playwright；dramatist

惧 动 fear；dread：毫无所～ *not cowed in the least；fearless*

【惧内】〈书〉henpecked

【惧怕】fear；dread

【惧色】a look of fear：面无～ *look undaunted*

据 Ⅰ 动 ❶ occupy；seize：盘据 ❷ rely on；depend on：～险固守 *take advantage of a natural barrier to put up a strong defence* Ⅱ 介 according to；on the grounds of：～报道 *according to (press) reports*；*it is reported that* / ～我看 *as I see it*；*in my opinion* / ～我所知 *as far as I know* Ⅲ 名 evidence；certificate：证据

【据称】it is said；they say；allegedly

【据传】a story is going around that；rumour has it that

【据此】on these grounds；in view of the above；accordingly

【据点】strongpoint；fortified point；stronghold

【据理力争】argue strongly on just grounds

【据守】guard；be entrenched in：～交通要道 *guard vital lines of communication*；*be entrenched in communication centres* / 掘壕～ *dig in*；*entrench oneself*

【据说】it is said；they say；allegedly：～他在那里干得不错。*They say he is doing quite well there.* / 这场事故～是由于疏忽造成的。*The accident was allegedly due to negligence.*

【据为己有】take forcible possession of；appropriate

【据悉】it is reported：～，他将于明天辞职。*He is reportedly going to resign tomorrow.*

距 Ⅰ 名 ❶ distance：行距 ❷ spur (of a cock, etc.) Ⅱ 动 be apart (or away) from；be at a distance from：天津～北京约有一百二十公里。*Tianjin is about 120 km from Beijing.* / ～今已有十年。*That was ten years ago.*

【距离】❶ distance：保持一个～ *keep one's distance*；*keep at a distance* ❷ be apart (or away) from；be at a distance from：他的看法和你有～。*His opinion differs from yours.*

飓 (构词成分)见下

【飓风】hurricane

锯 Ⅰ 名 saw：一把～ *a saw* Ⅱ 动 cut with a saw；saw：～木头 *saw wood*

【锯齿】sawtooth

【锯床】sawing machine：圆盘～ *circular sawing machine*

【锯末】sawdust

【锯木厂】sawmill；lumber-mill

【锯条】saw blade

【锯屑】sawdust

【锯子】〈方〉saw

聚 动 assemble；gather；get together：大家～在一起商量商量。*Let's get together and talk it over.* / 咱们找个地方～～。*Let's find a place to have a get-together.*

【聚氨酯】(又作'聚氨基甲酸酯') polyurethane

【聚宝盆】treasure bowl—a place rich in natural resources；cornucopia

【聚苯乙烯】polystyrene

【聚变】[物] fusion：核～ *nuclear fusion* / 受控～ *controlled fussion*

【聚变反应堆】[物] fusion reactor

【聚丙烯】polypropylene

【聚丙烯腈】polyacrylonitrile

【聚餐】dine together (usu. on festive occasions)；have a dinner party

【聚赌】get together to gamble

【聚光灯】spotlight

【聚光镜】condensing lens

【聚合】❶ get together ❷ [化] polymerization：定向～ *stereoregular (or stereotactic) polymerization* / ～反应 *polyreaction*

【聚合物】[化] polymer：工程～ *engineering polymers*

【聚会】❶ get together；meet：老战友～在一起，格外亲热。*The meeting of the old comrades-in-arms was extremely cordial.* ❷ get-together：他们每隔两个月搞一次～。*They have a get-together every two months.*

【聚积】accumulate；collect；build up：～军事力量 *build up military forces*

【聚集】gather；assemble；collect：机场上～着数千人，为代表团送行。*Thousands of people gathered at the airport to see the delegation off.*

【聚甲醛】polyformaldehyde

【聚歼】round up and annihilate；annihilate en masse

【聚焦】[物] focusing：指向～ *directional focusing*

【聚精会神】concentrate one's attention；be all attention：～地工作 *concentrate on one's work*；*be intent on one's work* / ～地听 *listen with rapt attention*

【聚居】inhabit a region (as an ethnic group)；live in a compact community：少数民族～的地区 *regions where minority nationalities live in compact communities* ◇ ～点 settlement

【聚敛】amass wealth by heavy taxation

【聚拢】gather together

【聚氯乙烯】polyvinyl chloride (PVC)

【聚醛树脂】aldehyde resin

【聚伞花序】[植] cyme

【聚沙成塔】many grains of sand piled up will make a pagoda—many a little makes a mickle

【聚四氟乙烯】polytetrafluoroethylene (PTFE)

【聚讼纷纭】argue back and forth without coming to an agreement；opinions differ widely；a welter of conflicting opinions

【聚碳酸脂】polycarbonate

【聚酰胺】polyamide：～塑料 *polyamide plastics*

【聚星】[天] multiple star

【聚乙烯】polyethylene；polythene

【聚乙烯醇】polyvinyl alcohol

【聚酯】polyester：～塑料 *polyester plastics*

【聚众】assemble a crowd；gather a mob：～闹事 *assemble a crowd to make trouble* / ～斗殴 *gath-*

er a mob to have brawls / ～赌博 *organize gambling parties*

踞 动 ❶ crouch; squat ❷ sit ❸ occupy: 盘踞

【踞守】同〖据守〗

遽 Ⅰ 副 hurriedly; hastily: ～下结论 *pass judgment hastily* Ⅱ 形 frightened; alarmed: 惶遽

【遽然】〈书〉suddenly; abruptly: ～变色 *suddenly change countenance*

juān

涓 名〈书〉a tiny stream

【涓滴归公】every bit goes to the public treasury; turn in every cent of public money

【涓涓】〈文〉trickling sluggishly: ～流水 *a sluggish trickle of water*

捐 动 ❶ relinquish; abandon ❷ contribute; donate; subscribe: 我向基金会～了一笔钱。*I have donated some money to the foundation.*

【捐款】❶ contribute money ❷ contribution; donation; subscription

【捐弃】〈书〉relinquish; abandon: ～前嫌 *bury old grudges*

【捐躯】sacrifice one's life; lay down one's life

【捐税】taxes and levies

【捐献】contribute (to an organization); donate; present: 他把全部藏书～给图书馆。*He presented his whole collection of books to the library.*

【捐赠】contribute (as a gift); donate; present: 向图书馆～图书 *present books to a library*

【捐助】offer (financial or material assistance); contribute; donate

【捐资】contribute funds to: 为希望工程～ *contribute funds to Project Hope* ◇ ～办学 donate money for school

娟 形〈书〉beautiful; graceful: 婵娟

【娟秀】〈书〉beautiful; graceful: 字迹～ *beautiful handwriting; a graceful hand*

圈 动 ❶ shut in a pen; pen in: 把羊群～起来 *herd the sheep into the pens* / 别老～在书房里。*Don't shut yourself up in your study.* ❷〈口〉lock up; put in jail: 犯人都～起来了。*The prisoners were locked up.* ——另见 juàn; quān

镌 动〈书〉engrave: ～碑 *engrave a stone tablet*

【镌刻】〈书〉engrave

juǎn

卷 Ⅰ 动 ❶ roll up: 把竹帘子～起来 *roll up the bamboo screen* / ～起袖子就干 *roll up one's sleeves and pitch in* ❷ sweep off; carry along: 一个大浪把小船～走了。*A huge wave swept the boat away.* / 汽车飞驰而过，～起一阵尘土。*A car sped past, raising a cloud of dust.* Ⅱ 名 cylindrical mass of sth.; roll: 把书裹成一个～儿寄出去。*Roll up the book and take it to the post.* Ⅲ 量 roll; spool; reel: 一～手纸 *a roll of toilet paper* / 一～软片 *a roll of film* / 一～铺盖 *a roll of bedding*

【卷笔刀】pencil sharpener

【卷层云】[气] cirrostratus

【卷尺】tape measure; band tape: 布～ *cloth (or linen) tape* / 钢～ *steel tape*

【卷发】curly hair; wavy hair ◇ ～器 curler

【卷积云】[气] cirrocumulus

【卷铺盖】❶ pack up and quit ❷ get the sack

【卷绕】[纺] winding: ～机 *take-up machine*

【卷刃】(of a knife blade) be turned (or twisted): 你把我的刀拿去干什么啦？都卷了刃儿了！*What have you been doing to my knife? The blade's all turned.*

【卷入】be drawn into; be involved in: ～漩涡 *be drawn into a whirlpool* / ～一场纠纷 *be involved in a dispute*

【卷舌辅音】[语音] retroflex consonant

【卷舌元音】[语音] retroflex vowel

【卷逃】abscond with valuables

【卷筒】reel ◇ ～纸 web

【卷土重来】stage a comeback

【卷尾猴】(weeping) capuchin; weeping monkey

【卷心菜】〈方〉cabbage

【卷须】[植] tendril

【卷烟】❶ cigarette ❷ cigar ◇ ～纸 cigarette paper

【卷扬机】hoist; hoister

【卷叶蛾】(又作'卷叶虫') leaf roller

【卷云】[气] cirrus

【卷轴】reel: 天线～ *aerial reel* ——另见 juànzhóu

juàn

卷 名 ❶ book: 手不释卷 ❷ chapter, section, or volume; fascicle: 这个图书馆藏书十万～。*This library has 100,000 volumes.* /《新大英百科全书》共三十～。*The New Encyclopaedia Britannica is complete in 30 volumes.* ❸ examination paper: 交卷 ❹ file; dossier: 查～ *look through the files* ——另见 juǎn

【卷轴】〈书〉scroll ——另见 juǎnzhóu

【卷子】❶ examination paper: 看～ *mark examination papers* ❷ a handwritten copy in scroll form

【卷宗】❶ folder ❷ file; dossier

倦 形 weary; tired: 疲倦

【倦容】a tired look: 面有～ *look tired*

【倦色】a tired look

【倦意】a feeling of tiredness: 他滔滔不绝地讲，好像毫无～。*He talked on and on, apparently not feeling in the least tired.*

【倦游】〈书〉weary of wandering and sightseeing:

～归来 *be back home, sated, from pleasure excursions*

绢 名 thin, tough silk

【绢本】silk scroll

【绢纺】silk spinning

【绢花】silk flower

【绢画】classical Chinese painting on silk

【绢丝】spun silk (yarn): ～纺绸 *spun silk pongee* / ～织物 *spun silk fabric*

【绢网印花】[纺] screen printing: ～法 *silk-screen process*

隽 形〈书〉meaningful

【隽永】〈书〉meaningful: 语颇～，耐人寻味。*The remarks are meaningful and thought-provoking.*

眷 Ⅰ名 family dependant: 女眷 Ⅱ动〈书〉have tender feeling for: 眷顾

【眷顾】〈书〉regard with tenderness; be concerned about

【眷恋】〈书〉be sentimentally attached to (a person or place)

【眷念】〈书〉think fondly of; feel nostalgic about

【眷属】family dependants

圈 名 pen; fold; sty: 把羊轰到～里去。*Put the flock in the fold.* ——另见 juān; quān

【圈肥】barnyard manure

juē

撅 动 ❶ stick up: ～着尾巴 *sticking up the tail* / ～嘴 *pout (one's lips)* ❷〈口〉break (sth. long and narrow); snap: 把树枝～成两段 *break the twig in two*

jué

决 Ⅰ动 ❶ decide; determine: 表决 ❷ execute a person: 枪决 ❸ (of a dyke, etc.) be breached; burst: 溃决 Ⅱ副 (used before a negative) definitely; certainly; under any circumstances: ～非恶意 *be entirely without malice; bear no ill will whatsoever* / ～不退让 *will under no circumstances give in* / 不达目的～不罢休。*We'll never give up until the goal is reached.*

【决标】select the winning tender

【决策】❶ make policy; make a strategic decision: 运筹～ *devise strategies* ❷ policy decision; decision of strategic importance: 战略～ *strategic decision* ◇ ～分析 dicision analysis; ～机构 policy-making body; ～人 policy-maker; ～树 decision tree

【决出】contest (prizes); fight for: 今天将～三块金牌。*Three golds will be contested and awarded today.*

【决堤】breach (or burst) a dyke

【决定】❶ decide; resolve; make up one's mind: 一时～不了 *cannot make up one's mind for the moment; be unable to come to a decision for the moment* ❷ decision; resolution: 通过一项～ *pass a resolution* ❸ determine; decide: 存在～意识。*Man's social being determines his consciousness.* / ❹ decisive: ～因素 *decisive factor; determinant*

【决定论】[哲] determinism

【决定权】power to make decisions: 有最后～ *have the final say*

【决定性】decisiveness: ～的胜利 *a decisive victory* / 起～作用 *play a decisive part (or role)*

【决斗】❶ duel ❷ decisive struggle

【决断】❶ make a decision ❷ resolve; decisiveness; resolution: 他很有～。*He shows great resolve.* / 你要有～，你认为怎么办好就怎么办。*You must be resolute and do what you think best.*

【决计】❶ have decided; have made up one's mind: 我～把工作干完再走。*I have decided to get the work done before I leave.* ❷ definitely; certainly: 那样办～没错儿。*We definitely can't go wrong if we do it that way.* or *There is absolutely nothing wrong with doing it that way.*

【决口】(of a dyke, etc.) be breached; burst: 河～了。*The river burst its banks.*

【决裂】break with; rupture: 这样她就和我～了，彼此再没有见面。*With that she broke off with me, and we were never to see each other again.*

【决然】〈书〉❶ resolutely; determinedly: ～返回 *turn back resolutely* ❷ definitely; unquestionably; undoubtedly: 那～不是我的错。*That's definitely not my fault.*

【决赛】[体] finals

【决胜】decide the issue of the battle; determine the victory ◇ ～局 [体] deciding game (or set); ～球 deciding ball

【决死】life-and-death: ～的斗争 *a life-and-death struggle; a last-ditch fight*

【决算】final accounts; final accounting of revenue and expenditure

【决心】determination; resolution: 下定～ *make up one's mind; be resolute; be determined* / 有～，有信心 *have both determination and confidence* ◇ ～书 written pledge; statement of one's determination

【决一雌雄】fight to see who is the stronger; fight it out

【决一胜负】fight it out

【决一死战】fight to the death; fight to a finish

【决议】resolution: ～草案 *a draft resolution*

【决意】have one's mind made up; be determined: 他～要走。*He's made up his mind to quit.*

【决战】decisive battle; decisive engagement

诀 Ⅰ名 ❶ rhymed formula: 口诀 ❷ knack; tricks of the trade: 秘诀 Ⅱ动 bid farewell; part: 永诀

【诀别】bid farewell; part (usu. with the implication that there is little likelihood of meeting again)
【诀窍】secret of success; key to success; tricks of the trade; knack: 炒菜的～主要是拿准火候儿。*By and large, the key to success in stir-frying is proper control of time and temperature.*
【诀要】同〖诀窍〗

抉 动〈书〉pick out; single out: 抉择
【抉择】〈书〉choose: 作出～ *make one's choice*
【抉摘】〈书〉❶ choose ❷ expose and censure: ～弊端 *expose and censure malpractices*

角 Ⅰ名 ❶ role; part; character: 他在这出戏里演哪个～儿? *What's his role in this play?* ❷ type of role (in traditional Chinese drama): 丑角 ❸ actor or actress: 名～ *a famous actor or actress* Ⅱ动 contend; wrestle: 口角 ——另见 jiǎo
【角斗】wrestle ◇ ～场 wrestling ring
【角力】have a trial of strength; wrestle
【角色】❶ role; part: 她在这部电影里演哪个～? *What part does she play in that film?* / 扮演了不光彩的～ *play a contemptible role* ❷ type of role (in traditional Chinese drama) ◇ ～扮演游戏［计］roles play games
【角逐】contend; tussle; enter into rivalry

觉 Ⅰ动 ❶ sense; feel: 下过这场雪,就～出冷来了。*After the snow it is really cold.* / 身上～着不舒服 *not feel well* ❷ wake (up); awake: 如梦初～ *as if waking from a dream* ❸ become aware; become awakened: 他的意思你还没～出来吗? *Haven't you figured out what he meant yet?* Ⅱ名 sense; feel: 触～ *touch; sense of touch; tactile sensation* / 视～ *sight; sense of sight* / 听～ *hearing; hearing; sense of hearing; auditory sensation* / 味～ *taste; sense of taste; taste sensation* / 嗅～ *smell; sense of smell; smell perception* ——另见 jiào
【觉察】detect; become aware of; perceive: 她～到这里面有问题。*She sensed there was something wrong.*
【觉得】❶ feel: 一点儿也不～累 *not feel tired at all* ❷ think; feel: 我～应该先跟他商量一下。*I think we should consult him first.* / 我～他这几天情绪不好。*I have a feeling that he's been in low spirits these last few days.*
【觉悟】❶ consciousness; awareness; understanding: 阶级～ *class consciousness* ❷ come to understand; become aware of; become politically awakened: 他～到了改造世界观的重要性。*He has come to see the importance of remoulding his world outlook.*
【觉醒】awaken

绝 Ⅰ动 ❶ cut off; sever: ～其后路 *cut off his retreat* / 掌声不～ *prolonged applause* ❷ exhausted; used up; finished: 法子都想～了。*All possible ways have been tried.* or *All possibilities have been exhausted.* Ⅱ形 ❶ desperate; hopeless: 绝境 ❷ unique; superb; matchless: 她发的那球真～。*Her serve was a beauty.* ❸ leaving no leeway; making no allowance; uncompromising: 他尽管不同意,但是没把话说～。*He disagreed, but he didn't say anything definitive.* Ⅲ副 ❶ extremely; most: ～大多数 *most; the overwhelming majority* / ～好的机会 *an excellent opportunity* ❷ (used before a negative) absolutely; in the least; by any means; on any account: ～无此意 *have absolutely no such intentions* / ～非偶然 *by no means fortuitous* / ～不可粗心大意 *must on no account be negligent*
【绝版】out of print
【绝笔】❶ last words written before one's death ❷ the last work of an author or painter
【绝壁】precipice
【绝唱】the peak of poetic perfection: 堪称千古～ *rank as a poetic masterpiece through the ages*
【绝处逢生】be unexpectedly rescued from a desperate situation
【绝代】〈书〉unique among one's contemporaries; peerless: 才华～ *unrivalled talent* / ～佳人 *a woman of matchless beauty*
【绝地】❶ a danger spot: 这里左边是悬崖,右边是深沟,真是个～。*A precipice on the left side and a deep gully on the right—a veritable danger spot.* ❷ hopeless situation; dead end; impasse: 陷于～ *come to a dead end*
【绝顶】❶ extremely; utterly: ～聪明 *extremely intelligent* / ～愚蠢的行为 *the height of folly* ❷〈书〉peak; summit
【绝对】❶ absolute: ～多数 *absolute majority; overwhelming majority* / ～优势 *absolute predominance; overwhelming superiority* ❷ absolutely; perfectly; definitely: ～可靠 *absolutely reliable* / 你～不能去。*You absolutely can't go.* ◇ ～担保 absolute guaranty; ～地租 absolute rent; ～高度 absolute altitude; ～观念［哲］absolute idea; ～继承权 absolute inheritance ; ～量度［物］absolute measurement; ～零度［物］absolute zero; ～贫困化 absolute impoverishment; ～平均主义 absolute equalitarianism; ～权威 absolute authority; ～湿度［气］absolute humidity; ～温度［物］absolute temperature; ～音乐 absolute music; ～真理［哲］absolute truth; ～值［数］absolute value; ～主义［哲］absolutism
【绝后】❶ without offspring (or issue) ❷ never to be seen again: 空前绝后
【绝户】❶ without offspring (or issue) ❷ a childless person
【绝活】one's best skill: 内画山水是王师傅的～。*In-bottle landscape painting is Master Wang's unique skill.*
【绝技】unique skill; consummate skill
【绝迹】disappear; vanish; be stamped out: 猛犸在史前时期就～了。*Mammoths became extinct in prehistoric times.*

【绝交】break off relations (as between friends or countries)
【绝经】menopause
【绝境】❶ isolated condition ❷ hopeless situation; impasse; blind alley; cul-de-sac: 濒于～ *face an impasse*
【绝口】❶ (only used after 不) stop talking: 骂不～ *heap endless abuse upon; pour out unceasing abuse* ❷ keep one's mouth shut: ～不提 *never say a single word about; avoid all mention of*
【绝路】❶ block the way out; leave no way out: 这个办法要是还不行，那可就绝了路了。*If this proves to be no solution, then there can be no solution.* ❷ road to ruin; blind alley; dead end; impasse: 自寻～ *court destruction; bring ruin upon oneself* / 走上～ *come to a dead end (or impasse)*
【绝伦】〈书〉 unsurpassed; unequalled; peerless; matchless: 精美～ *exquisite beyond compare; superb*
【绝密】top-secret; strictly confidential: ～文件 *top-secret papers* / ～情报 *top-secret information*
【绝妙】extremely clever; ingenious; excellent; perfect: ～的一招 *a masterstroke* / ～的讽刺 *a supreme (or perfect) irony*
【绝命书】❶ suicide note ❷ note written on the eve of one's execution
【绝情】heartless; cruel: ～忘义 *ungrateful and heartless* / 夫妻之间不要说这种～的话。*It's not for a husband or wife to make such heartless (or cruel) remarks.*
【绝热】[物] heat insulation: ～材料 *heat-insulating material* / ～冷却 *adiabatic cooling* / ～曲线 *adiabatic curve; adiabatics* / ～压缩 *adiabatic compression*
【绝色】〈书〉(of a woman) exceedingly beautiful; of unrivalled beauty
【绝食】go on a hunger strike; fast
【绝收】total crop failure
【绝望】give up all hope; despair: ～情绪 *feeling of despair* / ～的挣扎 *desperate struggle*
【绝无仅有】the only one of its kind; unique
【绝育】[医] sterilization
【绝缘】❶ cut all ties with sth.: 我与酒～了。*I have stopped drinking.* ❷ [电] insulation: ～材料 *insulating material; insulant* / ～体 *insulator* / ～线 *covered wire* / ～纸 *insulating paper* / ～子 *insulator*
【绝招】(又作'绝着') ❶ unique skill ❷ unexpected tricky move (as a last resort)
【绝症】incurable disease; fatal illness
【绝种】(of a species) become extinct; die out

倔 形 (limited to use in 倔强) ——另见 juè
【倔强】stubborn; unbending

掘 动 dig: ～井 *dig a well*
【掘获】dig up: ～黄金 *dig up gold*
【掘进】[矿] driving; tunnelling: 平巷～ *drifting* / 快速～ *quick tunnelling* / 全断面～ *full-face tunnelling*
【掘墓人】gravedigger
【掘土机】excavator; power shovel

崛 动〈书〉rise abruptly
【崛起】〈书〉❶ (of a mountain, etc.) rise abruptly; suddenly appear on the horizon ❷ rise to prominence: 吴淞口畔，一座新的钢铁城正在～。*At Wusong a new city of steel is emerging on the horizon.*

厥 Ⅰ 动 faint; lose consciousness; fall into a coma: 昏厥 Ⅱ 代〈书〉his or her; its; their: ～后 *thereafter* / ～父 *his or her father*

谲 动〈书〉cheat; swindle: 诡谲
【谲诈】cunning; crafty

蕨 名 brake (fern)
【蕨类植物】pteridophyte

橛 名 a short wooden stake; wooden pin; peg
【橛子】a short wooden stake; wooden pin; peg

爵 名 the rank of nobility; peerage: 封～ *confer a title (of nobility) upon*
【爵禄】〈书〉 ranks and stipends; titles and stipends; dignities and emoluments: 财贿不以动其心，～不以移其志。*Rich bribes serve not to move him, nor do dignities and emoluments deflect his purpose.*
【爵士】❶ knight ❷ Sir: 约翰·史密斯～ *Sir John Smith*
【爵士音乐】jazz
【爵位】the rank (or title) of nobility

蹶 动 ❶ fall ❷ suffer a setback: 一蹶不振

矍 形〈书〉looking around in alarm
【矍铄】〈书〉hale and hearty

嚼 动 (limited to use in 咀嚼 and 过屠门而大嚼) ——另见 jiáo

攫 动 seize; grab: ～为己有 *seize possession of; appropriate*
【攫取】seize; grab: ～别国的资源 *grab the resources of other countries* / ～暴利 *rake in exorbitant profits*

juè

倔 形 gruff; surly: 这老头儿脾气～。*That old man is rather surly.* ——另见 jué
【倔头倔脑】blunt of manner and gruff of speech

jūn

军 名 ❶ armed forces; army; troops: 日～ *Jap-*

anese troops ❷ army (consisting of two or more divisions)：第一～ *the First Army* / 全歼敌人一个～ *wipe out an enemy army*

【军备】armament；arms：～控制 *arms control* / ～限制 *arms limitation* ◇ ～竞赛 armament (or arms) race

【军博】(〈略〉全称为'中国人民革命军事博物馆') Military Museum of the Chinese People's Revolution

【军操】military drill

【军车】military vehicle

【军刀】soldier's sword；sabre

【军地两用人才】PLA men trained to be competent for both military and civilian services

【军队】armed forces；army；troops ◇ ～标号 military symbols

【军阀】warlord：～战争 *war among warlords* / ～作风 *warlord ways*；*warlord style* ◇ ～主义 warlordism

【军法】military criminal code；military law：～从事 *punish by military law* ◇ ～审判 court-martial

【军方】the military

【军费】military expenditure

【军分区】military subarea

【军风纪】soldier's bearing and discipline

【军服】military (or army) uniform；uniform

【军港】naval port

【军歌】army song

【军工】❶ (〈略〉见〖军事工业〗) war industry：～生产 *war production* ❷ military project

【军功】military merit；military exploit ◇ ～章 medal for military merit

【军官】officer

【军管】military control ◇ ～会(〈略〉全称为'军事管制委员会') military control commission

【军棍】(in former times) a cane for corporal punishment in the army

【军国主义】militarism：～者 *militarist* ◇ ～主义化 militarization

【军号】bugle

【军徽】army emblem

【军婚】marriage of serviceman or servicewoman：他犯有破坏～罪。*He is found guilty of disrupting the marriage of a serviceman.*

【军火】munitions；arms and ammunition：～工业 *munitions industry*；*armament industry* / ～舰 *ammunition ship* ◇ ～库 arsenal；～商 munitions merchant；arms dealer；merchant of death

【军机】❶ military plan：贻误～ *delay (or frustrate) the fulfilment of a military plan* ❷ military secret：泄漏～ *leak a military secret*

【军籍】military status；one's name on the army roll：保留～ *retain one's military status* / 开除～ *strike sb.'s name off the army roll*；*discharge sb. from the army*

【军纪】military discipline

【军舰】warship；naval vessel

【军阶】(military) rank；grade

【军界】military circles；the military

【军垦】reclamation of wasteland by an army unit ◇ ～农场 army reclamation farm；army farm

【军礼】military salute

【军力】military strength

【军粮】army provisions；grain for the army ◇ ～库 military grain depot；army granary

【军列】military train

【军龄】length of military service：他的～比我长。*He has served in the army longer than I have.*

【军令】military orders：颁布～ *issue a military order*

【军令如山】military orders are like mountains (i.e. are unalterable and must be obeyed)

【军令状】a promise to get a job done, failing which one is willing to accept a severe penalty

【军旅】〈书〉armies；troops：～生涯 *life in the army*；*soldiering* / ～之事 *military matters*

【军马】army horse ◇ ～场 army horse-breeding farm；army horse ranch

【军帽】army cap；service cap

【军民】the army and the people；soldiers and civilians；military and civilian：～关系 *the relations between the army and the people*；*army-people relations* / ～联防 *army-civilian joint defence* / ～共建 *joint efforts by the army and people*

【军品】military products

【军旗】army flag；colours；ensign

【军旗礼】colours salute

【军企】military-run enterprise

【军情】military (or war) situation：刺探～ *spy out military secrets*；*gather military intelligence*

【军区】military region；(military) area command：各大～ *the greater military areas* / ～司令部 *the headquarters of a military area command*

【军权】military leadership；military power

【军犬】a police dog used for military purposes

【军人】soldier；serviceman；armyman：～大会 *soldiers conference (of a company)*

【军容】soldier's discipline, appearance and bearing：整饬～ *strengthen army discipline and maintain required standards for appearance and bearing*

【军嫂】honorific appellation for the wives of military personnel

【军师】〈旧〉war counsellor；military adviser

【军士】noncommissioned officer (NCO)

【军事】❶ military affairs ❷ military：～表演 *display of military skills* / ～部署 *military deployment*；*disposition of military forces* / ～演习 *military manoeuvre*；*war exercise* / ～优势 *military superiority* ◇ ～法庭 military tribunal (or court)；～工业 war industry；～管制 military control；～管制委员会 military control commission；～化 militarize；place on a war footing；～基地 military base；～家 strategist；～科学 military science；～体育 military sports；～条令 military manuals

【军事学】military science：～家 *military scientist*

【军事学院】military academy (or institute)
【军售】arms sale：该地区为一大潜在的～市场。*This region is a potentially large market for arms sales.*
【军属】soldier's dependants；armyman's family
【军团】army group
【军威】military might：～大振。*The might of the army was made felt.*
【军委】the Military Commission of the Central Committee of the Communist Party of China
【军务】military affairs；military task：～繁忙 *be busy with military affairs*
【军衔】military rank：～制度 *system of military ranks*
【军饷】〈旧〉soldier's pay and provisions
【军校】military school；military academy
【军械】ordnance；armament：～员 *armourer* ◇ ～处 ordnance department；～库 ordnance depot；arms depot；armoury
【军心】soldiers' morale：动摇～ *shake the army's morale* / ～大振。*The morale of the troops has been greatly raised.*
【军需】❶ military supplies ❷〈旧〉quartermaster ◇ ～库 military supply depot；～品 military supplies；military stores
【军训】military training
【军衣】military (or army) uniform；uniform
【军医】medical officer；military surgeon
【军营】military camp；barracks
【军运】military transport：～任务 *military transport task*
【军用】for military use；military：～地图 *military map* / ～飞机 *warplane；military aircraft* / ～机场 *military airfield* / ～列车 *military train* / ～物资 *military supplies；matériel*
【军援】military aid
【军乐】martial (or military) music ◇ ～队 military band
【军长】army commander
【军政】❶ military affairs and politics ❷ military administration ❸ army and government：～当局 *civil and military authorities* / ～关系 *the relations between the army and the government*
【军政府】military government
【军职】official post in the army；military appointment
【军中无戏言】there is no room for levity in the army
【军种】(armed) services
【军转民】conversion from military to civilian production
【军装】military (or army) uniform；uniform

均 Ⅰ形 equal；even：人口分布不～。*The population is unevenly distributed.* Ⅱ副 without exception；all：各项准备工作～已就绪。*All the preparatory work has been completed.*
【均等】equal；impartial；fair：机会～ *equal opportunity*
【均分】divide equally；share out equally：这批建筑材料由三个单位～。*This lot of building materials will be shared out equally among three units.*
【均衡】balance；equilibrium：走钢丝的演员举着一把伞，保持身体的～。*The tightrope walker kept her balance by holding up an umbrella.* / 国民经济的～发展 *the balanced (or harmonious) development of the national economy*
【均衡论】[哲] the theory of equilibrium
【均势】balance of power；equilibrium of forces；equilibrium；parity：保持(打破)～ *keep (upset) the balance of power*
【均摊】share equally：～费用 *share the expenses equally*
【均一】even；uniform；homogeneous ◇ ～性 [化] homogeneity
【均匀】even；well-distributed：～的呼吸 *even breathing* / ～撒播 *even broadcasting of seeds* / 今年的雨水很～。*Rainfall has been fairly well-distributed this year.* ◇ ～混合物 [化] homogeneous mixture
【均沾】share (interests, etc.) equally；have equal access to (advantages)：利益～ *even share of benefits*

君 名 ❶ monarch；sovereign；supreme ruler ❷〈书〉(used as a title) Mr.：张～ *Mr. Zhang* / 张刘二～ *Messrs. Zhang and Liu* / 诸～ *gentlemen (used in addressing a group)* ❸〈书〉(used in direct address) you；sir：祝～早安。*Good morning, sir.*
【君权】monarchical power；royal prerogative
【君王】monarch；sovereign；emperor
【君主】monarch；sovereign ◇ ～国 monarchical state；monarchy；～立宪 constitutional monarchy；～制 monarchy；～专制 autocratic monarchy；absolute monarchy
【君子】a man of noble character；a man of virtue；gentleman
【君子国】the Land of Gentlemen (an imaginary land free from deceit and avarice)
【君子兰】scarlet kafirlily (Clivia miniata)
【君子协定】gentlemen's agreement
【君子之交淡如水】the friendship of a gentleman is insipid as water

龟 (构词成分)见下 ——另见 guī
【龟裂】❶ (of parched earth) be full of cracks：长期干旱，田地～。*There has been no rain for a long time and the earth is full of cracks.* ❷ (of skin) chap

菌 名 ❶ fungus ❷ bacterium ——另见 jùn
【菌核】sclerotium
【菌苗】[医] bacterial vaccine；vaccine
【菌丝】[植] hypha
【菌血症】bacteraemia

皲 (构词成分)见下
【皲裂】〈书〉(of skin) chap

jùn

俊 Ⅰ 形 handsome; pretty：这小伙子长得挺～的。*That lad is very handsome.* / 这孩子长得多～哪。*What a pretty little child!* Ⅱ 名 of outstanding talent：俊杰

【俊杰】a person of outstanding talent; hero

【俊美】pretty

【俊男倩女】handsome men and beautiful women

【俊气】pretty：那个小姑娘长得挺～。*That little girl is very pretty.*

【俊俏】〈口〉pretty and charming

【俊秀】pretty; of delicate beauty

【俊雅】〈书〉refined and elegant

郡 名［史］prefecture

浚 动 dredge：～渠 *dredge a canal*

【浚泥船】dredger

峻 形 ❶（of mountains）high：～岭 *a lofty mountain range* ❷ harsh; severe; stern：严峻

【峻峭】high and steep

骏 名 fine horse; steed

【骏马】fine horse; steed

菌 名 mushroom ——另见 jūn

【菌子】〈方〉mushroom

竣 动 complete; finish

【竣工】(of a project) be completed：这座大楼已提前～。*The building has been completed ahead of schedule.*

K

kā

咖 (构词成分)见下 ——另见 gā

【咖啡】coffee

【咖啡伴侣】coffee mate

【咖啡杯】coffee cup

【咖啡馆】coffee house；café

【咖啡壶】coffee pot

【咖啡色】coffee (colour)

【咖啡因】(又作'咖啡硷')［药］caffeine

喀 象 noise made in coughing or vomiting

【喀嚓】a cracking or snapping sound：～一声，树枝断了。*The branch broke with a snap.* or *The branch snapped.*

【喀尔巴阡山】the Carpathians

【喀麦隆】Cameroon ◇ ～人 Cameroonian

【喀秋莎】katyusha rocket launcher

【喀斯特】［地质］karst：～地形 *karst topography*

kǎ

卡 Ⅰ 动 ❶ block；check：～住通往海港的公路 *block the road to the seaport* / 会计及时～住了这笔不必要的开支。*The accountant checked this unnecessary spending in good time.* ❷ clutch；choke：～脖子 *seige sb. by the throat* Ⅱ 名 ❶〈略〉见〖卡路里〗❷〈略〉见〖卡片〗——另见 qiǎ

【卡巴胂】［药］carbarsone

【卡宾枪】carbine

【卡车】lorry；truck

【卡尺】〈略〉见〖游标卡尺〗

【卡介苗】［药］BCG vaccine (Bacille Calmette-Guérin) ◇ ～注射 BCG injection

【卡拉 OK】karaoke

【卡路里】［物］calorie

【卡那霉素】［药］kanamycin

【卡片】card：借书～ *library card* / ～目录 *card catalogue* / ～索引 *card index* ◇ ～分类机 card sorter；～柜 card cabinet

【卡其】［纺］khaki

【卡钳】［机］callipers：内外～ *combination callipers*

【卡式录像带】video cassette

【卡塔尔】Qatar ◇ ～人 Qatari

【卡特尔】［经］cartel

【卡通】❶ caricature；cartoon ❷ another name for 动画片

咔 (构词成分)见下

【咔叽】同〖卡其〗

【咔唑】［化］carbazole

咯 动 cough up：把鱼刺～出来 *cough up a fishbone* ——另见 gē

【咯痰】cough up phlegm

【咯血】［医］spit blood；haemoptysis

胩 名［化］carbylamine；isocyanide

kāi

开 Ⅰ 动 ❶ open：～锁 *open a lock*；*unlock* / 门～了。*The door opened.* ❷ make an opening；open up：墙上～了个窗口。*A window was made in the wall.* ❸ open out；come loose：花都～了。*The flowers are all open.* / 扣儿～了。*The knot has come untied.* ❹ (of a frozen river) thaw out：等河～了坐船走。*Wait until the river is open and then go by boat.* ❺ lift (a ban, restriction, etc.)：开禁 ❻ start or operate (a machine, car, ship, plane, etc.)；turn on (a light, radio, TV, etc.)：～机器 *operate a machine* / ～汽车 *drive a car* / ～飞机 *fly (or pilot) an airplane* / ～灯 *turn on a light* / 把汽船～到对岸去。*Steer the motorboat over to the opposite bank.* ❼ (of a train, bus, ship, etc.) leave；start：火车几点～？*What time does the train leave?* / 校车快～了。*The school bus is about to start.* ❽ (of troops) set out；move：部队正往前线～去。*The troops are moving to the front.* ❾ start or run (a factory, school, store, etc.)；set up：～工厂 *set up a factory* / ～茶馆 *run a teahouse* / 他～了一个饭馆。*He has opened a restaurant.* ❿ hold (a meeting, exhibition, etc.)：～运动会 *hold an athletic meet* / ～舞会 *give a dance* / 舞会～了一夜。*The dance lasted all night.* ⓫ make a list of；write out：把你需要的东西～个单子。*Make a list of the things you need.* / ～一张支票 *write out a cheque* / ～介绍信 *write a letter of introduction* ⓬ pay (wages, fares, etc.)：～工资 *pay wages* ⓭ boil：水～了。*The water is boiling.* ⓮ (indicating separation or dissemination) open；apart；away；widely：躲～！*Get out of the way!* / 站～！*Stand aside!* / 把门推～。*Push the door open.* / 把书翻～。

Open the book. ⓯ (indicating the beginning and continuation of an action)：一见到亲人他就哭～了。*He began to cry the moment he saw his own people*. / 冻得他哆嗦～了。*He was shivering with cold*. Ⅱ **名** (used to express a ratio between two things considered as parts of a whole which is 10)：二八～ 2∶8 / 大家认为他的功过是三七～。*The general assessment of his work is 70% achievements and 30% mistakes*. Ⅲ **量** ❶ [刷] division of standard size printing paper：四开 / 八开 ❷carat：十四～金 14-*carat gold*

【开办】start or run (a factory, school, store, etc.); set up：～训练班 *start a training course* ◇～费 initial cost

【开本】[刷] format; book size：八～ *octavo* / 十六～ 16 *mo* / 三十二～ 32 *mo*

【开编】begin the compilation of (books)

【开标】open sealed tenders

【开播】❶ initiate broadcast：电视台明天～《三国演义》。*The Romance of the Three Kingdoms will start showing tomorrow on TV*. ❷ [农] start sowing

【开采】mine; extract; exploit：～煤炭 *mine coal* / ～石油 *recover petroleum* / ～天然气 *tap (or extract) natural gas*

【开衩】vent (at the bottom of a coat at the sides or back); branch; slit：中间～*centre vent*/ 旁边 *side vent(s)* / 你新做的大衣开不开衩? *Do you want any vent in your new overcoat?*

【开场】(of a performance, etc.) begin; start：他们到剧院时，戏已经～了。*The play had already begun when they got to the theatre*.

【开场白】❶ prologue (of a play) ❷ opening (or introductory) remarks

【开车】❶ drive or start a car, train, etc.：～的时候精神要集中。*You should concentrate when driving*. ❷ set a machine going

【开诚布公】frank and sincere; open-hearted：～地谈一谈 *speak frankly and sincerely* / 我希望大家～，把问题摆到桌面上谈清楚。*I hope that we can all be perfectly honest about the matter and put all our cards on the table for a frank discussion*.

【开诚相见】deal with sb. in all sincerity; treat sb. open-heartedly; be frank and open

【开除】expel; discharge：～出党 *expel from the Party* / ～学籍 *expel from school* / ～公职 *discharge sb. from public employment; take sb.'s name off the books*

【开锄】begin tilling land for the year

【开船】set sail; sail：～时间 *sailing time; hour of sailing*

【开创】start; initiate：～新局面 *create a new situation; open up a new prospect* / ～社会新风尚 *initiate a new social custom*

【开春】beginning of spring (usu. referring to the first month of the lunar year)

【开裆裤】open-seat (or split) pants (for children)

【开刀】❶〈旧〉behead; decapitate：～问斩 *execution by decapitation* ❷〈口〉perform or have an operation; operate or be operated on：给病人～ *operate on a patient* / 他得了阑尾炎，～了。*He had an operation for appendicitis*. ❸ make sb. the first target of attack：拿某人～ *make an example of sb*.

【开导】help sb. to see what is right or sensible; help sb. to straighten out his wrong or muddled thinking; enlighten：他一时想不通，你～～他好吗? *He hasn't come round yet. Could you try and straighten him out?*

【开倒车】back the car—turn back the clock：开历史倒车 *try to reverse the trend of history; try to turn back the wheel of history*

【开道】❶ clear the way ❷〈方〉make way

【开顶风船】〈字〉sail against the wind;〈喻〉run counter to the mainstream of thought or conduct：不怕～ *unafraid to run counter to the mainstream*

【开动】❶ start; set in motion：火车～了。*The train was starting*. / ～机器 *start a machine* / ～宣传机器 *set the propaganda machine in motion* / ～脑筋 *use one's brains* ❷ move; march

【开冻】thaw; unfreeze

【开端】beginning; start：良好的～ *a good beginning* / 两国关系新的～ *a new turn in the relations between the two countries*

【开恩】show mercy; bestow favours

【开发】develop; open up; exploit：～自然资源 *exploit natural resources* / ～合作 *cooperation in development* / 智力～ *tapping intellectual resources* ◇～区 Open Economic Zone；～软件 develop software；～市场 explore market；～中心 development centre

【开饭】serve a meal：～了。*The meal's ready*. or *Time to eat!* / 食堂什么时候～? *When does the cafeteria serve meals?*

【开方】❶ (又作'开方子') write out a prescription ❷ [数] extraction of a root; evolution

【开房间】〈方〉rent a room in a hotel (esp. for a secret liaison)

【开放】❶ (of flowers) come into bloom ❷ lift a ban, restriction, etc. ❸ open to traffic or public use：新建的港口已向外轮～。*The new port has been opened to foreign ships*. ❹ be open (to the public)：星期日图书馆照常～。*The library is open on Sundays as well as on weekdays*. ❺ be open (to the outside world)：～政策 *the policy of opening to the outside world; the open policy* ◇～城市 a city open to foreigners; open city；～骨折[医] open (or compound) fracture

【开放式系统】open system

【开放型】open; export-oriented

【开缝】crack; fracture

【开赴】move (or march) to; be bound for：～前线 *march to the front*

【开杆】[体] start (game, e.g. billiard game)

【开工】❶ (of a factory, etc.) go into operation：～不足 *be operating under capacity* / 新厂～了。

The new factory has gone into operation. ❷ (of work on a construction project, etc.) start：水库工程～了。*Construction of the reservoir has started.* ◇ ～率 utilization of capacity

【开关】[电] switch：分档～ *step switch* / 通断～ *on-off switch* / ～厂 *switchgear plant*

【开关灯头】switch socket

【开馆】open (library, art gallery, etc.) to the public

【开罐器】can opener

【开锅】〈口〉(of a pot) boil

【开国】found a state：～大典 *founding ceremony (of a state)* / ～元勋 *founders of a state*

【开航】❶ become open for navigation：又一条新航线～了。*Another new air route has been opened up.* / 运河～了。*The canal is now open.* ❷ set sail：去武汉的船上午八点～。*The boat for Wuhan sails at 8 a.m..* / ～日 *sailing day*

【开河】❶ (of a frozen river) thaw out ❷ construct a canal

【开合桥】bascule bridge; folding bridge

【开后门】open the "backdoor"—give sb. special advantage (or privilege)：利用职权～ *abuse one's powers to secure advantages for others*

【开户】open (or establish) an account (with a bank) ◇ ～银行 bank of deposit

【开花】❶ blossom; bloom：木兰要～了。*The magnolias are beginning to blossom.* / 二踢脚在空中开了花。*The double-bang firecracker exploded in the air.* ❷ split (like a flower blooming)：这只鞋～儿了。*The shoe has split open.* ❸ feel happy or smile happily：心里乐开了花 *burst with joy; feel elated* ◇ ～结果 blossom and bear fruit—yield positive results

【开花馒头】split-top steamed bun

【开花期】[植] florescence

【开化】❶ become civilized ❷〈方〉thaw; unfreeze

【开怀】to one's heart's content：～畅饮 *drink (alcohol) to one's heart's content; go on a drinking spree* / ～大笑 *laugh heartily*

【开荒】open up (or reclaim) wasteland

【开会】hold or attend a meeting：我要～去。*I'm going to a meeting.* / 他正在～。*He's at a meeting.* / 现在～。*Let's start the meeting.*

【开荤】(esp. of a person with a religious belief) begin or resume a meat diet; end a meatless diet

【开火】open fire：准备！～！(*word of command*) *Ready, fire!* / 前线～了。*Fighting has started at the frontlines.*

【开伙】❶ run a mess or cafeteria ❷ provide food

【开豁】❶ open and clear：雾气一散，四处都显得十分～。*With the lifting of the mist, the view opened up.* ❷ with one's mental outlook broadened：听了报告，他的心里更～了。*After hearing the report, his mind opened up.* or *The report widened his horizons.*

【开机】❶ start a machine ❷ start shooting a film, TV play, etc.

【开价】state or quote a price

【开架】open shelves (as in a supermarket, from which customers select goods) ◇ ～式 open shelves

【开讲】begin lecturing or story-telling

【开奖】draw lottery in public and announce winner

【开胶】come unglued：我的鞋底～了。*The sole of my shoe came unglued.*

【开戒】break an abstinence (from smoking, drinking, etc.)

【开禁】lift a ban

【开镜】start shooting (film)

【开局】opening (of a chess game, etc.)

【开具】〈书〉write out (a certificate, etc.)：～清单 *write out a detailed list* / 由所在单位～证明。*A certificate is to be provided by the organization one belongs to.*

【开卷】❶〈书〉open a book; read ❷ (of examinations) open-book：～考试 *an open-book examination*

【开卷有益】reading is always profitable

【开掘】dig：～运河 *dig a canal* / ～新的矿井 *open up a new mine*

【开课】❶ school begins; begin classes：学校九月一日～。*School will begin on September 1st.* ❷ (chiefly in college) give a course; teach a subject：你下学期开什么课？*Which subjects are you going to teach next term?* or *What courses are you offering next term?*

【开垦】open up (or reclaim) wasteland; bring under cultivation：～荒山 *bring barren hills under cultivation*

【开口】❶ open one's mouth; start to talk：难以～ *find it difficult to bring the matter up* / 没等我～，他就抢先替我说了。*Before I could open my mouth, he hastened to speak on my behalf (or he went ahead and said it for me).* ❷ put the first edge on a knife

【开口闭口】every time one opens one's mouth; whenever one speaks

【开口销】split pin

【开口子】❶ (of a dyke) break; burst ❷ (of the skin) chap：天气干冷，我的手都开了口子了。*The cold, dry weather made my hands get chapped.*

【开快车】step on the gas; speed up the work

【开矿】open up a mine; exploit a mine

【开阔】❶ open; wide：～的广场 *an open square* / ～的原野 *wide open fields* / ～的天空 *the wide open sky* / ～的前额 *a broad forehead* ❷ tolerant; broad-minded：他是一个思想～而又活泼愉快的人。*He's a broad-minded, energetic and cheerful person.* ❸ widen：～路面 *widen a road* ◇ ～地 [军] open terrain; open ground; unenclosed ground

【开阔眼界】broaden one's outlook (or horizons)

【开朗】❶ open and clear：我们在密林中穿行，约数百米，便豁然～。*We pushed ourselves through the thick forest for a few hundred metres and then reached an open space.* ❷ sanguine; optimistic：

性情～ *of a sanguine disposition; always cheerful* / 今晚上她的心情似乎特别～。*Tonight she seems to be in an especially cheerful mood.*

【开犁】start the year's ploughing

【开例】create a precedent：如果从你这里～，以后事情就不好办了。*If we allow you to set this precedent, it will create difficulties for us afterwards.*

【开脸】❶〈旧〉(of a girl on the eve of marriage) remove the fine hairs on the face and neck and tidy up hairline at temples ❷ carve the face of a statue

【开列】draw up (a list); list：～如下 *as listed below* / ～名单 *draw up (or make out) a name list* / 按照～的项目进行 *work through the list of assignments*

【开裂】crack; fracture：湖面上的冰～了。*The ice on the lake fractured.*

【开溜】〈方〉sneak away; slink off; make oneself scarce

【开路】❶ open a way; blaze a trail：我在前面～，你们跟紧我。*I'll be in front blazing the trail, you follow close behind.* ❷［电］open circuit ◇ ～先锋 pathbreaker; trail-blazer; pioneer

【开绿灯】give the green light; give the go-ahead

【开门】❶ open the door：有人敲门，快～去。*Somebody's knocking at the door. Quick, go and open it.* ❷ (of a store) begin a day's business

【开门办学】open-door school management

【开门红】make a good beginning; get off to a good start

【开门见山】come straight to the point：他说话喜欢～，不绕弯子。*He likes to speak candidly, and not beat about the bush.*

【开门揖盗】open the door to robbers—invite disaster by letting in evildoers

【开明】enlightened：～人士 *enlightened persons*

【开幕】❶ the curtain rises：戏已经～了。*The opera has begun.* ❷ (of a meeting, exhibition, etc.) open; inaugurate：展览会明天～。*The exhibition will open tomorrow.* / 大会今天上午～了。*The conference was inaugurated this morning.* ◇ ～词 opening speech (or address); ～式 opening ceremony

【开拍】start shooting (a film)

【开盘】give the opening quotation (on the exchange)：～汇率 *opening exchange rate* / ～价格 *opening price; opening quotation* ◇ ～行市 opening quotation; ～叫价 opening call

【开炮】❶ open fire with artillery; fire：向敌人猛烈～ *fiercely open fire on the enemy* ❷ fire criticism at sb. or sth.：他在会上对这种现象又开了炮。*At the meeting he unleashed a great deal of criticism against this trend.*

【开辟】open up; start：～航线 *open an air or sea route* / ～专栏 *start a special column (in a newspaper, etc.)*

【开票】❶ open the ballot box and count the ballots ❷ make out an invoice, receipt, voucher, etc.

【开屏】(of a peacock) spread its tail; display its fine tail feathers

【开启】open：这种灭火器的开关能自动～。*The switch on this kind of fire extinguisher opens up automatically.*

【开枪】fire with a rifle, pistol, etc.; shoot：～射击 *open fire* / ～还击 *return fire*

【开腔】begin to speak; open one's mouth：他半天不～。*For a long time he didn't utter a word.* or *He kept silent for a long while.* / 大家都还没说话，他先～了。*He opened his mouth first, before anyone else had spoken.*

【开窍】❶ have one's ideas straightened out：他一听这么说，就～了。*He straightened his ideas out as soon as the matter was explained to him.* ❷ (of a child) begin to know things

【开球】kick off (in soccer) ◇ ～一方 service side

【开刃儿】put the first edge on (a knife or a pair of scissors); sharpen for the first time：这把刀刚～，快极了。*This knife has just got its first edge and is extremely sharp.*

【开山】❶ cut into a mountain (for quarrying, etc.)：～劈岭 *open up a mountain* ❷ unseal a closed mountain for a period of time ❸［宗］(佛教) build the first temple on a famous mountain

【开山祖师】(又作'开山老祖') builder of the first temple on a famous mountain—the founder of a religious sect, a school of thought, etc.

【开设】❶ open (a shop, factory, etc.); set up：～店铺 *set up a store* ❷ offer (a course in college, etc.)：～音乐欣赏课 *give (or offer) a course in music appreciation*

【开审】start the trial; sit at session：～日期 *hearing time* / 本庭明日上午九时～。*This law court will be in session at 9 o'clock tomorrow morning.*

【开始】❶ begin; start：阅兵式～了。*The military review has begun.* / ～生效 *take effect; come into effect (or force)* ❷ initial stage; beginning; outset：一种新的工作，～总会遇到一些困难。*You always run into some difficulties at the beginning of any new job.*

【开市】❶ (of a shop) reopen after a cessation of business ❷ conduct the first transaction of a day's business ◇ ～价 opening quotation

【开释】release (a prisoner)

【开水】❶ boiling water ❷ boiled water

【开司米】(又作'开士米') cashmere

【开台】begin a theatrical performance：戏已～。*The performance has begun.*

【开膛】cut open the chest (of a pig, chicken, etc.); draw：杀猪～ *slit a pig's throat and cut open its chest*

【开天窗】❶ syphilis nose start festering ❷ put in a skylight—leave a blank in a publication to show that sth. has been censored

【开天辟地】the creation of heaven and earth—the beginning of history

【开庭】［法］open a court session; call the court to order：～审理 *hold a hearing* / 下月～。*The court sits next month*.

【开通】❶ remove obstacles from; dredge; clear: ～河道 *dredge a river* / 坚冰已经打破,航道已经～。*The ice has been broken and the river route is open*. ❷ open-minded; liberal; enlightened: 老大爷上夜校以后,脑筋更～了。*After attending evening classes Grandpa became more open-minded*.

【开头】❶ begin; start: 我们的学习刚～。*We've only just begun our study*. / 请你先开个头儿。*Would you make a start?* ❷ beginning; start: 你从一～就错了。*You've been wrong from the start*.

【开脱】absolve; exonerate: ～罪责 *absolve sb. from guilt or blame* / 替某人～ *plead for sb*.

【开拓】❶ open up: 在荒原上～出大片农田 *open up large areas of wasteland and turn them into farmland* ❷ [矿] developing; opening: ～巷道 *development opening* / ～进尺 *tunnelling footage* ◇ ～市场 explore markets; ～型人才 talent with pioneering style; pioneering talent; ～者 pioneer

【开挖】excavate: ～机械 *excavating machinery*

【开外】over; above: 他看起来有 40～。*He looks over forty*. / 东西相距 60 里～ *over sixty li from east to west*

【开玩笑】crack a joke; joke; make fun of: 他是跟你～呢,你别当真。*He was only joking. Don't take it seriously*. / 这可不是～的事情。*This is no joking matter*.

【开往】(of a train, ship, etc.) leave for; be bound for: ～广州的特快 *the Guangzhou express*

【开胃】❶ whet (or stimulate) the appetite: 这药吃了能～。*This medicine will improve your appetite*. ❷ 〈方〉 amuse oneself at sb.'s expense; make fun of sb.

【开销】❶ pay expenses: 我带的钱够一路～的。*I've brought enough money with me to cover the expenses of the trip*. ❷ expense: 日常的～ *daily expenses; running expenses* / 住在这儿～不大。*Living is cheap here*.

【开小差】❶ (of a soldier) desert ❷ be absent-minded; be woolgathering: 他一开会思想就～。*His mind wanders whenever he attends a meeting*.

【开小灶】〈字〉 kitchen where food is cooked in small quantities for a few people; 〈喻〉 special favor; special treatment; special consideration

【开心】❶ happy; joyous; elated: 他们去长城玩得很～。*They went on a trip to the Great Wall and enjoyed themselves very much*. ❷ amuse oneself at sb.'s expense; make fun of sb.: 他有一点儿结巴,别的孩子就拿他～。*Because he stammerd slightly, the other boys made fun of him*.

【开心果】pistachio

【开学】school opens; term begins: 九月一日～。*The term will begin on September 1*. / 开了学大家都要忙了。*Everybody will be busy when the new term begins*. ◇ ～典礼 school-opening ceremony

【开眼】(又作'开眼界') open one's eyes; widen one's view (or horizons); broaden one's mind: 这个展览会真叫人～。*The exhibition is a real eye-opener*.

【开演】(of a play, movie, etc.) begin: 今晚节目 7 点 30 分～。*The performance begins at 7:30 this evening*.

【开洋荤】〈方〉 have a new experience; see or eat sth. for the first time

【开业】❶ (of a shop, etc.) start business: 这家铺子明天～。*The store will open for business tomorrow*. ❷ (of a lawyer, doctor, etc.) open a private practice ◇ ～大吉 commence the business auspiciously

【开夜车】work late into the night; put in extra time at night; burn the midnight oil

【开音节】[语音] open syllable

【开营】(of summer camp, etc.) open

【开元音】[语音] open vowel

【开源节流】increase income and reduce expenditure; tap new sources of supply and reduce consumption

【开云见日】the clouds disperse and the sun shines forth—❶ darkness recedes and light dawns ❷ all misunderstanding has been dispelled

【开凿】cut (a canal, tunnel, etc.): 在山岩上～渠道 *hew a channel through stony mountains*

【开斋】❶ resume a meat diet ❷ [宗](伊斯兰教) come to the end of Ramadan

【开斋节】[宗](伊斯兰教) Lesser Bairam; the Festival of Fast-breaking

【开展】❶ develop; launch; unfold: ～体育活动 *develop an athletics program* / ～劳动竞赛 *launch an emulation drive* ❷ open-minded; politically progressive: 他思想很～。*He is very open-minded*. ❸ (of exhibition, etc.) open

【开战】❶ make war; open hostilities ❷ battle (against nature, conservative forces, etc.): 向穷山恶水～ *battle against barren hills and untamed rivers*

【开绽】come unsewn: 鞋后跟～了。*The shoe has split at the heel*.

【开张】❶ open a business; begin doing business: 那家新粮店～了。*The new grain store has opened for business*. ❷ conduct the first transaction of a day's business ❸ (of certain activities) begin; start

【开仗】make war; open hostilities

【开账】❶ make out a bill ❷ pay the bill (at a restaurant, hotel, etc.)

【开征】begin to levy (or collect) taxes

【开支】❶ pay (expenses): 这笔钱厂里不能～。*The factory shouldn't foot this bill*. ❷ expenses; expenditure; spending: 节省～ *cut down expenses; retrench* / 军费～ *military spending* ❸ 〈方〉 pay wages (or salaries): 我们每月五号～。*We get our pay on the 5th of every month*.

【开宗明义】make clear the purpose and theme from the very beginning: ～第一章 *in the first*

place; *first of all*
【开足马力】put into high gear; go full steam ahead; with the throttle wide open: 这条船～，向前行驶。*The ship was moving full steam ahead*.
【开罪】offend; displease

揩 动 wipe: ～汗 *wipe off sweat* / 把桌子～干净 *wipe the table clean*
【揩拭】clean; wipe
【揩油】get petty advantages at the expense of other people or the state; scrounge

锎 名 [化] californium (Cf)

kǎi

凯 形 triumphant (strains); victorious: 奏凯
【凯歌】a song of triumph; paean: 高唱～而归 *return amidst songs of triumph*
【凯旋】triumphant return: 大军～归来。*The army returned in triumph*.
【凯旋门】❶ triumphal arch ❷ Arc de Triomphe (in Paris); Arch of Triumph

铠 名 (a suit of) armour: 铁铠
【铠甲】(a suit of) armour
【铠装】[电] armour: ～电缆 *armoured cable*

慨 形 ❶ indignant: 愤慨 ❷ generous: 慨允 ❸ deeply toched: 感慨
【慨然】❶ with deep feeling: ～长叹 *heave a sigh of regret* ❷ generously: ～相赠 *give* (*as a present*) *generously*
【慨叹】sigh with regret
【慨允】readily consent; kindly promise

楷 名 ❶ model; pattern: 楷模 ❷ (in Chinese calligraphy) regular script: 大楷
【楷模】model; paragon; example
【楷书】(in Chinese calligraphy) regular script
【楷体】❶ 同〖楷书〗❷ block letter

kài

忾 名 〈书〉hatred: 敌忾

kān

刊 Ⅰ 动 ❶ print; publish: 创刊 ❷delete or correct: 刊误 Ⅱ 名 periodical; publication: 报刊 / 周刊
【刊登】publish in a newspaper or magazine; carry: ～广告 *print an advertisement*; *advertise* / 今天的《中国日报》～了两封读者来信。*Two letters to the editor were published in today's China Daily*.
【刊发】publish (in a newspaper or magazine)
【刊刻】inscribe
【刊授】teach through publications; give courses through periodicals: 世界语～招生。*Students will be enrolled to learn Esperanto mainly through publications*.
【刊头】masthead of a newspaper or magazine
【刊物】publication: 定期～ *periodical* (*publication*) / 内部～ *restricted publication*
【刊误】correct errors in printing ◇ ～表 errata; corrigenda
【刊行】print and publish
【刊印】❶ cut blocks and print ❷ compose and print
【刊载】publish (in a newspaper or magazine); carry: 报纸上～了几篇有关激光技术的文章。*The newspaper carried a few articles about laser technology*.

看 动 ❶ look after; take care of; tend: ～孩子 *look after children* / 他病很重，得有人～着。*He is seriously ill and needs someone to look after him*. ❷ keep under surveillance; keep an eye on: ～住他，别让这坏家伙跑了! *Keep an eye on that rascal. Don't let him run away*. / 这场比赛你要～住对方中锋。*Your job in this match is to mark the opponent's centre*. ——另见 kàn
【看场】guard the threshing floor (during the harvest season): 麦收季节要派人～。*We should send someone to guard the threshing floor during the wheat harvest season*.
【看管】❶ look after; attend to: 我去买票，你～一下行李。*You look after the luggage while I go to buy the tickets*. ❷ guard; watch: ～犯人 *guard prisoners* / 对于精神病人应严加～。*Mental patients should be subjected to strict surveillance*.
【看护】❶ nurse: ～病人 *nurse the sick* / 他伤得很重，要细心～。*He's seriously wounded and needs careful nursing*. ❷〈旧〉a hospital nurse
【看家】❶ look after the house; mind the house: 我明天出差，你好好看着家。*I'm going away on a business trip tomorrow. You stay home and mind the house*. ❷ outstanding (ability); special (skill): ～的武艺 *one's outstanding skill in martial arts* ◇ ～本领 one's special skill; one's stock-in-trade
【看家狗】〈旧〉watchdog—a person who takes care of the affairs and property of a landlord, high official, etc.
【看门】❶ guard the entrance; act as doorkeeper ❷ look after the house
【看青】keep watch over the ripening crops
【看守】❶ watch; guard: ～仓库 *guard a storehouse* / ～犯人 *guard prisoners* ❷ jailer; warder
【看守内阁】caretaker cabinet
【看守所】lockup for prisoners awaiting trial; detention house
【看押】take into custody; detain: ～俘虏 *detain prisoners* / 把犯罪分子～起来 *take the criminal into custody*

勘 动 ❶ read and correct the text of; collate:

校勘 ❷ investigate; survey: 勘察

【勘测】survey

【勘察】(又作'勘查') ❶ reconnoitre (an area for engineering or other purposes) ❷ [地质] prospecting

【勘探】exploration; prospecting: 磁法～ *magnetic prospecting* / ～地震学 *exploration seismology* / ～队 *prospecting team*

【勘误】correct errors in printing ◇ ～表 errata; corrigenda

龛 名 niche; shrine: 佛龛

【龛影】[医] niche (shown in an X-ray photograph)

堪 动 ❶ may; can: ～称佳作 *may be rated as a good piece of writing (or a fine work of art)* / ～当重任 *be capable of shouldering important tasks; can hold a post of great responsibility* ❷ bear; endure: 不堪一击

戡 动 suppress: ～平叛乱 *suppress (or put down) a rebellion*

【戡乱】suppress (or put down) a rebellion

kǎn

坎 名 ❶ bank; ridge: 田～儿 *a raised path through fields* ❷〈书〉pit; hole

【坎肩儿】sleeveless jacket (usu. padded or lined)

【坎儿井】an irrigation system of wells connected by underground channels used in Xinjiang; karez

【坎坷】❶ bumpy; rough: ～不平的道路 *a rough and bumpy road* ❷〈书〉full of frustrations: ～一生 *a lifetime of frustrations*

【坎子】mound; rise

侃 Ⅰ 形 ❶ upright and outspoken ❷ amiable; pleasant Ⅱ 动〈口〉chat idly; gossip

【侃大山】〈方〉chat idly; gossip

【侃价】bargain

【侃侃】〈书〉with assurance and composure: ～而谈 *speak with fervour and assurance*

砍 动 ❶ cut; chop; hack: 把树～倒 *fell a tree* / 这篇稿子太长,得～去一半。*The manuscript is too long and should be cut down by half.* ❷〈方〉throw sth. at: 拿砖头～狗 *throw a brick at a dog*

【砍刀】chopper

【砍伐】fell (trees): ～森林 *cut down trees in a forest; lumber*

【砍头】chop off the head; behead

莰 名 [化] camphane; bornane

槛 名 threshold: 门槛

kàn

看 动 ❶ see; look at; watch: ～电影 *see a film; go to the movies* / ～戏 *go to the theatre; see a play (or an opera)* / ～电视 *watch TV* / ～球赛 *watch a ball game* ❷ read (silently): ～报 *read a newspaper* / ～书 *read (a book)* ❸ think; consider: 你～她这个人可靠吗? *Do you think she's reliable?* / 你对这件事怎么～? *What's your view on this matter?* ❹ look upon; regard: 把人民的利益～得高于一切 *put the interests of the people above all else* ❺ see or consult (a doctor); treat (a patient or an illness): 李大夫把她的肺炎～好了。*Dr. Li has cured her of pneumonia.* / 有病就该去～。*You ought to go and see a doctor when you are ill.* ❻ look after: 衣帽自～。*Take care of your own hats and coats.* ❼ call on; visit; see: 我明天去～他。*I'll go and see him tomorrow.* / 有空我来～你。*I'll drop in on you when I have time.* ❽ depend on: 明天是不是打场,得～天气。*Whether we'll do the threshing tomorrow will depend on the weather.* ❾ mind; watch out: 别跑这么快! ～摔着! *Don't run so fast! Mind you don't fall.* ❿ (used after a reduplicated verb or a verb phrase) try and see (what happens): 试试～ *have a try* / 等一等～ *wait and see* / 尝尝～。*Just taste this.* ⓫ (used in exclamations to express surprise or rebuke, esp. in the phrase 看你 or 你看你): 你～你! 怎么满头大汗啊! *Look at yourself! How come you're bathed in sweat!* ——另见 kān

【看扁】underestimate; belittle: 别门缝里看人,把人家给～了。*Don't look at people with a jaundiced eye and make little of them!*

【看病】❶ (of a doctor) see a patient: 大夫出去～去了。*The doctor has gone out to see a patient.* / 王大夫～很认真。*Dr. Wang handles his cases with great care.* ❷ (of a patient) see (or consult) a doctor: 明天我要～去。*I'm going to see a doctor tomorrow.*

【看不过去】(又作'看不过')〈口〉cannot stand by and watch: 他这么虐待老人,真叫人～。*Nobody can stand his cruelty towards his own old parents.*

【看不起】〈口〉look down on; scorn; despise: 他太骄傲了,总～别人。*He is very proud and always holds others in contempt.*

【看菜吃饭,量体裁衣】fit the appetite to the dishes and the dress (or clothes) to the figure—act according to actual circumstances: 俗话说:"～"。我们无论做什么事都要看情形办理。*There is a proverb: "Fit the appetite to the dishes and the dress to the figure". Whatever we do must be done according to actual circumstances.*

【看成】❶ take sb. or sth. for; look upon as; regard as: 你把我～什么人了? *What do you take me for?* / 我把十块的票子～五块的了。*I mistook the ten-yuan bill for a five-yuan one.* ❷ be able to see or watch: 我有会,电影没～。*I had a meeting and wasn't able to see the film.*

【看出】make out; see: ～问题在哪里 *see where the trouble is* / 看不出真假 *cannot tell whether it is genuine or fake* / 我没～他的用意。*I failed to see his intention*.

【看穿】see through：小张一眼就～了他的诡计。*Xiao Zhang saw through his trick right off*.

【看待】look on (or upon)；regard；treat：我把他当朋友～。*I look on him as a friend*. / 矛盾要分主次，不能一律～。*We should distinguish between major and minor contradictions and not treat them all alike*.

【看到】catch sight of；see：拐个弯儿就可以～村子了。*The village will come into view at the next turn*.

【看得过去】(又作'看得过儿')〈口〉passable；just presentable：这手工做得不算很精细，但还～。*The workmanship is not too fine, but it's passable*.

【看得起】〈口〉have a good opinion of；think highly of：没有什么人～他。*Few people think highly of him*.

【看低】〈口〉look down on；belittle

【看跌】(of market prices) be expected to fall：这两天香港股票行情～。*Stock market quotations in Hong Kong are expected to fall in the next few days*.

【看法】❶ a way of looking at a thing；view：对这个问题有两种不同的～。*There are two different views on this question*. ❷ an unfavourable or a critical view of sb.：我对一个候选人有～。*I'm critical of one of the candidates*.

【看风使舵】〈贬〉steer according to the wind；trim one's sails：他这人善于～，所以官运亨通。*He was good at trimming his sails, so he had had a successful career as an official*.

【看风水】practise geomancy (for selecting a site for a tomb, house, etc.)

【看惯】be accustomed to the sight of；get used to the sight of：你看得惯他这样发脾气吗？*Can you put up with his bad temper*? / 这种浪费现象我们看不惯。*We hate to see such waste*.

【看好】have a good prospect (of winning, gaining, etc.)：赛前人们普遍～辽宁队。*Before the match most people expected the Liaoning team would win*. / 今年的西瓜市场～。*The prospects of this year's watermelon market are good*.

【看见】catch sight of；see：你～老张了吗？*Did you see Lao Zhang*? / 我看了好半天，可是什么也没～。*I looked for a while but didn't see anything*.

【看开】accept (or resign oneself to) an unpleasant fact (or situation)：伯母去世，你要～些，不要过分悲伤。*Auntie has passed away. Try to resign yourself to that fact and don't grieve too much*.

【看看】❶ look carefully；examine：你好好～，这都是上等的货色。*Look carefully. These are all of best (or high) quality*. ❷ soon；in a moment：～天色已晚，只好找了个地方住下。*Soon it became dark, so we had to find a place to stay for the night*.

【看来】it seems (or appears)；it looks as if：这活儿～今天可以做完。*It looks as if we'll be able to finish this job today*. / ～他还没有拿定主意。*Evidently he has not made up his mind yet*.

【看破】see through：～那些卑劣勾当 *see through those base tricks*

【看破红尘】see through the vanity of the world；be disillusioned with the mortal world

【看齐】❶ dress：向右(左)～！(*word of command*) *Dress right* (*left*), *dress*! ❷ keep up with；emulate：向先进工作者～ *emulate the advanced workers*

【看起来】it seems (or appears)；it looks as if：～要下雪。*It looks like snow*. / 他～很凶，其实心眼儿挺好的。*He looks fierce, but in fact he's kindhearted*.

【看轻】underestimate；look down on：我们不应～自己的力量。*We must not underestimate our own strength*.

【看热闹】watch the excitement；watch the fun：大伙儿在会上争得不可开交，他却在一旁～。*Everybody at the meeting was arguing excitedly while he stood by and watched the fun*.

【看人下菜】(又作'看人端菜'；'看人下菜碟儿')〈喻〉treat people according to their social status；be snobbish：他这号人～，势利得很。*He is a real snob, treating people discriminatorily*.

【看上】(又作'看上眼') take a fancy to；settle on：他～了一位漂亮的姑娘。*He's taken a fancy to a pretty girl*.

【看台】bleachers；stands

【看透】❶ understand thoroughly：这一着棋我看不透。*I don't quite understand this move*. ❷ see through：这个人我～了，没有什么真才实学。*I've seen through him；he's not a man of real learning*.

【看头】〈口〉sth. worth seeing or reading：这个展览会没什么～。*There is nothing much to see in the exhibition*. / 这部小说很有～。*This novel is well worth reading*.

【看图识字】learn to read with the aid of pictures

【看望】call on；visit；see：～老战友 *call on an old comrade-in-arms* / 这位老人很孤单，没有人来～。*The old man is lonely, and never has any visitors*.

【看相】read fortune (by face, palm lines, etc.)

【看笑话】amuse oneself by watching other people make fools of themselves；watch the fun；have a good laugh at：别吵了，让人家～。*Stop squabbling, will you? People will laugh at us*.

【看医生】see a doctor；consult a doctor

【看涨】(of market prices) be expected to rise

【看着办】do as one sees fit：需要买点什么，你～吧。*You may buy whatever you need, as you see fit*.

【看中】take a fancy to；settle on：这些布你～了哪块？—我一块都看不中。*Which of these materials have you settled on? —None of them catch my fancy*.

【看重】regard as important; value; set store by: 我非常～我们之间的友谊。*I value our friendship highly*.

【看做】(又作'看作') look upon as; regard as: 你把次要问题～主要问题了。*You have taken a minor question for a major one*.

【看座】〈旧〉(said to a servant, waiter, etc.) find a seat for the guest

瞰 动 look down from a height; overlook: 鸟瞰

kāng

康 名 well-being; health: 健康

【康拜因】combine (harvester)

【康采恩】[经] concern

【康复】restored to health; recovered: 病体～ *be restored to health* / 祝您早日～。*Hope you'll soon be well again*. or *I wish you a speedy recovery*. ◇ ～车 public bus reserved for the disabled; ～中心 health recovery centre

【康健】healthy; in good health

【康乐】happy and peaceful

【康乐中心】recreation centre

【康乐球】caroms

【康耐馨】carnation (a transliteration)

【康铜】constantan

【康庄大道】broad road; main road

慷 (构词成分)见下

【慷慨】❶ vehement; fervent: ～陈词 *present one's views vehemently* / ～的歌声 *fervent singing* ❷ generous; liberal: ～的援助 *generous aid* / 他为人～大方。*He is generous and free-handed*.

【慷慨悲歌】sing with solemn fervour

【康慨陈词】speak with fervour; speak with righteous indignation; present one's views vehemently

【慷慨激昂】impassioned; vehement: 他讲得～,非常感人。*His impassioned speech was very moving*.

【慷慨解囊】help sb. generously with money; give generously (of one's money)

【慷慨就义】go to one's death like a hero; die a martyr's death

糠 Ⅰ 名 chaff; bran; husk Ⅱ 形 (usu. of a radish) spongy: 这萝卜～了。*This radish has gone spongy*.

【糠秕】❶ chaff ❷ worthless stuff

【糠醛】[化] furfural: ～树脂 *furfural resin*

káng

扛 动 carry on the shoulder; shoulder: ～着锄头 *carry a hoe on one's shoulder* / ～枪 *shoulder a gun*; *bear arms* ——另见 gāng

【扛长活】(又作'扛长工') work as a farm labourer on a yearly basis

【扛竿】acrobatics on a bamboo pole

【扛活】(又作'扛大活') work as a farm labourer

kàng

亢 形 ❶ high: 高亢 ❷ haughty: 不亢不卑 ❸ excessive; extreme: 亢旱

【亢奋】extremely excited; stimulated

【亢旱】severe drought

【亢进】[医] hyperfunction: 甲状腺机能～ *hyperthyroidism*

伉 Ⅰ 动 (of a married couple) fit for each other; equal Ⅱ 形 high; mighty

【伉俪】〈书〉married couple; husband and wife: ～之情 *affection between husband and wife*

抗 动 ❶ resist; combat; fight: 喝点儿酒～～风寒。*Have a drink. It's good for preventing colds*. / 这羽绒服能挡风～冻。*This down jacket can resist wind and cold*. / 我～了他几句。*I said a few words to him in retort*. ❷ refuse; defy: 违抗 ❸ contend with; be a match for: 分庭抗礼

【抗癌】anticancer: ～药 *anticancer drugs*

【抗暴】fight against violent repression

【抗爆】[化] antiknock: ～剂 *antiknock (agent)* / ～汽油 *antiknock gasoline*

【抗辩】❶ contradict ❷ [法] counterplea; demurrer

【抗病】[农] disease-resistant: ～性 *disease resistance*

【抗磁性】diamagnetism

【抗倒伏】[农] resistant to lodging; lodging-resistant

【抗毒素】[医] antitoxin

【抗毒血清】antitoxin serum

【抗旱】fight (or combat) a drought: ～措施 *drought-relief measures* / ～品种 *drought-resistant variety*

【抗衡】contend with; match

【抗洪】fight (or combat) a flood

【抗坏血酸】ascorbic acid; vitamin C

【抗婚】refuse to marry the person chosen by one's family

【抗击】resist and fight back: ～侵略者 *resist the aggressors*

【抗拒】resist; defy: ～逮捕 *resist arrest* / 人的衰老死亡是不可～的。*Old age and death are inevitable*.

【抗菌素】[药] antibiotic

【抗拉强度】[机] tensile strength

【抗老剂】[化] antiager

【抗美援朝战争】the War to Resist U. S. Aggression and Aid Korea (1950—1953)

【抗命】defy orders; disobey

【抗热合金】heat-resisting alloy

【抗日战争】the War of Resistance Against Japan (1937—1945)
【抗渗】[水] impervious: ～试验 *impermeability test*
【抗生素】old name for 抗菌素
【抗霜】frost-resistant
【抗水性】water-resistance; water-resisting property
【抗税】refuse to pay taxes
【抗诉】[法] protest: ～书 *written protest* / ～案件 *protested case*
【抗体】[医] antibody ◇ ～酶 abzyme
【抗弯强度】[机] bending strength
【抗压强度】[机] compressive strength (or resistance)
【抗药性】[医] resistance to the action of a drug: 产生～ *become drug-fast (or drug-resistant)*
【抗议】protest: 我～! *I protest!* / 提出～ *lodge a protest* / ～集会 *a protest rally* ◇ ～照会 note of protest
【抗御】resist and guard against: ～外侮 *resist foreign aggression*
【抗原】[医] antigen
【抗灾】fight natural calamities
【抗战】❶ war of resistance against aggression ❷ 〈略〉见〖抗日战争〗
【抗张强度】同〖抗拉强度〗
【抗震】❶ anti-seismic capability: ～结构 *anti-seismic structure* ❷ take precautions against an earthquake; fight an earthquake: ～救灾工作 *earthquake relief work* ❸ 同〖抗爆〗
【抗争】take a stand against; resist: 以理～ *fight sb. with rational arguments*
【抗皱】anti-wrinkle: ～霜 *anti-wrinkle cream*

炕 名 kang; a heatable brick bed
【炕头】〈口〉❶ the warmer end of a kang ❷ the edge of a kang
【炕席】kang mat
【炕沿】〈口〉the edge of a kang
【炕桌儿】a small, short-legged table for use on a kang; a kang table

钪 名 [化] scandium (Sc)

kǎo

考 动 ❶ give or take an examination, test or quiz: ～大学 *take a college entrance examination* / 我～～你。*I'll give you a quiz.* or *Let me quiz you.* ❷ check; inspect: 考勤 ❸ study; investigate; verify: 待考
【考本】take the relevant exam in order to obtain a driver's license
【考查】examine or check (against a certain standard): ～学生成绩 *check students' work* / ～计划完成的情况 *check on the progress of a project*
【考察】❶ inspect; make an on-the-spot investigation: 科学～ *a scientific investigation* / ～团 *an investigation (or observation) group* ❷ observe and study: ～组 *a study group*
【考场】examination hall (or room)
【考点】location of an examination
【考订】examine and correct; do textual research
【考古】❶ engage in archaeological studies ❷ archaeology
【考古学】archaeology: ～家 *archaeologist*
【考核】examine; check; assess (sb.'s proficiency): 定期～ *a routine check* / ～飞行 *test flight; check out flight*
【考级】grade examination
【考究】❶ observe and study; investigate: 这问题很值得～。*We need to go into the matter seriously.* or *This problem merits serious attention.* ❷ be particular about; pay attention to; strive for: 穿衣服不必过于～。*One need not be overly particular about dress.* ❸ exquisite; fine: 用料～ *use choice materials* / 这本画册装订得很～。*This album is beautifully bound.*
【考据】textual criticism; textual research
【考卷】examination paper
【考虑】think over; consider: 让我～一下再答复你。*Let me think it over before I give you an answer.* / 这方面的情况你～了吗? *Have you taken this aspect of the matter into account?*
【考评】check and evaluate (ranking, results, etc.): 通过～决定干部升降 *determine promotions on cadre evaluation*
【考期】date of an examination
【考勤】check on work attendance: ～簿 *attendance record* / ～卡 *attendance card*
【考取】pass an entrance examination; be admitted to school or college (after an examination): 他今年没～,打算明年再考。*He failed the entrance examination this year, and will try again next year.*
【考生】a candidate for an entrance examination; examinee
【考试】❶ take an examination: 你们什么时候～? *When will you have the exam?* ❷ examination; test: 期中～ *mid-term exam* / 期末～ *final (or end-of-term) exam* / 他顺利地通过了～。*He's successfully passed the exam.*
【考题】examination questions; examination paper: 出～ *prepare an examination paper; set examination questions*
【考问】examine orally; question
【考务】examination affairs (administration): 要严格考务管理。*The administration of an examination should be strict.*
【考研】take the graduate school entrance exam
【考验】test; trial: 经受了严峻的～ *have stood a severe test* /她还不打算跟我结婚,说还要～～我。*She's not ready to marry me yet. She says she wants to test me some more.*
【考证】make textual criticism; do textual research
【考中】pass an examination; be admitted to (a college, etc.) through examination: ～北大数学系

pass the entrance examinations and be admitted to the Department of Mathematics of Peking University

拷 动 flog; beat; torture: 拷打

【拷贝】[电影] copy

【拷贝纸】copy (or copying) paper

【拷打】flog; beat; torture

【拷问】torture sb. during interrogation; interrogate with torture

烤 Ⅰ 动 bake; roast; toast: ～白薯 *baked sweet potatoes* / ～馒头 *toasted steamed buns* / 把湿衣裳～干 *dry wet clothes by a fire* / 在火边～～脚 *toast (or warm) one's feet by a fire* Ⅱ 形 scorching: 这炉子太～人。*This stove is really scorching.* / 太阳～得大地火辣辣的。*The earth, scorched by the sun, was burning hot.*

【烤电】[医] diathermy

【烤火】warm oneself by a fire: 围炉～ *sit around a fire*

【烤炉】oven

【烤面包】toast: 一片～ *a slice of toast*

【烤肉】roast meat; roast ◇ ～叉 spit; skewer

【烤箱】oven

【烤鸭】roast duck: 北京～ *roast Beijing duck*

【烤烟】flue-cured tobacco

【烤羊肉串】mutton shish kebab (a common snack food)

【烤炙】(sun or heat) scorch: 炎夏的太阳～着大地。*The hot summer sun is scorching the earth.*

栲 名 [植] evergreen chinquapin (Castanopsis)

【栲胶】tannin extract

kào

铐 Ⅰ 名 handcuffs Ⅱ 动 put handcuffs on; handcuff: 把犯人～起来。*Handcuff the criminal.*

犒 动 reward with food and drink: ～师 *reward an army with food and drink*

【犒劳】reward with food and drink: ～解放军 *reward the PLA soldiers with food and drink* / 吃～ *enjoy rewarded food and drink*

【犒赏】reward a victorious army, etc. with bounties

靠 动 ❶ lean against; lean on: 扁担～在门背后。*The shoulder pole is standing behind the door.* / 把梯子～在墙上 *lean a ladder against a wall* ❷ stand by the side of; get near; come up to: 船已经～码头了。*The ship has docked.* / 疗养院～海。*The sanatorium stands by the sea.* ❸ depend on; rely on: 他家里～他维持生活。*His family depended on him for support.* ❹ trust: 可靠

【靠岸】pull in to shore; draw alongside

【靠背】back (of a chair) ◇ ～椅 chair

【靠边】❶ keep to the side: ～! ～! *Make way! Move aside!* or *Mind your backs, please!* / 行人～走。*Pedestrians keep to the side of the road.* ❷ (be forced to) step down from one's post ❸ 〈方〉 reasonable; sensible: 这话说得还～儿。*That sounds more like it.* ◇ ～儿站 stand aside; get out of the way; (be forced to) leave the post; lose power

【靠不住】unreliable; undependable; untrustworthy: 这话～。*This story cannot be relied upon.* / 他的好朋友原来～。*His best friend proved to be untrustworthy.*

【靠得住】reliable; dependable; trustworthy: 这消息～吗? *Is the information reliable?* / 这个投资～。*This is a solid investment.*

【靠垫】cushion (for leaning on)

【靠近】❶ be close to; be near: 两人坐得十分～。*The two of them sat quite close together.* ❷ draw near; approach: 轮船慢慢地～码头。*The ship is gradually nearing the dock.* / ～些。*Come closer.*

【靠拢】draw close; close up: 向前～! (*word of command*) *Close ranks!*

【靠山】backer; patron; backing

【靠山吃山,靠水吃水】those living on a mountain live off the mountain, those living near the water live off the water—make use of local resources

【靠手】armrest

【靠枕】back cushion

kē

苛 形 harsh; severe; exacting: 他待人太～。*He treats people ungenerously.* / 对方提出的条件太～了。*The terms advanced by the other party are too harsh.*

【苛待】treat (inferiors) harshly

【苛捐杂税】exorbitant taxes and levies

【苛刻】harsh; severe; exacting: 这个条件太～,接受不了。*The terms are too harsh.* We cannot accept them.

【苛求】make excessive demands; be overcritical: 他的汉语底子差,对他不能～。*He has a poor grounding in Chinese, so don't make excessive demands of him.*

【苛细】〈书〉 severe and exacting

【苛性】[化] causticity ◇ ～钾 [化] caustic potash; ～碱 [化] caustic alkali; ～钠 [化] caustic soda

【苛杂】exorbitant taxes and levies

【苛责】criticize severely; excoriate

【苛政】harsh (or oppressive) government; tyranny

【苛政猛于虎】Tyranny is fiercer than a tiger.

珂 名 〈书〉 ❶ jade-like stone ❷ ornament on a bridle

科 名 ❶ a branch of academic or vocational

study：文科 / 理科 ❷ a division or subdivision of an administrative unit, etc.; section; department：我们～只有八个人。*There are only eight people in our section.* ❸［生］family：猫～动物 *animals of the cat family* / 松～ *the coniferous tree family*

【科班】❶ old-type opera school ❷ regular professional training

【科班出身】be a professional by training

【科幻】(〈略〉全称为'科学幻想') science fiction：～小说 *science fiction (novel)* / ～片儿 *science fiction film*

【科技】(〈略〉见〖科学技术〗) science and technology：～大学 *university of science and technology* / ～界 *scientific and technological circles* / ～术语 *scientific and technical terminology* / ～情报 *scientific and technological information*

【科技成果】scientific and technological achievements

【科技扶贫】help the poor areas with science and technology

【科技馆】museum of science and technology

【科技体制改革】reform of science and technology system

【科技咨询活动】scientific and technical consulting

【科教片儿】〈口〉popular science film; science and educational film

【科举】(又作'科甲') imperial examinations：～制度 *imperial examination system*

【科盲】〈字〉science illiterate; 〈喻〉have no or little knowledge of science

【科摩罗】the Comoros

【科目】❶ subject (in a curriculum); course ❷ headings in an account book

【科普】(〈略〉全称为'科学普及') popular science：～读物 *popular science books; popular science*

【科室】administrative or technical offices：～人员 *office staff; administrative personnel*

【科特迪瓦】Côte d'Ivoire

【科威特】Kuwait ◇ ～人 Kuwaiti

【科学】❶ science; scientific knowledge：自然～ *natural science* / ～工作者 *scientific worker; scientist* / ～实验 *scientific experiment* ❷ scientific：这种工作方法不～。*This working method is not scientific.* / ～种田 *scientific farming* ◇ ～共产主义 scientific communism; ～家 scientist; ～假设 scientific hypothesis; ～教育影片 popular science film; science and educational film; ～社会主义 scientific socialism

【科学技术】science and technology：～是第一生产力。*Science and technology are the primary productive forces.*

【科学院】academy of sciences

【科研】(〈略〉全称为'科学研究') scientific research：～机构 *scientific research institution* / ～考察船 *research ship* / ～人员 *scientific research personnel*

【科员】a member of an administrative section; section member

【科长】section chief

棵 量 (usu. for plants)：一～树 *a tree* / 一～大白菜 *a (head of) Chinese cabbage*

窠 名 nest; burrow：鸟在树上做～。*Birds make their nests in trees.*

【窠臼】〈书〉set pattern (usu. of writing or artistic creation)：摆脱前人的～，独创一格 *break free of conventions and create a style of one's own*

颗 量 (usu. for anything small and roundish)：一～珠子 *a pearl* / 一～黄豆 *a soya bean* / 他脸上的汗珠子一～～往下掉。*Beads of sweat were dripping down from his face.*

【颗粒】❶ anything small and roundish (as a bean, pearl, etc.); pellet：这些珍珠的～大小很整齐。*These pearls are uniform in size.* ❷ a grain (of rice, wheat, etc.)：～归仓 *every grain to the granary* / ～无收 *total crop failure* ◇ ～肥料 granulated fertilizer; pellet fertilizer; ～物质 particulate matter; ～细胞 granular cell

磕 动 ❶ knock (against sth. hard)：牙～掉了一颗 *have one's tooth knocked out* / 摔了一跤，脸上～破了皮 *fall and graze one's face* / 碗边儿～掉了一块。*The edge of the bowl was chipped.* ❷ knock sth. out of a vessel, container, etc.：～烟袋锅儿 *knock the ashes out of a pipe; empty out a pipe*

【磕磕绊绊】❶ (of a road) bumpy; rough ❷ (of a person) limping

【磕磕撞撞】walk unsteadily (when drunk or in a hurry); stumble (or stagger) along; reel

【磕碰】❶ knock against; collide with; bump against：这箱瓷器一路上磕磕碰碰的，碎了不少。*This box of porcelain has been bumped about all the way here and quite a few pieces got broken.*

【磕头】kowtow

【磕头碰脑】bump against things on every side (as in a room full of furniture); push and bump against one another (as in a crowd)：一大群人～地挤在一起看热闹。*A large crowd of people are pushing and jostling each other, trying to get a look at the excitement.*

瞌 (构词成分)见下

【瞌睡】sleepy; drowsy：一宿没睡，白天～得很。*I'm terribly sleepy today; I didn't sleep a wink last night.*

【瞌睡虫】❶ sleep-inducing insect (mentioned in traditional stories) ❷ a sleepy person

蝌 (构词成分)见下

【蝌蚪】tadpole

ké

壳 名 ❶〈口〉shell：鸡蛋～儿 *egg shell* / 核桃～儿 *walnut shell* / 子弹～儿 *bullet shell* ❷［机］

housing; casing; case: 拼合～ *split housing* / 涡轮～ *turbine casing* / 护～ *protective case* —— 另见 qiào

咳 动 cough: ～得很厉害 *cough badly; have a bad cough* / 她～了一晚上。*She coughed the whole night.* / 他～了一声,清了清嗓子。*He coughed in order to clear his throat.* ——另见 hāi

【咳嗽】cough: 感冒了就容易～。*A cold can easily cause a cough.* / 他听到轻轻的一声～。*He heard a quiet cough.* ◇ ～糖浆 cough syrup

kě

可 Ⅰ 动 ❶ approve: 许可 / 认可 ❷ can; may: 这篇文章～长～短,你看着办吧。*You can make this article either long or short, as you see fit.* ❸ need (doing); be worth (doing): 没有什么～担心的。*There is nothing to worry about.* ❹ fit; suit: 可心 / 可口 Ⅱ 连 but; yet; however: 文字虽短,～内容不错。*It's a short piece of writing, but it's meaningful in content.* / 我嘴里不说,心里～高兴极啦。*I said nothing, but felt extremely happy inside.* Ⅲ 副 ❶〈口〉(used for emphasis): 他～没说过这话。*He never said that.* / 我跑得～不快。*I'm by no means a fast runner.* / 他汉语说得～好啦! *He speaks excellent Chinese.* ❷ (used in a rhetorical question for emphasis): 都这么说,～谁见过呢? *So they say, but who has ever actually seen it?* ——另见 kè

【可爱】lovable; likable; lovely: 这花儿真～。*What a lovely flower!* / 湖水清得～。*The lake is beautifully clear.*

【可悲】sad; lamentable: 她的后半生实在太～了。*The latter half of her life was really too sad.*

【可比】comparable: ～价格 *comparable prices* / ～生产成本 *comparable production prices* / ～产品 *comparable products* / ～性 *comparability*

【可鄙】contemptible; despicable; mean: 行为～ *act in a contemptible way*

【可变】variable ◇ ～电容器 variable capacitor (or condenser); ～均衡器 variable equalizer; ～资本 [经] variable capital

【可怖】horrible; frightful

【可不】(又作'可不是'、'可不是吗')〈口〉exactly; right; that's just the way it is: 咱们该去看看老赵了。—～,好久没去了。*We should go to see Lao Zhao.* —*Right! It's been a long time since we last visited him.*

【可采储量】recoverable reserves (of petroleum)

【可操左券】be sure to succeed; be certain of success

【可拆】removable; detachable: ～装置 *detachable device*

【可乘之机】an opportunity that can be exploited: 不要给敌人以～。*Don't give the enemy a chance.*

【可持续发展】sustainable development

【可耻】shameful; disgraceful; ignominious: ～的行为 *shameful behaviour* / 人穷并不～。*Being poor is nothing to be ashamed of.*

【可待因】[药] codeine

【可的松】[药] cortisone

【可读性】readability

【可锻性】[冶] malleability; forgeability

【可锻铸铁】[冶] malleable (cast) iron

【可兑换】convertible: ～货币 *convertible currency (or money)* ◇ ～债券 convertible bond

【可歌可泣】move one to song and tears: ～的英雄事迹 *heroic and moving deeds*

【可耕地】arable land; cultivable land

【可观】❶ worth seeing: 这出戏大有～。*This play is well worth seeing.* ❷ considerable; impressive; sizable: 这个数目相当～。*This is a considerable figure.*

【可贵】valuable; praiseworthy; commendable: ～的品质 *fine qualities* / 她的～之处在于坚持真理。*Her finest quality lies in upholding the truth.* / 时间是最～的。*Time is of the essence.*

【可好】as luck would have it; by a happy coincidence: 我正想找他来帮忙,～他来了。*I was just about to seek his help when he turned up.*

【可恨】hateful; detestable; abominable: 他这人真～,老在背后说别人的坏话。*He's a most hateful person, always saying nasty things behind people's back.*

【可加工性】[机] machinability

【可嘉】laudable; praiseworthy: 其志～,其情可悯。*While his ambition is worthy of praise, his lot deserves sympathy.*

【可见】it is thus clear (or evident, obvious) that; it shows; that proves; so

【可见度】visibility

【可见光】[物] visible light

【可敬】worthy of respect; respected: 他是位～的老师。*He is a respected teacher.*

【可卡因】[药] cocaine

【可靠】reliable; dependable; trustworthy: ～消息 *reliable information* / 这个人很～。*This person is reliable (or trustworthy).*

【可可】cocoa

【可控硅】(又作'可控硅整流器') silicon controlled rectifier (SCR); thyristor

【可口】good to eat; nice; tasty; palatable: 这菜很～。*This dish is very tasty.*

【可口可乐】Coca-Cola; coke

【可乐】❶ laughable; funny; amusing: 那猴子的怪样真～。*The monkey's antics are really amusing.* ❷ cola (a type of non-alcoholic drink): 百事～ *Pepsi-Cola*

【可怜】❶ pitiful; pitiable; poor: 装出一付～相 *put on a pitiable look* / 他这付样子真～。*He looks so pitiful.* ❷ have pity on; pity: 他这是自作自受,没人～他。*Nobody feels sorry for him; he's got what he deserves.* ❸ (of quantity or quality) meagre; wretched; miserable; pitiful:

这一带雨水少得～。*There's terribly little rainfall in this area.* or *The rainfall is pitifully low in this area.*

【可怜巴巴】pitiable; pathetic

【可怜虫】pitiful creature; wretch

【可裂变物质】[物] fissile (or fissionable) material

【可恼】annoying; irritating

【可能】❶ possible; probable; likely: 惟一～的解释 *the only possible explanation* / 在～的条件下给予照顾 *give all the preferential treatment possible under the conditions* ❷ probably; maybe: 他～不知道。*He probably doesn't know.* / 她今天～会再来的。*Maybe she'll pop in again today.*

【可能性】possibility: 这种～不大。*The possibility is very small.* or *There isn't much possibility of that happening.*

【可逆】[冶] reversible ◇ ～反应 [化] reversible reaction

【可怕】fearful; frightful; terrible; terrifying: 做了一个～的梦 *had a terrible dream* / 真～! 他自杀了! *How dreadful! He committed suicide.*

【可欺】❶ gullible; easily duped ❷ easily cowed or bullied

【可气】annoying; exasperating: 这孩子刚换的衣服就弄脏了，真～! *The child just changed his clothes and now he's got them dirty again. How annoying!*

【可巧】as luck would have it; by a happy coincidence: 大家正念叨他，～他来了。*We were just talking about him when he turned up.*

【可亲】amiable; affable; genial

【可取】desirable: 他的意见没什么～的。*There is nothing desirable in his suggestion.* / 这个方案有～之处。*This plan has something to recommend.*

【可燃性】[化] combustibility; flammability

【可实现利润】[经] realisable profit

【可视电话】videophone; viewphone; picture telephone

【可是】❶ but; yet; however: 他嘴里不说，心里～想着呢! *He wouldn't say it, but he sure was thinking it!* ❷ (used for emphasis): 他～没说过这话。*He never said that.* / 说话～要算数的。*You can never go back on your word.* / 这鱼～新鲜的。*The fish is really fresh.*

【可塑性】plasticity ◇ ～炸药 plastic explosive

【可叹】it is regrettable; it is a pity: ～我年事已高，难以相助。*It is regrettable that I'm too old to help.*

【可贴现票据】bankable bill

【可望而不可即】within sight but beyond reach—unattainable; inaccessible

【可谓】〈书〉 one may well say; it may be said; it may be called: 老师对他的教育挽救～仁至义尽。*One may well say that the teacher has done his very best to educate and save him.*

【可恶】hateful; abominable; detestable: 他那样对待她，太～了。*It's hateful of him to treat her that way.*

【可惜】it's a pity; it's too bad: ～我去晚了一步，最精彩的节目已经演过了。*What a pity I was just too late for the best item on the programme.*

【可喜】gratifying; heartening: ～的成就 *gratifying achievements* / 取得了～的进展 *have made encouraging progress*

【可想而知】one can well imagine: 大家都不愿意接近他，他的为人～。*Everybody stays away from him. You can imagine what he is like.*

【可笑】laughable; ridiculous; ludicrous; funny: ～不自量 *ridiculously overrate oneself; make oneself ridiculous by overestimating one's ability* / 他说的话我觉得很～。*What he said struck me as funny.*

【可心】satisfying; to the satisfaction (or liking) of: 这件衣服买得挺～的，既合身，又便宜。*I'm satisfied with my clothing purchase. It's a good fit and cheap too.* / 这回倒可了他的心了。*It suited him perfectly this time.*

【可信】credible: ～性 credibility / 你看此事～程度如何? *How credible do you think the story is?*

【可行】feasible: 我看这个办法是～的。*I think this method is workable.* / 是否～，请斟酌。*Please consider whether or not this is feasible.*

【可行性】feasibility ◇ ～报告 feasibility report; ～研究 feasibility study

【可疑】suspicious; dubious; questionable: ～分子 *a suspect; a suspicious character* / 这案子有些～之处。*There are some questionable points in this case.*

【可以】❶ can; may: 这间屋子～住四个人。*This room can accommodate four people.* / 你～走了。*You may go.* ❷ be worth (doing): 这个问题很～研究一番。*This question is worth looking into.* / 这个展览我觉得倒还～一看，可他说不值得看。*I think the exhibition is worth a visit, but he doesn't think so.* ❸ passable; pretty good; not bad: 这篇文章写得还～。*This article is pretty good.* / 她的英语还～。*Her English is not at all bad.* ❹ terrible; awful: 他今天忙得真～。*He's awfully busy today.* / 你这张嘴真～! *What a sharp tongue you've got!*

【可有可无】not essential; not indispensable

【可遇不可求】sth. that can only be found by accident, and not through seeking

【可造之才】a person suitable for training; a promising (or hopeful) young person; a person with great potentialities

【可憎】hateful; detestable; abominable

【可支配收入】[经] disposable income

【可知性】[哲] knowability: 世界～ *knowability of the universe*

【可转换】[经] convertible: ～公司债券 *corporate convertible bonds*

【可转让】❶ transferable: ～权力 *transferable right* / 这种入场券～。*One must not give away such tickets of admission (to others).* ❷ negotiable: ～提单 *negotiable bill of lading* / ～证券 *negotiable securities* ◇ ～债券 [经] *negotiable securi-*

ties

渴 Ⅰ**形** thirsty：我有点～了。*I'm getting a little thirsty.* / ～死了 *be dying of thirst* / 这里有开水，～了请随便喝。*Here's some boiled water. Have some whenever you're thirsty.* Ⅱ**副** yearningly：渴念

【渴念】long for；yearn for；miss sb. very much

【渴盼】eagerly look forward to；earnestly hope

【渴求】eagerly desire；crave for：～进步 *earnestly strive for progress*

【渴望】thirst for；long for；yearn for：～自由 *long for freedom* / 她～着和这位作家见见面。*She's yearning to meet this writer in person.*

【渴想】long for；miss sb. very much

【渴仰】admire；look up to

kè

可 （构词成分）见下 ——另见 kě

【可汗】khan

克 Ⅰ**动** ❶ can；be able to：弗～如愿 *could not have it as one wished* / ～享 *be able to enjoy*；*be in good health* ❷ restrain：克己 ❸ overcome；subdue；capture (a city, etc.)：迭～名城 *capture one important city after another* ❹ digest：克食 ❺set a time limit：克期 Ⅱ**量** gram (g.)

【克当量】［化］gram equivalent

【克敌制胜】vanquish (or conquer) the enemy and win victory

【克分子】［化］gram molecule ◇ ～浓度［化］molarity；～体积［化］gram molecular volume

【克服】❶ surmount；overcome；conquer：～缺点 *overcome one's shortcomings* / ～困难 *surmount a difficulty* / ～私心杂念 *overcome selfish considerations* ❷〈口〉put up with (hardships, inconveniences, etc.)：这儿生活条件不太好，咱们先～点吧。*The living conditions here are not very good, but let's put up with them for a while.*

【克复】retake；recapture；recover：～失地 *recover lost territory*

【克格勃】KGB (the former Soviet State Security Committee)

【克己】restrain oneself

【克己奉公】be wholeheartedly devoted to public duty；work selflessly for the public interest

【克扣】embezzle part of what should be issued：～军饷 *pocket a portion of the soldiers' pay*

【克拉】carat

【克厘米】［物］gram-centimetre

【克里姆林宫】the Kremlin

【克隆】clone (transliteration)：～羊 *cloned sheep* / 湖南医科大学教授在国内首次～出了抑癌基因。*A professor at Hunan Medical University was the first in China to successfully clone a cancer inhibitor gene.*

【克罗的亚共和国】Republic of Croatia

【克期】set a date；set a time limit：～完工 *set a date for completing the work*

【克勤克俭】be industrious and frugal；be hardworking and thrifty

【克什米尔】Kashmir

【克食】help digestion

【克丝钳】combination pliers；cutting pliers

【克星】jinx；natural enemy：猫头鹰是鼠类的～。*The owl is the natural enemy of mice and rats.*

【克原子】［化］gram atom

【克制】restrain；exercise restraint：～自己的感情 *restrain one's passion* / 他非常生气，难以～。*He was so angry that he could hardly restrain himself.*

刻 Ⅰ**动** carve；engrave；cut：～图章 *engrave a seal* / ～蜡版 *cut stencils* / 他那满脸的皱纹好像～出来的。*The wrinkles covering his face seemed to be engraved.* Ⅱ**量** quarter (of an hour)：五点一～ *a quarter past five* Ⅲ**名** moment：此刻 Ⅳ**形** ❶ unkind；harsh：苛刻 ❷ in the highest degree：深刻

【刻板】❶ cut blocks for printing；carve printing blocks ❷ mechanical；stiff；inflexible：～地照抄 *copy mechanically*

【刻版】cut blocks for printing；carve printing blocks ◇ ～印刷 block printing

【刻本】block-printed edition：宋～ *a Song Dynasty block-printed edition*

【刻薄】unkind；harsh；mean：说～话 *speak unkindly*；*make caustic remarks* / 待人～ *treat people meanly* / 他为人～，人缘儿很坏。*He's mean and extremely unpopular.*

【刻不容缓】brook no delay；demand immediate attention；be of great urgency：大大加快我国国民经济发展的步伐，是～的。*Greatly accelerating the development of our national economy is a task which brooks no delay.*

【刻刀】burin；graver

【刻毒】venomous；spiteful：～的语言 *venomed remarks*

【刻度】graduation (on a vessel or instrument)：～盘 *graduated disc*；*dial* / ～瓶 *graduated bottle*

【刻骨】deeply ingrained；deep-rooted：～仇恨 *inveterate hatred*；*deep-seated hatred*

【刻骨铭心】be engraved on one's bones and heart—be remembered with deep gratitude

【刻花】engraved designs；carved designs

【刻画】depict；portray：鲁迅生动地～了阿Q这个形象。*Lu Xun vividly portrayed the character of Ah Q.*

【刻记】cut (stencils)：我一共～了十张蜡纸。*I cut ten stencils altogether.*

【刻苦】❶ assiduous；hardworking；painstaking：～学习 *study hard* / ～钻研 *study assiduously* / ～耐劳 *bear hardships and work hard* ❷ simple and frugal：生活～ *lead a simple and frugal life*

【刻意】be painstaking；be meticulous about；sedulously strive：～加工 *make painstaking refinements* / ～修饰 *be very meticulous about clothes or makeup*

【刻意求工】sedulously strive for perfection；be a scrupulous craftsman

【刻舟求剑】nick the boat to seek the sword (make a notch on the side of a moving boat to show where to look for the sword which has dropped overboard)—take measures without regard to changes in circumstances

【刻字】carve (or engrave) characters (on a seal, slabstone, etc.) ◇ ～社 seal-engraving shop

客 Ⅰ名 ❶ visitor；guest：家里来～了。*We have a guest at home.* / 他是哪村来的～？*Which village does the guest come from?* ❷ traveller；passenger：客舱 / 客车 ❸ travelling merchant：珠宝～ *jeweller* ❹ customer：乘客 / 房客 ❺ settle or live in a strange place；be a stranger：客居 ❻ a person engaged in some particular pursuit：政客 Ⅱ形 objective：客观

【客舱】passenger cabin

【客场】[体] (in basketball as between two competing teams) other team's home court；(in soccer) other team's home ground：～比赛 *away game—game played on the other team's court or ground* / 该队主场以3比1胜了对手，～以1比1打平。*The team defeated its rival three to one on home ground while tying it one to one in the away game.*

【客车】❶ passenger train：350次列车是～还是货车？*Is train No. 350 a passenger train or a cargo train?* ❷ bus：你坐大～还是小公共汽车？*Are you going to take a bus, or a minibus?*

【客船】passenger ship (or boat)：定期～ *liner*

【客串】(of an amateur singer, actor, etc.) play a part in a professional performance；be a guest performer

【客店】inn

【客队】[体] visiting team

【客饭】❶ a meal specially prepared for visitors at a cafeteria ❷ set meal；table d'hôte

【客房】guest room ◇ ～服务 room service

【客观】objective：～存在 *objective reality (or fact, existence)* / ～事物 *objective things (or reality)；objectively existing things* / ～条件 *objective conditions* ◇ ～规律 objective law or principle；～实在 objective reality；～世界 objective world；～唯心主义 objective idealism；～真理 objective truth；～主义 objectivism

【客户】customer：国内外～ *domestic and foreign customers* ◇ ～定金 customer's deposit

【客货船】passenger-cargo vessel

【客货两用汽车】notchback

【客机】passenger plane；airliner

【客籍】❶ a settler from another province ❷ the province into which settlers move

【客家】the Hakkas ◇ ～话 Hakka (dialect)

【客居】live abroad；live away from home：～他乡 *live away from one's native place* / 他现在～美国。*He lives in the United States now.*

【客流】the flow of passengers

【客轮】passenger ship (or liner)

【客满】❶ (of a theatre, cinema, etc.) have a full house；house full ❷ no vacancy (in a hotel)

【客票】passenger ticket

【客气】❶ polite；courteous：他对人很～。*He is very polite to people.* / 你怎么净说～话。*What are you making so many polite remarks for?* ❷ modest：您太～了。*You are being too modest.* or *You are too kind.* ❸ make polite remarks or act politely；be polite；be courteous：别～。(*to a guest*) *Please don't stand on ceremony.* or *Make yourself at home.* (*to the host*) *Please don't bother.*

【客人】❶ visitor；guest ❷ guest (at a hotel, etc.)；traveller ❸ 同〖客商〗

【客商】travelling trader

【客室】(又作'客屋') guest room

【客死】die in a strange land；die abroad

【客随主便】A guest should suit the convenience of the host or hostess.

【客套】❶ polite formula；civilities：我们是老朋友，用不着讲～。*As old friends we don't need to stand on ceremony.* / 他们见了面从来没有任何～。*There were never any formalities when they met.* ❷ make polite remarks；exchange greetings：他们～了几句，就坐下了。*After an exchange of greetings, they took their seats.* ◇ ～话 polite expressions or formulas (such as 劳驾，借光，慢走，留步，etc.)

【客体】[哲] object

【客厅】drawing room；parlour；living room；sitting room

【客源】source of tourists；potential customers or tourists：～丰富 *have no lack of potential customers (or tourists)*

【客运】passenger transport；passenger traffic ◇ ～列车 passenger train

【客栈】inn

【客座】❶ seat or place for a guest or client：～单间 *private room for a client* ❷ professional person invited to work temporarily in an institution：～研究员 *visiting research fellow* / ～演员 *puest star* / ～教授 *guest professor；visiting professor*

恪 副〈书〉scrupulous and respectful：～遵 *obey (orders, rules, etc.) with respect*

【恪守】〈书〉scrupulously abide by (a treaty, promise, etc.)：～中立 *observe a strict neutrality*

课 Ⅰ名 ❶class：一节物理～ *a class in physics；a physics class* / 我们星期六下午没～。*We don't have any classes on Saturday afternoon.* ❷ subject；course：这学期共有五门～。*We have five courses this term.* Ⅱ量 lesson：第一～ *Lesson One* / 这本教科书共有25～。*This textbook con-*

tains 25 *lessons*. Ⅲ 动 levy; collect; impose: ～以罚款 *impose a fine on sb.*; *fine sb.*

【课本】textbook

【课表】(又作'课程表') school timetable; class schedule

【课程】course; curriculum: 这学期我们的～很多。*We are taking a lot of courses this term.* / 我们的～安排得很紧。*We have a heavy course-load.*

【课间】break (between classes) ◇ ～餐 break-time snack (for pupils); ～操 setting-up exercises during the break between classes

【课件】courseware

【课时】class hour; period: 每周授课16～ *teach 16 periods a week*

【课税】❶ levy (or collect) taxes ❷ taxes ◇ ～价值 taxable value; ～品 dutiable goods

【课堂】classroom; schoolroom: ～教学 *classroom instruction (or teaching)* / ～讨论 *classroom discussion* / ～作业 *classwork*

【课题】❶ a question for study or discussion: 我们现在研究的～是光合作用。*Our current research topic is photosynthesis.* ❷ problem; task: 如何教育好独生子女,这给我们提出了新的～。*How to educate an only child is a new problem before us.*

【课外】extracurricular; outside class; after school: ～辅导 *instruction after class* / ～活动 *extracurricular activities* / ～阅读 *outside reading* / ～作业 *homework*

【课文】text (of a lesson)

【课业】lessons; schoolwork: 要好好用功,不可荒废～。*Study hard and never neglect schoolwork.*

【课余】after school; after class: 利用～时间进行义务劳动 *do voluntary labour after school*

【课桌】(school) desk

氪 名 [化] krypton (Kr)

嗑 动 crack sth. between the teeth: ～瓜子儿 *crack melon seeds* / 老鼠把箱子～破了。*A rat has eaten a hole in the box.*

溘 副 〈书〉 suddenly: ～逝 *pass away*; *die*

【溘然长逝】pass away; die

kēi

剋 动 〈口〉 scold or beat: 老师～了他一顿。*The teacher gave him a good scolding.*

kěn

肯 动 ❶ agree; consent: 我劝说了半天,他才～了。*He did not agree until I had talked to him for a long time.* ❷ be willing to; be ready to: ～干 *be willing to do hard work* / ～虚心接受意见 *be ready to listen to criticism with an open mind* / 青年人最～学习。*Young people are most eager to learn.*

【肯德基】Kentucky Fried Chicken

【肯定】❶ affirm; confirm; approve; regard as positive: 他的设计得到了总工程师的～。*His design was approved by the chief engineer.* ❷ positive; affirmative: ～的判断 *a positive assessment* / 他的回答是～的。*His answer is in the affirmative.* ❸ definite; sure: 请给我一个～的答复。*Please give me a definite answer.* / 他今天来不来,我不能～。*I'm not sure whether he will come today.* ❹ certainly; undoubtedly; definitely: ～按时送到 *guarantee punctual delivery* / 情况～是对我们有利的。*The situation is undoubtedly in our favour.*

【肯尼亚】Kenya ◇ ～人 Kenyan

垦 动 cultivate (land); reclaim (wasteland): ～了三亩地 *have cultivated 3 mu of land*

【垦荒】reclaim wasteland; bring wasteland under cultivation; open up virgin soil

【垦区】reclamation area

【垦殖】reclaim and cultivate wasteland

恳 Ⅰ 形 earnestly; sincerely: 勤恳 Ⅱ 动 request; beseech; entreat: 敬～ *respectfully request*

【恳辞】sincerely decline; earnestly beg off

【恳切】earnest; sincere: ～的要求 *an earnest request* / ～的态度 *a sincere attitude* / 言词～ *speak in an earnest tone*

【恳请】earnestly request: ～协助。*Your assistance is earnestly requested.* / ～出席会议。*We earnestly request your presence at the meeting.*

【恳求】implore; entreat; beseech: ～宽恕 *implore forgiveness* / ～的目光 *an imploring look*

【恳谈】talk sincerely; have a heart-to-heart conversation ◇ ～会 frank discussion meeting

【恳挚】〈书〉 earnest; sincere: 情意～ *show sincere feeling* / 词意～动人 *express oneself in moving words*

啃 动 gnaw; nibble: ～骨头 *gnaw a bone* / ～老玉米 *nibble at an ear of corn* / ～书本 *delve into books*

kēng

坑 Ⅰ 名 ❶ hole; pit; hollow: 挖一个～ *dig a pit* / 留神,那儿有个～儿。*Mind the hole over there.* ❷ tunnel; pit: 坑道 Ⅱ 动 ❶ 〈古〉 bury alive: ～杀 *execute sb. by burying him alive* ❷ entrap; cheat: 坑害

【坑道】❶ [矿] gallery ❷ [军] tunnel: ～工事 *tunnel defences (or fortifications)* / ～战 *tunnel warfare*

【坑害】lead into a trap; entrap

【坑坑洼洼】full of bumps and hollows; bumpy; rough: 一路上～的。*The road was bumpy and rough the whole way.*

【坑蒙拐骗】swindle
【坑木】[矿] pit prop; mine timber
【坑骗】entrap; cheat
【坑人】❶ entrap; cheat: 这家商店净～。*That store is a racket.* ❷〈方〉be upset (by a heavy loss)

吭 动 utter a sound or a word: 他坐在那儿一声不～。*He sat there without saying a word.* / 这么半天,他连～都没～一声。*For a long time he didn't even utter a sound.* ——另见 háng
【吭哧】❶ puff and blow: 他背起麻包～～地走了。*He heaved the sack on his back and staggered off, puffing and blowing from the strain.* ❷ work hard; toil: 她～了半天才把文章写出来。*She toiled a long time over her article.* ❸ hum and haw: 他～了好一会儿才说出来。*He hummed and hawed for quite a while before he finally came out with it.*
【吭声】utter a sound or a word: 你为什么不～? *Why do you keep silent?* / 没人敢～。*No one dared to speak.*

铿 象 the sound of clanging or clattering: 拖拉机走在路上～～地响。*Tractors clattered along the road.*
【铿锵】(of sound produced by the gong, piano, cymbals, etc.) rhythmic and sonorous: 音调～ *a rhythmic and sonorous tune* / 钢琴声～悦耳。*The piano produced a sonorous and pleasant melody.*

kōng

空 Ⅰ 形 empty; hollow; void: ～箱子 *an empty box* / 把抽屉腾～ *empty out a drawer* / 这棵树被虫子蛀～了。*This tree has been eaten hollow by worms.* / 书已销售一～。*All the books have been sold out.* Ⅱ 名 sky; air Ⅲ 副 for nothing; in vain: ～跑一趟 *make a journey for nothing; make a wasted trip* / ～忙 *make fruitless efforts* / 说了半天是～欢喜一场。*We spoke too soon, only to have our hopes dashed to pieces.* ——另见 kòng
【空靶】air (or aerial, airborne) target
【空包弹】[军] blank cartridge
【空舱费】[交通] dead freight
【空肠】[生理] jejunum
【空城计】the stratagem of the empty city —presenting a bold front to conceal a weak defence
【空挡】[机] neutral gear
【空荡荡】empty; deserted: 农忙季节,人都下地了,村子里显得～的。*In the busy season the village looked deserted when all the peasants had gone to the fields.*
【空洞】❶cavity: 肺～ *pulmonary cavity* ❷empty; hollow; devoid of content: ～的理论 *an empty theory* / ～的词句 *empty phraseology; empty rhetoric* / 这篇文章写得空空洞洞,没有什么内容。*The article is empty and hollow, devoid of substance.*
【空洞无物】utter lack of substance; devoid of content: ～的八股调 *a piece of stereotyped writing devoid of content*
【空对地导弹】air-to-ground guided missile
【空对空导弹】air-to-air guided missile
【空翻】[体] somersault; flip: 后～ *backward somersault; backflip*
【空泛】vague and general; not specific: ～的议论 *vague and general opinions; generalities* / 这篇评论语言干瘪,内容～。*The review is dull and devoid of content.*
【空防】air defence
【空腹】on an empty stomach: ～抽血 *a blood test taken on an empty stomach* / 此药需～服用。*This medicine is to be taken on an empty stomach.*
【空谷足音】the sound of footsteps in a deserted valley—unexpected good news
【空话】empty talk; idle talk; hollow words: 说～ *indulge in idle talk* / ～连篇 *pages and pages of empty verbiage*
【空怀】[牧] nonpregnant; barren
【空幻】visionary; illusory
【空寂】quiet and deserted
【空架子】mere skeleton (usu. referring to a piece of writing, an organization, etc.); bare outline
【空间】space: ～技术 *space technology* / ～科学 *space science* ◇ ～波 space wave; ～点阵 [物] space lattice; crystal lattice; ～技术 space technology; ～垃圾 space junk; ～速度 space velocity; ～天文学 space astronomy; ～医学 space medicine; aeromedicine; ～站 space station; ～知觉 [心理] space perception
【空降】land from the air; be airborne: ～地点 *landing area* ◇ ～兵 airborne forces; paratroops
【空姐】〈略〉见〖空中小姐〗
【空军】air force: ～部队 *air (force) unit* / ～基地 *air base* / ～司令部 *general headquarters of the air force; air command*
【空空如也】absolutely empty: 有些人喜欢夸夸其谈,其实肚子里却是～。*Some people have a glib tongue but an empty head.*
【空口】eat dishes without rice or wine; eat rice or drink wine with nothing to go with it: 别～吃饭不吃菜呀。*Don't only eat rice. Help yourself to what you like.*
【空口说白话】make empty promises; pay mere lip service
【空口无凭】a mere verbal statement is no guarantee: ～,立字为证。*Word of mouth being no guarantee, a written statement is hereby given.*
【空旷】open; spacious: ～的原野 *an expanse of open country; champaign* / 砍掉了这棵树,院里显着～点儿。*After cutting down the tree the courtyard seems more spacious.*
【空阔】open; spacious: 水天～ *a vast expanse of*

water and sky

【空廓】open；spacious：四望～ *spacious and open on all sides*

【空灵】free and natural；unconventionally graceful

【空论】empty talk：切不可只发～。*Don't just make a lot of empty remarks.*

【空门】Buddhism

【空名】❶ empty title；empty name ❷ undeserved reputation

【空难】air disaster；aviation accident；aeroplane crash

【空气】❶ air：湿～ *moist air* / 山上～稀薄。*Up in the mountains the air is thin.* ❷ atmosphere：会场上～紧张。*A tense atmosphere pervaded the meeting.* ◇ ～采样法 impingement；～过滤器 air filter；～加湿器 humidifier；～冷却 air-cooling；～力学 aeromechanics；～调节 air-conditioning；～调节器 air conditioner；～污染 air pollution；～压缩机 air compressor；～浴 air bath

【空气净化】air purification；air purge ◇ ～器 air purifier；～装置 air cleaner

【空前】unprecedented：～的规模 *an unprecedented scale* / ～的灾难 *an unprecedented catastrophe*

【空前绝后】unprecedented and unrepeatable；unique

【空勤】air duty：～人员 *aircrew*；*aircraft crew*；*flight crew*

【空嫂】middle-aged female flight attendants

【空身】carry no luggage；carry nothing

【空手】empty-handed：他想去买激光唱片的，结果～而还。*He went to buy some compact discs but came back empty-handed.*

【空谈】❶ indulge in empty talk ❷ empty talk；idle talk；prattle ◇ ～主义 phrase-mongering

【空调】〈略〉见〖空气调节〗；〖空气调节器〗

【空头】❶ (on the stock exchange) bear；shortseller ❷ nominal；phony：～文学家 *phony writer* / ～政治家 *armchair politician* / ～人情 *nominal friendship or lip service*；*empty favour* ◇ ～市场 bear market

【空头政治】phony polities；empty politicizing ◇ ～家 armchair politician

【空头支票】❶ dud (or rubber) cheque；bad cheque ❷ empty promise；lip service：他这回又给我开了张～。*His promises turned out to be empty again this time.*

【空投】air-drop；paradrop：～包 *parapack* / ～场 *dropping ground* / ～救灾物资 *air-drop relief supplies* (*to a stricken area*)

【空文】ineffective law，rule，etc. ——另见〖一纸空文〗

【空吸】［物］suction

【空袭】make an air attack (or raid)：这座城市遭到～。*The city was attacked from the air.* / 其后的三天，～的次数增加了。*In the next three days the air attacks increased.*

【空袭警报】air raid alarm：～器 *air raid siren*

【空想】❶ indulge in fantasy；daydream：别～了，还是从实际出发吧。*Stop daydreaming. Be realistic.* / ～家 *dreamer*；*visionary* ❷ unrealistic thought；fantasy；daydream：离开了客观现实的想像就成为～。*An imagination which is divorced from objective reality can only produce empty fantasies.*

【空想社会主义】utopian socialism：～者 *a utopian socialist*

【空心】(of trees，vegetables，etc.) become hollow inside：这棵柳树空了心了。*The willow tree has become hollow inside.* / 大白菜空了心了。*The cabbages have gone spongy.* ◇ ～长丝［化］fibre hollow filament；～面 macaroni；～砖 hollow brick

【空虚】hollow；void：生活～ *lead a life devoid of meaning* / 思想～ *lack mental or spiritual ballast*；*be spiritually barren* / 敌人后方～。*The enemy rear is weakly defended.*

【空穴】hole

【空穴来风】an empty hole invites the wind—weakness lends wings to rumours

【空邮】send a letter，etc. by airmail

【空域】airspace：战斗～ *combat airspace*

【空援】air reinforcement；assistance from the air

【空运】transport by air；airlift：～救灾物资 *airlift relief supplies* (*to a stricken area*) ◇ ～提单 air bill of lading

【空运货物】airfreight；air cargo

【空战】air battle；aerial combat

【空中】in the sky；in the air；aerial；overhead：～补给 *air-supply*；*air-resupply* / ～待战 *air alert* / ～加油 *air refueling*；*inflight refueling* / ～侦察 *aerial reconnaissance* / ～走廊 *air corridor*；*air lane* ◇ ～飞人［杂］flying trapeze；～花园 Hanging Gardens of Babylon (one of the ancient world's seven wonders)；～加油［航空］air refueling；in-flight refueling；air-to-air refueling；～劫持 aerial hijacking；～客车 airbus；～楼阁 castles in the air；～小姐 air hostess

【空重】［交通］empty weight

【空竹】diabolo：抖～ *play with a diabolo*

【空转】❶ (of a motor，etc.) idle；race：不要让马达～。*Don't race your motor.* ❷ (of a wheel) turn without moving forward；spin

kǒng

孔 Ⅰ 名 hole；opening；aperture：钥匙～ *keyhole* / 这座石桥有七个～。*This stone bridge has seven arches.* Ⅱ 量 for cave-dwellings：一～土窑 *a cave-dwelling*

【孔道】a narrow passage providing the only means of access to a certain place；pass

【孔洞】opening or hole in a utensil，etc.

【孔方兄】〈诙〉〈贬〉Brother Square Hole—money (so called from the appearance of a former coin which was pierced with a square hole)

【孔径】❶［物］aperture ❷［机］bore diameter

【孔孟之道】the doctrine of Confucius and Mencius

【孔庙】Confucian temple
【孔雀】peacock
【孔雀绿】peacock green; malachite green
【孔雀石】malachite (a mineral)
【孔隙】small opening; hole ◇～度［地质］porosity
【孔型】［冶］pass
【孔穴】hole; cavity

恐 Ⅰ**动** ❶ fear; dread: 惊恐 ❷ terrify; intimidate: 恐吓 Ⅱ**副** perhaps; probably; maybe: 消息～不可靠。*I'm afraid the information is not reliable.* / ～另有原因。*There may be some other reason behind it.*
【恐怖】terror; horror: ～分子 *terrorist* / ～手段 *terrorism* / ～电影(小说) *horror film* (*fiction*) / ～统治 *reign of terror* / ～的经历 *a terrifying experience* ◇～症［医］phobia; ～主义 terrorism
【恐高症】acrophobia
【恐吓】threaten; intimidate: ～信 *blackmailing letter*; *threatening letter* / 恐怖分子～说要杀死人质。*The terrorists threatened to kill the hostages.*
【恐慌】panic: ～万状 *panic-stricken* / 地震在全市引起了～。*The earthquake caused a panic in the city.*
【恐惧】fear; dread: ～不安 *be frightened and restless* / 他有～对手的心理。*He regarded his opponent with some apprehension.*
【恐龙】dinosaur
【恐怕】❶ fear; dread; be afraid of: 他～迟到,一早就起来了。*He got up earlier for fear of being late.* ❷ perhaps; probably; maybe: 他走了～有十来天了。*It's been almost ten days since he left.* / ～要下雨。*It looks like rain.*
【恐水病】同〖狂犬病〗

kòng

空 Ⅰ**动** leave empty or blank: 请把前面一排座位～出来。*Please leave the front row of seats vacant.* / 每段开头要～两格。*Leave two blank spaces at the beginning of each paragraph.* Ⅱ**形** unoccupied; vacant: ～房 *a vacant room* / 车厢里～得很。*There are many vacant seats in the carriage.* Ⅲ**名** ❶ empty space: 各行之间多留点～儿。*Leave a little more space between the rows.* ❷ free time; spare time: 有～儿到我这儿来。*Come over when you have time.* / 今天没～,改日再谈吧。*I'm busy today. Let's talk about it some other day.* ——另见 kōng
【空白】blank space: 填补科学技术上的～ *fill the gaps in science and technology* / ～表格 *blank form* / ～支票 *blank cheque* ◇～备书汇票 bill endorsed in blank; ～承兑 acceptance in blank; ～收据 blank receipt
【空白点】blank spot; gap; blank
【空当子】(又作'空当儿')〈口〉space; interval; gap: 从一个～挤过去 *squeeze through a gap* / 趁这～,我去把报纸拿来。*I'll go and fetch the newspapers during this break.*
【空地】vacant lot; open ground; open space: 咱们把砖卸在那边～上吧。*Let's leave the bricks on that patch of open ground over there.*
【空额】vacancy: ～已经补上了。*The vacancy has already been filled.*
【空格】blank space (on a form) ◇ ～键 space key
【空缺】vacant position; vacancy: 主任的～谁来补? *Who will fill in for the director?*
【空隙】space; gap; interval: 铁轨接头的地方都有一定的～。*There is a specified gap at every rail joint.*
【空暇】free time; spare time; leisure: 小王一有～就背英文单词。*Whenever he has a bit of spare time, Xiao Wang uses it to memorize English words.*
【空闲】❶ idle; free: 我们车间里的机器没有一台是～的。*None of the machines in our workshop are idle.* / 等你～的时候,咱俩谈谈心。*The next time you're free, let's have a heart-to-heart talk.* ❷ free time; spare time; leisure
【空余】free; vacant; unoccupied: ～的时间 *free time*; *spare time* / ～的房间 *unoccupied room*
【空子】❶ unoccupied place or time; gap; opening: 抽个～到我们这里来。*Do find time to come visit us.* ❷ chance or opportunity (for doing sth. bad): 他专门找～说风凉话。*He uses every opportunity to make sarcastic comments.* ——另见〖钻空子〗

控 **动** ❶ accuse; charge: 指控 ❷control; dominate: 遥控 ❸turn a container upside down to let the liquid trickle out: 把瓶子先～一～再装油。*Turn the bottle upside down to empty it before you fill it with oil.*
【控编】control staff size: 这个研究所用经济手段～,行政人员减少百余人。*The research institute used economic means to control the staff size and cut administrative staff by over a hundred.*
【控告】charge; accuse; complain: 向法院提出～ *file charges in court* / 向国家机关提出～ *lodge complaints with organs of state* / ～某人的罪行 *accuse sb. of a crime*
【控股公司】［经］holding company
【控诉】accuse; denounce: ～旧社会的罪恶 *condemn the evils of the old society* / ～人 *accuser*
【控制】control; dominate; command: ～人口增长 *control population growth* / ～货币发行 *control monetary issue* / ～局面 *have the situation under control* ◇ ～电路 control circuit; ～杆［计］joystick; ～数字［经］control figure; ～台 automation console
【控制论】［数］cybernetics

kōu

抠 Ⅰ**动** ❶ dig or dig out with a finger or sth.

pointed；scratch：在墙上～个洞 *drill a hole in the wall* / 把掉在缝里的豆粒～出来 *dig out the beans from the crevices* ❷ carve；cut：在镜框边上～点花儿 *carve a design on a picture frame* ❸ delve into；study meticulously：这本书用不着一字一句地～。*You needn't puzzle over every single word or phrase in the book*. Ⅱ 形 〈方〉stingy；miserly：这人真 ～！*How stingy he is*！

【抠门儿】〈方〉stingy；miserly

【抠字眼儿】pay too much attention to wording；find fault with the choice of words

眍 动 (of the eyes) sink in；become sunken：她病了一场，眼睛都～进去了。*Her illness made her look sunken-eyed*.

kǒu

口 Ⅰ 名 ❶ mouth (of a human being or animal)：口述 ❷ opening；entrance；mouth：瓶～ *the mouth of a bottle* / 碗～ *the rim of a bowl* ❸cut；hole：衣服撕了个～儿。*A hole was torn in the jacket*. / 茶碗缺了个～儿。*The rim of the teacup is chipped*. ❹the edge of a knife, etc.：刀卷～了。*The edge of the knife is turned*. Ⅱ 量 (for family members, pigs, knives, etc.)：一个五口之家 *a family of five* / 三～猪 *three pigs* / 一～钢刀 *a knife* / 一～井 *a well*

【口岸】port：通商～ *trading port* / 入境～ *port of entry*

【口白】❶ (in an opera) words spoken；spoken parts：她唱得不错，只是～不够清楚。*She sings well but does not speak clearly enough*. ❷ colourless lipstick (used to prevent the lips from being dry)

【口碑】public praise

【口碑载道】be praised everywhere

【口才】eloquence：他很有～。*He is an eloquent speaker*.

【口吃】stutter；stammer：他说话有点～。*He speaks with a slight stutter*.

【口齿】❶ enunciation：～清楚 *have clear enunciation* ❷ ability to speak：～伶俐 *be fluent and eloquent*

【口臭】bad breath；halitosis

【口传】instruct orally：～技艺 *pass on one's special skill orally* ◇ ～心授 oral teaching inspires true understanding

【口疮】aphtha

【口袋】❶pocket ❷bag；sack：纸～儿 *paper bag* / 面～ *flour sack*

【口德】restraint in one's speech；propriety of words：说话要注意～。*Use proper restraint when you speak*. / 年轻轻的，别说话不留～！*Don't hurt people with your loose tongue, young fellow*！

【口对口呼吸】［医］mouth-to-mouth breathing

【口风】one's intention or view as revealed in what one says：先探探他的～。*Sound him out first*.

【口服】❶profess to be convinced ❷take orally：不得～ *not to be taken orally* / ～避孕药 *oral contraceptive*；*the pill*

【口服心不服】pretend to be convinced

【口服液】oral liquid

【口福】〈诙〉gourmet's luck；the luck to get sth. very nice to eat：我们今天～可不浅。*We've really lucked out today in the food department*.

【口腹】food：不贪～ *not indulge one's appetite* ◇ ～之欲 the desire for good food

【口感】texture (of foods)：这种面条吃起来～好。*These noodles have a nice chewy texture*.

【口供】a statement made by the accused under examination

【口号】slogan；watchword：呼～ *shout slogans* / 提出～ *put forward a slogan* / 标语～ *posters and slogans*

【口红】lipstick

【口惠】lip service；empty promise ◇ ～而实不至 make a promise and not keep it；pay lip service

【口技】vocal mimicry；vocal imitation

【口角】(kǒujiǎo) corner of the mouth：～流涎 *slobber* ◇ ～炎［医］perlche——另见 kǒujué

【口紧】close-mouthed；tight-lipped

【口径】❶ bore；calibre：～155 毫米的大炮 *155mm. gun* ❷ requirements；specifications；line of action：～不合 *not meet the requirements* / 对～ *arrange to give the same story*；*give the same account by arrangement*

【口诀】a pithy mnemonic formula (often in rhyme)；mnemonic rhyme：珠算～ *abacus rhymes*

【口角】(kǒujué) quarrel；bicker；wrangle：这对小夫妻常常发生～。*The young couple often bicker with one another*. ——另见 kǒujiǎo

【口渴】thirsty

【口口声声】say again and again；keep on saying：他～说不知道。*He kept on pleading ignorance*.

【口溃疡】［医］canker sore

【口粮】grain ration

【口令】❶ word of command ❷ password；watchword；countersign：～问答 *challenge and reply*

【口蜜腹剑】honey-mouthed and dagger-hearted；honey on one's lips and murder in one's heart；hypocritical and malignant

【口气】❶ tone；note：严肃的～ *a serious tone* / 改变～ *change one's tone* / ～强硬的声明 *a strongly worded statement* ❷ manner of speaking：他的～真不小。*He talked big*. / 总经理的话～很硬。*The general manager spoke with firmness*. ❸ what is actually meant；implication：听他的～，好像感到为难。*Judging by the way he spoke, he seemed to be in an awkward situation*. ——另见〖探口气〗

【口器】mouthparts (of an insect)

【口腔】［生理］oral cavity：～卫生 *oral hygiene* ◇ ～学 stomatology；～医院 stomatological hospital

【口琴】mouth organ；harmonica

【口轻】❶ not too salty：我喜欢吃～的，请你少放点盐。*I prefer food that's not too salty. Please don't put too much salt in it.* ❷ be fond of food that is not too salty：他～。*He's fond of food that is not too salty.* ❸（又作'口小'）(of a horse, donkey, etc.) young：～的骡子 *young mules*

【口若悬河】let loose a flood of eloquence; be eloquent; speak volubly：这人～，一说就是一大套。*It seemed as if his flow of words would never stop.*

【口哨儿】whistling sound made through rounded lips：吹～ *whistle*

【口舌】❶ dispute or misunderstanding caused by gossip：～是非 *disputes and quarrels* ❷ talking round：费了很大的～才把他说服。*It took a lot of talking to convince him.* / 不必费～了。*You might as well save your breath.*

【口实】〈书〉a cause for gossip; handle

【口试】oral examination; oral test

【口是心非】say yes and mean no; say one thing and mean another

【口授】❶ teach or instruct orally：我国许多地方戏曲都是由民间艺人世代～而保存下来的。*Many of our local operas were preserved by folk artists who passed them down from generation to generation by word of mouth.* ❷ dictate：他写的这封信是他父亲～的。*The letter he wrote was dictated by his father.*

【口述】give an oral account：～全部经过 *give an oral account of what happened from beginning to end* ◇～记录机 dictating machine

【口水】saliva：流～ *slobber* / 他见了这些吃的直流～。*His mouth watered at the sight of all the food.*

【口说无凭】verbal statements are no guarantee：～，立此为据。*Verbal statements being no guarantee, a written agreement is hereby made.*

【口算】❶ chant out the result while doing mental calculation; calculate orally：举行～比赛 *hold a contest in oral calculation* ❷ poll tax

【口蹄疫】[牧] foot-and-mouth disease

【口条】pig's or ox's tongue (as food)

【口头】oral：～通知 *notify orally* / ～表决 *voice vote; vote by "yes" and "no"* / ～汇报 *oral report* / ～声明 *oral statement* ◇～语 pet phrase; habitual turn of phrase

【口头禅】pet phrase

【口头交】a casual acquaintance

【口头文学】folk tales, ballads, etc. handed down orally; oral literature

【口腕】[动] oral arm

【口味】❶ a person's taste：合～ *suit one's taste* / 不合～ *not be to one's taste* / 各人～不同。*Tastes differ.* / 京剧最合我的～。*Beijing opera suits my taste best.* ❷ the flavour or taste of food：这菜～不错。*This dish is tasty.* / 这些菜都是湖南～。*These are all Hunanese dishes.*

【口吻】❶ [动] muzzle; snout ❷ tone; note：玩笑的～ *jocular tone* / 以教训人的～ *in a lecturing tone*

【口误】❶ make a slip of the tongue ❷ a slip of the tongue; an oral slip

【口香糖】chewing gum

【口信】oral message：请你给我家捎个～，说我今晚不回家了。*Please tell my family that I'm not going home tonight.*

【口形】[语音] degree of lip-rounding

【口炎】[医] stomatitis

【口译】oral interpretation

【口音】❶ voice：她一听是她儿子的～，就赶紧出来了。*Recognizing her son's voice, she hurried out.* ❷ accent：说话带广东～ *speak with a Guangdong accent*

【口语】❶ spoken language ❷〈书〉slander; calumny

【口燥唇干】(talk until) the lips are dry and the mouth is parched

【口罩】gauze mask (worn over nose and mouth); surgical mask

【口重】❶ salty：我爱吃～的。*I like salty dishes.* ❷ be fond of salty food：我～。*I'm fond of salty food.*

【口诛笔伐】condemn both in speech and in writing

【口子】opening; hole; cut; tear：我手上拉的～快好了。*The cut on my hand is nearly healed.* / 袖子撕了个～。*There is a tear in the sleeve.*

kòu

叩 **动** ❶knock：～门 *knock at a door* ❷kowtow

【叩拜】kowtow

【叩击】(usu.〈喻〉) knock; beat; tap：她的诉说～着我的心弦。*Her narration tugged at my heartstrings.* / 回忆的浪花在她的心头～。*Sprays of recollections were lapping her mind.*

【叩见】〈书〉visit (one's superior); call on (one's superior)

【叩首】kowtow

【叩头】kowtow

【叩头虫】[生] click beetle; snapping beetle

【叩问】〈书〉make inquiries

【叩谢】kowtow in thanks; offer earnest thanks

【叩诊】[医] percussion：～锤 *percussion hammer*

扣 Ⅰ **动** ❶ button up; buckle：把衣服～上 *button (up) one's coat* / 把皮带～上 *buckle a belt* / 把门～上 *latch the door* / ～扣子 *do up the buttons* ❷ place a cup, bowl, etc. upside down; cover with an inverted cup, bowl, etc.：用碗把菜～上，免得凉了。*Cover the food with a bowl to keep it from getting cold.* ❸ detain; take into custody; arrest：把可疑分子～起来 *detain a suspect* ❹ deduct：～工资 *deduct a part of sb.'s pay* ❺ give a discount：打九～ *give a 10 per cent discount* ❻ smash or spike (a ball)：～球 *smash a ball* Ⅱ **名** ❶ knot：绳～儿 *a knot (in a rope)* /

系个～儿 *tie (or make) a knot* ❷button; buckle: 上衣掉了个～儿。*I lost a button off my coat.* / 带金属～儿的皮带 *a belt with a metal buckle*

【扣除】deduct: ～各种费用后,收入超过万元。*After deducting costs, the proceeds still exceeded 10,000 yuan.* / 从工资里～房租 *deduct rent from wages*

【扣发】withhold; hold: ～半年奖金 *hold sb.'s bonus for half a year*

【扣分】deduct mark; deduction of point

【扣篮】basketball dunk shot; over-the-rim shot

【扣留】detain; hold in custody; arrest: 把走私犯～起来 *detain the smuggler* / ～驾驶执照 *suspend a driving licence*

【扣帽子】put a (political) label on sb.: 批评要以理服人,不要乱～。*When criticizing people, we must try to convince them through reasoning, not just put labels on them.*

【扣球】[体] smashing; (to) smash

【扣人心弦】exciting; thrilling; breath-taking: 一场～的比赛 *an exciting match*

【扣杀】[体] smash or spike (a ball): 闪电般的～ *lightning smashes* / 大板～ *overpowering smashes (in table-tennis)*

【扣题】keep to the point; be relevant to the subject: 作文要～。*You should keep to the subject when writing an essay.*

【扣压】withhold; pigeonhole: ～稿件 *withhold a manuscript from publication*

【扣押】❶ detain; hold in custody: 被告在～中。*The accused is in custody.* / ～人质 *hold sb. hostage* ❷ [法] distrain; seize

【扣眼】buttonhole

【扣子】❶ knot ❷ button ❸ an abrupt break in a story to create suspense; a point of high suspense

寇 Ⅰ 名 bandit; invader; enemy: 海～ *pirate* / 敌～ *the (invading) enemy* Ⅱ 动 invade: 入寇

【寇仇】enemy; foe

筘 名 [纺] reed

kū

枯 形 ❶ (of a plant, etc.) withered: ～草 *withered grass* / ～叶 *dead leaves* ❷ (of a well, river, etc.) dried up: 枯井 ❸ dull; uninteresting

【枯草热】[医] hay fever

【枯肠】〈文〉impoverished mind

【枯干】dried-up; withered; wizened

【枯槁】❶ (of a plant, etc.) withered ❷ haggard: 形容～ *look haggard*

【枯涸】(of the source of a river) dry up

【枯黄】withered and yellow: 树叶逐渐～了。*The leaves are beginning to turn yellow.*

【枯寂】bored and lonely: 他们人多,虽然在沙漠中行进,也不感到～。*They travelled in a large group, so they didn't feel bored or lonely while passing through the desert.*

【枯竭】dried up; exhausted: 水源～。*The source has dried up.* / 财源～。*Financial resources were exhausted.*

【枯井】a dry well

【枯窘】〈书〉dried up: 文思～ *the source of one's inspiration has dried up; be devoid of inspiration; run out of ideas to write about*

【枯木逢春】spring comes to the withered tree—get a new lease of life

【枯涩】dull and heavy: 文字～ *a dull and heavy style (of writing)*

【枯瘦】emaciated; skinny: ～如柴 *skinny; be all skin and bones*

【枯水】low water ◇ ～期 dry season

【枯萎】withered: 这花已经～了。*The flower has withered.*

【枯叶蛾】lappet moth

【枯燥】dry and dull; uninteresting: 这本书那么～,谁高兴看呢? *This book is so dull. Who would ever want to read it?*

【枯燥无味】dry as dust; dry and dull: 群众不欢迎他们～的宣传。*The masses don't think much of their dry and dull propaganda.*

哭 动 cry; weep: ～了起来 *burst into tears*

【哭鼻子】〈口〉snivel: 输了可别～啊。*If you lose, don't go and start snivelling.*

【哭哭啼啼】weep and wail

【哭泣】cry; weep; sob

【哭腔】❶ (in traditional opera) sobbing tune ❷ speak with sobs (maybe pretending): 她带着～说别人冤枉她了。*She told in a sobbing tone how she had been wronged by others.*

【哭穷】go about telling people how hard up one is; complain of being hard up

【哭丧着脸】put on (or wear) a long face; go around with a long face: 想开点,别整天～。*Cheer up. Don't go around with such a sad look on your face all the time.*

【哭诉】complain tearfully; accuse while weeping; sob out

【哭天抹泪】〈贬〉wailing and whining; crying piteously

【哭笑不得】not know whether to laugh or to cry; find sth. both funny and annoying

窟 名 ❶ hole; cave: 石窟 ❷ den: 赌窟

【窟窿】❶ hole; cavity: 耗子～ *mouse-hole* / 鞋底磨了个～ *have worn a hole in the sole of one's shoe* ❷ deficit; debt

【窟窿眼儿】small hole: 这块木头上有好些虫蛀的～。*There're a lot of worm-holes in this piece of wood.*

骷 (构词成分)见下

【骷髅】❶ human skeleton ❷ human skull; death's-head

kǔ

苦 Ⅰ 形 bitter：这药～极了。*This medicine tastes very bitter.* Ⅱ 名 hardship；suffering；pain：～日子 *hard times* / 勘探队员以～为乐，以～为荣。*The prospectors feel it a joy and an honour to work under hard conditions.* Ⅲ 动 ❶cause sb. suffering；give sb. a hard time：这事可～了他了。*This matter really gave him a hard time.* ❷suffer from；be troubled by：～旱 *suffer from drought* Ⅳ 副 painstakingly；doing one's utmost：～劝 *earnestly advise (or exhort)* / 刚才你妹妹找你找～了。*Your sister was knocking herself out looking for you.*

【苦熬】go through years of suffering and hardship

【苦不堪言】(of a person) suffer untold misery and hardship；(of sth.) be indescribably painful (or miserable)；the misery or hardship is beyond words：这差事～。*This is a wretched job.*

【苦差】a hard and unprofitable job

【苦楚】suffering；misery；distress

【苦处】suffering；hardship；difficulty：你可不知道我当童养媳那时的～。*You don't know how I suffered as a child bride.*

【苦胆】common name for 胆囊

【苦干】work hard：～精神 *the spirit of hard work* / ～加巧干 *work hard and skilfully；work hard and use one's brain*

【苦工】❶ hard (manual) work；hard labour ❷ a person doing hard (manual) work

【苦功】hard work；painstaking effort：语言这东西，不是随便可以学好的，非下～不可。*The mastery of language is not easy and requires painstaking effort.* / 下～学习 *study hard*

【苦瓜】❶［植］balsam pear ❷〈喻〉bitter gourd：咱们俩是一根藤上的～。*We are two bitter gourds on the same vine.*

【苦果】bitter fruit—evil consequence；disastrous effect；bitter pill：自食～ *eat one's own bitter fruit；swallow one's own bitter pill；reap what one has sown*

【苦海】sea of bitterness；abyss of misery：脱离～ *get out of the abyss of misery* ◇ ～无边，回头是岸 the sea of bitterness has no bounds，repent and the shore is at hand

【苦寒】bitter cold

【苦尽甘来】the bitterness ends and the sweetness begins：直到解放，他们才～。*Only with liberation did their misery end and their happiness begin.*

【苦口】❶ (admonish) in earnest：～相劝 *earnestly advise (or exhort)* ❷ bitter to the taste

【苦口婆心】(admonish) earnestly and maternally

【苦苦】strenuously；hard；persistently：～思索 *think hard*

【苦苦哀求】entreat piteously；implore urgently

【苦劳】credit for hard work：勤勤恳恳地干了许多年，他没有功劳也有点～。*Having worked for so many years，he should be given some credit for hard work if not for merit (or good work).*

【苦乐】joy and sorrow；enjoyment and suffering；happiness and hardship：～人生 *jogs and sorrows of life* / ～与共 *share joy and sorrow；share weal and woe*

【苦力】coolie

【苦闷】depressed；dejected；feeling low：没有人理解她，她感到很～。*She was in a depressed state because no one understood her.*

【苦命】cruel fate；ill-fated life：～人 *a luckless person*

【苦难】suffering；misery；distress：～的深渊 *the abyss of misery* / ～的年代 *an era of suffering* / ～的家史 *the tragic history of one's family* ◇ ～深重 be in deep distress；be in the depth of misery

【苦恼】vexed；worried：受到一点挫折用不着～。*You shouldn't get frustrated just because of a few setbacks.* / 这个问题使人非常～。*This problem is extremely vexing.*

【苦肉计】the ruse of self-injury (inflicting an injury on oneself to win the confidence of the enemy)

【苦涩】❶ bitter and astringent ❷ pained；agonized；anguished：～的表情 *a pained look* / 他～地笑了笑。*He forced a smile.*

【苦水】❶ bitter water ❷ gastric secretion，etc. rising to the mouth ❸ suffering (in the old society)：她是在～里泡大的。*She grew up amidst suffering.* ——另见〖吐苦水〗

【苦思】think hard；cudgel one's brains

【苦思冥想】think long and hard；cudgel (or rack) one's brains (to evolve an idea)：他～了半天，还是拿不出什么主意来。*He racked his brains for a long time，but couldn't come up with any ideas.*

【苦痛】pain；suffering；agony

【苦头】❶bitter taste：这个井里的水带点～儿。*Water from this well has a slightly bitter taste.* ❷ suffering

【苦味酸】［化］picric acid：～盐 *picrate*

【苦夏】loss of appetite and weight in summer

【苦想】think hard

【苦笑】force a smile；make a wry smile

【苦心】trouble taken；pains：一片～ *troubles and pains taken for a good cause* / ～钻研 *do painstaking research*

【苦心孤诣】make extraordinarily painstaking efforts

【苦心经营】take great pains to build up (an enterprise，etc.)

【苦行】religion ascetic practices

【苦役】［法］hard labour；penal servitude

【苦于】❶ suffer from (a disadvantage)：～不识字 *be handicapped by illiteracy* / ～时间紧 *be hard pressed for time* ❷ be harder than；be worse off than

【苦战】❶ hard fighting；bitter battle ❷ wage an

arduous struggle; struggle hard

【苦中作乐】seek joy amidst sorrow; try to enjoy oneself despite one's suffering

【苦衷】difficulties that one is reluctant to discuss or mention: 应该体谅他的～。*Allowance must be made for his difficulties.* / 难言的～ *sth. which is too embarrassing or painful to talk about*

【苦竹】[植] bitter bamboo (Pleioblastus amarus)

【苦主】the family of the victim in a murder case

kù

库 名 warehouse; storehouse: 材料～ *warehouse for raw materials*

【库藏】have in storage: 图书馆～图书三十万册。*There are* 300,000 *books in the library.*

【库存】stock; reserve: 有大量～ *have a large stock of goods* / ～物资 *goods kept in stock; reserve of materials*

【库存管理】inventory control ◇ ～系统 inventory control system

【库房】storehouse; storeroom

【库克群岛】the Cook Islands

【库仑】[电] coulomb ◇ ～定律 [电] Coulomb's law

【库区】the area covered by a reservoir; reservoir; dam area: 三峡～ *the Three Gorge dam area*

【库容】storage capacity (of a reservoir, warehouse, etc.)

【库蚊】[动] culex

裤 名 trousers; pants: 长裤 / 短裤

【裤衩】underpants; undershorts

【裤裆】crotch (of trousers)

【裤兜】trouser pocket

【裤缝】seams of a trouser leg

【裤脚】❶ bottom of a trouser leg ❷ 〈方〉 trouser legs

【裤筒】〈方〉 trouser legs

【裤头】〈方〉 underpants; undershorts

【裤腿】trouser legs

【裤袜】panty hose

【裤线】creases (of trousers)

【裤腰】waist of trousers ◇ ～带 waist belt; band; girdle

【裤子】trousers; pants

酷 Ⅰ 形 ❶ cruel; oppressive: 残酷 ❷ cool Ⅱ 副 very; extremely: 酷寒 / 酷似

【酷爱】ardently love

【酷寒】bitter cold

【酷烈】〈书〉 ❶ cruel; fierce: ～的太阳 *the scorching sun* / ～的苦难 *severe sufferings* ❷ (of fragrance) very strong

【酷热】(of weather) extremely hot: 天气～ *sweltering hot weather* / 这是一个～的夏天。*It was an extremely hot summer.*

【酷暑】the intense heat of summer; high summer

【酷似】be the very image of; be exactly like

【酷刑】cruel (or savage) torture

kuā

夸 动 ❶ exaggerate; overstate; boast: 她把一点小事～得比天还大。*She's made a mountain out of a molehill.* ❷ praise: 人人都～她机灵。*Everyone praised her for her cleverness.*

【夸大】exaggerate; overstate; magnify: ～困难 *exaggerate the difficulties* / ～敌情 *overestimate the enemy* / 原来的数字被～了。*The original figures were inflated.*

【夸大其词】make an overstatement; exaggerate: 对已经取得的成绩不要～。*We shouldn't overstate our past achievements.*

【夸奖】praise; commend: 老师～他进步快。*The teacher praised him for his rapid progress.*

【夸克】[物] quark

【夸口】boast; brag; talk big

【夸夸其谈】indulge in exaggeration; indulge in verbiage

【夸脱】quart (one fourth of a gallon)

【夸耀】brag about; show off; flaunt: 她从不～自己。*She never brags.* / ～自己的见识 *show off one's knowledge and experience*

【夸赞】speak highly of; commend; praise

【夸张】❶ exaggerate; overstate: 你这样说未免太～了。*I'm afraid you've been exaggerating.* or *I'm afraid you've overstated the case.* / ～的语言 *inflated language; exaggerations* / 艺术～ *artistic exaggeration* ❷ hyperbole

kuǎ

垮 动 collapse; fall; break down: 这堵墙要～了。*The wall's going to collapse.* / 我身体结实，累不～。*I'm very strong; no amount of hard work can wear me down.* / 洪水冲～了堤坝。*The flood waters burst the dyke.*

【垮掉的一代】beat generation

【垮台】fall from power; collapse: 与人民为敌的人总是要～的。*Those who oppose the people will surely come to grief.*

kuà

挎 动 ❶ carry on the arm: ～着个篮子 *with a basket on one's arm* / ～着胳膊 *arm in arm* ❷ carry sth. over one's shoulder or around one's neck or at one's side: ～着照相机 *have a camera slung over one's shoulder*

【挎包】satchel

【挎兜】satchel

胯 名 hip

【胯骨】common name for 髋骨

跨 动 ❶ stride (forward or sideways): ～进大门 *step into a doorway* / 向前～一步 *take a step forward* / ～过小沟 *stride over a ditch* ❷ bestride; straddle: ～上战马 *mount* (*or bestride*) *a war-horse* ❸ cut across; go beyond: 亚洲地～寒、温、热三带。*Asia extends across the frigid, temperate and tropical zones.* /组织～地区的商品供应 *organize transregional commodity supplies*

【跨部门】trans-departmental

【跨地区】trans-regional; inter-regional: ～经济联合 *inter-regional economic integration* / ～经济实体 *trans-regional economic entity*

【跨度】[建] span

【跨国公司】transnational corporation; multinational corporation; multinational

【跨国银行】multinational bank

【跨行业】trans-sectoral

【跨栏赛跑】[体] hurdle race; the hurdles

【跨年度】go beyond the year: ～预算 *a budget to be carried over to the next year*

【跨世纪】extending into the next century: ～工程 *project that will not be completed until the next century; project that will extend into the next century*

【跨行业公司】conglomerate

【跨线桥】flyover; overpass

【跨院儿】(of a traditional Chinese compound house) house by the side of the main one; side house; side compound: 小～ *small adjacent house in a traditional courtyard or compound*

【跨越】stride across; leap over; cut across; span: ～几个历史阶段 *span several historical stages of development* / ～障碍 *surmount an obstacle*

kuài

会 (构词成分)见下 ——另见 huì

【会计】❶ accounting ❷ bookkeeper; accountant ◇ ～年度 fiscal (or financial) year; ～师 certified accountant; chief accountant; treasurer; ～事务所 accounting firm; ～制度 accounting system

快 Ⅰ 形 ❶ fast; quick; rapid; swift: 请别说得那么～。*Please don't speak so fast.* / 我的表～五分。*My watch is five minutes fast.* /他学东西～。*He learns quickly.* ❷ speed: 这车能跑多～? *How fast can this car go?* ❸ hurry up; make haste: ～上车吧! *Hurry up and get on the bus!* / ～点儿，车要赶不上了! *Come on, or we'll miss the bus!* / ～跟我走。*Quick, come with me.* ❹ quick-witted; nimble; clever: 他脑子～。*He's quick-witted.* or *He has a quick mind.* ❺ (of a knife, sword, etc.) sharp: ～刀 *a sharp knife* ❻ straight-forward; forthright; plainspoken ❼ pleased; happy; gratified: 不快 / 大快人心 Ⅱ 副 soon; before long: 他～回来了。*He'll be back soon.* / 这学期～结束了。*The term will be over before long.* / 火车～开了。*The train is about to leave.* / ～吃午饭了。*It's almost time for lunch.*

【快班】fast stream; accelerated class

【快板】[音] allegro

【快板儿】kuaibanr, rhythmic comic talk or monologue to the accompaniment of bamboo clappers; clapper talk

【快报】wall bulletin; bulletin

【快步】❶ walk at a quick pace ❷ [军] half step; trot ◇ ～舞 quickstep

【快餐】quick meal; fast food; snack: ～部 *quick-lunch counter; snack counter*

【快车】express train or bus ◇ ～道 fast traffic lane (on a street)

【快当】quick; prompt: 她做起事来又细心又～。*She's quick and careful.*

【快刀斩乱麻】cut a tangled skein of jute with a sharp knife; cut the Gordian knot

【快递】express delivery: ～邮件 *express mail*

【快感】pleasant sensation; delight: 觉着一阵～ *experience a sensation of pleasure*

【快干】quick-drying: ～漆 *quick-drying paint*

【快攻】quick attack (in ball games): 打～ *use the strategy of quick attack*

【快活】happy; merry; cheerful: 日子过得挺～ *live a happy life* / 孩子们～地打雪仗。*The children were enjoying a snowball fight.*

【快件】express delivery luggage, goods or mail: 寄～ *send sth. by express mail; check in luggage for express delivery*

【快捷】(of speed) quick; fast; nimble; agile: ～的步伐 *quick steps* / 信息传递～准确 *speedy and accurate transmission of information*

【快镜头】snapshot

【快乐】happy; joyful; cheerful: ～的微笑 *a happy smile* / ～的童年生活 *a happy childhood* / 节日过得很～。*The festival was spent joyfully.* / 小鸟在树上～地歌唱。*A little bird was singing happily in the tree.*

【快马加鞭】spur on the flying horse—at top speed; posthaste; whip and spur: 这项工作必须～地进行。*This work must be carried out at top speed.*

【快慢】speed: 这些按钮是管～的。*These buttons control the speed.* / 这条轮船的～怎么样? *What's the speed of this steamer?* or *How fast can this steamer sail?* ◇ ～针 regulator (in a clock or watch)

【快门】(camera) shutter: ～开关 *shutter release*

【快人】〈书〉straight person

【快事】a happening that gives great satisfaction or pleasure; delight: 引为～ *recall* (*an event*) *with great satisfaction* / 生平一大～ *one of the most delightful experiences in one's life*

【快手】quick worker; deft hand

【快书】quick-patter (rhythmic storytelling accompanied by bamboo or copper clappers): 山东～

Shandong clapper ballad

【快速】fast；quick；high-speed：～部队 *mobile force* (*or troops*，*units*) / ～掘进 *high-speed drivage* / ～切削 *high-speed cutting* ◇ ～存储器 rapid memory；～倒带 fast rewind；～进带 fast forward

【快艇】speedboat；motor boat；mosquito boat

【快慰】feel pleased with and derive comfort from sth.；be pleased：我们都为她的进步感到～。*We are all pleased with the progress she has made.*

【快信】express letter

【快婿】son-in-law after one's heart：东床～ *son-in-law after one's heart*；*ideal son-in-law* / 乘龙～ *ideal son-in-law with a promising future* (*or of a high position*)

【快讯】newsflash；flash

【快要】soon；before long：新年～到了。*It'll soon be the New Year.* / 酒～喝完了，再去拿些来。*Wine is about to run out. Go and get some more.*

【快意】pleased；satisfied；comfortable：微风吹来，我感到十分～。*A gentle breeze was blowing*，*and I felt refreshed.*

【快译通】electronic bilingual dictionary

【快硬水泥】［建］quick-hardening cement

【快照】snapshot

【快针】［中］swift insertion

【快中子】［物］fast (or high-speed) neutron

【快嘴】❶ one who readily voices his thoughts；one who is quick to articulate his ideas；a straight person ❷ one who has a loose tongue

块 Ⅰ 名 piece；lump；chunk：糖～儿 *hard candy* (*or fruit drops*) *or lumps of sugar* / 把肉切成～儿 *cut the meat into cubes* Ⅱ 量 ❶ piece；lump：两～肥皂 *two cakes of soap* / 一～面包 *a piece* (*or hunk*) *of bread* / 一～手表 *a wrist watch* ❷〈口〉(for gold or silver dollars，Renminbi，and certain paper money)：两～银洋 *two silver dollars* / 三～钱 *three yuan* / 一千～港币 1,000 *Hong Kong dollars*

【块根】［植］root tuber

【块规】［机］slip gauge；gauge block

【块茎】［植］stem tuber

【块码】block code

【块煤】lump coal

【块头】〈方〉(physical) build：他的～很大。*He's a big burly man.*

脍 〈书〉Ⅰ 名 meat chopped into small pieces；minced meat Ⅱ 动 chop meat or fish into small pieces

【脍炙人口】(of a piece of good writing，etc.) win universal praise；enjoy great popularity：一首～的唐诗 *an oft-quoted and widely loved Tang poem*

筷 名 chopsticks：牙～ *ivory chopsticks*

【筷子】chopsticks：竹～ *bamboo chopsticks*

kuān

宽 Ⅰ 形 ❶ wide；broad：～肩膀 *broad-shouldered* / ～边草帽 *broad-brimmed straw hat* / 眼界～ *have a broad outlook* / 这条马路很～。*This road is very wide.* ❷ generous；lenient ❸ comfortably off；well-off：他手头比过去～多了。*He's much better off than before.* Ⅱ 名 width；breadth：这条河有一里～。*This river is one li wide.* Ⅲ 动 ❶ relax；relieve：听说他的病情并不严重，我们的心就～多了。*We were greatly relieved to learn that his condition was not serious.* ❷ extend：限期能再～几天吗？*Can the deadline be extended a few more days?*

【宽波段天线】broadband antenna

【宽敞】spacious；roomy；commodious：～的房子 *a commodious house* / 新建的厂房又高大又～。*The newly-built factory building is tall and spacious.*

【宽畅】free from worry；happy

【宽绰】❶ spacious；commodious：这间屋子很～。*The room is spacious.* ❷ relaxed；relieved：听了他的话，我心里～多了。*When I heard him say that*，*I felt greatly relieved.* or *I felt a big load taken off my mind when I heard what he said.* ❸ comfortably off；well-off

【宽打窄用】budget liberally and spend sparingly

【宽大】❶ spacious；roomy：～的候车室 *a spacious waiting room* (*for bus*，*train*，*etc.*) / ～的窗户 *a big*，*wide window* ❷ lenient；magnanimous：受到～处理 *be dealt with leniently*；*be accorded lenient treatment*；*receive clemency* ❸ show leniency (towards an offender)

【宽待】treat with leniency；be lenient in dealing with：～俘虏 *give lenient treatment to prisoners of war*；*treat prisoners of war leniently*

【宽贷】pardon；forgive

【宽度】width；breadth：这料子的～是多少？*What is the width of this material?*

【宽幅】(of cloth，etc.) wide；broad：～布 *broad* (*or wide*) *cloth*

【宽广】broad；extensive；vast：～的田野 *a broad expanse of country* / 心胸～ *broad-minded*

【宽轨】broad gauge：～铁路 *broad-gauge railway*

【宽宏大量】large-minded；magnanimous

【宽厚】❶ thick and broad：～的胸膛 *a big and strong chest* ❷ tolerant and generous；honest and kind：待人～ *be generous towards others*

【宽解】ease sb.'s anxiety；ease sb. of his trouble：我生气的时候，妈妈总能设法～我。*When I'm angry*，*my mother can always think of a way to calm me down.*

【宽旷】extensive；vast：～的草原 *extensive grasslands*

【宽阔】broad；wide：～的林阴道 *a broad* (*or wide*) *avenue* / ～的大厅 *a spacious hall* / ～的

胸怀 *broad-mindedness*

【宽饶】forgive；show mercy；give quarter

【宽容】tolerant；lenient

【宽恕】forgive：请求～ *ask for forgiveness*

【宽松】〈口〉❶（of clothes）loose and comfortable ❷ not crowded：这个车厢比较～。*This carriage is not so crowded.* ❸ feel relieved；be free from worry ❹ comfortably off；ample；easy：手头～ *be in easy circumstances；be quite well-off at the moment*

【宽慰】comfort；console：你去～她几句。*Go and say something to comfort her.* / 这样一想，我心里才～了些。*This thought brought me a little comfort.*

【宽限】extend a time limit：～期 *days of grace；grace period* / ～一星期 *give a week's grace* / 请～几天。*Please extend the deadline a few days.*

【宽心】feel relieved：说几句～话 *say a few reassuring words* / 请喝杯茶，宽宽心。*Please have a cup of tea and relax yourself.*

【宽心丸儿】anxiety-relief pills—words that set sb.'s mind at ease；reassuring words：吃了～ *be reassured*

【宽衣】〈套〉take off your coat：天气热，请～。*It's hot. Do take your coat off.*

【宽银幕电影】wide-screen film

【宽裕】well-to-do；comfortably off；ample：经济～ *in easy circumstances；well-off* / 时间很～。*There's plenty of time yet.*

【宽窄】width；breadth；size：这块布做窗帘，～正合适。*This piece of cloth is just the right size for a curtain.*

髋（构词成分）见下

【髋骨】［生理］hipbone；innominate bone

kuǎn

款 Ⅰ形 ❶ sincere：款曲❷〈书〉leisurely；slow：款步 Ⅱ动 receive with hospitality；entertain：～客 *entertain guests* Ⅲ名 ❶section of an article in a legal document，etc.；paragraph：根据该条约的第六条第二～ *according to Article 6，Section 2 of the Treaty* ❷ a sum of money；fund：公款 ❸ the name of sender or recipient inscribed on a painting or a piece of calligraphy presented as a gift：上款

【款步】〈书〉walk with deliberate steps

【款待】treat cordially；entertain：～客人 *entertain guests* / 感谢你对我们的盛情～。*Thank you for the hospitality you have shown us.*

【款额】amount of money；sum of money：～巨大 *large amount（or sum）of money*

【款留】cordially urge（a guest）to stay

【款曲】〈书〉heartfelt feelings：互通～ *express feelings of mutual affection or friendship*

【款式】pattern；style；design：这些上衣的～都不错。*The styles of these coats are good.* / 这套家具～新颖。*This set of furniture is of a brand-new design.*

【款项】❶ a sum of money；fund ❷ sections and items（in a legal document，etc.）

【款爷】〈方〉moneybags；nouveau riche

【款子】〈口〉a sum of money：很大一笔～ *a huge sum of money* / 一笔汇来的～ *a remittance*

kuāng

匡 动 ❶〈书〉rectify；correct：～谬 *correct mistakes* ❷〈书〉assist；save：～我不逮 *help me to overcome my shortcomings*

【匡复】save the state

【匡救】deliver sb.（from evil）；rescue；save

【匡算】roughly estimate

【匡正】rectify；correct：～时弊 *correct the maladies of the times*

【匡助】help；assist

诓 动 deceive；hoax：我哪能～你？*How could I deceive you?*

【诓骗】（又作'诓哄'）deceive；hoax；dupe

哐 象 crash；bang：～的一声，脸盆掉在地上了。*The basin fell with a crash.*

【哐啷】crash：～一声把门关上 *bang the door shut*

筐 名 basket

【筐子】small basket

kuáng

狂 形 ❶ mad；crazy：发狂 ❷ violent：雨骤风～。*The wind blew hard and the rain came down in sheets.* / 股票价格～跌。*The stocks slumped.* ❸ wild；unrestrained：狂奔 ❹ arrogant；overbearing：这个人～得很。*That person is very arrogant.*

【狂傲】wildly arrogant；presumptuous

【狂暴】violent；wild：～的山洪 *raging mountain torrents*

【狂奔】run wildly；run like mad：他在街上～而去。*He ran wildly down the street.* / ～的马 *a bolting horse*

【狂飙】hurricane

【狂飙运动】Sturm and Drang；Storm and Stress（a German literary movement of the latter part of the 18th century）

【狂潮】（usu.〈喻〉）turbulent tidewater：革命的～ *turbulent revolutionary movement；unrestrained spread of the revolution*

【狂放】unruly or unrestrained

【狂吠】bark furiously；howl

【狂风】❶［气］whole gale ❷ fierce wind：～呼啸。*The wind howled.*

【狂风暴雨】violent storms：他们向敌人展开了～似的攻击。*They launched a furious whirlwind at-*

tack on the enemy.

【狂轰滥炸】wanton and indiscriminate bombing

【狂欢】revelry; carnival: ～节 *carnival* / ～之夜 *a night of revelry*

【狂澜】raging waves

【狂怒】furious; mad with rage

【狂犬病】hydrophobia; rabies

【狂热】fanaticism: ～的军备竞赛 *feverish armament race* / ～的信徒 *a fanatical follower; fanatic; zealot* / ～性 *fanaticism*

【狂人】❶ madman; maniac: 帝国主义战争～ *imperialist war maniacs* ❷ an extremely arrogant person

【狂人呓语】ravings of a madman

【狂妄】wildly arrogant; presumptuous: ～的野心 *a wild ambition* / 他太～了。*He is too arrogant*.

【狂妄自大】arrogant and conceited

【狂喜】wild with joy: 他们相见时～地拥抱起来。*When they met, they hugged each other in an ecstasy of delight*.

【狂想】❶ fancy; fantasy: 诗人的～ *poet's fantasy* / 突发～ *be struck with a fancy* ❷ vain hope; wishful thinking; illusion: 就你还想当电影明星? 简直是～! *You, a movie star? What a wild dream*! ◇ ～曲 [音] rhapsody; fantasia

【狂笑】laugh wildly; laugh boisterously

【狂言】ravings; wild language: 口出～ *talk wildly*

【狂野】violent and rough; wild and boorish: 那帮人～的笑声使他心惊胆颤。*He shuddered at the wild and hysterical laughter of that bunch*.

【狂躁】rash and impatient; indiscreet and hot-headed; restless with anxiety: 发出一阵阵～的叫声 *send out fits of restless and anxious cries* / 要沉住气,不要～。*Keep your head. Don't be rash and hot-headed*.

诳 (构词成分)见下

【诳骗】deceive; hoax; dupe

【诳语】(又作'诳话') lies; falsehood

kuàng

况 Ⅰ 名 condition; situation: 情况 Ⅱ 动 compare: 比～ *draw an analogy* / 以古～今 *draw parallels from history* Ⅲ 连 〈书〉 moreover; besides

【况且】moreover; besides; in addition: 这房子太贵,～地点也不适中。*The price is too high, and moreover, the house isn't in a suitable position*.

旷 Ⅰ 形 ❶ vast; spacious ❷ free from worries and petty ideas: 心旷神怡 ❸ loose-fitting: 螺丝～了。*The screw has come loose*. / 这身衣服她穿着太～了。*The dress sits loosely (or is too loose-fitting) on her*. Ⅱ 动 neglect or waste: ～日废时 *waste time*

【旷达】〈书〉 broad-minded; bighearted

【旷费】waste: ～时间 *waste one's time*

【旷工】stay away from (or miss) work without leave or good reason

【旷古】from time immemorial ◇ ～未闻 unheard-of; unprecedented

【旷课】be absent from school without leave; cut school: 旷一堂课 *cut a class*

【旷日持久】long-drawn-out; protracted; prolonged: ～的谈判 *long-drawn-out negotiations* / ～的战争 *a long-drawn-out war*

【旷世】〈书〉 unequalled in one's time; unrivalled; unique: ～功勋 *unique deeds* / ～之才 *a man of brilliance unequalled in his time*

【旷野】wilderness

【旷职】be absent from duty without leave or good reason

矿 名 ❶ ore (or mineral) deposit: 报～ *report where deposits are found* ❷ ore: 这里新发现了一种～。*A kind of ore has been discovered here recently*. ❸ mine: 他在～上工作。*He works at the mine*.

【矿藏】mineral resources: 中国～丰富。*China is rich in mineral resources*. / ～量 (ore) *reserves*

【矿层】ore bed; ore horizon; seam

【矿产】mineral products; minerals

【矿车】mine car; tub; tram

【矿尘】mine dust

【矿床】mineral (or ore) deposit; deposit: 金属～ *metalliferous deposit* / 层状～ *bedded deposit*

【矿灯】miner's lamp

【矿工】miner

【矿井】mine shaft or pit: ～火灾 *mine-shaft fire*

【矿坑】(mining) pit

【矿脉】mineral ore; mineral vein; lode

【矿棉】mineral wool

【矿苗】outcropping; outcrop; crop

【矿泥】sludge; slime; slurry

【矿区】mining area: ～铁路 *mine railway*

【矿泉】mineral spring: ～水 *mineral water*

【矿砂】ore in sand form

【矿山】mine (with its accompanying shafts, buildings, etc.): ～地压 *rock pressure* / ～工程图 *mine map* / ～机械 *mining machinery*

【矿石】ore ◇ ～收音机 crystal radio receiver (or set)

【矿田】ore field

【矿物】mineral: 伴生～ *associated mineral* / ～界 *mineral kingdom* ◇ ～学 mineralogy; ～油 mineral oil

【矿样】sample ore

【矿业】mining industry

【矿渣】slag: ～水泥 *slag cement* / ～砖 *slag brick*

【矿质肥料】mineral fertilizer

【矿柱】(ore) pillar

框 Ⅰ 名 frame; circle; case: 给照片配个～儿 *have a photo framed* Ⅱ 动 ❶ draw a frame round: 用红线把标题～起来 *frame the heading in red* ❷ restrict; restrain; bind: 不能～得太死

not make rigid restrictions
【框架】frame；framework：窗户的～ *a window frame* / 计划商品经济的～ *the framework for a planned commodity economy*
【框框】❶ frame；circle：他拿红铅笔在图片四周画了个～。*He drew a circle around the picture with a red pencil*. ❷ restriction；convention；set pattern：突破旧～的限制 *throw convention to the winds*
【框子】frame；rim：眼镜～ *rims of spectacles*

眶 名 eye socket：眼眶

kuī

亏 Ⅰ 动 ❶ lose (money, etc.)；have a deficit：做生意～了 *have lost money in business* / ～了二百元 *have a deficit of 200 yuan* ❷ deficient；short：～什么就买什么。*Buy what you're short of*. / ～你十块钱。*I owe you 10 yuan*. ❸ treat unfairly：你放心吧，～不了你。*Don't worry, we won't be unfair to you*. / 人不～地，地不～人。*The land won't fail people as long as people don't fail the land*. Ⅱ 副 ❶ fortunately；luckily；thanks to：～他提醒了我，要不我早忘了。*Luckily he reminded me; otherwise I'd have forgotten all about it*. ❷(used to show sarcasm)：～他说得出口！*And he had the nerve to say so!* / ～你还是个大学生呢，连这个都不懂。*For a college student, you ought to know better than that!*
【亏本】lose money in business；lose one's capital：～生意 *a losing proposition*
【亏仓】broken stowage
【亏产】fail to fulfil a production target (or quota)
【亏秤】❶ give short measure：这人买卖公道，从不～，也不多要钱。*The man is an honest tradesman. He never gives short measure nor overcharges his customers*. ❷ lose weight：这菜太湿，放两天就～好几斤。*As the vegetable is too moist, it will lose quite a few kilograms when stored for a couple of days*.
【亏待】treat unfairly；treat shabbily：我可从来没～过你。*I've never treated you unfairly*.
【亏得】❶ fortunately；luckily；thanks to：～大家帮忙，我们才按时把这活干完。*Thanks to everybody's help, we finished the job on time*. ❷ used to show sarcasm：～你长这么大，那么点事儿都不懂。*Fancy a big boy like you not understanding such a simple thing!*
【亏乏】short (of supplies)；deficient
【亏负】let sb. suffer；let sb. down：他没有～你的地方。*He didn't let you down in any way*.
【亏耗】loss by a natural process：货物在运输中的～ *losses incurred in the course of transportation*
【亏空】❶ loss money in business；be in debt：公司今年～不少。*The corporation lost a lot of money this year*. ❷ debt；deficit：弥补～ *meet (or make up) a deficit*；*make up (for) a loss*
【亏欠】have a deficit；be in arrears
【亏蚀】❶ eclipse of the sun or moon ❷ lose money in business；lose one's capital ❸ loss；wear and tear
【亏损】❶ loss；deficit：企业～ *loss incurred in an enterprise* ❷ general debility：久病而～ *be in general debility after a long illness* ◇ ～企业 money-losing enterprise
【亏心】have a guilty conscience：～事 *a deed that troubles (or weighs on) one's conscience* / 你说这话，不～吗？*Doesn't your conscience trouble you for saying that?*

岿 (构词成分)见下
【岿然】〈书〉towering；lofty：～屹立 *stand towering like a giant* ◇ ～不动 steadfastly stand one's ground

盔 名 helmet：钢盔
【盔甲】suit of armour

窥 动 peep；spy：窥视
【窥测】spy out：～时机 *bide one's time*
【窥测方向】see how the land lies；see which way the wind blows
【窥察】spy upon；pry about
【窥见】get (or catch) a glimpse of；detect：从他这首诗里可以～他的胸怀。*From his poem we can get a hint of his breadth of mind*.
【窥器】[医] speculum
【窥视】peep at；spy on：他发现一个形迹可疑的人向屋内～。*He spotted a suspicious character peeping into the house*. ◇ ～孔 peep hole
【窥伺】〈贬〉lie in wait for；be on watch for
【窥探】spy upon；pry about：～军事机密 *pry into military secrets*
【窥听】eavesdrop
【窥望】peep at；spy on

kuí

奎 名 the fifteenth of the twenty-eight constellations (二十八宿) into which the celestial sphere was divided in ancient Chinese astronomy (consisting of sixteen stars, said to be like a person striding, in Pisces)
【奎宁】[药] quinine

葵 名 certain herbaceous plants with big flowers：向日葵
【葵花】sunflower ◇ ～子 sunflower seeds
【葵扇】palm-leaf fan

喹 (构词成分)见下
【喹啉】[化] quinoline

魁 Ⅰ 名 chief；head：罪魁 Ⅱ 形 of stalwart build：魁梧
【魁首】(又作'魁元') a person who is head and shoulders above others；the brightest and best：

文章～ *outstanding writer of the day*
【魁伟】big and tall；stalwart
【魁梧】big and tall；stalwart：～的身躯 *be of great stature* / 身量～ *of great height and powerful build*；*tall and sturdy*

睽 动〈书〉go against；run counter to
【睽睽】stare；gaze

蝰 (构词成分)见下
【蝰蛇】viper

kuǐ

傀 (构词成分)见下
【傀儡】puppet：殖民主义者及其～ *colonialists and their stooges* (*or puppets*) / ～政府 *puppet government* / ～政权 *puppet regime*

kuì

匮 形〈书〉deficient：匮乏
【匮乏】(又作'匮缺')〈书〉short (of supplies)；deficient：物资～ *short of supplies* / 极度～ *a serious shortage in the supply* / 人口的激增引起资源的～。*The rapid increase in population caused a shortage of natural resources.*

溃 动 ❶ (of a dyke or dam) burst：溃决 ❷ break through (an encirclement) ❸ be defeated；be routed ❹ fester；ulcerate：溃烂
【溃败】be defeated；be routed
【溃不成军】(of troops) be utterly routed；break and scatter
【溃决】(又作'溃堤') (of flood waters) burst (a dyke, dam, etc.)：大坝～成灾。*The dam broke and caused a flood.*
【溃军】routed army
【溃烂】fester；ulcerate
【溃灭】(of a regime, etc.) crumble and fall
【溃散】(of troops) be defeated and dispersed
【溃逃】escape in disorder；fly pell-mell；flee helter-skelter
【溃退】beat a precipitate retreat
【溃疡】[医] ulcer

馈 动 make a present of：～以鲜果 *make a present of fresh fruit*
【馈电】[电] feed：交叉～ *cross feed* / ～线 *feed line*；*feeder*
【馈赠】(又作'馈送') present (a gift)；make a present of sth.

愦 形 muddled；dazed and confused；befuddled：昏愦
【愦乱】dazed and confused；befuddled

愧 形 ashamed；conscience-stricken：～无以报。*I feel ashamed of my inability to repay your favour.* / ～不敢当。*I really don't deserve such an honour.* or *You flatter me.*
【愧恨】ashamed and remorseful；remorseful：～交集 *be overcome with shame and remorse* / 内心深自～ *feel bitterly remorseful*
【愧疚】〈书〉feel remorseful and uneasy；be conscience-stricken
【愧色】a look (or an expression) of shame：面有～ *look ashamed* / 毫无～ *look unashamed* (*or unabashed*)

聩 形〈书〉deaf；hard of hearing：振聋发聩

kūn

坤 形 female；feminine：～鞋 *woman's shoes* / ～包 *lady's handbag*
【坤表】woman's watch

昆 名 ❶ elder brother：昆仲 ❷〈书〉offspring
【昆布】[中] kelp
【昆虫】insect：传病～ *insect vector*
【昆虫学】entomology；insectology：～家 *entomologist*
【昆仲】elder and younger brothers；brothers

醌 名 [化] quinone

kǔn

捆 Ⅰ 动 tie；bind；bundle up：～行李 *tie up one's baggage* / ～谷草 *bundle up millet stalks* / 把他～起来 *tie him up* / ～住手脚 *bound hand and foot* Ⅱ 量 bundle：一～柴禾 *a bundle of firewood*
【捆绑】tie up (usu. a person)；truss up；bind ◇ ～式 [军] cluster
【捆扎】tie up；bundle up：一定要把这批货物～好了。*Be sure to bundle the goods up firmly.*

kùn

困 Ⅰ 动 ❶ be stranded；be hard pressed：～于异乡 *be left stranded in a foreign land* / ～于酒色 *be addicted to wine and women* / 为病所～ *be afflicted with illness* ❷ surround；pin down：把敌人～死在据点里 *bottle up the enemy in his stronghold* Ⅱ 形 ❶ tired：困乏 ❷ sleepy：你～了就睡吧。*Go to bed if you feel sleepy.* / 孩子们～得眼睛都睁不开了。*The children were so sleepy that they could hardly keep their eyes open.*
【困补】(〈略〉全称为'困难补助') subsidy to those in financial difficulties：申请～ *apply for a grant-in aid on account of one's straitened circumstances*
【困顿】❶ tired out；exhausted ❷ be in financial straits

【困乏】❶ tired；fatigued ❷〈书〉financially difficult；straitened economically
【困惑】perplexed；puzzled：～的神色 *a perplexed look* / ～不解 *feel puzzled*
【困境】difficult position；predicament；straits：处于～ *be in a difficult position* / 陷于～ *fall into dire straits*；*find oneself in a tight corner*；*land oneself in a fix* / 摆脱～ *extricate oneself from a difficult position*
【困窘】❶ in straitened circumstances；in a difficult position；embarrassed ❷ poverty-stricken；destitute
【困倦】sleepy：昨晚没有睡好，现在感到十分～。*I feel very sleepy because I didn't sleep well last night.*
【困苦】(live) in privation：艰难～ *difficulties and hardships*
【困难】❶ difficulty：情况十分～。*Conditions are very difficult.* / ～重重 *be beset with difficulties* ❷ financial difficulties；straitened circumstances：生活～ *live in straitened circumstances* / ～户 *families with financial* (*or material*) *difficulties*
【困扰】perplex；puzzle：为一个难题所～ *be puzzled by a difficult question*
【困守】defend against a siege；stand a siege：～孤城 *be entrenched in a beseiged city*
【困兽犹斗】cornered beasts will still fight；beasts at bay will fight back

kuò

扩 动 expand；enlarge；extend：扩大
【扩充】expand；strengthen；augment：～实力 *expand* (*military or political*) *forces* / ～军备 *engage in arms expansion* / ～设备 *augment the equipment*
【扩大】enlarge；expand；extend：～政治影响 *extend political influence* / ～经营范围 *expand business scope* / ～相互间的经济技术合作 *extend mutual economic and technological cooperation*
【扩大化】broaden the scope；magnify：使错误没有～ *keep mistakes within bounds*
【扩大会议】enlarged meeting (or session，conference)
【扩大内需】to expand domestic demand
【扩大企业自主权】extend the decision-making power of enterprises
【扩大再生产】reproduction on an extended scale；extended (or expanded) reproduction
【扩股】enlarge the number of shares
【扩建】extend (a factory，mine，etc.)：～码头 *extend a wharf* ◇ ～工程 extension (project)
【扩军】engage in arms expansion：～备战 *engage in arms expansion and war preparations*
【扩孔】[机] reaming：～钻头 *reaming bit*；*reamer bit*
【扩散】spread；diffuse：～谣言 *spread rumours* / ～影响 *extend influence* / 不让废气～ *prevent the diffusion of waste gas* / 病菌～ *proliferation of germs*
【扩胸器】chest expander；chest developer
【扩音器】❶ megaphone ❷ audio amplifier
【扩印】make enlargements from a 135 (esp. colour) film
【扩展】expand；spread；extend；develop：五年内全省林地将～到 1,000 万亩。*The forest land of the province will be expanded to ten million mu within five years.* ◇ ～槽 [计] expansion slot
【扩张】❶ expand；enlarge；extend；spread：对外～ *expansionism*；*foreign aggrandizement* / ～野心 *expansionist ambitions* ❷ [医] dilate：血管～ *blood vessel dilatation*
【扩张器】[医] dilator
【扩张主义】expansionism：～分子 *expansionist*
【扩招】to increase enrollment：大学扩招是为了鼓励教育消费。

括 动 ❶ draw together (muscles，etc.)；contract：括约肌 ❷ include：概括
【括号】brackets (〔 〕，( )，〈 〉)
【括弧】parentheses
【括约肌】[生理] sphincter
【括注】an explanatory note in brackets

蛞 (构词成分)见下
【蛞蝓】[动] slug

阔 形 ❶ wide；broad；vast：辽阔 ❷ weal-thy；rich：他～起来了。*He's getting rich.*
【阔别】long separated；long parted：～多年的战友 *long-separated comrades-in-arms* / 我们已～多年了。*We've been apart for many years now.*
【阔步】take big strides：～前进 *advance with giant strides*
【阔绰】ostentatious；liberal with money：～的生活 *an extravagant life* / 他的日子过得很～。*He leads an extravagant life.*
【阔老】(又作'阔佬') a rich (old) man
【阔气】luxurious；extravagant；lavish：花钱～ *spend lavishly* / 摆～ *display* (*or parade*) *one's wealth*
【阔少】a rich man's son
【阔叶树】broadleaf tree

廓 Ⅰ 形 wide；extensive：寥廓 Ⅱ 名 outline：耳廓
【廓张】〈书〉expand；enlarge；extend；spread

L

lā

拉 动 ❶ pull; draw; tug; drag: ～弓 *draw a bow* / ～风箱 *work the bellows* / 他把我～到一边。*He drew me aside*. ❷ transport by vehicle; haul: 套车去～肥料 *get a cart ready to haul back the fertilizer* ❸ move (troops to a place): 把二班～到桥头 *move Squad Two to the bridge* ❹ play (certain musical instruments): ～小提琴(手风琴) *play the violin* (*accordion*) ❺ drag out; draw out; space out: ～长声音说话 *drawl* ❻ give (or lend) a helping hand; help: 他犯了错误,要～他一把。*He's made mistakes and we must help him*. ❼ drag in; implicate: 这是你自己做的事,为什么要～上别人? *It was all your own doing. Why drag in others*? ❽ draw in; win over; canvass: ～一派打一派 *draw in one faction and hit out at another* / ～选票 *canvass votes*; *canvass* ❾〈口〉empty the bowels: 又～又吐 *suffer from vomiting and diarrhoea* ——另见 lá

【拉拔】[机] drawing

【拉帮结伙】recruit people to form a faction; gang up; band together

【拉扯】〈口〉❶ drag; pull: 别～,让我走。*Don't hold me back. Let me go*. ❷ take great pains to bring up (a child): 你妈把你～到这么大可真不容易啊。*It wasn't at all easy for your mother to bring you up*. ❸ help; support; promote: 师傅见他有出息,愿意特别～他一把。*His instructor finds him promising and is willing to give him special help*. ❹ gang up with; rope in ❺ implicate; drag in: 干吗把我～进去? *Why drag me in*?

【拉出去】pull out; drag out: 把他～枪毙! *Lead him off to execution*!

【拉床】[机] broaching machine

【拉大旗作虎皮】use a great banner (of revolution, etc.) as a tiger-skin—deck oneself out and intimidate people

【拉刀】[机] broach

【拉倒】〈口〉forget about it; leave it at that; drop it: 你不同意,就～。*Since you don't agree, let's forget about it*.

【拉丁美洲】Latin America

【拉丁文】Latin (language)

【拉丁字母】the Latin alphabet; the Roman alphabet

【拉肚子】〈口〉suffer from diarrhoea; have loose bowels

【拉队伍】raise a force or contingent; form a band

【拉夫】pressgang; press people into service

【拉幅机】[纺] stenter; tenter

【拉杆】[机] pull rod; drag link; draw bar; tension link ◇ ～天线 telescopic antenna

【拉关系】〈贬〉try to establish a relationship with sb.; cotton up to: 拉亲戚关系 *claim kinship* / ～,走后门 *use personal connections and get in through the "back door"*

【拉后腿】hold sb. back; be a drag on sb.; be a hindrance to sb.

【拉花】garland: 纸～ *festoon*; *paper garland*

【拉环】ring-pull

【拉簧】[机] extension spring

【拉火绳】[军] lanyard

【拉家常】talk about everyday matters; engage in small talk; chitchat

【拉家带口】be burdened with a family

【拉架】try to stop people from fighting each other: 他们又打起来了,你去拉拉架。*They're fighting again. Go and stop them*.

【拉交情】〈贬〉try to form ties with; cotton up to

【拉锯】❶ work a two-handed saw ❷ be locked in a seesaw struggle: ～地带 *area which frequently changes hands in a war*; *scene of a seesaw battle* ◇ ～战 seesaw battle

【拉开】❶ pull open; draw back: ～抽屉 *pull the drawer open* / ～窗帘 *draw back the curtain* / ～枪栓 *pull back the bolt* (*of a rifle*) / ～架式 *get into a ready position* (*to fight*) ❷ increase the distance between; space out: 不要～距离! *Close up*! / 比分逐渐～了。*The gap between the scores gradually widened*.

【拉客】❶ (of inns, small restaurants, etc.) solicit guests or diners ❷ (of taxi drivers, pedicab riders, etc.) take on passengers ❸ (of prostitutes) solicit patrons

【拉拉扯扯】❶ pull (or drag) sb. about ❷ exchange flattery and favours; scratch each other's backs: 吃吃喝喝,～ *wining and dining and flattering each other*

【拉拉队】cheering squad; rooters

【拉力】pulling force: ～试验 *pull* (*or tension*) *test* ◇ ～器 chest-developer; chest-expander

【拉力赛】[体] rally

【拉链】zip fastener; zipper

【拉拢】draw sb. over to one's side; win over; rope in: 不要受坏人～。*Don't get roped in by bad people.* ◇ ～腐蚀 win someone over and corrupt him; win people over to one's side and corrupt them

【拉马克学说】[生] Lamarckism

【拉买卖】canvass business orders; drum up trade

【拉面】〈方〉同〖抻面〗

【拉模】[机] drawing die

【拉皮条】〈方〉act as a procurer or pimp

【拉平】bring to the same level; even up: 双方比分渐渐～。*The score gradually evened up.*

【拉纤】❶ tow (a boat) ❷ act as go-between

【拉撤】❶ draw in (or up) the net; haul in the net ❷ close in on (besieged forces)

【拉山头】form a faction

【拉屎】〈口〉have a bowel movement; shit

【拉手】(lāshǒu) shake hands

【拉手】(lāshou) handle (of a door, window, drawer, etc.)

【拉锁儿】zip fastener; zipper

【拉条】[机] brace; stay: 斜～ *batter brace* / 链～ *chain stay*

【拉脱维亚】Latvia ◇ ～人 Latvian; ～语 Latvian (language)

【拉稀】〈口〉have loose bowels; have diarrhoea

【拉下脸】❶ look displeased; pull a long face; put on a stern expression: 他听了这句话，立刻～来。*When he heard this, his expression became stern immediately.* ❷〈口〉not spare sb.'s sensibilities: 他办事大公无私，对谁也能～来。*He is perfectly fair and impartial and never tries to spare anybody's feelings.*

【拉下水】pull sb. into the water—get sb. involved in one's scheme; drag sb. into the mire; make an accomplice of sb.; corrupt sb.

【拉线】act as go-between

【拉线开关】pullswitch

【拉削】[机] broaching

【拉秧】uproot plants after their edible portions have been harvested

【拉杂】rambling; jumbled; ill-organized: 这篇文章写得太～。*This article is very badly organized.* / 我拉拉杂杂就谈这些吧。*I think I'll stop my rambling talk here.*

垃 (构词成分) 见下

【垃圾】rubbish; garbage; refuse: ～处理 *garbage disposal* / 焚化～ *refuse incineration*

【垃圾堆】rubbish heap; refuse dump; garbage heap: 把它扔到～里去。*Throw it on the rubbish heap.* / 被扫进了历史的～ *be swept onto the rubbish heap of history*

【垃圾发电】garbage power

【垃圾焚化炉】garbage furnace; refuse burner

【垃圾箱】dustbin; ash can; garbage can

邋 (构词成分) 见下

【邋遢】〈口〉slovenly; sloppy: 你怎么这样～? *How did you ever get so sloppy?*

lá

拉 动 slash; slit; cut; make a gash in: 把这块皮子～开 *slit the leather* / 手上～了个口子 *cut one's hand; get a cut in the hand* ——另见 lā

lǎ

喇 (构词成分) 见下

【喇叭】❶ popular name for 唢呐 ❷ brass-wind instruments in general or any of these instruments ❸ loudspeaker; horn (in a car)

【喇叭花】(white-edged) morning glory

【喇叭裤】flared trousers; bell-bottoms

【喇嘛】lama ◇ ～教 Lamaism; ～庙 lamasery

là

落 动 ❶ leave out; be missing: 这里～了两个字。*Two words are missing here.* ❷ leave behind; forget to bring: 我忙着出来，把书～在家里了。*I was in a hurry and left my book at home.* ❸ lag (or fall, drop) behind: ～下很远 *fall (or be left) far behind* / 谁也不愿意～在后面。*No one likes to lag behind.* ——另见 lào; luò

腊 名 ❶ an ancient sacrifice which took place each (lunar) year shortly after the winter solstice ❷ the twelfth lunar month: ～尽冬残。*The year is drawing to a close.* ❸ cured (fish, meat, etc., generally done in the twelfth lunar month) ——另见 xī

【腊八粥】laba porridge (rice porridge with beans, nuts and dried fruit eaten on the eighth day of the twelfth lunar month)

【腊肠】sausage

【腊梅】winter sweet (an ornamental shrub bearing sweet yellow flowers in winter)

【腊肉】cured meat; bacon

【腊味】cured meat, fish, etc.

【腊月】the twelfth month of the lunar year; the twelfth moon

辣 Ⅰ 形 ❶ peppery; hot: 这个辣椒～不～? *Is this pepper hot?* / 我爱吃～的。*I like hot foods.* ❷ vicious; ruthless: 心毒手～ *vicious and ruthless* / 口甜心～ *sweet words but a wicked heart* Ⅱ 动 (of smell or taste) burn; bite; sting: 切葱头～眼睛。*When you slice an onion it makes your eyes sting.* / ～得舌头发麻。*The hot taste burns the tongue.*

【辣根】horse radish

【辣酱】thick chilli sauce

【辣酱油】pungent sauce (similar to Worcestershire sauce)

【辣椒】hot pepper；chilli ◇ ～粉 chilli powder；～油 chilli oil

【辣手】❶ ruthless method；vicious device ❷〈方〉vicious；ruthless ❸〈口〉thorny；troublesome；knotty：这件事真～。*That's really a knotty problem.* or *That's a real hot potato.*

【辣丝丝】a little hot

【辣子】〈口〉hot pepper；cayenne pepper；chilli

蜡 名 ❶ wax ❷ candle：点一支～ *light a candle*

【蜡版】mimeograph stencil (already cut) ◇ ～术 cerography

【蜡笔】wax crayon ◇ ～画 crayon drawing

【蜡虫】wax insect

【蜡光纸】glazed paper

【蜡果】wax fruit

【蜡花】snuff

【蜡黄】wax yellow；waxen；sallow：面色～ *have a sallow complexion*

【蜡染】［纺］wax printing；batik

【蜡人】wax figure；waxwork

【蜡台】candlestick

【蜡丸】a wax-coated pill

【蜡像】wax figure；waxwork：～陈列馆 *waxworks museum*；*waxworks*

【蜡印】wax seal：打上～ *affix a wax seal (to a contract, etc.)*

【蜡纸】❶ wax paper ❷ stencil paper；stencil：刻～ *cut a stencil*

【蜡烛】(wax) candle

【蜡嘴雀】hawfinch

瘌（构词成分）见下

【瘌痢】〈方〉favus of the scalp

【瘌痢头】〈方〉a person affected with favus on the scalp

la

啦 助 a fusion of 了 and 啊：他早来～！*Why, he's been here a long time!* / 二组跟我们挑战～。*Look! Group B has sent us a challenge.* / 这回我可亲眼看见～！*This time I've actually seen it for myself.* / 她真来～？*Has she really come?*

lái

来 Ⅰ 动 ❶ come (to)：他今天～过两次。*He came twice today.* / 客人～了。*The guests are here.* ❷ cause to come；send here；bring：他～过两封信。*He's sent me two letters.* / 我们可以～两个人帮忙。*We can send two people over to help.* ❸ (used as a substitute for some other verb)：你歇歇，让我～吧。*You take a rest. Let me do it.* / 慢慢儿～，别忙。*Take it easy. No hurry.* / 我自己～吧，别客气。*Please don't bother. I'll do it myself.* ❹ (used with 得 or 不，indicating possibility or impossibility, capability or incapability)：上海话我说不～。*I don't speak Shanghai dialect.* / 这个歌我唱得～。*I can sing this song.* ❺ (used before a verb, indicating an intended or suggested action)：你去打水，我～生炉子。*You get some water and I'll light the stove.* / 我～问你。*Let me ask you.* ❻ (used after a verb or verbal expression) come in order to：我们支援你们～了。*We've come to help you out.* / 我们道喜～了。*We've come to congratulate you.* ❼ (used between a verbal expression and a verb or between two verbal expressions) in order to：大家想办法～解决。*Let's think of a way to solve the problem.* / 我们得尽一切力量～完成计划。*We must do all we can to implement the plan.* Ⅱ 形 future；coming；next：来年 Ⅲ 助 ❶ (used after a time expression, indicating a period of time that extends from the past up to the present)：一年～ *during the past year* / 这三年～ *over the last three years* / 几天～ *for the last few days* / 两千年～ *over the past 2,000 years* ❷ (used after a round number or after a numeral plus a measure) approximately；about；around：二十～个 *about 20* / 两米～高 *about two metres high*

【来宾】guest；visitor：接待～ *receive guests* ◇ ～席 seats for guests

【来不得】won't do；be impermissible：这是一个科学问题，～半点虚伪。*This is a matter of science, which permits no dishonesty.*

【来不及】there's not enough time (to do sth.)；it's too late (to do sth.)：今天我们～去看他了。*There's no time for us to go and see him today.*

【来到】arrive；come：雨季～了。*The rainy season has set in.* / 你们终于～了。*So here you are at last.*

【来得及】there's still time；be able to do sth. in time；be able to make it：赶快去，还～。*Go at once while there's still time.* / 我把车开快点还～。*We can make it if I drive a bit faster.*

【来得容易去得快】easy come, easy go

【来电】❶ incoming telegram or telephone call；your telegram or telephone call；your message：3月17日～悉。*Your message of March 17 received.* ❷ send a telegram or make a telephone call here：请～告知。*Please inform me by telegram.*

【来而不往非礼也】it is impolite not to reciprocate—one should return as good as one receives

【来犯】come to attack us；invade our territory：坚决消灭敢于～之敌。*Resolutely wipe out any enemy that dares to invade our territory.*

【来访】come to visit；come to call：认真对待人民群众来信～ *treat seriously the letters the people send in and the complaints they make when they call*

【来复枪】rifle

【来复线】rifling

【来稿】incoming manuscript；your manuscript

【来函】〈书〉incoming letter; your letter
【来回】❶ make a round trip; make a return journey; go to a place and come back: ～有多远? *How far is it there and back?* ❷ a round trip: 一天打两个～ *make two round trips in one day* ❸ back and forth; to and fro: 在房间里～走动 *pace up and down the room* / ～摇摆 *oscillate; vacillate* ◇ ～飞行 round-trip flight
【来回来去】back and forth; over and over again: ～地跑了好多趟 *run back and forth many times* / ～地说 *say sth. over and over again; repeat again and again*
【来回票】round-trip ticket; return ticket
【来件】communication or parcel received ◇ ～装配 assemble parts supplied by clients
【来劲】〈方〉❶ full of enthusiasm; in high spirits: 他越干越～儿。*The longer he worked at it, the more enthusiastic he became.* ❷ exhilarating; exciting; thrilling: 这样伟大的工程,可真～! *What a magnificent project! How thrilling!* ❸ jest with; annoy; offend: 你别跟我～。*I won't stand any nonsense from you.*
【来客】guest; visitor
【来历】origin; source; antecedents; background; past history: 查明～ *trace to the source; ascertain a person's antecedents*
【来历不明】(of things) of unknown origin; (of persons) of dubious background or of questionable antecedents
【来料加工】process materials supplied by customers; accept customers' materials for processing; customers' own materials made up (notice outside tailor's shop)
【来临】arrive; come; approach: 每当春天～,这里是一片绿油油的庄稼。*When spring comes, this place is an expanse of lush green crops.*
【来龙去脉】origin and development; the entire process: 请你把事情的～给我们讲一遍。*Please tell us the whole story from beginning to end.*
【来路】❶incoming road; approach: 六连挡住了敌人的～。*Company Six blocked the enemy's path of approach.* ❷ origin; antecedents: ～不正 *(of things) of questionable origin; (of persons) of* dubious background / ～不明的飞机 *unidentified aircraft*
【来年】the coming year; next year
【来去自由】have the freedom of entry and exit
【…来…去】(used with two identical or synonymous verbs) back and forth; over and over again: 飞来飞去 *fly back and forth* / 挑来挑去 *pick and choose* / 翻来覆去睡不着 *toss and turn in bed*
【来人】bearer; messenger: 收条请交～带回。*Please give the receipt to the bearer.*
【来日】the days to come; the future
【来日方长】there will be ample (or plenty of) time; there will be time for that
【来生】next life; afterlife
【来世】next life; afterlife
【来势】the force with which sth. breaks out; oncoming force: 这场雨～很猛。*The rainstorm broke with tremendous force.* / ～汹汹 *bear down menacingly*
【来苏】[药] lysol (a transliteration)
【来头】❶ connections; backing: 这个人～不小。*This guy has powerful backing.* ❷ the motive behind (sb.'s words, etc.); cause: 他这些话有～,是冲着我们说的。*He didn't say all that without cause; it was directed against us.*
【来往】❶ come and go: 街上～的人很多。*There are many people coming and going on the streets.* / ～的信件 *correspondence* ❷ dealings; contact; intercourse: 我跟他从来没有任何～。*I've never had any dealings with him.* ❸ have contact or dealings: 我跟他～过,但不很熟。*I've had dealings with him, but I don't know him very well.*
【来文】document received
【来信】❶ send a letter here: 到了那里就～。*Write to us as soon as you get there.* / 他好久没～了。*I haven't heard from him for a long time.* ❷ incoming letter; your letter: 十日～收到。*I have received your letter of the 10th.* / 人民～ *letters from the people*
【来样加工】process according to buyer's samples
【来意】one's purpose in coming: 说明～ *make clear what one has come for*
【来由】reason; cause: 没～ *without rhyme or reason* / 他讲了他学针灸的～。*He explained how he came to study acupuncture.*
【来源】❶ source; origin: 经济～ *source of income* / 税收～ *source of revenue* ❷ (followed by 于) originate; stem from: 知识～于实践。*Knowledge stems from practice (or experience).*
【来者不拒】refuse nobody; refuse nobody's request or offer
【来者不善,善者不来】❶ He who has come is surely strong or he'd never have come along. ❷ He who has come, comes with ill intent, certainly not on virtue bent.
【来着】(used at the end of affirmative sentences or special questions, indicating a past action or state): 你刚才说什么～? *What were you saying just now?* / 他去年冬天还回家～。*He was home only last winter.*
【来之不易】not easily come by; hard-earned: 我们的胜利～。*Our victory was hard-won.* / 每一粒粮食都～。*Every single grain is the result of toil.*
【来踪去迹】traces of sb.'s movements; traces of sb.'s whereabouts

莱

名 ❶ 同〖藜〗❷〈古〉fields lying fallow in rotation
【莱菔】radish ◇ ～子 [中] radish seed
【莱索托】Lesotho ◇ ～人 Mosotho (sing.); Basotho (pl.)

铼

名 [化] rhenium (Re)

lài

睐 动〈书〉❶ squint ❷ look at：青睐

赖 Ⅰ 动 ❶ rely；depend：～以生存的条件 *conditions on which persons or things rely (or depend) for existence* ❷ hang on in a place；drag out one's stay in a place；hold on to a place：～着不走 *hang on and refuse to clear out* ❸ deny one's error or responsibility；go back on one's word：～是～不掉的。*It's no good trying to deny it.* or *You simply can't deny it.* ❹ blame sb. wrongly；put the blame on sb. else：自己错了还～别人，这就不对了。*It's not right to blame others for one's own mistake.* ❺〈口〉blame：这事全～我。*I'm entirely to blame for that.* Ⅱ 形 ❶ rascally；shameless：赖皮 ❷〈口〉no good；poor：好的～的我都能吃。*I can eat anything, good or bad.*

【赖床】be feeling too lazy to get out of bed

【赖婚】repudiate a marriage contract

【赖皮】rascally；shameless；unreasonable：耍～ *act shamelessly*

【赖债】repudiate a debt

【赖账】❶ repudiate a debt ❷ go back on one's word

癞 名 ❶ leprosy ❷〈方〉favus of the scalp

【癞瓜】〈方〉another name for 苦瓜

【癞蛤蟆】toad

【癞蛤蟆想吃天鹅肉】a toad lusting after a swan's flesh—aspiring after sth. one is not worthy of

【癞皮狗】❶ mangy dog ❷ loathsome creature

【癞子】〈方〉❶ favus ❷ a person affected with favus of the scalp

籁 名 ❶ an ancient musical pipe ❷ sound；noise：万籁俱寂

lán

兰 名 ❶ 同〖兰花〗❷ 同〖兰草〗❸ (used in ancient texts) lily magnolia：～桨 *magnolia oars*

【兰草】fragrant thoroughwort (Eupatorium fortunei)

【兰花】cymbidium；orchid

【兰室】boudoir

岚 名〈文〉haze；vapour；mist：晓～ *morning mists*

拦 动 bar；block；hold back：别～着我，我一定得走。*Don't stop me；I must go.* / 他刚要说，我把他给～住了。*He was just about to speak when I stopped him.* / 一道河～住了我们的去路。*A river blocked our way.*

【拦挡】block；obstruct：～住敌人的去路 *block the enemy's way*

【拦道木】road fence；roadblock

【拦河坝】a dam across a river；dam

【拦洪坝】a dam for holding back floodwater；a dam for flood control

【拦击】❶ intercept and attack ❷［体］volley

【拦劫】waylay and rob；mug

【拦截】intercept：～增援的敌人 *intercept enemy reinforcements*

【拦路】block the way：～抢劫 *waylay；hold up*

【拦路虎】a road-blocking tiger—obstacle；hindrance：读科技书籍时，专门术语对我是个～。*In reading books on science and technology, I have trouble with technical terms.*

【拦网】［体］(排球) block

【拦蓄】retain (water)；impound：～洪水 *impound floodwater*

【拦腰】(hold) by the waist；(cut across) in the middle：～抱住 *seize sb. by the waist (or round the middle) from behind* / 大坝把河水～截断。*The dam cut the river in the middle.*

【拦鱼栅】fish screen

【拦阻】block；hold back；obstruct

栏 名 ❶ fence；railing；balustrade；hurdle：桥～ *the railing of a bridge* ❷ pen；shed：牛栏 ❸ column (of a page or of a table, or in a newspaper)：左～ *the left column* / 那条新闻占了两～。*That news takes up two columns.* / 体育～ *sports column* / 把这一～数字加起来。*Add up this column of figures.*

【栏杆】railing；banisters；balustrade：桥～ *the railing of a bridge*

【栏目】the heading or title of a column (in a magazine, etc.)

阑 Ⅰ 名 同〖栏〗❶ Ⅱ 动 同〖拦〗Ⅲ 形〈文〉(of time) late：岁～ *late in the year*

【阑珊】〈文〉coming to an end；waning：意兴～。*One's interest is flagging.*

【阑尾】［生理］appendix ◇ ～切除术 appendectomy；～炎 appendicitis

蓝 Ⅰ 形 blue Ⅱ 名 indigo plant

【蓝宝石】sapphire

【蓝本】❶ writing upon which later work is based；chief source ❷ original version (of a literary work)

【蓝筹股】［经］blue chip stocks；blue chips

【蓝靛】indigo

【蓝矾】［化］blue vitriol；cupric sulphate

【蓝晶石】［矿］kyanite；disthene

【蓝鲸】blue whale

【蓝领工人】blue-collar worker

【蓝皮书】blue book

【蓝铜矿】azurite；chessylite

【蓝图】blueprint：绘制～ *design a blueprint* / 新图书馆的～ *the blueprints of a new library* / 国家建设的～ *a blueprint for national reconstruction*

【蓝藻】blue green algae

谰 动〈书〉calumniate；slander

【谰言】calumny；slander：无耻～ *shameless slander*

澜 名 billows；waves：微～ *ripples*

褴（构词成分）见下

【褴褛】ragged；shabby

篮 名 ❶ basket ❷［体］（篮球）goal；basket：投篮

【篮板】［体］（篮球）backboard；bank

【篮板球】［体］（篮球）rebound：控制～ *control the rebounds* / 抓住～投篮入网 *grab the rebound and sink a basket*

【篮球】basketball：打～ *play basketball* / ～队 *basketball team* ◇ ～场 basketball court；～架 basketball stands

【篮圈】［体］（篮球）ring；hoop

【篮子】basket

镧［化］lanthanum（La）

lǎn

览 动 ❶ look at；see；view：游览 ❷ read：阅览

【览古】〈书〉visit historic sites：洛阳～ *a tour of the historic sites in Luoyang*

【览胜】〈书〉visit scenic spots

揽 动 ❶ pull sb. into one's arms；take into one's arms：母亲把孩子～在怀里。*The mother clasped the child to her bosom.* ❷ fasten with a rope，etc.：用绳子～上 *tie a rope around sth.* ❸ take on；take upon oneself；canvass：他把责任都～到自己身上。*He took all the responsibility on himself.* / ～买卖 *canvass business orders* ❹ grasp；monopolize：～权 *arrogate power to oneself*

【揽承】agree（or contract）to do a job

【揽活】take on work

缆 Ⅰ 名 ❶ hawser；mooring rope；cable：解～ *cast off*；*set sail* / 新船砍～下水。*The new ship cut her cable and slipped into the water.* ❷ thick rope；cable：电缆 Ⅱ 动 fasten（a boat）with a rope or cable：～舟 *moor a boat*

【缆车】cable car ◇ ～铁道 cable railway

【缆道】cableway

【缆索】thick rope；cable ◇ ～铁道 funicular railway；funicular

罱 Ⅰ 名 a kind of net used for fishing or for dredging up river sludge，etc. Ⅱ 动 dredge up：～河泥 *dredge up sludge from a river*

【罱泥船】a boat used in collecting river sludge for fertilizer

懒 形 ❶ lazy；indolent；slothful：你未免太～点儿了吧。*Aren't you being a bit too lazy?* / 你越不做事越～。*The less you do the lazier you get.* ❷ sluggish；languid：发懒

【懒虫】〈口〉lazybones

【懒怠】❶ lazy；indolent ❷ too lazy to：我这两天身体不太好，话也～说了。*I haven't felt too well for the last couple of days，and I don't have the energy to talk.*

【懒得】not feel like（doing sth.）；not be in the mood to；be disinclined to：天太热，我～出去。*It's too hot. I don't feel like going out.*

【懒惰】lazy

【懒骨头】〈口〉lazybones

【懒汉】sluggard；idler；lazybones

【懒散】sluggish；negligent；indolent：不要这样～，振作起来。*Don't be so sluggish. Pull yourself together.*

【懒洋洋】languid；listless：每到炎热的夏天，我就有点～的。*I always feel rather listless on hot summer days.*

【懒腰】见〖伸懒腰〗

làn

烂 Ⅰ 形 ❶ soft；mashed；pappy：牛肉烧得很～。*The beef is very tender.* or *The beef melts in your mouth.* / 豆子煮～了。*The beans are now soft enough to eat.* ❷ worn-out：衣服穿～了。*The clothes are worn-out.* / ～纸片 *scraps of paper* ❸ messy：烂账 Ⅱ 动 rot；fester：阴雨天要防止～秧。*In wet weather we must prevent the seedlings from rotting.* / 苹果都～了。*The apples are all rotten.* / 伤口～了。*The wound is festering.*

【烂糊】（of food）mashed；pulpy：老年人爱吃～面。*Old people like noodles cooked to a pulp.*

【烂漫】❶ bright-coloured；brilliant：山花～ *bright mountain flowers in full bloom* ❷ unaffected；natural

【烂泥】mud；slush：汽车陷在～里了。*The car is stuck in the mud.* / ～塘 *a muddy pond*

【烂熟】❶ thoroughly cooked ❷ know sth. thoroughly：台词背得～ *learn one's lines thoroughly*

【烂摊子】a shambles；an awful mess：新任首相得忙于收拾前任首相留下来的～。*The new prime minister will have a hard time clearing up the mess left by his predecessor.*

【烂账】❶ messy accounts：真是一本～。*The accounts are all in a mess.* ❷ uncollectable debts

【烂醉】dead drunk：喝得～ *be dead drunk* / ～如泥 *be dead drunk*；*be as drunk as a lord*

滥 Ⅰ 动 overflow；flood Ⅱ 副 excessive；indiscriminate：～施轰炸 *indiscriminate bombing*；*wanton bombing* / ～发钞票 *issue banknotes recklessly*；*inflate the paper currency* / ～发奖金 *distribute bonuses indiscriminately*

【滥调】hackneyed tune；worn-out theme

【滥伐】severe deforestation；denudation

【滥交】choose friends indiscriminately

【滥用】abuse；misuse；use indiscriminately：～经费 *squander funds* / 不要～成语典故。*We should not use proverbs and allusions indiscriminately*.

【滥用职权】abuse one's power；abuse one's authority or position

【滥竽充数】pass oneself off as one of the players in an ensemble—be there just to make up the number（used of incompetent people or inferior goods）

láng

郎 名 ❶ an official title in imperial times ❷（used in forming nouns designating certain classes of persons）：放牛～ *cowherd* ❸（used by a woman in addressing her husband or lover）my darling ——另见 làng

【郎才女貌】a brilliant young scholar and a beautiful woman—a fine couple

【郎舅】a man and his wife's brother：他们俩是～。*Those two are brothers-in-law*.

【郎君】〈旧〉（used in addressing one's husband）you

【郎中】〈方〉a physician trained in herbal medicine；doctor：江湖～ *quack doctor*；*mountebank*

狼 名 wolf

【狼狈】in a difficult position；in a tight corner：～逃窜 flee in panic；flee helter-skelter / 陷于～境地 *find oneself in a fix*；*be caught in a dilemma*（*or quandary*）/ 显出一副～相 *cut a sorry figure*

【狼狈不堪】in an extremely awkward position；in a sorry plight；in sore straits

【狼狈为奸】act in collusion（or cahoots）with each other

【狼奔豕突】run like wolves and rush like boars—tear about like wild beasts

【狼疮】［医］lupus

【狼狗】wolfhound

【狼毫】a writing brush made of weasel's hair

【狼嚎】the howl of a wolf

【狼獾】glutton

【狼藉】（又作'狼籍'）〈书〉in disorder；scattered about in a mess

【狼吞虎咽】wolf down；gobble up：他端起碗来，～地吃着，觉得又香又甜。*He took the mess and wolfed it down*，*finding it sweet and good*.

【狼心狗肺】rapacious as a wolf and savage as a cur；cruel and unscrupulous；brutal and cold-blooded；heartless and ungrateful

【狼烟四起】smoke signals rising on all sides—war alarms raised everywhere

【狼子野心】a wolf cub with a savage heart—have a wolfish nature；be full of wild ambitions

廊 名 porch；corridor；veranda：走廊

【廊檐】the eaves of a veranda

【廊子】porch；corridor；veranda

琅（构词成分）见下

【琅琅】a tinkling or jingling sound；the sound of reading aloud

榔（构词成分）见下

【榔头】hammer

锒（构词成分）见下

【锒铛】❶〈书〉iron chains ❷ a clanking or clanging sound：铁索～ *iron chains clanking*

【锒铛入狱】be put in chains and thrown into prison

lǎng

朗 形 ❶ light；bright：晴朗 ❷ loud and clear：朗诵

【朗读】read aloud；read loudly and clearly

【朗朗】the sound of reading aloud：书声～ *reading aloud in a clear voice*

【朗姆酒】rum（a transliteration）

【朗诵】read aloud with expression；recite；declaim：～诗歌 *recite poems*

làng

郎 见〖屎壳郎〗——另见 láng

浪 Ⅰ 名 wave；billow；breaker：～很大。*The waves are very high*. / 白～滔天 *white breakers leaping skywards* Ⅱ 形 unrestrained；dissolute：放浪

【浪潮】〈喻〉tide；wave：革命的～ *the tide of revolution* / 罢工～ *a wave of strikes*

【浪船】swingboat

【浪荡】❶ loiter about；loaf about ❷ dissolute；dissipated

【浪费】waste；squander；be extravagant：～时间 *waste time*；*fritter away one's time* / ～人力物力 *waste manpower and material resources* / 反对～，提倡节约 *combat waste and encourage economy*

【浪花】❶ the foam of breaking waves：～四溅 *the waves breaking and foaming* ❷ episodes in one's life：生活的～ *life's little episodes*

【浪迹】wander about；roam about：～江湖 *wander from place to place* / ～天涯 *rove all over the world*

【浪漫】❶ romantic：《梁山伯与祝英台》是个很～的爱情故事。*Liang Shanbo and Zhu Yingtai is a very romantic love story*. ❷ unconventional；bohemian；loose：她的生活很～。*She leads a loose life*.

【浪漫史】romance：他们俩的～在中学时代就开始了。*Their romance began in middle school*.

【浪漫主义】romanticism：～作家（诗人）*a roman-*

tic writer (*poet*) / ～诗歌 *romantic poetry* ◇ ～运动 the Romantic Movement (in western Europe in the early 19th century)

【浪人】❶ wanderer; vagrant ❷ ronin (in Japan)

【浪头】〈口〉❶ wave: 风大,～高。*The wind is strong and the waves are high*. ❷ trend

【浪涌】[电] surge: ～放电器 *surge arrester*

【浪子】prodigal; loafer; wastrel

【浪子回头】return of the prodigal son: ～金不换。*A prodigal who returns is more precious than gold*.

lāo

捞 动 ❶ scoop up from a liquid; dredge up; fish for; drag for: ～鱼 *fish with a net*; *net fish* / 在河里～水草 *dredge up water plants from the river* ❷ get by improper means: ～外快 *make extra money* / 他～了一大笔钱。*He made a killing*. / 他们能从这里～到什么好处呢? *What good can they get out of this*?

【捞本】win back lost wagers; recover one's losses; recoup oneself

【捞稻草】(try to) take advantage of sth.; (try to) make capital of sth.: 休想在这件事上～。*Don't imagine you can get anything out of it*.

【捞饭】rice boiled, strained and then steamed

【捞钱】make money (by quick or improper means)

【捞取】❶ scoop up from a liquid ❷ fish for; gain: ～政治资本 *fish for political capital*; *seek political advantage*

【捞外块】get extra income

【捞一把】〈贬〉reap some profit; gain some advantage

【捞油水】〈贬〉make a side profit; get a squeeze

【捞着】get the opportunity (of doing sth.): 那天的电影,我没～看。*I missed the film the other day*.

【捞资本】make political and economic "capital": 文化大革命中,他可捞足了资本。*He made plenty of political capital during the Cultural Revolution*.

láo

牢 Ⅰ 名 prison; jail: 坐牢 Ⅱ 形 firm; fast; durable: 绳子没系～。*The rope hasn't been tied fast*.

【牢不可破】unbreakable; indestructible: ～的友谊 *unbreakable friendship*

【牢房】prison cell

【牢固】firm; secure: 地基很～。*The foundations are very firm*.

【牢记】keep firmly in mind; remember well: 老师的教导我～在心。*I always bear in mind my teacher's instructions*.

【牢靠】❶ firm; strong; sturdy: 这堵墙不太～。*This wall is not very strong*. ❷ dependable; reliable: 办事～ *dependable* (*or reliable*) *in handling matters*

【牢牢】firmly; safely: 这一点你必须～记住。*You must keep this firmly in mind*.

【牢笼】❶ cage (〈喻〉); bonds: 冲破旧思想的～ *shake off the bonds of old ideas* ❷ trap; snare: 陷入～ *fall into a trap*; *be entrapped* ❸ entrap; ensnare ❹ confine; restrain: 为旧思想所～ *be shackled by old ideas*

【牢骚】❶ complaint; grumble: 他老发～。*He's always grumbling*. ❷ complain; grumble: 他～了半天。*He grumbled for a long time*.

【牢头】〈旧〉jailer

【牢稳】(of objects) stable; secure; firm: 梯子靠这儿比较～。*The ladder will be more secure here*.

【牢狱】prison; jail

劳 Ⅰ 动 ❶ work; labour: 操劳 ❷〈套〉(used in asking a favour of sb.) put sb. to the trouble of: ～你帮个忙。*Will you please do me a favour* (*or give me a hand*)? ❸ express one's appreciation (to the performer of a task); reward: 犒劳 Ⅱ 名 ❶ fatigue; toil: 积劳成疾 ❷ meritorious deed; service: 汗马之～ *distinctions won in battle*; *war exploits*

【劳保】❶ labour insurance: 吃～ *live on labour insurance allowances* ❷ labour safety: ～设施 *labour safety devices*

【劳动】❶ work; labour: ～创造世界。*Labour creates the world*. / 大家的～热情很高。*Everyone worked with great enthusiasm*. ❷ physical labour; manual labour: ～锻炼 *temper oneself through manual labour* ◇ ～保护 labour safety; ～保险 labour insurance; ～布 denim; ～定额 work norm; production quota; ～对象 subject of labour; ～法 labour law; ～服务公司 labor service company; manpower contractor; ～改造 reform (of criminals) through labour; ～观点 labour viewpoint (i.e. to view labour, esp. manual labour, with respect); attitude towards labour; ～号子 work song ; ～合同制 labour contract system ; ～教养 reeducation (of juvenile delinquents, etc.) through labour; ～节 Labour Day (May 1); ～竞赛 labour emulation; emulation drive; emulation campaign; ～立法 labour legislation; ～模范 model worker; ～强度 labour intensity; ～权 the right to work; ～人民 labouring people; working people; ～日 workday; working day; ～生产率 labour productivity; productivity; ～手段 means (or instruments) of labour; ～英雄 labour hero; ～者 labourer; worker; ～仲裁制度 labour arbitration system; ～资料 means (or instruments) of labour

【劳动力】❶ labour (or work) force; labour: ～调配 *allocation of the labour force* / ～不足 *short of manpower*; *shorthanded* ❷ capacity for physical labour: 丧失～ *lose one's ability to work*; *be rendered unfit for physical labour*; *be incapacita-*

ted；*be disabled* ❸ able-bodied person ◇ ～流动状况 degree of mobility within the labour force

【劳动密集型】labour-intensive：～产品 *labour-intensive products*

【劳顿】〈书〉fatigued；wearied：旅途～ *fatigued by a journey*；*travel-worn*

【劳而无功】work hard but to no avail；work fruitlessly

【劳方】labour（as opposed to capital or management）：～与资方 *labour and capital*

【劳改】(〈略〉见〖劳动改造〗) ◇ ～队 a group sentenced to reform through labour；～犯 a prisoner serving a sentence of reform through labour；～农场 reform-through-labour farm

【劳工】〈旧〉labourer；worker：～运动 *labour movement*

【劳驾】〈套〉excuse me；may I trouble you...；would you please...：劳您驾，替我写封信吧！*Would you be kind enough to write a letter for me?* / ～，挪挪窝儿行吗？*Excuse me, would you move over a bit?* / ～，请让让路。*Excuse me.*

【劳教人员】a person subjected to reeducation in a reform school

【劳苦】toil；hard work：不辞～ *spare no pains* / ～大众 *toiling masses*；*labouring people*

【劳苦功高】have worked hard and performed a valuable service

【劳累】tired；run-down；overworked

【劳力】❶ labour；labour force：～可能紧张一些，但我们一定努力完成任务。*We may be a little short of labour, but we'll do our best to fulfil the task.* / 合理安排～ *rational allocation of labour* ❷ labour with one's strength；work with one's brawn

【劳碌】work hard；toil：母亲操持家务，～一生。*My mother worked hard as a housewife all her life.*

【劳民伤财】exhaust the people and drain the treasury；waste money and manpower

【劳模】〈略〉见〖劳动模范〗

【劳师】〈书〉take greetings and gifts to army units

【劳师动众】mobilize too many troops —drag in lots of people（to do sth.）

【劳师远征】tire the troops on a long expedition

【劳什子】〈方〉nuisance

【劳损】[医] strain：肌腱～ *muscular strain*

【劳务】labour services：～输出 *export of labour services* / ～费 *service charge* / ～人员 *contract workers*（*sent abroad*）/ ～合作 *labour cooperation* ◇ ～市场 labour market；markets for labour service

【劳心】work with one's mind or brains

【劳心者治人，劳力者治于人】Those who work with their brains rule and those who work with their brawn are ruled.

【劳燕分飞】the shrike and the swallow flying in different directions—part from each other

【劳役】❶ penal servitude；forced labour ❷ corvée ◇ ～地租 rent paid in labour；labour rent

【劳逸】work and rest

【劳逸不均】uneven allocation of work

【劳逸结合】strike a proper balance between work and rest；alternate work with rest and recreation

【劳资】labour and capital：～关系 *relationship between labour and capital*；*labour-capital relationship* / ～两利 *be of benefit to both labour and capital* / ～纠纷 *labour trouble* / ～争议 *labour dispute* ◇ ～协议 labour agreement

唠（构词成分）见下

【唠叨】be garrulous；chatter：人老了，就爱～。*As one grows old, one tends to be garrulous.* / 唠唠叨叨说个不停 *chatter interminably*

痨 名 consumptive disease；tuberculosis；consumption：肺痨

【痨病】[中] tuberculosis；TB

铹 名 [化] lawrencium（Lw）

lǎo

老 Ⅰ 形 ❶ old（not young）：～妇人 *an old woman* / ～马 *an old horse* / ～树 *an old tree* / 他父亲很～了。*His father is very old.* ❷ experienced；veteran：～作家 *a veteran writer* ❸ old（not new）：～朋友 *an old friend* / ～部下 *a former subordinate* / ～厂 *an old factory* / ～机器 *an old machine* / ～地方 *the same old place* / ～习惯 *an old habit* ❹（of food）tough；overdone；well-done：牛肉太～。*The beef is too tough.* / 我喜欢吃～一点的牛排。*I like steak quite well-done.* Ⅱ 名 old people；a venerable old man：敬～ *show respect for the aged* Ⅲ 动（of vegetables）overgrown：菠菜不收就～了。*The spinach will be overgrown if we don't get it in now.* Ⅳ 副 ❶ for a long time：～没见你啊。*I haven't seen you for ages.* / 这屋子～不住人，有股霉味儿。*This room has been left vacant for a long time, so there is a mouldy smell.* ❷ always；all the time：他～跟我借钱。*He's always borrowing money from me.* / 他～那么干。*He does it all the time.* ❸ very：～早 *very early* / ～远 *far away* / ～长的胡子 *a very long beard* / 太阳已经～高了。*The sun is already high.* ❹（used as a prefix）（in terms of address before the surnames of acquaintances or friends to indicate intimacy or informality）：～王 *Lao Wang* ❺ in certain names of animals and plants：老虎 / 老玉米

【老百姓】〈口〉common people；ordinary people；civilians：这些活报剧～很欢迎。*These skits are popular with the man in the street.*

【老板】shopkeeper；proprietor；boss ◇ ～娘 shopkeeper's wife；proprietress

【老半天】〈口〉a long time：我等你～了。*I've been waiting for you for an awfully long time.*

【老伴儿】〈口〉（of an old married couple）husband or wife：我的～ *my old man or woman*

【老蚌生珠】an old oyster yielding a pearl—have a son born in one's old age
【老鸨】(又作'老鸨子') a woman running a brothel; procuress; madam
【老本】principal; capital: 把~输光 *lose one's last stakes* ——另见〖吃老本〗
【老兵】old soldier; army veteran
【老伯】uncle (used in addressing a friend of one's father or the father of one's friend)
【老财】〈方〉moneybags; landlord: 地主~ *landlord*
【老巢】nest; den; lair: 直捣土匪~ *swoop down on the bandits' den*
【老成】experienced; steady
【老成持重】experienced and prudent: 他~,不大随便发表意见。*He was experienced and reserved, and did not give his views on anything without due thought.*
【老处女】old maid; spinster
【老粗】(often used in self-deprecation) an uneducated person; a rough and ready chap
【老搭档】old partner; old workmate
【老大】❶ number one (in order of seniority, i.e. the eldest son, daughter, brother, or sister) ❷〈方〉the captain of a boat ❸ greatly; very: 心里~不高兴 *feel very annoyed*
【老大不小】have grown up and be no longer a child: 你也~的了,该懂点事了。*You are no longer a child and should show some sense.*
【老大哥】elder brother (a respectful form of address for a man older than oneself)
【老大姐】elder sister (a respectful form of address for a woman older than oneself)
【老大难】long-standing, big and difficult (problem): ~单位 *a unit with serious and long-standing problems* / ~的技术问题 *a knotty technical problem of long standing*
【老大娘】〈口〉(a polite form of address to an old woman, esp. a stranger) aunty; granny
【老大爷】〈口〉(a polite form of address to an old man, esp. a stranger) uncle; grandpa
【老当益壮】old but vigorous
【老道】〈口〉elderly Taoist priest
【老底】sb.'s past; sb.'s unsavoury background: 揭~ *dredge up some embarrassing facts about sb.'s past; drag the skeleton out of sb.'s closet*
【老弟】(a familiar form of address to a man much younger than oneself) young man; young fellow; my boy
【老调】hackneyed theme; platitude
【老调重弹】harp on the same string; play the same old tune
【老掉牙】very old; out of date; obsolete; antediluvian: 这部机器已经~了。*This machine is completely obsolete.*
【老而弥笃】the older one gets, the deeper one's love
【老干部】veteran cadre
【老公】〈方〉husband
【老公公】〈方〉❶ grandpa (used by children in addressing an old man) ❷ husband's father; father-in-law
【老古董】old fogey; fuddy-duddy
【老光】presbyopic: ~眼 *presbyopia* / ~眼镜 *presbyopic glasses*
【老规矩】old rules and regulations; convention; established custom or practice: 时代变了,那一套~不行了。*Times have changed, and the old way of doing things is no good any more.* / 照~办事 *do things in the same old way*
【老汉】❶ old man ❷ I (used by an old man)
【老好人】〈口〉Mr. Goody-goody (a benign and uncontentious person who is indifferent to matters of principle; one who tries never to offend anybody)
【老狐狸】old fox; crafty scoundrel
【老虎】tiger
【老虎凳】rack (an instrument of torture)
【老虎屁股摸不得】like a tiger whose backside no one dares to touch—not to be provoked
【老虎钳】❶ vise ❷ pincer pliers
【老虎头上蹭痒】scratch oneself against a tiger's head—court disaster
【老花】presbyopic ◇ ~镜 presbyopic glasses; ~眼 presbyopia
【老化】❶ [化] ageing ❷ (of cadres) become old: 干部~问题 *the problem of cadres becoming old and losing efficiency* ❸ (of knowledge, etc.) become outdated
【老话】❶ old saying; saying; adage: 中国有句~:世上无难事,只怕有心人。*There is an old Chinese saying: nothing in the world is difficult for one who sets his mind on it.* ❷ remarks about the old days: 咱们谈的这些~,年轻人都不大明白了。*What we are saying about the old days is incomprehensible to young people.*
【老皇历】last year's calendar—ancient history; obsolete practice
【老黄牛】willing ox—a person who is diligent and conscientious in serving the people
【老几】❶ order of seniority among brothers or sisters: 你是~? *Where do you come in the family?* or *Are you the oldest, the second or what?* ❷ (used in rhetorical questions to express disparagement): 你算~? *Who do you think you are?* / 我算~? *Who am I?* or *I'm a nobody.*
【老骥伏枥,志在千里】an old steed in the stable still aspires to gallop a thousand li—an old hero still cherishes high aspirations
【老家】native place; old home: 我~在山东。*My old home is in Shandong.* ——另见〖回老家〗
【老奸巨滑】a past master of machination and manoeuvre; a crafty old scoundrel; a wily old fox; an old hand at trickery and deception
【老茧】(又作'老趼') callosity; callus
【老江湖】〈旧〉a well-travelled, worldly-wise person; a person who has seen much of the world
【老将】veteran; old-timer

【老将出马，一个顶俩】When a veteran goes into action, he can do the job of two.
【老交情】long-standing friendship; an old friend
【老街坊】〈口〉old neighbour
【老辣】shrewd and ruthless
【老来俏】〈口〉an elderly woman who tries to make herself attractive
【老老实实】honestly; conscientiously; in earnest: 我们应该是～地办事；在世界上要办成几件事，没有老实态度是根本不行的。*We should do things honestly, for without an honest attitude it is absolutely impossible to accomplish anything in this world.*
【老泪纵横】(of an old person) be in tears
【老脸皮】a thick-skinned person
【老练】seasoned; experienced: 他比起过去来已经～得多了。*He's much more experienced and capable now than before.* / 她办事很～。*She is experienced and works with a sure hand.*
【老路】old road; beaten track: 咱们还是走那条～回家吧。*Let's go home the usual way.* / 走～ *follow the beaten track; slip back into the old rut*
【老妈子】(又作'老妈儿')〈旧〉amah; maidservant
【老马识途】an old horse knows the way; an old hand is a good guide
【老迈】aged; senile
【老毛病】〈口〉old trouble; old weakness: 我有个～，一到冬天就咳。*My cough is an old trouble. I get it every winter.* / 粗心大意是他的～。*Carelessness is an old weakness of his.*
【老谋深算】circumspect and far-seeing; experienced and astute
【老奶奶】❶ paternal great grandmother ❷ old granny (used by children in addressing an old woman)
【老脑筋】old (or outmoded) way of thinking: 你这～也该换换了。*It's high time you got rid of your old way of thinking.*
【老年】old age ◇ ～人 old people; the old; the aged; ～学 gerontology; ～医学 geriatrics
【老娘】❶〈旧〉mother ❷ I, your old mother (used by a harridan to refer to herself)
【老牛破车】an old ox pulling a rickety cart —making slow progress
【老牛舐犊】an old cow licking her calf—a parent doting on his or her child
【老农】old farmer; experienced peasant
【老牌】old brand: ～帝国主义 *old-line imperialism* / ～特务 *an old hand at espionage*
【老婆婆】〈方〉❶ granny (used by children in addressing an old woman) ❷ husband's mother; mother-in-law
【老婆】〈口〉wife
【老气】❶ mature and steady: 他年纪虽小却很～。*He's old for his years.* ❷ (of clothes) dark and old-fashioned
【老气横秋】❶ arrogant on account of one's seniority ❷ lacking in youthful vigour
【老前辈】one's senior; one's elder: 革命～ *a veteran of the revolution*
【老人】❶ old man or woman; the aged; the old ❷ one's aged parents or grandparents ◇ ～斑(又作'老年斑') senile plaque
【老人星】Canopus
【老人政治】gerontocracy
【老人家】〈口〉❶ a respectful form of address to an old person: 您～今年多大年纪了？*How old are you, granddad (or grandma)?* ❷ parent: ～都好吗？*How are your parents?*
【老弱】❶ the old and the young ❷ the old and the weak
【老弱病残】the old, weak, sick and disabled
【老弱残兵】old, weak and wounded troops; those who on account of old age, illness, etc. are no longer active or efficient
【老三届】senior high school graduates of the classes of 1966, 1967 and 1968
【老少】old and young: 这种杂志～咸宜。*This magazine suits the taste of both old and young.*
【老生常谈】commonplace; platitude; truism
【老师】teacher (sometimes used as a form of address)
【老师傅】master craftsman; experienced worker
【老实】❶ honest; frank: ～说，我很不赞成这个意见。*To be frank, I don't like the idea at all.* / ～回答我的问题。*Give me a straight answer.* / ～交待 *come clean; own up; make a clean breast of* ❷ well-behaved; good: 放～点！*Behave yourself!* or *None of your tricks!* / 这孩子可～了。*The child is as good as gold.* ❸〈婉〉simple-minded; naive; easily taken in
【老实巴交】〈方〉soft-spoken and timid
【老式】old style: ～家具 *old-fashioned furniture*
【老是】always; all the time: 他～犯错误。*He is always making mistakes.*
【老视眼】presbyopia
【老手】old hand; old stager; veteran: 干这一行他是～。*He is an old hand at the trade.* / 谈判～ *veteran negotiator*
【老鼠】mouse; rat
【老鼠过街，人人喊打】a rat running across the street, with everybody shouting, "Kill it!" (said of a person or thing hated by everyone)
【老死不相往来】grow old and die without having had any dealings with each other—never be in contact with each other
【老太太】❶ old lady; (in direct address) Venerable Madam ❷ (a polite term) your mother; his mother; my mother or grandmother
【老太爷】❶ elderly gentleman; (in direct address) Venerable Sir ❷ (a polite term) your father; his father; my father or grandfather
【老态龙钟】senile; doddering
【老天爷】(used in exclamations) God; Heavens: 我的～！*My goodness!* or *Good Heavens!* or *Good Gracious!*
【老头子】❶ old fogey; old codger ❷ my old man
【老外】〈口〉❶ layman ❷ foreigner

【老顽固】old stick-in-the-mud; old diehard; old fogey
【老王卖瓜,自卖自夸】Lao Wang selling melons praises his own goods—praise one's own work or wares
【老翁】〈书〉old man; greybeard
【老挝】Laos ◇ ～人 Laotian; ～语 Laotian (language)
【老乡】❶ fellow-townsman; fellow-villager ❷ a friendly form of address to a man in the countryside
【老小】grown-ups and children; one's family: 全村～ *the whole village, old and young* / 一家～ *the whole family*
【老兄】(a familiar form of address between male friends) brother; man; old chap
【老羞成怒】fly into a rage out of shame; be shamed into anger
【老朽】❶ decrepit and behind the times: 昏庸～ *old and stupid* / ～无能 *old and useless* ❷〈谦〉〈旧〉I (used by an old man)
【老学究】old pedant
【老眼光】old ways of looking at things; old views: 不能以～看新事物。*One mustn't judge new things by old standards.*
【老眼昏花】dim-sighted from old age
【老爷爷】❶ great grandfather ❷ grandpa (used by children in addressing an old man)
【老爷】❶ master; bureaucrat; lord: 做官当～ *act as lords and masters* / 采取～式的态度 *adopt a bureaucratic attitude* ❷〈旧〉a respectful address to a master by a servant ◇ ～兵 pampered soldier
【老一辈】older generation
【老一套】the same old stuff; the same old story: 他们的所谓新建议无非是～。*Their so-called new proposal is nothing but the same old stuff.* / 改变～的做法 *change outmoded methods*
【老鹰】black-eared kite; hawk; eagle
【老油条】同〚老油子〛
【老油子】wily old bird; old campaigner
【老于世故】versed in the ways of the world; worldly-wise
【老玉米】〈口〉❶ maize; Indian corn; corn ❷ (esp. boiled) ear of maize (or corn)
【老丈人】father-in-law
【老账】old debts; long-standing debts: ～未清,又欠新账。*While old debts are still unpaid, new ones are incurred.* ——另见〚翻老账〛
【老着脸皮】unabashedly; unblushingly
【老主顾】old customer; old client
【老资格】old-timer; veteran: ～的外交家 *a veteran diplomat* / 摆～ *flaunt one's seniority; put on the airs of a veteran*
【老子】〈口〉❶ father: ～英雄儿好汉 *the father a hero, the son a brave man; like father, like son* ❷ I, your father (said in anger or in fun): ～不吃你这一套! *I'll have none of your nonsense!*
【老子天下第一】think oneself the most important person in the world
【老字号】an old name in business —an old firm or shop
【老祖宗】ancestor; forefather

佬 名〈贬〉man; guy; fellow: 乡巴佬儿

姥 (构词成分)见下
【姥姥】❶〈方〉(maternal) grandmother; grandma ❷〈方〉midwife
【姥爷】〈方〉(maternal) grandfather; grandpa

铑 [化] rhodium (Rh)

lào

涝 动 (of land or crops): 庄稼～了。*The crops were waterlogged.*
【涝洼地】waterlogged lowland
【涝灾】damage or crop failure caused by waterlogging

烙 动 ❶ brand; iron: 给马～上印记 *brand a horse* / ～衣服 *iron clothes* ❷ bake in a pan: ～两张饼 *bake a couple of cakes*
【烙饼】a kind of pancake
【烙铁】❶ flatiron; iron ❷ soldering iron
【烙印】❶ brand (on cattle; usu.〈喻〉): 他的作品都有鲜明的时代～。*His works all bear a marked brand of the times.* ❷ brand (cattle; usu.〈喻〉): 这个教训已经～在我的心头,永远不会忘记。*This lesson is branded on my mind for ever.*

落 动 同〚落(luò) Ⅰ ❶❷❻❼❽〛, confined to use in the following ——另见 là; luò
【落价】fall (or drop) in price; go down in price
【落炕】〈方〉stay in bed with illness; be laid up
【落色】discolour; fade
【落枕】have a stiff neck (caused by cold or an awkward sleeping posture)

酪 名 ❶ junket ❷ thick fruit juice; fruit jelly: 红果～ *haw jelly* ❸ sweet paste made from crushed nuts; sweet nut paste: 核桃～ *walnut cream*
【酪氨酸】[化] tyrosine
【酪素】[化] casein: ～胶 *casein glue*
【酪酸】〈口〉butyric acid

lè

乐 Ⅰ 形 happy; cheerful; joyful: 我心里～开了花。*My heart swelled with happiness (or was filled with joy).* Ⅱ 动 ❶ be glad to; find pleasure in; enjoy: 幸灾乐祸 ❷〈口〉laugh; be amused: 他说的笑话把大家逗～了。*His joke amused everyone.* / 你～什么呀? *What are you laughing at?* or *What's the joke?* ——另见 yuè
【乐不可支】overwhelmed with joy; overjoyed

【乐不思蜀】so happy as to forget home and duty
【乐此不疲】always enjoy it; never be bored with it: 20 年前他对编词典产生了兴趣,从此~。*He began to be interested in dictionary-making 20 years ago, and since then has worked at it gladly and never tired.*
【乐得】readily take the opportunity to; be only too glad to: 既然如此,我们~在这儿多待几天。*In that case, we'll be only too glad to spend a few more days here.*
【乐而不淫】joy without wantonness
【乐观】optimistic; hopeful; sanguine: ~的看法 *an optimistic view* / ~的报道 *a sanguine report* ◇ ~主义 optimism; ~主义者 optimist
【乐果】Rogor (an insecticide)
【乐呵呵】buoyant; happy and confident: 他成天~的。*He's always cheerful and confident.*
【乐极生悲】extreme joy begets sorrow: ~,否极泰来。*When joy reaches its height, it is sorrow's turn; when ill luck reaches its limit, good luck comes in.*
【乐趣】delight; pleasure; joy: 生活中的~ *joys of life* / 要在工作中找到~,得先把工作做好。*Joy in work comes from mastery of work.*
【乐善好施】be given to doing charitable work
【乐事】pleasure; delight: 以助人为~ *find pleasure in helping others*
【乐陶陶】〈文〉(usu. used in rhymes) cheerful; happy; joyful
【乐天】carefree; happy-go-lucky ◇ ~派 optimist; a happy-go-lucky person
【乐天知命】submit to the will of Heaven and be content with one's lot
【乐土】land of happiness; paradise
【乐意】❶ be willing to; be ready to: ~帮忙 *be willing to help* ❷ pleased; happy: 他听了这话有点不~。*He seemed somewhat displeased with that remark.*
【乐于】be happy to; take delight in: ~助人 *be ready to help others*
【乐园】paradise; playground; amusement park: 人间~ *earthly paradise; paradise on earth* / 儿童~ *children's playground; children's amusement park*
【乐滋滋】〈口〉contented; pleased: 他听了这话心里~的。*He was quite pleased to hear this.*
【乐子】〈方〉❶ fun; pleasure: 闲得没事干,出去找个~。*Since we have nothing better to do, let's go out and have some fun.* ❷ a laughable matter: 你丢脸,人家瞧~。*You make a fool of yourself and others laugh at you.*

勒 动 ❶ rein in: ~马 *rein in the horse* ❷ force; coerce: ~交 *force sb. to hand sth. over* ——另见 lēi

【勒逼】force; coerce: 债主~她父亲立即还债。*The usurer forced her father to pay back the debt at once.*
【勒克司】[物] lux; metre-candle
【勒令】compel (by legal authority); order: ~交出赃物 *order sb. to surrender stolen goods* / ~退学 *order a student to leave school*
【勒派】force sb. to pay levies or do corvée labour
【勒索】extort; blackmail: ~钱财 *extort money from sb.*

lēi

勒 动 tie or strap sth. tight: 带子太松了,再~一~。*The strap is too loose. Tighten it up a bit.* / 背包带太紧,~得慌。*The pack straps are too tight. They cut into the flesh.* / ~紧裤带 *tighten the belt* ——另见 lè

【勒脚】[建] plinth

léi

累 (构词成分)见下 ——另见 lěi; lèi

【累累】❶〈书〉haggard; gaunt: ~若丧家之狗 *wretched as a stray cur* ❷〈书〉clusters of; heaps of: 果实~ *fruit growing in close clusters; fruit hanging heavy on the trees* ——另见 lěilěi
【累赘】❶ burdensome; cumbersome ❷ wordy; verbose: 这个句子太~。*That's a clumsy, involved sentence.* ❸ encumbrance; burden; nuisance: 行李带得多了,是个~。*Too much luggage is a nuisance.*

雷 名 ❶ thunder: 打~了。*It's thundering.* ❷ mine: 布雷

【雷暴】[气] thunderstorm ◇ ~雨 thunderstorm rain
【雷池】a river in ancient China (now confined to use in 不敢越雷池一步)
【雷达】radar: ~兵 *radar operator; radarman* / ~测距 *radar ranging* / ~干扰 *radar jamming* / ~跟踪 *radar tracking*
【雷打不动】not to be shaken by thunder—(of an arrangement or plan) not to be altered under any circumstances
【雷电】thunder and lightning: ~交作 *lightning accompanied by peals of thunder* ◇ ~计 ceraunograph
【雷动】thunderous: 欢声(掌声)~ *thunderous cheers (applause)*
【雷公】Thunder God
【雷公打豆腐,拣软的欺】the God of Thunder strikes the bean curd—bullies pick on the soft and weak
【雷汞】[化] mercury fulminate
【雷管】detonator; detonating cap; blasting cap; primer: 电~ *electric detonator*
【雷击】be struck by lightning
【雷厉风行】with the power of a thunderbolt and the speed of lightning—(carry out orders, policies, etc.) vigorously and speedily; vigorously

and resolutely：～地开展反对贪污浪费的斗争 *launch a vigorous, resolute struggle against corruption and waste*
【雷米封】［药］rimifon
【雷鸣】❶ thunder：～电闪。*It's thundering and lightning.* ❷ thunderous：～般的掌声 *thunderous applause*
【雷鸟】white partridge
【雷声】thunderclap；thunder：～隆隆 *the rumble (or roll) of thunder*
【雷声大，雨点小】loud thunder but small raindrops—much said but little done；much talk, little action
【雷霆】❶ thunderclap；thunderbolt ❷ thunder-like power or rage；wrath
【雷霆万钧】as powerful as a thunderbolt：以～之力 *with the force of a thunderbolt*
【雷同】❶ echoing what others have said ❷ duplicate；identical
【雷雨】thunderstorm
【雷雨云】［气］thundercloud
【雷阵雨】thunder shower

镭 名［化］radium (Ra)
【镭疗】radium therapy
【镭射】laser
【镭射气】［化］radium emanation
【镭射影碟】laser videodisc

lěi

垒 Ⅰ 动 build by piling up bricks, stones, earth, etc.：～一道墙 *build a wall* / ～猪圈 *build a pigsty* Ⅱ 名 ❶ rampart ❷ baseball；softball base
【垒球】softball：～棒 *softball bat*

累 Ⅰ 动 ❶ pile up；accumulate：日积月累 ❷ involve Ⅱ 形 continuous；repeated；running：/ ～戒不改 *refuse to mend one's ways despite repeated warnings* ——另见 léi；lèi
【累次】time and again；repeatedly
【累牍连篇】同〖连篇累牍〗
【累犯】❶ recidivism ❷ recidivist
【累积】accumulate：头八个月完成的工程量～起来，已达到全年任务的百分之九十。*The work done in the first eight months amounts to ninety per cent of the year's quota.* ◇ ～股本 cumulative capital stock；～亏损 accumulated deficit；～盈余 accumulated surplus
【累及】implicate；involve；drag in：～无辜 *involve the innocent*
【累计】❶ add up：全年实现利润～为223,000元。*Profits for the whole year add up to 223,000 yuan.* ❷ accumulative total；grand total
【累进】progression：～率 *graduated rates* / ～税 *progressive tax；progressive taxation*
【累累】❶ again and again；many times ❷ innumerable；countless：罪行～ *have a long criminal record；have committed countless crimes* ——另见 léiléi
【累卵】a stack of eggs—liable to collapse any moment；precarious ——另见〖危如累卵〗
【累年】for years in succession；year after year：～丰收 *have bumper harvests year after year*
【累世】for many generations；generation after generation

磊（构词成分）见下
【磊落】open and upright：胸怀～ *openhearted and upright*

蕾 名 flower bud；bud
【蕾铃】cotton buds and bolls

lèi

肋 名 ❶ rib ❷ costal region：两～ *both sides of the chest* / 左（右）～ *left (right) side of the chest*
【肋骨】rib ◇ ～切除术 costectomy
【肋间肌】intercostal muscle
【肋膜】pleura ◇ ～炎 pleurisy
【肋木】［体］stall bars
【肋条】〈方〉❶ rib ❷ pork ribs；spareribs

泪 名 tear；teardrop：欲哭无～ *in tearless grief*
【泪痕】tear stains：满脸～ *a face bathed in tears* / ～斑斑 *tear-stained*
【泪花】tears in one's eyes：她眼里闪烁着喜悦的～。*Her eyes glistened with tears of joy.*
【泪如泉涌】tears welling up in one's eyes；tears gushing from one's eyes
【泪如雨下】tears falling like rain
【泪水】tear；teardrop
【泪汪汪】(eyes) brimming with tears
【泪腺】lachrymal gland ◇ ～炎 dacryoadenitis
【泪眼】tearful eyes：～模糊 *eyes blurred by tears*
【泪液】tear
【泪盈盈】brimming with tears；tearful：她两眼～的。*Her eyes were brimming with tears.*
【泪珠】teardrop

类 Ⅰ 名 kind；type；class；category：这是另一～问题。*This is a problem of another kind.* Ⅱ 动 resemble；be similar to：类似
【类比】analogy：作历史的～ *draw a historical analogy*
【类别】classification；category：土壤的～ *classification of soil* / 属于不同的～ *belong to different categories*
【类地行星】［天］terrestrial planet
【类毒素】［中］toxoid
【类风湿性关节炎】rheumatoid arthritis
【类木行星】［天］Jovian planet
【类人猿】anthropoid (ape)
【类似】similar (to)；analogous (to)：保证不再发生～事件 *guarantee against the occurrence of similar incidents* / 我见过很多～这样的例子。*I*

have seen many instances similar to this.

【类推】analogize；reason by analogy：照此～ *on the analogy of this* / 其余～ *reason out the rest by analogy*

【类星体】［天］quasi-stellar object

【类型】type；category ◇ ～学 typology；～语言学 typological linguistics；linguistic typology

累 Ⅰ形 tired；weary；fatigued：我～了，想去睡觉了。*I'm tired and I want to go to sleep*. / 不怕苦，不怕～ *fear neither hardship nor fatigue* Ⅱ动 ❶tire；wear out；strain：这个活儿真～人。*This work really makes you tired*. / 我怕出去那么一趟会把我～坏了。*I'm afraid that trip will tire me out too much*. ❷work hard；toil：你～了一天，该休息了。*You've been working hard all day. You need a rest*. ——另见 léi；lěi

【累死累活】tire oneself out with backbreaking toil；work oneself to death

擂 名 a platform for martial contests；arena：打擂

【擂台】a platform for martial contests；ring；arena：摆～ *give an open challenge*

léng

棱 名❶ arris；edge：桌子～儿 *edges of a table* / 见～见角 *angular* ❷ corrugation；ridge：搓板的～儿 *ridges of a washboard*

【棱角】❶ edges and corners ❷edge；pointedness：他是个有～的人。*He has a forceful personality*. / 不露～ *keep a low profile* / 不要把～磨掉。*Don't draw in your horns*.

【棱镜】［物］prism：～分光 *prismatic decomposition*

【棱线】［军］crest line

【棱柱体】［数］prism

【棱锥体】［数］pyramid

lěng

冷 Ⅰ形 ❶ cold：今天真～。*It's really cold today*. / ～天 *the cold season*；*cold days* / 你～不～？*Do you feel cold*？❷cold in manner；frosty：他待人很～。*He is very cold towards people*. / 他～～地说了声"好吧"。*He said coldly*，"*All right*"！❸ unfrequented；deserted；out-of-the-way：冷清 ❹receiving little attention；unwelcomed：冷货❺shot from hiding：冷枪 Ⅱ动〈方〉(of food) cool：太烫了，～一下再吃。*It's too hot. Let it cool off before you eat it*.

【冷拔】［机］cold-drawing

【冷板凳】cold bench—an indifferent post or a cold reception ——另见〖坐冷板凳〗

【冷冰冰】❶ cold in manner；frosty：～的脸色 *a cold expression*；*frosty looks* / ～的态度 *an icy manner* / 对人～的 *be cold towards people* ❷ (of objects) ice-cold；icy：她的手～的。*Her hands are icy*.

【冷不防】suddenly；unexpectedly；without warning：～，他打了我一下。*Suddenly*，*without warning*，*he gave me a blow*. / 打他一个～ *take him unawares*；*catch him off guard*

【冷布】(cotton) gauze

【冷菜】cold dish

【冷餐】buffet：～招待会 *buffet reception*

【冷藏】refrigeration；cold storage ◇ ～车 (on a railway train) refrigerator car (or van)；～库 cold storage；freezer；～汽车 cold storage truck；～室 refrigerating compartment (in a refrigerator)；～箱 refrigerator；fridge

【冷场】❶ awkward silence on the stage when an actor enters late or forgets his lines ❷ awkward silence at a meeting

【冷嘲热讽】with freezing irony and burning satire；with biting sarcasm：鲁迅用～的杂文形式与黑暗统治势力作战。*Lu Xun used burning satire and freezing irony*，*cast in the form of essays*，*to do battle against the rule of the forces of darkness*.

【冷处理】［机］cold treatment

【冷床】［农］cold bed；cold frame

【冷脆】［冶］cold short

【冷待】treat coldly；cold-shoulder；slight

【冷淡】❶ cheerless；desolate ❷ cold；indifferent：反应～ *a cold response* / 对倡议表示～ *show indifference towards a proposal* / ～的态度 *a frigid manner* ❸ treat coldly；cold-shoulder；slight：他强打着精神说话，怕～了朋友。*He forced himself to perk up and make conversation so that his friend wouldn't feel he'd been given the cold shoulder*.

【冷冻】freeze：～精液 *frozen semen* / ～厂 *cold storage plant* ◇ ～干燥 freeze-dry；～机 refrigerator；freezer；～剂 refrigerant；～疗法 syrotherapy；cold therapy；～食品 frozen food；～室 freezer compartment (in a refrigerator)；freezer；～手术 cryosurgery

【冷锻】［机］cold forging；cold hammering

【冷锋】(又作'冷锋面')［气］cold front

【冷敷】［医］cold compress

【冷宫】❶ cold palace—a place to which disfavoured queens and concubines were banished ❷ limbo ——另见〖打入冷宫〗

【冷光】［物］cold light

【冷汗】cold sweat：出～ *be in a cold sweat*；*break out in a cold sweat*

【冷焊】［机］cold welding

【冷货】goods not much in demand；dull goods

【冷加工】［机］cold working

【冷箭】an arrow shot from hiding；sniper's shot

【冷静】sober；calm：头脑～ *sober-minded*；*level-headed*；*cool-headed* / 保持～ *keep calm*

【冷觉】sensation of cold；sense of cold

【冷峻】grave and stern：面色～ *a grave and stern face*

【冷酷】unfeeling；callous；grim：～的人 *a callous*

person / ～的现实 *grim reality*

【冷酷无情】unfeeling; cold-blooded

【冷冷清清】cold and cheerless; desolate: 不要只靠少数人～地做工作。*Do not rely on a mere handful of people working in quiet isolation.* / 会议开得～。*The meeting was very dull.*

【冷落】❶ unfrequented; desolate: 狭窄～的胡同 *an unfrequented narrow alley* ❷ treat coldly; cold-shoulder; leave out in the cold: ～了客人 *leave a guest out in the cold*

【冷铆】〔机〕cold riveting

【冷门】❶ a profession, trade or branch of learning that receives little attention ❷ an unexpected winner; dark horse: 那次比赛出了个～。*The contest produced an unexpected winner.* ——另见〖爆冷门〗

【冷漠】cold and detached; unconcerned; indifferent: ～的态度 *an indifferent attitude* / 他对人向来～。*He is always unconcerned about others.*

【冷凝】〔物〕condensation ◇ ～点 condensation point; ～器 condenser; ～物 condensate

【冷暖】changes in temperature—daily life: 注意～ *be careful about changes of temperature; take care of oneself*

【冷暖自知】one knows whether it's cold or warm without being told—one knows best by personal experience

【冷盘】cold dish; hors d'oeuvres

【冷僻】❶ deserted; out-of-the-way ❷ rare; unfamiliar: ～的字眼 *rarely used words* / ～的典故 *unfamiliar allusions*

【冷启动】cold start

【冷气】air conditioning: 这个剧院有～设备。*The theatre is air-conditioned.* ◇ ～机 air conditioner; ～团 cold air mass

【冷枪】sniper's shot ——另见〖打冷枪〗

【冷清】cold and cheerless; desolate; lonely; deserted: ～的秋夜 *a cold and cheerless autumn night* / 这里很～。*It's very quiet here.* / 他一个人住着很～。*He's very lonely, living all by himself.*

【冷却】become or make cool ◇ ～导管 cooling duct; ～剂 coolant; cooler; ～塔 cooling tower

【冷热病】❶〈方〉malaria ❷ capricious changes in mood; sudden waxing and waning of enthusiasm: 他的～又犯了。*He's in one of his moods again.*

【冷若冰霜】(usu. of women) as cold as ice; have an icy (or chilly) manner

【冷色】cool colour

【冷杉】fir

【冷射】make a sudden shot for the goal

【冷食】cold drinks and snacks: ～部 *cold drink and snack counter*

【冷霜】cold cream

【冷水】❶ cold water: ～浴 *cold bath* ❷ unboiled water: 喝～容易得病。*If you drink unboiled water, you're likely to get sick.* ——另见〖泼冷水〗

【冷水浇头】splashing the head with cold water—a rude shock; a bitter disappointment

【冷丝丝】a bit chilly: 晚风吹来，身上～的。*The night wind was blowing, and I felt a bit chilly.*

【冷飕飕】(of wind) chilling; chilly: 北风～地迎面吹来。*The north wind blew cold in my face.*

【冷笑】sneer; laugh grimly; grin with dissatisfaction, helplessness, bitterness, etc.

【冷血动物】❶ cold-blooded animal; poikilothermal animal ❷ an unfeeling person; a coldhearted person

【冷言冷语】sarcastic comments; ironical remarks: ～敲打人 *irritate people with sarcastic remarks*

【冷眼】❶ (with) a cold eye; (with) cool detachment: 他坐在墙角里，～观察来客的言谈举止。*He sat in a corner, watching with a cold eye how the guests were conducting themselves.* ❷ cold shoulder: ～相待 *give sb. the cold shoulder*

【冷眼旁观】look on with a cold eye

【冷饮】cold drink

【冷遇】cold reception; cold shoulder: 遭到～ *be given the cold shoulder; be left out in the cold*

【冷轧】〔冶〕cold rolling: ～钢 *cold-rolled steel* / ～机 *cold-rolling mill*

【冷战】❶ cold war ❷〈口〉shiver: 打～ *shiver with cold*

【冷铸】〔冶〕chill casting

lèng

愣 Ⅰ 形 ❶ dumbfounded; stupefied; dazed: 他一问，大家都～了。*When he asked the question, everybody was dumbfounded.* / 听到这消息，他～住了。*He was struck dumb by the news.* ❷〈口〉rash; blunt; brusque: 他很～。*He has a very blunt manner.* / 他说话很～。*He speaks very bluntly.* Ⅱ 副〈口〉forcefully insist on sth. without proof or basis: 我告诉他不能去，可是他～去。*I told him he couldn't go, but he just went.* / 明知不对，他～那么说。*He knew it was wrong, but he still went ahead and said it.*

【愣干】〈口〉do things recklessly (or rashly); persist in going one's own way: 要遵守操作规程，不能～。*You've got to observe the working regulations. You can't do things any way you like.*

【愣劲儿】〈方〉dash; pep; vigour: 这些小伙子真有股子～。*These boys are really full of pep.*

【愣神儿】〈方〉stare blankly; be in a daze: 他站在一旁～，不知道想些什么。*He stood by staring blankly, lost in thought.*

【愣头愣脑】rash; impetuous; reckless

【愣头儿青】〈方〉rash (or brusque) fellow; hothead

【愣着】not moving; in a daze: 快干吧，别～。*Get to work quickly; don't just stand there.*

lī

哩 (构词成分) 见下

【哩哩啦啦】〈口〉scattered; sporadic: ～下了一天雨。*It rained on and off all day.* / 跟上队伍,不要～的。*Close up, don't straggle along.*
【哩哩罗罗】〈口〉verbose and unclear in speech; rambling and indistinct: 他～说了半天,没有一句要紧的话。*He gibbered away for a long time, but said nothing of importance.*

lí

厘 量 ❶ centi-: 厘米 / 厘升 ❷a unit of interest rate, equal to 0.1% monthly interest, or 1% annual interest: 月利率五～七 0.57% *monthly interest* / 年利率七～二 7.2% *annual interest* ❸ a very small amount; a fraction; the least
【厘米】centimetre (cm.) ◇ ～波[电] centimetre wave; ～克秒单位 centimetre-gram-second unit (CGS unit)
【厘升】centilitre (cl.)

离 动 ❶ leave; part from; be away from: 她～家已经三年了。*She's been away from home for three years.* ❷ from (in giving distances): 车站～这儿三里地。*The railway station is three li from here.* / ～国庆节只有十天了。*National Day is only ten days away.* ❸ without; independent of: 发展工业～不了钢铁。*Industry cannot develop without steel.* / 他～不了酒。*He can't stay away from the bottle.*
【离岸价格】[经] free on board (FOB)
【离瓣花类】[植] choripetalae
【离别】part (for a longish period); leave; bid farewell: 我～故乡已经两年了。*It's two years since I left my hometown.*
【离不开身】be fully occupied or be very much needed and unable to leave for a moment: 这孩子淘得要命,大人一会儿也～。*The child is too naughty to be left alone even for a little while.*
【离队】leave the ranks; leave one's post: 擅自～ *leave one's post without permission*
【离格儿】go beyond what is proper; be out of place
【离合】separation and reunion
【离合器】[机] clutch
【离婚】divorce: 他们～了。*They divorced (or divorced each other).* / 她跟他～了。*She divorced him.* / ～证明书 *divorce certificate* ◇ ～率 divorce rate
【离间】sow discord; drive a wedge between; set one party against another
【离解】[化] dissociation
【离经叛道】depart from the classics and rebel against orthodoxy
【离境】leave a country or place ◇ ～签证 exit visa
【离境许可证】exit permit
【离开】leave; depart from; deviate from: 他已经～北京了。*He has left Beijing.* / ～本题 *stray from the subject; digress* / 离不开手儿 *be too busy with the job on hand; have one's hands full*
【离谱】go beyond what is proper; be out of place: 你开的价太～了。*The price you ask is unreasonable.*
【离奇】strange; odd; fantastic; bizarre: ～的故事 *a strange story* / ～的谎言 *a fantastic lie* / 这事儿很～。*This is a very odd business.*
【离弃】abandon; desert; forsake
【离群索居】live in solitude; live all alone
【离任】leave one's post: ～回国 *leave one's post for home* / 即将～的大使 *the outgoing ambassador*
【离散】(of relatives) be dispersed; be scattered about; be separated from one another: 解放前～了的母女终于重新团聚了。*Mother and daughter who were separated from each other before liberation have at long last been reunited.* ◇ ～系数 coefficient of dispersion
【离题】digress from the subject; stray from the point: 发言不要～。*Please keep to the subject.*
【离退休老人】retirees
【离心】❶ be at odds with the community or the leadership ❷ centrifugal: ～倾向 *a centrifugal tendency* / ～作用 *centrifugal effects* ◇ ～泵 centrifugal pump; ～机 centrifugal machine; centrifuge
【离心离德】torn by dissension and discord
【离心力】[物] centrifugal force
【离休】(of veteran cadres) retire: ～干部 *retired veteran cadres*
【离异】〈书〉divorce
【离辙】〈口〉off the track—off the beam; off the point
【离职】❶ leave one's job temporarily: ～学习 *leave one's job and join a study group* ❷ leave office; resign
【离中趋势】statistics dispersion
【离子】[物] ion: 阴～ *anion* / 阳～ *cation* / 氩～ *argon ion* ◇ ～泵 ionic pump; ～束 ion beam; ～淌度 ionic mobility; ～雾 ion-atmosphere
【离子交换】[化] ion exchange

狸 名 racoon dog
【狸猫】leopard cat
【狸藻】[植] bladderwort (Utricularia vulgaris)

梨 名 pear
【梨膏】pear syrup (for the relief of coughs)
【梨园】〈旧〉the Pear Garden—the theatre ◇ ～子弟〈旧〉students of the Pear Garden —operatic actors
【梨子】pear

犁 Ⅰ 名 plough Ⅱ 动 work with a plough; plough: 地已经～了两遍。*The fields have been ploughed twice.*
【犁壁】同〖犁镜〗
【犁底层】[农] plough sole; plough pan
【犁铧】ploughshare; share

黎 名〈书〉multitude; host
【黎巴嫩】Lebanon ◇ ～人 Lebanese
【黎民】〈书〉the common people; the multitude
【黎明】dawn; daybreak
罹 动〈书〉suffer from; meet with: ～病 *suffer from a disease*; *fall ill* / ～祸 *suffer misfortune*
【罹难】〈书〉❶ die in a disaster or an accident ❷ be murdered
篱 名 hedge; fence: 树～ *hedge*; *hedgerow*
【篱笆】bamboo or twig fence: ～墙 *wattled wall*
藜 名 lamb's-quarters
【藜芦】black false hellebore

lǐ

礼 名 ❶ ceremony; rite: 婚礼 ❷ courtesy; etiquette; manners: 失礼 ❸ gift; present: 这份～很重。*This is a generous gift*.
【礼拜】❶ religious service: 做～ *go to church*; *be at church* ❷〈口〉week: 下～ *next week* ❸〈口〉day of the week: 今天～几? *What day is it today?* ❹〈口〉Sunday: 今儿个～。*Today is Sunday*.
【礼拜天】〈口〉Sunday
【礼宾司】the Department of Protocol; the Protocol Department: ～司长 *Director of the Protocol Department*; *Chief of Protocol*
【礼单】a list of presents
【礼多人不怪】Nobody will blame you for being too polite.
【礼服】ceremonial robe or dress; full dress; formal attire
【礼花】fireworks display: 每逢国庆节晚上都要放～。*We always have a fireworks display on the evening of National Day*.
【礼节】courtesy; etiquette; protocol; ceremony: ～性拜访 *a courtesy call* / 社交～ *social etiquette*
【礼金】a gift of money
【礼帽】hat that goes with formal dress: 大～ *top hat*
【礼貌】❶ courtesy; politeness; manners: 有～ *be courteous*; *be polite* / 没～ *have no manners*; *be impolite* ❷ courteous; polite: 我觉得这么早就走不大～。*I don't think it'd be polite for us to leave so soon*. / ～语言 *polite language*
【礼炮】salvo; (gun) salute: 鸣～21 响。*A 21-gun salute was fired*.
【礼品】gift; present ◇ ～部 gift and souvenir department or counter (in a shop); ～店 gift shop
【礼聘】invite sb. cordially; enlist the service of sb. with rich gifts
【礼轻人意重】the gift is trifling but the feeling is profound; it's nothing much, but it's the thought that counts
【礼让】give precedence to sb. out of courtesy or thoughtfulness; comity: 国际～ *the comity of nations* / 中速行驶,安全～。*Drive at moderate speed*; *yield right of way for safety's sake*.
【礼尚往来】❶ courtesy demands reciprocity ❷ deal with a man as he deals with you; pay a man back in his own coin; give as good as one gets
【礼堂】assembly hall; auditorium
【礼物】gift; present: 他送了一份很重的～。*He gave a generous present*. / 一定得送他们点儿～才好。*We must send them some sort of gift*.
【礼贤下士】(of a ruler or a high minister) treat worthy men with courtesy
【礼仪】ceremony and propriety: 中国向被称为～之邦。*China has long been known as the "land of ceremony and propriety"*.
【礼义廉耻】propriety, righteousness, honesty, and a sense of shame (formerly upheld as 四维 the "four social bonds")
【礼遇】courteous reception: 受到～ *be accorded a courteous reception*
李 名 plum
【李代桃僵】❶ substitute one thing for another; substitute oneself for another person ❷ sacrifice oneself for another person; bear the blame for another person's mistake
【李子】plum
里 Ⅰ 名 ❶ lining; inside (of clothing): 衣服～儿 *the lining of a garment* / 这面是～儿,那面是面儿。*This is the inside, that is the outside*. ❷ inner ❸ neighbourhood: 邻里 ❹ native place: 故里 Ⅱ 量 currently called 市里, a traditional unit of length Ⅲ 介 in; inside: 往～走 *go inside* / 手～ *in one's hands* / 皮箱～ *in (or inside) the suitcase* Ⅳ 副 used after 这,那,哪 etc. to indicate a place: 这～ *here* / 那～ *there* / 县～发的通知 *a circular issued by the county authorities* / 家～没人。*There is no one at home*.
【里边】inside; in; within: 他们都在～。*They are all inside*. / 这～有问题。*There is something wrong here*. or *Something is wrong here*. / ～请! *Come on in, please!*
【里程】❶ mileage ❷ course of development; course: 革命的～ *the course of the revolution* ◇ ～标 milepost; ～表 odometer
【里程碑】milestone: 历史的～ *a milestone in history*
【里出外进】irregular; uneven: 他的牙长得～的。*His teeth are uneven*.
【里勾外联】in collusion with forces within and without
【里海】the Caspian Sea
【里脊】tenderloin
【里拉】lira (Italian monetary unit)
【里里外外】inside and outside: 屋子～都打扫得很干净。*The house has been given a thorough cleaning inside and out*. / ～一把手 *competent in*

all one does, both inside and outside the house

【里弄】〈方〉lanes and alleys; neighbourhood: 担任～工作 *work on the neighbourhood committee*

【里面】inside; interior: 宿舍～清洁豁亮。*It's clean and bright inside the dormitory.*

【里圈】[体] inner lane (of a running track)

【里手】❶ the left-hand side (of a running vehicle or machine) ❷ expert; old hand

【里通外国】have (or maintain) illicit relations with a foreign country

【里外】inside and outside: ～受敌 *face opposition within and without*

【里应外合】act from inside in coordination with forces attacking from outside; collaborate from within with forces from without

【里子】lining: 棉袄～ *the lining of a cotton-padded jacket*

俚 形 vulgar; rustic; unrefined

【俚俗】vulgar; rustic; unrefined

【俚语】slang

理 Ⅰ 名 ❶ texture; grain (in wood, skin, etc.): 木～ *the grain of wood* ❷ reason; logic; truth: 是他没～。*He's the one who's been unreasonable.* / 他讲的句句是～。*There is truth in every word he says.* ❸ natural science (esp. physics): ～学院 *college of science* Ⅱ 动 ❶ manage; run: ～家 *keep house; manage family affairs* ❷put in order; tidy up: 把书～一～。*Put the books in order.* / 把房间～一～。*Straighten up the room.* ❸ (usu. used in the negative) pay attention to; make a gesture or speak to: 别～那条狗。*Don't pay any attention to that dog.* / 他想跟我讲话,我没～他。*I ignored him when he tried to talk to me.*

【理财】manage money matters; conduct financial transactions ◇ ～家 financier

【理睬】(usu. used in the negative) pay attention to; show interest in: 没人～这事。*Nobody pays any attention to this matter.* / 不予～ *ignore; turn a deaf ear to; pay no heed to*

【理舱费】stowage charges

【理当】ought to; should: ～如此。*That's just as it should be.* or *It's only right and proper.*

【理短】be in the wrong; have no justification

【理发】❶ (of men) get a haircut; (of women) go to the hairdresser's: 我去理个发。(*of men*) *I'm going to get a haircut.* or (*of women*) *I'm going to the hairdresser's* (*or going to have my hair done*). ❷ give a haircut; do sb.'s hair: 我每月给他理一次发。*I give him a haircut once a month.* ◇ ～馆 barbershop; barber's; hairdresser's; ～师 barber; hairdresser; ～员 barber; hairdresser

【理工】science and engineering: ～科大学 *college* (*or university*) *of science and engineering*

【理化】physics and chemistry

【理会】❶ understand; comprehend: 不难～ *not difficult to understand* ❷ (usu. used in the negative) take notice of; pay attention to: 叫了他好几声,他都没～。*We called him several times, but he took no notice of us.*

【理货】freight forwarding; customs brokerage ◇ ～单 tally sheet; ～员 tallyman; tally clerk

【理解】understand; comprehend: 加深～ *deepen one's comprehension; acquire a better understanding* / 不可～ *incomprehensible; beyond one's comprehension*

【理解力】faculty of understanding; understanding; comprehension: ～强 *have good understanding* (*or comprehension*)

【理科】❶ science (as a field of study) ❷ science department in a college

【理亏】be in the wrong: 自知～ *know that one is in the wrong; realize that justice is not on one's side*

【理亏心虚】feel that one is not on solid ground

【理疗】physiotherapy: ～科医生 *physiotherapist*

【理论】theory; principle: 别空谈～。*Don't just talk about abstract principles.* / 你的意见～上我同意,但实际上恐怕行不通。*In theory, I agree with you, but I feel that your ideas would not work in practice.* ◇ ～家 theoretician; theorist

【理赔】settle claims; claims settlement: 欣丰棉纺厂遭遇特大火灾,保险公司～2000 万。*After the big fire, the Xinfeng Textile Factory received a settlement of 20 million yuan from insurance company.*

【理屈词穷】fall silent on finding oneself bested in argument; be unable to advance any further arguments

【理事】member of an executive council or of a board of directors; director; manager ◇ ～国 a member of the UN Security Council; ～会 executive council; board of directors; ～长 chairman of a board of directors or of an executive council

【理所当然】of course; as a matter of course; naturally: 他们的荒谬提案～地被否决了。*Of course their absurd proposal was rejected.*

【理想】❶ an ideal: 他的～很高。*He has high ideals.* / 你～中的丈夫是个什么样的人? *What's your ideal of what a husband should be?* ❷ be ideal: 天气很～。*The weather is ideal.* / 他找到了一个～的伴侣。*He found an ideal companion.* ◇ ～国 an ideal state; utopia; ～气体 [物] ideal gas; ～主义 idealism

【理性】❶ rational ❷ the rational faculty; reason: 失去～ *lose one's reason* ◇ ～认识 [哲] rational cognition; rational knowledge

【理学】❶ a rationalistic Confucian philosophical school that developed during the Song and Ming Dynasties, known to the West as Neo-Confucianism ❷ natural science: ～博士 *Doctor of Science* (*D. Sc.*) / ～硕士 *Master of Science* (*M. Sc.*)

【理应】ought to; should: 他有困难,我们～帮助。*He's in difficulties, and we ought to help him.*

【理由】reason; ground; argument: 有充分～相信 *have every reason to believe* / 没有～抱怨 *have no grounds for complaint* / 他提出的～不能成立。*His argument is untenable.*
【理喻】reason with sb.
【理直气壮】with justice on one's side, one is bold and assured: ～地回答 *reply with perfect assurance* / ～地予以驳斥 *justly and forcefully refute*
【理智】❶ reason; intellect: 丧失～ *lose one's reason; lose one's senses* / 碰到严重事情的时候,他的～总控制不住感情。*When confronted with a serious matter, his reason always gives way to emotion.* ❷ rational: ～点儿。*Do try to be rational.*

锂 名 [化] lithium (Li)
【锂云母】lepidolite; lithia mica

鲤 名 carp
【锂离子电池】lithum ion battery
【鲤鱼】carp
【鲤鱼钳】slip-joint pliers

lì

力 Ⅰ 名 ❶ [物] force ❷ power; strength; ability: 人力 / 理解力 ❸ physical strength: ～大无比 *of prodigious strength* Ⅱ 动 do all one can; make every effort: ～谏 *try all one can to remonstrate*
【力避】try hard to avoid or avert: ～嫌疑 *try hard to avoid suspicion*
【力臂】[物] arm of force
【力不从心】ability falling short of one's wishes; unable to do as much as one would like to
【力不胜任】be unequal to one's task; incompetent
【力场】[物] field of force
【力促】make every effort to promote: ～此事成功 *try hard to make it a success*
【力挫】defeat (the best) after many efforts: ～竞争对手 *beat the competition after tenacious effort*
【力度】❶[音] dynamics ❷strength; intensity: 加大改革的～ *step up the reform; increase the impact and momentum of reform*
【力戒】strictly avoid; do everything possible to avoid; guard against: ～浪费 *do everything possible to avoid waste* / ～骄傲 *guard against arrogance*
【力矩】[物] moment of force; moment: 合～ *resultant moment*
【力量】❶ physical strength: 这一脚～很大。*This is a powerful kick.* ❷ power; force; strength: 我一定尽我的～帮忙。*I'll certainly do everything in my power to help.* ❸ potency; efficacy; strength: 这种农药的～大。*This pesticide is strong.*
【力偶】[物] couple
【力排众议】prevail over all dissenting views; override all objections
【力气】physical strength; effort: 他的～不小。*He has great strength.* / 他连上楼的～都没有。*He hasn't even the strength to walk upstairs.* ◇ ～活 heavy work; strenuous work
【力求】make every effort to; do one's best to; strive to: 文字～精练。*Strive to be concise in writing.* / 我们～取得一致意见。*We'll do our best to reach a consensus.*
【力士】a man of great strength; strong man
【力所能及】in one's power: 在～的范围内 *within one's power*
【力图】try hard to; strive to: ～否认 *try hard to deny* / ～摆脱困境 *strive to get out of a predicament*
【力挽狂澜】do one's utmost to stem a raging tide or save a desperate situation; make vigorous efforts to turn the tide
【力学】mechanics: 波动～ *wave mechanics* / 断裂～ *fracture mechanics* / 生物～ *biomechanics*
【力争】❶ work hard for; do all one can to: ～主动 *do all one can to gain the initiative* / ～少花钱,多办事 *strive by every means to spend less and accomplish more* ❷ argue strongly; contend vigorously
【力争上游】aim high; strive for first place
【力作】major piece of writing; major article; well-written influential writing: 鲁迅的～ *Lu Xun's major works*

历 Ⅰ 动 go through; undergo; experience: 历尽 Ⅱ 形 all previous (occasions, sessions, etc.): 历年 / 历届 Ⅲ 副 covering all; one by one: ～访各有关部门 *have visited the departments concerned one by one* Ⅳ 名 calendar: 阴历 / 日历
【历程】course: 回顾我们党的战斗～ *look back on the course of the struggle of our Party*
【历次】all previous (occasions, etc.): 在～比赛中她都取得了优异的成绩。*She has done well in all past contests.*
【历代】successive dynasties; past dynasties: ～封建王朝 *the feudal dynasties of past ages* / ～名画 *famous paintings through the ages*
【历法】calendric system; calendar: 这国的～跟别国不一样。*This country has a different calendar.*
【历届】all previous (sessions, governments, etc.): ～全国人民代表大会 *all the previous National People's Congresses* / ～毕业生 *graduates of all previous years*
【历尽】have gone through a lof of: ～艰辛 *have gone through all kinds of hardships and difficulties* / ～沧桑 *have experienced various vicissitudes of life*
【历来】always; constantly; all through the ages: ～认为 *have invariably insisted; have consistently held; have always maintained*
【历来如此】this has always been the case
【历历】distinctly; clearly: 往事～在心头。*Past events remain fresh in my memory.*

【历历在目】come clearly into view; leap up before the eyes：追忆往事，～。*As I look back, scenes of the past leap before my eyes.*

【历年】❶ over the years：～的积蓄 *savings over the years* ❷ calendar year

【历任】❶ have successively held the posts of; have served successively as：他～连长、营长、团长、师长等职。*He successively held the posts of company, battalion, regiment and division commander.* ❷ successive：这家公司的～经理 *the successive managers of this company*

【历时】last (a period of time); take (a period of time)：手术～三个小时。*The operation took three hours.*

【历史】❶ history：中国～悠久。*China has a long history.* / 这件事早已成为～了。*That's past history already.* ❷ history (as a course of study)：他是研究～的。*His field is history.* ❸ personal records：～清白 *have a clean personal record* / 隐瞒自己的～ *conceal one's past record* / ～问题 *questions of a political nature in one's personal history* ◇ ～比较语言学 historical comparative linguistics; ～博物馆 history (or historical) museum; ～潮流 the tide of history; historical trend; ～地图 historical map (or atlas); ～观 view (or conception) of history; ～剧 historical play; ～人物 historical personage; historical figure; ～唯物论 historical materialism; ～唯物主义 historical materialism; ～唯心论 historical idealism; ～唯心主义 historical idealism; ～小说 historical novel; ～学家 historian; ～循环论(又作'～决定论') historicism; ～遗产 legacy of history; historical heritage

【历史性】historic; of historic significance：～胜利 *a historic victory*

【历书】almanac

【历数】count one by one; enumerate：～侵略者的罪行 *enumerate the crimes of the aggressors*

【历月】［天］calendar month

立 Ⅰ 动 ❶ stand：他在那儿～了半天了。*He has stood there for quite a while.* ❷ set or stand sth. up; erect：别横着放，～着放。*Don't lay it down, stand it up.* / 把梯子～起来。*Set up the ladder.* / ～碑 *set up (or erect) a monument* ❸ establish; found; set up：这是谁～的规矩？*Who established this rule?* / ～标兵 *make sb. the pacesetter; set up a model; set a good example* ❹ draw up; conclude：～合同 *conclude (or sign) a contract* / ～章程 *draw up rules and regulations* / ～遗嘱 *make a will* Ⅱ 形 upright; vertical; erect：立柜 Ⅲ 副 immediately; instantaneously：～见功效 *produce immediate results; feel the effect immediately*

【立案】❶ register; put on record ❷ ［法］place a case on file for investigation and prosecution：对该案予以～受理。*This case should be put on file for investigation and prosecution.*

【立场】position; stand; standpoint：丧失～ *depart from the correct stand* / ～坚定 *be steadfast in one's stand; take a firm stand*

【立春】the Beginning of Spring

【立德粉】［化］lithopone

【立等】wait for sth. to be done immediately：～回信 *wait for an immediate reply* / 本店设有快修部，～可取。*We have a quick repair service where repairs can be done on the spot.*

【立定】halt：～！(*word of command*) *Halt!*

【立定跳远】standing long jump

【立冬】the Beginning of Winter

【立法】make (or enact) laws; legislate：经济～ *economic legislation* / 行政～ *administrative legislation* ◇ ～机关 legislative body; legislature

【立法权】legislative power：全国人民代表大会行使国家～。*The National People's Congress exercises the legislative power of the state.*

【立方】❶ ［数］cube：二的～ *the cube of 2*; 2^3 ❷ 〈略〉见〖立方体〗❸ cubic metre; stere：一～土 *one cubic metre of earth* ◇ ～根［数］cube root; ～厘米 cubic centimetre; ～米 cubic metre; ～体 cube

【立竿见影】set up a pole and you see its shadow—produce instant results

【立功】render meritorious service; do a deed of merit; win honour; make contributions：立一等功 *win a first class merit citation* ◇ ～奖状 certificate for meritorious service; certificate of merit

【立功赎罪】do good deeds to atone for one's crimes

【立柜】clothes closet; wardrobe; hanging cupboard

【立候】〈书〉wait for sth. to be done immediately：～回音 *An immediate reply is requested.* or *Awaiting your prompt reply.*

【立户】❶ register for a household residence card; register for permanent residence ❷ (less common than 立户头) open an account with the bank

【立即】immediately; at once; promptly：判处死刑，～执行 *be sentenced to death and executed immediately*

【立交桥】❶ overpass; flyover ❷ motorway interchange

【立决】summary execution

【立克次氏体】［医］rickettsia

【立刻】immediately; at once; right away：我～就去。*I'll go right away.* / 铃声一响，教室里～安静下来。*As soon as the bell rang, the classroom quieted down at once.*

【立论】❶ set forth one's views; present one's arguments ❷ argument; position; line of reasoning

【立面图】［建］elevation (drawing)

【立秋】the Beginning of Autumn

【立射】［军］fire from a standing position

【立身处世】the way one conducts oneself in society

【立式】vertical; upright：～车床 *vertical lathe* / ～钻床 *upright drill; vertical drill*

【立誓】take an oath; vow

【立陶宛】Lithuania
【立体】❶ three-dimensional; stereoscopic ❷ [数] solid ◇～地图 three dimentional map; ～感 three-dimensional effect; ～化学 stereochemistry; ～几何 solid geometry; ～交叉 grade separation; ～角 [数] solid angle; ～模型 space model; ～派 cubism; ～图 hologram; ～图像 stereopicture; ～显示 three-dimensional display; ～显微镜 stereoscopic microscope; stereomicroscope; ～战争 three-dimensional warfare; triphibious warfare; ～照相机 stereoscopic camera; stereo camera
【立体电影】stereoscopic film; three-dimensional (or 3-D) film; cinerama: ～院 *stereoscopic cinema*
【立体声】stereophony; stereo: ～唱机 *stereo record-player*; *stereo* / ～唱片 *stereo record* / ～磁带 *stereotape* / ～收录机 *stereo radio-tape recorder*; *stereo tape recorder*; *stereo* / ～音响设备 *stereo component system*; *stereo*
【立夏】the Beginning of Summer
【立宪】constitutionalism: 君主～ *constitutional monarchy* / ～政体 *constitutional government*; *constitutionalism*
【立项】establish; decide upon a project: 大桥的～工作已经完成。*The bridge project has been decided upon.*
【立言】expound one's ideas in writing; achieve glory by writing
【立意】❶ be determined; make up one's mind ❷ conception; approach: 这幅画～新颖。*This painting shows an interesting new approach.*
【立于不败之地】establish oneself in an unassailable position; be in an impregnable position; be invincible: 不论时局发展的情况如何,我们均须作持久打算,才能～。*No matter how the situation develops, we must always calculate on a long-term basis, if our position is to be invincible.*
【立约】conclude a treaty; draw up an agreement (or a contract)
【立账】open an account
【立正】stand at attention: ～! (*word of command*) *Attention!*
【立志】resolve; be determined: ～改革 *be determined to carry out reforms*; *be resolved to institute reforms* / 他～要当一名宇航员。*He is determined to become an astronaut.*
【立轴】❶ vertical scroll of painting or calligraphy; wall scroll ❷ [机] vertical shaft; upright shaft
【立锥之地】(usu. used in the negative with 无) land just enough to stick an awl into: 无～ *have not even enough land to stick an awl into—very poor*
【立姿】[军] standing position
【立足】❶ have a foothold somewhere ❷ base oneself upon: ～于独立自主和自力更生 *be based on independence and self-reliance*
【立足点】❶ foothold; footing: 找不到～ *be unable to find a foothold* ❷ standpoint; stand
【立足之地】foothold; footing: 在社会上获得～ *gain a place in society*

历 形 ❶ strict; rigorous: ～禁 *strictly forbid* ❷ stern; severe: *历声*
【历兵秣马】同〖秣马历兵〗
【历鬼】an evil spirit
【历害】同〖利害〗
【历色】a stern countenance
【历声】in a stern voice
【历行】strictly enforce; rigorously enforce; make great efforts to carry out: ～节约 *practise strict economy*

吏 名 ❶〈旧〉a government clerk ❷ official; mandarin
【吏治】〈旧〉the administration of local officials: 澄清～ *bring order into the local administration*

沥 Ⅰ 动 rip; trickle: ～血 *drip blood* Ⅱ 名 drop: 余沥
【沥涝】waterlogging: ～成灾。*Waterlogging has caused serious damage.*
【沥青】pitch; asphalt; bitumen: 天然～ *natural asphalt*; *natural bitumen* / ～混凝土 *bituminous concrete*; *asphalt concrete* / ～基原油 *asphalt-base crude oil*
【沥水】waterlogging caused by excessive rainfall

丽 形 beautiful: 美丽
【丽人】〈书〉a beautiful woman; a beauty
【丽日】〈书〉bright sun
【丽质】beauty (of a woman): 天生～ *natural beauty*

励 动 encourage: 勉励
【励磁】[物] excitation ◇～机 exciter
【励精图治】(usu. of a ruler or prime minister) exert oneself to make the country prosperous

利 Ⅰ 形 ❶ sharp: ～爪 *sharp claws* ❷ favourable; smooth: 顺利 Ⅱ 名 ❶ advantage; benefit: 有利有弊 ❷ profit; interest: 连本带利 *profit as well as capital* Ⅲ 动 do good to; benefit: ～己～人 *benefit other people as well as oneself*
【利比里亚】Liberia ◇～人 Liberian
【利比亚】Libya ◇～人 Libyan
【利弊】advantages and disadvantages; pros and cons: 各有～ *there are both advantages and disadvantages*
【利钝】❶ sharp or blunt ❷ smooth going or rough: 成败利钝
【利多卡因】[药] lidocaine
【利福霉素】[药] rifamycin
【利福平】[药] rifampin (RFP)
【利改税】tax payments (made by state-owned enterprises) instead of profit deliveries to the state
【利滚利】at compound interest
【利害】❶ advantages and disadvantages; gains and

losses：不计～ *regardless of gains or losses* / ～冲突 *conflict of interests* / 有共同的～关系 *have common interests* ❷(of a wild animal or of one's temper, words, etc.) fierce; terrible：老虎比狮子还～。*Tigers are even fiercer than lions.* / 他这张嘴可～了。*He has a sharp tongue.* ❸(of a person) strict; stern; harsh：我们老师很～。*Our teacher is very strict.* / 我要给他点～。*I'll teach him a lesson.* ❹(of illness, heat, cold, etc.) intense; severe; terrible：他病得很～。*He is seriously ill.*

【利己主义】egoism

【利令智昏】be blinded by lust for gain

【利禄】〈书〉rank and wealth

【利率】rate of interest; interest rate

【利落】❶ agile; nimble; dexterous：动作～ *agile movements* / 手脚～ *dexterous; deft* / 说话不～ *speak slowly and indistinctly* ❷ neat; orderly：他做事干净～。*He is a neat worker.* ❸ settled; finished：事情已经办～了。*The matter is all settled.*

【利眠宁】[药] librium

【利尿】diuresis ◇ ～剂 diuretic

【利器】❶ a sharp weapon ❷ good tool; efficient instrument

【利钱】interest (on an investment)：付～ *pay interest*

【利权】economic rights (esp. of a country)：～外溢 *lose economic rights to foreigners*

【利刃】a sharp sword

【利润】profit ◇ ～分成 profits sharing; ～留成 retained profits; ～率 profit margin; ～税 profits tax

【利税】profit and tax

【利税分流】practice of separating profits and faxes

【利他主义】altruism

【利息】interest (on an investment)：～很高。*The interest is very high.* ◇ ～差额 interest spread; ～回扣 interest rebate; ～津贴 interest subsidization

【利血平】[药] reserpine

【利益】interest; benefit; profit：为大多数人谋～ *work for the interests of the vast majority of people* ◇ ～集团 interest group

【利用】❶ use; utilize; make use of：～废料 *make use of scrap material; turn scrap material to good account* ❷ take advantage of; exploit：～职权 *take advantage of one's position and power; exploit one's office* / 受人～ *be made use of; be a cat's-paw* / 互相～ *each using the other for his own ends* ◇ ～率 utilization ratio; ～外资 introducing foreign investment; utilizing foreign funds

【利用系数】utilization coefficient; utilization factor

【利诱】lure by promise of gain

【利于】be of advantage to; benefit

【利欲熏心】be obsessed with the desire for gain; be overcome by covetousness; be blinded by greed

例 Ⅰ 名 ❶ example; instance：举例 ❷ precedent：破例 ❸ case; instance：患这种病的33～中，21～有显著好转。*Out of the 33 cases of this disease, 21 showed marked progress.* ❹ rule; regulation：旧～ *an old rule* / 不在此～。*That is an exception.* Ⅱ 形 regular; routine：例会

【例会】regular meeting

【例假】❶ official holiday; legal holiday ❷〈婉〉menstrual period; period：她来～的时候总是不大舒服。*She always feels unwell at the start of her period.*

【例句】illustrative sentence; example sentence

【例如】for instance; for example (e.g.); such as：田径运动的项目很多，～跳高、跳远、百米赛跑等。*There are many track-and-field events, such as the high jump, the long jump, the 100-metre dash, etc.*

【例题】a problem designed to illustrate a principle or method (as in a mathematics book); example

【例外】❶ be an exception：世界各国都有环保问题，中国也不～。*The problem of environmental protection affects all countries, and China is no exception.* ❷ exception：什么事都有～。*There's an exception to everything.* / 那是～。*That's an exception.*

【例行公事】❶ routine; routine business ❷ mere formality

【例言】introductory remarks; notes on the use of a book

【例语】illustrative phrase; example word or phrase

【例证】illustration; example; case in point

【例子】example; case; instance：你给我举个～。*Give me an example.*

隶 Ⅰ 动 be subordinate to; be under：隶属 Ⅱ 名 a person in servitude：奴隶

【隶书】official script, an ancient style of calligraphy current in the Han Dynasty (206 B.C.—A.D. 220), simplified from xiaozhuan (小篆)

【隶属】be subordinate to; be under the jurisdiction or command of：直辖市是直接～国务院的市。*A province-level municipality is under the direct control of the State Council.*

栎 名 oak (Quercus) ——另见 yuè

荔 (构词成分) 见下

【荔枝】litchi; lichee

俪 Ⅰ 形 paired; parallel：俪句 Ⅱ 名 husband and wife; married couple：伉俪

【俪句】parallel sentences

【俪影】a photograph of a couple

莅 动〈书〉arrive; be present：～场 *be present on the occasion* / ～会 *be present at a meeting*

【莅临】〈书〉arrive; be present：敬请～指导。

Your presence and guidance are requested.

栗 Ⅰ名 chestnut Ⅱ动 tremble；shudder：战栗

【栗钙土】chestnut soil

【栗色】chestnut colour；maroon

【栗子】chestnut

砾 名 gravel；shingle

【砾石】gravel：～混凝土 *gravel concrete* / ～路 *gravel road*

【砾岩】［地质］conglomerate

粒 Ⅰ名 grain；granule；pellet：砂～儿 *grains of sand* / 盐～儿 *grains of salt* / 豆～儿 *beans* Ⅱ量 (for grainlike things)：一～砂 *a grain of sand* / 一～米 *a grain of rice* / 三～子弹 *three bullets* / 每服五～。*Dosage*：5 *pills each time*.

【粒度】［冶］size

【粒肥】〈略〉见〖颗粒肥料〗

【粒选】grain-by-grain seed selection

【粒状】granular：～物 *granules*

【粒子】［物］particle：～加速器 *particle accelerator* / ～束 *particle beam*

痢 名 dysentery

【痢疾】dysentery

liǎ

俩 数〈口〉❶ (a fusion of 两 and 个) two：咱～ *we two*；*both of us*；*the two of us* / 这种冰棍儿一块钱～。*You can get two of these popsicles for a yuan*. ❷ some；several：给他～钱儿。*Give him some money*. / 那么多事情，这么～人干不了。*There's so much to do that these few people can hardly cope*. or *There's too much work here for so few people*.

lián

连 Ⅰ连 link；join；connect：把这两条电线～起来。*Connect these two electric wires*. / 把零散的土地～成一片 *join together scattered pieces of land* Ⅱ副 continuously；in succession；one after another：他～说了三个钟头。*He spoke continuously for three hours*. / 他～着三天没来。*He hasn't come for three days in a row*. Ⅲ介 ❶including：～你一共十个人。*There are ten people, including you*. ❷(used correlatively with 也，都，etc.) even：～我都知道。*Even I know*. / 他～报也看不懂。*He can't even read a newspaper*. / 他～看都没看。*He didn't even look*. Ⅳ名［军］company：一营有三个～。*A battalion has three companies*.

【连本带利】both principal and interest；profit as well as capital

【连鬓胡子】〈口〉whiskers；full beard

【连词】〈语〉conjunction

【连带】related：人的作风和思想是有～关系的。*A person's work style is related to his ideology*. ◇～法律关系 joint legal relations

【连…带…】❶ (indicating the inclusion of two items)：连老带小一共23个人。*There are altogether* 23, *including the old people and children*. ❷ (indicating the simultaneous occurrence of two actions)：连说带比划 *talking and gesticulating* / 连蹦带跳 *hopping and skipping* / 连打带骂 *beating and cursing*

【连带责任】［法］joint liability

【连裆裤】child's pants with no slit in the seat

【连队】［军］company

【连发】［军］running fire：～枪 *repeating rifle*；*magazine gun* / ～射击 *burst* (*of fire*) / ～武器 *repeating firearms*

【连杆】［机］connecting rod

【连根拔】tear up by the roots；uproot

【连亘】(of mountain ranges) continue；extend：山岭～ *a continuous stretch of mountains*

【连拱坝】multiple-arch dam；multi-arch dam

【连拱桥】multiple-arch bridge；multi-arch bridge

【连贯】link up；piece together；hang together；be coherent：文章写得很不～。*This article is rather incoherent*. / 上下句意思要～。*Two consecutive sentences must hang together*. ◇～性 coherence；continuity

【连锅端】take all the pots and pans—take or get rid of the whole lot

【连环】a chain of rings ◇～画 a book (usu. for children) with a story told in pictures；picture-story book；～计 a set of interlocking stratagems；a series of stratagems；～图画 comic strips；comics

【连击】［体］double hit (in table tennis)；double contact (in volleyball)

【连枷】flail

【连接】join；link：把两条铁路～起来 *link up the two railway lines* / ～不断的山岭 *a continuous range of mountains* ◇～号 hyphen (-)

【连接线】［音］tie

【连襟】husbands of sisters：他们是～。*Their wives are sisters*. or *They are brothers-in-law*.

【连裤袜】panty hose

【连累】implicate；involve；get sb. into trouble

【连连】repeatedly；again and again：～点头 *nod again and again* (*to show agreement, etc.*) / 演出结束，观众～叫好。*At the end of the performance, the audience applauded again and again*.

【连忙】hastily；hurriedly；promptly：他～道歉。*He hastened to apologize*. / 听见有人叫他，他～去开门。*Hearing someone calling him, he hurriedly went to open the door*.

【连绵】continuous；unbroken；uninterrupted：阴雨～。*There was an unbroken spell of wet weather*. / ～起伏的山峦 *rolling hills*

【连年】in successive years；in consecutive years；for years running；for years on end：～丰收 *reap rich harvests for many years running*

【连皮】(weight of goods) including the packing; gross (weight): ～30斤。*It weighs 30 jin, including the packing.* or *The gross weight is 30 jin.*

【连篇】❶ throughout a piece of writing; page after page: 空话～ *pages and pages of empty verbiage* ❷ one article after another; a multitude of articles

【连篇累牍】lengthy and tedious; at great length: ～地发表文章 *publish one article after another*

【连谱号】[音] accolade; brace

【连任】be reappointed or reelected consecutively; renew one's term of office: ～部长 *be reappointed minister* / ～总统 *be reelected president*

【连日】for days on end; day after day: ～来 *for the last few days* / ～刮大风。*The wind blew hard for several days running.*

【连射】[军] running fire

【连声】say repeatedly: ～称谢 *say "thanks" repeatedly; thank sb. profusely* / ～称赞 *be profuse in one's praise*

【连锁】linked together ◇ ～比例 chain relative; ～反应 chain reaction; ～商店 chain stores

【连天】❶ for several days in a row; for days on end: ～连夜 *for days and nights* / ～阴雨。*It was cloudy and drizzly for days on end.* ❷ continuously; incessantly ❸ (of a mountain, the horizon, flames, etc.) touch the sky: 杀声～ *air-rending battle cries* / 天连水,水～。*The sky and the water seem to merge.*

【连同】together with; along with: 图纸～清单一并送去。*Send the blueprints along with the inventory.*

【连续】continuously; successively; in a row: ～作战 *continuous fighting; successive battles; consecutive operations* / ～爆破 *continuous demolition* ◇ ～光谱 [物] continuous spectrum; ～航次 consecutive voyages

【连续剧】serial

【连续性】continuity; continuance: 保持政策的～ *maintain the continuity of a policy*

【连选连任】be reelected and serve another term

【连夜】❶ the same night; that very night; all through the night: 我们～开车,赶回来了。*We drove far into the night and rushed back.* ❷ for nights on end

【连衣裙】a woman's dress; dress

【连阴天】cloudy weather for several days running

【连阴雨】an unbroken spell of wet weather

【连用】use consecutively; use together: 这两个词不能～。*These two words do not go together.*

【连载】publish in instalments; serialize: 长篇～ *serial (of a novel, etc.)*

【连长】company commander

【连珠】like a chain of pearls or a string of beads — in rapid succession: ～似的机枪声 *a continuous rattle of machine-gun fire*

【连珠炮】continuous firing; drumfire: 说话像～ *chatter away like a machine gun* / 像～似地向他提问 *bombard him with questions; fire questions at him*

【连缀】❶ join together; put together: 孤立地看,每一个情节都很平淡,～在一起,就有趣了。*When taken separately, each of the episodes is rather dull, but when linked together, they're very interesting.* ❷ [语音] cluster: 辅音～ *consonant cluster*

【连字号】hyphen (-)

【连奏】[音] legato

帘

名 ❶ flag as a shop sign: 水帘 ❷ (hanging) screen; curtain: 窗帘

【帘布】cord fabric (in tyres)

【帘幕】heavy curtain: ～低垂。*The curtain hung low.*

【帘栅管】[电子] screen-grid tube

【帘栅极】[电子] screen grid

【帘子】〈口〉(hanging) screen; curtain: 竹～ *a bamboo screen or curtain* / 窗～ *a window curtain*

【帘子布】同〖帘布〗

怜

动 ❶ sympathize with; pity: 同病相怜 ❷ love: 怜爱

【怜爱】love tenderly; have tender affection for: 这小姑娘惹人～。*The little girl is so lovable.*

【怜悯】pity; take pity on; have compassion for

【怜贫惜老】feel compassion for the aged and the poor

【怜惜】take pity on; have pity for: 决不～恶人。*We should never take pity on evil people.*

【怜香惜玉】show pity and tenderness to women

涟

名〈书〉❶ ripples ❷ continuous flow (of tears): 泣涕～～ *tears flowing continuously*

【怜漪】〈文〉wimpled waves; ripples

莲

名 lotus: 采～ *pick lotus*

【莲花】lotus flower; lotus

【莲花纹】lotus design

【莲藕】the lotus plant, or esp. its root: 种植～ *plant lotuses* / ～同根 *the lotus stems spring from the selfsame root — inseparable*

【莲蓬】seedpod of the lotus

【莲蓬头】〈方〉shower nozzle

【莲台】a Buddha's seat in the form of a lotus flower; lotus throne

【莲心】the heart of a lotus seed

【莲子】lotus seed

联

Ⅰ 动 ally oneself with; unite; join: 联盟 Ⅱ 名 antithetical couplet: 对联

【联邦】federation; union; commonwealth ◇ ～储备系统 Federal Reserve System; ～调查局 the (U.S.) Federal Bureau of Investigation (FBI); ～共和国 federal republic; federated republic; ～基金 federal funds; ～制 federal system; federalism

【联苯胺】[化] benzidine

【联播】radio hookup；broadcast over a radio network：新闻～ *news hookup* / ～节目时间 *network time*

【联产承包责任制】a system of contracted responsibility linking remuneration to output；a contract system with remuneration linked to output

【联产计酬】payment linked to output

【联单】receipts or other documents in duplicate

【联队】［军］wing（of an air force）

【联防】❶ joint defence；joint command of defence forces：军民～ *joint defence by army and militia*；*army-civilian defence* ❷［体］joint defence

【联管节】［机］pipe union；pipe coupling；union joint

【联管箱】［机］header：汽锅～ *boiler header*

【联合】❶ unite；ally：～一切可能～的力量 *ally oneself with all forces that can be allied with* ❷ joint；combined：～举办 *jointly organize or sponsor* / ～进攻 *launch a combined*（*or concerted*）*attack* ❸ combination；alliance；union；coalition：各派大～ *a grand alliance of all groups* / 专业性的生产～ *a combination of specialized productive undertakings* ❹［生理］symphysis：耻骨～ *symphysis pubis* ◇ ～兵种［军］combined arms；～采煤机 cutter-loader；combine；～词组［语］coordinative word group；～大企业 conglomerate company；～公报 joint communiqué；～公司 joint company；～股份公司 joint-stock company；～机 combine；～经营 joint venture；～开发 joint exploitation；～企业 an incorporated business enterprise；～商标 unite band；～声明 joint statement；～收割机 combine（harvester）；～王国 the United Kingdom；～行动 joint action；concerted action；～宣言 joint declaration；～演习［军］joint manoeuvre；joint exercise；～战线 united front；～政府 coalition government；～作战［军］combined operations

【联合国】the United Nations（U.N.）◇ ～安全理事会 the United Nations Security Council；～大会 the United Nations General Assembly；～秘书处 the United Nations Secretariat；～宪章 the United Nations Charter

【联合会】federation；union：妇女～ *women's federation* / 学生～ *students' union*

【联合体】an organic whole；association：农工商～ *an association of agricultural, industrial and commercial units*；*an agricultural-industrial-commercial association*

【联欢】have a social gathering；have a get-together：节日～ *gala celebrations* / 军民～ *get-together of soldiers and civilians* ◇ ～会 get-together；party；～节 festival；carnival；fiesta；～晚会（evening）party

【联机】［计］（又作'在线'）on-line：～服务 *online service* ◇ ～测试 online testing；～实时系统 on-line real-time system

【联接】❶ 同〖连接〗❷［电］connection；strapping

【联结】join；connect；link；bind：画一条直线把这两点～起来。*Draw a line to join the two points.* / 共同的目标把我们紧紧～在一起。*A common goal has bound us closely together.*

【联军】allied forces；united army

【联立方程】［数］simultaneous equations

【联络】❶ start or keep up personal relations；make or maintain contact or liaison：～感情 *start or keep up a friendship*；*strengthen the bonds of friendship* ❷ contact（between people）；liaison：失掉～ *lose contact* ◇ ～部 liaison department；～处 liaison office；～官 liaison officer；～网 liaison net；～员 liaison man；～站 liaison station

【联袂】〈书〉go（or come etc.）together：～而往 *go together* / ～而至 *arrive together*

【联盟】alliance；coalition；league；union：工农～ *alliance of the workers and peasants*；*worker-peasant alliance*

【联名】jointly signed；jointly：～发起 *jointly initiate*；*jointly sponsor* / ～上书 *submit a joint letter*

【联翩】in close succession；together：～而至 *come in close succession*；*arrive one after another*

【联赛】［体］league matches：足球～ *league football matches*

【联锁机构】［机］interlocking mechanism

【联体婴】Siamese twins

【联网】networking：计算机～已成为趋势。*The trend is towards computer networking.*

【联席会议】joint conference；joint meeting

【联系】❶ contact；touch；connection；relation：失去～ *lose contact* / 取得～ *get in touch with*；*establish contact with* / 保持～ *keep in contact*（*or touch*）*with* ❷ integrate；relate；link；get in touch with：理论～实际 *integrate theory with practice*；*apply theory to reality*

【联想】connect with mentally；associate with：提起大夫，小孩儿就～到打针、疼。*Children always associate the doctor with injections and pain.*

【联谊】keep up a friendship；strengthen the bonds of friendship：～会 *get-together*；*party*

【联姻】〈书〉（of two families）be related by marriage；form an alliance by marriage

【联营】joint venture：～公司 *integrated company*

【联运】through transport；through traffic：国际铁路～ *international railway through transport* / 火车汽车～ *train-and-bus coordinated transport* ◇ ～票 through ticket；～提单 through bill of lading

【联展】joint exhibition：计算机～ *joint exhibition of computers*（*by several vendors*）

【联轴节】［机］shaft coupling；coupling：刚性～ *rigid coupling* / 挠性～ *flexible coupling* / 万向～ *universal coupling*

廉

形 ❶ honest and clean：清廉 / 廉耻 ❷ low-priced；inexpensive；cheap：价廉物美

【廉耻】integrity and a sense of honour：不知～ *have no sense of shame*；*be shameless*

【廉价】low-priced；cheap：～书 *a cheap book* / ～

买进 *buy cheap* / ～出售 *sell at a low price; sell cheap* / ～劳动力 *cheap labour* / ～品 *cheap goods; bargain* ◇ ～部 bargain counter; ～抛售 distress sale; distress selling; ～商店 bargain shop

【廉洁】honest and clean; incorruptible: ～政府 *an honest and clean government*

【廉洁奉公】be honest in performing one's official duties

【廉明】(of officials) upright and incorruptible

【廉政】honest and clean government: ～建设 *building an honest and clean government*

鲢 名 silver carp

【鲢鱼】silver carp

臁 名 [生理] shank

镰 名 sickle

【镰刀】sickle

【镰鱼】Moorish idol (a fish)

liǎn

敛 动 ❶ hold back; restrain ❷ collect

【敛步】check one's steps; hold back from going

【敛财】accumulate wealth by unfair means

【敛迹】temporarily desist from one's evil ways; lie low

【敛容】〈书〉assume a serious expression

脸 名 ❶ face (of people or animals): 洗～ *wash one's face* ❷ the front part of sth.: 门脸儿 ❸ face (〈喻〉): ～上下不来 *haven't the face to do sth.*

【脸蛋儿】(usu. children's) cheeks; face: 小姑娘的～红得像苹果。*The little girl's rosy cheeks are like apples.*

【脸红】❶ blush (with shame or embarrassment) ❷ flush with anger; get excited; get worked up

【脸红脖子粗】get red in the face from anger or excitement; flush with agitation: 争得～ *get red in the face in the heat of the argument*

【脸颊】cheeks; face: 红润的～ *ruddy cheeks* / 泪珠儿顺着她的～直往下淌。*Tears streamed down her cheeks.*

【脸面】❶ face (〈字〉) ❷ face; self-respect; sb.'s feelings: 看我的～，不要生他的气了。*For my sake, don't get angry with him.* / 不顾～ *have no regard for face*

【脸盘儿】(又作'脸庞儿') the cast of one's face: 大～ *a big face* / 方～ *a square face*

【脸盆】washbasin; washbowl ◇ ～架 washstand

【脸皮】face (〈喻〉); cheek: ～厚 *thick-skinned; shameless* / ～薄 *thin-skinned; shy; sensitive* / 撕破～ *put aside all considerations of face*

【脸谱】types of facial makeup in operas

【脸色】❶complexion; look: ～红润 *a ruddy complexion* / 他这几天～不好。*He doesn't look well these days.* ❷ facial expression: 一看他的～，我就知道有了好消息。*I could see from the expression on his face that there was good news.*

【脸上无光】have lost face

【脸形】(又作'脸型') the shape of one's face; facial features: ～端正 *have regular features* / ～瘦长 *a thin and long face* / 圆圆的～ *a full (or round) face*

liàn

练 Ⅰ 名 white silk: 江平如～。*The river lies as smooth as silk.* Ⅱ 动 ❶boil and scour raw silk ❷ practise; train; drill: ～工夫 *practise one's skill* / ～气功 *do breathing exercises* / ～字 *practise calligraphy* / ～钢琴 *practise the piano* Ⅲ 形 experienced; skilled; seasoned: 老练

【练笔】❶ practise writing ❷ practise calligraphy

【练兵】train troops; drill soldiers ◇ ～场 drill ground; parade ground

【练操】(of troops, etc.) drill

【练队】drill in formation; drill for a parade

【练功】do exercises in gymnastics, wushu, acrobatics, etc.; practise one's skill

【练球】practise a ball game: 主队和客队在一起～。*The home team and the visitors are practising together.* / 赛前～ *warm-up (before a match)*

【练鹊】long-tailed flycatcher

【练武】❶ learn or practise martial arts ❷ learn or practise military skills

【练习】❶ practise: 要多～～。*You must practise some more.* / ～讲英语 *practise speaking English* ❷ exercise (in a book): 做～ *do exercises* / 交～ *hand in exercises* / 算术～ *arithmetic exercises* ◇ ～本 (又作'练习簿') exercise-book; ～曲 [音] étude; ～题 exercise problems; exercises

炼 动 ❶ smelt; refine: ～铅 *smelt lead* / ～糖 *refine sugar* ❷ temper (a metal) with fire ❸ weigh one's word; seek the right phrase: 炼句

【炼丹】(try to) make pills of immortality (as a Taoist practice)

【炼钢】make steel; smelt steel ◇ ～厂 steel mill; steelworks; ～工人 steelworker; ～炉 steelmaking furnace; steel-smelting furnace

【炼焦】make coke; coke ◇ ～厂 coking plant; cokery; ～炉 coke oven; ～煤 coking coal

【炼金术】alchemy

【炼句】try to find the best turn of phrase; polish and repolish a sentence

【炼乳】condensed milk

【炼铁】smelt iron ◇ ～厂 ironworks; ～炉 iron-smelting furnace; blast furnace

【炼油】❶ refine oil ❷ extract oil by heat: 炼猪油 *boil down fat to get lard* ❸ heat edible oil ◇ ～厂 (oil) refinery

【炼制】refine: 石油～ *petroleum refining*

恋 动 ❶ love (one of the opposite sex): 相～ *be in love with each other* ❷long for; feel attached to：～家 *reluctant to be away from home*；*be tied to home*

【恋爱】❶ romantic love；love affair：谈～ *be in love*；*have a love affair* ❷ be in love；have a courtship

【恋父情结】Electra complex

【恋母情结】Oedipus complex

【恋歌】love song

【恋旧】❶ yearn for one's native place；be filled with nostalgia ❷ 同〖怀旧〗

【恋恋不舍】be reluctant to part from；hate to see sb. go：老人～，把他们一直送到门外。*The old man hated (or couldn't bear) to see them go. He accompanied them to outside the door.*

【恋慕】have tender feelings towards；adore

【恋情】romantic love

【恋人】sweetheart；loved one；girlfriend or boyfriend

殓 动 put a body into a coffin；encoffin：入殓

【殓衣】graveclothes

链 Ⅰ 名 chain：铁链 Ⅱ 量 cable length (1/10 of a nautical mile)

【链扳手】chain wrench

【链钩】chain hook；sling

【链轨】caterpillar track (of a tractor)

【链锯】chain saw

【链轮】chain wheel；sprocket (wheel)

【链霉素】［药］streptomycin

【链球】［体］hammer：掷～ *hammer throw*

【链球菌】streptococcus

【链式反应】［化］chain reaction

【链套】chain case (of a bicycle)

【链条】❶ chain ❷ roller chain (of a bicycle)；chain

【链烃】［化］chain hydrocarbon

【链罩】chain guard (of a bicycle)；chain cover

【链子】❶ chain：铁～ *iron chain* ❷〈口〉roller chain (of a bicycle)；chain

楝 名 chinaberry

【楝树】chinaberry

潋（构词成分）见下

【潋滟】〈文〉❶ overflowing；inundating ❷ billowing；rippling

liáng

良 Ⅰ 形 good；fine：优良 Ⅱ 名 good people：除暴安良

【良材】❶ good timber ❷ able person

【良策】good plan；sound strategy

【良辰美景】a fine moment and a beautiful scene

【良导体】［物］good conductor

【良方】❶ effective prescription；good recipe ❷ good plan；sound strategy

【良港】a good harbour

【良好】good；well：～的开端 *a good beginning* / ～的习惯 *good habits* / ～的愿望 *good intentions*

【良机】〈书〉good (or golden) opportunity：莫失～。*Don't let this good opportunity slip.*

【良久】〈书〉a good while；a long time

【良能】intuitive ability；inborn ability

【良师益友】good teacher and helpful friend

【良田】good farmland；fertile farmland

【良心】conscience：有～ *have a conscience*；*be good-hearted* / 没～ *conscienceless*；*heartless*；*ungrateful* / ～上感到不安 *have an uneasy conscience*；*feel the pricks of conscience* / ～发现。*The conscience is moved.*

【良性】［医］benign：那个肿瘤检查出来是～的。*The tumour proved benign.*

【良性循环】a virtuous circle：国民经济的～ *a virtuous circle in the national economy*

【良性肿瘤】benign tumour

【良药】good medicine (usu.〈喻〉)：对症～ *the right remedy*

【良药苦口】good medicine tastes bitter：～利于病，忠言逆耳利于行。*Just as bitter medicine cures sickness, unpalatable advice benefits conduct.*

【良医】a skilful doctor

【良友】good friend

【良莠不齐】the good and the bad are intermingled

【良知】intuitive knowledge；innate knowledge

【良种】❶ (fine) improved variety：水稻～ *improved varieties of rice* ❷ fine breed：～马 *a horse of fine breed* ◇ ～场 seed multiplication farm

凉 形 ❶ cool；cold：～风 *cool breeze* / 天气忽然～了。*The weather has suddenly got cold.* / 饭～了。*The food's got cold.* ❷ discouraged；disappointed：一听这消息他就～了半截。*His heart sank at the news.* ——另见 liàng

【凉拌】(of food) cold and dressed with sauce：～生菜 *tossed salad* / ～面 *cold noodles in sauce*

【凉菜】cold dish

【凉粉】bean-starch noodles

【凉快】❶ nice and cool；pleasantly cool：这里～，坐下来歇会儿。*It's nice and cool here. Let's sit down and have a rest.* ❷ cool oneself；cool off：咱们到树荫下面去～一下吧！*Let's sit in the shade and cool off a bit.*

【凉棚】mat-awning；mat shelter

【凉气】cold air；chilly air：～袭人。*The cold air chills one to the core.*

【凉伞】sunshade；parasol

【凉爽】nice and cool；pleasantly cool：～的秋天 *pleasantly cool autumn days*

【凉水】❶ cold water ❷ unboiled water

【凉丝丝】coolish；rather cool；a bit cool

【凉飕飕】(of wind) chilly；chill

【凉台】balcony；veranda

【凉亭】wayside pavilion；summer house；kiosk

【凉席】summer sleeping mat (of woven split bamboo, etc.)

【凉鞋】sandals

梁 名 ❶ roof beam: 架～ *set a roof beam in place* ❷ bridge: 桥梁 ❸ ridge: 山梁 / 鼻梁

【梁桥】beam bridge

【梁上君子】gentleman on the beam—burglar; thief

椋 (构词成分) 见下

【椋鸟】starling

量 动 ❶ measure: ～身材 *take sb.'s measurements* / ～尺寸 *take sb.'s measurements* / ～体温 *take sb.'s temperature* ❷ appraise; evaluate; estimate: 打量 / 估量 ——另见 liàng

【量杯】measuring glass; graduate

【量度】measurement

【量角器】protractor

【量具】measuring tool

【量瓶】measuring (or graduated, volumetric) flask

【量热器】calorimeter

【量日仪】heliometer

【量筒】graduated (or volumetric, measuring) cylinder; graduate

【量图仪】map measurer

【量雪尺】snow scale

【量雪器】snow gauge

【量油尺】oil dip rod; dipstick

【量雨筒】precipitation gauge

粮 名 ❶grain; food; provisions: ～棉双丰收 *a bumper harvest of grain and cotton* ❷ grain tax paid in kind: 公粮

【粮仓】❶ granary; garner ❷ granary (〈喻〉); rice bowl: 东北是祖国的～。*The Northeast is the granary of the country.*

【粮草】army provisions; rations and forage (or fodder)

【粮店】grain shop

【粮库】grain depot

【粮秣】army provisions; rations and forage; grain and fodder ◇ ～库 ration depot

【粮票】food coupon; grain coupon

【粮食】grain; cereals; food ◇ ～产量 grain yield; ～储备 grain reserves; grain stock; ～供应 staple food supply; ～加工 grain processing; ～配给 grain ration; ～作物 cereal crops; grain crops

【粮油】grain and cooking oil

【粮栈】wholesale grain store; grain depot

【粮站】grain distribution station; grain supply centre

liǎng

两 Ⅰ 数 ❶(used before measure words and before 半,千,万,and 亿) two: ～匹马 *two horses* / ～个半月 *two and a half months* / ～千元 *two thousand yuan* ❷a few; some: 我想讲～句。*I'd like to say a few words.* / 这事过～天再说。*Let's leave it for a couple of days.* Ⅱ 名 both (sides); either (side): ～利 *benefit both; be good for both sides* / ～不吃亏。*Neither side suffers any loss.* Ⅲ 量 liang, currently called 市两, a traditional unit of weight

【两岸三地】three regions of China: Mainland, Taiwan (separated by the Taiwan Strait) and Hong Kong

【两败俱伤】both sides suffer (or lose); neither side gains

【两半儿】two halves; in half; in two: 碟子摔成～了。*The dish is broken in two.* / 把苹果切成～ *cut an apple in half*

【两边】❶both sides; both directions; both places: 这张纸～长短不齐。*The two edges of this piece of paper aren't even in length.* ❷ both parties; both sides: ～讨好 *try to please both sides* / ～都说好了,明天下午赛球。*The two teams have agreed to play the match tomorrow afternoon.*

【两边倒】lean now to one side, now to the other; waver: 墙上一棵草,风吹～。*A tuft of grass atop the wall sways right and left in the wind (a saying).*

【两便】be convenient to both; make things easy for both: 您甭等我了,咱们～。*Please don't wait for me. That might be more convenient for both of us.*

【两鬓斑白】greying at the temples

【两鬓苍苍】greying at the temples

【两重】double; dual; twofold: ～意义 *a double meaning* / ～任务 *a two-fold task*

【两次三番】(又作'三番两次') again and again; time and again; over and over again

【两次运球】[体](蓝球)double dribble

【两党制】two-party system; bipartisan system

【两抵】balance or cancel each other: 收支～。*Income and expenditure balance each other.* or *The account balances out.*

【两点论】the doctrine that everything has two aspects

【两耳不闻窗外事】both ears shut to what goes on outside the window: ～,一心只读圣贤书。*Both ears are shut to what goes on outside the window; the whole mind is concentrated on the sages' books (said, usu. disapprovingly, of one who is absorbed in study and oblivious of his surroundings).*

【两分法】application of the Marxist law that "one divides into two"

【两湖】the Two Hus—Hubei and Hunan Provinces

【两虎相斗,必有一伤】When two tigers fight, one is bound to get hurt.

【两回事】two entirely different things; two different matters: 严格要求和求全责备是～。*Being strict and being a nitpicker are two entirely different things.*

【两会】the National People's Congress and the Chinese Political Consultative Conference

【两极】❶ the two poles of the earth ❷［物］the two poles (of a magnet or an electric battery) ❸ two opposing extremes

【两极分化】polarize：贫富～ *the polarity between rich and poor*

【两件套】two-piece dress

【两脚规】❶ compasses ❷ dividers

【两可】both will do；either will do；could go either way：我去不去～。*It's all right with me whether I go or not.* / 成不成还在～。*Whether it will succeed or not—it could go either way.*

【两可之间】❶ either will do；not know which to choose ❷ both are possible；maybe，maybe not

【两口子】（又作'两口儿'）〈口〉husband and wife；couple：他们～都工作。*Both he and his wife work.*

【两码事】同〖两回事〗

【两面】❶ two sides；both sides；two aspects；both aspects：这张纸～都写满了字。*Both sides of the paper were covered with writing.* ❷ having a dual (or double) character；dual；double：～手法 *double-faced tactics*；*double-dealing*；*double game*

【两面光】(try to) please both parties

【两面夹攻】close in from both sides；make a pincer attack：受到～ *be under a pincer attack*；*be caught in a two-way squeeze*；*be caught in cross fire*

【两面派】double-dealer：耍～ *resort to double-dealing*；*be double-faced*

【两面三刀】double-dealing；double cross

【两面性】dual nature；duplicity；ambivalence

【两难】face a difficult choice；be in a dilemma：去也不好，不去也不好，真是～。*I'm in a dilemma as to whether to go or not.*

【两旁】both sides；either side：马路～都种着树。*There are trees on either side of the road.*

【两栖】amphibious ◇ ～部队 amphibious forces；amphibious units；～动物 amphibious animal；amphibian；～植物 amphibious plant；amphibian；～作战 amphibious warfare；amphibious operations

【两讫】［经］the goods are delivered and the bill is cleared

【两全】be satisfactory to both parties；have regard for both sides：～的办法 *measures satisfactory to both sides (or in both respects)*

【两全其美】satisfy both sides；satisfy rival claims

【两审终审制】［法］the system of the court of second instance being the court of last instance

【两世为人】barely escape with one's life；be lucky to have escaped death

【两手】dual tactics：作～准备 *prepare oneself for both eventualities*

【两条心】in fundamental disagreement；not of one mind

【两头】❶ both ends；either end：～尖 *pointed at both ends* / ～儿跑 *go back and forth between two places* ❷ both parties；both sides：～为难 *find it hard to please either party*；*find it difficult to satisfy two conflicting demands*

【两头落空】fall between two stools

【两头小，中间大】small at both ends and big in the middle；a few at each extreme and many in between；a few advanced，a few backward，but the majority middling

【两下子】（又作'两下'）❶ a few times：轻轻敲了～ *give a couple of raps (on sth.)* ❷ a few tricks of the trade：你真有～！*You really are smart!*

【两相情愿】by mutual consent；both parties being willing

【两厢】❶ wing-rooms on either side of a one-storey house ❷ both sides：站立～ *stand on either side*

【两相】［电］two-phase：～电动机 *two-phase motor*

【两小无猜】(of a little boy and a little girl) be innocent playmates

【两性】❶ both sexes ❷［化］amphiprotic；amphoteric ◇ ～关系 sexual relations；～花 hermaphrodite flower；～化合物 amphoteric compound；～胶体 amphoteric colloid；ampholytoid；～人 bisexual person；hermaphrodite；～生殖 bisexual reproduction

【两袖清风】(of an official) have clean hands；remain uncorrupted

【两伊战争】the Iran-Iraq War

【两翼】❶ both wings：鸟的～ *both wings of a bird* / 飞机的～ *both wings of an airplane* ❷［军］both wings；both flanks：～包抄 *double envelopment*

【两用】dual purpose：～炉子 *dual-purpose stove* / ～雨衣 *reversible raincoat* ◇ ～人才 dual-purpose personnel；～衫 同〖春秋衫〗

【两院制】two-chamber system；bicameral system；bicameralism

【两造】❶［法］both parties in a lawsuit；both plaintiff and defendant ❷〈方〉two crops：改一年～为一年三造 *change from two crops a year to three*

liàng

亮 Ⅰ 形 ❶ bright；light：屋里很～。*The room is very bright.* / 那个电灯很～。*That electric light is very bright.* / 天～了。*It's light already.* ❷ loud and clear：她的嗓子真～。*She has a resonant voice.* ❸ enlightened：你这一说，我心里头～了。*I find what you say most enlightening.* Ⅱ 动 ❶ shine：屋子里～着灯光。*Lights were shining in the room.* / 他把手电筒～了一下。*He flashed the torch on for a second.* ❷ make one's voice loud and clear：～起嗓子 *lift one's voice* ❸ show；reveal：～刀 *pull out a knife* / 他把工作证～了一下就进去了。*He showed his identity card and went in.*

【亮底】reveal the whole story；disclose one's plan，stand，views，etc.；put one's cards on the table

◇ ～牌〈字〉show one's cards (or hand);〈喻〉reveal one's true intention

【亮度】[物] brightness; brilliance: 星的～ *the brightness of a star* / 萤光屏～ *screen brilliance*

【亮光】light (〈反〉: darkness): 一道～ *a shaft of light* ◇ ～漆 lacquer polish

【亮红灯】〈字〉show the red light;〈喻〉forbid: 有关部门对此做法亮了红灯。*Authorities concerned have forbidden such a practice.*

【亮晶晶】glittering; sparkling; glistening: ～的星星 *glittering stars* / ～的露珠 *glistening dewdrops*

【亮堂】❶ light; bright: 这屋子又宽敞又～。*The room is light and spacious.* ❷ (of voice) loud and clear: 嗓门～ *have a resonant voice* ❸ clear; enlightened: 经过反复讨论,大家心里更～了。*After repeated discussions, we had a much better understanding of the whole thing.*

【亮相】❶ (in Beijing opera, dancing, etc.) strike a pose on the stage ❷ declare one's position; state one's views

凉 动 let sth. cool: ～一会儿再吃。*Let it cool off a bit before you eat it.* ——另见 liáng

谅 动 ❶forgive; understand: 本着互～互让的精神 *in the spirit of mutual understanding and mutual accommodation* ❷I think; I suppose; I expect: 前信～已收到。*I expect you have received my last letter.* / ～他也不会这样做。*I don't think he'd do that.*

【谅解】understand; make allowance for: 他很～你的苦衷。*He understands your difficulties.* / 达成～ *reach an understanding* ◇ ～备忘录 memorandum of understanding

辆 量 (for vehicles): 一～公共汽车 *a bus* / 三～大车 *three carts*

晾 动 ❶ dry in the air; air: 草垫子该～一～了。*The straw mattress needs to be aired.* ❷ dry in the sun; sun: ～衣服 *sun clothes; hang the wash out to dry* / 海滩上～着渔网。*Fishnets are spread out on the beach to dry.* ❸ neglect sb.: 我不喜欢玩儿牌。他们每次玩儿的时候都把我～在一边儿。*As I didn't like cards, I was left out in the cold every time they played.*

【晾干】dry by airing: 把衣服拿出去～。*Hang the clothes out to dry.* / 草药已经～了。*The medicinal herbs are dry now.*

【晾台】sun terrace (for drying clothes)

【晾烟】❶air-curing of tobacco leaves ❷ air-cured tobacco

【晾衣绳】clothesline

量 Ⅰ 名 ❶capacity for tolerance or for taking food or drink: 饭量 / 气量 ❷quantity; amount; volume: 出口～ *the volume of exports* Ⅱ 动 estimate; measure: 量力——另见 liáng

【量变】[哲] quantitative change

【量才录用】give sb. work suited to his (or her) abilities; assign jobs to people according to their abilities

【量词】[语] measure word (as 个、只、次、阵); classifier

【量纲】[物] dimension: ～分析 *dimensional analysis*

【量力】estimate one's own strength or ability (and act accordingly)

【量力而行】do what one is capable of; act according to one's capability

【量入为出】keep expenditures below income; live within one's means; cut one's coat according to one's cloth

【量体裁衣】cut the garment according to the figure—act according to actual circumstances

【量刑】[法] measurement of penalty

【量子】[物] quantum: 光～ *light quantum* ◇ ～化学 quantum chemistry; ～力学 quantum mechanics; ～论 quantum theory; ～生物学 quantum biology

靓 〈方〉beautiful; pretty; handsome

【靓女】〈方〉a pretty girl

【靓仔】〈方〉a handsome young man

踉 (构词成分) 见下

【踉跄】(又作'踉锵') stagger: 那个醉汉踉踉跄跄地在路上走着。*The drunk man staggered along the road.*

liāo

撩 动 ❶ raise or lift up (a part of sth. which is hanging): ～起帘子 *raise the curtains* / ～裙子 *lift (or hold up) the hem of one's skirt* ❷ sprinkle (with one's hand): 先～些水再扫地。*Sprinkle some water on the floor before sweeping it.* ——另见 liáo

liáo

辽 Ⅰ 形 distant; faraway: 辽远 Ⅱ 名 the Liao Dynasty (907—1125)

【辽阔】vast; extensive: ～的土地 *a vast expanse of land; vast territory* / 我国幅员～。*Our country has a vast territory.*

【辽远】distant; faraway: ～的边疆 *distant frontier regions* / 但见一行大雁正飞向～的天空。*A column of wild geese was seen flying into the distant sky.*

疗 动 treat; cure: 医疗 / 治疗

【疗程】course (or period) of treatment

【疗法】therapy; treatment: 化学～ *chemotherapy* / 新针～ *new acupuncture therapy* / 电休克～ *shock treatment*

【疗效】curative effect: 青霉素对肺炎有显著的～。*Penicillin is particularly effective against pneu-*

monia.

【疗养】recuperate; convalesce ◇ ～院 sanatorium; convalescent hospital (or home)

聊 Ⅰ 副 ❶ merely; just: ～表谢意 *just a token of gratitude; just to show my appreciation* ❷ a little; slightly: 聊胜于无 Ⅱ 动〈口〉chat; gab: 晚饭后咱们～～。*Let's have a chat after supper.* / 你们在～些什么? *What are you folks gabbing about?*

【聊备一格】may serve as a specimen

【聊赖】见〖百无聊赖〗

【聊且】tentatively; for the moment

【聊胜于无】better than nothing

【聊天(儿)】〈口〉chat; gab: 我们聊了半天天儿。*We chatted for a long time.* ◇ ～室[计]chat room

【聊以解嘲】make a feeble attempt to explain things away when ridiculed; in a feeble attempt to silence jeers

【聊以塞责】just to meet the bare requirements

【聊以自慰】just to console oneself

【聊以卒岁】just to tide over the year

寥 形 ❶few; scanty: 寥落 ❷silent; deserted

【寥廓】〈书〉boundless; vast: ～的天空 *the boundless sky*

【寥寥】very few

【寥寥可数】very few: 到会者～。*Very few people came to the meeting.*

【寥寥无几】very few: 号召自愿参加,但响应者～。*A call for volunteers was sent out, but very few people responded.*

【寥落】few and far between; sparse; scattered: 疏星～ *only a few solitary stars twinkling in the sky*

【寥若晨星】as sparse as the morning stars; few and far between

僚 名 ❶ official: 官僚 ❷ an associate in office: 同僚

【僚机】[军] ❶ wing plane; wingman ❷ wingman

【僚舰】[军] consort

【僚属】〈旧〉officials under sb. in authority; subordinates; staff

寮 名〈方〉small house; hut: 僧～ *a monk's cell (or hut)* / 茶～酒肆 *teahouses and wineshops*

【寮棚】shed; hut

撩 动 ❶tease; tantalize❷ provoke; stir up —— 另见 liāo

【撩拨】❶ tease; banter ❷ incite; provoke

【撩动】provoke; stir up: ～心弦 *tug at one's heartstrings; be heart-stirring*

【撩逗】tease; provoke: 他这两天好像心情不好,你别去～他。*He seems very moody these days. Don't tease him.*

【撩人】stirring; exciting; teasing: 春色～。*Spring's hues are teasing.*

嘹 (构词成分) 见下

【嘹亮】resonant; loud and clear: 歌声～。*The singing is loud and clear.* / ～的号角 *a clarion call*

獠 (构词成分) 见下

【獠牙】long, sharp, protruding teeth

缭 动 ❶ entangled: 缭乱 ❷ sew with slanting stitches: ～贴边 *stitch a hem; hem*

【缭乱】〈书〉confused; in a turmoil: 心绪～ *in a confused state of mind*

【缭绕】curl up; wind around: 炊烟～ *smoke curling up from kitchen chimneys* / 歌声～。*The song lingered in the air.*

潦 (构词成分) 见下

【潦草】❶ (of handwriting) hasty and careless; illegible: 字迹～。*The writing is illegible.* ❷ sloppy; slovenly: 干活儿～ *work in a slipshod way*

【潦倒】be frustrated; be down on one's luck

燎 动 burn

【燎泡】(又作'燎浆泡') blister raised by a burn or scald

【燎原】set the prairie ablaze: 革命的烈火已成～之势。*The flames of revolution are spreading far and wide.*

liǎo

了 Ⅰ 动 ❶ finish; conclude; settle; dispose of: 这事情还没～哇。*This matter hasn't been settled yet.* / 账也～了,我的心事也～了。*The debt is settled, and my worry is over.* ❷ (used after a verb plus 得 or 不) to a finish: 办得～ *can manage it* / 受不～ *cannot stand it* / 你骗不～我。*You can't fool me.* Ⅱ 副〈书〉(not) in the least: ～不相涉 *have nothing at all to do with it* Ⅲ 动 know clearly; understand: 明了

【了不得】❶ wonderful; terrific: 他真～。*He's really terrific.* / 一件～的大事 *a matter of the utmost importance* ❷ (used as complement after 得) extremely; awfully; terribly: 高兴得～ *be extremely happy* ❸ terrible; awful: 可～,他昏过去了! *Good God! He's fainted.* / 危险是有的,但并不是那么～。*There was danger, but it wasn't so serious.*

【了不起】amazing; terrific; extraordinary: ～的成就 *an amazing achievement* / 他真～。*He's really terrific.* / 没什么～。*There's nothing so terrific.*

【了得】(used, usu. after 还, in exclamations) horrible; terrible: 哎呀! 这还～! *Oh! How outrageous (or terrible, awful)!* / 过去要是遇到这样的大旱,那还～! *How terrible such a drought would have been in the past!*

【了结】finish; settle; wind up; bring to an end: ～一场纠纷 *settle a dispute; end a conflict*

【了解】❶ understand; comprehend: 我完全～你。*I understand you perfectly.* / 我很～你的困难。*I very much understand your difficulty.* ❷ find out; acquaint oneself with: 我们必须设法～全部情况。*We must try to find out about the whole situation.* ❸ understanding; comprehension: 我对市场经济的～很差。*My understanding of market economy is very limited.*

【了局】❶ end: 这就是故事的～。*This is how the story ends.* ❷ solution; settlement: 拖下去不是个～。*Putting things off is no solution.*

【了却】settle; solve: 这就～了我的一桩心事。*That settled a matter which had been weighing on my mind.*

【了然】understand; be clear: 真相如何,我也不大～。*I don't have a clear picture of the real situation either.*

【了如指掌】know sth. like the palm of one's hand; have sth. at one's fingertips: 他对这一带的地形～。*He knows the terrain of this locality like the back of his hand.*

【了事】dispose of a matter; finish up sth.; get sth. over: 这样就算～了吗? *Do you consider this done?* / 应付～ *deal with sth. in a perfunctory way*

钌 名 [化] ruthenium (Ru)

蓼 名 knotweed

【蓼科】[植] Polygonaceae

【蓼蓝】indigo plant

liào

料 Ⅰ 动 suppose; expect; anticipate: ～他不敢。*I don't think he dare.* / ～定敌军会有行动 *anticipate movements on the part of the enemy* Ⅱ 名 ❶ material; stuff: ～备足了没有? *Have we got enough material?* ❷ (grain) feed: 多给牲口加点～。*Put more grain in the fodder.* ❸ makings; material: 我不是唱歌的～。*I haven't got the makings of a singer.* / 凭他那块～也想当教授。*Even an oaf like him thinks he can be a professor.*

【料车】skip car; skip

【料到】foresee; expect: 没～他会来。*We didn't expect him to come.*

【料酒】cooking wine

【料理】❶ arrange; manage; attend to; take care of: ～家务 *manage household affairs* / 孩子们已能自己～生活。*The children can take care of themselves now.* ❷ cuisine; food: 日本～ *Japanese food*

【料理后事】make arrangements for a funeral

【料器】glassware

【料峭】〈文〉chilly: 春寒～。*There is a chill in the air in early spring.*

【料事如神】predict like a prophet; foretell with miraculous accuracy

【料想】expect; think; presume: 真是～不到的事情! *Who would have thought that would happen!*

【料子】❶ material for making clothes ❷〈方〉woollen fabric: ～裤 *trousers made of woollen fabric* / ～服 *suits of woollen cloth*

撂 动〈口〉❶ put down; leave behind: 把帘子～下来。*Let down the curtain.* / 他把东西都～在地下了。*He put everything down on the floor.* ❷ throw down; knock down; shoot down: 一枪就～倒一个敌人 *hit an enemy soldier with each shot*

【撂挑子】put down the load—give up one's responsibilities; quit one's job: 不该挨了批评就～。*It's bad to quit one's job just because one's been criticized.*

瞭 动 watch from a height or a distance

【瞭望】watch from a height or a distance; keep a lookout: 用望远镜～敌军阵地 *look at the enemy's position through field glasses* ◇ ～哨 lookout post; ～台 observation tower; lookout tower

镣 名 fetters: 脚镣

【镣铐】fetters and handcuffs; shackles; irons; chains: 戴上～ *be shackled; be in chains*

liē

咧 (构词成分) 见下——另见 liě

【咧咧】〈方〉❶ talk nonsense; blabber: 你瞎～什么? *What are you blabbering about?* ❷ (of a child) cry: 那个小孩儿老～。*That child is always crying.*

liě

咧 (构词成分) 见下——另见 liē

【咧嘴】draw back the corners of the mouth; grin: 疼得直～ *grin with pain* / 他咧着嘴笑。*His face broadened into a grin.* / 他尝了一口,直～。*He made a face when he tasted it.*

裂 动〈口〉(of two pieces joined together) come apart; open up: 衣服没扣好,～着怀 *with one's coat (or shirt) unbuttoned*——另见 liè

liè

列 Ⅰ 动 ❶ arrange; set out: ～出理由 *set out one's reasons (for sth.)* / ～表 *arrange (facts, figures, etc.) in tables or columns; tabulate* ❷ list; enter in a list: 代表姓名～后。*Listed below are the names of the delegates.* / ～入议程 *be*

placed on the agenda Ⅱ 名 ❶row; file; rank: 前列❷ kind; sort: 不在讨论之～ *not among the subjects to be discussed* Ⅲ 量 (for a series or row of things): 一～火车 *a train* Ⅳ 代 various; each and every: 列国
【列兵】[军] private
【列车】train: 旅客～ *passenger train* / 直达～ *through train* / 15 次～ *No. 15 train* ◇ ～调度员 train dispatcher; ～时刻表 train schedule; timetable; ～员 attendant (on a train); ～长 head of a train crew
【列当】[植] broomrape
【列岛】a chain of islands; archipelago
【列队】line up: ～欢迎 *line up to welcome sb.*
【列国】the various countries, states, or kingdoms: ～相争 *kingdoms warring against each other*
【列举】enumerate; list: ～大量事实 *cite numerous facts* / 计划中～了各种具体办法。*Various concrete measures were enumerated in the plan.*
【列宁主义】Leninism
【列强】〈旧〉the Great Powers: 打倒～! *Down with the imperialist Powers!*
【列氏温度计】the Réaumur thermometer
【列位】all of you; gentlemen; ladies and gentlemen: ～来宾 *all of you honoured guests*
【列席】attend (a meeting) as an observer or a nonvoting delegate; attend without voting rights ◇ ～代表 delegate without the right to vote; nonvoting delegate
【列阵】[电] array
【列支敦士登】Liechtenstein ◇ ～人 Liechtensteiner
【列传】biographies
【列祖列宗】successive generations of ancestors

劣 形 bad; inferior; of low quality: 优劣
【劣币】sinker
【劣等】of inferior quality; low-grade; poor: ～产品 *poor quality products; products of inferior quality* / ～人种 *an inferior race (a racist term)*
【劣根性】deep-rooted bad habits; an inherent weakness
【劣弧】[数] minor arc
【劣迹】misdeed; evil doing
【劣迹昭彰】have a notorious record
【劣马】❶ inferior horse; nag ❷ vicious horse; fiery steed
【劣绅】evil gentry
【劣势】inferior position; unfavourable situation: 处于～ *be in an inferior position*
【劣质】of poor (or low) quality; inferior: ～煤 *inferior coal; faulty coal*
【劣种】inferior strain (or breed, stock)

烈 Ⅰ 形 strong; violent; intense: ～酒 *a strong drink; hard liquor* / 两国之间的争夺愈演愈～。*The rivalry between the two countries is becoming increasingly acute.* ❷ staunch; upright; stern: 刚烈 Ⅱ 名 sacrificing oneself for a just cause: 先烈
【烈度】〈略〉见〖地震烈度〗
【烈风】[气] strong gale
【烈火】raging fire; raging flames: 熊熊的～ *a raging fire*
【烈火见真金】pure gold proves its worth in a blazing fire—people of worth show their mettle during trials and tribulations ——另见〖疾风知劲草〗
【烈士】❶ martyr: 革命～ *a revolutionary martyr* ❷ (in former times) a man of high endeavour; hero ◇ ～纪念碑 a monument to revolutionary martyrs; ～陵园 revolutionary martyrs' cemetery; martyrs' park; ～墓 the tomb of a revolutionary martyr
【烈属】members of a revolutionary martyr's family
【烈性】❶ spirited: ～汉子 *a man of spirited character* ❷ strong: ～酒 *a strong (or stiff) drink; hard liquor; spirits* / ～毒药 *deadly poison* / ～炸药 *high explosive*
【烈焰】raging flames; a roaring blaze

猎 动 hunt: ～虎 *tiger hunting*
【猎豹】cheetah
【猎场】hunting ground; hunting field
【猎刀】hunting knife
【猎狗】hunting dog; hound
【猎户】hunter; huntsman
【猎户座】[天] Orion
【猎获】capture or kill in hunting; bag: ～两三只野兔 *bag a couple of hares* / ～一头幼象 *trap a young elephant* ◇ ～物 bag
【猎奇】hunt for novelty; seek novelty
【猎潜艇】submarine chaser
【猎枪】shotgun; fowling piece; hunting rifle
【猎取】❶ hunt: 原始社会的人用粗糙的石器～野兽。*Primitive man hunted wild animals with crude stone implements.* ❷ pursue; seek; hunt for: ～个人名利 *pursue personal fame and gain* / ～廉价的声誉 *make a bid for cheap popularity*
【猎犬】hunting dog; hound
【猎人】hunter; huntsman
【猎头】〈口〉headhunter: ～公司 headhunter company
【猎艳】〈书〉❶ rack one's brains for ornate diction ❷ chase after pretty women
【猎鹰】falcon
【猎装】hunting suit; hunting outfit

裂 动 split; crack; rend: 杯子～了。*The cup's cracked.* / 地都干～了。*The earth was so dry that it cracked.* / 他的手冻～了。*His hands are chapped by the cold.* / ～成两半 *split in two* ——另见 liě
【裂变】[物] fission ◇ ～产物 fission product; ～武器 the fission type of weapon
【裂缝】❶crack; split: 墙上裂了一道缝。*The wall has cracked.* ❷rift; crevice; crack; fissure: 墙上

有一道～。*There is a crack in the wall.*

【裂果】[植] dehiscent fruit

【裂痕】rift; crack; fissure: 这块玻璃有一道～。*There is a crack in the glass.* / 他们之间一度有过～。*There was once a rift between them.*

【裂化】cracking (in the distillation of petroleum) ◇ ～炉 cracking still (or furnace, heater); ～气 cracked gas

【裂解】[化] splitting decomposition; splitting ◇ ～作用[化] splitting action

【裂开】crack open; split open: 盒子掉在地上～了。*The box fell on the ground and cracked open.* / 木板干得～了。*The board was so dry that it split open.*

【裂口】❶ crack; split: 堤上～了。*The dike has cracked.* / 他的手冻得～了。*His hands are chapped by the cold.* ❷ breach; gap; crack; split: 堤上的～越来越大。*The crack in the dike is getting wider.* ❸ vent (of a volcano) ◇ ～火山锥 breached cone

【裂纹】❶ crack (the sides being still together): 窗户上有一道～,是踢球踢的。*The window has a crack in it where the ball hit it.* ❷ crackle (on pottery, porcelain, etc.)

【裂隙】crack; crevice; fracture ◇ ～水 crevice water

【裂殖菌】schizomycete

趔 (构词成分) 见下

【趔趄】stagger; reel: 他～着走进屋来。*He staggered into the room.* / 他打了个～,摔倒了。*He reeled and fell.*

鬣 名 mane

【鬣狗】hyena; striped hyena

【鬣羚】serow

līn

拎 动〈方〉carry; lift: 他～着桶去打水。*He was carrying a bucket to fetch water.*

【拎包】〈方〉handbag; shopping bag; bag

lín

邻 Ⅰ 名 neighbour: 近邻 Ⅱ 形 neighbouring; near; adjacent: ～县 *a neighbouring county* / ～座 *an adjacent seat*

【邻邦】neighbouring country: 我们两国历来是友好的～。*Our two countries have always been good neighbours.*

【邻国】neighbouring country

【邻家】next-door family; next-door (or close) neighbour

【邻角】[数] adjacent angles

【邻接】border on; be next to; be contiguous to; adjoin: 西班牙～法国西南部。*Spain borders on the southwest of France.*

【邻近】❶ be near; be close to; be adjacent to: 我国东部跟朝鲜接壤,跟日本～。*In the east, our country adjoins Korea and is close to Japan.* ❷ neighbourhood; vicinity: ～没有医院。*There's no hospital in the neighbourhood.* / 学校～有商店。*There's a shop in the vicinity of the school.*

【邻居】neighbour

【邻里】❶ neighbourhood: ～服务所 *a neighbourhood service centre* ❷ people of the neighbourhood; neighbours

【邻位】[化] ortho-position: ～化合物 *orthocompound*

林 名 ❶ forest; woods; grove: 松～ *pine forest* ❷ a group of persons or things: 艺林 ❸ forestry: 农林

【林产】forest products

【林场】forestry centre (including tree nurseries, lumber camps, etc.); tree farm

【林带】forest belt: 防沙～ *a sand-break forest belt*

【林地】forest land; woodland; timberland

【林冠】[林] crown canopy; crown cover

【林海】immense forest

【林垦】forestry and land reclamation

【林立】(of masts, smokestacks, derricks, tall buildings, etc.) stand (in great numbers) like a forest: 港口樯桅～。*There is a forest of masts in the harbour.*

【林龄】[林] age of stand

【林木】❶ forest; woods: ～葱郁 *densely wooded* ❷ forest tree

【林檎】another name for 花红❶

【林区】forest zone; forest region; forest

【林涛】the soughing of the wind in forest trees

【林业】forestry ◇ ～工人 forest worker; forester

【林阴道】(又作'林阴路') boulevard; avenue

【林子】〈口〉woods; grove; forest

临 Ⅰ 动 ❶ face; overlook: ～街的窗子 *a window overlooking the street* / 东～大海 *border on the sea in the east* ❷ arrive; be present: 亲临 ❸ copy (a model of calligraphy or painting): ～画 *copy a painting* / ～帖 *practise calligraphy after a model* Ⅱ 介 on the point of; just before; be about to: ～睡 *just before going to bed; at bedtime* / 这本书是我～离开北京时买的。*I bought this book just before I left Beijing.*

【临本】copy (of a painting, etc.)

【临别】at parting; just before parting: ～合影 *have a group photo taken just before parting* / 作为～纪念 *as a parting souvenir* ◇ ～赠言 words of advice at parting; parting advice

【临产】about to give birth; parturient ◇ ～阵痛 labour pains; birth pangs

【临场】❶ when attending an examination; when participating in a contest: ～要沉着,不要慌。*Keep calm during the exam. Don't panic.* ❷ come personally to the site (or spot): ～指导 *come personally to give on-the-spot guidance*

【临床】clinical：～检查 *clinical examination* / ～教学 *clinical instruction* / ～经验 *clinical experience* / ～诊断 *clinical (or bedside) diagnosis* ◇ ～表现 clinical manifestation；～学 clinical medicine；～医生 clinician；～应用 clinical practice

【临到】❶ just before；on the point of：～开会，她还在准备发言。*She was still preparing her speech when the meeting began.* ❷ befall；happen to：这事如果～你的头上，你怎么办？*What would you do if it happened to you?*

【临机】face an emergency：～应变 *make changes as the situation demands；act according to the circumstances；be prepared for all contingencies* / ～立断 *make a quick decision as the situation demands*

【临界】［物］critical ◇ ～点 critical point；～角 critical angle；～态 critical state；～体积 critical size；～温度 critical temperature

【临近】close to；close on：～黎明 *close on daybreak* / ～太湖的一所疗养院 *a sanatorium close by Taihu Lake*

【临渴掘井】not dig a well until one is thirsty—start acting too late；make an eleventh-hour attempt

【临了】(又作'临末了')〈口〉finally；in the end：人人都想去，～只好由组长决定。*Everyone wanted to go. In the end the group leader had to decide.*

【临门】❶ come to the house：贵客～。*A distinguished guest came to the house.* ❷ facing the goal：～一脚 *(in football) shooting (at the goal) after breaking through the opponent's defence；go for the goal*

【临摹】copy (a model of calligraphy or painting)

【临盆】be giving birth to a child；be confined；be in labour

【临时】❶ at the time when sth. is needed or is expected to happen：你现在不准备，～怎么办呢？*If you don't prepare now, what will you do when the time comes?* ❷ temporarily；for the time being：我们～就用这个办法吧。*Let's use this method temporarily.* / ～凑合 *make do for the moment* ❸ temporary；provisional：～办法 *a temporary solution (or arrangement)；makeshift measures* / ～工作人员 *a temporary member of the staff* / ～舞台 *a makeshift stage* / ～协议 *a provisional (or interim) agreement* / ～议程 *a provisional agenda* ◇ ～代办 chargé d'affaires ad interim；～动议 extempore motion；～法庭 provisional court；～费用 interim (or incidental) expenses；～工 casual labourer；temporary worker；～户口 temporary residence permit；～协议 provisional agreement；～执照 temporary license；～证书 (in diplomacy) temporary credentials (or papers)；～政府 provisional (or interim) government；～主席 interim chairman

【临时抱佛脚】embrace Buddha's feet in one's hour of need—seek help at the last moment；make a frantic last-minute effort

【临死】on one's deathbed

【临头】befall；happen

【临危】❶ be dying (from illness) ❷ face death or deadly peril

【临危不惧】face danger fearlessly；betray no fear in face of danger

【临危授命】be ready to give one's life in times of national danger

【临刑】just before execution

【临渊羡鱼】stand by a pond longing for fish；one should take practical steps to achieve one's aims

【临阵磨枪】sharpen one's spear just before going into battle—start to prepare at the last moment

【临阵脱逃】desert on the eve of a battle；sneak away at a critical juncture

【临终】approaching one's end；immediately before one's death；on one's deathbed ◇ ～遗言 deathbed testament；last words

淋 动 pour；drench：他的衣服让雨～湿了。*His clothes were drenched by the rain.* / 日晒雨～ *sun-scorched and rain-drenched；exposed to the elements* ——另见 lìn

【淋巴】lymph ◇ ～球 lymphocyte；～肉瘤 lymphosarcoma；～液 同〖淋巴〗

【淋巴结】lymph node (or gland) ◇ ～炎 lymphnoditis

【淋漓】❶ dripping wet：大汗～ *dripping with sweat* / 鲜血～ *dripping with blood* ❷ (of a piece of writing or a speech) free from inhibition：痛快～ *impassioned and forceful*

【淋漓尽致】vividly and incisively；in great detail：刻画得～ *portray most vividly* / 揭露得～ *make a telling exposure* / 他这番表演，真可谓～。*He put on an act, which showed him up completely.*

【淋淋】dripping wet：湿～的衣服 *dripping wet clothes*

【淋洗】drip washing

【淋雨】get wet in the rain

【淋浴】shower bath；shower：洗～ *take (or have) a shower*

琳 名〈书〉beautiful jade

【琳琅】beautiful jade；gem

【琳琅满目】a superb collection of beautiful things；a feast for the eyes：展品～，美不胜收。*One is dazzled by the endless array of beautiful exhibits.* or *The exhibition is a feast for the eyes.*

粼 (构词成分) 见下

【粼粼】〈文〉(of water, stone, etc.) clear；crystalline：～碧波 *clear, blue ripples*

嶙 (构词成分) 见下

【嶙峋】〈书〉❶ (of mountain rocks, cliffs, etc.) jagged；rugged；craggy：怪石～ *jagged rocks of grotesque shapes* / ～的山峦 *craggy hills* ❷ (of a person) bony；thin：瘦骨～ *be terribly emaciated*

霖 名 continuous heavy rain：秋～ *autumn rains*

【霖雨】continuous heavy rain

辚（构词成分）见下

【辚辚】〈文〉the sound made by a running cart, chariot, etc.

磷 名［化］phosphorus（P）

【磷肥】phosphate fertilizer

【磷光】phosphorescence ◇ ～体 phosphor

【磷火】phosphorescent light; will-o'-the-wisp; jack-o'-lantern

【磷矿粉】ground phosphate rock

【磷酸】phosphoric acid ◇ ～铵 ammonium phosphate；～钙 calcium phosphate；～盐 phosphate

【磷虾】euphausiid shrimp

【磷脂】phosphatide ◇ ～酸 phosphatidic acid

鳞 名 scale（of fish, etc.）

【鳞次栉比】（of buildings）like fish scales and comb teeth; in tight rows; row upon row：江岸新建的仓库～。*Row upon row of newly built warehouses line the waterfront.*

【鳞甲】scale and shell（of reptiles and arthropods）

【鳞茎】［植］bulb

【鳞片】❶ scale（on fish or insects' wings）❷ bud scale

【鳞屑】scales of skin that peel off

【鳞爪】〈书〉scales and claws—small bits; fragments; odd scraps：《羊城～》*"Titbits from the City of Rams"*（*i.e. Guangzhou*）

麟 名〈书〉（〈略〉全称为'麒麟'）（Chinese）unicorn

【麟凤龟龙】the unicorn, the phoenix, the tortoise, and the dragon（formerly called the "four spiritually endowed beings"）—worthy men

【麟角凤嘴】the unicorn's horn and the phoenix's beak—rare treasures

lǐn

凛 形 ❶ cold：凛冽 ❷ strict; stern; severe：～遵 *strictly abide by* ❸ afraid; apprehensive：～于远行 *be afraid of going on a long journey*

【凛冽】piercingly cold：北风～，大雪纷飞。*The north wind was blowing cold; the snowflakes were flying.*

【凛凛】❶ cold：寒风～。*A cold wind chills.* ❷ stern; awe-inspiring

【凛然】stern; awe-inspiring：正气～ *awe-inspiring righteousness* / 态度～ *stern in manner* / 一副～不可侵犯的样子 *look stern and forbidding*

【凛若冰霜】look severe; have a forbidding manner

檩 名 purlin

【檩条】purlin

lìn

吝 形 stingy; mean; closefisted：悭吝

【吝啬】stingy; niggardly; miserly; mean

【吝啬鬼】miser; niggard; skinflint

【吝惜】grudge; stint：不～自己的力量 *spare no effort; stint no effort* / 不～钱财 *spare no expense*

赁 动 rent; hire：～一辆车 *hire a car* / 房屋出～ *house to let*

【赁费】rental fee; rent

【赁金】rental fee; rent

淋 动 strain; filter：用纱布把药～一下 *strain the herbal medicine with a piece of gauze* ——另见 lín

【淋病】gonorrhoea

【淋溶】［地质］leaching; eluviation

【淋溶层】leached horizon; eluvial horizon; eluvium

膦 名［化］phosphine

líng

伶 名〈旧〉actor：名～ *a famous actor* / 坤～ *actress*

【伶仃】left alone without help; lonely

【伶俐】clever; bright; quick-witted：口齿～ *be clever and fluent* / 这孩子真～！*What a clever child!*

【伶人】〈旧〉actor

【伶牙俐齿】have the gift of the gab; have a glib tongue; have a ready tongue

灵 Ⅰ 形 ❶ quick; clever; sharp：他耳朵很～。*He has sharp ears.* or *His hearing is very good.* / 他脑子很～。*His mind is very sharp.* ❷ efficacious; effective：这个药真～。*This medicine is very effective.* / 我们试了一下，果然很～。*We tried it out and it really worked.* Ⅱ 名 ❶ spirit; intelligence：英灵 ❷ fairy; sprite; elf ❸（remains）of the deceased; bier：～前摆着花圈。*Wreaths were laid in front of the coffin.*

【灵便】❶ nimble; agile：他虽然上了年纪，手脚倒还～。*Though getting on in years, he is still nimble.* ❷ easy to handle; handy：这把钳子使着真～。*This pair of pliers is really handy.*

【灵车】hearse

【灵床】❶ bier ❷ a bed kept as it was when the person was alive

【灵丹妙药】（又作'灵丹圣药'）a magic（or wonder）drug; a miraculous cure; panacea

【灵魂】soul：～不灭论 *the theory of the immortality of the soul* / 出卖～ *sell one's soul* ◇ ～深处 in one's innermost soul; in the depth of one's soul

【灵活】❶ nimble; agile; quick：手脚～ *dexterous and quick in action* / 脑筋～ *be quick-witted; have a supple mind* ❷ flexible; elastic：～多样的经营方式 *flexible and diversified forms of ope?ation* ◇ ～性 flexibility; elasticity; mobility

【灵机】sudden inspiration; brainwave
【灵机一动】have a brainwave：她～，想出了个好办法。*She had a brainwave and found a good solution.*
【灵柩】a coffin containing a corpse; bier
【灵快】nimble; agile
【灵猫】civet (cat)：大～ *zibet*
【灵敏】sensitive; keen; agile; acute：嗅觉～ *have an acute sense of smell* / 动作～ *be quick in one's movements* ◇ ～度 sensitivity
【灵牌】spirit tablet
【灵巧】dexterous; nimble; skilful; ingenious：一双～的手 *a pair of clever hands* / 她的健身操动作准确而～。*Her movements in callisthenics were precise and nimble.*
【灵台】❶〈书〉the mind; the heart ❷ a platform on which a coffin or a cinerary casket is placed
【灵堂】mourning hall
【灵通】❶ having quick access to information; well-informed：他消息特别～，*He is well-informed.* ❷〈方〉be of use (or help)
【灵童】[宗]（藏传佛教）soul boy：十世班禅的转世～ *the reincarmated soul boy of the 10th Panchen Lama*
【灵位】同〖灵牌〗
【灵犀】magic horn (i. e. rhinoceros horn with its threadlike white core, mentioned in old texts as having a high sensibility)
【灵效】(usu. of drugs) effective; efficacious
【灵性】intelligence (of animals)：这匹马很有～，能领会主人的意图。*This horse is very intelligent. He can sense what his master wants.*
【灵验】❶ efficacious; effective：这种药非常～。*This medicine is highly efficacious.* ❷ (of a prediction, etc.) accurate; right：天气预报果然～。*The weather forecast turned out to be accurate.*
【灵长目】[动] Primates：～动物 *primate*
【灵芝】magic fungus—glossy ganoderma (Ganoderma lucidum; used in medicine; formerly credited with miraculous powers and considered a symbol of good luck)

囹（构词成分）见下
【囹圄】（又作'囹圉'）〈书〉jail; prison：身陷～ *be behind prison bars; be thrown into prison*

玲（构词成分）见下
【玲珑】❶ (of things) ingeniously and delicately wrought; exquisite ❷ (of people) clever and nimble
【玲珑剔透】exquisitely carved; beautifully wrought：～的玉石雕刻 *exquisitely wrought jade carvings*

凌 Ⅰ 动 ❶ insult：盛气凌人 ❷ approach：凌晨 ❸ rise high; tower aloft：凌空 Ⅱ 名〈方〉ice (esp. in blocks or cone-shaped)
【凌波】〈文〉❶ dashing waves ❷ like treading the waves (said of a beautiful woman's graceful way of walking)：～微步 *walk with dainty steps*
【凌晨】in the small hours; before dawn：七月三日～ *in the small hours of July 3* / 火车将于明日～四时半到达。*The train arrives at half past four tomorrow morning.*
【凌迟】(in imperial times) the punishment of dismemberment and the lingering death (for heinous crimes)：～处死 *execute by the slow process*
【凌驾】place oneself above; override：决不能把个人～于群众之上。*One must never place oneself above the masses.*
【凌空】be high up in the air; soar or tower aloft：大桥～飞架两山之间。*High up in the air, a bridge spans the valley.*
【凌厉】swift and fierce：攻势～ *a swift and fierce attack* / 朔风～。*A north wind was blowing hard.*
【凌乱】in disorder; in a mess：～不堪 *in a fearful mess; in a state of utter confusion* / 头发～ *with hair dishevelled*
【凌日】[天] transit：金星～ *transit of Venus*
【凌辱】insult; humiliate：受到～ *be humiliated; suffer humiliation*
【凌霄花】Chinese trumpet creeper (Campsis grandiflora)
【凌汛】spring flood caused by melting river ice
【凌云】reach the clouds; soar to the skies

铃 名 ❶ bell：～响了。*The bell is ringing.* ❷ a thing like a bell：哑铃 / 棉铃 ❸〈略〉见〖蕾铃〗
【铃铛】small bell
【铃鼓】[音] tambourine
【铃兰】lily of the valley

陵 名 ❶ hill; mound ❷ tomb; mausoleum：谒～ *pay homage at sb.'s mausoleum*
【陵谷】hills and valleys：～变迁 *vicissitudes; ups and downs*
【陵墓】mausoleum; tomb
【陵寝】〈书〉emperor's or king's resting place; mausoleum
【陵园】funerary park; cemetery

羚 名 ❶ antelope; gazelle ❷ antelope's horn
【羚牛】takin
【羚羊】antelope; gazelle：大～ *oryx* ◇ ～角 antelope's horn (used in medicine)

聆 动〈书〉listen; hear：亲聆
【聆教】hear your words of wisdom (used in letters)
【聆听】〈书〉listen (respectfully)：～教导 *listen to sb.'s instructions*

菱 名 ling; waternut; water caltrop (Trapa natans)
【菱角】ling; waternut; water caltrop (Trapa natans)
【菱镁矿】magnesite
【菱铁矿】siderite
【菱锌矿】smithsonite

【菱形】diamond; rhombus; lozenge ◇ ～队形［军］diamond formation; ～六面体 rhombohedron

翎 名 plume; tail feather; quill: 孔雀～ *peacock plumes; peacock feathers*

【翎毛】❶ plume ❷ a type of classical Chinese painting featuring birds and animals

绫 名 a silk fabric resembling satin but thinner; twill-weave silk

【绫罗绸缎】silks and satins

【绫子】同〖绫〗

零 Ⅰ 形 fragmentary; fractional: 这种纸都是一本一本的,没有～的。*This kind of paper comes in pads; there are no individual sheets.* Ⅱ 名 fragment; fraction: 把～儿去了,就要个整数儿。*Round off that fraction to a whole number.* Ⅲ 数 ❶ (in expressions of time, age, money, weight, etc., used between two different denominations, even when these are consecutive if the excess is to be emphasized): 一年～三天 *one year and three days* / 一岁～五个月 *one year and five months old* / 五点～一分 5:01 (*five oh one*) ❷ (representing a final or a medial zero in serial numbers or in designations of years, in which each digit is spoken separately; now usu. replaced by ○): 二～五号 或 二○五号 *No.* 205 (*number two-oh-five*) / 一九八～年 或 一九八○年 (*the year*) 1980 (*nineteen eighty*) ❸ the number or figure ○; nought; zero; nil: 我在这方面的知识几乎等于～。*My knowledge of the subject is practically nil.* / 上半场的比分是二比～。*The score at half-time was two-nil* (*or two-nothing*). / ～比～ *no score; love all* ❹ the lowest point on a thermometer; zero: ～上(下)五度 *five degrees above* (*below*) *zero* / 摄氏～下十度 10 *degrees below zero centigrade; minus* 10 *degrees centigrade* Ⅳ 动 withered: 凋零

【零部件】spare parts; component parts

【零吃】〈口〉between-meal nibbles; snacks

【零点】00:00 hour; zero hour; midnight: ～三十分 00:30; *zero hour thirty; midnight thirty*

【零点方案】zero option

【零点人口增长】zero population growth

【零度】zero degrees: 今天的温度是～。*Today's temperature is zero.* / 气温降到了～。*The* (*atmospheric*) *temperature has fallen to zero.*

【零工】❶ odd job; short-term hired labour: 打～ *do odd jobs* ❷ odd-job man; casual labourer

【零花】❶ spend money on minor purchases: 你留着这点钱在路上～吧! *Keep this money for incidental expenses on the way.* ❷〈口〉pocket money: 妈妈给了他五块钱做～。*Mother gave him five yuan as pocket money.*

【零活儿】odd jobs: 他给这块儿的人做点～。*He does odd jobs for people around here.*

【零件】❶ part (of a machine): 这个马达少了一个～。*This motor has a part missing.* ❷ spare parts; spares

【零落】❶ (of plants) withered; stripped of leaves: 草木～。*The grass is withered and the trees are bare.* ❷ desolate; wretched; in reduced circumstances: 一片凄凉～的景象 *a desolate scene* ❸ scattered; sporadic: 村庄零零落落地散布在河边。*There are scattered villages along the river.*

【零卖】❶ sell retail; retail: 他们只批发,不～。*They do only wholesale, they don't sell retail.* ❷ sell by the piece or in small quantities: 这些茶具成套出售,不～。*These tea things are sold by the set, not separately.*

【零七八碎】❶ scattered and disorderly: ～的东西放满了一屋子。*The room is cluttered up with all kinds of things.* ❷ miscellaneous trifles; odds and ends: 桌上放着好些～儿。*There were various odds and ends lying about on the table.*

【零钱】❶ small change: 我要换点～。*I want to exchange this for some small change.* / 您能给我换十块钱的～吗? *Could you give me* (*small*) *change for a ten-yuan note?* ❷ pocket money

【零敲碎打】do sth. bit by bit, off and on; adopt a piecemeal approach: 把这事一气儿解决了吧,别～了。*Let's settle the matter at one stroke, not piecemeal.* or *Let's do this at one go, not bit by bit.*

【零散】scattered: 桌子上～地放着几本书。*Several books lie scattered on the desk.* / 把～的情况凑到一块儿 *piece together scraps of information*

【零时】同〖零点〗

【零食】between-meal nibbles; snacks: 他喜欢吃～。*He likes to eat between meals.*

【零售】❶ sell retail; retail ❷ sell by the piece or in small quantities: 这套家具不能～。*We can't sell this set of furniture by the piece.* ◇ ～店 retail shop (or store); ～额 turnover (from retail trade); ～价格 retail price; ～商 retail trader (or dealer); retailer; ～市场 retail market; ～网 retail network; ～总额 total volume of retail sales

【零碎】❶ scrappy; fragmentary; piecemeal: ～活儿 *odd jobs* / 这些～东西很占地方。*These odds and ends take up a lot of space.* ❷ odds and ends; oddments; bits and pieces: 她正在拾掇～儿。*She is tidying up the odds and ends.*

【零头】❶ the remaining sum beyond the round figure: ～不算,我们花了 20 元。*We spent 20 yuan, not counting the small change.* ❷ remnant (of cloth): 一块～布 *a remnant*

【零星】❶ fragmentary; odd; piecemeal: ～材料 *fragmentary material* / ～土地 *odd pieces of land* / 一些零零星星的消息 *some odd scraps of news* ❷ scattered; sporadic: ～小雨 *occasional drizzles; scattered showers* / 草地上零零星星地点缀着一些小花。*The lawn is dotted with little flowers.*

【零用】❶ spend money on minor purchases ❷ pocket money ◇ ～费 petty cash; ～钱 pocket money；～账 petty cash book；petty cash account

【零指数】[数] zero exponent

龄 名 ❶ age；years：年龄 ❷ length of time；duration：工龄

lǐng

令 量 ream (of paper) ——另见 lìng

岭 名 ❶ mountain；ridge：翻山越岭 ❷ mountain range：大(小)兴安～ *the Greater (Lesser) Xing'an Mountains*

【岭南】south of the Five Ridges (五岭)—the area covering Guangdong and Guangxi

领 Ⅰ 名 ❶ neck：引领而望 ❷ collar；neckband：把大衣～儿翻起来 *turn up one's coat collar* / 尖～儿 *V-shaped collar* ❸ outline；main point：要领 Ⅱ 量 (for mats)：一～席 *a mat* Ⅲ 动 ❶lead；usher：～兵打仗 *lead troops into battle* / 把客人～到餐厅去 *usher the guests into the dining hall* ❷ have jurisdiction over；be in possession of；be in sb.'s possession：占领 / 领土 ❸ receive；draw；get：～奖 *receive a prize (or an award)* / ～养老金 *draw one's pension* ❹ understand；comprehend；grasp：领会

【领班】❶ head a work group ❷ gaffer；foreman

【领唱】❶ lead a chorus ❷ leading singer (of a chorus)

【领带】necktie；tie：打～ *tie the necktie* / 把～解下来 *untie (or remove) the necktie* / 穿衬衫系～ *wear a shirt and tie* ◇ ～卡(又作'领带夹') tie clasp；tie clip；～扣针 tiepin

【领导】❶ lead；exercise leadership：担任～工作 *shoulder the responsibility of leadership；hold a leading position* ❷ leadership；leader：这个错误由我们～上负责。*We of the leadership must accept responsibility for this mistake.* ◇ ～班子 leading group；～潮流 lead the trend (tendency)；～地位 a position of leadership；status as a leader；～方法 method of leadership；～干部 leading cadre；～骨干 the backbone (or mainstay，key members) of the leadership；～核心 eading nucleus (or core)；～机关 leading body；～权 leadership；authority；overall control；～人 leader；～水平 the level of leadership；～小组 leading group；～艺术 the art of leadership；～者 leader；～作风 the work style of the leadership；leadership style；～作用 leading role

【领地】❶ manor (of a feudal lord)；domain ❷ territory

【领队】❶ lead a group：我们这次远足谁～？ *Who's going to lead us on the hike?* ❷ the leader of a group，sports team，etc. ◇ ～机 [军] lead aircraft

【领港】❶ pilot a ship into or out of a harbour；pilot ❷ (harbour) pilot

【领钩】hook and eye on the collar

【领海】territorial waters；territorial sea：～范围 *extent of territorial waters* / ～宽度 *breadth (or extent) of the territorial sea* / ～线 *boundary line of territorial waters*

【领航】❶ navigate；pilot ❷ navigator；pilot ◇ ～飞机 pathfinder aircraft；～员 navigator；pilot

【领会】understand；comprehend；grasp：我还没有～你的意思。*I still don't see your point.*

【领江】❶ navigate a ship on a river ❷ river pilot

【领教】❶〈套〉〈字〉receive instructions (used to express thanks for sb.'s advice or performance)：请你弹一个曲子，让我们～一下。*Could you oblige us by playing a tune?* ❷ ask sb.'s advice or opinion：有点儿小事向您～。*I'd like to ask you for advice about a small matter.* ❸ (used ironically)：他们的伎俩，我们早就～过了。*We've encountered their tricks before.* / 我叫你～～我的厉害！*See how I'm going to teach you a lesson!*

【领结】bow tie

【领巾】scarf；neckerchief ——另见〖红领巾〗

【领空】territorial sky (or air)；territorial air space

【领口】❶ collarband；neckband：这件毛衣～太小。*The neckband of the sweater is too small.* ❷ the place where the two ends of a collar meet：她～上别着一个宝石别针。*She wore a jewelled brooch at the neck of her dress.*

【领扣】collar button；collar stud

【领款】receive funds；draw money ◇ ～人 payee

【领路】lead the way：我在前面～。*I'll be in front leading the way.*

【领略】have a taste of；understand；appreciate：～川菜风味 *taste Sichuan dishes* / ～塞外风光 *see and appreciate the scenery north of the Great Wall*

【领情】feel grateful to sb.；appreciate the kindness：您的心意我～，但是礼物不能收。*I appreciate your kindness，but I can't accept your gift.*

【领取】receive；draw；get：～工资 *draw (or collect) one's pay* / ～办公用品 *get office supplies* / ～出入证 *receive one's pass*

【领事】[外交] consul：副～ *vice-consul* / 代理～ *pro-consul* ◇ ～裁判权 consular jurisdiction；～处(又作'领事部') consular section；～馆 consulate；～条例 consular act；～团 consular corps (c. c.)；～委任书 certificate of appointment of consul；consular commission；～协定 consular agreement；～证书 exequatur

【领受】accept (kindness，etc.)；receive：她怀着激动的心情～了同志们的慰问。*She was deeply moved by her comrades' comforting words.*

【领水】❶ inland waters ❷ territorial waters ◇ ～员 navigator；pilot

【领头】〈口〉take the lead；be the first to do sth.：我领个头，大家跟着一起唱吧。*I'll lead off，if everyone will join in.* ◇ ～羊 bellwether

【领土】territory：台湾是中国～。*Taiwan is Chinese territory.* ◇ ～扩张 territorial expansion；territorial aggrandizement；～完整 territorial integrity；～要求 territorial claim

【领舞】❶ lead a dancer ❷ leading dancer
【领悟】comprehend; grasp
【领先】be in the lead; lead: 她~登上了山顶。*She was the first to reach the top of the hill.* / 客队~五分。*The visiting team led by five points.*
【领衔】head the list of signers (of a document); be the first on a name list: 最近两部影片由他~主演。*He has starred in two recent films.*
【领袖】leader ◇ ~欲 the desire to be a leader
【领养】adopt (a child)
【领有】possess; own
【领域】❶ territory; domain; realm ❷ field; sphere; domain; realm: 上层建筑~ *the realm of the superstructure* / 社会科学~ *the domain of the social sciences* / 意识形态~ *the ideological sphere*
【领章】collar badge; collar insignia
【领主】feudal lord; suzerain
【领子】collar
【领罪】admit one's guilt; plead guilty

lìng

另 Ⅰ 副 ❶ in addition; besides: 买一打,~送半打。*If you buy a dozen, you get a half dozen free in addition.* ❷ in place of that: 我们得~想办法。*We have to try and find some other way.* / 全文~发。*The full text will be dispatched separately.* Ⅱ 代 (used with nouns) different; other: 那是~一回事。*That's another matter.* / 从一个极端跳到~一个极端 *jump from one extreme to another*
【另案】a separate case: 作~处理 *to be handled as a separate case*
【另册】the other register (反义词: 正册), a Qing Dynasty census book for listing disreputable people: 打入~ *list sb. as an undesirable*
【另当别论】should be regarded as a different matter
【另函】❶ a separate letter ❷ write another letter
【另寄】(又作'另邮') post (or mail) separately; post (or mail) under separate cover
【另起炉灶】set up another kitchen—make a fresh start; start all over again
【另请高明】find someone better qualified (than myself): 这事我恐怕干不了,你还是~吧。*I'm afraid I'm not equal to the job. You'd better try and find someone better qualified.*
【另外】❶ in addition; besides: 我虽然有一个,可是我还想~买一个。*Even though I already have one, I want to buy another one besides.* ❷ (used with nouns) different; other: 我还要跟你谈~一件事情。*There's another thing I want to talk over with you.* / ~两个人我不认识。*I don't know the other two people.*
【另行】(do sth.) separately: ~安排 *make separate arrangements* / ~通知 *issue a separate notice*
【另眼相看】❶ regard (or look up to) sb. with special respect; give sb. special treatment ❷ view sb. in a new, more favourable light; see sb. in a new light
【另议】discuss or negotiate separately

令 Ⅰ 动 ❶ order; command: ~即返家 *order sb. to return home at once* ❷ cause sb. to: ~人深思 *set sb. thinking; provide food for thought* / ~人鼓舞 *encouraging; heartening; inspiring* Ⅱ 名 ❶ order; command; decree: 下令 ❷ drinking game: 酒令 ❸ season 夏令 Ⅲ 形 ❶〈书〉good; excellent ❷〈尊〉your (used before certain relationship terms when referring to a member of a friend's family): ~兄 *your elder brother* / ~妹 *your younger sister* ——另见 lǐng
【令出如山】orders are like a mountain (i. e. cannot be changed and compel obedience)
【令箭】an arrow-shaped token of authority (used formerly in the army)
【令箭荷花】[植] nopalxochia
【令人齿冷】arouse scorn
【令人发指】get one's hackles up; make one bristle with anger
【令人喷饭】side-splitting; screamingly funny
【令人捧腹】set people roaring with laughter; make one burst out laughing
【令人神往】fire one's imagination; have a strong appeal for one
【令人作呕】make one sick; nauseating; revolting: 她那装模作样劲儿真~。*Her affectations make you sick.* / ~地吹捧 *nauseatingly extol*
【令行禁止】any order will be immediately carried out, any prohibition will be heeded

liū

溜 Ⅰ 动 ❶ slide; glide: 从山坡上~下来 *slide down a slope* ❷ sneak off; slip away: 从后门~出去 *slip out through the back door* / 他跟谁也没说就~了。*He sneaked off without telling anyone.* Ⅱ 形 smooth: 滑溜 ——另见 liù
【溜边】〈口〉keep to the edge (of a road, river, etc.)
【溜冰】❶ skate ❷〈方〉roller-skate; go roller-skating ◇ ~场 skating rink
【溜达】〈口〉stroll; saunter; go for a walk: 他在河边来回~。*He sauntered up and down the river bank.* / 吃完饭出去~~吧。*Let's go for a stroll after the meal.*
【溜光】〈方〉very smooth; sleek; glossy: 他的头发梳得~。*His hair is combed sleek.*
【溜号】〈方〉sneak away; slink off
【溜肩膀】❶ sloping shoulders ❷〈方〉lacking a proper sense of responsibility; irresponsible
【溜须拍马】smooth sb.'s beard and pat his horse's hindquarters—lick sb.'s boots; toady to; fawn on

【溜之大吉】sneak away; slink off; make oneself scarce

liú

刘 名 a surname

【刘海】bang; fringe: 她留着～。*She wears her hair in bangs.*

浏 形〈书〉(of water) clear; limpid

【浏览】glance over; skim through; browse: 这本书我只～过一遍。*I've only skimmed through (or glanced over) the book.* / ～各种报章杂志 *browse among newspapers and magazines* ◇ ～浏览器［计］browser

流 Ⅰ 动 ❶ (of liquid) flow: 水～得很快。*The water is flowing very fast.* /伤口～脓。*The wound is festering.* / ～汗 *perspire; sweat* / ～鼻涕 *have a runny nose* / ～泪 *shed tears* ❷ moving from place to place; drifting; wandering: 流通 ❸ spread; circulate: 流传 ❹ change for the worse; degenerate ❺ banish; send into exile: 流放 Ⅱ 名 ❶stream of water: 河流 ❷ sth. resembling a stream of water; current: 电流 ❸ class; rate; grade: 一～作家 *a first-class writer* / 一～作品 *a first-rate (literary) work*

【流弊】corrupt practices; abuses

【流产】❶ (of a woman) have a miscarriage; miscarry: 她上月～了。*She had a miscarriage last month.* / 她～过几次。*She has had several miscarriages.* ❷ (of a plan, etc.) miscarry; fall through: 他们的计划～了。*Their project miscarried.* / ～政变 *an abortive coup*

【流畅】(of writing) easy and smooth: 文笔～ *write with ease and grace* / 这篇文章读起来很～。*The essay reads very smoothly.*

【流程】❶ a distance travelled by a stream of water ❷ technological process ❸［矿］circuit: 破碎～ *crushing circuit* / 浮选～ *flotation circuit* ◇ ～图 flow chart; flow diagram

【流传】pread; circulate; hand down: 古代～下来的寓言 *fables handed down from ancient times*

【流窜】flee hither and thither: ～在山区的残匪不久都被消灭了。*The remaining bandits who fled to the hills were soon wiped out.* ◇ ～犯 criminal on the run

【流弹】stray bullet

【流动】❶ (of water, air, etc.) flow; circulate: 溪水缓缓地～。*The brook flowed sluggishly.* ❷ go from place to place; be on the move; be mobile: 促进人才的合理～ *facilitate a rational flow of trained personnel* ◇ ～存款 float deposit; ～费用 floating charge; ～货车 shop-on-wheels; ～人口 floating (or transient) population; ～商店 mobile shop; ～哨 person (or soldier) on patrol duty; patrol; ～售货 mobile sale; ～图书馆 travelling library; ～性 mobility; fluidity; ～支票 circulating cheque; ～资本 circulating capital; floating capital; working capital; ～资产 current assets; liquid assets; floating assets; ～资金 (又作'流动基金') circulating fund; operating fund; revolving fund

【流毒】❶ exert a pernicious (or baneful) influence: ～甚广 *exert a widespread pernicious influence* ❷ pernicious (or baneful) influence: 肃清～ *liquidate a pernicious influence*

【流芳百世】leave a good name for a hundred generations; leave a good name to posterity; win immortal fame; leave one's mark on history

【流放】❶ banish; send into exile ❷ float (logs) downstream

【流感】〈略〉见〖流行性感冒〗

【流寇】❶ roving bandits ❷ roving rebel bands

【流浪】roam about; lead a vagrant life: ～街头 *roam the streets* ◇ ～儿 waif; street urchin; ～汉 tramp; vagrant

【流离】〈书〉wander about as a refugee or vagrant

【流离失所】become destitute and homeless; wander about homeless

【流利】fluent; smooth: 她说一口～的英语。*She speaks fluent English.* / 文章写得～。*The article reads smoothly.*

【流里流气】rascally

【流连】be reluctant to leave; linger on

【流连忘返】enjoy oneself so much as to forget to go home; linger on with no thought of leaving; cannot tear oneself away: 展品琳琅满目,令人～。*The exhibition is absolutely fascinating—you can't tear yourself away.*

【流量】volume of flow; rate of flow; flow; discharge: 管道～ *flow of a pipe* / 河道～ *discharge of a river* / 交通～ *traffic flow* ◇ ～计 flowmeter

【流露】show unintentionally (one's thoughts or feelings); reveal; betray: 她不大～自己的感情。*She seldom shows her emotions.* /真情～ *a revelation of one's true feelings*

【流落】wander about destitute

【流落江湖】live a vagabond life

【流落他乡】lead a wretched life far from home; be stranded in a strange land

【流氓】❶ rogue; hoodlum; hooligan; gangster ❷ immoral (or indecent) behaviour; hooliganism; indecency: 耍流氓 ◇ ～集团 gang of hooligans (or hoodlums); criminal gang; ～无产者 lumpenproletariat; ～习气 hooliganism; ～行为 indecent behaviour; hooliganism

【流明】［物］lumen

【流年】❶〈文〉fleeting time: 似水流年 ❷ (in fortune-telling) prediction of a person's luck in a given year

【流年不利】an unlucky year

【流派】school; sect: 学术～ *schools of thought*

【流气】❶ rascally: 他这个人很～。*He's a regular rascal.* ❷ rascally behaviour; hooliganism

【流散】scatter; drift: 敦煌经卷现已大多～国外。

Most of the Dunhuang MSS are now scattered in various foreign countries. ◇ ～人口 drifting population

【流沙】shifting sands; drifting sands; quicksand

【流失】❶ run off; be washed away: 黄金储备～ *be a drain on gold reserves* / 堵住管道的漏洞,不让石油～ *stop up the leaks in the pipe so that no oil will seep through* ❷ (of students) drop out

【流逝】(of time) pass; elapse: 时光～。*Time passes*. / 随着时间的～,人们就会把这件事全忘了。*With the passage of time, the whole thing will be forgotten*.

【流水】❶ flowing water ❷ turnover (in business): 本月做了 15 万元的～。*We have had a turnover of* 150,000 *yuan this month*. or *We have turned over* 150,000 *yuan this month*. ◇ ～号 serial number; ～席 feast at which guests are served as they come; ～线 assembly line; ～账 day-to-day (bookkeeping) account; current account; ～作业 flow process; assembly line method; conveyer system

【流水不腐,户枢不蠹】Running water is never stale and a door-hinge never gets worm-eaten.

【流苏】tassels

【流速】❶ [机] velocity of flow ❷〈水〉current velocity ◇ ～仪 current meter (for use in water conservancy)

【流淌】(of liquid) flow

【流体】fluid ◇ ～动力学 hydrokinetics; hydrodynamics; ～静力学 hydrostatics; ～力学 hydromechanics; fluid mechanics; ～压力计 manometer

【流铁槽】[冶] iron runner

【流通】(of air, money, commodities, etc.) circulate: 打开窗户使室内空气～ *open the windows to increase the circulation of air in the room* / 货币(商品)～ *the circulation of money* (*commodities*) ◇ ～费用 circulation costs; ～管 [机] runner pipe; ～货币 currency; ～领域 the field of circulation; ～券 (in former times) paper money issued by a provincial bank to be circulated in a given area; ～手段 medium (or means) of circulation; ～证券 negotiable instrument

【流亡】be forced to leave one's native land; go into exile: 孙中山曾长期～海外。*Sun Yat-sen spent long years in exile abroad*. ◇ ～政府 government-in-exile

【流网】[渔] drift net

【流纹岩】rhyolite

【流线型】streamlined: ～汽车 *streamlined car*

【流星】❶ meteor; shooting star ❷ (in acrobatics) meteors: 火～ *fire-meteors* / 水～ *water-meteors* ◇ ～尘 meteoric dust; ～防护 [航天] meteoroid protection; ～群 meteor stream; meteor swarm; ～雨 meteor (or meteoric) shower

【流行】popular; prevalent; fashionable; in vogue: 这种发型很～。*This kind of hairdo is very popular*. / 这是当时～的论调。*This argument was prevalent at the time*. ◇ ～病 epidemic disease; ～病学 epidemiology; ～歌曲 pop song; pop music; pop; ～色 fashionable colour; ～文化 pop culture

【流行性】epidemic ◇ ～感冒 influenza; flu; ～脑脊髓膜炎 epidemic cerebrospinal meningitis; ～腮腺炎 mumps; ～乙型脑炎 epidemic encephalitis B

【流血】lose blood; shed blood; draw blood; bleed: 你的鼻子～了。*Your nose is bleeding*. / 他流了很多血。*He lost a lot of blood*.

【流言】rumour; gossip

【流言飞语】(又作'流言蜚语') rumours and slanders

【流言止于智者】rumours find no credence with a wise man

【流域】river valley; river basin; drainage area: 黄河～ *the Huanghe River* (*or Yellow River*) *valley* (*or basin*) / ～面积 *drainage area*

【流质】liquid diet (for patients): 半～ *semiliquid*

【流转】❶ wander about; roam; be on the move: ～四方 *wander all over the country* ❷ (of goods or capital) circulate ◇ ～税 turnover tax

留

动 ❶ remain; stay: 你～在原地。*Stay where you are*. / 会后你～一下。*Will you please remain after the meeting*. ❷ reside in a foreign country to study: ～日 *study in Japan* / ～美 *study in the U.S.* ❸ ask sb. to stay; keep sb. where he is: 他们一定要～我们吃午饭。*They pressed us to stay for lunch*. / 那我就不～你了。*In that case I won't keep you any longer*. ❹ pay attention to: 留心 ❺ reserve; keep; save: ～座位 *reserve a seat for sb*. / 把钱～起来,以后用。*Save the money for use later on*. ❻ let grow; grow; wear: ～胡子 *grow a beard* (*or moustache*) / ～小辫儿 *wear plaits* (*or braids*); *wear one's hair in plaits* (*or braids*) ❼ accept (sth. given); take: 我们的邻居想把五只小猫都给我们,我们只～了一只。*Our neighbours wanted to give us all of their five kittens, but we only took one*. ❽ leave behind: 给她～个条。*Leave a note for her*. / 请他～个地址。*Ask him to leave his address*.

【留步】〈套〉(said by departing guest to host) don't bother to see me out; don't bother to come any further

【留成】retain a portion (of earnings, profits, etc.): 利润(外汇)～ *retain a portion of the profits* (*foreign exchange*) *brought in* / ～利润(外汇) *retained profits* (*foreign exchange*)

【留存】❶ preserve; keep: 此稿～ *keep this copy on file* ❷ remain; be extant

【留待】wait till later: 那件事可以～明天再定。*The matter can wait until tomorrow*.

【留党察看】be placed on probation within the Party (as an inner-Party disciplinary measure)

【留得青山在,不怕没柴烧】(又作'留得青山在,不愁没柴烧') As long as the green hills last, there'll always be wood to burn.

【留点】[天] stationary point

【留后路】keep a way open for retreat; leave a way

out：给自己留条后路 *leave oneself a way out*；*leave oneself an option*

【留后手】leave room for manoeuvre

【留话】leave a message；leave word：他给你留了个话儿。*He left a message for you*.

【留级】(of pupils，etc.) fail to go up to the next grade (or year)；repeat the year's work；stay behind

【留局候领】(in postal service) poste restante；general delivery

【留空】leave a blank；leave a space in writing

【留兰香】[植] spearmint

【留利】retained profits

【留恋】❶ be reluctant to leave (a place)；can't bear to part (from sb. or with sth.)：临毕业时，同学们对学校都十分～。*As their graduation day drew near，the students felt reluctant to leave their school*. ❷ recall with nostalgia：～过去 *yearn for the past*

【留量】[机] allowance：机械加工～ *stock allowance*

【留门】leave a door unlocked or unbolted (in expectation of sb. during the night)

【留难】make things difficult for sb.；put obstacles in sb.'s way：他故意～。*He's being difficult on purpose*.

【留念】accept or keep as a souvenir：照相～ *have a photo taken as a memento*

【留鸟】resident (bird)

【留情】show mercy or forgiveness：对敌人毫不～ *show the enemy no mercy*；*give the enemy no quarter*

【留任】retain a post；remain (or continue) in office

【留神】be careful；take care：你留点儿神。*Be careful*. / 过马路要～。*Be careful when you cross the street*.

【留声机】gramophone；phonograph

【留守】❶ act for the emperor during his absence from the capital ❷ stay behind to take care of things；stay behind for garrison or liaison duty (after the main force has left) ◇ ～处 rear office；～人员 rear personnel

【留宿】❶ put up a guest for the night ❷ stay overnight；put up for the night

【留尾巴】leave loose ends：他做事老留个尾巴让我来收拾。*He always leaves some loose ends for me to clear up for him*.

【留校】remain at a school or university after graduation as a faculty member

【留心】be careful；take care：他开车非常～。*He is very careful when he's driving*. / ～别写错了。*Mind you don't write it wrong*. / ～听讲 *listen attentively to a lecture*

【留学】study abroad：他想～。*He wants to study abroad*. / 他～美国已经三年了。*He's been studying in the United States for three years*. ◇ ～生 student studying abroad；returned student

【留言】leave one's comments；leave a message ◇ ～簿 visitors' book

【留一手】hold back a trick or two (in teaching a trade or skill)

【留意】be careful；look out；keep one's eyes open：这是个细致活，稍不～就会出错。*This is a delicate job. If you let your mind wander for a single moment，you'll do it wrong*.

【留影】❶ take a photo as a memento；have a picture taken as a souvenir ❷ a picture taken as a souvenir

【留用】continue to employ；keep on ◇ ～人员 personnel (of the old regime) who were kept on after liberation

【留余地】allow for unforeseen circumstances；leave some leeway：咱们订计划时要留有余地。*When drawing up a plan，we should allow for unforeseen circumstances*.

【留职】retain one's post：～察看 *retain one's post on probation (as a disciplinary measure)* / ～停薪 *retain one's post with salaries suspended during a long leave of absence*

【留置权】[法] lien：对船货有～ *have a lien on the cargo*

【留种】reserve seed for planting；have seed stock ◇ ～地 seed-breeding field

琉 (构词成分) 见下

【琉璃】coloured glaze ◇ ～塔 glazed pagoda；～瓦 glazed tile

【琉球群岛】the Ryukyu Islands

硫 名 [化] sulphur (S)

【硫胺素】thiamin(e)

【硫代硫酸钠】sodium thiosulphate

【硫化】[化] vulcanize ◇ ～汞 mercuric sulphide；～剂 vulcanized agent；curing agent；～氢 hydrogen sulphide；～染料 sulphur dyes；～物 sulphide；～橡胶 vulcanized rubber；vulcanizate

【硫磺】(又作'硫黄') common name for 硫 ◇ ～泉 sulphur spring

【硫塑料】thioplast

【硫酸】sulphuric acid ◇ ～铵 ammonium sulphate；～盐 sulphate

馏 动 distil ——另见 liù

【馏出油】distillate oil

【馏份】[化] fraction；cut：轻(重)～ *light (heavy) fraction (or cut)*

榴 名 pomegranate

【榴弹】high explosive shell

【榴弹炮】howitzer

【榴莲】durian

【榴霰弹】shrapnel；canister (shot)；case shot

瘤 名 tumour

【瘤胃】rumen ◇ ～臌胀 bloat

【瘤子】〈口〉tumour

镏 (构词成分) 见下

【镏金】gold-plating：～银器 *gilded silverware*

liǔ

柳 名 willow

【柳暗花明】dark willows and blooming flowers—a beauteous scene; a new vista ——另见〖山穷水尽〗

【柳眉】(又作'柳叶眉') arched eyebrows (of a woman)

【柳琴】a plucked stringed instrument

【柳杉】cryptomeria

【柳条】willow twig; osier; wicker ◇ ~筐 wicker basket; ~帽 wicker safety helmet; ~箱 wicker suitcase (or trunk); ~制品 wickerwork; wicker

【柳絮】willow catkins

【柳腰】willowy (or slender) waist

【柳阴】the shade of a willow tree

【柳莺】willow warbler: 黄腰~ *yellow-rumped willow warbler*

绺 量 (for thread, hair, etc.) tuft; lock; skein: 一~丝线 *a skein of silk thread* / 一~头发 *a lock (or tuft, wisp) of hair*

liù

六 数 six: ~个班 *six classes* / ~班 *the sixth class; class 6* / 棉纺~厂 *No. 6 Cotton Textile Mill*

【六边形】hexagon

【六畜兴旺】the domestic animals are all thriving

【六分仪】sextant

【六根】(in Buddhism) the six roots of sensation—eye, ear, nose, tongue, body and mind: ~清净 *be free from human desires and passions*

【六害】the "six evils" (namely, prostitution, pornography, abduction and sale of women and children, gambling, drugs, and fraud associated with feudal and superstitious practices)

【六角车床】turret lathe

【六角形】hexagon

【六〇六】"606" or salvarsan (a remedy for syphilis commonly employed until the advent of antibiotics)

【六六六】BHC (benzene hexachloride)

【六面体】hexahedron

【六亲】the six relations (father, mother, elder brothers, younger brothers, wife, children); one's kin

【六亲不认】disown all one's relatives and friends

【六亲无靠】have no relatives or friends to depend on

【六神无主】all six vital organs failing to work properly—distracted; out of one's wits; at a loss what to do

【六十四开】[刷] sixty-fourmo; 64 mo

【六弦琴】guitar

【六一国际儿童节】International Children's Day (June 1)

【六月】❶ June ❷ the sixth month of the lunar year; the sixth moon

陆 数 six (used for the numeral 六 on cheques, etc. to avoid mistakes or alterations) ——另见 lù

溜 Ⅰ 名 ❶ swift current: 河里~很大。*The river has a strong current.* ❷ line; column; row: 一~平房 *a row of one-storeyed houses* / 一~松树 *a row of pines* ❸ surroundings; neighbourhood: 这~儿果木树很多。*There are plenty of fruit trees round our way.* ❹ rainwater from the roof ❺ eaves gutter Ⅱ 动 〈方〉fill (a crevice, fissure, etc.) ——另见 liū

【溜子】[矿] scraper-trough conveyer

碌 (构词成分) 见下——另见 lù

【碌碡】stone roller (for threshing grain, levelling a threshing floor, etc.)

遛 动 ❶ saunter; stroll: 出去~~。*Let's go for a stroll.* / ~大街 *stroll around the streets; go window-shopping* ❷ walk (an animal): ~狗 *walk a dog*

【遛达】同〖溜达〗

【遛马】walk a horse

【遛鸟】(of bird keepers) take caged birds out into the country (to eat insects or to listen to and learn the songs of their kind who are free to roam the skies)

馏 动 heat up in a steamer: 把凉馒头~一~ *heat up the cold steamed bread* ——另见 liú

lóng

龙 Ⅰ 名 ❶ dragon ❷ a huge extinct reptile: 恐龙 Ⅱ 形 the dragon as the symbol of the emperor; of the emperor: ~床 *the emperor's bed* / ~袍 *imperial robe*

【龙船】dragon boat (a dragon-shaped racing boat)

【龙胆】[植] rough gentian (Gentiana scabra) ◇ ~紫 gentian violet

【龙灯】dragon lantern

【龙飞凤舞】like dragons flying and phoenixes dancing—lively and vigorous flourishes in calligraphy; a flamboyant style of calligraphy

【龙凤呈祥】the dragon and the phoenix bringing prosperity—excellent good fortune

【龙宫】the palace of the Dragon King

【龙骨】❶ a bird's sternum ❷ [中] fossil fragments ❸ keel

【龙骨车】dragon-bone water lift; square-pallet chain-pump

【龙睛鱼】dragon-eyes (a species of goldfish with prominent eyes and a large tail)

【龙井】Dragon Well tea (a famous green tea produced in Hangzhou, Zhejiang Province)

【龙驹凤雏】dragon colt or young phoenix—a brilliant young man

【龙卷】[气] spout

【龙卷风】tornado

【龙口夺粮】snatch food from the dragon's mouth—speed up the summer harvesting before the storm breaks

【龙葵】[植] black nightshade

【龙门起重机】gantry crane

【龙门铣床】planer-type milling machine

【龙脑】[化] borneol; borneo camphor

【龙盘虎踞】a coiling dragon and a crouching tiger—a forbidding strategic point (usu. referring to the city of Nanjing)

【龙舌兰】century plant

【龙蛇混杂】dragons and snakes jumbled together—good and bad people mixed up

【龙生龙,凤生凤】dragons beget dragons, phoenixes beget phoenixes—each after its own kind

【龙潭虎穴】a dragon's pool and a tiger's den— a danger spot

【龙套】❶ costume with dragon designs, worn by groups of soldiers or attendants in traditional opera ❷ actor playing a walk-on part in traditional opera; utility man ——另见〖跑龙套〗

【龙腾虎跃】dragons rising and tigers leaping—a scene of bustling activity

【龙头】❶ tap; faucet; cock ❷〈方〉handlebar (of a bicycle) ❸ in the lead, playing the key role; leading: ～产品 *flagship product* / 发挥～作用: *play a leading role*; *serve as a powerhouse*

【龙头鱼】Bombay duck

【龙王】the Dragon King (the God of Rain in Chinese mythology)

【龙虾】lobster

【龙涎香】ambergris

【龙须菜】〈方〉asparagus

【龙须草】Chinese alpine rush (Eulaliopsis binata)

【龙须面】dragon whiskers noodles—long, thin noodles

【龙血树】dragon tree (Dracaena draco)

【龙牙草】hairyvein agrimony (Agrimonia pilosa)

【龙眼】[植] longan

【龙爪槐】Chinese pagoda tree

【龙争虎斗】fighting between a tiger and a dragon—a fierce struggle between well-matched opponents; a contest between giants

【龙钟】〈书〉decrepit; senile

【龙舟】dragon boat: ～竞渡 *dragon-boat regatta*; *dragon-boat race*

聋 形 deaf; hard of hearing: 他耳朵～。*He is deaf.*

【聋哑】deaf and dumb; deaf-mute ◇ ～人 deaf-mute; ～学校 school for deaf-mutes; ～症 deaf-mutism

【聋子】deaf person

笼 名 ❶ cage; coop: 鸟～ *birdcage* / 鸡～ *chicken coop* ❷ basket; container ❸ (food) steamer: 一～肉包子 *a steamerful of meat-filled buns* ——另见 lǒng

【笼鸟】cage bird

【笼屉】bamboo or wooden utensil for steaming food (composed of several tiers); food steamer

【笼头】headstall; halter

【笼子】(lóngzi) ❶ cage; coop ❷ basket; container ——另见 lǒngzi

隆 Ⅰ 形 ❶ grand: 隆重 ❷ prosperous; thriving: 兴隆 ❸ intense; deep: ～情厚谊 *profound sentiments of friendship* Ⅱ 动 swell; bulge: 隆起

【隆冬】midwinter; the depth of winter

【隆隆】rumble; boom: 雷声～。*The thunder rumbled.* / 炮声～。*The guns boomed.*

【隆起】swell; bulge: 他碰得前额～一个大包。*He got a bad bump on his forehead.*

【隆头鱼】wrasse

【隆重】grand; solemn; ceremonious: ～的典礼 *a grand ceremony* / 受到～的接待 *be accorded a grand reception*; *be given a red carpet reception*

lǒng

垄 名 ❶ ridge (in a field) ❷ raised path between fields

【垄断】monopolize: ～市场 *monopolize (or corner) the market* ◇ ～集团 monopoly group; ～价格 monopoly price; ～利润 monopolist profits; ～资本 monopoly capital; ～资本主义 monopoly capitalism; ～资产阶级 monopoly capitalist class

【垄沟】field ditch; furrow

【垄作】[农] ridge culture

拢 动 ❶ approach; reach: 我们快～工地了。*We are almost on the worksite now.* ❷ add up; sum up: 把账～一～ *sum up the accounts* ❸ hold (or gather) together: 把所有的书都～在一块。*Gather all the books together.* / 用绳子把柴火～住。*Tie the firewood in a bundle.* / 她把孩子～在怀里。*She held her child in her arms.* ❹ (used after verbs) bring together: 他笑得嘴都合不～了。*He grinned from ear to ear.* / 他们谈不～。*They talk but never get close to each other.* ❺ comb (hair): 我来给你～一～头发。*Let me comb your hair.*

【拢共】altogether; all told; in all: 买这么多东西, ～才花了十块钱。*It only cost ten yuan altogether to buy so many things.*

【拢头】comb hair

【拢子】a fine-toothed comb

笼 Ⅰ 动 envelop; cover: ～着手 *put each hand in the opposite sleeve* / 烟～雾罩 *be enveloped (or hidden) in mist* Ⅱ 名 a large box or chest; trunk ——另见 lóng

【笼络】win sb. over by any means; draw over; rope in: 他很会～人。*He is very good at buying* people's support.

【笼络人心】cultivate people's good will (by dispensing charity, favours, etc.)

【笼统】general; sweeping: 他的话说得很～。*He spoke in very general terms.* / 这么说未免太～了。*That statement is rather too sweeping.*

【笼罩】envelop; shroud: 晨雾～在湖面上。*The lake is shrouded in morning mist.* / 会场上～着一种悲痛的气氛。*A cloud of gloom hung over the meeting.*

【笼子】(lǒngzi) a large box or chest; trunk ——另见 lóngzi

lòng

弄 名〈方〉(usu. used in names of lanes) lane; alley; alleyway ——另见 nòng

【弄堂】〈方〉lane; alley; alleyway

lōu

搂 动 ❶ gather up; rake together: ～柴火 *rake up twigs, dead leaves, etc. (for fuel)* ❷ hold up; tuck up: ～起袖子 *tuck up one's sleeves* ❸ squeeze (money); extort: ～钱 *extort money* ❹〈方〉pull: ～扳机 *pull a trigger* ——另见 lǒu

【搂草机】rake

lóu

娄 Ⅰ 形〈方〉weak (physically): 他的身体可～啦。*He's very weak.* Ⅱ 动〈方〉(of melons, gourds, etc.) overripe and unfit to eat

【娄子】〈口〉trouble; blunder: 惹～ *stir up trouble* ——另见〖出娄子〗;〖捅娄子〗

楼 名 ❶ a storied building; tower: 教室～ *classroom building* / 黄鹤～ *Yellow Crane Tower* ❷ storey; floor: 一～ *(British) ground floor; (American) first floor* / 二～ *(British) first floor; (American) second floor* ❸ superstructure: 城楼

【楼板】floor; floorslab

【楼层】storey; floor: 每个～都有消火栓。*On every floor there is a fire hydrant.*

【楼道】corridor; passageway

【楼房】a building of two or more storeys

【楼面】[建] floor: ～面积 *floor area*

【楼上】upstairs: ～住的是一位退休老工人。*A retired worker lives upstairs.*

【楼梯】stairs; staircase; stairway: 一层～ *a flight of stairs* / 上(下)～ *go up (down) by the stairway* / ～平台 *landing (of stairs)*

【楼下】downstairs: 他住在～。*He lives downstairs.* / ～有人叫你。*Somebody is calling you downstairs.*

蝼 名 mole cricket

【蝼蛄】mole cricket

【蝼蚁】❶ mole crickets and ants ❷ nobodies; nonentities: ～尚且偷生,何况人乎? *Even the lowly cricket and ant cling to life, let alone a human being.*

耧 名 an animal-drawn seed plough; drill barrow; drill

lǒu

搂 动 hold in one's arms; hug; embrace: 她把孩子～在怀里。*She held the child in her arms.* ——另见 lōu

【搂抱】hug; embrace; cuddle: 小姑娘亲热地～着小猫。*The little girl cuddled her pet cat.*

篓 名 basket: 字纸篓

【篓子】basket

lòu

陋 形 ❶ plain; ugly: 丑陋 ❷ (of a dwelling-place) humble; mean: ～室 *a humble room* / ～巷 *a mean alley* ❸ vulgar; corrupt; undesirable: 陋习 ❹ (of knowledge) scanty; limited; shallow: 浅陋

【陋规】objectionable practices

【陋见】shallow (or superficial) views

【陋俗】undesirable customs

【陋习】corrupt customs; bad habits

漏 Ⅰ 动 ❶ leak: 水壶～了。*The kettle is leaking.* / ～雨了。*The rain is leaking in.* ❷ divulge; leak: 你千万不能把这个消息～出去。*You absolutely must not let this news leak out.* ❸ be missing; leave out by mistake: ～了一行。*A line is missing.* / 这一项可千万不能～掉。*Be sure not to leave out this item.* / 他抄～了三个字。*When he made the copy, he left out three words by mistake.* Ⅱ 名 water clock; hourglass: ～尽更残。*The night is waning.*

【漏报】fail to report sth.; fail to declare (dutiable goods)

【漏疮】anal fistula

【漏电】leak electricity

【漏洞】❶ leak: 检查一下管道有没有～。*Check and see if there is any leak in the pipe.* ❷ flaw; hole; loophole: 他的话里有许多～。*What he says is full of holes.*

【漏洞百出】full of loopholes: 他的话前后矛盾,～。*His argument is full of holes.*

【漏斗】funnel

【漏风】❶ leak air; not be airtight: 这个风箱～。*This bellows is not airtight.* ❷ speak indistinctly through having one or more front teeth missing

❸ (of information, secrets) leak out
【漏缝】crack; leak: 壶底有道～。*There is a crack in the bottom of the kettle.*
【漏光】leak light: 这个照相机～。*The camera has a light leak.*
【漏壶】(又作'漏刻') water clock; clepsydra; hourglass
【漏孔】small opening; hole
【漏勺】strainer; colander
【漏税】evade payment of a tax; evade taxation
【漏网】slip through the net; escape unpunished: 决不让一个犯罪分子～。*Don't let a single criminal escape.*
【漏网之鱼】a fish that has slipped through the net—fugitive; runaway
【漏子】❶〈口〉funnel ❷ flaw; hole; loophole
【漏嘴】let slip a remark; make a slip of the tongue ——另见〖说漏〗

瘘 (构词成分) 见下
【瘘管】fistula

镂 动 engrave; carve
【镂花】ornamental engraving
【镂刻】❶ carve; engrave: ～花纹 *engrave designs* ❷ impress deeply (on the mind); engrave: 这番情景将永远～在她的心中。*The scene would always be engraved on her memory.*
【镂空】pierced work; reticulated work; openwork; fretwork: ～的象牙球 *a pierced ivory ball* / ～套瓶 *a vase enclosed in a reticulated envelope (the whole fired in one piece)*

露 动〈口〉同〖露〗(lù) Ⅱ, limited to use in the following ——另见 lù
【露丑】make a fool of oneself in public
【露底】let the secret out
【露富】show one's wealth
【露脸】become known (by doing sth.); be successful; shine: 那次讲演他很～。*He made himself known when he made that speech.*
【露马脚】give oneself away; let the cat out of the bag
【露面】show one's face; make (or put in) an appearance; appear or reappear on public occasions: 他整天没～儿。*He didn't show up for a whole day.*
【露怯】〈方〉display one's ignorance; make a fool of oneself
【露头】❶ show one's head ❷ appear; emerge: 太阳刚～,我们就起来了。*The sun had hardly appeared when we got up.* ——另见 lùtóu
【露馅儿】let the cat out of the bag; give the game away; spill the beans: 别再保密了,你的话已经～了。*Don't try to keep it a secret any longer. You've already given the game away.*
【露相】〈方〉show one's true colours
【露一手】make an exhibition of one's abilities or skills; show off: 我来做鱼,给你们～。*Let me cook the fish and have a chance to show off.*

lú

卢 名 a surname
【卢比】rupee
【卢布】rouble
【卢瑟福】[物] rutherford
【卢森堡】Luxembourg ◇ ～人 Luxembourger
【卢旺达】Rwanda ◇ ～人 Rwandese

庐 名 hut; cottage: 茅庐
【庐山真面目】the true face of Lushan—the truth about a person or a matter
【庐舍】〈书〉house; farmhouse

芦 名 reed
【芦柴】reed stems
【芦丁】[药] rutin
【芦花】reed catkins
【芦荟】[植] aloe
【芦笙】a reed-pipe wind instrument, used by the Miao, Yao and Dong ethnic groups
【芦笋】common name for 石刁柏
【芦苇】reed ◇ ～荡 reed marshes
【芦席】reed mat

炉 Ⅰ 名 stove; oven; furnace: 新出～的烧饼 *baked sesame buns fresh out of the oven* Ⅱ 量 [冶] heat: 一～钢 *a heat of steel*
【炉衬】(furnace) lining: ～寿命 *lining durability*
【炉顶】[冶] furnace top; furnace roof
【炉灰】stove ashes
【炉火纯青】the stove fire (for making pills of immortality) begins to glow a pure blue—attain a high degree of perfection: 他画山水的技巧达到了～的地步。*He attained the acme of perfection in landscape painting.*
【炉料】[冶] furnace charge; furnace burden
【炉龄】[冶] furnace life
【炉门】the draft of a stove
【炉盘】stone or metal plate for standing a stove on as a precaution against fire
【炉前工】blast-furnace man; furnaceman
【炉身】[冶] (furnace) shaft; furnace stack
【炉台】stove top
【炉膛】the chamber of a stove or furnace
【炉条】fire bars; grate
【炉温】[冶] furnace temperature
【炉灶】kitchen range; cooking range
【炉渣】slag; cinder
【炉子】stove; oven; furnace: 生～ *light a stove*

鸬 (构词成分) 见下
【鸬鹚】cormorant

颅 名 cranium; skull
【颅骨】cranial bones
【颅腔】cranial cavity

鲈 名 perch

lǔ

卤 Ⅰ 名 ❶ bittern ❷［化］halogen ❸thick gravy used as a sauce for noodles, etc.：打～ *make such gravy* Ⅱ 动 stew (whole chickens or ducks, large cuts of meat, etc.) in soy sauce：～鸡 *pot-stewed chicken*
【卤菜】pot-stewed meat or fowl
【卤化】［化］halogenate ◇ ～物 halogenide；halide
【卤水】❶ bittern ❷ brine
【卤素】［化］halogen
【卤味】pot-stewed fowl, meat, etc. served cold
【卤虾油】shrimp sauce
【卤族】［化］halogen family

虏 Ⅰ 动 take prisoner Ⅱ 名 captive；prisoner of war.
【虏获】capture (men and arms)

掳 动 carry off；capture
【掳掠】pillage；loot

鲁 形 ❶ stupid；dull：愚鲁 ❷ rash；rough；rude：粗鲁
【鲁钝】dull-witted；obtuse；stupid
【鲁莽】crude and rash；rash：～行事 *act rashly*；*act without thought*
【鲁米那】［药］luminal (a transliteration)

橹 名 scull；sweep

镥 名［化］lutecium；lutetium (Lu)

lù

陆 动 land：水陆 ——另见 liù
【陆半球】the continental hemisphere；the land hemisphere
【陆稻】dryland rice；upland rice；dry rice
【陆地】dry land；land ◇ ～棉 upland cotton
【陆风】［气］land breeze
【陆海空】land, sea, and air：～三军 *the army, the navy, and the air force*；*the armed forces*
【陆军】ground force；land force；army ◇ ～武官 military attaché
【陆连岛】land-tied island；tombolo
【陆龙卷】［气］tornado；landspout
【陆路】land route：走～ *travel by land* / ～交通 *overland communication*；*land communication*
【陆上油田】onshore oil fields；inland oil fields
【陆生动物】terrestrial animal
【陆相】［地质］land facies ◇ ～沉积［地质］continental deposit
【陆续】one after another；in succession：代表们～到达。*The delegates arrived one after another*.
【陆运】land transportation
【陆战队】marine corps；marines

录 Ⅰ 动 ❶ record；write down；copy：记录 ❷ choose；employ；hire：录用 ❸ tape-record：报告已经～下来了。*The speech has been tape-recorded*. / 你给我～盘磁带，好吗？*Would you please copy a tape for me*？Ⅱ 名 record；register；collection：回忆录
【录播】make a recorded broadcast
【录放】record and play back
【录供】［法］take down a confession or testimony during an interrogation
【录取】enroll；recruit；admit：～新生五百名 *enroll 500 students* ◇ ～通知书 admission notice；～线 minimum passing marks for admission
【录像】videotape；video：他为婚礼录了像。*He videotaped (or videoed) the wedding ceremony*. ◇ ～机 video recorder；videotape recorder；video
【录像带】❶ videotape ❷ video cassette ❸ a videotape recording
【录音】❶ tape-record (sound)；record；tape：他的讲话已经录了音。*His speech has been recorded*. ❷ sound-recording：磁带～ *tape recording* / 放～ *play back the recording* ◇ ～报告 tape-recorded speech；～打字 audiotyping；～带 magnetic tape；tape；～电话 answering machine；～电话机 telegraphone；～放大器 recording amplifier；～机 tape recorder；cassette recorder；recorder；～胶片 recording film；～棚 sound recording studio；～摄影机 sound camera；～师 recordist；～室 recording room
【录用】employ；take sb. on the staff：这家公司从几百名应试者中～了五人。*The company took on five out of several hundred candidates*.

鹿 名 deer：公～ *stag*；*buck* / 母～ *doe* / 小～ *fawn*
【鹿角】deerhorn；antler
【鹿角菜】［植］siliquose pelvetia (Pelvetia siliquosa)
【鹿角胶】［中］deerhorn glue
【鹿圈】deer enclosure；deer pen
【鹿皮】deerskin
【鹿茸】［中］pilose antler (of a young stag)
【鹿肉】venison
【鹿死谁手】at whose hand will the deer die—who will win the prize；who will gain supremacy：不知～。*It's hard to tell who will emerge victor*.
【鹿苑】deer park

绿 同〖绿〗(lǜ), limited to use in the following ——另见 lǜ
【绿林】the greenwood—brigands；outlaws ◇ ～好汉 greenwood hero—brigand；outlaw

禄 名 official's salary in feudal China；emolument：俸禄
【禄位】official rank and salary

碌 形 ❶ (of a person) commonplace；mediocre：庸碌 ❷ busy：忙碌 ——另见 liù

【碌碌】❶ mediocre；commonplace ❷ busy with miscellaneous work：～半生 *plod away for half a lifetime*

【碌碌无能】devoid of ability；incompetent；mediocre

【碌碌无为】lead a vain and humdrum life

路 名 ❶ road；path；way：新开～ *a new road* / 上山的～ *a path up the mountain* ❷ journey；distance：～很远。*It's a long way.* / 一小时走二十里～ *cover 20 li an hour* ❸ way；means：我实在没～可走了。*I'm really at a dead end.* ❹ sequence；line；logic：思路 ❺ region；district：外～人 *nonlocal people* / 南～货 *southern products* ❻ route：三～进军 *advance along three routes* / 七～公共汽车 *No.7 bus* ❼ sort；grade；class：这一～人 *this sort of people* / 哪一～病？*What kind of disease is this?*

【路霸】highway overlord (people who demand money or services with little or no justification esp. of drivers using the section of highway or road under their control)：打～ *rid the roads of overlords*

【路拌】road mix ◇ ～路面 road-mixed pavement

【路边摊】roadside market

【路标】❶ road sign ❷［军］route marking；route sign

【路不拾遗】同〖道不拾遗〗

【路程】distance travelled；journey：三天～ *a three days' journey* / 走了 500 里的～ *have covered a distance of 500 li*

【路道】〈方〉❶ way；approach：他人倒聪明，就是～没有走对。*He's quite intelligent, but he doesn't have a correct approach to things.* ❷ behaviour：此人～不正。*The person's behaviour is questionable.*

【路灯】street lamp；road lamp

【路堤】embankment

【路段】a section of a highway or railway

【路费】travelling expenses

【路轨】❶ rail ❷ track

【路过】pass by or through (a place)：他每次～总要来看望他的老战友。*Every time he passes by, he drops in to see his old comrades-in-arms.*

【路基】roadbed；bed

【路见不平，拔刀相助】see injustice on the road and draw one's sword to help the victim—take up the cudgels for the injured party

【路劫】highway robbery；holdup；mugging

【路警】railway police

【路径】❶ route；way：～不熟 *not know one's way around* ❷ method；ways and means：成功的～ *the road to success*

【路口】crossing；intersection

【路矿】railways and mines

【路况】road conditions

【路面】road surface；pavement：柔（刚）性～ *flexible (rigid) pavement*

【路牌】street nameplate

【路堑】cutting (for a railway or highway)

【路人】passerby；stranger：视同路人

【路上】❶ on the road：～停着一辆车。*There is a car parking on the road.* ❷ on the way；en route：～不要耽搁。*Don't waste any time on the way.* / 我在回来的～碰见了他。*I came across him on my way back.*

【路数】❶ 同〖路子〗❷ a movement in martial arts：击剑的～ *thrusts in fencing* ❸ exact details；inside story

【路透社】(UK) Reuter's News Agency；Reuters

【路途】❶ road；way：他熟悉这一带的～。*He knows the roads in this district quite well.* ❷ way；journey：～遥远 *a long way to go；far away*

【路线】❶ route；itinerary：旅行的～ *the route of a journey* / 按规定的～进行越野比赛 *run the cross-country race over a set course* ❷ line：～错误 *errors of line*

【路遥知马力，日久见人心】As distance tests a horse's strength, so time reveals a person's heart.

【路障】roadblock；barricade：设置～ *set up roadblocks (or barricades)*

【路子】❶ way；approach；means：寻找解决问题的～ *seek ways to solve the problem* ❷ social connections；pull：～宽 *have many social connections；have a lot of pull* / 找～ *try to secure help from potential backers*

漉 动 seep through；filter

【漉网】vat-net (used in paper making)

辘 （构词成分）见下

【辘轳】well-pulley；windlass；winch

【辘辘】the rumbling sound of cart wheels：牛车发出笨重的～声。*The ox cart rumbled down the road.*

戮 动 ❶ kill；slay：杀戮 ❷〈书〉unite；join

【戮力同心】unite in a concerted effort；make concerted efforts

鹭 名 egret；heron：牛背～ *cattle egret* / 池～ *pond heron*

【鹭鸶】egret

麓 名〈书〉the foot of a hill or mountain：华山北～ *at the northern foot of Huashan Mountain*

露 Ⅰ 名 ❶ dew ❷ beverage distilled from flowers, fruit or leaves；syrup：果子露 Ⅱ 动 show；reveal；betray：～出原形 *reveal one's true colours；betray oneself* / 她脸上～出了笑容。*A smile appeared on her face.* ——另见 lòu

【露点】dew point：温度～差 *dew-point deficit* ◇ ～湿度表 dew-point hygrometer

【露骨】thinly veiled；undisguised；barefaced：说得十分～ *speak undisguisedly；speak in no equivo-*

cal terms / ～地干涉别国内政 *flagrantly interfere in the internal affairs of another country*
【露光计】［摄］exposure meter
【露脊鲸】right whale
【露酒】alcoholic drink mixed with fruit juice
【露脸】face time
【露水】dew
【露水夫妻】man and woman living together only for a short while without being married
【露宿】sleep in the open：～街头 *sleep in the street*
【露天】in the open (air)；outdoors：今晚电影在～演。*The film will be shown in the open air tonight*. ◇ ～电影 open-air cinema；～堆栈 open-air repository；open-air depot；～剧场 open-air theatre；～开采 opencast mining；～矿 opencut；opencast；open-pit；strip mine；～煤矿 opencut coal mine；～市场 open martet；～游泳池 out door or open-air swimming pool
【露头】［矿］outcrop；outcropping ——另见 lòutóu
【露头角】(of a young person) beginning to show ability or talent；budding
【露营】camp (out)；encamp；bivouac
【露珠】dewdrop

lǘ

驴 名 donkey；ass
【驴唇不对马嘴】donkeys' lips don't match horses' jaws—incongruous；irrelevant：这个比方有点～。*The analogy is rather farfetched*.
【驴打滚】a form of usury in the old society, the borrower having to pay interest on interest；snowballing usury
【驴脸】〈贬〉a donkey's face—a long face
【驴骡】hinny
【驴鸣犬吠】asses braying and dogs barking—a poor style of writing
【驴年马月】year of the donkey and month of the horse—a time that will never come (as there is no such year or month in the Chinese calendar)
【驴子】〈方〉donkey；ass

lǚ

侣 名 companion；associate：伴侣 / 情侣
【侣伴】同〖伴侣〗

旅 Ⅰ 动 travel；stay away from home：旅居 Ⅱ 名 ❶［军］brigade ❷ troops；force：军～之事 *military affairs*
【旅伴】travelling companion；fellow traveller
【旅差费】travelling expenses on a business trip
【旅程】route；itinerary；journey：登上～ *start on a journey*
【旅店】inn
【旅费】travelling expenses
【旅馆】inn；hotel
【旅进旅退】always follow the steps of others, forward or backward—have no views of one's own
【旅居】live away from one's native place；sojourn：～海外的侨胞 *Chinese nationals residing abroad*
【旅客】hotel guest；traveller；passenger：过往～ *travellers passing through*；*transients* ◇ ～登记簿 hotel register
【旅舍】〈书〉hotel
【旅途】journey；trip：～见闻 *what one sees and hears during a trip*；*traveller's notes* / 祝你～愉快。*Have a pleasant journey*. or *Bon voyage*.
【旅行】travel；journey；tour：他要～去了。*He's going travelling*. / 作长途～ *make a long journey* ◇ ～包 travelling bag；～车 station wagon；～袋 travelling bag；～剪 folding scissors；～闹钟 travelling clock；～社 travel service；travel agency；～团 touring party；～证 travel certificate；～支票 traveller's cheque；～指南 guidebook；～装 safari suit
【旅游】tour；tourism ◇ ～背包 packsack；～船 houseboat；～度假区 tourist holiday zone；～结婚 have a honeymoon trip；～热 travel fever；travel bug；～市场 tourist market；～鞋 sneakers；walking shoes；～业 tourist industry；tourism；～资源 tourism resources
【旅长】brigade commander
【旅资】travelling expenses

捋 动 smooth out with the fingers；stroke：～胡子 *stroke one's beard* / 把纸～平 *smooth out a piece of paper* ——另见 luō

铝 名［化］aluminium (Al)
【铝箔】aluminium foil
【铝合金】aluminium alloy
【铝胶】alumina gel
【铝热剂】thermite：～燃烧弹 *thermite bomb*
【铝土矿】bauxite

偻 形〈书〉hunchbacked；bent：伛偻

屡 副 time and again；repeatedly：～战～胜 *have fought many battles and won every one of them*；*score one victory after another* / ～遭打击 *repeatedly came under attack*
【屡次】time and again；repeatedly：他～打破全国纪录。*He repeatedly broke the national record*. / 我～告诉过你，你总是不听。*I've told you time and again, but you never listened*.
【屡次三番】again and again；over and over again；many times：我～提醒他要谨慎。*I've reminded him over and over again that he should be cautious*.
【屡见不鲜】common occurrence；nothing new：考试作弊～。*Cheating in examinations is a matter of common occurrence*.
【屡教不改】refuse to mend one's ways despite repeated disciplinary action
【屡屡】time and again；repeatedly：他写这篇回忆录的时候，～搁笔沉思。*While writing his reminiscences, again and again he laid down his pen*

and fell into meditation.

【屡试不爽】put to repeated tests and proved right：这种新杀虫药效果良好，～。*This new insecticide has proved effective every time it's been used.*

缕 Ⅰ名 thread：千丝万缕 Ⅱ副 detailed；in detail：缕述 Ⅲ量 wisp；strand；lock：一～烟 *a wisp (or curl) of smoke* / 一～麻 *a strand of hemp* / 一～头发 *a lock of hair*

【缕缕】continuously：村中炊烟～上升。*Wisps of smoke rose continuously from the village chimneys.*

【缕述】state in detail；give all the details；go into details (or particulars)：为了节省篇幅，恕不一一～。*For economy of space, I shall not go into details.*

膂 名〈书〉backbone

【膂力】muscular strength；physical strength；brawn

【膂力过人】possessing extraordinary muscular (or physical) strength

履 Ⅰ名 shoe：革履 ❷footstep：步履 Ⅱ动 ❶ tread on；walk on：履险如夷 ❷ carry out；honour；fulfil：履约

【履带】caterpillar tread；track：～式拖拉机 *caterpillar (or crawler) tractor*

【履历】❶ one's personal record (of education, work experience, and attainments)；antecedents ❷ (British) curriculum vitae (cv)；(American) résumé

【履历表】(British) curriculum vitae (cv)；(American) résumé

【履险如夷】go over a dangerous pass as if walking on level ground—cope with a crisis without difficulty

【履新】〈书〉❶ celebrate the New Year ❷ take up a new post

【履行】perform；fulfil；carry out：～诺言 *keep one's word；fulfil (or carry out) one's promise* / ～合同 *fulfil a contract* / ～手续 *go through the procedures* / ～职责 *do one's duty*

【履约】〈书〉keep a promise，pledge，agreement，appointment，etc.

lǜ

律 Ⅰ名 ❶ law；statute；rule：定律 / 规律 ❷ pitch-pipes used in ancient music Ⅱ动〈书〉restrain；keep under control：～己甚严 *be strict with oneself；exercise strict self-discipline*

【律师】lawyer；(British) barrister；(British) solicitor；(American) attorney：我想请个～来打这场官司。*I'm trying to employ a lawyer to handle the case.* ◇ ～事务所 lawyer's office

【律诗】regulated verse：五言～ *pentasyllabic (or five-syllable) regulated verse* / 七言～ *septasyllabic (or seven-syllable) regulated verse*

虑 动 ❶ consider；ponder；think over：考虑 ❷ concern；be anxious；worry：不足为～ *give no cause for anxiety*

率 名 rate；proportion；ratio：人口增长～ *the rate of population growth* / 圆周～ *the ratio of the circumference of a circle to its diameter* ——另见 shuài

绿 形 green：～叶 *green leaves* / 书皮儿是～的。*The book cover is green.* ——另见 lù

【绿宝石】emerald

【绿茶】green tea

【绿岛工程】green street island project

【绿灯】❶ green light (a traffic signal) ❷〈喻〉green light；permission

【绿地】greenery patches (in a town or city)

【绿豆】mung bean；green gram ◇ ～糕 a pastry made of mung bean flour；～芽 mung bean sprouts

【绿矾】[化] green vitriol

【绿肥】green manure ◇ ～作物 green manure crop

【绿化】make (a place) green by planting trees，flowers，etc.；afforest：～城市 *plant trees in and around the city* ◇ ～地带 greenbelt；～工程 landscape engineering

【绿卡】"green card" (USA)；permit of permanent residence

【绿蓝色】turquoise (blue)

【绿篱】hedgerow；hedge

【绿帽子】(又作'绿头巾') a green hat or turban—the state of being a cuckold：戴～ *be a cuckold*

【绿内障】another name for 青光眼

【绿泥石】chlorite

【绿茸茸】lush green：～的稻田 *a lush green rice paddy*

【绿色】green colour ◇ ～革命 the Green Revolution；～和平组织 Greenpeace；～食品 green food；～植物 green plants

【绿松石】turquoise

【绿头鸭】mallard

【绿茵】❶ a carpet of green grass；greensward ❷ green meadow：～场 (*green meadow*) *football field*

【绿油油】fresh green：～的麦苗 *fresh green wheat seedlings*

【绿藻】green alga

【绿洲】oasis

【绿柱石】beryl

氯 名 [化] chlorine (Cl)

【氯丙嗪】chlorpromazine；wintermine

【氯丁橡胶】chloroprene rubber

【氯仿】[化] chloroform

【氯化铵】ammonium chloride

【氯化钾】potassium chloride

【氯化钠】sodium chloride

【氯化物】chloride (e.g. 氯化钠 sodium chloride)

【氯喹】[药] chloroquine

【氯磷定】［药］pyraloxime methylchloride
【氯纶】［纺］polyvinyl chloride fibre
【氯霉素】chloromycetin；chloramphenicol
【氯气】chlorine
【氯噻酮】［药］chlorthalidone
【氯酸】chloric acid ◇ ～钾 potassium chlorate

滤 动 strain；filter：咖啡得～一～。*The coffee must be strained.* / 把水～一下再喝。*Filter the water before you drink it.*
【滤波器】［电］wave filter：带通～ *band-pass filter* / 高通～ *high-pass filter*
【滤光器】light filter；ray filter
【滤过性病毒】filterable virus
【滤器】filter：粗～ *strainer*
【滤色镜】［摄］(colour) filter
【滤液】filtrate
【滤纸】filter paper：定量(定性)～ *quantitative (qualitative) filter paper*

luán

峦 名〈书〉❶ low but steep and pointed hill ❷ mountains in a range

孪 名〈书〉twin：～子 *twin boys*
【孪生】twin：～姐妹 *twin sisters* / ～兄弟 *twin brothers* / ～子 *twin boys*

栾 名 goldenrain tree

挛 名 contraction：痉挛
【挛缩】contracture

鸾 名 a fabulous bird related to the phoenix
【鸾凤】❶ a married couple ❷ distinguished talents
【鸾飘凤泊】❶ free and powerful calligraphic style ❷ husband and wife separated ❸ men of worth neglected
【鸾翔凤集】a gathering of talented men

銮 名 a small tinkling bell
【銮驾】imperial carriage
【銮铃】tinkling bells on a carriage

luǎn

卵 名 ovum；egg；spawn
【卵白】white of an egg；albumen
【卵巢】ovary
【卵黄】yolk
【卵磷脂】lecithin
【卵生】oviparity ◇ ～动物 oviparous animal；ovipara
【卵石】cobble；pebble；shingle
【卵胎生】ovoviviparity ◇ ～动物 ovoviviparous animal；ovovivipara
【卵细胞】egg cell；ovum
【卵翼】〈贬〉cover with wings as in brooding；shield：在某人～之下 *under the aegis of sb.*；*be shielded by sb.*
【卵用鸡】a chicken raised for egg production (e.g. 来亨鸡 the Leghorn chicken)；layer
【卵子】ovum；egg

luàn

乱 Ⅰ 形 ❶in disorder；in a mess；in confusion：车站很～。*The station was in a state of disorder.* / 屋里很～，请你把它收拾一下。*The room is in a mess；please tidy it up.* ❷ in a confused state of mind；in a turmoil：我心里很～。*My mind is in a turmoil.* Ⅱ 名 ❶ disorder；upheaval；riot；unrest；turmoil：安史之～ *The Rebellion of An Lushan and Shi Siming* (755—763) ❷ illicit sexual relationships Ⅲ 动 throw into disorder；confuse；mix up Ⅳ 副 indiscriminate；random；arbitrary：各种木料～堆在一起。*Logs and planks of all shapes and sizes were jumbled together.* / 他在墙上～写。*He scribbled on the wall.*
【乱兵】❶ mutinous soldiers ❷ totally undisciplined troops
【乱点鸳鸯】❶ misarrangement of matches through wrong identification of couples ❷ misarrangement of personnel
【乱纷纷】disorderly；confused；chaotic：～的人群 *a tumultuous crowd* / 他心里～的。*He's rather disturbed.*
【乱坟岗】unmarked common graves；unmarked burial-mounds
【乱搞】❶bedhop ❷ bedhopping
【乱哄哄】in noisy disorder；in a hubbub；tumultuous；in an uproar：大家听到这个消息，～地议论起来。*The news set them arguing heatedly among themselves.*
【乱砍滥伐】fell trees indiscriminately；engage in destructive lumbering practices
【乱来】act foolishly or recklessly
【乱了营】〈方〉be thrown into confusion；be in disarray
【乱伦】commit incest
【乱蓬蓬】dishevelled；tangled；jumbled：～的头发 *dishevelled hair*；*tangled hair* / ～的茅草 *a jumbled mass of reeds*
【乱七八糟】at sixes and sevens；in great disorder；in an awful mess：他的屋子～的。*His room was in great disorder.* / 我心里～的，这会儿不想吃。*I don't feel like eating—my mind's in a whirl.*
【乱世】troubled times；turbulent days ◇ ～英雄 heroes in times of disorder
【乱说】speak carelessly or foolishly；talk in a scatterbrained way；talk nonsense；make irresponsible remarks：别～。*Don't talk nonsense.* / 当面不说，背后～ *gossip behind people's backs but say nothing to their faces*
【乱弹琴】act or talk like a fool；talk nonsense：这简直是～。*That's a lot of nonsense.* or *It's*

downright nonsense.

【乱套】〈方〉muddle things up; turn things upside down: 要是各行其是,那就～了。*If everyone acts as he pleases, everything will be in a muddle*.

【乱腾腾】confused; upset: 心里～的 *feel all hot and bothered*

【乱腾】confused; disorderly; restless

【乱糟糟】❶ chaotic; in a mess: 屋子里～的。*The room is in a mess*. ❷ confused; perturbed: 心里～的 *feel very perturbed*

【乱真】❶ (of fakes) look genuine: 他临摹的画足以～。*The copy he made of the painting can pass for an authentic*. ❷ [物] spurious: ～放电 *spurious discharge* / ～脉冲 *spurious pulse*

【乱子】disturbance; trouble; disorder

lüè

掠 动 ❶ plunder; pillage; sack: 我国许多珍贵文物被帝国主义者～走了。*Many of our cultural treasures have been plundered by imperialists*. ❷ sweep past; brush past; graze; skim over: 凉风～面。*A cool breeze brushed my face*. / 探照灯～过夜空。*The searchlights swept the night sky*.

【掠地飞行】minimum-altitude flight; treetop flight; hedgehopping

【掠夺】plunder; rob; pillage: 帝国主义～成性。*Imperialism is predatory by nature*. / ～别国领土 *seize the territory of another country*

【掠美】(又作'掠人之美') claim credit due to others: 这是她的高见,我不敢～。*It was her idea. I can't claim credit for it*.

【掠取】seize; grab; plunder: ～别国的资源 *plunder the resources of other countries*

【掠水飞行】wave-hopping

【掠影】❶ impressing gained after brief observation: 北京～ *brief look at Beijing* ❷ bird's-eye view; panaroma

略 Ⅰ 形 brief; sketchy: ～述大意 *give a brief account* / 这个提纲写得太～了。*This outline is rather too rough*. / ～读 *a cursory reading* Ⅱ 副 slightly; a little; somewhat: ～加修改 *make some slight changes; edit slightly* / ～有所闻 *have heard a little about the matter* / ～有出入 *vary slightly; there's a slight discrepancy* Ⅲ 名 ❶ summary; brief account; outline: 史略 ❷ strategy; plan; scheme: 策略 Ⅳ 动 ❶ omit; delete; leave out: ～去不提 *make no mention of; leave out altogether* / ～去细节 *leave out the details* ❷ capture; seize: 侵略

【略称】abbreviation; shortened form

【略见一斑】catch a glimpse of; get a rough idea of

【略略】slightly; briefly: 关于那个问题他只～说了几句。*He touched only briefly on that question*.

【略识之无】know only a few simple characters

【略图】sketch map; sketch

【略微】slightly; a little; somewhat: ～有点感冒 *have a slight cold; have a touch of flu* / 我脸擦破了,～流了点血。*I got a scratch on my face and it bled a little*.

【略语】abbreviation; shortening

【略知一二】have only a smattering of; know only a little

lūn

抡 动 brandish; swing: ～刀 *brandish a sword* / ～起大铁锤 *swing a sledgehammer*

lún

伦 名 ❶ human relations (esp. as conceived by feudal ethics): 天伦 ❷ logic; order: 伦次 ❸ peer; match: 绝伦

【伦巴】rumba (a dance)

【伦比】〈书〉rival; equal: 史无～ *unrivalled (or peerless, unequalled) in history*

【伦常】feudal order of importance or seniority in human relationships

【伦次】coherence; logical sequence: 文笔错杂,毫无～。*The writing is tangled, utterly lacking in coherence*.

【伦理】ethics; moral principles ◇ ～学 ethics

【伦琴】[物] rontgen (or roentgen) ◇ ～射线 [物] rontgen (or roentgen) rays

沦 动 ❶ sink: 沉沦 ❷ fall; be reduced to: ～于敌手 *fall into enemy hands* / ～为殖民地 *be reduced to the status of a colony*

【沦落】fall low; come down in the world; be reduced to poverty

【沦落街头】be driven onto the streets (to become a tramp, beggar, etc.); be reduced to beggary, vagrancy, etc.

【沦丧】be lost; be ruined: 道德～ *decay of morals*

【沦亡】(of a country) be annexed (or subjugated)

【沦陷】❶ (of territory, etc.) be occupied by the enemy; fall into enemy hands ❷ 〈书〉 submerge; inundate; flood; drown ◇ ～区 enemy-occupied area

轮 Ⅰ 名 ❶ wheel: 十～卡车 *ten-wheel truck* ❷ sth. resembling a wheel; disc; ring: 光～ *halo* ❸ steamboat; steamer: 巨轮 Ⅱ 动 take turns: 下一个就～到你了。*It will be your turn next*. / 今天～到我值班。*It's my turn to be on duty today*. Ⅲ 量 ❶ (for the sun, the moon, etc.): 一～红日 *a red sun* / 一～明月 *a bright moon* ❷ round: 第一～比赛 *the first round of the match* / 新的一～会谈 *a new round of talks*

【轮班】in shifts; in relays; in rotation: ～护理病人 *take turns tending the sick*

【轮唱】[音] round

【轮齿】teeth of a cogwheel

【轮虫】wheel animalcule; rotifer
【轮船】steamer; steamship; steamboat
【轮次】❶ order of turns ❷ number of turns or rounds
【轮渡】ferry
【轮番】take turns: 我们～给锅炉添煤。*We took turns stoking the furnaces.* / ～轰炸 *bomb in waves*
【轮换】rotate; take turns: 我们～着照料他。*We take turns looking after him.*
【轮回】[宗](佛教) samsara; transmigration
【轮机】❶ (〈略〉见〖涡轮机〗) turbine: 燃气～ *combustion gas turbine* / 冲压空气～ *ram-air turbine* ❷ motorship engine; engine ◇ ～室 engine room; ～员 engineer; ～长 chief engineer
【轮奸】(of two or more men) rape a woman in turn; gang-rape
【轮距】track; tread
【轮空】[体] bye: 他在第一轮比赛中～。*He drew a bye in the first round of the tournament.*
【轮廓】outline; contour; rough sketch: 先画个～，再画细部。*Draw an outline before you fill in the details.*
【轮流】take turns; do sth. in turn: 我们～到医院去看他。*We'll take turns going to the hospital to see him.* / 他俩～值夜班。*They work on night shifts in turn.*
【轮牧】rotation grazing
【轮生】[植] verticillate: ～叶 *verticillate leaves*
【轮式拖拉机】wheeled tractor
【轮胎】tyre: 防滑～ *antiskid tyre; nonskid tyre* / 双层～ *two ply tyre* / 翻制～ *retreaded tyre* ◇ ～帘子线 tyre cord; ～压力计 tyre pressure gauge
【轮辋】rim (of a wheel)
【轮休】❶ (of land) lie fallow in rotation ❷ have holidays by turns; rotate days off; stagger holidays
【轮训】training in rotation ◇ ～班 a training class operating on a rotating basis
【轮椅】wheelchair
【轮轴】❶ [物] wheel and axle ❷ wheel axle
【轮转】rotate
【轮转印刷机】rotary press
【轮子】wheel
【轮作】crop rotation: 粮棉～ *rotation of cereal crops and cotton*

lùn

论 Ⅰ 动 ❶ discuss; talk about; discourse: 讨论 / 辩论 ❷ mention; regard; consider: 别论 ❸ decide on; determine: 按质～价 *determine the price according to the quality* Ⅱ 名 ❶ view; opinion; statement: 高论 ❷ dissertation; essay: 《实践～》*On Practice* ❸ theory: 进化论 Ⅲ 介 by (a certain unit of measure); according to (a certain system or principle): 鸡蛋～斤卖。*Eggs are sold by the jin.* / ～小时给钱 *pay by the hour*
【论辩】argue; debate: ～有力。*The argument is strong.*
【论处】decide on sb.'s punishment; punish: 以违反纪律～ *be punished for a breach of discipline*
【论点】argument; thesis: 这篇文章～鲜明。*The argument set forth in the article is clear-cut.*
【论调】〈贬〉view; argument: 这种～是错误的。*Such views are erroneous.* / 荒谬的～ *an absurd argument*
【论断】inference; judgment; thesis: 作出～ *draw an inference*
【论功行赏】dispense rewards or honours according to merit; give people awards according to their contributions
【论据】grounds of argument; argument: ～不足 *insufficient grounds* / 有力的～ *strong argument; valid reasons*
【论理】❶ reason (with sb.): 我要跟他～。*I'll try and reason with him.* ❷ normally; as things should be: ～她早可以退休了，可是她仍然坚持工作。*She really ought to have retired long ago, but she's still working.* ❸ logic: 合乎～ *be logical; stand to reason*
【论述】discuss; expound: 本文准备就以下三个问题分别加以～。*This paper will take up the following three questions one by one.* / 精辟的～ *a brilliant exposition*
【论说】❶ exposition and argumentation ❷〈口〉normally; as things should be: ～这个会他应该参加，不知道为什么没有来? *Normally he ought to have attended the meeting. I wonder why he didn't come.* ◇ ～文 argumentation
【论坛】forum; tribune: 这是最近公众～上引起激烈争论的问题。*This question has caused heated controversy in recent forums of public opinion.*
【论题】[逻] proposition
【论文】thesis; dissertation; treatise; paper: 学术～ *an academic thesis (or paper)* / 科学～ *a scientific treatise*
【论文答辩】thesis defence: 我明天～。*I'm going to defend my thesis tomorrow.*
【论战】polemic; debate: 展开～ *launch a debate*
【论证】❶ demonstration; proof: 无可辩驳的～ *irrefutable proof* ❷ expound and prove: 文章～了改革的必要性。*The article proves the necessity of the reform.* ❸ grounds of argument
【论著】treatise; work; book
【论资排辈】arrange in order of seniority; give top priority to seniority in promotion
【论罪】decide on the nature of the guilt: 按贪污～ *be found guilty of corruption*

luō

捋 动 rub one's palm along (sth. long): ～起袖子 *push up one's sleeve* / ～掉树枝上的叶子 *strip a twig of its leaves* ——另见 lǚ

【捋胳膊】push up one's sleeve and show the arm
【捋虎须】stroke the tiger's whiskers—do sth. very daring; run great risks

啰（构词成分）见下

啰嗦（又作'啰唆'）❶ talkative; long-winded; wordy: 他说话太～。*He's far too long-winded.* ❷ overelaborate; troublesome: 这些手续真～。*All these formalities are overelaborate.*

luó

罗 Ⅰ名 ❶ a net for catching birds: 罗网 ❷ a kind of silk gauze Ⅱ动 ❶ catch (birds) with a net: 门可罗雀 ❷ collect; gather together: 搜罗 ❸ display; spread out: 星罗棋布 ❹ sieve; sift: ～面 *sift flour* / 把面再～一遍。*Sift the flour over again.* Ⅲ量 twelve dozen; a gross
【罗布麻】bluish dogbane (Apocynum venetum)
【罗得西亚】[地] Rhodesia
【罗浮宫】the Louvre (in Paris)
【罗锅】arched: ～桥 *arch bridge*
【罗锅儿】❶ hunchbacked; humpbacked ❷ hunchback; humpback
【罗汉】[宗](佛教) arhat, arahat, or arahant
【罗汉果】mangosteen
【罗汉松】yew podocarpus
【罗经】compass: 电～ *gyrocompass* / 磁～ *magnetic compass* / 航海～ *mariner's compass*
【罗口】rib cuff or rib collar; rib top (of socks)
【罗口灯泡】同〖螺口灯泡〗
【罗口灯头】同〖螺口灯头〗
【罗列】❶ spread out; set out: 厂房～在山坡上。*Factory buildings spread out over the hillside.* ❷ enumerate: 光～事实还不够，必须加以分析。*It's not enough just to enumerate the facts. You've got to analyse them, too.*
【罗马法】Roman law
【罗马尼亚】Romania ◇ ～人 Romanian; ～语 Romanian (language)
【罗马数字】Roman numerals
【罗马语族】[语] the Romance group of languages; Romance languages
【罗曼蒂克】romantic (a transliteration)
【罗盘】compass
【罗盘赌】roulette
【罗圈】the round frame of a sieve
【罗圈腿】❶ bowlegs; bandy legs ❷ bowlegged; bandy-legged
【罗裙】a skirt of thin silk; silk skirt
【罗网】net; trap
【罗帷】gauze curtain
【罗织】〈书〉frame up: ～诬陷 *frame sb. up* ◇ ～罪名 cook up charges; frame a case against sb.
【罗致】enlist the services of; secure sb. in one's employment; collect; gather together ◇ ～人才 enlist the services of able people

萝 名 trailing plants: 藤萝
【萝卜】radish ◇ ～干儿 dried radish
【萝芙木】[植] devilpepper

逻 动 patrol: 巡逻
【逻辑】logic: 研究～ *study logic* / ～上的错误 *an error in logic* / 这句话不合～。*This statement is illogical.* ◇ ～操作 logical operation; ～电路 logical circuit; ～记录 logical record; ～数据库 logical date base; ～思维 logical thinking; ～学 logic; ～主语 [语] logical subject

锣 名 gong
【锣槌】(gong) hammer
【锣鼓】❶ gong and drum ❷ traditional percussion instruments ❸ ensemble of such instruments with gongs and drums playing the main part
【锣鼓喧天】a deafening sound of gongs and drums

箩 名 a square-bottomed bamboo basket
【箩筐】a large bamboo or wicker basket

骡 名 mule
【骡马店】an inn with sheds for carts and animals
【骡子】mule

螺 名 ❶ spiral shell; snail ❷ whorl (in fingerprint)
【螺钿】（又作'螺甸'）mother-of-pearl inlay: ～漆盘 *lacquer tray inlaid with mother-of-pearl*
【螺钉】screw: 木～ *wood screw*; *screwnail* / 十字槽～ *Phillips screw*
【螺号】conch; shell trumpet
【螺距】[机] (screw) pitch; thread pitch
【螺口灯泡】screw-socket bulb; screw bulb
【螺口灯头】screw socket
【螺母】（又作'螺帽'）[机] (screw) nut: ～垫圈 *nut collar*
【螺栓】[机] (screw) bolt: 连接～ *binder bolt*; *connecting bolt* / 地脚～ *foundation bolt*
【螺丝】screw ◇ ～板牙 screw die; threading die; ～刀 screwdriver; ～钉〈口〉screw; ～扣 thread (of a screw); ～母 (screw) nut; ～起子 screwdriver
【螺蛳】spiral shell; snail
【螺纹】❶ whorl (in fingerprint) ❷ [机] thread (of a screw): 公制～ *metric thread* / 惠氏～ *Whitworth thread* ◇ ～刀具 threading tool; screw tool
【螺旋】❶ spiral; helix ❷ [物] screw ◇ ～桨（又作'螺旋推进器'）(screw) propeller; screw
【螺旋式】spiral: ～发展 *spiral development*; *developing in spirals* / ～军备竞赛 *arms race spiral* / ～通货膨胀 *inflation spiral*; *spiralling inflation*
【螺旋体】[微] spirochaeta

luǒ

裸 形 bare; naked; exposed

【裸背女裙】backless dress；sunback dress
【裸鲤】naked carp
【裸露】uncovered；exposed：～的煤层 *exposed coal seam* ◇ ～癖 exhibitionism
【裸麦】naked barley；highland barley
【裸体】naked；nude：一张～的照片 *a photograph (or picture) of a nude* ◇ ～画 a painting of a nude (esp. a nude woman)；～像 a nude figure or statue；nude
【裸线】bare wire
【裸眼】naked eye
【裸泳】skinny-dipping
【裸装货】nude cargo
【裸子植物】gymnosperm

luò

荦 形〈书〉prominent；outstanding：卓荦
【荦荦】〈书〉conspicuous；apparent；obvious
【荦荦大端】(又作'荦荦大者') major items；salient points

洛 名 ❶ a river in Shaanxi Province ❷ a river in Henan Province
【洛氏硬度】[物] Rockwell hardness
【洛阳纸贵】paper is dear in Luoyang (said of the wide circulation of a popular work)

络 Ⅰ名 ❶ sth. resembling a net ❷[中] subsidiary channels in the human body through which vital energy, blood and nutriment circulate Ⅱ动 ❶ hold sth. in place with a net：她头上～着一个发网。*She kept her hair in place with a net.* ❷ twine；wind：～纱 *winding yarn；spooling*
【络合】[化] complexing：～物 *complex compound*
【络离子】[化] complex ion
【络腮胡子】whiskers；full beard
【络纱】[纺] doff：～工 *doffer* / ～机 *doffer*
【络筒机】[纺] (high speed) cone winder；winding machine；winder
【络盐】[化] complex salt
【络绎不绝】in an endless stream：参观展览会的人～。*A continuous flow of visitors came to the exhibition.*

骆 名 a white horse with a black mane (mentioned in ancient texts)
【骆驼】camel
【骆驼刺】(又作'骆驼草') camel thorn
【骆驼队】camel train；caravan
【骆驼绒】camel hair cloth

落 Ⅰ动 ❶ fall；drop：有些棉桃～在地上了。*Some cotton bolls have fallen on the ground.* ❷ go down；set：潮水～了。*The tide is low (or out).* / 太阳～山了。*The sun has set.* ❸ lower：把帘子～下来 *lower the blinds* ❹ decline；come down；sink：～到这步田地 *come to such a pass* ❺ lag behind；fall behind：落伍 ❻ leave behind；stay behind：不～痕迹 *leave no trace* ❼ fall onto；rest with：这项任务～在我们肩上了。*The task was put on our shoulders.* ❽ get；have；receive：～褒贬 *be criticized；lay oneself open to censure* / 就这么办吧，我不怕～埋怨。*Let's do it that way, then. I don't mind taking the blame.* ❾ put pen to paper；write down：落款 Ⅱ名 ❶ whereabouts：下落 ❷ settlement：村落 ——另见 là；lào
【落榜】fail in an entrance examination；fail as a candidate
【落笔】put pen to paper；start to write or draw：写文章时，～之前要很好构思。*When you write you should think it all out before you put pen to paper.*
【落标】fail towin a bid；fail in an election or competition
【落泊】(又作'落魄')〈书〉❶ be in dire straits；be down and out ❷ untrammelled by convention；casual；unconventional
【落草】take to the greenwood；take to the heather；become an outlaw
【落差】❶ drop in elevation (between two points in a stream) ❷ head drop (in hydroelectric power plants)
【落潮】ebb tide
【落成】(of a building, etc.) be completed：大桥已经～，日内就可以正式通车。*The bridge has been completed and will be open to traffic in a few days.* ◇ ～典礼 inauguration ceremony (for a building, etc.)
【落锤】[机] drop hammer
【落得】get；end in：～一场空 *come to nothing；end up in smoke* / 搞阴谋诡计的人，必然要～可耻的下场。*Plotters come to no good end.*
【落底】❶〈方〉the end of a year or month：一月～要进行大扫除。*We shall have a thorough cleaning at the end of January.* ❷ feel at ease；have one's mind set at rest：事情办成了，咱们的心也就～了。*The matter was settled, and our minds were set at rest.*
【落地】❶ fall to the ground：人头～ *be killed (or beheaded)* ❷ (of a baby) be born：呱呱～ *come into the world with a cry；be born* ◇ ～车床 face lathe；～窗 French window；～灯 floor lamp；standard lamp
【落地生根】❶ [植] air plant；life plant ❷ take root；strike root
【落地式收音机】console (radio) set
【落点】❶ [体] placement (of a ball)：～准 *accuracy in placement* ❷ [军] point of fall
【落果】[农] premature drop
【落后】❶ be behind；fall behind；lag behind：谁也不甘心～。*Nobody is willing to be left behind.* ❷ backward；behind the times：他的思想很～。*His thoughts are very backward (or are far behind the times).* / ～地区 *backward areas；less developed areas* ◇ ～分子 backward elements
【落户】settle：在农村～ *settle in the countryside* /

他是十年前在这里落的户。*He settled down here ten years ago*.

【落花流水】like fallen flowers carried away by flowing water—in a sorry plight：敌人被打得～。*The enemy was utterly routed*.

【落花生】peanut；groundnut

【落花有意，流水无情】the waterside flower pining for love sheds petals, while the heartless brook babbles on—unrequited love

【落价】fall (or drop) in price：收音机～了。*The price of radios has gone down*.

【落脚】stay (for a time)；stop over；put up：找个地方～ *find a place to stay* / 在客店～ *put up at an inn* ◇ ～处 temporary lodging

【落井下石】drop stones on someone who has fallen into a well—hit a person when he's down

【落空】come to nothing；fail；fall through：希望～ *fail to attain one's hope* / 这事有～的危险。*There is a danger that nothing will come of it*.

【落款】write the names of the sender and the recipient on a painting, gift or letter；inscribe (a gift, etc.)

【落泪】shed tears；weep

【落铃】［农］shedding (or premature dropping) of cotton bolls

【落落大方】natural and at ease

【落落寡合】standoffish；unsociable；aloof：他性情孤傲，～。*He is proud and arrogant, holding himself aloof from the others*.

【落马】❶ fall off a horse ❷〈喻〉be defeated；lose a race

【落幕】the curtain falls；lower the curtain

【落难】meet with misfortune；be in distress

【落聘】not be hired or recruited；be turned down in one's job application：有许多人～。*Many were turned down*.

【落魄】〈书〉❶ in dire straits；down and out ❷(又作'落拓') untrammelled by convention；casual；unconventional

【落日】the setting sun

【落腮胡子】同〖络腮胡子〗

【落实】❶ practicable；workable：生产计划要订得～。*Production plans must be practicable*. ❷ fix (or decide) in advance；ascertain；make sure：交货时间还没有最后～。*The date of delivery hasn't been fixed yet*. ❸ carry out；fulfil；implement；put into effect：～政策 *implement a policy*

【落水】❶ fall into water：打救～儿童 *save a drowning child* ❷ fall into evil ways

【落水狗】dog in the water—a bad person who is down

【落俗】show poor taste

【落汤鸡】(of a person) like a drenched chicken；like a drowned rat；soaked through；drenched and bedraggled

【落体】［物］falling body：自由～ *freely falling body*

【落拓不羁】unconventional and uninhibited

【落网】(of a criminal) fall into the net—be caught；be captured：主犯已经～。*The chief criminal has been caught*.

【落伍】❶ fall behind the ranks；straggle；drop behind；drop out ❷ out of date；behind the times；backward：他的思维方式～了。*His way of thinking is out of date (or behind the times)*.

【落线】［军］line of fall

【落选】fail to be chosen (or elected)；lose an election

【落叶】❶ fallen leaves ❷［植］deciduous leaf ◇ ～树 deciduous tree；～松 larch

【落叶归根】同〖叶落归根〗

【落英】〈文〉❶ fallen or falling flowers ❷ new-bloomed flowers

【落英缤纷】petals falling in riotous profusion

【落座】take a seat (in restaurants, theatres, etc.)：各位观众请～，节目就要开始了。*Will all spectators be seated. The performance is going to start*.

摞 Ⅰ 动 pile up；stack up：把砖～起来 *stack up the bricks* / 他屋里的书一直～到屋顶。*The books in his room piled up to the ceiling*. Ⅱ 量 pile；stack：一～砖 *a pile of bricks* / 一～书 *a stack of books* / 一～碗 *a pile of bowls*

M

mā

妈 名 ❶〈口〉ma; mum; mummy; mother: 我～让你去。*Mother wants you to go to her.* / ～，再见。*Goodbye, Mum!* ❷ (a form of address for a married woman one generation one's senior): 姑妈 ❸ (used in an exclamation): 我的～呀! 钱包丢了。*Oh dear! I've lost my purse.* ❹〈旧〉a middle-aged or old maidservant (called together with her surname): 王～ *Nanny Wang*

【妈妈】〈口〉ma; mum; mummy; mother

抹 动 ❶ wipe: ～桌子 *wipe a table clean* / ～一把脸 *wipe one's face* ❷ rub sth. down; slip sth. off: 把帽子～下来 *slip one's cap off* ——另见 mǒ; mò

【抹布】rag (to wipe things with)

【抹脸】〈口〉be strict with sb. all of a sudden: 抹不下脸来 *find it difficult to be strict with sb.* (*for fear of hurting his feelings*)

麻 (构词成分)见下——另见 má

【麻麻黑】〈方〉(it is) dusk: 天～了，屋里逐渐模糊起来。*As dusk fell, the room got dimmer and dimmer.*

【麻麻亮】〈方〉(it is) just dawning; (day is) just beginning to break; just getting light: 天～ *at the crack of dawn*

摩 (构词成分)见下——另见 mó

【摩挲】(māsa) ❶ gently stroke; smooth sth. out with one's hands: 她肚子疼，你给她～～肚子。*She's got a stomachache. Massage her stomach for her.* ❷ do sth. in a careless and quick way: 你让他洗把脸，他好歹一～。*When you tell him to wash his face, he just gives it a wipe.* ❸ coax; humour: 你是怎么把他给～顺了的? *How did you get him to quiet down?* —— 另见 mósuō

má

麻 Ⅰ 名 ❶ general name for hemp, flax, etc. ❷ fibre of hemp, flax, etc. for textile materials: 这块手绢是～的。*This handkerchief is linen.* ❸ sesame: ～糖 *sesame candy* Ⅱ 形 ❶ rough; coarse: 这种纸一面光，一面～。*This paper is smooth on one side and rough on the other.* ❷ pocked; pockmarked; pitted; spotty: 得了天花，脸就～了。*Smallpox will leave pockmarks on the face.* / 铸件上有～点。*There are pits in the casting.* Ⅲ 动 feeling pins and needles; tingling; numb: 她坐得太久，腿都～了。*She'd been sitting so long that she felt pins and needles in her legs.* / 他手指头都冻～了。*The cold numbed his fingers.* ——另见 mā

【麻包】gunnybag; gunnysack; burlap sack; sack

【麻痹】❶［医］paralysis: 面部神经～ *facial paralysis* ❷ benumb; lull; blunt: ～人们的斗志 *lull* (*or blunt*) *people's fighting will* ❸ lower one's guard; slacken one's vigilance: ～粗心是产生事故的原因。*Carelessness is the cause of accidents.* / 思想～ *a slackening of vigilance; a decline in alertness*

【麻痹大意】lower one's guard and become careless; be off one's guard

【麻布】❶ gunny (cloth); sackcloth; burlap; hessian ❷ linen

【麻袋】gunnybag; gunnysack; burlap sack: ～片 *a piece of gunnysacking*

【麻刀】［建］hemp; hair: ～灰泥 *hemp-fibred plaster*

【麻烦】❶ troublesome; inconvenient: 这下可～了，我把钥匙锁在屋里了。*What a nuisance. I've locked my key in the room.* / 自找～ *ask for trouble* ❷ put sb. to trouble; trouble sb.; bother: 对不起，太～你了。*Sorry to have put you to so much trouble.*

【麻纺】the spinning of jute, hemp or flax

【麻风】［医］leprosy: ～病人 *leper*

【麻花】❶ fried dough twist ❷〈方〉(of clothes) wearing thin; worn out: 两只袖子都～了。*The sleeves are wearing thin.*

【麻花钻】［机］(fluted) twist drill

【麻黄】［植］Chinese ephedra (Ephedra sinica); mahuang

【麻黄硷】［药］ephedrine

【麻将】mahjong: ～牌 *mahjong pieces; mahjong tiles* / 打～ *play mahjong*

【麻酱】sesame paste

【麻辣辣】(of a pain) searing

【麻利】❶ quick and neat; dexterous; deft: 干活～ *work dexterously; be a quick and neat worker* ❷〈方〉quick; fast: 厂里开会，叫你～回去。*You've been asked to return quickly to attend a meeting in the factory.*

【麻脸】pockmarked face

【麻乱】confused (state of mind); in a turmoil: ～的情绪 *anxious state of mind* / 他的心里～极了。*His mind was in a turmoil.*

【麻木】❶ numb: 他手脚～了。*Both his hands and feet have gone numb.* ❷ apathetic; insensitive; lifeless: ～地生活 *lead an empty life* / 他年龄不大,思想却近乎～。*Though he is not old, his mind is already deadened.*

【麻木不仁】apathetic; insensitive; unfeeling

【麻婆豆腐】pockmarked grandma's beancurd — stir-fried beancurd in hot sauce

【麻雀】(house) sparrow: ～虽小,五脏俱全 *the sparrow may be small but it has all the vital organs—small but complete*

【麻纱】❶ yarn of ramie, flax, etc. ❷ cambric; haircords

【麻绳】rope made of hemp, flax, jute, etc.

【麻酥酥】slightly numb; tingling: 脚在冷水里冻得～的。*The cold water gave my feet a tingling feeling.*

【麻线】flaxen thread; linen thread

【麻药】anaesthetic: 上～ *apply an anaesthetic; administer anaesthesia*

【麻油】sesame oil

【麻疹】measles: 出～ *have measles*

【麻织品】fabrics of flax, hemp, etc.; linen fabrics

【麻子】❶ pockmarks: 他脸上有几点～。*He's got a few pockmarks on his face.* ❷ a person with a pockmarked face

【麻醉】❶ [医] anaesthesia; narcosis: 全身(局部、脊髓)～ *general (local, spinal) anaesthesia* / 药物～ *drug anesthesia* / 针刺～ *acupuncture anesthesia* / 中药～ *herbal anesthesia* ❷ [医] anaesthetize: 病人已经～过了,您可以动手术了。*The patient has been anaesthetized and you can operate now.* ❸ corrupt (sb.'s mind); poison: 用诲淫诲盗的电影～青年人 *poison young people's minds with films full of sex and violence* ◇ ～剂 anaesthetic; narcotic; ～品 narcotic; drug; ～师 anaesthetist

mǎ

马 Ⅰ [名] ❶ horse ❷ horse, one of the pieces in Chinese chess Ⅱ [形] big; large: 马蜂

【马鞍】(又作'马鞍子') saddle

【马鞍形】the shape of a saddle—a falling-off between two peak periods: 由于这次事故,我厂生产一度出现了～。*As a result of the accident, there was a temporary falling-off (or drop) in production at our factory.*

【马帮】a train of horses carrying goods; caravan

【马宝】[中] bezoar of a horse

【马鼻疽】[牧] glanders

【马鞭】horsewhip

【马表】stopwatch

【马鳖】common name for 水蛭

【马不停蹄】a horse galloping without a stop; non-stop: 我接到电报就赶来了,一路上可是～啊! *I hurried here as soon as I got your telegram and didn't waste a single minute on the way.*

【马槽】manger

【马车】❶ (horse-drawn) carriage ❷ cart

【马齿苋】[植] purslane

【马刺】spur

【马达】common name for 电动机

【马达加斯加】Madagascar ◇ ～人 Madagascan; ～语(又作'马尔加什语')Malagasy (language)

【马大哈】〈口〉❶ careless; forgetful: 他可真够～的了,自己丢了表,居然不知道。*How careless he is! He even doesn't know that he's lost his watch.* ❷ a careless person; scatterbrain: 他是个～,老忘锁门。*He's such a scatterbrain that he always forgets to lock the door.*

【马刀】sabre

【马到成功】be victorious the moment the battle steeds arrive—win success immediately upon arrival; gain an immediate victory; win instant success: 祝你～! *I wish you instant success!*

【马灯】barn lantern; lantern

【马镫】stirrup

【马丁炉】[冶] Martin furnace; open-hearth furnace; open hearth

【马兜铃】[植] birthwort

【马队】❶ a train of horses carrying goods; caravan ❷ a contingent of mounted troops; cavalry

【马尔代夫】Maldives ◇ ～人 Maldivian

【马尔加什语】(又作'马达加斯加语') Malagasy (language)

【马尔萨斯人口论】Malthusian theory of population

【马尔萨斯主义】Malthusianism

【马尔维纳斯群岛】Islas Malvinas; the Falkland Islands

【马耳他】Malta ◇ ～人 Maltese; ～语 Maltese (language)

【马贩子】horse dealer; coper

【马粪纸】strawboard

【马蜂】honet

【马蜂窝】hornet's nest ——另见〖捅马蜂窝〗

【马夫】〈旧〉groom

【马革裹尸】be wrapped in horsehide after death—die on the battlefield

【马褂】mandarin jacket (worn over a gown)

【马关条约】the Treaty of Shimonoseki (1895)

【马海毛】[纺] mohair

【马号】❶ public stable ❷ long-tubed bugle (used by cavalry)

【马赫数】(又作'马赫') [物] Mach number; Mach

【马赫主义】[哲] Machism: ～者 *Machist*

【马后炮】(a Chinese chess term used figuratively to mean) belated action or advice; belated effort: 切记不要使问题成了堆,才来一个总结,放～。*Make sure that you don't wait until problems pile up before making a reckoning — that would be firing belated shots.* / 我这个建议也许是～。*It's probably already too late for my suggestion to do any good.*

【马虎】(又作‘马糊’) careless; casual: ～了事 *get sth. done in a slapdash manner* / 这是件大事,不能～过去。*This is a serious matter. It shouldn't be handled in just any old way.*
【马甲】〈方〉a sleeveless garment; vest
【马脚】sth. that gives the game away ——另见〖露马脚〗
【马厩】stable
【马驹子】〈口〉foal; colt or filly
【马具】horse harness; horse gear
【马克】❶ mark (German monetary unit) ❷ markka (Finnish monetary unit)
【马克思列宁主义】Marxism-Leninism: ～者 *Marxist-Leninist*
【马克思主义】Marxism ◇ ～哲学 Marxist philosophy; ～者 Marxist; ～政治经济学 Marxist political economy
【马口铁】tinplate; galvanized iron
【马裤】riding breeches
【马裤呢】[纺] whipcord
【马拉犁】[农] horse-drawn plough
【马拉松】marathon: ～赛跑 *marathon race*; *marathon* / ～演说 *a marathon speech*
【马拉维】Malawi ◇ ～人 Malawian
【马来半岛】the Malay Peninsula
【马来西亚】Malaysia ◇ ～人 Malaysian
【马来语】Malay (language)
【马蓝】[植]acanthaceous indigo (Strobilanthes cusia)
【马里】Mali ◇ ～人 Malian
【马力】[物] horsepower (h. p.): ～小时 *horse-power-hour* (*hp-hr*)
【马立克派】[宗](伊斯兰教) the Malikite school (or sect)
【马列主义】〈略〉见〖马克思列宁主义〗
【马蔺】[植] Chinese small iris (Iris pallasii var. chinensis)
【马铃薯】potato: ～晚疫病 *late blight of potato*
【马六甲海峡】the Strait of Malacca
【马鹿】[动] red deer
【马路】road; street; avenue: 逛～ *stroll around the streets*; *go window-shopping* ◇ ～新闻 street-gossip; hearsay
【马骡】[动] mule
【马马虎虎】❶ careless; casual: 他的信我只是～地看了一下。*I merely glanced over his letter.* / 你最近工作有些～。*You've been slack in your work recently.* ❷ not very good; just passable; so-so; fair; not so bad: 你的游泳技术怎么样? —～,游不远。*Are you a good swimmer? —Just so-so. I can't swim far.*
【马奶】mare's milk
【马尼拉麻】another name for 蕉麻
【马匹】horses
【马屁】见〖拍马屁〗
【马屁精】sycophant; flatterer
【马其顿共和国】Republic of Macedonia
【马前卒】pawn; cat's-paw
【马钱子】[植] vomiting nut; nux vomica
【马枪】carbine
【马球】[体] equestrian polo; polo
【马赛克】[建] mosaic: ～铺面 *mosaic pavement*
【马上】❶ at once; immediately; straight away; right away: 我们～动手。*We'll start working straight away.* / 演出～就要开始了。*The performance will begin in a minute.* / ～集合! *Fall in immediately*! ❷ in the near future; soon: ～就要高考了。*The college entrance examinations are coming up soon.*
【马勺】ladle
【马失前蹄】make a mistake by accident; have an accidental setback: 谁没有个～的时候? *Who can always be free from setbacks and mistakes? or To err is human.*
【马首是瞻】(usu. used in) 唯某某之～ *take the head of sb.'s horse as guide—follow sb.'s lead*
【马术】horsemanship
【马蹄】❶ horse's hoof: ～声 *hoofbeat*; *clatter of a horse's hoofs*; *clip-clop* ❷〈方〉water chestnut
【马蹄表】round or hoof-shaped desk clock, usu. an alarm clock
【马蹄铁】❶ horseshoe ❷ U-shaped magnet; horseshoe magnet
【马蹄形】the shape of a hoof; U-shaped
【马桶】(又作‘马子’) ❶ nightstool; closestool; commode; chamber pot ❷ toilet
【马头琴】a bowed stringed instrument with a scroll carved like a horse's head, used by the Mongolians
【马尾松】masson pine
【马戏】circus: ～团 *circus troupe*
【马熊】同〖棕熊〗
【马靴】riding boots
【马仰人翻】同〖人仰马翻〗
【马缨丹】[植] lantana
【马缨花】another name for 合欢❷
【马蝇】horse botfly
【马扎】campstool; folding stool
【马掌】❶ cutin skin of a horse's hoof ❷ horseshoe
【马桩】hitching post
【马鬃】horse's mane

吗 (构词成分)见下——另见 ma
【吗啡】morphine

玛 (构词成分)见下
【玛瑙】agate
【玛雅人】Maya
【玛雅文化】the Mayan Culture
【玛祖卡】[音] mazurka

码 Ⅰ[名] ❶ a sign or thing indicating number: 页码 ❷ an instrument used to indicate number: 砝码 Ⅱ[量] ❶ (used to indicate the same thing or the same kind): 这是两～事。*They are two different matters.* / 你们说的是一～事。*You were talking about the same thing.* ❷(英美制长度单位) yard (yd.) Ⅲ[动] pile up; stack: ～砖 *stack bricks* / 把这些报纸～齐了。*Put these news-*

papers in a neat pile.

【码表】speedometer

【码头】❶ wharf; dock; quay; pier ❷〈方〉port city; commercial and transportation centre: 水陆～ *a port city where land and water transport service is highly developed* ◇ ～费 wharfage; dockage; ～工人 docker; stevedore; long-shoreman; ～交货 ex wharf (or pier, quay); ～税 pierage

【码洋】total price (of books): 这部词典第一版印刷一万册,～为一百万元。*The first edition of this dictionary has an impression of 10,000 copies and the total price is 1,000,000 yuan.*

【码子】❶ numeral ❷ counter; chip ❸〈旧〉(in financial circles) cash under one's control

蚂

(构词成分)见下 ——另见 mà

【蚂蟥】leech

【蚂蚁】ant

【蚂蚁搬泰山】ants can move Mount Taishan—the united efforts of the masses can accomplish mighty projects

【蚂蚁啃骨头】ants gnawing at a bone—a concentration of small machines on a big job; plod away at a big job bit by bit

【蚂蚁缘槐】ants on the locust tree—little people inflated with pride

mà

骂

动 ❶ verbally abuse; curse; swear; call names: ～人 *swear (at people)* / ～人话 *abusive language; swearwords; curse* / 他～我是笨蛋。*He called me an idiot.* ❷ condemn; rebuke; reprove; scold: 这样铺张浪费,没有一个人不～。*Such extravagance is an object of general condemnation.*

【骂街】shout abuses in public; call people names in public ——另见〖泼妇骂街〗

【骂骂咧咧】intersperse one's talk with curses; be foul-mouthed; be grumbling and swearing

【骂名】bad name; infamy: 留下千古～ *earn oneself eternal infamy*

【骂娘】abuse; curse; swear

蚂

(构词成分)见下 ——另见 mǎ

【蚂蚱】〈方〉locust

ma

吗

助 ❶ (used at the end of a question): 下午有会～? *Is there a meeting this afternoon?* / 你找我有事～? *Is there something you want to see me about?* / 明天他来～? *Will he come tomorrow?* ❷ (used to form a pause in a sentence before introducing the theme of what one is going to say): 特殊情况～,还得特殊对待。*Special cases, of course, need special consideration.* / 这件事～,其实也不能怪他。*This matter, actually, is not his fault.* ❸ used at the end of a rhetorical question: 你发这么大脾气像话～? *Aren't you ashamed of flying into such a rage?* / 你难道没看见我正忙着～? *Don't you see I'm busy at the moment?* / 这不是很明白的～? *Isn't this perfectly clear?* ——另见 mǎ

嘛

助 ❶ (indicating that sth. is obvious): 这也不能怪他,头一回做～。*He's not to blame. After all, it was the first time he'd done it.* / 这件事他是知道的～。*He's well aware of it.* / 他本来就不愿意去～,就不要勉强他了。*He just doesn't want to go. Don't force him.* / 有意见就提～,你怎么不提呀? *If you have any suggestions to make, by all means make them. What are you keeping quiet for?* ❷ (expressing a hope or giving advice): 喂,汽车开慢点～! *Hey, don't drive so fast!* / 既然你忙,就别去～。*Since you are busy, don't go then.* ❸ (used to form a pause in a sentence, calling listener's attention): 这个问题～,很简单。*As for this problem, it's really quite simple.* / 不让他去～,他有意见;让他去～,他又不去了。*If you don't let him go, he'll complain; but if you ask him to go, then he'll refuse to.* / 好～,那就快找他去吧。*O K. Go to him at once.*

mái

埋

动 ❶ cover up (with earth, snow, etc.); bury: 雪把这口井～起来了。*The well is buried in snow.* / ～地雷 *lay a mine* ❷〈口〉bury (a dead person): 莫扎特是～在穷人的乱葬岗子上的。*Mozart was buried in an unmarked pauper's grave.* ——另见 mán

【埋藏】lie hidden in the earth; bury: 这一带地下～着丰富的矿产。*There are rich mineral deposits in this region.* / 他向她倾诉～在心底的感情。*He revealed his innermost feelings to her.*

【埋存】bury: ～在心底 *buried deep in the heart*

【埋伏】❶ lie in ambush; ambush: 设下～ *lay an ambush* / ～了一部分兵力 *have part of the troops wait in ambush* / 中～ *fall into an ambush* ❷ hide; lie low ——另见〖打埋伏〗

【埋名】conceal one's identity; keep one's identity hidden; live incognito

【埋没】❶ cover up (with earth, snow, etc.); bury: 泥石流～了整个村庄。*The mud-rock flow submerged the whole village.* ❷ neglect; stifle: ～人才 *stifle real talents* / 瞧,这儿有重要的资料,差点给～了。*Look, here's some important source material we almost overlooked.*

【埋设】fit sth. underground: ～地雷 *lay a mine*

【埋汰】〈方〉❶ dirty: 看你那股～劲,不许你进屋。*Look, how dirty you are! You can't go inside.* ❷ insult or ridicule: ～人 *insult (or make fun of) sb.*

【埋头】immerse oneself in; be engrossed in: ～读

书 *bury oneself in one's studies* / ～业务 *engross oneself in vocational work*

【埋头苦干】quietly immerse oneself in hard work; quietly put one's shoulder to the wheel: 我就喜欢你们这股扎扎实实～的劲儿。*I like your down-to-earth and hardworking spirit*.

【埋头铆钉】countersunk rivet

【埋线疗法】[中] catgut embedding therapy (embedding a piece of catgut in a selected point to produce protracted stimulation)

【埋葬】bury (a dead person): 这里～着一位伟人。*A great man is buried here. or Here lies a great man.*

霾 名 [气] haze: 阴霾

【霾层】[气] haze layer

【霾线】[气] haze line; haze level

mǎi

买 动 buy; purchase: 我家～了台彩电。*We've bought a colour TV set.* / 这是人家送的,不是～的。*It is a present, not a purchase.* / ～东西 *buy things; go shopping* / 太贵了,～不起。*It's too expensive. I can't afford it.* / 三块钱～两个。*Three yuan will buy two pieces.*

【买办】comprador ◇ ～资产阶级 comprador bourgeoisie

【买单】to pay a bill; check: 小姐,～。*Waitress, bill please.*

【买椟还珠】keep the glittering casket and give back the pearls—show lack of judgment; make the wrong choice

【买方】the buying party (of a contract, etc.); buyer: ～市场 *a buyer's market*

【买关节】get round (law, rules, etc.) by bribery; offer bribes to facilitate one's operations

【买好】try to win sb.'s favour; ingratiate oneself with; play up to: 他使出浑身的解数向她～。*He did all he could to win her favour.*

【买家】purchaser; buyer; customer

【买价】buying price

【买进】buy in

【买空】[经] bull; buy long

【买空卖空】speculate (in stocks, etc.)

【买路钱】❶ paper money thrown on the road during a funeral procession ❷ toll money (formerly asked for by highwaymen)

【买麻藤】[植] sweetberry jointfir (Gnetum montanum)

【买卖】❶ buying and selling; business; deal; transaction: 做成一笔～ *make a deal* / ～人〈口〉*businessman; trader; merchant* / ～公平 *be fair in buying and selling; buy and sell at reasonable prices* / ～婚姻 *mercenary marriage* / ～亏本 *be out of pocket by the transaction* / ～兴隆。*Business is brisk.* ❷ (private) shop: 他原先在城里有个～。*He used to have a shop in the city.*

【买面子】have regard for sb.'s face; defer to sb.: 不是我不买你的面子,实在这事不好办。*I'd be happy to defer to your wishes, but there's really nothing I can do about it.* / 他买我的面子准同意。*He's sure to agree for my sake.*

【买期货】forward buying

【买入汇率】buying rate

【买通】bribe; buy over; buy off: ～官府 *bribe the local authorities (in old times)*

【买一送一】buy one item with another similar item presented free

【买账】(usu. used in the negative) acknowledge the superiority or seniority of; show respect for: 你摆架子,人家就不买你的账。*If you put on airs, people just won't go for it.*

【买主】buyer; customer

mài

迈 Ⅰ 动 step; stride: ～过门槛 *step over the threshold* / ～着矫健的步伐 *walk with vigorous strides* / ～开双脚,走向基层。*Get yourself moving and go down to the grass roots.* Ⅱ 形 advanced in years; old: 年迈 Ⅲ 名 ❶ mile (a transliteration): 这卡车一小时走七十～。*This truck can go 70 miles per hour (mph).* ❷ (mistakenly used by some drivers for) kilometre

【迈步】take a step; make a step; step forward: ～走向讲台 *step up to the platform* / 迈出第一步 *make the first step*

【迈方步】walk with measured steps; stride leisurely forward

【迈进】stride forward; forge ahead; advance with big strides: 他在学习上又～了一步。*He made further progress in his studies.*

麦 名 ❶ general name for wheat, barley, etc. ❷ wheat

【麦茬】wheat stubble: ～白薯 *sweet potatoes grown after the wheat harvest* / ～地 *a field of wheat stubble (ready for growing other crops)*

【麦当劳】MacDonald's (an American fast-food chain)

【麦地那】Medina

【麦冬】[中] the tuber of dwarf lilyturf (Ophiopogon japonicus)

【麦蛾】gelechiid (moth)

【麦尔登呢】melton (cloth)

【麦粉】flour

【麦麸】wheat bran

【麦秆虫】skeleton shrimp

【麦红吸浆虫】wheat midge

【麦加】Mecca

【麦角】[药] ergot

【麦秸】wheat straw ◇ ～画 woven straw patchwork

【麦精】malt extract: ～鱼肝油 *cod-liver oil with malt extract*

【麦克风】microphone (a transliteration); mike
【麦浪】rippling wheat; billowing wheat fields: ～翻滚。*The wheat bent before the wind in swaying billows.*
【麦粒肿】[医] sty
【麦芒】awn of wheat
【麦门冬】同〖麦冬〗
【麦苗】wheat seedling
【麦片】oatmeal: ～粥 *oatmeal porridge; oatmeal*
【麦淇淋】margarine (a transliteration, also called 人造黄油)
【麦秋】wheat harvest season: ～假 *wheat harvest vacation (for village schools)*
【麦乳精】extract of malt and milk
【麦收】wheat harvest
【麦穗】ear of wheat; wheat head
【麦芽】malt ◇ ～糖 malt sugar; maltose
【麦蚜】(又作'麦蚜虫') wheat aphid
【麦子】wheat

卖 动 ❶ sell: 大伏天西瓜～得快。*Watermelons sell fast during the dog days.* / 他的画～不出去。*He can't sell off his paintings.* ❷ betray (one's country or friends): 这件事我只跟你说,你可别把我给～了。*I'm telling this only to you. Don't give me away.* ❸ exert to the utmost; not spare: 卖劲儿 ❹ show off: 卖弄
【卖不动】not sell well; be unsalable: 这种次货～。*This kind of inferior goods doesn't sell.*
【卖唱】sing for a living
【卖大户】(又作'卖大号') (of a shop) profiteer by selling goods in great demand to individual buyers in batches
【卖呆】❶ pretend to be naive or stupid; feign stupidity ❷ 〈方〉(of a woman) stand idly at the gate and watch what's going on in the street
【卖恩】do sb. a favour for an ulterior motive
【卖儿鬻女】sell one's children
【卖方】the selling party (of a contract, etc.); seller: ～市场 *a seller's market*
【卖狗皮膏药】sell quack remedies; practise quackery; palm things off on people
【卖乖】show off one's cleverness: 得了便宜～ *pretend innocence and disinterest after succeeding in gaining some advantages; swagger and brag after having gained some advantages*
【卖关子】(stop a story at a climax to) keep the listeners in suspense; keep people guessing
【卖官鬻爵】sell official posts and titles
【卖国】betray one's country; turn traitor to one's country ◇ ～集团 traitorous clique; ～求荣 seek power and wealth by betraying one's country; turn traitor for personal gain; ～条约 traitorous treaty; ～行为 treasonable act; ～主义 national betrayal; ～贼 traitor (to one's country)
【卖好】curry favour with; ingratiate oneself with; play up to; fawn on: 谁有钱有势,他就向谁～。*He would fawn on anyone of wealth and position.*
【卖价】selling price
【卖劲儿】〈口〉exert all one's strength; spare no effort: 姑娘们干活真～。*The girls are really going all out in their work.*
【卖空】[经] short sales; sell short
【卖老】flaunt one's seniority; put on the airs of a veteran
【卖力】exert all one's strength; spare no effort; do all one can: 他干活一向很～。*He is always hard-working.*
【卖力气】❶ exert all one's strength; exert oneself to the utmost; do one's very best: 我再～也不容易讨她的好。*She is hard to please no matter how hard I try.* ❷ live by the sweat of one's brow; make a living by manual labour
【卖名】capitalize on one's reputation or prestige
【卖命】❶ work oneself to the bone for sb. ❷ die (unworthily) for: 这些士兵没有一个愿意为侵略战争～。*None of these soldiers wanted to die in a war of aggression.*
【卖弄】show off; parade: ～学问 *show off one's learning; parade one's knowledge* / ～小聪明 *show off one's smartness* / ～风情 *flirt and coquet* / ～风骚 *play the coquette*
【卖破绽】〈旧〉(in a fight or combat) feign an opening in order to hoodwink the opponent
【卖钱】sell for money: 这东西卖不了几个钱。*You can't get much for this if you sell it.*
【卖俏】play the coquette; coquette; flirt
【卖人情】show favours for one's own ends; win gratitude by favours
【卖身】❶sell oneself or a member of one's family: ～契 *an indenture by which one sells oneself or a member of one's family* ❷ 〈口〉sell one's body; sell one's soul
【卖身投靠】barter away one's honour for sb.'s patronage; basely offer to serve some reactionary bigwig
【卖相】〈方〉❶outward appearance; exterior; surface ❷ demeanour; bearing; manner: ～十足 *have poise*
【卖笑】(of a prostitute or a singing girl) show a smiling face and flirt: ～生涯 *make a living by prostitution*
【卖艺】make a living as a performer: 在街头～ *be a street-performer*
【卖淫】be a prostitute
【卖友】betray one's friend: ～求荣 betray friends to obtain promotion
【卖主】seller
【卖嘴】show off one's ability or good nature by trying to talk cleverly: 别～了,有本事练两下让我们开开眼。*Don't go on chatting about your skill but do a few stunts to entertain us.*
【卖座】(of a theatre, etc.) draw large audiences; (of a restaurant, teahouse, etc.) attract large numbers of customers: ～片 (*film*) *box-office success*

脉 名 ❶ arteries and veins ❷ pulse: 病人的～很

弱。*The patient's pulse was weak.* ❸ vein (of a leaf, etc.): 叶脉 ❹ sth. linking up to form a blood-vessel-like network: 山脉 ——另见 mò

【脉搏】pulse: 他的～每分钟一百次。*His pulse was one hundred beats per minute.* / 这部小说把握了我们时代的～。*The novel throbs with the pulse of our times.*

【脉搏计】sphygmometer

【脉冲】[物] pulse ◇ ～编码调制 pulse-code modulation (PCM); ～发生器 pulser; ～计数器 pulse counter; ～雷达 pulse radar; ～信号 pulse signal

【脉冲星】[天] pulsar

【脉动】[物] pulsation: ～式喷气发动机 *pulse-jet engine* ◇ ～电流 (又作'脉冲电流') pulsating current

【脉动星】[天] pulsating star

【脉管炎】[医] vasculitis

【脉络】❶ [中] general name for arteries and veins ❷ veins (of a leaf, etc.) ❸ train (or thread) of thought; sequence of ideas: 这篇文章结构严谨,～分明。*This article is closely knit and presents its ideas in a clear, logical way.*

【脉石】gangue (a mineral); veinstone: ～矿物 *gangue mineral*

【脉速】[医] rapid pulse

【脉息】pulse: ～微弱 *have a weak pulse* / 文学应与时代共～。*Literature should beat with the pulse of the times.*

【脉象】[中] pulse condition; type of pulse

【脉泽】[物] maser

【脉诊】[中] diagnosis by feeling the pulse

mán

埋 (构词成分)见下——另见 mái

【埋怨】blame; complain; grumble: 她总是～自己不好,从不抱怨别人。*She always puts the blame on herself, and never on others.* / 他的话里有～情绪。*There was a note of complaint in what he said.*

蛮 Ⅰ 形 rough; fierce; reckless; unreasoning: 野蛮 Ⅱ 名 an ancient name for the tribes in the south Ⅲ 副 〈方〉 quite; pretty: 这电影～好。*This is quite a good film.* or *This is a pretty good film.*

【蛮不讲理】be impervious to reason; persist in being unreasonable; wilful; obstinate: 他脾气很坏,而且～。*He's bad-tempered and wilful.*

【蛮缠】见〖胡搅蛮缠〗

【蛮干】act rashly; act recklessly; be foolhardy: 要苦干加巧干,不要～。*We should work hard and intelligently, not blindly.*

【蛮悍】boorish, rough: 态度～ *boorish attitude*

【蛮横】rude and unreasonable; arbitrary; peremptory: ～的态度 *an unreasonable attitude* / ～地拒绝合理建议 *arbitrarily reject reasonable proposals*

【蛮横无理】rude and unreasonable; arbitrary; peremptory: ～的要求 *peremptory demands*

【蛮勇】impetuous; valiant; bold: ～举动 *bold action* / ～的气势 *valiant manner*

蔓 (构词成分)见下——另见 màn; wàn

【蔓青】[植]turnip

馒 (构词成分)见下

【馒头】steamed bun; steamed bread

瞒 动 hide the truth from: 他怕妻子着急,把病情～着不说。*He didn't let his wife know about his illness for fear she'd worry.* / 不～你说 *to tell you the truth* / 这件事不能再～着他了。*We cannot keep him in the dark about this any longer.*

【瞒报】make a deceptive report

【瞒哄】deceive; pull the wool over sb.'s eyes: ～领导 *hide the truth from the leadership*

【瞒上欺下】deceive those above and bully those below

【瞒天过海】cross the sea by a trick—practise deception

鳗 名 eel

【鳗鲡】eel

mǎn

满 Ⅰ 形 ❶ full; filled; packed: ～～一卡车煤 *a full truckload of coal* / 这两个抽屉都～了。*Both drawers are full.* / 话不能说得太～、太绝。*One shouldn't speak in absolute terms, leaving no room for compromise.* / ～头大汗 *one's face streaming with sweat* / ～脑子封建思想 *be steeped in feudal ideology* ❷ satisfied: 不满 ❸ complacent; conceited: 自满 Ⅱ 动 ❶ fill: 再给你～上一杯。*Let me fill your glass once more.* ❷ expire; reach the limit: 年～十八的公民 *citizens who have reached the age of 18* / 他的服役期还没～。*His term of military service hasn't expired yet.* / 她学徒还不～一年。*It isn't a year yet since she became an apprentice.* / 假期已～。*The holidays are over.* Ⅲ 副 ❶ completely; entirely; perfectly: ～有信心 *be fully confident* / ～不是那么回事。*That wasn't the way it was at all.* / 我～以为他会同意的。*I had counted on him to agree with me.* ❷ quite; very: 这首歌～好听。*This song is quite pleasant.* / 您说的～对。*What you've said is quite right.* / 节目倒也～不错。*The performances were pretty good.* Ⅳ 名 the Man ethnic group (另见〖满族〗)

【满不在乎】not worry at all; not care in the least; give (or take) no heed: 他表面上装出一副～的样子,内心却是恐慌的。*Although feigning complete indifference, he was actually terrified.*

【满城风雨】(become) the talk of the town: 这件丑闻闹得～。*The scandal has created a sensation.*

【满打满算】reckoning in every item (of income or expenditure); at the very most：这项工程～有一百吨水泥就足够了。*We need* 100 *tons of cement at most for this project.*
【满登登】(又作'满满登登')〈口〉full：粮仓里装得～的。*The grainary was stuffed full of grain.*
【满额】fulfil the (enrolment, etc.) quota：我校今年招生已经～。*Our school has already fulfilled its enrolment quota for this year.*
【满分】full marks：体操比赛的～是十分。*The highest possible score in a gymnastics event is ten points.*
【满腹】be full of; have one's mind filled with：～狐疑 *filled with suspicion; extremely suspicious* / ～经纶 *an encyclopedic mind*
【满负荷】full load; full-loaded：～工作法 *full load working method*
【满贯】❶ reach the limit ❷ (in mahjong, card games, etc.) perfect score; slam：(*in bridge*) 小(大)～ *little or small (grand) slam*
【满怀】❶ have one's heart filled with; be imbued with：～豪情 *be filled with pride and enthusiasm* / ～热情 *be full of enthusiasm* ❷ (usu. used in) 撞了个～ *bump right into sb.* ❸ bear a full crop of young
【满口】(speak) unreservedly or profusely; be full of：～称赞 *praise profusely; be full of praises* / ～答应 *readily promise* / ～谎言 *spout lies* / ～脏话 *pour out dirty words*
【满满当当】〈口〉full to the brim：他吃了～三碗饭。*He ate three full bowls of rice.* / 挑着～的两桶水 *carry (or tote) two brimming buckets of water*
【满门】the whole family：～抄斩 (*in feudal China*) *execution of the entire family*
【满面】have one's face covered with：泪流～ *tears streaming down one's cheeks* / *glowing with health* / ～怒容 *red with anger* / ～笑容 *grinning from ear to ear; be all smiles*
【满面春风】beaming with satisfaction; radiant with happiness
【满目】meet the eye on every side：～荒凉。*A scene of desolation met the eye on every side.*
【满目疮痍】misery and suffering greets the eyes everywhere
【满脑子】have one's mind stuffed with
【满期】expire：租约～ *the expiration of a lease* / 进修～ *complete a refresher course*
【满腔】have one's bosom filled with：～仇恨 *burning with hatred* / ～怒火 *filled with rage* / ～热血 *full of patriotic fervor* / ～同情 *heartfelt sympathy* / ～的热血已经沸腾。*Our blood is boiling.*
【满腔热忱】filled with ardour and sincerity：～地接待顾客 *willingly wait on customers* / ～地提出建议 *propose in all earnestness*
【满腔热情】full of enthusiasm; whole-hearted：她～地投入工作。*She enthusiastically threw herself into the work.*
【满山遍野】同〖漫山遍野〗
【满身】have one's body covered with; be covered all over with：～油泥 *covered all over with grime* / ～是汗 *sweat all over; be soaked with sweat*
【满师】(of an apprentice) finish serving one's time; serve out one's apprenticeship：学徒三年～。*The apprenticeship requires three years of service.*
【满世界】〈方〉everywhere：你这孩子在家干点什么不好，～瞎跑什么？*Why run around everywhere, you naughty boy! Can't you find something useful to do at home?*
【满堂彩】(usu. used in) 得了个～ *bring the house down*
【满堂灌】(of a teacher) cram students; spoonfeed
【满堂红】❶ all-round victory; success in every field：今年我们厂是～，各项指标都提前完成了。*Our factory has had all-round success this year. All our targets have been fulfilled ahead of schedule.* ❷ common name for 紫薇
【满天】all over the sky：乌云～。*The sky is overcast with dark clouds.* / 鹅毛大雪～飞。*The snow is falling thick and heavy.* /
【满天星斗】a star-studded sky
【满头大汗】head covered with big drops of perspiration
【满心】have one's heart filled with：～欢喜 *be filled with joy*
【满眼】❶ have one's eyes filled with：他一连两夜没有睡，～都是血丝。*He didn't get any sleep for two successive nights, so his eyes were all bloodshot.* ❷ meet the eye on every side：～的山花 *mountain flowers greeting the eye everywhere*
【满意】satisfied; pleased; content：双方对会谈的结果表示～。*Both sides expressed satisfaction with the results of the talks.* / 大家对他的工作很～。*Everyone was pleased with his work.* / 她～地笑了。*She smiled with contentment.*
【满员】❶［军］be at full strength：保证主力部队经常～ *ensure that the main forces are always kept at full strength* ❷ (of a train, etc.) have all seats taken：二号车厢已经～。*No.* 2 *carriage is full.*
【满园春色】同〖春色满园〗
【满月】❶ a baby's completion of its first month of life：孩子明天就～了。*The baby will be a month old tomorrow.* ❷ full moon
【满载】be loaded to capacity; be fully loaded; be laden with：一辆～木材的卡车 *a truck fully loaded with timber*
【满载而归】come back with fruitful results; return from a rewarding journey
【满招损，谦受益】haughtiness invites disaster, humility receives benefit
【满洲】Manchuria (old name for 东北)
【满足】❶ satisfied; content; contented：～于现状 *be satisfied with the existing state of affairs; be content with things as they are* ❷ satisfy; meet

(needs, demands, etc.): ～人民的需要 *satisfy (or meet) the needs of the people* / 我们将尽可能地～你们的要求。*We'll do our best to meet your demands.*
【满族】the Man ethnic group; the Manchus
【满嘴】entire mouth: ～起疱 *one's lips are infected all over with boils* / ～喷粪〈讳〉*talk nonsense; shit*
【满座】have a capacity audience; have a full house: 这个剧演了一个月，场场～。*The play ran for a month to capacity audiences.*

螨 名 [动] mite

màn

曼 形 ❶ graceful: 轻歌曼舞 ❷ prolonged; long-drawn-out: 曼延
【曼丁哥语】Mande; Mandingo
【曼妙】〈文〉(of dancing) lithe and graceful
【曼声】(sing or recite in) lengthened sounds: ～吟诵 *recite in slow, measured tones* / ～而歌 *drawl out a song*; ～低语 *murmur slowly* / 她一面走，一面～地唱着。*She sang lazily as she strolled along.*
【曼陀林】[音] mandolin
【曼陀罗】[植] datura
【曼延】draw out (in length); stretch: ～曲折的羊肠小道 *a winding footpath stretching into the distance*

谩 形 disrespectful; rude
【谩骂】hurl invectives; fling abuse; rail: ～决不是战斗。*To hurl abuse is no way to fight.*

漫 Ⅰ 动 over flow; brim over; flood; inundate: 池塘的水～出来了。*The pool overflowed its banks.* / 水不深，只～过我脚面。*The water wasn't deep. It only came up to my ankles.* Ⅱ 形 ❶ be all over the place; be everywhere: ～江碧透。*The whole stream was emerald green.* ❷ free; unrestrained; casual: ～无目标 *aimless; at random* / ～无限制 *without any limit; with no restrictions whatsoever*
【漫笔】(usu. used as title of an essay) literary notes: 灯下～ (*literary*) *notes by the lamp—illuminating (literary) notes*
【漫不经心】careless; casual; negligent: ～地说 *speak in an offhand way* / 看他那～的样子，能把事情办好么? *He looks as if he couldn't care less, so I doubt he'll do a good job.*
【漫步】stroll; ramble; roam: ～街头 *stroll along the street*
【漫长】very long; endless: ～的海岸线 *a long coastline* / 在～的岁月中 *during the long years; over the years*
【漫反射】[物] diffuse reflection
【漫灌】❶ flood irrigation ❷ (of a flood) overflow (into an area)
【漫画】caricature; cartoon
【漫骂】use bad language against sb.; fling abuse
【漫漫】very long; boundless: 四野都是一眼望不到头的～白雪。*A boundless expanse of snow stretched out as far as the eye could see.*
【漫灭】wear away; efface; obliterate
【漫山遍野】all over the mountains and plains; over hill and dale: 战士们～地奔跑，去占领这个高地。*The soldiers began swarming across the countryside trying to occupy the height.*
【漫射】[物] diffusion ◇ ～光 diffused light; ～体 diffuser
【漫说】同〖慢说〗
【漫谈】(have an) informal discussion: ～国际形势 *have a free discussion about the world situation* / ～会 *informal discussion* / 听完报告咱们～一下吧。*After we've heard the report, we'll talk about it.*
【漫天】❶ filling the whole sky; all over the sky: ～大雾 *a dense fog obscuring the sky* / ～大雪 *whirling snow* / 黄土～。*A cloud of loess filled the whole sky.* ❷ boundless; limitless: ～大谎 *a monstrous lie*
【漫天要价】ask (or demand) an exorbitant price: ～，就地还钱。*The seller can ask a sky-high price; the buyer can make a rock-bottom offer.*
【漫无边际】❶ boundless: ～的海洋 *the boundless sea* ❷ straying far from the subject; rambling; discursive: ～的长篇大论 *a long-winded speech (or article); a long rambling talk*
【漫无止境】know no bounds; be without limit: 一个人的欲望是～的。*A man's desires know no bounds.*
【漫延】同〖曼延〗
【漫野】all over the plains
【漫游】❶ go on a pleasure trip; roam; wander: ～西湖 *go boating on (or roam around) the West Lake* ❷ [通信] roaming

蔓 (构词成分)——另见 mán; wàn
【蔓草】creeping weed
【蔓生植物】trailing plant
【蔓延】spread; extend: 火势～很快。*The fire spread quickly.* / 控制流行性感冒的～ *keep flu from spreading*

慢 Ⅰ 形 ❶ slow: 反应～ *be slow to react* / 他看书看得～。*He reads slowly.* / 他跑得～。*He's a slow runner.* / 病人恢复得很～。*The patient is making a slow recovery.* / 火车～～地驶进了车站。*Slowly the train pulled into the station.* ❷ supercilious; rude: 傲慢 Ⅱ 副 (used in imperative sentences, alone or before verbs): 你～点儿吃。*Don't rush through your meal.* / ～来，别着急。*Take your time and don't worry.* / 这事～点儿告诉他，等两天再说。*Don't tell him the news just now; wait a couple of days.*
【慢藏诲盗】failure to put things away properly is inviting theft

【慢车】slow train ◇ ～道 slow (traffic) lane (on a street); inside lane
【慢工出细活】slow work yields fine products
【慢火】slow fire; gentle heat
【慢件】package freight; ordinary mail
【慢镜头】slow motion
【慢慢腾腾】(又作'慢慢吞吞') loiteringly slow: 这样～地走,什么时候才能到啊? *If we walk at this snail's pace, when will we ever get there?*
【慢跑】jogging
【慢坡】gentle slope
【慢手慢脚】slow in doing something; slow moving
【慢说】let alone; to say nothing of: 他讲故事,～孩子,连大人都爱听。*Even the adults like to listen to his stories, to say nothing of the children.*
【慢速摄影】low-speed cinematography
【慢腾腾】(又作'慢吞吞') at a leisurely pace; unhurriedly; sluggishly: 你这么～的,什么时候能做完哪? *When will you ever finish the job if you go on at this pace?* / 他干什么都是～的。*He always works at a leisurely pace, no matter what he does.* / 说话～ *speak slowly*
【慢条斯理】slowly; leisurely; unhurriedly: 他说话做事总是～的。*He always speaks slowly and acts unhurriedly.*
【慢性】❶ chronic ❷ slow (in taking effect): ～毒药 *slow poison* ◇ ～病[医] chronic disease; ～支气管炎 chronic bronchitis
【慢性子】❶ phlegmatic temperament ❷ slowpoke; slowcoach
【慢悠悠】(又作'慢慢悠悠') unhurried; leisurely: ～地走着 *walk leisurely*
【慢中子】[物] slow neutron; low-speed neutron
【慢走】❶ don't go yet; stay; wait a minute ❷ (said by the host or hostess to a guest at departure) good-bye; take care

幔 名 curtain; screen: 布～ *cotton curtain*; 窗～ *window curtain*
【幔帷】heavy curtain
【幔帐】curtain; screen; canopy
【幔子】〈方〉curtain; screen

māng

牤 (构词成分)见下
【牤牛】〈方〉bull

máng

忙 Ⅰ 形 busy; fully occupied: 我这会儿～得很。*I'm very busy just now.* / 她～了一整天,为这些报告打字。*She was busy all day typing the reports.* / 这两天～不～? —～得团团转。*Are you busy these days? —Yes, I'm running round in circles.* / 她正～着做饭呢。*She's busying herself preparing the meal.* Ⅱ 动 hurry; hasten; make haste: 他～从里屋出来。*He came hurrying out of the inner room.* / 你～什么,再坐一会儿吧。*What's the hurry? Stay a bit longer.* / 别～于下结论。*Don't jump to conclusions.*
【忙不迭】hastily; hurriedly; in a hurry: ～地赔不是 *apologize in haste*
【忙乎】be busy; bustle about: ～了一天 *have been busy all day*
【忙活】❶ be busy with sth.: 你忙什么活? *What are you busy with?* ❷ an urgent piece of work; an urgent job: 这是件～,要先做。*This is an urgent piece of work. Do it first.* ❸ be busy; bustle about: 他们俩已经～了一上午了。*The two of them have been busy the whole morning.*
【忙里偷闲】snatch a little leisure from a busy life
【忙碌】be busy; bustle about: 为了全厂工人的生活,她成天～不停。*She's busy all day looking after the daily life of the workers in the factory.* / 忙忙碌碌 *as busy as a bee*
【忙乱】be in a rush and a muddle; tackle a job in a hasty and disorderly manner: 要克服～现象。*Don't work in a rush and get into a muddle.*
【忙忙叨叨】busy and flustered
【忙人】busy person: 他是个大～,哪有功夫上这儿来。*He's a busy man and certainly doesn't have the time to come here.*
【忙音】engaged signal; busy tone (in telephone)
【忙中有错】haste makes waste

芒 名 awn; beard; arista
【芒刺在背】feel prickles down one's back —feel nervous and uneasy
【芒果】[植] mango
【芒硝】[化] mirabilite; Glauber's salt
【芒种】❶ Grain in Beard—the 9th of the 24 solar terms ❷ the day marking the beginning of the 9th solar term

盲 形 blind
【盲肠】[生理] caecum ◇ ～炎 appendicitis; cecitis
【盲椿象】[动] plant bug
【盲从】follow blindly
【盲打】touch system: ～式打字 *touch-type*
【盲道】blind track—grooved track for the blind (along the middle of a sidewalk)
【盲点】[生理] blind spot; scotoma
【盲动】act blindly; act rashly ◇ ～主义 putschism
【盲干】act aimlessly or rashly: 这样一味～,结果非碰壁不可。*Such rashness is bound to land you in great difficulties.*
【盲流】unchecked flow of population (from the countryside to the cities)
【盲鳗】hagfish
【盲目】blind: 人口的～增长 *unchecked growth of the population* / ～崇拜 *worship blindly* / ～乐观 *be unrealistically optimistic* / ～投资 *blind investment* ◇ ～发展 pell-mell development; ～飞行 blind flight; instrument flying; ～轰炸 blind bombing; ～着陆 blind landing

【盲目性】blindness (in action)：去掉～，养成分析的习惯。*Stop acting blindly and cultivate the habit of analysis.*
【盲棋】blind chess (a chess game played by one person without looking at the chessboard against a number of individual opponents)
【盲区】[无] blind area
【盲人】blind person ◇ ～院 blind asylum
【盲人摸象】a group of blind men trying to size up an elephant, each mistaking the part he touches for the whole animal—take a part for the whole
【盲人瞎马】a blind man on a blind horse—rushing headlong to disaster; in for trouble
【盲文】❶ braille ❷ braille publication
【盲校】school for the blind
【盲哑教育】education for the blind and the deaf-mute
【盲障】[军] blindage
【盲字】braille

茫 形 ❶ boundless and indistinct：白茫茫 ❷ ignorant; in the dark：迷茫
【茫茫】boundless and indistinct; vast：～大海 *a vast sea* / ～草原 *the boundless grasslands* / ～一片白雾 *a vast expanse of fog* / 前途～ *bleak prospects*
【茫昧】〈书〉❶ dim; gloomy; blurred ❷ confused; uncomprehending; ignorant
【茫然】❶ ignorant; in the dark; at a loss：～无知 *be utterly ignorant; be in the dark* / ～不知所措 *be at a loss what to do; be at sea* / 显出～的神情 *look blank; wear a blank expression* ❷ frustrated; disappointed：她坐车走了，我～若失地站在那里。*She got on the bus and was gone, leaving me standing there with a feeling of loss.*
【茫无头绪】not know how to go about things; be in a hopeless muddle

硭（构词成分）见下
【硭硝】[化] mirabilite; Glauber's salt

mǎng

莽 Ⅰ 名 rank grass：草莽 Ⅱ 形 ❶〈书〉big; large; huge ❷ rash：鲁莽
【莽苍】(of scenery) blurred; misty：烟雨～ *a wast blur of mist and rain*
【莽汉】（又作'莽夫'）a boorish fellow; boor
【莽莽】❶ (of plant growth) lush; rank ❷ (of fields, plains, etc.) vast; boundless
【莽原】wilderness overgrown with grass
【莽撞】crude and impetuous; rash：～的小伙子 *a young harum-scarum* / 恕我～。*Forgive me for my bluntness.*

漭 （构词成分）见下
【漭漭】〈书〉vast; boundless

蟒 名 ❶ boa; python ❷〈略〉见〖蟒袍〗
【蟒袍】official robe worn by ministers during Ming and Qing Dynasties, with gold designs of pythons
【蟒蛇】boa; python

māo

猫 Ⅰ 名 cat：雄～ *tomcat* / 小～ *kitten* Ⅱ 动〈方〉hide oneself：他一听我们到来，就赶紧～起来了。*As soon as he heard us coming, he quickly hid himself somewhere.* ——另见 máo
【猫耳洞】[军] foxhole
【猫哭老鼠】(usu. used in) ～——假慈悲 *the cat weeping over the dead mouse—shed crocodile tears*
【猫腻】〈口〉cunning plot; underhand act; trick：正派人不玩～。*An honest person never plays tricks.* / 这事儿准有～。*There is something fishy behind this.*
【猫头鹰】owl
【猫熊】panda; giant panda
【猫眼】〈方〉peephole (fixed in a door); spyhole
【猫眼石】cat's eye (a mineral)

máo

毛 Ⅰ 名 ❶ hair; feather; down：这马长得一身好～。*The horse has a fine coat of hair.* / 桃子的皮上有细～。*A peach has downy skin.* ❷ wool：～袜 *woollen stockings* / 这件夹克衫是棉的还是～的？*Is this jacket cotton or woollen?* ❸ mildew; mould：长毛 ❹〈口〉mao, a fractional unit of money in China (＝1/10 yuan 元 or 10 fen 分)：一～钱 *one mao* / 这支铅笔几～钱？—四～。*How much is this pencil? —Four mao.* Ⅱ 形 ❶ semifinished：毛坯 ❷ gross：毛利 ❸ little; small：～贼 *petty thief; pilferer* ❹ careless; crude; rash：～头～脑 *rash; impetuous* ❺ panicky; scared; flurried：这下可把他吓～了。*This really made him scared.* / 她一考试就～。*She panicks whenever she takes an exam.* Ⅲ 动 ❶〈口〉(of currency) be no longer worth its face value; depreciate：钱～了。*Money has gone down in value.* ❷〈方〉get angry; lose one's temper：你可别再说他了，再说，他就要～了。*Don't scold him any more or he'll get angry.*
【毛白杨】[植] Chinese white poplar
【毛背心】woollen vest
【毛笔】writing brush
【毛边纸】（又作'毛边'）writing paper made from bamboo
【毛病】❶ trouble; mishap; breakdown：这架收音机有点～。*There's something wrong with the radio.* ❷ defect; shortcoming; fault; mistake：克服工作作风上的～ *overcome defects in one's work style* ❸ bad habit; shortcoming：他抽烟的～总也改不了。*He'll never give up his bad habit*

of smoking. ❹ illness：老～ *inveterate disease* / 他胃有～。*He has stomach trouble*. / 她有头疼的～。*She suffers from headaches*. ——另见〖出毛病〗

【毛玻璃】frosted glass；ground glass

【毛糙】rude；coarse；careless：这活做得太～。*That's rather crude work*.

【毛虫】(又作'毛毛虫') caterpillar

【毛刺】[机] burr

【毛地黄】[药] digitalis

【毛豆】young (or fresh) soya bean

【毛发】hair (on the human body and head) ◇ ～生长剂 hair-growing tonic

【毛纺】wool spinning：粗梳～ woollen spinning/ 精梳～ worsted spinning ◇ ～厂 woollen mill

【毛感】the feel of wool：这料子～强。*This cloth feels very much like wool*.

【毛葛】[纺] poplin

【毛茛】[植] buttercup

【毛骨悚然】with one's hair standing on end—absolutely terrified：令人～ *send cold shivers down one's spine*；*make sb.'s hair stand on end*；*be bloodcurdling*

【毛孩子】〈口〉a small child；a mere child

【毛蚶】〈方〉blood clam

【毛烘烘】hairy；furry

【毛焦火辣】burning with impatience；in a nervous state

【毛巾】towel ◇ ～布 towelling；～架 towel rail or rack

【毛巾被】(又作'毛巾毯') towelling coverlet

【毛举细故】(又作'毛举细务') bring up trifling matters

【毛孔】[生理] pore

【毛口】[机] burr：去～ *burring*

【毛裤】long woollen underwear；woollen pants

【毛拉】[宗](伊斯兰教) maula；mullah

【毛梾】[植] long-petioled dogwood (Cornus walteri)

【毛蓝】darkish blue：～土布 *dyed* (*or blue*) *nankeen*

【毛里求斯】Mauritius ◇ ～人 Mauritian

【毛里塔尼亚】Mauritania ◇ ～人 Mauritanian

【毛利】gross profit

【毛利人】Mauri

【毛料】woollen cloth；woollens

【毛驴】donkey

【毛毛雨】drizzle

【毛南族】the Maonan ethnic group, or the Maonans, inhabiting the Guangxi Zhuang Autonomous Region

【毛囊炎】folliculitis

【毛呢】woollen cloth (for heavy clothing)；heavy woollen cloth；wool coating or suiting

【毛坯】❶ semifinished product ❷ [机] blank

【毛皮】fur；pelt：～兽 *fur-bearing animal* ◇ ～大衣 fur coat

【毛片】❶ unprocessed film after shooting ❷ pornographic film or telefilm

【毛票】〈口〉banknotes of one, two or five jiao (角) denominations

【毛渠】sublateral canal；sublateral

【毛茸茸】hairy；downy：～的胸脯 *a hairy chest* / ～的小鸭子 *a downy little duck*

【毛瑟枪】Mauser

【毛纱】[纺] wool yarn：粗纺～ *woollen yarn* / 精纺～ *worsted yarn*

【毛石】[建] rubble：～混凝土 *rubble concrete*

【毛收入】gross income

【毛手毛脚】careless (in handling things)：他～地把杯子打了。*He clumsily knocked over his cup and broke it*.

【毛刷】brush

【毛丝】[纺] broken filament

【毛遂自荐】offer one's services as Mao Sui (of the Warring States Period) did—volunteer one's services

【毛损】gross loss

【毛笋】the shoot of mao bamboo (毛竹)

【毛毯】woollen blanket

【毛桃】wild peach

【毛细管】capillary ◇ ～水 [农] capillary

【毛细现象】[物] capillarity

【毛细血管】[生理] blood capillary

【毛虾】shrimp

【毛线】knitting wool：～针 *knitting needle* / 打～ *do knitting work*

【毛丫头】〈口〉a chit of a girl

【毛样】[刷] galley proof

【毛腰】〈方〉arch one's back：他毛着腰悄悄地溜过窗口。*He bent over and slipped by the window*.

【毛衣】woollen sweater；sweater；woolly

【毛蚴】[动] miracidium

【毛躁】❶ short-tempered；irritable：他的脾气很～。*He has a short temper*. ❷ rash and careless：他这个人做事从来就是毛毛躁躁的。*He always does things in a careless way*.

【毛泽东思想】Mao Zedong Thought

【毛毡】felt

【毛织品】❶ wool fabric；woollens ❷ woollen knitwear

【毛重】gross weight

【毛猪】[商] a live pig

【毛竹】mao bamboo

矛

名 lance；pike；spear

【矛盾】**名** ❶ [哲][逻] contradiction：～的普遍性(特殊性) *the universality* (*particularity*) *of contradiction* / ～的同一性(斗争性) *the identity* (*struggle*) *of opposites* / 主要(非主要)～ *principal* (*nonprincipal*) *contradiction* ❷ problem；conflict；contradiction：双方发生～已有多年。*The two sides have been in conflict for years*. / 他俩在闹～。*The two of them have fallen out*. / ～百出 *full of contradictions* ❸ contradict：他说的话前后～。*He was contradicting himself in what he said*. ❹ contradictory：这两种意见并不～。*These two views are not contradictory* (*or mutu-*

ally exclusive). / 他的心情很～。*His feelings were mixed*.
【矛盾律】[逻] the law of contradiction
【矛头】spearhead: ～所向 *the target of attack* / 漫画家把讽刺的～指向官僚主义。*The cartoonist directed his satire at the bureaucracy*.

茅 名 [植] cogongrass
【茅草】[植] cogongrass ◇ ～棚(又作'茅棚') thatched shed; thatched shack
【茅厕】[口] latrine; outhouse
【茅房】[口] latrine; outhouse
【茅膏菜】[植] sundew
【茅坑】❶ [口] latrine pit ❷ [方] latrine; outhouse
【茅庐】thatched cottage ——另见〖初出茅庐〗
【茅塞顿开】同〖顿开茅塞〗
【茅舍】[书] thatched cottage
【茅屋】thatched cottage

牦 (构词成分) 见下
【牦牛】yak

旄 名 ancient flag with yak's tail

猫 (构词成分) 见下 ——另见 māo
【猫腰】同〖毛腰〗

锚 名 anchor
【锚地】anchorage
【锚链】anchor chain; anchor cable ◇ ～孔 hawsehole
【锚雷】[军] mooring mine; moored buoyant mine
【锚爪】fluke (of an anchor)

蟊 名 an insect destructive to the roots of seedlings
【蟊贼】a person harmful to the country and people; pest

mǎo

卯 名 ❶ the fourth of the twelve Earthly Branches (地支) ❷ mortise ——另见〖干支〗
【卯时】the period of the day from 5 a. m. to 7 a. m.
【卯榫】mortise and tenon
【卯眼】mortise

昴 名 the eighteenth of the twenty-eight constellations (二十八宿) into which the celestial sphere was divided in ancient Chinese astronomy (consisting of seven stars in Pleiades)

铆 Ⅰ 动 fasten with a rivet; rivet Ⅱ 名 [机] riveting: 风动～ *pneumatic riveting*; 对接～ *butt riveting*; 搭接～ *lap riveting*
【铆钉】rivet: ～距 *rivet pitch* / 开口～ *bifurcated rivet*
【铆工】❶ riveting ❷ riveter
【铆机】riveter: 风动～ *pneumatic riveter* / 水力～ *hydraulic riveter*
【铆接】riveting; rivet joint
【铆劲儿】❶〈口〉make a sudden all-out effort: 几个人一～,就把大石头撬下坡去了。*With a sudden thrust, they sent the boulder rolling down the hillside*. ❷〈方〉have a trial of strength; compete; contest: 他跟我铆上劲儿了。*He's trying to get the upper hand of me*.

mào

茂 Ⅰ 形 ❶ luxuriant; exuberant; profuse: 繁茂 ❷ rich and splendid: 情文并～ *excellent in both content and language* Ⅱ 名 cyclopentadiene
【茂林修竹】thick forest of trees and tall bamboos
【茂密】(of grass or trees) dense; thick: ～的森林 *a dense forest*
【茂盛】(of plants) luxuriant; exuberant; flourishing: 庄稼长得很～。*The crops are growing luxuriantly*. / 枝叶～ *an exuberant growth of branches and leaves*

冒 Ⅰ 动 ❶ emit; send out (or up, forth); give off: ～泡 *send up bubbles; be bubbling* / 水壶正～着气。*The kettle is giving off steam*. / 泥浆从地下～出来。*Mud oozed from underground*. / 错误思想总是要～出来的。*Wrong ideas are bound to manifest themselves*. ❷ risk; brave: ～着风浪出海 *put to sea in spite of wind and wave; venture out on a stormy sea* / ～风险 *run risks* Ⅱ 副 ❶ boldly; rashly: ～猜一下 *make a bold guess; venture a guess* / 看见那人好像是老李,我～喊一声。*As he looked very much like Lao Li, I made bold as to call out to him*. ❷ falsely (claim, etc.); fraudulently: ～认 *lay a false claim to* / 那人～称是部长的亲戚。*The man falsely claimed to be a relative of the minister*.
【冒充】pretend to be (sb. or sth. else); pass (sb. or sth.) off as: ～内行 *pretend to be an expert; pose as an expert* / 用次品～正品 *pass off defective goods as certified goods* / 他～记者。*He passed himself off as a journalist*.
【冒顶】[矿] roof fall: 工作面～ *face fall* / 大～ *bulk caving*
【冒渎】〈书〉bother or annoy a superior
【冒犯】offend; affront: ～禁令 *violate a prohibition* / ～尊严 *offend sb's dignity*
【冒富】become better off; become better than the average: 改革初期,农民害怕被称作富裕户;今天以～而自豪。*In the early stages of reform, farmers were afraid to be considered well-off, but today they are proud of doing better than average*.
【冒汗】perspire; sweat: 他急得直～。*He was so worried that he kept sweating*.
【冒号】colon (:)
【冒火】burn with anger; get angry; flare up: 有话

好好说，冒什么火！*If you have something to say, then say it. No reason to get angry.*

【冒尖儿】❶ be piled high above the brim：筐里的土豆装得～了。*The basket is piled high with potatoes.* ❷ be a little over; be a little more than：十斤刚～ *a little over ten jin* ❸ stand out; be conspicuous：怕～ *be afraid of becoming too conspicuous* / 她就爱～。*She likes to be in the limelight.* or *She's too pushing.* ❹ begin to crop up：问题一～，就及时采取了措施。*Proper measures were taken as soon as the problem cropped up.*

【冒金星】see stars：我一头撞在门上，眼前直～。*I banged my head on the door and saw stars.*

【冒进】prematurely advance; advance rashly

【冒口】［机］rising head; riser

【冒领】falsely claim as one's own：虚报～ *fraudulent applications and claims*

【冒昧】〈谦〉make bold; venture; take the liberty：我可以～地提一个问题吗？*May I venture to ask a question?* / 这么晚了还来打搅您，真是太～了。*Is it too presumptuous of me to come and disturb you at this late hour?*

【冒名】go under sb. else's name; assume another's name：～顶替 *take another's place by assuming his name*

【冒牌】falsely use a well-known trade mark; be an imitation; be a fake：～货 *an imitation (of a well-known trade mark); pirated goods* ◇ ～社会主义 bogus (or sham) socialism; ～医生 a quack doctor

【冒失】rash; abrupt; reckless：说话～ *speak without due consideration* / 这样冒冒失失去找他可不好。*It's not appropriate to drop in on him so casually.* ◇ ～鬼 harum-scarum

【冒天下之大不韪】defy world opinion; risk universal condemnation; fly in the face of the will of the people

【冒头】begin to crop up：不良倾向一～就要抓住它。*Watch out for harmful tendencies and deal with them the moment they crop up.*

【冒险】take a risk; take chances：犯不上为这件事去冒那么大的险。*It's not worthwhile taking such a big risk over this job.* / 军事～ *military adventure* ◇ ～政策 adventurist policy

【冒险家】adventurer

【冒烟】❶ (of smoke) rise：烟囱正冒着烟。*Smoke was rising from the chimney.* ❷〈方〉get angry; flare up

【冒用商标】infringement

【冒雨】braving the rain; in spite of the rain

贸 名 trade：外贸

【贸促会】❶ (〈略〉全称为〖贸易促进会〗) trade promotion council; committee or board for promoting trade ❷ China Council for the Promotion of International Trade

【贸然】(又作'贸贸然') rashly; hastily; without careful consideration：～下结论 *draw a hasty conclusion; jump to a conclusion* / ～同意 *agree without careful consideration* / ～从事 *act rashly*

【贸易】trade：和别国进行～ *trade with foreign countries; do business with other countries* ◇ ～保护主义 trade protectionism; ～差额 balance of trade; ～赤字 trade deficits; ～额 volume of trade; turnover; ～法 trade act; ～港 trading port; commercial port; ～公司 trading corporation; ～伙伴 trade partner; ～禁运 commercial embargo; ～逆差 unfavourable balance of trade; ～顺差 favourable balance of trade; ～谈判 trade negotiation; ～条件 term of trade; ～往来 trade contacts; commercial intercourse; ～协定 trade agreement; ～议定书 trade protocol; ～战 trade war; ～中心 trade centre; ～总额 total volume of trade

耄 形〈书〉❶ octogenarian ❷ advanced in years

【耄耋】advanced in years：～之年 *old age (esp. from 70 to 90)*

帽 名 ❶ headgear; hat; cap：草帽 ❷ cap-like cover for sth.：笔帽

【帽顶】crown

【帽耳】earflaps (of a cap)

【帽徽】(又作'帽章') insignia (or badge) on a cap

【帽盔儿】skullcap

【帽舌】peak (of a cap); visor

【帽檐】(又作'帽沿') the brim of a hat

【帽子】❶ headgear; hat; cap：戴上(摘下)～ *put on (take off) a hat or cap* ❷ label; tag; brand：摘掉文盲的～ *rid oneself of the label of "illiterate"* ——另见〖戴帽子〗;〖扣帽子〗

貌 名 looks; appearance：美貌

【貌不惊人】be unprepossessing (or unimposing) in appearance; be of undistinguished appearance

【貌合神离】(of two persons or parties) be seemingly in harmony but actually at variance

【貌似】seem to be; appear to be：～公允 *be seemingly just and sound (or fair and equitable)* / ～公正 *pretend to be just and fair; put on an appearance of impartiality* / ～强大 *be seemingly powerful; be outwardly strong* / ～有理 *be apparently reasonable (but actually not)*

méi

没 Ⅰ 动〈口〉❶ not have; there is not; be without：他还～女朋友。*He doesn't have a girlfriend yet.* / 这儿～人。*There's nobody here.* / 她～钱了。*She has no more money.* ❷ be not so... as：我～你高。*I'm not so tall as you.* / 谁都～他会说话。*No one is as eloquent as he is.* ❸ less than; not more than：他去了～多大工夫。*He wasn't gone for long.* / 我家里～多大地方。*There isn't much space in my home.* Ⅱ 副 have not or did not：他来～来？—还～来呢。*Has he come yet? —Not yet.* / 她三天～来了。*She hasn't been here for three days.* / 你买了吗？—

～买。*Did you buy it?—No, I didn't.* / 银行昨天～开门。*The bank was closed yesterday.* —— 另见 mò

【没出息】not promising; good for nothing

【没词儿】〈口〉❶ can find nothing to say ❷ be at a loss for words; be stuck for an answer: 刚说了几句,他就～了。*After uttering a few sentences, he got stuck.*

【没错儿】〈口〉❶ I'm quite sure; you can rest assured: ～,准是小王告诉他的。*I'm quite sure it was Xiao Wang who told him about it.* / 电影七点的,是吗? —～。*The film begins at seven, doesn't it? —Yes, that's right.* ❷ can't go wrong: 照说明书做,准保～。*Just follow the directions. You can't go wrong.*

【没大没小】show no respect for one's elders: 这孩子真～的,在爷爷面前也这么说话! *The child really has no manners. Talking like that in front of his grandpa!*

【没得说】〈方〉❶ be on intimate terms; be cronies: 老弟,咱哥俩儿～。*My boy, we are buddies, aren't we?* ❷ really good; incomparably fine; perfect: 这东西的质量～。*This product is of very high quality.* / 这里的服务态度～。*The service here is excellent.*

【没法儿】〈口〉❶〈方〉most unlikely; absolutely impossible: 你～不知道。*You certainly know it.* ❷〈方〉beyond comparison: 今晚这场戏,～那么好的了。*The performance tonight was terrific.* ❸ 同〖没法子〗

【没法子】can do nothing about it; can't help it; there is no way out: 我当时手头紧,～,只好卖书。*I was hard up then, and had to sell off my books.*

【没骨头】weak-kneed; spineless

【没关系】〈口〉it doesn't matter; it's nothing; that's all right; never mind: 他来不来都～。*It doesn't matter whether he comes or not.*

【没规矩】not observing proper rules or manners; improper; inappropriate

【没好气儿】〈口〉be angry; be in a bad temper: 他一听这话就～。*He got angry as soon as he heard this.*

【没见过世面】green and inexperienced

【没见识】inexperienced and ignorant; unlearned and provincial

【没劲】〈口〉❶ weak: 浑身～ *feel very weak* ❷ uninteresting: 这电影真～。*This film is dull as ditchwater.*

【没精打采】listless; in low spirits; out of sorts; lackadaisical: 他～地坐在地上,低着头,不吱声。*He sat on the ground listlessly with his head hanging and said nothing.*

【没救】incurable; incorrigible; beyond remedy or hope: 医生认为这个病人～了。*The doctor considered the patient's case hopeless.*

【没空(儿)】have no time (for sth. or sb.): 我这两天很忙,～看电影。*I have been too busy for the past few days to go to the movies.*

【没脸】feel ashamed; feel embarrassed: ～见人 *be too ashamed (or embarrassed) to face anyone*

【没良心】without conscience; unconscionable; ungrateful

【没…没…】❶ (used before two synonyms to emphasize the sense of "without") ❷ (used before two antonyms to indicate that no distinction is made) ◇ 没老没少 overfamiliar (between old and young); 没深没浅 have no sense of propriety; 没皮没脸 have no sense of shame; 没羞没臊 shameless; have no sense of shame

【没门儿】〈方〉❶ have no access to sth.; have no means of doing sth.: 你能给我们弄几张戏票吗? ——我可～。*Can you get us some tickets for the performance? —You're asking the wrong person.* ❷ no go; nothing doing: 他想拉拢我? ～! *He wants to rope me in? Not a chance!* / 你别想蒙我,～! *You can't fool me. No way!*

【没命】❶ lose one's life; die: 要不是医生及时赶到,这小孩就～了。*The child would have died if the doctor hadn't come just in time.* ❷ recklessly; desperately; like mad; for all one's worth: 敌兵～地逃跑。*The enemy soldiers ran off as fast as their legs could carry them.*

【没跑儿】〈方〉beyond doubt; undoubtedly: 这次你输定了,～! *You're sure to lose this time.*

【没谱儿】〈方〉be unsure; have no idea: 下一步该怎么走还～呢。*We have no plan yet as to our next move.* / 这个计划行不行,他心里～。*He's not too sure whether the plan will work.*

【没轻没重】(speak) tactlessly or indiscreetly

【没趣】feel put out; feel snubbed: 咱们别理他,给他个～。*Let's pay no attention to him. Just ignore him.*

【没商量】irretrievable; irredeemable; irrevocable: 你一点儿不让步,这事～了。*If you refuse to make any concessions, the deal is off.*

【没什么】it doesn't matter; it's nothing; that's all right; never mind: 你怎么了? —～,有点头疼。*What's the matter with you? —Just a bit of a headache; nothing serious.*

【没事儿】❶ have nothing to do; be free; be at a loose end: 今晚～,我想去看电影。*I've got nothing to do this evening. I think I'll go to the film.* ❷ it doesn't matter; it's nothing; that's all right; never mind: 啃,踩了你的脚了。—～。*Sorry to have stepped on your toe. —That's all right.* / 他刚才还头疼来着,现在～了。*He was having a headache a moment ago, but he's all right now.*

【没事人】not care in the least; give (or take) no heed; be indifferent: 你怎么批评他,他还像个～似的。*However much you criticize him, he still looks unconcerned.* / 喝了一瓶酒,他跟～似的。*After drinking a whole bottle, he didn't even turn a hair.*

【没事找事】❶ ask for trouble; ask for it ❷ try hard to find fault; cavil

【没挑】faultless; perfect: 要说她的工作那是～了。

Her work is beyond reproach. / 他的英语真～。*He speaks perfect English*.
【没头案子】a criminal case without a clue for law enforcement officers to work on
【没头没脑】without rhyme or reason; abrupt: 他一到就～地把我们批评了一顿。*No sooner had he stepped in the door than he began criticizing us, for no reason at all*.
【没完】〈口〉have not finished with sb. (in quarrelling): 你等着吧,这事儿～! *Just wait. You haven't seen the end of this yet*! / 我跟他～! *I haven't finished with him yet*! or *I'll never let him off*!
【没完没了】endless; without end: 她这么～地唠叨,真是烦死人了。*Her endless chattering is really driving me up the wall*.
【没戏】〈方〉hopeless: 去黄山旅游的事～了。*Our trip to Huangshan Mountain is off*. / 他俩谈得怎样了? —～! *How is their talk going*? — *Nothing will come of it*!
【没想儿】〈口〉hopeless: 指挥病倒,这场演出恐怕～了。*I'm afraid the performance's off because the conductor's ill*.
【没心没肺】❶ simple-minded ❷ scatter-brained
【没心眼儿】careless; frank
【没羞】have no shame; be unabashed: 那么大的小子还哭,真～。*Tut, tut! Such a big boy crying*.
【没样儿】(又作'没好样')have no manners; be ill-mannered
【没意思】❶ bored: 一个人待在家里实在～。*I'm bored stiff staying at home all alone*. ❷ boring; uninteresting: 这本书～。*This book is boring*. ❸ (of people) petty: 这个人～。*He's a petty person*.
【没影儿】❶ disappear without a trace: 一转眼,他怎么就～了。*How could he disappear in just the blink of an eye*? / 他早就忘得～了。*He's clean forgotten it*. ❷ groundless; unfounded; fantastic: 这都是～的事,你怎么就相信了? *This is all nonsense. How can you take it so seriously*?
【没有】❶ not have; there is not; be without: 电影票早～了。*Tickets for the film were sold out quite a while ago*. / 屋里～人。*There isn't anyone in the room*. / 你说的这种事我们那儿是～的。*That kind of thing never happens at our place*. ❷ be not so ... as: 我弟弟～他聪明。*My younger brother is not so clever as he*. / 谁都～他跑得快。*No one can run as fast as he*. ❸ less than; not more than: 他来了还～三天就走了。*He was here less than three days*. / 这间屋子～十平方米。*This room is not more than* 10 *metres square*. ❹ have not or did not: 衣服还～干。*The clothes aren't dry yet*. / 我～着急,只是有点担心。*I'm not upset, but a bit worried*. / ～经过专业训练的业余歌唱家 *an untrained amateur singer*
【没有把握】(又作'没把握')not sure of; not confident
【没有出路】(又作'没出路')find oneself in a blind alley; without a way out
【没有的话】it's not true; nothing of the sort
【没有的事儿】nothing of the sort; it's impossible
【没有结果】come to nothing; with no result
【没有解决的问题】open question; suspended problem
【没有什么了不起】(又作'没什么了不起')not enough to; not so great; nothing to be impressed by
【没有说的】(又作'没说的')❶ really good: 这小伙子思想好,劳动好,真是～。*He's good in ideology and in work, a really fine young chap*. ❷ there's no need to say any more about it; it goes without saying: ～,这是我们应尽的责任。*It goes without saying that we should do it; it's our duty*. ❸ there's no need arguing; indisputable
【没有依靠】(又作'没依靠')with no support; have no backing
【没有种】(又作'没种')〈口〉gutless; cowardly
【没辙】〈口〉can find no way out; be at the end of one's rope: 她这么对付我,我完全～了。*The way she's been treating me—I really can't take it any more*. / 下一步该怎么办,我～了。*I have no idea what to do next*.
【没治】〈口〉❶ incurable; beyond hope: 这台机器坏了,～了。*This machine is beyond repair*. ❷ excellent; beyond description: 他的表演真～了。*His performance was first-rate indeed*. ❸ cannot do anything with sb.: 我真拿他～。*I simply can't do anything with him*.
【没主意】lose one's head; cannot make up one's mind

玫

(构词成分)见下
【玫瑰】rugosa rose; rose
【玫瑰红】rose-red
【玫瑰花茶】rose tea

枚

量 (for small-piece things): 三～纪念章 *three souvenir badges* / 一～古币 *an ancient coin* / 两～邮票 *two stamps*

眉

名 ❶ eyebrow; brow ❷ the top margin of a page: 书眉
【眉笔】eyebrow pencil
【眉端】❶ the space between the eyebrows: 愁上～ *be with a worried frown; have a worried look* ❷ the top of a page; top margin
【眉飞色舞】with dancing eyebrows and radiant face—enraptured; exultant: 小王听得～。*A look of delight came into Xiao Wang's face as he listened*. / 说起拿乒乓球冠军的事,他就～。*His face lights up whenever he speaks of the table tennis championship he's won*.
【眉峰】brows
【眉高眼低】an expression on the face: 看人～行事 *take one's cue from sb*.
【眉急】〈略〉见〖燃眉之急〗
【眉尖】brows: ～微微一皱 *knit the brows a little*

【眉睫】(as close to the eye as) the eyebrows and eyelashes：祸在～ *in imminent danger*
【眉开眼笑】be all smiles；beam with joy
【眉来眼去】make eyes at each other；exchange amorous glances；flirt with each other
【眉棱骨】superciliary ridge
【眉毛】eyebrow；brow
【眉毛胡子一把抓】try to grasp the eyebrows and the beard all at once—try to attend to big and small matters all at once
【眉目】❶ features；looks：～清秀 *have delicate features* ❷ logic (of writing)；sequence of ideas：这篇文章～清楚。*The article is clear and well-organized*. ❸ prospect of a solution；sign of a positive outcome：你托我办的事已经有点～了。*About that job you asked me to do, I'm beginning to get somewhere with it*. or *I'm getting on with what you asked me to do*. / 计划有了～。*The plan is beginning to take shape*.
【眉目不清】(of writing) not well organized
【眉目传情】flash amorous glances；make eyes at sb.
【眉批】notes and commentary at the top of a page
【眉清目秀】have delicate features；have finely chiselled features：那孩子生得～，十分俊雅。*The boy was remarkably handsome, with finely chiselled features*.
【眉梢】the tip of the brow：～间露出忧郁的神色 *a melancholy cast between the brows*
【眉头】brows：～紧锁 *frown severely*
【眉头一皱，计上心来】knit the brows and a plan (or stratagem) comes to one's mind：他寻思了半天，～。*He thought to himself for a while. He knit his brows heavily and at last a plan was born in his heart*.
【眉心】the space between the eyebrows
【眉眼】appearance；looks：小姑娘～长得很俊。*The little girl is very pretty*.
【眉眼高低】an expression on the face：你这人真不识～，谁都看得出她正发愁呢。*You should learn to read a person's thoughts from his face. Anyone can see she's worrying about something*.
【眉宇】〈文〉forehead；appearance
【眉月】eyebrow-shaped moon—the crescent moon；crescent

梅

名 plum
【梅毒】[医] syphilis
【梅红色】plum (colour)
【梅花】❶ plum blossom ❷〈方〉wintersweet
【梅花鹿】sika (deer)
【梅童鱼】baby croaker
【梅雨】[气] plum rains
【梅子】plum

媒

名 ❶ matchmaker；go-between：做媒 ❷ intermediary：触媒
【媒介】intermediary；medium；vehicle：空气是传播声音的～。*Air is a medium of sound*. / 传染疾病的～ *vehicle of disease*；*vector* ◇ 新闻～ news media
【媒婆】a woman matchmaker
【媒染】mordant dyeing ◇ ～剂 [化] mordant；～料 mordant dye
【媒人】matchmaker；go-between
【媒妁】〈书〉matchmaker ◇ ～之言 the good offices of a matchmaker ——另见〖父母之命，媒妁之言〗
【媒体】medium；media：多～ *multi-media*；新闻～ *news media*
【媒质】[物] medium：吸收～ *absorbing medium*

煤

名 coal：炉子上添点～。*Put some coal on the fire*. / 一块烧红的～ *a live (or hot) coal*
【煤仓】coal bunker
【煤层】coal seam；coal bed
【煤铲】coal shovel
【煤场】coal yard
【煤尘】coal dust：～爆炸 *coal-dust explosion*
【煤斗】coal scuttle；scuttle
【煤毒】carbon monoxide poisoning；gas poisoning
【煤酚皂溶液】〈药〉cresol and soap solution；saponated cresol solution；lysol
【煤矸石】gangue
【煤耗】coal consumption
【煤核儿】partly-burnt briquet；coal cinder
【煤化】carbonize
【煤灰】coal ash
【煤焦油】(又作'煤黑油') coal tar
【煤精】(又作'煤玉') black amber；jet
【煤矿】coal mine；colliery：～工人 *coal miner*
【煤轮】coal freighter
【煤末子】coal dust
【煤气】coal gas；gas：你们家烧～吗？*Do you use a gas stove at home*？◇ ～表 gas meter；～厂 gasworks；gashouse；～贮罐 gas (storage) holder；～灯 gas lamp；gas light；～管 gas pipe；～罐 gas tank；gas container；～机 gas engine；～炉 gas stove；gas furnace；～设备 gas fittings；～灶 gas range；gas cooker；～总管 gas main；～中毒 carbon monoxide poisoning；gas poisoning
【煤球】(egg-shaped) briquet
【煤炭】coal：～工业 *coal industry*
【煤田】coalfield：～地质学 *coal geology*
【煤系】[地质] coal measures
【煤屑】nickings
【煤烟】❶ smoke from burning coal ❷ (又作'煤烟子') coal soot；soot
【煤烟污染】coal-smoke pollution
【煤窑】coalpit
【煤油】kerosene；paraffin ◇ ～灯 kerosene lamp；～炉 kerosene stove
【煤渣】coal cinder ◇ ～路 cinder road；～跑道 cinder track
【煤砟子】a small piece of coal
【煤砖】(brick-shaped) briquet

楣

名 lintel (of a door)：门楣

酶 名 [生化] enzyme；ferment：消化～ *digestive ferment*
【酶原】[生化] zymogen；fermentogen
镅 名 [化] americium (Am)
霉 Ⅰ 名 mould；mildew Ⅱ 动 become mildewy；go moldy：这块饼～了。*The cake is moldy.* / 箱子里有股～味。*The inside of the trunk has a mildewy smell.*
【霉变】become mildewy；go moldy
【霉病】[农] mildew
【霉蠹】(of books) get mildewed and worm-eaten
【霉菌】[微] mould ◇ ～病 mycosis
【霉烂】mildew and rot：～食品 *mildewy and rotten food*
【霉天】early summer rains ——另见〖黄梅季〗
【霉头】〈方〉bad luck
【霉雨】同〖黄梅雨〗
糜 名 见下——另见 mí
【糜子】[植] broom corn millet

měi

每 Ⅰ 代 every；each；per：～星期五 *every Friday* / 节约～一分钱 *save every penny* / ～四小时服一次 *to be taken once every four hours* / ～两周开一次会 *hold a meeting every other week* Ⅱ 副 ❶ on each occasion；each time：～到上海，我总要去逛一下城隍庙。*I invariably visit the Town God's Temple when I go to Shanghai.* / ～逢春节，我都要去看老师。*I always go to see my teachers during the Spring Festival.* ❷ often：春秋佳日，～作郊游。*We often go for an outing in the country on fine days in spring and autumn.*
【每当】whenever；every time
【每逢佳节倍思亲】on festive occasions more than ever we think of our dear ones far away
【每个角落】every nook and cranny
【每况愈下】steadily deteriorate；go from bad to worse：他的病情～，治不好了。*His condition is getting steadily worse, and there is no hope of recovery.*
【每每】often：他们常在一起，～一谈就是半天。*They often got together, and when they did, they'd chat for hours.*
【每时每刻】all the time；at all times
【每下愈况】同〖每况愈下〗
美 Ⅰ 形 ❶ beautiful；pretty：她长得很～。*She's very pretty.* / 风景多～啊！*What beautiful scenery!* ❷ very satisfactory；good：～酒 *good wine* / 这鱼的味道很～。*The fish tastes quite good.* / ～～地吃了一顿 *have had an excellent dinner* / 日子过得挺～ *live quite happily* Ⅱ 动 ❶ beautify；prettify：美容 ❷〈方〉be pleased with oneself：夸了他两句，他就～得不得了。*Just a few words of praise made him exceedingly pleased with himself.* Ⅲ 名 ❶〈略〉见〖美洲〗 ❷〈略〉见〖美国〗
〖美编〗(〈略〉全称为'美术编辑') art editing
【美不胜收】so many beautiful things that one simply can't take them all in；more beauty than one can take in
【美餐】❶ tasty food；table delicacies ❷ eat and drink one's fill；have an excellent dinner
【美差】a cushy job；a pleasant task：你去桂林开会，这可是一趟～！*What a pleasant assignment you've got going to Guilin for the conference!*
【美钞】U. S. banknote；greenback
【美称】laudatory title；good name：四川向有天府之国的～。*Sichuan has always enjoyed the reputation of being "Nature's storehouse".*
【美传】a story passed on with approval
【美德】virtue；moral excellence：艰苦朴素是我们的传统～。*Hard work and plain living are traditional virtues of ours.*
【美吨】short ton
【美发】give beauty treatment to hair (cut or perm)；hair-styling：～厅 *hairdresser's shop*
【美感】aesthetic feeling；aesthetic perception；sense of beauty：舒伯特的艺术歌曲给人以～。*Art songs by Schubert give one sensuous pleasure.*
【美工】[电影] ❶ art designing ❷ art designer
【美观】pleasing to the eye；beautiful；artistic：房间布置得很～。*The room is artistically decorated.* / 这些花布设计得～大方。*The design of the cotton print is artistic and in good taste.*
【美国】the United States (U. S. A) ◇ ～佬〈口〉Yankee (U. S. citizen)；～人 American
【美好】fine；happy；glorious：～的日子 *happy days*；*a happy life* / ～的将来 *a glorious future* / ～的回忆 *happy memories* / ～的远景 *magnificent prospects* / 致以～的祝愿 *with best wishes*
【美化】beautify；prettify；embellish：～环境 *beautify the environment* / ～精神生活和物质生活 *enrich one's cultural and material life*
【美籍华人】Chinese American
【美金】同〖美元〗
【美劲儿】〈口〉❶ outward expression of joy or delight：瞧他这～。*Look how delighted he is.* ❷ joy；delight：工作之后，听点儿好音乐，那个～就别提啦。*What a delight it is to listen to some good music after work.*
【美景】beautiful scenery (or landscape)：～良辰 *beautiful scenery and pleasant morning*；*an enjoyable situation* / 西湖～ *the enchanting scenery of the West Lake*
【美酒佳肴】good wine and delicious dishes
【美拉尼西亚】Melanesia
【美利奴羊】Merino (sheep)
【美丽】beautiful：～富饶的国家 *a beautiful and richly-endowed country* / ～的小姑娘 *a pretty little girl*
【美轮美奂】(of building) tall and splendid；magnificent
【美满】happy；perfectly satisfactory：生活～ *lead*

a happy life / ～婚姻 *a happy marriage*; *conjugal happiness* / ～幸福的家庭 *a happy family*

【美貌】❶ good looks ❷ pretty; beautiful: ～的年轻女子 *a beautiful young lady*

【美梦】fond dream

【美妙】beautiful; splendid; wonderful: ～歌喉 *sweet voice* / ～的青春 *the wonderful days of one's youth* / 那家公司的经济情况很不～。*The financial situation of that company is anything but good.*

【美名】good name; good reputation: 英雄～天下扬。*A hero's good name spreads far and wide.* / 博得～ *win a good reputation*

【美男子】a handsome man

【美尼尔氏症】[医] Ménière's syndrome (or disease)

【美女】a beautiful woman

【美其名曰】call it by the fine-sounding name of; describe it euphemistically as

【美气】〈方〉comfortable; easy: 日子过得很～。*We're leading a very comfortable life.*

【美缺】an ideal vacancy; a well-paid post

【美人】a beautiful woman; beauty

【美人计】beauty trap: 定下～ *set a beauty trap*

【美人蕉】[植] canna; Indian shot

【美人鱼】mermaid

【美容】improve (esp. a woman's) looks: 她今天去做～了。*She went to the beauty parlour today.* ◇ ～师 beautician; ～手术 cosmetic surgery; ～术 cosmetology; beauty treatment; ～院 beauty parlour; beauty shop; ～专家 cosmetologist

【美声唱法】bel canto

【美食】good food; table delicacies ◇ ～家 gourmet; ～街 food street; restaurant row

【美术】❶ the fine arts; art: 工艺～ *industrial arts*; *arts and crafts*; ❷ painting; ◇ ～爱好者 lover of arts; ～革 fancy leather; ～工作者 art worker; artist; ～馆 art gallery; ～家 artist; ～明信片 picture (or pictorial) postcard; ～片 film cartoons; puppet films; ～人型 artist figurine; ～设计 artistic design; ～学校 art school; ～学院 academy of fine arts; ～展览会 art exhibition; ～字 artistic calligraphy; art lettering

【美谈】a story passed on with approval

【美味】❶ delicious food; delicacy ❷ delicious; dainty: ～小吃 *dainty snacks*

【美协】(〈略〉全称为'美术工作者协会') association of artists

【美学】aesthetics

【美言】put in a good word for sb.

【美艳】beautiful and voluptuous; gorgeous; glamorous

【美意】good intention; kindness: 谢谢您的～。*Thank you for your kindness.*

【美育】aesthetic education; art education

【美誉】good name; good reputation

【美元】(又作'美圆') American dollar; U. S. dollar ($) ◇ ～冲击 dollar shock; ～购买力 dollar's purchasing power

【美展】(〈略〉全称为'美术作品展览') art exhibition

【美中不足】a blemish in an otherwise perfect thing; a blemish in a thing of beauty: 这本小说很好,～的是结尾太冗长了。*This is a good novel, except for the long and tedious ending.*

【美洲】America ◇ ～虎 jaguar; ～狮 cougar; puma

【美滋滋】very pleased with oneself: 他被选中当队长,心里～的。*He was very pleased at being chosen to captain the team.*

镁 名 [化] magnesium (Mg)

【镁光】magnesium light: ～照明弹 *magnesium flare*

【镁砂】[冶] magnesia; magnesite

【镁砖】[冶] magnesia brick

mèi

妹 名 younger sister; sister: 兄～ *brother and sister* / 她是我小～。*She's my youngest sister.*

【妹夫】younger sister's husband; brother-in-law

【妹妹】younger sister; sister

【妹婿】〈书〉younger sister's husband; brother-in-law

【妹子】〈方〉❶ younger sister; sister ❷ a young girl

昧 Ⅰ 形 ignorant; stupid; foolish: 愚昧 Ⅱ 动 hide; conceal: ～着良心 (*do evil*) *against one's conscience*

【昧心】(do evil) against one's conscience: ～钱 *money obtained by dishonest means*

【昧于】be ignorant of; fail to understand: ～事实 *be ignorant of the facts*; *be unaware of the truth* / ～事理 *lack common sense*

寐 动 [书] sleep: 喜而不～ *too happy and excited to fall asleep*

媚 Ⅰ 动 fawn on; curry favour with; flatter; toady to: 谄媚 Ⅱ 形 charming; fascinating; enchanting: ～人的景色 *enchanting scenery*

【媚敌】curry favour with (or toady to) the enemy

【媚骨】obsequiousness: 没有丝毫的奴颜与～ *be free from all sycophancy or obsequiousness*

【媚上骄下】fawn on and please superiors while to be proudly contemptuous to inferiors

【媚世】try to please the public; play to the gallery

【媚俗】(of literary works) catering to the readership's poor taste: 文学不能媚俗。*Literature must not cater to the reader's poor taste.*

【媚态】❶ obsequiousness ❷ feminine charms

【媚外】fawn on (or toady to) foreign powers

【媚笑】a bewitching smile; an ingratiating smile

【媚眼】seductive eyes: 抛～ (*esp. of a woman*) *make eyes at sb.*; *throw amorous glances at sb.*

【媚悦】curry favor with; ingratiate oneself; court: ～部分人的庸俗趣味 *cater to the vulgar tastes of certain people*

魅 名 evil spirit; demon

【魅力】glamour; charm; enchantment; fascination: 艺术～ *artistic charm* / 音乐的～ *the magic of music*

【魅惑】charm; irresistible temptation; enchanting

mēn

闷 Ⅰ形 ❶ stuffy; close: 开开窗吧,屋里太～了。*Open the windows. It's too stuffy in here.* / 我觉得胸口～得慌。*I feel like I can't breathe.* / 这天儿真～。*It is very oppressive today.* ❷〈方〉(of a sound) muffled: 说话～声～气的 *speak in a muffled voice; won't come out with a clear statement* Ⅱ动 ❶ cover tightly: ～一会儿,茶味儿就出来了。*Let the tea draw for a while and the flavour will come out.* ❷ keep silent; say nothing: 你有什么事就说吧,别～在心里。*Speak out. Don't just brood over things.* ❸ shut oneself or sb. indoors: 别老～在屋里看书,出来活动活动。*Don't shut yourself indoors reading all day long. Come outside and stretch your legs.* ——另见 mèn

【闷气】stuffy; close ——另见 mènqi

【闷热】hot and suffocating; sultry; muggy: 我看快下雨了,天这么～。*I think it's going to rain—it's so sultry.*

【闷声不响】remain silent: 她～只管干活。*She kept silent, concentrating on her work.*

【闷头儿】(work hard) quietly or silently: ～干 *work doggedly in silence; plod away silently*

mén

门 Ⅰ名 ❶ door; gate; entrance: 校～ *school gate* / 炉～儿 *a stove door* / 柜～儿 *a cabinet door* / 请走南～。*Please use the south entrance.* ❷ valve; switch: 电门 ❸ way to do sth; knack: 我到钢厂劳动了一段时间,对炼钢摸着点～儿了。*After working in the steel mill for a while I got an inkling of how steel is made.* ❹ family: 张～王氏 *Mrs. Zhang, née Wang* ❺ (religious) sect; school (of thought): 佛门 ❻ relating to the teacher: 同门 ❼ class; category: 分门别类 ❽ [生] phylum: 亚～ *subphylum* / 脊椎动物～ *vertebrata* ❾ [计] computer gate: "与"～ *AND gate* / "非"～ *NOT gate* Ⅱ量 ❶ (for subjects of study, etc.): 两～功课 *two subjects; two courses* / 这～学问 *this subject of study* / 你选了几～课? *How many courses did you select?* / 掌握三～技术 *master three skills* ❷ (for cannons): 一～大炮 *a piece of artillery; a cannon; a gun* ❸ (for a marriage): 一～亲事 *a marriage* ❹ (for relatives): 一～亲戚 *a set of relatives*

【门巴族】the Moinba (Monba) nationality, or the Moinbas (Monbas), inhabiting the Xizang Autonomous Region

【门把】door knob; door handle

【门板】❶ door plank ❷ shutter: 上～儿 *put up the shutters*

【门鼻儿】bolt staple

【门钹】gate cymbal (nailed onto old-fashioned gates, with a ring-shaped knocker attached to it)

【门插关儿】(door) bolt

【门齿】front tooth; incisor

【门当户对】be well-matched in social and economic status (for marriage)

【门道】❶ gateway; doorway ❷〈口〉way to do sth.; knack: 技术革新的～很多。*There are all sorts of possibilities for technical innovation.* ❸ social connections; contacts: 他这个人～很粗。*He's a very well-connected man.*

【门第】family status: 诗书～ *an intellectual family*

【门吊】[机] gantry crane

【门吊儿】hasp and staple

【门丁】doorman; gatekeeper

【门洞儿】gateway; doorway

【门房】❶ gate house; janitor's room; porter's lodge ❷ gatekeeper; doorman; janitor; porter

【门风】ethics and moral standards that a family or a clan keeps

【门缝】a crack between a door and its frame or between two doors

【门岗】gate sentry

【门户】❶ door: ～紧闭 *with the doors tightly shut* / 小心～。*Watch the door and beware of intruders.* ❷ gateway; important passageway: 天津港是北京通往海洋的～。*The port of Tianjin is Beijing's gateway to the sea.* ❸ faction; sect: 门户之见 ❹ family: 兄弟分居,自立～。*The brothers have set up their own homes.* ❺ family status: ～相当 *families well-matched in social status*

【门户之见】sectarian bias; sectarianism

【门环子】knocker

【门将】goalkeeper (soccer, hockey, etc.)

【门捷列夫元素周期律】[化] Mendeleev's law

【门禁】entrance guard: ～森严 *with the entrances heavily guarded*

【门警】police or security guard at an entrance

【门镜】peep-hole (in a door)

【门径】access; key; way: 经过反复实验,他终于找到了节省原料的～。*Through repeated experiments he at last found the way to save raw materials.*

【门静脉】[生理] portal vein

【门槛】(又作'门坎') ❶ threshold ❷〈方〉way to do sth.; knack: 你不懂～。*You don't know the tricks.* / 他～精,不会上当。*He's too sharp to be taken in.*

【门可罗雀】you can catch sparrows on the doorstep—visitors are few and far between

【门客】a hanger-on of an aristocrat

【门口】entrance; doorway: 在～等候 *wait at the door (or gate)* / 走过学校～ *walk past the*

school entrance
【门框】doorframe
【门廊】[建] porch; portico
【门类】class; kind; category: 基础科学和技术科学这两大～ *the two major departments of basic and technical sciences*
【门帘】door curtain; portire
【门脸儿】❶ the vicinity of a city gate ❷ the facade of a shop; shop front ❸ shop
【门铃】doorbell
【门楼】an arch over a gateway
【门路】❶ way to do sth.; knack: 摸到一些～ *have learned the ropes; know one's way around* / 广开生产～ *tap new sources of production* / 广开就业～ *create job opportunities on an extensive scale* ❷ social connections (for securing jobs, etc.); pull: 找～ *solicit help from potential backers* / 办这种事，他有～。*He knows the right places to go to get this kind of job done.*
【门楣】❶ lintel (of a door) ❷ family status: 辱没～ *bring disgrace to one's family*
【门面】❶ the facade of a shop; shop front: 三间～ *a three-bay shop front* / 这家店铺～很大。*The shop puts on a very prosperous front.* ❷ appearance; facade: 支撑～ *keep up appearances; put up a front* ◇ ～话 formal and insincere remarks; lip service
【门钮】door knob; door handle
【门牌】❶ (house) number plate ❷ street number; house number: 你家～几号? *What's the street number of your house?*
【门票】entrance ticket; admission ticket: 不收～ *admission free*
【门前三包】system of three responsibilities in front of the gate (every unit or household along a street takes responsibility for cleanliness, order and planting greenery in front of their gate)
【门桥】[军] raft of pontoons; boat raft
【门球】[体] croquet
【门人】❶ pupil; disciple; follower ❷ a hanger-on of an aristocrat
【门神】door-god (whose pictures were often pasted on the front door of a house as a talisman in old China)
【门生】pupil; disciple; follower
【门市】retail sales: ～部 *retail department; sales department; salesroom*
【门闩】(door) bolt; (door) bar
【门厅】[建] entrance hall; vestibule
【门庭】❶ courtyard ❷ family status
【门庭若市】the courtyard is as crowded as a marketplace—❶ a much visited house ❷ the shop is doing booming business
【门徒】disciple; follower; adherent
【门外汉】layman; the uninitiated: 对于美术，我是个～。*Where the fine arts are concerned, I am only a layman.*
【门卫】entrance guard
【门牙】front tooth; incisor
【门诊】outpatient service ◇ ～病人 outpatient; clinic patient; ～部 clinic; outpatient department; ～时间 consulting hours
【门柱】doorpost

扪 动 〈书〉touch; stroke
【扪心自问】examine or search one's conscience: ～，我从来没有亏待过你。*I have searched my conscience, and believe I have never mistreated you.*
【扪诊】[医] palpation

钔 名 [化] mendelevium (Md)

mèn

闷 形 ❶ bored; depressed; in low spirits: 你一个人在这儿多～得慌，跟我们出去走走吧! *Don't you feel bored staying here all alone? Why not come out with us for a walk?* ❷ tightly closed; sealed: ～屋子住着憋气。*I feel suffocated in a tightly closed room.* ——另见 mēn
【闷沉沉】depressed; gloomy
【闷堵】suffocated; oppressed: 觉得胸口～ *feel a tightness in the chest*
【闷棍】见【打闷棍】
【闷葫芦】enigma; puzzle; riddle: 这几句没头没脑的话真把人装进～里了。*These abrupt remarks were really a puzzle to everyone.*
【闷酒】drinks taken alone to drown one's sorrows
【闷倦】bored and listless
【闷雷】❶ muffled thunder ❷ unpleasant surprise; shock
【闷闷不乐】depressed; in low spirits: 她～，满腹心事。*She was in low spirits and laden with anxiety.*
【闷气】the sulks: 生～ *be sulky; be in the sulks* ——另见 mēnqì
【闷子车】boxcar

焖 动 boil in a covered pot over a slow fire; braise: ～饭 *cook rice over a slow fire* / ～牛肉 *braised beef*

mēng

蒙 Ⅰ 动 ❶ cheat; deceive; dupe: 你～我! *You're kidding me!* / 一张假票子把他～了。*He was taken in by a forged note.* / 欺上～下 *deceive one's superiors and dupe one's subordinates* ❷ make a wild guess: ～对了 *make a lucky guess* Ⅱ 形 unconscious; senseless: 给打～了 *be knocked senseless* / 他觉得脑袋发～。*He felt his head swimming.* / 老师一问到这个问题，她就～了。*Her teacher's question baffled her.* ——另见 méng; měng
【蒙蒙亮】first glimmer of dawn; daybreak: 天～他就起床了。*He got up at the crack of dawn.*

【蒙骗】deceive；cheat；hoodwink；delude：～顾客 *cheat customers*

【蒙头转向】lose one's bearings；be utterly confused：情况这样复杂，我都有点儿～了。*In all this mass of facts, I've rather lost my bearings.*

méng

虻 名 horsefly；gadfly：牛虻

萌 动 sprout；shoot forth；bud；germinate

【萌动】❶ (of plants) sprout；shoot forth；germinate；bud ❷ start：春意～。*The breath of spring stirs.*

【萌发】［植］sprout；shoot forth；bud；germinate：茶树修剪后又～新枝。*The tea plants sprouted new buds after the pruning.*

【萌生】〈书〉come into being；arise：她的心底～出一个强烈的愿望。*There arose a strong desire in her heart.*

【萌芽】❶ sprout；shoot forth；bud；germinate ❷ rudiment；shoot；seed；germ：处于～状态 *in the embryonic stage*；*in the bud*

蒙 Ⅰ 动 ❶ cover：～上一层灰尘 *be covered with a layer of dust* / 她们头上都～着白毛巾。*They all covered their heads with white towels.* / ～住眼睛 *be blindfolded* / ～头睡大觉 *tuck oneself in and sleep like a log* ❷ receive；meet with：～大力协助，十分感谢。*Thank you very much for your kind help.* Ⅱ 名 ignorance；illiteracy 启蒙 ——另见 mēng；měng

【蒙蔽】hoodwink；deceive；hide the truth from；pull the wool over sb.'s eyes：不要被花言巧语所～。*Don't let yourself be fooled by honeyed words.*

【蒙导法】［生］mentor method

【蒙垢】〈书〉be subjected to humiliation；be humiliated

【蒙汗药】a narcotic believed to have been used by highwaymen, etc. to drug their victims；knockout drops

【蒙哄】deceive；hoodwink；swindle；cheat

【蒙混】deceive or mislead people：～过关 *get by under false pretences*

【蒙胧】half asleep；drowsy；somnolent：睡眼～ *eyes heavy with sleep*；*drowsy* / ～睡去 *doze off*

【蒙昧】❶ barbaric；uncivilized；uncultured：～时代 *age of barbarism* ❷ ignorant；benighted；unenlightened ◇ ～无知 unenlightened；benighted；childishly ignorant；～主义 obscurantism

【蒙蒙】drizzly；misty：～细雨 *a fine drizzle* / 烟雾～ *misty*

【蒙面盗】a masked bandit；a masked burglar

【蒙难】(of a revolutionary) be confronted by danger；fall into the clutches of the enemy

【蒙受】suffer；sustain：～耻辱 *be subjected to humiliation*；*be humiliated*

【蒙太奇】［电影］montage

【蒙头盖脸】cover one's head and face

【蒙羞而亡】die an ignominious death

【蒙冤】be wronged；suffer an injustice

【蒙在鼓里】be kept inside a drum—be kept in the dark：这事儿早就传扬开了，只有他还～。*The news has already got abroad*；*only he himself is still completely in the dark.*

盟 Ⅰ 名 ❶ alliance：结盟 ❷ league (an administrative division of the Nei Mongol Autonomous Region, corresponding to a prefecture) Ⅱ 形 sworn (brothers)：盟兄弟

【盟邦】an allied country；ally

【盟国】an allied country；ally

【盟军】allied forces

【盟誓】❶〈书〉an oath of alliance；a treaty of alliance ❷ take an oath；make a pledge：对天～ *swear by Heaven*

【盟兄弟】sworn brothers

【盟友】ally

【盟员】a member of an alliance (or league)

【盟约】an oath of alliance；a treaty of alliance

【盟主】the leader (or chief) of an alliance

朦 (构词成分) 见下

【朦胧】❶ (of moonlight) dim；hazy：月色～ *hazy moonlight* ❷ obscure；dim；hazy：～的景色 *a hazy view* / 烟雾～ *misty* / 暮色～ *in the gloaming*

【朦胧诗】obscure poems

měng

猛 Ⅰ 形 fierce；violent；energetic；vigorous：炮火很～。*There was heavy gunfire.* / 用力过～ *use too much strength*；*overexert oneself* / 在背上击一～掌 *give sb. a powerful shove in the back* Ⅱ 副 ❶ suddenly；abruptly：～吃一惊 *be startled* / 河水～涨。*The river suddenly rose.* / 产量～增 *a sharp increase in output* / 物价～涨(跌) *a sharp rise (fall) in prices* ❷ vigorously；with sudden force：～干 *work with vim and vigour* / 他一脚～射，球破门而入。*He sent the ball into the net with a powerful kick.* / ～冲～打 *fiercely charge and attack*

【猛不防】by surprise；unexpectedly；unawares：～后面有人推了他一下。*Suddenly someone gave him a push from behind.*

【猛打猛冲】go full blast ahead

【猛地】suddenly；abruptly：～往前一跳 *suddenly jump forward*

【猛不丁地】〈方〉suddenly；abruptly：火车～停住了。*The train came to an abrupt halt.*

【猛攻】onslaught；fierce attack

【猛虎】fierce tiger

【猛将】valiant general ◇ ～如云 a great many brave warriors

【猛进】push ahead vigorously；advance in quick and big strides：祝你学业～！*I wish you a rapid progress in your studies.*

【猛劲儿】〈口〉❶ a spurt of energy；dash：她一个～，就超过了跑在前面的人。*Putting on a spurt，she overtook all the other runners.* / 搬重东西要用～。*To lift heavy things，you need to use a sudden jerk of strength.* ❷ great vigour：这小伙子干活有股子～。*This young chap works with vim and vigour.*

【猛力】with sudden force：～扣杀 *smash*（*a ball*）*with all one's strength* / 把手榴弹～一甩 *throw a grenade with all one's might* / ～一拉 *pull with a jerk*

【猛厉】fierce；vigorous；violent：朔风～。*There was a fierce north wind.*

【猛烈】fierce；vigorous：～的炮火 *heavy shellfire* / 这里气候寒冷，风势～。*It's bitter cold and violently windy here.*

【猛犸】mammoth

【猛禽】bird of prey

【猛然】suddenly；abruptly：我～想起来了。*In a flash I remembered.* / ～一拉 *pull with a jerk* / ～回头 *hastily turn one's head*

【猛士】brave warrior

【猛兽】beast of prey

【猛醒】（又作'猛省'）suddenly wake up（to the truth）

【猛增】dramatic increase：销量～。*Sales volume has skyrocketed.* / 产值～。*Output value has skyrocketed.* / 赤字～。*The deficit has increased drastically.*

【猛鸷】hawk；eagle

【猛追】give a hot pursuit

蒙 名 the Mongol ethnic group ——另见 mēng；méng

【蒙古】Mongolia ◇ ～包 yurt；～人 Mongolian；Mongol；～人种 the Mongolian stock；～语 Mongolian（language）；Mongol（language）；～语族［语］the Mongolian group——另见〖内蒙古〗

【蒙古族】❶ the Mongolian ethnic group，or the Mongolians（or Mongols）of China ❷ the Mongolians（or Mongols）of Mongolia

【蒙栎】［植］Mongolian oak（Quercus mongolica）

锰 名［化］manganese（Mn）

【锰钢】manganese steel

【锰结核】［地质］manganese nodule

【锰矿】manganese mine

【锰铁】ferromanganese

蠓 名［动］midge；biting midge

懵 形 muddled；ignorant：～然无知 *be totally ignorant*

【懵懂】muddled；ignorant

mèng

孟 名 ❶ the first month of a season：孟春 ❷ the eldest among brothers

【孟春】the first month of spring

【孟德尔主义】［生］Mendelism

【孟冬】the first month of winter

【孟加拉】Bengal ◇ ～国 Bangladesh；～人 Bengalese；Bengali；～湾 the Bay of Bengal；～语 Bengali（language）

【孟浪】rash；impetuous；impulsive：不可～行事。*Don't act rashly.*

【孟秋】the first month of autumn

【孟什维克】Menshevik

【孟什维克主义】Menshevism

【孟夏】the first month of summer

【孟子】Mencius

梦 名 ❶ dream：昨晚我做了个可怕的～。*I had a terrible dream last night.* ❷ fancy；illusion：痴人说梦

【梦笔生花】dream that one's brush is blooming—begin to show one's literary brilliance

【梦话】❶ words uttered in one's sleep；somniloquy：昨晚我听见你说～。*I heard you talk in your sleep last night.* ❷ daydream；nonsense：六个月就能编一本词典？这简直是在说～！*To compile a dictionary within 6 months —that's just daydreaming!*

【梦幻】illusion；dream；reverie：～般的境界 *a dreamlike world*；*dreamland*

【梦幻泡影】pipe dream；bubble；illusion：一切希望都成了～。*All my hopes have come to nothing.*

【梦见】see in a dream；dream about：我～我母亲了。*I saw my mother in my dream.*

【梦境】dreamland；dreamworld；dream

【梦寐】dream；sleep：～难忘 *be unable to forget sth. even in one's dreams* / ～以求 *crave sth. so that one even dreams about it*；*long*（*or yearn*）*for sth. day and night*

【梦乡】dreamland：他太累了，一躺下就进入了～。*He was so tired that as soon as his head hit the pillow，he went off to dreamland.*

【梦想】❶ vain hope；wishful thinking：他以为她会嫁给自己的，这只是～而已。*His belief that she will marry him is only wishful thinking.* ❷ vainly hope；dream of：他居然得了冠军，这是连他自己都～不到的事。*His winning of the championship was something he'd never dreamt of before.*

【梦魇】nightmare

【梦遗】［医］nocturnal emission；wet dream

【梦呓】❶ sleeptalking；somniloquy ❷ rigmarole

【梦游症】（又作'梦行症'）somnambulism；sleepwalking

【梦之队】（又作'最佳组合'）dream team

mī

咪 (构词成分)见下

【咪咪】mew; miaow: 小猫一饿就～叫。*The kittens mewed when they were hungry.*

眯 动 ❶ narrow (one's eyes): ～着眼睛笑 *narrow one's eyes into a smile* / ～着眼睛瞧 *squint at* ❷〈方〉take a nap: ～一会儿 *take a short nap; have forty winks* ——另见 mí

【眯盹儿】〈方〉doze off; take a nap

【眯缝】narrow (one's eyes): 他不说话,只是～着眼睛笑。*He didn't say anything, but only narrowed his eyes into a smile.*

mí

弥 Ⅰ 动 ❶ fill; overflow: 弥漫 ❷ cover; fill: 弥缝 Ⅱ 副〈书〉more; still more; even more: 欲盖～彰 *try to cover sth. up only to make it more conspicuous*

【弥补】make up; remedy; make good: 无法～的损失 *an irreparable loss* / ～赤字 *make up (or meet) a deficit* / 学习别人的优点,～自己的不足 *learn from other people's strong points to counteract one's own weaknesses*

【弥缝】plug up holes—gloss over faults

【弥合】close; bridge: ～裂痕 *close a rift*

【弥勒】Maitreya

【弥留】〈书〉be dying: ～之际 *on one's deathbed*

【弥漫】fill the air; spread all over the place: 春意～。*Spring is very much in the air.* / 风雪～ *be in a blinding snowstorm*

【弥撒】[宗](天主教) Mass: 望～ *attend Mass; go to Mass*

【弥撒曲】[音] mass

【弥散】spread or diffuse in all directions

【弥天大谎】monstrous lie; outrageous lie

【弥天大罪】monstrous crime; heinous crime

【弥望无际】boundless horizon

迷 Ⅰ 动 ❶ be confused; be lost: ～了方向 *lose one's bearings; get lost* ❷ be fascinated by; be crazy about: 小伙子们～上了霹雳舞。*The youngsters became crazy about break dance.* ❸ confuse; perplex; fascinate; enchant: 景色～人。*The scenery is of enchanting beauty.* / 他让金钱～住了心窍。*He was obssessed by lust for money.* Ⅱ 名 fan; enthusiast; fiend: 足球～ *a soccer fan (or enthusiast)*

【迷不知返】go astray not knowing how to return

【迷彩】camouflage colors: ～服 *camouflage battledress*

【迷宫】labyrinth; maze

【迷航】(of a plane, ship, etc.) drift off course; lose one's course; get lost

【迷糊】❶ misted; blurred; dimmed: 这么多花布我都看～了。*I was simply dazzled by all these cotton prints.* ❷ dazed; confused: 睡～了 *be dazed with sleep* / 喝酒喝～了 *get tipsy* / 把人给弄～了 *make one feel muddled* / 我刚合上眼就迷迷糊糊地睡着了。*I dozed off as soon as I closed my eyes.* ❸ muddleheaded: 他这个人有点～。*He's somewhat muddleheaded.*

【迷幻】hazy and illusionary; fantastic: 这草木不生的世界被笼罩在～的雾里。*The barren place was cloaked in mysterious fog.*

【迷幻剂】psychedelic drug

【迷幻药】〈口〉acid; LSD (an illegal drug that makes you see things as more beautiful, strange, frightening etc. than usual, or see thing that do not exist)

【迷魂汤】(又作'迷魂药') ❶ sth. intended to turn sb.'s head; magic potion ❷ flattery

【迷魂阵】a scheme for confusing or bewildering sb.; maze; trap: 摆～ *lay out a scheme to bewitch sb.; set a trap*

【迷惑】puzzle; confuse; perplex; baffle: 感到～不解 *feel puzzled; feel perplexed* / 不要被假象所～。*Don't be misled by false appearances.*

【迷津】miss the ferry—stray from the right path: 指破～ *point out where sb. has gone astray*

【迷离】blurred; misted: 睡眼～ *eyes dim with sleep*

【迷离惝恍】indistinct; blurred

【迷恋】be infatuated with; madly cling to

【迷路】❶ lose one's way; get lost: 天太黑,我迷了路。*I lost my way because it was too dark.* ❷ go astray

【迷乱】dazed and confused; befuddled

【迷漫】boundless and indistinct; vast and hazy: 烟雾～ *be enveloped in mist; be covered in thick mist*

【迷茫】❶ vast and hazy: 大雪纷飞,原野一片～。*The vast plain was obscured by the falling flakes of snow.* ❷ confused; perplexed; dazed

【迷梦】pipe dream; fond illusion

【迷迷糊糊】in a daze, difficult to make out

【迷迷怔怔】dazed; confused: 睡得～的 *be dazed with sleep*

【迷你裙】miniskirt

【迷人】charming; fascinating; enchanting; bewitching

【迷失】lose (one's way, etc.): ～方向 *lose one's bearings; get lost*

【迷途】❶ lose one's way ❷ wrong path: 走入～ *go astray*

【迷途知返】recover one's bearings and return to the fold; realize one's errors and mend one's ways

【迷惘】be perplexed; be at a loss: ～的神色 *a perplexed look*

【迷雾】❶ dense fog ❷ anything that misleads people

【迷信】❶ superstition; superstitious belief; blind faith; blind worship ❷ have blind faith in;

make a fetish of：～权威 *have blind faith in authority*
【迷走神经】[生理] vagus (nerve)

谜 名 ❶ riddle；conundrum：猜谜儿 ❷ enigma；mystery；puzzle：他的死因现在还是一个～。*The cause of his death remains a mystery to this day*.
【谜底】❶ answer (or solution) to a riddle ❷ truth：揭开～ *find out the truth* (*of a matter*)
【谜团】doubts and suspicions：揭开～ *resolve doubts*
【谜语】riddle；conundrum

眯 动 (of dust，etc.) get into one's eye：沙子～了眼。*The dust has got into my eye*.——另见 mī

猕 (构词成分)见下
【猕猴】macaque；rhesus monkey
【猕猴桃】[植] kiwi fruit (Actinidia chinensis)

醚 名 [化] ether

糜 Ⅰ名 gruel or paste Ⅱ形 ❶ rotten：糜烂 ❷ wasteful：糜费
【糜费】spend extravagantly；waste：节约开支，防止～ *cut down expenses and avoid waste*
【糜烂】❶ rotten to the core；dissipated；debauched：生活～ *lead a dissipated* (*or fast*) *life* ❷ erosion
【糜烂性毒剂】[军] vesicant agent；blister agent

麋 名 elk
【麋羚】hartebeest
【麋鹿】mi-lu；David's deer

靡 形 extravagant；wasteful：奢靡——另见 mǐ
【靡费】同〖糜费〗

mǐ

米 Ⅰ名 ❶ (husked) rice ❷ shelled or husked seed：高粱米 Ⅱ量 metre
【米波】[无] metric wave
【米醋】rice vinegar
【米袋子】〈字〉rice sack；〈喻〉rice supply to the market：与丰富人民的"菜篮子"和"～"直接相关的农业科技开发项目 *agricultural projects directly related to the people's vegetable and grain supply*
【米饭】(cooked) rice
【米粉】❶ ground rice；rice flour ❷ rice-flour noodles
【米粉肉】steamed rice flour pork
【米泔水】water in which rice has been washed
【米糕】rice cake；rice pudding
【米黄】cream-coloured
【米价】the price of rice
【米酒】rice wine
【米糠】rice bran
【米老鼠】Mickey Mouse；mickey mouse
【米粒】grain of rice
【米粮川】rich rice-producing area：昔日穷山沟，今日～。*The barren gully of yesterday has become a granary*.
【米面】❶ rice and wheat flour ❷ ground rice；rice flour ❸ rice-flour noodles
【米色】cream-coloured
【米汤】❶ water in which rice has been cooked ❷ thin rice or millet gruel；rice water
【米线】〈方〉rice-flour noodles
【米象】[动] rice weevil
【米制】同〖国际公制〗
【米粥】congee；rice gruel
【米珠薪桂】rice is as precious as pearls and firewood as costly as cassia—exorbitantly high cost of living
【米烛光】[物] metre-candle；lux
【米蛀虫】❶ rice worm ❷ rice profiteer

弭 动 put an end to；stop；suppress；remove：消弭
【弭除】eliminate；dispel；remove；clear up：～成见 *dispel prejudices*
【弭患】〈书〉remove the source of trouble
【弭乱】put down a rebellion or stop a civil war

脒 名 [化] amidine

靡 Ⅰ动 blown away by the wind：披靡 Ⅱ副〈书〉not have；there is not；be without：～日不思 *not a day passes without one's thinking of sth. or sb*.
【靡丽】〈书〉❶ magnificent；resplendent ❷ luxurious；extravagant
【靡靡之音】decadent music

mì

泌 动 secrete：分泌
【泌尿科】[医] urological department
【泌尿器官】[生理] urinary organs
【泌尿系统】[生理] urinary system
【泌尿学】[医] urology

觅 动 look for；hunt for；seek：鸟雀经常在这里～食。*Birds often look for food here*.
【觅句】seek a telling line (for a poem)
【觅取】look for；hunt for；seek
【觅索词句】strive for phrases and sentences
【觅致人才】on the lookout for proper personnel

秘 Ⅰ形 secret；mysterious：诡秘 Ⅱ动 keep sth. secret；hold sth. back：秘而不宣 ——另见 bì
【秘宝】a rare treasure
【秘本】treasured private copy of a rare book
【秘传】hand down (a recipe，formula，etc.) from generation to generation in the family as a closely guarded secret
【秘而不宣】keep sth. secret；not let anyone in on

a secret

【秘方】secret recipe

【秘诀】secret (of success): 成功的～ *the secret of (or key to) one's success*

【秘密】❶ secret; clandestine; confidential ❷ sth. secret: 探索海底的～ *explore the secrets of the ocean bed* / 军事～ *a military secret* ◇ ～报告 a secret report; ～会议 secret meeting; closed-door session; ～活动 clandestine activities; ～警察 secret police; ～渠道 back channel; ～文件 secret papers; confidential document

【秘史】secret history (as of a feudal dynasty); inside story

【秘事】private affair; secret

【秘书】secretary ◇ ～处 secretariat; ～长 secretary-general

【秘闻】secret: 她知道宫中许多～ *She knows a lot of secrets of the court.*

密 Ⅰ 形 ❶ close; dense; thick: 这两行苗栽得太～了。*These two rows of seedlings are planted too close together.* / ～不透风 *airtight* / 枪声很～。*There was the sound of intensive gunfire.* ❷ intimate; close: 亲密 ❸ fine; meticulous: 周密 Ⅱ 副 secretly: ～通声息 *secretly communicate with each other* Ⅲ 名 [纺] density: 经密 / 纬密

【密报】❶ secretly report; inform against sb. ❷ a secret report

【密闭】airtight; hermetic: ～容器 *airtight container; hermetically-sealed chamber* ◇ ～集装箱 sealed container

【密布】be densely covered: 阴云～。*The sky was overcast.* or *Dark clouds were gathering.* / 礁石～ *be thick with reefs*

【密电】❶ secretly telegraph sb. ❷ cipher telegram ◇ ～码 cipher code

【密度】❶ density; thickness: 兵力～ *density of troops* / 火力～ *density (or volume) of fire* / 果树的～不宜太大。*Fruit trees should not be planted too close together.* ❷ [物] density ◇ ～计 densimeter

【密访】pay a secret visit; make investigation by traveling incognito

【密封】seal up; seal airtight; seal hermetically ◇ ～包装 air-tight wrapping; ～保存 preserve sth. by sealing it airtight; ～舱 sealed cabin; airtight cabin; ～垫圈 [机] sealing washer; ～机身 [航空] closed fuselage; ～压盖 [机] sealing gland

【密告】secretly report; inform against sb.

【密函告知】inform one by means of confidential letters

【密集】concentrated; crowded together: 人口～ *densely populated; thickly populated* / 对敌人进行～包围 *closely surround the enemy* ◇ ～队形 close formation; tight formation; ～轰炸 mass bombing; ～炮火 intensive bombardment; concentrated fire; massed fire; drumfire

【密集型】intensive: 技术～ *technology-intensive* / 劳动～ *labor-intensive*

【密件】a confidential paper or letter; classified matter; classified material

【密克罗尼西亚】Micronesia

【密林】thick (or dense) forest

【密令】❶ give a secret order or instructions ❷ secret order or instructions

【密码】cipher; cipher code; secret code ◇ ～电报 cipher telegram; ～机 cipher machine; cryptograph; ～术 cryptography; cryptology; ～锁 trick lock; ～箱 code box; ～学 cryptography; ～员 cryptographer

【密码子】[生] codon

【密密层层】packed closely layer upon layer (or ring upon ring); dense; thick: ～的人群 *a dense crowd*

【密密丛丛】(of grass or trees) dense; thick: ～的森林 *a dense forest*

【密密麻麻】〈口〉close and numerous; thickly dotted: 笔记本上写满了～的小字。*The notebook was filled with small, closely-written characters.*

【密密匝匝】同〖密匝匝〗

【密谋】conspire; plot; scheme: ～叛变 *conspire to defect* / ～政变 *plot a coup*

【密切】❶ close; intimate: ～配合 *act in close coordination* / ～相关 *be closely related* / ～联系群众 *maintain close ties with the masses* ❷ build (or forge, establish) close links (between two parties): 进一步～两国的关系 *build closer relations between the two countries* ❸ careful; intent; close: ～注视 *pay close attention to; watch closely*

【密商】hold private counsel; hold secret talks

【密使】secret emissary; secret envoy

【密室】a room used for secret purposes: 策划于～ *plot behind closed doors*

【密实】closely knit; dense; thick: 这件棉衣针脚做得真～。*This padded jacket is sewn tightly with small stitches.* or *The stitches on this padded jacket are small and close.*

【密谈】have a secret (or confidential, private) talk; talk behind closed doors

【密探】secret agent; spy

【密陀僧】[化] litharge; yellow lead

【密位】[军] mil

【密纹唱片】long-playing record; microgroove record

【密西西比河】the Mississippi

【密写情报】intelligence written in invisible ink, etc.

【密信】confidential letter; secret letter

【密友】close (or fast) friend; bosom friend

【密语通信】crypto-communication

【密约】secret agreement; secret treaty

【密云不雨】dense clouds but no rain—trouble is brewing

【密匝匝】〈口〉thick; dense

【密植】[农] close planting: 合理～ *rational close planting*

幂 名 ❶［数］power ❷〈书〉cloth cover
【幂级数】［数］power series
谧 形〈书〉quiet；still；tranquil
【谧静】〈书〉quiet；still；tranquil
蜜 Ⅰ 名 ❶ honey：蜂蜜 ❷ honey-like thing：糖蜜 Ⅱ 形 honeyed；sweet：甜蜜
【蜜蜂】honeybee；bee
【蜜柑】mandarin orange；tangerine orange
【蜜罐】honey jar；〈喻〉comfortable living conditions：我的孩子生活在优越的环境中，可以说是在～中长大的。*My child has always lived in comfort. He can be said to have grown up in a honey jar.*
【蜜饯】candied fruit；preserved fruit
【蜜橘】tangerine
【蜜蜡】beeswax
【蜜色】light yellow
【蜜甜】as sweet as honey；very sweet
【蜜丸子】［中］a bolus made of powdered Chinese medicine and honey
【蜜腺】［植］nectary
【蜜源】nectar source ◇ ～区（bee）pasture；～植物 nectariferous（or bee，honey）plant
【蜜月】honeymoon：度～ *spend*（*or be on*）*one's honeymoon*；*honeymoon*
【蜜枣】candied date or jujube
【蜜渍】candied；preserved in sugar
嘧（构词成分）见下
【嘧啶】［化］pyrimidine

mián

眠 Ⅰ 动 sleep：不～之夜 *a sleepless night*；*a white night* Ⅱ 名 dormancy：冬眠
【眠尔通】［药］miltown
绵 Ⅰ 名 silk floss：丝绵 Ⅱ 形 ❶ continuous：连绵 ❷ soft：软绵绵
【绵白糖】fine white sugar
【绵薄】〈套〉（my）meagre strength；humble effort：愿尽～。*I'll do what little I can.*
【绵长】（of time）very long：福寿～。*I wish you a happy and long life*（*said to an elderly person*）.
【绵绸】fabric made from waste silk
【绵亘】（of mountains，etc.）stretch in an unbroken chain
【绵里藏针】a needle hidden in silk floss—a ruthless character behind a gentle appearance；an iron hand in a velvet glove
【绵力】同〖绵薄〗
【绵绵】continuous；unbroken：秋雨～。*The autumn rain goes on and on.*
【绵邈】〈书〉faraway；remote：年代～ *of the remote past*；*age-old* / 道路～ *a long journey*；*a long way to go*
【绵软】❶ soft：～的羊毛 *soft wool* ❷ weak：觉得浑身～ *feel weak all over*
【绵延】be continuous；stretch long and unbroken：第二次世界大战后，局部战争一直～不断。*Local wars have been going on continually ever since the end of World War II.*
【绵羊】sheep
【绵纸】tissue paper
棉 Ⅰ 名 ❶ general name for cotton and kapok ❷ cotton：～纺织品 *cotton textiles* Ⅱ 形 cotton-padded；quilted：～大衣 *cotton-padded overcoat*
【棉袄】cotton-padded（or quilted）jacket
【棉被】a quilt with cotton wadding；cotton-wedded quilt
【棉布】cotton cloth；cotton
【棉纺】cotton spinning ◇ ～厂 cotton mill
【棉纺织品】cotton textiles
【棉凫】［动］cotton teal
【棉婚】cotton wedding anniversary—the 2nd wedding anniversary
【棉红铃虫】pink bollworm
【棉红蜘蛛】two-spotted spider mite
【棉猴儿】hooded cotton-padded coat；（knee-length）parka；anorak
【棉花】cotton ◇ ～签（cotton）swab；～蛆 pink bollworm；～胎 cotton wadding（for a quilt，etc.）；～套子 cotton wadding（for a quilt）
【棉花糖】cotton candy
【棉卷】［纺］lap
【棉枯萎病】fusarium wilt of cotton
【棉裤】cotton-padded trousers
【棉铃】cotton boll ◇ ～虫 bollworm
【棉毛机】interlock（knitting）machine
【棉毛裤】cotton（interlock）trousers（worn as underwear）
【棉毛衫】cotton（interlock）jersey（worn as underwear）◇ ～布 cotton interlock（fabric）
【棉帽】cotton-padded cap
【棉农】cotton grower
【棉袍子】cotton-padded robe
【棉绒】cotton velvet
【棉纱】cotton yarn ◇ ～头（cotton）waste
【棉毯】cotton blanket
【棉桃】cotton boll
【棉套】a cotton-padded covering for keeping sth. warm
【棉田】cotton field
【棉条】［纺］sliver ◇ ～桶 sliver can
【棉线】cotton thread；cotton
【棉鞋】cotton-padded shoes
【棉絮】❶ cotton fibre ❷ a cotton wadding（for a quilt，etc.）
【棉蚜虫】cotton aphid
【棉衣】cotton-padded clothes
【棉织品】cotton goods；cotton textiles；cotton fabrics
【棉籽】cottonseed

miǎn

免 动 ❶ excuse sb. from sth.; exempt; dispense with: ～试 *be excused from an examination* / ～服兵役 *be exempt from military service* / 互相～办签证协议 *mutual exemption of visas agreement* / 这些手续就～了。*We'll dispense with the formalities*. ❷ remove from office; dismiss; relieve: 他已被～去教育部长的职务。*He has been removed from his post as minister of education*. / 他工作太多,得给他～掉几项。*He's got too much to do. He should be relieved of some of his jobs*. ❸ avoid; avert; escape: ～于受灾 *avert a disaster* ❹ be not allowed: 闲人～进。*No admittance except on business*.

【免办签证】dispense with a visa

【免不得】be unavoidable; be bound to be

【免不了】be unavoidable; be bound to be: 在前进的道路上,～会有困难。*There are bound to be difficulties in the course of our advance*.

【免除】❶ prevent; avoid: 兴修水利,～水旱灾害 *build irrigation works to prevent droughts and floods* ❷ remit; excuse; exempt; relieve: ～债务 *remit a debt* / ～一项任务 *excuse sb. from a task; relieve sb. of a task* / ～处罚 *be exempt from (criminal) punishment*

【免得】so as not to; so as to avoid: 多问几句,～走错路。*Make some more inquiries so that you won't go the wrong way*. / 我再说明一下,～引起误会。*To avoid any misunderstanding, let me explain once again*.

【免费】free of charge; free; gratis: ～医疗 *free medical care* / ～入场 *admission free; be admitted gratis*

【免耕农业】till-less agriculture

【免冠】❶ take one's hat off (in salutation) ❷ without a hat on; bareheaded: 半身～正面相片 *a half-length, bareheaded, full-faced photo*

【免检】exempt from inspection; inspection-free

【免开尊口】please keep your mouth shut (i.e. not broach the ticklish topic)

【免赔条款】franchise clause

【免票】❶ free pass; free ticket ❷ free of charge: 身高不满一米的儿童～ *free of charge for children under a metre in height*.

【免试】❶ (又作'免考') be exempted from an examination (for admission to college or for promotion): ～入学 *be exempted from the entrance examination (to a school or college)* ❷ be exempted from a test

【免税】❶ exempt from taxation ❷ tax-free; duty-free ◇ ～货物 duty-free goods; ～利润 tax-free profits; ～期 tax holiday; ～商店 duty-free shop; ～投资 tax-free investment; ～物品 free goods; ～证券 tax-exempt securities

【免俗】(often used in the negative) act contrary to common practice: 未能～ *unable to break away from convention*

【免烫】[纺] easy-care; non-ironing

【免刑】[法] exempt from punishment

【免修】be excused from a college course

【免验】exempt from customs examination: ～放行 *pass without examination (P. W. E.)* ◇ ～证 laissez-passer

【免役】exempt from military service

【免疫】[医] immunity (from disease): 后天～ *acquired immunity* / 先天～ *congenital immunity* ◇ ～力 immunity (from disease); 〈喻〉immune to unhealthy ideas; ～球蛋白 immunoglobulin; ～体 immune body; ～性 immunity; ～证书 bill of health; ～治疗 immunization therapy

【免于公诉】[法] immunity from prosecution

【免予起诉】[法] exempt from prosecution: ～决定书 *decision to exempt from prosecution*

【免予处罚】remit

【免战牌】a sign used in ancient times to show refusal to fight

【免征】exempt from taxation

【免职】remove sb. from office; relieve sb. of his post

【免致后患】avoid causing future trouble

【免罪】exempt from punishment

勉 动 ❶ exert oneself; strive: 奋勉 ❷ encourage; urge; exhort: 互～ *encourage one another* / 自～ *spur oneself on* ❸ strive to do what is beyond one's power: 勉强

【勉力】exert oneself; try hard; make great efforts: ～为之 *exert oneself to the utmost; do one's best*

【勉励】encourage; urge: 他～学生努力学习。*He urged his students to work hard*.

【勉强】❶ manage with an effort; do with difficulty: 病人～喝了点粥。*With an effort the patient ate some gruel*. or *The patient forced himself to take a few mouthful of gruel*. ❷ reluctant; grudging: ～协助(许诺) *give reluctant assistance (a reluctant promise)* / ～同意 *reluctantly agree* / ～地笑了笑 *force a smile* / ❸ force sb. to do sth.: 要是他不愿意去,就不要～他。*If he doesn't want to go, don't force him to*. ❹ inadequate; unconvincing; strained; farfetched: 你的理由很～。*The reason you give is rather unconvincing*. ❺ barely enough: ～的多数 *a bare majority* / ～维持生活 *eke out a bare living; scrape along*

【勉为其难】undertake to do a difficult job as best one can; agree to do what one knows is beyond one's ability or power

娩 动 give birth to: 分娩

冕 名 crown (worn by an emperor, etc.): 加冕

湎 动 indulge; be given to

【湎于酒色】indulging in wine and lewdness

缅 形 remote; far back

【缅甸】Myanmar；Burma ◇ ～人 Myanmese；Burmese；～语 Myanmese (language)；Burmese
【缅怀】cherish the memory of；recall：～革命先烈 *cherish the memory of our revolutionary martyrs* / ～往事 *recall past events*
【缅邈】〈书〉remote；far back
【缅茄】［植］Shan pahudia (Pahudia xylocarpa)
【缅想】think of (past events)；recall

腼（构词成分）见下
【腼腆】shy；bashful：这孩子见了生人有点～。*The child is shy with strangers.*

miàn

面 Ⅰ 名 ❶ face：～带笑容 *with a smile on one's face* / ～无惧色 *not look at all afraid* / 看在我的～上，饶了他这一回吧。*Please let him off this time just for my sake.* ❷ surface；top；face：钟～ *clock face*；*dial* / ～儿磨得很光。*The surface has been polished shining bright.* ❸ side：这种纸一～光。*This kind of paper is smooth on one side.* / 这本书有多少～？*How many pages are there in this book?* ❹ the right side；cover；outside：书～儿 *the cover of a book* / 夹袄的～儿 *the outside of a lined jacket* / 这块布做里儿，那块布做～儿。*Use this piece of cloth for the lining and use that piece for the outside.* ❺ extent；range；scale；scope：知识～广(窄) *have a wide (narrow) range of knowledge* / 这次讨论涉及的～很广。*The discussion covered a wide range of topics.* ❻ wheat flour；flour：大米～ *rice flour* ❼ powder：药～儿 *medicinal powder* / 胡椒～儿 *ground pepper* ❽ noodles：一碗～ *a bowl of noodles* ❾ an entire area (as opposed to particular points)：部长下去蹲点了，～上的工作他让我来抓。*The minister has gone to work at a grass-roots unit and left me in charge of the ministry.* Ⅱ 动 face (a certain direction)：这房子～南坐北。*The house faces south.* Ⅲ 量 ❶ surface：立方体有六～。*A cube has six surfaces.* ❷ (for flat things)：一～镜子 *a mirror* / 两～旗子 *two flags* Ⅳ 副 personally；directly：～告 *tell sb. personally* Ⅴ (方位词后缀)(to a noun of locality)：前面/后面 Ⅵ 形 soft and floury：这块白薯真～。*This sweet potato is soft and floury.*
【面包】bread ◇ ～房 bakery；～干 rusk；～酵母 baker's yeast；～渣儿 breadcrumbs；crumbs
【面包车】minibus；small van
【面包果】［植］breadfruit
【面包师】baker
【面禀】report (to one's superior) in person
【面不改色】not change colour；remain calm；without turning a hair；without batting an eyelid：～心不跳 *remain absolutely calm*
【面茶】seasoned millet mush
【面陈】tell or explain in person
【面呈】submit in person
【面斥】give sb. a talking-to；reprove
【面辞】go to say good-bye to sb.；take leave of sb.
【面从后言】say yes to sb.'s face but begin to carp the moment his back is turned
【面带病容】one's face shows sickly countenance
【面带愁容】with a sad air
【面带笑意】one's face shows smiling mood
【面的】minibus taxi：打个～ *take a minibus taxi*
【面点】snacks made from wheat or rice flour
【面对】face；confront：～现实 *face reality*；*be realistic* / ～危险情况，镇定自若 *remain calm in the face of danger*
【面对面】facing each other；face-to-face；vis-à-vis：～地坐着 *sit face-to-face*；*sit vis-à-vis*
【面额】❶［经］denomination：各种～的纸币 *banknotes of different denominations* ❷ forehead
【面肥】❶ leavening dough；leaven ❷［农］top-dressing
【面粉】wheat flour；flour ◇ ～厂 flour mill
【面疙瘩】balls of dough：～汤 *dough ball soup* / 炒～ *fried dough balls*
【面革】upper leather
【面和心不和】remain friendly in appearance but estranged at heart
【面红耳赤】be red in the face；be flushed：争得～ *argue until everyone is red in the face*；*have a heated argument* / 羞得～ *blush with shame or shyness*
【面糊】❶ paste ❷〈方〉soft and floury：面条煮得太～了。*The noodles are cooked almost to a pulp.*
【面黄肌瘦】sallow and emaciated；lean and haggard
【面积】area：棉花种植～ *the acreage under cotton* / 展览会～为三千平方米。*The exhibition covers a floor space of 3,000 square metres.*
【面颊】cheek
【面交】deliver personally；hand-deliver
【面巾】〈方〉towel ◇ ～纸 face tissues
【面筋】gluten
【面具】mask：防毒～ *gas mask*
【面孔】face：和蔼(严肃)的～ *a kind (stern) face* / 板起～ *put on a stern expression* / 装出一副救世主的～ *assume the guise of a saviour*
【面料】material for making the outside (of a garment)
【面临】be faced with；be confronted with；be up against：～一场严重的危机 *be faced with a serious crisis* / 我们正～一场新的斗争。*A new struggle lies ahead of us.*
【面聆】hear sb.'s words of wisdom in person
【面貌】❶ face；features：他俩的～十分相似。*The two of them look very much alike.* ❷ appearance (of things)；look；aspect：精神～ *mental outlook (or attitude)* / ～一新 *take on a new look (or aspect)* / 一个国家的社会经济～ *the social and economic physiognomy of a country*
【面面观】comprehensive survey；full overview：中国保险市场～ *detailed overview of China's insur-*

ance market

【面面俱到】attend to each and every aspect of a matter：文章因篇幅有限，不可能讲得～。*Limitation of space forbids full treatment of the subject.* / 我没看到的，你都看到了，真是～。*You can see all the things that I can't；you don't miss a thing.*

【面面相觑】look at each other in blank dismay；gaze at each other in speechless despair

【面膜】face-pack；mask

【面目】❶ face；features；visage：～清秀 *of fine and delicate features* ❷ appearance (of things)；look；aspect ❸ self-respect；honour；sense of shame；face：愧无～见人 *feel too ashamed to face people*

【面目可憎】repulsive in appearance

【面目全非】be changed beyond recognition：照那样改动，～，就不是原来的《茶馆》了。*If the play is changed the way like that, it will be completely disfigured and no longer recognizable as the original Teahouse.*

【面目一新】take on an entirely new look；present a completely new appearance；assume a new aspect

【面目狰狞】ferocious features；a vile visage

【面嫩】❶ look younger than one's age ❷ shy；bashful；sensitive

【面庞】contours of the face；face：圆圆的～ *a round face*

【面盆】〈方〉❶ washbasin；washbowl ❷ bowl for kneading dough

【面皮】❶ face；cheek ❷ rapper (of dumpling)

【面洽】discuss with sb. face to face；take up a matter with sb. personally：有关事宜，请找张同志～。*For particulars, please go and see Comrade Zhang.*

【面前】in (the) face of；in front of；before：在事实～ *in the face of the truth* / 我们～困难还多，不可忽视。*There are still many difficulties ahead which we must not overlook.*

【面罄】〈书〉explain in detail personally

【面人儿】dough figurine

【面容】facial features；face：～消瘦 *look emaciated*

【面如死灰】look like dying embers —be deathly pale due to fright or poor health

【面如土色】look ashen；look pale：吓得～ *turn pale with fright*

【面色】❶ complexion：～苍白 *look pale* / ～红润 *have rosy cheeks；be ruddy-cheeked* ❷ facial expression：～忧郁 *have a melancholy look；look worried*

【面纱】veil

【面善】❶ look familiar：他很～。*He looks familiar to me.* ❷ affable；amiable：～心慈 *affable and kind-hearted*

【面商】discuss with sb. face to face；consult personally

【面上】general；overall：主持～工作 *manage the general work*

【面上无光】loss of prestige

【面神经】［生理］facial nerve

【面生】look unfamiliar：这个人～得很。*I don't think I've seen this person before.*

【面食】cooked wheaten food

【面试】interview

【面世】(of writing, product, etc.) come into existence；come out；be published：新产品年内可望～ *The new product is expected to come out within the year.*

【面授】instruct personally；classroom teaching：～机宜 *personally instruct sb. on the line of action to pursue；give a confidential briefing；brief sb. on how to act*

【面熟】look familiar：这人看着～，就是想不起来是谁。*That person looks familiar but I simply can't place him.*

【面谈】speak to sb. face to face；take up a matter with sb. personally

【面汤】❶ water in which noodles have been boiled ❷ noodles in soup ❸〈方〉hot water for washing face

【面条】noodles

【面团】dough

【面无人色】look ghastly pale：他惊恐得～，像僵了似的。*His face was ghastly and he seemed paralysed.*

【面向】❶ turn one's face to；turn in the direction of；face：～党旗庄严宣誓 *stand facing the Party flag and make a solemn vow* ❷ be geared to the needs of；cater to：～四个现代化 *be geared to the needs of the four modernizations* / ～基层 *cater to (or meet) the needs of grass-roots units* / ～出口 *be export-oriented*

【面相】〈书〉facial features；looks；appearance

【面谢】thank sb. in person

【面议】negotiate face to face；take up a matter with sb. personally

【面有菜色】look famished

【面有难色】show signs of reluctance or embarrassment

【面谕】〈书〉(of superiors or elders) instruct or tell sb. in person

【面誉背毁】praise sb. to his face and abuse him behind his back；praise openly and slander secretly

【面罩】face guard

【面值】❶ par value；face value；nominal value ❷ denomination

【面砖】［建］face brick

【面子】❶ outer part；outside；face：大衣的～ *the outside of an overcoat* ❷ reputation；prestige；face：保全～ *save face* / 撕破～ *cast aside all considerations of face；not spare sb.'s sensibilities* / 有～ *enjoy due respect* / 给～ *show due respect for sb.'s feelings* ❸ feelings；sensibilities：给某人留～ *spare sb.'s feelings* / 不顾～ *have no consideration for sb.'s feelings* ——另见〖驳面

子】;【买面子】

眄 动 give a sidelong glance

【眄视】〈书〉give a sidelong glance

miāo

喵 象 mew; miaow

miáo

苗 名 ❶ young plant; seedling: 麦～儿 *wheat seedling* / 这女孩看来是个游泳的好～～。*The girl is showing great promise as a swimmer.* ❷ the young of some animals: 鱼苗 ❸ vaccine: 卡介苗 ❹ sth. resembling a young plant: 火苗

【苗儿】〈方〉symptom of a trend; suggestion of a new development

【苗床】seedbed

【苗而不秀】put forth shoots that fail to flower—show great potentialities but fail to fulfil them

【苗木】[林] forestry nursery stock

【苗圃】nursery (of young plants)

【苗期】[农] seedling stage

【苗条】(of a woman) slender; slim: 身材～ *have a slim figure*

【苗头】symptom of a trend; suggestion of a new development: 他一看～不对就溜了。*He slipped off when he saw what was going to happen.*

【苗裔】〈书〉progeny; descendants; offspring

【苗子】❶〈方〉young plant; seedling ❷ young successor ❸〈方〉symptom of a trend; suggestion of a new development

【苗族】the Miao nationality, or the Miaos of China

描 动 ❶ trace; copy: ～图样 *trace designs; copy designs* ❷ touch up; retouch: ～眉 *pencil (or paint) one's eyebrows* / 练毛笔字,一笔是一笔,不要～。*In practising Chinese calligraphy, write with a sure hand — don't retouch.*

【描红】trace in black ink over characters printed in red (in learning to write with a brush)

【描画】draw; paint; depict; describe: ～出美好的前景 *paint a bright future*

【描绘】depict; describe; portray: 这幅画～了西湖的景色。*The painting gives a view of the West Lake.*

【描金】[工美] trace a design in gold

【描龙绣凤】do fine needlework

【描摹】depict; portray; delineate

【描述】describe: 详细～事情的经过 *describe what happened in great detail*

【描图】tracing ◇ ～员 tracer; ～纸 tracing paper

【描写】describe; depict; portray: ～一位优秀画家的成长过程 *describe how he grew up to be an outstanding painter*

【描写语言学】descriptive linguistics

瞄 动 concentrate one's gaze on; take aim: ～得准,打得狠 *take good aim and hit hard*

【瞄准】take aim; aim; train on; lay; sight: 练习～ *practise aiming* / ～靶心 *aim at the bull's-eye* ◇ ～环 ring sight; ～具 sighting device; (gun) sight; ～手 layer; pointer

miǎo

秒 量 second (= 1 / 60 of a minute)

【秒表】stopwatch; chronograph

【秒差距】[天] parsec

【秒立方米】[水] cubic metre per second

【秒针】second hand (of a clock or watch)

渺 形 ❶ (of an expanse of water) vast ❷ distant and indistinct; vague: ～无人迹 *remote and uninhabited* / ～若烟云 *as vague as mist* ❸ tiny; insignificant: ～不足道 *insignificant; negligible; not worth mentioning*

【渺茫】❶ distant and indistinct; vague: 他走后音信～。*We haven't heard from him since he left.* ❷ uncertain: 前途～ *have an uncertain future* / 希望～ *have slim hopes (of success)*

【渺若烟云】as vague as nist

【渺无人烟】uninhabited; without a trace of human habitation

【渺无音信】there has been no news whatsoever about sb.; never been heard of since

【渺小】tiny; negligible; insignificant; paltry: 个人的力量是～的。*The strength of an individual is insignificant.*

【渺远】faraway; distant; remote

淼 形〈书〉(of an expanse of water) vast: 浩淼

【淼茫】(of an expanse of water) stretch as far as the eye can see

邈 形〈书〉faraway; remote: 绵邈

【邈远】faraway; distant; remote

藐 Ⅰ 形 small; petty: 藐小 Ⅱ 动 slight; despise

【藐视】despise; look down upon: ～法律 *defiance of law* / ～法庭 *contempt of court*

【藐小】tiny; negligible; insignificant; paltry

miào

妙 形 ❶ wonderful; excellent; fine: ～极了! *Wonderful!* / 这主意真～。*That's an excellent idea.* ❷ ingenious; clever; subtle: 深得其中之～ *have got the trick of it; fully appreciate its subtlety* / 他回答得很～。*He made a clever answer.*

【妙笔】ingenious or exquisite writing: ～生花 *ingenious writing with exquisite description*

【妙不可言】too wonderful for words; most intriguing

【妙处】❶ ideal place；suitable location：西山是休养的～。*The Western Hills is an ideal place for rest and recuperation.* ❷ merit；advantage；fine point

【妙计】（又作'妙策'）an excellent plan；a brilliant scheme：想出一条～ *hit upon an excellent idea*

【妙境】fairyland；wonderland

【妙句】a beautiful sentence；a well-turned phrase

【妙诀】a clever way；an ingenious method

【妙龄】youthfulness（of a girl）：～少女 *a young lady* / 正当～ *be in the bloom of（a girl's）youth*

【妙论】an ingenious remark；a very clever remark

【妙品】❶ fine quality goods：调味～ *best-quality condiment* ❷ fine work of art

【妙棋】a clever（chess）move

【妙趣横生】full of wit and humour；very witty

【妙手回春】（of a doctor）effect a miraculous cure and bring the dying back to life

【妙手空空】❶ petty（or sneak）thief；pilferer ❷ not own a thing in the world；not have a thing to one's name

【妙算】wonderful foresight；accurate calculations

【妙药】efficacious medicine；wonder drug

【妙用】magical effect：小小银针，大有～。*A tiny acupuncture needle can work wonders.*

【妙语】witty remark；witticism：妙人～ *a clever person and his clever remarks* ◇ ～解颐 witty remarks that make people laugh；wisecracks that really tickle；～惊人 an unsurpassed beauty of expression；～如珠 a stream of witticism；～双关 a very clever pun

【妙在不言中】the charm lies in what is left unsaid

庙 名 ❶ temple；shrine：❷ temple fair：赶～ *go to the fair*

【庙号】posthumous title of an emperor

【庙会】temple fair；fair

【庙堂】❶ the Imperial Ancestral Temple ❷ imperial court

【庙宇】temple

【庙主】head priest of a temple

【庙祝】temple attendant in charge of incense and religious service；acolyte

miē

乜（构词成分）见下

【乜斜】❶ squint：他～着眼睛，眼角挂着讥诮的微笑。*He squinted with a sneering look in the corner of his eye.* ❷（of eyes）half-closed：～的睡眼 *half-closed eyes heavy with sleep*

咩 象 baa；bleat

miè

灭 动 ❶（of a light, fire, etc.）go out：火～了。*The fire has gone out.* / 灯突然～了。*All of a sudden the lights went out.* ❷ extinguish；put out；turn off：消防队很快就把火～了。*The fire brigade soon put out the fire.* / 请把烟～了。*Please stub out（or extinguish）your cigarette.* ❸ submerge；drown：灭顶 ❹ destroy；exterminate；wipe out：～蝇 *kill flies*

【灭茬】［农］clean stubble（fields）：～机 *stubble cleaner*

【灭虫宁】［药］bephenium

【灭此朝食】will not have breakfast until the enemy is wiped out—be anxious to finish off the enemy immediately

【灭滴灵】［药］metronidazole；flagyl

【灭顶】be drowned ◇ ～之灾 getting drowned

【灭火】❶ put out a fire；extinguish a fire ❷ cut out an engine ◇ ～剂 fire-extinguishing chemical（or agent）；～器 fire extinguisher

【灭迹】destroy the evidence（of one's evildoing）

【灭尽天良】destroy utterly one's conscience

【灭绝】❶ become extinct：现已～的动物 *extinct animals* ❷ completely lose

【灭绝人性】inhuman；savage；cannibalistic：～的暴行 *inhuman atrocities*

【灭绝种族】genocide

【灭口】do away with a witness or accomplice：杀人～ *silence a witness by killing him；kill sb. to prevent him from disclosing a secrect*

【灭门】exterminate an entire family ◇ ～之灾 the calamity of exterminating a family

【灭绦灵】［药］niclosamide

【灭亡】be destroyed；become extinct；die out：逃脱不了～的命运 *be doomed to destruction* / 汉朝的～使中国陷入了分裂的局面。*The downfall of the Han Dynasty brought China national disunity.*

【灭音器】muffler

【灭种】exterminate a race；commit genocide

【灭族】extermination of an entire family（a punishment in ancient China）

蔑 Ⅰ 动 slight；disdain：轻蔑 Ⅱ 副 nothing；none：～以复加 *in the extreme*

【蔑称】❶ call in contempt：我常被她～为傻瓜蛋。*I'm often scornfully referred to as a fool by her.* ❷ contemptuous name

【蔑视】despise；show contempt for；scorn：～某人 *hold sb. in contempt* / ～妇女 *look down upon women*

【蔑视法庭】［法］contempt of court

篾 名 ❶ thin bamboo strip ❷ the rind of reed or sorghum

【篾黄】the inner skin of a bamboo stem

【篾匠】a craftsman who makes articles from bamboo strips

【篾片】❶ thin bamboo strip ❷ old hanger-on；sycophant

【篾青】the outer cuticle of a bamboo stem

【篾条】bamboo strip

【篾席】a mat made of thin bamboo strips

mín

民 Ⅰ[名] ❶ the people：人民 ❷ a member of a nationality：回民 ❸ a person of a certain occupation：农民 / 牧民 ❹ civilian：军民 Ⅱ[形] of the people；folk：民歌

【民安国泰】The masses are in peace and the country is prosperous.

【民办】be run by the local people：～公助 *be run by the local people and subsidized by the state* ◇ ～教师 non-state employed teachers；～小学 a primary school run by the local people

【民变】mass uprising；popular revolt

【民兵】❶ people's militia；militia：～师 *a contingent of the people's militia* ❷ militiaman：女～ *militiawoman*

【民不聊生】the people have no means of livelihood；the masses live in dire poverty；the people are destitute：军阀混战，～。*Incessant fighting among the warlords made life impossible for the people.*

【民粹主义】populism

【民法】civil law ◇ ～典 civil code

【民防】civil defence

【民房】a house owned by a citizen；a private house

【民愤】popular indignation；the people's wrath：～极大 *have earned the bitter hatred of the people；have incurred the greatest popular indignation*

【民风】folkways；local traits ◇ ～淳朴 the people are simple，honest and unspoiled

【民富国强】The people live in plenty and the country is strong.

【民歌】folk song

【民工】a labourer working on a public project

【民国】the Republic of China (1912-1949)

【民航】〈略〉见〖民用航空〗

【民航机】civil aircraft；civil airplane

【民间】❶ among the people；popular；folk：～验方 *folk remedy；folk recipe* ❷ nongovernmental；people-to-people ◇ ～传说 popular legend；folk legend；folklore；～故事 folktale；folk story；～疾苦 hardships of the people；～纠纷 dispute among the people；～来往 nongovernmental contact；people-to-people exchange；～诗人 folk bard；～文学 folk literature；～舞蹈 folk dance；～艺术 folk art；～音乐 folk music；～协定 nongovernmental agreement；～组织 a nongovernmental organization

【民警】people's police；policeman or policewoman：女～ *people's policewoman*

【民居】local-style dwelling houses

【民康物阜】products abound and the people live in peace

【民力】financial resources of the people

【民萌】(又作'民氓') the masses of the people；the common people

【民气】the people's morale；popular morale

【民情】❶ condition of the people：熟悉地理～ *be familiar with the place and the people* ❷ feelings of the people；public feeling：不了解～ *fail to keep abreast of public feeling*

【民穷财尽】The people are impoverished and the nation's resources exhausted；the people are destitute and the national economy is in dire straits.

【民权】civil rights；civil liberties；democratic rights

【民权主义】the Principle of Democracy ——另见〖三民主义〗

【民生】the people's livelihood：国计～ *the national economy and the people's livelihood*

【民生凋敝】the people live in destitution：～、民怨沸腾、民变峰起的严重危机 *a grave crisis of mass impoverishment，seething discontent and widespread revolt*

【民生主义】the Principle of the People's Livelihood ——另见〖三民主义〗

【民事】[法] relating to civil law；civil ◇ ～案件 civil case；～法律关系 civil legal relationship；～法庭 civil court；～诽谤罪 civil libel；～管辖权 civil jurisdiction；～过失 civil negligence；～纠纷 civil litigation；～立法 civil legislation；～赔偿 civil compensation；～侵法权 law of tort；～上诉 civil appeal；～审判庭 the civil division of a people's court；civil court；～诉讼 civil action；～诉讼法 civil procedure act；～调解 civil mediation；～责任 civil liability

【民俗】folk custom；folkways ◇ ～学 folklore

【民团】civil corps (formerly，reactionary local armed forces organized by landlords)

【民心】popular feelings；common aspiration of the people：深得～ *enjoy the ardent support of the people* / ～所向 *where the popular will inclines；(what conforms to) the common aspiration of the people*

【民谚】common proverb

【民谣】folk rhyme (esp. of the topical and political type)

【民以食为天】The masses regard food as their heaven (i.e. as their prime want).

【民意】the will of the people；popular will：～测验 *public opinion poll；poll*

【民营】run by private citizens：转为～ *turn over to private management* / ～企业 *enterprise run by private citizens*

【民用】for civil use；civil ◇ ～产品 products for civil use；～航空 civil aviation；～机场 civil airport

【民怨沸腾】the people are boiling with resentment；seething popular discontent：军阀混战，～。*Warlords fought one another and popular grievances ran high.*

【民乐】music，esp. folk music，for traditional instruments ◇ ～队 traditional instruments orchestra；～合奏 ensemble of traditional instruments

【民运】❶ civil transport ❷ the army's propaganda and organizational work among the civilians during the revolutionary wars led by the Chinese Communist Party ❸ mass movement；mass campaign
【民贼】traitor to the people
【民宅】a private (or civilian) residence
【民政】civil administration ◇ ～机关 civil administration organ
【民脂民膏】flesh and blood of the people：反动政府搜刮～。*The reactionary government fed on the flesh and blood of the people*.
【民众】the masses of the people；the common people；the populace ◇ ～团体 people's organization；mass organization
【民主】❶ democracy；democratic rights ❷ democratic：他作风～。*He has a democratic workstyle*. ◇ ～党 the Democratic Party (in U. S.)；～改革 democratic reform；～革命 democratic revolution；～共和国 democratic republic；～集中制 democratic centralism；～人士 democratic personage；～生活 democratic life；～协商 democratic consultation
【民主党派】democratic parties
【民族】nation；nationality；ethnic group：国内各～的团结 *the unity of our various nationalities* ◇ ～败类 scum of a nation；～大家庭 the great family of nationalities；～大义 supreme interests of the nation；～动乱 ethnic unrest；～独立 national independence；～复兴 revival of nationhood；national rejuvenation；～革命 national revolution；～共同语 common national language；～解放运动 national liberation movement；～精神 national spirit；national pride；～利己主义 national egoism；～民主革命 national-democratic revolution；～歧视 ethnic discrimination；～气节 national integrity；～区域自治 regional autonomy of minority nationalities；regional national autonomy；～学 ethnology；～意识 national consciousness；～英雄 national hero；～杂居地区 multi-national area；～政策 policy towards nationalities；～资产阶级 national bourgeoisie；～自决 national self-determination；～自信心 national confidence；～自治 autonomy of minority nationalities；～自尊心 national pride；national self-respect；～尊严 national dignity
【民族主义】❶ nationalism ❷ the Principle of Nationalism ——另见〖三民主义〗

mǐn

泯 动 vanish；die out：永存不～ *be everlasting；be immortal* / 良心未～ *still have some conscience；not be devoid of conscience*
【泯灭】die out；disappear；vanish：难以～的印象 *an indelible impression*
【泯没】vanish；sink into oblivion；become lost：烈士的功绩永远不会～。*The contributions of the revolutionary martyrs will never be forgotten*.
【泯弃宿怨】disregard old grievances

抿 动 ❶ smooth (hair, etc.) with a wet brush：～了～头发 *give a few touches to one's hair (with a brush)* ❷ close lightly；furl；tuck：～着嘴笑 *smile with closed lips；compress one's lips to smile* / 水鸟儿一～翅膀，钻入水中。*The water bird tucked its wings and dived into the water*. ❸ sip：～一口酒 *take a sip of wine*
【抿子】a small hairbrush (used by a woman)

悯 Ⅰ 动 commiserate；pity：其情可～。*His case deserves sympathy*. Ⅱ 形 sorrow
【悯恻】〈书〉feel compassion for；pity
【悯惜】take pity on；have pity for
【悯恤】feel compassion for；pity

敏 形 quick；nimble；agile：～于应对 *quick at repartee*
【敏感】sensitive；susceptible：政治～性 *political sensitivity* / 他是一个对语言十分～的人。*He has a tremendous feeling for language*. ◇ ～度 susceptibility；～市场 sensitive market；～元件〔无〕sensitive element；sensor
【敏化】〔物〕sensibilization；sensitization：◇ ～剂 sensitizer；～纸 sensitized paper
【敏慧】bright；intelligent
【敏捷】quick；nimble；agile：动作～ *be quick in movement*
【敏锐】sharp；acute；keen：～的政治眼光 *keen political insight* / 目光～ *have sharp eyes；be sharp-eyed* / 听觉～ *have good (or sharp) ears* / 嗅觉～ *have a keen sense of smell*

míng

名 Ⅰ 名 ❶ name：一种～为九二〇的生长激素 *a growth hormone known as 920* / 他～叫张南。*His name is Zhang Nan*. or *He is called Zhang Nan*. ❷ excuse；false prentences：以出差为～游山玩水 *take a pleasure trip in the guise of a business trip* ❸ fame；reputation；renown：不为～，不为利 *seek neither fame nor gain* / ～闻中外 *be well-known both at home and abroad* Ⅱ 动 ❶ given name：这位同志姓李～大刚。*This comrade's surname is Li and his given name, Dagang*. ❷ express；describe：不可名状 Ⅲ 形 famous；celebrated；well-known；noted：～厨师 *a famous chef* / ～诗人 *a noted poet* / ～教授 *a well-known (or prominent) professor* Ⅳ 量 (for people)：十二～学生 *twelve students*
【名不副实】(又作'名不符实') the name falls short of the reality；be sth. more in name than in reality；be unworthy of the name or title：一个～的军事学家 *not a military expert in the real sense of the term*
【名不虚传】have a well-deserved reputation；deserve the reputation one enjoys；live up to one's

reputation
【名不正，言不顺】if names are not right，arguments will not be tenable
【名菜】famous dish；speciality dish：～谱 *menu of speciality dishes*
【名册】（又作'名籍'）register；roll：学生～ *students' register*；*students' roll* / 部队～ *muster roll* / 工作人员～ *personnel roll*
【名茶】famous brand of tea：龙井是我国的～。*Longjing* (*or Dragon Well*) *is a famous brand of tea in China*.
【名产】famous product：织锦是杭州的～。*Brocade is a famous product of Hangzhou*.
【名称】name (of a thing or organization)
【名城】a famous city：历史～ *a city famous for its historical associations*
【名垂青史】go down in history；be crowned with eternal glory
【名词】❶［语］noun；substantive ❷ term；phrase：化学～ *chemical term* ❸［逻］name
【名次】position in a name list；place in a competition：按比赛成绩排列～ *arrange the names of contestants in the order of their results*
【名存实亡】cease to exist except in name；exist in name only
【名单】name list：入伍～ *list of recruits*
【名额】the number of people assigned or allowed；quota of people：代表～ *the number of deputies to be elected or sent* / 招生～ *the number of students to be enrolled*；*planned enrolment figure*
【名分】a person's status
【名孚众望】prestige commands public confidence
【名副其实】the name matches the reality；be sth. in reality as well as in name；be worthy of the name：一个～的共产党员 *a Party member in the real sense of the term* / 这真是～的奇迹。*That's a veritable miracle*.
【名贵】famous and precious；rare：～药材 *rare medicinal herbs* / ～的字画 *priceless scrolls of calligraphy and painting*
【名过其实】be sth. more in name than in reality；have an undeserved reputation
【名号】person's official and courtesy names；person's name
【名家】❶ the School of Logicians (in the Spring and Autumn and Warring States Periods，770-221 B.C.) ❷ a person of academic or artistic distinction；famous expert；master
【名缰利锁】the fetters of fame and wealth
【名将】famous general；great soldier：足球～ *a football hero* (*or star*)
【名教】the Confucian ethical code
【名句】a well-known phrase；a much quoted line
【名款】the name of the painter or writer inscribed on a painting or a piece of calligraphy
【名利】fame and gain；fame and wealth：～思想 *desire for personal fame and gain* / 不求～ *not seek fame and gain*
【名利场】Vanity Fair
【名利双收】gain both fame and wealth
【名列前茅】be among the best of the successful candidates
【名流】distinguished personages；celebrities
【名落孙山】fall behind Sun Shan (who was last on the list of successful candidates)—fail in a competitive examination
【名门】an old and well-known family；a distinguished family；an illustrious family ◇ ～闺秀 daughter of an illustrious family；～望族 distinguished family；prominent family；～之后 descendant of an illustrious family
【名模】famous model
【名目】names of things；items
【名目繁多】a multitude of names (or items)；names of every description：解放前，苛捐杂税，～。*Before liberation there were exorbitant taxes and levies of every sort under the sun*.
【名牌】❶ famous brand：优质～商品 *famous-brand quality products* / 创～ *establish a brand* / ～香烟 *a famous brand of cigarettes* / ～产品 *best brands of products* / ～大学 *a prestigious university* ❷ nameplate；name tag
【名片】visiting card；calling card：留下～ *leave one's card*
【名气】〈口〉reputation；fame；name：有点～ *enjoy some reputation*；*be quite well-known*；*have made a name for oneself* / 她在我们这儿还小有～呢！*She's quite popular here*.
【名曲】a great musical composition；a masterpiece in music
【名人】famous person；eminent person；celebrity；notable：～墨迹 *original work by a famous calligrapher or painter* / 文化界～ *celebrities in cultural circles*
【名山大川】famous mountains and great rivers
【名山事业】commitment to literature
【名声】reputation；repute；renown：～很坏 *have an unsavoury reputation*；*be held in ill repute*；*be notorious*
【名胜】a place famous for its scenery or historical relics；scenic spot
【名胜古迹】places of historic interest and scenic beauty；scenic spots and historical sites
【名师出高徒】A great teacher produces a brilliant student.
【名手】a famous artist，player，etc.
【名数】❶［数］concrete number ❷ numeral-classifier compound (as 三斤，四尺二寸)
【名堂】❶ variety；item：这个坏家伙又在搞什么～？*What's that villain up to now*？❷ result；achievement：问了他半天也没问出个～。*I questioned him for a long time but couldn't get anything out of him*. ❸ what lies behind sth.；reason：墙角上的砖这么砌是有～的。*There's a reason for laying the corner bricks this way*.
【名头】〈方〉reputation；repute；renown
【名望】fame and prestige；good reputation；renown：有～的大夫 *a famous doctor*

【名位】fame and position

【名下】under sb.'s name; belonging or related to sb.: 这笔账就记在我～吧。*Charge these expenses to my account.* / 这事怎么搞到我～来了? *How could it be my fault?* or *How could it have anything to do with me?*

【名下无虚】deserve the reputation one enjoys; live up to one's reputation

【名言】well-known saying; celebrated dictum; famous remark

【名扬四海】become famous all over the world; be world-renowned

【名义】❶ name: 以会议执行主席的～ *in one's capacity as executive chairman of the conference* ❷ (usu. followed by 上) nominal; titular; in name: ～上裁军,实际上扩军 *disarmament in name, armament in reality* ◇ ～被告 nominal defendant; ～代理 ostensible agency; ～代理权 ostensible authority; ～当事人 nominal party; ～负债 nominal liability; ～工资［经］nominal wages; ～合伙人 nominal partner; ～汇价［经］nominal rate (of exchange); ～所得 nominal income; ～原告 nominal plaintiff

【名优】a famous actor or actress; ～产品 *famous quality products*

【名誉】❶ fame; reputation: ～好 *have a good reputation; be of high repute; be held in high esteem* ❷ honorary ◇ ～公民 honorary citizen; ～会员 honorary member; ～主席 honorary chairman; honorary president

【名噪一时】gain considerable fame among one's contemporaries

【名正言顺】the name is correct and what is said accords with reason—perfectly justifiable; fitting and proper

【名著】famous book; famous work: 文学～ *a famous literary work; a literary masterpiece*

【名状】(usu. used in the negative) give the right name for; describe: 难以～的奇花异草 *exotic flowers and rare plants that words fail to describe*

【名字】❶ name or given name: 您叫什么～? *What's your name?* or *May I know your name?* ❷ name (of a thing): 这种花的～很特别。*This flower has a peculiar name.*

【名作】(literary) masterpiece

明

Ⅰ **形** ❶ bright; brilliant; light: ～月 *a bright moon* / 天已微～。*Day is breaking.* ❷ clear; distinct: 真理愈辩愈～。*The more truth is debated, the clearer it becomes.* / ～心迹 *make one's intention clear; lay bare one's true feelings* / 问～来意 *ask what sb. has come for* ❸ open; overt; explicit: 有不同意见～着说。*Those who differ should air their views openly.* ❹ sharp-eyed; clear-sighted: 眼明手快 ❺ aboveboard; honest: 明人不做暗事 ❻ immediately following in time: ～春 *next spring* / ～晚 *tomorrow evening* Ⅱ **名** ❶ sight: 失明 ❷ the Ming Dynasty (1368-1644) Ⅲ **动** understand; know: ～是非 *know the difference between right and wrong; know right from wrong*

【明儿】〈口〉❶ tomorrow: ～见。*See you tomorrow.* ❷ one of these days; some day: ～你长大了,也开拖拉机好不好? *What about you becoming a tractor driver too when you grow up?*

【明暗】light and shade ◇ ～对照法［美］chiaroscuro

【明摆着】obvious; clear; plain: 这不是～的事儿吗? *Isn't this obvious?* or *Isn't it as clear as daylight?*

【明白】❶ clear; obvious; plain: 他讲得～易懂。*He spoke clearly and simply.* ❷ open; unequivocal; explicit: 有意见就～提出来。*If you have any opinions, state them openly.* / 你还是跟他讲～了好。*It would be best to be frank with him.* ❸ sensible; reasonable: 明白人 ❹ understand; realize; know: ～事理 *know what's what; have good sense* / 我不～你的意思。*I don't see what you mean.* / 我忽然～了。*The truth suddenly dawned on me.*

【明白人】a perceptive person; a sensible person: 他是个～,不会干什么傻事。*He is too sensible to do anything foolish.*

【明辨是非】make a clear distinction between right and wrong

【明察暗访】observe publicly and investigate privately—conduct a thorough investigation

【明察秋毫】have eyes sharp enough to perceive an animal's autumn hair—be perceptive of the minutest detail

【明察秋毫之末,而不见舆薪】be sharp-sighted enough to perceive the tip of an animal's autumn hair but unable to see a cartload of firewood—see the minute details but miss the major issue

【明畅】clear and lucid; lucid and smooth: 译文～。*The translation is clear and lucid.*

【明澈】bright and limpid; transparent: 湖水～如镜。*The lake is crystal-clear like a mirror.*

【明处】❶ where there is light: 你把相片拿到～来,让大家看个清楚。*Bring the photo to the light so we can see it better.* ❷ in the open; in public: 有话说在～。*If you've got anything to say, say it openly.*

【明达】sensible; understanding: ～公正 *sensible and fairminded*

【明打明】〈方〉clear; obvious; plain

【明灯】〈喻〉bright lamp; beacon

【明兜】patch pocket

【明断】〈书〉pass (fair) judgment

【明矾】(又作'明石') alum ◇ ～石 alumstone; alunite

【明沟】open drain

【明河】〈书〉the Milky Way

【明后天】tomorrow or the day after tomorrow

【明晃晃】gleaming; shining: ～的刺刀 *gleaming bayonets*

【明慧】〈书〉intelligent; bright; clever

【明火】❶ flame ❷ carry torches (esp. in a robbery)

【明火执仗】carry torches and weapons (in a robbery)—do evil openly

【明鉴】❶ a bright mirror; a clear mirror ❷〈套〉your brilliant idea; your penetrating judgment

【明胶】gelatin

【明净】bright and clean; clear and bright: ～的橱窗 *a bright and clean shop window*

【明镜】a bright mirror; a clear mirror: 湖水清澈，犹如～。*The lake is bright and clear like a mirror.* ◇ ～高悬 a clear mirror hung on high—an impartial and perspicacious judge

【明快】❶ lucid and lively; sprightly: ～的笔调 *a lucid and lively style* / 节奏～ *with sprightly rhythm* ❷ straightforward; forthright: ～的性格 *a forthright character* ❸〈方〉bright

【明来暗往】have overt and covert contacts with sb.

【明朗】❶ bright and clear: ～的月色 *bright moonlight* ❷ clear; obvious: 态度～ *take a clear-cut position; adopt an unequivocal attitude* / 听了报告,他心里～了。*The speech helped him to straighten out his thinking.* ❸ forthright; bright and cheerful: 这幅画色调～。*This picture is painted in bright, warm colours.*

【明理】❶ sensible; reasonable: ～的人 *a sensible person* ❷ an obvious truth or fact

【明丽】bright and beautiful: ～的秋色 *a bright and beautiful autumn scene*

【明亮】❶ well-lit; bright: 宽敞而～的教室 *a bright and spacious classroom* ❷ bright; shining: ～的眼睛 *bright eyes* ❸ become clear: 听了同志们这番解释,老张心里～了。*The comrades' explanation helped Lao Zhang to straighten out his thinking.*

【明了】❶ understand; be clear about: 你的意思我～。*I understand what you mean.* ❷ clear; plain: 简单～ *simple and clear; concise and explicit*

【明令】explicit order; formal decree; public proclamation: ～取谛 *proscribe by formal decree* / ～嘉奖 *issue a commendation; mention in a citation*

【明码】❶ plain code: ～电报 *plain code telegram* / 用～发报 *send a telegram in plain code* ❷ with the price clearly marked: ～售货 *put goods on sale with the prices clearly marked; sell at marked prices* ◇ ～标价 attach price-tags (to prevent overcharging or short-changing); ～实价 put goods on sale with wet prices clearly marked

【明媒正娶】be legally and formally married

【明媚】bright and beautiful; radiant and enchanting: ～的阳光 *bright and beautiful sunshine* / ～的早晨 *a glorious morning* / 河山～ *a land of enchanting beauty*

【明灭】now in view, now hidden; appearing and vanishing: 星光～。*The stars twinkled in the sky.*

【明明】obviously; plainly; undoubtedly: 这事～是他干的嘛！*This is obviously his doing.* or *There can be no doubt that it was he who did it.*

【明眸皓齿】(of a beautiful woman) have bright eyes and white teeth

【明目张胆】brazenly; flagrantly: ～地进行武装干涉 *brazenly commit armed intervention*

【明年】next year

【明枪暗箭】spear thrusts in the open and arrows shot from hiding—both open and covert attacks

【明枪易躲,暗箭难防】it is easy to dodge a spear thrust in the open, but difficult to guard against an arrow shot from hiding

【明确】❶ clear and definite; clear-cut; explicit; unequivocal: 目的～ *have a clear aim* / ～的立场 *a clear-cut stand* / 宪法～规定了公民的权利和义务。*The Constitution clearly defines the rights and duties of citizens.* ❷ make clear; make definite; clarify: 这篇社论进一步～了当前的中心任务。*The editorial further defined the key task for the present period.*

【明人不做暗事】An honest man does nothing underhand.

【明日】❶ tomorrow ❷ the near future

【明日黄花】chrysanthemums after the Double Ninth Festival—things that are stale and no longer of interest

【明睿】〈书〉wise and farsighted

【明升暗降】a promotion in appearance but a demotion in fact: 使某人～ *kick sb. upstairs*

【明十三陵】Tombs of Thirteen Emperors of the Ming Dynasty to the north of Beijing

【明示】explicitly instruct; clearly indicate

【明誓】同〖盟誓〗

【明说】speak frankly; speak openly: 我对你～了吧。*I'll be frank with you.* / 他嘴里虽没～,心里却有想法。*He didn't say anything definitely, although he had ideas of his own.*

【明太鱼】walleye pollack

【明天】❶ tomorrow ❷ the near future: 光辉灿烂的～ *a bright future*

【明文】(of laws, regulations, etc.) proclaimed in writing: ～规定 *stipulate in explicit terms; expressly provide*

【明晰】distinct; clear: 雷达荧光屏上出现了～的图像。*A distinct blip appeared on the radar screen.*

【明细账】subsidiary ledger

【明显】clear; obvious; evident; distinct: ～的优势 *clear superiority* / ～的改进 *distinct improvement* / ～的成效 *tangible result*

【明线】［电子］open-wire line; open wire: ～载波设备 *open-wire carrier equipment*

【明效】obvious results; telling (or marked) effects

【明效大验】clinching proof of effectiveness; telling (or marked) effects

【明信片】postcard

【明星】❶〈古〉Venus ❷ a famous performer; star: 电影～ *a film (or movie) star* / 足球～ *a football star* / 全～队 *an all-star team* ❸ old society lady; social butterfly

【明修栈道,暗渡陈仓】pretend to advance along one path while secretly going along another; do one thing under cover of another

【明眼人】a person with a discerning eye; a person of good sense

【明一套,暗一套】act one way in the open and another way in secret

【明莹】sparkling and crystal-clear; glittering and translucent: ～的金钢钻 *a sparkling diamond*

【明于观人,暗于察己】good at knowing others but poor at knowing oneself

【明于知人,昧于知已】have a good knowledge of others but a poor knowledge of oneself; understand others but not oneself

【明喻】simile

【明早】〈方〉❶ tomorrow morning ❷ tomorrow

【明哲保身】be worldly-wise and play safe

【明争暗斗】both open strife and veiled struggle; overt contention and covert struggle

【明正典刑】carry out a death sentence according to the law

【明证】clear proof: 西沙群岛自古即为我国领土,这些文物就是～。*These cultural relics are clear proof that the Xisha Islands have been China's territory since ancient times.*

【明知】know perfectly well; be fully aware ◇ ～故犯 knowingly violate (discipline, etc.); deliberately break (a rule, etc.); do sth. one knows is wrong; ～故问 ask while knowing the answer

【明知山有虎,偏向虎山行】go deep into the mountains, knowing well that there are tigers there—go on undeterred by the dangers ahead

【明志】show one's high ideals

【明智】sensible; sagacious; wise: 表现出～的态度 *show a sensible attitude*

【明珠】bright pearl; jewel

【明珠暗投】a bright pearl cast into darkness— ❶ a person of talent or a thing of value unrecognized ❷ a good person fallen among bad company

【明珠弹雀】shoot a pearl at the sparrow—the loss outweighs the gain; the game is not worth the candle

【明子】pine torch

鸣 动 ❶ (of birds, animals or insects) cry: 鸡～ *the crow of a cock* / 秋虫夜～ *autumn insects chirping at night* ❷ make a sound; ring: 我耳～。*My ears are ringing.* / ～笛 *blow a whistle* / ～鼓 *beat a drum* / ～礼炮二十一响 *fire a 21-gun salute* / 钟～三下。*The clock struck three.* ❸ express; voice; air: 鸣冤

【鸣不平】complain of unfairness; cry out against injustice

【鸣镝】whistling (or twanging) arrow (used in ancient times)

【鸣放】❶ fire a shot ❷ air one's views (through meetings, newspapers and other media)

【鸣金收兵】beat the gong and recall the troops—call off a battle

【鸣锣开道】beat gongs to clear the way (for officials in feudal times)—prepare the public for a coming event; pave the way for sth.

【鸣枪示警】fire a warning shot

【鸣禽】songbird; singing bird

【鸣谢】express one's thanks formally: ～启事 *a notice expressing one's thanks to benefactors (mentioned in the notice)*

【鸣冤】voice grievances; complain of unfairness ◇ ～叫屈 complain and call for redress; voice grievances

茗 名 ❶ tender tea leaves ❷ tea

冥 Ⅰ 形 ❶ dark; obscure ❷ deep; profound: 冥想 ❸ dull; stupid: 冥顽 Ⅱ 名 underworld; the nether world: 冥府

【冥钞】paper made to resemble bank notes and burned for the dead

【冥府】the nether world

【冥冥之中】in the unseen world

【冥器】funerary object; burial objects

【冥思苦想】同〖苦思冥想〗

【冥顽】[书] thickheaded; stupid: ～不灵 *dull and stupid; impenetrably thickheaded*

【冥王星】Pluto

【冥想】deep thought; meditation: 歌声把我带到对草原的～之中。*On hearing the song, I fell into a reverie about the grasslands.*

铭 Ⅰ 名 inscription: 墓志铭 Ⅱ 动 engrave: 铭刻

【铭感】[书] be deeply grateful: ～终身 *remain deeply grateful for the rest of one's life*

【铭记】❶ bear firmly in mind; always remember: ～在心 *always bear in mind* ❷ inscription; epigraph

【铭刻】❶ inscription: 古代～ *ancient inscription* ❷ be engraved on one's mind; be always remembered: 他的话深深～在我的心中。*His words were engraved on my mind.* ◇ ～学 epigraphy

【铭牌】[机] data plate; nameplate

【铭文】inscription; epigraph

【铭谢】show gratefulness

【铭心】be engraved on one's heart—be remembered with gratitude

【铭诸肺腑】be engraved on one's mind (or memory); be borne firmly in mind

瞑 (构词成分)见下

【瞑目】close one's eyes in death—die content

【瞑眩】[中] dizziness, nausea, etc. as a side effect of drugs

螟 名 snout moth's larva

【螟虫】snout moth's larva

【螟蛾】snout moth

【螟蛉】❶ corn earworm ❷ adopted son

mǐng

酩 (构词成分)见下

【酩酊】be dead drunk：～大醉 *be dead drunk*

mìng

命 Ⅰ名 ❶ life：～在旦夕 *be on the verge of death*；*be dying* ❷ lot；fate；destiny：他认为自己受苦是～苦。*He thought he had suffered because of his cruel fate.* / ～好 *be born under a lucky star* ❸ order；commandation：奉命 Ⅱ动 ❶ order；command：～其速归。*Order him to return immediately.* ❷ assign (a name，title，etc.)：命名

【命案】a case involving the killing of a person；homicide case

【命笔】〈书〉take up one's pen；set pen to paper：欣然～ *gladly set pen to paper*；*be happy to start writing*

【命不该绝】not be destined to die (said of a person who has had a narrow escape)

【命大】of extremely good fortune；very lucky：他空难余生，真是～。*He was extremely lucky to survive the air crash.*

【命定】be determined by fate；be predestined

【命根子】one's very life；lifeblood：孙子是她的～。*Her grandson is the very apple of her eye.*

【命令】❶ order；command：连长～一排担任警戒。*The company commander ordered the first platoon to keep watch.* ❷ order；commandation：下～ *issue an order* / 服从～ *obey orders* / ～式的口气 *a commanding tone* ◇ ～句［语］imperative sentence；～系统 command system；～主义 commandism

【命脉】lifeblood；lifeline：经济～ *economic lifelines* / 水利是农业的～。*Irrigation is the lifeblood of agriculture.*

【命门】［中］the gate of vitality，the area between the kidneys，generally regarded as the source of vitality，the function of which is to promote respiration，digestion，reproduction and the metabolism of body fluid

【命名】name (sb. or sth.)：～典礼(大会) *a naming ceremony* ◇ ～法 nomenclature

【命若悬丝】life as if hanging by a thread

【命数】destiny；fate；lot ◇ ～法［数］numeration

【命题】❶ assign a topic；set a question：～作文 *assign a subject for composition* ❷ proposition：～演算 *propositional calculus* ❸［逻］proposition

【命途多舛】suffer many a setback during one's life

【命意何在】where is the meaning

【命运】destiny；fate；lot：悲惨的～ *a tragic lot*

【命在旦夕】death may come any minute；be dying

【命之所招】be caused by fate

【命中】hit the target (or mark)；score a hit：她第一枪就～靶心。*Her first shot hit the bull's-eye.* ◇ ～率 percentage of hits；～目标 hit the target (or mark)；～偏差 deviation of impact

miù

谬 形 wrong；false；erroneous；mistaken

【谬传】a false report

【谬见】❶ a wrong view ❷〈谦〉my humble opinion

【谬奖】〈谦〉overpraise (me)

【谬论】fallacy；false (or absurd) theory；falsehood：驳斥～ *refute a fallacy*

【谬误】falsehood；error；mistake：真理是在同～作斗争中间发展起来的。*Truth develops through its struggle against falsehood.*

【谬种】❶ error；fallacy ❷〈诋〉scoundrel

【谬种流传】the dissemination of error：～，误人不浅。*The dissemination of error does people great harm.*

mō

摸 动 ❶ feel；stroke；touch：你～～刀口，看看快不快。*Try to feel the edge of the knife and see whether it is sharp.* / 这衣料～着很软。*The material feels soft.* / 她轻轻地～了～孩子的头。*She gently stroked the child's head.* ❷ feel for；grope for；fumble：在黑暗中～着下楼 *grope one's way down the stairs in the dark* / 他从床底下～出一双鞋来。*He fished out a pair of shoes from under the bed.* ❸ try to find out；feel out；sound out：你去～～他对这个问题的看法。*Go and sound him out on this matter.* / ～清敌情 *find out about the enemy's situation* / ～出一套种植水稻的好经验 *gain good experience in growing rice*

【摸不透】wonder；be puzzled

【摸彩】draw lot to determine the prize winners in a raffle or lottery

【摸到门路】have learned the ways of the trade

【摸底】❶ know the real situation：这事我不～，你可以问问别人。*I don't know much about this business. Please ask someone else.* ❷ try to find out the real intention or situation；sound sb. out：他是想摸我们的底。*He was trying to feel us out.*

【摸黑】〈口〉grope one's way on a dark night：～赶路 *press on with the journey at night* / 起早～地干 *work from morning till night*

【摸门儿】〈口〉learn the ropes；get the hang of sth.：这事初看起来不容易，可是过了几个星期你就能摸着门儿了。*It may seem difficult at first, but you'll get the hang of it after a few weeks.*

【摸清底细】get to the bottom of the story；ascertain the actual situation

【摸索】❶ grope; feel about; fumble: 在黑暗中～前进 *grope (or fumble) one's way in the dark* ❷ try to find out: ～种花生的规律 *try to find out the secret of peanut growing*
【摸透】get to know sb. or sth. very well: ～某人的脾气 *get to know sb. inside out*
【摸瞎】〈口〉grope one's way in the dark
【摸着石头过河】grope one's way across the river; act with caution in handling uncertain issues; tread carefully: 改革还处在探索阶段,要～,使其健康发展。*To ensure a healthy development of the reforms, we should be very cautious, for they are still at the exploratory stage.*

mó

馍 名 (又作'馍馍')〈方〉steamed bun; steamed bread

摹 动 copy; trace
【摹本】facsimile; copy
【摹仿】(又作'摹效')同〖模仿〗
【摹绘】[书] draw; paint; depict; describe
【摹刻】❶ carve a reproduction of an inscription or painting ❷ a carved reproduction of an inscription or painting
【摹拟】同〖模拟〗
【摹写】❶ copy; imitate ❷ describe; depict: ～人物情状 *depict characters in various situations*
【摹印】❶ copy and print ❷ a style of characters or lettering on ancient imperial seals
【摹状】depict; portray; delineate

模 Ⅰ 名 pattern; standard: 楷模 Ⅱ 动 imitate: 模仿 ——另见 mú
【模本】calligraphy or painting model
【模范】an exemplary person or thing; model; fine example: 劳动～ *model worker* ◇ ～共青团员 model member of the Communist Youth League; ～事迹 exemplary deeds; ～作用 exemplary role
【模仿】(又作'模效') imitate; copy; model oneself on: 这部机器是～上海的一种新产品制造的。*This machine is modelled on one recently made in Shanghai.* / 儿童的～能力特强。*Children are very imitative.*
【模糊】❶ blurred; indistinct; dim; vague: 字迹～了。*The writing was blurred.* / ～的景物 *a hazy scene* / 只有些～的印象 *have only a vague idea of sth.* ❷ blur; obscure; confuse; mix up: 泪水～了他的双眼。*Tears blurred his eyes.* or *His eyes were dim with tears.* ◇ ～经济学 fuzzy economics; ～理论 fuzzy theory; ～逻辑 fuzzy logic; ～数学 fuzzy mathematics
【模棱两可】equivocal; ambiguous: 采取～的态度 *take an equivocal attitude*
【模拟】imitate; simulate: 经过电子技术处理～立体声 (*of a record, etc.*) *be electronically reprocessed to simulate stereo* ◇ ～程序 simulation program; ～飞行[军] simulated flight; ～考试 mock examination; ～试验 simulated test; ～通信 analogue communication
【模式】pattern; model: ～化 *patterning*
【模数】(又作'模量') [物] modulus: 弹性～ *modulus of elasticity*
【模特】❶ [美] model ❷ model; dummy: 时装～ *dress model; fashion model* / 时装表演现在有中老年～。*Nowadays we find elderly models in fashion shows.*
【模型】❶ model: 宇宙飞船～ *a spaceship model* / 原尺寸～ *mock-up* ❷ mould; matrix; pattern: ～板 *mould plate* ◇ ～展品 scale model; replica

膜 名 ❶ membrane: 细胞膜 ❷ film; thin coating: 纸浆表面结了一层～。*A thin film formed on the surface of the pulp.*
【膜拜】prostrate oneself (before an idol or person); worship
【膜翅目】[动] Hymenoptera
【膜法】[环保] membrane method
【膜片】diaphragm

摩 动 ❶ rub; scrape; touch: 按摩 ❷ mull over; study: 揣摩 ——另见 mā
【摩擦】❶ rub: 轴颈在轴承上～。*The journal rubs against the bearing surface.* ❷ [物] friction: ～生热。*Friction generates heat.* ❸ clash (between two parties); friction: 制造～ *create friction* / 与某人发生～ *have a brush with sb.* / 工作中的～ *conflicts in work*
【摩擦力】[物] frictional force; friction
【摩擦抛光】[机] burnishing
【摩擦音】[语音] fricative
【摩擦桩】[建] friction pile
【摩登】modern; fashionable: ◇ ～家具 fashionable furniture; ～女郎 a fashionable girl
【摩电灯】dynamo-powered lamp (on a bicycle, etc.)
【摩顶放踵】wear the whole body smooth from head to foot—serve the interests of others at great self-sacrifice
【摩尔】[物] mole
【摩尔多瓦】Moldova
【摩尔法则】〈计〉Moore's Law
【摩尔根主义】[生] Morganism
【摩肩接踵】jostle each other in a crowd: 那天街上人特别多,真是～,川流不息。*That day the street was jam-packed with people coming and going all the time.*
【摩洛哥】Morocco ◇ ～人 Moroccan
【摩纳哥】Monaco ◇ ～人 Monacan
【摩拳擦掌】rub one's fists and palms—be eager for a fight; be itching to have a go: 战士们一个个～,准备战斗。*The soldiers were rolling up their sleeves for the battle.*
【摩丝】styling mousse; mousse
【摩挲】stroke; caress ——另见 māsa
【摩天】skyscraping: ～岭 *a mountain ridge tower-*

ing into the sky；*a towering mountain ridge*；*a cloud-capped mountain* / ～大楼 *skyscraper*

【摩托】motor ◇ ～车 motorcycle；motor bicycle；motorbike；～船（又作'摩托艇'）同〖汽艇〗；～化部队 motorized troops

磨 动 ❶ rub；wear：他的脚上～出了泡。*His feet were blistered from the rubbing.* / 没关系，就～破了一点皮。*Nothing serious. Just a graze.* / 袜子～破了。*The socks are worn into holes.* ❷ grind；polish：～剪子 *grind scissors*；*sharpen scissors* / ～大理石 *polish marble* / ～墨 *rub an ink stick against an inkstone*；*make ink for writing with a brush* ❸ wear down；wear out：他被这场病～得不成样子。*The illness has worn him down to a mere shadow of his former self.* ❹ trouble；pester；worry：这孩子可真～人。*What a little torment that child is!* / 他不答应，你就跟他～。*If he doesn't agree, just keep on at him until he does.* ❺ obliterate；die out：百世不～ *will endure for centuries* ❻ dawdle；waste time：快走吧，别再～时间了。*Stop dawdling and get going.* ——另见 mò

【磨版机】［刷］graining machine

【磨擦】同〖摩擦〗

【磨蹭】❶ rub (lightly)；stroke (gently)：他右脚轻轻地在地上～着。*He was scraping his right foot lightly on the floor.* ❷ move slowly；dawdle：别～了，快走吧。*Stop dawdling and get going.* ❸ pester；nag：我跟爸爸～了半天，他才答应明天带我到动物园玩去。*I kept on at my father until he promised to take me to the zoo tomorrow.*

【磨杵成针】见〖只要工夫深，铁杵磨成针〗

【磨穿铁砚】wear out an iron inkslab—study assiduously

【磨床】［机］grinding machine；grinder：内圆～ *internal grinder* / 外圆～ *cylindrical grinder*

【磨刀不误砍柴工】Sharpening the axe won't interfere with the cutting of firewood.

【磨刀石】whetstone；grindstone

【磨电灯】同〖摩电灯〗

【磨革】buff (leather)：～机 *buffing machine*

【磨工】［机］❶ grinding work：～车间 *grindery* ❷ grinder

【磨工夫】consume time：这活最～。*This is a time-consuming job.*

【磨光】polish：◇ ～玻璃 polished glass；～机 polishing machine；glazing machine

【磨耗】wear and tear

【磨合】❶ (of machines) grind in；wear in：新汽车正式启用前必须有一段～时间。*A new car must go through a period of breaking in before use.* ❷ adapt to each other

【磨砺】go through the mill；steel oneself；harden oneself；discipline oneself

【磨炼】put oneself through the mill；temper oneself；steel oneself：困难能～我们的意志。*Difficulties can temper our willpower.*

【磨料】abrasive；abradant

【磨灭】wear away；efface；obliterate：留下难以～的印象 *leave an indelible impression*

【磨墨挥毫】grind the ink and flourish the brush to write

【磨木机】paper making (wood) grinder：链式～ *caterpillar grinder* / 袋式～ *pocket grinder*

【磨难】tribulation；hardship；suffering：历经～ *have gone through all kinds of hardships*

【磨砂玻璃】同〖毛玻璃〗

【磨砂灯泡】frosted bulb

【磨舌头】〈方〉indulge in idle talk；argue pointlessly

【磨蚀】［地质］abrasion

【磨损】wear and tear：这台机器基本上没有什么～。*The machine shows scarcely any sign of wear and tear.*

【磨损留量】［机］wear allowance

【磨洗】wear away；corrode；erode：碑文经受了岁月的～。*The inscription on the stone had been worn away over the years.*

【磨削】［机］grinding：～裕量 *grinding tolerance*

【磨牙】❶ grind one's teeth (in sleep) ❷〈方〉indulge in idle talk；argue pointlessly：你别跟他～了。*Don't waste your time arguing with him.*

【磨洋工】dawdle over one's work；loaf on the job；lie down on the job：别～了，快把活干完。*Stop dawdling and finish your work.*

【磨嘴皮子】(又作'磨嘴')〈方〉❶ jabber；blah-blah：成天～不干活，还能建设好社会主义？*How can you build socialism if you just blah-blah and don't do a stroke of work?* ❷ do a lot of talking：我跟他磨了半天嘴皮子，也没能把他说服。*I failed to bring him around though I talked myself hoarse.* ❸ indulge in idle talk；argue pointlessly：我没功夫跟他～。*I can't afford to waste my time arguing with him.*

蘑 名 mushroom：鲜～ *fresh mushrooms*

【蘑菇】❶ mushroom ❷ worry；pester；keep on at：你别跟我～了，我还有急事呢。*Don't pester me. I've got something urgent to attend to.* ❸ dawdle；dillydally：你再这样～就赶不上火车了。*If you go on dawdling like this, you'll miss the train.* ◇ ～云 mushroom cloud (esp. from nuclear explosion)；～战术［军］the tactics of "wear and tear" (wearing the enemy down and then wiping them out)

魔 Ⅰ 名 evil spirit；demon；devil；monster：恶魔 Ⅱ 形 magic；mystic：魔力

【魔法】sorcery；witchcraft

【魔方】magic square

【魔怪】demons and monsters；fiends

【魔鬼】devil；demon；monster

【魔窟】den of monsters

【魔力】magical power；magic；charm

【魔球】magic ball

【魔术】magic；conjuring；sleight of hand ◇ ～演员 magician；conjurer；～师 magician

【魔头】❶ devil；demon；evil spirit ❷〈方〉wizard；sorcerer
【魔王】❶ Prince of the Devils；erlking ❷ tyrant；despot；fiend
【魔影】spectre：内战的～正威胁着那个国家。*The spectre of civil war was haunting the country.*
【魔芋】Amorphophallus rivieri
【魔掌】devil's clutches；evil hands：逃出敌人的～ *escape from the clutches of the enemy*
【魔杖】magic wand
【魔爪】devil's talons；claws；tentacles：斩断侵略者的～ *cut off the tentacles of the aggressors*

mǒ

抹 动 ❶ put on；apply；smear；plaster：～点雪花膏 *put on a little vanishing cream* / 面包上～点果酱 *spread some jam on a piece of bread* / ～药膏 *apply ointment* / 你～浆糊，我来贴布告。*You smear the wall with paste and I'll stick the notice on it.* ❷ wipe：～眼泪 *wipe one's eyes；be weeping* / 用手把嘴一～ *wipe one's mouth with the back of the hand* ❸ cross (or strike，blot) out；erase：把这一行字～了。*Cross out this line.* / ～掉磁带上的录音 *erase the recording from a tape* ——另见 mā；mò
【抹鼻子】〈方〉cry；weep
【抹脖子】cut one's own throat；commit suicide
【抹刀】trowel
【抹掉】erase；wipe away：～这个短语。*Cross out this phrase.*
【抹粉】apply face powder；〈喻〉prettify；whitewash：他不但不承认错误，反而替自己～。*He not only refused to admit his mistake but even tried to whitewash himself.*
【抹黑】blacken sb.'s name；throw mud at；bring shame on；discredit：他的所作所为简直是在给我们集体脸上～。*What he did is simply bringing shame on our collective.*
【抹零】count the small change (in a payment)
【抹杀】(又作'抹煞') blot out；obliterate；write off；deny：～成绩 *obliterate achievements* / 历史事实是～不了的。*The facts of history cannot be denied.*
【抹稀泥】〈方〉try to mediate differences at the sacrifice of principle；try to gloss things over
【抹香鲸】sperm whale
【抹一鼻子灰】suffer a snub；meet with a rebuff
【抹子】trowel

mò

末 名 ❶ tip；end：秋毫之末 ❷ nonessentials；minor details：本末倒置 ❸ end；last stage：明～农民起义 *the peasant uprisings towards the end of the Ming Dynasty* / 一学期的最～一天 *the last day of a school term* ❹ powder；dust：茶叶～儿 *broken tea leaves；tea dust* / 把药研成～儿 *grind medicinal herbs into powder* ❺ the role of a middle-aged man in traditional operas
【末班车】❶ last bus ❷〈口〉last chance or turn
【末代】the last reign of a dynasty：～皇帝 *the last emperor* (*of a dynasty*)
【末端】end；bottom
【末伏】❶ the last or third fu—the third hottest period of the year (10 days) ❷ the first day of the last or third fu (falling in early or mid August) ——另见〖三伏〗
【末技】a trifling skill；an insignificant stunt
【末节】minor details；nonessentials
【末了】last；finally；in the end：第五行～的那个字我不认识。*I don't know the last word of the fifth line.*
【末流】❶ the later and decadent stage of a school of thought，literature，etc. ❷ inferior；low-grade：～演员 *a minor actor or actress*
【末路】dead end；impasse：英雄～ *a hero in dire straits*
【末年】last years of a dynasty or reign
【末期】last phase；final phase；last stage：七十年代～ *in the late seventies*
【末日】❶［宗］(基督教) doomsday；Day of Judgment；Judgment Day：～审判 *Last Judgment* ❷ end；doom：封建王朝的～ *the end of a feudal dynasty*
【末梢】tip；end：鞭子的～ *the tip of a whip* ◇ ～神经［生理］nerve ending
【末世】last phase (of an age)：封建～ *the last years of feudalism*
【末尾】❶ end：信的～ *at the end of the letter* / 排队排在～ *stand at the end of a queue* ❷［音］fine；end
【末席】the least prominent seat at a dinner table
【末屑】bits；scraps；crumbs：面包～ *crumbs* (*of bread*)
【末业】(in ancient times) industry and commerce
【末叶】last years (of a century or dynasty)：十九世纪～ *the end of the 19th century；the late 19th century*

没 Ⅰ 动 ❶ sink；submerge：潜水艇很快就～入水中。*It was not long before the submarine submerged.* ❷ over flow；rise beyond：洪水几乎～过了大坝。*The flood nearly overflowed the dam.* / 水深～顶。*The water goes above a man's head.* / 雪深～膝。*The snow was knee-deep.* ❸ disappear；hide：出没 ❹ confiscate；take possession of：没收 Ⅱ 形 last；end：没世 ——另见 méi
【没齿不忘】(又作'没世不忘') will never forget to the end of one's days；remember for the rest of one's life
【没顶】be drowned：～水深 *The water goes above a man's head.*
【没骨画】boneless painting (i.e. painting without outline but with forms achieved by washes of ink and colour)

【没落】decline; wane: 这个文学流派从此日趋~。*This school of literature has since been on the wane*.
【没奈何】be utterly helpless; have no way out; have no alternative: 等了他好久也没来,~我只好一个人去了。*I waited for a long time, but he didn't show up, so I had to go alone*.
【没世】all one's life; lifelong
【没收】confiscate; expropriate: ~违禁物品 *confiscate contraband*
【没药】[中] myrrh
沫 名 foam; froth: 啤酒~ *froth on beer*; *the head on a glass of beer* / 肥皂~ *soapsuds*; *lather* / 有的啤酒~儿比较多。*Some beer has more froth than others*.
【沫子】foam; froth
茉 (构词成分)见下
【茉莉】[植] jasmine ◇ ~花茶 jasmine tea
抹 动 ❶ daub; plaster: ~墙 *plaster a wall*; *daub plaster on a wall* ❷ skirt; bypass: ~过林子 *skirt the edge of the forest* ——另见 mā; mǒ
【抹不开】同〖磨不开〗
【抹得开】同〖磨得开〗
【抹灰】[建] plastering: ~工 *plasterer*
陌 名 ❶ a path between fields (running east and west): 阡陌 ❷ road
【陌路】〈书〉 stranger (whom one passes in the street): 视同~ *treat like a stranger*; *cut sb. dead*
【陌生】strange; unfamiliar: ~人 *stranger* / 对这些年青人来说,养鹿是一件~的事情。*Breeding deer was something completely new for these young people*.
脉 (构词成分) 见下 ——另见 mài
【脉脉】affectionate; loving; amorous: 她~地注视着远去的儿子。*She followed with loving eyes the departing figure of her son*. / 含情~ *quietly sending the message of love* / 温情~ *full of tender affection*; *sentimental*
莫 Ⅰ 代 〈书〉 no one; nothing; none: ~之能御。*No one (or Nothing) can resist it*. Ⅱ 副 no; not: ~知所措 *not know what to do*; *be at a loss*
【莫不】there's no one who doesn't or isn't: ~为之感动。*There was no one who was unmoved*.
【莫不】同〖莫非〗
【莫测高深】unfathomable; enigmatic
【莫此为甚】A more flagrant instance has yet to be found.
【莫大】greatest; utmost: 感到~的光荣 *feel greatly honoured* / ~的侮辱 *a gross insult*
【莫非】*can it be that*; *is it possible that*: 今天她没来,~又生了病不成? *She is absent today. Can she be ill again*? / 听你的意思,~是我错了? *Do you mean to say that I'm in the wrong*?
【莫过于】nothing is more... than: 最大的幸福~此。*There's no greater happiness than this*. / 我国古代的伟大建筑,恐怕~万里长城了。*Of all the ancient Chinese buildings, the Great Wall is perhaps the greatest*.
【莫霍界面】[地质] Moho discontinuity; Moho
【莫可名状】that cannot be described
【莫可指数】beyond counting on one's fingers—countless; innumerable
【莫名】beyond description; indescribable; nameless: 一种~的紧张 *a nameless nervousness* / ~所以 *be unable to make head or tail of sth.*; *be baffled*
【莫名其妙】❶ be unable to make head or tail of sth.; be baffled: 他为什么讲这番话,真叫人~。*It is quite baffling why he should have made such remarks*. ❷ without rhyme or reason; inexplicable; odd: 她~地哭了起来。*Quite unaccountably she burst out crying*.
【莫逆】very friendly; intimate: 他们二人最称~。*The two of them have become the best of friends*. ◇ ~之交 bosom friends
【莫如】would be better; might as well: 与其你去,~他来。*It would be better for him to come than for you to go*. / 她想既然来了,~跟着进去看看。*Now that she'd come to the place, she thought she might as well go in with the others to have a look*.
【莫桑比克】Mozambique ◇ ~人 Mozambican
【莫为子孙作牛马】do no slave for your children
【莫信直中直,须防仁不仁】don't believe the honesty of the honest, be wary of the unkindness of the kind
【莫须有】unwarranted; groundless; fabricated; trumped-up: ~的罪名 *a fabricated charge*; *an unwarranted charge*
【莫衷一是】unable to agree or decide which is right ——另见〖众说纷纭〗
秣 Ⅰ 名 fodder: 粮秣 Ⅱ 动 feed animals
【秣马厉兵】feed the horses and sharpen the weapons—make preparations for war; prepare for battle
漠 Ⅰ 名 desert: 沙漠 Ⅱ 形 indifferent; unconcerned: 冷漠
【漠不关心】indifferent; unconcerned: 官长必须爱护士兵,不能~。*Officers must cherish their men and must not be indifferent to their well-being*.
【漠漠】❶ misty; foggy: 湖面升起一层~的烟雾。*A thick mist rose over the lake*. ❷ vast and lonely: 黄沙~ *a vast stretch of yellow sand*
【漠然】indifferent; apathetic; unconcerned: 这个作家对批评意见处之~。*The writer was indifferent to criticism*.
【漠视】treat with indifference; ignore; overlook; pay no attention to: 不能~群众的意见。*The masses' opinions must not be treated with indifference*.

寞 形 lonely；deserted：寂寞

蓦 副 suddenly

【蓦地】suddenly；unexpectedly；all of a sudden：黑暗里～窜出个人来。*Suddenly, somebody ran out of the darkness.*

【蓦然】suddenly：～想起 *suddenly remember*

墨 Ⅰ 名 ❶ China (or Chinese) ink；ink stick：～太稠了。*The ink is too thick.* ❷ pigment；ink：油墨 ❸ handwriting or painting：遗墨 ❹ learning：胸无点墨 Ⅱ 形 ❶ black；pitch-dark：墨黑 ❷〈书〉corrupt：墨吏

【墨宝】❶treasured scrolls of calligraphy or painting ❷〈套〉your beautiful handwriting

【墨斗】carpenter's ink marker

【墨斗鱼】popular name for 乌贼

【墨海】a big basin-like inkstone

【墨盒】ink box (for Chinese calligraphy or painting)

【墨黑】pitch-dark：一个～的夜晚 *one pitch-dark night*

【墨迹】❶ ink marks；ink stains：他衬衫上有～。*There were ink stains on his shirt.* ❷ sb.'s writing or painting：这是鲁迅的～。*This is Lu Xun's calligraphy.*

【墨迹未干】before the ink is dry：协议～，他们就把它撕毁了。*They tore up the agreement before the ink was hardly dry.*

【墨家】Mohist School (a school of thought in the Spring and Autumn and Warring States Periods, 770-221 B.C.)：～学说 *Mohism*

【墨晶】smoky quartz

【墨镜】sunglasses

【墨客】〈书〉literary men；men of letters

【墨吏】〈书〉corrupt officials

【墨绿】blackish green

【墨囊】ink sac (of a cuttlefish)

【墨守成规】stick to convention；stay in a rut

【墨守旧习】adhere to old customs

【墨水】❶ prepared Chinese ink ❷ ink：红(蓝)～ *red (blue) ink* ❸ book learning：他肚子里还有点儿～。*He's something of a scholar.* ◇ ～池 inkwell；～瓶 ink bottle；～台 inkstand

【墨西哥】Mexico ◇ ～人 Mexican；～湾 the Gulf of Mexico；～湾流 the Gulf Stream

【墨线】❶ the line in a carpenter's ink marker ❷ a line made by a carpenter's ink marker

【墨鸦】〈方〉cormorant

【墨鱼】popular name for 乌贼

【墨汁】prepared Chinese ink

【墨渍】ink blot；ink spot

默 Ⅰ 形 silent；tacit：～不作声 *keep silent* Ⅱ 动 write from memory：～生字 *write out the new words from memory*

【默哀】stand in silent tribute：全体起立～。*All rose and stood in silent tribute.* / ～三分钟 *observe three minutes' silence*

【默察】watch quietly

【默祷】pray in silence；say a silent prayer

【默悼】pay a silent tribute of memory (to the dead)

【默读】read silently

【默记】make a mental note；learn by heart；commit to memory

【默默】quiet；silent：～无言 *without saying a word*；*silently* / 一连几天，她总是这么～的，不理人。*She's been like that for days, silent and unapproachable.*

【默默无闻】unknown to the public；without attracting public attention：一生～ *remain in obscurity all one's life* / ～地工作 *work quietly and never show off*

【默念】❶read silently ❷think back；recollect；recall：～童年情景，如在昨日。*My childhood days passed through my mind as if they were yesterday.*

【默契】❶tacit agreement；tacit understanding：互相～ *have a perfect mutual understanding in doing sth.*；*coordinate by tacit agreement* / 这对双打选手配合～。*This pair of doubles played in perfect unison.* ❷ secret agreement：关于这个问题双方曾有～。*The two sides had a secret agreement on this question.*

【默然】silent；speechless：～无语 *fall silent*；*be speechless* / 二人～相对。*The two of them sat face to face in silence.*

【默认】give tacit consent to；tacitly approve；acquiesce in：～现状 *give tacit consent to the status quo*

【默示】❶ imply ❷ [法]tacit declaration ◇ ～承诺 implied promise；～承认 implied recognition；～担保 implied warrant；～放弃 implied waiver；～合同 implied contract；～批准 implied ratification；～特约条款 warranty implied；～条件 implied term；～同意 implied consent；～协定 implied agreement；～信托 implied trust；～异议 implied objection

【默书】write out a text from memory

【默诵】❶ read silently ❷ read silently to oneself from memory

【默算】❶ do mental arithmetic；do sums in one's heart ❷ calculate；figure；plan

【默想】think deeply；ponder over；reflect on

【默写】write from memory：她把这一课的生词～了一遍。*She wrote out from memory the new words in the lesson.*

【默许】tacitly consent to；acquiesce in

【默坐】sit quietly

磨 Ⅰ 名 mill；millstones：电～ *electric mill* Ⅱ 动 ❶ grind；mill：～麦子 *grind wheat* / ～面 *mill flour* ❷ turn round：把大车～过来。*Turn the cart round.* / 我几次三番劝他，他还是～不过来。*I had talked to him again and again, but he simply wouldn't come round.* ——另见 mó

【磨不开】(又作'抹不开')❶ feel embarrassed；be put out：本想说他两句，又怕他脸上～。*I hesita-*

ted to criticize him for fear of making him uncomfortable. ❷ unable to act impartially for fear of offending sb.; afraid of impairing personal relations: 他有错误,就该批评,有什么～的? *If he's made mistakes, you should criticize him and not let personal considerations get in your way*.

【磨得开】❶ not feel embarrassed; be at ease: 你这样说他,他脸上～吗? *Don't you think your sharp criticism would embarrass him?* ❷ not find it embarrassing (to do sth.): 你不答应她的请求,你～吗? *Don't you find it difficult to refuse her request?* ❸〈方〉be convinced; come round

【磨豆腐】❶ grind soya beans to make bean curd ❷〈方〉say sth. over and over again; repeat again and again

【磨坊】mill

【磨面机】flour-milling machine

【磨盘】❶ nether (or lower) millstone ❷〈方〉mill; millstones

【磨棚】grinding shed; mill shed

【磨扇】upper and lower millstones

【磨子】〈方〉mill; millstones

貘 名 [动] tapir

mōu

哞 象 (the sound made by an ox) moo; low; bellow

móu

牟 动 try to gain; obtain; seek: 牟利

【牟利】seek private (or selfish) interests; seek personal gain

【牟取】try to gain; seek; obtain: ～暴利 *seek exorbitant profits; reap staggering (or colossal) profits*

谋 Ⅰ 名 stratagem; plan; scheme: 计谋 Ⅱ 动 ❶ work for; seek: 为人民～福利 *work for the interests of the people* / ～独立,求解放 *seek independence and liberation* ❷ consult: 不谋而合

【谋财害命】murder sb. for his money

【谋臣】emperor's counsellor

【谋刺】plot to assassinate

【谋反】conspire against the state; plot a rebellion

【谋害】❶ plot to murder ❷ plot a frame-up against

【谋和】sue for peace

【谋划】plan; scheme; try to find a solution

【谋利】make a profit; seek gain

【谋虑】consider carefully; contemplate; deliberate

【谋略】astuteness and resourcefulness; strategy: 此人颇有～。*He is a man of resource and astuteness*.

【谋面】〈书〉meet each other or be acquainted with sb.: 我与此人素未～。*I never had the pleasure of meeting him*.

【谋篇】〈书〉plan a composition

【谋求】seek; strive for; be in quest of: ～独立 *strive for independence* / ～解决办法 *try to find a solution*

【谋取】try to gain; seek; obtain: 不能为了～暂时的利益而牺牲原则。*We mustn't seek temporary gain at the expense of principle*.

【谋杀】murder

【谋生】seek a livelihood; make a living: ～的手段 *a means of life*

【谋私】seek personal gain: 以权～ *use one's position and power to seek personal gain; abuse one's power for personal gain*

【谋图】premeditate

【谋士】adviser; counsellor

【谋事】❶ plan matters: ～不密 *leave loopholes in a plan* ❷〈旧〉look for a job

【谋事在人,成事在天】The planning lies with man, the outcome with Heaven; Man proposes, God disposes.

【谋算】❶ plan; scheme; try to find a solution ❷ scheme against sb. or for sth.; plot ❸ calculate; plan: 很有～ *be very calculating*

【谋议】〈书〉plan; scheme

【谋职】seek employment; try to find a job: 外出～ *go out to find a job*

眸 名 pupil (of the eye); eye: 凝眸

【眸子】pupil (of the eye); eye

mǒu

某 代 ❶ certain; some: ～日 *at a certain date* / 张～ *a certain person called Zhang* / 在～种程度上 *to some (or a certain) extent* / 在～种意义上 *in a sense* / 他老说～～～是他的朋友。*He's always saying that so-and-so is a friend of his*. ❷ (referring to oneself): 我李～不是干这种事的人。*Yours truly is not the sort of person to do a thing like that*.

【某某】so-and-so: ～同志 *comrade so-and-so* / ～学校 *a certain school* / ～人 *someone*

【某人】❶ a certain person; someone ❷ (referring to oneself): 我王～从来不说假话。*As for me, I've never told lies*.

mú

模 名 mould; matrix; pattern: 铜模 —— 另见 mó

【模板】❶ [建] shuttering; formwork ❷ [机] pattern plate

【模具】mould; matrix; pattern; die

【模压】mould pressing: ～胶底皮鞋 *leather shoes with moulded-on rubber soles* ◇ ～机 moulding press

【模样】❶ appearance; look: 那人是什么～? *What did that person look like?* / 这孩子的～像他妈妈。*The child takes after his mother.* / 这姑娘～儿真不错。*The young lady is quite pretty.* ❷ indicating a rough estimate of time or age: 我等了有半小时～。*I waited for about half an hour.* / 那男的有三十岁～。*The man was around thirty.*

【模子】mould; matrix; pattern; die: 一个～里铸出来的 *made out of the same mould; as like as two peas*

mǔ

母 Ⅰ 名 ❶ mother: ～女 *mother and daughter* / 老～ *one's old mother* ❷ one's female elders: 伯母 / 祖母 ❸ nut (so called because of the female screw thread): 螺母 Ⅱ 形 ❶ female (animal): ～象 *female (or cow) elephant* / 你的狗是公的还是～的? *Is your dog a he or a she?* / ～狼 *she-wolf* ❷ origin; parent: 母公司

【母爱】mother love; maternal love

【母本】[植] female parent: ～植株 *maternal plant*

【母畜】mother of a domestic animal; dam

【母带】master tape (audio or video)

【母蜂】queen bee

【母公司】parent company

【母狗】female dog; bitch

【母机】❶ machine tool ❷ mother aircraft; launching aircraft

【母鸡】hen

【母舰】mother ship

【母老虎】❶ tigress ❷ vixen; shrew; termagant

【母马】female horse; mare

【母牛】cow

【母亲】mother: ～节 *Mother's day*

【母权制】matriarchy

【母乳】breast milk; mother's milk: ～喂养 *breast-feeding*

【母山羊】she-goat; nanny goat

【母狮】lioness

【母体】[动] the mother's body; the (female) parent

【母系】❶ maternal: ～亲属 *maternal relatives* ❷ matrilineal; matriarchal: ～社会 *matrilineal society* / ～氏族制 *matriarchy*

【母线】❶ [电子] bus; bus bar ❷ [机] generatrix; generator

【母校】one's old school; Alma Mater

【母性】maternal instinct

【母羊】ewe

【母夜叉】an ugly and fierce woman; an ugly shrew

【母液】[化] mother liquor; mother solution

【母音】[语音] vowel

【母语】❶ mother tongue ❷ parent language; linguistic parent

【母株】[植] maternal plant; mother plant

【母猪】female pig; sow

【母子】mother and son: ～候车室 *waiting room (as in a railway station) for mothers with babies*

亩 量 currently called 市亩, a traditional unit of area: ～产量 *per mu yield* ——另见〖市亩〗

牡 形 male (of some birds and animals): ～牛 *bull* / ～雉 *male pheasant*

【牡丹】tree peony; peony

【牡蛎】oyster

拇 (构词成分)见下

【拇指】❶ thumb ❷ big toe

姆 名 wet nurse

【姆夫蒂】[宗] (伊斯兰教) mufti

【姆欧】[电] mho

mù

木 Ⅰ 名 ❶ tree: 树木 ❷ timber; wood: 松～ *pinewood* ❸ coffin: 棺木 Ⅱ 形 ❶ made of wood; wooden: ～制家具 *wooden furniture* / ～箱 *wooden box* / ～桥 *wooden bridge* ❷ simple; plain: 木讷 ❸ numb; wooden: 两脚都冻～了。*Both feet were numb with cold.* / 舌头～了,什么味儿也尝不出来。*My tongue has lost all its sense of taste.*

【木板】plank; board ◇ ～床 plank bed

【木版】[刷] block ◇ ～画 woodcut; wood engraving; ～印花 [纺] block printing; ～印刷 block printing

【木本水源】the root of a tree and the source of a stream—the root of a matter

【木本植物】[植] xylophyta; woody plant

【木笔】another name for 木兰

【木菠萝】[植] jackfruit

【木材】wood; timber; lumber: ～厂 *timber mill* / ～防腐 *wood preservation*

【木柴】firewood

【木醇】another name for 甲醇

【木醋酸】[化] pyroligneous acid

【木雕】wood carving ◇ ～泥塑 like an idol carved in wood or moulded in clay; as wooden as a dummy

【木牍】[考古] inscribed wooden tablet

【木蠹蛾】wood moth; carpenter moth

【木耳】an edible fungus (Auricularia auricula-judae)

【木筏】raft

【木芙蓉】(又作'木莲')[植] cotton rose (Hibiscus mutabilis)

【木工】❶ woodwork; carpentry ❷ woodworker; carpenter

【木工机械】woodworking machinery

【木瓜】❶ [植] Chinese flowering quince ❷〈方〉papaya

【木管乐器】woodwind instrument; woodwind

【木盒】tub
【木化石】(又作'木变石') petrified wood; woodstone
【木屐】clogs
【木简】[考古] inscribed wooden slip
【木浆】[纸] wood pulp: 化学～ *chemical wood pulp*
【木僵】numb; stiff
【木强】〈书〉upright; unyielding: ～敦厚 *upright and honest*
【木匠】carpenter
【木焦油】[化] wood tar
【木结构】[建] timber structure; wood construction
【木槿】[植] rose of Sharon
【木精】another name for 甲醇
【木刻】woodcut; wood engraving ◇ ～术 xylography
【木兰】[植] lily magnolia
【木立】stand motionless
【木料】timber; lumber
【木马】❶ [体] vaulting horse; pommelled horse ❷ (children's) hobbyhorse; rocking horse ◇ ～计 the stratagem of the Trojan horse; Trojan horse
【木棉】silk cotton; kapok
【木乃伊】mummy
【木讷】〈书〉simple and slow (of speech): ～寡言 *simple and reticent*
【木偶】❶ puppet; marionette ❷ wooden image; carved figure: 像～似地站着 *stand as still as a carved figure* ◇ ～片 puppet film; ～戏 (又作'木偶剧') puppet show; puppet play
【木排】raft
【木片】wood chip
【木器】wooden furniture; wooden articles
【木琴】[音] xylophone
【木然】stupefied: 神情～ *look stupefied*
【木人石心】a body of wood and a heart of stone—insusceptible; unfeeling
【木石】a lifeless thing; a senseless being: ～心肠 *heartless; unfeeling*
【木梳】wooden comb
【木薯】[植] cassava
【木栓】[植] phellem; cork
【木丝】wood wool ◇ ～板 [建] wood wool board
【木炭】charcoal ◇ ～画 charcoal drawing
【木通】[植] akebi
【木头木脑】wooden-headed; dull-witted
【木头】〈口〉wood; log; timber: 一块～ *a piece of wood* / ～桌子 *a wooden table* ◇ ～人儿 woodenhead; blockhead; slow coach
【木屋】log cabin
【木犀】(又作'木樨') ❶ [植] sweet-scented osmanthus ❷ egg beaten and then cooked: ～饭 *fried rice with scrambled eggs* / ～肉 *pork fried with scrambled eggs* / ～汤 *eggdrop soup*
【木锨】wooden winnowing spade
【木星】[天] Jupiter
【木已成舟】the wood is already made into a boat—what is done cannot be undone
【木俑】[考古] wooden figurine (used as a burial object)
【木鱼】wooden fish (a percussion instrument made of a hollow wooden block, originally used by Buddhist priests to beat rhythm when chanting scriptures)
【木贼】[植] scouring rush
【木质部】[植] xylem
【木质素】lignin

目 Ⅰ **名** ❶ eye: 注目 ❷ item: 项目 ❸ [生] order: 亚～ *suborder* ❹ a list of things; catalogue; table of contents: 书目 Ⅱ **动** look; regard: ～为奇迹 *regard as a miracle*
【目标】❶ objective; target: 发现～ *find the target* / 攻击～ *target (or objective) of attack* / 军事～ *military objective; military target* ❷ goal; aim; objective: 共同～ *a common goal (or objective)* / 我的生活～是当一名小提琴手。*My goal in life is to be a violinist.* ◇ ～程序 target program; ～语言 object language
【目不见睫】the eye can't see its lashes—lack self-knowledge
【目不交睫】not sleep a wink
【目不窥园】never take a peep into the garden—bury oneself in one's studies
【目不忍睹】cannot bear to look at
【目不识丁】not know one's ABC; be totally illiterate
【目不暇接】(又作'目不暇给') the eye cannot take it all in; too many things for the eye to take in
【目不邪视】not cast sidelong glances—❶ be upright and proper ❷ cold and detached; unconcerned; indifferent
【目不斜视】not look sideways; refuse to be distracted
【目不转睛】look with fixed gaze; regard with rapt attention: 歌唱演员们～地望着指挥。*The singers kept their eyes fixed on the conductor.* / 雷达兵～地注视着荧光屏。*The radarman's eyes were glued to the screen.*
【目测】range estimation
【目次】table of contents; contents
【目瞪口呆】gaping; dumbstruck; stupefied: 吓得～ *be struck dumb with fear*
【目的】purpose; aim; goal; objective; end: ～明确 *have a definite purpose* / ～与手段 *ends and means* / 怀着不可告人的～ *harbour evil intentions; have ulterior motives* ◇ ～地 destination; ～港 port of destination; ～论 [哲] teleology;
【目睹】see with one's own eyes; witness: 整个事件我都亲眼～。*I saw the incident from beginning to end with my own eyes.*
【目光】❶ sight; vision; view: ～短浅 *short-sighted* / ～锐利 *sharp-eyed; sharp-sighted* / ～远大 *farsighted; farseeing* ❷ gaze; look: ～呆滞 *one's eye-sight is restrained* / ～炯炯 *flashing eyes* / ～无神 *dull look* / 两人的～碰到一起。

Their eyes met.
【目光如豆】vision as narrow as a bean—of narrow vision; short-sighted
【目光如炬】❶ eyes blazing like torches—blazing with anger ❷ looking ahead with wisdom; far-sighted
【目击】see with one's own eyes; witness: ～其事 *witness the event* ◇ ～者 eyewitness; witness
【目见】see for oneself
【目镜】[物] eyepiece; ocular
【目空一切】consider everybody and everything beneath one's notice; be supercilious
【目力】同〖视力〗
【目录】❶ catalogue; list: 图书～ *library catalogue* ❷ table of contents; contents ◇ ～学 bibliography (as a science)
【目迷五色】dazzled by a riot of colour—bewildered by a complicated situation
【目前】at present; at the moment: ～形势 *the present (or current) situation* / ～的生产能力 *existing production capacity* / 到～为止 *up till the present moment; up till now; so far; to date*
【目清眉秀】(又作'眉清目秀') The eyes are clear and the eyebrows refined.
【目视飞行】[航空] visual flight
【目送】follow sb. with one's eyes; watch sb. go; gaze after: 她～着他的背影远去。*She gazed affectionately after his receding figure.*
【目无法纪】disregard (or flout) law and discipline; show contempt for the law
【目无全牛】(of an experienced butcher) see an ox not as whole (but only as parts to be cut)—be supremely skilled
【目无组织】disregard organizational discipline; defy the leadership of one's organization
【目无尊长】with no regard for one's elders and betters
【目眩】dizzy; dazzled: 灯光强烈，令人～。*The light is too dazzling.*
【目语】communicate with the eyes
【目指气使】order people about by a glare; be insufferably arrogant
【目中无人】consider everyone beneath one's notice; be supercilious; be overweening: 你看她神气的，简直是～。*Just look at the airs she's giving herself, looking down her nose at everybody.*

沐 动 wash one's hair: 栉风沐雨
【沐猴而冠】a monkey with a hat on—a worthless person in imposing attire
【沐雨栉风】同〖栉风沐雨〗
【沐浴】❶ have (or take) a bath ❷ bathe; immerse: 他们～在青春的欢乐里。*They revelled in the joy of youth.*

苜 (构词成分)见下
【苜蓿】[植] lucerne; alfalfa

牧 动 tend (sheep, cattle, etc.); herd: ～马 *herd horses* / ～羊 *tend sheep*
【牧草】herbage; forage grass
【牧场】grazing land; pastureland; pasture
【牧笛】reed pipe
【牧放】herd; tend; put out to pasture
【牧歌】❶ pastoral song; pastoral ❷ [音] madrigal
【牧工】hired herdsman
【牧马人】herdsman (of horses)
【牧民】herdsman
【牧区】❶ pastureland; pasture ❷ pastoral area
【牧犬】shepherd dog; sheep dog
【牧人】herdsman
【牧师】[宗](基督教) pastor; minister; clergyman
【牧童】shepherd boy; buffalo boy
【牧畜】同〖畜牧〗
【牧羊犬】shepherd dog; collie
【牧羊人】shepherd
【牧业】animal (or livestock) husbandry; stock raising; livestock farming
【牧主】herd owner (who owns livestock and pastures and hires herdsmen)

钼 名 [化] molybdenum (Mo)
【钼钢】molybdenum steel
【钼酸】molybdic acid ◇ ～铵 ammonium molybdate

募 动 ❶ raise; collect: ～款 *raise money (or fund)* ❷ enlist; recruit: ～兵 *recruit soldiers*
【募兵制】mercenary system
【募股】raise capital by floating shares
【募化】(of Buddhist monks or Taoist priests) collect alms
【募集】raise; collect: ～资金 *raise a fund*
【募捐】solicit contributions; collect donations

墓 名 grave; tomb; mausoleum
【墓碑】tombstone; gravestone
【墓道】❶ path leading to a grave; tomb passage ❷ aisle leading to the coffin chamber of an ancient tomb
【墓地】graveyard; burial ground; cemetery
【墓室】coffin chamber
【墓穴】coffin pit; open grave
【墓葬】[考古] grave: ～群 *graves*
【墓志】inscription on the memorial tablet within a tomb
【墓志铭】inscription on the memorial tablet within a tomb; epitaph

幕 名 ❶ tent: 帐幕 ❷ curtain; screen: ～启。*The curtain rises.* / ～落。*The curtain falls.* or *Curtain.* ❸ act (of a play): 第一～ *the first act; Act 1* / 一出三～五场的话剧 *a play in three acts and five scenes* ❹ office of a commanding general in ancient China or Japan: 幕府
【幕宾】(又作'幕客') ❶ 同〖幕僚〗❷ 同〖幕友〗
【幕布】❶ (theatre) curtain ❷ (cinema) screen
【幕府】office of a commanding general in ancient China or Japan
【幕后】behind the scenes; backstage: ～操纵 *pull*

strings (*or wires*) *behind the scenes* / ～活动 *behind-the-scenes activities*; *backstage manoeuvring* / ～人物 *wirepuller*; *backstage manipulator*

【幕间休息】interval (in a play, etc.); intermission

【幕僚】❶ aides and staff ❷ assistant to a ranking official or general in old China

【幕墙】screen wall (made of a series of screens, often with inlaid glass)

【幕天席地】have the sky as one's tent and the earth as one's mat—❶ take one's ease out in the open air ❷ have great breadth of view

【幕友】a private assistant attending to legal, fiscal or secretarial duties in a local yamen; private adviser

睦 形 peaceful; harmonious: 婆媳不～ *mother-in-law and daughter-in-law not getting along well*

【睦邻】good-neighbourliness: ◇ ～关系 good-neighbourly relations; ～政策 good-neighbour policy

慕 动 admire; yearn for: 爱慕

【慕光性】同〖趋光性〗

【慕名】out of admiration for a famous person (or a place): ～而来 *visit a place* (*or a person*) *out of admiration* / ～求见 *have respect for one's name and ask for an interview*

【慕尼黑】Munich ◇ ～协定 the Munich Agreement (1938); ～阴谋 the Munich conspiracy

【慕容】a two-character surname

暮 Ⅰ 名 dusk; evening; sunset: 薄暮 Ⅱ 形 towards the end; late: 岁暮

【暮霭】evening mist: 晚霞渐渐暗淡,～沉沉,野旷天低。*The sunset grew darker and darker; the evening mist became heavier. The vast fields were dim as far as the eye could see.*

【暮齿】〈书〉old age; one's later (or remaining) years

【暮春】late spring (the third month of the lunar year)

【暮鼓晨钟】the evening drum and the morning bell (in a monastery)—exhortations to virtue and purity

【暮景】❶ sunset scene; twilight ❷ life in old age; evening of one's life

【暮年】declining years; old age; evening of one's life

【暮气】lethargy; apathy: ～沉沉 lethargic; apathetic; lifeless

【暮秋】late autumn (the ninth month of the lunar year)

【暮色】dusk; twilight; gloaming ◇ ～苍茫 deepening dusk; spreading shades of dusk

【暮世】〈旧〉modern times; recent years

【暮岁】❶ towards the end of the year ❷ old age; one's later (or remaining) years

穆 形 solemn; reverent: 肃穆

【穆罕默德】Islam Mohammed (c. 570-632), founder of Islam

【穆民】believers in Islam

【穆斯林】Moslem; Muslim

N

ná

拿 Ⅰ 动 ❶ hold; take: ～去。*Take it.* / ～来。*Bring it here.* / 她手里～着一把扇子。*She's holding a fan in her hand.* / 把这些东西～走。*Take these things away.* / 不～枪的敌人 *enemies without guns* ❷ seize; capture: ～下敌人的碉堡 *capture the enemy's blockhouse* / 他们～住三个匪徒。*They captured three bandits.* ❸ have a firm grasp of; be able to do; be sure of: ～不准 *not be sure; feel uncertain* / 这事你～得稳吗? *Are you sure of it?* ❹ put sb. in a difficult position: 这件事你～不住人。*I don't think you can make things difficult by not doing the job.* / 他说不干了,想～我一把。*He said he wasn't going to do it and tried to put me in an awkward position.* ❺ (of a chemical agent, etc.) turn sth. bad: 这块木头让药水～白了。*The chemical agent has bleached the wooden block.* Ⅱ 介 ❶〈口〉by means of; with; by: ～尺量 *measure with a ruler* / ～事实证明 *prove with facts; cite facts to prove* / ～这个标准去衡量 *judge by this standard* ❷ (used in the same way as 把 bǎ Ⅳ): 不能～工作当儿戏。*You shouldn't treat your work as a trifling matter.* / 她要是一定要走,你又能～她怎么样? *If she insists on leaving, what can you do about it?* ❸(used with 来说,来讲,来看, etc.) as regards; as to: ～产品质量来讲 *as to the quality of the products* / ～英语水平来看,她比组里其他人要强些。*So far as English proficiency goes, she is better than the other members of the group.*

【拿办】apprehend and punish by law; arrest and bring to justice

【拿不出去】(又作'拿不出手') not be presentable: 我这笔字～。*My handwriting is not presentable.*

【拿不起来】cannot manage: 这样的工作他～。*He cannot manage this kind of work.*

【拿大顶】(又作'拿顶') stand on one's hands

【拿大头】❶ take the lion's share ❷ take sb. for a sucker; cheat sb. out of his money; fleece sb.: 我买这台录音机让人～了。*I've been had over this recorder I've bought.*

【拿刀动杖】take up swords and cudgels; start a fight with weapons

【拿得起,放得下】can take it up or put it down—be adaptable to circumstances

【拿得起来】can manage; can do: 样样农活她都～。*She can do every kind of farm work.*

【拿定主意】make up one's mind: 她一直拿不定主意。*She's been wavering all along.*

【拿获】apprehend (a criminal): 凶手被当场～。*The murderer was seized on the spot (or was caught red-handed).*

【拿架子】put on airs; assume great airs; throw one's weight around: 你拿什么架子? *Who do you think you are to put on such airs?*

【拿开】take away

【拿捏】〈方〉❶ be affectedly bashful: 有话快说,～个什么劲儿! *Out with it. Why be so shy and hesitant?* ❷ make things difficult for; put pressure on; threaten: 我就做错过那么一次,你就老用这个来～我。*That's the only mistake I made and you are always using it against me.*

【拿腔拿调】speak with an affected tone of voice

【拿腔作势】(又作'拿班作势') be affected or pretentious; act affectedly; strike a pose

【拿权】wield power; be in the saddle

【拿人】make things difficult for others; raise difficulties: 你这不是故意～吗? *Aren't you being difficult on purpose?*

【拿事】have the power to do sth. or to decide what to do: 父母都出门了,家里连个～的人也没有。*The parents are away; no one in the family can make a decision.*

【拿手】adept; expert; good at: 剪纸她很～。*She's good at making paper-cuts.* / ～菜 *a cook's best dishes; dishes one is particularly good at making*

【拿手好戏】❶the play that an actor does best:《贵妃醉酒》是她的～。*The Drunken Beauty was the play she did best.* ❷ one's speciality; one's forte: 游泳是她的～。*Swimming is her forte.* / 挑拨离间是他的～。*He makes a speciality of sowing discord.* or *He is a past master at sowing discord.*

【拿稳】hold steadily; predict with confidence

【拿印把子】hold the seal of authority—be in an important position; be in power

【拿着鸡毛当令箭】take a chicken feather for a warrant to issue orders —treat one's superior's casual remark as an order and make a big fuss about it

【拿主意】make a decision; decide: 究竟去不去,你自己～吧。*You'd better decide for yourself whether to go or not.*

【拿住】hold firmly; put under arrest

镎 名［化］neptunium (Np)

nǎ

哪 Ⅰ代 ❶ (used in questions) which; what：我们这里有两位姓张的，您要找的是～一位？*We've got two Zhangs here. Which one do you want to see?* / 你学的是～国语言？*What foreign language are you studying?* ❷ (used in statements to indicate sth. indefinite) whichever; any that：～天有空就请过来。*Come over any time you are free.* / 你最喜欢～件就拿～件。*Take whichever you like best.* Ⅱ副 (used in rhetorical questions to express negation)：～有这样的事？*Nothing of the sort (or kind)!*

【哪儿】❶ where：他上～去啦？*Where has he gone?* ❷ wherever; anywhere：～需要，我就上～去。*I'll go wherever I'm needed.* / ～都找不到他。*He is nowhere to be found.* ❸ (used in rhetorical questions to express negation)：我～知道他不吃牛肉。*How was I to know he didn't eat beef?*

【哪儿的话】〈套〉what are you saying; you shouldn't say that：太麻烦你了。——～。*Sorry to have caused you so much trouble. —You shouldn't say that.*

【哪个】❶ which：你们是～班的？*Which class are you in?* ❷〈方〉who：～在打电话？*Who's using the telephone?*

【哪会儿】〈方〉(又作'哪会子') ❶ when：你这篇文章～才能脱稿？*When can you get the draft ready?* ❷ whenever; any time：你要～来就～来。*Come any time you like.*

【哪里】❶ where：你是～人？*Where are you from?* / 你～不舒服？*What is the trouble with you?* or *Where do you feel the pain?* ❷ wherever; where：～最艰苦就在～干 *go and work where the work is hardest* ❸ (used in rhetorical questions to express negation)：我～知道他会改变主意的？*How could I know that he should change his mind?* ❹〈套〉(used as a polite reply to a compliment)：你对我们帮助很大。——～，～。*You gave us a lot of help. —It was nothing.* / 你的英语说得真好。——～，～。*You speak very good English. —I'm flattered.*

【哪门子】〈方〉(used to emphasize a rhetorical question)：好好儿的，你哭～？*Everything is all right. What on earth are you crying for?* / 他说的是～事呀！*What the hell is he talking about?*

【哪能】(used in rhetorical questions to express negation) how can; how could：我～干那种缺德事儿呢。*How could I play that sort of mean trick? It's the last thing I would do in the world!*

【哪怕】even; even if; even though; no matter how：～天气不好也要去。*We'll go even if it rains.* / ～是再大的困难我们也能克服。*However great the difficulties may be, we can overcome them.*

【哪些】which (ones); who; what：～是你的？*Which ones are yours?* / ～人出席这次会议？*Who will attend the meeting?* / 你们讨论了～问题？*What problems did you discuss?*

【哪样】❶ what kind; what：你要～颜色的？*What colour do you want?* ❷ whatever kind; whatever：我们这儿的毛线颜色齐全，你要～的就有～的。*We have knitting wool in a variety of colours. You can have whatever colour you want.*

【哪知】who would have thought：～他会出这样的丑？*Who would have thought he could make such a fool of himself?*

nà

那 Ⅰ代 that：～老头儿 *that old man* / ～时候 *at that time* / 我们说这道～的，不知不觉已到凌晨。*We talked about this and that, and without our realizing it, it was almost dawn.* Ⅱ连 then; in that case：你要想跟我们一块走，～就得快点。*If you're coming with us, you must hurry.* / ～我们就不再等了。*In that case, we won't wait any longer.*

【那边】there; over there：孩子们在～玩。*The children are playing over there.*

【那儿】〈口〉❶ 同〖那里〗❷ (used after 打，从，由) that time; then：打～起，她就用心念书了。*She's been studying hard since then.*

【那程子】〈方〉those days; that period：～我很忙，没有工夫来看你。*I was terribly busy those days and couldn't find time to come to see you.*

【那达慕】Nadam Fair, a Mongolian traditional fair

【那当儿】at that time; in those days

【那个】❶ that (one)：～孩子 *that child* / ～根本谈不到。*That's out of the question.* ❷〈口〉(used before a verb or adjective with exclamatory force)：瞧他们干得～欢哪！*See how they're throwing themselves into their work!* ❸〈口〉(used euphemistically as a predicative adjective)：你刚才的脾气也太～了。*The way you lost your temper was a little too—you know what I mean.*

【那会儿】〈口〉at that time; then：到～钢的产量将大大增加。*By that time the steel output will have greatly increased.* / 傍晚～下了一阵小雨。*Toward evening, there came a drizzly rain.*

【那里】that place; there：我刚从～回来。*I've just come from there.* or *I've just been there.* / 这星期天，老张～有个聚会。*There'll be a get-together at Lao Zhang's place this coming Sunday.*

【那么】(又作'那末') ❶ like that; in that way; so：你不该～做。*You shouldn't have done that.* or *You oughtn't to have acted the way you did.* / 她不好意思～说。*It embarrassed her to say that.* ❷ (used before numerals to indicate approximation) about; or so: 估计得走～三、四个钟头才能到。*I think it will take three or four hours to get there*. ❸ (used to connect a clause expressing a logical consequence to a conditional clause) then; in that case: 既然这样不行,～你打算怎么办呢? *Since that's impossible, what are you going to do?*

【那么点儿】〈口〉so little; so few: ～活儿,一天就可以干完了。*We can finish that little bit of work in a day*.

【那么些】so much; so many: 她一个人照料～孩子,真不容易。*She looks after all those kids by herself. That's not so easy*.

【那么着】〈口〉do that; do so: 他～是为了集体。*He did it for the collective*. / 你再～,我可要恼了。*If you do that again, I'll get angry*.

【那时】at that time; then; in those days: 从～以来 *since then; from that time on* / ～正是冬天。*It was wintertime then*.

【那些】those: ～苹果 *those apples* / ～饭店都是最近几年盖的。*Those hotels were all built in recent years*.

【那样】of that kind; like that; such; so: 他不像你～仔细。*He's not so careful as you are*. / 这点小事你怎么就急得～儿了。*Why let such trifles worry you so much?*

【那阵儿】(又作'那阵子')〈口〉during that period (of time); in those days; then: 大伙儿开会～,你上哪儿去了? *Where were you when we were all at the meeting?*

呐

(构词成分)见下

【呐喊】shout loudly; cry out: ～助威 *shout encouragement; cheer*

纳

动 ❶ receive; admit: 闭门不～ *refuse to admit; shut sb. out* ❷ accept: 采纳 ❸ enjoy: 纳凉 ❹ pay; offer: 纳税 ❺ sew close stitches (over a patch, etc.): ～鞋底子 *stitch soles (of cloth shoes)*

【纳彩】(of the bridegroom-to-be's family) present gifts to the girl's family at time of betrothal

【纳粹】Nazi: ～分子 *Nazi* / ～主义 *Nazism*

【纳呆】[中] indigestion and loss of appetite

【纳福】〈书〉(usu. of elderly people) enjoy a life of ease and comfort

【纳贡】pay tribute (to a suzerain or emperor)

【纳罕】be surprised; marvel: 朋友们都～我为什么近来沉默寡言。*My friends wondered why I had been so reticent recently*.

【纳贿】❶ take bribes ❷ offer bribes

【纳谏】〈书〉(of a sovereign, an elder or superior) accept an admonition; accept advice

【纳款】〈书〉surrender and pledge allegiance

【纳凉】enjoy the cool (in the open air)

【纳赂被控】be accused of receiving bribes

【纳闷】〈书〉feel puzzled; be perplexed; wonder: 家里一个人也没有,他心里很～。*He was surprised to find nobody at home*.

【纳米比亚】Namibia ◇ ～人 Namibian

【纳聘】同〖纳彩〗

【纳妾】take a concubine

【纳入】bring (or channel) into: ～正轨 *put sth. on the right course* / ～国家计划 *bring sth. into line with the state plan*

【纳纱制品】[工美] petit-point articles

【纳税】pay taxes ◇ ～年度 tax year; ～凭证 tax payment receipt; ～人 taxpayer; ～申报单 tax returns

【纳头】〈旧〉bow one's head (in greeting): ～便拜 *kneel down and kowtow at once*

【纳西族】the Naxi (Nahsi) ethnic group or the Naxis (Nahsis), inhabiting Yunnan Province

【纳降】accept the enemy's surrender

【纳新】take in the fresh—take in new members

衲

Ⅰ 动 patch up Ⅱ 名 patchwork vestment worn by a Buddhist monk

钠

名 [化] sodium (Na)

【钠长石】albite (a mineral)

【钠钙玻璃】(又作'钠玻璃') soda-lime glass

【钠汽灯】sodium lamp; sodium vapor

【钠缺乏】sodium deficiency

捺

Ⅰ 动 press down; restrain: ～着性子 *control one's temper* / 勉强～住心头的怒火 *barely manage to restrain one's anger* Ⅱ 名 right-falling stroke (in Chinese characters)

na

哪

助 (used in the same way as 啊, only after words ending with consonant n): 谢谢您～! *Thank you!* / 我没留神～! *I wasn't noticing*. / 加油干～! *Speed up!* or *Come on!*

nǎi

乃

〈书〉Ⅰ 动 be: 此～我国特产。*This is a special product of China*. / 失败～成功之母。*Failure is the mother of success*. Ⅱ 副 ❶ so; therefore: 因山势高峻,～在山腰休息片时。*It was a steep climb, so we rested for a while halfway up the hill*. ❷ only then: 惟虚心～能进步。*You can make progress only if you are modest*. / 今～知之。*I didn't know it until now*. Ⅲ 代 you; your: ～父 *your father*

【乃尔】〈书〉like this; to such an extent

【乃是】〈书〉be: 人民群众～真正的英雄。*The masses of the people are the true heroes*.

【乃至】〈书〉and even: 他精通英语、法语、德语、阿拉伯语～世界语。*He has a good command of English, French, German, Arabic and even Esperanto*.

奶

Ⅰ 名 ❶ breasts (of a female mammal);

mammae ❷ milk Ⅱ 动 suckle; breast-feed: ～孩子 *suckle (or breast-feed) a baby* / 他是奶妈～大的。*He was breast-fed by a wet nurse.*

【奶茶】tea with milk

【奶疮】common name for 乳腺炎

【奶粉】milk powder; powdered milk; dried milk: 冲一杯～ *make a cup of milk with milk powder* ◇ 全脂～ whole milk powder; 脱脂～ skimmed milk powder

【奶糕】a baby food made of rice-flour, sugar, etc.

【奶积】[中] indigestion of suckling babies due to improper breast-feeding

【奶酒】同〖奶子酒〗

【奶酪】cheese

【奶妈】(又作'奶母') wet nurse

【奶毛】foetal hair

【奶名】a child's pet name; infant name

【奶奶】〈口〉❶ (paternal) grandmother; grandma ❷ a respectful form of address for an old woman ❸〈方〉young mistress of the house

【奶娘】〈方〉wet nurse

【奶牛】milch cow; milk cow; cow

【奶皮】skin formed on boiled milk

【奶品】milk products; dairy products

【奶瓶】feeding bottle; nursing bottle; (baby's) bottle

【奶水】〈口〉milk: 她～足不足? *Has she got enough milk to nurse her baby?*

【奶糖】toffee

【奶头】〈口〉❶ nipple; teat ❷ nipple (of a feeding bottle)

【奶昔】milk shake

【奶牙】common name for 乳齿

【奶羊】milch goat

【奶油】cream ◇ ～蛋糕 cream cake; ～分离器 cream separator; ～泡夫 cream puff; ～色 cream-colored

【奶罩】brassiere; bra

【奶汁】milk

【奶子】❶〈口〉milk ❷〈方〉breasts ❸〈方〉wet nurse

【奶子酒】fermented (cow's or mare's) milk (used by Mongolians as an alcoholic drink)

【奶嘴】nipple (of a feeding bottle)

氖 名 [化] neon (Ne)

【氖灯】neon lamp; neon light; neon

【氖管】neon tube

【氖气】common name for 氖

nài

奈 Ⅰ 副 what; how; but: ～援军不至。*But unfortunately the reinforcements didn't arrive.* Ⅱ 动 bear; endure: ～不过 *unable to bear it*

【奈何】❶ (used in a rhetorical question) what alternative is there; what's to be done: 没～ *have no way out; have no choice; there is no alternative* ❷ how; why ❸ do sth. to (a person); cope with; deal with: 其奈我何? *What can they do to me?* / 谁也～他不得。*Nobody could do anything against him.*

耐 动 be able to bear or endure: ～穿 *can stand wear and tear; be endurable* / 这种料子很～洗。*This material washes well.* / 他再也～不住性子了。*He could no longer hold back his anger.*

【耐波力】seakeeping qualities (of a vessel)

【耐不住】unable to bear; unable to stand

【耐潮湿】humidity resistant

【耐烦】be patient: 谁～你的絮叨? *Who can bear the endless chatter of yours?*

【耐寒】cold-resistant: 耐严寒 *resistant to low temperature* ◇ ～性 cold resistance; winterhardiness; ～作物 cold-resistant crop

【耐旱】drought-enduring ◇ ～植物 drought-enduring plant

【耐航包装】seaworthy packing

【耐火】fire-resistant; refractory ◇ ～材料 refractory (material); fireproof material; ～衬砌 refractory lining; ～黏土 refractory clay; ～水泥 refractory cement; ～砖 refractory brick; firebrick

【耐久】lasting long; durable: ～力 *durability; endurance*

【耐苦】able to endure hardships

【耐劳】able to stand hard work; able to endure heavy labour

【耐力】endurance; staying power; stamina

【耐磨】(of metals) wear-resisting; wearproof ◇ ～合金钢 wear-resisting alloy steel; ～性 wearability; wear resistance; ～硬度 abrasion hardness

【耐热】heat-resisting; heatproof ◇～合金 heat-resisting alloy; ～性 heat resistance

【耐人寻味】afford food for thought: 他的话是很～的。*What he says gives one much food for thought.*

【耐蚀钢】corrosion-resisting steel

【耐受】bear; stand; endure

【耐水作物】water-tolerant crop

【耐酸】acidproof; acid-resisting ◇ ～缸器 acidproof stoneware; ～混凝土 acid-resisting concrete

【耐心】❶ patient; patiently: ～等待 *wait patiently* / 她做任何事都～得很。*She does everything patiently.* ❷ patience: 失去～ *lose one's patience; be out of patience*

【耐心烦】〈口〉patience: 伺候病人没有～可不行。*It needs great patience to nurse the sick.*

【耐性】patience; endurance

【耐印力】[刷] pressrun

【耐用】durable: 这种地毯经久～。*This kind of carpet is highly resistant to (or stands any amount of) wear and tear.*

萘 名 [化] naphthalene

【萘酚】naphthol

nán

男 名 ❶ man；male：～病房 *men's ward* / ～护士 *male nurse* / ～主人公 *hero* / ～学生 *boy student* / ～佣人 *manservant* ❷ son；boy：长～ *one's eldest son* ❸ baron：男爵

【男扮女装】a man disguised as a woman

【男傧相】best man

【男才女貌】the man is able and the woman is beautiful；an ideal couple

【男厕所】❶ men's lavatory（or toilet，room）❷（used to indicate a lavatory）Gentlemen；Men；Gents

【男大当婚，女大当嫁】Upon growing up，every male should take a wife and every female should take a husband.

【男单】［体］〈略〉见〖男子单打〗men's singles（of tennis，table tennis，etc.）

【男盗女娼】behave like thieves and whores；be out-and-out scoundrels：他满嘴仁义道德，满肚子～。*All his talk is of humanity，justice and morality，while in his heart there is nothing but greed and lust*.

【男低音】［音］bass

【男儿】man：好～ *a fine man* / ～本色 *the manliness of a man*

【男方】the bridegroom's or husband's side

【男高音】［音］tenor

【男耕女织】men plough the fields and women weave—an agricultural community's ideal of peace and order

【男孩儿】（又作'男孩子'）❶ boy ❷ son：她有一个～。*She's got a son*（*or boy*）.

【男婚女嫁】A man should take a wife and a woman a husband.

【男家】the bridegroom's or husband's family

【男角】male role（in a play，film，etc.）

【男爵】baron ◇ ～夫人 baroness

【男科】❶ andrologic department（of a hospital）：～大夫 *andrologic doctor* ❷ andrology

【男蓝】men's basketball game or team

【男男女女】men and women

【男女】❶ male and female；men and women：～青年 *young men and women* / ～同工同酬。*Men and women get equal pay for equal work*. ❷〈方〉sons and daughters ◇ ～混合双打 mixed doubles；～老少 men and women，old and young；～平等 equality of men and women；equality of the sexes；～有别 Males and females should be treated differently.

【男女关系】relations between the two sexes：不正当的～ *illicit sexual relations*（*between the two sexes*）

【男排】men's volleyball team

【男朋友】boyfriend

【男人】（nánrén）❶ man ❷ menfolk

【男人】（nánren）〈口〉husband

【男生】man student；boy student；schoolboy

【男声】［音］male voice：～合唱 *men's chorus*；*male chorus*

【男士】〈谀〉man；gentleman：下一场舞，由女士们邀请～们跳。*The next will be ladies' invitation dance*.

【男双】［体］〈略〉见〖男子双打〗men's doubles（of table tennis，tennis，etc.）

【男相】（of a female）look or behave like a man：她长得有些～。*She looks quite masculine*.

【男性】❶ the male sex ❷ man

【男中音】［音］baritone

【男装】menswear；men's clothing：有些女客穿着～。*Some of the women were dressed up in men's clothes*.

【男子】man；male：～单（双）打 *men's singles*（*doubles*）/ ～团体赛 *men's team event* / ～项目 *man's event*

【男子汉】a manly man；man：不像个～ *not manly*；*not man enough* / ～，大丈夫，一人做事一人当。*A man should have the courage to take the blame for what he does*.

南 名 south：城～ *south of the city* / ～屋 *a room with a northern exposure*

【南半球】the Southern Hemisphere

【南北】❶ north and south：～合击 *make a joint attack from north and south* ❷ from north to south：这个水库～足有五公里。*This reservoir extends a good five km. from north to south*.

【南北朝】the Northern and Southern Dynasties（420-589）

【南北对话】North-South dialogue（i. e. dialogue between developed countries in the Northern Hemisphere and developing countries in the Southern Hemisphere）

【南边】❶ south；the southern side ❷〈口〉the southern part of the country，esp. the area south of the Changjiang River；the South

【南部】southern part；south：～非洲 *southern Africa*

【南朝】the Southern Dynasties（420-589），namely，the Song Dynasty（宋，420-479），the Qi Dynasty（齐，479-502），the Liang Dynasty（梁，502-557）and the Chen Dynasty（陈，557-589）

【南斗】the Southern Dipper

【南方】❶ south ❷ the southern part of the country，esp. the area south of the Changjiang River；the South：住在～ *live in the South* ◇ ～风味 southern style；southern flavour；～话 southern dialect；～人 Southerner

【南方古猿】Australopithecus

【南非】South Africa

【南风】south wind

【南瓜】pumpkin；cushaw

【南国】〈文〉the southern part of the country；the South：～风光 *southern scenery*

【南海】the Nanhai Sea；the South China Sea

【南寒带】the south frigid zone
【南回归线】the Tropic of Capricorn
【南货】delicacies from south China (such as dried bamboo shoots, etc.)
【南箕北斗】something which enjoys empty name but serves no practical purposes
【南极】❶ the South Pole; the Antarctic Pole ❷ the south magnetic pole ◇ ～光［天］southern lights; aurora australis; ～圈 the Antarctic Circle; ～虾 another name for 磷虾; ～洲 the Antarctic Continent; Antarctica
【南柯一梦】a Nanke dream—a fond dream; an illusory joy
【南来北往】going north and south (said of heavy traffic or a bustling crowd)
【南粮北调】supply grain to the north from the south
【南美洲】South America
【南冕座】［天］Corona Australis
【南面】❶ face south—be a ruler (from the fact that the emperor sat facing south when holding court): ～称孤 *face south and call oneself the Lonely One—become a ruler* ❷ south; the southern side——另见〖北面〗❶
【南南合作】South-South cooperation (i. e. cooperation among developing countries in the Southern Hemisphere)
【南欧】Southern Europe
【南腔北调】(speak with) a mixed accent: 他说话～。*He speaks with a mixture of accents.*
【南曲】❶ southern tunes (tunes and melodies popular in the South during the Song, Yuan and Ming Dynasties) ❷ opera sung in southern tunes
【南三角座】［天］Southern Triangle
【南沙群岛】the Nansha Islands
【南十字座】［天］Cross; Crux; South Cross
【南式】(of) southern style: ～糕点 *southern-style pastry*
【南水北调】south water to north ◇ ～工程 projects for diverting water from the south to the north
【南斯拉夫】Yugoslavia ◇ ～人 Yugoslav
【南宋】the Southern Song Dynasty (1127-1279)
【南天极】［天］south pole; south celestial pole
【南天竹】［植］nandina
【南纬】south (or southern) latitude
【南味】of southern taste and flavour or food of southern taste and flavour
【南温带】the south temperate zone
【南下】go down south: 大军～ *large contingents of the army advancing south*
【南亚】South Asia ◇ ～次大陆 the South Asian Subcontinent
【南音】southern music—❶ a kind of ballad singing accompanied by dulcimer, pipa (琵琶), dongxiao (洞箫), etc., popular in the Zhujiang (Pearl River) Delta ❷ a type of classical music popular in Fujian Province
【南辕北辙】try to go south by driving the chariot north—act in a way that defeats one's purpose
【南乐】同〖南音〗❶
【南岳】the Southern Mountain (another name for 衡山 Mount Heng in Hunan Province) ——另见〖五岳〗
【南针】❶ compass ❷ a guide (to action)
【南征北战】fight north and south; campaign all across the country: 这是一支解放战争中经过～的英雄连队。*This is a heroic company which fought on many fronts in the Liberation War.*
【南竹】同〖毛竹〗

难 Ⅰ形 ❶ difficult; hard; troublesome: 很～想像 *it's hard to imagine* / 这道题～解。*This problem is hard to solve.* / 山路～走。*Mountain paths are hard to travel.* / 说起来容易，做起来～。*It's easier said than done.* ❷ hardly possible: 难免 / 难说 ❸ bad; unpleasant: 难吃 / 难看 Ⅱ动 put sb. into a difficult position: 这问题一下子把我～住了。*The question put me on the spot.*—— 另见 nàn
【难熬】hard to bear: 饥饿～ *can hardly bear (or stand) the hunger*
【难办之事】have a long row to hoe
【难保】❶ there is no guarantee; one cannot say for sure; it's hard to say: 今天～不下雨。*You can't say for sure that it won't rain today.* ❷ difficult to preserve, protect, defend, etc.: 地位～。*One's position is untenable.* / 性命～。*One's life is in danger.*
【难辨是非】difficult to discriminate between right and wrong
【难辨真伪】hard to distinguish between the true and false
【难缠】(of a person) unreasonable and hard to deal with
【难产】❶［医］difficult labour; dystocia ❷ (of a literary work, plan, etc.) be difficult of fulfilment; be slow in coming
【难吃】taste bad; be unpalatable
【难处】(nánchǔ) hard to get along (*or* on) with: 他只是脾气暴躁些，并不～。*He's a bit quick-tempered, but not difficult to get along with.*
【难处】(nánchu) difficulty; trouble: 他有他的～。*He has his difficulties.*
【难打交道】hard to deal with
【难当】❶ find it hard to shoulder (a responsibility, etc.): ～重任 *can hardly shoulder heavy responsibilities* ❷ hard to endure; unbearable; insufferable: 羞愧～ *be mortally ashamed*
【难倒】daunt; baffle; beat: 这个问题可把我～了。*This problem baffles (or beats) me.*
【难道】(used to give force to a rhetorical question): ～你忘了自己的诺言吗? *Can you have forgotten your promise?* / 这一点儿困难～我们还不能克服吗? *Can't we overcome even such small difficulties?*
【难得】❶ hard to come by; rare: ～的好机会 *a rare chance* / 这种草药很～。*This medicinal herb is hard to come by.* / 像他这样的人很～。*There*

aren't many like him. ❷ seldom; rarely: 她千年～看书。*She seldom, if ever, reads a book*.

【难点】a difficult point; difficulty; a hard nut to crack

【难度】degree of difficulty; difficulty: 这个杂技动作～很大。*This acrobatic feat is extremely difficult*.

【难割难舍】find it hard to part with (a person, place, etc.); be loath to tear oneself away

【难怪】❶ no wonder: ～找不到人,都开会去了。*No wonder you can't find anybody here; they're all away at a meeting*. ❷ understandable; pardonable: 他不大了解情况,搞错了也～。*You can hardly blame him for the mistake he made; he didn't know much about the situation*.

【难关】difficulty; crisis: 渡过～ *tide over a difficulty (or crisis)* / 攻克技术～ *break down a technical barrier; resolve key technical problems*

【难过】❶ have a hard time: 父亲失业,我们日子很～。*We had a hard time when father lost his job*. ❷ feel sorry; feel bad; be grieved: 他听到老师去世的消息,非常～。*He was deeply grieved to learn that his teacher had died*.

【难乎为继】hard to carry on or keep up: 尽管我们极为节省,生活仍～。*Though extremely frugal, we still found it hard to make both ends meet*.

【难解难分】❶ be inextricably involved (in a dispute); be locked together (in a struggle): 两军厮杀,～。*The two opposing armies are locked in battle*. ❷ be sentimentally attached to each other; can't bear to part

【难堪】❶ intolerable; unbearable: ～的话 *annoying remarks* / 天气闷热～。*It was terribly hot and sultry*. ❷ embarrassed: 感到～ *feel very much embarrassed* / 处于～的境地 *be in an extremely awkward (or miserable) situation*

【难看】❶ ugly; unsightly: 他听到这个消息,脸色变得很～。*When he heard the news, his face took on a ghastly expression*. ❷ shameful; embarrassing: 咱们在音乐会上要是演奏不好,那就太～了。*It would be a shame if we put on a bad performance at the concert*.

【难免】hard to avoid: 犯错误是～的,你认真改了就好了。*Mistakes are hard to avoid, but if you correct them conscientiously, things will be all right*. / 人们的看法有时～带片面性。*Sometimes people can't help being one-sided in their views*.

【难耐】hard to bear; unbearable: ～的不眠之夜 *a tormenting sleepless night*

【难能可贵】difficult of attainment, hence worthy of esteem; deserving praise for one's excellent performance or behaviour; estimable; commendable

【难人】❶ difficult; delicate; ticklish: 这种～的事,我办不了。*I cannot handle such a ticklish matter*. ❷ a person handling a delicate matter: 有麻烦我们帮助你,决不叫你做～。*We'll stand by you in case of trouble, and will never leave you holding the bag*.

【难色】a reluctant or embarrassed expression

【难上难】(又作'难上加难') extremely difficult; all the more difficult

【难舍难分】(又作'难分难舍') loath to part from each other: 两人依依惜别,～。*The two of them could hardly tear themselves away from each other*.

【难事】a difficult matter; sth. not easy to manage

【难受】❶ feel unwell; feel ill; suffer pain: 浑身疼得～ *be aching all over* / 胃里～ *feel queasy* ❷ feel unhappy; feel bad: 他知道事情做错了,心里很～。*He felt bad when he realized his error*.

【难说】it's hard to say; you never can tell: 他什么时候回来还很～。*No one can tell when he will return*.

【难说话】be difficult to talk with or deal with: 你那位上司真～。*That boss of yours is really a difficult person*.

【难逃法网】be unable to escape the net of justice

【难题】a difficult problem; a hard nut to crack; poser: 出～ *set difficult questions*

【难听】❶ unpleasant to hear: 这个曲子有点～。*This tune is not very pleasing to the ear*. ❷ offensive; coarse: 她在背后说了你很多～话。*She said a lot of mean things about you behind your back*. ❸ scandalous: 这事情说出去多～。*The story will create a scandal once it gets out*.

【难忘】unforgettable; memorable: ～的一课 *an unforgettable lesson* / ～的岁月 *memorable years* / 当时的情景令人～。*It was so impressive that it always remained fresh in my memory*.

【难为情】❶ abashed; embarrassed: 他听见别人这样夸他,感到很～。*He was very embarrassed to hear people speak so highly of him*. ❷ embarrassing; disconcerting: 答应吧,办不到;不答应吧,又有点～。*It is not feasible to comply, but a bit embarrassing to refuse*.

【难为】❶ embarrass; press: 她不会唱歌,就别～她了。*She can't sing. So don't press her to*. ❷ be a tough job to: 一个人拉扯大五六个孩子,真～了她。*It was quite a job for her to bring up half a dozen children all by herself*. ❸〈套〉(used to thank sb. for doing a favour): 机票也替我们买好了,真～你了。*It was really very kind of you to get the plane tickets for us*.

【难闻】smell unpleasant; smell bad

【难兄难弟】(nánxiōng-nándì) two of a kind; birds of a feather ——另见 nànxiōng-nàndì

【难言之隐】sth. which it would be awkward to disclose; sth. embarrassing to mention; a painful topic: 他似有～。*He seemed too embarrassed to say what was on his mind*.

【难以】hard to; difficult to: ～捉摸 *difficult to pin down; elusive; unintelligible* / ～想像 *unimaginable* / ～形容 *indescribable; beyond description* / ～预料 *hard to predict (or forecast)* / ～置信 *hard to believe*

【难以为继】同〖难乎为继〗
【难易】degree of difficulty：这些问题应该分别～有先有后逐个解决。*These problems should be tackled one by one in the order of difficulty.*
【难于】hard to；difficult to：时间太短，工程～完成。*It's hard to finish the project in such a short time.*
【难于启齿】have a bone in the throat；difficult to speak out one's mind
【难字】uncommon word；rarely used word

楠 （构词成分）见下
【楠木】［植］nanmu（Phoebe nanmu）
【楠竹】another name for 毛竹

nǎn

赧 形 blushing；shamefaced
【赧红】（of one's face）blush for shame；crimson from shame
【赧愧】〈书〉ashamed
【赧赧】blushing；shamefaced
【赧然】〈书〉blushing；shamefaced
【赧颜】〈书〉blush；be shamefaced

蝻 名 the nymph of a locust
【蝻子】the nymph of a locust

nàn

难 Ⅰ 名 calamity；adversity；misfortune；trouble：一方有～，八方支援。*When trouble occurs at one spot, help comes from all quarters.* / 多灾多～ *be dogged by misfortunes* Ⅱ 动 take to task；blame：非难 —— 另见 nán
【难胞】fellow countrymen in distress
【难民】refugee：～收容所 *a haven or shelter for refugees* / ～营 *refugee camp*
【难侨】fellow countrymen in distress overseas
【难兄难弟】（nànxiōng-nàndì）fellow sufferers —— 另见 nánxiōng-nándì
【难友】fellow sufferer

nāng

囔 （构词成分）见下
【囔囔】speak in a low voice；murmur

náng

囊 名 ❶ bag；pocket：药～ *medicine bag* / 背～ *knapsack* ❷ anything shaped like a bag：胆囊
【囊虫】cysticercus：～病 *cysticercosis*
【囊空如洗】with empty pockets；penniless；broke
【囊括】❶ include；embrace：～四海 *bring the whole country under imperial rule* ❷［体］win all：～锦标赛上的全部四块金牌 *pocket all the four gold medals at the championships*
【囊生】Tibetan household slave（or bondman，bondwoman）
【囊尾蚴】another name for 囊虫
【囊中物】sth. which is in the bag—sth. certain of attainment
【囊肿】［医］cyst

nǎng

攮 动 stab
【攮子】dagger

nāo

孬 形〈方〉❶ bad ❷ cowardly
【孬种】〈方〉coward

náo

挠 动 ❶ scratch：～痒痒 *scratch an itch* ❷ hinder：阻挠 ❸ yield；flinch：不屈不挠
【挠度】［建］deflection
【挠钩】long-handled hook
【挠人清梦】disturb one's dream
【挠头】❶ scratch one's head ❷ difficult to tackle：这可是件～的事。*This is a knotty problem.*
【挠性】［物］flexibility
【挠秧】［农］weed rice fields and loosen the soil around the seedlings

硇 （构词成分）见下
【硇砂】［化］sal ammoniac

蛲 （构词成分）见下
【蛲虫】pinworm ◇ ～病 enterobiasis

nǎo

恼 Ⅰ 动 angry；irritated；annoyed：再说我可要～了。*I'll be angry with you if you go on talking like that.* Ⅱ 形 unhappy；worried：烦恼
【恼恨】resent；hate：他的批评是为你好，你可别～他。*You shouldn't resent his criticism. He meant well.*
【恼火】annoyed；irritated；vexed：对于他那种听不进批评的态度，我们感到～。*We're annoyed at his not listening to criticism.*
【恼怒】angry；indignant；furious
【恼人】irritating；annoying：这件事真～。*It's really irritating.* / 春色～。*Spring's hues are teasing.*
【恼羞成怒】fly into a rage from shame；be shamed into anger

脑 名 ❶ brain：用～过度 *overtax one's brain* ❷

brains；mind；head：动手动～ *use one's hands and brains* ❸ essence：樟脑

【脑儿】❶ animal brains（as food）：猪～ *pig's brains* ❷ brain-like jellied food

【脑充血】［医］encephalemia

【脑出血】cerebral hemorrhage

【脑袋】〈口〉❶ head ❷ brains；mind

【脑袋瓜子】（又作‘脑袋瓜儿’）〈口〉❶ head ❷ brains；mind：他的～好使。*He's very clever*. or *He's got a clever mind*.

【脑电波】［生理］brain wave

【脑电图】［医］electroencephalogram（EEG）

【脑动脉】［生理］cerebral artery

【脑瓜子】〈方〉head

【脑海】brain；mind：多年前的旧事又重现在他的～里。*Memories of things long past flashed across his mind*.

【脑黄金】DHA（docosahexaenoic acid）

【脑积水】［医］hydrocephalus

【脑脊膜】meninges ◇ ～炎 meningitis

【脑脊髓炎】［医］encephalomyelitis

【脑脊液】［生理］cerebrospinal fluid（CSF）

【脑际】mind；memory：突然一个念头浮上～。*An idea flashed across my mind*.

【脑浆】brains：～迸裂 *have one's brains dashed out*

【脑筋】❶ brains；mind；head：动～ *use one's brains*（*or head*）❷ way of thinking；ideas：旧～ *a person who clings to old-fashioned ideas*；*an old fogey*

【脑壳】❶ skull ❷〈方〉head

【脑力】mental power；intelligence

【脑力劳动】mental work：逐步消灭～和体力劳动的差别 *gradually eliminate the distinction between mental and manual labour* ◇ ～者 mental worker；brain worker

【脑瘤】brain tumor：切除～ *remove a brain tumor*

【脑颅】brainpan；cranium

【脑满肠肥】heavy-jowled and potbellied（said of the idle rich）

【脑门子】〈口〉forehead；brow

【脑膜】［生理］meninx

【脑膜炎】［医］meningitis

【脑贫血】［医］cerebral anaemia

【脑桥】［生理］pons

【脑上体】［生理］pineal body

【脑勺子】〈方〉the back of the head

【脑神经】［生理］cranial nerve

【脑室】［生理］ventricles of the brain

【脑室造影】［医］ventriculography

【脑死亡】［医］brain death

【脑髓】brains

【脑瘫】brain failure；brain paralysis；stroke

【脑体倒挂】wage disparity between white-collar and blue-collar worker

【脑萎缩】encephalatrophy

【脑下垂体】［生理］pituitary body；pituitary gland；hypophysis

【脑血管造影】［医］cerebral angiography

【脑炎】［医］encephalitis；cerebritis：流行性乙型～ *epidemic encephalitis B*

【脑溢血】［医］cerebral haemorrhage

【脑震荡】［医］cerebral concussion；concussion

【脑汁】brains：绞尽脑汁

【脑子】❶brain ❷ brains；mind；head：没～ *have no brains* / ～灵活 *quick-witted*

瑙（构词成分）见下

【瑙鲁】Nauru ◇ ～人 Nauruan

nào

闹 Ⅰ［形］noisy：这屋里太～。*This room is too noisy*. Ⅱ［动］❶ make a noise；stir up trouble：叫孩子们别～了。*Tell the children to stop making a noise*（*or fooling around*）. / 又哭又～ *make a tearful scene* / 孙悟空大～天宫。*The Monkey King caused havoc in Heaven*. ❷ give vent（to one's anger，resentment，etc.）：闹脾气 / 闹情绪 ❸ suffer from；be troubled by：～眼睛 *have eye trouble* / ～嗓子 *have a sore throat* / ～虫灾 *suffer from insect pests* / ～矛盾 *be at loggerheads* / ～分裂 *engage in splittism* / 你最近瘦了，怎么～的？*How come you look so thin these days*？❹ go in for；do；make：～生产 *go in for production* / 把问题～清楚再发言。*Don't speak until you've got the thing clear in your mind*.

【闹别扭】be difficult with sb.；be at odds with sb.：两口子又在～了。*The couple are at odds with each other again*.

【闹病】〈口〉fall ill；be ill：这孩子体弱，爱～。*The child is weak and sickly*.

【闹不清】〈口〉cannot tell；be unclear about：我也～这里谁是负责人。*I'm not clear either who's in charge here*.

【闹场】a flourish of gongs and drums introducing a theatrical performance

【闹虫灾】suffer from insect pests

【闹得鸡犬不宁】cause such utter confusion as to make everybody nervous

【闹得满城风雨】cause a big scandal

【闹得头混脑胀】cause such utter confusion as to crave one crazy

【闹洞房】同〖闹房〗

【闹独立性】assert one's independence —refuse to obey the leadership

【闹肚子】〈口〉have diarrhoea；be suffering from loose bowels

【闹翻】fall out with sb.：他俩为了一点小事儿就～了。*They fell out with each other over some little thing*.

【闹翻天】raise hell；raise a rumpus

【闹房】（of friends and relatives）banter or tease the newlyweds on wedding night

【闹风潮】carry on agitation；stage strikes，demonstrations，etc.

【闹革命】carry out revolution；make revolution；

rise in revolution

【闹鬼】❶ be haunted ❷ play tricks behind sb.'s back; use underhand means

【闹哄哄】clamorous; noisy: 这里～的,我们另找个地方谈吧。*It's too noisy here, so let's find another place to talk.*

【闹哄】❶ make a noise; make a fuss ❷ (of a group of people) bustle about

【闹荒】(of peasants in former times) start famine riots

【闹饥荒】❶ suffer from famine ❷〈方〉be hard up; be short of money: 快到发工资那几天他就～。*He's always hard up before payday.*

【闹剧】farce

【闹乱子】cause trouble: 我担心他们再这么闹下去会闹出乱子来。*I'm afraid there will be trouble if they go on like that.*

【闹脾气】vent one's spleen; lose one's temper; be in a tantrum

【闹气】〈方〉be cross with sb.

【闹情绪】be disgruntled; be in low spirits: 为这件事他闹了好几天情绪。*He has been unhappy about this for quite a few days.*

【闹嚷嚷】noisy: 外面～的,什么事呀? *What's all that noise about outside?*

【闹嚷】clamour; make a racket; kick up a row

【闹市】busy streets; busy shopping centre; downtown area

【闹事】create a disturbance; make trouble: 上街～ *take to the streets and make trouble*

【闹腾】❶ make a noise; kick up a row ❷ talk and laugh boisterously

【闹笑话】make a fool of oneself; make a stupid mistake: 不懂装懂就会～。*If you pretend to know what you don't know, you'll only make a fool of yourself.*

【闹心】〈方〉❶ be vexed; be annoyed ❷ feel sick; feel queasy

【闹新房】同〖闹房〗

【闹性子】lose one's temper; be in a tantrum

【闹玄虚】purposely make a mystery of simple things; be deliberately mystifying

【闹意见】be on bad terms because of a difference of opinion; be at odds

【闹意气】feel resentful because something is not to one's liking; sulk: 你有意见就提出来,不要～。*If you have any complaint, don't just sulk; speak up.*

【闹着玩儿】〈口〉be joking: 他是跟你～的,你别当真。*He was joking. Don't take it seriously.*

【闹中取静】seek peace and quiet in noisy surroundings

【闹钟】alarm clock

【闹嘴】〈方〉quarrel; bicker: 他们俩怎么又～啦? *Why are they bickering again?*

nè

讷 形〈书〉slow (of speech): ～于言而敏于行 *slow of speech but quick in action*

něi

馁 形 ❶ hungry; famished: 冻馁 ❷ disheartened; dispirited: 气馁

【馁怯】〈书〉lose heart; lose courage; lose one's nerve

nèi

内 名 ❶ (used as a noun) inside; inner part or side: 入～ *go inside; enter* / 请勿入～。*No admittance.* / 共十人,儿童包括在～。*Altogether ten, children included.* / ～附照片。*Photos enclosed.* ❷ (used after a noun to indicate place, time, scope or limits) within; in; inside: 校～ *in the school; on campas* / 墙～ *within the walls* / 本月～ *within the month* / 最近几天～ *within these few days; in a few days* / 市～交通 *urban traffic* ❸ (used before a noun or verb in forming a compound word) inner; internal: 内室 / 内伤 / 内分泌 ❹ one's wife or her relatives: 内人 / 内弟

【内白】words spoken by an actor from offstage

【内宾】Chinese guest (as distinguished from 外宾 foreign guest)

【内部】❶ inside; interior; within: 在人民～ *among the people themselves* / ～装修 *interior decorations* / 堡垒是最容易从～攻破的。*The easiest way to capture a fortress is from within.* ❷ inside; restricted: ◇ ～参考 document to be read only by a certain circle of people; ～电影 film to be shown in limited circles; ～发行 (of newspapers, magazines or books) for restricted circulation; ～刊物 restricted publication; ～矛盾 inner contradictions; ～消息 inside information

【内查外调】make investigations both within and without

【内场】[体] (baseball, softball) infield ◇ ～手 infielder

【内臣】❶ chamberlain ❷ eunuch

【内城】inner city

【内出血】[医] internal haemorrhage (or bleeding)

【内存】[计] memory ◇ 常规～conventional memory; 扩充～ extended memory;

【内存储器】internal storage; internal memory

【内当家】〈方〉❶ wife ❷ the wife of one's master, employer or landlord

【内地】inland; interior; hinterland: ～城市 *inland city* / 我国的～ *the interior of our country*

【内弟】wife's younger brother; brother-in-law

【内电阻】[电] internal resistance

【内定】(of an official appointment) decided at the higher level but not officially announced: 听说他已～为下一任部长。*It is said that he has been*

designated as the incoming minister.
【内毒素】[医] endotoxin
【内耳】internal ear; inner ear
【内耳眩晕综合症】(又作'美尼尔综合症')[医] Ménière's syndrome; Ménière's disease
【内耳炎】[医] otitis interna
【内方外圆】square internally and round externally
【内分泌】[生理] endocrine; internal secretion ◇ ~系统 endocrine system; ~失调 [医] endocrine imbalance; endocrinopathy; ~腺 [生理] endocrine glands
【内封】title page
【内锋】[体] inside forward
【内服】taken by the mouth; oral: ~药,每日三次,每次一片 *an oral dose of 1 tablet, 3 times a day*
【内阁】cabinet ◇ 改组~ cabinet reshuffle; 影子~ shadow cabinet; ~大臣 cabinet minister; ~会议 cabinet council
【内功】(wushu 武术 or qigong 气功) exercises to benefit the internal organs
【内骨骼】endoskeleton
【内顾之忧】domestic worries; trouble at home
【内果皮】[植] endocarp
【内海】❶ inland sea ❷ continental sea
【内涵】[逻] intension; connotation
【内行】❶ be expert at; be adept in; know the ins and outs of: 对养蚕很~ *be expert at silkworm breeding* ❷ an expert; a dab hand; master: 充~ *pose as an expert*
【内耗】❶ energy consumed by a machine without getting any work done ❷ losses suffered in internal strife
【内河】inland river (or waters, waterway): ~航行权 *inland navigation rights* / ~运输 *inland water transport*
【内核】the crux of a matter
【内讧】internal conflict; internal strife; internal dissension
【内画壶】a bottle with painted designs inside
【内踝】the medial part of the ankle (where the lower end of the tibia is)
【内急】have to go to the toilet
【内寄生】[生] endoparasitism ◇ ~物 endoparasite
【内奸】a secret enemy agent within one's ranks; a hidden traitor
【内间】〈方〉inner room
【内监】eunuch
【内角】[数] interior angle; internal angle
【内接多边形】[数] inscribed polygon
【内接形】[数] inscribed figure
【内紧外松】be relaxed outwardly but vigilant or alert inwardly
【内景】indoor setting; indoor scene; interior
【内径】internal diameter; inside (or inner) diameter (ID): ~千分尺 *inside micrometer* ◇ ~规 internal gauge
【内疚】compunction; guilty conscience: ~于心 *feel compunction*; *have qualms of conscience*; *be conscience-stricken*
【内聚力】[物] cohesive force; cohesion
【内眷】female members of a family
【内卡钳】[机] inside callipers
【内科】(department of) internal medicine: a ~病房 *medical ward* / ~医生 *physician* / 你看~还是外科? *Do you want to see a physician or a surgeon?*
【内控】controlled from the inside (i. e., not allowing those on the outside to take part)
【内裤】briefs; knickers: 男~ *briefs*; *short pants*; *underpants*/ 女~ *women's panties*; *knickers*
【内窥镜】[医] endoscope: ~检查 *endoscopy*
【内涝】waterlogging
【内力】[物] internal force
【内流河】continental river
【内陆】inland; interior; hinterland ◇ ~边境 inland frontier area; ~国 landlocked country; ~海 inland sea; ~河 continental river; ~湖 inland lake; ~盆地 interior (or inland) basin
【内乱】civil strife; internal disorder
【内蒙古】Inner Mongolia
【内蒙古自治区】the Inner Mongolia Autonomous Region
【内幕】what goes on behind the scenes; inside story: ~消息 *inside information* ◇ ~交易 [经] insider trading
【内能】[物] internal energy; intrinsic energy
【内胚层】(又作'内胚叶') endoderm; entoderm
【内切圆】[数] inscribed circle (of a triangle); incircle
【内亲】relatives on one's wife's side; (a man's) in-laws
【内勤】❶ internal or office work (as distinguished from work carried on mainly outside the office) ❷ office staff
【内情】inside information (or story): 了解~ *be an insider*; *be in the know*
【内燃机】[机] internal-combustion engine
【内燃机车】diesel locomotive
【内热】[中] internal heat—disorders due to predominance of the yang (阳)
【内人】my wife
【内容】content; substance: ~和形式的统一 *unity of content and form* / 这次谈话的~牵涉面很广。*The talk covered a lot of ground*. ◇~提要 synopsis; résumé
【内伤】❶ [医] internal injury ❷ [中] disorder of internal organs caused by improper diet, fatigue, emotional strains, sexual excess, etc.
【内室】inner room; bedroom
【内水】inland waters
【内胎】inner tube (of a tyre)
【内廷】inner chambers in an imperial palace; imperial residence
【内外】❶ inside and outside; domestic and foreign: 长城~ *both sides of the Great Wall* / ~反动势力 *domestic and foreign reactionary forces* ❷ around; about: 五十年~ *in about fifty years* /

～交困 *beset with difficulties both at home and abroad* / ～有别 *keep inside information from outsiders or foreigners*

【内外夹攻】attack from both within and without：造成～的形势 *form a pincer movement from inside and out*

【内网】[计] intranet

【内务】❶ internal affairs ❷ daily routine tasks to keep the barracks, etc. clean and tidy：～条令 *routine service regulations* (*for barracks*) ◇～部 Ministry of Internal Affairs

【内吸磷】[农] demeton

【内线】❶ planted agent ❷ [军] interior lines：～作战 *fight* (*or operate*) *on interior lines* ❸ inside (telephone) connections：～自动电话机 *interphone*

【内详】name and address of sender enclosed

【内向】[心理] introversion：性格～ *be introverted by nature*；*be an introvert*

【内向型】domestically-oriented：满足国内市场的～经济 *domestically-oriented economy aimed at meeting the needs of the domestic market*

【内项】[数] the second or third term (in a proportion of four terms)；mean

【内销】sold inside the country；for the domestic market：出口转～ *exportable goods put on the domestic market*；*exportable goods sold on home market*

【内斜视】[医] esotropia；cross-eye

【内心】❶ heart；innermost being：～深处 *in one's heart of hearts* / 出自～的感谢 *heartfelt thanks* / 他～很矛盾。*He is torn by conflicting thoughts*. ❷ [数] incentre (of a triangle)

【内省】introspection：～心理学 *introspective psychology*

【内兄】wife's elder brother；brother-in-law

【内秀】be intelligent without seeming so

【内需】domestic demand (in a market)：扩大～ *to increase* (*expand*) *domestic demand*

【内焰】[化] inner flame

【内衣】underwear；underclothes

【内因】[哲] internal cause：唯物辩证法认为，外因通过～而起作用。*Materialist dialectics holds that external causes become operative through internal causes*.

【内应】a person operating from within in coordination with outside forces；a planted agent；a plant

【内应力】[机] internal stress

【内忧外患】domestic trouble and foreign invasion；internal disturbance and foreign aggression

【内在】inherent；intrinsic；internal；inner ◇～规律 inherent law；～联系 inner link；internal relations；～论 immanentism；～矛盾 inner (or inherent) contradictions；～美 inner beauty；～因素 internal factor

【内脏】internal organs；viscera

【内宅】inner chambers (for the womenfolk of a household)

【内债】internal debt；domestic loan

【内战】civil war

【内障】cataract or glaucoma

【内招】enroll students or recruit children of current employees：～做法容易造成员工素质下降。*The practice of internal enrolment of workers tends to lower the caliber of the personnel*.

【内争】internal strife

【内政】internal (or domestic, home) affairs：互不干涉～ *noninterference in each other's internal affairs*

【内侄】son of wife's brother；nephew

【内侄女】daughter of wife's brother；niece

【内痔】[医] internal piles；internal haemorrhoids

【内中】the inside：你不晓得～的奥秘。*You don't know the inside story*.

【内助】〈书〉wife (considered as a helpful companion)

【内装修】interior decoration：新房的～十分豪华。*The bridal chamber is sumptuously decorated*.

【内子】〈书〉my wife

【内阻】[电] internal resistance；inherent resistance

nèn

嫩 形 ❶ tender；delicate：～叶 *tender leaves* / 这肉炒得很～。*This stir-fried meat is very tender*. / 小孩子肉皮儿～。*Young children have delicate skin*. / 脸皮～ *shy*；*bashful* ❷ light：嫩绿 ❸ inexperienced；unskilled：～手 *a raw hand*；*a new hand*

【嫩红】pink；apricot pink

【嫩黄】light yellow

【嫩绿】light green；soft green

【嫩气】❶ delicate (or dainty) looks；youthfulness ❷ dainty-looking；youthful-looking

【嫩色】light colour；soft colour；pastel shade

【嫩生生】very tender；very delicate：一片～的秧苗 *a stretch of tender green rice shoots*

néng

能 Ⅰ 名 ❶ ability；capability；skill：技能 / 无能 ❷ [物] energy Ⅱ 形 able；capable：她可～呢，穿的衣服都是自己做的。*She's very capable. She makes all the clothes she wears*. Ⅲ 动 ❶ can；be able to；be capable of：她一分钟～打七十个字。*She can type 70 characters a minute*. / 他好多了，～下床了。*He's much better and can get up now*. / 我干这个工作～行吗？*Am I really fit for the job*？❷ (expressing possibility) can possibly：天这么晚了，他～来吗？*It's already very late. Can he possibly come tonight*？/ 这件事她～一点也不知道吗？*Could she know nothing of it*？or *Could she be completely in the dark*？❸ (used between 不…不 to express obligation, certainty or great probability)：不能不 ❹ (usu. used negatively or interrogatively) may; can; have the permission to：这儿～停车吗？—这儿不～停车。*Can we park here? — No. Parking is not allowed here.*

【能动】active; dynamic：人的～作用 *man's initiative (or dynamic role)* / 从感性认识到理性认识之～的飞跃 *the active leap from perceptual to rational knowledge*

【能动性】dynamic role; activity; initiative：自觉的～ *(man's) conscious dynamic role*

【能干】able; capable; competent：他是个很～的人。*He is a man of great ability.*

【能歌善舞】good at both singing and dancing

【能工巧匠】skilful craftsman; skilled artisan; dab hand

【能攻能守】be able to take the offensive as well as hold one's ground：这个队～。*The team is good at both attack and defence.*

【能够】can; be able to; be capable of：～独立工作 *be able to work on one's own* / 他～说三种外国语。*He can speak three foreign languages.* / 这河的下游～行驶轮船。*The lower reaches of the river are navigable for steamers.*

【能官能民】be ready to serve as an official or to be one of the common people

【能耗】energy consumption

【能级】[物] energy level：费密～ *Fermi level* / 基态～ *ground state level*

【能见度】visibility：地面～ *ground visibility*

【能力】ability; capacity; capability：～强 *have great ability; be very capable* / 培养学生的推理～ *develop the students' reasoning capacity* ◇ ～倾向 aptitude; ～水平 ability level

【能量】❶ [物] energy：～转化 *conversion of energy* / ～交换 *energy exchange* ❷ capabilities：他们人数很少，～很大。*Though few in number, they have enormous capacity for manoeuvre.*

【能量守恒律】the law of conservation of energy

【能耐】〈口〉ability; capability; skill：我有什么～呀，全靠各位撑腰呢！*What could I do without you people backing me up?*

【能骑善射】expert at horseback riding and shooting arrow

【能掐会算】tell fortunes; be able to predict the future course of events

【能屈能伸】be able to stoop or to stand; submit or assert oneself as the occasion requires; be adaptable to circumstances：大丈夫～。*A man among men is he who knows when to eat humble pie and when to hold his head high.*

【能人】able person

【能人背后有能人】For every able person there is always one still abler.

【能上能下】be ready to work either at the top or at the grass roots; be ready to accept a higher or a lower post：干部要～。*A cadre should be ready to take a lower as well as a higher post.*

【能诗善画】having superior abilities to write poetry and good in painting

【能事】(usu. used in combination with 尽) what one is particularly good at：竭尽挑拨离间之～ *stop at nothing to sow discord*

【能手】dab; expert; crackajack：木刻～ *a dab at wood engraving* / 技术革新～ *a crackajack at technical innovation* / 解决复杂问题的～ *a trouble-shooter*

【能说会道】have the gift of the gab; be a glib talker：他以～闻名于工商界。*He earned a reputation in business circles for having a ready and eloquent tongue.*

【能文能武】be versed in both polite letters and martial arts; be able to wield both the pen and the sword

【能言快语】eloquent and frank in speech

【能言善辩】eloquent, glib and quick-tongued in argument

【能源】the sources of energy; energy resources; energy：～短缺 *energy shortage*/ 可再生～ *renewable sources of energy* ◇ ～危机 energy crisis

【能愿动词】[语] modal verb

【能者多劳】able people should do more work (said when asking sb. to perform a service or do extra work); the abler one is, the more one should do：俗话说"～。"经理见你这样能干，就什么都交给你了。*As the saying goes, "The abler a man is, the busier he gets." It's because you're so capable that the manager leaves everything to you.*

【能者为师】let those who know teach

ní

尼

名 Buddhist nun

【尼庵】Buddhist nunnery

【尼泊尔】Nepal ◇ ～人 Nepalese; Nepali ; ～语 Nepali; Nepalese

【尼姑】Buddhist nun

【尼古丁】nicotine

【尼加拉瓜】Nicaragua ◇ ～人 Nicaraguan

【尼龙】nylon：～丝 *nylon yarn* / ～袜 *nylon socks*

【尼罗河】the Nile

【尼日尔】Niger ◇ ～人 Nigerois

【尼日利亚】Nigeria ◇ ～人 Nigerian

【尼亚加拉瀑布】Niagara Falls

泥

名 ❶ mud; mire ❷ sth. like paste or pulp：土豆～ *mashed potato* / 苹果～ *applesauce* —— 另见 nì

【泥巴】〈方〉mud; mire

【泥饭碗】clay rice-bowl(referring to insecure job)

【泥肥】[农] sludge (used as manure)

【泥封】[冶] lute

【泥工】〈方〉bricklayer; tiler; plasterer

【泥垢】dirt; grime：他满脸～。*His face was covered with dirt.*

【泥灰岩】[地质] marl

【泥浆】slurry; mud：钻井～ *drilling mud* / ～泵

slurry (or mud, slush) pump / ～工 mudman
【泥金】coating material made of powdered gold or other metals; golden paint: ～佛像 *a gilded Buddha*
【泥坑】mud pit; mire; morass: 陷入～ *get stuck in the mud; be bogged down in a quagmire*
【泥疗】[医] mud therapy
【泥煤】同〖泥炭〗
【泥泞】❶ muddy; miry: ～的道路 *a muddy road* / 雨后道路～。*The road is muddy after the rain.* ❷ mire; mud: 陷入～ *get stuck in the mire*
【泥牛入海】like clay oxen entering the sea —never to be heard of again; gone forever
【泥盆纪】the Devonian period (the 4th period of the Palaeozoic era, 350,000,000-400,000,000 years ago)
【泥盆系】the Devonian system
【泥菩萨过河,自身难保】like a clay idol fording a river—hardly able to save oneself (let alone anyone else)
【泥鳅】loach
【泥人】clay figurine: 彩塑～ *painted clay figurine*
【泥沙】silt
【泥沙俱下】mud and sand are carried along — there is a mingling of good and bad: 各种人都来参加,未免～,鱼龙混杂。*People of all descriptions flocked to join in, so inevitably the waters were muddied and the bad became mixed with the good.*
【泥石流】[地质] mud-rock flow
【泥水匠】bricklayer; tiler; plasterer
【泥塑】clay sculpture
【泥胎】an unpainted clay idol
【泥胎儿】unfired pottery
【泥潭】mire; morass; quagmire
【泥炭】peat
【泥塘】mire; bog; morass
【泥土】❶ earth; soil: 春天的原野散发着～的芳香。*In spring the fields give off the aroma of the earth.* ❷ clay
【泥腿子】bumpkin; clodhopper
【泥浴】[医] mud bath
【泥洼】marsh; mire
【泥瓦匠】bricklayer; tiler; plasterer
【泥岩】[地质] mudstone
【泥俑】clay figure buried with the dead; funerary clay figure; earthen figurine
【泥沼】mire; swamp; morass; slough
【泥足巨人】a colossus with feet of clay
【泥醉】dead drunk

呢 名 (cloth made of) wool; woollen cloth (for heavy clothing); heavy woollen cloth; wool coating or suiting: 格子～ *woollen check* / 厚～大衣 *heavy woollen overcoat*
【呢喃】(of swallows) twitter
【呢绒】woollen goods; wool fabric
【呢子】woollen cloth (for heavy clothing); heavy woollen cloth; wool coating or suiting

铌 名 [化] niobium (Nb)
【铌铁矿】columbite

霓 名 [气] secondary rainbow
【霓虹灯】neon lamp; neon light; neon ◇ ～广告牌 neon sign

鲵 名 salamander (an amphibian)

nǐ

拟 动 ❶ draw up; design; devise; draft: ～个计划 *devise a plan* / ～一个方案 *draw up a plan* ❷ intend; plan: ～于下月前往青岛 *plan to go to Qingdao next month* ❸ imitate: 模拟
【拟订】draw up; draft; work out: ～城市建设规划 *map out a programme for municipal construction*
【拟稿】prepare a draft; make a draft: 这一套规章是校长亲自拟的稿。*The principal himself drafted this set of rules.*
【拟古】model one's literary or artistic style on that of the ancients: ～之作 *a work modelled after the ancients*
【拟人】personification: 使之～化 *personify sth.*
【拟态】[动] mimicry; imitation
【拟议】❶ proposal; recommendation: 事实证明他的～是正确的。*Facts show that his recommendations were sound.* ❷ draw up; draft: 小组一致通过了她所～的意见书。*The group unanimously adopted the proposal she drew up.*
【拟于不伦】draw inapt parallels
【拟作】a work done in the manner of a certain author

你 代 ❶ you (second person singular): ～爸爸 *your father* / ～带了多少钱? *How much money do you have on you?* ❷ you (second person plural): ～方 *your side; you* / ～校 *your school* ❸ (referring to any person) you; one; anyone: 碰到这么一个人,～有什么办法? *What can you do with a person like that?* ❹ (used coordinately with 我 or 他 in parallel structures to indicate several or many people behaving the same way): 三个人～看看我,我看看～,谁也不说话。*The three of them kept looking at one another without saying a word.* / ～一言,我一语,大家谈得很热闹。*A lively conversation went on with everybody joining in.*
【你好】how are you; hello (a common form of greeting, used at any time of the day, requiring the same phrase as an answer; also used at the beginning of informal letters)
【你们】❶ you (second person plural): 这就是～的责任所在。*This is where your responsibility lies.* ❷〈口〉(used in the same way as 你❶❷): ～组最近情况怎么样? *How is your group getting along these days?*
【你死我活】life-and-death; mortal: ～的斗争 *a*

life-and-death struggle / 拼个～ *fight to the bitter end*

【你追我赶】try to overtake each other in friendly emulation

【你走你的阳关道,我过我的独木桥】 you take the open road, I'll cross the log bridge—you go your way, I'll go mine

nì

泥 Ⅰ 动 cover or daub with plaster, putty, etc.; putty; plaster: ～墙 *cover the crevices in a wall with mud* (*or plaster*) / 把窗玻璃用油灰～上 *fix a windowpane with putty* Ⅱ 形 stubborn; bigoted; obstinate: 拘泥 —— 另见 ní

【泥古】have bigoted belief in the ancients; obstinately follow ancient ways: ～不化 *stick to ancient ways to the letter*

【泥子】putty

逆 Ⅰ 形 ❶ contrary; counter; inverse; converse: ～反应 *inverse reaction*; *back reaction* ❷ traitorous; rebellious: ～贼 *rebel*; *traitor* / ～臣 *a traitorous vassal* Ⅱ 动 go against; disobey; defy: ～时代潮流而动 *go against the trend of the times* Ⅲ 副 beforehand; in advance: 逆料

【逆差】adverse balance of trade; trade deficit: 国际收支～ *an adverse* (*or unfavourable*) *balance of international payments*

【逆产】❶ a traitor's property ❷(又作'倒产')(of a baby) breech birth; breech delivery

【逆颤音】[音] inverted trill

【逆定理】[数] converse theorem

【逆耳】grate on the ear; be unpleasant to the ear: ～之言 *words or advice unpleasant to hear*

【逆反心理】rebellious psychology; psychology of aversion

【逆风】❶ go against the wind: ～行舟 *sail against the wind* / ～飞行 *make a head-wind flight* ❷ contrary wind; head wind

【逆光】[摄] backlighting

【逆火】(of an internal-combustion engine) backfire: ～式超音速轰炸机 *Backfire bomber*; *Backfire*

【逆经】[医] vicarious menstruation

【逆境】adverse circumstances; adversity: 身处～ *be in adverse circumstances*

【逆来顺受】meekly submit to oppression, maltreatment, etc.; resign oneself to adversity: 他一辈子老实、无能,对环境的压迫～。*All his life he had been simple, ineffective, docilely accepting the worst his environment had given him.*

【逆料】anticipate; foresee: 事态的发展不难～。*The course of events can be foreseen.*

【逆流】❶ go against the current: ～而上 *sail against the current* ❷ adverse current; countercurrent

【逆旅】inn; hotel: 宿于～ *stay at an inn*

【逆伦】〈书〉the violation of proper human relationships (e.g. parricide)

【逆事】❶ untoward incidents; mishaps ❷ rebellious acts

【逆水】(of a boat, etc.) go against the current

【逆水行舟】a boat sailing against the current: 学如～,不进则退。*Study is like sailing against the current: either you keep forging ahead or you keep falling behind.*

【逆温】[气] (temperature) inversion ◇ ～层 [气] inversion layer

【逆向】opposite direction: ～行驶 *drive in a direction not allowed by traffic regulations*

【逆行】❶ (of vehicles) go in a direction not allowed by traffic regulations; go in the wrong direction ❷ [天] retrograde motion

【逆运】adversity; misfortune; ill luck

【逆证】[中] a severe case with unfavourable prognosis

【逆转】take a turn for the worse; reverse; deteriorate: 形势突然～。*The situation suddenly deteriorated.*

【逆子】unfilial son

昵 形 close; intimate: 亲昵

【昵称】a term of endearment; pet name

匿 动 hide; conceal: 隐匿

【匿报】withhold information: ～实情 *withhold information on the actual situation*

【匿藏】conceal; hide; go into hiding

【匿伏】be in hiding; lurk

【匿迹】go into hiding; stay in concealment: ～海外 *go into hiding abroad*; *lie low abroad*

【匿名】anonymous ◇ ～信 an anonymous letter

【匿影藏形】hide from public notice; conceal one's identity; lie low

溺 动 ❶ drown: ～死 *be drowned* ❷ be addicted to: ～于酒色 *be given over to wine and woman*

【溺爱】spoil (a child); dote on (a child)

【溺水】drowning; sinking: 抢救～儿童 *rescue the drowning child* / ～身亡 *be drowned*

【溺婴】infanticide by drowning

【溺于酒色】given over to wine and wonen

【溺职】neglect of duty; dereliction

腻 形 ❶ greasy; oily: 这炖肉有点～。*This stew is a bit greasy.* / 汤太～了。*The soup is too oily.* ❷ be bored with; be tired of: 这些话我都听～了。*I'm tired of listening to all this.* ❸ meticulous: 细腻 ❹ sticky; grimy: 擦碗布粘手都～了。*The dish towel has got grimy.* ❺ intimate: ～友 *a very close friend*

【腻虫】common name for 蚜虫

【腻烦】❶ be bored; be fed up: 这本书我看了多少遍都不觉得～。*I never get bored reading and rereading this book.* ❷ loathe; hate: 我最～说大话的人。*I can't stand people who brag.*

【腻人】❶ be boring or tedious：他老重复那几个笑话，真～。*It's really boring to listen to his same old jokes.* ❷ (of food that is too greasy or sweet) make one sick

【腻味】❶ be bored；be fed up：这套节目真叫人～。*This programme is really boring.* ❷ hate；loathe：我最～肥肉，从来不吃。*I hate fatty pork and never eat any.*

niān

拈 动 pick up (with the thumb and one or two fingers)：从罐子里～出一块糖 *take a candy from the jar*

【拈花惹草】toy with flowers and grass —dally with women；philander

【拈阄儿】draw lots

【拈轻怕重】prefer the light to the heavy—pick easy jobs and shirk hard ones

蔫 Ⅰ 动 fade；wither；shrivel up；droop：菠菜～了。*The spinach is shrivelled up.* / 花儿晒～了。*The flowers drooped in the heat of the sun.* Ⅱ 形 listless；spiritless；droopy：这孩子有点～，怕是病了。*The child looks a bit listless. I'm afraid he's not well.*

【蔫巴】〈口〉fading；withering；shrivelling：稻秧都～了。*The rice seedlings were all shrivelled up.*

【蔫不唧儿】〈方〉❶ listless；droopy；sluggish ❷ quiet：别看他平时～的，打起仗来可像个小老虎。*Although he is usually rather quiet, he fights like a tiger in battle.*

【蔫不溜】(又作'蔫不出溜'；'蔫不悄儿')〈方〉quiet；silent

【蔫呼呼】weak-willed and indecisive

【蔫儿坏】〈方〉be inwardly vicious；behave in an underhand way：这人瞧着挺老实的，其实～。*He looks honest, but he is really crooked.*

【蔫蔫】〈方〉❶ quiet；silent ❷ listless；droopy；sluggish

【蔫头耷脑】with head hanging—dejected；listless；droopy

nián

年 Ⅰ 名 ❶ year：三～ *three years* / ～复一～ *year after year*；*year in year out* ❷ age：～过六十 *over sixty* (*years old*) ❸ a period in one's life：童年 / 老年 ❹ a period in history：近～来 *in recent years* / 明朝初～ *at the beginning of the Ming Dynasty* ❺ harvest：丰年 ❻ New Year：拜年 Ⅱ 形 annual；yearly：～产量 *annual output*；*annual yield* ❷ of or for New Year：年货

【年报】❶ annual (a book or magazine, often used in titles)：《文学～》*Literary Annual* ❷ annual report

【年辈】one's age and generation

【年表】chronological table

【年菜】dishes prepared for the lunar New Year (or Spring Festival)

【年产量】annual output；annual yield

【年成】the year's harvest：好～ *a good harvest* / ～不好 *a lean year*

【年初】the beginning of the year：去年～ *at the beginning of last year*

【年代】❶ age；years；time：～不详 *without date*；*sine anno* / ～久了，石碑上的字迹已经模糊了。*The inscriptions on the stone tablet have become blurred with the passage of time.* ❷ a decade of a century：八十～ *the eighties* / 二十世纪九十～ *the 1990's*

【年底】the end of the year

【年度】year (a yearly period fixed for a certain purpose)：财政～ *financial year*；*fiscal year* ◇ ～报告 annual report；～计划 annual plan；～结算 annual account；～决算表 annual statement；～收入 annual revenue；～统计表 annual returns

【年饭】同〖年夜饭〗

【年份】❶ a particular year：这两笔开支不在一个～。*These two expenditures were not incurred in the same year.* ❷ age；time：这件瓷器的～比那件久。*This piece of porcelain is older than that one.*

【年俸】annual salary；yearly pay

【年富力强】in the prime of life；in one's prime：～的干部 *young and energetic cadres*

【年高德劭】of venerable age and eminent virtue；of advanced years and known integrity；venerable

【年高望重】aged and in high standing

【年糕】New Year cake (made of glutinous rice flour)

【年庚】the time (year, month, day and hour) of a person's birth；date of birth

【年购买额】annual purchase (rate)

【年关】the end of the year (formerly time for settling accounts)

【年关荏苒】the quick passing of time

【年光】❶ time；years ❷ the year's harvest

【年号】reign title (a designation for the years when an emperor was on the throne)

【年华】time；years：～如矢 *the years glide swiftly along* / 虚度～ *idle away one's time*；*waste one's life*

【年画】New Year (or Spring Festival) pictures

【年会】annual meeting

【年货】special purchases for the Spring Festival：办～ *do Spring Festival shopping*

【年级】grade；year：大学三～学生 *third year university student* / 小学一～学生 *first grade primary school pupil*

【年纪】age：～轻 *young* / 你多大～了？*How old are you?*

【年假】❶ New Year holidays ❷ winter vacation ❸ annual leave

【年间】certain period (of a dynasty or reign)：光

绪～ *in the period of Emperor Guangxu*
【年检】annual inspection：汽车～ *annual inspection of motor vehicles*
【年鉴】yearbook；almanac：《中国～》(2000 年) *China Yearbook* 2000
【年节】the lunar New Year Festival；the Spring Festival
【年金】annuity
【年景】❶ the year's harvest：在正常～下 *in normal harvest years* ❷ holiday atmosphere of the Spring Festival
【年久日深】同〖年深日久〗
【年久失修】worn down by the years without repair
【年均】annual average：他们农场养的鸡每只～产蛋 240 个。*The hens raised on their farm each average 240 eggs a year.*
【年历】a calendar with the whole year printed on one sheet；single-page calendar
【年利】annual interest：～率 *annual interest rate*
【年龄】age：他参军还不够～。*He is too young to join the army.* / 从马的牙齿可以看出它的～。*You can tell a horse's age from its teeth.* / ～不饶人。*Age will show itself.* or *Age will tell.* ◇ ～结构 age structure；～群 age set；～性别组成 age-sex structure
【年龄组】age group：同～的人 *cohorts*
【年轮】[植] annual ring；growth ring
【年迈】old；aged：～力衰 *old and infirm*；*senile*
【年貌】age and appearance：两人～相当。*The two are well matched in age and appearance.*
【年末】the end of the year
【年年】every year；year after year
【年谱】chronological life
【年青】young
【年轻】young：～人 *young people* / ～力壮 *young and vigorous* / ～一代 *the younger (or rising) generation* / ～有为 *able and young*；*young and promising*
【年轻化】make...younger；become younger in average age
【年少】❶ young ❷ youngster；a young man：翩翩～ *an elegant young man* ◇ ～气盛 young and impetuous
【年深日久】with the passage of time；as the years go by：河里的泥沙淤积在这里，～便成了沙洲。*The bar was formed by the mud and sand deposited here over a long period of time.*
【年时】〈方〉last year：他们是～才结的婚。*They got married only last year.*
【年事】〈书〉age (of a person)：～已高 *be advanced in years*
【年岁】❶ age：上了～的人 *a person who is getting on in years* ❷ years：因为～久远，当时的具体情况已记不清了。*As it happened so many years ago, I don't remember the details.*
【年头】❶ year：他到武汉已经三个～了。*It's three years since he came to Wuhan.* ❷ years；a long time：她干这一行有～了。*She has been doing this sort of work for years.* ❸ days；times：那～ *in those days* ❹ harvest：今年～真好。*This year's harvest is very good indeed.*
【年息】annual interest
【年限】fixed number of years：学习～ *the number of years set for a course (of study)* / 工具使用～ *the service life of a tool*
【年薪】annual salary；yearly pay
【年夜】the lunar New Year's Eve ◇ ～饭 family reunion dinner on the lunar New Year's Eve
【年幼】young；under age：～无知 *young and ignorant*
【年愈不惑】have passed 40
【年月】❶ days；years ❷〈口〉times：太平～ *peaceful times*
【年增长系数】annual improvement factor
【年长】older in age；senior
【年终】the end of the year；year-end ◇ ～报告 year-end report；～分配 year-end distribution；～奖 year-end bonus；～结存 annual balance；～结账 year-end settlement of accounts；～评比 year-end appraisal of work
【年资】age and years of service；seniority

鲇

名 catfish
【鲇鱼】catfish

黏

形 sticky；glutinous：这浆糊不～。*This paste is not sticky enough.*
【黏儿】〈方〉gum；resin
【黏巴】sticky；gluey；gummy：手上有点儿～。*My hand is somewhat sticky.*
【黏虫】armyworm
【黏度】[化] viscosity：恩氏～ *Engler viscosity* ◇ ～计 viscosimeter
【黏附】adhere：～力 *adhesion* / ～体 *adherend*
【黏合】[化] bind；bond；adhere ◇ ～剂 binder；adhesive；bonding agent
【黏糊】❶ sticky；glutinous：粥熬得怪～的。*The rice gruel is well cooked.* ❷ languid；slow-moving
【黏胶】[化] viscose ◇ ～长丝 viscose filament yarn；～短纤维 viscose staple fibre；～丝 viscose；～纤维 viscose fibre
【黏结】cohere：～力 *cohesion*；*cohesive force* / ～性 *cohesiveness*
【黏菌】[微] slime mould；slime fungus
【黏米】❶ glutinous rice ❷〈方〉broomcorn millet
【黏膜】[生理] mucous membrane；mucosa ◇ ～炎 [医] mucositis
【黏土】clay：耐火～ *refractory clay* / ～矿物 *clay mineral* / ～岩 *clay rock*
【黏涎子】slaver；slobber
【黏涎】〈方〉tedious；dull
【黏性】stickiness；viscidity；viscosity ◇ ～油 viscous oil
【黏液】[生理] mucus ◇ ～性水肿 [医] myxoedema
【黏着】stick together；adhere ◇ ～语 [语] agglutinative language

niǎn

捻 Ⅰ 动 twist with the fingers：～线 *twist thread* / 把油灯～大些 *turn up the wick* (*of a lamp*) Ⅱ 名 sth. made by twisting：灯～儿 *lampwick*

【捻度】[纺] number of turns (or twists)；twist

【捻线机】[纺] twisting frame

【捻针】[中] twirling or rotating of the acupuncture needle

【捻子】spill (for lighting candles, lamps, etc.)；wick

碾 Ⅰ 名 roller and millstone；stone roller Ⅱ 动 grind or husk with a roller：～米 *husk rice* / ～得粉碎 *be crushed to powder*；*be crushed to pieces*；*be pulverized* / ～平 *flatten or level* (*with a roller*)；roll out

【碾场】〈方〉thresh or husk grain on a threshing ground

【碾槌】pestle

【碾坊】grain mill

【碾滚子】stone roller (for grinding or husking grain on a millstone)

【碾米厂】rice-hulling mill

【碾米机】rice mill (a machine)

【碾盘】a millstone upon which a stone roller is used

【碾碎】pulverize

【碾砣】同〖碾滚子〗

【碾子】roller and millstone；roller

撵 动 ❶ drive out；oust：把人～走 *drive sb. away* / ～下台 *oust from a leading position* ❷〈方〉catch up：我～不上他。*I couldn't catch up with him*.

niàn

念 Ⅰ 动 ❶ think of；miss：我们老～着你。*We miss you very much*. ❷ read aloud：她把上级的指示～给大家听。*She read out the directive from the higher authorities*. ❸ attend school：他～过中学。*He has been to middle school*. Ⅱ 名 thought；idea：杂念

【念白】spoken parts of a Chinese opera

【念叨】❶ talk about again and again in recollection or anticipation；be always talking about：他就是我们常常～的张大伯。*This is the Uncle Zhang we're always talking about*. ❷ talk over；discuss：我有个事儿跟大家～～。*I've got something to talk over with you*.

【念佛】chant the name of Buddha；pray to Buddha：吃素～ *be a reverent Buddhist and practise vegetarianism*

【念经】recite or chant scriptures

【念旧】keep old friendships in mind；remember old friends

【念念不忘】bear in mind constantly

【念念有词】❶ mutter incantations ❷ mumble

【念书】❶ read ❷ study

【念诵】❶ read aloud；chant：～诗文 *read aloud poems and essays* ❷ talk about (in recollection or anticipation)：老太太方才还在～呢，可巧你就来了。*Granny was just talking about you a minute ago, and here you are now*.

【念头】thought；idea；intention：当时他心中只有一个～，就是为祖国增光。*At that time he had only one thing in mind：to win credit for his country*.

【念咒】chant incantations

【念珠】beads；rosary

埝 名 a low bank between fields：打～ *build banks between fields*

niáng

娘 名 ❶ ma；mum；mother：爹～ *father and mother* ❷ a form of address for an elderly married woman：婶～ *wife of one's father's younger brother*；*aunt* ❸ a young woman：渔～ *a young fisherwoman*

【娘儿】〈口〉(followed by a numeral-classifier compound) mother and son or daughter；aunt and niece or nephew：～俩 *mother and son or daughter*

【娘家】a married woman's parents' home

【娘舅】〈方〉brother of one's mother；uncle

【娘儿们】❶〈口〉mother and son or daughter ❷〈方〉the womenfolk：咱～不比男的差。*We womenfolk are just as good as the men*. ❸〈方〉wife

【娘娘】❶ (used in speaking to or of an empress or an imperial concubine)：正宫～ *emperor's wife*；*empress* ❷ a name for certain guardian goddesses：子孙～ *Our Lady of Many Children*；*Goddess of Fertility* (*a patroness of marriage and giver of sons*) / ～庙 *Temple of the Goddess of Fertility*

【娘亲】mother

【娘胎】mother's womb：出了～ *be born* / 从～带来的记 *a birthmark*

【娘子军】a detachment of women；any contingent entirely made up of women

niàng

酿 Ⅰ 动 ❶ make (wine)；brew (beer)：酿酒 ❷ make (honey)：蜜蜂会～蜜。*Bees make honey*. ❸ lead to；result in：～祸 *lead to disaster* Ⅱ 名 wine：佳～ *good wine*

【酿成】lead to；bring on；breed：小错不改往往～大错。*Small mistakes left uncorrected will lead to big ones*.

【酿祸】create trouble; ferment disturbance

【酿酒】make wine; brew beer ◇ ～厂 winery; brewery; ～业 wine-making industry

【酿酶】[化] zymase

【酿母菌】another name for 酵母

【酿热物】ferment material

【酿造】make (wine, vinegar, etc.); brew (beer, etc.)

niǎo

鸟 名 bird

【鸟儿】a small bird; birdie

【鸟粪】❶ birds' droppings ❷ guano ◇ ～层 guano

【鸟害】bird pest

【鸟喙】beak; bill

【鸟尽弓藏】cast aside the bow once the birds are all killed—cast sb. aside when he has served his purpose

【鸟瞰】❶ get a bird's-eye view: ～全城 *get a bird's-eye view of the city* ❷ a general survey of a subject; bird's-eye view: 古代史～ *a general survey of ancient history* ◇ ～图 a bird's-eye view; an aerial view

【鸟类】birds (of any kind) ◇ ～学 ornithology

【鸟笼】birdcage

【鸟枪】❶ fowling piece ❷ air gun

【鸟枪换炮】change from fowling pieces into guns—become much better equipped; have much better conditions; improve greatly

【鸟兽】birds and beasts; fur and feather

【鸟兽散】见〖作鸟兽散〗

【鸟窝】(bird's) nest

【鸟为食亡,人为财死】Birds die in pursuit of food and human beings die in pursuit of wealth.

【鸟语花香】Birds sing and flowers give forth fragrance (as on a fine spring day).

【鸟篆】bird script (an ancient form of Chinese written characters, resembling birds' footprints)

【鸟嘴】beak; bill

茑 名 a kind of creeping plant

【茑萝】[植] cypress vine (Quamoclit pennata)

袅 形 slender and delicate

【袅袅】❶ curl upwards: 炊烟～。*Smoke is curling upward from kitchen chimneys*. ❷ wave in the wind: 垂杨～。*Drooping willows are dancing in the wind*. ❸ linger: 余音～。*The music lingered in the air long after the performance ended*.

【袅袅婷婷】[文] (of a girl or young woman) lithe, slim and supple; lissom and graceful

【袅娜】[文] ❶ (of plants) soft and slender: 春风吹拂着～的柳丝。*The slender willow twigs were swaying gently in the spring breeze*. ❷ (of a female figure) delicate and graceful; willowy

niào

尿 Ⅰ 名 urine Ⅱ 动 urinate; make water; piss: 这孩子～了我一身。*The baby has wetted my clothes*.

【尿崩症】[医] diabetes insipidus

【尿闭】[医] anuria

【尿布】diaper; napkin; nappy

【尿不湿】paper nappy; disposable diaper

【尿床】bed-wetting: 这孩子又～了。*The child wetted the bed again*.

【尿胆素】[医] urobilin: ～原 *urobilinogen*

【尿道】[生理] urethra: ～造影 *urethrography* ◇ ～炎 [医] urethritis

【尿毒症】[医] uraemia

【尿分析】urinalysis: 常规～ *routine urinalysis*

【尿肥】urine used as manure

【尿炕】wet the kang; wet the bed

【尿盆】chamber pot; urinal

【尿频】[医] frequent micturition

【尿少症】[医] oliguria

【尿失禁】[医] urinary incontinence; incontinence of urine

【尿素】[化] urea; carbamide

【尿素脱蜡】[油] urea dewaxing

【尿酸】[化] uric acid

【尿血】[医] haematuria

【尿潴留】[化] retention of urine

脲 名 同〖尿素〗

【脲醛塑料】[化] urea-formaldehyde plastics

niē

捏 动 ❶ hold between the finger and thumb; pinch: ～着鼻子 *stop one's nose with the fingers* / 把米里的虫子～出来 *pick the worms out of the rice* ❷ knead with the fingers; mould: ～泥人儿 *mould clay figurines* / ～饺子 *make dumplings* ❸ fabricate; make up: ～报 *fake a report*

【捏把汗】be breathless with anxiety or tension; be keyed up; be on edge: 看着他们表演杂技,我们都捏一把汗。*We were breathless as we watched the acrobats*. / 他在第一次登台之前着实捏了把汗呢。*He was all keyed up before making his first stage appearance*.

【捏合】put together; bring together: 他俩结婚缺乏感情基础,是双方家长硬把他们～在一起的。*Their marriage was not a love match; it was their parents who brought them together against their wishes*.

【捏合机】[化纤] kneading machine

【捏积】[中] a method of treating children's digestive disorders by kneading or massaging the muscles along the spine; chiropractic

【捏弄】❶ play with; fiddle with: 她一边说话,一边～着毛衣上的纽扣。*As she talked, she fiddled with the buttons on her sweater*. ❷ order about; manipulate: 我们不能由着别人～。*We shouldn't allow ourselves to be ordered about*. ❸ discuss in private: 这事他俩一～就那么办了。*The two of them discussed the matter in private and then got it all settled*.

【捏造】fabricate; concoct; fake; trump up: ～事实 *invent a story*; *make up a story* / ～罪名 *trump up charges* / ～数字 *conjure up figures* / 纯属～。*That's sheer fabrication*.

【捏闸】apply the handbrake

niè

涅 Ⅰ 名 alunite Ⅱ 动 dye sth. black

【涅白】opaque white

【涅槃】[宗](佛教)nirvana

啮 动 (of rodents) gnaw; nibble

【啮齿动物】rodent

【啮齿目】[动] Rodentia

【啮合】❶ clench the teeth ❷ (of gears) mesh; engage: 这个小齿轮和另外两个齿轮相～。*The pinion meshes with two other gear wheels*. / 这两个齿轮～在一起。*The two cogwheels are engaged*.

镊 Ⅰ 名 tweezers Ⅱ 动 pick up sth. with tweezers

【镊子】tweezers: 一把～ *a pair of tweezers*

镍 名 [化] nickel (Ni): ～箔 *nickel foil*

【镍币】nickel coin; nickel

【镍黄铁矿】pentlandite (a mineral)

【镍钢】nickel steel

颞 (构词成分)见下

【颞骨】[生理] temporal bone

【颞颥】[生理] temple

蹑 动 ❶ lighten one's steps; walk on tiptoe: 他～着脚走出病房。*He tiptoed out of the ward*. ❷ follow: 蹑踪 ❸〈书〉tread; step on; trample

【蹑悄悄】softly; quietly: 她～地拉开门闩,没有惊动任何人。*She unfastened the latch quietly without disturbing anybody*.

【蹑手蹑脚】walk gingerly; walk on tiptoe: 他～摸上楼来。*With light steps and soft movements of his hands he felt his way up the stairs*.

【蹑踪】follow the trail of; track

【蹑足】❶ walk with light steps: 他～走到门口。*He tiptoed to the door*. ❷〈书〉participate in; join: ～其间 *join a profession*; *follow a trade*; *associate with a certain type of people*

【蹑足不前】not move a step forward

【蹑足潜踪】walk stealthily

孽 名 evil; sin: 作孽 / 妖孽

【孽报】同〖业报〗

【孽海】同〖业海〗

【孽障】同〖业障〗

【孽种】❶〈旧〉the bane of one's existence ❷〈讳〉(said to one's descendant) vile spawn; unfilial son

【孽子】❶ son of a concubine ❷ an unfilial son; an unworthy descendant

nín

您 代〈尊〉you: 老师,～早! *Good morning, Sir*! or *Good morning, Ma'am*!

níng

宁 形 peaceful; tranquil: 宁静 ——另见 nìng

【宁静】peaceful; tranquil; quiet; calm: ～的夜晚 *a tranquil night* / 心里渐渐～下来 *calm down gradually*

【宁静致远】still water runs deep; leading a quiet life

【宁人息事】pacify people and settle matters

【宁日】peaceful days

【宁夏回族自治区】the Ningxia Hui Autonomous Region

【宁馨儿】〈书〉a lovely child

拧 动 ❶ twist; wring: ～麻绳 *twist hemp into rope* / 把衣服～干 *wring out wet clothes* ❷ pinch; tweak: ～了他一把 *give him a pinch* ——另见 nǐng

【拧成一股绳】twist into a rope—stick together; make joint efforts: 只要大伙儿～,没有克服不了的困难。*As long as we are united, there is no difficulty we cannot overcome*.

狞 形 (of facial expression) ferocious; hideous: 狰狞

【狞恶】fierce; ferocious: ～的嘴脸 *ferocious features* / ～可怖 *fierce and terrifying*

【狞视】stare fiercely at; fix one's sinister eyes on

【狞笑】grin hideously

柠 (构词成分)见下

【柠檬】lemon ◇ ～茶 lemon tea; ～黄 citrine; lemon-coloured; ～色 lemon yellow; ～水 lemonade; lemon squash; ～素 [化] citrin; vitamin P; ～酸 [化] citric acid; ～糖 lemon drops; ～油 lemon oil; ～榨汁器 lemon squeezer; ～汁 lemon juice

凝 动 ❶ congeal; coagulate; curdle; condense: 他的衬衣都被血～住了。*His shirt was congealed with blood*. / 用鲜血～成的战斗友谊 *militant friendship cemented with blood* ❷ with fixed attention: 凝思

【凝点】[物] condensation point

【凝冻】freeze: 河水～。*The river is frozen*.

【凝固】solidify: 蛋白质遇热会～。*Protein becomes solid when heated*. ◇ ～点 [物] solidifying

point；～汽油 napalm；～汽油弹 napalm bomb；～浴［纺］coagulating bath
【凝华】［物］sublimate：～核 *sublimation nucleus*
【凝灰岩】［地质］tuff
【凝集】（of fluids or gases）agglutinate ◇ ～素［化］agglutinin
【凝胶】gel
【凝结】congeal；coagulate；curdle；condense：湖面上～了一层薄冰。*A thin layer of ice formed over the lake*. ◇ ～剂［化］coagulant；～力 coagulability；～尾迹 contrail；condensation trail；～物 coagulum
【凝聚】❶（of vapour）condense；（of fluids）coagulate or curdle：荷叶上～着晶莹的露珠。*Glistening dewdrops have formed on the lotus leaves*. ❷［化］coacervation ◇ ～层 coacervate
【凝聚力】❶［物］cohesive force；cohesion ❷ cohesion（〈喻〉）：增强中华民族的～ *increase the cohesion of the Chinese nation*
【凝练】（of writing）concise；condensed；compact
【凝眸】〈文〉fix（or focus）one's eyes on；look with a fixed gaze：～远望 *gaze into the distance*
【凝神】with fixed（or concentrated，rapt）attention：～谛听 *listen with rapt attention*；*listen attentively*
【凝视】gaze fixedly；stare：我久久地～着那尊铜像。*I fixed my eyes on the bronze statue for a long time*.
【凝思】be lost in thought；meditate
【凝听】listen attentively（or intently）listen with rapt attention
【凝望】gaze or stare at：他～着她那逐渐远去的身影。*He couldn't tear his eyes away from her receding figure*.
【凝析油】［油］condensate
【凝血酶】thrombin；thrombase
【凝血药】［医］coagulant
【凝脂】［医］congealed fat（said of a woman's skin）：肤如～ *smooth*，*soft and glossy skin*
【凝滞】stagnant；unmoving；sluggish：～的目光 *dull*，*staring eyes*
【凝重】❶ dignified；imposing：神情～ *look dignified* ❷（of sound or voice）deep and forceful：他的声音～有力。*He has a deep*，*powerful voice*. ❸ deep；dense；thick：～的乌云 *heavy*（*or thick*）*black clouds*

nǐnɡ

拧 Ⅰ 动 ❶ twist；screw：～开瓶盖 *screw*（*or twist*）*the cap off a bottle* / ～上盖子 *screw a lid on* / ～紧螺丝 *tighten up a screw* ❷ differ；disagree；be at cross-purposes：两个人越说越～。*The more they talked*，*the more they disagreed*. Ⅱ 形 wrong；mistaken：他想说"小题大做"，说～了，说成"大题小做"。*He meant to say* "*make a mountain out of a molehill*，" *but he got it the wrong way round and said* "*make a molehill out of a mountain*". ——另见 nínɡ

nìnɡ

宁 Ⅰ 副 ❶ would rather：我～死也不投降。*I would rather die than surrender*. ❷〈书〉could there be：山之险峻，～有逾此？*Could there be a mountain more precipitous than this*？
【宁教我负天下人，休教天下人负我】I would rather betray the world than let the world betray me（a saying attributed to Cao Cao 曹操）
【宁可】would rather：～站着死，绝不跪着生 *would rather die on one's feet than live on one's knees* / ～小心一点的好。*Better safe than sorry*.
【宁肯】would rather
【宁缺毋滥】rather go without than have something shoddy—put quality before quantity
【宁死不屈】rather die than submit（or surrender）
【宁为玉碎，不为瓦全】rather be a broken piece of jade than a whole tile—better to die in glory than live in dishonour：万一失败，那就"～"。*In the event that we fail we'd rather fall to pieces like broken jade than remain intact as a worthless tile*.
【宁愿】would rather

佞 形 ❶ given to flattery：～人 *sycophant*；*toady* ❷ witty；wise：不佞
【佞臣】a sycophantic official or courtier

niú

牛 Ⅰ 名 ox；cattle：母～ *cow* / 公～ *bull* / 小～ *calf* Ⅱ 形 stubborn or arrogant：牛脾气 / 牛气
【牛蒡】［植］great burdock（Arctium lappa）
【牛蒡子】［中］the achene of great burdock
【牛鼻子】the nose（or muzzle）of an ox：牵牛要牵～。*We must lead an ox by the halter*.
【牛车】ox cart；bullock cart
【牛刀小试】a master hand's first small display
【牛痘】❶ cowpox ❷ smallpox pustule；vaccine pustule：种～ *give or get smallpox vaccination* ◇ ～苗（bovine）vaccine
【牛犊】calf
【牛顿】［物］newton（the standard metre-kilogram-second unit of force，named after Sir Isaac Newton）◇ ～万有引力定律 Newton's law of gravitation；～望远镜 Newtonian telescope；～运动定律 Newton's law of motion
【牛轭】oxbow；yoke
【牛轭湖】［地理］oxbow lake
【牛肺疫】pleuropneumonia（of cattle）
【牛粪】cow dung
【牛倌】cowherd；cowhand；oxherd；herd-boy
【牛鬼蛇神】monsters and demons—forces of evil；evil people of all descriptions
【牛黄】［中］bezoar
【牛角】ox horn ◇ ～画 horn mosaic；～制品 horn-

ware
【牛角尖】the tip of a horn—an insignificant or insoluble problem ——另见〖钻牛角尖〗
【牛劲】❶ great strength；tremendous effort：他费了～才把门打开。*He had to exert all his strength to open the door.* ❷ stubbornness；obstinacy；tenacity：这小伙子有股子～，干一件事就非干到底不行。*The lad is strong-willed；once he starts doing something，he won't leave off until he's finished it.*
【牛栏】cattle pen
【牛郎星】common name for 牵牛星
【牛郎织女】the Cowherd and the Weaver，characters in a Chinese folk story；〈喻〉husband and wife who live far apart and can only get together once in a while：为分居两地的～解决生活中的困难 *ease the daily difficulties encountered by couples who do not live and work in the same place*
【牛马】oxen and horses—beasts of burden：当～ *be a slave* / 过着～不如的生活 *live a life worse than that of beasts of burden*
【牛毛】ox hair：多如～ *as many as the hairs on an ox；countless；innumerable*
【牛毛细雨】drizzle；fine drizzling rain
【牛虻】gadfly
【牛奶】milk：鲜～ *fresh milk* ◇ ～场 dairy；～果仁巧克力 milk and nuts chocolate；～咖啡 white coffee；～糖 toffee
【牛腩】〈方〉sirloin；tenderloin
【牛排】beefsteak
【牛棚】cowshed
【牛皮】❶ cowhide；oxhide ❷ tough；tensile；pliable：牛皮糖 ❸ bragging：～大王 *braggart* / 吹～ *talk big*
【牛皮糖】sticky candy
【牛皮癣】［医］psoriasis
【牛皮纸】kraft (paper)
【牛脾气】stubbornness；obstinacy；bullheadedness
【牛气】〈方〉arrogant；overbearing
【牛肉】beef：～汁 *beef extract*
【牛舌鱼】tonguefish；tongue sole
【牛虱】ox louse
【牛市】bull market
【牛溲马勃】cheap but useful things
【牛头刨床】shaping machine；shaper
【牛头不对马嘴】horses' jaws don't match cows' heads—incongruous；irrelevant：他的回答简直是～。*His answer is completely off the point.*
【牛头马面】Ox Head and Horse Face (two demon attendants of the King of Hell)
【牛蛙】bullfrog
【牛尾】oxtail：～汤 *oxtail soup*
【牛尾鱼】flathead
【牛瘟】rinderpest；cattle plague
【牛膝】［中］the root of bidentate achyranthes (Achyranthes bidentata)
【牛饮】drink gallons
【牛蝇】common name for 牛虻
【牛油】butter
【牛仔裤】jeans
【牛仔帽】cowboy hat

niǔ

忸 (构词成分)见下
【忸怩】blushing；bashful
【忸怩作态】behave coyly；be affectedly shy：我讨厌她的～。*I'm sick of her affected manners.*

扭 动 ❶ turn round：他～过头来看了一下。*He looked over his shoulder.* ❷ twist；wrench：把树枝子～断 *twist a twig and break it* / 用力把门～开 *wrench the door open* ❸ sprain；wrench：～了筋 *wrench a tendon；sprain a muscle* / ～了腰 *sprain one's back* ❹ roll；swing：他走路一～一～的。*He walks with a rolling gait.* ❺ seize；grapple with：两人～在一起。*The two were grappling with each other.*
【扭摆】(of one's body) sway：她～着腰肢走过来。*She walked over swaying her hips.* ◇ ～舞 twist
【扭秤】［物］torsion balance
【扭打】wrestle；grapple
【扭动】sway；writhe：她走起路来～着腰肢。*She walks with a swaying motion.*
【扭干】wring dry
【扭角羚】another name for 羚牛
【扭结】twist together；tangle up
【扭亏为盈】turn losses into profits；turn an unfavourable balance into a favourable one
【扭亏增盈】make up deficits and increase surpluses；eliminate losses and increase profits
【扭力】［物］twisting (or torsional，torque) force
【扭力天平】torsion balance
【扭捏】❶ walk affectedly with a swing ❷ 她～了好半天才说出话来。*She affected embarrassment for quite a while before she spoke.*
【扭曲】twist；distort：地震发生后，铁路～得很厉害。*The railroad was twisted out of shape after the earthquake.*
【扭伤】sprain；wrench：～手腕 *sprain one's wrist*
【扭送】(of civilians) seize (a criminal，etc.) and deliver him to (the police)：把违法犯罪分子～公安部门 *seize the offender and hand him over to the public security authorities*
【扭头】❶ turn one's head away；turn away：她扭过头去，不理我。*She turned away and cut me dead.* ❷ turn (round)：他二话没说，～就走。*He just turned and walked off，without saying another word.*
【扭秧歌】do the yangko dance
【扭转】❶ turn round：他～身子，向车间走去。*He turned round and made for the workshop.* ❷ turn back；reverse：～局势 *turn the tide；reverse a trend* / ～被动局面 *put an end to a passive state of affairs；regain the initiative* / ～企业亏损 *eliminate enterprise losses*
【扭转乾坤】bring about a radical change in the sit-

uation; reverse the course of events

纽 名 ❶ handle; knob: 印纽 ❷ button: 衣～ *button* ❸ bond; tie: 纽带

【纽带】link; tie; bond: 友谊的～ *ties of friendship* / 商业是工农业之间的重要～。*Trade is an important link between industry and agriculture.*

【纽扣】button: 钉～ *sew a button on*

【纽眼】〈方〉buttonhole

【纽约】New York ◇ ～市 New York City; ～州 New York State

【纽子】button

狃 动 be bound by; be constrained by: ～于习俗 *be bound by custom*

niù

拗 形 stubborn; obstinate; difficult: 这老头子脾气很～。*He is a difficult old fellow.* —— 另见 ào

【拗不过】be unable to dissuade; fail to talk sb. out of doing sth.: 他这个人脾气犟,你可～他。*He is very obstinate; you won't be able to make him change his mind.*

nóng

农 名 ❶ agriculture; farming: 务～ *go in for agriculture* ❷ peasant; farmer: 菜农 / 贫农

【农产】❶ agricultural production: ～区 *agrarian area; rural district* ❷ agricultural products; farm produce: 这地区有丰富的～。*This district abounds in farm produce.*

【农产品】agricultural products; farm produce: ～加工工业 *farm products processing industry*

【农场】farm: 国营～ *state farm*

【农村】rural area; countryside; village: ～产业结构 *the structure production in rural areas* ◇ ～城市化 urbanization of villages; ～电气化 electrification of the countryside; rural electrification; ～集市 village fair; rural market; ～经济 rural economy; ～生活 rural life

【农贷】agricultural loans (or credits)

【农夫】farmer

【农妇】peasant woman

【农副产品】farm and sideline products: ～批发市场 *a wholesale market for farm and sideline products*

【农工】peasants and workers: 扶助～ *help the peasants and workers* ◇ ～商联合企业 integrated farm-industry-commerce enterprise

【农行】Agricultural Bank of China

【农户】peasant household

【农活】farm work

【农机】agricultural machinery; farm machinery

【农家】peasant family ◇ ～肥 farm manure; farmyard manure

【农具】farm implements; farm tools

【农科所】institute of agricultural science

【农垦】land reclamation and cultivation

【农历】the traditional Chinese calendar; the lunar calendar

【农林牧副渔】farming, forestry, animal husbandry, sideline production and fishery

【农忙】busy season (in farming)

【农贸市场】a market of farm produce (in urban areas)

【农民】peasant; peasantry ◇ ～阶级 the peasantry; ～企业家 farmer-entrepreneur; peasant entrepreneur; ～起义 peasant uprising; peasant revolt; ～协会 peasant association; ～意识 peasant mentality; ～战争 peasant war

【农膜】plastic sheeting for farm use

【农奴】serf ◇ ～制度 serf system; serfdom; ～主 serf owner

【农渠】field ditch

【农桑】farming and sericulture

【农舍】farmhouse; cottage

【农时】farming season: 不违～ *do farm work in the right season*

【农事】farm work; farming: ～繁忙 *busy with farm work*

【农田】farmland; cropland; cultivated land ◇ ～基本建设 capital construction on farmland; farmland capital construction; ～水利 irrigation and water conservancy; ～水利建设 construction of water conservancy works

【农隙】〈书〉slack season (in farming)

【农闲】slack season (in farming)

【农械】farm chemical apparatus (e.g. sprayer, duster)

【农学】agronomy; agriculture: ～家 *agronomist*

【农谚】farmer's proverb; farmer's saying

【农药】agricultural chemical; farm chemical; pesticide: 打～ *apply farm chemical (or pesticide)* / ～污染 *pesticide pollution*

【农业】agriculture; farming ◇ ～保险 agricultural insurance; ～地质学 agrogeology; ～工程学 agricultural engineering; ～国 an agricultural country; ～合作化 cooperative transformation of agriculture; agricultural cooperative (or cooperation) movement; ～化学 agricultural chemistry; agrochemistry; ～机械 agricultural machinery; farm machinery; ～机械人口 people engaged in agriculture; agricultural population; ～机械投入 agricultural input; ～集体化 the collectivization of agriculture; ～气象学 agricultural meteorology; agrometeorology; ～生产合作社 agricultural producers' cooperative; ～生物学 agrobiology; ～税 agricultural tax; ～现代化 modernization of agriculture; agricultural modernization; ～综合开发 comprehensive agricultural development; comprehensive exploitation of agriculture

【农业技术】agricultural technology; agrotechnique ◇ ～改造 the technical transformation of agriculture; ～推广站 station for popularizing agri-

cultural technique；～员 agrotechnician；～站 agrotechnical station
【农艺师】agronomist
【农艺学】agronomy
【农转非】change from rural to non-rural registration
【农作物】crops

浓 形 ❶ dense；thick；concentrated：～烟 *dense smoke；thick smoke* / ～墨 *thick，dark ink* / ～茶 *strong tea* / ～硫酸 *concentrated sulphuric acid* / ～云密布 *overcast with heavy clouds* ❷ (of degree or extent) great；strong：兴趣很～ *take a great interest in sth.* / 玫瑰花香味很～。*The rose has a heavy fragrance.* / 这幅画颜色太～。*The painting is too heavily coloured.*
【浓淡】deep or light—shade of colour：～适宜 *neither too deep nor too pale；just the right shade of colour*
【浓度】consistency；concentration；density：矿浆～ *pulp density* / 当量～ *equivalent concentration*
【浓厚】❶ dense；thick：～的云层 *thick clouds* ❷ strong；pronounced：～的地方色彩 *pronounced (or marked) local colour* / 会议充满着～的火药味。*The meeting smelt strongly of gunpowder.*
【浓积云】［气］cumulus congestus
【浓烈】strong；thick；heavy：香气～ *heavily scented* / ～的色彩 *rich，strong colours* / ～的乡土气息 *marked local colour*
【浓眉】heavy (or bushy，thick) eyebrows：～大眼 *heavy features*
【浓密】dense；thick：～的枝叶 *thick foliage* / 头发～ *thick hair*
【浓缩】［化］concentrate；enrich：～物 *concentrate* / ～铀 *enriched uranium*
【浓香】❶ giving off a strong fragrance：～的茅台酒 *Maotai with its rich distinctive fragrance* ❷ a strong fragrance：～袭人。*A strong fragrance assailed one's nose.*
【浓艳】rich and gaudy：色彩～ *in gaudy colours*
【浓荫】dense leafy shade：在一棵老橡树的～下 *in (or under) the thick leafy shade of an old oak tree* / ～蔽日。*The thick foliage seemed to blot out the sun.*
【浓郁】❶ (of perfume，fragrance，etc.) strong；rich：桂花发出～的香味。*Osmanthus blossoms give off (or exhale) a rich perfume.* ❷ dense；thick：～的松林 *a dense pine forest* ❸ strong；rich：色彩～ *in strong colours* / 表现～的兴趣 *show a great interest in sth.*
【浓重】dense；thick；strong：烟雾越发～了。*The smoke-laden fog became thicker still.* / 他画的花卉，设色十分～。*His paintings of flowers are distinguished by their rich colours.*
【浓妆】heavy makeup and gaudy dress：～艳抹 *richly attired and heavily made-up*

脓 名 pus
【脓包】❶［医］pustule ❷ a worthless fellow；good-for-nothing
【脓疮】running sore
【脓尿】［医］pyuria
【脓疱病】［医］impetigo
【脓胸】［医］pyothorax
【脓肿】［医］abscess：肝～ *liver abscess* / 阑尾～ *appendicular abscess*

nòng

弄 动 ❶ play with；fool with：小孩儿爱～沙土。*Children like to play with sand.* / 你别～闹钟了。*Stop fooling with that alarm clock.* ❷ do；manage；handle；get sb. or sth. into a specified condition：他把衣服～脏了。*He got his clothes dirty.* / 有些问题还需要～清楚。*Certain questions have yet to be clarified.* / ～得不好，就会前功尽弃。*If we don't do a good job now，all the work we've done will be wasted.* ❸ get；fetch：你去～点水来。*Go and get some water.* ❹ play：～手段 *play tricks* —— 另见 lòng
【弄潮儿】a seaman；a beach swimmer
【弄臣】a favourite courtier
【弄错】make a mistake；misunderstand：你～了。*You've got it wrong.*
【弄鬼】〈方〉play the devil—play tricks；hatch a plot
【弄好】❶ do well：把事情～ *do a good job* ❷ finish doing sth.：计划～了没有？*Is the plan ready?*
【弄坏】ruin；put out of order；make a mess of：把事情～ *make a mess of things*
【弄假】practise fraud；resort to trickery
【弄假成真】what was make-believe has become reality；what was said in fun is fulfilled in earnest
【弄僵】bring to a deadlock；deadlock
【弄巧成拙】try to be clever only to end up with a blunder；outsmart oneself
【弄清】make clear；clarify；gain a clear idea of；understand fully：～情况 *gain a clear idea of the situation；find out the real situation* / ～事实 *set the facts straight* / ～是非 *thrash out the rights and wrongs；distinguish right from wrong*
【弄权】manipulate power for personal ends
【弄死】put to death；kill
【弄通】get a good grasp of：认真看书学习，～基本原理。*Read and study conscientiously and get a good grasp of the basic principles.*
【弄虚作假】practise fraud；employ trickery；resort to deception：～，骗取荣誉 *seek honour through fraud and deception*
【弄脏】stain；soil；pollute；smudge；smear
【弄糟】make a mess of；mess up；bungle；spoil：他一插手，就把事情全都～了。*His meddling made a mess of everything.*

nú

奴 Ⅰ 名 bondservant；slave：女～ *a slave girl*；

a woman slave Ⅱ 动 enslave：奴役
【奴婢】slave girls and maidservants
【奴才】unkey；lackey：～相 *servile behaviour*；*servility*；*shameless fawning*
【奴化】enslave：～教育 *education aimed at enslavement* / ～政策 *policy of enslavement*
【奴隶】slave ◇ ～起义 slave uprising；～社会 slave society；～主 slave owner；slaveholder；～主义 slavishness；slavish mentality
【奴仆】servant；lackey
【奴使】〈书〉enslave；keep in bondage
【奴性】servility；slavishness
【奴颜婢膝】subservient；servile：他们对外～，甘心卖国求荣。*They bow and scrape like slaves to the foreigners, willing to sell the country for their own selfish ends.*
【奴颜媚骨】bowing and scraping；sycophancy and obsequiousness：～者向来就有，今后也永远会有。*There has ever been and ever will be found sycophancy on the side of power.*
【奴役】enslave；keep in bondage：受贫穷～ *be enslaved by poverty*

驽 Ⅰ 名 an inferior horse；jade Ⅱ 形（of a person）dull；incompetent：～才 *a person of puny intelligence*；*dullard*
【驽钝】〈书〉dull；stupid
【驽马】〈书〉an inferior horse；jade：～千里，功在不舍。*If a nag travels a thousand li, it's only through perseverance.*

nǔ

努 动 ❶ put forth（one's strength）；exert（one's effort）：～劲儿 *put forth all one's strength* ❷〈方〉injure oneself through overexertion：箱子太沉，你别扛，看～着。*Don't carry that heavy trunk, or you'll strain yourself.* ❸ protrude；bulge：～着眼睛 *with bulging eyes* / 小姑娘把嘴一～，不高兴了。*The little girl pursed her lips to show her dislike.*
【努力】make great efforts；try hard；exert oneself：尽最大～ *do one's utmost*；*do the best one can* / 大家再努一把力。*Let's make still greater efforts.* / 学好一门外语要作出极大的～。*It takes great effort to master a foreign language.*
【努嘴】pout one's lips as a signal：我向他努努嘴，让他先说。*I pouted my lips at him, hinting that he should speak first.*

nù

怒 Ⅰ 名 anger；rage；fury：～骂 *curse furiously* / 我一～之下狠狠地打了他一记耳光。*In a fit of anger I gave him a heavy slap on the cheek.* Ⅱ 形 forceful；vigorous；dynamic：怒火 Ⅲ 副 vigorously；violently；in rage：怒放
【怒不可遏】be beside oneself with anger；be in a towering rage；boil with rage：对待儿童如此残忍真使我～。*It made my blood boil to see such cruelty to children.*
【怒潮】❶（tidal）bore ❷ angry tide；raging tide：革命～汹涌澎湃。*The raging tide of revolution surges forward.*
【怒斥】angrily rebuke；indignantly denounce
【怒冲冲】in a rage；furiously：他把门一摔，～地走了。*He slammed the door and left in a huff.*
【怒发冲冠】bristle with anger；be in a towering rage（or passion）
【怒放】in full bloom：山花～。*The mountain flowers are in full bloom.*
【怒号】howl；roar：狂风～。*A violent wind is howling.*
【怒吼】roar；howl：雄狮～。*The lion roared.* / 示威群众的～震天动地。*The angry shouts of the demonstrators rent the air.*
【怒火】flames of fury；fury：满腔～ *be filled with fury* / 压不住心头的～ *be unable to restrain one's fury*；*be unable to control one's anger* / ～冲天 *a surge of great fury* / ～中烧 *be burning with anger（or wrath）*
【怒骂】curse in rage：～不休 *cursing angrily without stopping*
【怒目】❶ stare with anger：～而视 *stare angrily*；*look daggers at*；*glare at*；*glower at* ❷ glaring eyes；a fierce stare
【怒目横眉】同〖横眉怒目〗
【怒气】anger；rage；fury：～冲冲 *in a great rage* / ～冲天 *be in a towering rage（or passion）*；*give way to unbridled fury*；*be boiling with rage*
【怒容】an angry look：～满面 *a face contorted with anger*；*looking very angry*
【怒色】an angry look：面带～ *wear an angry look*
【怒视】glare at；glower at；scowl at
【怒涛】furious（or raging）billows：～澎湃 *billows raging with great fury*
【怒形于色】betray one's anger；look angry

nǚ

女 名 ❶ woman；female：～教师 *woman teacher* / ～医生 *woman doctor* / ～售货员 *saleswoman* / ～运动员 *sportswoman* / ～民兵 *militiawoman* / ～演员 *actress* / ～英雄 *heroine* / ～飞行员 *aviatrix* ❷ daughter；girl：儿女 ❸ the tenth of the twenty-eight constellations（二十八宿）into which the celestial sphere was divided in ancient Chinese astronomy（consisting of four stars in the shape of a sieve in Aquarius）
【女伴】female companion
【女扮男装】a woman disguised as a man
【女傧相】bridesmaid
【女厕所】❶ women's lavatory（or toilet）；ladies' room ❷（used as a sign for a public toilet）Ladies；Women

【女车】woman's bicycle；lady's bicycle
【女大十八变】There is no telling what a girl will look like when she grows up.
【女单】〈略〉见〖女子单打〗
【女低音】［音］alto
【女儿】daughter；girl
【女儿酒】〈方〉daughter's wine—wine made at a daughter's birth and kept underground until her wedding feast
【女儿墙】［建］parapet
【女方】the bride's side；the wife's side
【女飞行员】female pilot；aviatrix
【女服务员】stewardess；waitress；woman attendant
【女高音】［音］soprano
【女工】❶ woman worker ❷ needlework
【女孩儿】❶ girl ❷ daughter
【女皇】empress
【女监】prison for women criminals
【女将】❶ woman general ❷ a female dab，expert or mastermind
【女眷】the womenfolk of a family
【女角】a female role（in a play，film，etc.）
【女郎】a young woman；maiden；girl
【女垒】（〈略〉全称为'女子垒球队'）women's softball team
【女流】〈贬〉the weaker sex
【女能人】woman of exceptional ability；capable career woman
【女排】〈体〉❶（〈略〉全称为'女子排球队'）women's volleyball team ❷（〈略〉全称为'女子排球'）women's volleyball
【女朋友】girlfriend
【女气】effeminate
【女强人】a strong woman；a woman of exceptional ability
【女墙】（又作'女儿墙'）parapet wall；parapet
【女权】women's rights ◇ ～运动 feminist movement；～主义 feminism
【女人】woman；womenfolk
【女色】woman's beauty；feminine charms；woman as a sexual partner：好～ *be fond of women* / 不近～（*of men*）*be sexually continent*
【女神】goddess
【女生】woman student；girl student；schoolgirl
【女声】［音］female voice：～合唱 *women's chorus*；*female chorus*
【女士】（a polite term for a woman，married or unmarried）lady；madam：～们，先生们！*Ladies and gentlemen*！
【女式】women's（clothing）◇ ～衬衣 shimmy；～贴身内衣 lingerie
【女售货员】shopgirl；saleswoman
【女双】〈略〉见〖女子双打〗
【女王】queen
【女巫】witch；sorceress
【女性】❶ the female sex ❷ woman：新～ *modern women*；*emancipated women*
【女修道院】convent
【女婿】❶ son-in-law ❷〈口〉husband
【女演员】actress
【女英雄】heroine
【女招待】waitress
【女贞】［植］glossy privet（Ligustrum lucidum）
【女贞子】［中］the fruit of glossy privet
【女中音】［音］mezzo-soprano
【女中丈夫】as a man amongst the woman folks
【女主角】feminine lead；leading lady
【女主人】hostess
【女装】women's clothing；women's costume——另见〖男扮女装〗
【女子】woman；female ◇ ～单（双）打 women's singles（doubles）；～团体赛 women's team event；～项目 woman's event；～学校 girl's school
【女足】women's football team

钕 化 neodymium（Nd）

nuǎn

暖 Ⅰ 形 warm；genial：天～了。*It's getting warm*. Ⅱ 动 warm up：～一～手 *warm one's hands* / 雪里送炭～人心。*Sending charcoal in snowy weather warms the heart*.
【暖低压】［气］warm-core cyclone；warm-core low
【暖调】［工美］warm colour tone；warm tone
【暖房】❶ go to the bridal chamber on the eve of a wedding to offer congratulations ❷ call on sb. who has moved into a new home to congratulate him ❸〈方〉greenhouse；hothouse
【暖锋】［气］warm front
【暖阁】〈旧〉a partitioned-off section of a large room with a heating stove
【暖锅】〈方〉chafing dish
【暖烘烘】nice and warm
【暖呼呼】warm；nice and warm：～的南风 *the nice and warm southerly wind* / 听了这番话，我们大家心里～的。*The words warmed our hearts*.
【暖壶】❶ thermos flask；thermos bottle ❷ a teapot or waterpot with a cosy ❸ a metal or earthen hot-water bottle
【暖和】❶（of weather，environment，etc.）warm；nice and warm：炉子一着，屋子就～了。*The room became warm when the fire got going*. ❷ warm up：屋里有火，快进来～～吧！*There is a fire in here*；*come in and warm yourself up*.
【暖帘】quilted door curtain
【暖流】❶［地理］［气］warm current ❷ warm feeling：听了她的一番劝慰，一股～涌上我的心头。*Her soothing words left me with a glow in my heart*.
【暖瓶】〈方〉thermos flask；thermos bottle
【暖气】❶ steam or water heat；central heating ❷ central heating equipment ❸ a warm gas；warm air ◇ ～片 heating radiator；radiator
【暖气团】［气］warm air mass

【暖融融】nice and warm
【暖色】warm colour
【暖水瓶】thermos flask; thermos bottle
【暖洋洋】warm: ～的春风 *a warm spring breeze*

nüè

疟 名 malaria; ague —— 另见 yào
【疟疾】malaria; ague: 恶性～ *pernicious malaria*
【疟蚊】malarial mosquito
【疟原虫】plasmodium; malarial parasite

虐 形 cruel; tyrannical: 暴虐
【虐待】maltreat; ill-treat; tyrannize: ～俘虏是违反政策的。*Any maltreatment of prisoners of war is against our policy.*
【虐杀】cause sb.'s death by maltreating him; kill sb. with maltreatment
【虐政】tyrannical government; tyranny

nuó

挪 动 move; shift: 劳驾把桌子～到那边儿去。*Move the table over there, please.* / 会议～到下周了。*The meeting has been put off till next week.*
【挪东补西】make up deficiency at one place by drawing upon the surplus at the other
【挪动】move; shift: 往前～几步 *move a few steps forward* / 把车上东西捆好,免得车开快的时候～。*Fasten the load down to keep it from shifting at high speed.*
【挪借】borrow money for a short time; get a short-term loan
【挪威】Norway ◇ ～人 Norwegian; ～语 Norwegian (language)
【挪窝儿】〈方〉❶ move to another place: 这炉子真碍事,给它挪个窝儿。*The stove's in the way; let's move it to some other place.* ❷ move house; move
【挪用】❶ divert (funds): 不得～基本建设资金。*The fund earmarked for capital construction is not to be diverted to any other purpose.* ❷ misappropriate; embezzle: ～公款 *misappropriation (or embezzlement) of public funds*

nuò

诺 Ⅰ 动 promise: 许诺 Ⅱ 叹 yes: ～～连声 *keep on saying "yes"*
【诺贝尔奖金】Nobel prize
【诺亚方舟】Noah's Ark
【诺言】promise: 履行～ *fulfil one's promise; keep one's word* / 违背～ *break one's promise; go back on one's promise*

锘 名 [化] nobelium (No)

懦 形 cowardly; weak: 怯懦
【懦夫】coward; craven; weakling: ～懒汉思想 *the coward's and sluggard's way of thinking*
【懦弱】cowardly; weak: 性情～ *chicken-hearted; weak-kneed*

糯 名 glutinous (cereal)
【糯稻】glutinous rice
【糯米】polished glutinous rice ◇ ～酒 glutinous rice wine

O

ō

喔 叹 (expressing sudden realization)：～，原来是你干的！*Oh, so it was you who did it !* / ～，你也这么想！*Oh, so you feel the same way !* ——另见 wō

【喔唷】❶ (expressing surprise) oh：～，这么大的雹子！*Oh, what big hailstones!* ❷ (expressing pain) oh；ouch：～，好疼！*Ouch, it hurts!*

ó

哦 叹 (expressing doubt)：～，是这样的吗？*Oh? Is that so?* / ～！会有这样的事？*What! How can that be?* ——另见 ò

ǒ

噢 叹 (expressing surprise)：～！他竟会说出这样的话来？*Oh, could he really have said such a thing?* / ～！亩产都超千斤了？*What! The per-mu yield has topped 1,000 jin?*

ò

哦 叹 (expressing realization, understanding, etc.)：～，我懂了。*Oh! I see.* or *Oh! Now I understand.* / ～，我想起来了。*Ah, I've got it.* / ～！你是老王的弟弟。*Ah, so you're Lao Wang's brother.* ——另见 ó

ōu

讴 Ⅰ 动 sing Ⅱ 名 folk songs；ballads

【讴歌】〈书〉sing the praises of；celebrate in song；eulogize

【讴吟】〈书〉sing；chant

欧 名 ❶〈略〉见〖欧洲〗❷〈略〉见〖欧姆〗

【欧化】Europeanize；westernize

【欧椋鸟】［动］starling

【欧罗巴人种】the Caucasoid race；the white race

【欧姆】［物］ohm ◇ ～表 ohmmeter；～定律 Ohm's Law

【欧佩克】OPEC (transliteration for 石油输出国组织)

【欧鸲】［动］robin；redbreast

【欧氏管】［生理］Eustachian tube；auditory canal (named after B. Eustachio, an Italian anatomist)

【欧亚大陆】Eurasia

【欧洲】Europe

【欧洲经济共同体】the European Economic Community (E. E. C.)

【欧元】Euro(€)

殴 动 beat up；hit：～伤 *beat and injure；injure by beating* / 他挨了流氓一阵～打。*He got beaten up by some hooligans.*

【殴打】beat up；hit：互相～ *come to blows；exchange blows* / 被～致死 *be beaten to death*

【殴斗】have a fist fight；have fisticuffs

【殴辱】insult and beat up

【殴杀】beat to death

鸥 名 gull：海鸥

ǒu

呕 动 vomit；throw up

【呕吐】vomit；throw up；be sick：～不止 *keep vomiting*

【呕心】exert one's utmost effort (in creative work)：～之作 *a work embodying one's utmost effort*

【呕心沥血】shed one's heart's blood；take infinite pains；work one's heart out

【呕血】［医］haematemesis；spitting blood

偶 Ⅰ 名 ❶ image；idol：木偶 ❷ mate；spouse：择偶 Ⅱ 形 even (number)；in pairs：无独有偶 Ⅲ 副 ❶ by chance；by accident：旅途～遇故友 *chance to meet an old friend while travelling* ❷ once in a while；occasionally

【偶氮基】［化］azo group；azo radical

【偶氮染料】［化］azo dyes

【偶尔】once in a while；occasionally：我们～见面。*We see each other once in a long while.* / 她擅长山水画，～也画画油画。*She is especially good at traditional Chinese landscape painting, but occasionally she does oils too.*

【偶发】accidental；chance；fortuitous：～事件 *a chance occurrence*

【偶犯】casual offence
【偶感】❶ random thoughts (often used in titles of articles):《参观鲁迅故居～》*Random Thoughts on a Visit to Lu Xun's Former Residence* ❷ suddenly feel; occasionally feel: 昨日～不适。*I happened to be ill yesterday.*
【偶合】coincidence: 他们在这一点上见解一致完全是～。*It is a mere coincidence that they see eye to eye on this point.*
【偶或】occasionally; now and then; sometimes; once in a while
【偶然】❶ accidental; fortuitous; chance: ～事故 *an accident* / ～现象 *accidental (or fortuitous) phenomena* / ～误差 *accidental error* ❷ accidentally; by accident; by chance: ～遇见一位老朋友 *run into an old acquaintance; come across an old friend; meet an old friend by chance* ❸ once in a while; occasionally: 他不经常来,～来一次。*He does not come very often; he comes once in a while.*
【偶然性】[哲] contingency; fortuity; chance
【偶数】[数] even number
【偶数页】[刷] even page
【偶蹄动物】even-toed mammal; artiodactyl
【偶蹄目】[动] artiodactyla
【偶像】image; idol: ～崇拜 *idolatry* / ～化 *idolize*

耦 **动**〈书〉(of two persons) plough side by side
【耦合】[物] coupling: 机械～ *mechanical coupling* / ～电路 *coupled (or coupling) circuit* / ～系数 *coupling coefficient*

藕 **名** lotus root: 糖醋～片 *sliced lotus root cooked in sweet and sour sauce*
【藕断丝连】the lotus root snaps but its fibres stay joined—(of lovers, etc.) still in contact though apparently separated; separated but still in each other's thoughts
【藕粉】❶ lotus root starch ❷ lotus root paste (a semifluid food): 冲两碗～ *prepare two bowls of lotus root paste*
【藕荷】(又作'藕合') pale pinkish purple
【藕灰】pale pinkish grey
【藕节儿】joints of a lotus root
【藕煤】〈方〉honeycomb briquet
【藕色】pale pinkish grey

òu

沤 **动** soak; steep; macerate
【沤肥】❶ make compost ❷ wet compost; waterlogged compost
【沤麻】ret flax or hemp
【沤田】a waterlogged plot or field

怄 **动**〈方〉❶ be irritated; be annoyed ❷ irritate; annoy: 你是故意～我。*You are purposely annoying me.*
【怄气】be difficult and sulky: 怄了一肚子气 *have a bellyful of repressed grievances* / 不要～。*Don't sulk.*

P

pā

趴 动 ❶ lie on one's stomach; lie prone: ～在地上打靶 *lie on the ground for target practice* ❷ bend over; lean on: 他正～在桌子上画图。*He was bending over the desk, drawing.*

【趴伏】lie on one's stomach; lie prone: ～地上纹丝不动 *lie prone on the ground stock-still*

【趴架】(of houses) collapse; topple down

【趴窝】〈方〉❶ (of a hen) be sitting ❷ (of a female animal) lie on the ground ready to give birth ❸ (of a person) be broken in health: 他累～了。*He's utterly worn-out.* ❹ (of a machine, vehicle, etc.) break down; be out of order

啪 象 (the sound of clapping, slapping, a gunshot, etc.): ～的一声,瓶塞飞出来了。*The cork popped and flew out of the bottle.* / ～～两声枪响。*Bang, bang, went the gun.*

【啪嚓】(the sound of sth. crashing, hitting the ground, etc.): ～一声,碗掉在地上碎了。*The bowl dropped and broke with a crash.*

【啪嗒】patter: 打字机～～地响着。*The typewriter was clattering away.* / 雨点打在窗户上～～直响。*The rain went pitter-pattering against the windows.*

【啪唧】patter: 那孩子光着脚～～地跑。*The boy pattered along barefoot.*

pá

扒 动 ❶gather up; rake up: 把枯树叶～在一起 *rake together the dead leaves* ❷ stew; braise: ～羊肉 *stewed mutton* / ～鸡 *braised chicken* ——另见 bā

【扒窃】pick people's pockets

【扒手】pickpocket

爬 动 ❶ crawl; creep: 蛇正往洞里～。*The snake is crawling into a hole.* / 这小孩会～了。*The baby can crawl now.* / 有一条虫子在你背上～。*There is a worm creeping up your back.* ❷ climb; clamber; scramble: ～树(绳,山) *climb a tree (rope, mountain)* / 山崖陡峭,要手足并用,才～得上去。*The cliff is very steep. You'll have to clamber with both hands and feet to get to its top.* / 墙上～满了常春藤。*The wall is covered all over with ivy.*

【爬虫】old name for 爬行动物

【爬竿】[体] ❶ pole-climbing ❷ climbing pole

【爬高】❶ climb: 蹬梯子～ *climb a ladder* ❷ 同〖爬升〗

【爬格子】〈口〉crawl over squared or lined paper—write (esp. in order to make a living)

【爬灰】〈口〉scratching in the ashes—incest committed with one's daughter-in-law

【爬犁】〈方〉sledge; sleigh

【爬坡】❶〈字〉climb a mountain slope ❷〈喻〉aim high: 上半年出口～计划基本完成了。*Higher export goals for the first half year have generally been accomplished.*

【爬山虎】❶ [植] Boston ivy ❷〈方〉a sedan chair or litter to carry a person up a mountain

【爬升】(of an airplane, rocket, etc.) ascend; climb; gain altitude: 客机开始～。*The airliner began to gain altitude.*

【爬行】crawl; creep: 跟在别人后面一步一步地～ *trail behind others at a snail's pace*

【爬行动物】[动] reptile

【爬行主义】unadventurous; unwilling to take the initiative: ～受到强烈批评。*The stick-in-the-mud mentality was strongly criticized.*

【爬泳】[体] the crawl

【爬越】climb over: 请勿～此墙。*No climbing over this wall.*

耙 Ⅰ 名 rake: 木～ *wooden rake* Ⅱ 动 make smooth with a rake; rake: 把地～平 *rake the soil level* / 把稻草～拢成堆 *rake up the straw into a pile* ——另见 bà

【耙子】rake

pà

怕 动 ❶ fear; dread; be afraid of: ～蛇 *be afraid of snakes* / 很～艾滋病传染 *be in great fear of AIDS infection* / ～有什么用? *What's the use of being afraid?* ❷ cannot stand; will be affected by: 这种蓝布～晒。*This blue cloth will discolour through exposure to the sun.* / 这种表不～水。*This kind of watch is waterproof.* ❸ (expressing supposition, judgment, estimation, etc.) I am afraid (that); I suppose; perhaps: 事情～不那么简单。*I am afraid things are not that simple.* / 这生意～赚不了多少钱。*This doesn't* *seem a very profitable business, I'm afraid*. ❹ be afraid something might happen; feel anxious about; feel concerned for or about: 他～迟到,六点就动身了。*He started out at six for fear of being late*. / ～要下雨了,你最好带着伞。*It looks like rain, so better take your umbrella with you*. / 现在的女孩子大都～胖。*Most girls are afraid of being overweight*.

【怕老婆】be henpecked

【怕人】❶ dread to meet people; be shy: 这孩子有点～。*The child is a bit shy*. / 企鹅不～。*Penguins are not afraid of people*. ❷ frightening; terrifying; horrible: 山洞里黑得～。*It's frighteningly dark inside the cave*.

【怕三怕四】have all sorts of misgivings; be apprehensive of this and that

【怕生】(of a child) be shy with strangers

【怕事】be afraid of getting into trouble: 胆小～ *timid and overcautious*

【怕是】I guess; I suppose; perhaps; maybe: 你～有点不舒服吧? *You're feeling a bit unwell, aren't you*?

【怕死鬼】coward

【怕头】〈方〉sth. to be afraid of: 有啥～? *What's there to be afraid of*?

【怕羞】coy; shy; bashful: 这女孩子～。*She is a bashful girl*.

帕 名 handkerchief

【帕米尔高原】the Pamirs

pāi

拍 Ⅰ 动 ❶ clap; pat; beat: ～～他的肩膀 *pat him on the shoulder* / ～掉身上的土 *pat one's clothes to get the dust off* / ～桌子大骂 *strike the table and pour out a stream of abuse* / ～球 *bounce a ball* / ～～翅膀 *flap wings; beat wings* / 惊涛～岸 *mighty waves beating the shore* ❷ take (a picture); shoot: ～电影 *shoot (or make) a film* / 这部小说已～成电影了。*This novel has been made into a film*. / 今天天气不好,外景～不成了。*We can't shoot the outdoor scenes in this foul weather*. ❸ send (a telegram, etc.): ～电报 *send a telegram* ❹ 〈口〉flatter; fawn on: 一不会吹,二不会～ *not be given to bragging or toadying* Ⅱ 名 ❶ bat; racket: 乒乓球～ *ping-pong bat* / 网球～ *tennis racket* / 苍蝇～儿 *flyswatter* ❷ [音] beat; time: 一小节四～ *four beats in (or to) a bar* / 这歌是几～的? —是4/4～的。*What time is the song in? —It's in four-four time*.

【拍案】strike (or bang) the table (in anger, surprise, admiration, etc.) ◇ ～而起 smite the table and rise to one's feet in anger; ～叫绝 thump the table and shout "bravo!"

【拍巴掌】〈口〉clap one's hands

【拍板】❶ clappers ❷ beat time with clappers: 你来唱,我来～。*I'll beat time while you sing*. ❸ rap the gavel ❹ have the final say; give the final verdict: 这事儿得由厂长来～。*The factory director has the final say in this matter*. ◇ ～成交 strike a bargain; clinch a deal

【拍打】pat; slap: ～身上的雪 *pat (or beat) the snow off one's clothes* / 把地毯～一下 *beat the carpet; give the carpet a beating* / 波浪～着船舷 *waves lapping against the sides of the boat*

【拍发】send (a telegram): ～消息 *cable a dispatch or report*

【拍抚】pat, caress: 妈妈轻轻地～着儿子。*The mother gently patted her son*.

【拍号】[音] time signature

【拍击】(of waves) beat; run against: 巨浪～着礁石。*Huge waves dashed against the rocks*.

【拍节器】[音] metronome

【拍马屁】(又作'拍马')〈口〉lick sb.'s boots; flatter; soft-soap; play up to; fawn on: 他不是那种～的人。*He is no toady (or flatterer)*.

【拍卖】❶ auction: ～商 *auctioneer* / 交拍卖行～ *come under the hammer* ❷ selling off goods at reduced prices; sale ◇ ～场 auction market; ～行 auction house

【拍摄】take (a picture); shoot: ～一张照片 *take a photo* / ～特写镜头 *shoot a close-up* / 把舞剧～成电影 *film a dance drama* / 在～外景 *be on location*

【拍手】clap one's hands; applaud: ～叫好 *clap and shout "bravo!"*

【拍手称快】clap in high glee; clap and cheer (as on being avenged): 正义得到伸张,人民～。*Justice prevailing at last, people clapped their hands with joy*.

【拍戏】make a film; shoot a scene: 明天拍"记者招待会"这场戏。*Tomorrow we're going to film the press conference scene*.

【拍照】take a picture or have a picture taken; photograph: 我拍了十几张照。*I took about a dozen pictures*. or *I had a dozen pictures taken*.

【拍纸簿】(writing) pad

【拍子】❶ bat; racket: 羽毛球(网球)～ *badminton (tennis) racket* ❷ [音] beat; time: 打～ *beat time* / 二(三,四)～ *duple (triple, quadruple) time* / 单(复)～ *simple (compound) time*

pái

排 Ⅰ 动 ❶ arrange; put in order: ～座位 *arrange seats* / 把课桌椅～整齐 *put the desks and chairs in order* / 节目单已～好。*The programme has been arranged*. ❷ rehearse: 剧团正在～一出历史剧。*The troupe is rehearsing (for) a historical play*. ❸ exclude; eject; discharge: ～脓 *discharge pus* / 把水～出去 *drain the water away* ❹ push: ～门而出 *push the door open and go straight out* Ⅱ 名 ❶ row; line: 前排 ❷ [军] platoon ❸ raft：竹排❹（现多写作“派”）pie：苹果～ *apple pie* Ⅲ量 row；line：一～椅子 *a row (or line) of chairs* —— 另见 pǎi

【排班】arrange in order of shifts，runs，or classes and grades

【排版】［刷］composing；typesetting：机器～ *machine composition* / 照相～ *photocomposition*；*phototypesetting*；*photoset* / 程控～ *programmed composition* / 自动～ *automatic typesetting*；*automatic composition*

【排比】parallelism

【排笔】a broad brush comprising a row of pen-shaped brushes（for whitewashing，painting，picture colouring，etc.）

【排场】❶ ostentation and extravagance；pomp and ceremony：讲～ *go in for ostentation and extravagance* ❷ ostentatious and extravagant；sumptuous；lavish：他们的婚礼办得可～了。*Their wedding was a most ostentatious and extravagant affair*.

【排斥】repel；exclude；reject：同种电荷互相～。*Two like electric charges repel one another*. ◇～异己 discriminate against those who hold different views；exclude outsiders

【排除】get rid of；remove；eliminate：～路上积水 *drain the flooded streets* / ～障碍 *remove (or get over) an obstacle* / ～故障 *fix a breakdown* / 不能～这种可能性 *cannot rule out this possibility*

【排除万难】surmount every difficulty；conquer all obstacles

【排挡】gear（of a car，tractor，etc.）；stall；stand：小吃～ *snack stand*

【排队】form a line；line up；queue up：～买票 *line up for tickets* / ～上车 *queue up for a bus* / ～前进 *march in a column* / 把问题按轻重缓急排排队 *arrange the problems in order of importance and urgency*

【排队论】queuing theory

【排筏】bamboo or timber raft

【排放】❶ place（things）in proper order：书桌上～着台灯、文具和工具书。*The reference books，stationery and reading lamp are arranged in proper order on the desk*. ❷ discharge；let out；drain off：～废气 *discharge used steam or gas*

【排风扇】ventilating fan

【排骨】spareribs or spines

【排灌】irrigation and drainage：～设备 *irrigation and drainage equipment* / ～网 *irrigation and drainage network* / ～站 *irrigation and drainage pumping station*

【排行】seniority among brothers and sisters：他～第三。*He's the third child of the family*.

【排号】❶ row number（of seats in a theatre，etc.）❷〈口〉arrange in numerical order ❸〈方〉line up；queue up

【排洪】drain off floodwaters

【排挤】push aside；push out；squeeze out；elbow out：拉拢一些人，～一些人 *draw some in，push others out*

【排解】❶ mediate；reconcile：～纠纷 *mediate a dispute*；*reconcile a quarrel* ❷ 同〖排遣〗

【排拒】reject；repel；exclude：市场经济已不再受人们的～。*The concept of a market economy is no longer rejected by people*.

【排涝】drain flooded（or waterlogged）fields

【排雷】［军］removal of mines；mine clearance

【排立】stand in a line；line up：群众～在马路两侧欢迎贵宾。*People lined the streets to welcome the distinguished guests*.

【排练】rehearse：～节目 *have a rehearsal*

【排列】❶ arrange；range；put in order：～成行 *arrange in a row (or line，column)* / ～成四路纵队 *form a column of fours* / 按字母顺序～ *arrange in alphabetical order* ❷［数］permutation：～组合 *permutations and combinations*

【排卵】［生理］ovulate ◇～期 period of ovulation

【排难解纷】mediate a dispute；pour oil on troubled waters

【排尿】urinate；micturate ◇～困难［医］dysuria

【排炮】❶（artillery）salvo；volley of guns ❷ successive blastings（in mining，tunnelling，etc.）❸ remove or defuse a dud，or a charge of explosive that fails to explode when it should

【排气】［机］exhaust ◇～管 exhaust pipe

【排遣】divert oneself（from loneliness or boredom）：他闲得无聊，只好去看场电影～～。*As time lay heavily on his hands，he went to the cinema to divert himself*.

【排枪】volley of rifle fire

【排球】volleyball（the game or the ball）◇～场 volleyball court；～网 volleyball net；～柱 volleyball post

【排山倒海】topple the mountains and overturn the seas：以～之势 *with the momentum of an avalanche*；*with the force of a landslide and the power of a tidal wave*

【排射】volley（of fire）

【排笙】［音］a reed pipe wind instrument with a keyboard

【排水】❶ drain off（or away）water ❷ drainage ◇～工程 drainage works；～沟渠 escape canal；～管 drain pipe；～管道 drainage pipeline

【排水量】❶ displacement：～22,000吨的远洋轮船 *an ocean-going liner of 22,000 tons displacement* ❷ discharge capacity（of a spillway，etc.）

【排送】dispatch（vehicle）：每天～20辆货车去码头。*Every day 20 trucks are dispatched to the port*.

【排他性】exclusiveness：～集团 *exclusive bloc* / ～条约 *exclusive multilateral treaty*；*exclusive treaty*

【排坛】volleyball circles

【排头】the person at the head of a procession or formation；file leader：向～看齐！*Keep level with your file leader*!

【排头兵】❶ the soldier at the head of a formation ❷ pacesetter；pacemaker

【排外】exclusive；antiforeign：盲目～ *blind oppo-*

sition to everything foreign ◇ ～心理 xenophobia; ～主义 exclusivism; exclusionism; antiforeignism

【排尾】the last person in a row, procession or formation; the person at the end of a row, etc.

【排污】emit pollutants: 任意～会带来严重的环境问题。*Careless pollution will result in serious environmental problems*.

【排戏】rehearse a play: 排一出新戏 *rehearse a new play*

【排险】eliminate a danger

【排箫】[音] panpipes; Pan's pipes

【排泄】❶ drain rainwater, waste water, etc.: ～不畅 *drainage difficulty* ❷ excrete: ～粪便 *excrete faeces and urine* ◇ ～器官 excretory organs; ～物 excreta; excrement

【排序】sort, collate, rank, sequence, order

【排轧】〈喻〉push aside; squeeze out; outdo; get the best of: 同行们互相～。*People in the same occupation try to outdo each other*.

【排演】rehearse

【排椅】seats in a row

【排印】typesetting and printing: 在～中 *in the typesetting and printing stage* / 赶紧把这本书～出来。*Rush the book into print*.

【排忧解难】relieve sb. of worries and help solve his problems: 帮助乡镇企业～ *help township enterprises allay their worries and tide over their difficulties*

【排运】rafting

【排长】platoon leader

【排中律】[逻] the law of excluded middle

【排钟】[音] chimes

【排字】composing; typesetting: ～车间 *composing room* / ～工人 *typesetter*; *compositor* / ～机 *typesetter*; *composing machine* / ～架 *composing frame* / ～手托 *composing stick*

牌 名 ❶ plate; tablet: 车～儿 *number plate* (*on a vehicle*) / (衣帽间等的)号码～ *check* ❷ brand; make: 你用什么～的肥皂? *What brand of soap do you use*? / 你的汽车是什么～的? *What make is your car*? ❸ cards, dominoes, etc.: 一副扑克～ *a pack of playing cards* / 手里有一副好～ *have a good hand* / 该你出～了! *It's your turn*. or *Play your card*!

【牌匾】an inscribed board (fixed to a wall or the lintel of a door); tablet; plaque

【牌额】a horizontal inscribed board

【牌坊】memorial archway (or gateway)

【牌号】❶ the name of a shop; shop sign ❷ trademark

【牌价】❶ list price; posted price: 按～打八折出售 *goods sold at a discount of 20% off the list prices* ❷ (market) quotation: 外汇～ (*foreign*) *exchange quotations* / 开盘～ *an opening quotation* / 收盘～ *a closing quotation*

【牌九】paijiu, a game of Chinese dominoes: 推～ *play paijiu*

【牌局】a game at dominoes, mahjong, or cards; a gambling game

【牌例】sample card hands used for demonstrating plays (usu. bridge): 许多～都已介绍过了。*Many different plays have already been described*.

【牌楼】❶ pailou, decorated archway ❷ temporary ceremonial gateway

【牌品】personal style and attitude (of cardplayer)

【牌情】the cards one holds; a hand at cards: 隐瞒～是一种常用的手段。*Keeping one's hand secret is a frequent tactic*.

【牌手】participants in a bridge game: 这次参赛的～很多。*There are many participants in this bridge tournament*.

【牌位】memorial tablet (used in ancestral worship)

【牌艺】skill (usu. at bridge): 她～高超。*She is a very skillful bridge player*.

【牌照】license plate; license tag; license certificate; license

【牌证】❶ licence, certificate: 他的～批下来了。*His licence was approved*. ❷ badge: 他的～表明他是个警察。*The badge he wears shows he is a policeman*.

【牌子】❶ plate; sign: 存车～ *tally* (*for parking a bicycle*) ❷ brand; trademark: 老～ *old brand*; *well-known brand*

pǎi

迫 (构词成分) 见下 —— 另见 pò

【迫击炮】[军] mortar: ～弹 *mortar projectile*; *mortar shell*

排 (构词成分) 见下 —— 另见 pái

【排子车】a large handcart

pài

派 Ⅰ 名 ❶ political group, school of thought or art, etc.: 国会议员在这个问题上分成两～。*The Congressmen were divided into two opposing groups over this issue*. / 他是个乐天～。*He is an optimist*. ❷ style; manner and air: 气派 Ⅱ 量 ❶ (for political groups, schools of thought or art, etc.): 三～学者 *scholars of three different schools* / 各～政治力量 *the different political forces* (*or groups*) ❷ (used with the numeral 一, for scene, atmosphere, speech, etc.): 一～深秋景色 *a late autumn scene* / 一～北国风光 *an expanse of typical northern scenery* / 一～胡言! *A pack of nonsense*! / 一～谎言! *A pack of lies*! Ⅲ 动 send; dispatch; assign; appoint: ～代表团出席大会 *send a delegation to the conference* / ～他担任车间主任 *appoint him head of the workshop* / ～兵 *dispatch troops* / ～工作 *set sb. a task* / ～勤务 *assign fatigue duties*

【派别】group; sect; school; faction: 清教徒是十六、十七世纪英国新教徒中的一个～。*The Puritans were a sect of English Protestants in the 16th and 17th centuries.*

【派不是】put (or lay) the blame on sb.: 他自己不认错,还派别人的不是。*Instead of admitting his mistakes, he shifted the blame onto others.*

【派出机构】agency: 地区一级是省的～。*The organ of state power at the prefectural level is an agency of the provincial authorities.*

【派出所】local police station; police substation

【派对】(港台用法) party

【派发】assign to deliver: 请帖已～了。*The invitations have been sent out.*

【派饭】meals in peasant homes arranged for cadres, students, etc. temporarily staying at a village; arranged meals: 吃～ *board with different peasant families by arrangement*

【派购】(of the state) prescribe purchases (of farm produce); fix quantities for state purchase

【派活】assign sb. a task (usu. manual work): 今天派我什么活儿? *What work do you assign me today?*

【派款】impose levies of money

【派力斯呢】[纺] palace

【派遣】send; dispatch: ～代表团 *send a delegation* / ～驻外全权代表 *dispatch a plenipotentiary to a foreign country* ◇ ～国 the sending state; the accrediting state

【派生】derive: 由此～出来的问题 *the questions derived therefrom* ◇ ～词 [语]derivative

【派势】manner; momentum: 他好大的～。*He certainly has a grand manner.* / 经济迅猛发展的～令人倍受鼓舞。*Everyone is encouraged by the rapid momentum of economic growth.*

【派头】style; manner: 他～真不小! *He certainly puts on quite a show!*

【派系】groups or factions (within a political party, etc.): ～之争 *factional strife*

【派性】factionalism: 进行秘密的～活动 *engage in secret factionalist activities*

【派用场】put to use; turn to account: 这东西将来好派大用场。*It can be turned to good account in future.* / 这东西我派不上用场了。*I have no use for it any more.*

【派驻】❶ post; station: 在边境～重兵 *station large numbers of troops along the border* / ～国外 *be posted abroad* / ～北京的外国记者 *foreign correspondents resident in Beijing* ❷ [外交] accredit to: ～联合国的代表 *a representative accredited to the United Nations*

pān

攀 动 ❶ climb; clamber: ～着绳子往上爬 *climb up a rope hand over hand* ❷ seek connections in high places: 高攀 ❸ involve; implicate: 乱咬乱～ *make wild charges, while under interrogation, to implicate others*

【攀比】cite the cases of others in support of one's own claim; vie with; compete: 收入有差别,但是彼此没有～的心理。*There is difference in their income, but no jealousy of those who are better off.*

【攀缠】climb and intertwine: 墙上～着两种藤蔓。*Two vines intertwined over the wall.*

【攀扯】implicate (sb. in a crime)

【攀登】climb; clamber; scale: ～峭壁 *climb up a cliff* / ～科学技术新高峰 *scale new heights in science and technology* ◇ ～架 jungle gym (a playground apparatus for children to climb on)

【攀附】❶ (of a plant) climb (a support): 藤蔓～树木 *vines climbing trees* ❷ seek connections with (people of power and influence): ～权贵 *seek connections with those in power*

【攀高】❶ climb to a higher point ❷ make friends or claim ties of kinship with someone of a higher social position

【攀高枝儿】make friends or claim ties of kinship with someone of a higher social position

【攀交】make friends with people of a higher social position

【攀龙附凤】play up to people of power and influence; put oneself under the patronage of a bigwig

【攀亲】❶ claim kinship ❷ 〈方〉 arrange a match

【攀亲道故】claim ties of blood or friendship

【攀禽】[动] scansorial birds

【攀雀】[动] penduline tit

【攀升】climb; rise continuously: 日元继续～。*The Japanese yen is rising continuously.*

【攀谈】engage in small talk; have a chat: 两人边喝茶边～,十分投机。*They had a most congenial chat over tea.*

【攀岩】cliff-climbing as a competitive sport; rock-climbing

【攀缘】(又作'攀援') ❶ climb; clamber: ～而上 *climb up* ❷ climb the social ladder through pull ◇ ～植物 [植] climber; climbing plant

【攀越】climb up and over; scale; surmount: ～险峰 *scale a perilous peak*

【攀折】pull down and break off (twigs, etc.): 请勿～花木。*Please don't pick the flowers.*

pán

胖 形 〈书〉 easy and comfortable: 心广体胖 ——另见 pàng

盘 Ⅰ 名 ❶ an ancient washbasin ❷ a rather flat receptacle, as a tray, plate, dish, etc. 棋盘 ❸ market quotation; current price: 开盘 Ⅱ 动 ❶ coil (up); wind; twist: 把绳子～起来 *coil up the rope* / 把头发～成一个髻 *comb one's hair into a coil or bun* / 莫干山上下十八～。*There are 18 hairpin bends on the way up the Mogan Moun-*

tain. ❷ build (by laying bricks, stones, etc.): ～炕 *build a kang* / ～灶 *build a brick cooking range* ❸ check; examine; interrogate: 盘问 / 盘账 ❹ transfer the ownership of; make over to sb. else: 把整个厂连同设备～给人家 *transfer the ownership of the factory with all its equipment to another person* ❺ carry; transport: 从仓库往外头～东西 *carry things out of the warehouse* Ⅲ 量 ❶ (for dishes, millstones, etc.): 一～磨 *a pair of millstones* / 四～菜 *four dishes* / 一～电线 *a coil of wire* / 一～蚊香 *a coil of mosquito-repellent incense* ❷ [体] game; set: 下一～棋 *play a game of chess* / 以六比零胜了这一～ *win the set in six straight games*

【盘剥】practise usury: 重利～ *lend money at usurious rates*; *exploit by practising usury*

【盘菜】ready-to-cook dish of meat, vegetables, etc. (sold at the food market); assorted cold dishes

【盘查】(又作'盘察') interrogate and examine: 加设岗哨,～行人。*More sentries were posted to interrogate and examine the passersby*.

【盘缠】〈口〉money for the journey; travelling expenses

【盘秤】a steelyard with a pan

【盘存】take inventory: 商品～ *inventory of merchandise*

【盘道】winding mountain paths; bends

【盘点】check; make an inventory of: ～存货 *take stock*

【盘店】transfer the ownership of a shop with its merchandise and equipment to another person; transfer a business

【盘根错节】with twisted roots and gnarled branches—complicated and difficult to deal with; deep-rooted

【盘根究底】get to the heart of a matter; get to the bottom of things; inquire deeply into sth.: 她～问个没完。*She asked about everything in great detail*.

【盘古】Pan Gu, creator of the universe in Chinese mythology: 自从～开天地 *since Pan Gu separated heaven and earth*; *since the beginning of the world*

【盘管】[机] coil (pipe)

【盘桓】❶〈书〉stay; linger: ～终日 *linger about all day long* ❷ winding; coiling: 她梳了个～髻。*She wore her hair in a coil*. ❸ wind round and round; spiral up or down

【盘簧】[机] coil spring

【盘货】make an inventory of stock on hand; take stock: 今日～,停业半天。*Closed for half a day for stocktaking*.

【盘诘】cross-examine; interrogate: ～行迹可疑的人 *interrogate suspicious-looking persons*

【盘踞】(又作'盘据') illegally or forcibly occupy; be entrenched: 我军一举歼灭了～海岛的敌人。*At one stroke our troops wiped out the enemy who were entrenched on the island*.

【盘库】make an inventory of goods in a warehouse

【盘马弯弓】ride round and round bending one's bow—assume an impressive posture but take no action

【盘尼西林】penicillin (a transliteration, also called 青霉素)

【盘弄】play with; fiddle with; fondle

【盘绕】twine; coil; spiral; wreathe: 长长的藤葛～在树身上。*Long vines twine round the tree*.

【盘山】winding up a mountain: ～小道 *a winding mountain path*

【盘式磁带录像机】reel videotape recorder

【盘式录像磁带】reel videotape

【盘式录音磁带】reel audiotape

【盘算】calculate; figure; plan: 我们～了一下,产量将增加百分之五。*We figured that the output would increase by five per cent*.

【盘梯】winding staircase; spiral staircase

【盘条】[冶] wire rod

【盘头】❶ hair worn in a bun or coil: 梳着～ *wear one's hair in a bun or coil* ❷〈旧〉turban

【盘腿】cross one's legs: ～坐在炕上 *sit cross-legged on a kang*

【盘问】cross-examine; interrogate

【盘膝】cross one's legs: ～而坐 *sit cross-legged*

【盘香】incense coil

【盘旋】❶ spiral; circle; wheel: 雄鹰在空中～。*Eagles were wheeling in the air*. / 这件事在我脑子里～了好久。*I've been turning this over in my mind for a long while*. ❷ linger; stay: 他在暖房里～了半天才离开。*He lingered in the greenhouse for some time before he left*.

【盘羊】[动] argali

【盘账】check (or audit, examine) accounts

【盘整期】period of recovery, regrouping: 最近二至三年内,中国的房地产业发展将进入走出低迷后的～。*In the next two or three years, China's real estate sector will be recovering from a low period*.

【盘子】❶ tray; plate; dish ❷〈旧〉the market rate

【盘坐】sit cross-legged

磐 名 huge rock

【磐石】huge rock: ～般的团结 *rocklike unity*; *monolithic unity* ◇ ～之固 the firmness of a rock

蹒 (构词成分) 见下

【蹒跚】walk haltingly; limp; hobble

pàn

判 Ⅰ 动 ❶ distinguish; discriminate: 判别 ❷ judge; decide: ～卷子 *mark examination papers* ❸ sentence; condemn: ～五年徒刑 *be sentenced to five years' imprisonment* Ⅱ 副 obviously (different): 判然 / 判若两人

【判案】decide a case

【判别】differentiate; distinguish: ～真假 *distinguish the true from the false*

【判别式】[数] discriminant

【判处】sentence (sb.) to; condemn (sb.) to: 罪犯被～死刑。*The criminal was sentenced (or condemned) to death.*

【判词】[法] court verdict

【判定】judge; decide; determine

【判断】❶ judge; decide; determine: ～是非 *judge (or decide) what is right and what is wrong* / ～情况 *assess (or size up) the situation* / 你～得很正确。*Your judgment is sound.* / 你～错了。*You used bad judgment.* ❷ [逻] judgment ◇～词 [语] a grammatical term for the character 是, used as a link word to form a compound predicate with a noun or pronoun; ～力 the ability to judge correctly; judgment

【判罚】penalize (in a sports event): 所有犯规者都得到了～。*All those who broke the rules were penalized.*

【判分】give a mark; mark; score: 由评委～。*Judges will give them marks.*

【判官】a judge in Hades

【判据】[物] criterion

【判决】[法] pass judgment; pronounce (judgment): ～有罪(无罪) *pronounce sb. guilty (not guilty)*

【判决书】[法] court verdict; written judgment

【判例】[法] legal precedent; judicial precedent: 国际法～ *cases in international law* / ～法 *case law*

【判令】make a binding court decision on civil or economic cases: 在这个案件中,法庭～日方赔偿。*The court ordered the Japanese side to pay compensation in this case.*

【判明】clearly distinguish; ascertain: ～是非 *clearly distinguish right from wrong* / ～真相 *ascertain the facts* / ～责任 *establish responsibility (for what has happened)*

【判然】(of differences) noticeable; marked; striking: ～不同 *be markedly different*

【判若两人】have become quite a different person; no longer be one's old self

【判若云泥】(又作'判若天渊') be as far removed as is heaven from earth; be poles apart

【判刑】pass a sentence on; sentence sb. to: 判死刑 *pass a death sentence on sb.* / 他被判了五年刑。*He has been sentenced to five years' imprisonment.*

【判罪】declare guilty; convict

叛 动 betray; rebel against: ～匪 *rebels* / ～贼 *a traitor*

【叛变】betray one's country, party, etc.; turn traitor; turn renegade: ～投敌 *turn traitor and go over to the enemy*

【叛党】turn renegade, esp. from the Communist Party; betray one's party; turn traitor to one's party

【叛国】betray one's country; commit treason: ～罪 *high treason*

【叛教者】apostate; renegade

【叛军】rebel army; rebel forces; insurgent troops

【叛离】betray; desert; defect from; turn renegade

【叛乱】armed rebellion: 煽动～ *incite people to rise in rebellion*

【叛卖】betray; sell out: ～祖国 *betray one's country* / ～活动 *traitorous activity; acts of treason*

【叛逆】❶ rebel against; revolt against ❷ rebel: 封建礼教的～ *a rebel against feudal ethics*

【叛逃】desert and flee one's country; defect: ～者 *a defector; a deserter*

【叛徒】traitor; renegade; turncoat

盼 动 ❶ hope for; long for; expect: ～解放 *long for liberation* / ～复。*I await your reply.* ❷ look: 左顾右盼

【盼顾】look around; look left and right: 引领～ *crane one's neck to look around*

【盼念】look forward to seeing; long to see: 你母亲正日夜～着你呢! *Your mother misses you terribly and is longing to see you.*

【盼头】sth. hoped for and likely to happen; good prospects: 这事有～了。*This business is looking hopeful now.* or *Things are looking up.*

【盼望】hope for; long for; look forward to: ～生活改善 *long for better living conditions*

畔 名 ❶ side; bank: 河～ *river bank; riverside* / 湖～ *the shore of a lake* ❷ the border of a field

襻 Ⅰ 名 ❶ a loop for fastening a button: 纽襻 ❷ sth. shaped like a button loop or used for a similar purpose: 鞋～儿 *shoe strap* / 篮子～儿 *the handle of a basket* Ⅱ 动 fasten with a rope, string, etc.; tie: 用绳子～上 *fasten with a rope* / ～上几针 *put in a few stitches*

pāng

乓 象 a loud sudden noise made by gunfire, door-slamming, breaking of things, etc.; bang; pop; slam; crash: 门～地一声关上了。*The door slammed (or banged) shut.* / 听到～～两声枪响。*I heard two bangs of a gun.*

滂 形〈书〉(of water) rushing; gushing; pouring

【滂湃】(of water) roaring and rushing

【滂沛】〈书〉❶ (of water) surging; rushing ❷ (of rain) torrential; pouring; pelting: 大雨～。*The rain was pelting down.* ❸ powerful; of great momentum: 文辞～ *powerful writing*

【滂沱】torrential: 大雨～。*It's raining in torrents.* / 涕泗～ *let loose a flood of tears*

páng

彷 （构词成分）见下

【彷徨】walk back and forth, not knowing which way to go; hesitate

【彷徨歧途】hesitate at the crossroads

庞 Ⅰ[形] ❶ huge ❷ innumerable and disordered Ⅱ[名] the cast of one's face：面庞

【庞大】huge; enormous; colossal; gigantic：机构～ *an unwieldy organization* / ～的正规军 *a massive regular army* / ～的计划 *a grandiose plan*

【庞然大物】huge monster; colossus; giant

【庞杂】numerous and jumbled：议论～ *numerous and jumbled views* / 机构～ *cumbersome administrative structure*

旁 Ⅰ[名] side：马路两～ *both sides of the street* / 站在路～ *stand by the roadside* Ⅱ[形] other; else：还有～的建议吗？*Any other suggestions?* / 他没说～的话。*He didn't say anything else.* / ～的还要什么？*Do you want anything else?*

【旁白】aside (in a play)

【旁边】side：我坐在他～。*I sat by his side.* / ～有一棵树。*There is a tree nearby.*

【旁侧】side

【旁顾】attend to other matters：无暇～ *have no time to attend to other affairs*

【旁观】look on; be an onlooker：～者 *onlooker; bystander; spectator*

【旁观者清】the spectator sees most clearly; the onlooker sees the game best

【旁及】take up (along with sth. more important)：他专攻历史，～考古。*He is an historian, but also takes an interest in archaeology.*

【旁路】[电] bypass：～电容器 *bypass capacitor*

【旁落】(of power, etc.) pass into others' hands：大权旁落

【旁门】side door

【旁门左道】同〖左道旁门〗

【旁敲侧击】attack by innuendo; make oblique references

【旁人】other people：这个错误由我一人负责，跟～不相干。*I alone should be held responsible for the mistake; no one else has anything to do with it.*

【旁若无人】act as if there was no one else present—self-assured or supercilious

【旁听】be a visitor at a meeting, in a school class, etc.：我明天上午～你的课可以吗？*May I sit in on your lecture tomorrow morning?* ◇ ～生 auditor; ～席 visitors' seats; public gallery (at a Congressional session, etc.)

【旁通管】[机] bypass pipe

【旁系亲属】collateral relatives (or kinsmen); collaterals

【旁压力】[物] lateral pressure

【旁征博引】quote copiously to support one's thesis; be well documented

【旁证】circumstantial evidence; collateral evidence

【旁支】collateral branch (of a family)

膀 （构词成分）见下——另见 bǎng

【膀胱】(urinary) bladder ◇ ～镜 [医] cystoscope; ～炎 [医] cystitis; ～造影 [医] cystography

磅 （构词成分）见下——另见 bàng

【磅礴】boundless; majestic

螃 （构词成分）见下

【螃蟹】crab

pǎng

耪 [动] loosen soil with a hoe：～地 *hoe the field*

pàng

胖 [形] fat; stout; plump：他～起来了。*He's getting fat.* or *He's putting on weight.* ——另见 pán

【胖大海】[中] the seed of boat-fruited sterculia (Sterculia scaphigera)

【胖墩儿】〈口〉(esp. referring to children) roly-poly; fatty

【胖鼓鼓】fat; plump; full; bulging：～的脸蛋儿 *a chubby face* / 豆荚长得～的。*The pods are already full (or have grown very full).*

【胖乎乎】(of children) plump; chubby; pudgy：这个小孩的脸蛋～的。*This child has plump (or chubby) cheeks.* / 婴儿～的小手 *a baby's pudgy fingers*

【胖头鱼】bighead; variegated carp

【胖子】a fat person; fatty

pāo

抛 [动] ❶ throw; toss; fling：～球 *throw (or toss) a ball* / ～出一项欺骗性的提案 *dish out (or trot out) a phoney proposal* ❷ leave behind; cast aside：跑到第三圈，他已经把别人远远地～在后面了。*On the third lap he left the other runners far behind.* / ～进历史的垃圾堆 *be relegated to the garbage heap of history* ❸ 同〖抛售〗

【抛光】[机] polishing; buffing：摩擦～ *burnishing* / ～剂 *polishing compound; polish* / ～轮 *polishing wheel; buff*

【抛荒】❶ (of cultivated land) go out of cultivation; lie waste ❷ (of one's studies) be neglected; (of one's professional knowledge or ability) be wasted through disuse; get rusty

【抛空】[经] sell short; sell against the box; short sale：投资者～往往是为了赢利。*Investors often sell short for profit*.

【抛离】abandon; leave behind: ～亲生骨肉 *abandon one's own flesh and blood*

【抛锚】❶ drop anchor; cast anchor ❷ (of vehicles) break down: 汽车中途～了。*The car broke down on the way*.

【抛弃】abandon; forsake; cast aside: ～妻儿 *abandon one's wife and kids*

【抛却】cast aside; throw away: ～不切实际的幻想 *cast away unrealistic notions (or fanciful ideas)*

【抛洒】(又作'抛撒') spill; shed; scatter: 饭粒～满地。*Grains of cooked rice were scattered all over the floor*. / ～一腔热血 *shed one's blood (for a just cause)*

【抛射】project; catapult; launch ◇ ～体[物] projectile

【抛售】sell (goods, shares, etc.) in big quantities, usu. in anticipation of or in order to bring about a fall in price

【抛头颅,洒热血】shed one's blood and lay down one's life (for a just cause)

【抛头露面】〈贬〉reveal one's head and show one's face (formerly said of a woman showing herself in public, which was considered unbecoming; now said of sb. blatantly seeking publicity)

【抛物面天线】dish antenna

【抛物线】[数] parabola

【抛掷】〈书〉throw; cast

【抛砖引玉】〈套〉cast a brick to attract jade—offer a few commonplace remarks by way of introduction so that others may come up with valuable opinions

泡 Ⅰ名 sth. puffy and soft: 豆腐～儿 *beancurd puff* Ⅱ形 spongy: 这木料发～。*This wood is spongy*. Ⅲ量 (for number of excretions; slightly vulgar): 撒两～尿 *piss twice* / 拉一～屎 *have a shit* ——另见 pào

【泡货】〈方〉light but bulky goods

【泡桐】[植] paulownia

páo

刨 动 ❶ dig; excavate: ～个坑 *dig a hole (or pit)* / ～地 *dig the ground* / ～白薯 *dig (up) sweet potatoes* / 把树根～出来 *dig up the roots of the tree* ❷〈口〉(used with 去, 掉 or 了 as complement) exclude; subtract; not count: 十五天～去五天,只剩下十天了。*Fifteen minus five—there are only ten days to go now*. ——另见 bào

【刨除】exclude; subtract; not count

【刨分】deduct marks (or points) (for errors in a student's work): 他拼错了两个词,刨了四分。*He got four marks deducted for two spelling mistakes*.

【刨根】get to the root (or bottom) of the matter

【刨根问底】get to the root (or bottom) of things: 他这人就爱～。*He's never satisfied until he gets to the bottom of things*.

【刨煤机】coal plough

咆 动〈书〉(of beasts of prey) roar; howl

【咆哮】❶ (of beasts of prey) roar; howl ❷ (of humans) roar with rage: ～如雷 *be in a thundering rage* ❸ (of torrents) roar on; thunder away: 黄河在～。*The Huanghe River roars on*.

狍 名 [动] roe deer

【狍子】[动] roe deer

炮 动 [中] prepare herbal medicine by roasting or parching (in a pan): ～姜 *roasted ginger* ——另见 bāo; pào

【炮炼】[中] parch and refine medicinal herbs

【炮烙】the hot pillar (an ancient instrument of torture)

【炮制】❶ [中] the process of preparing Chinese medicine, as by parching, roasting, baking, steaming, soaking, simmering, etc. ❷〈贬〉concoct; cook up: ～反动纲领 *concoct a reactionary programme*

袍 名 robe; gown

【袍笏登场】dress up and go on stage (said contemptuously of an official or a political puppet taking office)

【袍子】robe; gown: 皮～ *fur robe*

pǎo

跑 动 ❶ run: 他～得很快。*He can run very fast*. / ～上前去迎接客人 *run forward to meet the guests* / 每天早晨练慢～ *do jogging every morning* / 火车在飞～。*The train is racing along*. ❷ run a race: ～百米 *run (or take part in) the 100-metre dash* / ～接力赛的第一棒 *run the first leg of the relay* / ～第二 *run second* ❸ run away; escape; flee: 别让坏蛋～了。*See that the scoundrel doesn't escape*. / 暴风雨快来了,你还是赶紧～吧! *A storm is coming up. You'd better cut and run*. ❹〈方〉walk; stroll: 他们通常吃过晚饭出去～～路。*They usually go for a stroll after supper*. / 我们～了五里路。*We walked five li*. ❺ run about doing sth.; run errands: ～材料 *run about collecting material* / 我～了好几家商店,才找到那种扳手。*I had to run around to several shops to get that wrench*. / 你这辆卡车一天能～几个来回? *How many round trips can your truck make in a day?* ❻ (of a liquid or gas) leak or evaporate: 哎哟,水管子～水了。*Oh, the pipe leaks!* / 车胎～气了。*The tyre is flat*. / 汽油～了半瓶。*Half the bottle of gasoline has evaporated*. ❼ (used as complement to a verb) away; off: 一枪把鸟儿都吓～了。*The shot scared away the birds*. / 桌上的纸叫风给刮～了。*The paper blew off the table*.

【跑表】stopwatch

【跑步】❶ run; march at the double: ～走!(*word of command*) *At the double, quick march!* / ～前进!(*word of command*) *Double time!* ❷ jogging (a form of physical exercise)
【跑车】❶ racing bicycle ❷ a trolley for conveying logs in a forest ❸ sports car ❹〈口〉(of train conductors) be on the job ❺ (of trolleys for hoisting coal in a mine) accidentally slide down
【跑驰】〈口〉run errands; be on the run; hurry here and there: 他白～了一整天,什么事也没办成。*He was on the run the whole day, but all for nothing.*
【跑单帮】travel around trading on one's own
【跑刀】race skates
【跑道】❶ runway (on an airfield) ❷ [体] track: 煤渣～ *cinder track* / 渣土～ *cinder and dirt track* / 塑料～ *plastic track*
【跑电】leakage of electricity
【跑光】[摄] (of a film) be exposed to light accidentally
【跑旱船】boat that runs on land (a folk dance performed by a girl gliding about with a cloth boat and a man making rowing movements with an oar, singing a rude ditty as they dance)
【跑江湖】wander about, making a living as a street-performer (e.g. an acrobat, fortune-teller, physiognomist, etc.)
【跑警报】run for shelter during an air raid
【跑了和尚跑不了庙】the monk may run away, but the temple can't run with him—a fugitive must belong to some place that can provide clues
【跑垒】[体] baserunning: ～员 *base runner*
【跑龙套】play a walk-on part; play a bit role
【跑马】❶ have a ride on a horse ❷ horse racing ◇ ～场 racecourse; the turf
【跑码头】travel from port to port as a trader; be a travelling merchant
【跑买卖】be a commercial traveller: 他跑过几年买卖。*He was a commercial traveller for a couple of years.*
【跑跑颠颠】bustle about; be on the go: 老大娘在服务站成天～的,给大伙办事。*The old lady is bustling about every day at the neighbourhood service centre, helping people do all sorts of things.*
【跑跑跳跳】skip along: 小姑娘～的上街去。*The little girl skipped down the street.*
【跑墒】[农] loss of moisture in soil (through evaporation): 使用塑料薄膜覆盖,可以防止～。*Plastic sheeting is used to cover the soil to prevent loss of moisture.*
【跑生意】同【跑买卖】
【跑堂】〈旧〉waiter (in a wineshop, small restaurant, etc.)
【跑题】digress from the subject; stray from the point
【跑腿】〈口〉run errands; do legwork: 我没干多少,就是跑跑腿儿。*I didn't do much, just a bit of running around.*
【跑外】act as a travelling agent or salesman: ～的 *a travelling agent or salesman*
【跑鞋】track shoes (either with spikes for use outdoors or with rubber soles for use indoors)

pào

泡 Ⅰ 名 ❶ bubble: 肥皂～儿 *soap bubbles* / 冒～儿 *send up bubbles; rise in bubbles* ❷ sth. shaped like a bubble: 手上起了～ *get (or raise) blisters on one's palm* Ⅱ 动 ❶ steep; soak: 把种子放在温水里～一下 *steep the seeds in lukewarm water* / 他是在苦水里～大的。*He was brought up in bitter misery.* ❷ dawdle: 别～时间了,快把工作做完! *Stop dawdling and finish your work!* ——另见 pāo
【泡病号】shun work on pretence of illness
【泡菜】pickled vegetables; pickles
【泡茶】make tea
【泡饭】❶ soak cooked rice in soup or water ❷ cooked rice reheated in boiling water; gruel from recooked rice
【泡沸石】[矿] zeolite
【泡蘑菇】〈口〉❶ play for time; use delaying tactics; stall: 别～了,咱们赶紧干吧。*No more dilly-dallying. Let's get going.* ❷ importune; pester: 别跟我～了,我们不能为你破例。*Stop pestering me. I can't make an exception for you.*
【泡沫】foam; froth: 啤酒～ *head (on a glass of newly poured beer)* ◇ ～包装 bubble wrap; ～玻璃 foam glass; foamed glass; ～混凝土 foam concrete; ～经济 bubble economy; ～灭火器 foam extinguisher; ～塑料 foamed plastics; ～橡胶 air foam rubber; ～浴 bubble bath
【泡泡纱】[纺] seersucker
【泡泡糖】bubble gum; chewing gum
【泡汤】❶ fall flat; fall through: 这样一来,这个月的计划就要～了。*In that case, this month's plan is bound to fall through.* ❷ dawdle; dilly-dally
【泡影】visionary hope, plan, scheme, etc.; bubble
【泡罩塔】[化] bubble-cap tower (or column)
【泡制】brew: 如法～ *do the same*

炮 名 ❶ big gun; cannon; artillery piece ❷ bombard (the earliest kind of cannon throwing stone balls) ❸ firecracker: 鞭炮 ❹ a blasthole filled with dynamite ❺ cannon, one of the pieces in Chinese chess ——另见 bāo; páo
【炮兵】artillery; artillerymen: ～部队 *artillery (troops)* / ～连 *battery* / ～阵地 *artillery position; gun emplacement*
【炮车】gun carriage
【炮弹】❶ (artillery) shell ❷〈旧〉cannon ball
【炮轰】(of artillery) bombard; shell: 午夜开始～敌军防线。*The artillery started bombarding the enemy lines at midnight.*
【炮灰】cannon fodder: 战争贩子们视士兵为～。

In the eyes of the warmongers, soldiers are nothing but cannon fodder.
【炮火】artillery fire; gunfire: 掩护～ (*artillery*) *fire cover* / ～支援 *artillery support* / ～准备 *artillery preparation*
【炮击】bombard; shell
【炮架】gun carriage; gun mount
【炮舰】gunboat ◇ ～外交 gunboat diplomacy; ～政策 gunboat policy
【炮口】gun muzzle; cannon's mouth: ～焰 *muzzle flash*
【炮楼】[军] blockhouse
【炮钎】rock drill
【炮声】report (of a big gun): ～隆隆。*Cannons boomed.*
【炮手】gunner; artilleryman
【炮栓】breechblock (of a big gun)
【炮塔】gun turret; turret
【炮台】a fortification with built-in cannons; battery
【炮膛】bore (of a big gun)
【炮艇】gunboat
【炮筒】barrel (of a big gun)
【炮筒子】a person who shoots off his mouth
【炮尾】gun breech
【炮位】emplacement
【炮眼】❶ porthole; embrasure ❷ blasthole; dynamite hole; borehole
【炮衣】gun cover
【炮战】artillery action (or engagement)
【炮仗】firecracker
【炮座】gun platform

疱 名 blister; bleb
【疱疹】❶ bleb ❷ herpes: 带状～ *herpes zoster*; *zoster* ◇ ～净 [药] idoxuridine

pēi

呸 叹 (used to express disdain, annoyance or stern disapproval) pah; bah; pooh: ～! 胡说八道! *Bah! That's nonsense!* / ～! 我才不信呢! *Pooh! I don't believe that!*

胚 名 [生] embryo
【胚层】[生] germinal layer: 内～ *entoderm* / 外～ *ectoderm* / 中～ *mesoderm*
【胚根】[植] radicle
【胚囊】[生] embryo sac
【胚盘】[动] blastodisc; germinal disc
【胚乳】[植] endosperm
【胚胎】❶ [动] embryo: ～移植 *embryo transfer*; *embryonic implantation* ❷ the beginning or rudimentary stage (of anything) ◇ ～学 embryology
【胚芽】❶ [植] plumule ❷ an undeveloped thing; the bud: 矛盾的～ *a contradiction in the bud*
【胚叶】同〖胚层〗
【胚轴】[植] plumular axis
【胚珠】[植] ovule
【胚子】❶ silkworm embryo ❷ 〈喻〉 egg; person: 他是个坏～。*He's a bad egg.* / 好～ *a good egg*

péi

陪 动 accompany; keep sb. company: 我～你到农场去。*I'll accompany you to the farm.* / ～外宾参观工厂 *show foreign visitors round a factory* / ～病人 *look after a patient*
【陪伴】accompany; keep sb. company: 老太太要找个人～。*The old lady wants someone to keep her company.* or *The old lady wants to find a companion.*
【陪绑】❶ be taken to the execution ground together with those to be executed as a form of intimidation ❷ (of an innocent person) be criticized or punished together with the guilty
【陪衬】❶ serve as a contrast or foil; set off: 红旗在雪山的～下，显得分外鲜艳。*The red flags stood out in sharp relief against the snow mountains.* ❷ foil; setoff
【陪床】(of an inpatient's family member, etc.) stay in the ward to look after the patient night and day
【陪都】an alternate or secondary capital; a provisional capital (e.g. Chongqing after the fall of Nanjing during the Anti-Japanese War)
【陪读】accompany a person studying at school; accompany a spouse studying abroad: 她们都希望走～这条路出国。*They all hope to go abroad by accompanying their spouses.*
【陪护】stay with and nurse: 大夫请她～病人。*The doctor asked her to stay and nurse the patient.*
【陪嫁】dowry
【陪酒】be a drinking partner
【陪客】a guest invited to a dinner party to help entertain the guest of honour
【陪练】one who trains or practices with top athletes; practice athlete: 他每天都要～好几个小时。*Every day he spends several hours training with top athletes.*
【陪审】[法] ❶ act (or serve) as an assessor (in a law case) ❷ serve on a jury ◇ ～团 jury; ～席 jury box; ～员 juror; juryman; ～制 jury system
【陪送】〈口〉 ❶ give as a dowry; dower ❷ dowry; ❸ include as a gift: 所有的磁带都随录音机～。*All the tapes are included as gifts with the tape recorder.* ❹ accompany: 学生们都由父母～到考场。*All the students were accompanied by their parents to the examination locations.*
【陪同】❶ accompany: ～前往参观 *accompany sb. on a visit* ❷ a responsible official accompanying an important visitor or visiting delegation ◇ ～人员 entourage ～团 hosting team; receptionist committee
【陪夜】stay with patient at night: 她今晚～。*She will stay with the patient tonight.*

【陪葬】❶ (of a wife, concubine or slave) be buried alive with the dead ❷ (of figurines or objects) be buried with the dead ❸ (of a wife or concubine after her death) be buried by the side of her husband's grave ◇ ～品 (又作'陪葬物') funerary objects, figurines, etc.

【陪住】(of an inpatient's family member, etc.) sleep in the ward to tend the patient

培 动 ❶ bank up with earth; earth up ❷ foster; train: ～干 *train cadres*

【培护】grow and protect: ～草地对城市环境非常重要。*Growing and maintaining lawns is very important for the urban environment.*

【培土】[农] hill up; earth up: 在玉米根部多培点儿土 *earth up the maize*

【培训】train (personnel): ～导游人员 *train tourist guides* / 在职～ *on-the-job training*

【培训班】training course: 暑期～ *summer vacation training course; summer school*

【培养】❶ cultivate (plants); culture (microorganisms): ～花卉 *cultivate flowers and plants* / 细菌～ *the culture of bacteria* ❷ foster, train, or develop (a certain spirit, ability, etc.) in sb.: 从小～好习惯 *develop good habits from childhood days* / ～学生自学能力 *train the students to study on their own* / 在老师的～教育下 *be nurtured and educated by the teachers* ◇ ～基 [生] culture medium; ～瓶 culture bottle

【培育】❶ help (young plants) grow by labour and care; cultivate; breed: ～小麦新品种 *breed new varieties of wheat* / ～树苗 *grow saplings* ❷ nurture and educate; bring up; rear: 孩子们在父母和老师的～下健康成长。*Nurtured and educated by their parents and teachers, the children are growing up healthy and strong.*

【培植】❶ cultivate (plants): ～中草药 *cultivate medicinal herbs* ❷ foster; train: ～人才 *train competent personnel* / ～私人势力 *build up one's personal influence*

【培种】cultivate (plants): ～芦笋 *cultivate asparagus*

赔 动 ❶ make good a loss; compensate; pay for; indemnify: 玻璃是我打碎的,由我来～。*I broke the glass, so I'll pay for it.* ❷ lose money in business; stand a loss: 去年我们～的钱,这一笔生意全赚回来了。*We have retrieved in this bargain all the money we lost last year.* / 你算算咱们是～是赚。*Balance the accounts and see if we have made any money.*

【赔本】sustain losses in business; run a business at a loss: ～生意 *a business run at a loss*

【赔补】make good a loss; make up a deficit

【赔不是】apologize: 是你错怪了她,你该给她赔个不是。*You should apologize to her for blaming her wrongly.*

【赔不起】be unable to make good a loss: 这本书要是丢了,你可～。*If ever this book got lost, you would never be able to make good the loss.*

【赔偿】❶ make good a loss; compensate; indemnify: ～损失 *compensate (or pay) for a loss* / 照价～ *compensate according to the cost* / 保留要求～的权利 *reserve the right to demand compensation for the losses* ❷ reparations (of a defeated state for war damage): 战争～ *war reparations; war indemnity* / 实物～ *reparations in kind* ◇ ～人 compensator; ～物 indemnity

【赔偿费】(又作'赔偿金') [法] (compensatory) damages

【赔错】acknowledge a mistake; apologize for one's wrongdoing: 我向您～来啦。*I've come especially to apologize to you.*

【赔垫】pay for sb. (usu. a large sum of money): 钱数太大,我可～不起。*I can't pay so much money for you.*

【赔话】say a word in apology

【赔款】❶ pay an indemnity; pay reparations: 割地～ *cede territories and pay reparations* ❷ indemnity; reparations: 庚子～ *the Boxer Indemnity*

【赔了夫人又折兵】give one's enemy a wife and lose one's soldiers as well—pay a double penalty (for attempting to gain an unfair advantage); instead of making a gain, suffer a double loss

【赔礼】make (or offer) an apology; apologize: ～道歉 *make a formal apology*

【赔钱】❶ sustain economic losses; lose money in business: ～的买卖 *a business run at a loss* ❷ pay for a loss; pay damages ◇ ～货 money-losing commodity

【赔小心】behave with great caution; act warily: 老板动不动就生气,在他面前说话,要赔点儿小心才好。*Our boss is easily offended, so be careful how you speak to him.*

【赔笑】(又作'赔笑脸') smile obsequiously, apologetically or appeasingly; smile an apologetic (or obsequious) smile

【赔账】❶ pay for the loss of cash or goods entrusted to one ❷ 〈方〉 lose money in business

【赔罪】apologize (for a wrong done to sb.); ask forgiveness for one's wrongdoing

锫 名 [化] berkelium (Bk)

pèi

沛 形 copious; abundant: ～然降雨。*A copious rain began to fall.*

佩 Ⅰ 名 an ornament worn as a pendant at the waist in ancient times: 玉～ *jade pendant* Ⅱ 动 ❶ wear (at the waist, etc.): ～玉 *wear a jade pendant at one's waist* / 腰～手枪 *carry a pistol in one's belt* ❷ admire: 他的国际主义精神十分可～。*His internationalist spirit is altogether admirable.*

【佩带】wear (at the waist, on the breast, etc.): ～徽章(肩章,臂章) *wear a badge (shoulder loops, an armlet)* / 胸前～奖章 *wear a medal on one's breast* ◇ ～式话筒 lapel mike; body mike

【佩刀】❶ wear a sword at the waist ❷ a sword worn at the waist

【佩服】esteem; admire: 他机智勇敢,令人～。*One must admire his resourcefulness and courage.*

【佩剑】[体] sabre: ～运动员 *sabre fencer; sabreur*

配 Ⅰ 动 ❶ join in marriage: 英雄～模范,真是美满姻缘。*A model worker married to a hero—this is really a good match.* ❷ mate (animals): 公驴～母马 *a male donkey mated with a mare* / ～马 *mate horses* ❸ mix according to a fixed ratio; compound: ～颜色 *mix colours (on a palette)* / 药～齐了。*The prescription has been made up.* / 这个食谱～得好。*This is a well-combined diet.* ❹ distribute according to plan; apportion: 配售 ❺ find sth. to fit or replace sth. else: ～钥匙 *have a key made to fit a lock* / ～眼镜 *have one's eyesight tested for glasses* / ～零件 *replace parts* ❻ match; harmonize with; be in harmony with: 颜色不～。*Those colours don't match.* / 粉红和浅蓝～在一起挺好看。*Pink and light blue go well together.* / 她的衬衣和裙子～不到一起。*Her blouse doesn't match her skirt.* ❼ deserve; be qualified; suit: 只有他们这样的人,才～称为先进工作者。*Only people like them deserve the name of advanced workers.* / 她不～当代表。*She is not qualified to be a representative.* ❽ exile; banish: 发配 Ⅱ 形 subordinate; supplementary; supporting: 配角

【配备】❶ provide (manpower or equipment); equip; fit out: 这些舰艇～有大口径炮。*These ships are fitted with large-calibre guns.* / 这个项目～的技术力量不足。*The project is not sufficiently provided with technical personnel.* / 这趟列车～的服务人员不够。*This train is undermanned.* ❷ dispose (troops, etc.); deploy: 从敌军～弱的地方插进去 *thrust in where the enemy deployment is weak* ❸ outfit; equipment: 现代化的～ *modern equipment* / 成套的～ *a complete outfit*

【配菜】❶ garnish food ❷ garnishes: 这个鱼就用黄瓜片作～。*Garnish the fish with cucumber slices.*

【配餐】❶ assorted foods for a meal ❷ prepared meal: 航空～ *airline meal*

【配餐室】pantry

【配电】[电] (power) distribution: ～线路 *distribution line* ◇ ～盘 [电] distributor; ～网 [电] distribution network

【配殿】side hall in a palace or temple

【配对】❶ pair; match: 这两只手套不～儿。*These two gloves don't match (or aren't a pair).* / 请你再给我找一只一模一样的花瓶,配成一对儿。*Please find me another vase exactly like this one to make a pair.* ❷ 〈口〉(of animals) mate; pair: 现在正是鸽子～的好时候。*It's high time to pair (or mate) the doves.*

【配额】quota: 出口～ *export quota*

【配发】❶ allocate: 书要到下月才能～。*The books will not be distributed until next month.* ❷ publish a related article: 这篇报道还～了一篇评论员文章。*A commentator's article was carried along with the news report.*

【配方】❶ fill (or make up) a prescription ❷ a formula for compounding a chemical or metallurgical product: 制皂～ *a formula for making soap* ❸ prescription

【配房】wing (of a house)

【配购】buy rations

【配股】[经] scrip issue

【配合】coordinate; cooperate; concert: ～作战 *coordination of military operations* / ～行动 *take concerted action* / 起～作用 *play a supporting role* ◇ ～饲料 mixed feed; compound feed

【配给】ration: ～证 *ration card (or book)* / ～制 *ration system; rationing*

【配件】❶ parts, fittings, or accessories: 合页之类门窗～ *door and window fittings such as hinges* / 管子～ *pipe fittings* ❷ replacement

【配角】❶ appear with another leading player; co-star with sb. ❷ supporting role; supporting actor: 当总经理的～ *play second fiddle to the general manager*

【配料】❶ mix ingredients according to a recipe; get materials ready (for the manufacture of sth.) in the right proportion ❷ [冶] burden: 高炉～ *blast-furnace burden* / ～表 *burden sheet* / ～计算 *burden calculation*

【配偶】〈书〉spouse: 外交官及其～ *diplomats and their spouses*

【配器】[音] orchestration

【配色】(pèisè) mix colours in the right proportion

【配色】(pèishǎi) 〈方〉match colours; harmonize colours: 室内装饰的～ *the matching of colours in interior decoration*

【配售】ration (at state price): 下个月起汽油实行～。*Gasoline will be rationed from next month.*

【配属】[军] place part of one's troops temporarily under the command of a subordinate officer

【配水闸】[水] distribution structure

【配套】❶ form a complete set or system: 就地生产,就地～ *manufacture complete sets of equipment locally* ❷ coordinated; complementary ◇ ～措施 coordinated measures; ～改革 complementary (or mutually-supporting) reforms; ～工程 auxiliary project; [水] conveyance system; ～器材 necessary accessories

【配伍】[医] compatibility of medicines: ～禁忌 *incompatibility*

【配戏】play a minor part (to support a leading actor): 他有幸为梅兰芳配过戏。*He had the honour of playing a supporting role in an opera starring Mei Lanfang.*

【配系】[军] system of disposition

【配演】perform supporting role in a play
【配药】❶ (of a pharmacist) make up a prescription; dispense a prescription ❷ have a prescription made up: 拿这张方子到中药房去配三副药。*Have three doses of this prescription made up at the Chinese pharmacy.*
【配页】[刷] gather (leaves of a book) in proper sequence for binding
【配音】dub (a film, etc.): 用汉语给外国电影～ *dub foreign films in Chinese* ◇ ～演员 dubber
【配乐】❶ select passages to serve as background music (for a film, play, radio programme, etc.) ❷ dub in background music: ～诗朗诵 *a poem recital dubbed in with background music* ◇ ～广播 dubbed-in radio programme
【配制】compound; make up: ～药剂 *compound medicines*
【配置】dispose (troops, etc.); deploy: 纵深～ *disposition in depth* / 生产力的合理～ *a rational distribution of productive forces*
【配种】[牧] breeding: ～率 *breeding rate* / ～站 *breeding station*
【配子】[生] gamete ◇ ～体 [植] gametophyte

辔 名 bridle: 鞍～ *saddle and bridle*
【辔头】bridle

pēn

喷 动 ❶ spurt; spout; gush: 喷泉向空中～水。*The fountain spurted water into the air.* / 石油从井口～了出来。*Oil gushed from the well.* / 火山不住地～出熔岩。*The volcano kept throwing up streams of lava.* ❷ spray; sprinkle: 给花～点水 *sprinkle some water on the flowers* / 往果树上～农药 *spray fruit trees with insecticide* ——另见 pèn
【喷薄】gushing; spurting ◇ ～欲出 (of the sun) emerge in all its splendour
【喷出岩】[地质] extrusive rock; extrusive
【喷灯】blowtorch; blowlamp
【喷发】erupt; throw out: 火山～ *volcanic eruption*
【喷饭】laugh so hard as to spew one's food; split one's sides with laughter
【喷放】spurt; spout: 烟火在夜空中～出五彩缤纷的火花。*Fireworks shot into the night sky, sending out colourful sparks.*
【喷粉器】[农] duster
【喷粪】〈讳〉use abusive language: 满嘴～ *shout filthy abuses; use foul language*
【喷灌】sprinkling irrigation; spray irrigation ◇ ～器 sprinkler
【喷壶】watering can; sprinkling can
【喷火器】[军] flamethrower
【喷溅】(of a liquid when being squeezed out) splash; spatter
【喷浆】[建] ❶ whitewashing ❷ guniting
【喷漆】spray paint; spray lacquer: ～枪 *paint spray gun; airbrush*
【喷气发动机】jet engine
【喷气式】jet-propelled ◇ ～飞机 jet plane; jet aircraft; jet
【喷气织机】air-jet loom
【喷枪】spray gun; airbrush
【喷泉】fountain
【喷洒】spray; sprinkle: ～农药 *spray insecticide*
【喷射】spray; spurt; jet: ～火焰 *spurt flames*
【喷水池】(artificial) fountain
【喷丝头】[纺] spinning jet; spinning nozzle: ～牵伸 *spinneret draft* / ～组件 *spinneret assembly*
【喷嚏】sneeze
【喷桶】〈方〉watering can; sprinkling can
【喷头】❶ shower nozzle ❷ sprinkler head
【喷吐】shoot out (flames, light, gas, etc.)
【喷雾】spray; atomize ◇ ～器 sprayer; atomizer
【喷泻】(of a liquid) shoot out; gush forth
【喷云吐雾】❶ (of a smoker) puff away ❷ (of a chimney, etc.) belch out smoke
【喷子】sprayer; spraying apparatus
【喷嘴】spray nozzle; spray head

pén

盆 Ⅰ 名 basin; tub; pot: 大大小小的～儿一大摞 *a pile of pots and basins of all sizes* Ⅱ 量 (for things held in a basin, tub, or pot): 几～花 *a few pots of flowers* / 一～热水 *a basin of hot water*
【盆地】[地理] basin: 柴达木～ *the Qaidam Basin* / 准噶尔～ *the Junggar Basin*
【盆花】potted flower
【盆景】potted landscape; miniature trees and rockery
【盆盆罐罐】pots and pans—household utensils
【盆腔】[生理] pelvic cavity ◇ ～炎 [医] pelvic infection
【盆浴】tub bath; tub
【盆栽】❶ grown (or cultivated) in a pot: ～葡萄 *a grapevine cultivated in a pot* ❷ potted flowers or miniature trees

pèn

喷 (构词成分) 见下 ——另见 pēn
【喷红】crimson: 她羞得满脸～。*Her face crimsoned from shame.*
【喷香】fragrant; delicious: 饭菜～。*The dishes smell delicious.*

pēng

怦 象 (of the heart) thumping; pit-a-pat: 他的心激动得～～直跳。*His heart was thumping with excitement.* / ～然心动 *one's heart goes pit-a-pat*

抨 动〈书〉impeach

【抨击】attack (in speech or writing); assail (with words); lash out at

砰 象 the sound of sth. falling heavily on the ground or striking against sth. else: ～的一声，门关上了。*The door banged shut.* / ～一声，木板倒下来了。*The plank fell on the ground with a thump.*

【砰然】with a bang; with a thump

烹 动 ❶ boil; cook in water; brew (tea, coffee, etc.) ❷ fry quickly in hot oil and stir in sauce: ～对虾 *quick-fried prawns in brown sauce*

【烹饪】cooking; culinary art: 擅长～ *be good at cooking; be a good cook*

【烹饪法】❶ cuisine; cookery ❷ recipe (for cooking)

【烹调】cook (dishes): 中国式～ *Chinese cooking; Chinese cuisine*

péng

朋 Ⅰ 名 friend: 良～ *good friend* / 宾～满座。*There was a houseful of guests.* or *Visitors filled all the seats.* Ⅱ 动〈书〉gang up: 朋比为奸

【朋比为奸】act in collusion; conspire; collude; gang up

【朋党】clique; cabal

【朋友】❶ friend: 广交～ *make many friends* ❷ boyfriend or girlfriend: 他有～了。*He has got a girlfriend now.*

棚 名 ❶ canopy or awning of reed mats, etc. ❷ shed; shack: 牲口～ *livestock shed* / 自行车～ *bicycle shed*

【棚车】❶［铁路］box wagon; boxcar ❷ covered truck

【棚户】〈方〉slum-dwellers; shack-dwellers

【棚架】trellis; frame for vines or climbing plants

【棚圈】covered pen (for animals)

【棚子】〈口〉shed; shack: 草～ *straw mat shed* / 马～ *horse shed*

蓬 Ⅰ 名［植］fleabane Ⅱ 形 fluffy; dishevelled: ～着头 *with dishevelled hair* Ⅲ 量 (for twiggy, leafy plants) clump; cluster: 一～竹子 *a clump of bamboo*

【蓬荜增辉】lustre lent to a humble house (said in thanks for a visit or a gift such as a scroll)

【蓬勃】vigorous; flourishing; full of vitality: 新生事物～兴起。*New things are springing up vigorously.*

【蓬蒿】〈方〉crowndaisy chrysanthemum

【蓬户】〈书〉a wicker door—a humble house

【蓬莱】a fabled abode of immortals: ～仙境 *fairyland*

【蓬乱】(of grasses, hair, etc.) fluffy and disorderly

【蓬门筚户】(a house with) a wicker door—a humble abode

【蓬蓬】(of grasses, shrubs, hair, beard, etc.) thick and disorderly

【蓬松】fluffy; puffy: ～的头发 *fluffy hair*

【蓬头垢面】with dishevelled hair and a dirty face; unkempt

硼 名［化］boron (B)

【硼砂】borax; sodium borate: ～玻璃 *borax glass*

【硼酸】boric acid

【硼酸盐】borate

鹏 名 roc

【鹏程万里】(make) a roc's flight of 10,000 li—have a bright future

澎 动 splash; spatter: ～了一身水 *be splashed all over with water*

【澎湖列岛】the Penghu Islands; the Penghus; (European name) the Pescadores

【澎湃】surge: 大海中波涛～。*Waves surge in the sea.*

篷 名 ❶ covering or awning on a car, boat, etc. ❷ sail (of a boat): 扯起～来 *hoist the sails*

【篷布】tarpaulin: 用～把货物盖上 *cover the goods with a tarpaulin*

【篷车】同〖棚车〗

【篷帐】tent

【篷子】awning (for protection from the sun, rain, wind, etc.)

膨 (构词成分) 见下

【膨大】expand; inflate

【膨化】(of rice, corn, etc.) popped: ～玉米 *popcorn* ◇ ～食品 dilated food; inflated food

【膨体纱】［纺］bulk yarn

【膨胀】expand; swell; dilate; inflate: 金属受了热就会～。*Metals expand when they are heated.* / 消费～ *inflated consumption; over-expanded consumption* ◇ ～计［物］dilatometer; ～系数［物］coefficient of expansion (or dilatation); ～性 expansibility

pěng

捧 Ⅰ 动 ❶ hold or carry in both hands: ～着一个西瓜 *hold a watermelon in both hands* / 她双手～着孩子的脸。*She cupped the child's face in her hands.* / 他～起水来喝了一大口。*He scooped up some water with his hands and took a big mouthful.* ❷ boost; exalt; extol; flatter: 把某人～上天 *praise sb. to the skies* Ⅱ 量 a double handful: 一～枣儿 *a double handful of dates*

【捧杯】❶〈字〉hold the cup (as a prize) ❷〈喻〉win the championship: 哪个队能～，现在还不清楚。*It is not clear which team will win the champion-*

ship.

【捧场】❶ be a member of a claque ❷ boost; sing the praises of; flatter: 无原则的～ *unprincipled praise*

【捧读】〈书〉〈套〉 have the pleasure of reading (your work)

【捧腹】split (or shake, burst) one's sides with laughter

【捧腹大笑】be convulsed with laughter; split one's sides with laughter

【捧哏】(of the supporting performer of a comic dialogue 相声) play the fool to help make people laugh

【捧角】try to build up an actor

【捧杀】kill with praise (over-praising leads to arrogance and complacency, and ultimately to failure): 不要～,也不要骂杀。*Do not destroy by either excessive praise or condemnation*.

【捧献】offer with respect: 人们～最好的食物,热烈欢迎解放军的归来。*People offered the best food to the PLA to welcome them back*.

pèng

碰 动 ❶ touch; bump: 这件精密仪器,你可别～。*Mind you don't touch this precision instrument*. / 把墨水瓶～翻了 *knock the inkbottle over* / 头～在门上 *bump one's head against the door* ❷ meet; run into: 在街上～到一个熟人 *run into an acquaintance in the street* / ～到困难 *run up against difficulties* / 我没～着他。*I didn't see him*. ❸ take one's chance: ～～机会 *take a chance*

【碰杯】clink glasses

【碰壁】run up against a stone wall; be rebuffed: 到处～ *run into snags and be foiled everywhere*

【碰钉子】meet with a rebuff; hit (or strike, run against) a snag: 如果我是你,我就不去碰这个钉子。*If I were you, I wouldn't run my head against a brick wall*. / 碰了个软钉子 *be mildly rebuffed*

【碰见】meet unexpectedly; run into: 你猜我昨晚在首都体育馆～谁了? *Who do you think I ran into at the Capital Stadium last night?*

【碰铃】a pair of hand-held bells played by striking together (used as a percussion instrument in traditional opera, etc.)

【碰面】meet: 明天我们还在这儿～。*Let's meet here again tomorrow*.

【碰碰车】bumper car

【碰碰船】bumper boat

【碰碰舞】slam dance

【碰巧】by chance; by coincidence: 我～也在那儿。*I happened to be there too*. or *It just so happened that I was there too*. / 正要送孩子上县医院,～医疗队到村里来了。*They were going to send the child to the county hospital when a medical team arrived in the village*.

【碰锁】spring lock

【碰头】meet and discuss; put (our, your, or their) heads together: 决定下次～的时间 *decide on the time of the next meeting* / 他们一～,很快就把问题解决了。*They put their heads together and promptly solved the problem*. ◇ ～会 brief meeting (mainly to exchange information)

【碰一鼻子灰】be snubbed; meet with a rebuff

【碰硬】boldly confront or challenge a powerful opponent; try to remove a formidable obstacle

【碰运气】try one's luck; take a chance

【碰撞】❶ collide; run into: 一辆卡车从后面～了我们的汽车。*A lorry ran into our car from behind*. ❷ offend; affront ❸ [物] collision; impact: 核～ *nuclear collision* / ～负载 *impact load*

pī

批 Ⅰ 动 ❶ slap: 批颊 ❷ scrape; pare; cut into slices: 片～ *slicing* ❸ criticize; refute: ～深～透 *criticize penetratingly and thoroughly* / 真理是～不倒的。*Truth cannot be overthrown by criticism*. ❹ write instructions or comments on (a report from a subordinate, etc.): ～文件 *write instructions on documents* Ⅱ 形 wholesale: ～购 *buy goods wholesale* Ⅲ 量 batch; lot; group: 新到的一～化肥 *a new lot of chemical fertilizer* / 一大～积极分子 *large numbers of activists* / 出动多～飞机 *dispatch wave after wave of planes*

【批办】issue (certificates, credentials, etc.): 每天他们都要～许多证明。*Every day they must issue many certificates*.

【批驳】❶ veto an opinion or a request from a subordinate body ❷ refute; criticize; rebut: 逐点予以～ *refute point by point*

【批捕】issue an arrest warrant: 在办理完～手续后,他们立即拘捕犯罪嫌疑人。*They detained the suspect soon after the warrant was issued*.

【批斥】refute, criticize: 一些散布谣言的人受到狠狠地～。*Those who spread rumors have been discredited and severely criticized*.

【批处理】[计] batch processing ◇ ～文件 [计] batch file

【批次】batch (of aircraft, etc.)

【批答】〈书〉 give an official, written reply to a subordinate body

【批点】mark words and phrases for special attention with dots or small circles and write comments

【批斗】criticize and denounce sb. (at a public meeting)

【批发】❶ wholesale: ～价格 *wholesale price* ❷ (of an official document) be authorized for dispatch: 那份电报是由副部长～的。*That telegram was authorized for dispatch by the vice-minister*. ◇ ～部 wholesale department; ～商 jobber; wholesaler; ～市场 wholesale business

【批复】give an official, written reply to a subordinate body
【批改】correct：～作业 *correct students' papers*
【批号】lot number; batch number
【批颊】〈书〉slap sb.'s face; box sb.'s ear
【批件】an official, written reply to a subordinate body
【批量】❶ (produce) in batches：～生产 *batch process*; *batch production* ❷ batch; lot：～小 *small lots* (*or batches*) / 大～生产 *mass production*
【批判】❶ criticize：～错误路线 *criticize the erroneous line* / ～会 *criticism meeting*; *criticism session* / ～文章 *critical article* ❷ critique：《哥达纲领～》*Critique of the Gotha Programme*
【批判地】critically; discriminatingly：～吸收 *critically assimilate*; *assimilate with discrimination*
【批判现实主义】critical realism
【批评】❶ criticize：～缺点和错误 *criticize shortcomings and mistakes* ❷ criticism：～与自我～ *criticism and self-criticism* / 党内～ *inner-Party criticism*
【批示】❶ write instructions or comments on a report, memorandum, etc. submitted by a subordinate ❷ written instructions or comments on a report, memorandum, etc. submitted by a subordinate
【批售】wholesale：这些桌子以每张 5 千元～。*These tables sell at wholesale for* 5,000 *yuan per piece*.
【批条】a note bearing a superior's instructions or comments
【批文】document bearing an official written response from senior authorities
【批销】见〖批售〗
【批语】❶ remarks on a piece of writing ❷ 同〖批示〗
【批阅】read over (official papers); read and amend or comment on (writings, texts, etc.)
【批注】❶ annotate and comment on ❷ annotations and commentaries; marginalia
【批转】write instructions or comments on a report submitted by a subordinate and refer it to those concerned
【批准】ratify; approve; sanction：～条约 *ratify a treaty* / 大会～了他的报告。*The congress approved his report*.
【批准书】instrument of ratification：互换～ *the exchange of instruments of ratification*.
【批准文号】sanction number

纰 动 (of cloth, thread, etc.) become unwoven or untwisted; be spoilt：线～了。*The thread came untwisted*.
【纰漏】a careless mistake; a small accident; slip：出了～ *made a small error*; *made a slip*
【纰缪】〈书〉error; mistake

坯 名 ❶ a base ready to be machined into a finished product; blank; clay mould：景泰蓝花瓶的铜～ *copper base for a cloisonné vase* ❷ unburnt brick; earthen brick; adobe ❸〈方〉semifinished product：面～儿 *cooked plain noodles*; *cooked but unseasoned noodles*
【坯布】[纺] unbleached and undyed cloth; grey cloth; grey
【坯革】crust leather
【坯件】❶ [机] blank：螺栓～ *bolt blank* ❷〈喻〉breed; strain：坏坯子 *bad egg*; *bastard*

披 动 ❶ drape over one's shoulders; wrap around：～着大衣 *have an overcoat draped over one's shoulders* / ～上衣服 *throw on some clothing* / ～上节日的盛装 *be colourfully decorated for the festival* / 一只～着羊皮的狼 *a wolf in sheep's clothing* ❷ open; unroll; spread out：～卷 *open a book* ❸ split open; crack：这根竹竿～了。*The bamboo pole has split*.
【披读】open (a book) and read
【披风】cloak
【披拂】〈书〉❶ wave; sway：微风吹来，枝叶～。*The trees are swaying in the light breeze*. ❷ (of a breeze) blow gently：春风～。*A gentle spring breeze is blowing*.
【披肝沥胆】open one's heart; be open and sincere; be loyal and faithful
【披挂】❶ put on a suit of armour：～上阵 *buckle on one's armour and go into battle* ❷ a suit of armour
【披红】drape a band of red silk over sb.'s shoulders (on a festive occasion or as a token of honour) ◇ ～戴花 have red silk draped over one's shoulders and a big red flower pinned on one's breast (as a token of honour)
【披坚执锐】buckle on one's armour and take up weapons—go forth to battle
【披肩】❶ cape ❷ shawl ◇ ～发 shoulder length hair
【披荆斩棘】break through brambles and thorns—hack one's way through difficulties
【披露】❶ publish; announce：要求不～姓名 *wish to remain anonymous* ❷ reveal; show; disclose：～肝胆 *open one's heart*; *be openhearted*
【披麻带孝】wear the hemp garments of mourning
【披靡】❶ (of grass, etc.) be swept by the wind ❷ be routed; flee：所向披靡
【披散】(of hair, mane, etc.) hang down loosely
【披沙拣金】sort out the fine gold from the sand—extract the essentials from a mass of material
【披头散发】with hair dishevelled; with hair in disarray; unkempt
【披星戴月】under the canopy of the moon and the stars—travel by night; work from before dawn till after dark
【披阅】open and read (a book); peruse：～群书 *peruse books of all sorts*; *read widely*

砒 名 arsenic

【砒霜】(white) arsenic

劈 动 ❶ split; chop; cleave: ～木柴 *chop wood; split logs* / ～成两半 *cleave sth. in two* / 这块木头好～。*This log splits easily*. ❷ right against (one's face, etc.): 大浪朝我们～面打来。*Huge waves came crashing almost on top of us*. ❸ (of lightning) strike: 老树让雷～了。*The old tree was struck by lightning*. ❹ [机] wedge ——另见 pǐ

【劈波斩浪】cleave through the waves

【劈刺】[军] sabre or bayonet fighting: ～训练 *bayonet drill*

【劈刀】❶ chopper ❷ [军] sabre fighting

【劈风斩浪】brave the wind and the waves—slash one's way through difficulties

【劈理】[矿] cleavage

【劈里啪啦】the successive sounds of crackling, etc.: 鞭炮～地响。*The firecrackers were crackling and spluttering*. / 敌人～乱打了一阵枪,就跑了。*The enemy fired off a few random shots and fled*.

【劈脸】right in the face: ～就是一巴掌 *slap sb. on the face* / 一块石头～向他打来。*A stone came hurtling towards his face*.

【劈啪】the sound of crackling, etc.: 把鞭子抽得～响 *crack a whip* / 孩子们劈劈啪啪地鼓起掌来。*The children began to clap their hands*.

【劈杀】(usu. of a man on horseback) slash at sb. (with a sword)

【劈山】level off hilltops; blast cliffs: ～造田 *level off hilltops and turn them into flat fields* / ～筑路 *blast cliffs to build highways or railways* / ～引水 *cleave hills and lead in water; cut through mountains to bring in water*

【劈手】make a sudden snatch: ～夺过枪来 *snatch a gun away from sb*.

【劈头】❶ straight on the head; right in the face: ～一拳 *hit sb. right on the head* / 他走到门口～撞上了老王。*As he reached the door, he bumped straight into Lao Wang*. ❷ at the very start: 他一进门～就问:"准备好了吗?" *The moment he entered the room he asked, "Is everything ready?"*

【劈头盖脸】right in the face: 倾盆大雨～地浇了下来。*The rain came pelting down*. / 记者们～向他提出许多问题。*The reporters fired a volley of questions at him*.

【劈胸】right against the chest: ～一把抓住 *grasp sb. by the front of his coat*

霹 (构词成分) 见下

【霹雷】〈口〉thunderbolt; thunderclap

【霹雳】thunderbolt; thunderclap ◇ ～舞 break dance

pí

皮 Ⅰ 名 ❶ skin; rind; peel: 香蕉～ *banana skin* / 土豆～ *potato peel* / 西瓜～ *watermelon rind* / 荞麦～ *buckwheat husk* / 擦破一块～ *scrape a bit of skin off* ❷ leather; hide; fur: ～靴 *leather boots* / ～大衣 *fur coat* ❸ cover; wrapper: 包袱～儿 *cloth-wrapper* ❹ surface: 飘在水～儿上 *float on the surface of the water* ❺ a broad, flat piece (of some thin material); sheet: 白铁～ *galvanized iron sheet; tinplate* ❻ rubber: 皮筋儿 Ⅱ 形 ❶ naughty: 这孩子真～! *What a naughty child!* ❷ case-hardened: 他老挨剋,都～了。*He gets scolded so often that he no longer cares*. ❸ soft and soggy: 花生～了。*The peanuts aren't crisp any more*.

【皮袄】fur-lined jacket

【皮包】leather handbag; briefcase; portfolio ◇ ～公司 briefcase company—an inadequately financed company, not credit-worthy; a fly-by-night company; ～生意 free riding

【皮包骨头】skinny: 瘦得～ *be a bag of bones; be all skin and bones*

【皮鞭】leather-thonged whip

【皮草】leather & fur: ～服装 *leather apparel; fur coat (or jacket)*

【皮层】❶ [生] cortex ❷ 〈略〉见〖大脑皮层〗

【皮尺】tape measure; tape

【皮带】❶ leather belt ❷ [机] (driving) belt: 交叉～ *cross belt* / 三角～ *triangle belt* / ～车床 *belt-driven lathe* / ～传动 *belt transmission* / ～运输机 *belt conveyer*

【皮带轮】(belt) pulley

【皮蛋】同〖松花蛋〗

【皮垫圈】[机] leather washer; leather packing collar

【皮筏】skin raft

【皮肤】skin ◇ ～病 skin disease; dermatosis; ～病学 dermatology; ～科 [医] dermatological department; dermatology; ～针 [中] cutaneous acupuncture; needles used in cutaneous acupuncture; ～真菌病 [医] dermatomycosis

【皮革】leather; hide

【皮辊花】[纺] lap waste

【皮猴儿】hooded fur overcoat; fur parka; fur anorak

【皮划艇】[体] canoeing (including kayaking): ～运动员 *canoeist*

【皮婚】leather wedding anniversary — the 3rd wedding anniversary

【皮货】furs; peltry: ～商 *fur dealer; furrier*

【皮夹子】(又作'皮夹儿') wallet; pocketbook

【皮匠】❶ cobbler ❷ tanner

【皮胶】hide glue

【皮筋儿】〈口〉rubber band ——另见〖跳皮筋儿〗

【皮具】leather products: 今年～流行。*This year leather products are popular*.

【皮开肉绽】the skin torn and the flesh gaping: 被打得～ *be bruised and lacerated (from flogging)*

【皮里阳秋】criticism kept to oneself: ～的笔法 *making well-covered or implicit remarks*

【皮毛】❶ fur: 貂皮是一种极贵重的～。*Marten is*

one of the most expensive furs. ❷ smattering; superficial knowledge: 略知～ *have only a superficial knowledge (of a subject)*

【皮棉】ginned cotton; lint (cotton)

【皮面】❶ outer skin; surface; outside ❷ leather cover

【皮囊】❶ leather bag ❷〈贬〉the human body

【皮内针】[中] intradermal needling (acupuncture by embedding the needle subcutaneously for one or several days)

【皮球】rubber ball; ball

【皮褥子】fur-lined mattress

【皮实】❶ sturdy: 这孩子真～,轻易不闹病。*He's a sturdy child. He hardly ever gets ill.* ❷ durable

【皮试】a test for allergies whereby allergens are injected into the skin

【皮糖】a sticky candy

【皮条】❶ leather strap ❷ 见〖拉皮条〗

【皮条纤】procurer; pimp

【皮艇】❶ [体] kayaking: ～运动员 *kayaker* ❷ kayak

【皮统子】(又作'皮桶子','皮桶儿') fur lining (for a jacket or an overcoat)

【皮下注射】[医] subcutaneous (or hypodermic) injection

【皮下组织】[生理] subcutaneous tissue

【皮线】rubber-insulated wire; rubber-covered wire

【皮箱】leather suitcase; leather trunk

【皮笑肉不笑】put on a false smile; smile hypocritically

【皮鞋】leather shoes ◇ ～油 shoe polish

【皮靴】leather boots

【皮炎】[医] dermatitis

【皮衣】❶ fur clothing ❷ leather clothing

【皮影戏】leather-silhouette show; shadow play

【皮张】hide; pelt

【皮掌儿】outsole

【皮疹】[医] rash

【皮之不存,毛将焉附】with the skin gone, what can the hair adhere to—a thing cannot exist without its basis

【皮脂腺】[生理] sebaceous glands

【皮纸】tough paper made from bast fibre of the mulberry or paper mulberry, etc.

【皮质】❶ [生理] cortex ❷〈略〉见〖大脑皮层〗

【皮重】tare

【皮子】❶ leather; hide ❷ fur

枇 (构词成分) 见下

【枇杷】loquat (the tree and its fruit)

毗 动〈书〉❶ adjoin; be adjacent to ❷ assist

【毗连】(又作'毗邻') adjoin; border on; be adjacent to: 江苏北部同山东～。*Northern Jiangsu borders on Shandong.* / ～地区 *contiguous zone* / ～性 *contiguity*

铍 名 [化] beryllium (Be)

疲 形 tired; weary; exhausted

【疲惫】❶ tired out; exhausted: ～不堪 *be in a state of utter exhaustion; be dog-tired* ❷ tire sb. out: 目的是～敌军。*The purpose was to tire out the enemy.*

【疲顿】〈书〉be tired out

【疲乏】同〖疲劳〗

【疲倦】tired and sleepy: 他连坐了两天火车,显得很～。*He looked quite worn-out after two days' train journey.*

【疲劳】❶ tired; fatigued; weary: 身心～ *be weary in body and mind* ❷ fatigue: 肌肉～ *muscular fatigue* / 精神～ *mental fatigue* ❸ [机] weakening of material subjected to stress; fatigue: 金属～ *metal fatigue* / 弹性～ *elastic fatigue* / ～强度 *fatigue strength* / ～试验 *fatigue test*

【疲劳综合征】exhaustion syndrome; fatigue syndrome

【疲软】❶ fatigued and weak: 两腿～ *be weak in the legs* ❷ [经] weaken; slump: 目前该国货币在外汇市场上显得～。*The currency of that country is weakening on foreign exchanges.*

【疲弱】tired and weak; frail and fatigued: 他拖着～的双腿缓慢地往前走。*He dragged his tired legs slowly along.*

【疲塌】(又作'疲沓') slack; negligent: 工作～ *be slack at one's work*

【疲于奔命】be tired out by too much running around; be kept constantly on the run; be weighed down with work: 使之～ *tire sb. out by keeping him or her on the run*

啤 (构词成分) 见下

【啤酒】beer: 黑～ *porter; brown ale; stout* / 生～ *draught beer* ◇ ～厂 brewery; ～罐 beer can; beer tin; ～花 [植] hops; ～桶 beer barrel

琵 (构词成分) 见下

【琵琶】pipa, a plucked string instrument with a fretted fingerboard

脾 名 spleen

【脾气】❶ temperament; disposition: ～很好 *have a good temper* / 摸熟机器的～ *get to know the characteristics of a machine* ❷ bad temper: ～大 *hot-tempered* / 发～ *lose one's temper; flare up*

【脾切除】[医] splenectomy

【脾胃】taste: 不合～ *not suit one's taste; not be to one's liking*

【脾胃相投】have similar tastes; have similar likes and dislikes

【脾性】〈方〉temperament; disposition; nature; habits and characteristics: 一个人有一个人的～。*People differ in temperament.*

【脾脏】spleen

【脾肿大】[医] splenomegaly

pǐ

匹 I 动 be equal to; be a match for: 世无其～

matchless; *peerless* Ⅱ 形 single; one: 单枪匹马 Ⅲ 量 ❶ (for horses, mules, etc.): 两～骡子 *two mules* / 三～马 *three horses* ❷ (for rolls of cloth or silk): 一～布 *a bolt of cloth*

【匹敌】be equal to; be well matched: 双方实力～。*The two sides are well matched.*

【匹夫】❶ an ordinary man ❷ an ignorant person ◇ ～之勇 reckless courage; foolhardiness

【匹夫有责】every one has the duty: 天下兴亡,～。*Every individual must hold himself responsible for the prosperity or decline of his country.*

【匹配】❶〈书〉mate; marry ❷ [电] matching: 阻抗～ *impedance matching* / ～变压器 *matching transformer*

【匹染】[纺] piece dyeing: ～色布 *piece-dyed cloth*

否 Ⅰ 形 bad; wicked; evil Ⅱ 动 censure: 臧否 ——另见 fǒu

【否极泰来】Out of the depth of misfortune comes bliss; The extreme of adversity is the beginning of prosperity.

痞 名 ❶ a lump in the abdomen ❷ ruffian; riffraff

【痞块】(又作'痞积')[中] a lump in the abdomen

【痞子】ruffian; riffraff

劈 动 ❶ divide; split: 把绳子～成三股 *split the rope into three strands* ❷ break off; strip off: ～白菜帮子 *strip the outer leaves off cabbages* ❸ split one's legs or fingers extremely wide apart ——另见 pī

【劈叉】do the splits

【劈柴】kindling; firewood

【劈账】share out proceeds according to a certain rate

癖 名 addiction; a weakness for: 嗜酒成～ *be addicted to drinking*

【癖好】a favourite hobby; a fondness for: 他有集邮的～。*His favourite hobby is stamp collecting.*

【癖习】an old habit

【癖性】natural inclination; proclivity; propensity

pì

屁 名 ❶ wind (from bowels): 放屁 ❷〈口〉nonsense; shit; rubbish: 这个电影好极了。—好个～! *This film is really good.—Shit!*

【屁股】❶〈口〉buttocks (of humans); bottom; behind; backside: 拍拍～就走了 *leave without a word of explanation*; *leave things in a mess* ❷ rump (of animals); haunch; hindquarters ❸ end; butt: 香烟～ *cigarette butt*

【屁滚尿流】(usu. used in) 吓得～ *be scared shitless*; *be frightened out of one's wits* (*or life*); *piss in one's pants* (*in terror*)

【屁话】shit; nonsense; rubbish

【屁事】a trifling matter; a mere nothing; nothing worth speaking of: 你爱怎么着就怎么着,关我～! *Do as you please. I don't care a damn.*

辟 Ⅰ 动 ❶ open up (territory, land, etc.); break (ground): 新～一座果园 *lay out a new orchard* / 另～专栏 *start a new column* (*in a newspaper, etc.*) ❷ refute; repudiate Ⅱ 形 penetrating; incisive: 精辟 ——另见 bì

媲 动 be equal to; be a match for

【媲美】compare favourably with; rival

僻 形 ❶ out-of-the-way; secluded: ～巷 *side lane* / ～处一隅 *live in a remote corner* ❷ eccentric: 怪僻 ❸ rare: ～字 *rare word*

【僻静】secluded; lonely: ～的地方 *a secluded place*

【僻壤】an out-of-the-way place

【僻性】eccentric character

【僻远】remote and out-of-the-way

譬 名 example; analogy

【譬如】for example; for instance; such as

【譬若】〈书〉for example; for instance; such as

【譬喻】metaphor; simile; analogy; figure of speech

piān

片 名 同〖片〗(piàn), limited to use in 片子, 相片儿, etc. ——另见 piàn

【片子】❶ a roll of film ❷ film; movie ❸ gramophone record; disc ❹ the negative of a roentgenogram ——另见 piànzi

扁 (构词成分) 见下 ——另见 biǎn

【扁舟】〈书〉small boat; skiff: 一叶～ *a small boat*

偏 Ⅰ 形 ❶ inclined to one side; slanting; leaning: 正东～北 *east by north* / 中间～右 (*take a position*) *right of centre* / 这一枪打～了。*That shot missed.* / 这个指标～低。*The target is on the low side.* ❷ partial; prejudiced: 偏爱 Ⅱ 副 wilfully; insistently; persistently: 他为什么～要那样做? *Why must he do it that way?* / 他～不听。*He simply wouldn't listen.* / 不该她去,她～要去。*She was not supposed to go but she insisted on going.*

【偏爱】have partiality for sth.; show favouritism to sb.

【偏安】(of a feudal regime) be content to retain sovereignty over a part of the country ◇ ～一隅 be content to exercise sovereignty over only a part of the country

【偏差】deviation; error: ～减为一毫米。*The deviation is reduced to one millimetre.*

【偏磁】bias ◇ ～电流 bias current

【偏方】[中] folk prescription

【偏废】do one thing and neglect another; emphasize one thing at the expense of another

【偏航】going off course；off-course；yaw

【偏好】（piānhǎo）〈方〉 it so happened that；as luck would have it：你告诉我他到外地去了，可～我昨天看到他了。*You told me he was out of town, but as it happened, I saw him yesterday.*

【偏好】（piānhào） have a special fondness for sth.；have a partiality for sth.：他对臭豆腐有特别的～。*He has a partiality for strong-smelling preserved bean curd.*

【偏护】be partial to and side with：不～任何一方 *show no partiality to either side*；*be impartial*；*be unbiased*

【偏激】extreme：意见～ *hold extreme views* / 他这个人比较～。*He tends to go to extremes.*

【偏见】prejudice；bias：我对他没有～。*I've no prejudice against him.*

【偏科】（of students） focus efforts on certain school subjects to the detriment of others：～现象 *tendency to focus on a few subjects*

【偏口鱼】同〖比目鱼〗

【偏枯】❶［中］hemiplegia ❷ lopsided（development）

【偏劳】〈套〉（used when asking sb. for help or thanking sb. for his help）：谢谢您，多～了。*Thanks for all your trouble.* / 请你～吧。*Can I trouble you to do it?*

【偏离】deviate；diverge：船～了航线。*The ship drifted off its course.*

【偏旁】character components or basic structural parts of Chinese characters（as 亻 in 住，囗 in 固，匚 in 匾，扌 in 拎，etc.）

【偏僻】remote；out-of-the-way：～的山区 *a remote mountainous district* / 地点～。*It is an out-of-the-way place.*

【偏偏】❶ wilfully；insistently；persistently：我们劝他不要那样做，可他～不听。*We tried to talk him out of it, but he just wouldn't listen.* ❷ contrary to expectations：他来找我，～我出差了。*I happened to be away on business when he came to see me.* / 事情的发展～同他的愿望相反。*Things turned out just the opposite to what he wanted.* ❸ only；alone：你为什么～不提这一点呢？*Why did you choose to omit this point?*

【偏颇】〈书〉biased；partial

【偏巧】it so happened that；as luck would have it：我们正找她，～她来了。*We were looking for her when she turned up.* / 我找他两次，～都不在家。*I called at his house twice, but he happened to be out each time.*

【偏食】❶［天］partial eclipse：日～ *partial solar eclipse* / 月～ *partial lunar eclipse* ❷ partiality for a limited variety of food；a one-sided diet

【偏瘫】［医］hemiplegia

【偏袒】be partial to and side with；give unprincipled protection to

【偏疼】〈口〉 favour one（child，etc.）more than the others

【偏题】a catch（or tricky）question（in an examination）

【偏听偏信】heed and trust only one side；listen only to one side；be biased

【偏头痛】［医］migraine

【偏西】（of the sun） move towards the west：太阳～了。*The sun is to the west.*

【偏向】❶ erroneous tendency；deviation：纠正～ *correct a deviation* ❷ be partial to；give unprincipled support or protection to

【偏心】❶ partiality；bias：她对小儿子有点儿～。*She makes rather a favourite of her youngest son.* ❷［机］eccentric：～凸轮 *eccentric cam*

【偏心轮】［机］eccentric wheel；eccentric

【偏心眼儿】（又作'偏心眼子'）〈口〉 prejudiced；partial：我看爷爷对弟弟是有～的。*I believe that grandpa is partial to my younger brother.*

【偏压】［电］bias voltage；bias：截止～ *cut-off bias* / ～电池 *bias battery*

【偏远】remote；faraway：～地区 *remote districts*

【偏振】［物］ polarization：光的～ *polarization of light* ◇ ～光［物］polarized light；～光镜 polariscope；～光显微镜 polarizing microscope

【偏正词组】［语］word group consisting of a modifier and the word it modifies

【偏执】stubbornly biased

【偏重】stress one aspect at the expense of another：学习只～记忆而忽视理解是不行的。*In studying one shouldn't stress memorization at the expense of comprehension.*

【偏转】［物］deflection

【偏坠】［中］swelling and hanging down of either of the testes（caused by orchitis，hernia，etc.）

翩

动〈书〉fly swiftly

【翩翩】❶ lightly（dance，flutter，etc.）：蝴蝶在花丛中～飞舞。*Butterflies are fluttering among the flowers.* ❷〈书〉 elegant：～少年 *an elegant young man*

【翩然】〈书〉lightly；trippingly：～而至 *come tripping down*

【翩若惊鸿】（of a beautiful woman）tripping lightly like a startled swan

【翩跹】〈文〉lightly；trippingly：～起舞 *dance with quick, light steps*；*dance trippingly*

篇

Ⅰ 名 ❶ a piece of writing：篇章 ❷ sheet（of paper，etc.）：歌～ *song sheet* / 单～油印材料 *mimeographed sheets* Ⅱ 量 （for paper，book leaves，articles，etc.）sheet；leaf；piece：三～纸 *three sheets*（*or pieces*）*of paper* / 一～文章 *a piece of writing*；*an article* / 这本书缺了一～。*One leaf is missing from this book.*

【篇幅】❶ length（of a piece of writing）：这篇文章～不太长。*This article is not very long.* ❷ space（on a printed page）：～有限 *have limited space* / 报纸用大量～报道了这次会议的情况。*The press gave the conference wide coverage.*

【篇目】table of contents；contents；list of articles

【篇章】sections and chapters；writings：～结构 *structure of an article*；*composition*

pián

便（构词成分）见下 ——另见 biàn

【便便】bulging；swelling：大腹便便

【便宜】❶ cheap：～货 *goods sold at bargain prices* / 价钱相当～。*It's a real bargain.* or *It's quite cheap.* ❷ unmerited advantages；unearned gains：占便宜 ❸ let sb. off lightly：这次～了他。*This time we have let him off lightly.* ——另见 biànyí

胼（构词成分）见下

【胼手胝足】callused hands and feet—a life of toil

【胼胝】callosity；callus

【胼胝体】［生理］corpus callosum

piàn

片 Ⅰ 名 ❶ a flat，thin piece；slice；flake：布～ *small pieces of cloth* / 牛肉～ *slices of beef* / 玻璃～ *bits and pieces of glass* / 碎纸～ *scraps of paper* ❷ part of a place：区西那一～归他管。*The western part of this district is in his charge.* Ⅱ 动 cut into slices：～肉片儿 *slice meat* / ～鱼片儿 *flake a fish* Ⅲ 形 incomplete；fragmentary；partial；brief：片言 Ⅳ 量 ❶（for slices，tablets，etc.）：一～面包 *a slice of bread* / 两～安眠药 *two sleeping tablets* ❷（for a stretch of land，a water surface，etc.）：一～土地 *a stretch of land* / 一～草地 *a tract of meadow* / 一～汪洋 *a vast sheet（or an expanse）of water* ❸（used with the numeral 一，for scene，atmosphere，sound，feeling，etc.）：一～丰收景象 *a vast countryside bringing in bumper crops* / 一～欢腾 *a scene of great rejoicing* / 一～脚步声 *a patter of footsteps* / 一～真心 *in all sincerity* ——另见 piān

【片段】part；passage；extract；fragment：谈话的～ *parts（or snatches）of a conversation* / 小说的一些～ *certain passages of a novel* / 生活的～ *an episode of sb.'s life*；*a slice of life*

【片断】❶ 同〖片段〗 ❷ fragmentary；incomplete：～的消息 *bits of information* / ～的回忆 *fragments of one's reminiscences*

【片盒】film magazine

【片簧】［机］leaf spring：多～ *multiple leaf spring*

【片剂】［药］tablet

【片甲不存】（又作'片甲不留'）not a single armoured warrior remains—the army is completely wiped out：杀得敌人～ *wipe out the enemy to a man*

【片假名】katakana（one of the written varieties of 假名，the other being 平假名）

【片儿警】〈口〉policeman responsible for a specific neighborhood；beat policeman

【片刻】a short while；an instant；a moment：稍待～ *wait a little while*

【片孔】film perforation；perforation

【片流】［物］laminar flow

【片麻岩】［地质］gneiss

【片面】❶ unilateral：～撕毁协议 *unilaterally tear up an agreement* / ～之词 *an account given by one party only*；*one party's version of an event，etc.*；*one person's word against another's* ❷ one-sided：～观点 *a lopsided（or one-sided）view* / ～地看问题 *take a one-sided approach to problems* / ～强调 *put undue emphasis on*

【片面性】one-sidedness：对人（事，形势）的看法有～ *see only one side of a person（thing，situation）*

【片盘】film spool；bobbin

【片商】movie distributor：这部电影立即引起了众多～的关注。*This film immediately caught the attention of many film distributors.*

【片石】slabstone；flagstone

【片时】a short while；a moment

【片梭织机】［纺］gripper loom

【片头】titles（in a film or a TV programme）；credits

【片瓦无存】not a single tile remains— be razed to the ground

【片言】a few words；a phrase or two：～可决 *can be settled in a few words*

【片言只语】（又作'片言只字'）（in）only a few words：断章取义地挑出～ *quote a phrase or two out of context*

【片岩】［地质］schist

【片艳纸】a machine-glazed paper（glossy on one side）

【片约】film contract（between an actor and a film producer）

【片纸只字】fragments of writing：档案中并无～提及此事。*There is no reference at all to this case in the files.*

【片子】❶ a flat，thin piece；slice；flake；scrap：铁～ *small pieces of sheetiron* ❷ visiting card ——另见 piānzi

骗 动 ❶ deceive；fool；hoodwink：受～ *be taken in*；*be deceived* / 这种花招～不了人。*Nobody will be fooled by such tricks.* ❷ cheat；swindle：～钱 *cheat sb. out of his（or her）money* ❸ swing（or leap）into the saddle；mount a horse

【骗供】trap（or trick）into making a confession：～是不合法的。*It is against the law to trick a person into making a confession.*

【骗局】fraud；hoax；swindle：和平～ *peace hoax（or fraud）*

【骗取】gain sth. by cheating；cheat（or trick，swindle）sb. out of sth.；defraud：～信任 *worm one's way into sb.'s confidence* / ～支持 *fool sb. into giving his support* / ～选票 *wangle votes*

【骗人】deceive people：～的幌子 *a camouflage*；*a smokescreen* / ～的勾当 *a fraudulent practice（or deal）*

【骗术】deceitful trick; ruse; hoax: 施行～ *perpetrate a fraud*

【骗子】swindler; impostor; cheat; trickster: 政治～ *a political swindler*

【骗宿】trick a person into staying in a hotel, guest house, etc

piāo

剽 Ⅰ 动 rob Ⅱ 形 nimble; swift

【剽悍】agile and brave; quick and fierce

【剽掠】plunder; loot

【剽窃】plagiarize; lift: ～行为 *plagiarism; plagiary* / ～者 *plagiarist*

【剽袭】plagiarize; lift

漂 动 float; drift: 树叶在水上～着。*Leaves were floating on the water.* / 小船顺流～去。*The boat drifted down the stream.* ——另见 piǎo; piào

【漂泊】lead a wandering life; drift: ～异乡 *wander aimlessly in a strange land*

【漂浮】❶ float: 湖面上～着几只小船。*A few boats are floating on the lake.* ❷ float or hover before the eyes or in the mind ❸ (of style of work) superficial; showy

【漂砾】[地质] erratic; erratic boulder

【漂流】❶ be driven by the current; drift about ❷ 同〖漂泊〗

【漂洋过海】travel far across the ocean (or sea)

【漂移】❶ drift ❷ [电子] drift: ～晶体管 *drift transistor*

【漂游】lead a wandering life; drift: 四处～ *wander from place to place*

缥 (构词成分) 见下

【缥缈】dimly discernible; misty: 虚无缥缈

飘 动 wave to and fro; float (in the air); flutter: 红旗～～。*Red flags are fluttering.* / 稻花～香。*The air was heavy with the aroma of the paddy fields.* / 外面～着小雪。*Outside it was snowing slightly.* / 随风～来一阵阵花香。*The scent of the flowers was wafted to us by the breeze.*

【飘尘】airborne dust

【飘带】streamer; ribbon

【飘荡】❶ drift; float; wave; flutter: 小船随波～。*The boat was drifting with the tide.* / 彩旗在风中～。*Coloured flags were flapping in the wind.* ❷ lead a wanderer's life; drift: 弃家避难,四处～ *flee from home and wander about seeking refuge*

【飘动】float (in the air or upon the waves); flutter; drift

【飘忽】❶ (of clouds, etc.) move swiftly; fleet ❷ mobile; uncertain: ～不定 *drift from place to place*

【飘零】❶ fading and falling; whirling and scattering: 黄叶～。*Brown leaves came whirling down.* ❷ wandering; adrift; homeless: ～一身 *a solitary wanderer*

【飘落】(又作'飘降') drift and fall slowly; descend slowly and lightly: 伞兵徐徐～。*The paratroopers descended slowly through the air.*

【飘飘然】smug; self-satisfied; complacent: 一听到恭维话,他就感觉～。*The least bit of praise goes to his head.*

【飘然】floating in the air: 浮云～而过。*Fleecy clouds floated past.* / 一对白天鹅～落在湖面上。*A pair of white swans glided down on to the surface of the lake.*

【飘洒】(piāosǎ) float in the air; drift with the wind: 天空～着雪花。*Snowflakes were swirling in the air.*

【飘洒】(piāosa) free and easy: 她那一手字写得好～! *What a graceful, facile hand she writes!*

【飘散】(of smoke, mist, etc.) drift away

【飘舞】wave in the wind: 到处～着彩旗。*Everywhere coloured banners are fluttering.*

【飘扬】wave; flutter; fly: 五星红旗迎风～。*The five-star red flag is fluttering in the wind.*

【飘摇】sway in the wind

【飘曳】sway: ～的柳枝 *swaying willow branches*

【飘移】drift

【飘逸】〈书〉possessing natural grace; elegant: 神采～ *have an elegant bearing*

【飘溢】drift about: 公园里～着花香。*In the park the fragrance of flowers drifted about in the air.*

【飘悠】drift leisurely: 几片树叶飘飘悠悠地落下来。*A few leaves fell floating to the ground.*

piáo

嫖 动 visit prostitutes; go whoring: 吃喝～赌 *wining and dining and whoring and gambling* / ～妓 *visit prostitutes*

【嫖客】brothel (or whorehouse) frequenter; whoremonger; whoremaster

瓢 名 gourd ladle; wooden dipper

【瓢虫】ladybug; ladybird

【瓢泼大雨】heavy rain; torrential rain; downpour

piǎo

漂 动 ❶ bleach: ～过的布特别白。*Cloth becomes much whiter when bleached.* ❷ rinse: 把衣服～干净 *give the clothes a good rinse* ——另见 piāo; piào

【漂白】bleach: ～棉布 *bleached cotton cloth* / ～机 *bleaching machine; bleacher* / ～率 *bleachability* ◇ ～粉 bleaching powder

【漂染】bleaching and dyeing

【漂洗】rinse

【漂洗槽】[化] potcher

瞟 动 look sidelong (or askance) at; glance sideways at: ～了他一眼 *cast a sidelong glance at him* / 她一面喝茶,一面用眼～他。*As she sipped her tea, she shot him glances.*

piào

票 名 ❶ ticket: 火车～ *train ticket* / 凭～入场。*Admission by ticket only.* ❷ ballot: 全～一致通过 *passed by unanimous vote* ❸ bank note; bill: 零～儿 *notes of small denominations; change* ❹ a person held for ransom by kidnappers; hostage: 赎～儿 *ransom a kidnapped person* ❺ amateur performance (of Beijing opera, etc.): 玩儿票 Ⅱ 量〈方〉一～货 *a shipment of goods* / 一～买卖 *a business transaction*

【票额】the sum stated on a cheque or bill; denomination; face value: 大～钞票 *notes of large denominations*

【票贩子】ticket scalper; tout

【票房】〈口〉booking office (at a railway station, airport, etc.); box office (at a theatre, stadium, etc.)

【票房价值】box-office value: 这部影片的～很高。*The film was a box-office success.*

【票房收入】box-office income; box-office receipts

【票根】counterfoil or stub (of a cheque, postal order, receipt, etc.); stub (of a ticket)

【票号】draft bank

【票汇】send bank drafts

【票价】the price of a ticket; admission fee; entrance fee: ～五元。*Admission five yuan.*

【票据】❶ bill; note: 应收(应付)～ *bills receivable (payable)* / 即期～ *a demand note* / 流通～ *negotiable instruments; negotiable papers* / 到期未付～ *overdue bill* ❷ voucher; receipt ◇ ～交换所 clearinghouse

【票面】face (or par, nominal) value: 各种～的邮票 *stamps of various denominations* ◇ ～价值 face value; par (value)

【票品】stamps, miniature sheets, first day covers, etc. collected by philatelists

【票券】ticket; coupon

【票箱】ballot box

【票选】elect (or vote) by ballot; vote for sb.

【票友】amateur performer (of Beijing opera, etc.)

【票源】supply of tickets (usu. illegal)

【票证】coupons

【票子】bank note; paper money; bill: 一大摞～ *a thick stack of bank notes*

漂 (构词成分) 见下 ——另见 piāo; piǎo

【漂亮】❶ handsome; good-looking; pretty; beautiful: ～的小伙子 *a handsome young man* / ～的小姑娘 *a pretty little girl* ❷ remarkable; brilliant; splendid; beautiful: 守门员这个球救得真～。*The goalie made a beautiful save.*

【漂亮话】fine words; high-sounding words: 说～没用,干出来才算。*It's not high-sounding words but actual deeds that really count.*

嘌 形〈书〉fast; speedy

【嘌呤】[化] purine

piē

氕 名 [化] protium (H^1)

撇 动 ❶ cast aside; throw overboard; neglect: 不能只抓一头,把别的事都～在一旁。*We should not just concentrate on one thing to the neglect of everything else.* ❷ skim: ～油 *skim off the grease* / ～沫儿 *skim off the scum* ——另见 piě

【撇开】leave aside; bypass: ～这个问题 *bypass this issue* / 咱们把次要问题～不谈了吧。*Let's leave aside questions of minor importance.*

【撇弃】cast away; abandon; discard

【撇清】whitewash oneself; plead innocence

瞥 Ⅰ 动 shoot a glance at; dart a look at: 他刚要插嘴,妈妈～了他一眼。*He was going to butt in when his mother darted a look of disapproval at him.* Ⅱ 名 a quick glance; a glimpse: 一瞥

【瞥见】get a glimpse of; catch sight of

【瞥视】cast a quick glance at

【瞥眼】in the twinkling of an eye; in an instant; in a flash

piě

苤 (构词成分) 见下

【苤蓝】[植] kohlrabi (the plant and its edible bulblike stem)

撇 Ⅰ 动 throw; fling; cast: ～手榴弹 *throw hand grenades* Ⅱ 名 left-falling stroke (in Chinese calligraphy) Ⅲ 量 (for things resembling the left-falling stroke): 两～浓眉,一双大眼 *two bushy brows over a pair of big eyes* / 两～小胡子 *two thin strokes of moustache* ——另见 piē

【撇嘴】curl one's lip (in contempt, disbelief or disappointment); twitch one's mouth: 这女孩儿～要哭。*The girl's mouth began to twitch; she was on the verge of tears.*

pīn

拼 动 ❶ piece together; join together: 把两块木板～起来 *join the two boards together* ❷ be ready to risk one's life (in fighting, work, etc.); go all out in work: ～到底 *fight to the bitter end* / 不畏强手,敢打敢～ *not fear a strong opponent but dare to stand up to him*

【拼版】[刷] makeup

【拼搏】struggle hard; exert oneself to the utmost;

go all out：勇于～ *have the courage to struggle against tremendous odds*

【拼刺】❶ bayonet drill；bayonet practice ❷ bayonet charge：和敌人～ *fight it out with the enemy with bayonets*

【拼刺刀】同〖拼刺〗❷

【拼凑】piece together；knock together；rig up：她把零碎花布～起来，给小闺女做了一件褂子。*She pieced together odds and ends of coloured cloth and made a jacket for her little girl.*

【拼攒】assemble (spare parts)：～一辆小汽车 *assemble parts into a car*

【拼接】piece together；join together

【拼劲儿】energy and determination：他很有～。*He has a lot of drive.*

【拼力】go all out；do one's utmost：～夺取金牌 *go all out to win the gold medal*

【拼命】❶ risk one's life；defy death；go all out regardless of danger to one's life：～精神 *the death-defying spirit* / 被围困的敌人摆出一副～的架势。*The encircled enemy seemed to be getting ready for a last-ditch stand.* ❷ exerting the utmost strength；for all one is worth；with all one's might；desperately：～奔跑 *run for all one is worth* / ～工作 *work with all one's might*

【拼排】［刷］compose and lay out：这篇文章～有错误。*There is something wrong in the composition and layout of this article.*

【拼盘】assorted cold dishes；hors d'oeuvres

【拼抢】scramble for；press on：他虽然病了，但仍参加了比赛，在场上～。*He was ill，but still joined the match and fought hard for the ball.*

【拼杀】battle fiercely：士兵们冲出城去，与侵略者～起来。*The soldiers charged out of the city and fiercely engaged the invaders.*

【拼死】risk one's life；defy death；fight desperately ◇ ～拼活 put up a life-and-death fight；exerting one's utmost；for all one is worth；desperately；～挣扎 wage a desperate struggle

【拼贴画】paste-up

【拼图游戏】jigsaw puzzle

【拼写】spell；transliterate：照汉语拼音方案～汉字 *transliterate Chinese characters into the Chinese Phonetic Alphabet* / ～测验 *spelling quiz* ◇ ～法 spelling；orthography；～检查 spelling check

【拼音】❶ combine sounds into syllables ❷ spell；phoneticize ◇ ～文字 alphabetic (system of) writing；～字母 phonetic alphabet；phonetic letters

【拼争】take on；face up to

【拼装】assemble；fit together

姘

动 have illicit relations with

【姘夫】(man) lover；paramour

【姘妇】kept woman；mistress；paramour

【姘居】live illicitly as husband and wife；cohabit

【姘头】paramour

pín

贫

形 ❶ poor；impoverished：～富不均 *unequal distribution of wealth* ❷ inadequate；deficient：贫油 ❸ garrulous；loquacious：他的嘴真～。*He is really too garrulous.*

【贫病交迫】suffer from both poverty and sickness；be plagued by poverty and ill health

【贫齿动物】edentate animal；edentate

【贫乏】❶ poor；needy；impoverished ❷ wretchedly lacking：经验～ *lack experience* / 语言～ *flat，monotonous language*

【贫富悬殊】a wide gap between the rich and the poor

【贫骨头】〈方〉❶ a person keen on petty gain ❷ a stingy person；niggard ❸ an idle chatterer；windbag

【贫寒】poor；poverty-stricken：～人家 *an impoverished family*

【贫化】［矿］dilution：矿石～ *ore dilution*

【贫瘠】barren；infertile；poor：～的土壤 *poor soil；impoverished soil*

【贫贱】poor and lowly；in straitened and humble circumstances ◇ ～之交 friends that have seen poverty together；friends in days of poverty；～之交不可忘。A man should not forget the friends he made when he was poor.

【贫苦】poor；poverty-stricken；badly off：～无告 *miserably poor and friendless*

【贫矿】lean ore：贫红铁矿 *low-grade red iron ore*

【贫困】impoverished；in pinching poverty；in straitened circumstances：生活～ *live in poverty* / ～化 *pauperization* ◇ ～地区 impoverished region；destitute or poor area；～户 poor family；family in poverty；～线 poverty line

【贫民】poor people；paupers：城市～ *the urban poor* ◇～窟 slum；～区 slum area；slum district

【贫气】❶ stingy；niggardly ❷ annoyingly garrulous

【贫穷】poor；needy；impoverished

【贫弱】(of a country) poor and weak

【贫血】［医］anaemia：再生障碍性～ *aplastic anaemia*

【贫油】oil-poor：～国 *an oil-poor country*

【贫嘴】garrulous；loquacious ◇ ～薄舌 be garrulous and sharp-tongued

频

Ⅰ 副 frequently；repeatedly：～来～往 *have frequent contacts with each other* Ⅱ 名［物］frequency：高频

【频传】(of good news，etc.) keep pouring in：喜讯～。*Good news kept pouring in.*

【频带】［物］frequency band

【频道】(TV) frequency channel；channel

【频发】take place (or happen) frequently

【频繁】frequently；often：交通事故日益～。*Traffic accidents are happening with increasing fre-*

quency.

【频率】❶［物］frequency：～范围 *frequency range* ❷ rate of recurrence；frequency ◇ ～发生器［物］frequency generator；～函数［数］frequency function；～理论 frequency theory；～调制（简称"调频"）frequency modulation（FM）

【频频】again and again；repeatedly：～举杯 *propose repeated toasts；drink toast after toast* / ～点头称是 *nod approval repeatedly*

【频仍】〈书〉frequent：外患～ *be subject to repeated foreign aggression*

pǐn

品 Ⅰ名 ❶ article；product：商品 ❷ grade；class；rank：～之最上者 *of the very best kind* ❸ character；quality：人品 / 品德 Ⅱ动 taste sth. with discrimination；sample；savour：～茶 *sample tea* / 这个人究竟怎么样，你慢慢就～出来了。*By and by you'll be able to figure out what sort of person he actually is.*

【品尝】taste；sample；savour：～我们的家乡风味 *try our local delicacies*

【品德】moral character

【品格】❶ one's moral character ❷ quality and style（of literary or artistic works）

【品红】❶ magenta；fuchsine（a dye）❷ purplish red

【品级】❶ official rank in feudal times ❷ grade（of products，commodities，etc.）：这种茶～高。*It's a high-grade tea.*

【品蓝】reddish blue

【品绿】malachite green；bamboo green

【品貌】❶ looks；appearance：～俊俏 *handsome and charming* ❷ character and looks；personality and appearance：～兼优的女郎 *a pretty girl of good character*

【品名】the name of an article；the name or description of a commodity

【品茗】sip tea（to judge its quality）；sample tea

【品目】the names or descriptions of goods：～繁多 *a wide variety of goods*

【品牌】brand（name）

【品评】judge；appraise；comment on

【品头论足】❶ make frivolous remarks about a woman's appearance ❷ find fault；be overcritical

【品脱】pint

【品位】❶［矿］grade ❷ quality（of products，listerary works，etc.）

【品味】❶ taste；sample；savour：请各位～一下我厂新出的特级啤酒。*Gentlemen，please sample this top-grade beer，our new product.* ❷ quality；flavour

【品系】［生］strain

【品行】moral conduct；behaviour：～端正 *having good conduct；weli-behaved*

【品性】one's nature and moral character：～高洁 *of noble nature and unsullied character*

【品学兼优】be a good student of good character；be a student of good character and fine scholarship

【品质】❶ character；intrinsic quality：道德～ *moral character* ❷ quality（of commodities，etc.）：～证明书 *certificate of quality* ◇ ～因数［电］quality factor

【品种】❶［生］breed；strain；variety：小麦优良～ *improved strains of wheat* ❷ variety；assortment：货物～齐全 *have a good assortment of goods*

pìn

聘 动 ❶ engage（a teacher，etc.）：～某人为顾问 *engage sb. as a consultant* / 受～为访问教授 *be engaged as a visiting professor* / 被～为名誉会长 *be invited to be honorary chairman* ❷〈书〉visit a state as an envoy：～使往来 *an exchange of state visits* ❸ betroth ❹〈口〉be married off；get married：张家快～姑娘了。*The Zhangs will soon marry their daughter off.*

【聘金】betrothal money for the bride's family

【聘礼】betrothal gifts（from the bridegroom's to the bride's family）；bride-price

【聘请】engage；invite：～一位工程师担任技校兼职教师 *get an engineer to act as a part-time teacher in the technical school*

【聘任】engage sb. as；appoint sb. to a position：听说他已被～为该医院院长。*It's said that he's been appointed the Director of the hospital.* ◇～制 system of appointment

【聘书】letter of appointment；contract

【聘用】employ；engage；appoint to a position

pīng

乒 ❶ 象 ping，a short high-ringing sound：～的一声枪响 *the crack of a rifle or pistol* ❷ 名〈略〉见〖乒乓球〗

【乒联】（〈略〉全称为'乒乓球联合会'）table tennis federation：国际～ *International Table Tennis Federation*

【乒乓】❶ rattling or clattering sound：雹子打在屋顶上～乱响。*Hailstones were rattling on the roofs.* ❷ table tennis；ping-pong

【乒乓球】❶ table tennis；ping-pong ❷ table tennis ball；ping-pong ball：～拍 *table tennis bat* / ～台 *table tennis table* / ～网 *table tennis net*

【乒赛】table tennis match or tournament

【乒坛】the table tennis circles

娉（构词成分）见下

【娉婷】〈文〉（of a woman）have a graceful demeanour

píng

平 Ⅰ〈形〉 flat; level; even; smooth: 桌面不～。*The table is not level.* / 把纸铺～ *smooth out the paper* / 让病人躺～ *help the patient to lie stretched out* Ⅱ〈动〉 ❶ make level or even; level: 把地～一～ *level the ground* ❷ be on the same level; be on a par; equal: 水涨得～了河岸。*The water rose until it was level with the banks.* / ～世界纪录 *equal a world record* ❸ make the same score; tie; draw: 双方打成十五～。*The two teams tied at 15-15.* / 这场足球赛最后踢～了。*The football game ended in a draw.* / 场上比分是七～。*The score is now seven all.* ❹ equal; fair; impartial: 平分 ❺ calm; peaceful; quiet: 经他一解释，老太太的气也就～了。*His explanation soothed the old woman's anger.* / ～民愤 *assuage popular indignation* / 为民～愤 *redress the grievances of the people* ❻ put down; suppress: ～叛 *put down a rebellion* ❼ average; common: 平日 Ⅲ〈名〉〈略〉见〖平声〗

【平安】safe and sound; without mishap; well: 全家～。*The whole family is well.* / 一路～! *Have a good trip!* or *Bon voyage!* ◇ ～无事 all is well; ～险［经］free of particular average (F. P. A)

【平白】for no reason; gratuitously: ～挨一顿骂 *get a scolding for no reason at all* ◇ ～无故 for no apparent reason

【平板】dull and stereotyped; flat: 文章写得太～。*The article is written in a flat style.* ◇ ～玻璃 plate glass; ～车 flatbed tricycle; flatbed

【平版】［刷］planographic plate: ～印刷 *planographic printing*; *planography*

【平暴】suppress a rebellion

【平辈】persons of the same generation

【平布】［纺］plain cloth

【平步青云】rapidly go up in the world; have a meteoric rise

【平舱费】trimming charges

【平槽】(of a river) rise as high as the banks; be level with the banks

【平产】show no increases in output

【平常】❶ ordinary; common: 这种现象很～。*This sort of thing is quite a common occurrence.* ❷ generally; usually; ordinarily; as a rule: 这个词儿～很少用。*This word is seldom used on ordinary occasions.*

【平车】❶［铁路］flatcar; platform wagon; platform car ❷ flatbed cart

【平川】level land; flat, open country; plain: 山区和～ *plains and mountain areas*

【平淡】flat; insipid; prosaic; pedestrian: ～无味的谈话 *an insipid (or a dull) conversation*

【平淡无奇】commonplace; prosaic; pedestrian: ～的文章 *a pedestrian piece of writing*

【平等】equality: 男女～ *equality between the sexes* / ～互利 *equality and mutual benefit* / ～协商 *consultation on the basis of equality* / ～待遇 *equal treatment* / ～待人 *treat others as equals* / 在～的基础上 *on an equal footing* / 各国主权～ *sovereign equality of all nations*

【平底】flat-bottomed (boat, etc.); low-heeled (shoe, etc.): ～船 *flat-bottomed boat*; *flatboat*; *punt* / ～鞋 *low-heeled shoes* / ～炒锅 *frying-pan*

【平地】❶ level the land (or ground); rake the soil smooth: 他一气儿平了十四亩地。*He levelled 14 mu of land at one go.* ❷ level ground; flat ground ◇ ～风波 a sudden storm on a calm sea—unforeseen trouble; ～机 land leveller; grader; road grader; ～楼台 (又作'平地起楼台') high buildings rise from the ground —start from scratch; ～木 同〖紫金牛〗; ～一声雷 a sudden clap of thunder—a sudden rise in fame and position; an unexpected happy event

【平电】ordinary telegram

【平定】❶ calm down: 他的情绪逐渐～下来。*He gradually calmed down.* ❷ suppress; put down: ～叛乱 *put down a rebellion*

【平峒】［矿］adit; tunnel

【平凡】ordinary; common: 在～的岗位上做出不～的成绩 *achieve extraordinary successes at an ordinary post*

【平反】redress (a mishandled case); rehabilitate

【平泛】(of writings) flat and superficial

【平方】❶［数］the second power (of a quantity); square: 三的～是九。*The square of 3 is 9.* ❷ square metre (sq. m.): 那间房有十二～。*The room has a floor space of 12 sq. m.* ◇ ～根［数］square root; ～公里 square kilometre (sq. km.); ～米 square metre (sq. m.)

【平房】❶ single-storey house; one-storey house ❷〈方〉a house with a flat plastered roof

【平分】divide equally; give or take equal shares; share alike: 两人～ *go halves*; *go fifty-fifty* / ～土地 *equal distribution of land* / ～兵力 *divide one's forces evenly* ◇ ～秋色 (of two parties) have equal shares (of honour, power, glory, etc.); ～线［数］bisector

【平伏】❶ calm down; subside; be pacified ❷ lie prostrate; lie flat

【平服】be convinced

【平复】❶ calm down; subside; be pacified: 事态～。*The situation has quietened.* ❷ be cured; be healed: 伤口～了。*The wound is healed.*

【平光】zero diopter; plain glass: ～眼镜 *plain glass spectacles*

【平巷】［矿］drift; level

【平和】gentle; mild; moderate; placid: 性情～ *be of gentle (or mild) disposition* / ～的语气 *a mild (or placid) tone*

【平衡】❶ balance; equilibrium: 收支～ *balance between income and expenditure* / 失去～ *lose one's balance*; *be in a state of imbalance* / 保持～ *maintain one's equilibrium*; *keep one's bal-*

ance / 在大国之间搞～ *balance between big powers* ❷ bring into or keep in equilibrium; balance: 咱们组的计划还要跟别的组～一下。*We'll have to fit in our plan with those of the other groups.* ◇ ～常数[化] equilibrium constant; ～价格 equilibrium price; ～觉[生理] sense of equilibrium; ～力 equilibrant; ～木[体] balance beam; ～器[机] balancer

【平滑】level and smooth; smooth

【平滑肌】[生理] smooth muscle; involuntary muscle

【平缓】❶ (of the terrain, flow of water, etc.) gentle; smooth: 地势～。*The terrain slopes gently.* ❷ mild; placid; gentle

【平击】[体] flush hit; plain hit

【平纪录】equal a record

【平假名】hiragana (one of the written varieties of 假名, the other being 片假名)

【平价】❶ stabilize prices ❷ stabilized (or normalized, moderate) prices ❸ par; parity: 汇兑～ *par of exchange* / 铸币～ *specie par* / 固定～ *fixed parity* ◇～商店 low-price shop; fair price shop

【平角】[数] straight angle; an angle of 180°

【平静】calm; quiet; tranquil: ～的夜晚 *a quiet night* / ～的海面 *a calm sea*

【平局】draw; tie: 比赛最后打成～。*The game ended in a draw.* / 场上屡次出现～。*The score was tied again and again.* / 扳成～ *equalize the score*

【平均】❶ average; mean: ～寿命 *average life span; life expectancy* / 按人口～计算收入 *per capita income* ❷ equally; share and share alike: ～分摊 *share out equally* ◇ ～利润[经] average profit; ～律[音] equal temperament; ～数 average; mean; ～值 average value; mean value; mean; ～主义 equalitarianism; egalitarianism

【平口钳】flat-nose pliers

【平旷】〈书〉(of land, fields, etc.) open and flat

【平列】place side by side; place on a par with each other

【平流】[气] advection ◇ ～层 stratosphere

【平炉】[冶] open-hearth furnace; open hearth; Martin furnace: ～钢 *open-hearth steel* / ～利用系数 *capacity factor of an open-hearth furnace* / ～炼钢法 *open-hearth process*

【平乱】put down a revolt; suppress a rebellion

【平落】(of prices) drop to normal

【平脉】[中] normal pulse

【平米】(〈略〉全称为〖平方米〗) square metre

【平面】[数] plane ◇ ～波[物] plane wave; ～几何 plane geometry; ～交叉[交通] grade crossing; level crossing; ～镜[物] plane mirror; ～磨床 surface grinding machine; ～图 plan; plane figure

【平面直角】flat square

【平民】the common people; the populace

【平年】❶ non-leap year; common year ❷ average year (in crop yield)

【平平】average; mediocre; indifferent: 成绩～。*The results are about up to the average.*

【平平当当】done smoothly; without a hitch

【平铺直叙】❶ tell in a simple, straightforward way ❷ speak or write in a dull, flat style

【平起平坐】sit as equals at the same table; be on an equal footing

【平权】(enjoy) equal rights

【平日】on ordinary days; ordinarily; usually

【平绒】[纺] velveteen

【平射】[军] flat (trajectory) fire◇ ～炮 flat fire gun; flat trajectory gun

【平身】❶ stand up after kowtowing ❷ stand up (said by an emperor to a kowtowing subject)

【平生】❶ all one's life; one's whole life: ～的志愿 *one's lifelong aspiration (or wish)* ❷ usually: 她～是很艰苦朴素的。*She usually lives simply (or frugally) and works hard.*

【平声】level tone (the first of the four tones in classical Chinese pronunciation, which has evolved into the high and level tone 阴平 and the rising tone 阳平 in modern standard pronunciation) ——另见〖四声〗

【平时】❶ at ordinary times; in normal times: 他～住在厂里，星期六才回家。*Ordinarily he sleeps at the factory and goes home only on Saturdays.* ❷ in peacetime: ～多流汗，战时少流血。*Losing more sweat in peacetime (training, etc.) means shedding less blood in war.*

【平时不烧香，急来抱佛脚】never burn incense when all is well but clasp Buddha's feet when in distress—do nothing until the last minute

【平视】look squarely (or directly); look straight ahead: 立正时两眼要～。*Keep your eyes straight when standing at attention.*

【平手】draw: 两队打了个～。*The two teams drew.*

【平水期】the period when a river is at its normal level

【平顺】smooth-going; plain sailing

【平素】usually: 他～就不爱说话。*He's usually very quiet.* or *He is a man of few words.*

【平台】❶ terrace ❷ platform: 钻井～ *drilling platform* ❸ [计] platform: 中文～ *Chinese platform* ❹ plateau: 一旦出口加工达到一个～，出口增长就会大大放慢。*Once export processing reaches a plateau, export growth will slow drastically.*

【平坦】(of land, etc.) level; even; smooth: 地势～ *smooth terrain*

【平添】add or give as an effect or a result: 这个新建的公园给市民～许多乐趣。*The new park is an important addition to the amenities of the town.*

【平头】❶ crew cut: 理～ *have a crew cut* ❷ (used to express round numbers) full; round; complete: ～二十年 *a full 20 years* / ～一打 *a round dozen* ◇ ～数〈方〉round figure (numbers given in tens, hundreds, thousands, etc.)

【平头正脸】have regular features

【平纹】[纺] plain weave: ～织物 *plain cloth*

【平稳】smooth and steady; smooth; stable: 机器运

转～。*The machine runs smoothly.* / 物价～。*Prices are stable.*

【平稳过渡】smooth transition

【平西】(of the sun) be setting：太阳已经～了，还这么热。*It's almost sunset, but it's still so hot.*

【平昔】in the past

【平息】❶ calm down；quiet down；subside：一场风波～了。*The tumult has subsided.* or *The trouble is over.* ❷ put down (a rebellion, etc.)；suppress：～暴乱 *put down a riot*

【平心而论】in all fairness；to give sb. his due：～，他工作还是比较认真的。*To give him his due, he is quite a conscientious worker.*

【平心静气】calmly；dispassionately：～地讨论 *calmly discuss*

【平信】❶ ordinary mail ❷ surface mail

【平行】❶ of equal rank；on an equal footing；parallel：～机关 *units (or organizations) of equal rank；parallel organizations* ❷ parallel：～线 *parallel lines* ❸ simultaneous；concurrent：～主权 *concurrent sovereignty* / ～领土管辖权 *concurrent territorial jurisdiction* ◇ ～联机［计］peer-to-peer network；～六面体［数］parallelepiped；～脉［植］parallel veins；～四边形［数］parallelogram；～作业 parallel operations；simultaneous operations

【平移】［物］translation：～运动 *translational motion*

【平议】❶ pass a fair judgment on ❷〈书〉appraise sth. through discussion

【平抑】stabilize：～物价 *stabilize prices；keep down prices*

【平易】❶ unassuming；amiable ❷ (of a piece of writing) easy；plain ◇ ～近人 amiable and easy of approach

【平庸】mediocre；indifferent；commonplace：才能～ *of limited ability*

【平鱼】another name for 鲳鱼

【平原】plain；flatlands

【平月】February of a non-leap year

【平匀】regular and steady；even and regular：呼吸～ *even and regular breathing*

【平仄】❶ level and oblique tones ❷ tonal patterns in classical Chinese poetry

【平展】❶ (of land, etc.) open and flat ❷ well smoothed out；unruffled；unwrinkled

【平整】❶ level (land)：他们～土地三万余亩。*They levelled over* 30,000 *mu of land.* ❷ neat；smooth；level

【平职】new position at the same administrative level as a former one：他经历了一次～调动。*He was given a horizontal transfer.*

【平装】paperback；paper-cover；paperbound：～本 *paperback (book)；paperbound edition*

【平装开关】［电］*flush switch*

【平足】*flatfoot*

评 动 ❶ comment；criticize；review：博得好～ *receive favourable comments；be well received* ❷ judge；appraise：你来～～谁说得对。*Now you be the judge and say which of us is right.* / 被～为劳动模范 *be chosen as a model worker*

【评比】appraise through comparison；compare and assess：～产品质量 *compare and appraise the quality of different products；make a public appraisal of the quality of different products*

【评定】pass judgment on；evaluate；assess：～技术职称 *grade technical personnel and give them appropriate titles*

【评断】judge；arbitrate：～是非 *judge between right and wrong；arbitrate a dispute*

【评分】give a mark；mark (students' papers, etc.)；score：裁判给他评多少分？*What did the judges score him?*

【评功】appraise sb.'s merits：～授奖大会 *a meeting to announce commendations and issue awards*

【评功摆好】enumerate sb.'s merits；speak of sb. in glowing terms

【评估】assess：资产～ *property assessment*

【评级】❶ grade (cadres, workers, etc.) according to work ❷ grade (products) according to quality

【评价】appraise；evaluate：高度～ *set a high value on；speak highly of；highly appraise*

【评奖】decide on awards through discussion

【评介】review (a new book, etc.)：新书～ *book review*

【评卷】mark examination papers

【评理】❶ judge between right and wrong；decide which side is right：谁是谁非，让大家来评个理。*Let others judge who is right and who is wrong.* ❷ reason things out；have it out：咱们得找他评评理。*Let's go and have it out with him.*

【评论】❶ comment on；discuss：请党外群众参加～党员 *ask non-Party people to join in the appraisal of Party members* ❷ comment；commentary；review：小～ *short comments* /《湘江～》*Xiangjiang Review* ◇ ～家 critic；reviewer；～员 commentator

【评判】pass judgment on；judge：～胜负 *decide who is the winner；judge between contestants* ◇ ～员 judge (in sports or speech contests, etc.)；adjudicator (in musical contests, etc.)

【评聘】assess and appoint to a position：大学教师职务～将制度化。*A system will be set up to assess and appoint university faculty.*

【评审】examine and appraise：～文艺作品 *make a critical examination and appraisal of literary works*

【评书】storytelling (by a professional storyteller)

【评述】commentary

【评说】comment on；appraise；evaluate

【评头论足】同〖品头论足〗

【评委】members of a selection committee

【评析】comment and analyse

【评选】choose through public appraisal：被～为先进工作者 *be chosen as an advanced worker*

【评议】appraise sth. through discussion；deliberate (a question) in a formal meeting

【评优】to appraise and select the most outstanding or the highest quality
【评语】comment; remark
【评阅】read and appraise (sb.'s writing, etc.)
【评职称】grant a technical or professional title (e.g. professor, associate professor, assistant professor; senior researcher, research fellow, etc.)
【评注】❶ make commentary and annotation ❷ notes and commentary
【评传】critical biography

坪 名 level ground: 草坪
【坪坝】〈方〉a level open space

苹 (构词成分)见下
【苹果】apple (the tree and its fruit) ◇ ～干 dried apple slices; ～酱 apple jam; ～酒 cider; applejack; ～泥 apple butter; ～脯 preserved apple; ～沙司 apple sauce; ～园 apple orchard
【苹果绿】apple green

凭 Ⅰ 动 ❶ lean on; lean against: ～几 *lean on a small table* ❷ rely on; depend on: ～我们的双手重建家园 *rebuild our home town with our own hands* ❸ go by; base on; take as the basis: 你～什么得出这个结论? *What do you base this conclusion on?* / 你不能～他嘴上说的就算数。*You can't take him at his word*. Ⅱ 名 evidence; proof: 口说无凭 Ⅲ 连 no matter (what, how, etc.): ～你跑多快,我也赶得上。*I'll catch up with you no matter how fast you run*.
【凭单】a certificate for drawing money, goods, etc.; voucher
【凭单付款】[经] pay cash on presentation of documents
【凭吊】visit (a historical site, etc.) and ponder on the past
【凭借】rely on; depend on: ～想像力 *draw on one's imagination* / 人类的思维是～语言来进行的。*Man thinks in words*.
【凭据】evidence; proof
【凭靠】rely on; depend on
【凭空】out of the void; out of thin air; without foundation; groundless
【凭空捏造】make something out of nothing; fabricate: 这完全是～。*This is a sheer fabrication*.
【凭栏】lean on a railing: ～远眺 *lean on the railing and gaze into the distance*
【凭恃】rely on; depend on: ～天险 *rely on natural barriers for defence*
【凭眺】gaze from a high place into the distance; enjoy a distant view from a height
【凭险】rely on natural barriers: ～据守 *hold fast to natural barriers as defences* / ～抵抗 *make use of a strategic vantage point to fight back*
【凭信】trust; believe: 不足～ *not to be trusted; not trustworthy*
【凭依】base oneself on; rely on; have something to go by: 无所～ *have nothing to go by*
【凭倚】lean on; lean against
【凭仗】rely on; depend on: 他们～着顽强不屈的精神克服了重重困难。*They overcame all kinds of difficulties by dint of an indomitable spirit*.
【凭照】certificate; permit; licence
【凭证】proof; evidence; certificate; voucher: 完税～ *tax payment receipt*

屏 Ⅰ 名 ❶ screen: 画屏 ❷ a set of vertically hung scrolls: 四扇～儿 *a set of four scrolls* Ⅱ 动 shield sb. or sth.; screen ——另见 bǐng
【屏蔽】❶ screen; shield: ❷ protective screen ❸ [物] screen: ～电缆 *screened cable* / ～天线 *screened antenna*
【屏蔽线】shielding line
【屏保】(〈略〉全称为'屏幕保护程序')[计] screensaver; screen saver
【屏风】screen
【屏极】[电子] plate: ～电路 *plate circuit*
【屏幕】[电子] screen: 电视～ *telescreen; screen*
【屏条】a set of vertically hung scrolls (usu. four in a row) of painting or calligraphy; a set of wall scrolls
【屏障】❶ protective screen: 燕山是北京的天然～。*The Yanshan Hills provide a natural defence for Beijing*. ❷ provide a protective screen for: ～中原 *provide a protective screen for the Central Plains*

瓶 Ⅰ 名 bottle; vase; jar; flask: ～～罐罐摆了一桌子。*The table was littered with bottles, flasks, jars, cans, and what not*. Ⅱ 量 the quantity contained in a bottle, vase, jar or flask: 两～牛奶 *two bottles of milk* / 一～草莓酱 *a jar of strawberry jam*
【瓶胆】glass liner (of a thermos flask)
【瓶颈】bottleneck: 我国的通讯事业曾经是严重制约国民经济发展的～。*China's telecommunications sector was a bottleneck in the growth of its national economy*.
【瓶装】bottled: ～奶粉 *bottled milk powder*
【瓶子】bottle; vase; jar; flask

萍 名 [植] duckweed
【萍水相逢】(of strangers) meet by chance like patches of drifting duckweed: 我们虽然～,可是我觉得你和我很谈得来。*Although we have only met by chance, I find we have a lot in common*.
【萍踪】〈书〉tracks (or whereabouts) of a wanderer ◇ ～浪迹 leaving no traces like duckweed and waves (said of persons who wander from place to place)

鲆 名 left-eyed flounder

pō

钋 名 [化] polonium (Po)

泊 名 lake: 罗布～ *Lop Nur* ——另见 bó

坡 Ⅰ名 slope：北～很陡。*The northern slope is very steep.* / 平～ *a slight (or gentle, gradual) slope* Ⅱ形 sloping; slanting：把板子～着放 *put the board on a slant* / 坑边挖得太陡了，再～一点。*The sides of the pit are too steep. Slope them a bit.*

【坡岸】a sloping bank

【坡地】hillside fields; sloping fields; land on the slopes：～梯田化 *terracing of the land on the slopes*

【坡度】the degree of an incline; slope; gradient：有三十来度～的一段山路 *a mountain path with a slope of about* 30 *degrees*

【坡跟】wedgies (of woman's shoe)

泼 Ⅰ动 sprinkle; splash; spill：先～点儿水再扫。*Sprinkle some water before you sweep.* / 互相～水 *splash water on each other* Ⅱ形 ❶ rude and unreasonable; shrewish：泼妇 ❷〈方〉bold and vigorous; daring and resolute：她干事儿可～了。*She is bold and resolute in her work.*

【泼妇】shrew; vixen; virago：～骂街 *like a shrew shouting abuse in the street*

【泼剌】the sound made by fish jumping in the water; splash; splosh

【泼辣】❶ rude and unreasonable; shrewish ❷ pungent; forceful：文章写得很～。*The article is written in a pungent style.* ❸ bold and vigorous; daring and resolute：她工作很～。*She is bold and vigorous in her work.*

【泼冷水】pour (or throw) cold water on; dampen the enthusiasm (or spirits) of

【泼墨】splash-ink, a technique of Chinese ink-painting：～山水 *splashed-ink landscape*

【泼水节】the Water-Splashing (or Water-Sprinkling) Festival of the Dais (傣族) and some other minority nationalities

【泼野】tough, fierce and unreasonable：～脾性 *harsh nature*

颇 Ⅰ形〈书〉inclined to one side; oblique：偏颇 Ⅱ副〈书〉quite; rather; considerably：～佳 *quite good* / 影响～大 *exert a considerable influence* / ～为费解 *rather difficult to understand* / ～不以为然 *highly disapprove of sth.* / 他说的～有道理。*There is a lot of sense in what he says.*

pó

婆 名 ❶ an old woman ❷ a woman in a certain occupation：媒婆 ❸ husband's mother; mother-in-law

【婆家】(又作'婆婆家') husband's family

【婆罗门】Brahman ◇～教 Brahmanism

【婆母】husband's mother; mother-in-law

【婆婆】❶ husband's mother; mother-in-law ❷〈方〉Grandmother ❸〈贬〉〈喻〉authorities or leaders who control their subordinate units too strictly：我们这个单位～多，难办事。*Our unit has too many bossy superiors, which makes things difficult.*

【婆婆妈妈】❶ like an old woman; old-womanish：你快点儿吧，别这么～的了。*Hurry up! Don't fuss like an old woman.* ❷ sentimental; mawkish; maudlin：他就是这么～的，动不动就掉眼泪。*He's such a sissy he easily breaks down and cries.*

【婆娑】whirling; dancing：杨柳～。*The willows dance in the breeze.*

【婆娑起舞】start dancing; begin to trip a measure

【婆子】❶〈贬〉woman ❷〈方〉wife ❸ a middle-aged or oldish woman servant

pǒ

叵 形〈书〉impossible

【叵测】〈贬〉unfathomable; unpredictable：世路窄狭，人心～。*Life's path is narrow and men's hearts are hard to fathom.*

钷 名［化］promethium (Pm)

笸 (构词成分) 见下

【笸箩】a shallow basket made of wicker or thin bamboo strips

pò

朴 名［植］Chinese hackberry (Celtis sinensis) ——另见 pǔ

【朴硝】mirabilite; Glauber's salt

迫 Ⅰ动 ❶ compel; force; press：～于形势 *under the stress of circumstances; under the pressure of events* / 为饥寒所～ *be driven (to do sth.) by cold and hunger* ❷ approach; go towards (or near)：迫近 Ⅱ形 urgent; pressing：从容不迫 ——另见 pǎi

【迫不得已】have no alternative (but to); be forced (or driven, compelled) to; (do sth.) against one's will

【迫不及待】unable to hold oneself back; too impatient to wait：他们都～地想知道发生了什么事。*They were too impatient to know what had happened.*

【迫促】❶ short; pressing：呼吸～ *be short of breath* ❷ urge; press; bring pressure on (sb. to do sth.)：在人们的～下，她才把这件事应承下来。*She was pressurized into agreeing to do it.*

【迫害】persecute; persecution：政治～ *political persecution*

【迫降】(pòjiàng) forced landing; distress landing——另见 pòxiáng

【迫近】approach; get close to; draw near：～敌人据点 *close in on the enemy stronghold* / ～胜利 *be nearing victory; come in sight of victory* / 行期～。*The day of departure is drawing near.* / 年

关～。*The end of the year is approaching when accounts must be settled.*

【迫令】force sb. to (do sth.)：被～停业三个月 *be forced to shut down for 3 months*

【迫切】urgent；pressing；imperative：～的需要 *an urgent need；a crying need* / ～的心情 *eager desire；eagerness* / ～性 *urgency*

【迫使】force；compel：～飞机降落 *force the plane down*

【迫视】look at from close-up；watch intently

【迫降】(pòxiáng) force sb. to surrender ——另见 pòjiàng

【迫在眉睫】❶ extremely urgent ❷ imminent

破 Ⅰ 形 ❶ broken；damaged；torn；worn-out：～碗 *a broken bowl* / ～衣服 *worn-out (or ragged, tattered) clothes* / ～房子 *a dilapidated (or tumbledown) house* / 我的手～了。*I've cut my hand.* ❷ paltry；lousy：这支～笔真气人！*This lousy pen really drives me mad!* / 这点～事两分钟就办完了。*To settle a simple matter like this won't take more than two minutes.* Ⅱ 动 ❶ break；split；cleave；cut：一～两半 *break (or split) into two* / ～开西瓜 *cut up the watermelon* / 把十元的票子～开 *break a ten-yuan note* ❷ get rid of；destroy；break with：大～天命观 *eradicate the concept of the mandate of heaven* / ～旧俗，立新风 *break with outmoded customs and establish new ones* / ～记录 *break a record* ❸ defeat；capture (a city, etc.)：大～敌军 *inflict a crushing defeat on the enemy* / 城～之日 *the day the city fell* ❹ expose the truth of；lay bare：看破

【破案】solve (or clear up) a case；crack a criminal case

【破败】ruined；dilapidated；tumbledown

【破冰船】icebreaker：原子～ *atomic icebreaker*

【破财】suffer unexpected personal financial losses；lose money

【破产】❶ bankruptcy：宣告～ *declare bankruptcy* / 银行～ *bank failure* ❷ go bankrupt；go broke；become insolvent：他的公司～了。*His company has gone broke.* ❸ come to naught；fall through；be bankrupt：他们的阴谋～了。*Their plot has fallen through.* ◇ ～法［法］insolvency law；law of bankruptcy

【破钞】同〖破费〗

【破除】do away with；get rid of；eradicate；break with：～迷信 *do away with superstitions or blind faith；topple old idols* / ～情面 *not spare anybody's feelings*

【破费】〈套〉spend money；go to some expense：你何必这么～呢？*Why must you go to this expense?* / 让你～了。*You really shouldn't have spent all this money (said when receiving a gift or a treat).*

【破釜沉舟】break the cauldrons and sink the boats (after crossing)—cut off all means of retreat；burn one's boats

【破格】break a rule；make an exception：～提升 *break a rule to promote sb.* / ～接待 *break protocol to honour sb.*

【破关斩将】(又作'破五关斩六将') break through numerous strategic passes and kill many defending generals—overcome a lot of difficulties and vanquish many opponents

【破罐破摔】smash a pot to pieces just because it's cracked—write off one's situation as hopeless and act recklessly

【破坏】❶ destroy；wreck：～桥梁 *destroy a bridge* ❷ do great damage to；disrupt；sabotage：～生产 *sabotage production* / ～团结 *disrupt unity；undermine unity* / ～名誉 *damage sb.'s reputation* / ～社会秩序 *undermine social order* / ～人权 *violate human rights* / ～和平 *breach of the peace* / 警惕敌人的～活动 *guard against enemy sabotage* ❸ change (a social system, custom, etc.) completely or violently：～旧世界，建设新世界。*Destroy the old world and build a new one.* ❹ violate (an agreement, regulation, etc.)；break：～停战协定 *violate an armistice agreement* ❺ decompose；destroy (the composition of a substance)：维生素 C 受热过度就会被～。*Vitamin C is destroyed when overheated.* ◇ ～分子 saboteur；～力 destructive power

【破货】loose woman

【破获】unearth；uncover：～一起凶杀案 *crack a murder case*

【破击】［军］attack and destroy；wreck；sabotage：～敌人的交通线 *wreck the enemy's communication lines*

【破解】analyse and explain

【破戒】❶ break a religious precept ❷ break one's vow of abstinence

【破镜重圆】a broken mirror joined together—reunion of husband and wife after an enforced separation or rupture

【破旧】old and shabby；worn-out；dilapidated：～的家具 *old, disreputable furniture*

【破旧立新】destroy the old and establish the new

【破口】❶ a cut (on one's hand, etc.)；a break (in a hedge, etc.)；a breach (in a wall, etc.)；a tear (in one's clothes, etc.) ❷ get a cut, break, breach, tear, etc.：手上破了个口儿 *got a cut on one's hand* / 袖子破了个口儿 *got a tear in one's sleeve* / 鞋底破了个口儿 *got a hole in the sole of one's shoe*

【破口大骂】shout abuse；let loose a torrent of abuse

【破烂】❶ tattered；ragged；worn-out：一家～的小工厂 *a small run-down factory* / 穿得～不堪 *be dressed in rags (or tatters)* ❷〈口〉junk；scrap：捡～ *search a garbage heap for odds and ends* ◇ ～货 worthless stuff；rubbish；trash

【破浪】cleave the waves；brave the waves：～前进 *cleave (or cut, plough) through the waves*

【破例】break a rule；make an exception

【破脸】turn against (an acquaintance or associate)；fall out：老夫妇俩相亲相爱，没有破过一回脸。*The old couple love each other dearly and have never quarrelled with each other*.

【破裂】burst；split；rupture；crack：外交关系的～ *break-off* (*or severance*, *disruption*) *of diplomatic relations* / 谈判～了。*The negotiations broke down*. / 他们两口子感情～了。*Their marriage has broken up*.

【破陋】run-down；dilapidated：小屋很～。*The hut is dilapidated*.

【破落】decline (in wealth and position)；fall into reduced circumstances；be reduced to poverty：～地主家庭 *an impoverished landlord family* ◇ ～户 a family that has gone down in the world

【破门】❶ burst (or force) open the door：～而入 *force open a door* ❷ (of the Christian Church) excommunicate sb. ❸ (in football, handball, ice hockey, etc.) score a goal

【破灭】be shattered；fall through；evaporate：他的幻想～了。*He was disillusioned*.

【破伤风】［医］tetanus

【破身】lose one's virginity；have one's first sexual intercourse

【破水】(of a woman about to give birth) one's water breaks

【破私立公】overcome selfishness and foster public spirit

【破碎】❶ tattered；broken：～的玻璃 *broken glass* ❷ smash (or break) sth. to pieces；crush ◇ ～机 crusher；breaker；～险［经］risk of breakage

【破损】damaged；worn；torn：这本书有几页已经～。*Some pages of the book are damaged*.

【破题儿第一遭】the first time one ever does sth.；the first time ever

【破体字】a non-standard or corrupted form of a Chinese character

【破涕为笑】one's tears giving way to smiles：她～，说："我真傻，怎么就没有想到这一点。" *She smiled through her tears, and said, "What a silly I am not to be aware of that!"*

【破天荒】occur for the first time；be unprecedented

【破土】❶ break ground (in starting a building project, etc.) ❷ start spring ploughing ❸ (of a seedling) break through the soil

【破网】score a goal

【破袭战】sabotage operations

【破相】(of facial features) be marred by a scar, etc.；disfigure

【破晓】dawn；daybreak：天将～。*Day is breaking*.

【破鞋】loose woman

【破颜】break into a smile

【破衣烂衫】ragged clothes；rags；tatters

【破译】decode；decipher

【破约】break one's promise

【破绽】❶ a burst seam ❷ flaw；weak point ◇ ～百出 full of flaws (or holes)

【破折号】dash (—)

【破竹之势】an irresistible force

魄 名 ❶ soul：魂魄 ❷ vigour；spirit：气魄

【魄力】daring and resolution；boldness：工作有～ *be bold and resolute in one's work*

pōu

剖 动 ❶ cut open；rip open：把鱼肚子～开 *cut open the belly of a fish* ❷ analyse；examine；dissect：～释 *analyse and explain*

【剖白】explain oneself；vindicate oneself：～心迹 *lay one's heart bare*

【剖腹藏珠】rip (or cut) open the stomach to hide a pearl—die for the sake of gain

【剖腹产】［医］Caesarean birth：～术 *Caesarean section* (*or operation*)

【剖腹自杀】(commit) hara-kiri

【剖解】analyse；dissect：～细密 *make a minute analysis*

【剖露】lay bare；strip bare；reveal

【剖面】section：横～ *cross section* / 纵～ *longitudinal section* ◇ ～图 sectional drawing；section

【剖明】analyse and make clear：～事理 *analyse the whys and wherefores* / ～心迹 *lay bare the true state of one's mind*

【剖尸】autopsy；post-mortem examination

【剖视图】cutaway view

【剖析】analyse；dissect：～问题的实质 *analyse the essence of the problem*

【剖心】open one's heart；lay bare one's true feelings；be completely open and sincere

pū

仆 动 fall forward；fall prostrate：前仆后继 ——另见 pú

扑 动 ❶ throw oneself on or at；pounce on：孩子一下子～到他妈的怀里。*The child threw himself into his mother's arms*. / 老虎～向山羊。*The tiger sprang on the goat*. / 他一下～在对手身上。*He threw himself at his adversary*. ❷ rush at；attack：直～匪徒的巢穴 *swoop down on the bandits' lair* / ～蝴蝶 *catch butterflies* ❸ throw oneself into (work, etc.)：一心～在集体事业上 *devote oneself heart and soul to the cause of the collective* ❹ flap；flutter：鸭子～着翅膀。*The duck flapped its wings*. ❺ dab (powder, etc.)：孩子浑身都～上了爽身粉。*The child was dabbed all over with talcum*. ❻〈方〉bend over：～在桌上看地图 *bend over a map on the desk*

【扑鼻】assail the nostrils：香气～。*A sweet smell greeted us*.

【扑哧】the sound of snorting or fizzing：～一笑 *snort with laughter*；*chortle*；*chuckle*

【扑打】(pūdǎ) swat：～蝗虫 *swat locusts*

【扑打】(pūda) pat；beat：～身上的尘土 *dust one's clothes*

【扑跌】❶ wrestling ❷ fall forward：他脚下一绊，～在地上。*He stumbled and fell forward*.

【扑冬】the sound of sth. heavy dropping on the ground；thump；thud：～一声，摔倒在地 *fall with a thump on the ground*

【扑尔敏】［药］chlorpheniramine

【扑粉】❶ face powder ❷ talcum powder ❸ apply powder：在脸上扑点儿粉 *powder one's face*

【扑击】❶ pounce on；fall on；set on：老鹰～鸡群。*An eagle swooped down and pounced on the chickens*. ❷ lap against；beat against：海浪～着岸边的礁石。*The sea beat against the rocky coast*.

【扑救】❶ put out a fire to save life and property ❷（in volleyball，football，etc.）diving save

【扑克】❶ playing cards：打～ *play cards* ❷ poker

【扑空】fail to get（or achieve）what one wants；fail to find a person where he is supposed to be；come away empty-handed：昨天我去找他，又～了。*Yesterday I went to see him，but again he wasn't home*.

【扑拉】❶ flap or spread（wings）：母鸡～着翅膀咕咕叫。*The hen cackled，flapping its wings*. ❷ pat；slap；whisk：～～身上的雪 *whisk the snow off one's clothes* ❸（of tears，sweat，etc.）roll down；trickle down：额头上的冷汗～～直往下淌。*Cold sweat kept rolling from his brow*.

【扑棱】（pūlēng）the sound of flapping of wings：～一声，飞起一只小鸟。*There was a flutter of wings and up flew a bird*.

【扑棱】（pūleng）flap：～着翅膀 *flapping its wings*

【扑落】❶ shake off；shake out of sth.：把口袋里的面粉～干净。*Shake all the flour out of the bag*. ❷〈书〉scattered about

【扑面】blow on（or against）one's face：春风～。*The spring wind caressed our faces*.

【扑灭】❶ stamp out；put out；extinguish：～火灾 *put out a fire* ❷ exterminate；wipe out：～蚊蝇 *wipe out mosquitoes and flies*

【扑热息痛】［药］paracetamol

【扑闪】❶ blink：她惊讶地～着她那两只大眼睛。*Her big eyes blinked with astonishment*. ❷〈方〉flap；flutter：小蜻蜓～～翅膀飞走了。*The little dragonfly fluttered its wings and flew off*.

【扑朔迷离】bewildering；confusing

【扑簌】（of tears）trickling down：她眼泪扑簌簌地往下掉。*Tears trickled down her cheeks*.

【扑腾】（pūtēng）the sound of a heavy fall；flop；thump；thud：～一声，包掉下来了。*The bundle fell with a thud*.

【扑腾】（pūteng）❶ move one's legs up and down in the water；flop：鱼在网里直～。*The fish flopped helplessly in the net*. ❷ throb；palpitate：他心里直～。*His heart was throbbing*. ❸〈方〉hustle；bustle；keep the ball rolling：这个人挺能～。*He's quite a go-getter*. ❹ spend freely；squander：没有几年，他把家产全～完了。*In just a few years，he squandered all his family property*.

【扑通】the sound of sth. heavy dropping into the water or to the ground；flop；thump；splash；pit-a-pat：～一声，掉进水里 *fall into the water with a splash* / 她的心～～地跳。*Her heart went pit-a-pat*.

【扑翼】flapping wing：～飞机 *flapping-wing aircraft；ornithopter*

铺 Ⅰ**动** ❶ spread；extend；unfold：～桌布 *spread a tablecloth* / ～地毯 *spread a rug on the floor* / 运动已经全面～开。*The movement is fully under way*. ❷ pave；lay：一条～砖的小路 *a path paved with bricks* / ～铁轨 *lay a railway track* / ～路面 *surface a road* Ⅱ**量**〈方〉（for 炕）：一～炕 *one heatable brick bed* / 全家四口人睡在一～炕上。*The family of four slept on one big brick bed*. ——另见 pù

【铺衬】small pieces of cloth used for patches

【铺床】make the bed

【铺地砖】❶ floor tile；paving tile ❷ tile the floor

【铺底资金】minimum capital；start-up fund；seed money

【铺垫】❶ bedding ❷ foreshadowing：这一段为故事的高潮作了～。*This passage foreshadows the climax of the story*.

【铺盖】（pūgài）spread（evenly）over：把草木灰～在苗床上。*Spread plant ash evenly over the seedbed*.

【铺盖】（pūgai）bedding；bedclothes

【铺盖卷儿】bedding roll；bedroll；luggage roll

【铺轨】lay a railway track：～机 *track-laying machine；tracklayer*

【铺炕】spread out the bedclothes on the kang；prepare the kang for sleep

【铺路机】paver

【铺平】❶ smooth out；spread sth. out smoothly：把床单～ *smooth out the sheet* ❷ make the ground，etc. level or even；level：把路面～ *level the road*

【铺平道路】pave the way（for sth.）：为两国之间恢复邦交～ *pave the way for the resumption of diplomatic relations between the two countries*

【铺砌】［建］pave

【铺设】lay；build（a road，railway，etc.）：～友谊之路 *open up a path of friendship*

【铺天盖地】blot out the sky and cover up the earth：暴风雪～而来。*The blizzard blotted out the sky and the earth*.

【铺叙】narrate in detail；elaborate：～事实 *elaborate on the facts*

【铺展】spread out；sprawl：蔚蓝的天空～着一片片的白云。*Fleecy clouds spread over the blue sky*.

【铺张】❶ extravagant：一次过分～的生日宴会 *a much too extravagant birthday party* ❷ exaggeration

【铺张浪费】extravagant and wasteful：反对～ *oppose extravagance and waste*

【铺张扬厉】❶ praise extravagantly ❷ indulge in

extravagance and ostentation

【铺植】sod; turf; plant: 斜坡～了草皮。*The slope has been turfed with grass.*

潽 动〈口〉(of a liquid) boil and spill over: 牛奶一煮开就会～出来。*Milk spills over as soon as it comes to boiling point.*

噗 象 puff: ～,一口气吹灭了蜡烛 *blow out a candle with one puff* / 子弹把尘土打得～～直冒烟。*Bullets whipped up the dust.*

【噗噜噜】(used to describe a flood of tears rolling down the cheeks): 听着她讲身世,很多人的眼泪～地直往下掉。*Tears trickled down the faces of many listeners when she told her story.*

pú

仆 名 servant: 男～ *manservant* / 女～ *maidservant* ——另见 pū

【仆从】footman; retainer; henchman ◇ ～国 vassal country

【仆人】(domestic) servant

【仆役】(domestic) servants

匍 (构词成分) 见下

【匍匐】(又作'匍伏') ❶ crawl; creep: ～前进 *crawl forward* ❷ (of plants) grow along the ground; creep; trail: 有些植物的茎～在地面上。*Some plants have trailing (or creeping) stems.* ◇ ～茎 [植] stolon; ～植物 [植] creeper

菩 (构词成分) 见下

【菩萨】❶ Bodhisattva: 观音～ *the Bodhisattva Guanyin* ❷ Buddha; deity; god ❸ a term applied to a kindhearted person

【菩萨心肠】the heart of a Bodhisattva—the bowels of compassion (or pity); the bowels of mercy; kindheartedness; mercifulness

【菩提】bodhi, supreme wisdom or enlightenment, necessary to the attainment of Buddhahood ◇ ～树 [植] pipal; bo tree; bodhi tree

脯 名 chest; breast ——另见 fǔ

【脯子】breast meat (of chicken, duck, etc.): 鸡～ *chicken breast*

葡 名 grape

【葡萄】grape: 一串～ *a bunch (or cluster) of grapes* / ～架 *grape trellis* / ～藤 *grapevine* / ～园 *vineyard*; *grapery* ◇ ～弹 [军] grapeshot; grape; ～干 raisin; ～酒 grape wine; wine; ～球菌 staphylococcus; ～胎 [医] hydatidiform mole; vesicular mole; ～糖 glucose; grape sugar; dextrose

【葡萄牙】Portugal ◇ ～人 Portuguese; ～语 Portuguese (language)

蒲 名 [植] cattail; reed mace; club grass

【蒲包】❶ cattail bag; rush bag ❷〈旧〉a gift of fruit or pastries (formerly packed in a cattail bag)

【蒲草】❶ the stem or leaf of cattail (or reed mace, club grass) ❷〈方〉dwarf lilyturf

【蒲公英】[植] dandelion

【蒲黄】[中] cattail pollen

【蒲葵】[植] Chinese fan palm

【蒲柳】[植] big catkin willow (Salix gracilistyla)

【蒲柳之姿】feel like a willow withering at the approach of autumn—suffer from poor health

【蒲绒】(又作'蒲茸') cattail wool, used for stuffing pillows

【蒲扇】Chinese fan palm fan (each made with a whole Chinese fan palm leaf)

【蒲式耳】bushel (=8 gallons)

【蒲团】cattail hassock used for kneeling; rush hassock

【蒲席】cattail mat; rush mat

镤 名 [化] protactinium (Pa)

pǔ

朴 形 simple; plain ——另见 pò

【朴厚】simple and honest: 心地～ *simple-minded and kindhearted*

【朴实】❶ simple; plain: 穿着很～ *be plainly dressed* ❷ sincere and honest; guileless: ～的工作作风 *a down-to-earth style of work* ◇ ～无华 simple and unadorned

【朴素】❶ (of colour, style, language, etc.) simple; plain: 他的诗～而感情真挚。*His poems are simple in style and imbued with true feelings.* ❷ (of one's living) frugal; thrifty; plain and modest: 艰苦朴素 ❸ naive; undeveloped: 朴素唯物主义

【朴素唯物主义】naive materialism

【朴直】honest and straightforward: 文笔～ *simple and straightforward writing*

【朴质】simple and unadorned; natural

圃 名 garden: 苗圃

普 形 general; universal: ～天下 *all over the world*; *everywhere in the world*

【普遍】universal; general; widespread; common: 有～意义 *be of universal significance* ◇ ～规律 universal law; ～性 universality; ～优惠制 generalized system of preferences (GSP); general preferential scheme; ～真理 universal truth

【普查】❶ general investigation (or survey): 常见病～ *general survey of common diseases* / 人口～ *census* ❷ [地质] reconnaissance survey

【普度】[宗](佛教) deliver all from torment ◇ ～众生 [宗](佛教) deliver all living creatures from torment

【普法】popularize knowledge of national laws (marriage, property, business contract, etc.): 北京正在开展～工作。*There is an effort in Bei-*

jing to inform ordinary citizens about national laws.

【普高】(〈略〉全称为'普通高级中学') regular senior middle school (different from a key senior middle school)

【普惠制】〈略〉见〖普遍优惠制〗

【普及】❶ be universalized in; be made popular among; be extensively spread: 这本书已经～全国。*This book has reached every part of the country.* ❷ popularize; disseminate; spread among the people: ～与提高相结合 *combine popularization with the raising of standards* / ～中等教育 *make secondary education universal* ◇ ～本 popular edition; ～教育 universal education

【普降】(of rain or snow) fall over a large area: 昨日华北～瑞雪。*A timely snow fell all over the north China area yesterday.*

【普教】general education (spec. secondary and primary school education)

【普鲁本辛】[药] propantheline (bromide); probanthine

【普鲁卡因】[药] procaine

【普什图语】Pushtu

【普特】pood (a Russian measure of weight equivalent to 16.38 kg.)

【普天同庆】The whole world (or nation) joins in the jubilation.

【普天之下】everywhere under the sun; all under heaven

【普调】make general readjustment (of price, wage, etc.)

【普通】ordinary; common; average: ～一兵 *an ordinary soldier; a soldier in the ranks; a rank-and-filer* / ～人 *the average person; the man in the street* ◇ ～法 [法] common law; ～股 [经] common stock; ～话 putonghua; Mandarin Chinese; common speech (of the Chinese language); standard Chinese pronunciation; ～税则 general tariff; ～心理学 general psychology; ～照会 diplomacy verbal note

【普选】general election: 成人～权 *adult suffrage* ◇ ～制 universal suffrage

【普照】illuminate all things: 阳光～大地。*The sun illuminates every corner of the land.*

谱 Ⅰ 名 ❶ a register or record for easy reference (in the form of charts, tables, lists, etc.): 食谱 ❷ manual; guidebook: 棋谱 ❸ music score; music: 根据这首歌的～配了一段新词。*New lyrics have been composed to the music of this song.* ❹ sth. to count on; a fair amount of confidence: 没谱儿 Ⅱ 动 set to music; compose (music): 把毛主席的诗词～成歌曲 *set Chairman Mao's poems to music*

【谱斑】[天] flocculus

【谱表】[音] stave; staff: 大～ *great stave*

【谱号】[音] clef: 高音～ *treble clef; G clef* / 中音～ *tenor clef; alto clef; C clef* / 低音～ *bass clef; F clef*

【谱架】music stand

【谱曲】set (words) to music; compose music for: 这首歌是谁谱的曲? *Who is the composer of the song?*

【谱系】pedigree

【谱写】compose (music): 这支曲子是在解放战争初期～的。*The tune was composed at the beginning of the War of Liberation.*

【谱制】compose: ～乐曲 *compose music; set to music*

【谱子】〈口〉music score; music

镨 名 [化] praseodymium (Pr)

蹼 名 web (that connects the digits of ducks, frogs, etc.)

【蹼趾】webbed toe

【蹼足】webfoot; palmate foot

pù

铺 名 shop; store; plank bed ——另见 pū

【铺板】bed board; bed plank

【铺底】shop fixtures

【铺户】shop; store

【铺面】shop front ◇ ～房 shop building

【铺位】bunk; berth

【铺子】shop; store

瀑 名 waterfall

【瀑布】waterfall; falls; cataract

曝 动〈书〉expose to the sun: 一曝十寒

【曝露】〈书〉expose to the open air

【曝气池】[环保] aeration tank

【曝晒】expose to the sun

Q

qī

七 数 seven：～公斤 *seven kilos* / ～个班 *seven classes* / ～班 *the seventh class*；*class 7* / ～路公共汽车 *No. 7 bus*

【七…八…】(used with verbs or nouns to indicate a large amount or great disorder)：七扭八歪 *crooked*；*uneven*；*irregular*

【七边形】heptagon

【七步之才】seven-pace talent—literary talent in ready play

【七颠八倒】at sixes and sevens；all upside down；topsy-turvy：我父亲死了以后，家里的事～。*Since my father's death all affairs at home have been in great confusion*.

【七级风】[气] force 7 wind；moderate gale

【七极管】[无] heptode

【七绝】(〈略〉全称为'七言绝句') a four-line poem with seven characters to a line and a strict tonal pattern and rhyme scheme；septasyllabic (or seven-syllable) quatrain

【七老八十】late seventies and early eighties—a very old person

【七零八落】scattered here and there；in disorder：～的几间破草房 *a few ramshackle huts scattered here and there* / 匪徒被打得～，四散奔逃。*Badly battered, the bandits fled in disorder*.

【七律】(〈略〉全称为'七言律诗') an eight-line poem with seven characters to a line and a strict tonal pattern and rhyme scheme；septasyllabic (or seven-syllable) regulated verse

【七拼八凑】throw together；piece together；knock together；rig up：用碎布～做成一个枕套 *make a pillowcase from odd pieces of cloth*

【七七八八】〈口〉mixed；assorted；miscellaneous：～的东西 *odds and ends*；*a medley* / ～的事情 *odd jobs*；*miscellaneous trifles*

【七巧板】seven-piece puzzle；tangram

【七窍】the seven apertures in the human head (i. e. eyes, ears, nostrils and mouth) ◇ ～生烟 fume with anger；foam with rage；be outraged

【七情】❶ the seven human emotions, namely, joy, anger, sorrow, fear, love, hate and desire ❷ [中] the seven emotional factors (joy, anger, melancholy, brooding, sorrow, fear and shock, considered to be the internal factors causing diseases)

【七鳃鳗】lamprey

【七色板】spectrum board

【七上八下】(又作'七上八落') seven buckets coming up and eight buckets going down—be agitated；be perturbed：他心里～的，不知怎么办才好。*He was so agitated that he didn't know what to do*.

【七十二变】seventy-two transformations (or metamorphoses)— countless changes of tactics

【七十二行】all sorts of occupations；every conceivable line of work

【七十七国集团】Group of 77；G77

【七手八脚】with everyone lending a hand：大伙儿～把他抬了出来。*Everybody lent a hand to carry him out*.

【七夕】the seventh evening of the seventh month (when the Herd-boy and the Weaving-girl are supposed to meet) ——另见〖牛郎织女〗

【七叶树】Chinese Horsechestnut (Aesculus chinensis)

【七一】July 1, anniversary of the founding of the Communist Party of China (1921)

【七月】❶ July ❷ the seventh month of the lunar year；the seventh moon

【七折八扣】various deductions

【七政仪】[天] orrery

【七嘴八舌】seven mouths and eight tongues —with everybody trying to get a word in；all talking at once：方案一公布，大家就～地议论开了。*The draft plan touched off a lively discussion the moment it was announced*；*everybody was eager to put in a word*. / 人们都围了上去，～，他不知听谁的好。*People crowded round him, all talking at once, so that he didn't know who to listen to*.

沏 动 infuse (with boiling water)：～茶 *infuse tea*；*make tea* / 用开水把糖～开。*Dissolve the sugar in the hot water*.

妻 名 wife

【妻弟】wife's younger brother；brother-in-law

【妻儿老小】parents, wife and children—a married man's entire family

【妻舅】wife's brother；brother-in-law

【妻离子散】breaking up or scattering of one's family ——另见〖天各一方〗

【妻室】〈书〉wife

【妻小】〈旧〉wife and children

【妻子】(qīzǐ) wife and children

【妻子】(qīzi) wife

桼 数 seven (used for the numeral 七 on cheques, etc., to avoid mistakes or alterations)

凄 形 ❶ chilly; cold: 风雨~~。*Cold, cold are the wind and the rain.* ❷ bleak and desolate: 凄凉 ❸ sad; wretched; miserable

【凄惨】wretched; miserable; tragic: ~的声音 *sad (or plaintive) cries* / ~的景象 *a heartrending sight* / 生活~ *lead a wretched existence; lead a miserable life*

【凄风苦雨】❶ wailing wind and weeping rain: ~,夜不能眠。*With the wind moaning and the rain pattering, I lay awake all night.* ❷ wretched circumstances; distress

【凄厉】sad and shrill: ~的叫声 *sad, shrill cries* / 风声~。*The wind was wailing.*

【凄凉】dreary; desolate; miserable: 满目~ *desolation all round* / 天景~ *lead a miserable and dreary life in old age*

【凄切】plaintive; mournful: 寒蝉~。*It was cold and the cicadas were chirping plaintively.*

【凄清】❶ slightly cold; cool: ~的月光 *cool moonlight* ❷ dreary; plaintive: 琴声~。*The qin was producing a plaintive tune.*

【凄然】〈书〉sad; mournful: ~泪下 *shed tears in sadness*

【凄酸】grieved; distressed; sorrowful: 心中一阵~ *feel a twinge at one's heart*

【凄婉】(of sound) plaintive but lovely; sadly moving: ~的笛声 *the plaintive tone of a flute*

【凄怨】sad; plaintive: ~的曲调 *a plaintive tune*

栖 动 ❶ (of birds) perch: 栖息 ❷ dwell; stay: 栖身

【栖身】stay; sojourn: 无处~ *have no place to stay*

【栖息】(of birds) perch; rest: 许多水鸟在岛上~。*A great number of water fowls dwell on the island.* ◇ ~地 habitat

萋 (构词成分) 见下

【萋萋】〈文〉luxuriant; lush

戚 名 ❶ relative: 亲戚 ❷ sorrow; woe

【戚友】friends and relatives

期 Ⅰ 名 ❶ a period of time; phase; stage: 第一~工程 *the first phase of the project* / 暑期班分两~,每~三周 *a summer school of two three-week sessions* ❷ scheduled time: 到期 Ⅱ 量 (for things scheduled by periods): 最近一~的《中国画报》*the current issue of China Pictorial* / 短训班办了三~。*The short-term training class has been run three times.* Ⅲ 动 ❶ make an appointment: 不期而遇 ❷ expect: 期待

【期待】expect; await; look forward to: 殷切地~你早日答复 *eagerly await your early reply* / 我们一直~着这一天。*We've been looking forward to this day for a long time.* / 老师用~的目光望着我们。*The teacher looked at us with expectant eyes.*

【期房】forward delivery housing

【期汇】[经] forward exchange

【期货】[经] futures: ~价格 *forward price* / ~合同 *forward contract; futures contract* ◇ ~交易 [经] futures; futures transaction; ~市场 futures market

【期冀】〈书〉ardently hope or expect

【期间】time; period; course: 就在这~ *during this time; in this very period* / 会议~ *in the course of the conference; during the conference* / 农忙~ *during busy farming seasons* / 他在住院~读了很多小说。*While in hospital, he read a lot of novels.*

【期刊】periodical: ~阅览室 *periodical reading room*

【期考】end-of-term examination; final (or terminal) examination

【期满】expire; run out; come to an end: 合同~ *the contract expires; on the expiration of the contract* / 服役~ *complete one's term of (military) service*

【期盼】expect; await; look forward to

【期票】promissory note; term bill

【期期艾艾】stammer; stutter: 他~地说不上话来。*He stammered and stuttered and couldn't utter a single coherent sentence.*

【期求】hope to get (or obtain)

【期望】❶ ardently hope or expect: 党和人民在~着我们。*The Party and the people place high hopes on us.* / 她~着和家人团聚。*She was looking forward to joining her family.* ❷ expectation: 我们决不辜负祖国对我们的~。*We will never disappoint our motherland in her expectations of us.*

【期望值】expectations: ~过高 *expectations that run too high*

【期限】allotted time; time limit; deadline: 规定一个~ *set a deadline; fix a target date* / 延长~ *extend the time limit* / ~快到了。*The deadline is drawing near.* / 必须在规定的~内完成这项工作。*The work must be finished within the allotted time.*

【期许】ardently hope or expect (usu. used of one's juniors)

【期颐】〈书〉a 100-year-old person; centenarian: ~之年 *in one's 100th year*

欺 动 ❶ deceive: 欺瞒 ❷ bully; take advantage of sb.: 软弱可欺 ❸ take advantage of (sb.'s weakness, etc.): 他~她老实。*He took advantage of her good nature.*

【欺负】❶ bully; treat sb. high-handedly; take advantage of sb.: 大国不应当~小国。*Big nations should not bully small ones.* / 别瞧谁老实就~谁。*Don't take advantage of a nice person when you see one.* ❷ take advantage of (sb.'s weakness, etc.): 他们~他年幼无知。*They took advantage of his youth and inexperience.*

【欺行霸市】bully fellow traders and dominate the market
【欺凌】bully and humiliate：受尽了～ *be subjected to endless bullying and humiliation* / 决不任人～ *never allow oneself to be trodden upon*
【欺瞒】hoodwink；dupe；pull the wool over sb.'s eyes
【欺瞒夹账】engage in fraud；falsify accounts；practise graft
【欺蒙】deceive；cheat；dupe；defraud
【欺弄】dupe；hoodwink：老太太受了他的～。*The old woman was duped by him.*
【欺骗】deceive；cheat；dupe：～世界舆论 *befuddle world opinion* / 这只能～那些不明真相的人。*This can only deceive those who do not know the truth.* or *This can only mislead those who are not aware of the facts.* / 你这是在～自己。*You're deceiving yourself.* / 揭露两面派的～性 *expose the duplicity of the double-dealers*
【欺人太甚】what a beastly bully；that's going too far；push people too hard
【欺人之谈】deceitful words；deceptive talk
【欺辱】bully and humiliate；insult
【欺软怕硬】bully the weak and fear the strong：大家骂他不公平，～。*Everybody lashed out at his unfairness, calling him a cowardly bully.*
【欺上瞒下】deceive one's superiors and delude (or dupe) one's subordinates
【欺生】❶ bully or cheat strangers：那儿的人～，见了外地人特横。*The people there are apt to cheat strangers；they're particularly rough on non-natives.* / 他们家那狗～，我一进院子它就叫。*Their dog is fierce towards strangers；he barks at me whenever I enter the courtyard.* ❷ (of horses, mules, etc.) be ungovernable by strangers：这马～，我一靠近它就尥蹶子。*This horse refuses to behave for strangers；he kicks at me whenever I approach him.*
【欺世盗名】gain fame by deceiving the public；fish for undeserved fame
【欺侮】bully and humiliate；treat sb. high-handedly：书评作者的批评没有必要这样～人。*The reviewer's criticism was unnecessarily insulting.* / 她让人～得直哭。*She was driven to tears by their bullying.*
【欺压】bully and oppress；ride roughshod over：～人民 *ride roughshod over the people*
【欺诈】cheat；swindle：这家商店经常～顾客。*This shop often swindles customers.*

缉 动 sew in close and joint stitches：～边儿 *sew the hem with close stitches* ——另见 jī

漆 Ⅰ 名 lacquer；paint：～盘 *lacquer tray* / 他用黑～把铁桌子漆了。*He painted the iron table with black lacquer.* Ⅱ 动 coat with lacquer；paint：把门～成深绿色 *paint the door dark green* / 把桌子再～一遍 *give the table another coat of paint* / 颜色～太深(浅) *paint a colour a bit too dark (light)* / ～厚(薄)些 *give a thick (thin) coat of paint*
【漆包线】enamel-insulated wire
【漆布】varnished cloth
【漆雕】同〖雕漆〗
【漆革】patent leather
【漆工】❶ lacquering；painting ❷ lacquerer；lacquer man；painter
【漆黑】pitch-dark；pitch-black：那是个～的夜晚。*It was a pitch-dark night.* / 屋子外面～一片。*Outside the house it was pitch-black.* / ～的头发 *jet-black hair*
【漆黑一团】❶ pitch-dark—utterly hopeless：把形势描绘成～ *paint a dark picture of the situation* ❷ be entirely ignorant of；be in the dark：这个问题在他心中还是～。*He is still completely in the dark about the matter.*
【漆画】lacquer painting
【漆匠】❶ lacquerware worker ❷ lacquerer；lacquer man；painter
【漆皮】❶ coat of paint ❷ shellac
【漆片】a coating agent which has to be dissolved in alcohol before use
【漆器】lacquerware；lacquerwork
【漆树】lacquer tree；varnish tree

嘁（构词成分）见下
【嘁哩喀喳】quick and efficient (in doing things)；snappy and clear-cut (in speaking)
【嘁嘁喳喳】the sound of chatter

槭 名 maple
【槭树】maple

蹊（构词成分）见下 ——另见 xī
【蹊跷】odd；strange；fishy：这事情有点～。*There is something fishy about it.*

qí

齐 Ⅰ 形 ❶ neat；even；uniform：把桌子摆～ *arrange the tables in an orderly way* / 剪得很～ *be evenly trimmed* / 这两根筷子长短不～。*These two chopsticks are not of equal (or uniform) length.* ❷ alike；similar：齐心 / 齐名 Ⅱ 动 be level with：水涨得～了岸。*The water has risen to the level of the river banks.* / 在～腰深的水里筑坝 *stand waist-deep in water building the dam* Ⅲ 介 even up at one point or along one line：把玉米秆～着根儿砍断 *cut the cornstalks right down to the roots* / ～着边儿画一道线 *draw a line along the edge* Ⅳ 副 ❶ together；simultaneously：男女老幼～动手。*Men and women, old and young, all pitched in.* / 万炮～发。*All the batteries fired at once.* ❷ all ready；all present：客人都来～了。*All the guests have arrived.* / 人到～了没有？*Is everybody here?* / 东西都预备～了。*Everything has been prepared.*
【齐备】complete；all ready：实验所需的东西都已

～。*The things necessary for the experiment are all ready.* / 万事～。*Everything is ready.* / 货色～。*Goods of every description are available.*
【齐步走】[军] quick march：～！(*word of command*) *Quick time, march!*
【齐唱】[音] singing in unison; unison
【齐齿呼】[语音] a class of syllables with i as the final (韵母) or a final beginning with i (e.g. 坚 jiān) ——另见〖四呼〗
【齐楚】neat and smart：衣冠～ *be smartly dressed*
【齐东野语】what folks say; popular report; unreliable words
【齐集】assemble; gather; collect：五大洲的朋友～在中国的首都北京。*Friends from the five continents gathered in the Chinese capital Beijing.*
【齐名】enjoy equal popularity; be equally famous
【齐明】[物] aplanatic ◇～成象 aplanatic image formation；～点 aplanatic foci；～镜 aplanat
【齐巧】〈方〉by chance; fortunately; as chance would have it：我上公园去，～她也在那儿。*She chanced to be in the park when I was there.*
【齐全】complete; having everything that one expects to find; all in readiness：尺码～ *have a complete range of sizes* / 登山队装备～。*The mountaineers are fully equipped.* / 新建的住宅设备～。*The new houses have all the necessary fittings.* / 这商店虽然小，货物却很～。*This store, though small, has a satisfactory variety of goods.*
【齐射】[军] salvo; volley
【齐声】in chorus; in unison：～回答 *answer in chorus* / ～欢呼 *cheer in unison*
【齐刷刷】even; uniform：～的一片麦子 *an even expanse of wheat*
【齐头并进】advance side by side; do two or more things at once：三路人马～。*The three columns advanced simultaneously.* / 这些工作要分轻重缓急，不要～。*These jobs should be arranged in order of priority and not done all at once.*
【齐心】be of one mind (or heart)：群众～了，一切事情就好办了。*When the masses are of one heart, everything becomes easy (or is easily accomplished).*
【齐心协力】work as one; make concerted efforts：我们大家～，一定能打败他们！*If we all pull together, there's no doubt we can beat them!*
【齐整】neat; uniform：运河两旁的柳树长得很～。*The canal is flanked by neat rows of willows.*
【齐奏】[音] playing (instruments) in unison; unison

祈 动 ❶ pray ❷ entreat：敬～指导。*We respectfully request your guidance.*
【祈祷】pray; say one's prayers：正在～ *be at one's prayer*
【祈求】earnestly hope; pray for：～上帝 *pray to God* / ～和平 *pray for peace*
【祈使句】[语] imperative sentence
【祈望】hope; wish
【祈雨】pray for rain

其 代 ❶ his (her, its, their)：～父 *his or her father* ❷ he (she, it, they)：劝～戒烟 *advise him (or her) to give up smoking* / 促～早日实现 *help bring it about at an early date* ❸ that; such：正当～时 *just at that time; at the opportune moment* / 查无～事。*Investigation shows that nothing of this sort has happened.* ❹ (referring to no definite person or thing) it：大请～客 *invite many guests to dinner; entertain lavishly* / 忘～所以 *forget all else*
【其次】❶ next; secondly; then：先看生产车间～，再参观托儿所。*Let's see the workshop first and then the nursery.* ❷ secondary：首要的问题已经解决，～的问题就比较好办了。*The secondary problems will be taken care of easily now that the main problem has been solved.* / 内容是主要的，形式还在～。*Content comes first, form second.*
【其后】later; after; afterwards
【其间】❶ between or among them; of them; in it ❷ during this or that time
【其乐无穷】find it a delight (or joy)：西湖赏月，～。*It is a delight to watch the moon rising over the West Lake.*
【其貌不扬】be unprepossessing (or unimposing) in appearance; be of undistinguished appearance
【其实】actually; in fact; as a matter of fact：～情况不是那样。*Actually, that is not the case.* / 这台机器看起来复杂，～不难掌握。*This machine looks complicated, but it's really not difficult to operate.*
【其它】(referring to things only) other; else
【其他】other; else：老李在这儿，～人呢？*Lao Li's here. Where are the others?* / 见到～人了吗？*Did you see anybody else?* / 除了小冯以外，～的人都去了。*Everybody went except Xiao Feng.* / 先拣重要的说，再说～。*Say what you think is most important first, then go on to other things.*
【其味无穷】have a marvellous flavour; be infinitely enjoyable
【其余】all the other (persons or things); the rest; the remainder：～的人马上就来。*The others will be here in a minute.* / 这个突击队只有三名男的，～都是女同志。*There are only three men in the shock team; the rest are women.*
【其中】among them; of them; in it：乐在～ *find pleasure in it* / 这篇论文我已经看过，～提出的问题值得重视。*I have read that paper. The questions it raises deserve serious attention.*

奇 Ⅰ 形 ❶ strange; queer; rare：希奇 ❷ remarkable; wonderful：奇书 Ⅱ 动 be surprised; be astonished：惊奇 Ⅲ 副 very; extremely：～痒 *itch terribly* / ～痛 *have a severe pain; be extremely painful* ——另见 jī
【奇兵】an army suddenly appearing from nowhere; an ingenious military move
【奇才】a rare talent; genius

【奇耻大辱】galling shame and deep humiliation; deep disgrace
【奇功】outstanding service：屡建～ *repeatedly perform outstanding service*
【奇怪】❶ strange; surprising; odd：真～，他们至今还一无所知。*It's really surprising that they should still be in the dark.* / 这个问题提得很～。*It's a strange question to raise.* / 各有各的爱好，没什么～。*Everyone has his or her own hobby. It's only natural.* ❷ feel surprised; wonder：他们都～你为什么要辞职。*They feel surprised at your resignation.* / 我～他怎么不来。*I wonder why he didn't come.*
【奇观】marvellous spectacle; wonder：自然界的～ *a marvellous natural phenomenon* / 世界七大～ *the seven wonders of the world*
【奇花异卉】(又作'奇葩异草') exotic flowers and rare herbs
【奇幻】fantastic; visionary：～的遐想 *fantastic reveries* / ～的景色 *visionary, kaleidoscopic scenes*
【奇货可居】a rare commodity worth hoarding
【奇迹】miracle; wonder; marvel：医学上的～ *a marvel of medical science*
【奇景】wonderful view; extraordinary sight：冰峰～ *a wonderful view of ice-capped peaks*
【奇妙】marvellous; wonderful; intriguing
【奇谋】a very clever strategy; an ingenius plan
【奇葩】exotic flowers：～斗妍 *exotic flowers vying for glamour* / 文苑～ *exotic flowers in the garden of literature—unusual literary works*
【奇缺】in great shortage
【奇人】❶ an eccentric person; eccentric ❷ a person of unusual ability
【奇事】a strange affair; an unusual phenomenon
【奇书】a remarkable book
【奇谈】a strange tale; an absurd argument：海外～ *strange tales from over the seas* ◇ ～怪论 a strange tale; an absurd argument
【奇特】peculiar; queer; singular：在沙漠地区常常可以看到一些～的景象。*In desert areas one often sees strange mirages.*
【奇文】❶ a remarkable piece of writing ❷ absurd writing
【奇文共赏】share the pleasure of reading a rare piece of writing
【奇闻】sth. unheard-of; a thrilling, fantastic story
【奇袭】surprise attack; raid
【奇效】extraordinary efficacy (of medicine)
【奇形怪状】grotesque or fantastic in shape or appearance：～的钟乳石 *stalactites of grotesque shapes*
【奇异】❶ unusual; strange; bizarre：～的动物 *rare animals* ❷ surprised; amazed; astonished; astounded：他们都用～的眼光看着我。*They all looked at me with astounded eyes.*
【奇遇】❶ happy encounter; fortuitous meeting ❷ adventure
【奇缘】relationship entered into unexpectedly; romance
【奇珍】a rarity or curio ◇ ～异宝 rare treasures
【奇志】high aspirations; lofty ideal
【奇装异服】exotic costume; bizarre dress; outlandish (grotesque) clothes; strange fashions; fancy clothes

歧 Ⅰ 名 fork; branch：歧路 Ⅱ 形 divergent; different：歧义
【歧出】(of the use of words, esp. technical terms in a book, etc.) conflicting and confusing; inconsistent
【歧管】[机] manifold
【歧黄】Chinese medicine ◇ ～之术 Chinese traditional medical science
【歧路】branch road; forked road ◇ ～亡羊 a lamb going astray at a fork in the road—go astray in a complex situation
【歧视】discriminate against：种族～ *racial discrimination* / ～妇女 *discriminate against women*
【歧途】wrong road：被引入～ *be led astray*
【歧义】being capable of various interpretations; ambiguity：有～ *be open to different interpretations; be equivocal* / 写文章要避免产生～。*One should try to avoid ambiguity in one's writing.*

颀 形〈书〉tall
【颀长】〈书〉tall：身材～ *tall in build*

脐 名 ❶ navel; umbilicus ❷ the abdomen of a crab
【脐带】umbilical cord
【脐风】[中] umbilical tetanus

畦 名 rectangular pieces of land in a field, separated by ridges, usu. for growing vegetables：我们种了两～萝卜。*We've grown two beds of radishes.*
【畦灌】[农] border method of irrigation
【畦田】an embanked field

崎 (构词成分) 见下
【崎岖】rugged：山路～不平。*The mountain path is rugged and uneven.* / 学习的道路是～不平的。*The road of learning is not smooth.*

骑 Ⅰ 动 ride (an animal or bicycle, etc.); sit on the back of：～马 *ride a horse; be on horseback* / ～车回家 *go home by bicycle* / 善～ *excel in horsemanship; be a good rider* / 这摩托车你～得怎么样？*How do you get on with the motorcycle?* Ⅱ 名 ❶ horse or horse rider：坐骑 ❷ cavalryman; cavalry：铁骑
【骑兵】cavalryman; cavalry ◇ ～部队 mounted troops; cavalry unit
【骑缝】a junction of the edges of two sheets of paper：在单据的～上盖印 *put a seal across the perforation between the two halves of a voucher*
【骑虎难下】he who rides a tiger is afraid to dismount—irrevocably but unwillingly committed;

unable to extricate oneself from a difficult situation

【骑虎之势】a case of one riding a tiger—an awkward predicament that one can neither manage nor get rid of

【骑警】horseback police

【骑马订】[刷] saddle stitching

【骑马找马】❶ sit on one horse and look for another—hold on to one job while seeking another ❷ sit on the very horse one is looking for—look for sth. that's right under one's nose

【骑墙】sit on the fence：～派 *fence-sitter*

【骑射】horsemanship and archery：善～ *excel in horsemanship and archery*

【骑士】knight；cavalier ◇ ～风度 knightly manner

【骑手】a good rider；horseman

【骑术】horsemanship；equestrian skill

棋 名 chess or any board game：下一盘～ *play a game of chess*

【棋布】scattered all over like men on a chessboard；spread all over the place

【棋锋】brilliance shown in playing chess：～犀利 *be a brilliant chess player*

【棋逢对手】(又作'棋逢敌手') meet one's match in a game of chess—be well-matched in a contest：～难相胜，将遇良才不敢骄。*When a general meets a worthy opponent, he won't dare to underestimate him.*

【棋高一着】be superior to one's opponent (in chess or otherwise)；outmatch one's opponent

【棋局】❶ a game of chess as it develops ❷〈旧〉chessboard

【棋路】chess tactics：～高明 *brilliant chess tactics*

【棋迷】chess fan；chess enthusiast

【棋盘】chessboard；checkerboard

【棋谱】chess manual

【棋圣】champion chess player；grand master

【棋手】chess player

【棋坛】chess circles

【棋艺】skill in playing chess：～精湛 *be a chess expert*

【棋友】fellow chess player；chess friend

【棋苑】chess circles

【棋峙】〈书〉be locked in a stalemate；each sticks to his own stand

【棋子】piece (in a board game)；chessman

蛴 (构词成分) 见下

【蛴螬】grub

旗 名 flag；banner；standard：旗杆上挂着一面～。*A flag is attached to the pole.*

【旗杆】flagpole；flag post

【旗鼓相当】be matched in strength；be well-matched：这两个队～，打得十分激烈。*The two teams were well-matched and the game was hotly contested.* / ～的对手 *an opponent worthy of one's steel*

【旗号】〈贬〉banner；flag：打着…的～ *flaunt the banner of...*

【旗舰】flagship

【旗开得胜】win victory the moment one's standard is raised；win victory in the first battle；win speedy success：我军在南进中～，声威大震。*In its southward drive our army won victory as soon as its banner was displayed and thus gained resounding fame.*

【旗袍】a close-fitting woman's dress with high neck and slit skirt；cheongsam；mandarin gown

【旗绳】halyard

【旗手】standard-bearer

【旗鱼】sailfish

【旗语】semaphore；flag signal：打～ *signal by semaphore；semaphore*

【旗帜】❶ banner；flag：五彩缤纷的～迎风飘扬。*Colourful flags are fluttering in the breeze.* ❷ stand；colours

【旗帜鲜明】have a clear-cut stand：我们必须坚持真理，而真理必须～。*We must firmly uphold the truth, and truth requires a clear-cut stand.*

【旗子】flag；banner；pennant

鳍 名 fin

【鳍脚】clasper ◇ ～动物 Pinnipedia；pinniped

麒 (构词成分) 见下

【麒麟】kylin；(Chinese) unicorn

【麒麟座】[天] Monoceros

qǐ

乞 动 beg (for alms, etc.)；supplicate：行乞

【乞哀告怜】beg for mercy；piteously beg for help

【乞丐】beggar

【乞力马扎罗山】Kilimanjaro

【乞怜】beg for pity (or mercy)

【乞灵】〈书〉resort to；seek help from

【乞盟】sue for peace

【乞免】beg for forgiveness：～一死 *beg for one's life*

【乞求】beg for；supplicate；implore：～宽恕 *beg for mercy (or pardon)* / ～的目光 *an imploring look* / 她～他饶了自己的儿子。*She implored him to spare her son.*

【乞食】beg for food

【乞讨】beg；go begging：沿街～ *go begging from door to door*

【乞降】beg to surrender

【乞援】ask for assistance；beg for aid

岂 副〈书〉(used to ask a rhetorical question)：这样做～不更实际些？*Wouldn't it be more practical to do it this way?* / 一国的内政～容别国干涉？*How can a country tolerate external interference in its internal affairs?*

【岂但】not only：这个僻字～我们不认识，恐怕连老教授们也未必知道。*Not only we don't know this obsolete character, even the old professors may* not know it.

【岂非】(used to ask a rhetorical question)：这样解释～自相矛盾？*Wouldn't it be self-contradictory to put it that way?*

【岂敢】〈套〉You flatter me；I don't deserve such praise or honour.

【岂能】(又作'岂可')(used to ask a rhetorical question)：～不辞而别？*How could you leave without saying good-bye?* / ～容许这种行为？*How could such behaviour be tolerated?*

【岂有此理】preposterous；outrageous；absurd：这个破录音机要那么多钱，真是～。*This lousy tape-recorder is outrageously expensive.*

【岂止】同〖岂但〗

企 动 ❶ stand on tiptoe ❷ anxiously expect sth.；look forward to

【企待】expect；await；look forward to

【企鹅】penguin

【企及】hope to reach；hope to attain

【企口】[建] tongue-and-groove：～接合 *tongue-and-groove joint*；*T and G connection* ◇～板[建] matched board

【企慕】admire；look up to

【企盼】hope for；look forward to；long for

【企求】desire to gain；seek for；hanker after：他一心只想把工作做好，从不～个人名利。*All he wanted was to do his job well；he never sought personal gain.*

【企图】attempt；try；seek：敌军～突围，但未得逞。*The enemy failed in his attempt to effect a break-through.* / ～掩盖事实 *try to conceal the facts* / ～推翻政府 *seek to overthrow the government* / 在这部作品中，作者～表现的主题并不突出。*The theme which the author has intended to bring forth in the book does not stand out.* / 别有～ *have an ulterior motive*

【企望】hope for；look forward to：我们都～有一个持久的和平。*We all hope for an enduring peace.* / 这是我们多年所～的。*This is what we have been looking forward to for years.*

【企羡】admire；look up to

【企业】enterprise；business：工矿～ *factories, mines and other enterprises* ◇～法人 legal entity；～管理 business management；～化 run an enterprise on a commercial basis；～集团 enterprise group；～家 entrepreneur；big businessman；～结构 the line-up of enterprises；～文化 enterprise culture；～形象 enterprise image；～自主权 the power of decision of enterprises

【企足而待】同〖翘足而待〗

启 动 ❶ open：～门 *open a door* / 幕～。*The curtain rises.* / 某某～ *to be opened by so-and-so；to so-and-so (written on an envelope of a personal letter)* ❷ start；initiate：启行 ❸ enlighten；awaken：启发 ❹〈书〉state；inform：某某～ *by so-and-so (closing words of a letter)*

【启程】set out；start on a journey：代表团已于昨日～赴日内瓦。*The delegation left for Geneva yesterday.*

【启齿】(又作'启唇'；'启口') open one's mouth；start to talk about sth.：我想问他借钱，但又觉得难以～。*I wanted to borrow money from him but found it difficult to bring the matter up.*

【启迪】〈书〉enlighten；inspire：我从这个残疾人取得的成就中得到～。*The achievement of the disabled person was an inspiration to me.*

【启动】❶ start (a machine, etc.)；switch on：这车没法儿～。*The car won't start.* ❷[计] boot up：他示范给我看如何进入和～操作系统。*He showed me how to log in and boot up the operating system.* ◇～区[计] boot sector；～资金[经] kick-off fund；start-up fund；seed money

【启发】arouse；inspire；enlighten：他常用这种方式～我们思考问题。*He often inspires us to ponder over questions this way.* / 要用～的方式讲课。*You should teach with the elicitation method.* / 我从他的工作方法中得到～。*I derived inspiration from his working method.*

【启发式】elicitation method (of teaching)；heuristic method

【启封】❶ unseal；break (or remove) the seal ❷ open an envelop or wrapper

【启航】set sail；weigh anchor：这艘货轮什么时候～？*When does the freighter set sail?*

【启蒙】❶ impart rudimentary knowledge to beginners；initiate：～老师 *the teacher who introduces one to a certain field of study* / ～课本 *children's primer* / 我做古诗是他启的蒙。*He was the teacher who introduced me to classical poetic composition.* ❷ enlighten；free sb. from prejudice or superstition

【启蒙运动】the Enlightenment

【启明星】literary name for 金星

【启示】enlightenment；inspiration；revelation：从他的经验中得到很多～ *gain a good deal of enlightenment from his experience；draw great inspiration from his experience* / 爱因斯坦的故事给了我很大的～。*The story of Einstein is a great inspiration to me.*

【启事】notice；announcement：招领～ *Found* / 征稿～ *a notice inviting contributions (to a magazine, newspaper, etc.)* / 寻物～ *Lost*

【启衅】start a quarrel；provoke discord；provoke dispute：两次世界大战都是德国军国主义者首先～的。*Both of the World Wars were instigated by a militarist Germany.*

【启行】set off on a journey

【启颜】(of a person's face) light up；smile；beam

【启用】start using (an official seal, etc.)

【启运】start shipment (of goods)

杞 名 the name of an ancient kingdom

【杞柳】purple willow；bitter willow (Salix sinopurpurea)

【杞人忧天】like the man of Qi who feared that the sky might fall—entertain imaginary or groundless fears：这岂不是～吗？*Isn't this a case of the man of Qi worrying lest the sky fall?* / 事情未必如他所说的那么可怕，也许完全是～。*Things may not be as bad as he says. Maybe he is merely imagining things.*

起 Ⅰ 动 ❶ rise；get up；stand up：～席 *rise from the table* / 早睡早～ *early to bed and early to rise* ❷ remove；extract；pull：～油 *remove grease stains* / ～瓶塞 *pull the cork from a bottle* / ～钉子 *draw out a nail* / ～雷 *clear mines* / 把画～下来 *take down a picture* ❸ appear；raise：脚上～水泡 *get blisters on one's feet* ❹ rise；grow：～风了。*The wind is rising.* / ～疑心 *become suspicious* / ～作用 *take effect* ❺ draft；work out：～稿子 *work out* (*or make*) *a draft* ❻ build；set up：～一堵墙 *build a wall* / ～伙 *set up a mess* ❼ start；begin：从今天～ *starting from today* ❽ draw；get：～护照 *get one's passport* ❾ (used after a verb preceded by 从 or 由)：从头讲～ *tell the story from the very beginning* / 从何说～？*What shall I say?* or *What's there to say?* ❿ upwards；up：她拿～皮包就走了。*She picked up her handbag and left.* / 我提不～这个重箱子。*I can't lift this heavy suitcase.* / 拿～武器 *take up arms* ⓫ (preceded by 得 or 不) up to a certain standard：买得(不)～ *can* (*can't*) *afford to buy* / 看得(不)～ *have a high* (*low*) *opinion of* Ⅱ 量 ❶ case；instance：两～大脑炎 *two cases of cerebritis* ❷ batch；group：分两～出发 *set out in two groups* (*or batches*)

【起岸】bring (cargo, etc. from a ship) to land

【起爆】detonate：准时～ *detonate on time* / ～帽 *detonating cap* / ～剂 *detonating agent*；*primer*

【起笔】❶ the first stroke of a Chinese character ❷ start a stroke in writing a Chinese character：～的时候要顿一顿。*One should pause when starting a stroke* (*of a Chinese character*).

【起兵】dispatch troops

【起驳】start shipment by lighter

【起步】start；move：这项研究尚属刚刚～阶段。*This research programme is still in its beginning stages.* / 沿海开放城市如何起好步？*How will the open coastal cities get a good start?*

【起步不公】unfair start

【起草】make a draft；draft；draw up：～文件 *draft* (*or draw up*) *a document* / ～人 *draftsman* / 这封信你来起个草吧。*Please make a draft copy of the letter.* ◇ ～委员会 drafting committee

【起承转合】introduction, elucidation of the theme, transition to another viewpoint, and summing up—the four steps in composing an essay

【起程】leave；set out；start on a journey：日内～前往广州 *leave for Guangzhou in a day or two*

【起初】originally；at first；at the outset：～我不同意他的做法，后来才觉得他是有道理的。*At first I didn't agree with his way of doing things, but later I realized that he was right.* / 这个工厂～很小。*The factory was originally very small.*

【起床】get up；get out of bed：他们已经～了。*They are already up.* / 我习惯六点～。*I am in the habit of getting up at six o'clock.* / 起了床还想睡。*After I got up I still felt like going back to sleep.*

【起床号】reveille：吹～ *sound the reveille*

【起道机】［铁路］track jack

【起点】❶ starting point：把成绩作为继续前进的新～ *take achievements as starting points for further progress* ❷ starting point (for a race) ◇ ～运费 minimum freight；minimum charge per bill of lading

【起电】electrification；charge：～盘 *electrophorus*

【起吊】lift by crane

【起钉钳】nail puller

【起动】(of a train, machine, etc.) start：我们到达车站时，火车正好～。*We arrived at the station just as the train was leaving.*

【起动机】starter

【起端】origin or beginning (of an event, etc.)

【起飞】❶ (of aircraft) take off：～全重 *all-up weight* ❷［经］takeoff：经济～ *economic takeoff* / 沿海城市的经济迅速～。*The economies of the coastal cities got off to a flying start.*

【起伏】rise and fall；undulate：凝望远处山峦～ *gaze at the mountain ranges rising and falling in the distance* / 微风中麦浪～ *a field of wheat undulating in the breeze* / 心潮～ *one's mind being in a tumult*

【起稿】make a draft；draft；draw up：报告是他起的稿。*He's the one who drafted the report.*

【起航】set sail；weigh anchor

【起哄】❶ (of a crowd of people) create a disturbance：起什么哄啊！都排好队一个个来。*What's all the disturbance about! Everyone line up and take turns.* ❷ (of a crowd of people) jeer；boo and hoot；tease clamorously

【起火】❶ catch fire；be on fire：房子～啦！*The house is on fire!* ❷ cook meals：他不愿意自己～，在食堂吃。*He doesn't want to do his own cooking. So he takes his meals in the cafeteria.*

【起货】take goods (from a warehouse)；unload (from a ship, etc.)

【起获】track down and recover stolen goods, etc.

【起急】〈方〉get impatient；lose one's patience：和老人说话不能～。*You shouldn't lose your patience when talking to old people.*

【起家】build up；grow and thrive；make one's fortune, name, etc.：这个大工厂是靠一台旧机床起的家。*The big factory has built itself up by starting with an old machine tool.*

【起见】(used in the pattern 为…起见 indicating purpose)：为醒目～，请排黑体字。*In order to make it stand out clearly, please print it in boldface type.*

【起降】(of aircraft) take off and land

【起劲】vigorous; energetic; enthusiastic: 干得很～ *work very energetically* / 孩子们～地学骑车。*The children enthusiastically learned to ride a bicycle.*

【起敬】show respect

【起居】daily life: ～有恒有助于身体健康。*To lead a regular life is conducive to good health.* / 孩子在托儿所饮食～都有规律。*Life in a nursery provides children with a strict daily regimen.* ◇～室 living room; sitting room

【起圈】remove manure from a pigsty, sheepfold, etc.

【起来】❶ stand up; sit up; rise to one's feet: 你～吃药吧。*Sit up and take your medicine.* / 有个小伙子～给老太太让了个座儿。*A youngster stood up and offered his seat to the old lady.* ❷ get up; get out of bed: 他们一～就下地了。*They went to work in the fields as soon as they got up.* ❸ rise; arise; revolt: ～反抗压迫 *rise against oppression* / ～捍卫真理 *come forward in defence of truth* ❹ upwards; up: 拿～ *pick up* / 他把孩子抱～。*He took the child up in his arms.* / 举起手来! *Hands up!* ❺ start to; become: 那回的事情! 你一提～我就生气。*Every time you (start to) mention that incident I get angry.* / 他这句话使我们大笑～。*This remark of his set us roaring with laughter.* ❻ (indicating completeness or effectiveness): 加～ *add up* / 锁～ *lock up* / 存～ *store away* / 合唱团组织～了。*The chorus has been organized.* ❼ when one comes to: 看～要下雨。*It looks like rain.* / 看～是不会有什么问题的。*By the look of it there won't be any problems.* / 听～颇有道理。*It sounds quite reasonable.* ❽ (forming a verbal topic): 说～容易,做～难。*It's easier said than done.*

【起立】stand up; rise to one's feet: ～欢迎 *rise to welcome sb.* / 全体～! *Everybody stands up!* ◇～表决 vote by sitting and standing

【起垄】[农] ridge: ～犁 *ridging plough*; *ridger*

【起落】rise and fall: 飞机～ *the takeoff and landing of an aircraft* / 心潮～ *one's mind being in a tumult*

【起落架】landing gear (of a plane); undercarriage: ～放下 *gear down*; *landing gear lowering* / ～收上 *gear up*; *landing gear raising*

【起码】❶ minimum; rudimentary; elementary: ～的要求 *minimum requirements* / ～的知识 *rudimentary knowledge*; *elementary knowledge* ❷ at least: 这项工程～要到五月才能完成。*This project can't be completed until May at the earliest.* / 参加测验的～有三千人。*At least 3,000 people took the test.*

【起毛】(of woollen cloth) pill: 海军呢爱～。*Navy cloth pills easily.*

【起锚】weigh anchor; set sail

【起名】give a name; name: 他们还没给孩子～呢。*They haven't given their baby a name yet.*

【起腻】〈口〉❶ feel sick: 我看见肥肉就～。*I feel sick whenever I see fat meat.* / 他的长篇大论真叫人～。*He bored everyone with his lengthy speech.* ❷ pester; annoy: 你少跟我～。*Stop pestering me with your silly questions.* / 这孩子老爱跟人～。*What a little torment that child is!*

【起跑】[体] start of a race: ～线 *starting line* (*for a race*); scratch line (for a relay race) / ～信号 *starting signal* / 在跑道上练～ *practise starts on a running track*

【起讫】the beginning and the end: 本书每篇各有头尾,自成～。*Each chapter is complete in itself, having beginning and end.* / 展览会的～日期为五月一日到二十日。*The exhibition lasts from May Ist to 20th.*

【起色】improvement; pickup: 她工作最近很有～。*Recently there's been a great improvement in her work.* / 经济情况有了很大的～。*The economy has picked up greatly.*

【起身】❶ get up; get out of bed: 他每天～后就做操。*He exercises everyday after getting up.* ❷ leave; set out; get off: 我将于下周～去重庆。*I'll leave for Chongqing next week.*

【起始】〈口〉❶ originate; stem from: 她喜欢花～于童年乡居期间。*Her interest in flowers stems from her childhood in the country.* ❷ at first; in the beginning: ～我不喜欢他,但很快改变了看法。*At first I didn't like him, but I soon changed my mind.*

【起事】start armed struggle; rise in rebellion

【起誓】take an oath; swear: 他～决不泄漏秘密。*He swore that he would not divulge the secret.*

【起首】at first; in the beginning; originally: ～我不会下棋。*I didn't know how to play chess at first.*

【起死回生】(of a doctor's skill) bring the dying back to life; snatch a patient from the jaws of death; raise sb. from the dead

【起诉】bring a suit (or an action) against sb.; sue; prosecute ◇～人 suitor; prosecutor; ～书 indictment; bill of complaint; bill of prosecution; ～意见书 opinion recommending prosecution; ～资格 standing to sue

【起算】reckon from (a stated point): 从现在～ *reckon from the present*

【起跳】[体] take off: ～板 *take-off board* / ～线 *take-off line* (*or mark*)

【起头】❶ start; originate: 这件事是谁起的头? *Who started all this?* / 我想织毛衣,可不会～。*I want to knit a sweater, but I don't know how to begin.* ❷ at first; in the beginning: ～她答应来的,后来有别的事不能来了。*At first she promised to come but then had another engagement and couldn't make it.* ❸ beginning: 我没听清楚,你从～儿再说一遍。*I didn't get what you said. Say it all over again from the beginning.*

【起网】[渔] (net) hauling: ～机 *net hauler*

【起息】[经] carry interest: ～日 *value date*; *date*

of value

【起先】at first; in the beginning: ～他反对,后来才同意了。*At first he was opposed to the idea, but later he came around.*

【起心】〈贬〉cherish certain intentions: ～不良 *cherish evil designs (or intentions)*

【起薪】probationary salary

【起行】leave; set out; start on a journey: 我即将～。*I am leaving soon.*

【起眼】(usu. used in the negative) attract attention

【起夜】get up in the night (to urinate): 少喝点水,免得～。*Don't drink so much, or you'll have to get up during the night.*

【起疑】become suspicious: 他的行动令人～。*His activities aroused my suspicion.*

【起义】rise in revolt; revolt: 农民～ *a peasant uprising* / 敌军纷纷～投诚。*Many enemy soldiers revolted and crossed over.*

【起义军】insurrectionary army

【起意】〈贬〉conceive a design

【起因】cause; origin: 事故的～ *the cause of the accident*

【起用】❶ reinstate (an official who has retired or been dismissed) ❷ call sb. to office; appoint sb. to an important position: 大胆～年轻干部 *boldly place young cadres in important positions*

【起源】❶ originate; stem from: 一切知识均～于劳动。*All knowledge originates from labour.* ❷ origin: 生命的～ *the origin of life*

【起运】start shipment: 货物业已～。*The goods are on their way.* / ～地点 *starting place for shipping; place of dispatch*

【起赃】track down and recover stolen goods

【起早贪黑】(又作'起早搭黑') start work early and knock off late; work from dawn to dusk

【起重车】derrick car

【起重船】crane ship

【起重机】hoist; crane; derrick: ～的起重能力 *the lifting (or hoisting) capacity of a crane* / 龙门～ *gantry crane* / 塔式～ *tower crane* / 门式～ *portal crane* / 移动式转臂～ *mobile jib crane*

【起皱】wrinkle; crease; crumple: 多晒太阳皮肤就会干燥～。*Too much sun dries the skin and it begins to wrinkle.* / 这种料子不～。*This material won't crease (or is crease-resistant).* / 这种合成纤维折叠以后也不～。*This synthetic fabric won't crumple when folded.* ◇ ～工艺 [纺] creping

【起子】❶ bottle opener ❷〈方〉baking powder ❸〈方〉screwdriver

绮 Ⅰ 名 figured woven silk material; damask Ⅱ 形 beautiful; gorgeous: 绮丽

【绮丽】beautiful; gorgeous: 春天的西湖显得格外～。*In spring the West Lake looks especially enchanting.* / 生活在她面前放出～的光彩。*Life was beckoning her with its fascinating beauty.*

qì

气 Ⅰ 名 ❶ gas: 沼气 ❷ air: 这球～儿挺足。*There's sufficient air in the ball.* / 自行车前带没～了。*The front tyre of the bike is flat.* ❸ breath: 停下来歇口～ *stop and catch one's breath* / 老太太已经没～了。*The old woman has stopped breathing.* / 长跑运动员需要～儿长。*Long-distance runners require plenty of stamina.* ❹ smell; odour: 香气 ❺ weather: 天气 ❻ airs; manner: 官气 ❼ spirit; morale: 朝气 ❽ bully; insult: 受气 Ⅱ 动 ❶ get angry; be enraged; be annoyed: ～得直哆嗦 *tremble with rage* / ～哭了 *be annoyed to tears* / ～坏了 *be beside oneself with rage* / ～出一场病来 *have an attack of illness caused by anger* ❷ make angry; enrage; annoy: 我故意～他一下。*I got him angry on purpose.* or *I was deliberately trying to annoy him.*

【气昂昂】full of mettle; full of dash

【气包子】〈口〉a person who has a quick temper or is quick to take offence

【气泵】air pump

【气不打一处来】be filled with anger: 一看见他那流里流气的样子,我就～。*As soon as I saw him, with his cocky manner and sleazy ways, I was just filled with anger and disgust.*

【气不过】cannot restrain one's anger; be beside oneself with rage: 我实在～,狠狠地说了他一顿。*I got mad and gave him a good talking-to.*

【气不平】(又作'气不公') be indignant over an injustice

【气藏】[油] gas pool

【气冲冲】furious; beside oneself with rage

【气冲牛斗】anger shooting up to the skies—in a towering rage; furious

【气冲霄汉】dauntless; fearless

【气喘】asthma: 阵发性～ *spasmodic asthma*

【气窗】transom (window); fanlight

【气粗】❶ rough; rude; boorish ❷ speak in a gruff voice

【气促】gasp for breath; be out of breath

【气垫】air cushion

【气垫车】hovercar

【气垫船】hovercraft

【气顶】petroleum gas cap: ～驱动 *gas-cap drive*

【气动】pneumatic: ～工具 *pneumatic tool*

【气度】❶ bearing; manner: 相貌威武,～不凡 *be extraordinarily dignified and impressive in appearance* / 他下棋的时候,镇定从容,很有～。*When he plays chess, he is calm and collected. He really has presence.* ❷ tolerance; magnanimity

【气短】❶ short of breath; panting: 快爬到山顶时,大家都感到～。*By the time we got near the top of the hill, we were all out of breath.* ❷ discouraged; disheartened: 失败并没有使他～。*He was not discouraged by failure.*

【气氛】surrounding feeling; atmosphere: 会谈是在亲切友好的～中进行的。*The talks were held in a cordial and friendly atmosphere.*

【气愤】indignant; furious: 对于这种蛮横态度,大家无不感到～。*Everybody was indignant at such an overbearing manner.* / 他听了这种不三不四的话非常～。*On hearing these frivolous remarks he became furious.*

【气腹】[医] ❶ pneumoperitoneum ❷〈略〉见〖人工气腹〗

【气概】lofty quality; mettle; spirit: 不畏强暴敢于斗争的英雄～ *the heroic spirit of daring to struggle against brute force*

【气缸】air cylinder; cylinder: ～套筒 *cylinder sleeve*

【气割】[机] gas cutting

【气根】(又作'气生根') [植] aerial root

【气功】qigong, a system of deep breathing exercises: ～师 *qigong master*

【气鼓鼓】fuming with anger; foaming with rage; furious

【气臌】[中] distension of the abdomen caused by accumulation of gas due to dysfunction of the spleen or to emotional factors

【气管】windpipe; trachea ◇ ～切开术 tracheotomy; ～炎 tracheitis

【气贯长虹】filled with a spirit as lofty as the rainbow spanning the sky; full of noble aspiration and daring

【气焊】gas welding

【气候】❶ climate: 他离开了重庆,因为～不适应。*He left Chongqing because the climate did not agree with him.* ❷ situation; climate: 政治～ *political climate* ◇ ～带 climate zone; ～图 climate chart; ～学 climatology; ～志 climatography

【气呼呼】in a huff; panting with rage: ～地离去 *go off in a huff*

【气化】gasify

【气话】words said in a fit of rage: 他说的是～。*He just said it to vent his anger.*

【气急】gasp for breath; be out of breath

【气急败坏】flustered and exasperated; utterly discomfited: 他～地跑回来把发生的事情告诉我们。*He ran back, panting and dismayed, to tell us what had happened.*

【气节】integrity; moral courage: 革命者坚贞不屈的～ *the unyielding integrity of a revolutionary*

【气结】〈书〉depressed; melancholy; gloomy

【气井】[油] gas well

【气绝】stop breathing—die: 登时～身亡 *die immediately*

【气厥】faint away; lose consciousness

【气可鼓而不可泄】Morale should be boosted, not dampened.

【气孔】❶ [植] stoma ❷ [动] spiracle ❸ [冶] gas hole ❹ [建] air hole

【气浪】blast (of an explosion)

【气冷】[机] air cooling: ～式发动机 *air-cooled engine*

【气力】effort; energy; strength: 学习外语要用很大的～才能学好。*It takes a lot of effort to learn a foreign language well.* / 我们得费很大～去完成这项工作。*We'll have to exert great efforts to accomplish the task.* / 他用出全身～向对手猛扑过去。*He pounced on the adversary with all his strength.* / 他不费什么～就办成了这事。*He got it done easily.* / 这事需要花费～。*This will take a lot of doing.*

【气量】tolerance; forbearance: ～大 *broad-minded; large-minded; magnanimous* / ～小 *narrow-minded* / ～大的人对这点小事是不会介意的。*Broad-minded people won't bother about such trifles.*

【气流】❶ air current; airflow; airstream ❷ [语音] breath ◇ ～纺纱 open-end spinning; jet spinning; ～干扰 interference in airflow; ～畸变 flow distortion

【气楼】a small ventilation tower on the top of a roof

【气轮机】〈略〉见〖燃气轮机〗

【气煤】gas coal

【气门】❶ (air) valve of a tyre ❷ [动] spiracle; stigma

【气门心】〈口〉❶ valve inside ❷ valve rubber tube

【气闷】❶ unhappy; worried; in low spirits ❷ feel suffocated (or oppressed)

【气密】airtight; gastight; gasproof ◇ ～接合 airtight joint; ～试验 air seal test (for an aircraft); leakage test

【气囊】❶ (of birds) air sac ❷ gasbag (of an aerostat)

【气恼】get angry; take offence; be ruffled: 我如果考试不及格,妈妈要～的。*Mother will get angry if I don't pass the exam.* / 她的话真叫我～。*Her words really offended me.*

【气馁】become dejected; be discouraged; lose heart: 他多次遇到挫折,但从不～。*He never lost heart despite repeated setbacks.*

【气逆】[中] circulation of vital energy in the wrong direction

【气派】imposing manner; dignified air: 那大会堂修建得好～。*That meeting hall is really imposing.* / 一家门面～的商店 *a store that has an imposing facade* / 他是个很有～的人。*He has an impressive bearing.*

【气泡】air bubble; bubble

【气喷】[油] gas blowout

【气魄】❶ boldness of vision; breadth of spirit; daring: 他办事很有～。*He's very bold and decisive in doing things.* ❷ imposing manner: 这首诗歌颂了黄河的伟大～。*This poem praises the grandeur of the Yellow River.*

【气枪】air gun; pneumatic gun

【气球】balloon: 彩色～ *coloured balloon*

【气圈】❶ [纺] balloon ❷ [气] aerosphere

【气色】complexion; colour: ～很好 *have a rosy complexion; have a good colour* / 她～不好,脸上

没什么血色。*She's very pale; there isn't much colour in her face.* / 他休养了一段时间，～好多了。*After taking time off to recuperate, he looks much healthier.*

【气盛】❶ overbearing; arrogant; aggressive ❷ (of writing) forceful; vigorous

【气势】momentum; imposing manner: ～雄伟的长城 *the imposing Great Wall* / 排球队以不可阻挡的～，直落三局击败对手。*The volleyball team overwhelmed their opponent in three straight games.* / 他动不动就对别人横加指责，～逼人。*He's always making unwarranted accusations against others. His manner is intolerably aggressive.*

【气势磅礴】of great momentum; powerful:《黄河大合唱》～。*The Yellow River Cantata is full of power and grandeur.* / 民族解放运动的洪流～，奔腾向前。*The tide of the national liberation movement is surging forward with great momentum.*

【气势汹汹】fierce; truculent; overbearing: 看起来～，实际上十分虚弱 *fierce in appearance but feeble in reality*

【气数】destiny; fate: ～已尽（*of a dynasty or regime*）*be nearing its fated end*

【气死人】driving one crazy; infuriating; exasperating: 这种事是气得死人的。*That sort of thing can be very exasperating.*

【气态】❶［物］gaseous state ❷〈书〉manner; bearing; air

【气体】gas ◇ ～打火机 gas lighter; ～动力学 aerodynamics; ～发生器 gas generator / ～分离器 gas separator; ～力学 pneumatics; ～燃料 gaseous fuel

【气田】gas field

【气筒】inflator; bicycle pump

【气头上】in a fit of anger; in a temper: 这是他～说的话，你不要在意。*He said that in a fit of anger. Don't take it to heart.* / 他正在～，谁的话都听不进去。*He's in a temper right now, and won't listen to anyone.*

【气团】［气］air mass: 冷～ *cold air mass* / ～变性 *air-mass modification*

【气吞山河】imbued with a spirit that conquers mountains and rivers; full of daring

【气味】❶ smell; odour; flavour: 有些花～浓郁。*Some flowers have strong fragrances.* / ～难闻。*The smell is awful.* ❷〈贬〉smack; taste: 这人满身的市侩～。*This man has the look of a sordid merchant written all over him.* / 有沙文主义～ *smack of chauvinism*

【气味相投】congenial to each other; be two of a kind

【气温】air temperature; atmospheric temperature

【气息】❶ breath ❷ flavour; smell: 一阵芬芳的～从花丛中吹过来。*A waft of sweet-smelling fragrance blew over from the flower bush.* / 这个剧具有强烈的生活～。*The play has the rich flavour of life (or is imbued with a strong smack of everyday life).* / 时代～ *the flavour of the times*

【气息奄奄】be breathing feebly; be at one's last gasp; be at the point of death; be sinking fast: 老人病了半年，现在已经是～了。*The old man has been ill for half a year and is about to breathe his last.*

【气象】❶ meteorological phenomena: ～观测 *meteorological observation* ❷ meteorology ❸ atmosphere; scene: 生气勃勃的新～ *a new and dynamic atmosphere* / 商店里很热闹，已经有过年的～了。*The shops are very lively. They already have a New Year atmosphere.* ◇ ～观测船 weather observation ship; ～观测站 weather observation station; ～火箭 meteorological rocket; ～台 meteorological observatory; ～图 meteorological map; ～卫星 meteorological satellite; weather satellite; ～学 meteorology; ～预报 weather forecast; ～员 weatherman

【气象万千】a scene majestic in all its variety: 远望群山，～。*Far in the distance mountains rise range after range in all their majesty.*

【气性】❶ temperament; disposition ❷ bad temper: ～大 *quick to take offence; hot-tempered*

【气汹汹】fuming with anger; foaming with rage; furious

【气胸】［医］pneumothorax

【气吁吁】（又作'气咻咻'）panting; gasping for breath: 他慢跑了一公里，～地直出汗。*After jogging a kilometre he was panting and sweating.* / 他冲进屋去，～地报告了这消息。*He dashed into the room and gasped out the message.*

【气虚】［中］deficiency of vital energy

【气旋】［气］cyclone

【气血辨证】［中］analysing and differentiating the pathological condition according to the function of vital energy and the state of the blood

【气压】atmospheric pressure; barometric pressure ◇ ～表 barometer; ～沉箱［建］pneumatic caisson

【气眼】❶［建］air hole ❷［冶］gas hole

【气焰】〈贬〉arrogance; bluster: ～万丈 *be swollen with arrogance* ◇ ～嚣张 be puffed up with pride

【气宇轩昂】have an impressive bearing: 身材高大，～ *tall and imposing-looking* / 此人～，不同流俗。*His dignified bearing marks him out from the common run of men.*

【气郁】［中］obstruction of the circulation of vital energy

【气韵】the spirit, character, tone, or style (in the broadest sense) of a work of art or literature: "～生动"论是中国艺术理论的基础。*The concept of "spirit-resonance life-movement" is the cornerstone of Chinese art theory.*

【气闸】air (or pneumatic) brake

【气质】❶ temperament; disposition ❷ qualities; makings: 他英勇无畏，表现了革命者的～。*He is brave and fearless. He has the makings of a revo-*

lutionary.
【气滞】[中] stagnation of the circulation of vital energy
【气肿疽】[牧] blackleg; black quarter
【气壮如牛】fierce as a bull: 表面上～,实际上胆小如鼠 *outwardly fierce as a bull, but inwardly timid as a mouse*
【气壮山河】full of power and grandeur; magnificent: 一篇～的宣言 *a magnificent manifesto*

讫 动 ❶ settled; completed: 收讫 ❷ end: 起讫

迄 Ⅰ 介 up to; till: 迄今 Ⅱ 副 (used before 未 or 无) so far; all along: ～无音信。*We have received no information so far.* / ～未见复。*Up to now we have received no reply.*
【迄今】up to now; to this day; to date; so far: 他的态度～并无明显的转变。*There has been no visible change in his attitude so far.* / 事情～还没作出决定。*To date, the matter hasn't yet been decided.*

汽 名 vapour; steam: 蒸汽
【汽车】automobile; motor vehicle; car: ～保险 *automobile insurance* / ～旅店 *motor hotel; motel* ◇ ～安全带 shoulder belt; ～吊 truck crane; ～队 motor transport corps; fleet of cars or trucks; ～工业 auto industry; ～库 garage; ～拉力赛 motor rally; ～旅馆 motel; ～制造厂 automobile factory; motor works
【汽船】steamship; steamer
【汽锤】steam hammer: 龙门～ *arch type steam hammer*
【汽灯】gas lamp
【汽笛】steam whistle; siren; hooter: 鸣～ *sound a siren*
【汽缸】[机] cylinder: ～组 *cylinder block*
【汽锅】Yunnan steaming pot: ～鸡 *steamed chicken, Yunnan style*
【汽化】vaporize: ～热 *heat of vaporization*
【汽化器】❶ [机] carburettor: ～回火 *backfiring in carburettor* / ～主射口 *carburettor main jet* ❷ [化] vaporizer
【汽机】❶ another name for 蒸气机 ❷〈略〉见〖汽轮机〗
【汽酒】light sparkling wine
【汽轮发电机】turbogenerator: 双水内冷～ *turbogenerator with inner water-cooled stator and rotor*
【汽轮机】steam turbine
【汽碾】(又作'汽碾子') [机] steamroller
【汽水】aerated water; soft drink; soda water
【汽提】petroleum strip: ～油 *stripped oil* / ～塔 *stripping tower*
【汽艇】motorboat
【汽油】petrol; gasoline; gas: 航空～ *aviation gasoline* / 凝固～ *napalm*

弃 动 throw away; discard; abandon: 敌军～城而逃。*The enemy abandoned the city and fled.*
【弃暗投明】forsake darkness for light—leave the reactionary side and cross over to the side of progress
【弃官】give up one's office; abandon official life
【弃甲曳兵】(of routed troops) throw away armour and trail weapons: ～而走 *flee pell-mell*
【弃旧图新】turn over a new leaf: 我们对待在工作中犯过错误的人采取规劝态度,使之翻然改进,～。*Our attitude towards any person who has made mistakes in his work should be one of persuasion in order to help him change and start afresh.*
【弃农经商】give up farm production and engage in trading; leave farm work behind to engage in trade
【弃权】❶ abstain from voting: 八票赞成,三票反对,一票～ *8 votes for, 3 against, and 1 abstention* ❷ [体] waive the right (to play); forfeit
【弃世】pass away; die
【弃婴】❶ abandon a baby ❷ foundling
【弃之可惜】hesitate to discard sth.; be unwilling to throw away ——另见〖食之无味,弃之可惜〗
【弃之如敝屣】cast away like a pair of worn-out shoes
【弃置】discard; throw aside: 这所老房子早就～不用了。*This old house was abandoned long ago.*

泣 Ⅰ 动 weep; sob: 哭泣 Ⅱ 名 tears: 饮泣
【泣不成声】choke with sobs: 说到伤心处,她～。*When she got to the saddest part of the story, her voice was choked with sobs.*
【泣诉】accuse while weeping; accuse amid tears: 她～了这些年来所受的苦。*She tearfully recounted the suffering she'd undergone in the past few years.*
【泣下如雨】shed tears like rain; weep copious tears

契 Ⅰ 名 contract; deed: 房契 Ⅱ 动 agree; get along well: 默契
【契合】agree with; tally with; correspond to: 与进化论相～ *agree with the theory of evolution*
【契机】❶ [哲] moment ❷ turning point; juncture: 当代青年思想变化的～ *a turning point in the thinking of present-day youth*
【契据】deed; contract; receipt
【契友】close friend; bosom friend
【契约】contract; deed; charter
【契纸】contract; deed

砌 动 build by laying bricks or stones: ～砖 *lay bricks* / ～墙 *build a wall (with bricks, stones, etc.)* / ～井壁 *build shaft lining*

跂 动〈书〉stand on tiptoe
【跂望】〈书〉stand on tiptoe to look forward to sb. or sth.

葺 动〈书〉❶ cover a roof with straw; thatch ❷ repair; mend: 修葺

器 Ⅰ 名 ❶ implement; utensil; ware: 电器 ❷

organ：生殖器 ❸ capacity；talent Ⅱ 动 think highly of (a person)：器重

【器材】equipment；material：照相～ *photographic equipment* / 线路～ *line materials*

【器官】organ；apparatus：消化～ *digestive organs* / 呼吸～ *respiratory apparatus*

【器官移植】transplant organ；organ transplant

【器件】parts of an apparatus or appliance：电子～ *electronic device*

【器具】utensil；implement；appliance：日用～ *household utensils*；*articles of daily use*

【器量】tolerance：～小 *narrow-minded*；*petty*

【器皿】household utensils；containers esp. for use in the house

【器物】implements；utensils

【器械】❶ apparatus；appliance；instrument：体育～ *sports apparatus* / 光学～ *optical instrument* ❷ weapon ◇ ～体操 gymnastics on or with apparatus

【器宇】〈书〉bearing；deportment：～不凡 *have extraordinary poise* ◇ ～轩昂 have a dignified appearance

【器乐】[音] instrumental music：～曲 *composition for an instrument*

【器质性】organic：～精神病 *organic psychosis* / ～耳聋 *organic deafness*

【器重】think highly of (one's juniors or subordinates)；regard highly：他工作能力强，上级很～他。*He is a capable worker，and his superiors think highly of him*.

憩 动〈书〉have a rest；rest：小憩

【憩息】(又作'憩歇')〈书〉have a rest；rest：我们～片刻，继续前进。*We went on after a short rest*.

qiā

掐 动 ❶ pinch；nip：你把玉米杈子～掉。*Pinch off the side shoots of the maize*. / 不要～花。*Don't pick (or nip off) the flowers*. / 请把烟卷～了。*Stub out your cigarette，please*. / 她～了我一把，好疼。*She pinched me，and it really hurt*. ❷ clutch：把人～死 *choke sb. to death*

【掐断】nip off；cut off：～电线 *disconnect the wire* / ～水源 *cut off the water supply*

【掐尖儿】❶ [农] topping；pinching：地里的西红柿该～了。*The tomato plants need topping now*. ❷ oust sb. from office：你别太突出了，小心别人掐你的尖儿。*Don't try to outshine others. They can oust you from office，mind you*. ❸ scrounge；squeeze

【掐诀】calculate on one's fingers (while chanting incantations)

【掐丝】[工美] wire inlay；filigree：景泰蓝花瓶上的～ *wire inlay on a cloisonné vase*

【掐算】count (or reckon) sth. on one's fingers：他细心～第一列火车即将通过的时刻。*He carefully figured out what time the first train would pass by*.

【掐头去尾】break off both ends；leave out the beginning and the end：这把芹菜～剩下不多了。*With both ends chopped off，there's not much left of this bunch of celery*. / 引用他这段话不能～。*If you quote a passage from him，you should quote it in full，not leave out the beginning and the end*.

【掐腰】(of a dress) have a waistline：这连衣裙是～的。*The dress has a waistline*.

qiǎ

卡 Ⅰ 动 wedge；get stuck：有东西～在抽屉里，拿不出来。*Something has got wedged inside the drawer，so I can't pull it out*. / 鱼刺～在他的嗓子里。*A fish bone sticks in his throat*. Ⅱ 名 ❶ clip；fastener：发卡 ❷ checkpost：关卡 ——另见 kǎ

【卡脖子】❶ seize sb. by the throat；grip sb.'s throat：他正要叫喊，那歹徒猛扑过来，卡住他的脖子。*He was about to call out when that ruffian dashed at him and gripped his throat*. ❷ have in a stranglehold；subdue：用经济制裁来卡别国的脖子 *apply economic sanctions against another country in an attempt to force it into submission*

【卡具】[机] clamping apparatus；fixture

【卡壳】❶ (of cartridge or shell case) jam ❷ get stuck；be held up；have a temporary stoppage：双方意见分歧，会谈卡了壳。*With both sides having differences of opinion，the discussions came to a halt*.

【卡口灯泡】bayonet-socket bulb

【卡口灯头】bayonet socket

【卡盘】[机] chuck

【卡子】❶ clip；fastener：头发～ *hairpin* ❷ checkpost

【卡钻】[油] jamming of a drilling tool；sticking of a tool

qià

洽 动 ❶ be in harmony；agree：意见不～ *have different opinions*；*not see eye to eye* ❷ consult；arrange with：接洽

【洽购】arrange or negotiate a purchase

【洽商】make arrangements with；talk over with：这事要和他们～。*You will have to talk this over with them*. / 旅游团成员在一起～日程。*The members of the tour group were arranging the itinerary together*.

【洽谈】consult；discuss together：双方～了贸易事宜。*Both sides held trade talks*. / 一些引进项目，正在～之中。*Several programmes for importation are under discussion*.

【洽谈会】talk；symposium：国际经济技术～ *inter-*

national economic and technical symposium / 贸易～ *trade talk*

【洽妥】have made an arrangement

恰 Ⅰ副 just; exactly: ～合时宜 *just appropriate to the occasion* / 左边锋疾射入网，～在此时鸣笛终场。*The outside-left sent the ball into the net with a fast shot just before the whistle blew for full time*. Ⅱ形 appropriate; proper: 恰当

【恰当】proper; suitable; fitting; appropriate: 这篇文章里，有的地方用词不～。*Words were used inappropriately in some parts of this essay*. / 这件事处理得很～。*This matter was taken care of properly*.

【恰到好处】just right (for the purpose or occasion)

【恰好】just right: 您穿的尺码的鞋我们～有。*We have just the size of shoes you wear*. / 我们赶到电影院，售票处～还有两张票。*We got to the cinema just in time to buy the last two tickets left at the box office*.

【恰恰】just; exactly; precisely: 这～是我想说的话。*That's exactly what I wanted to say*. / 把事情搞糟的不是别人，～就是你自己。*It was you, rather than anybody else, who made a mess of things*.

【恰恰舞】cha-cha(dance)

【恰巧】by chance; fortunately or unfortunately: 她正愁着怎么拿行李，～来了个搬运工人。*She was worrying about how to carry her baggage when a porter came*. / 路上～碰上大雨，淋得我浑身湿透。*Unfortunately I was caught in a heavy rain and got drenched from head to foot*.

【恰如】just like: 晚霞～一幅图画。*The evening glow is just like a painting*.

【恰如其分】apt; appropriate; just right: ～的评价 *an apt appraisal* / 给予～的批评 *give a balanced criticism* / 对成绩和缺点作～的估计 *make an appropriate estimate of the achievements and shortcomings*

【恰似】just like

髂 (构词成分) 见下

【髂骨】ilium

qiān

千 数 ❶ thousand ❷ a great amount of; a great number of: ～百条建议 *lots and lots of suggestions* / ～百年来的梦想 *an age-old dream*

【千儿八百】〈口〉a thousand or slightly less: 那东西相当贵，没个～是买不回来的。*It's quite expensive. You can't buy it for less than a thousand*.

【千变万化】ever-changing: 国际形势错综复杂，～。*The international situation is complex and changeable*. / 他躺在草地上望着天上～的云彩出神。*As he lay in the grass looking up at the sky, he was transfixed by the ever-changing cloud formations*.

【千不该万不该】really should not have (done sth.): ～，不该让他独自一人去游泳。*We really shouldn't have let him go to swim by himself*.

【千部一腔，千人一面】all of the same tone, all with the same feature—(usu. of literary compositions) stereotyped

【千层饼】multi-layer steamed bread

【千层底】layers of cloth firmly stitched together for soles of cloth shoes

【千差万别】differ in thousands of ways: 各地气候～。*Climate varies from place to place*. / 世界上～的事物 *the immense variety of things in the world*

【千疮百孔】同〖百孔千疮〗

【千锤百炼】❶ thoroughly tempered (or steeled); finely honed: 在艰苦环境中工作，经过～，他意志越来越坚强了。*Toughened by working under difficult conditions, his will-power became stronger*. ❷ (of literary works) be polished again and again; be revised and rewritten many times; be a finished product

【千刀万剐】(usu. used in a curse) be hacked to pieces; be made mincemeat of

【千电子伏】kiloelectron-volt (KeV)

【千恩万谢】express a thousand thanks; be eternally indebted

【千乏】［电］kilovar (KVAR)

【千方百计】in a thousand and one ways; by every possible (or conceivable) means; by hook or by crook: ～挖掘潜力 *try every possible way to tap potential* / ～掩盖错误 *use all one's ingenuity to cover up one's mistakes* / 他～地请好大夫给妻子看病。*He is doing all he can to find good doctors to treat his wife*.

【千分表】dial gauge; dial indicator

【千分尺】micrometer

【千夫】〈书〉numerous people

【千夫所指，无病而死】when a thousand people point accusing fingers at a man he will die even though not ill—it is dangerous to incur public wrath

【千伏】［电］kilovolt (Kv.): ～安 *kilovolt-ampere (KVA)*

【千古】❶ through the ages; eternity; for all time: ～遗恨 *eternal regret* ❷ (used in an elegiac couplet or on wreaths dedicated to the dead): 某某先生～！*Eternal repose to Mr. So-and-so!*

【千古奇闻】(也作'千古奇谈') a fantastic tale

【千古罪人】one who stands condemned through the ages

【千赫】kilohertz

【千呼万唤】a thousand calls; a thousand entreaties

【千回百转】full of twists and turns: 崎岖的山路～ *a rugged mountain path, twisting and turning; a tortuous mountain path*

【千家万户】innumerable households or families; every family: 物价问题关系到～。*Commodity prices affect the livelihood of every family*.

【千娇百媚】(of a woman) bewitchingly charming

【千斤】❶ a thousand jin—very heavy; weighty: ～重担 *an exceptionally heavy load* (*or responsibility*) ❷〈略〉见〖千斤顶〗❸[机] pawl

【千斤顶】hoisting jack; jack

【千金】❶ a thousand pieces of gold; a lot of money: ～难买 *not to be had even for* 1,000 *pieces of gold*; *not to be bought with money* ❷〈尊〉daughter (other than one's own)

【千军万马】thousands upon thousands of men and horses—a powerful army; a mighty force

【千军易得,一将难求】simpler by far to raise a thousand troops than find a single general to lead them

【千钧一发】a hundredweight hanging by a hair—in imminent peril: 在这～、万分危急的时候,援军到了。*In this moment of extreme crisis when everything was hanging by a single thread, the relief troops arrived.*

【千钧重负】a grave responsibility

【千卡】[物] kilocalorie (Kcal.)

【千克】kilogram (kg.)

【千里】a thousand li—a long distance or a vast expanse

【千里光】[植] climbing groundsel (Senecio scandens)

【千里驹】thousand-li colt—a son who is showing great promise

【千里马】a horse that covers a thousand li a day; a winged steed

【千里送鹅毛】a goose feather sent from a thousand li away (or from afar): ～,礼轻情意重。*The gift itself may be light as a goose feather; but sent from afar, it conveys deep feeling.*

【千里迢迢】from a thousand li away; from afar; (come) all the way from: 我们热烈欢迎～从海外专程前来参加纪念活动的各位先生。*We warmly welcome all those who made a special trip, travelling all the way across the seas to join us in the commemoration ceremonies.*

【千里眼】❶ farsighted person ❷〈旧〉telescope; field glasses

【千里姻缘一线牵】Two beings destined to marry each other, though a thousand li apart, are tied together as if by a thread; People a thousand li apart may be linked by marriage.

【千里之堤,溃于蚁穴】one ant-hole may cause the collapse of a thousand-li dyke—slight negligence may lead to great disaster

【千里之行,始于足下】A thousand-li journey is started by taking the first step.

【千虑一得】❶ 见〖愚者千虑,必有一得〗❷〈谦〉My observations may contain a grain of truth.

【千虑一失】见〖智者千虑,必有一失〗

【千枚岩】[地质] phyllite

【千米】kilometre (km.)

【千难万险】innumerable hazards and hardships: 纵有～,也挡不住英雄的登山队员。*Even myriad hardships and hazards can't stop the dauntless mountaineers.*

【千年虫】[计] millennium bug; Y2K (problem)

【千篇一律】stereotyped; following the same pattern: ～的论调 *stereotyped views* / 那些文章～,没有什么新东西。*Those articles repeat each other; they contain nothing new.*

【千奇百怪】all kinds of strange things; an infinite variety of fantastic phenomena: 七星岩里的石头～。*There are all kinds of strange stone formations in the Seven-star Cave.*

【千千万万】thousands upon thousands

【千秋】❶ a thousand years; centuries ❷〈尊〉birthday (other than one's own)

【千秋万代】throughout the ages; generation after generation; forever

【千日红】[植] globe amaranth

【千山万水】同〖万水千山〗

【千丝万缕】countless ties; a thousand and one links: 这两个国家的文化有着～的联系。*There are countless cultural ties between these two countries.*

【千头万绪】thousands of strands and loose ends; a multitude of things: 工作～,要理出个轻重缓急来。*With thousands of tasks on our hands, we should arrange them in order of priority.* / 心里～,不知从何说起。*There are so many thoughts welling up in my mind that I really don't know where to start.*

【千瓦】[电] kilowatt (KW): ～小时 *kilowatt-hour* (*KWh*)

【千万】❶ ten million; millions upon millions ❷ be sure to; must: 到达后～来信。*Be sure to write us when you get there.* / ～要小心啊! *Do be careful!* / 这事儿～不可掉以轻心。*We must under no circumstances take this lightly.*

【千辛万苦】innumerable trials and tribulations; untold hardships: 历尽～ *go through innumerable* (*or untold*) *hardships*

【千言万语】thousands and thousands of words: 她心里有～,可一句也说不出来。*Her heart was filled with unspoken words but she failed to utter a single one.* / ～也说不尽我感激之情。*No words can express my gratitude to you.*

【千载难逢】not occurring once in a thousand years; very rare: ～的机会 *a golden opportunity; the chance of a lifetime*

【千载一时】a chance that comes once in a thousand years—the chance of a lifetime; a rare opportunity: 这是～的好机会,不能错过。*This is the chance of a lifetime. Don't miss it.*

【千真万确】absolutely true

【千周】kilocycle (KC)

【千字节】[计] kilobyte (KB)

仟

数 thousand (used for the numeral 千 on cheques, etc. to avoid mistakes or alterations)

阡

名〈书〉a footpath between fields, running north and south

【阡陌】crisscross footpaths between fields: ～纵

横。*The paths crisscrossed in the fields.* / ～交通 *footpaths connecting with each other*

扦 名 a short slender pointed piece of metal, bamboo, etc.

【扦插】[农] make a cuttage

【扦子】❶ a slender pointed piece of metal, bamboo, etc. ❷ a sharp-pointed metal tube used to extract samples of grains, etc. from sacks

迁 动 ❶ move：这个工厂已～到内地。*The factory has moved to the interior.* ❷ change：变迁

【迁都】move the capital to another place：明成祖～北京。*Emperor Cheng Zu of the Ming Dynasty moved the capital to Beijing.*

【迁飞】(of birds) migrate：～途径 *flyway*

【迁户口】report to the local authorities for change of domicile; change one's residence registration

【迁就】accommodate oneself to; yield to：～姑息 *excessively accommodating; overlenient* / 他太～孩子了，要什么就给买什么。*He gives in to the child too much. Whatever she wants, he buys for her.* / 在小事情上互相～着点儿 *give in a little to each other over small matters*

【迁居】change one's dwelling place; move (house)：他已～到成都。*He has moved to Chengdu.* / 从城里～郊区的人越来越多。*The movement of people from the cities to the suburbs is on the increase.*

【迁离】move to another place

【迁流】〈书〉(of time) flow past：岁月～。*Time flows past.*

【迁怒】vent one's anger on sb. who's not to blame; take it out on sb.：你碰到不顺心的事也不该～于人啊。*If things haven't been going your way lately, you shouldn't take it out on others.*

【迁徙】move; migrate; change one's residence：人口～ *population migration* / 燕子秋天往南方～。*Swallows migrate south in autumn.*

【迁延】delay; defer; procrastinate：～时日 *cause a long delay; become long-drawn-out*

【迁移】move; remove; migrate：从城市～到农村 *move from urban to rural areas*

【迁移性】[动] animal migration

【迁葬】move a grave to another place

钎 名 drill rod; drill steel; borer

【钎子】hammer drill (for making holes in rock); rock drill

牵 动 ❶ lead along (by holding the hand, the halter, etc.); pull：～牛下地 *lead an ox to the fields* / 手～手 *hand in hand* ❷ involve：他不愿意～在这里头。*He didn't want to get involved in it.*

【牵鼻子】lead by the nose：你自己应该有个主意，不能叫别人牵着鼻子走。*You should make your own decisions, and not let others lead you by the nose.*

【牵缠】involve sb. or get sb. entangled

【牵肠挂肚】feel deep anxiety; be very worried; be on tenterhooks：好长时间收不到他的信，叫人～的。*I haven't heard from him for ages, so I'm getting extremely anxious.*

【牵扯】involve; implicate; drag in：这事～很多人。*A number of people have become involved in the matter.*

【牵掣】❶ hold up; impede：互相～ *hold each other up* / 抓主要问题，不要被枝节问题～住。*Let's focus our attention on the main problem and not get bogged down in minor issues.* ❷ 同〖牵制〗

【牵动】affect; influence：～全局 *affect the situation as a whole* / ～整个作战计划 *affect the overall operational plan*

【牵挂】worry; care：好好工作，不要～家中老小。*Do your work well and don't worry about us folks at home.* / 我家里都安顿好了，没有什么～了。*I've got everything settled at home; I'm free of worries now.*

【牵合】make a match; act as go-between

【牵就】同〖迁就〗

【牵累】❶ tie down：受家务～ *be tied down by household chores* ❷ implicate; involve (in trouble)：他怕这事说出来会～家庭，所以隐瞒了。*He was afraid that if he mentioned the matter it would implicate his family, so he kept it secret.*

【牵连】❶ involve (in trouble); implicate：清查同这次破坏活动有～的人和事 *investigate the individuals and incidents connected with the sabotage* / 这个案件～了很多人。*Many people were implicated in this case.* ❷ tie up with; integrate with

【牵牛花】(white-edged) morning glory

【牵牛星】the Herd-boy star—Altair

【牵强】forced (interpretation, etc.); farfetched：这些理由都很～。*These reasons are farfetched.*

【牵强附会】draw a forced analogy; make a farfetched (or irrelevant) comparison; give a strained interpretation：你这样解释这篇文章太～了。*Your interpretation of this essay is much too forced.*

【牵切纺】[纺] tow-to-yarn direct spinning

【牵涉】involve; drag in：这项决定～很多部门。*This decision involves many departments.* / 他的发言既然～到我，我就想讲几句。*Since he has dragged me into his speech, I'd like to say a few words.*

【牵伸】[纺] draft; drawing

【牵头】take the lead; lead off; be the first to do sth.：这件事得几个单位商量着办，谁来～？*Several units must discuss how to handle this matter. Who will lead off?* / 我只是牵个头，事情是大伙儿办的。*I took the lead, but the work was done by everyone.*

【牵头】❶ act as a go-between ❷ go-between

【牵系】link; join; connect

【牵线】❶ manipulate or control (from behind the scenes) ❷〈口〉act as a go-between：他们俩谈恋爱是我牵的线。*I acted as a go-between for them to meet and fall in love.* ◇ ～搭桥 act as a go-between；～人 wire-puller；go-between

【牵一发而动全身】pull one hair and you move the whole body—a slight move in one part may affect the whole situation

【牵引】❶ tow；draw：这条线上的列车都由电力机车～。*The trains on this line are all drawn by electric locomotives*. ❷［医］traction：～器 *tractor* ◇ ～车 tractor；tractor truck；～犁 trailed plough；～力［物］traction force；traction；pulling force；～能量 haulage capacity（of a locomotive，etc.）；～炮 towed artillery；～式滑翔机 towed glider

【牵制】（usu. used with reference to military operations）pin down；tie up；check；contain：～敌人 *pin down the enemy* / 这对敌人是一种～。*This is a kind of check on the enemy*. / ～行动 *containing action* / ～性攻击 *diversionary attack*

悭

（构词成分）见下

【悭吝】stingy；miserly：～人 *miser*；*niggard*；*skinflint*

铅

名 ❶［化］lead（Pb）❷ lead（in a pencil）；black lead

【铅白】［化］white lead

【铅版】［刷］stereotype

【铅笔】pencil ◇ ～刀 a small knife for sharpening pencils；pen-knife；～盒 pencil-case；～画 pencil drawing；～心 lead（in a pencil）；black lead

【铅玻璃】lead glass

【铅垂线】［建］plumb line

【铅锤】［建］plummet；plumb（bob）

【铅丹】［化］red lead；minium

【铅刀一割】a leaden knife can cut—a mediocre person can be put to some use

【铅粉】同〖铅白〗

【铅封】lead sealing

【铅黄】lead and yellow—collation（so called from the use in former times of lead and yellow ochre for making corrections in editing）

【铅球】［体］shot：推～ *shot put*；*putting the shot* / ～运动员 *shot-putter*

【铅丝】❶ galvanized wire ❷［电］lead wire

【铅条】❶［体］slug；lead ❷ lead（for a propelling pencil）

【铅印】letterpress（or relief，typographic）printing；stereotype

【铅直】vertical；plumb

【铅中毒】lead poisoning；saturnism

【铅坠】plummet

【铅字】type；letter：大号～ *large type* / ～面 *typeface* / ～盘 *type case*；*letter board* ◇ ～合金 type metal

谦

形 modest

【谦卑】humble；modest

【谦诚】modest and sincere

【谦辞】self-depreciatory expression；humble words

【谦恭】modest and courteous

【谦和】modest and amiable

【谦谦君子】a modest gentleman

【谦让】modestly decline：您来主持这个讨论最合适，不要～了。*You're just the person to chair the discussion. Don't decline out of modesty*. / 客人们互相～了一下，然后落了座。*The guests politely offered their seats to each other before finally settling down in them*.

【谦慎】modest and prudent

【谦顺】modest and deferential

【谦虚】❶ modest；self-effacing：别～了，我们知道你是这方面的行家。*Don't be so modest. We know you're an expert in this field*. ❷ make modest remarks：他～了一番，终于答应来做一次演讲。*After making a few modest remarks he finally agreed to come and give a talk*.

【谦虚谨慎】modest and prudent：保持～、不骄不躁的作风 *remain modest，prudent and free from arrogance and rashness in one's style of work*

【谦逊】modest；unassuming：他知识丰富，但总是保持～的态度。*He's a man of great knowledge，but he always maintains an attitude of modesty*.

签

Ⅰ 动 ❶ sign；autograph：～支票 *sign a cheque* ❷ make brief comments on a document：看完请～个意见。*After you've read it，please write down a few brief comments*. ❸（of sewing）tack：把袖口～上 *tack on a cuff* Ⅱ 名 ❶ bamboo slips used for divination or drawing lots：抽签 ❷ label；sticker：标签 ❸ a slender pointed piece of bamboo or wood：牙签

【签呈】a brief document submitted to a superior；memorial

【签到】register one's attendance at a meeting or at an office；sign in：我们一到办公室就得～。*We have to sign in when we arrive at the office*. / ～簿 *attendance book* / ～处 *sign-in desk*

【签订】conclude and sign（a treaty，etc.）：～条约 *sign a treaty* / ～合同 *sign a contract* / ～协定的各方 *the parties signatory to the agreement*

【签发】sign and issue（a document，certificate，etc.）：这种通行证由国防部负责～。*The Defense Department is responsible for the signing and issuing of this type of travel permit*.

【签名】sign one's name；autograph：她请这个电影明星在本子上签了个名。*She asked the movie star to sign his autograph in her notebook*. / ～盖章 *sign and affix one's seal*；*set one's hand and seal to* / 亲笔～的照片 *an autographed picture* / 来宾～簿 *visitors' book*

【签名运动】signature drive

【签收】sign after receiving sth.：挂号信须由收件人～。*A receipt for a registered letter is to be signed by the recipient*. or *A registered letter must be signed for by the recipient*. / 他不在，我代他～这些文件。*He's not here. I'll sign for these documents on his behalf*.

【签署】sign：联合公报是由双方代表团团长～的。*The joint communiqué is signed by the heads of both delegations*. / ～意见 *write comments and sign one's name* (*on a document*)

【签筒】❶ a tube-like holder of lot-sticks ❷ a sharp-pointed metal tube used to extract samples of grains, etc. from sacks

【签押】put one's signature or seal on an official document

【签约】sign a contract

【签证】❶ visa; visé: 入(出)境～ *entry* (*exit*) *visa* / 过境～ *transit visa* / 一次有效出入境～ *entry-exit visa valid for a single journey* / 多次往返有效的出入境～ *multiple entry-exit visa* / 团体～ *group visa* / 互免～ *mutual exemption of visas* ❷ grant a visa: ～机关 *visa office*

【签注】❶ attach a slip of paper to a document with comments on it; write comments on a document (for a superior to consider) ❷ write comments or points for attention on a certificate, book of tables, etc.

【签字】sign; affix one's signature: 本条约在～后立即生效。*This treaty shall come into force upon signature.* / 请作者在扉页上～ *ask the author to autograph the title page* / ～国 *signatory state* (*or power*); *signatory* / ～仪式 *signing ceremony*

【签子】〈口〉❶ bamboo slips used for divination or drawing lots ❷ a slender pointed piece of bamboo or wood

qián

前 Ⅰ名 ❶ front: ～院 *front courtyard* / 楼～ *in front of the building* / 将军胸～戴着所有的勋章。*The general was wearing all his medals on his chest.* ❷ forward; ahead: 朝～走 *go straight ahead* / 往～看 *look forward* ❸ ago; before: 这个故事发生在五百年～。*The story took place* 500 *years ago.* / 晚饭～ *before supper* ❹ first: 这次比赛的～三名 *the first three places in this competition* / ～五排 *the first five rows* Ⅱ形 ❶ preceding: ～一阶段 *the preceding stage* / ～资本主义 *precapitalism* ❷ former; formerly: ～校长 *former principal* (*of a school*) ❸ future: 前程

【前半场】同〖上半场〗

【前半晌】〈方〉before noon; morning

【前半生】(又作'前半辈子') the first half of one's life

【前半天】before noon; morning

【前半夜】the first half of the night (from nightfall to midnight)

【前辈】senior (person); elder; the older generation: 他们都是我的～。*They are all my seniors.* / 革命～ *revolutionaries of the older generation* / 在书法方面,你是我们的～。*You are our venerable senior in calligraphy.*

【前臂】forearm

【前边】同〖前面〗

【前不见古人,后不见来者】I look back—I do not see the ancients; I look ahead—can't see the generations to come

【前不着村,后不着店】with no village ahead and no inn behind—be stranded in an uninhabited area

【前叉】front fork (of a bicycle)

【前车之覆,后车之鉴】the overturned cart ahead is a warning to the ones behind

【前车之鉴】warning taken from the overturned cart ahead; lessons drawn from others' mistakes: 他们试验失败对我们是个～。*The failure of their experiment should be a warning to us.*

【前程】❶ future; prospect: 你的孩子又聪明又用功,一定～远大。*Your son is smart and diligent; he definitely has a bright future before him.* ❷ 〈旧〉a desired career or a high rank (sought after by an intellectual or official) ◇ ～似锦 splendid prospects; a glorious future; ～万里 bright prospects

【前池】[水] forebay

【前仇】old hatred; old grievance

【前导】❶ lead the way; march in front; precede ❷ a person who leads the way; guide: 以仪仗队为～ *with the guard of honour marching at the head*

【前敌】front line: 身临～ *come personally to the front* ◇ ～委员会 front committee; ～总指挥 frontline commander-in-chief

【前度刘郎】the young Master Liu of those days—a person who revisits a place

【前额】forehead

【前方】❶ ahead: 注视着～ *look* (*or gaze*) *ahead* / 大副发现船的左～有鲸鱼群。*The first mate sighted a herd of whales ahead to the left of the boat.* ❷ the front: 开赴～ *be dispatched to the front*

【前锋】❶ vanguard: 部队～已到达目的地。*The vanguard units have reached the destination.* ❷ [体] forward ❸[气] front: 冷空气的～已进入我省。*The cold front has reached this province.*

【前夫】❶ former husband (either divorced or dead); ex-husband ❷ late husband

【前赴后继】advance wave upon wave

【前儿个】(又作'前儿')〈口〉the day before yesterday

【前功尽弃】all that has been achieved is spoiled; all one's previous efforts are wasted: 成功的希望不大,还可能～。*There is small chance of success, and you risk all you have gained.*

【前滚翻】[体] forward roll

【前后】❶around (a certain time); about: 天亮～ *shortly before and after daybreak* / 1949 年～ *round* 1949 / 春节～ *around the Spring Festival* ❷ from beginning to end (in time): 从动工到完成,这项工程～只用了十个月。*The entire project, from beginning to end, took only ten months.* ❸ in front and behind: 房子～都有树。*There are trees both in front and at the back of the house.* / ～次序不要颠倒。*Don't get the order mixed up.* ❹ people or things of the same kind in succession：～三种版本 *three consecutive editions* / 你的～几封信都已收到。*I've received all your letters*.

【前…后…】❶（indicating one thing behind another, or one action after another）：前街后巷 *front street and back lane* / 前思后想 *think over again and again* ❷（indicating backward and forward movements）：前俯后仰 *bend forwards and backwards*

【前后夹击】make a simultaneous frontal and rear attack；attack from the front and the rear simultaneously

【前后脚儿】〈口〉almost simultaneously；one close behind another：他们俩～到的。*They arrived at almost the same time*.

【前呼后拥】with attendants crowding round

【前胡】［中］the root of purple-flowered peucedanum（Peucedanum decursivum）

【前脚】❶ the forward foot in a step：我～一滑，身体站不稳，就摔了。*As soon as my front foot slipped, I lost my balance and fell over*. ❷（used together with 后脚）no sooner...than；the moment（when）：你～走，他后脚就来了。*He arrived the moment you had left*.

【前进】advance；go forward；forge ahead：我们不能停留在现有的成绩上，要继续～。*We can't rest on our laurels；we must forge ahead*. / 生产飞跃～。*Production increases by leaps and bounds*.

【前景】❶ foreground（of a view, picture, photo, etc.）❷ prospect；vista；perspective：他的发现为利用当地资源开辟了广阔的～。*His discovery opened up a vast range of prospects for making use of local resources*.

【前臼齿】premolar teeth

【前倨后恭】first supercilious and then deferential；change from arrogance to humility

【前科】record of previous crime：这个罪犯是有～的。*This offender has a criminal record*.

【前空翻】［体］forward somersault in the air

【前来】come：今天他举行婚礼，许多同事～贺喜。*Today is his wedding day and many of his colleagues came to congratulate him*.

【前例】precedent：这样处理有～可援，不算咱们独创。*This is not a creation of ours. There are precedents to be cited*.

【前列】front row（or rank）；forefront；van：主席台～ *the front row on the rostrum* / 年轻力壮的小伙子们站在与洪水搏斗的最～。*The able-bodied young men were at the forefront in the fight against the flood*.

【前列腺】prostate（gland）◇～肥大 hypertrophy of the prostate；prostatomegaly；～素 prostaglandin；～炎 prostatitis

【前掠翼】buzzard-type wing（of a plane）

【前轮】front wheel（of a vehicle）；nosewheel（of a plane）

【前门】front door；front gate

【前门拒虎，后门进狼】drive the tiger from the front door and let a wolf in at the back—fend off one danger only to fall a prey to another

【前面】❶ in front；at the head；ahead：在房子～ *in front of the house* / ～有座位。*There're seats in the front rows*. / 走在队伍～ *march at the head of the column* ❷ above；preceding：～提到的原则 *the above-mentioned principle* / ～的一章 *the preceding chapter*

【前脑】forebrain

【前年】the year before last

【前怕狼，后怕虎】（又作'前怕龙，后怕虎'）fear wolves ahead and tigers behind—be full of fears：我们如果～。就什么事情也做不成。*We'll never get anywhere if we are plagued by all sorts of fears*.

【前排】front row：～座位 *front-row seats* / 在～就座 *be seated in the front rows*

【前炮】forward gun（on a ship）；bow-piece

【前仆后继】no sooner has one fallen than another steps into the breach：无数革命先烈为了共产主义事业～，英勇地献出了生命。*Countless revolutionary martyrs, one stepping into the breach as another fell, have fought and laid down their lives for the cause of communism*.

【前妻】❶ former wife（either divorced or dead）；ex-wife ❷ late wife（dead）

【前期】earlier stage；early days

【前前后后】❶ the whole story；the ins and outs：一件事情的～ *the ins and outs of a matter* ❷ from beginning to end（in time）：这次旅游～共一个月。*The tour took a whole month's time*.

【前桥】front axle（of a car）：～壳 *front axle housing*

【前情】❶ antecedent；cause ❷ old friendship；former affection

【前驱】forerunner；precursor；pioneer

【前驱期】［医］prodromal stage

【前人】forefathers；predecessors：～总结的经验 *experience summed up by our predecessors*

【前人栽树，后人乘凉】one generation plants the trees in whose shade another generation rests—profiting by the labour of one's forefathers；sweating for the benefit of future generations

【前任】predecessor：～书记 *former secretary* / 他的～ *his predecessor* / ～总统 *ex-president* / ～首相 *the former prime minister*

【前日】the day before yesterday

【前晌】〈方〉before noon；morning

【前哨】outpost；advance guard：与敌～接触 *skirmish with the enemy's advance guards*

【前哨战】［军］skirmish

【前身】predecessor：八路军的～是工农红军。*The Eighth Route Army grew out of the Workers' and Peasants' Red Army*.

【前生】（又作'前世'）previous incarnation；previous existence：他这是～注定的。*This was decided in his previous incarnation*.

【前事不忘，后事之师】past experience, if not forgotten, is a guide for the future；lessons learned from the past can guide one in the future

【前视图】［机］front view
【前束】toe-in (of a car)
【前思后想】think over again and again
【前所未闻】never heard of before：～的奇迹 *an unheard-of miracle* / 这样的怪事真是～。*I've never heard of such a strange thing before.*
【前所未有】never existed before；hitherto unknown；unprecedented：～的盛况 *an unprecedentedly grand occasion* / 遇到～的困难 *encounter greater difficulties than ever*
【前台】❶ proscenium ❷〈喻〉on the stage：有人在～表演，有人在幕后指挥。*Some appeared on the stage, while others pulled strings behind the scenes.*
【前提】❶［逻］premise：大（小）～ *major (minor) premise* ❷ prerequisite；presupposition：必要的～ *essential prerequisite* / 矛盾的一方各以其另一方为自己存在的～。*Each aspect of a contradiction presupposes the existence of the other aspect.*
【前天】the day before yesterday：～晚上 *the night before last*
【前厅】antechamber；vestibule
【前庭】［生理］vestibule ◇ ～炎 vestibulitis
【前头】同〖前面〗
【前途】future；prospect：这个事儿没有～。*This job has no future.* or *There are no prospects in this job.*
【前途茫茫】have a bleak future；have gloomy prospects：他感觉到自己～，往后的光景难混了。*He felt that his future was bleak and the days ahead would be trying.*
【前途无量】have boundless prospects；have unlimited possibilities
【前腿】foreleg
【前往】go to；leave for；proceed to：代表团已动身～日内瓦。*The delegation has left for Geneva.* / 他们将由西安～延安。*From Xi'an they will proceed to Yan'an.*
【前卫】❶［军］advance guard；vanguard ❷［体］halfback：左～ *left halfback*；*left half* ❸ fashionable；modern
【前无古人】without parallel in history；unprecedented
【前夕】eve：解放～ *on the eve of liberation*；*shortly before liberation* / 毕业～，学生们紧张地准备考试。*As graduation day drew near, the students were all anxiously preparing for their final exams.*
【前嫌】previous ill will；old grudge：～尽释。*All previous ill will has been removed.* or *We have agreed to bury the hatchet.*
【前线】frontline；front：上～ *go to the front* / 远离～ *far from the frontline*
【前项】［数］antecedent
【前言】preface；foreword；introduction：～说明如何使用这本词典。*The preface explains how to use the dictionary.* / 宪法的～ *the preamble to a constitution*
【前言不搭后语】utter words that do not hang together；talk incoherently；babble disconnected phrases
【前沿】［军］forward position：～阵地 *forward position* / ～指挥所 *forward command post* ◇ ～科学 frontier science
【前仰后合】rock (with laughter)：笑得～ *rock (or shake) with laughter*；*double up with mirth*
【前夜】同〖前夕〗
【前因后果】cause and effect；the entire process：这件事情的～已经调查得清清楚楚。*The entire matter, its cause and effect, has been fully cleared up through investigation.*
【前缘】predestined ties or relationship；foreordained affinity：咱俩结为夫妻，也是～。*It is our foreordained affinity that we should become husband and wife.*
【前院】front courtyard
【前兆】omen；forewarning；premonition：这次地震很突然，没有任何～。*The earthquake was very sudden. There'd been no warning signs whatsoever.*
【前者】the former
【前肢】forelegs (of an animal)；forelimbs
【前装炮】muzzle-loading gun；muzzleloader
【前缀】prefix
【前奏】prelude：德国入侵波兰是第二次世界大战的～。*The German invasion of Poland was a prelude to World War II.*
【前奏曲】［音］prelude

荨（构词成分）见下
【荨麻】［植］nettle

钳 Ⅰ 名 pincers；pliers；tongs：火钳 Ⅱ 动 ❶ grip (with pincers)；clamp ❷ restrain；limit：钳制
【钳工】❶ benchwork ❷ fitter
【钳口】❶ force sb. into silence；prevent sb. from talking ❷ shut up；keep silent：～无言 *keep one's mouth shut*；*hold one's tongue*；*say nothing*
【钳口结舌】keep one's mouth shut；hold one's tongue
【钳形】pincerlike：～攻势 *a pincer movement*；*a two-pronged offensive* / 形成～包围 *form a pincerlike encirclement*
【钳制】clamp down on；suppress：～舆论 *muzzle (or gag) public opinion*
【钳爪】chela (of a crab, lobster, etc.)
【钳子】pliers；pincers；forceps

虔 形 pious；sincere
【虔诚】pious；devout：～的佛教徒 *a pious adherent of Buddhism*；*devout Buddhist* / ～地祈祷上帝 *pray devoutly to God*
【虔敬】reverent：他听布道很～。*He gave reverent attention to the sermon.*

钱 名 ❶ copper coin；cash：铜钱 ❷ money：这个多少～？*How much is this?* ❸ fund；sum：这

笔～是专为保健事业用的。*This fund is earmarked for public health services.* / 买拖拉机的～ *the wherewithal to buy tractors* ❹ qian, currently called 市钱, a traditional unit of weight ——另见〖市钱〗

【钱包】wallet; purse

【钱币】coin ◇ ～学 numismatics

【钱财】wealth; money: 浪费～ *waste money*

【钱龙】[动] millipede

【钱迷心窍】be blinded by lust for money; money-grubbing

【钱能通神】Money will move the gods; Money opens the gates of heaven.

【钱庄】old-style Chinese private bank

掮 动〈方〉carry on the shoulder

【掮客】broker: 房地产～ *a real estate broker* / 他没什么原则,只是个政治～。*He has no principles; he's just a political broker.*

乾 Ⅰ 名 qian, one of the Eight Diagrams Ⅱ 形 male

【乾坤】heaven and earth; the cosmos; the universe: 云迷世界,雾罩～。*Clouds over the world; Mist shrouds the cosmos.* ——另见〖扭转乾坤〗

潜 Ⅰ 形 latent; hidden: 潜能 Ⅱ 副 stealthily; secretly; on the sly: 潜入

【潜藏】hide; go into hiding

【潜地导弹】submarine-launched missile aimed at objectives on land; sea-to-ground missile

【潜返】〈贬〉return secretly: 毒贩～城里,继续犯罪。*The drug-traffickers returned secretly to the city and continued their activities.*

【潜伏】hide; conceal; lie low: ～特务 *a hidden enemy agent* / ～的疾病 *an insidious disease* / ～着的危机 *a latent crisis* / 游击小分队在预定地点～下来。*The guerrilla detachment was lying low at the predetermined location.*

【潜伏期】[医] incubation period; latency period

【潜航】(of a submarine) submerge: ～深度 *submerged depth* / ～速度 *submerged speed*

【潜科学】science of the human embryo to detect early signs of talent

【潜力】latent capacity; potential; potentiality: 有很大～ *have great potentialities* / 充分发挥～ *fully bring out latent potentialities; bring the potential into full play* / 挖掘～ *exploit potentialities; tap potentials*

【潜流】[地质] undercurrent; underflow

【潜能】❶ [物] latent energy ❷ potential

【潜匿】hide; go into hiding

【潜热】[物] latent heat

【潜入】❶ slip into; sneak into; steal in: ～敌占区 *slip into the enemy-occupied area* / ～室内 *sneak into a room* ❷ dive (into water); submerge

【潜水】❶ go under water; dive: ～器 *scuba* / ～钟 *diving bell* ❷ [地质] phreatic water ◇ ～病 caisson disease; decompression sickness; ～艇 submarine; ～衣 diving suit; ～员 diver; frogman

【潜台词】❶ unspoken words in a play left to the understanding of the audience or reader ❷ what is actually meant (in one's speech); implication

【潜逃】abscond: 携公款～ *abscond with public funds*

【潜艇】submarine: ～探测器 *submarine detector*

【潜望镜】periscope

【潜心】with great concentration: ～研究科学 *apply oneself to scientific study with great concentration; devote oneself to the study of science*

【潜行】❶ move under water ❷ move stealthily; slink

【潜血】[医] occult blood (in the faeces): ～试验 *occult blood test*

【潜移默化】exert a subtle influence on sb.'s character, thinking, etc.; imperceptibly influence: 文艺对人们的思想起着～的作用。*Literature and art exert an imperceptible influence on people's thinking.*

【潜意识】the subconscious; subconsciousness

【潜隐】❶ hide; conceal: 她淡淡地一笑,笑里却～着悲哀。*She gave a faint smile, a smile tinged with sadness.* ❷〈书〉withdraw from society and live in solitude; be a hermit

【潜泳】underwater swimming

【潜鱼】pearlfish

【潜在】latent; potential: ～的意识 *subconsciousness* / 一股～的势力 *a potential force (of a group of people)* / 要想办法使每个人的～力量充分发挥出来。*We must find a way to allow everyone to realize their potential.*

【潜质】latent quality: 有～青年 *young person with potential*

【潜滋暗长】grow and develop imperceptibly

黔 形 short for Guizhou Province

【黔驴技穷】the (proverbial) Guizhou donkey has exhausted its tricks—at one's wit's end; at the end of one's rope

【黔驴之技】tricks of the (proverbial) Guizhou donkey—tricks not to be feared; cheap tricks

qiǎn

浅 形 ❶ shallow: ～水 *shallow water; shoal water* / ～～的一碗饭 *a partly-filled bowl of rice* / 这房子进深～。*The house is not deep.* ❷ simple; easy: 这篇课文很～。*This lesson is very easy.* ❸ superficial: 对问题的认识很～ *just have a superficial understanding of the problem* / 功夫～ *have superficial mastery of a skill* ❹ not intimate; not close: 交情很～ *not on familiar terms* ❺ (of colour) light; pale: ～蓝 *light blue* / ～黄 *pale yellow* / 这种毛线色儿太～。*The colour of this woollen yarn is too pale.* ❻ not long in time: 相处的日子还～ *have not been to-*

gether long / 他在这儿工作的日子～。*He's been working here for only a short time.*

【浅薄】shallow; superficial; meagre: 我读过他的几本书，内容～得很。*I've read some of his books — they're very shallow.* / 他的历史知识很～。*He has a very meagre knowledge of history.*

【浅尝辄止】stop after gaining a little knowledge; be satisfied with a smattering of knowledge

【浅成岩】[地质] hypabyssal rock

【浅淡】❶ (of colour) light; pale: ～的红色 *pale red* ❷ (of feeling) vague; faint: 她的声音流露出～的哀愁。*There was a tinge of sadness in her voice.*

【浅耕】shallow ploughing

【浅海】shallow sea; epeiric sea; epicontinental sea: ～水域 *the shallow waters along the coast*

【浅见】❶ superficial view: ～寡闻 *ignorant and ill-informed* ❷〈谦〉humble opinion: 依我～ *in my humble opinion*

【浅近】simple; plain; easy to understand: 这本书写得～易懂。*The language of this book is simple and easy to understand.*

【浅口鞋】shoes with low-cut uppers

【浅陋】meagre; mean: 学识～ *have meagre knowledge*

【浅明】simple; plain; clear; obvious: ～的道理 *a plain truth*

【浅色】light colour: ～的女衬衣 *a light-coloured blouse*

【浅释】(usu. used in book titles) simple explanation:《唐诗～》*Tang Poems with Simple Explanations*

【浅水池】the shallow end of a swimming pool; shallow pool

【浅说】(usu. used in titles of books and articles) elementary introduction:《无线电～》*An Elementary Introduction to Radio*

【浅滩】shoal; shallows

【浅谈】(usu. used in titles of books and articles) brief talk:《～被动语态》*A Brief Talk on the Passive Voice*

【浅显】plain; easy to read and understand: ～的道理 *a plain truth* / ～通俗的科学读物 *simple popular scientific literature*

【浅笑】smile

【浅学】having superficial knowledge; of little learning; ill-educated

【浅易】simple and easy: ～读物 *easy readings; easy-to-read literature*

【浅斟低唱】drinking leisurely and singing softly—a cultured way of enjoying oneself

【浅种】shallow sowing

遣 动 ❶ send; dispatch: 派遣 ❷ dispel; expel: 消遣

【遣词造句】choice of words and building of sentences; wording and phrasing

【遣返】repatriate: ～战俘 *repatriate prisoners of war*

【遣散】disband; dismiss; send away; lay off: 这个机构已撤消，人员已～。*The agency has been disbanded, and all its employees have been sent elsewhere.* ◇ ～费 severance pay

【遣送】send back; repatriate: 他因为没护照，被～回国。*He was sent back to his country because he had no passport.* / ～出境 *deport*

谴 动 condemn

【谴责】condemn; denounce; censure: 世界舆论～侵略者的挑衅。*World opinion condemned the aggressor's provocation.* / 他做了错事，受到良心的～。*He had done wrong, and his conscience plagued him for it.*

qiàn

欠 动 ❶ yawn: 哈欠 ❷ raise slightly (a part of the body): ～脚儿 *slightly raise one's heels* ❸ owe; be behind with: ～租 *be behind with the rent* / 我～他十块钱。*I owe him ten yuan.* / 我还～图书馆一本书。*I still owe the library a book.* ❹ not enough; lacking; wanting: 文字～通。*The writing is not altogether grammatical.* or *The wording is some-what awkward.* / 说话～考虑 *be too free with one's tongue*

【欠安】(of an aged person or a VIP) feeling unwell; indisposed; under the weather: 爷爷今天身体～。*Grandpa is not feeling very well today.*

【欠产】fall short of the production target; have a shortfall in output: 今年非但没超产，还欠了产。*Not only did we not exceed this year's production target, we even fell short of it.*

【欠单】accommodation bill or note; IOU

【欠付工资】back pay; back wages

【欠火】have not been cooked or heated long enough; undercooked: 这些馒头～。*These buns haven't been steamed long enough.*

【欠佳】not good enough; not up to the mark: 身体～ *not feel well; be under the weather*

【欠款】❶ owe a debt: 这家公司～数百万，倒闭了。*This company was several million yuan in debt and went bankrupt.* / 他欠了银行的款。*He owes money to the bank.* ❷ money that is owing; arrears; balance due: 银行限期要公司还清～。*The bank demanded that the company repay its debt within the prescribed time limit.*

【欠情】owe sb. a debt of gratitude; be indebted to sb.: 人家帮了那么些忙，也没好好谢谢，总觉得～儿。*He helped us so much, and we never even thanked him properly. We feel indebted to him.*

【欠缺】❶ be deficient in; be short of: 我们的经验还很～。*We are still lacking in experience.* ❷ shortcoming; deficiency: 我们的工作还有很多～。*There are still many shortcomings in our work.*

【欠伸】stretch oneself and yawn

【欠身】raise oneself slightly; half rise from one's

seat：他～向进来的客人打招呼。*He rose slightly to greet the visitor.* / 主人给他端来一杯茶，他欠了欠身说："谢谢。"*His host brought him a cup of tea, and half rising from his seat, he said, "Thank you."*

【欠税】default on or be in arrears with tax payments

【欠条】(又作'欠据') a bill signed in acknowledgement of debt; IOU

【欠妥】not proper：措词～ *not properly worded* / 这件事你办得～。*You didn't handle the matter properly.*

【欠息】debit interest

【欠项】liabilities

【欠薪】❶ delay paying a salary：工厂欠了我们两个月的薪。*The factory still owes us two months' salary.* ❷ back pay; overdue salaries

【欠债】owe a debt; run into debt：他非但没有积蓄，还欠着债呢。*He not only has no savings but is also in debt.* / 他欠了很多债。*He is heavily in debt.*

【欠账】❶ owe a debt; run into debt ❷ bills due; outstanding accounts

【欠资】postage due：～信 *postage-due letter* / ～邮件 *postage-due mail*

【欠揍】〈口〉need a spanking：你太淘气了，真是～。*You're being awfully naughty. You need a good spanking.*

纤 名 a rope for towing a boat; tow line：拉纤 ——另见 xiān

【纤夫】boat tracker

【纤路】towpath; towing path; track road

【纤绳】towline; towrope

茜 (构词成分) 见下

【茜草】[植] madder

【茜素染料】alizarin dyes

倩 Ⅰ 形〈书〉pretty; handsome Ⅱ 动〈书〉ask sb. to do sth.：～人执笔 *ask sb. to write on one's behalf*

【倩男倩女】smartly dressed men and women

【倩影】beautiful image (of a woman); picture (of a beautiful woman)

【倩装】(a woman's) beautiful dress

堑 名 moat; chasm：天堑

【堑壕】[军] trench; entrenchment：～工事 *entrenchment works* / ～战 *trench warfare*

嵌 动 inlay; embed; set：～花的地面 *a mosaic pavement* / 桌面上～着象牙雕成的花。*The table is inlaid with an ivory flower-pattern.*

歉 Ⅰ 名 apology：道歉 Ⅱ 形 crop failure：以丰补～ *make up for a crop failure with a bumper harvest*

【歉疚】having a guilty conscience：让你代我受过，甚感～。*You took the blame for me, which troubles my conscience deeply.*

【歉年】lean year

【歉然】apologetic：～一笑 *give an apologetic smile*

【歉收】crop failure; poor harvest：因遭天灾而～ *have a bad harvest due to natural disaster*

【歉意】apology; regret：表示～ *offer an apology; express one's regret* / 谨致～。*Please accept my apologies.*

qiāng

抢 动〈书〉bump against：呼天抢地 ——另见 qiǎng

呛 动 choke：吃饭吃～了 *choke over one's food* / 他喝得太猛，～着了。*He took a big gulp and almost choked.* / 他游泳时～了一口水。*He choked on a mouthful of water while swimming.* / 米粒～进他气管里去了。*A grain of rice got stuck in his windpipe.* ——另见 qiàng

枪 名 ❶ rifle; gun; firearm ❷ a thing which is shaped or functions like a gun：焊枪 ❸ spear：红缨枪

【枪靶】(shooting) target

【枪把】the small of the stock; pistol grip

【枪毙】execute by shooting：这几个罪犯该～。*These criminals should be shot.*

【枪刺】bayonet

【枪带】(rifle) sling

【枪弹】❶ cartridge ❷ bullet

【枪法】marksmanship：她～高明。*She is a crack shot.*

【枪放下】(word of command) Order arms!

【枪杆】(又作'枪杆子') rifle; gun; arms：拿起～儿上前线 *take up arms and go to the front* / ～子里面出政权。*Political power grows out of the barrel of a gun.*

【枪管】barrel (of a gun)

【枪机】rifle bolt

【枪架】rifle rack

【枪决】execute by shooting：死刑用～的方法执行。*The death penalty is to be executed by means of shooting.*

【枪口】muzzle：把～对准靶子 *aim a gun at the target*

【枪林弹雨】a forest of guns and a hail of bullets—heavy fire：冒着～冲锋陷阵 *charge under a hail of bullets; charge under heavy fire* / 新闻记者出入于～，采集前方战讯。*The reporters gathered news of the front amidst heavy fire.*

【枪榴弹】rifle grenade

【枪炮】firearms; arms; guns

【枪杀】shoot dead

【枪伤】bullet wound

【枪上肩】(word of command) Shoulder arms!

【枪声】report of a gun; shot; crack：听到远处的～ *hear gunshots in the distance*

【枪手】(qiāngshǒu) ❶ marksman; gunner ❷〈旧〉spearman
【枪手】(qiāngshou) one who sits for an examination in place of another person
【枪栓】rifle bolt
【枪膛】bore (of a gun)
【枪替】sit for an examination in place of another person
【枪托】(rifle) butt; buttstock
【枪乌贼】squid
【枪械】firearms
【枪眼】❶ embrasure; loophole ❷ bullet hole
【枪鱼】marlin
【枪支】firearms: ～弹药 *firearms and ammunition*
【枪子儿】〈口〉❶ cartridge ❷ bullet; shot

戗 动 ❶ go in an opposite direction: 他老爱跟人～着说,真叫人生气。*He's always ready to argue, much to our annoyance.* ❷ clash; be at loggerheads with: 他们说～了,吵起来啦。*Their views clashed and this eventually led to a quarrel.*
【戗风】against the wind: ～行船 *sail against the wind*
【戗顺不吃】〈方〉yield neither to coercion nor to persuasion

戕 动〈书〉kill
【戕害】injure; harm
【戕贼】injure; undermine: ～身体 *undermine (or ruin) one's health*

腔 名 ❶ cavity (in human or animal bodies): 胸腔 ❷ tune; pitch: 唱走了～儿 *sing out of tune* ❸ accent: 山东～ *Shandong accent* ❹ speech: 开腔
【腔肠动物】coelenterate
【腔调】❶ tune: 京剧的～ *tunes of Beijing opera* ❷〈贬〉tone of voice: 他讲起话来一副十足的流氓～。*He speaks like a genuine gangster.* ❸ accent; intonation: 听他说话的～像是河南人。*Judging from his accent, he is probably from Henan.*
【腔骨】〈方〉spinal joints of pigs, sheep, etc. (for food)

蜣 (构词成分) 见下
【蜣螂】dung beetle

锵 象 a clanging or clanking sound: 锣声～～。*Gongs clanked.*

镪 (构词成分) 见下
【镪水】popular name for 强酸

qiáng

强 I 形 ❶ strong; powerful: 身～体壮 *strong and healthy* / 能力很～ *very capable* / 责任心～ *have a strong sense of responsibility* / ～冷空气 *a strong cold air current* ❷ better: 我们的劳动条件一年比一年～。*Our working conditions are getting better each year.* ❸ slightly more than; plus: 三分之一～ *slightly more than one third* II 副 by force: ～取 *take by force* ——另见 jiàng; qiǎng
【强半】〈书〉more than half; greater part; most
【强暴】❶ violent; brutal: ～的行为 *an act of violence* ❷ ferocious adversary: 不畏～ *defy brute force*
【强大】big and powerful; powerful; formidable: ～的人民解放军 *the powerful People's Liberation Army* / 阵容～的代表团 *strong delegation; big high-ranking delegation* / 这种植物具有～的生命力。*This kind of plant has great vitality.*
【强盗】robber; bandit: ～行为 *banditry; robbery* / ～头子 *gang boss; ringleader* / 法西斯～ *fascist bandits*
【强盗逻辑】gangster logic
【强的松】[药] prednisone
【强敌】formidable opponent or enemy
【强点】strong point: 我们应当学习他们的～来弥补自己的弱点。*We should learn from their strong points to offset our weak ones.*
【强调】stress; emphasize; underline: 不适当地～情况特殊 *lay undue stress on special circumstances* / 必须～产品质量。*Emphasis must be placed on the quality of the products.* / 不要～客观原因。*Don't overemphasize the influence of objective forces.*
【强度】intensity; strength: 钢的～ *the strength of the steel* / 辐射～ *radiation intensity*
【强渡】[军] fight one's way across a river; force a river: 1935年5月,红军～大渡河。*The Red Army forced its way across the Dadu River in May, 1935.*
【强风】[气] strong breeze
【强干】capable and experienced
【强攻】take by storm; storm: ～敌人阵地 *storm the enemy position*
【强固】strong; solid: ～的工事 *strong fortifications* / 为国家工业化打下～的基础 *lay a solid (or firm) foundation for the industrialization of the country*
【强国】powerful (or strong) nation; power: 把我国建设成为社会主义的现代化～ *build China into a modern, powerful socialist country*
【强悍】fierce; intrepid; doughty
【强横】rude and unreasonable; tyrannical; surly; arrogant: 他态度～,没法跟他讲理。*He is too surly to reason with.*
【强化】strengthen; intensify; consolidate: ～国家机器 *strengthen the state apparatus* / ～麦乳精 *fortified extract of malt and milk* / 英语～训练班 *an intensive English training course*
【强化基因】enhancer gene
【强击机】attack plane
【强记】(qiángjì)〈书〉have a retentive memory ——另见 qiǎngjì

【强加】impose；force：任何一方不得把自己的意志～给对方。*No party may impose its will on the other party.*
【强加于人】impose (one's views, etc.) on others：不要把你的意见～。*Don't force your views on others.*
【强奸】violate (a woman)；rape
【强奸民意】defile public opinion
【强碱】[化] alkali；strong base
【强健】strong and healthy：体魄～ *be physically strong；have a strong constitution*
【强将手下无弱兵】There are no poor soldiers under a good general.
【强劲】powerful；forceful：～的海风 *a strong wind from the sea*
【强劳动力】an able-bodied labourer
【强力霉素】[药] doxycycline
【强梁】brutal；tyrannical；surly：不畏～ *defy brute force*
【强烈】❶ strong；intense；violent：～的求知欲 *a strong thirst for knowledge* / ～的仇恨 *intense hatred* / ～反对 *strongly oppose* / ～谴责 *vehemently condemn* / 提出～抗议 *lodge a strong protest；protest strongly* / ～地震 *a violent earthquake* ❷ clear-cut；distinct；striking；sharp：这张照片黑白分明，显出～的对比。*The distinction between black and white in this photo creates a sharp contrast.*
【强令】arbitrarily give orders：～执行 *arbitrarily give orders to carry out sth.*
【强龙不压地头蛇】a powerful dragon cannot crush a snake in its old haunts—even a powerful man cannot crush a local bully
【强弩之末】an arrow at the end of its flight—a spent force
【强拍】[音] strong beat；accented beat：次～ *subsidiary strong beat*
【强权】power；might：～即公理——这是帝国主义的逻辑。*Might is right—that is the logic of imperialism.* / ～终于向正义低头。*Power gave way to justice at last.* ◇ ～外交 power diplomacy；～政治 power politics
【强人】❶ strong man ❷ (又作'强徒')〈旧〉robber；bandit
【强溶剂】[化] strong solvent
【强身】build up a good physique；improve one's health
【强盛】(of a country) powerful and prosperous
【强手】❶ a very capable person ❷ a master player；a topnotch athlete；ace
【强似】(又作'强如') be better than；be superior to：今年的秋收～去年。*This year's autumn harvest is better than last year's.*
【强酸】[化] strong acid
【强袭】take by storm；storm
【强项】❶〈书〉resolute and unbending；upright and unyielding ❷ [体] strong point (of an athlete or a team)
【强心剂】cardiac stimulant；cardiotonic
【强行】force：～闯入 *force one's way in* / ～登陆 *force a landing* / ～通过一项议案 *force a bill through*
【强行军】forced march
【强压】suppress；stifle：～住心中怒火 *suppress one's anger*
【强毅】resolute and steadfast；staunch
【强硬】strong；tough；unyielding：措词～的声明 *a strongly worded statement* / 提出～抗议 *lodge a strong protest* / ～路线 *tough line；hard line* / ～的态度 *an uncompromising stand* / ～派 *hardliner*
【强有力】strong；vigorous；forceful：采取～的行动 *take vigorous action*
【强于】be better than：我们队略～对方。*Our team is slightly better than the opponent.*
【强占】forcibly occupy；seize
【强者】the strong and valiant；a survivor：她是生活中的～。*She is unbeaten by the difficulties and hardships of life.*
【强震】[地质] strong shock：～区 *meizoseismal area*
【强直】[医] rigidity
【强制】force；compel；coerce：～措施 *compulsory (or mandatory) measure* / ～劳动 *forced labour* / ～手段 *compulsory means；coercive measure* / 法院～他缴纳五百元罚款。*The court compelled him to pay a 500 yuan fine.*
【强中自有强中手】however strong you are，there's always someone stronger
【强壮】strong；sturdy；robust：他身体～。*He's strong and healthy.*
【强壮剂】roborant；tonic
【强子】[物] hadron

墙

名 wall
【墙报】wall newspaper
【墙壁】wall
【墙倒众人推】when a wall is about to collapse，everybody gives it a shove—everybody hits a man who is down
【墙根】the foot of a wall
【墙角】corner formed by two walls：～石 *a cornerstone*
【墙脚】❶ the foot of a wall ❷ foundation ——另见〖挖墙脚〗
【墙裙】[建] dado
【墙头】❶ the top of a wall ❷ a short，low enclosing wall
【墙头草，随风倒】grass atop a wall swaying in the wind—a person who follows the crowd
【墙垣】〈书〉wall
【墙纸】wallpaper

蔷

(构词成分) 见下
【蔷薇】rose：～科 *the rose family*

樯

名〈书〉mast

qiǎng

抢 动 ❶ rob; loot: ～银行 *rob a bank* ❷ snatch; grab: 他把信～了过去。*He snatched away the letter.* ❸ vie for; scramble for: ～球 *scramble for the ball* / ～干重活 *vie with each other for the hardest job* / 孩子们～着要排第一个。*The children jostled with each other for the first place in line.* ❹ rush: 他～步上前接过了客人手上的行李。*He rushed over and took the luggage from his guest's hands* ❺ scrape; scratch: 把锅底～～ *scrape the bottom of the pot* / 磨剪子～菜刀 *sharpen scissors and kitchen knives* / 他摔了一跤,膝盖上～去了一块皮。*He fell and scraped his knee.* ——另见 qiāng

【抢白】tell off; dress down; rebuff: 我劝他别生气,反被他～了一顿。*I tried to pacify him, but got a rebuff for my pains.*

【抢答】vie for the opportunity of answering questions (esp. in oral knowledge contests): 百科知识～比赛 *general knowledge oral contest (where speed and accuracy win points)*

【抢点】❶ (of a train, etc.) make up time (in order to keep on schedule) ❷ (of a football striker, etc.) race to a favourable position

【抢渡】speedily cross (a river): 河水可能暴涨,得立即～。*The river may suddenly rise. We must make a swift crossing immediately.*

【抢夺】snatch; wrest; seize: ～胜利果实 *seize the fruits of victory*

【抢饭碗】〈口〉 fight for a job; snatch sb. else's job: 这儿只有一个打字员的名额,有好几个人抢这饭碗呢。*There is only one opening here for a typist, and quite a few people are competing for the position.*

【抢购】rush to purchase (anticipating inflation or scarcity): ～风潮 *panic purchasing; panic buying spree* / 这个商店来了一批新式毛衣,一上午就被～一空。*The store received a shipment of new-style sweaters, which were all sold out in one morning.*

【抢劫】rob; loot; plunder: 有四个人今天早上～了银行。*Four men robbed the bank this morning.* / 把商店～一空 *ransack a store*

【抢截】[体] intercept

【抢镜头】❶ (of a cameraman) fight for a vantage point from which to take a news picture: 这次上山考察熊猫生活,他抢下了很多珍贵的镜头。*During this expedition to study the life of the giant panda, he took a lot of valuable snapshots.* ❷ steal the show; be fond of being in the limelight: 她就喜欢～,出风头。*She loves to steal the show and be the centre of attention.*

【抢救】rescue; save; salvage: ～病人 *give emergency treatment to a patient; rescue a patient* / ～无效。*All rescue measures proved ineffectual.* / ～工作 *rescue work* / ～组 *rescue party*

【抢掠】loot; sack; plunder: 在地震灾区进行～的人将被枪决。*Anyone found looting in the earthquake-stricken area will be shot.* / 入侵者到处烧杀～。*The invaders burned, killed and plundered wherever they went.*

【抢拍】seize the opportunity to take pictures; grab the photo opportunity; photograph real-life scenes

【抢亲】(又作'抢婚') ❶ a marriage ceremony in which the bridegroom pretends to kidnap his bride ❷ steal, kidnap or force a woman to be one's wife

【抢青】rush a harvest of ripening crops (in anticipation of bad weather)

【抢市】rush (goods) to the market (to get a better price); grab the market: 要严格上市西瓜质量,不～。*The quality of water melons coming on the market must be strictly controlled; there must be no attempt to grab the market (by selling unripe melons).*

【抢墒】hurry to sow seeds while the soil is still moist

【抢生意】compete for business

【抢时间】race against time: 农活有季节性,必须～。*Farm work is seasonal, so we must race against time.*

【抢收】rush in the harvest; get the harvest in quickly: 天气很快会变,得赶快～。*The weather is bound to change soon. We must get the harvest in quickly.*

【抢手】(of goods) in great demand: ～货 *goods in great demand* / 如今,高档化妆品在市场上最～。*Nowadays high-grade cosmetics are the most popular items on the market.*

【抢先】try to be the first to do sth.; anticipate; forestall: 部队～占了那座桥。*The troops have anticipated the enemy and seized the bridge.* / 一个个进来,别～。*Come in one at a time. Don't rush in all at once.*

【抢险】rush to deal with an emergency (e.g. a breach in an embankment, a cave-in, etc.): 河堤决口后马上派出了工程队去～。*The river dyke sprang a leak, and the construction brigade was immediately sent to deal with it.*

【抢修】rush to repair; do rush repairs: 线路正在～,半小时后恢复供电。*The line is being rush-repaired and the power supply will return to normal in half an hour.*

【抢眼】noticeable; conspicuous; spectacular: 这幅广告牌很～。*The billboard is eye-catching.*

【抢运】rush to transport

【抢占】❶ race to control; seize; grab: ～制高点 *race to control a commanding point* ❷ unlawfully occupy: 这家工厂～了附近学校的一块地。*The factory unlawfully built on a piece of land which belongs to a nearby school.*

【抢种】rush-plant: ～晚稻 *rush-plant the late rice*

【抢嘴】〈方〉 ❶ try to get the first word in; try to be heard above the rest: 按次序发言,别～。*We will take turns speaking, so don't all try to speak at once.* ❷ rush to eat up the food

羟（构词成分）见下

【羟基】[化] hydroxyl (group)：～化物 *hydroxylate*

强 动 make an effort; strive：～作镇静 *make an effort to appear composed; try hard to keep one's composure* / ～不知以为知 *pretend to know what one does not know* ——另见 jiàng; qiáng

【强逼】compel; force：我并不想来，是被～着来的。*I didn't want to come; I was forced to.*

【强辩】defend oneself by sophistry; argue against all reason; argue stubbornly or obstinately

【强词夺理】use lame arguments; resort to sophistry; reason fallaciously：他在人行道上骑车撞了人，还～说人家没给他让路。*He hit a pedestrian while riding his bicycle on the pavement, but still he offered the lame excuse that the person didn't make way for him.*

【强记】(qiǎngjì) force oneself to memorize; learn by rote：这几课书我并没弄懂，考试全得靠～。*I didn't understand these lessons, so I had to rely on sheer memorization to pass the exam.* ——另见 qiángjì

【强留】force sb. to stay on：愿意退出的决不～。*Those who want to drop out are free to do so.*

【强迫】compel; force; coerce：～命令 *resort to coercion and commandism* / ～敌机降落 *compel the enemy plane to land* / 不要～我同意你的意见。*Don't force me to agree with you.*

【强求】insist on; impose：各地情况不同，不能～一律。*No uniformity should be imposed since conditions vary from place to place.*

【强人所难】try to make sb. do what he is unwilling or unable to：各人有各人的嗜好，不要～。*Everybody's got their own interests; you mustn't try and force people into doing things they don't want to.*

【强使】compel; force

【强笑】❶ force a smile ❷ a forced smile

【强颜欢笑】put on an air of cheerfulness; try to look happy

【强作解人】pretend to be in the know

襁（构词成分）见下

【襁褓】swaddling clothes：从～中抚育成人 *bring sb. up from infancy* / 我们的新计划还只是在～中呢。*Our new plan is still in its infancy.*

qiàng

呛 动 irritate (respiratory organs)：炸辣椒的味儿～鼻子。*The smell of red pepper being fried irritates the nose.* / 烟把我～着了。*The smoke almost choked me.* ——另见 qiāng

炝 动 ❶ boil (meat or vegetables) in water for a while, then dress with soy, vinegar, etc. ❷ fry sth. quickly in hot oil, then cook it with sauce and water

qiāo

悄（构词成分）见下 ——另见 qiǎo

【悄悄】quietly; on the quiet：我～地披上大衣，带上门出去。*Quietly, I put on my coat and went out, closing the door after me.* / 他～儿地跟我全说了。*He told me everything on the quiet.*

【悄悄话】whisperings (esp. between husband and wife, lovers, etc.)

跷 Ⅰ 动 ❶ lift up (a leg); hold up (a finger)：～着腿坐着 *sit with one's legs crossed* / 他～起大姆指说"好，好！"*He made a thumbs-up sign and said, "Good, good!"* ❷ stand or walk on tiptoe：～着脚走路 *walk on tiptoe* / 他～起脚往人群里看。*He stood on tiptoe to scan the crowd.* Ⅱ 名 stilts：踩着～扭秧歌 *do the yanko dance on stilts*

【跷跷板】seesaw：玩～ *play on a seesaw*

敲 动 ❶ knock; beat; strike：～门 *knock at the door* / 钟刚～过四点。*The clock has just struck four.* ❷〈口〉overcharge; fleece sb.：给～去五块钱 *be stung for five yuan* / 他提了工资，我们～了他一顿饭。*His pay has been raised, so we made him treat us to a dinner.*

【敲边鼓】speak or act to assist sb. from the sidelines; back sb. up：你可以在会上提出这建议，我在旁边给你～。*You present this proposal at the meeting and I'll back you up from the sidelines.*

【敲打】❶ beat; rap; tap：锣鼓～得很热闹。*Drums and gongs were beating boisterously.* ❷〈方〉say sth. to irritate sb.：冷言冷语～人 *irritate people with sarcastic remarks* ❸ pressurize and supervise sb.：这孩子老得大人～着点，不然就不好好做功课。*The boy needs constant prodding from his parents, otherwise he won't get his homework done.*

【敲定】nail down; make the final decision

【敲骨吸髓】break the bones and suck the marrow—suck the lifeblood; be a cruel, bloodsucking exploiter

【敲击】beat; rap; tap

【敲警钟】sound the alarm bell —sound a warning：这次事故给我们敲了警钟，今后必须严格制度。*The accident sounded a warning against a relaxation of the rules.*

【敲门砖】a brick picked up to knock on the door and thrown away when it has served its purpose—a stepping-stone to success

【敲丧钟】sound the funeral bell：民族独立运动敲响了殖民主义的丧钟。*The national independence movement sounded the death knell of colonialism.*

【敲小鼓】beat a little drum—feel uneasy or nervous
【敲诈】extort; blackmail; racketeer: ～钱财 *extort money* / 他想利用这种丑闻～我。*He tried to use the scandal to blackmail me*. ◇ ～勒索 extort; blackmail; racketeer
【敲竹杠】❶ fleece sb.; daylight robbery: 那家饭店真是～! *They really fleeced us at that hotel!* ❷ blackmail: 他知道我们的秘密,就借此敲我们的竹杠。*He knows our secret and is holding it over us*.

锹 名 spade: 一把～ *a spade* / 一～煤 *a shovelful of coal* / 挖一～深 *dig a spade's depth; dig a spit deep*

缲 动 hem with invisible stitches: 给裙子～边 *hem a skirt*

橇 名 sledge; sled; sleigh: 雪橇

qiáo

乔 Ⅰ 形 tall: 乔木 Ⅱ 动 disguise: 乔装
【乔林】[林] high forest
【乔模乔样】in an artificial or affected manner
【乔木】arbor; tree
【乔其纱】[纺] georgette
【乔迁】move to a better place get a promotion ◇ ～之喜 congratulations on your new home
【乔装】disguise: ～成商人 *disguise oneself as a merchant* ◇ ～打扮 disguise oneself; masquerade

侨 Ⅰ 动 live abroad: 侨居 Ⅱ 名 a person living abroad: 华侨
【侨办】(〈略〉全称为'华侨事务办公室')Office of Overseas Chinese Affairs
【侨胞】countrymen (or nationals) residing abroad; overseas compatriots
【侨汇】overseas remittance; immigrant remittance ◇ ～券 overseas remittance coupon
【侨居】live abroad: ～国 *country of residence* / 他在国外～了三十年。*He lived abroad for thirty years*. / 他是英国人,～中国。*He is British but lives in China*.
【侨眷】relatives of overseas Chinese who remain in the homeland
【侨民】a national of a particular country residing abroad: ～社会 *foreign community*
【侨生】❶ children of overseas Chinese born abroad ❷ overseas Chinese studying in China
【侨属】同〖侨眷〗
【侨务】affairs concerning nationals living abroad; overseas Chinese affairs
【侨乡】village or town inhabited by relatives of overseas Chinese and returned overseas Chinese
【侨资】capital investments of overseas Chinese: ～企业 *overseas Chinese enterprise*

荞 (构词成分) 见下
【荞麦】buckwheat

桥 名 bridge: 木～ *a wooden bridge* / 石～ *a stone bridge* / 铁～ *an iron bridge*
【桥洞】〈口〉bridge opening
【桥墩】(bridge) pier
【桥拱】bridge arch
【桥涵】bridges and culverts
【桥孔】bridge opening
【桥梁】bridge: 在河上架设～ *build a bridge across a river* / 这本双语词典起着沟通两国文化的～作用。*This bilingual dictionary serves as a bridge between the cultures of the two nations*.
【桥楼室】bridge house
【桥牌】bridge (a card game): 打～ *play bridge*
【桥式起重机】bridge crane; overhead travelling crane
【桥塔】[建] bridge tower
【桥台】[建] abutment
【桥头】either end of a bridge
【桥头堡】❶ [军] bridgehead ❷ [建] bridge tower
【桥堍】either end of a bridge
【桥支座】bridge seat

翘 动 ❶ raise (one's head): 翘首 ❷ become warped: 木板～了。*The board has warped*. —— 另见 qiào
【翘盼】eagerly look forward to
【翘企】〈书〉raise one's head and stand on tiptoe—eagerly look forward to: 不胜～ *look forward to sth. with eager anticipation*
【翘首】〈书〉raise one's head and look: ～星空 *look up at the starry sky*
【翘足而待】wait on tiptoe—expect sth. to happen soon
【翘足引领】stand on tiptoe and crane one's neck—eagerly look forward to

谯 (构词成分) 见下
【谯楼】〈书〉❶ watchtower ❷ drum tower

憔 (构词成分) 见下
【憔悴】wan and sallow; thin and pallid: 这姑娘脸色～,眼皮浮肿。*The girl's face looks wan and sallow, and her eyelids are swollen*.

樵 名 ❶〈方〉firewood ❷〈书〉gather firewood
【樵夫】〈旧〉woodcutter; woodman

瞧 动 〈口〉look; see: 等着～吧。*Wait and see*. / ～书 *read a book* / 东～西～ *look about* / 你～着办吧。*You can do as you see fit*. / 他～朋友去了。*He went to see his friend*.
【瞧病】〈口〉❶ (of a patient) see (or consult) a doctor ❷ (of a doctor) see a patient
【瞧不起】look down on; despise
【瞧不上眼】consider beneath one's notice; turn one's nose up at: 这些茶具,我一套也～。*Of all these tea sets, there's not one that I consider*

worth a second look.

【瞧得起】have a good opinion of; think highly of

【瞧惯】同〖看惯〗

【瞧哈哈儿】〈口〉have a good laugh over (sb.'s misfortune); gloat over

【瞧见】see; catch sight of: 你在图书馆～我弟弟了吗? —没～。*Did you see my brother in the library? —No, I didn't.*

【瞧热闹】同〖看热闹〗

【瞧上】❶ have a chance to see: 人们围着看熊猫, 我挤不进去,一眼也没～。*People crowded round the panda and I couldn't squeeze in, so I didn't get a chance to see it.* ❷ to one's liking: 你～了这姑娘,可人家不一定瞧得上你。*You've taken a liking to the girl, but she won't necessarily take a liking to you.*

qiǎo

巧 形 ❶ skilful; ingenious; clever: ～匠 *a skilled (or clever) workman* / 他的手艺很～。*His workmanship is excellent.* / 你嘴～,你去说他准听。*You're a clever talker and he'll listen to you if you try to persuade him.* ❷ cunning; deceitful; artful: 花言巧语 ❸ opportune; coincidental: 太～了,我一出家门就来了一辆出租汽车。*It was most opportune that a taxi arrived just as I was leaving the house.*

【巧辩】argue skilfully or plausibly

【巧夺天工】wonderful workmanship (or superb craftsmanship) excelling nature

【巧妇难为无米之炊】the cleverest housewife can't cook a meal without rice—one can't make bricks without straw

【巧妇鸟】wren

【巧干】work ingeniously; do sth. in a clever way: 你光是苦干是达不到指标的,得～才行。*You can't meet the standards only by working hard; you have to do the work in a clever way.*

【巧合】coincidence: 他俩同年,生日又是同一天,真是～。*What a coincidence it is that they were born in the same year and on the same day.*

【巧计】clever device; artful scheme

【巧劲儿】〈方〉❶ knack; trick: 常常练习,慢慢就找着～了。*Do it often, and in time you'll learn the trick.* ❷ coincidence: 我正要去找他,他就来了,真是～。*What a coincidence that I was just going to see him when he came.*

【巧克力】chocolate: 果仁～ *nut chocolate* / 酒心～ *whisky heart chocolate* / ～饼干 *chocolate biscuit*

【巧立名目】invent all sorts of excuses; concoct various pretexts: ～搜刮民财 *extort people's wealth under all sorts of pretexts* / ～滥发奖金 *invent excuses to give out extravagant bonuses*

【巧妙】ingenious; clever: ～的战术 *ingenious tactics* / 他用的方法很～。*The method he uses is very clever.*

【巧取豪夺】secure (sb.'s belongings, rights, etc.) by force or trickery

【巧舌如簧】have a smooth tongue like the reed of a wind instrument—have a glib tongue

【巧事】coincidence

【巧手】a dab (or deft) hand; being clever with one's hands; dexterity: 她是个绣花～。*She's a dab hand at embroidering.* / ～儿什么都会做。*A deft hand can do just about anything.*

【巧思】ingenious or brilliant conception

【巧言令色】clever talk and an ingratiating manner

【巧遇】encounter by chance

悄 形 ❶ silent or low-voiced: 低声～语 *speak in a low voice* ❷〈文〉sad; worried; sorrowful ——另见 qiāo

【悄静】quiet; still; silent

【悄没声儿】〈方〉silent or low-voiced: 她说起话来～的,可唱起歌来是条女高音甜嗓子。*Her voice is very low when she speaks, but she has a lovely soprano singing voice.*

【悄然】〈文〉❶ sad; worried; sorrowful: ～泪下 *shed tears in sorrow; shed sad tears* ❷ quiet; soft: ～无声。*All was quiet.*

【悄声】a low voice; whisper: 他～地告诉我窗外有人在偷听。*He whispered to me that there was an eavesdropper outside the window.*

雀 名 sparrow: 家雀儿 ——另见 què

【雀盲眼】〈方〉night blindness; nyctalopia

qiào

壳 名 shell; hard surface: 甲壳 ——另见 ké

【壳菜】mussel

【壳斗】[植] acorn-cup; cupule

【壳质】[生化] chitin

俏 形 ❶ pretty; smart-looking; handsome: 打扮得真～ *be smartly dressed* / 瞧她这～模样! *Look how pretty she is!* ❷ sell well; be in great demand: 俏货

【俏货】goods in great demand

【俏丽】handsome; pretty

【俏皮】❶ good-looking; smart-looking: 她穿上那套新衣服,显得很～。*She looks very smart in her new dress.* ❷ witty; clever: 他讲的话很～。*What he said was very clever.*

【俏皮话】❶ witty remark; witticism; wisecrack ❷ sarcastic remark ❸ 同〖歇后语〗

【俏销】(of commodities) sell well; be in great demand; have a ready market: 这种产品～国外。*This kind of product sells well in foreign markets.*

窍 名 ❶ aperture; hole: 七窍 ❷ a key to sth.: 诀窍

【窍门】key (to a problem); knack: 找～ *try to find the key to a problem; try to get the knack of doing sth.*

峭 形 ❶ high and steep; precipitous: 陡峭 ❷ severe; stern

【峭拔】❶ (of a mountain) high and steep ❷ (of style of writing) vigorous: 笔锋～ *have a vigorous style of writing*

【峭壁】cliff; precipice; steep

【峭寒】(esp. of early spring) chilly

【峭立】rise steeply

翘 动 stick up; hold up; bend upwards; turn upwards: ～起拇指 *hold up one's thumb* / 你的头发～起来了,要梳一梳。*A lock of your hair is sticking up. Go and comb it.* ——另见 qiáo

【翘板】同〖跷跷板〗

【翘辫子】〈诙〉kick the bucket: 袁世凯刚刚登上皇帝的宝座就～了。*Yuan Shikai had just taken the throne when he kicked the bucket.*

【翘尾巴】be cocky; get stuck-up: 别一有成绩就～。*Don't get cocky when you've achieved something.*

撬 动 prize; pry: ～石头 *pry (or lift) up a stone* / ～起箱子盖 *prize (or pry) the top off a box* / 用撬杠把锁着的门～开 *pry open the locked door with a crowbar*

【撬杠】(又作'撬棍') pinch bar; crowbar; pry

鞘 名 sheath; scabbard: 剑～ *(sword) scabbard* / 刀出～ *take the knife out of the sheath* ——另见 shāo

【鞘翅】[动] elytrum

qiē

切 Ⅰ 动 cut; slice: ～菜 *cut up vegetables* / ～肉 *slice meat* / ～开西瓜 *cut a watermelon open* / ～成两半 *cut sth. into halves* Ⅱ 名 [数] tangency ——另见 qiè

【切变】[物] shear

【切布机】paper making rag cutter (or chopper)

【切菜机】vegetable-chopper; vegetable-cutter

【切槽】[机] grooving

【切齿机】[机] gear cutting machine

【切除】[医] excise; resect: ～脂肪瘤 *resect (or remove) a lipoma* / ～扁桃腺 *remove tonsils* / 全(部分)～ *total (partial) excision*

【切磋】learn from each other by exchanging views: 比赛后两国篮球运动员聚在一起,～球艺。*The basketball players of the two countries got together and swopped pointers after the match.*

【切磋琢磨】carve and polish—learn from each other by exchanging views

【切点】[数] point of tangency; point of contact

【切断】cut off: ～敌人后路 *cut off the enemy's retreat* / ～电源 *cut off the electricity supply*

【切分音】[音] syncopation

【切腹自杀】commit hara-kiri; commit seppuku

【切糕】a kind of cake made of glutinous rice, sold in sliced pieces

【切割】cut metal (by lathes, etc.)

【切开】[医] incise: ～引流 *incision and drainage*

【切口】(qiēkǒu) the side margin of a page in a book ——另见 qièkǒu

【切块】stripping and slicing (food)

【切力】[物] shearing force; shear: 横～ *transverse shear*

【切面】❶ cut noodles; machine-made noodles ❷ [数] tangent plane ❸ 同〖剖面〗

【切片】❶ cut into slices ❷ [医] section (of organic tissues): ～检查 *section for microscopic examination*

【切片机】❶ slicer ❷ [纺] chipper ❸ [医] microtome

【切线】[数] tangent (line)

【切削】[机] cut: 粗～ *rough cut*

【切纸机】paper cutting machine; paper cutter

qié

茄 名 eggplant; aubergine ——另见 jiā

【茄泥】mashed eggplant (a dish)

【茄子】eggplant; aubergine

qiě

且 Ⅰ 副 ❶ just; for the time being: 你～等一下。*Just wait a little while.* / 这事～放一下。*Let the matter rest for the time being.* / ～不说中文期刊,外文期刊也订了不少。*Lots of periodicals in foreign languages have been subscribed to, not to mention those in Chinese.* ❷ 〈方〉for a long time: 这种钢笔～使呢。*These fountain pens last a long time.* / 他～来不了呢。*He's a long time coming.* or *It'll be a while yet before he gets here.* Ⅱ 连 〈书〉❶ even: 死～不惧,况困难乎! *Even death holds no fears for us, to say nothing of difficulties.* ❷ both...and...: 既高～大 *both tall and heavy set; both high and wide* / 她工作既快～好。*She works quickly and well.*

【且慢】wait a moment; not so soon; not so fast: ～,听我把话说完。*Wait a minute, let me finish what I have to say.* / ～高兴! 他答应我们的要求是有条件的。*Don't rejoice too soon! He agreed to our request only on certain conditions.*

【且…且…】(used with monosyllabic verbs) while; as: 他们一路上且谈且走。*All the way they talked as they walked.*

qiè

切 Ⅰ 动 correspond to: 译文不～原意。*The translation does not quite correspond to the original.* Ⅱ 形 ❶ be close to: 亲切 ❷ eager; anxious: 心切 Ⅲ 副 be sure to: ～勿迟延。*Be*

sure not to delay. / ～不可自以为是。*One should never be presumptuous and opinionated.* ——另见 qiē

【切齿】gnash one's teeth (in hatred): ～痛恨 *gnash one's teeth in hatred* / 令人～ *make one bristle with anger*

【切当】proper; suitable; fitting; appropriate: 用词～ *well-chosen wording; appropriate use of words*

【切肤之痛】keenly felt pain

【切骨】(of hatred) deep; bitter

【切合】suit; fit in with: 计划要～实际。*Plans should be geared to actual circumstances.* / ～人民的需要 *fit in with the needs of the people* / ～实际的办法 *a practical approach*

【切己】of immediate concern to oneself

【切记】be sure to keep in mind; must always remember: 妈妈的嘱咐,你要～在心。*You must never forget what your mother told you.*

【切忌】must guard against; avoid by all means: ～主观片面。*Be careful to avoid being subjective and onesided.* / ～生冷 *cold and raw food strictly forbidden (often found in directions for prepared Chinese medicines)*

【切近】❶ close to: 这样解释比较～作者原意。*This interpretation seems to be closer to the author's original meaning.* ❷ close; near: 要实现一个崇高的目标,必须从～处做起。*To achieve a lofty goal, we must proceed from what is close at hand.*

【切口】(qièkǒu) the secret language of underworld gangs or of certain professions ——另见 qiēkǒu

【切脉】[中] feel the pulse

【切盼】(又作'切望') eagerly look forward to; wait impatiently for

【切切】❶ be sure to: ～不可骄傲。*Be sure not to become conceited.* or *Guard against arrogance by every means.* ❷ eager; urgent; earnest: ～请求 *urgently request* ❸ 同〖窃窃〗

【切身】❶ of immediate concern to oneself or sb.: 物价影响到千家万户的～利益。*Prices affect the immediate interests of every family.* ❷ personal; first-hand: ～体验 *personal experience* / 他在山区工作过,对那里缺医少药的情况有～体会。*He has worked in mountainous areas before, and has first-hand knowledge of the lack of doctors and medicine there.*

【切实】❶ feasible; practical; realistic: ～有效的办法 *practical and effective measures* / ～可行的计划 *a feasible (or realistic) plan* ❷ conscientious; earnest: ～改正错误 *correct one's mistakes in real earnest* / 切切实实地工作 *do one's job conscientiously*

【切题】keep to the point; be relevant to the subject: 写文章要～。*When writing, keep to the subject.*

【切诊】[中] pulse feeling and palpation, one of the four methods of diagnosis ——另见〖四诊〗

【切中】hit (the mark): 她的批评～要害。*Her criticism struck home.* / 文章～时弊。*The article hit hard at the ills of the time.*

妾 名 ❶ concubine ❷ a form of self-address formerly used by a wife when speaking to her husband

怯 形 timid; cowardly; nervous: 胆怯

【怯步】draw back (in fear); hang back: 殿堂幽黑阴森,令人～。*The caverous hall, dark and gloomy, was uninviting.*

【怯场】have stage fright: 他～,在台上一句话也说不出来。*He was suffering from stage fright and could not utter a word.*

【怯懦】timid and overcautious

【怯弱】timid and weak-willed: 她生性～,没有主见。*She has a timid and weak-willed nature and has no definite views of her own.*

【怯生】〈方〉shy with strangers: 这孩子～,客人一抱他就哭。*The baby is shy with strangers and will cry whenever a guest holds him.*

【怯生生】in a timid manner

【怯声怯气】speak in a timid manner; speak haltingly

【怯头怯脑】uncouth; lumpish; countrified

【怯阵】❶ feel nervous when going into battle; be battle-shy ❷ 同〖怯场〗

窃 Ⅰ 动 steal; pilfer: 偷窃 Ⅱ 副 secretly; surreptitiously; furtively: 窃笑

【窃案】larceny; burglary

【窃夺】usurp; grab

【窃钩者诛,窃国者侯】He who steals a belt buckle pays with his life; he who steals a state gets to be a feudal lord.

【窃国】usurp state power: ～大盗 *arch usurper of state power*

【窃据】usurp; unjustly occupy: ～要职 *usurp a high post; unjustly occupy a high post*

【窃密】steal secret information; steal secrets

【窃窃】low (voice); whispering ◇ ～私议 exchange whispered comments; ～私语 talk in whispers; whisper

【窃取】usurp; steal; grab: ～别人的劳动果实 *grab (or seize) the fruits of other people's labour*

【窃听】eavesdrop; wiretap; tap; bug: ～电话 *tap a telephone* / 他怕有人～,不敢在电话里说。*He was afraid of being bugged, and didn't dare to talk over the phone.* / 他在窗外～屋里人谈话。*He hid just outside the window and eavesdropped on the conversation going on inside the room.*

【窃听器】tapping device; listening-in device; bug: 装～ *bug (a room, etc.)* / 拆除～ *debug (a room, etc.)*

【窃笑】laugh secretly; laugh up one's sleeve

【窃贼】thief; burglar; pilferer

挈 动 ❶ take along; carry: 他～眷返回故里。*He went back to his native place, taking his family along with him.* ❷ lift; raise; take up: 提纲

挈领

【挈带】take along; carry

惬 形〈书〉be satisfied: 惬意

【惬意】be pleased; be satisfied

锲 动〈书〉carve; engrave

【锲而不舍】keep on chipping away—work with perseverance: 学习要有～的精神。*Study requires perseverance.*

qīn

亲 Ⅰ名 ❶ parent: 双亲 ❷ blood relation; next of kin: ～兄弟 *blood brother* ❸ relative: 近亲 ❹ marriage; match: 说亲 ❺ bride: 迎亲 Ⅱ形 close; intimate; dear: 我和大姐最～。*My eldest sister is very dear to me.* Ⅲ副 in person; oneself: 亲眼 Ⅳ动 kiss: 她～了～孩子的脸。*She kissed the child on the cheek.* ——另见 qìng

【亲爱】dear; beloved: ～的同志们 *dear comrades* / ～的祖国 *one's beloved country*

【亲本】[生] parent: 轮回～ *recurrent parent*

【亲笔】❶ in one's own handwriting: 这信是他～写的。*This letter is in his own hand.* / ～信 *a personal, handwritten message (or letter); an autograph letter* / ～签名 *one's own signature; autograph* ❷ one's own handwriting: 这是他的～。*This is his handwriting.*

【亲代】[生] parental generation

【亲睹】see with one's own eyes; see for oneself

【亲骨肉】one's own flesh and blood (i.e. parents and children, brothers and sisters)

【亲和力】[化] affinity

【亲近】be close to; be on intimate terms with: 这两人很～。*Those two are on intimate terms.* / 他对人热情诚恳,大家都愿意～他。*As he is warmhearted and sincere, everyone wants to be friends with him.*

【亲眷】〈方〉❶ one's relatives ❷ family dependants

【亲口】(say sth.) personally: 这是他～告诉我的。*He told me this himself.*

【亲历】〈书〉have a personal experience of sth.

【亲临】come or go to a place personally: ～指导 *come personally to give guidance* / ～现场 *be on the spot* / 将军～前线指挥。*The general directed the battle personally at the front.*

【亲和】affable; genial

【亲聆】go in person to listen to (instructions): ～教诲 *go in person to listen to sb.'s instructions*

【亲密】close; intimate: ～的战友 *a close comrade-in-arms* / 他俩非常～。*The two of them are on very intimate terms.*

【亲密无间】be on intimate terms

【亲昵】very intimate; affectionate: ～的称呼 *an affectionate form of address*

【亲朋】relatives and friends; kith and kin: ～故旧 *relatives and old acquaintances*

【亲戚】relative: 我们两家是～。*Our two families are relatives.* / 一门～ *a set of relatives*

【亲切】❶ cordial; kind: ～的关怀 *kind attention; loving care* / ～的谈话 *a cordial conversation* / 他的话我们感到很～。*What he said touched our hearts.* ❷ close; intimate; dear

【亲情】affection between family members

【亲热】affectionate; intimate; warmhearted: 我们都～地称她为大姐。*We all affectionately refer to her as our elder sister.* / ～地问长问短 *make warmhearted inquiries (about sb.'s health, etc.)*

【亲人】❶ one's parents, spouse, children, etc.; one's family members: 他除母亲外,没有别的～。*His mother is the only other member of his family.* ❷ dear ones; those dear to one: 感谢～解放军 *thank our beloved Liberation Army*

【亲如手足】(又作'亲如兄弟') as close as brothers

【亲如一家】as dear to each other as members of one family

【亲善】close and friendly (between countries): ～关系 *good will*

【亲身】personal; firsthand: ～经历 *personal experience; firsthand experience*

【亲生】❶ be sb.'s own child (i.e. not an adopted one): 小明是她～的。*Xiao Ming is her own child.* ❷ one's own (children or parents): ～子女 *one's own children* / ～父母 *one's own parents (i.e. not foster parents or stepparents)*

【亲事】marriage: 他的～快成了吧? *Is he going to get married soon?*

【亲手】with one's own hands; personally; oneself: 这些是他～种的树。*Those are the trees he planted with his own hands.* / 你～做一做。*Do it yourself.*

【亲疏】(of relatives or social connections) close or distant: 不分～ *whether close or distant*

【亲属】kinsfolk; relatives

【亲痛仇快】(又作'亲者痛,仇者快') sadden one's own folk and gladden the enemy

【亲王】prince

【亲吻】kiss

【亲信】❶ close and trustful ❷〈贬〉trusted aide (or follower)

【亲眼】with one's own eyes; personally: 这是我～看见的。*I saw it with my own eyes.* / 我们～看到了贵国人民对中国人民的友好情谊。*We have seen for ourselves how friendly the people of your country are towards the people of China.*

【亲友】relatives and friends; kith and kin

【亲缘】[生] affinity

【亲自】personally; in person; oneself: ～动手 *personally take a hand in the work; do the job oneself* / ～拜访 *make a personal call* / 你～去看看。*Go and see for yourself.*

【亲族】members of the same clan

【亲嘴】kiss

侵 Ⅰ动 invade; intrude into; infringe upon: 入侵 Ⅱ形 approaching (daybreak): 侵晨

【侵彻力】[军] penetrativeness (of a bullet)

【侵晨】approaching daybreak; towards dawn

【侵犯】encroach on; infringe (upon); violate: ～人权 *infringe upon human rights* / ～著作权 *infringe a copyright* / ～领土和主权 *violate a country's territorial integrity and sovereignty*

【侵害】encroach on; make inroads on: 同～公民权利的行为作斗争 *fight against any infringement of the rights of citizens*

【侵略】aggression; invasion: ～别国 *commit aggression against another country* / ～国 *aggressor (nation)* / ～军 *aggressor troops; invading army* / ～行为 *act of aggression; aggression* / ～战争 *war of aggression* / ～者 *aggressor; invader*

【侵权】[法] tort: 他被卷进了这场～案。*He was involved in a tort case.* / ～行为 *tort; act of tort* / ～行为的赔偿责任 *tort liability*

【侵权行为】[法] tort

【侵染】(of germs, bacteria, or viruses) infect

【侵扰】invade and harass: ～边境 *harass a country's frontiers; make border raids*

【侵入】invade; intrude into; make incursions into: ～领海 *intrude into a country's territorial waters* / 外国资本的～ *the invasion of foreign capital* / 病菌已～肺部。*Germs have invaded the lungs.*

【侵人犯规】[体] (of basketball) personal foul

【侵入岩】[地质] intrusive rock; irruptive rock

【侵蚀】❶ corrode; erode: 风雨的～ *erosion by wind and rain* / 各种酸类～金属。*Acids erode (or eat into) metals.* / 资产阶级思想的～ *the corrosive influence of bourgeois ideology* / 细菌～人体。*Germs invade the human body.* / ～性 *corrodibility* ❷ seize (property) in secret and bit by bit: ～公款 *embezzle public funds; help oneself to public money*

【侵蚀土】eroded soil

【侵吞】❶ embezzle; misappropriate: ～公款 *embezzle public funds* / ～社会财富 *appropriate social property* ❷ swallow up; annex: ～别国领土 *annex another country's territory*

【侵袭】make inroads on; invade and attack; hit: 台风～沿海地区。*The typhoon hit the coastal areas.*

【侵晓】approaching daybreak; towards dawn

【侵占】❶ invade and occupy: ～别国领土 *invade and occupy another country's territory* ❷ seize; embezzle: ～公有土地 *seize public land* / ～国家收入 *embezzle state revenue*

钦 Ⅰ动 admire; respect: 钦佩 Ⅱ副 by the emperor himself: 钦定

【钦差】imperial envoy; imperial commissioner

【钦差大臣】❶ imperial commissioner; imperial envoy: ～林则徐 *(Imperial) Commissioner Lin Zexu* ❷ a nickname for a representative of the higher authorities: "～"满天飞 "*imperial envoys" rushing here, there, and everywhere*

【钦定】(of a book, etc.) made by imperial order

【钦服】esteem; admire

【钦敬】admire and respect

【钦佩】admire; esteem: 表示～ *express admiration for* / 他们坚持科学实验的精神令人～。*Their persistence in scientific experiment commands admiration.*

【钦羡】admire and respect

qín

芹 名 celery

【芹菜】celery

秦 名 ❶ one of the Warring States ❷ the Qin Dynasty (221-207 B.C.) ❸ a name for modern Shaanxi

【秦艽】[植] large-leaved gentian (Gentiana macrophylla)

【秦晋之好】the amity between Qin and Jin (sealed by a marriage alliance between the two royal houses)—a marriage alliance between two families: 两家结了～。*The two families formed a marriage alliance.*

【秦楼楚馆】towers of Qin and pavilions of Chu—quarters of pleasure; courtesans' quarters

【秦皮】[中] the bark of ash (Fraxinus bungeana)

【秦腔】Shaanxi opera, popular in the northwestern provinces

【秦越】as far apart as Qin and Yue—have no dealings with each other

琴 名 ❶ general name for certain musical instruments: 小提琴 ❷ qin, a seven-stringed plucked instrument in some ways similar to the zither

【琴拨】plectrum

【琴凳】music stool

【琴剑飘零】〈旧〉(of a scholar) wander from place to place

【琴键】key (on a musical instrument)

【琴马】[音] bridge (of a stringed instrument)

【琴鸟】lyrebird

【琴棋书画】lute-playing, chess, calligraphy, and painting—accomplishments of a scholar of the old school

【琴瑟不调】the qin and the se are not in harmony—discord between husband and wife; an uncongenial marriage

【琴瑟和谐】the qin and se are in harmony —husband and wife living in harmony; wedded bliss

【琴师】stringed instrumentalist

【琴弦】string (of a musical instrument)

【琴心剑胆】the sentiments of the lute (qin) and the spirit of the sword—a cultivated mind animated with a chivalrous spirit

禽 名 birds

【禽龙】iguanodon

【禽兽】birds and beasts—inhuman：～行为 *brutish acts*；*bestial acts*

勤 Ⅰ形 ❶ diligent；industrious；hardworking：辛勤 ❷ frequent；regular；constant：衣服要～洗～换。*Clothes should be changed and washed regularly*. / 夏季雨水～。*Rain is frequent in summer*. Ⅱ名（office，school，etc.）attendance：值勤

【勤奋】diligent；assiduous；industrious：学习～ *be diligent in one's studies* / 他一天到晚都在～地工作着。*He buries himself in his work from morning till night*.

【勤工俭学】part-work and part-study system；work-study programme

【勤俭】hardworking and thrifty：～过日子 *live industriously and frugally*；*lead an industrious and thrifty life* ◇ ～持家 be industrious and thrifty in running a household；～建国 build up the country through thrift and hard work

【勤恳】diligent and conscientious

【勤快】〈口〉diligent；hardworking：她真～，一会儿也不闲着。*She is diligent and keeps herself busy all the time*.

【勤劳】diligent；industrious；hardworking：～勇敢的中国人民 *the valiant and industrious Chinese people* / ～的双手 *an untiring pair of hands*

【勤勉】diligent；assiduous：～好学 *diligent and eager to learn*

【勤朴】industrious and thrifty

【勤王】〈书〉❶ come to the rescue of the king：发兵～ *send troops to save the throne* ❷ do one's best to serve the throne

【勤务】❶（public）duties；service ❷ a person who does logistic duties

【勤务兵】orderly

【勤务员】❶ odd-jobman（in an army unit or government office）❷（used in）人民的～ *a servant of the people*

【勤学苦练】study diligently and train hard

【勤杂工】odd-jobman；handyman

【勤杂人员】personnel regularly doing certain odd jobs（in an army unit or government office）；odd-jobmen

【勤政廉政】be diligent and honest in one's work

擒 动 capture；catch；seize：生擒

【擒拿】arrest；capture；catch

【擒贼先擒王】to catch brigands，first catch their king：射人先射马，～。*Aim at the rider's horse*：*the king of brigands first to justice bring*.

【擒纵轮】[机] escape wheel

噙 动 hold in the mouth or the eyes：～着烟袋 *hold a pipe between one's lips* / ～着眼泪 *eyes brimming with tears*

qǐn

寝 Ⅰ动 sleep：废寝忘食 Ⅱ名 ❶ bedroom：就寝 ❷ coffin chamber：陵寝

【寝车】sleeping car；sleeping carriage；sleeper

【寝宫】❶ sleeping quarters of the emperor and empress ❷ coffin chamber in an imperial mausoleum

【寝具】bedding

【寝食】eating and sleeping—daily life ◇ ～不安 feel uneasy even when eating and sleeping；be worried waking or sleeping

【寝室】room（in a dormitory）

qìn

沁 动 ooze；seep；exude：他的额上～出了汗珠。*His forehead was oozing sweat*.

【沁人心脾】gladdening the heart and refreshing the mind；mentally refreshing；refreshing：空气清新，～。*The air was pure and fresh*；*it seeped into my heart*. / 肖邦的夜曲～。*Chopin's nocturnes are heart-stirring*.

【沁润】（of liquid，aroma，etc.）soak into；permeate through；penetrate to：春雨～着大地。*The spring rain was soaking into the earth*.

qīng

青 Ⅰ形 ❶ blue or green：曲终人不见，江山数峰～。*The song is ended*，*no one is to be seen*. *On the river the mountain peaks are so blue*! ❷ black：青布 ❸ young（people）：青年 Ⅱ名 green grass or young crops：踏青

【青布】black cloth

【青菜】❶ general name for 蔬菜 ❷ another name for 小白菜

【青草】green grass

【青出于蓝】（usu. used in）～而胜于蓝 *blue comes from the indigo plant but is bluer than the plant itself—the pupil surpasses the master*

【青春】youth；youthfulness：把～献给祖国 *dedicate one's youth to serving one's country* / 充满着～的活力 *be bursting with youthful vigour* / 老厂恢复了～。*The old factory has regained its old vigour*.

【青春饭】job for young persons only：吃～ *hold a job that lasts only as long as one's youth*

【青春偶像】adolescent idol

【青春期】puberty；adolescence

【青瓷】celadon（ware）

【青葱】verdant；fresh green：～的竹林 *a verdant grove of bamboo* / ～的草地 *fresh green grassland* / 窗外长着几棵竹子，～可爱。*The bamboos just outside the window are green and lovely*.

【青翠】verdant；fresh and green：～的西山 *the verdant green Western Hills*（*in Beijing*）/ 雨后，垂柳显得格外～。*The weeping willows looked fresher and greener after the rain*.

【青豆】green soya bean

【青工】(〈略〉全称为'青年工人') young workers
【青光眼】[医] glaucoma
【青果】〈方〉Chinese olive
【青蒿】[植] Artemisia apiacea
【青红皂白】black and white; right and wrong —— 另见〖不分青红皂白〗
【青花瓷】blue and white porcelain
【青黄不接】when the crop is still in the blade and the old stock is all consumed—temporary shortage: 这个系正处在～的时期,青年教师大部分还没有成长起来。*This department is in a period of crisis right now, because most of the young teachers are still inexperienced.*
【青椒】green pepper
【青筋】blue veins: 他额角上暴起了～。*Blue veins stood out on his temples.*
【青稞】(又作'青稞麦') ❶ highland barley (grown in Xizang and Qinghai) ❷ the seed of highland barley
【青睐】〈书〉favour; good graces: 获得某人的～ *find favour in sb.'s eyes; be in sb.'s good graces*
【青莲色】pale purple; heliotrope
【青楼】〈文〉blue mansions—pleasure quarters; courtesans' quarters
【青绿】dark green: ～的松林 *a dark green pine forest*
【青盲】[中] glaucoma
【青梅】green plum
【青梅竹马】green plums and a bamboo horse—a girl and a boy playing innocently together; a man and a woman who had an innocent affection for each other in childhood
【青霉素】penicillin
【青面獠牙】green-faced and long-toothed—terrifying in appearance: 露出～的凶相 *reveal the ferocious features of an ogre*
【青苗】young crops; green shoots of (food) grains
【青年】youth; young people: ～时代 *one's youth* / ～人 *young people; youth* / ～学生 *young students; student youth* / ～一代 *the younger generation*
【青年节】〈略〉见〖五四青年节〗
【青纱帐】the green curtain of tall crops: 游击队利用～作掩护。*The guerrillas used the green curtain of tall crops as cover.*
【青山】green hills; blue mountains
【青山不老,绿水长存】The blue mountains do not grow old, the green waters always remain.
【青山绿水】blue mountains and green waters—beautiful scenery
【青少年】teen-agers; youngsters: ～犯罪 *juvenile delinquency*
【青史】annals of history: 永垂～ *go down in the annals of history* / ～留名 *have a place in history*
【青丝】〈文〉black hair (of a woman or girl): 一缕～ *a thread of black hair*
【青饲料】greenfeed; green fodder
【青松】pine
【青蒜】garlic leaves
【青苔】moss
【青檀】[植] wingceltis (Pteroceltis tatarinowii)
【青天】❶ the blue sky ❷ the clear sky (a respectful sobriquet for a clean and upright official): 老百姓管包公叫包～。*The people called Lord Bao "Bao the Clear Sky".*
【青天白日】❶ bright and sunny ❷ broad daylight
【青铜】bronze ◇ ～器 bronze ware; ～时代 the Bronze Age
【青蛙】frog
【青虾】freshwater shrimp
【青香薷】[中] Chinese mosla (Mosla chinensis)
【青葙】[植] feather cockscomb (Celosia argentea)
【青葙子】[中] the seed of feather cockscomb
【青杨】Cathay poplar (Populus cathayana)
【青蝇】greenbottle (fly)
【青鱼】black carp
【青郁】verdant and luxuriant: ～的竹林 *dense bamboos*
【青云】high official position or rapid official advancement ◇ ～直上 rapid advancement; a meteoric rise; ～志 high aspirations
【青贮】[农] ensiling: ～饲料 *ensilage; silage*

轻 Ⅰ 形 ❶ of little weight; light: 油比水～。*Oil is lighter than water.* / 身～如燕 (*of a high jumper, gymnast, etc.*) *as light as a swallow* ❷ (of load, equipment, etc.) small or simple: 轻武器 ❸ small in number, degree, etc.: 他年纪很～。*He is very young.* / 她的病很～。*Her illness is not at all serious.* / 工作很～ *have a light workload* / 伤势较～ *have a slight injury* / 她睡觉～。*She is a light sleeper.* ❹ not serious; relaxing; light: 轻音乐 ❺ not important: 责任～ *carry a light responsibility* / 关系不～ *have an important bearing on sth.* Ⅱ 副 ❶ gently; softly: ～～地说 *speak in a soft voice; whisper* / ～拿～放。*Handle gently.* / 她走路脚步～。*She walks with a light step.* / 病人睡着了,～点儿! *Be quiet! The patient is asleep.* ❷ rashly: 轻信 Ⅲ 动 belittle; make light of: 轻财重义
【轻磅纸】lightweight paper
【轻便】❶ light; portable: ～铁道 *light railway* / ～桥 *portable bridge* / ～自行车 *lightweight bicycle; light roadster* ❷ easy and convenient: 这种旅行包携带～。*This travelling bag is easy and convenient to carry.*
【轻薄】(usu. of a man towards a woman) given to philandering; frivolous
【轻财重义】value friendship more than money; be generous and charitable
【轻车简从】同〖轻装简从〗
【轻车熟路】drive in a light carriage on a familiar road—do sth. one knows well and can manage with ease
【轻淡】❶ faint; dim: ～地一笑 *give a faint smile* ❷ casual; random: 有人只是～地谈起这件事。*Someone casually mentioned it.*
【轻敌】take the enemy lightly; underestimate the

enemy：～思想 *tendency to take the enemy or the opponent (in a game) lightly*

【轻而易举】easy to do：编一本词典并不是～的事。*Compiling a dictionary is no easy task.* / 我们～地就把对手打败了。*We beat our opponents hands down.*

【轻纺工业】textile and other light industries

【轻放】put down gently：易碎物品，小心～！*Fragile! Handle with care!*

【轻风】［气］light breeze

【轻浮】frivolous；flighty；light：举止～ *behave frivolously* / ～的行为 *frivolous conduct*

【轻歌曼舞】soft music and graceful dances

【轻工业】light industry

【轻核】［物］light nucleus

【轻混凝土】lightweight concrete

【轻活】light work；soft job

【轻机关枪】light machine gun

【轻健】spry and light；nimble；brisk：步履～ *walk at a brisk pace；be spry in one's steps*

【轻捷】spry and light；nimble：他跨着～的脚步回家去。*He walked home with brisk steps.*

【轻金属】light metal

【轻举妄动】act rashly；take reckless action：这件事非同小可，不能～。*This is no trivial matter；make no move without careful thought.*

【轻看】look down upon；belittle

【轻口薄舌】❶ speak unkindly；make caustic remarks；be sharp-tongued ❷ make improper remarks

【轻快】❶ brisk；spry：她迈着～的步子走向公园。*She walked at a brisk pace towards the park.* ❷ lighthearted；lively：～的曲调 *a lively tune*

【轻狂】extremely frivolous

【轻量级】［体］lightweight

【轻慢】treat sb. without proper respect；slight

【轻描淡写】touch on lightly；mention casually：要认真检查自己的错误，不要～。*You should criticize your own mistakes earnestly, and not just touch on them lightly.* / 他～地说，"打了两场球都不费力就赢了。" *He said casually, "We won both games easily."*

【轻蔑】despise；scorn；disdain；be contemptuous：她用～的目光扫了他一眼。*She cast a contemptuous glance at him.*

【轻诺寡信】make promises easily but seldom keep them

【轻泡货】［交通］light cargo

【轻炮兵】light artillery

【轻飘】light；buoyant：～的柳絮 *buoyant willow catkins*

【轻飘飘】light；buoyant：垂柳～地摆动。*Willow branches were swaying lightly.* / 她高兴地走着，脚底下～的。*She tripped joyfully along, as if treading on air.*

【轻骑】❶ light cavalry ❷ moped ◇ ～兵 light cavalry

【轻巧】❶ light and handy：这录音机真～。*This is a handy tape recorder.* / 她身子很～，舞跳得好。*Her figure is slim and light, so she makes a good dancer.* ❷ dexterous；deft：他操纵机器动作非常～。*He operates the machine dexterously.* / 她的自由体操动作～，姿势优美。*She did her floor exercises with agility and grace.* ❸ simple；easy 你说得倒～。*You talk as if it were a simple matter.*

【轻取】win an easy victory (in a game)；beat easily；win hands down：～第一局 *win the first game easily (or without effort)* / 北京队以5：0～客队。*The Beijing team won an easy victory by beating the visiting team* 5：0.

【轻柔】soft；gentle：～的枝条 *pliable twigs* / ～的声音 *a gentle voice* / 第一小提琴奏出第一主题，旋律～动听。*The first violins introduced the first theme, a soft and beautiful melody.*

【轻纱】fine gauze

【轻伤】slight (or minor) wound；flesh wound：～不下火线 *not leave the frontline on account of minor wounds* / ～员 *ambulant patient (or case)；walking wounded*

【轻生】make light of one's life—commit suicide

【轻声】❶ in a soft voice；softly：～低语 *speak softly；whisper* ❷［语音］neutral tone：普通话中的"了、着、的"等虚词和做后缀的"子、头"等字都念～。*In putonghua, particles like le, zhe, and de and suffixes like zi and tou are all in the neutral tone (or are all toneless).*

【轻省】〈方〉❶ relaxed：如今添了个助手，你可以稍微～点。*Now that you have an assistant, you can relax a little.* ❷ light：这个箱子挺～。*This box is very light.*

【轻世傲物】full of conceit and defiant of convention

【轻视】belittle；look down on；underrate：～妇女 *look down on women* / ～小学教师的作用 *underestimate the role of primary school teachers*

【轻手轻脚】gently；softly：护士出来进去都～的，怕惊醒病人。*The nurse moved around very softly so as not to wake the patient.*

【轻率】rash；hasty；indiscreet：～的态度 *reckless attitude* / ～从事 *act rashly* / 你这样处理太～了。*It was indiscreet of you to handle it that way.*

【轻水】［化］light water

【轻松】light；relaxed：～的工作 *light work；soft job；cushy job* / ～地打败对手 *beat one's opponent with ease* / 我们过了一个～愉快的暑假。*We had a happy and relaxed summer vacation.*

【轻瘫】［医］paresis

【轻佻】frivolous；flippant；giddy：举止～ *flippant (or skittish) behaviour*

【轻微】light；slight；trifling；to a small extent：～的伤亡 *light casualties* / ～的头痛 *a slight headache* / ～的损失 *a trifling loss*

【轻武器】light arms；small arms

【轻闲】❶ not busy；leisurely ❷ easy or light (work)

【轻泻剂】laxative
【轻信】be credulous; readily place trust in; readily believe: 不要～谣言。*Give no credence to rumours.* / 重证据，不能～口供。*Lay stress on evidence and do not readily believe confessions.*
【轻型】light-duty; light: ～机械 *light-duty machinery* / ～飞机 *light aircraft*
【轻言细语】speak in a soft, gentle voice
【轻易】❶ easily: 胜利成果不是～得来的。*The fruits of victory were not easily won.* ❷ lightly; rashly: 不要～地下结论。*Don't draw hasty conclusions.* or *Don't jump to conclusions.* / 他不～发表意见。*He does not express an opinion rashly.*
【轻音乐】light music
【轻盈】❶ slim and graceful; lithe; lissom: ～的舞步 *graceful steps (in dancing)* / 她的自由体操动作～优美。*Her movements in free gymnastics are lithe and graceful.* ❷ lighthearted; relaxed: 笑语～ *talk and laugh merrily and lightheartedly*
【轻油】light oil
【轻于鸿毛】lighter than a goose feather ——另见〖重于泰山，轻于鸿毛〗
【轻重】❶ weight: 这两只箱子～不一样。*These two boxes do not weigh the same.* ❷ degree of seriousness; relative importance: 根据病情～决定病人是否住院。*Whether a patient is to be hospitalized depends on how serious the case is.* ❸ propriety: 这个人说话不知～。*That man doesn't know the proper way to talk.*
【轻重倒置】put the trivial above the important; stress trifles and overlook matters of moment
【轻重缓急】relative importance or urgency; order of priority: 分～解决问题 *solve problems in order of priority* / 工作应分～。*Work should be done in order of importance and urgency.*
【轻重量级】[体] light heavyweight
【轻舟】〈文〉a small light boat; skiff
【轻装】❶ light packs: ～就道 *travel light* / ～前进 *march with light packs* / ～上阵 *go into battle with a light pack* ❷ light equipment: ～部队 *a lightly equipped army*
【轻装简从】(of an important person) travel with little luggage and few attendants—travel light
【轻嘴薄舌】(又作'轻口薄舌') have a caustic and sharp tongue
【轻罪】[法] misdemeanour; minor offence (or crime): ～重判不对，重罪轻判也不对。*It is wrong to deal with a minor offence as if it were a major one and vice versa.*

氢 名 [化] hydrogen (H)
【氢弹】hydrogen bomb ◇ ～头 hydrogen warhead; H-warhead
【氢氟酸】[化] hydro-uoric acid
【氢化】[化] hydrogenation: ～裂解 *hydrocracking* / ～酶 *hydrogenase* / ～物 *hydride*
【氢气】hydrogen ◇ ～球 hydrogen balloon
【氢氰酸】[化] hydrocyanic acid
【氢氧】[化] oxyhydrogen: ～焰 *oxyhydrogen flame* ◇ ～吹管 oxyhydrogen blowpipe; ～化物 [化] hydroxide

倾 Ⅰ 动 ❶ incline; lean; bend: 向左～ *incline to the left* / 身子向前～ *bend forward; lean forward* ❷ collapse: 大厦将～ *a great mansion on the point of collapse* ❸ overturn and pour out; empty: ～其所有 *give away all one has* ❹ do all one can; use up all one's resources: ～全力把工作做好 *exert oneself to the utmost to do the work well* Ⅱ 名 deviation; tendency: "左"倾
【倾巢】(of the enemy or bandits) turn out in full force (or strength) ◇ ～出动 (of the enemy or bandits, etc.) turn out in full force (or strength)
【倾城】❶ the whole city or town: ～而出，迎接国宾。*The whole town turned out to welcome the state guests.* ❷ 同〖倾国倾城〗
【倾倒】(qīngdǎo) ❶ topple and fall; topple over ❷ greatly admire: 为之～ *be infatuated with sb.; be overwhelmed with admiration for sb.*
【倾倒】(qīngdào) tip; dump; empty; pour out: ～垃圾 *dump rubbish* / 他猛一使劲儿就把一车土都～到沟里了。*With a heave he emptied a wheelbarrow of earth into the ditch.*
【倾点】[化] pour point; flow point
【倾动】move and win admiration: ～一时 *cause a great sensation; create a furore*
【倾耳】prick up one's ears: ～细听 *prick up one's ears and listen carefully*
【倾覆】overturn; topple; capsize
【倾国倾城】(of a woman) lovely enough to cause the fall of a city or a state; devastatingly beautiful; exceedingly beautiful
【倾家荡产】lose a family fortune; be reduced to poverty and ruin
【倾角】❶ [物] dip ❷ [数] inclination ❸ [地质] dip angle ◇ ～测量仪 dipmeter
【倾慕】have a strong admiration for; adore: 彼此～ *have a strong admiration for each other*
【倾囊相助】empty one's purse to help; give generous financial assistance
【倾盆大雨】heavy downpour; torrential rain; cloudburst: 赶上一场～ *be caught in a downpour* / 下起了～。*The rain was pelting down.* or *It was raining cats and dogs.*
【倾洒】(of snow, tears, etc.) pour down or forth: 天空～着鹅毛大雪。*Big snowflakes are pouring down from the sky.* / 他一腔心血都～在这部词典里。*In carrying out this dictionary project he spat out, so to speak, the blood of his heart.*
【倾诉】pour out (one's heart, troubles, etc.): ～衷肠 *pour out one's heart; reveal one's innermost feelings*
【倾谈】have a good, heart-to-heart talk
【倾听】listen attentively to; lend an attentive ear to: ～群众的意见 *listen attentively to the views of the masses*

【倾吐】say what is on one's mind without reservation：～衷情 *unbosom oneself* / ～苦水 *unburden oneself of one's grievances*

【倾箱倒箧】turn out all one's boxes and suitcases—give away all one has

【倾向】❶ tendency；trend；inclination；deviation：政治～ *political inclination* / 要注意一种～有可能掩盖另一种～。*One must be alive to the possibility that one tendency may conceal another.* ❷ be inclined to；prefer：这两种方案我～于第一种。*Of the two plans, I prefer the first.*

【倾向性】tendentiousness：他的发言是有～的。*His statement was frankly tendentious.*

【倾销】sell goods at a very low price；dump：～货物 *dump goods*

【倾斜】tilt；incline；slope；slant：我国地势大致从西北向东南～。*Generally speaking, the terrain of China slopes from northwest to southeast.* / 地面微微向南～。*The land inclines gently to the south.* / 这墙有点～。*The wall is a little out of the perpendicular.* ◇ ～度 gradient；～面 inclined plane

【倾斜角】❶ bank angle (of an airplane) ❷ 同〖倾角〗

【倾斜政策】preferential policy；affirmative policy

【倾泻】come down in torrents：山水～而下，汇成洪流。*Streams rushed down the mountain and converged into a torrent.*

【倾卸】tip；dump；empty；pour out

【倾卸汽车】dump truck；tipper

【倾心】❶ admire；adore ❷ cordial；heart-to-heart：～交谈 *have a heart-to-heart talk*

【倾心吐胆】pour out one's heart；unburden one's heart；unbosom oneself

【倾轧】engage in internal strife；jostle against each other：互相～ *try to do each other down*

【倾注】❶ pour into：几股山泉～到深潭里。*Several mountain streams pour into the pool.* ❷ throw (energy, etc.) into：把全部心血～到工作中去 *throw all one's energy into one's work* / 她把全部的爱～在独生子身上。*She poured all her affection on her only son.*

卿 名 ❶ a minister or a high official in ancient times ❷ an emperor's form of address for a minister ❸ a term of endearment formerly used between husband and wife or among close friends

【卿卿我我】(of lovers) whisper sweet nothings to one another；bill and coo

清 Ⅰ 形 ❶ unmixed；clear：～水 *clear water* ❷ distinct；clarified：说不～ *hard to explain* / 数不～ *countless* / 问～底细 *make sure of every detail*；*get to the bottom of the matter* ❸ quiet：冷清 ❹ just and honest：清官 ❺ pure：清醇 Ⅱ 副 completely；thoroughly：还清 Ⅲ 动 ❶ settle；clear up：账～了吗？*Has the account been settled (or cleared up)?* ❷ clean up；purge：～政治，～思想，～组织，～经济 *clean things up in the fields of politics, ideology, organization and economy* ❸ count：～一～行李的件数 *count the pieces of luggage and see how many there are*

【清白】pure；clean；stainless：历史～ *have a clean personal record* / ～无辜 *innocent*

【清仓】make an inventory (or checkup) of warehouses

【清册】detailed list：固定资产～ *an inventory of fixed assets*

【清茶】❶ green tea ❷ tea served without refreshments

【清查】❶ check：～户口 *check on household occupant*；*check residence cards* / ～仓库 *make an inventory (or checkup) of a warehouse* ❷ ferret out (counterrevolutionaries, etc.)；uncover；comb out

【清产核资】general checkup on enterprise assets

【清偿】pay off；clear off：～债务 *pay off (or clear off) debts*

【清场】clear out (or clean up) a gathering place (theatre, arena, athletic field, etc.)

【清唱】sing opera arias (without makeup and acting)

【清唱剧】［音］oratorio

【清澈】(又作'清彻') limpid；clear：～的池塘 *a limpid pool* / 湖水～见底。*The lake water is so clear that you can see to the bottom.*

【清晨】early morning

【清除】clear away；eliminate；get rid of：～垃圾 *clear away the rubbish* / ～障碍 *remove obstacles* / 把某人～出党 *clear sb. out of the Party*

【清楚】❶ clear；distinct：字迹～ *written in a clear hand* / 发音～ *a clear pronunciation* / 头脑～ *a clear head* / 他的话说得不～。*He didn't speak clearly.* or *What he said was ambiguous.* ❷ be clear about；understand：这个问题你～不～？*Do you understand this question or not?* / 我真不～他为什么这样做。*I really can't understand why he has done this.*

【清创术】［医］débridement

【清醇】pure (in taste or smell)：酒味～可口。*The wine is pure and smooth to the palate.*

【清脆】clear and melodious：～的歌声 *clear and melodious singing*

【清单】detailed list；detailed account：货物～ *a detailed list of goods*；*inventory* / 列一个～ *make a detailed list*

【清淡】❶ light；weak；delicate：～的绿茶 *weak green tea* / ～的花香 *the delicate fragrance of flowers* ❷ not greasy or strongly flavoured；light：～的食物 *light food* ❸ dull；slack：生意～。*Business is slack.*

【清党】purge (a political party)；carry out a purge

【清道】❶ sweep the streets ❷ clear the way (for a high official in imperial times)

【清道夫】〈旧〉scavenger；street cleaner；street sweeper

【清点】check；make an inventory；sort and count：

～物资 *make an inventory of equipment and materials* / ～货物 *take stock* / ～战利品 *check and sort out spoils of war*

【清炖】boiled in clear soup (without soy sauce): ～鸡 *stewed chicken without soy sauce*

【清芬】〈书〉❶ delicate fragrance; faint scent ❷ moral integrity; nobility of character

【清风】cool breeze; refreshing breeze: ～徐来,水波不兴。*A cool breeze blew gently, without starting a ripple.*

【清福】the happiness of a leisurely, retired life

【清高】aloof from politics and material pursuits

【清稿】❶ make a fair (or clean) copy ❷ fair (or clean) copy

【清歌妙舞】clear singing, exquisite dancing

【清官】〈旧〉honest and upright official

【清官难断家务事】Even an upright official finds it hard to settle a family quarrel.

【清规】monastic rules for Buddhists

【清规戒律】❶ regulations, taboos and commandments for Buddhists or Taoists ❷ restrictions and fetters: 过多的评头品足,数不尽的～ *endless carping and countless taboos*

【清锅冷灶】the pot is empty and the stove is cold—(of a house, restaurant, etc.) deserted; unfrequented

【清寒】❶ poor; in straitened circumstances: 家境～ *come of an impoverished (or poor) family* ❷ cold and clear: 月色～ *clear, cold moonlight*

【清还】clear up and pay back (debts, etc.)

【清火】[中] relieve inflammation or internal heat

【清剿】clean up; suppress; eliminate: ～土匪 *clean up bandits; suppress bandits*

【清教徒】[宗](基督教) Puritan

【清洁】clean: 整齐～ *clean and tidy* / 人人要注意～卫生。*Everybody should pay attention to sanitation and hygiene.* ◇ ～袋 sick bag; ～队 cleaning squad; ～工人 sanitation worker; street cleaner; ～剂 cleanser; detergent; ～提单 clean bill of lading

【清结】❶ settle (or square) accounts; balance the books ❷ bring to an end; wind up; settle

【清劲风】[气] fresh breeze

【清净】peace and quiet: 怕麻烦,图～ *fear trouble and seek peace and quiet*

【清静】quiet: 咱们找个～的地方谈谈。*Let's find a quiet place to chat.*

【清口】tasty and refreshing

【清苦】(esp. of scholars or teachers) poor; badly off: 生活～ *live in poverty*

【清蜡】[油] paraffin removal

【清朗】❶ cool and bright: ～的天气 *clear and bright weather* ❷ loud and clear; resounding: ～的声音 *a loud and clear sound*

【清冷】❶ chilly: 一个～的秋夜 *a chilly autumn night* ❷ deserted; desolate: 夜已深了,街上十分～。*It was late at night and the streets were quite deserted.*

【清理】put in order; check up; clear; sort out: 把房间～～ *put the room in order; clean up the room* / ～物资 *check up on equipment and materials* / ～债务 *clear up debts* / ～仓库 *take stock; make an inventory of warehouse stocks* / ～档案 *put the archives in order; sort out documents*

【清廉】honest and upright; free from corruption: ～的官吏 *an honest and incorruptible official*

【清凉】cool and refreshing: ～饮料 *cold drink; cooler* / 你的批评对我是一服很好的～剂。*Your criticism had a sobering effect on me.*

【清凉油】cooling ointment; essential balm

【清亮】clear and resounding; resonant: 嗓音～ *a resonant voice*

【清棉】[纺] scutching: ～机 *scutcher* / ～间 *blowing room*

【清明】❶ clear and bright: 月色～ *clear and bright moonlight* ❷ sober and calm: 神志～ *be in full possession of one's faculties* ❸ (of government or administration) well ordered; well regulated ❹ Pure Brightness—the 5th of the 24 solar terms ❺ the day marking the beginning of the 5th solar term (April 4, 5, or 6; traditionally observed as a festival for worshipping at ancestral graves, technically known as "sweeping the graves" 扫墓) ——另见『节气』,『二十四节气』

【清喷漆】[化] clear lacquer

【清贫】(usu. of scholars or teachers) poor; badly off: 家道～ *be a person of scanty means*

【清平】peaceful; tranquil: ～世界 *times of peace and prosperity*

【清漆】varnish: 透明～ *clear varnish*

【清讫】payment received; paid

【清泉】cool spring (water)

【清热法】[中] antipyretic method (using medicines of a cold nature to treat acute febrile diseases)

【清热药】antipyretic

【清扫】thoroughly clean up; give a thorough clean-up

【清瘦】〈婉〉thin; lean; spare: 你病后略见～。*You look rather thin after your illness.*

【清爽】❶ fresh and cool: 晚风吹来,十分～。*The evening breeze is cooling and refreshing.* ❷ relieved; relaxed: 事情解决了,我心里也～了。*Now that the matter is settled, I feel relieved.* ❸〈方〉clean and tidy

【清水墙】[建] dry wall

【清水衙门】plain water yamen

【清算】❶ clear (accounts); square ❷ settle accounts; expose and criticize ◇ ～协定 clearing agreement; ～银行 clearing bank; ～账户 clearing account

【清谈】❶ pure conversations—intellectual discussions on lofty and nonmundane matters ❷ idle talk; empty talk: ～不能解决问题。*Idle talk solves no problems.*

【清汤】clear soup; light soup; consommé

【清汤寡水】(of a dish) watery and tasteless; dishwater

【清婉】(of voice) clear and sweet

【清晰】distinct; clear: 她发音～。*Her pronunciation is clear*. / 远山的轮廓～可见。*The outlines of the distant hills are clearly discernible*.

【清晰度】❶(TV) clarity ❷(sound) articulation

【清洗】❶ rinse; wash; clean: ～炊具 *clean cooking utensils* ❷ purge; comb out: 把腐化堕落分子～出去 *comb out the degenerates*

【清闲】at leisure; idle: 我干这个工作几乎没有～的时候。*I have very little leisure time in this job*. / 他过不惯～的退休生活。*He finds it difficult to get used to the idle life of retirement*.

【清香】delicate fragrance; faint scent: 晨风吹来野花的～。*The morning breeze carried with it the scent of wild flowers*.

【清心寡欲】purify one's heart and reduce the number of one's desires; be pure of heart and have few desires

【清新】pure and fresh; fresh: 雨后空气～。*The air was pure and fresh after the rain*. / 文字～ *written in a refreshingly lucid style*

【清醒】❶ clear-headed; sober: 保持～的头脑 *keep a clear (or cool) head; keep sober-minded* / 现实使他～过来。*The reality has sobered him up*. ❷ regain consciousness: 病人已经～过来。*The patient has come to*.

【清秀】delicate and pretty: 面貌～ *of fine, delicate features* / 山水～ *beautiful landscape*

【清选机】[农] cleaner

【清雅】elegant; refined: 风格～ *in an elegant style*

【清样】[刷] final proof; foundry proof

【清夜】the stillness of night ◇ ～扪心 examine one's conscience in the stillness of night; ～自思 be deep in thought in the stillness of night

【清一色】❶ all of one suit (in playing mahjong); flush ❷ all of the same colour; uniform; homogeneous: 运动员～地穿着红色运动服。*The players were all dressed alike in red sports suits*.

【清音】[语音] voiceless sound

【清幽】(of a landscape) quiet and beautiful

【清越】(of sound) clear and melodious; clear and far-reaching: 歌声～。*The singing was clear and melodious*.

【清运】clear; remove: 他们正在～垃圾。*They are clearing away the refuse*.

【清早】〈口〉 early in the morning; early morning: 他们一～就干活去了。*They went out to work early in the morning*.

【清账】square (or clear) an account

【清真】❶〈书〉 simple and unadorned; plain ❷ Islamic; Muslim ◇ ～点心 Muslims' cakes (without pork fat); ～食堂 Muslims' canteen; ～寺 mosque

【清蒸】steamed in clear soup (usu. without soy sauce): ～鱼 *steamed fish*

【清整】level (land): ～场地 level the ground

【清正】upright and just: 为官～ *be an upright and just official; be upright in performing one's official duties*

【清浊】❶ pure and impure; good and bad ❷ [语音] voiceless and voiced sounds

蜻

(构词成分) 见下

【蜻蜓】dragonfly

【蜻蜓点水】like a dragonfly skimming the surface of the water—just touch on sth. lightly without going into it deeply: 做调查工作不能～,要深入实际。*To make an investigation, one should go into matters deeply, not just scratch the surface*.

鲭

名 mackerel

qíng

情

名 ❶ feeling; affection; sentiment: 热情 ❷ love; passion: 爱情 ❸ sexual passion; lust: 情欲 ❹ favour; kindness: 求情 ❺ situation; circumstances; condition: 军情

【情爱】love (esp. between man and woman): ～甚笃 *be deeply in love with each other*

【情报】intelligence; information ◇ ～机关 intelligence agency; ～人员 intelligence personnel; intelligence agent; ～系统 intelligence channel

【情不可却】It would be ungracious not to accept (an invitation, etc.).

【情不自禁】cannot refrain from; cannot help (doing sth.); be seized with a sudden impulse to: ～地流下泪来 *cannot refrain from tears* / ～地笑起来 *can't help laughing* / ～地嚷起来 *shout beside oneself with excitement*

【情操】sentiment: 培养共产主义的～ *foster communist values*

【情场】the arena of love; the tournaments of love: ～得意 *be lucky in love* / ～失意 *be frustrated in love* / ～老手 *womanizer*

【情痴】love maniac

【情敌】rival in love

【情调】sentiment; emotional appeal: 不健康的～ *unhealthy sentimentalism* / 这首曲子充满了哀伤的～。*The music is full of pathos*. / 这位学者的书斋～高雅。*The scholar's study gives the impression of a man of simple, refined tastes*.

【情窦初开】(of a young girl) first awakening (or dawning) of love

【情分】mutual affection: 朋友～ *friendship* / 兄弟～ *fraternity; brotherhood* / 两家做了几辈子邻居,素来～好。*The two families have been neighbours for generations and have all along been on amicable terms*.

【情夫】an illicit lover of a married woman; lover

【情妇】an illicit lover of a married man; mistress

【情感】emotion; feeling

【情歌】love song

【情话】❶〈书〉 intimate words; heart-to-heart talk ❷ lovers' prattle; whispers of love; sweet nothings: ～绵绵 *whispering sweet nothings*

【情怀】feelings

【情急智生】hit on an idea in a moment of desperation
【情节】❶ plot：这个剧本～很复杂。*The play has a very complicated plot.* / ～紧凑 *a tightknit* (*or well-knit*) *plot* ❷ circumstances：根据～轻重，分别给予处理。*Each will be dealt with according to the seriousness of his case.*
【情结】［心理］emotional ties；deep emotions associated with something
【情景】scene；sight；circumstances：兴奋热烈的～ *an exhilarating scene* / 感人的～ *a moving sight* ◇～教学法 situational teaching method；～喜剧 sitcom；situation comedy
【情景交融】(of literary works) feeling and setting happily blended
【情境】circumstances；situation
【情况】❶ circumstances；situation；condition；state of affairs：～不明。*The situation is not clear.* / 在这种～下 *under these circumstances；such being the case* / 根据具体～ *in accordance with specific conditions* / 在许多～下 *in many cases* ❷ military situation：前线有什么～？*How is the situation at the front?* / 前面有～，做好战斗准备。*There's enemy activity ahead. Prepare for combat.*
【情郎】(girl's) lover；sweetheart
【情理】reason；sense：不近～ *unreasonable；irrational* / ～难容 *incompatible with the accepted code of human conduct；contrary to reason；absurd*
【情侣】sweethearts；lovers
【情面】feelings；sensibilities：留～ *spare sb.'s feelings* / 不顾～ *have no consideration for sb.'s feelings* / 对错误一定要揭发，不讲～。*The mistakes must be exposed without sparing anyone's sensibilities.*
【情趣】❶ temperament and interest：他们二人～相投。*The two of them are temperamentally compatible* (*or congenial*). ❷ interest；appeal：这首诗写得很有～。*This poem is very charming.*
【情人】sweetheart；lover
【情人节】Valentine's Day
【情人眼里出西施】a lover sees a Xishi in his beloved；in the eyes of the lover，his beloved is a beauty；beauty is in the eye of the beholder
【情杀】murder for love
【情商】(〈略〉全称为'情绪智商') EQ；emotional intelligence quotient
【情诗】love poem
【情事】(usu. used in legal documents) the facts；the phenomena
【情势】situation；circumstances；trend of events：～危急。*The situation is critical.* / 对～作出估计 *size up the situation*
【情势不变】diplomacy rebus sic stantibus
【情书】love letter
【情思】❶ tender regards；affection；goodwill ❷ state of mind；mood
【情死】die for love
【情愫】(又作'情素')〈书〉❶ feeling；sentiment：朝夕相处，增加了他们之间的～。*Thrown together，their feelings for each other grew.* ❷ real sentiment；innermost feeling
【情随事迁】feeling change with circumstances
【情态】spirit；mood：生动地描绘了儿童的～ *depict children's spirit vividly*
【情态动词】［语］modal verb
【情同手足】like brothers；with brotherly love for each other：两国人民～。*Our two peoples are bound together by ties of fraternal friendship.*
【情投意合】find each other congenial：两人说得～，只恨相见之晚。*They found so much in common that they regretted not having met earlier.*
【情网】snares of love：堕入～ *be caught in the snares of love*
【情文并茂】(of writing) excellent in both content and language
【情见乎辞】sincerity shines through the words
【情形】circumstances；situation；condition；state of affairs：两地～大不相同。*Conditions in the two places differ greatly.* / 大家看了这种～，非常气愤。*People felt indignant at this state of affairs.* / 这是一方面的～。*This is one side of the picture.*
【情绪】❶ morale；feeling；mood；sentiments：～高涨。*Morale is high.* / ～不高 *be in low spirits* / 全团战斗～高昂。*The whole regiment is in fine fighting fettle.* ❷ depression；moodiness；the sulks：有点儿～ *rather sulky*
【情义】ties of friendship，comradeship，etc.：姐姐待他很有～。*His elder sister is very affectionate towards him.* / 阶级～ *class love*
【情谊】friendly feelings；friendly sentiments：战斗～ *militant bonds of friendship* / 兄弟～ *brotherly affection*
【情意】tender regards；affection；goodwill：深厚的～ *deep affection*
【情由】the hows and whys：不问～ *without asking about the circumstances or causes*
【情有可原】excusable；pardonable
【情欲】sexual passion；lust
【情愿】❶ be willing to：他很～付这个价钱。*He's quite willing to pay the price.* ❷ would rather；prefer：她～粉身碎骨，也不在敌人面前屈服。*She would rather be cut to pieces than yield to the enemy.*
【情致】interest；appeal
【情种】person of the sentimental type，especially one who easily falls in love
【情状】state of affairs；situation；condition

晴 形 fine；clear：天～了。*It's clearing up.*
【晴好】warm and fine
【晴和】warm and fine：天气～。*It's a fine，warm day.*
【晴间多云】fine with occasional clouds
【晴空万里】a clear and boundless sky；the vast clear skies

【晴朗】fine；sunny：天气～。*It's a sunny day*.
【晴丝】gossamer
【晴天】fine day；sunny day
【晴天霹雳】a bolt from the blue：噩耗传来，犹如～。*The grievous news came as a bolt from the blue*.
【晴雨表】weatherglass；barometer

氰 名［化］cyanogen；dicyanogen
【氰钴胺】［药］cyanocobalamin；vitamin B_{12}
【氰化】cyaniding ◇ ～法 cyanidation；～钾 potassium cyanide；～物 cyanide
【氰酸】cyanic acid

擎 动 prop up；hold up；lift up：众擎易举
【擎天柱】a man in a responsible position；mainstay

qǐng

苘（构词成份）见下
【苘麻】［植］piemarker

顷 Ⅰ量 qing，currently called 市顷，a traditional unit of area Ⅱ副 ❶〈书〉just；just now：～接来信。*I have just received your letter*. ❷〈书〉a little while：少顷——另见〖市顷〗
【顷刻】in a moment；in an instant；instantly：～之间 *in a twinkling*；*in no time* / ～瓦解 *collapse instantly*

请 动 ❶ request；ask：～他进来。*Ask him in*. / ～你多加指导。*It is hoped you will give us guidance*. / ～人来修机器 *get sb. to repair the machine*；*get the machine repaired* ❷ invite；engage：～医生 *send for a doctor* / ～总工程师来讲课 *invite the chief engineer to give a lecture* ❸〈套〉please：～坐。*Won't you sit down*? or *Please be seated*. / ～安静。*Be quiet*，*please*. / ～速回信。*Please reply as soon as possible*.
【请安】pay respects to sb.；wish sb. good health
【请便】do as you wish；please yourself：你要是想现在去，那就～吧。*Well*，*if you want to leave now*，*go ahead*.
【请调】ask to be transferred to another post：～报告 *a written request for a transfer*（*to another post*）
【请功】ask the higher level to record sb.'s meritorious deeds
【请假】ask for leave：请三天假 *ask for three days' leave* / 因病～一天 *ask for a day's sick leave*
【请假条】written request for leave（of absence）
【请柬】〈书〉invitation card
【请见】〈书〉request an audience；ask for an interview
【请教】ask for advice；consult：我们想～你几个问题。*We wish to consult you on a few questions*. / 向小麦专家～ *consult a wheat expert* / 虚心向群众～ *learn modestly from the masses*
【请君入瓮】kindly step into the vat—have a taste of what you intended for others
【请客】stand treat；invite sb. to dinner；entertain guests；give a dinner party
【请命】❶ plead on sb.'s behalf ❷〈旧〉ask（the higher authorities）for instructions
【请求】ask；request：～宽恕 *ask for forgiveness* / ～贷款 *make a request for a loan* / 答应～ *compile with a request*
【请示】ask for（or request）instructions：向上级～ *ask the higher authorities for instructions* / 事前～，事后报告 *ask for instructions beforehand and submit reports afterwards*
【请帖】invitation card；invitation：发～ *send out invitations*
【请问】❶〈套〉excuse me；please：～，到火车站怎么走？*Excuse me*，*but could you tell me how to get to the station*? ❷ we should like to ask；it may be asked；one may ask：～，要不是改革开放，我们的经济建设能有今天吗？*I'd like to ask*，*without reform and the open policy*，*could our economic development be what it is today*?
【请勿】please don't：本室书籍～携出室外。*Please don't take the books out of this room*. / ～吸烟。*No smoking*. / ～入内。*No admittance*. / ～践踏草地。*Keep off the lawn*.
【请降】beg to surrender
【请缨】〈书〉request a cord from the emperor（to bind the enemy）—submit a request for a military assignment：～杀敌 *request to be sent to the front*；*volunteer for battle*
【请援】ask for support or aid
【请愿】present a petition；petition ◇ ～书 petition
【请战】ask for a battle assignment ◇ ～书 a written request for a battle assignment
【请罪】admit one's error and ask for punishment；apologize

qìng

庆 Ⅰ动 celebrate；congratulate：～丰收 *celebrate a bumper harvest* Ⅱ名 occasion for celebration：国庆
【庆大霉素】gentamicin
【庆典】celebration；a ceremony to celebrate：盛大～ *grand celebrations*
【庆父不死，鲁难未已】until Qing Fu is dead，the crisis in（the state of）Lu will not end—there will always be trouble until the one who causes it is gone
【庆功会】victory meeting
【庆贺】congratulate；celebrate：～胜利 *celebrate the victory* / ～老张得奖 *congratulate Lao Zhang on winning the award*
【庆幸】rejoice：值得～的事 *a matter for rejoicing* / 可～的是，这次车祸无人死亡。*Happily*，*no one was killed in the car accident*.
【庆祝】celebrate：～国庆 *celebrate National Day* ◇ ～大会 celebration meeting

亲（构词成分）见下 ——另见 qīn

【亲家】❶ parents of one's daughter-in-law or son-in-law ❷ relatives by marriage ◇～公 son's or daughter's father-in-law; ～母 son's or daughter's mother-in-law

磬 名 ❶ chime stone ❷ inverted bell (a Buddhist percussion instrument)

罄 动〈书〉use up; exhaust: ～其所有 *empty one's purse*; *offer all one has*

【罄尽】〈书〉with nothing left; all used up

【罄竹难书】(of crimes) too many (or numerous) to record

qióng

穷 Ⅰ 形 poor; poverty-stricken: 他家很～。*His family is very poor*. Ⅱ 动 limit; end: 技穷 Ⅲ 副 ❶ thoroughly: 穷究 ❷ extremely: 穷奢极欲

【穷兵黩武】use all one's armed might to wage wars of aggression; wantonly engage in military ventures

【穷愁潦倒】be penniless and frustrated

【穷当益坚】The greater the adversity, the stronger the will.

【穷光蛋】〈口〉pauper; poor wretch

【穷极无聊】❶ be utterly bored ❷ absolutely senseless; disgusting

【穷家富路】One should be frugal at home but well equipped for a journey.

【穷尽】limit; end: 学问是没有～的。*There is no limit to learning*.

【穷开心】❶ enjoy oneself despite poverty ❷ seek joy amidst sorrow; try to enjoy oneself despite one's suffering

【穷寇】hard-pressed enemy; tottering foe ◇～勿追 don't pursue a beaten enemy

【穷苦】poverty-stricken; impoverished

【穷困】poverty-stricken; destitute; in straitened circumstances: 陷入～的境地 *be reduced to destitution*

【穷年累月】for years on end; year after year

【穷期】termination; end: 战斗正未有～。*The struggle will go on and on*.

【穷人】poor people; the poor

【穷日子】days of poverty; straitened circumstances: 我们要把富日子当～过。*We're well off now, but we should still live as if we were poor*.

【穷山恶水】barren mountains and unruly rivers; barren hills and untamed rivers

【穷奢极欲】(又作'穷奢极侈') (indulge in) luxury and extravagance; (live a life of) wanton extravagance: 过着～的生活 *wallow in luxury*

【穷酸】(of a scholar) poor and pedantic

【穷途】straitened circumstances; destitution ◇～潦倒 at the end of one's tether; desperate; ～末路 be in an impasse; have come to a dead end

【穷乡僻壤】a remote, backward place; remote hinterland: 从通商口岸直至～ *from the trading ports to the remote hinterland*

【穷相】appearance or manner suggestive of abject poverty

【穷形尽相】❶ describe in minute, vivid detail ❷ appear in all one's ugliness

【穷凶极恶】extremely vicious; utterly evil; atrocious; diabolical: ～的敌人 *most vicious enemy* / 一副～的样子 *with the look of a fiendish brute*

【穷原竟委】get to the bottom of the matter; make a thorough (or exhaustive) inquiry into sth.

【穷源溯流】同〖穷原竟委〗

【穷则思变】Poverty gives rise to a desire for change.

【穷追猛打】hotly pursue and fiercely attack

穹 名〈书〉❶ vault; dome ❷ the sky: 苍穹

【穹苍】〈书〉the vault of heaven; the firmament; the sky; the heavens

【穹顶】[建] dome

【穹隆】〈书〉vault; arched roof ◇～构造 [地质] dome structure

【穹形】vaulted; arched: ～的屋顶 *a vaulted roof*

茕 形〈书〉❶ solitary; alone ❷ dejected

【茕茕】〈书〉all alone; lonely

【茕茕孑立,形影相吊】standing all alone, body and shadow comforting each other

琼 名〈书〉fine jade: ～阁 *a jewelled palace*

【琼浆】〈文〉jadelike wine; good wine

【琼楼玉宇】a richly decorated jade palace; a magnificent building

【琼脂】agar-agar; agar: ～培养基 *agar medium* / ～酸 *agaric acid* / ～糖 *agarose*

qiū

丘 名 ❶ mound; hillock: 荒～ *a barren hillock* ❷ grave: 坟丘

【丘比特】Cupid, Roman god of love

【丘陵】hills: ～起伏 *a chain of undulating hills* / ～地带 *hilly country*; *hilly land*

【丘脑】[生理] cerebral ganglion

【丘鹬】[动] woodcock

【丘疹】[医] papule

秋 名 ❶ autumn; fall(美): 一九八五年～ *Autumn*, 1985 / ～雨 *autumn rain* ❷ harvest time: 麦秋 ❸ year: 千秋万代 ❹ a period of (usu. troubled) time: 多事之秋

【秋波】autumn ripples—the bright and clear eyes of a beautiful woman: 暗送～ (*of a woman*) *cast amorous glances*; *make eyes*; *ogle*

【秋播】autumn sowing

【秋地】fields waiting for autumn sowing

【秋分】❶ the Autumn Equinox—the 16th of the 24

solar terms ❷ the day marking the beginning of the 16th solar term (Sept. 22, 23, or 24)
【秋风】autumn wind ◇ ～过耳 like autumn wind passing by the ear—unnoticed; unheeded; ～扫落叶 the autumn wind sweeping away fallen leaves—carry everything before one
【秋高气爽】autumn (sky) high and air brisk—the autumn sky is clear and the air is bracing (a set phrase for describing fine autumn weather)
【秋耕】autumn ploughing
【秋海棠】begonia
【秋毫】autumn hair or newly-grown down—sth. so small as to be almost indiscernible: 明察秋毫
【秋毫无犯】(of highly disciplined troops) not commit the slightest offence against the civilians; not encroach on the interests of the people to the slightest degree: 大军所到之处，～。*Wherever the troops went, they inflicted not the slightest harm on the people.*
【秋毫之末】the tip of an autumn hair—a minute, almost indiscernible particle
【秋后的蚂蚱】a grasshopper at the end of autumn—nearing its end: 敌人像～，蹦跶不了几天啦。*Like a grasshopper at the end of autumn, the enemy is on his last legs.*
【秋后算账】square accounts after the autumn harvest—wait until after a political movement is over to settle accounts with the leadership or the masses
【秋季】autumn; fall(美): ～作物 *autumn crops*
【秋景】❶ autumn scenery ❷ autumn harvest
【秋老虎】a spell of hot weather after the Beginning of Autumn (立秋)
【秋凉】cool autumn days: 等～再去吧。*Don't go there until the cool autumn days.*
【秋令】❶ autumn ❷ autumn weather: 冬行～。*The winter weather is like autumn.*
【秋千】swing (a seat for swinging): 打～ *have a swing*
【秋色】autumn scenery: ～宜人 *charming autumn scenery*
【秋收】❶ autumn harvest: 农民们都在忙着～。*The farmers are all busy with autumn harvest.* ❷ autumn crops
【秋水】autumn waters—limpid eyes (of a woman)
【秋水仙】[植] meadow saffron; autumn crocus ◇ ～素 [药] colchicine
【秋天】autumn; fall(美)
【秋汛】autumn floods
【秋游】autumn outing
【秋庄稼】autumn crops

蚯 (构词成分)见下
【蚯蚓】earthworm

楸 [植] Chinese catalpa

qiú

囚 Ⅰ 动 imprison: 被～ *be thrown into prison* Ⅱ 名 prisoner; convict: 死囚
【囚车】prison van; prisoners' van
【囚犯】prisoner; convict
【囚房】prison cell
【囚禁】(又作'囚困') imprison; put in jail; keep in captivity
【囚牢】〈旧〉prison; jail
【囚笼】(wooden) prisoner's cage used in imperial China
【囚室】prison cell
【囚首垢面】with unkempt hair and dirty face
【囚徒】prisoner; convict
【囚衣】prison garb

犰 (构词成分)见下
【犰狳】[动] armadillo

求 动 ❶ beg; request; entreat; beseech: ～你帮个忙，行吗? *May I ask you a favour?* ❷ strive for: ～进步 *strive for further progress* / ～解放 *strive for liberation* / 生物都有～生存的本能。*All living beings are endowed with an instinct for survival.* ❸ seek; try: ～学问 *seek knowledge* / 不～名利 *not seek fame and gain* ❹ demand
【求爱】pay court to; court; woo
【求成】hope for success
【求大同，存小异】seek common ground on major issues while reserving differences on minor ones
【求告】implore; entreat; supplicate
【求告无门】have nowhere to turn to for help
【求根】[数] extract a root
【求购】offer to purchase
【求过于供】demand exceeds supply
【求和】❶ sue for peace ❷ (in ball games or chess) try to equalize the score; try for a draw ❸ [数] summation
【求婚】make an offer of marriage; propose
【求积仪】[数] planimeter
【求见】ask to see (one's superior or a VIP); request an interview; beg for an audience
【求教】ask for advice: 登门～ *call on sb. for counsel; come to seek advice* / 不懂的事要向别人～。*Ask other people about things that you do not know.*
【求解】find the solution (of a mathematical problem); solve a problem
【求借】ask sb. for a loan
【求救】ask sb. to come to the rescue; cry for help: 发出～的信号 *signal an SOS; send a GMDSS*
【求偶】seek a spouse
【求乞】beg: 沿门～ *go begging from door to door*
【求签】divine by drawing lots in a temple
【求亲】seek a marriage alliance
【求亲告友】ask for favours (usu. loans) from relatives and friends
【求情】plead; intercede; ask for a favour; beg for leniency: 向他～ *plead with him* / 为某人～ *intercede for sb.; beg (for mercy) on sb.'s behalf* / ～告饶 *beg for leniency and mercy*

【求全】❶ demand perfection ❷ try to round sth. off：委曲求全
【求全责备】demand perfection；nitpick：对人不要～。*Don't demand perfection of others*. or *Don't nitpick at others*.
【求饶】beg for mercy；ask for pardon
【求人】ask sb. for help
【求人不如求己】Self-help is better than help from others；God helps those that help themselves.
【求生】seek survival：动物都有～的本能。*All animals have an instinct to seek survival*.
【求胜】strive for victory：～心切 *be anxious to gain victory*
【求实精神】matter-of-fact attitude；realistic approach：把革命热情和～结合起来 *combine revolutionary fervour with a realistic spirit*
【求田问舍】desire nothing but a homestead—have no high aims in life
【求同存异】seek common ground while reserving differences
【求仙】❶ seek immortality ❷ seek divine advice
【求贤若渴】(of a ruler) eagerly seek after men of worth and ability
【求降】beg to surrender；hang out (or hoist) the white flag
【求学】❶ go to school；attend school ❷ pursue one's studies；seek knowledge
【求爷爷告奶奶】〈口〉beg grandpas and entreat grandmas—go about begging for help
【求医】seek medical advice；see a doctor
【求雨】pray for rain
【求援】ask for help；request reinforcements
【求战】❶ seek battle；provoke battle ❷ ask to go into battle：战士们～心切。*The men are itching for action*.
【求证】seek to prove；seek evidence or verification
【求之不得】all one could wish for；most welcome：这对他真是～的事情。*This is just what he wants*. / 这是～的好机会。*This is a most welcome opportunity*. / 给王师傅当徒弟，他真是～。*He was only too glad to be an apprentice to Master Worker Wang*.
【求知】seek knowledge：～欲 *thirst (or craving) for knowledge*
【求值】[数] evaluation
【求职】look for a job；find a job；apply for a job：在广州，～很难。*In Guangzhou, it is difficult to find a job*.
【求助】turn to sb. for help；seek help：他理屈词穷，只好～于诡辩。*As he had a weak case and could not defend himself, he had to resort to sophistry*.

泅 动 swim
【泅渡】swim across
【泅水】swim
【泅泳】(又作'泅游') swim

酋 名 ❶ chief of a tribe ❷ chieftain (of bandits, invaders, etc.)
【酋长】❶ chief of a tribe ❷ sheik(h)；emir ◇～国 sheikhdom；emirate

球 名 ❶ sphere；globe：球体 ❷ ball (used in games)：传～ *pass a ball* ❸ anything shaped like a ball：雪球 ❹ ball game；match：看～去。*Let's go to watch the game*. ❺ the globe；the earth：地球
【球场】a ground where ball games are played；(volleyball, basketball, tennis, badminton, etc.) court；(football, baseball, softball, etc.) field
【球胆】bladder (of a ball)
【球队】(ball game) team
【球风】sportsmanship shown in ball games：他在足球场上～一直很好。*His behaviour on the football pitch has always been very sportsmanlike*.
【球罐】[油] sphere
【球果】[植] cone
【球茎】[植] corm
【球茎甘蓝】[植] kohlrabi
【球菌】coccus
【球类运动】ball games
【球路】tactics in ball games：～多变 *play with a variety of strokes (as in tennis)*
【球门】[体] goal：～柱 *goalpost*
【球迷】(ball game) fan：足～ *football fan*
【球面】spherical surface ◇～车床 [机] spherical turning lathe；～镜 [物] spherical mirror；～天文学 spherical astronomy；～投影 stereographic projection
【球磨床】[机] ball grinder
【球磨机】[机] ball mill
【球墨铸铁】[冶] nodular cast iron
【球拍】(又作'球拍子') ❶ (tennis, badminton, etc.) racket ❷ (table-tennis) bat
【球赛】ball game；match
【球手】ballgame player
【球坛】the ball-playing world；ball-playing circles；ball-players：～盛会 *a grand gathering of (table tennis, etc.) players* / ～新手 *a new player；a newcomer to the tournament*
【球体】spheroid
【球团矿】[冶] pellet
【球王】"ball king", a champion or superstar in a certain ball game
【球网】net (for ball games)
【球窝节】[机] ball-and-socket joint
【球鞋】gym shoes；tennis shoes；sneakers
【球心】centre of sphere
【球星】ball-game star；star
【球形】spherical；globular；round
【球艺】skills in playing a ball game；ball game skills
【球轴承】[机] ball bearing

遒 形〈书〉powerful；forceful
【遒劲】〈书〉powerful；vigorous：笔力～ *vigorous*

strokes in calligraphy / 苍老～的古松 *a sturdy old pine tree*

【遒媚】〈书〉(of calligraphy) vigorous and graceful

巯 名 (又作'巯基') [化] mercapto

裘 名 〈书〉fur coat：狐裘

qū

区 Ⅰ 名 ❶ area；district；region：山区 ❷ an administrative division：这个～高等院校很多。*There are many institutions of higher learning in this district.* Ⅱ 动 distinguish；classify；subdivide：区分

【区别】❶ distinguish；differentiate；make a distinction between：把两者～开来 *differentiate one from the other* / ～对待 *deal with each case on its merits；deal with different things or people in different ways* / ～好坏 *distinguish between good and bad* ❷ difference：这两个词在意义上没有～。*There is no difference in meaning between the two words.*

【区分】differentiate；distinguish：～母牛和公牛 *differentiate a cow from a bull* / ～两个历史时代 *mark off two historical epochs*

【区划】division into districts：行政～ *administrative divisions*

【区徽】regional emblem：香港特别行政区～ *emblem of Hong Kong Special Administrative Region*

【区间】lap，section of a route，line：从A到B～的电线杆断了。*Electricity poles between A and B are down.*

【区间车】a train or bus travelling only part of its normal route

【区块】block：划分合作～ *demarcate blocks for cooperation*

【区旗】flag of a certain administrative region：香港特别行政区的～ *flag of the Hong Kong Special Administrative Region*

【区区】trivial；trifling：～小事，何足挂齿。*Such a trifling thing is hardly worth mentioning.* / ～之数，不必计较。*Such a trifling amount of money isn't worth bothering about.*

【区时】[天] zone time

【区域】region；area；district：～间合作 *inter-regional cooperation* ◇ ～会议 regional conference；local conference；～自治 regional autonomy

【区域性】pertaining to a region：～公约 *regional convention (or pact)* / ～同盟 *regional alliance* / ～问题 *a matter of regional significance* / ～战争 *regional war*

【区长】head of a district (as in a city)

曲 Ⅰ 形 ❶ bent；curved：弯腰～背 *with one's back bent* ❷ wrong；unjustifiable：是非曲直 Ⅱ 动 bend：～肱而枕 *bend one's arm and rest the head on it* Ⅲ 名 ❶ bend (of a river，etc.)：河曲 ❷ leaven；yeast —— 另见 qǔ

【曲别针】paper clip

【曲柄】[机] crank：～摇杆机构 *crank and rocker mechanism*

【曲柄钻】brace drill

【曲尺】carpenter's square

【曲拱】arch：～石桥 *an arched stone bridge*

【曲古霉素】trichomycin

【曲棍球】❶ field hockey；hockey ❷ hockey ball

【曲解】misinterpret (usu. deliberately)；twist：这话意思很明确，不可能～。*These remarks are so clear that there can be no room for misinterpretation.* / 你～了他的意思。*You've misrepresented his meaning.*

【曲尽其妙】bring out (a quality，point，etc.) in a subtle and skilful way

【曲颈甑】[化] retort

【曲径】winding path

【曲径通幽】a winding path leads to quiet seclusion

【曲里拐弯】〈口〉winding；zigzag：～的胡同 *a winding lane* / 树林里的小路～儿的。*The path zigzags through the woods.*

【曲流】[地质] meander

【曲率】[数] curvature

【曲率计】exometer

【曲霉】aspergillus

【曲面】curved surface；camber：内～ *negative camber* / 外～ *positive camber*

【曲奇】cookie

【曲曲弯弯】winding；meandering：山坳里尽是些～的羊肠小道。*There are a lot of winding footpaths in the col.* / 这河～地流过峡谷。*The river meanders through the gorges.*

【曲射】[军] curved fire：～弹道 *curved trajectory* / ～炮 *curved-fire gun*

【曲室】secret chamber

【曲突徙薪】bend the chimney and remove the fuel (to prevent a possible fire)—take precautions against a possible danger

【曲线】❶ [数] curve ❷ sth.，esp. a human body，or part of it having the shape of a curve：她衣服非常合体，显出了她身材优美的～。*Her suit was so well tailored that it accentuated her graceful figure.* ◇ ～板 curve ruler；～球 [体] (垒球) curve ball；～图 diagram (of curves)；～运动 [物] curvilinear motion

【曲意逢迎】go out of one's way to curry favour

【曲折】❶ tortuous；winding：沿着池塘有一条～的小路。*There's a winding path following the edge of the pond.* ❷ complicated：这个剧本情节很～。*The play has a very complicated plot.* ❸ complications：这件事情里面还有不少～。*There are many complications in this matter.*

【曲直】right and wrong：～不分 *not distinguish between right and wrong*

【曲衷】〈书〉heartfelt emotion；inner feelings

【曲轴】[机] crankshaft；bent axle：～磨床 *crankshaft grinding machine* / ～箱 *crankcase*

驱 动 ❶ drive (a horse, car, etc.): 驱车 ❷ expel; disperse: ～云防雹 *disperse clouds in order to prevent a hailstorm* ❸ run quickly: 驰驱

【驱策】❶ drive; whip on ❷ order about: 任人～ *allow oneself to be ordered about*

【驱车】drive a vehicle: ～前往 *drive (in a vehicle) to a place*

【驱虫剂】insectifuge; anthelmintic

【驱虫药】anthelmintic; vermifuge

【驱除】drive out; get rid of; repel: ～蚊蝇 *repel mosquitoes and flies*

【驱动】[机] drive: ～齿轮 *driving gear*

【驱动器】[计] driver: 硬盘～ *hard (disc) driver* / 软盘～ *soft driver*

【驱赶】❶ drive (a cart, etc.) ❷ drive away; brush away: ～苍蝇 *brush away flies; whisk flies off* / ～麻雀 *shoo away sparrows*

【驱寒】dispel cold; warm oneself up: 喝点酒驱驱寒 *have a drink to warm oneself up*

【驱蛔灵】[药] piperazine citrate

【驱迫】order about; force; compel

【驱遣】❶〈书〉drive away; banish; expel ❷ order about; drive ❸ dispel; get rid of: ～别情 *dispel the sad feeling of parting*

【驱散】disperse; dispel; break up: ～人群 *disperse a crowd* / 阳光～了薄雾。*The sun dispelled the mist.*

【驱使】❶ order about: 供～ *be ordered about; be at sb.'s beck and call* / 奴隶主把奴隶当作牛马任意～。*The slave owners drove their slaves as they drove their cattle.* ❷ prompt; urge; spur on: 为好奇心所～ *be prompted by curiosity*

【驱邪】exorcise (or drive out) evil spirits

【驱逐】drive out; expel; banish: ～侵略者 *drive out the aggressors* / ～出境 *deport; expel*

【驱逐舰】destroyer

屈 Ⅰ 动 ❶ bend; bow; crook: ～臂 *crook one's arm* ❷ subdue; submit: 不屈 Ⅱ 名 wrong; injustice: 叫屈 Ⅲ 形 in the wrong

【屈才】do work unworthy of one's talents

【屈从】submit; yield: ～于外来压力 *yield to pressure from outside*

【屈打成招】confess to false charges under torture: 他的口供是～，不足为证。*His confession was forced out of him and can't be used as evidence.*

【屈服】(又作'屈伏') subdue; submit; yield; knuckle under: ～于外界的压力 *yield to pressure from outside* / 严刑拷打并未使她～。*Torture failed to make her submit.*

【屈光度】dioptre

【屈驾】〈套〉condescend (or be kind enough) to make the journey: 明日请～来舍一叙。*Would you be kind enough to visit me tomorrow?*

【屈就】〈套〉condescend to take a post offered: 要是您肯～，那是太好了。*It'd be very kind of you to condescend to take this post.*

【屈居】be forced to accept a place (or position): 他以四秒之差～第二。*He was forced into second place by only four seconds.*

【屈理】unreasonable; unfair; unjust: 不要做～的事。*Don't do anything unreasonable.*

【屈辱】humiliation; mortification

【屈氏体】[冶] troostite

【屈死】be wronged and driven to death; be persecuted to death

【屈膝】go down on one's knees; bend one's knees ◇～投降 go down on one's knees in surrender; knuckle under

【屈心】〈口〉have a guilty conscience: 你做出这样的事～不～哪? *Don't you feel guilty about doing this kind of thing?* or *Has your action never given you a twinge of conscience?* / 这种～的事我不干。*I wouldn't do a mean thing like that.*

【屈折语】[语] inflexional language

【屈肢葬】[考古] flexed burial

【屈指】count on one's fingers: ～已经八年啦。*Come to think of it, eight years have already passed.*

【屈指可数】can be counted on one's fingers —very few

【屈尊】condescend

祛 动 dispel; remove; drive away

【祛除】dispel; get rid of; drive out: ～疑虑 *dispel one's misgivings* / ～邪魔 *drive out (or exorcize) evil spirits*

【祛风】[中] dispel the wind; relieve rheumatic pains, colds, etc.

【祛风湿药】medicine for rheumatism

【祛暑】drive away summer heat

【祛痰】make expectoration easy: ～剂 *expectorant*

【祛疑】〈书〉remove suspicion or doubts

【祛瘀活血】[中] remove blood stasis and promote blood circulation

蛆 名 maggot

【蛆虫】❶ maggot ❷ a shameless (or base) person

躯 名 the human body: 身躯

【躯干】[生理] trunk; torso

【躯壳】the body (as opposed to the soul); outer form

【躯体】body; stature

趋 动 ❶ hasten; hurry along: ～前 *hasten forward* / 疾～而过 *hurry past* ❷ tend towards; tend to become: 局势～于稳定。*The situation is tending towards stability.* / 他们的意见～于一致。*They are reaching unanimity.* ❸ (of a goose or snake) pop the head and bite people

【趋避】〈书〉avoid; dodge: ～路旁 *dodge to one side of the road; get out of the way*

【趋奉】(又作'趋承') toady to; fawn on

【趋附】ingratiate oneself with; curry favour with: ～权贵 *curry favour with bigwigs*

【趋光性】[生] phototaxis

【趋热性】[生] thermotaxis

【趋势】trend; tendency: 世界历史的总～任何人也改变不了。*No one can change the general trend of world history*.
【趋向】❶ tend to; incline to: 财政情况日益～好转。*The financial situation is taking a favourable turn*. ❷ trend; tendency; direction: 总～ *general trend*
【趋向动词】[语] directional verb
【趋性】[生] taxis
【趋炎附势】(又作'趋炎附热') curry favour with the powerful; play up to those in power
【趋药性】[生] chemotaxis
【趋之若鹜】go after sth. like a flock of ducks; scramble for sth.

蛐 (构词成分)见下
【蛐蛐儿】〈方〉cricket (an insect)

黢 形 black; dark
【黢黑】pitch-black; pitch-dark: 两手净是墨,～的。*Both hands are black with ink*. / 山洞里～,什么也看不见。*The cave is pitch-dark. You can't see anything*.

嚁 象 chirping of a cricket

qú

渠 名 canal; ditch; channel
【渠道】❶ irrigation ditch ❷ medium of communication; channel: 通过外交～ *through diplomatic channels* / 利用多种资金～ *make use of funds from various channels* / 商品流通～不畅。*The commodity circulation is poor*.
【渠灌】canal irrigation
【渠首工程】[水] headwork

qǔ

曲 名 ❶ qu, a type of verse for singing, which emerged in the Southern Song and Jin Dynasties and became popular in the Yuan Dynasty ❷ song; tune; melody: 高歌一～ *lustily sing a song* ❸ music (of a song): 作曲 ——另见 qū
【曲调】tune (of a song); melody
【曲高和寡】highbrow songs find few singers; too highbrow to be popular
【曲剧】opera derived from ballad singing
【曲牌】the names of the tunes to which qu (曲) are composed——另见〖曲❶〗
【曲谱】❶ music score of Chinese operas ❷ a collection of tunes of qu (曲) ——另见〖曲❶〗
【曲式】[音] musical form
【曲艺】quyi, folk art forms including ballad singing, story telling, comic dialogues, clapper talks, cross talks, etc.
【曲终奏雅】a grand finale
【曲子】song; tune; melody

取 动 ❶ take; get; fetch: 请把灯泡～下来。*Please take the bulb off*. / 她回去～行李去了。*She's gone back to fetch her luggage*. / 我来～自行车。*I came to get (or collect) my bike*. / 上银行～钱 *go and draw some money from a bank* ❷ aim at; seek: 取乐 ❸ adopt; assume; choose: ～慎重态度 *adopt a cautious attitude* / ～个吉利 *for good luck*
【取保】[法] go bail for one: ～释放 *be released on bail; be bailed out* / 对被告人～候审 *allow a defendant to obtain a guarantor and await trial out of custody*
【取材】draw materials: 就地～ *make use of (or draw on) local materials* / 这本小说～于炼钢工人的生活。*This novel has drawn its material from the life of steel workers*.
【取长补短】learn from others' strong points to offset one's own weaknesses: 互相学习,～ *learn from each other to make up deficiencies*
【取代】replace; substitute for; supersede; supplant: 这家航空公司目前正在用波音747～DC 10。*The airline is currently replacing its DC10s with Boeing747s*.
【取代衍生物】[化] substitution derivate
【取道】by way of; via: 代表团将～巴黎回国。*The delegation will come back to China by way of Paris*.
【取得】gain; acquire; obtain: ～胜利 *gain (or win) a victory* / 通过实践～经验 *gain experience through practice* / ～有关方面同意 *obtain the consent of those concerned*
【取缔】outlaw; ban; suppress: ～投机倒把 *ban speculation and profiteering* / ～反动会道门 *ban reactionary secret societies* / 走私必须～。*Smuggling must be suppressed*.
【取而代之】replace sb.; supersede sb.
【取法】take as one's model; follow the example of
【取法乎上,仅得乎中】aim high or you may fall below the average
【取经】❶ go on a pilgrimage for Buddhist scriptures:《西游记》讲唐僧往西天～的故事。*The Journey to the West tells how the Tang monk went to the Western Heaven to acquire scriptures*. ❷ learn from sb. else's experience: 到兄弟厂去～ *go to other factories (of the same kind) to learn from their experience*
【取精用弘】(又作'取精用宏') select the finest from a vast quantity
【取景】find a view (to photograph, paint, etc.) ◇～器 viewfinder (on a camera)
【取决】(usu. followed by 于) be decided by; depend on; hinge on: 消费的增长～于生产的增长。*The increase in consumption depends on the increase in production*.
【取快一时】derive momentary pleasure
【取乐】seek pleasure; find amusement; amuse oneself; make merry: 饮酒～ *drink and make merry*

【取力器】power takeoff (of a car)

【取名】give a name to; be named: 给孩子取个名儿 *choose a name for a child; give a name to a child* / 此处可～玫瑰园。*This place may be called Rose Garden.*

【取闹】❶ kick up a row; make trouble ❷ amuse oneself at sb.'s expense; make fun of

【取暖】warm oneself (by a fire, etc.): 烤火～ *warm oneself (or keep warm) by the fire*

【取平】make even; even up: 墙上挂的两张画应该～。*The two pictures on the wall must be aligned.*

【取齐】❶ make even; even up: 先把两张纸～了再裁。*Even up the edges of the two sheets of paper before you cut them.* / 去年我们队的产量不如他们,今年已经～了。*Last year our team's output was less than theirs, but this year we've caught up with them.* ❷ assemble; meet each other: 下午三点我们在门口～。*We'll assemble at the gate at 3 o'clock in the afternoon.*

【取枪】[军] take arms: ～!(*word of command*) *Take arms!*

【取巧】resort to trickery to serve oneself or avoid a difficulty

【取容】try to please; ingratiate oneself with sb.

【取舍】accept or reject; make one's choice: 对技术资料进行分析后决定～ *analyse all the technical data first and then decide what to use*

【取胜】win victory; score a success: 以多～ *win victory through numerical superiority*

【取水口】[水] water intake

【取向】orientation: 确定发展～ *determine the direction of development*

【取消】(又作'取销') cancel; call off; abolish: ～一次会议 *cancel (or call off) a meeting* / ～会员资格 *deprive sb. of his membership* / ～决定 *rescind a decision* / ～禁令 *lift a ban* / 被～比赛资格 *be disqualified from the contest*

【取消主义】liquidationism

【取笑】ridicule; make fun of; poke fun at: 别～人家生理上的缺陷。*Don't make fun of someone's physical handicap.* / 她的嘴真损,老～人。*She has a really sharp tongue—always ridiculing people.*

【取信】win the confidence (or trust) of the others

【取信于民】win the people's confidence (or trust)

【取样】take a sample: ～检查 *take a sample to inspect*

【取悦】try to please; ingratiate oneself with sb.: ～于人 *ingratiate oneself with sb.*

【取证】collect evidence

【取之不尽,用之不竭】inexhaustible

【取之于民,用之于民】What is taken from the people is used for the people.

娶 动 marry (a woman): ～媳妇儿 *take a wife* / 三十不～(*of a man*) *be unmarried at thirty*

【娶妻】take a wife

【娶亲】(of a man) get married

龋 (构词成分)见下

【龋齿】❶ dental caries ❷ decayed tooth

qù

去 Ⅰ 动 ❶ go; go to (a place): 我～。*I'll go.* / 他已经～了。*He has already gone.* / 他～了三天,还没回来。*He's been away for three days, and hasn't come back yet.* / 昨天已经～了三个人。*Three people went there yesterday.* ❷ cause to go; send there: 我给他～过两封信。*I sent him two letters.* / 给她～个电话。*Give her a call.* / 已经～了一个电报。*A telegram has been sent (to him).* / 我们只～了个代表。*We only sent a representative.* ❸ remove; get rid of: ～头屑 *get rid of dandruff* / 汽油能～油迹。*Gas is good for taking out oil stains.* / ～了皮再吃。*Peel it before you eat it.* ❹ (used before and / or after a verb) go in order to; be going to (do sth. there): 你们～研究研究,看该怎么办。*Go and make a study of it, and see what's the best thing to do.* / 这件事我～办吧 *Let me (go and) arrange this.* / 你别管,让他自己～想办法。*Don't bother, let him figure it out for himself.* ❺ (used between two verbal expressions, and / or after the second expression) in order to (do sth. there): 他回家吃饭～了。*He went home to eat.* / 他提了一桶水～浇花。*He took a bucket of water to water the flowers.* / 用辩证唯物主义的观点～观察事物 *look at things from a dialectical-materialist point of view* ❻〈书〉be apart from in space or time: 两地相～40 里。*The two places are 40 li apart.* / ～今五十年 *50 years ago* ❼ (used after verbs of motion, indicating motion away from the speaker) thither; there; away: 上楼～ *go upstairs* / 回家～ *go home* / 谁把我的笔拿～了? *Who's taken my pen away?* ❽ (used after certain verbs to express the idea of detachment, separation, or loss): 把多余的枝叶剪～。*Cut off the unnecessary twigs and branches.* / 这些琐碎事情占～了他不少时间。*Such small things take up a lot of his time.* Ⅱ 形 just gone or elapsed: ～秋 *last autumn* / ～冬今春 *last winter and this spring*

【去病】prevent or cure a disease

【去处】❶ place to go; whereabouts: 有谁知道他的～? *Who knows his whereabouts?* ❷ place; site: 这是一个风景优美的～。*This is a beautiful place.* / 北戴河是个避暑的好～。*Beidaihe is a nice summer resort.*

【去磁】[物] deperm; demagnetize; degauss: ～器 *degausser; demagnetizer*

【去粗取精】discard the dross and select the essential

【去垢剂】detergent

【去火】[中] reduce internal heat; relieve inflammation or fever: 消痰～ *reduce phlegm and in-*

ternal heat

【去留】go or remain (or stay):～由你。*You can go or stay, as you like.*

【去路】the way along which one is going; outlet:挡住敌人的～ *block the enemy's way* / 给洪水找到～ *find an outlet for the flood*

【去敏灵】[药] tripelennamine

【去年】last year:～十二月 *last December* / ～此时 *this time last year*

【去声】[语音] ❶ falling tone (the third of the four tones in classical Chinese pronunciation) ❷ falling tone (the fourth of the four tones in modern standard Chinese pronunciation)

【去世】(of grown-up people) die; pass away:他爷爷是前年～的。*His grandfather died the year before last.* / 听说你父亲上个月～了,我很难过。*I'm sorry to hear that your father passed away last month.*

【去势】[牧] castrate; emasculate

【去暑】drive away summer heat

【去岁】last year

【去痛定】[药] piminodine esylate

【去伪存真】get rid of the false and retain the true

【去污粉】household cleanser; cleanser

【去向】the direction in which sb. or sth. has gone:不知～ *be nowhere to be found* / 这个人～不明。*The whereabouts of this man is unknown.*

【去雄】[植] emasculate; castrate

【去杂去劣】[农] roguing

【去职】no longer hold the post

阒 形〈书〉quiet; still:～无一人。*All was quiet and not a soul was to be seen.*

【阒然】〈书〉quiet; still:～无声 *very quiet; absolutely still* / 四野～。*All was quiet on the vast expanse of open ground.*

趣 Ⅰ名 interest; delight:兴趣 Ⅱ形 interesting

【趣事】an interesting episode; an amusing incident

【趣谈】interesting tale usu. in title of book, article, etc.:《美国风情～》*Interesting Tales of the United States*

【趣味】❶ interest; delight:～无穷 *be of infinite interest; afford the greatest delight; be fascinating* / 这个职业很有～。*It's a very interesting occupation.* ❷ taste; liking; preference:～高雅 *refined taste; good taste*

【趣闻】interesting hearsay or news

觑 动〈书〉look; gaze:面面相觑

【觑视】〈书〉look; gaze

quān

悛 动〈书〉repent; make amends:怙恶不悛

圈 Ⅰ名 ❶ circle; ring:我到外面转了一～。*I've been out for a walk.* / 孩子们围成一～。*The children gathered around in a circle.* / 我们的飞机降落前在机场上空绕～儿。*Our plane circled the airport before landing.* ❷ circle; group:他不是～里人。*He doesn't belong to the inner circle.* or *He's not on the inside.* Ⅱ动 ❶ enclose; encircle:用篱笆把菜园～起来 *enclose the vegetable garden with a fence* ❷ mark with a circle:把那个错字～了。*Mark the wrong word with a circle.* ——另见 juān; juàn

【圈闭】petroleum trap:地层～ *stratigraphic trap* / 背斜～ *anticlinal trap*

【圈点】❶ punctuate (with periods or small circles) ❷ mark words and phrases for special attention with dots or small circles

【圈定】draw a circle around sth. to show approval or selection

【圈梁】[建] girth

【圈套】snare; trap:设下～ *set a trap for sb.* / 中～ *play into sb.'s hands* / 他的诺言是个～,我可不上这个当。*His promises are a trap and I won't be taken in.*

【圈椅】round-backed armchair

【圈阅】draw a circle around one's name on a document submitted for approval to show that one has read it; tick off one's name listed on a circular, notice, etc. after reading it

【圈占】enclose and occupy (land); seize possession of (land)

【圈子】circle; ring:大家围成一个～站着。*They stood in a circle.* / 他的生活～很小。*He moves in a very small circle.* ——另见〖兜圈子〗;〖绕圈子〗

quán

权 Ⅰ动〈书〉weigh:～其轻重 *weigh the relative importance (of two or more things)* Ⅱ名 ❶ power; authority:企业有～自行安排某些技术改造项目。*The enterprises are entitled to undertake certain projects for technological transformation.* ❷ right:你有～发言。*You have the right to speak.* / 我们无～干涉她的婚姻自由。*We don't have the right to interfere with her freedom of choice in marriage.* ❸ an advantageous position:制空权 ❹ expediency:权诈 Ⅲ副 tentatively; for the time being:～充 *act temporarily as; serve as a stopgap for*

【权变】adaptability (or flexibility) in tactics; acting according to circumstances; tact

【权便】expedient

【权标】fasces

【权柄】power; authority:掌握～ *be in power; be in the saddle*

【权贵】influential officials; bigwigs

【权衡】weigh; balance:～利弊 *weigh the advantages and disadvantages; weigh the pros and cons*

【权衡轻重】weigh the relative importance (of two or more things)

【权力】❶ power; authority:一切～属于人民。

All power belongs to the people. / 国家～机关 *organs of state power* / ～下放 *transfer* (*or delegate*) *power to lower levels* ❷ scope of power; extent of authority; jurisdiction: 行使会议主席的～ *exercise the functions of chairman of a conference*; *invoke the authority of chairman of a conference*

【权利】right: 劳动的～ *the right to work* / 受教育的～ *the right to education*

【权谋】(political) tactics; trickery

【权能】powers and functions

【权钱交易】deal between power and money

【权且】tentatively; for the time being: ～如此办理。*This is to be carried out as an interim measure*. / 屋子太小，今晚～住一宿，明天再想办法。*Small as this room is, let's just make do with it for the night and look for another place tomorrow*.

【权势】power and influence

【权术】〈贬〉political trickery; shifts in politics: 玩弄～ *play politics*

【权威】❶ authority; authoritativeness: ～著作 *an authoritative book* / ～的植物学家 *an authority on botany* ❷ a person of authority; authority: 学术～ *an academic authority* / 这是物理学界的～著作。*This is an authoritative book in the field of physics*.

【权威人士】authoritative person; authoritative sources

【权限】limits of authority; jurisdiction; competence: 在法律规定的～内 *within the limits of one's authority as prescribed by law* / 确定委员会的～ *define the competence* (*or terms of reference*) *of the committee*

【权宜】expedient

【权宜之计】an expedient measure; makeshift (device); stopgap

【权益】rights and interests: 经济～ *economic rights and interests*

【权欲】a lust for power ◇ ～熏心 be overcome with a lust for power

【权责】power and responsibility; rights and duties

【权诈】trickery; craftiness

【权杖】staff of authority (as carried by political or religious leaders)

全 Ⅰ 形 ❶ complete: 这家铺子货物的品种很～。*This store has a wide assortment of goods*. / 这套邮票～不～? —不～，差一张。*Is this set of stamps complete? —No, it's one piece short*. / 资料收集得比较～。*The data collected is quite comprehensive*. ❷ whole; entire; full; total: ～世界 *the whole world* / ～人类 *all mankind* / ～中国 *the whole of China*; *all over China* / ～(交响)曲共分四个乐章。*The symphony is in 4 movements*. Ⅱ 动 make complete; keep intact: 两全其美 Ⅲ 副 entirely; completely: ～错了 *completely wrong*; *all wrong* / 这事～怪我。*It's entirely* (*or all*) *my fault*. / 我们一家～去了。*My whole family went*. / 他讲的话我～记下来了。*I took down all he said*.

【全豹】the whole picture; the overall situation: 未窥～ *fail to see the whole picture*; *fail to grasp the overall situation*

【全部】whole; complete; total; all: 要求赔偿～损失 *demand full compensation for the loss incurred* / ～歼灭入侵之敌 *wipe out the invading enemy to the last man* / 他们～是学生。*All of them are students*.

【全才】versatile person; all-rounder: 文武～ *be versed in both civil and military affairs* / 他是个体育～，网球，篮球，游泳，样样来得。*He's a good all-rounder who likes tennis, basketball, and swimming*.

【全场】❶ the whole audience; all those present: ～爆发出一片欢呼声。*The audience broke out into cheers*. ❷［体］full-court; all-court: ～紧逼 *all-court press*; *full-court press*

【全称】full name (of a thing)

【全程】whole journey; whole course: 自行车比赛～120 公里。*The whole course of the bicycle race is 120 kilometres*.

【全等】［数］congruent: ～形 *congruent figures*

【全动机翼】all-moving wing (of an aircraft)

【全都】all; without exception: 村里男女老少～出来欢迎贵宾。*The whole village, men and women, old and young, turned out to welcome the distinguished visitors*. / 去年栽的树～活了。*All the trees planted last year have survived*.

【全方位】comprehensive; all-inclusive: ～开放格局 *pattern of all round opening up* / 为了适应世界经济的发展，我们要敞开大门，进行～开放。*In order to adapt to the developing world economy, we should open up in all areas*. / ～外交政策 *all-round foreign policy*

【全反射】［物］total reflection

【全份】complete set: ～表册 *a complete set of lists and forms*

【全副】complete; full: ～武装 *fully armed*; *in full battle array*

【全国】the whole nation (or country); nationwide; countrywide; throughout the country: ～人民 *the people of the whole country*; *the people throughout the country*; *the whole nation* / ～上下 *the whole nation from the leadership to the masses*

【全国人民代表大会】the National People's Congress (NPC)

【全国性】nationwide; countrywide; national: ～报纸 *a national newspaper*; *a newspaper with a nationwide circulation*

【全国一盘棋】coordinate all the activities of the nation like moves in a game of chess; take the whole country into account

【全乎】〈口〉complete: 这商店虽小，货物倒是很～。*Small as it is, the store has a wide assortment of goods*.

【全会】plenary meeting; plenary session; plenum: 十一届三中～ *the Third Plenary Session of the Eleventh Central Committee (of the Chinese Communist Party)*

【全集】complete works; collected works:《鲁迅～》*The Complete Works of Lu Xun*

【全家福】〈方〉❶ a photograph of the whole family ❷ hotchpotch (as a dish)

【全价】real price; full price

【全歼】annihilate; wipe out: ～残敌 *wipe out the remnants of the enemy forces to the last man*

【全景】panorama; a full view; a whole scene: 西湖～ *a full view of the West Lake* ◇ ～宽银幕电影 cinepanoramic; ～摄影机 panoramic camera

【全局】the overall situation; the situation as a whole: 影响～ *affect the overall situation* / 胸有～ *with the situation as a whole in mind*

【全军】❶ the whole (or entire) army: ～指战员 *the officers and men of the whole army* / ～运动会 *army-wide sports meet* ❷〈书〉preserve military strength

【全军覆没】the whole army overwhelmed—a complete failure: 这一仗第一师～。*The First Division was practically wiped out in the battle.*

【全开】[刷] a standard-sized sheet: 一张～的宣传画 *a full-size poster (or billboard)*

【全劳动力】(又作'全劳力') an able-bodied farm worker

【全力】with all one's strength; all-out; sparing no effort: ～支持 *support with all one's strength; spare no effort to support; give all-out support* ◇ ～爬升 full climb (of an aircraft); ～以赴 go all out; spare no effort

【全貌】a complete picture; a full view: 从这里可以看到大桥的～。*You can get a view of the whole bridge from here.* / 弄清问题的～ *try to get a complete picture of the problem*

【全面】overall; comprehensive; all-round: ～规划 *overall planning* / ～总结 *a comprehensive summing-up* / ～经验 *extensive experience* / ～崩溃 *a total collapse; débâcle* / ～进攻 *an all-out attack* / ～战争 *a full-scale war* / ～落实党的各项政策 *implement the Party's policies in an all-round way* / ～地看问题 *look at problems all-sidedly*

【全苗】[农] a full stand: 保证棉花～ *ensure a full stand of cotton shoots*

【全民】the whole (or entire) people; all the people: ～总动员 *general mobilization of the nation*

【全民公决】referendum

【全民皆兵】an entire nation in arms; every citizen being a soldier

【全民所有制】ownership by the whole people: ～企业 *enterprises owned by the whole people*

【全名】❶ full name (of a person, i. e. family name plus given name) ❷ 同〖全称〗

【全能】[体] all-round: ～运动员 *an all-round athlete; an all-rounder* / ～冠军 *an all-round champion* / 获得女子～冠军 *win the women's individual all-round title* / 五项～运动 *pentathlon* / 十项～运动 *decathlon*

【全年】annual; yearly: ～收入 *annual income* / ～平均温度 *mean annual temperature* / ～雨量 *yearly rainfall*

【全盘】whole; all; overall: ～考虑 *give overall consideration to* / ～接受 *give a total and uncritical acceptance to* / ～否定 *completely negate; totally repudiate* / ～西化 *wholesale Westernization* / ～电气化(机械化) *overall electrification (mechanization)*

【全票】❶ full ticket ❷ all the votes; a unanimous vote: 他以～当选。*He was elected by a unanimous vote.*

【全屏幕】[计] full screen ◇ ～编辑 full-screen editing; ～方式 full-screen mode

【全勤】full work attendance (without a single day off during a specified period)

【全球】the whole world: ～战略 *global strategy* / 在～范围内 *on a global scale* ◇ ～定位系统 global positioning system (GPS); ～化 globalization; ～通信系统 Globecom (Global Communication system)

【全权】❶ full powers; plenary powers: ～证书 *full powers* ❷ full responsibility: 企业的经营管理由国家委托经理～负责。*Managers will be entrusted by the state with full responsibility for the management and operation of their enterprises.*

【全权代表】plenipotentiary

【全然】completely; entirely: ～不了解情况 *be completely ignorant of the situation* / ～不计后果 *in utter disregard of the consequences* / ～不顾个人安危 *give no thought to one's own safety*

【全日制】full-time; full-day ◇ ～教育 full-time schooling; ～学校 full-time school

【全色】[摄] panchromatic: ～乳剂 *panchromatic emulsion*

【全色胶片】(又作'全色片') panchromatic film

【全身】the whole body; all over (the body): ～不适 *general malaise* / ～发抖 *shake (or shiver) all over* / ～湿透 *be soaked to the skin* / ～是伤 *be covered with cuts and bruises* / ～检查 *a general physical checkup* ◇ ～麻醉 general anesthesia; ～像 full-length picture

【全神贯注】concentrate one's attention on; be absorbed (or engrossed) in; be preoccupied with: 她～地听着。*She listened with rapt attention.* or *She was all ears.* / 下棋需要～。*Chess requires great concentration.*

【全胜】❶ complete victory: 大获～ *win a complete victory* ❷ [体] win every match; be all-victorious

【全盛】(of a historical period) flourishing; in full bloom

【全食】[天] total eclipse: ～带 *path of total eclipse; belt (or zone) of totality*

【全始全终】see (or carry) sth. through; stick to

sth. to the very end

【全视图】full view; general view

【全数】total number; whole amount: 我们已～付讫。*We have paid the whole amount.*

【全速】full (or maximum, top) speed: ～前进 *advance at full speed* / 这车～每小时120公里。*The car has a maximum speed of 120 kilometres an (or per) hour.*

【全损】[经] total loss ◇ ～险 [经] total loss only (T. L. O.)

【全套】a complete set: ～设备 *a complete set of equipment* / 你这贝多芬交响曲唱片是～的吗? *Are your records of Beethoven's symphonies a complete set?*

【全体】all; entire; whole: ～起立,长时间鼓掌。*There was a long standing ovation.* / 内阁～辞职。*The cabinet resigned en bloc.* / 看问题,不但要看到部分,而且要看到～。*In approaching a problem one should see the whole as well as the parts.*

【全天候】all-weather: ～飞机 *all-weather aircraft* / ～公路 *all-weather road*

【全托】put one's child in a boarding nursery: 你的孩子是日托还是～? *Is your child in a day nursery or a boarding nursery?* or *Does your child board at the nursery or go home in the evening?* ◇ ～托儿所 boarding nursery

【全文】full text: ～如下。*The full text follows.* / ～记录 *verbatim record* /《人民日报》～发表了总理的讲话。*Renmin Ribao published the Premier's speech in full.*

【全息电影】holographic movie

【全息照相】hologram: 激光～ *laser hologram* / ～存储器 *holographic memory* / ～术 *holography*

【全线】❶ all fronts; the entire length: 边界～ *the entire length of the boundary* / ～出击 *launch an attack on all fronts* / 敌人已～崩溃。*The enemy was put to rout all along the line.* ❷ the whole line (of a railway or highway): 这条铁路已～通车。*The whole railway line has been opened to traffic.*

【全心全意】whole-heartedly; heart and soul: ～为人民服务 *serve the people wholeheartedly* / ～投身到工作里边,你的生活就会充实和快乐。*If you set your whole mind and heart on your work, your life will be full and happy.*

【全新】completely new; brand-new: ～的设备 *brand-new equipment*

【全新世】[地质] the Recent Epoch

【全休】❶ a complete rest: 大夫建议～一星期。*The doctor prescribed a complete rest of one week.* ❷ a long-term sick leave

【全音】[音] whole tone

【全音符】[音] whole note; semibreve

【全责】all responsibility: 他对这起事故负～。*He bears all responsibility for the accident.*

【全知全能】omniscient and omnipotent

【全脂奶粉】whole milk powder

【全自动】full automation

诠 动〈书〉annotate; give explanatory notes

【诠释】annotate; give explanatory notes

【诠注】provide notes and commentary

泉 名 ❶ spring (a small stream): 温泉 ❷ the mouth of a spring; spring ❸ an ancient term for coin: ～币 *ancient coin*

【泉华】[地质] sinter

【泉水】spring water; spring

【泉眼】the mouth of a spring; spring

【泉源】❶ fountainhead; springhead; wellspring ❷ source: 智慧(力量)的～ *source of wisdom (strength)*

拳 Ⅰ 名 ❶ fist: 挥～ *shake one's fist* / 打了一～ *give a punch* ❷ boxing; pugilism: 一套～ *a shadow boxing set* / 练～ *practise shadow boxing* Ⅱ 动 curl; twist; bend: 老大娘～着腿坐在炕上。*The old woman sat on the kang with her legs curled up.*

【拳不离手,曲不离口】The boxer's fist must stick to its task, and the singer's mouth no rest must ask; Practice makes perfect.

【拳打脚踢】cuff and kick; beat up

【拳击】boxing; pugilism: ～台 *boxing ring* / ～运动员 *boxer; pugilist*

【拳脚】Chinese boxing

【拳曲】curl; twist; bend: ～的头发 *curly hair*

【拳拳】〈书〉sincere: ～之忱 *sincere intention; sincerity*

【拳拳服膺】❶ always bear in mind ❷ have a sincere belief in

【拳师】boxing coach; pugilist

【拳术】Chinese boxing

【拳坛】boxing circles; the boxing world

【拳头】fist: 举起～喊口号 *raise one's fist and shout slogans* / 医生为他清理伤口时他疼得直攥～。*He clenched his fists in agony as the doctor cleaned the wound.*

【拳头产品】competitive products

【拳王】boxing champion; lord of the ring

痊 动 fully recover from an illness

【痊愈】fully recover from an illness; be fully recovered: 她还没有～。*She's not recovered yet.* / 希望你早日～。*I wish you a speedy recovery.* / 伤口～后,他又返回了前线。*After his wound healed, he went back to the front.*

蜷 动 curl up; huddle up: 小猫在沙发上～作一团睡觉。*The kitten was sleeping curled up on the sofa.*

【蜷伏】curl up; huddle up; lie with the knees drawn up: 他喜欢～着睡觉。*He likes to sleep with his knees drawn up.* or *He likes to sleep curled up on his side.*

【蜷曲】curl; coil; twist: 一条蛇在草丛里～着。*A snake lay coiled in the grass.* / 他把两腿～起来做

了个前滚翻。*Drawing up his knees against his chest, he did a forward roll.*
【蜷缩】roll up; huddle up; curl up: 刺猬一受到攻击就～成一团。*A hedgehog rolls itself into a ball when attacked.*

醛 名［化］aldehyde
【醛酸】［化］aldehydic acid
【醛糖】［化］aldose
【醛酯】［化］aldehydo-ester

鬈 形 ❶(of hair) curly; wavy: ～发 *curly hair* ❷(of hair) beautiful
【鬈曲】［纺］crimp; crinkle; curl: ～羊毛 *crimpy wool; crinkled wool*

颧（构词成分）见下
【颧骨】cheekbone: ～突起 *have prominent cheekbones*

quǎn

犬 名 dog
【犬齿】canine tooth
【犬马之劳】serve like a dog or a horse: 效～ *serve one's master faithfully; be at sb.'s beck and call* / 若蒙不弃，愿效～。*Should I be fortunate enough not to be rejected, I would render such humble services as I could.*
【犬儒】cynic
【犬儒主义】cynicism
【犬牙】❶ canine tooth ❷ fang (of a dog)
【犬牙交错】jigsaw-like; interlocking: 形成～的状态 *form a jagged, interlocking pattern* / ～的战争 *a war of jigsaw pattern*
【犬子】〈谦〉my son

quàn

劝 动 ❶ advise; urge; try to persuade: ～他戒烟 *advise him to give up (or quit) smoking* / ～他休息 *urge him to take a rest* / 我～了半天，他就是不听。*I spent a long time trying to talk him round, but he just wouldn't listen.* / 我们～他别去了。*We tried to persuade him not to go.* ❷ encourage: 劝学 ❸ comfort: 他心里不好受，你去～～吧。*He's feeling bad; please go and say a few words to comfort him.*
【劝导】try to persuade; advise; induce: 耐心～ *try patiently to talk sb. round* / 经过同志们～，他终于想通了。*With the help of his comrades, he has finally straightened things out in his mind.*
【劝返】persuade somebody to return: ～外地人回乡 *persuade people from the provinces to return home*
【劝告】❶ advise; urge; exhort: 我～她开车要小心。*I urged her to drive carefully.* / 医生～他注意休息。*The doctor advised him to have a good rest.* ❷ advice; exhortations: 她不顾我们的一再～。*She disregarded our repeated exhortations.* / 小王听从了我的～，把烟戒了。*Xiao Wang has taken my advice and given up (or quitted) smoking.*
【劝和】try to persuade two parties to become reconciled; mediate
【劝化】❶［宗］(佛教) urge to do good ❷ 同〖募化〗
【劝驾】urge sb. to accept an invitation or a post
【劝架】try to reconcile parties to a quarrel or to stop people from fighting each other; mediate
【劝解】❶ help sb. to get over his worries, etc.: 大家～了半天，她才消气了。*It was some time before we succeeded in pacifying her.* ❷ mediate; make peace between; bring people together: 他们吵架了，你去～～下。*They've had a quarrel. You try and patch things up between them.*
【劝戒】admonish; expostulate: 他把我当成亲兄弟一样，时时～我，帮助我。*He treats me like his own brother and often gives me advice and help.*
【劝酒】urge sb. to drink (at a banquet)
【劝勉】advise and encourage: 互相～ *help and encourage each other*
【劝募】solicit contributions by persuasions
【劝善】encourage people to do good
【劝说】persuade; advise: 我们已经～过他，叫他放弃原来的计划。*We've talked him out of his original plan.* / 他听从了我的～。*He gave in to my persuasion.*
【劝退】persuade somebody to quit (because of incompetence)
【劝慰】console; soothe
【劝降】induce to capitulate
【劝学】encourage learning
【劝业场】〈旧〉bazaar
【劝诱】induce; prevail upon
【劝止】同〖劝阻〗
【劝阻】dissuade sb. from; advise sb. not to: 你最好～他别那样干。*You'd better try to talk him out of doing that.* / 看到损害群众利益的行为，我们就要进行～。*Whenever we see a person doing something antisocial, we should try to stop him.*

券 名 certificate; ticket: 入场券

quē

炔 名［化］alkyne: 乙炔
【炔雌醇】［药］ethinyloestradiol

缺 Ⅰ 动 ❶ be short of; lack: ～人 *be short of hands* / 这本书～两页。*Two pages are missing from this book.* / 这些条件～一不可。*Not a single one of these conditions can be dispensed with.* / 我们队可不能～了小林。*Our team can't do without Xiao Lin.* ❷ be absent: 人都到齐了，一个不～。*No one is absent. Everybody's here.* Ⅱ

形 incomplete; imperfect: 残缺 Ⅲ 名 vacancy; opening: 空缺

【缺编】❶ understaffed: 这家医院～。*The hospital is understaffed.* ❷ 同〖缺额〗

【缺档】be in short supply; be out of stock

【缺德】mean; wicked; rotten: 做～事 *do sth. mean; play a mean trick* / 他这样做可真～。*It's wicked of him to act like that.* / 这样对待她真～。*What a rotten thing to do to her!*

【缺点】shortcoming; defect; weakness; drawback: 克服工作中的～ *overcome shortcomings in one's work* / 这种药的主要～是败胃。*The chief drawback of this medicine is that it spoils your appetite.*

【缺额】vacant position; vacancy: 他们厂按编制还有 50 名～。*Their factory is still 50 people short of its quota of workers.*

【缺乏】be short of; lack; be in want of: ～劳动力 *be short of labour power* / ～经验 *lack experience* / ～战斗力 *have poor fighting capacity* / ～资源 *be deficient in resources* / ～证据 *want of proof*

【缺钙】［医］acalcerosis; calcium deficiency: ～症 *calcifames; acalcerosis*

【缺憾】regrettable imperfection; regret

【缺货】be in short supply; be out of stock

【缺斤短两】give short weight: 这铺子卖东西老是～。*That shop always gives short weight (or short-weights its customers).*

【缺刻叶】［植］incised leaf

【缺课】be absent from school; miss a class: 缺了三课 *miss three lessons* / 给一个因病～的学生补习功课 *give extra help to a pupil who has missed some classes on account of illness*

【缺口】❶ breach; gap: 篱笆上有个～。*There is a gap in the fence.* / 碗边儿上碰了个～儿。*The bowl has a broken edge.* / 从敌人的侧翼打开一个～ *make a breach in the enemy's flank* ❷［机］notch

【缺漏】gaps and omissions: 弥缝～ *fill in gaps and supply omissions*

【缺门】gap (in a branch of learning, etc.): 这本书填补了词典学方面的重大～。*This book fills a major gap in lexicography.*

【缺欠】❶ shortcoming; defect; weakness ❷ lack; be short of

【缺勤】absence from duty (or work): 因病～ *be on sick leave* ◇ ～率 absence rate; absentee rate

【缺少】lack; be short of; be in want of: ～零件 *lack spare parts* / ～人手 *be short of hands; be shorthanded* / 不可～的条件 *indispensable conditions*

【缺市】in short supply

【缺损】❶ damaged; worn; torn ❷［医］physiological defect; physiological deficiency

【缺铁性贫血】iron-deficiency anaemia

【缺位】❶ (of a position) be vacant ❷ a vacant position; vacancy

【缺席】absent (from a meeting, etc.): 因事～ *be absent through being otherwise engaged* / 他这学期从没～过。*He has never been absent from class this term.* / ～者 *absentee* ◇ ～判决［法］judgment by default; ～审判［法］trial by default; ～投票 absentee voting; absentee vote; absentee ballot

【缺陷】defect; drawback; flaw; blemish: 生理～ *a physical defect* / 这个计划有些～。*The plan has some shortcomings.* / 精神上有～的人不能作证人。*Those with mental handicaps cannot be witnesses.*

【缺心眼儿】❶ simple-minded; scatterbrained ❷ dull-witted; mentally deficient; retarded

阙 名〈书〉fault; error

【阙如】〈书〉deficient; wanting; lacking: 竟告～ *be found wanting*

【阙疑】leave the question open

qué

瘸 动〈口〉be lame; limp: 左腿～了 *be lame in the left leg* / 一步一～ *walk with a limp* / 他扭了脚腕子，站起来～着走了。*After he twisted his ankle, he got up and limped away.*

【瘸腿】〈口〉lame: ～的人 *lame person; cripple*

【瘸子】〈口〉lame person; cripple

què

却 Ⅰ 动 ❶ step back: 退却 ❷ drive back; repulse: 却敌 ❸ decline; refuse: 推却 ❹ (used after a verb to indicate completion of an action): 冷却 Ⅱ 副 but; yet: 她有许多话要说，一时～什么也说不出来。*She had a lot to say, but at the time she was unable to utter a word.* / 文章虽短～很有力。*The essay is short but forceful.* / 这样推理很周全，～说服不了我。*The logic is sound, and yet it does not convince me.*

【却病】〈书〉prevent or cure a disease ◇ ～延年 prevent illness and prolong life

【却步】step back (in fear or disgust); hang back: 不要因为困难而～。*Don't hang back in the face of difficulties.*

【却敌】repulse the enemy

【却说】we were telling you... (a stock phrase used by traditional storytellers when resuming narration where they left off)

【却之不恭】〈套〉(said when receiving a gift) it would be impolite to decline: ～，受之有愧。*To decline would be disrespectful but to accept is embarrassing.*

雀 名 sparrow——另见 qiǎo

【雀斑】freckle

【雀鲷】［动］damselfish

【雀麦】［植］bromegrass; brome

【雀鹰】sparrow hawk

【雀跃】jump for joy：欢呼～ *shout and jump for joy*

【雀噪】〈贬〉enjoy loud fame：名声～一时 *enjoy fleeting fame*

确 Ⅰ形 true；real；authentic：正确 Ⅱ副 really；indeed：～有其事。*It's a fact*. or *It really happened*.

【确保】ensure；guarantee：～安全生产 *ensure safety in production* / ～质量 *guarantee quality* / 要～适时播种。*Be sure to do the sowing in good time*. / ～不发生类似事件 *ensure against the occurrence of similar incidents*

【确定】❶ define；fix；determine：～会议宗旨 *define the aims of the conference* / ～时限 *fix a time frame* / ～开会的日期和地点 *determine* (*or fix*) *the time and place for a meeting* / ～任务 *set the tasks* ❷ definite：～的答复 *a definite reply* / ～不移的结论 *an incontestable conclusion* / ～的时间 *a fixed time*

【确乎】really；indeed：这办法～有效。*This method is really effective*. / 他～非常聪明。*He is very clever indeed*.

【确乎不拔】firm and unshakable；unswerving；unflinching

【确立】establish：～社会主义制度 *establish the socialist system*

【确论】a sound assertion；a just argument

【确切】❶ definite；exact；precise：～的日期 *an exact date* / ～的解释 *a clear and unambiguous explanation* / 下个～的定义 *give a precise definition* / 用词～ *precise wording* ❷ true；reliable；sure：～的保证 *a sure guarantee*

【确认】affirm；confirm；acknowledge：参加会议的各国～了这些原则。*The participating countries affirmed these principles*. / ～这一经济合同无效。*The economic contract was confirmed to be void*. ◇ ～书［法］letter of confirmation

【确实】❶ true；reliable：～的消息 *reliable information* / ～的数字 *exact figures* / 把发生的事说得确确实实 *give an accurate and detailed account of what has happened* ❷ really；indeed：这～是个很好的建议。*This is really a very good suggestion*. / 他～来过。*Yes, he did come*.

【确守】strictly or scrupulously abide by：～信义 *act in strict good faith*

【确数】exact figures；exact amount

【确信】❶ firmly believe；be convinced；be sure：我们～正义的事业一定会胜利。*We firmly believe that a just cause is bound to triumph*. ❷ reliable information

【确凿】conclusive；authentic；irrefutable：～的事实 *irrefutable facts* / 证据～，不容抵赖。*The evidence is conclusive and brooks no denial*. ◇ ～不移 well established and irrefutable

【确诊】make a definite diagnosis；diagnose：他的病尚未～。*No diagnosis has as yet been made of his disease*.

【确证】❶ prove conclusively or positively：我们可以～他的论断是错误的。*We can prove conclusively that his assertion is wrong*. ❷ proof positive；conclusive or irrefutable evidence：在～面前他不得不承认自己的罪行。*When confronted with conclusive evidence, he had to admit his guilt*.

鹊 名 magpie

【鹊报】the cry of the magpie—a good omen

【鹊巢鸠占】the turtledove occupies the magpie's nest—one person seizes another person's place, land, etc.

【鹊起】〈书〉❶ act according to circumstances；do as one sees fit；use one's discretion ❷ (of fame) spread；rise

【鹊桥】Magpie Bridge：～相会 *Magpie Bridge meeting—the reunion of husband and wife* (*or lovers*) *after a long separation* ——另见〖牛郎织女〗

【鹊鸲】magpie robin

榷 动 discuss：商榷

qūn

逡 动〈书〉shrink from

【逡巡】〈书〉hesitate to move forward；hang back：～不前 *hesitate to make a move*

qún

裙 名 ❶ skirt：绸～ *a silk skirt* ❷ sth. like a skirt：围裙

【裙带】❶ belt (as a decoration for a skirt or dress) ❷ connected through one's female relatives：通过～关系 *with the help of one's female relatives*；*through petticoat influence* ◇ ～风 petticoat influence；～官 an official who owes his position to petticoat influence

【裙裤】culottes

【裙子】skirt

群 Ⅰ名 crowd；group：人群 Ⅱ量 (for people or animals) group；herd；flock：一～小孩 *a group of children* / 一～人 *a crowd of people* / 一～牛 *a herd of cattle* / 一～羊 *a flock of sheep* / 一～狼 *a pack of wolves* / 一～蜜蜂 *a swarm of bees*

【群策群力】pool the wisdom and efforts of everyone

【群岛】archipelago

【群雕】a group of statues

【群芳】❶ beautiful and fragrant flowers：～竞艳 *flowers vying with each other in beauty* ❷ a group of beauties or artists：艳压～ *the queen of beauties* ◇ ～之冠 the queen of flowers—the reigning beauty

【群峰】connected mountain peaks：～耸立 *mountain peaks towering into the sky*

【群婚】group marriage；communal marriage

【群集】gather；assemble：人们～在广场上。*People gathered together in the public square.*

【群件】［计］groupware

【群居】living in groups；gregarious；social ◇ ～动物 social animal；～昆虫 social insect

【群控制】group control

【群龙无首】a host of dragons without a head—a group without a leader

【群落】［生］❶ community：～交错区 *ecotone* ❷ building complex；cluster of buildings：古建筑～ *group of ancient buildings* / 商业～ *shopping complex*

【群魔乱舞】a host of demons dancing in riotous revelry—rogues of all kinds running wild

【群起】all rise（to do sth.）：～响应 *all rise to respond*

【群起而攻之】all rise（or turn）against sb.

【群青】［化］ultramarine

【群轻折轴】a load of many light things can break the axle of a cart—minor offences unchecked may bring disaster

【群情】public sentiment；feelings of the masses：～振奋。*Everyone is exhilarated.* / ～激昂。*Public feeling was aroused（or ran high）.*

【群山】connected hills（or mountains）：～环绕 *be surrounded by hills*

【群书】all kinds of books；a wide variety of books：博览～ *be well-read*

【群体】❶［生］colony ❷ groups：企业～ *groups of enterprises*

【群威群胆】mass heroism and daring：～，英勇杀敌 *display mass heroism and daring in destroying the enemy*

【群言堂】a conference hall where everyone is allowed to have his say—rule by the voice of the many：我们提倡"～"，反对"一言堂"。*We advocate "letting everyone have his say" and oppose the practice of "what I say goes".* ——另见〖一言堂〗

【群英会】a gathering of heroes；a conference of outstanding workers

【群众】❶ the masses：～大会 *mass rally* / ～监督 *surveillance by the masses* / ～心理 *mass psychology* / ～意愿 *the popular will* ❷ non-Party ❸ a member of the rank and file ◇ ～工作 mass work；～关系 one's relations（or ties）with the masses；～观点 the mass viewpoint；～路线 the mass line；～团体 mass（non-government）organization；～运动 mass movement；mass campaign；～组织 mass（non-government）organization；people's organization

【群众性】of a mass character：～体育活动 *mass sports activities* / 中国气象工作的一个重要特点是它的～。*Mass participation is a prominent feature of meteorological work in China.*

R

rán

然 Ⅰ形 right; correct: 不以为然 Ⅱ副 so; like that: 尽然 Ⅲ连〈书〉but; nevertheless; however: 此事虽小,～亦不可忽视。*This is a minor point, but it must not be overlooked*. Ⅳ(构词成分,副词或形容词后缀): 忽然

【然而】but; however; yet: 这篇文章写得不错,～还可以改进。*The composition is all right, there is room for improvement, however*. / 我失败了,～还要试试。*I have failed, yet I shall try again*.

【然后】then; after that; afterwards: 我们先研究一下,～再决定。*We'll consider the problem carefully before coming to any decision*. / 我们看了一场电影,～就回家了。*We saw a film, and after that we went home*.

【然诺】〈书〉promise; pledge: 重～ *be serious about making and keeping a promise; stand by one's word*

髯 名 whiskers; beard: 美～ *a beautiful beard*

【髯口】artificial beard or whiskers worn by traditional opera actors

燃 动 burn; ignite; light: ～灯 *light a lamp* / ～起一堆篝火 *light a bonfire* / ～起革命的烈火 *spark off (or kindle) the flames of revolution*

【燃炽】burn; smolder: 他眼中～着热情。*Passion smolders in his eyes*. / 一种奇怪的想法在我脑中～。*A strange idea has been nagging me*.

【燃点】❶ kindle; set fire to; light; ignite: ～灯笼 *light a lantern* / 木柴太湿,～不着。*The wood is too wet to kindle*. ❷[化] ignition (or burning, kindling) point

【燃放】set off (fireworks, etc.): ～爆竹 *set off firecrackers*

【燃耗】fuel consumption

【燃料】fuel: 标准～ *ideal fuels* / 低热值～ *low-calorie fuels* ◇ ～比[冶] fuel ratio; ～电池 fuel cell; ～动力工业 fuel and power industry; ～库 fuel depot; fuel reservoir

【燃煤】coal for fuel

【燃眉之急】as pressing as a fire singeing one's eyebrows—extremely urgent: 敌兵入侵,边界有～。*The enemy had started to invade the land and the situation on the border was very critical*.

【燃气轮机】gas turbine: ～发电厂 *gas turbine power station*

【燃气热水器】gas water heater

【燃烧】❶ burn; kindle: 干柴容易～。*Dry wood burns easily*. / 怒火～ *burning with rage* / 革命的烈火在～。*The flames of revolution are raging*. ❷[化] combustion; inflammation: ～性能 *combustibility* ◇ ～弹 incendiary bomb; ～剂 incendiary agent; ～瓶 frangible grenade; Molotov cocktail; ～室[机] combustion chamber; blast chamber; combustor

【燃油】fuel oil

【燃油泵】fuel pump

【燃油炉】fuel burner

rǎn

冉 (构词成分)见下

【冉冉】〈书〉❶ (of hair, twigs, etc.) hang down softly ❷ slowly; gradually: 一轮红日～升起。*A red sun slowly rose*.

染 动 ❶ dye: 把一块布～成绿色 *dye a piece of cloth green* / 我们的战旗是烈士的鲜血～红的。*Our standard is dyed with the blood of our martyrs*. ❷ catch (a disease); acquire (a bad habit, etc.): ～上了痢疾 *have caught dysentery* / ～上了赌博的恶习 *have contracted the bad habit of gambling* / 母亲不允许我们～上一点坏习惯。*Mother doesn't allow us to acquire any bad habits*. ❸ soil; contaminate: 污染 ❹ add details to a painting, etc.: 渲染

【染病】catch (or contract) an illness; be infected with a disease

【染毒】[军] contaminate: ～区域 *contamination area*

【染发】dye the hair

【染坊】dyehouse; dye-works

【染缸】dye vat; dyejigger

【染患】catch (an illness); contract (a disease); be infected: ～了传染病 *contract an infectious disease*

【染料】dyestuff; dye

【染色】dye; colour: ～性 *dyeability* ◇ ～剂 colouring agent; ～体[生] chromosome; ～质[生化] chromatin

【染液】dye liquor

【染印法】film dye transfer process: ～彩色电影 *colour film made by the dye transfer process*

【染指】take a share of sth. one is not entitled to; encroach on: ～别国资源 *encroach on the resources of other countries* / 国家神圣领土不容他人～。*Our territory is sacred and inviolable.*
【染指甲】paint the fingernails: 染了红指甲 *paint the fingernails red*
【染指择肥】dip one's finger in the pie and claim the lion's share

rāng

嚷 (构词成分)见下 ——另见 rǎng
【嚷嚷】〈口〉❶ make a noise; make an uproar: 谁在那儿～? *Who's making all that noise over there?* / 屋里一片乱～。*The room was in an uproar.* ❷ make widely known: 这件事,你可别～。*Don't breathe a word about this.* / 要是～出去,对咱俩都没好处。*Letting this out wouldn't do either of us any good.*

ráng

禳 动〈书〉avert (a misfortune or disaster) by prayers
【禳解】〈书〉avert (a misfortune or disaster) by prayers
瓤 名 ❶ pulp; flesh; pith: 橘子～ *the pulp of a tangerine* / 西瓜～ *the pulp (or flesh) of a watermelon* ❷ the interior part of certain things
【瓤子】pulp; flesh; pith

rǎng

壤 名 ❶ soil: 土壤 ❷ earth: 霄壤 ❸ area: 接壤
【壤土】[农] loam
攘 动〈书〉❶ reject; resist: 攘外 ❷ seize; grab: 攘夺 ❸ push up one's sleeves: 攘臂
【攘臂】〈书〉push up one's sleeves and bare one's arms (in excitement or agitation): ～高呼 *raise one's hands and shout*
【攘除】〈书〉get rid of; weed out; reject: ～奸邪 *get rid of crafty and evil people* / ～奸凶 *eliminate treacherous people*
【攘夺】〈书〉seize; grab: ～政权 *seize state power* / ～王位 *usurp the throne*
【攘善】〈书〉claim credit due to others
【攘外】resist foreign aggression
嚷 动 ❶ shout; yell; make an uproar: 别～了,人家都睡了。*Stop yelling, people are sleeping.* / 他在窗外～了几嗓子。*He shouted several times outside the window.* ❷〈口〉make a noise; make an uproar ——另见 rāng
【嚷叫】shout; yell; make an uproar

ràng

让 Ⅰ 动 ❶ give way; give ground; yield; give up: 各不相～。*Neither is willing to give ground.* / 我～了他两步棋。*I let him have the first two moves (in a chess game).* / 幸亏我～得快,要不早给那辆自行车撞倒了。*Luckily I dodged in time, or I'd have been knocked down by the bike.* ❷ invite; offer: ～茶 *offer sb. tea* / 把客人～进里屋 *invite guests into the inner room* ❸ let; allow; make: ～我想一想。*Let me think it over.* / 大夫不～她起来。*The doctor told her to stay in bed.* / 他～我把这个消息转告你。*He told me to pass the message on to you.* ❹ let sb. have sth. at a fair price: 我把激光唱机按原价～给他了。*I've turned my CD player over to him at the original price.* Ⅱ 介 (used in a passive sentence to introduce the doer of the action): 台布～墨水给染了。*The table cloth got stained with ink.* / 庄稼～大水冲跑了。*The crops were washed away by the flood.* / 行李～雨淋湿了。*The luggage got wet in the rain.* / 她～小刘给气跑了。*Xiao Liu made her so angry that she left in a huff.*
【让步】make a concession; give in; give way; yield: 准备作出某些必要的～ *be prepared to make some necessary concessions* / 不向无理要求～ *not yield to any unreasonable demand* / 最大限度的～ *the greatest (or maximum) concession* / 两人争吵了半天,谁也不肯～。*The two of them quarrelled for a long time; neither was willing to give in.*
【让渡】transfer the possession of; alienate: 资源不得～。*Resources are not subject to alienation.*
【让价】(of a seller) agree to reduce the price asked
【让开】get out of the way; step aside; make way: 车来了,快～。*A car is coming. Quick, get out of the way.* / 他挡着道,可又偏不～。*He was blocking the road and wouldn't make way.*
【让利】concession ◇ ～促销 promote (or stimulate) sales by cutting profits; ～销售 cut-price sales
【让路】make way for sb. or sth.; give way; give sb. the right of way: 大家让让路。*Please get out of the way, everybody.* / 你们的工程得给重点工程～。*Your project will have to make way for the main project.*
【让球】concede points (in ball games): 教练员让了小李五个球。*The coach conceded Xiao Li five points.*
【让位】❶ resign sovereign authority; abdicate: 谁领导无方,谁就得～。*Those who don't make good leaders should give up their positions.* ❷ offer (or give up) one's seat to sb.: 请为这位孕妇让个位! *Please give your seat up to this pregnant lady.* ❸ yield to; give way to; change into: 经过大家的努力,困难的局面终于～于顺利的局面。*As a result of collective effort, the difficult situ-*

ation changed into a favourable one.

【让贤】relinquish one's post in favour of sb. better qualified

【让枣推梨】offer dates and decline pears—show brotherly love

【让账】(of friends eating out) insist on paying the bill

【让座】❶ offer (or give up) one's seat to sb.：他给一位抱孩子的妇女让了座。*He eagerly offered his bus seat to a woman carrying a baby*. ❷ invite guests to be seated：他给客人又是～，又是让茶。*He eagerly invited the guests to be seated and offered them tea*.

ráo

饶 Ⅰ 形 rich；plentiful：～有风趣 *full of wit and humour* Ⅱ 动 ❶ have mercy on；let sb. off；forgive：下回可不能轻～了你。*We won't let you off so easily next time*. / 他说话不～人。*He has a sharp tongue*. ❷ give sth. extra；let sb. have sth. into the bargain：给你～上一个。*I'll let you have one more*. / 有两个人就够了，不要把他也～在里头。*Two people will be enough；there is no need to drag him along，too*. Ⅲ 连〈口〉although；in spite of the fact that：这孩子，～怎么说他也不听。*That child！Whatever you said，he simply wouldn't listen*. / ～这么让着他，他还不满意。*No matter how many concessions I made，he still wasn't satisfied*.

【饶命】spare sb.'s life：他跪在地上，直求～。*He knelt down begging to be spared*.

【饶舌】❶ too talkative；garrulous ❷ say more than is proper；shoot off one's mouth

【饶恕】forgive；pardon：请求～ *ask for forgiveness*

【饶头】〈口〉a small item given away free (in business transactions)；extra：这个小的是个～。*This little one is an extra*.

【饶沃】〈书〉(of soil) fertile；rich

桡 名 oar

【桡动脉】[生理] radial artery

【桡骨】[生理] radius

rǎo

扰 动 ❶ harass；trouble：干扰 ❷〈套〉trespass on sb.'s hospitality：我～了他一顿饭。*He kindly entertained me to dinner*.

【扰动】be in turmoil；be turbulent

【扰乱】harass；disturb；create confusion：～治安 *disturb public order* / ～市场 *disrupt the market* / ～军心 *undermine the morale of an army* / ～思路 *interrupt a train of thought* / ～睡眠 *disturb sb.'s sleep* / ～视线 *interfere with sb.'s view*

【扰民】disturb people；bother，inconvenience inhabitants：搬迁严重污染～的企业 *relocate enterprises that are heavy polluters and disturb local inhabitants*

【扰攘】hustle and bustle；noisy confusion；tumult：下课铃一响，教室里一片～的声音。*As soon as the bell rang，the classroom was in noisy confusion*.

rào

绕 动 ❶ wind；coil：～线 *wind thread* / 把铁丝～成圈 *coil wire；wind wire into a coil* ❷ move round；circle；revolve：地球～着太阳转。*The earth moves (or revolves) round the sun*. / 运动员～场一周。*The athletes marched around the arena*. ❸ make a detour；bypass；go round：～过暗礁 *bypass hidden reefs；steer clear of submerged rocks* / 你必须明确回答这个问题，想～是～不过去的。*You must give a definite answer to the question. There's no getting round it*. ❹ confuse；baffle；befuddle：你的话把他～住了。*What you said confused him*. / 我一时～住了，账目没算对。*I got confused and didn't work out the accounts correctly*.

【绕脖子】〈方〉❶ beat about the bush；speak or act in a roundabout way：你简单地说吧，别净～。*Just speak simply. Don't beat about the bush*. ❷ involved；knotty；tricky：这句话太～了。*This sentence is too involved*. / 这道题真～。*This is a very tricky question*.

【绕道】(又作'绕路') make a detour；go by a roundabout route：前面有个水库，我们得～过去。*There's a reservoir ahead. We'll have to make a detour*. / 你不要一遇困难就～走。*Don't always try to skirt round difficulties*.

【绕口令】tongue twister

【绕梁】(of the sound of singing) linger；reverberate

【绕圈子】❶ circle；go round and round ❷ take a circuitous route；make a detour：他想从她家门口经过，特地绕了一个圈子。*He made a detour to pass the house where she lived*. ❸ 同〖绕弯子〗

【绕弯儿】❶〈方〉go for a stroll (or walk)：他刚吃完晚饭，在院子里～。*He's just had his supper and is taking a stroll in the courtyard*. / 我出去绕个弯儿就回来。*I'm going out for a walk and will be back soon*. ❷ 同〖绕弯子〗

【绕弯子】talk in a roundabout way；beat about the bush：有话直说，别～。*If you have anything to say，say it. Don't beat about the bush*.

【绕行】❶ make a detour；bypass：道路施工，车辆～。*Detour. Road under repair*. ❷ move round；circle

【绕远儿】go the long way round：那样走可就～了。*If you take that route，you'll be going the long way round*.

【绕组】[电] winding：双线～ *bifilar winding*

【绕嘴】(of a sentence，etc.) not be smooth；be

difficult to articulate：这句话很～。*This sentence is a tongue twister*.

rě

惹 动 ❶ invite or ask for (sth. undesirable)：～麻烦 *ask for trouble*；*invite trouble* / 不要把他～翻了。*Don't touch off his temper*. ❷ offend；provoke；tease：我～不起他。*I cannot afford to offend him*. / 我可没～他呀！*I said nothing to provoke him*. or *I did nothing to provoke him*. ❸ attract；cause：～人注意 *attract attention* / ～人讨厌 *make a nuisance of oneself* / 他的话把大家～得哈哈大笑。*His words set everybody roaring with laughter*.

【惹火烧身】stir up a fire only to burn oneself—court disaster；ask for trouble

【惹祸】court disaster；stir up trouble：这都是我惹的祸。*It was I who started all the trouble*.

【惹乱子】court disaster；stir up trouble

【惹恼】make sb. angry；offend

【惹气】get angry：不值得为这点小事～。*It's senseless to get angry over such a trifle*.

【惹事】stir up trouble；make trouble

【惹是生非】provoke a dispute；stir up trouble：他是一个怕～的人。*He was the kind of man who would avoid becoming involved in tittle-tattle at all costs*.

【惹眼】〈方〉conspicuous；showy

rè

热 Ⅰ 名 ❶ heat：摩擦产生～。*Friction produces heat*. ❷ fever；temperature：这孩子有～。*The child is running a fever*. ❸ craze；fad：卡拉 OK～ *intense popular interest in karaoke*；*karaoke craze* / 旅游～ *travel craze* Ⅱ 形 ❶ hot：～水 *hot water* / 三伏天很～。*During the dogdays it's very hot*. ❷ ardent；warmhearted：亲热 ❸ envious；eager：眼热 ❹ in great demand；popular：～货 *goods in great demand*；*goods which sell well* ❺ thermal；thermo-：热中子 / 热核 Ⅲ 动 heat up；warm up；warm：把汤～一～ *heat up the soup*

【热爱】ardently love；have deep love (or affection) for：～自己的工作 *love one's work* / ～人民 *have deep love for the people* / 他从小就～科学。*He has loved science since childhood*. / ～生活 *have a keen sense of the joy of life*；*enjoy the pleasures of life with gusto*

【热拔】［机］hot drawing

【热病】［中］acute disease accompanied by fever

【热补】vulcanize (tyre, etc.)

【热潮】great mass fervour；upsurge：掀起群众性体育锻炼的～ *unfold a vigorous mass campaign for sports and physical training*

【热忱】zeal；warmheartedness；enthusiasm and devotion：革命～ *revolutionary zeal* / 对同志对人民极端的～ *extreme warmheartedness towards one's comrades and the people* / ～地致敬 *warmly pay tribute to sb*.；*send warm regards to sb*.

【热诚】warm and sincere；cordial：～欢迎 *cordially welcome* / ～地希望 *sincerely hope* / 张先生一向对人～。*Mr. Zhang is always warm and sincere towards others*.

【热处理】［机］heat (or thermal) treatment：～钢 *heat-treated steel* ◇ ～炉 heat-treated furnace

【热脆性】［冶］hot-shortness；red-shortness

【热带】the torrid zone；the tropics ◇ ～草原 *savanna*；～风暴 tropical storm；～气旋 tropical cyclone；tropical revolving storm；～鱼 tropical fish ～植物 *tropical plant*；～作物 tropical crops；

【热导体】［物］heat conductor

【热得快】immersion heater；element

【热点】❶ hot spot：旅游～ *a tourist hot spot* ❷ ［物］hot spot ❸ central issue；point at issue：讨论的～ *focus of discussion* ❹ arousing general interest：～问题 *a topic of general interest*

【热电】［物］pyroelectricity；thermoelectricity ◇ ～厂 heat and power plant；～偶 thermocouple；～体 pyroelectrics；～效应 pyroelectric effect；～学 pyroelectricity

【热电子】thermelectron

【热电阻】thermal resistance

【热度】❶ degree of heat；heat：物体燃烧需要一定的～。*The burning of an object requires a certain degree of heat*. ❷〈口〉fever；temperature：你～降下去了吗？*Has your temperature come down?*

【热风炉】［冶］hot-blast stove

【热敷】［医］hot compress

【热辐射】［物］heat (or thermal) radiation

【热功当量】［物］mechanical equivalent of heat

【热狗】hot dog

【热固塑料】thermosetting plastic

【热管】heat pipe

【热锅上的蚂蚁】an ant on a hot pan—restless：他等着选举的结果，像～。*He was waiting for the results of the elections*, *restless as an ant on a hot pan*.

【热合】heat seal

【热核】thermonuclear ◇ ～爆炸 thermonuclear explosion；～弹头 thermonuclear warhead；～反应［物］thermonuclear reaction；～反应堆［物］thermonuclear reactor；～技术 thermonucleonics；～武器 thermonuclear weapon

【热烘烘】very warm：炉火很旺，屋里～的。*With the stove burning cheerfully*, *it's very warm in the room*. / 天热极了，风吹过来都使人感到～的。*It's so hot that even the wind feels hot*.

【热乎乎】(又作'热呼呼') warm：他的手～的。*His hands are warm*. / 心里感到～的 *feel it heartwarming*

【热乎】(rèhu)(又作'热呼') 同〖热和〗

【热火朝天】buzzing (or bustling) with activity；in

full swing：工地上一派～的景象。*The construction site was bustling with activity*.

【热火】(rèhuo) ❶ showing tremendous enthusiasm; exciting：广场上锣鼓喧天，场面可～啦！*The square, resounding with the roll and clang of music, presented a scene of noisy hilarity.* ❷ 同〖热和〗

【热货】hot commodity; commodities that command a ready market are in great demand and sell well：变冷货为～ *make dead stock sell like hot cakes; turn dead stock into hot sellers* / 女装中的～ *hot items in women's wear*

【热和】(rèhuo)〈口〉❶ nice and warm; warm：饭菜还～。*The food is still warm.* / 炕上真～。*The kang is warm and cosy.* ❷ warm and friendly; pally; chummy; thick：他们一见面就很～。*They chummed up with each other the moment they met.* / 他们谈得很～。*They had a very agreeable chat.*

【热机】[机] heat engine

【热寂】[物] heat death

【热加工】[冶] hot-working; hot work

【热扩散】[物] thermal diffusion

【热辣辣】burning hot; scorching：太阳晒得人～的。*The sun feels scorching hot.* / 他听了大家的批评，觉得脸上～的。*After hearing everybody's criticism, he felt his cheeks burning.*

【热浪】[气] heat wave; hot wave

【热泪】hot tears; tears of joy, sorrow or gratitude：她激动得两眼含着～。*She was so moved that hot tears filled her eyes.* ◇～盈眶 one's eyes brimming with tears

【热力】[机] heating power ◇～学 thermodynamics

【热恋】be passionately in love; be head over heels in love

【热量】[物] quantity of heat：～单位 *thermal (or heat) unit*

【热量计】calorimeter

【热烈】warm; enthusiastic; animated：～的祝贺 *warm congratulations* / ～欢迎 *warmly welcome* / ～欢送 *give sb. a warm send-off* / 进行～的讨论 *have a lively discussion*

【热裂化】[油] thermal cracking

【热流】❶ [气] thermal current ❷ warm current：我感到一股～传遍全身。*I felt a warm current coursing through my body.*

【热门】arousing popular interest; popular：赶～ *follow a craze* / ～学科 *a popular subject of study* / ～话题 *a subject of great topical interest; a topical subject*

【热门货】goods which are in great demand or sell well; hot item：彩电供不应求，成了～。*The supply of colour TV sets can't keep up with the demand. They've become a hot item.*

【热敏电阻】[电] thermal resistor; thermistor

【热闹】❶ lively; bustling with noise and excitement：～的菜市场 *a food market bustling with activity; a busy food market* / 晚会很～。*It was a very lively evening party.* / 大家热热闹闹玩了个痛快。*Everyone had a terrific time.* ❷ liven up; have a jolly time：你说个笑话让大伙儿～～吧。*Tell us a joke to liven things up.* / 那天他们聚在一起～了一番。*That day they got together and had a jolly time.* ❸ a scene of bustle and excitement; a thrilling sight：节日里街上有～看。*There will be lots of fun to watch in the streets during the holidays.* ——另见〖看热闹〗

【热能】[物] heat (or thermal) energy

【热喷喷】steaming hot

【热启动】[计] warm boot (or start)

【热气】steam; heat：壶里开始冒～了。*The kettle's just on the boil.* / 人多～高，干劲大。*More people mean more enthusiasm and more energy.*

【热气球】fire balloon; hot air balloon

【热气腾腾】❶ steaming hot：～的馒头 *steaming hot buns* ❷ seething with activity：春耕生产搞得～。*The spring ploughing is going full steam ahead.*

【热气田】geothermal area

【热切】fervent; earnest：～的愿望 *earnest wish; fervent hope* / ～希望各位提出宝贵意见。*We earnestly hope that you will give us your valuable criticisms and suggestions.*

【热情】❶ enthusiasm; zeal; warmth：爱国～ *patriotic zeal* / 工作～ *enthusiasm for work* / 他充满～地陈述了自己的意见。*He expressed his views with a great deal of warmth.* ❷ warm; fervent; enthusiastic; warmhearted：～接待 *warmly receive; give sb. a warm reception* / ～支持这个倡议 *fervently (or enthusiastically) support this proposal*

【热情奔放】bubbling with enthusiasm

【热情洋溢】permeated (or brimming) with warm feeling; glowing with enthusiasm：一封～的感谢信 *a warm letter of thanks* / ～的讲话 *a speech brimming with warm feeling*

【热身】warm-up：～操练 *warm-up exercises* ◇～赛 [体] warm-up game

【热释光】[考古] thermoluminescence (TL) (an archaeological dating technique)

【热水袋】hot-water bottle (or bag)

【热水瓶】〈口〉thermos bottle (or flask); thermos; vacuum bottle (or flask)

【热水器】hot water heater; geyser：电(燃气)～ *electric (gas) geyser*

【热塑塑料】[化] thermoplastic

【热塑性】[化] thermoplasticity

【热汤面】noodles in hot soup

【热腾腾】steaming hot：～的汤面 *steaming hot noodles in soup* / 太阳落了山，地上还是～的。*The sun had set, but the ground was still very hot.*

【热天】hot weather; hot season; hot days

【热望】fervently hope; ardently wish

【热污染】[环保] thermal pollution

【热线】❶ (telephone) hot line ❷ busy passenger or freight route：旅游～ *popular tourist route*

【热像仪】［电子］thermal imaging system

【热销】(of goods) sell well; be in great demand

【热心】enthusiastic; ardent; earnest; warmhearted: ～为顾客服务 *warmheartedly serve the customers* / ～科学 *eager to promote science* / ～传授技术 *make earnest efforts to pass on one's skill*

【热心肠】〈口〉❶ warmheartedness ❷ a warmhearted (or sympathetic) and helpful person

【热性肥料】［农］hot manure

【热学】heat (a branch of physics)

【热血】warm blood—righteous ardour: ～青年 *ardent youth* / 甘洒～为人民 *be ready to shed one's blood for the people*

【热血动物】warm-blooded animal; warm blood

【热血沸腾】one's blood boils; burning with righteous indignation

【热压】［化］hot pressing

【热药】［中］medicines of a hot or warm nature; tonics and stimulants

【热饮】hot drink

【热源】［物］heat source

【热轧】［冶］hot-rolling: ～机 *hot-rolling mill*

【热战】hot war; shooting war

【热障】［物］heat barrier

【热证】［中］heat symptom-complex; febrile symptoms

【热值】［物］calorific value

【热挚】passionate; ardent; impassioned: ～的情感 *passion*

【热中】(又作'热衷')❶ hanker after; crave: ～于个人名利 *hanker after personal fame and gain* ❷ be fond of; be keen on: ～于溜冰 *be very fond of skating* / ～于跳迪斯科 *be crazy about disco dancing*

【热中子】［物］thermal neutron

rén

人 名 ❶ human being; person; people: 昨天有三个～来找你。*Three people came to see you yesterday.* / 他家有几口～? *How many people are there in his family?* / 今天星期天,商店里～很多。*Today is Sunday. The stores are full of people.* ❷ an adult human being: 成人 ❸ other people; other(s): 自己做错了事,不应该怪～。*When one has done something wrong one should not blame it on others.* / 这个座位有～吗? *Is this seat occupied (or taken)?* ❹ (used rhetorically in place of the first personal pronoun, often expressing displeasure): 别小看～! *Don't look down on me!* / 真叫～着急。*It really worries me.* ❺ a person considered as a worker or employee: 我们这里正缺～。*We are shorthanded at the moment.* ❻ the physical, psychological, or moral quality or condition of a given individual: 只要她～好,漂亮不漂亮没关系。*So long as she has a nice personality, it makes no difference whether she is pretty or not.* / 他～在那儿,心可想着别的事。*He was there all right, but his mind was elsewhere.* ❼ everybody; each; all: ～所共知 *be known to everybody (or all)* ❽ used as a suffix: 四川～ *a native of Sichuan* / 工～ *worker*

【人儿】❶ figurine ❷〈方〉personality; character: 他～很不错。*He's a very nice man.*

【人本主义】［哲］humanism

【人不犯我,我不犯人】if others let me alone, I'll let them alone: ～,人若犯我,我必犯人。*We will not attack unless we are attacked; if we are attacked, we will certainly counterattack.*

【人不可以貌相】never judge a person by his appearance; you can't judge people by appearances

【人不为己,天诛地灭】Unless a man looks out for himself, Heaven and Earth will destroy him; everyone for himself and the devil take the hindmost.

【人不知,鬼不觉】without a soul knowing anything about it

【人才】(又作'人材')❶ a person of ability; a talented person; talent; qualified personnel: 难得的～ *a person of extraordinary ability* / 科技～ *qualified scientists and technicians* / 管理～ *management personnel* ❷〈口〉handsome appearance: 有几分～ *be rather good-looking* ◇ ～辈出 people of talent coming forth in large numbers; ～出众 a person of exceptional ability or striking appearance; ～断层 lack of talent; temporary shortage of trained personnel to replace the older generation; ～荟萃 a galaxy of talent; ～济济 an abundance of capable people; a galaxy of talent; ～交流 exchange of talent; ～交流会 talent fair; the personnel exchange meeting; ～交流中心 personnel exchange center; talent exchange centre; ～库 brain bank; brain trust; talent bank; ～流动 flow (or mobility) of trained personnel; ～市场 employment market; ～外流 brain drain; ～学 talent studies; talentics

【人财两空】lose both a person and money (as a man does when his mistress runs away from him with his money and valuables)

【人潮】stream of people

【人臣】minister; subject

【人称】❶［语］person: 第一～ *the first person* / 不定～ *indefinite person* ◇ ～代词［语］personal pronoun ❷ be called; be named

【人次】person-time: 参观展览会的总共约有二十万～。*Admissions to the exhibition totalled about 200,000.*

【人丛】crowd (of people)

【人大】(〈略〉全称为'全国人民代表大会') the National People's Congress ◇ ～常委会 the Standing Committee of the National People's Congress; ～代表 a deputy to the National People's Congress

【人代会】People's Congress at different levels (county, municipality)

【人道】❶ humanity; human sympathy ❷ human;

humane：战俘应受到～待遇。*Prisoners of war should receive humane treatment*. ◇～主义 humanitarianism

【人地生疏】be unfamiliar with the place and the people; be a complete stranger

【人丁】population; number of people in a family ◇～兴旺 have a growing family; have a flourishing population

【人盯人防守】[体] man-to-man defence

【人定胜天】Man can conquer nature; Man will triumph over nature.

【人堆儿】〈口〉crowd (of people)

【人多势众】overwhelm with numerical strength; dominate by sheer force of numbers

【人多嘴杂】many people, many words; the more people, the more talk

【人而无信,不知其可】If a man does not keep his word, what is he good for?

【人犯】〈旧〉the accused or people implicated in a crime：一干～ *the defendants and the implicated*

【人贩子】trader in human beings

【人防】(〈略〉全称为'人民防空') people's air defense; civil air defense

【人非木石】man is not made of wood or stone—man is not feelingless

【人非圣贤,孰能无过】Men are not saints, how can they be free from faults; To err is human.

【人份】person-portion; person-share：麻疹疫苗三十万～ *doses of measles vaccines for* 300,000 *persons*

【人粪尿】[农] night soil; human wastes (or excrement)

【人逢喜事精神爽】joy puts heart into a man

【人浮于事】more staff (or hands) than needed; overstaffed

【人格】❶ personality; character; moral quality：～高尚 *have a noble character*; *have moral integrity* ❷ human dignity：污辱～ *insult human dignity* / 这事千真万确,我以～担保。*On my honour, I swear it is true*. ◇～化 personify

【人工】❶ man-made; artificial ❷ manual work; work done by hand ❸ manpower; man-day：修建这条渠道不需要很多～。*It won't take a lot of manpower to construct this irrigation canal*. / 修这所房子用了多少～？*How many man-days were put in on repairing the house*? ◇～繁殖[农] artificial propagation; ～放顶[矿] artificial caving; ～孵化 artificial incubation; ～更新 forestry artificial regeneration; ～合成蛋白质 synthetic protein; ～合成结晶胰岛素 synthetic crystalline insulin; ～呼吸 artificial respiration; ～湖 man-made lake; ～降水 artificial precipitation; ～降雨 artificial rainfall; ～流产 induced abortion; ～免疫 artificial immunization; ～气腹[医] (artificial) pneumoperitoneum; ～气胸[医] (artificial) pneumothorax; ～器官 artificial organ; ～肾 artificial kidney; ～授粉[农] artificial pollination; ～授精[动] artificial insemination; ～心肺机 heart-lung machine; ～选择[生] artificial selection; ～智能 artificial intelligence

【人工岛】man-made island; artificial island

【人公里】passenger-kilometre

【人海】a sea of faces; a huge crowd (of people)：茫茫～ *a blurry sea of faces*; *a vast sea of people* ◇～战术 "tactics of human sea"—a big increase in the labour force

【人和】human unity; support of the people; unity and coordination within one's own ranks：天时不如地利,地利不如～。*Heaven's favourable weather is less important than Earth's advantageous terrain, and Earth's advantageous terrain is less important than human unity*.

【人话】〈诋〉human speech; sensible talk：你怎么不说～？*Aren't you capable of human speech*? / 他这还算～。*What he says is at least human speech*.

【人欢马叫】people bustling and horses neighing—a busy, prosperous country scene

【人寰】〈书〉the human world; man's world; the world

【人祸】man-made calamity

【人机对话】man-machine interaction

【人际关系】interpersonal relationships

【人迹】human footmarks (or footprints); traces of human presence：我在这原始森林里走了三天三夜,不见～。*I walked in the primeval forest for three days and nights without seeing any traces of human presence*.

【人迹罕至】without human trace; uninhabited; untraversed：～的地区 *an untraversed region*

【人家】(rénjiā) ❶ household; family：这个村子有百十户～。*There are a hundred or so families in this village*. / 那条路上找不到一户～。*No house can be seen on that road*. ❷ the family of a girl's fiancé：她有了～儿了。*She is engaged to be married*.

【人家】(rénjia) ❶ a person or persons other than the speaker or hearer：～都不怕,就你怕。*No one else is afraid. It's only you who are afraid*. / ～能做到的,我们也能做到。*What other people can do we can do, too*. or *If other people can do it, so can we*. ❷ with the person or persons referred to in a near context, roughly equivalent to the third personal pronoun：把信给～送去。*Take the letter to him (her, them)*. ❸ (used before a nominal expression, usu. with liveliness of feeling)：说干活,咱们可比不上～年轻的。*As for work, we can't compare with those young people*. ❹ (used rhetorically in place of the first personal pronoun, often playfully expressing displeasure)：你走慢点儿行不行,～跟不上啊！*Would you slow down*? *I can't keep up*! / 原来是你呀,差点儿没把～吓死！*Oh, it's only you*! *You almost scared me to death*.

【人间】the human world; man's world; the world：～乐园 *earthly paradise*; *paradise on earth* / ～奇迹 *a man-made miracle* ◇～地狱 hell on earth；～天堂 heaven on earth

【人件】[计] humanware

【人杰】〈书〉outstanding personality

【人杰地灵】the greatness of a man lends glory to a place

【人尽其才】make the best possible use of men：～，地尽其利，物尽其用。*Our human, land and material resources should be used to the best advantage.*

【人均】per capita：～耕地面积 *per capita area of cultivated farmland* / ～住房面积 *the average per capita living space* / ～国民收入 *per capita national income* / ～国民生产总值 *per capita gross national product (GNP)*

【人孔】[建] manhole

【人口】❶ population：～稠密的地区 *densely populated area; thickly inhabited district* / ～众多（稀少）*have a very large (a sparse) population* ❷ number of people in a family：他们家～不多。*There aren't many people in their family.* ◇ ～爆炸 population explosion；～出生率 fertility rate；～动态统计 vital statistics；～动态学 population dynamics；～分布 population distribution；～过剩 over population；～基数 population base；～结构 population structure；～金字塔 population pyramid；～老化 aging of population；～密度 density of population；population density；～普查（population）census；～死亡率 mortality rate；～统计 population statistics；～统计学（又作'人口学'）demography；～意识 awareness of population problem；～增长 population growth；～质量 population quality；～自然增长率 natural growth rate of population；～组成 population composition

【人困马乏】the men weary, their steeds spent—tired out；exhausted：在地里干了一天，大家都～。*After a day's hard work in the fields, they were completely exhausted.*

【人来疯】〈方〉(of a child) show off his liveliness before visitors

【人浪】（又作'墨西哥浪潮'）[体] Mexican wave

【人老珠黄不值钱】in old age, one is like a pearl whose lustre has faded—no longer held in esteem

【人类】mankind；humanity：～起源 *the origin of mankind; the origin of the human species* / ～进步 *human progress* ◇ ～工程学 human factors engineering；～学 anthropology；～语言学 anthropological linguistics

【人类灵魂工程师】engineers who shape human souls—teachers, writers, artists, etc：文学艺术家们要切实负起～的伟大使命。*Writers and artists should realize their great responsibility as those who shape people's minds and souls.*

【人力】manpower；labour power：～资源 *human resources* / 非～所及 *be beyond human power*

【人力车】❶ a two-wheeled vehicle drawn or pushed by a man ❷〈旧〉rickshaw

【人流】❶ stream of people：不尽的～涌向天安门广场。*An endless stream of people swarmed towards Tian'anmen Square.* ❷（〈略〉全称为'人工流产'）induced abortion

【人龙】long queue：买票的～ *long queue for buying tickets*

【人伦】human relations (according to feudal ethics)

【人马】forces；troops：全部～已安全渡江。*All the troops have crossed the river safely.* / 我们编辑部的～比较整齐。*Our editorial department is well-staffed.*

【人马座】[天] Sagittarius

【人满为患】overcrowded with people；overstaffed

【人们】people；men；the public：草原上的～ *people of the grasslands* / ～都说她能干。*People say she is very capable.*

【人面兽心】the face of a man but the heart of a beast—a beast in human form

【人面桃花】her face and the peach-blossoms—the pinings of a lover

【人民】the people ◇ ～币 Renminbi (RMB, Chinese monetary unit)；～大会堂 the Great Hall of the People；～代表大会 people's congress；～法院 people's court；～防空 people's air defence；civil air defence；～公社 people's commune；～检察院 people's procuratorate；～警察 the people's police；～来信 letters from the masses；～民主专政 people's democratic dictatorship；～内部矛盾 contradictions among the people；～陪审员 [法] people's assessor；～群众 the masses；～日报 Renmin Ribao；the People's Daily；～团体 mass organization；people's organization；～武装部 people's armed forces department (of a county, etc.)；～性 (in literary and artistic works) popular or folk character；feeling for the people；affinity to the people；～英雄纪念碑 the Monument to the People's Heros；～战争 people's war；～阵线 popular front；～政府 the People's Government

【人命】human life：～案子 *a case of homicide or manslaughter* / 一条～ *a violent death*

【人命关天】a case involving human life is one of supreme importance：～，非同儿戏。*Taking someone's life is a serious crime, it's no joking matter.*

【人命危浅，朝不虑夕】be sinking fast；be dying

【人莫予毒】no one dare harm me—be supercilious

【人偶】image；figure：真人一般大的～ *lifesize figures*

【人怕出名猪怕壮】Fame portends trouble for men just as fattening does for pigs.

【人配衣服马配鞍】Clothes make the man as the saddle makes the horse；Clothes make the man.

【人品】❶ moral standing；moral quality；character：～很好 *be a person of excellent character* ❷〈口〉looks；bearing

【人弃我取】I pick up what others discard—I have my own views and tastes

【人强马壮】both men and horses are strong—❶ a

strong, combat effective army ❷ a strong working force

【人墙】[体](足球) wall: 筑～ *set a wall*

【人琴俱亡】The man and his lute are both dead (a lament for the death of a friend).

【人勤地不懒】Where the tiller is tireless the land is fertile.

【人情】❶ human feelings; human sympathy; sensibilities: 他很重～,朋友的事总是愿意帮忙。*He sets a great store on friendship, and is always willing to help his friends.* ❷ human relationships: ～之常 *be natural and normal (in human relationships)* ❸ favour: 做个～ *do sb. a favour* / 空头～ *an empty promise* ❹ gift; present

【人情冷暖】social snobbery

【人情礼】gift presented to obtain a favor

【人情练达】experienced in the ways of the world: 世事洞明皆学问,～即文章。*A grasp of mundane affairs is genuine knowledge, and worldly wisdom is true learning.*

【人情世故】worldly wisdom: 不懂～ *not know the ways of the world; not know how to deal with people*

【人情味】human touch; human interest: 他这个人,一点～都没有。*That chap! He has no human feelings whatsoever.* / 这故事很有～。*The story is warmly human.*

【人情债】a debt of gratitude

【人穷志不短】poor but proud; poor but ambitious

【人穷志短】Poverty chills ambition.

【人权】human rights; rights of man

【人群】crowd; throng; multitude

【人人】everybody; everyone: ～都说这孩子机灵。*Everybody says the child is smart.* ◇ ～为我,我为～ all for one and one for all

【人人自危】Everyone finds himself in danger; Everyone feels insecure.

【人山人海】huge crowds of people; a sea of people: 广场上～。*The square was a sea of people.*

【人身】living body of a human being; person: ～不可侵犯 *inviolability of the person* ◇ ～安全 personal safety (or security); ～保护令 habeas corpus; ～保险 life insurance and insurance against accidents; ～攻击 personal attack; ～伤害 personal injury; ～事故 personal injury caused by an accident; ～自由 freedom of person; personal freedom

【人参】ginseng

【人神共愤】(of a great outrage) arouse the great indignation of both men and gods

【人生】life: ～旅程 *life-long journey* / ～两件宝,双手和大脑。*There are two treasures in human life—hands and brains.* ◇ ～观 outlook on life; ～如寄 man's life is like a traveller's stay; ～如梦 life is but a dream; ～一世,草生一春 man has but one life, grass sees but one spring; life is short; ～朝露 life is like the morning dew; ～哲学 philosophy of life

【人生地不熟】be unfamiliar with the place and the people; be a stranger in a strange place

【人生七十古来稀】Man's life from of old has rarely reached seventy; Men who reach the age of seventy have always been a rarity.

【人声】voice: 远处传来～。*Voices came from afar.* or *Voices were heard in the distance.* ◇ ～鼎沸 a hubbub of voices; a babel of voices

【人士】personage; public figure: 爱国～ *patriotic personage* / 官方～ *official quarters* / 体育界～ *figures in the sports world* / 文艺界～ *people of literary and art circles*

【人氏】people native to a place: 你是哪里～? *Where do you come from?* or *What is your native place?* / 当地～ *a native-born*

【人世】this world; the world: 不在～ *be no longer living; be no longer in the land of the living* / 不久于～ *be dying* ◇ ～沧桑 tremendous changes in this world of ours; ～间 this world; the world

【人事】❶ human affairs; occurrences in human life ❷ personnel matters: ～安排 *arrangement of personnel* / ～更迭 *change of personnel* ❸ ways of the world: 不懂～ *not know the ways of the world* ❹ consciousness of the outside world: 他昏迷过去,～不知。*He fainted and lost consciousness.* ❺ what is humanly possible: 尽～ *do what is humanly possible; do one's best* ❻〈婉〉sexual awareness or passion; the facts of life: 渐省～ *begin to have some understanding of the facts of life* ◇ ～处 personnel division; ～档案 personal file (or dossier); ～调动 transfer of personnel; ～关系 organizational affiliation; ～管理 personnel management; ～制度 personnel system

【人手】manpower; hand: ～太少 *short of hands; shorthanded* / ～已经够了,别派人去了。*They have enough hands. Don't send any more people there*

【人手一册】everyone has a copy: 书不多不少,刚好～。*There are just enough books for everyone to have one copy, no more, no less.*

【人寿保险】life insurance

【人寿年丰】The land yields good crops and the people enjoy good health.

【人丝斜纹绸】rayon twill

【人死如灯灭】A man dies the way a lamp goes out. a

【人梯】❶ human ladder (as used in assaulting a fortress) ❷ a person who helps another to rise to success: 他甘当～,言传身教,培养青年一代。*He is devoted to educating the younger generation, teaching by precept and example, content to be, so to speak, a rung of the human ladder.*

【人体】human body: ～模型 *manikin* ◇ ～生物钟 biological clock; ～特异功能 extrasensory perception

【人同此心,心同此理】On this matter people feel and think alike.

【人头】❶ the number of people: 按～分 *distribute according to the number of people* ❷ relations with people：～熟 *know a lot of people* ◇ ～费 fee per person；～税 poll tax；capitation

【人望】〈书〉prestige；popularity

【人微言轻】The words of the lowly carry little weight.

【人为】artificial；man-made：～疆界线 *artificial boundary line* / ～的障碍 *an artificially imposed obstacle* / 这些困难完全是～的。*These difficulties were purely man-made.*

【人为刀俎，我为鱼肉】be meat on sb.'s chopping block—be at sb.'s mercy

【人为地貌】[军] culture features

【人为嬗变】[物] artificial transmutation

【人为万物之灵】Man of all creatures is the one endowed with intelligence.

【人为财死，鸟为食亡】Men will die for wealth, as birds for food.

【人味儿】humanness；humanity：他竟连点～都没有。*There's really nothing human about him.* / 有了这个知心朋友，他才觉出点～。*Not until he had this understanding friend did he have his first taste of warm humanity.*

【人文景观】place of cultural interest

【人文科学】the humanities；humane studies

【人文主义】humanism

【人无远虑，必有近忧】he who gives no thought to difficulties in the future is sure to be beset by worries much closer at hand

【人五人六】be affected；strike poses

【人物】❶ figure；personage：领袖～ *a leading personage*；*a leading public figure* / 英雄～ *a heroic figure*；*a hero or heroine* ❷ person in literature；character：典型～ *a typical character* / ～塑造 *characterization* ◇ ～表 a list of characters (in a play or novel)；characters；～画 figure painting；～像 bust (sculpture)

【人像】portrait；image；figure ◇ ～靶 silhouette target

【人心】❶ popular feeling；public feeling；the will of the people：～安定。*The public is quiet.* ❷ human feelings；human reason：他并不是没有～的人。*He's not unfeeling.* ◇ ～不古 public morality is not what it used to be (i.e. has degenerated)；～不足蛇吞象 a man who rests content with nothing is like a snake trying to swallow an elephant；～隔肚皮 different hearts in different breasts—it's hard to tell what's going on in the minds of other people；people should always be on guard against one another；～惶惶 popular anxiety；～齐，泰山移 the people all working with one will can move Mount Tai；a people united can move mountains；～如面 men's hearts are as different as their faces；～丧尽 lose (or forfeit) all popular sympathy；～所向 popular sentiment；the feelings of the people；～向背 whether the people are for or against；the feelings of the people ——另见〖得人心〗

【人行道】pavement；sidewalk

【人行横道】pedestrian crosswalk；pedestrian crossing；zebra crossing

【人性】(rénxìng) human nature；humanity：具体的～ *human nature in the concrete*

【人性】(rénxing) normal human feelings；reason：不通～ *unfeeling and unreasonable*

【人性论】the theory of human nature

【人熊】〈口〉brown bear

【人选】person selected：物色适当～ *try to find a suitable person (for a job)* / 决定秘书长的～ *decide who is to be secretary-general* / 他是可以考虑的～。*He's an eligible candidate for the job.*

【人烟】signs of human habitation：没有～ *uninhabited* / 几十里不见～。*No trace of human habitation could be seen for dozens of li.* ◇ ～稠密 densely populated；populous；～稀少 be sparsely populated

【人言可畏】The voice of the people is something to fear；Gossip is a fearful thing.

【人言啧啧】There is a good deal of unfavourable comment.

【人仰马翻】men and horses thrown off their feet—badly battered；thrown into confusion

【人样】❶ proper human appearance；proper behaviour：脏得不像个～ *be awfully dirty* / 那孩子惯得一点～都没有。*That child is terribly spoiled.* ❷ a successful person：不混出个～来，不要回来见我。*Don't come back and see me until you've got something to show for your efforts.*

【人要脸，树要皮】Face is as important to man as the bark is to the tree.

【人以群分】见〖物以类聚，人以群分〗

【人影儿】❶ the shadow of a human figure：窗帘上有个～。*Someone's silhouette appeared on the window curtain.* ❷ the trace of a person's presence；figure：她看见一个～在黑暗中消失了。*She caught sight of a figure disappearing into the darkness.* / 我等了半天，连个～也不见。*I waited a long time but not a soul turned up.*

【人有脸，树有皮】(又作'人有面，树有皮') a man has a face just as a tree has bark—a man has a sense of shame

【人欲】〈书〉human desires

【人欲横流】unbridled indulgence of human desires and passions；universal decadence

【人员】personnel；staff：全体～ *the entire personnel*；*the whole staff* / 机关工作～ *office workers* / ～不足 *understaffed*；*undermanned*

【人缘儿】relations with people；popularity：～好 *be very popular*；*enjoy great popularity* / 有～ *enjoy great popularity*

【人猿】anthropoid (ape)

【人云亦云】echo the views of others；have no views of one's own

【人造】man-made；artificial；imitation：～宝石 *artificial jewel*；*imitation jewel* ◇ ～冰 artificial ice；～地球卫星 artificial earth satellite；sputnik；～革 imitation (or artificial) leather；leatherette；～光 artificial light；～黄油 margarine；～浪 artificial wave；～毛 artificial wool；man-made feather；～棉 artificial cotton；staple rayon；～丝 artificial silk；rayon；～卫星 man-made satellite；～纤维 man-made fibre；～橡胶 artificial rubber；synthetic rubber；～羊毛 artificial wool

【人证】［法］testimony of a witness

【人证物证】［法］human testimony and material evidence：～俱在 *availability of eye-witnesses and material evidence*

【人之常情】what is natural and normal（in human relationships）：初次相会，说话不多，也是～。*To say very little at the first meeting is natural and normal.*

【人之将死，其言也善】Good are the words of a dying man.

【人治】rule by men（〈反〉法治）

【人质】hostage：把某人作～ *take（or hold）sb. hostage* / 释放～ *free a hostage*

【人中】［中］the vertical groove on the median line of the upper lip；philtrum

【人种】ethnic group；race ◇ ～学 ethnology

【人字呢】［纺］herringbone

【人自为战】each man fighting all by himself

壬 名 the ninth of the ten Heavenly Stems（天干）

仁 Ⅰ 名 ❶ benevolence；kindheartedness；humanity：～者人也。*Benevolence is humanity.* / ～心 *kindheartedness* ❷ kernel：坚果的～儿多半可以吃。*The kernel of a nut is usually eatable.* Ⅱ 形 sensitive：麻木不仁

【仁爱】kindheartedness；benevolence；humanity

【仁慈】benevolent；merciful；kind：～的老人 *a kind old man*

【仁德】kindheartedness；benevolence；humanity

【仁弟】〈套〉（usu. used in a letter to a male friend younger than oneself or to a former male student）my dear friend

【仁厚】honest and kindhearted

【仁人君子】benevolent gentlemen；public-spirited people

【仁人志士】同〖志士仁人〗

【仁兄】〈套〉（usu. used in a letter to a male friend）my dear friend

【仁义】benevolence and uprighteousness

【仁义道德】humanity，justice and virtue；virtue and morality.

【仁者见仁，智者见智】the benevolent see benevolence and the wise see wisdom—different people have different views

【仁政】policy of benevolence；benevolent government：施～ *apply a policy of benevolence*

【仁至义尽】do everything called for by humanity and duty；do what is humanly possible to help；be magnanimous

rěn

忍 动 ❶ bear；endure；tolerate；put up with：相～相安 *be tolerant towards and live in peace with one another* / 他～着剧痛，继续工作。*He continued to work despite the intense pain.* / 你就～着点吧。*You will just have to put up with it.* / ～着眼泪 *hold back one's tears* ❷ be hardhearted enough to；have the heart to：残忍

【忍冬】［植］honeysuckle

【忍饥挨饿】endure the torments of hunger

【忍俊不禁】cannot help laughing

【忍耐】exercise patience；exercise restraint；restrain oneself：你还是～一点吧，否则要吃亏的。*You'd better restrain yourself a little or you'll come to grief.*

【忍气吞声】swallow an insult；submit to humiliation；stifle one's indignation：～地过日子 *manage to get by swallowing insults and humiliations*

【忍让】exercise forbearance；be forbearing and conciliatory

【忍辱负重】endure humiliation in order to carry out an important mission

【忍受】bear；endure；stand：～艰难困苦 *endure hardships* / 热得难以～ *unbearably hot*

【忍痛】very reluctantly：～牺牲 *reluctantly give up*

【忍痛割爱】part reluctantly with what one treasures：文章太长，最后一段你必须～。*The article is much too long，so you must cut the last section however painful it may be.*

【忍无可忍】be driven beyond（the limits of）forbearance；come to the end of one's patience：他们欺人太甚，我们～。*Their provocations have gone beyond the limits of forbearance.*

【忍心】have the heart to；be hardhearted enough to：他不～拒绝他们的要求。*He didn't have the heart to（or couldn't bear to）turn down their request.*

【忍者】ninja

【忍住】bear；endure：～悲痛 *bear sadness* / 她真想哭，但还是～了。*She was on the verge of crying but then held her tears back.* / 把这鸡眼切除了吧，再疼我也忍得住。*Please excise the corn. I can stand the pain.* / 他忍不住大笑起来。*He couldn't help bursting into laughter.*

荏 Ⅰ 名 another name for 白苏 Ⅱ 形〈书〉weak；weak-kneed：色厉内荏

【荏苒】〈书〉（of time）elapse quickly or imperceptibly；slip by：光阴～，转瞬又是一年。*Time zipped by and the year was soon over.*

【荏弱】〈书〉weak；feeble；delicate

rèn

刃 Ⅰ 名 ❶ the edge of a knife，sword，etc.；blade：这刀没～儿了。*This knife is blunt.* or *The knife has lost its edge.* ❷ sword；knife：利刃 Ⅱ 动 kill with a sword or knife：手刃

【刃具】［机］cutting tool

【刃口】the edge of a knife, sword, etc.

认 动 ❶ recognize; know; make out; identify: ～笔迹 *try to recognize handwriting* / 自己的东西,自己来～。*Come and pick out your own things.* / 他的字真难～。*His handwriting is barely legible.* or *His handwriting is hard to read.* ❷ enter into a certain relationship with; adopt: ～师傅 *apprentice oneself to sb.* / ～她作闺女 *adopt her as a daughter* ❸ admit; recognize; own: ～个不是 *offer an apology; apologize* ❹ undertake to do sth.: ～捐五十元 *undertake to contribute 50 yuan; subscribe 50 yuan* / ～公债 *subscribe for (government) bonds* ❺ (followed by 了) accept as unavoidable; resign oneself to: 这东西一定得买,价钱贵一点我也～了。*I simply must buy it, even if I have to pay a little more for it.* / 这事是我吃亏,但我也～了。*I've resigned myself to losing out this time.*

【认出】recognize; make out; identify: 她戴着那顶帽子,我没～她来。*I didn't recognize her in that hat.* / 她又病又老,模样变得都认不出来了。*Illness and age had changed her appearance beyond recognition.*

【认错】acknowledge a mistake; admit a fault; offer (or make) an apology: 他既然～了,就原谅他一次吧。*Since he has made an apology, forgive him just this once.* / 给你妈认个错。*Go and apologize to your mother.*

【认得】know; recognize: 这位同志你～吗? *Do you know this comrade?* / 这地方我已经不～了。*I can no longer recognize the place.* / 你～回家的路吗? *Can you find your way home?*

【认敌为友】take a foe for a friend

【认定】❶ firmly believe; maintain; hold ❷ set one's mind on

【认罚】be ready to pay the penalty

【认购】offer to buy; subscribe: ～公债 *subscribe for (government) bonds*

【认可】approve: 得到领导的～ *be approved by the leadership* / 点头～ *nod approval*

【认领】claim: 拾得钱包一个,希望失主前来～。*Purse found. Will the owner please come to claim it?*

【认命】accept fate; resign oneself (or be resigned) to fate: 我总是不走运,只好～了。*I'm always having bad luck! I suppose I'll just have to resign myself to fate.*

【认赔】admit an obligation to pay (for damage done, etc.); agree to pay compensation

【认亲】❶ become related by marriage ❷ claim a family connection

【认清】see clearly; recognize; get a clear understanding of: ～形势 *get a clear understanding of the situation* / ～问题的性质 *grasp the nature of the problem* / ～是非 *make a clear distinction between right and wrong*

【认人】(of a baby) can recognize people: 这孩子才三个多月,就开始～了。*The baby is only a little over 3 months and it can already recognize people.*

【认生】(of a child) be shy with strangers

【认识】❶ know; understand; recognize: 你在哪儿～她的? *Where did you get to know her?* / 他不～这种草药。*He doesn't recognize this kind of medical herb.* / ～世界,改造世界 *understand the world and change it* ❷ understanding; knowledge; cognition: 感性(理性)～ *perceptual (rational) knowledge* / 我们都谈了对这件事的～。*We all said what we thought about the matter.* ◇ ～过程 process of cognition; ～论 theory of knowledge; epistemology; ～能力 cognitive ability; ～水平 level of understanding

【认输】admit defeat; throw in (or up) the sponge; give up

【认死理】(又作'认死扣儿') stubborn; as obstinate as a mule

【认为】think; consider; hold; deem: 大家～这个建议是可行的。*We all think (or consider) this proposal feasible.* / 你～怎样? *What do you think of it?* / 这件事我们～有必要跟你们说清楚。*We deem it necessary to make this clear to you.*

【认贼作父】take the foe for one's father; regard the enemy as kith and kin

【认账】acknowledge a debt (or an account); admit what one has said or done: 错了就要～。*If you're wrong, you should admit it.* / 自己说的话,怎么不～? *How can you go back upon your word?*

【认真】❶ conscientious; earnest; serious: ～对待 *deal seriously with* / 给予～的考虑 *give serious consideration to* / ～的自我批评 *an earnest self-criticism* ❷ take seriouly; take to heart: 我是说着玩儿的,你怎么就认起真来了? *I was only joking. Why take it seriously (or to heart)?*

【认证】[法] ❶ legalize; attest; authenticate: ～签字 *attest a signature* / ～文件 *authenticated document* / ～者 *authenticator* ❷ attestation; authentication ◇ ～机构 notified bodies

【认知心理学】cognitive psychology

【认准】set one's mind on

【认字】know or learn how to read: 我这个旧社会的文盲,今天也～了。*I was an illiterate in the old society, but now I can read.* / 这孩子才五岁,可他已经能认不少字了。*The boy is only five, but he has already learned quite a few characters.*

【认罪】admit one's guilt; plead guilty: ～悔过 *plead guilty and repent*

任 I 动 ❶ assign sb. to a post; appoint: 新～的厂长 *the newly appointed director of the factory* ❷ assume a post; take up a job: ～军长 *hold office as an army commander* ❸ undertake; bear: 任劳任怨 ❹ let; allow; give free reign to: ～其泛滥 *let it (e.g. a flood, etc.) spread unchecked* / ～你挑选一个。*Choose any one you like.* / 衣服的花色很多,～你选择。*There are* *clothes of all different designs and colours for you to choose from.* Ⅱ 名 official post; office: ～满 *expiration of one's term of office* / ～内 *during one's term (or tenure) of office* Ⅲ 量 (for the number of terms served on an official post): 他做过两～大使。*He has twice been ambassador.* Ⅳ 连 no matter (how, what, etc.): ～我们怎样劝说,他也不听。*No matter how hard we tried to persuade him, he wouldn't listen.* / 东西放在家里,～怎么也丢不了。*As long as we leave these things in the house, they can't possibly get lost.*

【任便】as you like; as you see fit: 你来不来～。*You may come or not as you see fit.*

【任从】同〖任凭〗

【任何】any; whichever; whatever: 我们能战胜～困难。*We can overcome any difficulty.* / 没有～理由拒绝这个建议。*There's no reason whatsoever to turn down this suggestion.* / ～一方 *either party; any of the parties*

【任教】be a teacher; teach: 在一所大学～ *teach at a university* / 他～多年了。*He has been a teacher for many years.*

【任课】teach (at a school)

【任劳任怨】work hard regardless of criticism; willingly bear the burden of office

【任免】appoint and remove (or dismiss): 国务院依照法律的规定～行政人员。*The State Council appoints and removes administrative personnel according to the provisions of the law.* / ～事项 *appointments and removals*

【任命】appoint: ～某人为校长 *appoint sb. president (of a university)* / 他被～为驻瑞典大使。*He was appointed ambassador to Sweden.*

【任命状】letter of appointment; commission: 外交人员～ *diplomatic commission*

【任凭】❶ allow; let (sb. do as he pleases): 要去要留,～你自己。*You may go or stay as you please.* / 这事不能～他一人决定。*This shouldn't be left entirely to his discretion.* ❷ no matter (how, what, etc.): ～问题多复杂,我们也能搞清楚。*We can solve the problem no matter how complicated it is.* ❸ even if; even though: ～江水冷得钻心,工人们仍然坚持下水操作。*The workers still kept on working in the river even though the water was icy cold.*

【任凭风浪起,稳坐钓鱼船】sit tight in the fishing boat despite the rising wind and waves—hold one's ground despite pressure or opposition

【任期】term of office; tenure of office: 主席～已满。*The term of the Presidency has expired.*

【任期制】tenure system

【任其自流】leave sth. to take its own course

【任其自然】give free rein to; let nature take its course

【任情】let oneself go; to one's heart's content; as much as one likes

【任人】let people (do sth. without restrictions): 公开展览,～参观 *an open exhibition, free to all visitors*

【任人唯亲】appoint people by favouritism

【任人唯贤】appoint people on their merits; appoint people according to their ability and political integrity

【任人宰割】(cannot but) allow oneself to be trampled upon

【任事】❶ have a job; be employed ❷ take up a task: 他勇于～。*He never hesitates to take up a task.*

【任所】office

【任务】assignment; mission; task; job: 接受～ *receive (or accept) an assignment* / 我们保证完成～。*We guarantee to fulfil (or complete) our mission.* / ～重,时间紧。*The task is hard and we are pressed for time.*

【任务观点】get-it-over-and-done-with attitude; perfunctory attitude

【任务提示】briefing

【任性】wilful; self-willed; wayward; headstrong: 她是个～的孩子。*She is a wilful child.*

【任意】wanton; arbitrary; wilful: ～诬蔑 *wantonly vilify* / ～捏造事实 *indulge in pure fabrication* / ～欺负别人 *bully people at will* ◇ ～常数〔数〕arbitrary constant; ～球〔体〕(足球) free kick; (手球) free throw

【任用】assign sb. to a post; appoint

【任职】hold a post; be in office: ～财政部 *work (or hold a post) in the Ministry of Finance* / 在～期间 *during one's tenure of office*

【任重道远】the burden is heavy and the road is long—shoulder heavy responsibilities

妊 动〈书〉be pregnant: ～五月 *be five months pregnant*

【妊妇】pregnant woman

【妊娠】gestation; pregnancy: 输卵管～ *tubal pregnancy* ◇ ～反应 morning sickness; ～期 period of gestation; gestational period

纫 动 ❶ thread a needle: 老太太眼花了,～不上针。*The old lady's vision had become blurred, so she couldn't thread the needle.* ❷ sew; stitch: 缝纫

韧 形 pliable but strong; tenacious; tough

【韧带】〔生理〕ligament

【韧度】tenacity

【韧劲】indomitableness; dauntlessness; tenacity; persevering spirit; perseverance

【韧力】indomitable will; indomitable spirit; persevering spirit; unyielding will: 百折不挠的～ *unyielding will in the face of setbacks*

【韧皮部】〔植〕bast; phloem

【韧皮纤维】〔植〕bast fibre

【韧性】toughness; tenacity

rēng

扔 动 ❶ throw; toss; cast: ～手榴弹 *throw a*

hand grenade / ～球 *throw (or toss) a ball* / 敌机～了几颗炸弹。*The enemy plane dropped a few bombs*. ❷ throw away; cast aside: 把它～了吧。*Throw it away*. / 被～进历史的垃圾堆 *be relegated to (or tossed on to) the rubbish heap of history* / 这事他早就～在脖子后边了。*He'd clean forgotten about it*.

【扔掉】throw away: 这条鱼都臭了,～算了。*The fish smells; throw it away*.

【扔弃】abandon; discard; cast aside

【扔下】abandon; put aside; leave behind: 敌人～武器逃跑了。*The enemy dropped their weapons and took to their heels*. / 这工作我不能～不管。*I can't leave the work half-finished*.

réng

仍 Ⅰ动 remain: 一～其旧 *remain the same* Ⅱ 形〈书〉frequent: 频仍 Ⅲ副 *still; yet*: ～有效力 *be still effective; be still in force* / ～须努力 *must continue to make efforts* / 他的病～不见好。*He's not yet recovered from his illness*. or *He's shown no sign towards recovery*.

【仍旧】❶ remain the same: 修订版体例～。*The style will still be the same for the revised edition*. ❷ still; yet: 他虽然遇到许多挫折,可是意志～那样坚强。*His determination remains as strong as ever despite all the setbacks he has encountered*. / 他～是十年前的老样子。*After ten years, he still looked the same*.

【仍然】still; yet: 补一补,这件衣服～可以穿。*You can still wear the clothes if you have them mended*. / 等了半天,她～没有到。*We've been waiting a long time for her, but she still hasn't arrived*. / 至今我们～没有得到回音。*As yet, we have received no answer*. / 他把信看完,～装在信封里。*He put the letter back into the envelope after he'd read it*.

rì

日 Ⅰ名 ❶ sun: 烈日 ❷ daytime; day: 终日 ❸ day: 一～,老王来我家。*One day, Lao Wang came to my place*. / 多～不见了,你好吗? *Haven't seen you for a long time. How are you?* ❹ time: 春～ *springtime; spring* Ⅱ副 daily; every day; with each passing day: 产量～增。*Output is going up every day*. / 天气～暖。*It's getting warmer and warmer*.

【日班】day shift: 上～ *be on day shift*

【日报】daily paper; daily: 《人民～》*Renmin Ribao (the People's Daily)* / 《中国～》*China Daily*

【日本】Japan ◇ ～海 the Sea of Japan; ～人 Japanese

【日薄西山】the sun is setting beyond the western hills—declining rapidly; nearing one's end

【日不暇给】be fully occupied every day; be pressed for time

【日常】day-to-day; everyday; daily: ～工作 *day-to-day work; routine duties* / ～事务 *routine business* / ～生活 *everyday life; daily life* / ～用语 *words and expressions for everyday use* / 这些都是～必须用的东西。*These are all the things needed for daily use*.

【日场】day show; daytime performance; matinée: ～电影 *daytime film show* / 他们每星期演六个夜场,三个～。*They do six evening performances and three matinées every week*.

【日程】programme; schedule: 访问～ *itinerary of a visit* / 工作～ *work schedule; programme of work* / ～很紧 *a tight (or crowded) schedule* / 提到～上来 *place (or put) sth. on the order of the day*

【日程表】schedule

【日出】sunrise: 看～ *watch (or see) the sunrise*

【日出而作,日入而息】begin work at sunrise and rest at sunset—life in primitive society

【日戳】❶ date stamp; dater ❷ datemark

【日耳曼人】Germanic people

【日耳曼语】Germanic language

【日珥】[天] prominence

【日工】❶ daywork ❷ day labour ❸ day labourer

【日光】sunlight; sunbeam ◇ ～灯 fluorescent lamp; daylight lamp; ～疗法 heliotherapy; ～浴 sunbath

【日晷】(又作'日规') sundial

【日后】in the future; in the days to come: 这东西～可能用得着。*We may find it useful in future*. or *It may come in handy someday*. / 你现在不下功夫,～会吃苦头的。*If you don't work hard now, you'll suffer for it later*.

【日积月累】accumulate over a long period: 每天学一点,～也能学不少。*Learn a little every day and in time you'll have learned a lot*.

【日记】diary: 记～ *keep a diary* / 工作～ *work diary; daily account of one's work* ◇ ～本 diary; ～账 journal; daybook

【日间】in the daytime; during the day: ～气温比夜间高多了。*The temperature was much higher in the daytime than at night*.

【日间不做亏心事,半夜敲门不吃惊】He who has done nothing shameful by day need not be alarmed by a knock at the door by night.

【日见】with each passing day; day by day: ～好转 *get better every day* / ～衰败 *decline day by day*

【日渐】with each passing day; day by day: ～强壮 *get stronger and stronger* / ～进步 *make steady progress*

【日界线】international date line; date line

【日经指数】[经] Nikkei Index

【日经-道琼斯平均指数】[经] Nikkei-Dow Jones Average

【日久】with the passing of time; in (the) course of time

【日久见人心】time reveals a person's heart; it

takes time to know a person ——另见〖路遥知马力，日久见人心〗

【日久天长】after a considerable period of time：由于水的不断侵蚀，～就形成了一个大溶洞。*As a result of continuous water erosion, in the course of time a huge cave was formed.*

【日就月将】achieve something every day and make progress every month—many a little makes a mickle

【日均】average per day；daily average：～贸易额 *daily average turnover*

【日理万机】attend to numerous affairs of state every day；be occupied with a myriad of state affairs

【日历】calendar ◇ ～手表 calendar watch

【日落】sunset

【日冕】[天]（solar）corona ◇ ～仪 coronagraph

【日暮】evening；nightfall；dusk：～归来，城内已万家灯火。*When we returned at dusk, the lights of the city had come on.*

【日暮途穷】the day is waning and the road is ending—approaching the end of one's days；be on one's last legs；be at the end of one's rope

【日内】in a few days；in a day or two；in a couple of days：大会将于～举行。*The meeting will take place in a few days.* / ～将有一场暴风雨。*There will be a heavy storm in a day or two.*

【日内瓦】Geneva

【日期】date：起程的～定了吗？*Has the departure date been fixed?* / 信上的～是六月二日。*The letter is dated June 2.* / 开会的～是六月二十一日到二十七日。*The congress will be in session from June 21st to June 27th.*

【日前】a few days ago；the other day

【日趋】with each passing day；gradually；day by day：市场～繁荣。*The market is becoming brisker day by day.* / 环境污染问题～严重。*Environmental pollution is an increasingly serious problem.*

【日日夜夜】day and night；night and day：在～的紧张抢修中，他一直没有休息过。*During the round-the-clock rush repair job, he never took a rest.*

【日上三竿】the sun is three poles high—it's late in the morning（usu. referring to getting up late）

【日射】[气] insolation ◇ ～表 actinometer；～病[医] sunstroke；insolation

【日食】[天] solar eclipse：日环食 *annular eclipse* / 日偏食 *partial solar eclipse* / 日全食 *total solar eclipse*

【日坛】the Altar to the Sun（in Beijing）

【日托】day care：这个托儿所只有～。*This is only a day nursery.* / 你的孩子是全托还是～？*Does your child board at the nursery or go home in the evening?*

【日托托儿所】day nursery

【日息】per diem interest；daily interest

【日心说】[天] heliocentric theory

【日新月异】change with each passing day：社会主义建设使祖国面貌～。*Our socialist construction is changing the face of the land day by day.*

【日薪】daily wage；per diem

【日夜】day and night；night and day；round the clock：～警惕地守卫着边疆 *vigilantly guard the borders day and night* / 我们厂～三班倒。*Our factory operates round the clock on three shifts.* ◇ ～商店 a shop open night and day；a round-the-clock shop；a day-and-night-service shop

【日以继夜】night and day；round the clock

【日益】increasingly；day by day：矛盾～尖锐。*The contradictions are becoming increasingly acute.* / 我们的队伍～壮大。*Our ranks are growing stronger day by day.*

【日用】❶ daily expenses ❷ of everyday（or daily）use ◇ ～必需品 daily necessities；household necessities；～工业品 manufactured goods for daily use；～品 articles of everyday use；～器具 household utensils；articles of everyday use；～小商品 small articles of everyday use

【日语】Japanese（language）

【日元】yen（Japanese moneytary unit）

【日月】❶ life；livelihood：解放前的～可真不好过啊！*What a hard life we had before liberation!* ❷ the sun and the moon ◇ ～重光 the sun and the moon shining again—back to peace and prosperity after a dark period；～如梭 the sun and the moon shuttle back and forth—how time flies；～星辰 the sun, the moon and the stars；the heavenly bodies

【日晕】[气] solar halo

【日杂】sundry goods；general merchandise；daily household supplies：～小商品 *every day household goods*

【日照】sunshine：～计 *sunshine recorder* / ～时间 *sunshine time*

【日志】daily record；journal：工作～ *daily record of work* / 航海～ *logbook；log*

【日中】〈书〉noon；midday

【日子】❶ day；date：这个～好不容易盼到了。*The day we have been looking forward to has come at long last.* / 定一个～ *fix a date* / 街上怎么这么多人，今天是什么～？*Why are there so many people in the streets? What's the occasion?* ❷ time：他走了有些～了。*He's been away for some time.* / 这些～我校师生在工厂实习。*The teachers and students of our school have been doing field work at a factory recently.* ❸ life；livelihood：勤俭过～ *lead an industrious and frugal life* / ～越来越不好过。*Things are getting harder and harder.*

róng

戎 名〈书〉army；military affairs：投笔从戎

【戎马】〈书〉army horse

【戎马倥偬】burdened with pressing military duties

【戎马生涯】army life；military life

【戎装】（又作'戎服'）〈书〉martial attire

荣 Ⅰ动 grow luxuriantly; flourish: 春～冬枯 *grow in spring and wither in winter* Ⅱ形 prosperous; thriving; flourishing: 繁荣 Ⅲ名 honour; glory: ～立一等功 *be cited for meritorious service, first class* / 以艰苦为～ *take pride in working under difficult conditions*
【荣光】honour; glory
【荣归】return in glory: ～故里 *return in glory to one's old home after becoming famous or rich*
【荣华富贵】glory, splendour, wealth and rank; high position and great wealth: 享不尽的～ *enjoy untold wealth and high honour*
【荣获】get or win sth. as an honour: ～冠军 *win the championship* / ～一枚奖章 *be awarded a medal*
【荣枯】❶ (of plants) flourishing and withering ❷ rise and fall (or decline)
【荣任】be honoured with a post
【荣辱】honour or disgrace ◇ ～与共 (of friends) share honour or disgrace, weal or woe
【荣升】be honoured by promotion to a higher post
【荣退】❶ retire from or leave a post with merit; honorable discharge ❷ general term for army veterans: 胸前戴满勋章的～军人 *medalled army veterans*
【荣幸】be honoured: 我们应邀访问贵国,感到非常～。*We feel greatly honoured by your invitation to visit your country.* / 如蒙光临,不胜～。*We shall be greatly honoured by your gracious presence.* / 今天很～能参加你们的晚会。*It is a great honour to be with you at this evening party.* / 那天,我～地参加了国宴。*I had the honour of attending the state banquet the other day.*
【荣耀】honour; glory
【荣膺】〈书〉be honoured with a post or decoration
【荣誉】honour; credit; glory: ～感 *a sense of honour* / 为祖国赢得～ *win honour for one's country* / 爱护集体的～ *cherish the good name of the collective* / 应得的～ *an honour that one well deserves*
【荣誉军人】disabled soldier (wounded in revolutionary war)

茸 Ⅰ形 (of grass, etc.) fine and soft; downy: 毛茸茸 Ⅱ名 young pilose antler: 鹿茸
【茸长】long and untidy (hair, grass, etc.): 头发～ *long, untidy hair*
【茸茸】(of grass, hair, etc.) fine, soft and thick; downy: 绿草～ *a carpet of green grass* / 这孩子长着一头～的头发。*The boy has a head of soft, thick hair.*

绒 名 ❶ fine hair; down: 鸭绒 ❷ cloth with a soft nap or pile on one or either side: 丝绒 ❸ fine floss for embroidery
【绒布】flannelette; cotton flannel
【绒花】[工美] velvet flowers, birds, etc.
【绒画】painting on velvet
【绒裤】sweat pants
【绒毛】❶ fine hair; down; villus ❷ [纺] nap; pile
【绒面革】suède (leather)
【绒毯】flannelette blanket
【绒头绳】❶ wool (for tying pigtails) ❷〈方〉knitting wool
【绒线】❶ floss for embroidery ❷〈方〉knitting wool: ～衫 *woollen sweater*
【绒线刺绣】crewelwork
【绒绣】[工美] woollen needlepoint tapestry; woollen embroidery: ～地毯 *finished needlepoint carpet*
【绒衣】sweat shirt

容 Ⅰ动 ❶ hold; contain: 这个礼堂能～一千人。*The auditorium can hold a thousand people.* or *The auditorium has a seating capacity of 1,000.* / 这座大桥可～四辆卡车并列通行。*The bridge can take four lorries a breast.* ❷ tolerate: ～人之过 *be tolerant of others' mistakes* / ～不得不同意见 *cannot tolerate dissenting views* ❸ permit; allow: 详情～后再告。*Permit me to give the details later.* / 请～我考虑几天再作决定吧! *Please give me a few days to consider before I make my decision.* Ⅱ名 ❶ facial expression: 笑容 ❷ appearance; looks: 仪容
【容错软件】[计] fault-tolerant software
【容光】facial expression; bearing
【容光焕发】one's face glowing with health: ～的脸颊 *a striking, radiant face*
【容华】〈文〉features and complexion; looks: ～绝代 *of unrivalled beauty*
【容积】volume
【容积吨】measurement ton
【容量】capacity: 这个油箱的～为300加仑。*The tank has a capacity of 300 gallons.*
【容留】give shelter to; take sb. in; keep: 我们不能～他这样不老实的人。*We can't keep a dishonest man like him here.*
【容貌】facial features; appearance; looks: ～端庄 *have a pleasant appearance* / 她的～已大不如前了。*She had lost her looks.*
【容纳】hold; have a capacity of; accommodate: 会议室能～五十人。*The meeting room can hold 50 people.* / 他不能～不同意见。*He can't tolerate dissenting views.*
【容器】container; vessel
【容情】(usu. used in the negative) show mercy
【容人】regard people with kindly tolerance; tolerant towards others; magnanimous; broad-minded: 他心胸狭窄,容不下人。*He is narrow-minded and intolerant.*
【容忍】tolerate; put up with; condone: 我们不能～这种浪费现象。*We cannot tolerate such waste.* / 采取～和克制的态度 *adopt a tolerant and restrained attitude*
【容色】facial expression; countenance: ～自若 *keep an easy countenance; appear composed* / 忧

虑不安的～ *a worried look*

【容身】take shelter：这种地方，简直让人无法～。*You simply can't take shelter in a place like this.*

【容身之地】a place to stay：四海飘零，无～。*I drifted from one place to another with nowhere to rest.*

【容受】❶ hold；contain ❷ endure；put up with

【容恕】tolerate；forgive

【容物】〈书〉tolerant；forbearing；magnanimous：不能～ *be intolerant*；*be unforbearing*

【容限】[物] tolerance；allowance：光学～ *optical tolerance*

【容许】❶ tolerate；permit；allow：～新闻自由 *toleration of free press* / ～宗教自由 *religious toleration* / ～别人把话说完 *allow others to finish what they want to say* / 侵犯别国主权是绝不～的。*It is absolutely impermissible to encroach upon the sovereignty of a country.* ❷〈书〉perhaps；possibly：此类事件，十年前～有之。*Such things might possibly have happened ten years ago.* ◇ ～负载[电] allowable load；～收缩量 shrinkage allowance

【容蓄】hold；contain；accumulate：～泥沙 *accumulated sand and mud*

【容颜】appearance；looks

【容易】❶ easy：先做～的题。*Do the easy problems first.* / 说起来～做起来难。*It's easier said than done.* / 今天的幸福来得不～。*The present happy life didn't come about easily.* ❷ likely；liable；apt：他～生病。*He often gets ill.* / 这～引起误会。*This is liable to cause misunderstanding.* / 人们～把这两个问题混淆起来。*People are apt to confuse the two issues.*

【容重】[水] unit weight

【容装】appearance and dress：她几分钟内整好了～。*She tidied her face and clothes in a few minutes.*

溶 动 dissolve：樟脑～于酒精而不～于水。*Camphor dissolves in alcohol, but not in water.* / ～西画之长于国画之中 *apply the strong points of Western painting to traditional Chinese painting*

【溶洞】limestone cave

【溶化】dissolve：盐在水里很快就～。*Salt dissolves quickly in water.*

【溶汇】❶ dissolve and mix；❷ mingle；merge：演员的心和观众的心相通了，感情～到一起了。*Actors and audience seemed to beat with the same heart and their emotions became one.*

【溶剂】[化] solvent

【溶胶】[化] sol

【溶解】dissolve：这种物质在水中不会～。*This substance does not dissolve in water.* ◇ ～度 solubility；～热 heat of solution；～物 dissolved matter

【溶菌素】[医] bacteriolysin

【溶媒】同『溶剂』

【溶没】fade into；become invisible；dissolve：他的身影～在苍茫的夜色中。*He faded into the darkness.* / 飞鸟终于脱出了我的视线，～于天空之中。*The bird eventually flew out of sight and disappeared in the vast skies.*

【溶溶】〈文〉broad：江水～。*The river is broad and gentle.* / 月色～ *a flood of moonlight*

【溶蚀】[地质] corrosion

【溶性油】[化] soluble oil

【溶血】[医] haemolysis

【溶液】(又作'溶体') [化] solution：实在～ *real solution* / 当量～ *normal solution*

【溶质】[化] solute

【溶注】〈喻〉absorb：～心血 *involve time and effort*

熔 动 melt；fuse；smelt：～焊 *fusion welding*

【熔池】[冶] (molten) bath

【熔点】[物] melting (or fusing, fusion) point

【熔断】[电] fusing：～器 *fuse (box)*

【熔化】melt：纯铁加热到摄氏1,535度就～。*Pure iron melts at 1,535 ℃.* ◇ ～炉 melting furnace；～期[冶] melting stage；～速率[冶] melting rate

【熔剂】[冶] flux

【熔接】[冶] weld

【熔结】fuse；combine：他们的友情是在战斗中～起来的。*Their friendship was forged in battle.*

【熔解】[物] fuse；fusion：～热 *heat of fusion*

【熔炼】smelt：闪速～ *flash smelting* ◇ ～炉 smelting furnace

【熔炉】❶ smelting furnace ❷〈喻〉crucible；furnace：革命～ *the furnace of revolution*

【熔融】melt ◇ ～纺丝[纺] melting spinning；～挤压法[化纤] extrusion by melting

【熔岩】[地质] lava

【熔铸】found；cast：～生铁 *cast pig iron* ◇ ～工 smelter

榕 名 [植] small-fruited fig tree；banyan

蝾 (构词成分) 见下

【蝾螈】[动] salamander；newt

融 Ⅰ 动 ❶ melt；thaw：春雪易～。*Spring snow soon melts.* ❷ blend；fuse；be in harmony：交融 Ⅱ 名 circulation (of money, etc.)：金融

【融合】mix together；fuse；merge：铜与锡的～ *the fusion of copper and tin*

【融和】pleasantly warm；genial：天气～。*The weather is pleasantly warm.*

【融化】(of ice, snow, etc.) melt；thaw：湖上的冰已经～了。*The ice on the lake has already melted.* / 雪已开始～。*The snow is beginning to thaw.*

【融会】(又作'融汇') mix together；fuse；merge

【融会贯通】achieve mastery through a comprehensive study of the subject；gain a thorough understanding of the subject through mastery of all relevant material

【融解】melt；thaw：山顶的积雪～了。*The snow on*

the mountain top has melted.

【融洽】harmonious; on friendly (or good) terms: 干群关系很～。*The relations between the cadres and the masses are harmonious.* / 他们俩相处得十分～。*The two of them are on very good terms (or are getting on very well together).*

【融融】〈书〉❶ happy and harmonious: 老战友欢聚一堂,其乐～。*When old comrades-in-arms meet, their happiness knows no bounds.* ❷ warm: 春光～。*Spring fills the air with warmth.*

【融通】circulate: 聚集和～资金 *collect and circulate funds*

【融资】[经] finance; extend credit: 贸易～ *trade financing* / ～总额 *total financing* / ～租赁 *capital leasing*

rǒng

冗 Ⅰ形〈书〉❶ superfluous; redundant: 冗词 ❷ full of trivial details: 冗杂 Ⅱ名 busyness: 拨冗

【冗笔】superfluity in writing or painting; unnecessary touches or strokes

【冗长】tediously long; lengthy; long-winded; prolix: ～的讲演 *a long and tedious speech*

【冗词】superfluous words (in a piece of writing) ◇～赘句 redundant words and expressions

【冗繁】(of affairs) many and diverse; miscellaneous: ～的琐事 *small fussy affairs*

【冗员】redundant personnel: 裁减～ *reduce redundant personnel*

【冗杂】❶ (of writing) lengthy and jumbled ❷ (of affairs) miscellaneous

【冗赘】verbose; diffuse

róu

柔 Ⅰ形 ❶ soft; supple; flexible: ～枝嫩叶 *supple twigs and tender leaves* ❷ gentle; yielding; mild: 温柔 Ⅱ动 soften: 柔麻

【柔板】[音] adagio

【柔肠】soft heart: ～寸断 *be broken-hearted*

【柔道】judo

【柔和】soft; gentle; mild: ～的光线 *soft light* / ～的声音 *a gentle (or mild) voice; a soft sound* / 她的性情很～。*She has a very mild disposition.*

【柔滑】soft and smooth; satiny; creamy

【柔静】gentle and quiet

【柔麻】soften jute, hemp, etc.

【柔曼】❶ soft; gentle: ～的旋律 *a melody of serene beauty; a lyrical tune* ❷ soft and smooth; satiny; creamy ❸ good-looking; gorgeous

【柔美】soft and graceful: 音色～ *sweet tone colour* / ～的舞姿 *graceful dance*

【柔媚】gentle and lovely; genial; lovable: ～的晚霞 *the soft glow of sunset*

【柔绵】mellow (taste): 酒味～醇净。*The wine taste smooth and mellow.*

【柔嫩】tender; delicate: ～的幼芽 *tender sprouts* / ～的柳条 *delicate willow twigs*

【柔能克刚】the soft can overcome the hard

【柔懦】timid and overcautious; weak-willed: ～的性格 *have a weak character; be weak-kneed*

【柔情】tender feelings; tenderness: ～蜜意 *tender affection*

【柔情似水】tender feelings like water—be deeply attached; be passionately devoted

【柔情侠骨】a tender heart and a chivalrous spirit

【柔韧】pliable and tough

【柔茹刚吐】bully the weak and fear the strong

【柔软】soft; lithe: ～的垫子 *a soft cushion*

【柔软体操】callisthenics

【柔润】soft and smooth; delicate: ～的皮肤 *soft complexion; delicate skin* / ～的嗓音 *a sweet, mellow voice*

【柔弱】weak; delicate: 性格～ *have a weak character; be meek and mild*

【柔术】jujitsu

【柔顺】gentle and agreeable; meek: 性情～ *of gentle disposition; meek and mild*

【柔荑花序】[植] catkin; ament

【柔婉】soft and mild: ～的语调 *a mild tone*

【柔细】soft and fine: ～的柳条 *delicate willow twigs*

【柔心弱骨】soft heart and weak bone—soft; mild; meek

【柔鱼】squid

【柔中有刚】firmness cloaked beneath gentleness; an iron hand in a velvet glove

揉 动 ❶ rub: 别～眼睛。*Don't rub your eyes.* / ～一～腿 *rub one's legs* ❷ knead; roll: ～面 *knead dough* / 把泥～成小球 *roll the earth into small balls* / 把信～成一团 *crumple a letter into a ball* ❸〈书〉bend; twist

【揉搓】rub: 他怕～坏了课本,包了书皮。*He was afraid that his textbook would get worn, so he put a cover on it.*

糅 动 mix; mingle: 杂糅

【糅合】form a mixture (usu. of things which don't blend well); mix: ～莎士比亚戏剧和京剧二者的艺术形式 *blend the artistic form of Shakespeare with that of Beijing opera*

蹂 (构词成分) 见下

【蹂躏】trample on; ravage; make havoc of; devastate: 遭到～ *suffer devastation, oppression, outrages, etc.* / ～人权 *a gross violation of human rights* / ～妇女 *violate a woman*

鞣 动 tan: 这皮子～得不够熟。*The hide isn't properly tanned.*

【鞣料】tanning material: ～浸膏 *tanning extract*

【鞣酸】[化] tannic acid; tannin

ròu

肉 名 ❶ meat (esp. pork); flesh: 她不吃～。*She does not eat meat.* / 许多动物的～可以吃。*The flesh of many animals is eatable.* / 掉～ *lose flesh* / 身上没有～ *be skinny* ❷ pulp; flesh (of fruit): 冬瓜～厚。*A white gourd is rich in pulp.* ❸ (as prefix) intended for human consumption

【肉包子】steamed bun with meat stuffing

【肉饼】ground-meat pie; meat pie

【肉搏】fight hand-to-hand ◇ ～战 hand-to-hand fight (or combat); bayonet fighting (or charge)

【肉畜】livestock raised for meat

【肉垂】[动] wattle

【肉苁蓉】[中] saline cistanche (Cistanche salsa)

【肉店】butcher's (shop)

【肉丁】diced meat: 辣子～ *diced pork with hot pepper*

【肉冻】meat jelly; aspic: 鸡～ *chicken in aspic*

【肉豆蔻】[中] nutmeg

【肉嘟嘟】plump; chubby; pudgy: ～的小手 *plump little hands*

【肉墩墩】stocky

【肉感】sex appeal; sexiness: 她穿起那条牛仔裤非常～。*She looks very sexy in those jeans.*

【肉鸽】meat pigeon; table pigeon

【肉冠】[动] comb

【肉桂】[植] cinnamon tree; Chinese cinnamon tree; cassia-bark tree (Cinnamomum cassia)

【肉红】flesh-coloured; pale red

【肉鸡】(又作'肉用鸡') table hen; table chicken; broiler

【肉酱】meat pulp; minced meat

【肉类加工厂】meat processing factory

【肉瘤】[医] sarcoma

【肉麻】nauseating; sickening; disgusting: ～的吹捧 *fulsome praise* / 这种话听着真～。*It's sickening to hear this kind of talk.*

【肉马】meat horse

【肉末】minced meat; ground meat

【肉牛】store cattle; beef cattle; meat cattle; stocker

【肉排】steak

【肉泡眼】eyes with fleshy eyelids; pouchy eyes

【肉皮】pork skin

【肉皮儿】〈方〉human skin; complexion: ～细嫩 *soft complexion; delicate skin*

【肉片】sliced meat

【肉禽】table poultry

【肉色】yellowish pink; flesh-coloured; flesh-tinted: ～袜子 *flesh-tinted stockings*

【肉身】[宗](佛教) the mortal body

【肉食】(ròushí) carnivorous: ～动物 *carnivorous animal; carnivore*

【肉食】(ròushi) meat: 老太太吃素,从不碰～。*The old lady is a vegetarian and never touches meat.*

【肉食品】meat product: ～加工厂 *meat processing factory*

【肉丝】shredded meat (esp. pork): ～面 *noodles with shredded pork*

【肉松】dried meat (esp. pork) floss

【肉穗花序】[植] spadix

【肉袒】〈书〉strip off the upper garments (in begging forgiveness)—make a humble apology

【肉汤】broth

【肉体】the human body; the flesh

【肉头】〈方〉soft and fleshy: 这孩子的手多～! *What plump little hands the child has!*

【肉兔】table rabbit

【肉丸子】meatball

【肉馅】meat stuffing; chopped (or ground) meat

【肉星儿】tiny bits of meat: 这菜里连个～都没有。*There is not a speck of meat in this dish.*

【肉刑】corporal punishment

【肉芽】[医] granulation

【肉眼】naked eye: ～看不见细菌。*Bacteria are invisible to the naked eye.*

【肉眼凡胎】a very mundane person; a commonplace and ignorant person

【肉眼泡儿】eyes with fleshy eyelids; pouchy eyes

【肉羊】mutton sheep

【肉用仔鸡】(又作'肉用童子鸡') broiler

【肉欲】〈贬〉carnal desire

【肉汁】gravy; (meat) juice

【肉制品】meat products

【肉中刺】见〖眼中钉,肉中刺〗

【肉猪】slaughter pig; hog; porker; pork pig: 小型～ *small hog; light porker* / 中型～ *medium porker*

【肉赘】wart

rú

如 Ⅰ 动 ❶ in compliance with; according to: 如命 ❷ like; as; as if: 湖水～镜。*The lake is like a mirror.* / ～上所述 *as described above* / ～你所说 *as you've said* / 十年～一日 *persevere for ten years as if it were one day* ❸ (used in the negative) can compare with; be as good as: 不如 ❹ surpass; exceed: 光景一年强～一年。*The situation is getting better year by year.* ❺ for instance; such as; as: 唐朝有很多大诗人,～李白、杜甫、白居易等。*The Tang Dynasty produced a host of great poets, such as Li Bai, Du Fu and Bai Juyi.* Ⅱ 连 if; in case (of); in the event of: ～处理得当,问题不难解决。*The problem will not be difficult to solve, if properly handled.* / ～有火警,将玻璃击碎。*In case of fire, break the glass.* (a notice) / ～发生此种情况,我们即诉诸法律。*In that event, we would take the matter to court.*

【如臂使指】have a perfect command of sth.

【如常】as usual: 一切～。*Things are as usual.* / 病人起居～了。*The patient was beginning to live a normal life.*

【如出一口】as if from one mouth—with one voice; unanimously
【如出一辙】be exactly the same; be no different from each other; be cut from the same cloth
【如此】so; such; in this way; like that: ～勇敢 *so brave* / ～聪明的孩子很少见。*Such an intell-ingent child is rarely seen.* / 他来得～之快,完全出乎意料。*I never expected him to get here so soon.* / 他的脾气向来～。*He has always been so.* or *He's always like this.*
【如此等等】and so on and so forth
【如此而已】that's what it all adds up to: ～,岂有他哉! *And that's all there is to it!*
【如此这般】thus and thus; thus and so: 他～嘱咐了我一番。*He told me that thus and so was to be done, in such and such a manner.* / 他把这计算机的功能～地跟我说了一遍。*He went through all the computer's functions with me.*
【如次】be as follows: 其理由～。*The reasons are as follows.*
【如堕五里雾中】as if lost in a thick fog; utterly mystified
【如堕烟海】as if lost on a misty sea; all at sea; completely at a loss
【如法炮制】prepare herbal medicine by the prescribed method—follow a set pattern; follow suit
【如故】❶ as before ❷ like old friends
【如果】if; in case (of); in the event of: ～不是他指引的话,我们就迷路了。*If it weren't for him, we would have gone astray.* / ～发生火警,拨 119 电话。*In case of fire, dial 119.* / ～下雨,联欢会将在室内举行。*In the event of rain, the party will be held indoors.*
【如何】how; what: 此事～办理? *How are we to handle this matter?* / 他不知～是好。*He didn't know what to do.* / 这个电影你觉得～? *How do you like the film?* or *What do you think of the film?*
【如虎添翼】like a tiger that has grown wings — with might redoubled
【如花似锦】like flowers and brocade—❶ beautiful (scenery) ❷ bright (future): 前程～ *have a bright (or glorious) future*
【如花似玉】like flowers and jade—(of a woman) young and beautiful
【如火如荼】like a raging fire: 全国掀起了～的改革热潮。*Reform is catching on like fire throughout the country.*
【如获至宝】as if one had found a priceless treasure: 他终于弄到了这本书,真是～。*When he at last managed to get a copy of the book, he felt as if he'd found a priceless treasure.*
【如饥似渴】as if thirsting or hungering for sth.; with great eagerness: ～地寻求真理 *seek truth with great eagerness*
【如箭在弦】同〖箭在弦上,不得不发〗
【如胶似漆】stick to each other like glue or lacquer; remain glued to each other; be deeply attached to each other
【如今】nowadays; now: ～很少有人用毛笔了。*Few people use writing brushes nowadays.*
【如来】[宗](佛教) Tathagata
【如狼牧羊】like a wolf shepherding sheep—(of an oppressive official) ride roughshod over the people
【如狼似虎】as ferocious as wolves and tigers; like cruel beasts of prey
【如雷贯耳】(又作'如雷灌耳') reverberate like thunder: 久闻大名,～。*Your exalted name has long resounded in my ears.*
【如临大敌】as if faced with a formidable foe
【如临深渊,如履薄冰】as though on the brink of an abyss, as though treading on thin ice—acting with extreme caution
【如芒在背】同〖芒刺在背〗
【如梦初醒】as if awakening from a dream—beginning to see the light: 一席话,说得他～。*This conversation made him suddenly see the light.*
【如命】〈套〉in compliance with your instructions
【如鸟兽散】scatter and flee like birds and beasts; flee helter-skelter; be utterly routed
【如牛负重】like an ox carrying a heavy load: 彼等债务丛集,～。*Their debts piled up like loads on the backs of oxen.*
【如期】as scheduled; by the scheduled time; on schedule: 会议将～召开。*The conference will be convened as scheduled.* / 任务已～完成。*The assignment has been completed according to schedule.* / 货物～运到。*The goods arrived on schedule.*
【如其】if; in case (of); in the event of: ～无人接待,你可改日再去。*If nobody is there to receive you, go again another day.*
【如泣如诉】(of music or singing) querulous and plaintive
【如日方升】rising like the morning sun—have bright and boundless prospects
【如日中天】like the sun at high noon—at the apex (or zenith) of one's power, career, etc.
【如入鲍鱼之肆】(usu. used in) ～,久而不闻其臭 *it's like staying in a fish market and getting used to the stink—long exposure to bad surroundings or bad company accustoms one to evil ways*
【如入无人之境】like entering an unpeopled land—smashing all resistance; meeting no resistance
【如入芝兰之室】(usu. used in) ～,久而不闻其香 *it's like entering a room full of fragrant orchids and getting used to the sweet smell—associating with people of noble character accustoms one to good ways*
【如若】〈书〉if; in case (of); in the event of: ～不信,请拭目以待。*If you don't believe it, wait and see.* / 此事宜立刻进行,～不然则将坐失良机。*We'd better do it right now, or else we'll miss this golden opportunity.*
【如丧考妣】(look) as if one had lost one's parents—(look) utterly wretched
【如上】as above: ～所述 *as stated (or mentioned)*

above

【如实】go strictly by the facts：～地反映情况 *report the situation accurately*；*reflect things as they really are* / ～汇报 *give a true account of what happened*；*report to sb. on the actual situation*

【如释重负】(feel) as if relieved of a heavy load：她写完采访，松了一口气，觉得～。*After she finished writing up the interview, she heaved a sigh as if relieved of a heavy burden.*

【如数家珍】as if enumerating one's family treasures—show thorough familiarity with a subject：他对故宫设计讲解甚详，～。*His description of the layout of the Imperial Palace was so detailed that it was as if he were enumerating the heirlooms of his own family.*

【如数】exactly the number or amount：～偿还 *pay back in full* / ～到齐 *all present and correct*

【如汤沃雪】like melting snow with hot water—easily done

【如同】like；as：待我们～亲人一样 *treat us like their kith and kin* / 大厅里亮得～白昼。*It is as bright as daylight in the great hall.*

【如闻其声，如见其人】(so vividly described that) You seem to see and hear the person.

【如下】as follows：这个计划的要点～。*The main points of the plan are as follows.* / 全文～。*The full text follows.* / 发表～声明 *make the following statement*

【如像】like；as

【如心】after one's own heart；to one's liking

【如许】〈书〉❶ so；such；in this way；like that：泉水清～。*The spring water is so clear.* ❷ so much；so many：枉费～工力 *have wasted so much labour*

【如蚁附膻】like ants clinging to sth. rank—swarming after unwholesome things or attaching oneself to influential people

【如意】❶ find sth. satisfactory or as one wishes；be gratified：祝万事～。*May everything turn out as you wish.* ❷ ruyi，an S-shaped ornamental object，usu. made of jade，formerly a symbol of good luck

【如意算盘】smug calculations；wishful thinking：打～ *indulge in wishful thinking* / 打乱了他的～ *upset his smug calculations*

【如影随形】like the shadow following the person—closely associated with each other

【如鱼得水】like a stranded fish put back into water (said of one in his proper surroundings or having got a great aid)

【如愿】have one's wish fulfilled：最后他得到了博士学位，总算如了愿。*He obtained a doctor's degree and thus had his wish fulfilled.*

【如愿以偿】have one's wish fulfilled；achieve (or obtain) what one wishes

【如云】cloudlike；many；full of：奴仆～ *full of servants*

【如之奈何】what's to be done

【如醉如痴】as if intoxicated and stupefied

【如坐针毡】feel as if sitting on a bed of nails；be on pins and needles；be on tenterhooks

茹 动〈书〉eat：～素 *be a vegetarian*

【茹苦含辛】同〖含辛茹苦〗

【茹毛饮血】(of primitive man) eat the raw flesh of birds and beasts

铷 名［化］rubidium (Rb)

儒 名 ❶ Confucianism；Confucianist ❷〈旧〉scholar；learned man：老～ *an old scholar*

【儒艮】［动］dugong

【儒家】the Confucianists

【儒将】scholar-general

【儒商】scholar-businessman

【儒雅】〈书〉scholarly and refined：～风度 *a scholarly bearing*

濡 动〈书〉❶ immerse；moisten ❷ linger

【濡染】immerse；imbue

【濡湿】soak；make wet

嚅（构词成分）见下

【嚅嚅】hesitate in speech；hem and haw；mutter and mumble

孺 名 child

【孺子】〈书〉child

【孺子可教】You could be taught，young man；The boy is worth teaching.

【孺子牛】a herd boy's willing ox—a servant of the people ——另见〖横眉冷对千夫指，俯首甘为孺子牛〗

蠕 动 wriggle；squirm

【蠕虫】worm；helminth ◇ ～学 helminthology

【蠕动】❶ wriggle；squirm ❷［生理］peristalsis ❸［地质］creep

【蠕蠕】wriggling；squirming：～而动 *move along by wriggling*

rǔ

乳 Ⅰ 名 ❶ breast；mamma：乳房 ❷ milk (in general)：炼乳 ❸ any milk-like liquid Ⅱ 动 give birth to Ⅲ 形 newborn (animal)；sucking：乳猪

【乳白】milky white；cream colour：～灯泡 *opal bulb* / ～玻璃 *opal glass*；*opalescent glass*；*milk glass*

【乳钵】mortar (a vessel)

【乳齿】milk tooth；deciduous tooth

【乳畜】milch livestock

【乳蛾】［中］acute tonsillitis

【乳儿】a nursing infant；suckling

【乳房】❶ breast；mamma ❷ udder

【乳峰】(young women's) rounded breasts

【乳化】［化］emulsify：～剂 *emulsifying agent*；*emulsifier*

【乳化液】［化］emulsion：水包油～ *oil-in-water emulsion* / 油包水～ *water-in-oil emulsion*
【乳化原油】emulsified crude oil
【乳剂】［化］emulsion ◇ ～层 emulsion layer
【乳胶】［化］emulsion ◇ ～漆 emulsion paint；latex paint
【乳疽】［中］intramammary abscess
【乳酪】cheese
【乳糜】［生理］chyle ◇ ～尿 chyluria
【乳名】infant name；child's pet name
【乳母】wet nurse
【乳牛】dairy cattle；milch cow ◇ ～场 dairy farm
【乳酸】lactic acid ◇ ～钙 calcium lactate
【乳糖】milk sugar；lactose ◇ ～酶 lactase
【乳头】❶ nipple；teat；mammilla ❷ papilla：视神经～ *optic papilla* / ～状瘤 *papilloma*
【乳腺】［生理］mammary gland ◇ ～癌 breast cancer；～炎 mastitis
【乳香】［植］frankincense
【乳臭】smelling of milk—childish
【乳臭未干】still smell of one's mother's milk—be young and inexperienced；be wet behind the ears
【乳燕】young swallow
【乳罩】brassiere；bra
【乳汁】milk (in general)
【乳脂】butterfat ◇ ～糖 toffee；taffy
【乳制品】dairy products：～工业 *dairy industry*
【乳猪】sucking pig；suckling pig
【乳浊液】［化］emulsion

辱 Ⅰ 名 disgrace；dishonour：羞辱 Ⅱ 动 ❶ bring disgrace (or humiliation) to；insult：折辱 ❷ bring disgrace on；be a disgrace to：辱没 ❸〈书〉〈套〉be indebted (to sb. for a kindness)：～承指教。*I am very grateful to you for your advice*.
【辱骂】abuse；call sb. names；hurl insults
【辱命】disgrace a commission；fail to accomplish a mission：出使～ *fail to accomplish one's diplomatic mission* / 幸不～。*I trust that you will accomplish your mission*.
【辱没】bring disgrace to；be unworthy of：～门楣 *bring disgrace to one's family* / ～先进集体的光荣称号 *prove unworthy of the honourable title of an advanced group*

rù

入 Ⅰ 动 ❶ go into；enter：部队凯旋～城。*The army made a triumphal entry into the city*. / 长江流～东海。*The Changjiang River empties into the Donghai Sea*. / 时已～冬。*Winter has set in*. ❷ join；be admitted into；become a member of：你孩子～了托儿所没有？——～了。*Is your child at a nursery？—Yes, she is*. ❸ conform to；agree with：入时 Ⅱ 名 ❶〈略〉见『入声』❷ income：岁入
【入不敷出】income falling short of expenditure；unable to make ends meet
【入仓】be stored in a barn；be put in storage
【入场】entrance；admission：凭票～。*Admission by ticket only*. / 运动员在乐曲声中列队～。*The athletes marched into the arena to the sound of music*. ◇ ～券 (admission) ticket；～式 march-in ceremony
【入超】unfavourable balance of trade；import surplus
【入党】join or be admitted to a political party (esp. the Chinese Communist Party)
【入档】file (away)：把材料～ *file the materials* / 事情已～了。*The matter is already on file*.
【入定】［宗］(佛教) sit in meditation (a technique for mental self-discipline)
【入肚】swallow；consume：一大碗面，他一会儿功夫就都～了。*He consumed a big bowlful of noodles in no time*. / 三杯酒～，他来了精神，话也多了。*After downing three glasses, he became lively and talkative*.
【入耳】pleasant to the ear：不～的话 *unpleasant words*
【入伏】the fu days begin；the hottest days of the year begin：明天～。*The fu days begin tomorrow*. or *From tomorrow we'll be having the hottest days of the year*. / ～以来，常有阵雨。*Since the fu days began, there have been frequent showers*.
【入港】❶［交通］enter a port ❷ (of conversation) in full agreement；in perfect harmony：二人谈得～。*The two of them are deep in conversation and in perfect agreement with one another*.
【入股】buy a share；become a shareholder
【入骨】to the marrow
【入国问禁】on entering a country, inquire about its prohibitions (or taboos)
【入海口】estuary；entry to the sea
【入户】❶ go to sb.'s place；call at sb.'s house ❷ obtain a residence permit
【入画】suitable for a painting；picturesque：桂林山水，处处可以～。*Every bit of Guilin scenery is worth painting*.
【入会】join a society, association, etc.
【入伙】❶ join a gang；join in partnership ❷ have one's meals at a canteen or mess hall：在食堂～ *eat at one's mess*
【入籍】be naturalized：入中国籍 *be naturalized in China；become a Chinese citizen*
【入寂】(of Buddhist monks or nuns) pass away；die
【入教】embrace a religion
【入静】［宗］(of Taoists) sit still (a technique for achieving mental calm and conserving energy)
【入境】enter a country：办理～手续 *go through the entry formalities* ◇ ～登记 entrance registration；～口岸 port of entry；～签证 entry visa
【入境问俗】on entering a country, inquire about its customs
【入口】❶ enter the mouth：难于～ *have a nasty*

taste / 此药不可～。*This medicine is not to be taken orally*. ❷ (of foreign goods or goods from another place) be transported into; import ❸ entrance: 车站～ *entrance to the station*

【入寇】invade (a country); intrude

【入库】be put in storage; be laid up: 粮食都已～。*All the grain has been put in storage*. or *All the grain is already in the granary*.

【入款】income; receipts

【入殓】put a corpse in a coffin; encoffin

【入列】[军] take one's place in the ranks; fall in

【入流】qualified: 他是个不～的电影演员。*He is not a qualified film (or movie) actor*.

【入门】❶ cross the threshold; learn the rudiments of a subject: 学英语～并不难,学好可不容易。*Rudimentary English is easy to acquire, but mastery of the language is quite difficult*. ❷ (usu. used in book titles) elementary course; ABC; primer:《汉语～》*Gateway to Chinese* /《英语语法～》*Elementary English Grammar*

【入梦】❶ fall asleep ❷ (of a person) appear in one's dream

【入迷】be fascinated; be enchanted: 他们的精彩表演使观众看得入了迷。*The audience was fascinated by their superb performance*. / 看书看～了 *be engrossed in a book* / 大家听他讲故事,都听得～了。*Everybody listened to his story with rapt attention*.

【入魔】be infatuated; be spellbound: 她做诗入了魔了。*She's got poetry mania*.

【入木三分】❶ (of calligraphy) written in a forceful hand: 这位书法家的书法苍劲有力,～。*This calligrapher writes a forceful hand, with bold and vigorous strokes*. ❷ penetrating; profound; keen: 这位经济学家的分析真是～。*The economist's analysis was really penetrating*.

【入暮】towards evening; at nightfall; at dusk: ～时分 *at dusk; at twilight*

【入侵】invade; intrude; make an incursion; make inroads: 消灭一切敢于～的敌人 *wipe out all enemies who dare to invade our country*

【入情入理】fair and reasonable: 她的建议～。*Her suggestion is fair and just*.

【入射点】incidence point

【入射角】[物] angle of incidence; incident angle

【入射线】[物] incident ray

【入神】❶ be entranced; be enthralled: 他越说越起劲,大家越听越～。*As he talked with more and more gusto, we came more and more under his spell*. ❷ superb; marvellous: 这幅画画得真是～。*This painting is really superb*. or *This is a marvellous picture*.

【入声】entering tone (the fourth of the four tones in classical Chinese pronunciation, still retained in certain dialects)

【入时】(of clothes) fashionable; modish; à la mode: 打扮～ *be fashionably dressed*

【入世不深】lack experience of life; not be socially experienced

【入室】〈书〉become well advanced in scholarship or highly proficient in a profession: ～弟子 *an initiated pupil*

【入室操戈】attack sb. with his own spear in his own house—turn sb.'s words or argument against himself

【入手】start with; begin with; proceed from; take as the point of departure: 解决问题要从调查研究～。*To solve a problem, one has to start with investigation*.

【入睡】go to sleep; fall asleep: 他晚上工作时间长了就不容易～。*He can't get to sleep easily if he works long hours at night*. / 吃了这种镇静剂很快就能～了。*You'll fall asleep soon after you take this sedative*.

【入土】be buried; be interred: 快～了 *have one foot in the grave*

【入团】join or be admitted to the Chinese Communist Youth League

【入托】start going to a nursery: 办理小孩～手续 *enrol a child in a nursery*

【入微】in every possible way; in a subtle way: 演员的表情细腻～。*The actor performed with great delicacy and sensibility*.

【入围】enter or be selected for the next round of competition: 初赛～的中国选手竟有5名。*As many as five Chinese contestants have qualified through the preliminaries for the next round of competition*.

【入味】❶ tasty: 菜做得很～。*The dish is very tasty*. ❷ interesting: 这出戏我们越看越～。*The more we watched the play, the more it aroused our interest*.

【入伍】enlist in the armed forces; join up

【入席】take one's seat at a banquet, ceremony, etc.: 主人请大家～。*The host invited everyone to go in and be seated*.

【入乡随俗】同〖随乡入乡〗

【入选】be selected; be chosen

【入学】❶ start school: ～年龄 *school age* / 我国儿童六、七岁～。*In our country children start school at the age of six or seven*. ❷ enter a school; 从～到毕业 *from entrance to graduation* / ～考试 *entrance examination*

【入眼】pleasing to the eye: 这些衣服没有一件她看得～的。*None of these clothes are to her liking*. / 你这种行为真让人看不～。*Your conduct is most unseemly*.

【入眼货】sth. (esp. goods) pleasant to the eye or to one's liking: 现在市场繁荣,到处都有～。*The market is flourishing, and there are so many things to attract the buyer*.

【入药】[中] be used as medicine: 陈皮可以～。*Dried tangerine peel can be used as (Chinese) medicine*.

【入夜】at nightfall: ～,工地上灯火通明。*When night fell the construction site was ablaze with light*.

【入狱】be put in prison; be sent to jail

【入院】be admitted to hospital; be hospitalized: 办理～手续 *fill out forms for admittance to a hospital*
【入账】enter an item in an account; enter into the account book
【入蛰】(of animals) go into hibernation
【入主出奴】academic sectarianism or bigotry
【入赘】marry into and live with one's bride's family
【入座】take one's seat (esp. at a feast)

溽 形〈书〉humid; damp
【溽热】humid and hot; muggy
【溽暑】sweltering summer weather: ～炎夏 *a sweltering hot summer*

缛 形 elaborate; cumbersome: 繁文缛节

蓐 名〈书〉straw mat or mattress: 坐蓐

褥 名 cotton-padded mattress: 被褥
【褥疮】[医] bedsore
【褥单】(又作'褥单子') bed sheet
【褥套】❶ bedding sack ❷ mattress cover
【褥子】cotton-padded mattress

ruǎn

软 形 ❶ soft; flexible; supple; pliable: ～椅 *a soft chair* / 柳条很～。*Willow twigs are pliable*. ❷ soft; mild; gentle: 你对他～了些。*You've been a bit soft with him*. / 他话说得太～了。*He spoke too mildly*. / 她看儿子哭了,心～了下来。*When she saw her son cry, her heart softened*. ❸ weak; feeble: 他两腿发～。*His legs felt weak (or like jelly)*. / 最近以来,爷爷的身子骨儿越来越感到～了。*Grandfather has been getting feebler lately*. ❹ poor in quality, ability, etc.: 货色～ *poor-quality goods* / 工夫～ *inadequate skill* ❺ easily moved or influenced: 他心肠～。*He is tender-hearted*.
【软包装】foods sold in soft packages
【软币】❶ paper money; paper currency; note ❷ soft currency
【软磁盘】[计] diskette; floppy disk
【软蛋】❶ soft-shelled egg ❷〈方〉coward
【软刀子】soft knife—a way of harming people imperceptibly
【软钉子】soft nail—a mild (or tactful) refusal or refutation
【软缎】soft silk fabric in satin weave
【软腭】[生理] soft palate
【软耳朵】soft ear—a credulous person
【软风】[气] light air
【软腐病】[农] soft rot
【软钢】mild steel; soft steel
【软膏】ointment; paste
【软骨头】a soft bone—a weak-kneed person; a spineless person; a coward
【软骨】[生理] cartilage
【软骨病】osteomalacia
【软骨鱼】cartilaginous fish
【软管】flexible pipe or tube; hose: 铠装～ *armoured hose*
【软罐头】foods packed in carton containers
【软焊】soft soldering; soldering
【软化】❶ soften: 使硬水～ *soften hard water* / 他对我态度逐渐～。*He gradually softened towards me*. ❷ win over by soft tactics: ～政策 *soft tactics* ❸ bate (leather)
【软话】soft words (spoken to express apology, ask pardon, show sympathy, etc.)
【软和】〈口〉❶ soft: ～的褥子 *a soft mattress* ❷ gentle; kind; soft: 给老太太说几句～话儿。*Say some kind words* (or *Say something nice*) *to please the old lady*.
【软件】[计] software ◇ ～包 software package
【软禁】put (or place) sb. under house arrest
【软科学】soft science
【软拷贝】soft copy (data not printed out on paper)
【软款】soft; lithe
【软麻工艺】[纺] bruising (of flax); batching (of jute)
【软媚】gentle and lovely; genial; lovable
【软锰矿】pyrolusite
【软绵绵】❶ soft: ～的枕头 *a soft pillow* / 这支歌～的。*This song is too sentimental*. ❷ weak: 她病好了,但身体还是～的。*She is well now, but she still feels weak*.
【软磨】use soft tactics: ～硬抗 *use both hard and soft tactics*
【软木】cork (bark of the oak tree): ～塞 *cork (as a stopper)*
【软能源】renewable energy
【软泥】[地质] ooze
【软盘】[计] diskette; floppy disk
【软片】(a roll of) film
【软弱】weak; feeble; flabby: 他病后身体～无力。*His illness has left him weak*. / 领导～ *weak leadership* / 他太～,不会保护自己的权利。*He is too weak to defend his rights*.
【软弱可欺】be weak and easy to bully: 不要把我们的克制当作～。*Don't mistake our restraint for weakness*.
【软弱无能】weak and incompetent; effete; ineffectual
【软设备】another name for 软件
【软食】soft diet; soft food; pap
【软式网球】soft tennis
【软水】soft water
【软酥酥】limp; weak; soft
【软糖】soft sweets; jelly drops
【软梯】〈口〉rope ladder
【软体动物】mollusk
【软体动物学】malacology
【软通货】soft currency
【软卧】〈略〉见〖软席卧铺〗
【软席】soft seat or berth; cushioned seat or berth;

～车厢 *railway carriage* (*or car*) *with soft seats* (*or berths*)

【软席卧铺】sleeping carriage with soft (or cushioned) berths

【软线】[电] flexible cord

【软性】softness; gentleness; lightness: ～读物 *light reading*

【软饮料】soft drink

【软硬不吃】yield neither to persuasion nor to coercion

【软硬兼施】use both hard and soft tactics; couple threats with promises; use the stick and the carrot

【软语】soft words

【软玉】nephrite (a mineral)

【软玉温香】soft fragrance and warmth—feminine charm

【软炸】(in Chinese cooking) soft-fry

【软脂】[化] palmitin

【软脂酸】[化] palmitic acid; palmic acid

【软着陆】soft landing: 宇宙飞船在月球上～。*The spacecraft made a soft landing on the moon.* / ～航天器 *soft landing spacecraft*

【软组织】[生理] soft tissue

ruǐ

蕊 名 stamen or pistil: 花蕊

ruì

蚋 名 buffalo gnat; blackfly

锐 Ⅰ 形 ❶ sharp; keen; acute: 尖锐 ❷ rapid; sudden: ～进 *rapid advance* Ⅱ 名 vigour; fighting spirit: 养精蓄锐

【锐不可当】can't be held back; be irresistible: 以～之势 *with irresistible force* / 我军攻势迅猛, ～。*Our attack was so swift and violent that nothing could withstand it.*

【锐减】sharp fall (or decline); sudden drop

【锐角】[数] acute angle

【锐利】❶ sharp-edged; sharp-pointed; sharp; keen: ～的匕首 *a sharp dagger* / ～的武器 *a sharp* (*or powerful*) *weapon* / ～的攻势 *a spirited attack* ❷ penetrating; incisive; sharp; keen: 眼光～ *sharp-eyed*; *sharp-sighted* / ～的笔锋 *a sharp pen*; *a vigorous style*

【锐敏】(of senses or insight) keen; sharp: ～的嗅觉 *a keen sense of smell* / ～的眼光 *sharp-eyed*; *keen-sighted*

【锐气】dash; drive: 表现了青年人的～ *show the dashing spirit of young people* / 这场比赛咱们一定得赢,不能挫了～。*We've got to win the game, otherwise we'll lose our momentum.*

【锐眼】sharp eyes

【锐意】〈书〉firm; resolute; determined; be bent on: ～革新 *be bent* (*or keen*) *on reform*

瑞 形 auspicious; lucky

【瑞典】Sweden ◇ ～人 Swede; the Swedish; ～语 Swedish (language)

【瑞士】Switzerland ◇ ～人 Swiss

【瑞香】[植] winter daphne (Daphne odora)

【瑞雪】timely snow; auspicious snow: 华北各省普降～。*Every province in North China has had an auspicious snowfall.*

【瑞雪兆丰年】a timely snow promises a good harvest; a snow year, a rich year

睿 形〈书〉farsighted; having foresight

【睿哲】〈书〉wise and farsighted

【睿智】〈书〉wise and farsighted

rùn

闰 名 [天] intercalation

【闰年】leap (or intercalary) year

【闰日】leap (or intercalary) day

【闰月】intercalary month in the lunar calendar; leap month

润 Ⅰ 形 moist; smooth; sleek: 这个条幅墨色很～。*This scroll is written in dark full-bodied ink.* Ⅱ 名 profit; benefit: 利润 Ⅲ 动 ❶ moisten; lubricate: 喝点儿水～一～嗓子。*Drink some water to moisten your throat.* ❷ embellish; touch up: 润色

【润笔】❶ (of a writing brush) dip in ink ❷〈旧〉remuneration for a writer, painter or calligrapher

【润肠】[中] lubricate the intestines; ease constipation

【润肺】[中] moisten the lungs—make expectoration easy

【润肤露】skin lotion; skin moisturizer

【润滑】lubricate: ～系统 *lubricating system*; *lubrication system* ◇ ～油 lubricating oil; lubrication oil; ～脂 (lubricating) grease

【润色】polish (a piece of writing, etc.); touch up: 这篇文章需要～一下。*This essay needs polishing.*

【润湿】❶ moist; damp: ～的泥土 *damp soil* ❷ soak; infiltrate: 露水～了他的衣服。*His clothes were soaked with dew.*

【润饰】同〖润色〗

【润燥】[中] moisten the respiratory tract, skin, etc.

【润泽】❶ moist; smooth; sleek: 这匹马全身～有光。*The horse's coat was sleek and glossy.* / 雨后荷花显得更加～了。*After the rain the lotus flowers looked fuller.* ❷ moisten; lubricate: 用油～轮轴 *oil an axle*

ruò

若 Ⅰ 动〈书〉(usu. used in set phrases) as if;

like：若有所失 Ⅱ 连〈书〉if：～不刻苦钻研，如何取得成果？*How can we achieve anything if we don't work hard?*

【若虫】[动] nymph

【若非】〈书〉if not；were it not for：～亲身经历，岂知其中甘苦。*You cannot appreciate the difficulty except through personal experience.*

【若干】❶ a certain number or amount：～年 *a number of years* / ～次 *several times* / 地区 *certain areas* ❷ how many；how much：共得～？*How many in all?* or *What is the sum total?*

【若何】how；what：结果～，还不得而知。*The outcome is not known yet.* or *I'm unable to find out how things have come out.*

【若即若离】be neither close nor distant；maintain a lukewarm relationship；keep sb. at arm's length

【若明若暗】have an indistinct (or blurred) picture of；have a hazy (or vague) notion about

【若是】if：我～他，决不会那么办。*If I were him, I wouldn't have done it that way.*

【若无其事】as if nothing had happened—calm；indifferent：急着等你帮忙，你怎么还～？*How can you remain indifferent when your help is urgently needed?*

【若要人不知，除非己莫为】If you don't wish anyone to know what you've done, it is better not to have done it in the first place.

【若隐若现】appear indistinctly：山峰在云雾中～。*The mountaintops loom through the clouds.*

【若有所失】feel as if something were missing；look distracted

【若有所思】seem lost in thought；look pensive：他凝视着远方，～的样子。*He gazed into the distance and seemed lost in thought.*

偌

代 such；so

【偌大】〈旧〉of such a size；so big：～的地方 *such a big place* / ～年纪 *so old*；*so advanced in years*

弱

形 ❶ weak；feeble：他身体很～。*He is very weak.* / 由～变强 *go from weakness to strength* / 他年纪虽老，干活并不～。*Old as he is, he works energetically.* / 他的语法～。*He's weak in grammar.* ❷ young：老弱 ❸ inferior：她的能力并不比别人～。*She's no less capable than the others.* / 这个队的防守～于对方。*This team's defence is not as good as the opponent's.* ❹ (following a fraction or decimal) a little less than：三分之一～ *a little less than one-third*

【弱不禁风】too weak to withstand a gust of wind；extremely delicate；fragile

【弱不胜衣】(of a woman) too frail to bear the weight of one's clothes

【弱点】weakness；weak point；failing：性格上的～ *weaknesses of character*

【弱冠】〈书〉a young man of around twenty (an age when man in ancient China started wearing hats)

【弱化】weaken；deplete：教育，特别是基础教育的～是令人担忧的一个问题。*The erosion of education, and of elementary education in particular, is an issue of grave concern.*

【弱碱】[化] weak base

【弱旅】weak team (esp. sports)：济南队虽为～，但踢得顽强。*The Jinan Football Team, though weak, played with determination.* (〈反〉劲旅)

【弱脉】[中] weak pulse

【弱拍】[音] weak beat；unaccented beat

【弱肉强食】the weak are the prey of the strong—the law of the jungle

【弱视】[医] weak-sighted；weak vision；poor eyesight

【弱手】❶ unskilled；poor ability (of person) ❷ weak opponent

【弱酸】[化] weak acid

【弱听】hard of hearing；hearing-impaired：～班 *class for the hearing-impaired*

【弱项】event in which one does poorly esp. sports：足球目前尚是我国体育的～。*Football is still a weak sport in our country.*

【弱小】small and weak：～的婴儿 *a small and weak baby* / ～民族 *small and weak nations*

【弱音器】[音] mute；sordine

【弱智】mentally deficient；retarded：～儿童 *a retarded child*

箬

(构词成分) 见下

【箬帽】(又作'箬笠') a broad-rimmed conical bamboo hat worn by peasants, fishermen, etc., as protection against sun and rain

【箬竹】[植] indocalamus

S

sā

仨 数〈口〉(not used with measure words) three：给我来～。*Give me three.* / 我们(哥儿)～ *we three (brothers)*；*the three of us*

【仨瓜俩枣】three melons and two dates —only a few small things；mere trifles

撒 动 ❶ cast；let go；let out：撒网 / 把手～开 *let go one's hold* ❷〈贬〉throw off all restraint；let oneself go：撒酒疯 ——另见 sǎ

【撒旦】[宗](基督教) Satan

【撒刁】act in a slick and shameless way

【撒疯】(又作'撒风') ❶ behave atrociously ❷ vent one's anger

【撒哈拉沙漠】the Sahara (Desert)

【撒欢儿】〈方〉gambol；frisk

【撒谎】〈口〉tell a lie；lie：当面～ *tell a barefaced lie*；*lie in one's teeth*

【撒娇】act like a spoiled child；act spoiled

【撒酒疯】be drunk and act crazy；be roaring drunk

【撒赖】make a scene；act shamelessly；raise hell

【撒尿】〈方〉piss；pee

【撒泼】be unreasonable and make a scene

【撒气】❶ (of a ball, tyre, etc.) leak；go soft；get a flat：后胎～了。*The back tyre has got a puncture.* or *The back tyre is flat.* ❷ vent one's anger or ill temper：你别拿我～嘛。*Don't take it out on me.*

【撒手】let go one's hold；let go：你拿稳，我～了。*Hold it tight. I'll let go.* / ～不管 *wash one's hands of the business*；*refuse to have anything more to do with the matter*

【撒手锏】an unexpected thrust with the mace—one's trump card

【撒腿】take to one's heels；beat it：～就跑 *make off at once*；*scamper*

【撒网】❶ cast a net；pay out a net ❷ invite relatives and friends to weddings, funerals, etc. with the intention of collecting presents

【撒丫子】(又作'撒鸭子')〈口〉take to one's heels；beat it：～就跑 *beat it double-quick*

【撒野】act wildly；behave atrociously

sǎ

洒 动 sprinkle；spray；spill；shed：～农药 *spray pesticide* / 别把汤～了。*Don't spill the soup.* / 甘～热血为人民 *willingly shed one's blood for the people*

【洒家】〈旧〉(used by men) I

【洒泪】shed tears：～告别 *take a tearful leave*

【洒落】❶ drip；trickle down：一串串汗珠～在地上。*Drops of sweat trickled down to the ground.* ❷ 同〖洒脱〗

【洒扫】sprinkle water and sweep the floor；sweep：黎明即起，～庭除。*Rise at dawn and sweep the courtyard.*

【洒水车】watering car；sprinkler

【洒脱】(of one's speech, deportment, etc.) free and easy；unrestrained

撒 动 ❶ scatter；sprinkle；spread：～农药 *dust crops with an insecticide* / ～种 *sow seeds* ❷ spill；drop：她把～在路上的麦粒儿扫到一块儿。*She swept up the grains of wheat that had spilled on the ground.* ——另见 sā

【撒播】[农] broadcast sowing；broadcast ◇ ～机 broadcast seeder；broadcaster

【撒肥机】fertilizer distributor；manure spreader

【撒粉】[农] dusting ◇ ～器 duster

【撒漫】spending freely；squandering：他是个～的主儿。*He's a spendthrift.*

【撒施】[农] scatter or spread fertilizer over the fields；broadcast fertilizer

sà

卅 数 thirty

飒 (构词成分)见下

【飒然】〈书〉soughing；whistling：有风～而至。*A soughing wind sprang up.*

【飒飒】sough；rustle：秋风～。*The autumn wind is soughing through the trees.*

【飒爽】〈书〉of martial bearing；valiant

【飒爽英姿】同〖英姿飒爽〗

脎 名 [化] osazone

萨 (构词成分)见下

【萨尔瓦多】El Salvador ◇ ～人 Salvadoran

【萨克管】[音] saxophone

【萨克号】[音] saxhorn

【萨拉热窝】Sarajevo

【萨摩亚】Samoa ◇ ～人 Samoan；～语 Samoan

(language)
【萨其马】a kind of Manchu candied fritter

sāi

塞 Ⅰ 动 fill in; squeeze in; stuff: 箱子不太满，还可以再～点东西。*There is still room in the suitcase to squeeze a few more things in.* / 把窟窿～住。*Stop that hole.* / 水管～住了。*The water-pipe is clogged up.* Ⅱ 名 stopper: 木～ *stopper; plug; spigot* ——另见 sài; sè
【塞规】[机] plug gauge
【塞满】fill up; stuff full
【塞牙】(of food) get stuck between the teeth
【塞子】stopper; plug; spigot; cork

腮 名 cheek
【腮帮子】〈口〉cheek
【腮颊】cheek
【腮托】[音] chin rest (of a violin or viola)
【腮腺】[生理] parotid gland
【腮腺炎】[医] parotitis; mumps

噻 (构词成分)见下
【噻吩】[化] thiophene
【噻唑】[化] thiazole

鳃 名 gill; branchia
【鳃瓣】gill lamella
【鳃盖】gill cover

sài

塞 名 a place of strategic importance ——另见 sāi; sè
【塞尔维亚-克罗地亚语】Serbo-Croatian
【塞拉利昂】Sierra Leone ◇ ～人 Sierra Leonian
【塞内加尔】Senegal ◇ ～人 Senegalese
【塞浦路斯】Cyprus ◇ ～人 Cypriot
【塞舌尔】Seychelles ◇ ～人 Seychellois
【塞外】north of the Great Wall; beyond the Great Wall: ～江南 *lush southern-type fields north of the Great Wall*
【塞翁失马】the old frontiersman losing his horse—a blessing in disguise: ～,安知非福? *Just like the old frontiersman losing his horse, who knows but that this may be a blessing in disguise?*

赛 Ⅰ 名 match; game; competition; contest: 足球～ *football match* (*or game*) Ⅱ 动 ❶ have a competition: 咱俩～一～看。*Let's have a competition.* / 要～出水平，也要～出风格。*We must give a good account of ourselves and display fine sportsmanship as well.* ❷ be comparable to; surpass: 我这萝卜～梨。*These radishes of mine taste as good as pears.*
【赛场】competition ground; arena for competition: 球迷们纷纷拥入～。*The fans crowded into the competition venue.*
【赛车】[体] ❶ cycle racing; motorcycle race; automobile race ❷ racing vehicle
【赛程】❶ distance in a sports event: 比赛的最后 300 米～ *the final 300 meters of the race* ❷ competition schedule: ～将重新排定。*The competiton schedule will be rearranged.*
【赛池】competition pool
【赛次】round of competition: 3 个～ *three rounds of competition*
【赛地】venue of sports event
【赛段】leg of a long-distance race; section: 昨天的行程在这次汽车拉力赛中～最长。*Yesterday's leg was the longest of this motor rally.*
【赛风】sportsmanship; competition: 运动员们都表现出了良好的～。*The athletes all showed good sportsmanship.*
【赛过】overtake; be better than; surpass; exceed: 此处风光～江南。*The scenery here surpasses that south of the lower reaches of the Changjiang River.*
【赛季】competition season; playing season
【赛况】the events during a competition: 报道世界杯足球赛～ *cover the World Cup Football Championship*
【赛力散】[农] phenylmercuric acetate (PMA)
【赛璐玢】cellophane
【赛璐珞】celluloid
【赛马】horse racing
【赛跑】race: 长距离～ *long-distance race* / 一百米～ *100-metre dash* / 越野～ *cross-country race*
【赛区】zone (of a large-scale sports competition); conference (U.S.): 亚洲～ *Asian zone*
【赛事】competition; match; contest; game: 由于～频繁，影响了足球队的冬训。*The frequent matches disrupted the winter training of the football team.*
【赛势】proceedings at a competition: 昨日～平平。*Yesterday's contest was uneventful.*
【赛艇】[体] ❶ rowing ❷ racing boat; shell
【赛制】competition rules

sān

三 Ⅰ 数 three Ⅱ 形 more than two; several; many: ～弯九转 *(full of) twists and turns*
【三八妇女节】March 8, International Women's Day
【三八红旗手】woman pacesetter
【三八式】38-rifle (a Japanese rifle made in the 38th year of Showa 昭和): 一支～ *a 38-rifle*
【三百六十行】all trades and professions; all walks of life
【三胞胎】triplets
【三宝】❶ three treasures; three precious things ❷ [宗](佛教) Triratna; the triad of the Buddha, the dharma, and the sangha
【三北】Three Northern Regions (Northwest Chi-

na, North China and Northeast China)
【三倍体】[生] triploid
【三边形】another name for 三角形
【三不管】come within nobody's jurisdiction; be nobody's business
【三部曲】rilogy
【三槽出钢】[冶] three-trough steel tapping technique
【三叉戟】a three-pronged spear; trident ◇ ～飞机 Trident
【三叉神经】[生理] trigeminal nerve
【三岔路口】(又作'三岔口') a fork in the road; a junction of three roads
【三产】(〈略〉全称为'第三产业') tertiary industry; service industry
【三长两短】unexpected misfortune; sth. unfortunate, esp. death: 万一他有个～ *if anything untoward should happen to him; in case he should die*
【三朝元老】minister to three emperors —an official who stays in power under different regimes: 他许家是～。改朝换代,改不了他许家的天下。*The Xus have been ranking officials in three succeeding regimes. Dynasties may change, but the Xus' power never wanes.*
【三重】triple; threefold ◇ ～唱 [音] (vocal) trio; ～奏 [音] (instrumental) trio
【三春】〈书〉the three spring months
【三次方程】[数] cubic equation
【三从四德】the three obediences and four virtues (for a woman according to Confucian ethics)—obedience to father before marriage, to husband after marriage, and to son after husband's death; morality, proper speech, modest manner, and diligent work
【三寸不烂之舌】a little lithe tongue; an eloquent tongue; a silver tongue
【三寸金莲】three-cun lily feet (formerly, men's laudatory term for women's bound feet)
【三大差别】the three major distinctions (between town and country, industry and agriculture, physical and mental labour)
【三大球】three games played with large balls (football, basketball and volleyball)
【三代】three generations (i. e. of father, son, and grandson)
【三等兵】(U. S. Army) basic private; (U. S. Navy) apprentice seaman; (U. S. Air Force) airman third class
【三等秘书】diplomacy third secretary
【三点式】bikini
【三叠纪】[地] the Triassic Period
【三叠系】[地] the Triassic System
【三度空间】three-dimensional space
【三段论】(又作'三段论法') [逻] syllogism
【三对六面】the presence of the two interested parties plus a third disinterested party as a witness
【三法】[中] the three therapeutic methods of traditional Chinese medicine (i. e. diaphoresis, emetic measures, purgation and diuresis)
【三番五次】(又作'三番两次') again and again; time and again; over and over again; repeatedly
【三方】tripartite: ～会谈 *tripartite talks*
【三废】the three wastes (i. e. waste gas, waste water, and industrial residue): 从～中回收和提取大量有用物质 *salvage large quantities of useful materials from the three wastes*
【三分】❶ 30%; a little; somewhat: 谁都怕他～。*Everybody is a little afraid of him.* / ～长相,七分打扮 *three parts natural beauty, seven parts clothing and makeup* ❷ divided into three parts; split into three
【三分球】[体] (篮球) three pointer; trey
【三分像人,七分像鬼】look more like a ghost than a human being
【三伏】❶ the three fu—the three hottest periods of the year (i. e. 初伏, 中伏, and 末伏; altogether 30 or 40 days) ❷ the third fu (another name for 末伏)
【三副】[航海] third mate; third officer
【三纲五常】the three cardinal guides (i. e. ruler guides subject, father guides son, and husband guides wife) and the five constant virtues (i. e. benevolence, righteousness, propriety, wisdom and fidelity) as specified in the feudal ethical code
【三个臭皮匠,赛过诸葛亮】three cobblers with their wits combined surpass Zhuge Liang the master mind—the wisdom of the masses exceeds that of the wisest individual
【三个面向】Three Orientations (education oriented to the needs of modernization, of the world and of the future.)
【三更半夜】in the dead of night
【三宫六院】the three palaces and six chambers—the imperial harem
【三姑六婆】women of dubious character making a living by dishonest means (e. g. women matchmakers, sorceresses, etc.)
【三顾茅庐】make three calls at the thatched cottage (as Liu Bei did when he sought the aid of Zhuge Liang, a master strategist then living in seclusion)—repeatedly request sb. to take up a responsible post
【三光政策】the policy of "burn all, kill all, loot all" (once pursued by the Japanese invaders in China)
【三好】Triple A (A in ideology and moral character, A in studies, A in health) ◇ ～学生 Triple-A pupil (title of merit)
【三合板】three-ply board; plywood
【三合土】(又作'三和土') a mixture of lime, clay, and sand to which water is added (used in building)
【三合星】[天] triple star
【三核苷酸】[生化] trinucleotide
【三化螟】[农] yellow rice borer
【三级风】[气] force 3 wind; gentle breeze

【三级火箭】three-stage rocket
【三级跳远】[体] hop, step and jump; triple jump
【三极管】[无] triode：充气～ *gas-filled triode* / 晶体～ *transistor*
【三季稻】triple cropping of rice
【三家村】a three-family village—a very small remote village
【三驾马车】❶ a carriage drawn by a team of three horses ❷ troika; triumvirate
【三尖瓣】[生理] tricuspid valve
【三尖瓣狭窄】[医] tricuspid stenosis
【三缄其口】with one's lips sealed
【三江平原】the Three-River Plain, referring to the vast alluvial plain formed by convergence of the waters from the three rivers Songhuajiang, Heilongjiang and Wusulijiang in Northeast China
【三焦】[中] the three visceral cavities housing the internal organs：～辨证 *analysing and differentiating diseases according to the pathological changes in the three visceral cavities*
【三角】❶ triangle ❷ [数] trigonometry ◇ ～板 set square; ～测量 triangulation; trigonometrical survey; ～鲂 [动] triangular bream; ～枫 [植] trident maple (Acer buergerianum); ～关系 triangular relationship; ～函数 trigonometric function; ～肌 [生理] deltoid; ～巾 sling; ～裤 panties; briefs; ～恋爱 love triangle; eternal triangle; ～旗 pennant; pennon; ～湾 estuary; ～形 triangle; ～学 [数] trigonometry; ～债 a tripartite cycle of debt; triangle of debt; ～洲 delta
【三角铁】❶ [音] triangle ❷ angle iron
【三脚架】tripod
【三脚猫】a jack of all trades
【三教九流】❶ the three religions (i.e. Confucianism, Taoism and Buddhism) and the nine schools of thought (i. e. the Confucians, the Taoists, the Yin-Yang, the Legalists, the Logicians, the Mohists, the Political Strategists, the Eclectics and the Agriculturists) ❷ various religious sects and academic schools ❸〈贬〉people in various trades; people of all sorts
【三节棍】a cudgel of three linked sections; three-section cudgel
【三九天】(又作'三九') the third nine-day period after the winter solstice—the coldest days of winter
【三句话不离本行】can hardly open one's mouth without talking shop; talk shop all the time
【三军】❶ the three armed services ❷〈旧〉the army
【三K党】Ku Klux Klan
【三棱尺】three-square rule; triangular scale
【三棱镜】[物] (triangular) prism
【三连冠】win the championship three times in succession; triple crown
【三连音符】[音] triplet
【三联单】triplicate form
【三磷酸腺甙】[药] adenosine triphosphate (ATP)
【三令五申】repeatedly give injunctions：县里曾～，干什么都得按法律办事。*The county repeatedly enjoined that everything must be done according to law*.
【三六九等】various grades and ranks：车子有～，各有各的用处。*There are all kinds of vehicles; each has its own use*. / 把工作分成～ *regard different kinds of work as indications of rank or grade*
【三氯杀螨砜】[农] tetradiphon; tedion
【三轮车】(又作'三轮儿') tricycle; pedicab
【三轮摩托车】motor tricycle
【三轮汽车】three-wheeled automobile (or motorcar)
【三昧】❶ [宗] (佛教) samadhi ❷ secret; knack：深得其中～ *master the secrets of an art*
【三秒区】[体] (篮球) 3-second area or zone
【三民主义】the Three Principles of the People (i. e. Nationalism, Democracy and the People's Livelihood; put forward by Dr. Sun Yat-sen)
【三明治】sandwich
【三年五载】from three to five years —in a few years
【三朋四友】a lot of friends
【三七】[中] pseudo-ginseng (Panax pseudo-ginseng var. notoginseng)
【三亲六故】relatives, friends and acquaintances
【三秋】[农] ❶ the three autumn jobs (of harvesting, ploughing and sowing) ❷〈书〉the three autumn months ❸〈书〉three years：一日不见，如隔三秋
【三权分立】separation of the three powers (i. e. the legislative, executive and judicial powers)
【三人成虎】the testimony of three men creates a tiger in the market—repeated false reports will lead one astray
【三人行,必有我师】where there are three men walking together, one of them is bound to be able to teach me something
【三三两两】in twos and threes; in knots：旅客～在月台上等车。*Passengers were waiting in knots on the platform*.
【三色版】[刷] three-colour halftone; three-colour block ◇ ～印刷 trichromatic printing
【三色堇】[植] pansy
【三生】[宗] (佛教) the three lives—the present life, the previous life, and the next life
【三生有幸】consider oneself most fortunate (to make sb.'s acquaintance, etc.)
【三十二分音符】[音] demisemiquaver; thirty-second note
【三十二开】[刷] thirty-two mo; 32mo
【三十六计,走为上计】Of the thirty-six strategems, the only choice is to run away; The only thing to do now is to quit.
【三熟制】[农] triple-cropping system
【三水铝矿】gibbsite
【三思】think thrice—think carefully：事关重大，请你～。*It's a matter of great importance. I would advise you to think carefully*.

【三思而行】(又作'三思而后行') think thrice before you act; look before you leap: 万一遇上个什么事儿,要～! *If anything happens, think well before you act!*
【三…四】❶ expressing confusion: 颠三倒四 / 丢三落四 ❷ expressing repetition: 推三阻四
【三天打鱼,两天晒网】go fishing for three days and dry the nets for two —work by fits and starts; lack perseverance
【三天两头】〈口〉every other day; almost every day: 他～地来找她。*He comes to see her almost every day.*
【三通】❶ [机] tee; tee joint ❷ direct links across the Taiwan Straits between mainland China and Taiwan Province for mail, trade, and air and shipping services
【三通管】three-way pipe
【三头对案】(又作'三曹对案') the confrontation of the three parties (i. e. the plaintiff, the defendant and the witness) in court
【三头六臂】(with) three heads and six arms—superhuman powers
【三推六问】〈旧〉a good many interrogations
【三围】three vital measurements (chest, waist, and hips)
【三维空间】同〖三度空间〗
【三位一体】❶ [宗] (基督教) the Trinity ❷ three forming an organic whole; three in one; trinity
【三五成群】in threes and fours; in knots: 街头巷尾人们～,议论纷纷。*People were seen standing about in knots on street corners, talking and arguing.*
【三峡】Three Gorges ◇ ～工程 Three Gorges Dam Project
【三下五除二】three-down-five-reject-two—neat and quick
【三夏】[农] ❶ the three summer jobs (of planting, harvesting and field management) ❷〈书〉the three summer months
【三鲜】three delicacies (a combination of delicacies such as sea slug, squid, shrimp, chicken, etc., used as the ingredients of a dish): ～汤 *soup with three delicacies* / 炒～ *stir-fried three delicacies*
【三弦】sanxian, a three-stringed plucked instrument
【三项全能运动】[体] triathlon
【三相】[电] three-phase ◇ ～变压器 three-phase transformer
【三硝基甲苯】[化] trinitrotoluene (TNT)
【三小球】three games played with small balls (table tennis, badminton and tennis)
【三心二意】be of two minds; shilly-shally; be half-hearted: 别～了,就这样办吧。*Don't shilly-shally. Just go ahead and do it.* / 我做事从来不～。*I'm not a person of two minds.*
【三言两语】in a few words; in one or two words: 这事不是～能说清楚的。*The matter can't be explained in a few words.*
【三氧化物】[化] trioxide (e.g. 三氧化二砷 arsenic trioxide)
【三叶虫】(古生物) trilobite
【三月】❶ March ❷ the third month of the lunar year; the third moon
【三灾八难】(children's) various illnesses and ailments
【三战两胜】[体] the best of three games
【三只手】〈方〉pickpocket
【三趾鹑】[动] button quail
【三资企业】(〈略〉全称为'中外合资,中外合作,外商独资') foreign investment enterprises (Chinese-foreign equity joint ventures, Chinese-foreign cooperative joint ventures, wholly foreign-owned enterprises)

叁 [数] three (used for the numeral 三 on cheques, etc. to avoid mistakes or alterations)

sǎn

伞 [名] umbrella; sth. shaped like an umbrella: 降落伞
【伞兵】paratrooper; parachuter
【伞兵部队】parachute troops; paratroops
【伞齿轮】[机] bevel gear
【伞伐】[林] shelterwood cutting
【伞房花序】[植] corymb
【伞降】parachuting; chuting: 新兵已完成～训练任务。*The recruits have completed their parachuting training program.*
【伞投】drop by parachute; parachute; chute: ～炸弹 *parachute bomb; parabomb* / ～照明弹 *parachute flare*
【伞形花序】[植] umbel
【伞形科】[植] carrot family

散 Ⅰ [动] come loose; fall apart; not hold together: 背包～了。*The blanket roll has come loose.* / 木箱～了。*The wooden box fell apart.* / 麦包～了。*The sack of wheat has spilled.* Ⅱ [形] scattered: 这个村的农民住得很～。*The peasants in this village live rather far apart from one another.* Ⅲ [名] [中] medicine in powder form; medicinal powder ——另见 sàn
【散兵】[军] skirmisher ◇ ～壕 fire trench; ～坑 foxhole; pit; ～线 skirmish line
【散兵游勇】stragglers and disbanded soldiers
【散打】[体] a style of wrestling
【散工】同〖零工〗——另见〖散工〗sàngōng
【散光】astigmatism ◇ ～眼镜 astigmatic glasses
【散户】[经] individual investors
【散货】bulk cargo ◇ ～船 bulk freighter
【散记】random notes; sketches; sidelights: 《农村～》*Village Sketches*
【散剂】[药] powder; pulvis
【散架】〈口〉fall apart; fall to pieces: 别再装了,大车快～了。*Don't put any more on the cart, or it'll break.* / 我的胳膊腿像散了架似的。*I feel as*

if all my limbs are falling apart (or are out of joint).

【散居】live scattered：游击队员～在老乡家里。*The guerrillas lived scattered among the villagers.*

【散客】walk-in

【散乱】in disorder：～的头发 *dishevelled hair* / 桌子上～地放着各种文具书籍。*Books and writing materials were scattered about on the desk.*

【散漫】❶ undisciplined；lax in discipline；slack；careless and sloppy：克服～性 *overcome slackness (or laxness in discipline)* ❷ unorganized；scattered：～无组织的状态 *a disorganized state of affairs*

【散曲】non-dramatic songs

【散射】[物] scattering ◇ ～粒子 scattering particles；～通信 scatter communication；～线 scattered rays

【散套】a sequence of sanqu (散曲) songs within a particular musical mode

【散体】prose style free from parallelism；simple，direct prose style

【散文】prose ◇ ～诗 prose poem

【散养】free-range raising of poultry，cattle，etc.：机械化养鸡不同于～。*Mechanized chicken farming is different from free-range farming.*

【散装】unpackaged；loose packed；in bulk：～饼干 *loose cookies* ◇ ～货物 bulk cargo；bulk freight；～汽油 petrol (or gasoline) in bulk；～水泥 bulk cement；～运输 bulk transportation

sàn

散 动 ❶ break up；disperse：会还没有～。*The meeting is not over yet.* / 大家别走～了。*Let's not get separated.* / 今天星期六，早点～吧。*It's Saturday today. Let's stop a bit earlier.* / 乌云～了。*Dark clouds dispersed.* ❷ distribute；disseminate；give out：～传单 *give out handbills；distribute leaflets* ❸ dispel；let out：请打开门窗～～烟。*Please open the door and windows to let the smoke out.* ❹〈方〉sack：旧社会资本家随便～工人。*In the old days，the capitalists sacked workers at will.* ——另见 sǎn

【散播】disseminate；spread：～种子 *broadcast (seeds)* / ～谣言 *spread rumours*

【散布】❶ spread；disseminate；distribute：～流言蜚语 *spread slanderous rumours* ❷ be scattered here and there：羊群～在山坡上吃草。*A flock of sheep are grazing here and there on the hillside.*

【散步】take a walk；go for a walk；go for a stroll

【散场】(of a show，performance，etc.) be over：电影～了。*The movie is over.*

【散发】❶ send out；send forth；diffuse；emit：花儿～着清香。*The flowers sent forth a delicate fragrance.* ❷ distribute；issue；give out：～传单 *distribute leaflets* / 作为正式文件～ *be circulated as an official document*

【散会】(of a meeting) be over；break up：宣布～ *declare the meeting over* / 一直到中午才～。*The meeting didn't end until noon.*

【散伙】❶ (of a group，body or organization) dissolve；disband ❷〈口〉(of lovers or a married couple) break up：他们吵了一架，～了。*They quarrelled and broke up.*

【散开】spread out or apart；disperse；scatter：看热闹的群众～了。*The crowd，which had gathered to watch the fun，dispersed.*

【散落】❶ fall scattered：花瓣～了一地。*The ground was scattered with fallen petals.* ❷ be scattered：草原上～着数不清的牛羊。*Countless cattle and sheep were scattered over the grasslands.* ❸ scatter and disappear

【散闷】divert oneself from boredom

【散热】❶ dissipate heat ❷ radiate heat ◇ ～管 cooling tube；radiating pipe；～片 cooling fin；radiating fin (or rib)；～器 radiator

【散失】❶ scatter and disappear；be lost；be missing：防止图书～ *prevent any loss of library books* ❷ (of moisture，etc.) be lost；vaporize；dissipate

【散水】[建] apron

【散摊子】(又作'散摊儿')〈口〉(of a group，body or organization) dissolve；disband；break up：他们合伙经营的铺子不久就～了。*Their partnership soon broke up.*

【散戏】(of a show，play，opera，etc.) be over

【散心】drive away one's cares；relieve boredom

【散佚】(又作'散轶') be scattered and lost；be no longer extant：他的著作～殆尽。*His writings are practically all scattered and lost.* or *Practically none of his works are still extant.*

【散逸】❶ (of a gas，etc.) escape；leak：气体向外～。*The gas is escaping.* ❷ [物] dissipation：热～ *heat dissipation* ❸ 同〖散佚〗

sāng

丧 名 funeral；mourning ——另见 sàng

【丧服】mourning apparel

【丧家】family of the deceased

【丧礼】obsequies；funeral

【丧乱】〈书〉disturbance and bloodshed；tragic disaster

【丧门星】❶ a woman who brings ill luck to her husband's family ❷ anyone who brings ill luck

【丧事】funeral arrangements

【丧葬】burial；funeral：～费 *funeral expenses*

【丧钟】funeral bell；death knell；knell：敲响殖民主义的～ *sound the death knell of colonialism*

桑 名 white mulberry；mulberry (tree)

【桑巴】samba (a Brazilian dance)

【桑白皮】[中] the root bark of white mulberry

【桑蚕】silkworm：～丝 *mulberry silk*

【桑寄生】[中] parasitic loranthus (Loranthus parasiticus)

【桑那浴】sauna bath
【桑皮纸】mulberry (bark) paper
【桑葚】(又作'桑葚子') mulberry (the fruit)
【桑树】white mulberry; mulberry (tree)
【桑榆】〈文〉❶ waning day; evening ❷ the west (where the sun sets): 失之东隅,收之桑榆 ❸ the evening of life; old age
【桑榆暮景】the evening of life; old age
【桑园】mulberry field
【桑梓】〈文〉one's native place

sǎng

搡 动 〈方〉push violently: 把他～了个跟头 *push him over*

嗓 名 ❶ throat; larynx ❷ voice
【嗓门】voice: 提高～ *raise one's voice* / ～大 *have a loud voice*
【嗓音】voice: 他～洪亮。*He has a resonant voice.* or *His voice carries well.*
【嗓子】❶ throat; larynx: ～疼 *have a sore throat* ❷ voice: ～好 *have a good voice* / 他的～哑了。*He's lost his voice.*
【嗓子眼儿】〈口〉throat

sàng

丧 动 lose ——另见 sāng
【丧胆】be terror-stricken; be smitten with fear
【丧魂落魄】(又作'丧魂失魄') driven to distraction; shaken to the core: 吓得～ *be scared out of one's wits*; *be frightened out of one's life*
【丧家之犬】a homeless dog; a stray cur: 惶惶如～ *as scared as a stray cur*; *as pitiful as a lost pup*
【丧尽天良】utterly devoid of conscience; conscienceless; heartless
【丧命】meet one's death; get killed
【丧偶】〈书〉be bereaved of one's spouse (esp. one's wife); have lost one's wife or husband
【丧气】(sàngqì) feel disheartened; lose heart; become crestfallen: ～话 *demoralizing words*
【丧气】(sàngqi)〈口〉be unlucky; be out of luck; have bad luck
【丧权辱国】humiliate the nation and forfeit its sovereignty; surrender a country's sovereign rights under humiliating terms: ～的条约 *a treaty of national betrayal and humiliation*
【丧生】(又作'丧身') meet one's death; lose one's life; get killed
【丧失】lose; forfeit: ～信心 *lose confidence* / ～时机 *miss the opportunity* / ～立场 *depart from the correct stand*
【丧亡】meet one's death
【丧心病狂】frenzied; frantic; perverse: ～地进行破坏活动 *carry on frenzied wrecking activities*

sāo

搔 动 scratch: ～痒 *scratch oneself to relieve itching*; *scratch where it itches*
【搔到痒处】scratch where it itches—hit the nail on the head
【搔首】scratch one's head
【搔首踟蹰】scratch one's head in perplexity
【搔首弄姿】〈书〉(of a woman) stroke one's hair in coquetry; posture and preen oneself
【搔头】❶ scratch one's head (in perplexity) ❷ perplexing: 这案件头绪纷纭,很是～。*This case is most complicated and perplexing.* ❸〈古〉hairpin; hair clasp: 玉～ *a jade hairpin*

骚 Ⅰ 动 disturb; upset: 骚乱 Ⅱ 名〈书〉literary writings: 骚人 Ⅲ 形 coquettish
【骚动】❶ disturbance; commotion; ferment: 那几位工会领袖的被囚禁,在全国范围内引起了～。*The imprisonment of the union leaders caused a commotion right through the country.* ❷ be in a tumult; become restless: 人群～起来。*The crowd was in a tumult.*
【骚货】〈讳〉tart
【骚客】〈书〉poet
【骚乱】disturbance; riot
【骚扰】harass; molest: ～活动 *harassment*
【骚人】〈书〉poet
【骚人墨客】literary men; men of letters

缫 动 reel silk from cocoons; reel
【缫丝】silk reeling; filature ◇ ～厂 reeling mill; filature; ～机 reeling machine; filature

臊 名 the smell of urine or of the fox, skunk, etc.; foul smell ——另见 sào
【臊气】foul smell; stink

sǎo

扫 动 ❶ sweep; sweep away: ～雪 *sweep away the snow* / ～街 *sweep the streets* ❷ eliminate; clear away: 扫雷 / 扫盲 ❸ pass quickly along or over; sweep: 他向听众～了一眼。*He swept his eyes over the audience.* / 探照灯光～过夜空。*The searchlights swept across the night sky.* ❹ put all together: 扫数 ——另见 sào
【扫边】play a minor role (in a traditional opera)
【扫除】❶ cleaning; cleanup: 院子要天天～。*The courtyard should be cleaned up every day.* ❷ clear away; remove; wipe out: ～一切害虫 *sweep away all pests*; *away with all pests* / ～文盲 *eliminate (or wipe out) illiteracy*
【扫荡】mop up: 粉碎敌人的～ *smash the enemy's mopping-up operations*
【扫地】❶ sweep the floor ❷ (of honour, credibility, etc.) reach rock bottom; reach an all-time

low；be dragged in the dust：名誉～ *be thoroughly discredited* / 威信～ *be shorn of one's prestige*

【扫地出门】sweep the garbage out—drive out the whole family with nothing except the clothes they have on

【扫地以尽】〈喻〉be swept clean；be swept out：他的体面威风，～。*Every bit of his dignity and prestige was swept into the dust.*

【扫毒】anti-drug campaign

【扫黄】anti-porn campaign（confiscate pornographic and obscene books，periodicals and movies，etc. from the market）

【扫雷】mine-sweeping（or clearance）◇～舰 minesweeper；～器 mine-sweeping apparatus

【扫路车】street sweeper

【扫盲】（〈略〉全称为'扫除文盲'）eliminate（or wipe out）illiteracy：～班 *literacy class* / ～运动 *campaign to eliminate illiteracy；anti-illiteracy campaign*

【扫描】［电子］scanning：行～ *line scanning* / 飞点～ *flying-spot scanning* / ～仪 *scanner*

【扫灭】mop up；wipe out：～小股残敌 *mop up the last few groups of the enemy*

【扫墓】（又作'扫坟'）sweep a grave—pay respects to a dead person at his tomb

【扫平】put down；crush；suppress：～叛乱 *put down a rebellion*

【扫清】clear away；get rid of：～官僚主义作风 *do away with bureaucracy* ◇～道路 clear the path；pave the way

【扫射】［军］strafe

【扫视】（of one's eyes or glance）sweep：我从左到右～了一遍。*My eyes swept from left to right.*

【扫数】the total number；the whole amount：～入库 *all put in storage* / ～还清 *all paid off*

【扫榻】〈书〉sweep the bed clean（in expectation of a visitor）：～以待。*We are looking forward to your visit.*

【扫尾】wind up；round off：～工作 *rounding-off work*

【扫兴】have one's spirits dampened；feel disappointed：真叫人～！*How disappointing!*

【扫雪车】snowplough

嫂 名 ❶ elder brother's wife；sister-in-law：二～ *second brother's wife* / 表～ *cousin's wife* ❷（a form of address for a married woman about one's own age）sister：桂英～ *Sister Guiying*

【嫂夫人】〈尊〉（a form of address for a friend's wife）your wife：内子嘱笔敬问～好。*My wife has asked me to send regards to yours.*

【嫂嫂】〈方〉❶ elder brother's wife；sister-in-law ❷（a form of address for a married woman about one's own age）sister：王家～ *Sister Wang*

【嫂子】〈口〉elder brother's wife；sister-in-law

sào

扫（构词成分）见下——另见 sǎo

【扫帚】broom

【扫帚眉】bushy eyebrows

【扫帚星】❶ common name for 彗星 ❷〈讳〉a person（esp. a woman）who brings ill luck；jinx

瘙 名〈古〉scabies

【瘙痒】itch

臊 形 shy；bashful：～得满脸通红 *blush scarlet* ——另见 sāo

sè

色 名 ❶ colour：～香味俱佳 *look good，smell good，and taste good* ❷ look；countenance；expression：喜色 ❸ kind；description：各～人等 *people of every description；all kinds of people* ❹ scene；scenery：景色 ❺ quality（of precious metals，goods，etc.）：成色 ❻ feminine charms：姿色 / 好色 ——另见 shǎi

【色不迷人人自迷】Lust does not blind，one blinds oneself.

【色彩】❶ colour；hue：～鲜明 *in bright colours；bright-coloured* ❷ characteristic quality；flavour；colour：地方～ *local colour* / 文学～ *literary flavour* / 感情～ *emotional colouring*

【色层谱】［物］chromatogram

【色差】❶［物］chromatic aberration；chromatism ❷［纺］off colour；off shade

【色丹岛】Shikotan

【色胆】the lengths to which one will go for sex：～包天 *will go to any lengths for sex；be utterly reckless in sex*

【色淀】［纺］（colour）lake：绯红～ *crimson lake*

【色调】tone；hue：暖～ *warm tones*

【色度计】［物］colorimeter：光电～ *photoelectric colorimeter*

【色光】chromatic light；coloured light

【色鬼】lecher；sex maniac：老～ *a lecherous old man；an old dirty man*

【色基】［化］colour base

【色觉】colour vision ◇～检查表 colour test cards

【色卡】colored card：流行色～ *cards painted in fashionable colours*

【色拉】同〖沙拉〗

【色狼】man with excessive sexual desire；lecher

【色厉内荏】fierce of mien but faint of heart；threatening in manner but cowardly at heart

【色盲】［医］achromatopsia；colour blindness ◇～表 colour test cards

【色迷迷】look erotic；have lust in the eyes：他～地看着她。*He looked at her，his eyes becoming hazy with lust.*

【色品】［物］chroma；chromaticity

【色谱】color spedrum；chromatograph ◇～法 chromatography；～分析 chromatographic analysis

【色情】sex ◇～电影 blue movie；pornographic film；～狂 erotomania；sex mania；～文学 erotica；～文艺 erotology；～文艺作者 erotologist；

～作品 pornography
【色球】［天］chromosphere
【色散】［物］chromatic dispersion
【色色】every kind：～俱全。*All sorts of things are kept in stock.*
【色授魂与】Beauty yields and passion quickens.
【色衰爱弛】Passion cools as beauty fades.
【色素】［生理］pigment ◇ ～沉着［医］pigmentation；～痣 mole
【色相】❶［宗］（佛教）form and aspect ❷ feminine charms：出卖～ *sell her charms* ❸ the colours of the spectrum—red，orange，yellow，green，blue，indigo，and violet
【色艺】looks and skills（of a female entertainer）：～俱佳 *be remarkable for both looks and skills*
【色欲】sexual urge；lust
【色泽】colour and lustre：～鲜明 *bright and lustrous*
【色织厂】［纺］yarn-dyed fabric mill
【色值】color content：这种白糖，～低。*This white sugar has a low color content.*
【色纸】coloured paper
【色痣】pigmented mole（or nevus）

涩 形 ❶ puckery；astringent：这柿子～不～？*Are these persimmons puckery?* ❷ unsmooth；hard-going：推子发～了，该上油了。*This pair of hair-clippers doesn't work smoothly. It needs oiling.* ❸ hard to understand；obscure：艰涩
【涩脉】［中］a weak，thready，uneven pulse
【涩滞】（of style of writing）not smooth

啬 形 stingy；miserly：吝啬
【啬刻】〈方〉stingy；miserly

铯 名［化］cesium（Cs）

塞（构词成分）见下——另见 sāi；sài
【塞擦音】［语音］affricate
【塞音】［语音］plosive；stop
【塞责】not do one's job conscientiously；perform one's duties perfunctorily

瑟 名［音］se（a twenty-five-stringed or sixteen-stringed plucked instrument，somewhat similar to the zither）
【瑟瑟】❶（of the wind）rustling ❷（of a person）trembling
【瑟缩】curl up and shiver with cold；cower

sēn

森 形 ❶ full of trees：森林 ❷〈书〉multitudinous；in multitudes：森罗万象 ❸ dark；gloomy：阴森
【森林】forest：～抚育 *tending of woods* / ～火灾 *forest fire* / ～资源 *forest reserves* ◇ ～覆盖率 percentage of forest cover；～学 forestry
【森罗殿】the Hall of Darkness（another name for 阎王殿）
【森罗万象】all-embracing；all-inclusive
【森然】❶（of tall trees）dense；thick：林木～ *thickly wooded with tall trees* ❷ awe-inspiring
【森森】❶（of trees）dense；thick；luxuriant：松柏～ *dense pine and cypress trees* ❷ ghastly；eerie
【森严】stern；strict；forbidding：门禁～ *with the entrance carefully guarded* / 等级～ *be rigidly stratified；form a strict hierarchy*

sēng

僧 名 Buddhist monk；monk
【僧道】Buddhist monks and Taoist priests
【僧多粥少】同〚粥少僧多〛
【僧伽罗语】Sinhalese
【僧侣】monks and priests；clergy
【僧侣主义】［哲］fideism
【僧尼】Buddhist monks and nuns
【僧人】Buddhist monk
【僧俗】clergy and laity
【僧徒】（又作'僧众'）Buddhist monks
【僧院】Buddhist temple；Buddhist monastery

shā

杀 Ⅰ 动 ❶ kill；slaughter ❷ fight；go into battle：～出重围 *fight one's way out of a heavy encirclement* ❸ weaken；reduce；abate：～～敌人的威风 *deflate the enemy's arrogance* / 风势稍～。*The wind abated.* ❹〈方〉smart：碘酒涂在伤口上真～得慌。*Iodine smarts when it is put on a cut.* ❺ take off；counteract：白菜馅里放点盐～一～水 *put some salt in the chopped cabbage to draw out the water* Ⅱ 副（used after a verb）in the extreme；exceedingly：笑～人 *absolutely ridiculous；terribly funny* / 闷～人 *bored to death* / 气～ *hopping mad*
【杀虫剂】insecticide；pesticide
【杀虫药】insecticide；pesticide
【杀敌】fight the enemy；engage in battle：苦练～本领 *practise hard to master combat skills* / 英勇～ *be brave in battle；fight heroically*
【杀敌致果】（of a soldier）fight gallantly（or valiantly）and win glory on the battlefield
【杀风景】spoil the fun；be a wet blanket
【杀害】murder；kill；slaughter：千千万万的平民百姓在战争中惨遭～。*Thousands upon thousands of civilians were slaughtered during the wars.*
【杀回马枪】make a backward thrust at one's pursuer；give sb. a backward thrust；wheel around and hit back
【杀机】murderous intentions
【杀鸡取卵】kill the hen to get the eggs；kill the goose that lays the golden eggs
【杀鸡吓猴】（又作'杀鸡给猴看'）kill the chicken to frighten the monkey—punish someone as a

warning to others
【杀鸡焉用牛刀】why use an oxcleaver to kill a chicken; why break a butterfly on the wheel
【杀价】beat a seller down：这架收录机卖主要价250元，我～杀到200元。*The seller was asking 250 yuan for the tape recorder, but I beat him down to 200.*
【杀戒】prohibition against taking life (one of the ten Buddhist prohibitions)
【杀菌】destroy harmful microorganisms; disinfect; sterilize ◇ ～剂 germicide; bactericide; ～纸 antiseptic paper; bactericidal paper
【杀戮】massacre; slaughter：惨遭～ *be massacred in cold blood*
【杀卵剂】［农］ovicide
【杀掠】massacre and plunder
【杀螨剂】［农］acaricide; miticide
【杀灭】kill; wipe out; eliminate; exterminate; slay：～病源微生物 *eliminate disease-causing micro-organisms*
【杀气】❶ an aura of death; a murderous look：满面～ *with murder in one's face* ❷ vent one's spleen：你有委屈就说出来，不该拿别人～。*Get it off your chest if you feel you've been wronged. Don't take it out on others.*
【杀气腾腾】murderous-looking; ferocious
【杀青】finalize a manuscript
【杀人】❶［法］homicide ❷ kill a person ◇ ～犯 homicide; murderer or manslayer; ～狂 homicidal maniac
【杀人不见血】kill without spilling blood—kill by subtle means
【杀人不眨眼】kill without batting an eyelid; kill without blinking an eye：一伙满身鲜血的～的刽子手 *a gang of blood-stained executioners, who slaughter people without blinking*
【杀人放火】murder and arson：～，无恶不作 *commit murder, arson and every crime imaginable*
【杀人如麻】kill people like flies
【杀人越货】kill a person and seize his goods; rob and kill
【杀伤】kill and wound; inflict casualties on：这种炮弹～力很强。*This is a powerful antipersonnel shell.*
【杀伤弹】fragmentation bomb; antipersonnel bomb
【杀身成仁】die to achieve virtue—die for a just cause
【杀身之祸】fatal disaster：遭～ *meet with a fatal disaster*
【杀生】［宗］(佛教) take animal life
【杀手】killer
【杀鼠剂】rat poison; raticide
【杀头】behead; decapitate
【杀退】put to flight
【杀一儆百】execute one as a warning to a hundred
【杀婴】infanticide

沙 Ⅰ 名 ❶ sand; grit ❷ sth. resembling sand; sth. granular or powdery：豆沙 Ⅱ 形 (of voice) hoarse; husky
【沙坝】sandbar
【沙包】❶ sand dune ❷ sandbag
【沙暴】sandstorm
【沙蚕】clam worm
【沙场】battlefield; battleground：久经～ *be a seasoned soldier—be experienced*
【沙尘】dust and sand in the air：卡车驶过，扬起一片～。*The lorry raised a cloud of dust as it drove by.*
【沙船】a large junk
【沙袋】sandbag
【沙丁鱼】sardine
【沙俄】tsarist Russia; czarist Russia
【沙发】sofa; settee：单人～ *(upholstered) armchair* / 三人～ *three-seater settee* ◇ ～床 studio couch; sofa bed
【沙岗】sand hill
【沙锅】earthenware pot; casserole：～豆腐 *tofu (or bean curd) en casserole*
【沙果】［植］Chinese pear-leaved crabapple
【沙海】sea of sand; huge expanse of desert
【沙狐】corsac (fox)
【沙化】desertification
【沙荒】sandy wasteland; sandy waste
【沙皇】tsar; czar：～政府 *the tsarist government*
【沙鸡】sandgrouse
【沙金】placer gold; alluvial gold
【沙坑】❶ sandpit ❷［体］jumping pit
【沙拉】salad
【沙梨】［植］sand pear
【沙里淘金】wash grains of gold out of the sands—extract the essential from a large mass of material; get small returns for great effort
【沙砾】grit; gravel
【沙龙】salon：学术～ *academic salon* / 文学～ *literary salon*
【沙罗周期】［天］saros
【沙门氏菌】Salmonella
【沙漠】desert ◇ ～化 desert encroachment; desertification; desertization; ～气候 desert climate; ～植被 desert vegetation; desert cover
【沙盘】［军］sand table：～作业 *sand table exercise*
【沙丘】(sand) dune：流动～ *moving dunes*
【沙瓤】mushy watermelon pulp
【沙沙】rustle：风吹树叶～响。*The leaves rustled in the wind.*
【沙参】［中］the root of straight ladybell (Adenophora stricta)
【沙司】sauce
【沙滩】sand beach ◇ ～车 dune buggy; ～排球 beach volleyball; ～椅 beach chair
【沙特阿拉伯】Saudi Arabia ◇ ～人 Saudi Arabian
【沙文主义】chauvinism
【沙哑】hoarse; husky; raucous：声音～ *have a husky voice*
【沙眼】trachoma
【沙浴】❶ sand bath (of birds) ❷［医］sand bath

【沙枣】［植］narrow-leaved oleaster (Elaeagnus angustifolia)
【沙蚤】sand hopper
【沙洲】shoal；sandbank
【沙蠋】lugworm
【沙柱】dust devil；sand column
【沙锥】［动］snipe
【沙子】❶ sand；grit ❷ small grains；pellets：铁～ *iron pellets*；*shot*
【沙嘴】［地质］sandspit

纱 名 ❶ yarn：棉纱 ❷ gauze；sheer：铁纱
【纱包线】cotton-covered wire
【纱布】gauze
【纱厂】cotton mill
【纱橱】screen cupboard
【纱窗】screen window；screen
【纱灯】gauze lantern
【纱锭】［纺］spindle
【纱巾】gauze kerchief
【纱罗】［纺］gauze
【纱线】yarn
【纱罩】❶ gauze or screen covering (over food) ❷ mantle (of a lamp)

杉 名［植］China fir (limited to use in the following entry words) ——另见 shān
【杉篙】fir pole (used for building a scaffold or for punting a boat)
【杉木】fir wood

刹 动 put on the brakes；stop；check：把车～住 *stop (or brake) a car* / ～住歪风 *check an unhealthy tendency* ——另见 chà
【刹把】［机］brake crank
【刹车】❶ stop a vehicle by applying the brakes；put on the brakes ❷ stop a machine by cutting off the power；turn off a machine ❸ bring to a halt：未经批准的项目，必须立即～。*All projects started without permission must be stopped immediately*. ❹ the brakes

砂 名 sand；grit
【砂布】emery cloth；abrasive cloth：刚玉～ *corundum cloth*
【砂浆】mortar：石灰～ *lime mortar* / 水泥～ *cement mortar*
【砂礓】［地质］conglomerate
【砂矿】placer deposit；placer：～开采 *placer mining*；*alluvial mining*；*placering*
【砂轮】［机］emery wheel；grinding wheel；abrasive wheel ◇ ～机 grinder
【砂囊】gizzard (of birds)
【砂壤土】sandy loam
【砂糖】granulated sugar
【砂土】sandy soil；sand
【砂箱】［冶］sandbox；moulding box
【砂心】［冶］core
【砂型】［冶］sand mould ◇ ～铸造 sand casting
【砂岩】sandstone
【砂眼】［冶］sand holes；blowholes
【砂样】［油］drilling mud cuttings
【砂纸】abrasive paper；sand paper：玻璃～ *glass paper* / 金刚～ *emery paper*
【砂质岩】arenaceous rock

痧 名［中］acute diseases such as cholera and sunstroke
【痧子】〈方〉measles：出～ *have measles*

煞 动 ❶ stop；halt；check；bring to a close：～住脚 *stop short* / 文章写到这里还～不住。*The article can't very well end here*. ❷ tighten：～一～腰带 *tighten one's belt* ——另见 shà
【煞笔】❶ concluding lines of an article；ending of a piece of writing ❷ write the final line of an article, letter, etc.
【煞车】❶ firmly fasten a load (on a vehicle)；lash down ❷ 同〖刹车〗
【煞尾】❶ finish off；round off；wind up：事情不多了，马上就可以～。*There isn't much work left*；*we're winding up*. ❷ final stage；end；ending：这出戏的～很带劲。*The play has a powerful ending*.

鲨 名 shark
【鲨鱼】shark

shǎ

傻 形 ❶ stupid；muddleheaded：你真～，他这点意思都听不出来。*How stupid you were. You should have known what he was driving at*. / 吓～了 *be dumbfounded*；*be stunned* ❷ think or act mechanically：别一个劲儿～干，要讲究方法。*Don't just keep slogging away. Pay attention to method*.
【傻瓜】(又作'傻蛋') fool；blockhead；simpleton ◇ ～照相机 fully automatic camera
【傻呵呵】〈口〉simple-minded；silly；foolish：别看他～的，心里可有数。*Maybe he doesn't look very clever, but he knows what's what*.
【傻乎乎】〈口〉simple-minded；silly；foolish：小孩子抿了抿嘴唇，～地笑了。*The child puckered up her lips and began to smile innocently*.
【傻话】stupid talk；foolish words；nonsense
【傻劲儿】〈口〉❶ stupidity；foolishness ❷ sheer enthusiasm；doggedness：不能光靠～，得找窍门。*Enthusiasm alone won't do. You've got to work skilfully*. / 这小伙子干活有股～。*That youngster works with a will*.
【傻乐】〈方〉laugh foolishly；giggle；smirk
【傻里瓜唧】〈方〉foolish；stupid
【傻冒儿】〈口〉〈诙〉❶ fool；blockhead；idiot ❷ foolish；stupid
【傻气】〈诙〉foolish；stupid
【傻头傻脑】❶ foolish-looking ❷ muddleheaded
【傻小子】〈诙〉silly lad
【傻笑】laugh foolishly；giggle；smirk

【傻眼】〈口〉be dumbfounded；be stunned：他一看考题就～了。*When he saw the examination questions he got a nasty shock.*

【傻样】〈口〉foolish look：看你这～，还不快过来和大家打招呼。*Don't stand there looking so foolish. Come over and say hello to everybody.*

【傻子】fool；blockhead；simpleton

shà

厦 名 a tall building；mansion：高楼大厦

歃 动〈书〉suck

【歃血】smear the blood of a sacrifice on the mouth—an ancient form of swearing an oath

【歃血为盟】swear an oath of alliance by smearing the mouth with the blood of a sacrifice

煞 Ⅰ名 evil spirit；goblin Ⅱ副（used before a verb or adjective）very ——另见 shā

【煞白】ghastly pale；deathly pale；pallid：脸色～ *look deathly pale*

【煞费苦心】cudgel one's brains；take great pains：～地寻找借口 *cudgel one's brains to find an excuse* / 他们为了攻克技术难关，可真是～。*They took great pains to solve the technical problems.*

【煞神】demon；fiend

【煞有介事】make a show of being in earnest；pretend to be serious（about doing sth.）

霎 名 a very short time；moment；instant

【霎时间】（又作'霎时'）in a twinkling；in a split second；in a jiffy

【霎眼】in a moment；in a twinkling

shāi

筛 Ⅰ名 sieve；sifter；screen Ⅱ动 sift；sieve；screen；riddle：～面 *sieve flour*；*sift flour* / ～煤 *screen coal* / ～砂砾 *riddle gravel* / ～煤渣 *sift cinders*

【筛法】［数］sieve method

【筛分】screening；sieving：～机 *screening machine*

【筛管】［植］sieve tube

【筛号】screen size；screen mesh；mesh number

【筛糠】〈口〉shiver：吓得直～ *shiver with fear*；*shake in one's shoes*

【筛洗】dress and wash（coal，etc.）

【筛选】❶ 同〖筛分〗❷ select

【筛子】a sieve；sifter；screen：粗～ *riddle*

shǎi

色 名〈口〉colour：这布掉～吗？*Will this cloth fade?* ——另见 sè

【色子】dice：掷～ *play dice*；*throw dice*

shài

晒 动 ❶（of the sun）shine upon：日～雨淋 *be exposed to the sun and rain* / 这里～得慌。*There's too much sun here.* ❷ dry in the sun；bask：～粮食 *dry grain in the sun* / ～被子 *air a quilt* / 他的脸～黑了。*His face is tanned.* / 放在太阳底下～～。*Leave it to dry in the sun.*

【晒场】sunning ground（for drying grain，etc.）

【晒垡】［农］sun the earth which has been ploughed up；sun the upturned soil

【晒台】flat roof（for drying clothes，etc.）

【晒太阳】sunbathe；bask in the sun：让孩子们尽量多～。*Take the children out to get as much sun as possible.*

【晒图】make a blueprint；blueprint ◇ ～员 blueprinter；～纸 blueprint paper

【晒像框】printing frame

【晒烟】sun-cured tobacco

【晒盐】evaporate brine in the sun to make salt

shān

山 名 ❶ hill；mountain：一座高～ *a high mountain* ❷ anything resembling a mountain：冰山 ❸ a bunch of straw in which silkworms spin cocoons：蚕上～了。*The silkworms have gone into the straw bundles to spin their cocoons.* ❹ gable

【山坳】col

【山包】〈方〉a small hill

【山崩】landslide；landslip

【山崩地裂】mountains collapsing and the earth cracking up（said of a cataclysm or of deafening noises）

【山苍子】［中］the fruit of a cubeb litsea tree（Litsea cubeba）

【山茶】［植］camellia

【山产】mountain products（mainly with economic value such as medicinal materials，wild fruits and nuts，furs，etc.）

【山城】mountain city：～重庆 *the mountain city Chongqing*

【山重水复】mountains multiply and streams double back：～疑无路，柳暗花明又一村。*Mountains multiply，streams double back—I doubt there's even a road；Willows cluster darkly，blossoms shine—another village ahead!*

【山川】mountains and rivers—land；landscape

【山鹑】partridge

【山慈姑】［植］edible tulip

【山村】mountain village

【山丹】［植］morningstar lily（Lilium concolor）

【山道年】［药］santonin

【山地】❶ mountainous region；hilly area；hilly country ❷ hillside field ◇ ～车 mountain bike

【山顶】the summit (or top) of a mountain; hilltop
【山顶洞人】Upper Cave Man
【山东梆子】Shandong clapper opera
【山东快书】Shandong clapper ballad
【山洞】cave; cavern
【山豆根】[植] subprostrate sophora (Sophora subprostrata)
【山风】[气] mountain breeze
【山峰】mountain peak
【山旮旯儿】〈方〉a faraway hilly area; an out-of-the-way place in the mountains; a remote mountain area
【山冈】low hill; hillock
【山高水长】(of nobility of character) as high as the hills and as long as the rivers—of lasting influence
【山高水低】unexpected misfortune; sth. unfortunate, esp. death: 万一有个~ *in the event of sb.'s death*
【山高水远】❶ the mountains are high and the rivers far away—a long distance ❷ 同〖山高水低〗
【山歌】folk song (sung in the fields or in mountain areas during or after work)
【山根】the foot of a hill
【山梗菜硷】[药] lobeline
【山沟】❶ gully ❷ ravine; (mountain) valley ❸ a remote mountain area
【山谷】mountain valley; ravine
【山国】a mountainous country; a hilly region
【山河】mountains and rivers—the land of a country: 祖国的锦绣~ *our beautiful land*
【山核桃】❶ hickory ❷ hickory nut
【山洪】mountain torrents: ~暴发。*Torrents of water rushed down the mountain.*
【山回路转】同〖峰回路转〗
【山火】mountain fire
【山货】❶ mountain products (such as haws, chestnuts and walnuts) ❷ household utensils made of wood, bamboo, clay, etc.
【山鸡】〈方〉pheasant
【山鸡椒】[植] cubeb litsea tree (Litsea cubeba)
【山脊】ridge (of a mountain or hill)
【山涧】mountain stream
【山椒鸟】minivet
【山脚】the foot of a hill
【山口】mountain pass; pass
【山里红】[植] large-fruited Chinese hawthorn
【山梁】ridge (of a mountain or hill)
【山林】mountain forest; wooded mountain: ~地区 *mountain and forest region*; *wooded and hilly lands*
【山陵】〈书〉❶ hills ❷ tombs of emperors
【山岭】a chain of mountains
【山路】mountain path: ~崎岖不平。*The mountain path is rough and rugged.*
【山麓】the foot of a mountain; piedmont: ~丘陵 *foothills*
【山峦】a chain of mountains; a multipeaked mountain: ~起伏 *undulating hills*; *rolling hills*
【山脉】mountain range; mountain chain
【山猫】leopard cat
【山毛榉】[植] beech
【山门】❶ the gate of a Buddhist temple ❷ Buddhism
【山盟海誓】同〖海誓山盟〗
【山民】mountain people; hillmen
【山姆大叔】Uncle Sam
【山奈】(又作'山萘')[化] cyanide
【山南海北】❶ south of the mountains and north of the seas—far away; far and wide: ~他哪儿都到过。*He has travelled far and wide.* ❷ discursive; rambling: 他们~地扯了一阵。*They talked about everything under the sun.*
【山炮】mountain gun; mountain artillery
【山坡】hillside; mountain slope; hillslope
【山墙】gable
【山清水秀】(又作'山明水秀') green hills and clear waters—picturesque scenery
【山穷水尽】where the hills and streams end—at the end of one's rope (or tether, resources)
【山区】mountain area
【山泉】mountain spring
【山雀】tit
【山人】recluse; hermit (formerly often used by scholar-officials as a form of self-address)
【山水】❶ water from a mountain: 一股~汩汩而下。*A stream gurgles down the mountain.* ❷ mountains and rivers; scenery with hills and waters: 桂林~甲天下。*The scenery of Guilin is the best under heaven.* ❸ traditional Chinese painting of mountains and waters; landscape painting; landscape
【山水画】mountains-and-waters painting; landscape painting; landscape
【山水相连】be linked by common mountains and rivers: 两国~。*The two countries are joined by common mountains and rivers.*
【山桃】mountain peach
【山田】hillside plot
【山桐子】[植] idesia
【山头】❶ hilltop; mountain top ❷ mountain stronghold; faction: 拉山头 ❸ gable
【山头主义】mountain-stronghold mentality (a type of sectarianism)
【山外有山】there's always a mountain beyond a mountain—there's always something better; nothing can be perfect
【山窝】(又作'山窝窝') an out-of-the-way mountain area
【山西梆子】Shanxi clapper opera (another name for 晋剧)
【山系】[地质] mountain system
【山险】difficult mountain terrain
【山乡】mountain village; mountain area
【山响】deafening; thunderous: 鼓擂得~ *drums beating thunderously* / 北风刮得门窗乒乒乓乓~。*The doors and windows are rattling noisily in the north wind.*

【山魈】❶［动］mandrill（Mandrillus sphinx）❷ mountain elf
【山鸦】chough
【山崖】cliff
【山羊】❶ goat ❷［体］buck ◇ ～胡子 goatee；～绒 cashmere
【山腰】halfway up the mountain
【山肴野蔌】mountain meats and wild vegetables
【山摇地动】同〖地动山摇〗
【山药】［植］Chinese yam
【山雨欲来风满楼】the wind sweeping through the tower heralds a rising storm in the mountains; the rising wind forebodes the coming storm
【山峪】mountain valley
【山芋】〈方〉sweet potato
【山鹬】woodcock
【山岳】lofty mountains：～地区 *mountainous region* ◇ ～冰川 mountain glacier；alpine glacier
【山楂】（又作'山查'）❶（Chinese）hawthorn ❷ haw：～酱 *haw jelly* ◇ ～糕（又作'山查糕'）haw jelly cake
【山寨】mountain fastness；a fortified mountain village
【山珍海味】（又作'山珍海错'）delicacies from land and sea；dainties of every kind
【山中无老虎，猴子称大王】when the tiger is away from the mountain，the monkey proclaims himself king
【山茱萸】［中］the fruit of medicinal cornel（Cornus officinalis）
【山庄】❶ mountain villa ❷ mountain village
【山子】（又作'山子石儿'）〈方〉rockery
【山嘴】［地质］spur

芟

名 ❶ mow（grass）❷ weed out；eliminate

【芟除】❶ mow；cut down：～杂草 *weeding* ❷ delete：～繁冗的词句 *delete the unnecessary words and sentences*

杉

名［植］China fir ——另见 shā

删

动 delete；leave out：这一段可以～去。*This paragraph can be left out.* / ～掉不必要的细节 *cut out the unnecessary details*

【删除】delete；strike（or cut，cross）out
【删繁就简】simplify sth. by cutting out the superfluous
【删改】delete and change；revise：稿子几经～才定下来。*The draft was revised several times before it was finalized.*
【删节】abridge；abbreviate：本报略有～ *slightly abridged by our editorial staff* ◇ ～本 abridged edition；abbreviated version；～号 ellipsis；suspension points；ellipsis dots（……）（...）
【删略】leave out；omit
【删削】delete；cut out；strike out

衫

名 unlined upper garment：衬衫

姗

（构词成分）见下

【姗姗】walk slowly like a woman ◇ ～来迟 be slow in coming；be late

钐

名［化］samarium（Sm）

珊

（构词成分）见下

【珊瑚】coral ◇ ～虫 coral polyp；coral insect；～岛 coral island；～礁 coral reef

栅

（构词成分）见下——另见 zhà

【栅极】［电子］grid：抑制～ *suppressor grid*

舢

（构词成分）见下

【舢板】（又作'舢舨'）sampan

扇

动 ❶ fan：～火 *fan a fire* / ～扇子 *fan oneself*；*use a fan* ❷ slap（sb. on the face）：～他一耳光 *slap him on the face* ——另见 shàn

【扇动】flap：～翅膀 *flap the wings*
【扇风耳】protruding ears；flappy ears
【扇风机】ventilating fan
【扇阴风，点鬼火】fan the winds of evil and spread the fires of turmoil—foment trouble

煽

动 ❶ fan（a fire）：把炉火～旺点儿 *fan the fire to make it burn brighter* ❷ incite；instigate；stir up：煽惑

【煽动】instigate；incite；stir up；whip up：～暴乱 *incite rebellion* / ～派性 *whip up factionalism* / ～群众闹事 *stir up trouble among the masses*
【煽风点火】fan the flames；in flame and agitate people；stir up trouble
【煽惑】incite；agitate：～人心 *agitate people by demagogy*
【煽情】incite（or stir up）emotions

潸

形〈文〉in tears；tearful

【潸然】〈文〉in tears；tearful：～泪下 *tears trickling down one's cheeks*
【潸潸】〈文〉in tears；tearful：不禁～ *can't keep back one's tears* / 热泪～ *tears streaming down one's cheeks*

膻

名 the smell of mutton：这羊肉不～。*This mutton hasn't got a strong smell.*

shǎn

闪

Ⅰ 动 ❶ dodge；get out of the way：他要打我，我一～，他没打着。*He wanted to hit me，but I dodged and he missed.* ❷ twist；sprain：～了腰 *sprain one's back* ❸ flash；sparkle；shine：远处灯光一～。*There was a flash of light in the distance.* / 灯一～就灭了。*The light flashed and then went out.* / ～金光 *emit golden rays* / 这时我脑子里～过一个念头。*At this moment an idea flashed through my mind.* ❹〈方〉leave behind：你去的时候叫我一声，可别把我～下。*Please call for me when you go；don't leave me behind.* Ⅱ 名 lightning：打闪

【闪爆弹】flash-band；stun grenade
【闪避】dodge；sidestep：～不及 *too late to dodge*
【闪长岩】diorite
【闪挫】［中］sudden strain or contusion of a muscle；sprain
【闪点】［化］flash point
【闪电】lightning ◇ ～战 lightning war；blitzkrieg；blitz
【闪动】flash；twinkle；flicker：灯光～。*Lights flashed.* / 夜空中群星～。*Stars twinkled in the night sky.* / 墙上有个人影在～。*The shadow of a person was flickering on the wall.*
【闪躲】dodge；evade
【闪光】❶ a flash of light：流星像一道～，划破黑夜的长空。*With a flash，the meteor shot across the night sky.* ❷ gleam；glisten；glitter：露珠在晨曦中～。*Dewdrops glistened in the morning light.*
【闪光灯】❶［摄］flash lamp；flashlight；photo flash ❷ flashlight（used for signals）
【闪光同步】［摄］flash synchronization
【闪击】launch（or make）a surprise attack ◇ ～战 lightning war；blitzkrieg；blitz
【闪开】get out of the way；jump aside；dodge：车来了，快～！*Look out！There's a bus coming.*
【闪亮】sparkling；glittering；glistening：她说话的时候，眼眶里含着～的泪珠。*As she spoke，her eyes glistened with tears.*
【闪米特人】Semite
【闪念】an idea which flashes through one's mind
【闪闪】sparkling；glistening；glittering：～的红星 *a sparkling red star* / 天空中电光～。*Lightning flashed in the sky.*
【闪射】glitter；shine；radiate：向四周～光芒 *radiate rays of light in all directions*
【闪身】❶ dodge：侦察兵一～机警地躲过了敌人的探照灯。*The scout dodged nimbly and evaded the enemy's searchlight.* ❷ move sideways：～进门 *walk sideways through the door*
【闪失】mishap；accident：要是有个～，怎么办呢？*What if anything should go wrong?*
【闪石】amphibole
【闪烁】❶ twinkle；glimmer；glisten：她的眼睛里～着喜悦的泪花。*Her eyes glistened with tears of joy.* ❷ evasive；vague；noncommittal：他闪闪烁烁，不做肯定的答复。*He hummed and hawed，giving no definite reply.* or *He was evasive and noncommittal.*
【闪烁计数器】scintillation counter
【闪烁其词】speak evasively；hedge
【闪现】flash before one：英雄的形象～在我的眼前。*The image of the hero flashed before my eyes.*
【闪锌矿】（zinc）blende；sphalerite
【闪眼】〈方〉dazzling：～的阳光 *the dazzling sunlight*
【闪耀】glitter；shine；radiate：繁星～ *glittering stars* / 他两眼～着刚毅的光芒。*His eyes flashed with resolution.*
【闪熠】〈书〉glitter；shine；radiate：灯火～ *lights glittering*
【闪音】［语音］flap
【闪语族】the Semitic group（including Arabic，Hebrew，etc.）
【闪蒸】［油］flash vaporization：～塔 *flash tower*
【闪灼】glitter；shine；radiate：灯烛～ *lamps and candles shining brightly*

睒 动 blink；twinkle：这孩子一～眼就不见了。*The boy vanished in the twinkling of an eye.*

shàn

讪 Ⅰ 动 mock；ridicule Ⅱ 形 embarrassed；awkward；shamefaced：脸上发～ *look embarrassed*
【讪谤】〈书〉slander；malign；calumniate
【讪讪】embarrassed；awkward；shamefaced：他觉得没趣，只好～地走开了。*Feeling he was not wanted，he walked away looking embarrassed.*
【讪笑】ridicule；mock；deride

疝 名 hernia：腹股沟～ *inguinal hernia* / 脐～ *umbilical hernia*
【疝带】［医］truss
【疝气】hernia

苫 动 cover with a straw mat，tarpaulin，etc.：要下雨了，快把麦子～上。*Quick！Cover up the wheat. It's going to rain.*
【苫布】tarpaulin
【苫席】mat cover

扇 Ⅰ 名 ❶ fan：电扇 ❷ a sliding，hinged or detachable flat part；leaf：八～屏风 *an eight-leaf screen* Ⅱ 量 for doors，windows，etc.：一～门 *a door* / 两～窗子 *two windows* ——另见 shān
【扇贝】［动］scallop；fan shell
【扇车】winnowing machine；winnower
【扇骨子】the ribs（or mount）of a folding fan
【扇面儿】the covering of a fan
【扇形】❶ fan-shaped：队伍到达开阔地便成～摆开阵势。*The troops fanned out as they reached open ground.* ❷［数］sector ◇ ～齿轮 sector（or segment）gear
【扇坠】fan pendants
【扇子】fan：一把～ *a fan* / 扇（shān）～ *fan oneself；use a fan*

善 Ⅰ 形 ❶ good；virtuous：心怀不～ *harbour ill intent（or evil intentions）* ❷ satisfactory；good：～策 *a wise policy；the best policy* ❸ make a success of；perfect：善始善终 ❹ kind；friendly：相～ *be kind and helpful to each other* Ⅱ 动 ❶ be good at；be expert（or adept）in：不～经营 *not good at management* / ～观风色 *quick to see which way the wind blows—very shrewd* ❷ be apt to：善变 Ⅲ 副 well：善为说辞
【善罢甘休】（usu. used in the negative）leave the

matter at that; let it go at that: 敌人这一仗打败了,但决不会～的。*The enemy will not take their defeat lying down*.

【善本】reliable text; good edition: ～书 *rare book*

【善变】be apt to change; be changeable

【善处】〈书〉deal discreetly with; conduct oneself well

【善待】treat sb. well

【善感】(of a person) sensitive

【善果】good fruit—the rewards of good deeds: 行善事,结～。*Good deeds bear good fruit*.

【善后】deal with problems arising from an accident, etc.: 处理火灾的～问题 *deal with the aftermath of the fire*

【善举】〈书〉a philanthropic act or project

【善类】〈书〉(usu. used in the negative) good people: 此人行迹诡秘,定非～。*Secretive as he is, he cannot possibly be a good man*.

【善良】good and honest; kind-hearted: ～的人们 *good and honest people*; *people of goodwill* / 心地～ *kind-hearted*

【善邻】〈书〉be a good neighbour: ～政策 *good-neighbour policy*

【善男信女】Buddhist devotees

【善人】philanthropist; charitable person; welldoer

【善始善终】start well and end well; do well from start to finish; see sth. through

【善事】charitable deeds; good deeds

【善忘】be forgetful; have a short memory

【善为说辞】put in a good word for sb.

【善心】mercy; benevolence: 发～ *show kindness*

【善意】❶ goodwill; good intentions: 出于～ *out of goodwill*; *with the best intentions* / ～的批评 *well-meaning criticism* ❷［经］bona fide ◇ ～第三者 bona fide third party; ～合约 bona fide contract; ～买方 bona fide purchaser; ～原告 bona fide claimant; ～执票人 bona fide holders

【善有善报,恶有恶报】Good is rewarded with good, and evil with evil.

【善于】be good at; be adept in: ～应对 *be good at repartee* / ～交际 *be good at socializing*

【善战】be good at fighting; be skilful in battle

【善终】❶ die a natural death; die in one's bed ❷ end well

【善自保重】take good care of oneself

【善自为谋】know how to look after oneself

禅

动 abdicate ——另见 chán

【禅让】abdicate and hand over the crown to another person

【禅位】abdicate the throne

骟

动 castrate (an animal); geld (a male animal) or spay (a female animal): ～马 *castrate a horse or a castrated horse*

缮

动 ❶ repair; mend: 修缮 ❷ copy; write out: ～清 *make a fair copy*

【缮写】write out; copy

擅

动 ❶ arrogate to oneself; do sth. on one's own authority: ～作主张 *make a decision without authorization* ❷ be good at; be expert in: 不～辞令 *lack facility in polite or tactful speech*

【擅长】be good at; be expert in; be skilled in: ～歌舞 *be good at singing and dancing*

【擅离职守】leave one's post without permission

【擅自】do sth. without authorization: 任何一方不得～修改合同。*Neither party may unilaterally modify the contract*. / ～行动 *act presumptuously*

膳

名 meals; board: 在食堂用～ *have one's meals at the mess*

【膳费】board expenses

【膳食】meals; food: 流质～ *liquid diet* / 半流质～ *semiliquid diet*

【膳宿】board and lodging: ～自理 *be responsible for one's own board and lodging*

嬗

动〈书〉transmute; transform

【嬗变】❶〈书〉evolution ❷［物］transmutation: 自然～ *natural transmutation* / 感生～ *induced transmutation*

赡

Ⅰ 动 support; provide for: ～家养口 *support a family* Ⅱ 形〈书〉sufficient; abundant: 力不～ *beyond one's strength*

【赡养】support; provide for: ～父母 *support one's parents* ◇ ～费 payment for support of one's parents

鳝

名 eel; finless eel

shāng

伤

Ⅰ 名 wound; injury: 刀～ *a knife wound* / 浑身是～ *be covered with cuts and bruises* / ～好了。*The wound has healed*. Ⅱ 动 ❶ injure; hurt: 被汽车撞～ *be knocked down and injured by a car* / 摔～ *fall and hurt oneself* ❷ be distressed: 伤怀 ❸ get sick of sth.; develop an aversion to sth.: 这孩子吃糖吃～了。*The child has got sick of eating sweets*. ❹ be harmful to; hinder: 有～国体 *discredit one's country* / 无～大体 *not matter much*

【伤疤】scar

【伤悲】sad; sorrowful

【伤兵】wounded soldier

【伤病员】the sick and wounded; noneffectives

【伤残】wounded and disabled

【伤残人】disabled person; handicapped: ～奥运会 *Special Olympics* (*for the handicapped*)

【伤风】catch cold; have a cold

【伤风败俗】offend public decency; corrupt public morals

【伤感】sick at heart; sentimental

【伤害】injure; harm; hurt: 不要～益鸟。*Don't*

harm beneficial birds. / ～自尊心 *injure* (*or hurt*) *one's pride*; *hurt one's self-respect*

【伤寒】❶［医］typhoid fever; typhoid ❷［中］diseases caused by harmful cold factors; febrile diseases; fevers

【伤耗】damage: 这筐苹果刨去～还有四十斤。*There are still forty jin of apples in this basket after taking out the damaged ones*.

【伤痕】scar; bruise

【伤痕文学】trauma literature

【伤怀】〈书〉sad; grieved; broken-hearted

【伤筋动骨】be injured in the tendons or bones: 他虽然浑身青肿，但并未～。*Although badly bruised all over, he had broken no bones*.

【伤科】［中］(department of) traumatology

【伤口】wound; cut: 洗～ *bathe a wound*

【伤脑筋】knotty; troublesome; bothersome: ～的问题 *a knotty problem*; *a headache* / 老下雨，真～。*It's a nuisance the way it keeps on raining*.

【伤气】❶〈方〉feel frustrated; feel disheartened ❷［中］sap one's vitality

【伤情】❶ the condition of an injury or wound ❷ sick at heart; sentimental; sad; sorrowful: 听了这话，他有点～。*When he heard this, he felt rather sad*. ❸ hurt sb.'s feelings: 这会～的。*This will be very hurtful*.

【伤人】❶ hurt sb.'s feelings ❷ inflict injuries ❸ injure the health: 忧能～。*Anxiety can wear you out*.

【伤神】❶ overtax one's nerves; be nerve-racking ❷ sad; grieved

【伤生】be injurious to life

【伤食】［中］dyspepsia caused by excessive eating or improper diet

【伤势】the condition of an injury or wound: ～很重 *be seriously injured or wounded*

【伤天害理】offend against Heaven and reason—atrocious; outrageous

【伤痛】❶ grieved; distressed ❷ the pain of an injury or wound

【伤亡】injuries and deaths; casualties: ～惨重 *suffer heavy casualties* / ～人数 *the number of casualties*

【伤亡报告】［军］returns of losses

【伤心】sad; grieved; broken-hearted: 伤透了心 *feel extremely heartbroken* / ～落泪 *shed sad tears*; *weep in grief*

【伤心惨目】too ghastly to look at; tragic (scene)

【伤心事】a heartbreaking affair; a painful memory; an old sore

【伤员】(usu. used among army personnel) wounded personnel; the wounded

商 Ⅰ 动 discuss; consult: 共～大计 *discuss matters of vital importance* Ⅱ 名 ❶ trade; commerce; business: 经商 ❷ merchant; trader; businessman; dealer: 盐～ *salt dealer* ❸［数］quotient

【商标】trademark ◇ ～法 trademark law; ～权 trademark rights; ～注册 trademark registration

【商埠】〈旧〉commercial (or trading) port

【商场】market; bazaar; department store

【商船】merchant ship; merchantman ◇ ～队 mercantile marine; merchant marine

【商店】shop; store

【商调】(of one organization) negotiate with another organization for the transfer of one of its cadres ◇ ～函 letter for negotiated transfer

【商定】decide through consultation; agree: 经～ *it has been decided through consultation that* / 已～的条款 *the provisions already agreed upon*

【商队】a company of travelling merchants; trade caravan

【商法】［法］commercial law

【商贩】small retailer; pedlar

【商港】commercial port

【商贾】〈书〉merchant

【商行】trading company; commercial firm

【商号】shop; store; business establishment

【商会】chamber of commerce

【商机】business opportunity

【商计】have discussions or consultations: 决定再作～ *decide to have further discussions*

【商检】(〈略〉全称为'商品检验') commodity inspection: ～局 *bureau of commodity inspection*

【商借】negotiate to borrow: ～7万元资金发展旅游业 *negotiate to borrow 70,000 yuan for developing tourism*

【商界】business circles; commercial circles

【商量】consult; discuss; talk over: 这事可以～着办。*That can be settled through discussion*. / 咱们得找主任～一下。*We ought to talk it over with the director*.

【商路】trade route

【商旅】travelling merchants

【商贸】commerce; trade: ～企业 *commercial company*; *trading company*

【商棚】peddler's stall; makeshift stall for selling goods

【商品】commodity; goods; merchandise ◇ ～拜物教 commodity fetishism; ～包装 commodity package; ～菜 market vegetables; (U.S.) truck vegetables; ～房 commercial housing; ～化 commercialization; ～交易会 trade fair; commodities fair; ～经济 commodity economy; ～粮 commodity grain; marketable grain; ～流通 commodity circulation; ～生产 commodity production; ～推销员 commercial travelers (CT); ～销售市场 outlet for goods; ～住宅 commercial residential building

【商洽】arrange with sb.; take up (a matter) with sb.

【商情】market conditions: ～预测 *business forecasting* ◇ ～晴雨表 business barometer

【商榷】discuss; deliberate: 这一点值得～。*This point is open to question*. / 提出几点意见，与诸位～。*Here are a few points I wish to discuss with you*.

【商人】businessman；merchant；trader
【商厦】department store；emporium
【商社】business organization
【商事法院】commercial court
【商数】［数］quotient
【商谈】exchange views；confer；discuss；negotiate：～递交国书事宜 *discuss matters relating to the presentation of credentials*
【商讨】discuss；deliberate over：就发展两国关系进行有益的～ *hold useful discussions on developing relations between the two countries*
【商亭】kiosk；stall
【商务】commercial affairs；business affairs ◇ ～参赞 commercial counsellor；～代表 commercial representative；trade representative；～旅行 business travel；～秘书 commercial secretary；～套房 service apartment；～卫星 commercial satellite；～专员 commercial attaché
【商务午餐】business lunch
【商务中心】business centre
【商业】commerce；trade；business ◇ ～城 commercial city；～广告 commercial advertising；～交易法 law of commercial transactions；～街 shopping street；～区 business quarter；commercial district；business district；～网 commercial network；network of trading establishments；～心理学 business psychology；～信贷 commercial credit；～银行 commercial bank；～中心 commercial centre；trading centre；shopping centre；～周期 business cycle；～资本 commercial capital；merchant capital
【商议】confer；discuss
【商用】commercial use：这项新技术目前只有少数国家实现～。*This new technology is commercially available in only a few countries.* ◇ ～计算机 business computer
【商誉】［经］goodwill；commercial standing；business reputation：保持和提高已建立的～ *maintain and improve an established business reputation*
【商约】commercial treaty
【商载】commercial transport（of passengers，cargo，etc）：这种飞机最大～为4.7吨。*The maximum capacity of this aircraft is 4.7 tons.*
【商展】commodity exhibition；commodity display；commodity show
【商战】❶ trade war ❷〈喻〉business competition
【商酌】discuss and consider；deliberate over：这个问题尚待～。*This matter needs further discussion and consideration.*

墒 名［农］moisture in the soil：抢～ *lose no time in sowing while there is sufficient moisture in the soil*
【墒情】soil moisture content
【墒土】newly-tilled moist soil：保住～ *preserve the moisture in the soil*

熵 名［物］entropy

shǎng

晌 名 ❶ part of the day：前半～ *morning* / 晚半～ *dusk* ❷〈方〉noon：歇～ *take a midday nap*（*or rest*）
【晌饭】〈方〉❶ midday meal；lunch ❷ extra meal in the daytime during the busy farming season
【晌觉】〈方〉afternoon nap
【晌午】midday；noon：～饭 *midday meal*；*lunch* / ～觉 *afternoon nap*

赏 Ⅰ 动 ❶ grant（or bestow）a reward；award：国王～给那个士兵一匹马。*The king awarded the soldier a horse.* ❷ view and admire；delight in viewing；feast one's eyes on：赏月 ❸ recognize；appreciate：赞赏 Ⅱ 名 reward；award：领～ *receive an award*
【赏赐】❶ grant（or bestow）a reward；award：～他很多钱 *give him a lot of money as a reward* ❷ a reward；an award：得到许多～ *be given a handsome reward*
【赏罚】rewards and punishments：有赏有罚 *duly mete out rewards and punishments*
【赏罚分明】be fair in meting out rewards and punishments；be discriminating in one's rewards and punishments
【赏罚严明】be strict and fair in meting out rewards and punishments
【赏光】〈套〉used when requesting sb. to accept an invitation：务请～。*We request the pleasure of your company.*
【赏鉴】appreciate and evaluate（a work of art）：～名画 *appreciate and evaluate a famous painting*
【赏金】money reward；pecuniary reward
【赏脸】〈套〉honour me with your presence：我想请你跟你夫人明天吃晚饭，你肯不肯～？*I'd like to invite you and your wife to dinner tomorrow. May I have the honour?*
【赏钱】tips
【赏识】recognize the worth of；appreciate：主编很～他这篇文章。*The editor in chief thinks highly of this article of his.* / 这个奴才深得其主子的～。*That flunkey was in his master's good graces.*
【赏玩】admire the beauty of sth.；delight in；enjoy；fondle：～山景 *enjoy mountain scenery* / ～古董 *fondle antiques*
【赏析】appreciate and analyze；study carefully：茅盾的这篇文章值得～。*This article of Mao Dun's merits careful study.*
【赏心乐事】happy moods and pleasurable things
【赏心悦目】find the scenery pleasing to both the eye and the mind
【赏雪】enjoy a beautiful snow scene
【赏月】enjoy a beautiful full moon

shàng

上 Ⅰ〈形〉❶ (used before a noun) upper (in position or quality); higher; better; superior: ～半截 *the upper half* / 在书架的最～一层放着 *lie on the top shelf* / 中～水平 *above the average; better than the average* ❷ most recent; last; former: ～次 *last time* / ～星期四 *last Thursday* / ～个世纪 *the last century* / ～一季度 *the previous quarter* / ～两批 *the last two groups* ❸ first (of sth. divided into two or three parts): ～半学期 *the first half of the term* / 二十世纪～半叶 *the first half of the 20th century* / ～一段 *the preceding (or above, foregoing) paragraph* Ⅱ〈动〉❶ come or go up; ascend: ～山 *go or climb up a mountain* / ～楼 *go or come upstairs; ascend the stairs* / 溯流而～ *sail or go upstream* ❷ get on (a conveyance); mount; board: ～公共汽车 *get on a bus* / ～飞机 *board a plane* / ～船 *go aboard a ship; go on board* ❸ go to; leave for: 你～哪儿? *Where are you going?* / 我明天～南京。*I'm leaving for Nanjing tomorrow.* / 我～卫生室。*I'm going to the clinic.* ❹ forge ahead; go ahead: 快～,投篮! *Go ahead. Quick! Shoot!* / 见困难就～ *advance where there are difficulties to overcome* ❺ (used in stage directions) appear on the stage; enter: 二战士左～。*Enter left two soldiers.* ❻ [体] enter the court or field: 换人! 三号下,四号～。*Substitution: Player No. 4 for No. 3.* / 这一盘你～。*You play this game.* ❼ fill; supply; serve: 上水 / 上菜 ❽ place sth. in position; fix: ～刀具 *fix a cutting tool* / 步枪都～了刺刀。*All the rifles have bayonets fixed on them.* / 我正在～螺丝呢。*I'm fixing the screws in place.* ❾ apply; paint; smear: ～药膏 *apply ointment* / 给门窗～漆 *paint the door and windows* / 给机器～油 *oil (or grease) the machine* ❿ be put on record; be carried (in a publication): 小王的先进事迹都～了电视了。*Xiao Wang's model deeds have been reported on TV.* ⓫ wind; screw; tighten: 表该～了。*The watch needs winding.* / 螺丝没有～紧。*The screw hasn't been tightened.* ⓬ be engaged (in work, study, etc.) at a fixed time: 我今天～中班。*I'm on the middle shift today.* / 她～大学了。*She's now in college.* / 明天的语文课还～不～? *Shall we have our Chinese lessons tomorrow or not?* ⓭ up: 跑～楼 *run upstairs* / 登～山顶 *reach the summit* / 爬～河堤 *climb up to the top of the dyke* / 飞～蓝天 *soar into the sky* / 踏～非洲的土地 *set foot on African soil* ⓮ (indicating the attainment of an objective): 锁～门 *lock the door; lock up* / 买～电视机了 *have bought a TV* / 她当～会计了。*She's become an accountant.* / 还没吃～饭呢。*I haven't eaten yet.* / 你跟他接～头了吗? *Have you got in touch with him?* ⓯ (indicating that an action has started): 她爱～了我。*She's fallen in love with me.* / 他俩已聊～天了。*The two of them are having a good chat.* ⓰ (indicating an amount, value or extent reached or to be reached): 我们没说～几句话车就开了。*We had barely enough time to exchange a few words before the train started.* ⓱ up to; as many as: ～百辆小汽车 *up to a hundred cars* / 出席人数已～万。*There are as many as ten thousand present.* or *There is an attendance of 10,000 or so.* Ⅲ〈介〉❶ on: 脸～ *on one's face* / 山顶～ *at the mountaintop* / 墙～ *on the wall* ❷ within (a certain area): 世界～ *in the world* / 课堂～ *in class* / 报纸～ *in the newspapers* / 会～ *at the meeting* ❸ in (some aspect): 事实～ *in fact* / 历史～ *in history* / 理论～ *in theory; theoretically* / 在数量～占优势 *excel in numbers* ❹ at (the age of): 他五岁～死了父亲。*His father died when he was five years old.* / 张大爷六十岁～得了孙子。*Uncle Zhang got his first grandson at sixty.* ❺ formerly, referring to the emperor ❻ (used alone, esp. in contrast to 下) above: 这个词是旧时下对～的称呼。*This word was used in the old days to address one's superiors.* ❼ (used after a preposition) up; upward: 往～看 *look up (at sth.)* / 向～拉 *pull it up* / 这头朝～ *this side up* / 向～反映情况 *report the situation to the higher-ups*

【上班】go to work; start work; be on duty: 下午不～。*We'll take the afternoon off.* or *No work this afternoon.* / ～时间 *work hours; office hours*

【上半场】first half (of a game, concert, etc.): ～比分多少? *What was the score at half time?*

【上半晌】〈口〉morning: ～我哪儿也没去啊。*I didn't go anywhere this morning.*

【上半身】the upper part of the body; above the waist

【上半夜】before midnight

【上绑】truss sb. up

【上报】❶ appear in the newspapers: 我们厂上了报了。*The newspaper carries a story about our factory.* ❷ report to a higher body; report to the leadership: 这件事应当立即～公安部,不容延误。*This matter should be reported, without delay, to the Ministry of Public Security.*

【上辈】❶ ancestors ❷ the elder generation of one's family; one's elders

【上辈子】❶ ancestors ❷ previous existence

【上臂】the upper arm

【上膘】(of animals) become fat; fatten

【上宾】distinguished guest; guest of honour: 待为～ *be treated as a distinguished guest*

【上不封顶,下不保底】impose "no ceiling or lower limit" on bonuses

【上不着天,下不着地】touch neither the sky nor the ground—be suspended in midair

【上菜】serve the dishes (of food): 上了好几道菜。

Several courses were served.
【上苍】Heaven；God
【上操】go out to drill；be drilling
【上策】the best plan；the best way out；the best thing to do
【上层】upper levels；upper strata：～人士 *upper circles*
【上层建筑】superstructure：文化艺术属于～。*Culture and art belong to the realm of the superstructure.*
【上层路线】the upper-level line：走～ *take the upper-level line—get things done through the personal influence of the higher-ups*
【上层社会】upper strata of society；upper-class society
【上谄下骄】obsequious towards one's superiors and arrogant towards one's inferiors
【上场】❶ appear on the stage；enter：学生甲～。*Enter Student A.* ❷［体］enter the court or field；join in a contest：双方运动员都已经～。*Players of both teams have entered the court.* / 今天该谁～？*Who's playing today?* ◇ ～门 entrance (of a stage)
【上乘】first-class：～之作 *first-class work*
【上床】go to bed；get into bed
【上窜下跳】run around on sinister errands
【上达】reach the higher authorities：下情～ *make the situation at the lower levels known to the higher levels*
【上代】the previous generation；former generations
【上当】be taken in；be fooled；be duped：这回我可不～啦！*I won't be taken in this time.* / 我们不上那个当。*We won't walk into that trap.*
【上灯】light the lamp；light up：～时分 *lighting-up time*
【上等】first-class；first-rate；superior：～货 *first-class goods* / ～料子 *high-quality material*
【上等兵】private first class
【上低音号】［音］baritone
【上帝】God (in Christianity)
【上吊】hang oneself
【上调】(shàngdiào) ❶ transfer sb. to a post at a higher level ❷ transfer goods，funds，etc. to a unit at a higher level ——另见 shàngtiáo
【上冻】freeze：一定要在～以前把地基打好。*We've got to finish the foundations before the ground freezes.*
【上颚】❶ mandible (of certain arthropods) ❷ the upper jaw or maxilla (of vertebrates)
【上方空间】superjacent air space
【上房】main rooms (usu. facing south，within a courtyard)
【上访】apply for an audience with the higher authorities to appeal for help：～人员 *visitors from the localities appealing to the higher authorities for help*
【上坟】visit a grave to honour the memory of the dead
【上粪】apply manure to the fields
【上风】❶ windward：咱们到烟的～头去吧。*Let's get to windward of the smoke.* or *Let's go upwind of the smoke.* ❷ advantage；superior position；upper hand：占上风
【上峰】〈旧〉superior；boss：～的命令 *orders from above*
【上浮】(usu. temporarily) rise；raise：厂里效益好，他们的工资也跟着～。*Their wages rise along with the improvement of economic returns of their factory.*(〈反〉'下浮')
【上纲】raise to the higher plane of principle：这个问题上不了纲。*That's not a matter of principle.*
【上岗】go to one's post；go on duty
【上告】❶ complain to the higher authorities or appeal to a higher court ❷ report to one's superior
【上工】go to work；start work：夜班十点钟～。*The night shift starts at* 10.
【上供】❶ offer up a sacrifice；lay offerings on the altar ❷ give presents to the higher-ups expecting favours in return
【上钩】rise to the bait；swallow the bait；get hooked
【上古】ancient times；remote ages ◇ ～史 ancient history
【上光】❶ glazing；polishing ❷［摄］ferrotyping ◇ ～机 glazing machine；glazer；～蜡 wax polish
【上轨道】get on the right track；begin to work smoothly：生产已～。*Production is proceeding smoothly.*
【上好】first-class；best-quality；tip-top：～烟叶 *best-quality tobacco*
【上颌】［生理］the upper jaw；maxilla
【上呼吸道】［生理］the upper respiratory tract ◇ ～感染 infection of the upper respiratory tract
【上回】last time
【上火】❶［中］suffer from excessive internal heat (with such symptoms as constipation，conjunctivitis and inflammation of the nasal and oral cavities) ❷〈方〉get angry
【上货】❶ get in stocks；replenish stocks ❷ replenish the goods shelves
【上机】operate computers
【上级】❶ higher level：～党委 *a Party committee of the higher level* / ～机关 *higher authorities；a higher body* / ～领导 *a leading body at a higher level* ❷ higher authorities；one's superior：报告～ *report to the higher authorities；report to one's superior* / 他是我的老～。*He is my old chief.*
【上佳】excellent；good；admirable；first-class；praiseworthy：在举重锦标赛中，小李有～表现。*Young Li made a good showing in the weight-lifting championship.*
【上家】(in mahjong，card games，etc.) the player whose turn comes just before
【上浆】❶ starching (of clothes) ❷［纺］dressing (of yarn，fabrics，etc.)

【上将】(U. S. & Brit. Army, U. S. Air Force, U. S. & Brit. Marine Corps) general; (U. S. & Brit. Navy) admiral; (Brit. Air Force) air chief marshal

【上交】hand in (or over) to sb. above oneself; pass on to the higher authorities

【上胶】[刷] sizing

【上焦】[中] the part of the body cavity above the diaphragm housing the heart and lungs

【上缴】turn over (revenues, profits, surplus materials, etc.) to the higher authorities: 多余器材应该~。*Surplus equipment should be turned over to the higher authorities*. ◇ ~利润 that part of the profits turned over to the state

【上街】❶ go to the street; go shopping: ~看看 *go window-shopping* / 我陪妈妈上了一趟街。*I went shopping with my mother*. ❷ take to the streets; go on to the streets: ~游行(示威) *take to the streets (to demonstrate)*

【上届】previous term or session; last: ~毕业生 *last year's graduates*

【上界】the world above; the abode of the gods

【上紧】〈口〉lose no time (in doing sth.); hasten; speed up: 葡萄快熟了,得~准备收摘了。*The grapes will soon be ripe. Let's speed up our preparations for the grape harvest*.

【上进】go forward; make progress: 不求~ *not strive to make progress* ◇ ~心 the desire to do better; the urge for improvement

【上劲】energetically; with gusto; with great vigour: 越干越~儿 *work with increasing vigour (or gusto)* / 越说越~儿 *get more and more excited as one talks*

【上课】❶ attend class; go to class: 你昨天怎么没来~? *Why didn't you come to class yesterday*? ❷ conduct a class; give a lesson (or lecture): 学校八点开始~。*Classes begin at 8*.

【上空】in the sky; overhead: 五星红旗在天安门广场~高高飘扬。*The Five-Star Red Flag flies high above Tian'anmen Square*.

【上口】❶ be able to read aloud fluently: 孩子们把这首诗念了又念,现在都能琅琅~了。*The children have read the poem several times, and can all recite it quite fluently now*. ❷ be suitable for reading aloud; make smooth reading: 这段文字太艰深,不易~。*The passage is too difficult and doesn't lend itself to reading aloud*.

【上跨交叉】[交通] overpass

【上款】❶ the name of the recipient (as inscribed on a painting or a calligraphic scroll presented as a gift) ❷ the name of the addressee (of a letter or package)

【上蜡】[纺] waxing

【上来】❶ begin; get started: 一~就没劲 *be boring right from the start* ❷〈书〉to sum up (the aforesaid): ~所言 *to sum up the aforesaid* ❸ come up: 游了半天了,快~歇会儿吧。*You've been swimming a long time now. Come out and have a rest*. ❹ come up to a place or state regarded as higher or above: 他是刚从基层~的。*He's just come from a grass-roots unit*. ❺ up (here): 把箱子抬~ *bring the trunk up* ❻ (indicating success in doing sth.): 这个问题你答得~吗? *Can you answer this question*? / 看他面熟,名字可叫不~。*I know his face but I can't recall his name*. ❼ indicating an increase in degree: 暖气片慢慢热~了。*Little by little the radiators got warmer*. / 天色黑~了。*It is getting dark*.

【上联】the first line of a couplet

【上梁】❶ put the beams in place (in building a wooden house) ❷ (of bicycles) cross bar; top tube ❸ (of buildings) upper beam

【上梁不正下梁歪】if the upper beam is not straight, the lower ones will go aslant—when those above behave unworthily, those below will do the same

【上列】listed above; above-listed; the above: ~各项 *the items listed above*; *the above-listed items*

【上流】❶ upper reaches (of a river) ❷ belonging to the upper circles; upper-class ◇ ~社会 high society; polite society

【上路】set out on a journey; start off

【上马】❶ mount (or get on) a horse: ~! (*word of command*) *To horse*! ❷ start (a project, etc.): 这项工程明年~。*The project will start next year*.

【上门】❶ come or go to see sb.; call; drop in; visit: 他好久没~了。*It's a long time since he last called*. / 送货~ *deliver goods to the doorstep* ❷ shut the door (or lock up) for the night; bolt the door ❸ marry into and live with one's bride's family ◇ ~服务 door-to-door service; ~女婿 live-in son-in-law; ~推销员 knocker

【上面】❶ above; over; on top of; on the surface of: 飞机在云层~飞行。*The plane flew above the clouds*. / 运河~架了一座桥。*A bridge has been built across the canal*. ❷ above-mentioned; aforesaid; foregoing: ~所举的例子 *the above-mentioned example* / ~这几条理由 *the aforesaid reasons* / ~几个发言 *the speeches you've just heard*; *the previous speeches* ❸ higher authorities; higher-ups: ~有指示。*There are instructions from above*. ❹ aspect; respect; regard: 他在外语~下了很多功夫。*He has put a lot of effort into his study of foreign languages*. ❺ the elder generation of one's family; the elders

【上年】last year

【上年纪】be getting on in years; be stricken in years: 奶奶上了年纪,腿脚不那么灵便了。*Granny is stricken in years and isn't so surefooted as before*.

【上牌子】apply for a license

【上盘】[矿] hanging wall

【上皮】[生理] epithelium ◇ ~癌 epithelioma; ~组织 [生理] epithelial tissue

【上品】highest grade; top grade: 茅台是酒中~。*Maotai is a top-grade spirit*.

【上坡路】❶ an uphill road; an upward slope: 他们

沿着那条十分陡峭的～爬上去。*They climbed by the very steep ascent*. ❷ upward trend; steady progress

【上铺】upper berth

【上气不接下气】gasp for breath; be out of breath

【上情】feelings or wishes of the higher authorities: ～下达 *make the wishes of the higher authorities known to those below*

【上去】❶ go up: 登着梯子～ *go up (on) a ladder* / 车来了,咱们～吧。*Here comes the bus. Let's get on*. ❷ rise to a place or state regarded as higher or above: 我们提的这些意见上得去吗? *Could the suggestions we raised reach the higher authorities*? ❸ up (there): 计划已经交～了。*The plan has been sent up to the higher-ups*. / 把国民经济搞～ *push the national economy forward* ❹ (indicating adding or fixing): 又铺了一床褥子～ *add another mattress to the bed* / 螺丝拧～了。*The screws have been driven in*.

【上圈套】fall into sb.'s trap

【上染率】[纺] dye-uptake

【上任】❶ take up an official post; assume office ❷ predecessor

【上色】(shàngsè) best-quality; top-grade: ～茶叶 *top-grade tea*

【上色】(shàngshǎi) colour (a picture, map, etc.)

【上上】❶ the highest; the very best: ～策 *the best plan* ❷ before last: ～星期 *the week before last*

【上上下下】high and low; old and young; everybody

【上身】❶ the upper part of the body: 光着～ *be stripped to the waist* / 他～穿一件土布衬衫。*He's wearing a shirt of handwoven cloth*. ❷ upper outer garment; shirt; blouse; jacket: 姑娘们穿着白～,花裙子。*The girls are wearing white blouses and bright-coloured skirts*. ❸ start wearing: 天冷了,羽绒服该～了。*It's getting cold. We'd better start wearing our down jackets*.

【上升】❶ move upward: 一缕炊烟袅袅～。*A wisp of smoke is curling up from the kitchen chimney*. ❷ rise (to a higher point, degree, rank, etc.); ascend: 气温～。*The temperature is going up*. / 生产持续～。*Production is rising steadily*. ◇ ～角 [航空] angle of climb (or ascent); ～气流 ascending air; up current; ～失速 [航空] advance stall; ～转弯 [航空] pull-up turn

【上声】[语音] ❶ rising tone (the second of the four tones in classical Chinese pronunciation) ❷ falling-rising tone (the third of the four tones in modern standard Chinese pronunciation) ——另见〖四声〗

【上士】(U. S. Army) sergeant first class; (Brit. Army) staff sergeant; (U. S. Navy) petty officer first class; (Brit. Navy) chief petty officer; (U. S. Air Force) technical sergeant; (Brit. Air Force) flight sergeant; (U. S. Marine Corps) technical sergeant or staff sergeant; (Brit. Marine Corps) colour sergeant

【上市】❶ go (or appear) on the market: 西红柿大量～。*There are plenty of tomatoes on the market*. / 这是刚～的苹果。*These apples have just come in*. ❷ go to market: 我～买菜去啦。*I'm going to market*. ❸ [经] (of companies) go public; be listed ◇ ～公司 listed companies; ～股票 listed stock; ～证券 listed securities

【上视图】[机] top view

【上手】❶ left-hand seat; seat of honour ❷ 同〖上家〗❸ (of work, etc.) get started: 今天的活一～就很顺利。*Today's work went smoothly from the outset*. / 那场球一～就打得那么别扭。*Everything went wrong from the beginning of that match*.

【上首】seat of honour

【上书】submit a written statement to a higher authority; send in a memorial

【上述】mentioned above; above-mentioned; aforementioned; aforesaid: 达到～目标 *achieve the aforementioned objectives*

【上水】❶ feed water to a steam engine, radiator (of an automobile), etc.: 给水箱～ *fill the tank with water* ❷ upper reaches (of a river) ❸ sail upstream: ～船 *an upstream boat* ◇ ～道 water-supply line

【上税】pay taxes

【上司】superior; boss: 顶头～ *one's immediate superior*

【上诉】[法] appeal (to a higher court): 提出～ *lodge an appeal* ◇ ～法院 court of appeal; appellate court; ～权 right of appeal; ～人 appellant

【上溯】❶ go upstream ❷ trace back: ～到公元前一世纪 *trace back to the 1st century B.C.*

【上算】paying; worthwhile: 烧煤气比烧煤～。*It's more economical to use gas than coal*.

【上岁数】〈口〉be getting on in years

【上锁】lock: 门上了锁。*The door was locked*.

【上台】❶ go up onto the platform; appear on the stage: 她～演奏了两支钢琴曲子。*She went up onto the platform and played two piano pieces*. ❷ 〈贬〉assume power; come (or rise) to power

【上膛】❶ [军] (of a gun) be loaded: 子弹上了膛。*The gun is loaded*. ❷ common name for 腭

【上套】❶ harness a draught animal (to a cart, etc.) ❷ fall into a trap

【上体】〈书〉the upper part of the body

【上天】❶ go up to the sky; fly sky-high: 我们又有一颗卫星～了。*Another of our satellites has gone up*. ❷ 〈婉〉go to Heaven—die ❸ Heaven; Providence

【上天无路,入地无门】there is no road to heaven and no door into the earth—no way of escape; in desperate straits

【上调】(shàngtiáo) raise (prices) ——另见 shàngdiào

【上头】(shàngtóu) go to head (of liquor)

【上头】(shàngtou) 同〖上面〗

【上吐下泻】throw up on top and purge down below; suffer from vomiting and diarrhoea; have loose bowels and vomit

【上推下卸】pass the buck both up and down; shift the blame on to one's superiors or on to one's subordinates

【上网】[计] go on-line; connect to the Internet: 本地～费用为每小时 3 元。*The local fee for Internet connection is 3 yuan per hour.*

【上尉】(U. S. & Brit. Army, U. S. Air Force, U. S. & Brit. Marine Corps) captain; (U. S. & Brit. Navy) lieutenant; (Brit. Air Force) flight lieutenant

【上文】foregoing paragraphs or chapters; preceding part of the text: 见～ *see above*

【上无片瓦,下无插针之地】have neither a tile above one's head nor an inch of land beneath one's feet—be utterly destitute

【上午】morning; forenoon

【上西天】go to the Western Paradise—die

【上下】❶ high and low: 全军～ *the whole army, officers and men alike* / ～通气 *full communication between the higher and lower levels* / ～一条心。*The leadership and the rank and file are of one mind.* ❷ from top to bottom; up and down: ～打量 *look sb. up and down; scrutinize sb. from head to foot* ❸ relative superiority or inferiority ❹ (used after round numbers) about; or so; or thereabouts: 四十岁～ *about forty years old; forty or so* ❺ go up or down: 山上修了公路,汽车～很方便。*With the completion of the highway up the mountain, cars can easily go up and down.*

【上下其手】practise fraud; manoeuvre for some evil end; get up to tricks

【上下水】water supply and sewage: 厨房的～有点问题。*There is something wrong with the kitchen's water supply and drains.*

【上下文】context: 根据～确定词义 *tell the meaning of a word from its context*

【上弦】❶ tighten the spring of; wind (up): 我的钟该～了。*My clock needs winding.* ❷ [气] first quarter (of the moon) ◇ ～月 the moon at the first quarter

【上线】❶ raise ordinary matters to the higher plane of political struggle ❷ reach the admission test scores: 今年师范院校报名者中～的很少。*This year normal schools and teachers colleges have only a few applicants who reached the admission test scores.*

【上限】the upper limit; the maximum permissible or prescribed

【上香】burn joss sticks (before an idol or a spirit tablet)

【上相】come out well in a photograph; be photogenic

【上校】(U. S. & Brit. Army, U. S. Air Force, U. S. & Brit. Marine Corps) colonel; (U. S. & Brit. Navy) captain; (Brit. Air Force) group captain

【上心】set one's heart on sth.

【上新世】[地质] the Pliocene Epoch

【上刑】put to torture; torture

【上行】❶ (of trains) going to the capital from any part of the country; up; upgoing: ～列车 *up train* ❷ (of boats) going upstream; upriver: ～船 *an upstream boat* ❸ (of documents) sent to the upper levels: ～公文 *documents sent to the upper levels*

【上行下效】subordinates follow the example of their superiors; those below follow the (usu. bad) example of those above; if a leader sets a bad example, it will be followed by his subordinates

【上旋】[体] top spin

【上选】the choicest; the most select

【上学】go to school; attend school; be at school: 没有～的机会 *have no chance of going to school* / 这孩子～了没有? *Is the child at school?*

【上旬】the first ten-day period of a month

【上压力】[物] upward pressure

【上演】put on the stage; perform: 国庆节将～几个新戏。*Several new plays will be performed on National Day.* / 人民剧场今晚～什么节目? *What's on at the People's Theatre this evening?*

【上衣】upper outer garment; jacket

【上议院】upper house; (Brit.) the House of Lords: ～议员 *Lords; temporal and spiritual peers of Parliament*

【上瘾】be addicted (to sth.); get into the habit (of doing sth.): 吸毒上了瘾 *be addicted to drugs; be a drug addict* / 他抽烟抽上了瘾。*He's got into the habit of smoking.* / 这种药吃久了会～。*This medicine is habit-forming.* / 她看侦探小说看～了。*She's developed a yen for detective stories.*

【上映】show (a film); screen: 近日将有几部新片～。*A number of new films will be shown in the next few days.*

【上游】❶ upper reaches (of a river): ～国家 *an upstream country* ❷ advanced position: ～无止境。*One can always aim higher.*

【上有天堂,下有苏杭】Up above there is Paradise, down here there are Suzhou and Hangzhou.

【上有政策,下有对策】The higher authorities have policies and the localities have their counter measures.

【上载】[计] upload

【上灶】do the cooking

【上涨】rise; go up: 河水～。*The river has risen.* / 物价～。*The prices are going up.*

【上账】make an entry in an account book; enter sth. in an account

【上阵】go into battle; take part in a match; pitch into the work: ～杀敌 *go to the front to fight the enemy* / 今天比赛谁～? *Who's going to play in tonight's match?*

【上肢】upper limbs

【上装】❶ make up (for a theatrical performance) ❷〈方〉upper outer garment; jacket

【上座】the seat of honour

【上座】❶（of restaurants）draw customers；（of theatres，etc.）draw an audience：戏园子里～已达八成。*The theatre is already 80% full*. ❷ be a draw；be a box-office success：这出戏可～了。*This play is a great draw*.

【上座率】attendance；occupancy；box office sales：京剧的～比若干地方戏低很多。*Peking Opera as a whole has far smaller audiences than local shows*.

尚 Ⅰ 动 esteem；value；set great store by：尚武 Ⅱ 副〈书〉still；yet：～待进一步讨论 *pending further discussion* / 为时～早。*It is still too early*. or *The time is not yet ripe*. / 此事～未解决。*The matter remains to be settled*. or *The problem is not resolved as yet*.

【尚方宝剑】the emperor's sword（the bearer of which is invested with discretionary powers）—a symbol of delegated power

【尚且】（used in the negative，followed by a negative with even greater force of denial）（not）even ...（let alone ...）：大人～举不起来，何况小孩子。*Even grown-ups can't lift it，to say nothing of children*.

【尚书】❶ a high official in ancient China ❷ minister（in the Ming and Qing Dynasties）

【尚武】encourage a military or martial spirit ◇ ～精神 a military or martial spirit

shāo

烧 Ⅰ 动 ❶ burn：干柴好～。*Wood burns better*（*or more easily*）*when dry*. / 这台锅炉～油。*This furnace burns oil*. / 咱们把这些废纸～掉吧。*Let's burn up all this waste paper*. ❷ cook；heat：～一点水 *heat up some water* / 水～开了。*The water is boiling*. / ～炭 *make charcoal* / ～砖 *bake*（*or fire*）*bricks* ❸ stew after frying or fry after stewing：～茄子 *stewed eggplant* / 洋葱～排骨 *spareribs stewed in onion and sauce* ❹ roast：～乳猪 *roast suckling pig* ❺ run a fever；have a temperature：病人～得厉害。*The patient's running a high fever*. or *The patient has a high temperature*. ❻ damage or injure by excessive or improper use of fertilizer：上的肥太多，把根儿都～坏了。*Overfertilization burned the roots*. / 这几棵苗全～了。*These seedlings are all burnt*. Ⅱ 名 fever：～退了。*The fever is down*.

【烧包】〈方〉be drunken with success；have a swollen head

【烧杯】beaker（used in the laboratory）

【烧饼】sesame seed cake

【烧饭】〈方〉do the cooking；cook food；prepare a meal

【烧锅】（liquor）distillery

【烧化】❶ cremate ❷ burn（paper，etc. as an offering to the dead）

【烧荒】burn the grass on waste land

【烧毁】destroy by fire；burn up：～秘密文件 *burn up the secret documents*

【烧火】make a fire；light a fire；tend the kitchen fire：我烧的火，她做的饭。*She did the cooking while I lit and tended the fire*.

【烧鸡】roast chicken

【烧碱】［化］caustic soda

【烧结】sintering；agglomeration；agglutination ◇ ～厂 sintering plant；～法［冶］sintering process；～剂［化］agglutinant

【烧酒】spirit（usu. distilled from sorghum or maize）；colourless spirit

【烧烤】barbecue ◇ ～架 barbecue grill

【烧料】imitation frosted glass（used to make lamps and handicrafts）

【烧麦】（又作'烧卖'）a steamed dumpling with the dough gathered at the top

【烧毛】［纺］singeing：煤气～ *gas singeing*

【烧瓶】flask（used in the laboratory）

【烧伤】［医］burn（an injury）：治疗大面积～ *treat extensive burns* / 三度～ *third-degree burns*

【烧蚀】［宇航］ablation

【烧香】burn joss sticks（before an idol）

【烧心】❶［医］heartburn ❷〈方〉（of cabbages）turn yellow at the heart

【烧纸】❶ burn paper money for the dead ❷ paper money burnt as an offering to the dead

【烧炙】burn：探询丈夫情况的强烈欲望～着我。*I burned with the desire to ask after my husband*.

【烧灼】burn；scorch；singe

捎 动 take along sth. to or for sb.；bring to sb.：请把这张报～给她。*Take this paper to her, please*. / 我给你孩子～来一点花生。*I've brought your children some peanuts*.

【捎带】incidentally；in passing：你上书店的话，～给我买张世界地图。*If you happen to be going to the bookshop，please get me a map of the world*.

【捎话】take a message to sb.：请你给她捎个话。*Please pass on this message to her*.

【捎脚】pick up passengers or goods on the way；give sb. a lift

梢 名 the thin end of a twig，etc.；tip：鞭～ *whiplash* / 辫～ *the end of a plait*

【梢头】❶ the tip of a branch ❷［林］top log

稍 副 a little；a bit；slightly；a trifle：～加修改 *make slight changes*；*make a few alterations* / 这大衣～长了一点。*The coat is a bit too long*. —— 另见 shào

【稍稍】a little；a bit；slightly；a trifle：～休息一下 *take a brief rest*；*take a breather*

【稍胜一筹】同〖略胜一筹〗

【稍微】a little；a bit；slightly；a trifle：～搁点盐 *put in a little salt* / 今天～有点冷。*It's rather chilly today*.

【稍为】同〖稍微〗

【稍许】同〖稍微〗

【稍纵即逝】transient; fleeting: ～的机会 *a fleeting opportunity*

筲 名 pail (usu. made of bamboo strips or wood); bucket

艄 名 ❶ stern ❷ rudder; helm: 掌～ *be at the helm*

【艄公】❶ helmsman ❷ boatman

鞘 名 whiplash ——另见 qiào

sháo

勺 名 spoon; ladle: 一把长柄～ *a ladle; a dipper*

【勺子】ladle; scoop

芍 (构词成分)见下

【芍药】Chinese herbaceous peony

韶 形〈书〉splendid; beautiful

【韶光】〈文〉❶ beautiful springtime ❷ glorious youth

【韶华】同〖韶光〗

【韶秀】〈文〉delicate and pretty

shǎo

少 Ⅰ形 few; little; less: 以～胜多 *defeat the many with the few* / ～花钱,多办事。*Get more done on less money.* / ～走弯路 *avoid detours* / ～吃多餐 *have many meals but little food at each* Ⅱ动 ❶ be short; lack: 我们还～两把椅子。*We're still two chairs short.* / 缺医～药 *be short of doctors and medicine* ❷ lose; be missing: 看看～不～人。*See if anyone is missing.* / 这里肯定～了一个字。*Surely, there's a word missing here.* / 羊群里～了几只羊。*A few sheep have been lost from the flock.* ❸ stop; quit: ～废话! *Stop talking rubbish!* / ～来这一套。*Cut it out.* or *Quit that!* / ～给我装蒜! *Stop pretending!* Ⅲ副 a little while; a moment: 请～候。*Wait a moment, please.* ——另见 shào

【少安毋躁】keep calm, don't get excited; don't be impatient, wait a while

【少不得】cannot do without; cannot dispense with: 学科学,参考书是～的。*Reference books are indispensable in scientific studies.* / 这事～还要麻烦您。*We may have to trouble you again about this.*

【少不了】❶ cannot do without; cannot dispense with: 这次比赛～你。*We can't do without you for this match.* ❷ be bound to; be unavoidable: 准备仓促,演出～会有缺点。*The performance has been arranged at short notice, so it's bound to have shortcomings.* ❸ can't be only a few or only a little; must be a lot: 困难看来～。*It looks as if there are going to be a lot of difficulties.*

【少得了】(used in rhetorical questions) can do without; can dispense with: 今天的晚会还～你吗? *You must come to the party this evening. We can't do without you.*

【少而精】smaller quantity, better quality; fewer but better: 教学内容要～。*Teaching content should be concise.* / 办事机构要～。*The executive organs should be smaller but more efficient.*

【少见】❶〈套〉(a form of greeting) I haven't seen you for a long time; I have seen very little of you these days—I'm very glad to see you again ❷ seldom seen; infrequent; rare: 这种事情太～了! *This is indeed something rare.*

【少见多怪】The less a man has seen, the more he has to wonder at; Ignorant people are easily surprised: 用不着～。*There's nothing to be surprised at.* / 也许是我～。*Maybe it was all due to my own ignorance.*

【少刻】after a little while; a moment later

【少量】a small amount; a little; a few

【少慢差费】fewer, slower, poorer and more costly: 这种方法～。*This method will get fewer and poorer results, and progress will be slower and costs higher.* or *That's an inefficient and expensive method.*

【少陪】〈套〉(an apology for taking leave of sb.) if you'll excuse me; I'm afraid I must be going now

【少顷】〈书〉after a short while; after a few moments; presently

【少时】after a little while; a moment later; soon

【少数】a small number; few; minority: ～人 *a small number of people; a few people; the minority* / ～服从多数。*The minority is subordinate to the majority.*

【少数党】a minority party; minority

【少数民族】minority nationality; ethnic minority: ～地区 *areas inhabited by the minority nationalities; minority nationality regions*

【少许】〈书〉a little; a few; a modicum

【少有】rare; few and far between: 现在这种人真是～。*Men like that are few and far between these days.*

shào

少 Ⅰ形 young: 男女老少 Ⅱ名 son of a rich family; young master: 阔少 ——另见 shǎo

【少白头】❶ be prematurely grey ❷ a young person with greying hair

【少不更事】young and inexperienced; green: ～者 *a greenhorn*

【少东家】(a form of address formerly used by an employee to his employer's son or by a tenant-peasant to his landlord's son) young master

【少儿】children and early teenagers: ～书刊 *books for children and young teenagers*

【少妇】young married woman
【少管所】correction institution for juveniles；reform school；juvenile penitentiary
【少将】(U.S. & Brit. Army，U.S. Air Force，U.S. & Brit. Marine Corps) major general；(U.S. & Brit. Navy) rear admiral；(Brit. Air Force) air vice marshal
【少奶奶】❶ (a form of address formerly used by servants of the house) young mistress ❷〈旧〉〈尊〉your or sb. else's daughter-in-law
【少男少女】unmarried young men and women：处于青春临界点的～ *young people at the critical age of puberty*
【少年】❶ early youth (from about ten to sixteen)：打从～时代我们就是好朋友了。*We have been close friends since early youth.* ❷ boy or girl in early teens；juvenile：～运动员 *juvenile athletes* / ～单打 *boys' or girls' singles* ◇ ～读物 books for young people；juvenile books；～犯 juvenile delinquent；～犯管教所 见〖少管所〗；～犯罪 juvenile delinquency；～宫 Children's Palace；～先锋队 Young Pioneers；～之家 Children's Centre；Children's Club
【少年老成】❶ an old head on young shoulders；young but mature ❷ an old young man；a young person lacking in vigour and drive
【少年班】juvenile college class
【少女】young girl
【少尉】(U.S. & Brit. Army，U.S. Air Force，U.S. & Brit. Marine Corps) second lieutenant；(U.S. Navy) ensign；(Brit. Navy) acting sub-lieutenant；(Brit. Air Force) pilot officer
【少先队】〈略〉见〖少年先锋队〗
【少先队员】Young Pioneer
【少相】young-looking：他长得～，岁数儿可不小了。*He looks much younger than his age.*
【少校】(U.S. & Brit. Army，U.S. Air Force，U.S. & Brit. Marine Corps) major；(U.S. & Brit. Navy) lieutenant commander；(Brit. Air Force) squadron leader
【少爷】❶ (a form of address formerly used by servants of the house) young master ❷〈旧〉〈尊〉your or sb. else's son
【少爷脾气】behaviour of a spoilt boy
【少壮】young and vigorous
【少壮不努力，老大徒伤悲】If one does not exert oneself in youth，one will regret it in old age；Laziness in youth spells regret in old age.
【少壮派】the up-and-coming

劭 Ⅰ 动〈书〉encourage；urge；exhort Ⅱ 形 excellent；admirable：年高德劭

哨 Ⅰ 名 ❶ sentry post；post：观察～ *observation post* ❷ a whistle：吹～儿 *blow a whistle* Ⅱ 动 (of birds) warble；chirp
【哨兵】sentry；guard
【哨岗】sentry post (where a sentinel is posted)
【哨卡】a frontier sentry post or a strategic sentry post
【哨所】sentry post；post：前沿～ *forward post*；*outpost* / 边防～ *frontier guard post*
【哨位】sentry post
【哨子】whistle

稍 (构词成分) 见下——另见 shāo
【稍息】[军] stand at ease：～！(*word of command*) *At ease!*

潲 动 ❶ (of rain) slant in：东边～雨。*The rain is driving (or slanting) in from the east.* ❷〈方〉sprinkle：往菜上～水 *sprinkle the vegetables with water*

shē

奢 形 ❶ luxurious；extravagant：奢侈 ❷ excessive；inordinate；extravagant：奢望
【奢侈】luxurious；extravagant；wasteful：生活～ *live in luxury*
【奢侈品】luxury goods；luxuries ◇ ～税 luxury tax
【奢华】luxurious；sumptuous；extravagant：陈设～ *be luxuriously furnished*
【奢靡】extravagant and wasteful
【奢求】extravagant claims；excessive demands；unreasonable demands
【奢望】extravagant hopes；wild wishes：我对此不抱～。*I entertain no high hopes in this regard.*
【奢想】extravagant hopes；wild wishes

猞 名 (构词成分) 见下
【猞猁】lynx

赊 动 buy or sell on credit
【赊购】buy on credit ◇ ～商店 tally shop
【赊欠】buy or sell on credit：购买我店家具，可以先付半数货款，～部分在三个月内付清。*You can always buy our furniture on credit if you can pay half the price now and the rest in three months.*
【赊销】sell on credit
【赊账】❶ a system of buying or selling on credit；the credit system：概不～。*No credit given.* ❷ outstanding bills or accounts：还有几笔～未清。*There are some bills still outstanding (or unpaid).* ❸ have outstanding bills or accounts：准许赊三个月的账 *allow people 3 months' credit* / 赊了一千元的账 *have an outstanding account of 1,000 yuan*

shé

舌 名 ❶ tongue (of a human being or animal) ❷ sth. shaped like a tongue：鞋～ *the tongue of a shoe* ❸ the tongue of a bell；clapper
【舌敝唇焦】talk till one's tongue and lips are parched；wear oneself out in pleading，expostulating，etc.

【舌根】the root of the tongue ◇ ～音［语音］velar
【舌耕】〈书〉make a living by teaching
【舌尖】the tip of the tongue ◇ ～后音［语音］blade-palatal；～前音［语音］dental；～音［语音］apical；～中音［语音］blade-alveolar
【舌剑唇枪】同〖唇枪舌剑〗
【舌面后音】another name for 舌根音
【舌面前音】［语音］dorsal
【舌鳎】［动］tonguefish；tongue sole
【舌苔】［中］coating on the tongue；fur
【舌头】❶ tongue ❷ an enemy soldier captured for the purpose of extracting information：侦察兵抓了个～。*The scouts took a prisoner to get information*. ——另见〖吐舌头〗
【舌下神经】［生理］hypoglossal nerve
【舌下腺】［生理］sublingual gland
【舌炎】glossitis
【舌蝇】tsetse fly (or tzetze fly)；tsetse (or tzetze)
【舌战】❶ have a verbal battle with；argue heatedly with：～群儒 *have a heated dispute with a group of scholars* ❷ a hot dispute；a verbal battle：一场～ *a heated dispute*；*a battle royal*
【舌状花】［植］ligulate flower

折 动 ❶ break；snap：扁担～了。*The shoulder pole broke*. / 他们太使劲，把绳子拉～了。*They pulled the rope so hard that it snapped*. ❷ lose money in business ——另见 zhē；zhé
【折本】lose money in business：～生意 *a losing business*；*a bad bargain*
【折秤】damage and loss to goods (such as vegetables, fruits, etc.) in the course of reweighing
【折耗】damage and loss (to goods during transit, storage, etc.)

蛇 名 snake；serpent
【蛇莓】［植］mock-strawberry
【蛇皮管】flexible conduit
【蛇丘】［地质］esker
【蛇头】❶ snake head ❷ coyote；ringleader of organized illegal immigration
【蛇蜕】［中］snake slough
【蛇纹石】serpentine (a mineral)
【蛇无头不行】a snake cannot move without its head—nothing can be accomplished without a leader
【蛇蝎】snakes and scorpions—vicious people：毒如～ *as vicious as a viper*
【蛇蝎心肠】as venomous as snakes and scorpions
【蛇行】〈书〉move with the body on the ground；crawl
【蛇形】snakelike；S-shaped
【蛇足】feet added to a snake by an ignorant artist—sth. superfluous ——另见〖画蛇添足〗

shě

舍 动 ❶ give up；abandon：～此别无他法。*There is no other way than this*. or *This is the only way*. ❷ give alms；dispense charity ——另见 shè
【舍本逐末】attend to trifles and neglect essentials
【舍不得】hate to part with or use；grudge；begrudge：我～你。*I hate to leave you*. or *I hate to lose you*.
【舍得】be willing to part with；not grudge：你～把这本书送给他吗？*Are you willing to give the book to him?*
【舍得一身剐，敢把皇帝拉下马】He who fears not being cut to pieces dares to unhorse the emperor.
【舍己救人】sacrifice oneself to save sb. else
【舍己为人】sacrifice one's own interests for the sake of others
【舍近求远】(又作'舍近图远')seek from afar what lies close at hand；forgo what is close at hand and seek what is far afield
【舍车保帅】give up a chariot to save the marshal (in Chinese chess)—make minor sacrifices to safeguard major interests
【舍命】risk one's life；sacrifice oneself
【舍命陪君子】I would throw in my lot with you, sir, at the risk of my life (said jocularly when agreeing to join sb. in some activity).
【舍弃】give up；abandon：～亲生骨肉 *abandon one's own flesh and blood*
【舍入】［数］rounding off
【舍身】give one's life；sacrifice oneself：～救人 *give one's life to rescue sb.*；*sacrifice oneself to save others*
【舍生取义】lay down one's life for a just cause：～，虽死何辞？*Nothing shall prevent me from dying for righteousness*.
【舍死忘生】disregard one's own safety；risk one's life
【舍我其谁】if I can't do it, who can；who but myself can do it

shè

设 Ⅰ 动 ❶ set up；establish；found：总部～在北京。*The headquarters was established in Beijing*. / 指挥所～在前沿阵地上。*the command post was set up in a forward position*. ❷ work out；设计 ❸［数］given；suppose；if：～长方形的宽是 x 米。*Suppose the width of a rectangle is x metres*. / ～$x=1$ *Given*：$x=1$ Ⅱ 连〈书〉if；in case：～有困难，当助一臂之力。*You can count on me to help in case of difficulty*.
【设备】equipment；installation；facilities：电气～ *electric (or electrical) installations* / 旅馆～齐全。*The hotel is well appointed*. / ～利用率 *utilization rate of equipment and installations* ◇ ～保养 equipment maintenance；～检修 equipment examine and repair；～完好率 rate of equipment in good condition；～租赁 equipment leasing
【设备齐全】fully equipped

【设辞】〈书〉excuse；pretext

【设点】(of a firm) set up a retail outlet：在各大城市～ *set up retail outlets in every major city*

【设定】set：～压力 *setting pressure* ◇～值 set a value；[电] set point

【设法】think of a way；try；do what one can：我们乐队正在～找个小提琴手。*Our orchestra is trying to find a violinist*.

【设防】set up defences；fortify；garrison：层层～ *set up defences in depth* / ～地带 *fortified zone*

【设伏】〈书〉lay an ambush

【设岗】❶ post a sentry：在门口设了岗，检查出入证。*A sentry was posted at the entrance to check the passes*. ❷ create a post (job, position)：因人～ *create a job in order to accommodate a person*

【设计】❶ design；plan：～一种新机器 *design a new machine* / ～一座水坝 *project a dam* / ～版面 *lay out a printed page* ❷ work out a plan or scheme：～陷害 *plot a frame-up*；*frame* ◇～洪水 [水] design flood；～能力 design capacity；～图 design drawing；～院 designing institute

【设计师】❶ designer❷ architect

【设计吃水】[航海] designed draft

【设立】establish；set up；found：～新的机构 *set up a new organization*

【设色】fill in colours on a sketch；lay paint on (canvas)；colour：～柔和 *painted in quiet colours*

【设身处地】put oneself in sb. else's position：你只要～想想他的处境，就可以理解他为什么会有那种表现。*If you put yourself in his place, you may realize why he acted as he did*.

【设施】installation；facilities：防洪～ *flood control installations* / 军事～ *military installations* / 医疗～ *medical facilities*

【设想】❶ imagine；envisage；conceive；assume：从最坏的可能来～ *anticipate the worst*；*prepare for the worst* / ～你自己处在他的境遇中会怎么办? *Imagine yourself to be in his place. What would you do then*? ❷ tentative plan；tentative idea：这些只是我们的初步～。*Those are just our tentative ideas*. ❸ have consideration for：为群众～ *take the interests of the masses into consideration* / 多为青少年～ *give much thought to the needs of the younger generation*

【设宴】give a banquet；fête：设喜(寿)宴 *give a wedding (birthday) feast* / 设午(晚)宴 *give a midday (evening) banquet*

【设营】[军] quarter；encamp ◇～地 camp site；～队 quartering party

【设障】place obstacles；make trouble；complicate matters：个别人公开挑衅，个别人暗中～。*Some were openly challenging, others made trouble behind the scenes*.

【设置】❶ set up；establish：～专门机构 *set up a special organization* / 课程～ *courses offered in a college or school*；*curriculum* ❷ put up；install：实验室里～了闭路电视。*A closed circuit TV system has been installed in the laboratories*. / 给会议～重重障碍 *place all sorts of obstacles before the conference* ❸ [计] configuration；setup

【设座】choose a place to give a banquet：当晚总经理～国际饭店宴请外宾。*In the evening the General Manager gave a banquet at the International Hotel in honour of the foreign guests*.

社 名 ❶ an organized body；agency；society：报社 ❷ (specifically) people's commune：～办企业 *commune-run enterprise* ❸ the god of the land, sacrifices to him or altars for such sacrifices：春～ *spring sacrifice*

【社工】❶ social work ❷ social worker

【社会】society；community：人类～ *human society* / 国际～ *international community* ◇～安全网 social safety net；～保险 social insurance；～保障 social security；～保障制度 social security system；～财富 wealth of society；public wealth；～党 Socialist Party；～地位 social position；social status；～调查 social investigation；social survey；～发展史 history of social development；history of development of society；～分工 division of labour in society；～分配 distribution of social wealth；～福利 social welfare；public welfare；～环境 social environment；～活动 social activities；public activities；～基础 social base；social basis；～经济制度 socio-economic system；～科学 social sciences；～民主党 Social Democratic Party；～民主主义 social democracy；～名流 noted public figures；～青年〈婉〉unemployed youth；～实践 social practice；～协商对话制度 a social system of consultation and dialogue (between groups of people with varied social interests)；～学 sociology；～学家 sociologist；～治安 public order；～制度 social system；～总产品 aggregate social product；～总产值 gross domestic product；GDP；total output value；～总供给 total social supply；～总需求 total social demand

【社会办学】all sectors of society giving support to school education

【社会传真】reality show；reality program

【社会风气】social morals

【社会福利院】social welfare institute (orphanage, old people's home)

【社会公德】social ethics

【社会公正】social justice

【社会工作】❶ work outside one's regular job, done for the community；community work ❷ professional work (〈反〉'家务' housework)：妇女走出家庭参加～，已经蔚然成风。*Women working outside the home have become quite common*. ❸ social work

【社会关系】❶ human relations in society；social relations ❷ one's social connections；relatives and friends：她有很多～在海外。*Many of her relatives and friends are residing abroad*.

【社会化】socialization：公共福利事业应该～。*Public welfare services should be socialized*. ◇～

大生产 large-scale socialized production；～服务体系 socialized service system

【社会集团】organized grouping；collective：～购买力 *intstitutional purchasing power*

【社会集资】fund raising from various sectors of society

【社会生活】social activity：这本书涉及～的各个方面。*The book touches on all aspects of social activity*.

【社会生物学】sociobiology

【社会团体】public organization

【社会效益】social benefits；beneficial social effects；social returns：精神产品尤其要注意～。*Special attention should be paid to the social benefits of products which stimulate the intellect*.

【社会心理学】social psychology

【社会语言学】sociolinguistics

【社会主义】socialism ◇～初级阶段 preliminary stage of socialism；the primary stage of socialism；～道路 socialist road；～法制 socialist legality；socialist legal system；～改造 socialist transformation；～革命 socialist revolution；～建设 socialist construction；～所有制 socialist ownership；～制度 socialist system

【社会主义公有制】socialist public ownership

【社会主义精神文明】socialist spiritual civilization

【社会主义市场经济】socialist market economy

【社稷】the altars to the gods of earth and grain — the state；the country ◇～之臣 a loyal servant of the dynasty's sacred altars；a bulwark of the state

【社交】social intercourse；social contact；social life：要为男女青年开展～活动创造条件。*Opportunities should be provided for social intercourse between young men and women*.

【社科】(〈略〉全称为'社会科学') social sciences：～院 *Academy of Social Sciences*

【社论】editorial；leading article；leader：一篇占有整版篇幅的～ *a full-page editorial*

【社评】〈旧〉editorial

【社区】community ◇～发展 community development；～服务 community service；～文化 community culture

【社区学院】community college

【社群】community；social group；social：～型的动物 *social animal* / ～需要 *community needs*

【社团】mass organizations

【社戏】village theatrical performance given on religious festivals in old times

【社员】a member of a society，club，etc.：合作社～ *cooperative member* / 摄影社～ *a member of a photographers' club*

舍 Ⅰ 名 ❶ house；shed；hut：牛～ *cowshed* ❷〈谦〉my place：敝～ *my place* Ⅱ 代〈谦〉(used before relatives younger than or junior to oneself) my：～弟 *my younger brother* / ～侄 *my nephew* ——另见 shě

【舍间】〈谦〉my humble abode；my house；my place：请到～去谈谈，吃顿便饭，如何？*Would you care to come with me to my place for a chat and have something to eat?*

【舍监】〈旧〉the warden of a school dormitory

【舍利】(又作'舍利子')［宗］(佛教) relics left after the cremation of Buddhas or saintly monks (deposited in stupas for worship)

【舍利塔】a pagoda for Buddhist relics；stupa

【舍亲】〈谦〉my relative；a relative of mine

【舍下】〈谦〉my humble abode；my house；my place

【舍营】［军］billeting

涉 动 ❶ wade；ford：～水过河 *wade across a river*；*ford a stream* ❷ go through；experience：涉险 ❸ involve：涉嫌

【涉笔】wet the brush—start writing or painting

【涉笔成趣】(of a writer or painter) produce good work as soon as the brush touches paper (or as soon as he sets his brush to paper)

【涉及】involve；relate to；touch upon：双方的分歧～一些重大原则性问题。*The differences between the two sides involve major matters of principle*.

【涉猎】do desultory reading；read cursorily：有的书必须精读，有的只要稍加～即可。*Some books are for intensive study and some are for cursory reading*.

【涉禽】［动］wading bird；wader

【涉世】gain life experience：～不深 *have scanty experience of life*；*have seen little of the world*

【涉讼】be involved in a lawsuit

【涉外】concerning foreign affairs or foreign nationals：～活动 *activities involving foreign countries or nationals* / ～经济法规 *laws and regulations governing business relations with foreigners* ◇～案件 criminal case involving foreign elements；～宾馆 hotel concerning foreign affairs or foreign nationals；～婚姻 marriage between Chinese and foreigners

【涉嫌】be suspected of being involved；be a suspect：他因～此案而被传讯。*He was cited for suspected involvement in this law case*. / ～人犯 *suspects in a crime*

【涉险】go through dangers

【涉足】〈书〉set foot in：～其间 *set foot there*

射 动 ❶ shoot；fire：能骑善～ *be a good horseman as well as a crack shot*；*be known for one's equestrian skill and marksmanship* / ～进一球 *kick the ball into the goal*；*score a goal* ❷ discharge in a jet；jet；spout：注射 ❸ send out (light，heat，etc.)：探照灯～出一道道强光。*The searchlights projected powerful beams of light*. ❹ allude to sth. or sb.；insinuate：影射

【射程】range (of fire)：有效～ *effective range*

【射弹】projectile

【射电天文学】radio astronomy

【射电望远镜】radio telescope

【射干】［植］blackberry lily

【射击】❶ shoot; fire: 向敌人～ *fire at the enemy* ❷［体］shooting ◇ ～场 shooting range; ～地境 sector of fire; ～孔 embrasure
【射箭】❶ shoot an arrow ❷［体］an archery: ～手 *archer*
【射角】angle of fire
【射界】area (or field) of fire; firing area
【射精】［生理］ejaculation ◇ ～管［生理］ejaculatory ducts
【射孔】［油］perforation
【射猎】hunting with bow and arrow or firearms
【射流】［物］efflux: ～喷口 *efflux nozzle* ◇ ～技术 fluidics
【射门】［体］shoot (at the goal) ◇ ～手 goal getter
【射频】［电子］radio frequency ◇ ～放大器 radio frequency amplifier
【射手】❶ shooter; marksman; archer: 机枪～ *machine gunner* ❷ goal getter
【射水鱼】archer fish
【射速】firing rate
【射线】［物］ray ◇ ～病 radiation sickness; ～疗法 radiotherapy
【射影】projection

赦 动 remit (a punishment); pardon
【赦令】order of pardon or amnesty
【赦免】remit (a punishment); pardon
【赦罪】absolve sb. from guilt; pardon sb.

摄 动 ❶ absorb; assimilate ❷ take a photograph of; shoot: ～下几个珍贵的镜头 *take some superb shots* ❸〈书〉conserve (one's health) ❹ act for
【摄动】［气］perturbation
【摄理】hold an office in an acting capacity
【摄谱仪】［物］spectrograph
【摄取】❶ absorb; assimilate; take in: ～营养 *absorb nourishment* ❷ take a photograph of; shoot: ～几个镜头 *take several shots*
【摄生】〈书〉conserve one's health; keep fit
【摄食】(of animals) feed: ～行为 *feeding behaviour*
【摄氏温度计】centigrade thermometer; Celsius thermometer
【摄像】make a video recording (with a video camera or TV camera)
【摄像机】video camera; television camera: 录像～ *video camera* / 电视～ *television camera; TV camera*
【摄行】〈书〉act for another
【摄影】❶ take a photograph: ～留念 *have a souvenir photograph taken* / 航空～ *aerial photography* / 红外～ *infrared photography* / 风景～ *landscape photography* ❷ shoot a film; film: 全景(内景,外景)～ *panoramic (interior, exterior) shooting* ◇ ～记者 press photographer; cameraman; ～棚 film studio; ～师 photographer; cameraman; ～室 photographic studio; photo studio; ～展览 photographic exhibition; photo exhibition
【摄影机】camera: 电影～ *motion-picture camera; cinecamera; cinematograph* / 立体～ *stereoscopic camera*
【摄政】act as regent
【摄政王】prince regent
【摄制】film produce: 北京电影制片厂～ *produced by the Beijing Film Studio* / ～组 *production unit*

慑 动〈书〉fear; be awed: ～于其淫威 *be cowed by his despotic power*
【慑服】❶ submit in fear; succumb ❷ cow sb. into submission

麝 名 ❶ musk deer ❷〈略〉见〖麝香〗
【麝牛】musk-ox
【麝鼠】muskrat
【麝香】musk

shēn

申 动 state; express; explain: 重申
【申办】apply for permission to do sth.; bid
【申报】❶ report to a higher body ❷ declare sth. (to the Customs): 出国人员必须向海关～其携带出境的外币。*Travellers leaving the country must declare the amount of foreign currency they are taking with them.*
【申辩】defend oneself; explain oneself; argue (or plead) one's case: 被告有权～。*The accused has the right to defend himself.*
【申斥】rebuke (usu. one's subordinates); reprimand: 小孩不听话,不要一味～。*Don't scold your children every time they don't listen to you.*
【申令】issue orders: ～全国 *issue orders to all parts of the country*
【申明】declare; state; avow: ～自己的立场 *state one's position* / ～理由 *give one's reason for doing sth.* / 公开～ *openly avow*
【申请】apply for; file an application: 向…～ *make an application to; lodge (or file) an application with; present a petition to* / ～入(出)境签证 *apply for an entry (exit) visa* ◇ ～国 applicant country; ～人 applicant; ～书 (written) application; petition
【申述】state; explain in detail: ～立场 *state one's position* / ～来意 *explain the purpose of one's visit* / 作进一步的～ *make further observations*
【申诉】appeal: 向上级提出～ *appeal to the higher authorities*
【申讨】openly condemn; denounce: ～反动派的罪行 *denounce the crimes of the reactionaries*
【申谢】acknowledge one's indebtedness; express one's gratitude
【申雪】❶ appeal for redress of a wrong ❷ redress a wrong: 多年的冤狱终于得到了～。*The long-standing wrong was at last redressed.*
【申冤】❶ redress an injustice; right a wrong ❷

appeal for redress of a wrong

伸 动 stretch; extend: ～胳臂 *stretch one's arms* / ～舌头 *stick out one's tongue* / 两臂平～ *extend (or stretch, spread) one's arms horizontally* / 跳水时腿要～直。*When you dive you must keep your legs straight.*

【伸大姆哥】hold up one's thumb (in praise)

【伸开】stretch out: 把胳臂～。*Stretch out your arms.*

【伸懒腰】stretch oneself

【伸手】❶ stretch (or hold) out one's hand: 他～去拿碗。*He reached for the bowl.* ❷ ask for money, honour, gifts, etc.: 一见美差就～ *try to seize any cushy job that comes along* ❸ have a hand in; poke one's nose into; meddle in

【伸手不见五指】so dark that you can't see your hand in front of you; pitch-dark: 天黑得～,我深一脚浅一脚,摸索着往前走。*It was pitch-dark. I stumbled along, groping my way.*

【伸缩】❶ stretch out and draw back; expand and contract; lengthen and shorten: 这架照像机的镜头可以前后～。*The lens of this camera can be pulled back and forth.* ❷ flexible; elastic; adjustable: 这些规定～性很大。*These regulations are quite elastic (or flexible).* / 没有～余地 *leave one no latitude* ◇ ～缝[建] expansion joint; ～三角架 extension tripod

【伸缩性】flexibility; elasticity

【伸头探脑】stretch one's neck to see (or find out); peep; spy

【伸腿】❶ stretch one's legs ❷ step in (to gain an advantage) ❸〈口〉kick the bucket; turn up one's toes

【伸延】extend; stretch: 街道沿着港湾～。*The streets run along the bay.*

【伸腰】straighten one's back; straighten oneself up

【伸引】extend: 我们的谈话向更细微的问题～开去。*Our conversation extended to more subtle questions.*

【伸展】spread; extend; stretch: 草原一直～到遥远的天边。*The prairie stretches to the distant horizon.*

【伸张】uphold; promote: ～正气,打击歪风 *promote healthy tendencies and combat unhealthy ones* ◇ ～正义 uphold justice

身 Ⅰ 名 ❶ body: ～肢 *body and limbs* / ～负重伤 *be seriously injured (or wounded)* ❷ life: 舍身 ❸ oneself; personally: 你～为组长,应当负起责任来。*As group leader, you should take charge.* ❹ one's moral character and conduct: 修身 ❺ the main part of a structure; body: 树～ *trunk* / 船～ *the body of a ship; hull* Ⅱ 量 (for clothes) suit: 一～新衣服 *a new suit*

【身败名裂】lose all standing and reputation; bring shame and ruin upon oneself; be utterly discredited: ～,遗臭万年 *bring ruin and eternal shame on oneself*

【身板】〈方〉body; bodily health: ～儿挺结实 *have a strong physique*

【身边】❶ at (or by) one's side: 他在专家～工作,进步很快。*Working at the side of the experts, he has made rapid progress.* ❷ (have sth.) on one; with one: ～没带钱 *have no money on one* / 她～总是带着药箱。*She never goes anywhere without her medical kit.*

【身不由己】involuntarily; under compulsion; in spite of oneself: 车子突然一停,他～地向前一扑。*When the bus came to a sudden stop, he jerked forward involuntarily.*

【身材】stature; figure: ～矮小 *short and slight of stature* / ～苗条 *have a slender (or slim) figure* / ～魁梧 *of great height and powerful build; tall and sturdy*

【身长】❶ height (of a person) ❷ length (of a garment from shoulder to hemline)

【身段】❶ (woman's) figure ❷ (dancer's) posture

【身份】❶ status; capacity; identity: 不合～ *incompatible with one's status* / 以官方(私人,个人)～发言 *speak in an official (a private, a personal) capacity* ❷ honourable position; dignity: 有失～ *be beneath one's dignity* / 符合其～ *befitting his position* ❸〈方〉the quality of a thing

【身份证】identity card; identification card; ID card; ID

【身高】height (of a person): 他～一米八。*He is 180 centimetres in height.*

【身故】(of a person) die: 因病～ *die of an illness*

【身后】after one's death

【身怀六甲】be with child; be pregnant

【身价】❶ social status ❷ the selling price of a slave

【身价百倍】a meteoric rise in social status: 一夜之间～ *have a sudden rise in social status*

【身教】teach others by one's own example

【身教胜于言教】Example is better than precept.

【身经百战】have fought a hundred battles: ～的老战士 *a veteran who has fought countless battles; a battle-tested veteran; a seasoned fighter*

【身历】experience personally: ～其境 *personally go through (or experience) the situation*

【身量】〈口〉height (of a person); stature: 她～不高。*She's not tall.*

【身临其境】be personally on the scene: 这个场面写得很生动,使人有～之感。*The scene is so vividly portrayed that the reader feels as if he is participating.*

【身强力壮】(of a person) strong; tough; sturdy

【身躯】body; stature: 健壮的～ *a sound body* / ～高大 *tall of stature*

【身上】❶ on one's body: ～穿一件白衬衫 *wear a white shirt* / 我～不舒服。*I'm not feeling well.* / 希望寄托在青年人～。*Our hopes are placed on the young people.* ❷ (have sth.) on one; with one: ～没带笔。*I haven't got a pen with me.* / ～有零钱吗? *Have you got any change on you?*

【身世】one's (unfortunate) life experience; one's (hard) lot: ～凄凉 *have had a sad life*

【身手】skill; talent: ～不凡 *be of no ordinary talent; display consummate skill*

【身首异处】be beheaded

【身受】experience personally: ～其害 *personally experience its baneful influence (or evil effects)*

【身体】❶ body: 保持～平衡 *keep one's balance* ❷ health: 注意～ *look after one's health* / 她最近～怎么样? *How is she these days?*

【身体力行】earnestly practise what one advocates; practise what one preaches

【身体素质】physique; constitution: ～好 *have a strong constitution*

【身外之物】external things; mere worldly possessions: 功名到底是～,德行才是要紧的。*Fame and fortune are external things after all; it's goodness that really counts.*

【身无长物】同〖别无长物〗

【身先士卒】lead one's men in a charge; charge at the head of one's men

【身心】body and mind: ～健康 *sound in body and mind; physically and mentally healthy*

【身形】figure (of person):～瘦长 *tall and thin*

【身影】a person's silhouette; form; figure: 一个高大的～ *a tall figure*

【身孕】pregnancy: 她有了三个月的～。*She is three months pregnant.*

【身在福中不知福】not appreciate the happy life one enjoys; Growing up in happiness, one often fails to appreciate what happiness really means.

【身正不怕影子斜】a man standing straight doesn't worry about his shadow slanting—an upright man fears no gossip

【身子】〈口〉❶ body: 光着～ *be naked* / ～不大舒服 *not feel well* ❷ pregnancy: 有了七个月的～ *be seven months pregnant*

【身子骨儿】〈方〉one's health; physique: 爷爷的～还挺结实。*Grandpa's enjoying good health.* or *Grandpa's still going strong.*

【身姿】manner of holding oneself; carriage; posture; figure: 她的～非常苗条。*She has a slender figure.*

呻

(构词成分) 见下

【呻吟】groan; moan: 痛得直～ *moan and groan with pain* / 伤员的～ *the moans of the wounded*

绅

名 ❶ girdle (worn by ancient officials and literary men) ❷ gentry

【绅士】gentleman; gentry

【绅士协定】同〖君子协定〗

参

名 ginseng ——另见 cān; cēn

砷

名 [化] arsenic (As)

莘

(构词成分) 见下

【莘莘】〈书〉numerous: ～学子 *a great number of disciples; large numbers of students*

深

Ⅰ 形 ❶ deep: 一口～井 *a deep well* / 雪～过膝 *knee-deep snow* / 林～苔滑。*The forest is thick and the moss is slippery.* ❷ hard to understand; difficult; abstruse; profound: 这本书给孩子们看太～了。*The book is too difficult for children.* ❸ thoroughgoing; penetrating; profound: 问题想得很～ *think deeply about a question* / 功夫～ *have put in a great deal of effort* ❹ (of relations or feelings) close; intimate: 交情～ *be very close; be on intimate terms* / 他们之间的感情已经很～了。*They are already deeply in love with each other.* ❺ (of colour) dark; deep; rich: ～蓝 *dark blue* / ～红 *deep red; crimson* / 颜色太～。*The colour is too dark (or deep).* ❻ far on in the day, night, season, etc.; late: 夜～了。*It was in the dead of night (or late at night).* Ⅱ 名 depth: 测量水～ *sound (or plumb) the depth of the water* / 这间大厅有三米宽、五米～。*This hall is 3 m. wide and 5 m. deep (or 3 m. in width and 5 m. in depth).* / 这山洞有多～? *What is the depth of the cave?* Ⅲ 副 very; greatly; deeply: ～知 *know very well; be fully (or keenly) aware* / ～受感动 *be deeply moved; be greatly touched* / ～感不安 *be greatly disturbed; be very much worried* / ～表同情 *show deep (or profound) sympathy* / ～得人心 *enjoy immense popular support* / ～恐出事 *be terribly afraid that something may go wrong*

【深奥】abstruse; profound; recondite: ～的哲理 *abstruse philosophy; a profound truth*

【深闭固拒】obstinate and perverse

【深不可测】unfathomable; enigmatic: 她～地微微一笑。*She gave an enigmatic smile.*

【深藏若虚】hide what one has and act as if one had nothing—be modest about one's talent or ability; not be given to boasting or showing off

【深层结构】[语] deep structure

【深长】(of meaning, intention, etc.) profound

【深沉】❶ deep: 暮色～。*The dusk is deepening.* / ～的哀悼 *deep grief over sb.'s death* ❷(of sound or voice) low-pitched; deep; dull: 大提琴～的音调 *the deep notes of a cello* ❸ undemonstrative; reserved: ～的微笑 *a knowing smile; a significant smile* / 这人很～。*He's a deep one.*

【深成岩】[地质] plutonic rock; plutonite

【深仇大恨】bitter and deep-seated hatred; profound hatred

【深处】depths; recesses: 在密林～ *in the depths (or recesses) of the forest* / 在内心～ *in the depth (or innermost recesses) of one's heart* / 在灵魂～ *in one's innermost soul* / 在思想～ *in one's heart of hearts*

【深度】❶ degree of depth; depth: 测量河水的～ *sound the depth of the river* ❷ profundity; depth; thoroughness: 他的发言缺乏～。*His speech lacks depth.* ❸ advanced stage of development: 向生产的～和广度进军 *boost production both in depth and in breadth*

【深度计】depth gauge

【深更半夜】at dead of night; in the depth (or dead) of night; in the middle of the night: 你打哪儿来? ～的! *Where have you come from so late at night?*

【深耕】[农] deep ploughing

【深沟高垒】deep trenches and high ramparts; strong defence

【深广】deep and broad: 影响～ *be of wide and profound influence* / 见识～ *be of wide experience and deep knowledge*

【深闺】boudoir

【深海】deep sea ◇ ～采矿 deep-sea mining; ～测量 bathymetry; ～带 abyssal zone; ～鱼 deep-sea fish; ～资源 deep-sea resources

【深厚】❶ deep; profound: ～的感情 *deep (or profound) feelings* ❷ solid; deep-seated: ～的基础 *a solid foundation*

【深呼吸】deep breathing

【深化】deepen: 认识的～ *deepening of cognition* / 矛盾的～ *intensification of a contradiction*

【深加工】downstream processing; intensive processing: ～产品 *down-stream products; high value added products*

【深交】deep friendship: 他们彼此还谈得来,虽然并没有～。*They get along quite well, though they are not close friends.*

【深究】go into (a matter) seriously; get to the bottom (of a matter): 对这些小事不必～。*These are small matters and you don't have to go into them seriously.*

【深居简出】live in the seclusion of one's own home

【深刻】deep; profound; deep-going: ～地阐明 *expound profoundly* / 给某人留下～的印象 *make a deep impression on sb.*

【深空】[物] deep space

【深密】deep; thick; dense: 他脸上皱纹～。*His face is creased with deep wrinkles.*

【深明大义】be deeply conscious of the righteousness of a cause; be clear on matters of principle

【深谋远虑】think deeply and plan carefully; be circumspect and far-sighted

【深浅】❶ depth: 你去探一下这条小河的～,看能不能蹚水过去。*Go and find out how deep the stream is and whether we can wade across.* ❷ shade (of colour): 颜色～不同 *of different shades* ❸ proper limits (for speech or action); sense of propriety: 说话没个～ *speak without thought and often inappropriately*

【深切】❶ heartfelt; deep; profound: ～关怀 *be deeply concerned about; show profound concern for* / ～怀念 *dearly cherish the memory of* ❷ keen; penetrating; thorough: ～地感受到 *keenly realize* / ～地理解 *understand thoroughly*

【深情】deep feeling; deep love: 她～地望着她母亲的遗像。*She gazed with deep feeling at the portrait of her deceased mother.*

【深情厚谊】profound sentiments of friendship; profound friendship

【深秋】late autumn

【深入】❶ go deep into; penetrate into: ～实际 *go deep into the realities of life* / ～生活 *plunge into the thick of life* ❷ thorough; deep-going: 做～细致的思想工作 *conduct thoroughgoing and painstaking ideological work* / ～进行调查研究 *make a thorough investigation and study*

【深入浅出】explain the profound in simple terms

【深入人心】strike root in the hearts of the people

【深山】remote mountains: ～老林 *remote, thickly forested mountains*

【深深】deeply; keenly; profoundly: ～地鞠个躬 *make a deep bow* / ～地吸一口气 *take a deep breath* / ～感到友情的温暖 *keenly feel the warmth of sb.'s friendship*

【深水】deep water ◇ ～港 deepwater port; ～码头 deepwater wharf; ～炸弹 depth charge; depth bomb

【深思】think deeply about; ponder deeply over: 这难道不值得～吗? *Is this not worth pondering?* or *Does this not call for deep thought?* / 这个问题值得我们～。*This matter gives us much food for thought.*

【深思熟虑】careful consideration: 这个决定是他们经过～后作出的。*Their decision was made after careful consideration.*

【深邃】❶ deep: ～的山谷 *a deep valley* ❷ profound; abstruse; recondite: 寓意～ *have a profound message*

【深谈】discuss thoroughly; go deeply into: 这个问题我没同他～。*I didn't go deeply into the matter with him.*

【深透】deep and thorough: 问题必须分析～。*We must make a deep and thorough analysis of the problem.*

【深味】profound meaning or significance: 他从老张的笑意里捉摸出了～。*He sees profound meaning behind Lao Zhang's smile.*

【深文周纳】apply the law with the utmost severity and make sb. appear guilty

【深恶痛绝】hate bitterly; abhor; detest

【深信】be deeply convinced; firmly believe

【深省】(又作'深醒') wake up to a sharp awareness of the truth: 发人深省

【深夜】late at night; in the small hours of the morning: 工作到～ *work far into the night*

【深意】profound meaning: 领会文章的～ *grasp the profound meaning of the article*

【深渊】abyss: 苦难的～ *the abyss of suffering (or misery)*

【深远】profound and lasting; far-reaching: 具有～的历史意义 *have profound historic significance* / 影响～ *have a far-reaching influence*

【深造】take a more advanced course of study or training; pursue advanced studies: 送到体育学院～ *be sent to the Institute of Physical Culture for further training* / 出国～ *pursue advanced studies abroad*

【深宅大院】imposing dwellings and spacious courtyards

【深湛】profound and thorough：～的著作 *a profound work* / 功夫～ *consummate skill*

【深挚】deep and sincere：～的友谊 *deep and sincere friendship*；*intimate friendship*

【深重】very grave；extremely serious：危机～ *be in the grip of a crisis*

shén

什

什（构词成分）见下 ——另见 shí

【什么】❶（used before a noun or by itself）what：你找～？*What are you looking for?* / 你找～人？*Who are you looking for?* / 你的理想是～？*What is your ideal in life?* ❷ something；anything：我想吃点～。*I'd like to have something to eat.* / 我讲不出～新鲜玩意儿。*There won't be anything new in my story.* ❸（used before 也 or 都）any；every：他～都不怕。*He's afraid of nothing.* / 时间比～都宝贵。*Time is more precious than anything else.* ❹（used correlatively with another 什么）whatever：冰箱里有～，咱们就吃～。*We'll eat whatever we can find in the fridge.* / 我有～说～，绝对没有保留。*I'll just say what's on my mind, withholding nothing.* ❺（expressing anger，surprise，censure or negation）：～！没有水？*What! No water?* / ～！都九点了，车还没有来！*What's happened? It's 9 o'clock and the taxi isn't here yet!* ❻（expressing disapproval or disagreement）：～不懂！装糊涂就是了。*What do you mean—not understand? You're just pretending.* / 年轻～呀，我都五十多了。*Young indeed! I'm past 50 already.* ❼ things like；such as；and so on；and what not：～乒乓球啊，羽毛球啊，篮球啊，他都会玩。*He can play table tennis，badminton，volleyball，anything.*

【什么的】（used after a series of items）things like that；and so on；and what not：他不喜欢打篮球～，就爱下个围棋。*He doesn't go in for basketball and things like that；what he's really keen on is go.*

神

神 Ⅰ 名 ❶ god；deity；divinity：～鬼 *gods and ghosts* ❷ spirit；mind：耗～ *take up one's energy* / 双目有～ *have a pair of piercing eyes* ❸ expression；look：眼神 Ⅱ 形 ❶ supernatural；magical；miraculous：～投手 *sharpshooter*（*in basketball*）；*superb shooter*（*or scorer*）❷〈方〉smart；clever：这孩子真～！*What a smart child!* / 这家伙～了！*This fellow is incredible!*

【神不守舍】be out of one's wits；be distracted

【神不知鬼不觉】unknown to god or ghost—without anybody knowing it；with great secrecy：她想起那天晚上，～地，他突然在她背后出现。*She recalled that evening when he had sprung up behind her as if from nowhere.*

【神采】demeanour；mien；countenance：他的眼睛充满了喜悦的～。*His eyes beamed with joy.*

【神采奕奕】glowing with health and radiating vigour

【神出鬼没】come and go like a shadow；appear and disappear mysteriously.

【神道】❶ the way of the gods ❷〈口〉gods；deities；divinities ❸ aisle leading to the coffin chamber of an ancient tomb；tomb passage ❹（又作'神道教'）Shinto（the native religion of Japan）；Shintoism

【神甫】（又作'神父'）Father（a title of respect for a Roman Catholic priest）

【神怪】gods and spirits

【神乎其神】fantastic；wonderful；miraculous：吹得～ *laud sth.*（*or sb.*）*to the skies*

【神乎】（shénhu）strange；odd；sensational；fantastic：他越说越～。*As he talked，his story became more and more fantastic.*

【神化】deify

【神话】mythology；myth；fairy tale

【神魂】state of mind；mind：～不安 *be distracted*；*have the jitters*

【神魂不定】be distracted；be deeply perturbed

【神魂颠倒】be infatuated：他叫那个女人给弄得～了。*He lost his head over that woman.*

【神机妙算】a superb strategy，a miracle of foresight；wonderful foresight in military operations，etc.

【神交】❶ friends with mutual understanding and admiration ❷ friendship grown out of mutual admiration without the friends ever having met

【神经】nerve：脑(感觉，交感)～ *cranial*（*sensory*，*sympathetic*）*nerve* / ～紧张 *be nervous*；*be jittery* / ～坚强 *have strong nerves*；*have iron nerves* / 刺激了他的～ *got on his nerves*；*gave him the nerves* ◇ ～错乱 mental disorder；～毒气 nerve gas；～官能症 neurosis；～节 ganglion；～科学 neuroscience；～末梢 nerve ending；～衰弱 neurasthenia；～索 nerve cord；～痛 neuralgia；～外科 neurosurgery；～系统 nervous system；～细胞 同〖神经元〗；～纤维 nerve fibre；～性皮炎 neurodermatitis；～炎 neuritis；～遗传学 neurogenetics；～语言学 neurolinguistics；～元（又作'神经原'）neuron；nerve cell；～战 war of nerves；～质 nervousness；～中枢 nerve centre

【神经病】❶ neuropathy ❷ mental disorder；nervous disorder；neurosis ❸ mentally disordered；neurotic：这家伙有点～。*That chap's not quite right in the head.*

【神经过敏】❶ neuroticism ❷ neurotic；oversensitive

【神来之笔】an inspired work；a stroke of genius

【神力】superhuman strength；extraordinary power

【神聊】indulge in idle and empty talk：他俩只要一见面，就天南海北地～起来。*Whenever they met，they would start chattering away about everything under the sun.*

【神灵】gods；deities；divinities

【神秘】mysterious; mystical: ～人物 *a mysterious person*; *a person shrouded in mystery* ◇ ～化 make a mystery of; mystify; ～主义 mysticism

【神妙】wonderful; marvellous; ingenious: ～的笔法 *wonderful style of writing*; *ingenious brushwork*

【神明】gods; deities; divinities: 我死而有知,必当诉之～。*If my spirit survives after death, I will certainly take my case to the gods.*

【神女】goddess

【神炮手】crack gunner

【神品】❶ a sublime work (usu. said of a painting or a piece of calligraphy) ❷ holy orders

【神奇】magical; mystical; miraculous: ～的效果 *miraculous effect*; *magical effect*

【神气】❶ expression; air; manner: 他脸上显出得意的～。*He had an air of complacency.* / 他说话的～特别像他爸爸。*He is very much like his father in the way he speaks.* ❷ spirited; vigorous: 小明带上红领巾多～。*Xiaoming looks quite impressive with his red scarf.* ❸ putting on airs; cocky; overweening: 呵!他倒～起来了。*Humph! What airs he gives himself!* / 你～什么? *What makes you think you're so wonderful?* or *You've got nothing to be cocky about.*

【神气活现】very cocky; high and mighty: 看她那个～的样子,真叫人受不了。*Look how she gives herself airs. It's really unbearable.*

【神气十足】looking very dignified; putting on grand airs; looking triumphant: 他～地走在前边。*He was proudly marching in the fore.*

【神枪手】crack shot; expert marksman; sharpshooter

【神情】expression; look: 露出愉快的～ *look happy*; *wear a happy expression* / ～尴尬 *look embarrassed*

【神曲】[中] medicated leaven

【神权】❶ religious authority; theocracy ❷ rule by divine right

【神人】❶ spiritual being; Taoist immortal ❷ a man of distinguished appearance

【神色】expression; look: ～不对 *look queer* / ～慌张 *look flustered* ◇ ～自若 be perfectly calm and collected; show composure and presence of mind

【神社】❶ place of worship; shrine; altar ❷ a Shinto shrine; jinja

【神神道道】〈方〉odd; fantastic; bizarre: 这人～的。*He's very odd.*

【神圣】sacred; holy: ～职责 *sacred duty*

【神思】state of mind; mental state: ～不定 *be distracted* / 定一定～ *manage to collect oneself* ◇ ～恍惚 be distracted; be distraught; be in a trance

【神似】be alike in spirit; be an excellent likeness: 不仅形似,而且～ *be alike not only in appearance but also in spirit* / 他画的奔马,栩栩如生,极其～。*The galloping horses he paints are extremely lifelike.*

【神速】marvellously quick; with amazing speed: 收效～ *yield marvellously quick results* / ～地向前挺进 *advance with lightning speed*

【神算】miraculous foresight; marvellous prediction

【神态】expression; manner; bearing; mien: ～悠闲 *look perfectly relaxed* / 看她的～像舞蹈演员。*From the way she carries herself she must be a dancer.*

【神通】magic power; remarkable ability

【神通广大】have vast magic powers; possess unusual powers; be infinitely resourceful

【神童】child prodigy

【神往】be carried away; be rapt; be charmed

【神威】martial prowess; invincible might: 人民军队的～ *the martial prowess of the people's army*

【神位】spirit tablet

【神仙】❶ supernatural being; celestial being; immortal ❷ a person who has the power of clairvoyance or who is free from worldly cares ◇ ～葫芦 [机] chain block; ～鱼 angelfish

【神像】the picture or statue of a god or Buddha

【神效】magical effect; miraculous effect

【神学】theology ◇ ～博士 Doctor of Divinity (D.D.); ～院 theological seminary

【神医】highly skilled doctor; miracle-working doctor

【神异】❶ gods and spirits ❷ magical; mystical; miraculous

【神鹰】[动] condor

【神勇】extraordinarily brave; superhumanly brave

【神游】〈书〉make a spiritual tour; range in fancy

【神韵】romantic charm (in literature and art)

【神职人员】clergy; clergymen

【神志】consciousness; senses; mind: ～清醒 *be in one's right mind*; *remain fully conscious* / ～昏迷 *have lost consciousness*; *be in a state of delirium*

【神州】the Divine Land (a poetic name for China)

钟 名 [化] arsonium

shěn

审 Ⅰ 形 careful; meticulous: 审视 Ⅱ 动 ❶ examine; go over: ～稿 *go over a manuscript or draft and give comments* ❷ interrogate; try: ～案 *try a case* ❸ 〈书〉know; be aware of: 未～其详 *not know the details*

【审办】try, hear (a case): 法院受理～民院案件。*The court accepts and will hear civil suits.*

【审查】examine (plans, proposals, credentials, etc.); investigate: ～属实。*The fact was established after investigation.* / ～经费 *check up on the funds*

【审察】❶ closely observe; closely examine ❷ investigate

【审处】❶ try and punish: 交由人民法院～ *hand*

over to the people's court for trial ❷ deliberate and decide

【审订】examine and revise; revise: ～教材 *revise teaching materials* / 请李教授～此稿。*Ask Professor Li to make a critical examination of this manuscript (or to revise this manuscript).*

【审定】examine and approve; examine and finalize: 计划已由委员会～。*The plan has been examined and approved by the committee.*

【审读】read and evaluate (a manuscript); read: 拼版样已经审稿人～通过。*The page proofs have been read and approved by the responsible reader.*

【审改】examine and revise (a manuscript); revise ◇ ～本 a draft for examination and revision (before printing)

【审核】verify; check: ～预算 *verify a budget* / ～存货清单 *check an inventory list*

【审计】audit: 进行～ *conduct an audit* / 事前～ *pre-emptive audit* / 事后～ *programme result audit* ◇ ～机构 auditing bodies; ～员 auditor; ～长 auditor general

【审校】❶ check and revise ❷ reviser

【审结】[法] complete legal procededings; decide (a case); close a case

【审看】❶ view movies, TV and theatrical programmes, etc. (before public showing) ❷ scrutinize; examine carefully: 他究竟是何许人物,还得细细～。*We still need to study him carefully to find out what kind of man he is.*

【审理】[法] try; hear: ～案件 *try a case; hear a case* / ～诉讼案 *adjudicate a litigation*

【审美】appreciation of the beautiful: ～能力 *aesthetic judgment* ◇ ～观 aesthetic conceptions; aesthetic standards

【审判】bring to trial; try: 受到人民的～ *be tried by the people* / 由军事法庭～ *be court-martialled* / ～经济案件 *try economic cases* ◇ ～程序 judicial procedure; ～机关 judicial organ; ～权 judicial authority; jurisdiction; ～员 judge; judicial officer; ～长 presiding judge

【审批】examine and approve; examine and give instructions: 报请上级～ *submit to the higher level for examination and approval*

【审片】review of a film by the censor: 通过～ *pass through censor review*

【审评】❶ examine, appraise (quality of products) ❷ evaluate (performance)

【审慎】cautious; careful; circumspect: ～从事 *steer a cautious course* / ～地考虑问题 *think over a problem carefully* / ～乐观 *cautious optimism; guarded optimism*

【审时度势】judge the hour and size up the situation: 他是一位善于～、多谋善断的经理人员。*He is a resourceful and resolute manager who can make a correct assessment of the situation.*

【审视】look closely at; examine closely: 他～再三,未置可否。*He examined it closely over and over again, but still declined to give any comment.*

【审听】review music programme or performance before public showing

【审问】interrogate; question: 正在进行～。*The interrogation is going on.*

【审讯】[法] ❶ hearing: 法官对离婚案的双方当事人各给予一次～。*The judge gave a hearing to both parties of the divorce case.* ❷ interrogate; hear; try: ～俘虏 *interrogate prisoners of war*

【审验】examine and verify: 在进行机动车检验的同时～驾驶员 *test the driver and vehicle at the same time*

【审议】(of a deliberative body, a committee, etc.) review; deliberate: 重新～提案 *make a critical reexamination of the proposal* / 这个纲要草案已发给你们,请～。*The draft outline (of the plan) is now submitted to you for review.* ◇ ～机构 deliberative body

【审阅】examine carefully and critically: 聘请专家～稿件并提出意见 *get some specialists to go over the manuscript and give comments and criticisms* / 此讲话记录未经本人～。*These notes of the speech have not been checked and approved by the speaker.*

哂

动〈书〉smile

【哂笑】❶〈书〉laugh at; ridicule ❷ smile: ～不语 *smile but say not a word*

谂

动〈书〉❶ know; be aware of ❷ advise; urge

【谂熟】know sth. or sb. well; be familiar with; have an intimate knowledge of

婶

名 ❶ wife of father's younger brother; aunt ❷ a form of address for a woman about one's mother's age; aunt; auntie: 张大～ *Aunt Zhang*

【婶母】wife of father's younger brother; aunt

【婶子】〈口〉wife of father's younger brother; aunt

shèn

肾

名 [生理] kidney

【肾功能试验】kidney function test

【肾功能衰竭】renal failure; kidney failure

【肾结石】[医] kidney stone; renal calculus

【肾亏】[中] renal weakness

【肾囊】[中] scrotum

【肾上腺】[生理] adrenal gland; adrenal ◇ ～素 adrenaline

【肾下垂】nephroptosis

【肾炎】nephritis

【肾移植】kidney transplant; renal transplant

【肾盂】[生理] renal pelvis ◇ ～肾炎 pyelonephritis; ～炎 pyelitis

【肾脏】kidney

甚

副 ❶ very; extremely: 知者～少。*Very few people know about it.* ❷ more than: 他的病情恶化,日～一日。*His condition got worse and*

worse. or *His condition steadily deteriorated*.
【甚高频】[无] very high frequency (VHF)
【甚为】very; extremely: ～痛快 *find it most satisfying* / 两人～亲密。*They are quite intimate*.
【甚嚣尘上】cause a great clamour: 所谓和战问题竟闹得～。*A great clamour arose around the question of peace or war*.
【甚至】(又作'甚至于') ❶ even to the extent that: 他忙得～好几夜没睡觉。*He was so busy that he didn't even go to bed for several nights*. ❷ (go) so far as to; so much so that: 他对同志们的批评置若罔闻,～反唇相讥。*He not only ignored the criticism of his comrades but went so far as to be sarcastic*.

胂 名 [化] arsine

渗 动 ooze; seep: 包扎伤口的绷带上～出了血。*Blood oozed out of the dressing*. / 雨水都～到地里去了。*The rain all seeped into the ground*.
【渗沟】sewer
【渗坑】seepage pit
【渗漏】seepage: ～损失 *seepage loss*
【渗滤】[化] percolation filtration; percolation ◇ ～白土 [油] percolation clay; ～器 percolator
【渗入】❶ permeate; seep into: ～地下 *permeate the ground*; *seep into the ground* ❷ 〈贬〉(of influence, etc.) penetrate; infiltrate
【渗色】[纺] bleeding
【渗碳】[冶] carburization; cementation ◇ ～钢 carburizing steel; ～体 cementite
【渗透】❶ [物] osmosis ❷ permeate; seep: 雨水～了泥土。*The rain permeated the soil*. / 每一件产品都～了工人的心血。*Every product embodies the painstaking effort of the workers*. ❸ infiltrate: 经济～ *economic infiltration* ◇ ～性 permeability; ～压 osmotic pressure; ～战术 infiltration tactics

慎 形 careful; cautious: 保守国家机密,～之又～。*One cannot be too careful in guarding state secrets*. / 不～ *carelessly*
【慎密】cautious and meticulous
【慎言慎行】be cautious in speech and in conduct
【慎重】cautious; careful; prudent; discreet: 采取～的态度 *adopt a prudent policy* / 处理这件事必须～。*The matter has to be handled with great care*.

蜃 名 clam
【蜃景】同〖海市蜃楼〗

瘆 动 horrify: ～人 *making one's flesh creep*; *horrifying* / ～得慌 *be horrified*

shēng

升 Ⅰ 动 ❶ rise; hoist; go up; ascend: 东方红,太阳～。*In the east the sky is red. The sun is rising*. ❷ promote: ～教授 *get promoted to professor* / ～到领导岗位 *be promoted to positions of leadership* Ⅱ 量 litre (l.): 三～啤酒 *three litres of beer*
【升班】〈口〉go up (one grade in school)
【升船机】ship lift
【升调】[语音] rising tune or tone
【升格】raise; promote; upgrade: 将外交关系～为大使级 *upgrade diplomatic relations to ambassadorial level*
【升汞】[化] mercuric chloride
【升官】be promoted ◇ ～发财 win promotion and get rich; (be out for) power and money
【升号】[音] sharp (♯)
【升华】❶ [物] sublimation ❷ raising of things to a higher level; distillation; sublimation: 艺术是现实生活的～。*Art is the distillation of life*. ◇ ～干燥 lyophilization
【升级】❶ go up one or more grades: 连升三级 *be promoted three grades in succession* ❷ escalate: 战争～ *escalation (of a war)* ❸ (of product) update, upgrade: 产品的～换代 *replace (outmoded) products and upgrade the line*
【升级换代】(of manufactured goods) updating and upgrading
【升降】go up and down ◇ ～舵 [航空] elevator; ～机 elevator; lift; ～奖惩 promotion and demotion, reward and punishment
【升力】[航空] lift: ～特性 *lift efficiency*
【升幂】[数] ascending power: ～级数 *ascending power series*
【升平】peace: ～世界 *peaceful world*; *peaceful life*
【升旗】hoist (or raise) a flag: ～仪式 *flag-raising ceremony*
【升迁】be transferred and promoted
【升势】rally; upswing: 股票价格在经历了连续7个交易日的强劲～之后,于2月10日告跌。*After rising sharply for seven consecutive trading days, stock prices fell on February 10*.
【升水】[经] premium ◇ ～率 premium rate
【升堂入室】pass through the hall into the inner chamber—have profound scholarship; become highly proficient
【升腾】(of flames, gas, etc.) leap up; rise: 火焰～。*The flames leapt up*. / 山头上～起白蒙蒙的雾气。*A thick mist rose over the hilltop*.
【升天】go up to Heaven—die
【升温】❶ rise in temperature ❷ 〈喻〉rise in enthusiasm, etc.: 股票热继续～。*The passion for stocks continues to grow*.
【升限】[航空] ceiling: ～高度 *ceiling height*
【升学】go to a school of a higher grade; enter a higher school ◇ ～率 the proportion of students entering schools of a higher grade
【升压】[电] step up; boost ◇ ～变压器 step-up transformer; ～器 booster
【升值】[经] ❶ revalue ❷ appreciate

生 Ⅰ 动 ❶ give birth to; bear: ～孩子 *give*

birth to a child ❷ be born; come into existence: 她～下来不多日子,她妈就死了。*Her mother died soon after she was born*. ❸ grow: ～芽 *sprout* ❹ be afflicted with; get; have: ～疖子 *get boils* / ～冻疮 *get chilblains* ❺ light (a fire): ～炉子 *light a stove* Ⅱ 名 ❶ life; living: 谋生 ❷ pupil; student: 留级～ *a pupil who is repeating the year's work* ❸ intellectual; scholar: 书生 ❹ male role (one of the four main roles in traditional opera) ❺ noun suffix, used in names of occupations or stations of persons: 医～ *doctor* Ⅲ 形 ❶ alive; living: 生龙活虎 / 生擒 ❷ unripe; green: ～的苹果 *a green apple* / 这些桃子还是～的。*The peaches are not ripe yet*. ❸ raw; uncooked: ～肉 *raw meat* / 黄瓜可以～吃。*Cucumbers can be eaten raw*. ❹ unprocessed; unrefined; crude: 生石膏 ❺ unfamiliar; unacquainted; strange: 刚到这里,工作还很～。*I've only just come here. I'm still not familiar with the work*. ❻ stiff; mechanical: 生凑 Ⅳ 副 (used before certain words indicating feeling or perception) very; much: ～疼 *very painful*

【生搬硬套】copy mechanically, disregarding specific conditions; apply or copy mechanically

【生变】trouble arises: 日久～。*Delay means trouble*.

【生病】fall ill

【生不逢辰】(又作'生不逢时') be born out of one's time; be born at the wrong time

【生财】develop financial resources; make money ◇ ～有道 know how to make money; have the knack of making money

【生菜】❶ romaine lettuce; cos lettuce ❷ lettuce ❸ row vegetable

【生产】❶ produce; manufacture: 新车间已投入～。*The new workshop has gone into operation*. / 坚守～岗位 *stick to one's post on the production front* ❷ give birth to a child: 她快～了。*She'll be having her baby.* or *She's expecting her baby*. ◇ ～成本 cost of production; manufacturing cost; ～大队 production brigade; ～单位 production unit; ～队 production team; ～方式 mode of production; ～工具 tool of production; ～关系 relations of production; production relations; ～过剩 overproduction; ～合作社 producers' cooperative; ～建设兵团 production and construction corps; ～劳动 productive labour; ～力 productive forces; ～率 productivity; ～手段 means of production; ～要素 essential factors of production (e. g. trained personnel, funds, technologies, resources, etc.); ～责任制 production responsibility system; ～资料 means of production; ～总值 total output value

【生产线】production line; assembly line

【生辰】birthday

【生成】❶ come or bring into being; generate; produce: 碳酸钙加热分解,～氧化钙和二氧化碳。*The thermal decomposition of calcium carbonate produces calcium oxide and carbon dioxide*. ❷ be born with; be gifted with: 他～的一个塌鼻子。*He was born with a flat nose*. ◇ ～物[化] product; resultant; ～语法[语] generative grammar

【生词】new and unfamiliar words (to the student)

【生凑】mechanically put together (disconnected words and phrases); arbitrarily dish up (unrelated facts)

【生存】subsist; exist; live: 鱼离开了水是不能～的。*Fish cannot live without water*. ◇ ～竞争 struggle for existence; ～空间 living space; ～权 right of existence; right to subsistence

【生旦净丑】the male role, the female role, the painted-face role, and the comic role (the four main roles in traditional opera)

【生地】❶ (又作'生地黄') [中] the dried rhizome of rehmannia (Rehmannia glutinosa) ❷ virgin soil; uncultivated land

【生动】lively; vivid; vital: ～的描写 *a lively description*

【生动活泼】lively; vivid and vigorous: ～的语言 *vivid language* / 这次会开得～。*It was a lively meeting*.

【生而知之】be born wise; be born with knowledge; have innate knowledge

【生分】estranged; not as close as before: 很久不来往,就显得～了。*Not having seen each other for so long, we don't feel so close any longer*.

【生父】one's own father

【生根】take root; strike root: 在群众中～开花 *take root and blossom among the masses*

【生光】[气] third contact (of a total solar or lunar eclipse)

【生花妙笔】a brilliant pen; a brilliant style of writing

【生还】come back alive; survive: 无一～。*None survived*.

【生荒】[农] virgin soil; uncultivated land

【生活】❶ life: 日常～ *daily life* / 政治～ *political life* ❷ live: 一个人脱离了社会就不能～下去。*One cannot live cut off from society*. ❸ livelihood: ～困难 *be badly off* / 关心群众的～ *be concerned with the well-being of the masses* / ～出路 *a chance to earn a living* / ～用品 *articles for daily use* ❹ 〈方〉 work (of workers, peasants, or handicraftsmen): 勤勤恳恳做～ *work diligently at one's job; do conscientious work* ◇ ～必需品 necessaries of life; daily necessities; ～补助 extra allowance for living expenses; ～方式 way of life; life style; ～费 living expenses; cost of living; ～福利 welfare; welfare benefits; ～环境 surroundings; environment; ～经验 experience of life; ～来源 source of income; ～能力 [生] viability; ～水平 living standard; ～条件 living conditions; ～习惯 habits and customs; ～细节 trifling matters of everyday life; domestic trivia; ～周期 [生] life cycle; ～资料 means of subsistence; means of livelihood

【生活关】the test of rigorous living conditions: 过好～ *prove oneself able to lead a rigorous life*;

stand the test of a rigorous life

【生活救济】hardship relief assistance; relief

【生活作风】❶ life style ❷〈婉〉behavior with the opposite sex (usu. considered immoral): 人们都说他有～问题。*It is widely believed that his life style is morally questionable.*

【生火】make a fire; light a fire

【生机】❶ lease of life: 一线～ *a slim chance of survival; a gleam of hope* ❷ life; vitality: 春天来了,田野里充满了～。*Spring has come and the fields are full of life.* ◇ ～盎然 full of life; overflowing with vigour; exuberant

【生计】means of livelihood; livelihood: 另谋～ *try to find some other means of livelihood*

【生姜】〈口〉ginger

【生津】[中] promote the secretion of saliva or body fluid

【生境】[生] habitat

【生就】be born with; be gifted with: ～一张利嘴 *have the gift of the gab*

【生客】an unfamiliar guest; stranger

【生恐】be very much afraid; fear greatly: 他～掉队,在后面紧跟。*Afraid of falling behind, he was trying hard to keep up.*

【生拉硬拽】❶ drag sb. along against his will ❷ stretch the meaning

【生来】from birth: 这孩子身体～就结实。*The child was born strong.*

【生老病死】birth and old age, sickness and death—the lot of man

【生冷】raw or cold food: 忌食～。*Avoid eating anything raw or cold.*

【生离死别】part never to meet again; part for ever

【生理】physiology ◇ ～反应 physiological reaction; ～缺陷 physiological defect; physiological deficiency; ～学 physiology; ～盐水[药] physiological saline; normal saline; ～作用 physiological action

【生力军】❶ fresh and combat-worthy troops ❷ fresh activists; new force: 文艺战线上的一支～ *a vital new force on the art and literary front*

【生灵】〈书〉the people

【生灵涂炭】the people are plunged into an abyss of misery: 战祸复发,～。*War broke out again, plunging the people into misery and suffering.*

【生龙活虎】doughty as a dragon and lively as a tiger—brimming (or bursting) with energy; full of vim and vigour: 小伙子们干起活来真是～。*The lads work with furious energy.*

【生路】means of livelihood; way out: 另谋～ *try to find another job; look for a new means of livelihood* / 杀出一条～ *fight one's way out (of an encirclement)*

【生猛】〈方〉alive and jumping vigorously

【生米煮成熟饭】the rice is cooked—what's done can't be undone

【生命】life: ～不息,战斗不止 *fight as long as one has a breath in one's body; go on fighting till one breathes one's last* ◇ ～科学 life science; ～科学家 life scientist; ～特征 vital signs

【生命力】life-force; vitality: 具有强大的～ *have great vitality*

【生命率】vital rates

【生命现象】biological phenomena: 用放射性同位素示踪技术探讨～ *apply radioisotopic tracers to study biological phenomena*

【生命线】lifeline; lifeblood: 铁路、公路是经济繁荣的～。*Railways and highways are a lifeline to a prosperous economy.*

【生命银行】organ depository (where human organs are stored, e.g. eyes, skin, blood, etc.)

【生母】one's own mother

【生怕】be very much afraid; fear greatly: 她轻轻地走进卧室,～惊醒了孩子。*She went into the bedroom softly so as not to wake her child* (or *lest she should wake her child*).

【生皮】rawhide; (untanned) hide

【生啤酒】draught beer

【生僻】(of words, expressions, etc.) uncommon; rare: ～的字眼 *rarely used words* / ～的典故 *obscure allusions*

【生平】all one's life: ～事迹 *one's life story* / 作者～简介 *a brief account of the author's life; a biographical note on the author* / ～第一次 *the first time in one's life*

【生漆】raw lacquer

【生气】❶ take offence; get angry: 她常无缘无故～。*She often gets angry over nothing.* ❷ vim; vitality: 有～ *energetic; dynamic; vigorous* / 毫无～ *lethargic* ◇ ～勃勃 dynamic; vigorous; full of vitality

【生前】before one's death; during one's lifetime: ～愿望 *unrealized wish (of a person who has passed away)* / ～友好 *friends of the deceased*

【生擒】capture alive ◇ ～活捉 capture alive; take prisoner

【生趣】joy of life; pleasures of life

【生人】❶ stranger ❷ be born: 他是1949年～。*He was born in* 1949.

【生日】birthday: 今天是他的～。*Today is his birthday.* / 过～ *celebrate a birthday*

【生色】add colour to; add lustre to; give added significance to: 老师们的演出,为英语晚会～不少。*The teachers' performance made the English evening more enjoyable.*

【生涩】(of language) jerky; choppy; not smooth

【生杀予夺】hold power over sb.'s life and property; have sb. completely in one's power

【生身父母】one's own parents

【生生世世】generation after generation; for generations

【生石膏】plaster stone

【生石灰】quick lime

【生事】make trouble; create a disturbance: 这人脾气很坏,容易～。*He has a bad temper and often makes trouble.*

【生手】new hand; green hand

【生疏】❶ not familiar: 我对这个地方并不算～。

I'm no stranger here. / 我对这项工作很～。*I don't know much about the job.* ❷ out of practice; rusty: 他的英文有点～了。*His English is getting rusty.* ❸ not as close as before: 多年不来往,我们的关系～了。*We haven't been in touch with each other for years, so we're not as close as we used to be.*

【生水】unboiled water

【生丝】raw silk

【生死】life and death: 一场～斗争 *a life-and-death struggle*

【生死存亡】life or death, survival or extinction: ～的斗争 *a life-and-death struggle* / 这个国家到了～的关头。*That country has reached a point where its very existence is at stake.*

【生死关头】a juncture when one's life is at stake; a moment when one's fate hangs in the balance; a critical juncture

【生死攸关】of vital importance: ～的问题 *a matter of life and death; a matter of vital importance*

【生死与共】share a common destiny; go through thick and thin together: ～的战友 *comrades-in-arms through thick and thin*

【生死之交】friends that are ready to die for each other

【生态】organisms' habits, modes of life and relation to their environment; ecology ◇ ～爆炸 ecological explosion; ～变异 ecocline; ～工程 eco-engineering; ～经济学 eco-economics; ～旅游 ecotourism; ～灭绝 ecocide; ～农业 eco-agriculture; ～平衡 ecological balance; eco-equilibrium; ～屏障 ecological protective screen; ～破坏 ecocide; ～圈 ecosphere; ～退化 ecological degradation; ～危机 ecological crisis; ecocrisis; ～系统 ecosystem; ～效益 ecological benefits; ～型 ecotype; ～学 ecology

【生态环境】ecological environment: ～保护 *protection of ecological environment*

【生态旅游】ecotourism

【生态群】[生] cline

【生铁】pig iron

【生土】immature soil

【生吞活剥】swallow sth. raw and whole—accept sth. uncritically: 不要～地搬用外国的经验。*It's no good taking over the experience of foreign countries uncritically.*

【生物】living things; living beings; organisms: 超显微～ *ultramicroscopic organisms* / 浮游～ *plankton* / 寄生～ *parasites* ◇ ～层 biosphere; ～传感器 biosensor; ～磁学 biomagnetics; ～带 biozone; ～地理学 biogeography; ～电流 [生理] bioelectric current; ～发生律 biogenetic law; recapitulation theory; ～防治 [农] biological control; ～工程 bioengineering; ～固氮 biological nitrogen fixation; ～耗氧量 biological oxygen demand; ～合成 biosynthesis; ～化学 biochemistry; ～技术 biotechnology; biological engineering; ～碱 [化] alkaloid; ～量 biomass; ～伦理学 bioethics; ～膜 biomembrane; ～气候学 bioclimatology; ～区 biotic division; ～圈 biosphere; ～群落 biocommunity; ～生态学 bioecology; ～体 organism; ～天文学 bioastronomy; ～武器 同〖细菌武器〗; ～物理学 bio-physics; ～学 biology; ～岩 biogenic rock; biolith; ～遥测器 biopack; ～战 [军] biological warfare; ～制品 biological product; ～钟 biological clock; biochronometer; living clock

【生物电脑】biocomputer

【生物多样性】biodiversity

【生息】❶ bear interest: ～资本 *interest-bearing capital* ❷ live; exist: 自古以来,我们的祖先就劳动、～、繁殖在这块土地上。*From ancient times our forefathers have laboured, lived and multiplied on this land.* ❸ propagate; multiply; procreate

【生橡胶】(又作'生胶') raw rubber; caoutchouc

【生肖】any one of the names of 12 symbolic animals associated with a 12-year cycle, often used to denote the year of a person's birth: 他～属鼠。*He was born in the year of the rat* (*i.e.* 1936, 1948, 1960, 1972, 1984 or 1996).

【生效】go into effect; take effect; become effective: 自签字之日起～ *go into effect from the date of signature* / 在互换批准书以后立即～ *come into force immediately on exchange of the instruments of ratification* / ～条款 *entry-into-force clause*

【生性】natural disposition: ～活泼 *have a lively disposition*

【生锈】get rusty: 永不～的螺丝钉 *a screw that never rusts*

【生涯】career; profession: 舞台～ *a stage career* / 操笔墨～ *write for a living* / 政治～ *a political career*

【生养】〈口〉give birth to; bear (children): 她结婚多年没有～。*She's been married for years but is still childless.*

【生药】crude drug; dried medicinal herbs

【生药学】pharmacognosy

【生疑】be suspicious

【生意】(shēngyì) tendency to grow; life and vitality: ～盎然 *full of life*

【生意】(shēngyi) business; trade: ～兴隆。*Trade is brisk.* or *Business is booming.* ◇ ～经 the knack of doing business; shrewd business sense

【生硬】❶ (of writing) not smooth; not polished; crude ❷ stiff; rigid; harsh: 态度～ *be stiff in manner*

【生油】unboiled oil

【生油层】[油] source bed

【生鱼片】sashimi

【生育】give birth to; bear: 不能～ *be unable to have children; be sterile* / 她已过了～年龄。*She is past her child-bearing age.* ◇ ～低谷 baby bust; ～高峰 baby boom; peak population growth; ～率 fertility rate

【生源】source of students; number of applicants: ～枯竭。*Source of students has dried up.*

【生源说】[生] biogenesis

【生造】coin (words and expressions): 不要～谁也不懂的词语。*Do not coin words and expressions that nobody can understand.* ◇ ～词 coinage

【生长】❶ grow: 小麦～良好。*The wheat is growing well.* or *The wheat is doing fine.* ❷ grow up; be brought up: 他～在武汉。*He was born and brought up in Wuhan.* ◇ ～点 [植] growing point; ～激素 growth hormone; ～率 growth rate; ～轮 growth ring; ～期 growth period; growing period

【生殖】reproduction: 无性～ *asexual reproduction* / 有性～ *sexual reproduction* / 营养体～ *vegetative reproduction* ◇ ～洄游 breeding migration (of some fish); ～孔 gonopore; ～率 reproduction rate; ～泌尿系统 urogenital system; ～器 reproductive organs; genitals; ～系统 reproductive system; ～腺 gonad

【生猪】live pig; pig; hog; pork on the hoof

【生字】characters or words new to the student; new characters or words ◇ ～表 list of new words (attached to a textbook)

声 Ⅰ 名 ❶ sound; voice: 脚步～ *the sound of footsteps* / 小～说话 *speak in a low voice* / 高～朗读 *read aloud* ❷ the initial of a Chinese syllable: 声母 ❸ tone: 四声 ❹ reputation: 声誉 Ⅱ 动 make a sound: 不声不响 Ⅲ 量 (for sounds): 我喊了他两～。*I called to him twice.* / 我听见一～炮响。*I heard the sound of a cannon going off.*

【声辩】argue; justify oneself; explain away: 为自己的行为～ *try to justify oneself for one's conduct* / 不容他人～ *not allow others to present their arguments*

【声波】[物] sound wave; acoustic wave

【声部】[音] part (in concerted music): 歌唱～分女高音、女低音、男高音、男低音。*Soprano, alto, tenor and bass constitute the four vocal parts.*

【声称】profess; claim; assert: ～已打破僵局 *claim to have broken the deadlock*

【声带】❶ [生理] vocal cords ❷ soundtrack (on a film)

【声道】sound track; sound channel

【声调】❶ tone; note: ～激昂 *in an impassioned tone* / ～低沉 *in a low, sad voice* ❷ [语音] the tone of Chinese characters ——另见〖四声〗

【声东击西】make a feint to the east and attack in the west

【声价】reputation: ～甚高 (*of a person*) *be held in high repute; be held in high esteem*

【声控】sound-activated; sound-controlled

【声浪】voice; clamour: 抗议的～ *a wave of protest*

【声泪俱下】shedding tears while speaking; in a tearful voice: 他～地诉说了自己的不幸遭遇。*Tears streamed down his cheeks as he recounted his unhappy experience.*

【声门】[生理] glottis

【声名】reputation

【声名狼藉】have a bad name; be notorious; be utterly discredited

【声明】❶ state; declare; announce: 他正式～他不是候选人。*He announced officially that he was not a candidate.* ❷ statement; declaration: 联合～ *joint statement*

【声母】[语音] the initial of a syllable

【声纳】[物] sonar (sound navigation and ranging)

【声囊】vocal sac (of tailless amphibians, such as frogs)

【声能学】[物] sonics

【声旁】[语] the phonetic element of a Chinese pictophonetic character

【声谱】[物] sound spectrum ◇ ～仪 sound spectrograph

【声气】information: 互通～ *exchange information; keep in contact with each other*

【声强】[物] sound intensity

【声情并茂】(of a singer) be remarkable for both voice and expression

【声色】voice and countenance

【声色俱厉】stern in voice and countenance

【声色犬马】music and women, keeping dogs and riding horses—sensual pleasures

【声势】prestige and power; fame and influence; impetus; momentum: 造成革命～ *build up a revolutionary momentum*

【声势浩大】great in strength and impetus; powerful and dynamic: 他觉得他的队伍实力坚强,～。*He was confident of the unyielding strength and formidable superiority of his troops.* / ～的游行 *a huge and grand parade*

【声嘶力竭】be hoarse and exhausted; shout oneself hoarse; shout oneself blue in the face

【声速】[物] speed of sound: 这种新型战斗机的巡航速度为～的二倍。*The cruising speed of this new type of fighter is twice the speed of sound (or is Mach two).*

【声讨】denounce; condemn: 愤怒～恐怖主义者的罪行 *indignantly denounce the crimes of the terrorists*

【声讨会】denunciation meeting

【声望】popularity; prestige: 在群众中享有很高的～ *enjoy great prestige among the masses*

【声威】renown; prestige ◇ ～大震 gain great fame and high prestige

【声息】❶ (usu. used in the negative) sound; noise: 没有一点～。*Not a sound is heard.* ❷ information: ～相闻 *keep in touch with each other*

【声响】sound; noise: 这发动机～太大。*This motor makes too much noise.* / 瀑布奔泻,发出巨大的～。*The waterfall came down with a rush and a roar.*

【声学】acoustics: 建筑～ *architectural acoustics* / 几何～ *ray acoustics; geometrical acoustics*

【声言】profess; claim; declare: 她～从此以后决不再过问此事。*She declared that from now on she would wash her hands of this business.*

【声音】sound; voice: 震耳欲聋的～ *an ear-split-*

ting sound / 她的～很高。*She has a high-pitched voice*.

【声音识别系统】sound recognition system

【声誉】reputation；fame；prestige：维护国家的～ *defend the honour of one's country* / 在国内外享有很高的～ *enjoy great prestige both at home and abroad*

【声冤】voice grievances；complain and call for redress

【声援】express support for；support：～被压迫民族的正义斗争 *support the oppressed nations in their just struggles*

【声乐】[音] vocal music

【声韵学】同〖音韵学〗

【声张】(usu. used in the negative) make public；disclose：不要～。*Don't let it out*. / 事情还没弄清楚，先别～。*The matter has not been clarified yet, so don't breathe a word of it to anyone for the time being*.

牲 名 ❶ domestic animal ❷ animal sacrifice

【牲畜】livestock；domestic animals ◇ ～车 [铁路] livestock wagon；stock wagon；stock car；～肥 animal manure

【牲粉】[化] animal starch；glycogen

【牲口】draught animals；beasts of burden；livestock ◇ ～贩子 cattle dealer；～棚 stock barn；livestock shed

笙 名 [音] sheng, a reed pipe wind instrument

【笙歌】〈文〉music and singing

甥 名 sister's son；nephew

【甥女】sister's daughter；niece

shéng

绳 Ⅰ 名 rope；cord；string：一条细～ *a string* / 一根钢～ *a steel cable* / 这条～又粗又结实。*This rope is thick and strong*. Ⅱ 动 restrict；restrain：～以纪律 *enforce discipline upon sb*.

【绳鞭技】[杂] (doing) tricks with a whip；(performing) feats with a whip

【绳技】[杂] rope walking or dancing；tightrope walking or slack rope walking

【绳锯木断】a rope can cut through a log；little strokes fell great oaks

【绳捆索绑】truss up；bind；tie up

【绳墨】❶ carpenter's line marker ❷〈书〉rules and regulations：拘守～ *stick to the rules*

【绳趋尺步】conform to every rule and regulation；toe the line

【绳索】thick cord；rope：尼龙～ *a rope made of nylon* / 砍断旧制度套在人民身上的～ *cut the bonds forced on the people by the old system*

【绳套】❶ loop：绞架上的～ *a hangman's noose* ❷ lasso

【绳梯】rope ladder

【绳之以法】prosecute and punish according to law；bring to justice

【绳子】cord；rope；string

shěng

省 Ⅰ 动 ❶ economize；save：～着点用 *use sparingly* / ～时间 *save time* / ～掉不少麻烦 *save a lot of trouble* / 能～的就～ *economize wherever possible* / 我一个月～不下几个钱。*I can't save much from my monthly wages*. ❷ omit；leave out：这两个字不能～。*These two characters cannot be omitted*. / ～一道工序 *eliminate one step from the process* Ⅱ 名 province：江苏～ *Jiangsu Province* / ～长 *governor of a province* / ～人民代表大会 *provincial people's congress* ——另见 xǐng

【省便】convenient；timesaving or laboursaving：用洗衣机洗衣服就～多了。*A washing machine will save us a lot of time*.

【省部级】at the provincial and ministerial level：～以上的科技成果 *scientific and technological achievements recognized at or above the provincial and ministerial level*

【省城】〈口〉provincial capital：我上～去办点事。*I'm going to the provincial capital on business*.

【省吃俭用】skimp and save；live frugally：我～把他送进学校念书。*By saving on food and clothes, I managed to send him to school*.

【省得】so as to save (or avoid)：你就住在这儿吧，～天天来回跑。*Better stay here to avoid going back and forth every day*

【省份】(not to be used in names of provinces) province：台湾是中国的一个～。*Taiwan is one of China's provinces*.

【省府】provincial government

【省工省钱】save both labour and money

【省会】provincial capital：湖南省的～是长沙。*Changsha is the provincial capital of Hunan*.

【省界】provincial boundaries

【省劲】同〖省力〗

【省力】(又作'省力气') save effort；save labour：这种耕作方法～不少。*This method of farming saves a lot of labour*.

【省略】❶ leave out；omit (on purpose)：这一段与主题关系不大，满可以～。*This irrelevant paragraph may well be left out*. ❷ [语] be understood：这个句子的主语～了。*The subject of the sentence is understood*. ◇ ～号 ellipsis；suspension points；ellipsis dots (……) (...)；～句 [语] elliptical sentence

【省钱】save money；be economical：每月省点钱 *save some money each month*

【省却】save：抄近路走可以～将近一公里。*Taking the short cut will save us nearly a kilometre*. / ～不少麻烦 *save a lot of trouble*

【省时省力】save both time and labour

【省事】save trouble；simplify matters：你工作要仔细，不能只图～。*You should be conscientious in your work, and not just try to save yourself trouble.*

【省属】directly under the jurisdiction of a provincial government

【省委】provincial Party committee：～书记 *secretary of a provincial Party committee*

【省辖市】city under the jurisdiction of a province

【省心】save worry：孩子进了托儿所，我～多了。*Having the child in kindergarten saves me a lot of worry.*

【省优】(of product) up to quality standards set by the province：获得～称号 *rated a top quality product by the province*

【省油的灯】〈方〉〈字〉lamp that does not burn much oil；〈喻〉person who knows his place and stirs up no trouble (usu. in a negative sentence)：他可不是一盏～。*You just watch, he is going to make waves.*

【省直】directly under the Party committee or government of a province：～机关 *offices directly subordinate to both the provincial Party committee and government*

shèng

圣 Ⅰ形 holy；sacred：圣地 Ⅱ名 ❶ emperor：圣上 ❷ the greatest master of a certain art or skill：棋圣 ❸ saint；sage：圣贤

【圣餐】[宗](基督教) the Lord's Supper；the Holy Communion；Eucharist

【圣诞】[宗](基督教) Christmas (the birthday of Jesus Christ)：～前夜 *Christmas Eve (Dec. 24)* / 恭祝～，并贺新禧 *With Best Wishes for a Merry Christmas and a Happy New Year* ◇ ～节 Christmas Day (Dec. 25)；～卡 Christmas card；Xmas card；～老人 Santa Claus；～树 Christmas tree

【圣地】❶ religion the Holy Land (or City) ❷ a sacred place；shrine

【圣多美和普林西比】São Tomé and Príncipe

【圣父】❶ [宗](基督教) Holy Father—God ❷ [宗](罗马天主教) Holy Father (a title of the Pope)

【圣公会】[宗](基督教) the Anglican Church

【圣公宗】[宗](基督教) Anglicanism；the Anglican Church

【圣火】sacred fire：奥运～ *the Olympic torch*

【圣洁】holy and pure

【圣经】the Holy Bible；the Bible；Holy Writ；the (Holy) Scriptures

【圣经贤传】Confucian classics

【圣灵】[宗](基督教) the Holy Spirit；the Holy Ghost

【圣灵节】[宗](基督教) Whitsunday

【圣卢西亚】Saint Lucia

【圣马力诺】San Marino ◇ ～人 San Marinese

【圣明】august wisdom (formerly used in adulation of the Roman emperor Augustus)

【圣母】❶ female deity；goddess ❷ Catholicism Christianity the (Blessed) Virgin Mary；the Madonna：～像 *Madonna* /《～颂》*Ave Maria*

【圣人】❶ sage；wise man ❷ the Sage (a title of respect for Confucius)

【圣人无常师】Sages have no constant teachers；A sage has more than one teacher.

【圣上】Your Majesty；His Majesty

【圣手】a master of a certain skill

【圣水】❶ sacred water credited with curative or exorcising powers ❷ holy water for religious uses

【圣体】[宗](基督教，天主教) holy bread

【圣贤】sages and men of virtue

【圣药】efficacious medicine：灵丹～ *miraculous cure；panacea*

【圣谕】imperial decree

【圣战】[宗](伊斯兰教) jihad；a holy war；crusade

【圣旨】imperial edict：你把他的话当成～啦？*Do you take everything he says as seriously as you would an imperial edict?*

【圣子】[宗](基督教) Holy Son—Jesus Christ

胜 Ⅰ动 ❶ win：这次比赛谁～了？*Who won this match?* / 我队以四～两负一平的成绩获得亚军。*Our team finished second with four wins, two defeats and one tie.* ❷ defeat：我～了他。*I defeated him.* / 以少～多 *use a small force to defeat a large one* / 战而～之 *fight to win* ❸ (often followed by 于, etc.) surpass；be superior to；get the better of：事实胜于雄辩 ❹ be equal to；can bear：力不能～ *beyond one's ability* Ⅱ形 superb；wonderful；lovely：胜景

【胜败】victory or defeat；success or failure

【胜败乃兵家常事】For a military commander, winning or losing a battle is a common occurrence；Victory or defeat is a common thing for the soldier.

【胜不骄，败不馁】not made dizzy with success, nor discouraged by failure

【胜地】a famous scenic spot：避暑～ *a famous summer resort*

【胜负】victory or defeat；success or failure：战争的～ *the outcome of a war* / ～未定。*Victory hangs in the balance.*

【胜过】be better than；be superior to：实际行动～空洞的言辞。*Action speaks louder than words.*

【胜迹】a famous historical site

【胜景】wonderful scenery

【胜境】a scenic spot；a beautiful place：名山～ *famous mountains and scenic spots；places of scenic beauty*

【胜利】❶ victory；triumph：充满了～的信心 *be fully confident of victory* ❷ successful；triumphant：～会师 *triumphantly join forces* / ～完成任务 *successfully carry out one's task* ◇ ～果实 fruits of victory；～者 victor；winner

【胜面】(in games such as weichi or go chess) the chance of winning：如果发挥正常，他的～比较大。*If he plays normally, he stands a good chance of winning*

【胜券】confidence in victory：操～ *be sure to win*

【胜任】be competent；be qualified；be equal to：～工作 *be competent at a job*；*prove equal to the task* ◇ ～愉快 be fully competent；prove more than equal to the task

【胜如】同〖胜似〗

【胜似】be better than；surpass

【胜诉】win a lawsuit (or court case)

【胜算】〈书〉a stratagem which ensures success：操～ *be sure of success*

【胜友】〈书〉good friends

【胜仗】victorious battle；victory：打～ *win a battle*；*score a victory*

盛 Ⅰ 形 ❶ flourishing；prosperous：桃花开得很～。*The peach trees are in full bloom.* or *The peach blossoms are out.* ❷ vigorous；energetic：火势很～。*The fire is raging.* / 年轻气～ *young and aggressive* ❸ magnificent；grand：盛举 ❹ abundant；plentiful：盛意 ❺ popular；common；widespread：学术气氛很～。*An academic atmosphere prevails.* Ⅱ 副 greatly；deeply：～夸 *praise highly* ——另见 chéng

【盛产】abound in；teem with：～煤铁 *abound in coal and iron* / ～石油 *be rich in oil* / ～鱼蟹 *teem with fish and crabs*

【盛传】be widely known；be widely rumoured

【盛大】grand；magnificent：～的欢迎 *a rousing welcome* / ～的招待会 *a grand reception* / ～的游行 *a mammoth parade*

【盛典】a grand ceremony (or occasion)：皇帝的大婚～ *the grand wedding ceremony of the emperor*

【盛服】〈书〉full dress；splendid attire；rich dress

【盛会】distinguished gathering；grand meeting：团结友谊的～ *a grand gathering of unity and friendship* / 体育～ *a magnificent sports meet*

【盛极一时】be in fashion (or vogue) for a time；be all the rage

【盛季】peak period；busy season：草莓～ *strawberry season* / 旅游～ *tourist season*

【盛举】grand occasion (or event)

【盛开】(of flowers) be in full bloom；flourish：百花～。*Flowers are in full bloom.*

【盛况】grand occasion；spectacular event ◇ ～空前 an exceptionally (or unprecedentedly) grand occasion

【盛名】great reputation ◇ ～之下，其实难副 A high reputation is hard to live up to.

【盛年】the more robust years of one's life；the prime of life

【盛怒】be very angry；be in a rage：他在～之下，做了件鲁莽的事。*He did something rash in a moment of anger.*

【盛气凌人】domineering；arrogant；overbearing：～的样子 *imperious bearing*

【盛情】great kindness；boundless hospitality：受到～款待 *be accorded lavish hospitality* ◇ ～难却 it would be ungracious not to accept your kindness

【盛秋】the height of autumn；midautumn

【盛世】flourishing age；heyday

【盛事】grand occasion；great event

【盛暑】sweltering summer heat；very hot weather

【盛衰】prosperity and decline；rise and fall；ups and downs ◇ ～荣辱 prosperity and decline，glory and humiliation；rise and fall；ups and downs；vicissitudes of life

【盛夏】the height of summer；midsummer

【盛行】be current (or rife，rampant)；be in vogue ◇ ～一时 be in vogue；prevail for a time

【盛宴】(又作'盛筵') a grand banquet；a sumptuous dinner

【盛意】great kindness；generosity：衷心感谢您的一片～。*I heartily appreciate your great kindness to me.*

【盛誉】great fame；high reputation：中国丝绸在世界上素有～。*Chinese silk has long been famous all over the world.*

【盛赞】highly praise；speak of sb. in glowing terms

【盛装】splendid attire；rich dress：穿着节日的～ *be dressed in one's holiday best*

剩 形 surplus；remnant：我只～五块钱了。*I've only five yuan left.* / ～货 *surplus goods* / ～菜～饭 *leftovers* / 所～无几。*There is not much left.*

【剩磁】[物] residual magnetism

【剩下】be left (over)；remain：～多少？ *How much is left (over)?* / ～的敌军已经被我们消灭了。*We have wiped out the remaining enemy troops.*

【剩余】surplus；remainder：收支相抵，略有～。*The reckoning up of revenue and expenditure shows a small surplus.* ◇ ～产品 surplus products；～价值 surplus value；～劳动 surplus labour；～物资 surplus materials

shī

尸 名 corpse；dead body；remains：兽～ *carcass*

【尸骨】(又作'尸骸') bones of the dead

【尸横遍野】a field littered with corpses

【尸检】autopsy

【尸居余气】be a living corpse；be at one's last gasp；be at the point of death；be as good as dead

【尸腊】a dead body naturally dried and preserved

【尸身】corpse；dead body；remains

【尸首】a dead body of a human being

【尸体】corpse；carcass

【尸体解剖】autopsy；postmortem (examination)

失 Ⅰ 动 ❶ lose：～而复得 *lost and found again* / ～民心 *lose the support of the people* / 得大于～。*Gains outweigh losses.* / 不要～了信心。*Don't lose confidence.* ❷ miss；let slip：良机莫

～。*Don't let slip this good chance*. ❸ not act according to; neglect; violate: 失信 / 失敬 ❹ lose control of: 失手 / 失禁 / 失态 ❺ err; have a slip; be defective in: ～之于烦琐 *have the defect of being too detailed* Ⅱ 名 slip; mistake; defect; mishap: 惟恐有～ *fear that there may be some mishap*

【失败】❶ be defeated; lose (a war, etc.): 遭到了可耻的～ *meet with ignominious defeat* ❷ fail: 这项试验～了不止一次。*The experiment has failed more than once*. ◇ ～情绪 defeatist sentiments; ～为成功之母 failure is the mother of success; ～主义 defeatism

【失标】fail in bidding; fail to win the tender: 竞争中的～者 *a loser in a bid for tender*

【失策】❶ err in tactics, scheming or planning; do sth. unwise: 这样做非常～。*It was a very unwise move*. ❷ an error (in tactics, etc.)

【失察】neglect one's supervisory duties

【失常】not normal; odd: 举止～ *act oddly* / 精神～ *be distraught*; *not be in one's right mind*

【失宠】〈贬〉fall into disfavour; be out of favour; be in disgrace

【失传】not be handed down from past generations; be lost: 一种～的艺术 *a lost art*

【失聪】become deaf: 双耳～ *become deaf in both ears*

【失措】lose one's presence of mind; lose one's head: 茫然～ *be at a loss what to do*

【失单】a list of lost or stolen articles (or property)

【失当】improper; inappropriate: 这个问题处理～。*This problem was not properly handled*.

【失盗】be robbed or burgled: ～事件 *a robbery or burglary*

【失道寡助】An unjust cause finds scant (or little) support ——另见〖得道多助,失道寡助〗

【失地】lost territory: 收复～ *recover lost territory*

【失掉】❶ lose: ～理智 *lose one's senses* / ～联系 *lose contact with* / ～权力 *be stripped of power* / ～民心 *lose popular support* ❷ miss: ～机会 *miss a chance* / ～战机 *fail to grasp a good opportunity to engage the enemy*

【失分】(in competition) lose points: 连连～ *lose many points in a row*

【失和】fail to keep on good terms; become estranged: 弟兄俩～有好几个月了。*The brothers have been estranged for months*.

【失衡】off balance; out of balance: 经济过热,各部门严重～。*The overheated economy has caused serious imbalance between various sectors*.

【失魂落魄】driven to distraction: 吓得～ *be scared out of one's wits*; *be frightened out of one's life*

【失火】catch fire; be on fire: 昨天城里～。*There was a fire in town last night*.

【失机】lose the opportunity; miss the chance

【失计】同〖失策〗

【失记】〈书〉forget

【失检】be indiscreet: 言语～ *be indiscreet with one's tongue*; *be indiscreet in one's speech*

【失脚】lose one's footing; slip: ～跌倒 *lose one's footing (or balance) and fall*

【失节】❶ forfeit one's integrity; be disloyal ❷ (of a woman, according to feudal morality) lose one's chastity

【失禁】lose control over one's bladder or rectum functions; be unable to restrain one's natural discharges; suffer from incontinence: 大小便～ *suffer from incontinence of faeces and urine*; *be doubly incontinent*

【失惊】be startled; be shocked: 她～地叫了起来。*Greatly startled, she cried out*.

【失敬】〈套〉sorry I didn't recognize you; excuse me for my lack of manners

【失控】get out of control; get out of hand: 物价～ *a runaway increase in prices*

【失口】make a slip of the tongue: 我～冒犯了她。*I let slip some remark that offended her*.

【失礼】❶ commit a breach of etiquette: 舅舅做寿,我们要是不去,人家会怪我们～的。*If we don't go to our uncle's birthday party, people will consider it a breach of etiquette*. ❷〈套〉excuse me for my impropriety, lack of manners, etc.: 对不起,～了。*Pardon me for my lack of manners*.

【失利】suffer a setback (or defeat): 军事上的～ *military reverses* / 在这场乒乓球比赛中我方第一盘～。*Our side lost the first game of the table-tennis match*.

【失恋】be disappointed in a love affair; be jilted: ～的痛苦 *the bitter taste of disappointed love*

【失灵】(of a machine, instrument, etc.) not work or not work properly; be out of order: 开关～了。*The switch is out of order*. / 他的听觉有点～了。*His hearing is getting worse*.

【失落】lose; drop: 我实在想不起来那块头巾可能～在什么地方。*Really I can't recall where I could have dropped my kerchief*.

【失落感】feeling of being lost or neglected

【失迷】lose one's way; lose one's bearings

【失密】give away official secrets due to carelessness: 怎么失的密? *How did the secret leak out?* / 一起后果严重的～事件 *a leakage of secrets likely to entail grave consequences*

【失眠】(suffer from) insomnia: 病人昨夜～。*The patient had a sleepless night last night*.

【失明】lose one's sight; go blind: 双目～ *lose the sight of both eyes*

【失能性毒剂】[军] incapacitating agent

【失陪】〈套〉excuse me, but I must be leaving now

【失窃】have things stolen; suffer loss by theft

【失去】lose: ～知觉 *lose consciousness* / ～信心 *lose confidence* / ～时效 *be no longer effective*; *cease to be in force* / ～控制 *get out of hand*; *get out of control*

【失群】stray from one's flock: 迷途～ *be lost and left behind*

【失散】be separated from and lose touch with each

other；be scattered：手稿的后一部分～了。*The last part of the manuscript is lost.*

【失色】❶ be discoloured；lose colour：这些壁画已年久～。*These murals have been discoloured with the passage of time.* ❷ turn pale：众人惊愕～，无一应对。*All those present turned pale and none dared to say anything in reply.*

【失闪】mishap；unexpected danger：他觉得累了就停止练习，怕有～。*He stopped practising when he felt tired for fear of accidents.*

【失墒】［农］(of soil) loss of moisture：土地～严重。*There is a serious loss of soil moisture.*

【失身】(of a woman) lose one's virginity or chastity

【失神】❶ inattentive；absent-minded：我有点～，没有听到他最后那段讲话。*I was somewhat absent-minded and missed the last part of his speech.* ❷ out of sorts；in low spirits：～地望着窗外发呆 *stare blankly out of the window feeling low*

【失慎】❶ not cautious；careless：我一时～，把一杯牛奶碰洒了。*I inadvertently upset a glass of milk.* ❷〈书〉cause a fire through carelessness

【失声】❶ ejaculate (involuntarily)；burst out：～喊叫 *exclaim outright* / ～大笑 *burst out laughing；burst into laughter* ❷ lose one's voice：痛哭～ *be choked with tears；cry oneself hoarse*

【失时】miss the season；let slip the opportunity：播种不能～。*Don't miss the sowing season.*

【失实】inconsistent with the facts；inaccurate：传闻～。*The rumour was unfounded.* / 报道～。*The report was inaccurate.*

【失势】lose power and influence；fall into disgrace

【失事】(have an) accident：飞机～ *aviation accident；aeroplane crash*

【失手】❶ lose control of one's hand；accidentally drop sth., hurt sb., etc.：小王和小李练剑的时候，小王～刺伤了小李的左臂。*When Xiao Wang was practising fencing with Xiao Li, he accidentally wounded Xiao Li in the left arm.* ❷ suffer defeat in competition：女排～并不奇怪。*It is no surprise that the women's volleyball team was defeated.*

【失守】(of a city, etc.) fall

【失水】dehydration

【失溲】［中］lose control over one's bladder functions；incontinence of urine

【失速】［航空］stall：～滑翔 *stalled glide*

【失算】miscalculate；misjudge；be injudicious

【失所】become homeless；be displaced：～平民 *displaced civilians*

【失态】lose control of oneself；misbehave；forget oneself：酒后～ *forget oneself in one's cups*

【失调】❶ imbalance；dislocation：供求～ *imbalance of supply and demand* / 经济～ *economic dislocation* / 比例～ *disproportion* / 雨水～ *abnormal rainfall* ❷ lack of proper care (after an illness, etc.)：产后～ *lack of proper care after childbirth* ❸［无］maladjustment；detuning

【失望】❶ lose hope；lose heart：他们失败多次，但是并没有完全～。*They failed time and again, but they never gave up hope.* ❷ disappointed：感到～ *be disappointed* / 令人～ *disappointing* / 我们对你太～了。*We are utterly disappointed with (or in) you.*

【失物】lost article；lost property ◇ ～招领处 Lost and Found Office；Lost Property Office

【失误】error；fault；muff：判断～ *an error in judgment；a misjudgment* / 接球～ *muff (or fumble) a ball* / 发球～ *a serving fault*

【失陷】(of cities, territory, etc.) fall；fall into enemy hands

【失效】❶ lose efficacy；lose effectiveness；cease to be effective：这药已～了。*The medicine no longer has any effect.* / 使水雷～ *deactivate mines* ❷ (of a treaty, an agreement, etc.) be no longer in force；become invalid：自动～ *automatically cease to be in force* / 条约的～ *voidance (or voidness) of a treaty*

【失笑】laugh in spite of oneself；cannot help laughing

【失谐】［无］detuning；mismatching

【失信】break one's promise；go back on one's word ◇ ～于民 (of a government) lose the confidence of the people

【失修】(of houses, etc.) be in bad repair；fall into disrepair：年久～ *have long been out of repair；have been neglected for years*

【失序】disorder；loss of order：取向～ *orientation disorders*

【失学】be deprived of education；be unable to go to school；be obliged to discontinue one's studies

【失血】lose blood：～过多 *excessive loss of blood*

【失言】make an indiscreet remark；make a slip of the tongue：酒后～ *make an indiscreet remark under the influence of alcohol* / 别生气，我是一时～。*Don't get sore；I didn't mean anything by that remark.*

【失业】lose one's job；be out of work；be unemployed ◇ ～保险 unemployment insurance；～救济 unemployment relief；～率 rate of unemployment；～者 the unemployed；the jobless

【失仪】❶ forget one's manners：我怕喝多了酒会～。*I am afraid I might forget myself in my cups.* ❷ a breach of etiquette

【失宜】〈书〉inappropriate：处置～ *handle improperly*

【失意】have one's aspirations, plans, etc. thwarted；be frustrated；be disappointed：情场～ *be frustrated in love*

【失音】［医］aphonia；loss of voice

【失迎】〈套〉fail to meet (a guest)：～！～！*Excuse me for not meeting you at the gate.* / 昨天～了，很抱歉。*Sorry I was out when you called yesterday.*

【失语症】［医］aphasia

【失约】fail to keep an appointment

【失责】dereliction of duty
【失着】❶ make a careless (or an unwise) move ❷ a careless move; an unwise move
【失真】❶ (of voice, images, etc.) lack fidelity; not be true to the original ❷［无］distortion: 频率～ *frequency distortion*
【失之东隅,收之桑榆】lose in the east and gain in the west—make up on the roundabouts what one loses on the swings
【失之毫厘,谬以千里】同〖差之毫厘,谬以千里〗
【失之交臂】just miss the person or opportunity: 机会难得,幸勿～。*Don't let slip such a golden opportunity.*
【失职】❶ neglect one's duty ❷ dereliction of duty
【失重】［物］weightlessness; zero gravity
【失主】owner of lost property
【失踪】(usu. of people) be missing: 伤亡之外,尚有多人～。*In addition to the killed and wounded, many are missing.*
【失足】❶ lose one's footing; slip: ～落水 *slip and fall into the water* ❷ take a wrong step in life: ～青少年 *juvenile delinquents*

师 Ⅰ 名 ❶ teacher; tutor master ❷ model; example: 师表 ❸ a person skilled in a certain profession: 工程师 / 厨师 ❹ (a term of respect for a monk or nun) master; mother: 法师 ❺ of one's master or teacher: 师母 ❻［军］division: 步兵～ *infantry division* ❼ troops; army: 正义之～ *an army fighting for a just cause* Ⅱ 动〈书〉model oneself after: 师承,师法
【师表】〈书〉a person of exemplary virtue
【师部】［军］division headquarters
【师承】〈书〉❶ have studied under (a teacher, usu. with reference to a particular school of thought or learning); be a disciple of ❷ transmission from master to disciple: 这些艺人各有自己的～。*These artists have inherited the traditions of their respective masters.*
【师出无名】dispatch troops without just cause
【师道尊严】dignity of the teaching profession
【师德】professional ethics of the teaching profession
【师弟】❶ junior (male) fellow apprentice ❷ the son of one's master (younger than oneself) ❸ father's (male) apprentice (younger than oneself)
【师法】❶ model oneself after (a great master); imitate ❷ knowledge or technique handed down by one's master
【师范】❶ teacher-training; (pedagogical): ～大学 *normal university* / ～学院 *teachers' college; teacher training college* ❷〈略〉见〖师范学校〗❸〈书〉a model to be followed
【师范学校】normal school
【师父】❶ 同〖师傅〗❷ (a term of respect for a monk or nun) master; mother
【师父领进门,修行在个人】The master initiates the apprentices, but their skill depends on their own efforts; The master teaches the trade, but the apprentice's skill is self-made.
【师傅】❶ master worker (a qualified worker as distinct from an apprentice) ❷ a respectful form of address for a skilled worker ❸〈口〉a form of address for any stranger
【师公】❶ master's master ❷ sorcerer
【师姐】❶ senior (female) fellow apprentice ❷ the daughter of one's master (older than oneself) ❸ father's (female) apprentice (older than oneself)
【师老兵疲】an army worn-down and war-weary
【师妹】❶ junior (female) fellow apprentice ❷ the daughter of one's master (younger than oneself) ❸ father's (female) apprentice (younger than oneself)
【师母】the wife of one's teacher or master
【师娘】〈口〉the wife of one's teacher or master
【师生】teacher and student: ～关系 *relations between teachers and students; teacher-student relations*
【师事】〈书〉treat sb. with the respect due to a teacher
【师徒】master and apprentice
【师团】［军］division
【师心自用】be opinionated
【师兄】❶ senior (male) fellow apprentice ❷ the son of one's master (older than oneself) ❸ father's (male) apprentice (older than oneself)
【师兄弟】male apprentices of the same master; fellow apprentices
【师训】teacher's instructions: 遵从～ *follow the teacher's instructions*
【师友】teachers and friends
【师长】❶ (a term of respect) teacher ❷［军］division commander
【师直为壮】An army fighting for a just cause has high morale.
【师专】(〈略〉全称为'师范专科学校') teacher training school; normal school; (two-year) teachers' college
【师资】persons qualified to teach; teachers: ～力量不足 *shortage of teachers* / 培训～ *train teachers*

虱 名 louse
【虱子】louse

诗 名 poetry; verse; poem
【诗歌】poems and songs; poetry: ～朗诵 *recitation of poems; poetry readings*
【诗话】❶ poetry talks ❷ vernacular stories interspersed with poems
【诗集】collection of poems; poetry anthology
【诗经】The Book of Songs ——另见〖五经〗
【诗句】verse; line
【诗剧】drama in verse; poetic drama
【诗礼之家】a highly cultured household; a family of scholars
【诗律】prosody

【诗篇】❶ poems：这些～抒发了作者的革命豪情。*These poems express the revolutionary fervour of the poet*. ❷ an inspiring story；epic：我们时代的壮丽～ *a magnificent epic of our era* / 英雄的～ *a heroic epic*
【诗情画意】a quality suggestive of poetry or painting；poetic charm：她的舞姿袅娜，富有～。*She danced with poetic grace*.
【诗穷而后工】Poverty makes for poetic excellence；Only a poet in adversity is apt to develop skill.
【诗人】poet
【诗社】poets' club
【诗圣】poet-sage (an epithet for Du Fu 杜甫)
【诗书】Confucian classics：出身～门第 *come from a family of scholars*
【诗坛】poetry circles；world of poetry；the circle of poets
【诗仙】poet-immortal (an epithet for Li Bai 李白)
【诗兴】urge for poetic creation；poetic inspiration；poetic mood：～大发 *feel a strong urge to write poetry*；*be in an exalted*，*poetic mood*
【诗意】poetic quality or flavour：饶有～ *rich in poetic flavour*；*very poetic*
【诗韵】❶ rhyme (in poetry) ❷ rhyming dictionary
【诗中有画，画中有诗】there are pictures (i. e. a pictorial imagination) in poetry and poetry (i.e. a poetic imagination) in pictures；evoke painting in poetry and poetry in painting
【诗作】poetical works

狮 名 lion：一头雄～ *a lion* / 一头母～ *a lioness*
【狮身人面像】sphinx
【狮头鹅】lion-headed goose (a fine breed of goose)
【狮子】lion
【狮子鼻】pug nose
【狮子搏兔】(like) a lion pouncing on a hare—go all out even when fighting a weaker enemy or tackling a minor problem
【狮子狗】pug-dog
【狮子头】large meatball (usu. deep-fried before being braised with vegetables)
【狮子舞】lion dance (a popular folk dance)
【狮子座】[天] Leo

施 动 ❶ bring (or put) into effect；execute；carry out：略～小技 *hatch a little scheme* / 他们一计不成，又～一计。*Their first ruse having failed*，*they tried another*. ❷ bestow；grant；hand out：～恩于人 *bestow favours on others* ❸ exert；impose：～压力 *exert pressure on sb*. ❹ use；apply：～底肥 *apply fertilizer to the subsoil*
【施放】discharge；fire：～催泪弹 *fire tear-gas shells* / ～烟幕 *lay a smokescreen*
【施肥】spread manure；apply fertilizer
【施工】carry out construction or large repairs：加紧～ *speed up the construction or repairs* / 道路～，车辆绕行。*Detour*. *Road Under Repair*. / ～现场 *construction site* / ～单位 *unit in charge of construction* / ～人员 *builders*；*constructors* ◇ ～缝[建] construction joint；～图 working drawing
【施加】exert；bring to bear on：～压力 *bring pressure to bear on sb*.；*put pressure on sb*. / ～影响 *exert one's influence on sb*.
【施教】teach；educate；instruct：因材施教
【施礼】make a bow；salute
【施力点】[物] point of application
【施舍】give alms；give in charity：乞求～ *beg for alms* / 靠别人～过日子 *survive on handouts*
【施事】[语] the doer of the action in a sentence；agent
【施威】exhibit one's power；show severity
【施洗】[宗](基督教) administer baptism：给某人～ *baptize sb*.
【施行】❶ put (laws，rules，regulations，etc.) into force；enforce；implement：本条例自公布之日起～。*These regulations come into force upon promulgation*. ❷ perform；administer；apply：～急救 *administer* (*or apply*) *first aid* / ～手术 *perform a surgical operation*
【施药】❶ prescribe ❷ give medicine to the poor free of charge
【施用】use；employ：～化肥 *use chemical fertilizer*
【施与】grant (money，gifts，etc.) to sb.；bestow (favours) on sb.
【施斋】provide (itinerant) monks with free food
【施展】put to good use；give free play to：～本领 *put one's ability* (*or talent*) *to good use* / 把全部技术都～出来 *give full play to one's technical competence*
【施政】the management of government affairs；administration：～纲领 *administrative programme* / ～方针 *administrative policy*
【施脂粉】apply cosmetics：薄～ *apply a light make-up*
【施粥】provide free porridge for the poor
【施主】(monks' or nuns' form of address for a layman) patron

湿 形 wet；damp；humid：小心点，别～了衣裳。*Be careful*! *Don't get your clothes wet*. / 别穿那双袜子，还～着呢。*Don't wear those socks*，*they're still damp*.
【湿痹】[中] arthritis with fixed pain caused by dampness
【湿病】[中] diseases caused by dampness
【湿答答】dripping wet
【湿度】humidity；moisture：空气～ *air humidity* / 土壤的～ *moisture content* (*or capacity*) *in soil*
【湿度表】humidometer
【湿法冶金】hydrometallurgy
【湿纺】[纺] wet spinning
【湿乎乎】(又作'湿呼呼') damp；moist；humid：近来天气老是～的。*It has been rather humid these last few days*. / 这条毛巾还有点～的。*This tow-*

el is still damp.

【湿津津】moist with sweat; sweaty

【湿淋淋】dripping wet; drenched: 身上浇得～的 get dripping (or soaking, sopping) wet; be soaked to the skin / ～的衣服 sopping wet clothes

【湿漉漉】(又作'湿渌渌') moist; damp

【湿蒙蒙】(of the air) damp; moist: 清晨有点雾，空气～的。It was a misty morning, and the air was moist.

【湿气】[中] eczema or fungus infection of hand or foot

【湿热】damp and hot

【湿润】moist: ～的土壤 damp soil / 空气～ humid air / 她眼睛～了。Her eyes were moist with tears.

【湿水货】water-damaged goods

【湿透】wet through; drenched: 汗水～了他的衣服。His clothes are drenched with sweat.

【湿选】[矿] wet separation

【湿疹】eczema

蓍 名 [植] alpine yarrow (Achillea alpina)

嘘 叹 hush; sh: ～，别作声! Sh! (or Hush!) Keep quiet! ——另见 xū

shí

十 Ⅰ 数 ten: ～倍 ten times; tenfold Ⅱ 形 topmost: ～成 100 per cent

【十八般武艺】skill in wielding the 18 kinds of weapons—skill in various types of combat: ～，样样精通 be skilful in using each and every one of the 18 weapons; be versatile

【十八层地狱】the eighteenth hell—the lowest depths of hell ——另见〖打入十八层地狱〗

【十步芳草】(〈略〉全称为'十步之内，必有芳草') fragrant grass is to be found within ten paces—talent is close at hand

【十大功劳】[中] Chinese mahonia (Mahonia fortunei)

【十滴水】[药] "10 drops" (a popular medicine for summer ailments)

【十冬腊月】the tenth, eleventh and twelfth months of the lunar year; the cold months of the year

【十恶不赦】guilty of unpardonable evil; unpardonably wicked: 一群青面獠牙、～的人 a horde of fiendish monsters who perpetrate every conceivable crime and are unpardonably wicked

【十二分】more than 100 per cent; extremely: 感到～的满意 be more than satisfied / 我有～的把握。I am more than 100 per cent sure.

【十二级风】[气] force 12 wind; hurricane

【十二门徒】[宗](基督教) the 12 apostles of Jesus Christ

【十二平均律】[音] twelve-tone equal temperament

【十二生肖】(又作'十二属相') the 12 symbolic animals associated with a 12-year cycle ——另见〖生肖〗,〖属相〗

【十二月】❶ December ❷ the twelfth month of the lunar year; the twelfth moon

【十二指肠】[生理] duodenum ◇ ～溃疡 duodenal ulcer

【十方】[宗](佛教) the ten positions (i.e. the four cardinal points 东、西、南、北, the intermediate points 东南、西南、东北、西北, and above and below 上、下)

【十分】very; fully; utterly; extremely: ～高兴 be very pleased; be elated / ～难过 feel very sorry; feel very bad / ～宝贵 most valuable / ～有害 extremely harmful

【十个指头有长短】the fingers are unequal in length—you can't expect everybody to be the same

【十行俱下】take in ten lines at a glance—read rapidly

【十级风】[气] force 10 wind; whole gale

【十佳】ten best individuals or units: ～运动员 the top-ten athletes

【十戒】[宗](佛教) the Ten Prohibitions

【十诫】[宗](基督教) the Ten Commandments; the Decalogue

【十进制】[数] the decimal system

【十六分音符】[音] semiquaver; sixteenth note

【十六进制】hexadecimal system

【十六开】[刷] sixteenmo; 16mo

【十目所视，十手所指】with many eyes watching and many fingers pointing—one cannot do wrong without being seen

【十拿九稳】(又作'十成九稳') ninety per cent sure; practically certain; in the bag: 这事情，我们是～了。We have the matter well in hand. / 这生意～赚钱。This is a business where we can be sure of making money.

【十年寒窗】ten years' study at a cold window—a student's long years of hard study

【十年九不遇】not occur once in ten years; be seldom seen

【十年树木，百年树人】It takes ten years to grow trees, but a hundred to rear people.

【十全十美】be perfect in every way; be the acme of perfection; leave nothing to be desired: 世上没有～的人。No man is perfect.

【十室九空】nine houses out of ten are stripped bare—the aftermath of war, natural calamities, etc.

【十四行诗】sonnet

【十万八千里】a distance of one hundred and eight thousand li; poles apart: 离题～ miles away from the subject; completely off the point

【十万火急】most urgent; posthaste; express

【十项全能运动】[体] decathlon

【十羊九牧】nine shepherds for ten sheep—too many bosses

【十一】October 1, National Day of the People's Republic of China

【十一级风】[气] force 11 wind; storm

【十一月】❶ November ❷ the eleventh month of the lunar year; the eleventh moon
【十月】❶ October ❷ the tenth month of the lunar year; the tenth moon
【十之八九】(又作'十有八九') in eight or nine cases out of ten; most likely: ～他是误会了。*Most likely there is some misunderstanding on his part.*
【十指连心】the fingers are linked to the heart—what happens to children is of vital interest to parents
【十字镐】pick; pickaxe; mattock
【十字花科】[植] the mustard family
【十字架】the Cross: 背上～ *take up one's cross*
【十字街头】crisscross streets; busy city streets
【十字军】❶ the Crusades (11th-13th centuries) ❷ crusade ❸ crusader
【十字路口】crossroads; intersection: 徘徊在～ *hesitate at the crossroads*
【十足】❶ pure: ～的黄金 *pure gold* ❷ 100 per cent; out-and-out; sheer; downright: 干劲～ *full of energy* / ～的强权政治 100% (*or naked*) *power politics*
【十足类】[动] Decapoda; decapods

什 Ⅰ 量〈书〉(used in fractions or multiples) ten: ～一 *one tenth* / ～百 *tenfold or hundredfold* Ⅱ 形 assorted; varied; miscellaneous: 什物 ——另见 shén

【什件儿】giblets: 炒～ *fried giblets*
【什锦】assorted; mixed: ～饼干 *assorted biscuits* / ～奶糖 *assorted toffees*
【什物】articles for daily use; odds and ends; sundries
【什叶派】[宗](伊斯兰教) Shiah; Shiites

石 名 ❶ stone; rock ❷ stone inscription

【石斑鱼】grouper (a fish)
【石板】❶ slabstone; flagstone; flag ❷ slate (for writing on)
【石版】[刷] stone plate
【石碑】stone tablet; stele
【石笔】slate pencil
【石壁】cliff; precipice
【石材】stone used in construction and masonry
【石菖蒲】grass-leaved sweetflag (Acorus gramineus)
【石沉大海】like a stone dropped into the sea—disappear for ever; never to be seen or heard of again
【石担】[体] stone barbell
【石刁柏】asparagus (Asparagus officinalis)
【石雕】❶ stone carving ❷ carved stone
【石碓】a treadle-operated tilt hammer for hulling rice
【石墩】a block of stone used as a seat
【石方】cubic metre of stonework: 一百万～ *one million cubic metres of stonework*
【石坊】stone memorial archway (or gateway)
【石膏】❶ gypsum; plaster stone ❷ [医] (for a broken bone) plaster cast; cast: 他的腿上了～。*He had a plaster cast on his leg.* ◇ ～绷带 plaster bandage; ～床 plaster bed; ～夹板 plaster splint; ～像 plaster statue; plaster figure
【石工】❶ masonry ❷ stonemason; mason
【石拱桥】stone arch bridge
【石河】stone river; rock stream
【石斛】❶ noble dendrobium (Dendrobium nobile) ❷ [中] the stem of noble dendrobium
【石花菜】agar (a seaweed)
【石花胶】agar-agar
【石化】(〈略〉全称为'石油化学') petrochemistry: ～工业 *petrochemical industry*
【石化作用】[地质] petrifaction
【石灰】lime: 生～ *quick lime* / 熟～ *slaked lime* ◇ ～华 travertine; tufa; ～浆 lime white; ～砂浆 lime mortar; ～石 limestone; ～水 limewash; ～岩 limestone; ～窑 limekiln; ～质砂岩 calcareous sandstone
【石鸡】chukar (a partridge)
【石级】a flight of stone steps
【石匠】stonemason; mason
【石决明】[中] the shell of abalone or sea-ear
【石刻】❶ carved stone ❷ stone inscription
【石窟】rock cave; grotto ◇ ～寺 cave temple
【石块】stone block; rock
【石蜡】paraffin wax: ～油 *paraffin oil*
【石栗】candlenut tree
【石料】stone as material
【石林】stone forest
【石硫合剂】[化] lime sulfur
【石榴】pomegranate ◇ ～红 garnet (colour); ～裙 pomegranate-red skirt—feminine charms (used esp. in the phrase); ～石 garnet (a mineral)
【石龙子】skink (a lizard)
【石绿】malachite green (a green pigment made of malachite, often used in traditional Chinese painting)
【石煤】bone coal
【石棉】asbestos ◇ ～板 [建] asbestos board; ～布 asbestos cloth; ～衬里 [机] asbestos lining; ～瓦 [建] asbestos shingle; asbestos tile
【石墨】graphite ◇ ～铀堆 graphite-uranium pile
【石磨】millstones
【石楠】Chinese photinia
【石脑油】naphtha
【石女】[医] a woman with a hypoplastic vagina
【石破天惊】heaven-shaking—(of a message, opinion, etc.) remarkably original and forceful
【石器】❶ stone implement; stone artifact ❷ stone vessel; stoneware
【石器时代】the Stone Age
【石青】azurite blue (a blue pigment made of azurite, often used in traditional Chinese painting)
【石蕊】❶ reindeer moss (Cladonia rangiferina) ❷ [化] litmus ◇ ～试纸 [化] litmus paper
【石首鱼】sciaenoid; sciaenid
【石蒜】short-tube lycoris (Lycoris radiata)

【石笋】［地质］stalagmite

【石锁】［体］a stone dumbbell in the form of an old-fashioned padlock

【石炭】〈古〉coal ◇ ～纪［地质］the Carboniferous Period；～酸［化］carbolic acid；～系［地质］the Carboniferous System

【石头】stone；rock：～砌的墙 *a stone wall* / 心里好像一块～落了地 *feel as though a load has been taken off one's mind*

【石头子儿】〈口〉cobblestone；cobble；pebble：男孩子们爱往池塘里扔～。*The boys like to throw pebbles* (*or stones*) *into the pond*.

【石印】lithographic printing；lithography ◇ ～机 lithographic press；～石 lithographic stone；～油画 oleograph；～纸 lithographic paper

【石英】quartz ◇ ～玻璃 quartz glass；～电子表 quartz watch；～电子钟 quartz clock；～卤钨灯［摄］quartz tungsten halogen lamp；～岩 quartzite

【石油】petroleum；oil ◇ ～地质学 petroleum geology；～工业 oil industry；petroleum industry；～管路 petroleum pipeline；～化工厂 petrochemical works；～勘探 petroleum prospecting；～沥青 petroleum pitch；～美元 petrodollars；～气 petroleum gas；～输出国组织 the Organization of Petroleum Exporting Countries (OPEC)；～运移 oil migration

【石钟乳】同〖钟乳石〗

【石竹】China pink (Dianthus chinensis)

【石柱】stone pillar

【石子儿】cobblestone；cobble；pebble：～路 *cobblestone road*；*cobbled road*

【石作】masonry

识 Ⅰ 动 know：一字不～ *not know a single character—absolutely illiterate* Ⅱ 名 knowledge：见多识广

【识别】distinguish；discern；spot：～真伪 *distinguish true from false*；*distinguish between genuine and sham* / 善于～干部 *know how to judge cadres* / ～骗子 *spot a swindler* / ～伪装的敌人 *see through enemies in disguise*

【识别力】discernment

【识大体，顾大局】have the cardinal principles in mind and take the overall situation into account

【识货】know all about the goods；be able to tell good from bad；know what's what

【识破】see through；penetrate：～骗局 *see through a fraud*

【识趣】know how to behave in a delicate situation；be sensible；be tactful

【识时务者为俊杰】Whosoever understands the times is a great man；A wise man submits to circumstances.

【识途老马】an old horse who knows the way—a person of rich experience；a wise old bird

【识文断字】be able to read；be literate

【识相】〈方〉be sensible；be tactful：你还是～点，赶快走吧。*You'd better be sensible and quit*.

【识羞】(usu. used in the negative) have a sense of shame：他对我撒了谎还不～。*He feels no shame for having lied to me*.

【识字】learn to read；become literate：他识几个字。*He can read a little*. ◇ ～班 literacy class；～课本 reading primer；elementary reader

时 Ⅰ 名 ❶ a long period of time；times；days ❷ fixed time：按时 ❸ season：农时 ❹ time of day；hour；o'clock：上午八～ *at 8 o'clock in the morning*；*at 8 a.m.* ❺［语］tense：过去～ *the past tense* ❻ opportunity；chance：待～而动 *bide one's time* Ⅱ 形 current；present：时下 Ⅲ 副 now and then；occasionally；from time to time：～有发生 *occur from time to time*

【时弊】ills of the times

【时病】❶ ills of the times ❷ seasonal disease

【时不可失】Don't let slip an opportunity.

【时不时】〈方〉often；time and again

【时不我待】Time and tide wait for no man.

【时差】❶ differences of local time between places belonging to different time zones ❷［天］equation of time

【时差反应】jet lag；jet fatigue

【时常】often；frequently：我们～玩儿牌。*We often play cards*.

【时辰】❶ one of the 12 two-hour periods into which the day was formerly divided before the introduction of western chronology；double-hour：约莫半个～ *about an hour* ❷ the time for sth；opportunity

【时代】❶ times；age；era；epoch：电子～ *the era of electronics* / 新～的凯歌 *a paean of triumph to the new age* ❷ the times；our age；the day；the present era：～精神 *the spirit of our age*；*the spirit of the times* / ～感 *sense of the times*；*climate of an era* ❸ a period in one's life：从青年～到老年～ *from youth to old age*

【时而】❶ from time to time；sometimes：天上～飘过几片薄薄的白云。*Every now and then fleecy clouds floated across the sky*. ❷ (used reduplicatively) now... now...；sometimes... sometimes...：这天气变化无常，～晴天，～下雨！*What changeable weather, fine one moment, raining the next!*

【时分】the time of；the time when：黄昏～ *at dusk*；*at twilight* / 深夜～ *in the dead of night*

【时乖命蹇】be born under an evil star；have the hand of fate against one；fall on bad times

【时光】❶ time：～不早了。*It's getting late*. ❷ times；years；days：他一生中最好的～白白浪费了。*He wasted the best years of his life*.

【时过境迁】Things have changed with the lapse of time.

【时候】❶ (the duration of) time：农忙的～ *a busy farming season* ❷ (a point in) time；moment：现在是什么～了？*What time is it?* / 就在这～ *just at this moment*

【时机】opportunity；an opportune moment：等待

～ *wait for an opportunity*; *bide one's time* / 错过最有利的～ *let slip a golden opportunity* / ～不成熟。*Conditions are not yet ripe*.

【时计】[天] chronometer

【时价】current price; prevailing price: 本店售价略低于～。*Our listed prices are slightly lower than the current prices*.

【时间】❶ (the concept of) time: ～与空间 *time and space* ❷ (the duration of) time: ～到了。*Time!* or *Time's up*. / 办公～ *office hours* / 不给对手喘息的～ *give your opponent no breathing space* / ～掌握得好 *beautiful timing* ❸ (a point in) time: 北京～十九点整 *19 hours Beijing time* ◇ ～表 timetable; schedule; ～词 [语] time word; ～性 seasonality; timeliness; topicality; ～知觉 [心理] time perception

【时间滞后】time lag

【时角】[天] hour angle

【时节】❶ season (marked by certain weather conditions, activities, etc.): 春耕～ *the season for spring ploughing* / 秋收～ *harvest time* ❷ a particular time; occasion: 解放那～她才十二岁。*She was only twelve at the time of liberation*.

【时局】the current political situation

【时刻】❶ a point of time; hour; moment: 欢乐的～ *a time of rejoicing* / 幸福的～ *a happy moment* / 在此关键～ *at this crucial hour* ❷ constantly; always: ～准备保卫祖国 *be ready to defend the country at any moment*

【时刻表】timetable; schedule: 火车～ *railway timetable*; *train schedule*

【时来运转】one's luck turns in the fullness of time

【时令】season: ～已交初秋。*It is already early autumn*.

【时令病】seasonal disease: 冬春之交是～流行的季节。*Seasonal diseases are prevalent when winter is changing into spring*.

【时令不正】unseasonable weather

【时髦】fashionable; stylish; in vogue: ～的服装 *fashionable clothes* / 赶～ *follow the fashion*

【时评】news commentary; editorial

【时期】a particular period

【时起时伏】now rise, now fall; have ups and downs

【时穷节乃见】integrity (or loyalty) shines out in time of woe

【时区】time zone

【时日】time: 如若假以～,试验必获成功。*Given time, the experiment is sure to yield results*.

【时尚】fashion; fad ◇ ～迷 fashioniata

【时时】often; constantly: ～想到 *often recall or think about*

【时…时…】now... now...; sometimes... sometimes...: 镜头时远时近 *sometimes long shots and sometimes close-ups*

【时世】times; age: 艰难～ *hard times*

【时势】the current situation; the trend of the times; the way things are going ◇ ～造英雄 The times produce their heroes.

【时事】current events; current affairs: ～述评 *current events survey*

【时速】speed per hour: ～高达三百公里。*It has a top speed of 300 km per hour*.

【时态】[语] tense

【时务】current affairs; the current situation; the trend of the times

【时下】at present; right now

【时鲜】(of vegetables, fruits, fishes, etc.) in season: ～果品 *fresh fruits and nuts* / 新到草莓,是上好的～货。*We've got tip-top strawberries just in season*.

【时限】time limit: 在规定的～内 *within the prescribed time*

【时象】current social phenomena: 九十年代新～ *social phenomena of the 90s*

【时效】❶ effectiveness for a given period of time ❷ [法] prescription ❸ [冶] ageing

【时效硬化】[冶] age-hardening

【时新】stylish; trendy: ～的式样 *up-to-date style*

【时兴】(又作'时行') fashionable; in vogue; popular: 这种式样已经不～了。*This design* (*or style*) *is no longer in vogue* (*or is out of fashion now*).

【时宜】what is appropriate to the occasion

【时移俗易】customs change with the times

【时疫】epidemic

【时运】luck; fortune

【时运不济】have bad luck; be down on one's luck: 她跟着丈夫离开了家乡,后来～,他又病死了。*She left home to go with her husband, but as ill luck would have it he fell sick and died*.

【时针】❶ hands of a clock or watch ❷ hour hand (of a clock or watch)

【时政】〈旧〉the political situation of the time

【时值】[音] duration; value

【时至今日】at this late hour; even to this day: ～,回想起来仍然难过。*Even now the thought of it agonizes me*.

【时钟】clock

【时装】❶ fashionable dress; the latest fashion ❷ contemporary costume ◇ ～表演 fashion show; modelling; ～博览会 fashion fair; ～店 fashion house; ～模特儿 fashion model; ～设计师 fashion designer

实 Ⅰ 形 ❶ solid: 里面是～的。*It's solid*. / 地基要砸～。*The foundations must be tamped solid*. ❷ true; real; actual: ～利 *actual* (*or tangible*) *benefits* / ～有其事。*It's a fact*. Ⅱ 名 ❶ reality; fact: 名不副实 ❷ fruit; seed: 开花结～ *blossom and bear fruit*

【实报实销】reimburse the amount actually spent; be reimbursed for what one spends

【实逼处此】be forced to do so by the circumstances; There's no alternative under the circumstances.

【实诚】〈口〉honest; trustworthy: ～话 *honest words*

【实词】[语] notional word; full word

【实打实】real; true; honest; genuine: ～的本领 *real skill; genuine skill* / ～地说吧 *to tell the truth; honestly*

【实弹】❶ (of a gun or cannon) be loaded: 荷枪～ *carry a loaded rifle* ❷ [军] live shell; live ammunition: ～射击 *live firing; firing practice; range practice* / ～演习 *practice with live ammunition*

【实地】on the spot: ～考察 *on-the-spot investigation*

【实繁有徒】there is no lack of people of that ilk

【实感】thoughts and feelings acquired from personal experience; true feelings

【实干】get right on the job; do solid work: ～、苦干加巧干 *work hard, conscientiously and resourcefully* ◇ ～家 man of action; one who is conscientious and down-to-earth; mover and shaker

【实干精神】down-to-earth; unflashy

【实话】truth: 说～ *tell the truth* ◇ ～实说 speak frankly; talk straight; not mince matters

【实惠】❶ material benefit: 从中得到～ *really benefit from it* ❷ substantial; solid: 让顾客吃到经济～的饭菜 *serve the customers inexpensive but substantial meals*

【实际】❶ reality; practice: 从～出发 *proceed from actual conditions; be realistic* / ～上 *in fact; in practice; in reality; actually* ❷ practical; realistic: ～经验 *practical experience* / 你这种想法不～。*This idea of yours is unrealistic.* ❸ real; actual; concrete: ～的例子 *a concrete instance* / ～情况 *the actual situation; reality* / ～收入 *real income* ◇ ～工资 real wages; ～汇价 effective exchange rate; ～控制线 [军] line of actual control; ～行动 practical action; ～增长 [经] growth in real terms

【实绩】actual results; tangible achievements: 这本文集是他近年来创作上的～。*These collected writings embody the fruits of his creative labours in recent years.*

【实价】actual price

【实践】❶ practice: 学习语言需要大量～。*It requires much practice to learn a language.* ❷ put into practice; carry out; live up to: ～诺言 *keep one's word; make good one's promise* / ～自己的主张 *put one's ideas into practice* ◇ ～出真知 genuine knowledge comes from practice; ～性 practicality; practicalness

【实景】actual setting; location (movies): ～拍摄 *shoot on location*

【实据】substantial evidence; substantial proof

【实况】what is actually happening: 电视转播群众大会～ *televise a mass rally; live telecast of a mass rally* ◇ ～录音 on-the-spot recording; live recording; ～转播 televise live; live broadcast; live telecast

【实力】actual strength; strength: 国家经济～ *national economic strength* / 国防～ *national defence capabilities* / 军事～ *military strength* / ～相当 *match each other in strength; be well matched in strength* ◇ ～地位 position of strength; ～政策 policy of force

【实例】living example; example: 用～说明 *illustrate with examples*

【实录】〈书〉a faithful record: 这本日记是他晚年生活的～。*This diary is a faithful record of his declining years.*

【实脉】[中] forceful pulse

【实模铸造法】[冶] cavityless casting

【实盘】[经] firm offer ◇ ～交易 firm bargain

【实情】the true state of affairs; the actual situation; truth: 你得讲～。*You must tell the truth.*

【实情实理】the actual situation and the real reason: 他说的都是～。*What he says is perfectly true and reasonable.*

【实权】real power

【实生苗】[农] seedling

【实施】put into effect; implement; carry out: 九年制义务教育正在逐步～。*The system of nine-year compulsory education is being implemented.* /监督宪法的～ *supervise the enforcement of the constitution*

【实时】[计] real-time ◇ ～操作 real-time operation; ～处理 real-time processing

【实事】practical things: 只说空话，不干～ *indulge in empty talk and do nothing practical*

【实事求是】seek truth from facts; be practical and realistic: ～的态度 *a realistic approach* / ～的工作作风 *a practical and realistic style of work* / ～的批评 *criticism based on facts*

【实数】❶ the actual amount or number ❷ [数] real number

【实说】to tell the truth; frankly speaking; frankly

【实体】❶ [哲] substance ❷ entity: 一个独立的政治～ *an independent political entity*

【实体法】[法] substantive law

【实物】❶ material object; object: 纪念馆展出了许多图片和～。*The memorial hall displays many photographs and objects.* ❷ goods or produce instead of money: 以～代替 *in kind* ◇ ～地租 rent in kind; ～工资 wages in kind; ～幻灯机 epidiascope; ～交易 barter; ～税 tax paid in kind

【实习】(of students or trainees) practise (what has been learnt in class); exercise one's skill in; do fieldwork: 在中学～ *do practice teaching at a middle school* / 去煤矿～ *go on a field trip to a coal mine* / 进行护理～ *do practice nursing* ◇ ～工厂 a factory for training students in practical skills; ～教师 student teacher; trainee teacher; ～生 trainee; ～医生 intern

【实现】realize; fulfil; carry out; bring about: ～自己的理想 *realize one's ideal* / ～自己的诺言 *fulfil one's promises*

【实像】[物] real image

【实效】actual effect; substantial results: 讲求～

strive for substantial results / 注重～ *emphasize practical results*

【实心】❶ sincere; honest: ～话 *words spoken from one's heart* ❷ solid: 这种车胎是～的。*These tyres are solid.* ◇ ～球[体] medicine ball; ～实意 honest and sincere

【实心眼儿】❶ honest and serious-minded ❷ an honest and serious-minded person

【实行】put into practice (or effect); carry out; practise; implement: ～精兵简政的政策 *put into effect the policy of better staff and simpler administration* / ～经济改革 *carry out economic reforms*

【实性人】an honest and sincere person

【实学】real learning; sound scholarship: 有虚名而无～ *have a false reputation and no real learning*

【实言】truth: ～相告 *to tell you the truth*

【实验】experiment; test: 做～ *do (or carry out) an experiment; make a test* ◇ ～动物 animal used as a subject of experiment; ～室 laboratory; ～心理学 experimental psychology; ～员 laboratory technician; ～组 experimental group

【实业】industry and commerce; a large-scale industry or business ◇ ～家 industrialist

【实业银行】industrial bank

【实用】practical; pragmatic; functional: 既美观,又～ *not only beautiful, but also practical (or useful)* ◇ ～美术 applied fine arts; ～文〈旧〉practical writing (as in official documents, notices, receipts, etc.); ～主义[哲] pragmatism

【实在】(shízài) ❶ true; real; honest; dependable: ～的本事 *real ability* / 心眼儿～ *honest; trustworthy* / 他这个人可～了。*He is an honest and truly dependable man.* ❷ indeed; really; honestly: ～太好了。*Very good indeed.* / 我～不知道。*Honestly I don't know.* / ～抱歉! *I'm really sorry!* ❸ in fact; as a matter of fact: 他装懂,～并没懂。*He pretends to understand, but as a matter of fact he doesn't.*

【实在】(shízai)〈方〉(of work) well-done; done carefully: 工作做得很～! *The work is well-done.*

【实在论】[哲] realism

【实则】actually; in fact; in reality

【实战】actual combat: ～训练 *exercises under battle conditions* ◇ ～演习 combat exercise with live ammunition

【实证】authentic proof; substantial evidence ◇ ～主义[哲] positivism

【实症】[中] a case of a physically strong patient running a high fever or suffering from such disorders as stasis of blood, constipation, etc.

【实至名归】Fame follows merit.

【实质】substance; essence: 问题的～ *the crux of the matter; the central point at issue*

【实质性】substantive; substantial: ～条款 *substantive provision* / 取得～进展 *make substantial progress*

【实字】full word; content word

【实足】full; solid: 这袋麦子～一百斤。*This sack of wheat is a full* 100 *jin.* / 我～等了两个钟头。*I waited for two solid hours.*

【实足年龄】exact age (i. e. age in completed years)

拾

Ⅰ 动 ❶ pick up (from the ground); collect: ～到一个钱包 *picked up a purse* / ～柴 *collect firewood* / ～麦穗儿 *glean (stray ears of) wheat* ❷ tidy up; put in order: 收拾 Ⅱ 数 ten (used for the numeral 十 on cheques, banknotes, etc. to avoid mistakes or alterations)

【拾掇】❶ tidy up; put in order: 我们把屋子～一下。*Let's tidy up the room.* ❷ repair; fix: 这机器有点毛病,你给～一下好吗? *Something is wrong with the machine. Will you help me fix it?* ❸〈口〉settle with; punish

【拾荒】glean and collect scraps (to eke out an existence)

【拾金不昧】not pocket the money one picks up

【拾零】(usu. used in headlines) news in brief; titbits; sidelights

【拾取】pick up; collect: 在海滩上～贝壳 *collect shells on the beach*

【拾人牙慧】pick up phrases from sb. and pass them off as one's own

【拾物】a lost article found

【拾物招领处】Lost and Found Office; Lost Property Office

【拾遗】❶ appropriate lost property: 路不拾遗 ❷ make good omissions (often used in book titles): 《本草纲目～》*Supplementary Amplifications of the "Compendium of Materia Medica"*

【拾遗补阙】make good omissions and deficiencies

【拾音器】[电] pickup; adapter

食

Ⅰ 动 eat: 多～蔬菜。*Eat plenty of vegetables.* Ⅱ 名 ❶ meal; food: 丰衣足食 ❷ food for animals; feed: 小猫出去找～儿了。*The kittens are out looking for food.* / 鸡～没剩多少了。*There is only a little feed left for the chickens.* ❸ for cooking; edible: 食油 ❹ eclipse: 日食 —— 另见 sì

【食变星】[天] eclipsing variable

【食不甘味】eat without relish: 寝不安席,～ *sleep fitfully and eat without relish*

【食不果腹】have not enough food in one's belly; go hungry

【食不厌精,脍不厌细】eat no rice but is of the finest quality, nor meat but is finely minced—be very particular about one's food

【食草动物】herbivorous animal; herbivore

【食虫动物】insectivorous animal; insectivore

【食虫植物】insectivorous plant; insectivore

【食道】同〖食管〗

【食而不化】eat without digesting—read without understanding

【食而不知其味】eat without knowing the taste of what one is eating—read without understanding

【食饵】(fish) bait

【食粪】coprophagy ◇ ～动物 coprophagous animal
【食腐动物】saprophagous animal; scavenger; saprozoic
【食古不化】swallow ancient learning without digesting it
【食管】[生理] esophagus ◇ ～癌 cancer of the esophagus; ～炎 esophagitis
【食火鸡】cassowary
【食积】[中] dyspepsia; indigestion
【食既】[天] the second contact of a total eclipse; the beginning of totality ——另见〖食相〗
【食具】eating utensils; tableware
【食客】❶ a person sponging on an aristocrat; a hanger-on of an aristocrat ❷ a customer of a restaurant
【食粮】grain; food: ～供应 *food supplies* / 精神～ *spiritual food*
【食量】capacity for eating; appetite: ～大(小) *have a big (small) appetite*
【食疗】food therapy; diet therapy
【食糜】chyme (the pulp to which the food is reduced in the stomach)
【食品】foodstuff; food; provisions: 罐头～ *tinned (or canned) food* ◇ ～保藏 food preservation; ～部 food department; ～厂 bakery and confectionery; food products factory; ～袋 plastic bag for storing food; doggy bag; ～工业 food industry; ～公司 food company; ～加工 food processing; ～街 food bazaar; restaurant row; ～商店 provisions shop; ～添加剂 food additive; ～质量管理 quality control of food
【食品规则】Codex Alimentarius (the code of laws governing food standards, food hygiene, additives, etc.)
【食品结构】composition of diet
【食谱】cookbook; recipes
【食人俗】cannibalism
【食肉动物】carnivorous animal; carnivore
【食肉寝皮】(want to) eat sb.'s flesh and sleep on his skin—(want to) see the person one hates destroyed
【食肉植物】carnivorous plant; insectivorous plant; insectivore
【食色性也】appetite for food and sex is nature
【食少事烦】eat too little and does too much—cannot last long
【食甚】[天] the maximum phase of an eclipse; the middle of a total eclipse ——另见〖食相〗
【食宿】board and lodging
【食堂】dining room; mess hall; canteen
【食糖】sugar
【食蚊鱼】mosquito fish
【食物】food; eatables; edibles ◇ ～链 food chain; ～摄入 [动] food intake; ～污染 food pollution; ～中毒 food poisoning
【食相】[天] the phases of an eclipse: 日(月)偏食时,有三个～:初亏、食甚、复圆。*A partial solar (lunar) eclipse goes through three phases: the first contact, the maximum phase, and the last contact.*
【食性】[动] feeding habits; eating patterns
【食血动物】sanguivorous (or haematophagous) animal
【食言】go back on one's word; break one's promise: 你放心,他从不～。*I assure you he is as good as his word.*
【食言而肥】fail to make good one's promise; break faith with sb.
【食盐】table salt; salt
【食蚁兽】anteater
【食用】❶ used for food ❷ edible: ～植物 *edible plants* / ～植物油 *edible vegetable oil*
【食用色素】food colouring
【食油】edible oil; cooking oil
【食欲】appetite: 促进～ *stimulate (or whet) the appetite; be appetizing*
【食欲不振】❶ have a jaded appetite; have a poor appetite ❷ [医] anorexia
【食之无味,弃之可惜】hardly worth eating but not bad enough to throw away
【食指】index finger; forefinger
【食茱萸】[植] ailanthus prickly ash (Zanthoxylum ailanthoides)
【食租衣税】(of officials) live on taxes and levies

蚀 动 ❶ lose: 亏蚀 ❷ erode; corrode: 锈能～铁。*Rust corrodes iron.*
【蚀本】lose one's capital ◇ ～生意 a business running at a loss; a losing proposition; an unprofitable venture (or undertaking)
【蚀财】lose money or property
【蚀耗】loss; wear and tear
【蚀刻】etching: ～法 *etching* / ～玻璃 *etched glass*

鲥 名 hilsa herring; reeves shad
【鲥鱼】hilsa herring; reeves shad

shǐ

史 名 ❶ history: 国际关系～ *history of international relations* ❷ official historian in ancient China
【史不绝书】History is full of such instances.
【史册】(又作'史策') history; annals: 在民族解放斗争～上写下灿烂的篇章 *add an illustrious page to the annals of national liberation struggles*
【史抄】extracts from history
【史官】official historian in ancient China; historiographer
【史话】stories about historical events
【史籍】同〖史书〗
【史记】Records of the Historian (written by Sima Qian 司马迁 of the Han Dynasty)
【史迹】historical site or relics
【史料】historical data; historical materials
【史略】outline history; a brief history
【史评】commentary on historical events or historical records

【史前】prehistoric：～时代 *prehistoric age* (*or times*) ◇ ～考古学 prehistoric archaeology；～学 prehistory
【史诗】epic
【史实】historical facts：这些故事大多有～根据。*Most of these stories are founded on historical facts.* ◇ ～剧 documentary drama
【史书】history；historical records：据～记载 *according to historical records*
【史无前例】without precedent in history；unprecedented：～的壮举 *an unprecedented feat*
【史学】the science of history；historical science；historiography：～家 *historian*；*historiographer*

矢

Ⅰ 名 arrow：飞～ *flying arrow* Ⅱ 动 vow；swear：矢志不移
【矢车菊】[植] cornflower (Centaurea cyanus)
【矢口否认】flatly deny
【矢口狡赖】quibble and prevaricate, refusing to admit one's guilt；persistently quibble and deny one's errors
【矢量】[数][物] vector：切变～ *shear vector* / 风～ *wind vector* / ～分析 *vector analysis* ◇ ～字库 [计] vector font
【矢石】arrows and stones (ancient weapons)：～如雨 *a rain of arrows and stones*
【矢志】pledge one's devotion (to a cause)：～于科学 *pledge to devote one's life to the advancement of science*
【矢志不移】(又作'矢志不渝') vow to adhere to one's chosen course

豕

名 〈书〉 pig

使

Ⅰ 动 ❶ send；tell sb. to do sth：～人去打听消息 *send sb. to make inquiries* ❷ use；employ；apply：我们早就～上电脑了。*We've been using computers for quite a long time.* / 心往一处想，劲往一处～ *with everyone's thoughts and efforts directed towards one goal* ❸ make；cause；enable：修改原计划，～之适合于新的情况 *revise the original plan so as to gear it to the needs of the new situation* / 他的话并不～人感到意外。*What he said was not surprising.* Ⅱ 名 envoy；messenger：出使
【使绊儿】(又作'使绊子') ❶ trip sb. up in wrestling ❷ injure sb. by underhand methods：他当面说得好听，背后会给你～。*He will say nice things to your face and then give you a stab in the back.*
【使不得】❶ cannot be used；useless；unserviceable：这笔尖坏了，～了。*This nib's broken—it can't be used.* ❷ be impermissible；be undesirable：你病刚好，干这种重活可～。*You've just been ill；you mustn't do such heavy work.*
【使不惯】not used to using：我～刀叉。*I'm not used to using a knife and fork.*
【使不了】cannot use；unable to use：这玩艺儿我～。*I can't use this gadget.*
【使出】use；exert：～全副本领 *use all one's resources* ◇ ～浑身解数 use all one's skill；do all that one is capable of
【使得】❶ can be used；be usable：这个汽筒～使不得？*Does this pump work all right?* ❷ be workable；be feasible：这个主意倒还～。*That's rather a good idea.* / 你不去如何～？*It won't do if you don't go.* ❸ make；cause；render：～家喻户晓 *make it known to everyone*
【使馆】diplomatic mission；embassy：～工作人员 *the staff of a diplomatic mission*；*embassy personnel* / ～区 *diplomatic quarter*
【使坏】(又作'使坏水儿')〈口〉be up to mischief；play a dirty trick
【使唤】❶ order about：爱～人 *be in the habit of ordering people about*；*be bossy* ❷〈口〉use；handle：这匹马不听生人～。*This horse won't obey a stranger.*
【使节】diplomatic envoy；envoy：各国驻华～ *diplomatic envoys to China*；*heads of diplomatic missions in China* / 特别～ *envoy extraordinary* / ～旅行 *diplomatic tour*
【使劲】exert all one's strength：～干活 *work hard* / ～蹬车 *pedal (a bicycle) furiously* / ～划桨 *strain at the oars* / 有使不完的劲 *have inexhaustible energy* / 再使把劲 *put in more effort*；*put on another spurt*
【使君子】[中] the fruit of Rangoon creeper (Quisqualis indica)
【使力】exert all one's strength
【使领馆】diplomatic and consular missions；embassies and consulates
【使命】mission：历史～ *historical mission*
【使女】maidservant；housemaid；chambermaid；maid
【使气】lose one's temper；get angry
【使钱】spend money；use money：很会～ *spend (or use) one's money wisely*；*turn one's money to good account* / 甭想～买通我。*Don't think you can buy me over.* / 有使不完的钱 *be rolling in money*
【使徒】[宗](基督教) apostle
【使团】diplomatic mission；diplomatic corps：～长 *Dean of the Diplomatic Corps*；*Doyen of the Diplomatic Mission*
【使性子】get angry；lose one's temper
【使眼色】tip sb. the wink；wink
【使役】work (an animal)：注意牲口的～和繁殖。*Attention must be paid to the proper use and the breeding of animals.*
【使用】use；employ；apply：善于识别人和～人 *know how to judge men and use men* / ～种种手段 *resort to every possible means* ◇ ～额 the amount of disbursement；～价值 [经] use value；～率 rate of utilization；～面积 usable floor area；～权 [法] right of use；right to use a thing；～寿命 service life (of machines, etc.)；～说明书 operation instructions；user's manual
【使者】emissary；envoy；messenger：他是一位和

平～。*He is an ambassador of peace.*

始 Ⅰ 动 begin; start: 不知～于何时 *not know exactly when this came into being* Ⅱ 副 〈书〉 only then; not... until: 坚持学习，～能不断进步。*Steady progress can only be the result of persistent study.* or *Only persistent study yields steady progress.*

【始创】initiate; originate

【始而】〈书〉at first; originally; at the start: ～不解，继而恍然。*At first I didn't catch on; then I suddenly saw the light.*

【始料】originally expected: ～所不及 *unexpected; unforeseen*

【始乱终弃】(of a man) seduce and then abandon

【始末】beginning and end—the whole story: 事情的～ *the whole story*

【始新世】[地理] the Eocene Epoch

【始业】〈书〉the beginning of the school year: 秋季～。*The school year begins in autumn.*

【始终】from beginning to end; from start to finish; all along; throughout: 会谈～在友好的气氛中进行。*The talks proceeded in a friendly atmosphere from beginning to end.*

【始终不懈】unremitting; untiring

【始终不渝】unswerving; consistent; steadfast: ～地支援各国人民的正义斗争 *steadfastly support and aid the just struggles of the people of all countries*

【始终如一】constant; consistent: ～地站在革命人民一边 *consistently side with the revolutionary people*

【始祖】first ancestor; earliest ancestor

【始祖鸟】palaeontology archaeopteryx

【始作俑者】the man who first made tomb figures—the creator of a bad precedent

驶 动 ❶ sail; drive: ～入港口 *sail into the harbour* / 火车～出车站。*The train pulled out of the station.* ❷ (of a vehicle, etc.) speed: 疾～而过 *speed by; fly past*

屎 名 ❶ excrement; faeces; dung; droppings: 鸡～ *chicken droppings* / 牛～ *cow dung* ❷ secretion (of the eye, ear, etc.): 耳屎

【屎壳郎】〈方〉dung beetle

shì

士 名 ❶ scholar ❷ soldier; armyman: 士兵 ❸ noncommissioned officer: 上士 / 下士 ❹ a person trained in a certain field: 护士 ❺ (commendable) person: 勇士 ❻ bodyguard, one of the pieces in Chinese chess

【士兵】rank-and-file soldiers; privates

【士大夫】scholar-officials (in imperial times)

【士女】young men and women

【士气】morale: 鼓舞～ *boost morale* / ～低落 *sagging morale*

【士为知己者用，女为悦己者容】A gentleman acts on behalf of an understanding friend, as a woman makes herself beautiful for her lover.

【士卒】soldiers; privates

氏 名 ❶ family; clan: 张～兄弟 *the Zhang brothers* ❷ used after a married woman's maiden name: 李王～ *Mrs. Li, née Wang* ❸ (used after the surname of a famous person): 《吕～春秋》*Master Lü's Spring and Autumn Annals* / 摄～温度计 *Celsius thermometer*

【氏族】clan: ～公社 *clan commune* / ～社会 *clan society* / ～制度 *clan system*

市 名 ❶ market: 米～ *rice market* ❷ city; municipality: 天津～ *the City of Tianjin; Tianjin municipality* / ～内交通 *city traffic* / ～中心 *the heart of the city; city centre; downtown* ❸ pertaining to the traditional Chinese system of weights and measures: 市尺 / 市斤

【市场】marketplace; market; bazaar: ～竞争日益加剧 *increasingly intense market competition* / 这种错误理论在群众中的～越来越小。*This erroneous theory finds less and less support among the people.* ◇ ～调研 market survey; ～份额 market share; ～规则 market mechanism; ～价格 market price; ～价值 market value; ～行情 market quotation; ～机制 market mechanism; ～经济 market-oriented economy; market economy; ～竞争 market competition; ～调节 regulation by market forces; ～透明度 market transparency; ～信息 market information; ～业务 marketing functions; ～预测 market forecasting

【市秤】the traditional Chinese scale of weights

【市尺】chi, a traditional unit of length, equivalent to 0.333 metre (米) or 1.094 feet (英尺)

【市寸】cun, a traditional unit of length, equal to 0.1 chi (市尺), and equivalent to 3.333 centimetres (厘米) or 1.312 inches (英寸)

【市撮】cuo, a traditional unit of capacity, equal to 0.001 sheng (市升), and equivalent to 1 millilitre (毫升) or 0.002 pint (品脱)

【市石】dan, a traditional unit of capacity, (esp. for grain), equal to 100 sheng (市升), and equivalent to 100 litres (升) or 176 pints (品脱)

【市担】dan, a traditional unit of weight, equal to 100 jin (市斤), and equivalent to 50 kilograms (公斤) or 110.25 pounds (磅)

【市斗】dou, a traditional unit of capacity, equal to 10 sheng (市升), and equivalent to 10 litres (升) or 17.60 pints (品脱) or 2.2 gallons (加仑)

【市分】❶ fen, a traditional unit of length, equal to 0.01 chi (市尺), and equivalent to 0.333 centimetre (厘米) or 0.131 inch (英寸) ❷ fen, a traditional unit of weight, equal to 0.001 jin (市斤), and equivalent to 0.5 gram (克) or 0.175 ounce (盎司) ❸ fen, a traditional unit of area, equal to 0.1 mu (市亩), and equivalent to 0.667 are (公亩) or 79.73 square yards (平方码)

【市府】(〈略〉全称为'市政府') the municipal government

【市合】ge, a traditional unit of capacity, equal to 0.1 sheng (市升), and equivalent to 0.1 litre (升) or 0.176 pint (品脱)

【市毫】❶ hao, a traditional unit of length, equal to 0.0001 chi (市尺), and equivalent to 0.0333 millimetre (毫米) or 0.0013 inch(英寸) ❷ hao, a traditional unit of weight, equal to 0.00001 jin (市斤), and equivalent to 5 milligrams (毫克) or 0.075 grain (谷)

【市花】city flower: 牡丹是洛阳的～。*The peony is the city flower of Luoyang.*

【市话】(〈略〉全称为'市内电话') local telephone call

【市集】❶ fair ❷ small town

【市价】market price; ruling price

【市郊】suburb; outskirts

【市斤】jin, a traditional unit of weight, each containing 10 liang (市两) or 16 old liang (旧市两) and equivalent to 0.5 kilogram (公斤) or 1.102 pounds (磅)

【市井】〈书〉 marketplace; town ◇ ～小人〈贬〉 philistine; ～之徒〈贬〉philistine

【市侩】sordid merchant: ～习气 *sordid merchants' ways; philistinism*

【市厘】❶ li, a traditional unit of length, equal to 0.001 chi (市尺), and equivalent to 0.333 millimetre (毫米) or 0.013 inch (英寸) ❷ li, a traditional unit of weight, equal to 0.0001 jin (市斤), and equivalent to 5 centigrams (厘克) or 0.771 grain (谷) ❸ li, a traditional unit of area, equal to 0.01 mu (市亩), and equivalent to 0.667 square metre (平方米) or 0.797 square yard (平方码)

【市里】li, a traditional unit of length, equal to 150 zhang (市丈), and equivalent to 0.5 kilometre (公里) or 0.311 mile (英里)

【市立】municipal: ～学校 *municipal school* / ～医院 *city hospital*

【市两】❶ liang, a traditional unit of weight, equal to 0.1 jin (市斤), and equivalent to 50 grams (克) or 1.763 ounces (盎司) ❷ old liang (旧市两), equal to 0.0625 jin (as 16 old liang make 1 jin), and equivalent to 31.25 grams (克) or 1.102 ounces (盎司)

【市面】market conditions; the state of trade; business: ～繁荣。*Trade is flourishing.* or *Business is brisk.* / ～萧条。*Business is slack.*

【市民】city residents; townspeople; urban inhabitants

【市亩】mu, a traditional unit of area, equal to 60 square zhang (平方市丈), and equivalent to 6.667 ares (公亩) or 0.165 acre (英亩)

【市钱】qian, a traditional unit of weight, equal to 0.01 jin(市斤), and equivalent to 5 grams (克) or 0.176 ounce (盎司)

【市情】❶ special characteristics of a city: 全国～调查 *investigation of all the cities in the country* ❷ market conditions

【市顷】qing, a traditional unit of area, equal to 100 mu (市亩), and equivalent to 6.667 hectares (公顷) or 16.474 acres (英亩)

【市区】city proper; urban district

【市容】the appearance of a city: 参观～ *go sightseeing in the city; have a look around the city*

【市勺】shao, a traditional unit of capacity, equal to 0.01 sheng (市升), and equivalent to 1 centilitre (厘升) or 0.018 pint (品脱)

【市升】sheng, a traditional unit of capacity, equivalent to 1 litre (升) or 1.76 pints (品脱) or 0.22 gallon (加仑)

【市丝】❶ si, a traditional unit of length, equal to 0.00001 chi (市尺), and equivalent to 3.333 microns (微米) ❷ si, a traditional unit of weight, equal to 0.000001 jin (市斤), and equivalent to 0.5 milligram (毫克) or 0.0075 grain (谷)

【市售】available on the market: ～国产胶卷 *Chinese-made film available on the market*

【市属】directly under the jurisdiction of a municipal government: ～工厂 *factory under the municipal government*

【市委】municipal Party committee

【市长】mayor

【市盈率】[经] price-earnings ratio: 上海市场平均～达44倍。*The average price-earnings ratio on the Shanghai stock market is 44.*

【市丈】zhang, a traditional unit of length, equal to 10 chi(市尺), and equivalent to 3.333 metres (米) or 3.65 yards (码)

【市镇】small towns; towns

【市政】municipal administration: ～当局 *municipal authorities* ◇ ～工程 municipal works; municipal engineering

【市制】the traditional Chinese system of weights and measures (with chi 市尺 as its basic unit of length, jin 市斤 as its basic unit of weight, and sheng 市升 as its basic unit of capacity)

示

示 动 show; notify; instruct: 盼速～知。*I hope you will notify me soon.* / ～悉。*Your letter has been received.*

【示波管】[电子] oscilloscope tube

【示波器】[电子] oscillograph; oscilloscope

【示范】set an example; demonstrate: 我先给大家～一下。*I'll first show you how to do it.* / ～飞行 *demonstration flight* / ～农场 *a demonstration farm; a pilot farm*

【示功器】[机] indicator

【示功图】[机] indicator card; indicator diagram

【示警】give a warning; warn

【示例】give typical examples; give a demonstration

【示人】show sth. to others; let others have a look at sth.

【示弱】give the impression of weakness; take sth. lying down

【示威】❶ demonstrate; hold a demonstration: ～

群众 *demonstrators* ❷ put on a show of force; display one's strength
【示威游行】demonstration; parade; march
【示意】signal; hint; motion: ~他出去 *motion to him to go out* / 以目~ *give a hint with the eyes; tip sb. the wink*
【示意图】❶ sketch map: 边界东段~ *a sketch map showing the eastern sector of the boundary* / 架设天线的~ *illustrated instructions for installing antennae* ❷［机］schematic diagram; schematic drawing
【示众】publicly expose; put before the public: 游街~ *parade sb. through the streets*
【示踪测定】［物］tracer determination
【示踪物】［物］tracer
【示踪元素】［物］tracer element
【示踪原子】［物］labelled atom; tagged atom; tracer

世 名 ❶ lifetime; life: 一~ *all one's life* ❷ generation: 第七十~后裔 *descendants of the 70th generation* ❸ from generation to generation; through generations: ~爵 *hereditary rank or nobility* ❹ (used in terms of address among old family friends): ~伯(叔) *uncle (friend of one's father)* ❺ age; era: 当今之~ *at present; nowadays* ❻ the world: 公之于~ *make known to the world; reveal to the public* ❼［地质］epoch
【世仇】❶ family feud ❷ ancient enemy
【世传】be handed down through generations: ~秘方 *a secret recipe handed down from generation to generation*
【世代】❶ years; ages ❷ for generations; from generation to generation; generation after generation: 他家~务农。*He comes from a long line of farmers.* ◇ ~交替［生］alternation of generations; ~相传 pass on from generation to generation
【世道】the manners and morals of the time: 唉！别提那吃人的旧~了。*Hm! Let's not talk about that man-eat-man society.* ◇ ~人心 the ways of the world and public sentiment
【世风】〈书〉public morals: ~日下。*Public morals are declining day by day.*
【世故】(shìgù) the ways of the world
【世故】(shìgu) worldly-wise: 这人相当~。*This chap is rather a smooth character.*
【世纪】century ◇ ~末 end of the century; fin-de-siècle
【世家】an old and well-known family; an aristocratic family: 音乐~ *a family of musicians* / ~子弟 *descendants of an aristocratic family*
【世间】❶ in this world ❷ in society
【世交】❶ friendship spanning two or more generations ❷ old family friends: 王家跟李家是~。*The Wangs and the Lis are old family friends.*
【世界】❶ world: 全~ *the whole world* / ~大事 *world events* / ~冠军 *world champion* / ~纪录 *world record* ❷［宗］(佛教) the universe: 大千世界 ❸ field; sphere; domain; realm: 内心~ *a person's inner world* / 科学~ *the domain of sciences* / 禽鸟~ *the feathered world* ◇ ~博览会 World's Fair; ~大战 world war; ~观 world outlook; ~末日［宗］(基督教) Doomsday; Day of Last Judgment; ~人权宣言 Universal Declaration of Human Rights (Dec. 10, 1948); ~时［天］universal time; ~语 Esperanto; world language; ~主义 cosmopolitanism
【世界音乐】world music
【世界银行】World Bank
【世局】the world situation
【世面】various aspects of society; society; world; life: 见过~ *have seen the world; have experienced life*
【世乒赛】(〈略〉全称为'世界乒乓球锦标赛') World Table Tennis Championship
【世情】worldly affairs; social trends: 不懂~ *unsophisticated*
【世人】common people
【世上】in the world; on earth
【世上无难事,只怕有心人】Nothing in the world is difficult for one who sets his mind on it.
【世事】affairs of human life
【世事洞明皆学问,人情练达即文章】A grasp of mundane affairs is genuine knowledge, and understanding of worldly wisdom is true learning.
【世俗】❶ common customs: ~之见 *common views* ❷ secular; worldly
【世态】the ways of the world: ~人情 *the ways of the world*
【世态炎凉】warmth or coldness is the way of the world—people are friendly or unfriendly, depending on whether one is successful or not
【世途】experiences in life: ~坎坷 *a life full of frustrations*
【世外桃源】the Land of Peach Blossoms—a fictitious land of peace, away from the turmoil of the world; a haven of peace
【世务】current affairs; the trend of the times: 不达~ *show no understanding of the times*
【世袭】hereditary: ~财产 *hereditary property; patrimony* / ~制度 *the hereditary system*
【世系】pedigree; genealogy
【世象】variety of life: ~漫画 *cartoons on many different subjects; great variety of cartoons*
【世谊】〈书〉friendship spanning generations

仕 名 ❶ be an official; fill an office ❷ bodyguard, one of the pieces in Chinese chess
【仕宦】〈书〉be an official; be in government service: ~之家 *an official family* / ~子弟 *sons of an official family*
【仕进】〈书〉pursue an official career: 不求~ *give up all thought of an official career*
【仕路】〈书〉an official career
【仕女】❶ a maid in an imperial palace; maid of honour ❷ painting traditional Chinese painting

of beautiful women

【仕途】〈书〉an official career：～多蹇 *an official career fraught with difficulties and danger*

式 名 ❶ type；style：雷锋～的人物 *people of the Lei Feng type* ❷ pattern；form：程式 ❸ ceremony；ritual：开幕式 ❹ formula：分子式 ❺［语］mood；mode：叙述～ *indicative mood*

【式样】style；type；model：各种～的服装 *clothes in different styles* / ～美观 *graceful-looking；stylish*

【式子】❶ posture：他的太极拳～摆得好。*The postures he assumes when doing taijiquan exercises are correct and graceful.* ❷ formula：列出这道代数题的～。*Write down the formula for this algebraic problem.*

似（构词成分）见下——另见 sì

【似的】used after a noun，pronoun，or verb to indicate similarity：像雪～那么白 *as white as snow* / 他仿佛睡着了～。*He seems to be asleep.*

试 Ⅰ 动 try；test：～一～ *have a try* / ～穿 *try on (a garment，shoes，etc.)* / ～～绳子结实不结实 *test the strength of a rope* / ～产 *trial production* Ⅱ 名 examination；test：口试

【试办】run an enterprise，etc. as an experiment；run a pilot scheme

【试表】〈口〉take sb.'s temperature

【试播】trial broadcast or trial telecast

【试产】trial production；test run：铜厂昨日投料～。*The copper mill performed a trial-production run yesterday.*

【试唱】try out a song

【试车】test run (of a machine，car，etc.)；trial run

【试车投产】go into trial production

【试穿】try on clothes；clothes fitting

【试点】❶ make (conduct) an experiment；make experiments；conduct tests at selected points；launch a pilot project：进行以税代利的～ *conduct experiments in substituting taxes for delivery of profits* ❷ a place where an experiment is made；experimental unit ◇ ～班 experimental class (in a teaching experiment)

【试电笔】［电］test pencil

【试读】probationary study：学校要求他先～一学期。*The school put him on probation for one semester.*

【试飞】test flight；trial flight：～驾驶员 *test pilot*

【试工】(of a worker or servant) be hired or engaged on a probational basis；be on probation：～期间 *during the probation or trial period*

【试管】test tube ◇ ～婴儿 test-tube baby

【试航】❶ trial voyage or flight；shakedown cruise or flight；trial run ❷ shake down (a ship or an aeroplane)

【试婚】trial marriage

【试机】test-run a machine

【试剂】［化］reagent

【试讲】give a trial lecture；dry run

【试金石】touchstone

【试镜头】screen test：导演让他～。*The director gave him a screen test.*

【试卷】examination paper；test paper

【试刊】trial publication of a newspaper or periodical：该报～成功，现已正式发行。*The newspaper has been formally issued after its successful trial publication.*

【试射】［军］fire for adjustment；trial fire；test-launch

【试试手】have a try at sth

【试探】(shìtàn) probe or explore (a question)：～宇宙的奥秘 *probe the secrets of the universe*

【试探】(shìtan) sound out；feel out：～一下他对这个问题的看法 *sound him out about the question*

【试探性】trial；exploratory；probing：～攻击 *probing attack* / ～谈判 *exploratory talks* ◇ ～气球 trial balloon

【试题】examination questions；test questions

【试图】attempt to (do sth.)；try to (do sth.)

【试问】we should like to ask；it may well be asked；may we ask

【试想】(used in reasoning with sb.) just think：～你这样干下去会有好结果吗？*Just think. Will it do you any good if you go on like this?*

【试销】❶ place goods on trial sale ❷ trial sale：～专柜 *trial sale counter*

【试行】try out：先～，再推广 *first try out，then popularize*

【试选样品】［机］pilot model

【试演】❶ trial performance (of a play，etc.)；preview；trial run ❷ give a trial performance or a preview (of a play，etc.)；(of a play，etc.) have a trial run

【试验】trial；experiment；test：水力～ *hydraulic test* / 进行反坦克武器～ *try out antitank weapons* ◇ ～场 proving ground；testing ground；～农场 experimental farm；～性工厂 pilot plant

【试验田】❶［农］experimental plot；experimental field ❷ a trial undertaking

【试样】❶ sample；specimen：岩石～ *rock sample* ❷ try on a partly finished garment ❸ try on：需要～的衣服 *apparel that needs to be tried on*

【试营业】open on a trial basis；in trial operation or service

【试映】preview (of a film)

【试用】❶ try out：我想～一下。*I want to try it out.* ❷ on probation：～人员 *person on probation；probationer* / ～期 *probation period* ◇ ～本 trial edition (an edition put out to solicit comments)；～品 trial products

【试运转】［机］test run；running-in

【试纸】［化］test paper：石蕊～ *litmus test paper* / 万用～ *universal test paper* / 姜黄～ *turmeric test paper*

【试制】trial-produce；trial-manufacture：一种新的

播种机～成功了。*A new seeding machine has been successfully trial-produced.*

【试种】plant experimentally：～水稻 *growing rice on a trial basis*

势 名 ❶ power；force；influence：权势 ❷ momentum；tendency：以排山倒海之～ *with the momentum of an avalanche* ❸ the outward appearance of a natural object：山～ *the lie of a mountain* ❹ situation；state of affairs；circumstances：～难从命。*Circumstances make it difficult for me to comply with your request.* ❺ sign；gesture：手势 ❻ male genitals：去势

【势必】certainly will；be bound to：饮酒过度，～影响健康。*Excessive drinking will undoubtedly affect one's health.*

【势不可挡】irresistible：革命的潮流汹涌澎湃，～。*The revolution is surging forward irresistibly.*

【势不两立】be mutually exclusive；be extremely antagonistic；be irreconcilable

【势成骑虎】like riding a tiger—a situation from which it is hard to extricate oneself ——另见〖骑虎难下〗

【势均力敌】match each other in strength：双方～。*The two sides are evenly matched.* / 一场～的比赛 *a close contest*

【势力】force；power；influence：壮大～ *expand one's forces* ◇ ～范围 sphere of influence

【势利】snobbish：～小人 *snob* ◇ ～眼 snobbish attitude；snobbishness；snob

【势难从命】circumstances make it difficult for me to comply with your request

【势能】［物］potential energy

【势如累卵】be in a very perilous position；hazardous like a pile of eggs

【势如破竹】like splitting a bamboo；like a hot knife cutting through butter；with irresistible force：～，所向披靡 *smash all resistance and advance victoriously everywhere*

【势所必然】inevitably；as a matter of course

【势态】situation；state：道德力量的崩溃，使～更加严重。*The collapse of moral values has made the situation worse.*

【势头】❶ impetus；momentum：风的～越来越大。*It blew harder and harder.* ❷〈口〉tendency；the look of things：他见～不对，转身就走。*Sensing that the odds were against him, he immediately turned back.*

【势焰】〈贬〉influence and power：～万丈 *aggressively powerful*

【势在必行】be imperative（under the circumstances）：此项改革～。*This reform must be enforced.*

事 Ⅰ 名 ❶ matter；affair；thing；business：没你的～。*It's not your business.* / 这是怎么回～？*What's this all about?* ❷ trouble；accident：出事 ❸ job；work：她找到～儿了。*She's got a job.* ❹ responsibility；involvement：这件案子里还有他的～呢。*He was involved in the case too.* / 有我什么～，干吗怪我？*Why put the blame on me? It has nothing to do with me.* Ⅱ 动 ❶〈书〉wait upon；serve：～父母 *wait upon one's parents* ❷ be engaged in：不～生产 *lead an idle life*

【事半功倍】get twice the result with half the effort

【事倍功半】get half the result with twice the effort

【事必躬亲】see（or attend）to everything oneself；take care of every single thing personally

【事变】❶ incident：七七～ *the July 7 Incident of* 1937 ❷ emergency；exigency：准备应付可能的突然～ *be prepared against all possible emergencies* ❸ the course of events；events：研究周围～的联系 *look into the relations of events occurring around one*

【事不关己，高高挂起】let things drift if they do not affect one personally；stand aloof from things on the ground that they are no concern of one's

【事不宜迟】We must lose no time in doing it；We must attend to the matter immediately；This matter needs immediate attention.

【事出有因】There is good reason for it；It is by no means accidental.

【事到临头】when things come to a head；when the situation becomes critical；at the last moment：你如果没有思想准备，～就会抓瞎。*If you don't anticipate what may happen, you'll find yourself at a loss when something crops up.*

【事典】encyclopedia：经济～ *source book on economics*

【事端】disturbance；incident：挑起～ *provoke incidents* / 制造～ *create disturbances*

【事非经过不知难】you never know how hard a task is until you have done it yourself

【事功】〈书〉achievement：急于～ *be desirous of achievement*

【事故】accident；mishap：责任～ *accident arising from sb.'s negligence*

【事过境迁】The affair is over and the situation has changed；The incident is over and the circumstances are different.

【事后】after the event；afterwards：不要老是只作～的批评。*Don't get into the habit of criticizing only after the event.*

【事后诸葛亮】be a Zhuge Liang only after something unpleasant has happened—be wise after the event

【事机】❶ affairs that should be kept secret ❷ situation

【事迹】deed；achievement：英雄～ *heroic deeds*

【事假】leave of absence（to attend to private affairs）；compassionate leave：请两小时～ *ask for two hours leave of absence*

【事件】incident；event：流血～ *a bloody incident* / 二十世纪最伟大的～ *the greatest event in the 20th century*

【事理】reason；logic：明白～ *be reasonable*；*be sensible*

【事例】example；instance：典型～ *a typical case*

【事略】biographical sketch; short biographical account

【事前】before the event; in advance; beforehand: ～请示,事后报告 *ask for instructions in advance and submit reports afterwards*; *ask for instructions beforehand and report back afterwards*

【事情】affair; matter; thing; business: ～的真相 *the truth of the matter*; *the facts of the case* / ～也真巧 *as luck would have it* / ～是这样的。*It happened like this*.

【事实】fact: 与～不符 *not tally with the facts* / ～恰恰相反。*The facts are just the opposite*. or *The opposite is the case*. / ～如此。*This is how things are* (*or stand*).

【事实上】in fact; in reality; as a matter of fact; actually: ～的承认 *de facto recognition*

【事实胜于雄辩】facts are stronger than rhetoric; facts speak louder than words

【事事】❶ everything: ～都要从人民的利益出发。*In whatever we do, our primary concern should be the interests of the people*. ❷〈书〉be engaged in some work or business

【事态】state of affairs; situation: ～严重。*The situation is serious*.

【事体】〈方〉matter; affair

【事无具细】(take part in) all kinds of work, no matter how big or trivial; all matters, big and small; all matters, whether important or trivial

【事务】❶ work; routine: ～繁忙 *have a lot* (*of work*) *to do* / ～性工作 *routine work*; *daily routine* ❷ general affairs: ～科 *the general affairs section* ◇ ～所 office; ～员 office clerk; ～主义 routinism

【事物】thing; object: ～都是一分为二的。*Everything divides into two*.

【事先】in advance; beforehand; prior: ～做好准备 *get everything ready beforehand* / ～跟他们打个招呼。*Notify them in advance*.

【事先声明】advance directive

【事项】item; matter: 注意～ *matters needing attention*; *points for attention*

【事业】❶ cause; undertaking; career: ～顺利 *have a successful career* / 文化教育～ *cultural and educational undertakings* ❷ institution; facilities: 集体福利～ *collective welfare facilities or services* / 公用～ *public utilities* ◇ ～单位 institution; ～费 operating expenses; ～家 entrepreneur; ～心 devotion to one's work; dedication

【事宜】(usu. used in official language) matters concerned; arrangements: 商谈有关建馆～ *discuss matters relating to the establishment of the embassy*

【事由】❶ the origin of an incident; particulars of a matter: 把～交代明白 *give all the particulars about the incident* ❷ (used in official language) main content ❸〈方〉job; work: 找～ *hunt for a job*

【事与愿违】Things turn out contrary to one's wishes.

【事在人为】It all depends on human effort; Human effort is the decisive factor: 他们能够做到那样,我们难道就做不到吗? ～嘛。*If they could achieve so much, why can't we? Everything depends upon men's efforts*.

【事主】the victim of a crime

侍 动 wait upon; attend upon; serve: 服侍

【侍从】〈旧〉attendants; retinue

【侍从副官】aide-de-camp (A. D. C.); aide

【侍奉】support and wait upon (one's elders): ～父母 *support and wait upon one's parents*

【侍候】wait upon; look after; attend: ～病人 *look after a patient* / ～少爷 *wait upon the young master*

【侍立】be in attendance: ～两旁 *stand on either side in attendance*

【侍弄】〈方〉tend with care (crops, domestic animals, etc.)

【侍女】maidservant; maid

【侍卫】❶ guard ❷ imperial bodyguard

【侍养】support and wait upon (one's elders)

【侍应生】〈旧〉a young attendant or odd-jobber (in banks, etc.)

【侍者】attendant; servant; waiter

视 动 ❶ look at: 注视 ❷ regard; look upon: ～为莫大光荣 *regard as a great honour* / ～如仇敌 *look upon sb. as one's enemy* ❸ inspect; watch: 视察

【视差】[物] parallax

【视察】❶ inspect: 去外地～工作 *be on an inspection tour* ❷ watch; observe: ～地形 *survey the terrain* ◇ ～团 inspection team; inspectorate; ～员 inspector

【视场】field of vision (or view)

【视唱】sightsinging; sing from a musical score ◇ ～练耳 solfeggio

【视窗】[计] Windows (software)

【视地平】[天] apparent horizon

【视点】point of view; perspective: 东方人的～和思维方式 *an Oriental perspective and way of thinking*

【视而不见】look but see not; turn a blind eye to; close (or shut) one's eyes to: 这是事实,不能～。*These are facts and you can't just ignore them*. ◇ ～,听而不闻 look but see not; listen but hear not; turn a blind eye to and a deaf ear to; take no notice of; pretend not to see or hear

【视感】visual sense; visibility

【视轨道】[天] apparent orbit

【视角】angle of view; visual angle

【视界】field of vision; visual field

【视景】what comes into a driver's or a pilot's view as the vehicle or the craft proceeds

【视觉】[生理] visual sense; vision; sense of sight ◇ ～像 visual image; ～印象 eye impressions; visual impressions; ～暂留 persistence of vision

【视力】vision; sight: ～测验 *eyesight test* / ～好

（差）*have good（poor）eyesight* ◇ ～表 visual chart
【视亮度】［天］apparent brightness
【视盘】video disc
【视频】［物］video frequency
【视如敝屣】regard as worn-out shoes—cast aside as worthless
【视如粪土】look upon as filth and dirt；consider as beneath contempt
【视如寇仇】regard as an enemy
【视若草芥】regard as worthless
【视若无睹】take no notice of what one sees；shut one's eyes to；turn a blind eye to；ignore
【视神经】［生理］optic nerve
【视事】〈旧〉（of officials）attend to business after assuming office；assume office
【视死如归】look upon death as going home；look death calmly in the face；face death unflinchingly
【视听】seeing and hearing；what is seen and heard：组织学生旅行参观，以广～ *arrange for touring trips and visits so as to broaden the students' views*
【视听教材】audio-visual materials；audio-visuals
【视听教具】audio-visual aids
【视听教学】audio-visual instruction
【视同等闲】regard sb. or sth. as unimportant；treat lightly or casually
【视同儿戏】treat（a serious matter）as a trifle；trifle with
【视同路人】regard as a stranger；treat like a stranger
【视图】［机］view：前～ *front view* / 侧～ *side view* / 上～ *top view*
【视网膜】［生理］retina
【视网膜脱离】detachment of retina
【视网膜炎】retinitis
【视为畏途】regard as a dangerous road to take；be afraid to undertake
【视线】line of vision；view；line of sight（in surveying）：请观众脱帽，以免挡住别人的～。*Spectators are requested to take off their hats so as not to block others' view.*
【视星等】［天］apparent magnitude
【视学】〈旧〉educational inspector
【视野】field of vision（or view）：广阔的～ *a wide field of vision* / 开拓～ *broaden one's vision*
【视译】sight translation
【视阈】［生理］visual threshold
【视紫质】［生理］visual purple
【视众】TV viewers：～的反映 *reaction of TV viewers*；*TV-audience reaction*

饰 Ⅰ名 decorations；ornaments：窗～ *window decorations* Ⅱ动 ❶ adorn；dress up；polish；cover up：修饰 / 文过饰非 ❷ play the role of；act the part of；impersonate：她在《白毛女》里～喜儿。*She played Xi'er in The White-haired Girl.*
【饰词】excuse；pretext
【饰物】❶ articles for personal adornment；jewelry ❷ ornaments；decorations
【饰演】play the role of；act the part of；play

室 名 ❶ room：有一～一套的，也有两～一套的。*There are one-room flats as well as two-room flats.* ❷ a room as an administrative or working unit：资料～ *reference room* / 档案～ *files room*
【室内】indoor；interior：～运动 *indoor sport* / ～装饰 *interior decoration* ◇ ～健身脚踏车 exercycle；～植物 house plant
【室内剧】studio production；indoor drama
【室内乐】［音］chamber music ◇ ～队［音］chamber orchestra
【室女座】［天］Virgo
【室外】outdoor；outside：～活动 *outdoor activities*

恃 动 rely on；depend on：～势欺人 *use one's power to bully people*
【恃才傲物】be inordinately proud of one's ability；be conceited and contemptuous
【恃强凌弱】use one's strength to bully the weak

拭 动 wipe away；wipe：～泪 *wipe away tears*
【拭除】wipe or brush sth. off：～镜面上的灰尘 *wipe the dust off the mirror*；*dust the mirror*
【拭目以待】wait and see；wait expectantly（for sth. to happen）

柿 名 persimmon
【柿饼】dried persimmon
【柿蒂】［中］the calyx and receptacle of a persimmon
【柿霜】［中］powder on the surface of a dried persimmon
【柿子】persimmon
【柿子椒】sweet pepper；bell pepper

是 Ⅰ形 correct；right：你说得～。*What you said is right.* / 应当早做准备才～。*To make early preparations is the right thing to do.* Ⅱ叹（used in affirmative answers）yes；right：～，我们一定完成任务。*Right, we will fulfil the task.* / ～，我就去。*Yes, I'll go right away.* Ⅲ代〈书〉this；that：～日天气晴朗。*It was fine that day.* / 由～可知 *from this you can see* / 如～ *like this* Ⅳ动 ❶（used like "be" before nouns or pronouns to identify, describe or amplify the subject）：我～个医生。*I am a doctor.* / 他真心爱的～你。*You are the girl he is truly in love with.* / 这小孩～白皮肤，黄头发。*That child is a blond.* ❷（used after nouns denoting place or position to express existence）：前面～一片稻田。*There is a stretch of rice fields ahead.* / 他满身～汗。*He is sweating all over.* / 遍地～鲜花。*The place is strewn with flowers.* ❸（used with 的 at the end of the sentence, to indicate category, characteristic, etc.）：那儿的房屋～木头的。*The houses there are built of wood.* / 我～教书的。*I am a teacher.* ❹（used before the subject to stress it）：

～谁告诉你的？*Who told you?* / 花瓶～我妹妹摔破的。*It was my sister who broke the vase.* ❺ (used after a verb or adjective plus 的, to stress the predicate)：说的正～你。*It's you we are talking about.* / 麻烦的～他生病来不了。*The trouble is he's taken ill and can't come at all.* / 可惜的～把这么多时间全浪费了。*It's a pity we've wasted so much of our time.* ❻ used before the object, adverbial, etc. which is to be stressed：字写成这样,～因为毛笔不好。*It was all because my brush was no good that I wrote the characters so poorly.* / 好好的一次郊游搞成这样子,都～你！*It was all your fault that the outing became such a flop.* ❼ pronounced with stress; used to indicate certainty：天气～冷。*It is cold indeed.* / 他的工作效率～高。*He is really efficient.* / 她～不知道。*Really she doesn't know.* / 他～去了。*He did go.* ❽ be just right：这场雨下的～时候。*This rain has come at just the right time.* / 工具放的不～地方。*The tools are not put in the right place.* ❾ (used before nouns at the beginning of the sentence, followed by 都 or 就) every; all; any：～什么种子,就开什么花。*Each kind of seed produces its own flowers.* / ～什么样的老师,就教出什么样的学生。*Like teacher, like student.* ❿ (used together with 就 or 总, to indicate actuality)：事实总～事实,谁也否认不了的。*A fact is a fact, which no one can deny.* / 不懂就～不懂,不要装懂。*If you don't know, there you stand. Don't pretend to know what you don't.* ⓫ (used in a clause of concession)：这东西旧～旧,可还能用。*Yes, it's old, but it can still be used.* / 诗～好诗,就是长了点。*It is a good poem all right, but it's a bit too long.* ⓬ (used in two parallel clauses to indicate mutual exclusiveness)：他～他,我～我,我们毫不相干。*He is he, I am I; we have nothing to do with each other.* ⓭ (used in two or three parallel clauses to indicate thoroughness or excellence of performance)：他演得真好,表情～表情,身段～身段,做功～做功。*He is a marvellous actor; his facial expressions, bodily movements and gesticulations are all the best that can be expected.* ⓮ (used in yes-no questions)：你～不～明天去游泳？or 你～明天去游泳不～？*Are you going swimming tomorrow?* ⓯ (used in alternative questions)：你～累了还～病了？*Are you tired or ill?* / 你～坐火车呢,还～坐汽车？*Are you going by train or by bus?*

【是的】yes; right; that's it

【是非】❶ right and wrong：明辨～ *distinguish clearly between right and wrong* ❷ quarrel; dispute：惹起～ *provoke a dispute; stir up trouble*

【是非曲直】rights and wrongs; truth and falsehood：不问～ *not bother to look into the rights and wrongs of a case* / 根据事情本身的～进行裁断 *decide the case on its merits*

【是非自有公论】The public will judge the rights and wrongs of the case; Public opinion is the best judge.

【是否】whether or not; whether; if：～符合实际 *whether or not it corresponds to reality*

【是古非今】praise the past and condemn the present

【是可忍,孰不可忍】If this can be tolerated, what else cannot?

【是味儿】〈口〉❶ (of food) have the right flavour; taste good：这个汤不～。*This soup doesn't have the right flavour.* ❷ (of a person) feel good：听了他那番话,我心里可真不～。*I was really upset to hear those words of his.*

【是样儿】〈口〉look right or good：这把椅子不～。*This chair doesn't look quite right.* / 衣服做得很～。*This suit is of a very nice cut.*

适 Ⅰ 形 ❶ fit; suitable; proper：～于儿童阅读的书籍 *books suitable for children* ❷〈书〉just; right：～因此故 *just for this very reason* / ～逢休假。*It happened to be a holiday.* ❸ comfortable; well：感到不～ *not feel well* Ⅱ 动 go; follow; pursue：无所适从

【适才】〈旧〉just now

【适当】suitable; proper; appropriate：～的工作 *suitable work* / ～的安排 *proper arrangement* / ～调整 *appropriate readjustment* / ～时机 *an opportune moment; the right moment* / 到～的时候 *in due course*

【适得其反】run counter to one's desire; be just the opposite to what one wished：多施肥能增产,但肥料过多会～。*More fertilizer will raise the output, but too much will lead to just the opposite.*

【适度】appropriate measure; moderate degree：～的体育活动有利于病人恢复健康。*A moderate amount of physical exercise will help improve the patient's health.* / 长短～ *be the right length*

【适航性】airworthiness (of a plane); seaworthiness (of a ship)

【适合】suit; fit：～当地情况 *be suited to local conditions* / 她～做教师。*She's fit for teaching.*

【适婚】of marriageable age：～青年 *young men and women of marriageable age*

【适间】just now; a moment ago

【适可而止】stop before going too far; know when or where to stop; not overdo it：初练长跑要～,不能过量。*A beginner at long-distance running must know when to stop and not overdo it.*

【适量】an appropriate amount or quantity：加一小匙盐,糖～。*Add a teaspoon of salt, and some sugar to taste.*

【适龄】of the right age：～儿童 *children of school age* / ～青年 *young people old enough to join the army*

【适时】at the right moment; in good time; timely：～的号召 *a timely call* / ～播种 *begin sowing in good time*

【适销】salable：～商品 *salable goods*

【适销对路】salable and in good demand; marketable：生产～、质量好的产品 *produce popular products of good quality*

【适宜】suitable；fit；appropriate；favourable：他～做卫生工作。*He's suitable for public health work.* / 创造～的经济和社会环境 *create a favourable economic and social environment*

【适应】suit；adapt to；adjust to；conform to：～需要 *meet the needs of* / ～时代的要求 *keep abreast of the times* / ～环境 *adapt oneself to circumstances* ◇ ～性［生］adaptability；～症［医］indication

【适用】be suitable；be applicable：这项原则并非～于一切情况。*This rule does not apply in all cases.* ◇ ～性 applicability

【适者生存】［生］survival of the fittest

【适值】〈书〉just when；as it happens：昨日来访，～外出，憾甚。*Unfortunately you happened to be out when I called yesterday.*

【适中】❶ moderate：雨量～ *moderate rainfall* ❷ well situated：招待所地点～。*The hostel is well situated.*

逝 动 ❶ pass：时光易～。*Time passes quickly.* ❷ die；pass away：病～ *die of illness*

【逝世】pass away；die

舐 动〈书〉lick

【舐犊情深】the cow fondly licking her calf—parental love

铈 名［化］cerium（Ce）

弑 动〈书〉murder（one's sovereign or parent）：～君 *regicide* / ～父 *patricide*

释 动 ❶ explain；elucidate：解释 ❷ clear up；dispel：释疑 ❸ let go；be relieved of：如释重负 ❹ release；set free：～俘 *set prisoners free；release prisoners*

【释放】❶ release；set free：要求～政治犯 *demand the release of political prisoners* ❷［物］release：～出能量 *release energy*

【释怀】（usu. used in the negative）dispel from one's bosom；dismiss from one's mind：当年离别的情景使我久久不能～。*I kept recalling the scene of our parting.*

【释迦牟尼】Sakyamuni，the founder of Buddhism（c. 565 B.C.-486 B.C.）

【释卷】put a book aside；leave off reading：这本书妙趣横生，令人不能～。*This book is so interesting that you can't put it aside once you start reading it.* ——另见〖手不释卷〗

【释然】〈书〉feel relieved；feel at ease

【释文】annotations（often used in book titles）

【释疑】clear up（or remove）doubts；dispel suspicion

【释义】explain the meaning（of a word，sentence，etc.）

嗜 动 have a liking for；be addicted to：～酒 *be addicted to drink*

【嗜好】❶ hobby ❷ addiction；habit

【嗜痂之癖】（又作'嗜痂成癖'）a depraved taste

【嗜杀成性】bloodthirsty；sanguinary：～的法西斯匪徒 *bloodthirsty fascists*

【嗜血】bloodthirsty；bloodsucking

誓 Ⅰ 动 swear；vow；pledge：～报此仇 *swear vengeance* / ～将革命进行到底 *vow to carry the revolution through to the end* Ⅱ 名 oath；vow：发誓

【誓不罢休】（又作'誓不甘休'）swear not to stop；swear not to rest：不达目的，～。*We'll never stop until we reach our goal.*

【誓不两立】swear not to coexist with sb.；resolve to destroy sb. or die in the attempt；be irreconcilable

【誓词】oath；pledge

【誓师】❶ a rally to pledge resolution before going to war ❷ take a mass pledge：～大会 *a meeting to pledge mass effort；an oath-taking rally*

【誓死】pledge one's life；dare to die：～保卫祖国 *pledge to fight to the death in defending one's country；be ready to die in defence of one's country*

【誓死不二】pledge to be true to death

【誓言】oath；pledge：履行～ *fulfil a pledge*

【誓愿】vow

【誓约】vow；pledge；solemn promise

噬 动 bite：吞噬

【噬菌体】［生］bacteriophage；phage

【噬脐莫及】（又作'噬脐何及'）one cannot bite one's own navel—it is too late to repent

螫 动〈书〉sting

【螫针】stinger（of insects，etc.）；sting

shōu

收 Ⅰ 动 ❶ receive；accept：请～下作为纪念。*Please accept this as a souvenir.* / 学校今年又～了一批研究生。*The college has enrolled another group of research students this year.* ❷ put away；take in：～工具 *put the tools away* / 洗的衣服～了没有？*Have you brought in the washing?* ❸ collect：～水电费 *collect water and electricity bills* / ～税 *collect taxes* / ～废品 *collect scrap* ❹ bring to an end；stop：时间不早了，今天就～了吧。*It's getting late. Let's call it a day.* ❺ restrain；control：孩子玩得心都～不回来了。*The boy can't get his mind off play.* ❻ harvest；gather in：～庄稼 *harvest（or gather in）crops* / 一亩稻子～了八百斤。*The rice yield was 800 jin per mu.* Ⅱ 名 money received；receipts；income：税收

【收报机】telegraphic or radiotelegraphic receiver

【收编】incorporate into one's own forces

【收兵】withdraw（or recall）troops；call off a battle：不获全胜，决不～。*We will not withdraw our forces till complete victory.*

【收藏】collect and store up：～古画 *collect old paintings* / ～粮食 *store up grain* ◇ ～家 collector (of books, antiques, etc.)

【收操】bring drill to an end

【收操号】a bugle call to dismiss；recall：吹～ *sound the recall*

【收场】❶ wind up；end up；stop：他的话匣子一打开，就不容易～。*Once he opens his trap, he just never stops.* / 这件事不好～。*It's hard to wind this matter up.* ❷ end；ending；denouement：圆满的～ *a happy ending*

【收车】return the vehicle to the garage, terminal, etc. and knock off

【收成】harvest；crop：从来没有过的好～ *a record harvest* / ～不好 *poor harvests；crop failures*

【收存】receive and keep：这些重要文件要～好。*These important documents must be kept in a safe place.*

【收到】receive；get；achieve；obtain：～一封信 *receive a letter* / ～良好效果 *achieve good results*

【收订】receive and process subscriptions

【收发】❶ receive and dispatch ❷ dispatcher

【收发报】transmit and receive telegrams：管～ *be in charge of transmitting and receiving telegrams；be a telegraph operator* ◇ ～机 transmitter-receiver；transceiver

【收发室】office for incoming and outgoing mail

【收方】［经］debit side；debit

【收费】collect fees；charge ◇ ～厕所 pay toilet；～电话 pay phone；～公路 toll road

【收费电视】subscription television；pay television

【收风】call prisoners in after letting them out for exercise

【收服】(又作'收伏') subdue；reduce to submission

【收复】recover；recapture：～失地 *recover lost territory* / ～城市 *recapture a city*

【收港】(of ships) return to harbour

【收割】reap；harvest；gather in：～小麦 *gather in the wheat* ◇ ～机 harvester；reaper

【收工】(usu. of those who work in the fields or on construction sites) stop work for the day；knock off；pack up：该～了。*It's time to knock off.* / 我们今天下午五点半～。*We stop work at 5:30 this afternoon.*

【收购】purchase；buy：～价格 *purchasing (or procurement) price* ◇ ～站 purchasing station (or centre)

【收归】take back (rights, ownership, etc.)：～国有 *nationalize*

【收回】❶ take back；call in；regain；recall：～发出的文件 *recall the documents which have been issued* / ～投资 *recoup capital outlay* ❷ withdraw；countermand：～建议 *withdraw a proposal* / 我～我的话。*I take back what I said.*

【收回成命】countermand (or retract) an order；revoke a command

【收活】❶ accept orders for repairs or processing ❷〈方〉stop work for the day；knock off；pack up

【收货人】consignee

【收获】❶ gather (or bring) in the crops；harvest：春天播种，秋天～ *sow in spring and reap in autumn* ❷ results；gains：一次很有～的访问 *a most rewarding visit* ◇ ～量 harvest yield；yield；crop

【收集】collect；gather：～民间验方 *collect time-tested folk prescriptions*

【收监】take into custody；put in prison

【收件人】addressee；consignee

【收缴】take over；capture：～敌人的武器 *take over the enemy's arms*

【收紧】tighten up

【收据】receipt ◇ ～簿 receipt book

【收看】watch television；look in

【收口】❶ (of a wound) close up；heal：刀伤～了。*The sword wound has healed.* ❷ (in knitting) cast off；bind off：注意～别太紧。*Be careful not to cast off (or bind off) too tightly.*

【收款机】popular name for 现金出纳机

【收款人】payee

【收揽】❶〈贬〉draw over to one's side：～民心 *try to win the support of the people* ❷ keep in one's grasp

【收礼】accept gifts

【收敛】❶ weaken or disappear：她的笑容突然～了。*Her smile suddenly disappeared.* ❷ restrain oneself：碰了钉子以后，他～些了。*He has pulled in his horns since that setback.* / 他继续胡作非为，毫无～。*Unrelentingly he pursued his course of evil.* ❸［数］convergence ❹［医］astringent：～剂 *astringent (a drug)*

【收殓】lay a body in a coffin

【收留】take sb. in；have sb. in one's care

【收拢】❶ draw sth. in：把网～ *draw the net in* ❷〈贬〉draw over to one's side：～人心 *try to win people's support by every artifice*

【收录】❶ employ；recruit；take on：～几个职员 *recruit some office workers* ❷ include：这篇文章已～在他的选集里。*This essay is included in his selected works.* ❸ listen in and take down；take down；record：～新闻广播 *take down the news from the radio；make a recording of the news broadcast*

【收录机】radio-tape recorder；radio-cassette recorder

【收罗】collect；gather；enlist：～人才 *recruit qualified personnel* / ～资料 *collect data*

【收买】❶ purchase；buy in：～旧书 *buy used books* ❷ buy over；bribe：他们是想～你啊。*They are trying to buy you over.*

【收买人心】buy popular support

【收纳】receive；take in

【收盘】closing quotation (on the exchange, etc.)：～汇率 *closing rate* / ～价格 *closing price*

【收票员】ticket collector

【收起】pack up；cut out；stop：～你们那一套高调

吧！*Cut out your high-sounding talk*！/～你那套鬼把戏！*None of your dirty tricks*！

【收讫】❶ payment received；paid ❷（on a bill of lading，an invoice，etc.）all the above goods received；received in full

【收清】received in full

【收取】receive；collect：～手续费 *collect service* （*or handling*）*charges*

【收容】take in；accept；house：～伤员 *take in wounded soldiers* /～难民 *house refugees*

【收容所】collecting post：难民～ *refugee camp*

【收入】❶ income；revenue；receipts；earnings；proceeds：财政～ *state revenue* /总～ *gross income* ❷ take in；include：修订版～许多新词语。*Many new words and phrases have been included in the revised edition*. ◇～税 income tax

【收审】detain for interrogation

【收市】（of markets or stores）close for the day

【收视率】（of TV program）viewing rate；rating：这部电视连续剧开播后不久，～便跃居首位。*Shortly after the TV serial was first aired*，*it shot to the top of the ratings*.

【收拾】❶ put in order；tidy；clear away：把工具～一下。*Put the tools in order*. /～屋子 *tidy up the room* /～床铺 *make the bed* /～碗筷 *clear away the bowls and chopsticks*；*clear the table* ❷ get things ready；pack：～药箱 *get one's medical kit ready*；*pack one's medical kit* /～行李 *pack one's luggage*；*pack up one's things* ❸ repair；mend：～鞋子 *mend shoes* ❹〈口〉settle with；punish：早晚我们要～这个坏蛋。*We'll settle with the scoundrel one of these days*.

【收拾残局】clear up the mess；pick up the pieces

【收受】receive；accept；take：～贿赂 *take bribes*

【收束】❶ bring together；collect：把心思～一下 *get into the frame of mind for work* ❷ bring to a close：写到这里，我的信也该～了。*I think it is about time I wound up this letter*. ❸ pack（for a journey）

【收缩】❶ contract；shrink：金属遇冷就会～。*Metals contract as they become cool*. /这种布下水后要～。*This kind of cloth shrinks when it's washed*. ❷ concentrate one's forces；draw back：敌人～到几个据点里。*The enemy drew back into a few fortified points*. ❸［生理］systole

【收缩压】systolic pressure

【收摊儿】pack up the stall—wind up the day's business or the work on hand

【收条】receipt

【收听】listen（in）：～天气预报 *listen in to a weather forecast* /～新闻广播 *listen to the news broadcast* /你的收音机能～多少电台？*How many stations can you get on your radio set*？

【收尾】❶ bring to a conclusion；wind up：我们正在做～工作。*We are winding up the job*. ❷ ending（of an article，etc.）：这个剧本～太没劲。*The ending of the play is rather too tame*.

【收文】incoming dispatches ◇～簿 register of incoming dispatches

【收效】yield results；produce effects；bear fruit：～显著 *bring notable results* /～甚微 *produce very little effect*

【收心】❶ get into the frame of mind for work or study；concentrate on more serious things ❷ have a change of heart

【收信人】the recipient of a letter；addressee

【收押】take into custody；detain

【收养】take in and bring up；adopt：～孤儿 *adopt an orphan* ◇～人 adoptive parents

【收益】income；profit；earnings；gains

【收益率】［经］income rate：投资～ *investment income rate*

【收音】❶ radio reception：这里～情况良好。*Radio reception is good here*. ❷ acoustics（of an auditorium，etc.）

【收音机】radio（set）；wireless（set）：便携式～ *portable radio* /落地式～ *console set*

【收载】record：书中～了许多濒于失传的民谣。*The book has recorded a number of folk ballads that were in danger of being lost*.

【收摘】pick（fruit，etc.）：～棉花 *pick cotton*

【收展】take down the exhibits；collect and put away exhibits

【收账】❶ charge to an account ❷ collect debts

【收针】（in knitting）decrease stitches；bind off；cast off

【收支】revenue and expenditure；income and expenses：～平衡。*Revenue and expenditure are balanced*. /～相抵 *break even*

【收支逆差】balance of payments deficit

【收执】❶（of a certificate，etc.）be issued to the person concerned for safekeeping ❷ receipt（issued by a government agency）

【收治】accept for treatment：儿童医院一年来已～病人近3,000人。*Nearly three thousand patients were admitted into the Children's Hospital over the past year*.

【收住】hospitalize：这是今天～的病人。*This patient was admitted to hospital today*.

shǒu

手 Ⅰ 名 ❶ hand：双～捧着 *hold in both hands* /～把～地教 *take a person in hand and teach him how to do a job* /～织的毛衣 *a hand-knitted woollen sweater* ❷ a person doing or good at a certain job：拖拉机～ *tractor driver* /机枪～ *machinegunner* Ⅱ 形 handy；convenient：Ⅲ 副 personally Ⅳ 量（for skill or dexterity）：他写一～好字。*He writes a fine hand*. /他真有两～。*He really knows his stuff*. Ⅴ 动 have in one's hand；hold：人手一册

【手背】the back of the hand

【手笔】❶ a famous person's own handwriting or painting：这一题词是鲁迅先生的～。*This inscription is in Lu Xun's own handwriting*. ❷ literary skill：大～ *a well-known writer*；*a master*

【手臂】❶ arm ❷ a reliable helper：他是队长的得力～。*He's the team leader's right-hand man*.

【手边】on hand；at hand：我～没有现钱。*I don't have any cash on hand*.

【手表】wristwatch

【手不释卷】always have a book in one's hand；be very studious；be a diligent reader

【手册】❶ handbook；manual：教师～ *teacher's manual* ❷ record book；workbook：劳动～ *worker's book*

【手抄】❶ write by hand；handwrite ❷ hand-written ◇ ～本 handwritten copy

【手车】handcart；pushcart；barrow

【手锤】light hammer

【手戳】〈口〉private seal；signet

【手挡】(car) stick shift；manual transmission

【手到病除】illness departs at a touch of the hand (said as a tribute to a doctor or a troubleshooter)

【手到擒来】(又作'手到擒拿') just stretch the hand and bring it back—very easy：要打赢他们还不是～? *Surely we can beat them hands down*!

【手倒立】[体] handstand

【手底下】同〖手下〗

【手电筒】electric torch；flashlight

【手段】❶ means；medium；measure；method：达到目的的一种～ *a means to an end* / 高压～ *high-handed measures* / 强制～ *coercive method*；*coercion* / 利用合法的斗争～ *utilize the legal form of struggle* / 艺术～ *artistic medium* ❷ trick；artifice：采用种种～ *resort to all sorts of tricks*；*use every artifice* ❸ skill；finesse：她应付那件事情很有～。*She managed that situation with great finesse*.

【手法】❶ skill；technique：国画的传统～ *traditional technique of Chinese painting* / 艺术表现～ *means of artistic expression* ❷ trick；gimmick：两面～ *dual tactics* / 惯用～ *habitual* (*or customary*) *practice*

【手风琴】accordion：六角～ *concertina*

【手扶拖拉机】walking tractor

【手感】[纺] feel：～柔软 *have a soft feel*

【手稿】original (or holograph) manuscript；manuscript

【手工】❶ handwork：这件上衣的～做得很细。*This jacket is a fine piece of handwork*. ❷ by hand；manual：～操作 *done by hand*；*manual operations* ❸charge for a piece of handwork：你这件大衣～多少? *How much did you pay for the tailoring of this overcoat*?

【手工工具】hand tools

【手工业】handicraft industry；handicraft：～者 *handicraftsman*

【手工艺】handicraft art；handicraft ◇ ～工人 craftsman；artisan；～品 articles of handicraft art；handicrafts

【手鼓】a small drum similar to the tambourine (used by the Uygur and other nationalities)

【手机】[通信] mobile phone；cellular phone

【手疾眼快】quick of eye and deft of hand

【手记】❶ write down notes or records ❷ written notes or records

【手技】❶ handicraft；craftsmanship ❷ acrobatics juggling；jugglery

【手迹】sb.'s original handwriting or painting

【手脚】❶ movement of hands or feet；motion：～利落 *nimble*；*agile* ❷ underhand method；devious device；trick：一定是有人从中弄了～。*Someone must have juggled things*. ◇ ～不干净 sticky-fingered；dishonest in money matters

【手巾】❶ towel ❷〈方〉handkerchief ◇ ～架 towel rack

【手紧】❶ closefisted；tightfisted ❷ be short of money；be hard up

【手劲儿】muscular strength of the hand

【手锯】handsaw

【手卷】hand scroll

【手绢】handkerchief

【手铐】handcuffs：带上～ *be handcuffed*

【手快】deft of hand：变戏法得～。*A juggler must have deft fingers*.

【手拉葫芦】[机] chain block

【手拉手】hand in hand

【手雷】[军] antitank grenade

【手力千斤顶】[机] hand jack

【手令】an order personally issued by sb. in command

【手榴弹】[军] hand grenade；grenade

【手笼】muff

【手炉】handwarmer

【手轮】[机] handwheel

【手慢】slow with one's hands；slow in movements；slow-moving

【手忙脚乱】in a rush；in a flurry：我先去厨房通知一声，免得临时～。*I'm going to the kitchen to warn them so that they'll not have to rush about at the last moment*.

【手面】〈方〉the extent of one's spending：你～太阔了，要节约一点才好。*You spend too freely. You should be more thrifty*.

【手模】fingerprint

【手拿把掐】(又作'手拿把攥') in the bag；a sure thing

【手帕】同〖手绢〗

【手旗】[军] handflag；semaphore flag

【手气】luck at gambling，card playing，etc.：他今天打牌的～好得出奇。*He's marvellously lucky at cards tonight*.

【手钳】hand vice；pliers

【手枪】pistol；handgun ◇ ～慢加速比赛 [体] centre-fire pistol；～速射 [体] rapid-fire pistol

【手枪套】holster

【手巧】skilful with one's hands；nimble-fingered；deft；dexterous

【手勤】diligent；industrious；hardworking：这徒弟～脚快。*This apprentice is keen and quick in his work*.

【手轻】have gentle hands；not use too much force；

handle gently：那位护士的手很轻。*That nurse has very gentle hands*.

【手球】［体］❶ handball (a game) ❷ handball (the ball) ❸ handball (a foul in sports)

【手刃】stab to death；kill with one's own hand

【手软】be irresolute when firmness is needed；be softhearted：对这种坏人可不能～。*We must not be soft on such scoundrels*.

【手刹车】hand brake

【手生】lack practice and skill；be out of practice

【手势】gesture；sign；signal：打～ *make a gesture*；*gesticulate* ◇ ～语 sign language

【手书】❶ write in one's own hand ❷ personal letter：顷接～。*I have just received your letter*.

【手术】surgical operation；operation：大（小）～ *major* (*minor*) *operation* / 动～ *perform or undergo an operation* / 高频电刀～ *high frequency electrotomy* ◇ ～刀 scalpel；～包 surgical kit；～室 operating room；operating theatre；～台 operating table

【手松】free with one's money；free-handed；open-handed

【手套】❶ gloves；mittens ❷ baseball gloves；mitts

【手提】portable ◇ ～包 handbag；bag；～打字机 portable typewriter；～电话 mobile phone；cellular phone；～电脑 portable computer；～箱 suitcase

【手头】❶ right beside one；on hand；at hand：放在～待用 *place right beside one in case of need* / ～工作挺多 *have a lot of work on hand*；*have one's hands full* ❷ one's financial condition at the moment：～紧 *be short of money*；*be hard up* / ～宽裕 *be in easy circumstances*；*be quite well off at the moment*

【手推车】同〖手车〗

【手推婴儿车】pushchair；light baby carriage

【手腕】❶ trick；artifice：耍～ *play tricks*；*use artifices* / 他很有～。*He's quite crafty*. ❷ skill；finesse；tactics：外交～ *diplomatic skill* (*or finesse*) / 政治～ *political tactics*

【手腕子】wrist

【手纹】the lines of the palm

【手无寸铁】bare-handed；unarmed；defenceless

【手无缚鸡之力】lack the strength to truss a chicken—physically very weak

【手舞足蹈】dance for joy

【手下】❶ under the leadership (or guidance, direction) of；under：他在我～工作，就得听我的。*He has to listen to me since he is working under me*. ❷ at hand：东西不在～。*I haven't got the thing with me*. ❸ at the hands of sb.：我曾两次败在她～。*I have been defeated by her twice*. ❹ one's financial condition at the moment：他每到月底，～就紧了。*He usually gets hard up by the end of the month*. ◇ ～败将 one's vanquished foe；one's defeated opponent；～留情 show mercy；be lenient；make allowances for (when dealing out punishment to sb.)；～人 one's subordinate；servant

【手相】palmistry：看～ *practise palmistry* / ～术士 *palmist*

【手携手】hand in hand

【手写】❶ write by hand；handwrite；write in one's own hand ❷ handwritten；written in one's own hand ◇ ～体 handwritten form；script

【手心】❶ the centre of the palm ❷ control：这事儿全捏在他～里。*He's got the matter in the palm of his hand*.

【手续】procedures；formalities：办～ *go through formalities* / ～不完备 *have not completed the formalities*

【手续费】service charges；handling charges；commission

【手癣】tinea manuum；fungal infection of the hand

【手眼通天】exceptionally adept in trickery

【手痒】❶ one's fingers itch ❷ have an itch to do sth.

【手摇泵】hand pump

【手摇发电机】hand generator

【手艺】❶ craftsmanship；workmanship：～高 *be highly skilled* ❷ handicraft；trade：跟师傅学～ *learn the trade from a master*

【手艺人】craftsman

【手淫】❶ masturbation；self-abuse ❷ masturbate

【手印】❶ an impression of the hand ❷ thumb print；fingerprint：按～ *put one's thumb print on* (*a document, etc.*)

【手语】sign language；dactylology

【手谕】〈旧〉personally written orders or instructions

【手札】〈书〉personal letter

【手闸】hand brake

【手章】private seal；signet

【手掌】palm (of the hand)

【手掌心】〈口〉❶ the centre of the palm ❷ control：我怎么也跳不出他的～。*No matter how hard I tried, I could never free myself from his control*.

【手杖】walking stick；stick

【手折】〈旧〉❶ a record book in accordion form ❷ an account book in accordion form

【手诊】diagnose by observing signs on a patient's palm

【手植】personally plant (a tree, etc.)：此树系周恩来～。*This tree was planted by Zhou Enlai*.

【手纸】toilet paper

【手指】finger ◇ ～甲 finger nail；～头〈口〉finger；～头肚儿 the inner side of the fingertip；～字母 manual alphabet (used by deaf-mutes)；deaf-and-dumb alphabet

【手重】use too much force：她上药时～了些。*She pressed the wound a bit too hard when dressing it*.

【手镯】bracelet

【手足】❶ movement ❷ brothers：～之情 *brotherly affection* ◇ ～无措 all in a fluster；at a loss what to do

【手钻】hand drill

守 动 ❶ guard; defend: ～城 *defend a city* / ～球门 *keep goal* / ～住阵地 *hold the position* ❷ keep watch: ～了一夜 *keep watch for the whole night* / ～着伤员 *watch over (or look after) the wounded* ❸ observe; abide by: ～纪律 *observe discipline* / ～规矩 *behave well* / ～信用 *keep one's promise; be as good as one's word* / ～着老一套 *stick to the old practice* ❹ close to; near: ～着水的地方要多养鱼。*Where there is water nearby, make a special effort to breed fish.*

【守备】perform garrison duty; be on garrison duty; garrison ◇ ～部队 garrison force; (holding) garrison

【守财奴】miser

【守场员】[体] fielder (in baseball, softball or cricket)

【守车】(British) guard's van; (American) caboose

【守成】〈书〉maintain the achievements of one's predecessors

【守敌】the enemy holding a fortress or a strategic point

【守法】abide by (or observe) the law; be law-abiding ◇ ～户 law-abiding firm

【守寡】remain a widow; live in widowhood

【守恒】[物] conservation: 能量～ *conservation of energy* / 动量～ *conservation of momentum* ◇ ～定律 [物] conservation law

【守候】❶ wait for; expect: ～着前线的消息 *wait for news from the front* ❷ keep watch: ～在病人身旁 *keep watch by the patient's bedside*

【守护】guard; defend ◇ ～神 guardian spirit; tutelary spirit; patron saint

【守活寡】be a grass widow

【守家】❶ look after the house; mind the house ❷ maintain what has been achieved or acquired by one's forefathers

【守节】(of a woman in former times) remain unmarried after the death of her husband or her betrothed

【守经达权】be mindful of principles but act according to circumstances; consider expediency as well as principle

【守旧】adhere to past practices; stick to old ways; be conservative ◇ ～派 old-liners; conservatives

【守军】defending troops; defenders

【守口如瓶】keep one's mouth shut; breathe not a single word; be tight-mouthed; be tight-lipped

【守垒员】[体] baseman (in baseball or softball)

【守灵】stand as guards at the bier; keep vigil beside the coffin

【守门】❶ be on duty at the door or gate: ～人 *gatekeeper; doorkeeper* ❷ [体] keep goal ◇ ～员 goalkeeper (in football, ice hockey, etc.)

【守身如玉】keep oneself as pure as jade—preserve one's honour or integrity

【守时】be on time; be punctual

【守势】defensive: 采取～ *be on the defensive*

【守岁】stay up late or all night on New Year's Eve; see the Old Year out and the New Year in

【守土】〈书〉defend the territory of one's country: ～有责 *be duty-bound to defend the territory of one's country*

【守望】keep watch ◇ ～台 watchtower; ～相助 (of neighbouring villages, etc.) keep watch and help defend each other; give mutual help and protection

【守卫】guard; defend

【守孝】observe a period of mourning for one's deceased parent

【守信】keep one's word

【守业】maintain what has been achieved by one's forefathers or predecessors; safeguard one's heritage: 创业难,～更难。*If it is difficult for a man to set up a business, it is even more so for his heirs to keep it up.*

【守夜】keep watch at night; spend the night on watch

【守约】❶ abide by an agreement ❷ keep an appointment

【守则】rules; regulations: 工作～ *work regulations*

【守正不阿】be strictly just and impartial

【守职】stand fast at one's post; be faithful in the discharge of one's duties

【守株待兔】stand by a stump waiting for more hares to come and dash themselves against it—trust to chance and strokes of luck

首 Ⅰ 名 ❶ head: 回首 ❷ leader; head; chief: 元首 Ⅱ 形 first: ～批 *the first batch* Ⅲ 量 (for songs and poems): 一～歌 *a song* /《唐诗三百～》300 *Tang Poems*

【首播】broadcast by TV or radio for the first time: 这条消息～后不到一小时,世界各地电台和电视台便纷纷转播。*Less than an hour following its first transmission, the news was reported by radio and TV stations across the world.* ◇ ～式 ceremony for the first broadcast of a radio or TV; première program

【首倡】be the first to advocate; initiate; start: ～改革 *be the first to advocate reform*

【首车】first bus (of a regular bus service)

【首创】originate; initiate; pioneer: ～精神 *creative initiative; pioneering spirit*

【首次】for the first time; first: ～航行 *maiden (or first) voyage* / ～公演 *first (or opening) performance; premiere*

【首当其冲】be the first to be affected (by a disaster, etc.); bear the brunt

【首都】capital (of a country)

【首恶】chief criminal; principal culprit

【首发】first issue (of book, magazine, stamp, etc.); give out or hand out something for the first time: ～式 *ceremony for the first issuing of (book, magazine, stamp, etc.); first distribution*

【首犯】chief criminal; principal culprit

【首飞】first test-flight of a new model of aircraft;

maiden flight

【首府】❶ (in former times) head prefecture (the prefecture in which a provincial capital was located) ❷ the capital of an autonomous region or prefecture：呼和浩特是内蒙古自治区的～。*Huhhot is the capital of the Inner Mongolia Autonomous Region.* ❸ the capital of a dependency or colony

【首富】(又作'首户') the wealthiest family in the locality；the richest person

【首告】report (an offender)；inform against (an offender)

【首功】the first-class merit

【首航】maiden voyage or flight

【首级】chopped-off head (in battle, etc.)

【首届】the first occasion, term, session, etc.：～毕业生 *the first class of graduates*

【首肯】nod approval；nod assent；approve；consent

【首领】❶〈书〉head and neck ❷ chieftain；leader；head

【首脑】head：政府～ *head of government*

【首屈一指】come first on the list；be second to none：老王的棋艺在我们单位是～的。*Lao Wang is the best chess player in our unit.*

【首任】the first to be appointed to an office：～驻中国大使 *the first ambassador accredited to China*

【首日封】the first day cover (an envelope with a commemorative stamp and postmark affixed on the first day of issue of a set of commemorative stamps)

【首善之区】the best of places (i.e. the capital of a country)

【首饰】❶ (originally) head ornaments ❷ jewels；jewelry：她戴很多～。*She wears a lot of jewelry.* ◇ ～店 jewelry store；～盒 jewel case

【首鼠两端】be in two minds；shilly-shally

【首陀罗】Sudra

【首尾】❶ the head and the tail；the beginning and the end：～不能相顾。*The vanguard is cut off from the rear.* ❷ from beginning to end：我对这个问题的看法是～一贯的。*I have always been consistent in my views on this subject.*

【首位】the first place：放在～ *put in the first place；place before everything else；give first priority to* / 居于～ *rank first*

【首乌】[中] the tuber of multiflower knotweed (Polygonum multiform)

【首乌藤】[中] the vine of multiflower knotweed (Polygonum multiform)

【首席】❶ seat of honour：坐～ *be seated at the head of the table；be in the seat of honour* ❷ chief：～代表 *chief representative or delegate* / ～秘书 *principal secretary* / ～顾问 *chief adviser*

【首先】❶ before all others；first：～发言 *speak first* ❷ in the first place；first of all；above all：～，我问你这个。*First, let me ask you this.*

【首相】prime minister

【首演】the first (or opening) performance；premiere

【首要】of the first importance；first；chief：～的事先办。*First things first.* / ～任务 *the most important task* / ～问题 *a question of the first importance* / 把这个问题放在～位置上 *give first priority to this issue*

【首要分子】[法] ringleader

【首映式】premiere (of a film)

【首战告捷】win in the very first battle or game

【首长】leading cadre；senior officer：团～ *senior officers of the regiment*

【首座】❶ seat of honour (at a banquet) ❷ abbot

shòu

寿 名 ❶ long life；old age：福～ *good fortune and long life* ❷ life；age：长寿 ❸ birthday：祝寿 ❹〈婉〉funerary

【寿比南山，福如东海】May your age be as the southern mountain and your happiness as the eastern sea (said as birthday congratulations to an elderly person).

【寿材】a coffin prepared before one's death；coffin

【寿辰】birthday (of an elderly person)

【寿酒】birthday wine；birthday feast

【寿礼】birthday present (for an elderly person)

【寿联】birthday couplets；birthday scrolls

【寿面】birthday noodles；longevity noodles

【寿命】life span；life：现代医学延长了人的～。*Modern medicine has increased man's life span.*

【寿司】sushi

【寿桃】❶ peaches offered as a birthday present ❷ peach-shaped birthday cakes

【寿险】life insurance

【寿星】❶ the god of longevity ❷ an elderly person whose birthday is being celebrated

【寿穴】a grave prepared before one's death

【寿筵】birthday feast

【寿衣】graveclothes；shroud；cerements

【寿终】die of old age ◇ ～正寝 die in bed of old age；die a natural death

受 动 ❶ receive；accept：～教育 *receive an education* / 这种新产品很～欢迎。*The new product has been well received.* ❷ suffer；be subjected to：～损失 *suffer losses* / ～压迫 *suffer oppression* / ～监督 *be subjected to supervision* / ～法律制裁 *be dealt with according to law* ❸ stand；endure；bear：真够～的。*This is really hard to put up with.* or *It's really unbearable.* ❹ be pleasant：～听 *be pleasant to hear*

【受不了】cannot stand (or endure)：我冻得～。*I can't stand the cold.* / 今天可真热得～。*It's unbearably hot today.*

【受不起】dare not accept；not deserve：我可～你的重礼。*I don't deserve such expensive gifts from* you.

【受潮】be affected with damp：这屋子阴，东西容易～。*The room gets no sun and things easily become damp.*

【受宠】be in sb.'s favour

【受宠若惊】be overwhelmed by an unexpected favour；feel extremely flattered

【受酬】accept a reward

【受挫】be foiled；be baffled；be thwarted；suffer a setback

【受得了】can stand (or endure)：再苦再累我也～。*I can stand even greater hardships than this.*

【受敌】be attacked by the enemy：四面～ *be attacked on all sides*

【受罚】be punished

【受粉】［植］be pollinated

【受害】suffer injury；fall victim；be affected：～的一方 *the aggrieved (or injured) party* ◇～不浅 suffer not a little；suffer a lot；～者 victim；sufferer

【受寒】catch a chill；catch cold

【受旱】suffer from drought；be drought-stricken

【受话号码】called number；receiving number

【受话器】(telephone) receiver

【受话人】receiver (of telephone call)

【受欢迎的人】［外交］persona grata

【受贿】accept (or take) bribes

【受惠】receive benefits

【受惠国】［外交］beneficiary country；beneficiary

【受夹板气】be blamed by both parties

【受奖】be rewarded：立功者～。*Those who perform deeds of merit shall be rewarded.*

【受教】receive instruction；learn from sb.；study under sb.

【受戒】［宗］(佛教) be initiated into monkhood or nunhood

【受尽】suffer enough from；suffer all kinds of；have one's fill of：～反动派的折磨 *suffer all kinds of tortures at the hands of the reactionaries*

【受惊】be frightened；be startled

【受精】be fertilized：体内(外)～ *internal (external) fertilization* / 异体～ *cross-fertilization* / 自体～ *self-fertilization*

【受精卵】zygote：～移植 *zygote transplant*

【受窘】be embarrassed；be in an awkward position

【受看】❶ pleasant to look at；good-looking：这块头巾挺～的。*This scarf looks quite nice.* ❷ honourable；creditable：孩子没出息，做父母的脸上也不～。*If the boy proves to be no good, it will mean a loss of face for his parents.*

【受控】controlled：～过程 *controlled process*

【受苦】suffer (hardships)；have a rough time：咱们俩都是受过苦的。*Both of us have suffered hardships.*

【受苦受难】live in misery；have one's fill of sufferings

【受款人】payee

【受累】(shòulěi) get involved on account of sb. else

【受累】(shòulèi) be put to much trouble；be inconvenienced：他为了我们大家，可没少～。*He's been put to no little trouble for our sake.*

【受冷】catch cold

【受理】［法］❶ accept (a case) ❷ deal with，handle

【受凉】catch cold

【受领】accept (an assignment，etc.)；appreciate (kind thoughts，etc.)：～任务 *accept an assignment* / 你们的心意我～了，东西可不能收下。*I appreciate your kindness but must decline the gift.*

【受命】receive instructions or assignments

【受难】suffer calamities or disasters；be in distress：战争～者 *war victims*

【受骗】be deceived (or fooled，cheated，taken in)

【受票人】drawee

【受聘】❶ (of a girl) accept betrothal gifts ❷ accept an appointment (to a post)：他～为男排主教练。*He was appointed head coach of the men's volleyball team.*

【受气】be bullied；suffer wrong ◇～包 a person whom anyone can vent his spite upon；one who always gets blamed (or takes the rap)

【受穷】suffer poverty；live in poverty：她不愿～。*She doesn't like being poor.*

【受屈】be wronged

【受权】be authorized：新华社～发表如下声明。*Xinhua News Agency is authorized to issue the following statement.* /我～处理此事。*I am empowered (or authorized) to deal with this matter.*

【受让人】［法］assignee

【受热】❶ be heated：物体～则膨胀。*When matter is heated, it expands.* ❷ be affected by the heat；have heatstroke (or sunstroke)

【受辱】be insulted；be disgraced；be humiliated

【受伤】be injured；be wounded；sustain an injury：头部受重伤 *sustain a severe head injury*

【受赏】be awarded

【受审】stand trial；be tried；be on trial

【受事】［语］a word denoting the receiver of an action (not necessarily an object，as in 饭准备好了 "Dinner is ready，" where 饭，the subject，denotes the receiver of the action)

【受暑】suffer from heatstroke (or sunstroke)

【受胎】become pregnant；be impregnated；conceive ◇～率［牧］conception rate

【受托】be commissioned；be entrusted (with a task)：受朋友之托买一块手表 *be asked to buy a watch for a friend* / ～照看房子 *be entrusted with the care of a house* ◇～国［外交］mandatory power；～人［法］trustee；fiduciary

【受洗】［宗］(基督教) be baptized；receive baptism

【受降】accept a surrender

【受刑】be tortured；be put to torture

【受训】receive (or undergo) training

【受业】〈书〉❶ receive instruction ❷ (in letters to one's teacher) I，your pupil

【受益】profit by；benefit from；be benefited：这本书使我～不浅。*This book has benefited me a great deal.* ◇ ～人［法］beneficiary

【受用】（shòuyòng）benefit from；profit by；enjoy：终身～ *benefit from sth. all one's life* ◇ ～不尽 benefit from sth. all one's life

【受用】（shòuyong）〈方〉（usu. used in the negative）feel comfortable：今天身体有点不～。*I feel a bit under the weather today.*

【受援】receive aid ◇ ～国［外交］recipient country

【受阅】be reviewed：这个飞机中队多次圆满完成～任务。*This squadron has successfully fulfilled many review assignments.*

【受孕】become pregnant；be impregnated；conceive

【受灾】be hit by a natural adversity（or calamity）：～地区 *disaster area*；*stricken*（*or afflicted*，*affected*）*area*

【受之有愧】I don't deserve it；I am not worthy of it ——另见〖却之不恭〗

【受制】❶ be controlled：～于人 *be under others' control* ❷ endure hardships，tortures，rough conditions，etc.；suffer

【受众】readers，listeners and viewers reached by the mass media；audience

【受主】［电子］acceptor

【受阻】be obstructed；meet with obstruction：撞车事故使交通～。*A car crash held up the traffic.*

【受罪】endure hardships，tortures，rough conditions，etc.；have a hard time：大热天穿这么厚的衣服，真～！*It's really awful to be wearing such heavy clothes on a hot day like this.*

狩 名〈书〉hunting（esp. in winter）

【狩猎】hunting：～专业队 *professional hunting team*

兽 Ⅰ 名 beast；animal：驯～ *tame wild animals* Ⅱ 形 beastly；bestial：兽行

【兽环】animal-head knocker（on doors of old-type houses）

【兽力车】animal-drawn vehicle（or cart）

【兽王】the king of beasts—the lion

【兽行】brutal act；brutality

【兽性】brutish nature；barbarity

【兽医】veterinary surgeon；veterinarian；vet ◇ ～学 veterinary science；veterinary medicine；～站 veterinary station

【兽疫】epizootic disease；epizootic ◇ ～学 epizootiology

【兽欲】animal（or bestial）desire：发泄～ *gratify one's animal desires*

授 动 ❶ award；vest；confer；give：～旗 *present*（*sb. with*）*a flag* / ～以全权 *vest sb. with full authority* ❷ teach；instruct：函授

【授粉】［植］pollination

【授计】confide a stratagem to sb.；tell sb. the plan of action

【授奖】award（or give）a prize：～仪式 *prizegiving ceremony*；*medal-awarding ceremony*

【授精】insemination

【授课】give lessons；give instruction

【授命】❶〈书〉give（or lay down）one's life ❷ give orders：～组阁 *authorize sb. to form a cabinet*

【授权】empower；authorize：～新华社发表声明 *authorize Xinhua News Agency to make a statement* ◇ ～书［法］letter of authorization；letter of attorney

【授时】❶［天］time service ❷（formerly of the government or the emperor）issue the official calendar ◇ ～信号 time signal

【授受】grant and receive；give and accept：男女～不亲。*In giving and receiving，man and woman should not touch each other*（*according to Confucian rules of etiquette*）.

【授位】confer a degree：～典礼 *degree-awarding ceremony*

【授衔】confer a title or a military rank

【授勋】confer orders or medals；award a decoration：～仪式 *medal-conferring ceremony*

【授业】〈书〉impart knowledge；give instruction

【授艺】teach a trade or skill

【授意】incite（or get）sb. to do sth.；inspire：他这样干，是谁～的？*Who got him to do that？* or *Who put him up to it？*

【授予】confer；award：～学位 *award a degree*

售 动 ❶ sell：～票 *sell tickets* / ～完 *be sold out* ❷〈书〉make（one's plan，trick，etc.）work；carry out（intrigues）：其计不～。*His plan didn't work.*

【售后服务】after-sale service

【售货】sell goods ◇ ～机 vending machine；～员 shop assistant；salesclerk

【售价】selling price；price

【售卖】sell

【售票处】ticket office；booking office（at a railway station）；box office（at a theatre，cinema，etc.）

【售票口】wicket

【售票员】ticket seller；（bus，tram，etc.）conductor；booking-office clerk；box-office clerk

绶 名 a silk ribbon attached to an official seal or a medal

【绶带】同〖绶〗

【绶带鸟】paradise flycatcher

瘦 形 ❶ thin；emaciated：他长得很～。*He is very thin.* / 脸～ *be thin in the face* ❷ lean：～肉 *lean meat* ❸ tight：这件上衣腰身～了点。*The coat is a bit tight at the waist.* ❹ not fertile；poor：～土薄田 *poor soil and barren land*

【瘦长】long and thin；tall and thin；lanky：他是～个儿。*He's a tall，lean chap.* or *He's a spindlelegs.*

【瘦高挑儿】❶ a tall and slender figure ❷ a tall，

slender person
【瘦骨嶙峋】all skin and bones
【瘦果】[植] achene
【瘦煤】lean coal; meagre coal
【瘦缺】(〈反〉肥缺) an unprofitable post
【瘦肉形】lean meat species
【瘦弱】thin and weak; emaciated; frail
【瘦小】thin and small: 身材～ *slight of figure* (*or stature*)
【瘦削】very thin; gaunt; bony: ～的面孔 *a haggard face*
【瘦子】a lean (or thin) person

shū

书 Ⅰ 动 write: 振笔直～ *take up the pen and write vigorously* Ⅱ 名 ❶ style of calligraphy; script ❷ book: 一本关于中国历史的新～ *a new work on Chinese history* ❸ letter ❹ document
【书包】satchel; schoolbag
【书包带】book strap (used by schoolchildren)
【书报】books, newspapers, and periodicals ◇ ～亭 newsstand
【书背】the back of a book; spine; backbone
【书本】book: ～知识 *book learning*; *book knowledge*
【书不尽言】I have much more to say than I can write in this letter (used at the end of a letter).
【书场】a place of entertainment where quyi(曲艺) performances are given
【书虫】〈书〉 pedant; bookworm
【书橱】bookcase (often with glass doors)
【书呆子】pedant; bookworm
【书挡】bookend
【书到用时方恨少】It is when you are using what you have learned from books that you wish you had read more books than you have.
【书店】bookshop; bookstore; bookseller's
【书法】penmanship; calligraphy ◇ ～家 calligrapher; calligraphist
【书房】study
【书扉】title page
【书稿】manuscript
【书柜】同〖书橱〗
【书函】❶ slipcase ❷ letters; correspondence
【书后】postscript (by the author or sb. else)
【书画】painting and calligraphy
【书籍】books; works; literature: 军事～ *military literature*
【书脊】spine (of a book); backbone
【书记】❶ secretary: 党委～ *secretary of the Party committee* / 总～ *general secretary* ❷ clerk ◇ ～处 secretariat
【书架】bookshelf; a set of bookshelves; bookcase
【书简】(又作'书柬') letters; correspondence
【书经】The Book of History ——另见〖五经〗
【书局】publishing house; press; book company: 中华～ *the Zhonghua Book Company*
【书卷】〈书〉 books ◇ ～气 bookishness; scholarliness
【书刊】books and periodicals
【书壳】slipcase
【书口】fore-edge (or foredge)
【书库】stack room
【书林】〈书〉 a forest of books—a treasury of books
【书录】bibliography
【书眉】the top of a page; top margin
【书面】written; in written form; in writing: ～材料 *written material* / ～通知 *written notice*
【书面合同】contract in writing; written contract
【书面语】written language; literary language
【书名】the title of a book; title ◇ ～号 punctuation marks used to enclose the title of a book or an article (《 》); ～页 title page
【书目】booklist; title catalogue: 参考～ *a list of reference books*; *bibliography*
【书皮】❶ book cover: 塑料～ *a plastic cover* / 布面烫金～ *a cloth gilt cover* ❷ dust cover ◇ ～纸 paper for covering books
【书评】book review
【书签】❶ a title label pasted on the cover of a Chinese-style thread-bound book ❷ bookmark
【书社】❶ 〈旧〉 literary club ❷ publishing house
【书生】intellectual; scholar
【书生气】bookishness; a bookish cast of mind: 不要～十足。*Don't be so bookish and unrealistic.*
【书生之见】a bookish approach; a pedantic view
【书市】book fair
【书摊】bookstall; bookstand
【书套】slipcase
【书体】style of calligraphy
【书亭】book-kiosk; bookstall
【书童】page boy
【书屋】〈文〉 study
【书香】(of a family) having literary or intellectual fame: ～人家 *a literary* (*or intellectual*) *family*; *a family of scholars* / 他家世代～。*He comes from a long line of scholars.*
【书香门第】a literary (or intellectual) family; a family of scholars
【书写】write: ～标语 *write slogans*; *letter posters* ◇ ～纸 writing paper
【书心】type area (of a book page)
【书信】letter; written message: 常有～往来 *keep up a regular correspondence*
【书信电】letter cable
【书信体】epistolary style: ～小说 *epistolary novel*
【书页】book page; printed page
【书院】(in former times) academy of classical learning
【书札】〈书〉 letters; correspondence
【书斋】a study
【书展】book exhibition
【书证】[法] evidence in writing; written evidence (that supports or verifies facts in a case)
【书桌】desk; writing desk

抒 动 express; give expression to; convey: 抒发

【抒发】express; voice; give expression to: 这一唱段～了一个开拓者的壮志豪情。*This aria conveys the determination and lofty ideals of a pioneer (or pathbreaker).*
【抒怀】pour out one's heart; unburden one's heart
【抒情】express (or convey) one's emotion ◇ ～散文 lyric prose; ～诗 lyric poetry; lyrics
【抒写】express in writing; write of; describe: 这篇文章～了他在日内瓦工作时的一些感受。*The article describes how he felt while working in Geneva.*

枢 名 pivot; hub; centre
【枢机】❶ (in former times) a key government post or office ❷〈书〉a vital element
【枢机主教】cardinal (of the Roman Catholic Church)
【枢密院】privy council
【枢纽】pivot; hub; axis; key position: ～作用 *a pivotal role* / 交通～ *a hub of communications* / 水利～工程 *a key water control (or water conservancy) project*
【枢要】〈书〉the central administration

叔 名 ❶ father's younger brother; uncle ❷ (a form of address for a man about one's father's age) uncle: 刘大～ *Uncle Liu* ❸ husband's younger brother: ～嫂 *brother-in-law and sister-in-law*
【叔伯】relationship between cousins of the same grandfather or great-grandfather: ～兄弟 *first or second cousins on the paternal side; cousins*
【叔父】father's younger brother; uncle
【叔母】wife of father's younger brother; aunt
【叔叔】〈口〉❶ father's younger brother; uncle ❷ (a child's form of address for any young man one generation its senior) uncle
【叔子】husband's younger brother; brother-in-law
【叔祖】(paternal) grandfather's younger brother; granduncle (or great-uncle)
【叔祖母】wife of (paternal) grandfather's younger brother; grandaunt (or great-aunt)

殊 Ⅰ 形 ❶ different ❷ outstanding; special; remarkable: 待以～礼 *receive sb. with unusual ceremony* Ⅱ 副〈书〉very much; extremely; really: ～觉歉然 *feel most regretful* / ～难相信 *very difficult to believe; hardly credible*
【殊不知】little imagine; hardly realize: 我以为他还在北京，～他已经走了。*I thought he was still in Beijing. I never dreamt that he had already left.*
【殊功】distinguished service; outstanding achievement
【殊荣】special honours
【殊深轸念】express deep solicitude; feel deeply concerned
【殊死】❶ desperate; life-and-death: ～的搏斗 *a life-and-death struggle* / 作～战 *fight to the death; fight a last-ditch battle; put up a desperate fight* ❷〈古〉the penalty of decapitation
【殊途同归】reach the same goal by different routes
【殊勋】〈书〉outstanding merit; distinguished service: 屡建～ *rendered one distinguished service after another*

倏 副〈书〉suddenly; quickly: 羊城一别，～已半年。*Six months have passed in a flash since we parted in the City of Rams (i.e. Guangzhou).*
【倏地】suddenly; quickly: 他～刹住了车。*He brought the car to a sudden stop.*
【倏尔】〈书〉suddenly; quickly: ～不见 *suddenly (or quickly) disappear*
【倏忽】suddenly; quickly: ～不见 *suddenly (or quickly) disappear*
【倏然】〈书〉suddenly; abruptly: ～一阵暴雨。*A rainstorm came on suddenly.*

淑 形 ❶ (of a woman) refined; pure; virtuous ❷ (of a woman) beautiful; lovely
【淑德】female virtue
【淑静】(of a woman) refined and gentle
【淑美】virtuous and beautiful; refined and beautiful
【淑女】a fair maiden; a virtuous maiden; a noble lady

梳 Ⅰ 名 comb: 木～ *a wooden comb* Ⅱ 动 comb (one's hair, etc): ～头发 *comb one's hair*
【梳辫子】❶ braid one's hair ❷ sort out matters, problems, etc: 先把问题梳梳辫子，再研究解决办法。*First sort out and classify the problems, then try to find solutions to them.*
【梳理】❶［纺］carding ❷ comb out (one's hair); dress (one's hair): 她坐在镜前，～长发。*She sat in front of the mirror, combing out her long hair.*
【梳棉】［纺］comb and parallel cotton fibers prior to spinning; card ◇ ～机［纺］carding machine; card
【梳头】comb one's hair
【梳洗】wash and dress ◇ ～用具 toilet articles
【梳妆】dress and make up ◇ ～打扮 deck oneself out; dress smartly; be dressed up; ～台 dressing table
【梳子】comb: 一把～ *a comb*

舒 Ⅰ 动 stretch; unfold; spread; smooth out Ⅱ 形〈书〉easy; leisurely
【舒畅】happy; entirely free from worry: 心情～ *have ease of mind; feel happy*
【舒服】❶ comfortable: 这把椅子又软又～。*This chair is soft and comfortable.* ❷ be well: 她今天不大～。*She isn't well today.* / 我浑身不～。*I feel sore all over.*
【舒缓】❶ slow and unhurried; leisurely: 动作～ *slow and unhurried in one's movements* ❷ relaxed; mild: 语调～ *in a mild tone* ❸ (of a slope) gentle; gradual: ～的斜坡 *a gentle slope*
【舒筋活络】［中］stimulate the circulation of the

blood and cause the muscles and joints to relax

【舒卷】〈书〉(of clouds or smoke) curl and uncurl; roll and unroll; roll back and forth: 白云～。*White clouds massed and scattered.*

【舒快】comfortable and relaxed; refreshed: 洗完蒸汽浴,我觉得浑身～。*After the sauna bath I felt completely refreshed.*

【舒眉展眼】smiling eyes; a beaming face

【舒气】❶ get one's breath; catch one's breath: 到了半山腰,我们坐下来舒舒气。*Halfway up the hill, we sat down to catch our breath.* ❷ relax; have a breathing space: 险情排除了,大家才算舒了口气。*We didn't get a breathing space until the crisis was over.* ❸ relieve one's feelings; let off steam: 他只知道发牢骚～。*He's given to fussing and grumbling as a way of relieving his feelings.*

【舒散】❶ stretch and flex: ～一下筋骨 *stretch oneself; flex one's limbs; relax one's muscles* ❷ shake off one's fatigue or cares

【舒适】comfortable; cosy; snug: ～的生活 *a comfortable life* / 房间不大,但很～。*The rooms are not big but they're very cosy.*

【舒适带】comfort zone (the range of temperature considered comfortable for most people, generally 20℃-24℃)

【舒松】relieved and relaxed

【舒泰】free from worries; comfortable and at ease: 心里好～ *feel completely relaxed*

【舒坦】comfortable; at ease

【舒心】〈方〉comfortable; happy

【舒展】❶ unfold; extend; smooth out: 荷叶～着,发出清香。*The lotus leaves are unfolding, sending forth a delicate fragrance.* / 问题解决了,老人家紧锁的眉头也～了。*Once the problem was solved, the old man's knitted brows became smooth again.* ❷ limber up; stretch: ～一下筋骨 *limber up one's muscles and joints*

【舒张】[生理] diastole ◇ ～压 [医] diastolic pressure

疏 Ⅰ 动 ❶ dredge (a river, etc.) ❷ disperse; scatter Ⅱ 形 ❶ thin; sparse; scattered: ～林 *sparse woods* / ～～的几根胡子 *a sparse beard* / 几点～星 *a few scattered stars* ❷ (of family or social relations) distant; not familiar: 亲～ *close and distant* ❸ negligent: ～于职守 *negligent of one's duties* / ～于防范 *neglect to take precautions* ❹ scanty

【疏不间亲】casual acquaintances should not come between near relatives

【疏财仗义】同〖仗义疏财〗

【疏淡】❶ sparse; thin: 白云～ *thin white clouds* / ～的眉毛 *thin eyebrows* ❷ drift apart; become estranged: 由于志趣不同,他俩的关系渐渐～了。*Pursuing different interests, they gradually drifted apart.*

【疏导】❶ dredge: ～淮河 *dredge the Huai River* ❷ remove obstructions: ～交通 *relieve traffic congestion*

【疏港】clear out a harbour

【疏果】[农] fruit thinning

【疏忽】carelessness; negligence; oversight: ～大意就可能引起事故。*Carelessness is liable to cause accidents.*

【疏花】[农] flower thinning

【疏剪】prune (trees, branches, etc.)

【疏解】❶ mediate ❷ relieve (traffic congestion, etc.)

【疏浚】dredge: ～水道 *dredge the waterways* / ～港口 *dredge a harbour*

【疏开】[军] extend; disperse; deploy: ～队形 *dispersed formation; extended order; open order (or formation)*

【疏懒】careless and lazy; indolent

【疏朗】❶ thinly scattered; sparse: 夜空中闪烁着疏疏朗朗的几点星光。*A few scattered stars were twinkling in the night sky.* ❷ cheerful; optimistic: 心胸渐渐～了 *be cheering up*

【疏理】〈书〉put in order; sort out: ～古籍 *reorganize ancient texts*

【疏漏】careless omission; slip; oversight: 计划匆促拟成,难免有～之处。*The plan was drawn up in haste, so there are bound to be oversights and omissions.*

【疏落】sparse; scattered: ～的村庄 *scattered villages*

【疏密】density; spacing: ～不匀 *of uneven density* / 花木栽得～有致。*The flowers and trees are artistically spaced.*

【疏苗】seedling thinning

【疏浅】❶ crude and superficial: 思虑～ *immature and superficial thinking* ❷ (of relationship) distant: 我和他关系～。*He and I are not close friends.*

【疏散】❶ sparse; scattered; dispersed: ～的村落 *scattered villages* ❷ evacuate; disperse: 我们要做好地震预报工作,以便及时～人口。*We must do a good job of predicting earthquakes so that we can disperse the population in time.*

【疏失】careless mistake; remissness

【疏松】❶ loose: 土质～。*The soil is porous.* ❷ loosen: ～土壤 *loosen the soil*

【疏通】❶ dredge: ～田间的排水沟 *dredge the irrigation ditches in the fields* ❷ mediate between two parties

【疏挖】dredge: ～河道 *dredge a river*

【疏远】drift apart; become estranged: 我们两个人越来越～了。*We have become more and more estranged.*

输 动 ❶ transport; convey: 油管把原油从油田直接～往港口。*The pipeline carries crude oil direct from the oil field to the harbour.* ❷〈书〉contribute money; donate ❸ lose; be beaten; be defeated: ～了一局 *lost one game in the set*

【输出】❶ send out: 血液从心脏～,经血管分布全身。*Blood is pumped by the heart through the blood vessels to all parts of the body.* ❷ export：资本～ *export of capital* ❸［电］computer output：～端数 *fan-out* / ～功率 *output power* / ～数据 *data-out*

【输电】transmit electricity：这个发电站已开始向山区～。*The power station has begun to transmit electricity to the mountain area.* ◇ ～网 power transmission network；grid system；～线路 transmission line

【输家】loser（in a gambling game）

【输将】〈书〉contribute；donate：慷慨～ *make generous donations*

【输精管】［生理］spermatic duct；seminal duct ◇ ～结扎术 vasoligation；～炎 deferentitis

【输理】be in the wrong：你输了理，还有什么可辩的？*You are in the wrong. Why argue?*

【输卵管】［生理］oviduct；Fallopian tube ◇ ～结扎术 tubal ligation；～炎 salpingitis

【输尿管】［生理］ureter ◇ ～炎 ureteritis

【输钱】lose money（in gambling）：他输了十块钱。*He lost ten dollars（in gambling）.*

【输入】❶ bring in；introduce：～新思想 *the influx of new ideas* ❷ import：～粮食 *import grain* / ～限额 *import quota* ❸［电］computer input：～计算机三百万字 *input 3,000,000 characters* / ～端数 *fan-in* / ～功率 *input power* / ～数据 *data-in* / ～员 *data operator*

【输沙率】［水］silt discharge

【输送】carry；transport；convey：卡车把货物～到边疆地区。*Commodities are transported to border areas by truck.* / ～新鲜血液 *infuse new blood* ◇ ～带 conveyer belt；～机 conveyer

【输血】❶ blood transfusion ❷ give aid and support；bolster up；give sb. a shot in the arm：这等于是给侵略者～打气。*This is tantamount to giving the aggressor a shot in the arm.* ◇ ～者 blood donor

【输氧】oxygen therapy

【输液】［医］infusion

【输赢】❶ victory or defeat：两个球队要较量一番，非见个～不可。*The two teams are determined to fight it out.* ❷ winnings and losses（in gambling）：他们常打麻将，而且～很大。*They were always playing mahjong, and the winnings and losses were very high.*

【输油管】petroleum pipeline

蔬

名 vegetables

【蔬菜】vegetables；greens；greenstuff：～栽培 *vegetable growing；vegetable farming*

【蔬果】vegetables and fruits

shú

秫

名 kaoliang；sorghum

【秫秸】kaoliang stalk；sorghum stalk

【秫米】husked sorghum

【秫秫】〈方〉kaoliang；sorghum

孰

代〈书〉❶ who；which：～胜～负？*Who wins and who loses?* / ～是～非？*Which is right and which is wrong?* ❷ what：是可忍，孰不可忍

赎

动 ❶ redeem；ransom：把东西～回来 *redeem a pledge* ❷ atone for（a crime）

【赎当】redeem sth. pawned；take sth. out of pledge；redeem a pledge

【赎价】ransom price；ransom

【赎金】ransom money；ransom

【赎买】redeem；buy out

【赎身】（of slaves or prostitutes）redeem（or ransom）oneself；buy back one's freedom

【赎刑】redeem sb. from punishment by paying a ransom

【赎罪】atone for one's crime：立功～ *perform meritorious services to atone for one's crime* ◇ ～券 indulgence（of the Roman Catholic Church in medieval times）；～日［宗］（犹太教）Yom Kippur；Day of Atonement

塾

名 old-type private school；family school：私塾

【塾师】the tutor of an old-type private school；a private tutor

熟

形 ❶ ripe：西红柿～了。*The tomatoes are ripe.* / 一年两～ *two crops a year* ❷ cooked；done：～肉 *cooked meat* / 饭～了。*The rice is done.* ❸ processed：～铜 *wrought copper* / ～皮子 *tanned leather* ❹ familiar；well acquainted：这个地方我很～。*I'm familiar with this place.* / 这口音听起来很～。*The voice sounds familiar.* / 这条路他最～。*He knows this route best.* ❺ skilled；experienced；practised：熟手 ❻ deeply；thoroughly：睡得很～ *sleep soundly*

【熟谙】〈书〉be familiar with；be good at：～水性 *be an expert swimmer*

【熟菜】cooked food；prepared food

【熟道】familiar road（or route）

【熟地】❶ cultivated land ❷（又作'熟地黄'）［中］prepared rhizome of rehmannia（Rehmannia glutinosa）

【熟化】cultivate（land）；till：～地 *cultivated land；tillable land*

【熟荒】（又作'熟荒地'）［农］once cultivated land；abandoned cultivated land

【熟记】learn by heart；memorize；commit to memory

【熟见】（of things）commonly seen：人所～，不足为奇。*A familiar sight is nothing to be surprised at.*

【熟客】frequent visitor

【熟练】skilled；practised；proficient：～工人 *skilled worker* / 他枪法很～。*He's a good shot.*

【熟料】fired refractory material；grog；clinker

【熟路】a familiar road（or route）；a beaten track

【熟门熟路】a familiar road and a familiar door—things that one knows well

【熟能生巧】Skill comes from practice; Practice makes perfect.
【熟年】a year of good harvests; bumper year
【熟漆】lacquer
【熟人】acquaintance; friend
【熟石膏】plaster of Paris; plaster
【熟石灰】slaked lime
【熟食】prepared food; cooked food
【熟视无睹】pay no attention to a familiar sight; turn a blind eye to; ignore: 对不良倾向决不能～。*We must not turn a blind eye to unhealthy tendencies.*
【熟识】be well acquainted with; know well: 我们交往不多，不太～。*We haven't met often and don't know each other very well.*
【熟手】old hand; practised hand
【熟睡】sleep soundly; be fast asleep
【熟丝】［纺］boiled-off silk
【熟思】ponder deeply; consider carefully; deliberate
【熟铁】wrought iron
【熟土】［农］mellow soil
【熟悉】know sth. or sb. well; be familiar with; have an intimate knowledge of: 他对这工作不～。*He is new to the task.* / ～内情 *know the ins and outs of the matter; know the inside story of; be in the know*
【熟习】be skilful at; have the knack of; be practised in: ～业务 *be practised (or well versed) in one's field of work* / ～蔬菜的栽培法 *have the knack of growing vegetables*
【熟橡胶】vulcanized rubber
【熟语】idiom; idiomatic phrase
【熟知】know very well; know intimately
【熟字】words already learned; familiar words

shǔ

黍 名 broomcorn millet (Panicum miliaceum)
【黍子】broomcorn millet (Panicum miliaceum)

属 Ⅰ名 ❶ category: 金属 ❷［生］genus: 小麦和燕麦是同科的，但不同～。*Wheat and oats are of the same family, but of different genera.* ❸ family members; dependants: 军属 Ⅱ动 ❶ be under; be subordinate to: 这些厂～地方领导。*These factories are run by the local authorities.* / 所～单位和部门 *subordinate units and departments* ❷ belong to: 我们两国同～第三世界。*Both our countries belong to the Third World.* ❸ be: 查明～实 *prove to be true after investigation* / 实～无理 *be really unreasonable* ❹ be born in the year of (one of the 12 symbolic animals associated with a 12-year cycle): 她比我小一岁，是～牛的。*She is one year younger than I am; she was born in the year of the ox.* ——另见 zhǔ
【属地】possession; dependency
【属国】vassal state; dependent state
【属下】subordinates: 我是他的～。*I'm one of his subordinates.* or *I work under him.*
【属相】popular name for 生肖
【属性】attribute; property
【属于】belong to; be part of: 西沙群岛～中国。*The Xisha Islands belong to China.*

暑 名 heat; hot weather: 中暑
【暑假】summer vacation (or holidays)
【暑期】summer vacation time: ～训练班 *summer course* / ～学校 *summer school*
【暑气】summer heat; heat
【暑热】hot summer weather
【暑天】hot summer days; dog days
【暑瘟】［中］febrile diseases in summer, including encephalitis B, dysentry, malignant malaria, etc.

署 Ⅰ名 government office; office: 公署 Ⅱ动 ❶ make arrangements for; arrange: 部署 ❷ handle by proxy; act as deputy: 署理 ❸ put one's signature to; sign: 请在信后～上你的名字。*Please sign this letter.*
【署理】handle by proxy; act as deputy: ～部务 *handle the ministry's affairs during the minister's absence*
【署名】sign; put one's signature to: 全组同志都在信上署了名。*The letter was jointly signed by all the comrades of the group.* ◇ ～人 the undersigned; ～文章 a signed article

数 动 ❶ count: 从一～到十 *count from 1 to 10* / ～～看一行有多少棵苗。*Count and see how many seedlings there are in a row.* ❷ be reckoned as exceptionally (good, bad, etc.): 全班～他个儿最高。*He is the tallest in the class.* ❸ enumerate; list: 历～其罪 *enumerate the crimes sb. has committed* ——另见 shù; shuò
【数不过来】too many to be counted; innumerable: 参观的人多得～。*There were innumerable visitors.*
【数不清】countless; innumerable: 天上有～的星星。*There are countless stars in the sky.*
【数不胜数】innumerable; incalculable; countless
【数不着】(又作'数不上') not count as outstanding, important, etc.: 论游泳技术，在我们厂里可～我。*I don't count as a good swimmer in our factory.*
【数得着】(又作'数得上') be reckoned as outstanding, important, etc.: 在我们村里，他是～的养猪能手。*He is one of the outstanding pig-breeders of our village.*
【数典忘祖】give all the historical facts except those about one's own ancestors; forget one's own origins; be ignorant of the history of one's own country
【数伏】beginning of the three fu(三伏), the three hottest ten-day periods of the year; beginning of the hottest days of the year

【数黑论黄】(又作'数黄道黑') talk irresponsibly; gossip
【数葫芦道茄子】rattle on; talk endlessly
【数九】beginning of the nine nine-day periods following the Winter Solstice; beginning of the coldest days of the year
【数九寒天】the coldest days of the year
【数来宝】rhythmic storytelling to clapper accompaniment
【数落】❶ scold sb. by enumerating his wrongdoings; rebuke; reprove: 把他～一顿 *give him a good scolding* ❷ enumerate; cite one example after another
【数米而炊】count the grains of rice before cooking them—fuss over small things; be miserly
【数数儿】count; reckon: 孩子们在学～。*The children are learning how to count.*
【数说】❶ enumerate ❷ scold; rebuke; reprove
【数一数二】count as one of the very best; rank very high: 他在连里是～的射手。*He is one of the very best marksmen in his company.*

蜀 名 short for Sichuan province
【蜀锦】Sichuan brocade
【蜀葵】hollyhock (Althaea rosea)
【蜀犬吠日】a dog of Shu, a misty region, barking at the sun—an ignorant person making a fuss about something that he alone finds strange
【蜀绣】Sichuan embroidery

鼠 名 mouse; rat
【鼠辈】mean creatures; scoundrels
【鼠标】[计](又作'鼠标器')mouse
【鼠疮】[中] scrofula
【鼠窜】scamper off like a rat; scurry away like frightened rats
【鼠胆】as timid as a mouse; chicken-hearted
【鼠肚鸡肠】petty; narrow-minded
【鼠害】a plague of rats; damage caused by rats
【鼠耗】wastage of grain, etc. caused by rats
【鼠夹】mousetrap
【鼠笼】squirrel cage ◇ ～式电动机 squirrel-cage motor
【鼠目寸光】a mouse can see only an inch; see only what is under one's nose; be short-sighted
【鼠窃狗偷】filch like rats and snatch like dogs—play petty tricks on the sly
【鼠曲草】affine cudweed (Gnaphalium affine)
【鼠咬热】rat-bite fever
【鼠疫】the plague

薯 名 potato; yam
【薯莨】dye yam (Dioscorea cirrhosa)
【薯芋类作物】tuber crops
【薯蓣】Chinese yam (Dioscorea batatas)

曙 名〈书〉daybreak; dawn
【曙光】the first light of morning; dawn 胜利的～ *the dawn of victory*
【曙色】the light of early dawn: 从窗口透进了灰白的～。*The pale light of early dawn slanted in through the window.*

shù

术 名 ❶ art; skill; technique ❷ method; tactics——另见 zhú
【术科】technical courses offered in military or physical training (〈反〉学科)
【术士】❶ a Confucian scholar ❷ magician
【术语】technical terms; terminology: 军事～ *military terms* / 医学～ *medical terminology*

戍 动 defend; garrison: ～边 *garrison the frontiers*
【戍楼】garrison watchtower
【戍守】defend; garrison: ～边疆 *garrison the frontiers*
【戍卒】garrison soldiers (at the frontiers)

束 Ⅰ 动 ❶ bind; tie: 腰～皮带 *wear a belt round one's waist* ❷ control; restrain: 拘束 Ⅱ 量 bundle; bunch; sheaf: 一～鲜花 *a bunch of flowers* / 一～稻草 *a sheaf of straw*
【束缚】tie; bind up; fetter: ～手脚 *bind sb. hand and foot; tie sb.'s hands; hamper the initiative of* / ～生产力 *fetter the productive forces*
【束射管】[电子] beam tube
【束身】❶ control oneself; restrain oneself ❷ bind oneself: ～归罪 *bind oneself with rope and surrender oneself to justice*
【束手】have one's hands tied; be helpless ◇ ～待毙 fold one's hands and await destruction; helplessly wait for death; resign oneself to extinction; ～就擒 allow oneself to be seized without putting up a fight; ～束脚 be over-cautious; ～无策 be at a loss what to do; feel quite helpless; be at one's wit's end
【束之高阁】tie sth. up and place it on the top shelf—lay aside and neglect; shelve; pigeonhole
【束装】〈书〉pack up (for a journey): ～就道 *pack up and start off*

述 动 state; relate; narrate: 略～其经过 *relate briefly how it happened; give a brief account of the matter* / 简～如下。*A brief account is as follows.*
【述评】review; commentary: 每周时事～ *weekly review of current affairs*
【述说】state; recount; narrate
【述职】report on one's work; report: 大使已回国～。*The ambassador has gone back for consultations.*

树 Ⅰ 名 tree: 苹果～ *apple tree* Ⅱ 动 ❶ plant; cultivate: 十年树木,百年树人 ❷ set up; establish; uphold: ～正气 *uphold (or foster) healthy tendencies* / ～雄心 *have lofty ambitions; aim high*

【树碑立传】erect a monument to sb. and write his biography—build up sb.'s public image：这本所谓回忆录，实际上是为他自己～的。*These so-called memoirs are, in fact, an attempt on his part to build up his own image.*
【树杈】（又作'树杈子'）crotch (of a tree)
【树丛】grove；thicket
【树大根深】a big tree with deep roots (said of an influential person or a huge organization)
【树大招风】a tall tree catches the wind —a person in a high position is liable to be attacked
【树倒猢狲散】when the tree falls the monkeys scatter—when an influential person falls from power, his hangers-on disperse
【树敌】make an enemy of sb.；set others against oneself；antagonize：～太多 *make too many enemies*；*antagonize too many people*
【树墩】（又作'树墩子'）tree stump；stump
【树蜂】wood wasp
【树干】tree trunk；trunk
【树高千丈，叶落归根】a tree may grow a thousand zhang high, but its leaves fall back to the roots—a person residing away from home eventually returns to his native soil
【树挂】common name for 雾凇
【树冠】crown (of a tree)
【树胶】gum (of a tree)
【树懒】［动］sloth
【树立】set up；establish：～榜样 *set an example* / ～远大理想 *foster a lofty ideal* / ～正确的世界观 *acquire a correct world outlook*
【树林】（又作'树林子'）woods；grove
【树苗】sapling
【树木】trees generally
【树皮】bark ◇ ～画 bark picture
【树鼩】［动］tree shrew
【树梢】the tip of a tree；treetop
【树身】tree trunk；trunk
【树蛙】tree frog
【树丫】（又作'树桠'）crotch (of a tree)
【树阴】the shade of a tree
【树欲静而风不止】the tree may crave calm, but the wind will not drop—things take their own course regardless of one's will
【树栽子】〈口〉sapling
【树枝】branch；twig
【树脂】resin ◇ ～酸 resinic acid；～整理［纺］resin finishing
【树种】❶ kinds of trees：阔叶～ *broad-leaved trees* / 针叶～ *coniferous trees* ❷ seeds of trees：采集～ *gather the seeds of trees*
【树桩】（又作'树桩子'）tree stump；stump
【树籽】seeds of trees

竖

Ⅰ 形 vertical；upright；perpendicular：画一条～线 *draw a vertical line* Ⅱ 动 set upright；erect；stand：～旗杆 *erect a flagpole* / 这杆子我～不起来。*I can't get the pole to stand up.* Ⅲ 名 ❶ vertical stroke (in Chinese characters)："王"字的写法是三横一～。*The character 王 is composed of one vertical and three horizontal strokes.* ❷〈书〉a young servant
【竖笛】［音］recorder
【竖井】［矿］(vertical) shaft
【竖立】erect；set upright；stand：门前～着一根旗杆。*A flagpole stands outside the gate.*
【竖起】hold up；erect：～大拇指 *hold up one's thumb in approval*；*thumbs up* / ～一面大旗 *hoist a huge banner* / ～耳朵听 *prick up one's ears*
【竖琴】［音］harp
【竖蜻蜓】〈方〉handstand
【竖子】〈书〉❶ boy；lad ❷ mean fellow；fellow

恕

Ⅰ 名 consideration for others；forbearance Ⅱ 动 ❶ forgive；pardon；excuse：～罪 *pardon an offence*；*forgive a sin* ❷〈套〉excuse me；beg your pardon
【恕不奉陪】excuse me (for not keeping you company)
【恕难从命】we regret that we cannot comply with your wishes

庶

Ⅰ 形 multitudinous；numerous Ⅱ 名 of or by a concubine (as distinguished from the legal wife)：～出 *be born of a concubine*
【庶民】〈书〉the common people；the multitude
【庶人】〈书〉commoners；the common people：夺去爵位，废为～ *be deprived of one's rank and reduced to the status of commoner*
【庶务】〈旧〉❶ general affairs；business matters ❷ a person in charge of business matters

数

Ⅰ 名 ❶ number；figure：代表人～ *the number of delegates* / ～以万计 *number tens of thousands* ❷［数］number：小数 / 整数 ❸［语］number：单数 / 复数 ❹ fate；destiny Ⅱ 数 several；a few：～百人 *several hundred people* / ～小时后 *a few hours later* ——另见 shǔ；shuò
【数词】［语］numeral
【数额】a fixed number；a definite amount：超出～ *exceed the number fixed*
【数据】data：科学～ *scientific data* ◇ ～处理 data processing；～传输 data communications；data transfer；～存储系统 data-storage system；～恢复 data recovery；～加密 data encryption；～库 data base；data bank
【数控】numerical control (Nc)：总体～ *total numerical control*
【数理化】（〈略〉全称为'数学、物理、化学'）mathematics, physics, and chemistry
【数理逻辑】mathematical logic
【数理统计学】mathematical statistics
【数量】quantity；amount：～和质量并重 *stress both quantity and quality* / 在～上占优势 *be superior in numbers*；*have numerical superiority*
【数量词】［语］numeral-classifier compound (e.g. 一次"once", 两套"two sets")

【数列】an ordered series of numbers
【数码】❶ numeral：罗马～ *Roman numerals* ❷ number；amount ❸ digital ◇～磁带 digital tape；～电视 digital television；～摄像机 digital video camera；～照相机 digital camera
【数目】number；amount
【数目字】同〖数字〗
【数学】mathematics：～家 *mathematician*
【数值】［数］numerical value ◇～天气预报 numerical weather forecast
【数制】a system of computation（based on the number 2，as the binary system 二进制，or on the number 10，as the decimal system 十进制）
【数轴】［数］number axis
【数珠】［宗］(佛教) beads
【数字】❶ numeral；figure；digit ❷ quantity；amount：不要单纯追求～。*Don't just go after quantity*. ◇～计算机 digital computer；～控制 numerical control（Nc）；～控制系统 numerical control system；～小键盘［计］numeric keypad
【数字地球】Digital Earth
【数字化】digitalization
【数字显示】digital display or presentation

漱 动 rinse（the mouth）；gargle
【漱口】rinse the mouth；gargle：用盐水～ *gargle with salt water* ◇～杯 a glass or mug for mouth-rinsing or teeth-cleaning；tooth glass；～剂 gargle

shuā

刷 Ⅰ 名 a brush：油漆～ *paintbrush* Ⅱ 动 ❶ clean with a brush；brush；scrub：～鞋 *brush shoes* / ～地板 *scrub the floor* / ～锅 *clean*（*or scour*）*a pot* ❷ paint，daub，paste up，etc. with a brush：用石灰浆～墙 *whitewash a wall* / ～标语 *paste up posters* ❸〈口〉eliminate；remove：那个队直到半决赛才给～下来。*That team was not eliminated until the semifinals*. Ⅲ 象 swish；rustle：玉米叶子被风吹得～～响。*The corn leaves rustled in the wind*. ——另见 shuà
【刷拉】a swishing sound：～一声，树上飞走一只鸟儿。*Swish! A bird flew out of a tree*.
【刷洗】scrub；scour：～地板 *scrub the floor* / ～锅碗 *scour the pots and pans*
【刷新】❶ renovate；refurbish：～门面 *repaint the front*（*of a shop，etc.*）；*put up a new shopfront* ❷ outdo；surpass：～纪录 *break*（*or better*）*a record* / 一再～生产纪录 *shatter the production records again and again* ❸［计］refresh
【刷牙】brush（or clean）one's teeth
【刷子】brush：一把～ *a brush* / 鞋～ *shoe brushes*

shuǎ

耍 动 ❶〈方〉play：叫孩子们到院子里～去。*Tell the children to go and play in the courtyard*. / 这可不是～的！*It's no joke!* ❷ play with；flourish：～刀 *flourish a sword*；*give a performance of swordplay* ❸ play（tricks）：～鬼把戏 *play dirty tricks* / ～两面派 *resort to double-dealing*；*be double-faced*
【耍把戏】❶ give an acrobatic performance；perform juggling feats ❷ play tricks
【耍笔杆】wield a pen；be skilled in literary tricks：他光会～，碰到实际问题就束手无策。*He knows only how to wield a pen and is helpless in the face of practical problems*.
【耍逗】play with；tease：～孩子 *tease children*
【耍猴儿】❶ put on a monkey show ❷ make fun of sb.；tease；kid：别以为我拿你～，我说的可都是实话。*Don't think I'm kidding you. I'm telling the truth*.
【耍花腔】cheat by glib talk；speak guilefully
【耍花招】❶ display showy movements in wushu（武术），etc. ❷ play（or get up to）tricks：别～了！*None of your tricks!* / 你这是耍的什么花招？*What are you up to?* or *What sort of game are you playing?* / 他又在～了。*He is up to his tricks again*.
【耍滑】（又作'耍滑头'）try to shirk work or responsibility；act in a slick way
【耍奸】同〖耍滑〗
【耍赖】（又作'耍赖皮'）act shamelessly；be perverse
【耍流氓】behave like a hoodlum；take liberties with women；act indecently
【耍闹】have horseplay
【耍弄】make fun of；make a fool of；deceive
【耍排场】parade one's wealth；go in for ostentation and extravagance
【耍盘子】［杂］plate-spinning；disc-spinning
【耍脾气】get into a huff；put on a show of bad temper
【耍贫嘴】〈方〉be garrulous
【耍钱】〈方〉gamble
【耍人】make fun of others；poke fun at others；make a fool of sb.
【耍手段】（又作'耍手腕'）use artifices；play tricks
【耍手艺】make a living as a craftsman
【耍态度】lose one's temper；get into a huff
【耍坛子】［杂］juggling with jars；jar balancing act
【耍威风】make a show of authority；throw one's weight about；be overbearing
【耍无赖】act shamelessly；be perverse
【耍笑】❶ joke；have fun ❷ make fun of；play a joke on：他喜欢～人。*He delights in making fun of others*.
【耍心眼儿】exercise one's wits for personal gain；be calculating；pull a smart trick
【耍嘴皮子】❶ talk glibly；be a slick talker ❷ mere empty talk；lip service

shuà

刷（构词成分）见下 ——另见 shuā

【刷白】〈方〉white; pale: 月亮把田野照得～。*The fields turned white under the moon.* / 听到这个不幸的消息,他的脸立刻变得～。*He turned pale when he heard the bad news.*

shuāi

衰 动 decline; wane: 体力渐～ *get weaker physically* / 风势渐～。*The wind was dying down.* / 懒则～。*Laziness leads to debility.*

【衰败】decline; wane; be at a low ebb

【衰敝】〈书〉decline; wane; be at a low ebb: 国力～。*National strength is on the wane.*

【衰变】[物] decay: 核～ *nuclear decay*

【衰草】withering grass: ～败叶 *withering grass and fallen leaves*

【衰减】❶ weaken; fail; diminish: 我的记忆力日见～。*My memory is failing fast.* ❷ [电] attenuation: ～器 *attenuator*

【衰竭】[医] exhaustion; prostration: 心力～ *heart failure*

【衰老】old and feeble; decrepit; senile: 一年不见,他明显地～了。*He's visibly aged and weakened since I saw him last a year ago.*

【衰落】decline; be on the wane; go downhill: 到了公元五世纪,罗马帝国迅速～。*The Roman Empire rapidly waned in power in the 5th century.*

【衰弱】❶ weak; feeble: 心脏～ *have a weak heart* ❷ weaken; diminish in strength: 攻势已经～。*The offensive is losing momentum.*

【衰颓】weak and degenerate

【衰退】fail; decline: 视力～。*One's eyesight is failing.* / 记忆力～ *be losing one's memory* / 经济～ *economic recession*

【衰亡】become feeble and die; decline and fall; wither away: 罗马帝国的～ *the decline and fall of the Roman Empire*

【衰朽】〈书〉feeble and decaying; decrepit: ～的王朝 *a decadent dynasty* / ～残年 *a decrepit old age*

摔 动 ❶ fall; tumble; lose one's balance: 他～了好多次才学会骑自行车。*He fell off many times before he learned to ride a bicycle.* / 他把腿～断了。*He had a fall and broke his leg.* ❷ hurtle down; plunge: 飞机～下来了。*The plane plunged to the ground.* ❸ cause to fall and break; break: 我不小心把玻璃杯～了。*I accidentally broke a glass.* ❹ cast; throw; fling: 把帽子往床上一～ *throw one's cap onto the bed* ❺ 同〖摔打〗

【摔打】❶ beat; knock: 把扫帚上的泥～～。*Beat the dirt off the broom.* ❷ rough it; temper oneself: 青年人应该到艰苦的环境中去～～。*Young people should temper themselves in difficult circumstances.*

【摔跟头】❶ tumble; trip and fall ❷ trip up; come a cropper; make a blunder

【摔跤】(又作'摔交') ❶ tumble; trip and fall: 他摔了一跤,把腿给摔折了。*He had a fall and broke his leg.* ❷ trip up; come a cropper; make a blunder ❸ [体] wrestling: ～运动员 *wrestler*

shuǎi

甩 动 ❶ move backward and forward; swing: ～着胳膊 *swinging one's arms* / ～鞭子 *crack a whip* / 小女孩一跑,辫子就来回～动。*The girl's pigtails swing to and fro as she runs.* / 他袖子一～就走了。*He flung up his hands in impatience and walked off.* ❷ throw; fling; toss: ～手榴弹 *throw hand grenades* ❸ leave sb. behind; throw off: 他加快速度,一会儿就把别的运动员都～在后头了。*Quickening his pace, he soon left all the other runners behind.* / 他的女朋友把他～了。*His girl-friend gave him the brush-off.*

【甩车】uncouple railway coaches from the locomotive; uncouple

【甩掉】throw off; cast off; shake off; get rid of: ～包袱 *cast off a burden; get a load off one's back* / ～尾巴 *throw off a pursuer; throw off a tail*

【甩干】spin-dry (laundry in an automatic washing machine); tumble-dry

【甩开膀子】go all out; go full steam ahead: ～抓生产 *go all out to increase production*

【甩脸子】〈方〉pull a long face

【甩卖】disposal of goods at reduced prices; markdown sale; reduction sale

【甩手】❶ swing one's arms ❷ refuse to do; wash one's hands of: 这事该你负责,你可不能～不管。*You can't wash your hands of this. It's your responsibility.*

【甩手掌柜】"hand-off" boss—boss who merely gives general instructions but keeps his hands off any practical work; "do-nothing" guy

【甩线】fishing line

【甩子】(shuǎizǐ) 〈口〉(of fish, insects, etc.) lay eggs: 青蛙正在～。*The frogs are spawning.*

【甩子】(shuǎizi) fly whisk; whisk

shuài

帅 Ⅰ 名 ❶ commander in chief: 统帅 / 挂帅 ❷ commander in chief, the chief piece in Chinese chess Ⅱ 形 ❶ beautiful; graceful; smart: 他的字写得真～。*He writes a beautiful hand.* / 他的双杠动作可～了! *His movements on the parallel bars were very graceful.* ❷ handsome; elegant: 这小伙子长得真～! *What a handsome strapping young man!*

【帅旗】the flag of a commander in chief

【帅气】handsome; elegant

【帅印】the seal of a commander in chief

率 Ⅰ 动 ❶ lead; command: ～师东征 *lead*

troops on an eastern expedition / ～众前往 *go (to a place) at the head of many people* ❷〈书〉follow; obey: 率由旧章 Ⅱ 形 ❶ rash; hasty: 草率 ❷ frank; straightforward: 坦率 Ⅲ 副〈书〉generally; usually: 大～如此。*This is usually the case.* ——另见 lǜ

【率常】〈书〉usually; generally: ～如此。*This is usually the case.*

【率尔】〈书〉rashly; hastily: 不可～应战。*We should not rashly accept battle.* ◇ ～操觚 write at random

【率领】lead; head; command: ～代表团 *lead (or head) a delegation* / 这支部队由他～。*This unit is under his command.*

【率然】hastily; rashly: ～回答 *give a rash answer*

【率先】take the lead in doing sth.; be the first to do sth.

【率由旧章】act in accordance with set rules; follow the beaten track

【率真】forthright and sincere

【率直】straightforward; unreserved; blunt

shuān

闩 Ⅰ 名 door bolt; latch: 上～ *fasten with a bolt or latch* Ⅱ 动 fasten with a bolt or latch: 把门～上 *bolt the door*

拴 动 tie; fasten: 把马～在树上 *tie (or tether) a horse to a tree* / ～根绳子晒衣服 *put up a clothes line* / 把船～住。*Make the boat fast.*

【拴绑】tie up; bind up

【拴缚】tie up; bind up

栓 名 ❶ bolt; plug: 枪栓 / 消火栓 ❷ stopper; cork

【栓剂】[医] suppository

【栓皮】cork (the outer bark of a kind of oak tree)

【栓皮栎】oriental oak (Quercus variabilis)

【栓塞】[医] embolism: 静脉～ *venous embolism* / 肺(脑)～ *pulmonary (cerebral) embolism*

【栓子】[医] embolus

shuàn

涮 动 ❶ rinse: 把衣服～一～。*Rinse the clothes.* / 把这瓶子～一下。*Give this bottle a rinse.* ❷ scald thin slices of meat in boiling water; instant-boil ❸〈方〉deceive; fool: 你别～我啦。*Don't try to fool me.*

【涮锅子】instant-boil slices of meat and vegetables in a chafing dish

【涮羊肉】❶ instant-boil slices of mutton in a chafing dish ❷ instant-boiled mutton; Mongolian fire pot

shuāng

双 Ⅰ 形 ❶ two; twin; both; dual: ～目失明 *blind in both eyes* / ～发动机飞机 *a twin-engined plane* / 粮食、棉花～丰收 *bumper harvests of both grain and cotton* ❷ (〈反〉单 "odd") even: 双数 / 双号 ❸ double; twofold: ～份 *double the amount; twice as much* Ⅱ 量 (for shoes, socks, chopsticks, etc.) pair: 一～鞋 *a pair of shoes* / 一～袜子 *a pair of socks*

【双胞胎】twins

【双边】bilateral: ～关系 *bilateral relations*

【双层】double-deck; having two layers; of two thicknesses: ～桥 *double-decker bridge* / ～床 *double-deck bed; double-decker; bunk bed* / ～火车(公共汽车) *double-decker* / ～玻璃窗 *double window*

【双重】double; dual; twofold: ～任务 *a double (or dual) task* / ～标准 *a double standard* / ～领导 *dual leadership* / ～公民身份 *dual citizenship* ◇ ～代表权 dual representation; ～国籍 dual (or double) nationality; ～间谍 double agent; ～人格〈贬〉dual personality

【双唇音】[语音] bilabial consonant; bilabial (i.e. p, b, m in Chinese)

【双打】[体] doubles: 男子(女子)～ *men's (women's) doubles* / 男女混合～ *mixed doubles*

【双方】both sides; the two parties: 缔约国～ *both signatory states; the contracting parties* / ～各执一词。*Each side persisted in its own views.* / ～同意 *by mutual consent*

【双峰驼】two-humped camel; Bactrian camel

【双幅】double width: 这块料子是单幅的还是～的? *Is this material single or double width?*

【双缸洗衣机】twin-tub washer

【双杠】[体] parallel bars

【双宫丝】[纺] doupion silk

【双挂号】registered mail requiring the receivers receipt

【双关】having a double meaning ◇ ～语 pun

【双管】double-barrelled: ～猎枪 *double-barrelled shotgun*

【双管齐下】paint a picture with two brushes at the same time—work along both lines

【双轨】double track: ～铁路 *double-track railway*

【双轨制】double-track system

【双号】even numbers (of tickets, seats, etc.)

【双簧】(又作'双镄') a two-man act, with one acting in pantomime and another hiding behind him doing all the speaking or singing: 唱～ *give a two-man comic show; collaborate*

【双簧管】[音] oboe

【双季稻】double cropping of rice; double-harvest rice

【双交】[农] double cross

【双料】of reinforced material; extra quality: ～脸盆 *special quality basin; extra good quality basin*

【双轮】❶ [体] double round: 五十米～射箭 *50-metre double round archery event* ❷ two-wheeled: ～马车 *a two-wheeled cab or hansom* / ～车 *two-wheeler* ◇ ～双铧犁 two-wheeled double-shared plough

【双面】two-sided；double-edged；double-faced；reversible：～刀片 *a double-edged razor blade* ◇～绣 double-faced embroidery；～摇纱机 double reeling frame；～印刷机 perfecting press；perfector；～织物 reversible cloth；reversibles
【双名】two-character given name
【双目显微镜】binocular microscope
【双亲】(both) parents；father and mother
【双球菌】diplococcus
【双曲面】[数] hyperboloid：单叶～ *hyperboloid of one sheet* / 双叶～ *hyperboloid of two sheets*
【双曲线】[数] hyperbola
【双全】complete in both respects；possessing both：父母～。*Both parents are alive*.
【双人床】double bed
【双人房】double-bedded room；twin-bedded room
【双人舞】a dance for two performers；pas de deux
【双日】even-numbered days (of the month)
【双身子】〈口〉a pregnant woman：她不是发胖，是～。*She isn't really getting fat；she is with child (or she's in the family way)*.
【双生】twin：～姐妹 *twin sisters* / ～兄弟 *twin brothers* / ～子 *twins*
【双声】[语] alliterative compound (a compound consisting of two syllables with the same initial consonant；e.g. 踟蹰，回环)
【双声道】double audio frequency line
【双手】both hands：我举～赞成。*I'm all for it*.
【双数】even numbers
【双双】in pairs
【双糖】[化] disaccharide
【双体船】catamaran
【双筒望远镜】binoculars；field glasses
【双喜】double happiness ◇～临门 a double blessing has descended upon the house
【双下巴】double chin
【双响】double-bang firecracker (which goes off twice—once on the ground, and then again in the air)
【双向】two-way：～交通 *two-way traffic* / ～通信 *two-way communication* ◇ ～飞碟射击 [体] skeet shooting；～开关 two-way switch
【双向选择】two-way selection (referring to employers and employees choosing each other in a job market)
【双薪】double pay：工作量加倍的发给～ *give double pay for double work*
【双星】❶ [天] double star ❷ Altair and Vega (另见〖牛郎织女〗)
【双姓】two-character surname (e.g. 欧阳，司徒)
【双修日】two-day weekend；double rest day
【双学位】double BA degree
【双语制】bilingualism
【双眼井】a twin-mouthed well
【双眼皮】double-edged eyelid
【双氧水】[药] hydrogen peroxide solution
【双翼机】biplane
【双音节词】[语音] disyllabic word；disyllable
【双鱼座】[天] Pisces
【双元音】[语音] diphthong
【双月刊】bimonthly (magazine)
【双职工】man and wife both at work；working couple
【双周刊】biweekly (magazine)；fortnightly
【双绉】[纺] crêpe de Chine
【双子叶植物】[植] dicotyledon
【双子座】[天] Gemini
【双座】two-seater；double-seater：～飞机 *two-seater aircraft*

霜 Ⅰ 名 ❶ frost (the white powdery substance) ❷ frostlike powder：糖～ *icing；frosting* Ⅱ 形 white；hoar：～鬓 *grey (or hoary) temples*
【霜冻】frost (the frozen condition)
【霜害】frost injury；frost：受～的农作物 *frosted crops*
【霜花】❶ frostwork ❷ (soft) rime
【霜降】❶ Frost's Descent—the 18th of the 24 solar terms ❷ the day marking the beginning of the 18th solar term (Oct. 23 or 24, when hoarfrost descends and is likely to bring the first film of ice)
【霜霉病】[农] downy mildew
【霜期】frost season
【霜叶】frosty leaves—autumn maple leaves

孀 名 widow
【孀妇】〈书〉widow
【孀居】〈书〉be a widow；live in widowhood

shuǎng

爽 Ⅰ 形 ❶ bright；clear；crisp：神清目～ *uplifting to the mind and the eye* ❷ frank；straightforward；openhearted：豪爽 ❸ feel well：身体不～ *not feel well* Ⅱ 动 deviate：毫厘不爽
【爽脆】❶ (of sounds or voices) sharp and clear ❷ frank；straightforward ❸ quick；brisk ❹ (of food) crisp and tasty
【爽口】tasty and refreshing
【爽快】❶ refreshed；comfortable：洗完澡身上～多了 *feel much refreshed after a bath* ❷ frank；straightforward；outright：为人～ *be frank and straightforward* ❸ with alacrity；readily：办事～ *work readily and briskly*
【爽朗】❶ bright and clear：深秋的天空异常～。*In late autumn the sky is crystal clear*. ❷ hearty；candid；frank and open；straightforward：～的笑声 *hearty laughter* / ～的性格 *a frank and open personality*
【爽利】brisk and neat；efficient and able：办事～ *be brisk and neat in one's work*
【爽亮】❶ loud and clear；resounding；sonorous ❷ cheerful；sanguine
【爽目】pleasing to the eye
【爽然若失】not know what to do；be at a loss
【爽身粉】talcum powder
【爽声】(in) a loud and clear voice：～笑了

laughed aloud

【爽信】〈书〉fail to keep one's promise; break one's promise; go back on one's word

【爽性】may just as well: 没多少活了,～干完了再休息。*There isn't much work left. We might as well finish it before we have a rest.*

【爽约】〈书〉fail to keep an appointment; break an appointment

【爽直】frank; straightforward; candid

shuí

谁 代(又读 shéi) ❶ who: 他是～? *Who is he?* / 他在跟～说话? *Who is he talking to?* / 这是～的意见? *Whose idea is this?* ❷ (used in rhetorical questions) who: ～不说他好? *Who wouldn't speak well of him?* ❸ someone; anyone: 有～能帮助我就好了。*If only someone would help me!* / 我没跟～说话。*I didn't talk to anyone.* / 你要找～吗? *Are you looking for someone?* ❹ (used before 都 or 也) everyone; anyone: ～都喜欢他。*Everybody likes him.* / ～也不要。*Nobody wants it.* ❺ (repeated in two phrases) whoever: ～先到,～先吃。*Whoever arrives first will eat first.* / 大家看～合适就选～。*You may elect whoever you think is suitable.* ❻ (used both before and after a verb, indicating that one person does sth. to another): ～先到～等着。*Whoever arrives first should wait for the other.* / 他们俩～也说不服～。*Neither of them could convince the other.*

【谁知】(又作'谁知道') who knows; who would have thought: 我只是开个玩笑,～她竟当真了。*I was only joking, who would have thought she would take it seriously.*

shuǐ

水 Ⅰ名 ❶ water: 请给我一杯～。*Give me a glass of water, please.* ❷ river: 汉～ *the Han River* ❸ a general term for rivers, lakes, seas, etc.; water: ～陆运输 *land and water transportation* / ～平如镜。*The surface of the water is as smooth as a mirror.* ❹ a liquid ❺ extra charges or incomes Ⅱ量 washing (of a garment): 这件衬衫洗了三～了。*This shirt has gone through three washings.*

【水坝】dam

【水半球】[地理] water hemisphere

【水饱儿】〈方〉feel bloated after eating much liquid food: 喝了两大碗粥,落了个～。*I gulped down two big bowls of porridge and felt terribly bloated.*

【水泵】water pump

【水笔】❶ a stiff-haired writing brush or water-colour paintbrush ❷〈方〉fountain pen

【水标】water gauge

【水表】water meter

【水鳖】[植] frogbit (Hydrocharis morsus-ranae)

【水滨】waterside; waterfront

【水兵】seaman; sailor; bluejacket

【水波】wave; ripple: 清风徐来,～不兴。*A cool wind blew gently, without starting a ripple.*

【水玻璃】[化] water glass

【水彩】watercolour ◇ ～画 watercolour (painting); ～颜料 watercolours

【水仓】[矿] sump

【水草】❶ water and grass: 逐～而居 (*of nomads*) *live where there is water and grass; rove about seeking water and grass* ❷ waterweeds; water plants

【水虿】[动] the nymph of the dragonfly, etc.

【水产】aquatic products: ～丰富 *abound in aquatic products* / ～资源 *aquatic resources* ◇ ～品 aquatic product; ～养殖 aquaculture; ～业 aquatic products industry

【水车】❶ waterwheel (for raising water or driving machinery) ❷ watercart; water waggon

【水城】waterside town

【水程】journey by boat; voyage: 一百公里的～ *a 100-kilometre journey by boat*

【水池】pond; pool; cistern

【水池子】❶ 同〖水池〗❷ sink

【水尺】[水] water gauge

【水处理】[化] water treatment

【水到渠成】when the water comes, a channel is formed—when conditions are ripe, success is achieved

【水道】❶ water course ❷ waterway; water route: 这次去上海,我想打～走。*This time I'll go to Shanghai by water.* ❸ lanes in a swimming pool

【水稻】paddy (rice); rice ◇ ～插秧机 rice (or paddy) transplanter; ～土 rice (or paddy) soil

【水滴石穿】dripping water wears through rock; little strokes fell great oaks

【水底电缆】submarine cable; subaqueous cable

【水地】❶ irrigated land ❷ paddy field

【水电】❶〈略〉见〖水力发电〗❷ water and electricity: ～供应 *water and electricity supply*

【水电费】charges for water and electricity

【水电站】〈略〉见〖水力发电站〗

【水貂】[动] mink

【水痘】[医] varicella; chicken pox; water pox

【水碓】water-powered trip-hammer (for husking rice)

【水飞蓟】[植] milk thistle (Silybum marianum)

【水肥】liquid manure

【水粉】❶〈方〉soaked noodles made from beans or sweet potatoes ❷ a cosmetic made from face powder and glycerine

【水粉画】painting gouache

【水分】❶ moisture content: 吸收～ *absorb moisture* ❷ exaggeration: 这个数字有～。*This figure is inflated.* / 这份报告有～。*This report is somewhat exaggerated.*

【水缸】water vat

【水工建筑物】hydraulic structure
【水沟】ditch；drain；gutter
【水垢】scale；incrustation：除去锅炉里的～ *scour out a boiler*
【水臌】［中］ascites
【水管】waterpipe
【水柜】❶ water tank ❷〈方〉cistern；reservoir ❸〈旧〉counter（in a shop）
【水果】fruit ◇ ～罐头 tinned（or canned）fruit；～软糖 fruit jelly；～糖 fruit drops
【水合】［化］hydration ◇ ～水 hydrate water；～物 hydrate
【水红】bright pink；cerise
【水壶】❶ kettle ❷ canteen ❸ watering can
【水葫芦】［植］water hyacinth
【水花】spray
【水患】flood；inundation
【水荒】water shortage
【水火】❶ fire and water—two things diametrically opposed to each other ❷ extreme misery：拯救人民于～之中 *save the people from untold miseries* ◇ ～不相容 be incompatible as fire and water；～地 an area afflicted alternately with drought and waterlogging；～无情〈口〉floods and fires have no mercy
【水货】smuggled goods
【水鸡】❶ water bird ❷ frog ❸ a drenched chicken；a drowned rat：淋得～似的 *be soaked through；be drenched and bedraggled*
【水碱】scale；incrustation
【水浇地】［农］irrigated land
【水饺】boiled dumplings
【水解】［化］hydrolysis ◇ ～产物 hydrolysate；～蛋白［药］protein hydrolysate；～质 hydrolyte
【水晶】crystal；rock crystal ◇ ～包 a steamed dumpling stuffed with diced pig fat and sugar；～玻璃 crystal（glass）；～宫 the Crystal Palace（of the Dragon King）；～棺 crystal sarcophagus；～体［生理］crystalline lens
【水井】well
【水景】waterscape：优美的～ *beautiful waterscape*
【水警】water police；coastal guard
【水具】glassware for drinking water
【水军】waterborne troops（in former times）
【水坑】puddle；pool；water hole：臭～ *cesspool；cesspit*
【水库】reservoir
【水牢】water dungeon
【水老鸦】（又作‘水老鸹’）cormorant
【水涝】waterlogging ◇ ～地 waterlogged land
【水雷】［军］（submarine）mine：敷设～ *lay mines（in water）*
【水冷】water-cooling：～式发动机 *a water-cooled engine* / ～系统 *water-cooling system*
【水力】waterpower；hydraulic power ◇ ～发电 hydraulic power generation；～发电站 hydroelectric（power）station；hydropower station；～开采［矿］hydraulic mining；hydraulicking；～学 hydraulics；～资源 hydroelectric resources（or potential）；waterpower resources
【水利】❶ water conservancy：～设施 *water conservancy facilities* ❷ irrigation works；water conservancy project：兴修～ *build irrigation works* ◇ ～工程 irrigation works；water conservancy project（or works）；～工程学 hydraulic engineering；～灌溉网 irrigation network；～化 bring all farmland under irrigation；～枢纽 key water control project；～资源 water resources
【水帘】cascade；waterfall
【水疗】hydropathy；hydrotherapy ◇ ～法［医］Hydrotherapy
【水淋淋】dripping wet
【水灵】〈方〉❶（of fruit，greens，etc.）fresh and juicy ❷（of appearance）bright and beautiful；radiant and vivacious：两只～的大眼睛 *a pair of bright，beautiful eyes*
【水流】❶ rivers；streams；waters：在我国，一切矿藏、～都属于全民所有。*In China，all mineral resources and waters are the property of the whole people.* ❷ current；flow：～湍急（迟缓）*rapid（sluggish）flow；rushing current*
【水流星】［杂］spinning bowls of water；water meteors
【水溜】eaves gutter
【水龙】（又作‘水龙带’）fire hose；hose
【水龙骨】［植］wall fern；golden locks
【水龙卷】［气］waterspout
【水龙头】（water）tap；faucet；bibcock：开（关）～ *turn on（off）the tap* / 用后将～关紧。*Don't leave the tap running after use.*
【水漉漉】wet；damp
【水陆】❶ land and water：～并进 *proceed by both land and water；conduct a combined operation by army and navy* ❷ delicacies from land and sea：～俱陈 *a feast with dainties of every kind* ◇ ～交通线 land and water communication lines；～联运 water-land transshipment；～联运码头 a dock for joint land and water transport service；～两用 amphibious；～两用车 amphibian；～两用飞机 amphibious aircraft；～坦克 amphibious tank；～运输 transportation by land and water
【水路】waterway；water route：由上海到武汉可以走～。*One can travel from Shanghai to Wuhan by water.*
【水铝矿】gibbsite（a mineral）
【水绿】light green
【水轮】waterwheel ◇ ～泵（water）turbine pump；～泵站（water）turbine-pump station；～发电机 water turbogenerator
【水轮机】hydraulic（or water）turbine
【水落管】［建］downspout；downpipe；water-spout；fallpipe
【水落石出】when the water subsides the rocks emerge—the whole thing comes to light：把事情辩个～ *argue a matter out* / 我们一定要把这事弄个～。*We must get to the bottom of this matter.*
【水煤气】［化］water gas

【水门】water valve
【水锰矿】manganite (a mineral)
【水米无交】❶ have no relations or contact with each other ❷ (of officials) be upright and accept no gifts from the people
【水密】[机] watertight
【水密桃】honey peach
【水面】❶ the surface of the water ❷ the area of a body of water
【水磨】(shuǐmó) polish with a waterstone
【水磨功夫】patient and precise work; painstaking work
【水磨石】[建] terrazzo: ～地面 *the terrazzo floor*
【水墨画】painting ink and wash; wash painting: 中国～ *Chinese ink and wash*
【水磨】(shuǐmò) ❶ watermill ❷ grind grain, etc. fine while adding water: ～年糕 *New Year cake made from finely ground rice flour*
【水母】[动] jellyfish; medusa
【水能载舟,亦能覆舟】while the waters can bear the boat, they can also sink it
【水泥】cement ◇ ～标号 strength of cement; cement grade; ～厂 cement plant; ～船 concrete boat; plastered boat; ～瓦 cement tile
【水碾】water-powered roller (for grinding grain)
【水鸟】aquatic bird; water bird
【水牛】(water) buffalo; ～儿〈方〉snail
【水暖】❶ hot water central heating system ❷ water supply and heating: ～设备 *water supply and heating installations* ◇ ～工 plumber
【水泡】bubble
【水疱】blister: 脚上打了～ *get blisters on one's feet*
【水培法】water culture; hydroponics
【水瓢】(gourd) water ladle
【水平】❶ horizontal; level: ～梯田 *level terraced field; level terrace* ❷ standard; level: 生活～ *living standard* / 文化～ *standard of education; cultural level* / 认识～ *level of one's understanding* ◇ ～飞行 horizontal (or level) flight; ～轰炸 [军] horizontal (or level) bombing; ～贸易 [经] horizontal trade; ～面 level surface; level; ～线 level line; level; ～仪(又作'水准器') level; spirit level
【水汽】water vapour; steam
【水汽浓度】[气] vapour concentration
【水枪】[矿] giant; (hydraulic) monitor: 水采～ *hydraulic giant*
【水橇】water ski: ～运动 *water skiing*
【水禽】[动] waterfowl; water bird
【水情】[水] regimen
【水球】[体] water polo
【水曲柳】[植] Manchurian ash (Fraxinus, mandshurica)
【水渠】ditch; canal
【水圈】[地质] hydrosphere
【水溶液】[化] aqueous solution
【水乳交融】as well blended as milk and water—in complete harmony: 好的翻译可以使宾主谈得～。*A competent interpreter can help bring about a meeting of minds like milk mingling with water.*
【水杉】[植] metasequoia (Metasequoia glyptostroboides)
【水上】on or above water: ～飞行 *overwater flight* ◇ ～芭蕾 water ballet; ～飞机 seaplane; hydroplane; ～居民 boat dwellers; ～运动 aquatic sports; water sports
【水筲】a pail made of wood or bamboo strips; bucket
【水蛇】[动] water snake
【水蛇腰】a very slender waist
【水深火热】deep water and scorching fire—an abyss of suffering; extreme misery
【水生动物】aquatic animal
【水生植物】water (or aquatic) plant; hydrophyte
【水声学】[物] marine acoustics
【水师】waterborne forces (in former times)
【水虱】[动] beach louse
【水蚀】erosion by the action of running water
【水势】the flow of water; the rise and fall of flood-water: 密切注意～ *keep a close eye on the flow of the water* / ～有所减退。*The flood subsided (or abated) a little.*
【水手】seaman; sailor ◇ ～长 boatswain
【水刷石】[建] granitic plaster
【水松】[植] China cypress (Glyptostrobus pensilis)
【水塔】water tower
【水獭】[动] otter
【水潭】puddle; pool
【水塘】pool; pond
【水体】waters; body of water: ～藻类 *algae suspended in the water (not rooted)*
【水天一色】the water and the sky blended in one colour (said of a vast body of water)
【水田】paddy field; paddy ◇ ～犁 paddy plough; ～耙 paddy harrow
【水桶】pail; bucket
【水头】❶ [水] head ❷ flood peak; peak of flow
【水土】❶ water and soil: 植树可以保持～。*Tree-planting helps to conserve water and prevent soil erosion.* ❷ natural environment and climate: ～不服 *unaccustomed to the climate of a new place; not acclimatized* ◇ ～保持 water and soil conservation; ～流失 soil erosion
【水汪汪】❶ full of water; very wet: 刚下过大雨,地里～的。*A heavy rain had fallen, and the fields were flooded.* ❷ (of children's or young women's eyes) bright and intelligent
【水网】a network of rivers, rivulets, lakes and ponds: ～地带 *an area crisscrossed with rivers, rivulets, lakes and ponds*
【水位】water level: 高(低)～ *high (low) water level* / 地下～ *water table; groundwater level* ◇ ～计 fluviograph
【水文】hydrology: ～测验 *hydrologic survey* / ～工作者 *hydrologist* / ～资料 *hydrological data* ◇ ～地理学 hydrography; ～地质学 hydrogeology;

～队 hydrological team；～年鉴 Water Year Book；～气象学 hydrometeorology；～图 hydrological map；～学 hydrology；～预报 hydrologic forecast；～站 hydrometric station；hydrologic station

【水污染】water pollution；water contamination

【水螅】［动］hydra

【水系】river system；hydrographic net

【水下】under water：～导弹 *submarine-based missile*

【水仙】［植］narcissus（the plant and its flower）

【水险】marine insurance

【水线】waterline

【水乡】a region of rivers and lakes

【水箱】water tank

【水泻】［医］watery diarrhoea

【水泄不通】not even a drop of water could trickle through；be watertight：挤得～ *be packed with people* / 围得～ *be so closely besieged that not a drop of water could trickle through*

【水榭】waterside pavilion

【水星】［天］Mercury

【水性】❶ ability in swimming：这姑娘的～很好。*This girl is a good swimmer*. ❷ the depth，currents and other characteristics of a river，lake，etc. ❸（of a woman）of easy virtue

【水性杨花】（of a woman）of easy virtue；a woman of loose morals；easy to seduce

【水袖】water sleeves（double white-silk sleeves attached to the cuffs of a costume，used in traditional Chinese opera）

【水锈】❶ scale；incrustation ❷ watermark（in water vessels）

【水选】seed or ore selection by immersion

【水靴】water boots

【水循环】hydrologic cycle；water cycle

【水压】hydraulic（or water）pressure ◇ ～机 hydraulic press

【水烟】shredded tobacco for water pipes：抽～ *smoke a water pipe* ◇ ～袋 water pipe

【水杨】［植］bigcatkin willow

【水杨酸】［化］salicylic acid ◇ ～钠 sodium salicylate

【水舀子】dipper；ladle；scoop（for water）

【水翼船】hydrofoil

【水银】［化］mercury；quicksilver ◇ ～灯 mercury-vapour lamp；～气压表［气］mercury（or mercurial）barometer；～温度计［气］mercury（or mercurial）thermometer；～柱 mercury column

【水印】（又作'水印木刻'）watercolour block printing；watermark

【水莹莹】（of eyes，etc.）radiant and crystal-clear；bright and clear

【水有源，树有根】every river has its source and every tree its roots—everything has its origin

【水域】waters；water area；a body of water：内陆～ *inland waters* / 国际～ *an international body of water*；*international waters*

【水源】❶ the source of a river；headwaters；waterhead：黄河的～ *the headwaters of the Yellow River* ❷ source of water：寻找～ *seek new sources of water*

【水运】water transport ◇ ～码头 a port handling river or ocean cargo

【水灾】flood；inundation

【水栽培】hydroponics；water culture

【水葬】water burial

【水蚤】water flea

【水藻】algae

【水泽】a region of rivers，lakes and marshes

【水闸】sluice；water gate

【水战】a battle on water

【水涨船高】when the river rises the boat goes up：通货一膨胀，物价就涨，～嘛。*Prices rise in proportion to inflation，like boats going up with the level of the water*.

【水针疗法】［中］acupuncture therapy with medicinal injection；liquid acupuncture

【水蒸气】steam；water vapour

【水至清则无鱼，人至察则无徒】water which is too clean has few fish；he who is too critical has few friends—one should not demand absolute purity

【水质】water quality ◇ ～保护［环保］water quality protection

【水蛭】leech

【水中捞月】fish for the moon—make impractical or vain efforts

【水肿】［医］oedema；dropsy

【水珠】（又作'水珠子'）〈口〉a drop of water

【水柱】water column

【水准】level；standard：高（低）于一般～ *above*（*below*）*average* ◇ ～点 bench mark；～面 level surface；level plane；～仪 surveyor's level

【水渍险】［经］with particular average（W. P. A.）

【水族】aquatic animals

【水族馆】aquarium

shuì

说 动 try to persuade：游说 ——另见 shuō

税 名 tax；duty：营业～ *business tax* / 进口（出口）～ *import*（*export*）*duty*

【税额】the amount of tax to be paid

【税法】tax law

【税负】tax burden：减轻～ *ease the tax burden*

【税后】after-tax：～承包 *after-tax contracting* / ～还贷 *after-tax payment of loans* / ～利润 *after-tax profit*

【税基】tax base

【税金】同〖税款〗

【税款】tax payment；taxation

【税率】tax rate；rate of taxation；tariff rate

【税目】tax items；taxable items

【税前】pre-tax；before tax：～还贷 *deduct loan principal payment from pre-tax profits*

【税收】tax revenue ◇ ～政策 tax policy
【税务局】tax bureau
【税务员】tax collector
【税源】source of taxes：防止～流失 *check the loss of tax sources*
【税则】tax regulations
【税政】tax administration
【税制】tax system；taxation：累进～ *progressive taxation*
【税种】tax category

睡 动 sleep：他～了。*He's gone to bed.* / 他～着了。*He's asleep.* / 一～就～到大天亮 *sleep like a log till broad daylight* / 他～得早起得也早。*He goes to bed early and gets up early.*
【睡袋】sleeping bag
【睡觉】sleep：该～了。*It's time to go to bed.* / 睡午觉 *take a nap after lunch* / 睡懒觉 *get up late；sleep in；sleep late*
【睡裤】pyjama trousers
【睡莲】[植] water lily
【睡帽】nightcap
【睡梦】sleep；slumber：一阵敲门声把他从～中惊醒了。*He was roused from sleep by a heavy pounding on the door.*
【睡眠】sleep：～不足 *not have enough sleep* ◇ ～疗法 [医] physiological sleep therapy
【睡魔】extreme sleepiness
【睡袍】nightgown；nightdress；nightie
【睡乡】dreamland：进入～ *fall asleep*
【睡醒】wake up
【睡眼惺忪】eyes still heavy with sleep；eyes still fogged with sleep
【睡衣】nightclothes；pyjamas
【睡椅】reclining chair；deck chair
【睡意】sleepiness；drowsiness：有几分～ *feel somewhat sleepy；be drowsy*

shǔn

吮 动 suck：～奶 *suck milk*
【吮吸】suck：～手指头 *suck fingers*
【吮痈舐痔】lick sb.'s ulcers and piles—debase oneself in trying to please sb. important or powerful

shùn

顺 Ⅰ 介 ❶ in the same direction as；with：～流而下 *go downstream* / ～时针方向 *clockwise* ❷ along：～着这条道儿走。*Follow this road.* / 水～着渠道流进地里。*Water runs along the channel to the fields.* Ⅱ 动 ❶ arrange；put in order：这篇文章还得～一～。*This essay needs polishing.* / 把这些讲义～一～，不要放得乱七八糟的。*Please put these teaching materials in order and don't leave them in a mess.* ❷ obey；yield to；act in submission to：他不对嘛，怎么能～着他呢？*How can we do as he wishes when he's obviously wrong?* ❸ fall in with；suit；agree with：顺意 ❹ (used at the close of a letter) take the opportunity to：～颂大安。*With best wishes for your health.* Ⅲ 形 (of writings) smooth；readable；clear and well-written Ⅳ 副 in sequence：顺延
【顺坝】[水] longitudinal dike
【顺便】(do sth.) in addition to what one is already doing，without much extra effort：你去图书馆的时候，～把我这本书还了吧。*When you go to the library，please return this book for me.*
【顺差】favourable balance；surplus：贸易～ *favourable balance of trade* / 国际收支～ *favourable balance of payments；balance of payments surplus*
【顺产】[医] natural labour
【顺畅】smooth and easy；unhindered：病人的呼吸渐渐～了。*The patient is beginning to breathe more easily.* / 保障城乡物资的～交流 *ensure the smooth flow of goods and materials between urban and rural areas*
【顺磁】[物] paramagnetic：～共振 *paramagnetic resonance* / ～性 *paramagnetism*
【顺次】in order；in succession；in proper sequence：按问题的轻重缓急～解决 *dispose of the problems one by one in order of importance and urgency*
【顺从】be obedient to；submit to；yield to
【顺带】同〖顺便〗
【顺当】〈口〉smooth；without a hitch；plain sailing：不可能每一件事都那么～。*Not everything could be that plain sailing.*
【顺导】guide or steer (a movement，etc.) along its proper course
【顺道儿】同〖顺路〗
【顺丁橡胶】[化] butadiene rubber
【顺耳】pleasing to the ear：不要只爱听～的话。*You shouldn't just listen to what pleases you.*
【顺访】visit (a place，person，etc.) on the way：总理在出访西欧归途中～了意大利。*On the journey back from his official visits to Western Europe，the Premier visited Italy in transit.*
【顺风】❶ have a favourable wind；have a tail wind：～行船 *sail with the wind* ❷ favourable wind；tail wind ◇ ～吹火 take advantage of favourable conditions；～转舵〈贬〉trim one's sails；take one's cue from changing conditions
【顺风耳】❶ a person in traditional Chinese novels who can hear voices a long way off ❷ a well-informed person
【顺服】obey；be obedient；be docile
【顺竿儿爬】take one's cue from sb. and say everything to please him
【顺光】[摄] frontlighting
【顺和】genial；gentle；affable
【顺脚】❶ (do sth.) on the way or without going out of one's way ❷ be a direct route：这么走太绕远儿，不～。*If you go that way，you'll be tak-*

ing a roundabout and much longer route.

【顺境】easy or favourable circumstances：身处～ *be in easy or favourable circumstances*

【顺口】❶ read smoothly：稿子经过这样一改，念起来就～多了。*After being touched up, the essay reads more smoothly*. ❷ say offhandedly：他也不想想就～答应了。*He agreed without thinking*. ❸〈方〉suit one's taste：这鱼我吃着很～。*I like the taste of this fish*. / 不知我这些菜你吃来～不～？*I wonder if my dishes are to your taste*.

【顺口搭音】echo what others say; chime in with others

【顺口溜】doggerel; jingle

【顺理成章】(of a statement, argument, etc.) logical; well reasoned

【顺利】smooth; successful; without a hitch：工作正在～进行。*The work is going on smoothly*. / 会议进行得很～。*The meeting went off without a hitch*.

【顺路】❶ on the way：我昨天回家时～去看了看李大爷。*I dropped in at Uncle Li's on my way home yesterday*. ❷ be a direct route：到王家庄这么走不～。*This is not the most direct route to Wangjiazhuang Village*.

【顺势】❶ take advantage of an opportunity (as provided by an opponent's reckless move)：他向旁边一闪，～把敌人摔倒了。*He dodged the enemy's assault and threw him to the ground*. ❷ conveniently; in passing

【顺势疗法】[医] homoeopathy

【顺手】❶ smooth; without a hitch; without difficulty：事情办得相当～。*It was done without a hitch*. ❷ conveniently; without extra trouble：出去时请～关上门。*Would you close the door when you go out*? ❸ (do sth.) as a natural sequence or simultaneously：我们扫完院子，～把房间也扫一扫好了。*After sweeping the courtyard, we might as well clean the rooms*. ❹ handy; convenient and easy to use：这把扳子使起来挺～。*This spanner is very handy*.

【顺手牵羊】lead off a goat in passing —pick up sth. on the sly; walk off with sth.

【顺水】downstream; with the stream ◇ ～人情 a favour done at little or no cost; ～推舟 push the boat along with the current—make use of an opportunity to gain one's end

【顺遂】(of things) go well; go smoothly

【顺藤摸瓜】follow the vine to get the melon—track down sb. or sth. by following clues

【顺心】be satisfactory：诸事～。*All is well*. / 他父亲晚年过得挺～。*His father spent the evening of his life in happiness*.

【顺行】[天] direct motion

【顺序】❶ sequence; order：文物按年代～展出。*The cultural relics are displayed in chronological sequence*. / 按字母～排列 *in alphabetical order* ❷ in proper order; in turn

【顺延】postpone：运动会定于六月四日举行，遇雨～。*The sports meet is scheduled for June 4th—subject to postponement in case of rain*.

【顺眼】pleasing to the eye：看着不～ *be offensive to the eye; be an eyesore*

【顺应】comply with; conform to：～历史发展的潮流 *conform to the historical trend of the times; go with the tide of historical development*

【顺证】[中] a serious case which improves steadily

【顺之者昌，逆之者亡】Those who submit will prosper, those who resist shall perish.

【顺嘴】同〖顺口〗

瞬 名 wink; twinkling

【瞬时】instantaneous ◇ ～速度 instantaneous velocity; ～性 instantaneity; ～值 instantaneous value

【瞬息】twinkling：～间 *in the twinkling of an eye*

【瞬息万变】undergoing a myriad changes in the twinkling of an eye; fast changing：股票市场～。*There are so many unpredictable fluctuations on the stock exchange*.

shuō

说 Ⅰ 动 ❶ speak; talk; say：他会～法语。*He speaks French*. / 请～慢一点儿。*Please speak more slowly*. / ～得多做得少 *talk much but do little* / 你～得很对。*What you say is quite true*. / 那未免～得太轻了。*That's putting it too mildly*. ❷ explain：他～了又～，我还是不懂。*He explained and explained, but I still couldn't understand*. / 我一～他就明白了。*I told him how and he caught on at once*. ❸ scold：他父亲～了他一顿。*His father gave him a scolding (or talking-to)*. ❹ act as matchmaker：给他～个媳妇儿 *find a wife for him* ❺ refer to; indicate：你的话是～谁呢？*Who did your remarks refer to*? Ⅱ 名 theory; teachings; doctrine：著书立说 ——另见 shuì

【说白】spoken parts in an opera

【说不得】❶ unspeakable; unmentionable ❷ scandalous ❸〈方〉have no say; have to comply

【说不定】perhaps; maybe：～她已经走了。*Maybe she's already left*. / ～要下雨。*It looks as if it might rain*.

【说不过】cannot outspeak sb.; cannot match sb.'s eloquence

【说不过去】cannot be justified or explained away：条件这样好，再不增产，可～。*With such favourable conditions, we'll have no excuse if we fail to increase output*.

【说不好】be unable to say for certain; not be certain; can't say：我～她肯不肯来我们这儿工作。*I can't say whether she would like to come and work here or not*.

【说不来】❶ cannot get along (with sb.)：我跟他～。*I don't see eye to eye with him*. ❷〈方〉not know how to put it

【说不清】be unable to explain clearly：到底发生了

什么事,谁也～。*Nobody can explain clearly what really happened.*

【说不上】❶ cannot say; cannot tell: 他也～问题在哪儿。*He can't put his finger on what's wrong.* / 我～他来不来。*I can't say whether he is coming or not.* ❷ not worth mentioning: 这些材料～有什么史料价值。*These materials can't be said to have much value as historical records.*

【说不下去】be unable to finish what one is saying

【说曹操曹操就到】mention Cao Cao and there he is—talk of the devil (and he will appear)

【说长道短】gossip: 在她身上找不出一点让人家～的地方。*There was not a single thing about her that one could find fault with.*

【说唱】a genre of popular entertainment consisting mainly of talking and singing, e.g. comic dialogue, dagu (大鼓), etc.

【说穿】tell what sth. really is; reveal; disclose: ～了,无非是想推卸责任。*To put it bluntly, this is shifting responsibility.*

【说辞】excuse; pretext

【说大话】brag; boast; talk big

【说到底】in the final analysis; at bottom: 偏差和片面性的产生,～,是主观认识脱离客观实际。*In the final analysis, wrong and one-sided thinking is caused by the separation of subjective thinking from objective reality.*

【说到钱,便无缘】To speak of a loan is to put an end to friendship.

【说到做到】do what one says; match one's deeds to one's words; live up to one's word

【说道】(shuōdào) say (the words quoted): 少先队员～:"我们要向雷锋叔叔学习。"*"We must learn from Uncle Lei Feng," said the Young Pioneer.*

【说道】(shuōdao)〈方〉❶ say; tell: 你把刚才听到的广播给大家～～。*Tell us what you heard over the radio just now.* ❷ talk over; discuss: 我跟他～～再作决定。*I'll talk it over with him before I make a decision.* ❸〈方〉what lies behind sth.; reason: 他为什么突然改变主意,这里头肯定有～。*There must be a reason for his sudden change of mind.*

【说得过去】be justifiable; be passable: 他的英语发音还～。*His English pronunciation is passable.*

【说得来】❶ can get along; be on good terms: 找一个跟他～的人去动员他。*Get someone who is on good terms with him to try and persuade him.* ❷ have a glib tongue

【说定】settle; agree on: 这件事基本上已经～了。*The matter is as good as settled.*

【说东道西】chatter away on a variety of things

【说短论长】gossip

【说法】(shuōfǎ) expound Buddhist teachings

【说法】(shuōfa) ❶ way of saying a thing; wording; formulation: 换一个～ *say it in another way* / 这个意思可以有两种～。*This idea can be formulated in two different ways.* ❷ statement; version; argument: 那种～是不对的。*That's a false statement.* / 关于那件事,各人～不同。*Different people have different versions of the incident.*

【说服】persuade; convince; prevail on; talk sb. over: 要耐心～他。*Talk to him patiently to bring him round.* / 她的话很有～力。*What she says is very convincing.*

【说好】come to an agreement or understanding: 我已经跟他～了,明天一块儿去看足球赛。*I've arranged to go with him to tomorrow's football match.*

【说好说歹】use every possible argument to convince sb.

【说合】❶ bring two (or more) parties together: ～亲事 *make a match* ❷ talk over; discuss ❸ 同〖说和〗

【说和】mediate a settlement; compose a quarrel: 你去给他们～～。*Try to patch things up between them, will you?*

【说黑道白】criticize irresponsibly or thoughtlessly

【说话】❶ speak; talk; say: 还是让事实来～吧。*Let the facts speak for themselves.* / ～算数 *honour one's word; mean what one says* ❷ chat; talk: 我找他～儿去。*I'd like to have a chat with him.* / 我们正说着话,他进来了。*We were talking when he came in.* ❸ gossip; talk: 你这样干,别人当然要～。*Considering what you've done, it's natural that people should be talking.*

【说黄道黑】同〖数黑论黄〗

【说谎】tell a lie; lie

【说教】❶ deliver a sermon; preach ❷ preachify

【说开】❶ explain clearly: 你还是把事情的原委跟他～了,免得他猜疑。*You'd better explain clearly to him how all this came about, so as not to leave him in doubt.* ❷ (of words or expressions) be in current use: 这个词儿已经～了,大家都懂得。*This word is in current use, and everybody understands it.*

【说客】❶ a person often sent to win sb. over or enlist his support through persuasion ❷ a persuasive talker

【说来】come to speak of it: ～都是老朋友。*Come to speak of it, we are all old friends.* ◇ ～话长 it's a long story; ～说去 repeat over and over again

【说理】❶ argue; reason things out: 咱们找他～去。*Let's go and reason things out with him.* ❷ (usu. used in the negative) listen to reason; be reasonable: 你这个人～不～? *Won't you listen to reason?* or *How could you be so unreasonable?*

【说漏嘴】let slip a remark; make a slip of the tongue: 我一句话说漏了嘴,把事情捅出去了。*I made a slip of the tongue and gave the show away.*

【说媒】act as a matchmaker

【说明】❶ explain; illustrate: ～机器的用法 *explain how a machine works* / 举例～ *illustrate by examples* / ～理由 *give reasons* ❷ show; prove: 事实充分～这种做法是正确的。*The results show clearly that this procedure is correct.* ❸ explana-

tion; directions; caption: 图片下边附有～。*There is a caption under the picture.*
【说明书】(a booklet of) directions; (technical) manual; synopsis (of a play or film)
【说明文】expository writing; exposition
【说破】lay bare; reveal
【说破嘴】talk till one is hoarse; talk oneself hoarse: 你～他也不会听你的。*He won't listen to you even if you talk yourself hoarse.*
【说千道万】keep on stating one's point
【说亲】act as a matchmaker
【说情】plead for mercy for sb.; intercede for sb.
【说三道四】make irresponsible remarks
【说啥】〈口〉no matter what one says: ～他也不会同意的。*No matter what you say to him, he won't agree.*
【说时迟,那时快】in the twinkling of an eye; in an instant
【说是】be said to; be supposed to; they say: ～留学生,可不知道他在哪儿留的学。*He is said to have studied abroad, but I don't know what country he studied in.*
【说书】storytelling
【说死】fix definitely; make it definite: 咱们～了,六点钟见面。*Let's make it definite—we'll meet at 6 o'clock.* / 咱们先别～吧。*Let's leave the question open for the present.*
【说头儿】❶ something to talk about: 问题已经解决了,没什么～了。*Now that the problem is solved, nothing remains to be said.* ❷ excuse: 你批评他,他总有～。*Whenever you criticize him, he always has an excuse.*
【说妥】come to an agreement
【说戏】(of a film or play director) explain (to one or more actors) how a part or a scene is to be acted
【说闲话】❶ gossip; grumble: 有意见当面提,别在背后～。*If you have any complaints, make them openly. Don't grumble behind our backs.* ❷ chat: 她常来我家说个闲话什么的。*She often drops in to have a chat.*
【说项】put in a good word for sb.; intercede for sb.
【说笑】chatting and laughing: 这时满屋子的人又说又笑,兴高采烈。*The room was then full of people chatting animatedly and laughing.*
【说一不二】mean what one says; stand by one's word: 老班长是～的,他答应的事一定能办到。*The old squad leader is a man of his word; he never makes a promise he cannot keep.*
【说着玩儿】be joking; not be serious in saying sth.
【说嘴】❶ brag; boast: 咱们谁也别～。*Let's not have any boasting.* ❷〈方〉argue; quarrel: 好跟人～ *like to quarrel with people*

shuò

烁 形 bright; shining: 闪烁
【烁亮】dazzling; brilliant; resplendent: 电灯把大街照得～。*The street was ablaze with lights.*
【烁烁】glitter; sparkle

铄 动〈书〉❶ melt (metal, etc.) ❷ waste away; weaken
【铄石流金】(hot enough to) make rocks and metals melt—sweltering

朔 名 ❶ new moon ❷ the first day of the lunar month ❸ north: ～方 *the North* / ～风 *north wind*
【朔日】the first day of the lunar month
【朔望】the first and the fifteenth day of the lunar month; syzygy
【朔望月】[气] lunar month; lunation; synodic month
【朔月】new moon

硕 形 large: ～大 *very large*
【硕大无朋】of enormous size; huge; gigantic: 整个地球可以想像为一块～的磁石。*The earth may be thought of as a gigantic magnet.*
【硕果】rich fruits; great achievements: ～累累 *numerous significant achievements*
【硕果仅存】the sole rare survival
【硕士】master: ～学位 *master's degree*
【硕学通儒】a wise and learned scholar

数 副 frequently; repeatedly ——另见 shǔ; shù
【数见不鲜】be a common occurrence; be nothing new
【数脉】[中] rapid pulse (of more than 90 beats per minute)

蒴 名 capsule: 芝麻～ *sesame capsule*
【蒴果】[植] capsule

sī

司 Ⅰ 动 take charge of; attend to; manage: 各～其事。*Each attends to his own duties.* / 各种组织要各～其职。*Let each of the various organizations perform its own functions.* Ⅱ 名 department (under a ministry): 外交部礼宾～ *the Protocol Department of the Ministry of Foreign Affairs*
【司泵员】pump man; pumper
【司乘人员】drivers and attendants (on a bus or train)
【司舵】❶ be at the helm; steer a boat ❷ helmsman; steersman
【司法】administration of justice; judicature ◇ ～部门 judicial department; judiciary; ～机关 judicial organ; ～鉴定 expert testimony (or evidence); ～权 judicial powers
【司号】[军] ❶ sound a bugle ❷ bugler; trumpeter ◇ ～员 [军] bugler; trumpeter
【司机】driver; chauffeur: 火车～ *engine driver*;

locomotive engineer
【司空见惯】a common sight；a common occurrence
【司令】commander；commanding officer ◇ ～部 headquarters；command；～台 review stand；～员 commander；commanding officer
【司炉】stoker；fireman
【司马昭之心，路人皆知】Sima Zhao's ill intent is known to all—the villain's design is obvious
【司售人员】bus drivers and conductors (ticket collectors)
【司务】❶ a petty official in charge of miscellaneous duties (in Ming and Qing times) ❷ craftsman；workman：厨～ *cook* ◇ ～长 mess officer；company quartermaster
【司线员】［体］linesman
【司药】pharmacist；druggist；chemist
【司仪】master of ceremonies
【司钻】(head) driller：副～ *assistant driller*

丝 Ⅰ〖名〗❶ silk ❷ a threadlike thing：蜘蛛～ *a thread spun by a spider*；*cobweb* / 铜～ *copper wire* / 把土豆切成细～儿 *cut the potatoes into fine shreds*；*shred the potatoes* ❸ a tiny bit；trace：一～不差 *not a bit of difference* / 她脸上没有一～笑容。*There isn't a trace of a smile on her face.* / 一～风也没有。*There isn't a breath of air.* Ⅱ〖量〗a thread or shred of：一～亮光 *a thread of light* / 这盘菜里一～儿肉也见不着。*Not a single shred of meat can you find in this dish.*
【丝虫】filaria (a parasitic worm) ◇ ～病 filariasis
【丝绸】silk cloth；silk ◇ ～之路［史］the Silk Road
【丝带】silk ribbon；silk braid；silk sash
【丝杠】［机］guide screw；leading screw ◇ ～车床 leading screw lathe
【丝糕】steamed millet or corn cake
【丝瓜】towel gourd；dishcloth gourd ◇ ～络 loofah；vegetable sponge
【丝光】the silky lustre of mercerized cotton fabrics ◇ ～机 mercerizing range；～纱线 mercerized yarn
【丝毫】(usu. used in the negative) the slightest amount or degree；a bit；a particle；a shred；an iota：拿不出～证据 *cannot provide a shred of evidence* / ～不差 *not err by a hair's breadth*；*tally in every detail*；*be just right*
【丝极】［电子］filament
【丝萝】〈文〉the bond of marriage：永结～ *seal an everlasting bond of marriage*
【丝绵】silk floss；silk wadding
【丝绒】velvet；velour
【丝丝入扣】(mostly of a writing or artistic performance) (done) with meticulous care and flawless artistry
【丝丝拉拉】off and on；intermittently：小雨～地下了几天。*It has been drizzling off and on for days.*
【丝袜】silk stockings (or socks)
【丝网】［刷］silk screen ◇ ～印刷 screen printing；～印刷机 screen process press
【丝弦】❶ silk string (for a musical instrument) ❷ a Hebei provincial opera
【丝线】silk thread (for sewing, embroidery, etc.)；silk yarn
【丝织品】❶ silk fabrics ❷ silk knit goods
【丝竹】❶ traditional stringed and woodwind instruments：～乐 *ensemble of such instruments* ❷ music
【丝状】filiform
【丝锥】［机］tap：粗制～ *taper tap* / 中～ *second tap* / 精～ *bottoming tap*

私 〖形〗❶ personal；private：～信 *personal* (*or private*) *letter* ❷ selfish：无私 ❸ secret；private：～话 *confidential talk* ❹ illicit；illegal：～卖违禁品 *illicit sale of contraband goods*
【私奔】elope
【私弊】corrupt practices
【私藏】❶ a private collection ❷ keep or possess illegally：～枪支 *possess firearms illegally*
【私产】private property
【私娼】unlicensed (or unregistered) prostitute
【私仇】personal enmity (or grudge)：报～ *satisfy a personal grudge*
【私党】a personal clique or faction
【私邸】private residence (of a high-ranking official)
【私底下】in private；in secret
【私法】［法］private law
【私贩】smuggle；traffic in contraband goods
【私房】(sīfáng) a privately owned house or building；private residence
【私房】(sīfang) ❶ private savings：～钱 *private savings of a family member* ❷ confidential：谈～话 *exchange confidences*
【私访】(of officials) go incognito among the people to make investigations
【私愤】personal spite：泄～ *vent personal spite*
【私股】private shares (in a joint state-private enterprise)
【私孩子】〈口〉a child born out of wedlock；illegitimate child
【私函】private letter
【私活】private job done during work hours instead of in one's spare time：这个车间里没有人利用上班时间干～。*No one in this workshop uses work hours to do private jobs.*
【私货】smuggled goods；contraband goods
【私家】privately owned or engaged：～车 *private car* / ～车道 *drive*；*driveway* / ～侦探 *private detective*；*private investigator*
【私见】❶ personal prejudice ❷ personal opinion
【私交】personal friendship
【私立】privately run；private：～学校 *private school*
【私利】private (or selfish) interests；personal gain：图～ *pursue private ends*；*seek personal*

gain / 不谋～ *seek no personal gain*

【私了】settle privately; settle out of court: 这事你看是～还是公了? *Would you prefer to settle the matter in court or out of court?*

【私囊】private purse: 饱～ *line one's pockets; feather one's nest*

【私念】selfish motives (or ideas)

【私情】personal relationships: 不徇～ *not swayed by personal considerations*

【私人】❶ private; personal: ～访问 *private visit* / ～关系 *personal relations; personal connections* ❷ one's own man: 任用～ *fill a post with one's own man; practise nepotism* ◇ ～代表 personal representative; ～经济 private sector of the economy; ～劳动[经] individual labour; ～秘书 private secretary; ～企业 private enterprise

【私商】❶ privately owned shop ❷ businessman; merchant; trader

【私设公堂】set up an illegal court; set up a kangaroo court

【私生活】private life: 别打听别人的～。*Don't pry into the private life of others.*

【私生子】a child born out of wedlock; illegitimate child

【私事】private (or personal) affairs

【私塾】old-style private school

【私逃】abscond

【私通】❶ have secret communication with: ～敌人 *have secret communication with the enemy* ❷ have illicit intercourse; commit adultery

【私图】one's personal scheme or attempt

【私下】(又作'私下里') in private; in secret: ～商议 *discuss a matter in private*

【私相授受】privately give and privately accept; illegally pass things between individuals; make an illicit transfer: 拿公家的东西～ *illicit transfer of public property*

【私心】selfish motives (or ideas); selfishness ◇ ～杂念 selfish ideas and personal considerations; selfish considerations

【私刑】illegal punishment (meted out by a kangaroo court); lynching

【私行】do sth. in a private capacity or on one's own initiative: ～释放 *set sb. free without official sanction*

【私蓄】personal or private savings

【私营】privately owned; privately run (or operated); private: ～工商业 *privately owned industrial and commercial enterprises* / ～企业 *private enterprise* / ～经济 *the private sector of the economy*

【私有】privately owned; private: 绝不能把公家财产占为～。*One should never make public property one's private possession.* ◇ ～财产 private property; ～观念 private ownership mentality; ～化 privatization; denationalization; ～制 private ownership (of means of production)

【私语】❶ whisper ❷ confidence

【私欲】selfish desire

【私运】smuggle: ～毒品 *smuggle drugs*

【私章】personal seal; signet

【私自】privately; secretly; without permission: 本阅览室参考书不得～携出。*No reference books are to be taken out of the reading room without permission.*

咝 象 (the sound of flying shells and bullets) whistle: 子弹～～～地从头顶上飞过。*Bullets whistled overhead.*

思 Ⅰ 动 ❶ think; consider; deliberate: 多～ *think more* ❷ think of; long for: ～亲 *think of one's parents with affection* Ⅱ 名 thought; thinking: 文思 / 哀思

【思潮】❶ trend of thought; ideological trend: 文艺～ *trends of thought in art and literature* ❷ thoughts: ～起伏 *disquieting thoughts surging in one's mind*

【思忖】〈书〉ponder; consider

【思凡】(of an immortal or of a monk or a nun) long for the world; yearn for the company of the opposite sex

【思过】ponder over one's mistakes; make an introspection into one's faults

【思旧】think fondly of past times or old acquaintances

【思考】think deeply; ponder over; reflect on: ～问题 *ponder a problem* / 独立～ *think things out for oneself; think independently*

【思恋】think fondly of; long for: ～故土 *think fondly of one's native land*

【思量】consider: 反复～ *turn sth. over and over in one's mind*

【思路】train of thought; thinking: 打断～ *interrupt one's train of thought* / 她的～很清楚。*She thinks very clearly.*

【思虑】consider; contemplate; deliberate: 他～周到。*He considers everything carefully.*

【思慕】think of sb. with respect; admire

【思念】think of; long for; miss: ～战友 *long for one's comrades-in-arms*

【思如泉涌】ideas teeming in one's mind

【思索】think deeply; ponder: 用心～ *do some hard thinking* / 周密地～ *consider carefully* / 我一夜没睡着,反复～这个问题。*I lay awake all night, turning the problem over and over in my mind.*

【思维】❶ thought; thinking: ～方式 *mode of thinking* ❷ think; consider: 再三～ *think over and over again*

【思贤若渴】(of a ruler) thirst for (or long for) the assistance of wise men

【思乡】be homesick

【思想】thought; thinking; idea; ideology: ～自由 *freedom of thought* / 有～准备 *be mentally prepared* / ～内容好 *have good ideological content* / 解除～顾虑 *free one's mind of misgivings* / ～跟不上 *lag behind in one's understanding* ◇ ～包袱

sth. weighing on one's mind; ～动向 ideological trend; ～斗争 ideological struggle; mental struggle (or conflict); ～方法 method (or mode, way) of thinking; ～改造 ideological remoulding; ～高度 ideological plane; intellectual level; ～疙瘩 mental block; hang-up; ～根源 underlying causes of words and deeds; ～工作 ideological work; ～家 thinker; ～检查 check on one's thinking; examine one's wrong ideas; ～僵化 rigid thinking; inflexibity of thought; ～教育 ideological education; ～禁区 ideologically forbidden zone; ～境界 ideological level; ～觉悟 political consciousness (or awareness); ～烙印 ideological imprint; deep influences on (one's) thinking; ～路线 ideological line; ～体系 ideological system; ideology; ～问题 a problem arising from erroneous thinking; ideological problem; ～武装 ideological weapon; ～性 ideological content (or level); ～修养 ideological cultivation (degree of ideological sophistication); ～意识 ideology; ～政治工作 ideological and political work; ～作风 one's way of thinking, workstyle, and life-style

【思想库】think tank, brain trust ——另见〖智囊团〗

【思绪】❶ train of thought; thinking: ～纷乱 *a confused state of mind; a confused train of thought* ❷ feeling: ～不宁 *feel perturbed*

斯 Ⅰ 代 〈书〉 this: ～时 *at this moment* / ～人 *this person* / 余生于～，长于～。*I was born and brought up here.* Ⅱ 连 〈书〉 then; thus

【斯堪的纳维亚半岛】the Scandinavian Peninsula

【斯拉夫人】Slav

【斯里兰卡】Sri Lanka ◇ ～人 Sri Lankan

【斯洛伐克】Slovakia ◇ ～人 Slovak; Slovakian; ～语 Slovak (language)

【斯瓦希里语】Swahili (language)

【斯威士兰】Swaziland ◇ ～人 Swazi

【斯文】(sīwén) 〈书〉 ❶ culture ❷ men of letters; scholars; literati ◇ ～败类 scum of the literati; ～扫地 scholarly dignity swept into the dust

【斯文】(sīwen) refined; gentle: 他说话挺～的。*He's a soft-spoken person.*

锶 名 [化] strontium (Sr)

厮 副 with each other; together: 厮混

【厮缠】pester: 孩子～住他爹妈要买个机器人。*The boy kept pestering his parents for a toy robot.*

【厮打】wrestle; grapple; tussle

【厮混】fool around (or about) with sb.; play around (or about) with sb.: 他整天和一些不三不四的人～。*He fools around all the time with some rather dubious fellows.*

【厮闹】play; romp; frolic: 在马路上～打逗是很危险的。*It is very dangerous to play in the street.*

【厮拼】fight; battle it out: 我们别参与，让他们俩去～。*We should not get involved but let the two of them fight it out.*

【厮杀】fight at close quarters (with weapons)

【厮熟】be well acquainted; know each other well; become close: 那残疾孩子渐渐和我～起来了。*The handicapped child became close to me.* / 他们两人已经很～了。*They are already very close.*

撕 动 tear; rip: 把信～开 *rip open a letter* / ～得粉碎 *tear to shreds* / 从日历上～下一页 *tear a page from the calendar* / ～下假面具 *tear off the mask; unmask* / 上衣～了。*The jacket is torn.*

【撕毁】tear up; tear to shreds: ～协定(条约) *tear up an agreement (a treaty); tear an agreement (a treaty) to shreds*

【撕票】(of kidnappers) kill the hostage

【撕破】tear; rip: 这种料子容易～。*This material tears easily.* / 衬衫～了。*The shirt is torn.*

【撕破脸】put aside all considerations of face; not spare sb.'s sensibilities

【撕纸】paper-tear picture (folk art): ～不动刀剪，仅用手去撕。*Paper-tear pictures are not made with knife or scissors but by tearing with the hands.*

嘶 Ⅰ 动 〈书〉 neigh: 人喊马～ *men shouting and horses neighing* Ⅱ 形 hoarse: 声嘶力竭

【嘶喊】shout; yell

【嘶叫】❶ shout; yell; scream: 她吓得尖声～起来。*She shrieked (or screamed) with terror.* ❷ (of horses) neigh; whinny; (of donkeys) bray

【嘶鸣】(of horses, donkeys, etc.) neigh; whinny; bray: 战马～。*The war-horses neighed.*

【嘶哑】hoarse: 他讲话过多，嗓子都～了。*He has talked himself hoarse.*

sǐ

死 Ⅰ 动 die; be dead: 这次车祸～了五人。*The accident took five people's lives.* / ～一般的寂静 *a deathly stillness* / 被打～ *be beaten to death* / 我差点没笑～。*I just about died laughing.* Ⅱ 副 ❶ to the death: 死战 ❷ extremely; to death: 高兴～了 *be extremely happy* / 累～了 *be tired to death; be dog-tired* / 渴得要～ *be parched with thirst; be dying for a drink* / ～咸～咸的 *terribly salty* / ～沉～沉的 *awfully heavy* / ～顽固 *die-hard* ❸ (used before verbs in the negative) stubbornly; adamantly; unyieldingly: ～不改悔 *be absolutely unrepentant; be incorrigible* / ～不要脸 *be dead to all feelings of shame; be utterly shameless* Ⅲ 形 ❶ implacable; deadly: 死对头 ❷ fixed; rigid; inflexible: ～规矩 *a rigid rule* / ～教条 *lifeless dogma* ❸ impassable; closed: 把漏洞堵～ *plug the holes; stop up loopholes* / 窗户钉～了。*The window has been nailed fast.*

【死板】rigid; stiff; inflexible: 动作～ *stiff movements* / 表情～ *an expressionless face* / 办事～ *work in a mechanical way* / ～的公式 *stereotyped formula*

【死别】be parted by death; part forever

【死不瞑目】not close one's eyes when one dies—die with a grievance or everlasting regret；die discontent

【死不死，活不活】❶ those that should die，do not，those that are alive live poorly；benefit no one：这个政策搞得企业～的。*This policy is making it difficult for all enterprises*. ❷〈字〉neither dead nor living；〈喻〉dejected；listless；dispirited：你看他那个～的样子。*Look how dejected he is*!

【死产】[医] stillbirth

【死沉】silent as the grave；still as death：战地一片～的气氛。*A deathlike silence reigned over the battlefield*.

【死沉沉】❶ heavy as lead；extremely heavy ❷ silent as the grave；still as death ❸ glum；sullen；gloomy：脸色～的 *look glum*；*put on a sullen countenance*

【死党】sworn followers；diehard followers

【死得其所】die a worthy death：我们为人民而死，就是～。*When we die for the people it is a worthy death*.

【死等】wait indefinitely：我们不能在这里～，应该派人去打听一下，看出了什么事。*We can't wait here indefinitely. We should send someone to find out what's happened*.

【死敌】deadly enemy；mortal enemy；implacable foe

【死地】a fatal position；deathtrap

【死读书】study mechanically；rely on book learning rather than practical experience；be bookish

【死对头】deadly enemy；irreconcilable opponent

【死而后已】until one's dying day；to the end of one's days ——另见〖鞠躬尽瘁，死而后已〗

【死工夫】hard persevering work；sheer hard work：你想通过考试，不下～是不行的。*You won't pass the exam unless you put in some real hard work*.

【死光】❶ death ray ❷ all die

【死鬼】(usu. used in cursing or jocularly) devil：你这个～，刚才跑到哪儿去了？*You devil*！*Where have you been all this while*？

【死海】the Dead Sea

【死耗】news of sb.'s death

【死胡同】blind alley；dead end

【死缓】[法]（〈略〉全称为'判处死刑、缓期二年执行'）death sentence with a two-year reprieve and forced labour；stay of execution

【死灰】cold ashes (of an extinguished fire)；dead ashes；burnt-out cinders

【死灰复燃】〈贬〉dying cinders glowing again—resurgence；revival

【死活】❶ life or death；fate：不顾人民～的政府早晚要被人民推翻。*A government which doesn't give a thought to the welfare of the people will sooner or later be overthrown*. ❷〈口〉anyway；simply：他～不让我走。*I wanted to go*，*but he simply wouldn't hear of it*.

【死火山】extinct volcano

【死机】[计] hang；hang-up

【死记】memorize mechanically；learn by rote；learn without comprehension ◇ ～硬背 memorize mechanically；learn by rote；learn without comprehension

【死忌】death anniversary

【死寂】〈书〉deathly stillness：夜深了，山谷里一片～。*As night wore on*，*a deathly silence filled the valley*.

【死角】❶ [军] dead angle；dead space ❷ a spot as yet untouched by a trend，political movement，etc.

【死结】a fast knot

【死劲儿】〈口〉❶ all one's strength；all one's might：大家用～推，才把车子推出泥坑。*Using all their strength*，*they pushed the cart out of the mud*. ❷ with all one's strength (or might)；with might and main；for all one's worth：～跑 *run for all one's worth* / ～盯住他 *watch him closely*

【死静】deathly silent；deathly still

【死扣儿】a fast knot

【死库容】[水] minimum volume of water a reservoir must have for normal operation

【死拉活拽】〈口〉drag sb. along against his will；drag by force

【死老虎】a dead tiger—a man who has lost his power and influence

【死里逃生】escape by the skin of one's teeth；have a narrow escape；barely escape with one's life

【死力】❶ all one's strength：出～ *exert one's utmost effort* ❷ with all one's strength：～抵抗 *resist with might and main*；*fight tooth and nail*

【死路】❶ blind alley ❷ the road to ruin (or destruction)

【死马当做活马医】doctor a dead horse as if it were still alive—make every possible effort；not give up for lost

【死面】unleavened dough

【死命】❶ doom；death：制敌于～ *send the enemy to his doom*；*have the enemy by the throat* ❷ desperately：～挣扎 *struggle desperately*

【死难】die in an accident or a political incident (esp. for a just cause)：～烈士 *martyr*

【死脑筋】one-track mind

【死皮赖脸】thick-skinned and hard to shake off；brazen and unreasonable

【死棋】❶ a dead piece in a game of chess ❷ a hopeless case；a stupid move

【死气沉沉】lifeless；spiritless；stagnant

【死气白赖】〈方〉pestering people endlessly

【死契】irrevocable title deed

【死囚】convict sentenced to death；convict awaiting execution

【死球】[体] dead ball

【死去活来】〈口〉half dead；only half alive；hovering between life and death：被打得～ *be beaten half dead*；*be beaten within an inch of one's life*；*be brutally beaten* / 哭得～ *cry oneself half dead*; *cry one's heart* (*or eyes*) *out*

【死伤】the dead and the wounded; casualties

【死神】Death (personified)

【死生有命,富贵在天】Life and death are a matter of Destiny; Wealth and honour depend on Heaven.

【死尸】corpse; dead body

【死守】❶ defend to the death; defend to the last; make a last-ditch defence: ～阵地 *defend the position to the last* ❷ obstinately cling to; rigidly adhere to

【死水】stagnant water

【死说活说】〈口〉beg and beg; try every means to persuade: 我～也没说动她的心。*In spite of all my persuasions, she remained unmoved.*

【死胎】[医] stillborn foetus; stillbirth

【死土】[农] dead soil

【死亡】death; doom: 挣扎在～线上 *struggle for existence on the verge of death* ◇ ～率 death rate; mortality

【死无对证】be totally devoid of evidence (because of the death of the principal witness, etc.); the witness, if any, is dead; dead men tell no tales

【死无葬身之地】die without a place for burial—come to a bad end

【死心】drop the idea forever; have no more illusions about the matter: 你还是死了这条心吧。*You'd better give up the idea altogether.*

【死心塌地】be dead set; be hell-bent: ～跟他走的只是一小撮。*Only a handful of people were dead set on following him.*

【死心眼儿】❶ stubborn; as obstinate as a mule ❷ a person with a one-track mind

【死信】❶ dead letter ❷ news of sb.'s death

【死刑】[法] death penalty; death sentence; capital punishment

【死讯】news of sb.'s death

【死因】cause of death: 查明他的～ *find out the cause of his death*

【死硬】❶ stiff; inflexible ❷ very obstinate; diehard ◇ ～派 diehards

【死有余辜】(used when denouncing a person guilty of the most heinous of crimes) Even death would be too good for him; Even death would not expiate all his crimes.

【死于非命】die an unnatural (or a violent) death: 他遭敌人杀害,～。*He died a violent death, murdered by an enemy.*

【死战】❶ a life-and-death struggle or battle ❷ fight to the death

【死仗】tough (or hard-fought) battle

【死者】the dead; the deceased; the departed

【死症】incurable disease

【死猪不怕开水烫】a dead pig fears not scalding water—be impervious to; oblivious of; know no better

【死罪】capital offence (or crime)

sì

巳 [名] the sixth of the twelve Earthly Branches (地支)

【巳时】the period of the day from 9 a.m. to 11 a.m.

四 [数] four

【四倍体】[生] tetraploid

【四边】(on) four sides: ～儿围着篱笆 *with a fence running all round*

【四边形】quadrilateral

【四不像】❶ [动] David's deer; mi-lu ❷ nondescript; neither fish nor fowl

【四重唱】[音] (vocal) quartet

【四重奏】[音] (instrumental) quartet: 弦乐～ *string quartet*

【四出】go hither and thither; go from place to place; go around: ～寻求资助 *go around seeking financial support*

【四处】all around; in all directions; everywhere: ～逃窜 *flee in all directions* / ～奔走 *go hither and thither* / ～寻找 *search high and low; look into every hole and corner*

【四大】[宗] (佛教) the four elements—earth, water, fire, and wind

【四叠体】[生理] corpora quadrigemina

【四方】❶ the four directions (north, south, east, west); all sides; all quarters: ～响应。*Response came from every quarter.* ❷ square; cubic: 一个～的盒子 *a square box* / 一块四四方方的木头 *a wooden cube*

【四方步】leisurely and measured steps

【四分五裂】fall apart; be rent by disunity; be all split up; disintegrate: 内部～。*The ranks are all split up* (*or disintegrating*).

【四分音符】[音] crotchet; quarter note

【四个现代化】the Four Modernizations (i.e. of industry, agriculture, defence, and science and technology)

【四顾】look around (or about): ～无人 *look around and find no one in sight*

【四海】the four seas; the whole country; the whole world ◇ ～升平 peace in the world; ～为家 make one's home wherever one is; ～之内皆兄弟 within the four seas all men are brothers

【四害】the four pests (i.e. rats, bedbugs, flies and mosquitoes)

【四合院儿】siheyuanr, a compound with houses around a square courtyard; quadrangle

【四呼】[语音] the four classes of syllables (set up according to the form of the final 韵母; i.e. 开口呼, 齐齿呼, 合口呼, and 撮口呼)

【四胡】[音] sihu, a four-stringed bowed instrument

【四化】〈略〉见〖四个现代化〗

【四环素】[药] tetracycline

【四级风】［气］force 4 wind；moderate breeze
【四极管】［无］tetrode
【四季】the four seasons：昆明～如春。*In Kunming it's like spring all the year round.*
【四角号码】the four-corner system（a system of classifying Chinese characters）
【四脚八叉】（lie）sprawling
【四脚朝天】（fall）on one's back
【四近】neighbourhood；vicinity
【四开】［刷］quarto ◇ ～本 quarto
【四邻】one's near neighbours ◇ ～八舍 all the neighbours；the neighbours all around
【四六风】［医］umbilical tetanus of newborn babies（frequently occurring on the 4th to 6th day after birth）
【四面】（on）four sides；（on）all sides：～包围敌人 *completely encircle the enemy forces* ◇ ～八方 all directions；all quarters；all around；far and near；～出击 hit out in all directions；～楚歌 be besieged on all sides；be utterly isolated；be in desperate straits；find oneself under fire from all quarters；～受敌 be exposed to enemy attacks on all sides
【四平八稳】❶ very steady；well balanced：文章写得～。*It's a well-balanced piece of writing.* ❷ overcautious and lacking in initiative：办事～ *be on the safe side in doing things；play safe*
【四起】rise from all directions：掌声～。*Applause broke out all around.*
【四人帮】the Gang of Four
【四散】scatter（or disperse）in all directions
【四舍五入】［数］round up or down；round off
【四声】the four tones of modern standard Chinese pronunciation（i.e. 阴平"－"，阳平"ˊ"，上声"ˇ"，and 去声"ˋ"）
【四时】the four seasons：～鲜果 *fresh fruits of every season*
【四时八节】the four seasons and the eight periods—throughout the year
【四书】the Four Books，namely，The Great Learning（《大学》），The Doctrine of the Mean（《中庸》），The Analects of Confucius（《论语》），and The Mencius（《孟子》）
【四体不勤，五谷不分】can neither toil with one's four limbs nor tell the five cereals apart
【四通八达】extend in all directions：公路～。*Highways radiate in all directions.* / 全省交通运输～。*Transport and communication lines link up all parts of the province.*
【四外】all around（esp. in the open）：～无人。*Not a soul was to be seen all around.*
【四围】on all sides；all around：这村子～都是菜地。*All around the village are vegetable fields.*
【四维】❶〈书〉the four directions（i.e. northeast，southeast，northwest and southwest）❷［中］the four limbs ❸［物］four-dimensional
【四维空间】［物］space-time；space-time continuum
【四下里】（又作'四下'）all around：～一看，都是果树。*Looking around，one can see a vast stretch of fruit trees.*
【四项基本原则】the Four Cardinal Principles（i.e. keeping to the socialist road，and upholding the people's democratic dictatorship，leadership by the Communist Party，and Marxism-Leninism and Mao Zedong Thought）
【四言诗】four-character verse
【四仰八叉】同〖四脚八叉〗
【四野】the surrounding country；a vast expanse of open ground：～茫茫，寂静无声。*All is quiet on the vast expanse of open ground.*
【四月】❶ April ❷ the fourth month of the lunar year；the fourth moon
【四则】［数］the four fundamental operations of arithmetic（i.e. addition，subtraction，multiplication and division）
【四战之地】a place open to attack from all directions
【四诊】［中］the four methods of diagnosis（i.e. observation 望，auscultation and olfaction 闻，interrogation 问，and pulse feeling and palpation 切）
【四肢】the four limbs；arms and legs
【四周】（又作'四周围'）all around；on all sides
【四足动物】quadruped；tetrapod
【四座】all the people present：语惊～ *words that startle all present*

寺

名 temple：少林～ *the Shaolin Temple*
【寺院】temple；monastery

似

Ⅰ 动 ❶ be similar；look like：相似 ❷ seem；appear：～属可行 *seem to be feasible* Ⅱ 介（used in a comparative）than：生活一年强～一年。*Life is getting better every year.*
【似曾相识】seem to have met before
【似…非…】（each followed by the same word）look like but be not quite；smack of：似懂非懂 *have only a hazy notion；not quite understand* / 她似笑非笑。*There's a faint smile on her face.*
【似乎】as if；seemingly：他的意思～另有所指。*It seems he was referring to something else.*
【似是而非】apparently right but actually wrong；specious；plausible：～的说法 *a specious argument*
【似水流年】Time passes swiftly like flowing water；Youth slips away like flowing water.

祀

动 offer sacrifices to the gods or the spirits of the dead：～孔 *offer sacrifices to Confucius* / ～祖 *offer sacrifices to one's ancestors*

伺

动 watch；await ——另见 cì
【伺服】［电子］servo：～传动 *servo drive* / ～放大器 *servo amplifier*
【伺机】watch for one's chance：～而动 *wait for the opportune moment to go into action*
【伺隙】wait for a chance；watch for an opportunity：～越狱 *wait for an opportunity to break pris-*

on

饲 Ⅰ 动 raise; rear Ⅱ 名 forage; fodder; feed

【饲槽】feeding trough

【饲草】forage grass

【饲料】forage; fodder; feed: 猪～ *pig feed* / ～加工厂 *feed-processing plant* ◇ ～粉碎机 feed (or fodder) grinder; ～作物 forage (or fodder, feed) crop

【饲喂】feed or raise (animals)

【饲养】raise; rear: ～家禽 *raise* (*or rear*) *poultry* / ～牲畜 *raise livestock* ◇ ～场 feed lot; dry lot; farm; ～员 stockman; poultry raiser; animal keeper

驷 名〈书〉❶ a team of four horses ❷ horse

【驷不及舌】a team of four horses cannot over-take the tongue—what is said cannot be unsaid

【驷马】〈书〉a team of four horses

俟 动〈书〉wait: ～机进攻 *wait for an opportunity to attack* / 一～准备就绪,即行公开展出。*The exhibition will be opened as soon as everything is in order.*

【俟河之清,人寿几何】How long does a man live, that he can wait for the River to run clear? (said in despair of realizing one's hopes; the River referring to the Yellow River)

嗣 Ⅰ 动 succeed; inherit: ～位 *succeed to the throne* Ⅱ 名 heir; descendant: 无～ *heirless; without issue*

【嗣后】〈书〉hereafter; subsequently; afterwards; later on

肆 Ⅰ 形 wanton; unbridled: 放肆 Ⅱ 数 four (used for the numeral 四 on cheques, etc. to avoid mistakes or alterations) Ⅲ 名〈书〉shop

【肆口大骂】let loose a torrent of abuse

【肆虐】indulge in wanton massacre or persecution; wreak havoc

【肆无忌惮】unbridled; unscrupulous; impertinent: ～地攻击 *make unbridled attacks*

【肆意】wantonly; recklessly; wilfully: ～歪曲事实 *wantonly distort the facts* / ～践踏别国主权 *wilfully trample upon other countries' sovereignty* / ～侮辱 *resort to wanton insults*

sōng

松 Ⅰ 名 ❶ pine (tree) ❷ dried meat floss; dried minced meat: 猪肉～ *dried minced pork* Ⅱ 形 ❶ loose; slack: 这里的土质很～。*The soil here is very loose.* / 你的鞋带～了。*Your shoelace has come loose.* / 绳子太～了。*The rope is too slack.* ❷ not be hard up: 现在手头～些 *be better off* ❸ light and flaky; soft: 这点心～脆可口。*The pastry is light and crisp.* / 这种木料太～,做家具不合适。*The wood is too soft for making furniture.* Ⅲ 动 ❶ loosen; relax; slacken: ～一～螺丝 *loosen the screw a little bit* ❷ untie; unfasten; release: 松绑

【松绑】❶ untie a person: 给囚犯～ *untie the prisoner* ❷ relax restrictions

【松弛】❶ limp; flabby; slack: 肌肉～ *flaccid muscles* ❷ lax: 纪律～ *lax discipline*

【松貂】pine marten

【松动】❶ become less crowded ❷ not hard up: 银根较之上月有所～。*Money is not so tight as it was last month.* ❸ become flexible; show flexibility; relax: 他的口气有点～。*He has become a bit more flexible.* / 两国关系有所～。*Relations between the two countries have moved forward.*

【松果腺】(又作'松果体')同〖脑上体〗

【松花蛋】(又作'皮蛋') a kind of preserved egg

【松缓】relax; ease up; mitigate: 紧张的空气～了一些。*The tense atmosphere has eased up a little.*

【松鸡】capercaillie; grouse

【松焦油】pine tar

【松节油】turpentine (oil)

【松紧】❶ degree of tightness ❷ elasticity ◇ ～带 elastic cord; elastic

【松劲】relax one's efforts; slacken (off): ～情绪 *slack mood*

【松口】❶ relax one's bite and release what is held ❷ be less unyielding; soften; relent: 最后大夫～了,同意她出院。*Finally the doctor relented and allowed her to leave the hospital.*

【松快】❶ be less crowded: 搬走一张桌子,屋里～多了。*With a desk moved out, there's much more space in the room.* ❷ feel relieved: 吃了药以后身上～多了。*I feel much better after taking the medicine.* ❸ relax: 干了一天活,～～吧。*After the day's work, let's relax a bit.*

【松毛虫】pine moth

【松明】pine torch

【松气】relax one's efforts: 在节骨眼上决不能～。*At this critical juncture we must not relax our efforts.*

【松球】pinecone

【松仁】pine nut kernel

【松软】soft; spongy; loose: ～的表土 *spongy topsoil* / ～的羊毛 *fluffy wool*

【松散】(sōngsǎn) ❶ loose; porous: 文章结构～。*The article is loosely organized.* ❷ inattentive

【松散】(sōngsan) relax; take one's ease: 屋里太闷热,出去～～吧。*It's too hot and stuffy in here. Let's go out for a breath of air.*

【松手】loosen one's grip; let go: 抓紧了,别～。*Hold it tight and don't let go.*

【松鼠】squirrel

【松树】pine tree; pine

【松松垮垮】❶ not solid or firm; unsteady ❷ slack; sluggish

【松塔】❶〈方〉pinecone ❷〔中〕the cone of lacebark pine

【松涛】the soughing of the wind in the pines

【松土】loosen the soil; scarify the soil ◇ ～机

loosener; scarifier

【松闲】not busy; slack: 秋收一完,农活就～点了。*After the autumn harvest comes the slack season*.

【松香】rosin; colophony ◇ ～油 retinol; rosin oil

【松懈】❶ lax; slack: 工作～ *be slack in one's work* / 管理～ *loose management* ❷ relax; slacken: ～斗志 *relax one's will to fight*

【松蕈】pine mushroom

【松鸦】jaybird; jay

【松烟】pine soot

【松烟墨】Chinese ink or ink stick made from pine soot; pine-soot ink or ink stick

【松针】pine needle

【松脂】rosin; pine resin

【松子】❶ pine nut ❷〈方〉pine nut kernel

【松嘴】〈口〉❶ relax one's bite and release what is held ❷ be less unyielding; soften; relent

sǒng

怂 形〈书〉alarmed and panicky; terrified

【怂恿】instigate; incite; egg sb. on; abet

悚 形〈书〉terrified; horrified

【悚然】terrified; horrified: 毛骨悚然

耸 Ⅰ 形 towering; lofty Ⅱ 动 alarm; shock: 耸听

【耸动】❶ raise (one's shoulders); shrug ❷ stir up; rouse: ～视听 *create a sensation*

【耸肩】shrug one's shoulders

【耸立】tower aloft: 人民英雄纪念碑～在天安门广场上。*The Monument to the People's Heroes towers aloft on Tian'anmen Square*.

【耸人听闻】deliberately exaggerate so as to create a sensation: ～的谣言 *a sensational rumour* / 这不是～,而是铁的事实。*This is not alarmist talk, but a hard fact*.

【耸入云霄】tower to the skies: ～的高山 *a high mountain towering to the skies*

【耸身】jump; leap: ～跳过水沟 *leap across the ditch*

【耸听】deliberately exaggerate so as to create a sensation

sòng

讼 动 ❶ bring a case to court ❷ dispute; argue

【讼案】lawsuit

【讼词】legal cases: 包揽～ *engage in pettifoggery*

【讼棍】legal pettifogger; shyster

【讼师】legal pettifogger

【讼事】lawsuit; litigation

宋 名 the Song Dynasty (960-1279)

【宋词】ci poetry of the Song Dynasty

【宋锦】Song brocade (a brocade modelled on the Song-style silk fabric famed for its rich, colourful and elegant designs)

【宋体字】Song typeface, a standard typeface

送 动 ❶ deliver; carry: ～信 *deliver a letter* / ～医～药上门 *deliver medical care right to the patient's home* / 给我们～来好消息 *bring us good news* ❷ give as a present; give: 姐姐～我一本书。*My sister gave me a book*. ❸ see sb. off or out; accompany; escort: ～她回家 *see her home* / 到车站～人 *see sb. off at the station* / 把客人～到门口 *see a guest to the door*; *walk a guest to the gate*

【送别】同〖送行〗

【送殡】attend a funeral; take part in a funeral procession

【送达】deliver: 他们每天都把报纸及时～各家各户。*Every day, they deliver the newspapers promptly to each household*.

【送风机】[机] forced draught blower; blower

【送话器】microphone

【送还】give back; return

【送货】deliver goods: ～上门 *deliver goods right to the doorstep of a customer*; *deliver to domicile*

【送检】submit (products) for inspection to product-testing authorities: 产品一次～合格率有所提高。*The proportion of products passing their first inspection has risen*.

【送交】deliver to; hand over to: 把犯罪分子～人民法院审判 *hand the criminal over to the people's court for trial*

【送旧迎新】see out the old and welcome the new

【送客】see a visitor out

【送礼】give sb. a present; present a gift to sb.: 请客～ *give dinners or send gifts (in order to curry favour)*

【送命】lose one's life; get killed; go to one's doom

【送气】[语音] aspirated ◇ ～音 aspirated sound; aspirate (e.g. Chinese p, t, k, c, ch, q)

【送亲】(of the bride's kinsfolk) escort the bride to the groom's home or the wedding hall

【送人】give away; present someone with: 他的画从不～。*He never gives away his paintings*.

【送人情】❶ do favours at no great cost to oneself ❷〈方〉make a gift of sth.

【送丧】attend a funeral; take part in a funeral procession

【送上门】〈喻〉deliver to the doorstep: ～的买卖你还不做? *A business right at the door, and you refuse to do it?*

【送审】submit to a higher level for approval or revision

【送死】〈口〉court death

【送往迎来】see off those who depart and welcome those who arrive; speed the parting guests and welcome the new arrivals: 负责～事宜 *be in charge of arrangements for receiving and seeing off guests*

【送瘟神】send away the god of plague —get rid of sb. or sth. undesirable

【送信儿】〈口〉send word; go and tell: 我已经给他～,让他马上来看你。*I have sent him word to come and see you at once.* / 你哥从东北回来了,去给你妈送个信儿。*Go and tell your mother that your brother has come back from the Northeast.*

【送行】❶ see sb. off; wish sb. bon voyage ❷ give a send-off party

【送修】send for repair: 冰箱坏了,应～去。*The refrigerator has broken down and needs to be sent for repair.*

【送养人】donors for adoption

【送葬】take part in a funeral procession

【送展】(send and) put on display: 从～的作品看,中国油画有明显的发展。*The paintings on display show that Chinese oil paintings have developed remarkably.*

【送终】attend upon a dying parent or other senior member of one's family; bury a parent

诵 动 ❶ read aloud; chant ❷ recite ❸ state; recount; narrate

【诵读】read aloud; chant

【诵习】〈书〉chant and study: ～经典 *read and study the classics*

颂 Ⅰ 动 ❶ praise; extol; eulogize; laud: 歌颂 ❷ express good wishes (in letters): 敬～大安 *wishing you good health* Ⅱ 名 song; ode; paean; eulogy: 《延安～》*Ode to Yan'an*

【颂词】❶ complimentary address; panegyric; eulogy ❷ a speech delivered by an ambassador on presentation of his credentials

【颂歌】song; ode

【颂古非今】eulogize the past and condemn the present

【颂扬】sing praises of; laud; extol; eulogize

sōu

溲 动〈书〉urinate

【溲血】[中] haematuria

搜 动 ❶ look for: 搜集 ❷ search: 什么也没～着。*Nothing was found in the search.*

【搜捕】track down and arrest

【搜查】search; ransack; rummage ◇ ～证 search warrant

【搜肠刮肚】rack one's brains: ～地想办法 *rack one's brains for a way out*

【搜刮】(又作'搜括') extort; plunder; expropriate; fleece

【搜集】hunt high and low for; collect; gather: ～标本 *collect specimens* / ～情报 *gather information; collect intelligence* / ～证据 *search for evidence*

【搜剿】track down and exterminate

【搜救】search-and-rescue: 这家公司专门从事～遇险船舶和飞机。*This company specializes in search-and-rescue of vessels and aircraft in distress.*

【搜罗】hunt high and low for (persons or things); collect; gather; recruit: ～人才 *recruit qualified persons; scout for talent*

【搜求】seek; search for; hunt for: ～古书 *hunt high and low for ancient books*

【搜身】search the person; make a body search; frisk

【搜索】search for; hunt for; scout around: ～失踪船只 *search for missing boats* / ～前进 *advance and reconnoitre*

【搜索飞行】scouting flight

【搜索引擎】[计] search engine

【搜索枯肠】rack one's brains (for fresh ideas or apt expressions)

【搜寻】search for; look for; hunt for; seek: ～失踪人员 *hunt high and low for the missing (persons)*

【搜腰包】search sb.'s pockets; search sb. for money and valuables

嗖 象 whiz: 汽车～的一声从他身边开过。*The car whizzed by him.*

馊 动 turn sour; become spoiled: 饭菜～了。*The food has spoiled.* or *The food smells a bit off.*

【馊点子】stupid suggestion; lousy idea: 谁出的这个～? *Who made this stupid suggestion?*

【馊主意】stupid suggestion; lousy idea: 别出～! *Stop making stupid suggestions!*

艘 量 (for boats or ships): 两～油船 *two tankers* / 四～巡洋舰 *four cruisers*

【艘次】vessel-time (total number of operations in which vessels or ships are involved): 建港一年来,共为506～进行导航。*Since the port opened one year ago, it has provided navigation services 506 vessel-times.*

sǒu

叟 名 an old man: 邻～ *the old man who lives next door*

嗾 Ⅰ 象 a whistling sound made as a signal to a dog Ⅱ 动〈书〉whistle to a dog

【嗾使】instigate; abet

sòu

嗽 动 cough: 干～ *a dry cough*

sū

苏 Ⅰ 名 [植] perilla; beefsteak plant Ⅱ 动 revive; come to: 死而复～ *come back to life*

【苏必利尔湖】Lake Superior

【苏打】［化］soda；soda ash；sodium carbonate：～饼干 *soda biscuit*；*soda cracker*
【苏丹】❶ sultan ❷ the Sudan ◇ ～人 Sudanese
【苏里南】Surinam ◇ ～人 Surinamese
【苏联】the Soviet Union（1917-1990）
【苏门答腊】Sumatra
【苏门羚】［动］serow
【苏铁】［植］sago cycas（Cycas revoluta）
【苏维埃】soviet：地方各级～ *the local and regional soviets* / 最高～ *the Supreme Soviet*
【苏醒】revive；regain consciousness；come to；come round：他昏迷了一个多小时才～过来。*He remained unconscious for more than an hour before he came to*.
【苏伊士运河】the Suez Canal
【苏子】perillaseed

酥 Ⅰ 形 ❶ crisp；short：～糖 *crunchy candy* ❷（of a person's limbs）limp；weak；soft Ⅱ 名 shortbread：杏仁～ *almond shortbread*
【酥脆】crisp：～的饼干 *crisp*（*or short*）*biscuit*
【酥麻】limp and numb：两腿～ *one's legs feeling weak and numb*
【酥软】（of the body）limp；languid
【酥松】（of soil，etc.）loose；porous；（of pastries，etc.）flaky；crisp：～的土壤 *porous soil* / ～的薄脆饼干 *flaky crackers*
【酥胸】soft and white breasts（of a woman）
【酥油】butter ◇ ～茶 buttered tea

sú

俗 Ⅰ 名 ❶ custom；convention：陈规旧～ *old habits and customs* ❷ secular；lay：僧俗 Ⅱ 形 ❶ popular；common：玉蜀黍～称棒子。*Corn is commonly called bangzi*. ❷ vulgar：俗气
【俗白】simple and clear：将深邃的哲理融入～的寻常情景之中 *profound philosophic principles embodied in simple*，*ordinary experiences*
【俗不可耐】unbearably vulgar
【俗话】〈口〉common saying；proverb：～说 *as the saying goes*
【俗家】❶（used by a monk or nun）my parents' home ❷ layman：～打扮 *in a layman's attire*
【俗名】popular name；local name
【俗气】vulgar；in poor taste：她穿得很～。*The clothes she wears are in poor taste*.
【俗人】❶ layman（as distinguished from 出家人）❷ a vulgar person；philistine
【俗套】conventional pattern；convention
【俗体字】nonstandard forms of characters
【俗文学】popular literature（as novels，ballads，etc.）
【俗务】everyday matters；routine business：～缠身 *be tied up with routine business*
【俗物】a vulgar or uncouth person
【俗语】common saying；folk adage
【俗字】同〚俗体字〛

sù

夙 形〈书〉❶ early in the morning：夙兴夜寐 ❷ long-standing；old：～志 *long-cherished ambition*
【夙仇】❶ long-time enemy ❷ long-standing enmity
【夙敌】old enemy
【夙日】generally；usually；ordinarily：～过往甚密 *usually have close contact with each other*
【夙世】previous incarnation：～因缘 *a relationship predestined from a previous incarnation* / ～冤家 *predestined enemies*
【夙兴夜寐】rise early and retire late—hard at work night and day
【夙夜】day and night：～不寐 *not sleep a wink day and night*
【夙夜匪懈】work tirelessly day and night
【夙愿】a long-cherished wish：～得偿 *a long-cherished wish fulfilled*

诉 动 ❶ tell；relate；inform：告诉 ❷ complain；accuse：～委屈 *pour out one's grievances* ❸ appeal to；resort to：上诉
【诉苦】complain；vent one's grievances；pour out one's woes
【诉说】（又作'诉述'）tell；relate；recount：～苦衷 *recount one's worries and difficulties*；*tell one's troubles*
【诉讼】［法］lawsuit；litigation：法律～ *judicial proceedings* / ～案件 *lawsuit* / 民刑～ *civil and criminal lawsuits* / 对某人提出～ *take*（*or start*）*legal proceedings against sb*. / 撤销～ *withdraw an accusation*；*drop a lawsuit* ◇ ～代理人 agent ad litem；legal representative；～当事人 litigant；～地点 venue of trial；～法 procedural law；～豁免 immunity from suit；～权利 procedural rights；～条例 rules of procedure
【诉冤】complain of injustice；air one's grievances
【诉诸武力】resort to force；appeal to arms
【诉状】［法］〈旧〉plaint；indictment：向法院提出～ *file a plaint at court*

肃 Ⅰ 形 ❶ respectful：肃立 ❷ solemn：严肃 Ⅱ 动 eliminate；clean up；mop up：肃反
【肃毒】eliminate drug addiction，drug trafficking and other related illegal activities：～行动 *anti-drug action*
【肃反】elimination of counterrevolutionaries
【肃静】solemn silence：全场～无声。*A solemn silence reigned*.
【肃立】stand as a mark of respect：奏国歌时全场～。*All stood as the band struck up the national anthem*. or *Everyone stood when the national anthem was played*. / ～默哀 *stand in silent mourning*
【肃穆】❶ solemn and quiet；solemn and respect-

ful：纪念会气氛～。*The commemoration meeting was permeated with a solemn atmosphere.* ❷ respectful and congenial

【肃清】eliminate；clean up；mop up：～敌军残部 *mop up the remnants of the enemy* / ～流毒 *liquidate a pernicious influence*

【肃然起敬】be filled with deep veneration：使我～ *call forth in me a feeling of profound respect*

【肃杀】〈书〉(of autumn or winter) stern；harsh：秋气～。*The breath of autumn is harsh and raw.*

【肃贪】eliminate corruption：～是一场政治斗争。*Eliminating corruption is a political struggle.*

素 Ⅰ 形 ❶ white；unbleached and undyed：～幡 *white streamers* ❷ plain；simple；quiet：～色 *plain colour* ❸ native：素性 Ⅱ 名 ❶ vegetable：三荤一～ *three meat dishes and one vegetable dish* ❷ basic element；element：色素 Ⅲ 副 usually；habitually；always：～不往来 *have never had anything to do with each other*

【素白】plain and white：～手绢 *a plain white handkerchief*

【素不相识】have never met；not be acquainted with each other

【素材】source material (of literature and art)；material：搜集小说～ *gather material for a novel*

【素菜】vegetable dish

【素餐】❶ a vegetarian meal ❷ be a vegetarian ❸〈书〉not work for one's living；eat the bread of idleness

【素常】usually；habitually；ordinarily：～他到十二点钟才睡觉。*Ordinarily he doesn't go to bed until twelve o'clock.*

【素淡】plain；quiet：衣着～ *be plainly (or quietly) dressed*

【素点】vegetarian light refreshments；cakes and pastries made to Muslim taste：元宵～ *vegetarian snacks for the Lantern Festival*

【素服】plain white clothes (esp. as mourning apparel)

【素混凝土】plain concrete

【素洁】white and pure

【素净】plain and neat；quiet：一套～的蓝衣服 *a plain blue suit* / 花色～ *a pattern in quiet colours* / 穿着～ *be plainly and neatly dressed*

【素酒】❶ wine served with vegetarian food ❷〈方〉a vegetarian feast

【素来】always；usually：他～是严格遵守纪律的。*He always strictly observes discipline.*

【素昧平生】have never met before；have never made sb.'s acquaintance：我同他～。*I have never had the honour of making his acquaintance.* or *I know nothing about him.* / 一个～的人 *a complete stranger*

【素面】❶ vegetarian noodles ❷ in ones's natural state or features

【素描】❶ sketch ❷ literary sketch

【素日】generally；usually：他～不爱说话。*He is usually very quiet.*

【素食】❶ vegetarian food；vegetarian diet ❷ be a vegetarian：～者 *a vegetarian*

【素数】[数] prime number

【素席】vegetarian feast

【素心】❶ one's real intention；one's true will：与～相违 *go against one's true will* ❷ clean and honest；pure in heart：他是个～人。*He is a simple and honest one.*

【素馨】[植] jasmine

【素性】one's natural instincts；one's true disposition (or temperament)

【素雅】simple but elegant；plain and in good taste：房间布置～。*The room is simply and tastefully furnished.*

【素养】accomplishment；attainment：艺术～ *artistic accomplishment*

【素因子】[数] prime factor

【素油】vegetable oil

【素愿】a long-cherished desire，wish，or aspiration

【素质】❶ character；quality：提高部队的军政～ *enhance the military and political quality of the troops* ❷ [心理] diathesis

【素质教育】quality-oriented education；education aimed at all-round development (of students)

速 Ⅰ 形 fast；rapid；quick；speedy：收效甚～ *produce quick results；have a speedy effect* Ⅱ 名 speed；velocity：音速 Ⅲ 动〈书〉invite：不速之客

【速成】attain a goal in a much shorter time than usual；gain a quick mastery of a course or subject：～教学法 *a quick method of teaching* / 英文打字～ *a speeded-up teaching programme of English typing*

【速成班】accelerated course；crash course

【速冻】quick-freeze：～饺子 *quick-frozen dumplings* / ～对虾 *quick-frozen fresh prawns*

【速递】deliver directly and rapidly；send out by express mail：～业务 *express mail service* / ～公司 *express mail company*

【速度】❶ [物] speed；velocity：匀～ *uniform velocity* / 轨道～ *orbital velocity* ❷ [音] tempo ❸ speed；rate；pace；tempo：加快～ *increase the speed* / 生产～ *the tempo of production* / 经济发展的～ *the rate of economic development* / 工业化的～ *the pace of industrialization*

【速度滑冰】[体] speed skating

【速度计】speed indicator；speedometer

【速记】shorthand；stenography ◇ ～员 stenographer

【速决】quick decision ◇ ～战 a quick battle

【速率】speed；rate：冷却～ *rate of cooling*

【速溶】instant：～咖啡 *instant coffee* / ～奶粉 *instant milk powder*

【速射】[军] rapid fire ◇ ～炮 quick-firing gun；quick-firer

【速生林】fast-growing woods (or timber forests)

【速生丰产林】fast-growing，high-yield woods (or timber forests)

【速胜】quick victory
【速调管】［无］klystron
【速效】❶ quick results ❷ quick-acting ◇ ～肥料 quick-acting fertilizer
【速效感冒胶囊】quick-cold-relieving capsule
【速效洗涤剂】quick-acting detergent
【速写】❶ sketch ❷ literary sketch
【速战速决】fight a quick battle to force a quick decision

宿 Ⅰ 动 lodge for the night；stay overnight：夜～古刹 *stay in an ancient temple for the night；make an overnight stay in an ancient temple* Ⅱ 形〈书〉❶ long-standing；old：～志 *a long-cherished ambition* ❷ veteran；old：宿将——另见 xiǔ
【宿弊】a long-standing abuse：～一清。*The long-standing abuses are all rooted out.*
【宿娼】go whoring；visit prostitutes
【宿仇】long-standing enmity
【宿处】lodgings；accommodation：我不知道她的～。*I don't know where she's staying.*
【宿敌】old enemy
【宿根】［植］❶ perennial root ❷ biennial root
【宿疾】chronic complaint；old trouble
【宿将】veteran general
【宿命论】［哲］fatalism：～者 *a fatalist*
【宿舍】hostel；living quarters；dormitory：学生～ *students' hostel (or dormitory)* / 职工～ *living quarters for staff and workers*
【宿营】(of troops) take up quarters；camp：～地 *temporary quarters for soldiers；camping site*
【宿营车】❶ trailer caravan；home on wheels ❷ dormitory car (of a long-distance train for its attendants to sleep in)
【宿缘】predestined relationship
【宿怨】old grudges；old scores
【宿愿】long-cherished wish
【宿主】［生］host：中间～ *intermediate host* / 终～ *final host*

粟 名 foxtail millet；millet (Setaria italica)
【粟米】〈方〉maize；Indian corn；corn
【粟子】〈方〉millet

溯 动 ❶ go against the stream：～流而上 *go upstream* ❷ trace back；recall：回溯
【溯源】trace (back) to the source

塑 动 model；mould：～一尊佛像 *mould a statue of Buddha*
【塑封】plastic-coated：～文件夹 *plastic-coated documents folder*
【塑胶】plastic cement：～跑道 *plastic cement race track*
【塑炼】plasticate ◇ ～机 plasticator
【塑料】plastics：通用～ *general-purpose plastics* / 氟～ *fluoroplastics* ◇ ～薄膜 plastic film；plastic sheeting；～胶布带［电］plastic adhesive tape；～热合机 plastic welder；～贴面板 plastic veneer；～印版 plastic (printing) plate；～炸弹 plastic bomb
【塑料袋】plastic bag
【塑像】statue
【塑性】［物］plasticity ◇ ～炸药 plastic bomb；high-explosive plastics
【塑造】❶ model；mould：～一座石膏像 *mould (or model) a plaster figure* ❷ portray：～一个女警察的英雄形象 *portray a heroic policewoman*

嗉（构词成分）见下
【嗉子】❶（又作'嗉囊'）crop (of a bird)：鸡～ *chicken crop* ❷〈方〉tin or porcelain wine flask

簌（构词成分）见下
【簌簌】❶ rustle：风吹树叶～响。*The leaves are rustling in the wind.* ❷ (of tears) streaming down

suān

酸 Ⅰ 名［化］acid Ⅱ 形 ❶ sour；tart：～梨 *sour pear* / ～果 *tart fruit* / 牛奶～了。*The milk has turned sour.* ❷ sick at heart；grieved；distressed：大娘鼻子一～，流下泪来。*The old woman felt a twinge in her nose and she began to weep.* ❸ pedantic；impractical：～秀才 *an impractical old scholar；a priggish pedant* Ⅲ 动 tingle；ache：腰～背痛 *have a pain in the back；have a backache*
【酸鼻】have a sting in the nose；feel like crying：令人～ *make one feel like crying*
【酸不唧】〈方〉❶ slightly sour or tart；sourish；tartish：这草莓～的，挺好吃。*These strawberries have a slightly sour taste；they taste quite nice.* ❷ tired and feeling weak；exhausted；worn-out：浑身～的 *worn-out and aching all over*
【酸不拉唧】〈方〉unpleasantly sour
【酸不溜丢】〈方〉unpleasantly sour
【酸菜】pickled Chinese cabbage；Chinese sauerkraut
【酸处理】［油］acid treatment；acidation
【酸楚】grieved；distressed；miserable
【酸度】［化］acidity
【酸酐】［化］acid anhydride
【酸解】［化］acidolysis
【酸刻】sharp-tongued；sarcastic；acebic：他的话太～了，叫人受不了。*He has an acid tongue and says very hurtful things.*
【酸苦】bitterness；misery；hardship：历尽～ *have experienced all kinds of hardships* / 心头一阵～ *feel a twinge at the heart*
【酸辣酱】chutney，an Indian condiment made of fruits or vegetables，vinegar，spices，sugar，etc.
【酸辣汤】vinegar-pepper soup
【酸溜溜】❶ sour；pungent ❷ tingle；ache：走了一天路，我的腿肚子～的。*My legs ached after I'd been walking all day.* ❸ sad；mournful ❹ envious；green with envy ❺ pedantic；priggish

【酸马奶】koumiss
【酸梅】smoked plum; dark plum ◇～汤 sweet-sour plum juice
【酸奶】(又作'酸牛奶') yoghurt; sour milk
【酸软】aching and limp: 四肢～ *one's limbs all aching and limp*
【酸涩】❶ (of smell, taste, feeling) sour and bitter: ～的棠梨 *sour birchleaf pears* / ～的眼泪 *stinging tears* / 她鼻尖～，泪水盈盈。*Her nose twitched and tears filled her eyes.* ❷ sad; grieved; sick at heart: 我忍着身上的寒冷和心头的～回答他。*Cold and sick at heart, I answered him.* / 在甜蜜中品尝着～ *taste the sadness in the happiness*
【酸式盐】[化] acid salt
【酸疼】(of muscles) ache
【酸甜】sweet and sour
【酸甜苦辣】sour, sweet, bitter, hot —joys and sorrows of life
【酸痛】ache: 浑身～ *ache all over*
【酸味】tart flavour; acidity
【酸文假醋】priggish; prudish
【酸洗】[冶] pickling; acid pickling ◇～试验 [化] acid washing test
【酸心】❶ be grieved; feel sad: 这出戏看了叫人～。*It was heartrending to see the play.* ❷ suffer from heartburn
【酸性】[化] acidity: ～染料 *acid dye* ◇～反应 acid reaction; ～试验 acid test; ～岩 acidic rock
【酸雨】acid rain
【酸枣】wild jujube
【酸值】[化] acid value

suàn

蒜 名 garlic: 一辫～ *a braid of garlic* / 一头～ *a bulb of garlic*
【蒜瓣儿】garlic clove
【蒜黄】blanched garlic leaves
【蒜苗】garlic bolt
【蒜泥】mashed garlic
【蒜薹】the flower stalk of garlic (edible when tender)
【蒜头】the head (or bulb) of garlic

算 Ⅰ 动 ❶ calculate; reckon; compute; figure: ～～旅行的费用 *calculate the cost of a journey* / 能写会～ *good at writing and reckoning* / 请你～一～我该付多少钱。*Please reckon up how much I must pay.* ❷ include; count: ～上你，一共十个人。*There'll be ten people, including you.* / 把我也～上。*Count me in.* ❸ plan; calculate: 失算 ❹ guess; think; suppose: 我～他今天该动身了。*I suppose he'll have started (or be starting) today.* ❺ consider; regard as; count as: 他可以～一个车把势。*He can be counted as a carter.* ❻ carry weight; count: 我一个人说的不～，还得大伙儿说。*It's not just what I say, but what we all say, that counts.* / 你怎么刚说了又不～了？*You just made a promise and now you've gone back on it!* ❼ (followed by 了 le) let it be; let it pass: ～了，别说了。*That's enough! Let it go at that.* or *Forget it.* / 他不愿意去就～了吧，咱们反正去。*If he doesn't want to go, he doesn't need to. We'll go anyway.* Ⅱ 副 at long last; in the end; finally: 现在～把情况弄清楚了。*At long last we have got things clear.* or *We've finally sized up the situation.* / 问题～解决了。*The problem is finally solved.*
【算尺】slide rule
【算得】regard as; count as: 你有这样一位贤内助，可～幸福的了。*You can well count yourself fortunate in having such a good wife.*
【算法】[数] algorithm
【算卦】tell sb.'s fortune or divine by using the Eight Trigrams (八卦) ——另见〖八卦〗
【算计】❶ calculate; reckon: ～一下全部收入 *count up all one's earnings* / 让我～～，看够不够。*Let me figure it out and see if it will be enough.* ❷ consider; plan: 我正～着要上北京去。*I am planning a trip to Beijing.* ❸ expect; figure: 我～他昨天回不来，果然没回来。*I thought he wouldn't come back yesterday, and he didn't.* ❹ scheme; plot: 暗中～别人 *secretly scheme against others*
【算旧账】settle an old account; settle an old score: 我要同他算一笔旧账。*I've got an old score to settle with him.*
【算命】fortune-telling: 那瞎子自称会给人～。*The blind man claimed that he could tell people's fortunes.* ◇～先生 fortune-teller
【算盘】❶ abacus ❷ calculation; plan; scheme: 他满口答应了这件事，是有他自己的～的。*In agreeing so readily, he had an axe to grind.*
【算盘子儿】beads of an abacus
【算式】mathematical formula or equation
【算是】at last: 这一下你～猜着了。*At last you've guessed right.* / 我们的计划～实现了。*At last our plan has materialized.*
【算术】arithmetic: 做～ *do sums* ◇～级数 arithmetic progression; arithmetic series; ～平均值 arithmetic mean
【算数】count; hold; stand: 个别情况不～。*Isolated instances do not count.* / 这条规定仍然～。*This rule still holds (or stands).* / 我们说话是～的。*We mean what we say.*
【算题】arithmetic problem; mathematical exercise
【算学】❶ mathematics ❷ arithmetic
【算账】❶ do (or work out) accounts; balance the books; make out bills: 他每十天算一次账。*He does his accounts every ten days.* ❷ square (or settle) accounts with sb.; get even with sb.: 以后再找这坏蛋～。*We'll get even with the scoundrel later.* or *We'll make the scoundrel pay for this.*
【算子】[数] operator: 微分～ *differential operator*

suī

尿 名 urine：这孩子又尿（niào）了一泡～。The child has pissed again! ——另见 niào

【尿脬】（又作'尿泡'）〈方〉bladder

虽 连〈书〉though；although；even if：问题～小，但很典型。*The question is small but typical.* / ～死犹荣 *honoured though dead；have died a glorious death*

【虽然】（often used correlatively with 但是，可是，etc.）though；although：他～在北京住了十来年了，可是家乡口音一点没改。*Though he has lived in Beijing for ten years or so，he still speaks with a heavy accent.*

【虽说】though；although：～我已认识他很久了，但我并不了解他。*I don't know him very well，though I've known him for a long time.*

【虽死犹生】live on in spirit

【虽则】though；although

suí

绥 〈书〉Ⅰ 形 peaceful Ⅱ 动 pacify

【绥靖】pacify；appease ◇ ～政策 policy of appeasement

随 动 ❶ follow；come or go along with：～我来。*Follow me.* or *Come along with me.* ❷ comply with；adapt to：只要你们做得对，我都～着。*So long as what you do is right，I'll go along with you.* ❸ let（sb. do as he likes）：去不去～你。*Whether you go or not is up to you.* ❹ along with（some other action）：随手 ❺〈方〉look like；resemble：她长得～她母亲。*She looks like her mother.* or *She takes after her mother.*

【随笔】❶ informal essay ❷ jottings

【随便】❶ do as one pleases：随你的便。*Do as you please.* / ～吃吧。*Help yourself.* ❷ casual；random；informal：～闲谈 *chat*；*chitchat* / ～说了几句 *make some casual remarks* / 我只是～问问。*I was just asking.* ❸ careless；slipshod：说话～ *not be careful about the way one talks* ❹ wanton；wilful；arbitrary：～撕毁协议 *wantonly tear up an agreement* ❺ anyhow；any：～什么时候来都行。*Come any time you like.*

【随波逐流】drift with the tide（or current）；go with the stream

【随常】ordinary；common；everyday：～的衣服 *everyday clothes*

【随处】everywhere；anywhere：这种树在这一带～可见。*This kind of tree can be seen everywhere in these parts.*

【随从】❶ accompany or follow（one's superior）；attend ❷（又作'随从人员'）retinue；suite；entourage

【随大溜】drift（or swim）with the stream；follow（or conform to）the trend；do as others do

【随带】❶ going along with：书籍一包，～书信一封。*Accompanying the parcel of books is a letter.* ❷ have sth. taken along with one：～行李两件 *two pieces of luggage which a passenger takes along with him*

【随地】anywhere；everywhere：不要～乱扔东西。*Don't litter.*

【随动件】［机］follower：凸轮～ *cam follower*

【随访】（of doctors，etc.）follow up a case by regular visits to or correspondence with a patient

【随份子】❶ contribute one's share of a group gift ❷ present a gift of money for a wedding，funeral，etc.

【随风倒】bend with the wind—be easily swayed（by whichever side has more power or influence）

【随风转舵】同〖顺风转舵〗

【随感】random thoughts：《旅欧～》*Random Thoughts on Travels in Europe*

【随行就市】（of prices）fluctuate in line with market conditions

【随和】amiable；obliging：脾气～ *have an amiable disposition*

【随后】soon afterwards：你先走，我～就去。*You go first. I'll follow.* or *You go ahead. I'll be there right away.*

【随机】❶［统计］random ❷［数］stochastic ◇ ～变数［统计］random variable；～抽样［统计］random sampling；～存取存储器［计］random access memory（RAM）；～过程［数］stochastic process

【随机应变】do as the changing circumstances demand；suit one's actions to changing conditions；act according to circumstances

【随即】soon after that；immediately；presently：他挂了电话，～出门。*He went out as soon as he hung up.*

【随军】go along with an army ◇ ～记者 war correspondent；～家属 camp family（i.e. an army officer's family allowed to settle at an army camp）

【随口】speak thoughtlessly or casually；blurt out whatever comes into one's head：～答应 *say "yes" absent-mindedly*；*agree without thinking*

【随迁】（of spouse or dependents）change and register permanent residence along with the head of the household when this person moves to a new locality

【随群】do as everybody else does；follow the crowd

【随人俯仰】be at sb.'s beck and call；follow sb. servilely

【随身】（carry）on one's person；（take）with one：他～没有带钱。*He had no money on him.* / ～衣服 *clothes for change taken along during a trip*

【随身听】walkman；personal stereo

【随身行李】accompanying luggage；carry-on items

【随声附和】echo what others say；chime in with others

【随时】❶ at any time; at all times: 你～都可以来。*Come any time (or whenever) you like.* or *You are welcome at all times.* ❷ whenever necessary; as the occasion demands: ～纠正错误 *correct mistakes as soon as they occur*

【随时随地】at all times and all places: ～都要注意卫生。*Pay attention to hygiene at all times and all places.*

【随侍】〈书〉❶ attend (or wait) upon one's elders and betters ❷ personal attendant

【随手】conveniently (when doing sth.); without extra trouble: 出门时～关灯。*Turn the light off as you go out.* / ～关门。*Shut the door after you.*

【随顺】be obedient to; comply with; yield to

【随俗】comply with convention; follow the customs; do as everybody else does

【随…随…】each 随 followed by a verb, indicating that the latter action immediately follows the former: 随叫随到 *be on call at any hour* / 雪随下随化。*The snow melted as it fell.*

【随同】be in company with; be accompanying: ～代表团出国访问 *accompany a delegation on a visit abroad*

【随喜】❶ [宗](佛教) join in charitable and pious deeds ❷ join in an enjoyable activity ❸〈旧〉visit a temple

【随乡入乡】wherever you are, follow local customs; when in Rome do as the Romans do

【随想曲】[音] caprice; capriccio

【随心】❶ follow one's inclinations ❷ find sth. satisfactory; be gratified ◇ ～所欲 follow one's inclinations; have one's own way; do as one pleases

【随行】❶ accompany or follow sb. on a trip ❷ retinue; suite; entourage

【随行人员】entourage; suite; party: 总统及其～ *the President and his entourage*

【随宜】as one sees fit: 请～改动。*Please make alterations as you see fit.*

【随意】at will; as one pleases: ～抽查 *random check* / 请各位～! *Make yourselves at home, everybody!*

【随意肌】[生理] voluntary muscle

【随遇而安】feel at home wherever one is; be able to adapt oneself to different circumstances

【随遇平衡】[物] indifferent equilibrium

【随员】❶ suite; retinue; entourage ❷ diplomacy attaché ◇ ～领事 diplomacy attaché consul

【随葬物】(又作'随葬品') funerary objects; burial articles

【随展】(of staff) travel with the exhibits on an exhibition tour: 产品在外地巡展时,公司没派一名～人员。*The company did not send anyone with the products on exhibition tour in the provinces.*

【随着】along with; in the wake of; in pace with: ～时间的推移 *as time goes on; with the lapse (or passage) of time*

suǐ

髓 名 ❶ [生理] marrow: 脊髓 ❷ [植] pith

suì

岁 Ⅰ 名 ❶ year: ～末 *the end of the year* / 辞旧～,迎新年 *ring out the Old Year and ring in the New* ❷〈书〉the year's harvest: 歉岁 Ⅱ 量 year (of age): 三～女孩儿 *a three-year-old girl; a little girl three years old* / 这匹马两～口。*This horse is two years old.*

【岁差】[天] precession of the equinoxes

【岁出】annual expenditure (in a state budget)

【岁寒三友】the three plant friends who thrive in cold weather—the pine, the bamboo, and the plum

【岁寒知松柏】only when the year grows cold do we see the qualities of the pine and the cypress; adversity reveals virtue

【岁暮】〈书〉the close of the year: ～天寒。*Cold weather sets in as the year draws to its close.*

【岁入】annual income (in a state budget); revenue

【岁首】〈书〉the beginning of the year; the first month of the lunar year

【岁数】〈口〉age; years: 老大爷,您多大～了? *How old are you, Grandpa?* / 我是上了～的人了。*I'm getting on in years.*

【岁月】years: 艰苦斗争的～ *years of arduous struggle* / ～不等人。*Time and tide wait for no man.*

祟 Ⅰ 名 an evil spirit; ghost Ⅱ 动 haunt and plague

遂 Ⅰ 动 ❶ satisfy; fulfil: 遂愿 ❷ succeed: 所谋不～ *fail in an attempt* Ⅱ 副〈书〉then; thereupon: 病人服药后腹痛～止。*The patient's stomachache stopped after he took the medicine.*

【遂心】after one's own heart; to one's liking: ～如意 *be perfectly satisfied*

【遂意】to one's liking

【遂愿】have one's wish fulfilled

碎 Ⅰ 动 break to pieces; smash: 碗掉地下就～了。*The bowl smashed on the floor.* Ⅱ 形 ❶ broken; fragmentary: ～玻璃 *bits of broken glass* / ～布 *oddments of cloth* ❷ garrulous; gabby: 嘴太～ *talk too much; be a regular chatterbox*

【碎步儿】(又作'碎步子') quick short steps

【碎尸万段】tear the body to thousands of pieces (said when swearing to destroy sb.)

【碎石】[建] crushed stone; broken stone; macadam ◇ ～混凝土 [建] crushed stone concrete; ～机 stone crusher; ～路 broken stone road; macadam road; macadam

【碎屑岩】clastic rock

【碎音】[音] acciaccatura
【碎纸机】shredder
【碎嘴子】〈方〉❶ chatter; jabber; prate: 两句话能说完的事就别犯～了。*Don't talk on and on* (*or jabber away*) *when you can say it in a few words*. ❷ a garrulous person; chatterbox

隧 (构词成分) 见下
【隧道】tunnel ◇ ～管 [电子] tunneltron; ～效应 [电子] tunnel effect
【隧洞】tunnel

燧 名 ❶ flint ❷ beacon fire (in ancient China)
【燧石】flint ◇ ～玻璃 flint glass

邃 形〈书〉❷ remote (in time or space): ～古 *remote antiquity* ❸ deep; profound
【邃密】❶ deep: 屋宇～。*The houses were deep and spacious*. ❷ profound: ～的理论 *a comprehensive and profound theory*

穗 名 ❶ the ear of grain; spike: 麦穗 ❷ tassel; fringe: 黄～红罩的宫灯 *red-shaded palace lanterns fringed with yellow tassels*
【穗选】[农] ear selection (i.e. seed selection done ear by ear)
【穗状花序】[植] spike
【穗子】❶ the ear of grain; spike ❷ tassel; fringe: 有～的旗 *a banner fringed with tassels*

sūn

孙 名 ❶ son's son; grandson ❷ generations below that of the grandson: 玄孙 ❸ relatives belonging to grandson's generation: 外孙
【孙女】son's daughter; granddaughter
【孙女婿】granddaughter's husband; grandson-in-law
【孙悟空跳不出如来佛的掌心】like the Monkey King who cannot jump out of Buddha's palm—be unable to get out of sb.'s control
【孙媳妇】grandson's wife; granddaughter-in-law
【孙子兵法】The Art of War by Sunzi
【孙子】son's son; grandson

sǔn

笋 名 bamboo shoot
【笋鞭】the subterranean stem of bamboo
【笋干】air-dried (cooked) bamboo shoots
【笋瓜】winter squash
【笋鸡】young chicken; broiler
【笋尖】tender tips of bamboo shoots

损 Ⅰ 动 ❶ decrease; lose: 增～ *increase and decrease* ❷ harm; damage: 有益无～ *can only do good, not harm* / 以～人开始,以害己告终 *begin with injuring others and end up ruining oneself* ❸〈方〉speak sarcastically; deride: 他爱～人。*He delights in making caustic remarks*. / 说话别太～。*Don't be so sarcastic*. Ⅱ 形〈方〉mean; shabby: 这法子真～。*That's a mean trick*.
【损兵折将】suffer heavy casualties
【损德】injure one's virtue (by misdeeds)
【损公肥私】seek private gain at public expense; feather one's nest at public expense
【损害】❶ do harm to; damage; impair: ～庄稼 *damage crops; be harmful to crops* / ～健康 *impair one's health* / 在光线不好的地方看书,容易～视力。*Reading in poor light is bad for one's eyes*. ❷ harm; injury; damage: 造成严重～ *do great harm to; inflict serious damage on* / 重大～ *substantial damage*
【损耗】❶ loss; wear and tear: 摩擦～ *friction loss* ❷ [经] wastage; spoilage: 运输过程中造成的～ *damage and spoilage incurred during transportation* ◇ ～费 cost of wear and tear; ～率 [经] proportion of goods damaged
【损坏】damage (objects): ～公物要赔。*Pay for public property you damage*.
【损毁】damage or destroy: 数万株树木遭～。*Tens of thousands of trees were damaged or destroyed*.
【损人利己】harm others to benefit oneself; benefit oneself at the expense of others
【损伤】❶ harm; damage; injure: 不要～群众的积极性。*Don't dampen the enthusiasm of the masses*. ❷ loss: 敌军兵力～很大。*The enemy forces suffered heavy losses*.
【损失】❶ lose: ～殆尽 *nearly lost everything* ❷ loss; damage: 遭受重大～ *suffer* (*or sustain*) *heavy losses*
【损益】❶ increase and decrease: 斟酌～ *consider making necessary adjustments* ❷ profit and loss; gains and losses: ～相抵。*The gains offset the losses*. ◇ ～比 profit and loss ratio; ～表 profit and loss account; ～计算书 profit and loss statement

隼 名 falcon

榫 名 tenon
【榫头】tenon
【榫眼】mortise
【榫子】同〖榫头〗

suō

娑 (构词成分) 见下
【娑罗树】sal tree (Shorea robusta)

莎 (构词成分) 见下
【莎草】nutgrass flatsedge (Cyperus rotundus)

唆 动 instigate; abet: 教唆
【唆弄】incite; instigate: ～是非 *sow discord*
【唆使】instigate; abet: ～者 *instigator*; *abettor*

桫 (构词成分) 见下

【桫椤】［植］spinulose tree fern（Cyathea spinulosa）

梭 名 shuttle：无～织机 *shuttleless loom*

【梭镖】spear：～队 *spear corps*

【梭梭】［植］sacsaoul（Holoxylon ammodendron）

【梭巡】〈书〉move around to watch and guard；patrol to and fro

【梭鱼】（redeye）mullet

【梭子】❶ weaver's shuttle ❷ cartridge clip ❸ a clip（of bullets）：打了一～子弹 *fire a whole clip of ammunition*

【梭子蟹】swimming crab

【梭子鱼】barracuda

羧 名［化］carboxyl

【羧基】［化］carboxyl；carboxyl group

【羧酸】［化］carboxylic acid

蓑 名 alpine rush or palm-bark rain cape

【蓑草】（又作'蓑衣草'）〈方〉Chinese alpine rush（Eulaliopsis binata）

【蓑衣】alpine rush or palm-bark rain cape

缩 动 ❶ contract；shrink：热胀冷～ *expand with heat and contract with cold* / 这种布下水不～。*This cloth won't shrink when it's washed.* ❷ draw back；withdraw；recoil：他把身子一～。*He shrank back（in shame，horror，etc.）.* / 冷得～成一团 *huddle oneself up with cold* / 敌人～回去了。*The enemy has drawn back.*

【缩编】（of troops，government organs，etc.）reduce the staff

【缩脖子】draw back one's neck—draw back；shrink back：碰上困难就～ *shrink from difficulty*

【缩尺】reduced scale；scale ◇ ～图 scale drawing

【缩短】shorten；cut down；cut short：～学制 *shorten the period of schooling* / ～距离 *reduce the distance；narrow the gap* / 把报告～一半 *cut a report down to half its length*

【缩短战线】contract the front—narrow the scope of an activity

【缩放仪】pantograph

【缩合】［化］condensation ◇ ～反应 condensation reaction；～物 condensation compound

【缩减】reduce；cut；trim；retrench：～开支 *reduce（or cut）spending* / ～军费 *cut back military expenditure*

【缩聚】［化］condensation polymerization ◇ ～物 condensation polymer

【缩略语】abbreviation；abbreviated expression

【缩手】❶ draw back one's hand ❷ shrink（from doing sth.）

【缩手缩脚】❶ shrink with cold ❷ be overcautious

【缩水】（of cloth through wetting）shrink：毛织品泡在热水里就～。*Wool shrinks when soaked in hot water.* or *Hot water shrinks wool.*

【缩水率】shrinkage：～高达每10米15公分 *a shrinkage of 15cm in a length of 10m.*

【缩头虫】bamboo worm

【缩头缩脑】❶ be timid；be fainthearted ❷ shrink from responsibility

【缩微】microform ◇ ～技术 microphotography；～胶卷 microfilm；～胶片 microfiche；microcopy；～照片 microfilm；microphotograph

【缩小】❶ reduce（in width，size，scope，etc.）；lessen；narrow；shrink：～范围 *reduce the scope；narrow the range* / 逐步～城乡差别 *gradually reduce the distinction between town and country* ❷ be reduced；shrink：他的毛衣放到热水里一洗就～了。*His sweater shrank when he washed it in hot water.*

【缩写】❶ abbreviation ❷ abridge ◇ ～本 abridged edition（or version）

【缩写签字】initials

【缩印】reprint books in a reduced format

【缩影】epitome；miniature

suǒ

所 Ⅰ 名 ❶ place：住所 ❷ office；bureau；institute：派出所 Ⅱ 量（for houses，schools，hospitals，etc.）：一～房子 *a house* / 两～学校 *two schools* / 这～医院 *this hospital* Ⅲ 助〈书〉（used before a verb to form a noun construction）what，that which，those whom，etc. ❶ noun or pronoun＋所＋verb ⓐ（used with 的 to modify a noun）：我～认识的人 *the people I know* / 大家～提的意见 *the opinions various people put forward* ⓑ（used with 的 as a noun）：他～说的未必确实。*What he says is not necessarily true.* / 我～知道的就这些。*That's all I know.* ⓒ（used as a noun without 的，esp. when the verb is monosyllabic）：尽我～能 *do all I can* / 据你～说 *from what you say* ❷ 所＋verb ⓐ（used with 的 to modify a noun）：～用的方法 *the methods which are used* / ～需的费用 *the necessary expenses* ⓑ（used with 的 as a noun）：～需的并不多。*What is needed is not much.* / ～考虑的正是这一点。*That's just what we have under consideration.* ⓒ（used as a noun without 的，esp. in set phrases in which the verb is monosyllabic）：～见～闻 *what one has seen and heard* / 各尽～能 *from each according to his ability* ❸ 为 or 被＋noun or pronoun ＋所＋ verb（expressing a passive meaning）：为人～笑 *be laughed at by other people* / 被表面现象～迷惑 *be misled by outward appearances* ❹ 所＋ verb（used as the object of 有 or 无）ⓐ as the object of 有：有～创造 *create something or other* / 有～准备 *be prepared in some way or other* ⓑ as the object of 无，esp. in set phrases：无～准备 *need do nothing in preparation for it* / 无～用心 *not give serious thought to anything*

【所部】〈书〉troops under one's command：此炮兵师为李将军～。*This artillery division is under General Li's command.*

【所长】(suǒcháng) what one is good at; one's strong point; one's forte: 有～必有所短。*Where you are strong on one thing, you are weak on another.*

【所答非所问】not give a direct answer to a question; not answer to the point; give an irrelevant answer

【所得】what one has gained or acquired; gains; earnings; income: 略有～ *have gained something* / ～大于所失。*The gains offset the losses.* or *We have gained more than we have lost.*

【所得税】income tax

【所费不赀】incur a considerable or great expense: 工程浩大,～。*The project is on such a gigantic scale that the cost is hard to calculate.*

【所罗门群岛】Solomon Islands

【所属】❶ what is subordinate to one or under one's command: 外交部～单位 *the organizations under the Foreign Ministry* ❷ what one belongs to or is affiliated with: 向～派出所填报户口 *apply to (or register with) the local police station for residence*

【所谓】❶ what is called; what is known as ❷ so-called: 他的～朋友都背弃了他。*All his so-called friends deserted him.*

【所向披靡】(of troops) carry all before one; sweep away all obstacles; send the enemy fleeing helter-skelter

【所向无敌】be all-conquering; be ever-victorious; break all enemy resistance: 其声势之浩大,威力之猛烈,简直是～的。*Its influence has been so great and its impact so powerful that it is invincible wherever it goes.*

【所向无前】carry all before one; be irresistible

【所学非所用】be employed in a job not in one's line: 可惜他～。*Pity he's employed in a job not in his line.*

【所以】❶ as a result; so; therefore: 天太冷,～我不去了。*It's too cold, so I'm not going.* ❷ the reason why: 我们～没有去,是因为我们得到通知太晚了。*The reason why we didn't go was that we were notified too late.* ❸ that's why: 我和他在一起工作过两三年,这就是我～对他比较熟悉的原因。*He and I have worked together for a couple of years. That's why I know him pretty well.* ❹ 〈口〉 that's just the reason; that's just the point: ～呀,要不我怎么会这么说呢? *That's just the point; otherwise I wouldn't have said it.*

【所以然】the reason why; the whys and wherefores: 他说了半天还是没说出个～来。*He talked a lot but made you none the wiser.*

【所有】❶ own; possess: 这些乐器属学校～。*These musical instruments belong to the school.* ❷ possessions: 尽其所有 ❸ all: 把～的劲儿都使出来 *exert all one's strength*

【所有格】[语] the possessive case

【所有权】proprietary rights; ownership; title

【所有制】system of ownership; ownership: 生产资料～ *the system of ownership of the means of production*

【所在】❶ place; location: 那是个风景优美的～。*It is a picturesque place (or a lovely scenic spot).* ❷ where sb. or sth. is: 这是我们的力量～。*That is where our strength lies.* or *Herein lies our strength.* / ～单位 *the organization one belongs to*

【所在地】location; seat; site

【所在多有】be found almost everywhere

【所长】(suǒzhǎng) the head of an office, institute, etc.: 研究所～ *the director of a research institute* / 托儿所～ *the head of a nursery*

【所致】be caused by; be the result of: 这次事故是由于疏忽～。*The accident was the result of (or was due to) negligence.*

【所作所为】one's behaviour or conduct: 看他平时的～,就可以想见他在这种场合的表现。*Just look at his usual behaviour and you can imagine how he will behave on this occasion.*

索

Ⅰ 名 ❶ a large rope: 麻～ *a hempen rope* / 船～ *a ship's rigging* Ⅱ 动 ❶ search: 遍～不得 *search high and low for sth. in vain* ❷ demand; ask; exact: ～债 *demand payment of a debt* Ⅲ 形 〈书〉 ❶ all alone; all by oneself: 离群索居 ❷ dull; insipid: 索然

【索酬】demand reward

【索道】cableway; ropeway: 在河上架起～ *throw a cableway across the river* / 高架～ *telpher*

【索贿】extort bribes: 利用迁办户口～的案件 *case involving extortion of bribes for changing residence permits* / ～受贿 *solicit (or accept) bribes*

【索价】ask (or demand) a price; charge: ～极高 *demand an exorbitant price*

【索解】seek an answer or explanation: ～人生的意义 *ponder the meaning of life*

【索马里】Somalia ◇ ～人 Somali; ～语 Somali (language)

【索寞】(又作'索莫','索漠')〈书〉❶ down-hearted; dejected; dispirited: 神情～ *look dejected* ❷ lonely; desolate: 岛上杂草丛生,异常～。*The island was overgrown with weeds and looked extremely desolate.*

【索赔】claim damages; claim an indemnity ◇ ～人 claimant; ～条款 claim clause; ～通知 notice of claim; ～信 letter of claims

【索桥】chain bridge; cable bridge

【索取】ask for; demand; exact; extort: ～样品 *ask for a sample* / ～巨额赔款 *extort a huge indemnity*

【索然】dull; dry; insipid: 兴致～ *uninterested; bored stiff*

【索然寡味】(又作'索然无味') flat and insipid

【索索】❶ a rustling sound: 微风吹动树叶～作响。*The leaves rustled in the breeze.* ❷ trembling: 他吓得脸色苍白,～发抖。*He turned ashen pale and trembled with fear.*

【索性】simply; just; might as well: 既然已经做了,～就把它做完。*Since you have started the job, you might as well finish it*.

【索要】ask for; claim; demand

【索引】index: 卡片～ *card index* / 书名～ *title index* / 作者～ *author index* / 标题～ *subject index*

唢 (构词成分) 见下

【唢呐】suona horn, a woodwind instrument

琐 形 trivial; petty

【琐事】trifles; trivial matters: 家庭～ *household affairs*

【琐碎】trifling; trivial: 摆脱这些～的事,多抓些大问题。*Don't get bogged down in these trivialities; try to grasp the essentials*.

【琐闻】bits of news; scraps of information

【琐细】同〖琐碎〗

【琐屑】〈书〉trifling; trivial

【琐杂】petty and involved: 理财是一件～的事情。*Managing money matters is messy and troublesome*.

锁 Ⅰ 名 ❶ lock: 门上加了一把～。*An extra lock has been fixed on the door*. ❷ lock and chains; chains: 枷锁 Ⅱ 动 ❶ lock (up): ～门 *lock a door* / ～在保险箱里 *be locked up in a safe* / 双眉紧～ *with knitted brows* ❷ lockstitch: ～眼 *do a lockstitch on a buttonhole* / ～边 *lockstitch a border*

【锁匙】〈方〉key

【锁骨】[生理] clavicle; collarbone

【锁国】见〖闭关锁国〗

【锁簧】[机] locking spring

【锁匠】locksmith

【锁紧】[机] locking: 自～ *self-locking*

【锁链】(又作'锁链子') ❶ chain ❷ shackles; fetters; chains

【锁阳】[中] Chinese cynomorium (Cynomorium songaricum)

【锁钥】❶〈喻〉key: 解决问题的～ *a key to the problem* ❷ strategic gateway (to an important centre or a major city)

T

tā

它 代 it：这杯牛奶你喝了～。*Drink up this glass of milk.* / 有个东西在黑影里蹲着，我也看不清～到底是猫还是狗。*Some animal was crouching in the shadow. I couldn't make out whether it was a cat or a dog.* / 这些画报我都看过了，你把～拿去吧。*I've finished with these pictorials. You can take them away.*

【它们】they or them (plural of 它)

他 代 ❶ he or him：～刚才给你送票来了。*He came just now with a ticket for you.* / 谁没有票，问～要。*Anyone without a ticket can ask him for one.* / ～俩 *the two of them* ❷ (used for either sex when the sex of a person is unknown or unimportant)：从远处看不出～是男的还是女的。*I can't tell whether it's a man or a woman from a distance.* ❸ (used before a person's name for emphasis)：这事儿成与不成就看～老张了。*The success or failure of this all depends on no one else but Lao Zhang.* / 老王～也提前到了。*Lao Wang also came a bit early.* ❹ (used as a meaningless mock object)：好好睡～一觉 *have a good sleep* / 咱们喝～几杯去。*Let's go and have a few drinks.* / 你写～两三本书就出名了。*If you can publish a couple of books, you'll become famous.* ❺〈书〉other; another; some other：别无～求 *have no other request* / 留作～用 *reserve for other uses* / 调往～处 *be transferred to another place* / 此人早已～去。*He has long since left.*

【他动词】同〖及物动词〗

【他妈的】〈讳〉damn it; blast it; to hell with it：～！又下雨了！*Damn it! It's raining again.* / 我～才不干呢！*I'll be damned if I will!*

【他们】❶ they or them (referring to people)：～刚来，你找～去。*They've just come. You may go and see them now.* / ～俩(仨) *the two (three) of them* ❷ (used before or after a noun or nouns for emphasis)：～弟兄都是钳工。*The two brothers are fitters.* / 赵先生、钱先生～都下班走了。*Both Mr. Zhao and Mr. Qian have left the office for the day.* ❸ (used after the name or title of a person to mean "and the others")：队长～都在体育馆里练球。*The captain and his team (or men) are in the gym practising.*

【他人】another person; other people; others：关心～比关心自己为重 *be more concerned about others than oneself*

【他日】〈书〉some other time or day; some day：～再来看望。*I'll call on you again some other time.*

【他杀】[法] homicide

【他乡】a place far away from home; an alien land ◇ ～遇故知 meet an old friend in a distant land

她 代 she or her：～好久没来这儿了。*She hasn't been here for a long time.* / 我明天找～去。*I'm going to see her tomorrow.*

【她们】(used when the referent is feminine) they or them

铊 名 [化] thallium (Tl)

趿 动 同〖趿拉〗

【趿拉】wear cloth shoes with the backs turned in; shuffle about with the backs of one's shoes trodden down：别～着鞋走路。*Don't walk around with the backs of your shoes turned in.* or *Don't use your shoes as slippers.*

【趿拉儿】〈方〉slippers

【趿拉板儿】〈方〉wooden slippers; clogs

溻 动〈方〉(of clothes, etc.) become soaked with sweat：天太热，我衣服都～了。*It's too hot and my clothes become soaked with sweat.*

塌 动 ❶ collapse; fall down; cave in：墙～了。*The wall collapsed.* / 地震的时候～了几间房。*Several houses collapsed during the earthquake.* / 没什么好怕的，天不会～下来。*There's nothing to be afraid of. The sky won't fall down.* ❷ sink; droop：～鼻梁 *a flat nose* / 花儿晒～秧了。*The flowers drooped in the hot sun.* ❸ calm down; settle down：～下心去 *set one's mind at ease; settle down to (work, etc.)*

【塌方】❶ cave in; collapse：大坝出现～。*A section of the dam has caved in.* ❷ landslide; landslip

【塌架】❶ (of a building, etc.) collapse; topple down ❷ fall from power

【塌落】cave in; collapse：天花板～了，打在他们身上。*The ceiling caved in on them.*

【塌实】❶ steady and sure; dependable：工作～ *be a steady worker; be steadfast in one's work* ❷ free from anxiety; having peace of mind：等事情办完，我就觉得～了。*I'll be able to put my mind at rest when the matter is settled.* / 睡得很

～ *enjoy a deep, quiet sleep; have a good, sound sleep*

【塌台】fall from power; collapse

【塌陷】subside; sink; cave in: 这座房子的地基～了。*The foundations of this building have subsided.*

踏 (构词成分)见下——另见 tà

【踏实】同〖塌实〗

tǎ

塔 名 ❶ Buddhist pagoda; pagoda ❷ tower: 水塔 ❸〔化〕column; tower: 氧化～ *oxidizing column (or tower)* / 蒸馏～ *distillation column (or tower)*

【塔吊】tower crane

【塔夫绸】taffeta

【塔吉克斯坦】Tadzhikistan: ～人 *Tajik*

【塔吉克族】the Tajik ethnic group, or the Tajiks

【塔楼】❶ tower ❷ turret

【塔轮】〔机〕cone pulley; stepped pulley

【塔式起重机】同〖塔吊〗

【塔斯社】TASS—official news agency of the former Soviet Union, merged with the Russian Telegraphic Information Agency in 1992 and renamed Itar-Tass

【塔塔尔族】the Tatar ethnic group, or the Tatars

【塔台】〔航空〕control tower

【塔钟】tower clock; turret clock

獭 名 otter: 水獭

鳎 名〔动〕sole

tà

拓 动 make rubbings from inscriptions, pictures, etc. on stone tablets or bronze vessels ——另见 tuò

【拓本】a book of rubbings

【拓片】rubbing (from a stone tablet or bronze vessel)

沓 动〈书〉crowded; repeated——另见 dá

【沓乱】numerous and disorderly: ～的脚步声 *the clatter of footsteps*

挞 动〈书〉flog; whip: 鞭挞

【挞伐】〈书〉send armed forces to suppress; send a punitive expedition against

嗒 形〈书〉frustrated

【嗒然】〈书〉dejected; despondent; depressed

【嗒然若丧】deeply despondent; mournful and dejected

【嗒丧】in low spirits; dejected; despondent: ～着脸 *wear a sad look; put on a long face*

榻 名 a long, narrow and low bed; couch: 竹～ *bamboo couch* / 藤～ *rattan (or cane) couch*

【榻榻米】tatami—Japanese mattress placed on the floor

踏 动 ❶ step on; tread; stamp: 把火～灭 *tread out a fire* / ～上贵国的土地 *set foot on the soil of your country* / 勘探队～遍了祖国的山山水水。*The prospecting team has traversed the length and breadth of the land.* ❷ go to the spot (to make an investigation or survey): 踏勘 ——另见 tā

【踏板】❶ treadle; footboard; footrest: 缝纫机～ *the treadle of a sewing machine* ❷ footstool (usu. placed beside a bed) ❸〔音〕pedal (of a piano, etc.): 强音～ *damper (or loud) pedal* / 弱音～ *soft pedal*

【踏步】❶ mark time; march in place ❷〈方〉a flight of steps; steps leading up to a house, etc.

【踏歌】singing accompanied by stamping of feet, or rhythmic dancing

【踏勘】❶ make an on-the-spot survey (of a railway line, construction site, etc.) ❷〈旧〉(of an official) make a personal investigation on the spot

【踏看】go to the spot to make an investigation

【踏破铁鞋无觅处，得来全不费工夫】you can wear out iron shoes in fruitless searching, and yet by a lucky chance you may find the lost thing without even looking for it; fancy finding by sheer luck what one has searched for far and wide

【踏青】walk on the green grass—go for an outing in early spring

【踏雪】walk in the snow

【踏月】walk in the moonlight

蹋 动 step on; tread ——见〖糟蹋〗

tāi

苔 (构词成分)见〖舌苔〗——另见 tái

胎 名 ❶ foetus; embryo: ～形 *the form of the foetus* / 有了～了 *become (or be) pregnant* / ～掉了 *have a miscarriage* ❷ padding; stuffing; wadding: 棉花胎 ❸ roughcast (in the making of china, cloisonné, etc.): 泥胎儿 ❹ tyre: 内胎/外胎 ❺ birth: 头～ *first baby; firstborn* / 一～十五只小猪 *fifteen piglets at a litter (or at one farrow)*

【胎动】movement of the foetus which can be felt by the mother

【胎儿】❶ (human) foetus ❷ foetus (of a domestic animal)

【胎发】foetal hair; lanugo

【胎记】birthmark

【胎教】foetal training (improving the environment of the foetus, through the pregnant mother engaging in activities such as reading, listening to music, enjoying art, etc. to ensure healthy foetal development)

【胎里坏】a born villain
【胎毛】foetal hair; lanugo
【胎膜】foetal membrane
【胎盘】placenta
【胎气】nausea, vomiting and oedema of legs during pregnancy; pregnancy complications
【胎生】[动] viviparity: ～动物 *viviparous animal*; *vivipara*
【胎位】[医] position of a foetus
【胎痣】birthmark: 她脸上有颗红色的～。*She has a red birthmark on her face.*
【胎座】[植] placenta

tái

台 Ⅰ 名 ❶ platform; stage; terrace: ～上坐着主席团。*Seated on the rostrum was the presidium.* ❷ anything shaped like a platform, etc.: 窗台 ❸ stand; support: 灯台 ❹ special telephone service: 查号台 ❺ broadcasting station: 电视台 ❻ table; desk: 写字台 ❼〈略〉见〖台湾〗 Ⅱ 代〈尊〉〈书〉your: ～启 *for your information* (*used after the name of the addressee on an envelope*) / ～鉴 *for your inspection* (*used after the name in the salutation of a business letter*) Ⅲ 量 ❶ (for certain machinery, apparatus, instruments, etc.): 一～打字机(计算机、拖拉机) *a typewriter* (*computer*, *tractor*) ❷ (for a whole performance on the stage): 一～戏(话剧、歌舞) *a performance* (*modern drama*, *song and dance performance*)
【台胞】compatriots in or from Taiwan
【台本】a playscript with stage directions
【台布】tablecloth
【台步】(in traditional opera) stage walk: 梅兰芳的～非常优美。*Mei Lanfang's stage walk was very graceful.*
【台秤】❶ platform scale; platform balance ❷〈方〉counter scale
【台词】actor's lines
【台灯】desk lamp; table lamp; reading lamp
【台地】❶ [地质] platform; tableland ❷ [军] mesa
【台独】independence of Taiwan (proposition of a handful of people in Taiwan attempting to split Taiwan from China)
【台风】❶ typhoon: 强～ *a violent typhoon* / ～眼 *typhoon eye* ❷ an actor's demeanour on the stage: ～稳健 *a calm and steady stage demeanour*
【台甫】〈尊〉〈书〉your honoured style (used in asking sb.'s courtesy name): ～? *May I ask your honoured style?*
【台虎钳】[机] bench vice
【台阶】❶ a flight of steps; steps leading up to a house, etc. ❷ chance to extricate oneself from an awkward position: 给他个～下吧。*Give him an out.* ❸ [矿] bench: 上～ *upper bench* ——另见〖下台阶〗
【台历】desk calendar
【台面】❶ [电子] mesa: ～型晶体管 *mesa transistor* ❷〈方〉on the table; aboveboard; in public ❸〈方〉winnings and losses (in gambling)
【台钳】[机] bench clamp
【台球】❶ billiards ❷ billiard ball
【台商】businessman from Taiwan
【台湾】Taiwan (Province)
【台钟】〈方〉desk clock
【台柱子】❶ star or leading member (of a theatrical troupe) ❷ soul member (of an organization); mainstay; pillar
【台资】Taiwan capital; investment from Taiwan
【台子】❶〈口〉platform; stage ❷〈方〉table; desk ❸ billiard table ❹ table tennis table; ping-pong table
【台钻】[机] bench drill

抬 动 ❶ lift; raise: ～胳膊 *raise one's arm* / 把桌子～起来 *lift* (*up*) *the table* ❷ (of two or more persons) carry: ～担架 *carry a stretcher*
【抬秤】huge steelyard (usu. worked by three persons, with two lifting the steelyard on a shoulder pole and the third adjusting the weight)
【抬杠】❶〈口〉argue for the sake of arguing; bicker; wrangle: 他俩抬起杠来就没完。*Those two can go on arguing for hours and hours.* ❷〈旧〉carry a coffin on stout poles
【抬高】raise; heighten; enhance: ～声誉 *raise sb.'s reputation* / ～物价 *force up commodity prices* / 打击别人～自己 *attack others so as to build oneself up*
【抬价】force up commodity prices
【抬肩】half the circumference of the sleeve where it joins the shoulder
【抬轿子】carry sb. in a sedan chair—flatter (rich and influential people); sing the praises of; boost
【抬举】praise or promote sb. to show favour; favour sb. ——另见〖不识抬举〗
【抬手】❶ raise one's hand ❷ be magnanimous; not be too hard on sb.; make an exception in sb.'s favour: 这事只要您抬抬手,就过去了。*I'll get off if you will make an exception in my case.*
【抬头】❶ raise one's head: ～一看 *look up* ❷ gain ground; look up; rise ❸ begin a new line, as a mark of respect, when mentioning the addressee in letters, official correspondence, etc. ❹ [经] (on receipts, bills, etc.) name of the buyer or payee, or space for filling in such name
【抬头纹】wrinkles on one's forehead

苔 名 [植] liverwort ——另见 tāi
【苔藓动物】bryozoan
【苔藓植物】bryophyte
【苔原】[地理] tundra

薹 名 ❶ [植] a kind of sedge ❷ the bolt of garlic, rape, etc.

tài

太 Ⅰ形 ❶ highest; greatest: 太空 ❷ remotest: 太古 ❸ more or most senior: ～老伯 *granduncle*; *great-uncle* Ⅱ副 ❶ excessively; too; over: 你车开得～快,不安全。*You're driving too fast for safety.* / 那～过分了。*That's going too far.* / 这座城市人口～多。*The city is over-populated.* ❷(used to express admiration or exclamation with 了 at the end of the sentence): 她的发音～好了。*Her pronunciation is excellent.* / 长城～伟大了。*The Great Wall is really great.* / 我～感激你了。*I feel very much indebted to you.* ❸ (used before another adverb 不 to emphasize negation): 这～不好了。*It's very bad.* / 你～不虚心了。*You're being immodest.* ❹ (used after 不 to soften the tone of negation): 不～好 *not very good* / 这车看起来不～漂亮,可就是快。*The car isn't much to look at, but it's fast.* / 他不～愿意结交新朋友。*He's hesitant about making new friends.*

【太白星】Grand White (old name for 金星)

【太仓一粟】a grain of millet in a granary—a drop in the ocean

【太阿倒持】hold the sword by the blade—surrender one's power to another at one's own peril

【太妃糖】taffy; toffee

【太公】〈方〉great-grandfather

【太公钓鱼,愿者上钩】like the fish rising to Jiang Taigong's hookless and baitless line—a willing victim letting himself be caught

【太古】remote antiquity

【太古代】[地质] the Archean (or Archaeozoic) Era

【太后】mother of an emperor; empress dowager; queen mother

【太极】the Supreme Ultimate ◇ ～拳 taijiquan, a system of physical exercises that emphasizes balance, coordination, and effortlessness in movements, designed for attaining bodily or mental control and wellbeing and also as an art of self-defence; ～图 Diagram of the Supreme Ultimate

【太监】(court) eunuch

【太空】the firmament; outer space ◇ ～步 space walk dance (imitation of walking in space); ～城 cosmograd; ～船 a space craft; space ship; ～服 spacesuit; ～人 astronauts; cosmonauts; ～时代 the space age; ～站 space station

【太庙】the Imperial Ancestral Temple

【太平】peaceful and tranquil; having good social order and without war ◇ ～盛世 times of peace and prosperity; the piping times of peace

【太平花】Beijing mockorange (Philadelphus pekinensis)

【太平间】mortuary

【太平门】exit (of a building, etc.)

【太平鸟】waxwing

【太平梯】fire escape

【太平天国】the Taiping Heavenly Kingdom

【太平无事】all is well

【太平洋】the Pacific (Ocean)

【太婆】〈方〉great-grandmother

【太上皇】❶ a title assumed by an emperor's father who abdicated in favour of his son ❷ overlord; supersovereign; backstage ruler

【太上老君】Most Exalted Lord Lao (a Taoist deity, identified with Lao Zi 老子)

【太甚】too far; to the extreme: 欺人～。That's going too far.

【太师椅】an old-fashioned wooden armchair

【太岁】❶ the Master of the Year (an ancient name for 木星) ❷ Taisui; the God of the Year: ～头上动土 *break ground where Taisui (a god) presides—defy the mighty* ❸〈贬〉a nickname for the most powerful man in a locality: 镇山～ *the Lord of the Mountain (a brigand chief)* / 花花～ *the King of Lechers*

【太太】❶ Mrs.; madame: 王～ *Mrs. Wang; Madame Wang* ❷ the mistress of a household; madam; lady ❸ (usu. preceded by a personal pronoun) wife: 我～ *my wife* ❹〈方〉(paternal) great-grandmother or great-grandfather

【太虚】〈文〉the great void; the universe ◇ ～幻境 in a state of visionary and emptiness

【太学】the Imperial College (in feudal China)

【太阳】❶ the sun: ～光 *the sun's rays; sunshine; sunlight* ❷ the sun's rays; sunshine; sunlight: 晒～ *bask in the sun* / 今天～很好。*It's a lovely sunny day.* ◇ ～常数 solar constant; ～灯[医] sunlamp; sunlight lamp; ～地儿 a place where there is sunshine; sunny spot; ～电池 solar cell; ～风 solar wind; ～辐射[气] solar radiation; ～光谱[物] solar spectrum; ～黑子 sunspot; ～活动周 solar cycle; ～历 solar calendar; ～炉 solar furnace; ～帽 sun helmet; topee; ～目视镜 helioscope; ～能 solar energy; ～年 another name for 回归年; ～系 the solar system; ～灶 solar energy stove; solar cooker

【太阳镜】sunglasses

【太阳鸟】sunbird

【太阳穴】the temples

【太爷】❶ (paternal) grandfather ❷〈方〉(paternal) great-grandfather

【太医】❶ an imperial physician ❷〈方〉medical man; doctor

【太阴】❶〈方〉the moon ❷[天] lunar ◇ ～历 lunar calendar; ～年 lunar year; ～月 lunar month; lunation

【太子】prince; crown prince

态 名 ❶ form; appearance; condition: 形态 ❷ [物] state: 气态 ❸〈语〉voice: 语态

【态度】❶ manner; bearing; how one conducts oneself: ～大方 *have an easy manner* / ～和蔼 *amiable; kindly* / ～恶劣 *behave badly* /他今天～有些异常。*He is not his usual self today.* ❷ attitude；approach：劳动～ *attitude towards labour* —— 另见〖要态度〗

【态势】state；situation；posture：战略～ *strategic situation* / 军事～ *military posture*

肽 名 [化] peptide

钛 名 [化] titanium (Ti)

【钛白】(又作'钛白粉')[化] titanium white；titanium dioxide

【钛铁矿】ilmenite

泰 形 ❶ safe；peaceful：康泰 ❷ extreme；most

【泰斗】Mount Tai and the North Star —an eminent scholar，musician，artist，etc.：音乐界的～ *the prince of musicians* / 京剧～ *the foremost actor of Beijing opera*

【泰国】Thailand ◇ ～人 Thailander；Thai；～语 Thai (language)

【泰然】calm；composed；self-possessed ◇ ～处之 take sth. calmly；bear sth. with equanimity；～自若 behave with perfect composure；be self-possessed

【泰山】❶ Mount Tai (in Shandong Province) ❷ a symbol of great weight or import：有眼不识泰山 ❸〈旧〉wife's father；father-in-law ◇ ～北斗 Mount Tai and the North Star (a respectful epithet for a person of distinction)；～压顶 bear down on one with the weight of Mount Tai；～压卵 like Mount Tai bearing down on an egg — with overwhelmingly superior force

酞 名 [化] phthalein

tān

坍 动 collapse；fall；tumble：土墙～了。*The earthen wall collapsed.*

【坍圮】〈书〉cave in；collapse

【坍塌】cave in；collapse

【坍台】〈方〉❶ (of enterprises，etc.) collapse；fold ❷ fall into disgrace；lose face

贪 动 ❶ embezzle；practise graft；be corrupt：贪污 ❷ have an insatiable desire for：～女色 *be fond of women*；*be a womanizer* / 他～吃，这回把肚子吃坏了。*He's a glutton*；*he ate himself sick this time.* ❸ covet；hanker after：～安逸 *seek ease and comfort* / ～大求全 *go in for grandiose projects*

【贪杯】be excessively fond of drinking；love a drop too much

【贪财】be greedy for money；be a money-grubber

【贪大求洋】concentrate on grandiose projects and advanced technologies without considering actual conditions

【贪得无厌】be insatiably avaricious

【贪多嚼不烂】bite off more than one can chew

【贪多务得】greedy and acquisitive

【贪官污吏】corrupt officials；venal officials

【贪婪】avaricious；greedy；rapacious：～的目光 *greedy eyes*

【贪恋】be reluctant to part with；hate to leave；cling to：～舒适的生活 *be reluctant to give up ease and comfort*

【贪便宜】eager to get things on the cheap；keen on gaining petty advantages

【贪色】be fond of women；be a womanizer

【贪生怕死】cravenly cling to life instead of braving death；care for nothing but saving one's skin；be mortally afraid of death

【贪天之功】arrogate to oneself the merits of others；claim credit for other people's achievements

【贪图】seek；hanker after；covet：～安逸 *seek ease and comfort* / ～小利 *covet small advantages*；*hanker after petty gains*

【贪玩】be too fond of play

【贪污】embezzle；practise graft；be corrupt：～分子 *a person guilty of corruption*；*grafter*；*embezzler* ◇ ～盗窃 graft and embezzlement；～腐化 corruption and degeneration；corruption

【贪污受贿】embezzlement and bribe-taking；corruption

【贪小失大】covet a little and lose a lot；seek small gains but incur big losses

【贪心】❶ greed；avarice；rapacity ❷ greedy；avaricious；insatiable；voracious：～不足 *insatiably greedy*

【贪赃】take bribes；practise graft ◇ ～枉法 take bribes and bend the law；pervert justice for a bribe

【贪嘴】greedy (for food)；gluttonous

滩 名 ❶ beach；sands：海滩 ❷ shoal：～多水急 *with many shoals and rapids*

【滩头堡】[军] beachhead

【滩羊】a kind of sheep known for its fine thick wool

摊 Ⅰ 名 vendor's stand；booth；stall：水果～儿 *fruit stand*；*fruit stall* / 报～ *news-stand*；*news stall* Ⅱ 动 ❶ spread out：把豆子～开晒一晒 *spread the beans out to dry in the sun* / 书～了一桌子。*Books are strewn all over the desk.* / 把事情～到桌面上来谈 *put the problems on the table and thrash them out* ❷ fry batter in a thin layer：～煎饼 *make pancakes* ❸ take a share in：每人～五元钱。*Each person will contribute 5 yuan.* ❹ (of unpleasant things) befall；happen to：～上这种事真倒霉！*What luck to have this happen to me！* Ⅲ 量 (for paste or thick liquid)：一～稀泥 *a mud puddle* / 一～血 *a pool of blood*

【摊车】pedlar's stand and cart

【摊点】stand；booth：夜市～ *night market booth*

【摊贩】street pedlar

【摊鸡蛋】omelette

【摊开】spread out：～双手 *spread out one's hands* / 把问题～来谈 *discuss the questions with all cards on the table*

【摊牌】lay one's cards on the table; show one's hand (or cards); have a showdown: 迫使对方～ *force one's opponent to show his hand*; *force a showdown*

【摊派】apportion (expenses, work, etc.)

【摊晒机】[农] tedder

【摊手】loosen one's grip; let go

【摊售】(of a vendor's stand) sell goods; set up a stall

【摊位】vendor's stand; booth; stall

【摊子】❶ vendor's stand; booth; stall: 菜～ *vegetable stall* (*or stand*) ❷ the structure of an organization; setup: ～铺得太大 *do sth. on too large a scale*

瘫 动 be physically paralysed: 吓～了 *be paralysed with fright* / 他～了两年了。*He's been paralysed for two years.*

【瘫痪】❶ paralysis; palsy: ～病人 *paralytic* ❷ (of transportation, etc.) be paralysed; break down; be at a standstill: 交通运输陷于～。*Transportation was at a standstill.*

【瘫软】(of arms, legs, etc.) become weak and limp: 被告一听到判决,浑身都～了。*On hearing the verdict, the defendant collapsed.*

【瘫子】a person suffering from paralysis; paralytic

tán

坛 名 ❶ altar: 天坛 ❷ a raised plot of land for planting flowers, etc.: 花坛 ❸ platform; forum: 讲坛 ❹ circles; world: 文坛 ❺ earthen jar; jug: 一～醋 *a jar of vinegar* / 酒～ *a wine jug*

【坛坛罐罐】pots and pans—personal possessions: 不怕打烂～ *not be afraid of having one's pots and pans smashed—not fear loss of possessions or destruction of property*

【坛子】*earthen jar*; *jug*

昙 形 cloudy; overcast

【昙花】broad-leaved epiphyllum (Epiphyllum oxypetalum) ◇ ～一现 flower briefly as the broad-leaved epiphyllum; last briefly; be a flash in the pan

谈 Ⅰ 动 talk; chat; discuss: 他～了自己的看法。*He offered his personal views.* / 第一次见面他们就～得很投机。*They had a most agreeable chat when they first met.* / 我们好好～～。*Let's have a good chat.* Ⅱ 名 what is said or talked about: 奇谈

【谈不到】(又作'谈不上') out of the question: 没有政治上的独立,就～经济上的独立。*Without political independence, you can't begin to talk about economic independence.*

【谈不来】not get along well

【谈得到】(又作'谈得上') take into consideration: 有了组合音响才～买激光唱片。*I can only consider buying a CD after I've bought a hi-fi set.*

【谈得来】get along well

【谈锋】volubility; eloquence: ～甚健 *talk volubly*; *be a good talker*; *have the gift of the gab*

【谈何容易】easier said than done; by no means easy

【谈虎色变】turn pale at the mention of the tiger—turn pale at the mere mention of something terrifying

【谈话】❶ talk; chat; discuss: 进行亲切友好的～ *have a cordial and friendly conversation* ❷ statement: 发表书面～ *make a written statement*

【谈家常】talk about everyday matters; engage in small talk; chitchat

【谈论】discuss; talk about: 同学们纷纷～着今天发生的事。*The students are all talking about what happened today.*

【谈判】negotiate; hold talks: 开始～ *enter into* (*or open*) *negotiations with* / 重开～ *resume the talks* / 举行～ *hold talks* (*or negotiations*) / 贸易～ *trade negotiations* (*or talks*) ～桌 *conference table*

【谈情说爱】be courting; talk love

【谈天】(又作'谈闲天') chat; make conversation ◇ ～说地 talk of everything under the sun

【谈吐】style of conversation: ～不俗 *talk in good taste*

【谈笑】talk (or chat) and laugh ◇ ～风生 talk and laugh cheerfully (or merrily)

【谈笑自若】go on talking and laughing as if nothing had happened: 沉着镇静,～ *go on talking and laughing without turning a hair* / 临危不惧,～ *talk and laugh imperturbably in face of danger*

【谈心】heart-to-heart talk

【谈兴】mood for conversation: ～正浓 *be having an animated conversation*

【谈言微中】speak tactfully but to the point; make one's point through hints

弹 Ⅰ 动 ❶ shoot (as with a catapult, etc.); send forth: ～石子 *shoot pebbles with a catapult* ❷ fluff; tease: ～棉花 *fluff* (*or tease*) *cotton* (*with a bow*) ❸ flick; flip: ～烟灰 *flick the ash off a cigarette* / 把帽子上的灰尘～掉 *flick the dust off a hat* ❹ play (a stringed musical instrument); pluck: ～钢琴 *play the piano* / ～琵琶 *pluck the pipa* ❺ spring; leap: 球从篮板上～回来。*The ball rebounded from the backboard.* / 从跳板上～起来 *leap from the springboard* ❻ accuse; impeach: 弹劾 Ⅱ 形 elastic: 弹性 ——另见 dàn

【弹拨】play (a stringed musical instrument); pluck ◇ ～乐器 plucked string (or stringed) instrument; plucked instrument

【弹词】❶ storytelling (esp. in Suzhou dialect) to the accompaniment of stringed instruments ❷ script for this kind of storytelling

【弹冠相庆】congratulate each other in anticipation

of fat jobs (upon hearing of a mutual friend's appointment to a high post); congratulate each other on the prospect of getting good appointments

【弹劾】impeach (a public official)

【弹花机】cotton fluffer

【弹簧】spring：回动～ *return spring* / 保险～ *relief spring* ◇ ～秤 spring balance；～床 spring bed；～钢 spring steel；～铰链 spring hinge；～门 swing door；～圈 spring coil；～锁 spring lock

【弹力】elastic force；elasticity；resilience；spring：失去～的橡皮圈 *a perished rubber band* ◇ ～尼龙 stretch nylon；elastic nylon；～纱 stretch yarn；～袜 stretch socks

【弹球】(play) marbles

【弹射】❶［军］launch (as with a catapult)；catapult；shoot off；eject ❷〈书〉pick faults and criticize；censure：～利病 *pick faults* ◇ ～器 ejector；catapult；～座舱 ejection capsule；～座椅 ejection (or ejector) seat

【弹跳】bounce；spring：～力好 *have a lot of spring* ◇ ～板［体］springboard

【弹涂鱼】mudskipper

【弹性】elasticity；resilience；spring：又软又有～的地毯 *soft and springy carpets* / 这种毛～大，拉力强。*This wool possesses high resilience and tensile strength.* / 球的～符合标准。*The balls reach the specifications for bounce.* ◇ ～分析 elastic analysis；～极限 elastic limit；～计 elastometer；～抗［物］elastic reactance；～塑料 elastoplast；～体 elastomer；～外交 elastic diplomacy

【弹压】suppress by force；quell

【弹指】snap one's fingers—(of time) quickly pass：～光阴 *time zipping by* / ～又过了三四年。*So another three or four years quickly passed.* ◇ ～之间 during the snapping of the fingers—in a flash；in the twinkling of an eye；in an instant

【弹奏】play (a stringed musical instrument)；pluck

痰 名 phlegm；sputum

【痰迷心窍】blinded judgement

【痰桶】〈口〉spittoon

【痰盂】spittoon；cuspidor

潭 名 ❶ deep pool；pond：水潭 ❷〈方〉pit；depression

【潭第】〈书〉〈尊〉your house

【潭府】〈书〉❶ a deep pool ❷〈尊〉your house

檀 名 wingceltis (Pteroceltis tatarinowii)：青檀

【檀板】hardwood clappers

【檀香】［植］white sandalwood；sandalwood ◇ ～木 sandalwood；～扇 sandalwood fan；～油 sandalwood oil；～皂 sandal soap

【檀香山】Honolulu

tǎn

忐 (构词成分)见下

【忐忑】perturbed；mentally disturbed ◇ ～不安 uneasy；fidgety；restless

坦 形 ❶ level；smooth：平坦 ❷ calm；composed：坦然 ❸ open；candid：坦率

【坦白】❶ honest；frank；candid：～对你说 *to be frank with you*；*frankly speaking* ❷ confess；make a confession；own up (to)：彻底～交代 *make a clean breast of (one's crimes)* / ～从宽，抗拒从严 *leniency to those who confess their crimes and severity to those who refuse to*

【坦诚】frank and sincere；frank and open：～相见 *deal with sb. in all sincerity*；*treat sb. openheartedly*

【坦荡】❶ broad and level ❷ magnanimous；bighearted：胸怀～ *have largeness of mind*；*be open-hearted and aboveboard*

【坦克】(又作'坦克车') tank：～手 *tankman*

【坦然】calm；unperturbed；having no misgivings：～无惧 *calm and fearless* ◇ ～自若 calm and confident；completely at ease

【坦桑尼亚】Tanzania ◇ ～人 Tanzanian

【坦率】candid；frank；straightforward：双方～地交换了意见。*The two sides had a frank exchange of views.*

【坦途】〈喻〉level road；highway：攀登科学高峰，既无捷径，又无～。*There are neither shortcuts nor easy paths to the heights of science.*

【坦挚】frank and sincere；frank and open

袒 动 ❶ leave (the upper part of the body) uncovered；be stripped to the waist or have one's shirt unbuttoned：袒胸露臂 ❷ give unprincipled protection to；shield；shelter：偏袒

【袒护】give unprincipled protection to；be partial to；shield：～一方 *be partial to one side* / 公然～ *openly shield* / 你别～他。*Don't make excuses for him.*

【袒露】expose；uncover

【袒胸露臂】exposing one's neck and shoulders；décolleté

钽 名［化］tantalum (Ta)

毯 名 blanket；rug；carpet：毛毯

【毯子】blanket

tàn

叹 动 ❶ sigh：～一声 *heave a sigh* ❷ exclaim in admiration；acclaim；praise：～为奇迹 *admire and praise sth. as a wonderful achievement*

【叹词】〈语〉interjection；exclamation

【叹服】gasp in admiration：令人～ *compel (or command) admiration*

【叹气】sigh；heave a sigh：叹了一口气 *heave a sigh*

【叹赏】admire；express admiration for：～不绝 *express profuse admiration (for)*

【叹为观止】acclaim (a work of art, etc.) as the acme of perfection
【叹息】〈书〉heave a sigh

炭 名 ❶ charcoal ❷〈口〉coal
【炭棒】crayon
【炭化】carbonize
【炭画】charcoal drawing; charcoal
【炭火】charcoal fire
【炭精】❶ general name for charcoal products ❷〈口〉general name for artificial charcoal and graphite ◇ ～棒 carbon stick; ～灯 arc lamp; arc light
【炭疽】[医] anthrax ◇ ～病 [农] anthracnose
【炭盆】charcoal brazier
【炭窑】charcoal kiln

探 Ⅰ 动 ❶ try to find out; explore; sound: ～情况 *try to find out how the situation is* / 他用竹竿～了～河水的深浅。*He used a bamboo pole to sound the river*. ❷ visit; pay a call on: 探视 ❸ stretch forward: 探身 Ⅱ 名 scout; spy; detective: 密探
【探宝】❶ hunt for treasure ❷ prospect for mineral deposits: 深山～ *prospect in the mountains* / 海底～ *explore the deep sea resources*
【探病】visit a sick person or a patient
【探测】survey; sound; probe: ～海底情况 *survey the seabed* / ～水深 *take soundings* / ～悬崖高度 *gauge the height of a bluff* ◇ ～器 sounder; probe; detector; ～气球 sounding ballon
【探查】look over; examine; scout: ～敌情 *gather intelligence about the enemy*
【探察】watch; look carefully at; observe: ～地形 *survey the terrain*
【探端知绪】investigate the beginning and know the end
【探访】❶ seek by inquiry or search: ～民间秘方 *seek out secret medicinal recipes from among the people* ❷ pay a visit to; visit: ～亲友 *visit one's relatives and friends*
【探风】make inquiries about sb. or sth.; fish for information
【探戈】tango (a transliteration)
【探花】title conferred on the one who won third place in the highest imperial examination in the Ming and Qing Dynasties
【探家】make a brief trip home: 你抽空探一回家。*Find time to make a trip home*.
【探监】visit a prisoner (usu. a relative or a friend)
【探井】❶ [矿] prospect (or test) pit; exploring (or exploratory) shaft ❷ [油] test well; exploratory well: 野猫～ *wildcat*
【探究】make a thorough inquiry; probe into: ～原因 *look into the causes*
【探看】❶ visit: ～病人 *visit a sick person or a patient* ❷ look about; watch: 四处～ *look around*
【探空】[气] sounding: ～气球 *sounding balloon*
【探口气】ascertain (or find out) sb.'s opinions or feelings; sound sb. out
【探矿】go prospecting; prospect
【探雷】detect (or locate) a mine: ～器 *mine detector*
【探路】explore the way
【探明】❶ ascertain; verify: 已～的煤储量 *proven (or known) coal deposits* ❷ get a clear understanding of sth.; find out: ～来访者的用意 *try to find out what the visitor has come for*
【探囊取物】(like) taking sth. out of one's pocket—as easy as winking; as easy as falling off a log
【探亲】go home to visit one's family or go to visit one's relatives: 到故乡～访友 *return to one's homeland to visit one's relatives and friends* ◇ ～假 home leave
【探求】seek; pursue; search after (or for): ～真理 *seek truth*
【探伤】[冶] detect a flaw (or crack): ～仪 *flaw detector*
【探身】lean forward: 他～去听她在说些什么。*He leaned forward (or over) to hear what she was saying*.
【探视】visit: ～病人 *visit a patient* ◇ ～时间 visiting hours (in a hospital)
【探索】explore; probe: ～宇宙的秘密 *probe (or explore) the secrets of the universe*
【探讨】inquire into; probe into; delve into: 从不同角度对问题进行～ *approach a subject from different angles*
【探听】try to find out; make inquiries: ～下落 *inquire about the whereabouts of sb. or sth.* / ～人家的私事 *pry into other people's private affairs*
【探头】pop one's head in; crane one's neck: 有人从门口探进头来。*Somebody popped his head in at the door*. / ～张望 *crane one's neck and look around*
【探头探脑】pop one's head in and look about: 他正乘着凉，只见一个人～在那里张望。*He was enjoying the cool breeze, when all at once he saw a man stealthily spying*.
【探望】❶ look about: 我在车站上四处～，哪儿也找不到那位朋友。*I looked all around the station but couldn't find my friend anywhere*. ❷ call on sb. (usu. from afar); visit; see: 回国～亲友 *return to one's home country to visit relatives and friends*
【探问】❶ make cautious inquiries about: 他们一再～此事。*They inquired about the matter time and again*. ❷ inquire after
【探悉】ascertain; learn; find out: 从有关方面～ *learn from those concerned*
【探险】explore; make explorations; venture into the unknown ◇ ～队 exploring (or exploration) party; expedition; ～家 explorer
【探信】〈口〉make inquiries about sb. or sth.; fish for information
【探寻】seek; pursue; search after (or for)
【探询】make cautious inquiries about

【探鱼仪】fish detector；fish-finder
【探照灯】searchlight：～的灯光 *searchlight beam*
【探针】［医］probe
【探知】get to know；find out；learn
【探子】❶〈旧〉scout ❷ a thin tube used to extract samples of food grains，etc.

碳 名［化］carbon（C）
【碳酐】［化］carbonic anhydride
【碳钢】同〖碳素钢〗
【碳黑】［化］carbon black
【碳化】carbonize ◇ ～钙 calcium carbide；～硅 carborundum；silicon carbide；～物 carbide
【碳精】［电］pure carbon ◇ ～棒 carbon stick（or rod）；～电极 carbon electrode；baked carbon
【碳氢化合物】hydrocarbon
【碳 14 测年法】［考古］C14 dating（another name for 放射性碳素测年法）
【碳刷】［电］carbon brush
【碳水化合物】carbohydrate
【碳丝】［电］carbon filament ◇ ～灯 carbon lamp
【碳素钢】carbon steel
【碳酸】carbonic acid ◇ ～钙 calcium carbonate；～钠 sodium carbonate；soda；～气 carbon dioxide；chokedamp；～氢钠 sodium bicarbonate；baking soda；～盐 carbonate

tāng

汤 名 ❶ hot water；boiling water：温汤浸种 ❷（usu. used as part of a place name）hot springs ❸ water in which sth. has been boiled：饺子～ *jiaozi water* / 姜～ *ginger tea* ❹ soup；broth：鸡～ *chicken soup* / 三菜一～ *soup and three other courses* / 喝点儿～吧。*Have some soup*. ❺ a liquid preparation of medicinal herbs；decoction：柴胡～ *a decoction of Chinese thorowax root*（*with other ingredients*）
【汤包】steamed dumplings filled with minced meat and gravy
【汤池】❶ 见〖金城汤池〗❷ hot water bathing pool（in a public bath-house）
【汤匙】tablespoon；soupspoon
【汤罐】a jug（fitted in an old-style kitchen range）used for heating up water
【汤锅】❶ a butcher's cauldron in a slaughterhouse ❷ slaughterhouse
【汤壶】metal or earthenware hot-water bottle
【汤剂】［中］decoction（of herbal medicine）
【汤加】Tonga ◇ ～人 Tongan
【汤料】soup stock ：固体～ *soup cubes* / 浓缩～ *concentrated soup*
【汤面】noodles in soup
【汤泉】〈古〉hot spring ◇ ～沐浴 bathe in a hot spring
【汤勺】soup ladle
【汤头】［中］a prescription for a medical decoction：～歌诀 *medical recipes in jingles*；*prescriptions in rhyme*
【汤碗】soup bowl
【汤药】［中］a decoction of medicinal ingredients
【汤圆】（usu. stuffed）dumplings made of glutinous rice flour served in soup

蹚 动 wade；ford：～水过河 *wade*（*across*）*a stream* / ～了一脚泥 *get one's feet muddy through wading*

táng

唐 名 the Tang Dynasty（618-907）：～诗 *Tang poetry*
【唐花】hothouse flower
【唐人街】Chinatown
【唐三彩】［考古］trio-coloured glazed pottery of the Tang Dynasty；Tang tricolour
【唐唐大国】a great powerful nation
【唐突】〈书〉❶ rudely offend sb.；blaspheme；profane：～古人 *profane an ancient sage* / 出言～ *make a blunt remark* / ～的行动 *a presumptuous act* / 恕我～。*Excuse me if I'm being too blunt*. ❷ pass oneself off as；pass sth. off as
【唐突陈说】make a statement unceremoniously

堂 Ⅰ 名 ❶the main room of a house：堂屋 ❷ a hall（or room）for a specific purpose：课堂/ 食堂 ❸〈旧〉court of law；a principal hall in a yamen ❹ relationship between cousins，etc. of the same paternal grandfather or great-grandfather：～兄弟（*male*）*cousins on the paternal side*；*cousins* Ⅱ 量（for furniture，classes，and in old use for trials）：每天上四～课 *have four classes every day* / 过了两～ *have been through two sessions*（*of a trial*）
【堂而皇之】❶ openly and legally ❷ do sth. in grand style
【堂鼓】a barrel-shaped drum，high and narrow（used in traditional operas）
【堂倌】〈旧〉waiter
【堂皇】grand；stately；magnificent：富丽堂皇
【堂上】❶ one's parents ❷〈旧〉（a term of address to magistrates or judges）Your Honour
【堂堂】❶ dignified；impressive：相貌～ *dignified in appearance*；*impressive-looking* ❷（of a man）having high aspirations and boldness of vision ❸ imposing；awe-inspiring；formidable
【堂堂正正】❶ impressive or dignified：他身材高大结实～的，不愧是个山东大汉。*He was a credit to the big men of Shandong with his height and solidity*. ❷ open and above-board
【堂屋】❶ central room（of a one-storey Chinese traditional house consisting of several rooms in a row）❷ principal rooms（in a courtyard，usu. facing south）

棠 名 同〖棠梨〗
【棠棣】［植］❶ Chinese bush cherry ❷ a kind of

white poplar
【棠梨】birchleaf pear (Pyrus betulaefolia)

塘 名 ❶ dyke; embankment: 河塘 ❷ pool; pond: 鱼塘 ❸ hot-water bathing pool: 澡塘
【塘肥】pond sludge used as manure
【塘醴】[动] sleeper
【塘泥】pond sludge; pond silt
【塘堰】(又作'塘坝')a small reservoir (in a hilly area)

搪 动 ❶ ward off; keep out: ～风 *keep out the wind* / ～饥 *allay one's hunger* ❷ evade; do sth. perfunctorily: ～账 *put off a creditor* / ～差事 *perform a duty perfunctorily* ❸ spread (clay, paint, etc.) over; daub: ～炉子 *line a stove with clay*
【搪瓷】enamel: ～茶缸 *enamel mug* ◇ ～钢板 [建] enamelled pressed steel; ～器皿 enamelware
【搪塞】stall sb. off; do sth. perfunctorily; put sb. off: ～他几句 *stall him off with a vague answer* / ～差事 *perform a duty perfunctorily*

樘 名 [建] door or window frame

膛 名 ❶ thorax; chest: 这小鸡儿的～肥。*The chick has a plump breast.* ❷ an enclosed space inside sth.; chamber: 这炉子的～儿大。*The stove has a large chamber.*
【膛线】rifling

糖 名 ❶ sugar: 咖啡里少搁点儿～。*Don't put too much sugar in the coffee.* / 你喝茶搁～吗? *Do you take sugar in your tea?* ❷ sweets; candy; sweetmeats: 一袋～ *a bag of sweets* / 吃块～。*Have a candy.* ❸ another name for 碳水化合物
【糖包】steamed bun stuffed with sugar
【糖厂】sugar refinery
【糖醋】sugar and vinegar; sweet and sour ◇ ～排骨 sweet and sour spareribs; ～鱼 fish in sweet and sour sauce
【糖果】sweets; candy; sweetmeats: ～店 *sweet shop; candy store; confectionery*
【糖葫芦】sugarcoated haws on a stick
【糖化】[化] saccharification: ～饲料 *saccharified pig feed; fermented feed*
【糖姜】sugared ginger; ginger in syrup
【糖浆】❶ medicinal syrup: 咳嗽～ *cough syrup* ❷ syrup (for making candy, etc.)
【糖精】saccharin; gluside
【糖类】[化] carbohydrate
【糖量计】[化] saccharometer; saccharimeter
【糖料作物】sugar crop
【糖萝卜】❶〈口〉beet ❷〈方〉preserved carrot
【糖酶】[化] carbohydrase
【糖蜜】molasses; treacle
【糖尿病】diabetes: ～患者 *diabetic*
【糖人儿】sugar figurine
【糖三角】steamed bun in triangular shape stuffed with sugar
【糖食】sweet food; sweets
【糖水】syrup: ～桔子(荔枝) *tangerines (lichees) in syrup*
【糖蒜】garlic in syrup; sweetened garlic
【糖稀】malt sugar; maltose
【糖衣】sugarcoating: 这种药片有～。*These pills are sugarcoated.* ◇ ～炮弹 sugarcoated bullet
【糖原】(又作'糖元')[化] glycogen

镗 动 [机] bore
【镗床】[机] boring machine; boring lathe; borer: 坐标～ *jig boring machine*
【镗刀】[机] boring cutter; boring tool
【镗孔】[机] bore hole; boring

螳 名 mantis
【螳臂当车】a mantis trying to obstruct a chariot—overrate oneself and try to hold back an overwhelmingly superior force
【螳螂】mantis ◇ ～捕蝉,黄雀在后 the mantis stalks the cicada, unaware of the oriole behind—covet gains ahead, unaware of danger behind

tǎnɡ

倘 连〈书〉if; supposing; in case: ～有不测 *in case of accidents; if anything untoward should happen*
【倘或】〈书〉if; supposing; in case
【倘来之物】an unexpected gain; windfall
【倘能如此】if this can be done
【倘能如愿】if one can satisfy his wishes
【倘若】if; supposing; in case: 你～有空,请到我家来谈谈。*Please come to my place for a chat if you have time.*
【倘使】同〖倘若〗

淌 动 drip; shed; trickle: ～眼泪 *shed tears* / ～口水 *let saliva dribble from the mouth; slaver; slobber* / 伤口～血。*Blood trickled from the wound.* / 他脸上～着汗水。*Sweat was dripping from his face.* / 这桶漏水,～了一地。*The pail leaked, so water ran all over the place.*

躺 动 lie; recline: ～下歇歇 *lie down and rest a while* / 他正～床上呢。*He's lying in bed.* / 不要～在过去的成绩上睡大觉。*Don't rest content with past achievements.* or *Don't rest on your laurels.*
【躺倒不干】stay in bed—refuse to shoulder responsibilities any longer
【躺柜】a long low box with a lid on top; chest
【躺椅】deck chair; sling chair

tànɡ

烫 Ⅰ 动 ❶ scald; burn: 让开水～着了 *be scal-*

ded by boiling water / ～了个泡 *get a blister through being scalded* (or *burnt*) ❷ heat up in hot water; warm: ～酒 *heat wine* (*by putting the container in hot water*) / ～澡 *take a hot bath* / ～脚 *bathe one's feet in hot water* ❸ iron; press: ～衣服 *iron* (or *press*) *clothes* ❹ perm; have one's hair permed: 她头发刚～过。*She just got her hair permed*. Ⅱ 形 very hot; scalding; boiling hot: 这汤真～! *This soup is boiling hot*!

【烫发】give or have a permanent wave; perm: 她烫了发显得精神了。*Her new permanent makes her look perky*.

【烫金】[刷] gild; bronze: 布面～ *cloth gilt* ◇ ～机 gilding press; bronzing machine

【烫蜡】polish with melted wax; wax (a floor, etc.)

【烫面】dough made with boiling water: ～饺 *steamed dumplings* (*made of dough prepared with boiling water*)

【烫伤】[医] scald

【烫手】❶ burn (or scald) the hand: 热得～ *so hot that it burns* (*or scalds*) *one's hand*; *scalding to the touch* / 钱不～。*Money doesn't burn the hand—the more money, the better*. ❷ troublesome; knotty: 这事有些～。*This is a sticky business*.

趟 Ⅰ 量 ❶ (for a round trip): 这辆卡车昨天往工地跑了三～。*Yesterday the truck made three trips to the construction site*. / 这一～来,是专给你们送好消息的。*I've come to bring you a piece of good news*. ❷ (for a single trip of a train): 刚开出一～列车。*A train has just left*. / 一下子到了好几～车,站台上挤满了人。*A number of trains arrived almost at the same time, and the platforms were crowded*. ❸ (for a street or things arranged in a row): 一～街 *a street* / 两～桌子 *two rows of tables* / 几～大字 *a few lines of big characters* Ⅱ 名 sth. that is going on: 跟不上～ *lag behind*

tāo

叨 动 ❶〈书〉〈套〉be unworthy of the honour: ～在知己,幸勿见怪。*Having the honour, though I am unworthy of it, to be counted among your intimate friends, I hope that you will not take offence*. (*an apology in a classical-style letter*) ❷ be favoured with; get the benefit of: 叨光 ——另见 dāo

【叨光】〈套〉be much obliged to you: 有劳你们二位,我只能～了。*You two will have to do all the work. I'm much obliged to you*.

【叨教】〈套〉thank you for your advice

【叨扰】〈套〉thank you for your hospitality

涛 名 great waves; billows: 波涛/ 松涛

绦 名 silk ribbon; silk braid

【绦虫】tapeworm; cestode: ～病 *taeniasis*; *cestodiasis*

【绦子】silk ribbon; silk braid

掏 动 ❶ draw out; pull out; fish out: ～手枪 *draw a pistol* / ～炉灰 *clear the ashes from a stove* / ～鸟窝 *take young birds or eggs out of a nest*; *go bird's-nesting* / ～耳朵 *pick one's ears* / ～蛐蛐儿 *catch crickets* / 这顿饭是他～的钱。*He footed the bill for the meal*. ❷ dig (a hole, etc.); hollow out; scoop out: 在墙上～一个洞 *make a hole in the wall* ❸ steal from sb.'s pocket: 他的皮夹子被～了。*His wallet was stolen* (*by a pickpocket*).

【掏槽】[矿] cutting

【掏底】try to find out the real intention or situation

【掏心】from the bottom of one's heart: 说句～的话,你真不该发那么大脾气。*To be frank, you shouldn't have lost your temper like that*.

【掏腰包】〈口〉❶ pay out of one's own pocket; foot a bill: 这顿饭我～。*This meal is on me*. ❷ pick sb.'s pocket

滔 动 inundate; flood

【滔滔】❶ torrential; surging: 白浪～ *whitecaps surging* ❷ keeping up a constant flow of words

【滔滔不绝】pouring out words in a steady flow: 口若悬河,～ *talk on and on in a flow of eloquence*

【滔天】❶ (of billows, etc.) dash to the skies: 波浪～ *waves running high* ❷ heinous; monstrous: ～罪行 *monstrous crimes*

【滔天大罪】a monstrous crime; a heinous crime; a towering crime

韬 Ⅰ 名〈书〉❶ sheath or bow case ❷ the art of war: 韬略 Ⅱ 动 hide; conceal: 韬晦

【韬光养晦】hide one's capacities and bide one's time

【韬晦】conceal one's true features or intentions; lie low

【韬略】military strategy

饕 形〈书〉be greedy for money or food

【饕餮】❶ taotie, a mythical ferocious animal ❷ a fierce and cruel person ❸ voracious eater; glutton; gourmand

【饕餮纹】[考古] taotie design

táo

逃 动 ❶ run away; escape; flee: 从监狱里～出去 *escape from prison* / ～出虎口 *flee from the jaws of death* ❷ evade; dodge; shirk; escape: 逃债

【逃奔】run away to (another place)

【逃避】escape; evade; shirk: ～现实 *try to escape*

reality / ～斗争 *evade struggle* / ～责任 *shirk responsibility* / ～困难 *avoid* (*or dodge*) *a difficulty*

【逃兵】army deserter; deserter

【逃窜】run away; flee in disorder: 敌军狼狈～。*The enemy troops fled helter-skelter*.

【逃遁】flee; escape; evade: 警察跟踪追击，罪犯无处～。*Being hotly pursued by the police, the criminal could find no refuge*.

【逃犯】escaped criminal or convict

【逃荒】flee from famine; get away from a famine-stricken area

【逃汇】evade foreign exchange control; avoid the foreign exchange controls of the state; illegal dealings in foreign currency

【逃婚】run away from an arranged marriage

【逃命】run (or flee, fly) for one's life

【逃难】flee from a calamity (esp. a war); be a refugee: 抗日战争爆发后他家从无锡～到了上海。*When the War of Resistance Against Japan broke out, his family fled from Wuxi to Shanghai*.

【逃匿】escape and hide; go into hiding

【逃跑】run away; flee; take flight; take to one's heels ◇ ～主义 flightism (the advocacy or practice of running away from the battlefield or from difficulties in revolutionary struggle)

【逃票】steal rides

【逃散】become separated in flight

【逃生】flee (or run, fly) for one's life; escape with one's life

【逃税】evade (or dodge) a tax ◇ ～人 tax dodger; ～手段 tax shelter

【逃脱】succeed in escaping; make good one's escape; get clear of: 不法分子～不了法律的制裁。*The lawbreakers will never escape punishment according to law*.

【逃亡】become a fugitive; flee from home; go into exile: 1927 年他～日本。*In* 1927 *he went into exile in Japan*.

【逃学】play truant; cut class

【逃逸】〈书〉escape; run away; abscond ◇ ～速度 space escape velocity

【逃债】dodge (or avoid) a creditor

【逃之夭夭】decamp; make one's get-away; slip away; show a clean pair of heels

【逃走】run away; flee; take flight; take to one's heels

【逃罪】escape responsibility for an offence (or crime); get away with it

桃

名 ❶ peach ❷ a peach-shaped thing

【桃符】❶ peachwood charms against evil, hung on the gate on lunar New Year's Eve in ancient times ❷ Spring Festival couplets

【桃脯】preserved peach

【桃红】pink

【桃红柳绿】red peach flowers and green willows—a spring scene

【桃花】peach blossom

【桃花心木】mahogany

【桃花汛】(又作'桃汛') spring flood

【桃花鱼】minnow

【桃花运】❶ a man's luck in love affairs: 走～ *be lucky in love affairs* ❷ good luck

【桃李】peaches and plums—one's pupils or disciples: ～盈门 *have many disciples* ◇ ～满天下 have pupils everywhere (usu. said in praise of a teacher)

【桃李不言，下自成蹊】the peach and the plum do not speak, yet a path is worn beneath them—a man of true worth attracts admiration

【桃仁】❶ [中] peach kernel ❷ walnut meat; shelled walnut

【桃腮杏眼】peach-like cheeks and almond-shaped eyes—the beauty of a woman

【桃色】❶ pink colour ❷〈婉〉illicit love and sex: ～案件 *legal cases involving love and sex*

【桃树】peach (tree)

陶

Ⅰ 名 pottery; earthenware: 彩陶 Ⅱ 动 ❶ cultivate; mould; educate: 熏陶 ❷ make pottery: 陶冶 Ⅲ 形 contented; happy: 乐陶陶

【陶瓷】pottery and porcelain; ceramics: ～工 *potter* / ～业 *ceramic industry*; *ceramics* ◇ ～片 [考古] potsherd; ～学 ceramics

【陶管】[建] earthenware pipe

【陶匠】potter

【陶钧】〈书〉❶ potter's wheel ❷ train (talents)

【陶粒】[建] ceramsite: ～混凝土 *ceramsite concrete*

【陶器】pottery; earthenware

【陶然】happy and carefree

【陶陶】happy; carefree

【陶土】potter's clay; pottery clay; kaolin

【陶文】[考古] inscription on pottery

【陶冶】❶ make pottery and smelt metal ❷ exert a favourable influence (on a person's character, etc.); mould: ～性情 *mould a person's temperament*

【陶俑】[考古]pottery figurine

【陶铸】〈书〉❶ mould; cast ❷ train (talents)

【陶醉】be intoxicated (with happiness, etc.); revel in: 她的歌声使我～。*Her song made me feel intoxicated*. / 我们不能～于已取得的成绩。*We mustn't let success go to our heads*.

淘

Ⅰ 动 ❶ wash in a pan or basket: ～米 *wash rice* ❷ clean out; dredge: ～阴沟 *clean out a drain* (*or sewer*) / ～茅房 *remove night soil from a latrine* / ～井 *dredge a well* ❸ tax (a person's energy) Ⅱ 形 〈方〉naughty; mischievous: 这孩子特～。*The child is very naughty*.

【淘金】wash (for gold); pan

【淘箩】a basket for washing rice in

【淘气】❶ naughty; mischievous: ～鬼 *a mischievous imp*; *a regular little mischief* ❷〈方〉get angry

【淘沙拣金】wash the sand for gold; choose or search for the very best

【淘汰】❶ eliminate through selection or competition：她～了两名种子选手。*She's knocked two seeded players out of the running*. ❷ die out; fall into disuse：这种机器已经～了。*This kind of machine is already obsolete*. ◇ ～赛［体］elimination series

萄 （构词成分）见〖葡萄〗

tǎo

讨 动 ❶ send armed forces to suppress; send a punitive expedition against：征讨 ❷ denounce; condemn：声讨 ❸ demand; ask for; beg for：去跟老张～点墨汁。*Go and ask Lao Zhang for some Chinese ink*. ❹ marry (a woman)：～老婆 *take a wife*; *get married* ❺ incur; invite：～了个没趣儿 *court a rebuff*; *ask for a snub* ❻ discuss; study：商讨

【讨伐】send armed forces to suppress; send a punitive expedition against

【讨饭】beg for food; be a beggar：他爸爸以前讨过饭。*His father used to be a beggar*.

【讨好】❶ ingratiate oneself with; fawn on; toady to; curry favour with：～领导 *curry favour with the leadership* ❷ (usu. used in the negative) be rewarded with a fruitful result; have one's labour rewarded：这个工作怎么干也讨不了好儿。*No matter how hard you work on this job, it's always a thankless task*. ——另见〖费力不讨好〗

【讨还】get sth. back ◇ ～血债 demand payment of a blood debt; make sb. pay for his bloody crimes

【讨价】ask (or name) a price

【讨价还价】bargain; haggle

【讨教】ask for advice

【讨论】discuss; talk over：这件事我们得～～。*We must talk it over*. ◇ ～会 discussion; symposium

【讨便宜】seek undue advantage; try to gain sth. at the expense of others; look for a bargain

【讨巧】act artfully to get what one wants; get the best for oneself at the least expense; choose the easy way out

【讨情】〈方〉plead for sb.; beg sb. off：～告饶 *plead for leniency*; *beg for pardon*

【讨扰】〈套〉trespass on sb.'s hospitality

【讨嫌】disagreeable; annoying：这孩子真讨人嫌。*That child is a nuisance*.

【讨厌】❶ disagreeable; disgusting; repugnant; repulsive：～的天气 *abominable weather* / 每天刮风，真～！*It's been windy every day. What a nuisance*! ❷ hard to handle; troublesome; nasty：气管炎是很～的病。*Tracheitis is a nasty illness*. ❸ dislike; loathe; be disgusted with：他是个老油子，谁都～。*He's a wily old bird. Everybody is disgusted by his behaviour*.

【讨债】demand the payment of a debt or loan

【讨债鬼】❶ a child dying young ❷ a person difficult to deal with or shake off

tào

套 Ⅰ 动 ❶ harness (a draught animal); hitch up (a draught animal to a cart)：我去～牲口。*I'll go and harness the beast* ❷ cover with; slip over; encase in：～上毛衣 *slip on a pullover* / 把枕套～上 *put the pillow in the pillowcase* / ～上罩衣 *put on a dustcoat* ❸ overlap; interlink：生产上一个环节～一个环节 *a closely linked succession in the production chain* ❹ put a ring, etc. round; tie：～上救生圈 *put on a life buoy* / 用绳子～一只狼 *catch a wolf with a lasso* ❺ model on (or after); copy：～公式 *apply a formul* ❻ coax a secret out of sb.; pump sb. about sth.：拿话～他 *coax the secret out of him*; *trick him into telling the truth* / ～口供 *trick the accused into confession* ❼ try to win (sb.'s friendship)：套交情 ❽ cut the thread (of a screw) with a die or tap Ⅱ 名 ❶ sheath; case; cover：毛笔～ *cap of a writing brush* / 沙发～ *slipcover for a sofa*; *sofa cover* / 给电视机加上一个～儿 *put a cover on the TV set* ❷ knot; loop; noose：拴个～儿 *tie a knot*; *make a loop* / 活～儿 *slipknot*; *running knot* ❸ the bend of a river or curve in a mountain range：河套 ❹ traces; harness：牲口～ *harness for a draught animal* ❺ convention; formula：客套 Ⅲ 量 (for books, furniture, rooms, methods, remarks, etc.) set; suit; suite：一～书 *a set of books* / 一～唱片 *a set of phonograph records* / 一～邮票 *a set of stamps* / 一～房间 *a suite of rooms or a flat* / 一～唱腔 *a score of voices* (*in a Chinese opera*) / 他讲了一大～客气话。*He made a lot of polite remarks*. Ⅳ 形 that which covers (other garments, etc.)：套鞋

【套版】❶［刷］register ❷ 同〖套色版〗

【套包】(又作'套包子') collar (for a horse)

【套裁】make suitable arrangements on one piece of cloth so that two or more jackets, dresses, etc. can be cut out of it

【套菜】semi-finished dish

【套餐】set meal; table d'hôte

【套车】harness a draught animal to a cart：我得～去拉农药。*I must get the cart ready to haul back the pesticide*.

【套服】suit (of clothes)

【套购】fraudulently purchase (state-controlled commodities); illegally buy up ◇ ～外汇 arbitrage; illegally procure foreign exchange with state authorization; ～证券 arbitrage of stocks and shares;

【套管】［油］casing pipe; casing：～程序 *casing programme*

【套话】❶ polite formula; conventionality ❷ stereotyped expressions

【套换】buy or get (goods, etc.) by illegal means: ～外汇 *engage in arbitrage* (*of foreign exchange*); *arbitrage*

【套汇】❶ buy foreign exchange by illegal means ❷ engage in arbitrage (of foreign exchange); arbitrage ◇～汇率 arbitrage rate; ～交易 arbitrage transaction;

【套间】❶ a small room opening off another; inner room ❷ apartment; flat

【套交情】try to get in good with sb.

【套近乎】〈贬〉try to be friendly with sb.; try to chum (or pal) up with sb.; cotton up to sb.: 他总想跟人家～,可就是没人理他这茬儿。*He always tries to cotton up to others, but no one pays any attention to him.*

【套裤】trouser legs worn over one's trousers; leggings

【套路】a series of skills and tricks in wushu (武术)

【套马】lasso a horse

【套曲】[音] divertimento: ～形式 *cyclical* (*or cycle*) *form*

【套色】[刷] chromatography; colour process ◇～版 process plate; colourplate; 木刻 coloured woodcut

【套衫】pullover

【套数】❶ a sequence of songs, dramatic (戏曲) or non-dramatic (散曲), with one rhyme and a common set of melodies ❷ a series of skills and tricks in wushu (武术), etc. ❸ conventional (or stereotyped) remark; conventionality

【套索】lasso; noose

【套套】〈方〉ways; tricks: 他的～可多了。*He is very resourceful.*

【套筒】[机] sleeve; muff: ～扳手 *box spanner* (*or wrench*); socket wrench / ～联轴节 *muff coupling*

【套鞋】overshoes; rubbers; galoshes

【套袖】oversleeve

【套印】[刷] chromatography: 彩色～ *process printing* / ～本 *chromatograph edition*

【套用】apply mechanically; use indiscriminately: 不能到处～这个公式。*This formula cannot be applied indiscriminately.*

【套语】polite formula; conventionality

【套种】(又作'套作') interplant: 实行间作～ *adopt intercropping and interplanting*

【套装】同〖套服〗

【套子】❶ sheath; case; cover: 照相机～ *camera case* / 沙发～ *slipcover for a sofa*; *sofa cover* / 唱片～ (*phonograph*) *record sleeve* ❷ conventional (or stereotyped) remark; conventionality: 俗～ *a conventional pattern* ❸〈方〉cotton padding (or wadding); batting: 棉花～ *cotton padding* ❹ snare; trap

tè

特 Ⅰ 形 special; particular; unusual; exceptional: 奇特 Ⅱ 副 ❶ for a special purpose; specially: 他～为此事而来。*He's come specially for this purpose.* ❷ very; especially: 这个医生扎针～灵。*That doctor is very good at giving acupuncture treatment.* Ⅲ 名 secret agent; spy: 敌特 Ⅳ 连〈书〉but; only

【特别】❶ special; particular; out of the ordinary; distinctive: ～开支 *special expenses* ❷ especially; particularly: 工作～努力 *be especially hardworking* ❸ for a special purpose; specially: 他临走时～去向女主人道谢。*He made a point of thanking his hostess before he left the party.* ◇～背书 special endorsement; ～法 [法] special law; ～股息 special dividend; ～会议 special meeting; special session; ～监护病房 intensive care unit (ICU); ～快车 express train; express; special express; ～提款权 special drawing rights (SDR); ～条款 special clause; ～行政区 special administrative region; ～许可证 special license

【特产】special local product; speciality; specialty: 东北～ *specialities* (*or special local products*) *of the Northeast*

【特长】what one is skilled in; strong point; speciality: 绘画不是他的～。*Painting is not his strong point.*

【特此】(used in a document or formal letter) hereby: 定于明天上午八点在礼堂开会,～通知。*It is hereby announced that there will be a meeting in the auditorium at 8 tomorrow morning.*

【特大】especially (or exceptionally) big; the most: ～喜讯 *excellent news*; *most welcome news* / ～丰收 *an exceptional bumper harvest* / 百年未遇的～干旱 *the worst drought in a century*

【特等】special grade (or class); top grade: ～舱 *stateroom*; *de luxe cabin*

【特地】for a special purpose; specially: 我们是～来向您学习育秧的。*We came specially to learn from you how to raise rice seedlings.*

【特点】characteristic; distinguishing feature; peculiarity; trait: 生理～ *physiological characteristics*

【特定】❶ specially designated (or appointed): ～的人选 *a person specially designated for a post* ❷ specific; specified; given: 在～的条件下 *under given* (*or specified*) *conditions*

【特氟隆】[化] teflon

【特工】secret service: ～人员 *special agent*; *secret service personnel*

【特惠】indulgence: ～待遇 *preferential treatment* / ～关税 *preferential tariff* / ～条款 *preferential clause* / ～制度 *preferential system*

【特混舰队】(naval) task force

【特级】special grade (or class); superfine / ～茉莉花茶 *superfine jasmine tea* / ～教师 *teacher of a special classification* / ～战斗英雄 *special-class combat hero*; *combat hero special grade*

【特急】extra urgent: ～电 *extra urgent telegram*; *flash message*

【特辑】❶ special number (or issue) of a periodical ❷ a special collection of short films

【特技】❶ stunt；trick：～跳伞 *trick parachuting* ❷ film special effects：～镜头 *trick shot*

【特技飞行】［军］stunt flying；aerobatics

【特技演员】stunt man；stunt woman

【特价】special offer；bargain price：～出售 *sell at a bargain price*

【特警】special police；special policeman

【特刊】special issue (or number)；special：国庆～ *special National Day issue*

【特快】❶ express ❷［交通］〈略〉见〖特别快车〗

【特困户】destitute household

【特立独行】independent in mind and action

【特立尼达和多巴哥】Trinidad and Tobago

【特例】a special case

【特命全权大使】ambassador extraordinary and plenipotentiary

【特命全权公使】envoy extraordinary and minister plenipotentiary

【特派】specially appoint：～员 special commissioner/ ～记者 *special correspondent*；*accredited journalist*

【特批】with special approval or authorization

【特遣部队】task force

【特区】special zone (where special political and economic policies are implemented)：经济～ *special economic zone* (*SEZ*)

【特屈儿】［化］tetryl

【特权】privilege；prerogative：～地位 *privileged position* ◇ ～阶层 privileged stratum；～思想 the idea that prerogatives and privileges go with position；the "special privilege" mentality

【特色】characteristic；distinguishing feature (or quality)：艺术～ *artistic characteristics*

【特设】ad hoc：～委员会 *ad hoc committee*

【特赦】❶ grant a special pardon ❷ grant a special amnesty：～战犯 *grant a special amnesty to war criminals* ◇ ～令 a decree (or writ) of special pardon or amnesty

【特使】special envoy

【特殊】special；particular；peculiar；exceptional：～情况 *an exceptional case*；*special circumstances* ◇ ～化 (esp. of leading cadres) become privileged；～教育 special education (for disabled or mentally retarded people)；～性 particularity；peculiarity；specific characteristics

【特斯拉】［物］tesla

【特务】❶ special task (or duties)：～营 *special task battalion* ❷ special (or secret) agent；spy：～活动 *espionage* ◇ ～机关 secret service；espionage agency；～组织 secret service；spy organization

【特效】specially good effect；special efficacy：～药 *specific drug*；*specific*；*effective cure*

【特写】❶ feature article or story；feature ❷ film close-up：～镜头 *close-up* (*shot*)

【特形演员】typecast actor

【特性】specific property (or characteristic)：坚硬是金刚钻的～。*Hardness is a property of diamonds*.

【特许】specially permit：～证书 *special permit*；*letters patent*

【特许经营商店】franchise store

【特压】［化］extreme pressure：～添加剂 *extreme pressure additive*

【特邀】specially invite：～代表 *a specially invited representative*

【特异】❶ exceptionally good；excellent；superfine：成绩～ *an excellent record* (*or performance*)；*extraordinary results* ❷ peculiar；distinctive：～的风格 *distinctive style* ◇ ～功能 extraordinary powers；～体质(又作'特异质')［医］idiosyncrasy

【特意】同〖特地〗

【特有】peculiar；characteristic：表现出青年～的热情 *display the characteristic enthusiasm of youth* / 这是广东人～的一种说法。*This is an expression peculiar to people from Guangdong*.

【特约】engage by special arrangement：这一期我们～钱教授写了一篇书评。*For this issue we have specially requested Professor Qian to write a book review*. ◇ ～稿 special contribution (to a publication)；～记者 special correspondent；～经售处 special sales agency；～评论员 special commentator；～维修店 special repair shop；～演员 guest actor；～撰稿人 special contributor

【特召】special admission to an organization or team，exceptional admittance：海霞 15 岁被～入武汉篮球队。*At the age of 15，Haixia was specially admitted to the Wuhan Basketball Team*.

【特征】characteristic；feature；trait：面部～ *facial characteristics* / 地理～ *geographical features* / 民族～ *national traits*

【特指】refer in particular to：我们所说的"小老虎"是～我们的副班长王发奋。*The "Little Tiger" we're talking about is our deputy squad leader Wang Fafen*.

【特制】specially made (for specific purpose or by special process)

【特种】special type；particular kind：～技术部队 *special technical units* ◇ ～战争 special warfare；～兵 special technical troops；～工艺 special arts and crafts；special handicraft products (of a particular place)

téng

疼 动 ❶ ache；have a pain；be sore：胃～ *have a stomachache* / 嗓子～ *have a sore throat* / 腿～ *have a pain in the leg* / 浑身都～ *be aching all over* / 你那个牙还～吗？*Does your tooth still hurt*? ❷ love dearly；be fond of；dote on：奶奶最～小孙子。*Granny dotes on her little grandson*. / 这孩子怪招人～的。*This child is really lovable*.

【疼爱】love dearly；be fond of；dote on：做父母的

都～自己的孩子。*All parents love their children*. / 他就是特别～圆圆。*He just dotes on Yuanyuan*.

【疼痛】pain；ache；soreness

【疼惜】love tenderly；have tender affection for

誊 动 transcribe (by hand)；copy out：她在～一封信。*She's copying out a letter*. / 这稿子太乱，要～一遍。*This draft is too messy. It must be recopied*. / 照底稿～一份 *make a clean copy of the draft*

【誊录】transcribe (by hand)；copy out：～文稿 *copy out a manuscript*

【誊清】make a clean copy of：～稿 *a clean* (*or fair*) *copy*

【誊写】transcribe (by hand)；copy out：把这篇文章连同我的修改部分～出来。*Copy out the article, including all the corrections I have made*. ◇～版［刷］stencil；～钢版 steel plate for cutting stencils；～蜡纸 stencil paper；～油墨 stencil ink

【誊印社】mimeograph service

腾 动 ❶ gallop；jump；prance：～身而过 *jump over sth*. ❷ rise；soar：升腾 ❸ make room；clear out；vacate：～出自己的房子给客人住 *vacate one's own room to put up a visitor* / 给新来的人～个地方 *make room for a newcomer* / ～出时间学英语 *try and find time to learn English* ❹ (used after certain verbs to show repeated actions)：翻腾

【腾达】〈书〉❶ rise；soar ❷ make rapid advances in one's career；rise to power and position

【腾飞】❶ fly swiftly upward；soar ❷ make rapid advance；develop rapidly：祖国在～。*Our country is developing rapidly*.

【腾空】soar；rise high into the air；rise to the sky：五彩缤纷的礼花～而起。*Colourful fireworks shot into the sky*.

【腾挪】❶ transfer (funds, etc.) to other use：专款专用，不得任意～。*Funds earmarked for specific purposes are not to be transferred at will*. ❷ move sth. to make room：把仓库里的东西～一下，好装水泥。*Move the things in the storehouse to make room for the cement*.

【腾腾】steaming；seething：烟雾～ *hazy with smoke*；*smoke-laden* / 烈焰～ *raging flames*

【腾越】jump over：～障碍 *jump over obstacles*

【腾云驾雾】❶ (of mythical beings) ride the clouds and mount the mist ❷ feel giddy (or dizzy)

藤 名 ❶ cane；rattan：～制品 *rattan work* / ～椅 *cane chair*；*rattan chair* / ～盔 *rattan helmet* ❷ vine：西瓜～ *watermelon vine*

【藤本植物】liana；vine

【藤黄】［植］❶ garcinia ❷ gamboge

【藤萝】［植］Chinese wistaria (Wisteria sinensis)

【藤牌】cane (or rattan) shield；shield

【藤条】rattan

tī

体 (构词成分)见下——另见 tǐ

【体己】❶ intimate；confidential：～人 *a person one can confide in*；*bosom friend* / ～话 *things one says only to one's intimates*；*words spoken in confidence* ❷ private (savings)：～钱 *private savings of a family member*

剔 Ⅰ 动 ❶ clean with a pointed instrument；pick：～指甲 *clean the fingernails* / ～骨头 *pick a bone* ❷ pick out and throw away；reject：把烂梨～出去 *pick out the rotten pears* Ⅱ 名 rising stroke (in Chinese characters)

【剔除】reject；get rid of：继承文化遗产要吸取精华，～糟粕 *absorb the essence and reject the dross in inheriting the cultural legacy*

【剔红】carved lacquerware

梯 名 ❶ ladder；steps；stairs：楼梯 ❷ shaped like a staircase；terraced：梯田

【梯次队形】［军］echelon formation

【梯度】［物］gradient

【梯队】❶［军］echelon formation；echelon ❷ a group of persons of one level or grade in an organization, kept for use if needed

【梯恩梯】［化］trinitrotoluene (TNT)：～当量 *TNT equivalent*

【梯级】stair；step

【梯己】同〖体己〗

【梯田】［农］terraced fields；terrace：修～ *build terraced fields*；*terrace mountain slopes*

【梯形】❶［数］trapezoid；trapezium ❷ ladder-shaped

【梯形翼】［航空］trapezoidal wing；tapered airfoil

【梯子】ladder；stepladder

锑 名［化］antimony；stibium (Sb)

踢 动 ❶ kick：一脚把门～开 *open the door with a kick*；*kick the door open* / 把凳子～翻 *kick over a stool* / 小心这马～人！*Be careful! This horse kicks*. / ～开绊脚石 *kick away a stumbling block* ❷ play (football)；kick：～足球 *play football* / ～进一个球 *kick* (*or score*) *a goal* / 他～中锋。*He plays centre forward*.

tí

提 Ⅰ 动 ❶ carry (in one's hand with the arm down)：手里～着个篮子 *carry a basket in one's hand* / 我去～壶水来。*I'm going to fetch a kettle of water*. ❷ lift；raise；promote：从井里～水 *draw water from a well* /把某人～到领导岗位上去 *promote sb. to a position of leadership* ❸ shift to an earlier time；move up a date：把会议的日期往前～ *move the date of the meeting up*

❹ put forward; bring up; raise: ～方案 *suggest (or propose) plans* / 把事情～到会上去讨论 *take (or submit) the matter to the meeting for discussion* / 把计划生育～到议事日程上来 *put family planning on the agenda* ❺ draw (or take) out; extract: 银行里的这笔款子你～了没有? *Have you drawn the money from the bank?* / 我到车站～行李去。*I'm going to collect my luggage at the station.* ❻ summon (a prisoner) for interrogation: ～犯人 *fetch a prisoner for interrogation* ❼ mention; refer to; bring up: 别再～那件事了。*Don't bring that up again.* / 论文有几处～到了《实践论》。*The paper contains several references to On Practice.* Ⅱ 名 ❶ dipper: 油提 ❷rising stroke (in Chinese characters) ——另见 dī

【提案】motion; proposal; draft resolution: ～国 *sponsor country (of a resolution); sponsor* / ～审查委员会 *motions examination committee*

【提拔】promote: ～某人担任领导工作 *promote sb. to a position of leadership*

【提包】handbag; shopping bag; bag; valise

【提笔】take up one's pen; start writing

【提倡】advocate; promote; encourage; recommend: ～晚婚和计划生育 *advocate late marriage and family planning* / ～说普通话 *promote the use of putonghua* / 这种做法值得～。*This method deserves recommendation.*

【提成】deduct a percentage (from a sum of money, etc.); draw a percentage ◇ ～额 unit; ～费 royalties; ～工资制 deduction wage system

【提出】put forward; advance; pose; raise: ～建议 *put forward a proposal; make a suggestion* / ～一种新的理论 *advance a new theory* / ～程序问题 *raise a point of order* / ～警告 *give (or serve) a warning* / ～抗议 *lodge a protest*

【提纯】purify; refine: ～器 *purifier* ◇ ～复壮 [农] purification and rejuvenation

【提词】[戏] prompt: 他忘了台词,还得让人～。*He forgot his lines and had to be prompted.* / 我来～。*I'll be the prompter.*

【提单】bill of lading (B / L): 直达～ *direct bill of lading* / 联运～ *through bill of lading*

【提兜】handbag; bag; valise

【提督】a provincial commander in imperial China

【提法】the way sth. is put; formulation; wording: 他们不同意你对这个问题的～。*They take exception to the way you put the question.* / 这是个新的～。*This is a new formulation.* / 这只是个～问题。*This is just a matter of wording.*

【提干】❶ make sb. a cadre ❷ promote a cadre to a higher position

【提纲】outline: 写发言～ *make an outline for a speech*

【提纲挈领】take a net by the headrope or a coat by the collar—concentrate on the main points; bring out the essentials: 我来～地谈一谈。*I'll just touch briefly on the essentials.*

【提高】raise; heighten; enhance; increase; improve: ～水位 *raise the water level* / ～警惕 *enhance (or heighten, sharpen) one's vigilance* / ～认识 *deepen one's understanding* / ～勇气 *pluck up one's courage*

【提供】provide; supply; furnish; offer: ～援助 *give aid; provide assistance* / ～贷款 *offer a loan*

【提行】[刷] begin a new line (in writing or printing)

【提盒】a tiered lunchbox with several round compartments one above the other and a handle

【提花】jacquard weave: ～枕巾 *a jacquard pillow cover* / ～织机 *jacquard loom*

【提货】pick up goods; take delivery of goods: 到火车站～ *pick up goods at the railway station* ◇ ～单 同〖提单〗

【提及】speak of; talk about; refer to; mention: 这部小说文学史上从未～。*The novel has received no mention in any history of literature.*

【提价】raise the price, markup

【提交】submit (a problem, etc.) to; refer to: 将决议草案～大会讨论 *submit the draft resolution to the congress for discussion*

【提款】draw money (from a bank)

【提篮】hand-basket

【提炼】extract and purify; abstract; refine: 从矿石中～金属 *extract (or abstract) metal from ore* / 将生活素材～加工 *refine the literary raw material gathered from life*

【提留】retain part of total revenue or resources for use in one's own unit

【提名】nominate (for election): ～某人为代表 *nominate sb. for representative* ◇ ～奖 nomination

【提起】❶ mention; speak of: ～这个爱乐乐团没有一个不夸的。*No one ever mentions the Philharmonic Orchestra without praising it.* ❷ raise; arouse; brace up: ～精神 *raise one's spirits; brace oneself up*

【提前】❶ shift to an earlier date; move up (a date); advance: 总攻的时间～了。*The time for the general offensive has been moved up.* ❷ do sth. in advance or ahead of time: ～召开大会 *convene the congress before the due date* ◇ ～量 [军] lead

【提挈】〈书〉❶ lead; take with one; marshal: ～全军 *marshal all one's (military) forces* ❷ guide and support; give guidance and help to

【提亲】(又作'提亲事') propose a marriage alliance

【提琴】[音] the violin family: 大～ *violoncello* / 低音～ *double bass* / 小～ *violin* / 中～ *viola*

【提请】submit sth. to: ～大会批准 *submit to the congress for approval* / ～大家注意 *call everybody's attention to sth.*

【提取】❶ draw; pick up; collect: ～银行存款 *draw money from a bank; withdraw bank deposits* / 到车站～行李 *pick up (or collect) one's* luggage at the railway station ❷ extract; abstract; recover: 从油页岩中～石油 *extract oil from shale* ◇ ～器 extractor; ～塔 extraction column

【提神】refresh oneself; give oneself a lift: 喝杯茶提提神 *refresh oneself with a cup of tea*

【提审】❶ bring (a prisoner) before the court; bring (sb. in custody) to trial; fetch (a detainee) for interrogation ❷ review (a case tried by a lower court)

【提升】❶ promote: ～他当排长 *promote him to be platoon leader* ❷ hoist; elevate: ～机 *hoist; elevator*

【提示】point out; prompt: 请把学习重点向大家～一下。*Please brief us on the main points to be studied.* / 如果她忘了台词,你就给她～一下。*Prompt her if she forgets her lines.* ◇ ～符 [计] prompt

【提味】render palatable (by adding condiments); season: 搁点儿味精提提味～。*Add a little MSG to make it more flavourful.*

【提问】(esp. of a teacher) put question to; quiz: 老师～以后,他答不上来。*The teacher put the question to him, but he couldn't answer it.*

【提线木偶】marionette

【提箱】suitcase

【提携】❶ lead (a child) by the hand ❷ guide and support; give guidance and help to

【提心吊胆】have one's heart in one's mouth; be on tenterhooks: 他对考试结果感到～的。*He was on tenterhooks about the result of the exam.*

【提醒】remind; warn; call attention to: 如果我忘了,请你～我一下。*Please remind me in case I should forget.*

【提选】select; choose: ～耐旱品种 *select drought-resistant varieties*

【提要】précis; summary; abstract; epitome; synopsis: 论文～ *abstract of the thesis* / 本书内容～ *capsule summary of the book*

【提议】❶ propose; suggest; move: 我～为两国人民的友谊干杯。*I propose a toast to the friendship between the peoples of the two countries.* / 我～现在休会。*I move the meeting be adjourned.* ❷ proposal; motion: 大会一致通过了他们的～。*The meeting unanimously adopted their proposal.*

【提早】shift to an earlier time; be earlier than planned or expected: ～出发 *set out earlier than planned* / ～通知一声 *notify in advance*

【提制】obtain through refining; distil; extract

啼 动 ❶ cry; weep aloud: 哭哭啼啼 ❷ (of certain birds and animals) crow; caw; screech: 鸡～。*Cocks crow.* / 月落乌～。*The crows caw when the moon goes down.*

【啼号】cry loudly; wail

【啼饥号寒】wail with hunger and cold; cry out from hunger and cold

【啼哭】cry; wail

【啼鸣】(of birds) crow; caw

【啼笑皆非】not know whether to laugh or cry; find sth. both funny and annoying

鹈 (构词成分)见下

【鹈鹕】pelican

题 Ⅰ 名 topic; subject; title; problem: 讨论～ *topic for discussion* / 这道～我没答对。*I didn't give the correct answer to the problem.* Ⅱ 动 inscribe: ～诗一首 *inscribe a poem (on a painting, fan, wall, etc.)* / 某某～ *(an inscription) by so-and-so*

【题跋】❶ preface and postscript ❷ short comments, annotations, etc. on a scroll (of painting or calligraphy); colophon

【题材】subject matter; theme: ～范围 *range of subjects* / 这是写小说的好～。*This is good material for a novel.*

【题词】❶ write a few words of encouragement, appreciation or commemoration ❷ inscription; dedication ❸ foreword

【题花】title design

【题解】❶ explanatory notes on the title or background of a book ❷ key to exercises or problems

【题库】examination question bank

【题名】❶ inscribe one's name; autograph: ～留念 *give one's autograph as a memento* ❷ autograph ❸ title (of an article, etc.)

【题目】❶ title; subject; topic: 辩论的～ *subject (or topic) for a debate* ❷ exercise problems; examination questions

【题签】❶ write the title of a book on a label to be stuck on the cover ❷ a label with the title of a book on it

【题外话】digression; what is mentioned in passing

【题旨】❶ the meaning of the title of an article ❷ the theme of a literary work

【题字】❶ write a few words of commemoration (on an autograph album, etc.) ❷ inscription; autograph: 书上有作者亲笔～。*The book is autographed by the author.*

醍 (构词成分)见下

【醍醐】〈古〉clarified butter; ghee (used by Buddhists as a metaphor for the perfect truth of Buddha)

【醍醐灌顶】❶ be filled with wisdom; be enlightened ❷ suddenly feel refreshed

蹄 名 ❶ hoof: 马有四个～儿。*A horse has four hoofs.* ❷ trotter: 猪～ *pig's trotters*

【蹄筋】tendons of beef, mutton or pork: 红烧～ *tendons stewed in soy sauce*

【蹄膀】〈方〉the upper part of a leg of pork

【蹄子】❶〈口〉hoof ❷〈方〉upper part of a leg of pork

tǐ

体 Ⅰ 名 ❶ body or part of the body: 肢体 ❷

substance or state of a substance：固体 ❸ style；form：文体 ❹ typeface：注解你要排什么～？*What typeface would you like the notes to be printed in?* ❺ system：政体 ❻ style of calligraphy：你写的什么～？*What style of calligraphy do you do?* ❼〈语〉aspect (of a verb) Ⅱ 动 personally do or experience sth.；put oneself in another's position：身体力行——另见 tī

【体壁】[动] body wall

【体裁】types or forms of literature

【体操】gymnastics ◇ ～表演 gymnastic exhibition (or display)；～服 gym outfit (or clothes, suit)；～馆 gymnastic stick；～器械 gymnastic apparatus；～运动员 gymnast

【体察】experience and observe：虚心～情况 *be ready to look into matters with an open mind；not be prejudiced in sizing up situations* / ～下情 *try to understand what is going on at the lower levels*

【体罚】corporal (or physical) punishment

【体格】physique；build：～强壮 *of strong physique (or constitution)；of powerful build* ◇ ～检查 physical examination；health checkup

【体会】❶ know (or learn) from experience；realize：他深深～到这友情的温暖。*He deeply felt the warmth of the friendship.* ❷ knowledge；understanding：深有～ *have an intimate knowledge of sth.* / 谈谈我个人的～。*I'll say a few words about my personal experience (or understanding).*

【体积】volume；bulk：～大 *bulky* / 容器的～ *the volume of a container* ◇ ～膨胀 [物] volume expansion

【体检】〈略〉见〖体格检查〗

【体力】physical (or bodily) strength；stamina；physical power：增强～ *build up one's strength* / 消耗～ *be a drain on one's (physical) strength；consume (or sap) one's strength* / 下半时队员们显得～不支。*The players showed signs of tiredness during the second half.* ◇ ～劳动 physical (or manual) labour

【体例】stylistic rules and layout；style：印刷～ *style sheet；stylebook*

【体谅】show understanding and sympathy for；make allowances for：充分～人家的困难 *make full allowances for their difficulties* / 她是很～人的。*She is quite understanding.*

【体貌】one's figure and features—general physical appearance

【体面】❶ dignity；face：维持～ *keep up appearances* ❷ honourable；creditable：不～的行为 *disgraceful (or disreputable) conduct* ❸ good-looking：长得～ *be handsome* / 你要出去的话得穿～一些。*You're not going out unless you're decently dressed.*

【体魄】〈书〉physique：强壮的～ *strong (or powerful) physique；vigorous health* / 锻炼～ *go in for physical training*

【体腔】[生理] body cavity

【体虱】[动] body louse

【体式】❶ form of characters or letters：汉语拼音字母有手写体和印刷体两种～。*There are two forms of the Chinese phonetic alphabet, the cursive and the printed.* ❷〈书〉form of literary works：词和律诗～不同。*Ci poems are different in form from lüshi poems.*

【体视】[物] stereo：～显微镜 *stereomicroscope* / ～望远镜 *stereotelescope*

【体饰】body piercing

【体态】posture；carriage：～轻盈 *have a graceful carriage*

【体坛】the sports world；sports circles

【体贴】show consideration for；give every care to：～病人 *show a patient every consideration* / 他对妻子很～。*He's very considerate of his wife.* ◇ ～入微 look after with great care；care for with great solicitude；show every possible consideration；be extremely thoughtful

【体统】decorum；propriety；decency：有失～ *be disgraceful；be scandalous* / 他这样无理取闹，成何～！*He's being difficult on purpose and it's so unseemly!* ——另见〖不成体统〗

【体外受精】external fertilization

【体温】(body) temperature：～过低 *hypothermia* / 给孩子量～。*Take the child's temperature.* ◇ ～计 (clinical) thermometer

【体无完肤】❶ have cuts and bruises all over the body；be a mass of bruises：被打得～ *be beaten black and blue* ❷ be thoroughly refuted or exposed；be scathingly criticized；be torn to pieces (or shreds)

【体系】system；setup

【体现】embody；incarnate；reflect；give expression to：这个提案～了发展中国家的利益和要求。*This proposal reflects the interests and demands of the developing countries.*

【体形】bodily form；build

【体型】❶ type of build or figure ❷ somatotype

【体恤】understand and sympathize with；show solicitude for

【体恤衫】T-shirt

【体癣】[医] ringworm of the body

【体循环】[生理] systemic circulation；greater circulation

【体验】learn through practice；learn through one's personal experience：～生活 *observe and learn from real life*

【体液】body fluid；humour

【体育】❶ physical culture；physical training：～锻炼 *physical training* / 今天下午有一节～课。*We'll have an hour of PE (physical education) this afternoon.* ❷ sports：～活动 *sports activities* / ～器械 *sports apparatus* ◇ ～场 stadium；～彩票 sports lottery；～道德 sportsmanship；～馆 gymnasium；gym；～节目主持人 sportscaster；～界 sports circles；the sporting world；～疗法 physical exercise therapy；～设施 sports facilities；～用品 sports goods (or requisites)；～运动

sports：～中心 sports center

【体征】［医］sign

【体制】system (of organization)；structure：国家～ *state system* / 管理～ *managerial system*

【体制改革】restructuring；structural reform：经济～ *economic restructuring* / 政治～ *political structural reform*；*political restructuring*

【体质】physique；constitution：增强～ *build up health* / 他们的～都很好。*They all have good physiques.* / 各人的～不同，对疾病的抵抗力也不同。*People's constitutions differ；so does their resistance to disease.*

【体重】(body) weight：～增加 *put on weight*；*gain weight* / ～减轻 *lose weight* / 她～60公斤。*She weighs 60 kilograms.*

tì

屉 名 ❶ a food steamer with several trays；steamer tray：～帽 *the lid (or cover) of a steamer* / 一～馒头 *a trayful of steamed buns* / ～跟锅不合适。*The steamer tray doesn't fit into the pot.* ❷ drawer：三～桌 *three-drawer desk*

【屉子】❶ (one of) a set of removable trays (in furniture or a utensil) ❷〈方〉drawer

剃 动 shave：～胡子 *have a shave*；*shave oneself*

【剃刀】razor

【剃度】［宗］(佛教) tonsure

【剃光头】have one's head shaved—score no points (in games)：我们队给对方剃了个光头，五比〇。*Our team blanked the other, 5-0.*

【剃头】❶ have one's head shaved ❷ have one's hair cut；have a haircut

【剃须膏】shaving cream

涕 名 ❶ tears：痛哭流涕 ❷ mucus of the nose；snivel：鼻涕

【涕泪】❶ tears ❷ tears and snivel

【涕零】shed tears

【涕泣】〈书〉weep

【涕泗】〈书〉tears and snivel ◇ ～交流 tears and snivel streaming down at the same time—crying piteously；～滂沱 be drenched with tears and snivel

倜 (构词成分)见下

【倜傥】〈书〉elegant；free and easy

替 Ⅰ 动 take the place of；replace；substitute for：这里的工作谁也～不了谁。*We cannot substitute for one another in our work here.* / 三号上场，～下五号。*Player No.3 for No.5.* / 他身体不好，快去把他～下来。*He's not well. Go and replace him at once.* Ⅱ 介 for：～别人买火车票 *buy a train ticket for sb.* / ～顾客着想 *think about the interests of the customers* / 大家都～你高兴。*We all feel happy for your sake.* / 别～我担心。*Don't worry about me.*

【替班】take sb. else's place (in a work shift)

【替补】substitute for：～队员 *substitute (player)*；*reserve (player)*

【替代】substitute for；replace；supersede：用石油～煤 *replace coal with petroleum*；*substitute petroleum for coal*

【替工】❶ work as a temporary substitute ❷ a temporary substitute (worker)：找一个～ *find a substitute*；*get a replacement*

【替换】replace；substitute for；displace；take the place of：教练决定让3号～8号。*The coach decided to replace player No. 8 with No. 3.* / 带上一套～的衣服。*Take a change of clothes with you.*

【替角儿】understudy

【替身】❶ substitute；replacement；stand-in ❷ scapegoat ◇ ～演员 stunt man；stunt woman

【替死鬼】〈口〉scapegoat；fall guy

【替天行道】right wrongs in accordance with heaven's decree (a slogan often used by leaders of peasant uprisings)

【替罪羊】scapegoat

嚏 (构词成分)见下

【嚏喷】〈书〉sneeze

tiān

天 Ⅰ 名 ❶ the sky；the heavens：明朗的～ *a clear sky* / 太阳一出满～红。*The sky is aglow with the rising sun.* ❷ day：每～ *every day* / 开学第二～ *on the second day of the new term* / 夏天～长夜短。*In summer the days are long and the nights short.* ❸ a period of time in a day：五更～ *around four in the morning* / ～不早啦。*It's getting late.* ❹ season：冷～ *the cold season*；*cold days* ❺ weather：下雨～ *wet (or rainy) weather* / ～越来越冷了。*It's getting colder and colder.* / ～晴了，咱们走吧。*It's cleared up now. Let's go.* ❻ nature：人定胜天 ❼ God；Heaven：～知道！*God knows!* / ～哪！*Good Heavens!* Ⅱ 形 ❶ natural；inborn；innate：天性 ❷ overhead：天桥

【天安门】Tian An Men (the Gate of Heavenly Peace)：～广场 *Tian'anmen Square*

【天崩地坼】(又作'天崩地裂') heaven felling and earth rending—violent political or social upheavals

【天边】horizon；the ends of the earth；remotest places：～的渔帆 *the sails of the fishing boats that appear on the horizon*

【天兵】troops from heaven—an invincible army

【天不怕，地不怕】fear neither Heaven nor Earth；fear nothing on earth；nothing daunted

【天才】genius；talent；gift；endowment：这孩子有音乐～。*The child has musical talent (or a gift for music).* / 爱因斯坦是个伟大的科学～。*Einstein was a great scientific genius.* ◇ ～论 the

theory of innate genius
【天蚕】giant silkworm；wild silkworm ◇ ～蛾 giant silkworm moth
【天长地久】enduring as the universe；everlasting and unchanging
【天长日久】同〖日久天长〗
【天车】［机］overhead travelling crane；shop traveller
【天成佳偶】a good match as of made in heaven
【天秤座】［天］Libra
【天窗】［建］skylight ——另见〖开天窗〗
【天赐】be bestowed by heaven：～我也！*This is indeed a godsend*！
【天从人愿】Heaven grants man's wish；by the grace of God
【天大】as large as the heavens；extremely big：～的好事 *an excellent thing* (*or event*) / ～的面子 *a mark of special favour* / ～的笑话 *a colossal absurdity*
【天道】❶〈旧〉the natural laws；heavenly laws ❷〈方〉weather
【天敌】［生］natural enemy
【天底】［天］nadir
【天底下】〈口〉in the world；on earth：～哪有这种道理！*Nobody on earth would reason that way*. or *How preposterous*！
【天地】❶ heaven and earth；world；universe：炮声震动～。*The earth shook with the roar of guns*. ❷ field of activity；scope of operation：开辟科学研究的新～ *open up a new field for scientific research* ◇ ～不容 a towering crime or a sinner that neither god nor men can forgive；～良心 can say in all honesty；must point out in all fairness
【天地头】［刷］top and bottom margins of a page；upper and lower margins of a page
【天帝】the Lord of Heaven
【天电】［电］atmospherics；static：～干扰 *static disturbances*
【天顶】［天］zenith
【天鹅】swan：小～ *cygnet* / ～绒毛 *swansdown*
【天鹅绒】velvet
【天鹅座】［天］Cygnus
【天蛾】hawkmoth；sphinx
【天翻地覆】heaven and earth turning upside down：～的变化 *earthshaking* (*or tremendous*) *changes*
【天方夜谭】❶ The Arabian Nights ❷ a cock-and-bull story；a most fantastic tale
【天分】natural gift；talent；special endowments：～高 *gifted*；*talented*
【天府之国】(usu. referring to Sichuan Province) Nature's storehouse—a land of abundance；a land of plenty
【天赋】❶ inborn；innate；endowed by nature ❷ natural gift；talent；endowments ◇ ～人权论 the theory of natural rights
【天干】the ten Heavenly Stems，used as serial numbers and also in combination with the twelve Earthly Branches（地支）to designate years，months，days and hours
【天罡】〈古〉❶ the Big Dipper ❷ the handle of the Big Dipper ◇ ～星［天］the Big Dipper
【天高地厚】as high as the heavens and as deep as the earth—❶ (of kindness) profound；deep ❷ complexity of things ——另见〖不知天高地厚〗
【天高皇帝远】heaven is high and the emperor far away—❶ justice is tardy ❷ one may do whatever one wishes without fear of interference
【天高气爽】the sky is clear and the air is crisp—fine autumn weather
【天各一方】(of relatives or friends) each in a different corner of the world：妻离子散，～ *a family torn asunder，each member in a different corner of the world*
【天公】the ruler of heaven；God ◇ ～不作美 Heaven is not cooperative；the weather isn't cooperating
【天公地道】absolutely fair：在我看来，她这样处理真是～。*In my opinion，the way she disposed of the matter was perfectly fair and reasonable*.
【天宫】heavenly palace (in mythology)
【天沟】［建］gutter
【天国】❶［宗］(基督教) the Kingdom of Heaven；paradise ❷ utopia
【天寒地冻】the weather is cold and the ground is frozen
【天河】common name for 银河
【天黑】❶ deepening dusk；dusk ❷ dark
【天候】［气］weather
【天花】［医］smallpox
【天花板】ceiling (of a room)
【天花粉】［中］the root of Chinese trichosanthes (Trichosanthes kirilowii)
【天花乱坠】flowers cascading from the sky—an extravagantly colourful description：吹得～ *give an extravagant account of*；*make a wild boast about*
【天皇】❶ the Son of Heaven—the emperor ❷ the emperor of Japan；Mikado
【天昏地暗】❶ murky heavens over a dark earth；dark all round：～，日月无光。*There was gloom above and darkness below，with the rays of the sun and the moon completely shut out*. ❷ in a state of chaos and darkness
【天机】❶ nature's mystery；something inexplicable ❷ God's design；secret：泄漏～ *give away a secret* / 一语道破～ *lay bare the secret of sth. with one remark* ◇ ～不可泄漏 God's design must not be revealed to mortal ears；Heaven's secrets must not be divulged；don't say a word about it to a soul
【天极】［天］celestial pole
【天际】〈文〉horizon
【天经地义】(in line with) the principles of heaven and earth—right and proper；perfectly justified：给国家纳税是～的事。*It's only right and proper that we should pay taxes to the state*.
【天井】❶ small yard；courtyard ❷ skylight ❸

［矿］raise：通风～ *air raise*
【天空】the sky；the heavens
【天籁】〈文〉sounds of nature（i. e. the sound of the wind or flowing waters，the call of the bird，etc.）
【天蓝】sky blue；azure
【天狼星】［天］Sirius
【天朗气清】the sky is clear and the air is fresh
【天理】❶ heavenly principles—feudal ethics as propounded by the Song Confucianists ❷（divine）justice◇ ～难容 an intolerable injustice；～昭彰 Heaven's laws are fully manifest
【天良】conscience：～发现 *be stung by conscience*；*be conscience-stricken*
【天亮】daybreak；dawn：～以前赶到 *get there before daybreak*
【天灵盖】top of the skull；crown（of the head）
【天龙座】［天］Draco
【天伦】〈书〉the natural bonds and ethical relationships between members of a family ◇ ～之乐 family happiness
【天罗地网】nets above and snares below—tight encirclement：布下～ *spread a dragnet from which there is no escape*；*cast an escape-proof net*
【天麻】［中］the tuber of elevated gastrodia（Gastrodia elata）
【天马行空】a heavenly steed soaring across the skies—a powerful and unconstrained style（of writing，calligraphy，etc.）
【天明】daybreak；dawn
【天命】God's will；the mandate of heaven；destiny；fate
【天幕】❶ the canopy of the heavens ❷ backdrop（of a stage）
【天南地北】❶ far apart：他们哥儿俩～，见一次面不容易。*The two brothers live so far apart they don't often get a chance to see each other*. ❷ from different places or areas：来自～ *come from different parts of the country*（*or from all over the country*）
【天南海北】❶ all over the country ❷ discursive；rambling：～地谈起来 *start chattering away about this and that*；*start a bull session*；*talk about everything under the sun*
【天年】❶ a natural span of life；one's allotted span：尽其～ *die a natural death*；*live one's full span* ❷〈方〉the year's harvest ❸〈方〉times；age；era
【天牛】［动］longicorn；long-horned beetle
【天怒人怨】the wrath of God and the anger of men；widespread indignation and discontent
【天女】（in Buddhist mythology）a female deva；a heavenly maiden：《～散花》*The Heavenly Maiden Scattering Flowers*（*an operatic dance drama*）
【天疱疮】［建］pemphigus
【天棚】❶［建］ceiling ❷ awning or canopy，usu. made of reed matting and bamboo poles
【天平】balance；scales
【天平动】［天］libration
【天气】weather：～要变。*The weather is changing*. / ～转晴。*It's clearing up*. ◇ ～图 weather map；synoptic chart；～形势预报 weather prognostics；～学 synoptic meteorology；～预报 weather forecast
【天堑】natural moat（usu. referring to the Changjiang River）：长江～ *the natural moat of the Changjiang River*
【天桥】overline bridge；platform bridge；overhead walkway
【天琴座】［天］Lyra
【天青】reddish black
【天穹】the vault of heaven
【天球】［天］celestial sphere
【天球赤道】［天］celestial equator
【天球仪】celestial globe
【天球子午圈】［天］celestial meridian
【天球坐标】［天］celestial coordinates
【天然】natural：～财富 *natural resources*（*or wealth*）◇ ～堤 natural levee；～港 natural harbour；～更新 forestry natural regeneration；～免疫［医］innate immunity；native immunity；natural immunity；～牧地 natural pasture
【天然气】natural gas：干～ *dry gas*；*poor gas* / 湿～ *wet gas*；*rich gas*
【天壤之别】as far apart as heaven and earth；worlds（or poles）apart；a world of difference
【天日】the sky and the sunlight ——另见〖暗无天日〗；〖重见天日〗
【天若有情天亦老】If Heaven has feelings，Heaven too will become aged.
【天色】colour of the sky；time of the day as shown by the colour of the sky；weather：～已晚。*It's getting dark*. / ～突变。*The weather suddenly changed*.
【天神】god；deity
【天生】born；inborn；inherent；innate：本事不是～的，是锻炼出来的。*Ability is not innate，but comes through practice*. / 他～聋哑。*He was born a deaf-mute*.
【天生桥】natural bridge
【天时】❶ weather；climate：～不正 *abnormal weather* / 庄稼活儿一定要趁～，早了晚了都不好。*Farming should be done in season，neither too early nor too late*. ❷ timeliness；opportunity
【天使】angel
【天书】❶ a book from heaven—abstruse or illegible writing：对我来说，这本书就跟～一样难懂。*To me this book is as difficult as a book from heaven*. or *This book is all Greek to me*. / 这封信字迹太潦草，像～似的。*This letter is as illegible as hieroglyphics*. ❷ imperial edict（in ancient China）
【天数】predestination；fate
【天塌地陷】❶ 同〖天崩地坼〗❷ serious；grave；critical
【天坛】the Temple of Heaven（in Beijing）
【天堂】paradise；heaven
【天梯】very tall ladder on high buildings and struc-

tures

【天体】[天] celestial body ◇ ～光谱学 astrospectroscopy; ～力学 celestial mechanics; ～物理学 astrophysics; ～演化学 cosmogony; ～照相仪 astrograph

【天天】every day: ～锻炼身体 *do physical training every day*

【天条】Heaven's commandments

【天庭】the middle of the forehead: ～饱满,地角方圆 *a full forehead and a strong square jaw (auspicious features according to physiognomy)*

【天头】the top (or upper) margin of a page

【天外】beyond the highest heavens—far, far away

【天王】heavenly king—❶ an epithet for the emperor ❷ a name for certain deities (e.g. the Pagoda-bearing Heavenly King 托塔天王)

【天王星】[天] Uranus

【天网恢恢,疏而不漏】the net of Heaven has large meshes, but it lets nothing through; the mills of God grind slowly, but they grind exceedingly small; justice has a long arm; the guilty can never escape Heaven's justice

【天威】〈书〉heavenly might

【天文】astronomy ◇ ～单位 astronomical unit; ～导航 astronavigation; celestial navigation; ～馆 planetarium; ～年历 astronomical yearbook; astronomical almanac; ～时 astronomical time; ～台 (astronomical) observatory; ～仪 astroscope; ～照相术 astrophotography; ～制导 celestial guidance; ～钟 astronomical clock

【天文数字】astronomical figure; enormous figure

【天文望远镜】astronomical telescope

【天文学】astronomy: 航海～ *nautical astronomy* / 恒星～ *stellar astronomy* / 空间～ *space astronomy* / 球面～ *spherical astronomy* / 射电～ *radio astronomy* / ～家 *astronomer*

【天无二日,民无二王】there cannot be two kings for the people just as there cannot be two suns in the heavens

【天无绝人之路】Heaven never seals off all the exits—there is always a way out

【天下】❶ land under heaven—the world ❷ rule; domination: 打～坐～ *conquer and rule the country* ◇ ～大乱 great disorder under heaven—a state of great confusion; ～大势 the momentum of history; historical trends; ～大治 great order throughout the land; a well ordered world; ～第一 the first under heaven—unequalled; peerless; ～奇闻 a most fantastic tale; a very strange story; the most absurd thing in the world; ～太平 peace reigns under heaven; the world (or the country) is at peace; ～为公 the whole world as one community; ～文章一大抄 all writings under heaven are nothing but copyings; ～乌鸦一般黑 all crows under the sun are black—evil people are bad all over the world; ～无不散的宴席 there never was a feast but the guests had to depart—all good things must come to an end; ～无敌 invincible; ever-victorious; all-conquering; ～无难事,只怕有心人 nothing in the world is difficult for one who sets his mind on it; ～无双 unparalleled in the world; unique; without equal; matchless

【天仙】❶ goddess ❷ a beautiful young woman; a beauty

【天仙子】[中] henbane seed (Hyoscyamus niger)

【天险】natural barrier

【天线】aerial; antenna: 定向～ *beam (or directional) antenna* / 拉杆～ *telescopic antenna*

【天象】astronomical phenomena; celestial phenomena: 观测～ *observe the heavenly bodies; astronomical observation* ◇ ～仪 planetarium

【天晓得】〈口〉God (or Heaven) knows: ～他在那儿待了多久。*He stayed there God knows how long.*

【天蝎座】[天] Scorpio; Scorpius

【天行赤目】[中] red and swollen eyes; conjunctivitis

【天性】natural instincts; nature: ～聪明 *be intelligent by nature*

【天幸】a providential escape; a close shave (or call)

【天旋地转】(feel as if) the sky and earth were spinning round; dizzy: 昏沉沉,只觉得～ *feel faint and dizzy as if the earth were spinning round*

【天涯】the world's end; the remotest corner of the earth ◇ ～海角 the ends of the earth; the remotest corners of the earth

【天衣无缝】a seamless heavenly robe—flawless: 这篇文章,论证严密～。*The article is close-knit and its argument flawless.*

【天意】God's will; the will of Heaven: 事在人为,不存在什么～。*There is no such thing as the will of Heaven. It is man that decides everything.*

【天鹰座】[天] Aquila

【天有不测风云】a storm may arise from a clear sky—something unexpected may happen any time: ～,人有旦夕祸福。*Storms gather without warning and bad luck befalls men overnight.* or *In nature there are unexpected storms and in life unpredictable vicissitudes.*

【天宇】❶ the sky; the heavens ❷ 〈文〉land under heaven—the world

【天渊】〈书〉high heaven and deep sea; poles apart ◇ ～之别 同〖天壤之别〗

【天灾】natural disaster (or calamity): 遭受～ *suffer natural disasters* ◇ ～人祸 natural and man-made calamities

【天葬】celestial burial (by which bodies are exposed to birds of prey)

【天造地设】created by nature; heavenly; ideal: 我看他二人恰是一对～的夫妻。*I think they will make a perfect match.* / 莫扎特的作品好似～,自然形成。*Like a work of Nature, a work by Mozart seems inevitable as it stands.*

【天真】innocent; simple and unaffected; artless; naive: ～活泼的女孩子 *an artless, vivacious girl* / ～的幻想 *a naive delusion* ◇ ～烂漫 innocent and artless; simple and unaffected

【天之骄子】God's favoured one—an unusually lucky person

【天知道】God (or Heaven) knows

【天职】bounden duty; vocation: 保卫国家是军人的～。*Safeguarding the country is a soldier's bounden duty*.

【天轴】❶［机］line shaft ❷［天］celestial axis

【天诛地灭】(used in cursing or taking vows) be destroyed by heaven and earth; stand condemned by God: 我要是说谎,～! *May heaven strike me down if I lie*!

【天竺】ancient name for 印度

【天竺鲷】cardinal fish

【天竺葵】fish pelargonium (Pelargonium hortorum)

【天竺鼠】guinea pig; cavy

【天主教】Catholicism: ～会 *the Roman Catholic Church* / ～徒 *Catholic*

【天资】natural gift; talent; natural endowments

【天姿国色】reigning beauty; a woman of matchless beauty

【天子】the Son of Heaven—the emperor

【天字第一号】number one; A1

【天尊】celestial worthy (the title of some deities in the Taoist pantheon): 元始～ *the Celestial Worthy of the Original Beginning (controlling time past)*

【天作孽,犹可违;自作孽,不可活】 when Heaven sends down calamities, there is hope of weathering them; when man brings them upon himself, there is no hope of escape

【天作之合】a heaven-made match (used in congratulations on marriage)

添 动 ❶ add; increase: ～煤 *add (or put in more) coal; stoke* / ～衣服 *put on more clothes* / ～一碗饭 *have one more bowl of rice* / ～了几根白头发 *have grown a few more white hairs* / 给你们～麻烦了。*Sorry to have troubled you*. ❷〈方〉have a baby: 她最近～了个女孩儿。*She recently had a daughter*.

【添补】replenish; get more: 需要～机器零件 *need a fresh supply of machine parts*

【添丁】〈旧〉have a baby (esp. a boy) born into the family

【添加剂】［化］additive

【添枝加叶】(又作'添油加醋') add colour and emphasis to (a narration); add highly coloured details to (a story); embellish (a story)

【添置】add to one's possessions; acquire: ～家具 *buy more furniture*

【添砖加瓦】do what little one can to help

tián

田 名 ❶ field; farmland; cropland: 犁～ *plough a field* / 在～里劳动 *work in the fields*; *work on the land* ❷ an open area abounding in some natural product; field: 煤田

【田鳖】giant water bug; fish killer

【田产】(property in the form of) land; landed property; estate

【田地】❶ field; farmland; cropland ❷ wretched situation; plight: 你怎么落到这步～! *How did you get into such a plight*?

【田凫】［动］lapwing

【田埂】a low bank of earth between fields; ridge

【田鸡】common name for 青蛙

【田间】❶ field; farm ❷ countryside ◇ ～持水量［农］field capacity; ～管理 field management; ～劳动 field labour; farm work

【田菁】［植］sesbania

【田径】track and field; athletics ◇ ～队 track and field team; ～赛 track and field meet; ～赛项目 track and field events; ～运动 track and field sports; athletics; ～运动员 athlete

【田猎】〈书〉go hunting

【田鹨】［动］paddy-field pipti

【田螺】river snail

【田亩】general name for 田地❶

【田契】title deed for farmland; land deed

【田赛】［体］field events

【田舍】〈书〉❶ farm ❷ farmhouse ❸ a farming family

【田鼠】vole: 普通～ *field vole*

【田野】field; open country: 广阔的～ *a vast field*; *a vast expanse of farmland*

【田园】fields and gardens; countryside: ～生活 *idyllic life* / ～风光 *rural scenery* ◇ ～诗 idyll; pastoral poetry; ～诗人 pastoral poet

【田庄】country estate

恬 形〈书〉❶ quiet; tranquil; calm: 恬适 ❷ not care at all; remain unperturbed

【恬不知耻】not feel ashamed; have no sense of shame; be shameless

【恬淡】indifferent to fame or gain

【恬静】quiet; peaceful; tranquil

【恬美】quiet and happy

【恬谧】〈书〉quiet; peaceful; tranquil

【恬然】unperturbed; calm; nonchalant: 处之～ *remain unruffled*

【恬适】〈书〉quiet and comfortable

钿 名〈方〉❶ coin ❷ money: 几～? *How much is it*? ❸ fund; sum: 车～ *(bus, train or taxi) fare*

甜 形 ❶ sweet; honeyed: 这西瓜好～哪! *This watermelon is really sweet*! / 她话说得很～。*Her words were honeyed*. ❷ (of sleep) sound: 睡得真～ *have a sound (or sweet) sleep*; *sleep soundly*

【甜菜】❶ beet: 糖～ *sugar beet* / ～糖 *beet sugar* ❷ beetroot

【甜点】sweet snacks; sweets

【甜瓜】muskmelon

【甜美】❶ sweet; luscious: 味道～ *taste sweet*; *have a sweet taste* / ～多汁的桃儿 *luscious and juicy peaches* ❷ pleasant; refreshing: ～的生活 *a happy life* / 睡了个～的午觉 *have a refreshing nap after lunch*

【甜蜜】sweet; happy: ～的回忆 *happy* (*or sweet*) *memories*

【甜面酱】(又作'甜酱') a sweet sauce made of fermented flour

【甜食】sweet food; sweets: 他爱吃～。*He has a sweet tooth.* or *He likes sweet things.*

【甜水】❶ fresh water: ～井 *fresh water well* ❷ sugar water—happiness; comfort: 这孩子是在～里长大的。*The child's grown up in happy times*

【甜睡】sleep soundly; be fast asleep

【甜丝丝】❶ pleasantly sweet: 这个菜～儿的。*This dish is sweet and delicious.* ❷ quite pleased; gratified; happy: 心里感到～的 *feel quite pleased* (*or happy*)

【甜头】❶ sweet taste; pleasant flavour ❷ good; benefit (as an inducement): 尝到～ *become aware of the benefits of*; *come to know the good of*

【甜味】sweet taste: 有点～ *taste sweet*; *have a sweet taste*

【甜言蜜语】sweet words and honeyed phrases; fine-sounding words: 他们的～不过是引鱼上钩的诱饵罢了。*Their honeyed words are nothing but bait to hook the fish.*

填 动 ❶ fill; stuff: 往坑里～土 *fill a pit with earth* / ～枕芯 *stuff a pillow* ❷ write; fill in: ～表 *fill in a form* / 别～错日期。*Don't fill in the wrong date.*

【填报】fill in a form and submit it to the leadership: 每周～工程进度 *make a weekly progress report on a project*

【填补】fill (a vacancy, gap, etc.): ～缺额 *fill a vacancy* / ～亏空 *make up a deficit*

【填充】❶ fill up; stuff ❷ fill in the blanks (in a test paper) ◇ ～塔[石油] packed column (or tower)

【填词】fill in the words to fit a given tune—compose a ci poem by choosing a tune and then writing words to it

【填方】[建] fill

【填房】❶ marry a widower ❷ a second wife a widower marries

【填空】❶ fill a vacant position; fill a vacancy ❷ fill in the blanks (in a test paper)

【填料】[机] packing; stuffing; filling; filler: ～函 *gland box*; *stuffing box*

【填密】[机] packing: 液压～ *hydraulic packing* / ～函 *packing box*

【填平】fill and level up: ～弹坑 *fill up bomb craters*

【填塞】stop up; block up: ～洞隙 *stop up a loophole*

【填写】fill in; write: ～表格 *fill in a form*

【填鸭】❶ force-feed a duck ❷ a force-fed duck ◇ ～式教学法 cramming (or forced-feeding) method of teaching

【填字游戏】crossword puzzle

tiǎn

腆 Ⅰ 形 sumptuous; rich Ⅱ 动 〈方〉 protrude; thrust out: ～着胸脯 *stick out one's chest*

舔 动 lick; lap: ～～嘴唇 *moisten one's lips with the tongue* / 这孩子～了一下蛋卷冰淇淋。*The child licked his ice cream cone.*

【舔犊情深】very affectionate toward one's children

【舔屁股】〈粗〉 lick one's ass; lick sb's boot; fawn servilely

tiāo

挑 Ⅰ 动 ❶ choose; select; pick out: ～个好日子举行婚礼 *choose a propitious day for the wedding* / ～最好的作种子 *select the best for seeds* / 把那筐西红柿～一～。*Pick over that basket of tomatoes.* ❷ nitpick; be hypercritical; be fastidious: ～毛病 *find fault* / 他讲的话你就别～错儿了。*Stop picking holes in what he said.* ❸ carry (or tote) on the shoulder with a pole; shoulder: ～着一担菜 *carrying two baskets of vegetables on a shoulder pole* / ～水点种 *carry* (*or fetch*) *water for dibbling* (*seeds, young plants, etc.*) / ～起领导生产的重担 *shoulder the heavy load of leadership in production* Ⅱ 量 (for a load carried on a shoulder pole): 一～水 *two buckets of water carried on a shoulder pole* ——另见 tiǎo

【挑刺儿】〈方〉 find fault; pick holes; be captious: 他就爱～。*He's always finding fault with people.*

【挑肥拣瘦】pick the fat or choose the lean—choose whatever is to one's personal advantage

【挑拣】pick; pick and choose: 挑挑拣拣 *be choosy*

【挑礼】quibble about etiquette; reproach sb. with a faux pas

【挑三拣四】❶ pick and choose; be choosy ❷同〖挑剔〗

【挑食】be very choosy about what one eats

【挑剔】nitpick; be hypercritical; be fastidious: 总的来说,这个计划是好的,我们不应过于～。*On the whole it's a good plan and we shouldn't nitpick.*

【挑选】choose; select; pick out: 百货商店有很多童装可供～。*The department store has a large selection of children's clothes.*

【挑眼】〈方〉 be fastidious (about etiquette, etc.)

【挑字眼儿】find fault with the choice of words; quibble: 我可是随便说的,你别～。*I said it just off the cuff, so don't get hung up on my choice of words.*

【挑子】carrying pole with its load; load carried on

a shoulder pole

tiáo

条 Ⅰ名 ❶ twig：这棵葡萄长出了许多新～。*This grapevine has grown many new twigs*. ❷ a long narrow piece；strip；slip：把一块布撕成～ *tear a piece of cloth into strips* ❸ a brief informal note：经理不在，请你给他留个～吧。*The manager is out. Will you leave a note for him please?* ❹ item；article：这项条约的正文共八～。*The main body of the treaty consists of eight articles*. ❺ order：有条不紊 Ⅱ量 ❶（for long or narrow or thin things）：一～床单 *a bed sheet* / 两～鱼 *two fish* / 三～船 *three ships* / 一～大街 *an avenue* / 一～肥皂 *a bar of soap* / 一～香烟 *a carton of cigarettes* / 一～裤子 *a pair of trousers* ❷（for certain nouns）：一～好汉 *a brave man* / 两～新闻 *two pieces（or items）of news* / 四～建议 *four proposals* / 一～妙计 *a brilliant scheme* / 三～人命 *three human lives*

【条案】a long narrow table

【条播】［农］drilling ◇ ～机 seed drill；drill

【条凳】bench

【条分缕析】make a careful and detailed analysis

【条幅】a vertically-hung scroll of painting or calligraphy；a wall scroll

【条钢】bar iron

【条规】rules；regulations

【条痕】［矿］streak

【条件】❶ condition；term；factor：自然～ *natural conditions* / 贸易～ *terms of trade* / 利用有利的～ *make use of the favourable factors* ❷ requirement；prerequisite；qualification：提出～ *list the prerequisites；put forward the requirements* ◇ ～刺激［生理］conditioned stimulus；～反射［生理］conditioned reflex；～句 conditional clause

【条款】clause（in a formal document）；article；provision：法律～ *legal provision*

【条理】proper arrangement or presentation；orderliness；method：她工作很有～。*She is a methodical worker*. / 这篇文章～清楚。*The article is well-organized*.

【条例】regulations；rules；ordinances：组织～ *organizational rules*

【条令】［军］regulations：内务～ *routine service regulations（for barracks）*

【条目】❶ clauses and subclauses（in a formal document）❷ entry（in a dictionary）

【条绒】同〖灯心绒〗

【条鳎】［动］striped sole

【条条框框】rules and regulations；regulations and restrictions；conventions and taboos：～太多，办事效率不高。*There are too many regulations and restrictions, and that makes it impossible to get things done quickly*.

【条文】article（in laws and regulations）；clause：～范例 *standard clause*

【条纹】stripe；streak：斑马身上有～。*A zebra has stripes on its body*. ◇ ～布 striped cloth；stripe

【条形码】bar code；（U. S.）Universal Product Code（UPC）

【条锈病】［农］stripe rust；yellow rust

【条约】treaty；pact

【条子】❶ strip：纸～ *a narrow strip of paper；a slip of paper* ❷ a brief informal note ❸〈方〉gold bar

迢（构词成分）见下

【迢迢】far away；remote：千里～ *from a thousand li away；from afar*

调 动 ❶ suit well；fit in perfectly：失调 ❷ mix；adjust：牛奶里加点糖～一下。*Mix some sugar into the milk*. / ～工资 *adjust wages（usu. upwards）* / ～房子 *change accommodations（usu. to improve conditions）* ❸ mediate：调解 ❹ provoke；tease；tantalize：调笑 ❺ incite；instigate；sow discord：调唆 ——另见 diào

【调处】mediate；arbitrate：～争端 *arbitrate a dispute；act as mediator*

【调挡】［机］gear shift

【调房】adjust housing；housing exchange：参加～的居民 *residents who have participated in housing adjustment schemes*

【调幅】［无］amplitude modulation；AM：～广播 *AM broadcast*

【调羹】spoon

【调和】❶ be in harmonious proportion：这两种颜色配得很～。*These two colours blend well*. ❷ mediate；reconcile：从中～ *mediate；act as mediator* ❸（usu. used in the negative）compromise；make concessions：两国的边界争端看来没有～的余地。*There seems to be no room for compromise in the border dispute between the two countries*. ◇ ～漆 ready-mixed paint

【调护】take care of a patient during convalescence；nurse：病人需要特别～。*The patient needs special care during his convalescence*.

【调级】adjust a wage scale（usu. upwards）

【调剂】❶ make up（or fill）a prescription ❷ adjust；regulate：～劳动力 *redistribute labour power* / 外汇～市场 *foreign exchange swap market* / 外汇～中心 *foreign currency swap center* / 自我～ *self-adjustment* / 市场～和计划～ *regulate by market mechanism and by planning* ◇ ～库存 buffer stock

【调价】readjust（or modify）prices

【调浆】［纺］size mixing

【调焦】［摄］focusing：～镜头 *focusing lens*

【调教】❶ look after and guide（children）❷ feed and train（domestic animals）

【调节】regulate；adjust：～水流 *regulate the flow of water* / 对货币的流通不断进行～ *constantly readjust the amount of money in circulation* / 市场～ *market regulation* / 空气～器 *air condi-*

tioner ◇ ～器 regulator；conditioner

【调解】mediate；make peace：～家庭纠纷 *mediate in (or patch up) a family quarrel*

【调经】[中] regulate the menstrual function

【调侃】ridicule；jeer at；deride

【调控】regulate and control：市场的～作用 *regulatory role of the market*

【调理】❶ nurse one's health；recuperate：精心～ *nurse with great care；careful nursing* ❷ take care of；look after：～牲口 *look after livestock* ❸ subject sb. to discipline ❹〈方〉make fun of；play tricks on；tease

【调料】condiment；seasoning；flavouring

【调弄】❶ make fun of；tease ❷ arrange；adjust ❸ instigate；stir up

【调配】mix；blend：～颜色 *mix colours* ——另见 diàopèi

【调皮】❶ naughty；mischievous：～的孩子 *a naughty child* ❷ unruly；tricky：～的牲口 *skittish beasts* ❸ insincere；scheming ◇ ～捣蛋 mischievous；troublesome；making trouble

【调频】[无] frequency modulation；FM：～广播 *FM broadcast*

【调情】flirt

【调色】mix colours ◇ ～板 palette；～刀 palette knife；painting knife；～碟 colour mixing tray

【调试】[计] debug

【调速器】[机] governor

【调唆】incite；instigate

【调停】mediate；intervene；act as an intermediary：对争端进行～ *mediate (or intervene in) a dispute*

【调味】flavour；season：加点生姜调调味 *flavour (or season) food with some ginger* ◇ ～品 condiment；seasoning；flavouring

【调戏】take liberties with (a woman)；assail (a woman) with obscenities

【调弦】tune a stringed instrument

【调笑】make fun of；poke fun at；tease

【调协】coodinate；harmonize；bring into line

【调谐】❶ harmonious ❷ radio tune：～范围 *tuning range* / ～旋钮 *tuning knob*

【调压器】[电] voltage regulator

【调养】take good care of oneself (as in poor health or after an illness)；build up one's health by rest and by taking nourishing food；be nursed back to health

【调音】[音] tune：为钢琴～ *tune a piano*

【调匀】mix well：和面时，水跟面粉要～。*When you make dough, you must mix flour and water well*

【调整】adjust；regulate；revise：～价格 *readjust (or modify) prices* / ～供求关系 *regulate (or readjust) supply and demand* ◇ ～杆 [机] adjusting rod；～器 [机] adjuster

【调治】recuperate under medical treatment

【调制】[无] modulation：～间隙 *modulation gap*

笤 (构词成分)见下

【笤帚】whisk broom；small broom

tiǎo

挑 Ⅰ 动 ❶ push sth. up with a pole or stick；raise：把帘子～起来 *raise the curtain* / ～眉毛 *raise one's eyebrows* / ～大拇指 *hold up one's thumb (in approval)* / ～灯笼 *hang a lantern (from a pole)* ❷ poke；pick：～火 *poke a fire* / ～刺 *pick out a splinter* / ～破水泡 *prick a blister with a needle* / 把问题～开来说吧。*Let's put all the cards on the table.* ❸ stir up；instigate：～事 *stir up trouble；sow discord* / 这口舌是他～起来的。*It was he who stirred up the quarrel.* Ⅱ 名 rising stroke (in Chinese characters) ——另见 tiāo

【挑棒游戏】jackstraws

【挑拨】instigate；incite；sow discord：～是非 *foment discord* / ～民族关系 *sow dissension among the various nationalities* ◇ ～离间 sow discord；foment dissension；incite one against the other；drive a wedge between

【挑大梁】play a leading role；shoulder the main responsibility：中国队把新人放在"～"的位置上。*The Chinese team put the new players in key positions on the team.*

【挑灯】❶ raise the wick of an oil lamp ❷ hang a lantern from a pole：～夜战 *fight by torchlight (in ancient times) or continue working by lamplight*

【挑动】❶ give rise to；lead to；touch off；arouse：～是非 *give rise to (or touch off) a dispute* ❷ provoke；stir up；incite：～内战 *provoke civil war*

【挑逗】provoke；tease；tantalize

【挑花】cross-stitch work

【挑明】no longer keep it back；let it all out；bring it out into the open

【挑起】provoke；stir up；instigate：～边境冲突 *provoke a border conflict (or clash)*

【挑唆】incite；abet；instigate：警惕有人在背后～。*Beware of people stirring up trouble behind the scenes.*

【挑头】take the lead；be the first to do sth.：～提意见 *be the first to make suggestions* / 这是你挑的头儿吧？*You started all this, didn't you?*

【挑衅】provoke：提出～性的问题 *raise provocative questions*

【挑战】❶ throw down the gauntlet；challenge to battle：～的口吻 *a provocative tone* / 接受～ *take up the gauntlet；accept a challenge* ❷ challenge to a contest：他向我～，下一盘围棋。*He challenged me to a game of weiqi (go chess).* ◇ ～书 a letter of challenge；challenge

tiào

眺 动 look into the distance from a high place：

远眺

【眺望】look into the distance from a high place

粜 动 sell (grain)

跳 动 ❶ jump; leap; bounce: 高兴得～起来 *jump for (or with) joy* / ～下自行车 *jump off a bicycle* / ～过一条沟 *leap over a ditch* / 他～过了二米的高度。*He cleared two metres in the high jump.* / 球在篮框上～了一下滚入篮内。*With one bounce on the ring the ball rolled into the basketball net.* ❷ move up and down; beat: 他激动得心直～。*His heart was throbbing with excitement.* / 我眼皮老是～。*My eyelids keep twitching all the time.* ❸ skip (over); make omissions: 从第一页～到第五页 *jump from page 1 to page 5* / ～过了三页 *skip over three pages* / ～一针 *drop a stitch (in knitting)*

【跳班】(of pupils) skip a grade

【跳板】❶ gangplank ❷ springboard; diving board

【跳板跳水】[体] springboard diving

【跳槽】(又作'跳槽子') jump the manger—❶ (of a horse, etc.) leave its own manger to eat at another ❷ throw up one job and take on another; job-hop

【跳虫】springtail; snowflea

【跳弹】[军] ricochet: ～轰炸 *ricochet bombing; skip bombing*

【跳到黄河洗不清】be unable to cleanse oneself even if one plunges into the Yellow River—find it hard to clear oneself (of a charge)

【跳动】move up and down; beat; pulsate: 只要我的心脏还在～,我就要为人民工作。*As long as my heart still beats, I will go on working for the people.*

【跳发球】[体] jump-serving

【跳房子】(又作'跳间') ❶ play hopscotch ❷ hopscotch

【跳高】high jump: ～运动员 *high jumper*

【跳行】❶ skip a line (in reading or transcribing) ❷ start a new paragraph ❸ change one's profession (or occupation, trade)

【跳级】(of pupils) skip a grade

【跳脚】stamp one's foot: 气得～ *stamp with rage*

【跳井】drown oneself in a well

【跳栏】hurdle race; the hurdles

【跳雷】[军] bounding mine

【跳楼货】distress merchandise

【跳梁小丑】buffoon; clown; a contemptible scoundrel

【跳马】[体] ❶ vaulting horse ❷ horse-vaulting

【跳皮筋儿】(又作'跳猴皮筋儿') rubber band skipping; skipping and dancing over a chain of rubber bands

【跳棋】Chinese checkers; Chinese draughts

【跳球】[体] jump ball

【跳伞】❶ parachute; bale (or bail) out ❷ [体] parachute jumping: ～运动员 *parachutist; parachuter* ◇ ～区 parachute drop zone; ～塔 parachute tower

【跳绳】rope skipping; jump rope

【跳虱】〈方〉flea

【跳鼠】jerboa

【跳水】[体] diving: ～表演 *diving exhibition* / 面对池反身～ *reverse dive* / 向前(后)～ *front (back) dive* / 面对板向内～ *inward dive*

【跳台】diving tower; diving platform

【跳台跳水】[体] platform diving: 高(低)难度～ *variety (plain) high diving*

【跳舞】❶ dance (as a performance) ❷ dance (socially or in a ballroom)

【跳箱】[体] ❶ box horse; vaulting box ❷ jump over the box horse

【跳鞋】a kind of leather shoes specially made for high jumping or long jumping

【跳远】long jump; broad jump

【跳月】moon dance (a festive dance performed in the moonlight by young people of the Miao and Yi ethnic groups)

【跳跃着陆】[军] rebound landing

【跳蚤】flea ◇ ～市场 flea market; swap market

【跳闸】[电] trip; tripping: 自动～ *automatic tripping* / ～装置 *tripgear*

tiē

帖 形 ❶ submissive; obedient: 服帖 ❷ well-settled; well-placed: 妥帖——另见 tiě; tiè

【帖服】〈书〉docile; obedient; submissive

【帖子】[计] post

贴 Ⅰ 动 ❶ paste; stick; glue: ～邮票 *stick on a stamp* / ～海报 *put up a playbill* / ～膏药 *apply a (medicated) plaster to* / ～上胶布 *stick on a piece of adhesive tape* / 请把这几张纸～在一块儿。*Please paste these sheets of paper together.* ❷ keep close to; nestle closely to: ～墙站着 *be standing against the wall* / 这孩子紧紧～在妈妈身边。*The child was nestling closely to its mother.* ❸ subsidize; help (out) financially: 我每月～他十块钱。*I help him out by giving him 10 yuan each month.* Ⅱ 名 subsidies; allowance: 米～ *food allowance* Ⅲ 量 (for medicated plaster): 一～膏药 *a piece of (medicated) plaster*

【贴边】hem (of a garment)

【贴饼子】❶ bake corn or millet cakes on a pan ❷ corn or millet cakes so baked

【贴补】❶ subsidize (one's relatives or friends); help (out) financially: ～家用 *help out with the family expenses* ❷ use stored material or savings to cover daily needs or expenses: 还有存的料子～着用,现在先不买。*Make do with the piece of cloth we've got on hand. You don't have to buy something new.*

【贴兜】patch pocket

【贴花】[纺] appliqué

【贴画】❶ pinup picture (e. g. a New Year pic-

ture, a picture poster, etc.) ❷ matchbox picture
【贴换】〈旧〉trade sth. in (for); trade in
【贴己】❶ intimate; close; confidential: ～朋友 *a person one can confide in; bosom friend* ❷〈方〉private savings: ～钱 *private savings of a family member*
【贴金】❶ cover with gold leaf (or gold foil); gild ❷ touch up; prettify: 别尽往自己脸上～了。*Don't put feathers in your own cap.* or *Don't go blowing your own trumpet.*
【贴金漆】gold size
【贴近】press close to; nestle up against: 那孩子～他身边,轻声说了几句话。*The child nestled up against him and murmured a few words.*
【贴面舞】cheek-to-cheek dancing
【贴面砖】[建] furring brick
【贴切】(of words) apt; suitable; appropriate; proper: 这个比喻很～。*This metaphor is very appropriate.* / 措词～ *aptly worded; well-put*
【贴身】❶ next to the skin: ～衣服 *underclothes; underclothing* ❷〈旧〉constantly accompanying: ～丫鬟 *a maidservant who constantly accompanies her mistress; personal maid* ◇ ～警卫 bodyguard
【贴水】[经] ❶ pay an agio ❷ agio
【贴题】relevant; pertinent; to the point: 着墨不多,但是十分～ *brief but very much to the point* / 你的话不～。*What you say is irrelevant (or beside the point).*
【贴体】(of clothes) fit
【贴息】[经] ❶ pay interest in the form of a deduction when selling a bill of exchange, etc. ❷ interest so deducted; discount
【贴现】discount (on a promissory note): ～率 *discount rate* ◇ ～经纪人 discount broker; ～银行 discount bank
【贴现市场】discount market
【贴心】intimate; close: ～朋友 *a person one can confide in; bosom friend* / ～话 *words spoken in confidence*

萜 名 [化] terpene

tiě

帖 Ⅰ 名 ❶ invitation: 请帖 ❷ note; card Ⅱ 量〈方〉(for herbal medicine): 一～药 *a dose (or draught) of herbal medicine* ——另见 tiē; tiè
【帖子】❶ invitation ❷ note; card

铁 Ⅰ 名 ❶ [化] iron (Fe) ❷ arms; weapon: 手无寸铁 Ⅱ 形 ❶ hard or strong as iron: 铁拳 ❷ resolved; determined: 铁心 ❸ indisputable; unalterable: ～的事实 *hard fact; ironclad evidence* / ～的纪律 *iron discipline* ❹ severe looking; serious expression: 在训练场上,教练总是～着脸。*On the training field, the coach always wore a serious look.* ❺〈口〉close; intimate: 误会消除后,两人的关系更～了。*With the misunderstanding cleared up, the two became even closer.*
【铁案如山】a case borne out by ironclad evidence; an ironclad case
【铁板】iron plate; sheet iron
【铁板钉钉】that clinches it; that's final; no two ways about it
【铁板一块】a monolithic bloc: 不要以为这帮人是～,他们是可以分化的。*Don't think this gang is monolithic—it can be split up.*
【铁笔】❶ a cutting tool used in carving seals, etc. ❷ stylus for cutting stencils; stencil pen
【铁箅子】❶ grate (of a stove) ❷ gridiron; grill
【铁壁铜墙】同〖铜墙铁壁〗
【铁饼】❶ discus throw ❷ discus
【铁蚕豆】roasted broad bean
【铁杵磨成针】见〖只要功夫深,铁杵磨成针〗
【铁窗】❶ a window with iron grating ❷ prison bars; prison ◇ ～风味 prison life; life behind bars
【铁磁共振】[物] ferromagnetic resonance
【铁磁性】ferromagnetism
【铁搭】〈方〉an iron rake with three to six teeth
【铁打】iron-forged—unshakable: ～的江山 *unshakable state power*
【铁道】railway; railroad ◇ ～兵 railway corps; ～炮兵 railway artillery
【铁电现象】[物] ferroelectricity
【铁定】ironclad; fixed; unalterable: ～的事实 *hard fact; ironclad evidence*
【铁饭碗】iron rice bowl—a secure job
【铁杆儿】❶ stubborn; inveterate; dyed-in-the-wool: ～汉奸 *out-and-out traitor* ❷ of guaranteed high yield; surefire: ～庄稼 *guaranteed high-yielding crop*
【铁哥们】〈口〉very close friends (usu. young men)
【铁工】❶ ironwork ❷ ironworker; blacksmith
【铁公鸡】iron cock (from which no feathers can be plucked)—a stingy person; miser
【铁箍】iron hoop
【铁骨铮铮】firm and unyielding
【铁观音】a variety of oolong (乌龙) tea
【铁管】iron pipe; iron tube
【铁轨】rail(s) (for trains, etc.); tracks
【铁柜】strongbox; safe
【铁合金】ferroalloy
【铁黑】[化] ❶ iron oxide black ❷ iron black
【铁红】[化] iron oxide red
【铁花】[工美] ornamental work of iron; iron openwork
【铁画】[工美] iron picture: ～银钩 *vigorous flourishes (or strokes) (in calligraphy); forceful strokes*
【铁环】iron hoop: 滚～ *trundle a hoop; play with a hoop*
【铁蒺藜】[军] caltrop
【铁甲】❶ mail; armour ❷ [军] armour for vessels, vehicles, etc. ◇ ～车 同〖装甲车〗; ～舰 同

〖装甲舰〗

【铁将军把门】General Iron guarding the door—the door is padlocked

【铁匠】blacksmith；ironsmith ◇ ～铺 smithy；blacksmith's shop

【铁脚板】iron soles—toughened feet

【铁军】iron army—invincible army

【铁铠】同〖铁甲〗❶

【铁矿】❶ iron ore ❷ iron mine ◇ ～石 iron ore

【铁力木】［植］ferreous mesua（Mesua ferrea）

【铁链】iron chain；shackles

【铁路】railway；railroad：～运输 *railway transportation*；*railway*（*or rail*）*transport*；*shipping by rail* / ～电气化 *railway electrification* ◇ ～干线 trunk railway；～公路两用桥（railway and highway） combined bridge；road and rail bridge；～路基 railway bed；～网 railway network；～线 railway line

【铁马】〈文〉iron-clad（or armoured）horses—strong mounted forces ——另见〖金戈铁马〗

【铁门】❶ iron gate ❷ grille

【铁面无私】impartial and incorruptible；strictly impartial

【铁皮】iron sheet：白～ *tinplate*；*galvanized iron sheet* / 黑～ *black sheet*（*iron*）

【铁骑】〈文〉armoured horses—strong cavalry

【铁器】ironware ◇ ～时代 the Iron Age

【铁锹】spade；shovel

【铁青】ashen；livid；ghastly pale：气得脸色～ *turn livid with rage*

【铁拳】iron fist—powerful striking force

【铁人】iron man—a person of exceptional physical and moral strength

【铁纱】wire gauze；wire cloth

【铁砂】❶ iron sand ❷ shot（in a shotgun cartridge）；pellets

【铁杉】Chinese hemlock（Tsuga chinensis）

【铁石心肠】be ironhearted；have a heart of stone；be hardhearted；be heartless

【铁树】❶ sago cycas（Cycas revoluta）❷ common name for 苏铁

【铁树开花】the iron tree in blossom—sth. seldom seen or hardly possible

【铁水】molten iron

【铁丝】iron wire ◇ ～网 wire netting；wire meshes；wire entanglement

【铁素体】［冶］ferrite

【铁算盘】iron abacus—❶ careful calculation and strict budgeting ❷ an astute businessman；a financial wizard

【铁索】iron chain；cable ◇ ～吊车 cable car；～桥 chain bridge

【铁塔】❶ iron tower；iron pagoda ❷［电］pylon；transmission tower

【铁蹄】iron heel—cruel oppression of the people

【铁桶】metal pail（or bucket）；drum：包围得～似的 *be tightly encircled*

【铁腕】❶ iron hand：～人物 *an ironhanded*（*or despotic*，*tyrannical*）*person*；*strong man or iron lady* ❷ strong rule（over a country）

【铁锨】shovel；spade

【铁线订书机】wire stitcher；wire stitching machine

【铁线蕨】（又作'铁线草'）［植］venus-hair fern（Adiantum capillarus-veneris）

【铁线莲】［植］cream clematis（Clematis florida）

【铁屑】❶ iron filings ❷ iron chippings and shavings

【铁心】❶be unshakable in one's determination：～务农 *be a very determined farmer* ❷［电］（iron）core

【铁锈】rust

【铁盐】molysite

【铁陨石】iron meteorite

【铁砧】anvil

【铁证】ironclad proof；irrefutable evidence ◇ ～如山 a mass of ironclad evidence；irrefutable，conclusive evidence

【铁中铮铮】the finest of metals—an outstanding person

tiè

帖 名 a book containing models of handwriting or painting for learners to copy：看着～写字 *practise calligraphy after a model* ——另见 tiē；tiě

tīng

厅 名 ❶ hall（for holding meetings，concerts，receiving guests，etc.）：休息～ *lounge*（*in a hotel*，*theatre*，*etc.*）；*foyer* / 这个（门）～很大。*This*（*entrance*）*hall is very spacious.* / 人民大会堂台湾～ *Taiwan Room in the Great Hall of the People* ❷ a department in a big government organization，such as a ministry；office：办公厅 ❸ a government department at the provincial level：教育～ *the Education Department*

听 Ⅰ 动 ❶ listen；hear：请仔细～。*Please listen carefully.* / ～广播 *listen to the radio* / 打开收音机～～新闻。*Let's turn on the radio and listen in to the news.* / 我没～过这样好的音乐。*I've never heard such beautiful music before.* / 请～我说完。*Please hear me out.* ❷ heed；obey；listen to：～我的没错儿。*Do as I say and you won't go wrong.* / 我劝他别去，他不～。*I advised him not to go，but he wouldn't listen.* / 她要～了我的话，哪儿会有今天。*If she'd listened to me，things would be different today.* ❸ administer；manage：听政 ❹ allow；let：听凭 Ⅱ 量〈方〉tin；can：三～咖啡 *three tins of coffee* / 六～啤酒 *six cans of beer*

【听便】do as one pleases：去留～。*You may go or stay as you please.*

【听差】〈旧〉manservant；office attendant

【听从】obey; heed; comply with: ～指挥 *obey orders* / ～吩咐 *be at sb.'s beck and call; do sb.'s bidding* / ～劝告 *accept sb.'s advice* / ～召唤 *answer sb.'s call*

【听而不闻】hear but pay no attention; turn a deaf ear to

【听风是雨】hear the wind and mistake it for the rain—believe rumours

【听骨】[生理] ear bones

【听候】wait for (a decision, settlement, etc. from higher authorities): ～分配 *wait for one's job assignment* / ～上级指示 *pending further instructions from the higher authorities*

【听话】heed what an elder or superior says; be obedient: 这孩子不～。*The child won't do as he is told.* or *The child doesn't behave himself.* / ～,做功课去。*Be a good boy (or girl). Go and do your homework.*

【听话儿】wait for a reply: 你的要求我们正在研究,过几天～。*We're considering your request and will give you a reply in a few days.*

【听见】hear: 我～有人敲门。*I heard a knock at the door.* / 她说的什么你～了吗? *Did you catch what she said?*

【听讲】listen to a talk; attend a lecture: 一面～,一面记笔记 *take notes while listening to a lecture*

【听觉】sense of hearing

【听课】❶ visit (or sit in on) a class ❷ attend a lecture

【听力】❶ hearing (ability): 经过针刺恢复了～ *regain one's hearing after receiving acupuncture treatment* ❷ aural comprehension (in language teaching)

【听命】❶ take orders from; be at sb.'s command: ～于人 *be at sb.'s beck and call* ❷ 同〖听天由命〗

【听凭】allow; let (sb. do as he pleases): ～别人的摆布 *be at the mercy of others*

【听其言而观其行】listen to a person's words and watch his deeds; judge people by their deeds, not just by their words

【听其自然】let things take their own course; let matters slide

【听取】listen to: 经常～群众的意见 *constantly heed the opinions of the masses* / ～汇报 *hear (listen to) reports (from below); debrief*

【听任】〈书〉allow; let (sb. do as he pleases): 不能～黄色书刊充斥市场。*We cannot allow pornographic books to flood the market.*

【听神经】[生理] auditory (or acoustic) nerve

【听说】❶ be told; hear of: 我听人说她到南方去了。*I hear she has gone to the South.* / 这种事我们从来没～过。*We've never heard of such a thing.* ❷〈方〉heed what an elder or superior says; be obedient

【听天由命】submit to the will of Heaven; resign oneself to one's fate; trust to luck: 得了这种病只好～。*When you get this kind of disease, there's nothing you can do but put yourself in the hands of God.*

【听筒】❶ (telephone) receiver ❷ headphone; earphone ❸ [医] stethoscope

【听头儿】worth listening to: 这段唱腔有～。*This aria is a joy to listen to.*

【听戏】go to the opera (esp. Beijing opera)

【听写】dictation: 教师让学生～。*The teacher gave the pupils (a piece of) dictation.*

【听信】❶ wait for information ❷ believe what one hears (usu. sth. incorrect or one-sided); believe

【听诊】[医] auscultation ◇ ～器 stethoscope

【听政】(of a monarch or regent) hold court; administer affairs of state ◇ ～会 hearing

【听之任之】let sth. (undesirable, evil, etc.) go unchecked; take a laissez-faire attitude; let sb. have his own way; let matters drift: 对于损害群众利益的事情,我们不能～。*We cannot shut our eyes to things that harm the interests of the masses.*

【听众】audience; listeners

【听装】〈方〉tinned; canned: ～奶粉 *tinned milk powder*

烃 名 [化] hydrocarbon: 开链～ *open chain hydrocarbon* / 闭链～ *closed chain hydrocarbon*

【烃气】[化] hydrocarbon gas

tíng

廷 名 the court of a feudal ruler; the seat of a monarchical government: 清～ *the Qing government*

【廷杖】flogging with a big stick at court (a punishment in ancient China)

亭 名 ❶ pavilion (in a park or beside a road for people to rest): 八角～ *octagonal pavilion* ❷ stall; kiosk: 书亭

【亭亭如盖】(of a tree) standing straight with a canopy of leaves

【亭亭玉立】❶ (of a girl) fair, slim and graceful ❷ (of a tree, etc.) tall and straight

【亭子】pavilion (in a park or beside a road for people to rest)

庭 名 ❶ hall ❷ front courtyard; front yard ❸ law court: 开庭

【庭训】〈书〉paternal instructions and admonitions

【庭园】flower garden; grounds

【庭院】courtyard

【庭长】the president of a law court; presiding judge

停 Ⅰ 动 ❶ stop; cease; halt; pause: 雨～了。*The rain has stopped.* / 演奏完序曲之后,乐队～下来又调了调音。*After the overture, the orchestra stopped to tune up again.* / 蟋蟀叫个不～。*The crickets were chirruping ceaselessly.* ❷ stop over; stay：我在杭州～了五天。*I stopped over at Hangzhou for five days*. / 火车在这些小站都只～一分钟。*The train stops only for one minute at these small stations*. ❸ (of cars) be parked; (of ships) lie at anchor; (of a dead body or coffin) be placed：门口～着一辆奔驰牌轿车。*Parked in front of the gate was a Benz sedan*. / 汽车～在哪儿？*Where can we park the car*? Ⅱ 形 ready; settled：停妥 Ⅲ 量〈口〉part (of a total); portion：十～儿有九～儿是好的。*Nine out of ten are good*.

【停摆】(of a pendulum) come to a standstill; stop：钟～了。*The clock's stopped*.

【停办】stop a business; close down：这个学校已经～三年了。*The school has been closed down for three years*.

【停泊】anchor; berth：这个码头可以～五十多艘轮船。*The docks can berth over fifty vessels*. ◇～处 berth; anchorage; roads; roadstead

【停产】stop production

【停车】❶ stop; pull up：下一站～十分钟。*At the next station we'll have a ten-minute stop*. ❷ park (a car)：此处不准～！*No Parking*! ❸ (of a machine) stall; stop working：机器～了，得加点油。*The machine's stalled. It needs oiling*. ◇～场 car park; parking lot; parking area

【停当】ready; settled：一切准备～。*Everything's ready*. or *All set*.

【停电】❶ cut off the power supply; have a power failure ❷ power cut; power failure; blackout

【停顿】❶ stop; halt; pause; be at a standstill：交通陷于～。*The traffic was at a standstill*. / 水库工程～了好些年。*The reservoir project has been suspended for quite a few years*. ❷ pause (in speaking)：念到这里要～一下。*When you've read up to here, you pause*.

【停放】❶ park (a vehicle)：人行道上不准～自行车。*Don't park bicycles on the pavement*. ❷ place (a coffin)

【停飞】grounding of aircraft

【停工】stop work; shut down：～待料 *work being held up for lack of material*

【停航】suspend air or shipping service：班机因气候恶劣～。*The regular flight is suspended on account of bad weather*.

【停火】cease fire：～协议 *cease-fire agreement*

【停机坪】aircraft parking area; parking apron

【停刊】stop publication (of a newspaper, magazine. etc.)

【停靠】(of a train) stop; (of a ship) berth：六艘万吨货轮可以同时在这个码头～。*Six 10,000-ton freighters can berth at this dock*. ◇～港 port of call

【停课】suspend classes：那天学校～了。*Classes were suspended that day*.

【停灵】keep a coffin in a temporary shelter before burial; rest the coffin temporarily

【停留】stay for a time; stop; remain：代表团在延安～了一周。*The delegation stayed in Yan'an for a week*.

【停留时间】[环保] retention period

【停球】[体] stop the ball

【停赛】❶ (of a match or sports meet) stop; halt; ❷ be temporarily disqualified from contests

【停食】[中] gastric disorder; indigestion

【停售】suspend sale of：～劣质产品 *stop the sale of inferior quality goods*

【停水】cut off the water supply; cut off the water：明天上午八点至下午三点～。*There will be no water tomorrow from 8 am to 3 pm*.

【停妥】be well arranged; be in order：事情已商议～。*The matter has been discussed and satisfactorily arranged*.

【停息】stop; cease：暴风雨～了。*The storm has subsided*.

【停歇】❶ close a business; go out of business ❷ stop; cease：从上午八点工作到下午两点一直没有～ *work nonstop from 8 am until 2 pm*. ❸ stop for a rest; rest：队伍在小树林里～。*The troops rested in a grove*.

【停薪留职】leave without pay：3年前，他～创办了自己的研究所。*Three years ago, he took leave without pay and set up his own research institute*.

【停学】stop going to school; drop out of school

【停业】❶ stop doing business：修理内部，暂时～。*Closed temporarily for repairs*. ❷ close a business; go out of business

【停战】armistice; truce; cessation of hostilities：～谈判 *armistice talks* (*or negotiations*) / ～协定 *armistice; truce agreement*

【停职】suspend sb. from his duties：～反省 *be temporarily relieved of one's post for self-examination*

【停止】stop; cease; halt; suspend; call off：～工作 *stop working* / ～营业 *business suspended* / ～前进！*Halt*! / ～敌对行动 *cease hostilities* / ～供水 *cut off the water supply; cut off the water*

【停滞】stagnate; be at a standstill; bog down：那几年国民经济处于～状态。*The national economy stagnated in those years*.

【停滞不前】stagnant; at a standstill：他们的国民经济～。*Their national economy is stagnant*. / 会谈～。*The negotiations have bogged down* (*or reached a stalemate*).

霆 名 thunderbolt：雷霆

tǐng

挺 Ⅰ 动 ❶ stick out; straighten up (physically)：～胸 *throw out one's chest; square one's shoulders* / ～起腰杆 *straighten one's back; straighten up* / 他～着脖子，气呼呼的样子。*His neck stiffened and he seemed to be in a huff*. ❷ endure; stand; hold out：他肝疼得厉害，都～不住了。

The pain in his liver was too sharp for him to endure. Ⅱ 形 ❶ straight; erect; stiff: 直挺挺 ❷ outstanding; prominent; extraordinary Ⅲ 副 〈口〉 very; rather; quite: ～好 *very good* / 今天～冷。*It's rather* (*or pretty, quite*) *cold today*. / 分量～轻的。*It's rather light*. / 他讲得～生动的。*His talk was quite lively*. Ⅳ 量 (for machine guns): 轻重机枪六十余～ *over sixty heavy and light machine guns*

【挺拔】❶ tall and straight: ～的白杨 *tall, straight poplars* ❷ forceful: 笔力～ *forceful strokes in handwriting or drawing*

【挺杆】[机] tappet: 阀门～ *valve tappet* / ～间隙 *tappet clearance*

【挺进】(of troops) boldly drive on; press onward; push forward: 向前～ *press onward*

【挺举】[体] clean and jerk

【挺立】stand upright; stand firm: 几棵青松～在山坡上。*Several pine trees stand erect on the hillside*.

【挺身】straighten one's back: ～反抗 *stand up and fight; stand up to* (*an enemy, reactionaries, etc*.) ◇ ～而出 step forward bravely; come out boldly

【挺尸】〈讳〉 lie sleeping like a corpse

【挺秀】tall and graceful

【挺直】❶ straighten (the body or a part of it): 走路腰板儿要～。*Keep your back straight when you walk*. ❷ straight; erect

铤

副 〈书〉 (run) quickly

【铤而走险】take a risk in desperation; make a reckless move

艇

名 light boat: 汽艇

tōng

通

Ⅰ 动 ❶ open; through: 路～了。*The road is now open*. ❷ open up or clear out by poking or jabbing: ～炉子 *poke the fire* / 用铅丝～烟嘴儿 *poke a piece of wire through a cigarette holder to clean it* ❸ lead to; go to: 这趟列车直～昆明。*This train goes straight to Kunming*. or *This is a through train to Kunming*. ❹ connect; communicate: 两个房间是～着的。*The two rooms are connected* (*or open into each other*). / 互～情报 *exchange information* ❺ notify; tell: 互～姓名 *each telling his name to the other* / ～消息 *tell sb. the news; let sb. know* / ～个电话 *give sb. a ring; call* (*or phone*) *sb. up* ❻ understand; know: 他～三种语言。*He knows three languages*. Ⅱ 名 authority; expert: 日本～ *an expert on Japan* / 中国～ *an old China hand; Sinologue* Ⅲ 形 ❶ logical; coherent: 这个句子是～的，不必改了。*This is a coherent sentence. It needs no correction*. ❷ general; common: 共通 ❸ all; whole: ～观全局 *take an overall view of the situation* Ⅳ 量 〈书〉 (for letters, telegrams, etc.): 一～电报 *a telegram* / 手书两～ *two personal letters* ——另见 tòng

【通报】❶ circulate a notice: ～表扬(批评) *circulate a notice of commendation* (*criticism*) ❷ circular: 关于情况的～ *a circular on the situation* ❸ bulletin; journal: 《科学～》*Science Bulletin* / 《经济～》*Economic Journal* ❹ notify or report to (one's superior or master)

【通便剂】[医] laxative; cathartic

【通病】common failing; common fault

【通才】all-round (or versatile) person; universal genius

【通常】❶ general; usual; normal: ～的方法 *usual way* / ～情况下 *under normal conditions* ❷ generally; usually; ordinarily; as a rule: 我～六点钟起床。*I generally get up at six o'clock*

【通畅】❶ unobstructed; clear: 大便～ *free movement* (*of the bowels*) / 血液循环～ *free circulation of the blood* ❷ easy and smooth: 文字～ *smooth writing*

【通车】❶ (of a railway or highway) be open to traffic ❷ have transport service

【通称】❶ be generally called; be generally known as: 汞～水银。*Mercury is generally known as quicksilver*. ❷ a general (or common) term

【通达】understand things; be sensible or be reasonable: 见解～ *hold sensible views; show good sense*

【通道】thoroughfare; passageway; passage

【通敌】collude (or collaborate) with the enemy; have illicit relations with the enemy

【通电】❶ set up an electric circuit; electrify; energize: ～的铁丝网 *electrified* (*or live*) *wire entanglements* ❷ publish an open telegram (making known one's political views): ～全国 *publish an open telegram to the nation* ❸ circular (or open) telegram: 大会～ *the circular telegram of the conference*

【通牒】diplomatic note: 最后～ *ultimatum*

【通都大邑】a large city; metropolis

【通读】❶ read over (or through) ❷ acquire a good knowledge of; have a good grasp of

【通兑】circulate, exchange: 这种支票，可以在全国范围内随时～或交换。*This kind of check can be cashed or exchanged at any time anywhere in the country*.

【通分】[数] reduction of fractions to a common denominator

【通风】❶ ventilate; aerate: 把窗子打开通通风。*Open the windows to ventilate the room*. or *Open the windows to let in some fresh air*. ❷ be well ventilated: 这屋里不～。*This room is badly ventilated* (*or is stuffy*). / 炉子不～。*The stove doesn't draw well*. ❸ divulge information ◇ ～报信 furnish secret information; tip sb. off; ～机 ventilator; fanner; ～井 ventilation shaft; air shaft; ～口 air vent; vent

【通告】❶ give public notice; announce ❷ public

notice; announcement; circular

【通共】in all; altogether; all told: 我们～十八个人。*There are eighteen of us altogether.*

【通关节】get round (laws, rules, etc.) by bribery

【通过】❶ pass through; get past; traverse: 电流～导线。*Electricity passes through the wires.* / 我们要打开局面就必须～这一关。*We must overcome this obstacle to open a new phase in our work.* ❷ adopt; pass; carry: ～宪法 *adopt a constitution* / 以压倒多数～ *be passed by an overwhelming majority* / 这个提案已一致～。*The motion was carried unanimously.* ❸ ask the consent or approval of: 这个问题要～群众才能做出决定。*No decision can be made on this matter until the masses have been consulted.* ❹ by means of; by way of; by; through: ～外交途径处理 *to be dealt with through diplomatic channels*

【通航】be open to navigation or air traffic: ～水域 *navigable waters* / 北京与拉萨之间已～了。*There is now air service between Beijing and Lhasa.*

【通红】very red; red through and through: 孩子的脸冻得～。*The child's face was bright red from the cold.* / 她羞得满脸～。*She blushed scarlet with shyness.*

【通话】❶ converse ❷ communicate by telephone ◇ ～计时器 peg count meter; ～时间 air time

【通婚】be (or become) related by marriage; intermarry

【通货】[经] currency; current money ◇ ～贬值 depreciation; ～紧缩 deflation; ～膨胀 inflation; ～膨胀率 rate of inflation

【通缉】order the arrest of a criminal at large; list (sb.) as wanted; put (sb.) on the wanted list: 下～令 *issue a wanted circular*

【通奸】commit adultery

【通经】❶ [中] stimulate the menstrual flow (by emmenagogues or acupuncture) ❷ be well versed in Confucian classics

【通栏】the layout of a page of a book or a periodical without columns: ～标题 *banner* (*or streamer*) *headline*; *banner*

【通览】take an overall view of (a situation, etc.)

【通力】put in a concerted effort: ～合作 *make a concerted* (*or united*) *effort*; *give full cooperation to*

【通例】❶ general rule; usual practice: 星期天休息是学校的～。*It is a general rule that schools close on Sundays.* ❷ 〈书〉 universal law

【通亮】well-illuminated; brightly lit: 火光～。*The flames lit up brightly.*

【通量】[物] flux

【通令】❶ issue a circular (or general) order: ～嘉奖 *issue an order of commendation* ❷ circular (or general) order

【通路】❶ thoroughfare; passageway; route: 将兵力集结于敌军必经的～两侧 *concentrate forces on both sides of the route the enemy is sure to take* ❷ way; channel

【通论】❶ a well-rounded argument ❷ (usu. used in book titles) a general survey: 《地震学～》 *General Seismology*

【通脉】[中] ❶ promote blood circulation by invigorating vital energy ❷ promote lactation

【通名】❶ introduce oneself ❷ a general (or common) term

【通明】well-illuminated; brightly lit: 灯火～ *be ablaze with lights*; *be brightly lit*

【通年】throughout the year; all the year round

【通盘】overall; all-round; comprehensive: ～计划 *overall planning* / ～估计 *an all-round estimate*

【通票】through ticket

【通铺】同〖统铺〗

【通气】❶ ventilate; aerate: 粘土结构紧,不容易～。*Clayey soils are dense and poorly aerated.* ❷ be in touch (or communication) with each other; keep each other informed: 各单位要经常～。*The various work units must keep in touch with each other.* / 这件事你得跟他通个气。*You should let him know of this matter.* ◇ ～孔 air vent; vent

【通窍】understand things; be sensible or reasonable: 道理讲得很明白,可他就是不～。*The reason was explained to him clearly, but he couldn't see it.*

【通情】❶ understanding and considerate; reasonable ❷ communicate the affection between a man and a woman ◇～达理 showing good sense; understanding and reasonable; sensible

【通权达变】act as the occasion requires; adapt oneself to circumstances; follow a flexible course of action

【通融】❶ stretch rules, get around regulations, etc., to accommodate sb.; make an exception in sb.'s favour: 这事可以～。*We can make an exception in this case.* ❷ accommodate sb. with a short-term loan: 我想跟你～二十块钱。*I wonder if you can lend me 20 yuan.*

【通商】(of nations) have trade relations: 订立～条约 *conclude a trade treaty*; *sign a treaty of commerce* / ～口岸 *trading port*

【通身】the whole body: ～是汗 *sweat all over*

【通史】comprehensive history; general history: 中国～ *general history of China*

【通式】[化] general formula

【通顺】(of writing) clear and coherent; smooth: 文理～ *coherent writing* / 这个句子不～。*This sentence doesn't read smoothly.*

【通俗】popular; common: ～易懂 *easy to understand* / 拿一句～的话来讲 *to use a common expression* ◇ ～读物 books for popular consumption; popular literature; ～化 popularize

【通体】the entire body or mass: 水晶～透明。*Crystal is entirely transparent.*

【通天】❶ exceedingly high or great: ～的本事 *exceptional ability*; *superhuman skill* ❷ direct access to the highest authorities

【通条】❶ (stove) poker ❷ cleaning rod (for a

gun)

【通通】all; entirely; completely: 唱片～卖完了。*The discs are all sold out*. / ～拿去吧。*Take away the lot*. or *Take them all*.

【通途】〈书〉thoroughfare: 天堑变～ *a deep chasm turned into a thoroughfare*

【通脱木】[植] rice-paper plant (Tetrapanax papyriferus)

【通宵】all night; the whole night; throughout the night: 干了个～ *work all night* ◇ ～达旦 all night long; all through the night

【通晓】thoroughly understand; be well versed in; be proficient in: ～几种文字 *have a good command of several languages*

【通心粉】macaroni

【通信】communicate by letter; correspond: 他经常跟我们～。*He often writes to us*. ◇ ～保密 [军] communication (or traffic) security; ～兵 signal corps (or unit, troops); signalman; ～处 mailing address; ～鸽 homing pigeon; carrier pigeon; ～连 [军] signal company; ～联络 [军] signal communication; communications and liaison; ～犬 messenger dog; ～枢纽 signal (or communication) centre; ～卫星 communications satellite; telecommunication satellite; ～员 messenger; orderly

【通行】❶ pass (or go) through: 自由～ *can pass freely*; *have free passage* / 停止～ *closed to traffic* / 此巷不～ *Blind Alley*; *Dead End*; *No Thoroughfare* ❷ current; general: 这是全国～的办法。*This is the current practice throughout the country*. / 这项规定在一些地区仍然～。*This regulation is still in force in some districts*. ◇ ～费 toll; ～能力 traffic capacity; ～权 right of way; ～税 transit duty;

【通行证】pass; permit; safe-conduct; laissez-passer: 边境～ *border pass* / 军事～ *military pass* / 临时～ *provisional pass*

【通性】general character; generality

【通讯】❶ communication: 无线电～ *radio* (*or wireless*) *communication* / ～方法 *means of communication* / ～设备 *communication apparatus* (*or equipment*) ❷ news report; news dispatch; correspondence; newsletter: 新华社～ *Xinhua dispatches* / ～报导 *news report*; *news dispatch*; *news story* / ～文学 *reportage* ◇ ～录 address book; ～社 news agency; news (or press) service; ～网 communication network; ～线路 communication line; ～员 reporter; (press) correspondent

【通用】❶ in common use; current; general: ～语种 *commonly used languages* / 国际会议～的语言 *languages used at international conferences* / 全国～教材 *national textbooks* ❷ interchangeable: 这两个词可以～。*These two words are interchangeable*. ◇ ～货币 current money; ～货币单位 current money unit; ～机械厂 universal machine works; ～计算机 general-purpose computer; ～商业语言 common business oriented language; ～月票 a monthly ticket for all urban and suburban lines

【通邮】accessible by postal communication

【通则】general rule

【通知】❶ notify; inform; give notice: 预先～ *give advance notice* / 请马上～他。*Please notify him immediately*. or *Please let him know at once*. ❷ notice; circular: 发出～ *send out* (*or dispatch*) *a notice* ◇ ～书 notice; [商] advice note

tóng

同 Ⅰ 形 same; alike; similar: ～年级 *of the same grade* Ⅱ 动 be the same as: "词典"～"辞典"。"词典" *is the same as* "辞典". Ⅲ 副 together; in common: 和工人～吃、～住、～劳动 *eat, live and work together with the workers* / 我们两国～属第三世界。*Both our countries belong to the Third World*. Ⅳ 介 ❶ (used to indicate accompaniment, relationship, involvement, etc.) with: 我～你一起去。*I'll go with you*. / 这～你没有关系。*This has nothing to do with you*. / 这件事～他有牵连。*He was implicated in the affair*. ❷ (used to introduce the recipient of an action): 他上午来～我告别了。*He came to say good-bye to me this morning*. / 他～我商量下一步该怎么办。*He consulted with me about what we should do next*. ❸ (used to show comparison): ～去年相比,产量增加了百分之二十。*Output has increased by 20% over last year*. ❹ 〈方〉for: 这封信我一直～你保存着。*I've kept this letter for you all this time*. / 别着急,我～你想个办法。*Don't worry. I'll find a way out for you*. Ⅴ 连 and: 老师～学生 *teachers and students*

【同班】❶ be in the same class: ～同学 *classmate* ❷ classmate

【同伴】companion

【同胞】❶ born of the same parents: ～兄弟(姐妹) *full brothers* (*sisters*) ❷ fellow countryman; compatriot: 台湾～ *our compatriots in Taiwan*

【同辈】of the same generation

【同病相怜】those who have the same illness sympathize with each other —fellow sufferers commiserate with each other

【同步】❶ [物] synchronism: 载波～ *carrier synchronization* ❷ in step with; in pace with: ～增长 *grow in step with*; *grow in pace with* ◇ ～电动机 [电] synchronous motor; ～回旋加速器 [物] synchrocyclotron; ～计算机 synchronous computer; ～加速器 [物] synchrotron; ～卫星 〈略〉见『地球同步卫星』

【同仇敌忾】share a bitter hatred of the enemy; be bound by a common hatred for the enemy

【同窗】❶ study in the same school ❷ schoolmate

【同床异梦】share the same bed but dream different dreams—be strange bedfellows

【同党】❶ belong to the same political faction or party ❷ fellow member of a political faction or party

【同道】❶ people cherishing the same ideals and following the same path; people having a common goal ❷ people of the same trade or occupation

【同等】of the same class, rank, or status; on an equal basis (or footing): ～重要 *of equal importance* / ～对待 *put on an equal footing* ◇ ～学力 the same educational level

【同恶相济】(又作'同恶相求') the wicked help the wicked

【同犯】accomplice

【同房】❶〈婉〉(of husband and wife) sleep together; have sexual intercourse ❷ of the same branch of a family

【同分异构体】[化] isomer

【同甘共苦】share weal and woe (or comforts and hardships, joys and sorrows): 与人民群众～ *share the comforts and hardships of the masses*

【同感】the same feeling (or impression): 老张认为这部小说的人物写得很成功，我也有～。*Lao Zhang feels—and so do I—that the characters of this novel are very well drawn.*

【同庚】〈书〉of the same age

【同工同酬】equal pay for equal work; equal remuneration for work of equal value: 男女应当～。*Men and women should enjoy equal pay for equal work.*

【同功酶】[生化] isoenzyme

【同归于尽】perish together; end up in common ruin

【同行】(tóngháng) ❶ of the same trade or occupation ❷ people of the same trade or occupation ——另见 tóngxíng

【同好】people having similar interests or tastes

【同呼吸，共命运】share a common fate; throw in one's lot with sb.

【同化】❶ assimilate (ethnic groups, etc.) ❷ [语音] assimilation ◇ ～政策 the policy of national assimilation (as pursued by reactionary rulers); ～作用 [生] assimilation

【同伙】❶ work in partnership; collude (in doing evil) ❷ partner; confederate

【同居】❶ live together: 父母死后，他和叔父～。*After his parents died, he lived with his uncle.* ❷ cohabit

【同类】of the same kind

【同僚】〈旧〉colleague; fellow official

【同龄】of the same age or about the same age: 和新中国～ *born in the same year as the New China* ◇ ～人 contemporary

【同流合污】wallow in the mire with sb.; associate with an evil person; go along with sb. in his evil deeds

【同路】go the same way: 咱俩～，一块儿走吧。*Come along with me. I'm going that way too.* ◇ ～人 fellow traveller

【同盟】alliance; league: 结成～ *form (or enter into) an alliance* ◇ ～罢工 joint strike; ～军 allied forces; allies; ～条约 treaty of alliance

【同盟国】❶ ally; allied nations ❷ the Central Powers (during World War I) ❸ the Allies (during World War II)

【同名】of the same title or name: 根据～小说摄制的电影 *a film based on a novel of the same name* / 他与我～。*He is my namesake.*

【同谋】❶ conspire (with sb.) ❷ confederate; accomplice ◇ ～犯 [法] accessory

【同年】❶ the same year ❷〈方〉of the same age ❸ candidates who passed the imperial examinations in the same year

【同期】❶ the corresponding period: 他们第一季度的钢产量超过了历史～的最高水平。*Their steel output in the first quarter of the year was higher than their previous record for the period.* ❷ the same term (in school, etc.): 我和他～毕业。*I graduated the same time as he.*

【同前】ditto; idem

【同衾共枕】(of husband and wife) share the same quilt and pillow—sleep together

【同情】sympathize with; show sympathy for: 博得～ *win sympathy* ◇ ～心 sympathy; fellow feeling

【同人】(又作'同仁') colleagues

【同上】ditto; idem

【同生死，共患难】share weal and woe

【同声】in chorus; in unison: ～欢呼 *cheer in unison* / ～呼喊 *shout in chorus (or in unison)*

【同声传译】simultaneous interpretation: 有七种语言的～设备 *be provided with facilities for simultaneous interpretation in seven languages*

【同声相应，同气相求】like attracts like

【同时】❶ at the same time; simultaneously; meanwhile; in the meantime: ～发生 *happen at the same time; coincide; concur* / ～存在 *exist simultaneously; exist side by side; coexist* ❷ moreover; besides; furthermore: 任务艰巨，～时间又很紧迫。*The task is arduous; besides, there's not much time.*

【同事】❶ work in the same place; work together: 我们～已经多年。*We've worked together for years.* ❷ colleague; fellow worker: 老～ *an old colleague*

【同室操戈】members of one family drawing swords on each other—fratricidal strife; internal strife; internecine feud

【同素异形】[化] allotropy: ～体 *allotrope; allotropic substance*

【同岁】of the same age: 我们两人～。*We two are the same age.*

【同榻】〈书〉sleep in the same bed; share a bed

【同位角】[数] corresponding angles

【同位素】[化] isotope: 放射性～ *radioisotope* / ～分离 *isotope separation* / ～扫描器 *radioisotope scanner* / ～探伤仪 *isoscope*

【同位语】〈语〉appositive

【同温层】❶ stratosphere ❷ old name for 平流层
【同屋】❶ share a room ❷ roommate
【同系物】［化］homologue
【同乡】a person from the same village, town or province; a fellow villager, townsman or provincial ◇ ～会 an association of fellow provincials or townsmen
【同心】❶ concentric ❷ with one heart ◇ ～度［机］concentricity; ～同德 be of one heart and one mind; be dedicated to the same cause; ～协力 work in full cooperation and with unity of purpose; work together with one heart; make concerted efforts; ～圆［数］concentric circles
【同行】(tóngxíng) travel together ——另见 tóngháng
【同性】❶ of the same sex ❷ of the same nature or character: ～的电互相排斥。*Two like electric charges repel each other.*
【同性恋】homosexuality; homosexual: ～者 *homosexual; gay*(男性); *lesbian*(女性)
【同姓】of the same surname: 他与我～。*He is my namesake.*
【同学】❶ be in the same school; be a schoolmate of sb.: 我和他同过三年学。*I studied in the same school with him for three years.* ❷ fellow student; schoolmate ❸ a form of address used in speaking to a student
【同学录】schollmates' address book
【同样】same; equal; similar: ～的方法 *the same method* / ～情况下 *under similar circumstances* / ～地懂得 *know equally well* / 他说英语和法语～流利。*He speaks English and French with equal fluency.*
【同业】❶ the same trade or business ❷ a person of the same trade or business
【同一】same; identical: 向～目标前进 *advance towards the same goal* / 抱～观点的人 *those who hold identical views*
【同一律】［逻］the law of identity
【同一性】［哲］identity
【同义词】synonym
【同意】agree; consent; approve: 我的意见你～吗? *Do you agree with me?* / 他～这项建议。*He consented to the proposal.* / 父母不～我的婚事。*My parents don't approve of my marriage.*
【同音词】homonym; homophone
【同余】［数］congruence: ～数 *congruent numbers*
【同源多倍体】［生］autopolyploid
【同志】comrade: 李～ *Comrade Li* / ～们辛苦了。*You comrades have been working hard.* / 致以～的敬礼 *with comradely greetings*
【同种】of the same race
【同舟共济】cross a river in the same boat—pull together in times of trouble
【同轴】［电］coaxial: ～电缆 *coaxial cable*
【同宗】of the same clan; have common ancestry: 同姓不～ *of the same surname, but not the same clan*
【同族】❶ 同〖同宗〗❷ 同〖同种〗

彤 形〈文〉red
【彤云】〈文〉❶ red clouds ❷ dark clouds: ～密布。*Dark clouds were gathering.* or *The sky was overcast.*

茼 (构词成分)见下
【茼蒿】［植］crowndaisy chrysanthemum

桐 名［植］❶ paulownia ❷ Chinese parasol (tree); phoenix tree ❸ tung oil tree; tung tree
【桐油】tung oil
【桐油树】common name for 油桐

铜 名［化］copper (Cu)
【铜氨液】cuprammonia
【铜铵人造丝】［纺］cuprammonium (or copper) rayon
【铜板】〈方〉copper coin; copper
【铜版】［刷］copperplate ◇ ～画 copperplate etching (or engraving); copperplate; ～印刷 copperplate printing; ～印刷机 copperplate press; etching press; ～纸 art (printing) paper
【铜币】copper coin; copper
【铜臭】the stink of money—profits-before-everything mentality: 满身～ *stinking (or filthy) with money; filthy rich*
【铜鼓】bronze drum
【铜管乐】music for or played by a brass band
【铜管乐队】brass band
【铜管乐器】brass-wind instrument; brass instrument; brass wind; brass
【铜壶滴漏】［考古］copper clepsydra
【铜活】❶ brass or copper fittings, accessories, etc. ❷ work in copper; coppersmithing
【铜匠】coppersmith
【铜筋铁骨】copper muscles and iron bones—strongly built; robust
【铜镜】［考古］bronze mirror
【铜蓝】［矿］covellite; indigo copper
【铜绿】［化］verdigris
【铜模】［刷］matrix; (copper) mould ◇ ～雕刻机 matrix cutting machine
【铜牌】bronze medal; bronze
【铜器】bronze, brass or copper ware ◇ ～时代 the Bronze Age
【铜钱】copper cash
【铜墙铁壁】a bastion of iron—an impregnable fortress
【铜丝】copper wire
【铜像】bronze statue
【铜元】(又作'铜圆') copper coin; copper
【铜子儿】〈口〉copper coin; copper

童 Ⅰ 名 ❶ child: 顽童 ❷〈旧〉boy servant: 书童 Ⅱ 形 ❶ virgin: 童男 / 童女 ❷ bare; bald: 童山
【童便】［中］boys' urine (the urine of boys under 12, used in cases of hemorrhage and extravasated blood)
【童工】❶ child labour ❷ child labourer

【童话】children's stories；fairy tales
【童伶】boy actor (in traditional opera)
【童男】virgin boy
【童年】childhood
【童女】maiden；virgin
【童仆】〈书〉❶ houseboys ❷ menservants；servants
【童山】bare hills：～秃岭 *bare hills and mountains* ◇ ～濯濯 bare and barren hills；hills denuded of vegetation
【童声】child's voice：～合唱 *children's chorus*
【童叟】children and old men—the old and the young ◇ ～无欺 (a shop sign) neither old nor young cheated (i.e. honest with all customers)
【童心】child's heart；childlike innocence ◇ ～未泯(of a grown-up，esp. an aged person) still preserve traces of childishness or childlike innocence
【童星】child star
【童养媳】a girl taken into the family as a daughter-in-law-to-be；child daughter-in-law；child bride
【童谣】children's folk rhymes
【童贞】virginity (esp. of a woman)；chastity
【童真】child's simplicity or innocence
【童稚】❶ child ❷ child's naivety
【童装】children's wear (or clothing)
【童子】boy；lad
【童子鸡】〈方〉young chicken；broiler
【童子军】boy scouts：女～ *girl scouts*

酮 名［化］ketone
【酮化】［化］ketonize

瞳 名 pupil (of the eye)
【瞳孔】［生理］pupil：放大～ *have one's pupils dilated* ◇ ～开大［医］mydriasis；～缩小［医］myosis
【瞳人】(又作'瞳仁') common name for 瞳孔

tǒng

统 Ⅰ 名 ❶ interconnected system：传统 / 系统 ❷any tube-shaped part of an article of clothing, etc：皮统子 Ⅱ 动 gather into one；unite：由老李～管 *be under Lao Li's overall leadership* Ⅲ 副 all；together：这些东西～归你用。*You have all these things at your disposal*.
【统舱】steerage (passenger accommodation)：～旅客 *steerage passenger* / 坐～ *travel steerage*
【统称】❶ be called by a joint name：武昌、汉口和汉阳常～为武汉。*The cities of Wuchang，Hankou and Hanyang are often referred to as Wuhan*. ❷ a general designation；a general term (or name)
【统筹】plan as a whole：～全局 *take the whole situation into account and plan accordingly* / ～规划 *overall planning* ◇ ～兼顾 unified planning with due consideration for all concerned；making overall plans and taking all factors into consideration
【统共】altogether；in all：我们小组～七个人。*There are altogether seven people in our group*.
【统购统销】state monopoly for purchase and marketing (of grain，cotton，etc.)
【统计】❶ statistics：～资料 *statistical data* / 据不完全～ *according to incomplete statistics* (*or figures*) ❷ add up；count：～出席人数 *count up the number of people present* (*at a meeting，etc*.) ◇ ～地图 statistical map；～力学 statistical mechanics；～数字 statistical figures；statistics；～图表 statistical graph (or chart，table)；～推断［数］statistical inference；～学 statistics (a science)；～员 statistician
【统考】(〈略〉全称为'统一考试') a general examination with a common test paper for all students from different schools
【统领】❶ command；lead ❷ commander；leader
【统配】state controlled allocation of vital commodities (grain，oil，coal，etc.)：～物资 *state allocated goods*
【统铺】a wide bed for a number of people (as in barracks，hostels，etc.)
【统属】subordination：彼此不相～。*Neither is subordinate to the other*.
【统帅】❶ commander in chief；commander ❷ command ◇ ～部 supreme command
【统率】command：～三军 *command the country's armed forces*
【统统】all；entirely；completely：把杂草～除掉 *get rid of all the weeds* / ～讲出来 *make a clean breast of it*
【统辖】have under one's command；exercise control over；govern
【统销】state monopoly of marketing of vital commodities：～粮 *grain marketed only by the state*
【统一】❶ unify；unite；integrate：～思想 *seek unity of thinking；reach a common understanding* / ～行动 *seek unity of action；coordinate actions；act in unison* ❷ unified；unitary；centralized：～(的)领导 *unified leadership* / ～的意见 *consensus of opinion* / ～的多民族的国家 *a unitary multi-national state* ◇ ～发票 uniform invoice；～价格 uniform price；～体［哲］entity；unity；～性［哲］unity；～战线 united front
【统战】〈略〉见〖统一战线〗
【统治】rule；dominate：反动～ *reactionary rule* / 占～地位 *occupy a dominant position* / ～者 *ruler* ◇ ～阶级 ruling class
【统制】control：严格～军用物资 *exercise strict control over military supplies*

捅 动 ❶ poke；stab：在硬纸盒上～个洞 *poke a hole in the cardboard box* / 把炉子～～ *give the fire a poke* / 用刺刀～ *stab with a bayonet* ❷ touch；push；nudge：他用胳膊肘～了我一下。*He gave me a nudge*. ❸ disclose；give away；let out：谁把秘密给～出去了？*Who gave away* (*or let out*) *the secret*? / 他是个直性子，把看到的事

儿都～出来了。*He's a straightforward man, and told everything he'd seen.*

【捅娄子】get (oneself or others) into trouble through a blunder; make a blunder; make a mess of sth.

【捅马蜂窝】stir up a hornet's nest; bring a hornets' nest about one's ears

桶 名 ❶ tub; pail; bucket; keg; barrel: 汽油～ *petrol drum* / 一～牛奶 *a pail of milk* / ～装啤酒 *barrelled beer*; *draught beer* ❷ barrel (of petroleum)

筒 名 ❶ a section of thick bamboo: 竹筒 ❷ a thick tube-shaped object: 笔筒 / 邮筒 ❸ any tube-shaped part of an article of clothing, etc.: 袜筒

【筒管】[纺] bobbin

【筒状花】[植] tubular flower

【筒子】tube or tube-shaped object: 枪～ *barrel of a gun*

【筒子楼】building design (usu. dormitory) characterized by a long corridor running the length of the building with rooms on both sides

tòng

恸 名 〈书〉deep sorrow; grief: 大～ *weep (or cry) bitterly*; *wail*

【恸哭】wail; cry one's heart out

通 量 ❶ a complete course or spell of activity in playing certain musical instruments: 擂鼓三～ *beat the drum in three rolls* / 唢呐已经吹过两～。*The suona horn has blared in two rounds.* ❷ (used after the numeral 一) an instance of doing sth. unpleasant: 胡说一～ *talk as much nonsense as one likes* / 闹了一～ *kick up a row* / 乱讲一～ *make irresponsible remarks* / 发一～牢骚 *give out a torrent of grumbles* ——另见 tōng

痛 Ⅰ 动 ache; pain: 肚子～ *have a stomachache* / 嗓子～ *have a sore throat* / 觉得很～ *feel a great deal of pain* / ～不～? *Does it hurt?* Ⅱ 名 sadness; sorrow: 悲痛 Ⅲ 副 extremely; deeply; bitterly: 痛哭

【痛不欲生】be so grieved as to wish one were dead

【痛陈】state or present in strong terms: ～民间疾苦 *give an accusing account of the people's sufferings*

【痛斥】bitterly attack; scathingly denounce: ～谬论 *sharply denounce a fallacy*

【痛楚】pain; anguish; suffering

【痛处】sore spot; tender spot: 触及～ *touch sb.'s sore spot*; *touch sb. on the raw*

【痛打】give a good thrashing; beat soundly

【痛定思痛】recall a painful experience; draw a lesson from a bitter experience

【痛风】[医] gout

【痛改前非】sincerely mend one's ways; thoroughly rectify one's errors

【痛感】keenly feel: ～自己知识不足 *keenly feel one's lack of knowledge*

【痛恨】hate bitterly; utterly detest

【痛悔】bitterly repent; deeply regret; be filled with remorse

【痛击】deal a severe blow; deliver a telling blow

【痛歼】wipe out; annihilate

【痛经】[医] dysmenorrnoea

【痛觉】[生理] sense of pain

【痛哭】cry (or weep) bitterly; wail: ～失声 *be choked with tears* ◇ ～流涕 weep bitter tears; cry one's heart out

【痛苦】pain; suffering; agony: 精神上的～ *mental agony* / 关心病人的～ *be concerned about the sufferings of the patient*

【痛快】❶ very happy; delighted; joyful: 感到从来没有过的～ *be filled with joy as never before* / 图一时的～ *seek momentary gratification* ❷ to one's heart's content; to one's great satisfaction: 喝个～ *drink one's fill* / 玩个～ *have a wonderful time* / 这个澡洗得真～。*I had a very refreshing bath.* ❸ simple and direct; forthright; straightforward: 说话很～ *speak simply and directly*; *not mince matters* / 她这人～,心里有什么就说什么。*She is frank and says what's on her mind.* / 他～地答应了。*He readily agreed.*

【痛快淋漓】impassioned and forceful

【痛骂】severely scold; roundly curse

【痛切】with intense sorrow; most sorrowfully: ～反省 *examine oneself with feelings of deep remorse*

【痛诉】give a bitter account

【痛惜】deeply regret; deplore: 我们都为失去一个好同志而感到～。*We all deeply regretted the loss of such a good comrade.*

【痛心】pained; distressed; grieved: 他对自己的错误感到很～。*He keenly regretted his mistake.*

【痛心疾首】with bitter hatred: 他～地说:"我上了这个坏家伙的当。" *"I was duped by that villain!" he said, his voice filled with hate.*

【痛痒】❶ sufferings; difficulties: 关心群众的～ *be concerned with the well-being of the masses* ❷ (usu. used in the negative) importance; consequence: 无关痛痒 ◇ ～相关 share a common lot

【痛饮】drink one's fill; drink to one's heart's content

【痛阈】[医] threshold of pain

【痛责】severely rebuke; castigate

tōu

偷 Ⅰ 动 ❶ steal; pilfer; make off with: 有人把我的雨衣～走了。*Someone has made off with my raincoat.* ❷ drift along: 偷安 ❸ find (time): 偷空 Ⅱ 副 stealthily; secretly; on the sly: 他没跟人说就～着跑了。*He sneaked off without telling*

anyone.
【偷安】seek temporary ease：苟且～ *seek only temporary ease and comfort*
【偷盗】steal；pilfer
【偷渡】slip out of a blockade in a water area；run a blockade
【偷工减料】do shoddy work and use inferior material；scamp work and stint material；jerry-build
【偷汉子】（又作'偷汉'）（of a married woman）have illicit relations with a man；commit adultery
【偷换】substitute one thing for another surreptitiously：～概念 *play tricks with concepts*
【偷鸡不着蚀把米】try to steal a chicken only to end up losing the rice；go for wool and come back shorn
【偷鸡摸狗】❶ steal chickens and dogs—pilfer ❷（of a man）always having affairs with women
【偷奸取巧】seize every chance to gain advantage by trickery；be opportunistic
【偷看】steal a glance；peek；peep：捂上眼睛，别～。*Cover your eyes and don't peek.*
【偷空】take time off（from work to do sth. else）；snatch a moment
【偷懒】loaf on the job；be lazy
【偷老婆】（of a man）have an affair with sb.'s wife；commit adultery
【偷垒】（in baseball and softball）steal a base；steal
【偷梁换柱】steal the beams and change the pillars—perpetrate a fraud
【偷漏】evade tax；defraud of taxes：～农业税 *evade agricultural taxes*
【偷跑】［体］jump the gun
【偷窃】steal；pilfer
【偷情】carry on a clandestine love affair
【偷生】drag out an ignoble existence
【偷税】evade taxes
【偷天换日】steal the sky and put up a sham sun—perpetrate a gigantic fraud
【偷听】eavesdrop：～别人谈话 *eavesdrop on a conversation*
【偷偷】stealthily；secretly；covertly；on the sly（or quiet）：～地溜走 *sneak away* / ～地瞧了一眼 *steal a glance at* / ～告诉他 *tell him on the quiet* / 这些孩子～地抽烟。*The boys smoked on the sly.*
【偷偷摸摸】furtively；surreptitiously；covertly
【偷袭】sneak attack；sneak raid；surprise attack
【偷闲】❶ snatch a moment of leisure：忙里偷闲 ❷〈方〉loaf on the job；be idle
【偷眼】steal a glance；take a furtive glance：他～看了一下母亲的神色。*He stole a glance at his mother's face.*
【偷营】make a surprise attack on an enemy camp；raid an enemy camp
【偷越】cross（a border，etc.）illegally or steathily：～封锁线 *run a blockade*；*slip through a cordon*
【偷嘴】take food on the sly

tóu

头 Ⅰ 名 ❶ head ❷ hair or hair style：您理什么～？*How shall I cut your hair?* / 这～理得好。*That's a good haircut.* ❸ top；end：村西～ *the west end of a village* / 这条胡同儿走到～就是60号。*No. 60 is at the end of the lane.* ❹ beginning or end：你这故事讲到什么时候才是个～儿呀！*When ever will you finish your story?* ❺ remnant；end：蜡～儿 *candle end* / 铅笔～儿 *pencil stub*（*or stump*）❻ chief；head；leader：头儿 ❼ side；aspect：他们是一～儿的。*They are on the same side.* / 事情不能只顾一～。*We mustn't pay attention to only one aspect of the matter.* ❽（noun suffix added to a noun，verb，or adjective）：木头 / 看头 / 甜头 ❾（noun suffix added to a word of locality）：上头 / 下头 / 前头 Ⅱ 数 first：头等 / 头号 Ⅲ 量 ❶（for certain domestic animals）：三十～牛 *thirty head of cattle* / 两～骡子 *two mules* ❷（for garlic）：一～蒜 *a bulb of garlic* ❸（after the numeral 一，for a marriage）：那一～亲事怎么样了？*What about the marriage?* / 他许过我一～亲事。*He's promised me a wife*（*husband*）. Ⅳ 形 ❶（used before a numeral）first：～一遍 *the first time* / ～半场比赛 *the first half of a game* / ～三天 *the first three days* / ～两排位子 *the two front rows of seats* / 他跑了个百米～一名。*He came in first in the 100-metre dash.* ❷〈方〉（used before 年 or 天）previous；last：头年 ❸ leading Ⅴ 介 before；prior to：～五点就得动身 *have to start before*（*or by*）*five* / ～吃饭要洗手。*Wash your hands before meals.* / ～鸡叫我就起来了。*I got up before cockcrow.*
【头儿】〈口〉head；chief；leader；boss：她是我们组的～。*She is the head of our group.* / ～，有火柴没有？*Have you got a match，boss?*
【头版】front page（of a newspaper）：～新闻 *front-page news*
【头半天】forenoon；morning
【头彩】first prize in a lottery：中～ *win first prize in a lottery*
【头筹】first；championship：先拔～ *come out first*；*win the first championship*
【头寸】［经］❶ money market；money supply：～紧（松）。*Money is tight*（*easy*）. ❷ cash
【头道贩子】one who purchases goods directly from the producer and sells them to the retailer at a profit；middleman ——另见〖二道贩子〗
【头灯】［矿］head lamp
【头等】first-class；first-rate：～重要任务 *a task of primary importance* / ～舱 *first-class cabin* / ～品 *first-rate*（*or top-quality*）*goods*
【头等大事】a matter of prime importance；a major event：这两件事，是目前咱们的～。*Both are of paramount importance to us today.*
【头顶】the top（or crown）of the head

【头发】hair (on the human head) ◇ ～夹子 hairpin

【头盖骨】[生理] cranium; skull

【头功】greatest service; highest merit: 立～ *render the greatest service; acquire the highest merit*

【头骨】[生理] skull; cranium

【头号】❶ number one; size one: ～字 *size one type* / ～敌人 *number one enemy; archenemy* ❷ first-rate; top quality

【头花】[工美] headdress flower

【头昏】dizzy; giddy: 我～。*I feel dizzy.* or *My head is swimming.* ◇ ～脑胀 feel giddy (or dizzy); feel one's head swimming; ～眼花 feel giddy (or dizzy); feel one's head swimming

【头奖】first prize (in a contest, etc.): 得～ *win first prize*

【头角】brilliance (of a young person); talent ◇ ～峥嵘 (of a youth) brilliant; very promising; outstanding

【头巾】scarf; kerchief

【头盔】(steel) helmet

【头里】❶ in front; ahead: 老张在～。*Lao Zhang is in front.* / 您～走,我马上就来。*Please go ahead. I won't be a minute.* / 她事事都走在～。*She takes the lead in everything.* ❷ in advance; beforehand: 咱们把话说在～。*Let's make this clear in advance.* ❸ before; ago: 十年～ *ten years ago*

【头脸】❶ head and face ❷ face; features ❸ reputation; prestige: 有～的人 *a prominent figure*

【头领】〈旧〉chieftan; leader; head

【头颅】head

【头鲈鱼】silver-spotted grunt

【头面人物】a prominent figure; a big shot; a bigwig

【头名】first place (in a contest, etc.)

【头目】head of a gang; ringleader; chieftain: 小～ *head of a small group in a gang*

【头脑】❶ brains; mind: 她很有～。*She has plenty of brains.* / 不用～ *not use one's head* / ～简单 *simple-minded; seeing things too simply* / ～清醒 *clearheaded; sober-minded* / 有政治～ *be politically-minded* ❷ main threads; clue: 摸不着～ *cannot make head or tail of sth.* ❸〈口〉chieftain; leader; head

【头年】❶ the first year ❷〈方〉last year or the previous year

【头帕】〈方〉scarf; kerchief

【头皮】❶ scalp: 搔～ *scratch one's head* ❷ dandruff; scurf: 他的上衣肩上白白的净是～。*The shoulders of his jacket were white with dandruff.*

【头破血流】one's head covered with bumps and bruises—be badly battered; be beaten; be crushed: 在事实面前碰得～ *bump one's head against a wall of hard facts*

【头纱】gauze kerchief worn on a woman's head

【头上长疮,脚底流脓——坏透了】with boils on the head and feet running with pus—rotten from head to foot; rotten to the core

【头生】firstborn

【头虱】head louse

【头式】hair style; hairdo; coiffure

【头饰】head ornaments

【头水】❶ (of goods) of the best quality; top-quality: ～货 *first-rate (or top-quality) goods* ❷ (of utensils) be used for the first time ❸ be washed for the first time: 这件衣服刚洗了～就缩了好多。*This coat shrank badly in the first wash.*

【头胎】firstborn

【头套】actor's headgear

【头疼】(have a) headache

【头疼脑热】a headache and a slight fever; a slight illness

【头条新闻】front-page headline: 成为各报的～ *hit (or make) front-page headlines in the press; be the top story of the paper*

【头痛】(have a) headache: ～得厉害 *have a bad headache* / 这件事真让我～。*This business is a headache for me.*

【头痛医头,脚痛医脚】treat the head when the head aches, treat the foot when the foot hurts—treat the symptoms but not the disease; take stopgap measures; apply palliative remedies

【头头儿】〈口〉head; chief; leader; boss

【头头是道】clear and logical; systematic and orderly; closely reasoned and well argued; coherent and cogent: 他说得～。*What he said was clear and logical.*

【头陀】mendicant Buddhist monk

【头衔】title (a sign of rank, profession, etc.)

【头像】head (portrait or sculpture)

【头屑】dandruff; scurf: 有的洗发香波能去～。*Some shampoos help to get rid of scurf (or dandruff).*

【头绪】main threads (of a complicated affair): ～太多 *have too many things to attend to* / 理出个～来 *get things into shape*

【头癣】favus of the scalp

【头雁】the wild goose that leads the flock flying in formation

【头羊】bellwether

【头油】hair oil; pomade

【头晕】dizzy; giddy: ～目眩 *have a dizzy spell; be afflicted with vertigo*

【头针疗法】[中] head-acupuncture therapy

【头重脚轻】top-heavy and unsteady

【头状花序】[植] capitulum; head

【头子】〈贬〉chieftain; chief; boss: 土匪～ *bandit chief*

【头足动物】cephalopod

投 动 ❶ throw; fling; hurl: ～手榴弹 *throw a hand grenade* ❷ put in; drop: 把信～进邮筒 *drop a letter into the pillar-box* ❸ throw oneself into (a river, well, etc. to commit suicide): 投河 ❹ project; cast: 树影～在窗户上。*The tree cast its shadow on the window.* / 把眼光～到来访

者身上 *cast one's eyes on the visitor* ❺ send; deliver ❻ go to; join ❼ fit in with; agree with; cater to: 意气相投

【投案】give oneself up (or surrender oneself) to the police: ～自首 *surrender oneself to the police or judicial department*

【投保】insure; take out an insurance policy: 为这批货物～了十万元 *insure the merchandise for 100,000 yuan* ◇ ～单 insurance application (from); insurance cover note; ～方 policy-holder; ～价值 insured value; ～人 applicant; policy holder

【投奔】go to (a friend or a place) for shelter: ～亲戚 *seek refuge with relatives; go to one's relatives for help*

【投笔从戎】cast aside the pen and join the army—renounce the pen for the sword; give up intellectual pursuits for a military career

【投币电话】coin telephone

【投币式自动售货机】slot machine

【投鞭断流】(of a vast and mighty army) could fling its whips into a river and stem its flow

【投标】submit a tender; enter a bid

【投镖】❶ dart; dart throwing ❷ throw a dart

【投产】(of a factory) go into operation; put into production

【投诚】(of enemy troops, rebels, bandits, etc.) surrender; cross over: 向人民～ *cross over to the side of the people*

【投弹】❶ drop a bomb ❷ throw a hand grenade ◇ ～高度 release altiude; ～角 dropping angle; ～器 bomb rack control; bomb release mechanism; ～手 bombardier; grenadier

【投敌】go over to the enemy; defect to the enemy

【投递】deliver: ～信件 *deliver letters* / 无法～,退回原处。*Undeliverable, returned to sender.* / 无法～的信 *dead letter* ◇ ～员 postman; letter (or mail) carrier; mailman

【投放】❶ throw in; put in: ～鱼饵 *throw in the bait* ❷ put (money) into circulation; put (goods) on the market: 这个新产品已～市场。*This new product has been put on market.*

【投稿】submit a piece of writing for publication; contribute (to a newspaper or magazine): 欢迎～。*Contributions are welcome.* / 我给《英语学习》投了篇稿。*I submitted an article to the English Language Learning.*

【投合】❶ agree; get along: 他们俩脾气很～。*The two of them are quite congenial.* ❷ cater to: ～顾客的口味 *cater to the tastes of the customers*

【投河】drown oneself in a river

【投机】❶ congenial; agreeable: 谈得很～ *talk very congenially; have a most agreeable chat* ❷ speculate ❸ seize a chance to seek private gain; be opportunistic ◇ ～倒把 engage in speculation and profiteering; ～倒把分子 speculator; profiteer; ～分子 opportunist; political speculator; ～取巧 seize every chance to gain advantage by trickery; be opportunistic; ～商 speculator; profiteer

【投寄】send (a letter, etc.) by post; post

【投井】drown oneself in a well

【投考】sign up for an examination: ～大学 *sign up for a college entrance examination*

【投靠】go and seek refuge with sb.: ～亲友 *go and seek refuge with one's relatives and friends*

【投篮】[体](篮球) shoot (a basket): 远(近)距离～ *long (close-in) shot* / 跳起～ *jump up and shoot* / ～不准 *inaccurate shooting* / ～不中 *miss the basket* / 钩手～ *hook shot* / 单手～ *one-hand shot*

【投票】vote; cast a vote: 我投了他一票。*I cast (or gave) my vote for him.* / ～赞成 *vote for; vote in favour of* / ～反对 *vote against* / ～表决 *decide (or vote) by ballot* / 无记名～ *secret ballot* / 去投票处～ *go to the polls* ◇ ～日 polling day; ～箱 ballot box; ～站 polling booth (or station); the polls

【投其所好】cater to sb.'s likes (or tastes)

【投枪】javelin; (throwing) spear

【投亲】go and live with relatives; seek refuge with relatives: ～靠友 *go and seek refuge with one's relatives and friends*

【投入】❶ absorbed: 她在比赛中非常～。*She displayed remarkable concentration in the contest.* ❷ input: 实物～ *input in kind* / 现金～ *input in cash* / ～少,见效快 *less investment and quicker returns* ❸ put into; throw into: ～运行 *put into operation; go into operation* / ～某人的怀抱 *nestle in the arms of...*

【投射】❶ throw (a projectile, etc.); cast ❷ project (a ray of light); cast: 金色的阳光～到平静的海面上。*The sun cast its golden rays on the calm sea.* / 周围的人都对他～出惊异的眼光。*All those around him looked at him with amazement.*

【投身】throw oneself into; join: ～到事业中去 *throw oneself into a career*

【投生】❶ be reincarnated in a new body; be reborn ❷ seek a livelihood outside one's home town

【投师】seek instruction from a master: ～访友 *learn from a master and call on friends to exchange knowledge or skills*

【投石问路】throw a stone to clear the road

【投手】(in baseball and softball) pitcher: ～犯规 *balk*

【投鼠忌器】hesitate to pelt a rat for fear of smashing the dishes—hold back from taking action against an evil-doer for fear of involving or harming good people

【投诉】❶ appeal: ～法院 *appeal to a court* ❷ (of a customer) complain

【投宿】seek temporary lodging; put up for the night: ～客栈 *put up at an inn for the night*

【投胎】reincarnation

【投桃报李】give a plum in return for a peach—return present for present; exchange gifts

【投纬】［纺］ picking
【投降】 surrender；capitulate ◇ ～派 capitulators；capitulationist clique；～主义 capitulationism
【投药】 offer medicine（to take）
【投医】 seek medical advice；go to a doctor
【投影】 projection：极～ *polar projection* / 墨卡托地图～ *Mercator（map）projection* ◇ ～几何学［数］projective geometry；～图［机］projection drawing
【投缘】 find each other congenial；hit it off：两人一见面就～。*The two of them hit it off as soon as they met*. / 两人越谈越～。*As they talked，they warmed up to each other*.
【投掷】 throw；hurl：～标枪（铁饼、手榴弹）*throw a javelin（discus，hand grenade）*
【投置】 throw oneself into；join
【投注】 throw（energy，etc.）into：把全副精力～到工作里 *throw all one's energies into one's work*
【投资】 ❶ invest：～工矿企业 *invest in industrial and mining enterprises* ❷ money invested；investment：国家～ *state investment* ◇ ～保护 investment protection；～场所 outlet for investment；～额 amount of capital invested；～公司 investment company；～环境 investment environment；investment climate；～基金 investment funds；～决策 investment decision；～市场 investment market；～收益 income from（or on）investment；～银行 investment bank；～债券 investment bond

tòu

透 Ⅰ 动 ❶ pass through；seep through；penetrate：～过现象看本质 *see through the appearance to get at the essence* / 血从绷带里～了出来。*Blood seeped out through the bandage*. / 阳光～过窗户照进来。*Sunlight came in through the windows*. / 这双鞋不～水。*These shoes are waterproof*. ❷ tell secretly；let out；reveal：～消息 *tell sb. news on the quiet* / 只听他～了一句半句的，详细情况还不清楚。*I only heard the fragmentary information he let out. Details are still unknown*. ❸ appear；show：白里～红 *white touched with red* / 他脸上～出幸福的微笑。*A happy smile appeared on his face*. / 她的一双大眼睛～着机灵。*Her large eyes show intelligence*. Ⅱ 副 fully；completely；thoroughly：恨～ *be full of hatred for sb.；bitterly hate* / 天已经黑～了。*It was completely dark*. / 道理讲得很～ *thoroughly explain one's reasons；drive the point home*
【透彻】 penetrating；thorough：她把问题分析得很～。*She made a penetrating analysis of the problem*. / 有～的了解 *have a thorough understanding*
【透翅蛾】［动］clearwing（moth）
【透底】 reveal the exact details
【透顶】〈贬〉thoroughly；downright；in the extreme；through and through：反动～ *downright reactionary；out-and-out reactionary* / 腐败～ *thoroughly corrupt；rotten to the core；decadent in the extreme*
【透风】 ❶ let in air；ventilate：打开窗户透透风 *open the window and let in some air* / 这门关不严，有点～。*This door doesn't fit very tightly and the wind blows through*. ❷ dry in the air；air ❸ divulge a secret；leak：这个人嘴很紧，一点风也不透。*The man was closemouthed and didn't drop a hint*.
【透骨】 ❶（of cold air）chill one to the bone；be piercing：冷得～ *be chilled to the bone* ❷ deep；profound；penetrating：看得～ *a keen observation；a penetrating analysis*
【透汗】 a good sweat：出一身～ *break into a sweat；sweat all over*
【透话】 drop a hint；hint；suggest：他～要买这所房子。*He hinted that he would buy the house*.
【透镜】［物］lens：分光～ *beam-splitting lens* / 复合～ *compound lens*
【透亮】 ❶ bright；transparent：这间房子又向阳，又～。*This room is sunny and bright*. ❷ perfectly clear：经你这么一说，我心里就～了。*Thanks to your explanation，it's clear to me now*.
【透亮儿】 allow light to pass through：这个暗室有点～。*This darkroom lets in light*.
【透漏】 divulge；leak；reveal：消息～出去了。*The news has leaked out*.
【透露】 divulge；leak；disclose；reveal：～风声 *leak（or disclose）information* / 真相～出来了。*The truth has come to light（or has come out）*.
【透明】 transparent；diaphanous：～度 *transparency；diaphaneity* / ～的纱巾 *a diaphanous veil* ◇ ～计 diaphanometer；～胶 adhesive tape；～漆 celluloid paint；clear lacquer；～体［物］transparent body；～纸 cellophane paper；cellophane
【透辟】 penetrating；incisive；thorough：～的分析 *a penetrating analysis*
【透平机】（又作'透平'）another name for 涡轮机
【透气】 ❶ ventilate：屋子太闷了，打开窗子透透气。*The room is too stuffy. Open the windows and let some air in*. ❷ breathe freely：透不过气来 *feel suffocated* ❸ leak（or disclose）information；drop a hint；tip off
【透热性】［物］diathermancy；diathermaneity
【透射】 ❶（of light）pass through ❷［物］transmission：定向～ *regular transmission* / ～比 *transmittance* / ～率 *transmissivity*
【透视】 ❶ perspective ❷［医］fluoroscopy；roentgenoscopy ❸ see through ◇ ～图 perspective drawing
【透水层】［地质］pervious bed；permeable stratum
【透心儿】 to the core；to the marrow：冷风吹了我个～凉。*The cold wind chilled me to the bone*. / 我一听他变卦了，马上就觉得～凉。*I felt bitterly disappointed when I heard that he had changed his mind*.

【透信】leak (or disclose) information; drop a hint; tip off: 如果有什么变化,你事先给我透个信儿。*If there should be any changes, please let me know beforehand.*

【透雨】saturating (or soaking) rain; soaker

【透支】❶ banking overdraw; make an overdraft: ～的账户 *overdrawn account* ❷ expenditure exceeds revenue; overspend ❸〈旧〉draw one's salary in advance

tū

凸 形 protruding; raised: ～花银瓶 *a silver vase with a raised floral design* / ～面 *convex*

【凸岸】[地质] convex bank

【凸版】[刷] relief printing plate: ～轮转机 *rotary letterpress machine* / ～印刷 *letterpress; relief (or typographic) printing*

【凸轮】[机] cam: 推动～ *actuating cam* / 急升～ *quick lift cam* / ～轴 *cam shaft*

【凸面镜】(又作'凸镜')[物] convex mirror

【凸透镜】[物] convex lens

【凸缘】[机] flange: 环状～ *collar flange* / 接头～ *joint flange* / 管～ *pipe flange*

秃 形 ❶ bald; bare: 他的头开始～了。*He's getting (or going) bald.* / ～山 *bare (or barren) hills* / ～树 *bare trees; defoliated trees* ❷ blunt; without a point: 铅笔～了。*The pencil is blunt.* ❸ incomplete; unsatisfactory: 这篇文章的结尾显得有点～。*This article seems to end rather lamely.*

【秃笔】bald writing brush—poor writing ability; low skill at composition: 我这支～不行,得找个笔杆子。*I'm no good at writing; you'll have to find someone who is.*

【秃疮】〈口〉favus of the scalp

【秃顶】❶ bald ❷ bald head

【秃发病】alopecia

【秃鹫】cinereous vulture

【秃头】❶ bareheaded; hatless ❷ bald head ❸ shaven head

【秃子】❶ baldhead; baldpate ❷〈方〉favus of the scalp

突 Ⅰ 动 ❶ dash forward; charge: ～入敌阵 *charge into enemy positions* ❷ projecting; sticking out Ⅱ 副 suddenly; abruptly; unexpectedly: 气温～降。*The temperature suddenly dropped.* Ⅲ 名〈书〉chimney

【突变】❶ sudden change: 认识过程中的～ *a sudden change in the process of cognition* ❷ [哲] leap ❸ [生] mutation: 自发～ *spontaneous mutation* / ～体 *mutant*

【突出】❶ break through: ～重围 *break through a tight encirclement* ❷ protruding; projecting; sticking out: 眼球～ *bug-eyed* / ～的岩石 *projecting rocks* ❸ outstanding; prominent: ～的成就 *outstanding achievements* / 他的优点和缺点都很～。*His virtues are as conspicuous as his defects.* ❹ give prominence to; stress; highlight: 他的发言没有～重点。*In his speech he failed to stress the main points.* / 她老想～自己。*She always tries to push herself forward.* or *She is very pushy.* ◇ ～部 [军] salient

【突飞猛进】advance by leaps and bounds; advance with seven-league strides; make giant strides: 生产力～的发展 *the rapid development of the productive forces*

【突击】❶ make a sudden and violent attack; assault ❷ make a concentrated effort to finish a job quickly; do a crash job: ～任务 *rush job; shock work* ◇ ～点 point of assault; ～队 shock brigade; ～手 shock worker; ～战术 shock tactics

【突尼斯】Tunisia ◇ ～人 Tunisian

【突破】❶ break through; make (or effect) a breakthrough: 医学上的～ *a medical breakthrough* ❷ surmount; break; top: ～难关 *break the back of a tough job* / ～定额 *overfulfil a quota* ❸ (in football, etc.) break through a defence ◇ ～地区 [军] area of penetration (or breakthrough); ～点 [军] breakthrough point; point of penetration; ～口 [军] breach; gap

【突起】❶ break out; suddenly appear: 战事～。*Hostilities broke out.* ❷ rise high; tower: 奇峰～。*Peaks tower magnificently.*

【突然】❶ sudden; abrupt; unexpected: ～死亡 *sudden (or unexpected) death* / 听到这消息我感到～。*The news took me by surprise.* / 准备对付一切～事变 *prepare for all eventualities (or contingencies)* ❷ suddenly; abruptly; unexpectedly: ～哭起来 *burst into tears* / 灯～都灭了。*Suddenly the lights went out.* ◇ ～袭击 surprise attack; sudden onslaught

【突如其来】arise suddenly; come all of a sudden; appear out of nowhere

【突突】她的心～地跳。*Her heart went pit-a-pat.* / 汽艇～地驶入港口。*The motorboat chugged its way into the harbour.*

【突围】break out of an encirclement

【突兀】❶ lofty; towering: ～的山石 *towering crags* / 怪峰～。*A grotesque peak thrusts itself towards the sky.* ❷ sudden; abrupt; unexpected: 事情来得这么～,使他简直不知所措。*It all happened so suddenly he didn't know what to do.*

【突袭】surprise attack

tú

图 Ⅰ 名 ❶ picture; drawing; chart; map: 制图 ❷ intention; intent ❸ scheme; plan; attempt: 另作他～ *find another way out; work out a different scheme* Ⅱ 动 pursue; seek: ～私利 *pursue private ends* / ～一时痛快 *seek momentary satisfaction*

【图案】*pattern; design*: 几何～ *geometrical pat-*

tern ◇ ～操 callisthenic performance forming patterns

【图板】drawing board

【图版】plate（for printing photos，maps，illustrations，etc.）

【图报】seek ways to return sb.'s kindness

【图表】chart；diagram；graph

【图财害命】同〖谋财害命〗

【图钉】drawing pin；thumbtack

【图符】［计］icon

【图画】drawing；picture；painting ◇～文字［语］picture writing；pictography；～纸 drawing paper

【图鉴】（usu. used in book titles）illustrated（or pictorial）handbook：《中草药～》*Pictorial Handbook of Chinese Medicinal Herbs*

【图解】❶ diagram；graph；figure：用～说明 *explain through diagrams* ❷［数］graphic solution：～法 *graphic method*

【图景】view；prospect：展现出一幅壮丽的～ *open up a magnificent prospect*

【图卷】picture scroll

【图例】legend（of a map，etc.）；key

【图谋】plot；scheme；conspire ◇～不轨 plot sth. unlawful；engage in conspiratorial activities

【图片】picture；photograph：～展览 *photo*（*or picture*）*exhibition* / ～说明 *caption*

【图谱】a collection of illustrative plates；atlas

【图穷匕首见】（又作'图穷匕见'）when the map was unrolled，the dagger was revealed—hidden intentions are revealed in the end

【图书】books：～资料 *books and reference materials* / ～目录 *catalogue of books*；*library catalogue*

【图书馆】library：～馆长 *librarian*（*in charge of a library*）/ ～管理员 *librarian*（*a library worker*）◇ ～学 library science

【图腾】totem ◇ ～崇拜 totem worship；totemism

【图文并茂】（of a book，magazine，etc.）both pictures and texts are excellent

【图文传真】fax

【图像】picture；image ◇ ～识别［电子］pattern recognition

【图形】❶ graph；figure ❷〈略〉见〖几何图形〗

【图样】pattern；design；draft；drawing：机器～ *a draft for a machine*

【图章】seal；stamp

【图纸】blueprint；drawing：建筑物的～ *drawing of a building*

涂 动 ❶ spread on；apply；smear：～漆 *apply a coat of paint*；*paint* / ～点软膏 *apply some ointment* / 给机器部件～油 *smear machine parts with grease* ❷ scribble；scrawl：别在墙上乱～。*Don't scribble*（*or scrawl*）*on the wall*. ❸ blot out；cross out：～掉几个字 *cross out a few words*

【涂层】coat；coating：减磨～ *friction coat* / 反雷达～ *antiradar coating*

【涂改】alter：～无效 *invalid if altered*

【涂改液】correction fluid

【涂画】scribble；scrawl；daub

【涂料】coating；paint：防腐～ *anticorrosive paint* / 耐火～ *refractory coating*

【涂抹】❶ daub；smear；paint ❷ scribble；scrawl：信笔～ *doodle*

【涂片】［医］smear：血～ *blood smear*

【涂饰】❶ cover with paint，lacquer，colour wash，etc. ❷ daub（plaster，etc.）on a wall；whitewash

【涂刷】apply paint，etc. with a brush

【涂炭】〈书〉mud and ashes—utter misery；great affliction；misery and suffering ——另见〖生灵涂炭〗

【涂写】scribble；scrawl；doodle：墙上净～着名字。*The wall was scribbled over with names*. / 禁止～！*No scribbling*！

【涂鸦】〈谦〉poor handwriting；scrawl；chicken tracks

【涂泽】〈书〉gloss over；whitewash

【涂脂抹粉】apply powder and paint—prettify；whitewash：为自己～ *try to whitewash oneself*

荼 名〈古〉❶ a bitter edible plant ❷ the white flower of reeds，etc.

【荼毒】〈书〉afflict with great suffering；torment ◇ ～生灵 plunge the people into the depths of suffering

【荼蘼】［植］roseleaf raspberry（Rubus rosaefolius var. Coronarius）

途 名 way；road；route：～中 *on the way*；*en route*

【途程】〈喻〉road；way；course：人类进化的～ *the evolution of the human species*

【途经】by way of；via：～武汉前往广州 *go to Guangzhou by way of Wuhan*

【途径】way；channel：寻找消除分歧的～ *seek ways to eliminate differences*

徒 Ⅰ 名 ❶ apprentice；pupil：学徒 ❷ follower；believer：信徒 ❸〈贬〉people of the same faction：党徒 ❹〈贬〉person；fellow：歹徒 ❺（prison）sentence；imprisonment：徒刑 Ⅱ 形 empty；bare：徒手 Ⅲ 副 ❶ on foot ❷ merely；only：～具形式 *be a mere formality* / 不～无益，反而有害 *not only useless*，*but harmful* ❸ in vain；for nothing；to no avail：～自惊扰 *frighten oneself for no apparent reason*；*become needlessly alarmed*

【徒步】on foot：～旅行 *travel on foot*

【徒弟】apprentice；disciple

【徒费唇舌】waste one's breath：我的主意已定，你别～了。*I've made up my mind*，*you're wasting your breath*.

【徒工】apprentice

【徒唤奈何】utter unavailing cries of despair

【徒劳】make a futile effort；work fruitlessly：去跟他争辩是～的。*It would be futile to argue with* him.

【徒劳往返】make a futile journey; hurry back and forth for nothing

【徒劳无功】(又作'徒劳无益') make a futile effort; work to no avail

【徒乱人意】(of a statement, argument, etc.) can only confuse people's minds

【徒然】❶ in vain; for nothing; to no avail: ～耗费精力 *waste one's energy (or effort)* ❷ merely; only: 如果那么办,～有利于敌人。*To do that will only be to the advantage of the enemy.*

【徒手】bare-handed; unarmed ◇ ～操 free-standing exercises

【徒孙】disciple's disciple

【徒刑】[法] imprisonment; (prison) sentence: 判三年～ *sentence sb. to three years' imprisonment*

【徒有虚名】have a false (or unearned, undeserved) reputation

【徒长】[农] excessive growth (of branches and leaves); spindling

【徒子徒孙】❶ disciples and followers ❷ hangers-on and their spawn

屠 动 ❶ slaughter (animals for food) ❷ massacre; slaughter: 屠杀

【屠场】slaughterhouse

【屠刀】butcher's knife

【屠夫】❶〈旧〉butcher ❷ a ruthless ruler

【屠户】〈旧〉butcher or butcher's

【屠龙之技】the art of butchering dragons—an art of a high order but of little value

【屠戮】〈书〉massacre; butcher; slaughter

【屠杀】massacre; butcher; slaughter: 军阀～罢工工人。*The warlords butchered the strikers.*

【屠宰】butcher; slaughter: ～牲畜 *slaughter animals; butcher fat stock* ◇ ～场 slaughterhouse; ～率 dressing percentage; ～税 tax on slaughtering animals

tǔ

土 Ⅰ 名 ❶ soil; earth: 一把～ *a handful of soil* / ～坷拉 *a lump of earth; clod* / 用～把种子盖上 *cover seeds with earth* / ～台 *an earthen platform* / 他鞋上都是～。*There's dust all over his shoes.* ❷ land; ground: 国土 / 领土 ❸ (crude) opium: 烟土 Ⅱ 形 ❶ local; native: 他穿着那件大褂显着～得很。*He looks very rustic in his gown.* / 他说的是很～的北京话。*He speaks with a broad Beijing accent.* ❷ homemade; indigenous: ～办法 *indigenous methods* / ～杂肥 *farmyard manure* ❸ unrefined; unenlightened: 土里土气

【土坝】earth-filled dam; earth dam

【土包子】clodhopper; (country) bumpkin

【土豹】[动] buzzard

【土崩瓦解】disintegrate; crumble; fall apart; collapse: 陷于不可挽救的～的状态 *be hopelessly disintegrated*

【土鳖】[动] ground beetle

【土拨鼠】[动] marmot

【土布】handwoven (or handloomed) cloth; homespun cloth

【土产】❶ produced in a locality ❷ local (or native) product

【土地】❶ land; soil: 肥沃的～ *fertile land; good soil* ❷ territory: 我国～辽阔,资源丰富。*Our country has a vast territory and abundant resources.* ❸ (又作'土地爷','土地老') local god of the land; village god: ～庙 *a tiny temple housing the village god* ◇ ～报酬递减律 the law of diminishing returns; ～法 land law; agrarian law; ～分红 dividend on land shares; ～改革 land reform; agrarian reform; ～集中 concentration of landholdings; ～使用费 land use charge; ～使用权 land-use right; ～使用税 land-use tax; ～税 land tax; ～征用 expropriation of land; ～证 land certificate; land deed; ～制度 land system

【土豆】〈口〉potato

【土耳其】Turkey ◇ ～人 Turk; ～语 Turkish (language); ～浴 Turkish bath

【土法】indigenous method; local method: ～上马 *get on the job with local methods*

【土方】❶ cubic metre of earth ❷ earthwork: ～工程 *earthwork* ❸ [中] folk recipe

【土房】an adobe house

【土匪】bandit; brigand

【土豪】local tyrant ◇ ～劣绅 local tyrants (or bullies) and evil gentry

【土话】local, colloquial expressions; local dialect

【土皇帝】local despot; local tyrant

【土黄】colour of loess; yellowish brown

【土货】local product; native produce

【土家族】the Tujia (Tuchia) ethnic group, or the Tujias (Tuchias)

【土炕】heatable adobe sleeping platform; adobe kang

【土库曼斯坦】Turkmenistan ◇ ～人 Turkman

【土老冒儿】(又作'土冒儿')〈口〉clodhopper; (country) bumpkin

【土里土气】rustic; uncouth; countrified

【土路】dirt road

【土霉素】[药] terramycin; oxytetracycline

【土木】building; construction ◇ ～工程 civil engineering

【土坯】sun-dried mud brick; adobe

【土气】❶ rustic style ❷ rustic; uncouth; countrified

【土丘】mound; hillock

【土壤】soil: 多腐植质的～ *humus-rich soil* ◇ ～学 soil science; pedology

【土生土长】locally born and bred; born and brought up in the locality

【土石方】cubic metre of earth and stone

【土司】❶ system of appointing national minority hereditary headmen in the Yuan, Ming and Qing Dynasties ❷ such a headman

【土特产】(collective name for 土产 and 特产) special local product; speciality
【土头土脑】rustic; uncouth; countrified
【土豚】[动] earth pig
【土卫】[天] satellite of Saturn; Saturnian satellite
【土温】[农] soil temperature
【土星】Saturn: ～光环 *Saturn's rings*
【土腥气】(又作'土腥味儿') the smell of soil
【土洋并举】use both indigenous and foreign methods; use both traditional and modern methods; use both simple and sophisticated methods
【土洋结合】combine indigenous and foreign methods; combine traditional and modern methods; combine simple and sophisticated methods
【土音】local accent
【土语】local, colloquial expressions; local dialect
【土葬】burial (of the dead) in the ground
【土造】make sth. with local methods: ～手榴弹 *grenades of local make*
【土政策】local policy (regulations of a locality or a government department designed to further its own interests and more often than not running counter to the state policy)
【土质】the quality and composition of the soil: ～肥沃 *the fertility of the soil*
【土冢】grave mound
【土著】original inhabitants; aboriginals; aborigines
【土专家】self-taught expert; local expert
【土族】the Tu nationality, or the Tus

吐 动 ❶ spit: ～核儿 *spit out the pips, stone or pits* / 蚕～丝。*Silkworms spin silk.* / 机枪～着火舌。*The machine gun was spitting fire.* ❷ say; tell; pour out: ～实 *tell the truth* / ～怨气 *vent one's grievances* ——另见 tù

【吐刚茹柔】bully the weak and fear the strong
【吐根】[植] ipecac (Cephaelis ipecacuanha) ◇ ～素(又作'吐根硷')[药] emetine
【吐故纳新】exhale the old and inhale the new; get rid of the stale and take in the fresh
【吐口】❶ tell truth ❷ put forward a claim; make a demand
【吐苦水】pour out one's grievances (or bitterness)
【吐露】reveal; tell ◇ ～真情 unbosom oneself; come out with the truth
【吐气】❶ feel elated after unburdening oneself of resentment; feel elated and exultant: 扬眉吐气 ❷ 同『送气』
【吐弃】spurn; cast aside; reject
【吐舌头】put (or stick) out one's tongue
【吐绶鸡】turkey
【吐穗】[农] earing (up); heading (of cereal plants)
【吐痰】spit; expectorate: 不准随地～! *No Spitting!*
【吐絮】[农] opening of bolls; boll opening
【吐字】(of an actor in traditional opera) enunciate: ～清楚 *enunciate clearly*

钍 名 [化] thorium (Th)

tù

吐 动 ❶ vomit; throw up: 恶心要～ *feel sick; feel like vomiting (or throwing up)* / 病人不断地～。*The patient was vomiting repeatedly.* ❷ give up unwillingly; disgorge: 吐赃 ——另见 tǔ

【吐酒石】[药] tartar emetic
【吐沫】saliva; spittle; spit
【吐血】spitting blood; haematemesis
【吐泻】vomiting and diarrhoea
【吐赃】disgorge ill-gotten gains

兔 名 hare; rabbit

【兔唇】[医] harelip
【兔毫】a writing brush made of rabbit's hair
【兔死狗烹】kill the hounds for food once the hares are bagged—eliminate trusted aids when they have outlived their usefulness
【兔死狐悲】(usu. used in) ～,物伤其类 *the fox mourns the death of the hare—like feels for like*
【兔狲】[动] steppe cat
【兔脱】〈书〉run away like a hare; escape; flee
【兔儿爷】a clay figurine with the head of a rabbit (children's toy at the Mid-Autumn Festival)
【兔崽子】〈诉〉brat; bastard
【兔子】hare; rabbit
【兔子不吃窝边草】a rabbit doesn't eat the grass near its own hole (for its own protection)—a villain doesn't harm his nextdoor neighbours
【兔子尾巴长不了】〈贬〉the tail of a rabbit can't be long—won't last long

tuān

湍 〈书〉Ⅰ 形 (of a current) rapid; torrential Ⅱ 名 rapids; rushing waters: 急湍

【湍急】(of a current) rapid; torrential: 水流～。*The current is swift.*
【湍流】❶〈书〉swift current; rushing waters; torrent; rapids ❷ [物] turbulent flow; turbulence

tuán

团 Ⅰ 形 round; circular: 团扇 Ⅱ 动 ❶ roll sth. into a ball; roll: ～纸团儿 *roll paper into a ball* / ～药丸 *roll pills* ❷ unite; conglomerate: 团结 Ⅲ 名 ❶ group; society; organization: 剧团 / 乐团 ❷ [军] regiment ❸ (〈略〉全称为『中国共产主义青年团』) the Communist Youth League of China; the League: ～籍 *League membership* ❹ sth. shaped like a ball: 把面揉成一个～ *knead dough into a ball* / 缩成一～ *curl up into a ball* ❺ dumpling Ⅳ 量 (for sth. in the shape of a ball): 一～毛线 *a ball of wool* / 一～面 *a lump* of dough

【团拜】gather together to exchange greetings (as on New Year's Day)

【团队】group; corps; team: ～精神 *team spirit* / ～协作 *teamwork*

【团粉】cooking starch

【团伙】gang; band; clique: 流氓～ *a gang of hooligans* (*or hoodlums*)

【团结】unite; rally: ～一致 *unite as one* / ～就是力量。*Unity is strength.* / ～、紧张、严肃、活泼。*Be united, alert, earnest and lively.*

【团聚】❶ reunite: 全家～ *family reunion* ❷ unite and gather

【团课】League class; League lecture

【团矿】[冶] nodulizing; briquetting

【团粒】[农] granule: ～结构 *granular structure*

【团脐】❶ broad and rounded abdomen of a female crab ❷ female crab

【团扇】a round fan

【团体】organization; group; team ◇ ～操 group callisthenics; ～冠军 team title; ～票 group ticket; ～赛 team competition

【团团】round and round; all round: ～围住 *surround completely*; *encircle* ◇ ～转 round and round

【团鱼】soft-shelled turtle

【团员】❶ member: 代表团～ *a member of a delegation* ❷ a member of the Communist Youth League of China; League member

【团圆】❶ reunion (of family members): 全家～ *family reunion* / ～饭 *family reunion dinner* ❷ round: 这男孩儿～脸。*The boy has a round face.*

【团圆节】Family Reunion Festival (another name for 中秋节)

【团藻】[植] volvox

【团长】❶ [军] regimental commander ❷ head (or chief, chairman) of a delegation, troupe, etc.

【团子】dumpling: 糯米～ *dumpling made of glutinous rice* / 菜～ *cornmeal dumpling with vegetable stuffing* / 饭～ *rice ball*

【团坐】(of a group of people) sit in a circle: 围炉～ *sit around a fire*

tuī

推 动 ❶ push; shove: ～车 *push a cart* / ～了他一下 *give him a push* / 把门～开 *push* (*or shove*) *the door open* / 把竹排～进河里 *shove* (*or push*) *the bamboo raft into the river* / 把子弹～上膛 *ram a cartridge into the rifle chamber* ❷ turn a mill or grindstone; grind: ～点白面 *grind some wheat into flour* ❸ cut; pare: 用刨子～光 *make smooth with a plane*; *plane* / ～个光头 *have one's head shaved* ❹ push forward; promote; advance: 把运动～向高潮 *push the movement to a climax* ❺ infer; deduce: 类推 ❻ push away; shirk; shift: 不要把重担子～给人家。*Don't shift burdensome tasks onto others.* ❼ put off; postpone: 这项工作得抓紧，不能老是往后～。*We have to get on with this job, we can't put it off day after day.* / 往后～几天 *postpone for a few days* ❽ elect; choose: ～他担任小组长 *elect him group leader*; *choose him to be group leader* ❾ hold in esteem; praise highly

【推刨】〈方〉plane (a carpenter's tool)

【推本溯源】trace the origin; ascertain the cause

【推波助澜】make a stormy sea stormier; add fuel to the flames: 煽风点火，～，极尽挑拨离间之能事 *fan the flames, add fuel to the fire and do one's utmost to incite one against the other*

【推测】infer; conjecture; guess: 根据～ *by inference* / 不过是～而已 *mere guesswork*; *nothing but conjecture*

【推陈出新】weed through the old to bring forth the new ——另见〖百花齐放，推陈出新〗

【推诚相见】deal with sb. in good faith; treat sb. with sincerity

【推迟】put off; postpone; defer: ～作出决定 *defer making a decision*

【推斥】[物] repulsion: ～力 *repulsive force*

【推崇】hold in esteem; praise highly: ～备至 *have the greatest esteem for*

【推出】introduce; put out; present: ～新产品 *put out a new product*

【推辞】decline (an appointment, invitation, etc.); derive (sth. from sth.)

【推戴】〈书〉support sb. assuming leadership

【推挡】[体] (乒乓球) half volley with push

【推导】derivation (in math, physics, etc.); derive (sth. from stk.)

【推倒】❶ push over; overturn: 把他～在地 *shove him to the ground* ❷ repudiate; cancel; reverse: 这个计划不切实际，要～重来。*The plan is not practical and has to be replaced with a new one*

【推定】❶ elect; choose ❷ infer; deduce

【推动】push forward; promote; give impetus to: ～工作 *push the work forward*; *expedite the work* / ～社会向前发展 *propel the society forward* / ～力 *motive* (*or driving*) *force*

【推断】infer; deduce: 经过周密的调查和分析才能作出正确的～。*Correct inferences can be drawn only from careful investigation and analysis.*

【推度】infer; conjecture; guess

【推而广之】likewise; in the same way

【推翻】❶ overthrow; overturn; topple ❷ repudiate; cancel; reverse: ～协议 *repudiate an agreement* / ～原定计划 *cancel the original plan*

【推杆】[机] push rod

【推故】give (or find) a pretext; make an excuse: 他～不去开会。*He excused himself from the meeting.*

【推广】popularize; spread; extend: ～普通话 *popularize the common spoken Chinese*

【推及】spread to; reach by analogy

【推己及人】put oneself in the place of another; treat other people as you would like to be treated; be considerate

【推挤】❶ push and shove: 人们～着上了公共汽车。*There was a lot of pushing and shoving to get on the bus.* ❷〈书〉push out; squeeze out; elbow out

【推荐】recommend: 向青年～优秀的文学作品 *recommend outstanding literary works to the youth*

【推进】❶ push on; carry forward; advance; give impetus to: 把两国之间的友好关系～到一个新阶段 *carry the friendly relations between the two countries to a new stage* ❷［军］move forward; push; drive: 战线再次向前～。*The battlefront has again moved forward.* ◇ ～剂 propellant; ～力 propulsive force; driving power; ～器 propeller

【推究】examine; study: ～事理 *study the whys and wherefores of things*

【推举】❶ elect; choose: 大家～他到大会发言。*They chose him to speak on their behalf at the meeting.* ❷［体］clean and press; press: ～一百三十七公斤 *press 137 kilograms*

【推理】［逻］inference; reasoning: 用～方法 *by inference* / 类比～ *reasoning from analogy*

【推力】thrust: 螺旋桨～ *propeller thrust* / 喷气发动机～ *jet thrust*

【推论】inference; deduction; corollary

【推磨】turn a millstone

【推拿】［中］massage

【推敲】weigh; deliberate: ～词句 *weigh one's words; seek the right word* / 这个提法是经过反复～的。*This formulation was worked out after repeated deliberation.* / 他写的东西经得起～。*His writings can stand close scrutiny.*

【推求】inquire into; ascertain: ～地面沉降的原因 *inquire into the causes of surface subsidence*

【推却】refuse; decline: 他要请我吃饭，我～了。*I declined his invitation to dinner.*

【推让】decline (a position, favour, etc. out of modesty)

【推人犯规】［体］pushing (in basketball, etc.)

【推三阻四】decline with all sorts of excuses; give the runaround

【推说】❶〈方〉offer as an excuse (for not doing sth.); plead ❷ infer; deduce

【推算】calculate; reckon: 日食发生的时间可以～出来。*The time when a solar eclipse will occur can be calculated.*

【推涛作浪】stir up (or make) trouble; create disturbances

【推头】〈口〉❶ cut sb.'s hair (with clippers) ❷ have a haircut

【推土机】bulldozer

【推推搡搡】push and shove: 大家慢慢走，别～的。*Take it easy, don't push and shove.*

【推托】offer as an excuse (for not doing sth.); plead: 她～嗓子疼，不肯唱。*Pleading a sore throat, she refused to sing.*

【推脱】evade; shirk: ～责任 *evade (or shirk) responsibility*

【推挽】❶〈书〉recommend (sb. for a post) ❷［电］push-pull: ～电路 *push-pull circuit*

【推委】(又作'推诿') shift responsibility onto others

【推问】investigate; cross-examine

【推想】imagine; guess; reckon

【推销】promote sales; market; peddle: ～商品 *promote the sale of goods* / ～员 *salesman*

【推销术】salesmanship; selling techniques

【推卸】shirk (responsibility): ～责任，委过于人 *shirk responsibility and shift the blame onto others*

【推心置腹】repose full confidence in sb.; confide in sb.: ～地交换意见 *have a confidential (or heart-to-heart) exchange of views*

【推行】carry out; pursue; practise: ～新的政策 *pursue a new policy* / ～学分制 *introduce a credit system*

【推选】elect; choose

【推移】❶ (of time) elapse; pass: 随着时间的～ *with the lapse (or passage) of time; as time goes on (or by)* ❷ (of a situation, etc.) develop; evolve ◇ ～质［水］bed load

【推知】know by inference; deduce

【推重】have a high regard for; hold in esteem

【推子】〈口〉hair-clippers; clippers

tuí

颓 形 ❶ ruined; dilapidated ❷ declining; decadent: 衰颓 ❸ dejected; dispirited: 颓丧

【颓废】dispirited; decadent: ～情绪 *decadent sentiments* / ～派 *the decadent school; the decadents*

【颓风】depraved customs; corrupt morals

【颓坏】ruined; dilapidated

【颓靡】downcast; dejected; crestfallen

【颓然】〈书〉dejected; disappointed

【颓丧】dejected; dispirited; listless: 敌军士气～。*The enemy is demoralized.*

【颓势】declining tendency: 挽回～ *retrieve oneself from an inferior position; turn the tide in one's favour*

【颓唐】dejected; dispirited

【颓朽】rotten; decayed

【颓运】〈书〉adversity; misfortune

tuǐ

腿 名 ❶ leg: 他～长。*He has long legs.* ❷ a leglike support: 桌子(椅子)～ *legs of a table (chair)* ❸ ham: 火腿

【腿肚子】〈口〉calf (of the leg)

【腿脚】legs and feet—ability to walk: ～不灵便 *have difficulty walking* / 这位老奶奶的～还很利落。*This old lady still moves briskly.*

【腿快】quick-footed; swift-footed

【腿懒】disinclined to move about; lazy about paying visits
【腿勤】be tireless in running around; love to run around
【腿腕子】ankle

tuì

退 动 ❶ move back; retreat: 他往后~了几步。*He stepped back a few paces.* or *He backed up several steps.* / 敌人已经~了。*The enemy has retreated.* / ~一步说 *even if that is so; even so* ❷ cause to move back; withdraw; remove: 把子弹~出来 *remove a cartridge from the breech of a gun; unload a gun* ❸ withdraw from; quit: 退党 ❹ decline; recede; ebb: 潮水~了。*The tide has receded.* or *The tide is on the ebb.* ❺ fade: 退色 ❻ return; give back; refund: 把这份礼~掉。*Return this gift.* / 空瓶不~。*Empty bottles are not refundable.* ❼ cancel; break off: ~掉订货 *cancel an order (for merchandise)*
【退避】withdraw and keep off; keep out of the way
【退避三舍】retreat ninety li—give way to avoid a conflict
【退兵】❶ retreat; withdrawal: 传令~ *order a retreat* ❷ force the enemy to retreat: ~之计 *a plan for repulsing the enemy*
【退步】❶ lag (or fall) behind; retrogress: 这孩子功课~了。*The boy's not doing so well in his studies as he used to.* / 他思想上~了。*He has slipped back ideologically.* ❷ room for manoeuvre; leeway: 留个~ *leave some room for manoeuvre; leave some leeway*
【退场】❶ (of atheletes) withdraw from the arena (as after the opening ceremony); march off the arena ❷ (of an audience) leave the theatre (as when a play ends)
【退潮】ebb tide; ebb
【退出】withdraw from; secede; quit: ~组织 *withdraw (or resign) from an organization* / ~比赛 *withdraw from a competition; scratch* / ~历史舞台 *step down from the stage of history*
【退磁】demagnetize
【退党】withdraw from (or resign, quit) a political party
【退敌】repulse (or repel) the enemy
【退格键】[计] backspace key
【退耕】let lie fallow; not plant crops: ~还林 *let cultivated land revert to woodland*
【退关】(of an exporter, etc.) cancel a declaration (of goods already cleared by customs)
【退股】withdraw shares (from a joint-stock company)
【退关】(of and exporter, etc) cancel a declaration (goods already cleared by customs)
【退化】❶ [生] degeneration ❷ degenerate; deteriorate; retrograde
【退还】return: ~公物 *return public property* / ~抗议照会 *reject a protest note*
【退换】exchange (or replace) a purchase: 货物出门,概不~。*Goods sold are not returnable.*
【退回】❶ return; send (or give) back: ~押金 *return a deposit* / 无法投递,~原处。*Undeliverable, returned to sender.* / 原稿已经~。*The manuscript has been sent back.* ❷ go (or turn) back: 道路不通,我们只得~。*Finding the road impassable, we had to turn back.*
【退婚】break off an engagement
【退火】[冶] annealing
【退伙】❶ 〈旧〉 withdraw from a secret society or underworld gang ❷ cancel an arrangement to eat at a mess; withdraw from a mess
【退货】return goods (or merchandise): ~退钱 *return merchandise for a refund*
【退居】❶ retire from a prominent position and take (a less important one): ~二线 *withdraw to the second line of duty—retire from active life and take up a nominal post (usu. in a consultant capacity)* ❷ be reduced to (a lower rank): 该厂产品已~第二位。*The products of that factory have dropped to second place now.*
【退路】❶ route of retreat: 切断敌军~ *cut off the enemy's retreat* ❷ room for manoeuvre; leeway: 留个~ *leave some leeway*
【退赔】return what one has unlawfully taken or pay compensation for it
【退票】❶ return a ticket; get a refund for a ticket ❷ a returned (or unused) ticket: 等~ *look for a returned (or unused) ticket*
【退钱】refund: 这鞋如果不合适,商店管~。*If the shoes do not wear well, the shop will refund your money.*
【退亲】同〖退婚〗
【退却】❶ [军] retreat; withdraw: 战略~ *strategic retreat* ❷ hang back; shrink back; flinch
【退让】make a concession; yield; give in: 稍微~一点 *give in a little* / 决不~一步 *never yield an inch* / 在原则问题上从不~ *never make concessions on matters of principle*
【退热】同〖退烧〗
【退色】fade: 这种布~吗? *Will this cloth fade?* or *Is this cloth colourfast?*
【退烧】❶ bring down (or allay) a fever ❷ (of a person's temperature) come down: 他已经~了。*His fever is gone.* or *His temperature has come down.* ◇ ~药 antipyretic
【退守】withdraw and stand on the defensive
【退税】[经] drawback
【退缩】shrink back; flinch; cower: 在困难面前从不~ *never flinch from difficulty*
【退庭】withdraw from the court
【退团】withdraw from a youth league; give up league membership
【退位】give up the throne; abdicate
【退伍】retire or be discharged from active military service; be demobilized; leave the army: ~军人

demobilized soldier；*ex-serviceman*；*veteran*
【退席】❶ leave a banquet or a meeting ❷ walk out：～以示抗议 *walk out in protest*
【退闲】〈书〉go into retirement
【退省】〈书〉introspection；self-questioning；self-examination
【退休】retire ◇ ～工人 retired worker；～金 retirement pay；pension；～年龄 retirement age
【退学】leave school；discontinue one's schooling：因病～ *leave school owing to bad health* / 勒令～ *order to quit school*
【退役】retire or be released from military service (on completing the term of reserve) / ～军官 *retired officer* / ～军人 *ex-serviceman*
【退赃】give up (or surrender，disgorge) ill-gotten gains
【退职】resign or be discharged from office；quit working
【退走】retreat；withdraw

蜕 Ⅰ 动 slough off；exuviate；moult Ⅱ 名 exuviae：蛇蜕
【蜕变】❶ change qualitatively；transform；transmute ❷［物］decay：感生～ *induced decay* / 自发～ *spontaneous decay*
【蜕化】❶ slough off；exuviate ❷ degenerate ◇ ～变质 become morally degenerate
【蜕皮】［动］cast off (or shed) a skin；exuviate

褪 动 ❶ take off (clothes)；shed (feathers) ❷ (of colour) fade —— 另见 tùn
【褪色】同〖退色〗

tūn

吞 动 ❶ swallow；gulp down：把药丸～下去 *swallow the pills* / 一口～掉 *gobble up in one go*；*devour in one gulp* ❷ take possession of；annex：独吞
【吞并】annex；gobble (or swallow) up
【吞吃】❶ swallow；gulp down ❷ embezzle；misappropriate
【吞金】swallow gold (to commit suicide)
【吞灭】conquer and annex (a country)
【吞没】❶ embezzle；misappropriate：～巨款 *misappropriate a huge sum* ❷ swallow up；engulf：小船被波浪～了。*The little boat was engulfed in the waves.*
【吞声】〈书〉gulp down one's sobs；dare not cry out
【吞食】swallow；devour：大鱼～小鱼。*Big fish devour small fish.*
【吞蚀】❶ embezzle；misappropriate ❷ corrode；erode
【吞噬】swallow；gobble up；engulf：洪水～了整个村庄。*The flood waters engulfed the whole village.*
【吞噬细胞】［生理］phagocyte
【吞噬作用】［生理］phagocytosis
【吞吐】swallow and spit—take in and send out in large quantities：这个港口一年可～三千万吨货物。*This port can handle up to* 30,000,000 *tons of cargo a year.*
【吞吐量】handling capacity (of a harbour)；the volume of freight handled
【吞吞吐吐】hesitate in speech；hem and haw；mutter and mumble：有话说清楚，不要～。*You've got to speak up clearly. No humming and hawing.*
【吞咽】swallow；gulp down：他嗓子疼得厉害，～有困难。*His throat was so painful that he could hardly swallow.* / 他话到嘴边，却又～下去了。*He was on the point of saying something when he checked himself.*
【吞云吐雾】swallow clouds and blow out fog—smoke (opium or cigarette)
【吞占】❶ embezzle；misappropriate ❷ invade and occupy；seize

tún

屯 Ⅰ 动 ❶ collect；store up：～粮 *store up grain* ❷ station (troops)；quarter (troops)：驻～ Ⅱ 名 village (often used in village names)：皇姑～ (*in Liaoning Province*)
【屯兵】station troops
【屯集】assemble；collect
【屯聚】(of troops，etc.) concentrate；assemble
【屯垦】station troops to open up wasteland
【屯田】have garrison troops or peasants open up wasteland and grow food grain (a policy pursued by feudal rulers since the Han Dynasty)
【屯扎】station (troops)；quarter (troops)
【屯驻】同〖驻屯〗

囤 动 store up；hoard：～货 *store goods* ——另见 dùn
【囤积】hoard for speculation；corner (the market)：～小麦 *corner the wheat market* ◇ ～居奇 hoarding and cornering；hoarding and profiteering
【囤聚】store up (goods)

臀 名 buttocks
【臀部】buttocks：在～打一针 *give or have an injection in the buttock*
【臀尖】pork rump
【臀鳍】［动］anal fin
【臀疣】［动］monkey's ischial callosities；monkey's seat pads

tùn

褪 动 ❶ slip out of sth.：褪下一只袖子 *slip one's arm out of one's sleeve* ❷〈方〉hide sth. in one's sleeve：～着手 *hide one's hands in sleeves* ——另见 tuì
【褪去】take off (clothes，etc.)

【褪套儿】❶ break loose; free oneself; get oneself free: 狗褪了套儿跑了。*The dog broke loose and ran away*. ❷ shake off responsibility

tuō

托 Ⅰ 动 ❶ hold in the palm; support with the hand or palm: ～着盘子 *hold a tray on one's palm* / 两手～腮 *cup one's chin in one's hands* ❷ serve as a foil (or contrast); set off: 衬托 ❸ ask; entrust: ～人买书 *ask sb. to buy books for one* / ～人照看孩子 *leave a child in sb.'s care* / 这事就～给她吧。*Let's leave the matter to her*. / 我想～你给他捎点东西。*I'd like you to take something to him*. ❹ plead; give as a pretext: 托病 ❺ rely upon; owe to: 托庇 Ⅱ 名 sth. serving as a support: 花托 Ⅲ 量 [物] torr (a unit of pressure)

【托儿】〈口〉a partner of a street pedlar or shopkeeper who pretends to be a customer and lures people into buying; salesperson's decoy

【托庇】rely upon one's elder or an influential person for protection

【托病】plead illness

【托词】(又作'托辞') ❶ find a pretext; make an excuse: ～谢绝 *decline on some pretext* ❷ pretext; excuse; subterfuge: 他说有事,不过是～。*He said he was busy, but that was just an excuse*.

【托大】❶ give oneself airs; be self-important; be conceited and arrogant ❷〈旧〉careless; negligent

【托儿所】nursery; child-care centre; crche

【托福】❶〈套〉(usu. responding to greetings) thanks to you: 托您的福,我身体好多了。*I'm much better now, thank you*. ❷ rely upon; owe to: 托共产党的福,我们才能过上今天的好日子。*We owe our happy life to the Communist Party*. ❸ transliteration of TOEFL : ～考试 *Test of English as a Foreign Language (TOEFL)*

【托付】entrust; commit sth. to sb.'s care: 我们把这任务～给他了。*We have entrusted him with the task*.

【托孤】(usu. of a dying emperor) entrust his young son to the care of a minister

【托故】give (or find) a pretext; make an excuse: ～早退 *leave early under some pretext*

【托管】(又作'托管制') trusteeship ◇ ～国 trustee state; trustee; ～理事会 Trusteeship Council; ～领土 trustee territory; ～区 trust area; ～制度 trusteeship system; trusteeship

【托灰板】[建] hawk

【托架】[机] bracket: 发动机～ *engine bracket* / ～臂 *bracket arm*

【托拉斯】[经] trust

【托里拆利真空】[物] Torricellian vacuum

【托洛茨基主义】Trotskyism

【托门子】solicit help from potential backers; gain one's end through pull

【托梦】(of the ghost of one's kith and kin) appear in one's dream and make a request

【托名】do sth. in sb. else's name

【托盘】(serving) tray

【托人情】(又作'托情') ask an influential person to help arrange sth.; gain one's end through pull; seek the good offices of sb.

【托身】❶ find a place to live in ❷ seek a living

【托生】reincarnation; transmigration

【托收】collection: ～汇票 *bill for collection*; ～款项 *items sent for collection*; ～票据 *collection bill; short bill*

【托叶】[植] stipule

【托运】consign for shipment; check: 你的行李～了吗? *Have you checked your baggage?* ◇ ～单 booking note; ～人 consignor; ～物 consignment

【托嘱】entrust

【托子】base; support: 花瓶～ *vase support (or holder)*

拖 动 ❶ pull; drag; haul: ～地板 *mop the floor* / 把身体～垮 *wear oneself down* / 火车头～着十二个车皮。*The locomotive was pulling (or drawing) twelve carriages*. ❷ delay; drag on; procrastinate: 再～就太晚了。*Don't delay any more, or it'll be too late*. / 这件工作～得太久了。*This work has been dragging on far too long*.

【拖把】(又作'拖布') mop

【拖车】trailer

【拖船】❶ tugboat; tug; towboat ❷〈方〉a wooden boat (towed by a tugboat)

【拖带】traction; pulling; towing

【拖儿带女】be burdened with children

【拖后腿】(又作'拖腿') hinder (or impede) sb.; hold sb. back; be a drag on sb.: 孩子要到西藏去工作,你可别～。*The kid wants to go and work in Xizang; you shouldn't try to hold him back*.

【拖家带口】(又作'拖家带眷') be burdened with a family

【拖拉】dilatory; slow; sluggish: ～作风 *dilatory style of work* / 她工作从不～。*She never puts off her work*.

【拖拉机】tractor: ～厂 *tractor plant* / ～手 *tractor driver* / ～站 *tractor station*

【拖累】❶ encumber; be a burden on: 受家务～ *be tied down by household chores* / 子女过多是个～。*Too many children are a burden*. ❷ implicate; involve

【拖泥带水】messy; sloppy; slovenly: 办事要利落,不要～。*Do things deftly, not sloppily*.

【拖欠】be behind in payment; be in arrears; default: ～税款 *be in arrears with tax payment*

【拖三拉四】(又作'拖三阻四') put off one's work with all sorts of excuses; give the runaround

【拖沓】dilatory; sluggish; laggard

【拖堂】(of a teacher) not dismiss class when time is up: 下课铃打了,老师还在滔滔不绝地～。*The teacher was still holding forth after the bell had rung*.

【拖网】trawlnet；trawl；dragnet：～渔船 *trawler*

【拖尾巴】❶ 同〖拖后腿〗❷ leave a project，etc. unfinished；leave loose ends：问题要彻底解决，不要拖个尾巴。*The problem must be solved once for all，without leaving any loose ends.*

【拖鞋】slippers

【拖延】delay；put off；procrastinate：期限快到，不能再～了。*The deadline is drawing near；we can't delay any more.* / ～时间 *play for time；stall（for time）*◇～战术 dilatory（or delaying，stalling）tactics

【拖曳】pull；tow；draw

【拖油瓶】〈贬〉❶（of a widow）remarry and take her children to her second husband's home ❷ such children

【拖债】be behind in paying one's debt；be in arrears with one's debt：不～ *pay one's debt in time*

脱 动 ❶（of hair，skin）shed；come off：他脸晒～皮了。*His face is peeling because of sunburn.* / 头发～光了 *lose all one's hair；become bald* ❷ take off；cast off：～鞋（衣服）*take off one's shoes（clothes）* ❸ escape from；get out of：逃脱 ❹ miss out（words）：这一行里～了三个字。*Three characters are missing in this line.* ❺〈书〉neglect；slight：轻脱

【脱靶】miss the target in shooting practice

【脱班】❶ be late for work ❷（of a bus，train，etc.）be behind schedule

【脱产】be released from production or one's regular work to take on other duties：～学习一年 *be released from work for one year's study*

【脱出】deviate from；shake off；break away from：～常轨 *break away from normal practice；break precedent* / ～被动局面 *regain the initiative*

【脱发】［医］loss of the hair；alopecia

【脱肛】［医］prolapse of the anus

【脱稿】（of a manuscript）be completed：这本书已～，即可付印。*The book is completed and is ready for printing.*

【脱钩】break off relations；cut ties

【脱轨】be derailed：火车～了。*The train was derailed.*

【脱滑】try to shirk work or responsibility；act in a slick way

【脱货】be in short supply；be out of stock

【脱缰之马】a runaway horse—uncontrollable；running wild：通货膨胀如～ *runaway inflation*

【脱胶】❶（of parts joined with gum or glue）come unglued；come unstuck：这件橡皮雨衣～了。*The rubber of this raincoat has disintegrated.* ❷［化］degum：生丝～ *degumming of silk*

【脱节】come apart；be disjointed；be out of line with：管子焊得不好，容易～。*Faultily welded piping is apt to come apart.* / 理论与实践不能～。*Theory must not be divorced from practice.*

【脱臼】同〖脱位〗

【脱壳机】huller；sheller

【脱空】❶ come to nothing；fail；fall through：希望～ *fail to attain one's hope* ❷〈方〉tell a lie；lie；resort to deception：～汉 *liar*

【脱口而出】say sth. unwittingly；blurt out

【脱蜡】［油］dewaxing

【脱离】separate oneself from；break away from；be divorced from：～群众 *cut oneself off from the masses；be divorced from the masses* / ～实际 *lose contact with reality；be divorced from reality*

【脱离速度】［航天］second cosmic velocity ——另见〖宇宙速度〗

【脱粒】［农］❶ threshing ❷ shelling ◇～机 thresher；sheller

【脱磷】［化］dephosphorization

【脱硫】［化］desulphurization；sweetening：～原油 *sweet crude*

【脱漏】be left out；be omitted；be missing：～一针 *drop a stitch（in knitting）*

【脱落】drop；fall off（or away）；come off：毛发～ *lose（one's）hair* / 门的把手～了。*The door handle has come off.* / 墙上油漆已经～了。*The paint on the wall has peeled off.* / 蕾铃～ *shedding of young bolls*

【脱盲】become literate

【脱毛】lose hair or feathers；moult；shed：那只骆驼刚脱了毛。*That camel has just shed.*

【脱帽】take off（or raise）one's hat（in respect）：～致敬 *take off one's hat in salutation* / ～默哀 *bare one's head and mourn in silence*

【脱模】［冶］drawing of patterns

【脱泡】［纺］deaeration：～桶 *deaerator*

【脱坯】mould adobe blocks

【脱贫】shake off poverty；lift oneself out of poverty：～致富 *shake off poverty and build up a fortune*

【脱期】（of a periodical）fail to come out on time

【脱氢】［化］dehydrogenation

【脱色】❶ decolour；decolourize：～剂 *decolourant；decolourizer* ❷ fade

【脱涩】take away the puckery taste（from persimmons）；depuckerise

【脱身】get away；get free；extricate oneself：我事情太多，脱不开身。*I have so much to do that I just can't get away.* / 他跳上一辆汽车脱了身。*He jumped into a car and made his escape.*

【脱手】❶ slip out of the hand：他用力一扔，石块～飞了出去。*With a powerful fling he sent the stone flying.* ❷ get off one's hands；dispose of；sell：这些货不好～。*These goods are difficult to dispose of.*

【脱水】❶［医］deprivation（or loss）of body fluids；dehydration：严重～ *serious dehydration* ❷［化］dehydration；dewatering ◇～机 hydroextractor；whizzer；～蔬菜 dehydrated vegetables

【脱俗】free from vulgarity；refined

【脱榫】be out of joint

【脱胎】❶ emerge from the womb of；be born out of：这部小说～于民间传说。*This novel has been developed out of a folk story*. ❷ a process of making bodiless lacquerware：～漆器 *bodiless lacquerware*

【脱胎换骨】be reborn；cast off one's old self；thoroughly remould oneself：得到～的改造 *cast off one's old self and take on a new self*；*make a change in one's very nature*

【脱逃】run away；escape；flee

【脱兔】〈书〉a fleeing hare—fast speed：动如～ *as quick as a fleeing hare*

【脱位】［医］dislocation

【脱险】escape（or be out of）danger：经过抢救，孩子～了。*The child was out of danger after the emergency treatment*.

【脱销】out of stock；sold out：这本书～了。*The book is out of stock*. or *The book is sold out*.

【脱卸】shirk（responsibility）

【脱氧】［化］deoxidation；deoxidization：～剂 *deoxidizer*；*deoxidant* ◇ ～核糖［生化］deoxyribose；～核糖核酸［生化］deoxyribonucleic acid（DNA）

【脱衣舞】striptease

【脱颖而出】the point of an awl sticking out through a bag—talent revealing itself

【脱羽】（of birds）moult

【脱证】［中］exhaustion of vital energy at the critical stage of an illness

【脱脂】de-fat；degrease ◇ ～剂 degreasing agent；～棉 absorbent cotton；～奶粉 de-fatted milk powder；nonfat dried milk；～乳 skimmed milk；～纱布 absorbent gauze

tuó

驮 动 carry（or bear）on the back：这头驴子能～三袋粮食。*This donkey can carry three sacks of grain*. ——另见 duò

【驮畜】pack animal

【驮筐】pannier

【驮马】pack horse

陀（构词成分）见下

【陀螺】top（a toy）：抽～ *whip a top*

【陀螺仪】［航空］gyroscope；gyro

驼 Ⅰ 名 camel：骆驼 Ⅱ 形 hunchbacked；humpbacked：老爷爷的背～了。*The grandpa's back has become bent*.

【驼背】❶ hunchback；humpback ❷ hunchbacked；humpbacked

【驼峰】❶ hump（of a camel）❷［交通］hump：～调车场 *hump yard* / ～调车法 *hump switching*

【驼铃】camel bells

【驼鹿】elk；moose

【驼绒】❶ camel's hair ❷ camel hair cloth

【驼色】the colour of camel's hair；light tan

【驼子】〈口〉hunchback；humpback

沱 名 ❶〈方〉a small bay in a river（often used in place names）

【沱茶】a bowl-shaped compressed mass of tea leaves

坨 Ⅰ 动（of cooked wheaten food）stick together：面条～了。*These noodles are sticking together*. Ⅱ 名 同〖坨子〗

【坨子】❶ lump：泥～ *a lump of mud*；*clod* ❷ heap：盐～ *salt mound*

柁 名［建］girder

鸵 名 ostrich

【鸵鸟】ostrich ◇ ～政策 ostrich policy；ostrichism

鼍 名（又作'鼍龙'）［动］Chinese alligator

tuǒ

妥 形 ❶ appropriate；proper：请～为保存。*Please look after it carefully*. / 以上意见～否，请指示。*Please indicate whether you consider the above views sound or not*. ❷（usu. used after a verb）ready；settled；finished：款已备～。*The money is ready*. / 事已办～。*The matter has been settled*.

【妥当】appropriate；proper：办得很～ *well handled*；*quite well done*

【妥靠】reliable；dependable

【妥善】appropriate；proper；well arranged：～安排 *make appropriate arrangements* / 问题比较复杂，需要～处理。*The problem is rather complicated and needs careful and skilful handling*.

【妥帖】appropriate；fitting；proper：看来这段译文不十分～。*That doesn't seem to be an apt translation*. / 办事～ *manage things properly*；*handle matters well*

【妥协】come to terms；compromise：达成～ *reach a compromise* / ～性 *a tendency towards compromise*（*or accommodation*）

椭（构词成分）见下

【椭率】［数］ellipticity

【椭面】［数］ellipsoid

【椭圆】［数］ellipse ◇ ～截面 oval cross section；～星云［天］elliptical nebula；～柱面 elliptic cylinder；～锥面 elliptic cone

tuò

拓 动 open up；develop：拓宽 ——另见 tà

【拓地】〈书〉extend（or expand）territory

【拓荒】open up virgin soil；reclaim wasteland：～者 *pioneer*；*pathbreaker*；*trailblazer*

【拓宽】widen：～业务 *extend one's business*

【拓落】〈书〉❶ be frustrated；be disappointed ❷ broad；extensive；vast

【拓扑学】［数］topology

【拓展】expand；spread；extend；develop

【拓殖】plant a colony；colonize

唾 Ⅰ 名 saliva；spittle Ⅱ 动 ❶ spit ❷ spit (to show one's contempt)

【唾骂】spit on and curse；revile：为世人所～ *be the opprobrium of the community*

【唾沫】saliva；spittle ◇ ～星子 a spray of saliva

【唾弃】cast aside；spurn：逆历史潮流而动的人终将被人民所～。*Those who go against the trend of history will be cast aside by the people.*

【唾手可得】extremely easy to obtain

【唾涎】saliva；spittle

【唾液】saliva；spittle ◇ ～腺（又作'唾腺'）salivary gland

【唾余】idle talk；casual remarks：拾人～ *repeat other people's casual remarks*

W

wā

洼 Ⅰ 形 hollow; low-lying: 这地太～,不适于种棉花。*This is low-lying land and not suitable for cotton.* Ⅱ 名 low-lying area; depression: 水～儿 *a waterlogged depression*

【洼地】depression; low-lying land

【洼陷】(of ground) be sunken; be low-lying

挖 动 dig; excavate: ～井 *dig (or sink) a well* / ～隧道 *excavate a tunnel* / ～塘泥 *scoop up sludge from a pond* / ～煤 *mine coal* / ～防空洞 *dig an air-raid shelter*

【挖补】mend by replacing a damaged part

【挖槽机】[机] groover

【挖兜】inset pocket

【挖耳】〈方〉❶ pick one's ears (to get rid of the wax) ❷ earpick

【挖方】[建] ❶ excavation (of earth or stone) ❷ cubage of excavation

【挖沟机】ditcher; trencher; trench digger

【挖掘】excavate; unearth: ～古物 *excavate ancient relics* / ～地下宝藏 *unearth buried treasure*

【挖掘机】(又作'挖土机') excavator; navvy: 迈步式～ *walking excavator* / 履带式～ *caterpillar excavator* / 索斗～ *dragline excavator*

【挖空心思】〈贬〉rack one's brains: ～为自己辩护 *rack one's brains trying to justify oneself*

【挖苦】speak sarcastically or ironically: 那话是～我的。*That was a dig at me.* ◇ ～话 ironical remarks; verbal thrusts

【挖泥船】dredger; dredge

【挖潜】(〈略〉全称为'挖掘潜力') tap the latent power (or potentialities)

【挖墙脚】〈口〉sap the wall; undermine the foundation; cut the ground from under sb.'s feet: 你把我们最好的教师都弄走了,你这是在挖我们系的墙脚。*You've taken away our best teachers, so you're undermining the foundation of the department.*

【挖肉补疮】同〖剜肉补疮〗

【挖树机】tree mover

哇 象 the sound of crying or vomiting: ～的一声哭了起来 *burst out crying* ——另见 wa

【哇啦】(又作'哇喇') hullabaloo; uproar; din: 老师叫学生别那么～～的。*The teacher told the pupils to stop making such a hullabaloo.*

【哇哇】the crying of a child, the cawing of a crow, etc.

蛙 名 frog

【蛙人】frogman

【蛙式打夯机】frog rammer

【蛙泳】[体] breaststroke: ～蹬腿 *frog kick*

wá

娃 名 ❶ baby; child ❷〈方〉newborn animal: 鸡～ *chick* / 猪～ *piglet*

【娃娃】baby; child: 胖～ *a chubby child* ◇ ～床 crib; cot; ～亲 the betrothal of a little boy and a little girl arranged by parents of both sides

【娃娃鱼】giant salamander

wǎ

瓦 Ⅰ 名 tile: 无棱～ *plain tile* Ⅱ 形 made of baked clay Ⅲ 量 [电]〈略〉见〖瓦特〗——另见 wà

【瓦房】tile-roofed house

【瓦釜雷鸣】an earthen crock sounding like thunder—an unworthy man in a high position

【瓦工】❶ bricklaying, tiling or plastering ❷ bricklayer; tiler; plasterer

【瓦棺】earthen coffin (used in ancient times)

【瓦罐】earthen jar

【瓦匠】bricklayer; tiler; plasterer

【瓦解】disintegrate; collapse; crumble: ～敌军 *disintegrate the enemy forces* / ～士气 *sap morale*

【瓦块】(又作'瓦片') fragments of tiles; broken tiles

【瓦楞】❶ rows of tiles on a roof ❷ corrugated ◇ ～铁皮 corrugated sheet iron; ～纸 corrugated paper; ～子 (又作'瓦垄子') [动] blood clam

【瓦砾】rubble; debris: 成了一片～ *be reduced to rubble*

【瓦亮】very bright: 锅擦得锃光～的。*The pot was polished shining bright.*

【瓦圈】rim (of a bicycle wheel, cart wheel, etc.)

【瓦全】见〖宁为玉碎,不为瓦全〗

【瓦舍】❶ tile-roofed house ❷ pleasure quarters in cities in Song and Yuan times

【瓦时】［电］watt-hour
【瓦斯】gas：～爆炸 *gas explosion* / ～筒 *gas cylinder* / ～弹 *gas bomb*；*gas shell*
【瓦特】［电］watt：～计 *wattmeter*
【瓦砚】tile inkslab
【瓦窑】tile kiln

wà

瓦 动 cover (a roof) with tiles；tile ——另见 wǎ
【瓦刀】(bricklayer's) cleaver
袜 名 socks；stockings；hose
【袜带】suspenders；garters
【袜底儿】sole of a sock
【袜套】ankle socks；socks
【袜筒】the leg of a stocking
【袜子】socks；stockings；hose

wa

哇 助 (used in place of 啊 a after a word ending in u or ao)：你怎么还不走～？*Why haven't you gone yet, eh?* / 你好～？*Well, how are you?* ——另见 wā

wāi

歪 Ⅰ 形 ❶ askew；crooked；inclined；slanting：～戴帽子 *have one's hat on crooked* / 这堵墙有点～。*This wall is a little out of the perpendicular.* / 小女孩儿～着头聚精会神地听故事。*The little girl listened attentively to the story with her head tilted to one side.* ❷ devious；underhand；crooked：～点子 *evil ideas*；*devil's advice* ❸ 〈方〉domineering；bossy：他在乡下～得很。*He is a local bully.* Ⅱ 动 〈方〉recline to take a rest
【歪词儿】worthless talk；defamatory talk
【歪打正着】hit the mark by a fluke；score a lucky hit
【歪道】❶ evil ways；depraved life；vice：走～ *lead a depraved life*；*abandon oneself to evil ways* ❷ evil ideas；devil's advice
【歪风】evil wind；unhealthy trend：打击～，发扬正气 *combat evil trends and foster a spirit of uprightness* ◇ ～邪气 evil winds and noxious influences；unhealthy trends and evil practices
【歪理】false reasoning
【歪路】crooked ways；underhand ways；dishonest practices
【歪门邪道】同〖邪门歪道〗
【歪扭】twisted；awry：他的嘴有些～。*His mouth was a little twisted.*
【歪七扭八】crooked；askew；shapeless and twisted：～地写几个字 *scrawl a few words*
【歪曲】❶ distort；misrepresent；twist：～事实 *distort the facts* / 事实不容～。*The facts brook no distortion.* / ～作者原意 *misrepresent the author's meaning* / ～别人的话 *twist people's words* ❷ crooked；askew；aslant
【歪诗】inelegant verses；doggerel
【歪歪倒倒】❶ rickety；shaky：这椅子～。*This chair is rather rickety.* / 那醉汉～地走着。*The drunk man reeled along.* ❷ uneven；irregular；untidy：他那～写的也算是字？*Does he call that scribble handwriting?*
【歪歪扭扭】crooked；askew；shapeless and twisted：字写得～ *write a poor hand*；*scrawl*；*scribble*
【歪斜】crooked；askew；aslant

wǎi

崴 Ⅰ 形 rugged (mountain path) Ⅱ 动 sprain；twist：把脚～了 *sprain one's ankle*

wài

外 Ⅰ 名 ❶ outer；outward；outside：窗～ *outside the window* ❷ a role for old men in traditional opera Ⅱ 形 ❶ other：外埠 ❷ foreign；external：外国 ❸ (relatives) of one's mother，sisters or daughters：外孙 ❹ unofficial：外传 ❺ not of the same organization，class，etc.；not closely related：见外 Ⅲ 副 besides；in addition；beyond：预算～的开支 *extra-budgetary expenditure* / 计划～的项目 *projects not included in the plan*
【外办】〈略〉见〖外事办公室〗
【外邦】〈书〉foreign country
【外币】foreign currency：～汇票 *foreign currency bill* / ～申报单 *foreign currencies declaration* / ～折合率 *foreign currency conversion rate*
【外边】❶ outside；out：到～散步 *go out for a walk* / 咱们上～去谈，好不好？*Let's go outside to talk, shall we?* ❷ a place other than where one lives or works：她儿子在～工作。*Her son works somewhere away from home.* ❸ exterior；outside：行李卷儿～再裹一层塑料布。*Wrap a plastic sheet round the bedroll.*
【外表】outward appearance；exterior；surface：～美观 *have a fine exterior*；*look nice* / 事物的～ *the outward appearance of things* / 从～看人 *judge people by appearances*
【外宾】foreign guest (or visitor)
【外部】❶ outside；external：事物的～联系 *external relations of things* / ～世界 *the external world* ❷ exterior；surface
【外埠】towns or cities other than where one is
【外财】extra income
【外层空间】outer space：～导弹 *outer-space missile*
【外差】［电］heterodyne：超～ *superheterodyne*
【外场】❶ sociable：她是个～人儿，人头儿挺广。

She's a good mixer and has a large circle of acquaintances. ❷ outfield (in baseball and softball): ～手 *outfielder*

【外钞】foreign bank note

【外出】go out: 他有事～，我没见到他。*He had gone out on business so I didn't see him.* ◇ ～血［医］external haemorrhage

【外带】❶ outer cover (of a tyre); tyre: ～和里带都扎穿了。*The tyre and the inner tube are both punctured.* ❷ as well; besides; into the bargain: 这个厂生产农业机械，～修理农具。*This factory, which produces agricultural machinery, repairs farm tools as a sideline.*

【外待】treat sb. as a stranger or an outsider

【外道儿】〈口〉stranger; outsider

【外道】〈口〉over-polite: 我们都是老同学，你还～什么? *We are all old classmates so why stand on ceremony?*

【外敌】foreign enemy

【外地】parts of the country other than where one is: 代表团将在首都访问三天，然后再到～游览。*The delegation will pay a three-day visit to the capital before leaving for other parts of the country.*

【外电】dispatches from foreign news agencies: 据～报导 *according to reports from foreign news agencies*

【外调】❶ transfer (materials or personnel) to other localities: ～物资 *materials allocated for transfer to other places* ❷ go out to another work unit to make investigations

【外毒素】［医］exotoxin

【外耳】external ear ◇ ～道 external auditory meatus; ～炎 otitis externa

【外翻足】［医］talipes valgus

【外藩】vassal state

【外分泌】［生理］exocrine; external secretion: ～腺 *exocrine gland*

【外敷】［医］apply (ointment, etc.) ◇ ～药 medicine for external application

【外感】［中］diseases caused by external factors: ～风寒 *be affected by the cold; have a cold*

【外港】outport

【外公】〈方〉(maternal) grandfather

【外功】exercises to benefit the muscles and bones

【外观】outward appearance; exterior: 这座大楼～很美。*This is a fine-looking building.*

【外国】foreign country: ～朋友 *foreign friends* / 到～学习 *go abroad to study* ◇ ～管辖权 foreign jurisdiction; ～货（又作'外货'）foreign goods; imported goods; ～军事基地 foreign military base; ～人 foreigner; alien; ～语 foreign language; ～驻华机构 foreign institutions in China; ～驻华使领馆 foreign diplomatic and consular missions in China; ～租界 foreign settlement; foreign concession

【外果皮】［植］exocarp

【外行】❶ layman; nonprofessional ❷ lay; unprofessional: 种庄稼他可不～。*He's no amateur in farming.* / 我对股票很～。*I'm quite ignorant about stocks.* / ～话 *lay language; a mere dabbler's opinion*

【外号】nickname

【外话】〈方〉unduly polite words that a friend is not expected to say

【外患】foreign aggression

【外汇】foreign exchange: ～官价 *official exchange rate* / ～管理 *(foreign) exchange control* / ～行情 *exchange quotations* / ～牌价 *foreign exchange rate* / ～平价 *par of exchange; exchange parity* / ～收入 *foreign exchange earnings (or income)* / ～收入留成 *retention of a share of the foreign currency earned* ◇ ～储备 foreign exchange reserve; ～兑换券（又作'外汇券'）foreign exchange certificate (FEC); ～负债 foreign exchange liabilities; ～管制 foreign exchange control; foreign exchange restrictions; ～管制法规 forign exchange control regulations; ～交易 foeign exchange transactions; ～结存 foreign exchange balance; foreign exchange surplus; ～率 foreign exchange rate; ～牌价 foreign exchange quotations; foreign exchange rate; ～平准基金 exchange stabilization fund; ～期货交易 forward exchange transaction; ～倾销 exchange dumping; ～升水 exchange premium; ～市场 foreign exchange market ～贴水 exchange discount; ～业务 foreign exchange policy; ～营业许可证 foreign-exchange business licence; ～预算 foreign exchange budget; ～政策 foreign exchange policy; ～资产 foreign exchange assets

【外活】〈方〉❶ orders taken by factories or craftsmen ❷ work taken in by housewives

【外祸】foreign aggression

【外籍】foreign nationality: ～工作人员 *foreign personnel*

【外寄生物】ectoparasite

【外加】more; additional; extra: 给你们十份报纸，～三本小册子。*Here you are— ten copies of the newspaper, plus three pamphlets.*

【外加电压】applied voltage

【外家】❶ maternal grandparents' home ❷ mistress; concubine; kept woman ❸ house for a mistress or concubine

【外间】❶ outer room ❷〈书〉the external world; outside circles

【外交】diplomacy; foreign affairs: 通过～途径解决 *be settled through diplomatic channels* ◇ ～部 ministry of foreign affairs; foreign ministry; ～部长 minister of (or for) foreign affairs; foreign minister; ～程序 diplomatic procedure; ～辞令 diplomatic language (or parlance); ～大臣 Foreign Secretary (in Britain); ～代表 diplomatic agent (or representative); ～法 diplomatic law; ～官 diplomat; ～惯例 diplomatic practice; diplomatic usage; customary diplomatic practice; ～护照 diplomatic passport; ～豁免权 diplomatic immunity; ～机关 diplomatic establishments; ～家 diplomat; ～界 diplomatic circles; ～礼节

diplomatic protocol (or etiquette); ～签证 diplomatic visa; ～使节 diplomatic envoy; ～使团 diplomatic mission; ～谈判 diplomatic negotiation; ～特权 diplomatic prerogative (or privilege); ～途径 diplomatic channels; ～团 diplomatic corps; ～文书 diplomatic papers; ～衔 diplomatic rank; ～信使 diplomatic courier; ～邮袋 diplomatic pouch; diplomatic bag; ～邮件 diplomatic mail; ～语言 diplomatese; diplomatic language; ～政策 foreign policy; ～制裁 diplomatic sanction

【外交关系】diplomatic relations: 建立大使级的～ *establish diplomatic relations at ambassadorial level* / 断绝～ *sever (or break off) diplomatic relations* / 恢复～ *resume diplomatic relations* / 中止～ *suspend diplomatic relations* / ～升格 *upgrade diplomatic relations* / ～降格 *downgrade diplomatic relations*

【外角】[数] exterior angle

【外教】(〈略〉全称为'外籍教员') foreign teacher

【外接圆】[数] circumscribed circle; circumcircle

【外界】❶ the external (or outside) world: 对～的认识 *knowledge of the external world* ❷ outside: 顶住～的种种压力 *withstand all kinds of outside pressure*

【外借】lend out: 工具书恕不～。*Reference books are not for lending.* / 电话不～。*This telephone is not for public use.*

【外景】outdoor scene; a scene shot on location; exterior: 拍摄～ *film the exterior*; *shoot a scene on location*

【外径】[机] external diameter; outside (or outer) diamete ◇ ～千分尺 outside micrometer

【外舅】〈书〉wife's father; father-in-law

【外科】[医] surgical department: ～病房 *surgical ward* / ～手术 *surgical operation*; *surgery* / ～医生 *surgeon* ◇ ～学 surgery

【外壳】outer covering (or casing); shell; case: 热水瓶～ *the outer casing of a thermos flask* / 电池～ *battery case*

【外寇】invading army; aggressor troops

【外快】extra income: 捞～ *make extra money*

【外来】outside; external; foreign: ～干涉 *outside interference*; *foreign (or external) intervention* ◇ ～户 a household from another place; nonnative; ～语 word of foreign origin; foreign word; loanword

【外力】❶ outside force ❷ [物] external force

【外流】outflow; drain: 美元～ *dollar outflow* / 黄金～ *gold bullion outflow*

【外路】from outside; not local: ～货 *imported goods* / ～人 *stranger*; *outsider*

【外露】reveal; show: 他感情从不～。*He never reveals his true feelings.*

【外卖】takeout; takeaway; carry-out

【外贸】〈略〉见〖对外贸易〗◇ ～部 ministry of foreign trade; ～经营 foreign trade management; ～中心 foreign trade centres

【外貌】appearance; exterior; looks: 不要以～取人。*Don't judge people by their appearance.*

【外面】(wàimiàn) outward appearance; exterior; surface

【外面】(wàimian) outside; out: 今天我们要在～吃饭。*We'll eat (or dine) out today.*

【外面儿光】deceptively smooth appearance; outward show: 做事要考虑实际效果,不能追求～。*In handling matters, we must pay attention to actual results and not try to be flashy.*

【外胚层】[生] ectoblast; ectoderm; epiblast

【外婆】〈方〉(maternal) grandmother

【外戚】relatives of a king or emperor on the side of his mother or wife

【外企】(〈略〉全称为'外资企业') foreign enterprise

【外强中干】outwardly strong but inwardly weak; strong in appearance but weak in reality

【外侨】(〈略〉全称为'外国侨民') foreign national; alien ◇ ～身份 alienism

【外切形】[数] circumscribed figure

【外勤】❶ work done outside the office or in the field (as surveying, prospecting, news gathering, etc.): 跑～ *do fieldwork*; *run errands* ❷ field personnel

【外倾】[心理] extroversion

【外圈】[体] outer lane; outside lane

【外燃机】external-combustion engine

【外人】❶ stranger; outsider: 别客气,我又不是～。*Don't stand on ceremony. I'm no stranger.* / 不足为～道 *not to be mentioned to outsiders* / 你说吧,这里没～。*Speak up. You're among friends.* ❷ foreigner; alien

【外柔内刚】soft outside but hard inside—outwardly yielding but inwardly firm

【外伤】an injury or wound; trauma: ～性休克 *traumatic shock* ◇ ～学 traumatology

【外商】(〈略〉全称为'外国商人') foreign businessman; foreign merchant ◇ ～独资企业 exclusively foreign-owned enterprises; sole foreign invested enterprises

【外生殖器】external genital organs

【外省】provinces other than where one is; other provinces

【外甥】❶ sister's son; nephew ❷〈方〉daughter's son; grandson ◇ ～打灯笼—照舅(旧) the nephew carrying a lantern to give light to his uncle—the same as before (a pun on 照舅 and 照旧)

【外甥女】❶ sister's daughter; niece ❷〈方〉daughter's daughter; granddaughter

【外史】unofficial history; informal history

【外事】foreign affairs; external affairs: ～活动 *external public functions* ◇ ～办公室 office of foreign affairs; foreign affairs office; ～局 bureau of foreign affairs, foreign affairs bureau; ～口〈口〉a collective name for all government organs that have to do with foreign affairs

【外事组】❶ foreign affairs section ❷ a section dealing with foreign personnel and foreign visitors

【外室】❶ mistress; concubine; kept woman ❷

house for a mistress or concubine
【外孙】daughter's son; grandson
【外孙女】daughter's daughter; granddaughter
【外胎】outer cover (of a tyre); tyre
【外逃】❶ flee to some other place ❷ flee the country: ～出境 *run out of the country* / ～分子 *deserter; escapee*
【外套】❶ overcoat ❷ loose coat; outer garment
【外听道】[生理] external auditory meatus
【外头】outside; out: 这事儿～全知道了。*Even those on the outside know about it.* / 夏天我常在～睡。*In summer I often sleep outdoors.*
【外围】periphery: 首都～ *the periphery of the capital* ◇ ～防线 outer defence line; ～设备 peripheral equipment; ～组织 peripheral organization
【外文】foreign language
【外屋】outer room
【外侮】foreign aggression; external aggression: 抵御～ *resist foreign aggression*
【外务】❶ matters outside one's job ❷ foreign affairs; external affairs
【外务大臣】minister of (or for) foreign affairs; foreign minister
【外务省】the Ministry of Foreign Affairs (as in Japan)
【外县】counties other than where one is; other counties
【外线】❶ [军] exterior lines: ～作战 *fight on exterior lines; exterior-line operations* ❷ outside (telephone) connections
【外乡】another part of the country; some other place: ～口音 *a nonlocal accent* / 他是～人。*He is not from these parts.*
【外向】[心理] extroversion ◇ ～型经济 export-oriented economy
【外销】for sale abroad or in another part of the country: ～产品 *products for export; articles for sale in other areas*
【外心】❶ unfaithful intentions (of husband or wife) ❷ [数] circumcentre
【外星人】extraterrestrial being (ET)
【外形】appearance; external form; contour
【外姓】(people) not of the same surname
【外延】[逻] extension
【外焰】[化] outer flame
【外衣】❶ coat; jacket; outer clothing; outer garment ❷ semblance; appearance; garb
【外因】[哲] external cause
【外阴】[生理] vulva ◇ ～炎 vulvitis
【外引内联】introduce funds, equipment, technology or qualified personel from abroad or other parts of the country, and establish domestic or local connections
【外用】[药] external use; external application: ～药水 *lotion* / 只能～ *for external use only*
【外语】foreign language
【外域】〈书〉foreign lands
【外遇】extramarital relations: 她怀疑她丈夫有～。*She suspected her husband of carrying on with some other woman.*
【外圆内方】round outside but square inside—outwardly gentle but inwardly stern
【外援】foreign aid; outside help; external assistance
【外运】transport out to other places or countries: 晋煤～ *transport coal out of Shanxi*
【外在】external; extrinsic: ～因素 *external factor* ◇ ～性 externalism
【外债】external debt; foreign debt
【外长】〈略〉见〖外交部长〗
【外罩】outer garment; dustcoat; overall
【外痔】external piles (or haemorrhoids)
【外传】unofficial life history; unauthorized biography
【外资】foreign capital: 引进～ *absorb foreign capital* / ～流入 *foreign capital inflow* ◇ ～企业 foreign enterprise
【外子】〈旧〉my husband
【外族】❶ people not of the same clan ❷ foreigner; alien ❸ other nationalities
【外祖父】(maternal) grandfather
【外祖母】(maternal) grandmother

wān

弯 Ⅰ 形 curved; tortuous; crooked: ～～的月牙儿 *a crescent moon* / 累累的果实把树枝都压～了。*Clusters of fruit weighed the branches down.* Ⅱ 动 bend; flex: ～着腰插秧 *bend over to transplant rice* Ⅲ 名 turn; curve; bend: 这胡同有个～儿。*There's a curve in the lane.*
【弯度】curvature
【弯弓】〈书〉draw a bow; bend a bow
【弯路】❶ crooked road; tortuous path ❷ roundabout way; detour: 少走～ *avoid detours* / 由于缺少经验,我们工作走了～。*Owing to lack of experience we took a roundabout course in our work.*
【弯曲】winding; meandering; zigzag; crooked; curved: 一条～的山间小道 *a winding mountain path* / 一根～的木棍 *a crooked stick*
【弯子】(又作'弯儿') bend; turn; curve ——另见〖绕弯子〗

剜 动 cut out; gouge out; scoop out: 把苹果烂的地方～掉。*Scoop out the rotten part of the apple.* / 凶残的奴隶主～掉了奴隶的双眼。*The brutal slave owner gouged out the slave's eyes.*
【剜肉补疮】(又作'剜肉医疮') cut out a piece of flesh to cure a boil—resort to a remedy worse than the ailment; resort to a stopgap measure detrimental to long-term interests

湾 Ⅰ 名 ❶ a bend in a stream: 河～ *river bend* ❷ gulf; bay: 渤海～ *Bohai Bay* / 波斯～ *the Persian Gulf* Ⅱ 动 cast anchor; moor: 把船～在那边。*Moor the boat over there.*
【湾泊】anchor; berth

蜿（构词成分）见下

【蜿蜒】❶（of snakes, etc.）wriggle ❷ wind; zigzag; meander: 小溪～流过田野。*The stream winds through the fields.* / 小路～而上。*The path zigzagged upwards.*

豌（构词成分）见下

【豌豆】pea ◇ ～黄 pea-flour cake; ～象［动］pea weevil

wán

丸 名 ❶ ball; pellet ❷ pill; bolus: 每服两～ *take two pills each time*

【丸剂】pill

【丸药】pill (or bolus) of Chinese medicine

【丸子】❶ a round mass of food; ball: 肉～ *meatball* ❷ pill; bolus

纨 名〈书〉fine silk fabrics

【纨绔】〈书〉silk clothes—a rich family ◇ ～子弟 profligate son of rich parents; fop; dandy; playboy

【纨扇】round silk fan

完 Ⅰ 动 ❶ pay: 完税 ❷ run out; use up: 我们的煤快烧～了。*We're running out of coal.* / 听～别人的话 *hear sb. out* / 信纸用～了。*The writing pad is used up.* ❸ finish; complete; be over; be through: 我马上就～。*I'll be through soon.* / 会开～了。*The meeting is over.* / 下期续～ *to be concluded in the next issue* Ⅱ 形 intact; whole: 完好

【完备】complete; perfect: 一套～的工具 *a complete set of tools* / 指出不～之处 *point out the imperfections* / 设施～ *be equipped with all sorts of facilities*

【完毕】finish; complete; end: 第一期工程已经～。*The first phase of the project has been completed.* / 一切准备～。*Everything is ready.*

【完璧归赵】return the jade intact to the State of Zhao—return sth. to its owner in perfect condition

【完成】accomplish; complete; fulfil; bring to success (or fruition): ～任务 *complete one's mission; accomplish a task; discharge one's duty* / ～作业 *finish one's homework* / 他的论文～了。*He has finished off his thesis.*

【完蛋】〈口〉be done for; be finished: 要是银行不借钱,我们就～了。*If the bank refuses to lend us the money, we're finished.*

【完稿】finish a piece of writing; complete the manuscript

【完工】complete a project, etc.; finish doing sth.; get through: 这座桥一个月就～了。*It took only one month to complete the bridge.*

【完好】intact; whole; in good condition: ～无缺 *intact; undamaged* / 货物已到,～无损。*The goods have arrived in good condition.*

【完婚】〈书〉(of a man) get married; marry

【完结】end; be over; finish: 事情并没有～。*This is not the end of the matter.*

【完了】come to an end; be over

【完满】satisfactory; successful: 会议～结束。*The meeting came to a satisfactory close.*

【完美】perfect; consummate: ～的演奏 *give a perfect performance* ◇ ～无缺（又作'完美无疵'）perfect; flawless

【完密】careful; meticulous; deliberate

【完全】❶ complete; whole: 他话没说～。*He didn't give a full picture.* ❷ completely; fully; wholly; entirely; absolutely: ～错了 *be completely wrong* / ～不同 *be totally different; have nothing in common* / ～相反 *be the exact opposite* ◇ ～变态［生］complete metamorphosis; ～燃烧 complete combustion; ～叶［植］complete leaf

【完人】perfect man: 人无～。*No man is perfect.*

【完善】❶ perfect; consummate: 设备～ *very well equipped* ❷ make perfect; improve: ～教育制度 *improve the educational system*

【完胜】［体］win a perfect or complete victory (over sb.); thoroughly defeat

【完事】finish; get through; come to an end: 他们校对到深夜才～。*They didn't finish their proofreading until late at night.*

【完税】pay taxes

【完整】complete; integrated; intact: ～的工业体系 *an integrated (or all-round, comprehensive) industrial system* / 维护领土～ *safeguard territorial integrity*

玩 Ⅰ 动 ❶ play; have fun; amuse oneself: ～儿牌 *play cards* / 咱们～儿盘棋好吗? *Shall we have a game of chess?* 他是说着～儿的。*He only said it for fun.* or *He was only joking.* ❷ employ; resort to: ～邪的 *employ underhand means; not play fair* / ～手段 *resort to crafty manoeuvres; play tricks* ❸ trifle with; treat lightly: 玩世不恭 ❹ enjoy; appreciate: ～月 *enjoy a beautiful moonlight* / ～邮票 *make a hobby of collecting stamps* Ⅱ 名 object for appreciation: 古玩

【玩儿不转】〈口〉can't handle; can't manage: 要他领导这班人,根本～。*He's not up to the task of leading such a group.*

【玩法】trifle with the law

【玩忽】neglect; trifle with: ～职守 *neglect (or dereliction) of duty; be remiss in one's duty*

【玩话】joking remarks; joke: 他说的准是～吧? *I'm sure his remarks were meant jokingly, were they?*

【玩儿坏】〈方〉be up to mischief; play a dirty trick

【玩火】play with fire ◇ ～自焚 he who plays with fire will get burnt; whoever plays with fire will perish by fire

【玩具】toy; plaything: ～汽车 *toy car* / ～汽枪

popgun / ～店 *toyshop* / ～熊 *teddy bear*

【玩儿命】〈口〉❶ gamble (or play) with one's life; risk one's life needlessly: 在大街上撒把骑车简直是～。*To ride a bicycle in the street without holding the handlebars is simply to play with one's own life.* ❷ exerting the utmost strength; for all one is worth; with all one's might: ～地干 *work like hell*

【玩弄】❶ dally with: ～女性 *philander; dally with women* ❷ play with; juggle with: ～词句 *juggle with words; go in for rhetoric* ❸ resort to; employ: ～种种阴谋诡计 *resort to all sorts of schemes and intrigues* / ～新花招 *employ some new tricks* / ～两面派手法 *engage in double-dealing*

【玩偶】doll; toy figurine

【玩儿票】play a role in Beijing opera as an amateur

【玩儿去】〈口〉get away; clear off

【玩赏】enjoy; take pleasure (or delight) in: ～风景 *enjoy (or admire) the scenery*

【玩世不恭】thumb one's nose at the world; be cynical

【玩耍】play; have fun; amuse oneself

【玩儿完】〈口〉❶ be done for; be finished: 一场大火他的买卖全～了。*After the fire, his business was done for.* ❷ dead

【玩味】ponder; ruminate: 他的话很值得～。*His words are worth pondering.*

【玩物】plaything; toy

【玩物丧志】riding a hobby saps one's will to make progress; pursuit of petty pleasures thwarts high aims

【玩笑】❶ joke with; play a prank on: 他这是开～,你别认真。*He's only joking; don't take him seriously.* ❷ joke; jest; prank ——另见〖开玩笑〗

【玩意儿】(又作'玩艺儿')〈口〉❶ toy; plaything ❷ acrobatics, cross talks, ballad singing, magic, etc. ❸ thing: 新鲜～ *newfangled gadget* / 他手里拿的是什么～? *What's that thing in his hand?* / 他是什么～! *What kind of louse is he!* / 我早知道他不是个好～。*I know all along that he was no good.*

顽 形 ❶ stupid; dense; insensate: 冥顽 ❷ stubborn; obstinate: 顽敌 ❸ naughty; mischievous

【顽磁】[物] magnetic retentivity

【顽敌】stubborn enemy; inveterate

【顽钝】〈书〉❶ dull and obtuse; stupid; thickheaded ❷ lacking moral courage ❸ blunt

【顽梗】obstinate; perverse

【顽固】❶ obstinate; stubborn; headstrong: ～地坚持错误立场 *stubbornly cling to one's wrong position* ❷ bitterly opposed to change; die-hard ◇～不化 incorrigibly obstinate; ～分子 diehard; die-hard element; ～派 the diehards

【顽疾】chronic and stubborn disease; persistent ailment

【顽抗】stubbornly resist: 敌人再～就消灭它。*If the enemy continue to resist stubbornly, wipe them out.*

【顽劣】stubborn and stupid; stubborn and obstreperous

【顽皮】naughty; mischievous

【顽强】indomitable; staunch; tenacious: ～的精神 *indomitable spirit*

【顽石】hard rock; insensate stone

【顽石点头】the insensate stones nodding in agreement (said of persuasive powers)

【顽童】naughty boy; urchin

【顽癣】[中] stubborn dermatitis (e.g. neurodermatitis)

【顽症】chronic and stubborn disease; persistent ailment

烷 名 [化] alkane

【烷化】[化] alkanisation; alkylation: ～汽油 *alkylation gasoline*

【烷基】[化] alkyl: ～胺 *alkylamine*

wǎn

宛 Ⅰ 形 winding; tortuous Ⅱ 连〈书〉as if: 音容宛然

【宛然】as if: 这里山清水秀,～江南风景。*The scenery here has great charm, reminding one of the land south of the Changjiang River.*

【宛如】(又作'宛似';'宛若') just like: 欢腾的人群～大海的波涛。*The jubilant crowds are just like the surging waves of the sea.*

【宛延】〈书〉wind; zigzag; meander

莞 (构词成分)见下

【莞尔】〈书〉smile: 不觉～ *cannot help smiling*

挽 动 ❶ draw; pull: ～弓 *draw a bow* / 手～着手 *arm in arm* ❷ roll up: ～起袖子 *roll up one's sleeves* ❸ pull; draw: ～车 *pull (or draw) a cart or carriage* ❹ lament sb.'s death

【挽词】(又作'挽辞') memorial speech

【挽歌】dirge; elegy

【挽回】retrieve; redeem: ～败局 *retrieve a defeat* / ～面子 *save face* / ～劣势 *retrieve oneself from an inferior position; improve one's position* / ～损失 *retrieve a loss* / ～影响 *redeem (or retrieve) one's reputation*

【挽救】save; remedy; rescue: ～病人的生命 *save the patient's life* / 想出一个有效的～办法 *think out an effective remedy* / ～失足青少年 *make great efforts to reform juvenile delinquents*

【挽联】elegiac couplet

【挽留】urge (or persuade) sb. to stay: 再三～ *repeatedly urge sb. to stay; press sb. to stay*

【挽马】draught horse

【挽诗】elegy

惋 动〈书〉sigh

【惋伤】heave a sigh of grief
【惋叹】sigh mournfully; lament
【惋惜】feel sorry for sb. or about sth.; regret: 我把旧书全卖了,一直感到～。*I've always regretted selling all my old books*.

晚 Ⅰ 名 evening; night: ～风 *evening breeze* Ⅱ 形 ❶ far on in time; late: ～唐 *the late Tang Dynasty* / 睡得～ *go to bed late* / ～做总比不做好。*Better late than never*. / 现在去还不～。*It's still not too late to go*. ❷ younger; junior: 晚辈
【晚安】〈套〉good night
【晚班】night shift: 上～ *be on the night shift*
【晚报】evening paper
【晚辈】the younger generation; one's juniors
【晚餐】supper; dinner
【晚场】evening show; evening performance
【晚车】night train
【晚稻】late rice
【晚点】(of a train, ship, etc.) late; behind schedule: 火车～十五分钟。*The train is 15 minutes overdue*.
【晚饭】supper; dinner
【晚会】evening of entertainment; soirée; social evening; evening party: 除夕～ *New Year's Eve entertainment*
【晚婚】marry late; late marriage: 提倡～ *encourage late marriage*
【晚间】(in the) evening; (at) night: ～新闻 *evening news*
【晚节】integrity in one's later years: 保持革命～ *maintain (or uphold) one's revolutionary integrity in one's later years*
【晚景】❶ evening scene ❷ one's circumstances in old age: ～凄凉 *lead a miserable and dreary life in old age*
【晚礼服】evening dress; evening clothes
【晚年】old age; one's later (or remaining) years: 过着幸福的～ *spend one's remaining years in happiness*
【晚娘】〈方〉stepmother
【晚期】late period: ～作品 *sb.'s later works* / 他的病已到～。*His illness has reached an advanced stage*. / ～癌症 *terminal cancer*
【晚秋】❶ late autumn; late in the autumn ❷ late-autumn crops ◇ ～作物 late-autumn crops
【晚上】(in the) evening; (at) night: ～好。*Good evening*.
【晚生】〈旧〉〈谦〉I (used when speaking to an elder or a senior)
【晚熟】[农] late-maturing: ～品种 *late variety*
【晚霜】late frost
【晚霞】sunset glow; sunset clouds
【晚香玉】[植] tuberose
【晚宴】dinner party
【晚育】late childbirth: 晚婚～应予鼓励。*Late marriage and late childbirth should be encouraged*.

婉 形 ❶ mild and indirect; tactful ❷〈书〉gentle; gracious ❸〈书〉beautiful; graceful; elegant
【婉词】gentle words; euphemism
【婉辞】❶ 同〖婉词〗❷ graciously decline; politely refuse
【婉谢】graciously decline; politely refuse
【婉言】gentle words; tactful expressions: ～相劝 *gently persuade*; *plead tactfully* ◇ ～谢绝 graciously decline; politely refuse
【婉约】〈书〉❶ graceful and restrained ❷ subtle and concise
【婉转】❶ mild and indirect; tactful: 措词～ *put it tactfully* / 他那话虽然说得～,意见却很尖锐。*His remark, for all its mildness, is nevertheless a sharp criticism*. ❷ sweet and agreeable: 歌喉～ *a sweet voice*; *sweet singing*

绾 动 coil up: 把头发～起来 *coil one's hair* / ～个扣儿 *tie a knot*

碗 名 ❶ bowl: 摆～筷 *put out bowls and chopsticks for a meal*; *set (or lay) the table* ❷ bowl-like thing
【碗柜】kitchen cupboard
【碗盏】crockery; chinaware

wàn

万 Ⅰ 数 ten thousand Ⅱ 形 a very great number; myriad: ～事～物 *myriads of things*; *all nature* / ～里长空 *vast clear skies* Ⅲ 副 (used in the negative) absolutely: 你～不可去。*You absolutely may not go*. / 此事～不可泄漏出去。*Be sure not to let it out*.
【万儿八千】〈口〉ten thousand or a bit less
【万般】❶ all the different kinds ❷ utterly; extremely
【万般皆下品,惟有读书高】the worth of other pursuits is small, the study of books excells them all (a parodical reversed version runs: 万般皆上品,惟有读书糟 *all other callings now rank first, the study of books is last and worst*)
【万般无奈】have no alternative (but to): 她～,只好自寻短见。*She took her own life: there was no alternative*. or *As a last resort she took her own life*.
【万变不离其宗】change ten thousand times without leaving the original aim or stand; change time and again, yet stay much the same
【万不得已】out of absolute necessity; as a last resort: 他知道这只是～的办法。*He knew it was a last resort*. / 不到～,他不会亲自出马。*He never appeared personally unless it was absolutely essential*.
【万次闪光灯】[摄] multitime flash lamp
【万代】同〖万世〗
【万端】multifarious: 变化～ *multifarious changes*; *kaleidoscopic changes*
【万恶】extremely evil; absolutely vicious: ～之源 *the root of all evil*

【万方】❶ all places ❷ extremely；incomparably：仪态万方

【万分】very much；extremely：～感谢 *thank you very much indeed* / ～抱歉 *be extremely sorry*

【万夫莫当】more than a match for ten thousand men（said of a brave warrior）

【万福】〈旧〉a woman's bow；curtsy：道～ *make*（*or drop*）*a curtsy*；*curtsy*

【万古】through the ages；eternally；forever ◇ ～长存 last forever；be everlasting；～长青 remain fresh forever；be everlasting；～流芳 leave a good name that will live forever；achieve immortal fame；～千秋 through unnumbered ages；for eons

【万贯】ten thousand strings of cash—great wealth：他有～家财。*He is extremely wealthy*. or *He is a millionaire*.

【万国邮政联盟】Universal Postal Union

【万户侯】a marquis with a fief of 10,000 families—a high noble；a high official

【万花筒】kaleidoscope

【万机】a myriad of state affairs：日理万机

【万家灯火】a myriad twinkling lights（of a city）

【万箭穿心】（as if）ten thousand arrows have pierced the heart—in extreme grief

【万劫不复】lost forever；beyond redemption：陷于～之地 *be doomed forever*

【万金油】❶ a balm for treating headaches，scalds and other minor ailments ❷ Jack of all trades and master of none

【万钧】ten thousand jun—very heavy；very powerful：雷霆万钧

【万籁俱寂】all is quiet and still；silence reigns supreme

【万类】all creation；all living things

【万里长城】the Great Wall

【万里长征】a long march of ten thousand li

【万隆】Bandung：～会议 *the Bandung Conference*（1955）

【万马奔腾】ten thousand horses galloping ahead—all going full steam ahead

【万马齐喑】ten thousand horses standing mute—a lifeless atmosphere

【万难】❶ extremely difficult；utterly impossible：～照办 *impossible to do as requested* / ～同意 *can by no means agree* ❷ all sorts of difficulties：排除万难

【万能】❶ omnipotent；all-powerful ❷ universal；all-purpose：～材料试验机 *universal testing machine* / ～工具机 *all-purpose machine* / ～虎钳 *universal vice* / ～胶 *all-purpose adhesive*

【万能钥匙】skeleton key；master key

【万年】ten thousand years；all ages；eternity：遗臭万年 *leave a bad name for generations to come*

【万年历】perpetual calendar

【万年青】［植］❶ evergreen ❷ Japanese rohdea（Rohdea japonica）

【万念俱灰】abandon oneself to despair；be in the slough of despond

【万千】multifarious；myriad：变化～ *eternally changing*；*changing all the time* / 思绪～ *myriads of thoughts welling up in one's mind*

【万全】perfectly sound；surefire ◇ ～之计 a completely safe plan；a surefire plan

【万人坑】a pit of ten thousand corpses—a mass grave

【万人空巷】the whole town turns out（to celebrate or to welcome sb.）

【万世】all ages；generation after generation ◇ ～师表 the Model Teacher of a Myriad Ages（an honorific title for Confucius 孔子）

【万事】all things；everything：人生～ *everything in life* ◇ ～大吉 everything is just fine；everything goes off without a hitch；everything's O.K.；～亨通 everything goes well；～俱备，只欠东风 everything is ready，all we need is an east wind—all is ready except what is crucial；～起头难（又作'万事开头难'）everything's hard in the beginning；the first step is always difficult；～通 know-all

【万寿无疆】（may you enjoy）boundless longevity

【万水千山】ten thousand torrents and a thousand crags—the trials of a long and arduous journey

【万死】die ten thousand deaths ◇ ～不辞 willing to risk any danger（to fulfil a task）

【万岁】❶ long live：全世界人民大团结～！*Long live the great unity of the people of the world*！❷ the emperor；Your Majesty；His Majesty

【万万】❶（used in the negative）absolutely：我～没有想到。*This idea never occurred to me*. / 那是～不行的。*That's absolutely out of the question*. or *That won't do at all*. / 对此～不可大意。*You must under no circumstances take this lightly*. ❷ hundred million

【万无一失】no danger of anything going wrong；no risk at all；perfectly safe

【万物】the ten thousand things of creation；all things of creation all things on the earth

【万向】［机］universal：～阀 *universal valve* / ～联轴节 *universal coupling*

【万象】every phenomenon on earth；all manifestations of nature ◇ ～更新 all things take on a new aspect；everything looks new and fresh

【万幸】very lucky（or fortunate）；by sheer luck：他差点儿没淹死，真是～。*What luck he escaped being drowned*！

【万一】❶ just in case；if by any chance：～有人找我，就请他留个条。*If by any chance somebody comes to see me*，*ask him to leave a message*. ❷ what if：～这传闻是事实呢？*What if the rumour is true*？❸ contingency；eventuality：防备～ *be ready for all eventualities*；*be prepared for the worst* ❹ one ten thousandth；a very small percentage：笔墨不能形容其～。*It simply beggars description*.

【万应灵丹】cure-all；panacea

【万用电表】［电］avometer；multimeter

【万有引力】［物］（universal）gravitation；gravitational attraction ◇ ～定律 the law of universal gravitation

【万丈】lofty or bottomless：怒火～ *a towering rage；a fit of violent anger* ◇ ～高楼平地起 the loftiest towers are built up from the ground；great oaks from little acorns grow；～深渊 a bottomless chasm；abyss

【万众】millions of people；the multitude ◇ ～一心 millions of people all of one mind

【万状】in the extreme；extremely：危险～ *extremely dangerous*

【万紫千红】a riot (or blaze) of colour：百花盛开，～。*Flowers of all sorts are blooming in a riot of colour*.

腕 名 wrist

【腕儿】同〖大腕〗

【腕力】wrist strength

【腕子】wrist：手～ *wrist*

【腕足动物】brachiopod

蔓 名 a tendrilled vine：这棵黄瓜爬～了。*This cucumber plant is climbing*. ——另见 mán；màn

wāng

汪 Ⅰ 形〈书〉(of a body of water) deep and vast Ⅱ 动 (of liquid) collect；accumulate：汤里～着油。*There are blobs of fat in the soup*. Ⅲ 名〈方〉pond；pool Ⅳ 量 (for liquid)：一～雨水 *a puddle of rainwater* Ⅴ 象 bark；bowwow

【汪汪】❶ tears welling up；tearful：泪汪汪 ❷ bark；yap；bowwow：狗～地叫。*A dog is barking*. ❸〈书〉(of a body of water) vast；boundless

【汪洋】(of a body of water) vast；boundless：一片～ *a vast expanse of water* ◇ ～大海 a vast (or boundless) ocean

wáng

亡 Ⅰ 动 ❶ flee；run away：出亡 ❷ lose；be gone ❸ die；perish：阵亡 ❹conquer；subjugate：亡国 Ⅱ 形 deceased：～妻 *deceased wife* / ～友 *deceased friend*

【亡故】die；pass away；decease

【亡国】❶ subjugate a nation；let a state perish ❷ a conquered nation：～之民 *the people of a conquered nation* ◇ ～灭种 national doom and racial extinction；～奴 a slave without a country；a conquered people

【亡魂】soul of the newly deceased；ghost

【亡灵】soul of a deceased person；ghost；spectre

【亡命】❶ flee；seek refuge；go into exile ❷ desperate ◇ ～之徒 desperado

【亡羊补牢】mend the fold after the sheep is lost：～，犹未为晚。*It is not too late to mend the fold even after the sheep is lost*.

王 Ⅰ 名 ❶ king；monarch：国王 ❷ duke；prince：亲王 ❸ best or strongest of its kind：拳王 Ⅲ 形〈书〉grand；great：～父 *grandfather*

【王八】❶ tortoise ❷〈讳〉cuckold

【王八蛋】(又作'王八羔子')〈讳〉bastard；son of a bitch

【王朝】❶ imperial court；royal court ❷ dynasty：封建～ *feudal dynasties*

【王储】crown prince

【王道】kingly way；benevolent government

【王法】the law of the land；the law

【王府】palace of a prince

【王公】princes and dukes；the nobility：～大臣 *princes, dukes and ministers* / ～贵族 *the nobility*

【王宫】(imperial) palace

【王顾左右而言他】the king looked right and left, and spoke of other things

【王冠】imperial crown；royal crown

【王国】❶ kingdom ❷ realm；domain

【王侯】princes and marquises；the nobility

【王后】queen consort；queen

【王浆】royal jelly

【王母娘娘】the Lady Queen Mother (popular name for 西王母)

【王牌】trump card ◇ ～军 elite troops；crack units

【王权】monarchical power

【王室】❶ royal family：～成员 *a member of the royal family* ❷ imperial court；royal court

【王水】[化] aqua regia

【王孙】prince's descendants；offspring of the nobility ◇ ～公子 同〖公子王孙〗

【王位】throne：继承～ *succeed to the throne*

【王子】king's son；prince

【王族】persons of royal lineage；imperial kinsmen

wǎng

网 Ⅰ 名 ❶ net：一张～ *a net* / 捉蝴蝶的～ *a butterfly-net* ❷ network：铁路网 ❸ Internet Ⅱ 动 ❶ catch with a net；net：～鱼 *net a fish* ❷ cover or enclose as with a net：眼里～着红丝 *have bloodshot eyes*

【网吧】cyber café

【网点】a network of commercial establishments

【网兜】string bag

【网获量】[渔] haul

【网巾】hairnet

【网开一面】leave one side of the net open—give the wrongdoer a way out；be lenient

【网篮】a basket with netting on top

【网恋】cyber love

【网罗】❶ a net for catching fish or birds；trap ❷ enlist the services of：～人材 *enlist able men* / ～一小撮不法分子 *scrape together a handful of lawbreakers*

【网络】❶ network：开放式、～型的经济区 *an open*

and interconnected economic zone ❷［电］network：有源～ *active network* / 无源～ *passive network* ❸ Internet ◇ ～分析 network analysis；～服务器 network server

【网迷】web fan

【网屏】（又作'网版'）［刷］screen

【网球】❶ tennis：～场 *tennis court* / ～拍 *tennis racket* / 软式～ *soft tennis* ❷ tennis ball

【网上购物】E-shopping ◇～者 E-shopper

【网上交易】online transaction

【网坛】tennis circles

【网眼】（又作'网目'）mesh

【网页】［计］web page

【网友】cyber acquaintance

【网站】web site

【网址】［计］web site

【网状结构】netted texture

【网状脉】［植］netted（or reticulated）veins：～叶 *net-veined（or reticulate）leaf*

【网子】❶ net ❷ hairnet

枉

Ⅰ 形 crooked：矫枉过正 Ⅱ 动 ❶ twist；pervert：枉法 ❷ treat unjustly；wrong：～杀无辜 *kill an innocent person* Ⅲ 副 in vain；to no avail：～活了半辈子 *have wasted half a lifetime*

【枉尺直寻】bend the foot in order to straighten the yard—lose a little in order to gain a great deal

【枉道】❶ make a detour；go by a roundabout route ❷〈书〉curry favour by crooked means

【枉法】pervert（or bend）the law

【枉费】waste；try in vain；be of no avail：～工夫 *waste time and energy* ◇ ～唇舌 waste one's breath；～心机 hatch plots in vain；scheme to no avail

【枉己正人】be crooked yet try to set others straight

【枉然】futile；in vain；to no purpose：既然他不讲理，跟他争辩也是～。*It's no use arguing with him when he refuses to listen to reason.*

【枉死】die uncleared of a false charge；die a victim of injustice：～鬼 *wronged souls*

【枉自】futile；in vain；to no purpose：～讨论了那么多次，问题还是没解决。*We have discussed the problem several times but to no purpose.*

罔

Ⅰ 动〈书〉deceive Ⅱ 副〈书〉no；not：置若罔闻

往

Ⅰ 动 go：何～？ *Where are you going?* Ⅱ 介 in the direction of；towards；to：～东走去 *go in an eastward direction；go eastwards* / 劲～一处使 *all directing their efforts towards the same goal* ～前看 *look forward* Ⅲ 形 past；previous：往事

【往常】habitually in the past；as one used to do formerly：他～不这样。*He was not like that before.* / 他比～回来得晚。*He came back later than usual.*

【往返】go there and back；journey to and fro：～要多少时间？*How long does it take to go there and back?* / ～运费 *freight out and home* ◇ ～票 return ticket；round-trip ticket

【往复】❶ move back and forth；reciprocate：～泵 *reciprocating pump* / ～式发动机 *reciprocating engine* / ～运动 *reciprocating motion；alternating motion* ❷ contact；dealings；intercourse

【往后】from now on；later on；in the future：～我们要加倍努力。*From now on we'll redouble our efforts.* / ～的日子会更好。*As time goes on we'll live an even better life.*

【往还】contact；dealings；intercourse：经常有书信～ *write to each other regularly；keep in contact by correspondence*

【往来】❶ come and go ❷ contact；dealings；intercourse：贸易～ *trade contacts；commercial intercourse* / 他们俩～密切。*The two of them are in close contact.* or *They see a lot of each other.* ◇ ～账 current（or open，running）account

【往年】（in）former years：～人们不怎么外出旅游。*In former years people did not travel so much.*

【往前】before；formerly；in the past：～的事不要再提了。*Don't bring up those things of the past again.*

【往日】（in）former days；（in）bygone days：～这个地区全是些低矮的小房子。*In the past，all houses in this area were small and low.*

【往事】past events；the past：回忆～ *recollections of the past* ◇ ～如烟 past events have vanished like smoke

【往往】often；frequently；more often than not：这里春天～刮大风。*It often blows hard here in spring.*

【往昔】in the past；in former times

惘

动 feel frustrated；feel disappointed：怅惘

【惘然】frustrated；disappointed ◇ ～若失 feel lost

魍

（构词成分）见下

【魍魉】demons and monsters：魑魅魍魉

wàng

妄

形 ❶ absurd；preposterous：狂妄 ❷ presumptuous；rash：～作主张 *make a presumptuous decision* / ～加评论 *make improper comments*

【妄称】declare falsely or presumptuously

【妄动】rash（or reckless，ill-considered）action：轻举妄动

【妄断】draw a rash conclusion；jump to a conclusion

【妄加猜测】make wild guesses

【妄加指责】make rash criticism

【妄求】inappropriate request；presumptuous demand

【妄取】take sth. without authorization or permission

【妄说】talk irresponsibly；talk nonsense

【妄图】try in vain; vainly attempt:～打破一个缺口 *vainly attempt to make a breach*
【妄为】act recklessly or wildly:胆大妄为
【妄下雌黄】❶ make irresponsible comments ❷ make wrong corrections
【妄想】❶ vainly hope to do sth.:～挽回败局 *in a vain attempt to retrieve the defeat* ❷ vain hope (or attempt); wishful thinking ❸［医］delusion
【妄想狂】［医］paranoia:医生说他是～。*The doctor says that he is paranoiac.*
【妄言】❶ talk tactlessly; speak carelessly; make irresponsible remarks ❷ wild talk; rant
【妄言妄听】loose talk not to be taken seriously
【妄语】❶ tell lies; talk nonsense ❷ wild talk; rant
【妄自菲薄】belittle oneself; be unduly humble:不可骄傲自满,也不可～。*Be neither conceited nor excessively humble.*
【妄自尊大】have too high an opinion of oneself; be overweening; be self-important

忘 动 ❶ forget:他把这事全～了。*He forgot all about it.* or *He clean forgot about the whole thing.* / 别～了给我打电话。*Don't forget to phone me.* ❷ overlook; neglect:不要只看到事物的一面而～了另一面。*Don't look at only one aspect of the thing and neglect the other.*
【忘本】forget one's past suffering; forget where one's happiness comes from
【忘掉】forget; let slip from one's mind:我当时忙于工作,把这件事给～了。*I was so busy working it simply slipped my mind.*
【忘恩负义】devoid of gratitude; ungrateful
【忘乎所以】(又作'忘其所以')forget oneself:心血来潮,～ *be carried away by a sudden impulse; lose one's head in a moment of excitement* / 不要因为胜利而～。*Don't get swollen-headed because of victory.*
【忘怀】forget; dismiss from one's mind:当时的情景我久久不能～。*For a long time afterwards I could not get the scene out of my mind.* / ～得失 *not worried about personal gains or losses*
【忘记】❶ forget:我永远不会～我们初次见面的那一天。*I'll never forget the day we first met.* ❷ overlook; neglect:不能～自己的责任。*One mustn't neglect one's duties.*
【忘旧】forget old friends (after making new friends)
【忘年交】❶ friendship between generations ❷ good friends despite great difference in age
【忘情】❶ (usu. used in the negative) be unruffled by emotion; be unmoved; be indifferent:不能～ *be still emotionally attached* ❷ let oneself go:～地歌唱 *let oneself go and sing lustily*
【忘却】forget:一件～了的往事 *a forgotten event in one's past*
【忘我】oblivious of oneself; selfless:～地工作 *work selflessly; work untiringly*
【忘形】be beside oneself (with glee, etc.); have one's head turned:得意忘形
【忘性】forgetfulness:～大 *be forgetful; have a poor memory*

旺 形 prosperous; flourishing; vigorous:人畜两～。*Both men and livestock are flourishing.* / 屋中炉火烧得正～。*There was a roaring fire in the room.*
【旺炽】flaming; blazing:火焰～。*The fire was blazing.*
【旺季】peak period; busy season:西红柿～ *tomato season*
【旺盛】vigorous; exuberant:他精力～。*He is vigorous.* / 士气～ *have high morale* / ～的生命力 *exuberant vitality* / 麦子长势～。*Wheat is growing luxuriantly.*
【旺销】be in great demand; sell well
【旺月】busy month (in business)

望 Ⅰ 动 ❶ gaze into the distance; look over:登山远～ *climb a mountain and gaze far afield* / 放眼～去 *look ahead as far as the eye can reach* / ～了他一眼 *shoot a glance at him* ❷ call on; visit:拜望 ❸ hope; expect:～速归。*Hoping you'll return as soon as possible.* / ～回信。*Awaiting your reply.* Ⅱ 名 ❶ reputation; prestige:一乡之～ *a respected man in a township* ❷ resentment; enmity ❸ full moon ❹ the 15th day of a lunar month Ⅲ 介 to; towards:～我点点头 *nod to me* / ～他笑了笑 *smile at him*
【望板】［建］roof boarding
【望尘莫及】so far behind that one can only see the dust of the rider ahead —too far behind to catch up; too inferior to bear comparison
【望穿秋水】keep gazing anxiously till one's eyes are strained; await with great anxiety
【望断】〈书〉watch sth. in the distance until it vanishes
【望而却步】shrink back at the sight of (sth. dangerous or difficult); flinch; hang back:这座桥看来很不稳,行人都～。*The bridge looked so unsafe that the travellers all hung back in fear.*
【望而生畏】be terrified (or awed) by the sight of sb. or sth.:这位老教授态度严肃,令人～。*The old professor seemed stern and forbidding.*
【望风】be on the lookout (while conducting secret activities); keep watch
【望风而逃】flee at the mere sight of the oncoming force:敌军～。*The enemy fled pell-mell (or helter-skelter) before our army.*
【望风披靡】scatter at the mere sight of the oncoming force
【望江南】［植］coffee senna (Cassia occidentalis)
【望楼】watchtower; lookout tower
【望梅止渴】quench one's thirst by thinking of plums—console oneself with false hopes; feed on fancies
【望日】the 15th day of a lunar month
【望天田】fields on hill tops which depend on rains

for water

【望文生义】misinterpret words through taking them too literally

【望闻问切】见〖四诊〗

【望眼欲穿】keep gazing anxiously till one's eyes are strained; have long been looking forward with eager expectancy

【望洋兴叹】lament one's littleness before the vast ocean—bemoan one's inadequacy in the face of a great task

【望远镜】telescope：色球～ *chromospheric telescope* / 射电～ *radio telescope* / 双筒～ *binoculars; field glasses* / 天文～ *astronomical telescope* / 剧场用小～ *opera glasses*

【望月】full moon

【望诊】[中] observation of the patient's complexion, tongue, expression, behaviour, etc., one of the four methods of diagnosis ——另见〖四诊〗

【望子成龙】long to see one's son become a dragon (i.e. win success in the world); long to see one's son succeed in life

【望族】〈书〉distinguished family; prominent family

wēi

危 Ⅰ 名 ❶ danger; peril：居安思危 ❷ the twelfth of the twenty-eight constellations (二十八宿) into which the celestial sphere was divided in ancient Chinese astronomy Ⅱ 动 endanger; imperil：危害 Ⅲ 形 ❶ dying：病危 ❷〈书〉high; precipitous：～崖 *a precipitous cliff* ❸〈书〉proper：危坐

【危殆】〈书〉in great danger; in jeopardy; in a critical condition：病势～ *be dangerously ill; be critically ill*

【危地马拉】Guatemala ◇ ～马拉人 Guatemalan

【危笃】〈书〉critically ill; on the point of death

【危房】buildings that are ready to collapse; unsafe buildings

【危害】harm; endanger; jeopardize：～国家主权和领土完整 *endanger the sovereignty and territorial integrity of the state* / ～健康 *be detrimental to health* ◇ ～性 harmfulness; perniciousness

【危机】crisis：财政～ *a financial crisis* / ～重重 *bogged down in crisis; crisis-ridden* ◇ ～感 sense of crisis; ～四伏 danger lurks on every side

【危及】endanger：酒后开车～他人生命。*Drunk drivers endanger the lives of others.*

【危急】critical; in imminent danger; in a desperate situation：～关头 *critical juncture (or time, moment)* / 情况十分～。*The situation is desperate.* / 伤势～。*The wound may be fatal.* ◇ ～存亡 danger and crisis; ～存亡之秋 a most critical moment (for a nation)

【危境】a desperate situation

【危局】a dangerous (or critical, desperate) situation

【危惧】worry and fear; be apprehensive

【危楼】a high building; a high tower

【危难】danger and disaster; calamity：处于～之中 *be in dire peril*

【危迫】critical; in imminent danger; in a desperate situation

【危如累卵】as precarious as a pile of eggs; in an extremely precarious situation

【危亡】in peril; at stake：民族～的时刻 *when the nation's existence is in peril; when the fate of the nation hangs in the balance*

【危险】dangerous; perilous：冒生命～ *at the risk of one's life* / 脱离～ *out of danger* / 有电，～！*Danger! Electricity!* / ～地带 *danger zone* / ～人物 *a dangerous person; a danger* / ～信号 *danger signal* / ～工作津贴 *danger money* ◇ ～品 dangerous articles; dangerous goods; ～性 dangerous nature; danger; ～因素 hazardous factor

【危言耸听】(又作'危辞耸听') say frightening things just to cause alarm; exaggerate just to scare people：这不是～，而是历史多次证明了的真理。*This is not alarmist talk; it is a truth repeatedly borne out by history.*

【危在旦夕】in imminent danger; on the verge of death or destruction：生命～。*Death is expected at any moment.* / 该城～。*The city may fall at any moment.*

【危重】critically ill

【危坐】〈书〉sit bolt upright; sit properly：正襟危坐

威 Ⅰ 名 impressive strength; might; power：～震四方 *known far and wide for one's military prowess* Ⅱ 动 threaten by force：威逼

【威逼】threaten by force; coerce; intimidate ◇ ～利诱(又作'威胁利诱') alternate intimidation and bribery; combine threats with inducements; use both coercion and cajolery

【威风】power and prestige; might ◇ ～凛凛 have an awesome bearing; have a commanding presence; ～扫地 with every shred of one's prestige swept away—completely discredited ——另见〖抖威风〗

【威吓】intimidate; threaten; bully：证人受到～未能作证。*The witness was kept from testifying by intimidation.*

【威力】power; might：舆论的～ *the tremendous force of public opinion*

【威猛】brave and fierce

【威名】fame based on great strength or military exploits; mighty name; mighty reputation：～天下扬 *one's fame has spread far and wide*

【威尼斯】Venice

【威迫】同〖威逼〗

【威慑】terrorize with military force; deter：～力量 *deterrent force; deterrent* / ～均势 *balance of deterrence* / ～政策 *deterrent policy*

【威士忌】whisky
【威势】power and influence
【威望】prestige：崇高的～ *high prestige*
【威武】❶ might；force；power ❷ powerful；mighty：～雄壮 *full of power and grandeur* ◇ ～不屈 not to be subdued by force；unyielding in the face of force
【威胁】threaten；menace；imperil：～邻国的安全 *threaten* (*or menace*) *the security of a neighbouring country* / ～世界和平 *imperil world peace* / 受到战争～ *be menaced by war*
【威信】prestige；popular trust：他在群众中有很高的～。*He has high prestige among the masses*. / 有～的人 *men of prestige*；*prestigious people* ◇ ～扫地 with every shred of prestige swept away—completely discredited
【威严】❶ dignified；stately；majestic；awe-inspiring：将军的举止～。*The general had a dignified manner*. ❷ prestige；dignity：保持～ *keep up one's prestige*
【威仪】impressive and dignified manner

逶

(构词成分)见下
【逶迤】winding；meandering：～的山路 *a winding mountain path* / 这条铁路～在群山之中。*The railway winds its way through the mountains*.

偎

动 snuggle up to；lean close to：看电影时她～着他。*She snuggled up to him in the darkened cinema*.
【偎抱】hug；cuddle：小女孩～着她的洋娃娃。*The little girl cuddled her doll*.
【偎依】(又作'偎倚') snuggle up to；lean close to：孩子～在母亲的怀里。*The child snuggled up in its mother's arms*.

葳

(构词成分)见下
【葳蕤】〈文〉luxuriant (foliage)

煨

动 ❶ cook over a slow fire；stew；simmer：～牛肉 *stewed beef* ❷ roast (sweet potatoes, etc.) in fresh cinders

微

Ⅰ 形 ❶ minute；tiny；slight：相差甚～。*The difference is slight* (*or negligible*). / ～云 *thin clouds* / ～雨 *drizzle* / 我跟他～说了一下。*I just mentioned it to him*. ❷ profound；abstruse Ⅱ 动 decline：衰微 Ⅲ 量 one millionth part of；micro-：微米
【微安】[电] microampere：～计 *microammeter*
【微波】❶ ripples ❷ [电子] microwave ◇ ～炉 microwave oven
【微薄】meagre；scanty：收入～ *have a meagre income* / 尽我们～的力量。*We'll exert what little strength we have*. or *We'll do what little we can*.
【微不足道】too trivial or insignificant to mention；insignificant；inconsiderable；negligible：～的人物 *an insignificant figure*；*a nobody* / ～的损失 *a trivial loss*
【微程序设计】[计] microprogramming；microcoding
【微处理机】[计] microprocessor
【微词】(又作'微辞')〈书〉veiled criticism；complaints：观众对裁判的执法多有～。*The spectators muttered their disapproval of the judge's performance*.
【微代码】[计] microcode
【微电子技术】micro-electronic technology
【微雕】miniature sculpture
【微法拉】[电] microfarad
【微分】[数] differential：二项式～ *binomial differential* / ～法 *differentiation* / ～分析 *differential analysis* ◇ ～学 differential calculus
【微风】❶ [气] gentle breeze ❷ breeze
【微伏】[电] microvolt (μV)
【微服】(of officials) in disguise；in incognito：～私访 *travel incognito*
【微观】microcosmic ◇ ～经济学 microeconomics；～世界 microworld；microcosm；～物理学 microphysics；～现象 [物] microphenomenon
【微乎其微】very little；next to nothing：我一个人的力量是～的。*On my own I can do very little*. / 双方达成协议的可能性是～的。*There is hardly any possibility of the two parties reaching agreement*.
【微火】slow fire；gentle heat
【微机】(〈略〉全称为'微型电子计算机') microcomputer
【微积分学】[数] infinitesimal calculus；calculus
【微贱】humble；lowly：出身～ *be of humble origin*；*be from a humble background*
【微刻】miniature carving
【微粒】❶ particle ❷ [物] corpuscle ◇ ～体 [植] microsome
【微量】trace；micro-：～分析 *microanalysis* ◇ ～化学 microchemistry；～天平 microbalance；～元素 trace element
【微码】[计] microcode
【微米】micron (μ)
【微妙】delicate；subtle：关系～ *subtle relations*
【微末】trifling；insignificant：～的贡献 *an insignificant contribution*
【微气象计】micrometeorograph
【微热】[医] low-grade fever
【微弱】faint；feeble；weak：呼吸～ *faint breath* / 光线～ *faint light*；*glimmer* / 脉搏～ *feeble pulse* / ～的声音 *a thin voice* / ～的多数 *a slender majority*
【微生物】microorganism；microbe：～农药 *microbial pesticide* ◇ ～学 microbiology
【微调】[电子] fine tuning；trimming：～电容器 *trimmer* (*condenser*)；padder
【微微】❶ slightly；faintly：～一笑 *smile faintly* ❷ micromicro-；pico-：～法拉 *micromicrofarad*；*picofarad* / ～秒 *picosecond*
【微细】very small；tiny：～的血管 *very small blood vessels*
【微小】small；little：极其～ *infinitely small*；*infinitesimal* / ～的希望 *slender hopes* / ～的进步

meagre progress
【微笑】smile ◇ ～服务 service with a smile
【微行】travel incognito
【微型】miniature；mini-：～电路 microcircuit / ～化 *microminiaturization* / ～汽车 *minicar*；*mini* / ～照相机 *miniature camera*；*minicam* / ～计算机 *microcomputer* / ～小说 *mini-story*
【微血管】(blood) capillary
【微言大义】sublime words with profound meaning
【微恙】〈书〉slight illness；indisposition
【微音器】microphone
【微震】❶ slight shock ❷［地质］［物］microseism

巍 形 towering；lofty
【巍峨】towering；lofty：～的群山 *lofty mountains*
【巍然】towering；lofty；majestic；imposing：大桥～横跨在江上。*The bridge stands majestic astride the river*. ◇ ～屹立 stand lofty and firm；stand rock-firm
【巍巍】towering；lofty：～井岗山 *the towering Jinggang Mountains*

wéi

为 Ⅰ 动 ❶ do；act：敢作敢～ *be decisive and bold in action*；*act with daring* ❷ act as；serve as：选她～人民代表 *elect her a people's deputy* / 以此～凭。*This will serve as a proof*. / 有诗～证。*A poem testifies to that*. ❸ become：变沙漠～良田 *turn the desert into arable land* ❹ be；mean：一公里～二华里。*One kilometer is equivalent to two li*. Ⅱ 介 (used with 所 in a passive sentence)：～人民所爱戴 *be loved and respected by the people* / 不～表面现象所迷惑 *not be confused by superficial phenomena* Ⅲ 助 ❶〈书〉(used in a rhetorical question with 何)：何以家～? *What need have I of a home*? (*usu. said during a national crisis*) ❷ (used after an adjective to form an adverb)：大～高兴 *very happy* / 广～流传 *widely spread* ❸ (used after an adverb for emphasis)：极～重要 *extremely important*——另见 wèi
【为非作歹】do evil；commit crimes；perpetrate outrages：欺压百姓，～ *ride roughshod over the people and commit all sorts of crimes*
【为富不仁】be rich and cruel；be one of the heartless rich
【为害】cause harm；cause damage：腻虫～蔬菜。*Aphids are destructive to vegetables*.
【为患】bring trouble：洪水～ *suffer from floods*
【为难】❶ feel embarrassed；feel awkward：～的事 *an awkward matter* / 使人～ *embarrass sb*.；*put sb. in an awkward situation* ❷ make things difficult for：故意～ *deliberately make things difficult for sb*.
【为期】(to be completed) by a definite date：以两周～ *not to exceed two weeks* / 会议～三天。*The meeting is scheduled to last three days*. ◇ ～不远 the day is not far off
【为人】behave；conduct oneself：～正直 *be upright* ◇ ～处世 the way one conducts oneself in society；one's attitude towards life；～师表 be worthy of the name of teacher；be a paragon of virtue and learning
【为生】make a living：以狩猎～ *make a living as a hunter*
【为时过早】premature；too early；too soon：现在下结论～。*It's still too early to reach a conclusion*.
【为首】with sb. as the leader；headed (or led) by：以某某～的代表团 *a delegation headed* (*or led*) *by so-and-so*
【为数】amount to；number：～不少 *come up to a large number*；*amount to quite a lot* / ～不多 *have only a small number*
【为所欲为】act wilfully；do whatever one likes；have one's own way
【为伍】associate with：与坏分子～ *associate with bad elements*
【为限】be within the limit of；not exceed：费用以一百元～。*The expenses shall not exceed* 100 *yuan*.
【为止】up to；till：迄今～ *up to now*；*so far* / 到去年年底～ *up to the end of last year* / 一直等到他回来～ *wait till he returns* / 今天的讨论到此～。*That's all for today's discussion*.
【为重】attach most importance to：以大局～ *put the general interest first* / 以人民的利益～ *value the interests of the people above everything else*
【为主】give first place to；give priority to：以自力更生～，外援为辅 *rely mainly on one's own efforts while making external assistance subsidiary*

韦 名〈书〉leather
【韦编三绝】be diligent in one's studies
【韦伯】［物］weber (Wb)

圩 名 dyke；embankment：筑～ *build dykes*
【圩田】❶ low-lying paddy fields surrounded with dykes ❷ polder
【圩垸】protective embankments in lakeside areas
【圩子】protective embankments surrounding low-lying fields

违 动 ❶ disobey；violate：违法 ❷ be separated：久违
【违碍】taboo；prohibition
【违拗】defy (one's superiors or elders)；disobey
【违背】violate；go against；run counter to：～原则 *violate a principle* / ～人民的意志 *go against the will of the people* / ～自己的诺言 *go back on one's word* / ～历史事实 *be contrary to the historical facts*
【违法】break the law；be illegal：～行为 *illegal activities*；*unlawful practice* / ～失职 *transgression of the law and neglect of duty* ◇ ～必究 violators must be brought to justice；～乱纪 violate

law and discipline; break the law and violate discipline

【违反】violate; run counter to; transgress; infringe: ～政策 *run counter to the policy* / ～纪律 *violate discipline* / ～交通规则 *violate traffic regulations* / ～刑法 *commit a criminal offence* / ～事实 *fly in the face of facts*

【违犯】violate; infringe; act contrary to: ～纪律 *violation of discipline; breach of discipline*

【违禁】violate a ban: ～品 *contraband (goods)* / ～贸易 *illicit trade*

【违抗】disobey; defy: ～命令 *disobey orders; act in defiance of orders* / ～上级 *defy the higher leading body; defy one's superiors; be insubordinate*

【违例】[体] breach of rules; violation

【违令】disobey orders

【违逆】violate; go against; run counter to

【违误】(used in official documents) disobey orders and cause delay: 迅速办理,不得～。*This is to be acted upon without delay.*

【违宪】violate the constitution; be unconstitutional: ～行为 *an unconstitutional act*

【违心】against one's will; contrary to one's convictions: 做～事 *act against one's conscience* ◇ ～之论 words uttered against one's conscience; insincere talk

【违约】❶ break a contract; violate a treaty: ～责任 *liability for breach of contract* ❷ break one's promise; break off an engagement

【违章】break rules and regulations: ～行驶 *drive against traffic regulations* / ～冒险作业 *work in a risky way in violation of the rules*

围 Ⅰ 动 enclose; surround: 用篱笆把菜园子～上 *enclose the vegetable patch with a fence* / 团团～住 *completely surround; encircle; besiege* / ～着他问长问短 *gather round him, asking all sorts of questions* Ⅱ 名 all round; around: 周围 Ⅲ 量 arm span: 树大十～ *a tree trunk ten arm spans around*

【围脖儿】〈方〉muffler; scarf

【围捕】surround and seize; round up

【围城】❶ encircle (or besiege) a city ❷ besieged city

【围城打援】lay siege to a city to annihilate the enemy relief force; besiege the enemy in order to strike at his reinforcements

【围攻】❶ besiege; lay siege to: 停止～ *abandon a siege* ❷ jointly speak or write against sb.; jointly attack sb.: 遭到～ *come under attack from all sides; be caught in a cross fire*

【围观】(of a crowd of people) watch; look on: 一群人在那里～。*A crowd of people were looking on.* / ～的人群 *a crowd of onlookers*

【围湖造田】(build dykes to) reclaim land from a lake; reclaim lake bottom land and plant it to crops

【围护】go along with sb. to guard him

【围击】besiege; lay siege to

【围歼】surround and annihilate

【围剿】encircle and suppress

【围巾】muffler; scarf

【围聚】crowd around; gather round

【围垦】(build dykes to) reclaim land from marshes; enclose tideland for cultivation

【围困】besiege; hem in; pin down: 把敌人～在少数据点中 *pin down the enemy in a few strongholds*

【围猎】round up and hunt

【围拢】crowd around; gather round

【围棋】weiqi, a game played with black and white pieces on a board of 361 crosses; go

【围墙】enclosure; enclosing wall

【围裙】apron

【围绕】❶ encircle; go round: 月亮～着地球旋转。*The moon revolves round the earth.* ❷ centre on: ～中心任务安排其他工作 *arrange other work around the central task*

【围网】[渔] purse seine; purse net: ～渔船 *purse seiner; purse boat*

【围魏救赵】besiege Wei to rescue Zhao—relieve the besieged by besieging the base of the besiegers

【围岩】country rock; surrounding rock

【围堰】cofferdam; coffer

【围子】❶ defensive wall or stockade surrounding a village: 土～ *fortified village* ❷ curtain ❸ protective embankments surrounding low-lying fields

【围嘴儿】bib

【围坐】sit around sb. or sth.

桅 名 mast: 船～ *mast*

【桅灯】❶ mast head light; range light ❷ barn lantern

【桅顶】masthead

【桅杆】mast

【桅樯】mast

惟 Ⅰ 副 only; alone: ～你是问。*You'll be held personally responsible.* Ⅱ 连〈书〉but: 母已痊愈,～体力尚未恢复。*Mother's well now, but she hasn't fully recovered her strength yet.* Ⅲ 助〈书〉(used before a year, month or day): ～二月既望 *on the 16th of the second lunar month* Ⅳ 名 thinking; thought:

【惟独】only; alone: 他心里总是装着别人,～没有他自己。*His thoughts always turn to other people; hardly ever does he think of himself.*

【惟恐】for fear that; lest: ～落后 *for fear that one should lag behind* / 我几次提醒他,～他忘了。*I reminded him several times lest he should forget.* ◇ ～天下不乱 crave nothing short of nationwide chaos; desire to see the world plunged into chaos; desire to stir up trouble

【惟利是图】be bent solely on profit; be intent on nothing but profit; put profit first: ～的思想

profit-before-everything mentality

【惟妙惟肖】remarkably true to life; absolutely lifelike: 这幅画把儿童天真活泼的神态画得～。*This picture catches the innocent vivacity of children.*

【惟命是听】(又作'惟命是从') be at sb.'s bidding; be obedient to sb.

【惟其】〈书〉precisely because: ～知者甚少,故须多加宣传。*It's precisely because very few people know about it that we must publicise it.*

【惟我独尊】overweening; extremely conceited

【惟一】only; sole: ～出路 *the only way out* / ～继承人 *the sole heir*

【惟有】only; alone: 大家都愿意去,～他不愿意。*Everybody is willing to go except him.*

唯 副 only; alone ——另见 wěi

【唯成分论】the theory of the unique importance of class origin

【唯理论】[哲] rationalism

【唯美主义】aestheticism

【唯名论】[哲] nominalism

【唯能说】[物] energetics

【唯生产力论】theory that overemphasizes development of forces of production (ultra-left distortion of any attempts to increase production)

【唯我主义】[哲] solipsism

【唯武器论】the theory that weapons alone decide the outcome of war

【唯物辩证法】[哲] materialist dialectics

【唯物论】[哲] materialism

【唯物主义】[哲] materialism

【唯心论】[哲] idealism

【唯心主义】[哲] idealism

维 Ⅰ 动 ❶ tie up; hold together: 维系 ❷ maintain; safeguard; preserve: 维护 Ⅱ 名 [数] dimension: 三维空间

【维持】keep; maintain; preserve: ～秩序 *keep order; maintain order* / ～现状 *maintain the status quo; let things go on as they are* / ～生活 *support oneself or one's family* ◇ ～和平部队 peace-keeping force; ～原判 [法] affirm the original judgment

【维管束】[植] vascular bundle

【维护】safeguard; defend; uphold: ～国家主权 *defend state sovereignty* / ～民族尊严 *vindicate (or defend) national honour* / ～国际和平与安全 *maintain international peace and security*

【维纶】[纺] polyvinyl alcohol fibre

【维棉】[纺] vinylon and cotton blend

【维尼纶】(又作'维尼龙') vinylon

【维生素】vitamin: ～缺乏症 *vitamin-deficiency; avitaminosis* / ～过多症 *hypervitaminosis*

【维数】[数] dimension; dimensionality: ～论 *dimension theory*

【维他命】old name for 维生素

【维吾尔族】the Uygur (Uighur) ethnic group, or the Uygurs (Uighurs)

【维系】hold together; maintain: ～人心 *maintain popular morale*

【维新】reform; modernization

【维修】keep in (good) repair; service; maintain: ～房屋 *maintain houses and buildings* / ～汽车 *service a car* / 设备～ *maintenance (or upkeep) of equipment* / ～得很好 *be in good repair* / ～费 *maintenance cost; upkeep*

帷 名 bed-curtain

【帷幕】(又作'帷幔') heavy curtain

【帷幄】〈书〉army tent: 运筹帷幄

【帷帐】bed-curtain

【帷子】curtain: 床～ *bed-curtain*

wěi

伪 形 ❶ false; fake; bogus: 作伪 ❷ puppet; collaborationist: ～政权 *puppet regime*

【伪币】❶ counterfeit money; counterfeit (or forged) bank note; spurious coin ❷ money issued by a puppet government

【伪钞】counterfeit (or forged) bank note

【伪军】puppet army or soldier

【伪君子】hypocrite

【伪科学】pseudoscience

【伪劣】(of goods) fake, shoddy, of poor quality: 制售～药品 *make and sell inferior quality medicines*

【伪善】hypocritical: ～的言词 *hypocritical words* / ～者 *hypocrite*

【伪书】ancient books found to have been incorrectly dated, forged, or attributed to a wrong author; ancient books of dubious authenticity

【伪托】forge ancient literary or art works, or pass off modern works as ancient ones

【伪造】forge; falsify; fabricate; counterfeit: ～签名 *forge a signature* / ～证件 *forge a certificate* / ～账目 *falsify accounts* / ～历史 *fabricate history; falsify history* / ～货币 *counterfeit money; forge money* / ～的文件 *spurious (or fake, forged) document; pseudograph* ◇ ～品 counterfeit; forgery; ～罪 forgery

【伪证】[法] perjury; false evidence (or testimony): 那证人有意作～。*The witness intentionally gave false testimony.*

【伪撰】write an essay under sb. else's name (esp. that of a writer of the past)

【伪装】❶ pretend; feign: ～进步 *pretend to be progressive* / ～中立 *feign neutrality* ❷ disguise; guise; mask: 他～成传教士。*He disguised himself as a missionary.* / 假的就是假的,～应当剥去。*Sham is sham, and the mask must be stripped off.* ❸ [军] camouflage: ～工事 *camouflage works* / ～猎潜舰 *Q-boat* / ～网 *camouflage net; garnished net*

【伪足】[动] pseudopodium

伟 形 big; great: 魁伟

【伟岸】〈书〉tall and sturdy; stalwart; husky; strapping: 身材～ *tall and sturdy; of great height and powerful build*
【伟大】great; mighty: ～的事业 *a great undertaking* / ～的胜利 *a signal victory*
【伟哥】[医] Viagra—US brand name of medicine for sexual impotence or erectile dysfunction
【伟观】a grand (or magnificent) sight
【伟绩】great feats; great exploits; brilliant achievements
【伟人】a great man; a great personage: 当代的～ *a great man of our time*
【伟业】〈书〉great cause; exploit

苇 名 reed
【苇箔】reed matting
【苇丛】a clump of reeds
【苇塘】reed pond
【苇席】reed mat
【苇子】reed

纬 名 ❶ weft; woof ❷ [地理] latitude
【纬编】[纺] weft knitting: ～针织物 *weft-knitted fabric*
【纬度】[地理] latitude: 高(低)～ *high (low) latitudes*
【纬密】[纺] weft density
【纬纱】[纺] ❶ weft (yarn); woof; filling ❷ pick
【纬线】❶ [地理] parallel ❷ [纺] weft

尾 Ⅰ 名 ❶ tail ❷ the sixth of the twenty-eight constellations (二十八宿) into which the celestial sphere was divided in ancient Chinese astronomy (consisting of nine stars in the shape of a hook in Scorpio) ❸ tail-like part: 机尾 ❹ end: 排尾 ❺ remaining part; remnant: 扫尾 Ⅱ 量 (for fish): 两～鱼 *two fish*
【尾巴】❶ tail: 夹起～逃跑 *run away with one's tail between one's legs* / 夹着～做人 *tuck one's tail between one's legs; pull (or draw) one's horns in* ❷ tail-like part: 彗星～ *the tail of a comet* ❸ servile adherent; appendage: 你为什么老做别人的～,难道自己一点主见也没有? *Why are you always tailing behind others? Don't you have any ideas of your own?* ❹ remaining part ❺ a person shadowing sb.: 甩掉～ *throw off one's tail* ——另见〖拖尾巴〗
【尾巴主义】tailism
【尾大不掉】❶ leadership rendered ineffectual by recalcitrant subordinates ❷ (of an organization) too cumbersome to be effective
【尾灯】tail light; tail lamp
【尾骨】[生理] coccyx
【尾矿】[矿] tailings
【尾轮】tail-wheel (of an aircraft)
【尾期】last stage; last phase; final phase
【尾鳍】tail fin; caudal fin
【尾气】tail gas
【尾欠】❶ owe a small balance ❷ balance due
【尾声】❶ [音] coda ❷ epilogue: 序幕和～ *prologue and epilogue* ❸ end: 会谈已接近～。*The talks are drawing to an end.*
【尾数】odd amount in addition to the round number (usu. of a credit balance)
【尾水】[水] tail water
【尾随】tail behind; tag along after; follow at sb.'s heels: 孩子们～着巡回演出队走了好远。*The kids followed the mobile cultural troupe for quite a distance.*
【尾须】[动] cercus
【尾翼】tail surface (of an aircraft); empennage
【尾音】last or end syllable
【尾蚴】[动] cercaria
【尾追】in hot pursuit; hot on the trail of
【尾座】[机] tailstock

委 Ⅰ 动 ❶ entrust; appoint: 委托 ❷ throw away; cast aside: 委弃 ❸ shift: 委过于人 ❹〈书〉gather; accumulate; build up Ⅱ 形 ❶ indirect; roundabout: 委婉 ❷ listless; dejected: 委靡 Ⅲ 副〈书〉actually; certainly: ～系实情。*This is the true story.* Ⅳ 名 ❶ (〈略〉见〖委员〗) committee member ❷ (〈略〉见〖委员会〗) committee; commission; council ❸〈书〉end: 原委
【委顿】tired; exhausted; weary
【委过于人】put the blame on sb. else; shift the blame on to sb. else
【委决不下】hesitate to make a decision; be undecided
【委令】appointment
【委靡】listless; dispirited; dejected: 精神～ *listless; dispirited and inert* ◇ ～不振 dejected and apathetic; dispirited; in low spirits
【委内瑞拉】Venezuela ◇ ～人 Venezuelan
【委派】appoint; delegate; designate
【委培】sponsored training: ～生 *student who is sponsored by an organization*
【委弃】abandon; forsake; cast aside
【委曲】❶ (of roads, rivers, etc.) winding; tortuous ❷〈书〉ins and outs; all the details
【委曲求全】make concessions to achieve one's aim; compromise for the sake of the general interest
【委屈】❶ feel wronged; nurse a grievance: 诉～ *pour out one's grievances (or troubles)* ❷ put sb. to great inconvenience: 你只好～一点。*You'll have to put up with it.* / 对不起,～你了。*Sorry to have made you go through all this.* or *Sorry to have put you to such inconvenience.*
【委任】appoint: ～某人为首席顾问 *appoint sb. chief adviser* ◇ ～书 certificate of appointment; ～统治 mandate; ～统治地 mandated territory; ～状 certificate of appointment
【委身】submit to; give oneself to: ～事人 *submit oneself to the service of sb.*
【委实】really; indeed: 我～不知道。*I really don't know.* / ～不容易 *by no means easy*
【委托】entrust; trust: ～他负责这项工作 *entrust*

him with responsibility for the work / 这事就～你了。*I leave this matter in your hands*. ◇ ～代理 agency by agreement；～人［法］trustor；～商店 commission shop；commission house；～书 trust deed；power of attorney；～销售 sales on commission；～责任 fiduciary duty

【委婉】（又作'委宛'）mild and roundabout；tactful：～的语气 *a mild tone* / 他批评得很～。*He made his criticism very tactfully*. ◇ ～语 euphemism

【委员】committee member；member of a committee：中央～ *member of the Central Committee* ◇ ～长 chairman of a committee

【委员会】committee；commission；council：常务～ *permanent committee* / 筹备～ *preparatory committee* / 调查～ *committee of enquiry* / 国家计划～ *State Planning Commission* / 纪律检查～ *commission for inspecting discipline*

【委罪】put the blame on sb. else

娓（构词成分）见下

【娓娓】（talk）tirelessly：～不倦 *talk tirelessly* ◇ ～动听 speak most interestingly；～而谈 talk in a kindly and informal fashion

萎 动 wither；wilt；fade

【萎靡】同〖委靡〗

【萎蔫】［植］wilting

【萎缩】❶ wither；shrivel ❷ listless；dispirited；dejected ❸ （of a market，economy，etc.）shrink；sag ❹［医］atrophy：肝～ *hepatatrophy*；*atrophy of the liver* / 肌肉～ *muscular atrophy*；*amyotrophy*

【萎陷疗法】［医］collapse therapy

【萎谢】wither；fade

唯 象〈书〉yea ——另见 wéi

【唯唯诺诺】be a yes-man；be subservient

猥 形 ❶ numerous；multifarious：～杂 *miscellaneous* ❷ base；obscene；salacious；indecent

【猥辞】（又作'猥词'）obscene（or dirty，foul）language；obscenities

【猥贱】lowly；humble

【猥劣】〈书〉abject；base；mean

【猥陋】〈书〉base；mean；despicable

【猥琐】of wretched appearance

【猥屑】〈书〉base；mean；comtemptible；despicable

【猥亵】❶ obscene；salacious ❷ act indecently towards（a woman）

wèi

卫 动 defend；guard；protect：保家～国 *protect our homes and defend our country*

【卫兵】guard；bodyguard

【卫道】defend traditional moral principles

【卫道士】〈贬〉apologist

【卫队】squad of bodyguards；armed escort：～长 *captain of the guard*

【卫护】protect；guard

【卫矛】［植］winged euonymus（Euonymus alatus）

【卫冕】defend one's championship；defend one's title

【卫生】hygiene；health；sanitation：讲～ *pay attention to hygiene* / 个人～ *personal hygiene* / 喝生水，不～。*Drinking unboiled water is bad for the health*. / ～知识 *hygienic knowledge* ◇ ～带 sanitary belt；sanitary napkin；～队 medical unit；medical team；～防疫站 sanitation and antiepidemic station；～间 toilet（room）；～检疫 health quarantine；～巾 feminine napkin；～裤〈方〉sweat pants；～筷 hygienic chopsticks；～棉 cotton wool；～球（又作'卫生丸'）camphor ball；mothball；～设备 sanitary equipment；～室 clinic；～学 hygiene；hygienics；～衣〈方〉sweat shirt；～员 health worker；medical orderly；medic；～院 small hospital；～纸 toilet paper

【卫士】bodyguard

【卫戍】garrison：北京～区 *the Beijing Garrison Command* / ～部队 *garrison force*

【卫星】❶ satellite；moon：木星有几个～？*How many moons has the planet Jupiter*？❷ artificial satellite；man-made satellite：低轨～ *low altitude satellite* / 高轨～ *high altitude satellite* / 军用～ *military satellite* / 气象～ *weather satellite*；*meteorological satellite* / 通讯～ *telecommunications satellite* ◇ ～城 satellite town；～处理机 satellite processor；～导航 satellite navigation；～广播 satellite broadcast；～国 satellite state；satellite country；～天线 satellite antenna；～云图 satellite cloud picture

【卫星电视】television programs transmitted by satellite；satellite TV

为 Ⅰ 介 ❶ in the interest of；for：～大多数人谋利益 *work in the interests of the vast majority of people* ❷ because of：～我们的友谊干杯！*A toast to our friendship*！/ ～胜利而欢呼 *hail a victory* ❸ for the purpose of；for the sake of：～方便起见 *for the sake of convenience* / 不～名，不～利 *seek no personal fame or gain* ❹ to；towards：他～我送来一份请帖。*He's sent an invitation to me*. / 且～诸君言之。*Now I'll inform you about it*. Ⅱ 动〈书〉stand for；support ——另见 wéi

【为此】to this end；for this reason（or purpose）；in this connection：～而作出种种努力 *make every effort to that end* / ～，大会作出一项重要决定。*The conference made a very important decision in this connection*.

【为国捐躯】lay down one's life for one's country

【为何】why；for what reason

【为虎傅翼】（又作'为虎添翼'）give wings to a tiger—aid an evildoer

【为虎作伥】play the jackal to the tiger—help a villain do evil

【为了】for；for the sake of；in order to：～健康戒烟 *give up smoking for the sake of health* / ～准确起见，他再次核查数字。*To make sure，he checked all the figures over again.*

【为民除害】rid the people of an evil；rid the people of a scourge

【为民请命】plead in the name of the people；plead for the people：打着～的幌子 *pose as a spokesperson of the people*

【为人作嫁】sewing sb. else's trousseau—doing work for others with no benefit to oneself

【为什么】why；why (or how) is it that：你～没来？*Why didn't you come?*

【为我之物】［哲］thing-for-us

【为渊驱鱼，为丛驱雀】drive the fish into deep waters and the sparrows into the thickets—drive friends over to the side of the enemy

未

Ⅰ名 ❶ have not；did not：意犹～尽 *have not given full expression to one's views* / 走访～遇。*I called but you were out.* / 尚～恢复健康 *not yet recovered* (*from illness*)；not yet restored to health ❷ not：～知可否 *not know whether sth. can be done* Ⅱ名 the eighth of the twelve Earthly Branches (地支) ——另见〖干支〗

【未爆弹】［军］dud

【未必】may not；not necessarily：事情～会如此。*Things may not necessarily turn out that way.*

【未便】not be in a position to；find it hard to：～擅自处理 *cannot do it without authorization* / ～立即答复 *find it difficult to give an immediate reply*

【未卜先知】know without consulting the oracle—have foreknowledge

【未曾】have not；did not：～听说过 *never heard of it* / 历史上～有过的奇迹 *a miracle unprecedented in history*

【未尝】❶have not；did not：她一夜～合眼。*She didn't get a wink of sleep the whole night.* ❷ (used before a negative word，in making a guarded assertion)：这～不是好主意。*That might not be a bad idea.*

【未成年】not yet of age；under age ◇ ～人［法］minor

【未定】uncertain；undecided；undefined：行期～。*The date of departure is not yet fixed.* ◇ ～稿 (又作'未定草') manuscript not yet finalized；draft；～界 undefined boundary；undemarcated boundary；～之天 an unknown factor；uncertainty

【未敢苟同】〈书〉beg to differ；cannot agree：你的意见，我～。*I beg to differ.* or *I'm sorry but I don't agree.*

【未婚】unmarried；single ◇ ～夫 fiancé；～妻 fiancée

【未及】❶ there's not enough time (to do sth.)；it's too late (to do sth.)：他匆促起程，～向朋友告别。*He set out in such a haste that he didn't have time to say good-bye to his friends.* ❷ not touch upon；leave unmentioned：他只谈到了奏鸣曲的结构，而～于它的起源。*He only talked about the structure of the sonata without mentioning its origin.*

【未竟】unfulfilled；unaccomplished：～之志 *an unfulfilled ambition* / ～之业 *an unaccomplished task*

【未决】unsettled；outstanding：胜负～。*The outcome* (*of the battle or contest*) *is not yet decided.*

【未可】cannot：前途～限量 *have a brilliant future*

【未可厚非】not be altogether unjustifiable；give little cause for criticism

【未可乐观】give no cause for optimism；nothing to be optimistic about

【未来】❶ coming；approaching；next；future：～的一年 *the coming year*；*next year* / 在～的岁月中 *in the years to come* ❷ future；tomorrow：美好的～ *a glorious future* ◇ ～派 futurism；～学 futurology

【未老先衰】frail and failing before one's time

【未了】unfinished；outstanding：～事宜 *unsettled matters*；*unfinished business* / ～的心愿 *an unfulfilled wish*

【未免】❶ rather；a bit too；truly：这～太过份。*This is really going too far.* / 他的话～太多。*He's rather talkative.* ❷〈书〉unavoidable

【未能】fail to；cannot：～实现 *fail to materialize* / 阴谋～得逞 *be frustrated in one's plot*

【未能免俗】be unable to rise above the convention；cannot but follow conventional practice

【未然】见〖防患未然〗

【未时】the period of the day from 1 p.m. to 3 p.m.

【未遂】not accomplished；abortive：政变～。*The coup d'état aborted.* / 自杀～ *an attempted suicide* ◇ ～犯 one who attempts to commit a crime；～罪 attempted crime；attempt

【未完】unfinished：～待续 *to be continued*

【未亡人】the bereaved one (a form of self-address formerly used by a widow)

【未详】unknown：本书作者～。*The author of the book is unknown.*

【未雨绸缪】repair the house before it rains；provide for a rainy day；take precautions

【未知量】［数］unknown quantity

【未知数】❶［数］unknown number ❷ unknown；uncertain：这事能不能办成还是个～。*It's still uncertain whether this can be arranged.*

位

Ⅰ名 ❶ place；location：座位 ❷ position：名位 ❸ throne：即位 ❹［数］place；figure；digit：个～ *unit's place* / 十～ *ten's place* / 小数～ *decimal place* / 计算到小数点后五～ *calculate to five decimal places* / 四～数 *four-figure number*；*four-digit number* Ⅱ量〈套〉(for people)：各～代表！*Fellow Delegates!* / 今天我们家要来几～朋友。*We have some friends coming to see us today.*

【位次】❶ precedence；seating arrangement：～卡 *place card* ❷ rank
【位能】［物］potential energy
【位势米】［气］geopotential metre
【位移】［物］displacement
【位于】〈书〉be located；be situated；lie：～亚洲东部 *be situated in the eastern part of Asia*
【位置】❶ seat；place：地理～ *geographical position* / 在地图上找出西安的～ *locate Xi'an on a map* ❷ place；position：《红楼梦》在中国文学史上占有重要～。*A Dream of the Red Mansions occupies an important place in the history of Chinese literature.*
【位子】seat；place

味 Ⅰ 名 ❶ taste；flavour：～儿甜 *taste sweet* / 这糖有巧克力～儿。*The candy has a chocolate flavour.* ❷ smell；odour：香～儿 *a sweet smell*；*fragrance*；*perfume*；*aroma* / 臭～儿 *an offensive* (*or foul*) *smell*；*stench*；*stink* ❸ interest；delight：趣味 Ⅱ 动 distinguish the flavour of：细～其言 *ponder his words* Ⅲ 量 (for ingredients of a Chinese medicine prescription)：这个方子共有七～药。*The prescription specifies seven medicinal herbs.* or *Seven medicinal herbs are prescribed.*
【味道】taste；flavour：这个菜～很好。*This dish is delicious.* / 感冒的时候吃东西没有～。*When you have a cold, your food has very little flavour.* / 心里有一股说不出的～ *have an indescribable feeling* / 他的话里有点讽刺的～。*There's a touch of irony in his remarks.*
【味精】monosodium glutamate；gourmet powder；MSG
【味觉】sense of taste
【味蕾】［生理］taste bud
【味同嚼蜡】like chewing wax—insipid

畏 动 ❶ fear：不～强敌 *stand in no fear of a formidable enemy* ❷ respect：后生可畏
【畏避】avoid sth. out of fear；recoil from；flinch from
【畏光】［医］photophobia
【畏忌】have scruples；fear；dread
【畏惧】fear；dread：他和这位强手比赛并不感到～。*He played fearlessly against his strong opponent.*
【畏难】be afraid of difficulty：～情绪 *fear of difficulty*
【畏怯】cowardly；timid；chickenhearted
【畏首畏尾】be full of misgivings；be over-cautious
【畏缩】recoil；shrink；flinch：在困难面前从不～ *never shrink* (*or flinch*) *from difficulty*
【畏缩不前】(又作'畏葸不前') recoil in fear；hesitate to press forward；hang back
【畏途】〈书〉a dangerous road—a perilous undertaking：视为畏途
【畏友】an esteemed friend
【畏罪】dread punishment for one's crime：～潜逃 *abscond to avoid punishment* / ～自杀 *commit suicide to escape punishment*

胃 名 ❶ stomach ❷ the seventeenth of the twenty-eight constellations（二十八宿）into which the celestial sphere was divided in ancient Chinese astronomy (consisting of three stars in Musca Borealis)
【胃癌】cancer of the stomach；gastric carcinoma
【胃病】stomach trouble；gastric disease；gastropathy
【胃肠炎】gastroenteritis
【胃出血】gastric bleeding；gastric hemorrhage；gastrorrhagia
【胃穿孔】gastric perforation；stomach perforation
【胃蛋白酶】［生理］pepsin
【胃痉挛】gastrospasm
【胃镜】gastroscope：～检查 *gastrocopy*；*stomachoscopy*
【胃口】❶ appetite：～好 *have a good appetite* / 没有～ *have no appetite* ❷ liking：对～ *to one's liking* ——另见〖倒胃口〗
【胃溃疡】gastric ulcer
【胃扩张】dilatation of the stomach；gastrectasis
【胃粘膜】gastric mucosa ◇ ～疾病 gastric mucosa disease
【胃切除术】gastrectomy
【胃酸】hydrochloric acid in gastric juice：～过多 *hyperchlorhydria*；*hyperacidity* / ～过少 *hypochlorhydria*；*hypoacidity*
【胃痛】stomachache；gastralgia
【胃萎缩】lipogastry
【胃下垂】ptosis of the stomach；gastroptosis
【胃腺】［生理］gastric gland
【胃炎】gastritis
【胃液】［生理］gastric juice

谓 Ⅰ 动 ❶ say：或～ *someone says* ❷ call；name：此之～形式主义。*This is what is called formalism.* Ⅱ 名 meaning；sense：无谓
【谓词】［逻］predicate：～演算 *predicate calculus*
【谓语】〈语〉predicate

尉 名 officer
【尉官】a military officer above the rank of warrant officer and below that of major；a junior officer

喂 Ⅰ 叹 hello；hey：～，请接三一三号分机，*Hello, extension* 313, *please!* / ～，你的围巾快掉了。*Hey, your scarf is slipping off.* Ⅱ 动 feed：～猪 *feed pigs* / 给病人～饭 *feed a patient*
【喂料】feed (draught animals)
【喂奶】breast-feed；suckle；nurse
【喂养】feed；raise；keep：～家禽 *keep fowls*

猬 名［动］hedgehog

蔚 形〈书〉❶ luxuriant；grand ❷ colourful
【蔚蓝】azure；sky blue：～的天空 *a bright blue sky*

/ ～的海洋 *the blue sea*

【蔚然成风】become common practice；become the order of the day：学习外语～。*Studying foreign languages is the order of the day.*

【蔚为大观】present a splendid sight；afford a magnificent view：展出的美术作品，～。*There's a splendid array of works of art on display.*

慰 动 ❶ console；comfort：慰勉 ❷ be relieved：知你平安到达，甚～。*I am greatly relieved to learn that you have arrived safely.*

【慰安妇】"comfort woman"—Asian women enforced to satisfy the sexual desire of Japanese soldiers during World War Two

【慰抚】comfort；console；soothe

【慰藉】〈书〉comfort；console

【慰劳】bring gifts to，or send one's best wishes to，in recognition of services rendered

【慰留】urge sb. to stay on

【慰勉】comfort and encourage

【慰情胜无】a little comfort is better than none

【慰问】express sympathy and solicitude for；extend one's regards to；convey greetings to；salute：请向他们转达我们亲切的～。*Please convey to them our sincere solicitude.* ◇ ～袋 gift bag；～团 a group sent to convey greetings and appreciation；～信 a letter expressing one's appreciation or sympathy；～演出 a special performance as an expression of gratitude or appreciation

【慰唁】condole with sb.

wēn

温 Ⅰ 形 warm；lukewarm：～水 *lukewarm water* Ⅱ 动 ❶ warm up：把酒～一下 *warm up the wine* ❷ review；revise：～课 *review (or revise) one's lessons* Ⅲ 名 temperature：体温

【温饱】dress warmly and eat one's fill；have adequate food and clothing：终年劳累，不得～ *toil all the year round without enough to eat and wear* ◇ ～问题 problem of adequate (ample) food and clothing；～型 simply having adequate food and clothing

【温标】［物］thermometric scale：华氏～ *Fahrenheit's thermometric scale* / 摄氏～ *Celsius' thermometric scale* / 开氏～ *Kelvin's thermometric scale*

【温差】difference in temperature；range of temperature：这里白天和夜晚的～很大。*The temperature here varies greatly between day and night.* ◇ ～电［物］thermoelectricity；～电检波器 thermodetector；～电偶 thermoelectric couple；thermocouple

【温床】❶［农］hotbed ❷〈喻〉breeding ground；hotbed：官僚主义是贿赂和腐败的～。*Bureaucracy is a hotbed of bribery and corruption.*

【温存】❶ attentive (usu. to a person of the opposite sex) ❷ gentle；kind

【温带】temperate zone ◇ ～气候 temperate climate

【温度】temperature：室内（外）～ *indoor (outdoor) temperature*

【温度表】thermometer：摄氏～ *centigrade (or Celsius) thermometer* / 华氏～ *Fahrenheit thermometer*

【温度计】thermograph；thermometer

【温故知新】❶ gain new knowledge by reviewing old ❷ understand the present by reviewing the past

【温和】(wēnhé) ❶ temperate；mild；moderate：气候～ *a temperate climate* ❷ gentle；mild：性情～ *a gentle disposition* / 语气～ *a mild tone* ◇ ～派 moderates——另见 wēnhuo

【温厚】gentle and kind；good-natured

【温乎乎】warm；lukewarm：我不爱喝～的汤。*I hate lukewarm soup.*

【温乎】warm；lukewarm：烙饼还有点儿～。*The pancake is still warm.*

【温和】(wēnhuo) warm；lukewarm：汤还～呢。*The soup is still warm.* ——另见 wēnhé

【温觉】［生理］sense of heat

【温良】gentle and kindhearted

【温良恭俭让】temperate，kind，courteous，restrained and magnanimous

【温暖】warm：天气～ *warm weather* / 对同志像春天般～ *be as mild as spring towards one's comrades* / 他的一席话～了我的心。*What he said warmed my heart.*

【温情】❶ tender feeling ❷ too soft-hearted：你对他太～了。*You're too lenient with him.* ◇ ～脉脉 full of tendernes；～主义 excessive tender-heartedness；undue leniency

【温泉】hot spring

【温柔】(usu. of a woman) gentle and soft

【温柔敦厚】gentle and kind

【温柔乡】the land of warmth and tenderness—a place where a man can find solace in feminine charms

【温润】❶ gentle；kindly：～的面容 *a kindly face* ❷ mild (or temperate) and moist：气候～ *a temperate and moist climate*

【温湿计】hygrothermograph；thermohygrograph

【温室】hothouse；greenhouse；glasshouse；conservatory：～育苗 *nurse young plants in hothouses* ◇ ～效应 greenhouse effect

【温淑】〈书〉(of a woman) gentle and kind

【温顺】docile；meek：像小羊一般～ *as meek as a lamb*

【温汤】❶ lukewarm water ❷〈书〉hot spring

【温汤浸种】［农］hot water treatment of seeds

【温暾】〈方〉（又作'温吞'）❶ lukewarm；tepid：～水 *lukewarm water* ❷ (of language) not to the point；irrelevant

【温文尔雅】refined and cultivated

【温习】review；revise：～功课 *review one's lessons*

【温馨】soft and sweet；warm：～的春夜 *a soft spring evening* / ～的情谊 *warm friendship*

【温血动物】warm-blooded animal
【温驯】(of animals) docile; meek; tame
【温雅】gentle and refined: ～的少年 *a gentle and elegant young man*

瘟 Ⅰ 名 [中] acute communicable diseases Ⅱ 形 (of traditional opera) dull and insipid
【瘟病】[中] seasonal febrile diseases
【瘟神】god of plague
【瘟疫】pestilence

wén

文 Ⅰ 名 ❶ character; script; writing: 甲骨文 ❷ language: 英文 ❸ literary composition; writing: 文如其人 ❹ literary language: 这句话太～了,不好懂。*This sentence is too bookish to be readily intelligible*. ❺ culture: 文物 ❻ formal ritual: 虚文 ❼ certain natural phenomena: 天文 / 水文 Ⅱ 形 ❶ civilian; civil: 文职 ❷ gentle; refined: 文雅 Ⅲ 动 ❶ cover up; paint over: 文过饰非 ❷ tattoo: 文身 Ⅳ 量 (for copper cash): 一～钱 *a cash* / 一～不值 *not worth a farthing*
【文案】〈旧〉❶ official documents and correspondence ❷ secretary; clerk
【文本】text; version: 本合同两种～同等有效。*Both texts of the contract are equally valid*. ◇ ～编辑 [计] text editing
【文笔】style of writing: ～流利 *write in an easy and fluent style*
【文不对题】irrelevant; beside the point (or mark); wide of the mark
【文不加点】never make the slightest change in one's writing; have a facile pen
【文才】literary talent; aptitude for writing
【文采】❶ rich and bright colours ❷ literary grace; literary talent: 这个人很有～。*This is a man of unusual literary talent*.
【文昌鱼】lancelet
【文抄公】plagiarist
【文丑】(in traditional opera) a comedian in civil plays (文戏)
【文辞】(又作'文词') diction; language: ～优美 *exquisite diction; elegant language*
【文从字顺】readable and fluent
【文斗】verbal struggle; nonviolent struggle
【文牍】❶ official documents and correspondence ❷ 〈旧〉 secretary; clerk ◇ ～主义 red tape
【文法】❶ rules of composition and rhetoric ❷ old name for 语法
【文房】〈书〉 study (a room) ◇ ～四宝 the four treasures of the study (writing brush, inkstick, inkslab and paper)
【文风】style of writing: ～朴实 *a simple style of writing*
【文风不动】absolutely still
【文稿】manuscript; draft
【文告】proclamation; statement; message
【文革】〈略〉见〖无产阶级文化大革命〗
【文蛤】[动] clam
【文工团】song and dance ensemble; art troupe; cultural troupe
【文官】civil official
【文冠果】[植] shiny-leaved yellowhorn (Xanthoceras sorbifolia)
【文过饰非】conceal faults and gloss over wrongs; gloss over one's faults; cover up (or explain away) one's errors
【文豪】literary giant; great writer; eminent writer
【文化】❶ civilization; culture: ～侵略 *cultural aggression; cultural penetration* / ～渗透 *cultural infiltration* / ～遗产 *cultural heritage* / ～遗址 *a site of ancient cultural remains; remains of an ancient culture* ❷ education; culture; schooling; literacy: ～事业 *cultural establishments; cultural undertakings* / ～水平 *cultural level; educational level* ◇ ～参赞 cultural counsellor; cultural attaché; ～程度 cultural level; cultural standard; ～宫 palace of culture; cultural palace; ～馆(又作'文化站') cultural centre; ～机关 cultural institution; ～街 street with many cultural institutions and facilities; ～界 cultural circles; ～模式 cultural pattern; ～偶像 culture icon; ～人 intellectual; ～热 cultural craze; ～沙漠 cultural desert; ～市场 cultural market; ～用品 stationery; ～专员 cultural attaché; ～专制主义 cultural tyranny
【文火】slow fire; gentle heat: ～焖四十分钟 *simmer gently for forty minutes*
【文集】collected works
【文件】documents; papers; instruments: ～编号 *the reference or serial number of a document* / ～处理 *file processing; document handling* / ～袋 *documents pouch; dispatch case* / ～分析 *file analysis* / ～柜 *filing cabinet* / ～目录 *file catalog; file directory*
【文教】(〈略〉全称为'文化教育') culture and education: ～事业 *cultural and educational work; culture and education* ◇ ～界 cultural and educational circles
【文静】gentle and quiet
【文具】writing materials; stationery: ～店 *stationer's; stationery shop*
【文据】written pledge
【文科】liberal arts: ～学校 *liberal arts school* / ～院校 *colleges of arts*
【文库】(usu. used in book titles) a series of books issued in a single format by a publisher; library: 《万有～》*Everyman's Library*
【文莱】Brunei
【文理】unity and coherence in writing: ～不通 *illogical and ungrammatical; ungrammatical and incoherent* / ～通顺 *have unity and coherence; make smooth reading*
【文盲】an illiterate person; illiterate: 据统计,该国百分之十的人是～。*Ten per cent of the country is reckoned to be illiterate*.

【文庙】Confucian temple

【文明】❶ civilization；culture：～古国 *a country with an ancient civilization* ❷ civilized：～国家 *an civilized country* / ～经商 *do business with civility* / ～礼貌 *decorum*；*courtesy*；*manners* ◇～棍〈旧〉walking stick；stick；～戏〈旧〉early form of spoken drama（话剧）

【文墨】writing：粗通～ *barely know the rudiments of writing*

【文鸟】［动］mannikin

【文痞】literary prostitute

【文凭】diploma ◇～至上 credentialism

【文气】（wénqì）vigour of style

【文气】（wénqi）〈方〉gentle and quiet

【文契】contracts concerning the buying and selling of real estate，etc.

【文情并茂】（of writing）elegant in style and rich in sentiment

【文人】man of letters；scholar；literati ◇～画 literati painting；～无行 men of letters are lacking in moral character；～相轻 scholars tend to look down upon each other；～学士 scholars；men of letters

【文如其人】the writing mirrors the writer；the style is the man

【文弱】gentle and frail-looking：～书生 *a frail scholar*

【文山会海】a mountain of papers and a sea of meetings—the intricate routine that a leading cadre gets bogged down in

【文身】〈书〉tattoo

【文史】literature and history：～资料 *historical accounts of past events* ◇～馆 Research Institute of Culture and History

【文饰】❶ polish（a piece of writing）❷ gloss over（one's mistakes）；cover up

【文书】❶ document；official dispatch ❷ copy clerk

【文殊】［宗］（佛教）Manjusri

【文思】the thread of ideas in writing；the train of thought in writing：～敏捷 *have a ready pen*

【文坛】the literary world（or arena，circles）；the world of letters

【文韬武略】civil and military skills

【文体】❶ type of writing；literary form；style ❷ recreation and sports：～活动 *recreational and sports activities*

【文恬武嬉】（of a corrupt regime）the officials are indolent and the officers frivolous

【文武】civil and military：～官员 *civil and military officials* ◇～双全 be well versed in both polite letters and martial arts；adept with both pen and sword

【文物】cultural relic；historical relic：重点～保护单位 *major historical and cultural sites under state protection* ◇～保护 preservation of cultural relics；protection of historical relics

【文戏】（in traditional opera）civil plays（〈反〉武戏）

【文献】document；literature：历史～ *historical documents* ◇～记录片 documentary film

【文选】（usu. used in book titles）selected works；literary selections

【文学】literature：～家 *writer*；*man of letters*；*literati* / ～流派 *schools of literature* / ～批评 *literary criticism* / ～作品 *literary works* ◇～士 bachelor of arts（B. A.）；～语言 standard speech；literary language

【文雅】elegant；refined；cultured；polished：举止～ *refined in manner*

【文言】classical Chinese ◇～文 writings in classical Chinese；classical style of writing

【文以载道】The function of literature is to convey the Tao.

【文艺】literature and art：～作品 *literary and artistic works* / ～座谈会 *forum on literature and art* ◇～复兴 the Renaissance；～会演 theatrical festival；～节目 programme of entertainment；theatrical items；theatrical performance；～界 literary and art circles；the world of literature and art；～批评 literary or art criticism

【文友】literary friend

【文娱】（〈略〉全称为'文化娱乐'）cultural recreation；entertainment：～活动 *recreational activities*

【文苑】❶ the literary world（or arena，circles）；the world of letters ❷ literary and art circles；the world of literature and art

【文约】contract；deed

【文责】the responsibility an author should assume for his own writings；author's responsibility ◇～自负 the author takes sole responsibility for his views

【文摘】abstract；digest

【文章】❶ essay；article ❷ literary works；writings ❸ hidden meaning；implied meaning：话里有～。*There is an insinuation in that remark.* or *That's an insinuating remark.* / 其中大有～。*There is a lot behind all this.* ——另见〖做文章〗

【文职】civilian post：～人员 *nonmilitary personnel*

【文治】〈书〉civil administration

【文治武功】cultural and military achievements

【文质彬彬】gentle；urbane；suave：他举止大方，～，和蔼可亲。*He is composed，urbane，and affable.*

【文绉绉】genteel：说话～的 *speak in a genteel manner*；*be soft-spoken*

【文竹】［植］asparagus fern（Asparagus plumosus）

【文字】❶ characters；script；writing ❷ written language：～宣传 *written propaganda* / 有～可考的历史 *recorded history* ❸ writing（as regards form or style）：～清通 *lucid writing* ◇～处理机 word processor；～方程［数］literal equation；～改革 reform of a writing system（as in China）；～交 pen friends；literary friends；～学 philology；～游戏 play with words；juggle with terms

【文字狱】［史］imprisonment or execution of an author for writing sth. considered offensive by the imperial court; literary inquisition

【文宗】〈书〉an outstanding literary figure: 一代～ *the most outstanding literary figure of the time*

纹 名 lines; veins; grain: 皱纹

【纹理】veins; grain: 有～的大理石 *veined marble* / 这木头的～很好看。*This wood has a beautiful grain.*

【纹路儿】lines; grain

【纹饰】decorative pattern (on utensils); figure

【纹丝不动】absolutely still: 没有一点风,柳条儿～。*There wasn't a breath of wind and the willow twigs were perfectly still.*

【纹银】〈旧〉fine silver

闻 Ⅰ 动 ❶ hear: 耳闻 ❷ smell: 你～～这是什么味儿? *Smell this and see what it is.* / 我～到煳味儿了。*I can smell something burning.* Ⅱ 名 ❶ news; story: 要闻 ❷ reputation: 秽闻 Ⅲ 形 well-known; famous: 闻人

【闻达】〈书〉illustrious and influential; eminent: 不求～ *seek neither fame nor position*

【闻风而动】act without delay upon hearing the news; immediately respond to a call; go into action without delay

【闻风丧胆】become terror-stricken (or panic-stricken, terrified) at the news: 我军向前推进,敌人～。*The enemy trembled with fear on hearing of our advance.*

【闻过则喜】be glad to have one's errors pointed out

【闻鸡起舞】rise at cock's crow—diligent and self-disciplined

【闻见】(wénjiàn) what one sees and hears; knowledge; information

【闻见】(wénjian) ❶ notice by smell; smell: 我～了花香。*I smell the fragrance of a flower.* ❷ hear

【闻名】❶ well-known; famous; renowned: ～全国 *well-known throughout the country* / 世界～ *world-famous; world-renowned* ❷ be familiar with sb.'s name; know sb. by repute

【闻名不如见面】knowing a person by repute is not as good as meeting him face to face

【闻人】well-known figure; famous man; celebrity

【闻所未闻】hear what one has never heard before; unheard-of: 他们给我讲了很多～的事情。*They told me a lot of things I had never heard before.*

【闻悉】〈书〉hear; learn; be informed: ～贵体欠安,希早日康复。*I've heard you are slightly indisposed these days. I wish you a speedy recovery.*

【闻讯】hear the news: 消防队～赶到。*On hearing the alarm the fire brigade rushed to the scene.*

【闻一知十】learn one thing and know ten things—very intelligent

蚊 名 mosquito

【蚊虫】〈方〉mosquito

【蚊香】mosquito-repellent incense

【蚊帐】mosquito net: ～纱 *mosquito netting*

【蚊子】mosquito

wěn

刎 动 cut one's throat: 自刎

【刎颈之交】friends that are ready to die for each other: 两人相与为～。*The two men were such devoted friends that they would have died for each other.*

吻 Ⅰ 名 ❶ lips: 接吻 ❷ an animal's mouth Ⅱ 动 kiss: ～别 *kiss sb. good-bye*

【吻合】❶ be identical; coincide; tally: 意见～ *have identical views* / 他讲的情况和我听到的～。*His account tallies with what I heard.* ❷［医］connect by anastomosis

【吻合术】［医］anastomosis

紊 形 disorderly; confused: 有条不紊

【紊流】［物］turbulence; turbulent flow

【紊乱】disorder; chaos; confusion: 秩序～ *in a state of chaos* / 新陈代谢功能～ *metabolic disorder*

稳 Ⅰ 形 steady; firm: 把桌子放～ *make the table steady* / 坐～ *sit tight* / 她做事很～。*She is steady and reliable in doing things.* Ⅱ 副 surely; certainly: 这场比赛他～赢。*He is certain to win the game.*

【稳步】with steady steps; steadily: ～前进 *advance steadily; make steady progress*

【稳操胜券】be certain (or confident) of success

【稳产】stable yields: ～高产田 *land (or fields) with high, stable yields*

【稳当】❶ reliable; secure; safe: ～的办法 *a reliable method* ❷ steady; stable: 把梯子扶～。*Hold the ladder steady.*

【稳定】❶ stable; steady: 情绪～ *be in a calm, unruffled mood* / ～的多数 *a stable majority* ❷ stabilize; steady: ～物价 *stabilize commodity prices* / ～情绪 *set sb.'s mind at rest; reassure sb.* ◇ ～剂［化］stabilizer; ～平衡［物］stable equilibrium; ～装置 stabilization plant; stabilizer

【稳固】❶ firm; stable: ～的基础 *a firm (or solid) foundation* ❷ stabilize: ～政权 *stabilize a government*

【稳健】firm; steady: 迈着～的步子 *walk with firm steps* / 他这个人很～。*He's a steady person.* ◇ ～派 moderates

【稳流】［物］steady flow

【稳拿】be certain to win, achieve, etc.: 他～第一名。*He is certain to win first place.*

【稳如泰山】as stable as Mount Tai

【稳妥】(又作'稳帖') safe; reliable: ～的计划 *a safe plan*

【稳压器】voltage stabillizer; voltage regulator

【稳扎稳打】❶ go ahead steadily and strike sure blows (in war) ❷ go about things steadily and surely：事情要一步一步地、～地去进行。*The business should be conducted step by step, slowly and surely.*

【稳重】steady；staid；sedate：他年纪不大，说话做事都很～。*Young as he is, he is steady in what he says and what he does.*

【稳住阵脚】maintain (or secure) one's position；hold one's ground

【稳准狠】sure, accurate and relentless：～地打击 *strike surely, accurately and relentlessly at sb.*

wèn

问 动 ❶ ask；inquire：～路 *ask the way* / 不懂就～。*Ask when you don't know.* / 我～他为什么要那样做。*I asked him why he did it.* / 他在食堂～了一下开饭的时间。*He inquired about the meal times at the canteen.* ❷ ask after；inquire after：他信里～起你。*He asks after you in his letter.* ❸ interrogate；examine：审问 ❹ hold responsible：出了事惟你是～。*You'll be held responsible if anything goes wrong.* ❺ ask (sb.) for sth：我去～他借那本书。*I'll ask him to lend me the book.*

【问安】pay one's respects (usu. to elders)；wish sb. good health

【问案】try (or hear) a case

【问卜】divine by the Eight Trigrams

【问长问短】make detailed inquiries；inquire with concern about sb.'s well-being；ask about this and that：她见医生走出手术室，急忙上前～。*When she saw the surgeon coming out of the operating room, she stepped forward and asked many solicitous questions.*

【问答】questions and answers：～练习 *question-and-answer drills*

【问道于盲】ask a blind man the way—seek advice from one who can offer none

【问鼎】❶ inquire about the tripods—aspire after the throne；have monarchic ambitions ❷ compete for a championship；try to carry off the first prize：～桂冠 *win the victor's laurels*

【问寒问暖】inquire with concern about sb.'s well-being；be solicitous for sb.'s welfare

【问好】send one's regards to；say hello to：请代我向你父亲～。*Please give my regards to your father.* or *Remember me to your father.*

【问号】❶ question mark；interrogation mark (or point) (?) ❷ unknown factor；unsolved problem：致癌的真正原因还是个～。*The exact cause of cancer is still unknown.* / 他究竟有多大能力，还得打上一个～。*There is still some doubt as to his ability.*

【问候】send one's respects (or regards) to；extend greetings to：致以亲切的～ *extend cordial greetings*

【问话】ask about；inquire：老师要找你～。*The teacher wants to ask you some questions.*

【问津】〈书〉(usu. used in the negative) make inquiries (as about prices or the situation)

【问荆】［植］meadow pine (Equisetum arvense)

【问卷】questionnaire：关于妇女地位的～ *questionnaire on the status of women*

【问难】raise difficult questions for discussion

【问世】be published；come out：本书作者的一部新小说即将～。*A new novel by the same author will soon come out.*

【问事】❶ inquire；ask ❷ run affairs；be in charge：找他没有用，他现在已经不～了。*It's no use asking him. He is no longer in charge now.* ◇ ～处 inquiry office；information desk

【问题】❶ question；problem；issue：这是个用法～。*This is a matter of usage.* / ～是我们去还是不去。*The thing is shall we go or not.* / 那不是～之所在。*That's just not the issue.* ❷ trouble；mishap：那台车床出～了。*Something has gone wrong with that lathe.* / 一路上没出～。*The trip went off without mishap.*

【问心无愧】feel no qualms upon self-examination；have a clear conscience：你只要～，就不必感到不安。*You have nothing to worry about as long as you have a clear conscience.* / 我～。*I have done nothing to be ashamed of!*

【问心有愧】feel a twinge of conscience；have a guilty conscience

【问讯】inquire；ask ◇ ～处 inquiry office；information desk

【问斩】〈旧〉behead；decapitate

【问住】stump sb. with a question：我一句话就把他～了。*I stumped him with a question.* / 这下子你把我～了。*You've got me there.*

【问罪】denounce；condemn

wēng

翁 名 ❶ old man：渔翁 ❷ father ❸ father-in-law：翁姑

【翁姑】a woman's parents-in-law

【翁婿】father-in-law and son-in-law

【翁仲】stone statue placed in front of a tomb

嗡 象 drone；buzz；hum：蜜蜂～～地飞。*Bees are buzzing all around.*

wèng

瓮 名 urn；earthen jar：水～ *water jar* / 菜～ *a jar for pickling vegetables*

【瓮城】the enceinte of a city gate；a barbican entrance to a city

【瓮声瓮气】in a low, muffled voice

【瓮中之鳖】like a turtle in a jar—bottled up；trapped

【瓮中捉鳖】catch a turtle in a jar —go after an easy prey

蕹（构词成分）见下

【蕹菜】water spinach

wō

涡 名 whirlpool；eddy：水～ *eddies of water*

【涡虫】［动］turbellarian worm；turbellarian

【涡流】❶ the circular movement of a fluid；whirling fluid；eddy ❷［物］eddy current；vortex flow

【涡轮】turbine：～壳 *turbine casing* / ～叶片 *turbine blade* / ～轴 *turboshaft* ◇ ～发电机 turbogenerator；～机 turbine；～螺旋桨发动机 turboprop（engine）；～喷气发动机 turbojet（engine）

【涡旋】［气］vortex：大气～ *atmospheric vortex*

倭 名（old name for 日本）Japan

【倭瓜】〈方〉pumpkin；cushaw

【倭寇】［史］Japanese pirates（operating in Chinese coastal waters from the fourteenth to the sixteenth century）

莴（构词成分）见下

【莴苣】lettuce

【莴笋】asparagus lettuce

窝 Ⅰ 名 ❶ nest：燕子在我家房檐下做了个～。*The swallows built a nest under the roof of our house.* ❷ lair；den：土匪～ *bandits' lair*；*bandits' nest* ❸ a hollow part of the human body；pit：心口～ *the pit of the stomach* ❹〈方〉place：挪窝儿 Ⅱ 动 ❶ harbour；shelter：窝赃 ❷ hold in；check：窝火 ❸ bend：把铁丝～个圆圈 *bend the wire into a circle* / 别把画片～了。*Be careful not to bend（or crease）the picture.* Ⅲ 量（for animals）litter；brood：一～十只小猪 *ten piglets at a litter* / 一～小鸡 *a brood of chickens*

【窝憋】〈方〉❶ feel frustrated：事情没办好，心里老觉得～得慌。*I feel frustrated about having botched the job.* ❷ shut oneself indoors；stay at home ❸ narrow and small；poky：我这间卧室太～。*This bedroom is too poky for me.*

【窝脖儿】（又作'窝脖子'）〈方〉meet with a rebuff；strike a snag；be crossed

【窝藏】harbour；shelter：～罪犯 *give shelter to（or harbour）a criminal* / ～赃物 *conceal booty*

【窝匪】give shelter to（or harbour）a bandit

【窝工】enforced idleness due to poor organization of work；holdup in the work through poor organization

【窝火】be filled with anger：窝了一肚子火 *be filled with pent-up anger*；*be simmering with rage*；*be forced to bottle up one's anger*

【窝儿里斗】internal struggle；internal quarrels and fights

【窝儿里反】〈口〉internal strife；family quarrel

【窝儿里横】〈方〉a terror at home（but a coward outside）

【窝囊】❶ feel vexed；be annoyed：受～气 *be subjected to petty annoyances* / 这事办得真～。*That's really botched it up.* ❷ good-for-nothing；hopelessly stupid ◇ ～废〈方〉good-for-nothing；worthless wretch

【窝棚】shack；shed；shanty

【窝气】choke with resentment；feel injured and resentful：窝了一肚子气 *have pent-up grievances*

【窝窝头】（又作'窝头'）steamed bread of corn，sorghum，etc.

【窝赃】harbour stolen goods；conceal booty

【窝主】a person who harbours criminals，loot or contraband goods

喔 象 cock's crow：～～～！*Cock-a-doodle-doo!* ——另见 ō

蜗 名 snail

【蜗杆】［机］worm：～轴 *worm shaft*

【蜗居】〈书〉humble abode

【蜗轮】［机］worm gear；worm wheel

【蜗牛】snail

【蜗旋】spiral；helix：阶梯绕着中间的石柱～而上。*The stairs spiralled round the central pillar.*

wǒ

我 代 ❶ I or me ❷ we or us：～方 *our side*；*we* / ～军 *our army* ❸（used coordinately with 你 in parallel structures）one；anyone：大家你帮～，～帮你，很快就把活儿干完了。*With each one giving the other a hand，they soon got the job done.* ❹ self：自我 ❺（我的）my：～家 *my family* / ～母亲 *my mother* ❻（我们的）our：～国 *our country* / ～家 *our army*

【我辈】〈书〉we or us

【我见】my opinion：以我之见 *in my opinion*

【我们】we or us

【我行我素】persist in one's old ways（no matter what others say）；stick to one's old way of doing things

wò

沃 Ⅰ 形 fertile；rich：肥沃 Ⅱ 动 irrigate：～田 *irrigate farmland*

【沃壤】（又作'沃土'）fertile soil；rich soil

【沃野千里】a thousand li of fertile fields；a vast expanse of fertile land

肟 名［化］oxime

卧 Ⅰ 动 ❶ lie：仰卧 ❷（of animals or birds）crouch；sit ❸〈方〉poach（eggs）：～个鸡子儿 *poach an egg* Ⅱ 形 for sleeping in：卧室

【卧病】be confined to bed；be laid up

【卧舱】sleeping cabin

【卧车】❶ sleeping car；sleeping carriage；sleeper

❷ automobile; car; limousine; sedan
【卧床】❶ (of the old or the sick) lie in bed; be confined to bed: ～休息 rest in bed / ～不起 *bed-ridden; take to one's bed and never rise again* ❷〈方〉bed
【卧倒】drop to the ground; take a prone (or lying-down) position: ～! (*word of command*) *Lie down!* or *Hit the ground!*
【卧底】〈方〉be a planted agent
【卧房】bedroom
【卧佛】reclining Buddha (a huge statue of a recumbent Buddha)
【卧轨】lay oneself on the railway tracks (either to commit suicide or as a form of protest)
【卧具】bedding (provided on a train or ship)
【卧龙】sleeping dragon—a talent in obscurity
【卧铺】sleeping berth; sleeper
【卧射】[军] prone fire
【卧式】[机] horizontal: ～镗床 *horizontal boring machine* / ～发动机 *horizontal engine*
【卧室】bedroom
【卧榻】〈书〉bed
【卧榻之侧,岂容他人鼾睡】how can one tolerate people snoring at one's bedside? —how can one tolerate others encroaching on one's preserve?
【卧薪尝胆】sleep on brushwood and taste gall—undergo self-imposed hardships
【卧姿】[体] prone position

握 动 hold; grasp: ～笔 *hold a writing brush or pen*
【握别】shake hands at parting; part: ～以来,已逾三月。*It is more than three months since we parted.*
【握力】the power of gripping; grip ◇ ～器 [体] spring-grip dumb-bells
【握拳】make a fist; clench one's fist
【握手】shake hands; clasp hands ◇ ～言欢 hold hands and chat cheerfully (esp. in making up a quarrel)

硪 名 a flat stone or iron rammer with ropes attached at the sides

斡 动〈书〉revolve; spin; rotate
【斡旋】❶ mediate: 由于他从中～,双方的争端得到了解决。*Through his mediation the dispute between the two parties was settled.* ❷ [法] good offices

龌 (构词成分)见下
【龌龊】❶ dirty; filthy ❷ base; unprincipled: 卑鄙～ *sordid; foul* ❸〈书〉narrow-minded

wū

乌 Ⅰ 名 crow Ⅱ 形 black; dark: 乌云 —— 另见 wù
【乌鲳】[动] black pomfret
【乌尔都语】Urdu
【乌饭树】oriental blueberry (Vaccinium bracteatum)
【乌干达】Uganda ◇ ～达人 Ugandan
【乌龟】❶ tortoise ❷ cuckold ◇ ～壳 tortoiseshell;〈口〉enemy's pillbox or tank
【乌合之众】a disorderly band; a motley crowd; rabble; mob
【乌黑】pitch-black; jet-black
【乌桕】[植] Chinese tallow tree
【乌克兰】Ukraine ◇ ～人 Ukrainian; ～语 Ukrainian (language)
【乌拉尔】Ural ◇ ～山 the Ural Mountains; the Urals
【乌拉圭】Uruguay ◇ ～人 Uruguayan
【乌鳢】[动] snakehead; snakeheaded fish
【乌亮】glossy black; jet-black: ～的头发 *dark, glossy hair; raven locks*
【乌溜溜】(of eyes) dark and liquid: 一双～的眼睛 *sparkling, black eyes*
【乌龙茶】oolong (tea)
【乌龙球】[体] own goal (in football)
【乌梅】smoked plum; dark plum
【乌木】[植] ebony
【乌七八糟】❶ in a horrible mess; in great disorder ❷ obscene; dirty; filthy: 那本小说里全是些～的东西。*That novel is filled with filth.*
【乌纱帽】❶ black gauze cap (worn by feudal officials) ❷ official post: 丢～ *be dismissed from office*
【乌头】[中] the rhizome of Chinese monkshood (Aconitum carmichaeli)
【乌涂】❶ (of drinking water) lukewarm; tepid ❷ not clear-cut
【乌托邦】Utopia
【乌鸦】crow
【乌烟瘴气】a foul (or pestilential) atmosphere: 搞得～ *create a foul atmosphere; foul things up*
【乌药】[中] the root of three-nerved spicebush (Lindera strychnifolia)
【乌油油】shiny black: ～的头发 *black and glossy hair*
【乌有】〈书〉nothing; naught: ～乡 *Utopia* / 化为～ *come to nothing*
【乌鱼】another name for 乌鳢
【乌云】black clouds; dark clouds: ～遮天。*Black clouds blotted out the sky.* or *The sky was covered with dark clouds.*
【乌枣】smoked jujube; black jujube
【乌贼】[动] cuttlefish; inkfish
【乌孜别克族】the Ozbek (Uzbek) ethnic group, or the Ozbeks (Uzbeks)
【乌兹别克斯坦】Uzbekistan

污 Ⅰ 名 dirt; filth: 血污 Ⅱ 形 ❶ dirty; filthy; foul: 污泥 ❷ corrupt: 贪官污吏 Ⅲ 动 defile; smear: 玷污
【污点】stain; spot; blemish; smirch
【污毒】dirty and noxious

【污垢】dirt; filth
【污秽】〈书〉filthy; foul
【污迹】(又作'污痕')stain; smear; smudge
【污蔑】❶ 同〖诬蔑〗❷ defile; sully; tarnish
【污泥】mud; mire; sludge
【污泥浊水】filth and mire: 荡涤旧社会遗留下来的～ *clean up the filth left by the old society*
【污七八糟】in a filthy mess
【污染】pollute; contaminate: ～地带 *contaminated zone* ◇ ～报警系统 pollution warning system; ～等级 class of pollution; ～计数管 contamination counter; ～控制 pollution control; ～气象学 air pollution meteorology; pollution meteorology; ～物 pollutant; contaminant; ～源 pollution source; ～指示生物 pollution indicating organism
【污辱】❶ humiliate; insult ❷ defile; sully; tarnish
【污水】foul (or polluted, waste) water; sewage; slops: 生活～ *domestic sewage* / ～管 *sewage pipe*; *sewer (pipe)* / ～管道 *sewage conduit*; *sewer line* ◇ ～处理 sewage disposal; sewage treatment; ～处理系统 sewage disposal system; ～灌溉 sewage irrigation; ～净化 sewage purification; ～排放标准 sewage discharge standard
【污浊】(of air, water, etc.) dirty; muddy; foul; filthy

巫 名 shaman; witch; wizard
【巫婆】witch; sorceress
【巫师】wizard; sorcerer
【巫术】witchcraft; sorcery
【巫医】witch doctor

呜 象 toot; hoot; zoom: 轮船上的汽笛～～叫。*The ship's whistle kept hooting.* / 汽车～的一声飞驰而过。*The car zoomed past.*
【呜呼】❶〈古〉alas; alack ❷ die: 一命呜呼
【呜呼哀哉】❶ (formerly usu. used in funeral orations) alas ❷ dead and gone; all is lost
【呜咽】sob; whimper

诬 动 accuse falsely: 诬告
【诬告】(又作'诬控')lodge a false accusation against; bring a false charge against; trump up a charge against: ～案件 *frame-up*; *trumped-up case*
【诬害】injure by spreading false reports about; calumniate; malign
【诬赖】falsely incriminate: ～好人 *incriminate innocent people*
【诬蔑】slander; vilify; calumniate; smear
【诬陷】frame a case against; frame sb.

屋 名 ❶ house: 一座小～ *a small house* ❷ room: ～里坐。*Come in and sit down please.*
【屋顶】roof; housetop ◇ ～花园 roof garden
【屋脊】ridge (of a roof)
【屋架】roof truss
【屋面】roofing: 瓦～ *tile roofing* / ～板 *roof boarding*
【屋上架屋】build one house on top of another—needless duplication
【屋檐】eaves
【屋子】room: 三间～ *three rooms*

钨 名 [化] tungsten; wolfram (W)
【钨钢】wolfram steel; tungsten steel
【钨砂】tungsten ore
【钨丝】tungsten filament: ～灯 *tungsten lamp*

wú

无 Ⅰ 名 nothing; nil: 从无到有 Ⅱ 动 not have; there is not; without: ～一定计划 *without a definite plan* Ⅲ 副 not: ～碍大局 *not affect the situation as a whole* Ⅳ 连 regardless of; no matter whether, what, etc.: 事～大小,都有人负责。*Everything, big and small, is properly taken care of.*
【无伴奏合唱】a cappella
【无被选权】ineligible
【无比】incomparable; unparalleled; matchless: ～的优越性 *incomparable (or unparalleled) superiority* / ～的毅力 *tremendous determination* / ～英勇 *unrivalled in bravery* / ～愤怒 *furiously indignant*
【无边无际】boundless; limitless; vast: ～的大海 *a boundless ocean* / ～的沙漠 *a vast expanse of desert*
【无柄叶】[植] sessile leaf
【无病呻吟】❶ moan and groan without being ill; make a fuss about an imaginary illness ❷ adopt a sentimental pose (in writing or speech)
【无补】of no help; of no avail: 空谈～于实际。*Mere words won't help matters.* ◇ ～于事 of no avail
【无不】all without exception; invariably: 同志们对这种英勇行为～表示钦佩。*All the comrades, without exception, expressed great admiration for this heroic act.* / 大家～为之感动。*None were unmoved.*
【无产阶级】the proletariat ◇ ～文化大革命 the Great Proletarian Cultural Revolution (1966-1977); the Great Cultural Revolution; ～专政 dictatorship of the proletariat; proletarian dictatorship
【无产者】proletarian
【无常】❶ a demon regarded as the messenger of death ❷〈婉〉die: 一旦～万事休。*When death comes, everything is ended.* ❸ variable; changeable: 反复无常 / 变化无常
【无偿】free; gratis; gratuitous: ～援助 *aid given gratis (or gratuitously)* / 提供～经济援助 *render economic assistance gratis*; *give free economic aid*
【无偿付能力】bankruptcy
【无偿还义务】without recourse
【无偿债能力】insolvency

【无成】accomplish nothing：毕生～ *a life of utter failure*

【无耻】shameless；brazen；impudent：～谰言 *shameless slander* ◇ ～之徒 a person who has lost all sense of shame；a shameless person；～之尤 brazen in the extreme；the height of shamelessness

【无酬劳动】［经］unpaid labour

【无出其右】second to none；matchless；unequalled

【无从】have no way（of doing sth.）；not be in a position（to do sth.）：我们不了解情况，～答复这类问题。*As we do not know the facts，we are in no position to answer such questions.* / ～下手 *not know where to start；not know how to set about a job*

【无党派】without party affiliation；nonparty：～人士 *a public figure without party affiliation；nonparty personage*

【无道】not follow the Way；be without principles：～昏君 *an unprincipled，dim-witted ruler*

【无敌】unmatched；invincible；unconquerable ◇ ～于天下 unmatched anywhere in the world；invincible

【无底洞】a bottomless pit

【无地自容】can find no place to hide oneself for shame；feel too ashamed to show one's face；look for a hole to crawl into

【无的放矢】shoot an arrow without a target；shoot at random：批评要有针对性，不要～。*Criticism should have an aim；it shouldn't be undirected.*

【无调性】［音］atonality

【无冬无夏】be it winter or summer —throughout the year；all the year round

【无动于衷】aloof and indifferent；unmoved；untouched；unconcerned：对这种情况，我们不能～。*We cannot remain indifferent in such a situation.* / 他对我的忠告～。*He turned a deaf ear to my advice.*

【无独有偶】it is not unique，but has its counterpart

【无毒不丈夫】every real man has his venom；all great men are ruthless

【无度】immoderate；excessive：饮食～ *excessive*（*or immoderate*）*eating and drinking* / 挥霍～ *squander wantonly*

【无端】for no reason：～侮辱 *a gratuitous insult* / ～气恼 *become angry over nothing* / ～生事 *create a disturbance for no reason；wilfully make trouble*

【无恶不作】stop at nothing in doing evil；stop at no evil；commit all manner of crimes：杀人放火，～ *commit murder，arson and every crime imaginable*

【无法】unable；incapable：～应付 *unable to cope with；at the end of one's resources* / ～形容 *beyond description* / ～解脱的困境 *an inextricable dilemma* / 局势～控制。*The situation was out of control.*

【无法无天】defy laws human and divine；become absolutely lawless；run wild：～的人 *a lawless，ungovernable creature*

【无方】not in the proper way；in the wrong way；not knowing how：经营～ *mismanagement*

【无妨】there's no harm；may（or might）as well：你～试一试。*There's no harm in having a try.* / 我们～同他取得联系。*We might get in touch with him.*

【无纺织物】［纺］adhesive-bonded fabric

【无非】nothing but；no more than；simply；only：我想说的～是那么几句话。*What I want to say is no more than*（*or nothing but*）*this.*

【无风】［气］calm

【无风不起浪】there are no waves without wind；there's no smoke without fire

【无风带】［气］calm belt；calm zone

【无缝钢管】seamless steel tube（or pipe）：～厂 *seamless*（*steel*）*tubing mill*

【无氟冰箱】freon-free refrigerator

【无干】have nothing to do with：这事与你～。*It has nothing to do with you.* or *It's none of your business.*

【无功受禄】get a reward without deserving it

【无辜】❶ not guilty；innocent ❷ an innocent person

【无故】without cause or reason：不得～缺席。*Nobody may be absent without reason.*

【无怪】（又作'无怪乎'）no wonder；not to be wondered at：门是锁着的，～你打不开。*The door was locked. No wonder you couldn't open it.*

【无关】have nothing to do with：此事与他～。*It has nothing to do with him.* ◇ ～大局 not affecting（or having no bearing on）the general situation；insignificant；of little account；～宏旨 insignificant；minor；immaterial；～紧要 of no importance；immaterial

【无关痛痒】of no consequence；immaterial：～的自我批评 *irrelevant or superficial self-criticism* / ～的话 *comment without any bite；irrelevant or pointless remarks* / ～的文章 *innocuous articles*

【无官一身轻】happy is the man who is relieved of his official duties

【无规】［物］random：～介质 *random media* / ～取向 *random orientation*

【无轨电车】trackless trolley；trolleybus

【无国籍】absent nationality；stateless：～者 *a stateless person* / ～状态 *statelessness*

【无害】harmless：这种农药对农作物～。*This pesticide is harmless to crops.*

【无害通过】［法］innocent passage；inoffensive passage

【无何】〈书〉❶ soon；before long ❷ nothing else

【无核】nuclear-free；nonnuclear ◇ ～化 denuclearize；～区 nuclear-free zone；～武器国家（又作'无核国家'）nonnuclear country；～武器区 nuclear-weapon-free zone

【无后】without male offspring；without issue

【无后坐力炮】recoilless gun

【无花果】［植］fig

【无华】simple and unadorned：文章质朴～ *written*

in a simple style
【无话不谈】keep no secrets from each other; be in each other's confidence
【无机】[化] inorganic: ～界 *the inorganic world* ◇ ～肥料 inorganic fertilizer; mineral fertilizer; ～化合物 inorganic compound; ～化学 inorganic chemistry; ～酸 inorganic acid; ～物 inorganic substance; inorganic matter; ～盐 inorganic salts
【无稽】unfounded; fantastic; absurd ◇ ～之谈 an unfounded statement; fantastic talk; sheer nonsense
【无及】it's too late (to do sth.); there's not enough time (to do sth.): 后悔～ *too late to repent*
【无级】[机] stepless: ～调速 *stepless speed regulation* / ～变速装置 *stepless speed change device*
【无疾而终】(of an old person) pass peacefully away
【无几】very few; very little; hardly any: 所剩～。*There's very little left.* / 两人的年岁相差～。*The two are almost the same age.*
【无脊椎动物】invertebrate
【无计可施】have exhausted one's whole bag of tricks; at one's wits' end; at the end of one's resources
【无记名】❶ secret ❷ bearer ◇ ～股票 bearer shares; stock to bearer; ～投票 secret ballot; unsigned vote; ～债券 bearer bond; unregistered bond; ～支票 bearer check; bearer cheque
【无际】boundless; limitless; vast: 一望无际
【无济于事】not help matters; of no help; of no avail; to no effect: 在他病中医生们用了许多办法,但都～。*Many remedies were employed by the physicians in his sickness, but all were of no avail.*
【无家可归】wander about with no home to go to; be homeless
【无价之宝】a priceless treasure; an invaluable asset
【无坚不摧】overrun all fortifications; carry all before one; be all-conquering
【无间】〈书〉❶ not keeping anything from each other; very close to each other: 亲密无间 ❷ continuously; without interruption: 坚持户外锻炼,寒暑～ *keep on doing outdoor exercise all the year round*
【无疆】boundless; limitless: 万寿无疆
【无精打采】listless; in low spirits; out of sorts; lackadaisical: 许多人碰到下雨天就～。*Many people feel listless on rainy days.* / 他不时长吁短叹,～的。*He kept sighing and looked very downcast.*
【无拘无束】unrestrained; unconstrained; free and easy: 在～的气氛中 *in an unconstrained atmosphere* / 大家～地发表意见。*Everyone expressed his views freely.*
【无菌】[医] asepsis ◇ ～操作法 [医] aseptic manipulation; ～装罐 aseptic canning process
【无可比拟】incomparable; unparalleled; matchless; beyond compare: 有史以来～的大变化 *a tremendous change unparalleled in history*
【无可非议】irreproachable; blameless; beyond (or above) reproach; above criticism: 他的行为～。*His conduct is irreproachable (or beyond reproach).*
【无可奉告】no comment
【无可厚非】not be altogether unjustifiable; give little cause for criticism
【无可讳言】there is no hiding (or denying) the fact: 这些都是～的事实。*All these are undeniable (or indisputable) facts.*
【无可救药】同『不可救药』
【无可奈何】have no way out; be utterly helpless; have no alternative: 他虽然每日抱怨,也～了。*Grumble as he might, he had to put up with it.* / 我们～,只得应允。*We had no choice but to give in.*
【无可挽回】irretrievable; irredeemable; irrevocable: ～的损失 *an irretrievable loss*
【无可无不可】not care one way or the other: 对原则问题不应采取～的态度。*One should not take an indifferent (or nonchalant) attitude towards questions of principle.*
【无可争辩】indisputable; irrefutable: ～的事实 *an indisputable (or irrefutable) fact* / 这件事情是非分明,～。*The rights and wrongs of the case are perfectly clear and admit of no dispute.*
【无可置疑】indubitable; unquestionable: 证据充分,～。*The evidence is strong and admits of no doubt.*
【无孔不入】get in by every opening; seize every opportunity: 他是～,有空就钻。*He slips into every opening.* / 广泛的～的宣传 *widespread, all-pervasive propaganda*
【无愧】feel no qualms; have a clear conscience: ～于共产党员的称号 *be worthy of the name of a communist*
【无赖】❶ rascally; scoundrelly; blackguardly: 耍～ *act shamelessly* ❷ rascal
【无理】unreasonable; unjustifiable: ～要求 *unreasonable demands* / ～阻挠 *unjustifiable obstruction* / ～指责 *unwarranted accusations; groundless charges*
【无理方程】[数] irrational equation; radical equation
【无理取闹】wilfully make trouble; be deliberately provocative: 他简直是～。*He's being difficult on purpose.*
【无理式】[数] irrational expression
【无理数】[数] irrational number
【无力】❶ lack strength; feel weak: 四肢～ *feel weak in one's limbs* ❷ unable; incapable; powerless: 一个人是～完成这项任务的。*One person alone can't accomplish this task.* or *No one can do this job single-handed.*
【无量】measureless; immeasurable; boundless: 前途无量

【无虑】worry about nothing; be free from care

【无论】no matter what, how, etc.; regardless of: ～发生什么情况,你都要保持冷静。*Keep calm, whatever happens.*

【无论如何】in any case; at any rate; whatever happens; at all events: 你～得来一趟。*You've got to come, whatever happens.* / 我们～得把丢失的文件找到。*At all costs, we have to find the missing document.*

【无米之炊】cook a meal without rice; make bricks without straw ——另见〖巧妇难为无米之炊〗

【无冕王】a crownless king —reporter

【无名】❶ nameless; unknown ❷ indefinable; indescribable: ～的恐惧 *an indefinable feeling of terror* ◇ ～高地[军] an unnamed hill; ～氏 an anonymous person; ～帖 poison-pen letter; ～小卒 a nobody; nonentity; ～指 the third finger; ring finger; ～肿毒[中] nameless sore or boil

【无名英雄】❶ unknown hero; unsung hero ❷ unknown soldier: ～英雄纪念碑 *monument to the unknown fallen soldiers*

【无明火】(又作'无名火') flames of anger: ～起 *get angry; fly into a rage*

【无奈】❶ cannot help but; have no alternative; have no choice: 他出于～,只得表示同意。*He had no choice but to agree.* ❷ but; however: 他本想来的,～临时有会,来不了。*He had meant to come, but was prevented by an unexpected meeting.*

【无奈何】can do nothing about it: 他整天游手好闲,他母亲也无奈他何。*He just fools around all day long, and his mother can do nothing about it.*

【无能】incompetent; incapable: 教练～,该队屡遭败绩。*The coach was incompetent and the team suffered repeated defeats.*

【无能为力】powerless; helpless; incapable of action: 我对她不幸的遭遇非常同情,可惜～。*I sympathize with her in her misfortune, but I'm afraid I can do nothing to help.* / 这事我～。*That's beyond my power.*

【无期徒刑】life imprisonment: 判处～ *be sentenced to imprisonment for life; be given a life sentence*

【无奇不有】there is no lack of strange things

【无牵无挂】have no cares; be free from care

【无铅汽油】clear gasoline; unleaded gasoline

【无前】❶ unmatched; invincible; unconquerable: 所向无前 ❷ unprecedented: 成绩～ *an unprecedented succes*

【无巧不成书】without coincidences there would be no stories: 真是～,我的顶头上司就是被我在街上撞倒的那个人。*What a coincidence: My immediate superior was the man I had knocked down on the street.*

【无巧不巧】by coincidence; as it happens; as luck would have it: 我正要找他,他自己来了,真是～。*What a coincidence! He came just as I was looking for him.*

【无情】merciless; ruthless; heartless: ～的打击 *a merciless blow* / ～的事实 *harsh reality; hard facts* / 历史的辩证法是～的。*The dialectics of history is inexorable.*

【无穷】infinite; endless; boundless; inexhaustible: ～的烦恼和忧虑 *endless troubles and worries* ◇ ～无尽 inexhaustible; endless

【无穷大】[数] infinitely great; infinity

【无穷小】[数] infinitely small; infinitesimal

【无权】have no right: ～干预 *have no right to interfere* / ～享受豁免 *not be entitled to immunities* ◇ ～追索[法] without recourse

【无缺】intact; whole

【无人】❶ unmanned: ～驾驶飞机 *unmanned plane; pilotless plane; robot plane* ❷ depopulated: ～区 *a depopulated zone* ❸ self-service: ～售书处 *self-service bookstall* ◇ ～地带[军] no man's land; ～问津 nobody troubles to ask; nobody is interested

【无任】〈书〉extremely; immensely: ～感激 *be deeply grateful*

【无日】❶ all the time; not a single day: ～不在想念你。*Not a single day passed without my thinking of you.* ❷ soon; before long

【无伤大雅】not matter much; not affect things as a whole: 他以文才著称,虽然脾气有些古怪,但～。*His claim to fame rests on his literary talents. His eccentric behaviour is considered immaterial.*

【无上】supreme; paramount; highest: ～权力 *supreme power* / ～光荣 *the highest honour*

【无神论】atheism: ～者 *atheist*

【无生代】[地质] the Azoic Era

【无生物】inanimate object; nonliving matter

【无声】noiseless; silent: ～打字机 *noiseless typewriter* ◇ ～片 silent film; ～手枪 pistol with a silencer

【无声无息】unknown; obscure: 不甘心～地过一辈子 *hate to live out one's life unknown*

【无绳电话】cordless (phone)

【无师自通】learn sth. wihout a teacher; be self-taught

【无时无刻】all the time; incessantly: 我们～不在想念你。*You are constantly in our thoughts.* / 登山队员～不在和风雪搏斗。*The mountaineers had to fight the blizzard the whole time.*

【无事不登三宝殿】one never goes to the temple for no reason; I wouldn't come to you if I hadn't something to ask of you

【无事忙】busy oneself over nothing; make much ado about nothing

【无事生非】make trouble out of nothing; be deliberately provocative

【无视】ignore; disregard; defy: ～别国主权 *disregard the sovereignty of other countries* / ～我方的警告 *in defiance of our warning*

【无熟料水泥】[建] clinker-free cement

【无数】❶ innumerable; countless: 天上有～颗星星。*There are innumerable (or countless) stars in the sky.* ❷ not know for certain; be uncertain：这计划是否可行，我心中～。*I'm not too sure whether the plan will work.*

【无双】unparalleled；unrivalled；matchless：举世无双

【无霜期】frost-free period

【无水】［化］anhydrous：～酒精 *absolute alcohol* / ～溶剂 *anhydrous solvent* / ～酸 *anhydrous acid*

【无丝分裂】［植］amitosis

【无私】selfless；disinterested；unselfish：给予～的援助 *give (or render) disinterested assistance* / ～才能无畏。*Only the selfless can be fearless.*

【无损】❶ cannot harm；be harmless；will not lessen：有益～ *can only do good，not harm* ❷ intact；whole；in good condition：那包易碎物品寄到时完好～。*The fragile parcel arrived intact.*

【无梭织机】［纺］shuttleless loom

【无所不包】all-embracing；all-inclusive；all-encompassing

【无所不能】❶ omnipotent ❷ versatile：琴棋书画，～ *be equally adept in music，chess，calligraphy，and painting*

【无所不为】do all manner of evil；stop at nothing：匪徒烧杀掳掠，～。*Stopping at nothing，the bandits massacred，burned and looted.*

【无所不在】omnipresent；ubiquitous

【无所不知】omniscient

【无所不至】❶ penetrate everywhere：细菌活动的范围很广，～。*Bacteria are active practically everywhere.* ❷ spare no pains (usu. to do evil)；be capable of anything；stop at nothing：威胁利诱，～ *use intimidation，bribery and every other means*

【无所事事】be occupied with nothing；have nothing to do；idle away one's time：他们本来可以工作却～。*They were idling about when they might have been working.*

【无所适从】not know what to do；not know whom to turn to：领导意见分歧，群众～。*The leaders are divided，and the rank and file don't know whom to turn to.*

【无所畏惧】fearless；dauntless；undaunted

【无所谓】❶ cannot be called；not deserve the name of：这是随便说的，～什么批评。*It was a passing remark；I didn't mean it as a criticism.* ❷ be indifferent；not matter：采取～的态度 *adopt an indifferent attitude* / 你替他着急，他自己却好像～似的。*You are worried about him，but he himself doesn't seem to care.*

【无所用心】not give serious thought to anything ——另见〖饱食终日，无所用心〗

【无所作为】attempt nothing and accomplish nothing；be in a state of inertia

【无题】no title (used as a title for writings for which the author cannot find，or chooses not to give，a title)：～诗 *a poem without a title；titleless poem*

【无条件】unconditional；without preconditions：建议～地立即举行谈判 *propose that negotiations be held at once without preconditions* ◇ ～反射［生理］unconditional reflex；～投降 unconditional surrender；～转让 absolute conveyance

【无头公案】(又作'无头案') an intricate case without a clue；an unsolved mystery

【无土栽培】soilless culture

【无往不利】go smoothly everywhere；be ever successful：依靠党，依靠群众，工作就～。*Rely on the Party and the masses and you will succeed wherever you go.*

【无往不胜】ever-victorious；invincible

【无妄之灾】an unexpected calamity；an undeserved ill turn

【无望】hopeless：局势已经～。*The situation is hopeless.* / 康复～。*There is no hope of recovery.*

【无微不至】meticulously；in every possible way：他对青年的关怀～。*He takes the greatest care of the youth.*

【无为】(〈字〉"do nothing") inaction；nonaction (a basic concept in Taoism，understood as no unnatural action rather than complete passivity)：～而无不为。*Do nothing and everything is done.* / ～而治 *govern by noninterference*

【无尾礼服】dinner jacket；tuxedo

【无味】❶ tasteless；unpalatable ❷ dull；insipid；uninteresting：语言～ *insipid language；colourless language*

【无畏】fearless；dauntless

【无谓】meaningless；pointless；senseless：～的争吵 *a pointless quarrel* / ～的牺牲 *a meaningless (or senseless) sacrifice* / ～的话 *senseless talk；twaddle*

【无物】empty；devoid of substance：言之无物

【无误】no mistake；errorless：核查～ *checked and found correct*

【无息】interest-free：～贷款 *interest-free loan* / ～信贷 *interest-free credit*

【无隙可乘】no crack to get in by；no loophole to exploit；no weakness to take advantage of；no chink in one's armour

【无暇】have no time；be too busy：～顾及 *have no time to attend to* / ～他顾 *be too busy to attend to other things*

【无瑕】flawless：完美～ *perfect；flawless*

【无限】infinite；limitless；boundless；immeasurable：～光明的未来 *a future of incomparable brightness* / ～忠诚 *boundless loyalty；absolute loyalty；absolute devotion*

【无限大】同〖无穷大〗

【无限公司】unlimited company

【无限花序】［植］indefinite inflorescence

【无限期】indefinite duration：～罢工 *a strike of indefinite duration* / ～搁置动议 *shelve a motion sine die* / ～休会 *adjourn indefinitely；adjourn sine die*

【无限小】同〖无穷小〗

【无限制】unrestricted；unbridled；unlimited

【无线】wireless ◇ ～电报 wireless telegram；radiotelegram；～电话 radiotelephone；radiophone

【无线电】radio；wireless ◇ ～测向器 radio direction finder; radio goniometer; ～传真 radiofacsimile; ～导航 radio navigation～发射机 radio transmitter; ～干扰 radio jamming; ～跟踪 radio tracking; ～收发两用机 transceiver; ～收音机 radio receiver; ～探空仪 radiosonde; ～天文学 radio astronomy; ～通信 radio communication; wireless communication; ～遥测 radio telemetry; ～遥控 wireless remote control

【无效】of (or to) no avail; invalid; null and void: 医治～ *fail to respond to medical treatment* / 宣布合同～ *declare a contract invalid* (*or null and void*); *invalidate* (*or nullify*) *a contract* / 宣布选举～ *nullify an election* ◇ ～分蘖［农］ineffective tillering; ～劳动 fruitless labour; labour lost

【无懈可击】with no chink in one's armour; unassailable; invulnerable: 这篇文章论证周密,～。*The article is closely reasoned and the arguments are unassailable.*

【无心】❶ not be in the mood for: 他工作还没做完,～去看电影。*He was in no mood to go to the film, as he hadn't finished his work.* ❷ not intentionally; unwittingly; inadvertently: 他说这话是～的,你可别见怪。*Don't take offence. He didn't say it intentionally.*

【无行】〈书〉be a man of loose conduct: 文人无行

【无形】invisible; intangible: ～资产 *intangible asset* / ～利益 *intangible benefit* / ～损耗 *nonphysical wear*

【无形中】imperceptibly; virtually: 这～成了风气。*This has imperceptibly become a common practice.* / 他～成了我的助手。*He's virtually become my assistant.*

【无性】［生］asexual ◇ ～繁殖 vegetative propagation;cloning; ～生殖 asexual reproduction; ～世代 asexual generation; ～杂交 asexual (or vegetative) hybridization

【无休止】ceaseless; endless: ～地争论 *argue on and on*

【无须】(又作'无须乎') need not; not have to: ～顾虑 *need not worry* / ～细说。*It's unnecessary to go into details.*

【无需】(又作'无需乎') 同〖无须〗

【无涯】boundless; limitless: 一望～ *stretching beyond the horizon; boundless*

【无烟工业】smokeless industry (e. g. tourism , dlectronics, tele communications, etc.)

【无烟火药】smokeless powder; ballistite

【无烟煤】anthracite

【无烟区】a smokeless zone

【无言以对】have nothing to say in reply

【无颜见江东父老】cannot bear to see again the elders east of the river—be ashamed to go back to one's people after a defeat or failure

【无恙】〈书〉in good health; well; safe: 安然无恙 / 别来无恙

【无业】❶ be out of work; be unemployed ❷ have no property ◇ ～游民 vagrant

【无依无靠】have no one to depend on (or to turn to); be helpless: ～的孤儿 *a helpless orphan*

【无遗】nothing left: 破坏～ *be totally destroyed*

【无疑】beyond doubt; undoubtedly: 这种行为～是错误的。*Such conduct is undoubtedly wrong.* / 确凿～ *well established and irrefutable*

【无已】〈书〉❶ endlessly; incessantly: 赞叹～ *praise again and again; be profuse in praise* ❷ have no alternative but to; have to

【无以复加】in the extreme: 荒谬到了～的地步 *be absurd in the extreme*

【无以为生】have no means of livelihood; have no means of support

【无异】not different from; tantamount to; as good as: 这件复制品几乎与原作～。*The reproduction is almost as good as the original.* / 他撤回声明～于表示歉意。*The withdrawal of his statement is tantamount to an apology.*

【无益】unprofitable; useless; no good: 读这种无聊的东西非但～,而且有害。*Reading that trash is not only unprofitable but harmful.*

【无意】❶ have no intention (of doing sth.); not be inclined to: ～参加 *have no intention of joining* / ～于此 *not interested in that; not keen on it* ❷ inadvertently; unwittingly; accidentally: 他们在挖井时,～中发现了一些古代文物。*While digging a well they accidentally unearthed some ancient relics.*

【无意识】unconscious: ～的动作 *an unconscious act* (*or movement*)

【无翼鸟】kiwi

【无垠】〈书〉boundless; vast: 一望～的草原 *a boundless prairie*

【无影灯】［医］shadowless lamp

【无影无踪】without a trace: 那小偷早跑得～了。*The thief had disappeared without a trace.*

【无庸】need not ◇ ～讳言 no need for reticence; ～赘述 there is no need to go into details; it is pointless to belabour the obvious

【无用】useless; of no use

【无用能】［机］unavailable energy

【无忧无虑】free from care; free from all anxieties; carefree

【无由】〈书〉not be in a position (to do sth.); have no way (of doing sth.)

【无余】nothing left: 一览无余

【无与伦比】incomparable; unparalleled; peerless; unique; without equal: 他在地质学方面的贡献是～的。*His contribution in the field of geology was unparalleled.*

【无原则】unprincipled: ～纠纷 *an unprincipled dispute*

【无援】have no support; be cut off from help

【无缘】❶ have not the chance or luck (to do sth.): 久闻大名,但恨～拜识。*I have long been aware of your exalted name, and I regret never getting a chance to make your acquaintance.* / 我和酒～。*I never touch the bottle.* ❷ have no way (of doing sth.); not be in a position (to do sth.)

【无缘无故】 without cause or reason; without rhyme or reason; for no reason at all: 世上决没有～的爱,也没有～的恨。*There is absolutely no such thing in the world as love or hate without cause or reason.*

【无源】[无] passive: ～天线 *passive antenna*

【无源之水,无本之木】 water without a source, a tree without roots

【无韵诗】 blank verse

【无照】 without a licence: ～营业 *do business without a licence*

【无政府主义】 anarchism

【无知】 ignorant: 出于～ *out of ignorance*

【无止境】 have no limits; know no end: 科学的发展是～的。*The development of science has no limits.*

【无中生有】 purely fictitious; fabricated: 纯粹是～,当面造谣。*Nothing but rumours fabricated out of thin air and brazen lies.*

【无重力】 space agravic: ～状态 *null-gravity state*

【无着】 ❶ nowhere: 寻找～ *nowhere to be found; whereabouts unknown* ❷ unassured: 生活～ *have one's livelihood unassured*

【无足轻重】 of little importance (or consequence); insignificant: ～的人物 *a nobody; a nonentity* / 他们看不起我们,认为～。*They looked down upon us as of little importance.* / 此事～。*It's a matter of no consequence.*

【无阻】 without hindrance; unimpeded: 拿着这张通行证就可以通行～。*This pass will let you through.*

【无罪】 innocent; not guilty: ～释放 *set a person free with a verdict of "not guilty"*

【无坐力炮】 同〖无后坐力炮〗

毋 副〈书〉no; not: ～令逃逸。*You must not let him escape.*

【毋宁】 rather...(than); (not so much...) as: 与其固守,～出击。*Better to strike out than to entrench oneself in defence.*

【毋庸】 同〖无庸〗

吾 代〈书〉I or me; we or us: ～国 *my or our country*

【吾辈】〈书〉we or us

【吾人】〈书〉we or us

芜 Ⅰ 形〈书〉❶ overgrown with weeds: 荒芜 ❷ mixed and disorderly; miscellaneous: 芜词 Ⅱ 名 grassland

【芜词】 superfluous words

【芜菁】[植] turnip

【芜杂】 (of writing) mixed and disorderly; jumbled

梧 (构词成分)见下

【梧桐】 Chinese parasol (tree); phoenix tree

蜈 (构词成分)见下

【蜈蚣】 centipede

【蜈蚣草】 ciliate desert-grass (Eremochloa ciliaris)

鼯 (构词成分)见下

【鼯鼠】 flying squirrel

wǔ

五 Ⅰ 数 five: ～公斤 *five kilos* / ～个班 *five classes* / ～班 *the fifth class; class 5* / ～路公共汽车 *No. 5 bus* Ⅱ 名 [音] a note of the scale in gongchepu (工尺谱), corresponding to 6 in numbered musical notation

【五保户】 a household enjoying the five guarantees (childless and infirm old persons who are guaranteed food, clothing, medical care, housing and burial expenses)

【五倍子】[中] Chinese gall; gallnut ◇ ～虫 gall makers

【五边形】 pentagon

【五步蛇】 long-noded pit viper

【五彩】 ❶ the five colours (blue, yellow, red, white and black) ❷ multicoloured ◇ ～缤纷 colourful; blazing with colour

【五重唱】[音] (vocal) quintet

【五重奏】[音] (instrumental) quintet

【五大三粗】 big and tall; tall and stalwart; strapping

【五斗柜】(又作'五屉橱') chest of drawers

【五毒】 ❶ the five poisonous creatures (scorpion, viper, centipede, house lizard and toad) ❷ the "five evils"

【五短身材】 (of a man) squat

【五方】 the five directions (i.e. the four cardinal points and the centre)

【五方杂处】 (of a big city) be inhabited by people from all parts; have a mixed (or cosmopolitan) population

【五分制】 the five-grade marking system

【五更】 ❶ the five watches (or periods) of the night ❷ the fifth watch of the night; just before dawn: 起～,睡半夜 *retire at midnight and rise before dawn*

【五谷】 ❶ the five cereals (rice, two kinds of millet, wheat and beans) ❷ food crops ◇ ～不分 见〖四体不勤,五谷不分〗; ～丰登 an abundant harvest of all food crops; a bumper grain harvest

【五官】 ❶ [中] the five sense organs (ears, eyes, lips, nose and tongue) ❷ facial features ◇ ～端正 have regular features

【五光十色】 ❶ multicoloured; bright with many colours ❷ of great variety; of all kinds; multifarious

【五合板】 five-ply board; plywood

【五湖四海】 all corners of the land: 来自～ *hail from all corners of the country*

【五花八门】 multifarious; of a wide (or rich) variety

【五花大绑】 tie a person's hands behind his back with a rope that is looped round his neck

【五花肉】 streaky pork

【五级风】［气］force 5 wind；fresh breeze
【五极管】［电子］pentode
【五加】［植］slender acanthopanax（Acanthopanax gracilistylus）
【五加皮】❶［中］bark of the slender acanthopanax ❷ a medicinal wine made by soaking the bark of the slender acanthopanax in liquor
【五讲四美】Five Stresses and Four Points of Beauty
【五角大楼】the Pentagon
【五角星】five-pointed star
【五金】❶ the five metals（gold，silver，copper，iron and tin）❷ metals；hardware：～店 *hardware store* / ～商 *dealer in hardware*；*ironmonger*
【五经】the Five Classics，namely，The Book of Songs（《诗经》），The Book of History（《书经》），The Book of Changes（《易经》），The Book of Rites（《礼记》），and The Spring and Autumn Annals（《春秋》）
【五局三胜制】［体］best of give games；three out of five sets
【五绝】（〈略〉全称为‘五言绝句’）pentasyllabic（or five-syllable）quatrain
【五劳七伤】［中］general debility
【五里雾】thick fog—bewilderment
【五敛子】［植］carambola（Averrhoa carambola）the fruit of carambola；star fruit
【五律】（〈略〉全称为‘五言律诗’）pentasyllabic（or five-syllable）regulated verse ——另见〖律诗〗
【五氯硝基苯】［农］pentachloronitrobenzene；PCNB
【五伦】the five human relationships（i.e. between ruler and subject 君臣，father and son 父子，husband and wife 夫妇，brothers 兄弟，and friends 朋友）
【五马分尸】dismemberment by five horses—dividing up；sharing out
【五内】〈书〉viscera
【五内如焚】one's heart rent with grief；one's heart torn by anxiety
【五年计划】Five-Year Plan
【五日京兆】（of an official）not expecting to remain long in office；holding office only for a brief period
【五卅运动】the May 30th Movement（1925）
【五色】同〖五彩〗
【五色斑斓】a riot of colour
【五声音阶】［音］five-tone scale；pentatonic scale
【五十步笑百步】one who retreats fifty paces mocks one who retreats a hundred—the pot calls the kettle black
【五四青年节】Youth Day（May 4）
【五四运动】the May 4th Movement of 1919
【五体投地】prostrate oneself before sb.：佩服得～ *prostrate oneself before sb. in admiration*；*admire sb. from the bottom of one's heart*；*worship sb.*
【五味】❶ the five flavours（sweet，sour，bitter，pungent and salty）❷ all sorts of flavours
【五味子】［中］the fruit of Chinese magnoliavine（Schisandra chinensis）
【五线谱】［音］staff；stave
【五香】❶ the five spices（prickly ash，star aniseed，cinnamon，clove and fennel）❷ spices
【五香豆】spiced beans
【五项全能运动】［体］pentathlon
【五星红旗】the Five-Starred Red Flag（the national flag of the People's Republic of China）
【五星级】five-star：～旅馆 *a five-star hotel*
【五星上将】five-star general（referring to the U. S. General of the Army，Fleet Admiral and General of the Air Force）
【五行】the five elements（metal，wood，water，fire and earth）
【五言诗】a poem with five characters to a line ——另见〖古体诗〗；〖绝句〗；〖律诗〗
【五颜六色】of various（or all）colours；multicoloured；colourful：～的云霞 *clouds of many colours* / 一叠～的纸 *a heap of papers of various colours*
【五一国际劳动节】May 1，International Labour Day；May Day
【五音】［音］the five notes of the ancient Chinese five-tone scale
【五月】❶ May ❷ the fifth month of the lunar year；the fifth moon ◇ ～节（又作‘端午节’）the Dragon Boat Festival（the 5th day of the 5th lunar month）
【五脏】［中］the five internal organs（heart，liver，spleen，lungs and kidneys）◇ ～六腑 the internal organs of the body；the viscera
【五指】the five fingers（thumb，index finger，middle finger，third finger and little finger）
【五洲】the five continents；the whole world
【五子棋】gobang

午 名 ❶ noon；midday ❷ the seventh of the twelve Earthly Branches（地支）——另见〖干支〗
【午餐】midday meal；lunch ◇ ～肉（pork）luncheon meat
【午饭】midday meal；lunch
【午后】afternoon
【午间】noon；midday
【午觉】afternoon nap；noontime snooze
【午前】forenoon；before noon；morning
【午时】（又作‘午刻’）the period of the day from 11 a.m. to 1 p.m.
【午睡】❶ afternoon nap；noontime snooze ❷ take（or have）a nap after lunch
【午休】noon break；midday rest；noontime rest；lunch hour
【午宴】luncheon
【午夜】midnight

伍 Ⅰ 数 five（used for the numeral 五 on cheques，banknotes，etc. to avoid mistakes or alterations）Ⅱ 名 ❶ the basic five-man unit of the army in ancient China；army：入伍 ❷ company：羞与为伍

妩（构词成分）见下

【妩媚】(of a woman) lovely; charming：唐小姐～端正的圆脸，有两个浅酒窝。*On Miss Tang's charming, well-proportioned round face were two shallow dimples.*

忤 形 ❶ disobedient ❷ uncongenial：与人无～ *bear no ill will against anybody*

【忤逆】disobedient (to parents)

武 形 ❶ military：黩武 / 尚武 ❷ connected with boxing skill, swordplay, etc.：武术 ❸ valiant; fierce：威武

【武备】〈书〉defence preparations, specifically the condition of the armed forces and armaments

【武昌鱼】［动］blunt-snout bream (Megalobrama amblycephala)

【武丑】(in traditional opera) a comedian in military plays (武戏)

【武打】acrobatic fighting in Chinese opera or dance ◇ ～片 martial arts film; Kung-fu film

【武斗】resort to violence (in a debate, dispute, etc.)

【武断】arbitrary; subjective assertion：这样说太～了。*This is a subjective assertion.*

【武夫】❶ a man of great physical prowess ❷ soldier; military man

【武功】〈书〉military accomplishments (or achievements)

【武官】❶ military officer ❷ military attaché ◇ ～处［外交］military attaché's office

【武行】(in traditional opera) specialists in acrobatics (actors who take minor parts in military combats)

【武火】high heat (in cooking)

【武将】military officer; general

【武警】〈略〉见『武装警察』

【武力】❶ force ❷ military force; armed might; armed strength; force of arms：～镇压 *armed suppression*

【武林】(又作'武坛') martial arts circles

【武器】weapon; arms：放下～ *lay down one's arms* / 拿起～ *take up arms* ◇ ～禁运 arms embargo; ～库（又作'武库'）arsenal; armoury; ～装备 weaponry

【武师】a man versed in martial arts; martial arts master

【武士】❶ palace guards in ancient times ❷ man of prowess; warrior; knight ◇ ～俑 warrior figure

【武术】wushu, martial arts such as shadowboxing, swordplay, etc., formerly cultivated for self-defence, now a form of physical culture

【武戏】(in traditional opera) military plays (〈反〉文戏)

【武侠】a person adept in martial arts and given to chivalrous conduct (in olden times) ◇ ～小说 swordsman fiction; knight-errant fiction

【武艺】skill in wushu ——另见『武术』

【武职】military post

【武装】❶ arms; military equipment; battle outfit：全副～ *fully armed; in full battle gear* / ～人员 *armed personnel* ❷ armed forces：～夺取政权 *seizure of power by armed force* ❸ equip (or supply) with arms; arm：～到牙齿 *be armed to the teeth* ◇ ～部队 armed forces; ～冲突 armed clash; ～带 Sam Browne belt; ～斗争 armed struggle; ～干涉 armed intervention; ～警察 armed police; ～力量 armed power; armed forces; ～起义 armed uprising (or insurrection); ～泅渡 swim with one's weapons; swim in battle gear

侮 动 insult; bully：欺侮

【侮骂】abuse; call sb. names; hurl insults

【侮慢】slight; treat disrespectfully

【侮蔑】despise; look down on

【侮辱】insult; humiliate; subject sb. to indignities

捂 动 seal; cover; muffle：～鼻子 *cover one's nose with one's hand* / ～着耳朵 *stop one's ears*

【捂盖子】keep the lid on—try to cover up the truth (about a crime, etc.)

【捂捂盖盖】〈方〉try to cover up; hedge and dodge：有了错误不能～。*You shouldn't try to cover up your mistakes.*

舞 Ⅰ 名 dance：交谊舞 Ⅱ 动 ❶ move about as in a dance：手舞足蹈 ❷ dance with sth. in one's hands：舞剑 ❸ flourish; wield; brandish：挥舞

【舞伴】dancing partner

【舞弊】fraudulent practices; malpractices; irregularities; embezzlement：我们在清查账目时发现了他的～行为。*We discovered his irregularities while checking the accounts.*

【舞步】step (in dancing)

【舞场】dance hall; ballroom

【舞蹈】dance：～动作 *dance movement* / ～家 *dancer* / ～设计 *choreography*

【舞蹈病】［医］chorea

【舞动】wave; brandish

【舞会】dance; ball：举行～ *hold a dance*

【舞剑】perform a sword-dance

【舞剧】dance drama; ballet

【舞客】dance hall customer

【舞弄】wave; wield; brandish：～刀枪 *brandish swords and spears*

【舞女】dancing girl; dance-hostess; taxi dancer

【舞曲】dance music; dance

【舞台】stage; arena：～设计 *stage design* / ～效果 *stage effect* / ～艺术 *stagecraft* / 政治～ *political arena (or scene, stage)* / 在国际～上 *in the international arena* ◇ ～记录片 stage documentary

【舞厅】dance hall; ballroom

【舞文弄法】pervert the law by playing with legal phraseology

【舞文弄墨】engage in phrase-mongering

【舞艺】(又作'舞技') dancing skill

【舞姿】a dancer's posture and movements

wù

兀 形〈书〉❶ rising to a height; towering ❷ bald
【兀鹫】[动] griffon vulture
【兀立】stand upright
【兀自】still

乌 (构词成分)见下 ——另见 wū
【乌拉】leather boots lined with wula sedge
【乌拉草】[植] wula sedge

勿 副 (used in prohibitions, admonitions, etc.) do not; never: 请~入内 *No Admittance* / 请~吸烟。*No Smoking*.
【勿忘草】forget-me-not (Myosotis sylvatica)
【勿谓言之不预】do not say that you have not been forewarned; do not blame us for not having forewarned you
【勿以善小而不为,勿以恶小而为之】don't fail to do good even if it's small; don't engage in evil even if it's small

戊 名 the fifth of the ten Heavenly Stems (天干) ——另见〖干支〗

务 Ⅰ 名 affair; business: 公务 Ⅱ 动 be engaged in; devote one's efforts to: 务农 Ⅲ 副 must; be sure to: ~使大家明了这一点。*Be sure to make this point clear to everyone*. / ~请光临指导。*You are cordially invited to come and give guidance*.
【务必】must; be sure to: 你~在本周内去看望他一次。*Be sure to go and see him before the week is out*.
【务农】be engaged in agriculture; be a farmer
【务求】must; be sure to: 此事~妥善解决。*We must find a satisfactory solution to the problem*.
【务实】deal with concrete matters relating to work; be pragmatic: ~的政府 *a pragmatically-inclined government*
【务使】make sure; ensure: ~老年人得到适当照顾 *ensure that old people are properly cared for*
【务虚】discuss principles or ideological guidelines

芴 名 [化] fluorene

杌 名〈方〉a square stool
【杌子】〈方〉a square stool

坞 名 ❶ a depressed place: 船坞 ❷〈书〉a fortified building; castle

物 名 ❶ thing; matter: 公物 ❷ the outside world as distinct from oneself; other people: 待人接物 ❸ content; substance: 言之无物
【物产】products; produce
【物腐虫生】worms breed in decaying matter
【物故】〈书〉pass away; die
【物归原主】return sth. to its rightful owner
【物候学】phenology
【物化】〈书〉pass away; die
【物换星移】things change and the stars move—change of the seasons
【物极必反】things turn into their opposites when they reach the extreme
【物价】(commodity) prices: ~稳定。*Prices remain stable*. ◇ ~补贴 subsidies paid out to compensate for price rises; ~上涨 inflation of price; price rise; ~上涨指数 index of price rises; ~统计 statistics of prices ~政策 pricing policy; ~指数 price index
【物件】thing; article
【物尽其用】make the best use of everything; let all things serve their proper purpose
【物镜】[物] objective (lens)
【物理】❶ innate laws of things ❷ physics ◇ ~变化 physical change; ~化学 physical chemistry; ~疗法 physical therapy; physiotherapy; ~性质 physical property; ~诊断 physical diagnosis
【物理学】physics: 低温~ *low temperature physics* / 地球~ *geophysics* / 高能~ *high energy physics* / 固体~ *solide state physics* / 理论~ *theoretical physics* / 天体~ *astrophysics* / 应用~ *applied physics* / 原子~ *atomic physics* / 原子核~ *nuclear physics* ◇ ~家 physicist
【物力】material resources; materiel: 节约人力~ *use manpower and material resources sparingly*
【物美价廉】同〖价廉物美〗
【物品】article; goods: 贵重~ *valuables* / 零星~ *sundries; odds and ends* / 免税~ *duty-free articles* / 随身携带的~ *things carried on one's person* / 违禁~ *contraband* / 应上税~ *dutiable article* / 自用~ *personal effects*
【物色】look for; seek out; choose: ~这方面的人才 *look for qualified persons in this field*
【物伤其类】like feels for like ——另见〖兔死狐悲〗
【物体】body; substance; object: 运动~ *a body in motion* / 透明~ *a transparent substance (or object)*
【物象】❶ image ❷ visible phenomena
【物以类聚,人以群分】things of a kind come together, people of a mind fall into the same group; like attracts like; birds of a feather flock together
【物以稀为贵】When a thing is scarce, it is precious.
【物欲】material desires
【物证】material evidence
【物质】❶ matter; substance: ~形体有三种:气体、液体、固体。*All matter has one of three forms: gas, liquid, or solid*. ❷ material: ~财富 *material wealth* / ~储备 *reserve supply; stockpile* / ~条件 *material conditions or prerequisites* / ~享受 *material comforts* / ~资料 *material goods* ◇ ~不灭定律 the law of conservation of matter; ~刺激 material incentive; ~鼓励 material

reward; material incentive; ～基础 material base; ～生活 material life; ～世界 the material (or physical) world; ～文明 material civilization; ～性[哲] materiality; ～运动 the motion of matter

【物种】[生] species

【物主】owner (esp. of lost or stolen property)

【物资】goods and materials: ～调度 *distribution of materials* / ～管理 *handling of goods and materials* / ～交流 *interflow of commodities*

误 Ⅰ 动 ❶ mistake; error: ～把友谊当爱情 *mistake friendship for love* ❷ miss: ～了火车 *miss a train* ❸ hinder; impede: 生产学习两不～。*Neither production nor study is to suffer*. Ⅱ 副 by mistake; by accident: 误伤

【误差】error: ～不超过千分之三毫米 *with a tolerance of less than three-thousandths of a millimetre* / 平均～ *mean error*; *average error* / 仪器～ *instrumental error* / 概然～ *probable error* ◇ ～函数 error function; ～率 error rate

【误场】(of an actor) fail to turn up for the show

【误导】mislead; lead astray

【误点】late; overdue; behind schedule: 飞机～了。*The plane is overdue* (*or late*). / 火车～十分钟。*The train was ten minutes late* (*or behind schedule*).

【误工】❶ delay one's work ❷ loss of working time

【误国】endanger the realm

【误会】❶ misunderstand; mistake; misconstrue: 你～了我的意思。*You've mistaken my meaning*. ❷ misunderstanding: 小小的～ *a minor misunderstanding*

【误解】❶ misread; misunderstand: 你～了我的话。*You misunderstood what I said*. ❷ misunderstanding: 产生～ *produce misunderstanding* / 消除～ *clear up a misunderstanding*

【误期】exceed the time limit; be behind schedule: 这项工程～了。*The project is behind schedule*.

【误区】misunderstandings; the wrong region

【误人子弟】(of a teacher) harm the younger generation; lead young people astray

【误入歧途】go astray

【误杀】[法] manslaughter

【误伤】❶ accidentally injure ❷ accidental injury

【误信】wrongly believe; be misled

【误事】❶ cause delay in work or business; hold things up ❷ bungle matters

【误信】wrongly believe; be misled

【误诊】make a wrong diagnosis: ～病例 *missed case*

悟 动 realize; awaken: ～出其中的道理 *realize why it should be so*

【悟道】awake to the truth; attain enlightenment: ～之言 *enlightened views*

【悟解】understand; comprehend; grasp

【悟性】power of understanding; comprehension

恶 动 loathe; dislike; hate: 好～ *likes and dislikes* / 可～ *loathsome*; *hateful*——另见 ě; è

【恶寒】[中] aversion to cold

晤 动 meet; interview; see: 会晤

【晤面】(又作'晤见') meet; see

【晤谈】meet and talk; have a talk; interview

焐 动 warm up: 把被褥～热 *warm up the bedding* / 用热水袋～一～手 *warm one's hands with a hot-water bottle*

痦 (构词成分)见下

【痦子】[医] naevus; mole

骛 动 〈书〉 ❶ move about freely and quickly; sweep through the length and breadth ❷ go after; seek for: 好高骛远

雾 名 ❶ fog: 中午时分～就散了。*Around midday, the fog lifted*. ❷ fine spray: 喷雾器

【雾霭】〈书〉 fog; mist; vapour

【雾标】fog buoy

【雾沉沉】misty; foggy: 天气～的,我不得不开得很慢。*It was very foggy. I had to drive very slowly*.

【雾滴】[环保] droplet

【雾虹】fogbow

【雾化】atomize ◇ ～器 atomizer

【雾里看花】look at flowers in a fog—a blurred vision

【雾茫茫】misty; foggy: 山上～的,只看见一个模糊的轮廓。*The mountains were covered in thick mist and only a faint outline could be seen*.

【雾气】fog; mist; vapour

【雾凇】[气] (soft) rime: ～雾 *rime fog*

【雾腾腾】misty; foggy: 水面上～的。*There's cloud of mist over the water*.

鹜 名 〈书〉 duck: 趋之若鹜

X

xī

夕 名 ❶ sunset：夕阳 / 朝发夕至 ❷ evening; night：风雨之～ *a stormy night*

【夕晖】evening twilight

【夕烟】evening mist

【夕阳】the evening sun; the setting sun：～反照 *evening (or sunset) glow* ◇ ～产业(又作'夕阳工业')sunset industry

【夕照】the glow of the setting sun; evening glow

汐 名 tide during the night; nighttide

西 Ⅰ 名 west：～屋 *west room* / ～海岸 *the west coast* / 太原以～ *to the west of Taiyuan* / 往～去 *head west* Ⅱ 形 Occidental; Western：西服 / 西药

【西班牙】Spain ◇ ～人 a Spaniard; the Spanish; ～语 Spanish (language)

【西半球】the Western Hemisphere

【西北】❶ northwest ❷ northwest China; the Northwest (including Shaanxi, Gansu, Qinghai, Ningxia, and Xinjiang)

【西北风】northwest wind; northwesterly wind

【西边】同〖西面〗

【西伯利亚】Siberia

【西部】west ◇～片 western film; cowboy movie

【西餐】Western-style food ◇ ～馆 a restaurant which serves Western food

【西点】Western-style pastry

【西法】Western method：～洗染 *Western method of laundering and dyeing*

【西番莲】❶ passionflower ❷ dahlia

【西方】❶ the west ❷ the West; the Occident：～国家 *the Western countries*

【西非】West Africa

【西风】❶ west wind; westerly wind ❷ autumn wind ❸〈喻〉decaying influences ◇ ～带 westerlies

【西服】Western-style clothes; suit ◇～料 suiting

【西府海棠】[植] midget crabapple

【西瓜】watermelon

【西瓜子】watermelon seed

【西红柿】同〖番茄〗

【西湖】the West Lake

【西葫芦】[植] pumpkin; summer squash

【西化】be westernized：向西方学习不等于全盘～。*To learn from the West does not mean to be completely westernized.*

【西经】west longitude：～一百六十五度 *longitude 165°W.*

【西历】〈旧〉the Gregorian calendar

【西米】[植] sago

【西面】west：电影院～(*to the*) *west of the cinema* / 剧场在商店的～。*The theatre is to the west of the store.* / ～的窗子 *a window facing west*

【西南】❶ southwest ❷ southwest China; the Southwest (including Sichuan, Yunnan, Guizhou, and Tibet)

【西南风】southwest wind; southwesterly wind

【西欧】Western Europe

【西皮】one of the two chief types of music in traditional Chinese operas

【西撒哈拉】Western Sahara

【西萨摩亚】Western Samoa

【西沙群岛】the Xisha Islands

【西晒】(of a room) have a western exposure (hot on summer afternoons)

【西施】❶ the name of a famous beauty in the late Spring and Autumn Period ❷ a beautiful woman; a beauty：情人眼里出西施

【西式】Western style：～点心 *Western-style pastry*

【西天】❶ Western Heaven (ancient Chinese Buddhists-name for India) ❷ [宗](佛教) Western Paradise ——另见〖上西天〗

【西学】Western learning (a late Qing Dynasty term for Western natural and social sciences)

【西亚】(又作'西南亚') Southwest Asia

【西洋】the West; the Western world：～文学 *Western literature* ◇ ～画 Western painting; ～人 Westerner; ～参 American ginseng (Panax quinquefolium); ～史 history of the Western world (or Western countries)

【西洋景】(又作'西洋镜') ❶ peep show ❷ hanky-panky; trickery：拆穿～ *expose sb.'s tricks; strip off the camouflage*

【西药】Western medicine

【西医】❶ Western medicine (as distinguished from traditional Chinese medicine) ❷ a doctor trained in Western medicine

【西印度群岛】the West Indies

【西语】❶ Western languages：～系 *the Department of Western Languages* ❷〈略〉见〖西班牙语〗

【西乐】Western music

【西岳】the Western Mountain (another name for

华山 Mount Hua in Shaanxi Province）

【西藏】Tibet ◇～自治区 the Tibet Autonomous Region

【西装】Western-style clothes；suit

吸 动 ❶ inhale；breathe in；draw：～进新鲜空气 *inhale fresh air* / 深深～一口气 *draw a deep breath* ❷ suck（liquids）：～奶 *suck milk*；*nurse* / 蚊子～人血。*Mosquitoes suck human blood.* ❸ absorb；suck up：用粉笔把墨水～干 *blot ink with a piece of chalk* / 海绵～水。*A sponge absorbs water.* ❹ attract；draw to oneself：磁石～铁。*A magnet attracts iron.*

【吸尘器】dust catcher；dust collector：真空～ *vacuum cleaner*

【吸虫】fluke：肺～ *lung fluke* / 肝～ *liver fluke*

【吸毒】take addictive drugs；be addicted to a narcotic ◇～者 drug addict；narcotic addict

【吸附】［化］adsorb：～作用 *adsorption* / 活性炭～毒气和液体中的杂质。*Active carbon adsorbs poisonous gases and impurities in liquids.* ◇～剂 adsorbent；～器 adsorber；～水 adsorbed water

【吸管】straw

【吸力】suction；attraction：相互～ *mutual attraction* ◇～计 suction gauge

【吸墨纸】blotting paper

【吸纳】absorb；draw；attract：今年总共～社会游资 120 亿。12 *billion yuan of hot money has been absorbed this year.*

【吸奶器】breast pump

【吸泥泵】dredge pump

【吸盘】sucking disc（of certain animals）；sucker

【吸取】absorb；draw；assimilate：～水分 *absorb water* / ～精华 *absorb the quintessence* / ～教训 *draw a lesson*

【吸热】absorption of heat ◇～反应［化］endothermic reaction

【吸声】sound-absorbing；acoustic：～材料 *sound-absorbing material* / ～瓷砖 *acoustic tiles*

【吸湿】moisture-absorbing ◇～剂 hygroscopic agent；moisture absorbent；～性 hygroscopicity；moisture absorbency

【吸食】suck；take in（liquid foods，narcotic drugs，etc.）

【吸收】❶ absorb；suck up；assimilate；imbibe；draw：～养分 *assimilate nutriment* / ～水分 *suck up moisture* / ～知识 *absorb*（*or imbibe*）*knowledge* ❷ recruit；enrol；admit：我们决定～他为正式会员。*We have decided to admit him to full membership.* ◇～光谱［物］absorption spectrum；～剂 absorbent；～率 absorptivity；～塔［化］absorption tower；～作用 absorption

【吸吮】suck；absorb：婴儿在～母亲的奶汁。*The baby is nursing at its mother's breast.*

【吸铁石】magnet；lodestone

【吸血鬼】bloodsucker；vampire

【吸烟】smoke：他一天吸一包烟。*He smokes a pack of cigarettes a day.* / 严禁～。*No smoking.* ◇～室 smoking room

【吸音板】acoustic board

【吸音贴砖】acoustolith tile

【吸引】attract；draw；fascinate：～注意力 *attract attention* / 这部电影对观众很有～力。*This film has a strong appeal to the audience.* ◇～器［医］aspirator

【吸滞】（of plants）absorb and retain：一公顷松林一年可～灰尘约 36.4 吨。*One hectare of pine forest can retain 36.4 tons of dust annually.*

希 动 hope：敬～读者指正。*It is hoped that the readers will kindly point out our errors.* / ～准时到会。*Please get to the meeting on time.*

【希伯来语】Hebrew（language）

【希罕】❶ rare；scarce；uncommon：骆驼在南方是～的东西。*Camels are a rare sight in the south.* ❷ value as a rarity；cherish：你不～，我还～呢。*You may not cherish it，but I do.* / 谁～你的臭钱？*Who cares about your lousy money?* ❸ a rare thing；rarity：看～儿 *enjoy the rare sight of sth.* / 这么大的人参可是个～儿。*Such a big ginseng root is certainly a rarity.*

【希腊】Greece ◇～人 Greek；～语 Greek（language）；～正教 the Greek Orthodox Church；～字母 the Greek alphabet

【希奇】rare；strange；curious：十月下雪在这儿不是什么～的事。*Snow in October is nothing strange in this place.*

【希求】❶ hope for；wish for ❷ what one hopes or wishes for

【希世之珍】a rare treasure：故宫博物院收藏着许多～。*Many rare treasures are housed in the Palace Museum.*

【希图】harbour the intention of；intend to；attempt to：～蒙混过关 *try to wangle*；*try to get by under false pretences* / ～牟取暴利 *go after quick profits*

【希望】❶ hope；wish；expect：～你明天能来。*Hope you'll be here tomorrow.* ❷ hope；wish；expectation：他康复的～不大。*There is little hope of his recovery.* ❸ a person or thing on which hope is placed：青少年是我们的未来，是我们的～。*The youngsters are our future，our hope.*

昔 名 former times；the past：今胜于～。*The present is superior to the past.*

【昔年】〈书〉（in）former years

【昔日】（in）former days（or times）：～荒坡，今日良田。*The once barren hillsides are now good farmland.*

析 动 ❶ divide；separate：分崩离析 ❷ analyze；dissect；resolve：析义

【析出】❶ find（results）on analysis ❷［化］separate out

【析像管】［电子］image dissector

【析疑】〈书〉resolve a doubt；clear up a doubtful

point

【析义】analyse the meaning (of a word, etc.)

矽 名［化］silicon (Si)

【矽尘】silicious dust

【矽肺】［医］silicosis (a disease)

【矽钢】silicon steel

奚 (构词成分) 见下

【奚落】scoff at; taunt; gibe at：他就爱～人。*He's always gibing at (or making gibes about) others.* / 我被他～了一顿。*I was scoffed at by him.*

牺 名〈书〉a beast of a uniform colour for sacrifice; sacrifice：～牛 *sacrificial ox*

【牺牲】❶ a beast slaughtered for sacrifice; sacrifice ❷ sacrifice oneself; die a martyr's death; lay down one's life：英勇～ *die a heroic death* ❸ sacrifice; give up; do sth. at the expense of：～个人利益 *sacrifice one's personal interests* ◇ ～品 victim; prey

息 名 ❶ breath：战斗到最后一～ *fight to one's last breath* ❷ news：信息 ❸ interest：年息 / 无息

【息兵】cease fire

【息鼓】❶〈字〉stop beating the drum ❷〈喻〉(of sports competition) end：中国女子体操对抗赛～。*The Chinese Women's Gymnastic Meet has ended.*

【息交绝游】shut oneself in and cut oneself off from social life

【息怒】cease to be angry; calm one's anger

【息票】interest coupon

【息钱】interest (money)

【息肉】［医］polyp; polypus

【息事宁人】❶ patch up a quarrel ❷ give way to avoid trouble; gloss things over to stay on good terms：我们的人恐怕他们捣乱，为了～，便放他们进去了。*We were afraid they'd disturb the audience with the racket they were making, so we let them in, just to keep them quiet.*

【息息相关】(又作'息息相通') be closely linked; be closely bound up

【息影】(又作'息景')〈书〉retire into private life：～银坛 *retire from the screen*

【息战】cease fire; stop fighting

淅 动〈书〉wash rice

【淅沥】the sound of a light rain, a breeze, falling leaves, etc.：雨声～。*The rain went pitter-pattering.*

【淅飒】the sound of a light wind, rain, etc.：风吹得杨树叶淅淅飒飒直响。*The wind set the poplar leaves a-rustling.*

惜 动 ❶ cherish; value highly; use sparingly; care for tenderly：～寸阴 *value every bit of time; make good use of every moment* ❷ spare; grudge; stint：吝惜 ❸ have pity on; feel sorry for：惋惜

【惜别】be reluctant to part; hate to see sb. go：依依～ *be reluctant to part* / 老师们怀着～的心情，送走了毕业同学。*The teachers reluctantly parted with the graduates.*

【惜老怜贫】have compassion for the old and the poor

【惜力】be sparing of one's energy; not do one's best：小张干活从不～。*Xiao Zhang never spares himself in his work.*

【惜怜】feel sorry for; pity; sympathize; regret：他根本没有～体贴女人的习惯。*He is not used to showing consideration for women.*

【惜墨如金】(of a painter, calligrapher, or writer) use ink as if it were gold-work with scrupulous care：那些了不得的作家，谨严入骨，～，要把一生的作品，只删存一个或者三四个字。*Some important writers are so strict with themselves, so sparing of ink, that they like to pare down the work of a lifetime to three or four words.*

【惜指失掌】stint a finger and lose a hand —try to save a little only to lose a lot; spoil the ship for a ha'p'orth of tar

烯 (构词成分) 见下

【烯烃】［化］alkene

硒 名［化］selenium (Se)

悉 Ⅰ 形 all; entire：悉数 Ⅱ 动 know; learn; be informed of：熟悉

【悉力】go all out; spare no effort：定～相助。*I will do all I can to help you.*

【悉数】〈书〉all; every single one：～奉还 *return all that has been borrowed or taken away*

【悉听尊便】You are free to try anything you like.

晰 形 clear; distinct：清晰

翕 Ⅰ 形〈书〉amiable and compliant Ⅱ 动 furl; fold; shut：～张 *furl and unfurl; close and open*

【翕动】〈书〉(of lips, nostrils, etc.) open and close; quiver：他的嘴唇～着，可已经说不出话来。*He kept moving his lips but could not utter a word.*

【翕然】〈书〉(of opinions, actions, etc.) be in unison; be in harmony：舆论～。*Public opinion is unanimous.*

稀 形 ❶ rare; scarce; uncommon：物以稀为贵 / 稀少 ❷ sparse; scattered：月明星～。*The moon is bright and the stars are few.* / 他的头发长得特别～。*He has very thin hair.* ❸ watery; thin：粥太～了。*This gruel is too thin.* / 我想喝点儿～的。*I'd like to have some liquid food.*

【稀薄】thin; rare：山顶空气～。*The air at the top of the mountain is thin.*

【稀饭】rice or millet gruel; porridge

【稀客】a rare visitor

【稀拉】❶ sparse; scanty; thinly scattered：几根～

的枯草 *a few withered grass scattered here and there* ❷〈方〉slovenly; sloppy; slack: 作风～ *lax*

【稀烂】❶ completely mashed; pulpy: 肉煮得～。*The meat was cooked to a pulp*. ❷（又作'稀巴烂'）smashed to pieces (or smithereens); broken to bits: 鸡蛋掉在地上，摔了个～。*The egg fell on the ground and smashed*.

【稀里呼噜】〈口〉the sound of snoring, guzzling porridge, etc.: 他端起那大碗粥，～地喝起来。*He took up that big bowl of porridge and started guzzling it down at once*.

【稀里糊涂】❶ not knowing what one is about; muddleheaded: 这道算题他讲了两遍，我还是～的。*He explained the problem twice, but I was none the wiser*. ❷ careless; casual; perfunctory: 这个提案没经过认真讨论，就～地通过了。*The motion was carried perfunctorily, without any adequate discussion*.

【稀里哗啦】〈口〉❶ the sound of rain or of sth. falling down: 雨～下了起来。*The rain came down in sheets (or came pouring down)*. ❷ badly battered; broken to pieces; utterly shattered: 大厅里的摆设给打了个～。*All the furnishings in the hall were shattered into splinters*.

【稀落】❶ become sparse; be thinning: 她的头发～了。*Her hair is thinning out*. / 枪声～了。*The gunfire dwindled off*. ❷ sparse; scattered; thin: 小河边只有几株～的柳树。*There are only a few scattered willow trees by the stream*.

【稀缺】in short supply; scarce; in pressing demand: ～商品 *goods in short supply*

【稀少】few; rare; scarce: 人口～ *be sparsely populated* / 街上行人～。*There were few people in the street*.

【稀释】dilute: 应该把柠檬汁～一下。*You are supposed to dilute the lemon juice with water*. ◇～测定［化］dilution metering; ～剂［化］diluent; thinner

【稀疏】(of objects, sounds, etc.) few and scattered; few and far between; thin; sparse: ～的晨星 *a few scattered morning stars* / ～的头发 *thin hair; sparse hair*

【稀松】❶ sloppy; lax: 这活儿干得～。*This is sloppy work*. / 他们干起活儿来，哪个也不～。*When they set to work, not one of them is lax*. ❷ unimportant; trivial: 别把这些～的事放在心上。*Don't take such trivial matters to heart*. ❸ loose; porous: 这土够～的。*This soil is loose enough*.

【稀汤寡水】(of porridge, soup, etc.) watery; thin and tasteless

【稀土金属】［化］rare-earth metal

【稀土元素】［化］rare-earth element

【稀稀拉拉】（又作'稀稀落落'）❶ sparse; thinly scattered: 天上只有～的几颗晨星。*There were only a few scattered stars in the morning sky*. ❷ slack; remiss: 昨天的大会开得～，真没劲。*Yesterday's meeting was a dull affair*.

【稀有】rare; unusual: 十月下雪在这儿并不是～的事。*Snow in October is not unusual around here*. ◇～金属［化］rare metal; ～元素［化］rare element

犀 名 rhinoceros

【犀角】rhinoceros horn

【犀利】sharp; incisive; trenchant: ～的目光 *sharp eyes* / 谈锋～ *be incisive in conversation* / 文笔～ *have or wield a trenchant pen*

【犀鸟】hornbill

【犀牛】common name for 犀

溪 名 a small stream; brook; rivulet

【溪涧】mountain stream

【溪流】brook; rivulet

锡 名［化］tin; stannum (Sn)

【锡箔】tinfoil paper (formerly used as funeral offerings)

【锡匠】tinsmith

【锡金】Sikkim

【锡矿】tin ore

【锡兰肉桂】Ceylon cinnamon (Cinnamomum zeylanicum)

【锡石】［矿］cassiterite; tinstone

【锡杖】Buddhist abbot's staff

【锡纸】tinfoil; silver paper

熄 动 ❶ extinguish; put out: ～灯 *put out the light* ❷ (of a fire, light, etc.) go out; die out: 火～了。*The fire has gone out*.

【熄灯号】lights-out; taps

【熄风】［中］relieve dizziness, high fever, infantile convulsions, epilepsy, etc.

【熄火】❶ (of fuel, a stove, etc.) stop burning; die out ❷ (of an engine, etc.) stop working; go dead ❸ stop (fuel) from burning; stop (an engine, etc.)

【熄灭】(of a fire, light, etc.) go out; die out: 篝火～了。*The campfire died out*. / 把灯～ *put out the light*

熙 形 ❶ bright; sunny ❷ prosperous ❸ gay; merry

【熙和】❶〈书〉congenial and happy ❷ pleasantly warm; genial: ～的南风 *a genial wind from the south*

【熙熙攘攘】bustling with activity; with people bustling about: 马路上～的尽是人。*The pavement was packed with jostling crowds*.

蜥（构词成分）见下

【蜥蜴】lizard

嘻 象 the sound of merry laughter: ～～地笑 *giggle*

【嘻嘻哈哈】laughing and joking; laughing merrily; mirthful

膝 名 knee: 双～跪下 *kneel on both knees* / 左

（右）～ *the left* (*right*) *knee*

【膝盖】common name for 膝 ◇ ～骨 another name for 髌骨

【膝关节】knee joint

【膝腱】patellar tendon ◇～反射［生理］patellar reflex; knee jerk

【膝下】〈书〉❶ at one's knees (used in saying whether one has children or not)：～无子 *have no son* / ～一儿一女 *have a son and a daughter* ❷ (used in the salutations of letters to one's parents or grandparents)：父亲大人～ *Dear Father*

【膝内翻】out knee; bowleg

【膝上电脑】laptop computer

【膝外翻】in knee; knock knee

【膝痒搔背】not scratch at the itch; not scratch where it itches — fail to handle a matter properly; miss the point; miss fire

嬉 动〈书〉play; sport

【嬉闹】laugh and frolic：姑娘们～了好一阵。*The girls laughed and frolicked for a long time.*

【嬉皮士】hippie; hippy

【嬉皮笑脸】grinning cheekily; smiling and grimacing

【嬉耍】play; sport; frolic：孩子们光着脚在河边～。*The kids were playing barefoot by the riverside.*

【嬉戏】〈书〉play; sport：湖面上鸭群在～。*Ducks are sporting on the lake.*

【嬉笑】be laughing and playing：孩子们的～声 *the happy laughter of children at play*

【嬉笑怒骂】laughing merrily or cursing angrily：～，皆成文章。*Anything, from a merry laugh to an angry curse, can make good writing.*

【嬉游曲】［音］divertimento

蹊 名〈书〉footpath ——另见 qī

【蹊径】〈书〉path; way

蟋（构词成分）见下

【蟋蟀】cricket (an insect) ◇～草［植］yard grass

曦 名〈书〉sunlight (usu. of early morning)：晨曦

【曦光】morning sunlight

xí

习 Ⅰ动 ❶ practise; exercise; review：自习 / 复习 ❷ get accustomed to; be used to; become familiar with：～闻 *often hear* / 不～水性 *be not good at swimming* Ⅱ名 habit; custom; usual practice：积习

【习非成是】get used to what is wrong and regard it as right

【习惯】❶ be accustomed to; be used to; be inured to：这样潮湿的天气我实在不～。*I just can't get used to this damp weather.* ❷ habit; custom; usual practice：别养成抽烟的～。*Don't get into the habit of smoking.*

【习惯成自然】once you form a habit, it comes natural to you; habit becomes second nature

【习惯法】common law; customary law

【习见】commonly seen (thing or sight)：～的现象 *a common sight*

【习气】a bad habit; bad practice：官僚～ *habitual practice of bureaucracy; bad bureaucratic habits* / 流氓～ *hooliganism*

【习俗】custom; convention

【习题】exercises (in school work)

【习习】(of a wind) blow gently：微风～。*A gentle breeze is blowing.*

【习性】habits and characteristics：熊猫的～ *the habits and characteristics of the giant panda*

【习以为常】be used (or accustomed, inured) to sth.：渐渐地人们对这种现象也～了。*Gradually people got used to it.*

【习艺】learn a trade, skill, handicraft, etc.

【习用】habitually use

【习语】(又作'习用语') idiom

【习与性成】habit becomes second nature

【习字】practise penmanship; do exercises in calligraphy ◇～帖 copybook; calligraphy model

【习作】❶ do exercises in composition ❷ an exercise in composition, drawing, etc.

席 Ⅰ名 ❶ mat：一领～ *a mat* ❷ seat; place：入席 ❸ seat (in a legislative assembly)：该党在议会选举中失去了十五～。*That party lost 15 seats in the parliamentary election.* ❹ feast; banquet; dinner：宴席 Ⅱ量：一～酒 *a banquet* / 一～话 *a talk (with sb.); a conversation*

【席次】the order of seats; seating arrangement; one's place among the seats arranged：按指定～入座 *take one's assigned seat; sit down in one's place*

【席地】have a mat on the ground; (sit or lie) on the ground：～而坐 *sit on the ground*

【席间】at or during the feast：～宾主频频举杯。*Again and again the host and guests raised their glasses during the feast.*

【席卷】❶ roll up like a mat; carry everything with one; take away everything：～而去 *make off with everything that one can lay hands on* ❷ sweep across; engulf：暴风雨～大草原。*A blizzard swept across the prairie.*

【席梦思】Simmons (a transliteration); innerspring mattress

【席面】the dishes served at a feast

【席棚】mat shed; mat hoarding

【席位】seat (at a conference, in a legislative assembly, etc.)

【席子】〈方〉mat

袭 Ⅰ动 ❶ make a surprise attack on; raid：花气～人。*The fragrance of flowers assails one's nose.* ❷ follow the pattern of; carry on as before：因袭 / 抄袭 Ⅱ量〈书〉a suit or set (of clothes)：一～棉衣 *a set of cotton-padded clothes* (*consisting of trousers and a coat*)

【袭击】❶ make a surprise attack on; attack by surprise：沿海一带受到台风的～。*The coastal areas were hit by a typhoon*. ❷ a surprise attack; raid：敌人向我们发动了一次突然～。*The enemy launched a surprise attack on us*.

【袭取】❶ take by surprise ❷ take over (something that has long been used in the past)：后人～这个故事，写成了戏。*Later people adapted this story for the stage*.

【袭扰】[军] harass; attack repeatedly：～敌军 *harass the enemy troops*

【袭用】take over (something that has long been used in the past)：～古方 *take over an age-old recipe* / ～老谱 *follow old practice*

媳 名 daughter-in-law

【媳妇】❶ son's wife; daughter-in-law ❷ the wife of a relative of the younger generation：侄媳妇 / 孙媳妇

【媳妇儿】〈方〉❶ wife：你～ *your wife* ❷ a young married woman：这小～长得好标致！*How pretty this young woman is*!

檄 名 (a literary genre) a war proclamation setting forth the purpose of the expedition and enumerating the crimes of the enemy

【檄文】war proclamation

xǐ

洗 动 ❶ wash; bathe：～衣服 *wash clothes* / ～伤口 *bathe a wound*; *apply wash to a wound* / 袜子没～干净。*The socks have not been washed clean*. / 用肥皂～～手 *wash one's hands with soap* ❷ baptize：受洗 ❸ redress; right：～冤 *right a wrong*; *redress a grievance* ❹ kill and loot; sack：～城 *massacre the inhabitants of a captured city* ❺ [摄] develop; process：～胶卷 *develop an exposed film* / ～相片 *process a photo* / 照片～出来了。*The photos have been processed*. ❻ clear (a recording, etc.); erase：那段讲话的录音已经～了。*The recording of the talk has been erased*. ❼ shuffle (cards, etc.)：这牌没～开。*The cards weren't shuffled properly*.

【洗不掉】can't be washed off; can't wash out：衣服上的这块墨迹～。*I can't get rid of this ink stain on my coat*. or *This ink stain didn't wash out*.

【洗尘】give a dinner of welcome (to a visitor from afar)

【洗涤】wash; cleanse ◇ ～槽 washing tank; sink; ～剂 detergent; ～器 washing appliance; washer; scrubber; ～塔[化] washing tower

【洗耳恭听】listen with respectful attention

【洗发剂】shampoo

【洗剂】lotion; wash

【洗劫】loot; sack：屋子里的东西被匪徒们～一空。*The bandits made off with everything in the house*.

【洗井】[油] flushing

【洗礼】❶ baptism ❷ a severe test：炮火的～ *a baptism of fire* / 受过战斗的～ *have gone through the test of battle*

【洗脸盆】washbasin; washbowl

【洗练】(又作'洗炼') succinct; clear：文笔～。*The language is very succinct*. / 剧情处理得很～。*The plot is well-knit*.

【洗煤】coal washing ◇ ～厂 coal washery; coal cleaning plant

【洗面膏】(facial) cleansing cream

【洗脑筋】(又作'洗脑') ❶〈字〉wash brains; ❷〈喻〉ideological remoulding：～有什么不好？思想上有脏东西，为什么不把它洗掉？*What's so bad about brainwashing? If there are wrong ideas, why not wash them away*?

【洗牌】shuffle cards; make the pack：该你～了。*Your turn to make* (*the pack*).

【洗片】[摄] develop a film or process a photo ◇ ～机 developing machine

【洗钱】launder money; money laundering：那家伙是～老手。*That fellow is an old hand at laundering money*.

【洗染店】cleaners and dyers; laundering and dyeing shop

【洗手不干】❶ (of a thief, etc.) stop doing wrong and reform oneself ❷ wash one's hands of sth.

【洗手间】toilet; lavatory; washroom; rest room

【洗刷】❶ wash and brush; scrub：～地板 *scrub the floor* ❷ wash off; clear oneself of (opprobrium, stigma, guilt, etc.)：～耻辱 *clear oneself of opprobrium*

【洗涮】rinse：把蔬菜放在自来水龙头下～干净。*Give the vegetables a good rinse with running water*.

【洗头】wash one's hair; shampoo one's hair; have a shampoo

【洗碗机】dishwasher

【洗胃】[医] gastric lavage

【洗洗涮涮】laundering, washing of utensils and other household cleaning jobs

【洗心革面】turn over a new leaf; thoroughly reform oneself

【洗选】[矿] ore dressing (by washing)

【洗雪】wipe out (a disgrace); redress (a wrong)：～国耻 *wipe out a national disgrace*

【洗盐】[农] desalinization of soil by flooding or leaching

【洗眼杯】eyecup

【洗眼剂】[药] eyewash

【洗衣】wash clothes ◇ ～板 washboard; ～店 laundry; ～粉 laundry detergent (powder); washing powder; ～机 washing machine; ～刷 wash brush

【洗印】[摄] develop and print (photos); process ◇ ～机 (film) processor

【洗澡】have (or take) a bath; bathe：我刚洗完澡。

I've just had a bath. ◇ ～间 bathroom；～盆 bathtub；～堂 bath pool
【洗濯】〈书〉wash；cleanse

玺 名 imperial or royal seal：玉玺

徙 动 move from one place to another：迁徙
【徙居】move house：～内地 *move up-country*

铣 动 mill (metals) ——另见 xiǎn
【铣床】[机] milling machine；miller
【铣刀】[机] milling cutter
【铣工】❶ milling (work) ❷ miller；milling machine operator

喜 Ⅰ 动 ❶ happy；delighted；pleased：心中暗～ *secretly feel pleased* / ～不自胜 *be delighted beyond measure*；*be beside oneself with joy* ❷ be fond of；like；have an inclination for：～读书 *be fond of reading* / 猴子性～攀缘。*Monkeys have a natural inclination for climbing*. Ⅱ 名 ❶ a happy event (esp. wedding)；an occasion for celebration：喜事❷〈口〉pregnancy：有喜
【喜爱】like；love；be fond of；be keen on：～户外活动 *be keen on outdoor activities* / 这花真惹人～。*This flower is really attractive*.
【喜报】a bulletin of glad tidings
【喜冲冲】look exhilarated；be in a joyful mood
【喜出望外】be overjoyed (at an unexpected gain, good news, etc.)；be pleasantly surprised：听说我们队得了冠军，大家～。*We were overjoyed to hear that our team had won the championship*.
【喜从天降】a heaven-sent fortune；a heavenly blessing—an unexpected piece of good fortune；a gift from the gods
【喜好】like；love；be fond of；be keen on：她从小就～音乐。*She's been a music lover since childhood*.
【喜欢】❶ like；love；be fond of；be keen on：～看电视 *like watching TV* / 我～热闹。*I like company*. ❷ happy；elated；filled with joy：快把这好消息告诉奶奶，让她老人家～～。*Tell Grandma the good news quick. She'll be delighted to hear it*.
【喜酒】drinks offered to guests at a wedding；wedding feast：什么时候喝你们的～啊？*When's your wedding*? or *When do I wish you joy*? / 吃～ *attend a wedding feast or any other kind of wedding celebration*
【喜剧】comedy ◇ ～演员 comedian
【喜马拉雅山】the Himalayas
【喜眉笑眼】be all smiles；be smiling all over
【喜怒哀乐】happiness, anger, grief and joy—the gamut of human feeling
【喜怒无常】be subject to changing moods：他这个人～。*He is a man of moods*.
【喜期】the happy occasion—wedding day：～已近，得加紧准备。*You must speed up your preparations, as it will soon be your wedding day*.
【喜气】a cheerful atmosphere or countenance：满脸～ *a face beaming with joy*
【喜气洋洋】full of joy；jubilant：农民们～庆丰收。*The farmers are jubilantly celebrating their bumper harvest*.
【喜庆】❶ joyous；jubilant：在这～的日子里 *on this day of jubilation*；*on this happy occasion* ❷ a happy event or occasion
【喜鹊】[动] magpie
【喜人】give pleasure and satisfaction；be gratifying or satisfactory：取得～的成果 *achieve satisfactory results* / 形势～。*The situation is gratifying*.
【喜色】a happy expression；a joyful look：面有～ *wear a happy expression*
【喜上眉梢】be radiant with joy；look very happy
【喜事】❶ a happy event；a joyous occasion：瞧你这么高兴，有什么～？*You look so happy. What's the good news*? ❷ marriage；wedding：什么时候办～？*When will the marriage (or wedding) take place*?
【喜糖】wedding sweets (or candies)：吃～ *have wedding sweets-attend a wedding celebration*
【喜闻乐见】love to see and hear：人民大众～的作品 *literary and artistic works loved by the people*
【喜笑颜开】a face wreathed in smiles；a face lit up with pleasure：看着院子里堆成山的粮食，全家人都～。*Looking at the grain piled high in the courtyard, the whole family were wreathed in smiles*.
【喜新厌旧】love the new and loathe the old —be fickle in one's affections：唉，你们男人家，我是晓得的，都有～的毛病。*Ai! You men, I know you all have the same fault—off with the old love and on with the new*.
【喜形于色】a face lit up with pleasure；visibly pleased；beaming with happiness：男女老少，个个～。*Men and women, old and young, all beamed with happiness*.
【喜讯】happy news；good news；glad tidings
【喜洋洋】beaming with joy；radiant
【喜雨】a seasonable rain；a welcome fall of rain：普降～ *have a widespread seasonable rainfall*；*have a seasonable fall of rain over a wide area*
【喜悦】happy；joyous：怀着万分～的心情 *with a feeling of immeasurable joy* / 内心充满了～ *be filled with joy*
【喜滋滋】feeling greatly pleased；filled with joy：听到这好消息，她心里～的。*When she heard the good news, she was immensely pleased*.

禧 名 auspiciousness；happiness；jubilation：恭贺新禧

xì

戏 Ⅰ 动 ❶ play；sport：鸳鸯～水 *mandarin ducks sporting in water* / 二龙～珠 *two dragons playing with a pearl* ❷ make fun of；joke：戏言 Ⅱ 名 drama；play；show：古装～ *a drama in* *ancient costume* / 这场～演得很精彩。*It was a wonderful performance*.

【戏班】(又作'戏班子')〈旧〉theatrical troupe

【戏词】actor's part or lines

【戏法】conjuring; juggling; tricks; magic: ～人人会变,各有巧妙不同。*Many are the magicians, but each has his own tricks*.

【戏剧】drama; play; theatre: 现代～ *modern drama*; *the modern theatre* / ～评论 *dramatic criticism* ◇ ～家 playwright; dramatist; ～界 theatrical circles

【戏剧性】dramatic: 一起富有～的事件 *a dramatic event* / 政治局势发生了～变化。*Spectacular changes in the political situation are taking place*.

【戏路】(又作'戏路子') the range of character types that an actor can portray: ～宽(窄) *can portray a wide (narrow) range of character types*

【戏迷】theatre fan

【戏目】(theatrical) programme

【戏弄】make fun of; play tricks on; tease; kid: 你别老～人。*Don't you go playing tricks on others*.

【戏票】theatre ticket

【戏评】a review of a play

【戏曲】traditional opera: 地方～ *local operas* ◇ ～片 a screen adaptation of a traditional or local opera

【戏耍】tease; play tricks on

【戏台】〈口〉stage

【戏文】actor's part or lines

【戏谑】banter; crack jokes

【戏言】joking remarks; pleasantries

【戏院】theatre

【戏装】theatrical or stage costume

【戏子】〈旧〉〈贬〉opera singer; actor: 女～ *actress*

系 Ⅰ 名 ❶ system; series: 语系 ❷ department (in a college); faculty: 哲学～ *the department of philosophy* ❸ [地质] system: 奥陶～ *the Ordovician system* Ⅱ 动 ❶ (used with abstractions) relate to; bear on: 名誉所～ *have a direct bearing on one's reputation* / 成败～于此举 *stand or fall by this* ❷ tie; fasten; bind: ～马 *tether a horse to a hitching post* ❸ take into custody; put in prison: ～狱 *be put in prison* ❹ feel anxious; be concerned: 系念 ❺〈书〉be: 其母～山东人。*His mother is a native of Shandong*. / 纯～试验性质 *be purely experimental* / 确～实情 *be nothing but the truth* ——另见 jì

【系词】❶ [逻] copula ❷ [语] copulative verb; linking verb

【系恋】be reluctant to leave; can't bear to part (from sb. or with sth.)

【系列】series; set: 一～的问题 *a series of problems* / 一～政策 *a whole set of policies* / 运载～ *vehicle series* ◇ ～化 serialize; come out in serial form; ～片 serial; ～小说 novel series

【系念】〈书〉be anxious about; worry about; feel concerned about

【系谱】[生] family; genealogy ◇ ～树 [生] family tree

【系数】[数] coefficient: 光学～ *optical coefficient*

【系统】❶ system: 灌溉系统 / 财贸系统 ❷ systematic: 作～的研究 *make a systematic study* / ～地说明 *explain in a systematic way* / 有～地进行经济体制改革 *reform the economic structure systematically* ◇ ～分析 systems analysis; ～工程 systems engineering; ～化 systematize; systemize; ～科学 system science; ～论 systems theory; ～性 systematic nature; systematicness; system

细 形 ❶ thin; slender: ～铁丝 *thin wire* / 她们纺的线又～又匀。*The thread they spin is thin and smooth*. ❷ in small particles; fine: ～沙 *fine sand* / 玉米面磨得很～。*The corn flour has been ground very fine*. ❸ thin and soft: ～嗓子 *a thready voice* ❹ fine; exquisite; delicate: ～瓷 *fine porcelain (or china)* / 粗粮～作 *make delicacies out of coarse food grain* ❺ careful; meticulous; detailed: ～看 *examine carefully*; *scrutinize* / 工作做得～ *be meticulous in one's work* ❻ minute; trifling: 事无巨～ *all matters, big and small* / 分工很～ *have an elaborate division of labour*

【细胞】cell ◇ ～壁 cell wall; ～分裂 cell division; ～核 cell nucleus; ～膜 cell membrane; ～学 cytology; ～质 cytoplasm

【细布】muslin

【细部】detail (of a drawing)

【细长】long and thin; tall and slender: ～身材 *a tall and slender figure*

【细齿】[机] serration: ～拉刀 *serration broach* / ～螺母 *serrated nut*

【细大不捐】reject nothing, big or small

【细纺】[纺] finespun

【细高挑儿】〈方〉❶ a tall and slender figure ❷ a tall, slender person

【细工】fine workmanship

【细活】a job requiring fine workmanship or meticulous care; skilled work

【细火】slow fire; gentle heat: 用～烤十五分钟 *bake over a slow fire for* 15 *minutes*

【细嚼慢咽】chew carefully and swallow slowly; chew one's food well before swallowing it

【细节】details; particulars: 讨论计划的～ *discuss the details of a plan*; *go into the particulars of a plan* / 通过～描写来表现人物性格 *portray a character through the description of detail*

【细菌】germ; bacterium ◇ ～弹 B-bomb; bacteria bomb; ～肥料 bacterial fertilizer; ～农药 bacterial pesticide; ～武器 bacteriological weapon; ～性痢疾 bacillary dysentery; ～学 bacteriology; ～学家 bacteriologist; ～战 bacteriological warfare

【细粮】fine food grain (usu. referring to wheat flour and rice)

【细脉】[中] thready pulse

【细毛】fine, soft fur ◇ ～羊 fine-wool sheep

【细密】❶ fine and closely woven; close: 质地～ *of close texture* / 针脚～ *in fine close stitches* / ～

的纹理 *a close grain* ❷ meticulous; detailed: ～的分析 *a detailed analysis* / 现代企业分工～。*Modern enterprises have a fine division of labour*.

【细木工】❶ joinery ❷ joiner; cabinetmaker

【细目】❶ detailed catalogue ❷ specific item; detail

【细嫩】delicate; tender: ～的皮肤 *delicate skin* / 肉质～ *tender meat*

【细腻】❶ fine and smooth ❷ exquisite; minute: ～的描写 *a minute description* / ～的表演 *an exquisite performance*

【细皮白肉】(又作'细皮嫩肉') delicate skin and fair complexion: 一身～ *be delicate-skinned and fair-complexioned*

【细巧】exquisite; dainty; delicate: ～的图案 *an exquisite design*

【细情】details: 我不了解～,所以不好说。*I can't say for sure because I don't know the details*.

【细绒线】fingering yarn

【细柔】fine and soft; gentle and slender; fine-textured: ～的声音 *a fine, gentle voice* / ～的皮革 *soft and smooth leather*

【细软】jewelry, expensive clothing and other valuables: 席卷～,逃之夭夭 *make off with all the valuables one can lay hands on*

【细润】fine and glossy: 瓷质～。*The porcelain is fine and glossy*.

【细弱】thin and delicate; slim and fragile: ～的身子 *of slim and delicate build* / 声音～ *a feeble voice*

【细纱】[纺] spun yarn ◇ ～机 spinning frame

【细声细气】in a soft voice; soft-spoken: 他举止文雅,说话～的。*He is gentle and soft-spoken*.

【细石器】[考古] microlith ◇ ～文化 [考古] microlithic culture

【细水长流】❶ economize to avoid running short ❷ go about sth. little by little without a letup

【细说】(又作'细谈') recount or describe in detail; tell at length: ～分明 *give a clear and detailed account*

【细碎】in small, broken bits: ～的布片 *scraps of cloth* / ～的脚步声 *the sound of light and hurried footsteps*

【细挑】(又作'细条') tall and slender: ～个儿 *a tall, slender figure*

【细微】slight; fine; subtle: ～的声响 *a slight sound* / ～的动作 *a scarcely perceptible movement* / ～的变化 *slight (or subtle) changes* / ～差别 *a fine distinction; a subtle difference*

【细纹木】fine-grained wood

【细细儿】❶ very thin; very fine: 他把那些木棍儿都削得～的。*He pared each of the sticks down to a thin strip*. ❷ very careful: 你～想想,当时在场的都有哪些人? *Now think very carefully who were present at the time*.

【细小】very small; tiny; fine; trivial: ～的零件 *small parts (of a machine)* / ～的雨点 *tiny raindrops* / ～的事情 *trivial matters*

【细心】careful; attentive: ～观察 *carefully observe* / ～护理伤员 *nurse the wounded with care*

【细辛】[中] the root of Chinese wild ginger (Asarum sieboldi)

【细腰】slender waist (esp. of a woman)

【细雨】drizzle; fine rain

【细语】speak softly; whisper: 低声～ *speak in a soft low voice*

【细则】detailed rules and regulations:《中华人民共和国商标法实施～》*Rules for the Implementation of the Trademark Law of the People's Republic of China*

【细账】itemized account

【细针密缕】in fine, close stitches — (work) in a meticulous way

【细支纱】[纺] fine-count yarn

【细枝末节】minor details; nonessentials

【细致】careful; meticulous; painstaking: 她想得很～。*She thought it out in detail*. / 这活做得很～。*This is a careful piece of work*.

【细作】〈旧〉spy; secret agent

隙 名 ❶ crack; chink; crevice: 墙～ *a crack in the wall* / 云～ *a rift in the clouds* ❷ gap; interval: 农～ *interval between busy seasons in farming* ❸ loophole; opportunity: 乘隙 ❹ discord; rift: 嫌隙

【隙地】unoccupied place; open space

xiā

呷 动〈方〉sip: ～一口茶 *take a sip of tea*

虾 名 shrimp: ～群 *a shoal of shrimps*

【虾兵蟹将】shrimp soldiers and crab generals—ineffective troops; hopeless soldiers

【虾干】dried shrimps

【虾蛄】mantis shrimp

【虾酱】salted shrimp paste

【虾米】❶ dried, shelled shrimps ❷〈方〉small shrimps

【虾皮】(又作'虾米皮') dried, unshelled small shrimps

【虾仁】shelled fresh shrimps; shrimp meat

【虾油】shrimp sauce

【虾子】shrimp roe (or eggs): ～酱油 *shrimp-roe soy sauce* / ～豆腐 *bean curd stewed with shrimp roe*

瞎 Ⅰ 动 blind: ～了一只眼 *be blind in one eye* / 我真～了眼,把他当做好人了。*I was so blind as to take him for a gentleman*. Ⅱ 副 groundlessly; foolishly; to no purpose: ～讲 *speak groundlessly* / ～花钱 *spend money foolishly* / ～干 *go it blind* / ～猜 *make a wild guess* / ～费劲儿 *make a vain effort*

【瞎掰】〈口〉❶ talk nonsense ❷ do stupid things

【瞎扯】❶ talk groundlessly or irresponsibly; talk nonsense: 他尽～,别信他的。*He's just talking nonsense. Don't believe him.* ❷ talk at random about anything under the sun; waffle; natter: 她没说什么正经事,～了一通就走了。*She didn't talk about anything serious. She just chattered away for a while and left.*

【瞎吹】boast in the most fantastic of terms

【瞎话】untruth; lie: 说～ *tell a lie; tell a fib*

【瞎混】muddle along

【瞎聊】chat at random about anything under the sun; chat idly: 没事也不能整天地～啊。*Even if you are free, you still shouldn't waste your time chatting the whole day away.*

【瞎忙】(又作'瞎忙活') make a fuss about nothing: ～了几天,什么也没搞成。*For days we made ourselves busy but got nothing done.*

【瞎蒙】〈口〉make a wild guess: 他并不知道答案,全是～上的。*He didn't really know the answers. He just made a lucky guess.*

【瞎闹】(又作'瞎胡闹') ❶ act senselessly; mess about ❷ fool around; be mischievous: 赶快做作业,别～。*Hurry up and get your homework done; don't fool around.*

【瞎炮】ignited dynamite or a fired artillery shell that fails to explode; dud

【瞎说】talk groundlessly or irresponsibly; talk nonsense

【瞎指挥】issue confused orders; give arbitrary and impracticable directions; mess things up by giving wrong orders

【瞎诌】〈方〉make up wild stories; tell cock-and-bull stories

【瞎抓】do things without a plan; go about sth. in a haphazard way: 事先把要带的东西都准备好,免得临时～。*Get everything ready beforehand so that you won't be in a rush when it's time to leave.*

【瞎字儿不识】〈口〉cannot read a single word; be completely illiterate: 他从小没上过学,到现在～。*He's never had any schooling, and even now can't read a single word.*

【瞎子】〈讳〉a blind person

【瞎子点灯白费蜡】a blind person lighting a candle—a sheer waste

【瞎子摸象】the blind men sizing up the elephant—take a part for the whole

【瞎子摸鱼】a blind person groping for fish—act blindly

xiá

匣 名 a small box (or case); casket: 木～ *a wooden box (or case)* / 买两～点心 *buy two boxes of pastries*

【匣子】a small box (or case); casket: 梳头～ *a casket for hairdressing articles*

狎 动 be improperly familiar with; be too close with (usu. a woman)

【狎妓】visit prostitutes; go whoring

【狎客】a frequenter of brothels

【狎昵】be improperly familiar with

侠 Ⅰ 名 a person adept in martial arts and given to chivalrous conduct (in olden times) Ⅱ 形 having a strong sense of justice and ready to help the weak; chivalrous

【侠骨】〈书〉chivalry: ～义胆 *chivalry and loyalty*

【侠客】(又作'侠士') a person adept in martial arts and given to chivalrous conduct (in olden times)

【侠气】lofty sense of honour and courage; heroic spirit

【侠义】having a strong sense of justice and ready to help the weak; chivalrous: ～心肠 *a generous and gallant heart* / ～行为 *a chivalrous act* / ～之士 *a chivalrous man*

峡 名 (usu. used as part of a place name) gorge: 三门～ *the Sanmen Gorge* / 长江三～ *the Three Gorges on the Yangtze River*

【峡谷】gorge; canyon

【峡湾】[地理] fiord

狭 形 narrow: 坡陡路～。*The slope is steep and the path narrow.*

【狭隘】❶ narrow: ～的山道 *a narrow mountain path* ❷ (of mind, views, etc.) narrow and limited; parochial: ～的看法 *a narrow view* / 心胸～ *be narrow-minded* ◇～民族主义 narrow nationalism

【狭长】long and narrow: ～的山谷 *a long and narrow valley*

【狭路相逢】(of adversaries) meet face to face on a narrow path—come into unavoidable confrontation

【狭小】narrow and small; narrow: ～的阁楼 *a poky attic* / 气量～ *be intolerant; be narrow-minded*

【狭义】narrow sense

【狭窄】❶ narrow; cramped: ～的走廊 *a narrow corridor* / ～的胡同 *a narrow lane (or alley)* ❷ (of mind, experience, etc.) narrow and limited; narrow: 心地～ *be narrow*-minded / 见识～ *be limited in knowledge and narrow in experience* ❸ [医] stricture

遐 形〈书〉❶ far; distant ❷ lasting; long: ～龄 *advanced age*

【遐迩闻名】be known far and wide; enjoy widespread renown

【遐思】同〖遐想〗

【遐想】reverie; daydreaming: 满天的繁星会引起人们无边无际的～。*A star-studded sky induces fantastic reveries.*

瑕 名 ❶flaw in a piece of jade ❷ flaw; defect; shortcoming

【瑕不掩瑜】one flaw cannot mar the jade—small defects cannot obscure great virtues

【瑕疵】flaw; blemish
【瑕玷】〈书〉blemish; stain; defect
【瑕瑜互见】have defects as well as merits; have both strong and weak points

暇 名 free time; leisure: 有～望即来信。*Hope you'll write to me when you have time.*

辖 动 have jurisdiction over; administer; govern: 省～市 *a municipality (or city) under the jurisdiction of the provincial government* / 下～四个兵团 *have four army corps under its command*

【辖区】area under one's jurisdiction
【辖制】〈书〉control

霞 名 rosy clouds; morning or evening glow: 晚霞
【霞光】rays of morning or evening sunlight: ～万道 *a myriad of sun rays* / 彩云万朵,～四射。*Rays of sunlight shine through multihued clouds.*
【霞石】[矿] nepheline

黠 形〈书〉crafty; cunning: 狡黠

xià

下 Ⅰ名 ❶ (used alone, esp. in contrast to 上) below: 上有父母,～有儿女 *have parents above and children below—have a large family to take care of* ❷ (used after a preposition) down; downward: 往～看 *look down at sth.* / 他将帽沿向～拉了拉。*He pulled his hat down a little.* ❸ (used after a noun) under: 树～ *under a tree* / 山～ *at the foot of a hill* / 零～五度 *five degrees below zero* / 在月光～散步 *take a walk in the moonlight* ❹ (used before a noun) lower (in position, rank, or quality): 分为上、中、～三等 *divided into three grades: the upper, the middle and the lower* / 那本书在书架的最～一层。*The book is on the bottom shelf.* ❺ next (in time or order); latter; second: ～次 *next time* / ～礼拜 *next week* / ～个世纪 *next century* / ～两批 *the next two batches* / ～一班车 *the next bus or train* ❻ the second of two or the last of three: ～集 *Volume Two or Three; Vol. II or III* / ～半学期 *the second (or latter) half of the term* ❼ (indicating scope, state, condition, etc.): 在党的领导～ *under the leadership of the Party* / 在这种情况～ *in (or under) such circumstances* ❽ (used in certain time expressions): 时下 Ⅱ副 ❶ (used before a verb) downward; down: 防止圆木～滑 *prevent the logs from rolling down* ❷ down: 坐～ *sit down* / 躺～ *lie down* / 传～一道命令 *send down an order* / 走～楼 *go downstairs* ❸ (indicating the capacity for holding or containing): 坐得～ *can seat* / 坐不～ *cannot seat* / 这么多菜我吃不～。*I can't eat all this food.* Ⅲ动 ❶ come or go down from; descend: ～山 *descend the mountain; come or go down a mountain* / ～楼 *descend the stairs; go or come downstairs* / ～床 *get out of bed* / 顺流而～ *sail or go downstream* ❷ get off (a conveyance); alight: ～车 *get off a car or bus* / ～电梯 *get off an elevator* / ～飞机 *get off a plane; alight from a plane* ❸ (of rain, snow, etc.) come down; fall: ～雨 *rain* / ～雪 *snow* / ～雹子了。*It's hailing.* / ～霜了。*There is frost.* / 雪～得很大。*The snow is falling heavily.* or *It's snowing hard.* ❹ issue (an order, etc.); deliver; send out (an invitation, etc.): ～命令 *issue (or give) orders* / ～请帖 *send an invitation* / 我们早～过通知了。*We have already sent out notices.* ❺ go to (a place thought of as lower or below): ～地狱 *go down to hell* / ～馆子 *go and eat in a restaurant* ❻ leave (the stage, field, etc.); exit: 换人,四号～,三号上。*Substitution, No. 3 for No. 4.* ❼ put in (ingredients of food, fertilizer, poison, capital, etc.); cast: ～作料 *put in the condiments; add the ingredients* / ～面条 *put noodles in a pot of boiling water to cook; cook noodles in boiling water* ❽ play (a board game); make a move (in a board game): ～围棋 *play go* / 该你～了。*Your turn to make a move.* ❾ take down or off; dismantle; unload: 把纱窗～下来 *take the screen window off* / 船上的货还没～完。*The cargo hasn't all been unloaded yet.* ❿ give (a definition, conclusion, etc.): ～定义 *give a definition; define* / ～决心 *make a resolution; determine* / ～结论 *draw a conclusion* ⓫ apply; use: ～力气 *put forth strength; make an effort; exert oneself* / ～刀 *get a knife into sth.* ⓬ (of animals) give birth to; drop (a litter); lay (eggs): ～了一窝小猪 *give birth to (or drop) a litter of piglets* ⓭ capture (a city); take: 连～数城 *take several cities in succession* ⓮ give in: 相持不下 ⓯ get off (work); get out of (class): ～夜班 *come off night duty* / 早～课了。*The class has long been dismissed.* ⓰ (used in the negative) be less than: 参加大会的不～三千人。*No less than 3,000 people attended the conference.* Ⅳ量 ❶ (for verbs of action) stroke; time(s): 钟敲了三～。*The clock struck three times.* / 推了我一～ *gave me a push* ❷ (used after 两 or 几) what one is good at or capable of: 想不到他还有几～。*I never expected him to be so capable.* / 我就会这么两～。*That's all I can do.*

【下巴】❶ the lower jaw ❷ chin
【下巴颏儿】〈口〉chin
【下摆】the lower hem of a gown, jacket or shirt
【下拜】make obeisance; kneel down to pay respect; kowtow
【下班】get off work; knock off: 每天下午六点～。*We knock off at six p.m. every weekday.*
【下半辈子】the latter half of one's life; the rest of one's life
【下半场】second half (of a game, concert, etc.):

～，客队踢进了一个球。*The visiting team scored one goal in the second half of the game.*

【下半旗】fly a flag at half-mast

【下半晌】〈口〉afternoon：～我见她来着。*I saw her this afternoon.*

【下半身】the lower part of the body；below the waist

【下半天】afternoon：天气预报说～有雨。*The weather forecast predicts rain in the afternoon.*

【下半夜】the time after midnight；the latter half of the night

【下辈】❶ future generations；offspring ❷ the younger generation of a family

【下辈子】the next life

【下本钱】（又作'下本儿'）put in time，money and effort；make an investment：要舍得～培养人才。*Don't begrudge time，money and effort in training qualified personnel.*

【下笔】put pen to paper；begin to write or paint：不知如何～ *be at a loss as to how to begin writing or painting* / 想好了再～。*Think it out before you put pen to paper.*

【下笔成章】produce a piece of writing as soon as the pen is put to paper（said of a good and fast writer）

【下笔千言，离题万里】a thousand words flow from the pen，but ten thousand li away from the theme—write fast and at length but not to the point；long-winded and irrelevant

【下边】同〖下面〗

【下拨】（of governments or other organizations at higher levels）allocate and transfer（goods or funds）to units at lower levels：市政府强调指出，这次～的补贴款必须专款专用。*The Municipal Government stressed that the subsidies allocated must be used for their specified purposes only.*

【下不来】❶ cannot come down：她的体温～。*Her temperature won't come down.* ❷ cannot be accomplished；won't do：这道墙没有五千块砖～。*You can't build that wall with less than 5,000 bricks.* ❸ feel embarrassed：几句话说得他脸上～。*He was visibly embarrassed at the remarks.*

【下不来台】（又作'下不了台'）be unable to get out of an embarrassing situation；be unable to back down with good grace；be on the spot；feel embarrassed：给他一个～ *put him on the spot* / 你的话说得太重，弄得他～了。*Your remarks were much too harsh for him to swallow with good grace.*

【下不为例】not to be taken as a precedent；not to be repeated：就这一回，～。*Just this once.*

【下部】❶ the lower part ❷ the lower part of the body

【下操】❶ have drills：我们上午～，下午听课。*We have drills in the morning and lectures in the afternoon.* ❷ finish drilling：他刚～回来。*He's just back from drill.*

【下策】a bad plan；an unwise decision；the worst thing to do；a stupid move：为何出此～？*Why do you resort to such an unwise move?*

【下层】❶ lower levels：深入～ *go to lower-level units；go down to the grass-roots level* ❷ lower strata：～社会 *the lower strata of society*

【下场】（xiàchǎng）❶ go off stage；exit ❷ leave the playing field or court（in a game）

【下场】（xiàchang）an end that a person comes to，usu. bad；fate：遭到可耻～ *come to a disgraceful end；meet with an ignominious fate*

【下车伊始】the moment one alights from the official carriage—the moment one takes up a post；immediately on arrival at a new post

【下沉】sink；subside；submerge：潜水艇逐渐～。*The submarine gradually submerged.* / 地基～。*The foundations have subsided.*

【下乘】❶［宗］（佛教）同〖小乘〗❷ low order；inferior quality：～之作 *a literary or artistic work of low order or inferior quality*

【下厨房】go to the kitchen（i.e. to cook or to prepare a meal）：今天他要亲自～招待你们。*Today he'll treat you to a meal he cooks himself.*

【下处】one's temporary lodging during a trip：找到～了没有？*Have you found a lodging yet?*

【下穿交叉】［交通］underpass；undercrossing

【下船】❶ go ashore；disembark ❷〈方〉get down into a junk；go aboard

【下垂】❶ hang down；droop：她软弱无力，双手～。*Her hands hung limply.* ❷［医］prolapse：子宫～ *prolapse of the uterus；metroptosis*

【下次】next time；next

【下达】make known（or transmit）to lower levels：～作战命令 *issue orders of operation* / 任务已经～。*The task has been assigned.*

【下蛋】lay eggs：咱们的鸭子～了。*Our ducks are laying.*

【下等】of low grade or caste；inferior

【下等人】〈旧〉a person belonging to one of the lower social strata

【下地】❶ go to the fields：～劳动 *go to work in the fields* ❷ leave a sickbed：他病好多了，现在能～了。*He is getting much better now and can get up and move about a bit.*

【下调】（xiàdiào）transfer to a lower-level work unit ——另见 xiàtiáo

【下跌】（of water level，prices，etc.）fall；drop：黄河水位逐渐～。*The water level of the Yellow River is gradually falling.* / 导致物价急剧～ *cause a sharp drop in prices*

【下碇】cast anchor：船在九江～。*The ship anchored at Jiujiang.*

【下毒】put in poison

【下毒手】resort to cruel treachery；strike a vicious blow；lay murderous hands on sb.：背后～ *stab sb. in the back* / 对他～ *lay murderous hands on him；do him in*

【下颚】❶ maxilla（of certain arthropods）❷ the lower jaw or mandible（of vertebrates）

【下发】give（instructions，notice，etc.）to subordinates：放假通知已～到各单位。*The circular concerning holiday time has been sent to all units.*

【下法】[中] laxative (or purgative) remedy

【下凡】(of gods or immortals) descend to the world

【下饭】❶ go with rice：你这两个菜都不喜欢，拿什么～呀？*If you don't like either of the two dishes, what are you going to have with your rice?* ❷ go well with rice：这个菜下酒不～。*This dish goes well with wine, but not with rice.*

【下放】❶ transfer to a lower level：权力～ *transfer (or delegate) power to lower levels* / 企业～ *put an enterprise under a lower administrative level* ❷ transfer (cadres, etc.) to work at the grass-roots level or to do manual labour in the countryside or in a factory：～农村 *be transferred to work in the countryside*

【下风】❶ leeward：工业区一般都设在城市的～。*Industrial districts are generally situated to the leeward of the cities.* ❷ disadvantageous position：占～ *be at a disadvantage* / 暂时处于～ *be temporarily at a disadvantage*

【下岗】❶ come or go off sentry duty ❷ lay off：～工人 *laid-off worker*

【下岗分流】lay off works and reposition redundant personnel

【下工】come or go off work; stop work; knock off：今天～下得早。*We knocked off early today.*

【下工夫】(又作'下功夫') put in time and energy; concentrate one's efforts：在技术革新上狠～ *devote a lot of time and energy to technical innovation*

【下跪】kneel down; go down on one's knees

【下锅】put food in the pot or pan (ready to be cooked)：肉已～。*The pork is already in the pot.* / 无米～ *destitute of rice; starving*

【下海】❶ go to sea：～去游泳 *go swimming in the sea* ❷ (of fishermen) go fishing on the sea; put out to sea：～捕鱼 *go fishing on the sea* / 初次～，难免晕船。*You can't help being seasick on your first trip at sea.* ❸〈口〉(of people from other walks of life) go in for business; become a businessman：近年来，不少科技人员纷纷～经商。*Over the past few years, quite a number of scientific and technological workers have switched to doing business.*

【下颌】[生理] the lower jaw ◇ ～骨 lower jawbone

【下怀】one's heart's desire：正中下怀

【下回】next time

【下级】❶ lower level：～服从上级。*The lower level is subordinate to the higher level.* / ～军官 *a low ranking (or junior) officer* ❷ subordinate：帮助～解决工作中的问题 *help one's subordinates to solve the problems they encounter in their work*

【下家】(in mahjong, card games, or in wine games) the player whose turn comes next

【下嫁】(of a girl of high birth) marry a man of lower social status

【下贱】❶ of humble origin; low in social status ❷ low; mean; degrading：～女人 *a cheap woman*

【下降】descend; go or come down; drop; fall; decline：飞机开始～。*The plane began to descend.* / 气温显著～。*There was a marked drop in the temperature.*

【下焦】[中] the part of the body cavity below the umbilicus, housing the bladder, kidneys and bowels

【下脚】❶ get a foothold; plant one's foot：没有～的地方 *be unable to gain a footing (or foothold); have nowhere to plant one's foot* ❷ leftover bits and pieces：～棉 *cotton waste* ◇ ～货 unsalable leftover goods of inferior quality; ～料 leftover bits and pieces (of industrial material, etc.); scrap

【下届】the next session of a regular meeting; next (graduating class, etc.)：～会议 *the next session of the conference* / ～毕业生 *students graduating next year*

【下界】❶ the world of mortals; the world of man ❷ 同〖下凡〗

【下劲】exert oneself; go all out：他学习很～。*He works really hard.* / 要想成功就得下死劲干。*You have to go all out if you want to be a success.*

【下井落石】同〖落井下石〗

【下酒】❶ go with wine：买点花生米～ *buy some peanuts to go with the wine* ❷ go well with wine：这菜不～。*This dish doesn't go very well with wine.* ◇ ～菜 a dish that goes with alcoholic drinks

【下课】❶ get out of class; finish class：～后再去。*Go there after class.* / 现在～。*The class is dismissed.* or *The class is over.* ❷ be removed from a post; be made redundant

【下筷】apply one's chopsticks to the food—start eating

【下款】❶ the name of the donor (as inscribed on a painting or a calligraphic scroll presented as a gift) ❷ the signature at the end of a letter

【下来】❶ come down：梯子不牢，快～！*Come down at once! The ladder isn't steady.* ❷ come down to a place regarded as being lower or below：新任务～了。*A new task has fallen on us.* ❸ (of farm crops) be harvested：麦子已经～了。*The wheat has been harvested.* ❹ (of a period of time) be over; come to an end：一年～，他的技术大有提高。*After one year's work, his skills have improved a lot.* ❺ (indicating motion toward a lower or nearer position) down (here)：溪水从山上流～。*The stream flows down from the mountain.* ❻ (used after a verb of duration) up to the present; till the end (or finish)：古代流传～的寓言 *fables handed down from ancient times* ❼ (used after a verb, expressing completion or finality of an action)：风突然停了～。*The wind dropped all of a sudden.* / 剩～的就这

么些了。*This is all that's left*. ❽(used after an adjective, indicating increasing degree)：他的声音慢慢低了～。*His voice trailed off*. / 天色渐渐黑～。*It was getting darker and darker*.

【下里巴人】Songs of the Rustic Poor (folk songs of the state of Chu)—popular literature or art

【下联】the second (or latter) line of a couplet

【下列】listed below; following：应注意～几点。*Attention should be paid to the following points*.

【下令】give orders; order

【下流】❶ lower reaches (of a river)：黄河～ *the lower reaches of the Huanghe River* ❷ low down; mean; obscene; dirty：～的勾当 *a base act*; *a dirty deal* / ～的玩笑 *dirty (or obscene) jests*; *coarse jokes* / ～话 *obscene (or dirty, foul) language*; *obscenities*

【下落】❶ whereabouts：打听某人的～ *inquire about sb.'s whereabouts* / 失踪者至今还没有～。*We still have no idea of the whereabouts of those missing persons*. ❷ drop; fall：气球～的地点 *the place where the balloon has fallen*

【下马】❶ get down (or dismount) from a horse ❷ (of a project, plan, etc.) be discontinued; be given up：这项工程不能～。*This project should not be abandoned*.

【下马看花】(又作'下马观花') get off one's horse to look at the flowers—go deep into the realities of life and make thorough investigations

【下马威】severity shown by an official on assuming office; the severity of a newly-appointed official：给他个～ *deal him a head-on blow at the first encounter*

【下面】❶ below; under; underneath：大桥～ *under the bridge* / 图表～的说明 *the caption below the chart* ❷ the next in order; following：～该谁了？*Who's next*? / ～一个 *the next one* / 必须记住～几点。*The following points should be borne in mind*. ❸ lower level; subordinate：了解～的情况 *find out about how things are at the lower levels*

【下奶】stimulate or increase the secretion of milk (of nursing mothers)

【下品】of the lowest grade or quality

【下聘】(of the bridegroom-to-be's family) send betrothal gifts and money over to the bride

【下坡路】❶ a downhill path; a downhill journey ❷ decline：走～ *go downhill*; *be on the decline*

【下铺】lower berth; bottom berth

【下棋】play chess; have a game of chess

【下欠】❶ still owe (after paying part of one's debt)：～八百元 *with 800 yuan still owing* ❷ a sum still owing：全数还清，并无～。*The debt has been fully paid up. Nothing owing*.

【下情】❶ conditions at the lower levels; feelings or wishes of the masses or one's subordinates：不了解～ *not know what is going on at the lower levels* ❷〈旧〉〈谦〉the situation I am in; my feelings or wishes：还望体念～。*Hope you will give sympathetic consideration to my situation*.

【下去】❶ go down; descend：～看看是谁在敲门。*Go downstairs and see who's knocking at the door*. / 到站了，快～。*Here we are, let's get off at once*. ❷ go down to a place regarded as lower or below; step down (from the stage, platform, etc.)：你应该～了解一下情况。*You should go down there to size up the situation*. ❸ lessen; be reduced; go down：他的气还没～吗？*Hasn't he calmed down yet*? ❹(indicating motion toward a lower or farther position) down (there)：跳～ *jump down* / 从窗口扔～ *throw sth. down through the window* / 洪水退～了。*The flood has receded*. ❺ go on (doing sth.); continue：坚持～ *stick it out* / 她激动得说不～。*She was so overcome with emotion that she couldn't go on*. ❻ (used after an adjective, indicating increasing degree) develop; grow：看来天气还会冷～。*It seems it will get even colder*. / 她一天天地瘦～。*She's getting thinner every day*.

【下山】❶ go down a hill or mountain ❷ (of the sun) set; sink below the horizon：太阳已经～。*The sun has sunk in the west*.

【下身】❶ the lower part of the body ❷ private parts; genitals

【下生】be born

【下士】(U. S. & Brit. Army, Brit. Air Force, U. S. & Brit. Marine Corps) corporal; (U. S. Navy) petty officer third class; (Brit. Navy) petty officer second class

【下世】❶ next life ❷〈书〉leave this world—die

【下手】❶ (又作'下首') right hand side or seat; seat of lower priority：坐在主宾的～ *sit on the right hand of the guest of honour* ❷ 同〖下家〗❸ put one's hand to; start doing sth.; set about; set to：不知从何～ *not know where to start*; *not know how to set about a job* ❹〈口〉assistant; helper：打～ *act as assistant*

【下书】〈书〉deliver a letter

【下属】subordinate：他像使唤用人一样对待他的～。*He treated his subordinates like servants*.

【下水】(xiàshuǐ)❶ enter the water; be launched：又一艘新船～了。*Another new ship was launched*. / 新船～典礼 *the launching ceremony of a new ship* ❷ soak in water to shrink cloth or fabrics before use ❸ take to evil-doing; fall into evil ways：拖人～ *involve sb. in evildoing*; *drag sb. into the mire* ❹ going downstream; downriver：～船 *a downriver boat*

【下水】(xiàshui) tripe or chitterlings：猪～ *pig's tripe and chitterlings*

【下水道】sewer

【下榻】〈书〉stay (at a place during a trip)：～于新侨饭店 *stay at the Xinqiao Hotel*

【下台】❶ step down from the stage or platform ❷ fall out of power; leave office：被赶～ *be driven out of office*; *be thrown out* / 总统快～了。*The President will soon leave office*. ❸ (usu. used in the negative) get out of a predicament or an embarrassing situation：没法～ *be unable to back down with good grace* / 叫他下不了台 *put him on the spot*

【下台阶】get out of a predicament or an embarrassing situation：自己想法～ *try to find oneself a way out of a predicament* / 趁势～ *take an opportunity to back down with good grace*

【下体】〈书〉❶ the lower part of the body ❷ private parts；genitals

【下调】(xiàtiáo) adjust (prices，standards，quotas，etc.) downward：工业品价格大幅度～。*There has been a drastic downward adjustment of the prices of industrial goods*. ——另见 xiàdiào

【下帖】〈书〉send an invitation card

【下同】(used in annotation) similarly hereinafter；the same below

【下头】同〖下面〗❶❸

【下网】[计] off-line

【下文】❶ what follows in the passage，paragraph，article，etc.：～再作阐述 *be explained in the ensuing chapters or paragraphs* ❷ later development；outcome；sequel：事情并没有就此结束，还有～哩。*The matter didn't end there；there was a sequel to it*.

【下午】afternoon：～有场电影。*There's a movie this afternoon*. / ～见！*See you in the afternoon*!

【下弦】[天] last (or third) quarter (of the moon) ◇～月 the moon at the last (or third) quarter

【下限】the latest or minimum permissible；lower limit；prescribed minimum；floor level；floor：溶液比重不能低于～。*The specific gravity of the solution should be kept above the prescribed minimum*.

【下陷】be sunken；be hollow；form a depression：眼眶～ *with sunken eyes* / 双颊～ *with sunken cheeks* / 一下雨，地面～的地方就成了水坑。*Rain formed puddles in the depressions on the ground*.

【下乡】go to the countryside：～务农 *go in for farming in the countryside*

【下泻】❶ (of water) flow down：激流～不畅。*The torrents were impeded in their downflow*. ❷ (of prices，etc.) drop sharply：年初以来，美元对日元的汇价一路～。*Since the beginning of the year，there have been sharp drops in the dollar-yen conversion rate*. ❸ have loose bowels ——另见〖上吐下泻〗

【下行】❶ (of trains) going from the capital to any other part of the country；down：在中国，～列车编号用奇数。*In China，the down trains are given odd numbers*. ❷ (of boats) going downstream；downriver：～船 *a downstream boat* ❸ (of documents) being issued to the lower levels：～公文 *documents issued to the lower levels*

【下旋】[体] underspin；backspin：他擅长打～球。*He's good at cutting underspins*.

【下学】finish classes and leave school (for the day)：～后早点回家！*Come home right after school*!

【下旬】the last ten-day period of a month

【下咽】swallow (food or other things)：难以～ *find it hard to swallow*

【下药】❶ prescribe medicine：李大夫～比较重。*Dr. Li usually prescribes heavy doses*. ❷ put in poison

【下野】(of a ruler) retire from the political arena；be forced to relinquish power

【下议院】❶ lower house；lower chamber ❷ the House of Commons (the lower house of the British Parliament)

【下意识】subconsciousness：有一种～的恐惧 *have a subconscious fear* / 我～地感到要出事。*Subconsciously I felt something untoward was going to happen*.

【下游】❶ lower reaches (of a river)：长江～ *the lower reaches of the Changjiang (Yangtze) River* ❷ backward position：甘居～ *be resigned to being backward*

【下余】be left：除去成本，～多少？*How much is left after deducting the capital investment*? / ～部分 *the remaining part；the remainder；the rest*

【下狱】throw into prison；imprison

【下载】[计] download

【下葬】be interred；be buried

【下诏】issue an imperial edict：～大赦天下。*An imperial edict was given for an amnesty*.

【下肢】lower limbs；legs

【下中农】lower-middle peasant

【下种】sow (seeds)：麦子该～了。*It's time to sow wheat*.

【下注】lay down a stake (in gambling)：他在那匹马身上下了大注。*He staked a lot of money on that horse*.

【下箸】apply one's chopsticks to the food —start eating

【下装】remove theatrical makeup and costume

【下坠】[医] straining (at stool)；tenesmus

【下子】(used after 两 or 几) what one is good at or capable of：他打起篮球来还有两～。*He's no mean basketball player*.

【下钻】[油] run the drilling tool into a well：～速度 *drilling speed*

【下作】low-down；mean；obscene；dirty：那个老家伙太～。*That man is a mean old bird*.

吓

动 frighten；scare；intimidate：别～着孩子。*Be careful not to frighten the child*. / ～坏了 *be terribly frightened；be overcome with fear* / ～破了胆 *be scared out of one's wits* / 把我～一跳 *give me a start (or scare)* ——另见 hè

【吓唬】〈口〉frighten；scare；intimidate：别～她，她胆儿小。*Don't frighten her；she's rather timid*. / 他净～人。*He's always trying to intimidate people*.

【吓人】be frightening：山洞又黑又深，进去可真～。*It was really frightening to get into that deep and pitch dark cave*.

夏

名 summer

【夏播】summer sowing

【夏布】grass linen; grass cloth
【夏锄】summer hoeing and weeding
【夏管】field management in summer
【夏候鸟】summer resident (e. g. barn swallows, cuckoos, etc. in China)
【夏季】summer (season)
【夏枯草】[中] selfheal (Prunella vulgaris)
【夏历】the traditional Chinese calendar; the lunar calendar
【夏粮】summer grain crops
【夏令】❶ summertime: ～时装 *summer fashions* / ～商品 *commodities for summer use* ❷ summer weather: 春行～ *have summerlike weather in spring; see exceptionally warm days in spring* ◇ ～时 summer time; daylight-saving time; ～营 summer camp
【夏炉冬扇】stoves in summer and fans in winter—things that do not meet the needs of the time
【夏眠】aestivation (of certain animals)
【夏时制】the practice of adopting daylight-saving time in summer
【夏收】summer harvest: ～季节快到了。*It's about time for the summer harvest.* / ～作物 *summer crops*
【夏熟】ripen in summer: ～作物 *summer crops*
【夏天】summer: 这里的～特别热。*It's very hot here in summer.*
【夏娃】Eve (the first woman according to the Bible)
【夏衣】summer clothing; summer wear
【夏至】❶ the Summer Solstice—the 10th of the 24 solar terms ❷ the day marking the beginning of the 10th solar term (June 21 or 22, the longest day of the year)
【夏至点】the Summer Solstice (the northernmost point in the ecliptic reached by the sun about June 21 or 22)
【夏种】summer sowing
【夏装】summer clothing; summer wear

xiān

仙 名 celestial being; immortal: 仙人
【仙丹】elixir of life
【仙风道骨】the demeanour of a transcendent being
【仙姑】❶ female immortal (or celestial) ❷ sorceress
【仙鹤】❶ another name for 丹顶鹤 ❷ white crane (kept by immortals in Chinese mythology)
【仙鹤草】[中] hairyvein agrimony (Agrimonia pilosa)
【仙后座】[天] Cassiopeia
【仙境】fairyland; wonderland; paradise
【仙客来】[植] cyclamen
【仙女】female celestial; fairy maiden
【仙女座】[天] Andromeda
【仙人】celestial being; immortal
【仙人果】[植] prickly-pear cactus; prickly pear
【仙人球】[植] ball cactus
【仙人掌】[植] cactus
【仙山琼阁】a jewelled palace on the mountain of the immortals
【仙逝】〈婉〉pass away
【仙王座】[天] Cepheus
【仙姿】fairy-like beauty
【仙子】❶ female celestial ❷ celestial being; immortal

先 Ⅰ 副 ❶ earlier; before sb. else; before doing sth. else; first; in advance: 他比我～到。*He arrived earlier than I did.* / 我～说两句。*Let me say a few words first.* ❷ (used with a negative word "不", "别", etc.) for the time being; for the moment: 你～别走，我有话跟你说。*Don't leave yet, I want to have a word with you.* ❸ 〈口〉earlier on; before; at first: 你～怎么不告诉我呢? *Why didn't you tell me before?* / 他～说不去，后来却又改变了主意。*At first he refused to go, but later on he changed his mind.* Ⅱ 名 elder generation; ancestor: 祖先 Ⅲ 形 deceased; late
【先辈】elder generation; ancestors: 继承革命～的事业 *carry on the cause of the older generation of revolutionaries*
【先导】guide; forerunner; precursor: 错误常常是正确的～。*Error is often the precursor of what is correct.*
【先睹为快】consider it a pleasure to be among the first to read (a poem, article, etc.) or see (a play, ballet, etc.)
【先发制人】gain the initiative by striking the first blow; forestall the enemy: 采取～的手段 *take preemptive measures*
【先锋】vanguard; van: 打～ *fight in the van; be a pioneer* / ～模范作用 *exemplary vanguard role* ◇ ～队 vanguard
【先公后私】public interest comes before private or personal interests
【先河】the beginning of sth.: 开…之～ *be a forerunner of...*
【先后】❶ being early or late; priority; order: 这些事都该办，可也得有个～。*All these matters should be tackled, but they should be taken up in order of priority.* ❷ successively; one after another: 他～三次访美。*He visited America three times.*
【先见之明】prophetic vision; foresight: 缺乏～ *lack foresight*
【先进】advanced: ～单位 *advanced unit* / ～分子 *advanced element* / ～个人 *advanced individual* / ～经验 *advanced experience* ◇ ～工作者 advanced worker; ～集体 advanced group (or collective)
【先决】prerequisite: ～条件 *prerequisite; precondition* / 社会安定是社会发展的～条件。*Social order and stability is a prerequisite to social development.*
【先来后到】in the order of arrival; first come,

first served：请按～的次序排队。*Please line up in order of arrival*.

【先礼后兵】take strong measures only after courteous ones fail；try peaceful means before resorting to force

【先例】precedent：开～ *set* (*or create*) *a precedent* / 有～可援 *have a precedent to go by*

【先烈】martyr：革命～ *revolutionary martyr*

【先令】❶ shilling (a monetary unit of Britain until 1971) ❷ shilling (a monetary unit of Uganda, Kenya, Somalia and Tanzania) ❸ schilling (a monetary unit of Austria)

【先期】earlier than the date scheduled；earlier on；in advance：代表团的部分团员已～到达。*Some members of the delegation had arrived at an earlier date*.

【先前】before；previously：这孩子比～高多了。*The child is much taller than before*.

【先遣】sent in advance：～部队 *advance troops* (*or force*) / ～队 *advance party*

【先驱】pioneer；forerunner；harbinger：聂耳、冼星海是中国革命音乐的～。*Nie Er and Xian Xinghai were pioneers of China's revolutionary music*.

【先人】❶ ancestor；forefather ❷ my late father

【先人后己】put others before oneself；put other people's interest ahead of one's own

【先入为主】first impressions are strongest；prejudices die hard

【先入之见】preconception；preconceived idea；prejudice

【先声】first signs；herald；harbinger：一七八九年的法国革命是十九世纪各国资产阶级革命的～。*The French Revolution of* 1789 *heralded other bourgeois revolutions in the* 19*th century*.

【先声夺人】demoralize one's opponent by a show of strength；overawe people by displaying one's strength：湖南队～，一上场就连中三球。*The Hunan team got the better of their opponents by scoring three baskets in a row at the beginning*.

【先生】❶ teacher：要做人民的～，先做人民的学生。*To be a teacher of the people, one must first be their pupil*. ❷ Mister (Mr.)；gentleman；sir：总统～ *Mr. President* / 女士们，～们！*Ladies and Gentlemen*！❸ husband：她～出差去了。*Her husband is away on business*. / 我～不在家。*My husband is out*. ❹〈方〉doctor ❺〈旧〉(usu. used in) 账房～ *bookkeeper* / 算命～ *fortune-teller*

【先是】before this；originally

【先手】offensive position (in chess)：～棋 *an offensive move*

【先天】❶ congenital；inborn：～畸形 *congenital malformation* ❷〈哲〉a priori；innate：人的知识不是～就有的，而是从社会实践中来的。*Man's knowledge is not innate but comes from social practice*.

【先天不足】congenital deficiency；inborn weakness：这孩子体弱多病，医生说他～。*The child is always ailing. The doctor says he's congenitally deficient*.

【先天下之忧而忧，后天下之乐而乐】be the first to become concerned with the world's troubles and the last to rejoice in its happiness；be concerned before anyone else and enjoy oneself only after everyone else finds enjoyment

【先天性疾病】congenital disorders

【先天性免疫】congenital immunity

【先天性缺陷】birth defects

【先天性心脏病】［医］congenital heart disease

【先头】❶ ahead；in front；in advance：～部队 *an advance party of soldiers*；*vanguard* / 走在最～ *walk ahead of all other people* ❷ before；formerly；in the past：你～没说过这事。*You didn't mention this before*.

【先下手为强】he who strikes first gains the advantage；to take the initiative is to gain the upper hand：～，后下手遭殃。*He who strikes first prevails, he who strikes late fails*.

【先小人后君子】let's allow impoliteness to precede courtesy (said when discussing the terms of a deal)

【先行】❶ go ahead of the rest；start off before the others ❷ beforehand；in advance：～通知 *notify in advance* / 新产品将在本市～试销。*The new products will first be put on trial sale in this city*.

【先行官】commander of an advance unit or vanguard：铁路运输是国民经济的～。*Railway transportation is the vanguard of the national economy*.

【先行者】forerunner：纪念伟大的革命～孙中山先生！*Let us pay tribute to our great revolutionary forerunner, Dr. Sun Yat-sen*！

【先验】〈哲〉a priori：～知识 *a priori knowledge* ◇ ～方法 transcendental method；～论〈哲〉apriorism

【先斩后奏】execute sb. first and report to the emperor afterwards—act first and report afterwards

【先兆】omen；portent；sign；indication：地震的～ *indications of an impending earthquake* / 不祥的～ *ill omen* ◇ ～流产［医］early signs of miscarriage；threatened miscarriage；～子痫［医］preeclampsia

【先哲】a great thinker of the past；sage

【先知】❶ a person of foresight ❷ religion prophet

【先知先觉】❶ a person of foresight ❷ having foresight

纤 形 fine；minute：纤尘 ——另见 qiàn

【纤尘】fine dust

【纤尘不染】❶ without a speck of dust：室内窗明几净，～。*The room is bright and spotlessly clean*. ❷ untainted with evil thoughts or bad habits

【纤度】［纺］fibre number；size

【纤毫不爽】be extremely accurate；be free from the slightest error

【纤毛】［生］cilium：～运动 *ciliary movement*

【纤毛虫】[动] ciliate; infusorian

【纤巧】dainty; delicate: 这些精美的绣品都出自她那～的双手。*All these elegant embroideries are creations of her dainty and dexterous hands.*

【纤弱】slim and fragile; delicate: ～的身影 *a slim and frail figure*

【纤手】dainty (or delicate) hands (of a woman)

【纤维】fibre; staple: 天然(合成、人造)～ *natural (synthetic, man-made) fibre* / ～长度 *fibre length; staple* ◇ ～板 fibreboard; ～蛋白 [生化] fibrin; ～蛋白原 [生化] fibrinogen; ～光学 [物] fibre optics; ～集束 [化纤] collection of filaments; ～瘤 [医] fibroma; ～束 [化纤] tow; ～素 [化] cellulose; ～素分解菌 cellulose-decomposing bacterium; cellvibrio; ～植物 fibre plant

【纤悉无遗】with not a single detail left out

【纤细】very thin; slender; fine; tenuous: ～的头发 *fine hair* / ～的游丝 *tenuous gossamer*

【纤小】fine; tenuous

氙 名 [化] xenon

【氙灯】xenon lamp

籼 (构词成分) 见下

【籼稻】long-grained nonglutinous rice; indica rice

【籼米】polished long-grained nonglutinous rice; polished indica rice

掀 动 lift (a cover, etc.): ～门帘 *lift the door curtain* / ～掉盖子 *take the lid off* / 把对手～翻在地 *throw the opponent off his balance* / 把被子～起来 *pull the quilt off*

【掀动】❶ launch (a war) ❷ lift; start; set in motion: 春风～了她的衣襟。*The spring breeze lifted the edge of her blouse.* / 壶里的蒸汽把壶盖都～了。*The steam in the kettle is jiggling the lid.*

【掀风鼓浪】raise a storm—stir up trouble

【掀开】open; lift; draw: ～窗帘 *draw the curtains open* / ～锅盖 *lift the lid off the pot*

【掀起】❶ lift; raise: 一阵狂风～了她的大衣衣角。*A sudden gust lifted the corners of her overcoat.* ❷ surge; cause to surge: 大海～了巨浪。*Big waves surged on the sea.* ❸ set off (a movement, etc.); start: 就这个问题～了一场激烈的辩论。*This question set off a fierce debate.*

锨 名 shovel

酰 名 [化] acyl

鲜 Ⅰ 形 ❶ fresh: ～奶 *fresh milk* / ～蘑 *fresh mushrooms* / ～鱼 *fresh fish* ❷ bright-coloured; bright: 这块布颜色太～。*The colour of this cloth is too bright.* ❸ (of salty dishes or soup) delicious; tasty: 这汤味道很～。*The soup tastes delicious.* Ⅱ 名 ❶ delicacy: 尝尝～ *have a taste of a delicacy of the season* ❷ seafood; aquatic foods: 海鲜 ——另见 xiǎn

【鲜脆】(of fruits, melons and gourds) fresh and crisp: ～的苹果 *fresh, crisp apples*

【鲜果】fresh fruit

【鲜红】bright red; scarlet: ～的旗帜 *a bright red flag*

【鲜花】fresh flowers; flowers

【鲜活】❶ fresh and alive (of aquatic products, flowers, etc.): 那盆里的鱼还是～的。*The fish in that bowl are alive.* ❷ vivacious; lively: ～的个性 *lively personality*

【鲜货】fresh fruit, vegetables, or seafood, etc.

【鲜亮】(of colour) shining bright

【鲜美】❶ (of cooked food, fruit, etc.) delicious; tasty ❷ 〈书〉(of flowers, grass, etc.) fresh and pleasing: 芳草～。*There were scented grasses, fresh and pleasing to the eye.*

【鲜明】❶ (of colour) bright: 色彩～ *in bright colours; bright-coloured* ❷ clear-cut; distinct; distinctive: ～的对照 *a striking (or sharp) contrast* / ～的节奏 *strongly accented rhythms* / 主题～ *have a distinct theme*

【鲜嫩】fresh and tender: ～的藕 *fresh and tender lotus roots*

【鲜血】(red) blood

【鲜艳】(又作'鲜妍') bright-coloured; gaily-coloured: 颜色～ *in gay colours* / 穿着～的民族服装 *wearing bright-coloured national costume*

【鲜艳夺目】dazzlingly beautiful; resplendent: 那～的浆果,在绿叶的衬托下,显得格外娇妍。*The contrast of the bright, eye-catching red of the berries against the green of the leaves looked particularly charming.*

【鲜衣怒马】be dressed in fine clothes and ride on well-groomed horses—lead a luxurious life

xián

闲 Ⅰ 形 ❶ not busy; idle; unoccupied: 我这两天～着没事。*I've had nothing to do for the last couple of days.* ❷ not in use; unoccupied; lying idle: 别让机器～着。*Don't let the machine stand idle.* / 没有一辆车～着! *There's not a single free vehicle.* or *All the vehicles are in use.* ❸ having nothing to do with business: 闲谈 Ⅱ 名 spare or free time; leisure: 今天她不得～。*She has no time to spare today.*

【闲不住】refuse to stay idle; always keep oneself busy

【闲扯】chat; engage in chitchat: 你别在这儿～了,快回家去吧。*Don't hang around here and gab. Get yourself home, quick.*

【闲富】idle; surplus: 让一些～的人员返家待聘 *send redundant personnel home to await re-employment*

【闲工夫】spare time; leisure

【闲逛】saunter; stroll: 星期天在街上～的人比平时多。*On Sundays there are more people strolling along the streets than on weekdays.*

【闲话】❶ digression: ～少说,书归正传。*Enough of this digression; let's return to our story.* or

However, to continue the story. ❷ complaint; gossip: 别让人说咱们的～。*We mustn't give anyone cause for complaint.* / 她可不爱说人～。*She's not fond of gossip.* ❸〈书〉talk casually about; chat about: ～当年 *chat about bygone days*

【闲空】free time; spare time; leisure

【闲聊】chat: 她俩正在院子里～呢。*They are in the courtyard chatting.*

【闲气】anger about trifles: 我可没工夫生这份儿～。*I'm too busy to lose my temper over such a little thing.* or *I've no time to get angry about such a trivial matter.*

【闲钱】〈口〉spare cash

【闲情逸致】(be in) a leisurely and carefree mood; (have) the leisure and (be in the) mood for enjoyment: 大家都在紧张地工作着,谁还有～去跳舞呢! *Everybody is busy working and is in no mood for going to a dance.*

【闲人】❶ an unoccupied person; idler: 现在正是农忙季节,村里一个～也没有。*It's the busy season for farmers and nobody in the village is idle.* ❷ persons not concerned: ～免进。*No admittance except on business.* or *Admittance to staff only.* or *Employees only.*

【闲散】❶ free and at leisure; at loose ends ❷ unused; idle: ～资金 *idle capital* / ～土地 *scattered plots of unutilized land*

【闲时】leisure; free time

【闲事】❶ a matter that does not concern one; other people's business: 爱管～ *like to poke one's nose into other people's business* / 别管～! *Mind your own business.* or *None of your business.* ❷ an unimportant matter

【闲是闲非】idle gossip: 别人爱说个～的,随他们说去。*Some people like to engage in idle gossip. Don't pay any attention to them.*

【闲书】light reading

【闲谈】chat; engage in chitchat

【闲暇】leisure

【闲心】leisurely mood: 没有～管这种事 *be too busy to think about such matters; not be in the mood to bother about such matters*

【闲言碎语】❶ idle chatter; irrelevancies ❷ gossip; backbiting; groundless rumour; slander

【闲云野鹤】(like) drifting clouds and wild storks—free and unrestrained

【闲杂】without fixed duties: ～人员 *people without fixed duties; miscellaneous personnel*

【闲职】an extremely light and easy job; sinecure

【闲置】leave unused; let sth. lie idle; set aside: ～的机器 *idle machines* / ～资金 *idle funds*

贤 Ⅰ 形 ❶ virtuous and able; worthy: 贤明 ❷〈套〉(used in addressing people of the same or of a younger generation) Ⅱ 名 a worthy person; an able and virtuous person: 让～ *relinquish one's post in favour of sb. better qualified*

【贤达】a prominent and worthy personage: 社会～ *the worthies*

【贤惠】(又作'贤慧') (of a woman) virtuous; genial and prudent; kindhearted and understanding: 他有一位十分～的夫人。*He has a genial and devoted wife.*

【贤良】❶ (of a man) able and virtuous ❷ able and virtuous men

【贤明】wise and able; sagacious

【贤内助】❶〈套〉(said of another person's wife) a good wife: 大家都羡慕你有一位～。*Everybody envies you for having such a good wife.* ❷〈诙〉my better half; my good wife: 这是我的～。*This is my better half.*

【贤能】a virtuous and talented person

【贤妻】〈旧〉(a term of respect) my good (or worthy) wife

【贤妻良母】a good wife and loving mother

【贤人】a person of virtue (or merit); a person of outstanding worth

【贤淑】〈书〉(of a woman) virtuous, kind and genial

弦 名 ❶ bowstring; string ❷〈方〉spring (of a watch, etc.) ❸［数］chord ❹［数］hypotenuse ❺ the string of a musical instrument

【弦外之音】overtones; implication: 我懂得他的～:这事儿总工程师也有责任。*I'm quite aware of the overtones of what he was saying: the chief engineer should also be held responsible.*

【弦月】crescent or half moon

【弦乐队】string orchestra (or band); string ensemble

【弦乐器】stringed instrument

涎 名 saliva: 流～ *slobber; slaver; drool*

【涎皮赖脸】brazen; cheeky; shameless and loathsome

【涎水】〈方〉saliva

【涎着脸】be brazenfaced; be cheeky

咸 Ⅰ 副〈书〉all: ～受其益。*All benefited from it.* / 老少～宜 *suitable for old and young alike* Ⅱ 形 salted; salty: ～鱼 *salt fish* / ～蛋 *salted egg* / 菜太～了。*The dish is too salty.*

【咸菜】salted vegetables; pickles

【咸淡】degree of saltiness: 这汤的～正合适。*This soup tastes just right, neither too salty nor too flat.*

【咸肉】salted meat; bacon

【咸水】salt water ◇ ～湖 saltwater lake; ～鱼 saltwater fish

【咸盐】〈方〉table salt; salt

娴 形〈书〉❶ refined: 娴静 ❷ adept; skilled: 娴熟

【娴静】gentle and refined

【娴熟】adept; skilled: 弓马～ *adept in archery and horsemanship* / ～的技巧 *consummate skill*

【娴雅】(of a woman) refined; elegant: 举止～ *poised and elegant*

【娴于辞令】be skilled in the use of words; be gifted with a silver tongue

舷 名 the side of a ship or aircraft: 左舷 / 右舷

【舷边】gunwale; gunnel

【舷窗】porthole

【舷梯】❶ gangway ladder; accommodation ladder ❷ (boarding) ramp

衔 Ⅰ 动 ❶ hold in the mouth: ～着烟斗 *have a pipe between one's teeth* / 燕子～泥筑窠。*Swallows carry bits of earth in their bills to build nests*. ❷ harbour; bear: 衔恨 ❸〈书〉receive (orders, etc.): 衔命 ❹ link up; join: 衔接 Ⅱ 名 rank; title: 大使～常驻代表 *permanent representative with the rank of ambassador*

【衔恨】harbour resentment; bear a grudge: ～终生 *nurse a deep grudge to the end of one's days*

【衔接】link up; join: 大桥把两条公路～起来。*The bridge links up the two highways*.

【衔命】〈书〉carry out an order

【衔铁】[电] armature

【衔头】title (of a person by right of office, attainment, etc.)

【衔冤】nurse a bitter sense of wrong; have a simmering sense of injustice

嫌 Ⅰ 名 ❶ suspicion: 避嫌 ❷ ill will; resentment; enmity; grudge: 前嫌 Ⅱ 动 dislike; mind; complain of: ～麻烦 *not want to take the trouble; think it troublesome* / ～脏 *think sth. too dirty* / ～孩子吵 *think the children too noisy*

【嫌烦】find sth. annoying or trying: 老人很难侍候,但她从没嫌过烦。*The old man was very hard to please, but she never grew impatient waiting on him*.

【嫌弃】dislike and avoid; cold-shoulder: 不要～犯过错误的同志。*Don't cold-shoulder comrades who have made mistakes*.

【嫌恶】detest; loathe: 我们办公室里没有一个人不～他的。*There's no one in our office who doesn't detest him*.

【嫌隙】feeling of animosity; enmity; ill will; grudge

【嫌疑】suspicion: 有间谍～ *be suspected of being a spy* ◇ ～犯 suspect; ～分子 suspect

【嫌怨】grudge; resentment; enmity

xiǎn

险 Ⅰ 名 a place difficult of access; a narrow pass; defile: 无～可守 *have no tenable defence position; be strategically indefensible* Ⅱ 形 ❶ dangerous; perilous: 山又高又陡,而且雪深没膝,爬上去好～呀。*The mountain was high and steep, and the snow knee-deep. It was really dangerous to climb*. ❷ sinister; vicious; venomous: 阴险 Ⅲ 副 by a hair's breadth; by inches; nearly: ～遭不幸 *come within an ace of death* / 好～哪! *That was a near thing*!

【险隘】a strategic pass; defile

【险毒】sinister and vicious: 他的行动处处受到～刁滑的特务的监视。*His every move was followed by sinister and cunning spies*.

【险恶】❶ dangerous; perilous; ominous: 处境～ *be in a perilous position* / 病情～ *be dangerously ill* ❷ sinister; vicious; malicious; treacherous: ～的用心 *sinister (or vicious) intentions; evil motives*

【险峰】a perilous peak

【险境】dangerous situation: 脱离～ *be out of danger*

【险峻】dangerously steep; precipitous: 山峰～。*The mountains are precipitous*.

【险情】dangerous state or situation: 河水不断上涨,大堤出现～。*The river keeps rising and the dam is threatened*.

【险球】(mostly football) a near miss (goal): 守门员身手不凡,接连救起了几个～。*He's a very good goalkeeper and made several spectacular saves*.

【险区】danger zone

【险胜】win by a narrow margin: 以二十一比十九～ *win the game by the close score of 21-19*

【险滩】dangerous shoal; rapids

【险象环生】dangers lurking on all sides; beset (or surrounded) by perils

【险些】narrowly (escape from sth. untoward); just barely; nearly: ～掉到水里 *nearly fall into the water* / 马往旁边一闪,～把我摔下来。*The horse suddenly shied and I was nearly thrown off*.

【险要】strategically located and difficult of access

【险遭不测】have a near (or narrow) escape

【险诈】sinister and crafty

【险症】dangerous illness

【险阻】(of roads) dangerous and difficult: 崎岖～的山路 *a dangerous and difficult mountain path*

显 Ⅰ 形 ❶ be apparent; be obvious; be noticeable: 药的效果还不～。*The effect of the medicine is not yet noticeable*. ❷ illustrious and influential: 显达 Ⅱ 动 show; display; manifest: ～本领 *display one's skill* / 深色衣服不～脏。*Dark clothes do not show the dirt*.

【显出】show; reveal: 脸上～不耐烦的神色 *with impatience written on one's face* / 东方刚刚～鱼肚白。*Day was just breaking*.

【显达】illustrious and influential

【显得】look; seem; appear: 他～有点紧张。*He seems a bit nervous*.

【显而易见】obviously; evidently; clearly

【显赫】illustrious; celebrated: ～的战功 *illustrious war exploits* / 声势～ *have a powerful influence* / ～的名声 *great renown*

【显花植物】[植] phanerogam

【显见】be obvious; be self-evident; be apparent: ～的理由 *an obvious (or apparent) reason*

【显灵】(of a ghost or spirit) make its presence or power felt

【显露】become visible; appear; manifest itself: 随着乌云的消散,月亮逐渐～出来了。*As the dark clouds dispersed, the moon gradually came into view.*

【显明】obvious; manifest; distinct; marked: ～的道理 *an obvious truth* / ～的对照 *a sharp contrast* / ～的特点 *a distinct (or marked) characteristic*

【显目】conspicuous

【显能】show off one's talent or competence: 你在行家面前显什么能? *What have you to show off before those experts?*

【显然】obviously; evidently; clearly: 这～是另一码事。*That's obviously quite another matter.*

【显色染料】[化] developing dye

【显身手】display one's talent or skill

【显圣】(of the ghost of a saintly person) make its presence or power felt

【显示】❶ show; display; demonstrate; manifest: ～力量 *make a show of force; display one's strength* ❷ [油] show; indication: 石油(天然气)～ *oil (gas) shows* / 地面～ *surface indications*

【显微胶片】microfilm; microfiche; bibliofilm

【显微镜】microscope

【显微术】microscopy

【显微外科】microsurgery

【显微阅读机】microfilm viewer (or reader)

【显微照片】micrograph

【显微照相术】microphotography; photomicrography

【显现】manifest (or reveal) oneself; appear; show: 雾气逐渐消失,重叠的山峦一层一层地～出来。*As the mist lifted, the mountains revealed themselves one behind the other.*

【显像管】[电子] kinescope

【显效】❶ produce effects: 这种药～快。*This medicine produces quick results.* ❷ tangible results

【显形】show one's (true) colours; betray oneself

【显性】[生] dominance: ～性状 *dominant character*

【显眼】conspicuous; showy: 把布告贴在～的地方 *put up the notice in a conspicuous place* / 穿得太～ *be loudly (or showily) dressed*

【显要】❶ powerful and influential: ～人物 *an influential figure* ❷ an influential figure; an important personage; VIP

【显耀】❶ show off: ～自己的身份 *show off one's status* ❷ be of high repute: ～一时 *be highly renowned for a time*

【显影】[摄] develop ◇ ～机 developing machine; ～剂 developer; ～盘 developing dish; ～纸 developing-out paper

【显著】notable; marked; striking; remarkable; outstanding: 各报均以～地位刊载了这条消息。*This news was prominently featured in all the papers.*

铣 (构词成分) 见下 ——另见 xǐ

【铣铁】cast iron

鲜 副 seldom; rarely: ～见 *rarely seen; seldom met with* ——另见 xiān

藓 名 [植] moss

xiàn

见 动 show; appear; become visible: 图穷匕首见 ——另见 jiàn

苋 名 amaranth (a herbaceous plant)

【苋菜】three-coloured amaranth (Amaranthus tricolor)

县 名 county

【县城】county seat; county town

【县委】county Party committee

【县长】the head of a county; county magistrate

【县志】general records of a county; county annals

现 Ⅰ 名 cash; ready money: 付现 Ⅱ 副 (do sth.) in time of need; extempore: ～打的烧饼 *sesame cakes just out of the oven* / 他在晚会上～编了一首诗。*He improvised a poem at the evening party.* Ⅲ 形 ❶ present; current; existing: ～阶段 *the present stage* / ～况 *the existing (or present) situation* ❷ (of money, etc.) on hand: 现钱 / 现货 Ⅳ 动 show; appear; become visible: 她脸上～出一丝笑容。*A faint smile appeared on (or crept over) her face.* / ～原形 *show one's true colours*

【现案】recent case: 侦破重大～ *investigate important recent cases* (〈反〉'积案')

【现场】❶ scene (of an incident): 作案～ *the scene of a crime* / 保护～ *keep the scene (of a crime or accident) intact* ❷ site; spot: ～表演 *on-the-spot (or live) demonstration* / ～采访 *spot coverage* / ～会议 *on-the-spot meeting* / ～勘验 *inspection of the scene of a crime or accident* / ～指导 *on-the-spot guidance*

【现场办公】on-site handling of business: 市政府负责人曾几次上门～,当场拍板帮助解决问题。*Officials from the municipal government have been to the work-site several times and helped solve problems on-the-spot.*

【现成】ready-made: 买～衣服 *buy ready-made clothes; buy clothes off the peg* / 吃～的 *eat whatever is ready or prepared by others*

【现成饭】food ready for the table; unearned gain

【现成话】an onlooker's unsolicited comments; a kibitzer's comments: 说～ *kibitz*

【现存】extant; in stock: ～的手稿 *extant manuscripts* / ～物资 *goods and materials in stock*

【现代】❶ modern times; the contemporary age ❷ modern; contemporary: ～交通工具 *modern means of communication* / ～作家 *modern* (*or contemporary*) *writers* / ～题材 *contemporary themes* ◇ ～派 modernist school；～史 contemporary history；～舞 modern dance；～戏 drama with a contemporary theme；～艺术 modern art

【现代化】modernize：～企业 *modernized enterprise* / ～设备 *sophisticated equipment*

【现汇】[经] spot exchange：～汇率 *spot exchange rate* / ～价 *spot rate* / ～贸易 *trade by spot exchange* / ～业务 *spot exchange transaction*

【现货】merchandise on hand；spots：～价格 *spot price* / ～交易 *spot transaction*；*over-the-counter trading* / ～市场 *spot market*

【现浇】[建] cast-in-place；cast-in-situ：～混凝土 *cast-in-place* (*or cast-in-situ*) *concrete*

【现今】nowadays；these days

【现金】❶ ready money；cash：～付款 *cash payment*；*payment in cash* / ～交易 *cash transaction* / ～支出 *out-of-pocket expenses* ❷ cash reserve in a bank ◇ ～出纳机 cash register；～账 cash account；cash book

【现款】ready money；cash

【现钱】〈口〉ready money；cash

【现任】❶ at present hold the office of：她～工会主席。*At present she holds the position of chairman of the labour union.* ❷ currently in office；incumbent：～邮局局长过去是邮递员。*The present postmaster used to be a postman.*

【现身说法】advise sb. or explain sth. by citing one's own experience

【现时】now；at present

【现实】❶ reality；actuality：脱离～ *be divorced from reality*；*be unrealistic* / 面对～ *face the facts* / 理想变成了～。*A dream has come true.* ❷ real；actual：～生活 *real* (*or actual*) *life* / ～意义 *practical or immediate significance*

【现实主义】realism：～文学 *realistic literature* / ～者 *realist*

【现世】❶ this life ❷ lose face；be disgraced；bring shame on oneself：活～ *really disgraceful* (*or shameful*) ◇ ～报 retribution in this life

【现下】now；at present

【现象】appearance (of things)；phenomenon：社会～ *social phenomenon* / 向不良～作斗争 *combat unhealthy phenomena*

【现行】❶ currently in effect；in force；in operation：～法令 *decrees in effect* / ～规章制度 *rules and regulations in force* / ～政策 *present policies* ❷ (of a criminal) active

【现行犯】[法] active criminal (a criminal caught in, or immediately before or after the act)

【现形】reveal one's true features；betray oneself

【现眼】〈方〉make a spectacle (or fool) of oneself；lose face：丢人现眼

【现役】❶ active service；active duty：服～ *be on active service* ❷ on active service；on active duty；active：～军官 *officer on the active list* / ～年限 *term of active service* ◇ ～军人 a member of the armed forces in active service；serviceman

【现有】now available；existing：～材料 *materials now available* (*or on hand*)；*available information*

【现在】now；at present；today：我～不跟你争论。*I will not argue with you now.* / ～的年轻人可讲究穿着了。*Young people of today are particular about their clothing.*

【现状】present (or current) situation；status quo；existing state of affairs：研究这个国家的历史和～ *study the history and present condition of this country*

限

Ⅰ 名 limit；bounds：以年底为～ *set the end of the year as the deadline* Ⅱ 动 set a limit；limit；restrict：～你一个月完成。*You are allowed one month to finish the job.* / 人数不～。*There is no restriction* (*or limit*) *on the number of people.*

【限电】restrict use of electricity：拉闸～ *power cuts to limit consumption*

【限定】prescribe (or set) a limit to；limit；restrict：～时间完成 *prescribe a time limit for fulfilment*

【限度】limit；limitation：超过～ *go beyond* (*or exceed*) *the limit* / 最大(最小)～ *the maximum* (*minimum*) *limit* / 最高(最低)～ *the highest* (*lowest*) *limit*

【限额】norm；quota：～以上(以下)的工业企业 *above-norm* (*below-norm*) *industrial enterprises*

【限价】❶ fix the official price ❷ the (officially) fixed price：最高～ *the ceiling price* / 最低～ *the floor price*

【限量】limit the quantity of；set bounds to：前途不可～ *have boundless prospects*

【限令】order sb. to do sth. within a certain time：～某人于四十八小时内离境 *order sb. to leave the country within 48 hours*；*give sb. 48 hours' notice to leave the country*

【限期】❶ prescribe (or set) a time limit：～报到 *report for duty by the prescribed time* ❷ time limit；deadline：～已满。*The time limit has been reached.* / 给他三天～ *give him three days* (*to do sth.*)

【限于】be confined to；be limited to：～篇幅，来电不能一一登载。*As space is limited, it is impossible to publish all the messages we have received.*

【限制】❶ place (or impose) restrictions on；restrict；limit；confine：～数量 *limit to a number or amount* / ～发言时间 *restrict* (*or limit*) *the time allowed for a speaker* ❷ restriction；limit；confinement：年龄～ *age limit* / 受健康状况的～ *be handicapped by one's poor health* / 有一定的～ *have specified restrictions*

【限制性】restricted；restrictive：～会议 *restricted meeting*

线

Ⅰ 名 ❶ thread；string；wire：一根～ *a piece of thread* / ～团 *a ball of string*；*a reel of thread* / 铜～ *copper wire* / ～衣～裤 *cotton knitwear*

❷[数] line：直线 ❸ sth. shaped like a line, thread, etc.：光线 ❹ route；line：供应～ *supply route* (*or line*) / 铁道～ *railway line* / 沪宁～ *the Shanghai-Nanjing Railway* (*Line*) ❺ demarcation line；boundary：边界～ *boundary line* / 海岸～ *coastline* ❻ (political) line ❼ brink；verge：在死亡～上 *on the verge of death* / 在饥饿～上 *on the brink of starvation* ❽ clue；thread：案子的～儿断了。*The clue could not be followed up*. Ⅱ 量 (used with numeral — before abstract things, indicating very little)：一～希望 *a ray* (*or gleam*) *of hope*

【线虫】nematode ◇ ～病 nematodiasis

【线电压】[电] line voltage

【线段】[数] line segment

【线规】[机] wire gauge

【线间】[音] space

【线路】❶ [电] circuit；line：电话～ *telephone line* / ～工人 *wireman*；*lineman* ❷ communication line；route：公共汽车～ *bus line* / 航空～ *air route* ◇ ～图 [电] circuit diagram

【线呢】cotton suiting

【线膨胀】[物] linear expansion

【线圈】[电] coil：初级(次级)～ *primary* (*secondary*) *coil*

【线人】an inner connection；spy；informer

【线绳】cotton rope

【线速度】[物] linear velocity

【线索】clue；thread：破案的～ *clues for solving a case* / 关于他的下落，没有找到任何～。*No clues have been found as to his whereabouts*.

【线毯】a blanket woven of thick cotton yarn；cotton (thread) blanket

【线条】[工美] line；contour；figure：粗犷、雄浑的～ *bold and vigorous lines* / 这幅画的～非常柔和。*The lines of this painting are very soft*.

【线头】❶ the end of a thread：～上打个结 *secure the end of the thread with a knot* ❷ an odd piece of thread；a bit of thread

【线形动物】roundworm

【线形叶】[植] linear leaf

【线性】[数] linear：～方程 *linear equation* / ～规划 *linear programming* / ～函数 *linear function*

【线衣】cotton knitwear

【线轴儿】❶ a reel for thread；bobbin ❷ a reel (or spool) of thread

【线装】traditional thread binding (of Chinese books)：～本 *thread-bound edition* / ～书 *thread-bound Chinese book*

宪 名 ❶ statute ❷ constitution：制～ *draw up a constitution*

【宪兵】military police；military policeman；gendarme：～队 *gendarmerie*；*military police corps*

【宪法】constitution；charter：～草案 *draft constitution* / 中华人民共和国～ *the Constitution of the People's Republic of China*

【宪章】❶〈书〉follow the example of；model oneself on；learn from ❷〈书〉institutions, decrees and regulations ❸ charter：联合国～ *the United Nations Charter*

【宪政】constitutional government；constitutionalism

陷 Ⅰ 名 ❶ pitfall；trap：陷阱 ❷ defect；deficiency：缺陷 Ⅱ 动 ❶ get stuck or bogged down：～进泥里 *get stuck in the mud* / ～在日常事务堆里 *get bogged down in everyday routine* ❷ sink；cave in：深～的两颊 *sunken cheeks* / 他病了几天，眼睛都～进去了。*After being ill for a few days, his eyes became sunken*. ❸ frame (up)：～人于罪 *frame sb*. (*up*)；incriminate sb. ❹ (of a town, etc.) be captured；fall：城～之日 *the day the city fell*

【陷害】frame (up)；make a false charge against：～好人 *frame up an innocent person* / 政治～ *political frame-up*

【陷阱】pitfall；pit；trap；snare：布设～ *lay a trap*

【陷坑】pitfall；pit

【陷落】❶ subside；sink in；cave in：许多盆地都是因地壳～而形成的。*Many basins were formed by the subsidence of the earth's crust*. ❷ sink (or fall) into；land oneself in：～重围 *find oneself tightly encircled* / ～困境 *land oneself in a predicament*；*be put in a tight spot*；*be cornered* ❸ (of territory) fall into enemy hands：南京于1937年12月～。*Nanjing fell into enemy hands in December* 1937.

【陷入】❶ sink (or fall) into；land oneself in；be caught in；get bogged down in：～被动地位 *fall into a passive position* ❷ be lost in；be immersed in；be deep in：～沉思 *be lost in thought*；*be deep in meditation*

【陷入僵局】come to a deadlock；reach an impasse：谈判～。*The negotiations came to a deadlock*. or *The negotiations reached an impasse*.

【陷身】fall into；land in：～虎口 *fall into the tiger's mouth—fall into a very dangerous position*

【陷于】fall into (an unfavourable position)：双方谈判～僵局。*The talks between the two sides were in a deadlock*. / ～孤立 *find oneself isolated*

馅 名 filling；stuffing：饺子～儿 *stuffing for dumplings*

【馅儿饼】meat pie

羡 动 admire；envy：称羡

【羡慕】admire；envy：她很～我有这样一个好丈夫。*She envies me my good husband*.

献 动 ❶ offer；present；dedicate；donate：～哈达 *present a hada* (*a Tibetan ceremonial silk scarf*) / ～血 *donate blood* / 敬～花圈 *lay a wreath* ❷ show；put on；display：献殷勤 / 献技

【献宝】❶ present a treasure ❷ offer a valuable piece of advice or one's valuable experience ❸ show off what one treasures

【献策】offer advice；make suggestions

【献丑】〈谦〉(speaking of one's own performance)

show oneself up; show one's incompetence (or inadequacy): 一定要我唱,就只好～了。*Since you insist, I'll make a fool of myself and sing.*

【献词】congratulatory message: 新年～ *New Year message*

【献花】present flowers or bouquets

【献计】offer advice; make suggestions: 在技术革新中人人～献策。*Everyone suggested ways and means for technical innovation.*

【献技】show one's skill (in a performance)

【献礼】present a gift: 以优异成绩向国庆～ *greet National Day with new and outstanding successes*

【献媚】try to ingratiate oneself with; make up to

【献身】devote (or dedicate) oneself to; give one's life for: ～教育事业 *devote oneself to the cause of education*

【献血】donate blood: 无偿～活动 *blood donation*

【献艺】(of actors, singers, etc.) show one's skill; give a performance: 登台～ *go up on the stage and give a performance*

【献殷勤】do everything to please; pay attentions to; pay one's addresses to: 他不断地向姑娘～,倒把姑娘惹恼了。*His constant attentions annoyed the girl.*

腺 名 gland: 汗(泪、唾液)～ *sweat (lachrymal, salivary) gland*

【腺瘤】[医] adenoma

霰 名 [气] graupel

xiāng

乡 名 ❶ country; countryside; village; rural area: 城乡 ❷ native place; home village or town: 丝绸之～ *the home of silk* ❸ township (a rural administrative unit under the county)

【乡巴佬】〈贬〉(country) bumpkin

【乡愁】homesickness: ～满肠 *be overcome with homesickness*

【乡村】village; countryside; rural area: 那是一个边远的～。*That is a remote village.* / ～风格 *rustic style* / ～生活 *country life*

【乡规民约】local rules and regulations valid for the whole village

【乡间】in the village; in the country: ～小贩 *village pedlar* / ～别墅 *country villa*

【乡里】❶ home village or town ❷ fellow villagers or townsmen: 都是～乡亲的,有什么不好开口的。*As we are all fellow townsmen, there's nothing you can't bring up before us.*

【乡民】villagers; country people

【乡气】rustic; countrified; uncouth: 她的穿着有点～。*She looks rather rustic in the way she dresses.*

【乡亲】❶ a person from the same village or town; fellow villager or townsman ❷ local people; villagers; folks: 给～们办个示范性的养鸡场 *set up an exemplary poultry farm for the villagers*

【乡绅】country gentleman; squire

【乡思】homesickness; nostalgia

【乡俗】local customs; village customs: 按照～,他得叩三个头。*According to local customs, he had to kowtow three times.*

【乡土】native soil; one's native land; local: ～风味 *local flavour* / 富于～气息 *be imbued with local colour* ◇ ～观念 provincialism; ～文学 literary style that draws heavily on local subjects, customs and language; ～志 local records or annals

【乡下】countryside; village: ～来人了。*Someone is here from the village.*

【乡下人】country folk; country cousin; rustic: 我好像～头回进城,见啥都觉得新鲜。*I felt like a country bumpkin coming to town for the first time. Everything which met my eyes was a novelty.*

【乡音】accent of one's native place; local accent: 她说话～挺重的。*She speaks with a strong local accent.*

【乡邮】rural postal service ◇ ～员 rural postman

【乡镇】❶ villages and towns ❷ small towns in general ◇ ～企业 village and township enterprises

相 Ⅰ 副 ❶ each other; one another; mutually: ～见 *meet (each other)* / ～聚 *get together* / ～视而笑 *look and smile at each other* / 不～符合 *not tally with each other* ❷ (indicating an action performed by one person toward another): 实不～瞒 *to tell you the truth* / 他既然不愿意去,就不要～强。*Since he doesn't want to go, don't force him to.* Ⅱ 动 see for oneself (whether sb. or sth. is to one's liking): ～女婿 *take a look at one's prospective son-in-law* ——另见 xiàng

【相爱】be in love with each other

【相安无事】live in peace with each other

【相比】compare: 二者不能～。*There's no comparison between the two (of them).*

【相差】differ: 两者～无几。*There's hardly any difference between the two.*

【相称】(xiāngchèn) match; suit: 这两种颜色配在一起很～。*The two colours match very well.* / 这头巾跟你的年龄不～。*This kerchief doesn't suit a person of your age.*

【相称】(xiāngchēng) call each other; address each other (as ...): 以姐弟～ *address each other as brother and sister*

【相持】be locked in a stalemate: 双方已～很久。*The two sides have been locked in a stalemate for a long time.*

【相持不下】each sticks to his own stand; be locked in a stalemate: 双方～。*Neither side was ready to yield.*

【相处】get along (with one another): 不好～ *difficult to get along with* / ～得很好 *get on well with each other*

【相传】❶ tradition has it that...; according to

legend：～这里是当年孔明祭风处。*According to legend, this is where Kong Ming supplicated the wind.* ❷ hand down or pass on from one to another：世代相传

【相待】treat：以诚～ *treat another with all sincerity* / 拿他当朋友～ *treat him as a friend*

【相当】❶ match；balance；correspond to；be about equal to；be commensurate with：得失～。*The gains balance the losses.* / 两队实力～。*The two teams are about equal in strength.* ❷ suitable；fit；appropriate：他一时想不出～的字眼来。*At the time he couldn't think of a suitable word for it.* ❸ quite；fairly；considerably：～好 *fairly good* / 演出～成功。*The performance was quite a success.*

【相得益彰】each shining more brilliantly in the other's company；bring out the best in each other；complement each other

【相等】be equal：数量～ *be equal in amount (or quantity, number)*；*be numerically equal*

【相抵】offset；balance；counterbalance：收支～ *one's accounts balance*

【相对】❶ opposite to each other；face to face：～而坐 *sit opposite (or facing) each other*；*sit face to face* / 美是与丑～的。*Beauty is the opposite of ugliness.* ❷ relative：平衡是～的，不平衡是绝对的。*Balance is relative, imbalance is absolute.* ❸ relatively；comparatively：～稳定 *relatively stable* / ～地说 *comparatively speaking* ◇ ～高度 relative altitude (or height)；～湿度 relative humidity；～速度［物］relative velocity；～误差［数］relative error；～性 relativity；～运动［物］relative motion；～真理〈哲〉relative truth；～值 relative value；～主义〈哲〉relativism

【相对论】［物］the theory of relativity；relativity：广(狭)义～ *the general (special) theory of relativity*

【相对论性】［物］relativistic：～量子理论 *relativistic quantum theory* / ～物理学 *relativistic physics*

【相反】❶ contrary；opposite：结果与我们的愿望恰好～。*The result turned out contrary to our expectations.* ❷ on the contrary：他一点儿也不吝啬，～，没有比他更大方的了。*He is not stingy; on the contrary, no one could be more generous.*

【相反相成】things that oppose each other also complement each other；be both opposite and complementary to each other；oppose each other and yet also complement each other

【相仿】be similar；resemble each other；be more or less the same：内容～ *be similar in content* / 年纪～ *be about the same age*

【相逢】meet (by chance)；come across：想不到我和儿时好友竟在异国他乡～。*I never thought I would meet my childhood companion in a foreign land.*

【相符】conform to；tally (or agree) with；correspond to (or with)：报告与事实～。*The report tallies with the facts.* / 名实～。*The name corresponds to the reality.*

【相辅而行】be complementary to each other；proceed in coordination；go together

【相辅相成】supplement and complement each other

【相干】❶ (used in the negative or in a rhetorical question) have sth. to do with；be concerned with：这件事与她有什么～？*What has this to do with her?* ❷［物］coherent：～散射 *coherent scattering* ◇ ～性［物］coherence；coherency

【相告】inform (or tell) you：有要事～。*I have something important to tell you.* / 实话～ *to tell you the truth*

【相隔】be separated by；be apart；be at a distance of：～万里 *be thousands of li apart*；*be a long way away from each other* / ～多年 *after an interval of many years*

【相关】be mutually related；be interrelated：与此～的事物 *things correlated with this*

【相好】❶ be on intimate terms ❷ an intimate friend ❸ have an affair with ❹ lover or mistress

【相互】❶ mutual；reciprocal：～关系 *mutual relation*；*interrelation* / ～作用 *interaction*；*interplay* ❷ mutually；reciprocally；each other：～影响 *influence each other*；*interact* / ～支持 *support each other*

【相会】meet：我期待着在西安再一次和你～。*I'm looking forward to meeting you again in Xi'an.*

【相继】in succession；one after another：代表们～发言。*The delegates spoke one after another.*

【相见恨晚】regret not having met earlier：两人谈得情投意合，～。*The two found so much in common that they regretted not having met earlier.*

【相间】alternate with：黑白～ *black alternating with white*；*in black and white check*

【相交】❶ intersect：圆的直径必～于圆心。*Any two diameters of a circle intersect each other.* ❷ make friends with：～有年 *have been friends for years*

【相近】❶ close；near：地点～的两个学校 *two neighbouring schools* / 比分～。*The score was very close.* ❷ similar；about the same：两人性格～。*The two of them are similar in character.*

【相敬如宾】(of husband and wife) treat each other with the respect due to a guest

【相救】come to sb.'s rescue；save sb. from danger：拼死～ *risk one's life to help save sb.*

【相距】be separated by (a distance of ...)；be ... apart；be ... away from：两地～不到二公里。*The two places are less than two kilometres apart.*

【相连】be linked together；be joined：两地有铁路～。*The two places are linked by rail.* / 两国山水～。*The two countries are joined by common mountains and rivers.*

【相骂无好言，相打无好拳】there are no quarrels with nice words nor fights with weak blows

【相配】be well-matched；be a good match：小两口

儿很～。*The young couple are a perfect match*. / 她的打扮和她的年龄很不～。*Her clothes and her make-up do not fit her age*.

【相亲】size up a prospective mate in an arranged meeting

【相亲相爱】be friendly or on intimate terms：同学们～，关系十分融洽。*The students are very friendly and get on very well together*.

【相去无几】there is not much difference; pretty much the same

【相劝】try to persuade sb.; offer advice to sb.：尽管我好言～，她依然执意不从。*Though I tried hard to persuade her to do it, she flatly refused*.

【相濡以沫】(of stranded fish) moisten each other with spit—give one's meagre resources to help another in time of need

【相商】❶ consult each other ❷ consult you：有要事～。*I have something important to consult you about*.

【相生相克】mutual promotion and restraint between the five elements ——另见〖五行〗

【相识】❶ be acquainted with each other：此人似曾～。*It seems I've met him before*. ❷ an acquaintance：老～ *an old acquaintance*

【相思】pine with love; yearn for sb.'s love; languish with lovesickness

【相思病】lovesickness：害～ *be lovesick*

【相思鸟】red-billed leiothrix

【相思子】❶ jequirity (the plant) ❷ jequirity bean; love pea ❸ ormosia seed

【相似】resemble; be similar; be alike：兄弟俩面貌～。*The two brothers look alike*. / 历史往往有惊人的～之处。*Astonishing parallels can often be found in history*. ◇ ～形［数］similar figures

【相提并论】(usu. used in the negative) mention in the same breath; place on a par：两者不能～。*The two cannot be mentioned in the same breath*.

【相通】communicate with each other; be interlinked：这是两间～的屋子。*These are two communicating rooms*.

【相同】identical; the same; alike：我们在这个问题上观点～。*We have identical (or the same) views on this question*. / 两者毫无～之处。*The two have nothing in common*.

【相投】be congenial; agree with each other：兴趣～ *have similar tastes and interests; find each other congenial*

【相违】disagree; be opposed to each other：这种做法与我们的本意～。*This way of doing things runs counter to our original ideas*.

【相像】resemble; be similar; be alike：这两种花很～。*These two flowers are very much alike*.

【相信】believe in; be convinced of; trust; have faith in：～真理 *believe in truth* / ～自己的事业是正义的 *be convinced of the justice of one's cause*

【相形见绌】prove inferior by comparison; pale by comparison; be outshone：鬼见愁，名字听来令人生畏；但比起我们爬过的一些高山来，未免～了。*The Devil's Frown, despite its forbidding name, pales beside some of the mountains we have climbed*.

【相形之下】by contrast; by comparison

【相沿成习】become common practice through long usage

【相依】depend on each other; be interdependent：唇齿相依

【相依为命】depend on each other for survival：从此，母女俩～。*Since then the mother and the daughter had been dependent on each other for survival*.

【相宜】suitable; fitting; appropriate：在那个场合你说这样的话是不～的。*What you said on that occasion was not appropriate*.

【相异】different：语言～ *different languages* / 情况～ *different circumstances*

【相迎】welcome sb.：笑脸～ *give sb. a cheerful welcome*

【相应】corresponding; relevant; fitting; appropriate：随着工业的发展，对环境保护也采取了～的措施。*With the development of industry, appropriate measures have been taken to protect the environment*.

【相映成趣】set each other off and form a pleasing contrast; contrast pleasingly with each other：湖光塔影，～。*The lake's shimmer and the pagoda's reflection make a pleasing scene*.

【相与】❶ get along with sb.; deal with sb.：此人极难～。*That person is extremely difficult to get along with (or deal with)*. ❷ with each other; together：～大笑 *have a good laugh together*

【相遇】meet：我二人在美术馆偶然～。*We ran across each other in the art gallery*.

【相约】agree (on meeting place, date, etc.); reach agreement; make an appointment

【相赠】present to sb.; give as a present：她以亲笔签名的著作～。*She gave me an autographed copy of her book*.

【相知】❶ be well acquainted with each other; know each other well：～有素 *have known each other long* ❷ a bosom friend; a great friend

【相知恨晚】regret that one has not got to know sb. sooner

【相中】take a fancy to; settle on：这些姑娘当中他好像～了一个。*He seems to have taken a fancy to one of these girls*.

【相助】come to sb.'s help; aid：一人有难，众人～。*When one man is in difficulty, all come to his help (or aid)*.

【相撞】collide：两机～，同时坠毁。*Both planes crashed within seconds of a midair collision*. / 两车～。*The two vehicles had a head-on crash*.

【相左】〈书〉❶ fail to meet each other ❷ conflict with each other; fail to agree; be at odds with：意见～ *hold different views; be at variance*

香 Ⅰ 形 ❶ fragrant; sweet-smelling; aromatic;

scented：茉莉花好～！*What a sweet scent the jasmine flowers give off!* ❷ savoury；appetizing：这饭真～。*This rice is really appetizing.* / 炒什么菜啊？好～呀！*Mmm! What's cooking? It smells delicious.* ❸ with relish；with good appetite：吃得很～ *eat with relish；enjoy the food* / 昨晚没睡好，吃饭不～。*I have no appetite because I didn't sleep well last night.* ❹（of sleep）sound：她睡得正～呢。*She's sound asleep.* ❺ popular；welcome：这种摩托车在农村可～了。*This type of motorcycle is most popular in the countryside.* Ⅱ 名 ❶ perfume or spice：麝香 / 檀香 ❷ incense；joss stick：蚊香

【香案】a long altar on which incense burners are placed；incense burner table

【香槟酒】champagne

【香波】shampoo

【香菜】coriander

【香草】vanilla：～冰淇淋 *vanilla ice cream*

【香草醛】［化］vanillic aldehyde；vanillin；vanilla

【香肠】sausage

【香椿】❶ Chinese toon（Toona sinensis；the tree）❷ the tender，edible leaves and stems of Chinese toon（used as a vegetable）

【香醇】fragrant，rich（smell or taste）：～美酒 *rich，mellow wine* / 茶味～ *fragrant tea*

【香袋】sachet

【香榧】Chinese torreya（Torreya grandis）◇ ～子 Chinese torreya nut

【香粉】cosmetic powder

【香馥馥】strongly scented；richly fragrant

【香干】smoked bean curd

【香港】❶ Hong Kong（or Hongkong）Island ❷ the entire Hong Kong area（including Hong Kong Island，Kowloon 九龙 and the New Territories 新界）◇ ～特别行政区 the Hong Kong Special Administrative Region（HKSAR）

【香港脚】〈方〉Hong Kong foot；athlete's foot

【香菇】（又作'香菰'）Xianggu mushroom

【香瓜】muskmelon

【香蕉】banana

【香蕉苹果】a species of apple with a bananalike odor

【香蕉球】〈口〉（of soccer）curved shot

【香蕉水】［化］banana oil（used as a paint solvent）

【香精】essence：食用～ *flavouring essence* / 合成～ *compound essence* / ～油 *essential oil*

【香客】a worshipper at a Buddhist temple；a Buddhist pilgrim

【香料】❶ perfume ❷ spice ◇ ～厂 perfumery

【香炉】incense burner

【香茅】［植］lemongrass ◇ ～醛［化］citronellal；～油 citronella oil

【香喷喷】❶ sweet-smelling ❷ savoury；appetizing：一碗～的炖肉 *a bowl of savoury（pork）stew*

【香片】scented tea

【香蒲】［植］cattail

【香气】a sweet smell；fragrance；aroma：门一开，一阵～扑鼻而来。*The door opened and a sweet smell reached（or assailed）my nostrils.*

【香水】perfume；scent

【香甜】❶ fragrant and sweet：味道～ *taste and smell sweet* / ～的瓜果 *sweet melons and fruits* ❷（of sleep）sound：小伙子们劳动了一天，晚上睡得格外～。*The boys slept soundly after a day's work.*

【香蕈】another name for 香菇

【香烟】❶ incense smoke：～缭绕 *smoke coiling up from burning incense* ❷ cigarette：～盒 *cigarette case* / ～头 *cigarette butt（or end）*

【香艳】amorous；erotic：～小说 *an amorous novel*

【香油】sesame oil

【香鼬】［动］alpine weasel

【香鱼】［动］sweetfish；ayu

【香橼】［植］citron

【香云纱】［纺］gambiered Guangdong gauze

【香皂】perfumed（or scented）soap；toilet soap

【香獐子】popular name for 麝

【香脂】❶ face cream ❷ balm；balsam

厢 名 ❶ wing（usu. of a one-storeyed house）；wing-room：一正两～ *a central room with two wing-rooms* ❷ railway carriage or compartment；（theatre）box：车厢 / 包厢 ❸ the vicinity outside of a city gate

【厢房】wing（usu. of a one-storeyed house）；wing-room：东～ *the east wing*

箱 名 ❶ chest；box；case；trunk：大木～ *wooden trunk；chest* / 纸～ *cardboard box；carton* / 货～ *packing box* / 书～ *a box for books* ❷ anything in the shape of a box：风箱

【箱底】❶ the bottom of a chest：旧衣服都压～了。*The old clothes are stowed away at the bottom of the chest.* ❷ valuables stowed away at the bottom of the chest；one's store of valuables：她家～厚。*Her family has accumulated a large store of valuables.*

【箱子】chest，box，case，trunk，etc.

襄 动〈书〉assist；help：共～义举 *let everybody help to promote this worthy undertaking*

【襄理】assistant manager second to 协理（in a bank，business enterprise，etc. in former times）

【襄助】〈书〉assist

镶 动 ❶ inlay；set；mount：金～玉嵌 *inlaid with gold and jade* / ～宝石 *set gems；mount precious stones* / ～满口假牙 *have a full set of false teeth put in one's mouth* / 给窗子～玻璃 *glaze a window* ❷ rim；edge；border：给裙子～花边 *edge a skirt with lace* / 给镜子～上个框儿 *mount（or set）the mirror in a frame*

【镶板】［建］panelling

【镶边】edge；border；rim：她衣领上镶着一道红边。*The collar of her jacket is edged with red.* / 他的眼镜是镶金边的。*His glasses have gold rims.*

【镶嵌】❶ inlay；set；mount：～银丝漆器 *silver-*

inlaid lacquerware / ～细工 *inlaid work*; *marquetry* ❷ mosaic; tessellate: ～玻璃 *mosaic glass* / ～图案 *mosaic*; *tessellation* ◇～画 a picture or design made of mosaic; mosaic

【镶牙】put in a false tooth; insert an artificial tooth

xiáng

详 Ⅰ 形 detailed; minute: ～谈 *speak in detail* (*or at length*); *go into details* / ～述自己的论点 *elaborate one's thesis* Ⅱ 名 details; particulars: ～见附录。*For details, see the appendix*. Ⅲ 动 know clearly: 作者生卒年月不～。*The author's dates are unknown*.

【详备】detailed, complete: 例证～ *detailed examples* / 注释～ *thoroughly annotated*

【详尽】detailed and complete; exhaustive; thorough: ～的记载 *a detailed record* / ～的调查 *a thorough investigation*

【详密】elaborate; meticulous: ～的计划 *a meticulous plan*

【详明】full and clear: ～的注解 *full and clear annotations*

【详情】detailed information; details; particulars: 我不了解这件事的～。*I don't know the details of the matter*. / ～后报。*Details to follow*.

【详实】full and accurate: ～的材料 *full and accurate data* (*or material*)

【详图】detail drawing: 发动机～ *engine detail*

【详细】detailed; minute: ～的报导 *a detailed news report* / ～了解情况 *acquire detailed knowledge of the situation*

【详注】❶ annotate fully ❷ detailed annotations

降 动 ❶ surrender; capitulate: 宁死不～ *rather die than surrender* ❷ subdue; vanquish; tame: ～妖伏魔 *vanquish demons and monsters* ——另见 jiàng

【降伏】subdue; vanquish; tame: ～野马 *break in a wild horse* / 谁～得了那野小子? *Who could tame that unruly boy?*

【降服】yield; surrender and acknowledge allegiance

【降龙伏虎】subdue the dragon and tame the tiger—overcome powerful adversaries

【降旗】flag of surrender; white flag

【降顺】〈书〉yield and pledge allegiance to

祥 形 auspicious; propitious; lucky: 吉祥

【祥和】❶ happy and auspicious ❷ kind; benign

【祥云】auspicious clouds

【祥兆】good omen

翔 动 circle in the air: 翱翔

【翔实】full and accurate: ～的材料 *full and accurate data* / 她的叙述～可信。*The account she gave was full, accurate and reliable*.

xiǎng

享 动 enjoy: 享受

【享福】enjoy a happy life; live in ease and comfort: 我指望着老来能享点儿清福。*I'm looking forward to a peaceful, quiet and easy life in my old age*.

【享乐】lead a life of pleasure; indulge in creature comforts: ～思想 *preoccupation with pleasure-seeking*

【享乐主义】hedonism; pleasure-seeking

【享年】(of a deceased, generally old person) die at the age of; live to the age of: 他～七十四岁。*He died at the age of* 74.

【享受】❶ enjoy: ～公费医疗 *enjoy public health services* ❷ enjoyment; treat: 贪图～ *seek ease and comfort* / 看这样的好戏是一种艺术～。*A good play like this is an artistic treat*.

【享用】enjoy the use of; enjoy

【享有】enjoy (rights, prestige, etc.): ～崇高的威望 *enjoy high prestige*; *be held in esteem*

【享誉】enjoy good fame: ～海内外 *enjoy great prestige both at home and abroad*

响 Ⅰ 名 sound; noise: 一声炮～ *the report of a cannon* / 两～的爆竹 *double-bang firecrackers* Ⅱ 动 ❶ make a sound; sound; resound; ring: 锣～了。*The gong sounded*. / 电话铃～了。*The telephone rang*. / 扩音器不～了。*The loudspeaker's stopped working*. ❷ make sth. emit a sound; sound: 敲起鼓,～起锣 *sound the drum and the gong* Ⅲ 形 noisy; loud: 收音机开得太～了。*The radio's too loud* (*or noisy*).

【响板】[音] castanets

【响鼻】snort (of a horse, mule, etc.): 打～儿 *snort*

【响彻云霄】resound (or reverberate) across the heavens: 一曲～的凯歌 *a song of triumph that resounds across the heavens*

【响当当】❶ (of the sound made by a bell, a gong, etc.) loud and resounding ❷ (of a person) of resounding fame; outstanding; worthy

【响动】the sound of sth. astir: 夜很静,一点～也没有。*The night was quiet, and there was no sound of anything astir*.

【响度】[物] degree of loudness; volume

【响雷】❶ be thundering: ～了,暴风雨快来了。*It's thundering. There's a storm coming on*. ❷ a crash of thunder; thunderclap

【响亮】loud and clear; resounding; resonant; sonorous: ～的回答 *a loud and clear reply*; *an unequivocal reply* / ～的声音 *a resounding voice* / 一记～的耳光 *a heavy slap in the face*; *a smart box on the ear*

【响铃】jingle bell; cascabel: 小马的脖子上挂着一串～。*Round the neck of the pony is tied a string of jingle bells*.

【响器】[音] Chinese percussion instruments

【响声】sound; noise: 沙沙的～ *rustling sound*

【响尾蛇】rattlesnake

【响音】[语音] ❶ resonant (i.e. vowel, semivowel, or sonorant; e.g. ɑ, e, ou, j, w, m, n, ng, r, l) ❷ sonorant (e.g. m, n, ng, r, l)

【响应】respond; answer: 他们一提出倡议,我们就全力～。*As soon as they put forward the proposal, we responded with full support.*

飨 动〈书〉provide dinner for; entertain: ～客 *entertain a guest* / 以～读者 *offer to the readers*

想 动 ❶ think; ponder: ～问题 *think over a problem* / ～办法 *think of a way; try to find a solution (or a way out)* / 让我～一～。*Let me think it over.* or *Let me see.* ❷ think back; try to remember; recall; recollect: ～往事 *recall the past events* / 你好好～～钥匙搁哪儿了。*Think carefully, and see if you can remember where you put the key.* ❸ suppose; reckon; consider; think: 我～他今天不会来。*I don't think he'll be coming today.* / 你～他能买到票吗? *Do you think he can get the tickets?* ❹ want to; would like to; feel like (doing sth.): 你～看足球赛吗? *Do you want to see (or feel like seeing) a football match?* ❺ remember with longing; miss: 你走了以后,我们都很～你。*After you left, we all missed you.*

【想必】presumably; most probably (or likely): 他没有答复,～没有收到我的信。*No word from him yet; presumably he hasn't received my letter.*

【想不到】never expect; be unexpected: 这真是～的事! *This is something quite unexpected!* / 真～会在这儿见到你。*Fancy seeing you here!*

【想不开】take things too hard; take a matter to heart: 别为这些小事～。*Don't take such small things to heart.* / 她遭人遗弃,一时～就自杀了。*She was deserted by her lover, and in despair she took her own life.*

【想出】(object obligatory) think out; think up: 她～一条妙计。*She thought out a brilliant scheme.* / 想不出什么办法 *can't think up any solution to it*

【想出来】think out; think up: 这主意是谁～的? *Whose idea was this?* / 办法我是～了,就是不知道行不行。*I've thought out (or up) a plan, but I'm not sure whether it will work.*

【想当然】assume sth. as a matter of course; take sth. for granted: 我们不能凭～办事。*We must not act on assumptions.*

【想到】❶think of; call to mind: 忽然～一件重要的事情 *suddenly think of something important* ❷ expect sth. to happen; expect that sth. will happen: 我们没～你会来。*We didn't expect you (to come).*

【想得到】(usu. used in rhetorical questions) think; imagine; expect: 谁～会出事故? *Who would have thought there'd be an accident?*

【想得开】not take to heart; take philosophically; try to look on the bright side of things: 这老太太最～了。*This old lady always looks at the bright side of things.*

【想法】(xiǎngfǎ) think of a way; do what one can; try: ～给大伙儿弄点水喝喝。*Try and get some drinking water for everyone.*

【想法】(xiǎngfa) idea; opinion; what one has in mind: 把你的～给大家说说。*Tell us what you have in mind.*

【想方设法】do everything possible; try every means; try by hook or by crook: ～去打听消息 *try every means to find out what's happening*

【想家】be homesick: 我非常～。*I'm terribly homesick.*

【想见】infer; gather: 从这些事情上,你可以～他的为人。*From these instances you can gather what kind of person he is.*

【想来】it may be assumed that; presumably: 他的话～不是没有根据的。*I suppose what he says is not groundless.* / ～你都知道了。*Presumably you know all about it.*

【想念】remember with longing; long to see again; miss: 我们都很～你。*We all miss you very much.*

【想起】remember; recollect; recall; think of; call to mind: 你想得起他的原话吗? *Can you recall his exact words?* / 这人很面熟,可就是想不起他的名字。*He looks familiar to me, but I just can't think of his name.*

【想起来】remember; recollect; recall; think of; call to mind: 我～了,她当时在场。*Now I remember, she was present at the time.* / 隔了这么久,谁还想得起来呀! *No one can still remember after such a long time.*

【想入非非】indulge in fantasy; allow one's fancy to run wild

【想通】straighten out one's thinking; become convinced; come round: 我～了。*I've come round to the idea now.* / 我想不通他为什么说出那样的话来。*I can't figure out why he said that.*

【想头】〈口〉❶ idea: 老李有个～。*Lao Li's got an idea.* ❷ hope: 没什么～了。*There's no hope now.*

【想望】❶ desire; long for; yearn for: 他从小就～着当一名工程师。*He's longed to be an engineer ever since he was a child.* ❷〈书〉admire; look up to: ～其风采 *admire his elegant bearing*

【想像】❶ imagination: 完美无缺的人只存在于人们的～之中。*A flawless person exists only in imagination.* ❷ imagine; fancy; visualize: 难以～ *hard to imagine (or visualize)* / ～不到的困难 *unimaginable difficulties*

【想像力】the power (or faculty) of imagination; imagination: 激发人们的～ *fire people's imagination* / 充分发挥～ *give full play to one's imagination*

鲞 名 dried fish (with all insides taken out and

the body flattened)：鳗～ *dried eel*

xiàng

向 Ⅰ名 direction：风向 / 志向 Ⅱ动 ❶ face；turn towards：那间屋子～东。*That room faces east*. / 葵花～太阳。*Sunflowers turn towards the sun*. ❷ take sb.'s part；side with；be partial to：～理不～人 *stand by what is right, not by a particular person；side with whoever is right* Ⅲ介 to；towards；in the direction of：～上看 *look upward* / ～后撤 *withdraw* / 河水～东流去。*The river flows east*. Ⅳ副 all along；always：～无此例。*There's no precedent for this*. / 他对此～有研究。*He has always been doing research in this field*.

【向背】support or oppose：人心向背

【向壁虚构】(又作'向壁虚造') make up out of one's head；fabricate

【向导】❶ show sb. the way；lead sb. somewhere；act as a guide ❷ a guide；an escort：探险队急需一位～。*The exploring party needs a guide urgently*.

【向光性】[植] phototropism

【向后】towards the back；backward：～看 *look back* / ～转！(*word of command*) *About face*! or *About turn*! / ～转走！(*word of command*) *To the rear, march*!

【向来】always；all along：～如此。*It has always been so*. / 我～不抽烟。*I have never smoked*.

【向量】[数] vector：～分析 *vector analysis*

【向前】forward；onward；ahead：奋勇～ *forge ahead* / 科学的～发展 *the forward march of science* / ～看！(*word of command*) *Eyes front*! or *Ready, front*!

【向前看】look to the future；look forward：采取～的态度 *adopt a forward-looking attitude*

【向日葵】sunflower

【向日性】[植] heliotropism

【向上】upward；up：卡车沿着盘山公路～爬去。*The trucks climbed the twisting mountain road*.

【向上爬】❶ climb (up) ❷ seek personal advancement；be a social climber；be a careerist：有～的思想 *have the mentality of a careerist* (*or social climber*) / 一心～ *set one's mind on personal advancement*

【向水性】[生] hydrotropism

【向往】yearn for；look forward to：我终于登上了～已久的长城。*At long last, I climbed to the top of the Great Wall, which I had long been looking forward to seeing*.

【向下】downward；down：滑雪运动员飞快地～滑去。*The skiers sped down the slope*. / 他把帽沿～拉了拉。*He pulled the visor of his cap down a little*.

【向斜】[地质] syncline ◇ ～谷 [地理] synclinal valley

【向心力】[物] centripetal force

【向性】[生] tropism

【向阳】be exposed to the sun；have a sunny exposure：这间屋～。*The room has a southern exposure*. ◇ ～花〈文〉sunflower

【向右】towards the right：～转！(*word of command*) *Right face*! or *Right turn*! / ～转走！(*word of command*) *By the right flank, march*!

【向隅而泣】weep all alone in a corner；be left to grieve in the cold

【向着】❶ turn towards；face：～光明的未来前进 *advance towards a bright future* ❷〈口〉take sb.'s part；side with；be partial to：她说话在理，我就～她。*I take her part because she's right*.

【向左】towards the left：～转！(*word of command*) *Left face*! *or Left turn*! / ～转走！(*word of command*) *By the left flank, march*!

巷 名 lane；alley ——另见 hàng

【巷口】entrance to a lane

【巷尾】end of a lane

【巷战】street fighting

项 Ⅰ名 ❶ nape (of the neck) ❷ sum (of money)：进项 / 欠项 ❸ [数] term Ⅱ量 (for itemized things)：两～声明 *two statements* / 八～原则 *eight principles* / 一～一～地进行解释 *explain item by item* / 第五条第二款第三～ *article 5, clause 2, item 3*

【项背】a person's back：不可望其～ *cannot hold a candle to sb*.

【项背相望】walk one after another in close succession

【项链】(又作'项练') necklace

【项目】item：出口～ *goods for export；export items* / 基本建设～ *capital construction project*

【项圈】neckband (a band of gold or silver, worn around the neck as an ornament)；necklet

【项庄舞剑，意在沛公】performed the sword dance as a cover for his attempt on Liu Bang's life—act with a hidden motive

相 Ⅰ名 ❶ looks；appearance：一副可怜～ *a pitiful appearance；a sorry figure* ❷ bearing；posture：站没站～，坐没坐～ *not know how to stand or sit properly* / 这孩子睡～不好。*The child sleeps sprawled all over the bed*. ❸ photograph：照相 ❹ [物] phase：三～变压器 *three-phase transformer* / 调～ *phase modulation* ❺ chief minister：周瑜十三岁拜～。*Zhou Yu was given the post of chief minister when he was only 13 years of age*. Ⅱ动 ❶ look at and appraise：～马 *look at a horse to judge its worth* ❷〈书〉assist：～夫教子 *assist one's husband and teach one's children* ——另见 xiāng

【相册】photo album

【相机】❶ camera ❷ watch for an opportunity：～而动 *wait for an opportunity to act；bide one's time*

【相机行事】act as the occasion demands；do as one

sees fit
【相貌】facial features; looks; appearance: ～端正 *have regular features* / ～堂堂 *be elegant in appearance*
【相面】tell sb.'s fortune by reading his face; practise physiognomy
【相片】photo (of a person); snapshot
【相扑】[体] sumo (wrestling)
【相声】comic dialogue; cross talk: 说～ *perform a comic dialogue*
【相手术】palmistry
【相术】fortune-telling by studying facial features; physiognomy
【相纸】(photographic) printing paper; photographic paper

象 Ⅰ名 ❶ elephant ❷ elephant, one of the pieces in Chinese chess (象棋) ❸ appearance; shape; image: 印象 Ⅱ动 imitate: 象声
【象鼻】trunk; proboscis
【象鼻虫】weevil; snout beetle
【象皮病】[医] elephantiasis
【象棋】chess: 国际～ *chess* / 中国～ *Chinese chess*
【象声】[语] onomatopoeia ◇ ～词 onomatope
【象限】[数] quadrant ◇ ～仪 [天] quadrant
【象形食品】shaped food products, e. g. animal cookies
【象形文字】pictograph; hieroglyph
【象形字】pictographic character
【象牙】elephant's tusk; ivory: ～雕刻 *ivory carving (or sculpture)* / ～制品 *ivories*
【象牙海岸】the Ivory Coast
【象牙塔】❶〈字〉ivory tower; ❷〈喻〉aloofness from practical life; separation from the narsh realities of ordinary life
【象征】❶ symbolize; signify; stand for: 鸽子～和平。*The dove symbolizes peace.* ❷ symbol; emblem; token: 友谊的～ *emblem (or symbol) of friendship* ◇ ～性 symbolic; emblematic; token

像 Ⅰ动 ❶ be like; resemble; take after: 姐妹俩长得很～。*The two sisters are very much alike.* / 这孩子～他父亲。*The child takes after its father.* ❷ look as if; seem: ～要下雨了。*It looks like rain.* / ～是有人在敲门。*It sounds like somebody's knocking at the door.* ❸ such as; like: ～黄继光这样的英雄人物,将永远活在人民的心里。*Heroes such as Huang Jiguang will always live in the hearts of the people.* Ⅱ名 ❶ likeness (of sb.); portrait; picture: 画像 ❷ [物] image: 虚～ *virtual image* / 实～ *real image*
【像差】[物] aberration
【像话】(usu. used in the negative or in rhetorical questions) reasonable; proper; right: 真不～! *That's really the limit.* or *It's simply outrageous.*
【像模像样】up to the mark; presentable; decent
【像散】[物] astigmatism ◇ ～镜 [物] astigmatoscope; ～透镜 astigmatic lens
【像样】(又作'像样子') up to the mark; presentable; decent; sound: 这屋里连张～的桌子也没有。*There isn't even a decent table in this room.* / 他提不出～的理由来解释他的行动。*He couldn't give any sound reason for his action.*
【像章】badge (or button) with sb.'s likeness on it

橡 名 ❶ oak ❷ rubber tree
【橡浆】rubber latex
【橡胶】rubber: 天然～ *natural rubber* / 合成～ *synthetic rubber* / 海棉～ *foam rubber*
【橡胶草】[植] Russian dandelion; koksaghyz
【橡皮】❶ (vulcanized) rubber: ～胶水 *rubber cement* / ～手套 *rubber (operating) gloves* ❷ eraser; rubber ◇ ～版 [刷] rubber plate; ～船 rubber boat; ～膏 [医] adhesive plaster; ～筋 rubber band; ～泥 plasticine; ～图章 rubber stamp; ～线 [电] rubber-sheathed wire
【橡皮圈】❶ inflatable life preserver (for swimming learners) ❷ rubber ring or band (for binding or tying things together)
【橡实】(又作'橡子') acorn ◇ ～管 [电子] acorn tube

xiāo

枭 Ⅰ名 ❶ owl ❷ smuggler: 盐～ *salt smuggler (in former times)* / 毒～ *drugpusher* Ⅱ形 brave; valiant: ～将 *a brave general*
【枭首示众】cut off a person's head and hang it up as a warning to all
【枭雄】a fierce and ambitious person; a formidable man

削 动 ❶ pare (or peel) with a knife: ～苹果 *pare (or peel) an apple* / ～铅笔 *sharpen a pencil* / 把木棍再～细点儿。*Whittle the stick down a bit more.* ❷ [体] chop; cut: 这个球～得好漂亮! *What a beautiful chop!* ——另见 xuē
【削尖脑袋往里钻】try hard to worm one's way in
【削球】chop; cut: 他削得一手好球。*He's especially good at chopping.*

哓 (构词成分) 见下
【哓哓不休】argue (or talk) endlessly

骁 形 valiant; brave; spirited
【骁将】〈书〉a valiant general
【骁勇】〈书〉brave; valiant: ～善战 *brave and battlewise*

消 动 ❶ disappear; vanish: 火灭了,烟还没～尽。*The fire had gone out, but the smoke had not cleared yet.* / 红肿已～。*The swelling has gone down.* / 他的气～了。*He has cooled down.* ❷ cause to disappear; eliminate; dispel; remove: ～肿 *cause a swelling to go down* / ～烟除尘 *eliminate smoke and dust* / ～痰 *reduce* phlegm ❸ pass (time) in a leisurely way; while away (time): 消夏 ❹〈方〉(used after 不, 只, 何, etc.) need; take (time, etc.): 来回只～一个星期。*It takes only a week to get there and back.* / 只～几句话就可以说清楚。*A few words will be enough to make it clear.*

【消沉】downhearted; low-spirited; dejected; depressed: 意志～*demoralized; despondent* / 她近来有些～。*She's rather depressed these days.*

【消愁】dispel or allay worries: 借酒～ *try to drown one's worries in wine* ◇～解闷 divert oneself from boredom; dispel depression or melancholy

【消除】eliminate; dispel; remove; clear up: ～分歧 *eliminate (or iron out) differences* / ～顾虑 *dispel misgivings* / ～隐患 *remove a hidden danger*

【消毒】❶ disinfect; sterilize: 用酒精～ *sterilize in (or with) alcohol* / 用漂白粉～ *disinfect with bleaching powder* ❷ disinfected; sterilized; pasteurized: ～棉花 *sterilized cotton* / ～牛奶 *sterilized (or pasteurized) milk* ◇～剂 disinfectant

【消防】❶ fire fighting: ～设备 *fire-fighting equipment* / ～水龙 *fire hose* / ～演习 *fire drill* ❷ fire prevention and control: 普及基本的～知识 *spread among the people an elementary knowledge of fire prevention and control* ◇～车 fire engine; ～艇 fireboat; ～站 fire station

【消防队】fire brigade; fire department: ～员 *fireman; fire fighter*

【消费】consume: 城市建设～大量物资。*Urban construction consumes large stocks of material resources.* ◇～城市 consume city; ～合作社 consumer cooperative; ～基金 funds for consumption; ～结构 consumption patterns; ～品 consumer goods; ～水平 level of consumption; ～税 consumption tax; ～者 consumer; ～资料 means of subsistence; consumer goods

【消耗】consume; use up; deplete; expend: ～精力 *consume one's energy* ◇～热[医] hectic fever; ～战 war of attrition

【消化】❶ digest (food): 我～很好。*I have good digestion.* / ～功能紊乱 *disorders of digestion* ❷ think over and absorb; digest (knowledge): 帮助学生～所学的东西 *help the students digest what they have learnt* ◇～道 alimentary canal; digestive tract; ～酶 digestive enzyme; digestive ferment; ～器官 digestive organ; ～系统 digestive system; ～性溃疡 peptic ulcer; ～液 digestive juice

【消化不良】❶ indigestion: 我有点儿～。*I'm suffering from indigestion.* ❷[医] dyspepsia

【消火栓】fire hydrant

【消极】❶ negative: ～影响 *negative (or harmful) influence* ❷ passive; inactive: ～抵抗(防御) *passive resistance (defence)* / ～怠工 *be slack in work*

【消解】clear up; dispel; remove: 前嫌～, 和好如初。*With all past ill will dispelled, good relations were restored.*

【消弭】〈书〉put an end to (an evil); prevent: ～祸患 *put an end to a disaster* / ～水患 *eliminate the menace of floods; prevent floods*

【消灭】❶ perish; die out; pass away: 许多古生物早已～了。*Many prehistoric forms of life have long since died out.* / 自行～ *perish (or die out) of itself* ❷ eliminate; abolish; exterminate; wipe out: ～种族歧视 *put an end to racial discrimination*

【消磨】❶ wear down; fritter away: ～志气 *sap one's will* / ～精力 *fritter away one's energy* ❷ while away; idle away: ～时间 *kill time; pass the time* / ～岁月 *while away the time*

【消气】cool down; be mollified: 我向她赔个不是, 她也就消了气。*Her anger melted as soon as I said sorry.*

【消遣】❶ divert oneself; while away the time: 在火车上打扑克～ *beguile the train journey by playing cards* ❷ diversion; pastime: 下棋是我喜爱的一种～。*Playing chess is one of my favourite pastimes.*

【消融】(又作'消溶') (of ice or snow) melt; thaw: 冰雪～ *melting of ice and snow*

【消散】(of smoke, fog, odor, heat, etc.) scatter and disappear; dissipate: 晨雾～了。*The morning mist has lifted.* / 他脸上的愁容～了。*The worried expression has disappeared from his face.*

【消色差】[物] achromatism ◇～透镜[物] achromatic lens; achromat

【消声】diminish or eliminate noises ◇～器 muffler; ～室 anechoic chamber (of a recording room, TV studio, etc.)

【消失】disappear; vanish; dissolve; die (or fade) away: ～在浓雾中 *disappear in the dense fog* / ～在人群中 *be lost in a crowd* / 痛楚～了。*The pain subsided.*

【消食】help digestion: 山楂糕开胃～, 老少皆宜。*Haw jelly is good for both the old and the young because it whets one's appetite and helps digestion.*

【消逝】die (or fade) away; vanish; elapse: 一抹残霞渐渐在天边～。*A few stray rosy clouds were disappearing from the horizon.*

【消释】dispel (misunderstanding, misgivings, enmity, pain, etc.); clear up; dissipate: ～疑虑 *dispel misgivings* / ～前嫌 *dispel past grudges*

【消受】❶ (usu. used in the negative) enjoy (having sth.): 无福～ *not have the luck to enjoy; be unable to enjoy* ❷ endure, bear, or stand (hardship, ill treatment, etc.)

【消瘦】emaciated; thinning down: 身体一天天～下去 *be getting thinner every day* / 显得有点～ *look a bit emaciated*

【消暑】❶ spend a summer holiday ❷ relieve summer heat

【消损】❶ reduce bit by bit; decrease: 他的锐气～

了。*His dashing spirit has diminished*. ❷ fritter away

【消亡】wither away；die out

【消息】❶ news；information：本地～ *local news* / 头版～ *a front-page story* / 据新华社～ *according to a Xinhua dispatch* ❷ tidings；news：他至今毫无～。*We haven't had any news of him yet*. ◇ ～灵通人士 well-informed sources

【消夏】spend a summer holiday：到北戴河去～ *spend the summer at Beidaihe* / ～音乐会 *summer concert*

【消闲】fill one's spare time；while away the time：为了～，他学会了打麻将。*He's learned to play mahjong as a way to spend his spare time*.

【消炎】［医］diminish（or counteract，reduce）inflammation；dephlogisticate ◇ ～剂 antiphlogistic；～片 antiphlogistic tablets

【消夜】〈方〉❶ food（or refreshments）taken late at night；midnight snack ❷ have a midnight snack

【消灾】rid calamities：祈求神灵～降福 *pray to the gods to ward off calamities and send down blessings*

【消长】decrease and increase；growth and decline；wax and wane：双方力量的～ *the growth and decline of the relative strength of the two sides*

【消肿】❶ cause a swelling to go down：抹这种药膏可以～。*This ointment will reduce the swelling*. / 很快就会～的。*The swelling will soon go down*. ❷［医］detumescence

宵 名 night：今～ *tonight*

【宵禁】curfew：实行～ *impose a curfew* / 解除～ *lift a curfew*

【宵夜】同〖消夜〗❶

逍（构词成分）见下

【逍遥】free and unfettered

【逍遥法外】go scot-free；be（or remain）at large

【逍遥自在】free and unfettered；leisurely and carefree

萧 形 desolate；dreary：萧瑟

【萧墙】〈书〉the screen wall facing the gate of a Chinese house：～之内 *behind the screen wall*；*within one's home*

【萧墙之祸】trouble behind the screen wall—trouble at home；trouble from within；internal strife ——另见〖祸起萧墙〗

【萧瑟】（又作'萧飒'）❶ rustling in the air；soughing：秋风～。*The autumn wind is soughing*. ❷ bleak；desolate

【萧索】❶ bleak and dreary；dull and desolate：～的晚秋气象 *a bleak late autumn scene* ❷（of a person's mood）melancholy；depressed

【萧条】❶ desolate；bleak：一片～的景象 *a desolate scene on all sides* ❷［经］depression：市面～。*The market is dull*. / 生意～。*Business is bad*（*or slack*）. / 经济～ *economic depression*；*slump*

【萧萧】〈书〉❶ the sound of a horse neighing or whinnying ❷ the sound of a whistling wind，pattering rain，etc.

硝 Ⅰ 名 nitre；saltpetre Ⅱ 动 taw（animal skin）：～皮 *taw an animal skin into leather*

【硝化】［化］nitrify：～棉 *nitrocotton* ◇ ～甘油 nitroglycerine

【硝石】nitre；saltpetre：智利～ *Chile nitre*（*or saltpetre*）；*sodium nitre*

【硝酸】［化］nitric acid ◇ ～铵 ammonium nitrate；～甘油片［药］nitroglycerine tablets；～钾 potassium nitrate；～钠 sodium nitrate；～纤维素 nitrocellulose；cellulose nitrate；～盐 nitrate（e.g. 硝酸钾 etc.）

【硝烟】smoke of gunpowder：～滚滚 *billows of powder smoke* / 战场上空～弥漫。*Gun smoke filled the air over the battlefield*.

【硝盐】salt made from earth containing a comparatively high percentage of sodium chloride

销 Ⅰ 动 ❶ melt（metal）❷ cancel；annul：这笔账已经～了。*This item has been written off*（*the account*）. or *The score is settled*. ❸ sell；market：这种产品～得出去吗？*Are these products marketable*？/ 一天～不少货 *sell quite a lot of goods a day* ❹ expend；spend：开销 ❺ fasten with a bolt；bolt：把窗户～上！*Bolt the window，please*！Ⅱ 名 bolt；pin：门～ *door bolt*

【销案】close a case；bring a case to a close

【销户口】cancel one's residence registration：我销完户口就离开了北京。*I left Beijing after I had my name cancelled from the residence register*.

【销毁】destroy by melting，burning，etc.：～罪证 *destroy incriminating evidence* / ～核武器 *have the nuclear weapons destroyed*

【销魂】be overwhelmed with sorrow or joy；feel transported

【销假】report back after leave of absence

【销金窟】money squandering den（e.g. a brothel，gambling house，etc.）

【销量】the quantity（of goods）sold；sales made：本月～猛增。*This month has seen a sharp increase in sales*.

【销路】sale；market：～很好 *have a good sale*；*find a good market*；*sell well* / 没有～ *find no sale*（*or market*）

【销声匿迹】keep silent and lie low；disappear from the scene：这位大明星近来～，不知去向。*The renowned film star has of late disappeared from the scene and is nowhere to be found*.

【销蚀】corrode：～作用 *corrosion* ◇ ～剂 corrodent

【销势】sales momentum：自行车、黑白电视机的～已经逐渐低落。*Sales of bicycles and black-and-white television sets are already dropping*.

【销售】sell；market：～价格 *selling price* / ～量 *sales volume* / ～费用 *selling expenses* / ～净额

net sales / ～总额 *gross (or aggregate) sales*

【销行】sell; be on sale: ～各地 *be on sale everywhere* / ～百万册 *have sold a million copies* / 本地土产开始～国外。*We have commenced the sale of local products abroad.*

【销赃】dispose of stolen goods: 一定有人帮助窃贼～。*Somebody must have helped the thief sell the stolen goods.*

【销账】cancel or remove from an account; write off

【销子】pin; peg; dowel; bolt

潇 形 〈书〉(of water) deep and clear

【潇洒】(of a person's appearance, demeanour, carriage, etc.) natural and unrestrained: 举止～ *carry oneself with ease and natural poise* / 神情～ *look natural and unaffected*

【潇潇】❶ (of wind and rain) driving; whistling and pattering: 风雨～ *a driving wind and a heavy rain* ❷ drizzling; drizzly: ～细雨 *a fine, gentle drizzle*

箫 名 xiao, a vertical bamboo flute

霄 名 ❶ clouds: 云霄 ❷ sky; heaven: 九霄云外

【霄汉】〈文〉the sky; the firmament

【霄壤】heaven and earth

【霄壤之别】as far apart (or as different) as heaven and earth; a world of difference

嚣 动 clamour; hubbub; din: 叫嚣

【嚣张】rampant; arrogant; aggressive: ～一时 *run rampant (or wild) for a time* / 他也太～了。*He's really too aggressive.*

xiáo

淆 动 confuse; mix: 混淆

【淆惑】〈书〉confuse; bewider

【淆乱】❶ mixed and disorderly ❷ confuse; befuddle: ～视听 *befuddle the minds of the public*

xiǎo

小 Ⅰ 形 ❶ small; little; petty; minor: ～屋 *a small room or house* / ～河 a small river / ～姑娘 a little girl / ～国 a small country / ～事 a small matter / ～问题 a minor question / ～手术 a minor operation ❷ young: 他还～呢。*He's still young.* / 你也不～了。*You're not young any more.* / 她比我～。*She is younger than I am.* ❸ the last in order of seniority: ～儿子 the youngest son / 他是我的～弟弟。*He is my youngest brother.* ❹ 〈谦〉my; our: ～女 *my daughter* / ～店 *my store* ❺ (used before names of animals to indicate the young): ～鸡 *chick* / ～鸭 *duckling* / ～狗 *pup* / *puppy* / ～猫 *kitten*; *kitty* Ⅱ 副 of short duration: ～坐片刻 *sit for a while* Ⅲ 名 little ones; children: 一家大～ *the whole family; old and young*

【小白菜】a variety of Chinese cabbage; pakchoi

【小白脸儿】〈贬〉a young fair face—a handsome, effeminate young man

【小百货】small articles of daily use

【小摆设】little curios, handicrafts, statuettes, etc. placed on shelves and desks for decoration; bric-a-bracs; ornamental knick-knacks

【小报】small-sized newspaper; tabloid

【小报告】a little report—a secret report to the higher authority on the shortcomings or wrongdoings of sb: 打～ *tell on sb.*

【小辈】junior members of a family or of families more or less related

【小本经营】do business with little capital—go in for sth. in a small way

【小扁豆】lentil

【小便】❶ urinate; pass (or make) water; empty one's bladder ❷ urine ❸ penis ◇ ～池 urinal

【小辫儿】short braid; pigtail: 她梳着两条～。*She wears her hair in two pigtails.*

【小辫子】a mistake or shortcoming that may be exploited by others; vulnerable point; handle: 有～给人抓 *have vulnerable points that others may capitalize on*

【小标题】subheading; subhead

【小不忍则乱大谋】lack of forbearance in small matters upsets great plans

【小步舞曲】minuet(the music)

【小菜】❶ pickled vegetables; pickles ❷ dial; meat, fish and vegetable dishes; common dishes

【小菜儿】〈口〉something extremely easy to do or manage

【小册子】booklet; pamphlet

【小产】have a miscarriage

【小肠】[生理] small intestine

【小潮】neap tide

【小炒】stir-fry dish cooked in a small wok

【小车】❶ wheelbarrow; handbarrow; handcart; pushcart ❷ car; sedan

【小乘】Little Vehicle (a school of Buddhism); Hinayana

【小吃】❶ snacks; refreshments ❷ cold dishes (of western food) ◇ ～部 snack counter; ～店 snack bar; ～街 food street

【小丑】❶ clown; buffoon: 扮演～角色 *play the buffoon* ❷ a contemptible wretch; a vile character

【小葱】shallot; spring onion

【小聪明】〈贬〉cleverness in trivial matters; petty trick: 耍～ *play petty tricks* /有点儿～ *be clever in some small ways*

【小打小闹】on a small scale; in a small way

【小刀】pocket knife

【小道理】minor principle

【小道】a small lane; path

【小道(儿)消息】side-street news; grapevine news; hearsay: 那是他听来的～。*That's something he heard on the grapevine*.

【小调】❶ ditty；tune ❷［音］minor：A～协奏曲 *concerto in A minor*

【小动作】❶ mean and petty action；little trick or manoeuvre：搞～ *get up to little tricks* ❷ fidgety movements (made by schoolchildren in class)

【小豆蔻】cardamom；cardamon

【小肚鸡肠】petty；narrow-minded

【小肚子】popular name for 小腹

【小队】the lowest-level unit of a group organized for a particular purpose；team；squad：少先队～长 *a squad leader of the Young Pioneers*

【小额】small amount：～储蓄 small savings deposit

【小恩小惠】little or small favours；economic sops or bait

【小儿】❶ children ❷〈谦〉my son

【小儿科】❶ (department of) paediatrics：～医生 *paediatrician* ❷ trivial or insignificant in value or importance；petty；kid's stuff

【小儿麻痹症】infantile paralysis；poliomyelitis；polio

【小二】(又作'小二哥')〈旧〉a young waiter in a wineshop or an inn

【小贩】pedlar；vendor；hawker

【小费】tip；gratuity

【小腹】underbelly；lower abdomen

【小个子】a short person；a small fellow

【小工】unskilled labourer

【小姑】〈口〉❶ (又作'小姑子') husband's younger sister；sister-in-law ❷ one's youngest paternal aunt

【小鼓】［音］side drum；snare drum

【小褂】Chinese-style shirt (worn next to the skin)

【小广播】spreading of hearsay information；grapevine；bush telegraph

【小规模战争】miniwar

【小鬼】❶ little devil；a demon servant in Hell ❷ child；imp (a term of endearment used in addressing a child)

【小孩儿】(又作'小孩子')〈口〉child

【小号】❶ small size (of clothes, etc.)：～鞋 *small-size shoes* / 我要小一号的。*I want one size smaller*. ❷〈谦〉my (or our) store ❸ trumpet

【小户】❶ (又作'小户人家') a poor, humble family；a family of limited means and without powerful connections ❷ a small family

【小环境】❶ micro-environment ❷ local social environment：他们希望周围的～充满正气、友善和谅解。*They want the atmosphere to be positive, friendly and understanding*.

【小黄鱼】little yellow croaker

【小伙子】〈口〉a young man；lad；a young fellow (or chap)；youngster

【小集团】clique；faction

【小蓟】［中］field thistle (Cephatanoplos segetum)

【小家碧玉】a pretty girl of humble birth

【小家伙】kid：我那～调皮得很。*My kid is very naughty*.

【小家庭】a small family：建立～ *get married and set up one's own home*

【小家子气】(又作'小家子相') small-minded；petty：不要太～了！*Don't be so petty!* / 她的～很重。*Her small-town manners are unmistakable*.

【小脚】bound feet (of women in the old days)

【小轿车】sedan；car

【小节】❶ a small matter；trifle：生活～ *matters concerning personal life* ❷［音］bar；measure：～线 *bar line*；*bar*

【小结】❶ a brief sum-up；a preliminary or interim summary：期末～ *an end-of-term summary* ❷ summarize briefly：～一下前阶段的工作 *summarize briefly the work done in the previous stage*

【小姐】❶ a young (unmarried) lady ❷ Miss：张～ *Miss Zhang*

【小金库】private gold storage；self-concerned exchequer；unit-owned exchequer

【小舅子】〈口〉wife's younger brother；brother-in-law

【小看】〈口〉look down upon；underestimate；belittle：你不该这么～人。*You really shouldn't look down on people like this*

【小康】a relatively comfortable life：家道～。*The family was comfortably off*.

【小康之家】a family with a modest competence；a comfortably-off family

【小考】minor examination (i.e. quiz, test, midterm examination, etc.)

【小客车】minibus

【小口径】small-bore；small-calibre：～步枪 *small-bore rifle*

【小老婆】concubine

【小两口】〈口〉a young (married) couple：那～儿真是天生的一对儿。*That young couple were meant for each other*.

【小路】path；trail

【小萝卜】radish

【小买卖】small business：做～ *do small business*

【小麦】wheat ◇ ～赤霉病 wheat scab；～吸浆虫 wheat midge；～线虫 nematode of wheat (Anguina tritici)

【小卖部】❶ a small shop attached to a school, factory, theatre, etc. (selling cigarettes, confectionery, cold drinks, etc.) ❷ buffet；snack counter

【小猫熊】lesser panda

【小米】millet：～粥 *millet gruel* / ～面 *millet flour*

【小名】pet name for a child；childhood name：他～叫毛毛。*His childhood name is Maomao*.

【小命】〈口〉life：他差一点儿送了～。*He barely escaped with his life*.

【小拇指】〈口〉little finger

【小脑】［生理］cerebellun

【小鸟依人】an endearing little bird (said of a lovely young girl)

【小妞儿】〈口〉a young girl

【小牛肉】veal

【小农】small farmer ◇ ～经济 small-scale peasant economy；small-scale farming by individual owners

【小跑】trot; jog: 他是一溜～着来的。*He came jogging all the way here.*

【小朋友】❶ children: 幼儿园的～ *children of the kindergarten*/一群～ *a bunch of children* ❷ (a term of address used by an adult to a child) little friend; little boy or girl

【小便宜】small gain; petty advantage: 贪～ *go after petty advantages* / 占～ *gain petty advantages*

【小品】a short, simple literary or artistic creation; essay; sketch: 历史～ *a short historical essay* / 广播～ *a short piece for broadcasting* / 电视～ *a TV sketch*

【小品文】familiar essay; essay

【小评论】a short comment

【小气候】microclimate

【小憩】〈书〉take a short rest: 公园里辟有茶座,供游人～。*There are teahouses in the park where visitors can sit and relax.*

【小气】❶ stingy; niggardly; mean ❷〈方〉narrow-minded; petty

【小前提】[逻] minor premise (in a syllogism)

【小瞧】〈口〉look down upon; underestimate: 别～人,你能干的我也能干! *Now don't underestimate me. What you can do I can do too!*

【小巧玲珑】small and exquisite

【小青年】young people; boys and girls (about 20 years of age)

【小青瓦】small black tile (a name for the old-style curved roof-tile)

【小球藻】chlorella

【小区】small residential district, with shopping centers and various other amenities

【小曲儿】ditty; popular tune

【小觑】despise; look down upon; underestimate

【小圈子】❶ a small social circle; a narrow area of activity: 走出家庭的～ *come out of the narrow family circle* ❷ a small circle (or set) of people; a small clique: 搞～ *form a small clique*

【小犬座】[天] Canis Minor

【小人】❶ a small man ❷〈旧〉〈谦〉I (used by a man of low social position when speaking to his betters) ❸ a base person; a vile character; villain

【小人得志】small man intoxicated by success; a small man having greatness thrust upon him; villains holding sway

【小人书】〈口〉children's picture-story book

【小人物】an unimportant person; a nobody; cipher; nonentity

【小日子】the easy life of a small family (esp. of a young couple): 他们的～过得挺舒坦。*They lead a happy and snug life.*

【小商品】small commodities ◇ ～经济 small commodity economy

【小舌】[生理] uvula

【小生产】small (or small-scale) production ◇ ～者 small producer

【小狮座】[天] Leo Minor

【小时】hour

【小时候】〈口〉in one's childhood; when one was young: 这是他～照片。*These are his childhood photos.* /～,我们常在一块玩儿。*We used to play together when we were young.*

【小市民】a town-dweller of the lower middle class; urban petty bourgeois; plebeian; philistine: ～习气 *plebeian ways and habits*

【小事】trifle; petty thing; minor matter: 大事做不来,～又不做 *disdain minor assignments while being unequal to major ones*

【小试锋芒】display only a small part of one's talent or capability

【小手工业者】small handicraftsman

【小手小脚】❶ stingy; mean ❷ lacking boldness; timid; niggling

【小叔子】〈口〉husband's younger brother; brother-in-law

【小数】[数] decimal ◇ ～点 [数] decimal point

【小说】novel; fiction ◇ ～家 novelist; writer of fiction

【小厮】〈旧〉❶ a young male servant; page boy; page ❷ boy; a young lad

【小苏打】[化] sodium bicarbonate

【小算盘】small abacus-selfish calculations: ～打得精 *be very calculating; be very shrewd in looking after one's own interests*

【小提琴】violin

【小提琴手】violinist: 首席～ *concertmaster*

【小题大作】make a fuss over a trifle; make a mountain out of a molehill

【小天地】one's own little world: 不要把自己关在办公室的～里。*Don't confine yourself within the four walls of an office.*

【小艇】a small boat; dinghy; skiff (rowed or sailed by one person)

【小偷】petty (or sneak) thief; pilferer

【小偷小摸】pilfering

【小土地出租者】a lessor of small plots of land

【小团体主义】cliquism; small-group mentality

【小腿】shank; lower leg

【小巫见大巫】a minor magician in the presence of a great one —feel dwarfed; pale into insignificance by comparison: 我过去所受的那些委屈和刺激,比起他来,也只是～,算不得什么。*What little pain and adversity I've experienced so far is simply nothing compared to what he's gone through.*

【小五金】metal fittings (e.g. nails, wires, hinges, bolts, locks, etc.); hardware

【小先生】little teacher—a student playing the role of a teacher to his classmates

【小小说】(又作'微型小说') short story (about 1 000 Chinese characters, usually carried in the evening papers): ～只摄取生活中的一两个镜头,通过极简短的情节集中表现某个主题。*Short fiction has a simple plot, picks up only one or two scenes from life and focuses on a single theme.*

【小鞋】tight shoes—difficulties created, or unfair

treatment given, by one's boss or superior when he cannot punish openly——另见〖穿小鞋〗

【小写】❶ the ordinary form of a Chinese numeral (e.g. 一, 二, 三, as against 壹, 贰, 叁) ❷ a small letter; minuscule

【小心】take care; be careful; be cautious: ～火烛! *Guard against fire!* /～轻放! *Handle with care!* /过马路要～。*Be careful when crossing the street.* /～油漆! *Mind the wet paint!* ——另见〖赔小心〗

【小心谨慎】careful; cautious; discreet; prudent

【小心眼儿】narrow-minded; petty: 你也太～了, 为这点儿事还生气。*You are a bit too touchy to get angry about such a small thing.*

【小心翼翼】with the greatest of care; very cautiously: 她～地把门打开, 生怕把孩子惊醒。*She opened the door gently so as not to wake the baby.*

【小行星】[天] minor planet

【小型】small-size; small-scale; miniature: ～企业 *small enterprise* /～运动会 *a small-scale athletic meet* /～拖拉机 *baby (or small) tractor* /～照相机 *miniature camera* /～摄像机 *minicam* ◇～飞机 aviette; light aeroplane; ～公共汽车 minibus; ～跑车 kart

【小型张】a small sheet

【小熊座】[天] Ursa Minor

【小学】❶primary (or elementary) school ❷ philologiacl studies

【小学生】primary school pupil; schoolchild; schoolboy or schoolgirl: 甘当群众的～ *be willing to be a pupil of the masses*

【小循环】[生理] pulmonary circulation

【小样】[刷] galley proof (or a separate news item or an article in a newspaper)

【小业主】small (or petty) proprietor

【小夜曲】[音] serenade

【小姨】mother's youngest sister—aunt

【小姨子】〈口〉wife's younger sister; sister-in-law

【小意思】❶〈套〉a small token of one's regard: 这是我的一点儿～, 送给你做个纪念。*This is a token of my esteem—just a little keepsake for you.* ❷ a mere trifle; nothing important: 这种事～, 一两个小时就可以完。*This job is nothing to me. I can finish it in a couple of hours.*

【小音阶】[音] minor scale

【小引】a brief or short introductory note (to a poem, essay, etc.); foreword

【小雨】light rain; drizzle

【小灶】small mess—a mess hall where highergrade food is prepared and served to a restricted group of diners

【小账】〈口〉tip; gratuity

【小照】a small-sized photograph of oneself

【小指】little finger or toe

【小传】a brief biography; biographical sketch; profile

【小资产阶级】petty bourgeoisie

【小子】(xiǎozǐ)〈书〉❶ the younger male generation ❷〈旧〉a term of address used by seniors to juniors ❸〈旧〉I (a term referring to oneself, used by juniors to elders or to betters)

【小子】(xiǎozi)〈口〉❶ boy: 一个胖～ *a chubby little boy* / 他有两个孩子, 一个闺女, 一个～。*He has two children, one girl and one boy.* ❷〈贬〉bloke; fellow; guy: 这～真不是东西。*That guy is really despicable.*

【小字】❶ handwritten small characters ❷ childhood name

【小字辈】juniors; younger members; persons of lower status

【小卒】foot soldier: ～子 *a minor figure* /无名～ *a mere nobody*

【小组】a small group: 领导～ *the leading group* /～讨论 *group discussion* / ～委员会 *subcommittee* ◇～循环赛 group round robin

晓 Ⅰ名 dawn; daybreak: 拂晓 Ⅱ动 ❶ know: 谁人不知, 哪个不～? *Everybody knows.* ❷ let sb. know; tell

【晓畅】❶ be familiar with; have a deep understanding of: ～音律 *have a deep understanding of music* ❷ (of a piece of writing) smooth and explicit: 文笔～ *write in a smooth and clear style*

【晓得】know: 天～! *God knows!* /明天你要提早十分钟来啊! —～! *You must get here ten minutes earlier tomorrow.—I know.*

【晓示】tell explicitly; notify

【晓行夜宿】(of a person on a long journey) start at dawn and stop at dusk: 他～, 风尘仆仆, 一路来到陕西。*Travelling by day and resting by night, he came to the Province of Shaanxi, travel-worn and weary.*

【晓以大义】instil in sb.'s mind the righteousness of a cause

【晓以利害】(又作'晓以利弊') warn sb. of the possible consequences; impress on sb. the gains and losses involved

xiào

孝 名 ❶ filial piety; filial obedience: 尽孝 ❷ mourning apparel: 穿孝

【孝道】filial duty: 尽～ *fulfil one's filial duty to one's parents*

【孝服】❶ mourning apparel ❷ a conventional period of mourning (for a deceased eder member of one's family): ～已满。*The mourning period is over.*

【孝敬】❶ show filial respect to (one's elders) ❷ give presents to (one's elders or superiors) to show one's respect; pay a tribute of respect to: 他带了些南边的土产来～他奶奶。*He brought his grandmother some local produce from the south as a gift.*

【孝顺】show filial obedience: 她对父母十分～。*She is extremely filial towards her parents.*

【孝心】filial sentiments; filial devotion

【孝子】❶ a filial son; a dutiful son ❷ son in mourning
【孝子贤孙】worthy progeny; a fine son

肖 动 resemble; be like: 维妙维肖
【肖像】portrait; portraiture ◇ ～画 portrait-painting
【肖像权】protraiture right

哮 动 ❶ heavy breathing; wheeze: 哮喘 ❷ roar; howl: 咆哮
【哮喘】[医] asthma

效 Ⅰ名 effect: 见效 Ⅱ动 ❶ imitate; follow the example of: 上行下效 ❷ devote (one's energy or life) to; render (a service): 报效
【效法】follow the example of; model oneself on; learn from: 他治学严谨,值得～。*His meticulous scholarship is worthy of emulation.* or *We have much to learn form his meticulous scholarship.*
【效仿】imitate; follow the example of
【效果】❶ effect; result: ～不大 *not be very effective; produce little effect* / 取得良好的～ *achieve good results* ❷ [戏] sound and lighting effects
【效劳】work in the service of; work for: 乐于为您～。*I'm only too glad to offer you my services.*
【效力】❶ render a service to; serve: 为国～ *serve one's country* ❷ effect: 这药很有～。*The medicine is efficacious.*
【效率】efficiency: ～高 efficient/～低 inefficient/这项革新使工作～提高五倍。*The innovation raised (or increased) efficiency fivefold.*
【效命】go all out to serve sb. regardless of the consequences: ～疆场 *ready to lay down one's life on the battlefield*
【效能】efficacy; usefulness: 充分发挥水、肥的～ *make the best possible use of irrigation and fertilizer*
【效验】intended effect; desired result: 没有～ *prove ineffective; fall flat* / 这种方法具有明显的～。*This method produces tangible results.*
【效益】beneficial result; benefit: 灌溉～ *irrigation benefit* / 经济～ *economic returns (or results, benefits)* / 社会～ *social effect* / 投资～ *investment results* ◇ ～工资 efficiency-related wage
【效应】(physical or chemical) effect: 热～ *fuel factor; heat effect; thermal results* / 光电～ *photoelectric effect; electro-optic effect*
【效用】effectiveness; usefulness: 发挥明显的～ *show obvious effectiveness*
【效尤】knowingly follow the example of a wrongdoer
【效忠】pledge loyalty to; devote oneself neart and soul to: ～宣誓 *oath of allegiance*

校 名 ❶ school: 全～同学 *all students of the school* / ～办工厂 *school-run workshop; campus work-shop* ❷ field officer; field grade officer——另见 jiào
【校车】school bus
【校风】school spirit: 这所学校以具有良好的～闻名。*The school boasts of excellent school spirit.*
【校服】school uniform
【校官】[军] field officer; field grade officer
【校规】school regulations
【校花】campus belle
【校徽】school badge
【校刊】school publication; college journal
【校历】school calendar
【校内】on (the) campus
【校庆】the anniversary of the founding of a school or college
【校舍】schoolhouse; school building
【校外】outside school; outside the campus: 住～ *not live on the campus* ◇ ～辅导员 guest counsellor for schoolchildren's activities
【校外活动】after-school activities: ～站 *after-school activities club (or centre)* / ～辅导员 *after-school activities counsellor*
【校务】administrative affairs of a school or college
【校训】school motto
【校医】school doctor
【校友】alumnus or alumna: ～会 *alumni assocation*
【校园】campus; school grounds
【校长】❶ headmaster (of a middle or primary school); principal ❷ president (of a university, college, etc.); chancellor
【校址】the location of a school or college; school or college address

笑 动 ❶ smile; laugh: 哈哈大～ *laugh heartily; roar with laughter* / 真～死人 be terribly funny ❷ ridicule; laugh at: 他刚学,别～他。*He's just started learning. Don't laugh at him.*
【笑柄】laughing stock; butt; joke: 他这句话已成为～。*That remark of his has become a standing joke.*
【笑掉大牙】laugh one's head off: 叫人～ *ridiculous enough to make people laugh their heads off*
【笑哈哈】laughingly; with a laugh
【笑话】❶ joke; jest: 说～ *crack a joke* ❷ laugh at; ridicule: ～人 laugh at sb./咱们一定要赢,别让人～咱们。*We must win the game, and not give others any chance to laugh at us.*——另见〖闹笑话〗;〖看笑话〗
【笑话百出】make many stupid mistakes; make oneself utterly ridiculous
【笑里藏刀】hide a dagger behind a smile—with murderous intent behind one's smiles: 世界上多少人被他们的甜言蜜语所蒙蔽,而不知道他们～的可怕。*Quite a number of people have been fooled by their honeyed words, failing to see the murderous intent behind their smiles.*
【笑脸】smiling face: ～相迎 *greet with a genial smile*
【笑料】something funny or laughable; laughing stock; joke

【笑骂】❶ deride and upbraid; taunt ❷ scold in jest (or jokingly)
【笑眯眯】smiling; with a genial smile on one's face: 他老是～的。*He's always smiling.*
【笑面虎】a smiling tiger—an outwardly kind but inwardly cruel person
【笑纳】〈套〉 kindly accept (this small gift of mine): 送上薄酬,还望～。*Hope you will kindly accept this little remuneration we are sending you.*
【笑破肚皮】split one's sides with laughter
【笑气】[化] laughing gas; nitrous oxide
【笑容】smiling expression; smile: 慈祥的～ *a kindly smile* / ～满面 *be all smiles; have a broad smile on one's face*
【笑容可掬】be radiant with smiles
【笑谈】❶ laughing stock; object of ridicule: 传为～ *become a standing joke* ❷ a funny remark; joke; jest
【笑嘻嘻】grinning; smiling broadly
【笑星】comic star usu. outstanding comic dialogue performer: 这位～的独特表演风格给观众留下了深刻的印象。*The comic star with his unique style was a huge hit with his audience.*
【笑颜】smiling face: ～常开 *be always beaming with joy*
【笑逐颜开】beam with smiles; one's face wreathed in smiles: 张太太不由得～。*Mrs. Zhang couldn't restrain a smile of joy.*

啸 动 ❶ (of humans) make a whistling sound ❷ (of certain birds and animals) give a long, loud cry: 虎～ *tigers roaring (or growling)* / 鸟～ *birds screeching* ❸ (of the wind, the sea, etc.) howl; roar: 风～ *the wind howling* / 海水的～声 *the roaring of the sea* ❹ (of bullets, airplanes, etc.) whistle; whizz: 枪弹的～声 *the whistling of bullets* / 飞机尖～着飞过顶空。*A plane whizzed overhead.*
【啸聚】〈书〉 holler to each other and band together (or gang up)
【啸聚山林】holler to each other, form a band and take to the greenwood
【啸鸣】❶ whistle; whizz; screech; howl: 烈风～。*A strong wind was howling.* ❷ a loud, shrill and long sound: 汽笛的～把人们从睡梦中惊醒。*The wails of the siren woke the people out of their dreams.*

xiē

些 量 ❶ some; a few: 作了～改进 *have made some improvements* / 买～东西 *do some shopping* / 前～日子 *a few days ago; sometime ago* ❷ (used after adjectives) a little more; a little: 这个稍大～。*This is a little bigger.* / 我好～了。*I'm a little better.* / 请大声～! *Louder, please!*
【些微】slightly; a little; a bit: ～有点儿疼 *hurt slightly; be a bit painful* / 这颜色～深了一点。*The colour is a trifle too dark.*
【些许】a little; a few: ～礼物 *some small presents*

楔 名 ❶ wedge ❷ peg
【楔形文字】cuneiform characters (as of ancient Babylonia, Assyria, Persia, and some other areas of the Near East); sphenogram
【楔子】❶ wedge ❷ peg ❸ prologue or interlude in Yuan Dynasty drama ❹ prologue in some modern novels

歇 动 ❶ have a rest: ～一会儿 *have a short rest* / 累得我都～不过来了。*I'm completely done in.* ❷ stop (work, etc.); knock off: 咱们～会儿,喝杯茶。*Let's knock off for a cup of tea.* / 我已经～了一个礼拜没上班了。*I've been off from work for a week.*
【歇班】be off duty; have time off: 今天小王～。*Xiao Wang is off duty today.*
【歇顶】get a bit thin on top; be balding: 他年龄并不老,可是已经～了。*He is not old but is already balding.*
【歇伏】stop work during the hottest days of the year
【歇工】stop work; knock off: 今天我们早早就～了。*We stopped work early today.*
【歇后语】a two-part allegorical saying, of which the first part, always stated, is descriptive, while the second part, sometimes unstated, carries the message, e.g. 泥菩萨过河——自身难保 *like a clay idol fording a river—hardly able to save oneself (let alone anyone else)*
【歇脚】rest the feet—stop on the way for a rest: 咱们到那边荫凉地歇歇脚吧。*Let's stop for a rest in the shade over there.*
【歇气】have a short break: 歇口气儿 *stop for a breather; take (or have) a breather* / 他一连干了一天一夜没～。*He worked the whole day and night without a break.*
【歇晌】take a midday nap or rest
【歇斯底里】❶ [医] hysteria ❷ unnaturally excited or emotional; hysterical: ～大发作 *go into hysterics; become hysterical*
【歇息】❶ have a rest ❷ put up for the night; go to bed: 今晚就在我这儿～吧。*Stay here for the night.*
【歇业】close a business; go out of business

蝎 名 scorpion
【蝎虎】(又作'蝎虎子') gecko; house lizard
【蝎子】scorpion

xié

协 Ⅰ 形 joint; common: ～办 *do sth. jointly* Ⅱ 动 assist: 协理
【协办】help sponsor; assist in holding: 由文化部主办、美术家协会～的现代油画展 *an exhibition of*

contemporary oil paintings sponsored by the Ministry of Culture with the assistance of the Artists' Association of China

【协查】[法] help investigate (crime): 向有关单位发出～通知 *notify concerned units, calling for their assistance in the investigation*

【协定】❶ agreement; accord: 文化合作～ *agreement on cultural cooperation* ❷ reach an agreement on sth.; conclude a convention: 我们应该～一个共同的纲领。*We should reach an agreement on a common programme.* ◇ ～边界 conventional boundary; ～关税 conventional tariff

【协会】association; society: 中国人民对外友好～ *the Chinese People's Association for Friendship with Foreign Countries*

【协理】❶ assist in the management (of an enterprise, etc.) ❷ assistant manager (in a bank, business enterprise, etc.)

【协力】unite efforts; join in a common effort: ～进攻 *launch a joint assault*

【协商】consult; talk things over: 需要和有关部门～。*It's necessary to consult with the departments concerned.* ◇ ～会议 consultative conference; ～委员会 consultative committee or commission

【协调】❶ coordinate; concert; harmonize; bring into line: 一定要使我们的行动～起来。*We must coordinate our activities.* ❷ in a concerted way; balanced; harmonious; in tune: ～一致 *(work) in concert and harmony* / 比例关系逐渐趋于～。*The ratio is becoming more balanced.* ◇ ～委员会 coordination committee

【协同】work in coordination with; cooperate with: ～作战 *fight in coordination* / ～动作 *coordinated action*

【协议】❶ agree on: 一致～的文件 *a document unanimously agreed upon* / 双方～提高收购价格。*The two sides agreed to raise the purchasing price.* ❷ agreement: 达成～ *reach an agreement* / 口头～ *verbal agreement* / ～条款 *terms of agreement*

【协议离婚】consensual divorce

【协约国际法】conventional international law

【协助】assist; help; give assistance; provide help: 副总理～总理工作。*The Vice-Premiers assist the Premier in his work.*

【协奏曲】[音] concerto: 钢琴(小提琴)～ *piano (violin) concerto*

【协作】cooperate; coordinate; combine (in efforts): ～项目 *joint-operated project* / 双方～得很好。*The two sides cooperated harmoniously.*

邪 Ⅰ 形 evil; heretical; weird; irregular: 咱们按原则办事，决不搞～的歪的。*We'll stick to principles and never engage in irregularities.* Ⅱ 名 disaster (caused by supernatural beings): 中邪

【邪不胜正】(又作'邪不敌正') the evil will not triumph over the virtuous

【邪道】evil ways; a depraved life; vice: 走～ *lead a depraved life; abandon oneself to evil ways*

【邪恶】evil; wicked; vicious: ～的念头 *wicked thoughts*

【邪教】(evil) cult; herectic sect

【邪路】evil ways; vice: 走上～ *take to evil ways* / 把某人引向～ *lead sb. astray*

【邪门儿】❶〈方〉strange; odd; abnormal: 这天气真～，这时候还下雪。*What strange weather—snowing at this time of the year!* ❷ crooked ways; underhand means; dishonest practices (or methods)

【邪门歪道】crooked ways; underhand means; dishonest practices (or methods)

【邪魔】evil spirit; demon

【邪魔外道】❶ [宗](佛教) evil demons and heretics ❷ unorthodox ways; crooked ways and means

【邪念】an evil thought; a wicked idea: 他起了～。*A wicked idea came into his head.*

【邪气】a perverse trend; an evil influence: 使正气上升，～下降 *encourage healthy trends and check unhealthy ones*

【邪术】black magic; sorcery; witchcraft

【邪说】heresy; heretical ideas; fallacy

【邪心】同〚邪念〛

胁 Ⅰ 名 the side of the human body from the armpit to the waist Ⅱ 动 coerce; force: 威胁

【胁持】同〚挟持〛

【胁从】be an accomplice under duress: ～者 *reluctant (or unwilling) follower; accomplice under duress*

【胁肩谄笑】cringe and smile obsequiously; bow and scrape

【胁迫】coerce; force: 被～参与犯罪 *be coerced into participating in a crime*

挟 动 ❶ hold sth. under the arm ❷ coerce; force sb. to submit to one's will: 要挟 ❸ harbour (resentment, etc.): 挟仇

【挟持】❶ (usu. of bad people) seize sb. on both sides by the arms ❷ hold sb. under duress

【挟仇】harbour a grudge

【挟恨】harbour intense hatred

【挟天子以令诸侯】have the emperor in one's power and order the nobles about in his name; control the emperor and command the nobles

【挟嫌】〈书〉harbour resentment; bear a grudge: ～报复 *bear resentment against sb. and retaliate*

【挟制】take advantage of sb.'s weakness to enforce obedience; force sb. to do one's bidding

谐 Ⅰ 形 ❶ in harmony; in accord: 和谐 / 谐调 ❷ humorous: 诙谐 Ⅱ 动〈书〉come to an agreement; settle: 事～之后，即可动身。*We shall set out immediately once the matter is settled.*

【谐和】harmonious; concordant

【谐谑】banter: 语带～ *speak somewhat jokingly*

【谐谑曲】[音] scherzo

【谐调】harmonious; well-balanced

【谐音】❶ euphony ❷ [音] partials ❸ homophony

【谐振】［物］resonance：空腔～ *cavity resonance* ◇ ～腔［物］resonant cavity

偕 副 together with；in the company of

【偕老】(used in blessing newly-weds) live together to a ripe old age

【偕同】in the company of；accompanied by；along with

【偕行】❶ travel (or go) together：携手～ *go together hand in hand* ❷ coexist

斜 形 oblique；slanting；inclined；tilted：这根线～了。*The line is slanting.* / 柱子有点～。*The pillar is a little tilted.* / ～躺在沙发上 *recline on a sofa* / 把桌子～过来 *turn the table sideways* / ～着眼看人 *cast sidelong glances at sb.*；*look sideways at sb.*

【斜边】❶［数］hypotenuse ❷［机］bevel edge

【斜长石】plagioclase (a mineral)

【斜度】degree of inclination；gradient ◇ ～标 gradient sign

【斜对面】(又作'斜对过') opposite slightly to the right or left：车站在学校的～。*The station is almost opposite the school.*

【斜风细雨】gentle wind and light rain

【斜高】［数］slant height

【斜角】❶［数］oblique angle ❷［机］bevel angle ◇ ～规［机］bevel square

【斜井】❶［矿］inclined shaft；slope ❷ petroleum inclined well；slant hole

【斜路】wrong path：走到～上去 *go astray* / 正路不走走～ *turn from the right road and take the wrong one—give up an honest life for a dishonest one*

【斜率】［数］slope

【斜面】❶［数］inclined plane ❷［机］oblique plane；bevel (face)

【斜坡】slope

【斜射】❶ cast oblique rays (or beams) on：～的光线 *oblique light (or beams)* / ～的阳光穿过树丛，洒落在大道上。*The rays of the setting sun slanted through the trees onto the road.* ❷［军］oblique fire

【斜视】❶［医］strabismus ❷ look sideways；cast a sidelong glance：目不斜视

【斜视图】［机］oblique drawing

【斜体字】［刷］italics

【斜纹】［纺］twill (weave)

【斜纹布】［纺］twill；drill

【斜线】［数］oblique line ◇ ～号 slant (/)

【斜眼】❶［医］strabismus ❷ wall-eye or cross-eye；squint ❸ a wall-eyed or cross-eyed person

【斜阳】the setting sun

【斜照】❶ cast oblique rays (or beams) on ❷ the setting sun

【斜轴线】［数］oblique axis

携 动 ❶ carry；take along：～眷 *bring one's wife and children along* / ～款潜逃 *abscond with funds* / ～械投诚 *come over from the enemy's side bringing weapons* ❷ take (or hold) sb. by the hand：携手

【携带】carry；take along：～方便 *be easy to carry about* / 随身～的物品 *things carried on one's person*

【携手】join hands：～并进 *go forward hand in hand*

鞋 名 shoes

【鞋拔子】shoehorn

【鞋帮】upper (of a shoe)

【鞋带】shoelace；shoestring

【鞋底】sole (of a shoe)

【鞋垫】shoe-pad；insole

【鞋跟】heel (of a shoe)

【鞋匠】shoemaker；cobbler

【鞋扣】shoe buckle

【鞋刷】shoe brush

【鞋样】shoe pattern；outline of a shoe's upper and sole

【鞋油】shoe polish (or cream)

xiě

写 动 ❶ write：～封信 *write a letter* / ～得一手好字 *have good handwriting*；*write a good hand* / 这支笔不好～。*This pen doesn't write well.* ❷ compose；write (as an author，reporter，etc.)：～小说 *write a novel* / ～诗 *compose a poem* / ～日记 *make an entry in one's diary*；*keep a diary* ❸ describe；depict：～景 *describe the scenery* / ～人物的心理活动 *depict the characters' mental activities* / 这个人物叫他～活了。*His portrayal of the character is vivid and true to life.* ❹ paint；draw：写生

【写法】❶ style of writing；literary style：文体不同，～也不同。*Different types of writing call for different styles of writing.* ❷ style of handwriting；penmanship

【写稿】write for (or contribute to) a magazine，etc.：你给我们的晚报写篇稿好吗？*Will you write an article for our evening paper?*

【写生】［工美］sketch from life；do a still life painting；paint or sketch from nature：人物～ *portrait from life* ◇ ～画 sketch

【写实】write or paint realistically

【写意】［工美］freehand brushwork in traditional Chinese painting (characterized by vivid expression and bold outline)

【写照】❶ portray (a person or character)：传神～ *give a vivid and lifelike portrayal* ❷ portrayal；portraiture：真实的～ *a portrayal true to life*

【写真】❶ portray a person；draw a portrait ❷ portrait ❸ a true-to-life depiction；a faithful representation ❹ photograph

【写字间】〈方〉office

【写字楼】office building

【写字台】writing desk；desk；bureau

【写作】writing：从事～ *take up writing as one's career* / ～技巧 *writing technique* ◇ ～班子 writing group

血 名 blood：一滴～ *a drop of blood* / 一摊～ *a pool of blood* / ～的教训 *a lesson paid for* (*or written*) *in blood* ——另见 xuè

【血块】blood clot；clot

【血淋淋】❶ dripping with blood；bloody；gory ❷ grim；bitter；cruel：～的现实 *a grim reality* / ～的教训 *a bitter lesson*

【血丝】a trace of blood：由于睡眠不足，他两眼布满～。*His eyes are bloodshot because of lack of sleep.*

【血晕】(xiěyùn) contusion；bruise ——另见 xuèyùn

xiè

泻 动 ❶ flow swiftly；rush down；pour out：一泻千里 ❷ have loose bowels；have diarrhoea

【泻肚】have loose bowels；have diarrhoea

【泻湖】[地理] lagoon

【泻盐】Epsom salts；salts

【泻药】laxative；cathartic；purgative

泄 动 ❶ let out (a fluid or gas)；discharge；release：排泄 ❷ let out (a secret)；leak (news, secrets, etc.)：泄底 ❸ give vent to；vent：泄愤

【泄底】reveal or expose what is at the bottom of sth.

【泄愤】(又作'泄恨') give vent to one's pent-up anger：泄私愤，图报复 *try to revenge a personal grudge*

【泄洪】[水] release floodwater：开闸～ *open a sluice to release floodwater* ◇ ～道 flood-relief channel；floodway；～隧道 flood-discharge tunnel

【泄劲】lose heart；feel discouraged；be disheartened；slacken one's efforts：他近来有点～。*He has been a bit disheartened lately.*

【泄漏】❶ (of a fluid or gas) leak；escape ❷ (of a secret, etc.) leak；let out；divulge；give away：～秘密 *let out* (*or divulge, give away*) *a secret* / 消息已～出去了。*The news has leaked out.*

【泄露】let out；reveal：敌人无意中～了行动计划。*The enemy unwittingly revealed their plan of action.* / ～国家机密 *divulge a state secret*

【泄密】divulge a secret；betray confidential matters：～事件 (*a case of*) *leakage of a state or Party secret*

【泄气】❶ lose heart；feel discouraged；be disheartened：我不该说那些～话。*I shouldn't have made those discouraging* (*or pessimistic*) *remarks.* ❷ disappointing；frustrating；pathetic：这么矮他都跳不过去，真～！*He can't even jump that high. How pathetic!*

【泄水】[水] sluicing：～工程 *outlet work*

【泄水道】sluiceway

【泄水孔】outlet

【泄水闸】sluice gate；sluice

【泄殖腔】[动] cloacal chamber；cloaca

卸 动 ❶ unload；discharge；lay down：～担子 *lay down a burden* / ～牲口 *unhitch a draught animal* ❷ remove；strip：～零件 *remove parts from a machine；strip a machine* / 把门～下来 *lift a door off its hinges* ❸ get rid of；shirk

【卸车】unload (goods, etc.) from a vehicle；unload a truck, car, etc.

【卸货】unload (or discharge) a cargo；unload：这些船明天～。*The ships will unload* (*the cargoes*) *tomorrow.* ◇ ～港 [交通] port of discharge；unloading port

【卸磨杀驴】kill the donkey the moment it leaves the millstone—get rid of sb. as soon as he has done his job

【卸任】be relieved of one's office

【卸妆】(of a female) remove ornaments and formal dress

【卸装】(of an actor or actress) remove stage makeup and costume

屑 Ⅰ 名 bits；scraps；crumbs：纸～ *scraps of paper* / 煤～ (*coal*) *slack* / 金属～ *metal filings* / 面包～ *crumbs* (*of bread*) Ⅱ 形 trifling：琐屑 Ⅲ 动 (usu. used in the negative) consider sth. to be worth doing：不屑

【屑意】mind；take offence：毫不～ *not mind a bit*

械 名 ❶ tool；instrument：机械 ❷ weapon：持～抢劫 (*commit*) *armed robbery* ❸〈书〉fetters, shackles, etc.

【械斗】a fight with weapons between groups of people

谢 动 ❶ thank：～了又～ *thank again and again* / 多～。*Thanks a lot.* / 不用～。*Don't mention it.* ❷〈书〉make an apology；excuse oneself：～过 *apologize for having done sth. wrong* / ～病 *excuse oneself on grounds of illness* ❸ decline：谢绝 ❹ (of flowers, leaves) wither：凋谢

【谢忱】gratitude；thankfulness：承蒙协助，谨致～。*Allow us to express our thanks for your kindly help.*

【谢词】a thank-you speech

【谢顶】get a bit thin on top；be balding

【谢恩】(usually of a minister to an emperor) express gratitude for a favour

【谢绝】politely refuse；decline：～参观。*Not open to visitors.*

【谢客】❶ decline to receive visitors；not be seeing any visitors：闭门～ *not at home to visitors* ❷ thank a guest for his visit

【谢礼】a gift in token of gratitude；a return present

【谢幕】answer (or respond to) a curtain call

【谢世】〈书〉pass away; die

【谢天谢地】thank goodness; thank heaven: ～,你总算回来了! *Thank goodness, you're back at last!*

【谢谢】thank: ～! *Thanks!* or *Thank you!* / 请替我～他。*Please give my thanks to him.*

【谢意】gratitude; thankfulness: 预致～ *thank you in anticipation* / 谨致薄礼,聊表～。*Please accept this gift and my gratitude.*

【谢罪】apologize for an offence; offer one's apology for a fault

亵 Ⅰ 动 treat with irreverence; be disrespectful: 亵渎 Ⅱ 形 obscene; indecent: ～语 *obscene utterances; obscenities*

【亵渎】blaspheme; profane; pollute: ～神明 *a blasphemy against gods*

【亵衣】〈书〉underwear; underclothes

榭 名 a pavilion or house on a terrace: 水榭

懈 形 slack; lax: 松懈

【懈怠】slack; sluggish: 学习上不可～。*Don't slack off in your studies.*

【懈劲】relax one's exertions; lose one's drive; slack off

【懈气】relax one's exertions; lose one's drive; slack off

邂 (构词成分) 见下

【邂逅】〈书〉meet (a relative, friend, etc.) unexpectedly; run into sb.; meet by chance

蟹 名 crab

【蟹黄】the reddish-yellow crab meat (made up of the ovary and digestive glands)

【蟹钳】the crab's claws

【蟹青】greenish-grey (colour)

xīn

心 名 ❶ the heart ❷ heart; mind; feeling; intention: 羞耻之～ *sense of shame* / 伤人的～ *wound (or hurt) sb.'s feelings* / 你的～是好的,但是事情办得不好。*You meant well but you didn't handle the job well.* ❸ centre; core: 白菜～ *the heart of a Chinese cabbage* / 江～ *the middle of a river; halfway across the river*

【心爱】loved; treasured; dear to one's heart: ～的人 *one's beloved; loved one* / ～的东西 *treasured (or prized) possession*

【心安理得】feel at ease and justified; have an easy conscience; with mind at rest and conscience clear: 你能～地把全部责任都推到他一人身上吗? *Can you shift the blame onto him alone and yet have a clear conscience?*

【心瓣膜】[生理] heart valve

【心包】[生理] pericardium ◇ ～炎 pericarditis

【心病】❶ worry; anxiety: 这事老悬着,一直是他的～。*He has been worried by the unsolved matter all the time* ❷ sore point; secret trouble

【心搏】[生理] heartbeat

【心不在焉】absent-minded; inattentive; preoccupied (with sth. else): ～地听着 *listen absentmindedly* / 她拿起一本小说,～地看着。*She took up a novel to read, but could not concentrate.*

【心裁】idea; conception; mental plan: 独出心裁

【心肠】❶ heart; intention: ～软 *have a soft heart; be softhearted* / 好～ *kindhearted* / 他真是个热～, *He's a really warmhearted person!* ❷ 〈方〉state of mind; mood: 没～去看电影 *be in no mood to see a movie*

【心潮】a tidal surge of emotion; surging thoughts and emotions: 她～翻滚,无法入睡。*Her mind being in a tumult, she could not go to sleep.*

【心潮澎湃】feel an upsurge of emotion

【心驰神往】one's thoughts fly to (a place or person); have a deep longing for

【心慈手软】softhearted: 对怙恶不悛的犯罪分子不能～。*We should not be softhearted towards hardened criminals.*

【心粗气浮】hotheaded; thoughtless and impetuous

【心胆俱裂】be frightened out of one's wits; be terror-stricken: 吓得敌人～ *strike terror into the enemy's hearts*

【心得】what one has learned from work, study, etc.: 谈谈学习～ *talk about what one has gained from study*

【心底】the bottom of one's heart: 这是她出自～的话。*The words were spoken from her heart.*

【心地】a person's mind, character, moral nature, etc.: ～坦白 *candid; open* / ～单纯 *simple-minded* / ～善良 *good-natured; kindhearted* / ～光明 *always open and aboveboard*

【心电描记器】[医] electrocardiograph

【心电图】[医] electrocardiogram

【心动】❶ heartbeat ❷ 同〖动心〗◇ ～徐缓 [医] bradycardia; ～周期 [生理] cardiac cycle

【心动过速】[医] tachycardia: 阵发性～ *paroxysmal tachycardia*

【心耳】[生理] auricle (of the heart); auricular appendage

【心烦】be vexed; be perturbed: 这事真叫人～。*This is really a bother.* or *This is really upsetting.*

【心烦意乱】be terribly upset; be perturbed: ～,不知所从。*His mind was in such a turmoil that he did not know which way to turn.*

【心房】[生理] atrium (of the heart) ◇ ～纤颤 [医] atrial fibrillation

【心扉】the door of one's heart: 我愿意敞开自己的～,向你倾诉一切。*I wish to open my heart and tell you everything.*

【心浮】flighty and impatient; unstable

【心浮气躁】flighty and impetuous

【心服】be genuinely convinced; acknowledge (one's defeat, mistake, etc.) sincerely

【心服口服】be sincerely convinced: 我觉得他说的

有理,听得～。*All this made such good sense that I was won round completely.*

【心腹】❶ trusted subordinate; reliable agent ❷ confidential: 说～话 *tell sb. sth. in strict confidence; confide in sb.; exchange confidences* / ～事 *a secret in the depth of one's heart*

【心腹之患】disease in one's vital organs—danger from within; serious hidden trouble or danger

【心甘情愿】be most willing to; be perfectly happy to

【心肝】❶ conscience: 没～ *heartless* ❷ (a term of endearment mostly used with one's small children) darling; dear; sweetheart; honey

【心高气傲】(又作'心高气盛') ambitious and proud

【心广体胖】carefree and contented; fit and happy

【心寒】〈方〉be bitterly disappointed: 令人～ *chill the heart; be bitterly disappointing*

【心狠】cruel; merciless

【心狠手辣】cruel and ruthless; wicked and merciless

【心花怒放】burst with joy; be wild with joy; be elated

【心怀】❶ intention; purpose ❷ state of mind; mood ❸ harbour; entertain; cherish: ～不满 *feel discontented; nurse a grievance*

【心怀鬼胎】have evil intentions; have sinister motives

【心怀叵测】harbour unfathomable evil designs; have sinister intentions: 这个人～,对他的一举一动,都要严加提防。*That man has sinister designs. You must guard against his every move.*

【心慌】❶ be flustered; be nervous; get alarmed: 我考试的时候～。*I was nervous while I was taking the exam.* ❷〈方〉(of the heart) palpitate

【心慌意乱】be alarmed and confused; be nervous and flustered

【心灰意懒】be disheartened; be downhearted; be dispirited: 他连输三场,～。*Three defeats in a row dispirited him.*

【心机】thinking; scheming: 她年龄不大,但很有～。*Young as she is, she has a mind of her own.*

【心肌】[生理] cardiac muscle; myocardium ◇ ～梗塞(又作'心肌梗死')[医] myocardial infarction; ～炎 myocarditis

【心急】impatient; short-tempered

【心急火燎】burning with impatience; in a nervous state

【心急如焚】(又作'心急如火') burning with impatience: 他的全身滚热,～。*He was boiling hot all over, his mind tense with a great sense of urgency.*

【心计】calculation; scheming; planning: 工于～ *adept at scheming; very calculating* / 这个年轻人做事很有～。*This young chap does things intelligently.*

【心迹】the true state of one's mind; true motives or feelings: 表明～ *lay bare one's true feelings*

【心悸】❶ [医] palpitation ❷〈书〉be scared: 令人～ *terrifying; frightening*

【心焦】anxious; worried: 真叫人～! *This is really worrying!* / 我们等得好～! *How anxiously we waited!*

【心绞痛】[医] angina pectoris

【心惊胆战】tremble with terror; shake with fright; quake with fear

【心惊肉跳】be jumpy; have the jitters

【心境】state (or frame) of mind; mental state; mood: ～不好 *be in a bad mood* / ～非常愉快 *be in a very happy mood*

【心静】calm: ～自然凉。*So long as one keeps calm, one doesn't feel the heat too much.*

【心坎】❶ the pit of the stomach: 他把手放在～上。*He laid his hand on his heart.* ❷ the bottom of one's heart: 我从～里感谢您。*I thank you from the bottom of my heart.*

【心口】the pit of the stomach

【心口如一】say what one thinks; speak from the heart; be frank and forthright

【心宽体胖】见〖心广体胖〗

【心旷神怡】relaxed and joyful; carefree and happy

【心劳日拙】fare worse and worse for all one's scheming

【心理】mentality; psychology: 不要养成依赖别人的～。*Don't get into the habit of depending on others.* / ～因素 *psychological factor* ◇ ～病态 morbid state of mind; ～测验学 psychometry; ～分析 psychoanalysis; ～距离 psychological gap; ～疗法 psychotherapy; ～学 psychology; ～训练 psychological training; ～战 psychological warfare; ～治疗 psychotherapy

【心力】mental and physical efforts: 费尽～ *make strenuous efforts*

【心力交瘁】be mentally and physically exhausted

【心力衰竭】[医] heart failure

【心里】in the heart; at heart; in (the) mind: ～发闷 *feel constriction in the area of the heart* / ～不痛快 *feel bad about sth.*

【心里话】one's innermost thoughts and feelings: 说出自己的～ *give voice to one's innermost feelings* / 我看他没有说～。*I don't think he has come out with what's on his mind.*

【心连心】heart linked to heart: 我国各族人民～。*The hearts of the people of all our nationalities are linked to each other.*

【心灵】❶clever; intelligent; quick-witted: ～手巧 *clever and deft* ❷ heart; soul; spirit: ～深处 *deep in one's heart* / 在她幼小的～里 *in her childish heart*

【心领神会】understand tacitly; readily take a hint: 这个奴才对主子的意图～。*The lackey immediately understood what his master wanted.*

【心律】[医] rhythm of the heartbeat ◇ ～不齐 [医] arrhythmia

【心率】heart rate

【心乱如麻】have one's mind all in a tangle; be utterly confused and disconcerted; be terribly upset

【心满意足】be perfectly content (or satisfied)

【心明眼亮】see and think clearly；be sharp-eyed and clear-headed

【心目】❶ mood；frame of mind：以娱～ *to amuse oneself* ❷ memory：动人情景犹在～。*The moving scene remains* (or *is still*) *fresh in my memory*. ❸ mind；mental view：在某些人的～中 *in some people's eyes*

【心皮】［植］carpel

【心平气和】even-tempered and good-humoured；calm：～地交换意见 *exchange views calmly* / 有话～地讲。*Let's try to talk things over without getting excited*.

【心窍】capacity for clear thinking：权迷～ *be obsessed by a lust for power* / 他的话打开了我的～，我知道该怎么办了。*What he said cleared up my thinking and then I knew what to do next*.

【心切】eager；impatient；anxious：求胜～ *be anxious to gain victory* / 求官～ *seek office eagerly*

【心情】frame (or state) of mind；mood：～沉重 *with a heavy heart* / ～舒畅 *have ease of mind* / ～激动 *be excited*；*be thrilled* / ～不一样，感受也不同。*People in different frames of mind feel differently about things*.

【心如刀割】feel as if a knife were piercing one's heart：她听到这不幸的消息～。*The sad news stabbed her to the heart*.

【心如死灰】one's heart is like dead ashes—hopelessly apathetic

【心软】be softhearted；be tenderhearted

【心上】in the heart：这等小事你千万别搁在～。*Please don't take such trifles to heart*.

【心上人】person of one's heart；one's beloved

【心神】mind；state of mind：～不安 *feel uneasy* (*or restless*)；*be disturbed* ◇ ～不定 have no peace of mind；feel restless；be distracted

【心声】heartfelt wishes；aspirations；thinking：表达人民的～ *voice the aspirations of the people*

【心事】sth. weighing on one's mind；a load on one's mind；worry：了结一桩～ *take a load off one's mind* / 她好像有什么～似的。*She seems to have something on her mind*.

【心事重重】be laden with anxiety；be weighed down with care：他好像～。*He gave the impression of a man whose heart was heavy*.

【心室】［生理］ventricle ◇ ～纤颤［医］ventricular fibrillation

【心输出量】［生理］cardiac output

【心术】❶ intention；design：～不正 *harbour evil intentions* (*or designs*) ❷ calculation；scheming；planning：他是个有～的人。*He is a calculating person*.

【心死】one's will dies within one—see the futility of one's attempt

【心思】❶ thought；idea：坏～ *a wicked idea* / 他在想～。*He is pondering over something*. ❷ thinking：用～ *do a lot of thinking*；*think hard* / 白费～ *bother one's head for nothing* ❸ state of mind；mood：没有～去看戏 *not be in the mood to see a play*

【心酸】be grieved；feel sad：她的遭遇听了令人～。*Hers is a heart-rending story*.

【心算】mental arithmetic；doing sums in one's head

【心碎】be heartbroken：听到她的小妹妹的死讯，她的心都碎了。*She was heartbroken at the news of her little sister's death*.

【心态】mentality；psychology

【心疼】❶ love dearly：这样惯孩子不是～他。*Pampering a child like this is not loving him*. ❷ feel sorry；be distressed：这么浪费，叫人看了～。*It makes one's heart ache to see such waste*.

【心田】❶ heart ❷ intention

【心跳】palpitation：我有些～。*My heart is beating a bit too fast*. / 他吓得心直跳。*His heart jumped with fright*.

【心头】mind；heart：记在～ *bear* (*or keep*) *in mind* / ～恨 *rankling hatred* / ～火起 *burn with anger*

【心头肉】a dearly loved person or a treasured possession：孩子是她的～。*Her children are closest to her heart*.

【心窝儿】〈口〉❶ the pit of the heart or stomach：他一拳打在我～里，痛得我半天直不起腰来。*I doubled up with pain when he struck me in the pit of my stomach*. ❷ deep down in one's heart：他第一次把掏～的话都和她说了。*For the first time he told her all his innermost thoughts and feelings*.

【心无二用】one cannot keep one's mind on two things at the same time；one should concentrate on one thing at a time

【心细】careful；scrupulous：胆大～ *bold but cautious*

【心弦】heartstrings：动人心弦

【心想】think to oneself；think：我～他早晚总会来的。*I thought he would turn up sooner or later*.

【心向往之】yearning for sb. or sth.

【心心相印】have mutual affinity；be kindred spirits

【心胸】❶ breadth of mind：～开阔 *broad-minded*；*unprejudiced* / ～狭窄 *narrow-minded*；*intolerant* ❷ aspiration；ambition：他有～，有气魄。*He is a man of vision with high ambitions*.

【心虚】❶ afraid of being found out；with a guilty conscience ❷ lacking in self-confidence；diffident：对于这种生疏的工作，我感到～。*I don't know much about the job, and I'm diffident about my ability to do it properly*.

【心绪】state of mind：～烦乱 *emotionally upset*；*in an emotional turmoil*

【心绪不宁】in a disturbed state of mind；in a flutter

【心血】painstaking care (or effort)：费尽～ *expend all one's energies*

【心血管系统】［生理］cardiovascular system：～疾病和功能障碍 *cardiovascular system diseases and disorders*

【心血管造影】angiocardiography

【心血来潮】be prompted by a sudden impulse；be seized by a whim：～，忘乎所以 *forget oneself in an impulsive moment*；*be carried away by one's whims and act recklessly*

【心眼儿】❶ heart；mind：看到孩子们这么幸福，大家从～里感到高兴。*It warms the cockles of the heart to see the children so happy*. ❷ intention；a person's mind：～好 *good-natured*；*kindhearted* / 没安好～ *have bad intentions*；*be up to no good* ❸ intelligence；cleverness：他有～，什么事都想得周到。*He is alert and thoughtful*. / 长点～，别上人家的当。*Smarten up and don't be taken in*. ❹ unfounded doubts；unnecessary misgivings：～太多 *full of unnecessary misgivings*；*oversensitive* ❺ tolerance：～小 *oversensitive*；*petty* ——另见〖斗心眼儿〗

【心痒】have an itch for：一见那清凉的水，个个都～，巴不得马上跳下去。*When they saw the clear cool water, they all had an itch to dive in at once*.

【心仪】〈书〉admire；respect：～已久 *have long had a high regard for sb*.

【心疑】become or be suspicious

【心意】❶ regard；kindly feelings：这点礼物是我们大家的一点～。*This little gift is a token of our regard*. ❷ intention；purpose：你们不了解他的～。*You don't understand his intention*.

【心音】［生理］heart sounds；cardiac sounds：第一（第二）～ *the first* (*second*) *heart sound*

【心硬】hard-hearted；stony-hearted；callous；unfeeling

【心有灵犀一点通】hearts which beat in unison are linked

【心有余而力不足】one's ability falls short of one's wishes；the spirit is willing, but the flesh is weak

【心有余悸】one's heart still fluttering with fear；have a lingering fear

【心猿意马】a heart like a capering monkey and a mind like a galloping horse—restless；perturbed

【心愿】cherished desire；aspiration；wish；dream：这就了却了我的一桩～。*This serves to fulfil a cherished desire of mine*.

【心悦诚服】be completely convinced；feel a heartfelt admiration：她爸爸的一番话说得她～。*She was completely convinced by her father's arguments*.

【心杂音】［医］heart murmur

【心脏】❶ the heart：～搏动 *heartbeat* ❷ the central or most vital part of anything：首都是一个国家的～。*The capital is the heart of a country*. ◇～病 heart disease；～导管 cardiac catheter；～地带 heartland；～起搏器 (cardiac) pacemaker；～移植 heart transplant

【心照】understand without being told：彼此～ *have a tacit understanding with sb*.

【心照不宣】have a tacit understanding

【心直口快】frank and outspoken；straightforward and plain-spoken：他喜欢这个小伙子，～，有啥说啥。*He has always liked this straightforward, outspoken youngster*.

【心智】intelligence；wisdom

【心中】in the heart；in the mind：牢记～ *keep firmly in mind*

【心中无数】have no idea of how things stand；not know for certain：这计划是否可行，我～。*I'm not too sure whether this plan will work*.

【心中有数】know the score；have a pretty good idea of how things stand；know fairly well；know what's what：对计划执行情况～ *have a pretty clear idea of how the plan is being carried out*

【心轴】［机］mandrel：花键～ *splined mandrel*

【心拙口笨】dull-witted and slow-tongued

【心子】❶ centre (of sth.)；heart；core ❷〈方〉the heart of a pig, sheep, etc. as food

【心醉】be charmed；be enchanted；be fascinated

芯 名 rush pith：灯～ *lampwick*；*wick* ——另见 xìn

辛 形 ❶ hot (in taste, flavour, etc.)；pungent ❷ hard；laborious：艰辛 ❸ suffering：辛酸

【辛迪加】［经］syndicate

【辛苦】❶ hard；strenuous；toilsome；laborious：犁地这活儿很～。*Ploughing is hard work*. ❷〈套〉work hard；go to great trouble；go through hardships：这事恐怕还得～您一趟。*I'm afraid you'll have to take the trouble of going there to see about it*. ◇～费 trouble fee

【辛辣】pungent；hot；bitter：～的味道 *a sharp* (or *pungent*) *flavour* / ～的讽刺 *bitter irony*；*biting sarcasm*

【辛劳】work hard；toil：日夜～ *toil day and night* / 不辞～ *spare no pains*

【辛勤】industrious；hardworking：～劳动 *work hard*；*labour assiduously*

【辛酸】sad；bitter；miserable：～泪 *hot and bitter tears* / ～的往事 *sad* (*or poignant*) *memories*

【辛烷值】［化］octane number (or value)

【辛辛苦苦】take a lot of trouble；take great pains；work laboriously：她～地攒了几个钱。*She saved up some money with great difficulty*.

欣 形 glad；happy；joyful：～逢佳节 *on the happy occasion of the festival*

【欣然】〈书〉joyfully；with pleasure：～接受 *accept with pleasure* / ～同意 *gladly consent*；*readily agree*

【欣赏】appreciate；enjoy；admire：音乐～ *music appreciation* / ～风景 *enjoy* (*or admire*) *the scenery*

【欣慰】be gratified：我们对实验的成功感到～。*We were gratified at the success of the experiment*.

【欣悉】〈书〉be glad (or happy) to learn

【欣喜】glad；joyful；happy：听说王涛即将学成归国，～万分。*We are extremely glad to learn that*

Wang Tao will soon complete his studies abroad and return home.

【欣喜若狂】be wild with joy; go into raptures

【欣欣向荣】thriving; flourishing; prosperous: 一派～的景象 *a picture of prosperity*

【欣幸】be glad and thankful

锌 名［化］zinc (Zn)

【锌白】［化］zinc white

【锌版】［刷］zinc plate; zincograph ◇ ～印刷术 zincography

【锌钡白】［化］lithopone

【锌粉】［化］zinc powder

新 Ⅰ形 ❶ new; fresh; up-to-date: ～技术 *new (or up-to-date) technique* / ～品种 *a new variety* / 最～消息 *the latest news* / ～社会 *the new society* ❷ brand new; unused: ～笔 *a new pen* / ～衣服 *new clothes* ❸ recently married or just being married: ～女婿 *a man newly married to one's daughter; daughter's bridegroom* / ～媳妇 *a woman newly married to one's son; son's bride* Ⅱ副 newly; freshly; recently: ～建的工厂 *a newly built factory* / ～漆的门 *a freshly painted door* / 他是～来的。*He's a new arrival.*

【新兵】recruit; (Brit. Navy) ordinary seaman; (Brit. Air Force) aircraftsman

【新茶】newly picked and processed tea leaves

【新潮】new trend; new fashion: ～服装 *new fashions* ◇ ～新款 new fashion and new style

【新车展览】Motorama

【新陈代谢】❶［生］metabolism: 生物都有～，有生长、繁殖和死亡。*All living matter undergoes a process of metabolism: it grows, reproduces and perishes.* ❷ the new superseding the old: ～是宇宙间普遍的永远不可抵抗的规律。*The supersession of the old by the new is a general, eternal and inviolable law of the universe.*

【新仇旧恨】new hatred piled on old; old scores and new

【新词】new word; new expression: ～、新义，新用法 *new words, new meanings and new usages*

【新村】new residential quarter; new housing development (or estate)

【新大陆】the New World—the Americas

【新发行证券】new issue

【新房】bridal chamber

【新古典经济学】neoclassical economics

【新古典主义】neoclassicism

【新官上任三把火】a new official applies strict measures; a new broom sweeps clean

【新欢】new sweetheart (esp. a woman): 另结～ *be taken up with another woman*

【新婚】newly-married: ～夫妇 *a newly-married couple; newlyweds* / ～旅行 *go on a honeymoon trip*

【新纪录】a new record: 创造～ *set a new record*

【新纪元】a new era; a new epoch: 开创～ *usher in a new epoch; open a new era*

【新加坡】Singapore

【新交】a new acquaintance; a new friend: ～与故知 *old and new friends*

【新教】Protestantism ◇ ～徒 Protestant

【新近】recently; lately; in recent times

【新经济政策】New Economic policy

【新旧约全书】［宗］(基督教) the Old and New Testaments

【新居】new home; new residence

【新喀里多尼亚】New Caledonia

【新来乍到】newly arrived: ～，请多帮助。*I'm a newcomer here and would be glad to have your help.*

【新郎】bridegroom

【新老交替】replace old cadres with new ones

【新历】the new calendar—the Gregorian calender

【新马】Singapore and Malaysia

【新霉素】［药］neomycin

【新苗】❶〈字〉young plant; seedling ❷〈喻〉newly emerging, vigorous and promising talent: 中国足球队大力培养～。*The Chinese Football Team has been making vigorous efforts to train young talent.*

【新民主主义】new democracy ◇ ～革命 new-democratic revolution

【新名词】❶ new term; new expression ❷ vogue word; newfangled phrase: 满口～ *mouthing newfangled phrases*

【新年】New Year: ～好！*Happy New Year!* / ～献词 *New Year message*

【新娘】(又作'新娘子') bride

【新篇章】new page: 两国关系史上的～ *a new page in the history of relations between the two countries*

【新瓶装旧酒】old wine in a new bottle—the same old stuff with a new label

【新奇】strange; novel; new: ～的想法 *a novel idea* / 他初到矿山时，处处觉得～。*When he first got to the mine, everything struck him as new.*

【新秋】early autumn

【新区】newly developed area; newly added district

【新人】❶ people of a new type: 一代～在茁壮成长。*A new generation is reaching maturity.* ❷ new personality; new talent: 科学界涌现出了一批～。*A new batch of gifted people has emerged in the world of science.* ❸ bride and bridegroom ❹ bride

【新人新事】new people and new things: ～不断涌现。*New people and new things are constantly coming to the fore.*

【新任】❶ newly appointed: ～部长 *the newly appointed minister* ❷ new post: 赶赴～ *go to take up a new post*

【新生】❶ newborn; newly born: ～婴儿 *newborn (baby)* ❷ new life; rebirth; regeneration ❸ a new student or pupil ◇ ～代［地质］the Cenozoic Era; ～界［地质］the Cenozoic Erathem; ～力量 newly emerging force; new rising force; new force; ～事物 newly emerging things; new things

【新石器时代】the Neolithic Age; the New Stone Age

【新式】new type; latest type; new style: ～农具 *new types of farm implements*; *improved farm implements* / ～武器 *modern weapons*

【新手】a new hand; a raw recruit

【新书】❶ new book ❷ new title

【新四军】the New Fourth Army

【新文学】new-vernacular literature (promoted by the May 4th Movement in 1919)

【新闻】news: 头版～ *front-page news* (*or story*) / 简明～ *news in brief* / 电视～ *TV news* / ～简报 *news summary* / ～图片橱窗 *newsphoto display case* ◇ ～处 office of information; information service; ～导向 the guiding role of mass media; ～发布会 press conference; news releasing; ～发言人 news spokesman; ～封锁 news blackout; ～稿 press (or news) release; ～工作者 journalist; ～公报 press communiqué; ～广播 newscast; ～记者 newsman; newspaperman; reporter; journalist; ～检查 press censorship; ～界 press circles; the press; ～联播 news hookup; ～片 newsreel; news film; ～评论员 news analyst; ～人物 newsmaker; ～司 department of information (of the Foreign Ministry); ～通讯 newsletter; ～图片栏 news window; ～业 journalism; ～纸 newsprint; ～自由 press freedom

【新闻主持人】anchor

【新西兰】New Zealand ◇ ～人 New Zealander

【新媳妇儿】〈口〉bride

【新禧】good fortune for the new year: 恭贺～ *Happy New Year*

【新鲜】❶ fresh: 鱼有点不～了。*The fish is slightly off*. / 尝个～ *have a taste of what is just in season* ❷ new; novel; strange: ～经验 *new* (*or fresh*) *experience* / 这话真～。*That's a strange thing to say*. ◇ ～血液〈字〉fresh blood; 〈喻〉new addition to the membership; new blood

【新小说】nouveau roman

【新兴】new and developing; rising; burgeoning: ～势力 *the rising forces*; *the forces in the ascendant*

【新星】❶ [天] nova ❷ new star: 羽毛球～ *a new badminton star*

【新型】new type; new pattern: ～厨房用具 *modern cooking equipment*; *modern kitchenware*

【新秀】new star: 影坛～ *a new film* (*or movie*) *star*

【新义】new meaning

【新意】new meaning; new conception

【新颖】new and original; novel: 题材～ *original in choice of subject* (*or theme*) / 式样～ *in a novel style*

【新约】[宗] (基督教) the New Testament

【新月】❶ crescent (moon) ❷ [天] new moon (invisible to men)

【新月形沙丘】[地理] barchan

【新正】the first month of the lunar year

【新殖民主义】neocolonialism ◇ ～者 neocolonialist

【新制】new system

【新装】new clothes: 她正在试～。*She's trying on a new dress*. / 山村换～。*The mountain village takes on a new look*.

【新自由主义】neoliberalism

薪 名 ❶ firewood; faggot; fuel: 采木为～ *gather wood for fuel* ❷ salary: 加～ *increase* (*or raise*) *the salary*

【薪俸】salary; pay

【薪金】pay in money; salary

【薪尽火传】as one piece of fuel is consumed, the flame passes on to another—the torch of learning is passed on from teacher to student

【薪水】salary; pay; wages

【薪炭林】[林] fuel forest

馨 名〈书〉strong and pervasive fragrance: 如兰之～ *a strong and pervasive fragrance like the orchid's*

【馨香】〈书〉❶ fragrance: 桂花盛开,～四溢。*The osmanthus is in full bloom, filling the air with its fragrance*. ❷ the sweet smell of burning incense

xìn

芯 名 core ——另见 xīn

【芯子】❶ fuse (as in a firecracker); wick (as in a candle) ❷ the forked tongue of a snake

信 Ⅰ 形 true; real Ⅱ 名 ❶ confidence; trust; faith: 失信 ❷ sign; evidence: 信号 ❸ letter; mail: 写封～ *write a letter* ❹ message; word; information: 还没有～儿呢。*No news yet*. / 你到了那儿就给我来个～儿。*Please send me word of your arrival*. Ⅲ 动 ❶ believe: ～不～由你。*Believe it or not*. / 别～他的话。*Don't believe him*. / 我不～他能赢。*I don't believe he can win*. ❷ profess faith in; believe in: ～佛 *profess Buddhism* ❸ at will; at random; without plan: 信步

【信标灯】beacon light

【信步】take a leisurely walk; stroll; walk aimlessly

【信不过】distrust; have no trust in: 你是～我,所以不肯对我讲真话。*You are not telling me the truth because you don't trust me*.

【信差】〈旧〉❶ courier ❷ postman

【信贷】credit: 长期～ *long-term credit* / ～额度 *line of credit* / ～资金 *credit funds*; *funds for extending credit* ◇ ～担保 credit guarantee

【信道】information channel ◇ ～容量 channel capacity

【信得过】❶ trust: 你要是～我,就交给我去办。*If you trust me, let me do it for you*. ❷ trustworthy; dependable ◇ ～企业 "Trusted by the masses" enterprise

【信而有征】borne out by evidence

【信访】letters and calls
【信风】［气］trade winds；trades ◇ ～带 trade-wind zone
【信封】envelope
【信奉】believe in：～上帝 *believe in God* / ～伊斯兰教 *be a Moslem*
【信服】completely accept；be convinced：令人～的论据 *convincing argument*；*argument that carries conviction*
【信鸽】carrier pigeon；homing pigeon；homer
【信管】fuse：炸药～ *fuse in a blasting charge* / 触发～ *contact fuse*
【信函】letters
【信号】signal：灯光～ *light signal* / 识别～ *identification signal* ◇ ～兵 signalman；～刺激［心理］signal stimulus；～弹 signal flare；～灯 signal lamp；semaphore；～旗 signal flag；semaphore；～枪［军］flare pistol；signal pistol
【信汇】mail transfer（M/T）
【信笺】letter paper；notepaper
【信件】letters，papers，printed matter，etc.（sent either by post or by messenger）
【信教】profess a religion；be religious
【信口】speak thoughtlessly or casually：～说出 *blurt out* / ～回答 *answer casually*
【信口雌黄】make irresponsible remarks；wag one's tongue too freely：一个～的无赖 *a shameless liar and scoundrel*
【信口开河】（又作'信口开合'）talk irresponsibly；wag one's tongue too freely；talk at random
【信赖】trust；count on；have faith in：她是群众～的好干部。*She's a good cadre trusted by the masses.*
【信马由缰】❶ ride a horse without holding the reins ❷ stroll about aimlessly；act or do as one pleases
【信念】faith；belief；conviction：坚定的～ *a firm conviction* / 我的～决不会动摇。*Nothing can shake my belief.*
【信任】trust；have confidence in：得到人民的～ *enjoy the trust*（*or confidence*）*of the people* ◇ ～投票 vote of confidence；～危机 crisis of confidence
【信赏必罚】due rewards and punishments will be meted out without fail
【信使】courier；messenger：外交～ *diplomatic messenger* / ～证明书 *courier's credentials*
【信誓旦旦】pledge in all sincerity；vow solemnly
【信手】do sth. spontaneously or without much thought or effort：她抱起琵琶，～弹来，竟十分动听。*She took up the pipa and began to play，effortlessly and melodiously.*
【信手拈来】have the words at hand；have materials，etc. at one's fingertips
【信守】abide by；stand by：～协议 *abide by*（*or stand by*）*an agreement* / ～诺言 *keep a promise*；*be as good as one's word*
【信守不渝】be unswervingly true（to one's promise，etc.）
【信天翁】［动］albatross
【信条】article of creed（or faith）；creed；precept；tenet
【信筒】pillar-box；mailbox
【信徒】believer；disciple；follower；adherent；devotee：佛教～ *Buddhist*
【信托】trust；entrust ◇ ～公司 trust company；～基金 trust fund；～商店 commercial shop（or house，agent）；～投资公司 trust and investment corporation
【信物】authenticating object；token；keepsake
【信息】❶ information；news；message：～传递 *information transmission* / ～中心 *information centre* ❷［数］information ◇ ～产业 information industry；～处理 information processing；～反馈 information feedback；～高速公路 information super-highway；～革命 information revolution；～工程学 information engineering；～技术 information technology；～检索 information retrieval；～交换 information interchange；information switching；～科学 information science；～量 amount of information；information content；～论［数］information theory；～社会 information society；～体［生化］informosome；～网 information network；～学 information science；informatics；～资源 information resources
【信箱】❶ letter box；mailbox ❷ post-office box（P.O.B.）
【信邪】believe in dishonest practices or yield to evil forces：她是一个不～的正直女子。*She is an honest and upright person who will not go along with dishonest practices.*
【信心】confidence；faith：满怀～ *full of confidence* / 我对这药～不大。*I haven't much faith in this medicine.*
【信仰】faith；belief；conviction：政治～ *political conviction* / 宗教～ *religious belief* / ～自由 *freedom of belief* / ～危机 *credibility crisis*
【信以为真】accept sth. as true：因为他说得有凭有据，大家～。*Since his statement seemed well founded，all the others immediately accepted it.*
【信义】good faith；faith：有～ *act in good faith* / 无～ *be perfidious*
【信用】❶ trustworthiness；credit：他～好，完全可以信任。*His credit is good. You can trust him.* / 讲～ *keep one's word* / 失去～ *lose one's credit* ❷ credit：～贷款 *unsecured loan*；*loan on credit* ◇ ～报告 credit report；～合作社 credit cooperative；～卡 credit card；～债券 debenture stock；～证 letter of credit（L/C）
【信誉】prestige；credit；reputation：享有很高的国际～ *enjoy high international prestige*
【信噪比】signal-to-noise ratio（SNR）
【信札】letters
【信纸】letter paper；writing paper

衅

名 quarrel；dispute：寻衅
【衅端】〈书〉a cause for a quarrel or dispute

xīng

兴 Ⅰ 动 ❶ prosper; rise; prevail; become popular: 我们这儿不～这一套。*We don't go in for that sort of thing here.* / 现在又～超短裙了。*Miniskirts are coming into fashion again.* ❷ start; begin: 兴工 / 兴建 ❸ encourage; promote: 大～调查研究之风 *energetically encourage the practice of investigation and study* ❹〈书〉get up; rise: 晨～ *get up in the morning* ❺〈方〉(often used in the negative) permit; allow: 不～胡说! *None of your nonsense!* Ⅱ 副〈方〉maybe; perhaps: 明天他也～来,也～不来。*He may or may not come tomorrow.* ——另见 xìng

【兴办】initiate; set up: ～新型企业 *initiate enterprises of a new type*

【兴奋】❶ be excited: 他～过度,睡不着觉。*He was too excited to fall asleep.* ❷［生理］excitation

【兴奋剂】excitant; stimulant; dope ◇ ～检测中心 doping control centre

【兴奋性】excitability

【兴风作浪】stir up trouble; make trouble; fan the flames of disorder

【兴工】start construction: 破土～ *break ground and start construction*

【兴建】build; construct: 正在～一座大坝。*A dam is now under construction.*

【兴利除弊】promote what is beneficial and abolish what is harmful

【兴隆】prosperous; thriving; flourishing; brisk: 生意～。*Business is brisk.*

【兴起】❶ rise; spring up; be on the upgrade: 激光是六十年代初期～的一门新科学。*Laser is a new branch of science which rose in the early 1960s.* ❷〈书〉rise in excitement; be aroused

【兴盛】prosper; flourish; thrive; be in the ascendant: 国家～。*The nation is prosperous.* / 事业～。*Business is thriving.*

【兴师动众】move troops and stir up people-draw in many people (to do sth.): 这点小事,用不着～。*It's only a small matter; you needn't make a fuss about it and draw in a lot of people.*

【兴师问罪】send a punitive expedition

【兴衰】rise and decline; rise and fall

【兴替】〈书〉the rise of a power and its supersession by another; rise and fall: 朝代的～ *the rise and fall of a dynasty*

【兴亡】rise and fall (of a nation)

【兴旺】prosper; flourish; thrive: 他们的企业越办越～。*Their enterprise is growing more and more prosperous.*

【兴修】start construction (on a large project); start building (on an extensive scale): ～水利 *undertake new water conservancy projects*

【兴许】perhaps; maybe

【兴妖作怪】conjure up demons to make trouble—stir up trouble

星 名 ❶ star: 月明～稀。*The moon is bright and the stars are sparse.* ❷ heavenly body: 彗星 / 卫星 ❸ bit; particle

【星表】［天］star catalogue

【星辰】stars and constellations; the stars: 日月～ *the sun, the moon and the stars*

【星虫】sipunculid worm

【星等】［天］magnitude

【星斗】stars: 满天～ *a star-studded sky*

【星光】starlight: 在～下漫步 *go for a walk under the starlight* / 一个～闪烁的夜晚 *one starlit night*

【星号】asterisk (*)

【星火】❶ spark ❷ shooting star; meteor: 急如星火

【星火计划】the Spark Plan

【星火燎原】a single spark can start a prairie fire

【星际】interplanetary; interstellar ◇ ～飞船 spaceship; ～航行 interplanetary flight (or travel); interstellar flight (or travel); space flight (or travel); ～物质 interstellar medium

【星空】a starry sky; a star-studded sky; a starlit sky

【星罗棋布】scattered all over like stars in the sky or men on a chessboard; spread all over the place: 全国中小型水利工程～。*Small and medium-sized irrigation works spread all over the country.*

【星期】❶ week: 三个～ *three weeks* ❷ (used before 日,一,二,三,四,五,六,几) day of the week: 今天～几? *What day (of the week) is it today?* ❸〈略〉见〖星期日〗◇ ～二 Tuesday (Tues.); ～六 Saturday (Sat.); ～日 (又作'星期天') Sunday (Sun.); ～三 Wednesday (Wed.); ～四 Thursday (Thur. or Thurs.); ～五 Friday (Fri.); ～一 Monday (Mon.)

【星球】celestial body; heavenly body ◇ ～大战 Star-War

【星鲨】［动］gummy shark

【星探】talent scout

【星体】［天］celestial body; heavenly body

【星条旗】Stars and Stripes; the Star-Spangled Banner (the national flag of the U. S. A.)

【星图】［天］star chart; star map; star atlas

【星团】［天］star cluster

【星系】［天］galaxy: 总～ *metagalaxy* / ～团 *cluster of galaxies* ◇ ～天文学 extragalactic astronomy; ～晕［天］galactic halo

【星相】horoscope

【星象】configurations of the stars (formerly studied for their supposed influence on human affairs)

【星星】(xīngxīng) a tiny spot; speck: 天空晴朗,一～云彩也没有。*The sky is clear and bright without a speck of cloud.*

【星星点点】tiny spots; bits and pieces: 对于科学的最新成就我只是～知道一些。*I have only a scrappy knowledge of the latest scientific achievements.*

【星星之火,可以燎原】a single spark can start a prairie fire
【星星】(xīngxing)〈口〉star
【星夜】a starlit (or starry) night:～启程 *set out by starlight*; *set out in great haste*
【星移斗转】change in the positions of the stars—change of the seasons; passage of time
【星云】[天] nebula:旋涡～ *spiral nebula* / 银河～ *galactic nebula* / 蟹状～ *Crab Nebula* / 网状～ *network nebula* / ～团 *nebulous cluster*
【星占】divine by astrology; cast a horoscope ◇～术 astrology
【星震】[天] starquake
【星座】[天] constellation

惺(构词成分)见下
【惺忪】(又作'惺松')❶(of eyes) not yet fully open on waking up:睡眼～ *eyes still heavy with sleep*; *sleepy eyes* ❷〈书〉awake; conscious; clearheaded:不～ *not awake*; *still unconscious*
【惺惺】❶ clearheaded; awake ❷ wise; intelligent ❸ an intelligent person; a wise man
【惺惺作态】be affected; simulate (friendship, innocence, etc.)

猩 名[动] orangutan
【猩红】scarlet; bloodred:～的石榴花 *the fiery red pomegranate flowers*
【猩红热】scarlet fever; scarlatina
【猩猩】[动] orangutan ——另见〖大猩猩〗;〖黑猩猩〗
【猩猩草】[植] painted euphorbia (Euphorbia heterophylla)

腥 Ⅰ名 raw meat or fish:荤腥 Ⅱ形 having the smell of fish, seafood, etc.
【腥臭】stinking smell as of rotten fish; stench
【腥风血雨】a foul wind and a rain of blood—reign of terror
【腥气】❶ the smell of fish, seafood, etc.:一股子～ *a fishy smell* ❷ stinking; fishy:好～! *How stinky!*
【腥臊】stench
【腥膻】the smell of fish, mutton, etc.
【腥味儿】the foul smell of fish; a fishy smell

xíng

刑 名 ❶ punishment (inflicted for a crime); penalty; sentence:判刑 ❷ torture; corporal punishment:用刑
【刑场】execution ground
【刑罚】[法] penalty (for a criminal offence); punishment
【刑法】❶[法] penal code; criminal law ❷ corporal punishment; torture:动了～ *administer corporal punishment* / 受了～ *suffer corporal punishment*
【刑警】〈略〉见〖刑事警察〗
【刑具】instruments of torture; implements of punishment
【刑律】[法] criminal law:触犯～ *violate the criminal law*
【刑满释放】[法] be released upon completion of a sentence (or one's term)
【刑期】term of imprisonment; prison term:～已满 *have completed a term of imprisonment*; *have served one's sentence*
【刑事】[法] criminal; penal:～案件 *criminal case* / ～处分 *criminal sanction* / ～管辖权 *criminal jurisdiction* ◇～法庭 criminal court; ～犯 criminal offender; criminal; ～犯罪 criminal offence; criminal act; ～警察 criminal police; ～诉讼 criminal procedure; criminal suit; ～诉讼法 code of criminal procedure; criminal procedure law; ～责任 criminal responsibility; ～侦查 criminal investigation
【刑讯】inquisition by torture:～逼供 *extort a confession by torture*; *subject a criminal suspect to the third degree*

行 Ⅰ动 ❶〈书〉go; walk; travel:日～三千步 *walk three thousand steps a day (for exercise)* / 日～百里 *cover a hundred li a day* ❷ be current; circulate:发行 / 行销 ❸ do; perform; carry out:简便易～ *simple and easy to do* ❹ (used before a disyllabic verb, indicating the performance of some action):即～通知 *notify sb. at once* / 另～安排 *make separate arrangements* ❺ be all right; will do:咱们走着去,～不～? *Will it be all right if we go on foot?* / 没有铅丝,用绳子也～。*If there is no wire, a cord will do.* Ⅱ形 ❶ temporary; makeshift:行营 ❷ capable; competent:你看他干这工作～吗? *Do you think he is up to it?* / 不要认为只有自己才～。*Don't think you're the only capable one.*
【行百里者半九十】ninety li is only half of a hundred-li journey—the going is toughest towards the end of a journey; one must sustain one's effort when a task is nearing completion
【行板】[音] andante
【行不通】won't do (or work); will get nowhere:这个计划～。*This plan won't work.*
【行车】drive a vehicle:千万注意～安全。*Ensure safety in driving.* / ～时刻表 *a train or bus timetable*
【行成于思】a deed is accomplished through taking thought; success depends on forethought
【行程】❶ route or distance of travel:～一万多公里 *travel over 10,000 kilometres* ❷[机] stroke; throw; travel:活塞～ *piston travel* / 滑枕～ *ram stroke* / 偏心轮～ *throw of eccentric*
【行船】sail a boat; navigate:大运河有几段仍可以～。*The Grand Canal is still navigable in certain sections.*
【行刺】assassinate
【行道】〈旧〉preach one's doctrine; propagate one's belief

【行道树】trees that line a street

【行得通】will do (or work); be practicable: 这个主意～。*This idea will work*.

【行动】❶ move (or get) about: ～不便 *have difficulty getting about* / ～缓慢 *move slowly*; *be slowmoving* ❷ act; take action: ～起来 *go into action* / 按计划～。*Proceed according to plan*. ❸ action; operation: 军事～ *military operations* / ～纲领 *programme of action*

【行方便】make things convenient for sb.; be accommodating

【行宫】imperial palace for short stays away from the capital; temporary dwelling place of an emperor when away from the capital

【行好】act charitably; be merciful; be charitable; do a good turn: 您行行好,就饶了我这一回吧! *Please have a heart and let me off this time!*

【行贿】bribe; offer a bribe; resort to bribery

【行将】〈书〉be about to; be just going to; be on the verge of: ～就道 *be about to set out on a journey* / ～完工。*The project will soon be completed*.

【行将就木】be getting closer and closer to the coffin—be fast approaching death; have one foot in the grave

【行劫】commit robbery; rob

【行进】(usu. of troops) march forward; advance

【行经】❶[生理] menstruate; be in the period ❷ go (or pass) by: 火车～沈阳的时候,已是半夜了。*It was midnight when the train passed through Shenyang*.

【行径】〈贬〉act; action; move: 侵略～ *act of aggression* / 野蛮～ *barbarous act*

【行军】(of troops) march: ～警戒 *protection while on the move*; *security on the march* ◇ ～床 camp bed; camp cot; a lightweight folding bed; ～锅 field cauldron; ～壶 canteen; ～灶 field kitchen

【行乐】〈书〉indulge in pleasures; seek amusement; make merry

【行礼】❶ salute ❷〈方〉present gifts

【行李】luggage; baggage: 超重～ *excess luggage* / 手提～ *hand-luggage* ◇ ～标签 baggage tags; ～寄存处 left-luggage office; checkroom; ～架 luggage rack; baggage rack; ～卷儿 bedroll; bedding roll; bedding pack; ～票 luggage (or baggage) check

【行李车】❶ luggage van; baggage car ❷ luggage cart

【行囊】〈书〉travelling bag

【行骗】practise fraud; swindle; cheat: 用伪钞～ *cheat with counterfeit bank notes*

【行期】date of departure: ～已近。*The date of departure is drawing near*. / 推迟～ *postpone one's trip*

【行乞】beg one's bread; beg alms; beg

【行窃】steal; thieve: 在～时被抓住 *be caught in the act of stealing*

【行人】pedestrian; foot traveller: ～走便道。*Pedestrians, keep to the sidewalk* (or *footpath*)! / 公路上～稀少。*There were few pedestrians on the highway*.

【行若无事】behave as if nothing had happened

【行色】circumstances or style of departure: 以壮～ (*give a grand send-off, etc.*) *to enable sb. to depart in style*

【行色匆匆】be in a hurry to set out

【行善】do good; do kind deeds; practise philanthropy: ～人 *philanthropist*; *a charitable person*

【行商】itinerant trader; travelling merchant; pedlar

【行赏】give awards; dispense rewards or honours

【行尸走肉】a walking corpse—one who vegetates; an utterly worthless person

【行时】❶ (of a thing) be in vogue; be all the rage ❷ (of a person) be in the ascendant

【行使】exercise; perform: ～检察权 *exercise procuratorial authority* / ～职权 *exercise one's functions and powers* / ～主权 *exercise sovereignty*

【行驶】(of a vehicle, ship, etc.) go; ply; travel: 列车向南～。*The train is going south*. / 长江下游可以～万吨轮。*The lower reaches of the Changjiang River are navigable by* 10,000-*ton steamers*.

【行事】❶ act; handle matters: 按计划～ *act according to plan* ❷ behaviour; conduct: 言谈～ *speech and conduct*

【行署】〈略〉见〖行政公署〗

【行同狗彘】behave like dogs and pigs

【行头】❶ actor's costumes and paraphernalia ❷〈诙〉dress; clothing; apparel; outfit: 她的～可多了。*She has a large wardrobe*. / 新娘的～ *a bride's outfit* (*or apparel*)

【行为】action; behaviour; conduct: 正义的～ *righteous action* / 不法的～ *an illegal act* / ～不端 *dishonourable behaviour*; *bad conduct* ◇ ～科学 behavioral science; ～疗法 behavior therapy; ～模式 behavior patern; ～主义[心理] behaviourism

【行文】❶ style or manner of writing: 这篇作文～流畅。*This composition reads smoothly*. ❷ (of a government office) send an official communication to other organizations: 即将～各部委。*An official communication will soon be sent to all the ministries and commissions*.

【行销】be on sale; sell: ～全国 *be on sale throughout the country*

【行星】planet

【行星际】interplanetary: ～航行 *interplanetary flight* (*or travel*)

【行刑】carry out a death sentence; execute ◇ ～队 executioners; firing squad

【行凶】commit physical assault or murder; do violence

【行医】practise medicine (usu. on one's own)

【行营】field headquarters

【行云流水】(of style of writing) like floating clouds and flowing water—natural and spontaneous

【行政】administration：管～ *be in charge of administrative affairs* / ～部门 *administrative department*；*executive branch*；*administration* ◇～处分 administrative sanction；disciplinary sanction；～法规 administrative laws and regulations；～干预 administrative intervene；～公署 administrative office (within a province)；～管理 administration；～纠纷 administrative dispute；～拘留 administrative detention；～命令 administrative decree (or order)；～区 administrative area；～区划 division into administrative districts；～人员 administrative personnel (or staff)；～手段 administrative measures；～长官 chief executive

【行之有效】effective (in practice)；effectual：～的办法 *effective measures*

【行止】〈书〉❶ whereabouts：～不明 *whereabouts unknown* / ～无定 *there's no telling where sb. is* ❷ behaviour；conduct：～有亏。*His conduct has some shortcomings.*

【行装】outfit for a journey；luggage：整理～ *pack (for a journey)*

【行踪】whereabouts；track：～不定 *be of uncertain whereabouts*

【行走】walk：他在崎岖的山路上艰难地～着。*He was trudging laboriously on the rugged mountain path.*

形 Ⅰ 动 ❶ appear；look：喜形于色 ❷ compare；contrast：相形之下 Ⅱ 名 ❶ form；shape：鸡心～的胸针 *a heart-shaped brooch* ❷ body；entity：形影不离

【形变】[物] deformation：弹性～ *elastic deformation*

【形成】take shape；form：石灰岩经地下水长时期的侵蚀，～岩洞。*Caves are formed by the erosion of limestone by groundwater over many thousands of years.* ◇～层 [植] cambium

【形单影只】a solitary form，a single shadow-extremely lonely；solitary

【形而上学】[哲] metaphysics

【形骸】〈书〉the human skeleton；the human body

【形迹】❶ a person's movements and expression：不露～ *betray nothing in one's expression and movements* ❷ formality：不拘～ *without formality*；*not standing on ceremony*

【形迹可疑】of suspicious appearance；suspicious-looking：你进大楼时看到什么～的人没有？*Did you notice anyone suspicious-looking when you came into the building?*

【形容】❶〈书〉appearance；countenance：～枯槁 *look haggard* ❷ describe：难以～ *difficult to describe*；*beyond description* ◇～词 [语] adjective

【形容憔悴】wan-looking；thin and pallid

【形式】form；shape：艺术～ *art form* / 组织～ *organizational makeup* / 以公开信～提出建议 *put suggestions in the form of an open letter*

【形式逻辑】[逻] formal logic

【形式上】in form；formal：～的一致 *formal unity* / ～的独立 *nominal independence*

【形式主义】formalism

【形势】❶ terrain；topographical features：～险要 *strategically important terrain* ❷ situation；circumstances：～越来越好。*The situation is getting better and better.* / ～逼人。*The situation is pressing.* or *The situation demands immediate action.*

【形似】likeness in form or appearance；formal likeness (or resemblance)：绘画不仅要求～，而且要求神似。*Painters aim at a likeness not only in appearance, but also in spirit.*

【形态】❶ form；shape；pattern：社会经济～ *social-economic formation*；*the economic formation of society* ❷ [语] morphology

【形态学】❶ [生] morphology ❷ [语] morphology

【形体】❶ shape (of a person's body)；physique；body ❷ form and structure：汉字的～ *the form of Chinese characters*

【形同虚设】perform practically no function：这个机构～。*This organization is nothing but an empty shell.*

【形相】outward appearance；exterior；looks

【形象】❶ image；form；figure：图画教学通过～发展儿童认识事物的能力。*The use of pictures in classroom teaching helps children to understand things through images.* ❷ literary or artistic image；imagery：塑造英雄～ *create images of heroes and heroines*

【形象思维】thinking in (terms of) images：诗是运用～的。*Poetry conveys ideas by means of images.*

【形象设计师】image-spinner；imagemeister；image crafter

【形象塑造】image-building

【形销骨立】be all (or mere) skin and bones；be worn to a shadow of one's former self；be just a skeleton

【形形色色】of every hue；of all shades；of all forms；of every description：～的时髦衣裙 *fashionable dresses and skirts of every colour and design*

【形影不离】be inseparable as body and shadow；be always together

【形影相吊】body and shadow comforting each other—extremely lonely；sad and solitary

【形影相随】be as close as body and shadow；be always together

【形于辞色】show in one's words and expression：他欣喜之情，～。*There was joy in his words and on his face.*

【形状】form；appearance；shape：凤梨和苹果～不同。*A pineapple is different in shape from an apple.*

型 名 ❶ mould：砂型 ❷ model；type；pattern：人类血液分为 O～、A～、B～和 AB～四种血型。*Human blood is classified into four blood types* (*or blood groups*), *namely*, *type O*, *type A*, *type B and type AB*.

【型板】[机] template; templet

【型钢】[气] section steel; shape ◇ ～轧机 shape rolling mill

【型号】model; type: 他的车子是什么牌子、什么～的? *What make and model is his car?*

【型宽】moulded breadth

【型砂】moulding sand

【型深】moulded depth

【型心】[气] core: 干砂～ *baked core* / 粘土～ *loam core*

xǐng

省 动 ❶ examine oneself critically: 吾日三～吾身。*I daily examine myself on three points*. ❷ visit (esp. One's parents or elders): 省亲 ❸ become conscious; be aware: 不省人事 ——另见 shěng

【省察】examine oneself critically; examine one's thoughts and conduct

【省亲】pay a visit to one's parents or elders (living at another place)

【省视】❶ call upon; pay a visit to ❷ examine carefully; inspect

醒 动 ❶ regain consciousness; sober up; come to: 酒醉未～ *be drunk and not sobered up yet* / 他昏迷了三天,刚刚～过来。*He was unconscious for three days and has just come to*. ❷ wake up; be awake: 今天早晨我～得早。*I woke up early this morning*. / ～一～! *Wake up*! ❸ be clear in mind: 清醒 ❹ be striking; catch one's attention: 醒目

【醒酒】dispel the effects of alcohol; sober up: 浓茶可以用来～。*Strong tea can help to dispel the effects of alcohol*. / 吃个梨醒醒酒。*Have a pear to sober yourself up*.

【醒目】(of written words or pictures) catch the eye; attract attention; be striking to the eye: ～的标语 *eye-catching slogans* / ～的标题 *bold headlines*

【醒世】rouse the public; awaken the world: ～之言 *words to rouse the public*

【醒悟】come to realize (or see) the truth, one's error, etc.; wake up to reality

擤 动 blow (one's nose): ～鼻涕 *blow one's nose*

xìng

兴 名 mood or desire to do sth.; interest; excitement: 助兴 / 雅兴 ——另见 xīng

【兴冲冲】(do sth.) with joy and expedition; excitedly: 他～地跑进来,告诉我这个好消息。*He rushed into the room excitedly and told me the good news*.

【兴高采烈】in high spirits; excited; jubilant: 孩子们听说去动物园都～。*The children were all excited when they heard they were going to the zoo*.

【兴会】a sudden flash of inspiration; brain wave: 这首诗是乘一时的～写成的。*This poem was improvised on the spur of the moment*.

【兴趣】interest: 对文学产生了～ *become interested in literature* / 我对下棋不感～。*I'm not interested in chess*.

【兴头】enthusiasm; keen interest: 我们厂的工人对体育活动～可大了。*The workers of our factory are very keen on sport*.

【兴味】interest: 青少年们～盎然地阅读各种新出版的小说。*Teen-agers read the newly-published novels with keen interest*.

【兴味索然】have lost all interest in sth.; be bored stiff: 大凡一件事的性质由"消遣的"而变为"义务的",便觉得～。*Any pastime which is converted into an obligation loses its taste*.

【兴致】interest; mood to enjoy: 他对集邮的～很浓。*He's very much interested in collecting stamps*. ◇ ～勃勃 full of zest; in high spirits

杏 名 apricot

【杏脯】sun-dried sweetened apricot; preserved sweetened apricot

【杏红】yellowish pink; apricot pink

【杏核儿】〈口〉apricot stone

【杏黄】pinkish yellow; apricot (colour)

【杏仁】apricot kernel; almond

性 Ⅰ 名 ❶ nature: 天命之谓～。*What is God-given is called nature*. ❷ character; disposition: 性急 ❸ property; quality: 弹性 ❹ sex: ～的要求 *sexual desire* ❺〈语〉gender: 阳性 / 阴性 Ⅱ (a suffix designating a specified quality, property, scope, etc.): 科学～ *the state or quality of being scientific* / 综合～ *comprehensive* / 先天～ *congenital*

【性爱】love between the sexes; sexual love; love ◇ ～前奏 foreplay

【性别】sexual distinction; sex ◇ ～歧视 sexism; sexual discrimination; discrimination against women

【性病】venereal disease; V. D.

【性道德】sex morality

【性泛滥】sexploitation

【性感】sex appeal; sexiness: 那个女演员很～。*That actress has a lot of sex appeal* (*or is awfully sexy*).

【性格】nature; disposition; temperament: ～开朗 *have a bright and cheerful disposition* ◇ ～刻画 characterization; ～演员 character actor

【性革命】sexual revolution

【性激素】[生理] sex hormone

【性急】impatient; short-tempered

【性交】❶ sexual intercourse ❷ make love; have sex

【性教育】sex education
【性解放】sexual liberation
【性灵】❶〈书〉personality; temperament; character: 陶冶～ *mould a person's temperament, personality, etc.* ❷ intelligent; bright; brilliant: 我还不曾遇到过这样～的学生。*I've never had any student as brilliant as he is.*
【性命】life (of a man or animal): 差一点儿把～丢了 *nearly lose one's life; narrowly escape death*
【性命交关】(又作'性命攸关') (a matter) of life and death; of vital importance
【性能】function (of a machine, etc.); performance; property: ～试验 *performance test* / 反应堆～ *reactor behaviour* ◇ ～数据 performance data; ～指标 performance standards, or indicators
【性虐待狂】sadism
【性器官】[生理] sexual organs; genitals
【性情】disposition; temperament; temper: ～温柔 *have a gentle disposition* / ～暴躁 *have an irascible temperament; be short-tempered*
【性骚扰】sexual harassment
【性卫生】sex hygiene
【性腺】[生理] sexual (or sex) gland
【性心理学】sexual psychology
【性行为】sexual behaviour; sex act
【性学】sexology ◇ ～家 sexologist
【性欲】sexual desire (or urge): ～冲动 *sexual impulse; sexual excitement*
【性知识】sex knowledge
【性质】quality; nature; character: 弄清问题的～ *ascertain the nature of the problem*
【性状】shape and properties; properties; character: 土壤的理化～ *the physicochemical properties of soil* / 显性～ *dominant character* / ～分歧 *character divergence*
【性子】❶ temper: 使～ *get into a temper* / 这匹马的～很野。*This is a vicious horse.* ❷ strength; potency: 这药～平和。*This is a mild drug.* / 这酒的～很烈。*This liquor is very strong.*
【性自由】sexual freedom

幸 Ⅰ**形** fortunate; lucky: 荣幸 Ⅱ**动** ❶ rejoice: 庆幸 ❷〈书〉(I) hope; (I) trust: ～勿推却。*I hope that you will not refuse.* or *Pray do not refuse.* Ⅲ**副** fortunately; luckily: ～未成灾。*Fortunately it didn't cause a disaster.*
【幸而】luckily; fortunately: ～是你。*Luckily it was you and not anyone else.*
【幸福】❶ happiness; well-being: 人生的～ *happiness of life* / 祝你～。*I wish you happiness.* ❷ happy: ～的回忆 *happy memories*
【幸好】同〖幸亏〗
【幸会】〈套〉(a rather formal greeting) very pleased to meet you: 久仰,久仰!～,～! *I am most honoured to meet you after hearing so much about you!*
【幸亏】fortunately; luckily: ～我走得早,才没叫雨淋了。*Luckily I left early and wasn't caught in the rain.*
【幸免】escape by sheer luck; have a narrow escape: ～于难 *escape death by sheer luck; escape death by a hair's breadth*
【幸事】a piece of good fortune; a stroke of luck; blessing
【幸运】❶ good fortune; good luck ❷ fortunate; lucky
【幸运儿】fortune's favourite; lucky fellow: 她是个～。*She was born under a lucky star* (or *with a silver spoon in her mouth*).
【幸运号码】lucky number
【幸灾乐祸】take pleasure in (or gloat over) other people's misfortune

姓 **名** surname; family (or clan) name: 他～王。*He is surnamed Wang.* or *His surname is Wang.* / 您贵姓? —敝～陈。*May I know your surname? —(My surname is) Chen.*
【姓名】surname and personal name; full name
【姓氏】surname: 以～笔划为序 *arranged in the order of the number of strokes in the surnames*

悻 (构词成分) 见下
【悻然】enraged
【悻悻】angry; resentful: ～而去 *go away angry; leave in a huff*

xiōng

凶 Ⅰ**形** ❶ inauspicious; ominous: 凶兆 / 吉凶未卜 ❷ bad for crops; unproductive; threatened with famine ❸ fierce; ferocious: 这个人样子真～。*This chap looks really fierce.* ❹ terrible; fearful: 病势很～ *be terribly ill* / 闹得太～了! *What a terrific row!* / 这场雨来势很～。*The rain came down with a vengeance.* Ⅱ**名** act of violence; murder: 行凶
【凶暴】fierce and brutal
【凶残】❶ fierce and cruel; savage and cruel: ～成性 *be cruel by nature* ❷〈书〉a fierce and cruel person
【凶多吉少】bode ill rather than well; be fraught with grim possibilities
【凶恶】(of temper, appearance or behaviour) fierce; ferocious; fiendish
【凶犯】one who has committed homicide or mayhem; murderer
【凶悍】fierce and tough
【凶狠】❶ fierce and malicious ❷ powerful; vigorous: 拼抢～ *scramble furiously for a ball* / 射门～ *make powerful shots at the goal*
【凶狂】fierce; savage; ferocious
【凶猛】violent; ferocious: 山洪来势～。*The mountain torrents rushed down with a devastating force.* / 虎豹都是～的野兽。*Both tigers and leopards are ferocious beasts.*
【凶气】fierce manner; ferocious expression: 满脸

～ *with murder written on one's face*
【凶器】a tool or weapon for criminal purposes; a lethal weapon
【凶杀】homicide; murder: 这是一起～案。*This is a case of murder*.
【凶神】demon; fiend
【凶神恶煞】devils; fiends
【凶手】murderer; assassin; assailant (who has caused injury to sb.)
【凶险】❶ dangerous; perilous; critical: 病情～ *dangerously ill*; *critically ill*; *in a critical condition* / 情势～ *in a very dangerous situation* ❷ ruthless and treacherous
【凶相】ferocious features; fierce look; fiendish look: 一脸的～ *look fiendish*
【凶相毕露】look thoroughly ferocious; unleash all one's ferocity
【凶焰】ferocity; aggressive arrogance: ～万丈 *swell with aggressive arrogance*
【凶宅】a haunted house; an unlucky abode
【凶兆】ill omen; boding of evil

兄 名 ❶ elder brother: 胞～ *elder brother of the same parents* ❷ a courteous form of address between male friends: 王～,久违了! *Hi, Wang! Haven't seen you for ages!*
【兄弟】❶ brothers: ～二人都还没结婚。*Neither of the two brothers is married*. ❷ fraternal; brotherly: ～情谊 *fraternal affection* / ～般的团结 *fraternal solidarity*; *brotherly unity* ❸ younger brother ❹ a familiar form of address for a man younger than oneself: 大～,这件事就托你了。*And so, brother, I'll leave the matter in your hands*. ❺〈谦〉(used by a man, usu. in a public speech) I
【兄长】❶ a respectful form of address for an elder brother ❷ a respectful form of address for a male friend

匈 名〈古〉breast
【匈奴】Xiongnu, or the Huns, an ancient ethnic group in China
【匈牙利】Hungary ◇ ～人 Hungarian; ～语 Hungarian (language)

汹 (构词成分) 见下
【汹汹】〈书〉❶ the sound of turbulent waves: 波涛～ *roaring waves* ❷ violent; truculent: 来势～ *bear down menacingly* ❸ tumultuous; agitated: 议论～ *tumultuous debate*; *heated discussion*
【汹涌】surging; turbulent; tempestuous: 波涛～ *turbulent waves* / ～的洪水威胁着堤坝的安全。*The surging floodwaters threatened the dykes and dams*.
【汹涌澎湃】surging; turbulent; tempestuous: ～的历史潮流 *a tempestuous historical trend*

胸 名 ❶ thorax; chest; breast; bosom: 孩子把脸贴在母亲的～前。*The child buried its face in its mother's bosom*. ❷ mind; heart: 心胸 / 胸襟
【胸靶】chest silhouette (used as a target in shooting practice)
【胸部】thorax; chest: ～手术 *thoracic operation*
【胸骨】[生理] sternum; breastbone
【胸怀】❶ mind; heart: ～坦白 *openhearted*; *frank* / ～狭窄 *narrow-minded*; *small-minded* / ～宽广 *broad-minded* ❷ keep in the mind; cherish: ～大志 *cherish high ideals*; *have lofty aspirations*
【胸襟】mind; breadth of mind: ～开阔 *broad-minded*; *large-minded* / ～狭窄 *narrow-minded*; *small-minded*
【胸口】the pit of the stomach; chest: 我～疼得厉害。*I have severe pains in my chest*.
【胸膜】[生理] pleura ◇ ～炎 [医] pleurisy
【胸脯】chest; breast: 挺起～ *throw out one's chest* / 拍～保证 *strike one's chest as a gesture of guarantee or reassurance* / 鸡～ *chicken breast*
【胸鳍】pectoral fin
【胸腔】thoracic cavity; chest cavity
【胸墙】[军] breastwork; parapet
【胸膛】chest: 挺起～ *throw out one's chest*
【胸围】chest measurement; bust: 量～ *measure one's bust* / 他～90厘米。*He measures 90cm round the chest*.
【胸无城府】artless; simple and candid
【胸无点墨】unlearned; unlettered
【胸像】(sculptured) bust
【胸有成竹】have a well-thought-out plan, stratagem, etc.: 明年的生产计划,厂长已～。*The factory director has a well-thought-out plan for next year's production*.
【胸章】badge
【胸罩】brassiere; bra
【胸针】brooch
【胸椎】[生理] thoracic vertebra

xióng

雄 Ⅰ 形 ❶ male; (of plants) staminate: ～猫 *male cat*; *tomcat* / ～狮 (*male*) *lion* / ～冬青 *staminate* (*or male*) *holly* ❷ grand; imposing: 雄伟 ❸ powerful; mighty: 雄兵 Ⅱ 名 a person or state having great power and influence: 战国七～ *the seven powerful states of the Warring States Period*
【雄辩】❶ convincing argument; eloquent speech: 事实胜于雄辩 ❷ convincing; eloquent: 最～的莫过于事实。*Nothing is more convincing than facts*.
【雄兵】a powerful army: ～百万 *a million bold warriors*
【雄才大略】(a man of) great talent and bold vision; (a statesman or general of) rare gifts and bold strategy
【雄蜂】drone; male bee
【雄关】an impregnable pass
【雄厚】(of strength, resources, etc.) ample; rich;

solid；abundant：～的人力物力 *rich human and material resources* / 资金～ *abundant funds*

【雄花】［植］male flower；staminate flower

【雄黄】［矿］realgar；red orpiment

【雄浑】vigorous and firm；forceful：～的诗篇 *powerful poetry* / 笔力～ *vigour of strokes in calligraphy or drawing* / ～高亢的乐曲 *resounding music*

【雄鸡】cock；rooster：～报晓。*The cock heralds the dawn.*

【雄激素】［生理］androgen

【雄健】robust；vigorous；powerful：迈着～的步伐 *in vigorous strides*

【雄劲】vigorous and powerful：笔势～ *forceful strokes (in calligraphy)*

【雄赳赳】valiant；gallant

【雄跨】straddle，bestride：～黄河的青龙峡水电站 *the Qinglongxia Power Station that straddles the Yellow River*

【雄蕊】［植］stamen

【雄师】a powerful army；a mighty army

【雄图】a great ambition；a grandiose plan：～大业 *a grandiose and noble enterprise*；*a great cause*

【雄威】full of power and grandeur；strong and imposing；awe-inspiring

【雄伟】grand；imposing：～壮丽 *grand*；*magnificent*；*sublime* / ～的天安门 *the magnificent Tian An Men*

【雄文】profound and powerful writing；great works

【雄心】great ambitions；lofty aspirations

【雄心勃勃】very ambitious

【雄心壮志】lofty aspirations and high ideals：树立～ *set high aims and have lofty aspirations*；*set one's sights high*

【雄性】male

【雄性不育】［生］male sterility

【雄蚁】male ant；aner

【雄主】a ruler of great talent and bold vision

【雄壮】full of power and grandeur；magnificent；majestic：～的军乐 *majestic martial music*

【雄姿】majestic appearance；heroic posture：喷气式战斗机编队飞行的～ *the imposing sight of jet fighters flying in formation*

【雄姿英发】majestic and spirited；dashing and debonair

熊 Ⅰ名 bear：玩具～ *teddy bear* / 幼～ *bear cub* Ⅱ动〈方〉rebuke；upbraid；scold：挨了一顿～ *got a scolding*

【熊蜂】bumblebee

【熊猴】［动］Assamese macaque

【熊猫】panda (popular name for 猫熊)

【熊市】［经］bear marker

【熊心豹胆】bear's heart and leopard's gall—fearlessness；courage；guts

【熊熊】flaming；ablaze；raging：手持～燃烧的火炬 *bear a blazing torch in hand* / ～的烈火 *raging flames*

【熊掌】bear's paw (a rare delicacy)

xiū

休 Ⅰ动 ❶ stop；cease：争论不～ *argue ceaselessly* ❷ rest：～三个月的假 *take a three-month leave* ❸ (in former times) cast off one's wife and send her home：～妻 *put one's wife away* Ⅱ副 don't：～要胡言乱语！*Don't talk nonsense!* / 闲话～提。*No more of this digression.*

【休怪】don't blame：我们之间的问题解决不了，～我到法院去起诉。*Don't blame me for going to court since we can't settle it between us.*

【休会】adjourn：无限期～ *adjourn indefinitely (or sine die)* / 会议～一周。*The meeting was adjourned for a week.* / ～期间 *between sessions*；*when the meeting stands adjourned*

【休假】(of workers，students，etc.) have (or take，go on) a holiday or vacation；(of soldiers，personnel working abroad，etc.) be on leave or furlough：～一周 *have a week's holiday* / 回国～ *go home on furlough*

【休刊】suspend publication (of a newspaper or journal)

【休克】［医］shock：电～ *electric shock* / 病人～了。*The patient is suffering from shock.*

【休眠】［生］dormancy ◇ ～火山 dormant volcano；～期［生］rest period；～芽［植］resting (or dormant) bud

【休戚】weal and woe；joys and sorrows

【休戚相关】share joys and sorrows；be bound together by common interests：～，患难与共 *be bound by a common cause and go through thick and thin together*

【休戚与共】share weal and woe；stand together through thick and thin：～，生死相依 *share weal and woe，and stick together in life and death*

【休憩】have (or take) a rest；rest

【休市】off business；market closed；business suspended

【休息】have (or take) a rest；rest：～一会儿 *rest for a while*；*have a rest* / 幕间～ *intermission*；*interval* / 课间～ *break (between classes)* ◇ ～室 lounge；lobby；vestibule；foyer

【休闲】［农］lie fallow：～地 *fallow (land)* ◇ ～服 casual clothes

【休想】don't imagine that it's possible：你～逃脱。*Don't imagine you can get away.*

【休学】suspend one's schooling without losing one's status as a student

【休养】recuperate；convalesce：逐步扩充劳动者休息和～的物质条件 *gradually expand material facilities for the working people to rest and recuperate*

【休养生息】(of a nation) recuperate and multiply；rest and build up strength；rehabilitate：大战之后，各国都需要时间～。*After a great war，every country needs time to recuperate and multiply its*

population.
【休养所】sanatorium; rest home
【休业】❶ suspend business; be closed down: 今天～。*Closed today*. ❷ (of a short-term course, etc.) come to an end; wind up
【休战】truce; cease-fire; armistice: ～状态 (*state of*) *cease-fire*
【休整】rest and reorganization (of troops, etc.)
【休止】stop; cease: 这座火山已进入～状态。*The volcano is inactive*. ◇～符[音] rest

修 Ⅰ 动 ❶ embellish; decorate: 装修 ❷ repair; mend; overhaul: ～收音机 *repair a radio* / ～鞋 *mend shoes* ❸ write; compile: ～史 *write history* / ～县志 *compile the historical and other records of a county* ❹ study; cultivate: 自修 ❺ build; construct: ～铁路 *build a railway* / ～水库 *construct a reservoir* / ～渠 *dig irrigation ditches* ❻ trim; prune: ～指甲 *trim* (*or manicure*) *fingernails* / ～铅笔 *sharpen a pencil* Ⅱ 形 〈书〉long; tall and slender: 茂林～竹 *dense forests and tall bamboos*
【修补】❶ mend; patch up; repair; revamp: ～渔网 *mend fishing nets* / ～衣服 *patch clothes* / ～篱笆 *mend a fence* ❷ [医] repair
【修长】tall and thin; slender: ～身材 *a slender figure*
【修船厂】shipyard; dockyard
【修辞】rhetoric ◇～格[语] figures of speech; ～学[语] rhetoric
【修道】cultivate oneself according to a religious doctrine ◇～院 monastery or convent
【修订】revise: ～条约 *revise a treaty* / ～教学计划 *revise a teaching plan* / ～课本 *revise textbooks* ◇～本 revised edition
【修复】❶ repair; restore; renovate: 这段铁路已～通车。*This section of the railway has been repaired and reopened to traffic*. / ～有历史意义的建筑物 *renovate historic buildings* ❷ [医] repair (of destroyed cells or tissues)
【修改】revise; modify; amend; alter: ～计划 *revise a plan* / ～宪法 *amend* (*or revise*) *a constitution* / 小修小改 *minor alterations*
【修好】❶ 〈书〉foster cordial relations between states ❷ 〈方〉do good works
【修剪】prune; trim; clip: ～果枝 *prune fruit trees* / ～指甲 *trim one's fingernails*
【修建】build; construct; erect: ～机场 *build an airport* / ～纪念碑 *erect a monument* / ～桥梁 *construct a bridge*
【修脚】pedicure ◇～师 pedicurist
【修旧利废】repair and utilize old or discarded things
【修浚】dredge: ～河道 *dredge a river*
【修理】❶ repair; mend; overhaul; fix: 正在～ *be under repair* / 当场～，立等可取。*Repairs done while you wait*. ❷ prune; trim ◇～厂 fix-it shop; repair shop; ～行业 repairing trades
【修面】〈方〉shave; have a shave ◇～膏 shaving cream; ～刷 shaving brush
【修女】nun (of the Roman Catholic and Greek Orthodox churches); sister: 当～ *become a nun*; *enter a convent*
【修配】make repairs and supply replacements: ～车间 *repair and spare parts workshop*
【修葺】repair; renovate: ～一新 *take on a new look after renovation*; *be completely renovated*
【修缮】repair; renovate: ～房屋 *repair houses*
【修身】cultivate one's moral character
【修饰】❶ decorate; adorn; embellish: ～公园，准备迎接五一。*The parks are decorated for the May Day celebrations*. ❷ make up and dress up ❸ polish (a piece of writing): 请你把这篇稿子～一下。*Please polish this piece of writing*. ❹ [语] qualify; modify: 定语的作用是～或限制名词的。*An attribute is a word or phrase used to modify or limit the meaning of a noun*. ◇～剂 dressing agent; ～语[语] modifier
【修心养性】cultivate oneself through meditation
【修行】practise Buddhism or Taoism: 出家～ *become a Buddhist or Taoist monk or nun*
【修修补补】patch up; tinker
【修养】❶ accomplishment; training; mastery: 有艺术～ *be artistically accomplished* / 在文学上很有～ *be widely read in literature* ❷ accomplishment in self-cultivation; self-possession: 他无论做什么事总是非常稳重，不急躁，的确很有～。*He is always steady and reliable in whatever he does. He is really self-possessed*.
【修业】study at school: ～年限 *length of schooling* / ～期满 *one's term of schooling completed* ◇～证书 certificate for the completion of a course of study; certificate showing courses attended
【修造】build as well as repair: ～轮船 *build or repair ships*
【修整】❶ repair and maintain: ～农具 *repair and maintain farm implements* ❷ prune; trim: ～果树 *prune fruit trees*
【修正】❶ revise; amend; correct: 坚持真理，～错误 *uphold the truth and correct one's mistakes* / ～草案 *a revised draft* ❷ mutilate (Marxism-Leninism); revise ◇～案 amendment; ～角 aviation correction angle
【修正主义】revisionism: ～思潮 *revisionist trend* / ～者 *revisionist* / ～分子 *revisionist element*; *revisionist*
【修枝】prune ◇～剪 pruning scissors; pruning shears
【修筑】build; construct; put up: ～桥梁 *build bridges* / ～工事 *construct defences*; *build fortifications* (*or defence works*) / ～堤坝 *put up dykes*

羞 Ⅰ 形 shy; bashful: ～红了脸 *blush* Ⅱ 动 ❶ make sb. feel ashamed or embarrassed ❷ feel ashamed: 羞与为伍 Ⅲ 名 shame; disgrace: 遮羞
【羞惭】be ashamed: 满面～ *be shamefaced*
【羞耻】sense of shame; shame: ～之心 *sense of*

shame / 不知～ *lose all sense of shame*
【羞答答】(又作'羞羞答答') coy; shy; bashful
【羞愤】ashamed and resentful
【羞愧】ashamed; abashed: ～难言 *be ashamed beyond words* / ～地低着头 *hang one's head for shame*
【羞明】[医] photophobia
【羞恼】be angry and ashamed
【羞怯】shy; timid; sheepish: ～得说不出话来 *be too shy to utter a word*
【羞人】feel embarrassed or ashamed: 羞死人了 *simply die of shame; feel terribly embarrassed*
【羞辱】❶ shame; dishonour; humiliation ❷ humiliate; put sb. to shame
【羞涩】shy; bashful; embarrassed
【羞与为伍】feel ashamed to associate with sb.; think it beneath one to associate with sb.

xiǔ

朽 形 ❶ rotten; decayed: 枯木～株 *withered trees and rotten stumps* ❷ senile: 老朽
【朽败】decayed; rotten
【朽坏】decayed; rotten
【朽木】❶ rotten wood or tree ❷ a hopeless case; a good-for-nothing
【朽木粪土】rotten wood and worthless soil—a worthless person; useless stuff

宿 量 (used for counting nights): 住一～ *stay for one night* / 谈了半～ *chat till midnight* ——另见 sù

xiù

秀 Ⅰ 动 (of grain crops, etc.) put forth flowers or ears: ～穗 *put forth ears* Ⅱ 形 ❶ elegant; beautiful: 秀丽 ❷ excellent: 优秀
【秀拔】beautiful and forceful: 书法～ *a fine and forceful calligraphic style* / 文辞～ *elegant and forceful language*
【秀才】scholar; skilful writer: 他是我们班里的～。*He is the scholar in our class.*
【秀才不出门,能知天下事】without stepping outside his gate the scholar knows all the wide world's affairs
【秀而不实】flowering but bearing no fruit—fine in appearance but empty in substance
【秀丽】beautiful; handsome; pretty: 这个小姑娘长得很～。*This little girl is very pretty.* / ～的桂林山水 *the beautiful mountains and waters of Guilin*
【秀美】graceful; elegant: 书法～ *beautiful handwriting*
【秀气】❶ delicate; elegant; fine: 眉眼生得～ *have beautiful eyes* / 她的字写得很～。*She writes a beautiful hand.* ❷ (of manners) refined; urbane ❸ (of articles of use) delicate and well-made; exquisite: 这表可真～。*The watch is really exquisite.*
【秀色可餐】be a feast to the eye (usu. said of a very attractive woman, sometimes of beautiful scenery)
【秀外慧中】(又作'秀外惠中') beautiful and intelligent
【秀逸】(of style) free, easy and beautiful: 文辞～ *elegant, free-flowing language*

袖 Ⅰ 名 sleeve: 长(短)～ *long (short) sleeves* / ～长 *the length of the sleeves* Ⅱ 动 tuck inside the sleeve: 他～着手,踱来踱去。*He paced the floor, his hands tucked deep in his sleeves.* / ～刃 *hide a dagger in one's sleeve*
【袖标】armband or badge worn on the sleeve for identification
【袖口】cuff (of a sleeve): 衬衫～ *wristband*
【袖扣】cuff links
【袖手旁观】look on (or stand by) with folded arms; look on unconcerned: 看到损害国家财产的现象,不能～。*We must not stand by with folded arms when people damage state property.*
【袖套】oversleeve
【袖筒】sleeve
【袖章】armband; sleeve badge
【袖珍】pocket-size; pocket: ～字典 *pocket dictionary* / ～照相机 *vest-pocket camera* / ～潜艇 *midget submarine*
【袖珍本】pocket edition
【袖子】sleeve: 卷起～ *roll (or turn) up one's sleeves* / 一把抓住他的～ *seize him by the sleeve*

绣 Ⅰ 动 embroider: 她在围裙上～了一只小白兔。*She embroidered a little white rabbit on the apron.* / 那孩子的衣服上～着名字。*On the child's clothes is embroidered his name.* Ⅱ 名 embroidery
【绣工】❶ embroidery worker ❷ embroidery; embroidery work
【绣花】embroider; do embroidery: ～被面 *embroidered quilt cover* ◇ ～丝线 floss silk; embroidery silk; ～鞋 embroidered shoes; ～针 embroidery needle
【绣花枕头】a pillow with an embroidered case—an outwardly attractive but worthless person
【绣球】a ball made of rolled coloured silk
【绣球花】[植] big-leaf hydrangea (hydrangea macrophylla)
【绣像】❶ tapestry portrait; embroidered portrait ❷ exquisitely drawn portrait

臭 名 odour; smell: 纯空气是无色无～的。*Pure air is colourless and odourless.* ——另见 chòu

锈 Ⅰ 名 rust Ⅱ 动 become rusty: 门上的锁～住了。*The lock on the door is rusty and won't open.*
【锈病】[农] rust: 小麦秆～ *wheat stem rust*
【锈蚀】corroded by rust; spoilt by rust

溴 名［化］bromine (Br)
【溴化物】［化］bromide
【溴水】［化］bromine water
【溴酸】［化］bromic acid
嗅 动 smell; scent; sniff: 警犬～来～去，终于找到了踪迹。*The police dog scented about till he found the trail.* / 我们对任何东西都要用鼻子～～，鉴别其好坏。*We should take a sniff at everything and distinguish the good from the bad.*
【嗅觉】(sense of) smell; scent: ～很灵 *have a keen sense of smell* / 政治～灵敏 *be politically sharp*
【嗅神经】［生理］olfactory nerve

xū

吁 Ⅰ动〈书〉sigh: 长吁短叹 Ⅱ叹 (expressing surprise or amazement) why; oh ——另见 yū; yù
【吁吁】sound of breathing hard: 气喘～ *pant; puff hard sound of breathing hard*
须 Ⅰ动 ❶ must; have to: 我们～作出很大努力。*We'll have to make a great effort.* ❷〈书〉wait; await: ～我片刻。*Wait a moment for me.* Ⅱ名 ❶ beard; mustache: 留～ *grow a beard* ❷［动］palpus; feeler: 触须 ❸［植］tassel
【须发】beard and hair: ～皆白 *white hair and beard*
【须根】［植］fibrous root
【须眉】〈书〉beard and eyebrows—a man
【须要】must; have to: 做这项工作～细心。*This work needs to be done carefully.*
【须知】❶ one should know that; it must be understood (or borne in mind) that: ～胜利来之不易。*It must be borne in mind that the victory is hard-won.* ❷ points for attention; notice: 游览～ *tourist guide; information for tourists* / 旅客～ *notice to travellers, passengers, etc.*
【须子】❶［动］palpus; feeler: 虾～ *feelers of a shrimp* ❷［植］tassel: 玉米～ *tassels of maize*
虚 Ⅰ名 ❶ emptiness; void: 太虚 ❷ abstract; theory; guiding principles: 以～带实。*Let correct ideology guide practical work.* Ⅱ形 ❶ empty; void; unoccupied: ～位 *leave a seat vacant* ❷ diffident; timid: 胆～ *timid; milk-livered* / 心里有点～ *feel rather diffident* ❸ false; nominal: 虚名 / 虚构 ❹ humble; modest: 谦虚 ❺ weak; in poor health: 身体很～ *be very weak physically* ❻［物］virtual: ～阴极 *virtual cathode* Ⅲ副 in vain: 箭不～发。*Not a single arrow missed its target.*
【虚报】make a false report; report untruthfully: ～账目 *cook accounts; falsify accounts* / ～冒领 *make a fraudulent application and claim*
【虚词】［语］function word; form word
【虚度】spend time in vain; waste: 我们不能让青春～。*We must not let our youth slip idly by.* ◇ ～光阴 fritter away one's time; ～年华 idle away one's time; waste one's life
【虚浮】impractical; superficial: ～的计划 *an impractical plan* / 作风～ *have a superficial style of work*
【虚根】［数］imaginary root
【虚构】fabricate; make up: ～的情节 *a made-up story; a trumped-up story* / ～的人物 *a fictitious character* / 纯属～ *an out-and-out fabrication; a sheer fabrication*
【虚汗】abnormal sweating due to general debility
【虚怀若谷】have a mind as open as a valley—be extremely modest; be open-minded
【虚幻】unreal; illusory: ～的情景 *a mere illusion*
【虚晃一枪】feint a thrust with one's spear; make a feint
【虚假】false; sham: ～证明 *false testimony* / ～现象 *false appearance* / 我感到他对人有点～。*I don't think he is quite honest with people.*
【虚焦点】［物］virtual focus
【虚惊】false alarm: 受了一场～ *be the victim of a false alarm*
【虚夸】exaggerative; bombastic; boastful
【虚名】false reputation; undeserved reputation: 徒有～，并无实学 *have a false reputation and no real learning*
【虚拟】❶ invented; fictitious: 这个故事是～的。*This is a fictitious story.* ❷ suppositional ◇ ～存储器 virtual memory; ～地址 virtual address; ～市场 dummy market; ～语气［语］the subjunctive mood
【虚胖】puffiness
【虚情假意】a false display of affection; a hypocritical show of friendship
【虚荣】vanity: 不慕～ *not affected by vanity; not vain* / 爱慕～ *be vain* ◇ ～心 vanity
【虚弱】❶ in poor health; weak; debilitated: 病后身体很～ *suffer from general debility after an illness; be very weak after an illness* ❷ weak; feeble: 兵力～ *weak in military strength* / ～的本质 *inherent (or intrinsic) weakness*
【虚设】nominal; existing in name only: 形同虚设
【虚实】❶ false or true—the actual situation (as of the opposing side): 探听～ *try to find out about an opponent, etc.; try to ascertain the strength (of the enemy)* ❷ theoretical and practical: ～并举 *do both ideological and practical work*
【虚饰】❶ cover up or modify with false words: ～历史 *disguise historical facts* ❷ flashy; without substance: ～的文辞 *flashy, empty words*
【虚数】❶ unreliable figure ❷［数］imaginary number
【虚岁】nominal age
【虚脱】［医］collapse; prostration
【虚妄】unfounded; fabricated; invented: ～的故事 *a fabricated story*
【虚伪】sham; false; hypocritical: 这个人很～。

That chap is a hypocrite. / 他为人实在,没有一点～。*He is perfectly candid and never two-faced*.

【虚位以待】(又作'虚席以待') leave a seat vacant (or save a seat) for sb.: 宁可～,也不要让不称职的人滥竽充数。*We'd rather leave the place vacant than have someone incompetent fill the position*.

【虚文】❶ rules and regulations that have become a dead letter; dead letter ❷ empty forms: ～浮礼 *mere formalities*; *conventionalities*

【虚无】nihility; nothingness

【虚无缥缈】purely imaginary; entirely unreal; visionary; illusory

【虚无主义】nihilism: ～者 *nihilist*

【虚线】❶ dotted line or line of dashes ❷ [数] imaginary line

【虚像】[物] virtual image

【虚心】open-minded; modest: ～听取别人的意见 *listen to people's criticisms with an open mind*

【虚虚实实】the true mingled with the false; a mixture of truth and falsehood: 以～的战术使敌人疲于奔命 *tire out the enemy by feints and ambushes*

【虚应故事】do sth. perfunctorily as a mere form or routine

【虚有其表】look impressive but lack real worth; appear better than it is

【虚与委蛇】deal with sb. courteously but without sincerity; pretend politeness and compliance

【虚张声势】make an empty show of strength; bluff and bluster; be swashbuckling

【虚职】nominal position without authority or specific duties; redundant: 人浮于事、～过多 *overstaffed and with too many redundant positions*

需 Ⅰ 动 need; want; require: 所～物品 *goods in great need* / ～款甚巨 *require a big sum of money* Ⅱ 名 necessaries; needs: 军需

【需求】requirement; demand: 满足消费者的～ *supply consumer demand*; *meet the consumers' demands* ◇ ～膨胀 demand pull

【需要】❶ need; want; require; demand: 坏习惯一旦养成,～很长的时间才能根除。*A bad habit once contracted takes a very long time to uproot* (*or root up*). ❷ needs: 适应形势发展的～ *adapt oneself to the needs of the developing conditions*

嘘 Ⅰ 动 ❶ breathe out slowly: ～气 *exhale slowly* ❷ utter a sigh: 仰天而～ *staring up at the sky and sighing deeply* ❸ (of cooking fire, steam, etc.) come into contact with sth.; scald; burn: 掀笼屉时小心热气～着手。*Don't scald your hands when you open the steamer*. ❹ 〈方〉 hiss; boo: 把他～下台去 *hiss* (*or boo*) *him off the platform* Ⅱ 叹 sh; hush: ～! 轻一点儿,孩子们刚睡下。*Hush! The kids have just gone to bed*. ——另见 shī

【嘘寒问暖】inquire after sb.'s well-being; be solicitous about sb.'s health

墟 名 ruins: 废墟

xú

徐 副 〈书〉 slowly; gently: 清风～来。*A refreshing breeze was blowing gently*.

【徐步】〈书〉 walk slowly (or leisurely); stroll

【徐娘半老,风韵犹存】in middle age, attractive all the same—an attractive middle-aged woman

【徐徐】〈书〉 slowly; gently: 鲜艳的五星红旗～升起。*The bright Five-Star Red Flag slowly went up the pole*.

xǔ

许 Ⅰ 动 ❶〈书〉 praise: ～为佳作 *praise sth. as an excellent piece of work* ❷ promise: 他～过我一张票。*He promised me a ticket*. ❸ allow; permit: 每组只～去一个人。*Only one person is allowed from each group*. Ⅱ 副 ❶ maybe; perhaps: 他今天没来,～是生病了。*He didn't come today*; *perhaps he's ill*. ❷ (indicating a rough estimate): 年四十～ *about forty years old*

【许多】many; much; a great deal of; a lot of: 他讲的内容,～是我不知道的。*Much of what he said was new to me*. / 她好像一下子老了～。*She seems to have aged a lot*.

【许久】for a long time; for ages: 大家商量了～。*We talked things over for a long time*. / 我们～没有通信了。*We have not corresponded for ages*.

【许可】permit; allow: 凡是条件～的地方 *wherever conditions permit*

【许可证】license; permit: 出口～ *an export license*

【许诺】make a promise; promise: 他～过帮我解决困难。*He promised that he would help me out*.

【许配】(of a girl) be betrothed to sb. (in an arranged match): 她才满十岁就～人了。*She was betrothed to her husband when she was only ten*.

【许愿】❶ make a vow to a god: 烧香～ *burn incense and make vows* ❷ promise sb. a reward: 我给孩子许了愿,要是他这次考好了带他去海边玩。*I promised the child to take him to the seaside if he did well in the exam*.

诩 动 〈书〉 brag; boast: 自诩

栩 (构词成分) 见下

【栩栩】vivid; lively: ～欲活 *lifelike*; *to the life*

【栩栩如生】lifelike; to the life: 他画的奔马,～,极其神似。*The galloping horses he paints are extremely lifelike*.

醑 名 ❶〈书〉 fine wine ❷ [药] spirit; essence: 樟脑～ *camphor spirit* (*or essence*)

【醑剂】[药] spirit; essence

xù

旭 名〈书〉brilliance of the rising sun
【旭日】the rising sun
【旭日东升】the sun rising in the eastern sky—a display of youthful vigour and vitality

序 Ⅰ名 ❶ order; sequence: 顺序 / 程序 ❷ preface: 能否请您为这本书写一篇～? *Would you write a preface to this book?* Ⅱ动 arrange in order Ⅲ形 introductory; initial: 序幕
【序跋】preface and postscript
【序次】❶ order; sequence ❷〈书〉arrange in order
【序列】alignment; array: 战斗～ *battle array; battle order* ◇～分析 sequential analysis; ～记录 chronological record; ～账簿 chronological book; book of chronological entry
【序幕】❶ prologue (to a play) ❷ prologue (to a major event, etc.); prelude
【序曲】❶［音］overture ❷ prelude (to an event, action, etc.)
【序时账】accounting journal
【序数】ordinal number; ordinal
【序文】preface; foreword
【序言】preface; foreword

恤 动 ❶ pity; sympathize: 体恤 ❷ give relief; compensate: 抚恤
【恤金】pension for a person disabled while on duty; pension for the dependants of a person who died while on duty

叙 Ⅰ动 ❶ talk; chat: ～家常 *chitchat* ❷ narrate; recount; relate ❸ assess; appraise Ⅱ形 introductory; initial
【叙别】have a farewell talk
【叙旧】talk about the old days
【叙利亚】Syria ◇～人 Syrian
【叙事】narrate (in writing); recount ◇～歌剧 ballad opera; ～剧 epic theatre; ～曲［音］ballade; ～诗 narrative poem; ballade; ～文 narrative; narrative prose
【叙述】narrate (in speech or writing); recount; relate
【叙说】tell; narrate (in speech)
【叙谈】chat; chitchat

畜 动 raise (domestic animals) ——另见 chù
【畜产】livestock (or animal) products
【畜牧】raise (or rear) livestock or poultry: 从事～ *go in for animal husbandry*
【畜牧场】animal farm; livestock (or stock) farm
【畜牧业】animal husbandry; livestock husbandry; livestock farming
【畜养】raise (domestic animals)

酗 (构词成分) 见下
【酗酒】indulge in excessive drinking: ～滋事 *get drunk and create a disturbance*

绪 名 ❶ the beginning of a matter: 绪论 ❷ thread ends; remnants: ～余 *surplus; remnants* ❸ mental or emotional state: 心绪 ❹ task; cause; undertaking: 续未竟之～ *carry on an unfinished task; take up where another has left off*
【绪论】introduction
【绪言】introduction

续 Ⅰ形 continuous; successive: 连续 Ⅱ动 ❶ continue; extend; join: ～会 *extended session; follow-up meeting* / 这条绳子太短,再～上一截儿吧。*This piece of string is too short. Join another piece onto it.* ❷ add; supply more: 蒸锅要烧干了,赶快～水。*The steamer (on the fire) is nearly dry. Put some more water in it, quick.*
【续编】continuation (of a book); sequel
【续订】renew one's subscription (to a newspaper or magazine)
【续读】resume studies
【续断】［中］teasel root
【续航】(of an airplane or ship) continue (or pursue) a journey without refuelling ◇～力 endurance; flying range (of an airplane); cruising radius (of a ship)
【续集】continuation (of a book); sequel
【续假】extend one's leave of absence; extend leave: ～一星期 *have one's leave extended for another week*
【续借】renew (a library book)
【续篇】sequel
【续聘】renew (contract): 合同期满后,成绩显著者～。*Those who acquit themselves exceptionally well will have their contracts renewed.*
【续弦】❶ remarry after the death of one's wife ❷ a second wife (after the death of one's first wife)
【续约】❶ renew a treaty or contract ❷ a renewed treaty or contract; a supplementary contract

絮 Ⅰ名 ❶ (cotton) wadding ❷ sth. resembling cotton: 芦～ *(reed) catkin* Ⅱ动 wad with cotton: ～被子 *wad a quilt with cotton* / ～棉衣 *line (or wad) one's clothes with cotton* Ⅲ形 long-winded; garrulous
【絮叨】be long-winded; be garrulous; be wordy: 他老是～个没完,所以大家都烦他。*Everybody is fed up with his endless chatter.*
【絮棉】cotton for wadding

婿 名 ❶ son-in-law ❷ husband: 妹～ *younger sister's husband*

蓄 动 ❶ store up; save up: 蓄水 ❷ grow: ～须 *grow a beard* / ～发 *wear one's hair long* ❸ entertain (ideas); harbour: 蓄意
【蓄藏】save and preserve; lay in; lay up; store
【蓄电池】storage battery; accumulator ◇～车 accumulator vehicle

【蓄洪】store floodwater：～防旱 *store flood-water for use against a drought* / ～工程 *flood storage project* ◇ ～区 flood containment area；flood control area

【蓄积】store up；save up：～粮食 *store up grain*

【蓄谋】premeditate：～已久 *long premeditated* / ～迫害 *harbour a design of persecuting sb.*

【蓄水】retain (or store) water：在山坡上建池～ *dig ponds on the slopes to store water* ◇ ～池 cistern；reservoir

【蓄养】build up；accumulate：～力量 *build up (or accumulate) strength*

【蓄意】premeditated；deliberate：～挑衅 *premeditated provocation* / ～进行破坏 *deliberately sabotage* / ～干涉别国内政 *be bent on interfering in other countries' internal affairs*

【蓄志】harbour an ambition

煦 形〈书〉warm；balmy：和煦

xuān

轩 名 ❶ (formerly often used in names of studies, restaurants or teahouses) a small room or veranda with windows ❷ a high-fronted, curtained carriage used in ancient times ❸〈书〉window or door

【轩昂】dignified；imposing

【轩然大波】a great disturbance；a mighty uproar：没料到芝麻大的事儿竟会引起这样一场～。*Who could have thought that a trivial matter would cause such a stir (or cause so much agitation)?*

【轩轾】〈书〉high and low chariots—high or low；good or bad

宣 动 ❶ declare；proclaim；announce：～赦 *proclaim a general amnesty* ❷ lead off (liquids)；drain：宣泄

【宣布】declare；proclaim；announce：～独立 *declare (or proclaim) independence* / ～会议开始 *declare a meeting open；call a meeting to order* / ～无效 *declare sth. invalid (or null and void)*

【宣称】assert；declare；profess：被告～自己是无辜的。*The accused declared that he was innocent.* or *The accused pleaded not guilty.*

【宣传】conduct propaganda；propagate；disseminate；give publicity to：广为～ *give wide publicity to* / 做～要看对象。*In doing propaganda we must consider our audience.* ◇ ～队 propaganda team；～工具 instrument (or means) of propaganda or publicity；～工作者 propagandist；～画 picture poster；～机构 propaganda organ；～机器 propaganda machine；～品 propaganda (or publicity) material；～网 propaganda network；～员 propagandist

【宣传副页】tip-on

【宣读】read out (in public)：～中央文件 *read out a Central Committee document*

【宣告】declare；proclaim：～成立 *proclaim the founding of (a state, organization, etc.)* / ～无效 *declare sth. null and void* / ～破产 *declare bankruptcy；go bankrupt*

【宣讲】❶ explain and publicise (a policy, decree, etc.) ❷ preach (a religious doctrine)

【宣判】[法] pronounce judgment：～有罪 *pronounce sb. guilty* / ～无罪 *pronounce sb. not guilty；acquit sb. of a crime or charge*

【宣誓】take (or swear) an oath；make a vow；make a pledge：～就职 *take an oath of office；be sworn in；be sworn into office*

【宣泄】❶ lead off (liquids)；drain：～洪水 *drain off floodwaters* ❷ get sth. off one's chest；unbosom oneself：～心中的积郁 *give vent to one's pent-up feelings*

【宣叙调】[音] recitative

【宣言】declaration；manifesto：《共产党～》*Manifesto of the Communist Party* / 开罗～ *Cairo Declaration*

【宣扬】publicise；propagate；advocate；advertise：～好人好事 *give publicity to good people and their good deeds*

【宣战】declare war ◇ ～书 a declaration of war

萱（构词成分）见下

【萱草】day lily

【萱堂】formal honor your mother

喧 Ⅰ形 noisy Ⅱ副 noisily, loudly

【喧宾夺主】a presumptuous guest usurps the role of the host；the secondary supersedes the primary

【喧哗】❶ confused noise；hubbub；uproar：笑语～ *uproarious talk and laughter* / 门外一阵～。*There was a hubbub outside the door.* ❷ make an uproar；make a racket：请勿～。*Please keep quiet (a sign in a public place).*

【喧闹】noise and excitement；bustle；racket

【喧嚷】make an uproar；make a racket：人声～ *a hubbub of voices；loud confused voices* / 千万别把事情～出去呀！*For heaven's sake, don't spread it around!*

【喧扰】stir up a disturbance；make a commotion

【喧腾】noise and excitement；hubbub：广场上一片～。*A hubbub filled the square.*

【喧嚣】❶ noisy：～的车马声 *the noise of dense traffic* ❷ make a clamour；make a hullabaloo；raise a din：～鼓噪 *make a clamour；stir up a commotion*

【喧笑】❶ laugh loudly：大家～了一阵，对今天的胜利很是得意。*They all burst into loud laughter, very pleased with their victory that day.* ❷ loud laughter：孩子们不时发出阵阵的～。*Peals of laughter sounded from among the children.*

xuán

玄 形 ❶ black；dark：玄青 ❷ profound；abstruse ❸〈口〉unreliable；incredible：这话太～了。*That's a pretty tall story*.

【玄乎】〈口〉fantastic；incredible：说得那么～，有谁相信。*Who'd believe such a fantastic story*!

【玄机】［宗］（道教）arcane truth

【玄妙】mysterious；abstruse

【玄青】deep black

【玄孙】great-great-grandson；grandson of one's grandson

【玄武岩】［地质］basalt

【玄想】fancy；imagination

【玄虚】deceitful trick；mystery：故弄玄虚

【玄之又玄】the mystery of mysteries—extremely mysterious and abstruse

旋 Ⅰ动 ❶ revolve；circle；spin：旋绕 ❷ return；come back：凯旋 Ⅱ副〈书〉soon —— 另见 xuàn

【旋耕】rotary tillage ◇ ～机 rotary cultivator；rotocultivator

【旋光性】［物］optical rotation

【旋律】［音］melody

【旋毛虫】trichina

【旋木雀】tree creeper

【旋钮】knob

【旋桥】swing bridge

【旋绕】curl up；wind around：炊烟～。*Smoke is curling up from the kitchen chimneys*.

【旋塞】［机］cock：放水～ *drain cock* / 三通～ *three-way cock*

【旋涡】whirlpool；vortex；eddy

【旋涡星云】［天］spiral nebula

【旋翼机】rotary-wing aircraft；rotorcraft

【旋踵】〈书〉in the brief time it takes to turn round on one's heel—in an instant：～即逝 *vanish before one has time to turn round*；*disappear in the twinkling of an eye*

【旋转】revolve；gyrate；rotate；spin：顺时针方向～ *clockwise rotation* / 逆时针方向～ *counterclockwise rotation* / ～球 *a spinning ball*

【旋转餐厅】revolving restaurant

【旋转乾坤】effect a drastic change in nature or the established order of a country；be earth-shaking

【旋转天线】rotary antenna

悬 Ⅰ动 ❶ hang；suspend：～在空中 *suspend in midair* ❷ lift；raise：悬腕 ❸ feel anxious；be solicitous：悬念 ❹ imagine：悬拟 Ⅱ形 ❶ outstanding；unresolved：这事儿不能老～着，得抓紧解决。*We can't leave the matter unresolved any longer. Let's have it settled without delay*. ❷〈方〉dangerous：在快车道上骑自行车，可真～。*Cycling in the fast traffic lane is really dangerous*.

【悬案】❶ an unsettled law case ❷ an outstanding issue；an unsettled question

【悬臂】［机］cantilever ◇ ～梁 cantilever（beam）；～起重机 cantilever crane；～桥 cantilever bridge

【悬灯结彩】hang up lanterns and festoons；adorn with lanterns and coloured streamers

【悬吊】be suspended；hang：门上～着两个大红灯笼。*There were two big red lanterns hanging over the gate*.

【悬而未决】outstanding；unresolved：～的问题 *an outstanding question*

【悬浮】suspension：～染色 *suspension dyeing* ◇ ～固体［环保］suspended solid；～体 suspended substance；suspension

【悬隔】be separated by a great distance；be far apart：两地～。*The two places are far apart*. / ～千里 *be a thousand li apart*；*be a great distance apart*

【悬挂】❶ hang；suspend；fly（a flag）：～国旗 *fly the national flag of China* / 圣诞树上上下下～着亮晶晶的花彩。*Glistening trimmings were hung over the Xmas tree*. ❷ suspension（of a motor vehicle）◇ ～犁 mounted plough；～式滑翔［体］hang gliding；～式滑翔机 hang glider

【悬河泻水】a hanging river in flood—a flood of eloquence

【悬乎】〈方〉dangerous；unsafe：真～！她差点让汽车给撞了。*Whew, that was dangerous! She nearly got run over by the car*.

【悬胶】［化］suspensoid：～态 *suspensoid state*

【悬空】hang in the air—be unsettled；be impractical：这件事不能老～着，要抓紧解决。*Let's deal with the matter now*；*it's hung in the air too long*. ◇ ～通道 skywalk

【悬梁】hang oneself from a beam：～自尽 *commit suicide by hanging oneself from a beam*；*hang oneself*

【悬梁刺股】tie one's hair to a beam to keep from nodding off，or prod oneself awake with an awl in the thigh—study assiduously

【悬铃木】plane tree

【悬拟】fabricate；make up

【悬念】❶〈书〉be concerned about（sb. who is elsewhere）❷ suspense（felt as a story，play，etc. builds to a climax）：一篇充满～的侦探小说 *a suspenseful detective story*

【悬赏】offer（or post）a reward：～缉拿逃犯 *offer a reward for the capture of a runaway criminal*；*set a price on a runaway criminal's head*

【悬首示众】display sb.'s chopped-off head at a public place as a warning to all

【悬殊】a great disparity；a wide gap：力量～ *a great disparity in strength* / 众寡～ *a great disparity in numbers* / 贫富～ *a wide gap between the rich and the poor*

【悬索结构】［建］suspended-cable structure

【悬索桥】suspension bridge

【悬梯】hanging ladder

【悬腕】suspend the wrist

【悬想】imagine；fancy

【悬心】be on tenterhooks

【悬心吊胆】have one's heart in one's mouth；be on tenterhooks

【悬崖】overhanging（or steep）cliff；precipice

【悬崖勒马】rein in at the brink of the precipice—wake up to danger at the last moment

【悬崖峭壁】(又作'悬崖绝壁') sheer precipices and overhanging rocks; (perilous) cliffs and precipices

【悬雍垂】[生理] uvula

漩 名 whirlpool; eddy

【漩涡】同〖旋涡〗

xuǎn

选 Ⅰ 动 ❶ select; choose; pick: ～个好日子 *choose an auspicious day* / ～一种你喜欢的样式 *select a style that takes your fancy* ❷ elect: ～学生会主席 *elect a chairman of the student union* Ⅱ 名 selections; anthology: 诗～ *selected poems* / 民歌～ *selections of folk songs* / 散文～ *an anthology of prose*

【选拔】select; choose: ～运动员 *select athletes* / ～人才 *select talented people* ◇ ～赛 (selective) trial; ～委员会 selection board

【选本】anthology; selected works

【选材】❶ select a suitable person ❷ select suitable materials

【选定】decide on; fix: ～日期 *fix the date*

【选读】❶ pick out (pieces or passages) to read; read excerpts ❷ selected readings: 文学～ *selected readings in literature*

【选购】pick out and buy; choose from a variety of goods: 她为小女儿～了一件漂亮衣服。*She chose a pretty dress for her little daughter.*

【选集】selected works (or writings); selections; anthology:《现代戏剧～》*An Anthology of Modern Drama*

【选举】elect: 无记名投票～ *elect by secret ballot* / ～程序 *electoral procedure* (*or proceedings*) / ～单位 *electoral unit* / ～结果 *election results* (*or returns*) ◇ ～法 electoral law; ～权 the right to vote; franchise; ～人 voter

【选刊】❶ publish: 画报～了4幅人物彩色照片。*The pictorial has published four color photo portraits.* ❷ periodicals exclusively carrying selected writings

【选矿】ore dressing; mineral separation; beneficiation: ～厂 *ore dressing plant*; *concentration plant*

【选美】beauty contest

【选民】voter; elector: ～登记 *registration of voters* / ～名册 *voting register* / 全体～ *the constituency*; *the electorate* ◇ ～榜 list of eligible voters; ～证 elector's certificate; voter registration card

【选派】select; detail: ～代表参加会议 *depute sb. to attend a conference*; *select sb. as representative to a conference*

【选配】❶ provide: ～什么样的人进领导班子,群众有不可剥夺的发言权。*The masses have an inalienable right to have a say in what kind of people should be selected and appointed to the leading group.* ❷ select better breeds for reproduction; selective breeding

【选票】vote; ballot

【选聘】appoint to a position; engage or employ: ～教师 *select and employ teachers*

【选区】electoral (or election) district; electoral ward; constituency

【选曲】selected songs or tunes:《茶花女》～ *selected tunes from La Traviata*

【选取】select; choose

【选任】select (a suitable person) for a post

【选手】an athlete selected for a sports meet; (selected) contestant; player: 参加体操比赛的～有几百名。*There were hundreds of contestants in the gymnastics competition.*

【选送】select and recommend sb. (for a position or for admission to a school, etc.)

【选题】❶ select a title, subject or topic (for writing or research) ❷ the title, subject or topic selected

【选修】take as an elective course: 我们班大部分同学～欧洲史。*Most of the students of our class take European history as an elective course.* ◇ ～课 elective course; optional course

【选样】sampling; sample

【选用】select for employment or for use

【选育】❶ [农] seed selection: ～良种小麦 *develop improved varieties of wheat by selection* ❷ animal husbandry breeding

【选择】select; choose; opt: ～日期 *choose a date* / ～职业 *choose an occupation* / ～发型 *choose a hair style* / 没有～的余地 *have no choice at all* ◇ ～场地 [体] choice of ends; ～题 multiple-choice question; multiple-choice test; ～问句 [语] alternative question

【选种】seed selection

【选中】pick on; decide on; settle on: 她最后～了黄白条儿的那种料子。*Finally she decided on the white and yellow striped material.*

烜 形〈书〉❶ ablaze ❷ bright

【烜赫】of great renown and influence

【烜赫一时】have renown and influence for a time

癣 名 tinea; ringworm

xuàn

炫 动 ❶〈书〉dazzle: 光彩～目 *blindingly bright*; *with dazzling brightness* ❷〈书〉show off; display: 自～其能 *show off one's ability*

【炫弄】show off; display; parade: ～技巧 *show off one's skill*

【炫示】show off; display; parade: ～自己的知识 *parade one's knowledge*

【炫耀】make a display of; show off; flaunt: ～力量 *flaunt one's strength* / ～武力 *make a show of force* / ～自己的学问 *parade one's learning*

绚 形 gorgeous：绚丽

【绚烂】splendid；gorgeous：～的朝霞 *gorgeous morning clouds* / ～的杜鹃花 *splendid azaleas*

【绚丽】gorgeous；magnificent：～的景色 *magnificent scenery* / ～的鲜花 *gorgeous flowers* / 文采～ *literary brilliance*

【绚丽多彩】bright and colourful；gorgeous

眩 形〈书〉❶ dizzy；giddy：头晕目～ *feel dizzy* ❷ dazzled；bewildered：～于名利 *dazzled by the prospect of fame and wealth；obsessed with a desire for fame and wealth*

【眩目】dazzle the eyes

【眩晕】❶ dizziness：一阵～ *a fit of dizziness* ❷［医］vertigo

旋 Ⅰ 动 ❶ whirl ❷ cut or shape on a lathe，or pare with a knife：～根车轴 *shape a piece of steel into an axle on a lathe* / 给孩子～一个苹果吃。*Peel an apple for the child*. Ⅱ 副 at the time；at the last moment：～用～买 *buy for immediate use* ——另见 xuán

【旋床】［机］（turning）lathe

【旋风】whirlwind

【旋工】turner

渲 动 同〖渲染〗❶

【渲染】❶（in Chinese painting）add washes of ink or colour to a drawing ❷ play up；exaggerate；pile it on：～战争恐怖 *play up the horrors of war* / 一件小事情，用不着这么～。*No need to exaggerate a trifling matter like that*.

楦 Ⅰ 名 shoe last or hat block Ⅱ 动 shape with a last or block：～鞋 *last a shoe* / ～帽子 *block a hat*

【楦子】（又作'楦头'）shoe last or hat block

xuē

削 动（mainly as part of a compound word；otherwise pronounced xiāo）pare；whittle；cut：削减——另见 xiāo

【削壁】precipice；cliff

【削价】cut the price；lower the price：～处理 *disposal of goods at reduced prices；a clearance sale*

【削肩】sloping shoulders；drooping shoulders

【削减】cut（down）；reduce；slash；whittle down：～非生产性开支 *cut down nonproductive expenditures；cut back on nonproductive spending* / ～军费 *cut down military expenditures* ◇ ～关税 reduction in tariff

【削弱】weaken；cripple

【削铁如泥】cut through iron as if it were mud（said of an exceptionally sharp sword）

【削职】remove from office

【削足适履】cut the feet to fit the shoes

靴 名 boots：靴子

【靴筒】（又作'靴统'）the leg of a boot；bootleg

【靴子】boots

xué

穴 名 ❶ cave；den；hole：蚁～ *ant hole* / 匪～ *bandits-den* ❷ coffin pit ❸［中］acupuncture point；acupoint

【穴道】同〖穴位〗

【穴居人】cave dweller；troglodyte

【穴位】［中］acupuncture point；acupoint：～注射疗法 *therapy of point injection*

学 Ⅰ 动 ❶ study；learn：～文化 *acquire an elementary education；learn to read and write* / ～外语 *learn（or study）a foreign language* / ～游泳 *learn swimming* ❷ imitate；mimic：这孩子～他爸爸走路的样子。*The boy imitates his father's way of walking*. / ～鸡叫 *mimic the crowing of a cock* Ⅱ 名 ❶ learning；knowledge：博学 ❷ subject of study；branch of learning：数学 / 文学 ❸ school；college：上学

【学报】learned journal；journal：《清华～》*Qing Hua University Journal* /《中国考古～》*Chinese Journal of Archaeology*

【学潮】student unrest；campus upheaval

【学而不厌】have an insatiable desire to learn；be insatiable in learning

【学非所用】what one is doing has nothing to do with one's training

【学费】❶ tuition fee；tuition：交～ *pay tuition* ❷ a price for what one has learned to one's cost

【学分】credit：～制 *the credit system*

【学风】❶ academic atmosphere；academic discipline：那个学院以优良～著称。*That college is noted for its academic atmosphere and discipline*. / ～不正 *lack of academic discipline* ❷ style of study

【学府】seat of learning；institution of higher learning

【学富五车】have read five cartloads of books—be very learned

【学好】learn from good examples；emulate good

【学坏】❶ follow bad examples ❷（used with 了）be corrupted by bad examples

【学会】❶ learn；master：～多种外国语 *master quite a number of foreign languages* ❷learned society；society；institute：中国人民外交～ *the Chinese People's Institute of Foreign Affairs* / 物理～ *the Physics Society*

【学籍】one's status as a student；one's name on the school roll：保留～ *retain one's status as a student* / 取消～ *be struck off the school roll*

【学界】academic circles

【学究】pedant：～气 *pedantry*

【学科】❶ a branch of learning；discipline ❷ a

school subject; a course of study ❸ theoretical courses offered in military or physical training (〈反〉'术科')
【学理】scientific principle or theory
【学力】educational level; scholastic or academic attainments
【学历】record of formal schooling; academic credentials
【学龄】school age: ～儿童 *children of school age; school-age children* / ～前儿童 *preschool children; preschoolers*
【学名】❶ scientific name (e. g. Latin name for plants, etc.) ❷ formal name used at school (as distinguished from infant name or pet name at home)
【学路】❶ ways to run a school: 教育方面,要广开～。*In education, it is necessary to find as many ways as possible to provide educational opportunities*. ❷ ways of learning: 他知识渊博,～宽广。*He is extremely knowledgeable and well-versed in ways of learning*.
【学年】school (or academic) year: ～考试 *year-end examination*
【学派】school of thought; school
【学期】school term; term; semester
【学前教育】preschool education; infant school education
【学然后知不足】the more you learn, the less you feel you know
【学舌】❶ mechanically repeat other people's words; parrot; ape ❷〈口〉wag one's tongue spreading hearsay
【学生】❶ student; pupil: 医科～ *a medical student* / ～时代 *school days* / ～腔 *schoolboy or schoolgirl talk; classroom tone of a schoolboy or schoolgirl* ❷ disciple; follower ❸〈方〉boy; lad ◇ ～会 student union; student association; ～运动 student movement; ～证 student's identity card
【学时】class hour; period: 小学一～45分钟。*In primary schools, a class hour has 45 minutes* (or *a period is 45 minutes long*).
【学识】learning; knowledge; scholarly attainments: ～渊博 *have great learning; be learned* / ～浅薄 *have little learning*
【学士】❶ scholar ❷ a holder of the bachelor's degree; bachelor
【学术】systematic learning; science: ～领域 *sphere of learning* / 国际～交流活动 *international academic exchanges* / ～报告 *learned report; academic report* ◇ ～界 academic circles
【学说】theory; doctrine
【学徒】❶ apprentice; trainee ❷ serve an apprenticeship: 他跟一位木匠师傅学了三年徒。*He has served an apprenticeship of three years with* (*or to*) *a master carpenter*. ◇ ～工 apprentice
【学位】academic degree; degree: 硕士～ *master's degree* / 博士～ *doctor's degree; doctorate* / 名誉～ *an honorary degree*
【学问】❶ systematic learning; a branch of knowledge: 生物工程是一门新兴的～。*Bioengineering is an emergent branch of learning*. ❷ learning; knowledge; scholarship: ～高深的人 *a man of great learning; an erudite scholar*
【学无止境】Knowledge is infinite. There is no limit to knowledge.
【学习】study; learn; emulate: ～别人的长处,克服自己的弱点。*Emulate others' strong points and overcome one's own weaknesses*. ◇ ～动机 academic motivation; ～目的 aim of learning; ～系统 learning system
【学衔】academic rank (or title)
【学校】school; educational institution: 师范～ *teachers school; normal school* / 专业～ *specialized school; vocational school* / 高等～ *institution of higher learning*
【学业】one's studies; school work
【学以致用】study for the sake of application; study sth. in order to apply it
【学艺】❶ learn a craft or trade ❷ knowledge and skills
【学员】student (usu. of a college or a training course)
【学院】college; academy; institute: 师范～ *teachers training college* / 建筑工程～ *institute of civil engineering* / 美术～ *school of art*
【学者】scholar; a learned man; a man of learning
【学制】❶ educational (or school) system: ～改革 *reform in the school system* ❷ length of schooling: 缩短～ *shorten the period of schooling*
【学子】〈书〉student

噱 动〈方〉laugh: 发～ *make one laugh; excite laughter*
【噱头】〈方〉❶ words or act meant to amuse or to excite laughter: 这个丑角～真多。*That clown is full of amusing tricks*. / 卖弄～ *play to the gallery* ❷ tricks meant to deceive: 不要摆～! *Don't try any tricks!* or *None of your tricks!* ❸ funny; amusing; comical: 实在～ *really funny*

xuě

雪 Ⅰ 名 ❶ snow: 一场大～ *a heavy fall of snow* ❷ resembling snow; snowy: 雪白 / 雪亮 Ⅱ 动 wipe away (or off, out); clean: 雪耻
【雪白】snow-white; snowy white
【雪板】skis
【雪豹】[动] snow leopard; ounce (Panthera uncia)
【雪暴】snowstorm; blizzard
【雪崩】snowslide; avalanche ◇ ～效应 [物] avalanche effect
【雪车】sled; sledge; sleigh
【雪耻】avenge an insult; wipe out a disgrace or humiliation
【雪堆】snowbank; snow drift

【雪纺绸】［纺］chiffon
【雪糕】〈方〉ice cream
【雪恨】wreak vengeance；avenge
【雪花】snowflake
【雪花膏】vanishing cream
【雪花莲】［植］snowdrop
【雪花石膏】alabaster
【雪鸡】［动］snow cock
【雪茄】cigar
【雪里红】（又作'雪里蕻'）potherb mustard（Brassica cernua，a vegetable quite palatable when pickled）
【雪里送炭】同〖雪中送炭〗
【雪利酒】sherry
【雪莲】（又作'雪莲花'）snow lotus（Saussurea involucrata）
【雪亮】bright as snow；shiny：把自行车擦得～ *polish the bike till it has a good shine* / 灯光～ *dazzling lamplight*
【雪柳】［植］fontanesia（Fontanesia fortunei）
【雪盲】snow blindness
【雪泥鸿爪】marks left by goose claws in the snow—traces of past events
【雪片】〈喻〉snowflake：读者来信～似地飞向报社。*The newspaper office was swamped by a flood of readers-letters.*
【雪橇】sled；sledge；sleigh
【雪青】lilac（colour）
【雪球】snowball ——另见〖滚雪球〗
【雪人】❶ snowman：堆～ *make a snowman* ❷ the Abominable Snowman（a hairy manlike creature reported to live in the snows of the Himalayas）
【雪山】a snow-capped mountain；a snowy mountain
【雪上加霜】snow plus frost—one disaster after another
【雪上汽车】snowmobile ◇ ～运动［体］snowmobiling
【雪松】［植］cedar
【雪条】〈方〉ice-lolly；frozen sucker；popsicle
【雪冤】clear sb. of a false charge；redress a wrong
【雪原】snowfield
【雪杖】ski pole；ski stick
【雪中送炭】send charcoal in snowy weather—provide timely help

鳕 名 cod
【鳕鱼】cod

xuè

血 Ⅰ 名 blood：～从伤口流出来了。*Blood was flowing from the wound.* Ⅱ 形 ❶ related by blood：血亲 ❷ energetic and high-spirited：血性 ——另见 xiě
【血癌】a popular name for 白血病
【血案】a murder case；a bloody incident
【血本】principal；original capital
【血崩症】［医］metrorrhagia
【血沉】［医］erythrocyte sedimentation rate（ESR）
【血防】the prevention and cure of schistosomiasis（or snail fever）
【血管】blood vessel ◇ ～瘤［医］haemangioma；angioma；～硬化［医］vascular sclerosis；～造影［医］angiography
【血海】a sea of blood；bloodbath
【血海深仇】a huge debt of blood；intense and deep-seated hatred：我们誓死要报这～！*We swear to collect this blood debt!*
【血汗】blood and sweat；sweat and toil：～钱 *money earned by hard toil* / ～工厂 *sweatshop*
【血红蛋白】［生化］haemoglobin
【血花】spattered drops of blood
【血迹】bloodstain：～斑斑 *bloodstained*
【血痂】scab
【血浆】［生理］（blood）plasma
【血口喷人】make unfounded and malicious attacks upon sb.；venomously slander：你～，纯粹是造谣！*You're slinging mud at me—that's a pack of lies!*
【血库】［医］blood bank
【血亏】［中］anaemia
【血泪斑斑】full of blood and tears：～的家史 *a family history of blood and tears*
【血淋淋】dripping with blood；bloody
【血流成河】blood flowing like a river—bloodbath
【血流如注】blood streaming down
【血路】a bloody path；an escape route：杀出一条～ *open up a bloody path*；*cut an escape route*
【血脉】❶［中］blood vessels；blood circulation ❷ blood relationship；blood lineage：～相通 *be related by blood*
【血尿】［医］haematuria；blood in the urine
【血浓于水】blood is thicker than water
【血泊】a pool of blood：倒在～中 *lie in a pool of blood*
【血气】❶ animal spirits；sap；vigour：血气方刚 ❷ courage and uprightness：有～的青年 *a courageous and upright youth*
【血气方刚】full of animal spirits；full of sap；full of vigour and vitality
【血亲】blood relations
【血亲婚配】incest
【血清】［生理］（blood）serum ◇ ～病［医］serum sickness；serum disease
【血球】［生理］blood cell；blood corpuscle
【血染沙场】stain the battlefield with blood—die in battle
【血肉】flesh and blood；the human body
【血肉横飞】blood and flesh flying in every direction
【血肉模糊】be badly mangled
【血肉相连】as close as flesh and blood
【血肉之躯】the human body；flesh and blood
【血色】redness of the face；colour：她脸上几乎没有～。*She has very little colour.* / 她脸上逐渐恢复了～。*Little by little a healthy complexion came back to her face.*

【血色素】[生理] haemochrome
【血书】a letter (expressing one's determination, last wish, etc.) written in one's own blood
【血栓】[医] thrombus ◇ ～形成 [医] thrombosis
【血糖】[生理] blood sugar
【血统】blood relationship; blood lineage; extraction: 中国～的外国人 *foreign nationals of Chinese descent* / 德国～的美国人 *Americans of German extraction*
【血污】bloodstain
【血吸虫】blood fluke; schistosome ◇ ～病 [医] schistosomiasis; snail fever
【血细胞计数】[医] blood count
【血像】[医] blood picture; hemogram
【血小板】[生理] (blood) platelet ◇ ～病 [医] thrombocytopathy
【血腥】reeking of blood; bloody; sanguinary: ～的白色恐怖 *bloody white terror* / ～味 *smell of blood* / ～统治 *sanguinary* (or *bloodstained*) *rule*
【血型】[生理] blood group; blood type: ～分类 *blood grouping*; *blood typing*
【血性】courage and uprightness: ～汉子 *a courageous and upright man*
【血胸】[医] haemothorax
【血循环】[生理] blood circulation
【血压】blood pressure: 高～ *high blood pressure*; *hypertension* / 低～ *low blood pressure*; *hypotension* ◇ ～计 sphygmomanometer
【血样】blood sample; blood specimen
【血液】❶ (human) blood: 新鲜～ *fresh blood* ❷ lifeblood; lifeline: 石油是工业的～。*Petroleum is the lifeblood of industry.* ◇ ～病 [医] blood diseases
【血液透析】[医] haemodialysis ◇ ～器 haemodialyser
【血衣】a bloodstained garment; clothes covered with gore
【血印】bloodstain
【血友病】[医] haemophilia
【血雨腥风】wind and rain reeking of blood—a reign of terror; a bloodbath on a battlefield
【血缘】ties of blood; consanguinity; blood relationship
【血晕】(xuèyùn) [中] coma after childbirth due to excessive loss of blood——另见 xiěyùn
【血债】a debt of blood
【血债累累】have a mountain of blood debts
【血战】❶ a bloody (or sanguinary) battle: 一场～ *a bloody battle* ❷ fight a very fierce battle
【血战到底】fight to the last drop of one's blood; fight to the bitter end: 我们中华民族有同自己的敌人～的气概。*We Chinese have the spirit to fight the enemy to the last drop of our blood.*
【血肿】[医] haematoma

谑 动 〈书〉 crack a joke; banter; tease: 戏谑
【谑而不虐】tease without hurting or embarrassing; banter

xūn

勋 名 merit; meritorious service; achievement: 功勋
【勋绩】meritorious service; outstanding contribution
【勋爵】❶ a feudal title of nobility conferred for meritorious service ❷ Lord (in Great Britain)
【勋劳】meritorious service: 卓著～ *noted for meritorious service*
【勋章】medal; decoration

熏 动 ❶ expose to smoke or fumes; fumigate: 烟把厨房的墙壁～黑了。*The kitchen walls were blackened by cooking fumes.* / ～蚊子 *smoke out mosquitoes* / 臭气～天 *stink to heaven* ❷ treat (meat, fish, etc.) with smoke; smoke: 熏鱼 ❸ make fragrant with incense, etc.: 用茉莉花～茶叶 *scent tea with jasmine* ——另见 xùn
【熏干】smoke-dried beancurd
【熏鸡】smoked chicken
【熏笼】a frame placed over a brazier for drying things or over a censer for scenting clothes
【熏炉】censer
【熏染】exert a gradual, corrupting influence on: 受坏思想的～ *be gradually influenced by evil ideas*
【熏肉】smoked meat
【熏陶】exert a gradual, uplifting influence on; nurture; edify: 起～作用 *exert an edifying influence on*
【熏衣草】lavender (Lavandula angustifolia)
【熏鱼】smoked fish
【熏蒸】❶ sultry; sweltering; stifling; suffocating: 暑气～ *sweltering summer weather*; *stifling summer heat* ❷ [中] fuming or steaming—treating diseases with fumes as in moxibustion or with steam generated by boiling medicinal herbs ❸ fumigate ◇ ～剂 fumigant
【熏制】cure (meat, etc.) by smoking; smoke

醺 形 drunk: 微～ *tipsy*

xún

旬 名 ❶ a period of ten days: 按～计算 *calculate in ten-day periods* ❷ a period of ten years in a person's age (applied only to old persons): 八～老母 80-*year-old mother*
【旬刊】a publication appearing once every ten days

寻 动 look for; search; seek: ～人 *look for sb. missing* / ～物 *look for sth. lost*
【寻常】ordinary; usual; common: 不～ *unusual*; *out of the ordinary* / ～人家 *an ordinary family*
【寻的】[军] target-seeking; homing: ～导弹 *homing missile*

【寻短见】commit suicide; take one's own life
【寻访】look for (sb. whose whereabouts is unknown); try to locate; make inquiries about
【寻根究底】get to the bottom (or root) of things; inquire deeply into: 她最爱～，寻求事物隐蔽的、内在的缘由。*She liked to get to the root of a matter and find out its hidden and internal causes.*
【寻呼】page; bleep ◇ ～机 pager; bleeper; beeper
【寻花问柳】sport with flowers and willows—❶ enjoy a beautiful spring scene ❷ dally with prostitutes; visit houses of ill repute
【寻欢作乐】seek pleasure and make merry
【寻开心】〈方〉make fun of; poke fun at; joke: 别太认真了，她不过是在～罢了。*Don't take it too seriously. She is only joking.*
【寻觅】seek; look for: 这幅古画我们已～多年了。*We have been looking for this old painting for years.*
【寻求】seek; explore; go in quest of: ～打开僵局的途径 *explore possible paths for ending the stalemate* / 通过改革～出路 *seek (or find) a way out through reform*
【寻声】follow the sound (to find sb. or sth.): 我在远处听着像是你的说话声，所以就～而来了。*I heard a voice like yours at some distance from here, so I followed it and found you here.*
【寻事生非】seek a quarrel; stir up or make trouble
【寻死】❶ try to commit suicide; attempt suicide ❷ commit suicide
【寻死觅活】attempt suicide (usu. as a threat)
【寻思】think to oneself; think: 我～她最适合做这个工作。*I thought (or thought to myself) she was best suited for this job.*
【寻味】chew sth. over; ruminate; think over
【寻问】inquire about: 不断有人来～这件事。*People kept coming to inquire about that affair.*
【寻衅】pick a quarrel; provoke: ～滋事 *pick quarrels and stir up trouble*
【寻幽访胜】travel around visiting quiet and secluded scenic spots
【寻章摘句】cull phrases and cite passages; write in clichés
【寻找】seek; look for: ～失物 *look for lost articles* / ～真理 *seek truth*

巡 Ⅰ 动 patrol; make one's rounds: 巡逻 Ⅱ 量 a round of drinks: 酒过三～。*The wine has gone round three times.*
【巡边员】[体] linesman
【巡查】go on a tour of inspection; make one's rounds
【巡航】cruise: ～半径 *cruising radius* / ～速度 *cruising speed* ◇ ～导弹 cruise missile
【巡回】go the rounds; tour; make a circuit of: 剧团正在全国各地～演出。*The theatrical troupe is touring the country.* ◇ ～大使 roving ambassador; ～放映队 mobile film projection unit; ～剧团 touring theatrical troupe; touring company; ～医疗队 mobile medical team
【巡警】〈旧〉policeman
【巡礼】❶ visit a sacred land; go on a pilgrimage ❷ tour; sight-seeing
【巡逻】go on patrol; patrol: 执行～任务 *be on patrol duty*; *be on one's beat* ◇ ～队 patrol party; patrol; ～护卫舰 patrol escort; ～哨 roving sentry; patrol; patrol boat; ～线 patrol route
【巡视】❶ make (or be on) an inspection tour; tour: ～各地 *make an inspection tour of various places* ❷ cast one's eyes around
【巡洋舰】cruiser
【巡夜】go on night patrol; keep night watch
【巡弋】(of a warship) cruise

询 动 ask; inquire
【询问】ask about; inquire about: ～我们的学习情况 *ask us about our studies* / ～病状 *inquire about sb.'s illness*

循 动 follow; abide by: ～此前进 *proceed along this line* / ～例 *follow the usual practice*; *follow a precedent*
【循规蹈矩】observe rules, obey orders, etc. docilely; conform to convention; toe the line: 学生们都很～。*All the students conscientiously obeyed the rules of the school.*
【循环】circulate; cycle: ～不息 *move in endless cycles* / 四季的～ *the cycle of the seasons* ◇ ～论证 [逻] argue in a circle; ～赛 [体] round robin; ～系统 [生理] the circulatory system; ～小数 [数] recurring decimal; ～信用证 revolving letter of credit
【循环往复】move in cycles: ～，以至无穷 *repeat itself in endless cycles*
【循名责实】see that the reality matches the name: ～，这就是今天的工作。*Our present task is to create the reality that will fit the name.*
【循序】in proper order or sequence
【循序渐进】follow in order and advance step by step; proceed in an orderly way and step by step: ～地进行教学。*Instruction is given step by step.*
【循循善诱】be good at giving systematic guidance; teach with skill and patience

鲟 名 sturgeon

xùn

讯 Ⅰ 动 interrogate; question: 审讯 Ⅱ 名 information; news; message; dispatch: 据新华社～ *according to a Xinhua dispatch*
【讯号】radio signal; signal
【讯问】❶ ask about; inquire about: 向医生～病人的病情 *ask a doctor about the condition of a patient* / ～事情的原委 *inquire about all the details of a matter* ❷ interrogate; question: ～被告人

interrogate the defendant / ～案件 *hear* (*or try*) *a case*

训 Ⅰ 动 instruct; admonish; give sb. a lecture: 他没做作业,老师～了他一顿。*His teacher gave him a lecture for not doing his homework*. / 他专爱～人。*He's always lecturing people*. Ⅱ 名 ❶ instructions; teachings: 家训 ❷ standard; model; example: 不足为训

【训斥】reprimand; rebuke; dress down: 他数学不及格,受到爸爸的～。*He failed his maths examination and got a dressing-down from his father*.

【训词】admonition; instructions

【训导】instruct and guide ◇ ～长 (formerly in college) the dean of students

【训诂】exegetical studies (esp. of ancient texts); exegesis ◇ ～学 exegetics

【训话】give an admonitory talk to subordinates

【训练】train; drill: 这些警犬都受过很好的～。*All these police dogs are well trained*.

【训练班】training class; training course: 园艺 ～ *a training course in horticulture* / 短期 ～ *a short course of training*

【训练有素】have received a regular and thorough training; be well-trained: ～的运动员 *a well-trained athlete*

驯 Ⅰ 形 tame and docile: 这匹马很～。*This horse is very tame*. Ⅱ 动 tame; domesticate: 善于～虎 *good at taming tigers* / ～马 *break in a horse*

【驯服】❶ docile; tame; tractable: 猫是很～的。*Cats are very docile*. ❷ tame; break; domesticate: 这匹野马终于被～了。*The wild horse was finally broken in*.

【驯化】domesticate; tame: 鹿群经过～,可以放牧。*Deer can be tamed and trained to go out to pasture*.

【驯良】tractable; docile; tame and gentle

【驯鹿】[动] reindeer

【驯养】raise and train (animals); domesticate

汛 名 seasonal flood; high water: 伏～ *midsummer floods*

【汛期】flood (or high-water) season

【汛情】flood situation: ～严重。*The flood* (*situation*) *is serious*.

迅 形 fast; swift: ～跑 *run swiftly*

【迅即】immediately; at once: 此事望～处理。*It is hoped that immediate action will be taken on this matter*.

【迅疾】swift; rapid

【迅捷】fast; agile; quick

【迅雷不及掩耳】a sudden peal of thunder leaves no time to cover the ears—as sudden as a flash of lightning

【迅猛】swift and violent: 水势～异常。*The flood roared on, swift and violent*.

【迅速】rapid; swift; speedy; prompt: 动作～ *swift in action*; *quick-moving* / ～取得成效 *produce speedy results*

逊 Ⅰ 动 abdicate Ⅱ 形 ❶ modest: 出言不逊 ❷ 〈书〉 inferior: 稍～一筹 *be slightly inferior*

【逊色】be inferior: 毫无～ *be by no means inferior* / 其他玉雕跟这件相比大为～。*Other jade carvings pale beside this*.

【逊位】abdicate

徇 动 〈书〉 give in to; submit to; comply with

【徇情】〈书〉 act wrongly out of personal considerations; practise favouritism

【徇情枉法】bend the law to help one's friends or relatives

【徇私】同〖徇情〗

【徇私舞弊】do wrong to serve one's friends or relatives

殉 动 ❶ be buried alive with the dead ❷ sacrifice one's life for

【殉道】die for a cause ◇ ～者 martyr

【殉国】die (or give one's life) for one's country

【殉教】die for a religious cause

【殉难】die for a just cause or for one's country

【殉情】die for love

【殉葬】be buried alive with the dead: ～的奴隶 *slaves buried alive with their deceased masters* ◇ ～品 funerary object; sacrificial object

【殉职】die at one's post; die in the course of performing one's duty; die in line of duty

熏 动 〈方〉 be poisoned or suffocated by coal gas: 他被煤气～死了。*He died from suffocation by coal gas*. / 小心别让煤气～着。*Guard against coal gas poisoning*. ——另见 xūn

Y

yā

丫 名 bifurcation; fork

【丫鬟】slave girl; servant girl

【丫头】❶〈方〉girl ❷ slave girl

压 Ⅰ 动 ❶ press; push down; hold down; weigh down: ～扁 *press flat*; *flatten* / ～碎 *crush to pieces* / ～死 *crush to death* / ～坏 *damage by pressure* / 这盒子怕～。*This box won't stand much weight* ❷ keep under control; control; keep under; quell: 喝点热水把咳嗽～一～ *drink some hot water to ease a cough* / ～低嗓门 *lower one's voice*; *speak under one's breath* ❸ bring pressure to bear on; suppress; daunt; intimidate: 不受捧,不怕～ *withstand both flattery and pressure* / 别拿大帽子～人。*Don't you try to intimidate people by pinning labels on them*. ❹ approach; be getting near: 太阳～山了。*The setting sun was touching the hilltop*. ❺ pigeonhole; shelve: 这份公文～了不少时间。*This document was pigeonholed for quite some time*. ❻ risk (money); stake Ⅱ 名 pressure: 血压 ——另见 yà

【压不住】cannot keep under control: ～心头怒火 *cannot control one's anger* (*or hold back one's rage*)

【压仓物】[航海] ballast

【压场】❶ have a meeting, an audience, etc. well under one's control: 压不住场 *cannot hold the audience's attention* ❷ 同〖压台〗

【压秤】❶ be relatively heavy per unit volume: 干稻草不～。*Dry straw doesn't weigh much*. ❷ deduct a certain weight from the scale-weight for agricultural products such as cotton, food grains because of claimed excessive water content

【压船】ships backed up in the port due to delays in loading and unloading: 今年5月份,在港外待卸的货船,平均每天下降到276艘,比～最多的2月份减少77艘。*In May this year, the average number of cargo ships waiting to be unloaded in the harbor every day dropped to 276, 77 less than the record number in February*.

【压床】[机] press (machine): 手扳～ *arbor press*

【压倒】overwhelm; overpower; prevail over: ～一切的任务 *an overriding task* / 以～多数通过一项决议 *pass a resolution by an overwhelming majority*

【压得住】can keep under control: ～火 *can control* (*or hold down*) *one's anger*; *can control oneself*

【压低】lower; drop: ～声音说话 *speak in a lowered voice* / ～物价 *keep the prices down*

【压电】(又作'压电现象')[物] piezoelectricity ◇ ～晶体 [物] piezocrystal; piezoelectric crystal; ～拾音器 piezoelectric pickup; ～效应 piezoelectric effect

【压顶】bear down on one; weigh heavily on one: 乌云～。*Dark clouds hung overhead*.

【压锻】[冶] press forging

【压队】bring up the rear

【压服】force (or compel) sb. to submit: 解决思想问题只能靠说服,不能～。*Ideological problems can be solved only through persuasion, not by coercion*. / ～手段 *coercive measure*

【压盖】[机] gland ◇ ～填料 gland packing

【压港】cargo or ships being held up at a harbor

【压根儿】〈方〉ever; at all: 他～就没对过。*He has never been right*.

【压花玻璃】pattern glass

【压级】arbitrarily downgrade (by government purchase departments when assessing and buying farm produce or goods from farmers): 压秤、～是不允许的。*It is forbidden to arbitrarily downgrade agricultural products or claim high water content in them*.

【压级压价】press down the grade and price

【压挤】[机] extrude: 塑料从微孔～出来形成纤维。*Plastic material is extruded through very small holes to form fibres*. ◇ ～成形 [机] extrusion moulding

【压价】force prices down; demand a lower price: ～出售 *undersell*

【压惊】help sb. get over a shock (by entertaining him, etc.)

【压井】[油] kill the well

【压境】(of enemy troops) press on to the border: 大军～。*A large enemy force is bearing down upon the border*.

【压力】❶ [物] pressure: 大气～ *atmospheric* (*or barometric*) *pressure* ❷ overwhelming force; pressure: 外界～ *outside pressure* ◇ ～锅 pressure cooker; ～机 another name for 冲床; ～计 pressure gauge; manometer

【压裂】[油] fracture: 水力～ *hydraulic fracturing* ◇ ～车 fracturing unit truck

【压路机】road roller; roller

【压迫】❶ oppress；repress：～者 *oppressor* ❷ constrict：肿瘤～神经，引起疼痛。*The tumour constricts the nerves and causes pain*.

【压气】calm sb.'s anger：说几句好话给他压～。*Say a few agreeable words to calm him down*.

【压强】［物］intensity of pressure；pressure ◇ ～计 pressure gauge

【压青】［农］green manuring；green dressing

【压热效应】［物］piezocaloric effect

【压舌板】［医］tongue depressor

【压岁钱】money given to children as a lunar New Year gift

【压缩】❶ compress：空气是可以～的气体。*Air is a compressible gas*. ❷ condense；reduce；cut down：～开支 *cut down* (*or reduce*) *expenses*；*retrench* ◇ ～饼干 hardtack；ship biscuit (or bread)；pilot biscuit (or bread)；～机 compressor；～空气 compressed air

【压台】present a theatrical performance as the last item on a programme ◇ ～戏 the last item on a theatrical programme

【压条】［农］layering

【压痛】［医］tenderness：伤口好了，可是胳臂还有～。*The cut has healed*, *but my arm is still tender*.

【压下去】subdue；suppress；stifle；muffle：应该把这些流言蜚语～。*These rumors ought to be suppressed*.

【压线】［体］line ball

【压延】［机］mangle；roll；calender：～玻璃 *rolled glass* / ～机 *calender*；*mangler* / ～金属 *rolled metal* / ～能力 *rolling capacity*

【压抑】constrain；inhibit；depress；hold back：心情～ *feel constrained* (*or oppressed*) / 这部影片气氛比较～。*The film is rather depressing*. / 胸口感到～ *feel tight in the chest*

【压韵】rhyme：这两句不～。*These two lines don't rhyme*.

【压载舱】［航海］ballast tank

【压榨】❶ extract (juice, etc.) by pressure；press；squeeze：～甘蔗 *press sugarcane* ❷ oppress and exploit；extort (or exact) money from；squeeze；bleed ◇ ～机 squeezer；mangle

【压寨夫人】mistress of the fort (a sobriquet for the wife of a brigand chief)

【压阵】❶ 同〖压队〗❷ keep a situation well under one's control

【压植】［农］layer；propagate (a plant) by layering (burying plant stem in the ground to root)：她要把这些花枝～到路边。*She is going to layer these stems along the road*.

【压纸型机】［刷］stereotype press

【压制】❶ suppress；stifle；inhibit；repress：～批评 *suppress* (*or muzzle*) *criticism* / ～不同意见 *clamp down on* (*or stifle*) *differing opinions* ❷ ［军］neutralize (enemy fire by massive bombardment, etc.)：～射击 *neutralizing* (*or neutralization*) *fire* ❸ ［机］pressing：～砖坯 *make unfired bricks by pressing* / ～玻璃 *pressed glass* / ～茶 *pressed tea* ◇ ～板 pressboard

【压铸】［冶］die-casting

呀

Ⅰ 叹 (expressing surprise) ah；oh：～，下雪了！*Oh*, *it's snowing*！Ⅱ 象 creak：门～的一声开了。*The door opened with a creak*. ——另见 ya

押

Ⅰ 动 ❶ give as security；mortgage；pawn；pledge：以手表作～ *leave one's watch as security* ❷ detain；take into custody：拘押 ❸ escort：～行李 *escort luggage* / 把小偷～到派出所去 *escort the thief to the police station* / ～下去！*Take him away*. ❹ 同〖压〗, limited to use in 押宝，押队，押韵，etc. Ⅱ 名 signature or mark in lieu of signature：画押

【押宝】a gambling game, played with dice under a bowl；stake

【押车】escort goods on a train, truck, etc.

【押赌注】stake

【押队】bring up the rear

【押汇】loan secured from a bank by an exporter with the waybill of the export as mortgage

【押汇汇票】documentary bill(draft)

【押解】send (a criminal or captive) under escort；escort：～出境 *deport under escort*

【押金】cash pledge；deposit

【押款】［经］❶ borrow money on security；raise a mortgage ❷ mortgage loan；loan on security；secured loan

【押送】❶ send (a prisoner or captive) under escort；escort ❷ escort (goods) in transportation

【押尾】sign or mark in lieu of signature at the end of a document

【押运】escort (goods) in transportation

【押韵】同〖压韵〗

【押租】rent deposit

哑

同〖呀〗——另见 yǎ

【哑哑】❶ the cries of a crow ❷ the sound of a baby learning to speak；babble

鸦

名 crow (a bird)

【鸦片】opium ◇ ～战争 the Opium War (1840-1842)

【鸦雀】crow tit (a bird) ◇ ～无声 not a crow or sparrow is heard—silence reigns；all is quiet；no birds sing

桠

名 fork (of a tree)

【桠杈】❶ fork (of a tree)；crotch ❷ crotched；forked

鸭

名 duck 母～ *duck* / 公～ *drake* / 小～ *duckling*

【鸭蛋】❶ duck's egg ❷〈口〉zero (as a score or mark)；nought；goose egg ◇ ～脸 oval face；～青 pale blue；～圆〈方〉oval

【鸭儿梨】a fine species of pear grown in Hebei

Province

【鸭绒】duck's down; eiderdown; down: ～被 *eiderdown quilt*; *down quilt*

【鸭舌帽】peaked cap

【鸭行鹅步】walk in a slow, rocking manner; waddle

【鸭掌】duck's web (a delicacy)

【鸭胗】duck's gizzard (a delicacy)

【鸭跖草】［植］dayflower (Commelina communis)

【鸭子】〈口〉duck

【鸭嘴笔】drawing pen; ruling pen

【鸭嘴兽】platypus; duckbill; duckmole

yá

牙 名 ❶ tooth: 这颗～疼。*This tooth hurts*. / 孩子长～了。*The baby is teething*. ❷ tooth-like thing: 轮～ *cog* ❸ ivory: ～筷 *ivory chopsticks* / ～章 *ivory seal* ❹〈旧〉middleman; broker

【牙本质】［生理］dentine

【牙碜】❶ (of food) gritty ❷ (of language) coarse; jarring

【牙齿】tooth

【牙床】❶［生理］gum ❷ a richly carved ivory-inlaid bed

【牙雕】ivory carving

【牙粉】tooth powder

【牙缝】space between the teeth: 剔～ *pick one's teeth*

【牙缸】a mug for mouth-rinsing or tooth-cleaning; tooth mug

【牙膏】toothpaste

【牙根】gum: 咬紧～不说 *clench one's teeth and refuse to say anything*

【牙垢】tartar; dental calculus

【牙骨质】［生理］cementum; cement

【牙关】mandibular joint: ～紧闭 *lockjaw*

【牙冠】［生理］crown (of a tooth)

【牙花】(又作'牙花子')〈方〉❶ tartar; dental calculus ❷ gum

【牙慧】见〖拾人牙慧〗

【牙祭】an unusually good meal (with plenty of meat)

【牙具】tooth-cleaners (e. g. toothbrush, toothpaste, etc.)

【牙科】(department of) dentistry: ～诊疗所 *dental clinic* ◇ ～学 dentistry; ～医生 dentist; dental surgeon

【牙口】❶ the age of a draught animal as shown by the number of its teeth: 看一看～ *look at a draught animal's teeth to determine its age* ❷ the condition of an old person's teeth: 您这么大年纪,～可不错呀! *You've certainly got good teeth for your age*.

【牙买加】Jamaica ◇ ～人 Jamaican

【牙签】toothpick

【牙刷】toothbrush

【牙髓】［生理］dental pulp ◇ ～炎 pulpitis

【牙痛】toothache

【牙线】dental floss

【牙牙】the sound of baby talk; babble ◇ ～学语 babble one's first sounds; learn to speak

【牙医】〈略〉见〖牙科医生〗

【牙龈】［生理］gum; gingiva ◇ ～炎 gingivitis

【牙釉质】［生理］enamel

【牙质】❶ made of ivory: ～的刀把 *an ivory knife handle* ❷ 同〖牙本质〗

【牙周病】periodontosis

【牙周炎】periodontitis

芽 名 bud; sprout; shoot

【芽孢】［生］gemma (of a fungus)

【芽变】［植］bud mutation

【芽豆】sprouted broad bean

【芽接】bud grafting; budding

【芽眼】eye (the bud of a potato)

蚜 名 aphid; aphis; plant louse

【蚜虫】aphid; aphis; plant louse: 苹果～ *apple aphid* / 烟～ *tobacco aphid*

涯 名 ❶ water margin ❷ margin; limit: 天～海角

崖 名 ❶ precipice; cliff ❷ limit; bound; boundary: 崖略

【崖壁】precipice; cliff

【崖略】〈书〉outline; general idea

睚 名〈书〉the corner of the eye

【睚眦】〈书〉❶ an angry stare ❷ a small grievance: ～之怨 *a trifling (or trivial) grievance*

【睚眦必报】seek revenge just for an angry look

衙 名 yamen

【衙门】yamen, government office in feudal China: ～八字开,有理无钱莫进来。*The yamen gate is open wide; with right but no money, don't go inside*.

yǎ

哑 形 ❶ mute; dumb: 他又聋又～。*He's deaf and dumb*. ❷ hoarse; husky: ～嗓子 *a husky (or hoarse) voice* / 嗓子喊～了 *shout oneself hoarse* ❸ (of a shell, bomb, etc.) fail to explode: ～弹 *dud* ——另见 yā

【哑巴】❶ a dumb person; mute ❷ be dumb; keep mum: 你今儿个怎么～啦? *Why are you so silent today*? or *Have you lost your tongue*? ◇ ～亏 a grievance that one has to keep to oneself

【哑巴吃黄连,有苦说不出】a dumb person tasting bitter herbs—be unable to express one's discomfort; be forced to suffer in silence

【哑场】an awkward silence at a meeting

【哑剧】dumb show; pantomime: ～演员 *pantomimist*

【哑口无言】be left without an argument; be reduced to silence；be rendered speechless：他论辩有力，把对方说得～。*His forceful arguments silenced his opponent*.

【哑铃】［体］dumbbell

【哑谜】a puzzling remark；enigma；riddle：别给我们打～啦！*Don't keep us guessing*.

【哑然】❶〈书〉soundless；silent：～无声。*Silence reigns*. ❷〈书〉the sound of laughing：～失笑 *be unable to stifle a laugh*；*can't help laughing*

【哑语】同〖手语〗

雅 Ⅰ 形 ❶〈书〉standard；proper；correct：雅正 ❷ refined；elegant：你这房间的布置～得很。*Your room is furnished in excellent taste*. ❸〈尊〉your：雅意 Ⅱ 名 ❶ one of the three sections of The Book of Songs（《诗经》），consisting of festal songs sung at court during banquets and entertainment of guests ❷〈书〉acquaintance；friendship：无一日之～ *not have the pleasure of knowing sb*. Ⅲ 副 ❶ usually；often ❷ extremely；very much：～以为美 *really consider it beautiful*

【雅淡】simple and tasteful；quietly elegant：～梳妆 *be simply but tastefully dressed*

【雅尔塔】Yalta

【雅观】（usu. used in the negative）refined（in manner，etc.）；in good taste：很不～ *most unseemly*；*rather unsightly*

【雅号】❶〈尊〉your elegant name ❷〈诙〉nickname：我倒不晓得他还有这么一个～呢。*I never knew he had such a nickname*.

【雅静】❶ tastefully quiet：步入园中，使人顿感清幽～。*In the garden*，*there is an atmosphere of refined beauty and elegant quietness*. ❷ gentle and quiet：看她这样～，就是大家出身。*From her quiet poise*，*one can tell she is from an eminent family*.

【雅量】❶ magnanimity；generosity ❷ great capacity for liquor

【雅鲁藏布江】the Yarlung Zangbo（Yalu Tsangpo）River

【雅皮士】yuppie；yuppy（young，upwardly-mobile professional）

【雅趣】refined（or cultivated）tastes

【雅士】a refined scholar：文人～ *men of letters and refined scholars*

【雅俗共赏】（of a work of art or literature）appeal to all；suit both refined and popular tastes

【雅兴】an aesthetic mood：无此～ *not be in such a poetic mood*；*be in no mood for such things*

【雅意】❶ kindly thoughts ❷〈尊〉your kindness；your kind offer

【雅乐】（in ancient times）ceremonial music；court music

【雅正】❶〈书〉standard；correct ❷〈书〉upright；righteous ❸〈套〉（said when presenting sb. with a specimen of one's calligraphy，a copy of one's book，etc.）would you kindly point out my inadequacies

【雅致】refined；tasteful：陈设～ *tastefully furnished*

【雅座】private room（in a restaurant，etc.）

yà

轧 Ⅰ 动 ❶ roll；run over：把路面～平 *roll a road surface* / 被车～伤 *get run over and injured by a car* / ～碎 *crush to pieces* / ～棉花 *gin cotton* ❷ oust；squeeze out；push out：倾轧 Ⅱ 象 the sound of a machine running：缝纫机～～地响着。*The sewing machine was clicking away*. ——另见 gá；zhá

【轧板机】［冶］mangle

【轧场】❶ thresh grain on a threshing ground with a stone roller ❷ level a threshing floor with a stone roller

【轧光】［纺］calendering ◇ ～机［纺］calender

【轧花】［纺］cotton ginning：～厂 *cotton ginning mill* ◇ ～机 cotton gin

亚 Ⅰ 形 inferior；second：不～于人 *second to none*；*not inferior to anyone* Ⅱ 名 同〖亚洲〗

【亚当】Adam（the first man according to the Bible）

【亚得里亚海】the Adriatic（Sea）

【亚非经济合作组织】Afro-Asian Organization for Economic Co-operation

【亚砜】［化］sulphoxide

【亚急性】［医］subacute：～病 *subacute disease*

【亚军】second place（in a sports contest）；runner-up：他在百米赛跑中得了～。*He came second in the 100-metre dash*. or *He was runner-up in the 100-metre dash*.

【亚硫酸】［化］sulphurous acid

【亚麻】［植］flax（linum usitatissimum）◇ ～布 linen（cloth）；～精纺机［纺］flax spinning frame；～籽 linseed；flaxseed；～籽油 linseed oil

【亚马孙河】the Amazon（River）

【亚美尼亚】Armenia ◇ ～人 Armenian；～语 Armenian（language）

【亚平宁山脉】the Apennines

【亚热带】subtropical zone；subtropics；semitropics ◇ ～气候 subtropical climate

【亚速尔群岛】the Azores

【亚太】Asia-Pacific：～地区 *the Asian-Pacific region*

【亚铁】［化］ferrous：氯化～ *ferrous chloride*

【亚文化群】subculture

【亚细亚】Asia

【亚硝酸】［化］nitrous acid

【亚音速】［物］subsonic speed：～飞机 *subsonic aircraft*

【亚油酸】［化］linoleic acid

【亚运村】Asia Games Village（now a housing neighbourhood in Beijing）

【亚运会】（〈略〉全称为'亚洲运动会'）the Asian Games：第十一届～ *the 11th Asian Games*

【亚种】[生] subspecies
【亚洲】Asia ◇ ～四小龙 four little dragons of Asia—Taiwan, Hong Kong, the Republic of Korea and Singapore
【亚洲卫星】Asiasat

压（构词成分）见下 ——另见 yā
【压板】seesaw; teeterboard; teeter-totter
【压根儿】〈口〉(usu. used in the negative) from the start; in the first place; altogether: ～就不知道 *have had no idea from the start; not know anything about it*

砑 动 press and smooth (leather, cloth, paper, etc.); calender; mangle
【砑光】[机] calendering; mangling
【砑光机】[机] calender; mangle

氩 名 [化] argon (Ar)

揠 动〈书〉pull up; tug upward
【揠苗助长】try to help shoots grow by pulling them up—spoil things by excessive enthusiasm

ya

呀 助 (used in place of 啊 when the preceding word ends in sound a, e, i, o, or ü): 她是谁～? *Who is she?* / 快来～。*Come here, quick!* ——另见 yā

yān

咽 名 [生理] pharynx ——另见 yàn
【咽鼓管】[生理] Eustachian tube
【咽喉】❶ [生理] pharynx and larynx; throat ❷ strategic (or vital) passage; key junction (or link): 直布罗陀海峡是地中海通向大西洋的～。*The Straits of Gibraltar are the strategic passage between the Mediterranean and the Atlantic.* ◇ ～炎 sore throat; ～要地 strategic (or vital) passage; key junction (or link)
【咽峡炎】angina
【咽炎】pharyngitis

恹（构词成分）见下
【恹恹】〈书〉weak and weary through illness; rundown: ～欲睡 *feel weak and sleepy*

烟 Ⅰ 名 ❶ smoke ❷ mist; vapour: 烟雾 ❸ cigarette or pipe tobacco: 抽支～ *have a cigarette; have a smoke* / 一袋～的功夫 *time enough to smoke a pipeful of tobacco* ❹ opium: 烟土 ❺ the tobacco plant: 烟叶 Ⅱ 动 (of eyes) be irritated by smoke: 谁在这里生火啊? 都～得睁不开眼了。*Who's lighting the stove here? I can't even open my eyes for the smoke.*
【烟波】mist-covered waters ◇ ～浩渺 a vast expanse of misty, rolling waters
【烟草】the tobacco plant; tobacco: ～种植园 *tobacco plantation* ◇ ～专卖局 tobacco monopoly bureau
【烟尘】smoke and dust ◇ ～密度测定器 smokescope
【烟囱】chimney; funnel; stovepipe
【烟袋】a long-stemmed pipe or a water pipe ◇ ～杆儿 the stem of a pipe; ～荷包 tobacco pouch; ～嘴儿 the mouth-piece of a long-stemmed pipe
【烟袋锅】(又作'烟袋锅子') ❶ the bowl of a long-stemmed pipe; pipe bowl ❷ a long-stemmed pipe
【烟道】flue: ～尘 *flue dust* / ～气 *flue gas*
【烟蒂】cigarette end (or stub, butt, stump)
【烟斗】(tobacco) pipe ◇ ～架 pipe rack; ～丝 pipe tobacco
【烟缸】同〖烟灰缸〗
【烟鬼】❶ opium addict ❷ a heavy smoker
【烟锅】pipe bowl
【烟海】〈书〉a sea of fog or mist—vast and voluminous: *浩如烟海*
【烟盒】cigarette case
【烟花】❶〈书〉a lovely spring scene ❷〈旧〉prostitution: ～女 *prostitute* / ～巷 *a red-light district* ❸ fireworks ◇ ～炮竹 fireworks
【烟灰】tobacco or cigarette ash ◇ ～缸 ashtray
【烟火】❶ smoke and fire: 动～ *light a fire and cook* / 严禁～。*Smoking or lighting fires strictly forbidden.* ❷ cooked food: 不食人间～ *do not eat cooked food; live the life of an immortal* ❸ fireworks: 放～ *let off fireworks; put on a display of fireworks* ◇ ～探测器 smoke detector
【烟火食】cooked food
【烟碱】[化] nicotine: ～中毒 *nicotinism*
【烟晶】[地质] smoky quartz; smoky topaz
【烟具】smoking paraphernalia; smoking set
【烟卷儿】〈口〉cigarette
【烟煤】bituminous coal; soft coal
【烟民】〈诙〉smokers; tobacco users: 中国的"～"总数在全世界遥遥领先。*The total number of smokers in China is by far the largest in the world.*
【烟幕】smoke screen ◇ ～弹 smoke shell; smoke bomb; smoke screen
【烟屁股】〈口〉cigarette end (or stub, butt, stump)
【烟枪】opium pipe
【烟圈】smoke ring
【烟色】dark brown
【烟丝】cut tobacco; pipe tobacco
【烟酸】[化] nicotinic acid; niacin ◇ ～缺乏症 [医] pellagra
【烟筒】chimney; funnel; stovepipe
【烟头】cigarette end (or stub, butt, stump)
【烟突】〈书〉chimney; funnel; stovepipe
【烟土】crude opium
【烟雾】❶ smoke, mist, or vapour; a mixture of smoke and vapour: 厨房里～腾腾。*The kitchen is filled with steam and smoke.* ❷ smog: ～笼罩着那座城市。*The city was shrouded in a thick*

smog. ◇ ～弥漫 be full of smoke; be enveloped in mist

【烟消云散】vanish like smoke and disperse like clouds—completely vanish: 她方才那一阵兴奋又～了。*Her high spirits of a moment ago suddenly passed away like a breath of wind*. / 他紧张的心情,被我这一番笑谈,一下子冲得～了。*At my friendly jesting, his tension melted away*.

【烟叶】tobacco leaf; leaf tobacco

【烟瘾】a craving for opium; a craving for tobacco: 他～可大了。*He's a heavy smoker*. or *He smokes like a chimney*. / 他～发了。*He's dying for a smoke*.

【烟油子】tobacco tar; cigarette tar

【烟雨】misty rain

【烟云】smoke, mists and clouds

【烟柱】a column of smoke

【烟嘴儿】cigarette holder

殷

形〈书〉blackish red; dark red ——另见 yīn

【殷红】blackish red; dark red: ～的血迹 *blackish red bloodstains* / ～的鸡冠花 *the dark red cockscombs*

胭

(构词成分)见下

【胭脂】rouge ◇ ～红 carmine; famille rose

淹

Ⅰ 动 ❶ flood; submerge; inundate: 暴雨过后,整个村子的地都被水～了。*The heavy rains flooded all the fields of the village*. ❷ (of sweat, etc.) irritate the skin: 我胳肢窝被汗～得难受。*My armpits are tingling from sweat*. ❸〈书〉delay: 淹留 Ⅱ 形〈书〉wide: 淹博

【淹博】〈书〉wide; broad: 学识～ *have a wide (or broad) knowledge; be well-read; be learned*

【淹灌】[农] basin irrigation

【淹蹇】❶〈书〉be frustrated: 宦途～。*An official career is full of frustrations*. ❷ delay; hold up: 他老不回来,不知道什么事情～住了。*He isn't back yet. I wonder what's holding him up*.

【淹留】〈书〉stay for a long period

【淹埋】(of mud, sand, etc.) flow or blow over and cover completely: 一段铁路被淤泥～了。*A section of the railway was buried in mud*.

【淹没】submerge; flood; inundate; drown: 他的讲话被欢呼声～了。*His speech was drowned out by cheers*.

【淹死】be drowned

阉

动 castrate or spay: ～鸡 *capon* / ～牛 *bullock; steer* / ～羊 *wether* / ～猪 *barrow; hog*

【阉割】❶ castrate or spay ❷ deprive a theory, etc. of its essence; emasculate

【阉人】❶ a castrated person ❷ eunuch

湮

动〈书〉❶ fall into oblivion; bury in oblivion: 湮没 ❷ clog up; stop

【湮灭】bury in oblivion; annihilate

【湮没】❶ fall into oblivion; be neglected; be forgotten ❷ [物] annihilation: ～光子 *annihilation photon* ◇ ～无闻 sink into oblivion; fall into obscurity

腌

动 ❶ preserve in salt, sugar, etc.; pickle; salt: 剩下的肉可以～一下以后吃。*The rest of the meat can be salted down for later use*. / ～菜 *pickled vegetables; pickles* / ～鱼 *salted fish* / ～肉 *salted meat; bacon* ❷ marinate: 肉片要用黄酒、醋、酱油～过再炸。*Marinate the sliced pork in rice wine, vinegar and soy sauce before frying it*.

【腌制】make by pickling or salting: ～火腿 *make ham* / ～酱菜 *make pickles*

【腌渍】preserve in brine, vinegar, etc.; pickle: ～的黄瓜很爽口。*Pickled cucumbers are crisp and refreshing*. / 跑了一天的路,汗～得身上好难受。*After walking for a whole day, I was all sticky with sweat*.

嫣

形〈书〉handsome; beautiful

【嫣红】bright red

【嫣然】〈书〉beautiful; sweet: ～一笑 *give a charming (or winsome) smile*

yán

延

动 ❶ prolong; extend; protract: 蔓延 ❷ postpone; delay: 顺延 ❸〈书〉engage (a teacher, adviser, etc.); send for: ～医 *send for a doctor*

【延挨】delay; stall: ～时日 *play for time; stall (for time)*

【延爆炸弹】delayed action bomb

【延长】lengthen; prolong; extend: 会议～了三天。*The conference was prolonged for three more days*. / ～合同期限 *extend the contract period* ◇ ～号 [音] pause; ～时间 extra period; ～线 extension (or extended) line

【延迟】delay; defer; postpone: 展览会开幕的日期～了。*The opening of the exhibition has been postponed*. ◇ ～电路 [无] delay circuit; ～失真 [无] delay distortion

【延传】pass on; last; continue: 清河给沿岸人民带来的灾难世代～。*The Qinghe River has brought generations of disasters to the people living along its banks*.

【延宕】procrastinate; delay; keep putting off

【延发】[军] delayed action ◇ ～引信 delayed-action fuse; delay fuse

【延搁】delay; procrastinate: 这事已经～多天。*This matter has been delayed for quite a few days*.

【延后】postpone; put off; defer: ～上市 *delay putting on the market*

【延胡索】❶ [植] yanhusuo (Corydalis remota or Corydalis ambigua) ❷ [中]tuber of yanhusuo

【延缓】delay; postpone; put off: ～工作进度 *retard the progress of work*

【延揽】〈书〉enlist the services of：～人才 *enlist the services of able people*
【延年益寿】(of tonics, etc.) prolong life；promise longevity
【延聘】〈书〉engage；invite (sb. to do sth. in a particular capacity)：～某人为法律顾问 *engage sb. as one's legal adviser*
【延期】postpone；defer；put off：～付款 *defer payment* / 比赛因雨～。*The game was put off on account of rain.* / ～审理 *postponement of the hearing* ◇ ～偿付权［法］moratorium；～交货［经］back order；～交货通知单［经］back order memo
【延请】invite (sb. to do a particular job)；engage
【延伸】extend；stretch；elongate：铁路一直～到海边。*The railway line stretches right to the coast.* ◇ ～火力［军］creeping fire；lift fire；～率［冶］percentage elongation
【延绳钓】longline fishing；long-lining
【延时】［电子］delay
【延时摄影】time-lapse photography
【延寿】lengthen (or prolong) one's life
【延髓】［生理］medulla oblongata
【延误】incur loss through delay：～时机 *miss an opportunity because of a delay* / ～时日 *lose time*
【延性】［物］ductility
【延续】continue；go on；last：旱象～了半年之久。*The drought lasted for as long as six months.* ◇ ～性 continuity
【延音】［音］tenuto

言 Ⅰ名 ❶ speech；word：言语 / 有言在先 ❷ character；word：全书近二十万～。*It is a book of nearly 200,000 words.* Ⅱ动 say；talk；speak：～明 *state explicitly*；*clearly stipulate*
【言必信，行必果】insist on keeping one's word and seeing one's actions through to the end；always stand by one's word, and undertake nothing that one does not bring to achievement
【言必有中】when one speaks, one speaks to the point；whenever one says something one hits the mark
【言不及义】never say anything serious；talk frivolously
【言不尽意】I should like to say more (but I must bring my letter to a close)
【言不由衷】speak insincerely；speak with one's tongue in one's cheek
【言差语错】mistakes or slips in speaking：偶尔有个～，谁也不会责怪。*Nobody would blame you for an occasional slip of the tongue.*
【言传】explain in words：只可意会，不可言传 ◇ ～身教 teach by personal example as well as verbal instruction；teach by precept and example
【言辞】(又作'言词') one's words；what one says：～不逊 *make impertinent remarks*；*speak insolently*
【言定】decide；agree：他们～过了春节就动手。*They decided to start work immediately after the Spring Festival.*
【言多语失】(又作'言多必失') he who talks too much is prone to error
【言而无信】fail to keep faith；go back on one's word
【言而有信】be true to one's word；be as good as one's word
【言归于好】make it up (with sb.)；become reconciled
【言归正传】to come back to our story；to return to the subject
【言过其实】exaggerate；overstate
【言和】make peace；become reconciled；bury the hatchet：握手～ *shake hands and make it up*
【言简意赅】concise and comprehensive；compendious
【言教】teach by word of mouth；give verbal directions：～不如身教。*Example is better than precept.*
【言近旨远】simple words but deep meaning；simple in language but profound in meaning
【言路】channels through which criticisms and suggestions may be communicated to the leadership：堵塞～ *stifle criticisms and suggestions*
【言论】opinion on public affairs；expression of one's political views；speech：我们看一个人，不仅要听他的～，还要看他的行动。*We must judge a person not only by his words, but also by his deeds.* / ～自由 *freedom of speech*
【言情片】film with a romantic story；sentimental movie
【言情小说】a romantic or sentimental novel
【言人人殊】different people, different versions；each person tells a different story
【言三语四】make irresponsible remarks
【言声儿】utter a sound or a word：他不言一声儿。*He didn't say a word.*
【言说】put into words；say：一种难以～的心情 *an indescribable mood*
【言谈】the way one speaks or what he says：～举止 *speech and deportment*
【言听计从】listen to sb.'s words and follow his counsels；always follow sb.'s advice；act upon whatever sb. says；have implicit faith in sb.
【言外之意】what is actually meant；the real meaning；implication：体会其～ *read between the lines*
【言为心声】words are the voice of the mind；speech is the picture of the mind；what the heart thinks the tongue speaks：人的心理真是奇妙。～，一点不假。*A person's psychology is a subtle thing. How true it is that "words are echoes of the heart".*
【言行】words and deeds；statements and actions ◇ ～不一 the deeds do not match the words；one's actions do not square with one's promises；～录 records of the words and deeds (of a famous person)；～一致 the deeds match (or square with) the words；one's actions are in keeping with

one's promises; one's deeds are consistent with one's words; be as good as one's word

【言犹在耳】the words still ring (or reverberate) in one's ears

【言有尽而意无穷】the words come to an end, but the meaning is inexhaustible

【言语】❶ spoken language; speech: ～和文字 *spoken and written language* ❷〈方〉speak; talk; answer: 他这个人不爱～。*He is a man of few words*.

【言责】❶ a subject's responsibility of offering advice to the ruler ❷ responsibility for what one says

【言者无心,听者有意】a casual remark sounds significant to a suspicious listener; a careless word may reveal much to an attentive listener

【言者无罪,闻者足戒】blame not the speaker but be warned by his words; blame not the critic, heed what he says

【言者谆谆,听者藐藐】the speaker is earnest but the hearer is casual; the words are earnest but they fall on deaf ears

【言之成理】speak in a rational and convincing way; sound reasonable: 人家～,他无法驳斥。*He didn't see how he could turn down the suggestion which sounded plausible enough*.

【言之无物】(of speech or writing) be devoid of substance; be mere verbiage; be empty talk

【言之有据】speak on good grounds (or on good authority)

【言之凿凿】say sth. with certainty

【言重】overstate; exaggerate

严

Ⅰ形 ❶ tight: 把窗户关～了。*Shut the window tight*. / 他的嘴很～。*He is tight-mouthed*. ❷ strict; severe; stern; rigorous: 纪律要～。*Be strict in discipline*. / 高标准,～要求 *high standards and strict demands* / ～加批驳 *sternly refute* / ～是爱,松是害。*Strictness helps, indulgence spoils*. Ⅱ名〈书〉father

【严办】deal with severely; punish with severity

【严惩】punish severely: ～入侵之敌 *deal the invaders a crushing blow* ◇ ～不贷 punish without leniency; punish with severity

【严词】strong terms; stern words: ～谴责 *denounce in strong terms; sternly condemn* / ～拒绝 *give a stern rebuff; sternly refuse*

【严打】(〈略〉全称为'严厉打击刑事犯罪活动') crackdown on crime: 社会治安情况比"～"以前有明显好转。*Social order has greatly improved since the "crackdown on crime"*.

【严冬】a severe winter; a hard winter

【严防】be strictly on guard against; take strict precautions against

【严父】stern father; father ◇ ～慈母 stern father and compassionate mother

【严格】❶ strict; rigorous; rigid; stringent: 队长对我们要求很～。*Our team leader is very strict with us*. / ～说来 *strictly speaking* ❷ rigorously enforce: ～规章制度 *rigorously enforce rules and regulations*

【严固】(of defences) strong: 防守～。*The defences are strong*.

【严寒】severe cold; bitter cold

【严紧】tight; close: 窗户糊得挺～。*The windows are tightly sealed*.

【严谨】❶ rigorous; strict; careful and precise: ～的科学态度 *a rigorous scientific approach* ❷ compact; well-knit: 文章结构～。*The essay is well-knit*.

【严禁】strictly forbid (or prohibit): ～吸烟。*Smoking is strictly prohibited*.

【严峻】stern; severe; rigorous; grim: ～的考验 *a severe test; a rigorous test*

【严酷】❶ harsh; bitter; grim: ～的现实 *harsh reality* / ～的教训 *a bitter lesson* ❷ cruel; ruthless: ～的剥削 *cruel exploitation*

【严冷】❶ cold and stern: 板着～的面孔 *put on a cold, stern expression* ❷ bitter cold: ～的天气 *bitter cold weather*

【严厉】stern; severe: ～的措施 *severe (or stringent) measures* / ～声讨 *sternly (or strongly) denounce*

【严令】give strict orders: ～缉拿归案 *give strict orders to bring the criminal to justice*

【严密】tight; close: ～封锁 *impose a tight blockade* / ～监视 *put under close surveillance; keep close watch over* / ～防范 *take strict precautions against* ◇ ～拦网[体] wall blocking (in volleyball)

【严明】❶ strict and impartial: 赏罚～ *be strict and impartial in meting out rewards and punishments; give rewards and punishments impartially* / 纪律～ *observe strict discipline; be highly disciplined* ❷ strictly enforce (discipline): ～军纪 *enforce and maintain strict military discipline*

【严声】(speak) in a stern voice: ～喝问 *snap out one's questions* ◇ ～厉色 stern in voice and countenance

【严师】a strict teacher ◇ ～诤友 a strict teacher and a friend who will give unpalatable advice

【严实】〈方〉❶ tight; close: 她的嘴～着呢! *She has tight lips*. / 她那嘴可不～。*She has a loose tongue*. ❷ (hide) safely: 游击队把粮食藏～了才转移。*The guerrillas carefully hid their food grain before they moved on*.

【严守】❶ observe strictly: ～纪律 *observe strict discipline* / ～合同 *abide by a contract faithfully* ❷ guard closely: ～国家机密 *strictly guard state secrets*

【严霜】a severe (or heavy) frost: 一场～,把白菜秧儿都给冻坏了。*A severe frost killed the cabbage sprouts*.

【严丝合缝】fit together perfectly; join tightly; dovetail

【严肃】❶ serious; solemn; earnest: ～认真 *serious and conscientious* / ～地指出 *point out in all earnestness* ❷ strictly enforce：～党纪 *enforce Party discipline* / ～法制 *maintain the legal system*

【严刑】cruel torture：～逼供 *extort a confession by cruel torture* ◇ ～拷打 subject sb. to severe torture；cruelly beat up

【严以律己，宽以待人】(又作'严于责己，宽以待人') be strict with oneself and lenient towards others

【严阵以待】be in full battle array；stand in combat readiness

【严整】(usu. of troops) be in neat formation：军容～。*The troops are in gallant array*.

【严正】solemn and just；serious and principled；stern：～立场 *solemn and just stand* / 提出～抗议 *lodge a stern protest*

【严重】serious；grave；critical：～后果 *serious (or grave) consequences* / ～关头 *critical juncture* / 病情～ *be seriously ill* / 感到～不安 *feel grave concern*；*feel deeply disturbed*

芫

(构词成分)见下——另见 yuán

【芫荽】[植] coriander

沿

Ⅰ 介 along：～街栽着一排排法国梧桐。*Along the streets grow lines of plane trees*. / ～着海岸航行 *sail along the coast* Ⅱ 动 ❶ follow (a tradition, pattern, etc.)：世代相～ *be handed down from generation to generation* ❷ trim (with tape, ribbon, etc.)：～鞋口 *trim the top of a shoe* Ⅲ 名 edge；border：缸～儿 *the brim of a jar* / 沟～儿 *the edge of a ditch* / 河～ *riverside*

【沿岸】along the bank or coast；littoral or riparian：长江～ *along (the banks of) the Changjiang River* / 地中海～国家 *the littoral countries of the Mediterranean*

【沿边儿】trim (with tape, ribbon, etc.)：用白缎带在衣领上沿一道边儿 *trim the collar of a garment with white ribbon*

【沿革】the course of change and development；evolution：社会风俗的～ *the evolution of social customs*

【沿海】along the coast；coastal；littoral：～城市 *coastal cities* / ～岛屿 *offshore islands* / ～地区 *coastal areas*；*coastland* / ～国家 *coastal states (or countries)*；*littoral states (or countries)*

【沿江】along the river (esp. the Changjiang)；riparian；riverine

【沿阶草】[植] dwarf lilyturf

【沿例】follow the usual practice；follow the established precedents

【沿路】along the road；on the way：～林木成行，郁郁葱葱。*Along the road stand rows of green and luxuriant trees*.

【沿途】on the way；throughout a journey：这艘客轮～停靠五个码头。*This liner calls at five ports on her voyage*. ◇ ～贸易 way-port trade

【沿袭】carry on as before；follow：～陈规 *follow convention* / ～成说 *adopt an accepted theory*

【沿线】along the line (i. e. a railway, highway, air or shipping line)：铁路～的村镇 *villages and towns along the railway line*

【沿用】continue to use (an old method, etc.)：～原来的名称 *continue to use the old name*

炎

Ⅰ 形 scorching；burning hot：炎夏 Ⅱ 名 inflammation：发炎

【炎帝】Yan Di, also known as Shen Nong (神农), a legendary ruler ——另见〖炎黄〗；〖炎黄子孙〗

【炎旱】hot and dry：～的夏季 *a hot and dry summer*；*a scorching, droughty summer*

【炎黄】Yan Di and Huang Di (or the Yellow Emperor), two legendary rulers of remote antiquity

【炎黄子孙】descendants of Yan Di and Huang Di—the Chinese people

【炎凉】见〖世态炎凉〗

【炎热】(of weather) scorching；blazing；burning hot：冒着～ *braving the sweltering heat*

【炎暑】hot summer；sweltering summer days；dog days

【炎威】fierce heat

【炎夏】a torrid (or scorching) summer

【炎炎】scorching；sweltering；blazing：赤日～ *the scorching sun*

【炎症】inflammation

岩

名 ❶ rock：岩石 ❷ cliff；crag：七星～ *the Seven-Star Cliff (in Guilin)*

【岩岸】rocky coast

【岩壁】crag；cliff

【岩层】rock stratum；rock formation

【岩洞】grotto

【岩鸽】rock dove；rock pigeon

【岩画】rock painting

【岩浆】[地质] magma：～分异作用 *magmatic differentiation* / ～作用 *magmatism* ◇ ～岩 magmatic rock

【岩羚羊】[动] chamois (Rupicapra rupicapra Linnaeus)

【岩溶】[地质] karst ◇ ～地貌 karst features；karst topography

【岩石】rock ◇ ～力学 rock mechanics；～圈 lithosphere；～学 petrology

【岩相】[地质] lithofacies：～图 *lithofacies map*

【岩心】[地质] (drill) core：～回收 *core recovery* / ～样品 *core sample* ◇ ～筒 core barrel

【岩性学】[地质] lithology

【岩穴】cavern；cave：～之士 *a hermit*

【岩崖】cliff

【岩盐】rock salt；halite

【岩羊】[动] blue sheep；bharal (Pseudois nayaur Hodgson)

【岩样】❶ [地质] rock specimen ❷ [矿] core sample

研

动 ❶ grind；pestle：～成粉末 *grind into fine powder*；*pulverize by grinding* / ～墨 *rub an ink stick on an inkslab (to prepare ink for brush writing)* ❷ study：研读

【研钵】mortar (a vessel)

【研杵】pestle; grinder; pulverizer
【研订】develop: ～方案 *formulate a plan*; *develop a program*
【研读】study carefully: ～电影剧本 *make a careful study of the scenario*
【研究】❶ study; research: ～自然规律 *study the laws of nature* / 科学～ *scientific research* / 癌症病源～ *researches into the causes of cancer* ❷ consider; discuss; deliberate: 这些问题正在～。*These matters are under review* (*or consideration*). ◇ ～工作者 research worker; ～开发 research and development; R&D; ～密集型 research-intensive; ～生 postgraduate (student); graduate student; ～生院 graduate school; ～室 research room; ～所 research institute; ～员 research fellow; full professor (at research institutes); ～院 research institute; graduate school
【研磨】❶ grind; pestle ❷ abrade; polish: ～粉 *abrasive powder* / ～料 *abrasive* / ～器 *abrader*
【研拟】discuss and formulate; develop: ～新政策 *formulate a new policy*
【研评】examine, appraise: ～会 *appraisal meeting*
【研讨】deliberate; study and discuss ◇ ～会 symposium; seminar; ～小组 research group
【研习】study; research
【研修】do research work ◇ ～生 researcher
【研制】❶ develop (drugs, weapons, etc.): ～新式武器 *develop new weapons* ❷ [中] prepare medicinal powder by pestling

盐 名 ❶ table salt; salt: 加点儿～ *add a little salt* ❷ [化] salt (a product formed by the neutralization of an acid by a base): 酸式～ *acid salt* / 碱式～ *basic salt*
【盐巴】〈方〉table salt; salt
【盐层】salt deposit; salt bed
【盐场】saltern; saltworks
【盐池】salt pond
【盐分】salt content
【盐肤木】[植] Chinese sumac ◇ ～根皮 [中] the root bark of Chinese sumac
【盐罐】saltcellar; saltshaker
【盐湖】salt lake
【盐花】a little salt; a pinch of salt: 汤里搁点儿～儿。*Put just a little salt in the soup*.
【盐碱地】saline or alkaline land
【盐碱化】salinization or alkalinization (of soil); salinization of alkaline soil; alkalinization of saline soil
【盐碱土】saline or alkaline soil; salinized alkaline soil; alkalinized saline soil; saline-alkaline soil
【盐井】salt well; brine pit
【盐矿】salt mine
【盐卤】bittern
【盐瓶】saltcellar; saltshaker
【盐汽水】salt soda water
【盐泉】brine (or salt) spring
【盐霜】salt efflorescence
【盐水】salt solution; brine ◇ ～输液 [医] saline infusion; ～选种 seed sorting by salt water
【盐水鸭】salted duck
【盐酸】[化] hydrochloric acid
【盐滩】a beach for making sea salt
【盐田】salt pan; salina
【盐土】solonchak; saline soil
【盐析】[化] saltout: ～效应 *salting-out effect*
【盐业】salt industry
【盐液】saline solution ◇ ～比重计 (又作'盐重计') salinometer; salimeter
【盐渍土】salinized soil

阎 名〈书〉the entrance to a lane
【阎罗】[宗](佛教) Yama, King of Hell
【阎王】❶ Yama, King of Hell: 活～ *a living King of Hell*; *a devil incarnate* / 见～ *die* ❷ an extremely cruel and violent person ◇ ～殿 the Palace of the King of Hell; ～账 (又作'阎王债')〈口〉a usurious loan; shark's loan

筵 名 ❶〈书〉formerly, a bamboo mat spread on the floor for people to sit ❷ feast; banquet: 喜～ *a wedding feast*
【筵席】❶ seats arranged at a banquet ❷ feast; banquet

颜 名 ❶ face; countenance: 容颜 ❷ prestige; face: 无～见人 *not have the face to appear in public* ❸ colour: 颜料
【颜料】pigment; colouring: 天然～ *natural pigments* / 人造～ *artificial pigments*
【颜面】❶ face: ～神经 *facial nerve* ❷ prestige; face: 顾全～ *save face* / ～扫地 *lose face altogether*; *be thoroughly discredited*
【颜色】❶ colour: 你最喜欢什么～? *What colour do you like most*? ❷ countenance; facial expression: 给他一点～看看 *make it hot for him*; *teach him a lesson* ❸〈口〉pigment or dyestuff
【颜体】the Yan style (a calligraphic style created by Yan Zhenqing 颜真卿 of the Tang Dynasty)

檐 名 ❶ eaves: ～下 *under the eaves* ❷ ledge; brim: 帽檐
【檐沟】[建] eaves gutter
【檐子】〈口〉eaves

yǎn

奄 〈书〉Ⅰ 动 cover; include Ⅱ 副 all of a sudden; suddenly
【奄忽】〈书〉suddenly; all of a sudden; all at once
【奄奄】breathing feebly: 气息奄奄 ◇ ～一息 at one's last gasp; on the verge of death

俨 形〈书〉majestic; solemn; dignified
【俨然】〈书〉❶ solemn; dignified: 望之～ *look dignified* ❷ neatly arranged: 屋舍～ *houses set out in neat order* ❸ just like: 这孩子说起话来～是个大人。*This child speaks just like a grown-up*.

/ ～以恩人自居 *assume the airs of a benefactor*

【俨如】just like：～白昼 *as bright as day*

衍 Ⅰ 动 〈书〉spread out；develop；amplify：衍变 Ⅱ 形 redundant；superfluous：衍文 Ⅲ 名 〈书〉❶ low-lying flatland：广～沃野 *a broad expanse of fertile flatland* ❷ marsh；swamp；bog

【衍变】develop；evolve

【衍射】［物］diffraction：～角 *diffraction angle* / ～线 *diffracted ray*

【衍生】［化］derive ◇ ～物［化］derivative

【衍文】redundancy due to misprinting or mis-copying

掩 动 ❶ cover；hide：～口而笑 *hide one's smile* / ～鼻而过 *pass by (sth. nauseating) holding one's nose* ❷ shut；close：～卷 *close a book* / 虚～着门 *with the door left unlocked or unlatched* ❸〈方〉get squeezed (or pinched) while shutting a door, lid, etc.：小心门～了手。*Don't get your fingers caught in the door.* ❹ attack by surprise：～袭 *launch a surprise attack*

【掩蔽】screen；shelter；cover：高射炮上有树枝～着。*The antiaircraft guns were camouflaged with tree branches.* ◇ ～阵地［军］covered position

【掩藏】hide；conceal

【掩耳盗铃】plug one's ears while stealing a bell—deceive oneself；bury one's head in the sand

【掩盖】❶ cover；overspread：大雪～着田野。*The fields were covered with snow.* ❷ conceal；cover up：谎言～不了事实。*Lies cannot cover up (or conceal) the facts.*

【掩护】screen；shield；cover：他这样做，实际上是给他上司打～。*In so doing, he was actually trying to shield his boss.* ◇ ～部队［军］covering force；～火力［军］covering fire

【掩埋】bury：～尸首 *bury a corpse*

【掩泣】cover one's face with one's hands and start weeping

【掩人耳目】deceive the public；hoodwink people

【掩杀】〈书〉make a surprise attack；pounce on (the enemy)

【掩饰】cover up (faults, mistakes, etc.)；gloss over；conceal：～错误 *gloss over (or cover up) one's mistakes* / ～真实的意图 *conceal one's true intentions*

【掩体】［军］blindage；bunker：炮兵～ *emplacement*

【掩星】［天］occultation：月～ *lunar occultation*

【掩映】(of things screening part of each other from view) show off (each other)；set off (one another)：红楼翠竹交相～。*The red buildings and green bamboos set each other off.*

眼 Ⅰ 名 ❶ eye：左(右)～ *left (right) eye* / 我眯～了。*Something has got into my eye.* ❷ look；glance：瞪了他一～ *give him a hard look* / 瞥了他一～ *shoot a glance at him* / 一～就认出是她 *recognize her at first glance* ❸ a small hole；aperture：拿锥子扎个～儿 *pierce with an awl* / 打个～ *bore a hole* ❹ key point：节骨～儿 *critical juncture* ❺ (weiqi) trap ❻ an unaccented beat in traditional Chinese music：一板三～ *one accented and three unaccented beats in a bar* Ⅱ 量：两～井 *two wells*

【眼巴巴】❶ (expecting) eagerly；anxiously：大家～地盼着他回来。*We were eagerly looking forward to his return.* ❷ helplessly (watching sth. unpleasant happen)：他～地看着老鹰把小鸡抓走了。*He helplessly looked on when the hawk snatched the chick away.*

【眼白】〈方〉the white of the eye

【眼保健操】ocular exercises

【眼不见，心不烦】what the eye doesn't see the heart doesn't grieve for

【眼馋】cast covetous eyes at sth.；eye sth. covetously

【眼眵】gum (in the eyes)

【眼虫藻】(又作'眼虫') euglena (a green flagellate protozoan having a reddish eyespot)

【眼瞅着】〈方〉❶ see sth. happen：我～一根大梁掉下来把他砸死了。*I saw with my own eyes a girder fall and crush him to death.* ❷ soon；in no time：他～要红起来了。*He'll be a celebrity in no time.*

【眼底】❶ eyeground；the fundus of the eye (fundus oculi) ❷ in one's eyes；in sight：登楼一望，全城景色尽收～。*The top of the building commands a panoramic view of the city.* ◇ ～检查［医］funduscopy；～镜［医］funduscope；～照相机［医］fundus camera

【眼底下】❶ right before one's eyes ❷ at the moment

【眼点】eyespot (of a protozoan)；stigma

【眼福】the good fortune of seeing sth. rare or beautiful：～不浅 *be lucky enough to see sth.* / 一饱～ *feast one's eyes on sth.*

【眼干症】［医］xerophthalmia

【眼高手低】have high standards but little ability；be fastidious but incompetent

【眼观六路，耳听八方】have sharp eyes and keen ears；be observant and alert

【眼光】❶ eye：她的～锐利，什么事情都瞒不过她。*You can hide nothing from her sharp eyes.* ❷ sight；foresight；insight；vision：～远大 *far-sighted* / ～短浅 *shortsighted* / 政治～ *political foresight* / 历史～ *historical perspective*

【眼红】❶ covet；be envious；be jealous ❷ eyes burning with fury；be furious：仇人相见，分外眼红

【眼花】have dim eyesight；have blurred vision：耳不聋眼不花(*of an old person*) *be neither hard of hearing nor dim-sighted* ◇ ～缭乱 be dazzled

【眼犄角儿】〈方〉the corner of the eye；canthus

【眼疾手快】quick of eye and deft of hand

【眼尖】be sharp-eyed；have sharp eyes；have keen sight

【眼睑】［生理］eyelid

【眼见】soon；in no time：～就要立冬了。*It will be winter here very soon*.

【眼见得】〈方〉(of sth. unpleasant) be evident：病人～不行了。*It's clear that the patient won't pull through*.

【眼角】canthus；the corner of the eye

【眼睫毛】〈口〉eyelash

【眼界】field of vision (or view)；outlook：～不广 *have a narrow outlook* / 扩大～ *widen one's field of vision；broaden one's horizon*

【眼镜】eyeglasses；glasses；spectacles：一付～ *a pair of spectacles* / 戴～ *wear glasses* / 摘下～ *take off one's glasses* ◇ ～猴 tarsier；～框 rims (of spectacles)；spectacles frame；～蛇 cobra

【眼睛】eye：她那双～十分动人。*Her eyes are very beautiful*.

【眼看】❶ soon；in a moment：暴风雨～就要来了。*The storm will start any moment*. ❷ watch helplessly；look on passively：咱们哪能～着他走邪道不管呢？*How can we sit idly by and watch him go astray?*

【眼科】(department of) ophthalmology ◇ ～学 ophthalmology；～医生 oculist；ophthalmologist；eye-doctor

【眼快】be sharp-eyed (or sharp-sighted)；have sharp eyes；have keen sight

【眼眶】❶ eye socket；eyehole；orbit：他～里含着热泪。*His eyes were filled with tears*. ❷ rim of the eye：揉揉～ *rub one's eyes*

【眼泪】tears：流～ *shed tears* ◇ ～汪汪 eyes brimming with tears；in tears

【眼离】〈方〉have hallucinations；see things：牲口一～就惊了。*The animal shied the moment it began to see things*.

【眼力】❶ eyesight；vision：～好(差) *have good (poor) eyesight* ❷ judgment；discrimination：老支书看人很有～。*The old Party branch secretary is good at sizing people up*.

【眼里】in one's eyes；in one's view：看在～，记在心里 *bear in mind what one sees；see and heed* / ～有活 *see where there's work to be done；know where one can be of use* / 这点困难她根本不放在～。*She thinks nothing of a difficulty like that*.

【眼帘】〈文〉eyes：一片丰收的景色映入～。*A lively scene of farmers bringing in bumper crops greeted the eye*.

【眼量】perceptiveness：有～ *be perceptive*

【眼明手快】quick of eye and deft of hand；sharp-eyed and deft-handed

【眼明心亮】同〖心明眼亮〗

【眼内压】同〖眼压〗

【眼泡】upper eyelid：她～儿都哭肿了。*Her eyes were swollen from crying*.

【眼皮】(又作'眼皮子') eyelid：我～直跳。*My eyes kept twitching*. / 困得我上下～直打架。*I was so sleepy I couldn't keep my eyes open*. ◇ ～底下 (又作'眼皮子底下') 同〖眼底下〗；～子高 fastidious；hard to please；～子浅 short-sighted；shallow

【眼前】❶ before one's eyes：～是一片碧绿的稻田。*Before our eyes was a stretch of green paddy fields*. ❷ at the moment；at present；now：～利益服从长远利益 *subordinate immediate interests to long-term interests* / 胜利就在～。*Victory is at hand*. ◇ ～欢 pleasure of the moment；～亏 trouble right before the eyes

【眼球】eyeball

【眼圈】❶ eye socket；orbit：～红了 *be on the verge of tears* ❷ rim of the eye

【眼热】cast covetous eyes at sth.；eye sth. covetously：她见了那些珠宝怪～的。*She eyed those jewels covetously*.

【眼色】a hint given with the eyes；a meaningful glance；wink：使～ *tip sb. the wink；wink at sb.* / 看某人的～行事 *take one's cue from sb*.

【眼神】❶ expression in one's eyes：从他的～里，我能猜测到他的心事。*I can guess what's on his mind from the expression in his eyes*. ❷〈方〉eyesight：～不好 *have poor eyesight*

【眼生】look unfamiliar：来客很～。*I haven't seen the visitor before*.

【眼屎】〈方〉gum (in the eyes)

【眼熟】look familiar：这人看着很～。*That person looks familiar*.

【眼跳】twitching of the eyelid

【眼窝】eye socket；eyehole；orbit

【眼下】at the moment；at present；now：～正是秋收大忙季节。*We're right in the middle of the autumn harvest rush*.

【眼弦赤烂】[中] blepharitis

【眼线】❶ informer；stool-pigeon；finger man ❷ eye-liner

【眼压】intraocular pressure

【眼药】medicament for the eyes；eye ointment or eyedrops ◇ ～水 eyedrops

【眼印】eyeprint

【眼影】eye-shadow

【眼影粉】eye-shadow power；eye-shadow

【眼晕】dizziness (owing to defective vision)

【眼罩儿】❶ eyeshade ❷ blinkers (for a horse, donkey, etc.)

【眼睁睁】looking on helplessly or unfeelingly：咱不能～地看着庄稼被水淹了。*We can't just sit here and watch the crops being flooded*.

【眼中钉】a thorn in one's flesh (or side)

【眼中钉、肉中刺】a thorn in one's flesh (or side)

【眼珠子】❶ (又作'眼珠儿') eyeball ❷ the apple of sb.'s eye

偃 动〈书〉❶ fall on one's back：～卧 *lie supine；lie on one's back* ❷ lay down ❸ desist；cease：偃武修文

【偃旗息鼓】lower the banners and muffle the drums—cease all activities

【偃武修文】desist from war and encourage the arts of peace；desist from military activities and encourage culture and education

演 动 ❶ develop; evolve: 演变 ❷ deduce; elaborate: 演绎 ❸ drill; practise: 演算 ❹ perform; play; act; put on: ～电影 *show a film* / ～五场 *give (or put on) five performances*

【演变】develop; evolve: 从猿到人的～过程 *evolution from ape to man*

【演播】telecast (a play, performance, etc.) ◇ ～室 broadcast studio; television studio

【演唱】sing (in a performance)

【演唱会】concert

【演出】perform; show; put on a show: 登台～ *appear on the stage* / 首次～ *first performance or show; première (of a play, film, etc.); début (of an actor or actress)* / ～节目 *items on the programme; programme* ◇ ～本 acting version; playscript; script; ～单位 producer

【演化】evolution: 生物的～ *the evolution of living things*

【演技】acting; stage performance: 她的～好极了。*Her acting is excellent.*

【演讲】give a lecture; make a speech; lecture: ～比赛 *oratorical contest*

【演进】gradual progress; evolution

【演剧】act in a play

【演练】drill: ～场 *drill ground* / 地面～ *aviation ground drill*

【演示】demonstrate ◇ ～程序［计］demonstration program

【演说】❶ deliver a speech; make an address ❷ speech ◇ ～术 oratory

【演算】perform mathematical calculations

【演替】［生］succession: 植物～ *succession of plants*

【演武】practise traditional martial arts

【演习】manoeuvre; exercise; drill; practice: 军事～ *military manoeuvre; war exercise* / 民兵～ *militia drill* / 实弹～ *live ammunition manoeuvres* / 消防～ *fire drill*

【演戏】❶ put on a play; act in a play ❷ playact; pretend: 别再～了。*Stop playacting.*

【演义】historical novel; historical romance:《三国～》*The Romance of the Three Kingdoms*

【演艺】performing arts

【演绎】deduce ◇ ～法 the deductive method; deduction

【演员】actor or actress; performer: 挑选～ *choose the cast* / ～表 *the cast*

【演职员】general term for the performers and supporting staff of an artistic troupe

【演奏】give an instrumental performance; play a musical instrument (in a performance): ～琵琶 *play the pipa* / ～能手 *virtuoso* ◇ ～家 an accomplished performer (of a musical instrument)

鼹 名 mole (a small burrowing insectivorous mammal)

【鼹鼠】common name for 鼹

yàn

厌 动 ❶ be disgusted with; detest: 厌弃 ❷ be fed up with; be bored with; be tired of: 看～了 *have seen more than enough of sth.* / 吃～了 *be sick of eating sth.* ❸ be satisfied: 贪得无厌

【厌读】tired of school: 一部分学生有～倾向。*A certain number of students are tired of studying.*

【厌烦】be sick of; be fed up with: 这支小夜曲我听多少遍也不觉得～。*I never tire of listening to this serenade.*

【厌倦】be weary of; be tired of: 整天坐办公室,我早就～了。*I've long been tired of sitting in an office all day.*

【厌腻】be bored with; be tired of; be fed up with: ～流言飞语 *be tired of gossip; be fed up with rumors*

【厌弃】detest and reject; detest; loathe

【厌食症】［医］(esp. in young women) anorexia; anorexia nervosa

【厌世】be world-weary; be pessimistic

【厌恶】detest; abhor; abominate; be disgusted with: 他的所作所为实在令人～。*His behaviour is simply disgusting.* ◇ ～疗法［心理］aversion therapy

【厌学】见〖厌读〗

【厌氧微生物】anaerobe

【厌战】be weary of war; be war-weary: ～情绪 *war-weariness*

砚 名 inkstone; inkslab: 笔～ *writing brush and inkslab*

【砚池】inkstone; inkslab

【砚台】inkstone; inkslab

咽 动 swallow: ～一口水 *take a swallow of water* / 他话到嘴边又～了回去。*He was on the point of saying something when he checked himself.* / 她恐怕～不下这口气。*I don't think she can stomach (or swallow, take) an insult like that.* ——另见 yān

【咽气】breathe one's last; die: 爸爸刚～,几个子女就争开了遗产。*No sooner had the father died than the sons and daughters started to quarrel over the inheritance.*

宴 Ⅰ 动 entertain at a banquet; fête: ～客 *entertain guests at a banquet; give a banquet* Ⅱ 名 feast; banquet: 盛～ *a grand banquet; a magnificent feast* / 婚～ *wedding (or marriage) feast* Ⅲ 形 ease and comfort

【宴安鸩毒】seeking pleasure is like drinking poisoned wine; voluptuous comfort is poison

【宴会】banquet; feast; dinner party: 举行～ *give a banquet* / 主持～ *host a dinner party* ◇ ～厅 banquet hall

【宴请】entertain (to dinner); fête: ～贵宾 *entertain the distinguished guests*

【宴席】banquet; feast

艳 Ⅰ形 ❶ gorgeous; colourful; gaudy: 这布的花色太～了。*The cloth is too gaudy.* ❷ amorous: ～诗 *love poem in a flowery style* Ⅱ动〈书〉admire; envy: 艳羡

【艳福】a man's good fortune in love affairs: ～不浅 *have a lot of good fortune in love affairs; have a beautiful wife or girl friend*

【艳红】bright red: ～的阳光 *scarlet sunshine*

【艳丽】bright-coloured and beautiful; gorgeous: ～夺目 *of dazzling beauty* / 词藻～ *flowery diction*

【艳情】erotic: ～小说 *erotic fiction*

【艳如桃李,冷若冰霜】(of a woman) as beautiful as peach and plum blossoms, but as cold as frost and ice

【艳诗】erotic poetry

【艳史】erotic adventures; amorous adventures: 《隋炀帝～》*Merry Adventures of Emperor Yang of the Sui Dynasty*

【艳羡】〈书〉admire immensely

【艳阳天】bright spring day; bright sunny skies

【艳冶】〈书〉pretty and coquettish

【艳装】(又作'艳妆') gaudy attire

唁 动 extend condolences: 吊唁

【唁电】telegram (or cable) of condolence; message of condolence

【唁函】letter (or message) of condolence

验 Ⅰ动 ❶ examine; check; test: ～货 *check goods* / ～小便 *have a urine test* / ～护照 *examine (or check) a passport* ❷ prove effective; produce the expected result: 屡试屡～ *prove successful in every test* Ⅱ名 intended effect; desired result: 效验

【验钞机】a machine for checking paper money for counterfeits

【验潮器】[气] tide gauge

【验电器】electroscope

【验方】[中] proved recipe

【验关】customs examination

【验光】optometry

【验核】check; verify: ～装货单 *check the loading papers*

【验看】examine; inspect: ～护照 *examine a passport*

【验明正身】verify the identity of a convict prior to execution

【验讫】checked; examined

【验枪】[军] inspect arms

【验墒】check the moisture of the soil

【验尸】[法] postmortem; autopsy ◇ ～官 coroner

【验收】check and accept; check before acceptance; check upon delivery: 逐项～ *check item by item before acceptance* / ～单 *receipt (issued after examination and acceptance of goods)* / ～试验 *acceptance test*

【验收合格证】acceptance certificate

【验算】[数] checking computations: ～公式 *check formula*

【验血】blood test

【验证】verify: ～理论 *verify a theory*

【验资】check the capital of a business or organization

谚 名 proverb; saying; adage; saw: 谚语

【谚语】proverb; saying; adage; saw

焰 名 flame; blaze: 烈～ *blazing (or raging) flames*

【焰火】fireworks

雁 名 wild goose; goose

【雁过拔毛】pluck feathers from each goose as it passes by—squeeze whenever possible

【雁来红】[植] tricolour amaranth (Amaranthus tricolor)

堰 名 weir

【堰塞湖】[地理] barrier lake

酽 形 (of tea, etc.) thick; strong: 茶太～。*The tea's too strong.*

燕 名 swallow (a bird)

【燕巢幕上】a swallow nesting on a canopy—in a precarious position

【燕颔虎颈】a majestic and awe-inspiring appearance

【燕好】〈书〉(of husband and wife) be very fond of each other; be happily married: 百年～ *remain a devoted couple to the end of their lives*

【燕鸻】[动] pratincole; swallow plover

【燕麦】oats

【燕鸥】[动] tern

【燕雀】[动] brambling; bramble finch (Fringilla montifringilla)

【燕雀安知鸿鹄之志】how could a sparrow understand the ambitions of a swan? —the lofty aims of the great are beyond the understanding of the lowly

【燕雀处堂】swallows nesting in a hall that is about to be on fire—unaware of one's danger

【燕隼】[动] hobby

【燕尾服】swallowtail; swallow-tailed coat; tailcoat; tails

【燕窝】edible bird's nest

【燕鱼】[动] Spanish mackerel

【燕子】swallow

赝 形〈书〉counterfeit; spurious; fake: 赝品

【赝本】spurious edition or copy

【赝币】〈书〉counterfeit coin

【赝晶体】[物] pseudocrystal

【赝品】art forgery

yāng

央 Ⅰ动 entreat; beg: 我～你一件事。*May I ask*

a favour of you? Ⅱ 名 centre：中央
【央告】beg；plead；implore：苦苦～ *beg piteously*
【央求】beg；plead；implore：～宽恕 *beg for mercy* / 不管我怎么～，她就是不答应。*No matter how earnestly I pleaded with her，she wouldn't agree*.
【央托】entreat sb. to do sth.

泱 （构词成分）见下
【泱泱】〈书〉❶（of waters）vast ❷ grand；great；magnificent；glorious：～大国 *a great and proud country*

殃 Ⅰ 名 calamity；disaster；misfortune：遭殃 Ⅱ 动 bring disaster to：祸国殃民
【殃及】bring disaster to：这场暴风雪～数千牧民。*The snowstorm was a disaster to thousands of herdsmen*.
【殃及池鱼】见〖城门失火，殃及池鱼〗

秧 名 ❶ seedling；sprout：黄瓜～儿 *cucumber sprout* ❷ rice seedling：插秧 ❸ vine：白薯～ *sweet potato vine* ❹ young；fry：鱼～ *young fish*；*fry* / 猪～ *piglet*
【秧歌】yangge（dance），a popular rural folk dance：扭～ *do the yangge*
【秧鸡】［动］rail
【秧龄】the length of time rice seedlings grow in seedling beds until they are transplanted
【秧苗】rice shoot；rice seedling
【秧田】rice seedling bed
【秧子】同〖秧〗

yáng

羊 名 sheep：放～ *put sheep out to pasture*；*graze sheep* / ～叫 *baa*；*bleat*
【羊肠线】［医］catgut suture
【羊肠小道】a narrow winding trail；a meandering footpath：这条崎岖的～非常难走。*This bumpy*，*meandering byway is difficult to negotiate*.
【羊齿】［植］bracken；fern
【羊痘】［牧］sheep pox
【羊肚儿手巾】〈方〉towel
【羊肚蕈】［植］morel
【羊羔】❶ lamb ❷ the name of a wine
【羊倌】shepherd
【羊毫】writing brush made of goat's hair
【羊角锤】claw hammer
【羊角风】common name for 癫痫
【羊角面包】croissant；crescent-shaped roll；crescent
【羊脚碾】［建］sheepfoot roller
【羊圈】sheepfold；sheep pen
【羊毛】sheep's wool；wool；fleece ◇ ～衫 woollen sweater；cardigan；～套衫 pullover；～袜 woollen socks or stockings；～脂 lanolin；wool fat
【羊毛出在羊身上】after all，the wool still comes from the sheep's back—in the long run，whatever you're given，you pay for
【羊膜】［生理］amnion
【羊排】mutton chop；lamb chop
【羊皮】sheepskin：一双～靴子 *a pair of sheepskin boots* / 披着～的狼 *a wolf in sheep's clothing* ◇ ～纸 parchment
【羊群里头出骆驼】stand out like a camel in a flock of sheep
【羊绒】cashmere ◇ ～衫 cashmere sweater
【羊肉】mutton ◇ ～串 mutton cubes roasted on a skewer；shish kebab（or kabob）；shashlik
【羊水】［生理］amniotic fluid：～过多 *hydramnios*
【羊驼】alpaca（Lama alpacos）◇ ～毛 alpaca fibre
【羊痫风】common name for 癫痫
【羊质虎皮】a sheep in a tiger's skin—outwardly strong，inwardly weak

阳 Ⅰ 名 ❶（in Chinese thought）yang，the masculine or positive principle in nature（〈反〉"阴"）❷ the sun：阳光 ❸ south of a hill or north of a river：衡～ *Hengyang*（*a city situated on the south side of Hengshan Mountain*）/ 洛～ *Luoyang*（*a city situated on the north side of the Luohe River*）❹ male genitals Ⅱ 形 ❶ in relief：阳文 ❷ open；overt：阳沟 / 阳奉阴违 ❸ belonging to this world；concerned with living beings：阳间 ❹［物］positive：阳离子
【阳春】spring（season）◇ ～白雪 Spring Snow（melodies of the élite in the State of Chu）—highbrow art and literature；～面 noodles in a simple sauce
【阳地植物】sun plant
【阳电】positive electricity
【阳电子】同〖正电子〗
【阳奉阴违】overtly agree but covertly oppose；comply in public but oppose in private；feign compliance
【阳刚】manly；virile：～之气 *manliness*；*virility*
【阳沟】open drain；ditch
【阳关道】（又作'阳关大道'）a broad highway；a broad road；thoroughfare：你走你的～，我过我的独木桥。*You take the open road*，*I'll cross the log bridge—you go your way*，*I'll go mine*.
【阳光】sunlight；sunshine：～普照大地。*Sunlight floods the earth*. or *The sun illuminates every corner of the land*.
【阳极】［物］positive pole；positive electrode；anode：～板 *positive plate* / ～栅 *anode grid* / ～射线 *positive ray*
【阳间】this world
【阳离子】positive ion；cation
【阳历】❶ solar calendar ❷ the Gregorian calendar
【阳平】rising tone（the second of the four tones in modern standard Chinese pronunciation）
【阳畦】［农］seed bed with windbreaks；cold bed
【阳起石】actinolite（a mineral）
【阳伞】parasol；sunshade
【阳世】this world
【阳台】balcony or veranda
【阳痿】［医］impotence

【阳文】characters or designs cut in relief; relief
【阳性】❶［医］positive：～反应 *positive reaction* ❷［语］masculine gender ◇ ～植物 sun plant
【阳虚】［中］deficiency of yang; lack of vital energy

扬 动 ❶ raise：～手 *raise one's hand (and beckon)* / ～起灰尘 *raise (or kick up) a dust* / ～鞭催马 *flourish the whip to urge on the horse; whip one's horse on* ❷ throw up and scatter; winnow：～谷去糠 *winnow the chaff from the grain* ❸ spread; make known：宣扬
【扬长避短】show one's strong points and hide one's weaknesses; maximize favourable factors and minimize unfavourable ones
【扬长补短】bring out one's strengths to make up for one's weaknesses
【扬长而去】stalk off; swagger off
【扬场】［农］winnowing ◇ ～机 winnowing machine; winnower
【扬程】［水］lift：高～ *high lift* / 高～水泵 *high-lift pump* / 高～抽水站 *high-lift pumping station*
【扬帆】〈书〉hoist the sails; set sail
【扬幡招魂】fly a funeral banner to summon the soul—try to revive what is obsolete
【扬花】［农］(of cereal crops) be flowering
【扬眉吐气】feel proud and elated
【扬名】make a name for oneself; become famous：～天下 *become world-famous; become known throughout the country*
【扬旗】［铁路］semaphore
【扬弃】❶ develop what is useful or healthy and discard what is not ❷［哲］sublate
【扬琴】dulcimer
【扬清激浊】同〖激浊扬清〗
【扬声】❶ raise one's voice ❷ make public; disclose ❸〈书〉make a name for oneself; become famous
【扬声器】loudspeaker：高频～ tweeter / 低频～ woofer
【扬水】pump up water ◇ ～泵 lift pump; ～站 pumping station
【扬汤止沸】try to stop water from boiling by skimming it off and pouring it back—apply a palliative
【扬言】threaten (that one is going to take action)：～要进行报复 *threaten to retaliate*
【扬扬】triumphantly; complacently：意气～ *in buoyant spirits; elated (over success)* ◇ ～得意 be immensely proud with success; look triumphant; ～自得 be very pleased with oneself; be complacent
【扬誉】become famous; make a name for oneself：～全球 *become world-famous*
【扬州】Yangzhou (in Jiangsu Province)
【扬子鳄】［动］Chinese alligator

杨 名 poplar
【杨柳】❶ poplar and willow ❷ willow
【杨梅】［植］red bayberry (Myrica rubra)
【杨梅疮】〈方〉syphilis
【杨树】poplar
【杨枝鱼】pipefish

佯 动 pretend; feign; sham：～作不知 *feign ignorance; pretend not to know* / ～死 *feign death; play dead*
【佯嗔】pretend to be angry or displeased
【佯称】同〖佯言〗
【佯动】［军］make a feint
【佯攻】［军］feign (or simulate) attack; make a feint
【佯狂】〈书〉feign madness; pretend to be mad
【佯言】〈书〉allege falsely; tell lies; lie; pretend：～不知情 *pretend ignorance*
【佯装】〈书〉pretend; feign：～惊诧 *pretend to be surprised*

洋 Ⅰ 形 ❶ vast; multitudinous：洋溢 ❷foreign：～房 *Western-style house* ❸ modern：～办法 *modern methods* Ⅱ 名 ❶ocean：四大～ *the four oceans* ❷ silver dollar or coin：罚～一百元 *impose a fine of one hundred silver dollars*
【洋八股】foreign stereotyped writing; foreign stereotypes
【洋白菜】cabbage
【洋博士】foreign-trained Ph. D.; doctor educated abroad
【洋财】an unexpected big fortune; windfall money
【洋菜】common name for 琼脂
【洋插队】〈喻〉settle in a foreign country for further education (implying hardship)：出国"陪读"，犹如当年插队一样，只不过是～罢了。*Accompanying a spouse abroad is like settling in the countryside, the only difference being that it's in a foreign country instead of China.*
【洋场】metropolis infested with foreign adventurers (usu. referring to preliberation Shanghai)：～恶少 *rich young bully in a metropolis (in old China)*
【洋车】〈口〉rickshaw：拉～ *pull a rickshaw* / 拉～的 *rickshawman*
【洋瓷】〈口〉enamel：～器皿 *enamelware*
【洋葱】onion
【洋地黄】［植］digitalis (a Chinese medicine)
【洋粉】common name for 琼脂
【洋服】Western-style clothes
【洋橄榄】common name for 油橄榄
【洋镐】common name for 鹤嘴镐
【洋鬼子】foreign devil (a term used in preliberation China for foreign invaders)：假～ *imitation foreign devil—comprador, etc.*
【洋行】foreign firm (in preliberation China)
【洋红】carmine; crimson pigment
【洋槐】another name for 刺槐
【洋灰】popular name for 水泥
【洋火】〈口〉matches
【洋货】foreign goods; imported goods

【洋姜】〈口〉Jerusalem artichoke

【洋教条】❶ foreign tenets (doctrines, dogmas, creeds) ❷ dogmatic assertion or blind worship of foreign doctrines, theories or rules

【洋金花】[植] datura flower (Datura metel)

【洋泾浜】pidgin English; pidgin

【洋里洋气】in an ostentatious Western style

【洋流】[地质] ocean current

【洋奴】slave of a foreign master; flunkey of imperialism; worshipper of everything foreign: ～买办 *lackeys and compradors in the service of foreign bosses* / ～思想 *slavish mentality towards all things foreign* / ～哲学 *slavish comprador philosophy; blind worship of everything foreign*

【洋气】❶ foreign flavour; Western style ❷ in an ostentatious Western style: 穿着～ *be dressed in an ostentatious Western style; be stylishly dressed*

【洋钱】〈口〉silver dollar

【洋人】foreigner (usu. a Westerner)

【洋娃娃】(Western-style) doll

【洋为中用】make foreign things serve China: 利用外国工业技术来提高我们的劳动生产力就是～的一个例子。*When we use foreign industrial know-how to raise our labour productivity, we are making foreign things serve the needs of China.*

【洋务】〈旧〉foreign affairs ◇ ～运动 Westernization Movement

【洋相】见〖出洋相〗

【洋绣球】another name for 天竺葵

【洋洋】❶ numerous; copious: ～万言 *run to ten thousand words—be very lengthy* ❷ 同〖扬扬〗◇ ～大观 spectacular; grandiose; imposing; ～得意 同〖扬扬得意〗; ～洒洒 voluminous; of great length; ～自得 同〖扬扬自得〗

【洋溢】be permeated with; brim with: 宴会上～着团结友好的热烈气氛。*The banquet was permeated with a warm atmosphere of unity and friendship.*

yǎng

仰 动 ❶ face upward: ～着睡 *sleep on one's back* / ～头 *raise one's head; raise one's eyes* ❷ admire; respect; look up to: 瞻仰 ❸ rely on: 仰仗

【仰八叉】〈口〉(fall) on one's back: 摔了个～ *fall flat on one's back*

【仰角】[数] angle of elevation

【仰面】face upward: ～朝天 *lie on one's back* / ～倒下 *fall on one's back*

【仰慕】admire; look up to: 久已～盛名。*I have long been aware of your high fame.* or *I feel honoured to meet you.*

【仰人鼻息】be dependent on the whims of others; be slavishly dependent

【仰韶文化】the Yangshao culture (a Neolithic culture)

【仰食】〈书〉depend on another for food (or for one's living)

【仰视】look up: ～天空 *look up at the sky*

【仰首】〈书〉raise one's head ◇ ～伸眉 hold one's head high, feeling proud and elated

【仰天】look up to heaven: ～长叹 *look up to heaven and heave a deep sigh* / ～大笑 *laugh sardonically*

【仰望】❶ look up at: ～星空 *look up at the starlit sky* ❷〈书〉respectfully seek guidance or help from; look up to

【仰卧】lie on one's back; lie supine ◇ ～起坐 [体] sit-up

【仰屋兴叹】look up at the ceiling and sigh—be at the end of one's resources

【仰泳】[体] backstroke

【仰仗】rely on; look to sb. for backing (or support): 我们～你啦！*We rely on you.*

养 Ⅰ 动 ❶ support; provide for: ～家 *support a family* / 我从小没了父母，是姑姑把我～大的。*I lost my parents when I was a child, and was brought up by my aunt.* ❷ raise; keep; grow: ～鸭 *raise ducks* / ～鸟 *keep pet birds* / ～花 *grow flowers* ❸ give birth to: 她～了个儿子。*She gave birth to a boy.* ❹ form; acquire; cultivate: ～成良好的习惯 *cultivate good habits* ❺ rest; convalesce; recuperate one's health; heal: ～身体 *recuperate* / 你这回病得不轻，应该好好～～。*You've been seriously ill and should take a good rest.* ❻ let (one's hair) grow ❼ maintain; keep in good repair: 养路 Ⅱ 形 foster; adoptive: ～父(母) *foster father (mother)* / ～子(女) *adopted son (daughter)*

【养兵】maintain an army ◇ ～千日，用兵一时 maintain an army for a thousand days to use it for an hour

【养病】take rest and nourishment to regain one's health; recuperate: 他在家～呢。*He's recuperating at home.*

【养蚕】engage in sericulture ◇ ～业 sericulture

【养地】increase soil fertility (by fertilization, crop rotation, etc.)

【养儿防老，积谷防荒】just as one stores up grain against lean years, one rears children against old age

【养分】nutrient: 土壤～ *soil nutrient*

【养蜂】raise or keep bees; engage in apiculture (or beekeeping) ◇ ～场 apiary; bee farm; ～业 apiculture; beekeeping

【养汉】(of a woman) have a lover

【养虎遗患】to rear a tiger is to court calamity—appeasement brings disaster

【养护】❶ maintain; conserve: 道路～ *road maintenance* / 生物资源～ *conservation of living resources* ❷ curing: 混凝土～ *concrete curing*

【养活】〈口〉❶ support; feed: ～一家子 *support (or feed) a family* ❷ raise (animals): 他家～了上百头猪。*His family raises nearly a hundred pigs.* ❸ give birth to: ～孩子 *have a baby*

【养鸡场】chicken run；chicken farm
【养家活口】support one's family
【养精蓄锐】conserve strength and store up energy
【养老】❶ provide for the aged (usu. one's parents) ❷ live out one's life in retirement ◇ ～保险 endowment insurance；～金 old-age pension；～送终 look after one's parents in their old age and give them a proper burial after they die；～院 home for the old
【养廉】〈书〉(of government officials) nourish honesty—refrain from squeeze and graft
【养料】nutriment；nourishment：树根从土壤中吸取水分和～。*The roots of trees draw water and nourishment from the soil.*
【养路】maintain a road or railway：～道班 *road maintenance crew* ◇ ～费 road toll；road maintenance expense
【养马场】(horse) ranch
【养伤】nurse one's injuries or wounds
【养神】rest to attain mental tranquility；repose：闭目～ *sit in repose with one's eyes closed*
【养生】care for life；conserve one's vital powers；preserve one's health；keep in good health ◇ ～之道 how to care for life (or conserve one's vital powers)；how to maintain good health
【养兔场】rabbit warren
【养息】rest and take nourishing food to build up one's health；recuperate
【养性】nourish one's nature：修真～ *cultivate one's native sensibility and nourish one's inborn nature*
【养痈成患】(又作'养痈遗患') a boil neglected becomes the bane of one's life—leaving evil unchecked spells ruin
【养鱼】breed fish；engage in pisciculture ◇ ～池 fishpond
【养育】bring up；rear：～子女 *bring up children*
【养殖】breed (aquatics)：～海带 *cultivate kelp* / 淡水～ *freshwater aquiculture* / 海水～ *seawater aquiculture* ◇ ～珍珠 cultured pearl；～业 breeding industry
【养猪场】pig farm；piggery
【养尊处优】enjoy high position and live in comfort；live in clover

氧 名［化］oxygen (O)
【氧吧】oxygen bar (for oxygen therapy)
【氧合作用】［生理］oxygenation
【氧化】［化］oxidize；oxidate：～作用 *oxidation* ◇ ～还原酶［化］oxido-reducing enzyme；oxidoreductase；～剂 oxidizer；oxidant；～数 oxidation number；oxidation state；～态 oxidation state；oxidation number；～铁 ferric oxide；～物 oxide；～焰 another name for 外焰；～抑制剂 oxidation retarder (or inhibitor)
【氧气】oxygen：～炼钢 *oxygen steelmaking* ◇ ～袋 oxygen bag；～顶吹转炉 oxygen top-blown convertor；～面具 oxygen mask；～瓶 oxygen cylinder；～枪［冶］oxygen lance；～帐［医］oxygen tent；～罩 oxygen mask
【氧乙炔吹管】［机］oxyacetylene blowpipe

痒 形 itch；tickle：浑身发～ *itch all over* / 搔到～处 *scratch where it itches—hit the nail on the head* / 怕～ *ticklish*
【痒痒】〈口〉itch；tickle：蚊子咬得腿上直～。*The mosquito bites on my legs itch terribly.*

yàng

怏（构词成分）见下
【怏怏】disgruntled；sullen：～不乐 *unhappy about sth.；morose*

恙 名〈书〉ailment；illness：无恙
【恙虫】［动］tsutsugamushi mite
【恙虫热】tsutsugamushi disease；scrub typhus

样 Ⅰ 名 ❶ appearance；shape：这两支笔～儿差不多，色儿不一样。*These two pens are alike except that they're different colours.* / 几年没见，他还是那个～儿。*It's years since I last saw him, but he still looks the same.* ❷ sample；model；pattern：鞋样 / 样品 Ⅱ 量 kind；type：三～点心 *three kinds of pastries* / 商店虽小，各～货物俱全。*Small as it is, the shop stocks all kinds of wares.*
【样板】❶ sample plate ❷ templet ❸ model；prototype；example ◇ ～戏 (a term used during the Cultural Revolution) model opera
【样本】❶ sample book ❷［刷］sample；specimen：字体～ *type specimen book*
【样稿】sample manuscript
【样机】❶ prototype ❷ sample machine：这种～被一家外国公司买去了。*The samples of the machine have been sold to a foreign company.*
【样件】sample：工程师收集了各种地板～及技术资料。*The engineer has collected samples of various kinds of flooring as well as their technical specifications.*
【样款】pattern；style；sample
【样片】the sample copy of a film；(of a film) rushes
【样品】sample (product)；specimen
【样式】pattern；type；style；form：各种～的羊毛衫 *woollen sweaters in all styles*
【样书】［刷］final proof；sample book：作者看完～后，对封面设计十分满意。*After looking over the final proof, the author expressed pleasure at its cover design.*
【样图】master drawing
【样样】every kind；each and every；all：这孩子德、智、体～都好。*The child is developing in every way, morally, intellectually and physically.*
【样张】［刷］specimen page
【样子】❶ appearance；shape：这件大衣的～很好看。*This coat is well cut.* / 这活做得不像～。*This job has been done too crudely.* ❷ manner；

air：看他那高兴的～。*How happy he looks!* / 装出一副公正的～ *assume a righteous posture* (*or manner, air*) ❸ sample；model；pattern：衣服～ *clothes pattern* / 做出～来 *set an example* ❹〈口〉tendency；likelihood：天像是要下雨的～。*It looks like rain.*

漾 动 ❶ ripple：荡漾 ❷ brim over；overflow：碗里的汤快～出来了。*The soup in the bowl is brimming over.* / 她脸上～出了笑容。*Her face broadened into a smile.*

【漾动】ripple；flutter：她润泽白皙的脸上～着笑意。*A ripple of a smile crossed her smooth pale face.*

【漾奶】(of a baby) throw up milk

【漾溢】brim with；permeate with；fill with：市郊的原野上，～着一片山歌。*The open spaces around the town resonated with folk songs.*

yāo

幺 Ⅰ 数 one (used for the numeral 一 orally) Ⅱ 形〈方〉youngest (among brothers and sisters)：～妹 *youngest sister*

夭 动 die young

【夭殇】〈书〉die young

【夭亡】die young

【夭折】❶ die young ❷ come to a premature end：谈判中途～。*The negotiations came to a premature end.*

吆 (构词成分) 见下

【吆喊】cry out；call：他～了几声，也没人回答。*He called several times, but no one answered.*

【吆喝】❶ cry out；call；shout：走的时候～一声。*Give us a shout when it's time to leave.* ❷ cry one's wares：她头一次上街卖菜，不好意思～。*The first time she went out selling vegetables, she was too shy to cry out for customers.* ❸ loudly urge on (an animal)：牲口不听～。*The animal wouldn't obey its driver.*

【吆唤】cry out；call：你～几个小伙子来帮忙。*Call some of the boys over here to help.*

约 动〈口〉weigh in a balance (or on a scale)：给我～一公斤猪肉。*Weigh me out one kilo of pork.* / ～～多重。*See how much it weighs.* ——另见 yuē

【约克夏猪】Yorkshire (hog)

妖 Ⅰ 名 goblin；demon；evil spirit：妖魔 Ⅱ 形 ❶ seductive：妖里妖气 ❷ evil and fraudulent：妖术

【妖道】Taoist sorcerer or witch

【妖风】evil wind；noxious trend

【妖怪】monster；bogy；goblin；demon

【妖精】❶ evil spirit；demon ❷ seductress；siren

【妖里妖气】seductive；sexy：打扮得～的 *be seductively dressed*

【妖媚】seductively charming；bewitching；sexy

【妖魔】evil spirit；demon ◇ ～鬼怪 demons and ghosts；monsters of every description；all forces of evil

【妖孽】〈书〉❶ person or event associated with evil or misfortune ❷ evildoer

【妖娆】〈书〉enchanting；fascinating；bewitching

【妖人】sorcerer；enchanter

【妖声妖气】(又作'妖声怪气') speak in an affected voice and manner

【妖术】sorcery；witchcraft；black art

【妖妄】fantastic；absurd：～之说 *fallacy*

【妖物】evil spirit；monster

【妖言】heresy；fallacy ◇ ～惑众 spread fallacies to deceive people

【妖艳】seductive；bewitching

【妖冶】seductive；bewitching

要 动 ❶ demand；ask：要求 ❷ force；coerce：要挟 ——另见 yào

【要求】❶ ask；demand；require；claim；call for：～增加工资 *demand a raise in pay* / ～发言 *ask to be heard；ask for the floor* ❷ requirement；demand；claim：达到质量～ *fulfil quality requirements*

【要挟】coerce；put pressure on；threaten：对小国进行～ *use coercion against small nations*

腰 名 ❶ waist；the small of the back：齐～深 *waist-deep；up to the waist* / 弯～ *bend down；stoop* / ～酸腿疼 *aching back and legs* / 扭了～ *sprain one's back muscles* ❷ waist (of a garment)：裤～ *waist of trousers* ❸ pocket：我～里还有些钱。*I've still got some money in my pocket.* ❹ middle：半山～ *halfway up the mountain*

【腰板儿】❶ back：直起～ *straighten one's back* ❷ physique；build：他八十多了，～还挺硬朗。*He's well over eighty, but he's still quite strong.*

【腰包】purse；pocket：把钱装进自己的～ *pocket the money* ——另见〖掏腰包〗

【腰部】waist；the small of the back

【腰缠万贯】be loaded；be very rich

【腰带】belt；girdle

【腰带包】bum-bag

【腰杆子】(又作'腰杆儿') ❶ back：挺起～ *straighten one's back—be confident and unafraid* ❷ backing；support：～硬 *have strong backing*

【腰鼓】❶ waist drum ❷ waist drum dance

【腰果】cashew nut；cashew ◇ ～树［植］cashew (tree)

【腰花】scalloped pork or lamb kidneys：炒～ *stir-fried kidneys*

【腰肌劳损】strain of lumbar muscles；psoatic strain

【腰牌】sign fixed to the sides of public transport vehicles showing the route number or terminal

【腰身】waistline；waist；waist measurement；girth：她的～很细。*She has a slender waist.*

【腰酸背痛】have a sore waist and an aching back—

be aching all over

【腰痛】lumbago

【腰围】❶ waistline; waist measurement：你的～粗了。*Your waistline is getting bigger.* ❷ girdle

【腰眼】either side of the small of the back

【腰斩】❶ cutting sb. in two at the waist (a capital punishment in ancient China) ❷ cut sth. in half

【腰肢】waist：～纤细 *have a slim waist*

【腰椎】［生理］lumbar vertebra ◇ ～穿刺［医］lumbar puncture

【腰子】〈口〉kidney

邀 动 ❶ invite; ask：～几个朋友来打桥牌 *invite (or ask) some friends over for a game of bridge* ❷ solicit; seek：～准 *seek approval; ask permission* ❸ intercept：邀击

【邀宠】try to win sb.'s favour; curry favour with sb.

【邀功】〈书〉take credit for someone else's achievements：～请赏 *take credit and seek rewards for someone else's achievements*

【邀击】intercept (the enemy); waylay

【邀集】invite to meet together; call together：今天～大家来开个座谈会。*You have been invited here today to hold a forum.*

【邀买人心】buy popular support; court popularity

【邀请】invite：愉快地接受～ *accept an invitation with pleasure* ◇ ～国 host country; ～赛［体］invitational tournament; ～信 letter of invitation

【邀赏】ask to be rewarded for service rendered

yáo

尧 名 Yao, a legendary sage king in ancient China

【尧舜】Yao and Shun, legendary sage kings in ancient China—ancient sages

【尧天舜日】the days of Yao and Shun—the golden age of Chinese history (according to the Confucianists)

肴 名 meat and fish dishes：酒～ *wine and dainties*

【肴肉】a kind of cured pork

【肴馔】〈书〉sumptuous courses at a meal

窑 名 ❶ kiln：石灰～ *limekiln* ❷ (coal) pit：小煤～ *small coal pit* ❸ cave dwelling ❹〈方〉brothel

【窑变】kiln transmutation—the technique of making iridescent chinaware by the irregular application of glaze：～花瓶 *a flambé vase*

【窑洞】cave dwelling

【窑灰钾肥】flue ash potash

【窑姐儿】〈方〉prostitute

【窑子】〈方〉brothel

谣 名 ❶ ballad; rhyme：民谣 ❷ rumour：造谣

【谣传】❶ rumour; hearsay ❷ it is rumoured that; rumour has it that

【谣俗】〈书〉customs and habits; folkways

【谣言】rumour; unfounded report; groundless allegation：散布～ *spread (or circulate) rumours*

遥 形〈书〉distant; remote; far：千里之～ *at a distance of a thousand li; a thousand li away*

【遥测】telemetering：空间～ *space telemetry* ◇ ～计 telemeter; ～器 remote detector; ～术 telemetry; ～温度计 telethermometer

【遥感】［电子］remote sensing：红外～ *infrared remote sensing*

【遥控】remote control; telecontrol：～飞机 *remote control aircraft; telecontrolled airplane* / ～开关 *teleswitch* / ～器 *remote controller* / ～汽车 *remote-control car* ◇ ～力学 telemechanics

【遥望】look into the distance

【遥相呼应】echo each other at a distance; coordinate with each other from afar

【遥想】recall; recollect; reminisce：～当年 *reminisce about the good old days*

【遥遥】far away; a long way off：～相对 *stand far apart facing each other* ◇ ～领先 be far ahead; hold a safe lead; ～无期 not (realizable, etc.) within the foreseeable future

【遥远】distant; remote; faraway：～的将来 *the distant (or remote) future* / 路途～ *a long journey; a long way to go*

摇 动 shake; wave; rock; turn：～铃 *ring a bell* / ～扇子 *wave a fan* / ～辘轳 *turn a windlass* / ～橹 *scull; sweep* / 小狗～着尾巴跑了。*The little dog ran off wagging its tail.*

【摇摆】sway; swing; rock; vacillate：船身～。*The ship rocked.* / 左右～ *vacillate now to the left, now to the right* ◇ ～舞 swing; rock and roll; rock; ～乐 swing; swing music

【摇臂】［机］rocker (or rock, rocking) arm：～轴 *rocker shaft* / ～钻床 *radial drilling machine*

【摇船】row a boat

【摇床】［矿］table：选矿～ *cleaning table* / 粗选～ *roughing table*

【摇唇鼓舌】flap one's lips and beat one's tongue—wag one's tongue; engage in loose talk (to stir up trouble)

【摇荡】rock; sway

【摇动】❶ wave; shake：欢迎的群众～着花束。*The welcoming crowd waved their bouquets.* ❷ sway; rock：大树在狂风中～。*The big tree rocked in the strong wind.*

【摇滚乐】rock and roll; rock (music)

【摇撼】give a violent shake to; shake to the root or foundation; rock

【摇晃】rock; sway; shake：这椅子有点～。*The chair is a bit rickety (or shaky).* / 他病了很久，走起路来摇摇晃晃的。*He walked with faltering steps after a long illness.*

【摇奖】❶ lottery ❷ lot cast

【摇篮】cradle：她把孩子放在～里，把他摇睡着了。

She rocked the baby to sleep in the cradle. ◇ ～曲［音］cradle-song; lullaby; berceuse

【摇蜜】extract honey ◇ ～机 honey extractor

【摇旗呐喊】wave flags and shout battle cries—bang the drum for sb.

【摇钱树】a legendary tree that sheds coins when shaken—a ready source of money

【摇纱机】［纺］reeling frame

【摇摄】［摄］pan

【摇身一变】〈贬〉give oneself a shake and change into another form—suddenly change one's identity

【摇手】shake one's hand in admonition or disapproval

【摇头】shake one's head ◇ ～摆尾 shake the head and wag the tail—assume an air of complacency or levity; ～晃脑 wag one's head—look pleased with oneself; assume an air of self-approbation or self-satisfaction

【摇尾乞怜】wag the tail ingratiatingly—fawn obsequiously

【摇摇欲坠】tottering; crumbling; on the verge of collapse: 保守党政府～。*The Conservative Government was tottering.*

【摇曳】flicker; sway: ～的灯光 *flickering light*

【摇椅】rocking chair

瑶 名〈书〉precious jade; jasper: ～琴 *a lute with jasper mountings*

【瑶池】Jasper Lake (the dwelling-place of the Queen Mother of the West 西王母)

【瑶族】the Yao ethnic group, or the Yaos

yǎo

杳 形〈书〉distant and out of sight: ～无踪迹 *disappear without a trace; vanish*

【杳渺】(又作'杳眇')〈书〉distant and indistinct

【杳然】〈书〉quiet; still

【杳如黄鹤】leave like the yellow crane—leave never to return; be gone for ever

【杳无音信】there has been no news whatsoever about sb.; never been heard of since: 他走后～。*We have not heard from him since he left.* or *No word has come from him since he left.*

咬 动 ❶ bite; snap at: ～不动 *too tough to bite (or chew)* / ～一口 *take a bite* / 被蛇～了 *be bitten by a snake* ❷ grip; bite: 这个旧螺母～不住扣儿了。*This old nut won't bite (or grip).* / 双方比分一直～得很紧。*The score was very close throughout the match.* ❸ (of a dog) bark: 鸡叫狗～ *cocks crow and dogs bark* ❹ incriminate another person (usu. innocent) when blamed or interrogated: 别～好人。*Don't implicate the innocent.* ❺〈方〉corrode (metals); irritate (the skin): 我最怕漆～。*I'm allergic to paint.* or *My skin is allergic to paint.* / 这把刀埋在地里让土～了。*The knife had been buried in the ground and was corroded.* ❻ pronounce; articulate: 这个字他～不准。*He can't pronounce this word correctly.* ❼ be nitpicking (about the use of words): 咬字眼儿

【咬耳朵】〈口〉whisper in sb.'s ear; whisper

【咬合】(of gear wheels, etc.) interlock; engage; mesh

【咬紧牙关】grit (or clench) one's teeth; endure with dogged will: 他～忍受。*He gritted his teeth and resolved to hold out.*

【咬啮】gnaw: 恐惧和焦虑正～着她的心。*Fear and anxiety were gnawing at her heart.*

【咬舌儿】(又作'咬舌子') ❶ lisp ❷ lisper

【咬文嚼字】pay excessive attention to wording

【咬牙】❶ grit (or set, clench, gnash) one's teeth: 恨得直～ *gnash one's teeth in hatred* / 咬咬牙干下去 *go at it with set (or clenched) teeth* ❷ grind one's teeth (in sleep) ◇ ～切齿 gnash one's teeth

【咬住】❶ bite into; grip with one's teeth: 用嘴～绳子 *grip the rope with one's teeth* ❷ grip; take firm hold of; refuse to let go of: 别老～我那句话不放。*Don't keep nagging me about that remark of mine.*

【咬字儿】pronounce; articulate: 她～清楚。*Her articulation is clear.*

【咬字眼儿】be nitpicking on words

【咬嘴】be difficult to articulate; be awkward-sounding

窈（构词成分）见下

【窈冥】〈书〉❶ dim; dusky ❷ deep; profound; abstruse

【窈窕】〈书〉❶ (of a woman) gentle and graceful ❷ (of a palace, landscape, etc.) secluded

舀 动 ladle out; spoon up (or out); scoop up: ～汤 *ladle out soup*

【舀子】dipper; ladle; scoop

yào

疟（构词成分）见下 ——另见 nüè

【疟子】〈口〉malaria

药 Ⅰ 名 ❶ medicine; drug; remedy: 你吃过～了吗? *Have you taken your medicine yet?* / 这种～得有大夫处方才能买。*This drug is sold only on a doctor's prescription.* / 一种治高血压的新～ *a new remedy for high blood pressure* / 进口～ *imported drugs* ❷ certain chemicals: 杀虫～ *insecticide; pesticide* Ⅱ 动 ❶〈书〉cure with medicine: 不可救药 ❷ kill with poison: 把老鼠～死 *kill rats with rat poison*

【药补】build up one's health by taking tonic: ～不如食补。*Nourishing food is better than tonic.*

【药材】medicinal materials; crude drugs

【药草】medicinal herbs

【药茶】herb tea; medicated tea

【药厂】pharmaceutical factory
【药单】(medical) prescription
【药典】pharmacopoeia
【药店】drugstore；chemist's shop；pharmacy
【药方】prescription：开～ *write out a prescription*
【药房】❶ drugstore；chemist's shop；pharmacy ❷ hospital pharmacy；dispensary
【药费】expenses for medicine；charges for medicine
【药粉】(medicinal) powder
【药膏】ointment；salve
【药罐子】❶ a pot for decocting herbal medicine ❷ a chronic invalid
【药害】environmental damage caused by improper use of insecticides
【药衡】apothecaries' measure or weight
【药剂】medicament；drug ◇ ～师 pharmacist；pharmaceutist；druggist；～学 pharmaceutics；pharmacy
【药检】drug test：所有的运动员要进行～。*All athletes must take a drug test*.
【药箭】a poisoned arrow
【药劲儿】efficacy of a drug (or medicine)
【药酒】medicinal liquor
【药具】medication and device，spec. for contraception；contraceptives：安全、有效、简便、经济的避孕～ *safe，effective，convenient and cheap contraceptives*
【药理】❶ pharmacodynamics ❷ pharmacology ◇ ～学 pharmacology
【药力】efficacy of a drug (or medicine)：～发作。*The drug is taking effect*. / ～达不到。*The medicine was not potent enough to produce the desired effect*.
【药麻】［医］drug anaesthesia
【药棉】absorbent cotton
【药面儿】(medicinal) powder
【药捻儿】❶ fuse (for igniting an explosive charge) ❷ 同〖药捻子〗
【药捻子】a slender roll of medicated paper or gauze (to be inserted into wounds，boils，etc.)
【药农】a peasant who cultivates or collects medicinal herbs；medicinal herb grower or collector；herbalist
【药片】(medicinal) tablet
【药品】medicines and chemical reagents
【药瓶】medicine bottle
【药铺】herbal medicine shop
【药签】swab
【药膳】medicated food；food cooked with medicinal herbs
【药石】medicines and stone needles for acupuncture—remedies ◇ ～之言（又作'药言'）unpalatable but salutary advice
【药水】❶ liquid medicine；medicinal liquid ❷ lotion
【药丸】（又作'药丸子'）pill：大～ *bolus*
【药味】❶ herbal medicines in a prescription ❷ flavour of a drug
【药物】pharmaceuticals；materia medica；medicines；drugs ◇ ～过敏 drug allergy；～化学 pharmaceutical chemistry；～学 materia medica；pharmacognosy；～牙膏 medicated toothpaste；～中毒 drug poisoning
【药箱】medical kit；medicine-chest：急救～ *first-aid kit*
【药效】efficacy of a drug (or medicine)
【药性】property of a medicine：这种药～平和。*This medicine is quite mild*.
【药学】pharmacy
【药引子】［中］an ingredient added to enhance the efficacy of a dose of medicine；a medical supplement
【药用植物】medicinal plant
【药浴】［牧］dipping：羊～ *sheep dipping* / ～池 *dipping vat*
【药皂】medicated soap
【药渣】dregs of a decoction
【药疹】［医］drug rash；drug eruption
【药枕】medical pillow
【药政】pharmaceutical control and administration：～法 *pharmaceutical control law*

要 Ⅰ〔形〕important；essential：～事 *an important matter (or affair)* / 上述规定希严格执行为～。*It is imperative that the above rules be strictly observed*. Ⅱ〔名〕main points；essentials：择～记录 *note down the essential points* Ⅲ〔动〕❶ want；ask for；wish；desire：他～一架手风琴。*He wants an accordion*. / 这双鞋我还～呢。*I want to keep these shoes*. / 我～了两个菜。*I ordered two dishes*. ❷ ask (or want) sb. to do sth.：老大爷～我替他写封信。*The old man asked me to write a letter for him*. / 不是你～我来的吗？*Wasn't it you who asked me to come?* ❸ want to；wish to：这位先生～见总经理。*This gentleman wishes to see the general manager*. / 我还有几句话～说。*I'd like to say a few more words*. / 他～学游泳。*He wants to learn swimming*. ❹ must；should；it is necessary (or imperative，essential)：我～不～留下来？*Shall I stay?* / 这个问题～仔细考虑。*This question calls for careful consideration*. / 早点儿睡吧，明天还～起早呢。*Let's go to bed now. We'll have to get up early tomorrow morning*. ❺ shall；will；be going to：～下雨了。*It's going to rain*. / 天～黑了，快走吧。*It's getting dark. Let's hurry up!* / 他快～回来了。*He will soon be back*. ❻ need；take：这项任务～十天才能完成。*It will take ten days to get the work done*. / 这活儿～不了这么多人。*You don't need so many people for this job*. ❼ (used in comparisons to indicate an estimate)：你们～比我们辛苦得多。*You must have had a much tougher time than we did*. / 树阴底下比屋子里～凉快些。*It is cooler under the tree than in the room*. Ⅳ〔连〕❶ if；suppose；in case：我～赶不回来，你替我说一声。*In case I can't get back in time，please apologize for me*. /

这有什么可怕的，～我就不怕。*What is there to be afraid of? I wouldn't be afraid if I were you.* ❷（usu. used with 就 or 就是）or; either... or...：～就去跳舞，～就去听音乐，别处我不去。*Let's go either to the dance or to the concert. I won't go anywhere else.* ——另见 yāo

【要隘】strategic pass

【要案】important case：处理～ *handle a serious case*

【要不】（又作'要不然'）otherwise; or else; or：我得马上走，～就赶不上火车了。*I have to leave at once or I'll miss the train.*

【要不得】be no good; be intolerable：这种自私行为～。*Such selfish acts are not to be tolerated.*

【要不是】if it were not for; but for：～下雨，我们早就出门了。*We would have gone out long ago but for the rain.*

【要冲】communications centre (or hub)：军事～ *strategic point* / 兰州是西北交通的～。*Lanzhou is the communications hub of the Northwest.*

【要道】thoroughfare：交通～ *important line of communications; vital communications line*

【要得】〈方〉good; fine; desirable：这个办法～！*That's a good idea!*

【要地】important place; strategic point：徐州是历史上的军事～。*Xuzhou has been well known in history as a hotly contested strategic point.*

【要点】❶ main points; essentials; gist：抓住～ *grasp the main points* / 讲话的～ *the gist of a speech* ❷ key strongpoint：战略～ *strategic point*

【要犯】an important criminal

【要饭】beg (for food or money)：～的 *beggar*

【要害】❶ vital part; crucial point：～部位 *vital part* / ～部门 *key department* / 回避～问题 *evade the crucial question (or issue)* / 击中～ *hit home* / 抓住～ *scratch where it itches* ❷ strategic point：地处～ *be located at a strategic point*

【要好】❶ be on good terms; be close friends：她们俩从小就很～。*The two of them have been close friends since childhood.* ❷ be eager to improve oneself; try hard to make progress：这孩子很～。*The kid is eager to make progress.*

【要价】ask a price; charge：～过高 *demand an exorbitant price; ask too much* ◇ ～还价 bargain; haggle

【要件】❶ an important document ❷ an important condition

【要津】❶〈书〉key place ❷ key post：位居～ *hold a key post*

【要紧】❶ important; essential：我有点～的事儿跟他商量。*I have something urgent to discuss with him.* ❷ be critical; be serious; matter：他只受了点儿轻伤，没什么～的。*He was only slightly injured—nothing serious.* ❸〈方〉be in a hurry to; be anxious to：～去上班 *be in a hurry to go to work*

【要诀】important tricks of the trade; knack

【要脸】be keen on face-saving; care much about one's reputation

【要领】❶ main points; gist：不得要领 ❷ essentials (of an exercise in military or athletic training)：掌握～ *grasp the essentials*

【要略】outline; summary

【要么】（又作'要末'）or; either...or...：赶快给他发个电报，～挂个长途也行。*Send him a telegram at once, or call him long-distance.*

【要面子】be keen on face-saving; be anxious to keep up appearances

【要命】❶ drive sb. to his death; kill：这样短的期限，要了我的命，也完成不了定额。*I cannot fulfil the quota in such a short time even if I kill myself.* ❷ confoundedly; extremely; awfully; terribly：热得～ *awfully hot* / 渴得～ *terribly thirsty* ❸ a nuisance：真～，车胎又没气了。*What an awful nuisance. The tyre's flat again.* / 这姑娘可真～，火车都快开了，她还没影儿呢。*That girl is quite impossible. The train starts in a minute and there's still no sign of her.*

【要强】be eager to excel; be anxious to outdo others

【要人】very important person (VIP); important personage

【要塞】fort; fortress; fortification

【要事】an important matter：她说有～相商。*She says she has something important to consult you about.*

【要是】〈口〉if; suppose; in case：～下雨怎么办？*What if it rains?* or *Suppose it rains?* / ～别人，我才不管呢。*If it had been somebody else, I wouldn't have bothered myself.*

【要死】extremely; awfully; terribly：怕蛇怕得～ *be terribly afraid of snakes*

【要素】essential factor; key element

【要图】an important plan (or programme)

【要闻】important news; front-page story：～版 *the front page of a newspaper*

【要言不烦】terse; succinct; pithy

【要员】important official

【要账】demand payment of a debt; press for repayment of a loan; dun

【要职】an important post：身居～ *hold an important post*

【要旨】main idea; gist

钥（构词成分）见下 ——另见 yuè

【钥匙】key

鹞 名 sparrow hawk (another name for 雀鹰)

【鹞鹰】common name for 雀鹰

【鹞子】❶ common name for 雀鹰 ❷〈方〉kite

曜〈书〉Ⅰ 名 sunlight Ⅱ 动 shine; illuminate

耀 Ⅰ 动 ❶ shine; illuminate; dazzle：照耀 ❷ boast of; laud：夸耀 Ⅱ 名 honour; credit：荣耀

【耀斑】[天] solar flare

【耀武扬威】make a show of one's strength; swagger around; throw one's weight around: 表面上～,骨子里贪生怕死。*All bluff and bluster; in their bones they're afraid to die!*

【耀眼】dazzling: 车灯～。*The headlights are dazzling.* / ～的红旗 *bright red flags*

yē

耶 (构词成分) 见下

【耶和华】[宗](基督教) Jehovah (an Old Testament name for God)

【耶路撒冷】Jerusalem

【耶稣】(又作'耶稣基督') Jesus; Jesus Christ

【耶稣会】the Society of Jesus; the Jesuits

【耶稣教】Protestantism

掖 动 tuck in; thrust in between: 把被角～好 *tuck in the corner of the quilt* / 把衬衫～到裤子里边 *tuck one's shirt in* / 把纸条从门缝里～进去 *slip a note under the door* / 腰里～着枪 *with a pistol in one's belt* ——另见 yè

椰 名 [植] coconut palm; coconut tree; coco

【椰雕】[工美] coconut shell carving

【椰干】desiccated coconut; copra

【椰壳】coconut husk ◇ ～纤维 coir fibre; coir

【椰仁】coconut kernel; coconut meat ◇ ～干 desiccated coconut; copra

【椰蓉】fine coconut mash (used as a filling for cakes): ～月饼 *coconut moon cake (with such a filling)*

【椰丝】shredded coconut meat (used as a topping for cakes)

【椰油】coconut oil; coconut butter

【椰枣】[植] date palm; date

【椰子】❶ coconut palm; coconut tree; coco ❷ coconut (the fruit): ～肉 *coconut kernel; coconut meat* / ～糖 *coconut candy* / ～汁 *coconut milk*

噎 动 ❶ choke: 慢点吃,留神别～着。*Eat slowly. Be careful not to choke.* ❷〈方〉render sb. speechless by saying sth. blunt or rude; choke off: 他一句话就把她给～回去了。*She was just going to say something when that one remark of his choked her off.*

【噎嗝】[中] cancer of the esophagus

yé

爷 名 ❶〈方〉father: ～娘 *father and mother* ❷〈方〉grandfather ❸ (a respectful form of address for an elderly man) uncle: 李～ *Uncle Li* / 四～ *Fourth Uncle* ❹〈旧〉(a form of address for an official or rich man) sir; master; lord: 少爷 ❺ (a worshipper's form of address for a god): 土地～ *God of the Land* / 阎王～ *Yama, King of Hell*

【爷儿】〈口〉(often followed by 俩,几个,etc.) a senior male member of a family together with one or more junior members: ～俩并肩战斗。*Father and son fought side by side.*

【爷们】〈方〉❶ man or menfolk ❷ husband

【爷们儿】〈方〉a collective term for men of two or more generations

【爷儿们】〈口〉同〖爷们儿〗

【爷爷】〈口〉❶ (paternal) grandfather ❷ grandpa (a respectful form of address for any old man)

揶 (构词成分) 见下

【揶揄】〈书〉ridicule; deride: 她的微笑中带有一丝～。*There was a trace of derision in her smile.*

yě

也 Ⅰ 助〈书〉❶ (used at the end of a sentence, indicating an explanation or a judgment): 陈胜者,阳城人～。*Chen Sheng was a native of Yangcheng.* / 是不为～,非不能～。*This is a case of choosing not to, not of being unable to.* ❷ (used at the end of a question or counterquestion): 何～? *How is that?* or *Why so?* / 是可忍也,孰不可忍～? *If this can be tolerated, what else cannot?* Ⅱ 副 ❶ also; too; as well; either: 我妹妹～是售货员。*My sister is a shop assistant too.* / 你不去,我～不去。*If you're not going, I'm not going either.* ❷ (used for emphasis, often before a negative expression): 他病得一点～不想吃。*He is so ill that he doesn't feel like eating anything.* / 他忙得连饭～顾不上吃。*He is so busy that he can't even stop for a meal.* ❸ (used correlatively with 虽然,即使,etc.) still; yet: 我虽然没见过,～听人说过。*I've heard about it, though I have never seen it.* / 我即使干不了重活,～可以干点轻活嘛。*If I can't do heavy work, I can still do some light work.* ❹ (used in a hesitant or guarded statement): ～只好这样了。*We'll have to leave it at that.* / 这袋土豆～就一百公斤。*This sack of potatoes weighs a hundred kilos at most.* / 他的英语～还可以。*His English is passable.*

【也罢】❶ (used to express forbearance, resignation, etc.) well; all right: 这次不去～,下次可一定要让我去。*All right, I won't go this time but next time you must let me go.* ❷ (reduplicated) whether...or...; no matter whether: 刮风～,下雪～,他都坚持跑步。*He keeps up his jogging whether it's blowing or snowing.* / 你去～,不去～,反正是一样。*It makes no difference whether you go or not.*

【也好】❶ it may not be a bad idea; may as well: 说明一下～。*Better give an explanation.* ❷ (reduplicated) whether...or...; no matter whether: 学习～,劳动～,他都很积极。*He is enthusiastic about both study and physical labour.*

【也门】Yemen ◇ ～人 Yemeni; Yemenite

【也许】perhaps; probably; maybe: 他～病了。

Perhaps he's ill. / 我～来,～不来。*I may or may not come*.

【也…也…】❶ both...and...; either...or...: 也有好的,也有坏的。*There are both good ones and bad ones*. / 他也不抽烟,也不喝酒。*He neither smokes nor drinks*. ❷ no matter (whether, who, etc.): 天好我们也干,天不好我们也干。*We never stop working, rain or shine*. / 他左想也不是,右想也不是。*He just couldn't make up his mind either way*.

冶 动 smelt (metal): 冶金

【冶荡】lewd; lascivious

【冶金】metallurgy: ～工业 *metallurgical industry* ◇ ～学 metallurgy

【冶炼】smelt: ～操作 *smelting operation* / ～厂 *smeltery* / ～炉 *smelting furnace* / ～时间 *duration of heat*

野 Ⅰ 名 ❶ open country; the open: 野火 ❷ limit; boundary: 视野 ❸ not in power; out of office: 在野 Ⅱ 形 ❶ (of plants or animals) wild; uncultivated; undomesticated; untamed: ～花 *wild flowers* / ～狗 *homeless dogs* ❷ rude; rough: 说话太～ *use coarse language*; *speak rudely* / 动作太～ *rough play* ❸ unrestrained; abandoned; unruly: 放了几天假,这孩子的心都玩～了。*After the fun he's had during the holidays, the boy can't concentrate on his school work*.

【野菜】edible wild herbs

【野餐】picnic

【野草】weeds: ～丛生 *be overgrown (or choked) with weeds* ◇ ～闲花 weeds and wild flowers; mistress; prostitute

【野传】[体](棒球和垒球) wild throw: ～球 *passed ball*

【野炊】cook in the open air

【野地】wild country; wilderness

【野调无腔】coarse (or uncouth) in speech and manner

【野果】wild fruit

【野汉子】a woman's lover

【野合】〈书〉have illicit sexual relations; commit adultery

【野鹤闲云】同〖闲云野鹤〗

【野狐禅】[宗](佛教) heresy

【野火】prairie fire; bush fire ◇ ～烧不尽,春风吹又生 even a prairie fire cannot destroy the grass; it grows again when the spring breeze blows (said of what cannot be suppressed.)

【野鸡】❶ common name for 雉 ❷ streetwalker; unlicensed prostitute ◇ ～大学 diploma mill

【野景】wild scenery

【野菊花】mother chrysanthemum

【野驴】Asiatic wild ass; kiang

【野麻】❶ wild flax; wild hemp ❷ popular name for 罗布麻

【野马】❶ wild horse; untamed horse ❷ Przhevalski's horse (Equus przewalskii)

【野蛮】❶ uncivilized; savage ❷ barbarous; cruel; brutal: ～行为 *barbarous act*; *savage behaviour*

【野猫】❶ wildcat ❷ a stray cat ❸〈方〉hare

【野牛】wild ox (Bos gaurus)

【野炮】field gun; field artillery

【野蔷薇】[植] multiflora rose

【野趣】rustic charm

【野人】❶ an uncouth person; rustic ❷ savage; barbarian

【野生】wild; undomesticated; uncultivated; feral: ～植物 *wild plant* ◇ ～动物 wildlife

【野食儿】❶ animals' food picked up in the wilds ❷ ill-gotten (or illicit) gains

【野史】unofficial history

【野兽】wild beast; wild animal ◇ ～派 [工美] fauvism; brutalism

【野兔】hare

【野外】open country; field: 在～工作 *do fieldwork* / ～生活 *outdoor life* / ～演习 *field exercise* / ～作业 *fieldwork*; *field operation*

【野豌豆】[植] vetch (Vicia sativa)

【野味】game (as food)

【野心】wild ambition; careerism: 侵略～ *aggressive ambitions* ◇ ～勃勃 be overweeningly ambitious; be obsessed with ambition; ～家 careerist; ～狼 a vicious wolf—a person of evil ambitions

【野性】wild nature; unruliness: ～难驯 *untamable*

【野营】camp; bivouac: 出外～ *go camping* / ～训练 *camp and field training* ◇ ～车 camper

【野战】[军] field operations: ～仓库 *field depot* / ～工事 *fieldwork* ◇ ～军 field army; ～炮 fieldpiece; field gun; ～医院 field hospital

【野猪】wild boar (Sus scrofa)

yè

业 Ⅰ 名 ❶ line of business; trade; industry: 工业 ❷ occupation; profession; employment; job: 我家世代以农为～。*I come from a long line of farmers*. ❸ course of study: 结业 ❹ cause; enterprise: 创业 ❺ estate; property: 家业 ❻ [宗](佛教) karma; deed; action Ⅱ 动 engage in: ～农 *engage in farming* Ⅲ 副 already: ～已核实 *have already been verified*

【业报】[宗](佛教) retribution for sins

【业海】[宗](佛教) sea of retribution

【业绩】outstanding achievement: 医学界的最新～ *the latest achievements in medical science*

【业界】business circles

【业经】already: ～批准 *have been approved*

【业精于勤】mastery of work comes from diligent application; a subject is mastered through diligent study

【业师】one's (former) teacher

【业务】vocational work; professional work; business: 钻研～ *diligently study one's profession* / 恢复正常～ *resume normal business* ◇ ～范围

scope of business；～能力 professional ability (or proficiency)；～水平 professional skill；vocational level；～协定 business agreement；～学习 vocational study；～知识 professional knowledge

【业务班子】professional team；business team

【业务挂帅】put professional work in command；professional work comes first

【业务尖子】top-notch professional

【业余】❶ spare time；after-hours：～爱好 *hobby* / ～理论学习 *theoretical study after workhours* ❷ nonprofessional；amateur：～文艺工作者 *amateur literary and art workers* / ～剧团 *an amateur theatrical troupe* ◇ ～教育 spare-time education；～学校 spare-time school

【业余补习学校】spare-time continuation school

【业障】❶［宗］（佛教）retribution in this life for the sins of a previous existence ❷〈诋〉(said to one's children) medium of retribution

【业种】同〖孽种〗

【业主】owner (of an enterprise or estate)；proprietor

叶 名 ❶ leaf；foliage：红花绿～ *red flowers and green leaves* ❷ leaf-like thing：一～扁舟 *a small boat* ❸ 同〖页〗 ❹ part of a historical period：清朝末～ *the closing period of the Qing Dynasty* / 十九世纪中～ *(in) the middle of the 19th century*

【叶斑病】［农］leaf spot

【叶柄】［植］petiole；leafstalk

【叶蝉】leafhopper (an insect)

【叶蜂】sawfly (an insect)

【叶公好龙】Lord Ye's love of dragons—professed love of what one really fears

【叶红素】another name for 胡萝卜素

【叶猴】leaf monkey

【叶黄素】［生化］xanthophyll；lutein

【叶蜡石】pyrophyllite (a mineral)

【叶绿素】［生化］chlorophyll

【叶绿体】［生化］chloroplast

【叶轮】［机］impeller；vane wheel：～泵 *vane pump*

【叶落归根】the falling leaves settle on the roots—a person residing elsewhere finally returns to his ancestral home

【叶脉】［植］leaf vein

【叶片】❶ leaf blade ❷［机］vane：～式压缩机 *vane compressor*

【叶鞘】［植］leaf sheath

【叶肉】［植］mesophyll

【叶酸】［医］folic acid；folacin

【叶锈病】［农］leaf rust

【叶序】［植］phyllotaxy；leaf arrangement

【叶芽】［植］leaf bud

【叶子】leaf

【叶子烟】dried tobacco leaves

页 名 page or leaf：这本书掉了一～。*A leaf is missing from the book.* / 一本三百～的书 *a book of three hundred pages* / 打开新的一～ *open up a new chapter*

【页边】margin

【页理】the laminated structure of shale

【页码】page number

【页心】［刷］type page

【页岩】［地质］shale

【页岩油】shale oil

曳 动 drag；haul；tug；tow

【曳白】〈书〉hand in a blank paper in an imperial examination

【曳光穿甲弹】［军］armour-piercing tracer

【曳光弹】［军］tracer bullet or shell；tracer

【曳力】［物］drag force

【曳绳钓】［渔］trolling

【曳引】tow；tug

夜 名 night；evening：冬天昼短～长。*In winter the days are short and the nights long.* / 三天三～讲不完。*It would take days to tell it all.*

【夜班】night shift：值～ *be on night shift*

【夜半】midnight

【夜不闭户】doors are not bolted at night —law and order prevail ——另见〖道不拾遗〗

【夜餐】midnight snack

【夜叉】❶［宗］（佛教）yaksha (a malevolent spirit) ❷ a hideous，ferocious person

【夜长梦多】a long night is fraught with dreams—a long delay means trouble

【夜场】evening show；evening performance

【夜车】night train ——另见〖开夜车〗

【夜出动物】nocturnal animal

【夜大学】evening university

【夜工】night work；night job：打～ *work at night；do a night job*

【夜光杯】a cup of phosphorescent jade

【夜光表】luminous watch

【夜光虫】noctiluca

【夜光螺】green snail

【夜航】night flight or navigation

【夜合】❶ silk tree ❷〈方〉the tuber of multiflower knotweed (Polygonum multiflorum)

【夜壶】chamber pot

【夜间】at night：～行军 *march by night；night march* / ～施工 *carry on construction work at night* / ～演习 *night exercise* / ～战斗机 *night fighter*

【夜交藤】［中］the vine of multiflower knotweed (Polygonum multiflorum)

【夜禁】curfew

【夜景】night scene (or view)

【夜课】evening class

【夜空】the night sky：一道道探照灯光划破～。*Searchlight beams pierced the night sky.*

【夜来香】［植］cordate telosma

【夜阑人静】（又作'夜深人静'）in the dead of night；in the still (or quiet) of the night

【夜郎自大】ludicrous conceit of the King of Ye-

lang—parochial arrogance
【夜里】at night
【夜盲】［医］nyctalopia；night blindness
【夜猫子】〈方〉❶ owl ❷ a person who goes to bed late；night owl
【夜明珠】night-luminescent pearl
【夜幕】curtain (or veil) of night；gathering darkness：～降临。*Night has fallen.*
【夜尿症】enuresis；bed-wetting
【夜勤】night duty
【夜曲】［音］nocturne
【夜入私宅罪】［法］burglary
【夜色】the dim light of night：趁着～ *by starlight or moonlight* / ～苍茫 *in gathering dusk*
【夜生活】night life
【夜市】night market
【夜视仪】［军］night vision device (or instrument)
【夜啼】morbid night crying of babies
【夜晚】night
【夜望镜】［军］snooperscope
【夜袭】night attack (or raid)
【夜宵】(又作'夜消') food (or refreshments) taken late at night；midnight snack
【夜校】(又作'夜学') night (or evening) school
【夜行】❶ go out walking in the night；travel by night ❷ night flight or navigation ◇ ～军 night march
【夜夜】every night
【夜以继日】day and night；round the clock
【夜莺】nightingale
【夜鹰】nightjar；goatsucker
【夜游神】the legendary god on patrol at night—a person who is up and about at night；night owl
【夜战】❶［军］night fighting ❷ night work：打两个～ *put in two nights' work*
【夜总会】nightclub；cabaret

液 名 liquid；fluid；juice：溶液
【液肥】liquid manure (fertilizer)
【液化】liquefaction ◇ ～器 liquefier；～石油气 liquefied petroleum gas (LPG)；～天然气 liquefied natural gas (LNG)
【液化气】同〖液化天然气〗◇ ～罐 gas bottle
【液晶】liquid crystal ◇ ～显示 liquid crystal display (LCD)
【液晶电视】liquid crystal TV
【液冷】liquid cooling (or cooled)：～式内燃机 *liquid cooled engine*
【液力】［机］hydraulic：～变速箱 *hydraulic transmission box* / ～传动 *hydraulic power* / ～制动器 *hydraulic brake*
【液泡】［生理］vacuole
【液态】liquid state：～空气 *liquid air*
【液体】liquid ◇ ～比重计 hydrometer；～镜［天］liquid mirror；～燃料 liquid fuel
【液压】hydraulic pressure：～传动 *hydraulic transmission (or drive)* / ～联轴节 *hydraulic coupling* ◇ ～泵 hydraulic pump；～表 hydraulic pressure gauge；～传动装置 hydraulic transmission device；～机 hydraulic press

掖 动 ❶ support sb. by the arm ❷ help；assist；promote：奖掖 ——另见 yē

谒 动〈书〉call on (a superior or an elder person)；pay one's respects to：～陵 *pay homage at sb.'s mausoleum*
【谒见】call on (a superior or a senior in the clan hierarchy)；have an audience with

腋 名 ❶［生理］axilla；armpit ❷［植］axil
【腋臭】underarm odour
【腋毛】armpit hair
【腋窝】armpit
【腋芽】同〖侧芽〗

yī

一 Ⅰ 数 ❶ one：～匹马 *a horse* / ～瓶牛奶 *one bottle of milk* / ～万～ *eleven thousand* / 棉纺～厂 *No. 1 Cotton Mill* ❷ single；alone；only one：～枪就打中了目标 *hit the target with a single shot* / 你～个人行吗？*Can you manage all by yourself?* Ⅱ 形 ❶ same：意见不～。*Opinions differ.* / 这姑娘跟她妈妈～个模样。*The girl is the image of her mother.* / 这不是～码事。*They are not the same thing.* ❷ whole；all；throughout：～冬 *the whole winter；all winter；throughout the winter* / 他～脸的土。*His face was covered with dust.* / ～屋子的人都欢腾起来。*Everybody in the room was overjoyed.* ❸ concentrated；wholehearted：专心～意 *single-minded；concentrated* Ⅲ 副 ❶ every time：大家～提起那艰苦创业的日子，总有说不完的话。*Every time we talk about the hard pioneering days, we have so much to say that we can't get it all out.* ❷ also；otherwise：汞溴红～名红汞。*Merbromin is also known as mercurochrome.* ❸ (used before a verb or a verbal measure to indicate an action to be followed by a result)：～跳跳了过去 *get over in one jump* / 他～脚把球踢进了球门。*He kicked the ball into the goal.* or *He kicked a goal.* ❹ (used before a verb or an adjective, indicating the suddenness or thoroughness of an action or a change in the situation)：那马猛然～惊，直立起来。*All of a sudden the horse shied and reared in fright.* / 这部电影值得～看。*This movie is well worth seeing.* Ⅳ 助 ❶ (used in the middle of a reduplicated verb)：笑～笑 *give a smile* / 歇～歇 *have a rest* / 等～等 *wait a bit* / 出去走～走 *go out for a stroll* / 让我闻～闻。*Let me smell it.* ❷ (used between a verb and a verbal measure)：瞧～眼 *take a look* / 咳～声 *give a cough* / 咬～口 *take a bite* / 打他～巴掌 *give him a slap*
【一把手】❶ a party to an undertaking；a member；a hand：我们准备搭伙干，你也算上～吧。*We're going to pool our efforts. Shall we count you in?*

❷ very capable person：里里外外～ *good housekeeper and competent worker* ❸（of an institution）first in command，head，chief：不论做～，还是二把手、三把手，都要负起自己的责任来。*Whether first，second or third in command，each must assume his reponsibility*. ❹ a good hand：她干农活可真是～。*She is really good at farm work*. ❺ 同〖第一把手〗

【一把钥匙开一把锁】open different locks with different keys—use different methods to solve different problems

【一把抓】❶ take everything into one's own hands ❷ try to tackle all problems at once regardless of their relative importance

【一败涂地】fail completely；suffer a crushing defeat；be routed：我们有准备，决不会～。*We just can't possibly fail completely，after all the preparations we've made*.

【一班人】members of a squad—a small body of people working together：党委～ *the members of the Party committee*

【一般】❶ same as；just like：他们俩～高。*The two of them are the same height*. / 火车飞～地驰去。*The train flashed past like lightning*. ❷ general；ordinary；common：从～到具体 *from generalities to particulars* / ～工作人员 *ordinary personnel*；*an ordinary member of the staff*

【一般化】vague generalization：防止领导～ *avoid giving only vague，general directions*

【一般见识】（lower oneself to）the same level as sb.：别跟他～。*You don't want to bother yourself arguing with the likes of him*. / 由他便了，你也和他～。*Let him alone，that is all. Do you want to behave like him*?

【一斑】one spot（on a leopard）；one of a number of similar things ——另见〖管中窥豹，可见一斑〗

【一板一眼】following a prescribed（or set）pattern in speech or action；scrupulous and methodical：他办事总是那么～的。*He is always very methodical in his work*.

【一板正经】同〖一本正经〗

【一半】one half；half；in part：～以上 *more than half* / 把菜籽平分一下，给他们～儿，咱们留～儿。*Let's share the vegetable seeds with them，share and share alike*.

【一…半…】（used with synonymous words，forming a phrase implying not much or many or not a long time）：我只听到一句半句的。*What I heard was very fragmentary*. / 我去个一年半载就回来。*I'll be back within a year*.

【一半天】〈口〉in a day or two：过～就给你送回去。*I'll return it to you in a day or two*.

【一报还一报】retribution paid out in kind

【一辈子】all one's life；throughout one's life；as long as one lives；a lifetime：～也忘不了。*I won't forget as long as I live*.

【一本万利】a small investment brings a ten thousand-fold profit；make big profits with a small capital

【一本正经】in all seriousness；in dead earnest：装得～的样子 *assume a mock-serious manner*；*be sanctimonious*

【一鼻孔出气】〈贬〉breathe through the same nostrils—sing the same tune

【一笔勾销】write off at one stroke；cancel：我们的旧账可以～。*It's time we wrote off all our old scores*.

【一笔抹杀】blot out at one stroke；condemn out of hand；totally negate：这些成绩是不能～的。*These achievements cannot be gainsaid*.

【一臂之力】a helping hand：助我～ *lend me a hand*

【一边】❶ one side；side：两方面争论，总有～儿理屈。*In a dispute between two parties there is always one which is in the wrong*. ❷ either side：在他身旁，～儿站着一个保镖。*A bodyguard stood at either of his sides*. ❸ at the same time；simultaneously：他悠闲地往前走，～唱着歌儿。*He sang as he strolled leisurely along*. / ～喝茶，～聊天 *chat over a cup of tea*

【一边倒】❶ lean to one side；side with sb. without reservation ❷ predominate；enjoy overwhelming superiority

【一表人材】a man of striking appearance

【一并】along with all the others；in the lump：读者提出的几个疑问，现在～答复如下。*What follows is an answer to all the questions raised by the readers*.

【一病不起】take to one's bed and never leave it again；fall ill and die

【一波三折】full of twists and turns or ups and downs

【一波未平，一波又起】hardly has one wave subsided when another rises—one trouble follows another

【一…不…】❶（used with two verbs to indicate the unalterability of a situation）：一去不返 *gone never to return* / 一定不易 *unalterable* ❷（used with a noun and a verb）not a single；not the slightest：一字不漏 *without missing a single word* / 一笔不苟 *be scrupulous about every stroke*（*in writing or painting*）

【一不怕苦，二不怕死】fear neither hardship nor death

【一不做，二不休】carry it through，whatever the consequences；in for a penny，in for a pound：到这地步，～，我是打算拼一拼了！*Now that we've gone as far as this，we must either go the whole hog or else drop it altogether. I'm in favour of putting up a fight，myself*.

【一步登天】reach the sky in a single bound—attain the highest level in one step；have a meteoric rise

【一步一个脚印】every step leaves its print—work steadily and make solid progress

【一差二错】a possible mistake or mishap：万一有个～ *just in case there is a slip somewhere*；*just in case of accidents* / 他要是有个～，怎么办？

What if something happens to him?

【一刹】in an instant; in a split second; in the twinkling of an eye: ～间，布景换了。*In a twinkling the scene changed.*

【一刹那】见〖刹那〗

【一场春梦】a spring dream—a fleeting illusion

【一场空】all in vain; futile ——另见〖竹篮子打水一场空〗

【一场秋雨一场寒】a spell of autumn rain, and a spell of cold

【一唱百和】(又作'一倡百和') when one starts singing, the others join in—meet with general approval

【一唱一和】sing a duet; sing the same tune; echo each other

【一朝天子一朝臣】every new sovereign brings his own courtiers—a new chief brings in new aides

【一尘不染】not soiled by a speck of dust; spotless: 身居闹市，～ *remain uncontaminated amidst the temptations of a big city*

【一成不变】immutable and frozen; invariable; unalterable: 没有～的规则。*There is no hard-and-fast rule.*

【一程子】〈方〉a number of days

【一筹莫展】can find no way out; be at one's wits' end; be at the end of one's tether

【一触即发】may break out at any moment; be on the verge of breaking out: 形势～。*It's an explosive situation.*

【一触即溃】collapse at the first encounter

【一传】[体] first pass

【一传十，十传百】(of news) spread from one to ten, and from ten to a hundred—pass quickly from mouth to mouth; get around quickly

【一锤定音】set the tune with one beat of the gong—give the final word

【一锤子买卖】"once-for-all" deal—the one and only business deal to be made with sb. (from which the greatest possible advantage is to be derived)

【一词多义】polysemy

【一次】once: 我只跟他见过～面。*I've met him only once.* / 机器～试运成功。*The machine worked successfully on its first test run.* / ～或分期缴纳 *to be paid in a lump sum or in installments*

【一次方程】[数] linear equation

【一次付清】pay in one lump sum; pay a round sum

【一次函数】[数] linear function

【一次能源】primary energy

【一次性】❶ once only (without a second time): ～补助 *a lump-sum grant* ❷ disposable: ～筷子 *disposable chopsticks* / ～注射器 *disposable syringes* / ～尿布 *disposable nappies*

【一蹴而就】reach the goal in one step; accomplish one's aim in one move: 在中国这样一个幅员广大的国家里，要实现现代化，不可能～。*Modernization of a vast country like China cannot be done at one go.*

【一寸光阴一寸金】time is gold; time is precious

【一搭两用】one thing serving two purposes

【一打一拉】strike and stroke alternately; alternate hard and soft tactics; use the carrot and the stick

【一大早】〈口〉early in the morning: 他～就走了。*He left early in the morning.*

【一代】❶ a dynasty ❷ an era; the present age: ～英豪 *outstanding figures of our time* ❸ all one's life; a lifetime; a generation

【一带】the area around a particular place: 他是这～出名的猎手。*He is one of the most famous hunters around here.*

【一旦】❶ in a single day; in a very short time ❷ once; in case; now that: 他们多年相处，～分别，不免依依不舍。*After being together for years, they can't bear to part from each other.*

【一刀两断】sever at one stroke—make a clean break

【一刀切】cut it even at one stroke—make everything rigidly uniform; impose uniformity in all cases; prescribe a single solution for diverse problems

【一道】together; side by side; alongside: 学校、家长和社会～担负起教育下一代的责任。*School, parents and society share the responsibility of educating the younger generation.*

【一得之功】just an occasional, minor success: 不要沾沾自喜于～。*Don't feel self-satisfied over just a minor success.*

【一得之愚】〈套〉my humble opinion: ～，仅供参考。*This is my humble opinion, for what it's worth.*

【一等】first-class; first-rate; top-grade; topnotch: ～品 *first-rate (or top-quality) product* / ～奖 *first prize* / ～舱 *first class* ◇ ～功 Merit Citation, First Class; ～秘书[外交] First Secretary

【一等兵】(U.S. Army) private first class; (Brit. Army) lance corporal; (U.S. Navy) seaman first class; (Brit. Navy) leading seaman; (U.S. Air Force) airman first class; (Brit. Air Force) senior aircraftsman; (U.S. Marine Corps) private first class; (Brit. Marine Corps) marine first class

【一点儿】❶ a bit; a little: 请往右边移～。*Please move a little to the right.* / 还有～希望。*There is still a gleam of hope.* ❷ (used after 这么 or 那么, or with a negative expression) the least bit: ～也不累 *not feel the least bit tired* / ～都不知道 *have not the faintest idea*

【一点论】the doctrine that everything has only one aspect; the doctrine affirming only one aspect

【一点一滴】every little bit: ～地积累资料 *collect material bit by bit*

【一丁点儿】〈方〉a wee bit

【一定】❶ fixed; specified; definite; regular: 她一忙起来，吃饭睡觉都没有～的时间了。*When she gets really busy, she doesn't keep regular hours for eating or sleeping.* ❷ certainly; surely: 六点以前我～回家。*I shall certainly be home by six* o'clock. / 告诉他～不能说出去。*Tell him that under no circumstances is he to let it out*. ❸ given; particular; certain: 在～意义上 *in a certain sense* / 在～程度上 *to a certain degree* / 在～条件下 *under given conditions* ❹ proper; fair; due: 达到～水平 *reach a fairly high level* / 给以～的重视 *attach due importance to*

【一定之规】❶ a fixed pattern; a set rule ❷ one's own way

【一动】easily; frequently; at every turn: 他～就生气。*He takes offence easily*.

【一动不如一静】to stay put is better than to move (said when questioning the necessity of a move)

【一肚子】a stomachful of; full of: ～委屈 *be full of grievances*

【一度】❶ once: 一年～ *once a year; yearly; annually* ❷ on one occasion; for a time: 他因病～休学。*He stopped going to school for a time on account of illness*.

【一端】one aspect (or side) of the matter: 各执～ *each sticking to his own argument*

【一多半】the greater part: 一张双人床占了房间的～。*A double bed took up the greater part of the room*.

【一…而…】(used with two verbs to indicate that one action follows another as an immediate result): 一掠而过 *skim over* / 一怒而去 *go away in a temper; leave in anger* / 一饮而尽 *empty the glass at one gulp*

【一而再,再而三】*again and again; time and again; repeatedly*

【一二】*one or two; just a few; just a little*: 邀请～知己 *invite a few close friends*

【一二报数】[军] By twos, number!

【一发】❶ all the more; even more: 如果处理不当,就～不可收拾了。*If not handled properly, the situation will become even more hopeless*. ❷ together; along with all the others: 你把你的信留在这儿,等明天和我的信～寄出。*Leave your letter with me, and I'll post it together with mine tomorrow*.

【一发千钧】a hundredweight hanging by a hair—in imminent peril: 在这～的时刻 *at this critical moment*

【一帆风顺】plain sailing; smooth sailing

【一反常态】depart from one's normal behaviour; act out of character

【一方面】❶ one side: 这只是事情的～。*This is only one side of the matter*. ❷ on the one hand..., on the other hand...; for one thing..., for another...: 这场球打输了,～是由于对方实力较强,另～也是因为我们没有配合好。*We lost the game because, for one thing, our opponents were quite strong and, for another, our teamwork was poor*.

【一方有难,八方支援】When disaster strikes, help comes from all quarters.

【一分钱一分货】the higher the price, the better the quality; what price, what goods

【一分为二】one divides into two—everything has its good and bad sides; there are two sides to everything

【一风吹】scatter to the winds—dismiss all charges, etc.; cancel the whole thing

【一佛出世,二佛涅槃】(usu. used in) 被打得～ *be beaten half dead; be beaten within an inch of one's life*

【一夫当关,万夫莫开】if one man guards the pass, ten thousand cannot get through

【一夫多妻制】polygyny; polygamy

【一夫一妻制】monogyny; monogamy

【一概】one and all; without exception; totally; categorically: ～拒绝 *reject without exception* / ～排斥 *totally exclude* / 这些事情我～不知。*I know nothing whatever about these matters*.

【一概而论】(usu. used in the negative) treat (different matters) as the same: 不能～ *not to be lumped together*

【一干】all those involved: ～人犯 *the criminals and all those involved in the case*

【一干二净】thoroughly; completely: 把菜吃个～ *eat up all the food* / 忘得～ *clean (or completely) forget*

【一竿子到底】(又作'一竿子插到底') carry (a task or directive) right down to the grass-roots level; carry sth. through to the end

【一个巴掌拍不响】one hand alone can't clap—it takes two to make a quarrel: 有一个让着点,也吵不起来。～。*If only one of them were more easygoing, this would never have started. It takes two to make a quarrel*.

【一个和尚挑水吃,两个和尚抬水吃,三个和尚没水吃】one monk will shoulder two buckets of water, two monks will share the load, but add a third and no one will want to fetch water

【一个劲儿】continuously; persistently: 雨～地下。*It kept on raining*.

【一个萝卜一个坑】one radish, one hole—❶ each has his own task, and nobody is dispensable: 我们是～,腾不出人手来。*We're so busy that no one can be spared for any other work*. ❷ steady and reliable: 他是～的人,不会有什么闪失。*He is steady and reliable, so nothing'll go wrong*.

【一个心眼儿】❶ have one's heart set on sth.; devotedly; stubbornly ❷ be of one mind: 我们大家都是～。*We are all of one mind*.

【一共】altogether; in all; all told: ～多少人? *How many are there altogether?*

【一股劲儿】without a break; at one go; at a stretch: ～地干 *do sth. without a break*

【一股脑儿】(又作'一古脑儿')〈方〉completely; lock, stock and barrel; root and branch: 好!～告诉你罢。*All right, I'll tell you everything*. / 她兴奋得很,把要讲的话～都倒出来了。*She got so excited that she poured out all she had to say at once*.

【一鼓作气】press on to the finish without letup; get sth. done in one sustained effort

【一官半职】some official post or other

【一贯】consistent; persistent; all along: ～政策 *consistent policy*

【一贯制】❶ continuous education through junior and senior divisions without examinations between the two: 十年～ *ten-year continuous education, covering both primary and middle school* ❷ unchanged for a long time: 这些产品,无论造型还是颜色,都是几年或十几年～。*The models and colors of these products have remained the same for many years.*

【一棍子打死】knock sb. down at one stroke; finish off with one blow; completely negate: 对待犯错误的同志,要批评帮助,不能～。*Instead of bludgeoning our erring comrades, we should help them with criticism.*

【一锅端】❶〈字〉hold in a pot ❷〈喻〉bring everything out; speak out without reservation: 各式各样的意见,大的小的,对的和不对的,～地往外倒。*Ideas and thoughts, major or minor, correct or not were all aired without reservation.* ❸ eliminate, eradicate completely: 他们在刘邦去世时,就几乎被吕后～了。*After Liu Bang died, they were almost all killed by Empress Lü.*

【一锅粥】a pot of porridge—a complete mess; all in a muddle: 乱成～ *in a mess; in utter confusion*

【一锅煮】(又作'一锅烩') cook all things in one pot —treat different persons or things alike (or indiscriminately); cook different foods in one pot; treat identically: 西瓜都经过认真挑选,根据成熟度和个头大小分等出售,不搞"～"。*Watermelons should be sorted and priced by size and ripeness, not all mixed together.*

【一国两制】one country, two systems

【一国三公】a state with three rulers—a divided leadership

【一哄而起】(of a group of people) be roused to precipitate action; rush headlong into mass action

【一哄而散】break up (or disperse) in a hubbub

【一哄而上】impulsive, unthinking: 各地情况千差万别,改革可以有先有后,不应～。*Conditions vary from place to place, so the reforms may follow a different time schedule, nothing should be done impulsively or without careful thought.* ——另见〖一哄而起〗

【一呼百诺】have hundreds at one's beck and call

【一呼百应】hundreds respond to a single call

【一忽儿】同〖一会儿〗

【一环扣一环】one ring linked with another—a closely linked succession

【一晃】(yīhuǎng) flash: 窗外有个人影,～就不见了。*A figure flashed past the window.* ——另见 yīhuàng

【一晃】(yīhuàng) (of time) pass in a flash: ～几年又过去了。*Several years passed in a flash*

【一挥而就】a flourish of the pen and it's done: 提笔～ *finish* (*a piece of writing or a painting*) *at one go*

【一回生,二回熟】strangers at the first meeting, friends at the second; ill at ease the first time, at home the second; difficult the first time, easy the second

【一回事】❶ one and the same (thing): 他们所说的是～。*They were talking about the same thing.* ❷ one thing: 主观愿望是～,实际情况又是～。*Subjective wishes are one thing, objective reality is another.*

【一会儿】❶ a little while: 咱们歇～。*Let's rest for a while.* ❷ in a moment; presently: 我～就来。*I'll be coming in a moment. or I won't be a minute.* / ～地上就积起了一层雪。*Soon the ground was covered with a layer of snow.* ❸ now...now...; one moment...the next...: 天气～晴～阴。*The weather is now clear, now cloudy.*

【一级方程式赛车】(又作'F-1方程式赛车') Formula One (car racing)

【一级风】[气] force 1 wind; light air

【一级市场】[经] primary market

【一级战备】first-degree combat readiness

【一级准尉】(Brit. Army, Navy, Air Force & Marine Corps) warrant officer (Class I); (U.S. Army & Air Force) chief warrant officer; (U.S. Navy & Marine Corps) commissioned warrant officer

【一己】oneself: ～之私 *one's own selfish interests*

【一技之长】proficiency in a particular line (or field); professional skill; speciality

【一家之言】a distinctive doctrine or theory; an original system of thought

【一家子】❶ a family: 我们不是～。*We are not of the same family.* ❷ the whole family: ～都高兴极了。*The whole family was overjoyed.*

【一见倾心】fall in love at first sight

【一见如故】feel like old friends at the first meeting; hit it off well right from the start

【一见钟情】fall in love at first sight

【一箭双雕】hit two hawks with one arrow; kill two birds with one stone

【一箭之仇】the wrong of an arrow shot —a loss or defeat to be retrieved: 他们去年赢了我们,这回我们以二比一击败他们,报了～。*Last year they defeated us, but now we have got even with them by beating them* 2:1.

【一箭之地】as far as the arrow flies—a short distance: 他家离火车站不过～。*He lives only a short distance from the railway station.*

【一将功成万骨枯】a single general's reputation is made out of ten thousand corpses; what millions died that Caesar might be great

【一经】as soon as; once: 错误～发现,就应立即纠正。*Mistakes should be corrected as soon as detected.*

【一径】straight; directly; straightaway: 他一下车,～走进大厅,没和别人打招呼。*As soon as he got out of the car, he went straight into the hall without greeting anyone.*

【一…就…】no sooner... than...; the moment...; as soon as; at once: 这情况她一看就明白了。*She took in the situation at a glance.* / 他一接到通知就动身了。*He started off as soon as he got the message.*

【一举】one action; one stroke; one fell swoop: 成败在此～。*Success or failure hinges on this one action.* / ～成名 *become famous overnight; achieve instant fame*

【一举两得】gain two ends at once; kill two birds with one stone

【一举一动】every act and every move; every action: 我们新来乍到,得注意自己的～。*We're newcomers here and must be careful what we do.*

【一句话】in a word; in short

【一决雌雄】同〖决一雌雄〗

【一蹶不振】collapse after a single setback; be unable to recover after a setback

【一刻千金】one moment is worth a thousand pieces of gold—time is gold

【一客不烦二主】one guest should not bother two hosts (said when asking an additional favour of sb.)

【一孔之见】a peephole view; a narrow view; a very limited outlook: 有一种人,抱着一技之长和～,再也没有进步。*There are some people who, contented with a single skill or a peephole view, never make any progress.*

【一口】❶ a mouthful; a bite: 吸～气 *draw a breath* / 咬～ *take a bite* ❷ a manner of speech: 他讲～流利的英语。*He speaks fluent English.* ❸ with certainty; readily; flatly: ～断定 *arbitrarily assert; allege* / ～答应 *readily agree; readily promise* / ～回绝 *flatly refuse*

【一口吃不成胖子】you can't get fat on one mouthful—you must keep at it

【一口气】❶ one breath: 只要我还有～,就要为党和人民工作。*As long as there's a breath left in me, I'll work for the Party and the people.* ❷ in one breath; without a break; at one go; at a stretch: ～干完 *finish the work at one go*

【一口咬定】state categorically; assert positively; insist emphatically: 他～当时他不在现场。*He stated categorically that he was not at the scene of the crime.*

【一口钟】〈方〉mantle; cape; cloak

【一块儿】❶ at the same place: 两个人说不到～。*The two of them can never see eye to eye.* ❷ together: 老见他们俩在～。*The two of them are always seen together.*

【一块石头落地】the mind is at last set at rest: 听到她平安无事的消息,大家心里才～。*Not until they heard that she was safe and sound were their minds set at rest.*

【一来二去】in the course of frequent contact; in the course of time: 他们常在地里一块儿干活,～地也就熟了。*They often worked together in the fields, and in time they got to know each other quite well.*

【一览】general survey; bird's-eye view: 《北京名胜古迹～》*A Guide to the Historical Relics and Scenic Spots of Beijing* ◇ ～表 table; schedule; ～无余 take in everything at a glance

【一揽子】wholesale; package: ～计划 *package plan* / ～交易 *package deal*

【一浪接一浪】wave upon wave

【一劳永逸】by one supreme effort gain lasting repose—settle a matter once and for all: ～的解决办法 *a solution that holds good for all time; a permanent solution*

【一力】do one's best; do all one can: ～成全 *do one's best to help (sb. to achieve his aim)*

【一例】same; alike: ～看待 *treat in the same way*

【一连】in a row; in succession; running: ～下了三天雨。*It rained for three days running.*

【一连串】a succession of; a series of; a string of; a chain of: ～的事件 *a succession of events* / ～问题 *a series of questions*

【一连气儿】〈方〉in a row; in succession; running: 她～唱了四五个歌。*She sang four or five songs in a row.*

【一了百了】all troubles end when the main trouble ends: 一去世,他的苦恼就～了。*With his death all his woes ended.*

【一鳞半爪】odd bits; fragments: ～的情况 *odd bits (or scraps) of information*

【一流】❶ a kind; the same kind: 他属于抽象派～人物。*He belongs to the abstractionist school.* or *He is an abstractionist.* ❷ first-class; first-rate; top-notch: ～作家 *a first-class writer* / ～作品 *a first-rate work*

【一溜儿】〈方〉❶ a row: ～平房 *a row of one-storey houses* ❷ neighbourhood; vicinity: 他就住在那～。*He lives somewhere around there.* ❸ a short period of activity: 他～小跑来到村边。*He came running all the way to the village.*

【一溜风】like a gust of wind—very quickly

【一溜歪斜】〈方〉(walk, etc.) unsteadily in a zigzag: 他挑着一挑儿水,～地从河边走上来。*He wobbled up the slope from the river, carrying two buckets of water on a shoulder pole.*

【一溜烟】like a streak of smoke—very quickly: 小汽车～开走了。*The car sped off.* / 他～就没影儿了。*He disappeared in an instant (or a flash).*

【一路】❶ all the way; throughout the journey: ～上说说笑笑 *chat cheerfully all the way* / ～多保重。*Take care of yourself on the journey.* / 客队～领先。*The visiting team led from the beginning.* ❷ of the same kind ❸ go the same way; take the same route: 咱们是～吗? *Are we going the same way?* ❹ single file: ～纵队 *single column* / 成～纵队齐步走 *march (in) single file* ◇ ～货色(又作'一路货') the same sort of stuff; one of a kind; birds of a feather; ～平安(又作'一路顺风') have a pleasant journey; have a good trip; bon voyage

【一律】❶ same; alike; uniform: ～对待 *treat in the same way* (*or equally*) ❷ all; without exception: 国家不分大小,应该～平等。*All countries, big or small, should be equal* (*or on an equal footing*).

【一落千丈】drop a thousand zhang in one fall—suffer a drastic decline: 社会风气～。*Morals and manners have declined to an enormous extent*.

【一抹平】❶ the same; equal: 要按质定价,不能～。*The prices should be different, fixed according to quality*. ❷ level; smooth: 路修得～。*The road is very smooth*.

【一麻黑】(又作'一抹黑') pitch-dark: 山洞里～,什么也看不见。*It was pitch-dark in the cave; you couldn't see a thing*. / 人生地不熟,两眼～ *all alone and helpless in a strange place*

【一马当先】gallop at the head —take the lead; be in the forefront: 我们队长干什么活儿都是～。*Our team leader takes the lead in whatever work we do*.

【一马平川】a wide expanse of flat land; a wide stretch of flat country

【一脉相承】(又作'一脉相传') come down in one continuous line; can be traced to the same origin; in direct line of descent (or succession)

【一慢二看三通过】first slow down, then look around, and then cross (rhyme to remind drivers of safety when crossing an intersection)

【一毛不拔】unwilling to give up even a hair—very stingy

【一门心思】heart and soul; wholeheartedly: ～搞设计 *throw oneself wholeheartedly into designing*

【一秘】〈略〉见〖一等秘书〗

【一面】❶ one side: 这座房子朝南的～有两个窗户。*The house has two windows on the south side*. ❷ one aspect: 这只是问题的～。*This is only one aspect of the question*. ❸ at the same time; simultaneously: ～教,～学 *learn while teaching* ❹〈书〉have met once before: 未尝～ *have never met before* ◇ ～之词 the statement of only one of the parties; ～之交 (又作'一面之雅') have met only once; be casually acquainted; ～之缘 having met once (as ordained by fate)

【一鸣惊人】(of an obscure person) amaze the world with a single brilliant feat; set the world on fire

【一命归天】(又作'一命归阴') quit this world; pass away; die

【一命呜呼】die; kick the bucket; give up the ghost

【一模活脱】〈方〉cast in the same mould —exactly alike; as like as two peas

【一模一样】exactly alike; as like as two peas: 她长得跟她母亲～。*She's the image of her mother*.

【一木难支】同〖独木难支〗

【一目了然】be clear at a glance: 那门却是开着的,里面有几支枪、几把刀,～。*The gate was open, and you could see at a glance the number of guns and bayonets*.

【一目十行】take in ten lines at a glance—read rapidly

【一男半女】a son or a daughter; a child or two (usu. used in the negative, i. e. in the case of people who have no children)

【一年半载】in a year or so; in about a year: 这座桥～可望竣工。*Completion of this bridge is expected in a year or so*.

【一年到头】throughout the year; all the year round

【一年生】[植] annual: ～植物 *annual plant*; *annual*

【一年四季】throughout (the four seasons of) the year; all the year round

【一年之计在于春】the whole year's work depends on a good start in spring

【一念之差】a wrong decision made in a moment of weakness; a momentary slip with serious consequences

【一诺千金】a promise worth a thousand pieces of gold—a promise that can be counted on

【一拍即合】〈贬〉fit in readily; chime in easily

【一盘棋】❶〈字〉chess game ❷〈喻〉overall situation: 全国～ *activities of the nation seen as a whole*; *considerations and plans for the nation as a whole*

【一盘散沙】a sheet of loose sand —a state of disunity (formerly said of a country)

【一旁】one side: 他接过去,随手放在～。*He took it, and put it aside*. / 我们玩牌的时候,他站在～看着。*He stood by watching while we played cards*.

【一瞥】❶ a quick glance: 就在这～之间,我看出了她非常激动。*In a quick glance I noticed her agitation*. ❷ a glimpse; a brief survey: 《长城～》 *A Glimpse of the Great Wall*

【一贫如洗】penniless; utterly destitute

【一品】the highest official rank in imperial China: ～官 *highest-ranking official* / 当朝～ *highest court official*

【一品红】[植] poinsettia (Euphorbia pulcherrima)

【一平二调】equalitarianism and indiscriminate transfer of resources

【一瓶子不响,半瓶子晃荡】the half-filled bottle sloshes, the full bottle makes no sound—the dabbler in knowledge chatters away, the wise man stays silent

【一抔黄土】a handful of yellow earth—sth. utterly insignificant

【一暴十寒】(又作'一曝十寒') have one day's sun and then ten days' cold —work by fits and starts

【一妻多夫制】polyandry

【一齐】at the same time; simultaneously; in unison: ～努力 *make a concerted effort*

【一起】❶ in the same place: 住在～ *live in the same place* ❷together; in company: 我不跟他～走。*I won't go along with him*. ❸〈方〉altogether; in all: 这几件东西～多少钱? *How much is that altogether?* ❹〈方〉a batch of people: 那

～人刚走,这～人又到了。*This batch of people arrived as soon as the other batch left*.

【一气】❶ at one go; without a break; at a stretch: ～儿游了三千米 *swim three thousand metres at a stretch* ❷ of the same gang; hand in glove: 通同～ *act in collusion* ❸ a spell; a fit: 瞎闹～ *raise hell; kick up a row* / 胡吹～ *tell tall stories*

【一气呵成】❶ (of an essay) form a coherent whole; make smooth reading ❷ get sth. done at one go; carry sth. through without stopping

【一气之下】in a fury; in a fit of anger: 他～不辞而别。*Greatly angered, he left without saying good-bye*.

【一钱不值】not worth a penny; utterly worthless; mere trash

【一腔】be full of (zeal, grievances, etc.): ～热情 *be full of zeal* / ～冤仇 *be full of grievances*

【一窍不通】know nothing about (a subject); lack the slightest knowledge of; be utterly ignorant of: 我对原子核物理学～。*I'm out of my depth when it comes to nuclear physics*.

【一切】❶ all; every: 抓住～机会 *seize every opportunity* ❷ everything; all: ～向钱看 *put money above all else*

【一清二白】perfectly clean; blameless; unimpeachable

【一清二楚】perfectly clear: 他把情况打听得～。*He has found out all about it*.

【一清早】early in the morning

【一穷二白】poor and blank: 改变我国"～"的面貌 *lift our country from the state of "poverty and blankness"*

【一丘之貉】jackals from the same lair; birds of a feather

【一去不复返】gone never to return; gone for ever

【一犬吠影,百犬吠声】when one dog barks at a shadow a hundred others join in—blindly follow others

【一人得道,鸡犬升天】when a man attains the Tao, even his pets ascend to heaven —when a man gets to the top, all his friends and relations get there with him

【一任】〈书〉allow: 岂能～他胡作非为? *How can we let him run amuck?*

【一仍旧贯】stick to the old practice; follow the old routine

【一日不见,如隔三秋】one day apart seems like three years—miss sb. very much

【一日千里】a thousand li a day—at a tremendous pace; with giant strides: 当前电子工业的发展～。*At present the electronics industry is developing at a tremendous pace*.

【一日三秋】同〖一日不见,如隔三秋〗

【一日为师,终身为父】a teacher for a day is a father for a lifetime

【一日之长】a slight superiority: 争～ *strive for a slight superiority*

【一日之雅】(usu. used in) 无～ *not have the pleasure of knowing sb*.

【一如】just like; the same as: ～所见 *just like what we've seen* / ～所闻 *the same as what we've heard* ◇ ～既往 just as in the past; as before; as always

【一扫而光】(又作'一扫而空') make a clean sweep of; clear off; finish off; get rid of sth. lock, stock and barrel: 节日的气氛把他沉郁的心情～。*The festive atmosphere swept his melancholy thoughts clean away*.

【一色】❶ of the same colour ❷ of the same type; uniform: ～的瓦房 *tiled houses of a uniform style*

【一霎】in an instant; in a moment: ～间 *in a flash* / ～时 *in a flash*

【一闪念】a fleeting thought

【一晌】❶ a short time; a little while: 他坐了～就走了。*He sat for a while and went away*. ❷ 同〖一向〗 ❸ a period of time: 前～雨水太多了。*There was too much rain recently*.

【一上来】at first; at the beginning: ～就劲头十足 *be full of zest (or enthusiasm) from the very beginning*

【一身】❶ the whole body; all over the body: ～是泥 *be covered all over with mud* / ～是汗 *be sweating all over* ❷ a suit: ～新衣服 *a new suit of clothes* ❸ a single person: 独自～ *solitary; all alone* ◇ ～两役 hold two jobs at the same time; serve in a dual capacity; ～是胆 one's whole body is all pluck —know no fear; be absolutely fearless

【一神论】(又作'一神教') monotheism

【一审】[法] first instance: 法院～作出判决,认定他挪用公款不能退还的行为构成贪污罪。*The court convicted him in first instance and confirmed that his embezzlement of public funds without means to return them constituted a crime of corruption*.

【一生】all one's life; throughout one's life ◇ ～一世 all one's life; throughout one's life

【一声不响】not say a word; not utter a sound

【一失足成千古恨】one false step brings everlasting grief; a single slip may cause lasting sorrow; a moment's error can bring a lifelong regret

【一时】❶ a period of time: 此～彼～。*Times have changed*. ❷ for a short while; temporary; momentary: ～的多数 *a temporary majority* / 为～的表面现象所迷惑 *be misled by transient phenomena; be taken in by appearances* ❸ (used in pairs) now..., now...; one moment..., the next: 他的病～好～坏。*He'd be better for a while and then have a relapse*.

【一时半刻】(又作'一时半会儿') a short time; a little while: 他～还回不来。*He won't be back for a little while yet*.

【一时三刻】a short time; a little while: 要这么多钱,～叫我上哪儿去找哇? *Where can I find so much money in so short a time?*

【一时一刻】every moment: 我～也不能忘记这个教训。*I shall never forget this lesson*.

【一世】❶ all one's life; a lifetime：他～没出过远门。*All his life he's never been away from home*. ❷ age; era; times

【一式】the same form：～两份 *in duplicate* / ～三份 *in triplicate*

【一事无成】accomplish nothing; get nowhere

【一视同仁】treat equally without discrimination

【一手】❶ proficiency; skill：露～ *show off one's skill* / 业务上有～ *be proficient in one's own line; know one's stuff* / 他有～好手艺。*He's a real craftsman*. or *He's a master of his craft*. ❷ trick; move ❸ single-handed; all by oneself; all alone：这场争端是他们～挑起的。*The dispute was all started by them*.

【一手包办】keep everything in one's own hands; take everything on oneself

【一手交钱,一手交货】give me the case, and I'll give you the goods; COD (cash on delivery)

【一手遮天】shut out the heavens with one hand—hide the truth from the masses; hoodwink the public：他想～,颠倒是非,这只能是徒劳的。*He was merely wasting his time trying to hoodwink the people of the whole world and confound right with wrong*.

【一顺儿】in the same direction or order：村里新盖的房子,～都是朝南的。*The newly built houses in the village all face south*.

【一瞬】an instant; a flash; the twinkling of an eye：～即逝 *vanish in a flash*

【一丝不苟】not be the least bit negligent; be scrupulous about every detail; be conscientious and meticulous：她把眼睛睁得大大的,～地接着线头。*She strained to keep her eyes wide open and continued mending the broken threads with conscientious thoroughness*.

【一丝不挂】not have a stitch on; be stark naked

【一丝一毫】a tiny bit; an iota; a trace：没有～的差别 *without the least difference* / 这是死命令!不能改变～! *This is an order and it must be obeyed down to the last detail*.

【一塌刮子】〈方〉❶ all; entirely; completely ❷ in all; altogether

【一塌糊涂】in a complete mess; in an awful (or terrible) state：他把事情弄得～。*He has made a mess of the job*.

【一胎率】proportion of first-borns to total number of births during the same period, esp. important in China's one-child family policy：上海去年出生的孩子,～为 85.1%。85.1% *of the babies born in Shanghai last year were first-borns*.

【一潭死水】a pool of stagnant water—a stagnant or lifeless condition

【一体】❶ an organic (or integral) whole：融成～ *merge into an organic whole* ❷ all people concerned; to a man：上述各项望～遵照。*It is expected that the above stipulations will be observed by all*. ◇ ～化 integration

【一天】❶ a day：～二十四小时都有人值班。*There are people on duty round the clock*. ❷ one day (in the past) ❸〈方〉the whole day; all (the) day; from morning till night：忙碌了～ *have been busy all day*

【一天到晚】from morning till night; from dawn to dusk; all day long：～就是忙,不是工作,就是开会,还要学习。*I'm busy day and night, not only with work, but also with meetings or classes*.

【一条道儿跑到黑】follow one road until it's dark—cling obstinately to one course

【一条龙】❶ one continuous line：十几辆卡车排成～,向前开动。*A dozen trucks moved ahead one after another in a long line*. ❷ a connected sequence; a coordinated process：实行产、运、销～ *make production, transportation and marketing a coordinated process*

【一条心】be of one mind; be at one：众人～,黄土变成金。*If we're all of one heart and one mind, we can change clay into gold*.

【一通百通】master one and you'll master a hundred; grasp this and you'll grasp everything

【一同】together; at the same time and place：～出发 *set out together*

【一统】unify (a country)：大～ *a unified domain* ◇ ～天下 the whole empire under one ruler

【一头】❶ at the same time; simultaneously：他～走,～说。*He talked as he walked*. ❷ all of a sudden; all at once：我刚进门,便～撞见了他。*I bumped into him the moment I came in*. ❸ directly; headlong：～扎进水里 *plunge headlong into the water* ❹ a head：他比我高～。*He is a head taller than I am*. ❺ one end：扁担的～挑着篮子,另～挂着水罐。*A basket was being carried at one end of the shoulder pole, and a water pitcher at the other*. ❻〈方〉in a group; together：咱们玩桥牌,我们俩～,你们俩～。*Let's play bridge, we two against you two*.

【一头儿沉】〈方〉❶ heavy-at-one-end, a desk with a cupboard or drawers at one end ❷ be partial (in mediation)

【一吐为快】cannot rest until one has one's say

【一团和气】keep on good terms with everyone (at the expense of principle); keep on the right side of everyone

【一团漆黑】同〖漆黑一团〗

【一团糟】a complete mess; a chaotic state：他的事情～。*His affairs are in a mess*.

【一退六二五】(又作'一推六二五') evade or deny all responsibility

【一碗水端平】hold a bowl of water level—be impartial：处理争执要～,不能有偏向。*When settling a dispute, one must be fair to both sides*.

【一网打尽】catch the whole lot in a dragnet; round up the whole gang at one fell swoop

【一往情深】be deeply attached; be passionately devoted; be head over heels in love

【一往无前】press forward with an indomitable will：这个军队具有～的精神。*This army has an indomitable spirit*.

【一望无际】stretch as far as the eye can see;

stretch to the horizon：～的大草原 *a boundless stretch of grassland*

【一位论派】[宗](基督教) Unitarianism

【一味】blindly：～迁就 *make endless concessions; make one concession after another*

【一文不名】not have a penny to one's name; be penniless：她一天只吃了两个小烧饼，身上已经～。*She had only two small cakes for the whole day and had not a penny with her.*

【一文不值】not worth a farthing; utterly worthless; mere trash

【一问三不知】say "I don't know" to every question—not know a thing; be entirely ignorant：她是拿定了主意"不干己事不张口，一问摇头三不知"。*She's made up her mind not to open her mouth about matters that don't concern her, but to shake her head in answer to all questions.*

【一窝蜂】like a swarm of bees：孩子们～似地拥上来。*The children came swarming round.*

【一无可取】have nothing to recommend one; be worthless：这家饭馆儿除了价钱便宜之外，～。*This restaurant has nothing to recommend it except that it's cheap.*

【一无是处】without a single redeeming feature; devoid of any merit; having no saving grace：把他说得～ *make him out to be without a saving grace*

【一无所长】have no special skill

【一无所有】not own a thing in the world; not have a thing to one's name：我除了行李被褥之外，～。*Apart from clothes and bedding I have nothing.*

【一无所知】know nothing about; not have the least inkling of; be absolutely ignorant of：真奇怪，他们至今对那样重要的事还～。*It's really surprising that they should still be in the dark about such important events.*

【一五一十】(narrate) systematically and in full detail：他把事情～地都给同志们讲了。*He told his comrades the whole story exactly as it had happened.*

【一物降一物】one thing conquers another; everything has its superior

【一误再误】❶ make one error after another; keep on making mistakes ❷ make things worse by repeated delays：你这病要抓紧治，可不能～了。*You should go and see a doctor at once. You mustn't put it off any more.*

【一息尚存】so long as one still has a breath left; till one's last gasp：我只要～，就要努力为祖国工作。*I'll work hard for my country as long as I live.*

【一席话】what one says during a conversation：听君～，胜读十年书。*I profit more from one consultation with you than from ten years of reading.*

【一系列】a series of：～的事件 *a whole train of events* / ～措施 *a series of measures*

【一下】(又作'一下子') ❶ one time; once：亲～孩子的脸 *give the baby a kiss on the cheek* / 拍～他的肩膀 *give him a pat on the shoulder* ❷ in a short while; all at once; all of a sudden：灯～又亮了。*After a little while the lights went on again.* / 请等～。*Wait a minute, please.* / 这天气，～冷，～热。*Look at this weather. It's cold one moment and hot the next.*

【一线】❶ a ray of; a gleam of：～生机 *a slim chance of survival; a gleam of hope* ❷〈喻〉units or job directly involved in production and scientific research：领导几次建议他从～转到二线工作。*Those in leadership positions suggested several times that he transfer from a front line job to an advisory one.*

【一相情愿】(又作'一厢情愿') one-sided wish; one's own wishful thinking

【一向】❶ earlier on; lately：这～进步不小吧？*You must have made a lot of progress lately.* ❷ consistently; all along：她对工作～认真负责。*She's always been conscientious in her work.*

【一小撮】a handful：～战争贩子 *a handful of warmongers*

【一笑置之】dismiss with a laugh (or smile); laugh off

【一些】a number of; certain; some; a few; a little：有～事情我还不明白。*There are a few things that still puzzle me.* / 我想说的就这～。*That's all I wanted to say.*

【一泻千里】❶ (of a river) rush down a thousand li—flow powerfully ❷ (of a writer's style) bold and flowing

【一蟹不如一蟹】each crab is smaller than the one before—each one is worse than the last

【一心】❶ wholeheartedly; heart and soul：～为人民 *serve the people heart and soul* / 他～想上大学。*He is set on going to college.* ❷ of one mind; at one：全国～。*The country is of one mind.* ◇ ～一德 be of one heart and one mind; be dedicated to the same cause; ～一意 heart and soul; whole-heartedly

【一新】become something entirely new：房间已粉刷～。*The room has been whitewashed and become bright and tidy again.*

【一星半点】a tiny bit; a very small amount：这可是细活，不能有～差错。*This is a high precision job. There mustn't be the slightest slip.*

【一行】a group travelling together; party：代表团～十五人于昨日下午抵京。*The fifteen-person delegation arrived in Beijing yesterday afternoon.* / 副总理及其～ *the Vice-Premier and his party* / 总统及其～ *the President and accompanying officials*

【一宿】〈口〉one night：～没睡好 *not sleep well the whole night; not sleep a wink the whole night*

【一言不发】not say (or utter) a word; keep one's mouth shut：他在会上～。*He sat through the meeting without saying a word.*

【一言抄百总】to make a long story short; in a word; in short; in brief

【一言既出，驷马难追】a word once spoken cannot be taken back even by a team of four horses—

what is said cannot be unsaid

【一言难尽】it's hard to explain in a few words; it's a long story: 说来话长,其中底细,～。*It would take too long to tell you that in full*.

【一言堂】a conference hall where one person has all the say—what I say goes; one person alone has the say; one person lays down the law: 要搞"群言堂",不搞"～"。*Let all have a say, not just one*.

【一言为定】that's settled then: 你两人～,各无翻悔。*Now that you have both agreed to this, you must neither of you go back on your word*.

【一言以蔽之】sum up in a word

【一氧化碳】carbon monoxide: ～中毒 *carbon monoxide poisoning*

【一氧化物】[化] monoxide

【一样】the same; alike; as... as...: 哥儿俩相貌～,脾气也～。*The two brothers are alike in appearance and temperament*. / 谁去都～。*It won't make any difference who goes*.

【一叶障目,不见泰山】a leaf before the eye shuts out Mount Tai—have one's view of the important overshadowed by the trivial

【一叶知秋】the falling of one leaf heralds the autumn; it is a straw in the wind; a small sign can indicate a great trend

【一夜夫妻百夜恩】husband and wife for one night, love lingers on for a hundred nights

【一一】one by one; one after another: ～检查 *examine one by one* / 没时间～介绍 *have no time to go into details or cover everything*

【一…一…】❶ (used with two nouns) all; the whole of: 一生一世 *one's whole life*; *all one's life* ❷ each; every; single: 一言一行 *every word and deed* ❸ (used with two verbs similar in meaning, to indicate two successive actions): 一瘸一拐 *limping along* / 一蹦一跳 *skipping and hopping* ❹ (used with two verbs contrasting in meaning, to indicate the coordination or alternation of the two actions): 一问一答 *one asking and the other answering* ❺ (used with two words opposite in meaning, to indicate opposition or contrast): 一东一西 *one east, one west*; *poles apart* / 一长一短 *one short, one long*

【一衣带水】a narrow strip of water: ～的邻邦 *close neighbours separated by only a strip of water*

【一意孤行】cling obstinately to one's course; act wilfully; insist on having one's own way

【一应】all; everything: ～工具均已备齐。*All the tools are ready*.

【一应俱全】everything needed is there: 日用百货～。*All varieties of goods for daily use are available*.

【一拥而上】rush up in a crowd: 战士们跟在这勇敢的人后面,～,一下就冲上山峰。*Infected with his courage, the soldiers surged after him and at once charged up the heights*.

【一隅】a corner: ～之地 *a very small area* / ～之见 *a very narrow (or limited) view*

【一语道破】lay bare the truth with one remark; hit the nail on the head: ～其中奥秘 *lay bare the secret of sth. with one remark*

【一语破的】hit the mark with a single comment

【一语双关】a single phrase with a double meaning

【一元方程】equation with one unknown

【一元化】centralized; unified: 实行～的领导 *exercise unified (or centralized) leadership*

【一元论】[哲] monism

【一元酸】[化] monoacid; monoatomic acid

【一院制】unicameral (or one chamber) legislature

【一月】January

【一再】time and again; again and again; repeatedly: ～表示感谢 *express one's gratitude again and again*

【一…再…】(used with two identical verbs) repeatedly: 一错再错 *keep on making mistakes* / 一让再让 *make one concession after another* / 一拖再拖 *postpone again and again*

【一早】〈口〉early in the morning: 我明天～就告诉他。*I'll let him know first thing tomorrow morning*.

【一张一弛】tension alternating with relaxation

【一长制】system of one-man leadership; one-man authority

【一着不慎,满盘皆输】one careless move and the whole game is lost

【一朝】❶ in one day: ～覆亡 *collapse (or be toppled) in one short day* ❷ once: ～失足,悔恨终生。*A moment's error can bring a lifelong regret*.

【一朝被蛇咬,十年怕井绳】once bitten by a snake, one shies at coiled rope for ten years; he that hath been bitten by a serpent is afraid of a rope; once bitten, twice shy

【一朝一夕】in one morning or evening; overnight; in one day: 非～之功 *not the work of a single day*

【一针见血】pierce to the truth with one pertinent remark; hit the nail on the head: 他把我们的毛病讲得～。*He put his finger on our weak spot*.

【一枕黄粱】Golden Millet Dream—a brief dream or delusion of grandeur

【一阵】(又作'一阵子') ❶ a burst; a fit; a peal: ～掌声 *a burst of applause* / ～咳嗽 *a fit (or spasm) of coughing* / 一阵阵笑声 *peals of laughter* / ～狂风 *a violent gust of wind*; *a blast (of wind)* / ～枪声 *a burst of gunfire* / 脸上红～,白～ *one's face turning now red, now pale* ❷ a period of time; a spell: 这～尽下雨。*We've had a spell of rainy weather recently*. / 她病了好～了。*She has been ill for quite a long time*.

【一阵风】❶〈字〉gust of wind ❷〈喻〉short-lived (of work in general and a campaign in particular); capricious; unsteady: 他办事总是～。*He always does things by fits and starts*.

【一知半解】have a smattering of knowledge; have scanty (or half-baked) knowledge: 我对于国际事务只是～。*I have only a scanty knowledge of world affairs*.

【一直】❶ straight：～走 *go straight ahead*；*keep straight on* / ～往西走 *go straight towards the west* ❷ continuously；all along；always；all the way：雪～下了两天两夜。*It snowed for two days and nights on end*.

【一纸空文】a mere scrap of paper：协定如不执行，只是～。*An agreement, if not implemented, is a mere scrap of paper*.

【一致】showing no difference；identical；unanimous；consistent：观点～ *hold identical views*；*be of the same view* / 步调～ *march in step*；*act in unison* / 官兵～ *unity between officers and men* / ～行动 *concerted action* / 双方～认为 *both sides agree* (*that*...)

【一掷千金】stake a thousand pieces of gold on one throw—throw away money like dirt；spend money like water

【一柱擎天】one pillar supporting the sky —shouldering the heavy responsibility of high office

【一专多能】expert in one thing and good at many

【一准】〈口〉sure；surely；certainly：他～来吗？*Is he sure to come*?

【一字儿】in a row；in a line：靶场上～站着十名射手。*Ten marksmen stood in a row on the range*.

【一字褒贬】one word clearly expressing praise or censure—a strict, deliberate choice of words

【一字长蛇阵】single-line battle array：摆开～ *draw up in single-line formation*；*string out in a long line*

【一字千金】each word worth a thousand pieces of gold—a highly finished literary product

【一字师】one's single-correction teacher

【一字一板】(speak) calmly and clearly：他慢吞吞地从坐位上站起来，开始～地讲话。*He rose slowly from his chair and began to speak in a deliberate way*.

【一总】❶ altogether；all told；in all：～二十个人。*There are twenty people altogether*. ❷ all：那～是你的错儿。*It was all your fault*.

衣 名 ❶ clothing；clothes；garment：衣服 ❷ coating；covering：糖衣 ❸［中］afterbirth：胞衣 ——另见 yì

【衣胞】［中］(human) afterbirth

【衣钵】a Buddhist monk's mantle and alms bowl which he hands down to his favourite disciple；legacy：继承～ *inherit the mantle of sb*.

【衣不蔽体】be dressed in rags；have nothing but rags on one's back：过着～、食不果腹的生活 *have rags on one's back and little in one's belly*

【衣橱】wardrobe

【衣兜】pocket

【衣蛾】casemaking clothes moth

【衣分】［农］ginning outturn；gin turnout

【衣服】clothing；clothes

【衣钩】clothes hook

【衣冠】hat and clothes；dress：～不整 *be sloppily dressed* ◇ ～楚楚 be immaculately dressed；～禽兽 a beast in human clothing；brute；～冢 a tomb containing personal effects of the deceased, whose remains are either missing or buried elsewhere

【衣柜】wardrobe

【衣架】❶ coat hanger；clothes-rack ❷ clothes tree；clothes stand

【衣襟】the one or two pieces making up the front of a Chinese jacket

【衣锦还乡】(又作'衣锦荣归') go back to one's old home in silken robes (i.e. after acquiring wealth and honour)

【衣料】material for clothing；dress material

【衣领】collar

【衣帽架】clothes tree；clothes stand

【衣帽间】cloakroom

【衣衾】burial clothes

【衣衫】clothes：～不整 *not properly dressed*

【衣衫褴褛】shabbily dressed；out at elbows；in rags

【衣裳】〈口〉clothing；clothes

【衣食住行】food, clothing, shelter and transportation—basic necessities of life

【衣食足而知荣辱】when food and clothing are enough, men have a sense of honour and shame

【衣饰】dress and personal adornment；dress：～华丽 *be gorgeously dressed*

【衣物】clothing and other articles of daily use

【衣箱】trunk；suitcase

【衣鱼】silverfish；fish moth；bookworm

【衣装】❶ dress；attire ❷ clothes and luggage：整治～ *pack* (*for a journey*)

【衣着】clothing, headgear and footwear：～整洁 *be neatly dressed*

伊 代〈书〉he or she

【伊甸园】［宗］(基督教) the Garden of Eden；paradise

【伊克度】［药］ichthyol；ichthammol

【伊拉克】Iraq ◇ ～人 Iraqi

【伊朗】Iran ◇ ～人 Iranian

【伊人】〈书〉that person (referring esp. to a woman)

【伊始】beginning：就职～ *upon assuming office*

【伊斯兰教】Islam；Islamism：～国家 *Islamic country* ◇ ～历 the Moslem Calendar；～徒 Moslem

【伊蚊】yellow-fever mosquito

医 Ⅰ 名 ❶ doctor (of medicine)：边远农村缺～少药。*Remote rural areas are short of doctors and medicine*. ❷ medical science；medical service；medicine：她是学～的。*She studies medicine*. / ～用温度计 *clinical thermometer* Ⅱ 动 cure；treat：给牧民～病 *give medical treatment to herdsmen* / 把他的病～好 *cure him of his illness*

【医道】art of healing；medical knowledge；physician's skill：～高明 *be a highly skilled doctor*

【医德】medical ethics：～高尚 *be an ethical doctor*
【医风】style of work，medical practice
【医护】give medical treatment and nursing：～人员 *doctors and nurses*；*medical worker*，*health worker*
【医经】［中］ancient Chinese medical classics
【医科】medical courses in general；medicine：～大学 *medical university*
【医理】principles of medical science；medical knowledge：精通～ *have a profound knowledge of medicine*
【医疗】medical treatment：～卫生工作 *medical and health work* / ～机构 *medical establishment* （*or institution*） / ～器械 *medical apparatus and instruments* / ～事故 *unskilful and faulty medical or surgical treatment*；*malpractice* ◇ ～队 medical team；～辐射学 atomic（or radiological）medicine；～体育 medico-athletics；～站 medical station；health centre
【医密】confidentiality of medical records：为病人保守～ *patient case histories are confidential*
【医生】doctor；medical man：内科～ *physician* / 外科～ *surgeon* / 实习～ *intern* / 主治～ *doctor in charge* / 住院～ *resident doctor*
【医师】（qualified）doctor
【医士】practitioner with secondary medical school education
【医书】medical book
【医术】medical skill；art of healing：～高超 *have superb medical skill*
【医坛】medical circle
【医务】medical matters：～工作者 *medical worker* / ～人员 *medical personnel*（*or staff*，*workers*）；*public health worker*
【医务室】grass-roots health clinic，often small and equipped with basic facilities
【医务所】health clinic
【医学】medical science；medicine ◇ ～界 medical community；～文献 medical literature；～遗产 medical heritage；～科学院 academy of medical sciences
【医药】medicine：～常识 *general medical knowledge* / ～费 *medical expenses*（*or costs*）
【医院】hospital：儿童～ *children's hospital* / 综合性～ *general hospital*
【医治】cure；treat；heal：～战争创伤 *heal war wounds*
【医嘱】doctor's advice（or orders）：用量：遵～ *dosage*：*as directed by the physician*
【医助】assistant doctor（in the army）

依 Ⅰ 动 ❶ depend on：依靠 ❷ comply with；listen to；yield to：不能因为孩子小，就什么都～着他。*You shouldn't comply with every wish of his just because he is a child.* / ～着你该怎么办？*What do you suggest I should do?* / 我怎么劝，他还是不～。*No matter what I said，he just wouldn't listen.* Ⅱ 介 according to；in the light of；judging by：～我看 *in my view*；*as I see it* / ～当时情况来说 *in the light of the situation at the time*；*as matters then stood* / ～着我的性子，非揍他一顿不行。*If I had had my way，I would have given him a sound beating.*
【依傍】❶ depend on；rely on：互相～ *rely on each other* / 无可～ *without anyone to rely on* ❷ imitate；model oneself on：～前人 *model oneself on one's predecessors*
【依此类推】the rest may be inferred；and so on and so forth
【依次】in proper order；successively：他们～入座。*They take their seats in proper order.*
【依从】comply with；yield to：她坚持要单独去，我只好～她了。*Since she insisted on going alone，I had to comply.*
【依存】depend on sb. or sth. for existence：相互～ *be interdependent*
【依法】according to law；in conformity with legal provisions；in accordance with the law：～惩办 *punish according to law*；*deal with in accordance with the law*；*bring to justice*
【依附】depend on；attach oneself to；become an appendage to：～权贵 *attach oneself to bigwigs*
【依借】use；turn to advantage；draw on：他～自己的特殊地位，大发横财。*He took advantage of his special position to make huge ill-gotten gains.*
【依旧】as before；still：书房的陈设～未变。*The study is furnished as it was before.*
【依据】❶ according to；in the light of；on the basis of；judging by：～上述意见 *in accordance with the above views* ❷ basis；foundation：有～的 *well-founded* / 毫无～ *utterly baseless*（*or groundless*）
【依靠】❶ rely on；depend on：～自己的力量 *depend on one's own strength* ❷ something to fall back on；support；backing：生活有～ *have one's livelihood assured*
【依赖】rely on；be dependent on：～别人 *be dependent on others* / ～思想 *the dependent mentality* / ～性 *dependence*
【依恋】be reluctant to leave；feel regret at parting from
【依然】still；as before：～有效 *still hold good*；*remain valid* ◇ ～故我 I'm still my same old self；I'm just the same as before；～如故 remain as before；remain the same
【依山傍水】at the foot of a hill and beside a stream
【依顺】be obedient
【依随】agree to；yield to；comply with：孩子说什么她都～。*She agrees to whatever her child says.*
【依托】❶ rely on；depend on ❷ support；prop；backing：经济特区的建设没有国内其他地区作～是不行的。*The construction of special economic zones would have been impossible without the backing of the rest of the country.*
【依偎】snuggle up to；lean close to
【依稀】vaguely；dimly：～记得 *vaguely remember* / ～可见 *faintly*（*or dimly*）*visible*

【依循】follow; abide by

【依样画葫芦】draw a gourd according to the model—copy mechanically

【依依】❶〈文〉luxuriant：杨柳～。*The willows are fresh and green (or are spreading their shade).* ❷ reluctant to part：在此～惜别的时刻 *at this moment when we reluctantly bid farewell to each other* ◇ ～不舍 be reluctant to part; cannot bear to part

【依允】assent; consent：点头～ *nod assent*

【依仗】count on; rely on：～权势 *rely on one's power and position; count on one's powerful connections*

【依照】according to; in accordance with; in the light of：～情况而定 *decide as circumstances require* / ～法律规定的条件 *under conditions prescribed by law*

咿（构词成分）见下

【咿唔】the sound of reading aloud

【咿呀】❶ squeak; creak：咿咿呀呀的提琴声 *squeaky notes of a violin* ❷ prattle; babble

铱 名［化］iridium (Ir)

【铱金笔】iridium-point pen

【铱星】iridium satellite：中国成功地将美国摩托罗拉公司的两颗～送入轨道。*China has successfully put into orbit two iridium satellites owned by Motorola Corp. of the United States.*

壹 数 one (used as the numeral 一 on cheques, banknotes, etc. to avoid mistakes or alterations)

yí

仪 名 ❶ appearance; bearing：仪表 ❷ ceremony; rite：司仪 ❸ present; gift：贺～ *present for wedding, birthday, etc.* ❹ apparatus; instrument：仪器

【仪表】❶ appearance; bearing：～大方 *poised and graceful* ❷ meter：～板 *instrument panel; dashboard* / ～厂 *instrument and meter plant* ◇ ～堂堂 dignified in appearance; impressive-looking

【仪器】instrument; apparatus：精密～ *precision instrument* / 自记～ *recording instrument* / ～厂 *instrument plant* / ～制造工业 *instrument-making industry*

【仪容】looks; appearance：～俊秀，举止大方 *pretty and poised*

【仪式】ceremony; rite; function：宗教～ *religious rites* / 奠基～ *foundation stone laying ceremony*

【仪态】〈书〉bearing; deportment ◇ ～万方 (of a beauty) appear in all her glory

【仪仗】❶ insignia carried before the emperor ❷ flags, weapons, etc. carried by a guard of honour ◇ ～队 guard of honour; honour guard

夷 Ⅰ 形〈书〉smooth; safe：化险为夷 Ⅱ 动 ❶ raze：～为平地 *level to the ground; raze* ❷ exterminate; wipe out：～族 *extermination of an entire family (a punishment in ancient times)* Ⅲ 名 ❶ the name for ancient tribes in the east ❷〈旧〉foreign country; foreigner：～人 *foreigners*

宜 Ⅰ 形 suitable; appropriate; fitting：老幼咸～ *suitable (or good) for both young and old* Ⅱ 动 (usu. used in the negative) should; ought to：对孩子不～要求过高。*You shouldn't ask too much of a child.* / 讲演～短不～长。*A short speech is preferable to a long one.*

【宜人】pleasant; delightful：气候～ *pleasant (or delightful) weather* / 景物～ *attractive (or charming) scenery*

【宜于】be suitable for：这种土壤～种西瓜。*This kind of soil is good for growing watermelons.*

怡 形〈书〉happy; joyful; cheerful：心旷神怡

【怡和】〈书〉affable; genial

【怡情悦性】cheer the heart and compose the mind

【怡然】happy and contented

【怡然自得】be happy and pleased with oneself; feel a glow of happiness：热带小鱼在绿茵茵的水藻中～地游来游去。*Small tropical fish were swimming placidly to and fro in the green waterweed.*

【怡神】〈书〉soothe the spirit ◇ ～养性 soothe one's spirit and nourish one's nature

【怡悦】happy; joyous

饴 名 maltose; malt sugar

【饴糖】maltose; malt sugar

贻 动〈书〉❶ make a gift of sth.; present ❷ bequeath; leave behind; hand down

【贻贝】［动］mussel

【贻害】leave a legacy of trouble ◇ ～无穷 entail untold troubles; involve endless trouble

【贻患】leave a legacy of trouble

【贻人口实】provide one's critics with a handle; give occasion for talk

【贻误】affect adversely; bungle：～战机 *bungle the chance of winning a battle; forfeit a chance for combat* / ～青年 *mislead young people*

【贻笑大方】make a laughingstock of oneself before experts; incur the ridicule of experts

【贻训】teachings of the deceased

姨 名 ❶ mother's sister; maternal aunt; aunt ❷ wife's sister; sister-in-law：小姨子

【姨表】the relationship between the children of sisters (or maternal cousins); cousinship：～兄弟 *male maternal cousins* / ～姐妹 *female maternal cousins*

【姨夫】(又作'姨父') the husband of mother's sister (or one's maternal aunt); uncle

【姨姥姥】sister of one's maternal grandmother; great-aunt

【姨妈】〈口〉(married) maternal aunt; aunt

【姨母】(married) maternal aunt; aunt

【姨奶奶】❶ sister of one's paternal grandmother; great-aunt ❷〈口〉concubine

【姨娘】❶〈旧〉a term of address for father's concubine ❷〈方〉(married) maternal aunt; aunt

【姨太太】〈口〉concubine

胰 名 [生理] pancreas

【胰蛋白酶】[生化] trypsin

【胰岛】[生理] pancreas islet ◇ ～素 [医] insulin

【胰淀粉酶】[生化] amylopsin

【胰酶】[医] pancreatin

【胰腺】[生理] pancreas ◇ ～炎 pancreatitis

【胰液】[生理] pancreatic juice

【胰皂】〈方〉soap

【胰脂酶】[生化] pancreatic lipase; steapsin

【胰子】❶〈口〉pancreas (of pigs, sheep, etc.) ❷〈方〉soap

移 动 ❶ move; remove; shift: 把桌子～到那边去 *move the table over there* / ～沙造田 *create farmland by removing sand drifts* ❷ change; alter: 献身革命志不～ *dedicate oneself to the revolution with unshakable will*

【移调】[音] transposition: ～乐器 *transposing instrument*

【移动】move; shift: 冷气团正向南～。*A cold air mass is moving southward.* ◇ ～电话(又作'手机') cellular telephone; mobile phone; ～基期 shifting base period; ～加权平均法 moving weighted average method; ～均衡 moving equilibrium

【移动交换中心】[通信] mobile switching centre (MSC)

【移防】be shifted elsewhere for garrison duty

【移风易俗】change prevailing habits and customs; transform social traditions; reform the ways and manners of the people

【移行】(in English usage) divide a word with a hyphen at the end of a line

【移花接木】graft one twig on another —stealthily substitute one thing for another

【移交】❶ turn over; transfer; deliver into sb.'s custody: 那批仪器已经～给研究所了。*Those instruments have been turned over to the research institute.* ❷ hand over one's job to a successor: 他临走前把工作～给我了。*Before he left he handed over his job to me.*

【移居】move one's residence; migrate: ～国外 *emigrate to a foreign country* / ～我国 *immigrate into our country*

【移苗】transplant seedlings

【移民】❶ migrate; emigrate or immigrate ❷ emigrant or immigrant ◇ ～点 settlement; ～法 immigration laws

【移民局】immigration service (or office)

【移民签证】immigrant visa

【移送】turn over (suspects, legal files, etc.) to (appropriate judicial organs): 把拘留犯～市政法机关 *turn the detainee over to the city judiciary*

【移山倒海】move mountains and drain seas—exercise magic powers; transform nature: 用～之力 *make superhuman efforts*

【移时】〈书〉after a short while

【移天易日】(又作'移天换日') move the sky and change the sun—perpetrate a gigantic fraud

【移位】shift ◇ ～键 [计] shift key

【移徙】move; migrate: 牧民随牲畜～。*Herdsmen move about with their herds.*

【移项】[数] transposition

【移相器】[物] phase shifter

【移栽】transplant

【移植】❶ transplant: ～秧苗 *transplant seedlings* ❷ [医] transplant; graft: 做心脏～手术 *perform heart transplant surgery* ❸ adapt; transfer: 戏剧～节目 *items adapted from the theatre*

【移樽就教】take one's wine cup and go to sb.'s table to ask his advice—go to sb. for advice

遗 Ⅰ 动 ❶ lose: 遗失 ❷ involuntary discharge of urine, etc.: 梦遗 ❸ omit: 遗忘 ❹ leave behind; keep back; not give: 遗憾 ❺ leave behind at one's death; bequeath; hand down: 遗骨 Ⅱ 名 something lost: 路不拾遗 ——另见 wèi

【遗案】unsolved case

【遗笔】writings left behind by the deceased

【遗产】legacy; inheritance; heritage: 留下(继承)～ *bequeath (inherit) a legacy* / 历史～ *a legacy of history* / 文化～ *cultural heritage* ◇ ～承受人 legatee; ～税 inheritance tax; succession duty

【遗臭万年】leave a name that will stink to eternity; go down in history as a byword for infamy

【遗传】[生] heredity; inheritance: ～特征 *hereditary feature; heredity* ◇ ～病 hereditary disease; ～工程 [生] genetic engineering; ～基因 genetic genes; ～密码 genetic code; ～信息 hereditary (or genetic) information; ～学 genetics; ～学家 geneticist; ～因子 genetic factor; ～指纹鉴别 genetic fingerprinting; ～字母表 genetic alphabet

【遗存】❶ be left over; be handed down: 这些石刻～至今已千余年。*These stone inscriptions have been in existence for over a thousand years.* ❷ remnants; remains: 恐龙的化石～ *the fossil remains of a dinosaur*

【遗毒】evil legacy; harmful tradition; pernicious influence

【遗范】the example set by the deceased: ～犹存 *a shining example to posterity*

【遗风】customs which have been handed down: 太白～ *the ways of Taibai the Drinking Immortal (a common sign in wineshops)*

【遗腹子】a posthumous child

【遗稿】a manuscript left unpublished by the author at his death; a posthumous manuscript

【遗孤】orphan

【遗骨】remains (of the dead): 烈士～ *the remains of the martyrs*

【遗骸】remains (of the dead): 烈士～ *the remains of the martyrs*
【遗害】leave a legacy of trouble: ～后人 *bring calamity upon posterity*
【遗憾】regret; pity: 对此表示～ *express regret over the matter*
【遗恨】eternal regret
【遗患】leave a legacy of trouble: 养虎遗患
【遗祸】leave a legacy of trouble
【遗迹】historical remains; traces; vestiges: 古代村落的～ *the remains of ancient villages*
【遗教】teachings of the deceased
【遗精】[医] (seminal) emission
【遗老】❶ a surviving adherent of a former dynasty; an old fogy; an old diehard ❷〈书〉old people who have witnessed big social changes ◇ ～遗少 old fogies and young diehards; diehards old and young
【遗留】leave over; hand down: ～的痕迹 *surviving traces* / 草案中仍然～几个问题。*There are still a few points to clear up in the draft.*
【遗漏】omit; leave out: 重要～ *an important omission* / 名单上有～。*There are some names missing from the list.*
【遗命】last will; final charge
【遗墨】letters, manuscripts, scrolls of painting or calligraphy, etc. left behind by the deceased
【遗尿】[医] enuresis; bed-wetting
【遗篇】writings left behind by the deceased
【遗弃】❶ abandon; forsake; desert; walk out on: ～妻儿 *forsake one's wife and children* ❷ leave behind; cast away; abandon: 敌军～大批辎重。*The enemy abandoned (or left behind) large quantities of supplies.*
【遗容】❶ the looks of the deceased: 瞻仰～ *pay one's respects to the remains of sb.* ❷ a portrait of the deceased
【遗少】a young man with the mentality of an old fogy; a young diehard
【遗失】lose: ～声明 *lost property notice* / ～招领 *lost and found*
【遗事】❶ incidents of past ages ❷ deeds of those now dead
【遗书】❶ (usu. used in book titles) surviving works; posthumous works; collected writings published after the author's death ❷ a letter or note left by one immediately before death or suicide ❸〈书〉lost books
【遗属】members of the deceased's family; family dependants of the deceased
【遗孀】widow; relict
【遗体】remains (of the dead): 向～告别 *pay one's last respects to the remains*
【遗蜕】〈书〉remains (esp. of a Taoist priest)
【遗忘】forget: 他学过的知识,很多都已经～了。*He's forgotten much of what he learned.* ◇ ～症 amnesia
【遗物】❶ things left behind by the deceased ❷ relic: 这把石斧是旧石器时代的～。*This stone axe is a relic of the Old Stone Age.*
【遗像】a portrait of the deceased
【遗训】teachings of the deceased
【遗言】words of the deceased; (a person's) last words
【遗业】work left unfinished by one's predecessor or ancestor: 继承先人～ *carry on where one's ancestor left off*
【遗愿】unfulfilled wish of the deceased; last wish; behest
【遗赠】bequeath: ～物 *legacy; bequest*
【遗照】a photograph of the deceased
【遗址】site (where sth. was): 古城～ *the site of an ancient city*
【遗志】unfulfilled wish; behest; work bequeathed by the deceased: 继承先烈～ *carry out the behest of the martyrs; continue the work left by the martyrs*
【遗嘱】testament; will; dying words: 立～ *make (or draw up) a will* / 未立～ *intestate; will less* / ～检验 *probate* / ～执行人 *executor*
【遗著】posthumous work (of an author)
【遗作】posthumous work (of art or literature)

颐 Ⅰ **名**〈书〉chin or cheek Ⅱ **动**〈书〉nourish; take good care of one's health: 颐养
【颐和园】the Summer Palace (in Beijing)
【颐养】〈书〉keep fit; take good care of oneself: ～天年 *take good care of oneself so as to fulfil one's allotted life span*
【颐指气使】order people about by gestures; be insufferably arrogant

疑 Ⅰ **动** doubt; disbelieve; suspect: 深信不～ *unquestioningly believe; not have the slightest doubt* Ⅱ **形** doubtful; uncertain: 疑点 / 疑义
【疑案】a doubtful (or disputed) case; an open question; mystery
【疑兵】troops deployed to mislead the enemy; deceptive deployment (of soldiers)
【疑病】[医] hypochondriasis
【疑点】a doubtful (or questionable) point; an uncertain (or unclear) point: 这个案件还有几个～。*There are still a few questionable points in the case.*
【疑窦】〈书〉cause for suspicion; suspicion: 顿生～ *suddenly feel suspicious*
【疑惑】feel uncertain; not be convinced: ～不解 *feel puzzled; have doubts*
【疑惧】apprehensions; misgivings
【疑虑】misgivings; doubts: 消除心中的～ *clear one's mind of doubt; free sb. from doubts and misgivings*
【疑难】difficult; knotty: ～病症 *difficult and complicated cases (of illness)*
【疑念】suspicions; doubts
【疑神疑鬼】be terribly suspicious; be even afraid of one's own shadow
【疑似】doubtful: ～之词 *ambiguous words*

【疑团】doubts and suspicions：～顿释。*The suspicions were cleared up at once.*

【疑问】query；question；doubt：毫无～ *doubtless；without a doubt；without question* ◇ ～句〈语〉interrogative sentence

【疑心】suspicion：起～ *become suspicious* ◇ ～病 a suspicious frame of mind；～生暗鬼 suspicions create fantastic fears

【疑义】doubt；doubtful point：毫无～ *no doubt*

【疑云】misgivings or suspicions clouding one's mind：～消散。*The misgivings were dispelled.*

【疑阵】deceptive battle array to mislead the enemy；stratagem

yǐ

乙 Ⅰ名 the second of the ten Heavenly Stems（天干）Ⅱ数 second：～等 *second class；Class B* Ⅲ代（used for an unspecified person or thing）：某甲与某～ *Mr. A and Mr. B* / 甲方和～方 *the first party and the second party* / 甲队和～队 *team A and team B*

【乙胺】［化］ethylamine；aminoethane

【乙苯】［化］ethylbenzene；phenylethane

【乙醇】［化］ethyl alcohol；ethanol；alcohol

【乙肝】〈略〉见〖乙型肝炎〗

【乙醚】［化］ether

【乙脑】〈略〉见〖流行性乙型脑炎〗

【乙醛】［化］acetaldehyde；ethanal

【乙炔】［化］acetylene；ethyne：～焊 *acetylene welding*

【乙烷】［化］ethane

【乙烯】［化］ethylene

【乙烯基】［化］vinyl

【乙酰】［化］acetyl ◇ ～胆碱［生化］acetylcholine；～基［化］the acetyl group；～水杨酸［化］acetylsalicylic acid；［药］aspirin；～唑胺［药］acetazolamide；diamox

【乙型超声波】B-mode ultrasound（popularly called B超）

【乙型肝炎】［医］hepatitis B

【乙夜】the second watch（the second of the five two-hour periods into which the night was formerly divided，corresponding to around 10 p.m.）

【乙种粒子】［物］beta particle

【乙种射线】［物］beta ray

已 Ⅰ动 stop；cease；end：争论不～ *argue endlessly；be bogged down in endless argument* Ⅱ副 ❶ already：问题～解决。*The problem has already been solved.* / 雨季～过。*The rainy season is over.* / 为时～晚。*It's too late.* / ～成定局 *be a foregone conclusion* ❷〈书〉thereafter；afterwards ❸〈书〉too

【已故】deceased；late：～地质学家李四光 *the late geologist Li Siguang*

【已极】to the utmost；in the extreme：狂妄～ *extremely arrogant*

【已经】already：天～黑了。*It's already dark.*

【已决犯】［法］convicted prisoner；convict

【已然】be already so；have already become a fact：与其补救于～，不如防患于未然。*To forestall is better than to amend.* or *Prevention is better than cure.*

【已往】before；previously；in the past

【已知数】［数］known number

以 Ⅰ介 ❶ with；by means of：～诚相待 *treat sb. with all sincerity* / ～我之长，攻敌之短 *utilize our strong points to attack the enemy's weak points* ❷ according to：～时启闭 *open and close according to schedule* / ～此类推 *on the analogy of this* / ～到达先后为序 *in order of arrival* ❸ because of：不～失败自馁，不～成功自满 *not lose heart because of failure nor feel conceited because of success* / 何～知之？*How do you know?* ❹〈书〉at（a certain time）；on（a fixed date）：余～三月一日返。*I returned on March the first.* ❺（used before certain localizers to form compound localizers）：以前 / 以内 / 以上 ❻ in order to；so as to：～示区别 *so as to distinguish this from other cases* / ～应急需 *in order to answer an urgent need* Ⅱ连〈书〉and；as well as：淅沥～潇飒 *raindrops pattering and wind rustling* / 城高～厚。*The city wall is high and thick.*

【以暴易暴】replace one tyranny by another

【以备不虞】be prepared for any contingency

【以便】so that；in order to；so as to；with the aim of；for the purpose of：今天作好准备，～明天一早动身 *make preparations today for an early start tomorrow*

【以不变应万变】meet all changes by remaining unchanged—cope with a constantly changing situation by sticking to a fixed principle or policy

【以词害意】let the words interfere with the sense

【以此为戒】take this as a lesson；take warning from this

【以大欺小】the strong bullies the weak

【以德报怨】return good for evil；repay evil with good；requite ingratitude with kindness

【以点带面】fan out from point to area；use the experience of selected units to promote work in the entire area

【以毒攻毒】fight poison with poison；use poison as an antidote for poison

【以讹传讹】incorrectly relay an erroneous message（so that it becomes increasingly distorted）；spread an error or a falsehood：我是亲眼看见的，让我去对他们说说，免得～。*I am an eyewitness. Let me go and tell them so that they will not be wrongly informed.*

【以耳代目】rely upon hearsay instead of seeing for oneself

【以罚代刑】substitute administrative for legal penalties；mete out administrative penalties instead of prosecuting

【以防万一】be prepared for all contingencies; be ready for any eventuality: 也许不会下雨,不过还是带把伞,～。*It may not rain, but you'd better take an umbrella just in case.*

【以丰补歉】store up in fat years to make up for lean ones; have high-yield areas help low-yield areas

【以丰养廉】foster clean government by giving better pay to civil servants

【以干带学】use practical experience to promote learning

【以工代干】when a worker does a cadre's job

【以工代赈】provide work as a form of relief; give relief by providing labour

【以攻为守】use attack as a means of defence; attack in order to defend

【以古非今】disparage the present by extolling the past

【以寡敌众】pit few against many; fight against heavy odds

【以观后效】(lighten a punishment and) see how the offender behaves

【以后】after; afterwards; later; hereafter: 从今(那)～ *from now (then) on* / 别着急,～你会有机会去的。*Don't worry. You'll have a chance to go.*

【以及】as well as; along with; and: 党和国家领导人～各有关方面负责人 *Party and government leaders as well as responsible cadres of departments concerned*

【以己度人】judge others by oneself; measure others' corn with one's own bushel

【以假乱真】mix the false with the true; mix the spurious with the genuine

【以解倒悬】so as to relieve sb.'s distress

【以近】up to: 济南～的火车票 *train tickets up to Jinan*

【以进养出】promote exports by attracting foreign investment (through various forms of cooperation with foreign businessmen)

【以儆效尤】to warn others against following a bad example; as a warning to others

【以来】since: 长期～ *for a long time past* / 三年～ *in the past three years* / 自古～ *ever since the ancient times*

【以泪洗面】have a tearful face; wear a woebegone look

【以蠡测海】measure the sea with an oyster shell—make an appraisal in the light of limited knowledge

【以礼相待】treat sb. with due respect

【以理服人】convince by reasoning

【以力服人】force people to submit; dominate others by force

【以邻为壑】use one's neighbour's field as a drain—shift one's troubles onto others

【以卵投石】(又作'以卵击石') throw an egg against a rock—court defeat by fighting against overwhelming odds

【以貌取人】judge people solely by their appearance

【以免】in order to avoid; so as not to; lest: 仔细检查～出错 *check carefully to avoid mistakes*

【以内】within; less than: 本年度～ *within this year* / 五十人～ *less than fifty people*

【以偏概全】take a part for the whole

【以期】in the hope of: 这个问题必须反复讲,～引起各方面的重视。*This question must be brought up time and again in the hope of attracting universal attention.*

【以其昏昏,使人昭昭】try to enlighten others while in darkness oneself: ～,是不行的。*Those in darkness are in no position to enlighten others.*

【以其人之道,还治其人之身】deal with a man as he deals with you; pay sb. back in his own coin

【以前】before; formerly; previously: 我～没看过这个戏。*I've never seen this opera before.* / ～他当过理发员。*He used to be a barber.*

【以强凌弱】oppress the weak by sheer strength

【以求】in the hope of; in an attempt to: ～全胜 *in an attempt to achieve complete victory*

【以屈求伸】bend in order to straighten up —retreat in order to advance; make concessions to gain advantages

【以权谋私】seek personal gain by abusing one's position and authority; abuse power for personal gain

【以色列】Israel ◇ ～人 Israeli; Israelite; ～议会 Knesset

【以上】❶ more than; over; above: 五十人～ *over (or more than) fifty people* ❷ the above; the foregoing; the above-mentioned: 我完全同意～几位代表的发言。*I fully agree with the delegates who have already spoken.*

【以身试法】defy the law

【以身相许】(of a girl) pledge to marry sb.

【以身殉职】die at one's post: 他不幸～。*He died at his post, to our great sorrow.*

【以身作则】set a good example with one's own conduct; set an example

【以售其奸】in order to carry out an evil plot; to achieve a treacherous purpose: 利用别人的无知～ *take advantage of other people's ignorance to achieve one's treacherous purposes*

【以税代利】(of a state enterprise) replace profit delivery to the state by taxation; substitute taxation for profit delivery to the state

【以太】[物] ether ◇ ～网 Ether network

【以汤沃雪】melting snow with hot water—easily done

【以汤止沸】trying to stop water from boiling by adding boiling water to it—an ineffective measure

【以退为进】retreat in order to advance; make concessions in order to gain advantages

【以外】beyond; outside; other than: 长城～ *beyond the Great Wall* / 营房～ *outside the barracks* / 雾太大,五米～就看不见了。*There was such a heavy fog that one could not see further than five metres*.

【以往】before; formerly; in the past: 这里～是一片荒野。*This place used to be a vast expanse of wasteland*.

【以为】think; believe; consider: 我还～是她呢。*I thought it was her*. / 他～那样做比较好。*He considers it better to do it that way*.

【以…为…】take... as...; regard... as...: 以我为主 *take ourselves (or our side, our way, etc.) as the dominant factor; keep the initiative in our own hands* / 以姓氏笔划为序 *in the order of the number of strokes in the surnames*

【以文会友】make friends through literary activities

【以下】❶ below; under: 零度～ *below zero; subzero* / 三岁～儿童 *children under three* ❷ the following; hereafter: ～是代表名单。*The following is a list of the delegates*. / ～就来谈谈具体办法。*Now I'm coming to the concrete measures*.

【以销定产】plan production according to sales

【以小人之心,度君子之腹】gauge the heart of a gentleman with one's own mean measure

【以眼还眼,以牙还牙】an eye for an eye and a tooth for a tooth

【以一当十】pit one against ten

【以逸待劳】wait at one's ease for an exhausted enemy

【以远】beyond: 只售济南～的车票。*Only tickets for Jinan and beyond are available*.

【以远权】[交通] the right to extend a flying route; the right to fly beyond designated points

【以怨报德】return evil for good; repay good with evil; requite kindness with ingratitude; bite the hand that feeds one

【以正视听】in order to ensure a correct understanding of the facts

【以直报怨】meet resentment with upright dealing

【以至】❶ down to; up to: 团长、师长～军长都到这个连队来帮助总结经验。*Commanders of the regiment, the division and even the army came to this company to help sum up its experience*. ❷ (又作'以至于') to such an extent as to...; so...that...: 他工作非常专心,～连饭都忘了吃了。*He was so absorbed in his work that he even forgot his meals*.

【以致】(usu. referring to bad results) so that; with the result that; consequently; as a result: 小王平时训练不刻苦,～射击考核没有及格。*Xiao Wang didn't practise hard, so he failed the marksmanship test*.

【以资】as a means of: ～证明 *in testimony thereof; this is to certify that* / ～弥补 *to make up the deficit; to make up a shortage* / ～鼓励 *as an encouragement* / ～比较 *for the sake of comparison*

【以子之矛,攻子之盾】set a person's own spear against his own shield—refute sb. with his own argument

钇 名 [化] yttrium (Y)

迤 动 go (or extend) towards: 天安门～西是中山公园。*To the west of Tian An Men is Zhongshan Park*. ——另见 yí

【迤逦】winding; tortuous; meandering: 队伍沿着山道～而行。*The troops marched along the winding mountain path*.

蚁 名 ant

【蚁巢】ant nest

【蚁封】ant hill

【蚁后】queen (of an ant colony); gyne

【蚁丘】ant hill

酏 (构词成分) 见下

【酏剂】[药] elixir

倚 Ⅰ 动 ❶ lean on or against; rest on or against: ～栏远眺 *lean on the parapet and gaze into the distance* ❷ rely on; count on: ～势欺人 *take advantage of one's position to bully people* Ⅱ 形 〈书〉 biased; partial: 不偏不倚

【倚官仗势】rely on one's power and position; count on one's powerful connections

【倚靠】❶ lean on or against; rest on or against ❷ 同〖依靠〗

【倚赖】同〖依赖〗

【倚老卖老】take advantage of one's seniority or old age (to ignore manners, regulations, etc.); flaunt one's seniority

【倚马可待】can write at the side of a horse—can write very fast ——另见〖倚马千言〗

【倚马千言】dash off a thousand words at the side of a horse—write with great facility

【倚音】[音] appoggiatura

【倚仗】rely on; count on: ～权势 *rely on one's power and position; count on one's powerful connections*

【倚重】rely heavily on sb.'s service

椅 名 chair

【椅背】the back of a chair

【椅披】a colourful silk chair cover

【椅套】a slipcover for a chair

【椅子】chair

【椅子顶】[杂] balancing on a pyramid of chairs

旖 (构词成分) 见下

【旖旎】〈文〉 charming; enchanting: ～风光 *an enchanting scene*

yì

义 Ⅰ 名 ❶ justice; righteousness ❷ human ties; relationship: 情义 ❸ meaning; significance: 词～ *the meaning of a word* Ⅱ 形 ❶ righteous; equitable; just: ～行 *a righteous deed* ❷ adopted or adoptive: ～子(女) *adopted son (daughter)* /

～父(母) *adoptive father* (*mother*) ❸ artificial; false: ～发 *false hair*
【义兵】a righteous army: 举～ *raise an army to fight a just war*
【义不容辞】be duty-bound; have an unshirkable duty
【义齿】false tooth; artificial tooth
【义愤】righteous indignation; moral indignation: 激于～ *be stirred by righteous indignation* ◇ ～填膺 be filled with indignation
【义和团运动】the Yihetuan Movement
【义举】a magnanimous act undertaken for the public good; an undertaking in public interests
【义捐】donations for public welfare: ～门诊 *free consultations*
【义理】❶ reason and good sense ❷ argumentation (of a speech or essay)
【义卖】a sale of goods for charity or other worthy causes; (charity) bazaar
【义旗】the banner of an army fighting a just war; banner of righteousness: 举～ *raise the banner of righteousness*; *rise against injustice*
【义气】code of brotherhood; personal loyalty: 讲～ *be loyal* (*to one's friends*) / ～深重 *have a strong sense of obligation*
【义犬】a faithful dog
【义赛】benefit competition
【义师】an army fighting a just war; a righteous army: 兴～ *raise an army to fight for a just cause*
【义士】a high-minded or chivalrous person; a person who upholds justice; a righteous man
【义无反顾】honour permits no turning back; be duty-bound not to turn back
【义务】❶ duty; obligation: 公民的基本权利与～ *the fundamental rights and duties of citizens* / 条约规定的～ *treaty obligations* ❷ volunteer; voluntary: 我是来尽～的。*I've come to do voluntary service*. ◇ ～兵 compulsory serviceman; ～兵役制 compulsory military service; conscription; ～教育 compulsory education; ～劳动 voluntary labour; volunteer labour; ～植树运动 voluntary afforestation campaign
【义项】senses of a dictionary entry
【义形于色】with righteous indignation written on one's face
【义学】(in former times) a private or community-run school charging no tuition; free school
【义演】benefit performance
【义勇军】army of volunteers; volunteers ◇ ～进行曲 March of the Volunteers (the national anthem of the People's Republic of China)
【义诊】(of doctors) give free outpatient service to raise funds for charity or other worthy causes; benefit outpatient service
【义正词严】speak out sternly from a sense of justice; speak with the force of justice
【义肢】[医] artificial limb
【义冢】(in former times) a burial ground for the remains of unidentified persons

亿 数 a hundred million
【亿万】hundreds of millions; millions upon millions: ～人民 *hundreds of millions of people*; *the people in their hundreds of millions* / ～富翁 *billionaire*; *multimillionaire*
【亿万斯年】(for) billions of years; (for) aeons; time without end; eternity

忆 动 recall; recollect; remember: 回忆
【忆苦思甜】recall the sorrows of the past and savour the joys of the present; tell of one's sufferings in the old society and one's happiness in the new; contrast past misery with present happiness
【忆昔抚今】recall the past and compare it with the present; reflect on the past in the light of the present
【忆想】recall; recollect; call to mind: ～往事 *recollect the past*

艺 名 ❶ skill: 学艺 ❷ art: 文艺
【艺高人胆大】boldness of execution stems from superb skill
【艺妓】geisha (in Japan)
【艺林】the world of art; art circles
【艺龄】length of sb.'s stage career: 他有三十多年～。*He's been on the stage for over thirty years*.
【艺名】stage name (of an actor or actress)
【艺能】mastery of a skill or technique; technical ability; skill
【艺人】❶ actor or entertainer (in local drama, storytelling, acrobatics, etc.) ❷ artisan; handicraftsman
【艺术】❶ art: ～标准 *artistic criterion* / ～风格 *artistic style* / ～技巧 *artistry*; *craftsmanship* / ～形式 *artistic form*; *forms of art* / ～造诣 *artistic attainments* / 为～而～ *art for art's sake* ❷ skill; art; craft: 领导～ *art of leadership* ❸ conforming to good taste: 这个房间布置得很～。*The room is tastefully furnished*. ◇ ～化妆 artistic make-up; ～家 artist; ～节 Arts Festival; ～界 art circles; ～片 movie placing emphasis on artistic quality (〈反〉'娱乐片'); ～品 work of art; ～体操 sports rhythmic gymnastics; ～团 art ensemble; art troupe; ～性 artistic quality; artistry; ～造型 artistic design; ～指导 art director
【艺坛】art circles: ～新秀 *a new star in art circles*
【艺苑】the realm of art and literature; art and literary circles: ～奇葩 *exquisite works of art*

刈 动 mow; cut down: ～草 *mow grass*
【刈草机】mowing machine; mower
【刈除】cut off; root out; eradicate: ～杂草 *weeding*

议 Ⅰ 名 opinion; view: 异议 Ⅱ 动 discuss; exchange views on; talk over: 我们对各种方案都～了～。*We exchanged views on each of the different proposals*.
【议案】proposal; motion

【议程】agenda：会议有三项～。*There are three items on the agenda of the meeting.*
【议定】decide through consultation；agree on ◇ ～书 protocol
【议而不决】discuss sth. without reaching a decision；have a fruitless discussion
【议购】buy at negotiated prices
【议和】negotiate peace；carry on peace negotiations
【议会】parliament；congress；legislative assembly：召开(解散)～ *convene (dissolve) parliament* / ～党团 *parliamentary groups* ◇ ～制 parliamentarism；～走廊 lobby
【议价】❶ negotiate a price ❷ negotiated price
【议决】resolve after deliberation；pass a resolution
【议论】comment；talk；discuss：大发～ *speak at great length* / ～不休 *carry on endless discussions* ◇ ～纷纷 all sorts of comments；widespread comment
【议事】discuss official business：～规则 *rules of procedure；rules of debate* / ～日程 *agenda；order of the day*
【议题】item on the agenda；subject under discussion；topic for discussion
【议席】seat in a legislative assembly
【议销】sell at negotiated prices
【议员】member of a legislative assembly；assemblyman；(in Great Britain) Member of Parliament (MP)；(in U. S.) Congressman or Congresswoman
【议院】legislative assembly；parliament；congress
【议长】speaker (of a legislative body)；president：众议院～ *Speaker of the (U. S.) House of Representatives*
【议政】discuss affairs of government

亦 副〈书〉also；too：反之～然 *and the reverse is also true；and vice versa* / ～工～农 *be both worker and peasant*
【亦步亦趋】ape sb. at every step；imitate sb.'s every move；blindly follow suit
【亦即】that is；i.e.；namely；viz.
【亦且】〈书〉moreover
【亦庄亦谐】serious and comical at the same time；seriocomic

屹 形〈书〉towering like a mountain peak
【屹立】stand towering like a giant；stand erect
【屹然】towering；majestic：～不动 *stand firm and erect*

异 Ⅰ 形 ❶ different：～姓 *a different surname* ❷ strange；unusual；extraordinary：～兆 *a strange omen* / 奇才～能 *extraordinary talents and abilities* ❸ other；another：异日 Ⅱ 动 ❶ surprise：深以为～ *be greatly surprised* ❷ separate：离异
【异邦】a foreign country：漂泊～ *lead a wandering life in a foreign country*
【异步】[物] asynchronous ◇ ～传输方式 asynchronous transfer mode (ATM)；～电动机 induction motor；～发电机 asynchronous generator；～计算机 asynchronous computer；～通信接口 asynchronous communication interface
【异才】exceptional talents
【异彩】extraordinary (or radiant) splendour：戏剧舞台大放～。*New forms of traditional opera are blossoming in radiant splendour.*
【异常】❶ unusual；abnormal：～现象 *abnormal phenomena* / 神色～ *not be one's usual self* ❷ extremely；exceedingly；particularly：～危险 *extremely dangerous*
【异常期】anomalistic period
【异词】dissenting words
【异地】a place far away from home；a strange land
【异读】variant pronunciation
【异端】heterodoxy；heresy ◇ ～邪说 heresies；heretical beliefs；unorthodox opinions
【异构化】[化] isomerization
【异国】a foreign country (or land)：～情调 *an exotic atmosphere*
【异乎寻常】unusual；extraordinary：～地冷 *extraordinarily cold* / ～地热心 *unusually enthusiastic*
【异花传粉】[植] cross pollination
【异花受精】[植] allogamy；cross fertilization
【异化】❶ [哲] alienation ❷ [语] dissimilation
【异化作用】[生] dissimilation
【异己】dissident；alien：排除～ *discriminate against those who hold different views；get rid of dissidents*
【异教】paganism；heathenism ◇ ～徒 pagan；heathen
【异军突起】a new force suddenly coming to the fore
【异口同声】with one voice；in unison：大家～地称赞她献身教育事业的精神。*Everybody spoke in praise of her devotion to the cause of education.* / "好。"大家～说。"*Agreed," was the unanimous reply.*
【异类】❶〈旧〉foreign peoples ❷ a different class or species (of plants or animals)
【异曲同工】different tunes sung with equal skill—different approaches but equally satisfactory results
【异人】❶〈旧〉an extraordinary person (referring to a supernatural being or an immortal) ❷ another person
【异兽】strange animals；rare animals：珍禽异兽
【异说】❶ dissenting views；different views ❷ absurd remarks
【异体受精】❶ [动] cross-fertilization ❷ [植] allogamy；cross-fertilization
【异体字】a variant form of a Chinese character
【异同】❶ similarities and differences ❷〈书〉objection；dissent
【异外】unusual；exceptional：～舒畅 *feel unusually happy*
【异味】❶ a rare delicacy ❷ a peculiar smell

【异物】❶ foreign matter; a foreign body: 食管～ *a foreign body in the esophagus* ❷〈书〉a dead person; ghost: 化为～ *give up the ghost; die* ❸ a rare object

【异乡】a foreign land; a strange land

【异香】an unusually sweet smell; a rare perfume: ～扑鼻。*Strong whiffs of rare perfume assailed the nostrils.*

【异想天开】indulge in the wildest fantasy; have a most fantastic idea: 休要～。*Don't let your imagination run away with you.*

【异心】infidelity; disloyalty

【异形钢材】special-shaped steel

【异形管】[机] special pipe

【异性】❶ the opposite sex ❷ different in nature: ～的电互相吸引。*Unlike electric charges attract each other.*

【异烟肼】[医] isoniazid; rimifon

【异言】〈书〉dissenting words: 并无～ *raise no objection*

【异样】❶ difference: 多年没见了,看不出他有什么～。*We haven't seen each other for many years, but he doesn't look any different.* ❷ unusual; peculiar: 人们都用～的眼光打量他。*Everyone sized him up with curious eyes.*

【异议】objection; dissent: 提出～ *raise an objection; take exception to; challenge*

【异域】❶ a foreign country ❷ an alien land; a strange land ◇ ～情调 exotic romance

【异源多倍体】[生] allopolyploid

【异重流】density current

【异族】a different race or nation: ～通婚 *mixed marriages*

译 动 translate; interpret: ～成英语 *translate into English* / ～成电码 *coding* / ～成密码 *enciphering*

【译本】translated version (of a book); translation

【译笔】the quality or style of a translation: ～流畅。*The translation reads smoothly.*

【译电】❶ encode or encipher a telegram ❷ decode or decipher a telegram ◇ ～员 decoder; code clerk; cryptographer; ～组 code and cipher section

【译稿】the manuscript of a translation

【译介】translate and write an introduction to (a book)

【译码】decode; decipher ◇ ～器 decoder; decipherer

【译名】a translated term or name

【译配】translate and dub: 这部德国电影已～成广东话。*This German film has been dubbed into Cantonese.*

【译述】translate (or render) freely

【译文】translated text; translation: 把～跟原文核对一下 *check the translation against the original*

【译音】transliteration

【译员】interpreter

【译者】translator

【译制】dub (a film, etc.) ◇ ～片 a dubbed film

【译注】translate and annotate: ～古籍 *translate and annotate ancient books*

【译著】translations

【译作】translations

抑 Ⅰ 动 press down; restrain; repress; curb: ～价 *keep down the prices* Ⅱ 连〈书〉❶ or: 人欤,～鬼欤? *Is it a human being or is it a ghost?* ❷ but: 非惟天时,～亦人谋也。*It's not only a matter of Heaven-sent occasions but also a matter of human endeavour.*

【抑或】or: 不知他们是赞成,～是反对。*I wonder if they are for or against this.*

【抑菌作用】[医] bacteriostasis

【抑强扶弱】curb the strong and help the weak; uphold the weak against the strong

【抑且】〈书〉also; moreover; furthermore

【抑扬】(of sound) rise and fall; modulate ◇ ～顿挫 cadence; modulation in tone

【抑郁】depressed; despondent; gloomy: ～不平 *feel disgruntled* ◇ ～症 [医] depression

【抑止】hold in check; hold back: 眼泪～不住直往下流 *can't hold back one's tears*

【抑制】❶ restrain; control; check: ～自己的愤怒 *restrain one's anger* / ～自己的感情 *control one's emotion* ❷ [生理] inhibition ◇ ～剂 [化] inhibitor; ～神经 [生理] inhibitory nerve

呓 动 talk in one's sleep

【呓语】❶ talk in one's sleep ❷ crazy talk; ravings: 狂人～ *ravings of a madman*

邑 名 ❶ town; city ❷ county

役 Ⅰ 名 ❶ labour; service: 劳役 ❷ military service: 兵役 ❸ servant: 仆役 ❹ battle; campaign: 平型关之～ *the Battle of Pingxingguan (Sept. 1937)* Ⅱ 动 use as a servant: ～万物 *make all things serve man*

【役畜】draught animal; beast of burden

【役龄】enlistment age

【役使】work (an animal); use: 地主把长工当牛马一样～。*The landlord made the farmhands toil like beasts of burden.*

易 Ⅰ 形 ❶ easy: 不～解决 *not easy to solve* / 得来不～ *not easily won; hard-earned* / ～学 *easy to learn* / ～患感冒 *catch cold easily; be susceptible to colds* / ～涝地区 *areas liable to waterlogging* ❷ amiable: 平易 Ⅱ 动 ❶ change: ～地疗养 *go to another place for recuperation* / 数～寒暑。*Several years have passed.* ❷ exchange: 以物～物 *barter* / ～地而处 *change places with another person*

【易爆物】explosive substance

【易感者】[医] susceptible person; susceptible

【易货】barter ◇ ～汇兑 barter exchange; ～经济 barter economy; ～贸易 barter; barter trade; ～贸易协定 barter trade agreement; ～贸易制

barter system；～协定 an agreement on the exchange of commodities；barter agreement
【易经】The Book of Changes ——另见〖五经〗
【易拉罐】pop-top；pull-top；flip-top
【易燃物】combustibles；inflammables
【易熔点】［物］eutectic point
【易熔合金】［冶］fusible alloy
【易如反掌】as easy as turning one's hand over；as easy as falling off a log
【易手】change hands
【易性癖】transsexualism
【易于】be easy to：这件事～处理。*This is easy to manage*.
【易辙】〈书〉change one's course；strike out on a new path
【易帜】〈书〉change one's banner—change one's principles or allegiance
【易装癖】transvestite；trannie

驿 名 同〖驿站〗，now used mainly as part of a place name
【驿道】（又作'驿路'）post road
【驿站】（in former times）post station；courier station

奕 形〈书〉grand；great
【奕奕】❶ grand；great ❷ radiating power and vitality：神采奕奕

弈 Ⅰ名〈书〉weiqi，a game played with black and white pieces on a board of 361 crosses；go Ⅱ动 play chess：对弈
【弈林】chess-playing circles：～高手 *a master chess player*

疫 名 epidemic disease；pestilence：防疫
【疫病】epidemic disease
【疫苗】vaccine
【疫情】information about and appraisal of an epidemic；epidemic situation：报告～ *report epidemic diseases*
【疫区】an epidemic-stricken area

轶（构词成分）见下
【轶材】〈书〉talents above the average
【轶伦】〈书〉tower above one's generation；surpass one's contemporaries
【轶事】anecdote

益 Ⅰ名 benefit；profit；advantage：利益 Ⅱ形 beneficial：益虫 Ⅲ动 increase：延年益寿 Ⅳ副 all the more；increasingly：～觉困难 *find sth. increasingly difficult*
【益虫】beneficial insect
【益处】benefit；profit；good
【益发】（又作'益加'）all the more；even more
【益母草】［植］motherwort（Leonurus heterophyllus）
【益鸟】beneficial bird
【益友】friend and mentor

谊 名 friendship：～同手足 *be as close as brothers*

悒 形〈书〉sad；worried：～～不乐 *feel depressed*；*mope*
【悒闷】〈书〉depressed；dejected；in low spirits
【悒郁】〈书〉depressed；despondent；gloomy ◇ ～寡欢 同〖郁郁寡欢〗

逸 Ⅰ名 ease；leisure：有劳有～ *alternate work with rest* Ⅱ动 ❶ escape；flee：逃逸 ❷ be lost：～书 *ancient works no longer extant* ❸ excel：超逸
【逸乐】comfort and pleasure
【逸趣】refined interests or tastes
【逸散】escape；lose；disperse；～电子 escaped electron
【逸史】unofficial history
【逸事】anecdote
【逸闻】anecdote
【逸致】a carefree mood：闲情逸致

翌 形〈书〉immediately following in time；next：～日 *next day* / ～年 *next year*

溢 Ⅰ动 overflow；spill：河水四～。*The river overflowed*. Ⅱ形 excessive：～誉 *excessive praise*
【溢出】spill over；overflow
【溢额】surplus ◇ ～部分 surplus share；～再保险 surplus reinsurance
【溢洪道】［水］spillway
【溢价】premium：～发行股票 *float*（*or issue*）*stocks at a premium*
【溢流】overflow；brim over ◇ ～坝 water conservancy overfall dam；spillway dam
【溢美】〈书〉excessive praise；fulsome praise；undeserved praise
【溢于言表】（of feelings）show clearly in one's words and manner：愤激之情，～。*Indignation showed clearly in his words and manner*.

意 Ⅰ名 ❶ meaning；idea；thought：同意 ❷ wish；desire；intention：好意 ❸ suggestion；hint；trace：颇有秋～ *make one feel that autumn has set in* ❹〈略〉见〖意大利〗Ⅱ动 anticipate；expect：不意
【意大利】Italy ◇ ～人 Italian；～肉饼 pizza；～语 Italian（language）
【意会】perceive by intuition；sense：只可意会，不可言传
【意见】❶ idea；view；opinion；suggestion：交换～ *exchange ideas*（*or views*）；*compare notes* ❷ objection；differing opinion；complaint：我对这种办法很有～。*I strongly object to this method*. or *I take vigorous exception to this approach*. ◇ ～簿 visitors' book，customers' book，etc.；～箱 suggestion box
【意境】the mood of a literary work or a work of art

【意料】anticipate；expect：这是～中的事。*That's to be expected.*
【意念】idea；thought
【意气】❶ will and spirit：～高昂 *high-spirited* ❷ temperament ❸ personal feelings (or prejudice)：～之争 *a dispute caused by personal feelings* ◇ ～风发 high-spirited and vigorous；daring and energetic；～相投 be alike in temperament；be congenial；～用事 be swayed by personal feelings
【意识】❶ consciousness；awareness：法律～ *law awareness* / 宗教～ *religious consciousness* ❷ (usu. used with 到) be conscious (or aware) of；awake to；realize：他～到自己的责任了。*He is conscious of his responsibilities.* ◇ ～流［心理］stream of consciousness；～形态［哲］ideology；～域［心理］sphere of consciousness
【意思】❶ meaning；idea：这个词的～是什么？*What is the meaning of this word?* / 文章的中心～ *the central idea of an article* ❷ opinion；wish；desire：我的～是走着去。*In my opinion, (or I think) we should walk.* ❸ a token of affection, appreciation, gratitude, etc.：这不过是我的一点儿～，请收下吧。*Please accept this little gift as a token of my appreciation.* ❹ suggestion；hint；trace：天有点要下雨的～。*It looks like rain.* ❺ interest；fun：打桥牌很有～。*Bridge is a lot of fun.* / 他这个人没～。*He's dull.* ❻ (reduplicated) as a mere token：她要走了，咱们送她一条丝巾～～。*She's leaving. Let's give her a silk kerchief as a token of our friendship.*
【意态】mien；demeanor；bearing：～自若 *appear calm and at ease*
【意图】intention；intent：领会上级～ *understand the intentions of the higher organization*
【意外】❶ unexpected；unforeseen：～损失 *unexpected loss* / ～利润 *windfall profit* / 感到～ *be surprised；be taken by surprise* / 你太出乎我的～了！*You astound me!* ❷ accident；mishap：以免发生～ *so as to avoid accidents*
【意外风险】emergency risk
【意味】❶ meaning；significance；implication：我揣摩不透他那番话的～所在。*I can't figure out the implications of what he said.* ❷ interest；overtone；flavour：这首诗～无穷。*This is a poem of unlimited interest.* ◇ ～深长 having deep meaning；pregnant with meaning；of profound significance；～着 signify；mean；imply
【意下】❶ in the mind；in the heart：别人的闲话，她全不放在～。*She didn't take the idle gossip to heart at all.* ❷ opinion；idea；view：老兄～如何？*What do you think of it?* or *What's your opinion?*
【意想】imagine；expect：～不到的效果 *unexpected results*
【意向】intention；purpose：敌军～不明。*The enemy's intentions are not clear.* ◇ ～书 letter of intent
【意象】images；imagery
【意兴】interest；enthusiasm：～索然 *have lost all interest in sth.；be no longer interested in sth.* / ～勃勃 *be highly enthusiastic*
【意义】meaning；sense；significance：具有重大历史～的事件 *an event of historic significance* / 这样做没有～。*There's no point in doing that.* / 这个词有三个～。*This word has three distinct meanings.*
【意译】free translation
【意意思思】hesitate in speech
【意欲】intend to；want to：他～独自前去。*He intends to go all by himself.*
【意愿】wish；desire；aspiration：表达人民的～ *express the wishes of the people* / 这并不是我们的～。*This is not what we'd like to see.*
【意蕴】meaning；implication；connotation
【意在笔先】have an idea in the mind before starting writing or painting
【意在言外】the meaning is implied
【意旨】intention；wish；will：秉承某人的～ *in compliance with sb.'s wish*
【意志】will；willpower；determination：～消沉 *demoralized；despondent* / 锻炼～ *temper one's willpower* / 不以人的～为转移 *independent of man's will*
【意中人】the person one is in love with；the person of one's heart；the beloved one
【意中事】sth. that is to be expected

裔 名〈书〉❶ descendants；posterity：华裔 ❷ a distant land；a remote region：四～ *the borderlands；the frontiers*
【裔孙】〈书〉remote descendants

肄 动 study：肄业
【肄业】study in school or at college (usu. indicating without finishing one's education)：他曾在大学～二年。*He was in college for two years.*

缢 动〈书〉die or be put to death by hanging：自缢

毅 形 firm；resolute；staunch：刚毅
【毅力】willpower；will；stamina；tenacity：惊人的～ *amazing willpower* / 百折不回的～ *indomitable will*
【毅然】resolutely；firmly；determinedly ◇ ～决然 resolutely；determinedly

薏 (构词成分) 见下
【薏米】(又作'薏仁米') the seed of Job's tears
【薏苡】［植］Job's tears

臆 Ⅰ 名 the chest Ⅱ 副 subjectively：臆测
【臆测】conjecture；surmise；guess
【臆断】form a subjective judgment；assume
【臆度】〈书〉conjecture；surmise；guess
【臆见】a subjective view
【臆说】assumption；supposition

【臆造】fabricate (a story, reason, etc.); concoct

翼 Ⅰ名 ❶ the wings of a bird, an insect, etc. ❷ the wings of an aeroplane ❸ flank (of an army, etc.); wing (of a building): 从左右两～夹攻敌人 *attack the enemy on both flanks* / 主楼的两～ *the two wings of the main building* ❹ the twenty-seventh of the twenty-eight constellations (二十八宿) into which the celestial sphere was divided in ancient Chinese astronomy (consisting of twenty-two stars in Crater and Hydra) Ⅱ动 〈书〉assist (a ruler): ～助 *render assistance (to a ruler)*

【翼蔽】〈书〉shield; protect; screen

【翼侧】[军] flank: ～攻击 *flank attack* / ～迂回 *outflank*

【翼翅】wing

【翼护】shield sb. with one's own body

【翼手动物】[动] chiropter (e.g. the bat)

【翼手目】[动] Chiroptera

【翼型】[航空] wing section; aerofoil

【翼翼】〈书〉❶ reverent and cautious: 小心翼翼 ❷ in neat formation; in orderly array ❸ thriving; abundant

【翼指龙】pterodactyl (an extinct reptile)

【翼状胬肉】[医] pterygium

癔 (构词成分)见下

【癔病】[医] hysteria: ～患者 *hysteriac*

镱 名 [化] ytterbium (Yb)

yīn

因 Ⅰ动 ❶〈书〉follow; carry on: 因袭 ❷〈书〉rely on; accord with: ～病下药 *suit the medicine to the illness* / ～其自然 *let things take their natural course* Ⅱ名 cause; reason: 必有他～ *there must be some other reason* Ⅲ介 because of; as a result of: ～病请假 *ask for sick leave* / ～公牺牲 *die while on duty; die at one's post* / 会议～故延期。*The meeting has been postponed for some reason.* Ⅳ连 because: 他～有其他事情未能出席。*He was absent because he had other things to attend to.*

【因材施教】teach students according to their aptitude; suit the instruction to the student's level

【因此】so; therefore; for this reason; consequently: 雪融化时吸收热量,气温～下降。*Melting snow absorbs heat, and so makes the temperature drop.*

【因次】[物] dimension: ～分析 *dimensional analysis*

【因地制宜】take measures suited to local conditions; suit measures to local conditions: ～地进行密植 *carry out close planting in line with local conditions*

【因而】thus; as a result; therefore: 新机器的运转速度要快一倍,～会大大降低成本。*The new machines will work twice as fast, thus greatly reducing costs.*

【因果】❶ cause and effect: ～关系 *causality* / ～性 *causality* / ～倒置 *confuse cause and effect* ❷ [宗](佛教) karma; preordained fate ◇ ～报应 [宗](佛教) retribution; karma; ～律 the law of cause and effect; the law of causality (or causation)

【因祸得福】derive gain from misfortune; profit by misfortune

【因陋就简】make do with whatever is available; do things simply and thriftily: 实验室设备是不够理想,但我们只好～。*Our laboratory equipment isn't perfect, but we must make do.*

【因明】a system of Hindu logic

【因人成事】depend on others for success in one's work

【因人而异】vary with each individual: 疗效～。*The effect of the treatment varies with the individual.*

【因人设事】create a job to accommodate a person

【因人制宜】do what is suited to each individual; take measures suited to each person

【因时制宜】do what is suited to the occasion; take measures suited to the time

【因式】[数] factor (which is an algebraic expression): $a+b$ 和 a-b 都是 a^2-b^2 的～. $a+b$ *and* a-b *are both factors of* a^2-b^2. / ～分解 *factorization (into algebraic expressions)*

【因势利导】guide a matter along its course of development; adroitly guide action according to circumstances: ～,夺取胜利 *make the best use of the situation and guide the struggle to victory*

【因数】[数] factor (which is a whole number): 2、3、4 和 6 都是 12 的～。*2, 3, 4 and 6 are all factors of 12.* / ～分解 *factorization (into whole numbers)*

【因素】factor; element: 积极～ *positive factors* ◇ ～论 [哲] theory of factors

【因特网】(又作'国际互联网') Internet

【因为】❶ because: 我～事情太多,所以直到今天才来看你。*I didn't come and see you till today because I was terribly busy.* ❷ because of; on account of; owing to: ～天气的关系,飞机不能按时起飞。*Because of bad weather, the plane didn't take off on time.*

【因袭】follow (old customs, methods, rules, etc.); copy: ～前人 *follow in the footsteps of one's predecessors*

【因小失大】try to save a little only to lose a lot; penny wise and pound foolish; spoil the ship for a ha'p'orth of tar

【因循】❶ follow (old customs, etc.); continue in the same old rut: ～旧习 *follow the old customs* ❷ procrastinate: ～坐误 *sit back and allow the situation to deteriorate; procrastinate until it is too late* ◇ ～守旧 stick to old ways; follow the beaten track

【因噎废食】give up eating for fear of choking—refrain from doing what one should for fear of running a risk

【因由】〈口〉reason; cause; origin

【因缘】❶［宗］(佛教)principal and subsidiary causes; cause ❷ predestined relationship

阴 Ⅰ名 ❶ (in Chinese thought) yin, the feminine or negative principle in nature (〈反〉'阳') ❷ the moon: 阴历 ❸ shade: 树阴 ❹ north of a hill or south of a river: 华～ *Huayin* (*a county situated on the north side of Huashan Mountain*) / 江～ *Jiangyin* (*a county situated on the south side of the Changjiang River*) ❺ the back side: 碑～ *the back of a stone tablet* ❻ private parts (esp. of the female) Ⅱ形 ❶ overcast: 天～了。*The sky is overcast.* / 多云转～ *cloudy to overcast* ❷ in intaglio: 阴文 ❸ hidden; secret: 阴沟 ❹ sinister: 这个人真～。*This chap's very sinister.* ❺ of the nether world; of ghosts: 阴宅 / 阴间 ❻［物］negative: 阴极

【阴暗】dark; gloomy: ～的脸色 *a glum face* / ～的心理 *mentality marked by antipathy and gloom* ◇ ～面 the dark (or seamy) side of things

【阴部】［生理］private parts; genitals; pudenda

【阴曹】(又作'阴曹地府') the nether world; the Hades

【阴沉】cloudy; overcast; gloomy; sombre: 天色～。*The sky is cloudy (or grey).* / 脸色～ *have a sombre countenance; look glum*

【阴沉木】hard wood which has long been buried in earth

【阴唇】［生理］labia (of the vulva)

【阴错阳差】(又作'阴差阳错') a mistake or error due to a strange combination of circumstances

【阴丹士林】❶ indanthrone (a deep blue dye) ❷ a cotton cloth dyed with indanthrone

【阴道】［生理］vagina ◇ ～炎 vaginitis

【阴德】good deeds done in secret; hidden acts of merit: 积～ *accumulate hidden merit*

【阴地】a shaded place; shade ◇ ～植物 shade plant

【阴电】negative electricity

【阴毒】insidious; sinister and ruthless

【阴风】❶ a cold wind ❷ an ill (or evil) wind

【阴干】be placed in the shade to dry; dry in the shade

【阴功】同〖阴德〗

【阴沟】sewer; covered drain

【阴河】underground river

【阴黑】dark and gloomy; murky; sombre: 天色～。*The sky was dark and gloomy.*

【阴户】［生理］vaginal orifice

【阴魂】ghost; spirit; apparition ◇ ～不散 the ghost lingers on—the evil influence remains

【阴极】［物］negative pole; negative electrode; cathode: 冷～ *cold cathode* / ～激励 *cathode drive* ◇ ～射线［物］cathode ray

【阴间】the nether world; the Hades

【阴茎】［生理］penis: ～勃起 *penile erection*

【阴冷】❶ (of weather) gloomy and cold; raw ❷ (of a person's look) sombre; glum

【阴离子】another name for 负离子

【阴历】lunar calendar: ～正月 *the first month of the lunar year*

【阴凉】❶ shady and cool: 此药宜置于～处。*The medicine should be kept in a cool, dark place.* ❷ a cool place; shade: 找个～儿歇歇。*Let's have a rest in the shade.*

【阴霾】haze

【阴毛】［生理］pubes; pubic hair

【阴门】同〖阴户〗

【阴面】the shady side; the back side

【阴谋】❶ conspire; plot; scheme: ～复辟 *plot to restore the old order* / ～篡权 *scheme to usurp power* ❷ conspiracy; plot; scheme: ～诡计 *schemes and intrigues* / ～手段 *conspiratorial means* / 政变～ *a coup plot* / 外交～ *a diplomatic intrigue* ◇ ～集团 a conspiratorial clique (or group); ～家 schemer; intriguer; conspirator

【阴囊】［生理］scrotum

【阴平】high and level tone (the first of the four tones in modern standard Chinese pronunciation)

【阴燃】glow; smoulder: 这间宿舍因遗留火种～发生大火。*The dormitory building burned down when some smouldering cinders burst into flame.*

【阴森】gloomy; gruesome; ghastly: ～的树林 *a deep, dark forest* / ～可怕 *ghastly and bloodcurdling*

【阴生植物】同〖阴地植物〗

【阴盛阳衰】❶［医］Yin rises while Yang declines; the Yang forces recede in favour of the Yin forces ❷ the female being stronger and more powerful, or more numerous than the male

【阴虱】［动］crab louse

【阴湿】dark and damp

【阴私】shameful secret

【阴天】an overcast sky; a cloudy day

【阴文】characters or designs cut in intaglio; intaglio

【阴险】sinister; insidious; treacherous: ～毒辣 *sinister and ruthless*

【阴笑】a sinister smile: 他脸上露出一丝～。*A sinister smile crept over his face.*

【阴性】❶［医］negative: ～反应 *negative reaction* ❷［语］feminine gender

【阴虚】［中］deficiency of yin (insufficiency of body fluid), with irritability, thirst, constipation, etc. as symptoms

【阴阳】❶ (in Chinese thought) yin and yang, the two opposing principles in nature, the former feminine and negative, the latter masculine and positive ❷ ancient Chinese astronomy (esp. the study of the movements of the celestial bodies) ❸ occult arts (e.g. astrology, geomancy, etc.) ❹ 同〖阴阳生〗◇ ～历 lunisolar calendar; ～人 a bisexual person; hermaphrodite; ～生 yin-yang adept；～水［中］yin-yang water；～先生 geomancer

【阴阳怪气】❶（of a person's manner of speaking）mystifying；enigmatic；deliberately ambiguous ❷ eccentric；queer；cynical：他这个人～的。*He's a queer chap*. / 他来往的人都是有些～的。*The people he has to do with are all a rather peculiar lot*.

【阴阳家】❶ geomancer ❷ the Yin-Yang School or School of Naturalists（in the Warring States Period，475-221 B.C.）

【阴一套，阳一套】act one way in public and another in private；be engaged in double-dealing

【阴翳】〈书〉❶ be shaded or hidden by foliage：柳树～的河边 *river banks shaded by willows* ❷ with luxuriant foliage：桃李～ *peach and plum trees covered with luxuriant foliage*

【阴影】shadow：树木的～ *shadows of trees* / 肺部有～ *have a shadow on one's lungs*

【阴雨】overcast and rainy：～连绵 *cloudy and drizzly for days on end*；*an unbroken spell of wet weather*

【阴郁】gloomy；dismal；depressed：天色～。*The weather is gloomy*. / 心情～ *feel gloomy*（*or depressed*）

【阴云】dark clouds：～密布。*The sky is overcast*. or *The sky is covered with dark clouds*.

【阴宅】grave；tomb

【阴着儿】〈方〉a treacherous act

音 名 ❶ sound：噪音 / 口音 ❷ musical sound；note：这个～得延长一点儿。*The note must be held longer*. ❸ news；tidings：佳音 ❹ syllable：一字一～。*Each character stands for a syllable*.

【音爆】［航空］［航空］sonic boom

【音标】［语音］phonetic symbol；phonetic transcription

【音波】［物］sound wave

【音叉】tuning fork

【音长】the duration of a sound

【音程】［音］interval

【音带】audiotape：盒式～*audio cassette*

【音调】tone：～铿锵 *a ringing tone* ◇ ～失真 tonal distortion

【音读】pronunciation（of a character）

【音符】［音］note

【音高】［语］［音］pitch

【音阶】［音］scale

【音节】［语音］Syllable ◇ ～表 syllabary；～文字 syllabic language

【音控开关】voice-operated switch

【音量】volume（of sound）：～控制 *volume control*

【音律】［音］temperament

【音名】［音］musical alphabet

【音频】［物］audio frequency ◇ ～电话 tone telephone；～调制［无］voice modulation

【音强】intensity of sound

【音容】〈书〉voice and face（of sb. as recalled after his death）◇ ～宛在 the same voice and face seem still there（said as one thinks fondly of a dead person；usu. inscribed on a funeral banner）

【音色】tone colour；timbre

【音诗】［音］tone poem

【音素】old name for 音位 ◇ ～文字 old name for 音位文字

【音速】［物］velocity（or speed）of sound

【音位】［语音］phoneme ◇ ～文字［语］phonemic writing；～学［语］phonemics；phonology

【音箱】speaker；loudspeaker；amplifier

【音响】❶ sound；acoustics：～水雷 *sonic*（*or sound*，*acoustic*）*mine* / ～效果 *sound effects*；*acoustics* ❷〈略〉见〖组合音响〗◇ ～师 sound engineer

【音像】audiovisual；audio-video；sound and video recording：～产品 *audio-video product* ◇ ～出版社 audiovisual press（or publishing house）；～同步装置 moviola；movicola；～业 recording and video industry；～制品 audio-video product

【音效卡】［计］（又作'声卡'）audio card；sound card

【音信】（又作'音讯'）mail；message；news：互通～ *communicate with each other*；*be in correspondence with each other* / 他走后就一直没有～。*We have not heard from him since he left*.

【音型】［音］figure

【音译】transliteration

【音域】［音］range；compass；register

【音乐】music：学～ *study music* / ～形象 *musical image* ◇ ～电视 music TV（MTV）；～盒 music box；～会 concert；～家 musician；～疗法 music therapy；～门铃 music bell；music door-bell；～片 musical（film）；～厅 concert hall；～学 musicology；～学院 conservatory（of music）

【音乐茶座】music tea house

【音乐节】musical festival

【音乐剧】musical comedy

【音箱】sound box；speaker

【音韵】❶ harmonious sounds；rhyme and rhythm ❷ the initial，final and tone of a Chinese character

【音韵学】［语］phonology：～家 *phonologist*

【音障】［物］sound（or sonic）barrier

【音值】［语］value

【音质】❶ tone quality ❷ acoustic fidelity

【音准】［音］accuracy in pitch

茵 名 mattress：绿草如～ *a carpet of green grass*

【茵陈】［植］capillary artemisia（Artemisia capillaris）

【茵褥】〈书〉mattress

【茵茵】（of grass，etc.）lush；luxuriant：芳草～ *fragrant grass growing lush and long* / 一片～嫩绿的麦苗 *a stretch of lush*，*tender wheat seedlings*

洇 动（of ink）spread and sink in：这种纸写字容易～。*Ink blots on this paper*.

【洇色】diffusion or running of colouring matter; bleeding

姻 名 ❶ marriage: 婚姻 ❷ relation by marriage: ～兄弟 *brothers-in-law*

【姻亲】relation by marriage: ～关系 *relationship by marriage; affinity*

【姻缘】the happy fate which brings lovers together: 美满～ *a happy marriage; conjugal felicity*

殷 形〈书〉❶ abundant; rich: 殷实 ❷ eager; ardent: 期望甚～ *cherish high hopes* ❸ hospitable: 招待甚～ *offer cordial hospitality* ——另见 yān

【殷富】wealthy; well-off

【殷钢】[冶] invar

【殷切】ardent; eager: ～的期望 *ardent expectations*

【殷勤】eagerly attentive; solicitous: 受到～接待 *be accorded solicitous hospitality* ——另见〖献殷勤〗

【殷实】well-off; substantial: ～人家 *well-off families* / ～的商号 *a substantial firm* / 家道～ *be a man of substance*

【殷殷】ardent; sincere: ～期望 *entertain ardent hopes* / ～嘱咐 *enjoin sincerely*

铟 名 [化] indium (In)

yín

吟 Ⅰ 动 chant; recite: ～诗 *recite or compose poetry* Ⅱ 名 ❶ song (as a type of classical poetry):《秦妇～》*Song of a Qin Lady* ❷ the cry of certain animals or insects: 猿～ *monkeys squealing* / 蝉～ *cicadas stridulating*

【吟唱】sing; chant: ～毛泽东诗词 *chant Mao Zedong's poems*

【吟哦】recite (poetry) with a cadence; chant

【吟风弄月】(又作'吟风咏月') sing of the moon and the wind—write sentimental verse

【吟诵】chant; recite: ～唐诗 *recite a Tang poem*

【吟味】recite with relish; recite with appreciation: 反复～ *recite again and again in appreciation*

【吟咏】recite (poetry) with a cadence; chant

垠 名〈书〉boundary; limit: 无垠

淫 形 ❶ excessive: 淫雨 ❷ wanton: 乐而不淫 ❸ licentious; lewd; lascivious: 万恶～为首。*Lewdness is the worst of all vices.* ❹ obscene; pornographic: ～书 *pornographic books (or publications)* / ～画 *obscene pictures*

【淫辞】(又作'淫词') ❶〈书〉extravagant speech ❷ obscene language; lewd expressions

【淫荡】loose in morals; lascivious; licentious; lewd

【淫风】wanton customs; lascivious practices

【淫妇】a wanton woman; adulteress

【淫棍】libertine; womanizer; wolf

【淫秽】obscene; salacious; bawdy: ～书刊 *pornographic literature*

【淫乐】(yínlè) in sensual pleasures; gratify carnal desires ——另见 yínyuè

【淫乱】(sexually) promiscuous; licentious

【淫靡】❶ obscene; decadent: ～的歌曲 *obscene or decadent songs* ❷ extravagant: 风气～。*Extravagance has become a common practice.*

【淫威】abuse of power; despotic power

【淫猥】obscene

【淫邪】obscene and wicked; lewd and vicious

【淫亵】❶ obscene; salacious ❷ act indecently towards (a woman)

【淫刑】〈书〉❶ mete out excessive punishments ❷ excessive punishments

【淫羊藿】[植] longspur epimedium (Epime-dium macranthum)

【淫雨】excessive rains: ～成灾。*Excessive rains caused a flood.*

【淫欲】sexual desire; lust

【淫乐】(yínyuè)〈书〉decadent music; obscene music ——另见 yínlè

寅 名 the third of the twelve Earthly Branches (地支) ——另见〖干支〗

【寅吃卯粮】(又作'寅支卯粮') eat next year's food; anticipate one's income

【寅时】the period of the day from 3 a. m. to 5 a. m.

银 Ⅰ 名 [化] silver (Ag): 纯～ *pure silver* Ⅱ 形 ❶ relating to currency or money: 银行 ❷ silver-coloured: ～色 *silvery* / 红地～字 *silver characters on a red background*

【银白】silvery white ◇ ～杨 white poplar (Populus alba)

【银杯】silver cup

【银本位】[经] silver standard

【银币】silver coin

【银川】Yinchuan (capital of the Ningxia Hui Autonomous Region)

【银弹外交】"silver bullet" diplomacy; dollar diplomacy

【银锭】silver ingot

【银耳】tremella (Tremella fuciformis)

【银发】silver (or silvery) hair: 满头～ *silver-haired*

【银根】[经] money market; money: ～紧。*Money is tight. or The money market is tight.* / ～松。*Money is easy. or The money market is easy.* ◇ ～紧缩 tight money policy; limit the growth of money supply

【银汉鱼】[动] silverside

【银行】bank: ～储备金 *bank reserve* / 储备～ *reserve bank* / 储蓄～ *savings bank* / 外汇指定～ *authorized bank for dealing in foreign exchange* / ～存款 *bank deposit* / ～存折 *bankbook; passbook* / ～汇款 *bank remittance* ◇ ～承兑

banker's acceptance；～承兑票 banker's acceptance bill；～电汇 B.T.T（Bank Telegraph transfer）；～家 banker；～间贷款 inter-bank loan；～利率 bank rate；～信贷 bank credit

【银号】banking house

【银河】［天］the Milky Way ◇ ～系［天］the Milky Way system；the Galaxy；～星团［天］galactic cluster

【银狐】silver fox

【银灰】silver grey

【银婚】silver wedding

【银匠】silversmith

【银两】silver（used as currency）

【银幕】（motion-picture）screen；projection screen

【银鸥】［动］herring gull（Larus argentatus vegae）

【银牌】silver medal

【银票】（in former times）silver draft（a form of paper money）

【银屏】❶ fluorescent screen；luminescent screen；telescreen ❷ television；television circles：刘青登上了～。*Liu Qing has started his television career*.

【银器】silverware

【银钱】money

【银鼠】［动］snow weasel

【银条】silver bar

【银团】financial group formed by banks；bank association；banking consortium：～贷款 *syndicate loan*；*consortium loan*

【银屑病】［医］psoriasis

【银杏】［植］ginkgo；gingko

【银燕】silver swallow—aeroplane

【银洋】silver dollar

【银样镴枪头】a pewter spearhead that shines like silver—an impressive-looking but useless person

【银鱼】whitebait；salangid

【银圆】（又作'银元'）silver dollar

【银针】［医］acupuncture needle

【银质奖】silver medal

【银朱】vermilion：～涂料 *vermilion paint*

【银装】〈喻〉snow cover：巍巍群山披～。*The lofty mountains are blanketed with snow*.

【银子】silver；money

龈 名 gum

yǐn

引 动 ❶ draw；stretch：～弓 *draw a bow* ❷ lead；guide：～滦入津 *divert the water of the Luan River to Tianjin* ❸ leave：～避 *keep*（*or stay*，*steer*）*clear of*；*make way for* ❹ stretch out：引颈 ❺ induce；attract：劈柴太湿，火～不着。*The firewood is too wet to kindle*. ❻ cause；make：他这一句话～得大家笑起来。*His remark set everybody laughing*. ❼ quote；cite：～某人的话 *quote sb*. / ～自《中国日报》*quoted from China Daily* / ～书为证 *cite a book as proof*

【引爆】ignite；detonate：～装置 *igniter*

【引柴】（又作'引火柴'）kindling

【引产】［医］induce labour

【引出】draw forth；lead to：～正确的结论 *draw correct conclusions*

【引导】guide；lead：主人～贵宾们参观了车间。*The hosts showed the distinguished guests around the workshops*.

【引逗】❶ tantalize；tease ❷ lure；entice

【引渡】［法］extradite

【引而不发】（of a teacher of archery）draw the bow but not release the arrow—show people what to do without doing it for them

【引发】initiate；touch off；spark off；trigger off：那个事件～了一场暴乱。*The incident touched off*（*or sparked off*）*a riot*. ◇ ～剂［化］initiator

【引发价格】［经］trigger price

【引港】❶ pilot a ship（into or out of a harbour）❷ pilot（of a ship）

【引吭高歌】sing joyfully in a loud voice；sing heartily

【引航】同〖引水〗❶ ◇ ～员 another name for 引水员

【引号】quotation marks（“ ”）：双～ *double quotation marks*（“ ”）/ 单～ *single quotation marks*（‘ ’）

【引河】❶ irrigation channel ❷ diversion canal

【引火】light a fire：连～的木头片儿也找不到 *can't even find a piece of wood for kindling* ◇ ～烧身 draw fire against oneself—bring trouble on oneself；～线 fuse

【引见】present（a person）to another；introduce：他把我～给市长。*He presented me to the mayor*.

【引荐】recommend（a person）

【引进】❶ recommend（a person）❷ introduce from elsewhere：～新的小麦品种 *introduce new varieties of wheat* / ～技术装备 *import technology and equipment*

【引经据典】quote the classics；quote authoritative works

【引颈】crane one's neck：～四望 *crane one's neck to look around* / ～企待 *eagerly look forward to*

【引咎】〈书〉hold oneself responsible for a serious mistake；take the blame：～辞职 *take the blame and resign*

【引狼入室】invite a wolf into the house—open the door to an enemy

【引理】［数］lemma

【引力】［物］gravitation；gravitational force；attraction：核～ *nuclear attraction* / ～场 *gravitational field*

【引领】〈书〉crane one's neck to look into the distance—eagerly look forward to sth. ◇ ～而望 crane one's neck to see；eagerly look forward to

【引流】［医］drainage：十二指肠～ *duodenal drainage* ◇ ～管［医］drainage tube

【引路】lead the way

【引起】give rise to；lead to；set off；touch off；

cause; arouse: ～严重后果 *lead to grave consequences* / ～连锁反应 *set off a chain reaction* / ～公愤 *arouse* (*or touch off*) *public indignation*

【引桥】[交通] bridge approach

【引擎】engine: ～盖 *bonnet*; *hood*

【引燃管】ignitron

【引人入胜】(of scenery, literary works, etc.) fascinating; enchanting; bewitching: 把报纸办得～ *make the newspaper interesting and absorbing*

【引人注目】noticeable; conspicuous; spectacular: ～的横幅标语 *an eye-catching slogan on a banner* / ～的特点 *conspicuous features* / ～的变化 *spectacular changes*

【引入】lead into; draw into; introduce from elsewhere: ～圈套 *lure into a trap*; *ensnare* / ～新品种 *introduce new varieties* ◇ ～歧途 lead sb. onto a wrong path; lead sb. astray

【引申】extend (the meaning of a word, etc.): "兵"字的本义是武器,～为"战士"。*Originally* 兵 *meant "weapon" and has by extension come to mean "soldier"*. ◇ ～义 extended meaning

【引首】raise one's head; crane one's neck

【引述】quote sb.'s words; quote from sb.'s speech

【引水】❶ pilot a ship (through difficult waters, or into or out of a harbour) ❷ draw or channel water: ～灌田 *channel water into the fields* / ～上山 *draw water up a hill* ◇ ～工程 diversion works; ～员 pilot (of a ship)

【引头】take the lead: 只要你来引个头,这件事就好办了。*This can be easily arranged if you will take the lead*.

【引退】retire from office; resign

【引文】(又作'引语') quoted passage; quotation

【引线】❶ fuse ❷ go-between ❸ 〈方〉 sewing needle

【引信】detonator; fuse: 触发～ *contact fuse* / 延期～ *delay fuse*

【引言】foreword; introduction

【引以为耻】regard it as a disgrace; consider it shameful

【引以为憾】deem it regrettable

【引以为鉴】take warning from it

【引以为戒】(又作'引为鉴戒') draw a lesson (from a mistake, etc.); take warning

【引以为荣】regard it as an honour; take it as an honour

【引用】❶ quote; cite: 他在文章中～了鲁迅的话。*In his article he quoted Lu Xun*. ❷ recommend; appoint

【引诱】lure; entice; seduce: ～敌人进入伏击圈 *lure the enemy into a trap* / 企图用金钱和美女来～意志薄弱的人 *try to lure the weak-willed with money and women*

【引玉之砖】a brick cast to attract jade ——另见〖抛砖引玉〗

【引证】quote or cite as proof or evidence

【引种】(yǐnzhǒng) introduce a fine variety

【引种】(yǐnzhòng) plant an introduced variety

【引子】❶ [戏] an actor's opening words (either spoken or sung) ❷ [音] introductory music ❸ introductory remarks; introduction: 这一段话是下文的～。*This paragraph is an introduction to what follows*. / 我简单说几句做个～,希望大家多发表意见。*I'll just say a few words to start the ball rolling*. ❹ [中] an added ingredient (to enhance the efficacy of medicines)

【引座】usher: 顾客进来,服务～,递菜单。*The waiters usher customers to their tables and hand them menus*. ◇ ～员 usher

饮 Ⅰ 动 ❶ drink: ～茶 *drink tea* / ～酒 *drink wine or liquor* / 一～而尽 *drink it down in one gulp* ❷ keep in the heart; nurse: 饮恨 Ⅱ 名 ❶ drinks: 冷饮 ❷ [中] a decoction of Chinese medicine to be taken cold

【饮弹】〈书〉 be hit by a bullet: ～身亡 *be killed by a bullet*

【饮恨】〈书〉 nurse a grievance: ～而终 *die with a grievance in one's heart* ◇ ～吞声 swallow one's resentment and choke back one's sobs; endure insults and injuries

【饮料】beverage; drink (esp. a soft drink)

【饮片】[中] prepared herbal medicine in small pieces ready for decoction

【饮泣】〈书〉 weep in silence: ～吞声 *swallow one's tears*; *weep silent tears*

【饮食】food and drink; diet: 给病人规定～ *put a patient on a diet* / ～卫生 *dietetic hygiene* ◇ ～店 eating house; café; snack bar; ～疗法 [医] dietotherapy; ～业 the catering trade

【饮食男女】food, drink and sex —human prime wants

【饮水】drinking water; potable water ◇ ～器 drinking bowl; drinker; ～思源 when drinking water, think of its source—bear in mind where one's happiness comes from

【饮水不忘掘井人】when you drink the water, think of those who dug the well ——另见〖饮水思源〗

【饮用水】drinking water; potable water

【饮誉】have a good reputation; enjoy popularity: 我们的产品～全球。*Our products are popular all over the world*.

【饮鸩止渴】drink poison to quench thirst—seek quick relief regardless of the consequences

【饮子】同〖饮〗❷

隐 形 ❶ hidden from view; concealed: 隐蔽 ❷ latent; dormant; lurking: 隐患

【隐蔽】conceal; take cover: 公开的和～的活动 *overt and covert activities* / ～! *Take cover!* / ～运动 [军] *concealed movement* / ～阵地 *covered position*

【隐蔽色】[生] cryptic colour (or coloration)

【隐藏】hide; conceal; remain under cover: 她把负伤的战士～在地窖里。*She hid the wounded soldier in the cellar*.

【隐恶扬善】cover up sb.'s faults and publicize his

merits; hide sb.'s evil deeds and praise his good ones
【隐伏】lie concealed (or hidden); lie low: 小猫～在草丛里。*The cat lay hidden in the grass.* / 平静中～着危险。*Danger lurked where all was quiet.*
【隐睾症】[医] cryptorchidism
【隐含】imply
【隐函数】[数] implicit function
【隐花植物】[植] cryptogam
【隐患】hidden trouble; hidden danger; snake in the grass: 消除～ *remove a hidden peril*
【隐讳】avoid mentioning; cover up: 不要～自己的缺点。*One should not gloss over one's shortcomings.*
【隐晦】obscure; veiled: 文字写得很～ *be couched in ambiguous terms* ◇ ～曲折 (of a statement) veiled and roundabout
【隐疾】unmentionable disease
【隐居】live in seclusion; withdraw from society and live in solitude; be a hermit
【隐君子】〈诙〉retired scholar—drug addict; opium addict (a pun on 隐 "retired" and 瘾 "addicted")
【隐瞒】conceal; hide; hold back; cover up: ～错误 *conceal one's mistakes* / ～事实 *withhold the truth*; *hide (or hold back) the facts*
【隐秘】❶ conceal; hide: ～不说 *not disclose a secret* ❷ secret: 刺探～ *pry into sb.'s secrets*
【隐没】(又作'隐灭') hide and disappear: 东方露白,繁星～。*The east paled and the stars disappeared.*
【隐匿】〈书〉conceal; hide; go into hiding; lie low: ～罪证 *conceal criminal evidence*
【隐情】facts or circumstances one wishes to hide; secrets
【隐然】dim; faint: ～可见 *dimly visible* / ～可闻 *faintly audible*
【隐忍】bear patiently; forbear: ～不言 *forbear from speaking*
【隐射】insinuate; hint; throw out innuendoes
【隐身草】a person or thing acting as cover
【隐身术】disappearing act; vanishing act
【隐士】recluse; hermit
【隐私】one's secrets; private matters one wants to hide ◇ ～权 rights of privacy; privacy
【隐痛】secret anguish
【隐头花序】[植] hypanthodium
【隐退】go and live in seclusion; retire from political life
【隐显墨水】invisible ink
【隐现】be now visible, now invisible; be dimly visible: 水天相接,岛屿～。*The water merges with the sky; the islands are dimly visible.*
【隐形飞机】stealth aircraft
【隐形轰炸机】stealth bomber
【隐形失业】recessive unemployment
【隐形收入】invisible income; off-payroll income
【隐形眼镜】contact lens
【隐性】[生] recessiveness: ～性状 *recessive character*
【隐姓埋名】conceal one's identity; keep one's identity hidden; live incognito
【隐血】[医] occult blood
【隐隐】indistinct; faint: ～的雷声 *a distant roll of thunder* / ～可见 *faintly visible* / 感到～作痛 *feel a dull pain* ◇ ～绰绰 indistinct; faint
【隐忧】secret worry
【隐语】enigmatic language; insinuating language; riddle
【隐喻】metaphor
【隐约】indistinct; faint: ～可以听到远处传来的歌声。*We could faintly hear singing in the distance.* ◇ ～其词 use ambiguous language; speak in equivocal terms
【隐衷】feelings or troubles one wishes to keep to oneself

瘾 名 ❶ addiction; habitual craving: 他喝酒的～真大。*He's too fond of the cup.* ❷ strong interest (in a sport or pastime): 有球～ *have a passion for ball games* / 他看武侠小说都有～了。*He's crazy about swordsman fiction.*
【瘾头】addiction; strong interest: 你们游泳的～儿可真不小。*You people are certainly keen on swimming.*

yìn

印 Ⅰ名 ❶ seal; stamp; chop: 盖～ *affix a seal*; *stamp a seal* ❷ mark; trace; print: 脚印 Ⅱ动 ❶ print; engrave: ～书 *print books* / 这照片～得不清楚。*This photo is not well printed.* / 深深～在脑子里 *be engraved on one's mind* ❷ tally; conform: 印证
【印版】printing plate
【印本】printed copy
【印鼻】the knob (or handle) of a seal
【印次】[刷] impression
【印第安人】American Indian; Red Indian; Indian
【印地语】Hindi
【印度】India ◇ ～教 Hinduism; ～人 Indian; ～橡胶树 India rubber plant; India rubber tree (Ficus elastica); ～洋 the Indian Ocean
【印度尼西亚】Indonesia ◇ ～人 Indonesian; ～语 Indonesian (language)
【印度支那】Indo-China: ～半岛 *the Indo-Chinese Peninsula*; *Indo-China*
【印发】print and distribute: ～传单 *print and distribute leaflets*
【印盒】seal box
【印痕】mark; trace
【印花】❶ [纺] printing: ～丝绸 *printed silk* / ～布 *print* / ～厂 *printworks* / ～机 *printing machine* / ～棉布 *cotton print* / ～平布 *calico* ❷ 〈略〉见〖印花税票〗◇ ～税 stamp duty; stamp tax; ～税票 revenue stamp; fiscal stamp
【印记】❶ the seal or stamp of a government or-

ganization in old China ❷ the impression of a seal; trace; mark: 鲜红的～ *the red impression of a seal* / 鲜明的时代～ *a marked imprint of the times* ❸ impress deeply on one's mind

【印迹】trace; mark; vestige

【印加】Inca◇ ～人 Inca

【印鉴】a specimen seal impression for checking when marking payments

【印泥】red ink paste used for seals; Chinese vermilion seal paste

【印纽】the knob (or handle) of a seal

【印欧语】the Indo-European languages; Indo-European

【印染】printing and dyeing (of textiles): ～厂 *printing and dyeing mill*

【印绶】〈旧〉an official seal and the ribbon attached to it; an official seal

【印数】[刷] the number of copies of a book printed at one impression; impression: ～八万册 *an impression of 80,000 copies*

【印刷】printing: 这本书正在～中。*The book is in the press.* / 第一次～ *first impression* (*or printing*) / 立体～ *stereoscopic printing*; *three-dimensional printing* / 三色版～ *three-colour halftone* ◇ ～厂 printing house; ～错误 misprint; typographic error; ～电路 printed circuit; ～电路板 printed circuit board (PCB); ～工人 printing worker; printer; ～合金 type metal; ～品 printed matter; ～术 art of printing; printing; ～体 block letter; print hand; ～纸 printing paper

【印刷机】printing machine; press: 滚筒～ *cylinder press* / 轮转～ *rotary press* / 双面～ *perfecting press*; *perfector*

【印台】ink pad; stamp pad

【印纹陶文化】[考古] Stamped Pottery Culture

【印玺】imperial seal

【印相纸】photographic paper

【印象】impression: 这个城市给外宾们留下了深刻的～。*The city left a deep impression on foreign visitors.* ◇ ～派 impressionist school; impressionist; ～主义 impressionism

【印行】print and distribute; publish

【印油】stamp-pad ink

【印张】[刷] printed sheet (equal to a half sheet of printing paper)

【印章】seal; signet; stamp ◇ ～学 sigillography; sphragistics

【印证】confirm; corroborate; verify: 有待～ *yet to be confirmed*

【印制】print; duplicate (a painting, etc): 这是一张手绘的地图,而非～的。*This map is not machine printed but hand-drawn.*

茚 名 [化] indene

荫 Ⅰ 形 〈口〉sunless; damp and chilly: 朝北的屋子太～。*The rooms with a northern exposure are too damp and chilly.* Ⅱ 动 ❶〈书〉shelter; protect ❷ a hereditary rank or privilege granted sb. as a recognition of the services of his ancestors

【荫庇】shelter; protect; bless

【荫蔽】❶ be shaded or hidden by foliage: 野战医院～在树林中。*The field hospital lies hidden among the trees.* ❷ cover; conceal: ～集结 *concentrate under cover*

【荫凉】shady and cool: 大树下～得很。*It's very shady and cool under the tree.*

yīng

应 动 ❶ answer; respond: 喊他他不～。*I called him, but he didn't answer.* ❷ agree (to do sth.); promise; accept: 这事是我～下来的,由我负责吧。*I'm the one who took on the job, so let me take care of it.* ❸ should; ought to: ～享受的权利 *a right one is entitled to* / ～尽的义务 *one's bounden duty* / ～予考虑 *merit consideration* / 发现错误～立即纠正。*When a mistake is discovered, it should be corrected at once.* ——另见 yìng

【应当】should; ought to: ～不成问题。*There should be no problem.*

【应得】(well) deserved; due: ～的一份 *a due share* / ～的惩罚 *a deserved punishment*

【应分】part of one's job: 帮助顾客选购商品是我们售货员～的事。*It's part of our job as shop assistants to help customers choose what they want to buy.*

【应付票据】note payable

【应付押款】mortgage payable

【应付账款】[经] account payable

【应该】should; ought to: 你～知道。*You ought to know.* / 甭谢,这是我们～做的。*Don't mention it, we've only done our duty.*

【应届毕业生】graduating students or pupils; this year's graduates

【应名儿】❶ hold a title but have no real power or responsibility: 我当主席只是应个名儿。*I'm the chairman in name only.* ❷ only in name; nominally: 他们～是近亲,实际上不大来往。*Nominally they're close relatives, but they don't see much of each other.*

【应声】answer; respond: 我敲了一阵门,里边没有人～儿。*I knocked and knocked, but no one answered.* ——另见 yìngshēng

【应收税款】tax receivable

【应收押款】mortgage receivable

【应收账款】[经] account receivable

【应税商品】taxable good; dutiable commodity

【应许】❶ agree; promise: 他～明天来谈。*He agreed to come and talk it over with us tomorrow.* ❷ permit; allow: 谁～他把写字台搬走的? *Who gave him permission to take the desk away?*

【应有】due; proper; deserved: 发挥它～的作用 *play its proper role* / 做出～的贡献 *make a due* contribution ◇ ～尽有 have everything that one could wish for

【应允】assent; consent: 点头～ *nod assent*; *nod approval*

英 名 ❶〈文〉flower; petal: 落英 ❷ hero; outstanding person: 群英会 ❸〈略〉见〖英国〗

【英镑】pound sterling: ～结存 *sterling balance* ◇ ～区 the sterling area

【英才】a person of outstanding ability; a person of superior talents

【英尺】foot (a measure)

【英寸】inch

【英吨】long ton; gross ton

【英国】Britain; England: ～护照 *British passport* / ～文学 *English literature* / ～国民 *British national* / ～公民 *British subject* ◇ ～管[音] English horn; ～人 the British; Englishman or Englishwoman

【英豪】heroes; outstanding figures

【英魂】spirit of the brave departed; spirit of a martyr

【英吉利海】the English Channel

【英杰】heroes; outstanding figures

【英俊】❶ eminently talented; brilliant: ～有为 *brilliant and promising* ❷ handsome and spirited; smart: 一个～的小伙子 *a handsome young chap*

【英里】mile

【英联邦】the British Commonwealth (of Nations)

【英两】old name for 盎司

【英烈】❶ heroic; valiant: ～女子 *a heroic woman* ❷ heroic martyr ❸〈书〉brilliant achievement

【英灵】❶ spirit of the brave departed; spirit of a martyr ❷〈书〉a person of outstanding ability

【英名】heroic name; illustrious name

【英明】wise; brilliant: ～决策 *wise policy*; *brilliant policies of decisive and fundamental importance* / ～远见 *wisdom and foresight*; *sagacity (or acumen) and farsightedness*

【英模】(〈略〉全称为'英雄模范') heroic model; one who sets an example: 为～人物写报道 *report on heroes and exemplary people*

【英亩】acre

【英年】youthful years; youth

【英气】heroic spirit: ～勃勃 *full of heroic spirit*

【英特耐雄纳尔】Internationale (a transliteration)

【英文】English (language)

【英武】of soldierly (or martial) bearing

【英仙座】[天] Perseus

【英雄】❶ hero: 女～ *heroine* / ～本色 *the true quality of a hero* ❷ heroic: ～气概 *heroic spirit*; *mettle* ◇ ～所见略同 great minds think alike; ～无用武之地 a hero with no place to display his prowess —have no scope for the exercise of one's abilities

【英雄气短】brief is the spirit of a hero ——另见〖儿女情长〗

【英寻】fathom (= 6 feet)

【英勇】heroic; valiant; brave; gallant: ～奋斗 *fight heroically* / ～善战 *brave and skilful in battle*

【英语】English (language): 纯正～ *pure English*; 标准～ *standard English*; *King's (or Queen's) English*; ～国家 *English-speaking countries*; ～水平测验 *English Proficiency Test (EPT)*

【英制】the English system

【英姿】heroic bearing ◇ ～焕发 dashing and spirited; ～飒爽 valiant and heroic in bearing; bold and brave

莺 名 warbler; oriole

【莺歌燕舞】orioles sing and swallows dart —the joy of spring; a scene of prosperity

【莺声燕语】like an oriole trilling or a swallow twittering (said of a woman speaking in a sweet, delicate voice)

婴 名 baby; infant

【婴儿】baby; infant ◇ ～车 pram; baby carriage; stroller; pushchair; ～床 crib; cot; cradle; ～死亡率 infant mortality

【婴孩】baby; infant

【婴幼儿】infants and young children: ～心理学 *infant and child psychology*

罂 名〈书〉a small-mouthed jar

【罂粟】(又作'罂子粟')[植]opium poppy (Papaver somniferum): ～花 *poppy flower*

嘤 象〈书〉trill; chirp

【嘤鸣】❶ (of birds) trill; chirp ❷〈书〉friend seeking friend

【嘤其鸣矣,求其友声】a bird sings to call forth a mate's response

【嘤泣】sob

【嘤嘤】the sound of chirping, whispering, or sobbing: 鸟鸣～ *birds chirping* / ～啜泣 *sobbing*

缨 名 ❶ tassel: 红缨枪 ❷ sth. shaped like a tassel: 萝卜～儿 *radish leaves* ❸ ribbon

【缨帽】red-tasselled official hat (worn by Qing Dynasty officials)

【缨子】❶ ornamental tassels ❷ sth. shaped like a tassel: 萝卜～ *radish leaves*

樱 名 ❶ cherry ❷ oriental cherry

【樱唇】cherry lips (the red lips of a pretty woman)

【樱花】oriental cherry: 日本～ *Japanese flowering cherry*

【樱桃】cherry

鹦 (构词成分) 见下

【鹦哥】common name for 鹦鹉

【鹦哥绿】parrot green

【鹦鹉】parrot: 长尾～ *parakeet* / 虎皮～ *budgerigar* ◇ ～螺 nautilus; ～热 [医] psittacosis; parrot fever; ～学舌 repeat another person's words like a parrot; parrot

【鹦嘴鱼】parrot fish

鹰 名 hawk; eagle
【鹰鼻鹞眼】hawk-nosed and vulture-eyed—sinister and fierce-looking
【鹰钩鼻子】aquiline nose
【鹰犬】falcons and hounds—lackeys; hired thugs
【鹰隼】〈书〉hawks and falcons—brutal or fierce people
【鹰洋】Mexican silver dollar
【鹰爪毛儿】a kind of curly sheep's wool

yíng

迎 动 ❶ go to meet; greet; welcome; receive: 到门口去~客 *go to meet a visitor at the gate* / ~上前去同客人握手 *step forward to greet the guest and shake hands with him* / 喜~新春 *joyously see in the lunar New Year* ❷ move towards; meet face to face: ~着困难上 *meet difficulties head-on*
【迎宾】receive visitors: ~曲 *a tune of welcome*
【迎宾员】doorman
【迎春】(又作'迎春花') winter jasmine (Jasminum nudiflorum)
【迎风】❶ facing (or against) the wind: ~的一面 *the windward side* / ~飞翔 *fly against the wind* ❷ down the wind; with the wind: 彩旗~招展。*Coloured flags fluttered in the breeze.*
【迎合】cater to; pander to: ~低级趣味 *pander to low tastes* / ~上司意图 *cater to the wishes of one's superiors*
【迎候】await the arrival of: 在宾馆门口~一位贵宾 *await the arrival of the distinguished guest at the entrance of the guest house*
【迎击】meet (an approaching enemy) head-on
【迎接】meet; welcome; greet: ~新的挑战 *meet a new challenge* / ~新的一年 *usher in (or greet) the New Year*
【迎面】head-on; in one's face: ~走上去同他们打招呼 *step forward to greet them* / 微风~吹来 *a breeze blowing in one's face*
【迎亲】(of the bridegroom) send a party to meet the bride at the bride's home and escort her to the bridegroom's home for the wedding
【迎娶】(of a man) get married
【迎刃而解】(bamboo) splits as it meets the edge of the knife—(of a problem) be readily solved: 抓住了这个主要矛盾,一切问题就~了。*Once this principal contradiction is grasped, all problems can be readily solved.*
【迎头】head-on; directly ◇ ~赶上 try hard to catch up; ~痛击 deal a head-on blow
【迎新】❶ see the New Year in: 送旧迎新 ❷ welcome new arrivals: ~晚会 *an evening party to welcome newcomers*
【迎战】❶ [军] meet (an approaching enemy) head-on ❷〈喻〉(of sports) play; meet in competition; take on: 中国队首场~美国队。*The Chinese team will meet the US team in their first match.*

盈 动 ❶ be full of; be filled with: 丰盈 ❷ have a surplus of: 盈余
【盈亏】❶ profit and loss: ~包干 (*of enterprises*) *be responsible for their own profits or losses* ❷ the waxing and waning of the moon: 月有~。*The moon waxes and wanes.*
【盈利】同〖赢利〗
【盈利能力】profitability
【盈千累万】thousands and tens of thousands; thousands upon thousands
【盈盈】❶ clear; lucid: 荷叶上露珠~。*The lotus leaves glistened with dewdrops.* ❷ delicate; dainty: ~顾盼 *look about daintily (or gracefully)* ❸ brimming over: 喜气~ *brimming over with joy* ❹ graceful; lissom: ~起舞 *dancing gracefully*
【盈余】surplus; profit: ~两千元 *have a surplus of 2,000 yuan* / 略有~ *with a small favourable balance*

荧 形〈书〉❶ glimmering; shimmering; twinkling: 一灯~然。*A light is glimmering.* ❷ dazzled; perplexed: 荧惑
【荧光】[物] fluorescence; fluorescent light ◇ ~灯 fluorescent lamp; daylight lamp; ~粉 fluorescent powder; ~镜 fluoroscope; ~屏 fluorescent screen
【荧光管】fluorescent tube
【荧惑】❶〈书〉bewilder; confuse: ~人心 *confuse people's minds* ❷ the Sparkling Deluder (old name for 火星)
【荧幕】TV screen: 她初上~。*This is her TV debut.*
【荧屏】❶ 同〖荧光屏〗 ❷ television: 这个连续剧下周即可在~上和观众见面。*The serial will be on television next week.*
【荧荧】(of stars, lights, etc.) twinkling; glimmering: 明星~ *stars twinkling* / 一灯~。*A light is glimmering.*

莹 Ⅰ 名〈书〉jade-like stone Ⅱ 形 lustrous and transparent
【莹白】shining and white
【莹澈】lustrous and transparent; sparkling and crystal: ~的露珠 *sparkling dewdrops*
【莹洁】shining and clean
【莹莹】sparkling; glistening: 泪水~ *eyes glistening with tears*

营 Ⅰ 动 ❶ seek: 营利 ❷ operate; run: 营业 Ⅱ 名 ❶ camp; barracks: 安营 ❷ battalion: ~部 *battalion headquarters* / ~教导员 *battalion political instructor*
【营巢】(of birds) build a nest
【营地】campsite; camping ground
【营房】barracks
【营火】campfire ◇ ~会 campfire party; campfire
【营建】construct; build

【营救】succour; rescue
【营垒】❶ barracks and the enclosing walls ❷ camp: 革命～ *revolutionary camp*
【营利】seek profits
【营盘】〈旧〉military camp; barracks
【营舍】barracks
【营生】earn a living; make a living: 靠修鞋～ *earn a living as a cobbler*
【营私】seek private gain; feather one's nest ◇ ～舞弊 engage in fraud for selfish ends; practise graft
【营销】sell; market: 市场～的预测分析 *market sales projection and analysis* ◇ ～经理 marketing manager
【营养】nutrition; nourishment: 富于～ *nourishing; nutritious* / ～不良 *malnutrition; undernourishment* / ～过度 *overnutrition* ◇ ～钵 nutritive cube; ～级 trophic level; ～价值 nutritive (or nutritional) value; ～链 another name for 食物链; ～品 nutriment; ～师 dietitian; dietician; nutritionist; ～霜 nourishing cream; ～素 nutrient; ～学 nutriology; ～液 nourishing oral liquid
【营业】do business: 商店上午九时开始～。*The shops open at nine in the morning.* / 暂停～ *business temporarily suspended* / 照常～ *business as usual* / ～收入 *business income (or earnings, receipts)* / ～支出 *operating expenses* / ～项目 *business items* / ～执照 *business license* ◇ ～额 turnover; volume of business; ～时间 business hours; banking hours (of a bank); ～税 business tax; transactions tax; turnover tax; sales tax; ～员 shop employees (including buyers, travelling salespersons and shop assistants)
【营员】participant in a summer or winter camp
【营运】operation (of vehicles, ships, airliners, etc.): 这条新船即将投入～。*This new ship will soon go into operation.*
【营造】construct; build: ～防风林 *plant windbreak forests*
【营寨】〈旧〉military camp; barracks
【营长】battalion commander
【营帐】tent

萤 名 firefly; glowworm; lightning bug
【萤火虫】firefly; glowworm; lightning bug
【萤石】fluorite; fluorspar

萦 动〈书〉entangle; encompass: 琐事～身 *be preoccupied with trivialities; get bogged down in petty matters*
【萦怀】occupy one's mind
【萦回】hover; linger: ～脑际 *linger in one's mind*
【萦念】think of; long for: 回到日夜～的祖国 *return to one's sorely missed homeland*
【萦绕】hover; linger

楹 名 principal columns (or pillars) of a hall
【楹联】couplet written on scrolls and hung on the pillars of a hall

潆 (构词成分) 见下
【潆洄】swirl

蝇 名 fly; housefly
【蝇虎】a kind of spider that feeds on flies (Menemerus)
【蝇拍】flyswatter; flyflap
【蝇头】fly's head—very small; tiny: ～小楷 *small characters of the size of a fly's head; very small handwritten characters* ◇ ～小利 (又作'蝇头微利') a fly's head of profit; a pittance of profit; a petty profit
【蝇营狗苟】shamelessly seek personal gain
【蝇子】〈口〉fly; housefly

赢 动 ❶ win; beat: 这场比赛谁～了? *Who won the game?* / 我象棋下不～他。*I can't beat him at Chinese chess.* ❷ gain (profit)
【赢得】win; gain: ～独立 *win (or attain) independence* / ～长时间的掌声 *draw prolonged applause*
【赢利】profit; gain: ～五百万元 *net a profit of five million yuan*
【赢面】chance to win: 香港队仅存三分～。*The Hong Kong team has only a thirty percent chance to win.*
【赢余】同〖盈余〗

yǐng

颖 Ⅰ 名〈书〉❶ glume; grain husk ❷ tip (as of a writing brush); point Ⅱ 形 clever: 聪颖
【颖果】[植] caryopsis
【颖慧】〈书〉(of a teenager) clever; bright; intelligent
【颖悟】〈书〉(of a teenager) clever; bright

影 名 ❶ shadow: 树～ *the shadow of a tree* ❷ reflection; image: 湖光塔～ *a lake with the reflection of a pagoda in it* ❸ trace; sign; vague impression: 至今也没见他的～儿。*I haven't seen any sign of him yet.* / 他长得什么样,我早就忘得没～儿了。*I've clean forgotten what he looked like.* ❹ photograph; picture: 合影 ❺ film; movie: 影评
【影壁】❶ screen wall (facing the gate inside or outside a traditional Chinese courtyard) ❷ a wall with carved murals
【影城】video city
【影带】videotape of a TV programme, film, etc.; MTV tape
【影帝】king of the silver screen—most popular male movie star
【影碟】VCR disk; video disc
【影后】movie queen; most popular female movie star
【影集】photograph (or picture, photo) album
【影剧界】film and drama circles

【影剧院】theatre
【影迷】film (or movie) fan ◇ ～俱乐部 cineclub
【影片】film；movie：故事～ *feature film*
【影评】film review
【影射】allude to；hint obliquely at；insinuate：～攻击 *attack by innuendo*
【影视】(〈略〉全称为'电影电视') film and television：～新星 *a new film and TV star* ◇ ～界 film and TV circles；～音乐 movie and TV music
【影坛】film (or movie) circles
【影条】[纺] shadow stripes：～巴里纱 *shadow-stripe voile*
【影戏】❶ leather-silhouette show；shadow play ❷〈方〉film；movie
【影响】❶ influence；effect；impact：月亮对潮汐的～ *the influence of the moon on the tides* ❷ affect；influence：吸烟～健康。*Smoking affects health.* / ～质量 *impair the quality* / ～威信 *lower (or undermine) one's prestige* / ～工程进度 *hold up the project* ❸ hearsay；gossip：～之谈 *speaking from hearsay*
【影像】❶ image ❷〈旧〉portrait
【影星】film star；movie star
【影业】the film industry；the motion picture industry；the cinema：他毕生从事～。*He worked in the cinema all his life.*
【影印】photomechanical printing；photo-offset process：～版 *process plate* / ～本 *photo-offset copy；facsimile* / ～件 *photocopy* / ～照相机 *process camera* / ～制版 *photomechanical process*
【影影绰绰】vague；dim；indistinct：远处～地有一些小山。*A few hills loomed in the distance.*
【影院】(usu. used as part of the name of a cinema) cinema；movie (house)
【影展】❶ photo exhibition ❷ film exhibition
【影子】❶ shadow ❷ reflection ❸ trace；sign；vague impression：找了他半天，连个～也没见。*I looked for him a long time but never even caught a glimpse of him.* ◇ ～内阁 shadow cabinet

瘿 名 ❶ [中] goitre ❷ [植] gall
【瘿虫】gall insect

yìng

应 动 ❶ answer；respond；echo：山鸣谷～。*The valleys echo the sounds of the mountains.* ❷ comply with；grant：以～急需 *in order to fill an urgent need* / 为～广大读者需要 *to meet the needs of the broad reading public* / ～中国政府的邀请 *at the invitation of the Chinese government* ❸ suit；respond to：应景 ❹ deal with；cope with：从容～敌 *meet the enemy calmly* ——另见 yīng
【应变】❶ meet an emergency (or contingency)：～措施 *emergency measure* ❷ [物] strain：～硬化 *strain hardening* ◇ ～规 strain gauge；～计 strainometer
【应标】respond to offer of tender：～承包一家工厂 *contract to run a factory awarded by tender*
【应承】agree (to do sth.)；promise；consent：这件事他一口～下来了。*He agreed to do it without hesitation.*
【应酬】❶ have social intercourse with；treat with courtesy：不善～ *socially inept* / ～几句 *exchange a few polite words* / ～信件 *courtesy letter* ❷ a social engagement (e. g. dinner party, luncheon party, etc.)：今天晚上有个～。*I've been invited to dinner this evening.*
【应从】assent to；comply with：他点头～了大家的要求。*He nodded assent to our demands.*
【应答】reply；answer ◇ ～如流 (又作'应对如流') reply readily and fluently
【应电流】induced current
【应对】reply；answer：善于～ *be good at repartee*
【应付】❶ deal with；cope with；handle：准备～可能的突然事变 *be prepared against possible emergencies* / 定单过多，难于～。*We cannot cope with such a flood of orders.* ❷ do sth. perfunctorily；do sth. after a fashion：～事儿 *go through the motions* / 采取～的态度 *take a perfunctory attitude* ❸ make do：我这双凉鞋今年夏天还可以～过去。*I'll make do with these sandals for this summer.* ◇ ～裕如 (又作'应付自如') handle the situation with ease；be equal to the occasion；be master of the situation
【应合】❶ meet；suit；agree (of words, action)：～时代的呼声 *meet the demand of the times* ❷ accompany with sound or movement；echo；respond in concert with：～着船的摇动 rock with the boat
【应活儿】[口] take on service jobs (repairs, processing, etc.)：开展～业务 *provide services*
【应机】take an opportunity when it offers (or presents itself)：～立断 *make a quick decision when an opportunity presents itself*
【应急】meet an urgent need；meet an emergency (or contingency)：～措施 *emergency measure* / ～灯 *emergency light* / ～电源 *emergency power supply* / ～计划 *contingency plan；crash program*
【应接不暇】have more (visitors or business) than one can attend to：提出的问题太多，我真有点～了。*I could hardly cope with such a volley of questions fired at me.*
【应景】do sth. for the occasion：他本来不大会喝酒，可是在宴会上也不得不应个景儿。*He hardly ever drinks, but at banquets he doesn't mind drinking just a little for the occasion.* / ～诗 *occasional verses*
【应考】take (or sit for) an entrance examination：～的人很多。*Many sat for the examination.*
【应力】[物] stress
【应卯】answer the roll call at maoshi (卯时，i.e. 5 am—7 am)—put in a routine appearance

【应募】respond to a call for recruits; enlist; join up

【应诺】agree (to do sth.); promise; undertake

【应聘】accept an offer of employment: 她～到宁波大学执教。*She accepted a teaching post at Ningbo University.*

【应声】happen right at the sound of sth.: 鸟枪一响,野鸭～而落。*The wild duck fell at the report of the shotgun.* / 警官扣动扳机,逃犯～而倒。*The police officer pulled the trigger, and the fugitive fell at the bang.* ◇ ～虫 yesman; echo——另见 yīngshēng

【应时】❶ seasonable; in season: ～货品 *seasonable goods* / ～瓜果 *fruits of the season* / 西红柿正～。*Tomatoes are in season.* ❷ at once; immediately: 敌人一推门,地雷～就炸了。*No sooner had the enemy soldier pushed the door open than the mine exploded.*

【应试】同〖应考〗◇ ～教育 examination-oriented education

【应诉】respond to a charge: 被告人必须出庭～。*The accused must appear in court in response to the charge.*

【应许】promise; agree; permit: ～之地 *the Promised Land* (*Bible*)

【应选】be a candidate for election; be an election candidate; run for election

【应验】come true; be confirmed; be fulfilled: 他的话～了。*What he said has come true.*

【应邀】at sb.'s invitation; on invitation: ～派代表团参加庆祝活动 *send a delegation to attend the celebrations at sb.'s invitation*

【应用】❶ apply; use: 把理论～于实践 *apply theory to practice* ❷ applied: ～化学 *applied chemistry* / ～数学 *applied mathematics* ◇ ～程序 application program; ～科学 applied science; ～软件 application software; ～文 practical writing; ～研究 application study; applied scientific research

【应运而生】arise at the historic moment; emerge as the times demand

【应战】❶ meet an enemy attack: 沉着～ *meet the attack calmly* ❷ accept (or take up) a challenge ◇ ～书 a letter accepting a challenge

【应招】respond to a call for recruits or candidates

【应召】〈书〉respond to a call or summons ◇ ～女郎 call girl

【应诏】do sth. in response to an imperial decree

【应诊】(of a doctor) see patients

【应征】❶ be recruited: ～入伍 *be recruited into the army* ❷ respond to a call for contributions (to a publication): ～的稿件 *contributions to a periodical, etc. at the editor's public invitation*

【应准】approve: 他的请求未得～。*His request was not approved.*

映 动 reflect; mirror; shine: 朝霞～在湖面上。*The glory of the dawn is mirrored on the lake.* / 他的脸被炉火～得通红。*His cheeks shone red before the glowing oven.*

【映衬】❶ set off: 红墙碧瓦,互相～。*The red walls and green tiles set each other off beautifully.* ❷ antithesis

【映带】〈文〉enhance each other's beauty; set off each other: 湖光山色,～左右。*The lake and the hills side by side—each a foil for the other.*

【映山红】[植] azalea

【映射】shine upon; cast light upon: 阳光～在江面上。*The sun shines upon the river.*

【映托】set off; serve as a foil to

【映现】appear before one's eyes; show, manifest: 一幕难忘的情景,立即在他脑海～。*Unforgettable scenes flashed across his mind.*

【映照】shine upon; cast light upon

硬 形 ❶ hard; stiff; tough: ～铅笔 *a hard pencil* / ～领 *a stiff collar* / ～刷子 *a stiff brush* / 这根铁丝太～,弯不动。*The iron wire is too strong to bend.* ❷ strong; firm; tough; obstinate: 心肠～ *hardhearted* / 话说得很～ *express oneself in strong terms* / ～不承认错误 *obstinately refuse to admit one's error* / ～的不行来软的。*When hard tactics failed, soft methods were used.* ❸ manage to do sth. with difficulty: ～充好汉 *act the hero* / ～压住心头怒火 *choke down one's anger* / ～搬别人的经验 *copy other people's experience mechanically* ❹ good (quality); able (person): 货色～ *goods of high quality* / 牌子～ *a trademark of high standing; a prestigious trademark*

【硬邦邦】very hard; very stiff: 这个馒头～的,像块石头。*This steamed bun is as hard as rock.*

【硬包装】❶ hard packaging ❷ hard packaging material, such as tinplate can, glass bottle, etc.

【硬笔】pen with a hard point, spec. writing tools other than the traditional Chinese writing brush

【硬币】❶ coin; specie: 一个五分的～ *a five-fen piece* (*or coin*) / 用～支付 *payment in specie* ❷ hard currency

【硬边绘画】hard-edge

【硬撑】hold out or keep on in spite of difficulties: 有病不要～。*Don't force yourself to work when you are ill.*

【硬道理】inescapable truth; established truth

【硬顶】❶ resist stubbornly: 你对上级的指示不能这样～。*You cannot disobey orders from above like this.* ❷ contradict rudely: 你对长辈怎么老这样～? *Why are you always contradicting your elders so rudely?*

【硬度】[物] hardness: 维氏～ *Vickers hardness* ◇ ～计 sclerometer

【硬腭】[生理] hard palate

【硬功夫】great proficiency; masterly skill: 练就一身～ *acquire masterly skill through intensive training*

【硬骨头】hard bone—a dauntless, unyielding person: ～六连 *the Hard-Boned Sixth Company*

【硬骨鱼】bony fish

【硬汉】(又作'硬汉子') a dauntless, unyielding man; a man of iron

【硬化】❶ harden: 经久~ *age hardening* ❷ [医] sclerosis: 血管~ *vascular sclerosis* ❸ become rigid or inflexible in attitudes, opinions, etc.; ossify

【硬环境】material environment; infrastructure, spec. geographical conditions, buildings, communications, living facilites, etc. (〈反〉'软环境')

【硬件】[计] hardware

【硬结】❶ indurate; harden ❷ [医]scleroma

【硬拷贝】[计] hard copy

【硬科学】hard science: ~和软科学是借用计算机中的硬件和软件来命名的。*Hard science and soft science are named after computer hardware and software*. (〈反〉'软科学')

【硬朗】hale and hearty: 他七十多了,身子骨还挺~。*He's over seventy but still going strong*.

【硬煤】〈方〉hard coal; anthracite

【硬锰矿】psilomelane

【硬模】[机] die: ~铸造 *diecasting*

【硬木】hardwood: ~家具 *hardwood furniture*

【硬盘】[计] hard disk

【硬磐】[地质] hardpan

【硬碰硬】❶ confront the tough with toughness; meet force with force ❷ (of a job) demanding solid, painstaking work or real skill: 改山造田可是~的事。*To transform hills into fields is an extremely tough job*.

【硬皮病】[医] scleroderma; scleriasis

【硬皮书】[刷] hardback

【硬拼】fight recklessly

【硬气】〈方〉❶ strong-willed; firm; staunch; unyielding ❷ have no qualms; have an easy conscience: 她觉得自己挣的钱用着~。*She had no qualms about spending money she'd earned herself*.

【硬砂岩】[地质] greywacke

【硬石膏】anhydrite

【硬是】❶ actually (accomplish sth. extremely difficult): 民工们~打通了这座大山,修成了隧道。*The peasant labourers literally (or actually) hewed a tunnel through that rocky mountain*. ❷ just; simply: 医生嘱咐他卧床休息,可他~不听。*The doctor advised him to stay in bed, but he just wouldn't listen*.

【硬实】〈方〉strong; sturdy; robust: 别看他年过八十,身子骨儿还挺~。*Though over eighty, he's still going strong*.

【硬手】a skilled (or good) hand

【硬水】hard water

【硬说】stubbornly insist; obstinately assert; allege: 她~她不累。*She insisted that she wasn't tired*.

【硬挺】endure with all one's will; hold out with all one's might: 你牙疼别~着,快去治治吧。*Don't just try to put up with your toothache. Go and see the dentist*. / 那小伙子受了伤,还~着把活干完。*In spite of his injuries, the young man stuck it out*. / 这场官司叫他~了过来。*He barely survived the lawsuit*.

【硬通货】hard currency

【硬卧】〈略〉见〖硬席卧铺〗

【硬席】hard seats or berths (on a train) ◇ ~卧铺 sleeping carriage with hard berths; hard sleeper

【硬橡胶】hard rubber; ebonite; vulcanite

【硬性】rigid; stiff; inflexible: 至于具体做法,不作~规定。*As for the details of the procedure, we won't lay down any hard and fast (or rigid) rules*. ◇ ~指标 brass-tag indices

【硬玉】jadeite

【硬仗】a tough (or hard-fought) battle; a formidable task: 打~ *fight a hard battle* / 一支能打~的石油钻井队 *a drilling crew equal to the most formidable tasks*

【硬着头皮】toughen one's scalp—brace oneself; force oneself to do sth. against one's will: ~顶住 *brace oneself and bear it*; *hold out tenaciously* / 我~把这碗苦药喝了下去。*I forced myself to gulp down the bowl of bitter medicine*. / ~,装出不在乎的样子 *brazen it out and pretend that one does not care*

【硬脂】[化] tristearin; stearin

【硬脂酸】[化] stearic acid ◇ ~盐 [化] stearate

【硬脂油】[化] stearine oil

【硬纸板】hardboard; cardboard

【硬指标】a mandatory quota; an inflexible standard

【硬质合金】[冶] hard alloy; hard metal: ~刀具 *hard alloy cutter*; *hard metal tool*

【硬质塑料】[化] rigid plastics: 半~ *semirigid plastics*

【硬着陆】❶[航天] hard-land ❷[经]hard landing

【硬座】hard seat

yō

哟 叹 ❶ (expressing slight surprise): ~,你踩我的脚了。*Oh! You've stepped on my foot*. ❷ 见〖啊哟〗;〖哎哟〗——另见 yo

yo

哟 助 ❶ (used at the end of an imperative sentence): 用力拉~! *Heave ho*! ❷ (used as a syllable filler in a song): 呼儿嗨~! *Hu-er-hei-yo*! ——另见 yō

yōng

佣 Ⅰ 动 hire (a labourer): 雇佣 Ⅱ 名 *servant*: 女~ *woman servant*; *maid* ——另见 yòng

【佣妇】woman servant; maid

【佣工】hired labourer; servant

【佣人】(domestic) servant

拥 动 ❶ hold in one's arms; embrace; hug: 把孩子紧紧～在怀里 *hug the child tightly* ❷ gather around; wrap around: 病人～被而坐。*The patient sat wrapped in a quilt.* ❸ crowd; throng; swarm: 大门一开，人群一窝蜂似的往里～。*The crowd swarmed in as soon as the gate opened.* ❹ support: 军爱民，民～军。*The army cherishes the people and the people support the army.* ❺ have; possess: ～兵十万 *have an army of* 100,000 / ～书万卷 *possess a large collection of books*

【拥抱】embrace; hug; hold in one's arms: 两国选手热烈～，互致问候。*The players of the two countries warmly embraced and greeted each other.*

【拥戴】support (sb. as leader): 受到全国人民的～ *enjoy the support of the whole nation*

【拥护】support; uphold; endorse: 我们～这个决定。*We endorse this decision.*

【拥挤】❶ be crowded; be packed: 上下班时间，公共汽车特别～。*The buses are especially crowded during the rush hours.* ❷ push and squeeze: 不要～！*Don't push!*

【拥进】crowd into; swarm into

【拥军优属】(of civilians) support the army and give preferential treatment to families of revolutionary armymen and martyrs

【拥塞】jam; congest: 街道～ *streets jammed with traffic*

【拥吻】hug and kiss: 他热烈地～着我。*He gave me a warm hug and kiss.*

【拥有】possess; have; own: ～核武器 *possess nuclear weapons* / ～丰富的矿藏 *have rich mineral resources; abound in mineral resources*

【拥有率】possession rate: 如果～上升到15%，电视机的需求量将达到 4 000 万台左右。*If 15% of households have a TV set, the demand will be around 40 million.*

【拥政爱民】(of the army) support the government and cherish the people

痈 名 [医] carbuncle

【痈疽】ulcer

庸 Ⅰ 形 ❶ commonplace; mediocre: ～言～行 *commonplace words and deeds* ❷ inferior; second-rate: 平庸 Ⅱ 动 〈书〉(usu. used in the negative) need: 无～细述。*This needn't be related in detail.* or *There is no need to go into details.*

【庸才】〈书〉a mediocre person; a person of mediocre ability; mediocrity

【庸常】commonplace; mediocre: ～之才 *mediocre ability or a person of mediocre ability*

【庸夫】a mediocre person

【庸劣】inferior; low-grade

【庸碌】mediocre and unambitious: ～无能 *mediocre and incompetent*

【庸人】a mediocre person ◇ ～自扰 worry about imaginary troubles; alarm oneself needlessly

【庸俗】vulgar; philistine; low: 趣味～ *have vulgar (or unrefined) tastes* / ～化 *vulgarize; debase*

【庸医】quack; charlatan

【庸中佼佼】a giant among dwarfs

雍 名 〈书〉harmony

【雍和】harmony

【雍容】natural, graceful and poised: 态度～ *have a dignified bearing* ◇ ～大雅 display poise and refinement; ～华贵 (of a woman) elegant and poised; stately

慵 形 〈书〉weary; lethargic; languid

【慵惰】〈书〉lazy; indolent

【慵倦】(又作'慵困') tired and sleepy

【慵懒】〈书〉sluggish; indolent; lethargic

壅 Ⅰ 动 stop up; obstruct: 壅塞 Ⅱ 名 heap soil or fertilizer over and around the roots (of plants and trees): ～土 *hilling* / ～肥 *heap fertilizer around the roots*

【壅蔽】〈书〉hide from view; cover; conceal

【壅塞】be clogged up; be jammed; be congested: 水道～。*The waterway is blocked up.*

臃 形 〈书〉swelling

【臃肿】❶ too fat to move: 穿得太～ *be cumbersomely dressed; be encumbered by too much clothing* ❷ overstaffed: ～的机构 *overstaffed organizations*

yóng

喁 动 〈书〉a fish sticking its mouth out of the water

【喁喁】〈书〉❶ everyone looking up to sb. ❷ whisper: ～私语 *talk in whispers* / ～情话 *whisper tender words to each other*

yǒng

永 副 perpetually; forever; always: ～放光芒 *shine forever* / ～葆青春 *always keep one's spirit young; keep alive the fervour of youth* / ～不变心 *remain loyal till one's dying day*

【永别】part never to meet again; part forever; be parted by death

【永垂不朽】sb.'s memory will live forever; be immortal: 人民英雄～！*Eternal glory to the people's heroes!* or *Immortal are the people's heroes!* / ～的杰作 *a masterpiece that will live forever*

【永磁】[物] permanent magnetism ◇ ～发电机 magneto; ～体 permanent magnet

【永冻层】[地质] permafrost horizon

【永恒】eternal; perpetual: ～的真理 *eternal truth*

◇ ～运动［物］perpetual motion

【永久】permanent；perpetual；everlasting；forever；for good（and all）◇ ～磁铁 permanent magnet；～冻土 permafrost；～和平 perpetual（or everlasting）peace；～会员 permanent member；～性居民身份证 permanent identity card；～雪线 firn line；～中立 permanent neutrality；～主权 permanent sovereignty

【永诀】〈书〉part forever；be separated by death：蓉城一别，竟成～。*When we parted at Chengdu，I little thought that we were never to meet again in this world.*

【永眠】〈婉〉die；be dead

【永生】❶ eternal life ❷（usu. used in mourning for the dead）be immortal；live forever：～的战士 *immortal fighter*

【永生永世】for ever and ever

【永世】forever：～难忘 *will never forget it for the rest of one's life* / ～长存 *live forever；be everlasting；be immortal*

【永远】always；forever；ever：～记住我的劝告。*Always remember my advice.* / 我不想～住在这儿。*I don't plan to live here forever.*

【永志不忘】will forever bear in mind；will always cherish the memory of sb. or sth.

甬 名 ❶（又作'甬江'）a river in Zhejiang Province ❷ another name for 宁波 Ningbo（a city in Zhejiang Province）

【甬道】❶（又作'甬路'）a paved path leading to a main hall or a tomb ❷ corridor

泳 动 swim：仰泳 / 潜泳

【泳道】lane（in a swimming race）：他游的是第四～。*He swam in the fourth lane.*

【泳坛】swimming circles

【泳装】swim suit；swim wear；beach wear：比基尼～ *bikini*

咏 动 ❶ chant；intone：～诗 *chant poems* ❷ express or narrate in poetic form：《～梅》*Ode to the Plum Blossom*

【咏唱】chant；sing

【咏怀】singing from one's heart（a literary subgenre）：～诗 *poems of one's heart*（*in which the poet reveals his innermost feelings*）

【咏叹】intone；chant；sing ◇ ～调［音］aria

【咏赞】sing the praises of；praise

俑 名 wooden or earthen human figure buried with the dead in ancient times；tomb figure；figurine：陶～ *pottery figurine* / 武士～ *warrior figure*

勇 形 brave；valiant；courageous：越战越～ *one's courage mounts as the battle progresses*

【勇敢】brave；courageous：勤劳～的人民 *a brave and industrious people* / ～善战 *courageous and skilful in battle*

【勇冠三军】the bravest of the brave in the whole army；distinguish oneself by peerless valour

【勇猛】bold and powerful；full of valour and vigour：～前进 *march boldly forward*

【勇气】courage；nerve：鼓起～ *pluck up*（*or muster up*）*one's courage* / 见她满脸的不高兴，我没有～再问下去。*She looked so displeased that I didn't have the nerve to ask her further questions.*

【勇士】a brave and strong man；warrior

【勇往直前】march forward courageously；advance bravely

【勇武】valiant：～过人 *surpass others in valour；be surpassingly valorous*

【勇毅】brave and steadfast

【勇于】be brave in；be bold in；have the courage to：～负责 *be brave in shouldering responsibilities*

涌 动 ❶ gush；pour；surge：一排排巨浪向石滩～来。*Huge waves surged over the rocks.* / 大家都向外～。*The crowd was pouring out.* ❷ rise；spring；well；emerge：海上～出一轮红日。*A red sun rose above the sea.* / 多少往事～上心头。*Memories of the past welled up in my mind.*

【涌潮】tidal bore

【涌动】〈喻〉surge；billow：她的愿望在心里～。*Desires welled up in her heart.*

【涌进】pour into：人们从四面八方～广场。*Crowds of people poured into the square from all directions.*

【涌浪】turbulent waves

【涌流】flow rapidly；pour

【涌现】emerge in large numbers；spring up；come to the fore：新人新事不断～。*New people and new things are constantly emerging.*

【涌溢】gush out：清泉～ *crystal spring water gushing out*

蛹 名 pupa：蝶～ *chrysalis*

踊 动 leap up；jump up

【踊跃】❶ leap；jump：～欢呼 *leap and cheer* ❷ vying with one another；eagerly；enthusiastically：会上发言～。*People took the floor one after another.* / 今晚的晚会大家肯定会～参加的。*I'm sure everybody will be eager to come to this evening's party.*

yòng

用 Ⅰ 动 ❶ use；employ；apply：～双手 *use both hands* / 你会不会～计算机？*Do you know how to operate a computer?* / 把你的剪子借我～～，好吗？*May I use your scissors?* ❷（usu. used in the negative）need：不～开灯。*There's no need to turn on the light.* / 不～担心。*Don't worry.* ❸〈套〉eat；drink：请～茶。*Won't you have some tea，please.* Ⅱ 名 ❶ expenses；outlay：家用 / 零用 ❷ usefulness；use：有～ *useful*

/ 没～ *useless*; *worthless* / 有点～ *be of some use* Ⅲ 介 with: ～手掰 *break with one's hands* / ～剪子剪 *cut with scissors* / ～火烤 *bake over the fire* / ～水煮 *boil in water* / ～针刺麻醉做外科手术 *employ acupuncture anaesthesia in surgery*

【用兵】use military forces; resort to arms: 不得已而～ *have no alternative but to resort to arms* / 善于～ *be well versed in the art of war* ◇ ～如神 direct military operations with miraculous skill; be a superb military commander

【用不了】❶ have more than is needed: 把～的钱存在银行里 *put the spare money in the bank* ❷ less than: ～三天,他们就可以把地全部耕完。*They will finish ploughing the fields in less than three days.*

【用不着】❶ not need; have no use for: 活儿不多,～这么些人。*There aren't enough jobs for so many people.* ❷ there is no need to; it is not worthwhile to: ～为这些小事争论不休。*There's no need to keep arguing about such triflings.*

【用材林】commercial forest; timber forest

【用场】use: 有～ *be useful* / 没有～ *be useless* / 派大～ *be turned to good account* / 派新～ *be put to new uses*

【用出来】❶ use; exert: 他把吃奶的劲儿都～了。*He exerted his utmost strength.* ❷ become easier to handle with use; be broken in: 这台缝纫机刚买来的时候不好用,现在已经～了。*The sewing machine was rather hard to handle when it was bought, but now it has been broken in.*

【用处】use; good: 水库的～很多。*A reservoir has many uses.* / 不要扔掉,将来会有～。*Don't throw it away; it may come in handy.*

【用得了】need that much or many: 你要这么多钱,～吗? *Do you need all that money?*

【用得着】❶ find sth. useful; need: 这个材料没准儿会～,别扔掉。*This material may come in useful one day, so don't throw it away.* ❷ there is need to; it is necessary to; it is worthwhile to: ～派车去接他们吗? *Is it necessary to send a car for them?*

【用度】expenditure; expense; outlay: 他家人口多,～大。*He has a big family and many expenses.*

【用法】use; usage: ～说明 *directions (for use)* / 《英语～词典》*A Dictionary of English Usage*

【用非所长】what one is doing is not one's strong point

【用非所学】what one is doing has nothing to do with one's training

【用费】expense; cost

【用工】recruit and use (workers): ～制度 *the system of recruitment*

【用工夫】study or work hard; spend time and energy

【用功】hardworking; diligent; studious: ～读书 *be studious*; *study diligently*; *be diligent in one's studies*

【用惯】be accustomed to the use of: 欧美人用不惯筷子。*Westerners are not used to eating with chopsticks.*

【用户】consumer; user: 征求～意见 *ask for consumers' opinions* / 电话～ *telephone subscriber* ◇ ～电报 telex; ～界面[计] user interface; ～名[计] user ID; ～手册 user's manual; ～指南 user's guide

【用户终端】[计] user terminal

【用劲】exert oneself (physically); put forth one's strength: 大家一齐～,把大石头搬开了。*We all heaved together and removed the boulder.*

【用具】utensil; apparatus; appliance: 炊事～ *kitchen (or cooking) utensils* / 消防～ *fire-fighting apparatus* / 救生～ *lifesaving equipment* / 狩猎～ *hunting gear*

【用开】be widely used; become popular: 煤气灶这些年～了。*In the past few years the gas oven has become widely used.*

【用力】exert oneself (physically); put forth one's strength: ～把门推了一下 *give the door a hard push* / ～喊叫 *shout at the top of one's voice* / ～过度 *overexert oneself*

【用品】articles for use: 生活～ *articles for daily use*; *daily necessities* / 办公～ *things for office use*; *stationery*

【用人】❶ choose a person for a job; make use of personnel: 善于～ *know how to choose the right person for the right job*; *know how to make proper use of personnel*; *know how to employ people to the best advantage* / ～制度 *the system of personnel placement* / ～单位 *employing unit* ❷ need hands: 现在正是～的时候。*Now's the time when we are in need of personnel.* ❸ servant: 女～ *woman servant*; *maid*

【用上】be made use of; be put to use: 这些资料今天还都～了。*All these data proved useful today.* / 他主意倒不少,就是用不上。*He is full of ideas; none of them will work out, though.*

【用舍行藏】(又作'用行舍藏') go forward when employed and stay out of sight when set aside

【用事】❶ act: 意气用事 ❷〈书〉be in power: 奸臣～ *treacherous officials in power* ❸〈书〉make literary allusions

【用途】use: 橡胶的～很广。*Rubber has many uses.* / 一套设备,多种～ *one set of equipment serving many purposes*

【用武】use force; display one's abilities or talents: 大有～之地。*There's ample scope for one's abilities.*

【用项】items of expenditure; expenditures

【用心】❶ diligently; attentively; with concentrated attention: ～学习 *concentrate on one's studies*; *study diligently* / ～听讲 *listen attentively to a lecture* / ～思索 *think hard* ❷ motive; intention: ～险恶 *have vicious intentions*; *harbour sinister motives* ◇ ～良苦 have really given much thought to the matter; have expended much care and thought on sth.

【用刑】put sb. to torture; torture

【用以】in order to; so as to: 略举数例,～说明这一原理。*Here are a few examples to illustrate this principle.*

【用意】intention; purpose: ～很好 *with good intentions* / 你这是什么～? *Just what are you up to?* or *What's your game?* / 我说这话的～,只是想劝告他一下。*I said all that just to give him some advice.*

【用印】affix an official seal (to a document); seal (a document)

【用语】❶ choice of words; wording: ～不当 *inappropriate choice of words*; *incorrect wording* ❷ phraseology; term: 商业～ *commercial phraseology* / 外交～ *diplomatic terms*

佣 名 commission ——另见 yōng

【佣金】commission; brokerage; middleman's fee

yōu

优 Ⅰ 形 excellent: 择优 Ⅱ 名 actor or actress: 名优

【优待】❶ give preferential (or favoured, special) treatment: ～外宾 *give special consideration to foreign guests* / 学生半价～票 *special half-price tickets for students* ❷ preferential (or favoured, special) treatment: 我们受到了特别的～。*We were accorded preferential treatment.* ◇ ～券 complimentary ticket

【优等】high-class; first-rate; excellent: ～品 *high-class (or first-rate) product* / ～生 *top student*

【优点】merit; strong (or good) point; advantage; virtue: ～和缺点 *merits and demerits*; *virtues and defects*; *strong and weak points*

【优抚】(〈略〉全称为'优待和抚恤') give special care to disabled servicemen, and to family members of revolutionary martyrs and servicemen: 烈属～金 *allowance to the family members of revolutionary martyrs*

【优厚】munificent; liberal; favourable: 待遇～ *excellent pay and conditions*; *liberal wages and benefits*

【优弧】[数] major arc

【优化】optimize: ～产业结构 *optimize the industrial structure* ◇ ～组合 optimization grouping or regrouping

【优惠】preferential; favourable: ～贷款 *loan on favourable terms* ◇ ～差额 margin of preference; ～待遇 preferential treatment; favoured treatment; ～购货券 voucher; ～关税协定 preferential tariff agreement; ～国 avoured nation; ～价格 favoured price; ～期间 grace period; ～权 preferential rights; ～条件 favourable terms; concessional terms; ～条款 preferential clause; ～政策 preferential policy

【优价】❶ favorable (or concessional) rates; preferential prices; favorable prices ❷ higher prices: 优质～ *good products at high prices*

【优教】good education: ～是提高人口素质的重要措施。*Providing good education is important for improving population caliber.*

【优良】fine; good: 成绩～ *get good marks*; *make a good showing*

【优劣】good and bad; superior and inferior: 不分～ *make no distinction between the good and the bad*

【优伶】〈旧〉actor or actress

【优美】graceful; fine; exquisite: 风景～ *fine scenery* / 姿态～ *graceful postures* / ～的舞蹈动作 *graceful dance movements*

【优孟衣冠】the actor Meng in costume—act on the stage; imitate others

【优俳】〈古〉farce

【优人】同〖优伶〗

【优柔】❶〈书〉leisurely; unhurried ❷〈书〉gentle; amiable ❸ weak in character; hesitant ◇ ～寡断 irresolute and hesitant; indecisive

【优生学】[生] eugenics

【优生优育】bear and rear better children

【优胜】winning; superior: ～奖 *winning prize* / ～者 *winner*; *champion*

【优胜劣汰】(又作'优胜劣败') survival of the fittest; select the superior and eliminate the inferior

【优势】superiority; preponderance; dominant position: 军事～ *military superiority* / ～兵力 *superior force* / 占～ *occupy a dominant position*; *gain the upper hand*

【优先】have priority; take precedence: ～发展基础工业 *give priority to the development of the basic industries* / 必须～考虑的一个问题 *a question which claims precedence over all others*; *a first (or top) priority* ◇ ～股 preference shares; preferred shares; ～录取 priority of admission; ～权 priority; preference

【优闲】carefree; leisurely

【优秀】outstanding; excellent; splendid; fine: 成绩～ *get excellent results or marks* / ～人才 *talented persons* / ～选手 *topnotch player* / ～作品 *(literary or artistic) works of excellence*

【优选法】optimum seeking method; optimization

【优雅】graceful; elegant; in good taste: 客厅布置得十分～。*The drawing room was furnished with elegance and taste.* / 她弹的竖琴～动听。*She played the harp beautifully.*

【优异】excellent; outstanding; exceedingly good: 考试成绩～ *do exceedingly well in an examination*

【优游】〈书〉leisurely and carefree: ～岁月 *pass one's days in carefree leisure*

【优裕】affluent; abundant: 生活～ *be well-off*; *be well-to-do*; *live in affluence*

【优遇】give special treatment: 格外～ *accord ex-*

ceptionally good treatment

【优越】superior; advantageous: 处于～的地位 *be in an advantageous position* / ～条件 *favourable conditions* / 她总觉得自己比别人～。*She always considers herself superior to others*. ◇ ～感 sense of superiority; superiority complex; ～性 superiority; advantage

【优哉游哉】leisurely and carefree; leisurely and unhurried

【优质】high (or top) quality; high grade: ～混凝土 *quality concrete* / 提供～服务 *provide good service* / ～奖 *high-quality award* ◇ ～优价 high quality and high price

忧 Ⅰ **动** worry about; be worried: 忧国忧民 Ⅱ **名** sorrow; anxiety; concern; care: 无忧无虑

【忧愁】worried; troubled; depressed: 面容～ *look worried*

【忧烦】worried; vexed

【忧愤】worried and indignant

【忧国忧民】be concerned about one's country and one's people

【忧患】suffering; misery; hardship: 饱经～ *have gone through a good deal* ◇ ～余生 a person who has known adversity and sorrow

【忧惧】worried and apprehensive

【忧劳】care-laden and overworked: ～成疾 *fall ill from care and overwork*

【忧虑】❶ be worried; be anxious; be concerned: 为孩子的前途～ *worry about one's son's future* ❷ worry; anxiety: 无穷的～ *endless worries*

【忧闷】depressed; feeling low; weighed down with cares

【忧戚】〈书〉distressed; weighed down with sorrow; laden with grief

【忧容】a worried look: 面带～ *look worried*

【忧伤】distressed; weighed down with sorrow; laden with grief

【忧思】❶ be worried; be anxious ❷ troubled thoughts

【忧心】〈书〉a troubled heart ◇ ～忡忡 heavy-hearted; care-laden; weighed down with anxieties; ～如焚 burning with anxiety; extremely worried

【忧悒】〈书〉anxious and restless

【忧郁】melancholy; heavyhearted; dejected ◇ ～症〔医〕melancholia

呦 **叹** (expressing surprise): ～! 你怎么也来了? *Hey! Fancy seeing you here*.

【呦呦】〈书〉the cry of a deer

幽 Ⅰ **形** ❶ deep and remote; secluded; dim: ～林 *a secluded wood* ❷ secret; hidden: 幽怨 / 幽会 ❸ quiet; tranquil; serene: 幽深 ❹ of the nether world Ⅱ **动** imprison: 幽囚 Ⅲ **名** an ancient administrative district, comprising parts of modern Hebei and Liaoning

【幽暗】dim; dark; gloomy: ～的角落 *a dark corner* / ～的山谷 *a deep and gloomy valley*

【幽闭】〈书〉❶ put under house arrest ❷ confine oneself indoors

【幽愤】hidden resentment

【幽会】a secret meeting of lovers; a lovers' rendezvous; tryst

【幽寂】secluded and lonely

【幽禁】put under house arrest; imprison

【幽静】quiet and secluded; peaceful: 这里环境很～。*It's rather peaceful and secluded around here*.

【幽居】❶ live in seclusion ❷ a place of seclusion; retreat

【幽兰】〈文〉orchid

【幽蓝】dull blue

【幽灵】ghost; spectre; spirit

【幽美】secluded and beautiful: ～的庭院 *a secluded and beautiful courtyard*

【幽门】〔生理〕pylorus ◇ ～梗阻〔医〕pyloric stenosis

【幽冥】❶ dark; gloomy; sombre ❷ the nether world

【幽默】humour: 他很～。*He's full of humour*. or *He is very humorous*. ◇ ～大师 humorist; ～感 a sense of humour; ～曲〔音〕humoresque

【幽期】a secret meeting of lovers; a lover's rendezvous; tryst

【幽情】exquisite feelings: 发思古之～ *muse over things of the remote past*

【幽囚】imprison; put in jail; keep in captivity

【幽趣】the delightful serenity of seclusion

【幽深】(of forests, palaces, etc.) deep and serene; deep and quiet: ～的峡谷 *a deep gorge*

【幽思】❶ ponder; muse; meditate ❷ deep contemplation; melancholy brooding

【幽闲】❶ (又作'幽娴') (of a woman) gentle and serene ❷ 同〖悠闲〗

【幽香】a delicate (or faint) fragrance: 兰花～四溢。*The orchids give out a delicate fragrance*.

【幽雅】(of a place) quiet and tastefully laid out

【幽幽】❶ (of light or sound) faint: ～啜泣 *sob quietly* / ～的路灯 *dim street lamps* ❷〈书〉looming in the distance

【幽怨】hidden bitterness (of a young woman thwarted in love)

悠 Ⅰ **形** ❶ long-drawn-out; remote in time or space: 悠久 ❷ leisurely: 悠闲 Ⅱ **动**〈口〉swing: 他抓住绳子～了过去。*He held on to the rope and swung across*.

【悠长】long; long-drawn-out: ～的岁月 *long years*

【悠荡】swing (to and fro); sway (back and forth)

【悠久】long; long-standing; age-old: 历史～ *have a long history* / ～的文化 *a civilization (or culture) of long standing*

【悠然】carefree and leisurely: ～神往 *one's thoughts turn to things distant* ◇ ～自得 be carefree and content

【悠闲】leisurely and carefree: ～自在 *leisurely and*

carefree

【悠扬】(of music, etc.) rising and falling; melodious; mellifluous: ～的歌声 *melodious singing* / ～的小提琴声 *mellifluous notes flowing from the violin*

【悠悠】❶ long; long-drawn-out; remote: ～长夜。*The night seemed to drag.* ❷ leisurely; unhurried: ～自得 *carefree and content* ❸〈书〉absurd; preposterous: ～之谈 *a preposterous statement* ◇ ～荡荡 floating about; swinging to and fro;

【悠悠忽忽】❶ loitering languidly; lounging around ❷ be in a trance

【悠游】❶ move about unhurriedly: 有几艘小艇在湖面上～。*There were a few yachts sailing leisurely on the lake.* ❷ leisurely and carefree: ～自在 *leisurely and carefree*

【悠远】❶ a long time ago; long ago; distant: ～的往事 *events of the distant past* ❷ far off (or away); remote; distant: 山川～ *moun-tains and rivers far, far away*

【悠着】(又作'悠停着')〈方〉take things easy: ～点劲,别太猛了。*Take it easy* (*or Easy*)! *Don't go at it so hard.*

yóu

尤 Ⅰ副 particularly; especially: 这一点～为重要。*This is even more important.* / 此地盛产水果,～以梨桃著称。*The place abounds with fruit, especially pears and peaches.* Ⅱ形 outstanding: 择～ *pick out the best* / 拔其～ *select and promote those of outstanding ability* Ⅲ名 fault; mistake: 效尤 Ⅳ动 have a grudge against; blame: 怨天尤人

【尤伯杯】[体] Uber Cup

【尤其】especially; particularly: 我喜欢音乐,～喜欢古典音乐。*I love music, especially classical music.*

【尤甚】more so; especially so: 夏季多雨,七月下旬～。*We have abundant rains in summer, especially in the last ten days of July.*

【尤物】〈书〉❶ a rare thing ❷ an extraordinary person; a woman of great beauty

【尤异】〈书〉excellent; outstanding

由 Ⅰ名 cause; reason: 因由 / 理由 Ⅱ动 ❶ pass through; go by way of: 必由之路 ❷ be up to sb.; rest with sb.: 事不～己。*Things are beyond one's control.* or *Things are getting out of hand.* / ～着性子 *do as one pleases* Ⅲ介 ❶ by; through; via: ～边门出去。*Exit by the side door.* / ～此入内。*This way in.* or *Entrance.* / ～水路而来 *come by the water route* ❷ (done) by sb.: 这个钱该～我付。*This money should be paid by me.* / 这件事～他处理。*Leave it to him.* ❸ because of; due to: ～粗心大意造成的错误 *mistakes due to carelessness* ❹ by means of: 水～氢与氧化合而成。*Water is composed of hydrogen and oxygen.* / 代表～民主协商选举产生。*The representatives were elected after democratic consultation.* ❺ from: ～银川出发 *set off from Yinchuan* / ～点到面 *spread over a whole area from one point* / ～下而上 *from bottom to top; from the lower level upward; from below*

【由表及里】from the outside to the inside; from the surface to the centre

【由不得】❶ not be up to sb. to decide; be beyond the control of: 事到如今就～你了。*You have no choice in the matter at this late hour.* ❷ cannot help: ～笑了起来 *can't help laughing*

【由此】from this; therefrom; hence; thus: ～前进 *go forward from here* / ～看来 *judging from this; in view of this* / ～产生的一切后果 *all consequences arising therefrom* ◇ ～及彼 from one to the other; ～可见 thus it can be seen; this shows; that proves

【由俭入奢易,由奢入俭难】it is easy to go from frugality to extravagance, but difficult to go from extravagance to frugality

【由简及繁】from the simple to the complex

【由近及远】from the near to the distant

【由来】❶ origin; source: 分歧的～ *the origin of differences* ❷ up to now; so far: ～已久 *long-standing; time-honoured*

【由浅入深】from the easy to the difficult; from the elementary to the profound

【由头】pretext: 找～ *find a pretext*

【由于】❶ owing to; thanks to; as a result of; due to; in virtue of: ～健康关系 *on health grounds* / ～各种原因 *for various reasons* ❷ because; since: ～各人的观点不同,我们没有能够取得一致意见。*Since our points of view differ, we can't reach an agreement.*

【由衷】from the bottom of one's heart; sincere; heartfelt: 表示～的感激 *extend one's heartfelt thanks* ◇ ～之言 words from the bottom of one's heart; sincere words

邮 Ⅰ动 post; mail: 信～了吗? *Has the letter been posted* (*or mailed*)? / 我上月给家里～去二百元。*I remitted home 200 yuan by post last month.* Ⅱ名 postal; mail: 邮路 / 邮局

【邮包】postal parcel; parcel: ～保险 *parcel post insurance*

【邮差】〈旧〉postman

【邮车】postal (or mail) car

【邮船】ocean liner; liner; packet ship

【邮戳】postmark

【邮袋】mailbag; postbag; (mail) pouch

【邮递】❶ send by post (or mail) ❷ postal (or mail) delivery ◇ ～员 postman; mailman

【邮电】post and telecommunications ◇ ～局 post and telecommunications office

【邮发】distributed and delivered by the post office

【邮费】postage: ～免收 *post-free*

【邮购】mail-order: ～部 *mail-order department*

【邮汇】remit by post
【邮寄】send by post；post：～书籍 *send books by post*
【邮件】postal matter；post；mail：挂号～ *registered post* / 航空～ *air mail* / 小包～ *a postal packet* / 早班～几点到？*When does the morning post come in?* ◇ ～传输协定［计］simple mail transfer protocol（SMTP）；～服务器［计］mail server
【邮局】post office
【邮路】postal（or mail）route：～遍布全国。*A postal network now covers the whole country.*
【邮轮】同〖邮船〗
【邮票】postage stamp；stamp：一套纪念～ *a set of commemorative stamps* / 特种～ *special stamps*
【邮品】philatelic items（such as stamps，miniature sheets，first-day covers，etc.）
【邮亭】postal kiosk
【邮筒】pillar-box；postbox；mailbox
【邮箱】postbox；mailbox
【邮展】philatelic exhibition；stamp exhibition
【邮政】postal service ◇ ～包裹 postal parcel；～编码（British）postcode；（American）zip code；zip；～储蓄 postal savings deposit；～代办所 postal agency；～汇票 postal money order；postal order；～局 post office；～网 postal network；～信箱 post-office box（P. O. B.）
【邮资】postage：国内～ *postage paid for inland mail* / 国外～ *postage paid for overseas mail* / ～已付 *postage paid*；*postpaid*

犹 副〈书〉❶ just as；like：虽死犹生 ❷ still：～未定夺 *still undecided*；*not decided yet* / ～有可为 *can still do something about it*
【犹然】still；just as before：虽然时隔多年，那事他～记得很清楚。*After so many years，he still remembers it clearly.*
【犹如】just as；like；as if：灯火辉煌，～白昼。*The place was lit up as bright as day.*
【犹太复国主义】Zionism
【犹太教】Judaism：～教士 *rabbi* / ～教徒 *Judaist*；*Jew* / ～堂 *synagogue*
【犹太人】Jew
【犹疑】hesitate
【犹豫】hesitate；be irresolute：～不定 *hesitate*；*remain undecided* / 毫不～ *without the least hesitation* / 犹犹豫豫 *shilly-shally*
【犹豫不决】hesitate；remain undecided；be irresolute
【犹自】still：现在想起那件事，～叫人心惊肉跳。*Even to this day，I still shudder at the very thought of it.*

油 Ⅰ 名 oil；fat；grease；petroleum：摊鸡蛋要多放点～。*You have to put in more oil when making an omelet.* / 汽车该加～了。*The car's engine is in need of oil.* Ⅱ 动 apply tung oil，varnish，or paint：～门窗 *paint the doors and windows* Ⅲ 形 ❶ oily；greasy；stained or smeared with oil or grease：这炖肉太～了。*The stewed pork is too greasy.* / 你的上衣～了。*Your coat has got oil stains on it.* ❷ oily；glib：这家伙嘴～得很。*That fellow has a very glib tongue.* / 这个人～极了。*That chap is much too slippery*（*or tricky*）. / 他打麻将打得可～了。*He is an old hand at mahjong.*
【油泵】［机］oil pump
【油饼】❶ oilcake（as animal feed or fertilizer）❷ deep-fried dough cake
【油驳】oil barge
【油布】oilcloth；oilskin；tarpaulin
【油彩】greasepaint：演员们用～化装。*Actors and actresses make themselves up with greasepaint.*
【油菜】❶ rape（Brassica napus）：～籽 *rapeseed* ❷ Chinese cabbage（Brassica chinensis）
【油藏】oil deposit；oil pool：地层～ *stratigraphic oil pool* / 构造～ *structural oil pool* / 岩性～ *lithogical oil pool*
【油槽车】tank truck
【油层】oil reservoir；oil layer；oil horizon：～压力 *reservoir pressure* / ～动态 *reservoir behaviour*（*or performance*）
【油茶】❶ tea-oil tree；oil-tea camellia（Camellia oleifera）❷ a gruel of sweetened，fried flour ◇ ～面儿 flour fried in beef fat with sugar and sesame（for making youcha 油茶）
【油船】oil tanker；tanker；oil carrier
【油淬火】［机］oil hardening；oil quenching
【油灯】oil lamp
【油底子】〈口〉oil dregs
【油坊】oil mill
【油封】［机］oil seal
【油橄榄】（又作'油榄'）olive（Olea europaea）
【油膏】ointment
【油垢】greasy filth；greasy dirt
【油瓜】［植］large-fruited hodgsonia（Hodgsonia macrocarpa）
【油管】❶ oil pipe：铺设～ *lay oil pipes* ❷ oil tube：未下～的井 *untubed well* / ～深度 *tubing depth*
【油罐】oil tank；storage tank：～汽车 *oil car*（*or truck*）
【油光】glossy；shiny；varnished：把车子擦得～锃亮 *put a good shine on the car* ◇ ～水滑 smooth and shining；sleek
【油耗】oil consumption：降低汽车的～ *reduce the oil consumption of motor vehicles*
【油黑】glossy black：她的两条辫子～发亮。*She wears two glossy black braids.*
【油乎乎】oily；greasy：工作服～的。*The overalls are smeared with oil.*
【油壶】oilcan；oiler
【油葫芦】［动］a kind of field cricket（Gryllus testaceus）
【油花儿】drops of oil on the surface of soup；blobs of fat
【油滑】slippery；foxy
【油画】oil painting：画～ *paint in oils* ◇ ～色（又

作'油画颜料')oil colours；oils
【油灰】[建] putty
【油鸡】a fine breed of chicken with thick brownish feathers
【油迹】oil stains；grease spots：～斑斑 *covered with grease spots*
【油煎火燎】in a state of great agitation；in a stew
【油匠】同〖油漆工〗
【油井】oil well：钻一口～ *drill* (*or bore*) *a well*
【油锯】chain saw：～手 *chain-saw operator*
【油库】oil depot；tank farm：转运～ *oil terminal*
【油矿】❶ oil deposit ❷ oilfield
【油亮】(often reduplicated) glossy；shiny：刚下过雨,花草树木的叶子都是～～的。*The rain had just stopped, and the leaves of plants and trees all took on a beautiful sheen.*
【油料】oil-bearing seed；oilseed ◇ ～作物 oil-bearing crops；oil crops
【油绿】glossy dark green
【油轮】oil tanker；tanker；oil carrier
【油码头】oil jetty；oil wharf；tanker (loading) terminal
【油麦】同〖莜麦〗
【油毛毡】同〖油毡〗
【油门】❶ throttle ❷〈口〉accelerator：踩～ *step on the accelerator*
【油焖】braise：～茄子 *braised eggplant slices*
【油苗】[油] oil seepage
【油墨】printing ink：快干～ *quicksetting ink*
【油母页岩】同〖油页岩〗
【油泥】greasy filth：这表需要擦～。*The watch needs cleaning and oiling.*
【油腻】❶ greasy；fatty；oily：不爱吃～的东西 *not care for greasy* (*or fatty, oily*) *food* ❷ greasy food；fatty food；oily food
【油盘】food tray
【油票】❶ cooking oil coupon ❷ gasoline coupon
【油漆】❶ paint：一层～ *a coat of paint* / ～未干！*Wet paint!* or *Fresh paint!* ❷ cover with paint；paint：把大门～一下 *have the gate painted* ◇ ～工 painter
【油气】〈略〉见〖油田伴生气〗◇ ～比[油] oil-gas ratio；～界面[油] the interface of oil and gas；oil-gas interface
【油气田】oil and gas field：海上～ *offshore oil and gas field*
【油枪】[机] oil gun
【油腔滑调】glib：说起话来～ *speak glibly；have a glib tongue*
【油裙】kitchen apron；apron
【油然】❶ spontaneously；involuntarily ❷ (of clouds) gathering ◇ ～而生 (of a feeling) rise of itself；be produced of itself
【油溶性染料】oil-soluble dyes
【油润】glossy and sleek；wet and smooth：她有着一头乌黑～的秀发。*She has sleek and glossy hair.* / 雨后路面～,平滑如镜。*After the rain, the road surface was as smooth and shiny as a mirror.*
【油色】oil colours；oils
【油砂】oil sand：稠～ *heavy oil sand* / ～层 *pay sand*
【油石】oilstone (for sharpening cutting tools)
【油饰】cover or decorate with paint；paint；varnish：～一新 *freshly painted or varnished*
【油柿】wild kaki persimmon
【油刷】cover with paint or varnish；paint：～门面 *paint the shop front*
【油水】❶ grease：这个菜～太大。*This dish is too greasy.* ❷ pickings；profit：～不大 *not very profitable* / 捞到一点～ *pick up a few crumbs；make a profit*
【油松】Chinese pine (Pinus tabulaeformis)
【油酥】short；crisp；flaky：～点心 *short pastry*
【油酸】[化] oleic acid
【油提】oil-dipper
【油田】oilfield：～开发 *oilfield development* (*or exploitation*) / 多层～ *multi-pay oilfield* ◇ ～伴生气[油] associated gas；～气〈略〉见〖油田伴生气〗
【油条】deep-fried twisted dough sticks
【油桐】tung oil tree；tung tree (Aleurites fordii)
【油桶】oil drum
【油头粉面】sleek-haired and creamy-faced—heavily made-up；dressy or foppish
【油头滑脑】slick；smooth；oily：一个～的家伙 *a shifty-looking fellow*
【油汪汪】❶ dripping with oil；full of grease ❷ glossy；shiny
【油位】[机] oil level ◇ ～表 oil (level) gauge
【油污】greasy dirt：一个满身～的老工人 *an old worker covered all over with greasy dirt*
【油箱】fuel tank
【油香】a salted cake fried in sesame oil (a Moslem food)
【油鞋】〈旧〉oiled shoes (for wet weather)
【油星】(又作'油星子') 同〖油花儿〗
【油性】oiliness；greasiness
【油靴】oiled boots (for wet weather)
【油压】oil pressure ◇ ～泵 oil pressure pump；～表 oil pressure gauge；～传动 hydraulic transmission；～机 hydraulic press；oil press；～千斤顶 hydraulic jack；oil jack
【油烟】(又作'油烟子') lampblack；soot
【油椰子】another name for 油棕
【油页岩】oil-shale
【油衣】〈方〉oilskins
【油印】mimeograph：～一百份 *mimeograph a hundred copies* ◇ ～机 mimeograph；～蜡纸 stencil；stencil paper
【油油】〈书〉❶ glossy；shiny ❷ flowing smoothly and incessantly ❸ luxuriant and dense
【油浴】[化] oil bath
【油渣】❶ dregs of fat ❷ petroleum oil residue
【油炸】deep-fry：～土豆片 (*potato*) *chips；French fries* ◇ ～鬼〈方〉deep-fried dough strips or rings
【油毡】asphalt felt

【油脂】oil; fat: 植物～ *vegetable fat or oil* / 动物～ *animal fat or oil*; *tallow*; *grease*
【油纸】oilpaper
【油质颜料】oil pigment
【油子】❶ black sticky substance: 烟袋～ *tar inside a tobacco pipe* ❷〈方〉a foxy old hand
【油棕】[植] oil palm (Elaeis guineensis)
【油嘴】❶ glib ❷ a glib talker ❸ spray nozzle; spray head ◇ ～滑舌 glib-tongued

疣 名 [医] wart
【疣赘】❶ wart ❷ anything superfluous or useless

柚 (构词成分) 见下 ——另见 yòu
【柚木】teak; teakwood (Tectona grandis)

莜 (构词成分) 见下
【莜麦】[植] naked oats

铀 名 [化] uranium (U)
【铀后元素】[化] transuranium element; transuranium

蚰 名 见〖蚰蜒〗
【蚰蜒】common house centipede

游 Ⅰ 动 ❶ swim: 这条河太宽,我～不过去。*I can't swim across the river; it's too wide*. ❷ rove around; saunter; stroll; travel; tour: ～遍北京的山山水水 *visit all the scenic spots in Beijing* ❸〈书〉associate with: 交游 Ⅱ 形 moving about; roving; floating: 游资 / 游民 Ⅲ 名 part of a river; reach: 上游
【游伴】travel companion
【游标】[机] vernier; vernier scale: ～卡尺 *vernier calliper* / ～千分尺 *vernier micrometer*
【游程】❶ distance of swimming ❷ route of travel ❸ itinerary
【游船】pleasure-boat
【游春】go on a spring outing
【游词】(又作'游辞')〈书〉❶ unfounded remarks; a groundless statement ❷ joke; jest
【游荡】loaf about; loiter; wander
【游动】❶ move about; go from place to place: 白云在天空中徐徐～。*White clouds are slowly floating in the sky*. ❷ mobile; moving; roving: ～探照灯 *mobile floodlight* ◇ ～哨 a roving sentry; patrol
【游逛】go sightseeing; stroll about
【游魂】a wandering ghost
【游击】guerrilla warfare ◇ ～队 guerrilla forces; a guerrilla detachment; ～区 guerrilla area; ～战 guerrilla war; guerrilla warfare ——另见〖打游击〗
【游记】travel notes; travels
【游街】parade sb. through the streets: ～示众 *parade sb. through the streets to expose him before the public*
【游客】visitor (to a park, etc.); tourist; excursionist; sightseer
【游览】go sightseeing; tour; visit: ～长城 *visit the Great Wall* ◇ ～车 tourist coach; ～地 place for sightseeing; excursion centre; ～区 tourist area; ～图 tourist map
【游廊】covered corridor (linking two or more buildings); veranda
【游乐】make merry; amuse oneself: ～场所 *places of recreation* ◇ ～园 amusement park; pleasure ground (or garden); ～车 funabout
【游离】❶ dissociate; drift away: ～分子 *one who quits the collective* ❷ [化] free: ～酸 *free acid* / ～状态 *free state* ◇ ～电子 [物] free electron; ～基 [化] free radical
【游历】travel for pleasure; travel; tour: ～过很多地方 *have travelled extensively*
【游猎】go on a hunting trip
【游民】vagrant; vagabond
【游目骋怀】look as far as one's eyes can see and give free rein to one's thoughts and feelings
【游牧】move about in search of pasture; rove around as a nomad: ～部落 *nomadic tribe* / ～生活 *nomadic life*; *nomadism*
【游禽】[动] natatorial bird
【游人】visitor (to a park, etc.); sightseer; tourist: ～如织 *throngs of visitors*.
【游刃有余】handle a cleaver with skill —do a job with skill and ease; be more than equal to a task
【游山玩水】travel from one beauty spot to another; visit various scenic spots
【游手好闲】idle about; loaf: ～,不务正业 *idle about and do no decent work* / 别～的,干点正经活儿。*Stop fooling around, do some serious work*.
【游水】swim
【游说】go about selling an idea; go about drumming up support for an idea; go canvassing
【游丝】❶ gossamer ❷ [机] hairspring
【游艇】yacht; pleasure-boat
【游玩】❶ amuse oneself; play: 孩子们经常去海滨～。*The children often go to the beach to play*. ❷ go sightseeing; stroll about
【游戏】❶ recreation; game: 做～ *play games* ❷ play: 孩子们在公园里～。*The children are playing in the park*. ◇ ～机 (〈略〉全称为'电子游戏机') video game player; TV game player
【游侠】(in former times) roving brave; knight-errant
【游行】parade; march; demonstration: 节日～ *gala parade* / 抗议～ *protest march* / 饥饿～ *hunger march* / 举行～示威 *hold a demonstration* / ～队伍 *contingents of paraders or marchers*; *procession*
【游兴】interest in going on an excursion or sightseeing
【游移】(of attitude, policy, etc.) waver; vacillate; wobble: ～不定 *keep on vacillating* / ～于两者之间 *waver between the two*
【游弋】cruise: 在海上～ *cruise on the sea*
【游艺】entertainment; recreation: ～节目 *programme of musical and other performances* / ～室

recreation room ◇ ～会 an entertainment gathering (for watching performances and playing games)

【游泳】swim：去～ *go for a swim*；*go swimming* ◇ ～池 swimming pool；～馆 natatorium；～裤 bathing (or swimming) trunks；～帽 bathing (or swimming) cap；～衣 swimsuit；swimming suit (or costume)；bathing suit (or costume)

【游园】❶ visit a garden or park：陪外宾～ *accompany a foreign guest on a visit to a park* ❷ mass celebrations in parks◇ ～会 garden gathering；garden carnival；garden party

【游资】idle fund；idle money；floating capital

【游子】〈书〉a man travelling or residing in a place far away from home：慈母手中线，～身上衣。*The thread from a fond mother's hand is now in the jacket of her absent son.*

【游踪】the whereabouts of a traveller：～无定 *travel from place to place without a fixed plan or route*

鱿 名 squid

【鱿鱼】common name for 枪乌贼 ——另见〖炒鱿鱼〗

繇（构词成分）见下

【繇子】a bird used to lure other birds into a trap；decoy

yǒu

友 Ⅰ 名 friend：好～ *a good (or great) friend* / 敌～不分 *not distinguish between friend and foe* Ⅱ 形 friendly：友爱 / 友邦

【友爱】friendly affection；fraternal love：团结～ *fraternal unity* / 阶级～ *class brotherhood*

【友邦】friendly nation (or country)

【友好】❶ close friend；friend：生前～ *friends of the deceased* ❷ friendly；amicable：～往来 *friendly contacts (or exchanges)* / ～代表团 *goodwill mission* / ～协会 *friendship association* ◇ ～城市 cities of friendship；twin cities；sister cities；～邀请赛 friendship invitational tournament

【友军】friendly forces

【友邻】friendly neighbours；good neighbours

【友朋】〈书〉friends

【友情】friendly sentiments；friendship

【友人】friend：国际～ *foreign friend*

【友善】〈书〉friendly；amicable

【友谊】friendship：深厚的～ *profound friendship* / 建立～ *build (or forge) ties of friendship* ◇ ～杯 cup of friendship；～赛 friendly match；～商店 friendship store

有 Ⅰ 动 ❶ have；possess：她～热情，～朝气。*She is full of vigour and enthusiasm.* / ～百利而无一弊 *have every advantage and no drawback* ❷ there is；exist：屋里～人吗？*Is there anyone in the room?* / 这座位～人吗？*Is this seat taken?* / 树上～两只小鸟。*There are two birds in the tree.* ❸ (used in making an estimate or a comparison)：水～三米多深。*The water is more than 3 metres deep.* / 这条鱼～四公斤重。*This fish weighs about four kilos.* / 他～你这么高。*He is as tall as you.* ❹ (used to indicate sth. appearing or occurring)：一～问题就去解决 *deal with a problem as soon as it crops up* / 他～病了。*He is ill.* / 他～过肺病。*He has had TB before.* ❺ (used to express the idea of having plenty of)：～经验 *be experienced* / ～本事 *be capable* / ～了年纪 *be getting on in years* / 他很～学问。*He is quite a scholar.* ❻ (used with the meaning of "certain" or "some")：～一天我在街上碰见他了。*One day I ran into him in the street.* / ～些事还需要商量。*Certain things are still open to discussion.* ❼ (used after certain monosyllabic verbs, the combination functioning as a single word)：这家伙怀～不可告人的目的。*That fellow has an underhand scheme.* / 这种水果含～多种维生素。*This fruit contains vitamins.* Ⅱ 助 (used before certain verbs in polite formulas)：有劳 / 有请

【有碍】be a hindrance to；get in the way of；obstruct：～交通 *hinder traffic*

【有碍观瞻】be unsightly；offend the eye；be an eyesore

【有案可稽】(又作'有案可查') be a matter of record；be on record；be documented

【有板有眼】rhythmical；measured；orderly：他说话～。*Whatever he says is well presented.*

【有备无患】where there is precaution, there is no danger；preparedness averts peril：有备才能无患，无备必定吃亏。*If one is prepared, one will be safe; if not, one will suffer.* or *Preparedness ensures security; unpreparedness invites disaster.*

【有鼻子有眼儿】with every detail described：她说得～，就像真有那么一回事。*She described the whole thing in such vivid detail that it sounded quite real.*

【有产阶级】propertied class

【有偿】with compensation；compensated；paid：～技术转让 *compensated transfer of technology* / ～服务 *paid services* ◇ ～使用 paid use；～土地使用 paid land use；～新闻 paid news

【有成】〈书〉achieve success：双方意见已渐接近，谈判可望～。*Since the two sides are beginning to see eye to eye, we are hopeful that the talks will be a success.*

【有成果】productive；fruitful

【有酬劳动】[经] paid labour

【有错必纠】every wrong will be righted

【有待】remain (to be done)；await：～解决 *remain to be solved* / ～证明 *have yet to be proved* / ～研究 *await research*

【有袋类】[动] marsupial

【有道】have attained the Way；be accomplished in

the Way; adhere to principles of truth and right: ～之士 *a man who has attained the Way* (*or is accomplished in the Way*)

【有得】have learned sth.; have gained some knowledge: 学习～ *have profited from one's studies*

【有的】some: ～这样说,～那样说。*Some say one thing, some say another.*

【有的是】have plenty of; there's no lack of: 她～时间。*She has all the time in the world.*

【有底】know how things stand and feel confident of handling them; be fully prepared for what is coming: 他心里～,一点不慌。*He was not at all nervous, for he knew what to expect.*

【有的放矢】shoot the arrow at the target—have an object in view

【有点儿】❶ some; a little: 水壶里还～水。*There's still some water in the kettle.* ❷ somewhat; rather; a bit: ～反感 *feel a bit resentful; have a touch of resentment*

【有法必依】ensure that laws are observed: ～,执法必严,违法必究。*Laws must be strictly observed and enforced and lawbreakers must be punished.*

【有法不依】laws are ignored

【有法可依,有章可循】there are laws and regulations to go by

【有方】with the proper method; in the right way: 领导～ *exercise able leadership*

【有份儿】have a share; have taken a part in: 分红利她也该～。*She should also have a share of the profits.*

【有福同享,有祸同当】share joys and sorrows; share weal and woe; stick together through thick and thin

【有感】thoughts on sth. (usu. used in the title of a literary sketch)

【有功】have rendered great service; have performed meritorious service: ～部队 *troops with a fine record of service; meritorious army unit*

【有关】❶ have something to do with; have a bearing on; relate to; concern: 这件事与他～。*He has something to do with the matter.* / 这些问题都跟哲学～。*All these questions relate to philosophy.* / ～全局 *have a bearing on the situation as a whole* ❷ related; concerned; relevant; pertinent: ～部门 *the department concerned* / ～规定 *pertinent regulations*

【有光】❶ glazed: ～纸 *glazed paper* ❷ [纺] bright: ～人造丝 *bright rayon*

【有轨电车】tramcar; streetcar

【有鬼】there's something fishy: 这里面～。*There's something fishy about it.* or *One smells a rat here.* / 他心里～。*He's got a guilty conscience.*

【有过之无不及】go even farther than; outdo

【有害】harmful; pernicious; detrimental: 对健康～ *harmful* (*or detrimental*) *to one's health* / ～的影响 *pernicious effects*

【有行无市】(of a market) have only quotations but no actual trading

【有恒】persevering

【有会子】〈口〉quite a long while; quite some time: 他出去可～啦! *He's been out for quite a while.*

【有机】❶ [化] organic: ～酸 *organic acid* / ～盐 *organic salt* ❷ organic: ～的组成部分 *an organic part; a component part* ◇ ～玻璃 polymethyl methacrylate; plexiglass; perspex; ～肥料 organic fertilizer; manure; ～耕作 organic farming; organic gardening; ～合成 organic synthesis; ～化合物 organic compound; ～化学 organic chemistry; ～染料 organic dyestuff; ～体 organism; ～物 同〖有机化合物〗; ～物质 organic matter (or substance)

【有机可乘】There's an opportunity to take advantage of; There's a loophole that can be used.

【有计划】in a planned way; according to plan

【有价证券】negotiable securities; securities

【有奖储蓄】lottery-attached deposit

【有奖购物】lottery shopping

【有奖销售】lottery sales; prize-giving sales; sell goods with prize

【有奖债券】premium bond

【有教无类】in education there should be no class distinctions

【有禁不止】disregard prohibitions; ignore an interdiction

【有禁则止】observe a prohibition strictly; respect a taboo

【有救】can be saved (or cured, remedied): 好了,这病～了! *Thank goodness, we've found a cure for the disease.*

【有口皆碑】win universal praise; be universally acclaimed

【有口难分】(又作'有口难辩') find it hard to defend or vindicate oneself

【有口难言】cannot bring oneself to mention sth.; find it hard or embarrassing to bring up a matter

【有口无心】be sharp-tongued but not malicious: 他是～,你别见怪。*He didn't really mean what he said, so don't take it to heart.*

【有愧】feel qualms about sth.; have a guilty conscience

【有来有往】give-and-take; reciprocal

【有赖】depend on; rest on: 要实现这项革新,～于大家共同努力。*The success of the innovation depends on our concerted efforts.*

【有劳】〈套〉may I trouble you; sorry to bother you: ～您代我买本书。*May I trouble you to buy a book for me?* / 这件事～您了。*Sorry to have bothered you with this matter.*

【有了】〈口〉❶ (said when hitting upon an idea) I've got it. ❷〈婉〉be pregnant: 我～。*I'm going to have a baby.*

【有理】❶ reasonable; justified; in the right: 你讲的～。*What you say is quite reasonable.* ❷ [数] rational ◇ ～分式 [数] rational fraction; ～函数 [数] rational function; ～式 [数] rational formula; ～数 [数] rational number

【有理无情】❶ stick to the principle and disregard personal feelings ❷ for no apparent reason; without rhyme or reason

【有理走遍天下,无理寸步难行】with justice on your side, you can go anywhere; without it, you can't take a step

【有力】strong; powerful; forceful; energetic; vigorous: 提供～的证据 *provide strong evidence*; *furnish convincing proof* / 作出～的回答 *give a forceful answer* / ～地打击了歪风邪气 *hit hard at evil trends* / ～无处使 *have no outlet for one's surplus energy*

【有利】advantageous; beneficial; favourable: ～地形 *favourable terrain* / ～时机 *opportune time* / ～条件 *favourable conditions or terms* ◇ ～可图 have good prospects of profit; stand to gain; be profitable; ～无弊 have every advantage and not a single disadvantage; be advantageous in every respect; ～有弊 there are both advantages and disadvantages

【有例在先】there is a precedent for that

【有脸】❶ have prestige; command respect: 你～,这事得由你出面去调停。*You have prestige, and so are in a position to arbitrate*. ❷ have the face: 看你有什么脸见人。*I'd just like to see if you can face anyone*.

【有两下子】〈口〉have real skill; know one's stuff: 他干活又快又好,真～。*He works fast and well; he obviously knows his stuff*.

【有零】(used after round numbers) odd: 三十～ *thirty odd* / 一千～ *just over a thousand*

【有令不行,有禁不止,各行其是】go one's own way in disregard of orders and prohibitions; flout the rules

【有令则行】obey orders strictly

【有门儿】〈口〉❶ find the beginning of a solution; be hopeful (of success): 听他的口气,这事看来～了。*Judging by the way he spoke, he might get the matter off the ground now*. ❷ get the hang: 这活儿他干了几次,现在有点门儿了。*After several trials, he began to get the hang of the work*.

【有名】well-known; famous; celebrated: ～的科学家 *a celebrated scientist*

【有名无实】in name but not in reality; merely nominal; titular: 那个委员会～。*That committee exists only in name*.

【有名有姓】identifiable by both given name and surname—of established identity

【有目共睹】(又作'有目共见') be obvious to anyone who has eyes; be perfectly obvious: 他成就之大～。*The greatness of his achievements is obvious*.

【有目共赏】have a universal appeal; appeal to all alike

【有奶便是娘】whoever suckles me is my mother; submit to whoever feeds one; lick the hand of anyone who throws a few crumbs

【有你的】〈口〉❶ you really are something; good for you ❷ you'll get your deserts; you'll suffer for this

【有盼头】〈方〉sth. is hopeful

【有朋自远方来,不亦乐乎】Is it not a joy to have friends come from afar?

【有凭有据】fully substantiated; well-documented: 因为他说得～,大家信以为真。*Since his statement seemed well founded, we all accepted it*.

【有谱儿】have sth. to go by; have confidence: 做事儿～ *do things with confidence*; *know what one is doing*

【有期徒刑】[法] fixed-term imprisonment: 判～七年 *be sentenced to seven years' imprisonment*

【有其父,必有其子】like father, like son

【有气】be or get angry; take offence: 我越想越～。*The more I thought of it, the angrier I became*.

【有气儿】be breathing: 他还～,快叫救护车。*He's still breathing. Call an ambulance, quick*.

【有气无力】feeble; weak; faint; listless: 说话～ *speak in a faint (or feeble) voice* / 老人拄着拐棍儿,～地走开了。*The old man walked feebly away, supporting himself with a cane*.

【有钱】rich; wealthy◇ ～能使鬼推磨 with money you can make the devil turn the millstone; money makes the mare go

【有情】be in love: 你～,我有意。*You are all heart, and my heart is for you*. ◇ ～人 lovers; ～人终成眷属 lovers will be married; Jack shall have Jill, all shall be well

【有请】〈套〉ask the visitor in

【有求必应】respond to every plea; grant whatever is requested

【有求于】have to look to sb. for help; have a favour to ask of sb.: 他们以为我们～他们,所以要价越来越高。*Thinking we are asking favours of them, they are demanding more and more in return*.

【有去无还】gone never to return; gone forever

【有趣】interesting; fascinating; amusing: ～的故事 *an interesting story*

【有染】〈书〉have illicit sexual relations

【有扰】〈套〉thanks for your hospitality

【有人家儿】(of a girl) be engaged

【有日子】❶ for quite a few days; for days: 咱们～没见面了。*We haven't seen each other for quite a few days*. ❷ have fixed a date: 你们结婚～了没有? *Have you fixed the date for the wedding?*

【有如】just like; as if; as though

【有色】coloured: 戴着～眼镜看事情 *look at things through coloured spectacles—take a distorted view* ◇ ～金属 nonferrous metal; ～人种 coloured race (or people)

【有神论】theism: ～者 *theist*

【有生】(又作'有生以来') ever since one's birth: ～第一次 *the first time in one's life (or in all one's born days)*

【有生力量】effective strength; effectives

【有生之年】one's remaining years: 我今年八十岁了,希望能在～看到祖国统一的实现。*I'm eighty now. I hope I shall live to see the reunification of our country.*

【有声读物】audiobook

【有声片】sound film; talkie

【有声有色】full of sound and colour—vivid and dramatic: 他把他看到的情形～地描述了一番。*He gave a vivid and spirited description of what he had seen.*

【有声资料】voice data

【有失身份】beneath one's dignity

【有识之士】a person with breadth of vision; a man of insight

【有时】sometimes; at times; now and then: 他～也写几句诗。*Sometimes he writes a few lines of poetry*

【有史以来】since the beginning (or dawn) of history; throughout history: ～最大的陨石雨 *the biggest meteorite shower in history*

【有始无终】start sth. but not carry it through

【有始有终】carry sth. through to the end: 她做事总是～。*Once she starts a job, she goes through with it.*

【有事】❶ have a job; be employed: 她现在～了，待遇还不错。*She's got a job now, and is pretty well paid, too.* ❷ be occupied; be busy: 对不起，我这会儿～。*Sorry, I'm busy now.* ❸ have sth. happen; meet with an accident; get into trouble: 你放心，我看不会～的。*Don't worry, I don't think there'll be any trouble.* / 做好准备，一旦～，马上出动。*Get prepared so that you can set off immediately if something happens.* ❹ (used with 心里) have sth. on one's mind; be anxious; worry: 看他这几天愁眉苦脸的，心里一定～。*Just look at the worried look he's been wearing all these days. There must be something weighing on his mind.*

【有恃无恐】when one has something to fall back upon one has nothing to fear; feel secure in the knowledge that one has strong backing

【有数】❶ know exactly how things stand; have a definite idea of what one's doing: 你放心，怎么做我心里～。*Don't worry. I know what I'm doing.* ❷ not many; only a few: 只剩下～的几天了，得加把劲儿。*There are only a few days left. We must get a move on.*

【有说有笑】talk and laugh: 两人～。*The two of them talked and laughed together.*

【有丝分裂】[生] mitosis

【有所】to some extent; somewhat: 两国关系～改善。*The relations between the two countries have improved to some extent.*

【有所不为而后可以有所为】you must leave some things undone if you want to get others done; refrain from doing some things in order to be able to do other things

【有蹄动物】ungulate

【有天没日】(又作'有天无日') ❶ wanton; unbridled; outrageous: 他那些～的话简直听不得。*Those outrageous remarks of his were simply intolerable to the ear.* ❷ complete darkness—total absence of justice

【有条不紊】in an orderly way; methodically; systematically: ～地进行生产 *carry on production in a systematic fashion*

【有条有理】methodical; systematic; orderly

【有头无尾】have a beginning but no end; start sth. but not finish it; leave sth. unfinished; give up sth. halfway

【有头有脸】have prestige; command respect: 他在村里是个～的，说话很有分量。*He is a prestigious figure in his village and what he says carries a lot of weight.*

【有头有尾】have a beginning and an end; do sth. from beginning to end; start sth. and finish it: 他太激动了，没法把自己的事～地讲给大家听。*He was too excited to tell them his story from beginning to end.*

【有望】hopeful: 丰收～。*There's hope of a bumper harvest.*

【有为】promising: ～的青年 *a promising young person* / 年轻～ *young and promising*

【有味儿】❶ (of food) be tasty; be delicious: 这个酸辣汤真～。*This vinegar-pepper soup is so delicious.* ❷ (of food) smell bad; be off: 这个鱼～了，不能吃了。*This fish has gone off—we can't eat it.* ❸ be interesting; be meaningful: 这首诗越读越～。*The more you read this poem, the more meaningful you find it.*

【有闻必录】record whatever one hears

【有喜】〈口〉be pregnant; be expecting; be in the family way

【有戏】hopeful: 这事还～。*There is still hope.*

【有隙】❶〈书〉bear a grudge: 二人～。*They harbour a grudge against each other.* ❷ there is a loophole

【有隙可乘】there is a crack to squeeze through—there is a loophole to exploit

【有闲】have leisure: ～阶级 *the leisured classes; the idle rich*

【有限】limited; finite: 为数～ *limited in number; not many* ◇ ～公司 limited company; limited-liability company; ～花序 [植] definite inflorescence; ～级数 [数] finite progression; finite series; ～战争 limited war

【有线】wired: ～通讯 *wire communication* ◇ ～传真 wirephoto; ～电报 wire telegraph; ～电话 wire (or wired) telephone; ～电视 cable television; ～广播 wire (or wired) broadcasting; rediffusion on wire

【有效】efficacious; effective; valid: 这张车票三日内～。*This train ticket is good (or valid) for three days.* / 这个指示仍然～。*The directive still holds good.* ◇ ～分蘖 [农] effective tillering; ～功率 [电] effective power; useful power; ～荷载 useful load; ～库容 [水] effective storage; ～票 valid ballot paper; ～期 term (or period) of validity; time of efficacy; ～射程 effective range; ～数字 significant digits

【有些】❶ some：～人在看书，～人在谈天。*Some people were reading, some were talking.* ❷ somewhat；rather：～不满意 *be somewhat dissatisfied* / ～失望 *be rather disappointed*

【有心】❶ have a mind to；set one's mind on：我～去看看他，又怕打扰他。*I'd like to go and see him, but I don't want to disturb him.* ❷ intentionally；purposely：他是～说给你听的。*What he said was intended for you.* ◇ ～人 a person who sets his mind on doing sth. useful；a person with high aspirations and determination；an observant and conscientious person

【有形】tangible；visible；physical ◇ ～贸易 visible trade；～损耗 material loss；～资本 material capital；～资产 tangible assets；tangibles

【有性】[生] sexual：～孢子 *sexual spore* ◇ ～生殖 sexual reproduction；zoogamy；～世代 sexual generation；～杂交 sexual hybridization

【有幸】be lucky to；have the good fortune to：我们～再次相会。*We are happy to meet again.*

【有血有肉】lifelike；true to life；vivid：这个人物写得～。*The portrayal of the character is lifelike.* / 这篇报道～。*This news report is full of vivid details.*

【有言在先】make clear beforehand；forewarn：不是～，过时不候吗？*Wasn't it clearly understood that we wouldn't wait for anyone who was late?*

【有眼不识泰山】have eyes but not see Mount Tai；entertain an angel unawares：小人～！一时冒渎兄长，望乞恕罪！*I failed to recognize your eminence and I hope that you will forgive me for that blunder.*

【有眼无珠】have eyes but see not；possess no true discernment

【有一搭没一搭】〈口〉❶ trying to engage sb. in small talk；conversing for the sake of conversing ❷ not essential；not indispensable

【有一得一】no more，no less；just that much

【有一分热，发一分光】give as much light as the fuel can produce—do one's best，however little it may be

【有益】profitable；beneficial；useful：～的格言 *good popular maxims* / 作出～的贡献 *make valuable contributions*

【有意】❶ have a mind to；be inclined (or disposed) to：～帮忙 *be disposed to help* ❷ intentionally；deliberately；purposely：～歪曲 *deliberately distort* / ～刁难 *make things difficult for sb. on purpose*

【有意识】consciously：～地克服自己的缺点 *make conscious efforts to overcome one's weaknesses*

【有意思】❶ significant；meaningful：他说的话很～。*What he said was significant.* ❷ interesting；enjoyable：今天的晚会很～。*The performance this evening was most enjoyable.*

【有意无意】wittingly or unwittingly；consciously or unconsciously；by accident or design

【有影没影】groundless；unfounded：那些～的话很快传开了。*Such idle gossip spread quickly.*

【有勇无谋】have valour but lack strategy；be brave but not resourceful；be foolhardy

【有余】❶ have a surplus；have enough and to spare：粮食自给～ *have grain enough and to spare* ❷ odd：二十～ *twenty odd*

【有缘】be predetermined by fate；be predestined；have a bond；have an affinity：我们真～，又碰见了。*It's fate for us, we meet again.* / 你两个结为夫妻，是前世～。*Your union was predestined from a previous incarnation.*

【有缘千里能相会，无缘对面不相逢】If there is a bond between them，the two will meet across a thousand li；without a bond，they will not meet though face to face.

【有源】[电] active：～电路 *active circuit* / ～器件 *active device*；*active parts*

【有则改之，无则加勉】correct mistakes if you have made any and guard against them if you have not

【有增无已】ever-increasing；increasingly

【有朝一日】should the day come when...；if by chance...

【有职无权】hold a post but have no real power or authority；be a figurehead

【有职有权】hold both the post and the power；have the authority that goes with one's post；exercise the power that goes with one's post

【有志者事竟成】(又作'有志竟成') where there's a will there's a way

【有志之士】a person of noble aspirations；a person with lofty ideals

【有种】〈口〉have guts；be plucky；be gritty：～的站出来！*Let anyone who has guts step forward!*

【有助于】contribute to；be conducive to；conduce to：这次访问～增进我们两国人民的相互了解。*This visit has contributed to a better understanding between the peoples of our two countries.* / 体育锻炼～增强体质。*Exercise is conducive to good health.*

【有滋有味】❶ tasty；delicious ❷ with relish；avidly：他吃得～。*He ate with relish.*

【有嘴无心】同〖有口无心〗

【有罪】be guilty of a crime；be guilty

酉 名 the tenth of the twelve Earthly Branches (地支) ——另见〖干支〗

【酉时】the period of the day from 5 p.m. to 7 p.m.

莠 Ⅰ 名 [植] green bristle grass Ⅱ 形〈书〉bad；vicious；undesirable：良莠不齐

铕 名 [化] europium (Eu)

黝 形 black；dark

【黝黑】dark；swarthy：胳膊晒得～ *with sunburnt arms*

yòu

又 副 ❶ (used for an actual action) again：他～

来了。*Here he comes again*. / 我～到那儿去了。*I went there again*. / 他说了～说。*He said it over and over again*. ❷ also; in addition: 这个很好,～便宜。*This is very good, and inexpensive too*. / 天很黑,～下着雨,路更难走了。*On top of it being dark it was raining, which made the going even tougher*. ❸ (used between a whole number and a fraction) and: 一～二分之一 *one and a half* ❹ (used, sometimes in pairs, to indicate contrary actions or ideas): 他答应了来～不来。*He promised to come but didn't*. / 刚才太冷,现在～太热了。*Just a moment ago it was too cold, now it's too hot*. ❺ (used in a negative statement or a rhetorical question for emphasis): 这活儿～不重,我一个人顶得下来。*That's not a hard job. I'm sure I can manage it alone*. / 这样做～有什么好处呢? *What good is there in doing that?* ❻ (reduplicated, with verbs or adjectives) both ... and ...; not only ... but also ...: 坐飞机～快～舒服。*The plane is both quick and comfortable*. / 这儿的东西～便宜～好。*Things here are not only inexpensive but also good*. / ～哭～闹 *make a tearful scene*

【又打又拉】strike and stroke alternately; use both the carrot and the stick

【又红又专】both red and expert; both socialist-minded and professionally proficient; both politically conscious and professionally competent

【又及】postscript (PS)

【又惊又喜】be both startled and delighted; be pleasantly surprised

【又名】also called; alias; also known as

【又想当婊子,又想立牌坊】lead the life of a whore and want a monument put up to one's chastity

【又要马儿好,又要马儿不吃草】expect the horse to run fast but not let it graze; eat one's cake and have it

右 Ⅰ名 ❶ the right side; the right: 向～拐 *turn right* / 靠～走 *keep to the right* ❷ west: 山～ *areas west of the Taihang Mountains, specifically Shanxi Province* ❸ the right side as the side of precedence: 无出其右 Ⅱ形 the Right: 思想太～ *too far to the Right in thinking*

【右边锋】[体](足球) outside right; right wing

【右边】the right (or right-hand) side; the right

【右侧】同〖右边〗

【右舵】right standard rudder; right rudder

【右锋】[体](棒球) right forward

【右后卫】[体](足球) right back

【右面】the right (or right-hand) side; the right

【右内锋】[体](足球) inside right

【右派】the Right; the right wing; Rightist: 国民党～ *the right wing of the Kuomintang; the Kuomintang right-wingers*

【右前轮】off-front wheel (of a car)

【右前卫】[体](足球) right halfback; right half

【右倾】Right deviation: ～思想 *Right-deviationist thinking* ◇ ～机会主义 Right opportunism

【右手】❶ the right hand ❷ 同〖右首〗

【右手定则】[电] the right-hand rule

【右首】the right-hand side; the right: 他～坐着一位老大娘。*An old woman was seated on his right*.

【右袒】〈书〉 take sides with; be partial to

【右舷】starboard (of a ship)

【右旋】[化] dextrorotation: ～物质 *dextrorotatory substance* ◇ ～糖 [化] dextrose; glucose; grape sugar

【右翼】❶ [军] right wing; right flank ❷ the right wing; the Right: ～分子 *Rightist; Right-winger*

幼 Ⅰ形 young; under age: ～畜 *young animal; young stock* Ⅱ名 children; the young: 扶老携幼

【幼虫】larva

【幼雏】young bird; baby bird; nestling

【幼儿】child; infant ◇ ～家庭教师 baby tutor; ～教育 preschool education; ～园 kindergarten; nursery school; infant school

【幼功】skills (of actors, acrobats, etc.) acquired during childhood

【幼教】〈略〉见〖幼儿教育〗

【幼龄林】[林] young growth

【幼苗】seedling

【幼嫩】❶ tender; delicate: 婴儿～的皮肤 *a baby's delicate skin* ❷ immature; naive: 他太～,根本不懂人情世故。*He is too naive and knows nothing at all of the ways of the world*.

【幼年】childhood; infancy

【幼女】a young girl

【幼弱】young and delicate

【幼师】(〈略〉全称为'幼儿师范') preschool teachers training school

【幼时】childhood; infancy

【幼体】[生] the young; larva

【幼童】child

【幼小】young and small; immature: ～的心灵 *a childish heart*

【幼芽】young shoot; bud

【幼稚】❶ young ❷ childish; puerile; naive: ～可笑 *ridiculously childish* / ～的想法 *naive ideas* ◇ ～园 old name for 幼儿园

【幼稚病】❶ [心理] infantilism ❷ infantile disorder

【幼株】young plant; seedling

【幼子】❶ the youngest son ❷ young (and immature) son

佑 动 help; protect; bless

【佑护】protect; bless

【佑助】help; aid; assist

柚 名 [植] shaddock; pomelo (Citrus grandis) ——另见 yóu

【柚子】common name for 柚

囿 〈书〉 Ⅰ名 animal farm; enclosure; park: 鹿～ *deer farm; deer park* Ⅱ动 limited; hampered: ～于习俗 *be constrained by custom* / ～

于见闻 *be handicapped by lack of knowledge and experience*
【囿于成见】be blinded by prejudice

诱 动 ❶ guide; lead; induce: 诱导 ❷ lure; seduce; entice: ～良为娼 *induce innocent girls into prostitution*
【诱癌因素】carcinogen
【诱逼】(又作'诱迫') cajole and coerce
【诱变】[生] mutagenesis; mutagenicity ◇ ～处理 mutagenize; ～物质 mutagen matter; ～因素 mutagen; ～因子(又作'诱变剂')[生]mutagen; mutagenic agent; ～育种 mutation breeding
【诱变基因】mutator; mutator gene
【诱捕】trap (animals)
【诱虫灯】(又作'诱蛾灯') moth-killing lamp
【诱导】❶ guide; lead; induce: 这些问题可以～大家去思考。*These are thought-provoking questions.* ❷ [物] induce: ～作用 *induction* ◇ ～反应 [化] induced reaction
【诱敌深入】lure the enemy in deep
【诱饵】bait: 用金钱作～ *use money as bait*
【诱发】bring out (sth. potential or latent); induce; cause to happen
【诱供】trap a person into a confession; induce a person to make a confession: 既不～也不逼供。*Neither trickery nor coercion is used to secure confessions.*
【诱拐】abduct; carry off (a woman) by fraud; kidnap (a child)
【诱惑】❶ entice; tempt; seduce; lure: 用黄色书刊～青少年 *tempt the young with pornographic books and periodicals* ❷ attract; allure: 窗外是一片～人的景色。*The window commands a charming view.*
【诱奸】entice into unlawful sexual intercourse; seduce
【诱骗】inveigle; cajole; trap; trick: ～某人投赞成票 *cajole sb. into voting in one's favour*
【诱人】alluring; fascinating; captivating; enchanting: ～的景色 *captivating scenery*
【诱杀】trap and kill; lure to destruction: 用灯光～棉铃虫 *lure bollworms to their death with lamps*
【诱使】trick into; inveigle into; lure into: ～她上当受骗 *lure her into a trap* / ～犯罪 *entrapment*
【诱售法】bait-and-switch
【诱降】lure into surrender
【诱胁】cajole and coerce
【诱因】cause (esp. of an illness): 他这场病的～是着了凉。*His illness was brought on by a chill.*
【诱致】lead to; cause: ～堕落 *lead to one's degeneration* ◇ ～流动 induced flow; ～投资 induced investment

蚴 名 the larva of a tapeworm or the cercaria of a schistosome: 毛蚴 / 尾蚴

釉 名 glaze: 青～瓷器 *blue glazed porcelain* / ～里红 *underglaze red*
【釉彩玻璃】enameled glass
【釉工】glazer
【釉面砖】glazed tile
【釉陶】glazed pottery
【釉质】[生理] enamel
【釉子】glaze

鼬 名 [动] weasel
【鼬獾】[动] ferret badger

yū

迂 形 ❶ circuitous; winding; roundabout: ～道访问 *make a detour to call on sb.* ❷ clinging to outworn rules and ideas; pedantic: 这人有点～。*He's a bit of a pedant.*
【迂夫子】pedant
【迂腐】stubbornly clinging to outworn rules and ideas; pedantic: ～的见解 *pedantic ideas*
【迂缓】slow in movement; dilatory
【迂回】❶ circuitous; tortuous; roundabout: ～前进 *advance by a roundabout route* ❷ outflank: 向敌人左侧～ *outflank the enemy on the left* ◇ ～曲折 full of twists and turns; circuitous; tortuous; ～战术 outflanking tactics
【迂见】pedantic ideas
【迂阔】high-sounding and impracticable: ～之论 *impractical views*
【迂论】impractical views
【迂曲】tortuous; circuitous: ～的山路 *a tortuous mountain path*
【迂儒】a pedantic scholar; pedant
【迂拙】impractical and stupid

吁 象 a call to an animal to stop; whoa ——另见 xū; yù

淤 Ⅰ 动 become silted up; be choked with silt: 水渠里～了很多泥沙。*The channel is almost choked with silt.* Ⅱ 名 ❶ silt: 引～肥田 *fertilize the soil with silt* / 河～ *sludge from a riverbed* ❷ 同〖瘀〗
【淤地】alluvial plain ◇ ～坝[水] silt arrester
【淤淀】silt up: 河身～。*The river is silted up.*
【淤灌】[农] warping
【淤积】silt up; deposit: 洪水过后,地里～了一层泥浆。*When the flood subsided, it left a layer of mud in the fields.*
【淤泥】silt; sludge; ooze
【淤塞】silt up; be choked with silt: 航道～。*The waterway is silted up.*
【淤血】[医] extravasated blood
【淤滞】❶ (of the flow of a river, etc.) be retarded by silt; silt up ❷ [医] stasis (of blood or other bodily fluids): 静脉～ *venous stasis* / 尿～ *urinary stasis*

瘀 名 [中] stasis of blood: 活血化～ *reduce stasis and improve blood circulation*

【瘀斑】[医] ecchymosis
【瘀点】[医] petechiae
【瘀血】[中] stasis of blood

yú

于 介 ❶ (indicating time or place) in; on; at: 来信～十五日收到。*Your letter was received on the 15th.* / 此项工程将～三年内完成。*This engineering project is to be completed within three years.* ❷ (indicating direction): 求助～人 *ask people for help* / 热衷～集邮 *be keen on stamp collecting* ❸ (indicating giving or yielding to sb.): 腐朽的势力让位～新生的势力。*Decaying forces give way to new rising forces.* ❹ with regard to; concerning; to: 有利～提高产量 *be conducive to higher yields* / 这样～你自己不利。*It won't do you any good.* / 操之过急,～事无补。*It would be of no avail to act with undue haste.* ❺ (indicating beginning or origin) from: 黄河发源～青海。*The Yellow River rises in Qinghai Province.* / 认识来源～实践。*Knowledge comes from practice.* ❻ (indicating comparison): 不少～五千人 *no less than* 5000 *people* / 友谊贵～黄金。*Friendship is more precious than gold.* / 金星略小～地球。*Venus is a little smaller than the Earth.* ❼ (indicating the doer of an action) by: 主队败～客队。*The home team was defeated by the visiting team.* / 见笑～人 *be laughed at (by others)*

【于今】❶ up to the present; since: 延安一别,～十年。*It is ten years since we parted in Yan'an.* ❷ nowadays; today; now: 这城市建设得真快,～已看不出它原来的面貌了。*The city has been built up really fast; it's changed beyond recognition.*
【于是】(又作'于是乎') so; then; thereupon; hence
【于心不忍】not have the heart to; can't bear to
【于心有愧】have a guilty conscience; have something on one's conscience; feel ashamed

余 Ⅰ 形 ❶ surplus; spare; remaining: ～钱 *spare money (or cash)* / 收支相抵,尚～五十元。*After paying all the expenses, there is a balance of fifty yuan.* ❷ more than; odd; over: 五十～年 *fifty odd years* / 二百～公斤 *over* 200 *kilos* Ⅱ 名 beyond; after: 工作之～ *after working hours; after work*

【余波】the swell after a storm—repercussions: 这场纠纷～未平。*The trouble hasn't ended; there are still repercussions.*
【余存】balance; remainder: 核对销售数量和～数量 *check the amount of sales and stock*
【余党】remnants of an overthrown clique (or gang); remaining confederates
【余地】leeway; margin; room; latitude: 还有改进的～。*There is still room for improvement.*
【余毒】residual poison; pernicious vestige; pernicious influence: 肃清封建思想的～ *eliminate the pernicious influence of feudalist ideas*
【余额】❶ vacancies yet to be filled ❷ remaining sum; balance ◇ ～承前 balance brought forward
【余割】[数] cosecant
【余函数】[数] complementary function
【余晖】(又作'余辉') sunset glow; evening glow: 落日～ *the last rays of the setting sun; afterglow*
【余悸】lingering fear: 犹有～ *still have a lingering fear*
【余角】[数] complementary angle
【余烬】ashes; embers
【余可类推】the rest may be inferred by analogy
【余款】spare money (or cash)
【余力】surplus energy or strength: 不遗余力
【余粮】surplus grain: 把～卖给国家 *sell surplus grain to the state*
【余量】remnant; leftover
【余年】one's remaining years
【余孽】remaining evil element; leftover evil; surviving supporter of an evil cause: 封建～ *dregs of feudalism*
【余怒未息】(又作'余怒未消') be still angry; be still fuming
【余切】[数] cotangent
【余缺】surplus and deficiency: 互通有无,调剂～ *each making up the other's deficiency from his own surplus*
【余热】❶ surplus energy: 利用～取暖 *use surplus energy for heating purposes* ❷ old people's capacity for work: 发挥～ *do what one can in one's old age*
【余生】❶ the remainder of one's life; one's remaining years ❷ survival (after a disaster): 虎口余生
【余矢】[数] coversed sine (covers)
【余数】[数] remainder (after division)
【余头】〈口〉remainder
【余威】remaining prestige or influence
【余味】agreeable aftertaste; pleasant impression: ～无穷 *leave a lasting and pleasant impression or aftertaste*
【余隙】[机] clearance: 切屑～ *chip clearance*
【余暇】spare time; leisure time; leisure
【余下】remaining: ～的钱 *the remaining sum* / ～的同志 *the rest of the comrades; the other comrades*
【余弦】[数] cosine: ～定律 *the cosine law*
【余兴】❶ lingering interest; a wish to prolong a pleasant diversion ❷ entertainment after a meeting or a dinner party
【余因子】[数] complementary divisor
【余音】lingering sound (of music or singing): ～缭绕。*The music lingered in the air.* ◇ ～绕梁 the music lingering around the beams; the music lingering in the air long after the performance
【余勇可贾】with plenty of fight left in one; with strength yet to spare
【余震】[地质] aftershock

盂 名 a broad-mouthed receptacle for holding liquid; jar: 痰盂

【盂兰盆会】the Buddhist name of the Ghost Festival (on the 15th of the seventh lunar month)

鱼 名 fish: 两条～ *two fish*

【鱼白】❶ fish sperm; milt ❷ the whitish colour of a fish's belly—grey dawn: 东方一线～,黎明已经到来。*A streak of light in the east heralded the dawn.*

【鱼鳔】air bladder (of fish); swim bladder

【鱼叉】fish spear; fishgig; fish fork

【鱼池】fish pond

【鱼翅】shark's fin (a delicacy)

【鱼虫】water flea (used as fish feed)

【鱼唇】shark's lip (as food)

【鱼刺】fishbone: 剔掉～ *bone a fish*

【鱼大水小】a big fish in shallow water—a ponderous apparatus without sufficient resources for maintenance

【鱼肚】fish maw (as food) ◇ ～白 the whitish colour of a fish's belly— grey dawn

【鱼饵】(fish) bait

【鱼粉】fish meal

【鱼肝油】cod-liver oil

【鱼竿】fishing rod

【鱼缸】fish bowl; fish tank

【鱼钩】fishhook

【鱼狗】[动] kingfisher

【鱼贯】one following the other; in single file ◇ ～而入 enter in single file; file in

【鱼胶】❶ fish glue; isinglass ❷〈方〉air bladder; swim bladder

【鱼具】fishing tackle (or gear)

【鱼口】(又作'鱼口疔')[中] lymphogranuloma inguinale; climatic (or tropical) bubo

【鱼雷】torpedo: ～发射管 *torpedo tube* ◇ ～艇(又作'鱼雷快艇') torpedo boat

【鱼类学】ichthyology

【鱼鳞】fish scale; scale: 刮去～ *scale a fish* ◇ ～病(又作'鱼鳞癣') ichthyosis; fishskin disease; ～坑 pits arranged like fish scales, dug on mountain slopes for holding water or planting trees; fish-scale pits

【鱼龙】[考古] ichthyosaur

【鱼龙混杂】dragons and fishes jumbled together—good and bad people mixed up

【鱼篓】bamboo fish hamper

【鱼露】fish sauce

【鱼卵】(fish) roe

【鱼米之乡】a land of fish and rice—a well-watered place where fish and rice are abundant

【鱼苗】(fish) fry

【鱼目混珠】pass off fish eyes as pearls —pass off sth. sham as genuine

【鱼片】sliced fish meat

【鱼漂】cork on a fishing line; float

【鱼鳍】fin

【鱼群】a shoal of fish

【鱼肉】❶ the flesh of fish ❷ fish and meat: 人为刀俎,我为鱼肉 ❸ cut up like fish and meat—cruelly oppress: 反动官吏～百姓。*The reactionary officials savagely oppressed the people.*

【鱼石脂】[药] ichthammol; ichthyol

【鱼水】fish and water: 军民关系亲如～。*The army and the people are as inseparable as fish and water.* ◇ ～情 relationship between fish and water—close relationship; ～情深 be close as fish and water

【鱼死网破】either the fish dies or the net gets torn—a life-and-death struggle

【鱼塘】fish pond

【鱼藤】[植] trifoliate jewelvine (Derris trifoliata) ◇ ～精 [农] derris extract; ～酮 [农] rotenone

【鱼丸子】fish ball

【鱼网】fishnet; fishing net

【鱼尾号】boldface square brackets (【 】)

【鱼尾纹】crow's feet: 她的眼角已有几道明显的～。*At the corners of her eyes the crow's feet are quite noticeable.*

【鱼香肉丝】fish-flavoured shredded pork

【鱼腥草】[植] cordate houttuynia (Houttuynia cordata)

【鱼汛】fishing season

【鱼雁】〈文〉fish and wild geese—letters (from the legends of fish and wild geese as bearers of letters): 频通～ *often write to each other*

【鱼秧子】fingerling

【鱼鹰】❶ a large hawk that feeds on fish; fish hawk ❷ a diving bird leashed by fishermen to catch fish; cormorant

【鱼油】fish oil

【鱼游釜中】like fish swimming in a cooking pot—in imminent peril

【鱼圆】〈方〉fish ball

【鱼源】source of fish; breeding ground for fish

【鱼跃】fish dive: ～救球 *diving save*; *diving retrieve*

【鱼闸】fish lock

【鱼种】fingerling

【鱼子】(fish) roe ◇ ～酱 caviare

竽 名 an ancient wind instrument: 滥竽充数

谀 动〈书〉flatter: 阿谀奉承

【谀辞】(又作'谀词') flattering words; flattery

娱 Ⅰ 动 give pleasure to; amuse: 聊以自～ *just to amuse oneself* Ⅱ 名 joy; pleasure; amusement: 耳目之～ *pleasures of the senses*

【娱乐】amusement; entertainment; recreation: ～场所 *public place of entertainment* / ～活动 *recreational activities*; *recreation* / ～室 *recreation room*

【娱乐片】film or TV program for entertainment

隅 名 ❶ corner; nook: 城～ *the corner of a city wall* ❷ an outlying place; border: 海隅

渔 Ⅰ 名 fishing; fishery: 渔业 Ⅱ 动 take sth.

one is not entitled to：渔利

【渔叉】fish spear；fishgig；fish fork

【渔产】aquatic products

【渔场】fishing ground；fishery

【渔船】fishing boat

【渔村】fishing village

【渔夫】〈旧〉fisherman

【渔港】fishing port (or harbour)

【渔歌】fisherman's song

【渔钩】fishhook

【渔鼓】❶ a percussion instrument made of bamboo，used to accompany the chanting of folk tales ❷ 同〖渔鼓道情〗◇ ～道情 chanting of folk tales to the accompaniment of a bamboo percussion instrument

【渔火】lights on fishing boats

【渔获量】a catch (of fish)

【渔家】fisherman's family：～姑娘 *a fisherman's daughter*

【渔具】fishing tackle (or gear)

【渔捞】fishery

【渔利】❶ reap unfair gains；profit at others' expense ❷ easy gains；spoils

【渔猎】fishing and hunting

【渔轮】fishing vessel

【渔民】fisherman；fisherfolk

【渔区】fishing zone

【渔人】fisherman；fisherfolk ◇ ～之利 the fisherman's gains—profit reaped by a third party ——另见〖鹬蚌相争，渔人得利〗；〖坐收渔利〗

【渔网】fishnet；fishing net

【渔翁】an old fisherman

【渔线】fishing line；fishline

【渔乡】fish-farming area；fishing village

【渔汛】fishing season

【渔业】fishery：～区 *fishing zone* / ～协定 *fisheries agreement* / ～资源 *fishery resources*

【渔政】fish-farming operation

渝

动 (of one's attitude or feeling) change：忠贞不渝

腴

形 ❶ fat；plump：丰腴 ❷ fertile：膏腴

愉

形 pleased；happy；joyful；cheerful：面有不～之色 *wear an annoyed expression*；*look displeased*

【愉快】happy；joyful；cheerful：～的微笑 *a happy smile* / 祝你在中国逗留期间过得～。*I hope you'll have a pleasant stay in China.*

【愉乐】happy；joyful；cheerful：家庭融和～ *have a happy and harmonious family*

【愉悦】joyful；cheerful；delighted

逾

Ⅰ**动** exceed；go beyond：～额 *exceed the allowed amount* / 情～骨肉 *dearer than one's own flesh and blood* / 这位老人已年～七十。*The old man is over seventy.* Ⅱ**副**〈书〉even more：痛乃～甚。*Then the pain became even more acute.*

【逾常】out of the ordinary；unusual：欣喜～ *be overjoyed*

【逾分】excessive；undue：～的要求 *excessive demands*

【逾恒】〈书〉out of the common；unusual：勤奋～ *be exceedingly diligent*

【逾期】exceed the time limit；be overdue：～一星期 *be a week overdue*

【逾限】exceed the time limit；be overdue

【逾越】exceed；go beyond：～权限 *overstep one's authority* / ～界限 *go beyond the limit*；*go out of bounds* / ～常规 *depart from the usual practice*

【逾越节】［宗］Passover—a holiday in memory of the escape of the Jews from Egypt

愚

Ⅰ**形** foolish；stupid：愚笨 Ⅱ**动** make a fool of；fool：为人所～ *be fooled (or duped) by sb.* Ⅲ**代**〈谦〉I：～以为不然。*I beg to differ.* / ～兄 *your unworthy elder brother—I*

【愚笨】foolish；stupid；clumsy

【愚不可及】couldn't be more foolish；be hopelessly stupid；the height of folly

【愚蠢】stupid；foolish；silly：～无知 *foolish and ignorant*

【愚钝】slow-witted；stupid

【愚公移山】like the Foolish Old Man who removed the mountains—with dogged perseverance

【愚见】(又作'愚意')〈谦〉my humble opinion

【愚昧】ignorant；benighted：～落后 *ignorant and backward* ◇ ～无知 benighted；unenlightened；ignorant

【愚民】❶ ignorant people ❷ try to keep the people in ignorance；try to prevent the people from knowing the truth ◇ ～政策 policy of keeping the people in ignorance；obscurantist policy；obscurantism

【愚弄】deceive；hoodwink；make a fool of；dupe

【愚人】fool；simpleton ◇ ～节 All Fools' Day (April 1)；April Fool's (or Fools') Day

【愚妄】ignorant but self-important；stupid but conceited

【愚者千虑，必有一得】the greatest fool，in a thousand schemes，must hit once on the truth；even a fool occasionally hits on a good idea

【愚忠】blind devotion (to a master，ruler，etc.)

【愚拙】stupid and clumsy

瑜

名 ❶ fine jade；gem ❷ lustre of gems —virtues；good points：瑕不掩瑜

【瑜珈】(又作'瑜伽') yoga

榆

名 elm

【榆荚】elm seeds

【榆钱儿】〈口〉elm seeds

【榆树】elm tree；elm

【榆叶梅】flowering plum

虞

Ⅰ**名**〈书〉❶ supposition；prediction：以备不虞 ❷ anxiety；worry：兴修水利，水旱无～ *build irrigation works so as to have no worries about* *drought or flood* / 无冻馁之～ *be secure against hunger and cold* Ⅱ**动** deceive; cheat; fool: 尔虞我诈

【虞美人】[植] corn poppy

舆 Ⅰ**名**〈书〉❶ carriage; chariot: 舍～登舟 *change from a carriage to a boat* ❷ the part of a carriage for passengers or goods ❸ sedan chair: 彩～ *a decorated sedan chair* ❹ area; territory: 舆地 Ⅱ**形** public; popular: 舆论

【舆地】〈书〉land; territory

【舆论】public opinion: 作～准备 *prepare public opinion* / 大造～ *whip up opinion* / 国际～ *world opinion* ◇ ～工具 mass media; the media; ～界 the media; press circles

【舆论导向】spin control

【舆情】public sentiment; popular feelings: 洞察～ *know public sentiment well*

【舆图】〈书〉map

yǔ

与 Ⅰ**动** ❶ give; offer; grant: ～人方便 *give help to others; make things easy for others* / 信件已交～本人。*The letter has been given to the person concerned.* ❷〈书〉get along with; be on good terms with: 此人易～。*He is easy to get along with.* or *He is not difficult to approach.* / ～国 *friendly country; allied state* ❸ help; support: 与人为善 Ⅱ**介** ❶ (used to indicate involvement, relationship, etc.) with: 他～此事有关。*He has something to do with the matter.* ❷ (used to introduce the recipient of an action): ～困难作斗争 *strive to overcome difficulties* Ⅲ**连** and: 工业～农业 *industry and agriculture* /《战争～和平》*War and Peace*——另见 yù

【与虎谋皮】ask a tiger for its skin—expect sb. (usu. an evil person) to act against his own interests

【与君一夕话,胜读十年书】I have learnt much more from this evening's talk with you than I could have learnt from ten years of study.

【与其】(used correlatively with 不如 or 毋宁) rather than; better than: 你～坐车,不如坐船。*It's better for you to go by boat than by train.* / ～说是粗心大意,不如说是不负责任。*It's not so much carelessness as irresponsibility.*

【与人方便,自己方便】He who helps others helps himself.

【与人为善】well-intentioned; well-meaning: ～的批评 *well-meaning criticism*

【与日俱增】grow with each passing day; be steadily on the increase: 学习英语的人～。*The number of people learning English is on the increase.*

【与世长辞】depart from the world for ever; pass away

【与世浮沉】drift with the current of the times; swim with the tide

【与世无争】stand aloof from worldly strife; hold oneself aloof from the world

【与众不同】out of the ordinary; different from the common run

予 **动** give; grant; bestow: 免～处分 *exempt sb. from punishment*

【予夺】〈书〉❶ (the power) to give and take away: 生杀予夺 ❷ commend and depreciate

【予人口实】give people a handle

【予以】give; grant: ～表扬 *commend sb.* / ～照顾 *give preferential treatment*

宇 **名** ❶ eaves ❷ house: 庙宇 ❸ space; universe; world: ～内 *in the world*

【宇称】[物] parity: ～不守恒 *parity nonconservation* / ～守恒 *parity conservation*

【宇航】〈略〉见〖宇宙航行〗◇ ～员〈略〉见〖宇宙航行员〗

【宇宙】universe; cosmos ◇ ～尘 cosmic dust; ～飞船 spaceship; spacecraft; ～飞行 space flight; space travel; ～飞行员 astronaut; spaceman; cosmonaut; ～服 spacesuit; ～观 world view; world outlook; ～航行 space flight; space travel; ～航行学 astronautics; cosmonautics; ～航行员 astronaut; spaceman; cosmonaut; ～火箭 space rocket; ～空间 cosmic space; outer space; ～射线 (又作'宇宙线') cosmic rays; cosmic radiation; ～生物学 exobiology; ～速度 cosmic velocity (or speed); ～学 (又作'宇宙论') cosmology; ～站 space station

屿 **名** small island; islet: 岛屿

羽 **名** feather; plume

【羽缎】(又作'羽毛缎') sateen

【羽冠】crest (of a bird)

【羽化】❶ sprout wings—become an immortal: ～而登仙 *rise as an immortal on newly sprouted wings* ❷〈婉〉(used by Taoists) pass away; die ❸ [动] eclosion

【羽毛】feather; plume: 美丽的～ *beautiful plumage* ◇ ～丰满 become full-fledged; mature; ～画 feather patchwork; feather picture; ～扇 feather fan; ～未丰 unfledged; young and immature

【羽毛球】❶ badminton ❷ shuttlecock

【羽绒】fine soft feathers; eiderdown; down: ～被 *down quilt* / ～服 *down jacket*

【羽纱】camlet

【羽扇】feather fan: ～纶巾 *feather fan and silk kerchief*

【羽坛】badminton circles; the badminton world

【羽衣】❶〈书〉garment or robe made of feathers ❷ robe worn by a Taoist priest ❸ Taoist priest

【羽翼】❶ wing ❷ assistant

【羽族】birds

伛 〈书〉(构词成分) 见下

【伛偻】〈书〉❶ hunchbacked; humpbacked ❷ bow (to show respect)

雨 名 rain：天气预报说明天有～。*It will rain tomorrow according to the weather forecast*. / ～下得很大。*It's raining hard*.

【雨暴】［气］rainstorm

【雨布】waterproof cloth；waterproof

【雨层云】［气］nimbostratus

【雨滴】raindrop

【雨点】raindrop

【雨刮】windscreen（or windshield）wiper（of a car）

【雨过地皮湿】do sth. as a mere formality；go through the motions；do sth. perfunctorily or superficially

【雨过天晴】（又作'雨过天青'）the sun shines again after the rain—after gloom comes brightness

【雨后春笋】（spring up like）bamboo shoots after a spring rain：专业户像～一样蓬勃发展起来。*Specialized households sprang up like mushrooms*.

【雨后送伞】give sb. an umbrella after the rain has stopped—offer help when it's too late；offer help when it's no longer needed

【雨花石】yuhua pebbles（colourful fine-grained pebbles found in the Yuhuatai 雨花台 area at Nanjing）

【雨季】rainy season

【雨具】rain gear（i.e. umbrella，raincoat，etc.）

【雨帘】（又作'雨帘子'）同〖雨幕〗

【雨量】rainfall：～强度 *rainfall density* / ～站 *precipitation station*；*rainfall station* ◇ ～计 rain gauge；udometer

【雨露】❶ rain and dew ❷ favour；grace；bounty

【雨帽】❶ rain cap ❷ hood

【雨幕】a curtain of rain—a thick rain

【雨棚】［建］canopy

【雨情】rainfall（in a given area）

【雨区】rain area；rain field

【雨伞】umbrella

【雨势】the force of rain：～渐弱。*The rain gradually died down*.

【雨水】❶ rainwater；rainfall；rain：～足 *adequate rainfall* ❷ Rain Water—the 2nd of the 24 solar terms ❸ the day marking the beginning of the 2nd solar term ◇ ～管 another name for 水落管——另见〖节气〗；〖二十四节气〗

【雨丝】a very light rain

【雨蛙】［动］tree toad

【雨雾】misty rain

【雨鞋】galoshes；rubbers

【雨靴】rubber boots；rain boots

【雨烟】misty rain

【雨燕】［动］swift

【雨衣】raincoat；waterproof

【雨意】signs of approaching rain：颇有～。*It looks like rain*.

【雨云】［气］nimbus

【雨珠】raindrop

语 Ⅰ 名 ❶ language；tongue；words：汉语 ❷ nonlinguistic means of communicating ideas；sign；signal：手语 ❸ set phrase；proverb；saying：～云，"将欲取之，必先与之。" *As the saying goes*，"*Give in order to take*." Ⅱ 动 speak；say：低语

【语病】faulty wording or formulation（causing ambiguity）

【语词】words and phrases

【语调】［语］intonation

【语法】grammar

【语感】an instinctive feel for the language

【语汇】vocabulary：汉语的～是极其丰富的。*Chinese has a very rich vocabulary*.

【语惊四座】the words startle all present

【语境】❶ language environment；speech environment ❷［语］context

【语句】sentence

【语料】linguistic material ◇ ～库 corpus

【语流】flow of speech

【语录】recorded utterance；quotation：毛主席～ *quotations from Chairman Mao*

【语妙天下】speak with inimitable wit

【语气】❶ tone；manner of speaking：～友好 *a friendly tone* ❷［语］mood：祈使～ *imperative mood*

【语塞】be unable to utter a word（due to excitement，anger，etc.）：悲愤之下，一时～ *be speechless with grief and indignation*

【语失】make an indiscreet remark：言多语失

【语素】［语］morpheme

【语态】［语］voice：主动（被动）～ *active*（*passive*）*voice*

【语体】type of writing；style：口语～ *colloquialism* / 科学～ *scientific style of writing*

【语体文】prose written in the vernacular

【语文】❶ Chinese（as a subject of study or a means of communication）：他的～程度怎么样？*How good is his Chinese*？❷（〈略〉全称为'语言和文学'）language and literature

【语无伦次】speak incoherently

【语系】［语］family of languages；language family

【语序】［语］word order

【语训】speech therapy

【语焉不详】❶ not speak in detail；not elaborate ❷（of a statement）be rather too brief or sketchy

【语言】language ◇ ～隔阂 language barrier；～规范化 standardization of speech；～科学 linguistic science；～与文字 spoken and written language

【语言学】linguistics：比较～ *comparative linguistics*；普通～ *general linguistics*；应用～ *applied linguistics* ◇ ～家 *linguist*；*philologist*

【语义】semantic meaning

【语义学】semantics

【语意】meaning of one's words：～深长。*The words are full of meaning*.

【语音】❶ speech sounds ❷ pronunciation：她的～好。*She has good pronunciation*. / ～课 *phonetics class* ◇ ～学 phonetics

【语音信息】[通信] audiotext
【语音信箱】[通信] voice mail
【语用学】[语] pragmatics
【语域】[语] register (in stylistics)
【语源学】etymology
【语种】categories or families of languages
【语重心长】sincere words and earnest wishes：～的劝告 *earnest advice*
【语助词】(又作'语气助词')〈语〉an auxiliary word that indicates mood ——另见〖助词〗
【语族】branch：印欧语系日耳曼～ *the Germanic branch of the Indo-European language family*

yù

与 动 take part in; participate in：参与 ——另见 yǔ
【与会】participate in a conference：～国 *countries attending a conference; participating countries* / ～者 *conferee; participant*
【与闻】have a participant's knowledge of; be let into (a secret, etc.)：～其事 *have a participant's knowledge of a matter; be in the know*

玉 Ⅰ 名 jade Ⅱ 形〈书〉(of a person, esp. a woman) pure; fair; handsome; beautiful Ⅲ 代〈尊〉your：玉照
【玉版纸】a fine-quality writing paper
【玉帛】〈书〉jade objects and silk fabrics, used as state gifts in ancient China
【玉不琢,不成器】jade cannot be made into anything without being cut and polished—one cannot become useful without being educated
【玉成】〈套〉kindly help secure the success of sth. ◇～其事 kindly help make a success of it
【玉带】jade belt (worn by high-ranking officials in ancient China)
【玉雕】jade carving; jade sculpture：～工人 *jade carver*
【玉钩】❶ jade hook ❷〈文〉the crescent moon; the new moon
【玉皇大帝】(又作'玉帝') the Jade Emperor (the Supreme Deity of Taoism)
【玉洁】pure as jade：～的月亮 *the jade-pure moon* ◇～冰清 pure as jade and chaste as ice; pure and noble
【玉兰】[植] yulan magnolia (Magnolia denudata) ◇～片 dried slices of tender bamboo shoots
【玉立】〈书〉❶ slim and graceful ❷ steadfast to principles
【玉米】❶ maize; Indian corn; corn ❷ ear of maize (or corn) ◇～楂(又作'玉米楂子') hulled, coarsely ground corn (or maize); hominy; ～大斑病[农] leaf blight of corn; ～黑粉病[农] corn smut; ～花儿 popcorn; ～粒儿 kernel of corn; grain of corn; ～面 maize flour; cornmeal; ～螟 corn borer; ～脱粒机 maize sheller; ～芯 corncob; cob; ～粥 maize gruel
【玉女】the Jade Maiden ——另见〖金童玉女〗
【玉盘】❶ jade plate ❷〈文〉a bright full moon
【玉器】jade article; jade object; jadeware：～工厂 *jade workshop*
【玉人】❶〈古〉jade worker ❷ jade figure ❸〈文〉a handsome man or (esp.) a beautiful woman
【玉容】〈文〉beautiful face (usu. of a woman); good looks
【玉色】jade green; light bluish green
【玉石】〈口〉jade：这座人像是～的。*This statue is carved in jade.*
【玉石俱焚】jade and stone burned together—destruction of good and bad alike
【玉手】〈文〉jade hands—slender white hands (of a pretty woman)
【玉蜀黍】another name for 玉米
【玉树】同〖桉〗
【玉碎】be like a broken piece of jade—die in glory ——另见〖宁为玉碎,不为瓦全〗
【玉体】❶〈尊〉your person; your health ❷〈文〉jadelike frame—the naked body of a beautiful woman
【玉兔】〈文〉the Jade Hare—the moon：～东升。*The moon was rising in the east.*
【玉玺】imperial jade seal
【玉言】〈文〉〈尊〉your words
【玉液】〈文〉jadelike wine; good wine
【玉宇】❶ residence of the immortals ❷ the universe
【玉簪】❶ jade hairpin ❷[植] fragrant plantain lily (Hosta plantaginea)
【玉照】〈尊〉your photograph

驭 动 drive (a carriage)
【驭手】soldier in charge of pack animals; driver of a military pack train：炮车～ *gun-carriage driver*

芋 名[植] ❶ taro ❷ tuber crops：山芋
【芋艿】[植] taro
【芋头】[植] ❶ taro ❷〈方〉sweet potato

吁 动 appeal; plead：呼吁 ——另见 xū; yū
【吁请】implore; plead; petition
【吁求】implore; plead; petition

育 动 ❶ give birth to：生儿～女 *give birth to children; have children* ❷ rear; raise; bring up：～花 *cultivate flowers* / ～蚕 *raise silkworms* / ～婴 *feed and take care of babies* ❸ educate：德育
【育才】cultivate (or educate) people of ability
【育成品种】[农] improved variety
【育雏】raise young fowl ◇～器 brooder
【育儿袋】[动] brood pouch; marsupium
【育林】afforest：～区 *an afforested area*
【育龄】childbearing age：～妇女 *women of childbearing age*
【育苗】[农] grow (or raise) seedlings：～区 *nursery garden*

【育人】cultivate or foster talent；educate
【育性】［农］fertility
【育婴堂】foundling hospital
【育幼】raise an infant；child care：～机构 *child-care center*
【育种】［农］breeding：杂交～ *crossbreeding* / 作物～ *crop breeding* / ～家 *breeder*
【育珠】grow cultured pearls

郁 形 ❶ strongly fragrant：馥郁 ❷ luxuriant；lush ❸ gloomy；depressed：忧郁
【郁闭】［林］closing：林冠～ *canopy closure* / ～度 *canopy density*
【郁愤】worried and indignant：满腔～ *extremely worried and indignant*；*burning with anxiety*
【郁积】pent up：～的愤怒 *pent-up fury* / 仇恨～在心头 *hatred smouldering in one's bosom*
【郁结】pent up：～在心头的烦闷 *worries pent up inside one*
【郁金】［中］the root-tuber of aromatic turmeric (Curcuma aromatica)
【郁金香】［植］tulip (Tulipa gesneriana)
【郁闷】gloomy；depressed：～之感 *a feeling of oppression*
【郁血】［医］stagnation of the blood；venous stasis
【郁郁】〈书〉❶ elegant；refined：文采～ *displaying literary elegance* ❷ strongly fragrant ❸ lush；luxuriant ◇ ～不乐 depressed；melancholy；gloomy；～葱葱（又作'郁郁苍苍'）lush and green；～寡欢 depressed；melancholy；joyless
【郁蒸】〈书〉hot and suffocating；sultry；muggy

狱 名 ❶ prison；jail：～中的生活 *life in prison* ❷ lawsuit；case：冤狱
【狱警】prison guard；jailer

浴 动 bath；bathe：淋浴 / 日光浴
【浴场】outdoor bathing place：海滨～ *bathing beach*
【浴池】❶ common bathing pool (in a public bathhouse) ❷ public bathhouse；public baths
【浴缸】bathtub
【浴巾】bath towel
【浴具】bathroom facilities
【浴盆】bathtub
【浴室】bathroom or shower room
【浴血】bathed in blood；bloody：～奋战 *fight a bloody battle*
【浴液】liquid soap
【浴衣】bathrobe
【浴皂】toilet soap
【浴罩】plastic bathtub cover

峪 名 (usu. used as part of a place name) valley；ravine：嘉～关 *Jiayuguan* (*a mountain pass in Gansu Province*, *at the westernmost end of the Great Wall*)

预 Ⅰ 副 in advance；beforehand：预支 Ⅱ 动 take part in
【预报】forecast：天气～ *weather forecast* / 商情～ *commercial prediction*
【预备】prepare；get ready：～功课 *prepare lessons* / 你们～好了吗？*Are you all ready?* / 各就各位，～，跑！*Ready! Set! Go!* or *On your mark! Get set! Go!* ◇ ～党员 probationary Party member；～队 reserve force；reserves；～会议 preparatory meeting or conference；～金 reserve fund；～军 reserve army；～期 probationary period；～役［军］reserve duty (or service)；～役军人［军］reservist
【预卜】augur；foretell：～吉凶 *try to predict good or bad fortune*
【预测】calculate；forecast：～日蚀 *calculate an eclipse of the sun* / ～台风 *detect a typhoon*
【预产期】expected date of childbirth
【预处理】pretreatment
【预订】subscribe；book；place an order：～杂志 *subscribe to a magazine* / ～火车票 *book a train ticket* / ～旅馆 *make hotel reservations*
【预定】fix in advance；predetermine；schedule：在～时间 *at the fixed time* / 在～地点着陆 *make a landing in a predetermined area*
【预防】prevent；take precautions against；guard against：贯彻以～为主的医疗方针 *carry out the policy of putting prevention first in medical work* / 采取～措施 *take preventive measures* / ～火灾 *take precautions against fire* ◇ ～接种 preventive (or prophylactic) inoculation；～性拘留［法］preventive detention；～医学 preventive medicine
【预付】pay in advance：～费用 *advanced charges* / ～货款 *cash before delivery*
【预感】❶ premonition；presentiment：不祥的～ *an ominous presentiment* ❷ have a premonition
【预告】❶ announce in advance；herald ❷ advance notice：新书～ *notice on forthcoming books*；*books in preparation*
【预购】place an order or purchase in advance：～合同 *forward purchasing contract*
【预后】［医］prognosis：～良好 *favourable prognosis*
【预计】calculate in advance；estimate：大楼～十个月可以完工。*It is estimated that the building will be completed in ten months* ◇ ～到达时间［航海］estimated time of arrival (E. T. A.)
【预见】❶ foresee；predict：～不到的困难 *unforeseen difficulties* / 这是可以～到的。*This can be predicted*. ❷ foresight；prevision：英明的～ *brilliant foresight* / ～性 *foresight*；*farsightedness*
【预警】early warning：～系统 *early warning system* / ～雷达 *early warning radar* / ～飞机 *early warning plane*
【预科】preparatory course (in a college)
【预料】expect；predict；anticipate：今年的收成比人们～的要好得多。*This year's harvest was much better than expected* (*or anticipated*).

【预谋】premeditate; plan beforehand: ～杀人 *premeditated murder*; *murder with malice prepense*

【预期】expect; anticipate: 达到～的效果 *achieve the desired (or hoped-for) results* / 结果和～的相反。*The results are contrary to expectations.*

【预热】[机] preheat

【预赛】[体] preliminary contest; preliminary heats; preliminary; trial match

【预审】preliminary (or first) hearing

【预示】betoken; indicate; presage; forebode: 灿烂的晚霞～明天又是好天气。*The splendid evening glow in the sky means another fine day tomorrow.*

【预收】collect money in advance: ～定金 *collect a deposit*

【预售】(usu. train tickets) available for booking; sell in advance: ～处 *booking office* / ～票 *advance purchase ticket*; *tickets open to booking*

【预算】budget: ～经费 *budgetary resources* / ～赤字 *budget deficit* / ～结余 *budget surplus* / ～年度 *budget year* / ～收入 *budgetary receipts*

【预习】(of students) prepare lessons before class

【预先】in advance; beforehand: ～通知 *notify in advance* / ～声明 *state explicitly beforehand* / ～警告 *forewarn* / ～感谢 *thank sb. in anticipation*

【预想】anticipate; expect: 得到～的结果 *obtain the anticipated results*

【预选】preliminary election; primary election ◇ ～赛 [体] preliminaries

【预言】❶ prophesy; predict; foretell ❷ prophecy; prediction: 他的～得到了证实。*Things turned out as he predicted.*

【预言家】prophet

【预演】preview (of a performance or motion picture)

【预应力】[物] prestressing force: ～构件 *prestressed component*

【预约】make an appointment: 门诊～挂号 *have an appointment with a doctor*

【预兆】omen; presage; sign; harbinger: 吉祥的～ *an auspicious omen* / 胜利的～ *a harbinger of victory* / 下雨的～ *a sign of coming rain*

【预支】❶ pay in advance: 这本书我们要给作者～五万元稿费。*We'll give the author an advance of* 50,000 *yuan on this book.* ❷ get payment in advance: 我能～工资吗? *Can I have an advance on my salary?*

【预知】know beforehand

【预制】prefabricate: ～装配式房屋 *prefabricated house*; *prefab* ◇ ～板 prefabricated board; ～构件 [建] prefabricated components

【预祝】congratulate beforehand; wish: ～你取得成功。*I wish you success.*

欲 Ⅰ **名** desire; longing; wish: 食欲 Ⅱ **动** ❶ wish; want; desire: 从心所～ *follow what the heart desires* / ～言又止 *make as if to speak, and then stop* ❷ about to; just going to; on the point of: 摇摇欲坠

【欲罢不能】unable to stop even though one wants to; try to stop but cannot; cannot refrain from going on

【欲盖弥彰】the more one tries to hide, the more one is exposed; try to cover up a misdeed, only to make it more conspicuous; protest too much

【欲壑难填】greed is a valley that can never be filled; avarice knows no bounds

【欲火】the fire of lust; lewd desire: ～中烧 *burning with lewd desire*

【欲加之罪,何患无词】if you are out to condemn sb., you can always trump up a charge

【欲念】desire; wish; lust

【欲擒故纵】leave sb. at large the better to apprehend him; allow sb. more latitude first to keep a tighter rein on him afterwards

【欲求】desire; wish; lust

【欲取姑与】give in order to take; make concessions for the sake of future gains

【欲速则不达】haste brings no success; more haste, less speed

【欲望】desire; wish; lust

域 **名** land within certain boundaries; territory; region: 领域

【域名】[计] domain name: ～系统 *domain name system*; *DNS*

【域外】outside the country

【域中】inside the country

谕 **动** 〈书〉(of superiors or elders) instruct; tell: 面谕

【谕告】〈书〉(of superiors or elders) give explicit instructions (or directions); tell

【谕令】〈书〉order

【谕示】〈书〉(of seniors or elders) instruct

【谕旨】imperial edict

寓 Ⅰ **动** ❶ reside; live: 暂～友人处 *be staying with a friend* ❷ imply; contain: 这个故事～有深意。*This story contains a profound lesson.* or *The moral of the story is profound.* Ⅱ **名** residence; abode: 公寓

【寓教于乐】combine education with recreation; edutainment

【寓居】make one's home in (a place other than one's native place): 他晚年～上海。*He made Shanghai his home in his old age.*

【寓所】residence; abode; dwelling place

【寓言】fable; allegory; parable

【寓意】implied meaning; moral; message; import: ～深刻 *be pregnant with meaning*

【寓于】be contained in; reside in: 矛盾的普遍性即～矛盾的特殊性之中。*It is precisely in the particularity of contradiction that the universality of contradiction resides.*

裕 Ⅰ **形** abundant; plentiful: 富裕 Ⅱ **动** 〈书〉

make (a country or people) rich: 富国～民 *make one's country and people rich*

【裕固族】the Yugur (Yuku) ethnic group, or the Yugurs (Yukus)

【裕如】effortlessly; with ease: 应付～ *handle the situation with ease; be equal to the occasion*

遇 Ⅰ 动 ❶ meet: 我在路上没～着他。*I didn't see him on the way.* / ～雨 *be caught in a rain* ❷ treat; receive: 待遇 Ⅱ 名 chance; opportunity: 机遇

【遇便】when it's convenient; at sb.'s convenience

【遇刺】be attacked by an assassin: ～身死 *be assassinated*

【遇到】run into; encounter; come across: 在路上～一个老同学 *run into an old schoolmate on the way*

【遇害】be murdered

【遇见】meet; come across: ～一位朋友 *meet a friend*

【遇救】be rescued; be saved

【遇难】❶ die (or be killed) in an accident: 他在一次飞机失事中～。*He was killed in an air crash.* ❷ be murdered

【遇事】when anything crops (or comes) up: ～不慌 *be unruffled whatever happens* / ～和群众商量 *consult with the masses when problems arise*

【遇事生风】sow discord whenever possible

【遇险】meet with a mishap; be in danger; be in distress ◇ ～船只 ship in distress; ～信号 (又作'遇难信号') distress signal; SOS

【遇缘】as luck would have it; by chance; by a lucky coincidence

喻 Ⅰ 动 ❶ explain; make clear; inform: ～之以理 *reason with sb.; try to make sb. see reason* ❷ understand; know: 家喻户晓 Ⅱ 名 analogy: 比喻

御 Ⅰ 动 ❶ drive (a carriage): ～者 *carriage driver* ❷ manage; control: ～众 *rule or control the masses* / ～夫(妻) *control one's husband (wife)* ❸ resist; keep out; ward off: 防御 Ⅱ 形 of an emperor; imperial: 御宝

【御宝】imperial seal

【御笔】imperial brush—handwriting or painting of the emperor

【御赐】bestowed by the emperor

【御道】a road for the imperial carriage

【御敌】resist the enemy

【御夫座】[天] Auriga

【御寒】keep out the cold

【御花园】imperial garden

【御驾】imperial carriage: ～亲征。*The emperor personally led the expedition.*

【御览】❶ for the emperor's inspection ❷ books for the emperor's inspection

【御林军】❶ imperial guards ❷ 〈贬〉elite troops or crack units

【御膳】the food of the imperial household ◇ ～房 imperial kitchen

【御侮】resist foreign aggression

【御医】imperial physician; court physician

【御用】❶ for the use of an emperor ❷ serve as a tool; be in the pay of/ ～文人 *hired scribbler; hack writer*

【御苑】imperial garden or park

【御制】made by the emperor or by imperial order

誉 Ⅰ 名 reputation; fame: 名誉 Ⅱ 动 praise; eulogize: ～不绝口 *praise profusely; be full of praise*

【誉满全球】of world renown; famed the world over

愈 Ⅰ 动 ❶ heal; recover; become well: 痊愈 ❷ 〈书〉be better; excel: 彼～于此。*That one is better than this one.* Ⅱ 副 (used in duplicates) the more ... the more ...: ～多～好 *the more the better* / 山路～走～陡。*The mountain path becomes steeper and steeper as you go up.*

【愈合】(of a wound) heal: 伤口很快～了。*The wound healed quickly.*

【愈加】all the more; even more; further: 变得～模糊 *become even more indistinct*

【愈演愈烈】grow in intensity; become increasingly intense

鹬 名 sandpiper; snipe

【鹬蚌相争,渔人得利】when the snipe and the clam grapple, it's the fisherman who stands to benefit—it's the third party that benefits from the tussle

【鹬鸵】another name for 无翼鸟

yuān

鸢 名 [动] kite

【鸢尾】[植] iris

冤 Ⅰ 名 ❶ wrong; injustice: 含冤 ❷ feeling of bitterness; hatred; enmity: 结冤 Ⅱ 动 〈方〉kid; fool; pull sb.'s leg: 我不～你。*I'm not kidding.* Ⅲ 形 bad luck; loss; disadvantage: 白跑一趟,真～! *What bad luck, nothing came of my trip.*

【冤案】a case in which a person is unjustly charged or sentenced; an unjust case

【冤仇】rancour; enmity

【冤大头】a person who spends money wastefully and foolishly; squanderer; wastrel

【冤魂】the ghost of one who was wrongly put to death or was murdered

【冤家】❶ enemy; foe ❷ 〈旧〉(usu. used in dramas or folk songs) one's destined love; sweetheart; lover ◇ ～对头 opponent and foe; ～路窄 enemies are bound to meet on a narrow road—one can't avoid one's enemy (much as one wants to); ～宜解不宜结 better make friends than make enemies

【冤假错案】cases in which people were unjustly, falsely or wrongly charged or denounced; unjust, false and erroneous cases (esp. during the Cultural Revolution): 复查平反～ *re-examine cases involving unjust, false or wrong charges and reverse their verdicts*

【冤气】resentment; rancour: 一肚子～ *be resentful*

【冤情】facts of an injustice

【冤屈】❶ treat unjustly; wrong ❷ wrongful treatment; injustice: 受～ *be wronged; suffer an injustice*

【冤枉】❶ treat unjustly; wrong: 我是～的。*I was wrongly accused. or I am innocent.* / ～好人 *wrong an innocent person* ❷ not worthwhile; not repaying the effort: 在这件小事上,花那么多时间,真～。*It wasn't worthwhile to spend so much time on such a trifle.* / 花～钱 *waste money; not get one's money's worth* ◇ ～路 a longer way; a roundabout way; ～气 unjust treatment; mistreatment

【冤有头,债有主】every injustice has its perpetrator, every debt has its debtor

【冤狱】an unjust charge or verdict; a miscarriage of justice; frame-up: 平反～ *reverse an unjust verdict*

【冤冤相报】injury for injury

鸳

（构词成分）见下

【鸳鸯】❶ mandarin duck ❷ an affectionate couple

【鸳鸯房】❶〈字〉mandarin duck room or apartment ❷〈喻〉room or apartment reserved for newly married couples to rent temporarily before they find their own place: 有了～作为过渡性用房,他俩马上办了婚事。*They got married as soon as they obtained a mandarin duck apartment as their temporary home.*

【鸳鸯楼】❶〈字〉mandarin duck building ❷〈喻〉commercial apartment building specially reserved for newly-weds: 1984 年,首都建成了第一栋向大龄青年出售的～。*The first "mandarin duck building" with flats for sale to late-married couples was completed in Beijing in 1984.*

【鸳鸯座】love seat

渊

Ⅰ名 a deep pool Ⅱ形 deep: ～泉 *a deep spring*

【渊博】broad and profound; erudite: 学识渊博

【渊默】〈书〉profound (or deep) silence

【渊深】profound; deep; erudite

【渊薮】a gathering place of fish or beasts; den; haunt: 盗贼的～ *a den (or haunt) of bandits and thieves* / 罪恶的～ *a hotbed (or breeding ground) of crime; a sink of iniquity*

【渊源】origin; source: 历史～ *historical origins*

yuán

元

Ⅰ形 ❶ first; primary: 元月 ❷ chief; principal: 元首 / 元凶 ❸ basic; fundamental: 元素 Ⅱ名 unit; component: 单元

【元宝】a shoe-shaped gold or silver ingot used as money in feudal China

【元宝铁】[机] V-block

【元旦】New Year's Day

【元古代】[地质] the Proterozoic Era

【元古界】[地质] the Proterozoic Erathem

【元件】element; component; cell: 传输～ *transfer element* / 电光～ *electrooptic cell* / 电路～ *circuit component* / 敏感～ *sensor*

【元老】senior statesman; founding member (of a political organization, etc.)

【元年】the first year of an era or of the reign of an emperor

【元配】first wife

【元气】vitality; vigour: 大伤～ *undermine one's constitution; sap one's vitality* / 恢复～ *regain one's strength (or health, vigour)*

【元器件】components and parts (of an apparatus, etc.)

【元青】black: ～布 *black cloth*

【元曲】❶ Yuan songs ❷ Yuan drama

【元日】the first day of the first lunar month; the lunar New Year's Day

【元首】head of state

【元帅】❶ marshal; (Brit. Army) Field Marshal; (Brit. Air Force) Marshal of the Royal Air Force; (Brit. Navy) Admiral of the Fleet ❷ supreme commander (in ancient times)

【元素】❶ element ❷ [数][化] element: 稀有～ *rare element* / ～分析 *ultimate analysis* ◇ ～周期表 periodic table of elements

【元宵】❶ the night of the 15th of the 1st lunar month ❷ sweet dumplings made of glutinous rice flour (for the Lantern Festival)

【元宵节】the Lantern Festival (the 15th of the 1st lunar month)

【元凶】prime culprit; arch-criminal

【元勋】a man of great merit; founding father: 开国～ *founders of a state*

【元音】[语音] vowel

【元鱼】同〖鼋鱼〗

【元语言】metalanguage

【元月】❶ January ❷ the first month of the lunar year; the first moon

芫

（构词成分）见下——另见 yán

【芫花】lilac daphne

园

名 ❶ an area of land for growing plants: 葡萄～ *vineyard; grapery* / 苹果～ *apple orchard* ❷ a place for public recreation: 动物园 / 公园

【园地】❶ garden plot ❷ field; scope: 扩大文学创作的～ *broaden the scope of literary creation*

【园丁】❶ gardener ❷ school teacher

【园林】gardens; park

【园陵】tombs surrounded by a park; cemetery

【园圃】garden; ground used for growing vegetables, flowers or fruit

【园田】vegetable garden：耕作～化 *garden-style cultivation of farmland*；*intensive cultivation*

【园艺】horticulture；gardening：～家 *horticulturist* ◇ ～学 horticulture；gardening

【园子】orchard or garden：菜～ *vegetable garden*；*vegetable farm*

员 Ⅰ名 ❶ a person engaged in some field of activity：售货员 ❷ member：集体的一～ *a member of the collective* Ⅱ量 (for generals)：一～大将 *an able general*

【员额】specified number of personnel

【员工】staff；personnel：师生～ *teachers, students, administrative personnel and workers*

原 Ⅰ形 ❶ primary；original；former：～计划 *original plan* / ～单位 *the organization* (*or unit*) *one formerly belonged to* / ～有规定 *already existing provisions* ❷ unprocessed；raw：～矿石 *raw ore* Ⅱ动 excuse；pardon：情有可原 Ⅲ名 open country；plain；level：平原 / 草原

【原班人马】the old cast；the former staff

【原版】original edition (of a book, etc.)

【原本】❶ original manuscript；master copy ❷ the original (from which a translation is made) ❸ originally；formerly：他～住在山东。*Originally he lived in Shandong Province.*

【原材料】raw and processed materials：～消耗下降 *a drop in consumption of raw and other materials* / ～工业 *raw and semi-finished materials industries*

【原肠】［动］primitive gut；archenteron

【原虫】［动］protozoon

【原初】originally；formerly；at first：我～不同意，可很快就改变了主意。*At first I didn't agree, but I soon changed my mind.*

【原动力】motive power (or force)；motivity

【原防】［军］place where troops were originally stationed；original station or position (of a unit)

【原封】with the seal unbroken；intact：～退回 *return to the sender a parcel or letter unopened* ◇ ～不动 be left intact；remain untouched

【原稿】original manuscript；master copy

【原告】［法］(in civil cases) plaintiff；(in criminal cases) prosecutor

【原级】［语］positive degree

【原籍】ancestral home：他～广东。*His ancestral home is in Guangdong Province.*

【原价】original price

【原件】❶ original manuscript (of a document)；master copy ❷ the original (from which a replica is made)

【原教旨主义】fundamentalism

【原来】❶ original；former：～的计划 *the original plan* / 他还是住在～的地方。*He still lives in the same place.* ❷ originally；formerly；at first：我～抽烟，现在不抽了。*I used to smoke, but not now.* ❸ as a matter of fact；as it turns out；actually：这～是个骗局。*It turned out to be a fraud.* / ～是你呀！*So it's you.* / 你～是这样的朋友！*So that's the kind of friend you are!*

【原来如此】so that's how it is；so that's what's happened；I see

【原理】principle；tenet：根本的～ *a cardinal principle* / 数学的基本～ *fundamentals of mathematics*

【原谅】excuse；forgive；pardon：我来晚了，请～。*Please excuse me for being late.* / 不能～的错误 *an unpardonable mistake*

【原料】raw material

【原貌】original appearance (of things)：保存～ *keep sth. as it is*

【原煤】raw coal

【原棉】raw cotton：～等级 *grades of raw cotton*

【原木】log

【原任】❶ formerly held the post of ❷ predecessor

【原品】original

【原色】［物］primary colours

【原审】［法］first trial

【原声带】original sound tape

【原生动物】protozoon：～学 *protozoology*

【原生矿物】primary mineral

【原生林】(又作'原始林') primeval forest；virgin forest

【原生生物】protist

【原生植物】protophyte

【原生质】［生理］protoplasm

【原始】❶ original；firsthand：～记录 *original record* / ～资料 *firsthand information* (*or data*)；*source material* ❷ primeval；primitive：～人 *primitive man* / ～森林 *primeval forest*；*virgin forest* / ～细胞 *primordial cell* ◇ ～公社 primitive commune；～股［金］initial public offering；IPO；～积累 primitive accumulation；～群 primitive horde；～社会 primitive society

【原诉】［法］plaintiff's or prosecutor's accusation

【原索动物】protochordate；prochordate

【原糖】raw sugar

【原委】how a thing happened from beginning to end；the whole story；all the details：我来跟你说明事情的～。*I'll tell you the whole story.* / 不明～，妄加评论 *make presumptuous comments out of ignorance*

【原文】❶ the original (from which a translation is made)：我没看过这本书的～。*I have not read the book in the original.* ❷ original text：引用～要加引号。*Put quoted passages in quotation marks.* / ～如此 *sic* / 把抄件跟～核对一下 *check the copy against the original*

【原物】the original thing：～归还 *return the thing borrowed or taken*

【原先】❶ original；former：照～的计划做 *act according to the original plan* ❷originally；formerly；at first：我～以为他不会同意，没想到他居然答应了。*I thought that he would not agree, but to my surprise he said "Yes".*

【原线圈】［电］primary coil

【原形】original shape; the true shape under the disguise: 现～ *show one's true colours; betray oneself* ◇ ～毕露 be revealed for what one is; show one's true colours

【原型】model; prototype

【原盐】crude salt

【原样】❶ the same old way: 照～每月一号付房租。*As usual, rent is paid on the first day of each month.* ❷ original state; previous condition: 几年没见,你还是～,一点不见老。*It's years since I last saw you, but you still look the same as before and haven't aged at all.*

【原野】open country; champaign

【原义】original (or primary) meaning (of a word or phrase)

【原意】meaning; original intention: 这不是我们的～。*This was not our original intention.* or *This is not what we meant.*

【原因】cause; reason: ～和结果 *cause and effect* / 成功的～ *reasons for the success*

【原由】cause; reason

【原油】crude oil; crude: 含硫～ *sour crude* / 低硫～ *sweet crude* / 多蜡～ *waxy crude* / 无蜡～ *wax-free crude* / ～分馏塔 *crude fractionating tower* / ～裂化设备 *crude cracker*

【原原本本】from beginning to end: 我把这件事～讲给他们听了。*I told them the whole story exactly as it had happened.*

【原则】principle: ～问题 *a question (or matter) of principle* / ～分歧 *differences in principle* / 具有高度的～性 *be highly principled; have a strong sense of principle*

【原职】former post

【原址】former address

【原主】original owner (or proprietor)

【原注】original annotation

【原著】original work; original

【原装】intact; unopened; in the original package: ～进口 *imported in the original package*

【原状】original state; previous condition; status quo ante: 恢复～ *restore the status quo ante; restore to the former state*

【原子】atom: 标记～ *labelled atom* ◇ ～尘 fallout; ～弹 atom bomb; atomic bomb; A-bomb; ～动力船 atomic-powered ship; ～反应堆 atomic reactor; atomic pile; ～辐射 atomic radiation; ～核 atomic nucleus; ～价 valence; atomicity; ～键 atomic bond; ～结构 atomic structure; ～量 atomic weight; ～论 atomic theory; atomism; ～能 atomic energy; ～炮 atomic gun; ～时代 atomic age; ～团 atomic group; ～武器 atomic weapon; ～物理学 atomic physics; ～序数 (又作'原子序') atomic number; ～战争 atomic war (or warfare); ～钟 atomic clock

【原罪】[宗](基督教) original sin

【原作】original work; original: 译文保持了～的风格。*The translation reproduces the style of the original.*

袁

名 a surname

【袁头】(又作'袁大头') silver coins minted in the early years of the Republic of China with the head of Yuan Shikai on the obverse side

圆

Ⅰ 形 ❶ round; circular; spherical: ～孔 *a round hole* / ～锉 *round file* / 月～了。*The moon is full.* ❷ tactful; satisfactory: 他这话说得不～。*What he said was not very tactful.* Ⅱ 名 ❶ [数] circle ❷ yuan, the monetary unit of China, equal to 10 jiao or 100 fen ❸ a coin of fixed value and weight: 银圆 Ⅲ 动 make plausible; justify: 圆谎

【圆白菜】common name for 结球甘蓝

【圆材】roundwood; log

【圆场】mediate; help to effect a compromise: 打～ *mediate a dispute; smooth things over*

【圆成】help sb. to attain his aim

【圆唇元音】[语] round vowel

【圆顶】dome: 小～ *cupola*

【圆嘟嘟】(又作'圆敦敦') full and plump; chubby: ～的脸庞 *plump (or chubby) cheeks*

【圆钢】steel strip

【圆工】(又作'圆功') achieve the desired results; complete a project, etc.

【圆骨碌】good and round; rounded

【圆鼓鼓】rounded and bulging: 挺着～的肚子 *with a rounded, bulging belly*

【圆规】compasses: 一个～ *a pair of compasses* / 制图～ *drawing compasses* / 长杆～ *beam compasses*

【圆滚滚】good and round; rounded: ～的石子儿 *rounded pebbles* / ～的乳房 *rounded breasts* / ～的脸蛋儿 *a chubby face* / ～的小肥猪 *a podgy pigling*

【圆号】[音] French horn; horn

【圆和】❶ mediate (a dispute); help to effect a compromise ❷ flexible; accommodating ❸ mellow and full: 她的嗓音～洪亮。*Her sweet and mellow voice carries well.*

【圆乎乎】roundish: ～的脸颊 *plump (or chubby) cheeks* / 两眼睁得～的 *be round-eyed; with one's eyes opened wide*

【圆乎】roundish: 他中等个儿,～脸。*He is of medium height and has a roundish face.*

【圆滑】smooth and evasive; slick and sly: 他这个人太～。*He's a sly customer.*

【圆滑线】[音] slur

【圆谎】patch up a lie

【圆浑】〈书〉❶ (of voice) round and mellow: 这段唱腔流畅而～。*This aria is soft and melodious.* ❷ (of writing) natural and spontaneous

【圆活】❶ flexible; smooth: 说话～ *speak in a tactful way* / 办事～ *be flexible in handling a matter* ❷ mellow and full: 声音～ *a sweet, mellow voice*

【圆寂】[宗] (of Buddhist monks or nuns) pass away; die

【圆锯】[机] circular saw
【圆括号】parentheses; curves (( ))
【圆溜溜】good and round; rounded: ～的眼睛 *round eyes*
【圆颅方趾】round skull and square feet —human being
【圆满】satisfactory: ～成功 *complete success* / ～的答案 *a satisfactory answer*
【圆梦】同〖占梦〗
【圆盘】disc ◇ ～耙 disc harrow; ～犁 disc plough
【圆圈】circle; ring
【圆润】mellow and full: ～的嗓音 *a sweet, mellow voice* / 他的书法～有力。*He writes a round, vigorous hand.*
【圆鲹】[动] round scad
【圆熟】skilful; proficient; dexterous
【圆说】speak in defence of; argue in favour of; defend
【圆通】flexible; accommodating: 他为人～。*He's a very flexible person.*
【圆舞曲】waltz
【圆心】the centre of a circle
【圆心角】[数] central angle
【圆形】round; circular ◇ ～建筑 thoios; rotunda; ～剧场 amphitheatre
【圆凿方枘】like a square tenon for a round mortise—at variance with each other
【圆周】circumference ◇ ～角 [数] angle in a circular segment; ～接缝 [机] circumferential seam; ～率 ratio of the circumference of a circle to its diameter (π); ～运动 [物] circular motion
【圆珠笔】ball-point pen; ball-pen
【圆柱】[数] cylinder ◇ ～根 [数] cylindrical root; ～体 cylinder
【圆锥】circular cone; taper ◇ ～根 [植] conical root; ～花序 [植] panicle; ～曲线 [数] conic section; ～台 [数] frustum of a cone
【圆桌】round table ◇ ～会议 round-table conference; ～面 a detachable round tabletop (which can be put on a square table)
【圆子】〈方〉❶ dumpling (made of glutinous rice flour) ❷ (meat, fish, etc.) ball

援 动 ❶ pull by hand; hold: 援笔 ❷ quote; cite: 援例 ❸ help; aid; rescue: 求援
【援笔】〈书〉take up a pen: ～疾书 *take up a pen and write quickly*
【援兵】relief troops; reinforcements
【援建】provide assistance or aid in construction: 该省承担～非洲4个国家的糖厂。*The province has undertaken to provide assistance for building sugar refineries in four African countries.*
【援救】rescue; save; deliver from danger
【援军】relief troops; reinforcements
【援款】aid fund
【援例】quote (or cite) a precedent: 有例可援。*There's a precedent to quote.*
【援手】〈书〉aid; save; rescue
【援外】foreign aid: ～物资 *materials in aid of a foreign country*
【援引】❶ quote; cite: ～例证 *cite an example* / ～法律条文 *invoke a legal provision* ❷ recommend or appoint one's friends or favourites
【援用】quote; cite; invoke: ～成例 *cite a precedent* / ～条约 *invoke a treaty*
【援助】help; support; aid: 不附带条件的～ *aid with no strings attached* / 技术～ *technical assistance* / 国际～ *international support*

鼋 名 soft-shelled turtle
【鼋鱼】〈口〉soft-shelled turtle

源 名 ❶ source (of a river); fountainhead: 水源 ❷ source; cause: 货源
【源程序】[计] source program
【源代码】[计] source code
【源流】source and course (of a river, etc.); origin and development
【源泉】source; fountainhead; well-spring: 生活是文艺创作的～。*Life is the source of literary and artistic creation.*
【源头】fountainhead; source: 民歌是文学的一个～。*Folk songs are one of the sources of literature.*
【源源】in a steady stream; continuously: 大庆石油通过这条输油管～不断地流往北京。*Through this pipeline, crude oil flows from Daqing to Beijing in a steady stream.* ◇ ～本本 同〖原原本本〗; ～不绝 in an endless stream; continuously; ～而来 come in a steady (or continuous) stream
【源远流长】a distant source and a long stream—of long standing and well established: 我们两国人民的友谊～。*The friendship between our two peoples goes back to ancient times.*

猿 名 ape: 从～到人 *from ape to man*
【猿猴】apes and monkeys
【猿人】ape-man

缘 Ⅰ 名 ❶ reason: ～何到此? *What's your reason for coming here?* ❷ edge; fringe; brink: 外～ *outer fringe (or edge)* / 这个城市处于沙漠南～。*This city is located on the southern fringe of the desert.* ❸ predestined relationship: 姻缘 Ⅱ 介 along: ～溪而行 *walk along the stream*
【缘分】lot or luck by which people are brought together: 咱俩又在一起了，真是有～。*So we're together again. It must be fate.* / 烟、酒跟我没有～。*Smoking and drinking don't appeal to me.*
【缘故】reason; cause: 他这样生气，不知什么～。*I wonder what reason he had for getting so angry.*
【缘木求鱼】climb a tree to catch fish—a fruitless approach
【缘起】genesis; origin: 文章～ *the origins of literary forms*
【缘悭一面】it was never my good fortune to meet him
【缘由】cause; reason

辕 名 shafts of a cart or carriage
【辕马】horse in the shafts; shaft-horse
【辕门】the outer gate of a government office in ancient times
【辕子】〈口〉 shafts of a cart or carriage: 车～ *shafts of a cart*

yuǎn

远 Ⅰ 形 ❶ far away (in time or space); distant; remote: 别走～了。*Don't go far.* / ～在公元十一世纪,中国已使用火药。*Gunpowder was used in China as far back as the 11th century.* / 谁能看得这样～? *Who could have seen so far ahead?* ❷ distant (in relationship): 远亲 Ⅱ 副 by far; far and away: 这个问题～比那个重要。*This problem is far more important than that.* / ～不及 *far inferior to* / ～～超过 *far exceed* Ⅲ 动 keep away from; keep at a distance: 他这个人很危险,你最好～着他一点儿。*He is quite dangerous; you'd better keep away from him.*
【远程】long-range; long-distance ◇ ～登录 [计] remote login; telenet; ～导弹 long-range missile; ～火箭 long-range rocket; ～航行 long (sea) voyage
【远程教育】distance learning
【远处】a distant point or place: 我看见一个人从～走来。*I saw a man coming towards me from a long way off.*
【远大】long-range; broad; ambitious: 眼光～ *be farsighted; have a broad vision* / ～的理想 *lofty ideals*
【远道】a long way: ～而来 *come a long way; come from afar*
【远地点】[天] apogee
【远东】the Far East
【远渡】travel across a vast expanse of water: ～重洋 *travel all the way from across the oceans; travel across the oceans*
【远方】a distant place: ～的来客 *a guest from afar*
【远房】distantly related: ～亲戚 *a distant relative; remote kinsfolk*
【远隔重洋】be separated by vast oceans
【远古】remote antiquity; ancient times: 在～时代 *in remote antiquity*
【远海】distant sea waters
【远航】take a long (sea) voyage; sail to a distant place
【远话】a stranger's words: 近人不说～。*Friends don't speak like strangers.*
【远见】foresight; vision: 有～ *have breadth of vision; be farsighted*
【远见卓识】foresight and sagacity: ～的决策 *a farsighted policy decision*
【远交近攻】befriend distant states while attacking those nearby
【远郊】the outer suburbs; the remoter outskirts of a city
【远近】❶ far and near: ～闻名 *be known far and wide; be widely known* ❷ distance: 不论～我都去。*I'll go no matter how far it is.* / 这两条路～差不多。*The distance is about the same by either road.*
【远景】❶ distant view; long-range perspective; prospect: ～规划 *a long-range plan*
【远客】a guest from afar
【远路】❶ a long way: 走～ *go a long way; take a long journey* ❷ 同〖冤枉路〗
【远虑】foresight; long view
【远门】far away from home: 出～ *travel far away from home; go on a long journey*
【远谋】a long-term plan
【远年】many years ago; of long standing: ～陈酒 *aged wine*
【远期】at a specified future date; forward: ～汇价 *forward rate* / ～外汇 *forward exchange*
【远亲】distant relative (or relation); remote kinsfolk
【远亲不如近邻】a relative far off is less help than a neighbour close by; neighbours are dearer than distant relatives
【远日点】[天] aphelion
【远涉】make a long, arduous journey (esp. across the sea): ～重洋 *travel all the way from across the oceans; travel across the oceans*
【远射程炮】long-range gun
【远摄镜头】❶ film long shot ❷ telephoto lens
【远识】foresight; vision
【远视】[医] long sight; farsightedness; hyperopia; hypermetropia: ～眼镜 *spectacles for long sight; spectacles for the farsighted*
【远事记忆】long term memory (〈反〉'近事记忆')
【远水不解近渴】distant water can't quench present thirst—the aid is too slow in coming to be of any help
【远水救不了近火】distant water won't put out a fire close at hand—a slow remedy cannot meet an urgency
【远台】[体] (乒乓球) far from the table: ～防守 *long defence; far-from-table defence* / ～削球 *off-table chop*
【远眺】look far into the distance (from a high place)
【远图】a long-term plan
【远销】sell goods to distant places: ～海外 *find a good sale overseas; find a market abroad*
【远行】go on a long journey
【远扬】(of fame, reputation, etc.) spread far and wide: 声威～。*His mighty fame spread far and wide.*
【远洋】❶ ocean ❷ of the open sea beyond the littoral zone; oceanic ◇ ～航行 oceangoing voyage; ～货轮 oceangoing freighter; ～客轮(班轮) ocean liner; ～渔业 deep-sea (or pelagic) fishing; ～救助拖轮 oceangoing salvage tug
【远因】remote cause

【远缘杂交】［农］distant hybridization
【远月点】［天］apocynthion
【远在天边，近在眼前】seemingly far away，actually close at hand（said playfully to call attention to sb. or sth. right in front of sb.'s eyes）
【远征】expedition：～军 *expeditionary army*（*or force*）
【远志】❶ great and far-reaching ambition；high aspiration ❷［中］the root of the narrow-leaved polygala（polygala tenuifolia）
【远走高飞】fly far and high；be off to distant parts；flee to faraway places
【远足】pleasure trip on foot；hike；walking tour
【远祖】remote ancestor

yuàn

苑 名 ❶〈书〉enclosed ground for growing trees，keeping animals，etc.；gardens：御苑 ❷〈书〉centre（of art and literature，etc.）：文苑
【苑囿】animal farm（or park）

怨 Ⅰ 名 resentment；enmity：面有～色 *wear a resentful*（*or discontented*）*look* /《清宫～》*The Malice of Empire*（*a play*）Ⅱ 动 blame；complain：这件事～我。*I am to blame for this.*
【怨不得】❶ cannot blame：这件事～老李，都怪我。*Lao Li is not to blame for this. It's all my fault.* ❷ no wonder；so that's why：班车坏了，～他们迟到了。*The bus broke down. No wonder they were late.*
【怨愤】discontented and indignant
【怨怪】blame：他～我多嘴。*He blamed me for not keeping my mouth shut when I should.*
【怨恨】❶ have a grudge against sb.；hate ❷ resentment；grudge；enmity
【怨悔】repent remorsefully
【怨懑】discontented and indignant；resentful
【怨气】grievance；complaint；resentment：出～ *air one's grievances*；*vent one's resentment* / 一肚子～ *be full of complaints*（*or grievances*）
【怨声载道】cries of discontent rise all round；complaints（or voices of discontent）are heard everywhere
【怨天尤人】blame god and man—blame everyone and everything but oneself：唉声叹气，～ *groaning and sighing and cursing fate*
【怨言】complaint；grumble：人们对物价上涨颇有～。*There were a lot of complaints about the rising prices.*

院 名 ❶ courtyard；yard；compound：～里种了几棵枣树。*There are some jujube trees in the courtyard.* ❷ a designation for certain government offices and public places：法院 ❸ college；academy；institute
【院落】courtyard；yard；compound
【院墙】the walls that surround a house
【院士】academician
【院校】institutions of higher learning；colleges，universities and academic institutes：大专～ *universities and technical institutes* / 高等～ *institutions of higher learning*
【院子】courtyard；yard；compound：我们家有个～，孩子们可以在那里玩儿。*Our house has a yard for the children to play in.*

愿 Ⅰ 名 ❶ hope；wish；desire：平生之～ *one's lifelong wish* ❷ vow（made before Buddha or a god）：还愿 Ⅱ 动 be willing；be ready
【愿望】desire；wish；aspiration：她出国进修的～终于实现了。*Her wish to go abroad for advanced studies has at last come true.*
【愿心】a vow made to a god or Buddha
【愿意】❶ be willing；be ready：她～尽力帮忙。*She's willing to help in any way she can.* ❷ wish；like；want：他们～你留在这里。*They want you to remain here.*

yuē

约 Ⅰ 动 ❶ make an appointment；arrange：我想跟王经理～个时间谈谈。*I'd like to make an appointment with Mr. Wang，the manager.* / 我们～好下星期一碰头。*We agreed to meet next Monday.* ❷ ask or invite in advance：请～他来。*Please ask him to come.* / 我已～了王同志。*I've invited Comrade Wang.* ❸ restrict；restrain：约束 ❹［数］reduce：十分之五可以～成二分之一。*Five over ten can be reduced to one over two.* Ⅱ 名 pact；agreement；appointment：立约 Ⅲ 形 ❶ economical；frugal：节约 ❷ simple；brief：～言之 *in brief*；*in a word* Ⅳ 副 about；around；approximately：～五十人 *about fifty people* ——另见 yāo
【约旦】Jordan ◇ ～人 Jordanian
【约定】agree on；appoint；arrange：～会晤地点 *agree on a meeting place* / 在～的时间 *at the appointed time*
【约定俗成】established（or sanctioned）by popular usage；accepted through common practice
【约法】provisional constitution
【约法三章】agree on a three-point law —make a few simple rules to be observed by all concerned
【约访】request to discuss：建立～群众制度。*set up a system of inviting the public to come and discuss issues.*
【约分】［数］reduction of a fraction
【约合】invite to meet together；call together
【约会】❶ arrange a meeting；make an appointment：他们～过我，我没去。*They invited me，but I didn't go.* ❷ appointment；engagement；date：订个～ *make an appointment*
【约集】invite to meet together；call together
【约计】count roughly；come roughly to
【约见】make an appointment to meet（esp. a foreign diplomatic official）；ask for（or request）an

appointment with

【约略】❶ rough; approximate: ～的估计 *a rough (or approximate) estimate* ❷ roughly; approximately; about: 这件事我～知道一些。*I know something about the matter.*

【约莫】(又作'约摸') about; roughly: 现在～有十点钟。*It is about ten now.* / 我们等了～有一个小时的光景。*We waited for an hour or so.*

【约期】❶ fix a date; appoint a time: ～会谈 *fix a date to hold talks* ❷ appointment or engagement; the appointed time: 误了～ *fail to keep the appointment* ❸ the term or duration of an agreement: ～已满。*The contract has expired.*

【约请】invite; ask

【约束】keep within bounds; restrain; bind: 用纪律～自己 *keep oneself within the bounds of discipline*

【约束力】binding force: 本联合声明及其附件具有同等～。*This Joint Declaration and its Annexes shall be equally binding.*

【约数】❶ approximate number ❷ [数] divisor

【约谈】arrange talks

【约言】promise; word; pledge: 遵守～ *keep one's promise (or word)* / 违背～ *break one's*

yuě

哕 Ⅰ [象] the sound of vomiting Ⅱ [动] 〈口〉 vomit; throw up: 她刚吃完药,又都～出来了。*She threw up all the medicine she had just taken.*

yuè

月 Ⅰ [名] ❶ the moon ❷ month: 这孩子才两个～。*The baby is only two months old.* Ⅱ [形] ❶ monthly: 我的～收入为 3000 元。*My monthly income is 3000 yuan.* / ～产量 *monthly output* ❷ full-moon-shaped; round: 月饼

【月白】bluish white; very pale blue

【月白风清】a bright moon and a gentle breeze—a beautiful night

【月半】the 15th day of a month (esp. of a lunar nonth)

【月报】❶ monthly magazine; monthly: 《小说～》 *Short Story Monthly* ❷ monthly report

【月饼】moon cake (esp. for the Mid-Autumn Festival)

【月长石】[矿] moonstone

【月尘】[天] lunar dust

【月初】the beginning of the month

【月底】the end of the month

【月洞门】moon gate

【月度】monthly: ～计划 *a monthly plan*

【月份】month: 上～ *last month*

【月份牌】〈口〉 calendar

【月工】a labourer hired by the month

【月宫】the Lunar Palace (a legendary palace on the moon; also another name for the moon)

【月光】❶ moonlight; moonbeam ❷ 〈方〉 the moon

【月光花】large moonflower (Calonction aculeatum)

【月桂树】laurel; bay tree; bay

【月海】lunar maria

【月黑天】(又作'月黑夜') a moonless night

【月华】❶ moonlight: ～如水 *watery moonbeams; a flood of translucent moonlight* ❷ [气] lunar corona

【月季】Chinese rose

【月经】menses; menstruation; period ◇ ～不调 menoxenia; abnormal menstruation; ～带 sanitary belt (or napkin); ～过多 menorrhagia; excessive menstruation; ～周期 menstrual cycle

【月均】monthly average: ～收入 *monthly average income*

【月刊】monthly magazine; monthly

【月蓝】pale blue

【月老】同〖月下老人〗

【月历】monthly calendar

【月利】monthly interest: ～率 *monthly interest rate*

【月亮】the moon ◇ ～地儿 a place where there is moonlight; moonlit spot; ～门 moon gate

【月轮】full moon

【月门】moon gate

【月面行走】moonwalk

【月末】the end of the month

【月偏食】partial lunar eclipse

【月票】monthly ticket

【月琴】a four-stringed plucked instrument with a full-moon-shaped sound box

【月球】the moon: ～背面 *the far side of the moon* / ～轨道 *lunar orbit* ◇ ～探测 moon exploration; ～学 selenology

【月全食】total lunar eclipse

【月色】moonlight: 西湖～ *the moon over the West Lake*

【月石】[中] borax

【月食】(又作'月蚀') [天] lunar eclipse: 月全食 *total lunar eclipse* / 月偏食 *partial lunar eclipse*

【月尾】the end of the month

【月息】monthly interest

【月下老人】(又作'月下老儿') ❶ the Old Man of the Moon ❷ matchmaker

【月相】[天] phases of the moon (the four chief ones being 朔 new moon, 上弦 first quarter, 望 full moon, and 下弦 last quarter)

【月薪】monthly pay

【月牙】(又作'月芽') 〈口〉 crescent moon

【月岩】moon rock

【月夜】moonlit (or moonlight) night

【月晕】lunar halo

【月晕而风,础润而雨】a halo round the moon means wind; a damp plinth means rain—premonitory signs of future events

【月震】moonquake

【月中】the middle of the month
【月终】the end of the month
【月子】❶ month of confinement after giving birth to a child：她还没出～。*She's still in confinement.* ❷ time of childbirth；confinement：她的～是二月初。*She's expecting her baby at the beginning of February.*
【月子病】puerperal fever

乐 名 music：奏乐 ——另见 lè
【乐池】orchestra pit；orchestra
【乐段】［音］period
【乐队】orchestra；band ◇～指挥 conductor；bandmaster
【乐感】musicality；musical feeling；musical texture；tonal quality：富有～ *musical and sensitive*
【乐句】［音］phrase
【乐控喷泉】fountain display electronically synchronized to music
【乐理】［音］music theory
【乐律】［音］temperament
【乐迷】music lover
【乐谱】music score；music ◇～架 music stand
【乐器】musical instrument；instrument
【乐曲】musical composition；composition；music
【乐师】musician (who performs on a musical instrument)
【乐坛】the musical world；music circles
【乐团】❶ philharmonic society ❷ philharmonic orchestra
【乐舞】a dance with accompaniment
【乐音】musical sound；tone
【乐章】［音］movement

岳 名 ❶ high mountain：五岳 ❷ wife's parents：岳父
【岳父】(又作'岳丈') wife's father；father-in-law
【岳家】wife's parents' home
【岳母】wife's mother；mother-in-law

钥 名 key：锁钥 ——另见 yào

悦 Ⅰ 形 happy；pleased；delighted：大～ *feel very pleased* / ～色 *a pleased look (or expression)* Ⅱ 动 please；delight：悦耳
【悦耳】pleasing to the ear；sweet-sounding：～的音乐 *sweet (or melodious) music* / 歌声～。*The singing is pleasant.*
【悦服】heartily admire
【悦目】pleasing to the eye；good-looking

阅 动 ❶ read；go over：～报 *read newspapers* ❷ review；inspect：阅兵 ❸ experience；pass through：试行已～三月。*Three months have passed since we started to try this out.*
【阅报栏】showcase or bulletin board, erected in the street or parks where newspapers are displayed for the public to read
【阅兵】review troops：～场 *parade ground* / ～典礼 *dress parade* / ～式 *military review；parade*
【阅操】review soldiers at drill
【阅读】read：～杂志 *read magazines*
【阅卷】go over examination papers
【阅览】read ◇～室 reading room
【阅历】❶ see, hear or do for oneself：～过很多事 *have seen much of the world* ❷ experience：～浅 *having little experience；inexperienced*
【阅批】(of leading cadres) review and make written comments and instructions on an official document；read official papers
【阅世】〈书〉see the world：～渐深 *gain more and more experience of life*

钺 名 a battle-axe used in ancient China

跃 动 leap；jump：～上马背 *leap onto a horse* / 一～而起 *get up with a jump；jump up all of a sudden* / ～居世界首位 *leap to first place in the world*
【跃动】move up and down；quiver
【跃进】make (or take) a leap；leap forward：电子工业出现了～的局面。*The electronics industry is developing by leaps and bounds*
【跃居】jump or leap to a higher ranking：～世界前列 *leap into a leading position in the world；leap into the front ranks internationally.*
【跃马】spur the horse on
【跃迁】［物］transition：自发～ *spontaneous transition* / 俘获～ *capture transition* / ～概率 *transition probability*
【跃然】appear vividly
【跃然纸上】show forth in one's writing：义愤之情～。*Righteous indignation shows forth in his writing.*
【跃跃欲试】be eager to have a try；itch to have a go

越 动 ❶ get over；jump over：～墙而逃 *escape by climbing over the wall* ❷ exceed；overstep：～出范围 *overstep the bounds；exceed the limits* / ～出政策界限 *go beyond the bounds of policy* ❸ (of one's voice or emotion) be at a high pitch：清越
【越冬】live through (or survive) the winter ◇～作物 winter crop；overwintering crop
【越发】❶ all the more；even more：两年不见，这姑娘～长得标致了。*I haven't seen the girl for two years, and she's grown prettier than ever.* ❷ (used correlatively with a preceding 越 or 越是) (the more...) the more...：越是性急，～容易出差错。*The more impatient you are, the more mistakes you'll make.*
【越轨】exceed the bounds；transgress：～行为 *impermissible behaviour；transgression*
【越过】cross；surmount；negotiate：～戈壁沙漠 *cross the Gobi Desert* / ～障碍 *surmount obstacles* / ～激流险滩 *negotiate turbulent rivers and treacherous shoals*
【越级】❶ bypass the immediate leadership：～提

出申诉 *bypass the immediate leadership and present one's appeals and complaints to higher levels* ❷ (of personnel promotion) skip a grade or rank：～提升 *promote sb. more than one grade at a time*

【越加】all the more；even more

【越界】overstep the boundary；cross the border

【越境】cross the boundary illegally；sneak in or out of a country

【越橘】[植] cowberry

【越来越…】more and more：越来越好 *get better and better* / 发挥越来越大的作用 *play an increasingly important role*

【越礼】improper；indecorous

【越理】unreasonable

【越南】Vietnam ◇ ～人 Vietnamese；～语 Vietnamese (language)

【越权】exceed (or overstep) one's power or authority；ultra vires

【越位】[体] offside：裁判判进球无效，因为有个球员处在～位置。*The referee disallowed the goal because one of the players was offside.*

【越野】cross-country：～汽车 *cross-country (motor) vehicle* ◇ ～赛跑 cross-country race

【越铀元素】[化] transuranic element

【越狱】escape from prison；break prison：组织～ *organize a jailbreak* ◇ ～犯 prison breaker

【越…越…】the more... the more...：越多越好 *the more the better* / 越战越强 *grow stronger with the fighting* / 风越刮越大。*The wind was blowing harder and harder.*

【越俎代庖】exceed one's functions and meddle in other people's affairs；take sb. else's job into one's own hands

yūn

晕 Ⅰ 形 dizzy；giddy；faint (limited to use in 头晕，晕头晕脑，晕头转向，etc.) Ⅱ 动 swoon；faint：～了过去 *lose consciousness；faint；swoon* ——另见 yùn

【晕倒】fall in a faint；pass out

【晕糊】(又作'晕乎') dizzy；giddy：他才喝了一杯白兰地就～了。*One glass of brandy and he felt dizzy.*

【晕厥】[医] syncope；faint

【晕头晕脑】❶ dizzy；giddy ❷ muddleheaded

【晕头转向】confused and disoriented：这道算题真难，把我搞得～。*This mathematical problem is really difficult；it's got me confused.*

【晕眩】同〖眩晕〗

【晕晕忽忽】❶ dizzy；giddy ❷ muddleheaded

yún

云 Ⅰ 动 〈书〉 say：《诗》～："战战兢兢，如临深渊，如履薄冰。" *The Songs says："In fear and trembling，as if approaching a deep abyss，as if walking on thin ice."* Ⅱ 名 cloud

【云彩】〈口〉 cloud

【云层】cloud layer：在～上面飞行 *fly above the clouds*

【云顶】[气] cloud top

【云端】high in the clouds：飞机从～飞来。*A plane was coming down from behind the clouds.*

【云朵】flaky clouds

【云贵高原】the Yunnan-Guizhou Plateau

【云海】a sea of clouds

【云集】come together in crowds；gather；converge：各地代表～首都。*Representatives from all over the country gathered in the capital.*

【云谲波诡】bewilderingly changeable

【云开见日】同〖开云见日〗

【云量】[气] cloudiness

【云幂】[气] ceiling：～高度 *ceiling height* / ～气球 *ceiling balloon*

【云母】mica：～板岩 *mica-slate* / ～电容器 *mica condenser* / ～片 *mica sheet；sheet mica* / ～片岩 *mica schist；micacite*

【云泥之别】as far apart as clouds and mud—worlds (or poles) apart；a world of difference

【云霓】rain clouds

【云起龙骧】dragons rise as clouds gather—great men come to the fore when opportunity offers

【云气】thin，floating clouds

【云雀】skylark

【云散】disperse like the clouds：旧友～。*Old friends dispersed like the clouds.* ——另见〖烟消云散〗

【云山雾罩】❶ be enveloped in mist；misty ❷ rambling；discursive：他们在～地闲聊。*They were chatting aimlessly.* ❸ dazed；confused；muddled：这人～的，刚说过的事就忘了。*He's all in a muddle and doesn't even remember what he's just said.*

【云杉】[植] dragon spruce (Picea asperata)

【云室】[物] cloud chamber：威耳孙～ *Wilson (cloud) chamber*

【云梯】scaling ladder

【云天】the skies：高耸～ *rising to the skies* / 高峰直插～ *peaks towering into the clouds*

【云图】[气] cloud atlas；cloud chart；cloud picture

【云团】[气] cloud cluster

【云雾】cloud and mist；mist：拨开～见青天 *scatter the clouds and see the blue sky* ◇ ～天 soupy weather

【云霞】rosy clouds

【云消雾散】the clouds melt and the mists disperse—vanish into thin air

【云霄】the skies：响彻云霄

【云烟】cloud and mist；mist

【云涌】like surging clouds—in large numbers；in force：民工从四面八方～而来。*Volunteer workers arrived in force from different parts of the country.* / 才思～ *in a moment of literary effusion*

【云游】(of a Buddhist monk or a Taoist priest) wander about; roam about: ～天下 drift all around the country

【云雨】〈文〉the sport of cloud and rain —sexual intercourse

【云云】〈书〉and so on (used at the end of a direct or indirect quotation, implying that some words of the same purport are left unquoted): 他来信说读了不少新书，颇有心得～。*He wrote to say that he had read several new books and profited greatly from them.*

【云遮雾障】enveloped in mist; blurred; indistinct; hazy

【云蒸霞蔚】(又作'云兴霞蔚')(of scenery) magnificent

匀 Ⅰ形 even: 颜色涂得不～。*The colour is not evenly spread.* Ⅱ动 ❶ even up; divide evenly: 这两份多少不均，再～一～吧。*These two shares are not equal. Please even them up.* ❷ spare: 我们种子比较多，可以～给你们一些。*We've got more seeds than we need. We can spare you some.*

【匀称】well-proportioned; well-balanced; symmetrical: 身材～ *of proportional build* / 字写得～ *write a neat hand*

【匀兑】spare; share: 给某人～一间屋子 *spare sb. a room*

【匀和】(又作'匀乎')〈口〉even; neat; uniform

【匀净】uniform; even; neat: 这块布染得很～。*This cloth is evenly dyed.*

【匀脸】rub powder and paint evenly on one's face

【匀溜】〈口〉of the right size, thickness, consistency, etc.

【匀染】[纺] level dyeing: ～剂 *levelling agent*

【匀实】〈口〉even; neat; uniform

【匀适】even, regular: 打呼声音～ *sound of regular snoring*

【匀速运动】[物] uniform motion

【匀调】even; well-proportioned: 气息～ *even breathing* / 眉眼～ *have regular features*

【匀妥】even; equitable: 分配～ *be evenly (or equitably) distributed*

【匀细】even and fine; even and light: ～洁白的牙齿 *even and fine white teeth* / ～的鼾声 *even and light snoring*

【匀圆】nicely rounded: ～饱满的樱桃 *full and round cherries; plump cherries*

【匀整】neat and well spaced; even and orderly: 他的字写得很～。*His handwriting is very neat.*

芸 名[植] rue

【芸豆】kidney bean

【芸薹】[植] rape

【芸香】[植] rue

【芸芸】numerous; multitudinous

【芸芸众生】all living things; all mortal beings

耘 动 weed: 春耕夏～ *spring ploughing and summer weeding*

【耘锄】hoe (a farm tool)

【耘田】weed the fields

yǔn

允 Ⅰ动 permit; allow; consent: 不～ *refuse to consent* Ⅱ形 fair; just: 公允

【允差】permissible margin of error or disparity

【允承】agree or promise to do sth.; undertake: ～一项任务 *undertake a task*

【允从】consent to; assent to

【允当】proper; suitable

【允诺】promise; consent; undertake: 欣然～ *readily consent*

【允许】permit; allow: 不～任何破坏纪律的现象存在 *permit no breach of discipline* / 这是我国内政，不～任何外来干涉。*This is our internal affair which brooks no outside interference.*

【允许误差】[机] allowable (or permissible) error

【允许载荷】allowable load

【允准】approve; permit; allow

陨 动 fall from the sky or outer space

【陨落】(of a meteorite, etc.) fall from the sky or outer space

【陨灭】❶ fall from outer space and burn up ❷〈书〉meet one's death; perish

【陨石】[天] aerolite; stony meteorite: ～雨 *meteorite shower*

【陨铁】[天] meteoric iron; iron meteorite; siderite

【陨星】[天] meteorite: 石～ *aerolite; stony meteorite* / 铁～ *siderite; iron meteorite* / 石铁～ *siderolite; stony iron meteorite* / ～学 *meteoritics*

殒 动 perish; die

【殒灭】〈书〉meet one's death; perish

【殒命】〈书〉meet one's death; perish

yùn

孕 Ⅰ形 pregnant: 孕妇 Ⅱ名 pregnancy: 有～在身 *be pregnant; be in the family way*

【孕妇】pregnant woman

【孕期】[医] pregnancy; gestation

【孕穗】[农] booting: ～期 *boot stage*

【孕吐】vomiting during pregnancy; morning sickness

【孕育】〈喻〉give birth to; be pregnant with; breed: 黄河流域～了中国古代文明。*The Huanghe valley gave birth to ancient Chinese civilization.* / 局势中～着危险。*The situation is pregnant with grim possibilities.*

【孕震】[地质] tectonic stress; buildup of stress along a fault line that may eventually induce an earthquake: ～构造 *seismic structure*

运 Ⅰ 名 ❶ motion; movement: 运行 ❷ fortune; luck; fate: 幸运 Ⅱ 动 ❶ carry; transport; ship: ~货 *transport* (*or ship*) *goods* ❷ use; wield; utilize: 运笔

【运笔】wield the pen (in writing or painting): 他时而搁笔沉思,时而~如飞。*Now he was lost in thought, his pen laid down; now he was wielding the pen with rapid, vigorous strokes.* / 书法之道在于~。*Calligraphy is the way of the brush.*

【运程】[交通] haul

【运筹】draw up plans; devise strategies ◇ ~学 operational research; operations research

【运筹帷幄】plan strategies within a command tent: ~之中,决胜千里之外 *sit within a command tent and devise strategies that will assure victory a thousand li away*

【运动】❶ motion; movement: ~的物质 *matter in motion* / 行星的~ *the movement of a planet* ❷ sports; athletics; exercise: 室外~ *outdoor sports* / 散步也是一种~。*Walking is also a form of exercise.* ❸ (political) movement; campaign; drive: 竞选~ *election campaign* / 技术革新~ *a drive for technological innovation* ◇ ~病 motion sickness (carsickness, seasickness, etc.); ~场 sports (or athletic) ground; playground; stadium; ~服装 sportswear; ~会 sports meet; athletic meeting; games; ~健将 master of sports; sportsmaster; ~衫 sports shirt; ~神经同〖传出神经〗; ~学 [物] kinematics; ~医学 sports medicine; ~饮料 sportsdrink; ~员 sportsman or sportswoman; athlete; player; ~战 mobile war (or warfare); ~知觉 [心理] consciousness of motion

【运动量】amount of (physical) exercises

【运费】transportation expenses; freight; carriage: 到付~ *freight payable at destination* / ~表 *freight list* ◇ ~单 freight note; ~吨 freight ton; ~付讫 [经] carriage paid; ~率 freight rate; ~免付 carriage free; ~条款 freight clause; ~已付 freight (or carriage) paid; ~预付 freight prepaid; advanced freight

【运河】canal: ~税 *canal dues*

【运价】transport price

【运斤成风】whirl the hatchet with a noise like the wind—an uncanny feat

【运距】(〈略〉全称为'运输距离') load distance hauled; distance carried

【运力】❶ (〈略〉全称为'运输力量') transportation facilities ❷ (〈略〉全称为'运输能力') transport capacity

【运量】freight volume; traffic: 运能和~的矛盾 *gap between transport capacity and the freight volume* / ~较大的工业企业 *industrial enterprises requiring extensive transport services*

【运煤船】coal carrier; collier

【运能】transport capacity; carrying capacity

【运气】(yùnqì) (the art of) directing one's strength, through concentration, to a part of the body

【运气】(yùnqi) fortune; luck: 他~好,提升了。*He had the good fortune to be promoted.*

【运球】[体] (篮球、曲棍球) dribble; rumming ball

【运输】transport; carriage; conveyance: 陆上(水路)~ *land* (*water*) *transport*; *transport by land* (*water*) / 地面(空中)~ *surface* (*air*) *transport* ◇ ~部队 transportation troops; ~船 cargo ship; transport ship; ~队 transport corps (or team); ~方式 modes of transport; ~工具 means of transport; conveyance; ~公司 transport company; ~舰 transport ship; naval transport; ~里程 transport mileage; ~量 freight volume; ~能力 transport capacity; carrying capacity; ~网 transport network; ~业 transport service; carrying trade; transportation

【运输机】❶ [航空] transport plane; air-freighter ❷ [矿] conveyor

【运送】transport; ship; convey: ~物资 *ship* (*or transport*) *goods and materials*

【运算】[数] operation: 四则~ *the four fundamental operations of arithmetic* / 每秒钟~二百万次 *capable of 2,000,000 calculations per second* ◇ ~分析 operational analysis; ~器 [计] arithmetic unit; ~微积分 operational calculus; ~误差 arithmetic error

【运销】(commodity) transportation and sale

【运行】❶ move; be in motion: 列车~表 *train schedule* / 在轨道上~ *move in orbit* / 地球绕太阳~。*The earth revolves round the sun.* / 列车~时,请勿打开车门。*Don't open the door while the train is in motion.* ❷ operate; function: 推动经济~ *keep the economy functioning* ◇ ~机制 operating mechanism; operational mechanism

【运营】(of buses, ships, etc.) run; ply

【运用】use; wield; apply: ~你自己的判断力 *use your own judgment* / 成功地~外国先进经验 *make good use of the advanced experience of foreign countries*

【运用之妙,存乎一心】ingenuity in varying tactics depends on mother wit

【运用自如】handle very skilfully; have a perfect command of

【运载】deliver; carry ◇ ~工具 means of delivery; ~火箭 carrier rocket; launch vehicle; ~技术 delivery technology

【运转】❶ revolve; turn round: 行星绕着太阳~。*The planets revolve round the sun.* ❷ work; operate: 机器~正常。*The machine is running well.* / ~不灵 *not work well*; *be out of order*

【运作】function: 经济~ *functioning of the economy*

晕 Ⅰ 形 dizzy; giddy; faint: 他一坐汽车就~。*He feels dizzy* (*or sick*) *whenever he travels by car.* Ⅱ 名 [气] halo: 日晕 / 月晕 ——另见 yūn

【晕场】have stage fright; feel nervous and dizzy at an examination

【晕车】carsickness: 好~ *be liable to carsickness*

【晕船】suffer from seasickness
【晕高儿】〈方〉feel giddy when on a height
【晕机】suffer from airsickness
【晕针】[中] have a fainting spell during acupuncture treatment

酝〈书〉Ⅰ 动 ferment (wine) Ⅱ 名 wine
【酝酿】❶〈喻〉brew; ferment: 这场大辩论～已久。*This great debate has been brewing for a long time*. ❷ have a preliminary informal discussion; deliberate on: ～候选人名单 *consider and talk over the list of candidates* / 大家先～一下。*Let's have an exchange of views first*.

愠 形〈书〉angry; irritated: 愠色
【愠恼】angry; indignant; furious
【愠怒】be inwardly angry
【愠容】〈书〉angry look; irritated look
【愠色】〈书〉angry look; irritated look: 面有～ *look irritated*

韵 名 ❶ musical (or agreeable) sound: 琴～悠扬。*Sweet music was being played on the lute*. ❷ rhyme: 押韵 / 韵文 ❸ charm: 风韵
【韵白】❶ spoken parts in Beijing opera where the traditional pronunciation of certain words is slightly different from that in current Beijing dialect ❷ rhyming spoken parts in traditional opera
【韵调】musical tone
【韵腹】[语] the head vowel of a final ——另见〖韵母〗
【韵脚】the rhyming word that ends a line of verse; rhyme
【韵律】❶ metre (in verse) ❷ rules of rhyming; rhyme scheme
【韵律操】rhythmic gymnastics
【韵律学】prosody
【韵母】[语音] the final of a syllable
【韵目】rhyme classes (in traditional rhyming dictionaries)
【韵事】❶ literary or artistic pursuits, often with pretence to good taste and refinement ❷ romantic affair
【韵书】(traditional) rhyming dictionary
【韵头】another name for 介音 ——另见〖韵母〗
【韵尾】[语音] the ending of a final ——另见〖韵母〗
【韵味】lingering charm; lasting appeal: 她的唱腔很有～。*Her singing has a special pleasing quality about it*. / 这首诗～很浓。*This poem is charged with meaning and feeling*.
【韵文】literary composition in rhyme; verse
【韵语】rhymes
【韵致】charm; beauty: 水仙另有一种淡雅的～。*The narcissus has a quiet charm of its own*.

熨 动 iron; press: ～衣服 *iron (or press) clothes*
【熨斗】flatiron; iron: 电～ *electric iron*
【熨衣板】ironing board

蕴 动〈书〉accumulate; hold in store; contain
【蕴藏】hold in store; contain: 我国地下～着丰富的矿物资源。*Our country is rich in mineral resources*. / 这部百科全书～着丰富的信息。*This encyclopedia is a vast storehouse of information*. / ～量 *reserves; deposits*
【蕴涵】❶ (又作'蕴含')〈书〉contain: 这个故事虽然很短,但却～着深刻的哲理。*The story, short as it is, contains a profound philosophy*. ❷ [逻] implication
【蕴藉】〈书〉temperate and refined; cultured and restrained: ～的微笑 *a bland smile*
【蕴蓄】lie hidden and undeveloped; be latent

Z

zā

扎 动 tie; bind: ～小辫儿 *tie up one's plaits; plait one's hair; wear one's hair in plaits* / ～一根红头绳 *tie one's plait with a piece of red yarn* / 腰里～一条皮带 *tie a leather belt around one's waist* ——另见 zhā

【扎彩】hang up festoons

【扎制】make sth. by trussing or tying together: ～花圈 *assemble a wreath* / ～风筝 *make a kite*

匝 〈书〉Ⅰ 量 circle; circumference: 绕树三～ *circle a tree three times* Ⅱ 动 surround; encircle; revolve around Ⅲ 形 dense; full: 密密～～ *dense; thick*

【匝月】〈书〉a full month

咂 动 ❶ sip; suck: ～一口酒 *take a sip of wine* ❷ make clicks (of admiration, praise, etc.) ❸ taste (or savour) carefully

【咂嘴】make clicks (of admiration, praise, surprise, etc.)

zá

杂 Ⅰ 形 miscellaneous; sundry; mixed: ～事儿 *miscellaneous affairs* / ～而不乱 *mixed but not confused* / 到会的人很～。*A mixed bag of people attended the meeting*. Ⅱ 动 mix; mingle: 这片苹果树中～有几棵梨树。*There are a few pear trees scattered among these apple trees*.

【杂拌儿】❶ assorted preserved fruits; mixed sweetmeats ❷ mixture; miscellany; medley; hotchpotch

【杂草】weeds; rank grass: ～丛生 *be overgrown with weeds*

【杂处】(of people from different places) live together

【杂肥】miscellaneous fertilizers (e. g. urban refuse)

【杂费】❶ incidental (or miscellaneous) expenses; incidentals ❷ sundry fees (or charges); extras

【杂感】❶ random (or stray) thoughts ❷ a type of literature recording such thoughts

【杂股】[经]miscellaneous share

【杂环】[化] heterocycle; heterocyclic ring: ～化合物 *heterocyclic compound*

【杂烩】❶ a stew of various ingredients; mixed stew; hotchpotch ❷ mixture; miscellany; medley; hotchpotch

【杂活儿】odd jobs: 他在这家餐厅干～挣点钱。*He earns some money by doing odd jobs at the restaurant*.

【杂货】sundry goods; groceries: 日用～ *various household supplies* ◇ ～店(又作'杂货铺') grocery; sundry store; general store

【杂和菜】mixed stew (of leftovers)

【杂和面儿】maize flour mixed with a little soya bean flour

【杂记】❶ jottings; notes ❷ miscellanies (as a type of literature):《西京～》*Miscellany of the Western Capital*

【杂技】acrobatics ◇ ～团 acrobatic troupe; ～演员 acrobat

【杂家】the Eclectics, a school of thought flourishing at the end of the Warring States Period and the beginning of the Han Dynasty

【杂交】[生] hybridize; cross: 苹果与梨～ *cross the apple with the pear* / 通过～改良水稻品种 *improve paddy varieties through hybridization* ◇ ～后代 [生] filial generation; ～水稻 hybrid rice; ～玉米 hybrid (or crossbred) maize; ～育种 crossbreeding

【杂居】(of people of two or more nationalities) live together: 少数民族～地区 *an area inhabited by several minority nationalities*

【杂粮】food grains other than wheat and rice

【杂乱】mixed and disorderly; in a jumble; in a muddle: 抽屉里的东西很～。*The things in the drawer were all in a jumble*.

【杂乱无章】disorderly and unsystematic; confused and disorderly; chaotic: 无意义的、～的议论 *pointless, random talk* / 这篇报告～,文理不通。*This report is just a jumble of words, lacking logic and coherence*.

【杂乱信号】hash (in radio, radar or TV reception)

【杂念】distracting thoughts: 排除～ *banish distracting thoughts from one's mind*

【杂牌】a less known and inferior brand: ～货 *goods of an inferior brand* ◇ ～军 miscellaneous troops; troops of miscellaneous brands

【杂品】(又作'杂件') sundry goods; groceries

【杂七杂八】mixed; assorted; miscellaneous: 刀子、勺子之类～的东西 *a motley assortment of knives and ladles and so on*

【杂散】[物] stray: ～磁场 *stray magnetic field* /

～辐射 *stray radiation*

【杂色】❶ variegated; parti-coloured; motley ❷ an inferior brand

【杂食动物】omnivorous animal

【杂耍】variety show; vaudeville

【杂税】miscellaneous levies

【杂碎】chopped cooked entrails of sheep or oxen

【杂坛】acrobatics circles: ～新秀 *new stars in acrobatics*

【杂文】essay

【杂务】odd jobs; sundry duties

【杂音】❶ noise ❷［电］static ❸［医］murmur: 心脏～ *heart murmur*

【杂院儿】a compound occupied by many households

【杂志】❶ magazine: 订一份～ *subscribe to a magazine* ❷ (often used in book titles) miscellaneous notes; notes: 王念孙《读书～》*Wang Niansun's Miscellaneous Reading Notes* ◇ ～架 magazine rack

【杂质】❶ impurity: ～含量 *impurity content* / ～限度 *limit of impurities* ❷［化］foreign matter (or substance)

【杂种】❶［生］hybrid; crossbreed: ～猪 *crossbred pig* / ～狗 *mongrel dog* ❷〈诋〉bastard; son of a bitch ◇ ～不育性［生］hybrid sterility; ～优势［生］hybrid vigour; heterosis

砸 动 ❶ pound; tamp: 把地基～实 *tamp the foundations solid* / ～了脚 *have one's foot squashed* ❷ break; smash: 碗～了。*The bowl is broken.* / ～核桃 *crack walnuts* / ～碎锁链 *smash the shackles* / 把门～开 *smash (or ram) the door open* ❸〈方〉fail; fall through; be bungled: 考～了 *failed the test* / 事儿办～了。*The job was bungled.* / 戏演～了。*The performance was a fiasco.*

【砸饭碗】smash sb.'s rice bowl—make sb. lose his job; dismiss sb. from his job: 这可砸了我的饭碗了。*Now I've lost my job.*

【砸锅】〈方〉fail; fall through; be bungled

【砸锅卖铁】give away all one has

【砸碎】break into pieces; smash; shatter: 瓶子被～了。*The bottle was shattered to pieces.*

zǎ

咋 副〈方〉how; why: 情况～样? *How are things?* / 你看该～办? *What do you think we should do?* / 你～不去? *Why don't you go?* —— 另见 zhā; zhà

【咋个】〈方〉how; why: 你～没去上学? *Why didn't you go to school?*

zāi

灾 名 ❶ calamity; disaster: 一场大～ *a great calamity* / 去年有～。*There was a natural calamity last year.* ❷ personal misfortune; adversity: 没病没～ *good health and good luck; with one's health all right and luck not bad*

【灾变说】［地质］catastrophism

【灾害】calamity; disaster

【灾患】calamity; disaster: 屡经～ *suffer calamity after calamity*

【灾荒】famine due to crop failures: 去年他老家闹了～。*Famine hit his home district last year.*

【灾祸】disaster; calamity; catastrophe: ～临头。*A great disaster is befalling (or imminent).*

【灾民】victims of a natural calamity

【灾难】suffering; calamity; disaster; catastrophe: ～性的后果 *disastrous consequences* / 避免一场大～ *avert a catastrophe*

【灾难深重】disaster-ridden; calamity-ridden

【灾年】famine (or lean) year

【灾歉】crop failure due to natural disasters: 因～而被免征农业税 *be exempt from agricultural tax because of crop failure*

【灾情】the condition of a disaster: ～严重。*The losses caused by the disaster were serious.*

【灾区】disaster area: 地震～ *earthquake-stricken area* / 旱～ *drought-stricken area* / 水～ *flooded area* / 重～ *severely afflicted area*

【灾星】the star of calamity—sb. or sth. that brings disaster

甾 名［化］steroid

哉 助〈书〉❶ (used in exclamations): 诚～斯言! *How true that is!* ❷ (used with an interrogative word in asking a question or making a retort): 胡为乎来～? *Why has it come?* / 何～? *Why?* or *Wherefore?* / 有何难～? *What's so difficult about it?*

栽 Ⅰ 动 ❶ plant; grow: ～树 *plant trees* / ～花 *grow flowers* ❷ stick in; insert; plant: ～电线杆子 *erect a wire pole* ❸ force sth. on sb.; impose: ～上罪名 *frame sb.; fabricate a charge against sb.* ❹ tumble; fall: ～倒 *fall down* Ⅱ 名 young plant; seedling

【栽跟头】❶ tumble; fall ❷ come to grief; come a cropper: 他非常自负,到头来忘乎所以,栽了跟头。*He was very proud of himself until he overreached himself and came a cropper.*

【栽交】同〖栽跟头〗

【栽培】❶ cultivate; grow: 先进的～技术 *advanced cultivation techniques* / 棉花～ *the culture of cotton* / ～野生植物 *domesticate wild plants* ❷ foster; train; educate: 我们今天的成就离不开老师对我们的～。*We owe our success to the education and training our teachers gave us.* ❸ help advance sb.'s career; patronize ◇ ～品种 cultivar; ～植物 cultivated plant

【栽诬】falsely accuse; slander: 听到对他的种种～,他却能轻装上阵,真不容易。*How hard it must be for him to carry on working in the face of all the slander.*

【栽秧】transplant seedlings (as of tomatoes or eggplants)

【栽养】plant and cultivate：～防风林 *cultivate windbreaks* / 在这条公路两旁～的柳树正茁壮成长。*The willows planted on both sides of the road are growing well.*

【栽赃】❶ plant stolen or banned goods on sb. ❷ frame sb.; fabricate a charge against sb.

【栽植】plant; transplant：在山坡上～了树苗。*The hillside was planted with saplings.*

【栽种】plant; grow

【栽子】young plant; seedling：柳树～ *willow slips* / 桃树～ *peach seedlings*

zǎi

仔 名〈方〉❶ son ❷ young animal; whelp —— 另见 zǐ

宰 动 ❶ govern; rule：主宰 ❷ (in ancient times) warden; prefect ❸ slaughter; butcher：～猪 *butcher pigs* ❹〈口〉overcharge; soak; fleece; rip off：～人 *rip off sb.* / 这不是～人吗? *This is a rip-off.* / 挨～ *be ripped off* / 那家饭馆特～人。*They really fleeced us at that restaurant.*

【宰割】invade, oppress and exploit

【宰杀】slaughter; butcher

【宰牲节】another name for 古尔邦节

【宰相】prime minister (in feudal China); chancellor

【宰相肚里能撑船】a prime minister's heart is big enough to pole a boat in—a great person is large-hearted or magnanimous

载 Ⅰ名 year：一年半载 Ⅱ动 put down in writing; record：～入记录 *record in the minutes; place on record* / 据报～ *according to press reports* / 条约中～明 *be clearly stated in the treaty* ——另见 zài

【载入史册】be written into the annals of history; go down in history

崽 名〈方〉❶ son ❷ young animal; whelp

【崽子】〈讳〉whelp; bastard：狗崽子

zài

再 副 ❶ (for an action yet to take place or contemplated) again; once more; further：我叫他别～来,可他又来了。*I told him not to come again, but here he is again.* / 有工夫,请～来玩。*Please come again whenever you are free.* / 青春不～。*One's youth never returns.* / 良机难～。*Opportunity knocks but once.* ❷ (used before adjectives) more; -er：还有～大点儿的吗? *Have you got a bigger one?* / 声音～大一点。*Still louder, please.* / ～冷的天我也不怕。*I can stand colder weather than this.* / ～好不过了。*It couldn't be any better.* ❸ (used to indicate the continuing of a situation in conditional or suppositional clauses)：～不走我们就赶不上火车了。*We'll miss the train if we delay any longer.* ❹ (for a delayed action, preceded by an expression of time or condition) then; only then：你做完了功课～出去。*Finish your homework before you go out.* / 雨住了～走吧。*Let's leave when the rain stops.* / 这件事等明年～说。*This business can keep till next year.* ❺ in addition; on top of that：到会的有教职员工,～就是学生代表。*Present at the meeting were teachers, administrative personnel, and workers, and also representatives of the students.* ❻ ～…也 (followed by a negative expression) no matter how...still (not)：你～劝他也没有用。*No matter how hard you try, you can never persuade him.* / 他～卖力也升不了职。*No matter how hard he works, he'll never get promoted.*

【再版】❶ second edition ❷〈旧〉reprint; second impression

【再不】〈口〉or else; or：派老王去,～小李也行。*Send Lao Wang, or else Xiao Li.*

【再出口】[经] reexport

【再次】once more; a second time; once again：防止类似事件～发生 *prevent the occurrence of similar incidents*

【再度】once more; a second time; once again：～当选 *be reelected*

【再分配】[经] redistribution

【再会】goodbye; see you again

【再婚】remarry; marry again

【再嫁】(of a woman) remarry

【再见】goodbye; see you again

【再接再厉】make persistent efforts; continue to exert oneself：他们百折不挠,～,终于达到了目的。*The goal has been finally attained through their dauntless and persistent efforts.*

【再进口】[经] reimport

【再就业】re-employment：～服务中心 *re-employment service centre*

【再来一个】encore

【再起】recurrence; resurgence; revival：防止边境冲突～ *prevent the recurrence of border clashes*

【再三】over and over again; time and again; again and again; repeatedly：～再四 *over and over again* / ～考虑 *consider over and over again* / ～嘱咐 *bid or tell again and again*

【再审】❶ review ❷ [法] retrial

【再生】❶ be a second so-and-so (a well-known figure already dead)：他手艺真巧,简直是鲁班～。*His carpentry is really exquisite. He's another Lu Ban.* ❷ [生] regeneration ❸ reprocess; regenerate：～稻 *ratooning rice* / ～纤维素 *regenerated cellulose* / ～橡胶 *reclaimed (or regenerated) rubber* ◇ ～父母 one's second parent (said with gratitude of a person who has saved or spared one's life)；～检波器［无］regenerative detector；～障碍性贫血 aplastic anemia；～之德 the grace of rebirth；one's grateful acknowledgment

【再生产】［经］reproduction

【再说】❶ put off until some time later：这事先搁两天～。*Let's put the matter aside for a couple of days*. / 等他打定了主意～。*Wait until he's made up his mind*. ❷ what's more；besides：现在去找他太晚了，～我路也不熟。*It's too late to go and see him now；besides，I don't quite know the way*.

【再贴现】［经］rediscount

【再投资】［经］reinvest；plough back

【再现】(of a past event) reappear；be reproduced：～在眼前 *reappear before one's eyes* / 使红军过雪山的场面在银幕上～ *reproduce on the screen scenes of the Red Army crossing snowcapped mountains*

【再造】❶ give sb. a new lease of life ❷ restore lost limbs or any other body part implants made from macro-molecular materials：乳房～技术 *breast restructuring technique*

【再则】〈书〉moreover；furthermore；besides

【再者】〈书〉moreover；furthermore；besides

在 Ⅰ **动** ❶ exist；be alive：问题还～，并没有解决。*The problem still exists*. *It's not solved yet*. / 他父亲还～，母亲早就不～了。*His father is still alive*，*but his mother passed away long ago*. ❷ be at，in or on (a place)：你去那儿找他，他准～。*Go and see him*；*he must be there*. ❸ depend on；rest with：去不去～你自己。*It's up to you whether you go or not*. / 收不收他～学校领导。*Whether to admit him or not rests with the school authorities*. ❹ lie in；consist in：我们的希望～青年一代。*Our hopes lie in the younger generation*. / 这首诗妙～含蓄而不明言。*The appeal of this poem lies in suggestion rather than direct statement*. ❺ join or belong to an organization；be a member of an organization：～组织 *belong to a certain organization* ❻ be on the job or at the post：在职 Ⅱ **介** at，in，or on (a place or time)：阳光照射～水面上。*The sunlight fell on the water*. / 狗～地上打滚儿。*The dog rolled on the ground*. / ～我看来 *in my opinion*；*as I see it* / ～理论上 *in theory*；*theoretically* Ⅲ **副** (used to indicate action in progress)：他～看电视。*He's watching TV*. / 他～干什么？—他还～睡觉呢。*What's he doing*？—*He's still sleeping*. / 她～游泳。*She is swimming*.

【在案】be on record：记录～ *be put on record*；*be a matter of record* / 声明～ *have a statement placed on record*

【在编】(of personnel) be on the permanent staff；be on the regular payroll：～教师 *full-time faculty* / ～人员 *personnel on the permanent staff*；*personnel on the regular payroll*

【在场】be on the scene；be on the spot；be present：当时我没～。*I wasn't there at the time*.

【在岗】be at one's post；on duty：～警察 *policeman on duty*

【在行】be expert at sth.；know a job，trade，etc. well：他打草鞋很～。*He's good at weaving straw sandals*. / 她对计算机很～。*She knows a lot about computers*.

【在乎】❶ depend on；rest with：干不干～你自己。*It's up to you whether you do it or not* ❷ lie in；consist in：背景的作用～衬托。*The function of a background is to set off*. ❸ (usu. used in the negative) care about；mind；take to heart：难道你还～这几个钱？*Surely you won't grudge such a small sum*. / 人家会说你，你～不～？*Don't you care what people will say*？

【在即】near at hand；shortly；soon：完工～ *will soon be completed*；*be nearing completion* / 毕业～ *will soon be graduating* / 成功～。*Success is in sight*.

【在家】❶ be at home；be in：你爸～吗？*Is your father in*？/ 我们让她～好好休息。*We told her to stay home and have a good rest*. ❷ have not renounced the family and become a monk or nun：～人 *layman* ◇ ～办公 telecommuting

【在建】under construction：～项目 *projects under way*

【在劫难逃】if you're doomed，you're doomed；there's no escape

【在理】reasonable；sensible；right：这话说得～。*That's a perfectly reasonable statement*. / 她说得～，我当然听她的。*She's right*，*so of course I'll do what she says*.

【在内】included：邮费～ *postage included*

【在世】be living：他～的时候 *in his lifetime*

【在所不辞】will not refuse under any circumstances；will not hesitate to

【在所不惜】will not grudge；will never balk at

【在所难免】can hardly be avoided；be unavoidable：本词典虽非草率之作，但错误仍～。*This dictionary*，*despite the care exercised in compiling it*，*cannot in the nature of things be free from error*.

【在逃】［法］has escaped；be at large ◇ ～犯［法］escaped criminal；criminal at large；fugitive

【在天之灵】sb.'s soul in heaven (said when thinking fondly of a dead person)

【在外】excluded：这是饭钱，服务费～。*That is the price of the meal exclusive of service charge*.

【在望】❶ be visible；be in sight；be in view：山头隐隐～。*The mountain top was dimly visible*. ❷ will soon materialize；be in sight；be in the offing：胜利～。*Victory is in sight*.

【在位】❶ be on the throne；reign ❷ be at one's post

【在握】be in one's hands；be within one's grasp；be under one's control：大权～ *with power in one's hands* / 胜利～。*Victory is within grasp*.

【在下】〈谦〉I：～看来 *in my humble opinion*

【在先】(又作'在前') formerly; in the past; before
【在线】[计](又作'联机') on-line: ～服务网 *on-line service network*
【在心】feel concerned; mind; be attentive: 这事儿请您在点儿心。*Please keep an eye on the matter.*
【在学】be at school
【在押】[法] be under detention; be in custody; be in prison ◇ ～犯[法] criminal in custody; prisoner
【在野】not be in office; be out of office ◇ ～党 a party not in office
【在意】(usu. used in the negative) take notice of; care about; mind; take to heart: 这些小事他是不会～的。*He won't take such trifles to heart.*
【在业】employed; having a job: 不论在全民所有制单位、集体所有制单位工作或从事个体劳动,都应视为～人口。*Anyone employed by state or collective enterprises or self-employed should count as part of the working population.*
【在于】❶ depend on; rest with; be determined by: 最后怎么决定～你。*The final decision rests with you.* ❷ lie in; consist in: 战争的目的～消灭战争。*The aim of war is to eliminate war.* / 这项工程的问题不～进度,而～质量。*The question of this project is one not of speed but of quality.*
【在职】be on the job; be at one's post: ～训练 *in-service training; on-the-job training* / ～期间 *during one's tenure of office* ◇ ～干部 cadres at their posts; cadres at work; ～无业者 idled employee (from overstaffing, or from improved efficiency); ～研究生 cadres admitted to a postgraduate programme; ～总统 incumbent president
【在座】be present (at a meeting, banquet, etc.): ～的还有几位归国华侨。*Among those present were a few returned overseas Chinese.* / 有客人～,她没好意思说。*She was too embarrassed to bring it up in front of the guest.*

载 Ⅰ 动 ❶ carry; hold; be loaded with: 宇宙飞船正把他们～向月球。*The spaceship was carrying them to the moon.* ❷ be filled with: 风雪～途。*Whirling snow swept over the road.* Ⅱ 连 〈书〉 and; as well as; at the same time: ～笑～言 *talking and laughing* ——另见 zǎi
【载波】carrier wave; carrier: 三路～ *three-channel carrier* / ～电报 *carrier telegraphy* / ～电话机 *carrier telephone* / ～电流 *carrier current* / ～抑制 *carrier suppression*
【载歌载舞】festively singing and dancing: 人们～热烈欢迎贵宾。*Singing and dancing, people gave the distinguished guests a warm welcome.*
【载荷】load
【载货】carry cargo (or freight): ～吨位 *cargo tonnage* / ～甲板 *cargo deck* / ～容积 *cargo carrying capacity*
【载客】carry passengers
【载流子】[电] carrier; charge carrier
【载频】[无] carrier frequency: ～放大器 *carrier amplifier* / ～振荡器 *carrier oscillator*
【载人飞行器】manned vehicle
【载体】❶ [化] carrier: 催化剂～ *catalyst carrier* ❷ vehicle; medium: 语言是表达思想的工具,是信息的～。*Language is a vehicle for ideas and information.*
【载途】❶ encounter during a journey (snow, heavy wind, difficulties, etc.): 风雪～ *journey through a snow storm* ❷ route: 缩短～时间 *shorten the route*
【载誉】win honor or award: 代表团～而归。*The delegation returned with many honors.*
【载运】convey by vehicles, ships, etc.; transport; carry: 本市公共汽车每天～乘客十万左右。*The city buses carry about 100,000 passengers a day.*
【载重】load; carrying capacity: 这辆卡车～多少? *What's the carrying capacity of this truck?* ◇ ～表尺 deadweight scale; ～吨位 deadweight tonnage; ～量 loading capacity; deadweight capacity (of a ship, etc.); ～汽车 lorry; truck; ～线 load line; load waterline; ～线标志 load line mark; freeboard mark; Plimsoll mark
【载舟之水足以覆舟】The water that bears the boat is the same that swallows it.

zān

糌 名 (构词成分) 见下
【糌粑】zanba, roasted qingke barley (青稞) flour, a staple food of the Zang nationality
簪 Ⅰ 名 hairpin: 碧玉～ *emerald hairpin* Ⅱ 动 wear in one's hair: ～花 *wear flowers in one's hair*
【簪子】hair clasp

zán

咱 代 ❶ we or us (including both the speaker and the person or persons spoken to): ～班的人呢? *Where are our classmates?* ❷ 〈方〉 I or me: ～不会说英语。*I don't speak English.*
【咱们】❶ we or us (including both the speaker and the person or persons spoken to): ～商量一下。*Let's talk it over.* / ～三个 *the three of us* ❷ 〈方〉 I or me: ～是个大老粗,说话只会直来直去。*As I'm an uneducated person, I can only put this bluntly.* ❸ 〈方〉 you: ～别哭,妈出去一会儿就回来。*Don't cry, Mom will be back in a little while.*

zǎn

攒 动 accumulate; hoard; save: ～钱 *save (or scrape) up money* / 他把～的钱都买了书。*He spent all his savings on books.* ——另见 cuán

趱 动 ❶〈旧〉hurry (or rush) through：紧～了一程 *rush through one part of the journey* ❷ urge；hasten：～马向前 *urge on a horse*

zàn

暂 Ⅰ 形 of short duration：短暂 Ⅱ 副 temporarily；for the time being；for the moment：～别 *temporary separation* / ～不答复 *put off replying* / ～代 *act for sb.* / ～住 *stay temporarily* (*at a place*) / 工作～告一段落。*The work has been brought to a temporary close.*

【暂定】arranged for the time being；tentative；provisional：～议程 *tentative agenda* / ～办法 *provisional measures*；*tentative measures*

【暂缓】postpone；put off；defer：～成行 *postpone one's trip* / ～作出决定 *put off* (*or defer*) *making a decision*

【暂记账】suspense account

【暂且】for the time being；for the moment：讨论～告一段落吧。*Let's stop the discussion for the time being.*

【暂缺】❶ (of a post) be left vacant for the time being ❷ (of a commodity) be out of stock at the moment

【暂时】❶ temporary；transient：～的需要 *temporary needs* / ～现象 *transient phenomenon* ❷ temporarily；for the time being；for the moment：这事～就这样定了吧。*Let's make it a tentative decision.* / 他～来不了。*He can't come right away.*

【暂停】❶ suspend：～付款 *suspend payment* / 会议～，明天继续举行。*The meeting is adjourned till tomorrow.* ❷ sports time-out：要求～ *ask for time-out*

【暂行】provisional；temporary；interim：～条例 *provisional* (*or interim*) *regulations* / ～规定 *interim* (*or temporary*) *provisions* / 安理会～议事规则 *Provisional Rules of Procedure of the Security Council*

錾 Ⅰ 动 engrave on gold or silver；carve；chisel：～字 *engrave characters* / ～花 *carve flowers or patterns* Ⅱ 名 engraving tool；chisel

【錾刀】(engraver's) burin；graver

【錾子】chisel (for cutting stone)

赞 Ⅰ 动 ❶ support；favour；assist：赞助 ❷ praise；commend：盛赞 Ⅱ 名 eulogy：像～ *an inscription eulogizing the subject of a portrait* /《天安门～》*Ode to Tian An Men*

【赞比亚】Zambia ◇ ～人 Zambian

【赞不绝口】be profuse in praise；be full of praise

【赞成】❶ approve of；favour；agree with；endorse：咱们明天去郊游，你～吗？*How about going on an outing tomorrow?* / 我完全～。*I'm all for it.* / 他最不～你们这样搞。*He doesn't like the way you do it at all.* ❷〈书〉help sb. accomplish sth. ◇ ～票 affirmative vote

【赞服】appreciate；admire：～地点点头 *nod in appreciation*

【赞歌】song of praise；paean：一曲民族团结的～ *a paean of national solidarity*

【赞夸】praise；commend：～某人勤奋 *praise sb. for their diligence*

【赞美】praise；eulogize：他的大公无私受到人们的～。*He was praised for his selflessness.* ◇ ～诗 (又作'赞美歌')［宗］(基督教) hymn；psalm

【赞赏】appreciate；admire：对这一友好行动表示～ *express appreciation for this friendly act*

【赞颂】extol；eulogize；sing the praises of

【赞叹】gasp in (or with) admiration；highly praise：演员们的高超演技令人～。*People gasped with admiration at the superb skill of the performers.*

【赞同】approve of；agree with；endorse：这一主张得到普遍的～。*This proposition met with general approval* (*or acceptance*). / 我们～这项决议。*We subscribe to the resolution.*

【赞许】speak favourably of；praise；commend：值得～ *deserve commendation*；*be commendable*；*be worthy of praise*

【赞扬】speak highly of；praise；commend：他们的良好体育作风博得广泛的～。*Their fine sportsmanship won widespread acclaim.*

【赞谀】extravagant, exaggerated praise：老教授告诫他要经得住～，架得住批评。*The old professor cautioned him to hear both lavish praise and criticism with equanimity.*

【赞语】words of praise；praise

【赞誉】praise；acclaim；commend：这个厂的产品质量赢得了用户的～。*The factory has been commended by the consumers for the high quality of its products.*

【赞助】support；assistance：这次音乐会得到了多家公司的～。*The concert was under the auspices of various companies.*

zāng

赃 名 ❶ stolen goods；booty；spoils：分赃 ❷ bribes：贪赃

【赃官】a corrupt official

【赃款】money stolen, embezzled or received in bribes；illicit money

【赃物】❶ stolen goods；booty；spoils ❷ bribes

脏 形 dirty；filthy：～衣服 *dirty* (*or soiled*) *clothes*；*dirty linen* / ～水 *filthy water*；*slops*；*sewage* / 别把桌布弄～了。*Don't dirty the tablecloth.* ——另见 zàng

【脏病】popular name for 性病

【脏话】obscene (or dirty, foul) language；obscenities：他用～骂人。*He shouted obscenities at someone.*

【脏乱】(of a place) dirty and messy

【脏钱】〈口〉ill-gotten money
【脏土】rubbish；garbage
【脏污】❶ dirty：～的手 *dirty hand* / ～的思想 *dirty mind* ❷ stain；soil：与他这种人讲话，我还怕～了我的嘴呢。*By speaking to someone like him I shall only be fouling myself.*
【脏字】obscene word；swearword；dirty word：说话别带～。*Don't swear.*

臧 形〈书〉good；right
【臧否】〈书〉pass judgment (on people)：～人物 *pass judgment on people*

zàng

脏 名 internal organs of the body，usu. referring to the heart，liver，spleen，lungs and kidneys；viscera：心脏 ——另见 zāng
【脏器】internal organs of the body；viscera

葬 动 bury；inter：他～在西山。*He was buried in the Western Hills.*
【葬礼】funeral (or burial) rites；funeral
【葬身】be buried：～大海 *lose one's life in the sea*；*be drowned* ◇ ～鱼腹 become food for the fishes；be swept to a watery grave；be drowned
【葬送】ruin；spell an end to：封建婚姻制度～了她一生的幸福。*The feudal marriage system condemned her an unhappy married life.*
【葬仪】funeral：繁杂的～ *elaborate funeral rite*

藏 名 ❶ storing place；depository：宝藏 ❷ Buddhist or Taoist scriptures ❸〈略〉见〖西藏〗❹ the Zang ethnic group——另见 cáng
【藏传佛教】Tibetan Buddhism
【藏旱獭】Himalayan marmot
【藏红花】❶［植］saffron crocus (Crocus sativus) ❷［中］saffron
【藏蓝】purplish blue
【藏青】dark blue
【藏医】❶ Tibetan medicine ❷ physician practicing traditional Tibetan medicine
【藏族】the Zang (Tibetan) ethnic group or the Zangs (Tibetans)

zāo

遭 Ⅰ 动 meet with (disaster，misfortune，etc.)；suffer：几～挫折 *suffer repeated setbacks* / 惨～杀害 *be murdered in cold blood*；*be brutally killed* / ～人白眼 *be treated with disdain* / 你是～他骗了。*You have been taken in by him.* Ⅱ 量 ❶ round：用绳子绕两～ *wind the string around twice* ❷ time；turn：在这么多人面前讲话，我还是头一～。*This is the first time I have ever spoken to such a big audience.* / 一～生，两～熟。*Strangers at first meeting become familiar at the next.*
【遭到】suffer；meet with；encounter：～失败 *suffer (or meet with) defeat* / ～拒绝 *meet with refusal*；*be turned down*
【遭逢】meet with；come across；encounter：～盛世 *live in prosperous times* / ～不幸 *suffer misfortune*
【遭际】〈书〉❶ circumstances；lot ❷ meet with；encounter；run up against：～艰危 *be confronted with difficulties and dangers*
【遭劫】meet with catastrophe
【遭难】meet with misfortune；suffer disaster
【遭受】suffer；be subjected to；sustain：～损失 *sustain losses* / ～水灾 *be hit by floods*
【遭殃】suffer disaster；suffer
【遭遇】❶ meet with；encounter；run up against：～不幸 *meet with misfortune*；*have hard luck* ❷ (bitter) experience；(hard) lot：他后来的～我就不知道了。*I don't know what became of him later.* ◇ ～战 meeting engagement；encounter (action)；contact battle
【遭灾】be hit by a natural calamity
【遭罪】endure hardships，tortures，rough conditions，etc.；have a hard time

糟 Ⅰ 名 distillers' grains；grains Ⅱ 动 be pickled with grains or in wine：～鱼 *fish pickled with grains or in wine*；*pickled fish* Ⅲ 形 ❶ rotten；poor：这案板～了。*The chopping board is rotten.* / 他身体很～。*He is in very poor health.* ❷ in a wretched (or terrible) state；in a mess：把事情搞～了 *make a mess of sth.* / ～了，饭糊啦！*Damn it! The rice is burning!*
【糟糕】〈口〉how terrible；what bad luck；too bad：～，我把钥匙锁在屋里了。*Oh，no，I've locked the key in the room!* / 真～，误了火车啦！*What bad luck! We've missed the train.*
【糟行】(又作'糟坊') distiller
【糟践】〈方〉❶ waste；ruin；spoil：别～粮食。*Don't waste grain.* ❷ insult；trample on；ravage ❸ violate (a woman)；rape
【糟糠】distillers' grains，husks，chaff，etc.—foodstuffs for the poor
【糟糠之妻】the wife of one's "chaff and husks" days—a wife who has shared her husband's hard lot ◇ ～不下堂 the wife of one's "chaff and husks" days shall never go down from the hall；a wife who has shared her husband's hard lot must never be cast aside
【糟粕】waste matter；dross；dregs
【糟蹋】(又作'糟踏') ❶ waste；ruin；spoil：～粮食 *waste grain* ❷ insult；trample on；ravage：说话可不要这样～人。*You shouldn't talk about anyone like that.* ❸ violate (a woman)；rape
【糟心】vexed；annoyed；dejected：事情搞得这样，真～。*I'm really vexed (or It's a damned nuisance) things have turned out this way.*

záo

凿 Ⅰ 名 chisel Ⅱ 动 cut a hole；chisel or dig：～

一个窟窿 *bore a hole* / ～山劈岭 *tunnel through mountains and cut across ridges* / ～冰 *make a hole in the ice* / 把船～沉 *scuttle the ship* Ⅲ 形 〈书〉certain; authentic; irrefutable: 确凿

【凿井】❶ dig (or sink, bore) a well ❷［矿］shaft sinking; pit sinking: 冻结法～ *freeze sinking*

【凿空】〈书〉forced; farfetched: ～之论 *a farfetched argument*

【凿密】［机］caulking

【凿死理儿】〈方〉obstinate; stubborn; dogged

【凿岩】［矿］(rock) drilling: ～机 *rock drill*

【凿子】chisel

zǎo

早 Ⅰ 名 (early) morning: 从～到晚 *from morning till night* Ⅱ 副 ❶ long ago; as early as; for a long time: 我～就想来看你了。*I've been wanting to see you for a long time.* / ～在二十世纪初 *as early as the beginning of the twentieth century* ❷ early; in advance; beforehand: ～两天我还看见他的。*I saw him a couple of days ago.* / ～知如此,我就不回去了。*If I'd known this beforehand I would not have gone back.* / 电影离开演还～哩。*It's still quite a while before the film starts.*

【早安】good morning

【早班】morning shift: 上～ *be on the morning shift*

【早餐】breakfast

【早操】morning (setting-up) exercises

【早茶】morning tea

【早产】［医］premature delivery

【早场】morning show (at a cinema, theatre, etc.)

【早车】morning train or coach

【早晨】(early) morning

【早春】early spring; early in spring

【早稻】early (season) rice

【早点】(light) breakfast

【早饭】breakfast

【早慧】〈书〉(of a child) precocious

【早婚】marry too early: ～妨碍工作和学习。*Marrying too early hinders one's work and study.* ◇～早育 early marriage, early birth (discouraged in China for the sake of population control)

【早年】one's early years

【早期】early stage; early phase; early days; initial stage: ～作品 *sb.'s early works; the works of sb.'s earlier period* / ～食道癌 *early stage carcinoma of the esophagus*

【早起】get up early; rise early

【早秋】early autumn; early in autumn

【早日】at an early date; early; soon: 请～答复。*Your early reply is requested.* or *Please reply at your earliest convenience.* / 祝你～恢复健康。*I hope you'll get well soon.* or *I wish you a speedy recovery.* / ～完工 *complete the project as soon as possible*

【早上】(early) morning: ～好。*Good morning.*

【早市】❶ morning market ❷ morning business: 本店～供应豆浆。*We sell soya-bean milk in the morning.*

【早熟】❶［生理］precocity: ～的孩子 *a precocious child* ❷ early-maturing; early-ripe: ～品种 *early-maturing variety; early variety*

【早衰】［医］premature senility (or decrepitude); early ageing

【早霜】early frost

【早退】leave earlier than one should; leave early

【早晚】❶ morning and evening: ～各服一丸 *take one pill in the morning and one in the evening* ❷ sooner or later: 他～得去。*He'll have to go there sooner or later.* / 他～要栽跟头。*One of these days he will come a cropper.* ❸ time: 他一清早就走了,这～多半已经到家了。*He left early in the morning and should be home by now.* ❹〈方〉some time in the future; some day: 你～上城里来,到我们这里坐坐。*Drop in on us when you come to town.*

【早先】previously; before; in the past: 他～是中国驻悉尼总领事。*He was previously Chinese consul general in Sydney.* / 我～没见过他。*I haven't seen him before.*

【早泄】［医］premature ejaculation

【早已】long ago; for a long time: 他～打定主意了。*He made up his mind long ago.* / 你要的东西,我～给你买来了。*I've already bought all the things you want.*

【早早儿】as early as possible; well in advance: 既然要办,就～办。*Since we've decided to do it, let's do it as soon as possible.*

枣 名 jujube; (Chinese) date; tsao

【枣红】purplish red; claret

【枣泥】jujube paste

【枣树】jujube tree

【枣椰】date palm

【枣子】〈方〉Chinese date

蚤 名 flea: 跳蚤

澡 名 bath: 洗澡

【澡盆】bathtub

【澡堂】(又作'澡堂子') public baths; bathhouse

【澡塘】❶ common bathing pool (in a bathhouse) ❷ 同〖澡堂〗

藻 名 ❶ algae ❷ aquatic plants ❸ literary embellishment: 辞藻

【藻井】［建］sunk panel; caisson ceiling

【藻类学】algology: ～家 *algologist*

【藻类植物】algae

zào

灶 名 ❶ kitchen range; cooking stove ❷ kitchen; mess; canteen: 学生～ *students' dining room (or canteen)*

【灶间】〈方〉kitchen
【灶具】〈方〉cooking utensils
【灶君】同〖灶神〗
【灶神】kitchen god
【灶台】the top of a kitchen range
【灶膛】chamber of a kitchen range
【灶头】〈方〉kitchen range；cooking stove
【灶王爷】同〖灶神〗

皂 Ⅰ形 black：～鞋 *black shoes* Ⅱ名 ❶ yamen runner ❷ soap：香皂
【皂白】black and white—right and wrong：～不分 *make no distinction between right and wrong*
【皂化】［化］saponification：～剂 *saponifier*
【皂荚】（又作'皂角'）［植］Chinese honey locust
【皂片】soap flakes
【皂素】（又作'皂苷'）saponin
【皂洗机】［纺］soaper：平幅～ *open soaper*

造 Ⅰ动 ❶ make；build；create：～舆论 *create* (*or prepare*) *public opinion* / ～预算 *make* (*or draw up*) *a budget* / ～表 *draw up a form or list* / ～册 *compile a register* ❷ invent；cook up；concoct：～假账 *cook accounts* ❸ train；educate：深造 Ⅱ名 ❶［法］one of the two parties in a legal agreement or a lawsuit：两～ *both parties* (*in a lawsuit*) ❷〈方〉crop：早～ *early crops* / 一年三～ *three crops a year* ❸ achievements；attainments：造诣
【造币厂】mint (a place where money is made)
【造成】create；cause；give rise to；bring about：～既成事实 *bring about a fait accompli* / ～巨大损失 *cause enormous losses* / ～假象 *put up a facade*；*create a false impression*
【造船】shipbuilding ◇ ～厂 shipyard；dockyard；～工业 shipbuilding industry
【造次】〈书〉❶ hurried；hasty：～之间 *in one's hurry*；*in a moment of haste* ❷ rash；impetuous：～行事 *act rashly*
【造反】rise in rebellion；rebel；revolt
【造访】〈书〉pay a visit (or call)；call on：登门～ *call at sb.'s house*；*pay sb. a visit*
【造福】bring benefit to；benefit：～于人类 *bring benefit to mankind* / 为后代～ *benefit future generations*
【造化】〈书〉❶ the Creator；Nature；Creation：夺天地～之功 *rob Heaven and Earth of their creative powers* ❷ good luck；good fortune：有～ *be born under a lucky star*；*be lucky* / 好～！*What luck*！/ 真是天大的～！*What a stroke of good fortune*！
【造假】manufacture fake products；forge；counterfeit
【造假账】draw up false accounts
【造价】cost (of building or manufacture)：这种桥～比较低。*It costs less to build this kind of bridge.*
【造就】❶ bring up；train：～一代新人 *bring up a new generation* / ～良好的社会风气 *foster high standard of social conduct* ❷ achievements；attainments (usu. of young people)
【造句】make a sentence：～练习 *a sentence-making exercise*
【造块】［冶］agglomeration
【造林】afforestation：～面积 *afforestation* (*or afforested*) *area* ◇ ～学 silviculture
【造陆运动】［地理］epeirogenic (or epeirogenetic) movement；epeirogeny；epeirogenesis
【造孽】［宗］(佛教) do evil；commit a sin
【造山带】［地理］orogenic zone
【造山运动】［地理］orogenic movement；orogeny；orogenesis
【造物】the divine force that created the universe；Nature ◇ ～主［宗］(基督教) God；the Creator
【造像】statue
【造型】❶ modelling；mould-making：这些古代工艺品～优美。*These ancient art objects are beautifully shaped.* ❷ model；mould ❸［机］moulding：干砂～ *dry sand moulding* / 潮砂～ *green sand moulding* / 开砂～ *open sand moulding* ◇ ～板［机］mould board；～美观 attractive appearance；handsome appearance；～艺术 plastic arts
【造谣】cook up a story and spread it around；start a rumour ◇ ～惑众 fabricate rumours to mislead people；～生事 start a rumour to create trouble；stir up trouble by rumour-mongering；～诬蔑 rumour-mongering and mudslinging；calumny and slander；～中伤 spread slanderous rumours
【造诣】(academic or artistic) attainments：他是一位～很高的学者。*He is a scholar of great attainments.* / 她是一位很有～的歌唱家。*She's an accomplished singer.*
【造影】［医］radiography：支气管～ *bronchography*
【造渣】［冶］slag making；slag formation
【造纸】papermaking ◇ ～厂 paper mill；～机 paper machine
【造作】❶ make；manufacture ❷ affected；artificial

噪 动 ❶ (of birds, insects, etc.) chirp：蝉～ *the chirping of cicadas* / 群鸦乱～。*Crows were cawing.* ❷ make noise；make an uproar；clamour：鼓噪
【噪鹃】Chinese koel
【噪鹛】［动］laughing thrush
【噪闹】noisy；noise；racket；din：～的鸭叫声 *noisy quacking of ducks*
【噪嚷】cry；shout：别～了！*Stop shouting*！
【噪音】（又作'噪声'）noise：机器的～ *the noise of machinery* / 低～马达 *low-noise motor* ◇ ～污染 noise pollution；～抑制［无］noise suppression
【噪杂】noisy：人声～ *a hubbub of voices*

燥 形 dry
【燥裂】crack from dryness；chap：沙漠的风沙吹得他皮肤～。*His skin became chapped from the*

desert wind.

【燥热】hot and dry

躁 形 rash; impetuous; restless: 性子～ *quick-tempered*; *hot-tempered*

【躁动】move restlessly

【躁急】restless; uneasy

【躁狂】[医] mania: ～者 *a maniac*

zé

则 Ⅰ名 ❶ standard; norm; criterion: 准则 ❷ rule; regulation: 法则 Ⅱ动〈书〉imitate; follow: ～先烈之言行 *follow the example of the martyrs in word and deed* Ⅲ量 (for news, writing, etc.) piece; item: 新闻一～ *an item of news* / 寓言四～ *four fables* Ⅳ连〈书〉❶ (used to indicate cause, condition, etc.): 物体热～胀,冷～缩。*Objects expand when heated and contract when cooled*. / 不战～已,战～必胜。*Fight no battle unless victory is sure*. ❷ (used to indicate concession, contrast, etc.): 好～好,只是太贵。*It's good but too expensive*. / 今～不然。*However, things are quite different today*. Ⅴ助 (used to list reasons, preceded by 一,二,三, or 一,再,三): 这篇课文不合适,一～太长,二～太难。*This text is unsuitable. For one thing it's too long, for another it's too difficult*.

【则声】make a sound; utter a word: 不～ *keep silent*

责 Ⅰ名 duty; responsibility: 爱护公物,人人有～。*It is everybody's duty to take good care of public property*. Ⅱ动 ❶demand; require❷ question closely; call sb. to account: 责问 ❸ reproach; blame; reprove: 痛责 ❹ punish

【责备】reproach; blame; reprove; take sb. to task: ～的眼光 *a look of reproach* / 受到良心的～ *feel a prick of conscience*

【责编】❶ (又作'责任编辑') editor-in-charge; executive editor ❷ be an editor-in-charge; be in charge of editing: 10 年来,他已～了 60 余种图书。*Over the last ten years he has edited more than sixty kinds of books*.

【责成】instruct (sb. to fulfil a task); charge (sb. with a task); enjoin (sb. to do sth.): ～小组委员会提出报告 *instruct the subcommittee to submit a report*

【责打】punish by beating

【责罚】punish

【责怪】blame: 这事不应该～他。*He should not be blamed for this*.

【责令】order; instruct; charge: 这个饭馆因卫生差而被～停业。*The restaurant has been ordered to stop business for being unhygienic*.

【责骂】scold; rebuke; dress down: 老师～他不该考试作弊。*The teacher rebuked him for cheating in the exam*.

【责难】censure; blame: 受到各方面的～ *incur censure from various quarters*

【责任】❶ duty; responsibility: ～重大 *have a grave responsibility* / 先进的有～帮助后进的。*The advanced are duty-bound to help those lagging behind*. ❷ responsibility for a fault or wrong; blame: 追究～ *ascertain where the responsibility lies* / 你不应该把～推到别人身上。*You shouldn't shift the blame onto others*. ◇～保险 liability insurance; ～编辑 executive editor; ～感 (又作'责任心') sense of responsibility (or duty); ～事故 accident due to negligence; accident involving criminal or civil liability; ～田 responsibility field; ～限额 liability limit; ～预算 responsibility budget; ～制 system of job responsibility; ～状 responsibility contract

【责问】call (or bring) sb. to account: 小组长～他为何不来开会。*The group leader called him to account for his absence from the meeting*.

【责无旁贷】there is no shirking the responsibility; be duty-bound

【责有攸归】responsibility must rest somewhere

【责怨】blame; reproach: 老头的语气有些～。*The old man spoke in a somewhat reproachful tone*.

泽 Ⅰ名 ❶ pool; pond: 湖泽 ❷ lustre (of metals, pearls, etc.): 光泽 ❸〈书〉favour; beneficence Ⅱ形 damp; moist: 润泽

【泽国】〈书〉❶ a land that abounds in rivers and lakes ❷ inundated area: 全区尽成～。*The whole area became submerged*.

【泽泻】❶ [植] oriental water plantain (Alisma plantago-aquatica var. orientale) ❷ [中] the rhizome of such a plant

择 动 select; choose; pick: ～友 *choose friends* / 二者任～其一 *choose either of the two* / ～日起程 *fix a departure date* ——另见 zhái

【择伐】[林] selective cutting (or felling)

【择吉】select (or choose) an auspicious day (for a marriage, funeral, etc.): ～开张 *select an auspicious day for opening a business*

【择交】choose friends: 慎重～ *choose friends with care*

【择偶】choose a spouse

【择期】select a day or time : ～完婚 *select a day for the marriage ceremony*

【择善而从】choose and follow what is good

【择业】choose an occupation: 自行～ *select a job for oneself*; *choose one's job*

【择优】select the superior ones: ～录取 *employ (or enroll) on the basis of competitive selection*

啧 象 click of the tongue

【啧有烦言】there are a lot of complaints

【啧啧】❶ clicking the tongue; chattering ❷〈书〉chirping: 雀声～。*Sparrows were chirping*.

【啧啧称羡】(又作'啧啧称赞') click the tongue in admiration

zè

仄 Ⅰ 形 ❶ narrow ❷ uneasy; disturbed Ⅱ 名 同〖仄声〗

【仄声】［语音］oblique tones

zéi

贼 Ⅰ 名 ❶ thief ❷ traitor; enemy: 工贼 Ⅱ 形 ❶ crooked; wicked; evil; furtive: 贼心 ❷ crafty; sly; cunning; deceitful: 老鼠真～。*Rats are really cunning*. Ⅲ 副〈方〉(usu. used to show disapproval) extremely; disagreeably: ～冷 *terribly cold* / ～亮 *disagreeably glossy or dazzling*

【贼船】pirate ship: 上～ *board the pirate ship — join a reactionary faction or a criminal gang; go astray*

【贼喊捉贼】a thief crying "Stop thief"

【贼眉鼠眼】shifty-eyed; thievish-looking

【贼去关门】(又作'贼走关门') lock the door after the thief has gone; lock the stable door after the horse is stolen

【贼死】〈方〉extremely; utterly: 这么重的活儿把她累得个～。*The hard work completely exhausted her*.

【贼头贼脑】behaving stealthily like a thief; stealthy; furtive

【贼窝】thieves' den

【贼心】wicked heart; evil designs; evil intentions ◇ ～不死 refuse to give up one's evil designs

【贼星】popular name for 流星

【贼赃】stolen goods; booty; spoils

zěn

怎 副〈口〉why; how: 这样的好收成，我们～能不高兴呢? *How can we help rejoicing over such a good harvest?* / 你～不早说呀? *Why didn't you say so earlier?*

【怎么】❶ how; what; why: 我～没听说过这事儿? *How come I never heard of it?* / 你～啦? *What's the matter with you?* or *Why, is anything the matter?* / 你～搞的! *See what you've done!* ❷ in a certain way; in any way; no matter how: 不知道～一来我就滑倒了。*Somehow I slipped and fell*. / 他把～来～去都告诉了大家。*He told us everything, from beginning to end*. ❸ (used in the negative as an understatement) (not) very; (not) much; (not) quite; (not) too: 那个不～贵。*That's not very expensive*. / 他不～说话。*He doesn't talk much*. / 今天我不～舒服。*I'm not quite well today*. ❹ (used by itself at the beginning of a sentence to show surprise) what: ～，他还没来吗? *What? Isn't he here yet?* / ～连你都不知道! *What? Even you don't know it!*

【怎么得了】where will it all end; what a terrible thing it would be; this is one hell of a mess

【怎么样】❶ how; what: 你觉得～? *How are you feeling?* / 后来这孩子～了? *What became of the child?* / 你能把他～? *What can you do to him?* ❷ what's it like; how are things; what do you think: 四个菜，一个汤，～? *Four dishes and one soup — what do you think?* / 骑车去～? *How (or What) about going by bike?* ❸ in a certain way; in any way; no matter how: 人家～做，你也～做。*Do as everybody does*. / 我～做都不对。*No matter how I did it, I did it wrong*. ❹ (used in the negative as a mild understatement) (not) up to much: 这个电影不～。*The film isn't up to much*. / 她唱歌不～。*She's not much of a singer*.

【怎么着】❶ what to do; what: 看完戏我就回家，你打算～? *I'm going straight home after the play. What about you?* ❷ no matter what; whatever: ～都行。*It'll be all right whatever it is*. / 你不能想～就～。*You can't just do what (or as) you please*. ❸ (used by itself at the beginning of the sentence to show surprise) what: ～，你不去了? *What? You're not going?*

【怎样】❶ how; what: 你现在感觉～? *How are you feeling now?* / 这件事你～解释? *How do you explain it?* ❷ in a certain way; in any way; no matter how: 想想从前～，再看看现在～ *think of the past and look at the present* / 人家～做，你也～做。*Do as everybody does*.

zèn

谮 动〈书〉falsely charge; slander; calumniate: ～言 *slander; calumny*

zēng

曾 形 relationship between great-grandchildren and great-grandparents

【曾母暗沙】Zengmu Reef

【曾孙】great-grandson

【曾孙女】great-granddaughter

【曾祖】(paternal) great-grandfather

【曾祖母】(paternal) great-grandmother

憎 动 hate; detest; abhor: 憎恶

【憎称】derogatory name for sb. one hates or loathes

【憎恨】hate; detest

【憎恶】abhor; loathe; abominate: 有些人～现代艺术。*Some people loathe modern art*.

【憎厌】dislike: 她沉默着皱一皱眉头，露出一股极为～的神情。*Silently she frowned with a look of utter distaste*.

增 动 increase; gain; add: 产量猛～。*Output increased sharply*. / ～拨资金 *allocate more*

funds / ～兵 *throw in more troops*; *augment one's forces*; *reinforce*

【增白】［化］brighten ◇ ～剂［化］brightening agent; brightener; ～霜 fair complexion cream

【增补】augment; supplement: 该书内容有所～。*The book has been supplemented with new material*.

【增补本】an enlarged edition

【增产】increase production: ～节约 *increase production and practise economy*

【增充剂】［化］extender

【增订】revise and enlarge (a book) ◇ ～本 a revised and enlarged edition

【增多】grow in number or quantity; increase: 来华参观访问的外国朋友日益～。*More and more foreign friends come to visit China*.

【增防】［军］strengthen defences: 派出～部队 *send out defence reinforcements*

【增幅】degree of increase; rate of growth: 7月份,海关出口额达到今年～最高的一个月。*The export total this July showed the biggest monthly increase so far this year*.

【增高】❶ get higher; rise; increase: 正在建筑的电视发射台日见～。*The TV tower under construction is getting higher each day*. ❷ make higher; heighten; raise; increase: ～温室的温度 *raise the temperature of a hothouse*

【增光】add lustre to; do credit to; add to the prestige of: 为国～ *do credit to one's country*

【增加】increase; raise; add: ～积累 *increase accumulation* / ～收入 *increase income* / ～工资 *get a raise in pay* / ～困难 *add to the difficulties*; *multiply the difficulties* / ～体重 *put on weight* / ～抵抗力 *build up one's resistance to disease* ◇ ～值 value-added output

【增减】increase and decrease; fluctuate

【增进】enhance; promote; further: ～健康 *improve one's health* / ～食欲 *whet one's appetite*

【增刊】supplement (to a newspaper or periodical); supplementary issue

【增量】❶ increase: 投资～ *investment increase* ❷〈数〉increment; incremental quantity: ～参数 *incremental parameter* / ～计算机 *increment computer* / ～理论 *incremental theory*

【增强】strengthen; heighten; enhance: ～战斗力 *strengthen fighting capacity*; *increase combat effectiveness* / ～信心 *heighten one's confidence* / ～斗志 *raise (or heighten, boost) one's morale* ◇ ～塑料 reinforced plastics

【增色】add colour to; add beauty to: 这幅画给这间屋子～不少。*The picture adds beauty to the room*.

【增删】additions and deletions

【增设】establish an additional or new (organization, unit, course, etc.): ～一个新机构 *set up a new organization* / ～新课程 *establish a new course*; *offer a new course*

【增生】［医］hyperplasia; proliferation; multiplication

【增收】increase income; increase revenues: 增产～ *increase income along with increased production* / ～节支 *raise revenues and reduce expenditures*

【增塑剂】［化］plasticizer; plastifier

【增添】add; increase: ～设备 *get additional equipment* / ～力量和信心 *gain strength and confidence*

【增效剂】［化］synergist

【增页】text or pictures added to a periodical; supplement

【增益】❶ increase; raise; add ❷［电］gain: 高～ *high gain* / 分贝～ *decibel gain* / ～控制 *gain control*

【增盈】increase profit or profitability: 制定～目标 *fix a target for increased profits*

【增援】［军］reinforce: ～部队 *reinforcements*; *reinforcing units*

【增长】increase; rise; grow: 持续～ *sustained growth* / ～才干 *enhance (or develop) one's abilities* / ～知识 *broaden (or enrich) one's knowledge* ◇ ～率 rate of increase; growth rate

【增支】increase expenditure: 因物价上涨,我们医院今年的行政经费比去年～20%。*Due to inflation, administrative costs for our hospital rose by 20% over last year*.

【增值】❶［经］increase or rise in value; add value; increment: ～税 *value-added tax*; *VAT*; *duty on value added* / 产品～ *value-added on products* ❷［经］appreciate; appreciation: 美元～ *appreciation of US dollar* ❸〈喻〉increase in value: 知识的～与贬值 *the rise and fall in the value of knowledge*

【增殖】❶［医］hyperplasia; proliferation; multiplication: 细胞～ *proliferation of cells* ❷ breed; reproduce; multiply; propagate: ～耕牛 *breed farm cattles* ◇ ～率 animal husbandry rate of increase

【增砖添瓦】❶〈字〉add bricks and tiles (to the construction of a building) ❷〈喻〉make whatever contribution one can (to a cause)

【增资】increase salary: ～幅度 *the range of pay raise*

zèng

综 名［纺］heddle; heald: ～框 *heald frame* ——另见 zōng

锃 形〈方〉(of utensils, etc.) polished

【锃光瓦亮】〈方〉shiny

【锃亮】〈方〉shiny

甑 名 ❶ an ancient earthen utensil for steaming rice ❷ rice steamer ❸ a utensil for distilling water, etc.

【甑子】rice steamer

赠 动 give as a present; present as a gift: 此砚乃老友所～。*This inkstone is a present from an old friend of mine.*
【赠别】present a friend with gifts, poems, etc. at parting
【赠答】present each other with gifts, poems, etc.
【赠礼】❶ present sb. with a gift ❷ gift; present
【赠品】(complimentary) gift; giveaway
【赠券】gift coupons
【赠书】❶ present sb. with a book ❷ 同〖赠阅〗❸ complimentary copy
【赠送】give as a present; present as a gift: 向演员～花篮 *present a basket of flowers to the performers* ◇ ～仪式 presentation ceremony
【赠言】words of advice or encouragement given to a friend at parting
【赠予】(又作'赠与') present to; donate to ◇ ～国 donor country
【赠阅】(of a book, periodical, etc.) given free by the publisher ◇ ～本 complimentary copy

zhā

扎 动 ❶ prick; run or stick (a needle, etc.) into: 手指上～了一根刺 *prick one's finger on a thorn; have a splinter in one's finger* / ～一刀 *stab with a knife* ❷ 〈方〉 plunge into; get into: ～到人群里 *dash into the crowd* / 扑通一声,他～进水里去了。*He dived into the water with a splash.* / 一头～进书堆里 *bury oneself in books* ❸ be stationed; be quartered: 扎营 ——另见 zā
【扎堆儿】〈方〉 get together: ～聊天 *get together to gossip*
【扎耳朵眼儿】pierce the earlobe (in order to wear earrings)
【扎根】take root: ～于群众之中 *take root among the masses*
【扎花】〈方〉 embroider
【扎猛子】〈方〉 swim with the head kept submerged in water; dive
【扎实】❶ sturdy; strong ❷ solid; sound; down-to-earth: 工作很～ *do a solid job* / 这门基础课她学得很～。*She has a good grasp of this basic course.*
【扎手】❶ prick the hand: 树上有刺,留神～。*The tree is thorny. Mind you don't prick your hands.* ❷ difficult to handle; thorny: 这事真～。*This is really a hard nut to crack.*
【扎眼】❶ dazzling; offending to the eye; loud; garish: 这块布的颜色太～。*This cloth is too dazzling.* / 她穿得很～。*She's loudly dressed.* ❷ offensively conspicuous
【扎伊尔】Zaire ◇ ～人 Zairian
【扎寨】pitch a camp; camp: 安营扎寨
【扎针】[中] give or have an acupuncture treatment: 上医务室～ *go to the clinic for acupuncture treatment*

咋 (构词成分) 见下——另见 zǎ; zhà
【咋呼】(又作'咋唬')〈方〉 ❶ shout blusteringly ❷ show off; make a fuss: 甭听他瞎～。*Don't take any notice of him—he's just showing off.* / 他有点小事儿就爱～。*He's rather fussy about small things.*

渣 名 ❶ dregs; sediment; residue: 豆腐～ *soyabean residue (after making bean curd)* / 猪油～儿 *cracklings* ❷ broken bits: 饼干～儿 *biscuit crumbs*
【渣油】[油] residual oil; residuum: ～路 *residual-oil road*
【渣滓】dregs; sediment; residue: 溶液的～ *dregs of a solution* / 社会～ *dregs of society*
【渣子】〈口〉 ❶ dregs; sediment; residue ❷ broken bits: 点心～ *cake crumbs*

喳 Ⅰ 叹 aye (formerly used by servants to indicate polite attentiveness) Ⅱ 象 chirp; chatter: 喜鹊～～地叫。*Magpies were chattering.* ——另见 chā

揸 动 〈方〉 ❶ pick up sth. with the fingers ❷ spread one's fingers

楂 名 见〖山楂〗——另见 chá

zhá

札 名 ❶ thin pieces of wood used for writing on in ancient China ❷ 〈书〉 letter: 适奉大～。*I have just received your esteemed letter.*
【札记】reading notes

轧 动 roll (steel) ——另见 gá; yà
【轧钢】steel rolling: ～机 *rolling mill* ◇ ～厂 steel rolling mill
【轧辊】[冶] roll; roller: ～调整装置 *roll adjusting device*
【轧机】[冶] rolling mill: 二辊式～ *two-high mill* / 可逆式～ *reversing mill* / 连续式～ *continuous mill*
【轧制】[冶] rolling: ～钢 *rolled steel* / ～公差 *rolling tolerance*

闸 Ⅰ 名 ❶ floodgate; sluice gate ❷ brake ❸ 〈口〉 switch: 扳～ *operate a switch; switch on or off* Ⅱ 动 dam up a stream, river, etc.: ～住河水防洪 *dam up a river to control flooding*
【闸盒】fuse box
【闸流管】[电子] thyratron
【闸门】❶ sluice gate ❷ (ship) lock gate ❸ [机] throttle valve
【闸瓦】[机] brake shoe

炸 动 ❶ fry in deep fat or oil; deep-fry: 把花生～一～ *deep-fry the peanuts* / ～豆腐 *deepfried bean curd* / ～糕 *fried cake* ❷ 〈方〉 scald (as a way of cooking) ——另见 zhà

【炸酱】fried bean sauce (usu. with minced meat) ◇ ～面 noodles served with fried bean sauce

【炸土豆条】chips; French fries

铡 Ⅰ 名 hand hay cutter; fodder chopper Ⅱ 动 cut up with a hay cutter: ～猪草 *chop fodder for pigs*

【铡草机】hay cutter; chaffcutter

【铡刀】hand hay (or straw) cutter; fodder chopper

zhǎ

拃 Ⅰ 动 measure by handspans; span Ⅱ 量 span: 这块布有三～宽。*This cloth is three spans wide.*

眨 动 blink; wink: 眼睛一～ *blink (one's eyes)* / 他向我～了～眼。*He winked at me.*

【眨巴】〈方〉blink: 这孩子的眼睛直～,想是困了。*The child is blinking his eyes. He must be sleepy.*

【眨眼】very short time; wink; twinkle: 一～的工夫 *in the twinkling of an eye*

砟 名 tiny fragments of stone, coal, etc.: 炉灰～儿 *cinder*

【砟子】tiny fragments of stone, coal, etc.

zhà

乍 Ⅰ 副 ❶ first; for the first time: ～一听 *at first hearing* / ～看起来 *at first glance* / 天～晴。*The rain has just stopped.* ❷ suddenly; abruptly: 天气,冷～热。*The temperature changes abruptly.* Ⅱ 动 spread; extend: ～翅 *spread wings*

【乍得】Chad ◇ ～人 Chadian

【乍暖还寒】After suddenly getting warmer, it's turned cold again.

诈 动 ❶ cheat; swindle: ～人钱财 *swindle people out of their money; get money by fraud* ❷ pretend; feign: ～死 *feign (or fake) death; play dead* / ～败 *feign defeat* ❸ bluff sb. into giving information: 他是拿话～我。*He was trying to draw me out.*

【诈病】malinger; malingering ◇ ～者 malingerer

【诈称】jactitation ◇ ～者 jactitator

【诈唬】bluff; bluster

【诈骗】defraud; swindle ◇ ～犯 swindler

【诈降】pretend to surrender; feign surrender

【诈语】lie; falsehood; fabrication

咋 动 〈书〉bite ——另见 zǎ; zhā

【咋舌】〈书〉be left speechless or breathless (with wonder or fear): 杂技演员的惊险动作使观众为之～。*The acrobat's feat took the audience's breath away.*

炸 动 ❶ explode; burst: 暖瓶～了。*The thermos flask has burst.* ❷ blow up; blast; bomb: ～桥 *blow up a bridge* / ～毁 *blow up; blast to pieces; demolish* / 把障碍物～掉 *blast away the barriers* / ～平 *bomb flat* / ～沉 *bomb and sink* ❸〈口〉fly into a rage; flare up: 肺都气～了 *flare up; explode with rage* ❹〈方〉scamper; flee in terror: 炸窝 ——另见 zhá

【炸弹】bomb: ～坑 *bombcrater; crater* ◇ ～气球 balloon with bomb, often propaganda balloon

【炸锅】❶ oil spattering when food is fried ❷〈喻〉unrestrained anger; great dissatisfaction: 听到这一坏消息,全班同学马上就～了。*The whole class was in an uproar at the bad news.*

【炸胶】[化] blasting gelatine

【炸雷】〈方〉a clap of thunder

【炸窝】〈方〉scamper; flee in terror: 饭店着火,旅客炸了窝。*The guests stampeded out of the burning hotel.*

【炸响】explode; make cracking noise: 皮鞭子甩得～ *crack the whip*

【炸药】explosive (charges); dynamite ◇ ～包 pack (or satchel) of dynamite; explosive package; satchel charges

栅 名 railings; paling; bars: 木～ *paling; palisade* / 铁～ *iron railings; metal rails; iron bars* / 炉～ *grate* ——另见 shān

【栅栏】❶ railings; paling; bars ❷ [军] boom: ～网 *boom nets*

蚱 (构词成分) 见下

【蚱蜢】grasshopper

榨 Ⅰ 动 press; extract: ～甘蔗 *press sugar cane* / ～干血汗 *wring every ounce of sweat and blood out of sb.* Ⅱ 名 a press for extracting juice, oil, etc.

【榨菜】❶ mustard tuber (Brassica juncea var. tsatsai) ❷ hot pickled mustard tuber

【榨取】squeeze; extort: ～果汁 *squeeze juice out of oranges, etc.* / ～钱财 *extort money from sb.*

【榨油】extract oil: ～机 *oil press*

【榨汁机】juicer

zhāi

斋 Ⅰ 名 ❶ fast ❷ vegetarian diet adopted for religious reasons: 吃斋 Ⅱ 动 give alms (to a monk)

【斋饭】food given to Buddhist monks as alms

【斋戒】abstain from meat, wine, etc. (when offering sacrifices to gods or ancestors); fast ◇ ～节 Ramadan; the fast of Ramadan; ～沐浴 fast and ablution; fast and take a bath before a religious observance; ～日 fast day

【斋期】fast days; fast

【斋堂】dining hall in a Buddhist temple

【斋月】[宗](伊斯兰教) Ramadan; the month of fast

摘 动 ❶ pick; pluck; take off: ～棉花(苹果) *pick cotton (apples)* / ～花 *pluck flowers* / 把眼镜～下来 *take off one's glasses* ❷ select; make extracts from: 摘译 ❸ borrow money when in urgent need: ～几个钱救急 *borrow some money to meet an urgent need*

【摘报】make a summary report: 向领导～群众建议 *submit a summary report of suggestions from the grassroots*

【摘编】❶ select and edit; make extracts ❷ extracts

【摘抄】❶ take passages; make extracts; extract; excerpt ❷ extracts; excerpts: 雷锋日记～ *pages (or excerpts) from Lei Feng's diary*

【摘除】[医] excise: ～腹部肿瘤 *excise an abdominal tumour*

【摘登】publish excerpts (or extracts) of sth.: 今天报纸～了他的发言。*Today's paper carried excerpts of his speech.*

【摘发】publish an abstract of sth.: ～大会发言 *publish extracts of speeches given at a conference*

【摘桂】take the crown; win the title: A 战胜了 B 而～. *A defeated B and won the title.*

【摘记】❶ take notes: 报告很长,我只～了要点。*The report was rather long. I just jotted down the main points.* ❷ extracts; excerpts

【摘借】borrow money when in urgent need

【摘录】❶ take passages; make extracts; extract; excerpt ❷ extracts; excerpts: 文件～ *extracts from a document*

【摘棉铃机】[农] cotton stripper

【摘取】❶ obtain; get: ～金牌 *win a gold medal* ❷ quote: 他这是断章取义地～词句。*He is quoting out of context.*

【摘桃子】❶ pick peaches ❷〈喻〉steal the fruit of other's labor: 谢主任早不来,晚不来,偏挑我们实验成功这一天来露面,很明显是来～的。*Director Xie has chosen to make his appearance on the very day we have successfully completed our experiment. Clearly he has come to share the glory.*

【摘要】❶ make a summary: ～发表 *publish excerpts (or extracts) of sth.* ❷ summary; abstract; précis: 社论～ *the summary of an editorial*

【摘译】❶ translate selected passages: 一天内译完这份科研报告是不可能的,请你～重要部分吧。*It is impossible to translate the whole report in one day. Please just translate the more important passages.* ❷ translations of selected passages

【摘引】quote

【摘由】key extracts (of a document); résumé

zhái

宅 名 residence; house: 赵～ *the Zhaos' residence*

【宅第】a large house; mansion

【宅基】the foundations of a house; the site of a house

【宅门】❶ gate of an old-style big house ❷ family living in such a house

【宅院】a house with a courtyard; house

【宅子】〈口〉residence; house

择 动 同〖择〗(zé), limited to use in the following entry words ——另见 zé

【择不开】❶ unable to disentangle (or undo): 线乱成了一团,怎么也～了。*The thread is all in a tangle. I simply can't undo it.* ❷ cannot get away from: 一点儿工夫也～ *not have a moment to spare*

【择菜】trim vegetables for cooking

【择铺】(又作'择床')〈方〉be unable to sleep well in a new place

【择席】be unable to sleep well in a new place: 我从来不～。*I never have trouble sleeping in a strange place.*

zhǎi

窄 形 ❶ narrow: ～道 *narrow path* ❷ petty; narrow: 心眼儿～ *petty; oversensitive* ❸ hard up; badly off: 父亲死后,家里的日子过得挺～。*We were very hard up after my father died.*

【窄轨铁路】narrow-gauge railway

【窄小】narrow and small: 房屋～ *a small house*

zhài

债 名 debt: 一笔十万元的～ *a debt of 100,000 yuan* / 他的～还清了。*He was out of debt.*

【债户】debtor

【债款】loan

【债权】[法] creditor's rights ◇ ～国 creditor nation; ～人 creditor

【债券】bond; debenture: ～持有者 *bondholder* ◇ ～担保人 bond underwriter; ～发行 the issuance of debentures; ～价格 bond price; ～价值 bond value; ～交易 bond exchange; ～投资 bond investment; ～息票 bond coupons; coupon; ～溢价 bond premium; ～转让 transfer of bonds

【债台高筑】be heavily in debt; be up to one's ears in debt; be debt-ridden

【债务】debt; liabilities ◇ ～公司 debtor corporation; ～国 debtor nation; ～率 debt ratio; ～期 debt duration; ～人 debtor; ～咨询 debt counsel(l)ing

【债主】creditor ◇ ～权益 creditor's equity

寨 名 ❶ stockade ❷ stockaded village ❸〈旧〉camp: 营寨 ❹ mountain stronghold

【寨主】(in former times) brigand chief

【寨子】stockaded village

zhān

占 动 practise divination ——另见 zhàn

【占卜】practise divination; divine

【占卦】divine by means of the Eight Diagrams (八卦)

【占课】divine by tossing coins

【占梦】prognostication by dreams; oneiromancy

【占星】divine by astrology; cast a horoscope: ～术 *astrology*

沾 动 ❶ moisten; wet; soak: 泪～襟 *tears wet the front of one's jacket* ❷ be stained with: ～水 *get wet* / ～上了泥 *be stained with mud* ❸ touch: 他跑得真快,脚不～地似的。*He ran so fast that his feet seemed hardly to touch the ground*. / 烟酒不～ *touch neither tobacco nor alcohol* ❹ get sth. out of association with sb. or sth.: ～点便宜 *get a bargain*

【沾边】❶ touch on (or upon) only lightly: 他讲的那些话跟他的真实思想根本不～。*What he said wasn't at all what he was really thinking*. / 这事他也沾了点边儿。*He was involved in the affair to a certain extent*. ❷ be close to what it should be; be relevant: 你讲的一点也不～。*What you say is completely irrelevant*.

【沾光】benefit from association with sb. or sth.: 我们工厂每周放电影,附近小孩儿都～。*Kids in the neighbourhood enjoy the chance of seeing our factory's weekly film*.

【沾花惹草】同〖拈花惹草〗

【沾亲带故】be related somehow or other; have ties of kinship or friendship

【沾染】be infected with; be contaminated by; be tainted with: 伤口～了细菌。*The wound was infected with germs*. / ～市侩作风 *be contaminated by philistine ways* / ～坏习气 *be tainted with bad habits* ◇ ～区 contaminated area

【沾手】❶ touch with one's hand: 雪花一～就化。*Snowflakes melt as they fall on one's hand*. ❷ have a hand in: 看来这事他沾了手。*It seems that he has a hand in the matter*. / 这活儿她一～就会了。*She got the hang of the job the moment she started it*.

【沾污】❶ make dirty; dirty; soil ❷ contaminate

【沾沾自喜】feel complacent; be pleased with oneself: 不要～于一得之功。*Don't be complacent over an occasional success*. or *Don't feel self-satisfied over a minor success*.

毡 名 felt: ～帽 *felt hat*

【毡房】yurt

【毡条】〈方〉felt rug

【毡子】felt; felt rug; felt blanket

粘 动 glue; stick; paste: 把两块木片～在一起 *glue the two chips of wood together* / 把信封～上 *seal (up) an envelope* / 这糖不～牙。*This candy doesn't stick to your teeth*. ——另见 nián

【粘连】〔医〕adhesion: 瘢痕性～ *cicatricial adhesion*

【粘贴】paste; stick: 在墙上～标语 *paste slogans on the wall*

谵 形〈书〉rave; be delirious

【谵妄】〔医〕delirium

【谵语】〈书〉delirious speech; wild talk; ravings

瞻 动 look up or forward: 观瞻

【瞻顾】〈书〉look ahead and behind

【瞻念】look to; think of: ～前途 *think of the future*

【瞻前顾后】peer ahead and look behind — ❶ think over carefully ❷ be over-cautious and indecisive

【瞻赏】enjoy the sight of: 桂林以它秀丽的自然景观吸引了许多游客前往～。*Guilin attracts many tourists with its natural beauty*.

【瞻望】look forward; look far ahead: ～未来 *look to the future*

【瞻仰】(又作'瞻拜') look at with reverence: ～毛主席遗容 *pay one's respects to the remains of Chairman Mao*

zhǎn

斩 动 slay; chop; cut: ～敌将 *slay (or cut down) an enemy general* / 言降者～! *Whosoever mentions surrender dies*! / ～断侵略者的魔爪 *chop off the claws of the invaders*

【斩草除根】cut the weeds and dig up the roots—stamp out the source of trouble

【斩钉截铁】resolute and decisive; categorical: ～地拒绝 *give a round rebuff* / 他说得～。*He spoke with curt finality*.

【斩假石】〔建〕artificial stone; imitation stone

【斩尽杀绝】kill all; wipe out; exterminate

【斩首】behead; decapitate

展 Ⅰ 动 ❶ open up; spread out; unfold; unfurl: 风～红旗。*The red flags are fluttering in the wind*. / 舒眉～眼 *beam with joy* ❷ put to good use; give free play to: ～技 *give full play to one's skill* / 一～才华 *display one's talents* / 立大志,～宏图 *cherish high aspirations and carry out a great plan* ❸ postpone; extend; prolong: 展期 Ⅱ 名 exhibition: 画展

【展播】a special TV programme (to show the best productions); run (on TV, as in a festival): 举办电视专题片～周 *show a week of special TV films* / 迎春文艺节目～ *a Spring Festival art and literature TV programme*

【展翅】spread the wings; get ready for flight: ～高飞 *soar to great heights*

【展出】put on display; be on show (or view); exhibit: 展览会上～了各种各样的机床。*A good variety of machine tools are on display at the ex-*

hibition.
【展地】site of an exhibition：扩大～面积 *enlarge the exhibition space*
【展观】unroll and view a scroll painting：为～方便，他们将专门设计展室。*They will design a special hall for hanging and viewing scroll paintings*.
【展馆】exhibition center；exhibition hall
【展柜】showcase；display window
【展缓】postpone；extend；prolong：限期不得～。*The time limit is not to be extended*.
【展开】❶ spread out；unfold；open up：把地图～ *unfold the map* / 把队伍～ *deploy the forces* ❷ launch；unfold；develop；carry out：～攻势 *unfold an offen-sive* / 运动会的各项比赛已全面～。*The sports meet is now in full swing*.
【展览】put on display；exhibit；show：工业～ *industrial exhibition* / 菊花～ *chrysanthemum show* ◇ ～馆 exhibition centre（or hall）；～会 exhibition；～室 exhibition room；showroom
【展廊】exhibition gallery
【展露】reveal；show：～秘密 *reveal a secret* / ～丰姿 *show one's beauty*
【展卖】exhibit for sale：大～期间部分服装实行优惠价格。*During the exhibition some of the clothes were on sale*.
【展品】（又作'展览品'）exhibit；item on display：请勿触摸～。*Please do not touch the exhibits*.
【展评】display and appraise；exhibit and compare：新产品～会 *exhibition and evaluation of new products*
【展期】❶ extend a time limit；postpone：交易会～两天结束。*The fair will be extended for another two days*. ❷ duration of an exhibition；exhibition period
【展区】exhibition area；place of exhibition：改革后的美展每5年举办一次，按画种分别在全国各～举行。*Since the reforms，a national art exhibition has been held every five years，with different art forms on show in different parts of the country*.
【展示】open up before one's eyes；reveal；show；lay bare：～人物的内心世界 *reveal a character's inner world* ◇ ～会 exhibition；show
【展室】exhibition room；show room
【展售】exhibition sale：～部 *sales department*
【展台】showcase；booth；display counter
【展望】❶ look into the distance：登上山顶向四周～ *climb to the top of the mountain and get a view of the surrounding country* ❷ look into the future；look ahead：～未来 *look forward to the future* ❸ forecast；prospect：二十一世纪～ *prospects for the 21st century；the 21st century in prospect*
【展现】unfold before one's eyes；emerge；develop：到了工地，一派繁忙的景象～在我们眼前。*As we reached the construction site，a scene of bustling activity presented itself before our eyes*.
【展销】display and sell（goods）◇ ～会 commodities fair
【展性】［物］malleability
【展演】exhibition performance：本市将举办系列舞剧～。*The municipality will hold a dance festival*.
【展映】film festival：新片～周 *hold a week-long film festival*
【展阅】open and read：他拿出旧日朋友的书信，重新～。*He took out letters from his old friends and read them again*.

盏 Ⅰ名 a small cup：酒～ *a small wine cup* Ⅱ量（for lamps）：一～电灯 *an electric lamp*

崭 形 ❶〈书〉towering（over）❷〈方〉fine；swell：滋味真～！*How delicious*！
【崭露头角】（of a young person）begin to show one's brilliant talents；display remarkable ability or talent
【崭新】brand-new；completely new：穿一身～的制服 *wear a brand-new tunic suit* / ～的阶段 *a completely new stage*

搌 动 wipe or dab（with a soft dry object）to sop up liquid：纸上落了一滴墨水，快拿吸墨纸～～吧。*A drop of ink has fallen on the paper；blot it up quickly*.
【搌布】dishcloth；dish towel

辗（构词成分）见下
【辗转】❶ pass through many hands or places ❷ toss about（in bed）：～不能成眠 *toss and turn*（*in bed*）；*unable to go to sleep* ◇ ～反侧 toss about（in bed）；toss and turn；～流传 pass through many hands；spread from place to place；～相除法［数］division algorithm

zhàn

占 动 ❶ occupy；seize；take：～用不少时间 *take up much time* ❷ constitute；hold；make up；account for：～多（少）数 *constitute the majority*（*minority*）/ ～统治地位 *hold*（*or occupy*）*a dominant position* / ～世界第一位 *rank first in the world* ——另见 zhān
【占地】（of a garden，farm，etc.）cover an area of：故宫～72 公顷。*The Imperial Palace covers an area of 72 hectares*.
【占据】occupy；hold：～重要的战略地位 *occupy a position of strategic importance*
【占理】reasonable；sensible；right：她的话～，我们按她说的办。*She's right*. *We'll do what she says*.
【占领】capture；occupy；seize：～要塞 *capture a fort* / ～市场 *dominate the market* / ◇ ～军 occupation army；～区 occupied area
【占便宜】❶ gain extra advantage by unfair means；profit at other people's expense：别老想占我的便宜。*Don't always try to take advantage of me*. ❷ advantageous；favourable：你个子高，打篮球～。*A tall fellow like you has an advantage in*

playing basketball.

【占上风】get the upper hand; win an advantage; prevail: 我队下半场占了上风。*Our team gained the upper hand in the second half of the game*.

【占先】take precedence; take the lead; get ahead of: 上个月劳动竞赛,第一组～了。*The first team led all the others in last month's emulation drive*.

【占线】the line (of a telephone) is busy (or engaged) ◇ ～通道[电] active channel

【占小便宜】gain petty advantages; secure small advantages at other people's expense; make small gains at other people's expense

【占用】occupy and use; take up (time): 不能随便～耕地。*It is illegal to occupy cultivated land and put it to other uses without authorization*.

【占有】❶ own; possess; have: ～生产资料 *own the means of production* / ～第一手资料 *have firsthand data* ❷ occupy; hold: 商业在国民经济中～重要地位。*Commerce occupies an important place in the national economy*.

【占着茅坑不拉屎】sit on the (toilet) seat but not shit—hold on to a post without doing any work and not let anyone else take over; be a dog in the manger

战 Ⅰ 名 war; warfare; battle; fight: 淝水之～ *the battle of the Fei Shui (A.D. 383)*) Ⅱ 动 ❶ fight: ～而胜之 *fight and defeat the enemy* / 为保卫祖国而～ *fight to defend one's motherland* ❷ shiver; tremble; shudder: 寒战

【战败】❶ be defeated; be vanquished; suffer a defeat; lose (a battle or war): 敌军～了。*The enemy troops were defeated*. ❷ defeat; vanquish; beat ◇ ～国 vanquished (or defeated) nation

【战报】war communiqué; battlefield report

【战备】war preparedness; combat readiness: 加强～ *step up combat readiness* / ～观念强 *be prepared against war* / ～工作 *preparations against war* ◇ ～等级 degree of combat readiness; ～粮 grain stockpiled in case of war; ～行军 tactical march; tactical movement; ～状态 combat readiness

【战场】battlefield; battleground; battlefront: 开辟新～ *open another front* / 西北～ *the Northwest theatre* / 奔赴～ *go to the front*

【战车】war chariot

【战船】man-of-war; naval vessel; warship

【战刀】sabre

【战地】battlefield; battleground; combat zone: ～指挥部 *field headquarters* ◇ ～记者 war correspondent

【战抖】tremble; shiver; shudder

【战斗】❶ fight; battle; combat; action: 英勇～ *put up a heroic fight* / 进行了数十次～ *have fought scores of battles* / 作好～准备 *get ready for action; be combat ready* / 投入～ *go into battle* ❷ militant; fighting: ～的友谊 *militant friendship* / ～的诗篇 *militant poem* / ～岗位 *fighting post* / ～性 *militancy* ◇ ～轰炸机 fighter-bomber; ～机 old name for 歼击机; ～力 combat effectiveness (or strength, capability); fighting capacity; ～英雄 combat hero; ～员 fighter

【战端】the beginning of a war: 重启～。*War broke out again*.

【战法】strategies and tactics of war

【战犯】war criminal

【战俘】prisoner of war (P.O.W.): ～营 *prisoner-of-war camp* / ～收容所 *prisoner-of-war collecting post*

【战高温】fight the heat; work inspite of the heat

【战歌】battle song; fighting song

【战功】meritorious military service; outstanding military exploit; battle achievement: 立～ *distinguish oneself in action*

【战鼓】war drum; battle drum

【战国】the Warring States (475—221 B.C.)

【战果】results of battle; combat success; victory: 取得辉煌～ *achieve splendid results on the battlefield* / 扩大～ *exploit the victory (or success)*

【战壕】trench; entrenchment

【战后】postwar: ～时期 *postwar period*

【战火】flames of war: 海湾燃起了～。*Flames of war rose over the gulf*. ◇ ～纷飞 flames of war raging everywhere

【战祸】disaster of war

【战机】opportunity for combat: 丧失～ *miss the opportunity to win a battle*

【战绩】military successes (or exploits, feats); combat gains

【战舰】warship

【战将】warrior

【战局】war situation: ～大有好转。*The war situation has improved a lot*.

【战况】situation on the battlefield; progress of a battle

【战利品】spoils of war; captured equipment; war trophies (or booty)

【战例】a specific example of a battle (in military science): 有名的～ *a famous battle*

【战栗】tremble; shiver; shudder: 吓得全身～ *tremble all over with fear*

【战列舰】(又作'战斗舰') battleship

【战列巡洋舰】battle cruiser

【战乱】chaos caused by war; war

【战略】strategy: 保持实力作～上的撤退 *maintain military strength through strategic retreats* / 全球～ *global strategy* / ～部署 *strategic plan (or deployment, disposition)* ◇ ～家 strategist; ～学 science of strategy

【战马】battle steed; war-horse

【战幕】war curtain (*used esp. in*): 拉(揭)开～ *lift the war curtain—start a war or a match*

【战袍】(in former times) war robe; soldier's garb

【战前】prewar: ～时期 *prewar period* / ～动员 *mobilization before a battle*

【战区】war zone; theatre of operations

【战胜】defeat; triumph over; vanquish; overcome: ～敌人 *defeat (or vanquish) the enemy* / ～困难 *overcome (or surmount) difficulties* / ～自然灾害 *conquer natural disasters* / 甲队～乙队。*Team A beat Team B*. ◇ ～国 victorious nation

【战时】wartime: ～编制 *wartime establishment*; *war footing* / ～内阁 *wartime cabinet*

【战史】military history; war history

【战士】❶ soldier; man: 人民解放军～ *a PLA soldier (or man)* / 新～ *a new recruit* ❷ champion; warrior; fighter: 国际主义～ *champion of internationalism*

【战事】war; hostilities: ～结束 *conclusion of the war*; *termination of hostilities* / 大军渡江前暂无～。*There was a lull in the fighting before the army crossed the Yangtze*.

【战书】written challenge to war; letter of challenge: 下～ *deliver a letter of challenge*

【战术】(military) tactics: ～核武器 *tactical nuclear weapons* / ～训练 *tactical training* / ～演习 *tactical manoeuvre* / ～指挥员 *commander of a tactical operation* ◇ ～学 science of tactics

【战死】die (or be killed) in battle

【战天斗地】fight against heaven and earth; combat nature; brave the elements

【战位】[军] battle station: 坚持～ *hold one's battle station*

【战无不胜】invincible; ever-victorious; all-conquering ——另见〖攻无不克〗

【战线】battle line; battlefront; front: 长达五百公里的～ *a front of 500 kilometres* / 思想～ *the ideological front* / 在各条～上 *on every front of endeavour*; *on all fronts*

【战役】campaign; battle ～性的进攻 *offensive campaign* / ～指挥员 *commander of a campaign* ◇ ～学 science of campaigns

【战鹰】fighting eagle (an affectionate term for a fighter plane)

【战友】comrade-in-arms; battle companion: ～的情谊 *comradeship-in-arms* / 老～ *one's old comrade-in-arms*

【战云】war cloud: ～密布 *gathering war clouds*

【战战兢兢】trembling with fear; with fear and trepidation; gingerly: 敌军怕遭埋伏，～地向前移动。*Fearing an ambush, the enemy troops advanced cautiously*.

【战阵】battle array; battle scene: 久经～的士兵 *battle-hardened troops*

【战争】war; warfare: 挑起～ *provoke a war* / ～的双方 *the two sides in a war*; *both belligerents* / ～升级 *war escalation* / ～温床 *hotbed of war* / ～政策 *policy of war*; *bellicose policy* ◇ ～保险 war insurance; ～边缘政策 brink of war policy; brinkmanship; ～贩子 warmonger; ～机器 war machine; war apparatus; ～狂 war mania; war hysteria; ～学 polemology; ～状态 state of war

栈

名 ❶ warehouse: 货栈 ❷ inn: 客栈 ❸ shed; pen: 羊～ *sheep pen* ❹ 见〖栈道〗

【栈道】a plank roadway built along perpendicular rock-faces by means of wooden brackets fixed into the cliff

【栈房】❶ warehouse; storehouse ❷〈方〉inn

【栈桥】landing stage (in a port); loading bridge (at a railway station)

站

Ⅰ 动 stand; be on one's feet; take a stand: ～起来 *stand up*; *rise to one's feet* / 往后～～! *Stand back!* / 别拿椅子了，就～着看吧。*Don't bother to get chairs. Let's just stand and watch*. Ⅱ 名 ❶ stop; halt: 这车中途不～。*This bus makes no stops along the way*. / 东京是总统此次亚洲之行的第二～。*Tokyo is the President's second stop on his Asia trip*. ❷ station; stop: 我下一～下车。*I get off at the next stop*. ❸ station or centre for rendering certain services: 供应～ *supply centre*

【站不住脚】unable to stand one's ground; cannot be justified; impossible to defend

【站得高,看得远】stand high and see far; have vision; be far-sighted

【站队】line up; fall in; stand in line: 我们站好了队准备出发。*We lined up and got ready to start*.

【站岗】stand (or mount) guard; be on sentry duty; stand sentry: 站好最后一班岗 (*of one who is about to leave his job*) *continue working hard till the last minute*

【站柜台】serve as a shop assistant; a serve behind the counter

【站立】stand; be on one's feet: 他腿疼得厉害，几乎不能～。*His leg was so painful that he could hardly stand*.

【站票】ticket for standing room; standing ticket: ～观众 *standee* / 本处只售～。*Standing room only*.

【站哨】〈方〉stand (or mount) guard; be on sentry duty; stand sentry

【站台】platform (in a railway station) ◇ ～票 platform ticket

【站位】court position; playing position

【站稳】❶ come to a stop: 等车～了再下。*Don't get out until the car stops*. ❷ stand firm; take a firm stand: ～脚跟 *get a firm foothold*; *stand firm*

【站长】head of a station, centre, etc.: 火车站～ *stationmaster*

【站住】❶ stop; halt: ～，要不就开枪了! *Halt, or I'll fire!* / 谁? ～! *Who's that? Don't move!* ❷ stand firmly on one's feet; keep one's feet: 风刮得人都站不住了。*The wind was so strong that one could hardly keep one's feet*. ❸ stand (or hold) one's ground; consolidate one's position ❹ hold water; be tenable: 他的说法站不住。*His opinion doesn't hold water*.

【站住脚】❶ stop; halt: 他跑得太快，一下子站不住脚。*He was running too fast to stop suddenly*. ❷ stand (or hold) one's ground; consolidate one's position：我们向敌人猛烈攻击，打得他们站不住脚。*We attacked the enemy so fiercely that they couldn't hold their ground.* ❸ stay put：忙得站不住脚 *be so busy one can't stand still* ❹ hold water；be tenable：这些论点没有一个是站得住脚的。*None of these arguments are tenable.*

绽 动 split；burst：衣裳～线了。*The seam has split* (*or burst*).

【绽放】(of flowers) burst forth；burst into bloom

【绽裂】split open；burst open：棉桃～，露出雪白的棉花。*The cotton bolls burst open, revealing masses of snow-white fibres.*

【绽露】show；appear：人们的脸上～出幸福的笑容。*Happy smiles appeared on everyone's face.*

湛 形 ❶ profound；deep：精湛 ❷ crystal clear

【湛蓝】(of the sky，the sea，a lake，etc.) azure blue；azure：～的天空 *azure skies*

【湛清】limpid；clear：～的溪水 *a limpid stream*

颤 动 tremble；shiver；shudder：打颤 ——另见 chàn

【颤栗】同〖战栗〗

蘸 动 dip in (ink，sauce，etc.)：～墨水 *dip in ink* / 大葱～酱 *scallions dipped in thick sauce*

【蘸火】〈口〉quench

【蘸水钢笔】dip pen

zhāng

张 Ⅰ 动 ❶ open；spread；stretch：～开手 *open one's hand* / ～翅膀 *spread the wings* / ～网 *spread a net* / ～开双臂 *stretch out both arms* / ～弓 *draw a bow* / ～帆 *make sail；hoist sail* ❷ set out；display：大～筵席 *lay on a feast* ❸ magnify；exaggerate：夸张 ❹ look：张望 ❺ (of a shop) start business；set up：开张 Ⅱ 量：一～桌子 *a table* / 两～床 *two beds* / 一～纸 *a piece* (*or sheet*) *of paper* / 一～弓 *a bow* / 你这～嘴啊！*What a tongue you've got!* Ⅲ 名 the twenty-sixth of the twenty-eight constellations (二十八宿) into which the celestial sphere was divided in ancient Chinese astronomy (consisting of five stars in the shape of a drawn bow in Hydra)

【张榜】put up a notice；post a notice

【张本】❶ an anticipatory action ❷ a hint foreshadowing later developments in a story；an anticipatory remark

【张弛】tension and relaxation；tightness and looseness ——另见〖一张一弛〗

【张大】〈书〉magnify；exaggerate；publicize widely：～其词 *exaggerate；overstate* / ～其事 *publicize widely；play up*

【张灯结彩】be decorated with lanterns and coloured streamers；be decked with lanterns and bunting；be decked out and hung with lanterns；be gay with lanterns and decorations

【张挂】hang up (a picture，curtain，etc.)

【张冠李戴】put Zhang's hat on Li's head—attribute sth. to the wrong person or confuse one thing with another

【张皇】〈书〉alarmed；scared；flurried；flustered ◇ ～失措 be in a flurry of alarm；lose one's head；get into a panic

【张口结舌】be agape and tongue-tied；be at a loss for words：他被问得～，半天说不出话来。*He was stumped by the questions and remained tonguetied for a long time.*

【张狂】flippant and impudent；insolent

【张力】［物］❶ tension ❷ pulling force ◇ ～计 tensiometer

【张量】［数］tensor

【张罗】❶ take care of；get busy about：要带的东西早点儿收拾好，不要临时～。*Get your things ready in good time to avoid a last-minute rush.* ❷ raise (funds)；get together (money，etc.)：～一笔钱 *raise a sum of money* ❸ greet and entertain (guests)；attend to (customers，etc.)：她正忙着～客人。*She's busy looking after the guests.*

【张目】❶ open one's eyes wide：～注视 *watch wide-eyed* ❷ (usu. used in) 为某人～ *boost sb.'s arrogance；build up another*

【张三李四】Zhang，Li or anybody —any Tom，Dick or Harry

【张贴】put up (a notice，poster，etc.)：～海报 *put up posters* / ～通告 *post a notice* / 禁止～。*Post no bills.*

【张望】❶ peep (through a crack，etc.) ❷ look around：探头～ *crane one's neck and look around*

【张牙舞爪】bare fangs and brandish claws—make threatening gestures；engage in sabre rattling

【张扬】make widely known；make public；publicize：四处～ *publicize everywhere；spread (a story) all over the place*

【张应力】［物］tensile stress

【张嘴】❶ open one's mouth (to say sth.)：他正要～，一个年轻妇女抢先说了。*He was on the point of saying something when a young woman started to speak.* ❷ ask for a loan or a favour：我想找他帮忙，又不好意思～。*I would have liked him to give me a hand, but found it embarrassing to ask.*

章 名 ❶ chapter；section：全书共20～。*The book has twenty chapters.* ❷ order：杂乱无章 ❸ rules；regulations；constitution：规章 ❹ item；clause：约法三章 ❺ seal；stamp：刻个～ *engrave a seal* ❻ badge；medal：领章

【章程】❶ rules；regulations；constitution：会员～ *membership regulations* ❷〈方〉solution；way：我心里还没个准～。*I'm not sure yet what's the best way.*

【章法】❶ presentation of ideas in a piece of writing；art of composition：文章结构严谨，很有～。*The article is well organized and the ideas are skilfully presented*. ❷ orderly ways；methodicalness：他办事很有～。*He is quite methodical in his work*. / 碰到这样意外的事，他乱了～。*He was thrown off balance by such an unexpected turn of events*.

【章回体】a type of traditional Chinese novel with each chapter headed by a couplet giving the gist of its content

【章回小说】同〖章回体〗

【章节】chapters and sections

【章句】❶ chapters，sections，sentences and phrases in ancient texts ❷ syntactic and semantic analysis of ancient texts：～之学 *the philological study of ancient texts*

【章鱼】octopus

彰 Ⅰ 形 clear；evident；conspicuous：昭彰 Ⅱ 动 make known；display：表彰

【彰明较著】very obvious；conspicuous；easily seen

【彰善瘅恶】praise good and denounce evil；uphold virtue and condemn vice

【彰彰】clear；evident；conspicuous：～若是 *as clear (or obvious) as that* / ～在人耳目 *be clear for all to see*

獐 名 river deer

【獐头鼠目】with the head of a buck and the eyes of a rat—repulsively ugly and sly-looking

【獐子】river deer

樟 名 camphor tree

【樟蚕】a kind of wild silkworm (Eriogyna pyretorum)

【樟木】camphorwood

【樟脑】camphor

【樟脑丸】camphor ball；moth-ball

【樟脑油】camphor oil

【樟树】camphor tree

蟑（构词成分）见下

【蟑螂】cockroach；roach

zhǎng

长 Ⅰ 形 ❶older；elder；senior：比他年～ *older than him* / 他比我～一辈。*He belongs to my father's generation*. / 他比我～两岁。*He is senior to me by two years*. or *He is two years my senior*. ❷ eldest；oldest：～兄 *eldest brother* / ～女 *eldest daughter* Ⅱ 名 chief；head：科长 / 首长 Ⅲ 动 ❶ grow；develop：青年时期是～身体的时期。*Youth is the time of physical growth*. / 庄稼～得很旺。*The crops are growing very well*. ❷ come into being；begin to grow；form：～疮 *have a boil* / ～癌 *get cancer* / ～锈 *get rusty* / 孩子～牙了。*The baby is teething*. / ～叶子了。*The leaves are coming out*. / 桃树～虫了。*The peach tree is wormy*. ❸ acquire；enhance；increase：～见识 *increase one's knowledge*；*gain experience* / ～工资 *get an increase in salary*；*get a pay rise* (*or pay raise*) ——另见 cháng

【长辈】elder member of a family；elder；senior

【长膘】(of a domestic animal) get fat；put on flesh；flesh out

【长大】grow up；be brought up：我～了当医生。*I'm going to be a doctor when I grow up*.

【长房】the eldest branch of a family (i. e. that of the eldest son)

【长个儿】grow taller

【长官】〈旧〉senior officer or official；commanding officer

【长机】[军] lead aircraft；leader

【长进】progress：在学习上很有～ *make good progress in one's studies*

【长老】❶〈书〉elder ❷ (a respectful term of address for an old monk) elder

【长老会】[宗] the Presbyterian Church

【长毛】(zhǎngmáo)〈方〉become mildewed；be covered with mildew：馒头放久了就会～。*Steamed bread will go mouldy if kept long*. ——另见 chángmáo

【长肉】put on flesh；fill out：这孩子光长个儿，不～。*The child keeps growing taller but doesn't fill out*.

【长势】the way a crop is growing：作物～良好。*The crops are doing well*. / 棉花～喜人。*The cotton is coming along fine*.

【长孙】❶ eldest son's eldest son ❷ eldest grandson

【长相】〈口〉looks；features；appearance：～好 *be good-looking* / 看她们的～好像是姐儿俩。*They look like sisters*.

【长者】❶ elder；senior ❷ venerable elder

【长子】eldest son ◇ ～继承权 (right of) primogeniture；birthright

涨 动 (of water，prices，etc.) rise；go up：潮～了。*The tide is rising*. or *The tide is in*. / 火车票又～了。*Train fares are rising again*. ——另见 zhàng

【涨潮】rising tide；flood tide：正在～。*The tide is at the flood*.

【涨风】upward trend of prices：股市掀起了～。*There is an upswing of prices on the stock market*.

【涨幅】extent of price increase：上个月物价～是今年来最小的一个月. *Last month saw the smallest price increase of the year*.

【涨价】rise in price

【涨落】(of water，prices，etc.) rise and fall；fluctuate：潮水的～ *ebb and flow of the tide* / 价格的～ *fluctuations of prices*

【涨水】(of a river) rise；(of price) rise

掌 Ⅰ 名 ❶ palm：击掌 ❷ the bottom of certain animals' feet；pad；sole：鸭掌 ❸ shoe sole or heel：鞋子打前后～ *have a shoe soled and heeled* ❹ horseshoe：这匹马该钉～了。*It's time for the horse to be shod*. Ⅱ 动 ❶strike with the palm of the hand; slap: 掌嘴 ❷ hold in one's hand; be in charge of; control; wield: 掌权 ❸〈方〉mend (a shoe sole): ～鞋 *have a shoe sole mended* ❹〈方〉put in (salt, oil, etc.): ～点酱油 *put in some soy sauce* ❺〈方〉(used in the same way as 把 bǎ): ～门关上。*Close the door*.

【掌厨】be the chief cook; be in charge of cooking: 今天李主任亲自～,一定有喜事吧。*It must be a special occasion today for Director Li to do the cooking himself*.

【掌灯】❶ hold a lamp in one's hand ❷ light an oil lamp

【掌舵】❶ be at the helm; operate the rudder; take the tiller; steer a boat ❷ helmsman; steersman

【掌骨】[生理] metacarpal bone

【掌故】anecdotes: 文坛～ *literary anecdotes* / 他熟悉这座城市的～。*He knows a lot of historical anecdotes about this city*.

【掌管】be in charge of; administer: ～财政 *administer finances* / ～一个部门 *be in charge of a department* / 各项事务都有专人～。*Everything is taken care of by specially assigned people*.

【掌柜】(又作'掌柜的') ❶ shopkeeper; manager (of a shop) ❷〈方〉husband

【掌权】be in power; wield power; exercise control

【掌上明珠】a pearl in the palm—a beloved daughter: 女儿是他的～。*His daughter was the apple of his eye*.

【掌上型电脑】palm computer; palm held computer

【掌勺儿】(又作'掌锅','掌灶') be the chef: ～的 *chef*

【掌声】clapping; applause: 经久不息的～ *prolonged applause* ◇ ～雷动 thunderous applause

【掌握】❶ grasp; master; know well: ～一门外国语 *have a good command of a foreign language* / ～现代生产技能和科学知识 *master modern techniques of production and scientific knowledge* ❷ have in hand; take into one's hands; control: ～主动权 *have the initiative in one's hands* / ～自己的命运 *take one's destiny into one's own hands; be master of one's own destiny*

【掌心】❶ the centre (or hollow) of the palm ❷ control; influence: 他好像跳不出她的～。*He seems to be unable to break free from her control*.

【掌印】keep the seal—be in power

【掌子】❶(又作'掌子面')[矿] face; work area ❷ horseshoe

【掌嘴】slap sb.'s face; box sb.'s ears

zhàng

丈 Ⅰ 量 zhang, a unit of length ($3\frac{1}{3}$ metres) Ⅱ 动 measure (land): 春耕前要把地～完。*We must finish measuring the land before spring ploughing*. Ⅲ 名 ❶ senior; elder ❷ husband (used in certain kinship terms): 姑丈

【丈二和尚,摸不着头脑】you can't touch the head of the ten-foot monk —you can't make head or tail of it; be very much in the dark

【丈夫】❶ man: ～气概 *manliness* ❷ husband

【丈量】measure (land): ～土地 *measure land; take the dimensions of a field*

【丈人】wife's father; father-in-law

仗 Ⅰ 名 ❶〈书〉weaponry; weapons: 仪仗 ❷ battle; war: 那是这场战争中的最后一～。*That was the last battle of the war*. / 打好春耕这一～ *make a success of this spring ploughing* Ⅱ 动 ❶ hold (a weapon): ～剑 *hold a sword* ❷ rely on; depend on: 这事我一人干不了,全～大家帮忙。*I can't manage it on my own. I must rely on all of you for help*.

【仗势欺人】take advantage of one's own or sb. else's power to bully people; bully people on the strength of one's powerful connections or position; abuse one's power and bully people

【仗恃】rely on (an advantage)

【仗义】❶〈书〉uphold justice ❷ be loyal (to one's friends)

【仗义疏财】be generous in aiding needy people

【仗义执言】speak out from a sense of justice

杖 Ⅰ 名 ❶ cane; stick: 扶～而行 *walk with a cane* ❷ rod or staff used for a specific purpose: 擀面杖 Ⅱ 动 flogging with a stick (a punishment in ancient China)

帐 名 curtain; canopy: 蚊帐

【帐钩】bed-curtain or mosquito net hook

【帐幕】tent

【帐篷】tent: 搭(拆)～ *pitch (strike) a tent* ◇ ～拖车 tent-trailer

【帐子】❶ bed-curtain ❷ mosquito net

账 名 ❶ account: ～算出来没有? *Have you figured out the account?* / 从～上看我们超支了。*The accounts show we have spent more than we received*. ❷ account book: 一本～ *an account book* ❸ debt; bill: ～都还清了。*All of the debt was paid off*. / ～付了没有? *Have you paid the bill?*

【账簿】(也作'账本') account book

【账册】account book

【账单】bill; check: 服务员拿来了～。*The waiter came with the bill*.

【账房】〈旧〉❶ accountant's office ❷ accountant

【账号】number of a bank account

【账户】account: 非贸易～ *noncommercial account* / 在银行开立(结束)～ *open (close) an account with a bank*

【账款】funds on account; credit

【账面】as shown in an account book: ～价值 *book value* / ～利润 *book profit* / ～损失 *book loss* / ～盈余 *book surplus* / ～余额 *book balance* / ～债务 *book debt*

【账目】items of an account; accounts: 清理～ *square accounts* / 定期公布～ *publish the accounts regularly* / ～公开 *accounts open to public inspection* / ～不清。*The accounts* (*or books*) *are not in order*.

胀 动 ❶ expand; distend: 热～冷缩 *expand with heat and contract with cold* ❷ swell; be bloated: 我吃多了,肚子有点～。*I've overeaten and feel bloated*.

【胀闸】hub brake

涨 动 ❶ swell after absorbing water, etc.: 豆子泡～了。*The beans swelled up after being soaked*. ❷ (of the head) be swelled by a rush of blood: 气得～红了脸 *redden* (*or flush*) *with anger* ❸ be more, larger, etc. than expected: 上个月他钱花～了。*Last month he couldn't make ends meet*. ——另见 zhǎng

障 Ⅰ 动 hinder; obstruct: 障碍 Ⅱ 名 barrier; block: 路障

【障碍】❶ hinder; obstruct: ～物 *obstacle*; *barrier*; *entanglement* ❷ obstacle; obstruction; barrier; impediment: 两国正在进行的谈判遇到了～。*The current talks between the two countries have run into obstacles*. ◇ ～船 [军] blockship; ～赛跑 steeplechase; obstacle race

【障蔽】block; obstruct; shut out: ～视线 *obstruct one's view*

【障幕】screen; covering veil: 浓烟如～ *thick veil of smoke*

【障眼法】cover-up; camouflage: 玩弄～ *throw dust into people's eyes*

【障子】a barrier made of reeds, sorghum stalks or closely planted shrubs; hedge

幛 名 a large, oblong sheet of silk with an appropriate message attached, presented at a wedding, birthday or funeral

【幛子】同〖幛〗

嶂 名 a screen-like mountain peak

瘴 名 miasma

【瘴疠】communicable subtropical diseases, such as pernicious malaria, etc.

【瘴气】miasma

zhāo

招 Ⅰ 动 ❶ beckon: 他把手一～,要我跟上。*He beckoned me to follow*. ❷ recruit; enlist; enrol: 学校下学期～200人。*The school will enrol 200 pupils next term*. ❸ attract; incur; court: ～苍蝇 *attract flies* / ～灾 *court disaster*; *invite calamity* / ～人嫌 *incur odium* / ～人喜欢的孩子 *a charming* (*or lovable*) *child* ❹ provoke; tease: 这孩子爱哭,别～他。*He's a crybaby*. *Don't tease him*. ❺〈方〉infect; be contagious: 这病～人。*This disease is catching*. ❻ confess; own up: 犯人已经～了。*The prisoner has confessed*. / 他死也不肯～。*Nothing could make him own up*. Ⅱ 名 ❶ a move in chess ❷ 同〖招式〗

【招安】(of feudal rulers) offer amnesty and enlistment to rebels: 受～ (*of former rebels*) *accept amnesty and serve the ruler*

【招办】(〈略〉全称为'招生办公室') admissions office

【招标】invite tenders (or bids, public bidding) ◇ ～制 competive-bidding system

【招兵】recruit soldiers; raise troops ◇ ～买马 recruit men and buy horses—raise or enlarge an army; recruit followers

【招财进宝】let riches and treasures come into the house

【招待】receive (guests); entertain; serve (customers): 设宴～外宾 *give a dinner for* (*or in honour of*) *foreign guests* / ～客人 *entertain guests* / 谢谢你们的热情～。*Thank you for your kind hospitality*. / ～费 *entertainment allowance or expenses* ◇ ～券 complimentary ticket; ～所 guest house; hostel

【招待会】reception: 冷餐～ *buffet reception* / 举行～ *give* (*or hold*) *a reception*

【招风】catch the wind—attract too much attention and invite trouble ◇ ～耳 protruding ears; flappy ears

【招蜂引蝶】attract bees and butterflies —(of a woman) flirtatious

【招干】recruit cadres: ～条件 *qualifications for recruitment* / 张榜～ *open recruitment through advertisement*

【招工】advertise for workers; recruit workers ◇ ～提干 recruit workers and promote personnel

【招供】make a confession of one's crime; confess

【招股】raise capital by floating shares ◇ ～书 [经] prospectus (stocks and shares); ～章程 prospectus

【招雇】recruit; employ: ～农工 *recruit farm workers*

【招呼】❶ call: 那边有人～你。*Someone over there is calling you*. ❷ hail; greet; say hello to: 热情地打～ *greet warmly* ❸ notify; tell: ～他赶快来开会。*Tell him to come to the meeting at once*. / 你要是不去,事先打个～。*Let me know beforehand if you won't be going*. ❹ take care of: ～老人 *take care of old people* ❺〈方〉mind; take care: 路上有冰,～滑倒了。*The road is icy. Mind you don't slip*.

【招唤】summon; call: 把孩子～过来。*Call the boy over here*.

【招幌】shop sign (formerly signs and emblems denoting certain trades, e. g. barbershop, blacksmith, wine merchant, grain merchant, etc.)

【招魂】call back the spirit of the dead

【招集】call together; convene

【招架】ward off blows; hold one's own: ～不住 *be unable to hold one's own*; *unable to withstand* / 只有～之功,没有还手之力 *can only parry sb.'s blows without being able to hit back*

【招考】give public notice of entrance examination; admit (students, applicants, etc.) by examination

【招徕】solicit (customers or business); canvass: ～顾客 *solicit customers* / 以广～ *so as to have more customers*

【招揽】solicit (customers or business); canvass: ～主顾 *solicit customers* / ～生意 *canvass; seek business orders; drum up trade*

【招领】announce the finding of lost property: 失物～(*a notice*) *Found* / 拾物～处 *Lost and Found*

【招录】recruit; employ: ～通知 *recruitment notice; letter of employment*

【招募】recruit; enlist

【招纳】〈书〉recruit: ～贤士 *recruit men of worth*

【招女婿】take a man into the family as a son-in-law

【招牌】shop sign; signboard: 据说这～是一位名书法家写的。*This signboard is said to have been written by a famous calligrapher.* / 打着人道主义的～ *under the signboard of humanitarianism*

【招聘】❶ give public notice of vacancies to be filled; invite applications for jobs; advertise for (a secretary, teacher, etc.): ～技术工人 *advertise for skilled workers* ❷ want ad; wanted (for a job): ～会计一名 *Wanted: An Accountant*

【招亲】❶ 同〖招女婿〗❷ marry into and live with one's bride's family

【招请】❶ hire help ❷ invite: ～神女下凡 *invite a goddess to come down to earth*

【招惹】❶ provoke; incur; court: ～麻烦 *bring trouble* ❷〈方〉(usu. used in the negative) tease; provoke: 这人～不得。*You'd better not provoke that fellow.* ◇ ～是非 bring trouble on oneself

【招认】confess one's crime; plead guilty

【招商】invite outside investment

【招生】enrol new students; recruit students: ～制度 *enrolment system; admissions system* / ～简章 *school admission brochure*

【招式】movements in martial arts or traditional opera

【招事】bring trouble on oneself; invite trouble

【招收】recruit; take in: ～工人 *recruit workers* / ～大学生 *enrol new students in universities and colleges*

【招手】beckon; wave: 他～要我进去。*He beckoned me in.* / ～致意 *wave one's greetings; wave back in acknowledgement* / 胜利在向我们～。*Victory beckons.*

【招数】同〖着数〗

【招贴】poster; placard; bill ◇ ～画 pictorial poster (or placard)

【招贤】❶ (of a ruler) summon men of worth to serve their country ❷ call the able to service

【招降】summon sb. to surrender ◇ ～纳叛 recruit deserters and traitors

【招训】recruit and train: ～空中小姐 *recruit and train air stewardesses*

【招眼】eye-catching: 你这身儿打扮太～。*Your clothes are rather too loud.*

【招摇】act ostentatiously ◇ ～过市 swagger through the streets —blatantly seek publicity; ～撞骗 swindle and bluff; bluff one's way around

【招引】attract; induce: 灯光～蛾子。*Lights attract moths.*

【招怨】incur hatred

【招灾惹祸】court disaster; invite trouble: 这孩子老给大人～。*This child is always making trouble for his parents.*

【招展】❶ flutter; wave: 工地上红旗～。*Red flags fluttered over the construction site.* ❷ invite (institutes) to rent exhibition positions

【招致】❶ recruit (followers); scout about for (talents, etc.) ❷ incur; bring about; lead to: ～意外的损失 *incur unexpected losses* / ～失败 *cause defeat* / ～无穷后患 *lead to endless trouble*

【招赘】同〖招女婿〗

【招租】(house) for rent: 此屋～。*Room to let.*

昭 形 clear; obvious: 昭著

【昭布】make known to the public

【昭告】declare to the public

【昭然】clear; obvious

【昭然若揭】abundantly clear; all too clear

【昭示】make clear to all; declare publicly: ～全国 *declare to the whole nation*

【昭苏】〈书〉come to life; wake up: 大地回春,万物～。*Spring comes round, quickening all creation.*

【昭雪】exonerate; rehabilitate: 冤案得到了～。*The wrong has been righted.* or *The person wronged has been rehabilitated.*

【昭彰】clear; manifest; evident: 罪恶昭彰

【昭著】clear; evident; obvious: 成绩～ *have achieved signal successes*

着 Ⅰ 名 ❶ a move in chess: 妙～儿 *a clever move* / 走错一～ *make a false move; take a wrong step* ❷ trick; device; move: 这一～厉害。*That's a shrewd move.* / 他没～儿了。*He's at the end of his tether.* Ⅱ 动〈方〉put in; add: ～点儿盐 *put some salt in it* Ⅲ 副 all right; O.K.: ～,咱们就这么办。*O.K., that's what we'll do then.* ——另见 zháo; zhe; zhuó

【着数】(又作'着法') ❶ a move in chess ❷ a movement in wushu (武术) ❸ trick; device

朝 名 ❶ early morning; morning: 一朝一夕 ❷ day: 今朝 ——另见 cháo

【朝不保夕】not know at dawn what may happen by dusk; be in a precarious state

【朝不谋夕】(又作'朝不虑夕') be unable to plan one's day; be in a precarious state

【朝发夕至】start at dawn and arrive at dusk—a day's journey

【朝晖】morning sunlight: 祖国大地尽～。*This vast*

land of ours is glowing in the morning sun.

【朝令夕改】issue an order at dawn and rescind it at dusk; make unpredictable changes in policy

【朝露】〈文〉morning dew—ephemeral; transitory

【朝气】youthful spirit; vigour; vitality: 富有～ *be full of vigour* ◇ ～蓬勃 full of youthful spirit; full of vigour and vitality; imbued with vitality

【朝秦暮楚】serve (the State of) Qin in the morning and (the State of) Chu in the evening—be quick to switch sides; be fickle; be inconstant

【朝三暮四】blow hot and cold; chop and change

【朝思暮想】yearn day and night: 我～,连做梦也见到她。*I think about her from dawn to dusk; I see her even in my dreams.*

【朝夕】❶ morning and evening; from morning to night; day and night; daily: ～相处 *be together from morning to night; be closely associated* ❷ a very short time

【朝霞】rosy clouds of dawn; rosy dawn

【朝阳】(zhāoyáng) the rising sun; the morning sun ◇ ～产业(又作'朝阳工业') sunrise industry——另见 cháoyáng

zháo

着 动 ❶ touch; come in contact with: 我手上的烫伤一～水就疼。*The burns on my hand hurt when they get in contact with water.* ❷ be affected by (cold, etc.); be troubled with; suffer: 着凉 ❸ be ignited; be lit: 火～了。*The fire is lit.* / 炉子～得很旺。*The stove is going strong.* / 天黑了,路灯都～了。*It's dark, and the street lights are all on.* / 汽油一点就～。*Gasoline is highly inflammable.* ❹〈方〉fall asleep: 他困得很,一上床就～了。*He was so tired that he fell asleep the moment he got into bed.* ❺ (used as a complement to another verb) hitting the mark; succeeding in: 这回你可说～了。*This time you really hit the nail on the head.* / 灯点～了。*The lamp is lit.* / 他整夜翻来复去睡不～。*He tossed about all night, unable to get to sleep.* ——另见 zhāo; zhe; zhuó

【着风】be chilled by the wind: 我两个肩膀酸疼,想是夜里着了风。*My shoulders ache. I must have been chilled by the wind during the night.*

【着慌】get nervous; get alarmed; become flustered (or jittery); be thrown into a panic: 这下子他可～了。*At that point he panicked.*

【着火】catch fire; be on fire: ～啦! *Fire!* / 房子～了。*The house is on fire.* / 木头容易～。*Wood catches fire easily.*

【着急】get worried; get excited; feel anxious: 别～,安心养病。*Just take care of yourself and don't worry.* / 冷静点,别～。*Keep calm. Don't get excited.*

【着凉】catch cold; catch a chill: 外面有点冷,当心～。*It's chilly outside; be careful not to catch cold.*

【着忙】be in a hurry; be in a rush: 别～,还来得及。*Don't be in such a hurry; there's still time.*

【着迷】be fascinated; be captivated: 孩子们听故事都听得着了迷。*The children were spellbound by the story.* / 他对音乐着了迷。*He's crazy about music.*

【着魔】be bewitched; be possessed; crazy: 他着了魔似的站在那里不动。*He stood still like a man possessed.*

【着色】coloration: ～玻璃 *stained glass; pigmented glass* / ～橡胶 *tinted rubber*

zhǎo

爪 名 claw; talon ——另见 zhuǎ

【爪哇】Java

【爪牙】talons and fangs—lackeys; underlings

找 动 ❶ look for; try to find; seek: ～机会 *look for (or seek) an opportunity* / ～出路 *seek a way out* / 从世界观上～原因 *seek the cause (of an error) in a person's world outlook* / ～答案 *try to find the answer* ❷ want to see; call on; approach; ask for: 有人～你。*Someone wants to see you.* / 有人来～过我吗? *Did anyone ask for me?* / 明天再来～你。*I'll call on you again tomorrow.* ❸ give change: 她～我20元。*She gave me 20 yuan change (or in change).* / 甭～了。*(to a taxi driver, etc.) Keep the change.*

【找补】make up a deficiency: 请点一下,不够再～。*Count it, please. We'll make it up if there's any shortage.* / 这儿没焊好,再～两下。*The welding is faulty here. Let's touch it up.*

【找不开】have no small change for (money of a higher denomination): 对不起,你这张百元票子我～。*Sorry, I have no small change for your 100-yuan note.*

【找不自在】〈口〉ask for trouble; borrow trouble; bring trouble upon oneself: 你去劝他是～。*You are borrowing trouble if you try to persuade him.*

【找茬儿】find fault; pick holes; pick a quarrel: 他在～吵架。*He's trying to find some excuse and start a quarrel.*

【找对象】look for a partner in marriage

【找麻烦】❶ look for trouble; ask for trouble ❷ cause sb. trouble: 对不起,给你们～了。*I'm sorry to have caused you so much trouble.*

【找米下锅】❶〈字〉search for rice to cook ❷〈喻〉look for supplies of raw materials instead of waiting for state allocations

【找平】make level; level up or down: 右手边儿还差两层砖,～了再下班。*The right side needs two more layers of bricks. Let's lay them before knocking off for the day.*

【找婆家】look for a husband: 她今年28了,还没～。*She is twenty-eight this year, and still unmarried.*

【找齐】❶ make uniform; even up: 打埂得～。*The*

tops of ridges should be made even. ❷ make up a deficiency：先付一部分，差多少交货时～。*We'll pay you part of the sum now. The balance will be paid on delivery of the goods*.

【找钱】give change：售货员找了我钱。*The shop assistant gave* (*or handed*) *me my change*. / 这是找给你的钱。*Here's your change*.

【找事】❶ look (or hunt) for a job ❷ pick a quarrel

【找死】〈诋〉court death：你～啊！(*as said by a driver to another driver or a pedestrian trying to cut him off*) *What are you up to? Do you want to kill yourself?*

【找头】change (from money paid)：这是给你的～。*Here is your change*.

【找寻】❶ look for; seek ❷〈方〉find fault with; pick on：他爱～人。*He likes to pick on someone or other*.

沼 名 natural pond：池沼

【沼气】marsh gas; firedamp; methane; sewage gas; sludge gas：～池 *methane-generating pit; methane tank*

【沼泽】marsh; swamp; bog：～地 *marshland; swamp* / ～土 *bog soil*

zhào

召 Ⅰ 动 call together; convene; summon：号召 Ⅱ 名 (usu. used as part of a place name) temple; monastery

【召唤】call (usu.〈喻〉)：大草原在～着我们。*The grasslands are calling us*.

【召回】recall：～大使 *recall an ambassador* / ～国书 *letter of recall*

【召集】call together; convene：～会议 *call* (*or convene*) *a conference* ◇ ～人 convener

【召见】❶ call in (a subordinate) ❷ diplomacy summon (an envoy) to an interview

【召开】convene; convoke：～一次国际会议 *convene an international conference*

【召之即来】come as soon as called; be on call：～，来之能战，战之能胜。*Be ready to assemble at the first call and be capable of fighting and winning*.

兆 Ⅰ 名 sign; omen; portent：不祥之兆 Ⅱ 动 portend; foretell：瑞雪兆丰年 Ⅲ 数 ❶ million; mega- ❷ (in ancient times) a million millions; billion

【兆赫】[电子] megahertz (MHz); megacycle per second

【兆头】(又作'兆候') sign; omen; portent：好(坏)～ *a good* (*bad*) *omen* / 早晨有雾是晴天的～。*Mist in the morning is a sign of good weather*.

【兆位】megabit (Mb)

【兆周】[无] megacycle

【兆字节】[计] megabyte

诏 〈书〉Ⅰ 动 instruct Ⅱ 名 imperial edict

【诏令】imperial edict

【诏书】imperial edict

笊 (构词成分) 见下

【笊篱】a bamboo, wicker or wire strainer

照 Ⅰ 动 ❶ shine; illuminate; light up：车灯把大路～得通亮。*The headlights lit up the road*. / 拿手电～路 *light the way with a torch* ❷ reflect; mirror：～镜子 *look in the mirror* / 湖面～出了她的倒影。*Her image was reflected in the lake*. ❸ take a picture (or photograph); photograph; film; shoot：这镜头可不容易～。*This scene is by no means easy to shoot*. / 这张照片里我没～好。*I don't come out well in this photo*. ❹ take care of; look after：照看 ❺ notify ❻ contrast：对照 ❼ understand：心照不宣 Ⅱ 名 ❶ photograph; picture：小照 ❷ license; permit：禁止无～行车。*It is forbidden to drive without a license*. Ⅲ 介 ❶ in the direction of; towards：～这个方向走。*Go in this direction*. / 拿起茶碗～脸就打 *pick up a teacup and throw it in sb.'s face* ❷ according to; in accordance with：～他们的说法 *according to what they say* / ～规章办事 *act in accordance with the regulations* / ～我看，线路有毛病。*It seems to me there's something wrong with the circuit*.

【照搬】indiscriminately imitate; copy：全盘～人家的经验 *copy indiscriminately the experience of others*

【照办】act accordingly; act in accordance with; act upon; comply with; follow：你们提出的要求我们尽量～。*We'll try our best to comply with your request*.

【照本宣科】read item by item from the text; repeat what the book says

【照壁】(又作'照墙') a screen wall facing the gate of a house

【照常】as usual：～营业 *business as usual* / 遇雨比赛～进行。*The match will be played as scheduled in the event of rain*.

【照抄】❶ copy word for word：这个材料请你～一份。*Please make a copy of this material*. ❷ 同〖照搬〗

【照登】publish sth. as it is (i.e. without alterations)

【照度】[物] intensity of illumination; illuminance

【照发】❶ issue as before：女工产假期间工资～。*Women workers are entitled to maternity leave with full pay*. or *Women workers receive full pay during maternity leave*. ❷ approved for distribution (used for notices or circulars submitted for approval)

【照拂】〈书〉look after; care for; attend to：请惠予～。*Please be so kind as to take good care of him*.

【照顾】❶ give consideration to; show consideration for; make allowance(s) for：～实际需要 *consider actual needs* / ～他的困难 *take his dif-*

ficulties into account / 给予适当～ *give appropriate preferential treatment* ❷ look after; care for; attend to: ～伤员 *look after the wounded* ❸ (of a customer) patronize

【照管】look after; tend; be in charge of: ～孩子 *look after a child*; *mind a child* / ～机器 *tend a machine* / ～仓库 *be in charge of a storehouse*

【照葫芦画瓢】draw a dipper with a gourd as a model—copy; imitate

【照护】look after (patients, the wounded, etc.)

【照会】❶ present (or deliver, address) a note to (a government) ❷ note: 提出～ *present (or deliver, address) a note* / 交换～ *exchange notes* / 普通～ *note verbale* / 正式～ *formal note*; *official note*

【照价】according to the set (or arranged) price: ～付款 *pay according to the arranged price* / 如有损坏,～赔偿 *pay the full price for anything damaged*

【照旧】as before; as usual; as of old: 程序～。*The procedure remains unchanged*. / 参观改期,入场券～有效。*Visit postponed. Tickets remain valid*.

【照看】look after; attend to; keep an eye on: 她在幼儿园～孩子。*She looks after children in the kindergarten*. / ～病人 *attend to a patient* / 劳驾帮我～一下行李。*Will you please keep an eye on my luggage*.

【照理】according to reason; in the ordinary course of events; normally: ～他现在该来了。*He ought to be here by now*.

【照例】as a rule; as usual; usually: 那天早上,他～起得很早。*That morning he got up very early, as usual*.

【照料】take care of; attend to: 她把小女儿托给一位老大娘～。*She left her baby daughter in the care of an old woman*. / 你放心走吧,这里的事有我们～。*Don't you worry. We'll take care of everything while you're away*.

【照临】shine on; illuminate; light up: 曙光～大地。*The early sun bathes the land in light*.

【照猫画虎】draw a tiger with a cat as a model—copy sth. without catching its spirit

【照面】❶ (usu. used in the negative) put in an appearance; show up; turn up: 他始终不～。*He never showed up*. / 互不～ *avoid each other* ❷ encounter; come across: 打个～ *come face to face with sb.*; *run into sb*.

【照明】illumination; lighting: 舞台～ *stage illumination* / ～电路 *lighting circuit* / ～装置 *lighting installation* ◇ ～弹 flare; star shell; ～炮弹 illuminating shell

【照排】[刷] image composition; imaging: 激光～系统 *laser imaging system*

【照片儿】〈口〉photo

【照片子】take an X-ray; X-ray: 医生要给我的胸部～。*The doctor will take an X-ray of my chest*. / 我的胳膊得照个片子。*I must have my arm X-rayed*.

【照片】photograph; picture: 彩色～ *colour photograph* / 加印～ *print off copies from a negative*; *make copies of a print*

【照射】shine; illuminate; light up; irradiate: 用紫外线～ *irradiate with ultraviolet rays*

【照实】according to the facts: 情况怎样,你～说好了。*Tell us the truth about the situation*.

【照说】ordinarily; as a rule: ～我们早就应当通知你的。*We ought to have told you much earlier*.

【照相】(又作'照像') take a picture (or photograph); photograph: 我想照张相。*I want to have a picture taken*. / 缩微～ *microphotograph* ◇ ～版 process plate; ～簿 photo album; ～弹 [军] photo-flash bomb; flash bomb; ～复制 photocopy; ～馆 photo studio; ～排字 filmsetting; phototype setting; ～枪 [军] gun camera; ～纸 photographic paper; ～制版 photomechanical process; ～制图 photomap

【照相机】camera: 反射式～ *reflex camera* / 立体～ *stereoscopic (or stereo) camera* / 全景～ *panoramic camera* / 傻瓜～ *foolproof camera* / 小型～ *miniature camera*; *minicamera*; *minicam* / 折叠式～ *folding camera* / 制版～ *process camera*

【照样】❶ after a pattern or model: 照着样儿画 *draw after a model* / 照这个样儿做 *do it this way* ❷ in the same old way; as before; as usual: 没有他,我们～可以做。*We can do it without him, as we have before*.

【照妖镜】monster-revealing mirror; demondetector

【照耀】shine; illuminate: 灿烂的阳光～着祖国大地。*A bright sun is shining over our country*.

【照引】illuminate the way: 党像是一盏明灯,～着人们前进。*The Party leads the people, lighting the way forward like a lamp*.

【照应】❶ coordinate; correlate: 文章要前后～。*A composition must be well organized*. ❷ look after; take care of: 火车上乘务员对旅客～得很好。*The attendants on the train took good care of the passengers*.

【照章】in accordance with rules or regulations: ～罚款。*A fine will be imposed in accordance with the regulations*.

【照直】❶ (go) straight on: ～走就到学校了。*Go straight ahead and you'll find the school*. ❷ straight-forward; direct: 有话就～说。*Say directly what you have to say*.

【照准】❶ (used in official documents) request granted ❷ aim at: ～靶子射击 *aim at the target and fire* ◇ ～仪 [机] alidade

罩 Ⅰ 动 cover; overspread; wrap: 山坡上～着一层薄雾。*The mountain slope was wrapped in a thin mist*. / 棉袄外面～着一件蓝布褂儿 *wear a blue dustcoat over one's cotton-padded jacket* Ⅱ 名 ❶ cover; shade; hood; casing: 玻璃～ *glass cover* / 发动机～ (*engine*) *hood* / 保险～ *pro-*

tecting casing ❷ a bamboo fish trap ❸ a bamboo chicken coop

【罩袍】dust-robe；dust-gown；overall

【罩棚】an awning over a gateway or a courtyard

【罩衫】〈方〉overall；dustcoat

【罩袖】〈方〉oversleeve；sleevelet

【罩衣】(又作'罩褂儿') dustcoat；overall

【罩子】cover；shade；hood；casing

肇 动〈书〉❶ start；commence；initiate：肇始 ❷ cause (trouble, etc.)：肇事

【肇端】〈书〉beginning

【肇祸】cause trouble；cause an accident

【肇始】〈书〉start；commence；initiate

【肇事】cause trouble；create a disturbance：～者 *a person who has created a disturbance；trouble-maker*

zhē

折 动〈口〉❶ roll over；turn over：折跟头 ❷ pour back and forth between two containers：开水太烫，拿两个杯子～一～就凉了。*The water's boiling hot. Pour it from one cup to another to cool it.* ——另见 shé；zhé

【折跟头】turn a somersault

【折腾】〈口〉❶ turn from side to side；toss about：他～了好几个钟头才睡着。*He tossed about in bed for hours before he got to sleep.* ❷ do sth. over and over again：徒工把旧机器折了又安，安了又折，～了好多回。*The young apprentice again and again took the old machine apart and then put it together.* ❸ cause physical or mental suffering；get sb. down：牙疼真～人。*A toothache can get you down.* ❹ spend freely；squander：没多久他就把那份家产～光了。*It didn't take him long to squander away his family fortune.*

蜇 动 ❶ (of bees, wasps, etc.) sting：马蜂～人。*Wasps sting people.* ❷ smart；sting：碘酒擦在伤口上～得慌。*Iodine smarts when it is put on a cut.* / 切洋葱～眼睛。*When you slice an onion it makes your eyes sting.* ——另见 zhé

【蜇针】[动] sting；stinger

遮 动 ❶ hide from view；cover；screen：月亮给云彩～住了。*The moon was hidden by clouds.* / ～不住内心的喜悦 *cannot conceal one's delight* ❷ block；obstruct；impede：～道 *block the way* ❸ keep out：～风挡雨 *keep out wind and rain*

【遮蔽】❶ hide from view；cover；screen ❷ obstruct；block：～视线 *obstruct the view* ❸ [军] defilade：～物 *defilade* / ～阵地 *defiladed position*

【遮藏】hide；conceal；cover up

【遮丑】gloss over one's blemishes；hide one's shame；cover up one's defect

【遮挡】❶ shelter from；keep out：用帘子把窗户～起来 *cover the window with a curtain* ❷ a shelter；a cover

【遮断】[军] interdict：～射击 *interdiction fire*

【遮幅电影】a masked wide-screen film

【遮盖】❶ cover；overspread：山路全给大雪～住了。*The mountain paths were all covered by snow.* ❷ hide；conceal；cover up：错误总是～不住的。*Mistakes can never be hidden.*

【遮光罩】[摄] lens hood

【遮拦】block；obstruct；impede

【遮没】hide from view；cover；screen：山被浓雾～了。*The hills were covered in thick mist.*

【遮蓬】awning

【遮天蔽日】blot out the sky and the sun (said of a dense forest)

【遮天盖地】blot out the sky and cover up the earth (said of a snowstorm or sandstorm or of an invading army)

【遮羞】hush up a scandal；cover up one's embarrassment ◇ ～布 fig leaf

【遮掩】❶ cover；overspread；envelop：远山被云雾～着。*The distant hills were enveloped in clouds and mist.* ❷ cover up；hide；conceal：大胆承认错误，不要遮遮掩掩。*Admit your mistakes courageously. Don't try to cover them up.*

【遮眼法】cover-up；camouflage

【遮阳】sunshade ◇ ～板 [建] sunshading board；～帘 sunshade；sunbonnet

【遮阴】(又作'遮荫') shelter from heat or light；shade：～的树 *a shade tree*

zhé

折 Ⅰ 动 ❶ break；snap：～断一根树枝 *break off a branch* / ～断腿 *fracture (or break) one's leg* ❷ suffer the loss of；lose：损兵折将 ❸ bend；twist：曲折 ❹ turn back；change direction：边界由此～向西南。*From here the boundary turns southwestward.* ❺ be convinced；be filled with admiration：心～ *be deeply convinced；be filled with heartfelt admiration* ❻ convert into；amount to：这笔外币～成人民币是多少？*How much does this sum of foreign money amount to in Renminbi?* ❼ fold：把信～好 *fold the letter* / 把纸对～起来 *fold the sheet of paper in two* Ⅱ 名 ❶ discount；rebate：打八～ *give 20% discount；charge 80% of the original price* ❷ turning stroke (in Chinese characters) ❸ booklet in accordion form with a slipcase, used for keeping accounts, etc.；folder：存折 ——另见 shé；zhē

【折板结构】[建] folded plate structure

【折半】reduce (a price) by half；give 50% discount：按原价～出售 *sell at 50% discount；sell at half price*

【折变】〈方〉sell off (one's property)

【折布机】[纺] folding machine

【折尺】folding rule

【折冲】〈书〉repulse or subdue the enemy：～御侮

repel foreign aggression

【折纯】[化] (of chemical products) count only the active ingredients

【折叠】fold: 把报纸～好 *fold up the newspaper* ◇～床 folding bed; ～剪 folding scissors; ～伞 folding umbrella; ～椅 folding chair; ～翼飞机 folding-wing aircraft

【折兑】exchange (gold or silver) for money; convert

【折返】return; turn back (halfway)

【折服】❶ subdue; bring into submission; convince: 强词夺理不能～人。*You cannot convince people by sophistry.* ❷ be convinced; be filled with admiration: 令人～ *compel admiration*

【折光】(of water, glass, etc.) refract light ◇～度[物] dioptre

【折桂】pluck the cassia—❶ pass the imperial examinations ❷ carry off the first prize; win a championship

【折合】convert into; amount to: 把美元～成瑞士法郎 *convert dollars into Swiss francs* / 一英镑～成人民币是多少? *How much is a pound in terms of Renminbi?* or *How many Renminbi yuan to the pound?* / 水泥每包 50 公斤, ～100 市斤。*Each bag of cement weighs* 50 *kilogrammes, that is*, 100 *jin*.

【折回】turn back (halfway): 他刚走出不远又～来了。*He hadn't gone very far when he turned back.*

【折戟沉沙】broken halberds embedded in sand—reminder of a fierce battle or a beaten army

【折价】convert into money; evaluate in terms of money: ～退赔 *pay compensation at the market price*

【折旧】[经] depreciation (in value of property): ～费 *depreciation charge* / ～基金 *depreciation fund* / ～率 *rate of depreciation*

【折扣】discount; rebate: 这价钱已经打了～了。*This is the discounted price.* / 执行上级指示不打～ *carry out instructions to the letter*

【折门】[建] folding door; accordion door

【折磨】cause physical or mental suffering; torment: 受疾病的～ *suffer severely from a lingering illness*

【折让及回扣】allowance and rebate

【折扇】folding fan

【折射】[物] refraction: ～角 *angle of refraction* / *refraction angle* / ～率 *index of refraction* / *refracting power* / ～望远镜 *refracting telescope* / ～线 *refracted ray*

【折实】❶ reckon the actual amount after a discount ❷ adjust payment in accordance with the price index of certain commodities

【折寿】have one's allotted portion of life reduced by having or getting more than one deserves

【折算】convert: 把人民币～成法郎 *convert Renminbi into francs* / ～率 *conversion rate*

【折线】[数] broken line

【折腰】〈文〉bend one's back—bow in obeisance; cringe

【折页】[刷] folding: ～机 *folding machine*

【折账】pay a debt in kind

【折纸】paper folding

【折中】(又作'折衷') compromise: ～方案 *a compromise proposal*

【折衷主义】eclecticism

【折子】booklet in accordion form with a slipcase, used for keeping accounts, etc.

【折子戏】highlights from operas

哲 Ⅰ 形 wise; sagacious: 哲人 Ⅱ 名 wise man; sage: 先哲

【哲理】philosophic theory; philosophy: 这首诗富有～性。*This poem is philosophical.*

【哲人】〈书〉sage; philosopher

【哲学】philosophy: ～家 *philosopher*

蛰 动〈书〉hibernate

【蛰伏】❶ [动] dormancy; hibernation ❷ 同〖蛰居〗

【蛰居】〈书〉live in seclusion: ～书斋 *cloister oneself in one's study*

蜇 (构词成分) 见〖海蜇〗——另见 zhē

谪 动〈书〉❶ relegate a high official to a minor post in an outlying district (as a form of punishment in feudal times); banish; exile: 贬谪 ❷ (of immortals) be banished from Heaven ❸ censure; blame: 众口交～ *be censured by everybody*

【谪居】(of officials in former times) live in banishment

辙 名 ❶ the track of a wheel; rut ❷ direction of traffic: 戗～儿行驶 *drive in the wrong direction* (*against traffic regulations*) ❸ rhyme (of a song, poetic drama, etc.): 合辙 ❹〈方〉(usu. used after 有 or 没) way; idea: 没辙

【辙叉】[铁路] frog

【辙口】rhyme (of a song, poetic drama, etc.)

【辙乱旗靡】crisscross chariot tracks and drooping banners (said of an army in headlong flight)

zhě

者 助 ❶ (used after a verb or adjective, or a verb or adjective phrase to indicate a class of persons or things) one or those who; the thing or things which; -er: 译～ *translator* / 出版～ *publisher* / 符合标准～ *those which are up to standard* / 老～ *old man* / 大～ *the big one* / 前(后)～ *the former* (*latter*) / 贫(富)～ *the poor* (*rich*) ❷ (used after a noun phrase ending with 工作 "work" or 主义 "ism" to indicate the person or persons doing the stated work or holding the stated doctrine) -er; -ist: 医务工作～ *medical worker* / 马克思主义～ *Marxist* ❸〈书〉(used with the numbers 二、三、数，etc.)：二～ *these two things* / 三～ *these three things* / 两～缺一不可。*Neither is dispensable.* ❹〈书〉(used after a word, phrase, or clause to mark a pause, as in giving definitions)：仁～，人也；义～，宜也。(《中庸》) *Benevolence is acting like a human being; righteousness is doing what is right.*

锗 名［化］germanium (Ge)

赭 名 reddish brown; burnt ochre

【赭石】ochre (a mineral)

褶 名 pleat; crease：把衬衫上的～儿熨平 *iron the wrinkles out of the shirt*

【褶皱】❶［地质］fold：～作用 *folding* / ～山 *folded mountain* ❷ wrinkle (in the skin)

【褶子】❶ pleat：她的裙子有～。*Her skirt has pleats.* ❷ crease; fold; wrinkle：用熨斗把～烙平。*Iron out the wrinkles.* ❸ wrinkle (on the face)

zhè

这 代 ❶ this：～地方 *this place* / ～一回 *this time* / ～消息我知道了。*I've heard that news already.* or *Yes, so I've heard.* / ～就对了。*Now, you're on the right track.* or *Now, that's better.* ❷ now：他～才知道锻炼身体的好处。*Only now does he see the good of taking exercise.* / 我～就走。*I'm leaving right now.*

【这儿】〈口〉❶ here ❷ (used after 打,从 or 由 only) now; then：从～以后我再也没见着他。*Since then I haven't seen him again.*

【这般】such; so; like this：～仔细 *so careful* / ～大小 *this size; this big*

【这边】this side; here：到～来。*Come over here.* / 正义在我们～。*Justice is on our side.*

【这次】this time; present; current：～会议 *the present session* / ～运动 *the current movement (or campaign)*

【这等】like this; so; such：天下哪有～事? *How can there be such a thing?*

【这番】this; these：感谢你～好意。*I appreciate your kindness.*

【这个】❶ this one; this：～孩子真乖。*This child is a little dear.* / ～比那个沉。*This one is heavier than that one.* ❷〈口〉(used before a verb or adjective to give force to it) so; such：看见大象吹口琴,孩子们～乐啊! *When they saw the elephant blowing the mouth organ, the children roared with laughter.* ❸ (repeated to show hesitation)：他叫～～我想不起来了。*His name is... ah... I cannot remember.*

【这号人】〈方〉people of this sort：像他～,还是少跟他来往好。*You'd better have less to do with people of his sort.*

【这会儿】(又作'这会子')〈口〉now; at the moment; at present：～电话占线。*The line's busy at the moment.* / 去年～我还在深圳呢。*I was in Shenzhen at this time last year.*

【这里】here：我们～一年种两季稻子。*We grow two crops of rice a year here.*

【这么】(又作'这末') so; such; this way; like this：他就是～个人。*That's just like him.* / 那个句子应该～译。*The sentence should be translated this way.* / 大家都～说。*So they say.*

【这么点儿】such a little bit：～路一会儿就走到了。*It is so close, we can walk there in a short time.*

【这么些】so much; so many：～活儿,得有个人帮帮你吧? *Surely you need some help with so much work?*

【这么样】so; such; like this; this way：他老～说话吗? *Does he often talk like this?* / 要是～,事情会闹大的。*That would blow up the affair.*

【这么着】like this; so：～好。*It's better this way.* / 要是～,那我就去吧。*In that case, I'll go.*

【这山望着那山高】it's always the other mountain that looks higher; always think the grass is greener on the other side of the hill; never be happy where one is

【这些】(又作'这些个') these：～日子我们特别忙。*We've been particularly busy these days.*

【这样】so; such; like this; this way：如果你们觉得可以～办,就～办。*If you people feel this is the right thing to do, then do it.* / 一会儿～,一会儿那样 *now one way, now another* / 情况就是～。*That's how it is.*

【这样那样】this or that; of one kind or another; in one way or another：由于～的原因 *for this or that reason* / 存在～的分歧 *have differences of one kind or another* / ～的问题 *one question or another; various problems; all sorts of problems*

【这早晚儿】so late：～还去干什么! *It's too late to go.*

柘 名［植］three-bristle cudrania (Cudrania tricuspidata)

蔗 名 sugarcane

【蔗螟】sugarcane borer

【蔗农】sugarcane grower

【蔗糖】❶［化］sucrose：～酶 *sucrase* / ～蜜 *cane molasses* ❷ cane sugar

【蔗渣】bagasse

鹧 (构词成分) 见下

【鹧鸪】［动］Chinese francolin; partridge

【鹧鸪菜】zhegucai (Caloglossa leprieurii)

zhe

着 助 ❶ (added to a verb or adjective to indicate a continued action or state, often with the particle 呢 at the end of the sentence)：大门敞～。*The gate is wide open.* / 他穿～一身新衣服。*He is wearing new clothes.* / 雪正下～呢。*It's*

snowing. ❷ (in sentences beginning with a place word, added to the verb to indicate a resultant state, the verb plus 着 having the force of "there is"): 桌儿上放～好些东西。*There are a lot of things lying on the table*. / 墙上挂～一幅山水画。*On the wall hangs a landscape painting*. ❸ (verb plus 着 placed before another verb, indicating an accompanying action or state) ⓐ (verb plus 着 serving as an adverbial modifier): 他爱吃～饭看报。*He likes to read the newspaper while eating*. / 路不远,咱们走～去吧。*It's quite near, let's go there on foot*. ⓑ (verb plus 着 repeated, indicating that while one action is in progress the occurrence of another is expected): 她想～想～笑了起来。*She thought and thought and then burst out laughing*. / 我们走～走～天色已经暗了下来。*As we walked along, it began to grow dark*. ❹ (in imperative sentences, used after verbs or adjectives for emphasis, often with 点儿 added): 等～! *Wait*! / 慢～! *Hold it*! / 过马路看～点儿。*Mind how you cross the street*. ——另见 zhāo; zháo; zhuó

【着呢】(又作'着哩')〈口〉(used as an intensive at the end of a sentence, after adjectives or verbs that admit of differences of degree) very (much); quite; awfully: 他阔～。*He is awfully rich*. / 天儿冷～。*It's dreadfully cold*. / 那条路难走～。*The going is very hard over that road*.

zhēn

贞 Ⅰ 形 loyal; faithful: 坚贞 Ⅱ 名 (of women) chastity or virginity

【贞操】❶ chastity or virginity ❷ loyalty; moral integrity

【贞节】❶ loyalty; constancy ❷ chastity or virginity

【贞洁】chaste and undefiled

【贞烈】ready to die to preserve one's chastity

【贞女】a chaste girl; virgin

【贞淑】〈书〉chaste and gentle

针 Ⅰ 名 ❶ needle: 缝纫～ *sewing needle* ❷ stitch: 在袜子上缝两～ *sew (or put) a couple of stitches in a sock* / 织漏一～ *drop a stitch* / 伤口缝了四～。*The wound was closed with four stitches*. ❸ anything like a needle: 时针 ❹ injection; shot: 打针 Ⅱ 动 acupuncture: 针灸

【针鼻儿】the eye of a needle

【针布】[纺] card clothing

【针插不进,水泼不进】impenetrable and watertight (said of an exclusive group, etc.)

【针刺疗法】acupuncture treatment

【针刺麻醉】acupuncture anaesthesia: ～心脏手术 *heart surgery with acupuncture anaesthesia*

【针对】❶ be directed against; be aimed at; counter: 这个条约不～任何第三国。*The treaty is not directed against any third country*. ❷ in the light of; in accordance with; in connection with: ～儿童的特点进行教育 *educate children in accordance with their characteristics* / ～这种情况 *in view of this situation*

【针锋相对】give tit for tat; be diametrically opposed to: 进行～的斗争 *wage a tit-for-tat (or blow-for-blow) struggle against*

【针箍】〈方〉thimble

【针剂】[药] injection

【针尖】the point of a needle; pinpoint

【针尖大的窟窿,斗大的风】a big wind can blow through a small hole; a little leak can sink a great ship

【针尖对麦芒】a pin against an awl; diamond cut diamond

【针脚】stitch: 把～缝得密一些。*Make your stitches closer together*. / 顺着线头找～ *pick up clues*

【针灸】acupuncture and moxibustion: ～铜人 *a bronze figure marked with acupuncture points*

【针梳机】[纺] gill box

【针筒】syringe

【针头】[医] syringe needle

【针头线脑】odds and ends needed for sewing; needle and thread; sewing kit

【针尾鸭】[动] pintail

【针线】needlework: ～活儿 *needlework; stitching; sewing* / 学～ *learn how to do needlework* ◇ ～包 sewing kit

【针眼】❶ the eye of a needle ❷ pinprick ❸ [医] sty

【针鼹】[动] echidna; spiny anteater

【针药】medecine administered by injection

【针叶树】coniferous tree; conifer

【针织】knitting: ～外衣 *knitted (or knit) coat* / ～机 *knitting machine* ◇ ～厂 knitting mill; knit goods mill; ～品 knit goods; knitwear; hosiery

【针黹】〈书〉needlework

侦 动 detect; scout; investigate: 侦探

【侦办】investigate and prosecute: 依法～ *investigate and prosecute in accordance with the law*

【侦测】listen; monitor (e. g. radio communications): ～台 *listening and monitoring station*

【侦查】[法] investigate (a crime)

【侦察】reconnoitre; scout: 敌后～ *reconnoitre the enemy rear* / 进行～活动 *conduct reconnaissance* / ～敌情 *gather intelligence about the enemy* / ～飞行 *reconnaissance flight* ◇ ～兵 scout; ～部队 reconnaissance troops (or unit); scouting force; ～机 reconnaissance plane; scout; ～卫星 reconnaissance (or spy) satellite; ～员 scout

【侦错】[计] debug; debugger

【侦获】capture after investigation (criminal, etc.): ～走私犯 *capture the smuggler after an investigation*

【侦缉】track down and arrest

【侦看】watch; observe: 惯于～神色的警察 *policeman on the watch for suspicious signs*

【侦控】track down；track and monitor：～方案 *project of tracking and monitoring*

【侦破】investigate and uncover；detect；solve：～案件 *solve a case*；*crack a criminal case*

【侦探】❶ do detective work ❷ detective；spy

【侦探小说】detective story；detective fiction；crime novel：～作家 *writer of detective fiction*；*crime-writer*

【侦听】intercept (enemy radio communications)；monitor：～器 *detectaphone* / ～台 *intercept station*

【侦讯】investigation and interrogation：一个又一个～方案正在执行。*The investigation and interrogation projects are being carried out one by one.*

珍 Ⅰ 名 treasure：珍宝 Ⅱ 形 precious；valuable；rare：珍品 Ⅲ 动 value highly；treasure：珍惜

【珍爱】treasure；love dearly；be very fond of

【珍宝】jewellery；treasure：～馆 *Treasures Hall (in the Palace Museum)*

【珍本】rare edition；rare book

【珍藏】collect (rare books, art treasures, etc.)

【珍贵】valuable；precious：～药材 *valuable ingredients of traditional Chinese medicine* / ～的历史文物 *precious historical relics* / ～的纪念品 *precious mementos*

【珍品】treasure：艺术～ *art treasure*

【珍奇】rare：～的动物 *rare animals*

【珍禽异兽】rare birds and animals

【珍赏】treasure and delight in (curios, etc.)；highly value and appreciate

【珍视】value；prize；cherish；treasure：～我们两国人民之间的友谊 *treasure the friendship between the peoples of our two countries*

【珍玩】rare curios

【珍味】rare delicacies；dainties

【珍闻】news titbits；fillers：世界～ *world briefs (or miscellany)*

【珍惜】treasure；value；cherish：～时间 *value one's time* / ～人才 *value people of ability*

【珍稀】rare and precious：～动物 *rare animals* ◇ ～濒危物种 rare and endangered species

【珍馐】(又作'珍羞')〈书〉delicacies；dainties

【珍异】同〖珍奇〗

【珍重】❶ highly value；treasure；set great store by：我～你对我的信任。*I highly value the trust you place in me.* ❷ take good care of yourself：两人紧紧握手，互道～。*They clasped hands, each asking the other to take good care of himself.*

【珍珠】pearl ◇ ～贝 pearl shell；pearl oyster；～港 Pearl Harbour；～鸡 guinea fowl；～梅［植］false spiraea；～米〈方〉maize；(Indian) corn；～岩 pearlite

胗 名 gizzard：鸡～儿 *chicken's gizzard*

【胗肝儿】gizzard and liver (esp. chicken's or duck's)

帧 量 (for a picture, etc.)：一～油画 *an oil painting*

【帧脉冲发生器】framing pulse generator

【帧频】TV frame frequency；picture frequency

桢 名 ❶ hardwood ❷ terminal posts used in building a wall in ancient times

【桢干】〈书〉core member；backbone (element)

真 Ⅰ 形 ❶ true；real；genuine：～丝 *real silk* / 这幅宋人的画是～的。*This is a genuine Song painting.* / 我～的要走了。*It's true I'm leaving.* ❷ clear；unmistakable：你看得～么？*Can you see clearly?* / 字音咬得～ *pronounce words distinctly* Ⅱ 副 really；truly；indeed：我～不知道。*I really don't know.* / 他～信了。*He actually believed it.* / 时间过得～快。*How time flies!* / 演出～精彩。*The performance was just splendid.* Ⅲ 名〈略〉见〖真书〗

【真北】true north

【真才实学】real ability and learning；genuine talent：我决不计较学位，我只讲～。*I won't quibble about a degree. I'm only concerned with true talent and learning.*

【真诚】sincere；genuine；true：～的愿望 *a sincere wish (or desire)* / ～的友谊 *true friendship* / ～地执行协议 *implement the agreement in good faith*

【真传】be handed down in a direct line from the master

【真刀真枪】real swords and spears —the real thing：～地干起来 *start a shooting war*；*start in real earnest*

【真地平】［天］true horizon

【真谛】true essence；true meaning：人生的～ *the true meaning of life*

【真鲷】genuine porgy；red porgy

【真分数】［数］proper fraction

【真格的】〈口〉real；true：你别再装着玩儿啦，说～吧。*Stop joking and tell me the truth.* / ～，你到底去不去？*Seriously, are you going or not?* / 动～ *start a shooting war or do sth. in real earnest*

【真个】〈方〉really；truly；indeed：～了不起 *really wonderful*

【真果】［植］true fruit

【真话】the truth：你要说～。*You must tell the truth.*

【真迹】authentic work (of painting or calligraphy)

【真金不怕火炼】true gold fears no fire—a person of integrity can stand severest tests

【真菌】fungus

【真空】［物］vacuum：～过滤 *vacuum filtration* / ～技术 *vacuum technique* / ～吸尘器 *vacuum cleaner* / ～压铸 *vacuum die casting* ◇ ～包装 vacuum packaging；～成型机 a vacuum forming machine；～地带［军］no-man's-land；～管 同〖电子管〗

【真理】truth：坚持～，修正错误 *uphold the truth and correct mistakes*

【真面目】true features；true colours：认清其～ *see*

sb. in his true colours; know sb. for what he is / 露出～ reveal one's true colours; betray oneself

【真名实姓】real name

【真命】ordained by Heaven: ～之主 *an ordained ruler* / ～天子 *an ordained Son of Heaven*

【真皮】❶［生理］derma ❷ genuine leather

【真凭实据】genuine evidence; hard evidence; conclusive proof

【真漆】lacquer

【真枪实弹】real guns and bullets; live ammunition: 进行～的演习 *conduct exercises (or manoeuvres) with live ammunition*

【真切】vivid; clear; distinct: 这篇通讯写得～感人。*The report is vividly written and very moving.* / 看得～ *see clearly*

【真情】❶ the real (or true) situation; the facts; the actual state of affairs; truth ❷ true feelings; real sentiments: ～的流露 *a revelation of one's true feelings*

【真确】❶ true; real; authentic: ～的消息 *authentic (or reliable) news* ❷ clear; distinct

【真人】❶real person ❷true man (i.e. a man who has attained enlightenment or immortality; used esp. in official Taoist titles): 太乙～ *True Man of the Grand Unity* ◇ ～真事 real people and real events; actual persons and events

【真善美】the true, the good and the beautiful

【真实】true; real; authentic: ～记录 *authentic records* / ～感 *sense of reality* / ～性 *truthfulness; authenticity* / ～的故事 *a true story*

【真是】(又作'真是的') (used to express displeasure or annoyance): 下点雨就不让我们去,～。*Just because of a bit of rain we're not allowed to go. The idea!* / 你也～,连灯也不关,就走了。*Look at this! You didn't even turn off the light when you left.*

【真书】(in Chinese calligraphy) regular script

【真率】sincere; unaffected; straightforward

【真髓】essence

【真相】(又作'真象') the real (or true) situation; the real (or actual) facts; the actual state of affairs; truth: 掩盖～ *cover up the facts* / 弄清事情的～ *clarify the truth of the matter* ◇ ～大白 the whole truth has come out; the whole affair is now out in the open

【真心】whole-hearted; heartfelt; sincere: ～拥护 *give whole-hearted support to* / ～话 *sincere words* / 说～话 *speak from the bottom of one's heart* ◇ ～实意 genuinely and sincerely; truly and whole-heartedly

【真性】［医］genuine: ～痴呆 *genuine dementia* / ～血友病 *hemophilia vera*

【真真假假】the true mingled with the false; a mixture of truth and falsehood

【真正】genuine; true; real: ～的吉林人参 *genuine Jilin ginseng* / ～的朋友 *a true friend* / ～负起责任来 *shoulder the responsibilities in earnest* / ～有力量的是人民。*It's the people who are really powerful.*

【真知】genuine (or real) knowledge ◇ ～灼见 real knowledge and deep insight; penetrating judgment

【真值表】［物］truth table

【真挚】sincere; cordial: ～的友谊 *sincere friendship*

【真珠层】［动］pearly (or nacreous) layer

【真主】［宗］(伊斯兰教) Allah

砧 名 hammering block; anvil: 锻～ *smith anvil*

【砧板】chopping block

【砧骨】［生理］incus; anvil

【砧木】［农］stock

【砧子】〈口〉hammering block; anvil

斟 动 pour (tea or wine): 给她～一杯酒。*Pour her a glass of wine.*

【斟酌】consider; deliberate: 再三～ *consider carefully again and again* / ～词句 *weigh one's words* / ～办理 *act at one's discretion; act as one sees fit*

甄 动〈书〉discriminate; distinguish; examine: 甄选

【甄拔】select: ～人才 *select people of talent*

【甄别】❶ examine and distinguish; screen; discriminate ❷ reexamine a case

【甄选】select

榛 名［植］hazel

【榛鸡】hazel grouse

【榛莽】〈书〉luxuriant vegetation

【榛实】hazelnut

【榛子】❶ hazel ❷ hazelnut

箴 Ⅰ 动〈书〉admonish; exhort Ⅱ 名 a type of didactic literary composition

【箴言】〈书〉admonition; exhortation; maxim

臻 动〈书〉❶ attain (a high level): 交通日～便利。*Transportation and communications are becoming easier day by day.* / 方法日～完善。*The methods are being perfected.* ❷ reach; arrive: 百福并～。*May every blessing descend upon you!*

zhěn

诊 动 examine (a patient): 出诊

【诊病】diagnose a disease

【诊察】examine (a patient)

【诊断】diagnose: 物理～ *physical diagnosis* / 医生～这病是胸膜炎。*The doctor diagnosed the illness (or case) as pleurisy.* ◇ ～程序 diagnostic program; ～书 medical certificate; ～性测试 diagnostic test; ～性评价 diagnostic evaluation

【诊金】consultation fee; hospital fee

【诊疗】make a diagnosis and give treatment: ～器械 *medical instruments*

【诊脉】feel the pulse

【诊室】(又作'诊疗室') consulting room
【诊所】(又作'诊疗所') clinic; dispensary: 王医生开了一个私人～。*Dr. Wang runs a private clinic.*
【诊台】diagnostic table; examination table
【诊治】make a diagnosis and give treatment

枕 Ⅰ名 ❶ pillow ❷ [机] block: 转～ *swivel block* Ⅱ动 rest the head on: ～着胳臂睡觉 *sleep with one's head resting on one's arm*
【枕戈待旦】lie with one's head pillowed on a spear, waiting for day to break—be ready for battle; maintain combat readiness
【枕骨】[生理] occipital bone
【枕巾】a towel used to cover a pillow
【枕木】railway sleeper; tie
【枕套】(又作'枕头套') pillowcase; pillowslip
【枕头】pillow ◇ ～箱 pillow casket (a small box for valuables)
【枕席】❶ a mat used to cover a pillow; pillow mat ❷ bed
【枕心】(又作'枕头心儿') pillow (without the pillowcase)

轸 Ⅰ名 〈书〉 ❶ the cross board at the rear of an ancient carriage ❷ carriage ❸ the last of the twenty-eight constellations (二十八宿) into which the celestial sphere was divided in ancient Chinese astronomy (consisting of four stars in Corvus) Ⅱ形 〈书〉 sorrowful; distressed: ～悼 *mourn with deep grief*
【轸念】〈书〉 sorrowfully cherish the memory of sb.; think anxiously about: 殊深～ *express great solicitude for sb.*

疹 名 rash: 麻疹
【疹子】〈口〉 measles

缜 (构词成分) 见下
【缜密】careful; meticulous; deliberate: ～的计划 *a deliberate (or carefully thought-out) plan* / ～的分析 *a careful (or minute) analysis* / ～的研究 *a meticulous study*

zhèn

阵 Ⅰ名 ❶ battle array (or formation): 长蛇阵 ❷ position; front: 上阵 ❸ a period of time: 病了一～儿 *be ill for some time* / 那～儿 *in those days; then* / 这～儿 *these days; recently* Ⅱ量 short period; spell: 一～雨 *a spatter of rain* / 一～风 *a gust (or blast) of wind* / 一～寒潮 *a cold spell* / 一～咳嗽 *a fit (or spasm) of coughing* / 一～热烈的掌声 *a burst of warm applause*
【阵地】position; front: ～攻击(防御) *positional attack (defence)* / 前沿～ *forward position* / 思想～ *ideological front* ◇ ～战 positional warfare
【阵法】tactical deployment of troops
【阵风】a gust of wind
【阵脚】❶ front line: 压住～ *keep the troops in battle array; hold the line* ❷ position; situation; circumstances: 乱了～ *be thrown into confusion*
【阵列】[数] array ◇ ～处理机 array processor; ～机语言 array machine language (AML)
【阵容】❶ battle array (or formation) ❷ lineup: ～强大 *have a strong lineup* / 演员～整齐 *a well-balanced cast*
【阵势】❶ battle array (or formation); a disposition of combat forces: 摆开～ *deploy the ranks in battle array* ❷ situation; condition; circumstances
【阵痛】[医] ❶ labour pains; throes (of childbirth) ❷ growing pains; problems and discomfort caused by social dislocation as a result of rapid change
【阵图】a system of battle formations: 八～ *the Eightfold Maze*
【阵亡】be killed in action; fall in battle
【阵线】front; ranks; alignment: 民族统一～ *national united front*
【阵型】formation: 在这场足球比赛中,我队始终保持了4-3-3～。*Our team played in 4-3-3 formation throughout the match.*
【阵雪】snow shower
【阵营】a group of people who pursue a common interest; camp: 革命～ *a revolutionary camp*
【阵雨】shower

鸩 Ⅰ名 ❶ a legendary bird with poisonous feathers ❷ 〈书〉 poisoned wine: 饮鸩止渴 Ⅱ动 kill sb. with poisoned wine
【鸩毒】〈书〉 poisoned wine
【鸩酒】poisoned wine

振 动 ❶ shake; flap: ～翅 *flap the wings; flutter* / ～笔直书 *wield the pen furiously* ❷ rise with force and spirit; brace up: 精神为之一～ *feel one's spirits buoyed up* / 我军士气大～。*The morale of our troops was greatly boosted.*
【振笔直书】write with flying strokes; wield the pen furiously
【振臂】raise one's arm: ～高呼 *raise one's arm and shout (slogans, etc.)* ◇ ～一呼 raise one's arm and cry for action—issue a call for action; sound the trumpet call of action
【振翅高飞】flutter and soar high
【振荡】❶ [物] vibration ❷ [电] oscillation: 本机～ *local oscillation* / 寄生～ *parasitic oscillation* / ～电路 *oscillating circuit* / ～管 *oscillator valve* / ～器 *oscillator*
【振捣器】[建] vibrator
【振动】[物] vibration: 简谐～ *simple harmonic vibration* / 等时～ *isochronous vibration* / ～计 *vibrometer* / ～频率 *vibration frequency*
【振奋】❶ rouse oneself; rise with force and spirit; be inspired with enthusiasm: 人人～,个个当先 *everyone full of vigour, each one forging ahead* ❷ inspire; stimulate: ～士气 *boost (or raise)*

the morale (*of the troops*) / 令人～的消息 *heartening news* ◇ ～人心 inspire people; fill people with enthusiasm

【振幅】[物] amplitude (of vibration): 脉冲～ *pulse amplitude* / ～畸变 *amplitude distortion*

【振聋发聩】rouse the deaf, enlighten the benighted: 先生这番议论,真可谓之～。*Your arguments, sir, would make a deaf man hear and a blind man see.*

【振兴】develop vigorously; promote: ～中华 *rejuvenate China* / ～教育事业 *vitalize education* / ～工业 *vigorously develop industry*

【振振有词】speak plausibly and volubly (in self-justification)

【振作】bestir (or exert) oneself; display vigour: ～精神 *bestir oneself; brace* (*or cheer*) *up* / ～起来! *Brace up!* or *Pull yourself together!*

朕 Ⅰ **代** I, the sovereign; we (used by a royal person in proclamations instead of I) Ⅱ **名** 〈书〉 sign; omen

【朕兆】〈书〉 sign; omen; portent: 有～可寻。*There are signs for us to read.*

赈 **动** relieve; aid

【赈济】relieve; aid: ～灾民 *relieve the people in stricken areas; aid the victims of natural calamities*

【赈款】relief fund

【赈灾】relieve the people in stricken areas

震 Ⅰ **动** shake; shock; vibrate; quake: 他捶了一下桌子,杯子被～得跳起来。*He gave the table a thump which shook the cups.* Ⅱ **形** greatly excited; deeply astonished; shocked: ～骇 *shocked; stunned; astounded* Ⅲ **名** one of the Eight Trigrams (八卦)

【震波】[地质] seismic wave; earthquake wave: ～图 *seismogram*

【震颤】tremble; quiver ◇ ～性麻痹 paralysis agitans

【震旦纪】[地质] the Sinian Period

【震荡】shake; shock; vibrate; quake: 1976 年唐山大地震的时候北京都感到～。*Tremors were felt in Beijing when a great earthquake rocked Tangshan in* 1976.

【震动】shake; shock; vibrate; quake: 春雷～山谷。*Spring thunder shook the valley.* / 火车～了一下,开走了。*The train pulled out with a jerk.*

【震耳欲聋】deafening: ～的鞭炮声 *the deafening noise of firecrackers*

【震感】sensation of vibration and quaking (esp. earthquake): 这次地震云南各地普遍有～。*The earthquake was felt in many parts of Yunnan province.*

【震古烁今】(又作'震古铄今') surpassing the ancients and amazing contemporaries

【震骇】shock; appal; astonish

【震撼】shake; shock; vibrate: ～天地的英雄气概 *earthshaking heroism* ◇ ～人心 stirring; thrilling

【震级】magnitude (of an earthquake)

【震惊】shock; amaze; astonish; stun: 南京大屠杀～中外。*The Nanjing Massacre shocked the country and the whole world.*

【震怒】be enraged; be furious

【震情】situation after an earthquake: 地震灾区的～ *situation in the earthquake zone*

【震慑】awe; frighten

【震悚】〈书〉 tremble with fear; be terrified; be frightened

【震天动地】(又作'震天撼地') shake heaven and earth: 示威群众的怒吼～。*The angry shouts of the demonstrators rent the air.*

【震音】[音] tremolo

【震源】focus (of an earthquake)

【震灾】disaster caused by earthquake: ～中失去父母的孤儿 *children orphaned in the earthquake*

【震中】an epicentre: ～区 *epicentral area*

镇 Ⅰ **动** ❶ press down; keep down; ease: 镇纸 / 镇痛 ❷ calm; tranquil; at ease: 镇定 ❸ guard; garrison: 坐镇 ❹ cool with cold water or ice: 把西瓜放在冷水里～一～ *put the watermelon in cold water for a while to chill it* Ⅱ **名** ❶ garrison post: 重镇 ❷ town ❸ a comparatively large trading centre

【镇尺】paperweight (in the shape of a ruler)

【镇定】calm; cool; composed; unruffled: 神色～ *be calm and collected; show composure and presence of mind* / 保持～ *keep cool; remain calm; keep one's head*

【镇服】force sb. into submission

【镇静】calm; cool; composed; unruffled: 遇到紧急情况要～。*Keep calm in an emergency.* / 努力～下来 *compose oneself with an effort* ◇ ～钢 [冶] killed steel; ～剂 sedative; tranquillizer

【镇流管】[电] ballast tube

【镇流器】[电] ballast

【镇慑】cow sb. into submission

【镇守】guard (a strategically important place); garrison

【镇痛】❶ ease pain; relieve pain ❷ [医] analgesia: 针刺～ *acupuncture analgesia* / ～效果 *analgesic effect* ◇ ～剂 anodyne; analgesic; pain-killer

【镇压】❶ suppress; repress; put down: ～叛乱 *put down a rebellion* ❷ execute (a counterrevolutionary): 杀人犯已被依法～。*The murderer was executed according to law.* ❸ [农] rolling; compacting; tamping

【镇压器】[农] (land) roller

【镇长】town head

【镇纸】paperweight

【镇住】bring or keep sb. under control; reduce sb. to submission: 她第一次在音乐厅登台演出就把听众～了。*Her debut took the concert hall by storm.*

zhēng

正 名 the first month of the lunar year; the first moon：新正 ——另见 zhèng

【正旦】〈书〉the lunar New Year's Day

【正月】the first month of the lunar year; the first moon：～初一 *the lunar New Year's Day*

争 动 ❶ contend; vie; strive：～领导权 *contend for leadership* / 不～一日之短长 *not strive for temporary superiority* / 不～一城一地的得失 *not contend for a city or a piece of ground* (*in mobile warfare*) ❷ argue; dispute：你们在～什么？*What are you arguing about?*

【争霸】contend (or struggle) for hegemony; scramble (or strive) for supremacy：～世界 *contend for world domination* (*or hegemony*)

【争辩】argue; debate; contend：无休止的～ *an endless debate* / 真理不怕～。*Truth does not fear contention.*

【争长论短】squabble; argue

【争吵】quarrel; wrangle; squabble：无谓的～ *a pointless quarrel* / 激烈的～ *fierce* (*or bitter*) *wrangling* / ～不休 *bicker* (*or squabble*) *endlessly*

【争持】refuse to give in; stick to one's guns

【争宠】strive for sb's favour

【争斗】❶ fight ❷ struggle; contend

【争端】controversial issue; dispute; conflict：国际～ *an international dispute* / 边界～ *a border dispute* / 引起～ *give rise* (*or lead*) *to a dispute* / 挑起～ *provoke a dispute* / 解决～ *settle a dispute*

【争夺】fight (or contend, scramble) for; enter into rivalry with sb. over sth.; vie with sb. for sth.：～制高点 *fight* (*or contend*) *for possession of a commanding height* / ～市场 *scramble for markets*

【争分夺秒】race (or work) against time; make every minute and second count

【争风吃醋】fight for the affections of a man or woman

【争锋】fight for mastery; strive for a decisive victory

【争购】snap up (goods)：一时某些商品少了些，人们就忙着～。*When there is a shortage, people will snap up goods.*

【争光】win honour (or glory) for：为祖国～ *win honour for our homeland; bring credit to* (*or be a credit to*) *our country*

【争脸】(又作'争面子') try to win credit or honour

【争论】controversy; dispute; debate; contention：不同意见的～ *controversies over differing opinions* / 激烈的～ *a heated dispute* / ～不休 *an endless debate* / ～的双方 *the two contending sides* / ～之点 *the point at issue*

【争名夺利】strive (or scramble) for fame and gain：～，惟利是图 *scramble for fame and fortune and be interested only in personal gain*

【争鸣】contend

【争奇斗艳】(of flowers, etc.) vie with each other for glamour

【争气】try to make a good showing; try to win credit for; try to bring credit to：有人说妇女干不了这种工作，我们要争这口气。*Some people say women can't do this job, but we'll show them.*

【争抢】fight for; scramble for

【争取】strive for; fight for; win over：～时间 *race* (*or work*) *against time* / ～主动 *try to gain the initiative; contend for the initiative*；你能给我们杂志写点什么吗？—我～吧。*Can you write something for the magazine? —Well, I'll try.*

【争权夺利】scramble for power and profit; struggle for power

【争胜】compete for first place

【争讼】contest a lawsuit

【争先】try to be the first to do sth.：大家～发言。*Everyone tried to get the floor.* ◇ ～恐后 strive to be the first and fear to lag behind; vie with each other in doing sth.

【争雄】contend for supremacy

【争议】dispute; controversy：有～的地区 *a disputed area* / 有～的条款 *a contentious clause* / 一本有～的书 *a controversial book*

【争战】fight; war：连年～ *long years of war*

【争执】disagree; dispute; stick to one's position (or guns) ◇ ～不下 each stands (or holds) his ground; each sticks to his own stand; each sticks to his guns

怔 形 seized with terror; terrified; panic-stricken ——另见 zhèng

【怔忡】[中] palpitation

【怔营】〈书〉in a state of alarm (or trepidation)

【怔忪】〈书〉alarmed and panicky; terrified; panic-stricken; seized with terror

征 Ⅰ 动 ❶ go on a journey：征途 ❷ go on an expedition (or a campaign)：出征 ❸ levy (troops); call up; draft：征兵 ❹ levy (taxes); collect; impose：征粮 ❺ ask for; solicit：征稿 Ⅱ 名 ❶ evidence; proof：有实物可～。*There is solid evidence.* / 无～之言 *an unfounded assertion* ❷ sign; portent：特征

【征兵】conscription; draft; call-up：～年龄 *conscription age; age for enlistment* / ～站 *drafting centre* ◇ ～法 conscription (or draft) law; ～制 universal military service; conscription system

【征尘】〈文〉dust which settles on one during a journey

【征程】journey; march

【征答】question and answer game：有奖～比赛 *question and answer competition with prizes*

【征调】requisition; call up：～物资和人员 *requisition supplies and draft personnel*

【征伐】go on a punitive expedition

【征帆】〈书〉a ship on a long voyage

【征服】conquer；subjugate：～自然 *conquer nature* / ～黄河 *tame the Yellow River* / 她的歌声～了北京听众。*Her singing took Beijing by storm.*

【征稿】solicit contributions (to a journal, etc.)

【征歌】invitation to compose songs on a specific theme

【征购】requisition by purchase：粮食～ *grain purchases by the state* / ～任务 *state purchase quotas* / ～土地 *land acquisition*

【征管】levy (or collect) and administer (taxes)：负责税收～ *be responsible for tax administration*

【征候】sign：病人已有好转的～。*The patient shows signs of a turn for the better.*

【征婚】seek a marriage partner：～广告 *advertisement seeking a marriage partner*

【征集】❶ collect：～签名 *collect signatures (for an appeal)* / ～军粮 *collect grain for the army* / ～物资 *the acquisition of supplies* ❷ draft；call up；recruit：～新兵 *recruitment* / 战时～ *wartime draft*

【征借】seek to borrow：为举办画展向艺术家协会～油画 *borrow paintings from the Artists Association for a show*

【征粮】impose grain levies；collect grain taxes

【征马】battle steed；war horse

【征募】enlist；recruit

【征聘】同〖招聘〗

【征迁】relocate residents from locations to be used for construction of new buildings or factories：安置～农民的工作十分复杂。*It is a complicated process to relocate peasants from land designated for other uses.*

【征求】solicit；seek；ask for：广泛～群众意见 *consult the broad masses；solicit opinions from the general public* / ～意见稿 *an edition for soliciting comments；trial edition*

【征收】levy；collect；impose：～进口税 *impose import duties*

【征税】levy (or collect) taxes；taxation：～货物 *dutiable goods*

【征讨】go on a punitive expedition

【征途】the road to be travelled；journey：艰险的～ *a perilous journey* / 踏上～ *start on a journey；set out*

【征文】solicit articles or essays：～启事 *a notice soliciting contributions for a special issue, etc.*

【征象】sign；symptom

【征询】seek the opinion of；consult

【征引】quote；cite

【征用】take over for use；commandeer；requisition：～房屋 *requisition buildings*

【征战】go on an expedition (or a campaign)

【征召】❶ call up；enlist；draft；conscript：～入伍 *enlist in the army* ❷〈书〉appoint to an official position

【征兆】sign；omen；portent；indication：地震的～ *indications of an impending earthquake*

挣

(构词成分)见下 ——另见 zhèng

【挣扎】struggle：～着坐起来 *struggle to a sitting position*

峥

(构词成分)见下

【峥嵘】❶ lofty and steep；towering：山势～ *mountains towering high* ❷ outstanding；extraordinary ◇ ～岁月 memorable years (of one's life)

狰

(构词成分)见下

【狰狞】ferocious；savage；hideous

【狰狞面目】同〖面目狰狞〗

症

(构词成分)见下——另见 zhèng

【症瘕积聚】[中] a lump in the abdomen causing distension and pain

【症结】crux；crucial reason：这就是问题的～所在。*Therein lies the crux of the problem.*

睁

动 open (the eyes)：～开眼睛。*Open your eyes.*

【睁眼瞎】〈诙〉a blind person with eyes wide open—an illiterate

【睁一只眼,闭一只眼】turn a blind eye to sth.；wink at sth.

【睁着眼睛说瞎话】tell a bare-faced (or out-and-out) lie

铮

(构词成分)见下——另见 zhèng

【铮铮】clank；clang

筝

名 ❶ zheng, a 21- or 25-stringed plucked instrument in some ways similar to the zither ❷ 见〖风筝〗

蒸

动 ❶ evaporate：蒸气 ❷ steam：～饭 *steam rice* / 菜凉了,～一～吧。*The food is cold. Let's warm it up in the steamer.*

【蒸饼】steamed cake

【蒸发】evaporate：沸水～很快。*Boiling water evaporates rapidly.* ◇ ～计 evaporimeter

【蒸锅】a pot for steaming food；steamer

【蒸饺】steamed dumpling (with meat and vegetable stuffing)

【蒸烤】scorch；roast：暴日的～ *scorching sun*

【蒸馏】distillation：拔顶～ *topping distillation* / 常压～ *atmospheric distillation* / 真空～ *vacuum distillation* / ～器 *distiller；retort* / ～塔 *distilling tower (or column)* ◇ ～水 distilled water

【蒸笼】❶ food steamer (usu. made of bamboo) ❷ (of room etc.) very hot and sultry

【蒸馍】〈方〉steamed bun

【蒸呢】[纺] decatizing；decating

【蒸气】vapour ◇ ～软件[计] vaporware；～浴(又作'桑拿浴') sauna

【蒸汽】steam：～发生器 *steam generator* / ～供暖 *steam heating* / ～锅炉 *steam boiler* / ～机车 *steam locomotive* / ～绞车 *steam winch* ◇～锤

同〖汽锤〗；～机 steam engine；～浴 steam bath

【蒸球】paper making rotary spherical digester

【蒸腾】(of steam) rising：热气～ *steaming* ◇ ～作用［植］transpiration

【蒸蒸日上】becoming more prosperous every day；flourishing；thriving：一派～、欣欣向荣的景象 *a scene of prosperity*

zhěng

拯 动 save；rescue；deliver：～民于水火之中 *deliver the people from an abyss of misery*

【拯救】save；rescue；deliver：改善环境，～珍稀野生动物 *improve the environment to save rare wild animals*

整 Ⅰ 形 ❶ whole；complete；full；entire：～砖 *a whole (or an unbroken) brick* / ～夜 *the whole night*；*all night long* / 12点～ *twelve o'clock sharp* / 恰好～一年。*It's a year to the day*. ❷ in good order；neat；tidy：仪容不～ *untidy in one's appearance* / 衣冠不～ *slovenly in one's dress*；*not properly dressed* / ～然有序 *be in good order* Ⅱ 动 ❶ put in order；rectify：～一下领带 *adjust one's tie* ❷ repair；mend；renovate：～旧如新 *repair sth. old and make it as good as new* ❸ make sb. suffer；punish；fix：挨整 ❹〈方〉do；make；work：这东西我看见人～过，并不难。*I once saw someone do it. It's not very difficult*. / 绳子给～断了。*The rope was broken*.

【整版彩色印刷系统】［刷］full-page colour printing system

【整备】reorganize and outfit (troops)

【整编】reorganize (troops)

【整饬】❶ put in order；strengthen：～纪律 *strengthen discipline* ❷ in good order；neat；tidy：服装～ *neatly dressed*

【整除】［数］be divided with no remainder；divide exactly

【整党】consolidate the Party organization：～建党 *Party consolidation and Party building*

【整地】soil preparation (i. e. preparation of land for sowing or planting by ploughing, harrowing, levelling, etc.)

【整点】［数］integral point

【整队】dress the ranks；get (or bring) the ranks into orderly alignment；line up：～出发 *get the ranks in good order and set out*；*set out in orderly formation* / ～入场 *file into the arena*, *auditorium*, *etc*.

【整顿】rectify；consolidate；reorganize：～规章制度 *reestablish rules and regulations* / ～城市治安 *improve public order in the cities* / 我们的足球队要好好～一下。*Our football team needs a good shake-up*.

【整风】rectification of incorrect styles of work or thinking ◇ ～运动 rectification movement

【整改】rectify and reform

【整复】restore；restitution：～外科 *reparative surgery*；*plastic surgery*

【整个】whole；entire：～社会 *the whole of society* / ～国际形势 *the entire international situation* / 他把这件事～儿给忘了。*He clean forgot about that*. / ～说来 (*taken*) *as a whole*；*on the whole*；*by and large*

【整合】❶［地质］conformity ❷ integrate；consolidate；unify；unite

【整机】assembled machinery

【整纪】tighten discipline

【整洁】clean and tidy；neat；trim：房间收拾得很～。*The room is kept clean and tidy (or spick-and-span)*. / 衣着～ *be neatly dressed*

【整经】［纺］warping：分段～ *sectional warping* / ～机 *warping machine*

【整理】put in order；straighten out；arrange；sort out：～房间 *put a room in order*；*tidy a room* / ～桌上的东西 *straighten out the things on the table* / ～书架上的书 *rearrange the books on the shelves* / ～资料 *sort out the data*

【整料】material all in one piece for a given job

【整流】［电］rectification：～管 *rectifier tube* / ～子 *commutator* ◇ ～器［电］rectifier

【整齐】❶ in good order；neat；tidy：保持队伍～ *keep the ranks in good order* / 字写得清楚～ *clear and neat handwriting* ❷ even；regular：出苗～ *an even emergence of seedlings* / ～的牙齿 *regular teeth* / 迈着～的步伐 *march in step* / 这个篮球队阵容～。*This basketball team has a well-balanced lineup*.

【整齐划一】uniform

【整人】make sb. suffer；fix sb.

【整容】❶ tidy oneself up (i. e. have a haircut, a shave, etc.) ❷ face-lifting ◇ ～术 cosmetic operation；face-lifting

【整数】❶［数］integer；whole number ❷ round number；round figure

【整肃】〈书〉❶ strict；rigid：军容～ *soldiers drawn up in strict order* ❷ rectify；consolidate：～纪律 *strengthen discipline*；*enforce discipline*

【整套】a complete (or whole) set of：～设备 *a complete set of equipment* / 这就是他们的一～观点。*This is the sum total of their views*.

【整体】whole；entirety：从～上看形势 *view the situation as a whole* / ～的一个组成部分 *an integral part of the whole* / ～方案 *an overall plan*

【整体吊装】［建］integral hoisting；～观念 ❶ the concept of viewing the situation as a whole ❷［中］an organic conception of the human body, viewing its various parts as forming an organic whole

【整天】the whole day；all day；all day long：干了三～ *work for three whole days*

【整托】(又作'全托') put one's child in a boarding nursery：送～ *send (child) to a boarding nursery*

【整形】[医] plastic：～手术 *plastic operation* / ～外科 *plastic surgery*; *plastics*

【整修】rebuild; renovate; recondition：～水利工程 *rebuild water conservancy projects* / ～梯田 *reinforce terraced fields* / ～房子 *renovate a house*

【整训】train and consolidate (troops, etc.)

【整整】whole; full：～半小时 *a whole half hour* / ～两天 *two whole days* / ～一小时 *a full* (*or good*) *hour* / ～六公里 *a good six kilometres*

【整枝】[农] training; pruning：棉花～ *pruning of cotton plants* / 葡萄～ *training of vines*

【整治】❶ renovate; repair; dredge (a river, etc.)：～房屋 *renovate a house* / ～机器 *repair a machine* / ～航道 *dredge waterways* / ～河道 *the realignment of a river* ❷ punish; fix：这坏蛋得～一下。*That scoundrel needs to be punished.* ❸ do; work at：～饭菜 *prepare food* / ～庄稼 *field management*

【整装】get one's things ready (for a journey, etc.) ◇ ～待发 get ready for a journey or a march; be ready to start out

zhèng

正 Ⅰ 形 ❶ straight; upright：～前方 *straight ahead* / ～东(南、西、北) *due east* (*south*, *west*, *north*) / 把柱子扶～ *set the post upright* / 这幅画挂得不～。*This picture is not straight.* ❷ situated in the middle; main：正门 / 正厅 ❸ punctually; sharp：九点～ *at nine o'clock sharp* ❹ obverse; right：布的这一面是～的吗? *Is this the right side of the cloth?* / 这件茄克～穿反穿都可以。*You can wear this jacket inside out.* ❺ honest; upright：他作风不～。*His behaviour is not proper.* ❻ correct; right：路子走得～ *follow a correct path* ❼ (of colour, flavour, etc.) pure; right：～黄 *pure yellow* / 味儿不～ *not the right flavour* ❽ regular; standard：正楷 ❾ (〈反〉副 "secondary, vice-") principal; chief：～副主任 *director and deputy director* / ～驾驶员 *first pilot* (〈反〉副驾驶员 "*copilot*") ❿ (of figures, designs, etc.) regular：～八边形 *regular octagon* / ～多面体 *regular polyhedron* ⓫ [数] positive ⓬ [物] positive; plus：～晶体 *positive crystal* / ～离子 *positive ion*; *cation* Ⅱ 动 ❶ rectify; straighten; set right：把帽子～一～ *put one's cap straight* / 把领带～一～ *straighten one's tie* ❷ make right; correct：正误 / 正音 Ⅲ 副 ❶ just; right; precisely; exactly：～如上文所述 *just as mentioned above* / 大小～合适 *just the right size* / 我～要谈这个问题。*I'm just coming to that point.* ❷ just (doing sth.); just now：他～吃着饭呢。*He's eating just now.* / ～下着雨呢。*It's raining.* ——另见 zhēng

【正儿八经】〈方〉serious; earnest

【正版】(of a product) genuine

【正本】❶ original (of a document)：将～送存档案库 *deposit the original in the archives* ❷ reserved copy (of a library book)

【正本清源】radically reform; thoroughly overhaul：采取～的措施 *take measures for thorough-going reform*

【正比】direct ratio ◇ ～例 [数] direct proportion

【正步】[军] parade step; goose step：～走! (*word of command*) *Parade step, march!*

【正餐】❶ a regular meal served in a restaurant ❷ dinner

【正册】regular register

【正茬】the main crop (in crop rotation)

【正长石】orthoclase

【正长岩】syenite

【正常】normal; regular：两国关系～化 *normalization of the relations between the two countries* / 过～的生活 *lead a normal life* / 他的行为极不～。*His behaviour is far from normal.* / ～心搏 *regular heartbeats*

【正大】upright; honest; aboveboard：～的理由 *justifiable reasons* ◇ ～光明 open and aboveboard; just and honourable

【正当】(zhèngdāng) just when; just the time for：～春耕之时 *just the time for spring ploughing* ◇ ～年 in the prime of life; in one's prime; ～时 the right season or time

【正当】(zhèngdàng) ❶ proper; appropriate; legitimate：～收入 *legitimate income* / 通过～途径 *in proper ways*; *by appropriate means*; *through proper channels* ❷ (of behaviour, etc.) correct; proper：～的行为 *correct behaviour* ◇ ～防卫 legitimate defence; justified defence

【正道】❶ the right way (or course); the correct path：走～ *follow the correct path* ❷ the correct principle; the correct way

【正点】(of ships, trains, etc.) on schedule; on time; punctually：～运行 *running on schedule*

【正电】positive electricity

【正电荷】positive charge

【正电子】positive electron; positron

【正殿】main hall (in a palace or temple)

【正定霉素】[药] daunomycin

【正多边形】(又作'正多角形') [数] regular polygon

【正法】execute (a criminal)

【正反】positive and negative：～两方面的看法 *the pros and cons*

【正方】square：～盒子 *a square box* ◇ ～体 同〖立方体〗; ～形 square

【正房】❶ principal rooms (in a courtyard, usu. facing south) ❷ legal wife (as contrasted with concubine)

【正风】righteous style and practice：树立～ *affirm the honest and righteous*; *let the positive prevail* (〈反〉"歪风")

【正负电子对撞机】electron-positron collider

【正告】earnestly admonish; warn sternly; warn in all seriousness

【正割】[数] secant
【正宫】❶ empress's palace ❷ empress
【正骨】[中] bonesetting
【正规】regular; standard: ～部队 *regular troops; regulars* / ～化 *regularize; standardize* / ～学校 *regular school* / ～教育 *regular education* ◇ ～军 regular army; ～战 regular warfare
【正轨】the right (or correct) path: 纳入～ *lead onto the correct path; put on the right track*
【正果】[宗](佛教) the right fruit—the proper consequence of a regulated life in this world: 因为修行,得了～ *have attained the right fruit by self-cultivation*
【正好】❶ just in time; just right; just enough: 你来得～。*You've come just in time.* / 这双鞋我穿～。*This pair of shoes fits me nicely.* / 这～证明我们的做法是对的。*That only goes to prove that our approach is correct.* ❷ happen to; chance to; as it happens: 小王～从那儿路过。*Xiao Wang happened (or chanced) to be passing by.*
【正号】[数] positive sign; plus sign
【正话】❶ serious words: 他那个人就是玩笑话多,～少。*He often speaks in jest, and seldom says anything serious.* ❷ what one really means: 她正在气头上,那话怕是～反说吧! *She said that in a fit of anger, and it must surely have been the very opposite of what she really meant.*
【正火】[冶] normalizing
【正极】[电] positive electrode; positive pole; anode: ～板 *positive plate*
【正襟危坐】straighten one's clothes and sit properly
【正经】❶ decent; respectable; honest: ～人 *a decent person* ❷ serious: 钱必须用在～地方。*Money must be put to right uses.* / ～事儿 *serious affairs* / 谈～事 *talk business* / 说～的,你得注意点身体。*Seriously now, you ought to take more care of your health.* ❸ standard: ～货 *standard goods* ❹〈方〉really; truly; indeed: 这黄瓜长得还～不错呢! *The cucumbers are really doing fine.*
【正经八百】(又作'正经八摆')〈方〉serious; earnest: 这是～的事。*This is a serious matter.* or *This is no joke.*
【正剧】serious drama
【正角】同〖主角〗
【正楷】(in Chinese calligraphy) regular script
【正课】required courses (in college)
【正理】correct principle; valid reason (or argument); the right thing to do
【正梁】[建] ridge purlin
【正六面体】[数] regular hexahedron
【正路】the right way (or course); the correct path: 这才是～。*That's the correct thing to do.*
【正论】a just opinion
【正门】front door (or gate); main entrance
【正面】❶ front; frontage; facade: ～进攻 *frontal attack* / ～冲突 *head-on confrontation (or clash)* ❷ the obverse side; the right side: 牛皮纸的～ *the right side of kraft paper* / 硬币的～ *the obverse side of a coin* / 皮革的～ *the grain side of leather* ❸ positive: ～教育 *educate by positive measures or examples; positive education* ❹ directly; openly: 有问题请～提出来。*Please ask your question directly.* ◇ ～人物 positive character; ～图 同〖主视图〗
【正派】upright; honest; decent: ～人 *a decent person* / 他为人～。*He's honest and upright.*
【正片】❶ [摄] positive ❷ [电影] copy ❸ [电影] feature (film)
【正品】certified products (or goods); quality products (or goods)
【正气】❶ healthy atmosphere (or tendency): 发扬～ *encourage healthy trends; encourage standing up for what is right* ❷ [中] vital energy
【正桥】the main structure of a bridge
【正巧】❶ happen to; chance to; as it happens: 他们～带有仪器。*They happened (or chanced) to have their instruments with them.* ❷ just in time; in the nick of time; just at the right time: 你来得～,我们马上就要出发了。*You've come just in time. We're leaving immediately.*
【正切】[数] tangent
【正确】correct; right; proper: ～的答案 *a correct answer* / ～估计客观形势 *accurately appraise the objective situation* / ～的批评 *well-founded criticism* / ～性 *correctness; soundness; validity*
【正人君子】a man of honour; a man of integrity; gentleman: 打扮成～ *masquerade as a gentleman*
【正三角形】equilateral triangle
【正色】❶〈书〉pure colours ❷adopt a stern countenance: ～拒绝 *sternly refuse*
【正身】in person; not by proxy
【正史】history books written in biographical style ——另见〖纪传体〗
【正式】formal; official; regular: ～列入记录 *be officially placed on record* / 代表团的～成员 *a regular (or full) member of the delegation* / ～记录 *official records* / ～声明 *official statement* / ～文本 *official text*
【正视】face squarely; face up to; look squarely at: ～困难 *face difficulties squarely; face up to difficulties* / ～现实 *look reality in the face* / ～缺点 *acknowledge one's shortcomings* / 不～事实 *shut one's eyes to facts*
【正视图】同〖主视图〗
【正事】one's proper business: 现在咱们谈～。*Now let's talk business.*
【正室】❶ legal wife (as contrasted with concubine) ❷〈书〉the wife's eldest son
【正手】[体] forehand ◇ ～抽球 forehand drive; ～击球 forehand stroke; ～快抽 forehand fast drive; ～切击 forehand cut; ～球 forehand; forehand ball; ～握拍 forehand grip; ～削球 forehand chop; ～远抽 forehand long drive
【正数】[数] positive number
【正税】regular tax
【正态分布】statistics normal distribution

【正题】❶ subject (or topic) of a talk or essay：转入～ *come to the subject* / 离开～ *wander* (*or digress*) *from the subject* / 不离～ *stick to one's text* ❷［哲］thesis

【正体】❶ standardized form of Chinese characters ❷ 同〖正楷〗❸ block letter

【正厅】❶ main hall (in the middle) ❷ stalls (in a theatre)

【正统】❶ legitimism ❷ orthodox：～观念 *orthodox ideas* / ～派 *orthodox party or school*

【正投影】orthographic projection

【正文】main body (of a book, etc.); text：书的～ *the text of a book* / 词典～ *the main body of a dictionary; the dictionary proper*

【正屋】principal rooms (in a courtyard, usu. facing south)

【正午】high noon

【正误】correct (typographical) errors ◇ ～表 errata; corrigenda

【正弦】［数］sine ◇ ～波［物］sine wave

【正凶】［法］principal murderer

【正选】［体］(of athletes) key player on a team

【正言厉色】in a serious tone and with a solemn look

【正盐】［化］normal salt

【正颜厉色】serious and severe; with a stern look

【正眼】look straight：他和我说话时不敢～看着我。*He did not dare to look me straight in the face when he spoke.*

【正业】regular occupation; proper duties

【正义】❶ justice：主持～ *uphold justice* / 为～而战 *fight for justice* / ～之师 *an army dedicated to a just cause* ❷ just; righteous：～立场 *a just stand* / ～的事业 *a just cause* / ～的战争 *a just war* ❸ (formerly often used in book titles) orthodox or rectified interpretation (of ancient texts) ◇ ～感 a sense of what is right; a sense of justice (or righteousness)

【正音】❶ correct one's pronunciation ❷ standard pronunciation ◇ ～法［语音］orthoepy

【正应力】［物］direct stress

【正用】proper use：省了这笔钱作～多好。*Wouldn't it be better to save this money for more proper uses?*

【正院儿】main courtyard

【正在】in process of; in course of：他们～聊天。*They're having a chat.* / 许多问题～讨论。*Many questions are under discussion.*

【正直】honest; upright; fair-minded：～的人 *an honest person; a person of integrity*

【正职】❶ the position of the chief of an office, department, etc. ❷ full-time job or main occupation

【正治】［中］normal treatment, i.e. administering medicines of a cold nature to treat a febrile disease

【正中】right in the middle (or centre)：把茶具放在桌子～。*Put the tea-things right in the middle* (*or centre*) *of the table.*

【正中下怀】be just what one hopes for; fit in exactly with one's wishes

【正传】main story (of a novel, etc.); subject under discussion ——另见〖言归正传〗

【正字】❶ correct a wrongly written character or a misspelt word ❷ 同〖正楷〗❸ standardized form of Chinese characters ◇ ～法 orthography

【正宗】❶ orthodox school ❷ genuine：～川菜 *genuine Sichuan cooking*

【正座】central seats that directly face the stage; stalls

证

Ⅰ 动 prove; demonstrate：～几何定理 *demonstrate* (*or prove*) *a geometric theorem* Ⅱ 名 ❶ evidence; proof; testimony：以此为～ *take this as an evidence* ❷ certificate; card

【证词】testimony

【证婚人】chief witness at a wedding ceremony

【证监会】(〈略〉全称为'证券监督管理委员会')Securities Supervision Commission

【证件】credentials; papers; certificate：请出示～。*Please show your credentials* (*or papers*).

【证据】evidence; proof; testimony：搜集～ *collect evidence* / 提出～ *offer testimony*

【证明】❶ prove; testify; bear out：无数事实已～了这一点。*Countless facts have proved this point.* / 事实～我是对的。*The facts bear me out.* ❷ certificate; identification; testimonial：～文件 *certificate; testimonial; papers* ◇ ～书 certificate; testimonial

【证券】bond; security; negotiable securities：免税～ *tax-exempt* (*non-taxable*) *securities* ◇ ～镑 security sterling; ～包销人(承购人) underwriter; ～持有人 fund holder; ～存款 certificate deposit; ～抵押品 collateral security; ～兑换 exchange of securities; ～分析家 securities analyst; ～公司 security company; ～及投资 securities and investments; ～及投资损益 profit and loss on securities and investment; ～价格平均数 stock price average; ～交易 dealing in securities; stock swap; ～交易所 securities exchange; stock exchange; bourse; ～交易所交易 stock exchange transactions; ～交易所牌价 stock exchange list; ～交易所委员会 stock exchange committee; ～借款 security loan; ～金融公司 securities finance company; ～经纪人 underwriter; bill broker; ～买卖人协会 association of securities dealers; ～市场 stock market; bond market; market of (for) securities; security market; ～投资 investment securities; portfolio investment; ～投资分析 securities analysis; ～推销所 boiler room; ～销售书 prospectus; ～纸 loan; security paper

【证券委】(〈略〉全称为'证券管理委员会') Securities Administration Commission

【证实】confirm; verify; bear out：有待～ *remain to be confirmed* / ～一个科学上的假设 *verify* (*or bear out*) *a scientific hypothesis*

【证书】certificate; credentials：～审查委员会 *cre-*

dentials committee

【证物】［法］exhibit（produced in court as evidence）

【证言】testimony

【证章】badge

怔 动〈方〉stare blankly; be in a daze：那消息使她～住了。*She was stunned by the news*. —— 另见 zhēng

【怔神儿】〈方〉stare blankly; be in a daze

【怔怔】〈方〉stare blankly; be in a daze; be in a trance：～地站着 *stand there as if in a trance*; *stand there staring blankly*

诤 动〈书〉criticize sb.'s faults frankly; admonish; expostulate：诤友

【诤谏】〈书〉criticize sb.'s faults frankly

【诤言】〈书〉forthright admonition

【诤友】〈书〉a friend who will give forthright admonition

郑 名 one of the Warring states

【郑重】serious; solemn; earnest：态度～ *be serious in one's attitude* / ～表示 *earnestly declare*; *solemnly state* / ～声明 *solemnly declare* / ～其事 *seriously*; *in earnest*

政 名 ❶ politics; political affairs：政治 ❷ certain administrative aspects of government：邮政 ❸ affairs of a family or an organization：家政

【政变】coup d'état; coup：未遂～ *abortive coup d'état*

【政策】policy：～教育 *education in policy* / 提高～水平 *enhance the understanding of policy*

【政策性】policy-related; involving policy considerations：～补贴 *subsidies granted out of policy consideration* / ～亏损 *policy-related losses*

【政出多门】multiple leadership; conflicting policies resulting from clashing departmental interests; each department acting on its own; too many branches of an administration making decisions

【政党】political party

【政敌】political opponent

【政法】politics and law ◇ ～机构 procuratorial, judicial and public security organizations; ～学院 institute of political science and law

【政风】atmosphere in government bodies; the ideological and work styles of government officials; the attitude and efficiency of government functions.

【政府】government：～部门 *government departments* / ～官员 *government official* / ～机构 *government apparatus* / ～机关 *government bodies*（*or organizations*）/ ～人士 *government circles* / ～首脑 *head of government* ◇ ～补贴 government subsidy; ～间贷款 inter-government loans; ～特殊津贴 special government subsidies; ～债券 government bonds; ～职能 government functions

【政纲】（〈略〉见〖政治纲领〗）political programme; platform

【政工】（〈略〉见〖政治工作〗）❶ political work：～人员 *people engaged in political work* / ～组 *political working group* ❷ cadres responsible for political work; political cadre

【政工师】intermediate rank for people engaged in political work

【政纪】government discipline; administrative regulation's：遵守国法～ *abide by state laws and regulations*

【政绩】achievements in one's official career

【政见】political view：持不同～ *hold different political views* / 持不同～者 *dissident*

【政教分离】separation of religion from politics; separation of the church from the state

【政界】political circles; government circles：进入～ *enter politics* / 退出～ *withdraw from political life*

【政局】political situation; political scene：～稳定。*The political situation is stable*.

【政客】〈贬〉politician

【政令】government decree（or order）

【政论】political comment：～家 *political commentator*; *political writer* / ～文 *political essay*

【政企不分】no clear division of function between government and enterprise; confound functions of government and enterprise

【政企分开】draw a clear line between（or separate）the functions of the government and enterprise

【政情】political situation

【政权】political（or state）power; regime：革命～ *a revolutionary regime* ◇ ～机关 organs of state（or political）power

【政审】（〈略〉全称为'政治审查'）examine sb.'s political behaviour or record; political investigation; background check：～不合格 *fail a background check*

【政坛】political circles：～风云 *changeable political climate*; *political power games*; *political shifts*

【政体】system（or form）of government

【政委】〈略〉见〖政治委员〗

【政务】government affairs; government administration ◇ ～院 the Government Administration Council

【政协】〈略〉见〖政治协商会议〗

【政治】politics; political affairs：～舞台 *political arena*（*or stage*, *scene*）/ ～信仰 *political conviction*（*or belief*）/ ～性 *political nature* / ～嗅觉 *political sense of smell*; *political acumen*（*or sensitiveness*）◇ ～庇护 political asylum; ～避难 political refuge; political asylum; ～部 political department; ～动乱 political disturbance; ～犯 political offender; political prisoner; ～风波 political disturbances; ～家 statesman; ～教导员 political instructor（of a PLA battalion）; ～经济学 political economy; ～局 the Political Bureau;

～面目 political affiliation or back ground；～权利 political rights；～社会学 political sociology；～思想工作 political and ideological work；～素质 political caliber；～委员 political commissar (of a PLA regiment and above)；commissar；～协理员 political assistant (of a PLA regiment and above)；～协商会议 political consultative conference；～学 political science；government；～指导员 political instructor (of a PLA company)；～资本 political capital

挣 动 ❶ struggle to get free；try to throw off：～脱枷锁 *throw off the shackles* / 他把捆绑的绳子～开了。*He wrenched himself free from his bonds*. ❷ earn；make：～饭吃 *earn a living* / ～工资的 *wage earner* / 她～得挺多的。*She earns a high salary*. ——另见 zhēng

【挣揣】〈书〉struggle；strive hard

【挣命】struggle to save one's life

【挣钱】earn (or make) money：～糊口 *earn a living*

症 名 disease；illness：急症 ——另见 zhēng

【症候】❶ disease ❷ symptom

【症状】symptom：前驱～ *premonitory* (*or signal*) *symptoms* / 早期～ *early* (*or incipient*) *symptoms*

铮 形〈方〉(of utensils, etc.) polished：她把银匙擦得～亮。*She polished the silver spoons till they shone*. ——另见 zhēng

zhī

之 Ⅰ 代〈书〉❶ (used in place of an objective noun or pronoun)：影片情节十分悲惨，观众无不为～感动。*The film was so sad that none were unmoved*. / 将如～何? *What is to be done?* ❷ (used in certain set phrases without definite designation)：我们三个人我最年长，李次～，张又次～。*Of the three of us, I am the eldest, Li is younger, and Zhang is the youngest*. / 手之舞～，足之蹈～ *dance with joy* ❸ this or that：～子于归。*The maiden goes to her future home*. Ⅱ 助〈书〉❶ (used between an attribute and the word it modifies)：钟鼓～声 *the sound of drums and bells* / 原因～一 *one of the reasons* / 宝中～宝 *the treasure of treasures* / 一水～隔 *be separated only by a river* ❷ (used between the subject and the predicate in a S-P structure so as to make it nominalized)：如因势利导，则如水～就下，极为自然。*If we guide the matter along its course of development, it will proceed as naturally as water flows downwards*.

【之后】later；after；afterwards：从那～她没来过。*She hasn't been here since then*. / ～他又给我写了两封信。*Afterwards he wrote to me twice*.

【之乎者也】particles of literary Chinese—pedantic terms；literary jargon；archaisms：老学究满口～，教人半懂不懂。*The old pedant used so many archaisms that half of what he said was unintelligible*.

【之前】before；prior to；ago：在她动身～ *before* (*or prior to*) *her departure* / 这药在睡觉～吃。*Take the medicine before bedtime*.

支 Ⅰ 动 ❶ prop up；put up：～帐篷 *put up a tent* / 用两张凳子把木板～起来 *prop up the board with two stools* / 两手～着头 *rest one's head in both hands* ❷ protrude；raise：～着耳朵听 *prick up one's ears* / 他那两只虎牙朝两边～着。*His two upper canine teeth protrude*. ❸ support；sustain；bear：孩子疼得～不住了。*The child couldn't bear the pain*. ❹ send away；put sb. off：把他们～开 *put them off with excuses*；*send them away upon some pretext* / 这事甭～别人了，你自个儿去吧。*Don't send anyone else；better go yourself*. ❺ pay or draw (money)：～拨 *pay a sum of money or transfer a sum of money in payment* / 上银行～款 *go to the bank to draw money* Ⅱ 名 ❶ branch；offshoot：～店 *branch store* / 邮政～局 *branch post office* ❷〈略〉见〖地支〗 Ⅲ 量 ❶ (for long, thin, inflexible objects)：一～钢笔 *a pen* / 一～箭 *an arrow* / 一～香烟 *a cigarette* ❷ (for troops, fleets, etc.)：两～队伍 *two contingents of troops* / 一～舰队 *a fleet* ❸ (for songs or musical compositions)：一～曲子 *a tune* / 一～新歌 *a new song* ❹ (for the illuminating power of electric lights) watt：一个 40～光的灯泡 *a 40-watt bulb* ❺ (for the size or quality of yarn) count：60～纱 *60-count yarn* / 细(中)～棉纱 *fine* (*medium*) *count yarn*

【支边】support the border areas

【支部】branch (esp. of the Chinese Communist Party or the Chinese Communist Youth League)：～大会 *general membership meeting of the branch* / ～书记 *branch secretary*

【支撑】❶ prop up；sustain；support：病人～着坐了起来。*The patient propped himself up into a sitting position*. / 一家人的生活得由他～。*He has to support his whole family*. ❷［建］strut；brace ◇ ～点［军］strong point；centre of resistance

【支承】［机］support；bear：～点 *bearing point* / ～力 *supporting force* / ～圈 *backup ring*；*support ring*

【支持】❶ sustain；hold out；bear：他冻得～不住了。*He was so cold he couldn't hold out any longer*. ❷ support；back；stand by：在国际上得到越来越广泛的～ *enjoy wider and wider international support* / 我完全～这个建议。*I am all for this proposal*.

【支持率】favorability rating

【支出】❶ pay (money)；expend；disburse ❷ expenses；expenditure；outlay；disbursement：收入与～相抵。*The income balances the expenditure*.

【支点】［物］fulcrum

【支队】detachment：游击～ *a guerrilla detachment*
【支墩坝】[水] buttress dam
【支付】pay (money)；defray：～水电费 *pay for electricity and water* / ～手段 *means of payment* / ～协定 *payments agreement*
【支行】subbranch (of a bank)
【支护】strut；support (tunnels, walls)：木～ *wooden strut*
【支唤】〈方〉order about
【支架】support；stand；trestle：自行车～ *prop stand of a bicycle*
【支解】dismemberment：～一个国家 *dismember a country*
【支棱】〈方〉hold up；stick up：～着耳朵听 *prick up one's ears*
【支离】❶ fragmented；broken；disorganized ❷ (of writing) trivial and jumbled；incoherent ◇ ～破碎 torn to pieces；broken up；fragmented
【支流】❶ tributary；affluent：珠江的一条～ *a tributary of the Zhujiang River* ❷ minor aspects；nonessentials：看问题时，不要把～当作主流。*In considering a problem, one mustn't mistake the nonessentials for the essentials.*
【支脉】offshoot (of a mountain range)；branch range：天山的～ *a branch range of the Tianshan Mountains*
【支那】China (a transliteration, used in translations of Buddhist scriptures, and by the Japanese until recently)
【支派】❶ branch；sect；offshoot ❷ order；send；dispatch
【支配】❶ arrange；allocate；budget：合理～劳动力 *make a proper allocation of the labour force* / 善于～自己的时间 *be good at budgeting one's time* ❷ control；dominate；govern：受人～ *be controlled by others* / 受自然规律的～ *be subject to the laws of nature*
【支票】cheque；check：开～ *write a cheque* / 划线～ *crossed cheque* / 空白～ *blank cheque* / 空头～ *rubber cheque* / 来人～ *bearer cheque* / 保付～ *certified cheque* / 旅行～ *traveller's cheque*
【支气管】bronchus ◇ ～扩张 bronchiectasis；～性气喘 bronchial asthma；～炎 bronchitis
【支前】support the front
【支渠】branch (irrigation) canal
【支取】draw (money)：～存款 *draw one's deposit (from a bank)*
【支使】❶ order about：他老～人，我都烦了。*I'm tired of him ordering me about all the time.* ❷ send away；put sb. off
【支书】(〈略〉全称为'支部书记') secretary of a Party or League branch；branch secretary
【支枢】[机] pivot
【支数】[纺] number (of yarn)；count：纱线～ *yarn number*；*yarn size*
【支吾】prevaricate；equivocate；hum and haw ◇ ～其词 speak evasively；hum and haw
【支线】branch line；feeder (line)：铁路～ *feeder railway* / 公路～ *feeder highway*
【支援】support；assist；help：～灾区 *give aid (or send relief) to disaster areas* ◇ ～部队 support unit；supporting troops
【支柱】pillar；prop；mainstay：矿用～ *pit prop* / 国家的～ *pillar of the state* ◇ ～产业 pillar industries；～根[植] prop root

汁 名 juice：西瓜红瓤多～。*Watermelons have juicy red flesh.*
【汁水】〈方〉juice：这种果子～很多。*This fruit is juicy.*
【汁液】juice

只 Ⅰ 形 single；one only：只言片语 Ⅱ 量 (for boats, birds, some animals, some containers, and one of certain paired things)：一～船 *a boat* / 两～喜鹊 *two magpies* / 一～老虎 *a tiger* / 三～箱子 *three suitcases* / 两～手 *two hands* / 一～眼睛 *an eye* ——另见 zhǐ
【只身】alone；by oneself：～前往 *go there alone*
【只言片语】a word or two；a few isolated words and phrases：未留下～ *leave behind not even a single word*
【只字不提】not say a single word about sth.；not so much as mention sth.

芝 (构词成分) 见下
【芝加哥】Chicago
【芝兰】irises and orchids (symbolic of noble character, true friendship, or beautiful surroundings) ——另见〖如入芝兰之室〗
【芝麻】❶ sesame ❷ sesame seed ◇ ～官〈诙〉sesame official—petty official；～酱 sesame paste；～开花节节高 sesame stalks putting forth flowers notch by notch, higher and higher—(of living standards, etc.) rising steadily；～油 sesame-seed oil；sesame oil

吱 象 a creaking sound：门～地一声开了。*The door creaked open.*

枝 Ⅰ 名 branch；twig：柳～ *willow branches* Ⅱ 量 ❶ (for flowers with stems intact)：一～梅花 *a spray of plum blossoms* ❷ (for long, thin, inflexible objects)：一～步枪 *a rifle* / 三～钢笔 *three pens* / 一～蜡烛 *a candle*
【枝杈】branch；twig
【枝接】[农] scion grafting
【枝节】❶ branches and knots—minor matters：～问题 *a minor problem*；*a side issue* ❷ complication；unexpected difficulty：横生枝节
【枝蔓】branches and tendrils—complicated and confused
【枝条】branch；twig
【枝头】on a branch：～小鸟 *little birds on a branch*
【枝梧】(又作'枝捂')〈书〉prevaricate；equivocate；hum and haw
【枝桠】(又作'枝丫') branch；twig
【枝叶】❶ branches and leaves ❷ nonessentials；

minor details

【枝子】branch; twig

知 Ⅰ 动 ❶ know; realize; be aware of: 这话不～是谁说的。*We don't know who said this.* ❷ inform; notify; tell: 通知 ❸ administer; be in charge of: 知县 Ⅱ 名 knowledge: 求知

【知彼知己,百战不殆】Know the enemy and know yourself, and you can fight a hundred battles without defeat.

【知耻】have a sense of shame ◇ ～近乎勇 to know the things of shame is to be near to fortitude

【知道】know; realize; be aware of: 我不～这事儿。*I know nothing about it.* / 你的意思我～。*I know what you mean.* or *I see your point.*

【知底】know the inside story; be in the know

【知法犯法】knowingly violate the law; deliberately break the law

【知府】(in former times) prefect

【知根知底】know sb.'s background; know sb. thoroughly

【知更鸟】robin; redbreast

【知过必改】always correct an error when one becomes aware of it

【知会】〈口〉tell (orally): 你先去～他一声,让他早点儿准备。*Go and tell him so that he can get ready in time.*

【知己】❶ intimate; understanding: ～的朋友 *bosom (or intimate) friend* / 和他很～ *be on intimate terms with him* / ～话 *intimate words; heart-to-heart talk* ❷ bosom (or intimate) friend

【知交】bosom (or intimate) friend: 他和我父亲是～。*He is an intimate friend of my father's.*

【知觉】❶ consciousness: 失去～ *lose consciousness; pass out* / 恢复～ *recover consciousness; come to* ❷ [心理] perception

【知觉常性】[心理] perceptual constancies

【知了】cicada

【知名】well-known; noted; celebrated; famous: ～人士 *a well-known figure; celebrity* ◇ ～度 popularity

【知命】〈书〉❶ understand the Decree of Heaven ❷ (used esp. in): ～之年 *the age of fifty*

【知母】❶ [植] wind-weed (Anemarrhena asphodeloides) ❷ [中] rhizome of wind-weed

【知难而进】press forward despite difficulties; advance in the face of difficulties

【知难而退】beat a retreat in the face of difficulties; shrink back from difficulties

【知其不可为而为之】know it's no use, but keep on doing it; do what one knows is impossible

【知其然,不知其所以然】know that sth. is so but not why it is so; know the hows but not the whys

【知其一,不知其二】know only one aspect of a thing; have a one-sided view

【知青】〈略〉见【知识青年】

【知情】❶ know the facts of a case or the details of an incident; be in the know: ～不报 *fail to report what one knows of a case* / ～人 *person in the know; insider* ❷ feel grateful to sb.; appreciate the kindness: 你们的好意,我很～。*I'm very grateful to you for your kindness.* ◇ ～达理 reasonable; sensible

【知趣】know how to behave in a delicate situation; be sensible; be tactful: 你还是～一些,快走吧。*You'd better be sensible and quit.*

【知人善任】know one's subordinates well enough to assign them suitable jobs; know how to judge and use people

【知人之明】ability to appreciate a person's character and capability; a keen insight into a person's character: 有～ *know how to judge people; be a good judge of people*

【知人知面不知心】you may know a person's face but not his heart; one may know a person for a long time without understanding his true nature: 画虎画皮难画骨,～。*Painting a tiger's skin is easy, but not so the bones. A man's face one can know, but not his heart.*

【知事】〈旧〉(in former times) county magistrate

【知识】knowledge; intellect: ～渊博 *have a wide range of knowledge; be erudite; be learned* / 技术～ *technical know-how* / 书本～ *book learning* ◇ ～产权 intellectual property rights; ～产业 knowledge industry; ～界 intellectual circles; the intelligentsia; ～经济 knowledge economy; ～就是力量 knowledge is power; ～密集型产业 knowledge-intensive industry; ～青年 school leavers; school graduates; educated youth

【知识分子】intellectual; the intelligentsia: ～出身 *with an intellectual background*

【知疼着热】(又作'知冷知热') love sb. (esp. one's husband or wife) tenderly: 他需要一个～的人。*He needs the loving care of a woman.*

【知无不言,言无不尽】say all you know and say it without reserve

【知悉】know; learn; be informed of: 业已～ *have already learned of the matter* / 无从～ *have no way of finding out about it*

【知县】〈旧〉(in former times) county magistrate

【知晓】know; be aware of; understand

【知心】intimate; understanding: ～朋友 *intimate (or bosom) friend* / ～话 *intimate words; heart-to-heart talk*

【知行】[哲] knowing and doing: ～统一观 *the theory of the unity of knowing and doing* ◇ ～合一 the unity of knowledge and practice

【知音】a friend keenly appreciative of one's talents; an understanding friend: ～难觅。*It is difficult to find an understanding friend.*

【知遇】have found a patron or superior appreciative of one's ability: ～之恩 *a debt of gratitude for sb.'s recognition and appreciation*

【知政】knowledge of major state policies and activities

【知之为知之,不知为不知,是知也】To say you know when you know, and to say you do not when you

do not, that is knowledge.
【知子莫若父】No one knows a son better than his father.
【知足】be content with one's lot ◇ ～常乐 contentment brings happiness

肢 名 limb：四肢
【肢解】同〖支解〗
【肢体】❶ limbs ❷ limbs and trunk
【肢障】physical disability; handicap (of the limbs)

织 动 ❶ weave：～席 *weave (or make) a mat* ❷ knit：～毛衣 *knit a sweater*
【织补】darning; invisible mending
【织布】weaving cotton cloth; weaving：～工 *weaver* ◇ ～鸟 weaverbird
【织机】loom：多梭箱～ *multiple box loom*
【织锦】❶ brocade ❷ picture-weaving in silk：风景～ *landscape woven in silk* ◇ ～厂 brocade mill; ～缎 tapestry satin
【织女】❶〈旧〉weaving-girl; weaving-maid; girl weaver ❷ the Weaving-girl ◇ ～星 the Weaving-girl star—Vega
【织品】textile; fabric
【织袜机】hosiery machine
【织物】fabric：机织～ *woven fabric* / ～经纬密度 *thread count* / ～耐磨试验 *wear testing*
【织造】weaving ◇ ～厂 weaving mill
【织针】knitting needle
【织轴】[纺] beam (of a loom)

栀 (构词成分) 见下
【栀子】[植] Cape jasmine

脂 名 ❶ fat; grease; tallow：含～羊毛 *wool in the grease* ❷ rouge：脂粉
【脂肪】fat：动物～ *animal fat* / 植物～ *vegetable fat* ◇ ～肝 [医] fatty liver; ～酶 [生化] lipase; ～酸 (又作'脂酸') fatty acid; ～组织 [生理] adipose tissue
【脂粉】rouge and powder; cosmetics：薄施～ *apply a light make-up* ◇ ～气 womanlike ways; femininity
【脂膏】❶ fat; grease ❷ fruits of the people's labour; wealth of the people (见〖民脂民膏〗)
【脂瘤】[医] lipoma
【脂血症】lipemia; lipidemia
【脂眼鲱】[动] Pacific round herring

蜘 (构词成分) 见下
【蜘蛛】spider：～丝 *the thread of a spider web; cobweb* / ～网 *spider (or spider's) web; cobweb*
【蜘蛛抱蛋】[植] (common) aspidistra (Aspidistra elatior)

zhí

执 Ⅰ 动 ❶ hold; grasp：手～红旗 *hold (or carry) a red banner* ❷ take charge of; direct; manage：执教 ❸ stick to (one's views, etc.); persist：各执一词 ❹ carry out; observe ❺〈书〉catch; capture：战败被～ *be captured after being defeated in battle* Ⅱ 名 written acknowledgement：回执
【执棒】hold the baton; conduct music：这场音乐会是由谁来～？ *Who will be the conductor of the concert?*
【执笔】write; do the actual writing：这封信是集体讨论，由老王～的。*The letter was discussed by us all, but Lao Wang did the actual writing.*
【执鞭】〈书〉hold the teacher's pointer—be a teacher
【执导】direct a film or a play：这部片子是谁～的？ *Who directed the film?*
【执法】enforce (or execute) the law ◇ ～不严 laws are not strictly enforced; lax enforcement of laws; ～犯法 violation of the law by law enforcement officials; ～如山 enforce the law strictly
【执管】be in charge of
【执教】be a teacher; teach：他在北京外国语大学～多年。*He taught at Beijing Foreign Studies University for many years.*
【执迷不悟】obstinately stick to a wrong course; be perverse; refuse to come to one's senses
【执拗】stubborn; pigheaded; wilful
【执判】referee a contest：～比赛要公正。*The referee of a contest must be fair.*
【执勤】be on duty
【执行】carry out; execute; implement：～任务 *carry out a task; perform a mission* / ～命令 *execute an order* / ～纪律 *enforce discipline* / ～独立自主的外交政策 *pursue (or implement, follow) an independent foreign policy* ◇ ～机构 executive body; ～机关 executive organ; ～秘书 executive secretary; ～委员会 executive committee; ～员 [法] marshal; ～主席 executive (or presiding) chairman
【执意】insist on; be determined to; be bent on：她～不收彩礼。*She firmly refused to accept betrothal presents from her fiancé's family.*
【执掌】wield; be in control of：～兵权 *wield military power*
【执照】license; permit：驾驶～ *driver's license* ◇ ～税 tax on licenses
【执政】be in power; be in office; be at the helm of the state ◇ ～党 the party in power (or in office); the ruling (or governing) party
【执著】persistent; persevering：～地追求艺术上的完美 *strive perseveringly for artistic perfection*

直 Ⅰ 形 ❶ straight：街道又宽又～。*The streets are wide and straight.* / 把铁丝拉～ *straighten a piece of wire* ❷ vertical; perpendicular：～行的文字 *characters written from top to bottom* / 这屋子～里有六米，横里有三米。*The room is 6 metres in length and 3 in width.* ❸ just; upright：正直 ❹ frank; straightforward：～认不讳

admit frankly; *own up readily* / 我就～说了。*I'll speak very frankly*. ❺ stiff; numb: 天太冷，手指都冻～了。*It was so cold that my fingers were frozen stiff*. Ⅱ 动 straighten: ～起腰来 *straighten one's back*; *stand up straight* Ⅲ 名 vertical stroke (in Chinese characters) Ⅳ 副 ❶ directly; straight: 一～走 *go straight ahead* / ～奔火车站 *head direct for the railway station* / ～通港口 *lead directly to the harbour* / ～飞北京 *fly nonstop to Beijing* ❷ continuously: 新井～往外喷油。*Oil gushed continuously from the new well*. / 他冻得～哆嗦。*He was so cold that he kept shivering*. / 这个故事逗得她～乐。*The story tickled her fancy*. ❸ just; simply: 待他～如兄弟 *treat him just like a brother* / 疼得～像针扎一样 *feel a piercing pain*

【直白】❶ frank and honest: 有话～说。*Don't beat about the bush*. ❷ boring; flat: ～的演讲 *boring speech*

【直播】❶［农］direct seeding ❷ live radio or TV transmission; broadcast live: 现场～网球赛 *live broadcast of a tennis match*

【直拨电话】direct-dial telephone

【直布罗陀】Gibraltar ◇ ～海峡 the Strait(s) of Gibraltar

【直肠】［生理］rectum ◇ ～癌 carcinoma of the rectum; ～镜［医］proctoscope; ～炎 proctitis; rectitis; ～直肚〈口〉straightforward; frank

【直肠子】❶ straightforward; downright; forthright ❷ a straightforward person

【直尺】straightedge

【直齿轮】［机］straight gear

【直翅目昆虫】orthopteran

【直刺】❶ straight thrust (in fencing) ❷［中］perpendicular inserting (in acupuncture)

【直达】through; nonstop: ～车 *express*; *through train or through bus*

【直捣】drive straight on to: ～匪巢 *drive straight on to the bandits' den* ◇ ～黄龙 drive straight on to Huanglong (i.e. the enemy stronghold)

【直到】❶ until: 我们～昨晚才接到通知。*We didn't get the notice until last night*. ❷ up to: ～现在我们还没有接到正式通知。*We've received no official information about it up to now*.

【直道而行】follow the straight path—act with rectitude

【直根】［植］taproot

【直贡呢】［纺］venetian

【直勾勾】(stare) fixedly: 他～地望着我。*He stared fixedly at me*.

【直观】directly perceived through the senses; audio-visual: ～教具 *aids to object teaching*; *audio-visual aids* / ～教学 *object teaching* / ～教学课 *object lesson*

【直航】fly non-stop; direct route: 上海和纽约之间有～。*There are non-stop flights between Shanghai and New York*.

【直话】straightforward talk: ～直说 *speak frankly*

【直角】［数］right angle ◇ ～尺 square; ～三角形 right (or right-angled) triangle

【直接】direct; immediate: ～原因 *immediate cause*; *direct cause* / ～会晤 *meet sb. in person* ◇ ～宾语［语］direct object; ～经验［哲］direct experience; ～起飞 rolling (or follow-through) takeoff; rolling start; ～染料 direct dyes; ～任意球 free kick (in soccer); ～税 direct tax; ～推理 immediate reasoning; ～选举 direct election; ～着陆 straight-in landing

【直截】(又作'直捷') straightforward; blunt; point-blank ◇ ～了当 straightforward; blunt; point-blank

【直径】diameter: 大～ *major diameter* / 小～ *minor diameter*

【直觉】［心理］intuition ◇ ～主义［心理］intuitionism

【直来直去】frank and outspoken; blunt: 他是个～的人，说话有口无心。*He's a blunt man, often speaking sharply but meaning no harm*.

【直立茎】［植］erect stern

【直流电】direct current (D.C.)

【直露】forthright; explicit: 过于～的话恐怕谁也受不住。*Overly direct language is hard for anyone to accept*.

【直眉瞪眼】❶stare in anger; fume ❷ stare blankly; be in a daze; be stupefied: 他～地站在那里，也不说话。*He stood there staring blankly, saying nothing*.

【直拍握法】［体］(乒乓球)pen-hold grip

【直朴】forthright and uncomplicated: 张有田～诚实，说话不会拐弯。*Zhang Youtian is forthright, and never beats about the bush*.

【直射距离】［军］battle-sight range; point-blank range

【直升飞机】helicopter; copter: ～机场 *heliport* / ～母舰 *helicopter carrier* / ～运载 *helilift*

【直抒己见】state one's views frankly; be plainspoken

【直属】directly under; directly subordinate (or affiliated) to: 国务院～机关 *departments directly under the State Council*

【直率】frank; candid; straightforward: 你～地告诉我吧。*Now tell me frankly*.

【直爽】frank; candid; straightforward; forthright: 性格～ *forthright in character*

【直挺挺】straight; stiff; bolt upright: ～地站着 *stand ramrod straight* / ～地坐着 *sit bolt upright*

【直投】deliver directly: 在咱们乡连农民个人的邮件也已经～了。*In our village, even the farmers' personal mail is now delivered door-to-door*.

【直系亲属】directly-related members of one's family—parents, spouse and children

【直销】direct sale

【直辖】directly under the jurisdiction of ◇ ～市 municipality directly under the Central Government

【直线】❶ straight line: 两点之间以～为最短。*A straight line is the shortest distance between 2 points*. / ～距离 20 里 *twenty li as the crow flies*

/ ～飞行 *rectilinear* (*or straight*) *flight* ❷ steep; sharp (rise or fall): 捕鱼量～上升。*The total catch of fish has shot up*. ◇ ～加速器［物］linear accelerator; ～运动［物］rectilinear motion

【直心眼儿】〈口〉open; frank; straightforward

【直性子】❶ straightforward; downright; forthright ❷ a straightforward person

【直言】speak bluntly; state outright: 恕我～。*Excuse me for speaking bluntly*. ◇ ～不讳 speak without reservation; not mince words; call a spade a spade

【直译】word-for-word translation; literal translation

【直音】［语音］traditional method of indicating the pronunciation of a Chinese character by citing another character with the same pronunciation

【直展云】［气］cloud with vertical development

【直至】❶ until: 继续战斗，～胜利。*Keep on fighting till victory is assured*. ❷ up to: ～此时 *up to this moment*

侄

名 brother's son; nephew

【侄女】brother's daughter; niece

【侄女婿】husband of brother's daughter; niece's husband

【侄孙】brother's grandson; grandnephew

【侄孙女】brother's granddaughter; grandniece

【侄媳妇】wife of brother's son; nephew's wife

【侄子】(又作'侄儿') brother's son; nephew

值

Ⅰ 名 ❶ price; value ❷［数］value Ⅱ 动 ❶ be worth: 这～多少钱? *How much* (*or What*) *is this worth*? / 这只戒指～500 元。*This ring is worth* 500 *yuan*. ❷ happen to: 你上次来访，正～我外出。*I happened to be out when you called*. / ～此贵国 30 周年国庆之际 *on the occasion of the* 30*th anniversary of your National Day* ❸ be on duty; take one's turn at sth.

【值班】❶ be on duty: ～员 *person on duty* / 今天谁～? *Who's on duty today*? / 他值夜班。*He's on night duty*. or *He's on the night shift*. ❷ unsold merchandise on the shelf: ～菜 *unsold vegetables*

【值不当】〈方〉not be worthwhile

【值乘】(attendants) attend to needs of passengers (on plane, ship, train, etc.)

【值得】be worth; merit; deserve: ～买 *be worth buying* / ～赞许 *deserve commendation*; *be praiseworthy* / ～怀疑 *be open to doubt* / ～仔细考虑 *warrant careful consideration*

【值分布理论】［数］value distribution theory

【值钱】costly; valuable: 这张画～。*This is a valuable painting*. / 这些邮票不～。*These stamps are worthless*.

【值勤】(of armymen, policemen, etc.) be on duty; be on point duty: ～交通警 *policeman on point duty* / ～人员 *personnel on duty*

【值日】be on duty for the day; be one's turn to be on duty: ～表 *duty roster*; *rota* / ～生 *student on duty*

【值守】guard; watch over: 他见机房无人～，就溜了进去。*He sneaked into the engine-room when he found nobody on guard*.

【值星】(of army officers) be on duty for the week: 本周是王连长～。*Company commander Wang is the officer of the week*.

【值夜】be on night duty; be on the night shift

职

名 ❶ duty; job: 尽职 ❷ post; office: 在职 ❸ manage; direct: 职掌

【职别】official rank

【职称】the title of a technical or professional post (such as engineer, professor, lecturer, academician, etc.); professional title: 学术～和技术～ *academic and technical titles* ◇ ～等级 professional qualification; ～改革 the reform in professional titles; ～评定 the evaluation of professional titles

【职大】(〈略〉全称为'职业大学') workers' college: 上～ *enroll in the workers' college*

【职代会】(〈略〉全称为'职工代表大会') meeting of employee representatives: 执行～的决定 *carry out the decisions made by the meeting of employee representatives*

【职分】❶ duty ❷ official post; position

【职高】〈略〉见〖职业高中〗

【职工】❶ staff and workers; workers and staff members ❷〈旧〉workers; labour: ～运动 *labour movement*; *trade union movement* ◇ ～代表大会 the congress of workers and staff

【职级】rank

【职教】〈略〉见〖职业教育〗

【职能】function: 货币的～ *the functions of money* / ～部门 *functional department* (*in government*) / ～机构 *functional institution*

【职前教育】pre-job training

【职权】powers or authority of office: 行使～ *exercise one's functions and powers* / 超越～ *overstep one's authority*; *exceed one's powers* ◇ ～范围 limits (or scope) of one's functions and powers; terms of reference

【职守】post; duty: 忠于～ *be faithful in the discharge of one's duties*; *be devoted to one's duty*

【职位】position; post

【职务】post; duties; job: 履行～ *do* (*or perform*) *one's duties* / ～工资 *wages related to specific work posts* ◇ ～发明 service invention

【职衔】post and rank

【职业】occupation; profession; vocation: 从事各种～的人 *people of all occupations* / 他的～是医生。*He is a doctor by profession*. / 我们的～有保障。*Our jobs are secure*. ◇ ～病 occupational disease; ～道德 professional ethics; ～妇女 career woman; ～高中 vocational high school; ～过失 malpractice; ～教育 vocational schooling; vocational education; ～介绍所 job center; career service center; employment agency; ～杀手

bumpman; hit man; ～团体 professional organization; ～外交官 career diplomat; ～学校 vocational school; ～运动员 professional athlete; professional

【职员】office worker; staff member; functionary

【职责】duty; obligation; responsibility: 应尽的～ *bounden duty* / 神圣～ *sacred duty*

【职掌】〈书〉❶ be in charge of: ～财务 *be in charge of financial affairs* ❷ duty; charge

植 动 ❶ plant; grow: 植树 ❷ set up; establish: 植党营私

【植保】〈略〉见〖植物保护〗

【植被】[植] vegetation

【植党营私】set up a clique for one's own selfish interests

【植根】❶ take root ❷ lay a solid basis: 伟大的文学创作,总是～于人民生活。*Any great literary work is rooted in the life of ordinary people.*

【植苗】plant seedlings

【植皮】[医] skin grafting

【植绒】[纺] flocking

【植树】tree planting: ～造林 *afforestation* ◇ ～节 National Treeplanting Day (March 12)

【植物】plant; flora ◇ ～保护 plant (or crop) protection; ～病害 plant disease; ～检疫 plant quarantine; ～胶 vegetable gum or glue; ～界 plant kingdom; vegetable kingdom; ～净化 [环保] plant purification; ～区系 flora; ～群落 plant community; ～人 vegetable (a human being); comatose person; person in vegetative state; ～生长调节剂 [农] plant growth regulator; ～纤维 plant fibre; ～性神经 [生理] autonomic nerve; ～学 botany; ～油 vegetable oil; ～育种 plant breeding; ～园 botanical garden; ～志 flora

【植株】[农] plant

殖 动 breed; multiply: 生殖

【殖民】establish a colony; colonize: 非～化 *decolonize; decolonization* / ～国家 *colonialist power* / ～扩张 *colonial expansion* / ～战争 *colonialist war* ◇ ～地 colony; ～主义 colonialism

踯 (构词成分) 见下

【踯躅】〈书〉walk to and fro; loiter around: ～街头 *tramp the streets*

蹠 名 ❶ [生理] metatarsus ❷ 〈书〉sole of the foot ❸ 〈书〉tread

【蹠骨】[生理] metatarsal bones

zhǐ

止 Ⅰ 动 ❶ stop: ～痒 *stop or relieve itching* / 不达目的不～ *refuse to give up without attaining one's aim* ❷ close; end: 从本月十号起到十六号～ *from the 10th to the 16th of this month* Ⅱ 副 only: ～此一家。*This is the only shop.*

【止步】halt; stop; go no further: ～不前 *halt; stand still* / 游人～ *no visitors; out of bounds*

【止动机构】[机] stop motion (mechanism)

【止付】banking stop payment: ～通知书 *stop-payment notice*

【止境】end; limit: 科学的发展是没有～的。*There is no limit to the development of science.*

【止咳】relieve a cough ◇ ～糖浆 cough syrup

【止渴】quench one's thirst

【止痛】relieve pain; stop pain ◇ ～药 anodyne; analgesic; pain-killer

【止泻药】antidiarrheal

【止血】stop bleeding; stanch bleeding ◇ ～带 tourniquet; ～器 haemostat; ～药 haemostatic

只 副 only; just; merely: ～剩一个了。*There is only one left.* / 我～想问一个问题。*I have just one question.* / 这～是个时间问题。*It is merely a question of time.* ——另见 zhī

【只不过】only; just; merely: 这～是一种猜测。*It's just (or nothing but) a guess.* /我～拧了拧门把手,可它却掉了。*The door knob came off when I gave it a mere turn.*

【只此一家,别无分店】the only shop of this name—no branches anywhere (a shop sign warning of sham goods)

【只得】have no alternative but to; be obliged to; have to: 他们～把会议延期。*They had no alternative but to put the meeting off.* / 没有桥,我们～涉水过去。*As there was no bridge, we were obliged to wade across.*

【只读存储器】[计]read-only memory (ROM)

【只顾】❶ be only concerned with; just think of: 你别～自己。*Don't just think of yourself.* ❷ (do sth.) single-mindedly; just (do sth.): 他～赚钱。*He's just trying to make money.*

【只管】❶ by all means: 有意见～提出来。*Don't hesitate to put forward your suggestions if you have any.* / 你～干下去。*Go ahead by all means.* ❷ simply; just: 我的话你～相信,不会有错。*You must believe me simply on my word.*

【只好】have to; be forced to: 十点钟他还不来,～我一个人先去了。*By ten o'clock he still hadn't turned up, so I had to go by myself.*

【只可意会,不可言传】can be sensed, but not explained in words; can be apprehended but not expressed

【只是】❶ only; just; merely: 我说这个～开个玩笑罢了。*I said it merely as a joke.* / 随便你怎么问,他～不吭声。*No matter how you question him, he just kept silent.* ❷ except that; only; but: 他各方面都很好,～身体差些。*He's good in every respect except in health.* / 他想去,～去不了。*He wants to go , only he can't.*

【只听楼梯响,不见人下来】the stairs creak but no one comes down—much talk but no action

【只消】all one has to do is; you only need to: ～来个电话,货物马上送到。*Just give us a ring and the goods will be delivered without delay.*

【只许州官放火,不许百姓点灯】The magistrates are

free to burn down houses, while the common people are forbidden even to light lamps; One may steal a horse while another may not look over the hedge.

【只要】(usu. used correlatively with 就 or 便) if only; as long as; provided: ～你有钱就办得到。*You could do it if only you had the money.*

【只要功夫深,铁杵磨成针】if you work at it hard enough, you can grind an iron rod into a needle—perseverance spells success

【只有】❶ only; alone: ～他知道这事的内情。*He alone knows the inside story.* / ～在紧急情况下,才能动用这笔款项。*We can draw on the fund only in an emergency.* ❷ have to; be forced to: 你～采取这个办法了。*This is the only way open to you.*

【只争朝夕】seize the day, seize the hour; seize every minute; race against time

【只重衣衫不重人】only value the clothes and not the man himself; judge people by their clothes, not their qualities

旨 Ⅰ形〈书〉tasty; delicious Ⅱ动 purport; purpose; aim: ～在唤起民众 *for the purpose of arousing the masses* / ～在加快工程进度的措施 *measures aimed at speeding up the project* Ⅲ名 decree: 圣旨

【旨酒】〈书〉excellent wine

【旨趣】〈书〉purport; objective

【旨要】同〖指要〗

【旨意】decree; order: 你这样做是奉谁的～? *On whose orders did you do this?*

址 名 location; site: 地址

纸 Ⅰ名 paper: 一张～ *a piece (or sheet) of paper* Ⅱ量 (for letters, documents, etc.): 一～公文 *a document* / 单据三～ *three bills*

【纸板】paperboard; cardboard: ～盒(箱) *cardboard case or box; carton*

【纸版】[刷] paper mould; paper matrix

【纸包不住火】you can't wrap fire in paper—there is no concealing the truth; truth will out

【纸币】paper money; paper currency; note: 不兑现～ *fiat money*

【纸锭】paper ingots (burned as offerings to the dead)

【纸饭碗】❶ paper rice bowl ❷〈喻〉unstable job: 这个厂的合同制工人都曾担心"～"不牢靠。*All contract workers worry about the insecurity of their "paper rice bowl".*

【纸花】paper flower

【纸浆】paper pulp; pulp: ～板 *pulp board* / ～厂 *pulp mill* / ～筛滤器 *pulp strainer* / ～原材 *pulpwood* / ～制造机 *macerator*

【纸巾】paper towel; towel

【纸老虎】paper tiger: 一切反动派都是～。*All reactionaries are paper tigers.*

【纸捻】spill of rolled paper used to light a pipe, etc.; (paper) spill

【纸牌】playing cards

【纸钱】paper made to resemble money and burned as an offering to the dead

【纸上谈兵】fight only on paper; be an armchair strategist; engage in idle theorizing

【纸绳】paper string

【纸型】[刷] paper mould; paper matrix: ～干燥机 *scorcher*

【纸烟】cigarette

【纸鱼】silverfish; fish moth

【纸张】paper

【纸醉金迷】(a life of) luxury and dissipation

指 Ⅰ名 ❶ finger: 拇指 ❷ fingerbreadth; digit: 两～宽的纸条 *a strip of paper two fingerbreadths wide* / 下了四～雨。*We had about three inches of rain.* Ⅱ动 ❶ point at; point to: 时针～向12点。*The hour hand points to twelve.* / 他朝那个门～了～。*He pointed his finger at that door.* ❷ indicate; point out; refer to: ～出缺点 *point out sb.'s shortcomings* / 他的话不是～你说的。*His remarks were not directed at you.* ❸ depend on; count on: 一家子都～着我。*My wife and children depend on me.* / 他们就～着你帮忙哩。*They're counting on your help.* ❹ (of hair) stand: 发指

【指北针】compass

【指标】target; quota; norm; index: 招工～ *recruitment quota*

【指不定】〈方〉perhaps; maybe: 你甭等他了,他～来不来呢。*Don't wait for him; maybe he isn't coming.*

【指不胜屈】too many to be counted on the fingers; a great many

【指出】point out; lay one's finger on: ～某人的弱点 *lay one's fingers on sb.'s weak spot*

【指导】guide; direct: 教师正在～学生做实验。*The teacher was supervising his students in doing the experiment.* / ～思想 *guiding ideology* ◇ ～性计划 guideline plans; indicative plans; ～员 instructor

【指点】❶ give directions (or pointers, advice); show how (to do sth.): 教练耐心地～他们。*The coach patiently instructs them.* / 经他一～,我就全明白了。*A few pointers from him made it all clear to me.* ❷ gossip about sb.'s faults

【指定】appoint; assign: 在～地点见面 *meet at the designated place* /他被～为大会发言人。*He was named as the spokesman of the Conference.*

【指东话西】point to the east and talk west—make pointless comments; be irrelevant

【指法】[音] fingering

【指腹为婚】an antenatal (or prenatal) betrothal

【指供】force the accused to describe or admit to an offense that match the assumptions of the interrogator; lead the accused in to a confession; ask leading questions in an interrogation

【指骨】[生理] phalanx

【指航】navigate；guide the course

【指画】❶ point at；point to ❷ finger drawing

【指环】(finger) ring

【指挥】❶ command；direct；conduct：～一个连 *command a company*；*be in command of a company* / ～交通 *direct traffic* / ～乐队 *conduct an orchestra* ❷ commander；director ❸［音］conductor ◇ ～部 command post；headquarters；～舱 space command module；～车 command car；～刀 officer's sword；～官 commanding officer；commander；～若定 direct (work, etc.) with perfect ease；give competent leadership；～所 command post；～塔台 aviation control tower；～系统 command system；～员 commander

【指挥棒】❶ conductor's baton ❷ baton used by a policeman to direct traffic ❸〈喻〉direction and control：为什么盲目跟着别人的～转呢？*Why blindly follow another?*

【指鸡骂狗】point at the chicken and abuse the dog—point at one but abuse another；make oblique accusations

【指甲】nail：手～ *fingernail* / 脚～ *toenail* ◇ ～锉刀 nail file；～刀 nail clippers；～盖儿 nail；～花 popular name for 凤仙花；～心儿 nail；～油 nail polish

【指教】〈套〉give advice or comments：请多多～。*Kindly give us your advice.* / 望不吝～。*I hope you won't spare your comments.*

【指靠】depend on (for one's livelihood)；look to (for help)；count on：这件事我们就～你了。*We'll count on you for this.*

【指控】accuse；charge：有人～他纳贿。*He's been accused of taking bribes.*

【指令】❶ instruct；order；direct ❷ instructions；order；directive：～指标 *mandatory target* ❸ computer instruction ◇ ～性计划 mandatory plans

【指鹿为马】call a stag a horse—deliberately misrepresent

【指路明灯】〈喻〉beacon light；beacon

【指路牌】signpost；fingerpost；guidepost

【指名】mention by name；name：～攻击 *assail sb. by name* ◇ ～道姓 mention sb.'s name；name names

【指明】show clearly；demonstrate；point out：～两者之间的差别 *show clearly the difference between the two* / ～出路 *point the way out*

【指模】(又作'指摹') finger print or thumb print (used mostly by illiterates as a signature on official or legal papers)

【指墨】finger writing or painting：～作品展 *finger painting exhibition*

【指南】guide；guidebook

【指南车】an ancient Chinese vehicle with a wooden figure always pointing to the south

【指南针】compass

【指派】appoint；name；designate：双方各～一名大使级的首席代表。*Each side shall designate a senior representative, who shall be of ambassadorial rank.*

【指认】point out；identify：～缺点 *point out errors* / ～边界 *identify a boundary line*

【指日可待】can be expected soon；be just round the corner：胜利～。*Victory is just round the corner.*

【指桑骂槐】point at the mulberry and abuse the locust—point at one but abuse another；make oblique accusations

【指使】instigate；incite；put sb. up to sth.：揭露幕后～者 *expose the person behind the scenes*；*unmask the hidden instigator*

【指示】❶ indicate；point out：～前进的方向 *indicate the direction of advance* ❷ instruct：～部队立即出发 *instruct the troops to set out at once* ❸ directive；instructions：下达～ *give instructions* ◇ ～板 indicator board；～代词［语］demonstrative pronoun；～灯 pilot lamp (or light)；indicator lamp；～功率［机］indicated power；～剂［化］indicator；～器 indicator；～植物 indicator plant

【指事】［语］self-explanatory characters, e.g. 上 (above) and 下 (below)—one of the six categories of Chinese characters (六书)

【指手画脚】(又作'指手划脚') ❶ make gestures；gesticulate：～地高谈阔论 *talk volubly with animated gestures* ❷ make indiscreet remarks or criticisms

【指数】index number；index：～化 *indexation* / 综合～ *composite index* / 生活费～ *cost of living index* ◇ ～函数［数］exponential function；～律［数］index law

【指天画地】gesticulate excitedly；speak without restraint

【指头】❶ finger ❷ toe

【指头肚儿】〈方〉face of the fingertip

【指望】❶ look to；count on：别～他能帮你的忙。*You can't count on him for help.* ❷ prospect；hope：他这病还有～吗？*Is there still hope of his recovery?*

【指纹】❶ loops and whorls on a finger ❷ fingerprint ◇ ～学 dactylography

【指向】directional：～天线 *directional antenna* / ～植物 *compass plant*

【指要】〈书〉main idea；gist

【指引】point (the way)；guide；show：猎人～他通过了林区。*The huntsman showed him the way to pass through the forest.*

【指印】fingerprint；finger mark：按～ *make a fingerprint*

【指责】censure；criticize；find fault with：横加～ *make unwarranted charges* / 受到舆论的～ *be subjected to the censure of public opinion*

【指摘】censure；criticize；find fault with

【指战员】(collective name for 指挥员 and 战斗员) officers and men (of the PLA)

【指针】❶ indicator；pointer；needle ❷ guiding principle；guide：作为今后工作的～ *as a guide for future work* ❸［中］pressing with a finger (on an acupuncture point); finger-pressing

【指正】❶ point out mistakes so that they can be corrected ❷〈套〉make a comment or criticism: 请惠予~。*Please oblige me with your valuable comments.* or *Be kind enough to give me your opinion.*

枳 名 [植] trifoliate orange

【枳机草】同〖芨芨草〗

【枳壳】[中] dried fruit of citron or trifoliate orange

【枳实】[中] dried immature fruit of citron or trifoliate orange

咫 量 an ancient measure of length, equal to 8 cun (寸)

【咫尺】〈书〉very close: ~之间 *close at hand*

【咫尺天涯】(又作'咫尺千里') so near and yet so far—see little of each other though living close together

趾 名 ❶ toe ❷ foot

【趾高气扬】strut about and give oneself airs; be swollen with arrogance: ~,目中无人 *give oneself airs and look down one's nose at everybody*

【趾骨】metatarsal bones

【趾甲】toenail

酯 名 [化] ester

【酯化】[化] esterify

【酯酶】[生化] esterase

zhì

至 Ⅰ 动〈书〉arrive; reach: ~京之次日 *the day following my arrival at Beijing* / 有风飒然而~。*A gust of wind blew in.* Ⅱ 介 to; until: 从左~右 *from left to right* / 从早~晚 *from morning till night* / ~上月底为止 *up to the end of last month* Ⅲ 副〈书〉extremely; most: 是为~盼。*That is our sincerest hope.* / ~嘱。*See that you act accordingly.*

【至宝】most valuable treasure

【至诚】❶ complete sincerity: 出于~ *in all sincerity; from the bottom of one's heart* ❷ sincere; straightforward: ~的朋友 *a sincere friend*

【至迟】at (the) latest: 这条铁路~五月通车。*This railway will be opened to traffic in May at the latest.*

【至此】up to this point; at this stage: 事已~,后悔也没有用了。*There is no room for regret when matters have reached this stage.* or *Now it's done, regrets are no use.*

【至多】at (the) most: 他~不过40岁。*He's at most in his forties.* / 他不会来开会的,~只送一个书面发言来。*He isn't coming to the meeting. A written statement from him is all that we can hope for.*

【至高无上】most lofty; paramount; supreme: ~的事业 *most lofty undertaking* / ~的权力 *supreme power (or authority)*

【至关紧要】the most important; of the utmost importance

【至好】most intimate friend; best friend

【至极】to the utmost point; extremely: 他愤怒~。*His anger reached the boiling point.* or *He was extremely angry.* / 他真是可恨~。*He is unbearably hateful.*

【至交】most intimate friend; best friend

【至今】up to now; to this day; so far: 我~未得到他的答复。*So far I've had no reply from him.*

【至理名言】famous dictum; maxim; axiom

【至亲】very close relative; close kin: 骨肉~ *close kin; one's own flesh and blood* ◇ ~好友 close relatives and good friends

【至情】true feelings; real sentiments

【至若】〈书〉as for; as to

【至上】supreme; the highest: 艺术~ *put art above everything else*

【至少】at (the) least: 他并不了解我,~是了解得不全面。*He doesn't understand me, or at any rate not fully.* / ~可以说,这样处理不妥。*This is not the proper way to handle the matter, to say the least.* / 他~50岁了。*He's at least fifty.*

【至圣】the greatest sage—Confucius ◇ ~先师 the greatest sage and teacher—Confucius

【至死】unto death; till death: ~不屈 *not yield even unto death* ◇ ~不变 will not change even unto death; stick to one's course until the end of one's days; ~不悟 remain benighted to the end of one's days; be incorrigibly stubborn

【至言】pertinent remarks; profound words

【至友】most intimate friend; best friend

【至于】❶ as for; as to: ~其他问题,以后再说。*As for other matters, we'll take them up later.* ❷ go so far as to: 你要是早请大夫看,何~病成这样? *If you had seen the doctor earlier, you wouldn't be so seriously ill.*

【至尊】the most revered and respected—the emperor

志 Ⅰ 名 ❶ will; aspiration; ideal: ~坚如钢 *have an iron will; have a will of steel* ❷ records; annals: 《三国~》*History of the Three Kingdoms* / 《昌黎方言~》*A Survey of the Changli Dialect* ❸ mark; sign: 标志 Ⅱ 动 keep in mind: 永志不忘

【志哀】indicate mourning: 下半旗~ *fly a flag at half-mast as a sign of mourning*

【志大才疏】have great ambition but little talent; have high aspirations but little ability

【志得意满】enormously proud of one's success; smug; complacent

【志留纪】[地质] the Silurian Period

【志留系】[地质] Silurian

【志气】aspiration; ambition: 中国人民有~。*The Chinese people have high aspirations.*

【志庆】congratulate; celebrate: 公司开业~ *cele-*

brate the opening of a business

【志趣】aspiration and interest; inclination; bent: 她的～主要是在语言和文学方面。*Her main interests are language and literature.*

【志士】person of ideals and integrity: 爱国～ *a noble-minded patriot* ◇ ～仁人 people with high ideals

【志书】district annals; local histories

【志同道合】cherish the same ideals and follow the same path; have a common goal: 两人～,谈得投机,只恨相见之晚。*Having the same interests, they had a most agreeable chat. They only regretted that they had not met sooner.*

【志喜】offer congratulations (as on sb.'s wedding day)

【志向】aspiration; ideal; ambition: 青年人应有远大的～。*Young people should have lofty aspirations.*

【志愿】❶ aspiration; wish; ideal ❷ do sth. of one's own free will; volunteer ◇ ～兵 volunteer (soldier); ～军 people who volunteer to fight in another country; volunteers; ～书 application form

【志在必得】be determined to win: 我队参加这次锦标赛,～。*We are determined to come in first in the championships.*

治 Ⅰ 动 ❶ rule; govern; administer; manage: 统治 ❷ treat (a disease); cure: 他的病不久就～好了。*He was soon cured of his illness.* / ～好战争创伤 *heal the wounds of war* ❸ control; harness (a river): ～淮 *harness the Huai River* ❹ wipe out (injurious insects) ❺ punish: 他老是违反监规,非好好～～他不可。*He always violates the prison regulations and should be given a good punishment.* ❻ study; research: 专～宋史 *specialize in the history of the Song Dynasty* Ⅱ 名 ❶ order; peace: 治世 ❷〈旧〉seat of a local government: 治所

【治安】public order; public security: 维持～ *maintain public order* / 该市～情况良好(不好)。*Public order is good (poor) in that city.* / ～保卫委员会 *public security committee*

【治保】maintain law and order: ～办公室 *security department*

【治本】effect a permanent cure; get at the root (of a problem, etc.); take radical measures: 河流的～工程 *project for the permanent control of a river*

【治标】merely alleviate the symptoms of an illness; bring about a temporary solution (of a problem, etc.); take stopgap measures ◇ ～不治本 cure the symptoms, not the diseases — temporary medical relief; palliatives

【治病救人】cure the sickness to save the patient: 要以"～"的态度帮助犯错误的同志。*To help comrades who have made mistakes, we should adopt the approach of "curing the sickness to save the patient".*

【治国】administer (or run) a country; manage state affairs ◇ ～安民 run the country well and give the people peace and security

【治家】manage a household

【治理】❶ administer; govern: ～国家 *administer a country; run a state* ❷ harness; bring under control; put in order: ～河流 *harness a river; bring a river under control*

【治疗】treat; cure: 住院～ *be hospitalized* / ～效果 *therapeutic effect* / 她还在医院～。*She is still under treatment in hospital.* / 预防胜于～。*Prevention is better than cure.* ◇ ～学 therapeutics

【治丧】make funeral arrangements: ～委员会 *funeral committee*

【治沙】control sand

【治山治水】transform mountains and tame rivers

【治世】times of peace and prosperity

【治水】regulate rivers and watercourses; prevent floods by water control

【治所】〈旧〉seat of local government

【治外法权】extraterritoriality; exterritoriality; extrality

【治学】〈书〉pursue one's studies; do scholarly research: 他以～严谨著称。*He is noted for his meticulous scholarship.* / 实事求是才是～的正确态度。*To seek truth from facts is the correct approach in academic pursuits.*

【治愚】rid people of ignorance and backwardness

【治愈率】[医] cure rate

【治装】〈书〉purchase things necessary (esp. clothes) for a long journey

【治罪】punish sb. (for a crime)

帜 名〈书〉flag; banner: 旗帜

炙 动 broil; roast

【炙烤】scorch: 火辣的太阳～着大地。*The blazing sun scorches the earth.*

【炙酷】extremely hot (weather): ～的热风 *hot wind*

【炙晒】expose to the hot sun: 她让女儿到树荫下面去玩,躲开日光的直接～。*She told her daughter to play in the shade, out of the hot sun.*

【炙烧】roast; burn: 被愤怒的火焰～ *burn with anger*

【炙手可热】if you stretch out your hand you feel the heat (said of the imperative manner of a person with power)

质 Ⅰ 名 ❶ nature; character: 实质 ❷ quality: 按～分等 *grade according to quality* / ～的飞跃 *a qualitative leap* / ～优价廉 *high quality and low price* ❸ matter; substance: 木～纤维 *wood fibre* / 铁～的器具 *ironware* ❹〈书〉pledge: 以此为～ *with this as a pledge* Ⅱ 形 simple; plain: ～言之 *to put it bluntly* Ⅲ 动 ❶ question: 质疑 ❷〈书〉pawn: 以衣物～钱 *put one's clothes in pawn*

【质变】[哲] qualitative change: 部分～ *partial*

qualitative change
【质地】❶ quality of a material; texture; grain: ～细密 *of close texture*; *fine-grained* ❷ character; disposition
【质点】[物] particle
【质感】(art) sense of reality; real: 用头发绣花做工很细，用手摸来才有～。*Hair embroidery is so fine that one has to touch it to realize it's there.*
【质检】quality testing; quality inspection; quality control: 对产品要～，对人也要～。*Products need quality inspection, so do people.*
【质粒】[生] plasmid
【质量】❶ quality: ～好 *of high quality* / ～不高 *of low quality*; *inferior* / 提高～ *improve the quality* ❷ [物] mass: 相对论～ *relativistic mass* ◇ ～比 [物] mass ratio; ～标准 quality specification; ～第一 quality first; ～分级标准 quality classification standard; ～管理 quality management; quality control; ～监督 quality supervision; ～检验 quality inspection; ～控制 quality control; ～守恒 [物] conservation of mass; ～数 [物] mass number; nuclear number; nucleon number; ～作用定律 [物] law of mass action
【质料】material: 这套衣服的～很好。*This suit is made of very good material.*
【质难】blame; censure; reproach
【质能关系式】[物] mass-energy relation
【质朴】simple and unadorned; unaffected; plain: 文字～ *written in a simple style* / 为人忠厚～ *be simple and honest*; *be unsophisticated*
【质谱】[物] mass spectra: ～分析 *mass spectrographic analysis* ◇ ～仪 mass spectrometer; mass spectrograph
【质数】[数] prime number
【质问】question; interrogate; call to account: 提出～ *bring sb. to account*
【质心】[物] centre of mass
【质询】address inquiries to; ask for an explanation
【质言】〈书〉truthful words: ～之 *to put it in plain words*; *frankly speaking*
【质疑】call in question; query: 对他的说法提出～ *query (or question) the validity of his statement* ◇ ～问难 raise doubts and difficult questions for discussion
【质因数】[数] prime (number) factor
【质子】❶ (in feudal times) a prince sent to a neighbouring state to be held as hostage ❷ proton: ～轰击 *proton bombardment* / ～加速器 *proton accelerator*

制

Ⅰ 动 ❶ make; manufacture: 中国～ *made in China* ❷ work out; formulate: 制定 ❸ restrict; control: 限制 Ⅱ 名 system: 所有制
【制版】[刷] plate making: 平版～ *lithographic plate making*
【制备】[化] prepare: 氧的～ *preparation of oxygen*
【制币】standard national currency: ～厂 *mint*
【制表】❶ draw up a form or list ❷ statistics tabulation
【制裁】sanction; punish: 予以～ *mete out punishment to sb.*; *apply sanctions against sb.*
【制成品】finished products; manufactured goods; manufactures
【制导】control and guide (a missile, etc.): ～系统 *guidance system* / ～炸弹 *guided bomb*
【制订】work (or map) out; formulate: ～《汉语拼音方案》*work out The Scheme for the Chinese Phonetic Alphabet*
【制定】lay down; draw up; formulate; draft: ～操作规程 *lay down operating rules* / ～宪法 *draw up a constitution* / ～政策 *formulate a policy* / ～计划 *work out a plan* / ～法律 *make laws* / ～法令 *enact decrees*
【制动】apply the brake; brake ◇ ～火箭 retro-rocket; ～距离 transportation braking (or stopping) distance; ～器 brake; ～闸 damper brake
【制度】system; institution: 教育～ *system of education* / 奴隶～ *the institution of slavery*
【制伏】subdue; check; bring under control: ～敌人 *subdue the enemy* / ～风沙 *check wind and sand*
【制服】❶ uniform ❷ 同〖制伏〗◇ ～呢 uniform suiting (or coating)
【制高点】[军] commanding elevation (or point, ground, height)
【制革】process hides; tan: ～工人 *tanner* / ～厂 *tannery*
【制海权】[军] mastery of the seas; command of the sea
【制衡】check and balance: 失去～也是腐败现象产生的一个重要原因。*The lack of checks and balances is also an important cause of corruption.*
【制剂】[药] preparation: 标准～ *standard preparation*
【制空权】[军] control of the air; air domination
【制冷】refrigeration: ～循环 *refrigeration cycle* / ～剂 *refrigerant*
【制粒机】granulator
【制帽】uniform cap
【制霉菌素】nystatin
【制片】produce (a film): ～厂 *a film studio* / ～人 *producer*
【制品】products; goods: 奶～ *dairy products* / 黄麻～ *jute goods* / 竹～ *articles made of bamboo*; *bamboo articles*
【制胜】get the upper hand of; subdue: ～敌人 *subdue the enemy*
【制糖】refine sugar: ～厂 *sugar refinery*
【制图】charting; map-making; drafting: ～仪器 *drawing (or drafting) instrument* / ～员 *cartographer*; *draftsman* ◇ ～学 cartography
【制式】❶ standard model; prescribed method: ～警服 *standard policeman's uniform* / ～教练 *standard training* ❷ [电子] system: 中国电视采用的～为帕尔制。*Chinese television adopts PAL system.*

【制售】make and sell：一起～假药案 *a case involving the making and selling of fake drugs*
【制宪】draw up a constitution
【制销】［机］cotter
【制药】pharmacy：～厂 *pharmaceutical factory* ◇ ～学 pharmaceutics
【制音器】［音］damper
【制约】restrict；condition：受历史条件的～ *be restricted by historical conditions*
【制造】❶ make；manufacture：中国～的飞机 *China-made aircraft* ❷ engineer；create；fabricate：～纠纷 *create trouble；sow dissension* / ～紧张局势 *create tension* / ～分裂 *foment splits* / ～谣言 *fabricate rumours* (*or lies*) / ～假象 *put up a false front* ◇ ～商 manufacturer；～业 manufacturing industry
【制止】check；curb；prevent；stop：～流沙 *curb shifting sand* / ～通货膨胀 *check* (*or halt*) *inflation* / ～派别活动 *put an end to factional activities*
【制种】develop new seed strains：～技术 *techniques for developing new seed strains*
【制作】make；manufacture：～家具 *make furniture* / 精心～的银器 *elaborately wrought silverware*

栉 Ⅰ 名 〈书〉comb Ⅱ 动 comb (one's hair)：～发 *comb one's hair*
【栉比】〈书〉placed closely side by side (like the teeth of a comb)
【栉风沐雨】be combed by the wind and washed by the rain—travel or work in the open despite wind and rain
【栉沐】〈书〉wash and dress

峙 动〈书〉stand erect；tower：对峙
【峙立】stand towering

桎 名〈书〉fetters
【桎梏】〈书〉〈喻〉fetters and handcuffs；shackles：打碎精神上的～ *smash spiritual shackles*

致 Ⅰ 动 ❶ send；extend；deliver：～电 *send a telegram* / ～欢迎词 *deliver a welcoming speech；make an address of welcome* ❷ devote (one's efforts，etc.)：致力 ❸ incur；cause：致病 ❹ cause；result in：致使 Ⅱ 名 manner or style that engages attention or arouses interest：故事曲折有～。*The story with its many twists and turns is very intriguing*. Ⅲ 形 fine；delicate：细致
【致哀】pay one's respects to the dead：向革命烈士～ *pay one's respects to revolutionary martyrs*
【致癌】cause (or produce) cancer；be carcinogenic：～物质 *carcinogen；carcinogenic substance* / 吸烟能致肺癌。*Cigarette smoking can cause lung cancer*.
【致病】cause a disease：～菌 *pathogenic bacteria；germs*
【致残】cause disability or become disabled
【致辞】(又作'致词') make (or deliver) a speech：请来宾向大会～ *call upon a guest to address the conference* / 新年～ *New Year message*
【致富】become rich；make a fortune：劳动～ *become rich through sweat and toil*
【致函】write (a letter) to
【致贺】extend one's congratulations
【致敬】salute；pay one's respects to；pay tribute to：鸣礼炮21响～ *fire a 21-gun salute*
【致敬电】a message of greeting
【致力】devote oneself to；work for：～于中医学的研究 *devote* (*or dedicate*) *oneself to the study of traditional Chinese medical science*
【致密】fine and close；compact：～的观察 *careful* (*or close*) *observation* / 结构～ *fine and close in texture* ◇ ～结构［地质］compact texture
【致命】causing death；fatal；mortal；deadly：～的打击 *a deadly blow* / ～伤 *a mortal* (*or vital*) *wound* / ～的弱点 *fatal weakness*
【致使】cause；result in：由于地址字迹不清，～信件无法投递。*It is impossible to deliver this letter because the address is illegible*.
【致死】cause death or die：因伤～ *die of a severe wound* (*or injury*) / ～原因 *cause of death* / ～剂量 *lethal dose* ◇ ～性毒气 lethal gas
【致谢】express one's thanks (or gratitude)；extend thanks to：谨此～。*We hereby express our thanks*.
【致意】give one's regards (or best wishes)；present one's compliments；send one's greetings：点头(挥手)～ *nod* (*wave*) *a greeting* / 向欢呼群众挥手～ *wave to the cheering crowd in acknowledgement*
【致知】pursue knowledge；attain (or acquire) knowledge ——另见〖格物致知〗

秩 名 ❶〈书〉order：～然不紊 *orderly；shipshape* ❷〈书〉decade：七～寿辰 *the seventieth birthday* ❸ official rank in feudal times
【秩序】order；sequence：工作～ *sequence of work* / 守～ *observe order*

挚 形〈书〉sincere；earnest：真挚
【挚爱】true love：深情～ *deep love*
【挚诚】sincere；earnest
【挚厚】true，deep (feeling)：感情～ *deep feeling* / 交谊～ *deep friendship*
【挚切】sincere；earnest；cordial
【挚情】deep emotion；deep feeling
【挚热】sincere and warm；fervent
【挚深】true；genuine：感情～ *true feeling*
【挚意】❶ sincere wish ❷ sincerely；genuinely：他～要求你去。*He really wants to see you*.
【挚友】intimate friend；bosom friend

掷 动 throw；cast：～手榴弹 *throw a grenade*
【掷标枪】javelin throw
【掷弹兵】grenadier
【掷弹筒】grenade discharger；grenade launcher
【掷还】〈套〉please return (to the writer，etc.)：前

请审阅之件，请早日～为荷。*Please return at your earliest convenience the manuscript (or draft, material) submitted to you for approval.*

【掷界外球】throw-in (in football)

【掷弃】throw away; abandon; cast away.

【掷扔】throw; cast: 他猛一用力，将球～出好远。*With a sudden effort, he threw the ball a great distance.*

【掷铁饼】discus throw

窒〈书〉动 stop up; obstruct: 窒塞

【窒闷】close; stuffy

【窒热】stuffy; oppressive

【窒塞】stop up; block

【窒息】stifle; suffocate: ～而死 *be stifled to death* ◇ ～弹 stifling bomb; ～性毒气 asphyxiating (or choking) gas

痔 名 haemorrhoids; piles

【痔疮】haemorrhoids; piles

【痔漏】[医] anal fistula

滞 形 stagnant; sluggish: 停滞

【滞碍】block (up); obstruct

【滞尘】lay the dust; hold the dust down: 花草可以防风～。*Flowers and grass can cut down wind and dust.*

【滞呆】dull: 两眼～ *with a dull look in one's eyes; with lacklustre eyes*

【滞洪】flood detention; slow down flood waters: ～区 *detention basin; retarding basin; area for flood dispersal*

【滞后】❶ [物] hysteresis: ～效应 *hysteresis effect* / ～作用 *hysteresis* ❷ lag; delay: ～作用 *delayed effect*

【滞缓】slow; tardy; sluggish: 行动～ *act slowly* / 生产增长～ *a sluggish growth of production*

【滞留】be detained; be held up

【滞纳金】fine for delaying payment; fine for paying late; overdue fine

【滞泥】be a sticker for (form, etc.); rigidly adhere to (formalities, etc.) ❷ slow (in speech or action)

【滞涩】❶ slow; dull: 举止～ *slow in movements* / 目光～ *look dull* ❷ (of writing) unsmooth; obscure

【滞塞】block; obstruct; clog: 航运～。*The river traffic is held up.* / 他的思路～了。*His train of thought is interrupted.*

【滞销】unsalable; unmarketable: 消费品出现积压～现象。*There has appeared the problem of overstocking and sluggish sales of consumer goods.* ◇ ～货 unsalable (or slow-selling) goods

【滞育】[动] diapause

【滞胀】stagflation

痣 名 nevus; mole: 他脸上有一颗～。*He has a mole on his face.*

蛭 名 leech: 水蛭

【蛭石】vermiculite (a mineral)

智 名 wisdom; resourcefulness; wit: 智谋

【智残人】mentally-retarded person; mentally handicapped: ～体育代表团 *sports team made up of the mentally-retarded*

【智齿】(又作'智牙') wisdom tooth

【智多星】wizard—resourceful person; mastermind

【智慧】wisdom; intelligence: 吸取群众的～ *draw on the wisdom of the masses* / 勤劳～的人民 *the industrious and ingenious people*

【智力】intelligence; intellect: ～测验 *intelligence test* / ～竞赛 *quiz game* / ～开发 *tap (or develop) intellectual resources* / ～投资 *investment in brainpower* ◇ ～剥削 intellectual exploitation; brain drain; ～产业 white collar occupations where people do not engage in manual labor and resources are knowledge and expertise; ～结构 structure of talent in an institution; ～年龄 intellectual age; ～引进 bringing in talent from outside; hiring external scientific, technical, managerial and professional talent; introduction of foreign brainpower

【智利】Chile ◇ ～人 Chilean

【智略】wisdom and resourcefulness

【智谋】resourcefulness: 人多～高。*More people mean more ideas.*

【智囊】brain truster: ～人物 *brain truster; think tanker* ◇ ～团 brain trust; a think tank

【智能】❶ intellectual power; intellectual ability ❷ things that have intellect and ability of man ◇ ～机器人 intelligent robot; ～科学 intellectual science; ～人工 artificial intelligence;

【智能电话】smart phone

【智巧】brains and tact

【智穷才尽】at the end of one's resources; at one's wits' end

【智取】take (a fort, town, etc.) by strategy: 只可～，不可强攻。*The only way to take the enemy position is by strategy, not by forceful attack.*

【智商】intelligence quotient (IQ): ～高(低) *have a high (low) IQ*

【智童】child prodigy

【智勇双全】both intelligent and courageous; both brave and resourceful: ～的将军 *a brave and sagacious general*

【智育】intellectual education; intellectual development: 使学生在德育、～、体育几方面都得到发展 *enable the students to develop morally, intellectually and physically*

【智圆行方】resourceful and upright; flexible and principled

【智障】person afflicted with a mental deficiency: ～职工 *mentally retarded workers*

【智者千虑，必有一失】The wisest man, in a thousand schemes, must make at least one mistake; Even the wise are not free from error.

【智珠在握】be endowed with high native intelligence

置 动 ❶ place; put: 安～于案头 *be placed on one's desk* ❷ set up; establish; install: ～酒款待 *give a feast to entertain sb*. ❸ buy: ～一身衣服 *buy a suit or have one made to order* / ～一些家具 *buy some furniture*

【置办】buy (durables); purchase: ～家具 *buy furniture* / ～图书仪器 *procure books and instruments*

【置备】purchase (equipment, furniture, etc.)

【置产】buy property (esp. an estate)

【置放】put; lay up

【置换】[化] displacement; replacement

【置买】purchase; buy

【置评】(usu. used in the negative) comment on; discuss: 不予～ *give no comment*

【置若罔闻】turn a deaf ear to; pay no heed to: 我多次劝告,他都～。*I cautioned him many times but he paid no heed*.

【置身】place oneself; stay: ～于群众之中 *place oneself in the midst of the masses* / ～异域 *find oneself in the midst of a foreign people*

【置身事外】stay aloof from the affair; keep out of the business; refuse to be drawn into the matter

【置信】(usu. used in the negative) believe: 不可～ *not to be believed*; *unbelievable*

【置疑】(used in the negative) doubt

【置之不顾】leave out of account; ignore; disregard

【置之不理】ignore; brush aside; pay no attention to: 对于这种挑衅,我们不能～。*We cannot ignore such provocations*.

【置之度外】give no thought to; have no regard for: 把生死～ *face death with equanimity*

【置之脑后】banish from one's mind; ignore and forget

【置之死地而后快】will be content with nothing less than sb.'s destruction

【置之死地而后生】confront a person with the danger of death and he will fight to live

雉 名 pheasant

【雉堞】crenelation

【雉鸠】turtledove

稚 形 young; childish: 幼稚

【稚虫】[动] naiad

【稚嫩】❶ young and tender: ～的童音 *child's piping voice* / ～的脸蛋儿 *a delicate face* / ～的心灵 *an innocent heart* ❷ immature: 他的早期作品比较～。*His early works are relatively immature*.

【稚气】childishness: 一脸～ *innocent-looking*

【稚趣】childlike; innocent: 憨态可掬,～盎然 *shy and childlike*

【稚弱】childish and tender: ～的心灵 *a tender heart*

【稚拙】uncomplicated; unsophisticated: ～的造型 *simple shape* / ～的技巧 *simple skills*

【稚子】(innocent) child

zhōng

中 Ⅰ 名 ❶ centre; middle: 上、～、下 *upper, middle, lower* / 冀～ *central Hebei* ❷ China: 中文 ❸ in; among; amidst: 记在心～ *keep in mind* / 跳入水～ *jump into the water* ❹ middle; mid: 月中 ❺ medium; intermediate: 中号 ❻ mean; halfway between two extremes: 适中 ❼ intermediary: 作中 ❽ in the process of: 在修建～ *being built*; *under construction* / 历史在斗争～发展,世界在动荡～前进。*History develops in struggle and the world advances amidst turbulence*. Ⅱ 动 fit for; good for: 中看 Ⅲ 形 〈方〉 *all right*; *O. K.*: ～不～? *Is it all right?* / 这办法～! *This way works!* ——另见 zhòng

【中巴】〈口〉 medium-sized bus or coach; minibus

【中班】❶ middle shift; swing shift: 上～ *be on the middle shift*; *work the swing shift* ❷ the middle class in a kindergarten

【中板】❶ [冶] medium plate ❷ [音] moderato

【中饱】(又作'中饱私囊') batten on money entrusted to one's care; line one's pockets with public funds or other people's money; embezzle

【中保】middleman and guarantor

【中表】first cousin, child of father's sister or mother's sister or brother

【中波】medium wave

【中不溜儿】(又作'中溜儿')〈口〉 fair to middling; middling: 他不高不矮,个子～的。*He's neither tall nor short, but of middling height*.

【中部】central section; middle part: 在高原～ *in the middle part of the plateau*

【中餐】Chinese meal; Chinese food

【中草药】Chinese herbal medicine

【中策】the second best plan

【中层】middle-level: ～干部 *middle-level* (*or middle-ranking*) *cadres*

【中产阶级】middle class; middle bourgeoisie

【中场】[体] (足球) midfield

【中程】intermediate range; medium range: ～导弹 *intermediate-range missile*; *medium-range missile* / ～轰炸机 *medium bomber* / ～跑 *middle distance race*

【中垂线】[数] perpendicular bisector

【中词】[逻] middle term

【中档】medium quality at middling price: ～茶叶 *medium-quality tea*

【中道】❶ halfway; midway: ～而废 *give up halfway* / ～而行 *follow the middle course* ❷ 〈书〉 the golden mean (of the Confucian school)

【中稻】semilate rice; middle-season rice

【中等】❶ medium; moderate; middling: ～个儿 *of medium height* / ～城市 *medium-sized city* ❷ secondary: ～职业学校 *secondary vocational school* ◇ ～技术学校 secondary technical school; ～教育 secondary school education; ～师范学校 secondary normal school; ～职业技术教

育 secondary vocational and technical education；～专科学校 secondary specialized school；polytechnic school
【中点】[数] midpoint
【中东】the Middle East
【中短波】intermediate wave；medium-short wave
【中断】suspend；break off；discontinue：～谈判 *break off the negotiations (or talks)* / 两国关系～了好多年。*Relations between the two countries were suspended for many years*.
【中队】❶ [军] military unit corresponding to a company；squadron：歼击机～ *fighter squadron* ❷ a unit composed of several groups：交通～ *a detachment of traffic police*
【中耳】auris media；middle ear ◇ ～炎 otitis media
【中幡】[杂] flagpole-waving
【中饭】midday meal；lunch
【中非】Central Africa
【中分】❶ divide sth. equally into two halves ❷ part hair in the middle
【中锋】[体] centre forward (as in football)；centre
【中缝】❶ the column on the folding line of a newspaper, usu. reserved for advertisements or notices ❷ the line sewn down the back of a jacket
【中伏】❶ the middle or second fu—the second hottest period of the year (10 or 20 days) ❷ the first day of the middle or second fu (falling in late July)——另见〖三伏〗
【中耕】[农] intertill：～机 *cultivator* / ～作物 *intertilled crop*
【中共】(〈略〉全称为'中国共产党') the Communist Party of China
【中共中央】(〈略〉全称为'中国共产党中央委员会') the Central Committee of the Communist Party of China：～政治局 *the Political Bureau of the Central Committee of the Chinese Communist Party*
【中古】❶ the middle ancient times (in Chinese history, from the 3rd to the 9th century) ❷ medieval times；Middle Ages：～史 *medieval history*
【中国】China：～大陆 *China's mainland* ◇ ～共产党 the Communist Party of China (CPC)；the Chinese Communist Party；～共产主义青年团 the Communist Youth League of China；～话 the Chinese language；Chinese；～画 traditional Chinese painting；～科学院 the Chinese Academy of Sciences；Academia Sinica；～热 Sinomania；～人 Chinese；～人民解放军 the Chinese People's Liberation Army；～人民政治协商会议 the Chinese People's Political Consultative Conference (CPPCC)；～人民志愿军 the Chinese People's Volunteers；～社会科学院 the Chinese Academy of Social Sciences；～特色 Chinese characteristics；～通 China expert；～问题专家 China watcher；China expert；～字 Chinese characters；the Chinese written language
【中果皮】[植] mesocarp
【中号】medium size
【中和】[化][电] neutralization：～剂 *neutralizer*
【中华】❶ the Chinese nation ❷ China ◇ ～老字号 China's time-honored brand (shop)；～民族 the Chinese nation；～人民共和国 the People's Republic of China
【中级】middle rank；intermediate：～人民法院 *intermediate people's court*
【中继】[电] relay ◇ ～器 [电子] repeater；～线 trunk line；～站 relay station
【中间】❶ among；between：坐在他们两人～ *sit between the two of them* / 她是我们三人～最年轻的。*She is the youngest of us three*. ❷ centre；middle：～突破 *make a breakthrough at the centre (or in the middle)* / ～剥削 *middleman's exploitation* / ～道路 *middle road* / ～地带 *intermediate zone* ◇ ～阶层 intermediate strata；～力量 middle-of-the-road forces；intermediate forces；～派 middle-of-the-roaders；middle elements；intermediate sections (or forces)；～人 middleman；go-between；mediator；intermediary；～税 intermediate tax；～体 [化] intermediate；～线 [机] medium line；～消费者 intermediate consumer
【中坚】nucleus；hard core；backbone：～分子 *backbone elements* / 干部的～力量 *nucleus (or hard core) of cadres* / 社会～ *pillar of society*；*the salt of the earth*
【中将】(U. S. & Brit. Army, U. S. Air Force, U. S. & Brit. Marine Corps) lieutenant general；(U. S. & Brit. Navy) vice admiral；(Brit. Air Force) air marshal
【中焦】[中] the part of the body cavity between the diaphragm and the umbilicus housing the spleen, stomach, ect.
【中觉】afternoon nap；noontime snooze
【中介】intermediary；medium ◇ ～人 broker；matchmaker；intermediary；medium
【中介子】[物] neutretto
【中景】film medium shot
【中距离】[体] middle distance：～赛跑 *middle-distance race*
【中看】be pleasant to the eye ◇ ～不中吃 look nice but taste nasty；be pleasing to the eye but not to the taste
【中考】entrance examinations to secondary school, senior middle school, technical school and vocational high school：～升学率 *rate of admittance of students taking secondary school entrance exams*
【中栏】[体] intermediate hurdles
【中立】neutrality：守～ *observe neutrality* ◇ ～国 neutral state；～主义 neutralism
【中量级】[体] middleweight
【中林】[林] middle forest
【中流】midstream
【中流砥柱】a firm rock in midstream；mainstay

【中路】❶ mediocre in quality：～货 *mediocre goods* ❷ halfway；midway
【中落】(of family fortunes) decline；ebb
【中美洲】Central America
【中脑】mesencephalon；midbrain
【中年】middle age：～人 *a middle-aged person*
【中跑】[体] middle-distance race
【中胚层】mesoderm；mesoblast
【中篇小说】medium-length novel；novelette
【中频】[无] intermediate frequency
【中期】middle period：二十世纪～ *mid 20th century* / ～选举 *mid-term election*
【中青年】adultescent
【中秋节】the Mid-autumn Festival (15th day of the 8th lunar month)
【中人】❶ middleman；go-between；mediator；intermediary ❷ one of ordinary stature，appearance，ability，etc.；an average man
【中沙群岛】the Zhongsha Islands
【中山狼】the Zhongshan wolf in the fable —one who repays good with evil ——另见〖东郭先生〗
【中山陵】the Sun Yat-sen Mausoleum (in Nanjing)
【中山装】Chinese tunic suit：穿着一身灰色～ *in gray tunic and trousers*
【中生代】[地质] the Mesozoic Era；the Mesozoic
【中生界】[地质] the Mesozoic Erathem
【中师】〈略〉见〖中等师范学校〗
【中石器时代】Mesolithic Period；Middle Stone Age
【中士】(U. S. & Brit. Army，Brit. Air Force，U. S. & Brit. Marine Corps) sergeant；(U. S. Navy) petty officer second class；(Brit. Navy) petty officer first class；(U. S. Air Force) staff sergeant
【中世纪】Middle Ages
【中式】Chinese style：～服装 *Chinese-style clothing*
【中式盐】(又作'中性盐')[化] neutral salt
【中枢】centre：领导～ *leading centre* / 电讯～ *telecommunications centre* / 神经～ *nerve center* ◇ ～神经 central nervous system
【中碳钢】[冶] medium carbon steel
【中堂】❶ 同〖堂屋〗❷ central scroll of painting or calligraphy (hung in the middle of the wall of the main room)
【中提琴】viola
【中天】❶ in the sky：日丽～。*The sun was shining bright in the sky*. ❷ [天] culmination；meridian passage (or transit)
【中听】pleasant to the ear；agreeable to the hearer：他觉得这句话～。*He found these remarks very agreeable*.
【中途】halfway；midway：这趟公共汽车～不停。*This is a nonstop bus*. / 他原是学建筑的，～改行搞地质了。*At first he studied architecture，but later he switched to geology*.
【中途岛】Midway Island
【中土】❶ 同〖中原〗❷〈书〉China
【中外】China and foreign countries：～合资企业 *a Chinese-foreign joint venture* / ～合作企业 *Sino-foreign cooperative enterprises*
【中微子】[物] neutrino
【中纬度】middle latitudes
【中卫】[体](足球)centre halfback
【中位数】[数] median
【中尉】(U. S. Army，Air Force & Marine Corps) first lieutenant；(Brit. Army & Marine Corps) lieutenant；(U. S. Navy) lieutenant junior grade；(Brit. Navy) sublieutenant；senior commissioned branch officer；(Brit. Air Force) flying officer
【中文】the Chinese language；Chinese：～书刊 *books and magazines in Chinese*
【中午】noon；midday
【中西】Chinese and Western：～医结合 *combine traditional Chinese and Western medicine*
【中线】❶ [体] centre line (in basketball and volleyball)；halfway line (in football) ❷ [数] central line
【中校】(U. S. & Brit. Army，U. S. Air Force，U. S. & Brit. Marine Corps) lieutenant colonel；(U. S. & Brit. Navy) commander；(Brit. Air Force) wing commander
【中心】centre；heart；core；hub：在广场～ *at the centre of the square* / 抓住问题的～ *get to the heart of the matter* / 陆路交通的～ *hub of overland communications* ◇ ～城市 key city；～工作 central task；～环节 key link；central link；～问题 central issue；crucial question
【中心规】[机] centre gauge
【中心角】同〖圆心角〗
【中心思想】central idea；gist
【中心线】[机] centre line
【中心项】[哲] central term
【中新世】[地质] the Miocene Epoch
【中兴】resurgence (of a nation)；restoration (of a dynasty)
【中型】medium-sized；middle-sized：～词典 *a medium-sized dictionary* ◇ ～便携式电脑 luggable computer
【中性】❶ [化] neutral ❷ [语] Neuter ◇ ～反应 neutral reaction；～名词 neuter noun；～树脂 neutral resin；～土 neutral soil
【中性人】gender bender
【中学】middle school；high school：初(高)级～ *junior (senior) middle school* ◇ ～生 middle school student
【中旬】the middle ten days of a month：四月～ *the middle ten days of April*
【中央】❶ centre；middle：湖的～有一座亭子。*At the centre of the lake，there is a pavilion*. ❷ central authorities (of a state，party，etc.)：团～ *the Central Committee of the Youth League* / 发挥～和地方两个积极性。*Both central and local initiative should be brought into play*. / ～和地方企业并举 *simultaneous development of national and local enterprises* ◇ ～处理器[计] central processing unit (CPU)；～党校 the Party School

of the (CPC) Central Committee; ～电视台 China Central Television (CCTV); ～各部门 departments under the Party's Central Committee and the State Council; ～工作会议 the Central Working Conference; ～顾问委员会 the Central Advisory Commission; ～候补委员 alternate member of the Central Committee (of the Chinese Communist Party); ～机构 central organs (or institutions); ～集权 centralization (of authority); ～纪律检查委员会 the Central Commission for Discipline Inspection; ～军事委员会 the Central Military Commission; ～领导同志 leading comrades of the central authorities; ～情报局 the (U. S.) Central Intelligence Agency (CIA); ～全会 plenary session of the Central Committee; ～人民广播电台 Central People's Broadcasting Station of China(CPBS); ～条约组织 the Central Treaty Organization (CENTO); ～委员 member of the Central Committee (of the Chinese Communist Party); ～银行 central bank; national bank; ～直属机关 departments under the Party Central Committee

【中药】traditional Chinese medicine ◇ ～铺 shop (or store) of traditional Chinese medicines; Chinese pharmacy; ～学 traditional Chinese pharmacology

【中叶】middle period: 十九世纪～ *the mid-1800s*; *the middle of the 19th century*

【中衣】underpants; pants

【中医】❶ traditional Chinese medical science ❷ doctor of traditional Chinese medicine; practitioner of Chinese medicine ◇ ～学 traditional Chinese medicine; ～学院 college of traditional Chinese medicine; ～研究院 academy of traditional Chinese medicine

【中音号】［音］althorn; alto horn

【中庸】❶ the golden mean (of the Confucian school) ❷〈书〉of ordinary talent; common; mediocre) ◇ ～之道 the doctrine of the Golden Mean

【中用】(usu. used in the negative) of use; useful

【中游】❶ middle reaches (of a river) ❷ the state of being middling

【中雨】moderate rain

【中元节】the Festival of the Dead Spirits (15th day of the seventh lunar month when sacrifices are offered to the dead)

【中原】Central Plains (comprising the middle and lower reaches of the Huanghe River)

【中岳】the Central Mountain (another name for 嵩山 "Mount Song" in Henan Province)

【中云】［气］medium cloud

【中支】［纺］medium-counts: ～纱 *mediumcount yarn*

【中止】discontinue; suspend; break off ◇ ～发行 discontinue publishing; ～谈判 suspend (or break off) negotiations; ～射击 lift fire; ～外交关系 suspend diplomatic relations

【中指】middle finger

【中注管】［冶］running-gate

【中专】〈略〉见〖中等专科学校〗

【中转】change trains: ～环节 *intermediate link* / ～签字 *sign a transfer (for a railway passenger)* ◇ ～港 entrepot; ～站 transfer station

【中子】neutron ◇ ～弹 neutron bomb; ～反应堆 neutron reactor; ～态 neutron state; ～物理学 neutronics; ～星［天］neutron star; ～源 neutron source

忠

形 loyal; devoted; honest

【忠臣】official loyal to his sovereign

【忠诚】loyal; faithful; staunch: ～的朋友 *a loyal friend*

【忠告】❶ sincerely advise; admonish ❷ sincere advice; advice

【忠厚】honest and tolerant; sincere and kindly: 他为人～老实。*He is kindly and simple-hearted.*

【忠君爱国】be loyal to the sovereign and devoted to the country

【忠实】loyal; true; faithful: ～于原文 *true (or faithful) to the original* / ～的信徒 *a faithful disciple*

【忠顺】loyal and obedient; obedient: ～的奴仆 *a willing servant*

【忠孝】loyalty and filial piety: ～不能两全。*Loyalty and filial piety do not always complement each other.*

【忠心】loyalty; devotion: 表～ *express one's loyalty* ◇ ～耿耿 loyal and devoted; most faithful and true

【忠言】sincere advice; earnest advice ◇ ～逆耳 faithful words offend the ear; good advice jars on the ear ——另见〖良药苦口〗

【忠义】loyal and righteous

【忠勇】loyal and brave; faithful and courageous: ～之心 *loyalty and courage*

【忠于】true to; loyal to; faithful to; devoted to: ～职守 *be faithful in the discharge of one's duties*; *be devoted to one's duty*

【忠贞】loyal and steadfast: ～不屈 *staunch and indomitable* ◇ ～不渝 unswervingly loyal

终

Ⅰ **动** ❶ end; finish: 年终 ❷ die: ～其天年 *live one's full span* Ⅱ **副** eventually; after all; in the end: ～非良策。*It's not a good plan after all.* Ⅲ **形** whole; entire; all: ～其一生 *all his life*

【终场】❶ end of a performance or game: ～前一分钟，主队又攻进一球。*The host team scored another goal just before the final whistle.* ❷〈旧〉final session in an examination

【终底于成】succeed in the end

【终点】❶ terminal point; destination: 旅行的～ *destination of a journey* ❷［体］finish: ～线 *finishing line*; *finishing tape*; *terminal line*

【终点站】terminus; terminal

【终端】terminal: ～电缆 *terminal cable* ◇ ～局 terminal station (in postal service)

【终归】eventually; in the end; after all: 耍两面派

～不会有好下场。*Double-dealers will come to no good end*. 孩子～是孩子。*Children will be children*.

【终极】ultimate：～目标 *ultimate aim*

【终结】end; final stage

【终究】eventually; in the end; after all：一个人的力量～有限。*The strength of the individual is limited after all*.

【终局】end; outcome

【终老】spend one's remaining years till death：～故乡 *spend one's remaining years in one's hometown*

【终了】end (of a period)：学期～ *the end of the (school) term*

【终南捷径】a short cut to high office; the high road to fame or success

【终年】❶ (all) the year round; throughout the year：～积雪的高山 *mountains perennially covered with snow* ❷ the age at which one dies：他～78岁。*He died at the age of seventy-eight*.

【终曲】[音] finale

【终日】all day long; all day

【终身】lifelong; all one's life：～事业 *one's lifework* / 剥夺政治权利～ *be deprived of political rights for life* / ～职务 *life tenure* ◇ ～伴侣 lifelong companion—one's husband or wife; ～保险 perpetual insurance; ～大事 a great event in one's life (usu. referring to marriage); ～服务 lifelong service; ～教育 lifelong education; ～人寿保险 whole life insurance; ～职务制 lifelong tenure; lifelong position

【终审】[法] last instance; final judgment：～判决 *final judgement* / ～法院 *court of last instance* / ～权 *power of final adjudication*

【终生】all one's life：～难忘的教训 *a lesson for life*

【终霜】[气] latest frost

【终天之恨】lifelong regret; eternal regret

【终席】(of a dinner party or meeting) end; come to a close：没有等到～,他推说头疼,起身回家了。*Pleading a headache, he left for home before the dinner party ended*.

【终于】at (long) last; in the end; finally：她～到了,晚了将近半小时。*At long last she arrived, about half an hour late*.

【终止】❶ stop; end：～日期 *closing date* ❷ termination; annulment; abrogation：～条约通知书 *notice of termination of a treaty; notice of denunciation* ❸ [音] cadence

钟 Ⅰ 名 ❶ bell：这口铜～是明永乐初年铸造的。*The bronze bell was made in the early years of Yongle of the Ming Dynasty*. ❷ clock：～停了。*The clock has stopped*. ❸ time as measured in hours and minutes：六点～ *six o'clock* / 十分～ *ten minutes* Ⅱ 动 concentrate (one's affections, etc.)：钟情

【钟爱】dote on (a child); cherish

【钟摆】pendulum (of a clock)

【钟表】clocks and watches; timepiece：～店 *watchmaker's shop* / ～油 *watchmaker's oil*

【钟点】〈口〉❶ a time for sth. to be done or to happen：到～儿了,我们快走吧! *It's time; let's be off*. ❷ hour：我等了他一个～了。*I've been waiting for him for an hour*.

【钟鼎文】同〖金文〗

【钟灵毓秀】(of a place) pregnant with beauty and productive of talent

【钟楼】❶ bell tower; belfry ❷ clock tower

【钟鸣鼎食】partake of rich food in ding vessels to the accompaniment of music—affluency; extravagance：～之家 *a stately house (or mansion)*

【钟鸣漏尽】the morning bell is striking and the night is waning—be in one's declining years

【钟琴】[音] carillon

【钟情】be deeply in love

【钟乳石】[地质] stalactite

【钟头】〈口〉hour：这出戏演了三个半～。*The play lasted for three and a half hours*.

衷 名 inner feelings; heart：由衷

【衷肠】〈书〉words right from one's heart：畅叙～ *pour out one's heart*

【衷情】〈书〉heartfelt emotion; inner feelings：久别重逢,互诉～。*Meeting again after a long separation, they opened their hearts to each other*.

【衷曲】〈书〉heartfelt emotion; inner feelings：倾吐～ *pour out one's heart*

【衷心】heartfelt; wholehearted; cordial：～拥护 *give wholehearted support* / 表示～的祝贺 *extend cordial greetings* / ～感谢你的帮助。*I thank you for your help from the bottom of my heart*.

螽 (构词成分) 见下

【螽斯】[动] katydid; long-horned grasshopper

zhǒng

肿 Ⅰ 动 swell; be swollen：我的腿～了。*My legs are swollen*. Ⅱ 名 swelling：～消了一点。*The swelling has gone down a little*.

【肿骨鹿】palaeontology thick-jawed deer

【肿瘤】tumour：良(恶)性～ *benign (malignant) tumour* / ～医院 *tumour hospital*

【肿胀】❶ swelling ❷ [中] oedema and abdominal distension

种 Ⅰ 名 ❶ [生] species：本地～ *endemic species* / 外地～ *exotic species* / 老虎是猫科的一～。*The tiger belongs to the cat family*. ❷ race：黄种 / 白种 ❸ seed; strain; breed：麦～ *wheat seeds* / 这水稻是什么～? *What variety is this rice?* ❹ guts; grit：有种 Ⅱ 量 kind; sort; type：各～仪器 *all kinds of instruments* / 这～论调 *this sort of argument* / 四十～钢材 *forty types of rolled steel* / 一～现象 *a phenomenon* / 他有一～以前从未有过的感觉。*He had a kind of feeling that he'd never had before*. ——另见 zhòng

【种畜】breeding stock; stud stock
【种蛋】breeding eggs (allowed to hatch): 精选～ *choice breeding eggs*
【种肥】seed manure
【种间杂交】[农] interspecific hybridization (or cross)
【种类】kind; type; variety: 不同～的刀具 *cutters of different kinds* / ～繁多 *a great variety*
【种马】stud: ～场 *stud farm; stud*
【种内杂交】[农] intraspecific hybridization (or cross)
【种牛】bull kept for covering
【种禽】breeding fowl: ～厂 *large-scale breeding fowl farm*
【种仁】kernel
【种姓】caste (of India): ～制度 *caste system*
【种源】place of origin: 寻求稀有植物的～ *look for the origin of rare plants*
【种种】all sorts (or kinds) of; a variety of: 由于～原因 *for a variety of reasons* / 用～手段 *by hook or by crook; resort to every means (or trick)*
【种子】❶ seed: ～处理 *seed treatment* / ～清选机 *seed cleaner* / ～田 *seed-breeding field* / ～植物 *seed plant* ❷ [体] seeded player; seed: 被列为～ *be seeded* / ～选手 *seeded player; seed* ◇ ～队 [体] seeded team
【种族】race: ～平等 *racial equality* / 不分～和信仰 *irrespective of race or creed* ◇ ～隔离 racial segregation; apartheid; ～灭绝 genocide; ～歧视 racial discrimination; ～清洗 ethnic cleansing; ～主义 racism; racialism

踵 Ⅰ 名 〈书〉 heel: 接踵 Ⅱ 动 ❶ call in person: ～门道谢 *call in person to express one's thanks* ❷ follow close behind: 踵至
【踵事增华】carry on a predecessor's task and make a greater success of it; take over and carry forward
【踵武】〈书〉 follow in sb.'s footsteps; imitate; follow suit
【踵趾相接】follow the footsteps; one after another; in succession
【踵至】〈书〉 arrive upon the heels of another; arrive immediately after sb.

zhòng

中 动 ❶ hit; fit exactly: 射～靶心 *hit the bull's eye* / 你说～了。*You've hit it.* or *That's right.* / 打三枪～两枪,第三枪没有～。*Two shots out of three hit the target. The third shot missed the target.* ❷ be hit by; fall into; be affected by; suffer: ～煤气 *be gassed* / 他腿上～了一枪。*He got shot in the leg.* ——另见 zhōng
【中标】get (or win) the bid or tender
【中彩】win a prize in a lottery
【中弹】be hit by a bullet; get shot
【中的】hit the mark; hit the nail on the head: 批驳有力,语语～。*The refutation is forceful and every word hits home.*
【中毒】❶ be poisoned (usu. accidentally) ❷ poisoning; toxicosis: 食物～ *food poisoning*
【中风】suffer from a stroke of apoplexy: 死于～ *die of apoplexy*
【中计】play into sb.'s hands; fall into a trap; be taken in
【中奖】draw a prizewinning ticket (or win a prize) in a lottery; get the winning number in a bond
【中肯】❶ apropos; pertinent; to the point: ～的评语 *pertinent remarks* / 他的发言很～。*He spoke very much to the point.* or *His speech hit the nail on the head.* ❷ [物] critical: ～质量 *critical mass*
【中签】be the lucky number (in drawing lots, etc.)
【中伤】slander; malign; vilify: ～好人 *malign an innocent person*
【中试】pass a test, etc.
【中暑】❶ suffer heatstroke (or sunstroke); be affected by the heat ❷ heatstroke; sunstroke
【中选】be chosen; be selected
【中意】be to one's liking; take (or catch) the fancy of: 这些暖瓶,我一个都不～。*None of these thermosflasks is to my liking.*

众 Ⅰ 形 many; numerous: 众多 Ⅱ 名 crowd; multitude: 观众
【众多】multitudinous; numerous
【众寡悬殊】a great disparity in numerical strength
【众口难调】It is difficult to cater for all tastes.
【众口铄金】public clamour can confound right and wrong
【众口一词】with one voice; unanimously
【众目睽睽】with everybody watching: ～之下 *under the watchful eye of everyone; under the public gaze*
【众目昭彰】seen clearly by everyone; clear to all
【众怒难犯】one cannot afford to incur public wrath; it is dangerous to incur the anger of the masses
【众叛亲离】with the masses rising in rebellion and one's friends deserting; be opposed by the masses and deserted by one's followers; be utterly isolated
【众擎易举】with many people it's easy to lift a load—many hands make light work
【众人】everybody
【众人拾柴火焰高】when everybody adds fuel the flames rise high —the more people, the more strength
【众生】all living creatures
【众矢之的】a target of public criticism (or censure)
【众数】[数] mode
【众说纷纭】opinions vary; opinions are widely divided
【众所周知】as everyone knows; as is known to all;

it is common knowledge that：由于～的原因 *for reasons known to all*

【众望】people's expectations；popular confidence

【众望所归】enjoy popular confidence；command popular support

【众星拱月】a myriad of stars surrounding the moon—a host of lesser lights around the leading one

【众议员】representative (in Congress)；member of the House of Representatives；Congressman or Congresswoman

【众议院】House of Representatives (in the United States，Australia，Japan，etc.)；Chamber of Deputies (in Italy，Mexico，Chile，etc.)

【众志成城】unity of will is an impregnable stronghold；unity is strength

仲 形 ❶ the second month of a season：仲秋 ❷ the second among brothers：～兄 *the second eldest brother* ❸ middle；intermediate：仲裁

【仲裁】arbitrate：～法庭 *arbitration tribunal*；*court of arbitration* / ～人 *arbitrator* / ～书 *arbitration award* ◇ ～条款 arbitration clause；～通知书 arbitration notice；～协定 arbitration agreement；～委员会 arbitration commitee；board of arbitration

【仲春】second month of spring；the middle of spring

【仲冬】second month of winter；midwinter

【仲秋】second month of autumn；midautumn

【仲夏】second month of summer；midsummer

种 动 grow；plant；cultivate：～水稻 *grow rice* / ～庄稼 *grow (or plant) crops* / 过去这里的水田多数只～一季，现在全部～两季。*Most paddy fields here used to yield only one crop a year，but now they all yield two crops.* ——另见 zhǒng

【种地】till (or cultivate) land；go in for farming

【种痘】(又作'种牛痘') vaccinate sb. against smallpox：这孩子～了吗？*Has the baby been vaccinated?*

【种瓜得瓜，种豆得豆】plant melons and you get melons，sow beans and you get beans—as you sow，so will you reap

【种花】❶ cultivate (or grow) flowers ❷〈方〉vaccinate sb. against smallpox ❸〈方〉grow cotton

【种田】till (or cultivate) land；go in for farming

【种养】grow；cultivate：～果树 *grow fruit trees*

【种因】do things that will entail grave consequences

【种植】plant；grow ◇ ～园 plantation

重 Ⅰ 名 weight：这条鱼有三斤～。*This fish weighs three jin.* / 你多～？ *What's your weight?* Ⅱ 形 ❶ heavy；weighty；important：铁比木头～。*Iron is weightier than wood.* / 眉毛很～ *have thick eyebrows* / 工作很～ *have a heavy work load* ❷ considerable in amount or value：重金 ❸ deep；heavy；serious：情意～ *deep affection* / 私心很～ *extremely selfish* / 山东口音很～ *have a marked (or heavy) Shandong accent* / 病势很～ *be seriously ill* ❹ discreet：慎重 Ⅲ 动 lay stress on；attach importance to：～调查研究 *lay stress on investigation and study* ——另见 chóng

【重办】severely punish (a criminal)

【重兵】a large number of troops；massive forces：有～把守 *be heavily guarded*

【重柄】〈书〉great political power

【重臣】〈书〉minister (of a monarchy) holding an important post or shouldering heavy responsibilities；important official

【重惩】severely punish：～不贷 *punish with severity；punish without leniency*

【重酬】❶ generously reward ❷ a high (or handsome) reward

【重创】inflict heavy losses (or casualties) on；maul (heavily)

【重大】great；weighty；major；significant：～胜利 *a signal victory* / ～问题 *vital problem；major issue* / ～损失 *heavy losses* / 他有作案的～嫌疑。*There is a strong suspicion that he committed the crime.*

【重担】heavy burden；difficult task：敢挑～ *dare to shoulder heavy burdens (or responsibilities)* / 把～子留给自己 *take the difficult tasks for oneself*

【重地】important place (usu. not open to the public)：施工～，闲人免进。*Construction Site. No Admittance.* / 军事～ *a place of military importance*

【重典】〈书〉❶ severe punishment；heavy sentence ❷ important ancient books and records

【重点】❶［物］weight ❷ focal point；stress；emphasis：突出～ *make the focal (or key) points stand out (as in one's speech)* / ～工程 *major (or priority) project* / 今天～讨论技术革新问题。*Our discussion today will centre on technical innovation.* or *We'll focus our discussion today on technical innovation.*

【重点学校】key school，institute，or university

【重读】［语音］stress：～音节 *stressed syllable* / 非～音节 *unstressed syllable*

【重罚】severe punishment：对屡教不改者予以～ *severely punish repeated offenders*

【重犯】major criminal

【重负】heavy burden；heavy load

【重工业】heavy industry

【重过磷酸钙】double superphosphate

【重荷】heavy burden；heavy responsibilities：肩负～ *shoulder heavy responsibilities*

【重轰炸机】heavy bomber

【重话】hard words；harsh words：他俩结婚以来连句～都没有过。*Hardly a harsh word has passed between them ever since their marriage.*

【重活】heavy work

【重机关枪】heavy machine gun

【重价】high price：～收购古物 *offer high prices for antiques*

【重剑】［体］épée：～运动员 *épée fencer；épéeist*

【重奖】give ample rewards to：对有特殊贡献的，要给以～。*Those who have made outstanding contribution should be amply rewarded.*
【重金】a huge sum (of money)：～购买 *pay a high price for*
【重金属】［化］heavy metal
【重晶石】［矿］barite；heavy spar (a mineral)
【重力】gravity；gravitational force ◇ ～坝 gravity dam；～场 gravitational field；～秤 gravity balance；～加速度 acceleration of gravity；～水 gravitational water；free water；～选矿 gravity separation (or concentration)；～仪 gravity meter；gravimeter；～异常 gravity anomaly
【重利】❶ high interest ❷ huge profit
【重量】weight：～单 *weight list* (*or memo*) / ～证明书 *weight certificate*；*surveyor's report on weight*
【重量级】［体］heavyweight
【重男轻女】❶ regard men as superior to women ❷ prefer sons to daughters；preference of boys to girls
【重炮】heavy artillery；heavy artillery piece；heavy gun
【重切削】［机］heavy cut
【重氢】［化］heavy hydrogen；deuterium
【重任】important task；heavy responsibility：身负～ *be charged with important tasks*
【重伤】a severe injury：受～ *sustain* (*or receive*) *severe injuries*；*be severely injured*
【重商主义】mercantilism
【重赏】a high (or handsome) reward ◇ ～之下，必有勇夫 when a high reward is offered，brave fellows are bound to come forward
【重视】attach importance to；pay attention to；think highly of；take sth. seriously；value：～基础理论的研究工作 *pay great attention to basic theoretical research*
【重水】［化］heavy water
【重税】heavy (or oppressive) taxation
【重听】hard of hearing：他有点～，你说话得大点声儿。*You have to raise your voice for he is hard of hearing.*
【重头】significant；weighty ◇ ～厂家 important factory plant；～戏 traditional opera involving much singing and action；～作品 significant work；opus magnum
【重托】great trust：不辜负人民对我们的～ *justify the great trust placed in us by the people*
【重望】❶ good reputation ❷ high hopes；great expectations
【重武器】heavy weapons
【重心】❶［物］centre of gravity ❷ heart；core；focus：问题的～ *the heart of a matter*
【重刑】severe punishment；heavy sentence
【重型】heavy-duty；heavy ◇ ～机床 heavy-duty machine tool；～卡车 heavy-duty truck；heavy truck
【重压】heavy (or strong) pressure：树枝经不起雪的～，终于折断了。*Weighed down by snow, the twig broke off in the end.* / 承受着精神的～ *be under heavy mental pressure*
【重要】important；significant；major：～人物 *important figure*；*prominent personage*；*VIP* / ～关头 *critical juncture* / ～任务 *vital task*；*important mission* / ～原则 *cardinal principle* / ～政策 *major policy* / ～因素 *key factor* / ～性 *importance*；*significance*
【重音】❶［语音］stress；accent：句子～ *sentence stress* / 单词～ *word stress* / ～符号 *stress mark*；*accent* ❷［音］accent
【重用】put sb. in an important position：一直受到～ *have always been employed at high levels*
【重油】heavy oil
【重于泰山，轻于鸿毛】(of one's death) weightier than Mount Tai or lighter than a feather
【重元素】［化］heavy element
【重枣】reddish brown (like dried dates)
【重责】❶ heavy responsibility；important task ❷ severely reprimand or punish：～四十大板 *punish with* 40 *strokes of the rod*
【重镇】place of strategic importance：军事～ *a strategic post*
【重子】［物］baryon
【重罪】serious crime；felony

zhōu

州 名 ❶ an administrative division in former times ❷ (autonomous) prefecture

舟 名〈书〉boat：小～ *a small* (*or light*) *boat*
【舟车】〈书〉❶ vessel and vehicle ❷ journey ◇ ～劳顿 fatigued by a long journey；travel-worn
【舟楫】〈书〉vessels
【舟状窝】fossa navicularis；fossa scaphoidea
【舟子】〈书〉boatman

诌 动 fabricate (tales, etc.)；make up：胡诌

周 Ⅰ 名 ❶ circumference；periphery；circuit：运动员绕场一～。*The athletes made a circuit of the arena.* / 地球绕太阳一～是一年。*It makes a year when the earth finishes a circuit around the sun.* ❷ week：上～ *last week* ❸〈略〉见〖周波〗 Ⅱ 动 ❶ make a circuit；move in a circular course：周而复始 ❷ help out (the needy)；relieve：周济 Ⅲ 形 ❶ all；whole；all over；all around：周身 ❷ thoughtful；attentive：周到
【周报】a weekly newspaper or periodical；weekly：《北京～》*Beijing Review*
【周边】❶ periphery；❷ neighboring；surrounding：～国家 *surrounding countries* / ～外交 *foreign policy toward neighboring countries*
【周波】［电］cycle
【周长】girth；circumference；perimeter：湖的～12公里。*The lake is* 12 *kilometres in circumference.*
【周到】attentive and satisfactory；thoughtful；con-

siderate：安排得很～ *be satisfactorily arranged*；*be carefully worked out* / 照顾得很～ *take good care of sb.*；*look after sb. well*

【周而复始】go round and begin again；go round and round；move in cycles：四季更迭，～。*The seasons of the year make a cycle. When one cycle is completed, another begins.*

【周济】help out (the needy)；relieve

【周刊】a weekly publication (e. g. a magazine, a supplement to a newspaper, etc.)；weekly

【周流】circulate：血液～全身。*Blood circulates through the body.*

【周率】［物］frequency

【周密】careful；thorough：～的分析 *detailed analysis* / ～的计划 *well-conceived plan*

【周末】weekend

【周年】anniversary

【周期】period；cycle：～短，收益快 *short cycles and quick returns* ◇ ～表［化］periodic table；～律［化］periodic law

【周期性】periodicity；cyclicity：～循环 *periodic return* / ～经济危机 *periodic* (*or cyclical*) *economic crises*

【周全】❶ thorough；comprehensive：计划要尽量订得～些。*We should make the plan as comprehensive as we can.* ❷ help sb. attain his aim

【周身】the whole body；all over the body：～疼痛 *ache all over*

【周岁】one full year of life：今天孩子满～。*Today is the child's first birthday.*

【周围】around；round；about：环顾～ *look about*；*look around* / ～环境 *surroundings*；*environment*

【周围神经】［生理］peripheral nerves：～系统 *peripheral nervous system*

【周详】comprehensive；complete；careful：考虑～ *give careful consideration to*

【周旋】❶ circle round；spiral ❷ mix with other people；socialize：～于达官贵人之间 *move in high society* ❸ deal with；contend with：游击队长期在山区和侵略者～。*For a long time, the guerrillas fought the invaders in hilly country.*

【周延】［逻］distribution

【周游】travel round；journey round：～世界 *travel round the world* / ～各国 *travel to many countries*；*travel far and wide*

【周遭】the surrounding area：～静悄悄的，没有一个人。*It was very quiet all around with nobody in sight.*

【周章】〈书〉❶ be scared：～失措 *be flurried out of one's wits* ❷ trouble；effort：煞费～ *take great pains*；*spare no effort*

【周折】twists and turns；setbacks：这事恐怕要费一番～。*I'm afraid this business will cause us a good deal of bother.*

【周知】everybody knows or make known to all：特此通告～。*It is hereby announced that....*

【周转】❶［经］turnover：加速资本～ *speed up capital turnover* / ～率 *turnover rate* / ～资金 *working fund*；*revolving fund*；*circulating fund* / ～天数 *turnover period* ❷ have enough to meet the need：义务劳动的学生很多，土筐～不开。*We have many students here to do volunteer labour, but there aren't enough carrying baskets to go round.*

洲 名 ❶ continent ❷ islet in a river；sand bar

【洲际】intercontinental ◇ ～弹道导弹 intercontinental ballistic missile；～导弹 intercontinental missile

粥 名 gruel (made of rice, millet, etc.)；porridge；congee：小米～ *millet gruel*

【粥少僧多】little gruel and many monks—not enough to go round

zhóu

妯 （构词成分）见下

【妯娌】wives of brothers；sisters-in-law

轴 Ⅰ 名 ❶ axle；shaft：这～儿磨坏了。*The axle is worn.* ❷ axis：椭圆的长(短)～ *the major* (*minor*) *axis of an ellipse* ❸ spool；rod：画轴 Ⅱ 量 一～线 *a spool of thread* / 一～山水画 *a scroll painting of scenery*

【轴承】［机］bearing：～衬 *bearing bush* / ～钢 *bearing steel*

【轴对称】［数］axial symmetry

【轴距】wheelbase (of a vehicle)

【轴流泵】axial-flow pump；axial pump

【轴套】［机］axle sleeve

【轴瓦】［机］axle bush

【轴线】❶［机］axis：垂直～ *normal axis* ❷ spool thread；spool cotton

【轴向】［机］axial：～剖面 *axial section* / ～运动 *axial motion*

【轴心】❶［机］axle centre ❷ axis

【轴心国】Axis powers (i. e. Germany, Italy and Japan during World War II)；the Axis

【轴子】❶ roller (for a scroll of calligraphy or painting) ❷ (tuning) peg (or pin)

zhǒu

肘 名 elbow

【肘接】［机］toggle (or elbow) joint

【肘节】［机］toggle：制动～ *brake toggle*

【肘窝】crook of the arm

【肘腋】〈书〉elbow and armpit—close at hand

【肘腋之患】trouble coming from those closest

【肘子】❶ upper part of a leg of pork ❷ elbow

帚 名 broom：笤帚

zhòu

宙 名 time (conceived as past, present and future): 宇宙

绉 名 crape; crepe: 派力斯～ *palace crepe*

【绉布】cotton crepe; crepe

【绉纱】crape

咒 Ⅰ名 incantation: 念～ *chant incantations* Ⅱ动 curse; damn: 你别～我噢。*Don't you curse me.*

【咒骂】curse; swear; abuse; revile

【咒语】incantation

昼 名 daytime; daylight; day: ～伏夜出 *hide by day and come out at night*

【昼出动物】diurnal animal

【昼伏夜出】hide by day and come out by night

【昼夜】day and night; round the clock: ～看守 *keep watch round the clock*

皱 动 wrinkle; crease; crumple: 我的上衣在箱子里搁久了,～得不像样子。*My jacket has been in the suitcase so long that it's full of creases (or it's all creased).* / 这种料子爱～。*This material crumples easily.* / 注意别把地图弄～了。*Mind you don't crumple the map.*

【皱痕】fine wrinkle

【皱眉头】knit (or contract) one's brows; frown: 他看见有人吐痰,皱了皱眉头。*He frowned with displeasure when he saw someone spit.*

【皱胃】[动] abomasum

【皱纹】wrinkles; creases; lines: 他是满脸～。*His face is full of wrinkles.* or *He has many lines on his face.* / 眼角的～ *crow's-feet* ◇ ～法兰绒 crepe flannel; ～革 shrink leather; ～纸 crepe paper

【皱褶】fold; crease; wrinkle

【皱皱巴巴】(又作'皱巴巴') wrinkled; crumpled: 脸上～的 *a face full of wrinkles; having many lines on one's face* / 他那身衣服总是～的。*His suit is always full of creases.*

骤 Ⅰ动 (of a horse) trot Ⅱ形 sudden; abrupt: 一阵～雨 *a passing heavy shower* / 天气～变。*There was a sudden change of weather.* / 狂风～起。*A sudden gale struck.* / 雨疏风～。*The rain was light, the wind fierce.*

【骤然】suddenly; abruptly: ～离去 *leave abruptly* / ～一惊 *be startled; be stupefied*

zhū

朱 Ⅰ形 vermilion; bright red Ⅱ名 cinnabar

【朱笔】writing brush dipped in red ink (formerly used in marking students' papers or writing comments on official documents)

【朱陈之好】the union of two families

【朱唇皓齿】red lips and shining teeth— very pretty or handsome

【朱顶雀】redpoll (linnet)

【朱古力】同〖巧克力〗

【朱红】vermilion; bright red

【朱门】vermilion gates—red-lacquered doors of wealthy homes ◇ ～酒肉臭,路有冻死骨 behind the red doors meat and wine go to waste while out on the road lie the bones of the frozen

【朱墨】❶ red and black: ～套印 *printed in red and black* / ～本 *an edition of ancient books printed in red and black* ❷ ink made of cinnabar

【朱雀】rosefinch

【朱砂】cinnabar

【朱文】characters on a seal carved in relief

【朱颜】❶ beautiful face (of a woman) ❷ youthful colour

诛 动〈书〉❶ put (a criminal) to death: 伏诛 ❷ punish: 卖国贼人人得而～之。*Everybody has the right to punish traitors.*

【诛锄异己】wipe out (or liquidate) dissenters

【诛戮】〈书〉kill; put to death

【诛求】〈书〉make exorbitant demands; extort; exact: ～无厌 *demand greedily; be insatiably avaricious*

【诛求无已】make endless exorbitant demands

【诛心之论】penetrating criticism; exposure of sb.'s ulterior motives

侏 形〈书〉short and small

【侏罗纪】[地质] Jurassic Period

【侏罗系】[地质] Jurassic system

【侏儒】dwarf; midget; pygmy

珠 名 ❶ pearl: 明珠 ❷ bead: 算盘～ *beads on an abacus*

【珠蚌】pearl oyster

【珠宝】pearls and jewels; jewelry: ～店 *a jeweller's (shop)* / ～商 *jeweller*

【珠茶】a kind of green tea (the tea leaves looking like beads)

【珠翠】pearls and jade; ornaments made with pearls and jade

【珠光宝气】resplendent with jewels; bedecked with jewels

【珠光体】[冶] pearlite

【珠花】pearl head-ornaments

【珠玑】〈书〉❶ pearl; gem ❷ exquisite or excellent wording of a writing

【珠江】the Zhujiang River; the Pearl River

【珠帘】pearl-decorated screen or curtain; bead curtain

【珠联璧合】strings of pearls and girdles of jade—a perfect pair; a happy combination

【珠母】pearl oyster ◇ ～贝 pearl shell

【珠穆朗玛峰】Mount Qomolangma (known to the West as Mount Everest)

【珠算】reckoning by the abacus; calculation with

an abacus

【珠围翠绕】❶ (of a woman) be gorgeously dressed and richly ornamented ❷ be surrounded by attending maids

【珠圆玉润】round as pearls and smooth as jade—excellent singing or polished writing

【珠子】❶ pearl ❷ bead

株 Ⅰ 名 ❶ trunk of a tree; stem of a plant ❷ individual plant; plant: 幼株 Ⅱ 量 两～梨树 *two pear trees*

【株距】[农] spacing in the rows

【株连】involve (others) in a criminal case; implicate

【株式会社】(Japanese) limited company

诸 Ⅰ 形 all; various: 编辑部～同志 *all the comrades of the editorial department* / 自然科学～部门 *the various branches of natural science* Ⅱ 介 〈书〉 a fusing of 之于 or of 之乎: 付～(=之于)实施 *put into effect* / 数易其稿,而后公～(=之于)社会。*It went through several drafts before it was published*.

【诸多】〈书〉 (used for abstract things) a good deal; a lot of: ～不便 *quite a lot of trouble*; *rather inconvenient*

【诸公】〈套〉 (used in addressing a group of men) gentlemen

【诸侯】dukes or princes under an emperor

【诸君】〈套〉 (used in addressing a group of people) ladies and gentlemen; you

【诸如】such as

【诸如此类】things of that sort; and suchlike; and what not: ～,不胜枚举。*Such instances are too numerous to mention*.

【诸色】〈书〉 various; all kinds: ～人等 *all kinds of people*

【诸事】everything; every matter: 祝您～顺遂。*Hope everything goes well with you!* or *Wishing you every success!*

【诸位】〈套〉 (used in addressing a group of people) ladies and gentlemen; you: ～有什么意见,欢迎提出来。*You are welcome to put forward your views*.

【诸子百家】the various schools of thought and their exponents during the period from pre-Qin times to the early years of the Han Dynasty

猪 名 pig; hog; swine: 小～ *pigling*; *piglet* / 母～ *sow* / 公～ *boar*

【猪八戒倒打一耙】Pigsy striking backwards with his rake—make a counterattack or countercharge

【猪草】greenfeed for pigs

【猪场】pig farm; piggery

【猪丹毒】swine erysipelas; diamond-skin disease

【猪肚】pork tripe

【猪肝】pork liver ◇ ～色 liver-coloured; purplish red

【猪倌】swineherd

【猪獾】sand badger

【猪圈】pigsty; pigpen; hogpen

【猪苓】[中] umbellate pore fungus (Polyporus umbellata)

【猪笼草】[植] common nepenthes (Nepenthes mirabilis)

【猪猡】〈方〉 pig; swine

【猪苗】piglet; pigling

【猪囊虫病】pork measles

【猪排】pork chop

【猪皮】pigskin; hogskin

【猪气喘病】swine enzootic pneumonia

【猪肉】pork

【猪舍】pig (or hog) house

【猪食】pig feed; pigwash; swill: ～缸 (*pig*) *trough*

【猪蹄】pig's trotters

【猪头】pig's head: ～肉 *pieces of meat cut from a pig's head served as a cold dish to go with drinks*

【猪腿】leg of pork; ham

【猪瘟】swine fever; hog cholera

【猪窝】pigsty: 他的房间脏得像～。*His room is as dirty as a pigsty*.

【猪血】coagulated pig's blood used as a food

【猪腰子】pork kidney

【猪油】lard

【猪鬃】(hog) bristles

铢 量 an ancient unit of weight, equal to 1/24 liang (两)

【铢积寸累】accumulate little by little; build up bit by bit

【铢两悉称】carry the same weight; be exactly equal

蛛 名 spider: 蜘蛛

【蛛丝马迹】the thread of a spider and the trail of a horse—clues; traces: 此案有～可寻。*There are clues for solving the case*.

【蛛网】spider web; cobweb

【蛛形动物】arachnid

【蛛蛛】common name for 蜘蛛

zhú

术 (构词成分)见〖苍术〗——另见 shù

竹 名 bamboo: ～篓 *bamboo crate* (*or basket*) / ～林 *bamboo forest*; *groves of bamboo*

【竹板】bamboo clappers

【竹板书】story recited to the rhythm of bamboo clappers

【竹箅子】bamboo grid (to be put in a pot for steaming food)

【竹编】bamboo woven articles

【竹帛】bamboo slips and silk (used for writing on during ancient times); ancient books

【竹布】a light blue or white cotton cloth for making summer clothes

【竹材】bamboo used as lumber：用～代替木材 *substitute bamboo for wood*
【竹蛏】[动] razor clam；razor shell
【竹筹】bamboo chip
【竹雕】bamboo carving
【竹筏】bamboo raft
【竹竿】bamboo pole；bamboo
【竹黄】(又作'竹簧') handicraft articles made from bamboo with its green covering removed
【竹黄菌】[中] bamboo parasitic fungus
【竹鸡】bamboo partridge
【竹筴鱼】saurel；horse mackerel
【竹简】bamboo slip (used for writing on during ancient times)
【竹节】bamboo joint
【竹节虫】stick insect；walkingstick
【竹篮打水一场空】draw water with a bamboo basket—achieve nothing；all in vain
【竹篱茅舍】thatched cottage with bamboo fence—simple dwelling of a hermit
【竹帘】bamboo screen or curtain
【竹帘画】painting on a bamboo curtain
【竹马】❶ a bamboo stick used as a toy horse ❷ a bamboo horse used in a folk dance——另见〖青梅竹马〗
【竹马之交】friends from childhood days
【竹排】bamboo raft
【竹器】articles made of bamboo
【竹扦】bamboo spike
【竹笋】bamboo shoots
【竹筒】a thick bamboo tube
【竹筒倒豆子】pour beans out of a bamboo tube—withhold nothing：你就来个～，都说了吧。*Out with it—don't hold anything back.*
【竹头木屑】bamboo ends and wood shavings—things not of much value but of some use：～皆有用。*Bamboo ends and wood shavings all have their uses.*
【竹席】bamboo mat
【竹叶青】❶ green bamboo snake ❷ a kind of liquor
【竹椅】bamboo chair
【竹芋】[植] arrowroot
【竹枝词】❶ ancient folk songs with love as their main theme ❷ occasional poems in the classical style devoted to local topics
【竹纸】paper made from young bamboo
【竹子】bamboo

烛 Ⅰ名 candle：喜～ *wedding candles* Ⅱ动〈书〉illuminate；light up：火光～天。*Leaping flames lit up the sky.*
【烛光】[物] candlepower；candle
【烛花】snuff：剪～ *trim off the snuff (of a candle)*；*snuff*
【烛泪】*gutterings of a candle*
【烛台】*candlestick*
【烛心】(又作'烛芯') *candlewick*

逐 Ⅰ动 ❶ pursue；chase：追逐 ❷ drive out；expel：～出门外 *drive out of the door* Ⅱ介 one by one：～项 *item by item* / ～月 *month by month*
【逐步】step by step；progressively：～加以解决 *settle sth. step by step* / ～降低生产成本 *progressively reduce the production cost* / 战争正在～升级。*The war was escalating.*
【逐臭之夫】❶ an eccentric person；eccentric ❷ a person of depraved tastes—striving after fame and gain
【逐处】everywhere；in all respects
【逐格】frame by frame ◇ ～放映 stop frame projection；～摄影 single frame photography
【逐个】one by one：我们得～研究这些问题。*We must look into these matters one by one.*
【逐行倒相制】phase-alternation
【逐行扫描】line by line scan；progressive scanning
【逐渐】gradually；by degrees：天～暗下来了。*It's getting darker and darker.*
【逐客令】order for guests to leave：下～ *show sb. the door*
【逐鹿】〈书〉chase the deer—fight for the throne；bid for state power：群雄～ *feudal lords vying for the throne*；*powerful politicians fighting for supremacy*
【逐鹿中原】chase the deer on the Central Plains—try to seize control of the empire
【逐年】year by year；year after year：产量～增加。*Production has been increasing year after year.*
【逐日】day by day；every day：病情～好转。*The patient's condition is improving day by day.* ◇ ～保费 annual premium
【逐水】[中] relieve oedema or abdominal distension through diuresis or purgation
【逐条】item by item；point by point：～加以说明 *explain point by point*
【逐项定价】item pricing
【逐一】one by one：对这些规定～加以说明 *explain all these provisions one by one*
【逐字】word for word；verbatim：～记录 *verbatim record*
【逐字逐句】word by word and sentence by sentence；word for word：～的翻译 *a word-for-word (or literal) translation*

zhǔ

主 Ⅰ名 ❶ host：宾主 ❷ owner；master：～仆 *master and servant* / 企业～ *proprietor of an enterprise* ❸ person or party concerned：买主 / 事主 ❹ God；Lord ❺ Allah ❻〈方〉trunk card (in poker)：你有几张～？*How many trunk cards do you have?* Ⅱ形 main；primary：～航道 *main (or principal) channel* Ⅲ动 ❶ manage，direct；be in charge of：主管 ❷ indicate；signify、早霞～雨，晚霞～晴。*Rosy morning clouds indicate rain，and a rosy sunset means fine weather.* ❸ hold a definite view about sth.；advocate：我一

时心里没～。*For a moment I just didn't know what to do.*

【主儿】〈方〉❶ master；employer ❷ person of a specified type：他是个爱管闲事的～。*He is the busybody type.* ❸ a husband or fiancé：她快三十了，也该找～了。*She is about thirty and it's time she looked for a husband.*

【主板】［计］motherborad；mainboard

【主办】direct；sponsor：展览会将由农业部～。*The exhibition will be sponsored by（or held under the auspices of）the Ministry of Agriculture.*

【主笔】〈旧〉❶ editor in chief ❷ chief commentator

【主编】❶ chief editor（or compiler）；editor in chief ❷ supervise the publication of（a newspaper，magazine，etc.）；edit

【主宾】guest of honour：～席 *head table（for guests of honour）；seat for the guest of honour*

【主裁判】chief referee；head referee

【主菜单】［计］main menu

【主持】❶ take charge（or care）of；manage；direct：～日常事务 *take care of routine matters* ❷ preside over；chair：～讨论 *chair a discussion* ❸ uphold；stand for：～正义 *uphold justice*

【主持人】compère；host；hostess；interviewer；moderator；anchorman，anchorperson（of a news or talkshow program）

【主厨】❶ be the chef ❷ chef

【主词】［逻］subject term；subject

【主次】primary and secondary：我们干工作要分清～。*In our work we must differentiate what is primary from what is secondary.*

【主从】principal and subordinate：～关系 *the relationship between the principal and the subordinate*

【主单位】basic unit（as a standard of measurement）

【主刀】［医］❶ perform an operation：老医生让他的助手～。*The veteran surgeon asked his assistant to perform the operation.* ❷ operator

【主导】leading；dominant；guiding：起～作用 *play a leading role* / 占～地位 *occupy the leading position；hold sway* ◇ ～风［建］prevailing wind；～力量 the leading force；the main force；～思想 dominant ideas；guiding ideology；～主题［音］leitmotiv

【主调】❶［音］top melody of a homophonic piece ❷ keynote（of a speech，etc.）◇ ～音乐 homophony

【主动】❶ take the initiative；do sth. of one's own accord：争取～ *try to gain the initiative；contend for the initiative* ❷［机］driving：～齿轮 *driving gear* / ～轴 *driving shaft；driving spindle*

【主动脉】aorta ◇ ～弓 arch of aorta；～炎 aortitis

【主动语态】［语］active voice

【主队】［体］home team；host team

【主发动机】sustainer

【主伐】［林］final felling（or cutting）

【主犯】［法］prime culprit；principal criminal（or offender）；principal：～和从犯 *principal and accessories in a crime*

【主峰】the highest peak in a mountain range

【主妇】housewife；hostess

【主干】❶［植］trunk ❷ main force；mainstay

【主稿】be responsible for the first draft；be the chief writer（of a joint work）

【主格】［语］the nominative case

【主根】［植］main root；taproot

【主攻】［军］main attack ◇ ～部队 main attack force；～方面 main phase of attack；～方向 main direction of attack；～手［体］ace spiker（in volleyball）

【主顾】customer；client

【主观】subjective：～努力 *subjective efforts* / ～愿望 *subjective desire；wishful thinking* ◇ ～能动性［哲］subjective initiative；conscious activity；～唯心主义 subjective idealism；～主义 subjectivism

【主管】❶ be responsible for；be in charge of：～外事的副市长 *vice-mayor in charge of external relations* / ～机关 *competent authorities；responsible institution* ❷ person in charge：他是这项工程的～。*He is the person in charge of the project.*

【主和】advocate peace；be for a peaceful settlement：～派 *peace party*

【主婚】（usu. of the parents of the bride and the bride groom）preside over a wedding ceremony

【主机】❶［机］main engine；main processor ❷［军］lead plane；leader ❸［计］main body of a computer（compared with display and peripherals）❹［计］host computer

【主见】ideas or thoughts of one's own；one's own judgment；definite view：没有～ *have no definite views of one's own*

【主讲】be the speaker；give a lecture

【主将】chief commander；commanding general

【主焦点】［物］prime（or principal）focus

【主教】bishop

【主井】［矿］main shaft

【主句】〈语〉main（or principal）clause

【主角】leading role；lead；protagonist：在该片中演～ *play the lead in the film*

【主考】❶ be in charge of an examination ❷ chief examiner（in a school，etc.）

【主考官】official in charge of an imperial examination；chief examiner

【主客】❶ host and guest ❷ guest of honour

【主课】main subject；major course

【主力】main force；main strength of an army ◇ ～兵团 main formations；～队员 top players of a team；～舰 capital ship；～军 main（or principal）force

【主梁】［建］girder

【主粮】staple food grain

【主流】❶ trunk stream；mainstream：历史的～ *the mainstream of history* ❷ essential or main aspect; main trend: ～和支流 *principal and secondary aspects*

【主楼】main building in a complex: 由～和裙楼组成的业务大楼 *office building consisting of a main block and annexes*

【主麻】[宗](伊斯兰教) Djumah (Friday)

【主谋】❶ head a conspiracy; be the chief plotter ❷ [法] chief instigator

【主脑】❶ control centre; centre of operation ❷ leader; chief

【主权】sovereign rights; sovereignty: ～国家 *a sovereign state*

【主人】❶ master ❷ host: 女～ *hostess* ❸ owner: 房子的～ *the wowner of the house*

【主人公】leading character in a novel, etc.; hero or heroine; protagonist

【主人翁】❶ master: 有一种～感 *have a sense of being the master of one's own affairs* ❷ 同〖主人公〗

【主任】director; head; chairman: 教研室～ *chief of teaching and research section* / 内(外)科～ *head of the medical (surgical) department*

【主任委员】head of a committee

【主食】staple food; principal food

【主使】instigate; incite; abet

【主事】be in charge; take charge: 主不了事 *have no say; have no power of decision*

【主视图】front view; elevation

【主帅】同〖主将〗

【主诉】[医] patient's description of symptoms: 根据～作出的诊断 *diagnosis based on the patient's account of his symptoms*

【主题】theme; subject; motif; leitmotiv: 第一乐章第一～ *the first subject (or theme) of the first movement* ◇ ～歌 theme song; ～公园 theme park; ～音乐 theme music

【主体】❶ main body; main part; principal part: 一支以青年为～的突击队 *a shock force composed mainly of young people* / ～工程 *main project; principal part of a project* ❷ [哲] subject: ～和客体 *subject and object; the perceiver and the world*

【主位】❶ status of a sovereign ❷ seat of the host (at table)

【主谓词组】[语] subject-predicate word group

【主谓句】[语] subject-predicate sentence

【主文】[法] main body of a court verdict

【主文件】[计] master file

【主席】❶ chairman (of a meeting): 当～ *be in the chair; preside over a meeting* ❷ chairman or president (of an organization or a state)

【主席台】rostrum; platform: 登上～ *go up to the rostrum*

【主席团】presidium; bureau: ～成员 *bureau members; members of a presidium*

【主线】thread (of a novel, etc.)

【主项】(〈略〉全称为'主要项目') main project; main event: 今天我们只讨论工程的～设计。*Today we will confine ourselves to discussion of the design for the main project.*

【主心骨】❶ backbone; mainstay; pillar: 他是我们队里的～。*He is the mainstay of our team.* ❷ a definite view; one's own judgment: 他这个人没有～。*He has no judgment of his own.*

【主星】[天] primary (component) ◇ ～序 [天] main sequence

【主刑】[法] principal penalty

【主凶】prime (or chief) culprit (in a murder case); principal

【主修】❶ specialize (in a subject); major: ～科目 *major subjects* ❷ be responsible for the repair or overhaul (of a machine)

【主旋律】main melody; top melody; theme

【主演】act the leading role (in a play or film); star: 她～过许多影片。*She has starred in many films.*

【主要】main; chief; principal; major: ～理由 *main reasons* / ～对手 *chief opponent* / ～矛盾 *principal contradiction* / ～目的 *major objective* / ～因素 *primary factor*

【主页】[计] home page

【主义】doctrine; -ism: 资本主义 capitalism

【主意】❶ idea; plan: 好～! *That's a good idea.* / 人多～多。*More people mean a greater ferment of ideas.* ❷ decision; definite view: 打定～ *make a decision; make up one's mind* / 改变～ *change one's view (or mind)* / 拿不定～ *be in two minds (about sth.)* / 我一时没了～。*I was quite at a loss, then.* or *For a moment I just didn't know what to do.*

【主因】main reason; major cause

【主音】[音] keynote; tonic

【主语】[语] subject

【主宰】dominate; dictate; decide: ～自己的命运 *decide one's own destiny; be master of one's own fate*

【主战】advocate war: ～派 *war party*

【主张】❶ advocate; stand for; maintain; hold: ～自力更生 *advocate self-reliance* / ～改革 *favour reforms* ❷ view; position; stand; proposition: 这是我们一贯的～。*That has been our consistent stand.*

【主政】head the government: 新省长将于明天上午上任～。*The new governor will assume office tomorrow morning.*

【主旨】purport; substance; gist: 文章的～ *the gist of the article* ◇ ～演讲 keynote speech

【主治】[医] indications

【主治医生】physician-in-charge; doctor in charge of a case

【主轴】[机] main shaft; spindle: ～箱 *spindle box*

【主子】master; boss: ～和奴才 *the boss and his flunkey; master and servant*

拄 动 lean on (a stick, etc.): ～着拐棍走 *walk with a stick*

属 动 〈书〉❶ join; combine: ～文 *compose a*

piece of prose writing ❷ fix (one's mind) on; centre (one's attention, etc.) upon: 属望 —— 另见 shǔ

【属草】〈书〉draft (or draw up) a document

【属望】〈书〉centre one's hope on; look forward to; expect

【属意】fix one's mind on sb. (as one's choice, favourite, etc.)

【属垣有耳】walls have ears; beware of eavesdroppers

煮 动 boil; cook: ～鸡蛋 *boil eggs or boiled eggs* / ～饭 *cook rice*

【煮豆燃萁】burn beanstalks to cook beans —fratricidal strife

【煮呢】[纺] potting

嘱 动 enjoin; advise; urge: 叮嘱

【嘱咐】(又作'嘱告') enjoin; tell; exhort: 再三～ *exhort again and again; din sth. into sb.* / ～他保守秘密 *enjoin him to secrecy* / 临终～ *death-bed injunction* / 大夫～他好好休息。*The doctor told him to take a good rest.*

【嘱托】entrust: 她～我办这件事。*She entrusted me with the task.*

瞩 动 gaze; look steadily: 瞩目

【瞩目】〈书〉fix one's eyes upon; focus one's attention upon: 为世界所～ *attract worldwide attention*

【瞩望】〈书〉❶ look forward to: ～已久 *have been eagerly looking forward to it for a long time* ❷ gaze at; look long and steadily upon

zhù

伫 动〈书〉stand for a long while

【伫候】〈书〉stand waiting: ～佳音 *look forward to hearing good news from you*

【伫立】〈书〉stand still for a long while

苎 (构词成分) 见下

【苎麻】ramie

助 动 help; assist; aid: ～消化 *aid digestion* / ～一臂之力 *lend sb. a helping hand*

【助爆药】[军] booster charge; booster

【助残】help the handicapped: 开展～活动 *launch a campaign to aid the handicapped*

【助产】practise midwifery ◇ ～士 midwife

【助词】[语] auxiliary word, an unstressed form word which performs the grammatical functions of structure (as 的,地,得,所), of tense (as 了,着,过) or of mood (as 呢,吗;吧;啊); particle

【助动词】[语] auxiliary verb

【助耕】help in farmwork: 为孤老户组织～队 *organize farm aid for the aged and those who live alone*

【助攻】[军] holding (or secondary) attack: ～部队 *holding element*

【助工】(〈略〉见〖助理工程师〗) assistant engineer

【助剂】[纺] auxiliary

【助教】assistant professor (of a college faculty)

【助桀为虐】aid King Jie in his tyrannical rule—aid and abet the evil-doer

【助理】assistant: ～秘书长 *assistant secretary-general* ◇ ～编辑 assistant editor; ～导演 assistant director (of a film or play); ～工程师 assistant engineer

【助力】a helping hand; help; assistance

【助跑】[体] run-up; approach

【助燃】[化] combustion-supporting: ～气体 *combustion-supporting gas*

【助人为乐】find it a pleasure to help others; take pleasure in helping people

【助熔剂】flux

【助色团】[化] auxochrome

【助手】assistant; helper; aide

【助听器】audiphone; hearing aid; deaf-aid

【助推级】space booster

【助威】(又作'助阵') boost the morale of; cheer (for): 给我们的篮球队～ *cheer for our basketball team*

【助兴】liven things up; add to the fun

【助学】give financial aid to students ◇ ～金 stipend; grant-in-aid

【助益】benefit; help: 毫无～ *be of no help at all*

【助战】❶ assist in fighting ❷ bolster sb.'s morale

【助长】〈贬〉encourage; abet; foster; foment: ～侵略者的野心 *whet the ambitions of the aggressors* / ～歪风邪气 *encourage the evil trends*

【助纣为虐】aid King Zhou in his tyrannical rule—aid and abet the evil-doer

住 动 ❶ live; reside; stay: 我～这间屋。*I live in this room.* / 他～在北京。*He lives in Beijing.* / 对面没人～。*Nobody lives in the room opposite mine.* ❷ stop; cease: 雨～了。*The rain has stopped.* / 等风～了再走。*Don't go until the wind drops.* ❸ (used after a verb) firmly; to a stop: 拿～了,别撒手。*Hold tight. Don't let go.* / 悠扬的小提琴声把我吸引～了。*The beautiful notes of a violin held me spellbound.* / 这一下你可把我问～了。*You've got me there.*

【住持】[宗](佛教或道教) abbot

【住处】residence; dwelling (place); lodging; quarters: 找到～没有? *Have you found accommodation?*

【住读】(of a student) board at school

【住房】housing; lodgings: ～问题 *the housing problem; accommodation* ◇ ～面积 floor space; ～汽车 motor home; ～商品化 commercialization of housing; ～制度改革 housing system reform

【住户】household; resident: 院内有三家～。*There are three households in the compound.*

【住家】❶ (of one's family) live; reside in: 他在郊区～。*He lives with his family in the suburbs.* ❷ household; resident

【住口】shut up; stop talking: 你给我～! *Hold your tongue!*

【住声】stop talking, laughing, or crying: 他们有说有笑,老半天没有～。*They talked and laughed for a long time without stop.*

【住手】stay one's hand; stop: 他不做完不肯～。*He won't stop until he finishes the job.*

【住宿】stay; put up; get accommodation: 给客人安排～ *find lodgings* (*or arrange accommodation*) *for the visitors* / 大学生大部分在校～。*Most college students are boarders.*

【住所】dwelling place; residence; domicile: 固定～ *permanent dwelling place; domicile*

【住校】(of a student) board at school

【住院】be in hospital; be hospitalized: ～期间 *during one's hospitalization; while in hospital* / ～费 *hospitalization expenses* ◇ ～病人 inpatient; ～部 inpatient department; ～处 admission office (in a hospital); ～医生 resident (physician)

【住宅】residence; dwelling ◇ ～保险 residence insurance; ～建设 housing construction; ～区 residential quarters (or district); ～设计 housing design; ～小区 dwelling districts; housing district

【住址】address

【住嘴】stop talking: 老太太扯起东邻西舍的闲事,总是不～。*The old woman would keep on and on gossiping about her neighbours.*

注 Ⅰ 动 ❶ pour; fill: 大雨如注 ❷ concentrate; fix: 注视 ❸ annotate; explain with notes: 批注 ❹ record; register Ⅱ 名 ❶ stakes (in gambling): 下注 ❷ notes: 正文用大字,～用小字。*The text is to be in big type, the notes in small type.* Ⅲ 量 (for deals or sums of money): 一～交易 *a deal* / 一～钱 *a sum of money*

【注册】❶ register ❷ log-in ◇ ～处 registration office; registrar's office; ～会计师 certified public accountant; ～商标 registered trademark; ～资本 registered capital; ～证书 registration certificate

【注带】[纺] casting

【注定】be doomed; be destined: ～要失败 *be doomed to failure* / 命中～ *decreed by fate; predestined*

【注脚】(又作'脚注') footnote

【注解】❶ annotate; explain with notes ❷ (explanatory) note; annotation

【注明】give clear indication of: ～出处 *give sources* (*of quotations, etc.*) / 该表未～日期。*That form is undated.* / 本词典词类用下列方式～。*Parts of speech are labelled in the following way in this dictionary.*

【注目】gaze at; fix one's eyes on: 这个小县城成了全国～的地方。*The small town became the country's centre of attention.*

【注目礼】salute with eyes

【注入】❶ pour into; empty into: ～式教学法 *the spoon-feeding way of teaching; cramming* ❷ petroleum injection: ～井 *injection well*

【注射】[医] inject: 肌肉(皮下,静脉)～ *intramuscular* (*hypodermic, intravenous*) *injection* / ～器 *injector; syringe* / ～针头 *syringe needle*

【注视】look attentively at; gaze at: 久久～着陌生人的脸 *look fixedly at the stranger's face for a long time* / 密切～会议的进展 *closely follow the progress of the conference*

【注释】explanatory note; annotation: ～读物 *annotated readings*

【注水】petroleum water flooding: 边缘～ *edgewater flooding* / ～动态 *flood performance*

【注塑】mould plastics

【注文】explanatory notes; notes

【注销】cancel; write off: 把借条～ *cancel a written acknowledgment of a loan; cancel an I.O.U.* / 账已～。*The account has been written off.* / ～登记 *nullify the registration*

【注意】pay attention to; take note (or notice) of: 我没～他什么时候走的。*I didn't notice when he left.* / ～,马上就要点炮啦! *Look out! We're ready to blast.* / ～别摔倒。*Mind you don't fall.* / ～事项 *matters needing attention; points for attention* ◇ ～广度[心理] attention span; range of attention; ～力 attention

【注音】phonetic notation: 课文有～吗? *Is the text marked with phonetic symbols?*

【注音字母】(又作'注音符号') the national phonetic alphabet (in use before the publication of the Scheme for the Chinese Phonetic Alphabet)

【注油】❶ oiling; greasing ❷ fuel-injection

【注油枪】grease gun; oil gun

【注重】lay stress on; pay attention to; attach importance to: ～基本功的训练 *lay stress on basic training*

贮 动 store; save; lay aside: ～粮备荒 *store grain against a lean year*

【贮藏】store up; lay in: ～苹果 *store apples*

【贮存】store; keep in storage: ～期 *storage time*

【贮木场】timber depot; timber yard; lumber yard

【贮蓄】❶ store up; lay in; conserve: ～土壤养分 *conservation of soil nutrient* ❷ storage or saving

【贮运】storage and transportation

驻 动 ❶ halt; stay: 敌～我扰。*When the enemy halts, we harass him.* ❷ be stationed: 中国～埃及大使馆 *Chinese Embassy in Egypt* / ～京记者 *resident correspondent in Beijing* / ～外机构 *institutions stationed abroad*

【驻波】[物] standing wave

【驻地】❶ place where troops, etc. are stationed: 边防军～ *frontier guard station* ❷ seat (of a local administrative organ)

【驻防】be on garrison duty; garrison: ～福州 *garrison Fuzhou* / ～部队 *garrison* (*troops*)

【驻军】❶ station troops ❷ garrison troops; garrison

【驻守】garrison; defend
【驻屯】(of troops) be stationed; be quartered
【驻颜】〈书〉preserve youthful looks: ～有术 *possess the secret of preserving youthful looks*
【驻在国】state to which a diplomatic envoy is accredited
【驻扎】(of troops) be stationed; be quartered: ～重兵 *station a huge force*
【驻足】halt; stop; go no further: ～而观 *stop to watch*

炷 Ⅰ 名〈书〉wick (of an oil lamp) Ⅱ 动 burn: ～香 *burn a joss stick* Ⅲ 量 一～香 *a burning joss stick*

祝 动 express good wishes; wish: ～你健康。*I wish you the best of health.* / ～你旅途愉快。*Have a pleasant journey.* or *Bon voyage!*
【祝词】❶ congratulatory speech (at a ceremony, etc.); congratulations ❷ prayers at sacrificial rites in ancient times
【祝祷】(又作'祝告') pray; say one's prayers
【祝福】blessing; benediction: 为你～。*Blessings on you.*
【祝贺】congratulate: ～艺术家们演出成功 *congratulate the artists on their successful performance* / 向你～! *Congratulations!*
【祝酒】drink a toast; toast: 向来宾们～ *toast the guests* / 致～辞 *propose a toast* / 答谢～ *respond (or reply) to a toast*
【祝寿】congratulate (an elderly person) on his or her birthday
【祝愿】wish: 致以良好的～ *with best wishes*

柱 名 ❶ post; upright; pillar; column: 立一根～儿 *erect a post* ❷ sth. shaped like a column: 水柱 ❸ [数] cylinder
【柱础】stone base of a column; plinth
【柱顶】[建] capital
【柱廊】[建] colonnade
【柱面】[数] cylinder: 椭圆～ *elliptic cylinder*
【柱身】[建] shaft
【柱石】〈喻〉pillar; mainstay
【柱头】❶ [植] stigma ❷ [建] column cap; column head ❸〈方〉post; pillar
【柱状剖面】[地质] columnar section; geologic column
【柱子】post; pillar
【柱座】column base; plinth

疰 (构词成分) 见下
【疰夏】❶ [中] a summer disease, usu. contracted by children with symptoms of fever, loss of appetite, lassitude, etc. ❷〈方〉loss of appetite and weight in summer

著 Ⅰ 形 marked; outstanding: 卓著 Ⅱ 动 ❶ show; prove: 颇～成效 *prove rather effective* ❷ write: ～书 *write books* Ⅲ 名 book; work: 新～ *sb.'s latest work*
【著称】celebrated; famous: 以风景优美～ *be celebrated for its scenic beauty* / 杭州以西湖～于世。*Hangzhou is world-famous for its West Lake.*
【著录】put down in writing; record
【著名】famous; celebrated; well-known: ～论断 *a celebrated (or well-known) thesis*
【著书立说】write books to expound a theory; write scholarly works
【著述】❶ write; compile: 从事～ *be engaged in writing or compiling scholarly works* ❷ book; work: 主要～ *major works* ◇ ～等身 one's writings piled up to one's own height—be a prolific writer
【著者】author; writer
【著作】❶ work; book; writings: 古代医学～ *ancient books on medicine; ancient medical literature* ❷ write: 他一生～甚多。*He wrote many books during his lifetime.* or *He was a prolific author.* ◇ ～权 copyright (of the author)

蛀 Ⅰ 名 moth or any other insect that eats books, clothes, wood, etc.: 蛀虫 Ⅱ 动 (of moths, etc.) eat; bore through: 这件呢大衣给虫子～了。*This woollen coat is moth-eaten.*
【蛀齿】decayed tooth; dental caries
【蛀虫】insect that eats books, clothes or wood; moth; borer
【蛀心虫】同〖钻心虫〗

筑 动 build; construct: ～路 *construct a road* / ～堤 *build a dyke*
【筑巢】❶〈字〉build nest ❷〈喻〉build infrastructure: ～引凤 *build nest to attract phoenix—build infrastructure to attract investment domestic and foreign*
【筑埂机】[农] ridger
【筑室道谋】ask every passerby how to build one's house—have no idea or plan of one's own (and accomplish nothing)

铸 动 cast; found: ～钟 *cast a bell* / ～钱 *coin (or mint) money* / 这口钟是铜～的。*This bell is cast with bronze.*
【铸币】coin; specie ◇ ～权 mintage
【铸成大错】make a gross error (or stupendous mistake)
【铸错】commit blunders; make grave mistakes
【铸锭】ingot casting
【铸钢】cast steel
【铸工】❶ foundry work ❷ foundry worker; founder ◇ ～车间 foundry (shop); ～鼓风机 foundry fan
【铸件】cast; casting: 干砂～ *dry sand casting* / 压～ *die casting* / 冷硬～ *chill (or chilled) casting*
【铸模】mould for casting; matrix
【铸排机】[刷] composing machines
【铸石】cast stone; molten-rock casting; stone casting
【铸铁】❶ iron casting ❷ cast iron
【铸型】casting mould

【铸造】casting; founding: 无砂～ *sandless casting* / 蜡模～ *investment casting; lost wax casting* / ～车间 *foundry; casting shop*
【铸字】typefounding; typecasting: ～工场 *typefoundry* / ～工人 *typefounder* / ～机 *typecasting machine*

zhuā

抓 动 ❶ grab; seize; clutch: ～一把糖 *take a handful of sweets* / ～机会 *seize an opportunity* / 他～起帽子就往外走。*He grabbed (or snatched up) his cap and made for the door.* ❷ scratch: ～痒痒 *scratch an itch* / 猫把孩子的手～了。*The cat scratched the child's hand.* ❸ arrest; catch: ～小偷 *catch a thief* ❹ stress; pay special attention to: ～重点 *stress the essentials* / ～思想问题 *pay special attention to ideological problems* / ～苗头 *watch out for the first signs* ❺ take charge of; be responsible for: 他是～工会工作的。*He is in charge of trade union work.*
【抓辫子】同〖揪辫子〗
【抓捕】arrest; catch: ～逃犯 *arrest an escaped prisoner*
【抓不起来】❶ cannot get hold of or lift sth. ❷ cannot manage sth. (because of inability, etc.)
【抓差】draft sb. for a particular task; press sb. into service
【抓点】concentrate on work at selected units ◇ ～带面 draw experience from selected units to promote overall work
【抓丁】pressgang able-bodied men
【抓赌】(of police) break up a gambling party and arrest the participants
【抓耳挠腮】tweak one's ears and scratch one's cheeks (as a sign of anxiety or delight)
【抓夫】同〖拉夫〗
【抓哏】(of a comedian, etc.) throw in impromptu lines
【抓工夫】make good use of one's time; find time (to do sth.)
【抓好】do a good job of; make great efforts to: 你得把工作～。*You must do a good job of it.*
【抓获】catch (a criminal, etc.); capture; seize
【抓尖儿卖快】go out of one's way to curry favour
【抓紧】firmly grasp; pay close attention to: ～学习 *attend to one's studies in earnest; study hard* / ～时机 *seize (or grasp) the opportunity* / ～时间 *make the best use of one's time*
【抓阄儿】draw lots
【抓举】[体] snatch
【抓空子】find time (to do sth.)
【抓两头,带中间】grasp the two ends to bring along the middle—sustain the advanced and help the backward so as to encourage the vast majority to move along
【抓挠】〈方〉❶ scratch: ～几下就不痒了。*Scratch and it won't itch any more.* ❷ mess about: 好孩子,别～东西! *Don't mess things about, my child.* ❸ come to blows; fight: 他们俩又～起来了。*The two of them have got into a fight again.* ❹ prepare sth. hastily: 一下子来了这么多人吃饭,炊事员怕～不过来吧! *With so many people here all of a sudden for a meal, I wonder how the cook can hustle them up something to eat.* ❺ sb. or sth. that one can rely on: 最好派个负责人来,咱好有个～。*We should have someone sent here to take responsibility, so that we can turn to him with our problems.* ❻ solution to a difficulty: 事前要慎重考虑,免得发生问题时没～。*Think it over well beforehand so as to be prepared for all eventualities.*
【抓拍】❶ take a candid photograph (or picture) ❷ a candid photograph (or picture); candid
【抓破】injure or damage by scratching or clawing ◇ ～脸〈口〉scratch each other's face—quarrel openly
【抓人】arrest sb.; take sb. into custody: 抓了好些人。*A number of arrests were made.*
【抓瞎】〈口〉find oneself at a loss; be in a rush and muddle; be thrown off balance: 早点儿做好准备,免得临时～。*Arrange everything in advance so that you won't be in a rush at the last moment.*
【抓岩机】grab loader; grab
【抓药】❶ make up (or fill) a prescription of Chinese herbal medicine ❷ have a prescription of Chinese herbal medicine made up (or filled)
【抓周】the grabbing test on the occasion of a baby's first birthday
【抓住】❶ catch (or seize) hold of; grip: ～机遇 *grasp the opportunity* / ～要害 *scratch where it itches* ❷ catch; capture: ～个小偷 *catch a thief* ❸ grip sb.'s attention: 这出戏一开场就～了观众。*The play gripped the attention of the audience from the moment the curtain rose.*
【抓壮丁】pressgang able-bodied men

zhuǎ

爪 名 claw; talon ——另见 zhǎo
【爪儿】〈口〉❶ paw of a small animal ❷ foot of a utensil: 三～锅 *a pan standing on three feet*
【爪尖儿】pig's trotters; pettitoes
【爪子】〈口〉claw; paw; talon: 猫～ *a cat's paws* / 鹰～ *an eagle's talons*

zhuāi

拽 动〈方〉fling; throw; hurl: 把皮球～出去 *fling the ball out* ——另见 zhuài

zhuǎi

跩 动〈方〉waddle: 鸭子走起路来一～一～的。

Ducks waddle.

zhuài

拽 动 pull; drag; haul: 一把～住不放 *catch hold of sb. or sth. and not let go* ——另见 zhuāi

zhuān

专 Ⅰ 形 for a particular person, occasion, purpose, etc.; focussed on one thing; special: 心不～ *not concentrate (on any one thing)* / ～项贷款 *special-purpose loans* Ⅱ 动 monopolize: 专制

【专案】special case for investigation; case ◇ ～材料 material connected with a case; dossier; ～人员 person engaged in the examination of a case; ～组 special group for the examination of a case

【专长】speciality; special skill or knowledge: 学有～ *have specialized knowledge of a subject; be expert in a special field of study*

【专场】special performance; show intended for a limited audience: 相声～ *a performance of comic dialogues* / 学生～ *a special show for students*

【专车】a special train or car

【专诚】for a particular purpose; specially: ～拜访 *pay a special visit to sb.*

【专程】special trip: ～赴广州迎接贵宾 *make a special trip to Guangzhou to welcome the honoured guests*

【专电】special dispatch (sent by a reporter to a newspaper)

【专断】make an arbitrary decision; act arbitrarily

【专访】exclusive interview on a specific topic

【专攻】specialize in; do special research on: 他～空间技术。*He specializes in space technology.*

【专柜】special counter in shop (for specific products)

【专号】special issue (of a periodical): 小说～ *a fiction issue*

【专横】imperious; peremptory; domineering ◇ ～跋扈 imperious and despotic; arrogant and domineering

【专机】❶ special plane ❷ private plane

【专家】expert; specialist: 水稻～ *expert in rice-growing* / 眼科～ *ophthalmologist; eye specialist*; ◇ ～门诊 outpatient consultation by a specialist; ～系统 [计] expert system

【专刊】❶ special issue or column ❷ monograph

【专科】❶ special field of study; specialized subject; specialty ❷ 同〖专科学校〗◇ ～学校 college for professional training; training school; ～医生 (medical) specialist

【专控商品】controlled commodities (commodities controlled by the government): 这种汽车属～。*These kinds of automobiles are under special government control.*

【专款】special fund: ～专用 *earmark a fund for its specified purpose only*

【专栏】special column: 书评～ *book review column; book reviews* / 评论～ *opinion column; opion* ◇ ～作家 columnist

【专利】patent: ～品 *patent; patented article* ◇ ～法 patent law; ～费 patent fee; ～技术 patent technology; ～局 patent bureau; ～配方 patented formula; ～权 patent right; patent; ～申请 patent application; ～税 patent tax

【专列】(〈略〉全称为'专门列车') a special train; chartered trains for special uses: 运输煤炭的～ *special train for the transportation of coal*

【专卖】exclusive possession of the trade in some commodity; monopoly ◇ ～店 exclusive agency; franchised store

【专门】special; specialized: ～研究化学 *specialize in chemistry* ◇ ～机构 special agency; special organ; ～人材 people with professional skill; specialized personnel; ～人民法院 special people's court; ～术语 technical terms; nomenclature; ～知识 specialized knowledge; expertise; technical know-how

【专名】proper name

【专名号】a line under or beside a word to show that it is a proper noun (e.g. 西安, 诸葛亮)

【专权】arrogate all powers to oneself; monopolize power

【专人】person specially assigned for a task or job: 这项工作一定要有～负责。*Someone must be put in charge of the work.*

【专任】full-time; regular: ～教员 *full-time teacher*

【专属】exclusive ◇ ～经济区 exclusive economic zone; ～渔区 exclusive fishing zone; ～主权 exclusive sovereignty

【专题】special subject; special topic ◇ ～报告 report (or lecture) on a special topic; ～调查 investigation of a special subject; ～讨论 seminar; ～研究 monographic study; ～研讨会 symposium; ～著作 monograph; treatise

【专题广告片】informercial

【专线】❶ special railway line ❷ special telephone line; line for special use

【专项】assigned (to a use); dedicated; specialized: 国家～储备粮 *assigned national grain reserve* / ～训练 *specialized training* / ～资金 *dedicated fund*

【专心】concentrate one's attention; be absorbed: 学习必须～。*Study requires undivided attention.* ◇ ～致志 wholly absorbed; with single-hearted devotion

【专修】specialize in: ～数学 *specialize in mathematics* ◇ ～科 special (training) course

【专业】❶ special field of study; specialized subject; speciality; discipline: 该大学有 12 个系, 41 个～。*The university has 12 departments with 41 specialities.* ❷ specialized trade or profession; special line: 提供～服务 *offer professional service* ◇ ～队伍 professional contingent; ～户 a rural family that goes in for a special kind of production; specialized household; ～课 specialized course; ～人员 personnel in a specific field; ～生产会议 a conference on specialized trades; ～学校 vocational school; specialized school; ～银行 specialized bank; ～知识 professional knowledge

【专一】single-minded; concentrated: 心思～ *with concentrated attention* / 爱情～ *be constant in love*

【专营】exclusive sale rights; monopoly under exclusive government control: 化肥、农药实行～ *chemicals and pesticides sold by designated dealers*

【专用】for a special purpose: ～车床 *special-purpose lathe* / ～电话 *telephone for special use*

【专有】related to a particular person or thing: ～名词 *technical term; nomenclature*

【专员】❶ assistant director; (administrative) commissioner: 礼宾司～ *an assistant director of the Protocol Department* / 商务～ *commercial attaché* ❷ person specially assigned for a job

【专责】specific responsibility

【专政】dictatorship

【专政机关】organ of dictatorship

【专职】❶ sole duty; specific duty ❷ full-time: 他是工会的～干部。*He is a full-time cadre of the trade union.*

【专制】❶ autocracy ❷ autocratic; despotic: ～帝王 *autocratic monarch; despotic emperor* ◇ ～君主 autocrat; ～政府 autocratic government; ～政体 autocracy

【专注】concentrate one's attention on; be absorbed in; devote one's mind to: 心神～ *wholly absorbed; with single-hearted devotion*

【专著】monograph; treatise; a book on a special subject: 这是一本有关计算机的～。*This is a book about computers.*

砖 名 ❶ brick: ～房 *brick house* / ～墙 *brick wall* ❷ sth. shaped like a brick: 茶砖 / 煤砖

【砖茶】brick tea

【砖厂】brickfield; brickyard

【砖雕】carved brick; brick carving: 精制的室外～装饰 *ornamented on the exterior with finely carved bricks*

【砖红壤】laterite

【砖红壤性土】lateritic soil

【砖坯】unfired brick

【砖头】(zhuāntóu) fragment of a brick

【砖头】(zhuāntou)〈方〉brick

【砖窑】brickkiln

zhuǎn

转 动 ❶ turn; shift; change: ～败为胜 *turn defeat into victory* / ～弱为强 *transform (or grow) from weak to strong* / 晴～多云 *change from fine to cloudy; clear to cloudy* / 她～过头来和我说话。*She spoke to me over her shoulder.* ❷ pass on; transfer: 这封信请你～给他。*Please pass the letter on to him.* / 把她的邮件～寄到她的新地址 *forward her mail to her new address* ——另见 zhuàn

【转氨基酶】(又作'转氨酶') glutamic-pyruvic transaminase (GPT)

【转包】(又作'分包') subcontract: ～合同 *subcontract* / 这项工程已～给一家建筑公司。*The project has been subcontracted to a construction company.*

【转败为胜】turn defeat into victory

【转变】change; transform: ～立场 *change one's stand; shift one's ground* / 经过多次批评他仍无～。*He remains unrepentant after repeated criticism.* ◇ ～政府职能 transform the governmental function

【转播】relay (a radio or TV broadcast): ～台 *relay station*

【转产】(of a factory) switch to the manufacture of another line of products; change the line of production

【转车】change trains or buses; transfer to another train or bus

【转船】change to another ship; transship

【转达】pass on; convey; communicate: 请向他～我的问候。*Please give him my regards.*

【转道】make a detour; go by way of

【转递】pass on; transmit: 这信就由我～给他吧。*I'll pass on this letter to him.*

【转调】❶［音］modulation: 乐曲在这里～了。*At this point the music modulates.* ❷ (of a government employee, etc.) be transferred to another post; transfer: 办理人事～手续 *go through personnel transfer procedures*

【转动】(zhuǎndòng) turn; move; turn round: ～手腕子 *flex one's wrist* / 水龙头转不动。*The tap's stuck.* ——另见 zhuàndòng

【转发】transmit: 此件～全国。*This document is to be transmitted throughout the country.*

【转法】［军］facing

【转干】(of workers) be promoted to the position of a cadre (usu. administrative position)

【转岗】transfer (or switch) to another job; change jobs

【转港】route through one port to another

【转告】pass on (word); communicate; transmit: 他把这消息～了他的姐姐。*He passed on the news to his sister.*

【转关系】transfer the registration of Party membership, etc. from one unit to another

【转轨】❶〈字〉shift from one track to another ❷〈喻〉(of economy, production, etc.) undergo a fundamental change: ～经济 *economy in transition*

【转行】change profession; change jobs: 他是演员～后才任导演的。*He gave up his acting to become a director.*

【转化】change; transform: 将先进技术～为生产力

turn advanced technology into productive force

【转换】change; transform: ～方向 *change direction* / ～话题 *change the subject of conversation; switch the conversation to another subject* ◇ ～开关 change-over switch

【转机】❶ a favourable turn; a turn for the better: 他的病有了～。*The patient has taken a turn for the better.* or *His condition is improving.* ❷ change plane

【转基因】［生］transgenetic ◇ ～食品 genetically modified food

【转嫁】❶（of women）marry again; remarry ❷ shift; transfer: 把责任～给他人 *shift off one's responsibility; put the blame on someone else*

【转交】pass on; transmit: 来信请由中国大使馆～。*Address my mail care of（or c/o）the Chinese Embassy.*

【转角】street corner; corner

【转接器】adapter

【转口】transit: ～货物 *transit goods* / ～贸易 *entrepôt trade*

【转脸】❶ turn one's face ❷ in no time; in the twinkling of an eye: 他刚才还在这儿，怎么～就不见了？*He was here just now. How come he disappeared in a wink?*

【转录】make a copy of a pre-recorded cassette tape or videotape; copy; dub

【转卖】resell

【转念】reconsider and give up an idea; think better of: 他刚想开口，但一～，又不说了。*He was just going to speak when he thought better of it.*

【转让】transfer the ownership of; make over: 技术～ *technology transfer* ◇ ～人［法］assignor

【转入】change over to; shift to; switch to: ～地下 *go underground* / ～正常 *return to normal*

【转身】（of a person）turn round; face about

【转生】［宗］（佛教）reincarnation; transmigration

【转世】同〖转生〗

【转手】❶ pass on: 你就直接交给他，不必要我～了。*Give it directly to him; there is no need to do it through me.* ❷ sell what one has bought

【转述】report; relate sth. as told by another: 我只是～他的话。*I am merely reporting what he said.*

【转瞬】in the twinkling of an eye; in an instant; in a flash: ～间他就到了。*He arrived in the twinkling of an eye.*

【转送】❶ pass on; transmit on ❷ make a present of what one has been given

【转体】［体］turn; twist ◇ ～动作 rotational movement; ～两周 double turn; ～跳 turning leap; turning jump; ～跳水 twist dive

【转头】❶（of a person）turn round; face about ❷（of a car, etc.）make a U-turn ❸ repent

【转托】ask someone else to do what is asked of one: 你让我办的事，我已～老张了。*I've asked Lao Zhang to take care of the matter you spoke to me about.*

【转弯】turn a corner; make a turn: 邮局一～儿就是。*The post office is just round（or right around）the corner.* / 右～走！（*word of command*）*Right wheel!*（*to a rank*）*Right turn march!* or *Column right march!*（*to a column*）/ 给他们一个～的余地 *give them some leeway*

【转弯抹角】❶ full of twists and turns: 我们～地走了好一会才找到那个地方。*We had to take a tortuous route before we got to the place.* ❷ beat about the bush; speak in a roundabout way: 有什么意见就痛快说，别这么～的。*Say what you have to say and don't beat about the bush.*

【转弯子】❶ beat about the bush; speak in a roundabout way ❷ change one's position or get one's thinking straightened out

【转危为安】take a turn for the better and be out of danger; pull through

【转系】（of a college student）transfer from one department to another: 从物理系转经济系 *change（or switch）one's major from physics to economics*

【转向】(zhuǎnxiàng) ❶ change direction: ～装置 *steering gear* ❷ change one's political stand ◇ ～架 bogie（fitted under a railway carriage）——另见 zhuànxiàng

【转型】transformation; change the mode of production: ～期经济 *economy in transition*

【转学】（of a student）transfer from one school to another

【转眼】in the twinkling of an eye; in an instant; in a flash: 这孩子一～就不见了。*The child disappeared in the twinkling of an eye.* / ～间，一个月就过去了。*A month passed before we knew it.*

【转业】❶（of an armyman）be transferred to civilian work: ～军人 *armyman transferred to civilian work* / ～费 *decommission pay; military severance pay* ❷（of laid-off worker）transfer to a new occupation; move to a new area: ～培训 *retraining（for employment in another field）*

【转移】❶ shift; transfer; divert: ～兵力 *shift forces; transfer troops* / ～视线 *divert sb.'s attention* / ～目标 *distract people's attention from sth. or sb.* ❷ change; transform: ～社会风气 *change prevalent social customs* ❸［医］metastasis: 癌～ *the metastasis of a carcinoma* / ～性癌 *metastatic carcinoma*

【转义】transferred meaning（a collective name for extended meaning and metaphorical meaning）

【转引】quote from a secondary source

【转院】（of a patient）transfer from one hospital to another

【转运】❶ have a change of luck; luck turns in one's favour ❷ transport; transfer; transship: ～公司 *transport company; forwarding agency* / ～站 *transfer post*

【转韵】change rhyme（in a classic poem）

【转载】reprint sth. that has been published elsewhere; reprint ◇ ～权 right of reprint

【转赠】make a present of what one has been given

【转战】fight in one place after another

【转账】transfer accounts: ～凭单 *transfer docu-*

ment / 通过银行～结算 *make settlement by means of transfer between bank accounts*

【转折】❶ a turn in the course of events：戏剧性的～ *a dramatic turn* ❷ transition (of an essay)

【转折点】turning point

【转辙器】[铁路] switch

【转正】❶ (of a probationary member of the Communist Party of China) become a full member after completion of the probationary period ❷ (of a temporary worker) become a regular worker

【转注】[语] mutually explanatory or synonymous characters, e. g. 老 (old age) and 考 (long life, aged)—one of the six categories of Chinese characters (六书)

【转租】sublet；sublease

zhuàn

传 名 ❶ commentaries on classics：《左～》*The Zuo Commentary* (*on The Spring and Autumn Annals*) ❷ biography：名人～ *biographies of famous people* /《贝多芬～》*The Life of Beethoven* ❸ story or novel (usu. used in titles)：《白蛇～》*The Story of the White Snake* /《水浒～》*Water Margin or The Outlaws of the Marsh* /《新儿女英雄～》*Daughters and Sons*

【传记】biography

【传略】brief biography；biographical sketch

转 Ⅰ 动 turn；revolve；rotate：地球绕着太阳～。*The earth revolves round the sun*. / 你在这儿～来～去干什么？*What are you hanging around here for*？Ⅱ 量 revolution：每分钟2,000～ *2,000 revolutions per minute*；*2,000 r. p. m*. ——另见 zhuǎn

【转笔刀】pencil sharpener

【转碟】[杂] plate-spinning

【转动】(zhuàndòng) turn；revolve；rotate：经过修理，机器又～起来了。*The machine started working again after being put right*. ——另见 zhuǎndòng

【转筋】[中] ❶ have a cramp (esp. in the leg)；have a twisted muscle ❷ convulsion；spasm

【转炉】[冶] converter：～钢 *converter steel* / ～炼钢法 *converting process*

【转轮手枪】revolver

【转门】revolving door

【转盘】❶ turntable (as of a record player) ❷ sports giant stride ❸ [杂] disc-spinning ❹ petroleum rotary table：～速度 *rotary speed*

【转数】[机] revolution：每分钟～ *revolutions per minute* (*r. p. m.*) / 额定～ *rated revolution*

【转速】rotational speed ◇ ～计 tachometer

【转台】revolving stage

【转向】(zhuànxiàng) lose one's bearings；get lost：房子真大，我在里面简直转了向。*It was such a huge house that I got lost in it*. ——另见 zhuǎnxiàng

【转椅】swivel chair；revolving chair

【转悠】(又作'转游')〈口〉❶ turn；move from side to side：他眼珠一～就想出个主意。*He rolled his eyes and hit upon an idea*. ❷ stroll；saunter；take a leisurely walk：星期天我上街～了一下。*I strolled around the streets on Sunday*.

【转轴】axle

【转转】〈口〉take a short walk；go for a stroll：他要我陪他一块到厂里～。*He asked me to show him round the plant*.

【转子】rotor：～发动机 *Wankel engine*；*Wankel*

赚 Ⅰ 动 ❶ make a profit；gain：这家商行做出口生意～得可多了。*The firm made large profits from exports*. ❷〈方〉earn (money) Ⅱ 名〈口〉profit

【赚钱】make money；make a profit：～生意 *a profitable business*；*a paying proposition* (*or concern*)

【赚头】〈口〉profit

撰 动 write；compose：为报纸～稿 *write articles for a newspaper*

【撰述】❶ write；compile ❷ book；work

【撰文】write an article

【撰写】write (usu. short articles)：～评论文章 *write a commentary*

【撰著】write；compose

篆 Ⅰ 名 ❶ seal character (a style of Chinese calligraphy) ❷ seal Ⅱ 动 inscribe in such style：～额 *inscribe seal characters at the top of a tablet*

【篆刻】seal cutting

【篆书】seal character (a style of Chinese calligraphy, often used on seals)

【篆字】同〖篆书〗

zhuāng

妆 Ⅰ 动 apply makeup；make up：梳妆 Ⅱ 名 ❶ woman's personal adornments ❷ trousseau；dowry

【妆扮】dress up；attire；deck out

【妆点】decorate；dress up；deck out

【妆奁】trousseau；dowry

【妆饰】❶ adorn；dress up；deck out ❷ makeup

【妆梳】make up and dress up

【妆台】dressing table

庄 Ⅰ 名 ❶ village：王家～ *Wangjiazhuang Village* ❷ manor：庄园 ❸ a place of business：钱庄 ❹ banker (in a gambling game)：是谁的～？*Who's the banker*？Ⅱ 形 serious；grave；sedate：端庄

【庄户】peasant household：～人 *peasant* / ～人家 *peasant family*

【庄家】banker (in a gambling game)

【庄稼】crops：种～ *grow* (*or plant*) *crops* / 晚～

late crops ◇ ～地〈口〉cropland；fields；～汉〈口〉farmer；peasant；～活儿〈口〉farm work；～人〈口〉peasant；farmer

【庄严】solemn；dignified；stately：～隆重的场面 *a solemn, grand occasion* / ～地声明 *solemnly declare* / 态度～ *dignified in manner*

【庄园】manor

【庄重】serious；grave；solemn；sedate：法官神情分外～。*The judge looked grave.* / 他讲话语调～。*He spoke in a solemn tone.*

【庄子】〈口〉village；hamlet：他是我们～里的人。*He's one of our fellow villagers.*

桩 Ⅰ 名 stake；pile：木～ *wood stake* / 桥～ *bridge stake* Ⅱ 量 一～大事 *an important matter* / 一～买卖 *a business transaction*

【桩砦】［军］post obstacles

【桩子】stake；pile

装 Ⅰ 动 ❶ dress up；attire；deck；play the part (or role) of；act：她～老大娘真像。*She acted an old woman and really looked the part.* ❷ pretend；feign；make believe：她不是真哭，是～的。*She wasn't really crying；she was only pretending.* / ～出一副可怜相 *assume a pitiable look* / 不要不懂～懂。*Don't pretend to know what you don't know.* ❸ load；pack；hold：～车 *load a truck (or cart)* / ～箱 *pack a box；put sth. in a crate；crate* ❹ install；fit；assemble：给门～上锁 *fit a lock on the door* / ～个无线电 *assemble a radio set* Ⅱ 名 ❶ outfit；clothing：滑雪～ *skiing suits* ❷ stage makeup and costume：卸装

【装扮】❶ dress up；attire；deck out ❷ disguise；masquerade：～成朋友的敌人是最危险的。*The most dangerous enemy is one who disguises himself as a friend.*

【装备】❶ equip；fit out：～新式武器 *be equipped with modern weapons* ❷ equipment；outfit：军事～ *military equipment*

【装裱】mount (a picture, etc.)

【装病】pretend sickness；feign illness；malinger：他是～。*His illness is feigned.*

【装舱】stow the hold (with cargo)

【装船】shipment：分批～ *partial shipment*

【装点】decorate；dress；deck：大厅里～着花彩。*The hall was decorated with festoons.*

【装订】binding；bookbinding：布面～ *clothbound* / 皮面～ *bound in leather* / 硬面～ *hardbound* / ～车间 *bookbindery；bindery* / ～工人 *bookbinder* / ～机 *bookbinding machine；binding machinery*

【装疯卖傻】feign madness and act like an idiot

【装糊涂】pretend not to know；feign ignorance；play the fool

【装潢】(又作'装璜') ❶ mount (a picture, etc.)；decorate；dress ❷ decoration；mounting；packaging ◇ ～门面 do window dressing；put up a facade；keep up appearances

【装幌子】put up a front；maintain an outward show；keep up appearances

【装货】load (cargo) ◇ ～单 shipping order；～港 port of shipment；port of loading

【装机容量】［电］installed capacity

【装甲】❶ plate armour ❷ armoured：～列车 *armoured train* ◇ ～兵 armoured force (or troops)；～车 armoured car；armoured vehicle；～舰 ironclad (a warship)；～师 armoured division；～输送车 armoured carrier

【装假】pretend；feign；make believe

【装殓】dress and lay a corpse in a coffin

【装料】❶ feed (a machine) ❷［冶］loading；charging

【装聋作哑】pretend to be deaf and dumb；feign ignorance

【装门面】put up a front；maintain an outward show；keep up appearances

【装模作样】be affected；attitudinize；put on an act；behave in an affected way

【装配】assemble；fit together ◇ ～车间 assembly shop；fitting shop；～工 assembler；fitter；～件 assembly parts；～线 assembly line

【装腔】behave affectedly；be artificial ◇ ～作势 be affected or pretentious；strike a pose；put on airs

【装傻】act dumb；pretend not to know；pretend to be naive or stupid

【装设】install；fix；fit：～电灯 *install electric lights* / ～发动机 *install an engine*

【装神弄鬼】purposely make a mystery of simple things；be deliberately mystifying

【装饰】decorate；adorn；ornament；deck：～图案 *decorative pattern* ◇ ～布 upholstery fabrics；～品 ornament；～艺术 art deco；～音［音］grace note；grace；ornament

【装束】❶ dress；attire ❷〈书〉pack up (for a journey)

【装睡】pretend sleep；sham sleep

【装死】feign death；sham dead

【装蒜】〈口〉pretend not to know；feign ignorance

【装孙子】〈方〉❶ pretend to be helpless and miserable ❷ pretend not to know；feign ignorance

【装填】［军］load；ram

【装相】pretend；put on an act

【装卸】❶ load and unload：文明(野蛮)～ *careful (careless) loading and unloading* ❷ assemble and disassemble：他会～自行车。*He can take a bicycle apart and put it back again.* ◇ ～工 loader；stevedore；～时间 lay day

【装修】fit up (a house, etc.)：～门面 *fit up the front of a shop*

【装样子】put on an act；do sth. for appearance sake：这个选手看来沉着自信，其实是在～。*The player appeared calm and confident but it was just an act.*

【装药】［军］powder charge；filling

【装运】load and transport；ship：～货物 *ship cargo*

【装载】loading：～量 *loading capacity*

【装帧】binding and layout (of a book, magazine, etc.): 一本～精美的书 *a beautifully designed and bound book*

【装置】❶ install; fit: 仪器已经～好了。*The instrument has been installed.* ❷ installation; unit; device; plant ◇ 防护～ protective equipment; 减震～ damping device; 雷达～ radar installation; 磨煤～ coal-pulverizing plant; 配电～ power distribution unit; 自停～ automatic stop arrangement

【装作】pretend to be; disguise as: ～睡着了 *pretend to be asleep* / ～放羊的 *be disguised as a shepherd*

zhuàng

壮 Ⅰ 形 ❶ strong; robust: 他身体很～。*He is sturdy.* or *He has a strong physique.* ❷ magnificent; grand: 雄壮 Ⅱ 动 strengthen; make better: ～声势 *to lend impetus and strength; to make it appear more vigorous and impressive* / 以～观瞻 (*deck out a place*) *to make it more sightly*

【壮大】❶ grow in strength; expand; strengthen: 第三世界的～ *the growing strength of the Third World* ❷ thick and strong; bulky: 手脚～ *have thick and strong arms and legs*

【壮胆】build up sb.'s courage; boost sb.'s courage.

【壮丁】〈旧〉able-bodied man (subject to conscription)

【壮工】unskilled labourer

【壮观】grand (or magnificent) sight

【壮举】magnificent feat; heroic undertaking: 史无前例的～ *an unparalleled feat*

【壮阔】vast; grand; magnificent; grandiose: 规模～ *grand in scale*

【壮劳力】❶ strong labour power ❷ an able-bodied adult (esp. for farming)

【壮丽】majestic; magnificent; glorious: 一曲～的凯歌 *a stirring song of victory* / 山河～ *a land of glories*

【壮烈】heroic; brave: ～牺牲 *heroically give one's life; die a hero's death*

【壮美】majestic; magnificent

【壮苗】strong sprout

【壮年】the more robust years of a person's life (between thirty and fifty); prime of life

【壮士】brave man; heroic man; hero; warrior

【壮实】sturdy; robust: 一个～的小伙子 *a sturdy young chap*

【壮伟】grand; lofty; magnificent: ～的山峰 *lofty mountain peak*

【壮志】great aspiration; lofty ideal ◇ ～凌云 with soaring (or high) aspirations; ～未酬 with one's lofty aspirations unrealized

【壮族】the Zhuang (Chuang) ethnic group

状 名 ❶ form; shape: 其～不一 *of different forms* ❷ state; condition: 现状 ❸ account; record ❹ written complaint; plaint: 告状 ❺ certificate: 奖状

【状词】written complaint; plaint; indictment

【状况】condition; state; state of affairs: 健康～ *physical condition; state of health; health*

【状貌】appearance; form

【状态】state; condition; state of affairs: 固体～ *solid state* / 心理～ *state of mind / psychology* / 无组织～ *disorganized state of affairs* ◇ ～图 [冶] state diagram

【状语】[语] adverbial modifier; adverbial

【状元】❶ Number One Scholar, title conferred on the one who came first in the highest imperial examination ❷ the very best (in any field): 养鸡"～" *a champion chicken-raiser*

【状纸】〈旧〉official form for filing a lawsuit

【状子】〈口〉written complaint; plaint; indictment

撞 动 ❶ bump against; run into; strike; collide: ～墙 *bump against a wall* / ～钟 *toll* (*or strike*) *a bell* / 一辆卡车～坏了我们的汽车。*A lorry ran into our car and damaged it.* ❷ meet by chance; bump into; run into: 我不想见他,偏～上他了。*I tried to avoid him, but it was just my luck to bump into him.* ❸ rush; dash; barge: 横冲直撞 ❹ take one's chance: ～运气 *try one's luck; take a chance*

【撞车】❶ collision of vehicles ❷ clash of opinions or interests ❸ 〈口〉(of two meetings, etc.) clash: 这两个会～了。*The two meetings clash.*

【撞击】ram; dash against; strike: 波浪～着岩石。*The breakers dashed on the rocks.*

【撞见】meet or discover by chance; run across; catch sb. in the act

【撞骗】look about for a chance to swindle; swindle

【撞锁】❶ spring lock ❷ 〈口〉find that sb. is not home: 我昨儿晚上去你家串门,没想到～了。*I went to your place last night and found the door locked.*

【撞针】firing pin (in a firearm)

幢 量 〈方〉: 一～三层的楼房 *a three-storeyed building* ——另见 chuáng

zhuī

追 动 ❶ chase (or run) after; pursue: ～上他 *catch up with him* / 把比分～到 10 比 11 *close the margin to* 10－11; *catch up and bring the score to* 10－11 ❷ court (a woman); woo ❸ trace; look into; get to the bottom of: 他们决心一定要把这事的根底～出来。*They were determined to get to the bottom of the matter.* / ～穷根 *trace the root cause of one's poverty* ❹ seek; go after: 追名逐利 ❺ recall; reminisce ❻ do retroactively; act posthumously: ～授一级战斗英雄称号 *be posthumously awarded the title of*

Combat Hero Class 1
【追奔逐北】(又作'追亡逐北') give chase to a routed enemy
【追本溯源】(又作'追本穷源') trace to its source; get to the root of the matter
【追逼】❶ pursue closely (a fleeing enemy) ❷ press for (repayment); extort (a confession)
【追兵】pursuing troops
【追补】❶ 同〖追加〗❷ make up; remedy; make good: 不可～的损失 *an irretrievable loss*
【追捕】pursue and capture: ～逃犯 *pursue and capture an escaped prisoner*
【追查】investigate; trace; find out: ～事故原因 *investigate the causes of an accident*
【追悼】mourn over a person's death
【追悼会】memorial meeting
【追访】make a follow-up visit: 做原病人的～工作 *follow-up visits on former patients*
【追肥】top application; topdressing
【追风逐电】chase after wind and lightning—(of a train, etc.) run swiftly
【追赶】quicken one's pace to catch up; run after; pursue: ～世界先进水平 *measure up to advanced world levels*
【追根】get to the root (or bottom) of sth.: 这件事一定得～究底。*We must get to the root of the matter.*
【追怀】call to mind; recall; reminisce: ～往事 *reminisce about the old days*
【追回】(又作'追还') recover: ～赃物 *recover stolen goods*
【追悔】repent; regret: ～莫及 *too late to repent*
【追击】pursue and attack; follow up: ～敌人 *pursue and attack the enemy* / 战略～ *strategic pursuit* / ～战 *warfare of pursuit and attack*
【追缉】pursue and capture (an escaped criminal)
【追加】add to (the original amount): ～预算 *supplement a budget; make a supplementary budget* / ～税 *additional tax* ◇ ～保险 supplementary insurance; ～条款 rider clause; supplemental clause
【追歼】pursue and wipe out: ～残敌 *pursue and wipe out the remnants of the enemy forces*
【追剿】pursue and wipe out: ～队 *pursuit detachment*
【追缴】❶ demand payment (of tax arrears, etc.): ～税款 *demand tax arrears* ❷ recover: 犯罪分子非法所得的一切财物,应当予以～。*All articles of property illegally obtained by the criminal element shall be recovered.*
【追究】look into; find out; investigate: ～事故的责任 *investigate and affix the responsibility for an accident; find out who is to blame for an accident*
【追名逐利】seek (or be after) fame and wealth
【追求】❶ seek; pursue: ～真理 *seek truth; be in pursuit of truth* / ～名誉地位 *be after fame and position* / ～利润 *seek profits* ❷ court (a woman); woo
【追认】❶ subsequently confirm or endorse; recognize retroactively: ～一项法令 *subsequently endorse a decree* ❷ admit or confer posthumously: ～为共产党员 *be posthumously admitted as a member of the Communist Party*
【追授】confer a posthumous honor on: 老郭去世后,被～为"人民的好医生"的光荣称号。*Lao Guo was posthumously given the title "People's Doctor".*
【追述】*tell about the past; relate; recount*
【追诉】[法] *prosecute*
【追溯】trace back to; date from: 这个传说可以～到遥远的过去。*The legend goes (or can be traced) back to remote antiquity.*
【追随】follow: ～不舍 *follow sb. closely* / ～者 *follower; adherent; following*
【追索】❶ seek; pursue; explore ❷ demand; exact; extort: ～一笔旧账 *demand payment of an old debt* ◇ ～办法 means of recourse; ～财产者 recoverer; ～权 recourse; right of recourse; ～诉讼 recovery action
【追讨】demand payment of an old debt
【追问】(又作'追询') question closely; make a detailed inquiry; examine minutely: ～事实真相 *make detailed inquiries about the facts*
【追叙】❶ tell about the past; relate; recount ❷ narration of earlier episodes; flashback
【追寻】pursue; search; track down
【追询】inquire persistently: 事已至此,何必再～呢。*What's done is done, why keep on asking?*
【追忆】recollect; recall; look back: ～往事,历历在目。*As I look back, scenes of the past leap before my eyes.* / 年代太久,难以～。*It happened ages ago and I can't call it to mind.*
【追赃】order the return of stolen money or goods; recover stolen money or goods; make sb. disgorge the spoils
【追赠】confer posthumously (a title)
【追债】claim repayment of a debt: 他在广州办起了首家～公司。*He started the first claims company in Guangzhou.*
【追逐】❶ pursue; chase ❷ seek; quest: ～高额利润 *seek exorbitant profits*
【追踪】follow the trail of; track; trace

椎 名 vertebra: 脊椎
【椎骨】vertebra
【椎间盘】[生理] intervertebral disc ◇ ～突出症 protrusion of the intervertebral disc

锥 Ⅰ 名 ❶ awl ❷ anything shaped like an awl ❸ [数] cone Ⅱ 动 bore; drill: ～孔 *make a hole with an awl*
【锥处囊中】an awl in a bag—talent will reveal itself despite temporary obscurity
【锥刀之末】petty profits; small gains
【锥度】❶ coning; taper: ～规 *taper gauge* ❷ taper ratio
【锥栗】[植] chinquapin

【锥面】❶［数］conical surface ❷［矿］pyramidal face
【锥形】conical contour; cone; taper; pyramid
【锥指】〈书〉have a meagre knowledge of sth.; have a limited view of sth.
【锥子】awl

zhuì

坠 Ⅰ 动 ❶ fall; drop: ～马 *fall off a horse* / 飞机～入海中。*The plane crashed into the sea.* ❷ weigh down: 苹果把树枝～得弯弯的。*The branches were bending down with the weight of the apples.* or *The apples weighed the branches down.* Ⅱ 名 weight; a hanging object: 扇坠
【坠地】〈书〉(of a child) be born
【坠毁】(of a plane, etc.) fall and break; crash: 飞机在山中～。*The plane crashed in the mountains.*
【坠楼】❶ fall off a building ❷ commit suicide by jumping off a building
【坠落】fall; drop
【坠子】〈方〉❶ weight; plummet; pendant ❷ ear pendant

缀 动 ❶ sew; stitch: 你的袖子扯破了,我给你～上两针。*Your sleeve's torn. I'll put in a few stitches for you.* ❷ put words together correctly; compose: ～字成文 *put words together to produce a piece of writing* ❸ embellish; decorate: 天上～满了星星。*The sky was studded with twinkling stars.*
【缀合】put together; make up; compose
【缀辑】compile; edit: ～成书 *compile a book out of various materials*
【缀文】compose an essay; write a composition

惴 形〈书〉anxious and fearful
【惴栗】〈书〉tremble with fear; shudder
【惴惴不安】〈书〉be anxious and fearful; be alarmed; be on tenterhooks

赘 Ⅰ 形 superfluous; redundant: 赘言 Ⅱ 动 ❶ (of a man) go to live in the household of one's in-laws on getting married; (of the bride's parents) gain a son-in-law in such a manner ❷〈方〉be burdensome; be cumbersome: 孩子多了真～人。*It's really burdensome to have many children.*
【赘词】superfluous words; redundancy
【赘瘤】anything superfluous or useless
【赘述】give unnecessary details; say more than is needed: 不必一一～。*It is unnecessary to go into details.*
【赘婿】a son-in-law who lives in the home of his wife's parents
【赘言】❶ give unnecessary details; say more than needed: 不再～。*No more need be said.* ❷ superfluous words; redundancy
【赘疣】❶ wart ❷ anything superfluous or useless

zhūn

谆 形 earnest; sincere: ～嘱 *give earnest exhortations*
【谆谆】earnest and tireless ◇ ～教导 earnestly and tirelessly instruct; ～告诫 repeatedly admonish; tirelessly exhort

zhǔn

准 Ⅰ 动 ❶ allow; grant; permit: ～假两周 *grant sb. two weeks' leave* / 你要求调动工作,～了没有? *Has your request for a transfer been granted?* ❷ in accordance with; follow: ～前例处理 *to be settled by following precedent* Ⅱ 名 standard; norm; criterion: 以此为～ *take this as the standard (or criterion)* Ⅲ 形 ❶ accurate; exact: 投篮不～ *inaccurate shooting (in basketball)* / 这表走得～。*The watch keeps good time.* ❷ quasi-; para-: ～军事组织 *paramilitary organization* / ～单色光 *quasi-monochromatic light* Ⅳ 副 definitely; certainly: 我明天～去。*I'll certainly be there tomorrow.* / 他不～能来。*He'll not possibly come.*
【准儿】certain; sure: 心里有～ *feel sure; know what one is doing*
【准保】certainly; for sure: 你现在给他打电话,他～会来。*He will certainly come if you ring him up now.*
【准备】❶ prepare; get ready: 为会议～文件 *prepare documents for a meeting.* / 作最坏的～ *prepare for the worst* / ～阶段 *preparatory stage* ❷ intend; plan: 今年暑假我～回老家看看。*I intend to visit my native place this summer vacation.*
【准备活动】［体］warming-up exercise; limbering-up exercise
【准不动产】chattel real
【准得】certainly; for sure: 你看这黑云,今天～下雨。*Look at those dark clouds! It's sure to rain today.*
【准定】certainly; for sure: 明天我～来。*I'll certainly come tomorrow.*
【准分子激光】［物］quasi-molecular laser
【准话】definite message or answer: 什么时候定好日子,我再给您个～。*I'll give you a definite answer when we've fixed the date.*
【准将】(U. S. Army, Air Force & Marine Corps) brigadier general; (Brit. Army & Marine Corps) brigadier; (U. S. & Brit. Navy) commodore; (Brit. Air Force) air commodore
【准粒子】［物］quasi-particle
【准平原】paraplain
【准确】accurate; exact; precise: ～度 *degree of accuracy; accuracy* / ～性 *accuracy*

【准绳】criterion; yardstick: 以事实为根据,以法律为～ *take facts as the basis and the law as the criterion*
【准时】punctual; on time; on schedule: ～起飞 *take off at the scheduled time* / 请～出席。*Please be punctual.* or *You are requested to come on time.*
【准头】〈口〉accuracy (in speech, marksmanship, etc.): 枪法挺有～ *shoot well*; *be a good shot* / 他说话没有～。*You can't depend on what he says.*
【准尉】warrant officer ——另见〖一级准尉〗
【准信】definite message or answer: 你什么时候来,先给我个～。*Please let me know in advance exactly when you are coming.*
【准星】front sight (of a gun)
【准行】〈口〉there won't be any problem: 这事你去跟他说～。*If you go and talk to him there won't be any problem about his agreeing.*
【准许】permit; allow
【准予】grant; approve; permit: ～入境 *allow sb. to enter the country* / ～休假 *grant a leave*
【准则】norm; standard; criterion: 行为～ *code of conduct* / 外交～ *diplomatic norms* / 国际法的起码～ *elementary requirements of international law* / 热力学～ *thermodynamic criterion*
【准直】[物] collimation ◇ ～透镜 collimating lens; ～仪 collimator

zhuō

拙 形 ❶ clumsy; awkward; dull: 手～ *be all thumbs* / ～于言词 *be inarticulate*; *be clumsy in expressing oneself* ❷〈谦〉my: 拙荆
【拙笨】clumsy; dull; unskilful: 口齿～ *clumsy of speech*; *inarticulate*
【拙笔】〈谦〉my (poor) writing or painting
【拙稿】〈谦〉my (poor) writing; my (poor) work
【拙见】〈谦〉my (humble) opinion
【拙荆】〈旧〉〈谦〉my wife
【拙劣】clumsy; inferior: ～表演 *a clumsy performance*; *a bad show* / ～手法 *inferior tactics*; *clumsy trick* / 文笔～ *bad (or poor) writing*
【拙朴】simple and unadorned
【拙涩】clumsy and obscure: 译文～ *clumsy and obscure translation*
【拙直】straightforward and good-natured; simple and frank: 她生性～,待人热诚。*She is natural and warm-hearted.*
【拙著】〈谦〉my (poor) writing; my (poor) work
【拙嘴笨腮】(又作'拙嘴笨舌') clumsy-tongued; inarticulate
【拙作】〈谦〉my (poor) writing, painting, etc.; my (poor) work

捉 动 ❶ clutch; hold; grasp: ～笔 *hold a pen* / ～住不放 *seize hold of sb. or sth. and not let go* ❷ catch; capture: ～贼! *Stop thief!* / 小猫～到一只老鼠。*The little cat caught a rat.*
【捉刀】write (an article, etc.) for sb. else; ghostwrite ◇ ～人 ghostwriter
【捉奸】catch adulterers in the act
【捉襟见肘】when one pulls together one's lapels, one's elbows poke through the sleeves—have too many difficulties (esp. financial) to cope with
【捉迷藏】❶ hide-and-seek; blindman's buff ❷ be tricky and evasive; play hide-and-seek: 你就直说吧,不要跟我～了。*Get straight to the point. Don't beat about the bush.*
【捉摸】(usu. used in the negative) fathom; ascertain: ～不定 *difficult to ascertain*; *unpredictable*; *elusive*
【捉拿】arrest; catch: ～逃犯 *arrest an escaped prisoner* / ～归案 *arrest and bring a criminal to justice*
【捉弄】tease; make fun of; play tricks on

桌 Ⅰ 名 table; desk: 把它搁～上。*Put it on the table.* Ⅱ 量 三～客人 *three tables of guests (at a dinner party)* / 一～菜 *a table of dishes*
【桌布】tablecloth
【桌菜】prepared meals (fresh prepared foods which can be bought and cooked at home)
【桌面】top of a table; tabletop ◇ ～出版系统 desktop publishing (DTP); ～计算机 desktop computer
【桌面上】on the table; aboveboard; in public: ～的话 *polite and unimpeachable remarks* / 把问题摆到～来 *place problems on the table*; *bring problems out into the open*
【桌椅板凳】tables, chairs and benches—household furniture generally
【桌子】table; desk

zhuó

灼 Ⅰ 动 burn; scorch: 灼伤 Ⅱ 形 bright; luminous: 灼亮
【灼急】anxious; worried: ～的神色 *worried look* / 请勿过于～。*Don't be too anxious.*
【灼见】profound view; penetrating view: 真知灼见
【灼烤】burn; bake; scorch: 承受炎炎烈日的～ *exposed to the blazing sun*
【灼亮】bright; shining: ～的灯光 *bright lamplight*
【灼然】quite obvious; fairly clear: ～可见 *perfectly obvious*; *abundantly clear* / ～无疑 *indisputable*; *irrefutable*; *unquestionable*
【灼热】scorching hot
【灼伤】(of fire, acid, etc.) burn
【灼灼】〈书〉shining; brilliant: 目光～ *with keen, sparkling eyes*

卓 形 ❶ tall and erect: ～立 *stand upright* ❷ eminent; outstanding: 卓见
【卓尔不群】stand head and shoulders above all oth-

ers; be preeminent

【卓见】excellent opinion; brilliant idea

【卓绝】unsurpassed; extreme; of the highest degree: 英勇～ *extremely brave*

【卓然】outstanding; splendid; remarkable: 成绩～ *achieve outstanding results*

【卓识】judicious judgment; sagacity

【卓午】〈书〉high noon

【卓异】out of the ordinary; outstanding; unique; preeminent

【卓有成效】fruitful; highly effective: 进行了～的努力 *have made fruitful efforts*

【卓越】outstanding; brilliant; remarkable: ～的成就 *remarkable achievements* / ～的科学家 *a brilliant scientist*

【卓著】distinguished; outstanding; eminent: 该省农业机械化的工作成效～。*That province has achieved outstanding results in farm mechanization.*

茁 形 thriving

【茁壮】healthy and strong; sturdy: 小麦长得很～。*The wheat has grown sturdy.*

【茁壮成长】grow up strong and sturdy

浊 形 ❶ turbid; muddy: ～水 *turbid water* / ～流 *muddy stream* ❷ deep and thick: ～声～气 *in a deep, raucous voice* ❸ chaotic; confused; corrupted: 浊世

【浊点】[化] cloud point

【浊酒】unstrained wine or liquor

【浊气】foul smell

【浊世】❶〈书〉the corrupted world; chaotic times ❷ [宗](佛教) the mortal world

【浊物】〈诋〉absurd creature; insensitive creature; ignoramus

【浊音】[语音] voiced sound

酌 Ⅰ 动 ❶ pour out (wine); drink: 独～ *drink alone* ❷ consider; think over; use one's discretion: 请～加修改。*Make any alterations as you may think fit.* Ⅱ 名 a meal with wine

【酌办】act according to one's judgment; act at one's discretion; do as one thinks fit

【酌定】make a decision as one thinks fit; decide according to one's judgment: ～对策 *work out (or develop) countermeasures*

【酌减】discretionary reduction

【酌量】consider; deliberate; use one's judgment: 这事儿你～着办吧。*You can handle the matter as you think fit.*

【酌情】take into consideration the circumstances; exercise discretion in the light of the circumstances; use one's discretion: ～处理 *settle a matter as one sees fit; act at one's discretion*

【酌予】give sth. as one thinks fit: ～补助 *give some financial assistance*

着 Ⅰ 动 ❶ wear (clothes): 吃～不尽 *have as much food and clothing as one wants* ❷ touch; come into contact with: 附着 ❸ apply; use: 着墨 ❹ send: 请～人前来领取。*Please send someone here for it.* ❺ (used in official documents, expressing peremptory tone): 以上规定,～即施行。*The above regulations are to be enforced immediately.* Ⅱ 名 whereabouts: 无着 ——另见 zhāo; zháo; zhe

【着笔】put (or set) pen to paper; begin to write or paint: 不知如何～ *not know how to begin the writing or the painting*

【着力】put forth effort; exert oneself: ～描写 *concentrate one's efforts on depicting sb. or sth.; take great pains to describe*

【着陆】land; touch down: 飞机就要～了。*The plane is about to land.* or *The plane is going to touch down.* ◇ ～舱 space landing module

【着落】❶ whereabouts: 遗失的行李已经有～了。*The missing luggage has been found.* ❷ assured source: 这笔经费还没有～。*We still don't know where to get the funds from.* ❸ fall to sb.; rest with sb.: 这件事情就～在你身上了。*It falls to you to handle the matter.* ❹〈旧〉settle: ～停当 *all set; settled*

【着墨】apply ink to paper—write or paint: ～不多 *sketchily described or painted*

【着色】put colour on; colour: ～法 *colouring* / ～剂 *colouring agent; colouring material*

【着实】❶ really; indeed: 这孩子～讨人喜欢。*The child is really very cute.* ❷ severely: ～说了他一顿 *give him a good talking-to; lecture him severely*

【着手】put one's hand to; set about: 从调查研究～ *start with investigation and study*

【着先鞭】take precedence; take the lead; get ahead of

【着想】consider (the interests of sb. or sth.): 他是为你～才劝你不要去的。*It was for your good that he advised you not to go.*

【着眼】have sth. in mind; see (or view) from the angle of: ～于未来 *have one's eyes on the future* / 这些措施都～于建立一支庞大的科技队伍。*All these measures are aimed at building a huge contingent of scientists and technicians.* ◇ ～点 starting point; focus of attention; object in mind

【着意】act with care and effort; take pains: ～经营 *manage with diligent care*

【着重】stress; emphasize: ～指出 *emphatically point out* / 这里我想～地讲一个问题。*Here I would like to go into one question in particular.*

【着重号】mark of emphasis (as in 正是他本人)

【着装】❶ put on; wear ❷ clothing, headgear and footwear

啄 动 peck: 小鸡正在～米呢。*The chicks are pecking at the rice.*

【啄木鸟】woodpecker

琢 动 chisel; carve: 翡翠～成的小茶壶 *a small carved jadeite teapot* ——另见 zuó

【琢磨】(zhuómó) ❶ carve and polish (jade) ❷ improve (literary works); polish; refine ——另见 zuómo

镯 名 bracelet: 玉～ *jade bracelet*

【镯子】bracelet: 金～ *gold bracelet*

zī

吱 象 ❶ (of mice) squeak ❷ (of small birds) chirp; peep ——另见 zhī

【吱声】〈方〉utter sth.; make a sound: 我们问他几遍,他都没～。*We asked him several times, but couldn't get a peep out of him.*

孜 (构词成分) 见下

【孜孜】diligent; industrious; hardworking: ～以求 *diligently strive after; assiduously seek*

【孜孜不倦】diligently; assiduously; indefatigably

咨 动 consult; take counsel: 咨询

【咨文】❶〈旧〉official communication (between government offices of equal rank) ❷ report delivered by the head of a government on affairs of state; message: 总统～ *presidential message; president's message*

【咨询】seek advice from; hold counsel with; consult: 进行～服务 *provide consulting service* / 技术～ *technical consultation* / ～机关 *advisory body* / ～委员会 *consultative (or advisory) committee* ◇ ～公司 consulting company; ～热线 helpline

姿 名 ❶ looks; appearance: 姿色 ❷ gesture; carriage; posture: 舞姿

【姿容】looks; appearance: ～秀美 *good-looking; pretty*

【姿色】good looks (of a woman): 略有几分～ *be rather good-looking*

【姿势】posture; gesture: 直立的～ *an erect posture* / ～优美 *have a graceful carriage*

【姿态】❶ posture; carriage: 各种不同～的泥塑 *clay figures in various postures* ❷ attitude; pose: 以一个普通劳动者的～出现 (*of a senior cadre*) *appear among the masses as an ordinary worker*

资 Ⅰ 名 ❶ money; expenses: 投资 ❷ endowment; natural ability: 天资 ❸ qualifications; record of service: 年资 Ⅱ 动 ❶ subsidize; support: 资助 ❷ provide; supply: 可～对比 *provide a contrast*

【资本】❶ capital: ～的周转 *turnover of capital* / ～输出 *export of capital* / ～投入 *capital input* ❷ what is capitalized on; sth. used to one's own advantage: 你怎么能把集体取得的成绩看作个人的～? *How could you capitalize on what the group has achieved?* ◇ ～帝国主义 capitalist-imperialism; ～货物 capital goods; ～家 capitalist; ～市场 capital market

【资本主义】capitalism ◇ ～道路 the capitalist road; ～经济成份 capitalist sector of the economy; ～倾向 tendencies towards capitalism; ～社会 capitalist society; ～生产方式 capitalist mode of production; ～制度 capitalist system; ～自发势力 spontaneous capitalist forces

【资材】goods, materials and equipments

【资财】capital and goods; assets: 清点～ *make an inventory of the assets (of a factory, etc.)*

【资产】❶ property ❷ capital fund; capital ❸ [经] assets: 固定(流动)～ *fixed (liquid) assets*; 无形～ *intangible assets* ◇ ～冻结 freezing of assets; ～负债表 [经] statement of assets and liabilities; balance sheet

【资产阶级】the capitalist class; the bourgeoisie ◇ ～分子 bourgeois element; ～个人主义 bourgeois individualism; ～革命 bourgeois revolution; ～化 become bourgeoisified; ～民主 bourgeois democracy; ～民主革命 bourgeois-democratic revolution; ～权利 bourgeois right; ～世界观 bourgeois world outlook; ～思想 bourgeois ideas; bourgeois ideology; ～专政 the dictatorship of the bourgeoisie; ～自由化 bourgeois liberalization

【资方】those representing capital; capital: ～人员 *capitalists and their representatives* / ～代理人 *agent of the owner of a private enterprise; agent of a capitalist*

【资费】expenses

【资格】❶ qualifications: 具备必要的～ *have the requisite qualifications; be qualified* ❷ seniority: 他因～老而当选主席。*He was elected chairman by virtue of his seniority.* ◇ ～审查委员会 credentials committee; ～证书 credentials

【资金】fund; capital: ～短缺 *shortage of funds; capital shortage* / ～积累 *accumulation of funds* / ～市场 *capital market* / ～外流 *capital outflow*

【资力】financial strength: ～雄厚 *have a large capital; be financially powerful*

【资历】qualifications and record of service: 他的外交工作～很深。*He has a long record of diplomatic service.*

【资料】❶ means: 生产资料 ❷ data; material: 参考～ *reference material* / 搜集～ *gather material; collect data* / ～处理 *data processing* / ～室 *reference room*

【资深望重】one's reputation is distinguished

【资送】send sb. away with money provided: ～出国留学 *finance sb.'s education abroad*

【资信】capital and credit: ～评价 *credit rating*

【资信可靠】creditworthy

【资讯】data; information (used in Taiwan): 交换～ *exchange data and information* / 统计大陆经济～ *compile economic data from the Mainland*

【资用】[物] available: ～功 *available work* / ～假说 *working hypothesis*

【资源】natural resources; resources: ～丰富 *abound (or be rich) in natural resources* ◇ ～共享 share of resources; resource sharing; ～开发

resources development；～优化配置 optimum distribution of resources；～优势 resource advantages

【资质】natural endowments；intelligence：～庸下 *be a person of mediocre intelligence*

【资助】aid financially；subsidize

滋 Ⅰ 动 ❶ grow；multiply ❷〈方〉spurt；burst：水管裂缝了，直往外～水。*Water is spurting from the crack in the pipe.* / 电线～火。*Sparks are spurting out from the electric wire.* Ⅱ 副 more：为害～甚 *cause greater havoc than ever* Ⅲ 名 flavour；taste

【滋补】nourishing；nutritious：～食品 *nourishing food；nourishment* / 人参是～身体的名药。*Ginseng is well known for its tonic effect.*

【滋润】❶ moist：～的土地 *moist soil* / 皮肤～ *smooth skin* ❷ moisten：雨露～禾苗壮。*Moistened by rain and dew，young crops grow strong.* ❸〈方〉comfortable：你这小日子过得可够～的啊。*Your life is quite comfortable.*

【滋生】❶ multiply；breed；propagate：防止蚊蝇～ *prevent the breeding of flies and mosquitoes* ❷ cause；create；provoke：～事端 *cause trouble；create a disturbance*

【滋事】make (or stir up) trouble

【滋味】taste；flavour：这个菜很有～。*This dish tastes good.* / 心里不是～ *feel bad；be disturbed*

【滋养】❶ nourish：～身体 *be nourishing* ❷ nutriment；nourishment：丰富的～ *rich nutriment* ◇ ～品 nourishing food；nutriment；nourishment

【滋阴】[中] method of treating yin deficiency by reinforcing body fluid and nourishing the blood

【滋育】grow；multiply；breed：太阳～着万物生长。*The sun gives life to all things on earth.*

【滋长】grow；develop：防止～骄傲自满情绪 *guard against arrogance and conceit* / ～和平麻痹思想 *engender a false sense of security*

孳 动 multiply；propagate

【孳生】multiply；breed；propagate：～蚊蝇 *breed flies and mosquitoes*

辎 名 an ancient covered wagon

【辎重】impedimenta；supplies and gear of an army；baggage

锱 量 an ancient unit of weight，equal to one fourth of a liang（两）

【锱铢必较】haggle over every penny；dispute over every detail

龇 动〈口〉bare；show：～着牙 *bare one's teeth*

【龇露】(of teeth) protrude：～的牙齿 *protruding teeth*

【龇牙咧嘴】❶ show one's teeth；look fierce ❷ contort one's face (in agony)；grimace (with pain)

zǐ

子 Ⅰ 名 ❶ son；child：父与～ *father and son* / 他俩生有一～二女。*The couple have a son and two daughters.* ❷ person：男子 / 女子 ❸ ancient title of respect for a learned or virtuous man：先秦诸～ *the pre-Qin philosophers* ❹ 同〖子书〗❺ seed：结～儿 *bear seed；go to seed* / 这西瓜没～儿。*This melon is seedless.* ❻ egg：鱼子 ❼ sth. small and hard：棋子 ❽ copper coin；copper：一个～儿不值 *not worth a copper* / 一个～儿也没有 *penniless* ❾ viscount：子爵 Ⅱ 量 (used for sth. long and thin)：一～儿挂面 *a bundle of fine dried noodles* / 一～儿毛线 *a hank of knitting wool* Ⅲ 代〈书〉you：以子之矛，攻子之盾 Ⅳ 形 young；tender；small：子鸡

【子菜单】[计] submenu

【子城】a small city within a larger one

【子丑寅卯】the first four of the twelve Earthly Branches（地支）—in an orderly way；systematically：你倒～讲得像模像样的。*You've described the whole thing in such vivid detail that it sounds quite real.* / 他支吾了半天，也没有说出个～来。*He hummed and hawed for quite a while，failing to come out with a coherent story.*

【子畜】young animal；newborn animal

【子代】[生] filial generation：第一～ *the first filial generation*

【子弹】bullet；cartridge：步枪～ *rifle bullet* / 汽枪～ *air-gun pellet* / 练习～ *dummy cartridge* ◇ ～带 cartridge belt；bandoleer；～箱 cartridge box

【子弟】sons and younger brothers；juniors；children：职工～ *children of the workers and staff (of a factory，etc.)* ◇ ～兵 army made up of the sons of the people；our own army

【子房】[植] ovary

【子公司】subsidiary company；subsidiary

【子宫】uterus；womb ◇ ～颈 cervix (of womb)；～颈炎 cervicitis；～帽 cervical cap；～切除术 uterectomy；～脱垂 metroptosis；prolapse of uterus；～外孕 ectopic (or extrauterine) pregnancy

【子规】[动] cuckoo

【子鸡】chick

【子爵】viscount ◇ ～夫人 viscountess

【子粒】seed；grain；kernel；bean：～饱满 *full grains*

【子棉】unginned cotton

【子母】❶ son and mother ❷〈喻〉of similar relationship like a son and mother ◇ ～船 barge-carrier；LASH (lighter aboard ship)；～弹（又作'榴霰弹'）；～机 [军] composite aircraft；～扣儿 snap fastener；popper；～钟 synchronized clock

【子目】specific item；subtitle

【子囊】[植] ascus

【子女】sons and daughters；children；offspring

【子时】the period of the day from 11 p. m. to 1 a.m.
【子实】seed；grain；kernel；bean
【子书】philosophical works—one of the four traditional divisions of a Chinese library
【子嗣】son；male offspring
【子孙】children and grandchildren；descendants ◇～后代 descendants；posterity；coming generations；～满堂（of a person）be blessed with many children
【子午卯酉】from midnight to noon and from sunrise to sunset—❶ from beginning to end；from start to finish：问个～ *get to the bottom of things* ❷ reason；argument：他吭哧了半天，也没有说出个～。*He hummed and hawed for quite a while，failing to come out with any convincing argument*. ❸ result；achievement：没混出个～ *have accomplished nothing；have got nowhere*
【子午线】（又作'子午圈'）meridian（line）——另见〖本初子午线〗
【子午仪】meridian instrument
【子痫】［医］eclampsia
【子虚】〈书〉fictitious；unreal：事属～。*It is sheer fiction*. ◇ ～乌有 without foundation in fact；nonexistent；unreal；imaginary
【子叶】［植］cotyledon
【子夜】midnight
【子音】［语音］consonant
【子猪】pigling

仔 形（of domestic animals or fowls）young：仔鸡 ——另见 zǎi
【仔畜】newborn animal；young animal
【仔鸡】chick
【仔密】（of knitwear）close-knitted；（of textiles）close-woven
【仔细】❶ careful；attentive：～分析 *analyse carefully* / ～地研究文件 *pore over a document* ❷ be careful；look out：路很滑，～点儿。*Watch your step! The road is very slippery*. ❸〈方〉frugal；economical：日子过得～ *be frugal of one's expenses*
【仔猪】piglet；pigling

姊 名 elder sister；sister
【姊妹】elder and younger sisters；sisters ◇ ～城 sister city；～船 sister ship；～花 the two sisters；～篇 companion volume（or piece）

籽 名 seed：棉籽
【籽棉】同〖子棉〗

梓 Ⅰ 名［植］Chinese catalpa（Catalpa ovata）Ⅱ 动 cut blocks for printing

紫 形 purple；violet
【紫菜】［植］laver（Porphyra spp.）
【紫草】Asian puccoon；Chinese gromwell（Lithospermum erythrorrhizon）
【紫草茸】［中］shellac；lac
【紫癜】［医］purpura
【紫貂】sable（Martes zibellina）
【紫丁香】（early）lilac（Syringa oblata）
【紫毫】a writing brush made of rabbit's hair（which is dark purple）
【紫绀】［医］cyanosis
【紫河车】［中］dried human placenta
【紫红】purplish red
【紫花】pale reddish brown：～布 *nankeen（a kind of coarse cloth）*
【紫花地丁】［植］Chinese violet（Viola philippica；V. philippica ssp. munda）
【紫花苜蓿】alfalfa（Medicago sativa）
【紫胶】shellac；lac
【紫胶虫】lac insect（Laccifer lacca）
【紫荆】［植］Chinese redbud（Cercis chinensis）
【紫荆花】bauhinia flower：香港特别行政区的区徽是～。*The bauhinia flower is the emblem of the Hong Kong Special Administrative Region*.
【紫金牛】［植］Japanese ardisia（Ardisia japonica）
【紫堇】［植］corydalis（Corydalis edulis）
【紫禁城】the Forbidden City（in Beijing）
【紫羚羊】bongo
【紫罗兰】violet；common stock（Matthiola incana）
【紫茉莉】four-o'clock（Mirabilis jalapa）
【紫萍】duckweed（Spirodela polyrrhiza）
【紫杉】［植］（Japanese）yew（Taxus cuspidata）
【紫石英】amethyst
【紫苏】［植］purple perilla（Perilla frutescens var. crispa）
【紫穗槐】［植］false indigo（Amorpha fruticosa）
【紫檀】［植］red sandalwood；padauk（Pterocarpus indicus）
【紫藤】［植］Chinese wistaria（Wistaria sinensis）
【紫铜】red copper
【紫外线】ultraviolet ray：～灯 *ultraviolet lamp*
【紫菀】［植］aster（Aster tataricus）
【紫葳】another name for 凌霄花
【紫薇】［植］crape myrtle（Lagerstroemia indica）
【紫药水】common name for 龙胆紫
【紫云英】［植］Chinese milk vetch（Astragalus sinicus）
【紫涨】flushed；red in the face：看见他那气得～的脸，我真不知说什么好。*When I saw his angry red face，I didn't know what to say*.
【紫竹】black bamboo（Phyllostachys nigra）

zì

自 Ⅰ 代 self；oneself；one's own：～打耳光 *slap one's own face；contradict oneself* / ～顾～ *each for himself* Ⅱ 副 certainly；of course；naturally：～当努力 *will certainly do one's best* / 两人久别重逢，～有许多话说。*It was quite natural that they should have a lot to say to each other after such a long separation*. Ⅲ 介 from；since：～即日起生效 *become effective（as）from this date；with effect from（w.e.f.）* / ～数十元至几千元

不等 *ranging from tens to thousands of yuan* / ～远而近 *from far to near* / ～左而右 *from left to right*

【自爱】regard for oneself；self-respect

【自傲】❶ arrogant；conceited ❷ be proud of sth.；take pride in sth.

【自拔】free oneself（from pain or evildoing）；extricate oneself

【自白】make clear one's meaning or position；vindicate oneself ◇ ～书 a written confession

【自暴自弃】give oneself up as hopeless；have no urge to make progress；be resigned to one's backwardness

【自卑】feel oneself inferior；be self-abased：不自满，也不～ *be neither self-satisfied nor self-abased* ◇ ～感 inferiority complex；a sense of inferiority

【自备】provide for oneself：在本食堂用饭请～碗筷。*Will those who have their meals here please bring their own bowls and chopsticks.*

【自变数】（又作'自变量'）［数］independent variable

【自便】at one's convenience；as one pleases：听其～。*Let him do as he pleases.* / 请～。*Please do as you like.*

【自不待言】be self-evident；that goes without saying；that is taken for granted

【自不量力】overestimate one's strength or oneself；not know one's own limitations

【自裁】〈书〉commit suicide；take one's own life

【自惭】feel ashamed ◇ ～形秽 feel unworthy（of others' company）；have a sense of inferiority or inadequacy

【自测】test oneself；self-test

【自差】［电］autodyne：～收音机 *autodyne*（*radio receiver*）

【自嘲】laugh at oneself

【自沉】〈书〉drown oneself

【自称】call oneself；claim to be；profess：他～是孔子的后裔。*He claims to be a descendant of Confucius.* / ～不知情 *profess ignorance*

【自成一家】（in calligraphy，painting，sculpture，etc.）have a style of one's own；have a unique or original style

【自乘】［数］involution；squaring：七～得四十九。*The square of* 7 *is* 49. or 7 *squared is* 49.

【自持】❶ control oneself；restrain oneself；exercise self-restraint ❷ reserved；self-possessed

【自筹】collect or raise（funds，etc.）independently：～资金 *raise funds independently or funds raised independently*

【自出机杼】（of literary compositions）be original in conception

【自出心裁】think up an idea of one's own；make a new departure

【自吹自擂】blow one's own trumpet；crack oneself up

【自从】from；since：～去年秋天到现在 *from last autumn till now*；*since last fall*

【自打】〈方〉from；since

【自大】self-important；arrogant ◇ ～狂 megalomania

【自得】contented；self-satisfied：安闲～ *free and contented* ◇ ～其乐 derive pleasure from sth.；find enjoyment in sth.

【自动】❶ voluntarily；of one's own accord：～参加 *participate voluntarily* / ～帮忙 *make a spontaneous offer of help* ❷ automatic：～延长（*of a lease*，*etc.*）*be automatically extended* ◇ ～报价系统［经］automated quotation system；～补胎 tubeless seal tire；～步枪 automatic rifle；～除霜系统 automatic defrosting system；～传呼 auto call；～电话 automatic telephone；～柜员机 见〖自动提款机〗；～换梭织机 automatic shuttle-changing loom；～绢网印花机 automatic screen printing machine；～控制 automatic control；～门锁 autolock；～免疫［医］active immunity；～铅笔 propelling pencil；～售货机 vending machine；slot machine（in Britain）；～售票机 ticket vendor；～饲喂器 self-feeder；～提款机（又作'自动柜员机'；'自动取款机'）ATM（automatic teller machine）；cash machine；～线 transfer machine；～消磁 autodegauss；～音量控制 automatic volume control；～饮水器 automatic drinking bowl；～应答 automatic answer；～增益控制 automatic gain control；～诊断程序［计］automated conversion routine；～装配线 automatic assembly line；～装填炮 autoloading gun

【自动词】同〖不及物动词〗

【自动挡】（car）automatic gearshift；automatic transmission

【自动扶梯】escalator

【自动化】automate：工艺过程～ *process automation*

【自渎】〈书〉self-abuse；masturbation

【自发】spontaneous：～的斗争 *spontaneous struggle* / ～罢工 *wildcat strike*

【自肥】fatten oneself；enrich oneself by misappropriating funds or material；feather one's nest

【自费】at one's own expense：～出版 *vanity publication* / ～旅行 *travel at one's own expense* / ～生 *self-financing student*；*fee-paying student*

【自焚】burn oneself to death

【自封】❶ proclaim（or style）oneself：～为诗人 *proclaim oneself a poet*；*profess to be a poet* ❷ confine oneself；isolate oneself

【自负】❶ be responsible for one's own action，etc. ❷ think highly of oneself；be conceited：这个人很～。*This person is rather conceited.* ◇ ～盈亏（of an enterprise）assume sole responsibility for its profits or losses

【自甘堕落】wallow in degeneration；abandon oneself to vice

【自感应】［物］self-induction

【自高自大】self-important；conceited；arrogant

【自告奋勇】offer to undertake（a difficult or dangerous task）；volunteer（to do sth. difficult）：～参加突击队 *volunteer to join the shock team*

【自割】[动] autotomy

【自各儿】(又作'自个儿')〈方〉 oneself; by oneself: 我很忙,你~去,好吗? *I'm busy. Would you go there by yourself?*

【自供】confess ◇ ~状 confession

【自古】since ancient times; from time immemorial

【自顾不暇】be unable even to fend for oneself (much less look after others); be busy enough with one's own affairs

【自汗】[中] spontaneous perspiration (or sweating)

【自豪】have a proper sense of pride or dignity; be proud of sth.: ~感 *sense of pride*

【自花不稔性】[植] self-sterility

【自花传粉】[植] self-pollination

【自画像】self-portrait

【自毁】[军] self-destruction: 导弹~ *missile self-destruction*

【自己】❶ referring to the person mentioned earlier in the sentence: 我觉得~错了。*I felt that I was in the wrong.* ❷ oneself: 生~的气 *be angry with oneself* / ~动手 *use one's own hands; do-it-yourself (DIY)* ❸ closely related; own: ~弟兄 *one's own brothers* / ~家里 *one's own family*

【自己人】people on one's own side; one of us: 都是~,你别客气了。*You're among friends, so make yourself at home.*

【自给】self-sufficient; self-supporting: 粮食~有余 *be more than self-sufficient in grain* / ~经济 *self-supporting (or self-contained) economy* / ~率 *degree of self-sufficiency* ◇ ~自足 self-sufficiency; autarky

【自家】〈方〉 one or oneself: ~的小船 *one's own boat*

【自家人】〈方〉 people on one's own side; one of us

【自荐】recommend oneself (for a job); offer one's services

【自尽】commit suicide; take one's own life

【自净】[环保] self-purification

【自疚】feel compunction; have qualms of conscience

【自咎】blame oneself; rebuke oneself

【自救】save oneself; provide for and help oneself: 团结~ *get united for one's own salvation* / 生产~ *provide for and help oneself by engaging in production*

【自居】consider oneself to be; pose as: 以功臣~ *pose as one who has rendered great service; give oneself the airs of a hero*

【自决】self-determination ◇ ~权 right to self-determination

【自觉】❶ (usu. used in the negative) be conscious; aware of: 这种病初起时,患者每不~。*Those suffering from the disease are often unaware of it in the early stages.* ❷ on one's own initiative; conscious: 这女孩儿做作业挺~。*The girl does her homework on her own initiative.* / ~遵守纪律 *conscientiously observe discipline* ◇ ~性 (level of political) consciousness; ~症状 subjective symptoms; ~自愿 voluntarily; willingly; of one's own free will

【自绝】alienate oneself: ~于人民 *alienate oneself from the people*

【自掘坟墓】dig one's own grave; work for one's own destruction

【自控】❶ (〈略〉见〖自动控制〗) automatic control ❷ self-control: 培养孩子的~能力 *teach children self-control*

【自夸】sing one's own praises; crack oneself up

【自宽】comfort oneself; console oneself ◇ ~自解 comfort and relieve oneself

【自愧不如】(又作'自愧弗如') feel ashamed of one's inferiority

【自拉自唱】❶ accompany one's own singing ❷ hold forth all alone in defence of one's own views or proposals; second one's own motion

【自来】from the beginning; in the first place; originally

【自来水】running water; tap water

【自来水笔】fountain pen

【自理】take care of or provide for oneself: 伙食~ *make one's own eating arrangements* / 旅费~ *pay one's own travelling expenses*

【自力】do sth. through one's own efforts; rely on oneself

【自力更生】regeneration (or reconstruction) through one's own efforts; self-reliance

【自力霉素】[药] mitomycin C

【自立】stand on one's own feet; support oneself; earn one's own living: 我的孩子们现在都能~了。*My children are now self-supporting.*

【自量】estimate one's own ability or strength: 不知~ *overrate one's abilities*

【自流】❶ (of water, etc.) flow automatically; flow by itself ❷ (of a thing) take its natural course; (of a person) do as one pleases: 听其~ *let things drift along; let people act freely without leadership* ◇ ~灌溉 gravity irrigation; ~井 artesian well

【自留】reserve sth. for one's own use: ~资金 *funds an enterprise is entitled to retain* ◇ ~畜 livestock for personal needs; privately owned livestock; ~地 plot of land for personal needs; family plot; private plot

【自律】exercise self-discipline; self-management: 父母管教儿童的两大目标应是自尊和~。*Parents should teach their children self-respect and self-discipline.*

【自卖自夸】praise the goods one sells; indulge in self-glorification; blow one's own trumpet —— 另见〖老王卖瓜,自卖自夸〗

【自满】complacent; self-satisfied: ~情绪 *complacency; self-satisfaction*

【自明】self-evident; self-explanatory; obvious: 其理~。*The principle involved is obvious.*

【自鸣得意】show self-satisfaction; be very pleased with oneself; preen oneself

【自鸣清高】profess to be above politics and worldly considerations

【自鸣钟】striking clock；chime clock

【自命】consider oneself；regard oneself as ◇ ～不凡 consider oneself no ordinary being；have an unduly high opinion of oneself；think no end of oneself

【自谋出路】find one's own means of livelihood

【自谋职业】search for a job oneself；seek a job on one's own（as opposed being assigned by the government）（〈反〉'国家统一分配'）

【自馁】lose confidence；be discouraged

【自捻纱】［纺］self-twisted yarn

【自拍机】［摄］self-timer

【自喷井】［油］flowing well；gusher well

【自喷期】［油］flush stage；flowing life

【自欺欺人】deceive oneself as well as others：完全是～之谈 *a gross deception*

【自弃】give oneself up as hopeless；have no urge to make progress

【自谦】be modest：～之词 *self-deprecating remarks made as a gesture of politeness*

【自强不息】constantly strive to become stronger；make unremitting（or unceasing）efforts to improve oneself

【自轻自贱】demean oneself；belittle oneself；lack self-confidence and self-respect

【自取灭亡】court（or invite）destruction；take the road to one's doom

【自取其咎】bring blame on oneself；have only oneself to blame：你这是～。*You asked for it*.

【自然】(zìrán) ❶ natural world；nature：改造～ *transform nature* / ～条件 *natural conditions* ❷ natural：拍照时表情要～些。*Try to look natural for your photograph*. ❸ naturally；in the ordinary course of events：你先别问，到时候～明白。*Don't ask now. You'll understand in due course*. ❹ of course；naturally：只要努力，～会取得好成绩。*If you work hard, you're bound to get good results*. ◇ ～保护区 nature reserve；nature preservation zone；～辩证法 dialectics of nature；～博物馆 museum of natural history；～村 natural village；～地理 physical geography；～规律 natural law；law of nature；～环境 natural environment；～键盘［计］natural keyboard；～界 natural world；nature；～金属 native metal；～经济 natural economy；～科学 natural science；～类群［生］natural group；～力 natural forces；～免疫 同〖天然免疫〗；～区域 natural regions；～人［法］natural person；～神论 deism；～数［数］natural number；～死亡 natural death；～铜 native copper；～现象 natural phenomena；～形态 natural form；～选择 natural selection；～灾害 natural calamity（or disaster）；～增长率 natural growth；～主义 naturalism；～资源 natural resources（or wealth）

【自然而然】naturally；automatically；spontaneously；of oneself：这孩子发育快，～也就吃得多。*The boy is growing fast, so naturally he eats a lot of food*.

【自然】(zìran) at ease；natural；free from affectation：态度非常～ *be quite at ease* / 他不～地笑了一笑。*He forced a smile*.

【自燃】［化］spontaneous combustion（or ignition）

【自认】accept as unavoidable；resign oneself to：～晦气 *be resigned to one's bad luck；accept bad luck without complaint；grin and bear it*

【自如】〈书〉freely；smoothly；with facility：操纵～ *operate with facility* / 旋转～ *rotate or revolve freely*

【自若】〈书〉self-possessed；composed；calm and at ease：神志～ *appear calm and at ease；appear composed*

【自杀】commit suicide；take one's own life ◇ ～学 suicidology

【自伤】［法］self-inflicted injury；self-injury

【自上而下】from above to below；from top to bottom：军队中～的统一指挥 *unified command from above in the army*

【自身】self；oneself：～的物质利益 *one's own material benefits* ◇ ～难保 be unable even to protect or fend for oneself

【自生自灭】（of a thing）emerge of itself and perish of itself；run its course

【自食其果】eat one's own bitter fruit —reap what one has sown

【自食其力】support oneself by one's own labour；earn one's own living：～的劳动者 *working people living by their own labour*

【自食其言】go back on one's word；break one's promise；break faith with sb.

【自始至终】from beginning to end；from start to finish

【自视】consider（or think, imagine）oneself：～甚高 *think highly of oneself；be self-important*

【自恃】❶ over confident and conceited ❷〈书〉be self-assured for having sth. or sb. to rely on；count on；capitalize on：～有功 *capitalize on one's achievements* / ～有靠山 *count on sb.'s backing*

【自是】naturally；of course：久别重逢，～高兴。*It was of course a delight for them to meet again after such a long separation*.

【自首】❶（of a criminal）voluntarily surrender oneself；confess one's crime；give oneself up ❷ make a political recantation；surrender to the enemy：～变节 *recant and turn traitor* ◇ ～书 confession

【自述】an account in one's own words

【自说自话】〈方〉❶ act on one's own；decide for oneself ❷ talk to oneself；think aloud；soliloquize

【自私】selfish；self-centred

【自私自利】selfish：毫无～之心的精神 *the spirit of absolute selflessness*

【自诉】［法］private prosecution；action initiated by an injured party without the participation of the public prosecutor：～人 *private party who prosecutes a case by himself；party who initiates a*

private prosecution
【自讨苦吃】ask for trouble; bring trouble upon oneself
【自讨没趣】ask for a snub; court a rebuff
【自体不育性】［动］self-sterility
【自投罗网】cast oneself into the net; walk right into the trap; bite the hook; leap at the bait
【自卫】defend oneself; self-defence: ～能力 *the capacity to defend oneself* / ～行动 *an act in self-defence* / ～原则 *principle of self-defence* / ～战争 *war of self-defence* ◇ ～反击 fight (or strike) back in self-defence; ～军 self-defence corps
【自为阶级】［哲］class-for-itself
【自慰】❶ console oneself ❷〈婉〉masturbate
【自刎】commit suicide by cutting one's throat; cut one's throat
【自问】❶ ask oneself; examine oneself: 反躬自问 ❷ reach a conclusion after weighing a matter: 我～是花过不少力气的。*I flatter myself that I have spared no pains.*
【自我】(used before disyllabic verbs) self; oneself ◇ ～安慰 self-consolation; ～暗示［心理］self-suggestion; ～暴露 self-betrayal; self-exposure; ～辩解 self-justification; ～标榜 blow one's own trumpet; ～表现 self-expression; sing one's own praises; ～吹嘘 self-glorification; ～催眠 auto-hypnosis; ～改造 self-remoulding; ～观察［心理］self-observation; ～检查 self-examination; introspection; ～教育 self-education; ～解嘲 find excuses to console oneself; ～介绍 introduce oneself; ～批评 self-criticism; ～陶醉 be intoxicated with self-satisfaction; ～完善 self-improvement; ～牺牲 self-sacrifice; ～欣赏 self-appreciation; self-admiration; ～作古 be the founder (or originator) of sth.
【自习】(of students) study by oneself in scheduled time or free time: ～时间 *time for individual study*
【自下而上】from below: ～的监督 *supervision from below*
【自相残杀】(of persons within a group, party, etc.) kill each other; cause one another's death: ～的战争 *a fratricidal war*
【自相惊扰】alarm one's own group, etc.; create a disturbance within one's ranks; raise false alarms
【自相矛盾】contradict oneself; be self-contradictory: 他的话～。*What he says is self-contradictory.* / 你这不是～吗? *Aren't you contradicting yourself?*
【自销】(of a factory, etc.) sell goods through one's own channels
【自小】since childhood
【自卸卡车】dump truck; tip truck
【自新】turn over a new leaf; make a fresh start: 走上～的道路 *turn over a new leaf*
【自信】self-confident; confident: 有～心 *have self-confidence; be confident (or sure) of oneself* / 缺乏～ *lack confidence in oneself* / 她～自己能赢。*She is confident that she will win.* / 我～能够完成这项任务。*I'm sure I can fulfil the task.*
【自行】❶ by oneself: ～解决 *settle (a problem) by oneself* / ～安排 *arrange by oneself* / ～设计 *make designs of one's own* ❷ of oneself; of one's own accord; voluntarily: ～到来 *come of itself* ❸［天］proper motion
【自行车】bicycle; bike: 骑～ *ride a bicycle* / 骑～进城 *go down town by bike* ◇ ～棚 bicycle shed; ～赛 cycle racing; cycling
【自行车架】❶ bicycle frame ❷ bicycle stand (or rack)
【自行火炮】［军］self-propelled gun
【自行其是】go one's own way; act wilfully
【自省】examine oneself; examine one's ability, conduct, etc.
【自修】❶ (of students) study by oneself; have selfstudy ❷ study on one's own; study independently: ～法语 *teach oneself French*
【自许】❶ take pride in; pride oneself on ❷ call oneself; claim to be
【自诩】〈书〉praise oneself; crack oneself up; brag
【自序】(又作'自叙') ❶ author's preface; preface ❷ autobiographic note; brief account of oneself
【自选】［体］free; optional: ～手枪五十米赛 *free pistol 50 m.*
【自选动作】［体］optional exercise
【自选市场】(又作'超市'; '自选商场') supermarket
【自学】study on one's own; study independently; teach oneself: 培养～能力 *cultivate (or foster) one's ability to study independently* ◇ ～成才 be self-taught; ～课本 teach-yourself books
【自寻烦恼】worry oneself needlessly; bring vexation on oneself
【自寻死路】bring about one's own destruction
【自言自语】talk to oneself; think aloud; soliloquize
【自养生物】［生］autotroph
【自养植物】［植］autophyte; autotrophic plant
【自以为得计】be pleased with one's own scheming; think oneself smart
【自以为非】consider oneself in the wrong; recognize one's own fallibility
【自以为是】consider oneself (always) in the right; regard oneself as infallible; be self-opinionated
【自缢】〈书〉hang oneself: ～而死 *hang oneself*
【自用】❶〈书〉obstinately holding to one's own views; self-opinionated; self-willed: 愚而好～ *ignorant and self-willed* ❷ for private use; personal: ～物品 *personal effects; personal belongings*
【自由】❶ freedom; liberty: 公民～权 *civil liberties* ❷［哲］freedom: ～和必然 *freedom and necessity* ❸ free; unrestrained: ～讨论 *have a free exchange of views* ◇ ～电子 free electron; ～兑换［经］convertibility; ～泛滥 (of erroneous ideas, etc.) spread unchecked; run wild; ～放任 let people do what they like; let things go their own way; follow one's own inclinations; ～放任主义

laissez-faire；～港 free port；～化 liberalize；～汇率 free exchange rate；～价格 free price；～竞争 free competition；～联想［心理］free（or uncontrolled）association；～恋爱 freedom to arrange one's own marriage；free courtship；～贸易 free trade；～贸易区 free trade zone；free trade area；～民［史］freeman；～能［物］free energy；～软件［计］freeware；free software；～散漫 slack；lax in discipline；～诗 free verse；unorthodox verse；vers libre；～市场 free（or open）market；～体操 free exercise；floor exercise；free callisthenics；～王国［哲］realm of freedom；～意志 free will；～泳 freestyle（swimming）；crawl；～主义 liberalism；～撰稿人 free writer；～资本主义 non-monopoly capitalism；laissez-faire capitalism；～资产阶级 non-monopoly bourgeoisie；liberal bourgeoisie；～自在 leisurely and carefree；free and unrestrained；～组合规律［生］law of independent assortment

【自由职业】profession ◇ ～者 professional

【自幼】since childhood

【自娱】please oneself；amuse oneself：作诗～ *compose poems to please oneself*

【自育】［动］self-fertile

【自圆其说】make one's statement valid；justify oneself：这样解释能～吗？*Is this a plausible explanation?* / 不能～ *cannot offer a tenable argument；cannot justify oneself*

【自怨自艾】be full of remorse；repent

【自愿】voluntary；of one's own accord；of one's own free will：出于～ *on a voluntary basis；of one's free will*

【自在】（zìzài）free；unrestrained：日子过得挺～ *lead a free and easy life*

【自在】（zìzai）comfortable；at ease：身体有点不～ *feel a little out of sorts；not be quite oneself*

【自在阶级】［哲］class-in-itself

【自在之物】［哲］thing-in-itself

【自责】blame oneself；reprove oneself

【自找】suffer from one's own actions；ask for it：～麻烦 *be looking for trouble*

【自知之明】knowledge of oneself：人贵有～。*It is important to know one's own limitations.* or *Self-knowledge is wisdom.*

【自治】autonomy；self-government：～的权限 *autonomous jurisdiction* / ～条例 *regulations on the exercise of autonomy* ◇ ～机关 organ of self-government；～领 self-governing dominion；dominion；～区 autonomous region；～权 autonomy；～县 autonomous county；～州 autonomous prefecture

【自制】❶ made by oneself：这台铣床是我们厂～的。*This milling machine was made in our own plant.* ❷ self-control；self-restraint：失去～ *lose self-control*

【自重】❶ conduct oneself with dignity；be self-possessed：请～。*Please behave yourself.* ❷ dead weight：车皮～ *the dead weight of a wagon*

【自主】act on one's own；decide for oneself；keep the initiative in one's own hands：男女婚姻～。*Men and women shall marry the partners of their choice.* ◇ ～关税 autonomous tariff；～经营 be independent in management

【自主权】power to make one's own decisions：扩大企业的～ *enlarge the decision-making power of local enterprises*

【自助餐厅】cafeteria

【自传】autobiography

【自转】［天］rotation：地球的～ *the rotation of the earth* ◇ ～轴 axis of rotation

【自走式】self-propelled ◇ ～联合收割机 self-propelled combine harvester

【自足】self-satisfied；complacent；smug

【自尊】self-respect；self-esteem；proper pride：～感 *sense of self-respect*

【自作自受】suffer from one's own actions；stew in one's own juice：这是你～。*As you make your bed, so you must lie on it.* / 他这是～，没人可怜他。*Nobody feels sorry for him；he's got what he deserves.*

【自作聪明】think oneself clever（in making suggestions，etc.）；try to be smart（by acting on one's own，etc.）

【自作多情】proffer a love or affection which is not reciprocated

【自作主张】act on one's own；decide for oneself：这件事我们得请示，不能～。*We can't decide this for ourselves；we must ask for instructions.*

字 名 ❶ word；character：～形 *the form of a written character* / ～义 *meaning of a word* / 你这个～写得不对。*You wrote this character wrong.* ❷ pronunciation（of a word or character）：说话～～清楚 *pronounce every word clearly；have clear articulation* ❸ form of a written or printed character；style of handwriting；printing type：篆～ *seal character* / 黑体～ *boldface type* ❹ scripts；writings：专藏～，不藏画 *only collect scripts（or writings），not paintings* ❺ receipt；written pledge：收到款子，写个～儿给他。*Write him a receipt when you get the money from him.* ❻ a style（or name）taken at the age of twenty，by which a man is sometimes called：诸葛亮～孔明。*Zhuge Liang styled himself Kongming.*

【字标】slogan written in large characters

【字典】character dictionary（which defines only single characters，though including compounds as illustrative examples）

【字典纸】India paper；Bible paper

【字调】［语音］tones of Chinese characters ——另见〖四声〗

【字段】［计］field ◇ ～标记 fieldmark；～名 field name；～位移 field shifting

【字幅】horizontal or vertical scroll of calligraphy

【字符】character

【字符串】［计］string

【字号】font size；type size；word size

【字盒】[刷] (type) mould
【字画】calligraphy and painting
【字汇】glossary; wordbook; lexicon
【字迹】handwriting; writing: ～工整 *neat writing* / ～模糊 *illegible handwriting*
【字节】[计] byte
【字句】words and expressions; writing: ～通顺 *coherent and smooth writing*
【字据】written pledge (e. g. receipt, IOU, contract, etc.)
【字库】❶ word bank ❷ font bank; font collection
【字里行间】between the lines: 他的信～流露出畏难情绪。*His letter reveals, between the lines, that he's afraid of some difficulty.*
【字谜】a riddle about a character or word
【字面】literal: ～上的意思 *literal meaning* / 从～上看 *take (a word or expression) literally*
【字模】[刷] (type) matrix: 冲压～ *punched matrix* / ～雕刻机 *matrix cutting machine*
【字母】❶ letters of an alphabet; letter: 汉语拼音～ *the Chinese phonetic alphabet* / 英语～ *the English alphabet* / 大写～ *a capital letter* / 按～顺序排列 *be arranged in alphabetical order; be arranged alphabetically* ❷ (in phonology) a character representing an initial consonant (声母), as 明 míng for the initial m
【字母表】alphabet
【字幕】captions (of motion pictures, etc.); subtitles: 中文～ *Chinese subtitles (or captions)*
【字盘】[刷] case: 大写～ *upper case* / 小写～ *lower case*
【字体】❶ form of a written or printed character; script; typeface ❷ style of calligraphy ❸ [计] font; typeface
【字条】brief note; note: 他给我留了个～,是关于这次演出的。*He left me a note about the performance.*
【字眼】wording; diction: 玩弄～ *play with words* ——另见〖抠字眼儿〗;〖挑字眼儿〗
【字样】❶ model of written characters ❷ printed or written words (which succinctly inform, instruct, warn, etc.): 封面上有"初稿"～。*On the cover are the words "First Draft".*
【字斟句酌】choose one's words with care; weigh every word
【字纸】wastepaper with characters written or printed on it
【字纸篓】wastepaper basket
【字字珠玑】each word a gem (said in praise of sb.'s writing)

恣 Ⅰ 动 throw off restraint; do as one pleases: 得以自～ *be able to do as one likes (or indulge oneself)* Ⅱ 形 〈方〉 comfortable: ～得很 *very comfortable*
【恣情】❶ to one's heart's content; as much as one likes: ～欢笑 *laugh heartily* ❷ wanton; arbitrary; willful ◇ ～放纵 indulge in passions and run wild
【恣行无忌】act wilfully and unscrupulously; behave recklessly
【恣意】unscrupulous; reckless; unbridled; wilful: ～践踏 *wilfully trample on*
【恣意妄为】act wilfully and wildly; behave unscrupulously

渍 Ⅰ 动 ❶ steep; soak; ret: ～麻 *ret flax, jute, etc.* / 白衬衫被汗水～黄了。*The white shirt has yellowed with sweat.* ❷ be soiled (with grease, etc.): 她每天擦机器,不让～一点油泥。*She polishes the machine every day so that there's not a speck of dirt on it.* / 烟斗里～了很多油子。*The pipe is caked with tar.* Ⅱ 名 ❶ floodwater on low-lying land: 防洪排～ *prevention of floods and drainage of floodwater* ❷ 〈方〉 stain; sludge: 油～ *oil sludge* / 茶～ *tea stains*
【渍涝】waterlogging: ～的低洼地 *waterlogged low-lying land*
【渍染】dye: 血污～ *bloodstained*
【渍水】accumulated water

zōng

宗 Ⅰ 名 ❶ ancestor: 祖宗 ❷ clan: 同宗 ❸ sect; faction; school: 正宗 ❹ principal aim; purpose: 开宗明义 ❺ model; great master Ⅱ 动 (in academic or artistic work) take as one's model: 他的唱工～的是梅派。*In singing he takes Mei Lanfang as his model.* Ⅲ 量 一～心事 *a matter that worries one*
【宗祠】ancestral hall (or temple)
【宗法】patriarchal clan system: ～社会 *patriarchal society*
【宗教】religion ◇ ～法庭 the Inquisition (in European history); ～改革 the Reformation (in European history); ～戒律 religious taboo; ～派别 religious sect; ～信仰 religious belief; ～仪式 religious rites; ritual
【宗筋】[中] penis
【宗庙】ancestral temple (or shrine) of a ruling house
【宗派】faction; sect ◇ ～斗争 factional strife; ～活动 factional activities; sectarian activities; ～主义 sectarianism; factionalism
【宗谱】family tree; genealogical tree; genealogy
【宗亲】members of the same clan; clansmen
【宗师】master of great learning and integrity
【宗室】❶ imperial (or royal) clan ❷ imperial (or royal) clansman
【宗仰】〈书〉 hold in esteem: 海内～ *be held in esteem throughout the country*
【宗旨】aim; purpose
【宗主国】suzerain (state); metropolitan state
【宗主权】suzerainty
【宗族】❶ patriarchal clan ❷ clansman

综 动 put together; sum up: ～上所述 *to sum up* ——另见 zèng

【综观】make a comprehensive survey：～全局 *take a broad view of the situation*

【综合】❶ synthesize：～群众的意见 *synthesize (or sum up) the opinions of the masses* ❷ synthetical；comprehensive；multiple；composite：～的研究 *a synthetical (or comprehensive) study* ◇～保险 comprehensive insurance；～保险单 comprehensive policy；～报导（又作'综合报道'）comprehensive (or composite) dispatch；news roundup；～报告 comprehensive report；summing-up report；～病征（又作'综合征'）syndrome；～大学 university；～服务 comprehension service；～规划 unified plan；～国力 the overall strength of the country；～教学 integrated teaching；～考察 comprehensive survey；～利用 comprehensive utilization；multipurpose use；～平衡 overall balance；～性工厂 multiple-producing factory；～银行 universal bank；～语［语］synthetic language；～指数［经］composite index；～治理 tackle a problem in a comprehensive way

【综计】sum up；add up：合理化建议～有九个方面。*To sum up，the rationalization proposals fall into nine categories.*

【综括】sum up：～起来 *to sum up；to state succinctly*

【综述】summarize；sum up：来稿～ *a summary of readers' contributions*

棕 名 ❶ palm ❷ palm fibre；coir：棕毛

【棕绷】（又作'棕绷子'）wooden bed frame strung with crisscross coir ropes

【棕编】coir-woven articles

【棕黑】dark brown

【棕红】reddish brown

【棕黄】pale brown

【棕榈】palm ◇～酸 palmitic (or palmic) acid；～油 palm oil；palm butter

【棕毛】palm fibre：～蓑衣 *palm rain cape*

【棕壤】［农］brown earth

【棕色】brown：～森林土 *brown forest soil*

【棕绳】coir rope

【棕树】common name for 棕榈

【棕毯】coir-woven blanket

【棕熊】brown bear

【棕衣】palm-bark rain cape

踪 名 footprint；track；trace：跟踪

【踪迹】trace；track：他不见了，未留下任何～。*He disappeared without a trace.*

【踪影】(usu. used in the negative) trace；sign：我已好几天不见她的～了。*I haven't seen a trace of her for several days now.*

鬃 名 hair on the neck of a pig，horse，etc.：猪鬃

【鬃刷】bristle brush

zǒng

总 Ⅰ 动 assemble；put together；sum up：～起来说 *to sum up* / 把两笔账～到一块算 *settle the two accounts together* Ⅱ 形 ❶ general；overall；total：～产量 *total output* / ～趋势 *general trend* / ～根源 *root cause* / ～的说来 *generally speaking；by and large* ❷ chief；head；general：～头目 *chief boss；chieftain* Ⅲ 副 ❶ always；invariably：我一去那儿天～下雨。*It invariably rains when I go there.* / 我不是～在这儿。*I am not always here.* ❷ anyway；after all；eventually；sooner or later：问题～是要解决的。*The problem will be settled sooner or later.* / 你～会成功的。*You're bound to succeed.* / 他～还是个孩子，哪能像大人那样有力气？*After all，he's only a child. How can he possibly be as strong as a grown-up?* ❸ surely；certainly；probably：她说的你～不会相信吧？*You don't believe what she said，surely?* / 他～不大可能写这样一封信。*It's most unlikely that he should have written such a letter.*

【总罢工】general strike

【总编辑】editor in chief

【总部】general headquarters

【总裁】director-general (of a political party)；president (of a company)；governor (of a bank)

【总参谋部】the Headquarters of the General Staff

【总参谋长】chief of the general staff

【总产值】gross output value；total output value：工农业年～ *gross annual value of industrial and agricultural output (or production)*

【总承包商】general contractor

【总赤字】total deficit

【总代理】general agent

【总得】must；have to；be bound to：～想个办法 *have got to find a way out* / 他今天～来一趟。*He's bound to come today.*

【总店】main store (of a business)

【总动员】general (or total) mobilization

【总督】❶〈旧〉(in the Qing Dynasty) governor-general：两广～ *Governor-General of Guangdong and Guangxi* ❷ (in British colonies and dominions) viceroy；governor-general；governor：印度～ *(formerly) Viceroy of India* / 加拿大～ *Governor-General of Canada*

【总额】total：存款～ *total deposits* / 工资～ *total wages；payroll*

【总而言之】in short；in a word；in brief；to make a long story short：～，这电影我一点也不喜欢。*In short，I didn't like the film at all.*

【总方针】general policy；general principle：经济工作的～ *the general policy guiding economic work*

【总纲】general programme；general principles：中华人民共和国宪法～ *the General Principles of the Constitution of the People's Republic of China*

【总工程师】chief engineer

【总工会】federation of trade unions：中华全国～ *All-China Federation of Trade Unions*

【总公司】head office (of a corporation)

【总攻】［军］general offensive

【总供给】aggregate supply

【总共】in all; altogether; in the aggregate: ～约五千人 *about five thousand people in all*

【总管】❶ take overall responsibility ❷〈旧〉steward; butler

【总归】anyway; after all; eventually: 困难～是可以克服的。*Difficulties can after all be overcome.*

【总行】head office (of a bank)

【总和】sum; total; sum total: 头三个月产量的～ *the total output of the first three months*

【总后方】rear area (in wartime)

【总后勤部】the General Logistics Department

【总汇】❶ (of streams) come or flow together: ～入海 *flow into the sea together* ❷ confluence; concourse; aggregate: 人民是智慧的海洋,力量的～。*The people are a sea of wisdom and the aggregation of strength.*

【总机】❶ switchboard; telephone exchange ❷ operator

【总计】❶［数］grand total ❷ amount to; add up to; total: 观众～有十万人。*The audience totalled* 100,000. or *There were* 100,000 *spectators in all.*

【总监】inspector general; chief inspector

【总角】〈书〉a child's hair twisted in a knot—childhood ◇ ～之交 childhood friend

【总结】❶ sum up; summarize: ～经验 *sum up one's experience* ❷ summary; summing-up: 作～ *make a summary* / 哲学是关于自然知识和社会知识的概括和～。*Philosophy is the generalization and summation of the knowledge of nature and society.* ◇ ～报告 summary (or final, concluding) report; ～会 summing-up meeting

【总经理】general manager; president

【总经销】exclusive distribution

【总开关】master switch

【总括】sum up: ～起来 *to sum up; to state succinctly*

【总揽】assume overall responsibility; take on everything: ～大权 *have overall authority; assume a dominant role*

【总理】premier; prime minister: 国务院～ *the Premier of the State Council* / 副～ *Vice-Premier*

【总量】aggregate; total supply and demand ◇ ～控制 control aggregate supply and demand; control of aggregates; ～平衡 overall balance; ～调控 control of total supply and demand

【总领事】consul general ◇ ～馆 consulate general

【总路线】general line

【总论】introduction (at the beginning of a book)

【总目】general table of contents; general catalogue

【总平面图】general layout

【总评】general comment; overall appraisal

【总谱】［音］score

【总设计师】chief architect

【总书记】secretary-general; general secretary

【总数】total; sum total

【总司令】commander in chief

【总司令部】general headquarters

【总算】❶ at long last; finally: 会议一再延期,现在～开成了。*The meeting has come off at last, after being postponed again and again.* ❷ considering everything; all things considered; on the whole: 小孩子的字能写成这样,～不错了。*For a child's handwriting, it's quite good.*

【总体】overall; total ◇ ～规划 overall plan; ～设计 master design; ～水平 overall quality level; ～外交 total diplomacy; ～战略 total strategy; ～战争 total war

【总统】president (of a republic) ◇ ～府 presidential palace; the residence and / or office of a president; ～选举 presidential election; ～制 presidential government; presidential system

【总危机】general crisis

【总务】❶ general affairs ❷ person in charge of general affairs ◇ ～处 general affairs department; ～科 general affairs section; ～司 general service department

【总需求】aggregate demand

【总则】general rules; general principles; general provisions

【总闸门】petroleum master valve; master gate

【总长】(zǒngzhǎng) ❶ cabinet minister (a name used 1912-1927; now called 部长) ❷〈口〉(〈略〉全称为'总参谋长') chief of the general staff

【总账】general ledger

【总账单】master bill

【总政治部】the General Political Department

【总之】❶ in a word; in short; in brief: 我是既没工夫又没兴趣,～,我不干。*I have neither the time nor the inclination; in short, I refuse.* ❷ anyway; anyhow: 确切地址我记不清了,～是在颐和园附近。*I can't remember the exact address. Anyway, it's somewhere near the Summer Palace.*

【总支】general branch

【总值】total (or gross) value: 生产～ *total output value* / 进(出)口～ *gross import (export) value*

【总指挥】❶ commander in chief ❷ general director

【总指挥部】general headquarters

【总装】assemble a machine: 缩短～时间,以减少耗费 *cut costs by shortening assembly time*

【总状花序】［植］raceme

zòng

纵 Ⅰ 形 ❶ from north to south or from south to north: 纵贯 ❷ vertical; longitudinal; lengthwise: 纵深 / 纵剖面 Ⅱ 名〈略〉见〖纵队〗 Ⅲ 动 ❶ release; set free: 欲擒故纵 ❷ indulge; let loose; let oneself go: 纵声 ❸ jump up; jump into the air: 他向前一～,就把球接住了。*He leaped forward and caught the ball.* Ⅳ 连〈书〉even if; even though: ～有千难万险,也挡不住英勇的勘探队员。*Even though there are myriad hardships and hazards, they can't stop the dauntless pro-*

spectors.

【纵波】[物] longitudinal wave

【纵步】❶ stride：～向前走去 *stride forward* ❷ jump；bound：他一个～跳过了小河。*He crossed the brook in one big jump*.

【纵断面】同〖纵剖面〗

【纵队】❶ column；file：～队形 *column formation* / 一路～ *column of files*；*single file* / 二路～ *column of twos* ❷ a military unit during the War of Liberation，equivalent to an army；column

【纵隔】[生理] mediastinum：～炎 *mediastinitis*

【纵观】take a sweeping view；make a general survey：～全局 *make a general survey of the situation*

【纵贯】pass through from north to south or from south to north：～两省的铁路 *a railway passing through two provinces from north to south*

【纵横】❶ in length and breadth；vertically and horizontally：～数百里的山区 *a mountainous area several hundred li in length and breadth* ❷ with great ease；freely：笔意～ *write with great ease* ❸ sweep over；march over unhindered

【纵横捭阖】manoeuvre among various states or political groupings

【纵横驰骋】(of an army) move about freely and quickly；sweep through the length and breadth of：青年们可以在广阔的科学领域里～。*The length and breadth of the whole realm of science is open for our youth to explore and conquer*.

【纵横交错】crisscross：～的水渠 *a crisscross network of irrigation channels*

【纵虎归山】let the tiger return to the mountains—cause calamity for the future

【纵火】set on fire；commit arson：～犯 *arsonist*

【纵酒】drink to excess

【纵览】look far and wide；scan：～四周 *look all round* / ～群书 *read extensively*

【纵论】talk freely；have a wide-ranging discussion：～天下大事 *talk freely about world events*

【纵目】look as far as one's eyes can see：～四望 *look far into the distance in all directions*

【纵剖面】vertical section

【纵切面】同〖纵剖面〗

【纵情】to one's heart's content；as much as one likes：～歌唱 *sing to one's heart's content*；*sing heartily*

【纵然】even if；even though：～成功的希望不大，我们也要试试。*We will try even if there isn't much hope of success*.

【纵容】connive；wink at：受到～和庇护 *be winked at and shielded*

【纵射】[军] enfilade

【纵身】jump；leap：～一跳 *jump into the air*；*jump up* / ～上马 *leap onto a horse*

【纵深】[军] depth：向～发展 *develop in depth*

【纵声】at the top of one's voice：～大笑 *laugh heartily* / ～歌唱 *sing lustily*

【纵使】even if；even though

【纵视图】longitudinal view

【纵谈】talk freely：～国内外大好形势 *talk freely about the excellent internal and external situation*

【纵眺】look as far as one's eyes can see：～黄山景色 *scan the scenery of Huangshan*

【纵向】vertical；longitudinal；lengthwise ◇ ～合并 vertical consolidating；vertical merger；～结合 vertical integration (as of enterprises)

【纵欲】give way to one's carnal desires；indulge in sensual pleasures

【纵恣】〈书〉self-indulgent；undisciplined；wanton

【纵坐标】[数] ordinate

粽 (构词成分)见下

【粽子】a pyramid-shaped dumpling made of glutinous rice wrapped in bamboo or reed leaves (eaten during the Dragon Boat Festival)

zǒu

走 动 ❶ walk；go：～遍全国 *travel the length and breadth of the whole country* / ～前人没有～过的道路 *break new paths*；*take paths never trodden before* / 这船一小时～十五海里。*The ship makes 15 knots*. ❷ run；move：钟不～了。*The clock has stopped*. / 这个表～得很准。*This watch keeps good time*. / 打得赢就打，打不赢就～。*Fight when you can win*，*move away when you can't*. / 你这步棋～坏了。*You've made a bad move*. ❸ leave；go away：～开！*Get away*! or *Clear off*! / 我们该～了。*It's time for us to leave*. or *We must be off now*. / 他已经把蓝图拿～了。*He's taken the blueprint away*. ❹ visit；call on：他们两家～得很近。*The two families often visit each other*. ❺ through；from：咱们～这个门进去吧。*Let's go in through this door*. ❻ leak；let out；escape：～气了。*The gas is leaking*. or *The air is escaping*. ❼ depart from the original；lose the original shape，flavour，etc.：把原来的意思讲～了 *fail to get across the original meaning*

【走笔】〈书〉write rapidly：～疾书 *write rapidly (or swiftly)*

【走步】[体](篮球) walking

【走村串寨】go from village to village

【走刀量】[机] feed

【走道】❶ pavement；sidewalk ❷ path；walk；footpath

【走道儿】〈口〉walk：小孩子刚会～。*The baby has just learned to toddle*.

【走电】〈方〉leakage of electricity

【走调】out of tune：她唱歌爱～。*Her singing often gets out of tune*.

【走动】❶ walk about；stretch one's legs：病人能～了。*The invalid is able to get about now*. ❷ (of relatives and friends) visit each other：他们两家关系不错，常常～。*The two families are on good terms and often visit each other*.

【走读】attend a day school ◇ ～大学 private，self-financing day college；～生 day student；nonresident student

【走访】❶ interview；have an interview with：本报记者～了几位著名的小说家。*Our reporter interviewed several famous novelists*. ❷ pay a visit to；go and see：～在中国工作的外国专家 *pay visits to the foreign experts working in China*

【走风】let out a secret；leak out

【走钢丝】❶［杂］wirewalking ❷〈喻〉take risks：他向领导提出了辞职申请，这无异在～。*He was taking a risk when he handed in his resignation*.

【走狗】running dog；lackey；flunkey；stooge；servile follower

【走关节】get in through the back door；get round (laws，rules，etc.) by bribery

【走过场】do sth. as a mere formality；go through the motions；do sth. perfunctorily or superficially

【走红】(又作'走红运') have good luck；be in luck

【走后门】get in by (or through) the back door—get sth. done through pull；secure advantages through influence：～是不正之风，要杜绝。*The irregular practice of pulling strings and abusing influence must be stopped*.

【走火】❶［电］sparking ❷ (of firearms) discharge accidentally：他一时不慎，枪～了。*He wasn't careful and his rifle went off accidentally*. ❸ go too far in what one says；put sth. too strongly；overstate ❹ catch fire；be on fire：仓库～了。*The storehouse is on fire*.

【走江湖】wander from place to place and earn a living by juggling，fortune-telling，etc.；become a vagrant

【走廊】corridor；passage；passageway

【走漏】❶ leak out；divulge：～风声 *divulge a secret*；*leak information* ❷ smuggling and tax evasion

【走路】❶ walk；go on foot：孩子已经学会～了。*The baby has learned to walk*. / 你们是坐车去还是～去？*Will you go there by bus or on foot*? ❷ leave；go away

【走轮包】suitcase with wheels

【走马灯】running horse lantern (a lantern on the top band of which are decorative figures，which revolve as the hot air ascends)：人员不断更换，就像～似的。*Personnel were shifted about as often as if they were on a running horse lantern* (*or a merry-go-round*).

【走马疳】［医］noma；gangrenous stomatitis

【走马换将】change of command；reshuffle of personnel：领导班子～后，工作有了起色。*Things are looking up as a result of a reshuffle of the leading group*.

【走马看花】(又作'走马观花') look at flowers while riding a horse—gain a shallow understanding from a fleeting glance

【走马上任】go to one's post；take up (or assume) office

【走门路】(又作'走门子') solicit help from potential backers；gain one's end through pull

【走南闯北】journey north and south；travel widely：我～，也没见过这么能干的妇女。*I've been everywhere*, *but never have I seen a woman as capable as her*.

【走内线】take the inner line—use private influence to achieve one's end (e.g. seek sb.'s favour by approaching his confidants or members of his family)；go through private channels

【走娘家】(of a married woman) visit her parents' home

【走俏】(of goods) sell well；be in great demand

【走亲戚】call on relatives

【走禽】Cursores；cursorial birds

【走人】〈口〉go away；leave：叫他卷铺盖～。*Tell him to pack up and quit*.

【走色】lose colour；fade：这件衣服穿了两年了，还没有～。*The jacket hasn't lost colour though I've been wearing it for two years*.

【走扇】(of a door or window) won't shut properly (due to warping)

【走墒】evaporation of water in soil

【走神】(of one's attention) wander；be absent-minded：她一～漏了一针。*She dropped a stitch the moment her attention began to wander*.

【走绳】(又作'走索')［杂］ropedancing；ropewalking

【走失】❶ wander away；be lost；be missing：我们一起出去的，半路上他～了。*We went out together and he got lost on the way*. ❷ fail to keep；lose：译文～原意。*The original meaning is lost in the translation*.

【走时】(又作'走时运')〈方〉have good luck；be in luck

【走势】tendency：本产品价格～坚挺。*Such products tend to be expensive*.

【走兽】four-footed animals；quadrupeds；beasts

【走水】❶ leak water：房顶～了。*The roof is leaking*. ❷ (of water) flow；run：渠道～很通畅。*Water runs well in the canal*. ❸〈婉〉be on fire；catch fire

【走私】smuggle：～的货物 *smuggled goods*

【走题】(of a speech，etc.) digress from the subject；stray from the point：说话～ *speak beside the point*；*wander from the subject*

【走投无路】have no way out；be in an impasse；come to a dead end：逼得～ *be driven* (*or pushed*) *to the wall* / 穷困潦倒，～ *be down-and-out and have no place to turn*

【走味儿】lose flavour：茶叶～了。*The tea has lost its flavour*.

【走下坡路】go downhill；be on the decline

【走险】take a risk；make a reckless move

【走乡随乡】同〖随乡入乡〗

【走向】❶ run；trend；alignment：矿脉的～ *the run of the ore vein* / 海岸线～ *the trend of the coastline* ❷［地质］strike：～断层 *strike fault* / ～节理 *strike joint* ❸ move towards；head for；be on the way to：～反面 *change* (*or turn*) *into one's opposite* / ～死亡 *head for one's doom*; *go down to one's doom*

【走相】become deformed

【走形】be out of shape

【走形式】do sth. as a mere formality; go through the motions

【走穴】〈口〉(esp. of a performer) moonlight: 听说有的歌星～两个月,就收入40万元,是真的吗? *Is it true that some singers can make 400,000 yuan in two months by moonlighting in other shows?*

【走眼】see wrong: 拿着好货当次货,你可看走了眼了。*You've seen wrong. You took superior goods for inferior goods.*

【走样】lose shape; go out of form; be different from what is expected or intended: 这事让他给说～了。*His account presented a distorted picture of the matter.*

【走一步,看一步】take one step and look around before taking another—proceed without a plan, or with caution

【走油】(of oily food) go rancid

【走运】have good luck; be in luck: 祝你～。*Good luck to you.* or *Good luck!*

【走着瞧】wait and see: 咱们～! *We'll see (who's right).*

【走走】❶ take a stroll: 我们出去～吧。*Let's take a stroll.* ❷ come or go in a general sense: 有空常来～。*Drop in when you are free.*

【走卒】pawn; cat's-paw; lackey; stooge

【走嘴】make a slip of the tongue; let slip an inadvertent remark: 她说着说着就走了嘴。*As she talked on and on, she blurted the secret out.*

zòu

奏 动 ❶ play (music); perform (on a musical instrument): ～国歌 *play the national anthem* / ～哀乐 *play funeral music* / 当贵宾进入宴会厅时,乐队开始～迎宾曲。*The band struck up a tune of welcome when the distinguished guests entered the banquet hall.* ❷ achieve; produce: 奏效

【奏捷】win a battle; score a success: ～归来 *return in triumph*

【奏鸣曲】[音] sonata: 小～ *sonatina* ◇ ～式[音] sonata form

【奏效】prove effective; be successful; get the desired result: 这药服了马上～。*This medicine will have immediate efficacy.* / 这个办法能～吗? *Will this method work?*

【奏乐】play music; strike up a tune

揍 动 ❶〈口〉beat; hit; strike: 把他～一顿 *beat him up* / 挨～ *get a thrashing* ❷〈方〉smash; break: 他把碗给～了。*He smashed the bowl.* / 小心别把玻璃～了。*Be careful not to break the glass.*

zū

租 Ⅰ 动 ❶ rent; hire; charter: ～三间房 *rent three rooms* / ～一条小船 *hire a boat* / ～一架飞机 *charter a plane* ❷ rent out; let out; lease: 这块地已经～给人了。*This piece of land has been leased out.* Ⅱ 名 ❶ rent: 收～ *collect rent* ❷ land tax

【租船】[经] chartering ◇ ～代理 chartering agent; ～契约 charter party; charter; ～人 charterer; ～市场 chartering market

【租佃】(of a landlord) rent out land to tenants ◇ ～关系 tenancy relationship; ～制度 tenancy system

【租户】❶ tenant (of a building or part of it); lessee; leaseholder ❷ hirer (of a thing)

【租价】rent; rental

【租界】concession (in former times, a tract of land in a Chinese port or city supposedly on lease to, but actually seized by, an imperialist power and put under its colonial rule); settlement

【租借】rent; hire; lease ◇ ～地 leased territory; leasehold; ～人 leaseholder; lessee; tenant; hirer

【租金】rent; rental

【租赁】rent; lease; hire: ～服装和道具 *rent costumes and stage properties* ◇ ～合同 contract for lease; ～经营 leasing business; ～业 leasing trade

【租让】lease

【租书处】book rental

【租税】(in former times) land tax and other levies

【租用】rent; hire; take on lease: ～家具 *rent furniture* / ～礼堂 *hire a hall* / ～人 *leaseholder; lessee; tenant; hirer*

【租约】lease: ～什么时候到期? *When does the lease expire?* / 短期～ *short term tenancy*

【租债】rent and debt: 逼还～ *press for rent and debt payments*

【租子】〈口〉land rent; ground rent; rent

zú

足 Ⅰ 名 ❶ foot; leg: ～不出户 *never go out of one's room; stay indoors* / 自首至～ *from head to foot* ❷ leg (of certain utensils) Ⅱ 形 enough; ample; sufficient: ～吃～喝 *eat and drink to one's satisfaction* / 赚～了钱 *made plenty of money* / 工人们生产劲头很～。*The workers are full of drive in their work.* Ⅲ 副 ❶ fully; as much as: 路上～～走了两个钟头。*The journey took fully two hours.* / 从这里到邮局～有二里路。*It's a good two li from here to the post office.* ❷ (usu. used in the negative) enough; sufficiently: 无～挂齿 *not worth mentioning*

【足本】an unabridged version (of a novel, etc.)

【足不出户】never leave one's home
【足赤】pure gold; solid gold
【足够】enough; ample; sufficient: 我们对困难要有～的估计。*We must take full account of our difficulties.*
【足迹】footmark; footprint; track: 雪地上的～ *footprints (or tracks) in the snow*
【足见】it serves to show; one can well perceive: 他的发言内容丰富，～他是作了认真准备的。*His speech is substantial, which shows he took great pains to prepare it.*
【足金】pure gold; solid gold
【足谋寡断】resourceful but irresolute
【足球】❶ soccer; football: 踢～ *play soccer (or football)* ❷ football (the ball used in playing either soccer or American football): 美式～ *American football* / 英式～ *soccer; association football* ◇ ～队 football team; eleven; ～迷 football fan; ～运动员 footballer
【足色】(of gold or silver) of standard purity
【足坛】the football world: ～名将 *a football star* / ～劲旅 *a strong football team*
【足下】a polite form of address between friends (used mostly in letters): ～以为如何? *I wonder what you think of this.*
【足以】enough; sufficiently: 他挣的不多，但～应付生活所需。*He does not earn a large salary but it is adequate for his needs.*
【足音】(sound of) footsteps: 杂乱的～ *hurried footsteps*
【足银】pure silver
【足月】(of a foetus) born after the normal period of gestation; mature
【足智多谋】wise and full of strategems; wise and resourceful

卒 Ⅰ名 ❶ soldier; private: 士卒 ❷ servant: 走卒 ❸ pawn, one of the pieces in Chinese chess Ⅱ动 ❶ finish; end: ～其事 *finish the job; wind up the business* ❷ die: 病～ *die of illness* / ～于1986年 *died in* 1986 Ⅲ副 finally; at last: ～底于成 *finally achieve success*
【卒岁】〈书〉get through the year: 聊以～ *just to tide over the year*
【卒业】〈书〉graduate; finish a course of study
【卒子】❶〈旧〉rank-and-file soldier ❷ pawn, one of the pieces in Chinese chess

族 名 ❶ clan: 合～ *all the members of a clan; the whole clan* ❷ a death penalty in ancient China, imposed on an offender and his whole family, or even the families of his mother and wife ❸ race; ethnic group; nationality: 汉族 ❹ a class or group of things with common features: 猫～ *the cat tribe* / 碱土～ *alkaline earth family*
【族徽】emblem for a clan, tribe or nation
【族际】between nations: ～冲突 *inter-ethnic conflict* / ～协约 *agreement between nations*
【族类】the same clan (tribe, nation)
【族亲】members of a clan; clansmen
【族权】clan authority; clan power
【族人】clansman
【族长】clan elder; the head of a clan

zǔ

阻 动 hinder; block; obstruct: 拦阻 / 险阻
【阻碍】hinder; block; impede: ～交通 *block the traffic* / 遇到～ *meet with obstruction*
【阻车】hold up traffic; traffic jam: 南京长江大桥公路桥已超负荷，～现象经常发生。*Traffic jams are frequent on the Nanjing Yangtze Bridge because of its overload.*
【阻挡】stop; stem; resist; obstruct: 不可～的历史潮流 *an irresistible historical trend* ◇ ～犯规 [体] blocking
【阻断】stop; obstruct; block; cut off: 战争～了交通。*Communications have been cut by the war.*
【阻隔】separate; cut off: 山川～ *be separated by mountains and rivers*
【阻击】[军] block; check: ～战 *blocking action* / ～阵地 *blocking position*
【阻截】stop; obstruct; bar the way
【阻抗】[电] impedance ◇ 反射～ reflected impedance; ～匹配 impedance matching
【阻拦】stop; obstruct; bar the way: 他决心要走，我们也不好～。*As he was determined to go, we thought it better not to stop him.*
【阻力】❶ obstruction; resistance: 冲破各种～ *break through all kinds of obstructions* ❷ [物] resistance; drag: 空气～ *air resistance* / 摩擦～ *friction drag*
【阻留】be detained; be held up: ～误点的乘客 *held-up, delayed passengers*
【阻挠】obstruct; thwart; stand in the way; put a spoke in sb.'s wheel: 条约的履行受到了～。*The execution of the treaty was obstructed.*
【阻尼】[物] damping: ～器 *damper* / ～振荡 *damped oscillation*
【阻塞】block; obstruct; clog: 交通～。*The traffic is held up.* or *There's a traffic jam.*
【阻塞振荡器】blocking oscillator
【阻援】[军] hold off (or delay) enemy reinforcements
【阻止】prevent; stop; hold back: ～事态的恶化 *prevent the situation from deteriorating* / 别～他，让他去吧。*Don't try to stop him. Let him go.*

诅 动〈书〉curse; swear; wish sb. evil
【诅骂】curse; swear; abuse; revile
【诅咒】curse; swear; wish sb. evil; imprecate

组 Ⅰ动 organize; form: 改组 Ⅱ名 group: 20岁到30岁的年龄～ *the age group between* 20 *and* 30 Ⅲ量 set; series; battery: 两～发电机 *two generators* / 一～邮票 *a set of stamps*

【组胺】[化] histamine

【组办】organize; run: 该室内乐队由著名音乐家发起，社会～。*The Chamber Music Ensemble was sponsored by a well-known conductor, and is maintained by the community.*

【组编】put together (material); fit together: 抓住这个主题,把所有的材料～起来,成为一个整体。*Keep to the theme; put all relevant material together and work it into a unified, organic whole.*

【组成】form; make up; compose: 水的～ *the composition of water* / 每五个人～一组。*Every five persons constitute a group.* / 主席团由一百四十八位代表～。*The presidium consists of 148 delegates.*

【组成部分】component part; component; ingredient

【组队】form a team (usu. to take part in a competition): 各个工厂～参加比赛。*Each factory organized a team to take part in the competition.*

【组稿】(of editors) commission authors to write on given topics; solicit contributions

【组歌】suite of songs

【组阁】form (or set up, organize) a cabinet

【组合】❶ make up; compose; constitute: 各种政治力量的重新～ *a realignment of various political forces* ❷ association; combination: 词组是词的～。*A phrase is a group of words.* ❸ [数]combination ◇ ～车床 combined lathe; ～柜 large multi-use cabinet (for sound system, TV, books, etc.); ～家具 composite furniture; component furniture; ～理论 [数] combinatorial theory; ～体 [机] assembly; ～音响 hi-fi stereo component system; hi-fi (system, set, equipment); ～钻床 combination drilling machine

【组画】a series of paintings

【组件】[电] package; module: 微型～ *micromodule; module*

【组建】put together (a group); form: ～剧团 *put a theatre group together*

【组接】film montage; film editing

【组曲】[音] suite

【组台】organize a performance: 演员到外地～演出去了。*The actors are touring the provinces.*

【组态】[物] configuration: 平衡～ *configuration of equilibrium*

【组团】organize a performance group, touring group, etc.: 留美学子今夏～回国参观。*Chinese students in America are organizing travel groups to visit China this summer.*

【组织】❶ organize; form: ～劳力 *organize a labour force; organize labour power* / ～一个登山队 *form a mountaineering team* ❷ organization; organized system: 给予～处分 *take disciplinary measures against a member of an organization* / ～条例 *organic rules* / ～委员 *committee member in charge of organizational work* ❸ [纺] weave: 平纹～ *plain weave* / 斜纹～ *twill weave* / 缎纹～ *satin weave* ❹ [生理] tissue: 神经～ *nerve (or nervous) tissue* ◇ ～胺 同〖组胺〗; ～法 rules of organization; organic law; constituent act; ～关系 credentials showing membership in an organization; membership credentials; ～疗法 tissue therapy; histotherapy; ～生活 regular activities of an organization; ～行为学 organizational behaviorism; ～学 [生理] histology; ～液 [生理] tissue fluid

【组装】put together; assemble

【组字游戏】crossword puzzle

祖 名 ❶ grandfather: 祖父 ❷ ancestor: 远祖 ❸ founder (of a craft, religious sect, etc.); originator: 鼻祖

【祖辈】ancestors; forefathers; ancestry

【祖传】handed down from one's ancestors ◇ ～秘方 a secret prescription handed down in the family from generation to generation

【祖坟】ancestral grave

【祖父】(paternal) grandfather

【祖国】one's country; homeland; native land; motherland; fatherland

【祖籍】original family home; ancestral home; the land of one's ancestors

【祖居】❶ ancestral home ❷ 同〖祖籍〗 ❸ have one's ancestral home at; be a native of: ～绍兴 *be a native of Shaoxing*

【祖鲁语】Zulu (language)

【祖母】(paternal) grandmother

【祖母绿】emerald

【祖上】ancestors; forefathers; forbears

【祖师】(又作'祖师爷') ❶ the founder of a school of learning, a craft, etc. ❷ the founder of a sect of Buddhism or Taoism

【祖孙】grandparent and grandchild: ～三代 *three generations*

【祖先】ancestry; ancestors; forbears; forefathers

【祖宗】forefathers; ancestry; forbears: ～崇拜 *ancestor (or ancestral) worship*

【祖祖辈辈】for generations; from generation to generation: 我家～都是种地的。*Our family have been farmers for generations.* or *I come from a long line of farmers.*

zuān

钻 动 ❶ drill; bore: ～孔 *drill a hole* / ～木取火 *drill wood to make fire* ❷ get into; go through; make one's way into: ～进密林深处 *go deep into a forest* / 火车走这条线得～许多山洞。*The train has to pass through quite a few tunnels on this railway line.* / 月亮从云缝里～了出来。*The moon broke through the clouds.* ❸ study intensively; dig into: ～书本 *dig into books* / ～业务 *study one's trade; dig into one's job or a subject; work hard to perfect oneself professionally* ——另见 zuàn

【钻故纸堆】bury oneself in outdated writings; delve into musty old books

【钻劲】application to studies; studiousness：科研工作需要～，不能突击。*Scientific research demands close application rather than spurts of effort.*
【钻空子】avail oneself of loopholes (in a law, contract, etc.); exploit an advantage：不让对方～ *leave no loopholes for the other side to exploit* / 被人钻了空子 *be taken advantage of; be tricked*
【钻门子】〈口〉jockey for favours; manoeuvre for advantage
【钻牛角尖】(又作'钻牛角') ❶ take unnecessary pains to study an insignificant or insoluble problem; split hairs ❷ get into a dead end (or a blind alley)
【钻圈】[杂] jumping (or plunging) through hoops
【钻探】(exploration) drilling ◇ ～工 driller; ～机 drilling machine; ～设备 drilling equipment
【钻天柳】lombardy poplar (Populus nigra var. italica)
【钻天杨】Chosenia macrolepis
【钻头觅缝】(又作'钻天觅缝') worm oneself into every crack and crevice—try all possible means：他想长工资，～地往上巴结。*He wants a rise in his pay, and so he's currying favour with the boss by all possible means.*
【钻心】❶ (of pain, itching, etc.) unbearable：他感到浑身～的疼。*He was seized with sharp pains all over his body.* ❷ sneak in; infiltrate：～战术 *the tactic of taking the fortress from within*
【钻心虫】[动] borer
【钻研】study intensively; dig into：～国际法 *assiduously study international law* / ～技术 *perfect one's skill; master technique*
【钻营】curry favour with sb. in authority for personal gain; secure personal gain

躜 动 ❶ jump up ❷ dash forward：燕子～天。*The swallow dashed (or shot) through the air.*

zuǎn

纂 动〈书〉compile; edit：编纂
【纂修】compile; edit

zuàn

钻 Ⅰ 名 ❶ drill; auger：手摇～ *hand drill; drill* ❷ diamond; jewel：十九～的手表 *a 19-jewel watch* Ⅱ 动 bore; drill：在木头上～个眼 *bore a hole in wood* ——另见 zuān
【钻床】[机] drilling machine; driller：龙门～ *planer drilling machine*
【钻杆】[油] drill rod (or pipe)
【钻机】[油](drilling) rig; drilling machine：安装～ *rig up* / 拆卸～ *rig down* / 旋转～ *rotary rig*
【钻戒】diamond ring
【钻井】well drilling：构造～ *core drilling* / 海洋～ *offshore drilling* ◇ ～船 oil rig; ～队 drilling crew (or team); ～工人 driller; ～记录 drill log
【钻具】[油] drilling tool; drilling rig
【钻模】[机] (drill) jig：分度～ *indexing jig*
【钻石】❶ diamond ❷ jewel (used in a watch)
【钻塔】[矿] boring tower; derrick
【钻铤】[油]drill collar
【钻头】bit (of a drill)：装上～ *brace a bit* / 卸下～ *break out a bit* / 三牙轮～ *three cone bit*
【钻压】[油] bit pressure; bit weight

攥 动 hold; grip; grasp：手里～着一把斧子 *hold an axe in one's hand* / ～紧拳头 *clench one's fist* / 一把～住他的手 *clasp him by the hand*

zuǐ

嘴 名 ❶ mouth：闭上～ *keep one's mouth shut* / ～上说说而已 *pay lip service* / 你这张～啊！*What a tongue you've got!* ❷ anything shaped or functioning like a mouth：茶壶～儿 *the spout of a teapot* / 瓶～儿 *the mouth of a bottle*
【嘴巴】❶ mouth：张开～。*Open your mouth.* ❷〈口〉(usu. used in)：打～ *slap sb. in the face; box sb.'s ears*
【嘴笨】inarticulate; clumsy of speech
【嘴不饶人】fond of making sarcastic remarks
【嘴馋】fond of good food; greedy; voracious：他一见有好吃的东西就～。*He will start drooling at the sight of good food.*
【嘴唇】lip：上(下)～ *the upper (lower) lip* / 咬着～ *bite one's lips*
【嘴乖】(of children) clever and pleasant when speaking to elders：这小姑娘～，挺逗人喜欢。*What a dear little girl, talking so sweetly!*
【嘴尖】❶ sharp-tongued; cutting in speech：他这个人～，说的话真刺耳。*He's sharp-tongued and what he says is often very biting.* ❷ be choosy about what one eats：别～了，给你什么你就吃什么。*Don't be so choosy. Take what you're given.*
【嘴角】corners of the mouth：他～叼着一支烟走了进来。*He came in with a cigarette dangling from a corner of his mouth.*
【嘴紧】tight-lipped; closemouthed
【嘴啃泥】fall on one's face：他脚底一滑，摔了个～。*He slipped and fell on his face.*
【嘴快】have a loose tongue：她～，跟谁都会说。*She has a loose tongue and will tell everybody.*
【嘴懒】not inclined to talk much
【嘴脸】〈贬〉face; features; countenance：一副丑恶～！*What a hideous face!* / 他那副～真难看。*He had a very nasty look on his face.*
【嘴皮子】〈口〉〈贬〉lips (of a glib talker)：他那两片～可能说了。*He has a ready tongue.* or *He can argue on any side of any question.* ——另见〖要嘴皮子〗
【嘴贫】(又作'嘴频') loquacious; garrulous
【嘴勤】fond of talking; chatty
【嘴软】afraid to speak out：吃人～。*A guest can't*

speak against his host.

【嘴上没毛,办事不牢】A man too young to grow a beard is not dependable; A man with downy lips is bound to make slips.

【嘴松】have a loose tongue: 性直～ *have a candid nature and a loose tongue*

【嘴碎】loquacious; garrulous

【嘴甜】ingratiating in speech; smooth-tongued; honeymouthed

【嘴严】tight-lipped; closemouthed

【嘴硬】stubborn and reluctant to admit mistakes or defeats: 知道错了,就别～。*You know you're wrong, so don't stubbornly insist that you aren't*.

【嘴直】outspoken; plainspoken

【嘴子】❶〈方〉anything shaped or functioning like a mouth: 山～ *the tip of a foothill* ❷[音] mouthpiece (of a wind instrument)

zuì

最 副 ❶ (used before an adjective or a verb) most; -est: ～基本的条件 *fundamental prerequisites* / 他～不讲道理。*He's most unreasonable*. / 我～喜欢吃巧克力冰淇淋。*I like chocolate ice cream best*. ❷ (used before a noun of locality or a place word) farthest to or nearest (a place): ～上头 *farthest to (or nearest) the top; at the very top* / ～东头 *farthest to the east; at the very east end*

【最爱】favorite; fave

【最初】initial; first: ～阶段 *the initial stage* / ～的印象 *first impressions* / ～的计划 *the original plan; the first and earliest plan*

【最大公约数】[数] greatest common divisor

【最低】lowest; minimum ◇ ～纲领 minimum programme; ～价格 lowest price; bottom price; bedrock price; ～税率 minimum tariff

【最低限额】zero norm; nil norm

【最多】most; at (the) most; maximum: 这个礼堂～能容纳一千人。*This hall can hold a maximum of one thousand people*. / 这所学校学生～的时候有三千人。*The school's enrolment at its height reached* 3,000.

【最高】highest; supreme; tallest: ～国家权力机关 *the highest organ of state power* / 达到～峰 *reach the climax (or peak)*; reach a culminating point / 创造历史上～纪录 *hit an all-time high* ◇ ～点 statistics peak; ～纲领 maximum programme; ～国务会议 the Supreme State Conference; ～年产量 peak annual output; ～权力 supreme power; ～人民法院 supreme people's court; ～税率 maximum tariff; ～速度 maximum speed; ～统帅 supreme commander; ～限额 ceiling; ～限价 ceiling price

【最高级】❶ highest; summit: ～会谈 *top-level talks; summit talks* ❷〈语〉the superlative degree ◇ ～会议 summit meeting

【最好】❶ best; first-rate: ～的办法 *the best way* / 质量～ *best in quality* ❷ had better; it would be best: 你～今天把它搞完。*You'd better finish it today*. ◇ ～成绩 best result

【最后】final; last; ultimate: ～胜利 *final victory* ◇ ～冲刺[体] final spurt; ～条款 final provisions; final articles; ～通牒 ultimatum; ～议定书 final protocol; ～议事录 precés-verbal final

【最惠国】most-favoured-nation ◇ ～税率 most-favoured-nation rate; ～条款 most-favoured-nation clause

【最惠国待遇】most-favoured-nation (MFN) treatment; MFN trading status: 给以～ *accord (a country) most-favoured-nation treatment*

【最佳】❶[物] optimum: ～数 *optimum number* / ～谐振 *optimum resonance* ❷ the best: ～运动员 *the best athlete (or player)*

【最简单派艺术】minimal art ◇ ～家 minimal artist; minimalist

【最近】❶ recently; lately; of late: ～的消息 *the latest news; recent news* / ～一期的《英语学习》 *the current issue of English Language Learning* ❷ in the near future; soon: ～要上演许多新电影。*Many new films will be released soon*.

【最轻量级】[体] bantamweight

【最少】least; at (the) least; minimum: 他做的事～。*He did the least work*.

【最为】(used before disyllabic adjectives or verbs) most; extremely: ～重要 *most (or extremely) important*

【最小二乘法】[数] least square method

【最小公倍数】[数] least (or lowest) common multiple

【最新】latest; up-to-date ◇ ～产品 latest product; newest product; ～工艺 latest technology; ～技术 up-to-date technology; ～款式 latest fashion

【最优方法】optimization method

【最终】final; ultimate: ～结果 *the final outcome* ◇ ～消费者 ultimate consumer; ～用户 final user

罪 名 ❶ crime; guilt: 贪污～ *crimes of corruption* / 受贿～ *crimes of accepting bribes* / ～上加～ *be doubly guilty* ❷ fault; blame ❸ suffering; pain; hardship: 受罪

【罪案】details of a criminal case; case

【罪不容诛】even death cannot atone for the offence; be guilty of crimes for which even death is insufficient punishment

【罪错】(〈略〉全称为'罪行和过错') criminal offenses and errors: 犯有～的大部分人员是可以改邪归正的。*Most of those who have committed crimes are capable of turning over a new leaf*.

【罪大恶极】be guilty of the most heinous crimes

【罪恶】crime; evil: ～多端 *be guilty of all kinds of evil*

【罪恶昭彰】(又作'罪恶昭著') have committed flagrant crimes

【罪犯】criminal; offender; culprit

【罪该万死】be guilty of a crime for which one deserves to die ten thousand deaths; be guilty of a crime for which even death cannot atone

【罪过】❶ fault; offence; sin: 这是我的～。*It's my fault*. ❷〈谦〉thanks, but this is really more than I deserve

【罪魁】chief criminal (or culprit, offender); arch-criminal ◇ ～祸首 chief culprit (or offender); arch-criminal

【罪名】charge; accusation: 偷窃的～ *a charge of theft*

【罪莫大焉】There is no greater crime than this.

【罪孽】wrongdoing that brings retribution; sin: ～深重 *sinful*

【罪人】guilty person; offender; sinner: 历史～ *a person condemned by history*

【罪嫌】(〈略〉全称为'犯罪嫌疑') suspect: 叛国～ *suspected traitor*

【罪行】crime; guilt; offence: 他的～较轻。*His offence is a minor one*.

【罪有应得】One deserves one's punishment; The punishment fits the crime.

【罪责】responsibility for an offence: ～难逃 *cannot escape the responsibility for the offence (or crime); cannot get away with it*

【罪证】evidence of a crime; proof of one's guilt

【罪状】facts about a crime; charges in an indictment

醉 形 ❶ drunk; intoxicated; tipsy: 他喝～了。*He's tipsy*. or *He's had a drop too much*. ❷ (of some kinds of food) liquor-saturated; steeped in liquor: ～蟹 *liquor-saturated crab* / ～虾 *wine-soaked shrimp*

【醉鬼】drunkard; sot; inebriate

【醉汉】drunkard; drunken man

【醉酒】drunk; intoxicated: ～的人犯罪,应当负刑事责任。*An intoxicated person who commits a crime shall bear criminal responsibility*.

【醉拳】drunken boxing (a form of boxing with movements suggesting a drunken man reeling along)

【醉生梦死】live as if drunk or dreaming; lead a befuddled life

【醉翁之意不在酒】the Old Tippler's delight does not reside in wine—have other things in mind; have ulterior motives

【醉心】be bent on; be wrapped up in: 他～于数学的研究。*He's deeply engrossed in mathematical research*. / ～名利 *be infatuated with fame and gain*

【醉醺醺】sottish; drunk; tipsy

【醉言不较】do not find fault with drunken talk

【醉眼】〈书〉eyes showing the effects of drink: ～朦胧 *drunken and bleary-eyed*

【醉意】signs or feeling of getting drunk: 他已经有几分～了。*He is a bit tipsy*.

zūn

尊 Ⅰ 形 ❶ senior; of a senior generation: 尊长 ❷〈尊〉your: ～夫人 *your wife* / ～姓大名? *May I know your name*? Ⅱ 动 respect; venerate; honour: 自尊 Ⅲ 量 一～佛像 *a statue of a Buddha* / 五十～大炮 *fifty artillery pieces*

【尊称】❶ a respectful form of address; honorific title: "您"是"你"的～。您(*nín*) *is an honorific form for* 你(*nǐ* "*you*"). ❷ address sb. respectfully: 人们～他为郭老。*People respectfully called him the venerable Guo*.

【尊崇】worship; revere; venerate

【尊府】❶〈尊〉your residence; your home ❷〈书〉〈尊〉your father

【尊贵】honourable; respectable; respected: ～的客人 *an honoured guest*

【尊驾】〈尊〉you: 恭候～光临。*We request the pleasure of your company*.

【尊敬】respect; honour; esteem: ～父母 *honour one's parents* / ～的来宾们 *Distinguished Guests (a form of address)*

【尊命】〈尊〉your instructions

【尊容】distinguished face (usu. used ironically): 瞧他那副～,还打扮呢! *What a face he's got, and he pays so much attention to dress*.

【尊师爱生】respect the teacher and love the student; students respecting teachers and teachers loving students

【尊师重道】honour the teacher and revere his teachings

【尊严】dignity; honour: 国家～ *national dignity* / 维护法律的～ *guard the sanctity of the law*

【尊意】〈尊〉your opinion: 不知～如何? *I'd like to hear your opinion*.

【尊长】elders and betters

【尊重】❶ respect; value; esteem: 互相～ *respect each other* / ～群众的首创精神 *value the initiative of the masses* / ～科学 *have a high regard for science* ❷ serious; proper: 放～些! *Behave yourself*!

遵 动 abide by; obey; observe; follow: ～纪爱民 *observe discipline and cherish the people* / ～医嘱 *follow the doctor's advice*

【遵办】act in compliance with instructions

【遵从】defer to; comply with; follow: ～上级的指示 *in compliance with the directives of the leadership* / ～老师的教导 *follow the teacher's advice*

【遵命】〈套〉comply with your wish; obey your command: ～办理 *act in compliance with your instructions*

【遵守】observe; abide by; comply with: ～公共秩序 *observe public order* / ～时间 *be on time; be punctual* / ～法律 *abide by the law*

【遵循】follow; abide by; adhere to: ～和平共处的原则 *follow the principle of peaceful coexistence*

【遵照】obey; conform to; comply with; act in accordance with: ～上级的命令 *in obedience to orders from above*

zuō

作 名 workshop：木工～ *carpenters' workshop* / 洗衣～ *laundry* ——另见 zuò

【作坊】workshop：生产纺织品的～ *a workshop for manufacturing textiles*

zuó

昨 名 ❶ yesterday：昨天 ❷ the past

【昨儿】（又作'昨儿个'）〈口〉yesterday：～晚上 *yesterday evening*；*last night*

【昨日】yesterday

【昨天】yesterday

【昨晚】yesterday evening；last night

【昨夜】yesterday evening；last night

琢（构此成分）见下——另见 zhuó

【琢磨】（zuómo）think over；turn over in one's mind；ponder：～出个办法 *figure out a way*（*to do sth.*）/ 这件事她～了很久。*She pondered over the matter for a long time.* ——另见 zhuómó

zuǒ

左 Ⅰ 名 ❶ the left side；the left：～上方 *the upper left* / ～转弯 *turn to the left*；*turn left* ❷ east：山～ *areas east of the Taihang Mountains, specifically Shandong Province* ❸ the Left：凡有人群的地方，都有～、中、右。*Wherever there are masses of people they are invariably divided into the Left, the middle and the Right.* Ⅱ 形 ❶ queer；unorthodox；heretical ❷ wrong；incorrect：你想～了。*You're not thinking in the right way.* or *You've got a wrong idea.* ❸ different；contrary；opposite：相左

【左膀右臂】right-hand man；a capable assistant

【左边锋】［体］（足球）outside left；left wing

【左边】（zuǒ bian）the left；the left（or left-hand）side：房子～有一棵榆树。*There's an elm tree on the left of the house.*

【左不过】❶ anyway；anyhow；in any event：他说来说去，～是这么个意思。*He put it this way and that, but anyway that's what it boils down to.* ❷ only；merely；just：你怎么啦？—没什么，～有点头痛。*What's the matter with you?* —*Nothing serious. Just a slight headache.*

【左侧】同〖左边〗

【左道旁门】❶ heretical sect；heterodox school ❷ heresy；heterodoxy

【左舵】left standard rudder；left rudder：～十度！*Port 10 degrees!*

【左锋】［体］（篮球）left forward

【左顾右盼】glance right and left；look around：他～，像是在找人。*Casting glances here and there, he seemed to be looking for somebody.*

【左后卫】［体］（足球）left back

【左近】in the vicinity（or neighbourhood）；nearby：他就住在～。*He lives nearby.*

【左邻右舍】neighbours

【左轮】revolver

【左面】the left（or left-hand）side；the left

【左内锋】［体］（足球）inside left

【左派】❶ the Left；the left wing：～势力 *Left forces*；*forces of the Left* ❷ Leftist

【左撇子】left-handed person；left-hander；lefty

【左前卫】［体］（足球）left halfback；left half

【左倾】❶ left-leaning；progressive；inclined towards the revolution ❷ "Left" deviation ◇ ～空谈 "Left" phrasemongering；～机会主义 "Left" opportunism；～冒险主义 "Left" adventurism

【左手】❶ the left hand ❷ 同〖左首〗

【左首】the left-hand side；the left：坐在我的～ *sit on my left*

【左思右想】think over from different angles；turn sth. over in one's mind：她躺在床上～，一夜也没合眼。*She lay awake all night, thinking the matter over and over again.*

【左提右挈】❶ help each other；give mutual help ❷ guide and support；give guidance and help to

【左舷】port（of a ship）

【左性】（又作'左性子'）stubborn；pigheaded；wilful

【左翼】❶［军］left wing；left flank ❷ the left wing；the Left：～分子 *Leftist*；*Left-winger*

【左右】❶ the left and right sides：～摇摆 *vacillate now to the left and now to the right* ❷（used after a numeral）about；or so：八点钟～ *around eight o'clock* / 一个月～ *a month or so* / 价值十元～。*It's worth about* 10 *yuan.* ❸ master；control；influence：～局势 *be master of the situation* / 为人所～ *be controlled by sb.*；*fall under sb.'s influence* ❹ those in close attendance；retinue：屏退～ *order one's attendants to clear out* ❺〈方〉anyway；anyhow；in any case：我～闲着没事，就陪你走一趟吧。*Anyway I'm free now. Let me go with you.*

【左…右…】over and over again：*左劝右劝 try again and again to persuade sb.* / *左一条清规，右一条戒律 one taboo after another*

【左右逢源】❶ be able to achieve success one way or another ❷ gain advantage from both sides

【左右开弓】shoot first with one hand, then with the other；use both hands alternately in quick succession；be ambidextrous：～连续抽打 *attack with a volley of forehand and backhand smashes* / ～打人嘴巴 *slap sb. on both cheeks*

【左右手】right-hand man；*a capable assistant*

【左右为难】in a dilemma；in an awkward predicament

【左证】evidence；proof

【左支右绌】find it hard to cover expenses；be in straitened circumstances；have too many problems to cope with

佐 Ⅰ 动 assist：辅佐 Ⅱ 名 assistant

【佐餐】❶ be eaten together with rice or bread；go with rice or bread ❷ appetizing：～食品 *appetizers* / ～音乐 *music to accompany a meal*

【佐酒】〈书〉❶ drink with sb. ❷ (of food) go with wine：～佳肴 *delicacies that go with wine*

【佐料】同〖作料〗

【佐药】［医］adjuvant

【佐证】同〖左证〗

撮 量 (for hair) tuft：一～黑毛 *a tuft of black hair* / 一～山羊胡子 *a goatee* ——另见 cuō

【撮子】〈口〉tuft (of hair)：剪下一～头发 *cut off a tuft of hair*

zuò

坐 动 ❶ sit：请～。*Please sit down*. / 请进来～～。*Please come in and sit for a while*. / 我愿意站着，你～下吧。*I like to stand, you sit down*. / 他忽然～起来了。*He sat up suddenly*. ❷ travel by or on (any conveyance except those which one straddles)：～火车(公共汽车) *ride on a train* (*bus*) / ～火车(公共汽车)去 *go by train* (*bus*) / ～电梯上去 *go up by lift* / 进来～～。*Come in and sit down for a while*. ❸ (of a building) have its back towards：这所房子～北朝南。*This house faces south*. ❹ put (a pan, pot, kettle, etc.) on a fire：把壶～上 *put the kettle on* (*the fire*) ❺ (of a building) sink；subside：这个房子向后～了。*This house is beginning to slope backwards*. ❻ (of rifles, guns, etc.) recoil；kick back：坐力 ❼ bear；fruit：坐果 ❽ be punished：反坐

【坐班】keep office hours；keep set office hours (where staff are required to be in their offices during certain hours)

【坐标】［数］coordinate：～轴 *coordinate axis*

【坐不下】(of a vehicle, table, room, etc.) have not enough seats for (a certain number of people)；cannot seat：这车～这么多人。*This car can't seat so many people*.

【坐不住】cannot sit still；be restless；fidget：我们一听说有新任务，就～了。*When we learnt that we'd been given a new task, we just couldn't sit still any longer*.

【坐禅】［宗］(佛教) sit in meditation

【坐吃山空】if left to sit idle, one can even consume a mountain；sit idle and eat, and in time your whole fortune will be used up

【坐次】order of seats；seating arrangements

【坐得下】(of a vehicle, table, room, etc.) have seats for (a certain number of people)；seat

【坐得住】can sit still；can sit for long：她～，当编辑挺合适。*She has sedentary habits*；*she is fit to be an editor*.

【坐等】sit back and wait：～胜利 *sit back waiting for victory with folded arms*

【坐地分赃】(of a ringleader, criminal, receiver of stolen goods, etc.) take a share of the spoils without participating in the robbery

【坐垫】cushion

【坐而论道】sit back and pontificate

【坐骨】ischium ◇ ～神经 sciatic nerve

【坐观成败】wait to see what will come of another's venture；look on coldly；be a mere onlooker

【坐果】［农］bear fruit；fructify；fruit setting；fruition：～率 *fruition rate*

【坐化】(of Buddhist monks) pass away (or die) in a sitting posture

【坐监】(又作'坐监狱') be in prison；be in jail；be imprisoned

【坐禁闭】be placed in confinement (as a disciplinary measure)

【坐井观天】look at the sky from the bottom of a well—have a very narrow view

【坐具】a thing to sit on；seat

【坐困】be confined；be walled in；be shut up ◇ ～愁城 be walled in by one's own worries

【坐牢】be in prison；be in jail；be imprisoned：他坐了三年牢。*He's been in prison for three years*.

【坐冷板凳】sit on a cold bench—hold an unimportant post and be neglected；be kept waiting for an assignment or an audience with a VIP

【坐力】recoil (of a gun)；kick

【坐立不安】feel uneasy whether sitting or standing；be fidgety；be on tenterhooks

【坐落】(of a building) be situated；be located：我们工厂～在山脚下。*Our factory is located at the foot of a hill*.

【坐骑】saddle horse；mount

【坐蓐】〈书〉confinement in child-birth；lying-in

【坐山雕】［动］cinereous vulture

【坐山观虎斗】sit on top of the mountain to watch the tigers fight—watch in safety while others fight, then reap the spoils when both sides are exhausted

【坐失良机】let slip a golden opportunity；lose a good chance

【坐视不救】sit back and watch without going to the rescue

【坐收渔利】(又作'坐收渔人之利') reap the spoils of victory without lifting a finger；profit from others' conflict；reap third party profit ——另见〖鹬蚌相争，渔翁得利〗

【坐探】an enemy agent planted within one's own ranks

【坐位】❶ a place to sit；seat：留几个～ *reserve some seats* / 排～ *make seating arrangements* ❷ a thing to sit on；seat：给我搬个～儿来。*Get* (*or Fetch, Bring*) *me a seat*.

【坐卧不宁】(又作'坐卧不安') be unable to sit down or sleep at ease；feel restless；be on tenterhooks

【坐席】❶ take one's seat at a banquet table ❷ attend a banquet

【坐享其成】sit idle and enjoy the fruits of others' work; reap where one has not sown
【坐药】[中] suppository
【坐以待毙】sit still waiting for death; await one's doom; resign oneself to death: 与其～,不如先下手打他个措手不及。*It is better for us to go into action now and take the enemy by surprise, rather than wait passively until the enemy comes and seizes us.*
【坐以待旦】sit up and wait for daybreak
【坐月子】〈口〉confinement in childbirth; lying-in
【坐镇】(of a commander) personally attend to garrison duty; assume personal command
【坐庄】❶ be a resident buyer of a business firm ❷ be the banker or dealer (in a gambling game)

作 Ⅰ 动 ❶ rise; grow: 枪声大～。*Heavy firing broke out.* ❷ write; compose: ～诗 *compose a poem* / ～书一封 *write a letter* / ～画 *paint a picture* ❸ pretend; affect: 故～怒容 *pretend to be angry* ❹ regard as; take sb. or sth. for: 看作 / 作废 ❺ feel; have: 作呕 Ⅱ 名 writings; work: 新～ *a new work* / 成功之～ *a successful work*
【作案】commit a crime or an offence: ～时被捕 *be caught in the act; be caught red-handed*
【作罢】drop; relinquish; give up: 双方意见不一,事情只好～。*Since the two sides couldn't agree, the matter had to be dropped.*
【作保】be sb.'s guarantor; go bail for sb.; sponsor sb.
【作弊】practise fraud; cheat; indulge in corrupt practices
【作壁上观】watch the fighting from the ramparts—sit by and watch; be an onlooker (or bystander)
【作别】〈书〉bid farewell; take one's leave: 与亲友～ *take leave of one's relatives and friends*
【作词】write words (for a song): 李红～ *words by Li Hong*
【作答】answer
【作对】❶ set oneself against; oppose: 他没有理由和你～。*He has no reason to oppose you.* ❷ pair off in marriage
【作恶】❶ do evil: ～多端 *do all kinds of evil; be steeped in iniquity* ❷〈书〉gloomy; melancholy
【作伐】〈书〉act as matchmaker
【作法】❶ exercise magic ❷ (同〖做法〗) way of doing things; course of action; practice: 习惯～ *a habitual practice* ❸ technique of writing: 文章～ *technique of writing; art of composition*
【作法自毙】make a law only to fall foul of it oneself; be hoist with one's own petard; get caught in one's own trap
【作废】become invalid: 声明～ *declare invalid* / 宣布条约～ *declare a treaty null and void*
【作风】style; style of work; way: 工作～ *style of work* / ～正派 *be honest and upright in one's ways; have moral integrity*
【作复】write in reply; write back: 迟未～ *have not been able to reply sooner*
【作古】〈书〉〈婉〉die; pass away
【作怪】do mischief; make trouble: 保守思想在他们头脑中～。*Conservative ideas are doing mischief in their minds.*
【作害】(of birds and beasts) damage (crops, etc.); make havoc of
【作家】writer; author: 巴金是中国的著名～。*Ba Jin is a famous Chinese writer.* / 多产～ *a prolific writer (or author)* ◇ ～协会 the Writers' Union
【作假】❶ counterfeit; falsify ❷ cheat; play tricks ❸ behave affectedly
【作价】fix a price for sth.; evaluate: 合理～,公平交易 *fair pricing and square dealing* / 旧水泵～500元 *appraise the old pump at 500 yuan*
【作奸犯科】*violate the law and commit crimes; commit offences against law and discipline*
【作茧自缚】*spin a cocoon around oneself; get enmeshed in a web of one's own spinning*
【作践】(口语多读 zuó jian)〈口〉❶ spoil; waste: ～东西 *spoil things* ❷ run sb. down; disparage: 他这不是故意～人吗? *Didn't he say that just to run me down?* ❸ humiliate; insult
【作客】〈书〉sojourn: ～他乡 *sojourn in a strange land* ◇ ～思想 feeling of not belonging; guest mentality
【作困兽斗】fight like a cornered beast; fight back at bay
【作乐】make merry; enjoy oneself; have a good time
【作料】(口语多读 zuó liao) condiments; seasoning
【作乱】stage an armed rebellion
【作美】(usu. used in the negative) (of weather, etc.) help; cooperate; make things easy for sb.
【作难】❶ feel embarrassed; feel awkward; find oneself in a predicament ❷ make things difficult for sb.
【作鸟兽散】scatter like birds and beasts; flee helter-skelter; stampede
【作孽】do evil; commit a sin
【作弄】tease; make a fool of; play a trick on; poke fun at
【作呕】feel sick; feel like vomiting; be overcome by nausea
【作陪】help entertain the guest of honour; be invited along with the chief guest
【作品】works (of literature and art)
【作畦】[农] bedding: ～机 *bedder*
【作情】〈方〉❶ admire ❷ send gifts; make a gift of sth. ❸ mediate; arbitrate ❹ feel grateful to sb.; appreciate the kindness ❺ be affected or pretentious; strike a pose
【作曲】❶ write music; compose: 莫扎特五岁就开始～了。*Mozart began to compose when he was five years old.* ❷ write music (for a song): 王芳～ *music by Wang Fang* ◇ ～家 composer
【作如是观】view the matter in this light
【作色】show signs of anger; get worked up: 愤然

～ *flush with indignation*

【作数】count; be valid: 那条旧规定不～了。*That old rule doesn't hold any longer.* / 他讲的话作得了数。*What he says counts.*

【作死】(口语多读 zuōsǐ)〈诗〉seek death; take the road to ruin; look for trouble: 天这么冷不穿棉衣,你～呀! *Are you tired of life that you don't wear padded clothes in such cold weather?*

【作速】lose no time; hasten: ～处理 *deal with the matter as soon as possible; settle the matter quickly*

【作祟】❶ (of ghosts, spirits, etc.) haunt ❷ make mischief; cause trouble; exercise evil influence: 这都是利己主义在～。*All this trouble is caused by selfishness.*

【作痛】have a pain; ache: 周身的筋骨隐隐～ *feel a dull pain all over*

【作威作福】tyrannically abuse one's power; ride roughshod over others; act like a tyrant: 骑在人民头上～ *ride roughshod over the people; lord it over the people*

【作为】❶ conduct; deed; action: 从他的～可以看出他的态度。*From his deeds we can discern his attitude.* ❷ accomplishment; achievement: 这位新经理很有～。*The new manager is a dynamic and able man.* ❸ scope for one's abilities or talents: 大有作为 ❹ regard as; look on as; take as: 把那个～借口 *use it as an excuse* ❺ in the capacity, character, or role of; as: ～你的朋友,我得劝劝你。*As your friend, I have to give you some advice.*

【作伪】fake (works of art, cultural relics, etc.); make an imitation; forge

【作文】❶ (of students) write a composition ❷ composition

【作物】crop: 高产～ *high-yield crops; highly productive crop*

【作息】work and rest: 按时～ *work and rest according to schedule* ◇ ～时间表 daily schedule; work schedule; timetable

【作响】make a sound: 大车在路上辘辘～。*The cart rumbled on the road.* / 风吹树叶沙沙～。*The leaves rustled in the wind.*

【作兴】〈方〉❶ (usu. used in the negative) there's reason to; it's justifiable (or permissible) to: 可不～骂人。*It's not right to swear at people.* ❷ perhaps; possibly; maybe: ～要下雨。*Maybe it's going to rain.*

【作痒】have an itch; itch: 头皮～ *have an itch in one's scalp* / 全身～ *itch (or feel itchy) all over*

【作业】❶ school assignment: 做～ *do one's assignment* / 改～ *correct students' papers* ❷ work; task; operation; production: 水下～ *underwater operation* / 野外～ *fieldwork; field operation*

【作揖】(口语多读 zuōyī) make a slight bow with hands folded in front

【作用】❶ act on; affect: 外界事物～于我们的感官,在我们的头脑中形成印象。*External things act on our sense organs and give rise to impressions in our brains.* ❷ action; function: 化学～ *chemical action* / 心脏的～ *the function of the heart* ❸ effect: 起～ *be effective* / 起积极～ *play a positive role* / 不起～ *be ineffective; won't work* ❹ purpose; intention; motive: 他说那句话有什么～? *What was his purpose in saying that?* / 他那样说是有他的～的。*He had an axe to grind when he said that.*

【作用力】[物] acting force

【作战】fight; conduct operations; do battle: 英勇～ *fight heroically* / 大规模～ *conduct large-scale operations* / 积极对敌～ *active warfare against the enemy* ◇ ～部队 combat (or fighting) troops; ～部署 operational preparations; ～地图 battle map; operation map; ～方案 battle plan; line of action; ～方法 method of fighting; tactics in operations; ～方式 mode of operations; ～方针 concept of operations; operational principles; operational policy; ～基地 operational base; base of operations; ～技术 fighting technique; ～命令 combat (or operation) order; ～区域 theatre of war; ～线 battle line; ～效能 fighting efficiency; ～直升机 gunship; ～指挥部 operational headquarters

【作者】author; writer: ～赠 *From the author* / ～不详 *by an anonymous author; authorship unknown* / 本文～ *the present writer*

【作证】❶ be used as evidence ❷ testify; give evidence; bear witness: 在法庭上～ *bear witness in a law court*

座 Ⅰ 名 ❶ seat; place: 这个剧场有5,000个～儿。*The theatre seats 5,000.* ❷ stand; pedestal; base: 花瓶～儿 *vase stand* / 塑像～儿 *pedestal for a statue* ❸ [天] constellation: 大熊座 Ⅱ 量 (for mountains, buildings, and other similar immovable objects): 一～山 *a mountain* / 一～楼 *a building* / 一～桥 *a bridge* / 一～铜像 *a bronze statue*

【座舱】❶ passenger cabin (in an airliner) ❷ cockpit (of a fighter)

【座次】同『坐次』

【座号】seat number

【座机】sb.'s private plane

【座上客】guest of honour; honoured guest

【座谈】have an informal discussion

【座谈会】forum; symposium; informal discussion: 文艺～ *forum on literature and art*

【座位】a place to sit; seat: 这个体育馆有18,000个～。*The stadium seats 18,000.*

【座无虚席】all seats are occupied; there are no empty seats: 剧场内～。*There was a full house.*

【座右铭】motto; maxim

【座钟】desk clock

【座子】❶ stand; pedestal; base ❷ saddle (of a bicycle, motorcycle, etc.)

做 动 ❶ do; make; produce; manufacture: ～

结论 *pass a verdict*; *reach a conclusion* / ～长期打算 *plan on a long-term basis* / ～衣服 *make clothes* ❷ cook; prepare: ～菜 *cook a dish* ❸ do; act; engage in: ～好本职工作 *do one's best at one's own job* / 从点滴的事情～起 *start with little things* / 大事～不来,小事又不～ *be unable to do big jobs and look down on small ones* ❹ be; become: ～演员 *become an actor or actress*; *go on the stage* / 后来她～保育员了。*Later she became a child-care worker.* / 今天开会由你～主席。*You'll be the chairman at today's meeting.* ❺ write; compose: ～一首诗 *write a poem* ❻ hold a family (or home) celebration: 做寿 ❼ be used as: 这篇文章可以～教材。*This article may be used as teaching material.* / 树皮可以～造纸的原料。*Bark may be used as one of the raw materials for paper.* ❽ form or contract a relationship: ～朋友 *make friends with* / ～对头 *set oneself against sb.*

【做爱】make love

【做伴】keep sb. company: 我也来,和你做个伴儿。*I'll come too, and keep you company.*

【做操】do gymnastics; do callisthenics; do exercises

【做大】〈旧〉put on airs; give oneself airs

【做到】accomplish; achieve: 我们应当～增产不增人。*We should manage to increase production without taking on new hands.*

【做东】play the host; host sb.; act as host to sb.: 咱们找个馆子庆祝一下,我来～。*We should find a restaurant and celebrate a little. It is my treat.*

【做法】way of doing or making a thing; method of work; practice: 惯常的～ *the usual practice*; *the usual way of doing sth.*

【做饭】do the cooking; prepare a meal: ～的 *a cook*

【做工】❶ do manual work; work: 她在纺织厂～。*She works in a textile mill.* ❷ charge for the making of sth.: 这套衣服～十块钱。*The charge for the tailoring of this suit was ten yuan.* ❸ workmanship: ～精美 *of excellent workmanship*

【做官】be an official; secure an official position

【做鬼】play tricks; play an underhand game; get up to mischief

【做好人】try to be a good fellow; try to get along with everyone (often at the expense of principle)

【做好做歹】try every possible way to persuade sb. or to mediate

【做活儿】do manual labour; work: 他们一块儿在地里～。*They worked together in the fields.*

【做绝】leave no room for manoeuvre: 把事情～ *get things into an impasse*; *leave oneself no avenue of retreat*; *pass the point of no return* / 坏事～ *perpetrate every kind of villainy*

【做客】be a guest: 我昨天到一个老朋友家里去～。*I was a guest at an old friend's yesterday.*

【做礼拜】go to church; be at church

【做买卖】do business; carry on trade: 做成一笔买卖 *make a deal*; *strike a bargain* / ～的 *businessman*; *trader*; *merchant*

【做满月】celebrate a baby's birth when he is one month old

【做媒】be a matchmaker (or go-between)

【做梦】❶ have a dream; dream: 昨天我做了一个可怕的梦。*I had a terrible dream last night.* ❷ have a pipe dream; daydream: 他岂不是在～吗? *Isn't he just daydreaming?*

【做亲】❶ (of two families) become related by marriage ❷ get married

【做圈套】set a trap (to deceive sb.)

【做人】❶ conduct oneself; behave: 懂得如何～处世 *know how to conduct oneself in society* ❷ be an upright person

【做人情】do sb. a favour

【做生日】celebrate sb.'s birthday

【做生意】do business; carry on trade: 做成一笔生意 *make a deal*; *strike a bargain*

【做声】make a sound (as when speaking, coughing, etc.): 别～! *Keep quiet!*

【做事】❶ do work; do a deed; handle affairs: ～不能只凭动机,不问效果。*Actions shouldn't be guided solely by motive without any attention to effect.* ❷ work; have a job: 他没～。*He doesn't have a job.*

【做手脚】juggle things; put up a job

【做寿】celebrate the birthday (usu. of elderly people); hold a birthday party

【做文章】❶ write a composition ❷ make an issue of sth.; make a fuss about sth.: 抓住一点小事～ *seize on a trifle and make an issue of it*; *make a fuss about something trivial*

【做戏】❶ put on a play; act in a play ❷ playact; pretend

【做学问】engage in scholarship; do research: 他是～的人,不会做买卖。*He's a scholar and no businessman.*

【做样子】make a show; go through the motions

【做一天和尚撞一天钟】go on tolling the bell as long as one is a monk —do the least that is expected of one; take a passive attitude towards one's work

【做贼心虚】have a guilty conscience like a thief; have sth. on one's conscience: 他们推三阻四,正好暴露了他们～。*In making so many excuses, they revealed their own guilty conscience.*

【做针线】do needlework; sew: 她坐在窗口～。*She sat sewing by the window.*

【做主】❶ decide; take the responsibility for a decision: 我做不了主。*I am not in a position to decide.* / 只能做一半主 *have only half the say* ❷ back up; support

【做作】affected; artificial: 他老是那么～。*He's always affected.* or *He's never natural.* / 她唱得还可以,就是演得太～。*Her singing is all right, but her acting is overdone.*

附

英文字母开头的词语

AA制 go Dutch; have a Dutch treat (指聚餐付账时个人平摊出钱,或个人算个人的账的做法)

ABC ❶ [singular] the letters of the English alphabets as taught to children ❷ the basic facts about a particular subject ❸ American Broadcasting Corporation (美国广播公司)

AB型血 blood type AB

AI artificial intelligence (人工智能)

AIDS /eɪdz/ Acquired Immune Deficiency Syndrome (获得性免疫缺损综合症;爱滋病)

AOL American On-Line (美国在线)

APEC /ˈeɪpɛk/ the Asia Pacific Economic Co-operation forum (亚太经济合作论坛)

ASAP as soon as possible (尽快)

ATM automatic teller machine (自动柜员机)

A型血 blood type A

B&W black and white (黑白片)

B. A. Bachelor of Arts (文学士)

B. S. Bachelor of Science (理学士)

BBC British Broadcasting Corporation (英国广播公司)

BP机 beeper (无线传呼机)

B超 type-B ultrasonic (B型超声诊断)

B型血 blood type B

CAD /kæd/ computer-aided design (计算机辅助设计)

CCTV China Central Television Station (中国中央电视台)

CD compact disc (激光唱片)

CEO chief executive officer (首席执行官)

CFO chief financial officer (首席财务长官)

CIA Central Intelligence Agency (美国中央情报局)

CPU central processing unit (中央处理器)

CT computerized tomography (X射线电子计算机断层扫描)

DIY do it yourself (自己动手)

DJ disc jockey (原指广播或电视台的流行音乐节目主持人,现亦指酒吧、迪厅等处播放唱片者)

DNA deoxyribonucleic acid (脱氧核糖核酸)

DOS /dɒs/ Disk Operating System (磁盘操作系统)

DVD digital video disc (数字式激光视盘)

EMS Express Mail Service (邮政特快专递)

EQ emotion quotient (情商)

EU European Union (欧洲联盟;欧盟)

F－1赛车 Formula One, motor vehicle races featuring the best drivers and the fastest vehicles (一级方程式赛车)

FAQ frequently asked question (常见问题)

FBI Federal Bureau of Investigation (美国联邦调查局)

GATT General Agreement on Tariffs and Trade (关贸总协定)

GDP Gross Domestic Product (国内生产总值)

GM genetically modified (基因改性的;转基因的)

GMT Greenwich Mean Time (格林尼治标准时间)

GNP Gross National Product (国民生产总值)

GPS Global Positioning System (全球卫星定位系统)

GRE graduate record examination (美国研究生入学考试)

GSM global system for mobile communications (全球通)

HIV human immunodeficiency virus (人体免疫缺陷病毒;艾滋病病毒)

IBM International Business Machines (美国国际商用机器公司)

IC卡 intelligence card (智能卡)

ICQ I seek you (字面义为"我寻找你",实指网上寻呼机)

IDDD international direct distance dialing (国际长途直拨电话)

IE Internet Explorer (网络浏览器)

Ielts /ˈaɪlts/ International English Language Testing System (雅思:国际英语测试系统)

IMF International Monetary Fund (世界货币基金组织)

IP电话 Internet phone

IP卡 Internet phone card

IQ intelligence quotient (智商)

ISBN International Standard Book Number (国际标准图书编号)

ISDN Integrated Subscriber Digital Network (综

合业务数字网,俗称"一线通")
ISO International Organization for Standardization (国际标准化组织)
IT Information Technology (信息技术)
KB kilobyte, about one thousand bytes (千字节)
KTV karaoke television (演艺或餐饮场所的卡拉 OK 包厢)
LCD Liquid Crystal Display (液晶显示屏)
LD laser disc (激光视盘)
M. A. Master of Arts (文科硕士)
M. S. Master of Science (理科硕士)
MB megabyte (兆字节)
MBA master of business administration (工商管理学硕士)
MP3 MPEG Audio Layer 3 (原指数字音频压缩技术,后泛指该项技术压缩的音乐)
MTV music television (音乐电视)
MVP most valuable player (最优秀选手)
NATO /ˈneɪtəʊ/ North Atlantic Treaty Organization 北大西洋公约组织;北约
NGO Non-Government Organizations (非政府组织)
NMD National Missile Defence System (国家导弹防御系统)
OA office automation (办公自动化)
OPEC /ˈəupek/ Organization of Petroleum Exporting Countries (欧佩克;石油输出国组织))
O 型血 blood type O
PC personal computer (个人电脑)
Ph. D. Doctor of Philosophy (博士)
pH 值 pouvoir hydrogène (氢离子浓度指数)
PLO Palestine Liberation Organization (巴勒斯坦解放组织;巴解组织)
PR public relation (公共关系,公关)
RAM /ræm/ random access memory (随机存储器)
ROM /rɒm/ read-only memory (只读存储器)
RSVP Rèspondes, s'il vous plait; please answer or respond in writing or by telephone (请答复)
SOHO /səuhəu/ small office, home office (家庭办公室)
SOS ❶ used as a signal calling for help by a ship or a plane that is in danger (无线电紧急呼救信号) ❷ an urgent message that some one is in trouble and needs help (紧急求救)
TOEFL /ˈtəʊfl/ Test of English as a Foreign Language (托福:英语作为外语的考试)
TV television (电视)
T 恤衫 T-shirt (T 恤衫)
U. N. United Nations (联合国)
UNICEF/ˈjuːnɪsef/ the United Nations' children's Fund (联合国儿童基金组织)
UFO unidentified flying object (不明飞行物)
VCD video compact disc (激光视盘)
VCR video recorder (录像机)
VIP very important person
VOA Voice of America (美国之音)
WC water closet (厕所)
WHO World Health Organization (世界卫生组织)
WPS Word Processing System (文字操作系统)
WTO World Trade Organization (世贸组织)
WWW World Wide Web (互联网)
X 光 X-ray (爱克斯光)

* 这里收录的常见英文字母开头的词语,有的是借词,有的是外语缩略语,在语言中除标注音标的按音标发音外,其他均按英文字母音读。

附录一　世界各国家、地区、首都(或首府)及货币
Appendix 1　Countries, Regions, and Their Capitals and Currencies

国家、地区 Country, Region	首都、首府 Capital	货币 Currency	地理位置 Location
阿尔巴尼亚共和国 the Republic of Albania	地拉那 Tirana	列克 Lek	欧洲 Europe
阿尔及利亚民主人民共和国 the Democratic People's Republic of Algeria	阿尔及尔 Algiers	阿尔及利亚第纳尔 Algerian Dinar (AD)	非洲 Africa
阿富汗伊斯兰国 the Islamic State of Afghanistan	喀布尔 Kabul	阿富汗尼 Afghani (Af)	亚洲 Asia
阿根廷共和国 the Republic of Argentina	布宜诺斯艾利斯 Buenos Aires	比索 Peso	美洲 Americas
阿拉伯埃及共和国 the Arab Republic of Egypt	开罗 Cairo	埃及镑 Egyptian Pound	非洲 Africa
阿拉伯联合酋长国 the United Arab Emirates	阿布扎比 Abu Dhabi	迪拉姆 Dirham (Dh)	亚洲 Asia
阿拉伯叙利亚共和国 the Syrian Arab Republic	大马士革 Damascus	叙利亚镑 Syrian Pound	亚洲 Asia
阿鲁巴（荷） Aruba (Dutch)	奥兰也斯特德 Oranjestad	阿鲁巴弗罗林 Aruban Florin (AFI)	美洲 Americas
阿曼苏丹国 the Sultanate of Oman	马斯喀特 Muscat	阿曼里亚尔 Rial Omani (RO)	亚洲 Asia
阿塞拜疆共和国 Azerbaijani Republic	巴库 Baku	马纳特 Manat	亚洲 Asia
埃塞俄比亚联邦民主共和国 the Federal Democratic Republic of Ethiopia	亚的斯亚贝巴 Addis Ababa	比尔 Birr	非洲 Africa
爱尔兰共和国 the Republic of Ireland (Eire)	都柏林 Dublin	爱尔兰镑 Irish Pound (I£)	欧洲 Europe
爱沙尼亚共和国 the Republic of Estonia	塔林 Tallinn	爱沙尼亚克朗 Estonian Kroon	欧洲 Europe
安道尔公国 the Principality of Andorra	安道尔城 Andorra la Vella	西班牙比塞塔和法国法郎 Spanish Peseta & Franc	欧洲 Europe
安哥拉共和国 the Republic of Angola	罗安达 Luanda	新宽扎 New Kwanza	非洲 Africa
安圭拉（英） Anguilla (UK)	瓦利 Valley	东加勒比元 East Caribbean Dollar (EC $)	美洲 Americas
安提瓜和巴布达 Antigua and Barbuda	圣约翰 St. John's	东加勒比元 East Caribbean Dollar (EC $)	美洲 Americas

国家、地区 Country, Region	首都、首府 Capital	货币 Currency	地理位置 Location
奥地利共和国 the Republic of Austria	维也纳 Vienna	奥地利先令 Austrian Schilling	欧洲 Europe
澳大利亚联邦 the Commonwealth of Australia	堪培拉 Canberra	澳大利亚元 Australian Dollar ($A)	大洋洲及太平洋岛屿 Oceania and the Pacific Islands
巴巴多斯 Barbados	布里奇敦 Bridgetown	巴巴多斯元 Barbados Dollar	美洲 Americas
巴布亚新几内亚独立国 the Independent State of Papua New Guinea	莫尔兹比港 Port Moresby	基纳 Kina (K)	大洋洲及太平洋岛屿 Oceania and the Pacific Islands
巴哈马联邦 the Commonwealth of the Bahamas	拿骚 Nassau	巴哈马元 Bahamian Dollar (B $)	美洲 Americas
巴基斯坦伊斯兰共和国 the Islamic Republic of Pakistan	伊斯兰堡 Islamabad	巴基斯坦卢比 Pakistan Rupee	亚洲 Asia
巴拉圭共和国 the Republic of Paraguay	亚松森 Asuncion	瓜拉尼 Guarani (G)	美洲 Americas
巴勒斯坦 Palestine	耶路撒冷* Jerusalem		亚洲 Asia
巴林国 the State of Bahrain	麦纳麦 Manama	巴林第纳尔 Bahrain Dinar (BD)	亚洲 Asia
巴拿马共和国 the Republic of Panama	巴拿马城 Panama City	巴波亚 Balboa (B)	美洲 Americas
巴西联邦共和国 the Federative Republic of Brazil	巴西利亚 Brasilia	雷亚尔 Real	美洲 Americas
白俄罗斯共和国 the Republic of Belarus	明斯克 Minsk	白俄罗斯卢布 Belarus Rouble	欧洲 Europe
百慕大群岛（英） the Bermuda Islands (UK)	哈密尔顿 Hamilton	百慕大元 Bermuda Dollar (B $)	美洲 Americas
保加利亚共和国 the Republic of Bulgaria	索菲亚 Sofia	列弗 Lev	欧洲 Europe
北马里亚纳联合邦（美） the Commonwealth of the Northern Marianas (US)	塞班岛 Saipan Island	美元 US Dollar	大洋洲及太平洋岛屿 Oceania and the Pacific Islands
贝宁共和国 the Republic of Benin	波多诺伏 Porto-Novo	非洲法郎 African Franc (FA)	非洲 Africa
比利时王国 the Kingdom of Belgium	布鲁塞尔 Brussels	比利时法郎 Franc Belge (FB)	欧洲 Europe
秘鲁共和国 the Republic of Peru	利马 Lima	新索尔 New Sol	美洲 Americas
冰岛共和国 the Republic of Iceland	雷克雅未克 Reykjavik	冰岛克朗 Icelandic Krona (IKr)	欧洲 Europe

国家、地区 Country, Region	首都、首府 Capital	货币 Currency	地理位置 Location
波多黎各自由邦（美） the Commonwealth of Puerto Rico (US)	圣胡安 San Juan	美元 US Dollar ($)	美洲 Americas
波兰共和国 the Republic of Poland	华沙 Warsaw	兹罗提 Zloty (ZL)	欧洲 Europe
波斯尼亚和黑塞哥维那共和国 the Republic of Bosnia and Herzegovina	萨拉热窝 Sarajevo	第纳尔 Dinar	欧洲 Europe
玻利维亚共和国 the Republic of Bolivia	苏克雷 Sucre	玻利维亚诺 Boliviano (B)	美洲 Americas
伯利兹 Belize	贝尔莫潘 Belmopan	伯利兹元 Belizean Dollar (BZ $)	美洲 Americas
博茨瓦纳共和国 the Republic of Botswana	哈博罗内 Gaborone	普拉 Pula (P)	非洲 Africa
不丹王国 the Kingdom of Bhutan	廷布 Thimphu	努尔特鲁姆 Ngultrum (Nu)	亚洲 Asia
布基纳法索 Burkina Faso	瓦加杜古 Ouagadougou	非洲法郎 African Franc	非洲 Africa
布隆迪共和国 the Republic of Burundi	布琼布拉 Bujumbura	布隆迪法郎 Burundi Franc (Fbu)	非洲 Africa
朝鲜民主主义人民共和国 the Democratic People's Republic of Korea	平壤 Pyongyang	朝鲜元 Won	亚洲 Asia
赤道几内亚共和国 the Republic of Equatorial Guinea	马拉博 Malabo	非洲法郎 African Franc (FA)	非洲 Africa
大阿拉伯利比亚人民社会主义民众国 the Great Socialist People's Libyan Arab Jamahiriya (Libya)	的黎波里 Tripoli	利比亚第纳尔 Libyan Dinar (LD)	非洲 Africa
大不列颠及北爱尔兰联合王国 the United Kingdom of Great Britain and Northern Ireland	伦敦 London	英镑 Pound Sterling (£)	欧洲 Europe
大韩民国 the Republic of Korea	汉城 Seoul	韩元 Won	亚洲 Asia
丹麦王国 the Kingdom of Denmark	哥本哈根 Copenhagen	丹麦克朗 Danish Krone (DKr)	欧洲 Europe
德意志联邦共和国 the Federal Republic of Germany	柏林 Berlin	德意志马克 Deutsche Mark (DM)	欧洲 Europe
东萨摩亚（美） Eastern Samoa (US)	帕果帕果 Pago-Pago	美元 US Dollar	大洋洲及太平洋岛屿 Oceania and the Pacific Islands
多哥共和国 the Republic of Togo	洛美 Lomé	非洲法郎 African Franc (FA)	非洲 Africa
多米尼加共和国 the Dominican Republic	圣多明各 Santo Domingo	比索 Peso	美洲 Americas
多米尼克联邦 the Commonwealth of Dominica	罗索 Roseau	东加勒比元 East Caribbean Dollar (EC $)	美洲 Americas

国家、地区 Country, Region	首都、首府 Capital	货币 Currency	地理位置 Location
俄罗斯联邦 the Russian Federation	莫斯科 Moscow	卢布 Rouble (Ruble)	欧洲 Europe
厄瓜多尔共和国 the Republic of Ecuador	基多 Quito	苏克雷 Sucre	美洲 Americas
厄立特里亚国 Eritrea	阿斯马拉 Asmara	比尔 Birr	非洲 Africa
法兰西共和国 the Republic of France	巴黎 Paris	法郎 Franc	欧洲 Europe
法罗群岛(丹) the Faeroe Islands (Danish)	曹斯哈恩 Torshavon	法罗克朗 Faeroe Krone	欧洲 Europe
法属波利尼西亚 French Polynesia	帕皮提 Papeete	太平洋法郎 Pacific Franc	大洋洲及太平洋岛屿 Oceania and the Pacific Islands
梵蒂冈城国 the Vatican City State	梵蒂冈城 the Vatican City	意大利里拉 Italian Lira	欧洲 Europe
菲律宾共和国 the Republic of the Philippines	马尼拉 Manila	菲律宾比索 Philippine Peso	亚洲 Asia
斐济群岛共和国 the Republic of the Fiji Islands	苏瓦 Suva	斐济元 Fiji Dollar ($F)	大洋洲及太平洋岛屿 Oceania and the Pacific Islands
芬兰共和国 the Republic of Finland	赫尔辛基 Helsinki	芬兰马克 Finnish Markka (FIM)	欧洲 Europe
佛得角共和国 the Republic of Cape Verde	普拉亚 Praia	埃斯库多 Escudo (Esc)	非洲 Africa
冈比亚共和国 the Republic of Gambia	班珠尔 Banjul	达拉西 Dalasi	非洲 Africa
刚果共和国 the Republic of the Congo	布拉柴维尔 Brazzaville	非洲法郎 African Franc (FA)	非洲 Africa
刚果民主共和国 the Democratic Republic of Congo	金沙萨 Kinshasa	刚果法郎 Congolese Franc	非洲 Africa
哥伦比亚共和国 the Republic of Colombia	圣菲波哥大 Santa Fe Bogota	比索 Peso	美洲 Americas
哥斯达黎加共和国 the Republic of Costa Rica	圣何塞 San José	科朗 Colón	美洲 Americas
格林纳达 Grenada	圣乔治 St. George's	东加勒比元 East Caribbean Dollar (EC $)	美洲 Americas
格陵兰(丹) Greenland (Danish)	戈德霍普 Godthaab	丹麦克朗 Danish Krone (DKr)	欧洲 Europe
格鲁吉亚共和国 the Republic of Georgia	第比里斯 Tbilisi	拉里 Lari	亚洲 Asia
古巴共和国 the Republic of Cuba	哈瓦那 La Havana	比索 Peso	美洲 Americas

国家、地区 Country, Region	首都、首府 Capital	货币 Currency	地理位置 Location
瓜德罗普（法） Guadeloupe (French)	巴斯特尔 Basse-Terre	法国法郎 French Franc	美洲 Americas
关岛（美） Guam (US)	阿加尼亚 Agana	美元 US Dollar	大洋洲及太平洋岛屿 Oceania and the Pacific Islands
圭亚那（法） Guyana (French)	卡宴 Cayenne	法国法郎 French Franc	美洲 Americas
圭亚那合作共和国 the Cooperative Republic of Guyana	乔治敦 Georgetown	圭亚那元 Guyana Dollar	美洲 Americas
哈萨克斯坦共和国 the Republic of Kazakhstan	阿斯塔纳 Astana	坚戈 Tanga	亚洲 Asia
海地共和国 the Republic of Haiti	太子港 Port-au-Prince	古德 Gourde	美洲 Americas
豪兰、贝克和贾维斯岛（美） Howland, Baker and Jarvis Islands (US)		美元 US Dollar	大洋洲及太平洋岛屿 Oceania and the Pacific Islands
荷兰王国 the Kingdom of the Netherlands	阿姆斯特丹 Amsterdam	荷兰盾 Guilder or Florin (Fl)	欧洲 Europe
荷属安的列斯 Netherlands Antilles	威廉斯塔德 Willemstad	荷属安的列斯盾 Netherlands Antilles Guilder or Florin	美洲 Americas
洪都拉斯共和国 the Republic of Honduras	特古西加尔巴 Tegucigalpa	伦皮拉 Lempira	美洲 Americas
基里巴斯共和国 the Republic of Kiribati	塔拉瓦 Tarawa	澳大利亚元 Australian Dollar($A)	大洋洲及太平洋岛屿 Oceania and the Pacific Islands
吉布提共和国 the Republic of Djibouti	吉布提市 Djibouti	吉布提法郎 Djibouti Franc (DF)	非洲 Africa
吉尔吉斯共和国 Kyrghyz Republic	比什凯克 Bishkek	索姆 Som	亚洲 Asia
几内亚比绍共和国 the Republic of Guinea-Bissau	比绍 Bissau	比索 Peso	非洲 Africa
几内亚共和国 the Republic of Guinea	科纳克里 Conakry	几内亚法郎 Guinea Franc (GF)	非洲 Africa
加拿大 Canada	渥太华 Ottawa	加拿大元 Canadian Dollar (C$)	美洲 Americas
加纳共和国 the Republic of Ghana	阿克拉 Accra	塞迪 Cedi	非洲 Africa
加蓬共和国 the Republic of Gabon	利伯维尔 Libreville	非洲法郎 African Franc (FA)	非洲 Africa
柬埔寨王国 the Kingdom of Cambodia	金边 Phnom Penh	瑞尔 Riel	亚洲 Asia

国家、地区 Country, Region	首都、首府 Capital	货币 Currency	地理位置 Location
捷克共和国 the Czech Republic	布拉格 Prague	捷克克朗 Czech Crown	欧洲 Europe
津巴布韦共和国 the Republic of Zimbabwe	哈拉雷 Harare	津巴布韦元 Zimbabwe Dollar (Z $)	非洲 Africa
喀麦隆共和国 the Republic of Cameroon	雅温得 Yaoundé	非洲法郎 African Franc (FA)	非洲 Africa
卡塔尔国 the State of Qatar	多哈 Doha	卡塔尔里亚尔 Qatar Riyal (QR)	亚洲 Asia
开曼群岛(英) Cayman Islands (UK)	乔治敦 Georgetown	开曼元 Cayman Dollar	美洲 Americas
科摩罗伊斯兰联邦共和国 the Islamic Federal Republic of Comoros	莫罗尼 Moroni	科摩罗法郎 Comoros Franc	非洲 Africa
科特迪瓦共和国 the Republic of Cote d'Ivoire	亚穆苏克罗 Yamoussoukro	非洲法郎 African Franc (FA)	非洲 Africa
科威特国 the State of Kuwait	科威特城 Kuwait City	科威特第纳尔 Kuwait Dinar (KD)	亚洲 Asia
克罗地亚共和国 the Republic of Croatia	萨格勒布 Zagreb	库纳 Kuna	欧洲 Europe
肯尼亚共和国 the Republic of Kenya	内罗毕 Nairobi	肯尼亚镑 Kenya Pound (K£)	非洲 Africa
库克群岛(新) the Cook Islands (New Zealand)	阿瓦鲁阿 Avarua	新西兰元 New Zealand Dollar ($NZ)	大洋洲及太平洋岛屿 Oceania and the Pacific Islands
拉脱维亚共和国 the Republic of Latvia	里加 Riga	拉特 Lat	欧洲 Europe
莱索托王国 the Kingdom of Lesotho	马塞卢 Maseru	洛蒂 Loti	非洲 Africa
老挝人民民主共和国 the Lao People's Democratic Republic	万象 Vientiane	基普 Kip	亚洲 Asia
黎巴嫩共和国 the Republic of Lebanon	贝鲁特 Beirut	黎巴嫩镑 Lebanese Pound (£L)	亚洲 Asia
立陶宛共和国 the Republic of Lithuania	维尔纽斯 Vilnius	利塔斯 Litas (Lt)	欧洲 Europe
利比里亚共和国 the Republic of Liberia	蒙罗维亚 Monrovia	利比里亚元 Liberian Dollar (L $)	非洲 Africa
列支敦士登公国 the Principality of Liechtenstein	瓦杜兹 Vaduz	瑞士法郎 Swiss Franc (SF)	欧洲 Europe
留尼汪岛 Réunion	圣旦尼 Saint-Denis	法国法郎 French Franc	非洲 Africa
卢森堡大公国 the Grand Duchy of Luxembourg	卢森堡 Luxembourg	卢森堡法郎 Franc Luxembourgeois	欧洲 Europe
卢旺达共和国 the Republic of Rwanda	基加利 Kigali	卢旺达法郎 Rwanda Franc	非洲 Africa

国家、地区 Country, Region	首都、首府 Capital	货币 Currency	地理位置 Location
罗马尼亚 Romania	布加勒斯特 Bucharest	摩尔多瓦列伊 Moldovian Leu	欧洲 Europe
马达加斯加共和国 the Republic of Madagascar	塔那那利佛 Antananarivo	马达加斯加法郎 Madagascar Franc	非洲 Africa
马尔代夫共和国 the Republic of Maldives	马累 Male	拉菲亚 Rufiyaa	亚洲 Asia
马尔维纳斯群岛（福克兰群岛） Malvinas Islands (Falkland Islands)	斯坦利港 Stanley	福克兰镑 Falkland Pound	美洲 Americas
马耳他共和国 the Republic of Malta	瓦莱塔 Valletta	马耳他里拉 Malta Lira (LM)	欧洲 Europe
马拉维共和国 the Republic of Malawi	利隆圭 Lilongwe	马拉维克瓦查 Malawi Kwacha (K)	非洲 Africa
马来西亚 Malaysia	吉隆坡 Kuala Lumpur	林吉特 Ringgit	亚洲 Asia
马里共和国 the Republic of Mali	巴马科 Bamako	非洲法郎 African Franc (FA)	非洲 Africa
马其顿共和国 the Republic of Macedonia	斯科普里 Skopje	代纳尔 Denar	欧洲 Europe
马绍尔群岛共和国 the Republic of the Marshall Islands	马朱罗 Majuro	美元 US Dollar	大洋洲及太平洋岛屿 Oceania and the Pacific Islands
马提尼克（法） Martinique (French)	法兰西堡 Fort-de-France	法国法郎 French Franc	美洲 Americas
马约特岛(法) Mayotte (French)	扎乌兹 Dzaoudzi	法国法郎 French Franc	非洲 Africa
毛里求斯共和国 the Republic of Mauritius	路易港 Port Louis	毛里求斯卢比 Mauritius Rupee	非洲 Africa
毛里塔尼亚伊斯兰共和国 the Islamic Republic of Mauritania	努瓦克肖特 Nouakchott	乌吉亚 Ouguiya	非洲 Africa
美利坚合众国 the United States of America	华盛顿特区 Washington D. C.	美元 US Dollar (US $)	美洲 Americas
美属维尔京群岛 the Virgin Islands of the United States	夏洛特阿马利亚 Charlotte Amalie	美元 US Dollar	美洲 Americas
蒙古国 the State of Mongolia	乌兰巴托 Ulan Bator	图格里克 Tugrik	亚洲 Asia
蒙特塞拉特（英） Montserrat (UK)	普利茅斯 Plymouth	东加勒比元 East Caribbean Dollar (EC)	美洲 Americas
孟加拉人民共和国 the People's Republic of Bangladesh	达卡 Dhaka	塔卡 Taka	亚洲 Asia
密克罗尼西亚联邦 the Federated States of Micronesia	波纳佩 Ponape	美元 US Dollar	大洋洲及太平洋岛屿 Oceania and the Pacific Islands

国家、地区 **Country, Region**	首都、首府 **Capital**	货币 **Currency**	地理位置 **Location**
缅甸联邦 the Union of Myanmar	仰光 Yangon	缅元 Kyat	亚洲 Asia
摩尔多瓦共和国 the Republic of Moldova	基希讷乌 Kishinev	摩尔多瓦列伊 Moldovian Leu	欧洲 Europe
摩洛哥王国 the Kingdom of Morocco	拉巴特 Rabat	迪拉姆 Dirham	非洲 Africa
摩纳哥公国 the Principality of Monaco	摩纳哥 Monaco-Ville	法国法郎 French Franc	欧洲 Europe
莫桑比克共和国 the Republic of Mozambique	马普托 Maputo	梅蒂卡尔 Metical	非洲 Africa
墨西哥合众国 the United States of Mexico	墨西哥城 Mexico City	比索 Peso	美洲 Americas
纳米比亚共和国 the Republic of Namibia	温得和克 Windhoek	纳米比亚元 Namibia Dollar	非洲 Africa
南非共和国 the Republic of South Africa	比勒陀利亚 Pretoria	兰特 Rand (R)	非洲 Africa
南斯拉夫联盟共和国 the Federal Republic of Yugoslavia	贝尔格莱德 Belgrade	第纳尔 Dinar	欧洲 Europe
瑙鲁共和国 the Republic of Nauru	亚伦区 Yaren District	澳大利亚元 Australian Dollar ($A)	大洋洲及太平洋岛屿 Oceania and the Pacific Islands
尼泊尔王国 the Kingdom of Nepal	加德满都 Kathmandu	尼泊尔卢比 Nepalese Rupee (NR)	亚洲 Asia
尼加拉瓜共和国 the Republic of Nicaragua	马那瓜 Managua	科多巴 Córdoba	美洲 Americas
尼日尔共和国 the Republic of Niger	尼亚美 Niamey	非洲法郎 African Franc (FA)	非洲 Africa
尼日利亚联邦共和国 the Federal Republic of Nigeria	阿布贾 Abuja	奈拉 Naira (N)	非洲 Africa
纽埃（新） Niue (New Zealand)	阿洛菲 Alofi	新西兰元 New Zealand Dollar ($NZ)	大洋洲及太平洋岛屿 Oceania and the Pacific Islands
挪威王国 the Kingdom of Norway	奥斯陆 Oslo	挪威克朗 Norwegian Krone	欧洲 Europe
诺福克岛（澳） Norfolk Island (Australian)	金斯敦 Kingstown	澳元 Australian Dollar ($A)	大洋洲及太平洋岛屿 Oceania and the Pacific Islands
帕劳共和国 the Republic of Palau	科罗尔 Koror	美元 US Dollar	大洋洲及太平洋岛屿 Oceania and the Pacific Islands

国家、地区 **Country, Region**	首都、首府 **Capital**	货币 **Currency**	地理位置 **Location**
皮特开恩群岛（英） Pitcairn Islands Groups (UK)	亚当斯敦 Adamstown	新西兰元 New Zealand Dollar	大洋洲及太平洋岛屿 Oceania and the Pacific Islands
葡萄牙共和国 the Portuguese Republic	里斯本 Lisbon	埃斯库多 Escudo	欧洲 Europe
日本国 Japan	东京 Tokyo	日元 Yen	亚洲 Asia
瑞典王国 the Kingdom of Sweden	斯德哥尔摩 Stockholm	瑞典克朗 Swedish Krona	欧洲 Europe
瑞士联邦 the Confederation of Switzerland	伯尔尼 Bern(e)	瑞士法郎 Swiss Franc	欧洲 Europe
萨尔瓦多共和国 the Republic of El Salvador	圣萨尔瓦多 San Salvador	科郎 Colón	美洲 Americas
萨摩亚独立国 the Independent State of Samoa	阿皮亚 Apia	塔拉 Tala	大洋洲及太平洋岛屿 Oceania and the Pacific Islands
塞拉利昂共和国 the Republic of Sierra Leone	弗里敦 Freetown	利昂 Leone (L)	非洲 Africa
塞内加尔共和国 the Republic of Senegal	达喀尔 Dakar	非洲法郎 African Franc (FA)	非洲 Africa
塞浦路斯共和国 the Republic of Cyprus	尼科西亚 Nicosia	塞浦路斯镑 Cyprus Pound (Cyprus £)	亚洲 Asia
塞舌尔共和国 the Republic of Seychelles	维多利亚 Victoria	塞舌尔卢比 Seychelles Rupee	非洲 Africa
沙特阿拉伯王国 the Kingdom of Saudi Arabia	利雅得 Riyadh	沙特里亚尔 Saudi Riyal	亚洲 Asia
圣多美和普林西比民主共和国 the Democratic Republic of São Tomé and Principe	圣多美 São Tomé	多布拉 Dobra (Db)	非洲 Africa
圣赫拉拿岛(英) St. Helena (UK)	詹姆斯敦 Jamestown	圣赫拉拿镑 St. Helena Pound	非洲 Africa
圣克里斯托弗和尼维斯联邦 the Federation of St. Christopher and Nevis	巴斯特尔 Basseterre	东加勒比元 East Caribbean Dollar (EC)	美洲 Americas
圣卢西亚 St. Lucia	卡斯特里 Castries	东加勒比元 East Caribbean Dollar (EC)	美洲 Americas
圣马力诺共和国 the Republic of San Marino	圣马力诺 San Marino	意大利里拉 Italian Lira	欧洲 Europe
圣皮埃尔和密克隆群岛 St. Pierre & Miquelon Islands	圣皮埃尔 St. Pierre	法国法郎 French Franc	美洲 Americas
圣文森特和格林纳丁斯 St. Vincent & the Grenadines	金斯敦 Kingstown	东加勒比元 East Caribbean Dollar (EC)	美洲 Americas

国家、地区 Country, Region	首都、首府 Capital	货币 Currency	地理位置 Location
斯里兰卡民主社会主义共和国 the Democratic Socialist Republic of Sri Lanka	科伦坡 Colombo	斯里兰卡卢比 Sri Lanka Rupee	亚洲 Asia
斯洛伐克共和国 the Slovak Republic	布拉迪斯拉发 Bratislava	克朗 Slovak Crown	欧洲 Europe
斯洛文尼亚共和国 the Republic of Slovenia	卢布尔雅那 Ljubljana	托拉尔 Tolar	欧洲 Europe
斯威士兰王国 the Kingdom of Swaziland	姆巴巴纳 Mbabane	埃马兰吉尼 Emalangeni	非洲 Africa
苏丹共和国 the Republic of Sudan	喀土穆 Khartoum	苏丹镑 Sudanese Pound	非洲 Africa
苏里南共和国 the Republic of Suriname	帕拉马里博 Paramaribo	苏里南盾或弗罗林 Surinam Guilder or Florin	美洲 Americas
所罗门群岛 Solomon Islands	霍尼亚拉 Honiara	所罗门群岛元 Solomon Dollar	大洋洲及太平洋岛屿 Oceania and the Pacific Islands
索马里共和国 the Somali Republic	摩加迪沙 Mogadishu	索马里先令 Somali Shilling (So. Sh.)	非洲 Africa
塔吉克斯坦共和国 the Republic of Tadzhikistan	杜尚别 Dushanbe	塔吉克卢布 Tajik Rouble (Ruble)	亚洲 Asia
泰王国 the Kingdom of Thailand	曼谷 Bangkok	铢 Baht	亚洲 Asia
坦桑尼亚联合共和国 the United Republic of Tanzania	达累斯萨拉姆 Dar es Salaam	坦桑尼亚先令 Tanzania Shilling	非洲 Africa
汤加王国 the Kingdom of Tonga	努库阿洛法 Nukualofa	潘加 Pa'anga	大洋洲及太平洋岛屿 Oceania and the Pacific Islands
特克斯和凯科斯群岛（英） Turks and Caicos Islands (UK)	科伯恩城 Cockburn Town	美元 US Dollar	美洲 Americas
特立尼达和多巴哥共和国 the Republic of Trinidad & Tobago	西班牙港 Port of Spain	特立尼达和多巴哥元 Trinidad & Tobago Dollar	美洲 Americas
突尼斯共和国 the Republic of Tunisia	突尼斯 Tunis	突尼斯第纳尔 Tunisian Dinar (TD)	非洲 Africa
图瓦卢 Tuvalu	富纳富提 Funafuti	澳元和图瓦卢硬币 Australian or Tuvaluan Dollars	大洋洲及太平洋岛屿 Oceania and the Pacific Islands
土耳其共和国 the Republic of Turkey	安卡拉 Ankara	土耳其里拉 Turkish Lira (TL)	亚洲 Asia
土库曼斯坦 Turkmenistan	阿什哈巴德 Ashkhabad	马纳特 Manat	亚洲 Asia

国家、地区 Country, Region	首都、首府 Capital	货币 Currency	地理位置 Location
托克劳（新） Tokelau (New Zealand)		新西兰元 New Zealand Dollar	大洋洲及太平洋岛屿 Oceania and the Pacific Islands
瓦利斯和富图纳群岛（法） Wallis and Futuna Islands (French)	马塔乌图 Mata-Utu	太平洋法郎 Pacific Franc	大洋洲及太平洋岛屿 Oceania and the Pacific Islands
瓦努阿图共和国 the Republic of Vanuatu	维拉港 Port Vila	瓦图 Vatu	大洋洲及太平洋岛屿 Oceania and the Pacific Islands
危地马拉共和国 the Republic of Guatemala	危地马拉城 Guatemala City	格查尔 Quetzal	美洲 Americas
威克岛（美） Wake Island (US)		美元 US Dollar	大洋洲及太平洋岛屿 Oceania and the Pacific Islands
委内瑞拉共和国 the Republic of Venezuela	加拉加斯 Caracas	玻利瓦尔 Bolivar	美洲 Americas
文莱达鲁萨兰国 Negara Brunei Darussalam	斯里巴加湾市 Bandar Seri Begawan	文莱元 Brunei Dollar (Br $)	亚洲 Asia
乌干达共和国 the Republic of Uganda	坎帕拉 Kampala	乌干达先令 Uganda Shilling	非洲 Africa
乌克兰 Ukraine	基辅 Kyiv (Kiev)	格里夫纳 Hryvina	欧洲 Europe
乌拉圭东岸共和国 the Oriental Republic of Uruguay	蒙得维的亚 Montevideo	新比索 New Peso	美洲 Americas
乌兹别克斯坦共和国 the Republic of Uzbekistan	塔什干 Tashkent	苏姆 Sum	亚洲 Asia
西班牙王国 the Kingdom of Spain	马德里 Madrid	比塞塔 Peseta	欧洲 Europe
西撒哈拉 West Sahara	阿尤恩 Lá Youne		非洲 Africa
希腊共和国 the Hellenic Republic (or the Republic of Greece)	雅典 Athens	德拉克马 Drachma	欧洲 Europe
锡金 Sikkim	甘托克 Gangtok	印度卢比 Indian Rupee	亚洲 Asia
新加坡共和国 the Republic of Singapore	新加坡城 Singapore City	新加坡元 Singapore Dollar (S $)	亚洲 Asia
新喀里多尼亚（法） New Caledonia (French)	努美阿 Noumea	太平洋法郎 Pacific Franc	大洋洲及太平洋岛屿 Oceania and the Pacific Islands

国家、地区 Country, Region	首都、首府 Capital	货币 Currency	地理位置 Location
新西兰 New Zealand	惠灵顿 Wellington	新西兰元 New Zealand Dollar ($NZ)	大洋洲及太平洋岛屿 Oceania and the Pacific Islands
匈牙利共和国 the Republic of Hungary	布达佩斯 Budapest	福林 Forint	欧洲 Europe
牙买加 Jamaica	金斯敦 Kingstown	牙买加元 Jamaican Dollar (J $)	美洲 Americas
亚美尼亚共和国 the Republic of Armenia	埃里温 Yerevan	德拉姆 Dram	亚洲 Asia
也门共和国 the Republic of Yemen	萨那 Sana'a	里亚尔 Rial	亚洲 Asia
伊拉克共和国 the Republic of Iraq	巴格达 Baghdad	伊拉克第纳尔 Iraqi Dinar (ID)	亚洲 Asia
伊朗伊斯兰共和国 the Islamic Republic of Iran	德黑兰 Tehran	里亚尔 Rial	亚洲 Asia
以色列国 the State of Israel	耶路撒冷* Jerusalem	谢克尔 Shekel	亚洲 Asia
意大利共和国 the Italian Republic	罗马 Rome	里拉 Lira	欧洲 Europe
印度共和国 the Republic of India	新德里 New Delhi	卢比 Rupee	亚洲 Asia
印度尼西亚共和国 the Republic of Indonesia	雅加达 Jakarta	印尼盾 Indonesia Rupiah (Rp)	亚洲 Asia
英属维尔京群岛 the British Virgin Islands	罗德城 Road Town	美元 US Dollar	美洲 Americas
约旦哈希姆王国 the Hashemite Kingdom of Jordan	安曼 Amman	约旦第纳尔 Jordanian Dinar (JD)	亚洲 Asia
约翰斯顿岛（美） Johnston Atoll (US)		美元 US Dollar	大洋洲及太平洋岛屿 Oceania and the Pacific Islands
越南社会主义共和国 the Socialist Republic of Viet Nam	河内 Hanoi	越盾 Dong	亚洲 Asia
赞比亚共和国 the Republic of Zambia	卢萨卡 Lusaka	克瓦查 Kwacha	非洲 Africa
乍得共和国 the Republic of Chad	恩贾梅纳 N'Djamena	非洲法郎 African Franc (FA)	非洲 Africa
直布罗陀（英，西） Gibraltar (UK, Spanish)	直布罗陀城 the City of Gibraltar	直布罗陀镑和比塞塔 Pound & Peseta	欧洲 Europe
智利共和国 the Republic of Chile	圣地亚哥 Santiago	比索 Peso	美洲 Americas
中非共和国 the Central African Republic	班吉 Bangui	非洲法郎 African Franc (FA)	非洲 Africa

国家、地区 **Country, Region**	首都、首府 **Capital**	货币 **Currency**	地理位置 **Location**
中华人民共和国 the People's Republic of China	北京 Beijing	人民币元 Renminbi Yuan (RMB)	亚洲 Asia
中途岛（美） Midway Islands (US)		美元 US Dollar	大洋洲及太平洋岛屿 Oceania and the Pacific Islands

* 巴、以有争议。Disputed by Palestine and Israel.

附录二　中国国家机构、政协、政党和人民团体
Appendix 2　China's State Organs, CPPCC, Political Parties and People's Organizations

中国国家机关　China's State Organs

1.	**全国人民代表大会**	**National People's Congress (NPC)**
	主席团	Presidium
	常务委员会	Standing Committee
	办公厅	General Office
	秘书处	Secretariat
	代表资格审查委员会	Credentials Committee
	提案审查委员会	Motions Examination Committee
	民族委员会	Ethnic Affairs Committee
	法律委员会	Law Committee
	财政经济委员会	Finance and Economy Committee
	外事委员会	Foreign Affairs Committee
	教育、科学、文化和卫生委员会	Education, Science, Culture and Public Health Committee
	内务司法委员会	Committee for Internal and Judicial Affairs
	华侨委员会	Overseas Chinese Affairs Committee
	法制工作委员会	Commission of Legislative Affairs
	特定问题调查委员会	Committee of Inquiry into Specific Questions
	宪法修改委员会	Committee for Revision of the Constitution
2.	**中华人民共和国主席**	**President of the People's Republic of China**
3.	**中央军事委员会**	**Central Military Commission**
4.	**最高人民法院**	**Supreme People's Court**
5.	**最高人民检察院**	**Supreme People's Procuratorate**
6.	**国务院**	**State Council**
	(1)　**国务院部委**	**Ministries and Commissions Directly under the State Council**
	外交部	Ministry of Foreign Affairs
	国防部	Ministry of National Defence
	国家发展计划委员会	State Development Planning Commission
	国家经济贸易委员会	State Economic and Trade Commission
	教育部	Ministry of Education
	科学技术部	Ministry of Science and Technology

国防科学技术工业委员会	Commission of Science, Technology and Industry for National Defence
国家民族事务委员会	State Ethnic Affairs Commission
公安部	Ministry of Public Security
国家安全部	Ministry of State Security
监察部	Ministry of Supervision
民政部	Ministry of Civil Affairs
司法部	Ministry of Justice
财政部	Ministry of Finance
人事部	Ministry of Personnel
劳动和社会保障部	Ministry of Labour and Social Security
国土资源部	Ministry of Land and Resources
建设部	Ministry of Construction
铁道部	Ministry of Railways
交通部	Ministry of Communications
信息产业部	Ministry of Information Industry
水利部	Ministry of Water Resources
农业部	Ministry of Agriculture
对外贸易经济合作部	Ministry of Foreign Trade and Economic Cooperation
文化部	Ministry of Culture
卫生部	Ministry of Public Health
国家计划生育委员会	State Family Planning Commission
中国人民银行	People's Bank of China
国家审计署	State Auditing Administration

(2) **国务院办事机构** **Offices under the State Council**

国务院办公厅	General Office of the State Council
侨务办公室	Office of Overseas Chinese Affairs
港澳事务办公室	Hong Kong and Macao Affairs Office
台湾事务办公室	Taiwan Affairs Office
法制办公室	Office of Legislative Affairs
经济体制改革办公室	Office for Economic Restructuring
国务院研究室	Research Office of the State Council
新闻办公室	Information Office

(3) **国务院直属机构** **Departments Directly under the State Council**

海关总署	General Administration of Customs
国家税务总局	State Taxation Administration
国家环境保护总局	State Environmental Protection Administration
中国民用航空总局	Civil Aviation Administration of China (CAAC)
国家广播电影电视总局	State Administration of Radio, Film and Television
国家体育总局	State Physical Culture Administration
国家统计局	State Statistics Bureau

国家工商行政管理局	State Administration of Industry and Commerce
新闻出版署	Press and Publication Administration
国家版权局	State Copyright Bureau
国家林业局	State Forestry Bureau
国家质量技术监督局	State Bureau of Quality and Technical Supervision
国家药品监督管理局	State Drug Administration (SDA)
国家知识产权局	State Intellectual Property Office (SIPO)
国家旅游局	National Tourism Administration
国家宗教事务局	State Bureau of Religious Affairs
国务院参事室	Counsellors' Office of the State Council
国务院机关事务管理局	Government Offices Administration of the State Council
(4) **国务院直属事业单位**	**Institutions Directly under the State Council**
新华通讯社	Xinhua News Agency
中国科学院	Chinese Academy of Sciences
中国社会科学院	Chinese Academy of Social Sciences
中国工程院	Chinese Academy of Engineering
国务院发展研究中心	Development Research Centre of the State Council
国家行政学院	National School of Administration
中国地震局	China Seismological Bureau
中国气象局	China Meteorological Bureau
中国证券监督管理委员会	China Securities Regulatory Commission (CSRC)
(5) **部委管理的国家局**	**State Bureaux Administered by Ministries or Commissions**
国家粮食储备局(国家发展计划委员会)	State Bureau of Grain Reserve (under the State Development Planning Commission)
国家国内贸易局	State Bureau of Internal Trade
国家煤炭工业局	State Bureau of Coal Industry
国家机械工业局	State Bureau of Machine-Building Industry
国家冶金工业局	State Bureau of Metallurgical Industry
国家石油和化学工业局	State Bureau of Petroleum and Chemical Industries
国家轻工业局	State Bureau of Light Industry
国家纺织工业局	State Bureau of Textile Industry
国家建筑材料工业局	State Bureau of Building Materials Industry
国家烟草专卖局	State Tobacco Monopoly Bureau
国家有色金属工业局	State Bureau of Nonferrous Metal Industry
(以上由国家经贸委管理)	(all under the State Economic and Trade Commission)
国家外国专家局(人事部)	State Bureau of Foreign Experts Affairs (under the Ministry of Personnel)
国家海洋局(国土资源部)	State Oceanic Administration (under the Ministry of Land and Resources)
国家测绘局(国土资源部)	State Bureau of Surveying and Mapping (ditto)
国家邮政局(信息产业部)	State Post Bureau (under the Ministry of Information In-

	dustry)
国家文物局（文化部）	State Cultural Relics Bureau (under the Ministry of Culture)
国家中医药管理局(卫生部)	State Administration of Traditional Chinese Medicine (under the Ministry of Public Health)
国家外汇管理局(中国人民银行总行)	State Administration of Foreign Exchange (under the People's Bank of China)
国家出入境检验检疫局(海关总署)	State Administration for Entry-Exit Inspection and Quarantine (under the General Administration of Customs)

中国人民政治协商会议及其机构
The Chinese People's Political Consultative Conference (CPPCC) and Its Structure

中国人民政治协商会议全国委员会	**National Committee of the CPPCC**
中国人民政治协商会议全国委员会常务委员会	**Standing Committee of the National Committee of the CPPCC**
中国人民政治协商会议全国委员会办公厅	General Office of the CPPCC National Committee
专门委员会	Special Committees
提案委员会	Committee for Handling Proposals
经济委员会	Committee for Economic Affairs
人口资源环境委员会	Committee of Population, Resources and Environment
教科文卫体委员会	Committee of Education, Science, Culture, Health and Sports
社会和法制委员会	Committee for Social and Legal Affairs
民族和宗教委员会	Committee for Ethnic and Religious Affairs
文史资料委员会	Committee of Cultural and Historical Data
港澳台侨委员会	Committee for Liaison with Hong Kong, Macao, Taiwan and Overseas Chinese
外事委员会	Committee of Foreign Affairs
中国人民政治协商委员会地方委员会	CPPCC Local Committees

中国政党　Chinese Parties

中文名称 Name in Chinese	中文简称 Abbreviation	英文名称 Name in English

* 中国共产党	中共	Communist Party of China (CPC)
中国国民党革命委员会	民革	Revolutionary Committee of the Chinese Kuomintang
中国民主同盟	民盟	China Democratic League
中国民主建国会	民建	China Democratic National Construction Association
中国民主促进会	民进	China Association for Promoting Democracy
中国农工民主党		Chinese Peasants and Workers Democratic Party
中国致公党		China Zhi Gong Dang
九三学社		Jiu San Society
台湾民主自治同盟	台盟	Taiwan Democratic Self-Government League

* 中国共产党组织机构 Structure of the CPC

中国共产党中央委员会	Central Committee of the Communist Party of China (CCCPC)
中央政治局	Political Bureau of the Central Committee of the CPC
中央政治局常务委员会	Standing Committee of the Political Bureau of the CPC
中央书记处	Secretariat of the Central Committee of the CPC
中央军事委员会	Central Military Commission of the CPC
中央纪律检查委员会	Central Commission for Discipline Inspection of the CPC
中央办公厅	General Office, CCCPC
中央组织部	Organization Department, CCCPC
中央宣传部	Publicity Department, CCCPC
中央统一战线部	United Front Work Department, CCCPC
中央对外联络部	International Liaison Department, CCCPC
中央政法委员会	Committee of Political and Legislative Affairs, CCCPC
中央政策研究室	Policy Research Office, CCCPC
中央直属机关工作委员会	Work Committee for Offices Directly under the CCCPC
中央国家机关工作委员会	State Organs Work Committee of the CPC
中央台湾工作办公室	Taiwan Affairs Office, CCCPC
中央对外宣传办公室	International Communication Office, CCCPC
中央党校	Party School of the CPC
中央党史研究室	Party History Research Centre, CCCPC
中央文献研究室	Party Literature Research Centre, CCCPC
中央编译局	Compilation and Translation Bureau, CCCPC
中央外文出版发行事业局	China Foreign Languages Publishing and Distribution Administration
中央档案馆	Archives Bureau, CCCPC

人民团体 People's Organizations

测绘学会	Society of Geodesy, Photogrammetry and Cartography
地震学会	Seismological Society
国际金融学会	International Finance Society
国际战略问题学会	Institute for International Strategic Studies
海洋学会	Society of Oceanography
科普学会	Popular Science Society
全国少年儿童文化艺术委员会	National Council on Cultural and Art Work for Children
全国少年儿童工作协调委员会	National Children's Work Coordination Committee
全国史学会	China Society of History
宋庆龄基金会	Soong Ching Ling Foundation
中国奥林匹克委员会	Chinese Olympic Committee
中国笔会中心	Chinese Pen Centre
中国标准化协会	China Association for Standardization
中国残疾人福利基金会	China Welfare Fund for the Handicapped
中国出版协会	Chinese Publishers Association
中国道教协会	Chinese Taoist Association
中国电视艺术家协会	Chinese Television Artists Association
中国电影家协会	China Film Association
中国法律咨询中心	Chinese Legal Consultancy Centre
中国法学会	China Law Society
中国翻译工作者协会	Translators Association of China
中国佛教协会	Chinese Buddhists Association
中国福利会	China Welfare Institute
中国歌剧研究会	Chinese Opera Research Institute
中国共产主义青年团	Communist Youth League of China
中国国际法学会	Chinese Society of International Law
中国国际交流协会	Association for International Understanding of China
中国红十字会总会	Red Cross Society of China
中国会计学会	Chinese Accounting Society
中国基督教"三自"爱国运动委员会	Three-Self Patriotic Movement Committee of the Protestant Churches of China
中国基督教协会	China Christian Council
中国计量测试学会	Chinese Society for Measurement
中国金融学会	Chinese Monetary Society
中国考古协会	Archaeological Society of China
中国科学技术史学会	Chinese Society of Science and Technology History
中国科学技术协会	China Science and Technology Association

中国联合国教科文组织全国委员会	National Commission of the People's Republic of China for UNESCO
中国联合国协会	United Nations Association of the People's Republic of China
中国美术家协会	Chinese Artists Association
中国民间文艺家协会	China Society for the Study of Folk Literature and Art
中国企业管理协会	China Enterprise Management Association
中国曲艺家协会	Chinese Ballad Singers Association
中国人民保卫儿童全国委员会	Chinese People's National Committee for Defence of Children
中国人民对外友好协会	Chinese People's Association for Friendship with Foreign Countries
中国少年儿童基金会	Children's Foundation of China
中国少年先锋队	China Young Pioneers
中国摄影家协会	Chinese Photographers Society
中国书法家协会	Chinese Calligraphers Association
中国天主教爱国会	Chinese Patriotic Catholic Association
中国天主教教务委员会	National Administrative Commission of the Chinese Catholic Church
中国天主教主教团	Chinese Catholic Bishops College
中国文学艺术界联合会	China Federation of Literary and Art Circles
中国舞蹈家协会	Chinese Dancers Association
中国戏剧家协会	Chinese Dramatists Association
中国伊斯兰教协会	Chinese Islamic Association
中国音乐家协会	Chinese Musicians Association
中国杂技艺术家协会	Chinese Acrobats Association
中国政法学会	China Society of Political Science and Law
中国作家协会	Chinese Writers Association
中华全国妇女联合会	All-China Women's Federation
中华全国工商联合会	All-China Federation of Industry and Commerce
中华全国归国华侨联合会	All-China Federation of Returned Overseas Chinese
中华全国青年联合会	All-China Youth Federation
中华全国世界语联合会	All-China Esperanto League
中华全国台湾同胞联谊会	All-China Federation of Taiwan Compatriots
中华全国体育总会	All-China Sports Federation
中华全国新闻工作者协会	All-China Journalists' Association
中华全国总工会	All-China Federation of Trade Unions
中华医学会	Chinese Medical Association

附录三 中国历史年代简表
Appendix 3 A Brief Chinese Chronology

夏 Xia Dynasty			C. 2100— C. 1600 B. C.
商 Shang Dynasty			C. 1600— C. 1100B. C.
周 Zhou Dynasty	西周 Western Zhou Dynasty		1100—771B. C.
	东周 Eastern Zhou Dynasty	春秋 Spring and Autumn	770—476B. C.
		战国 Warring States	770—221B. C.
秦 Qin Dynasty			221—206B. C.
汉 Han Dynasty	西汉 Western Han		206B. C.—24A. D.
	东汉 Eastern Han		25—220A. D.
三国 Three Kingdoms	魏 Wei		220—265
	蜀汉 Shu Han		221—280
	吴 Wu		222—280
西晋 Western Jin Dynasty			265—316
东晋 Eastern Jin Dynasty			317—420
南北朝 Northern and Southern Dynasties	南朝 Southern Dynasties	宋 Song	420—479
		齐 Qi	479—502
		梁 Liang	502—557
		陈 Chen	557—589
	北朝 Northern Dynasties	北魏 Northern Wei	386—534
		东魏 Eastern Wei	534—550
南北朝 Northern and Southern Dynasties	北朝 Northern Dynasties	北齐 Northern Qi	550—577
		西魏 Western Wei	535—556
		北周 Northern Zhou	557—581
隋 Sui Dynasty			581—618
唐 Tang Dynasty			618—907
五代 Five Dynasties	后梁 Hou Liang		907—923
	后唐 Hou Tang		923—936
	后晋 Hou Jin		936—946
	后汉 Hou Han		947—950
	后周 Hou Zhou		951—960
宋 Song Dynasty	北宋 Northern Song Dynasty		960—1127
	南宋 Southern Song Dynasty		1127—1279
辽 Liao Dynasty			916—1125
金 Jin Dynasty			1115—1234
元 Yuan Dynasty			1271—1368
明 Ming Dynasty			1368—1644
清 Qing Dynasty			1644—1911
中华民国 Republic of China			1912—1949
中华人民共和国 People's Republic of China			1949—

附录四　中国各民族
Appendix 4　Ethnic Groups in China

中　文 in Chinese	汉语拼音 in Pinyin	英　文 in English	中　文 in Chinese	汉语拼音 in Pinyin	英　文 in English
阿昌族	Achang	Achang	傈僳族	Lisu	Lisu
白　族	Bai	Bai	珞巴族	Luoba	Lhoba
保安族	Bao'an	Bonan	满　族	Man	Manchu
布朗族	Bulang	Blang	毛南族	Maonan	Maonan
布依族	Buyi	Bouyei	门巴族	Menba	Monba
朝鲜族	Chaoxian	Korean	蒙古族	Menggu	Mongol
达斡尔族	Dawo'er	Daur	苗　族	Miao	Miao
傣　族	Dai	Dai	仫佬族	Mulao	Mulam
德昂族	De'ang	De'ang	纳西族	Naxi	Naxi
东乡族	Dongxiang	Dongxiang	怒　族	Nu	Nu
侗　族	Dong	Dong	普米族	Pumi	Primi
独龙族	Dulong	Derung	羌　族	Qiang	Qiang
俄罗斯族	Eluosi	Russian	撒拉族	Sala	Salar
鄂伦春族	Elunchun	Oroqen	畲　族	She	She
鄂温克族	Ewenke	Ewenki	水　族	Shui	Sui
高山族	Gaoshan	Gaoshan	塔吉克族	Tajike	Tajik
仡佬族	Gelao	Gelao	塔塔尔族	Tata'er	Tatar
哈尼族	Hani	Hani	土　族	Tu	Tu
哈萨克族	Hasake	Kazak	土家族	Tujia	Tujia
汉　族	Han	Han	佤　族	Wa	Va
赫哲族	Hezhe	Hezhen	维吾尔族	Weiwu'er	Uygur
回　族	Hui	Hui	乌孜别克族	Wuzibieke	Uzbek
基诺族	Jinuo	Jino	锡伯族	Xibo	Xibe
京　族	Jing	Gin	彝　族	Yi	Yi
景颇族	Jingpo	Jingpo	瑶　族	Yao	Yao
柯尔克孜族	Ke'erkezi	Kirgiz	裕固族	Yugu	Yugur
拉祜族	Lahu	Lahu	藏　族	Zang	Tibetan
黎　族	Li	Li	壮　族	Zhuang	Zhuang

附录五 中国法定计量单位简表

Appendix 5 Legal Units of Measurement of China

一、长度

Length

单位名称 Name	单位符号 Symbol	换算因数 Conversion Factors
微米 micron	μm	0.000 001m
毫米 millimetre	mm	0.001m
厘米 centimetre	cm	0.01m
分米 decimetre	dm	0.1m
米 metre	m	
十米 decametre	dam	10m
百米 hectometre	hm	100m
千米 kilometre	km	1 000m

二、面积

Area

单位名称 Name	单位符号 Symbol	换算因数 Conversion Factors
平方毫米 square millimetre	mm^2	$0.000\ 001m^2$
平方厘米 square centimetre	cm^2	$0.000\ 1m^2$
平方米 square metre	m^2	
平方百米(公顷) square hectare	hm^2	$10\ 000m^2$
平方千米(平方公里) square kilometre	km^2	$1\ 000\ 000m^2$

三、体积
Volume

单位名称 Name	单位符号 Symbol	换算因数 Conversion Factors
立方厘米 cubic centimetre	cm^3	0.000 001m^2
立方分米 cubic decimetre	dm^3	0.001m^3
立方米 cubic metre	m^3	

四、容量
Capacity

单位名称 Name	单位符号 Symbol	换算因数 Conversion Factors
毫升 millilitre	ml	0.001L
厘升 centilitre	cl	0.01L
分升 decilitre	dl	0.1L
升 litre	l	
千升 kilolitre	kl	1 000L

五、重量
Weight

单位名称 Name	单位符号 Symbol	换算因数 Conversion Factors
毫克 milligram	mg	0.000 001kg
克 gram	g	0.001kg
千克(公斤) kilogram	kg	
吨 ton	t	1 000kg

附：计量单位换算表

Conversion Tables of Units of Measurement

一、长度单位换算表

Conversion Table of Units of Length

单位名称	Name	折合法定计量单位 Conversion to the Legal Units of Measurement
市寸	*cun*	1*cun*=1/30m
市尺	*chi*	1*chi*=1/3m
市丈	*zhang*	1*zhang*=10/3m
市里	*li*	1*li*=500m
英寸	inch(in)	1 in=2.54cm=0.025 4m
英尺	foot(ft)	1 ft=0.304 8m
码	vard(yd)	1 yd=0.914 4m
英里	mile	1 mile≈1 609m

二、面积单位换算表

Conversion Table of Units of Area

单位名称	Name	折合法定计量单位 Conversion to the Legal Units of Measurement
平方英寸	square inch(in^2)	1 in^2=6 451 6cm^2
英亩	acre	1acre≈4 047m^2
公亩	are(a)	1a=100m^2
市亩	*mu*	1 *mu*=1/15hm^2=2 000/3m^2

三、重量单位换算表
Conversion Table of Units of Weight

单位名称	Name	折合法定计量单位 Conversion to the Legal Units of Measurement
钱	*qian*	1 *qain*=0.1 *liang*=5g
两	*liang*	1 *liang*=0.1*jin*=50g
市斤	*jin*	1 *jin*=500g
克拉 米制克拉	carat metric carat	1 carct 1metric carat =200mg=0.2g
盎司	ounce(oz)	1 oz≈28.35g
金衡盎司	ounce troy	1 ounce troy≈31.10g
磅	pound(lb)	1 lb=453.6g
短吨	short ton	1 short ton=2 000lb≈907kg
长吨 英吨	long ton ton	1 long ton 1ton =2 240lb≈1 016kg

四、容量单位换算表
Conversion Table of Units of Capacity

单位名称	Name	折合法定计量单位 Conversion to the Legal Units of Measurement
市斗	*dou*	1 *dou*=10L=10dm^3
市石	*shi*	1 *shi*=100L=100dm^3
美加仑	US gallon	1 US gallon≈3.79L
英加仑	UK gallon	1 UK gallon≈4.55L
美蒲式耳	US bushel	1 US bushel≈35.24L
英蒲式耳	UK bushel	1 UK bushel≈36.37L
美石油桶	US petroieum barrel	1 US petroleum barrel≈159L

附录六　中国、英国、美国军衔表
Appendix 6　Ranks in the Chinese, US and UK Armed Forces

陆军　Army

中国军衔 Rank in Chinese Armed Forces	美国军衔 Rank in US Armed Forces	英国军衔 Rank in UK Armed Forces
	General of the Army（五星上将）	Field Marshal（陆军元帅）
一级上将* General First Class		
上将 General	General	General
中将 Lieutenant General	Lieutenant General	Lieutenant General
少将 Major General	Major General	Major General
	Brigadier General （准将）	Brigadier （准将）
大校 Senior Colonel		
上校 Colonel	Colonel	Colonel
中校 Lieutenant Colonel	Lieutenant Colonel	Lieutenant Colonel
少校 Major	Major	Major
上尉 Captain	Captain	Captain
中尉 First Lieutenant	First Lieutenant	Lieutenant
少尉 Second Lieutenant	Second Lieutenant**	Second Lieutenant**
军士长 Master Sergeant	Command Sergeant Major**	
专业军士 Specialist Sergeant		
上士 Sergeant, First Class	Staff Sergeant	Staff Sergeant
中士 Sergeant	Sergeant	Sergeant
下士 Corporal	Corporal	Corporal
上等兵 Private, First Class	Private, First Class （一等兵）	Lance Corporal （一等兵）
列兵 Private	Private（二等兵） Basic Private（三等兵）	Private（二等兵） Recruit（新兵）

* 1955年中国首次颁布军官军衔时，还包括元帅(Marshal)、大将(Senior General)和大尉(Senior Captain)，但无一级上将。

** 英美军制少尉以下设有准尉(Warrant Officer, etc.)，而美国军士长在Command Sergeant Major以下还有数级，均与中国军衔不对应，此处略去。空、海军也有此种情况，从略。

海军 Navy

中国军衔 Rank in Chinese Armed Forces	美国军衔 Rank in US Armed Forces	英国军衔 Rank in UK Armed Forces
	Fleet Admiral (五星上将)	Admiral of the Fleet (海军元帅)
一级上将* Admiral，First Class		
上 将 Admiral	Admiral	Admiral
中 将 Vice Admiral	Vice Admiral	Vice Admiral
少 将 Rear Admiral	Rear Admiral	Rear Admiral
	Commodore (准将)	Commodore (准将)
大 校 Senior Captain		
上 校 Captain	Captain	Captain
中 校 Commander	Commander	Commander
少 校 Lieutenant Commander	Lieutenant Commander	Lieutenant Commander
上 尉 Lieutenant	Lieutenant	Lieutenant
中 尉 Lieutenant，Junior Grade	Lieutenant，Junior Grade	Sub-Lieutenant
少 尉 Ensign	Ensign	Acting Sub-Lieutenant
军士长 Chief Petty Officer	Master Chief Petty Officer	Fleet Chief Petty Officer (舰队上士)
专业军士 Specialist Petty Officer		
上 士 Petty Officer，First Class	Petty Officer，First Class	Chief Petty Officer
中 士 Petty Officer，Second Class	Petty Officer，Second Class	Petty Officer，First Class
下 士 Petty Officer，Third Class	Petty Officer，Third Class	Petty Officer，Second Class
上等兵 Seaman，First Class	Seaman，First Class (一等兵)	Leading Seaman(上等水兵) Able Seaman(一等水兵)
列 兵 Seaman，Second Class	Seaman Apprentice(二等兵) Seaman Recruit(三等兵)	Ordinary Seaman (二等水兵) Junior Seaman (新兵)

* 1955年中国首次颁布军衔时还包括海军大将(Senior Admiral)、海军大尉(Senior Lieutenant)，但无一级上将。

空军　Air Force

中国军衔 Rank in Chinese Armed Forces	美国军衔 Rank in US Armed Forces	英国军衔 Rank in UK Armed Forces
	General of the Air Force （五星上将）	Marshal of the Royal Air Force （皇家空军元帅）
一级上将* General，First Class		
上　将 General	General	Air Chief Marshal
中　将 Lieutenant General	Lieutenant General	Air Marshal
少　将 Major General	Major General	Air Vice Marshal
	Brigadier General（准将）	Air Commodore（准将）
大　校 Senior Colonel		
上　校 Colonel	Colonel	Group Captain
中　校 Lieutenant Colonel	Lieutenant Colonel	Wing Commander
少　校 Major	Major	Squadron Leader
上　尉 Captain	Captain	Flight Lieutenant
中　尉 First Lieutenant	First Lieutenant	Flying Officer
少　尉 Second Lieutenant	Second Lieutenant	Pilot Officer
军士长 Master Sergeant	Chief Master Sergeant	
专业军士 Specialist Sergeant		Technician** （技术军士）
上　士 Technical Sergeant	Technical Sergeant	Flight Sergeant
中　士 Staff Sergeant	Staff Sergeant	Sergeant
下　士 Sergeant	Sergeant	Corporal
上等兵 Airman，First Class	Airman，First Class （一等兵）	Senior Aircraftsman （一等兵）
列　兵 Airman，Second Class	Airman，Second Class（二等兵） Airman Basic（三等兵）	Leading Aircraftsman（二等兵） Aircraftsman（新兵）

* 1955年中国首次颁布军衔时无一级上将，而有空军大尉（Senior Captain）。

** 英空军中技术军士有两级：总技术军士（Chief Technician），在上士之下，中士之上；初级技术军士（Junior Technician）则在下士之下，上等兵之上。

附录七　中国法定假日和主要传统节日
Appendix 7　Official Holidays and Main Traditional Festivals in China

法定假日 *	**Official Holidays.**
元旦	New Year's Day (1 January, 1 day off)
春节	*see next table*
国际劳动妇女节	International Working Women's Day (8 March, $\frac{1}{2}$ day off for women)
国际劳动节	International Labour Day (1 May, 3 days off)
中国青年节	Chinese Youth Day (4 May, $\frac{1}{2}$ day off for youths of and above 14)
国际儿童节	International Children's Day (1 June, 1 day off for those below 14)
中国人民解放军建军节	Army Day (Anniversary of the Founding of the Chinese People's Liberation Army, 1 August, $\frac{1}{2}$ day off for those in active service)
国庆节	National Day (1 October, 3 days off)
传统节日	**Traditional Festivals**
春节	Spring Festival (*or* Chinese New Year's Day, 1st of the first lunar month, 3 days off)
元宵节	Lantern Festival (15th of the first lunar month, marking the end of the Chinese New Year celebrations with a display of colourful lanterns and eating of *yuanxiao*)
清明节	Pure Brightness Festival (marking the 5th seasonal division point and usually falling on the 5th or 6th of April, a traditional festival for commemorating the dead)
端午节	Dragon Boat Festival (5th of the fifth lunar month, celebrated by eating *zongzi* and holding dragon boat races)
中秋节	Mid-Autumn Festival (15th of the eighth lunar month, a traditional festival for family reunion, celebrated by eating moon cakes and enjoying the full moon)
重阳节	Double Ninth Festival (9th of the ninth lunar month, celebrated by climbing heights to enjoy nature and honouring elderly people)

* 自 1999 年 9 月 21 日生效。
Effective as from 21 September, 1999.

附录八　亲属关系

Appendix 8　Family Relationships

(1) 自己的家　One's Own Family

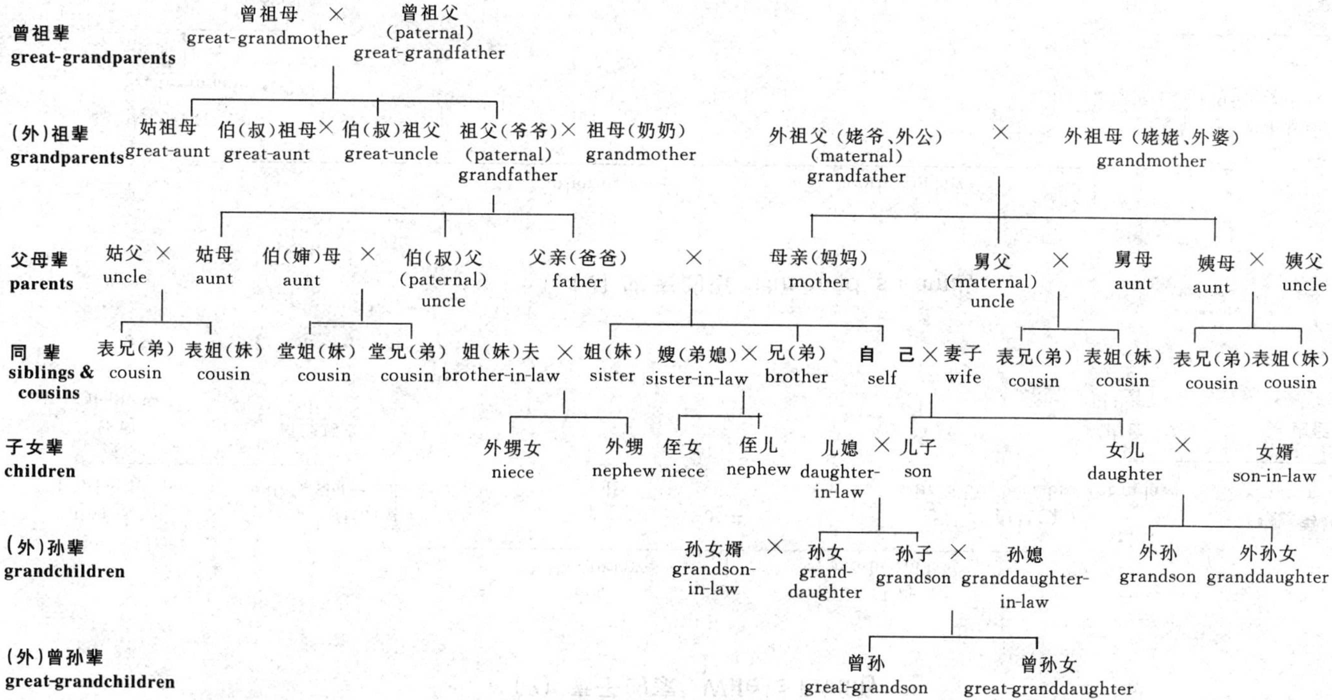

(2) 妻子的家 Wife's Family

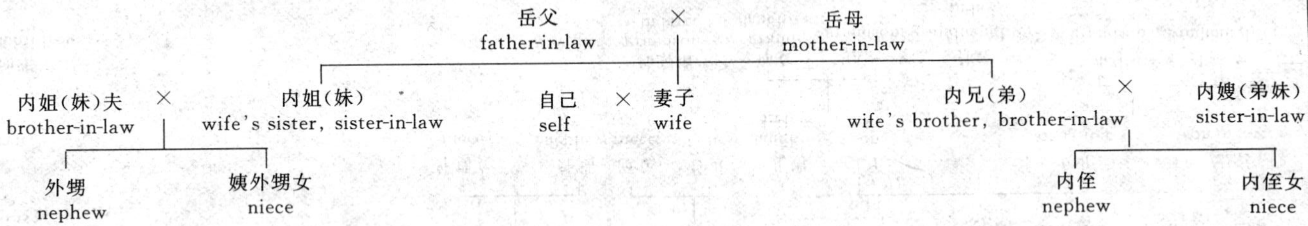

(3) 丈夫的家 Husband's Family

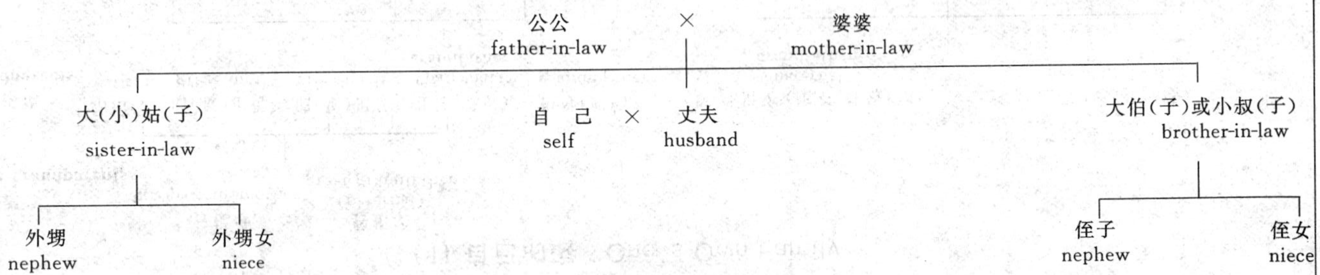

注：×＝嫁娶 married to

附录九　常见汉英分类词汇
Appendix 9　Categorized Vocabulary

1. 形状颜色 Shapes & Colours

形状 shapes

【圆形】round
【椭圆形】oval
【正方形】square
【长方形】rectangle；oblong
【三角形】triangle
【四边形】quadrangular
【六边形】hexagonal
【八边形】octagonal
【菱形】rhombus；lozenge
【球形】globular；globose
【圆柱形】cylindrical
【乳形】mammiform
【扁形】flat
【扁圆形】oblate
【随形】natural shape
【扇形】fan shape
【环形】annular
【月牙形】lune
【格子形】gridiron pattern
【梯形】trapezoid；trapezium
【锥形】cone
【工字形】shape like Chinese character “工”
【多边形】polygon
【桃形】peach shape
【灵芝形】*Lingzhi*（magic fungus）shape
【葫芦形】gourd shape
【海棠形】cherryapple shape
【荷叶形】lotusleaf shape
【菱花形】rhombus shape
【葵花形】sunflower shape
【梅花形】plumblossom shape
【簸箕形】dustpan shape
【米字形】shape like the Chinese character “米”
【凹面】（凹状）concave
【凸面】（凸状）convex
【角形】angular

颜色 colours

【红色】red
【深红】（绛红）crimson
【宝石红】ruby red
【豇豆红】peachbloom red；kidney bean red
【粉红】pink；soft red
【紫红】mauve；aubergine
【牡丹红】peony red
【海棠红】begonia red
【藏红】saffron
【珊瑚红】coral red
【桃红】peach red
【胭脂红】rouge；carmine
【铁红】iron red
【鲜红】fresh red；scarlet；bright red；blood red
【牛血红】ox blood red
【郎红】sang-de-boeuf；ruby red；*Langyao* red
【祭红】（霁红）sacrificial red；altar red；shiny red
【嫣红】bright red
【枣红】date-skin-red；jujube red；dark iron red
【抹红】overglaze red；spread red
【油红】oil red
【朱红】vermilion；satsuma red
【玫瑰红】roseate
【矾红】red from iron-oxide
【朱砂】cinnabar；mercury sulphide
【锑红】antimony red
【灰青红】ashes of roses；greyish pink
【火焰红】fiery red
【洋红】（品红）fuchsin；magenta；foreign red
【桔红】nacarat
【紫酱红】garnet red

【黄色】yellow
【橙黄】（桔黄）orange colour；orange yellow；salmon
【浅黄】（米黄）buff；millet-coloured；straw-coloured
【蛋黄】yolk yellow
【娇黄】bright yellow；light yellow
【鳝鱼黄】eel green；eel yellow
【柠檬黄】lemon yellow；citrine
【杏黄】apricot yellow
【樱桃黄】cherry yellow
【藤黄】rattan yellow；light bright yellow
【石黄】mineral yellow
【葵黄】sunflower yellow
【雄黄】cock yellow
【淡赭】pale umber

【赭墨】ochre ink
【赭黄】sienna
【赭石】umber；ochre
【黄褐】tan；ochre
【乳金】milk gold
【金黄】golden yellow
【锑黄】antimony yellow
【芥末黄】mustard yellow
【御黄】imperial yellow

【绿色】green
【孔雀绿】peacockgreen
【苹果绿】apple green
【瓜皮绿】cucumber green；water melon green
【鱼子绿】fishroe green
【松石绿】turquoise
【嫩绿】fresh green
【苍绿】gray green
【草绿】vegetation green；grass green
【菠菜绿】spinach green
【韭菜绿】chives green
【黛绿】dark green
【青绿】azurite and mineral green
【翠绿】emerald；kingfisher-blue
【墨绿】greenish black；blackish green
【石绿】mineral green
【铜绿】verdigris
【灰绿】sage green
【鹦鹉绿】parrot green
【粉绿】powder green
【淡绿】light green；green tint
【深绿】dark green
【苔点绿】mottled moss green
【蛇皮绿】snake skin green

【青色】blue；green
【黑色】black
【冬青】pale green；holly green
【葱青】（葱绿）onion green；emeraldblue
【飞青】speckled celadon；speckled green
【粉青】powder green；pale blue
【豆青】light-bluish-green；pea green
【影青】shadowy blue；mist colour；misty blue
【翠青】（翠绿）blue green；bright green；turquoise；kingfisher—blue
【鳝青】eel-green
【吹青】sprayed blue；powdered blue
【灰褐色】taupe
【鸭蛋青】pale blue
【靛青】（靛花）indigo blue
【浅青】light bluish green；pale greyblue
【灰青】bluish grey；greyish green；dark bluish grey

【回回青】Mohammedan blue；cobalt blue
【梅子青】plum green
【卵青】egg blue
【祭青】（霁青）sky clearing blue
【铅色】（铅灰色）leaden
【靛青】indigo
【花青】flower blue
【石青】mineral blue；azurite
【灰色】grey
【流青】watery blue

【蓝色】blue
【祭蓝】（霁蓝）sacrificial blue；the blue of the sky after rain
【浅蓝】pale blue
【碧蓝】azure
【淡蓝】light blue
【淡灰蓝】glaucous
【深蓝】dark blue
【月光蓝】lavender blue
【洒蓝】snowflake blue
【天蓝】（天青）skyblue；azure
【粉蓝】（粉青）powder blue；light blue；light greenish blue；the blue green of a duck's egg
【黛兰】dark blue
【紫罗兰色】violet

【紫色】purple
【棕色】（褐色）brown
【古铜色】bronze
【赤褐色】russet
【栗色】maroon
【蜜色】olive green colour；honey colour
【玫瑰紫】rose purple
【丁香紫】lilace purple
【茄皮紫】eggplant colour；eggplant purple；aubergine colour
【黛紫】dark purple
【酱紫】dark reddish brown
【藤萝紫】wistaria purple
【紫粉】purple pink
【白色】white
【牙白】ivory white
【月白】moon white
【甜白】sweet white；beautiful white
【乳白】milk white
【米色】beige
【银白】silver
【铅白】lead white
【珂粉】lime white
【铅粉】lead white
【锌白】zinc white
【奶油色】cream-colour

【淡】(浅) pale; light (of colours)

【暗】(深) dark; deep (of colours)

2. 动植物 Fauna & Flora

花草 flowers and herbs

【牡丹】peony; tree peony; *Mudan*
【芍药】peony; Chinese herbaceous peony
【金盏花】marigold
【万寿菊】calendula
【雏菊】(延命菊) daisy
【艾菊】tansy
【翠菊】China aster
【瓜叶菊】cineraria
【菊花】chrysanthemum
【水仙花】narcissus
【凤仙花】balsam; touch-me-not
【黄水仙】daffodil
【兰花】orchid; cymbidium
【白兰花】gardenia
【玉兰花】magnolia flower; *Yulan*
【菖兰】gladiola; gladiolus; sword grass
【铃兰】lily of the valley
【吊兰】pendulum orchid
【龙舌兰】agave; century plant
【君子兰】scarlet kafirlily; kaffir lily
【紫罗兰】violet
【紫罗兰花】gillyflower
【梅花】plum blossom
【腊梅】yellow plum; wintersweet
【月季花】monthly rose; Chinese rose
【玫瑰】rose
【荷花】(莲花) lotus; lotus flower
【芙蓉花】hibiscus; lotus
【木芙蓉】cottonrose hibiscus
【丁香花】clove; lilac
【蝴蝶花】iris
【大丽花】dahlia
【玉簪花】fragrant plantain lily; corfu lily; tuberose
【桅子花】gardenia
【金银花】(忍冬) honeysuckle
【山茶花】camellia
【桂花】sweet osmanthus
【香橙花】orange blossom
【茉莉花】white jasmine
【洋茉莉】heliotrope
【草茉莉】marvel of peru
【紫茉莉】four-o'clock flower
【罂粟花】poppy
【夜来香】cordate telosma
【晚香玉】tuberose
【桂竹香】gilly flower
【郁金香】tulip
【子午莲】(睡莲) water lily
【西番莲】dahlia; passionflower
【雪花莲】snowdrop
【雪片莲】snowflake
【旱金莲】nasturtium
【绣球花】(雪球花) guelderrose
【洋绣球】hydrangea
【草绣球】verbena
【萱花】day lily
【昙花】orchid cactus; queen of the night; broad-leaved epiphylum
【虞美人】corn poppy
【留兰香】spearmint
【瑞香】winter daphne
【美人蕉】canna; Indian shot
【一串红】scarlet sage; red sage; sagebrush
【一品红】poinsettia
【仙客来】(兔子花) cyclamen
【倒挂金钟】fuchsia
【吊钟花】canterbury bell
【石竹花】pink
【香石竹】(康乃馨) carnation
【麝香石竹】gilly flower
【美国石竹】sweet willow
【天竹葵】pelargonium; geranium
【金凤花】buttercup
【紫荆花】bauhinia
【金雀花】furze
【木棉花】kapok
【梨花】pear blossom
【杏花】apricot blossom
【桃花】peach blossom
【石榴花】pomegranate blossom
【秋海棠花】begonia
【鸡冠花】cockscomb
【葵花】sunflower
【牵牛花】morning glory
【樱花】cherry blossom
【樱草花】(报春花) primrose
【日本樱花】Japanese flowering cherry
【枇杷】loquat
【百合花】lily flower
【野百合】rattle
【杜鹃花】azalea
【夹竹桃】oleanlder; phlox
【野花】straw flower
【香橙花】orange blossom
【什样锦】gladiolus

【荼蘼】roseleaf raspberry
【蔷薇】rambler rose；hedge rose
【紫薇】crape myrtle
【栀子】cape jasmine
【鸢尾】iris
【毛茛】ivy buttercup
【指顶花】foxgloves
【绣线菊】meadow sweet
【紫藤】wistaria
【藤萝】wild climbing plant；creeper
【长春藤】ivy
【文竹】(天门冬) asparagus
【冬青】holly
【菖蒲】sweet sedge；calamus
【薄荷】mint
【仙人掌】cactus
【佛手】fingered citrus
【三色】pansy
【红叶】red autumnal leaves；red maple leaves
【芦苇】reed
【百日草】zinnia
【五指草】cinquefoil
【三叶草】clover
【燕草】larkspur
【熏衣草】lavender
【龙胆草】gentian
【龙须草】Chinese alpine rush；Eulaliopsis binata
【龙牙草】hairyvein agrimony；Agrimonia pilosa
【狼尾草】Chinese Pennisetum；Pennisetum alopecuroides
【狼把草】bur beggarticks
【狗尾草】green bristlegrass
【水草】water and grass；water plant
【水藻】(苲草) waterweed；alga
【海藻】kelp
【绿藻】green alga
【蓝藻】blue green alga
【爬山虎】Boston ivy；creeper
【兰草】fragrant thoroughwort
【乌拉草】Wula sedge
【香草】sweetgrass
【茜草】madder
【蟋蟀草】yard grass
【萱草】tawny daylily
【羊齿草】fern
【含羞草】touch-me-not；sensitive plant
【勿忘草】(玻璃草) forget-me-not
【凤尾草】brake
【酢浆草】wood sorrel；oxalis
【车前草】plantain
【金鱼草】snapdragon
【蒿草】wormwood
【益母草】(茺蔚) motherwort
【稗草】cockspur grass
【藓苔】moss
【杂草】weed
【蒲公英】dandelion
【浮萍】duckweed
【水浮莲】water lettuce
【芦花】fluffy ends of reed

树木 trees

【乔木】arbor；tree
【灌木】shrub；bush
【针叶树】conifer
【落叶树】deciduous tree
【常绿树】evergreen
【松树】pine
【雪松】cedar；white pine
【洋松】Oregon pine
【红松】Korean pine
【油松】Chinese pine
【落叶松】larch
【长青松】verdant pine
【马毛松】masson pine
【柏树】cypress
【云杉】spruce
【水杉】metasequoia
【柳杉】cryptomeria
【月桂树】laurel；bay tree；sweet wood
【柳树】willow；osier
【垂柳】(垂杨柳) weeping willow
【柽柳】tamarisk
【银柳】pussy willow
【白杨】(杨树) poplar；aspen
【赤杨】(桤木) alder
【榆树】elm
【梧桐树】paulownia tree；Chinese parasol tree；Chinese plane tree
【法国梧桐】plane tree；platan
【泡桐树】paulownia
【棕榈树】(葵树) palm
【橡树】(栋树) oak
【橡胶树】rubber tree
【栲树】evergreen chinquapin
【杉树】cedar
【枫树】maple
【榕树】banyan；banian
【樟树】camphor tree；camphor laurel
【桉树】eucalyptus
【枞树】fir
【龙爪槐】Chinese pagoda tree
【刺槐】(洋槐) locust tree
【槐树】Chinese scholar tree；locust tree
【铁树】sago cycas
【合欢树】silk tree

【梓树】catalpa
【椴树】linden
【漆树】lacquer tree；cashew
【木棉树】silk tree；cotton tree
【花楸树】sorb
【肉桂树】Chinese cassia tree
【槟榔树】areca
【桑树】mulberry
【桐油树】tung tree
【油棕】oil palm
【桧树】juniper
【白果树】（银杏树）gingko tree；ginkgo tree
【白桦】birch
【橄榄树】Chinese olive tree
【番木瓜树】papaya
【凤凰树】flametree
【油茶树】tea-oil tree
【冬青】holly；evergreen；ilex
【水曲柳】Manchurian tree
【山毛榉】beech
【荆棘】bramble；thistles and thorns
【菩提树】pipal tree；lime tree
【可可树】cacao tree
【椰子树】coconut palm tree
【果树】fruit tree
【海棠树】cherry-apple tree
【芭蕉树】banana tree
【李子树】plum tree
【梨树】pear tree
【石榴树】pomegranate tree
【葡萄树】vine
【柿子树】persimmon tree
【栗子树】chestnut tree
【核桃树】walnut tree
【无花果树】fig tree
【木瓜树】papaw
【樱桃树】cherry tree
【杏树】apricot tree
【桃树】peach tree
【苹果树】apple tree
【梅子树】prune tree
【枣树】date tree
【竹子】bamboo
【箬竹】indocalamus
【湘妃竹】（斑竹）mottled bamboo
【凤尾竹】（观音竹）fernleaf hedge bamboo
【乌竹】（紫竹）black bamboo
【毛竹】*Mao* bamboo
【淡竹】henon bamboo
【石竹】pink

鸟类 birds

【留鸟】resident bird
【候鸟】migratory bird
【夏候鸟】summer bird
【冬候鸟】winter bird
【水鸟】water bird；aquatic bird；waterfowl
【益鸟】beneficial bird
【害鸟】harmful bird；destructive bird
【家禽】fowl；poultry
【野禽】wild fowl
【水禽】waterfowl
【鸣禽】song bird；singing bird
【猛禽】bird of prey
【琴鸟】lyre bird
【青鸟】messenger bird of the goddess mother
【绶带鸟】paradise fly catcher
【雏鸟】young bird；nestling
【鸣鸟】finch
【孔雀】peacock
【鸳鸯】mandarin duck
【鹦鹉】parrot
【白鹦】cockatoo
【长尾小鹦鹉】parakeet
【金刚鹦鹉】macaw
【鹭鸶】egret；bittern
【鹌鹑】quail
【苍鹭】heron；hernshaw
【白鹭】egret
【白鹇】silver pheasant
【柳莺】willow warbler
【鹧鸪】partridge
【喜鹊】magpie
【夜莺】nightingale；bulbul
【金莺】（黄莺）oriole
【云雀】（百灵）lark
【丹顶鹤】red crowned crane
【白鹤】white crane
【信天翁】albatross
【杜鹃】（布谷鸟）cuckoo
【八哥】starling；mynah
【斑鸠】turtledove
【仙鹤】crane
【白头翁】grey starling；Chinese bulbul
【鸽子】pigeon；dove
【燕子】swallow
【大雁】wild goose
【画眉】thrush
【火烈鸟】flamingo
【屋鸟】Chinese jay
【鸨】bustard
【红尾鸲】redstart
【黄鹡鸰】yellow wagtail
【极乐鸟】bird of paradise
【九头鸟】a legendary bird with nine heads
【鸬鹚】cormorant

【照觉鸟】bullfinch
【鸸鹋】emu
【田凫】lapwing
【鹅】goose
【天鹅】swan
【企鹅】penguin
【翠鸟】kingfisher; halcyon
【鹪鹩】wren
【海鸥】seagull
【燕欧】tern
【海燕】petrel
【鹳】stork
【金丝雀】canary
【金翅雀】goldfinch; green finch
【山雀】tit; titmouse
【五十雀】nuthatch
【红雀】linnet
【蜂鸟】humming bird
【蜡嘴雀】hawfinch
【麻雀】sparrow
【鹬】snipe
【山鹬】woodcock
【鹰】eagle
【苍鹰】goshawk
【秃鹰】condor
【秃鹫】vulture
【隼】hawk; falcon
【猫头鹰】owl
【兀鹫】griffon vulture
【鸢】kite
【鸠】(斑鸠) turtle dove
【鸮】(鸱鸮) *Xiao* or *Chi Xiao*; owl
【枭】(鸺鹠) *Xiao* or *Xiu Liu*; owlet
【椋鸟】starling
【鹩哥】hill myna
【信鸽】carrier pigeon; homing pigeon
【乌鸦】corw
【白嘴鸦】rook
【大乌鸦】raven
【鸵鸟】ostrich
【啄木鸟】woodpecker
【穴鸟】jackdaw; daw
【知更鸟】robin
【火鸡】turkey
【雉】pheasant
【山鸡】black grouse; pheasant
【鹈鹕】(鱼鹰) pelican
【鸡】chicken
【公鸡】cock; rooster
【母鸡】hen
【小鸡】chick
【鸭】(母鸭) duck
【公鸭】drake
【小鸭】duckling
【填鸭】force-fed duck; crammed duck
【野鸭】wild duck; mallard

兽 animals

【猛兽】beasts of prey
【害兽】harmful animals
【野兽】wild animals; wild beasts
【牲畜】livestock
【耕畜】draught animals; farm animals
【家畜】domestic animals
【马】(公马) horse
【母马】mare
【小马】pony
【骡】mule
【驴】donkey; ass
【牛】cattle; ox
【公牛】ox; bull
【母牛】cow
【小牛】calf
【水牛】buffalo
【奶牛】milch cow
【菜牛】beef cattle
【野牛】bison; wild ox
【牦牛】yak
【耕牛】farm cattle
【犀牛】rhino; rhinoceros
【羚牛】takin
【麝香牛】musk ox
【羊】(绵羊) sheep
【公羊】ram
【母羊】ewe
【小羊】lamb
【山羊】goat
【羚羊】antelope; chamois
【小羚羊】gazelle
【大羚羊】oryx
【猪】pig; hog; swine
【公猪】boar
【母猪】sow
【小猪】pigling; piglet
【野猪】wild boar
【箭猪】porcupine
【狗】dog
【鬣狗】hyena
【狼狗】wolfhound
【猎狗】hunter; hound
【狮子狗】(哈巴狗) Peking poodle; Pekinese dog
【象】elephant
【虎】tiger
【美洲虎】jaguar
【狮】lion
【美洲狮】cougar; puma

【熊】bear
【黑熊】black bear
【北极熊】polar bear
【白熊】white bear
【棕熊】brown bear
【豹】leopard
【美洲豹】panther
【印度豹】(猎豹) cheetah
【猿】ape
【猩猩】orangoutang
【大猩猩】gorilla
【黑猩猩】chimpanzee
【狒狒】baboon
【猴】monkey
【金丝猴】golden haired monkey; snub nosed monkey
【猕猴】macaque; rhesus monkey
【长臂猿】gibbon
【獾】badger
【豺】jackal
【狼】wolf
【黄鼠狼】weasel
【狼獾】glutton
【狐狸】fox
【貂】marten; ermine; mink
【雪貂】ferret
【黑貂】sable
【角马】gnu
【斑马】zebra
【家兔】rabbit
【野兔】hare
【猫】cat
【小猫】kitten
【山猫】leopard cat; wildcat
【野猫】wild cat
【狸猫】leopard cat
【雄猫】tomcat
【雌猫】shecat
【骆驼】camel
【单峰骆驼】dromedary; onehumped camel
【双峰骆驼】bactrian camel; twohumped camel
【无峰骆驼】llama
【山魈】mandrill
【鹿】deer
【公鹿】stag; buck
【母鹿】doe
【小鹿】fawn
【长颈鹿】giraffe
【黄占鹿】(斑鹿) fallow deer
【梅花鹿】sika
【鼷鹿】chevrotain
【麋】elk
【麋鹿】David's deer
【麝】musk deer
【麋羚】hartebeest
【鬣羚】serow
【獐子】river deer
【狍子】roedeer
【熊猫】panda
【大熊猫】giant panda
【小熊猫】lesser panda
【猞猁】lynx
【松鼠】squirrel
【老鼠】rat; mouse
【袋鼠】kangaroo
【鼹鼠】mole
【田鼠】field mouse
【土拨鼠】marmot
【鼷鼠】house mouse
【鼢鼠】zokor
【黄鼠】desert rat; suslik
【蛇】snake
【大蛇】serpent
【蟒】boa; python; constrictor
【眼镜蛇】cobra
【响尾蛇】rattlesnake
【毒蛇】viper; asp; poisonous snake
【水蛇】water snake
【五步蛇】long-noded pit viper
【蝮蛇】viper
【蕲蛇】long-noded pit viper
【恐龙】dinosaur
【蛟龙】flood dragon
【鱼龙】ichthyosaur
【翼手龙】pterodactyl
【禽龙】iguanodon (an ancient big lizard)
【变色龙】chameleon
【蜥蜴】lizard
【壁虎】house lizard; gecko
【刺猬】hedgehog
【穿山甲】pangolin
【貘】tapir
【鸭嘴兽】platypus
【蝙蝠】bat

昆虫 insects

【益虫】beneficial insect
【害虫】injurious insect; destructive insect
【蝈蝈】katydid; longhorned grasshopper
【蟋蟀】cricket
【蜜蜂】bee
【蝉】cicada
【蝴蝶】butterfly
【蜻蜓】dragonfly
【螳螂】mantis
【蚱蜢】grasshopper

【蜘蛛】spider
【蟢子】tetragnatha
【蜗牛】snail
【蚯蚓】earthworm
【蝎子】scorpion
【蜈蚣】centipede
【蟑螂】cockroach
【蚕】silkworm
【蚊子】mosquito
【苍蝇】fly
【蚂蚁】ant
【蛾】moth
【萤火虫】firefly
【臭虫】bed-bug
【虱子】louse
【蚤】flea

水族 aquatic animals

【鱼】fish
【金鱼】goldfish
【龙睛鱼】telescope fish；dragoneyes fish
【鲤鱼】carp
【红鲤鱼】paradise fish of China
【鲢鱼】silver carp
【凤尾鱼】anchovy
【龙头鱼】bombay duck
【桂鱼】mandarin fish
【星鱼】star fish
【章鱼】octopus
【银鱼】ice fish
【草鱼】grass carp
【金枪鱼】tuna
【青鱼】herring；black carp；crucian
【黄花鱼】yellow croaker
【鲫鱼】（鲢鱼）silver carp；crucian
【鲨鱼】shark
【带鱼】hairtail；cutlass fish
【鲟鱼】sturgeon
【胖头鱼】big head；variegated carp
【鲫瓜子】gold carp
【大马哈鱼】salmon
【墨鱼】cuttlefish；inkfish
【鲮鱼】dace
【鲇鱼】catfish
【鲍鱼】abalone
【鲑鱼】salmon
【鳝鱼】（鳗鱼）eel
【娃娃鱼】giant salamander
【鱿鱼】squid
【比目鱼】flounder；halibut
【鲭鱼】mackerel
【鳕鱼】（鳘鱼）cod
【沙丁鱼】sardine
【河豚】swellfish；globefish
【泥鳅】loach；mud fish
【鳖】（甲鱼）turtle
【龟】tortoise
【海龟】sea-turtle
【鳄鱼】crocodile；alligator
【鲸】whale
【小虾】（河虾）shrimp
【大(对)虾】prawn；camaron
【龙虾】lobster
【蟹】crab
【海蟹】sea-crab
【河蟹】fresh-water crab
【海蜇】jelly fish
【海参】trepang；sea cucumber；sea slug
【蛤蜊】clam
【螺】conch
【海马】sea horse；hippocampus
【河马】hippopotamus；hippo
【河狸】beaver
【海豹】seal
【海狮】sea lion
【海象】walrus
【海豚】dolphin
【水獭】otter
【蟾蜍】toad
【青蛙】（蛤蟆）frog
【玳瑁】hawksbill turtle
【蝌蚪】tadpole
【海螺】sea conch
【田螺】fresh water snail
【蝾螈】salamander；newt
【砗磲】giant clam；tridacna

水果 fruits

【苹果】apple
【梨】pear
【京白梨】Beijing white pear
【雪梨】snow pear
【桃】peach
【杨桃】carambola
【蜜桃】honey peach；juicy peach
【樱桃】cherry
【油桃】nectarine
【猕猴桃】Chinese gooseberry
【蟠桃】flat peach
【杏】apricot
【蜜桔】mandarin orange
【红皮桔】（小桔）tangerine
【金桔】cumquat
【广柑】（橙子）orange
【柚子】pomelo；shaddock
【石榴】pomegranate

【番石榴】guava
【柿子】persimmon
【香蕉】banana
【芭蕉】plantain
【海棠果】cherryapple
【白果】(银杏) gingko
【葡萄】grape
【枇杷】loquat
【橄榄】olive
【花生】peanut
【栗子】chestnut
【荸荠】water chestnut
【杨梅】red bayberry
【草梅】strawberry
【枸橼】(香橼) citron
【椰子】coconut
【槟榔】betelnut
【榛子】hazelnut; filbert
【柠檬】lemon
【荔枝】litchi; lychee; lichee
【李子】(梅子) plum
【莲蓬】lotus pod
【莲子】lotus seed
【哈密瓜】*Hami* melon
【西瓜】watermelon
【香瓜】(甜瓜) muskmelon
【木瓜】(番木瓜) papaya; papaw
【白兰瓜】*Lanzhou* melon
【无子西瓜】seedless watermelon
【菠萝】pineapple
【木菠萝】(榴莲) jackfruit
【山楂】hawthorn; haw
【龙眼】(桂圆) longan
【桂圆肉】longan pulp
【红果】hill haw
【无花果】fig
【芒果】mango
【枣】date; jujube
【乌枣】smoked jujube; black jujube
【蜜枣】candied date; preserved date
【酸枣】wild jujube
【酸梅】smoked plum; dark plum
【蜜饯】candied fruit; preserved fruit; succade
【瓜子】melon seed
【桑葚】mulberry
【葡萄干】raisin
【甘蔗】sugar cane
【糖葫芦儿】sugared plums; sugared haws
【糖瓜儿】sugared melons
【糖人儿】sugar dolls
【糖耳朵儿】fried sweetmeat
【糖果】sweet; sweetmeats
【柿饼】dried persimmon

菜蔬、粮食作物及其他
vegetables, grains and others

【青菜】greens
【大白菜】Chinese cabbage
【圆白菜】(卷心菜) cabbage
【大头菜】rutabaga
【番茄】(西红柿) tomato
【扁豆】hyacinth beans; lentil
【油菜】cole; rape
【茄子】aubergine; eggplant
【大蒜】garlic
【洋葱】onion
【大葱】scallion; Chinese green onion; welsh onion
【青葱】shallot
【青蒜】leek
【木耳】edible fungus
【银耳】tremella; white fungus
【黄花菜】day lily
【苣荬菜】endive
【菜花】cauliflower
【菠菜】spinach
【空心菜】water spinach; swamp cabbage
【芹菜】celery
【苋菜】amaranth
【西葫芦】field pumpkin
【茴香】fennel; anise
【柿子椒】sweetbell redpepper
【辣椒】hot pepper
【胡椒】pepper
【生姜】ginger
【胡萝卜】carrot
【萝卜】radish
【菱角】water caltrop
【韭菜】Chinese chives; leek; fragrant-flowered garlic
【韭黄】hotbed chives
【甘蓝】wild cabbage
【野菜】edible wild herbs
【雪里红】potherb mustard
【芽菜】bean-sprout
【紫菜】laver; dried purple seaweed
【莲藕】lotus root
【竹笋】bamboo shoots
【冬笋】winter bamboo shoots
【莴苣】lettuce
【芋头】taro
【龙须菜】(芦笋) asparagus
【茭白】wild rice stem
【黄瓜】cucumber
【苦瓜】balsam pear
【菜瓜】snake melon
【冬瓜】wax gourd; white gourd
【丝瓜】vegetable sponge; sponge gourd; towel

gourd; dishcloth gourd
【南瓜】(倭瓜) pumpkin; cushaw
【蘑菇】mushroom
【冬菇】dried mushrooms
【马铃薯】(土豆) potato
【白薯】(甘薯) sweet potato
【木薯】cassava
【山药】Chinese yam
【谷】(粮) grain; cereal
【玉米】corn; maize
【高粱米】sorghum; *Gaoliang*
【谷】(小米) millet
【稻】(大米) rice
【黄米】glutinous millet
【江米】(糯米) glutinous rice; polished glutinous rice
【大麦】barley
【荞麦】buckwheat
【小麦】wheat
【莜麦】(油麦) naked oats
【燕麦】oats
【裸麦】(黑麦) rye
【红小豆】red beans
【菜豆】(芸豆) kidney beans; French beans
【豇豆】string beans; cowpea
【大豆】(黄豆) soya beans; soy
【绿豆】mung beans
【豌豆】peas
【蚕豆】broad beans
【芝麻】sesame seeds
【糠】chaff
【麸子】bran

附 录 十　数 字 的 用 法
Appendix 10　Usage of Numerals

(一) 基数词 cardinal numbers

1	one
2	two
3	three
4	four
5	five
6	six
7	seven
8	eight
9	nine
10	ten
11	eleven
12	twelve
13	thirteen
14	fourteen
15	fifteen
16	sixteen
17	seventeen
18	eighteen
19	nineteen
20	twenty
21	twenty-one
22	twenty-two
23	twenty-three
30	thirty
31	thirty-one
40	forty
50	fifty
60	sixty
70	seventy
80	eighty
90	ninety
100	one hundred
101	one hundred and one
200	two hundred
300	three hundred
400	four hundred
500	five hundred
600	six hundred
700	seven hundred
800	eight hundred
900	nine hundred
1000	one thousand
100 000	one hundred thousand
1 000 000	one million

(二) 序数词 ordinal numbers

第一	first
第二	second
第三	third
第四	fourth
第五	fifth
第六	sixth
第七	seventh
第八	eighth
第九	ninth
第十	tenth
第十一	eleventh
第十二	twelfth
第十三	thirteenth
第十四	fourteenth
第十五	fifteenth
第十六	sixteenth
第十七	seventeenth
第十八	eighteenth
第十九	nineteenth
第二十	twentieth
第二十一	twenty-first
第二十二	twenty-second
第二十三	twenty-third
第三十	thirtieth
第三十一	thirty-first
第四十	fortieth
第五十	fiftieth
第六十	sixtieth
第七十	seventieth
第八十	eightieth
第九十	ninetieth
第一百	(one) hundredth
第一百零一	(one) hundred and first
第二百	two-hundredth
第三百	three-hundredth
第四百	four-hundredth
第五百	five-hundredth
第六百	six-hundredth
第七百	seven-hundredth
第八百	eight-hundredth
第九百	nine-hundredth
第一千	(one) thousandth
第一万	ten thousandth
第一百万	(one) millionth

零（0）nought；zero；O

一百二十三（123）one hundred and twenty-three

一千三百（1 300）thirteen hundred；one thousand three hundred

二千（2 000）two thousand

四千五百零二（4 502）four thousand five hundred and two

三万六千（36 000）thirty-six thousand

四万五千七百八十九（45 789）forty-five thousand seven hundred and eighty-nine

五十万（500 000）five hundred thousand

三百一十二万四千五百（3 124 500）three million, one hundred and twenty-four thousand five

八百万（8 000 000）eight million

四千三百万（43 000 000）forty-three million

九亿（900 000 000）nine hundred million

十亿八千万（1 080 000 000）one billion and eighty million

一百亿（10 000 000 000）ten billion

三千亿（300 000 000 000）three hundred billion

五万亿（5 000 000 000 000）five million million

（三）分数 fractions

二分之一（1/2）one-half；a half

三分之一（1/3）one-third

四分之三（3/4）three-fourths

五分之一（1/5）one-fifth

五分之二（2/5）two-fifths

八分之七（7/8）seven-eighths

十分之一（1/10）one-tenth；a tenth

百分之一（1/100）one-hundredth；one percent

千分之一（1/1 000）one-thousandth

万分之一（1/10 000）one ten-thousandth

二又二分之一 two and one half；two and a half

四又三分之二 four and two-thirds

（四）百分比 percentages

百分之百（100%）one hundred per cent

百分之零点五（0.5%）point five per cent

百分之零点三七（0.37%）point three seven per cent

（五）小数 decimals

4.03 four point nought three；four point O three

7.005 seven point nought nought five；seven point O O five

45.21 forty-five point two one

（六）增加 go up by；shoot up by；rise by (to)；be raised by；increase by

双倍；加倍（to）double

象…一样多 as many as；as much as

增加百分之一 to increase by one-hundredth

增加百分之十 to increase by one-tenth

增加百分之五十 to increase by one-half

增加百分之七十 an increase of seventy per cent；an seventy-percent increase

是去年的二倍（即增加一倍）to be double that of last year

增加百分之百（即增加一倍或增加到原数的二倍）to increase by one hundred per cent；to double；to increase to twice as many (much) as

比 1978 年增加一倍以上 to be more than double the 1987 figure

是…的四倍 four fimes as many (much) as

是去年的五倍 to be five times that of last year；to increase fivefold compared with last year；to increase by 400 per cent over last year

比 1987 年增加了十多倍 to be a dozen times that of 1978

粮食产量从 1978 年的 30 万吨上升到 1983 年的 715 000 吨 grain output went up to 715 000 tons in 1983 from 300 000 tons in 1978

1983 年粮食产量为 38 728 万吨，是 1949 年的 3.42 倍 in 1983 the output of grain was 387.28 million tons, 3.42 times that of 1949

1983 年工农业总产值为 9 209 亿元，比 1982 年增加 10.2% the 1983 total combined output value of industry and agriculture was 920.9 billion *yuan*, 10.2 per cent higher than 1982

1979 至 1983 年间工农业总产值平均每年的增长率是 8.2% the average annual rate of increase of the total output value of industry and agriculture from 1979 through 1983 was 8.2 per cent

与 1949 年相比，大学生人数增加了 63%，中学生增加了 1.5 倍，小学生增加了 1.1 倍　compared with 1949, the number of university students increased by 63 per cent, that of secondary school students by 1.5 times, and that of primary school pupils by 1.1 times

（七）减少（下降）go down by；fall by (to)；reduce by

下降（减少）百分之六十　a reduction (fall) of sixty per cent

下降百分之一 to decrease by one-hundredth; to reduce by one-hundredth

下降百分之十(或十分之一) to decrease by ten per cent; to reduce by ten per cent; to reduce to nine-tenths; to be reduced to nine-tenths

下降百分之二十(或五分之一) to decrease by one-fifth; to reduce by one-fifth; to reduce to four-fifths; to be reduced to four-fifths

下降百分之二十五(或四分之一) to decrease by one quarter; to reduce by one quarter; to reduce to three-fourths; to be reduced to three-fourths

下降百分之五十(或一半) to decrease by one-half; to reduce by one-half; to reduce to one-half; to be reduced to one-half

(八) 不确指的数字 indefinite numbers

几个 some; a few; several; a number of

十几个 more than ten; over a dozen; no more than twenty

几十个 dozens of

几十年 decades

四十好几 well over forty

好几百个 hundreds of

成千上万 thousands of

几十万 hundreds of thousands of

数以百万计的 millions of

亿万(人) hundreds of millions of

(九) 时间 time

6:00 six o'clock;
six a. m. (上午); six p. m. (下午)

7:10 ten past seven; seven ten

8:15 a quarter past eight; eight fifteen

9:25 twenty-five past nine; nine twenty-five

10:30 half past ten; ten thirty

11:35 eleven thirty-five; twenty-five to twelve

12:45 twelve forty-five; a quarter to thirteen

13:50 thirteen fifty; ten to fourteen

14:57 fourteen fifty-seven; three to fifteen

15:00 fifteen

(十) 年月日 dates

1643 年 sixteen forty-three

1755 年 seventeen fifty-five

1898 年 eighteen ninety-eight

1900 年 nineteen hundred

1989 年 nineteen eighty-nine

2000 年 twenty hundred

三月八日 the eighth of March

五月一日 the first of May

七月二十三日 the twenty-third of July

一九四九年十月一日 the first of October, nineteen forty-nine

(十一) 电话号码 telephone numbers

117 one one seven

120 one two oh

699 six double-nine

2442 two double-four two

3271 three two seven one

893712 eight nine three seven one two

8123456 eight one two three four five six

(十二) 罗马数字 Roman numeral

1 I
2 II
3 III
4 IV
5 V
6 VI
7 VII
8 VIII
9 IX
10 X
11 XI
12 XII
13 XIII
14 XIV
15 XV
16 XVI
17 XVII
18 XVIII
19 XIX
20 XX
21 XXI
22 XXII
23 XXIII
24 XXIV
30 XXX
31 XXXI
32 XXXII
40 XL
41 XLI

42	XLII
50	L
51	LI
52	LII
60	LX
61	LXI
62	LXII
70	LXX
80	LXXX
90	XC
100	C
200	CC
300	CCC
400	CCCC;CD
500	D
600	DC
700	DCC
800	DCCC
900	CM
1000	M
2000	MM
2500	MMD

附录十一

Appendix 11 Per

原子序数 atomic number ← 24 Cr →
铬 ge →
英文名称 name in English ← chromium
51.9961(6) ↓ 原子量 atomic weight

族 Family 周期 Period	I_A	II_A	III_B	IV_B	V_B	VI_B	VII_B	
1	1 H 氢 qing hydrogen 1.00794(7)							
2	3 Li 锂 li lithium 6.941(2)	4 Be 铍 pi beryllium 9.0121823(3)						
3	11 Na 钠 na sodium 22.989768(6)	12 Mg 镁 mei magnesium 24.3050(6)						
4	19 K 钾 jia potassium 39.0983	20 Ca 钙 gai calcium 40.078(4)	21 Sc 钪 kang scandium 44.955910(9)	22 Ti 钛 tai titanium 47.88(3)	23 V 钒 fan vanadium 50.9415	24 Cr 铬 ge chromium 51.9961(6)	25 Mn 锰 meng manganese 54.93805(1)	26 Fe 铁 tie iron 55.847(3)
5	37 Rb 铷 ru rubidium 85.4678(3)	38 Sr 锶 si strontium 87.62	39 Y 钇 yi yttrium 88.90585(2)	40 Zr 锆 gao zirconium 91.224(2)	41 Nb 铌 ni niobium 92.90638(2)	42 Mo 钼 mu molybdenum 95.94	43 Tc 锝 de technetium [98]	44 Ru 钌 liao ruthenium 101.07(2)
6	55 Cs 铯 se cesium 132.90543(5)	56 Ba 钡 bei barium 137.327(7)	57—71 La—Lu 镧系 lanxi La group	72 Hf 铪 ha hafnium 178.49(2)	73 Ta 钽 tan tantalum 180.9479	74 W 钨 wu tungsten 183.85(3)	75 Re 铼 lai rhenium 186.207	76 Os 锇 e osmium 190.2
7	87 Fr 钫 fang francium [223]	88 Ra 镭 lei radium 226.0254	89—103 Ac—Lr 锕系 axi Ac group	104 Rf *铲 lu rutherfordi- um [261]	105 Db *钍 du dubnium [262]	106 Sg *𬭳 xi seaborgium [263]	107 Bh *𬭛 bo bohrium [262]	108 Hs 𬭶 hei hassium [265]

57—71 La—Lu 镧系 lanxi La group	57 La 镧 lan lanthanum 138.9055(2)	58 Ce 铈 shi cerium 140.115(4)	59 Pr 镨 pu praseodymi- um 140.90765(3)	60 Nd 钕 nü neodymium 144.24(3)	61 Pm *钷 po promethium [147]	62 Sm 钐 shan samarium 150.36(3)	63 铕 europ 151.9
89—103 Ac—Lr 锕系 axi Ac group	89 Ac 锕 a actinium 227.0278	90 Th 钍 tu thorium 232.0381	91 Pa 镤 pu protactinium 231.0359	92 U 铀 you uranium 238.0289	93 Np 镎 na neptunium 237.0482	94 Pu 钚 bu plutonium [244]	95 *镅 ameri [24

注 *的为人造元素
Those marked with * are man-made elements.

**原子量均采用国际标准数，末位数的准确度注于其后的圆括
Here listed are internationally acknowledged data on the a
noted in round brackets and those of the unnoted figures
most stable isotope of a given element.